The Concise Oxford Thesaurus

The Concise Oxford Thesaurus

Compiled by
Betty Kirkpatrick

Oxford
OXFORD UNIVERSITY PRESS
1997

Oxford University Press, Great Clarendon Street, Oxford OX2 6DP

Oxford New York
Athens Auckland Bangkok Bogota Bombay
Buenos Aires Calcutta Cape Town Dar es Salaam
Delhi Florence Hong Kong Istanbul Karachi
Kuala Lumpur Madras Madrid Melbourne
Mexico City Nairobi Paris Singapore
Taipei Tokyo Toronto

and associated companies in
Berlin Ibadan

Oxford is a trade mark of Oxford University Press

Published in the United States by
Oxford University Press Inc., New York

A–Z text © Oxford University Press 1995
Additional material © Market House Books 1995

First published 1995, and reissued 1997

Based on The Oxford Paperback Thesaurus, compiled by Betty Kirkpatrick
with additional material by Oxford University Press and Market House Books.

British Library Cataloguing in Publication Data
Data available

Library of Congress Cataloging in Publication Data
Data available
ISBN 0–19–860126–3

10 9 8 7 6 5 4 3 2 1

Printed in Great Britain by
The Bath Press, Bath

Guide to the Thesaurus

THE HEADWORDS

The text of the *Thesaurus* is organized under headwords, which are printed in bold type. The headwords are listed in strict alphabetical order. Many English words have two or more different acceptable spellings; in this book, the one used is the one regarded as being the most common. If two or more different forms are common, alternatives are given, for example:

> **cagey, cagy** *adjective* guarded, secretive, noncommittal, cautious, chary, wary, careful, shrewd, wily.

However, alternatives are not listed in all such cases. For instance, in British English many words ending in -ize can also be spelled with an -ise ending. Variants of this type have not been included.

PARTS OF SPEECH

Headwords are always followed by a label indicating the part of speech of the entry.

When a word has two or more different parts of speech, it is listed more than once with separate entries for each, for example:

> **captive** *noun take captives*...prisoner, prisoner-of-war, hostage....
>
> **captive** *adjective captive animals* imprisoned, incarcerated, locked up....

The order of parts of speech is based on usage, with the most common placed first. Not all possible parts of speech of a word are necessarily included as headwords. For example, many words that function as adjectives can also function as adverbs. These are included only when they have useful sets of synonyms.

HOMONYMS

Certain words have the same spelling but different meanings and different origins (etymologies). Such words, known as homonyms, are treated as separate headwords, even when they have the same part of speech. Homonym numbers are included in order to distinguish identical headwords with the same part of speech for the purposes of cross-referencing. For example:

> **bank¹** *noun a grassy bank* slope, rise, incline....
>
> **bank²** *verb bank an aircraft* tilt, slope, slant....
>
> **bank³** *noun borrow from the bank*...high-street bank, clearing bank....
>
> **bank⁴** *verb bank the money* deposit, save, save up....

If the headwords are identical but the parts of speech differ, there can be no ambiguity in cross references so homonym numbers are not used. This does not necessarily imply that the different part-of-speech entries have the same etymology.

THE ENTRIES

Each entry contains a list of words that are synonyms of the headword; i.e. the words can be used in place of the headword in most (although not all) contexts. When a word has more than one meaning, the different senses of the word are numbered. Example phrases (in italic type) indicate the particular sense and illustrate the use of the word. In some cases, two or more examples are given; these are separated by a vertical bar. For example:

> **assimilate** *verb* **1** *assimilate food/facts | assimilate people into a group* absorb, take in, incorporate, digest, ingest. **2** *assimilate your way of life to theirs* adapt, adjust, accustom, acclimatize, accommodate, become like/similar, blend in, fit, homogenize.

Note that a solidus (/) is used to separate alternative words in order to save space. The solidus applies only to the two words it separates; thus 'assimilate food/facts' can be read as 'assimilate food' and 'assimilate facts'.

GROUPS WITHIN SENSES

In general, the synonyms in an entry are separated by commas. However, there are cases in which the words fall naturally into two or more distinct groups, which are separated by a semicolon. There are various reasons for subdividing a sense in this way:

• **grammatical differences** Some of the words may function in a different way from others, for example:

> **briefing**...*recruits being given their briefing* brief, information, guidance, preparation; instructions, directions....

In this case the words *instructions* and *directions* have been grouped separately because they are plural nouns. There are other grammatical reasons why synonyms may be split into groups. For example, the headword may function as both a transitive and intransitive verb, whereas some of the synonyms may be intransitive only.

• **informal words** Words that are not used in standard formal English have been grouped at the end of lists and given the label *inf.* No distinction is made between colloquial, informal, and slang levels of usage. For example:

> **babble** *verb*...jabber, gibber, gabble, burble, chatter, mutter, mumble, prate, drivel, bleat, cackle; *inf.* rabbit, waffle, run on.

The label *inf.* applies to all the words following in the group.

• **restricted usage** Synonyms have been separated into labelled groups when they are used in different regions or in particular fields. For example:

> **baby** *noun holding a tiny baby* infant, newborn, child, babe, tiny tot; *inf* sprog; *Scots* bairn; *Med.* neonate.

A list of labels used in the *Thesaurus* is given later.

SUB-ENTRIES

Verb phrases are included as sub-entries under a main entry. For example:

> **call**...*call out in pain* cry, cry out, shout, exclaim...**call for** *this calls for a celebration*...need, require, be grounds for...**call off** *call off the dogs* order off, order away....

CROSS-REFERENCES

Cross-reference to main entries is indicated by small capitals. Where necessary, the part of speech and sense number are also given. For example:

> **barbaric** *adjective....See* BARBARIAN *adjective* 1

TABLES

Tables have been included throughout the book to give additional information for certain entries. These typically consist of lists of words that, while not strictly synonyms of the headword, are associated with it in some way. For example, at **dam** a table of notable dams is given; at **knife** a list of types of knife is shown.
References to the tables are given at the ends of entries. For example:

> **dam** *noun a river dam...See table.*
>
> **machete** *noun...See table at* KNIFE.

Certain headwords only refer to tables, i.e. there are no synonyms given. For example:

> **ballet** *noun. See table.*

ANTONYMS

Many entries contain a list of opposites. For example:

> **dally** *verb...*
> ***Opposites*** HURRY; HASTEN.

Words in small capitals are cross-references to other entries.

Abbreviations

The following labels have been used in the text:

Am.	American
Austral.	Australian
dial.	dialect
fml.	formal
inf.	informal
lit.	literary
Med.	Medicine
Tech.	Technical fields
vulg.	vulgar

Abbreviations for nationalities:

Afk.	Afrikaans
Afr.	African
Am.	American
Arab.	Arabic
Austral.	Australian
Belg.	Belgian
Brit.	British
Bulg.	Bulgarian
Can.	Canadian
Cz.	Czech
Da.	Danish
Du.	Dutch
Egypt.	Egyptian
Engl.	English
Flem.	Flemish
Finn.	Finnish
Fr.	French
Ger.	German
Gk	Greek
Icel.	Icelandic
Ind.	Indian
Ir.	Irish
It.	Italian
Jap.	Japanese
Mex.	Mexican
Norw.	Norwegian
NZ	New Zealand
Pers.	Persian
Pol.	Polish
Port.	Portuguese
Rom.	Roman
Russ.	Russian
S. Afr.	South African
S. Am.	South American
Scot.	Scottish
Sp.	Spanish
Sw.	Swedish
Turk.	Turkish

The Concise Oxford Thesaurus

abandon verb **1** *abandon one's wife* desert, leave, forsake, depart from, leave behind, cast aside, jilt; *inf.* run out on. **2** *abandon ship* leave, depart from, go away from, vacate, withdraw from, quit. **3** *abandon hope* give up, renounce, relinquish, dispense with, forgo, desist from, forswear. **4** *abandon a country to the enemy* yield, surrender, give up, cede, relinquish, abdicate, deliver up, resign. **5** *abandon smoking* stop, give up, cease, drop, forgo, desist from, dispense with, abjure; *inf.* kick, jack in, pack in. **6** *abandon oneself to despair* give way to, give oneself up to, yield to, indulge in, lose oneself to/in.
Opposites KEEP; RETAIN; CONTINUE.

abandon noun *behave with gay abandon* recklessness, lack of restraint/inhibition, unrestraint, carelessness, wildness, impulse, impetuosity, immoderation, wantonness.

abandoned adjective **1** *an abandoned wife* deserted, forsaken, cast aside. *See* ABANDON verb 1. **2** *an abandoned ship* vacated, evacuated, deserted, unoccupied, empty, unused. *See* ABANDON verb 2. **3** *abandoned behaviour* reckless, unrestrained, uninhibited, impetuous, wild, careless, wanton. **4** *an abandoned young man* dissipated, debauched, profligate, dissolute, immoral, corrupt, depraved, reprobate, wild, unrestrained, reckless, wanton.

abase verb *abase oneself before the emperor* | *abase one's servants* humiliate, humble, belittle, lower, degrade, disparage, debase, demean, discredit, mortify, bring low, demote, reduce.

abasement noun humiliation, belittlement, lowering, degradation, disparagement, debasement, mortification, demotion, reduction. *See* ABASE.

abashed adjective embarrassed, ashamed, shamefaced, mortified, humiliated, taken aback, disconcerted, nonplussed, discomfited, discomposed, perturbed, confounded, dismayed, dumbfounded, confused, put out of countenance, discountenanced.

abate verb **1** *the storm/pain abated* die down, lessen, ease, subside, let up, decrease, diminish, moderate, decline, fade, slacken, wane, ebb, alleviate, attenuate. **2** *trying to abate the pain* ease, lessen, decrease, diminish, moderate, soothe, relieve, dull, blunt, alleviate, mitigate, allay, assuage, palliate, appease, attenuate. **3** *attempts to abate the noise levels* decrease, reduce, lessen, lower, diminish.
Opposites INCREASE; INTENSIFY.

abatement noun **1** *the abatement of the wind* lessening, moderation, decrease, decline, ebb, alleviation, attenuation. *See* ABATE 1. **2** *the abatement of the pain* easing, decrease, moderation, relief, mitigation, assuagement, palliation, appeasement, attenuation. *See* ABATE 2.

3 *the abatement of noise levels* decrease, reduction, lowering. *See* ABATE 3.

abbey noun religious house; monastery, priory, cloister, friary, convent, nunnery, coenoby.

abbreviate verb shorten, reduce, cut, cut short/down, contract, condense, compress, abridge, truncate, clip, crop, shrink, constrict, summarize, abstract, précis, synopsize, digest.
Opposites LENGTHEN; EXPAND; ELONGATE.

abbreviation noun **1** *the abbreviation of his name* shortening, reduction, cutting, contraction, condensation, compression, abridgement. *See* ABBREVIATE. **2** *the abbreviation for the United Kingdom is UK* shortened form, contraction, abridgement.

abdicate verb **1** *the King abdicated in 1936* resign, stand down, retire, quit. **2** *abdicate the throne* give up, renounce, resign from, relinquish, abjure, cede; *Law* disclaim. **3** *abdicate all responsibility* give up, renounce, relinquish, abjure, repudiate, reject, disown, waive, yield, forgo, refuse, abandon, surrender, cast aside, drop, turn one's back on, wash one's hands of.

abdication noun **1** *abdication from the throne* giving up of, renunciation of, resignation from, relinquishment of, abjuration of, ceding of. **2** *abdication of responsibility* renunciation, relinquishment, abjuration, repudiation, rejection, waiving, refusal, abandonment, surrender. *See* ABDICATE 2.

abdomen noun stomach, belly, intestines; *inf.* tummy, tum, insides, guts, pot, paunch, corporation, maw, bread basket.

abdominal adjective gastric, intestinal, stomachic, visceral, coeliac, ventral.

abduct verb kidnap, carry off, run away/off with, make off with, seize, hold as hostage, hold to ransom; *inf.* snatch.

aberrant adjective deviant, deviating, divergent, anomalous, abnormal, irregular, atypical, freakish.

aberration noun **1** *a statistical aberration* deviation, divergence, anomaly, abnormality, irregularity, variation, freak. **2** *in a moment of aberration* abnormality, irregularity, eccentricity, deviation, straying, aberrancy. **3** *suffering from a mental aberration* disorder, disease, irregularity, instability, derangement, vagary.

abet verb assist, aid, help, support, back, second, encourage, promote, cooperate with, connive at, endorse, sanction, succour.

abeyance noun *the decision was in abeyance* a state of suspension/dormancy/latency, suspension, suspense, remission; *inf.* cold storage.

abhor verb detest, loathe, hate, abominate, feel aversion to, shrink/recoil from, dislike, execrate.
Opposites LOVE; ADMIRE; delight in (*see* DELIGHT).

abhorrent *adjective* detestable, loathsome, hateful, hated, abominable, repellent, repugnant, repulsive, revolting, disgusting, distasteful, horrible, horrid, heinous, obnoxious, odious, offensive, execrable; *inf.* yucky.

abide *verb* **1** *abide by the rules* keep to, comply with, observe, follow, obey, agree to, hold to, conform to, adhere to, stick to, stand by. **2** *I cannot abide them or their habits* stand, tolerate, bear, put up with, endure, stomach, suffer, accept, brook.

abiding *adjective* lasting, everlasting, eternal, unending, continuing, durable, constant, permanent, stable, enduring, persisting, unchanging, steadfast, immutable.
Opposites SHORT-LIVED; EPHEMERAL; TRANSITORY.

ability *noun* **1** *a person of outstanding ability* talent, competence, competency, proficiency, skill, expertise, expertness, adeptness, aptitude, dexterity, adroitness, qualification, cleverness, flair, gift, knack, savoir faire; *inf.* know-how. **2** *the ability to cope* capacity, capability, potential, potentiality, power, aptness, facility, faculty, propensity.
Opposites INABILITY; INCAPACITY.

abject *adjective* **1** *abject poverty* wretched, miserable, hopeless, pathetic, pitiable, piteous, stark, forlorn. **2** *an abject coward* base, low, vile, worthless, contemptible, debased, degraded, despicable, ignominious, mean. **3** *an abject apology* obsequious, grovelling, servile, cringing, snivelling, ingratiating, toadying, sycophantic, submissive.

abjure *verb* **1** *abjure a claim* give up, renounce, relinquish, retract, abandon, deny, abdicate, disclaim, disavow, forswear, renege on. **2** *abjure worldly pleasures* give up, renounce, relinquish, abandon, forswear, forgo, forsake, abstain from, refrain from, reject, repudiate, eschew, abnegate; *inf.* kick, jack in, pack in.

ablaze *adjective* **1** *the house was ablaze* on fire, burning, blazing, alight, flaming; *lit.* afire, aflame. **2** *the house was ablaze with lights* lit up, alight, gleaming, glowing, aglow, illuminated, brilliant, radiant, shimmering, sparkling, flashing, incandescent. **3** *ablaze with excitement/anger* passionate, aroused, excited, stimulated, animated, impassioned, ardent, fervent, frenzied.

able *adjective* *an able pupil* competent, capable, talented, skilful, skilled, clever, intelligent, accomplished, gifted, proficient, apt, fit, expert, adept, efficient, effective, qualified, adroit.
Opposites INCOMPETENT; INCAPABLE; INEPT.

able-bodied *adjective* healthy, in good health, fit, robust, strong, sound, sturdy, vigorous, hardy, hale and hearty, muscular, strapping, tough, powerful, mighty, rugged, burly, stalwart, staunch; in good shape, in tip-top condition.
Opposites INFIRM; FRAIL; FEEBLE.

ablution *noun* *perform one's ablutions* washing, cleansing, bathing, showering, scrubbing, purification; wash, bath, shower; *fml.* lavage, lavation.

abnegation *noun* **1** *monks leading a life of abnegation/self-abnegation* renunciation, self-denial, self-sacrifice, resignation, abstinence, temperance. **2** *the abnegation of a doctrine* giving up, renunciation, denial, rejection, relinquishment, abdication.

abnormal *adjective* unusual, strange, odd, peculiar, uncommon, curious, queer, weird, eccentric, extraordinary, unexpected, exceptional, irregular, unnatural, erratic, singular, atypical, non-typical, anomalous, deviant, deviating, divergent, aberrant; *inf.* oddball; *Am. inf.* off the wall, wacko.
Opposites NORMAL; REGULAR; TYPICAL.

abnormality *noun* **1** *the abnormality of their behaviour* unusualness, strangeness, oddness, eccentricity, unexpectedness, irregularity, singularity, atypicality, anomalousness, deviation, divergence, aberrance, aberration. **2** *X-rays showing a physical abnormality* irregularity, malformation, deformity, anomaly, flaw, deviation, aberration.

abode *noun* *welcome to my humble abode* home, house, place of residence/habitation, dwelling-place, domicile, dwelling, habitat; accommodation, habitation; quarters, lodgings; *inf.* pad.

abolish *verb* do away with, put an end to, end, stop, terminate, axe, eliminate, eradicate, exterminate, destroy, annihilate, stamp out, obliterate, wipe out, extinguish, quash, expunge, extirpate, annul, cancel, invalidate, nullify, void, rescind, repeal, revoke, vitiate, abrogate.
Opposites KEEP; RETAIN; MAINTAIN.

abolition *noun* ending, termination, elimination, extermination, destruction, annihilation, obliteration, extirpation, annulment, cancellation, nullification, invalidation, rescindment, repeal, revocation, vitiation, abrogation.

abominable *adjective* hateful, loathsome, detestable, odious, obnoxious, base, despicable, contemptible, damnable, cursed, disgusting, revolting, repellent, repulsive, offensive, repugnant, abhorrent, reprehensible, foul, vile, wretched, horrible, nasty, disagreeable, unpleasant, execrable; *inf.* yucky, god-awful.

abominate *verb* detest, loathe, hate, abhor, dislike, feel aversion/revulsion to, shudder at, recoil from.

abomination *noun* **1** *regard with abomination* detestation, loathing, hatred, aversion, antipathy, repulsion, abhorrence, repugnance, disgust, distaste, dislike; *fml.* odium, execration. **2** *the child/building is an abomination* atrocity, disgrace, horror, obscenity, curse, torment, anathema, bugbear, bête noir.

aboriginal *adjective* indigenous, native, original, earliest, first, ancient, primitive, primeval, primordial, autochthonous, autochthonal, autochthonic.

abort *verb* **1** *abort a pregnancy/foetus* terminate. **2** *the expectant mother aborted* miscarry, have a miscarriage. **3** *abort a space mission* call off, halt, stop, end, terminate, axe, arrest, nullify. **4** *the space mission aborted* come to a halt, end, terminate, fail.

3

abortion noun **1** *she had an abortion* termination, miscarriage, foeticide. **2** *the mission was an abortion* failure, non-success, fiasco, misadventure, disappointment, defeat.

abortive adjective *an abortive attempt/plan* failed, unsuccessful, non-successful, vain, futile, useless, worthless, ineffective, ineffectual, fruitless, unproductive, unavailing.
Opposites SUCCESSFUL; PRODUCTIVE; FRUITFUL.

abound verb **1** *weeds abound around here* be plentiful, proliferate, superabound, thrive, flourish. **2** *a river abounding with/in fish* be full of, overflow with, teem with, be packed/crowded/thronged/jammed with, be alive, swarm with; *inf.* be crawling/lousy with.

about preposition **1** *talk about it* with reference to, referring to, with regard to, regarding, concerning, with respect to, respecting, relating to, on, touching on, dealing with, with relevance to, connected with; *inf.* re. **2** *somewhere about here* near, nearby, close to, adjacent to, beside, around. **3** *about ten o'clock* approximately, roughly, nearly, in the neighbourhood of. **4** *dancing about the maypole* round, around, encircling, surrounding. **5** *travelling about the world* round, throughout, over, all over, in all parts, through. **6** *when you're about it* occupied with, concerned with, busy with. **about to** *they're about to die* on the point of, on the verge/brink of, going to, ready to, preparing to, soon to, intending to.

about adverb **1** *running and jumping about* around, here and there, to and fro, from place to place, hither and thither. **2** *it costs about £10* approximately, roughly, nearly, in the neighbourhood/region of. **3** *she's somewhere about* around, near, nearby, about the place, in the vicinity, hereabouts. **4** *turn the ship about* in the reverse/opposite direction, into reverse, backwards. **5** *a lot of 'flu about* around, in circulation, going on, in existence, current, prevailing, prevalent, happening, in the air. **6** *just about enough* nearly, almost, not quite, scarcely, barely.

above preposition **1** *above the horizon* over, higher than, on top of; atop. **2** *the rank above captain* over, higher than, superior to. **3** *a temperature above the average* over, higher than, greater than, more than, exceeding, in excess of, over and above, surpassing. **4** *above suspicion* beyond, not subject/liable/open to, superior to. **5** *prize honour above life* in preference to, more than, rather than, before, in favour of. **6** *above the bridge* upstream from, northwards of, north from. **above oneself** conceited, proud, arrogant, self-important; *inf.* cocky, stuck-up, big-headed.
Opposites BELOW; UNDER; BENEATH.

above adverb **1** *on the shelf above* overhead, on/at the top, on/at a higher place, high up; *fml.* on high. **2** *as stated above* earlier, previously, before, formerly.

above adjective *the above reference* aforementioned, aforesaid, preceding, earlier, foregoing, previous, prior.

above-board adverb/adjective *the deal was made above-board | an above-board discussion* honest, fair, open, frank, straight, overt, candid, forthright, unconcealed, unequivocal.

abrasion noun **1** *skin abrasions* graze, scrape, scratch, sore, ulcer, chafe. **2** *the abrasion of the rock* erosion, wearing down/away, corrosion, chafing, rubbing, scraping, excoriation.

abrasive adjective **1** *an abrasive substance* erosive, eroding, corrosive, chafing, rubbing, coarse, harsh. **2** *an abrasive manner* caustic, cutting, grating, biting, rough, harsh, irritating, sharp, nasty.

abreast adverb **1** *running abreast* side by side, alongside, level, beside each other, shoulder to shoulder. **2** *keeping abreast of the news/changes* up-to-date with, up with, in touch with, familiar/acquainted with, informed/knowledgeable about, conversant with, *au courant* with, *au fait* with.

abridge verb shorten, cut down, condense, contract, compress, abbreviate, reduce, decrease, diminish, curtail, truncate, lessen, trim, summarize, abstract, epitomize, synopsize, digest.

abridgement, abridgment, noun **1** *prepare an abridgement of the report* summary, synopsis, précis, abstract, outline, résumé, shortening, digest. **2** *the abridgement of a novel* shortening, cutting, condensation, contraction, reduction, summarization. See ABRIDGE.

abroad adverb **1** *go abroad on holiday* overseas, out of the country, to/in foreign parts, to/in a foreign country/land, beyond the seas. **2** *spreading the rumour abroad* about, widely, far and wide, everywhere, publicly, extensively, at large, forth, in circulation, circulating.

abrogation noun repeal, annulment, cancellation, countermanding, reversal, withdrawal, revocation, retraction, abolition, ending, quashing, scrapping, invalidation, nullification, voiding, repudiation, rescission.

abrupt adjective **1** *an abrupt ending* sudden, quick, hurried, hasty, swift, rapid, precipitate, headlong, instantaneous, surprising, unexpected, unanticipated, unforeseen. **2** *an abrupt manner* curt, blunt, brusque, short, terse, brisk, crisp, gruff, snappish, unceremonious, rough, rude. **3** *an abrupt slope* steep, sheer, precipitous, sudden, sharp; *fml.* declivitous. **4** *an abrupt style of writing* jerky, uneven, irregular, disconnected, discontinuous, broken, rough, inelegant.
Opposites GRADUAL; UNHURRIED; SMOOTH.

abscess noun ulcer, ulceration, boil, pustule, carbuncle, pimple, papule.

abscond verb run away, bolt, clear out, flee, make off, escape, take flight, fly, decamp, disappear, slip/steal/sneak away, take to one's heels, make a quick getaway, beat a hasty retreat, show a clean pair of heels, run for it; *inf.* do a bunk, do a moonlight flit, cut and run, skedaddle, skip, do a runner.

absence noun **1** *the teacher noted their absence* non-attendance, non-appearance, truancy, absenteeism. **2** *in the absence of proof* lack, want, non-existence, unavailability, deficiency, omission, default, need, privation.
Opposites PRESENCE; ATTENDANCE.

absent *adjective* **1** *absent overseas | absent from school* away, off, out, gone, missing, truant, lacking, unavailable, non-existent, non-attendant. **2** *an absent expression* absent-minded, distracted, preoccupied, daydreaming, dreaming, far-away, blank, empty, vacant, inattentive, vague, absorbed, abstracted, musing, unheeding, wool-gathering, *distrait*.

absent-minded *adjective* *an absent-minded professor* distracted, preoccupied, absorbed, abstracted, vague, inattentive, forgetful, oblivious, in a brown study, *distrait*. *See* ABSENT 2.

absolute *adjective* **1** *absolute trust* complete, total, utter, out and out, outright, perfect, entire, undivided, unqualified, unadulterated, unalloyed, downright, undiluted, solid, consummate, unmitigated. **2** *the absolute truth* certain, positive, definite, unquestionable, undoubted, unequivocal, decisive, unconditional, categorical, conclusive, confirmed, infallible. **3** *an absolute standard* fixed, independent, non-relative, non-variable, rigid, established, set, definite. **4** *absolute power* unlimited, unrestricted, unrestrained, unbounded, boundless, infinite, ultimate, total, supreme, unconditional, full, utter, sovereign, omnipotent. **5** *absolute monarch* despotic, dictatorial, autocratic, tyrannical, authoritarian, arbitrary, autonomous, sovereign.
Opposites QUALIFIED; CONDITIONAL; LIMITED.

absolutely *adverb* **1** *absolutely correct* completely, totally, utterly, perfectly, entirely, wholly, fully, thoroughly. **2** *absolutely the worst driver* certainly, positively, definitely, unquestionably, undoubtedly, without a doubt, unequivocally, unconditionally, conclusively, unreservedly. **3** *absolutely pouring down* positively, actually, in actual fact, really, in truth. **4** *ruling absolutely* despotically, dictatorially, autocratically, tyrannically, arbitrarily, unrestrictedly, totally, supremely, unconditionally, utterly, omnipotently. *See* ABSOLUTE 4, 5.

absolutely *interjection* *are you going? absolutely!* certainly, yes, indeed, of course, positively, naturally, without doubt, unquestionably.

absolution *noun* forgiveness, pardoning, exoneration, freedom, liberation, deliverance, remission, dispensation, condoning, vindication, exculpation; pardon, acquittal, reprieve, discharge, amnesty, release, delivery.

absolve *verb* **1** *absolve them from blame* acquit, exonerate, discharge, release, free, deliver, liberate, let off, clear, exempt, exculpate. **2** *absolve repentant sinners* forgive, pardon, excuse, reprieve, give amnesty to, give dispensation/indulgence to, clear, set free, vindicate. *Opposites* BLAME; CHARGE; CONDEMN.

absorb *verb* **1** *absorb liquid* soak up, suck up, draw up/in, take up/in, blot up, mop, sponge up, sop up. **2** *absorb food* consume, devour, eat up, swallow, assimilate, digest, ingest. **3** *absorb smaller companies* take in, incorporate, assimilate, appropriate, co-opt; *derog.* swallow up. **4** *absorb them | absorb their attention* occupy, engage, preoccupy, captivate, engross, monopolize, rivet.

absorbed *adjective* *absorbed in a book* occupied with, taken up with/by, engaged in, preoccupied with, engrossed in, immersed in, captivated by, riveted by.

absorbent *adjective* absorptive, porous, spongy, spongelike, permeable, pervious, penetratable, assimilative, receptive, soaking, blotting, sorbefacient.

absorbing *adjective* *an absorbing book* fascinating, gripping, interesting, captivating, engrossing, riveting, spellbinding, intriguing.
Opposites BORING; UNINTERESTING; DULL.

absorption *noun* **1** *absorption of liquid* soaking up, sucking up. *See* ABSORB 1. **2** *absorption of food* consumption, devouring, assimilation, ingestion. *See* ABSORB 2. **3** *absorption of small companies* incorporation, assimilation, appropriation, co-opting. *See* ABSORB 3. **4** *absorption of their attention* occupying, engagement, engaging, preoccupation, engrossment, monopolization, riveting, intentness, raptness, involvement. *See* ABSORB 4.

abstain *verb* **1** *abstain from voting* refrain, decline, forbear, desist, hold back, keep from, refuse, renounce, avoid, shun, eschew. **2** *most voted but I abstained* decline/refuse to vote. **3** *the young people drink but the parents abstain* be teetotal, take the pledge; *inf.* be on the wagon. *Opposites* join in (*see* JOIN); VOTE; INDULGE.

abstemious *adjective* moderate, temperate, abstinent, self-denying, austere, sober, self-restrained, ascetic, puritanical, non-indulgent, self-abnegating.

abstention *noun* *abstention from voting* abstaining, refraining, forbearing; desistance, refusal, renunciation, self-control, self-denial.

abstinence *noun* **1** *practise total abstinence* teetotalism, temperance, sobriety, nephalism. *See* ABSTAIN 3. **2** *abstinence from pleasure* refraining, forbearing, desistance, renunciation. *See* ABSTAIN 1.

abstract *adjective* **1** *beauty is abstract* theoretical, conceptual, notional, intellectual, metaphysical, philosophical. **2** *abstract art* non-representational, non-realistic, unrealistic. **3** *abstract theories of cosmology* complex, abstruse, recondite, obscure, deep.
Opposites ACTUAL; CONCRETE.

abstract *noun* *an abstract of/from a scientific paper* summary, synopsis, précis, résumé, outline, abridgement, condensation, digest.

abstract *verb* **1** *abstract metal from ore* extract, remove, take out/away, separate, detach, draw away, isolate. **2** *abstract goods from the shop* steal, rob, thieve, appropriate, make off with, filch, purloin; *inf.* pinch, nick. **3** *abstract a book* abridge, summarize, précis, condense, compress, shorten, cut down, abbreviate, contract, synopsize.

abstracted *adjective* **1** *an abstracted expression* absent-minded, distracted, preoccupied, far-away, inattentive, thoughtful, pensive, musing, absorbed, wool-gathering, absent, *distrait*. **2** *an abstracted book* abridged, summarized, condensed, compressed, abbreviated. *See* ABSTRACT *verb* 3.

abstraction *noun* **1** *the abstraction of metal from ore* extraction, removal, separation, detachment. *See* ABSTRACT *verb* 1. **2** *lost in abstraction* absent-mindedness, distraction, pre-occupation, daydreaming, inattentiveness, thoughtfulness, absorption. *See* ABSTRACTED 1. **3** *facts rather than an abstraction* concept, gener-ality, generalization, idea, theory, hypothesis, supposition, notion, presumption.

abstruse *adjective* obscure, deep, profound, complex, hidden, esoteric, mysterious, incom-prehensible, unfathomable, inscrutable, enig-matic, perplexing, puzzling, recondite, arcane, nebulous.

absurd *adjective* ridiculous, foolish, silly, idi-otic, stupid, nonsensical, senseless, inane, crazy, ludicrous, funny, laughable, comical, preposterous, farcical, hare-brained, asinine; *inf.* daft.

absurdity *noun* **1** *the absurdity of the situation* ridiculousness, foolishness, silliness, idiocy, stupidity, inanity, folly, incongruity, irrational-ity, ludicrousness, funniness, comedy, humour, joke, farce. *See* ABSURD. **2** *talking absurdities* nonsense, foolishness, rubbish, twaddle, gibberish, drivel, balderdash; *inf.* clap-trap, bunk.

abundance *noun* plenty, plentifulness, profu-sion, copiousness, amplitude, affluence, lavish-ness, bountifulness; *inf.* heaps, bags, stacks, loads, tons, oodles.
Opposites LACK; SCARCITY.

abundant *adjective* plentiful, large, great, huge, ample, well-supplied, well-provided, pro-fuse, copious, lavish, bountiful, teeming, over-flowing; *inf.* galore.

abuse *verb* **1** *abuse power/alcohol* misuse, mis-apply, misemploy, mishandle, exploit. **2** *abuse children* mistreat, maltreat, ill-use, ill-treat, manhandle, injure, hurt, harm, beat, damage, wrong, oppress, torture. **3** *abusing trespassers* insult, swear at, curse, scold, rebuke, upbraid, reprove, castigate, inveigh against, revile, vil-ify, vituperate against, slander.

abuse *noun* **1** *the abuse of power | alcohol abuse* misuse, misapplication, misemployment, mis-handling, exploitation. **2** *child abuse* mistreat-ment, maltreatment, ill-use, ill-treatment, manhandling, injury, hurt, harm, beating, damage, wronging, oppression, torture. **3** *guilty of political abuse* corruption, wrong-doing, wrong, misconduct, misdeeds, offence, crime, fault, sin. **4** *torrents of abuse* swearing, cursing, scolding, rebuke, upbraiding, reproval, invective, castigation, revilement, vil-ification, vituperation, defamation, slander; insults, curses, expletives, swear-words.

abusive *adjective* *abusive remarks | becoming abu-sive* insulting, rude, blasphemous, offensive, vulgar, vituperative, reproachful, reproving, derisive, scornful, castigating, slanderous, defamatory, opprobrious, calumniating.

abut *verb* adjoin, border, verge on, join, touch, meet, impinge on.

abutting *adjective* adjacent, next to, neigh-bouring, adjoining, contiguous, bordering, verging, joining, touching, meeting.

abysmal *adjective* *abysmal ignorance/poverty* extreme, utter, complete, thorough, profound, deep, endless, immeasurable, boundless, incal-culable, unfathomable, bottomless.

abyss *noun* **1** *a yawning abyss* chasm, gorge, cavity, void, pit, bottomless pit, hole, gulf, depth, ravine, canyon, crevasse. **2** *the abyss of despair* chasm, void, bottomless pit, hell, hell-hole; depths.

academic *adjective* **1** *academic considerations* educational, scholastic, instructional, pedagog-ical. **2** *of an academic turn of mind* scholarly, studious, literary, well-read, intellectual, eru-dite, learned, cultured, bookish, high-brow, pedantic, donnish, cerebral; *inf.* brainy. **3** *an academic rather than a practical solution* theoreti-cal, hypothetical, abstract, conjectural, notional, impractical, unrealistic, speculative, ivory-towerish.

academic *noun* scholar, lecturer, don, teacher, tutor, professor, fellow, bluestocking, book-worm, egghead, pedant, pedagogue.

accede *verb* **1** *accede to the request* agree to, consent to, accept, assent, acquiesce, endorse, comply with, go along with, concur, grant, yield to. **2** *accede to the throne* succeed to, assume, attain, come to, inherit.

accelerate *verb* **1** *the car accelerated* speed up, go faster, pick up speed; *inf.* open up. **2** *the process accelerated* speed up, go faster, hasten, hurry, quicken, advance rapidly. **3** *accelerate the process* speed up, hasten, quicken, expedite, step up, advance, forward, further, spur on, facilitate, precipitate, stimulate.
Opposites DECELERATE; slow down (*see* SLOW); DELAY.

acceleration *noun* **1** *the acceleration of the car* increased speed, speeding up; *inf.* opening up. **2** *the acceleration of the process* speeding up, has-tening, quickening, expedition, stepping up, advancement, forwarding, facilitation, precipi-tation, stimulation. *See* ACCELERATE 3.

accent *noun* **1** *a Scottish accent* pronunciation, intonation, enunciation, articulation, inflec-tion, tone, modulation, utterance. **2** *the accent on the first syllable* stress, emphasis, accentua-tion, force, beat, prominence; primary stress, secondary stress. **3** *the accent on comfort* emphasis, stress, prominence, importance, accentuation, priority, underlining, underscor-ing. **4** *an acute accent | an accent on the e* accent mark, mark, diacritic, diacritical mark, sign. *See table.*

ACCENTS AND DIACRITICAL MARKS	
acute	háček
breve	hamza
cedilla	macron
circumflex	tilde
diaeresis	umlaut
grave	

accent *verb* **1** *accent the first syllable* stress, put/ lay the stress on, emphasize, put/lay the emphasis on, put the force on, accentuate.

2 *accent the advantages* accentuate, emphasize, highlight, underline, draw attention. *See* ACCENTUATE 1.

accentuate *verb* **1** *the black dress accentuated her paleness* emphasize, stress, highlight, underline, draw attention to, give prominence to, heighten, point up, underscore, accent.
2 *accentuate the pulse of the music* stress, put the stress/emphasis on, emphasize, accent. *See* ACCENT *verb* 1.

accept *verb* **1** *accept the award* receive, take, take receipt of, get, gain, obtain, acquire, come by. **2** *accept the decision* accede to, agree to, consent to, acquiesce in, concur with, endorse, comply with, go along with, defer to, put up with, recognize, acknowledge, cooperate with, adopt, admit. **3** *accept the responsibility/project* take on, undertake, assume, bear, tackle, be responsible for. **4** *accept their story | accept what they say* believe, trust, credit, be convinced of, have faith in, count/rely on. **5** *never accepted as one of the family* welcome, receive, receive favourably, embrace, offer friendship to, integrate. **6** *accept the invitation* say yes to, reply in the affirmative, comply with.
Opposites REFUSE; REJECT; DENY.

acceptable *adjective* **1** *an acceptable present* welcome, agreeable, delightful, pleasing, desirable, satisfying, gratifying. **2** *a standard of work not acceptable* satisfactory, good enough, adequate, passable, admissible, tolerable.
3 *an acceptable risk* allowable, tolerable, admissible, bearable, supportable.
Opposites UNACCEPTABLE; unsatisfactory; UNDESIRABLE.

acceptance *noun* **1** *the acceptance of an award* receipt, receiving, taking, obtaining, acquiring. *See* ACCEPT 1. **2** *the acceptance of a decision* accedence, accession, acquiescence, endorsement, recognition, acknowledgement, adoption, admission. *See* ACCEPT 2. **3** *the acceptance of responsibility* undertaking, assumption, tackling, adoption. *See* ACCEPT 3. **4** *the acceptance of their story | acceptance of what they said* belief in, trust in, faith in, credibility, reliance on. *See* ACCEPT 4. **5** *acceptance as one of the family* welcome, welcoming, favourable reception, embracing, integration, approval, adoption. *See* ACCEPT 5. **6** *acceptances to an invitation* yes, affirmative reply, affirmation, confirmation, ratification.

accepted *adjective* **1** *an accepted opinion* approved, recognized, sanctioned, authorized, received, allowable, acceptable. **2** *the accepted manner of behaving* usual, customary, normal, expected, standard, conventional, recognized, acknowledged, established, traditional, confirmed.

access *noun* **1** *a building with a rear access | access to the building* entry, entrance, way in, means of entry/entrance; admittance, admission; approachability, accessibility; approach, means of approach; gateway, driveway, road, path, avenue, passage. **2** *access to the prison/ prisoner | access to secret information* admission, admittance, entrée, right of entry, permission/ opportunity to enter/reach/use; accessibility,

attainability. **3** *an access of anger* fit, outburst, attack, paroxysm, onset.

access *verb* *access the data/information* gain access to, retrieve, gain, acquire.

accessibility *noun* **1** *the accessibility of sources of entertainment* attainability, reachability, availability, approachability, achievability. *See* ACCESSIBLE 1. **2** *accessibility of the manager to the staff* approachability, availability, informality, friendliness, agreeableness, congeniality, affability, cordiality. *See* ACCESSIBLE 2. **3** *accessibility of information* comprehensibility, intelligibility, penetrability. *See* ACCESSIBLE 3.

accessible *noun* **1** *an accessible source of entertainment* attainable, reachable, available, approachable, obtainable, achievable; *inf.* get-at-able. **2** *accessible to the staff* approachable by, available, easygoing, informal, friendly, pleasant, agreeable, obliging, congenial, affable, cordial. **3** *accessible information* understandable, comprehensible, intelligible, penetrable, fathomable, graspable.
Opposites INACCESSIBLE; UNAPPROACHABLE.

accession *noun* **1** *accession to the throne/title* succession, inheritance. *See* ACCEDE 2. **2** *accession to the request/treaty* agreement, consent, acceptance, acquiescence. *See* ACCEDE 1. **3** *a recent accession to the museum collection* addition, increase, augmentation, increment, gain, enlargement, expansion, extension.

accessory *noun* **1** *his accessories in the raid* accomplice, associate, confederate, abettor, helper, assistant, partner. **2** *bicycle accessories* attachment, fitment, extra, addition, adjunct, appendage, supplement. **3** *accessories matching her outfit* adornment, finery, trimming, ornament, ornamentation, embellishment, trappings, fashion detail, frill; handbag, shoes, gloves, hat, belt, ribbon.

accessory *adjective* *an accessory part/factor* additional, extra, supplementary, contributory, subsidiary, ancillary, auxiliary, secondary, assisting.

accident *noun* **1** *an accident at work | an industrial accident* mishap, casualty, misfortune, misadventure, injury, disaster, tragedy, blow, catastrophe, calamity. **2** *the police were called to an accident* crash, collision; *inf.* smash, smash-up, pile-up. **3** *met by accident* chance, mere chance, fate, twist of fate, fortune, good fortune, luck, good luck, fortuity, hazard; *inf.* fluke.

accidental *adjective* **1** *accidental death | an accidental meeting* chance, occurring by chance/ accident, unintentional, unintended, inadvertent, unexpected, unforeseen, unlooked-for, fortuitous, unanticipated, unplanned, uncalculated, unpremeditated, unwitting, adventitious. **2** *an accidental consideration* non-essential, inessential, incidental, extraneous, extrinsic, supplementary, subsidiary, subordinate, secondary, accessory, irrelevant.
Opposites INTENTIONAL; CALCULATED.

accidentally *adverb* *killed/met accidentally* by accident, by chance, unintentionally, inadvertently, without design, unexpectedly, adventi-

tiously, unwittingly; *inf.* by a fluke. *See* ACCIDEN-
TAL 1.

acclaim *verb* **1** *acclaim his victory* applaud,
cheer, celebrate, salute, welcome, approve,
honour, praise, commend, hail, extol, laud,
eulogize, exalt. **2** *acclaim her queen* declare,
announce, proclaim, hail.

acclaim *noun returning to the acclaim of the crowd*
applause, ovation, praise, commendation,
approval, approbation, homage, tribute, extolment, laudation; cheers, congratulations, plaudits, bouquets, salutes, eulogies.

acclamation *noun* **1** *acknowledge the acclama-
tions of the crowd* applause, ovation, praise, salutation, welcome, homage, tribute, approval;
cheers, congratulations, plaudits. *See* ACCLAIM
noun. **2** *the acclamation of her as queen* declaration, announcement, proclamation, hailing.
3 *elected by acclamation* shouting, calling out,
oral vote, non-ballot; shouts.

acclimatization *noun acclimatization to the
heat* | *acclimatization to new conditions* adjust-
ment, adaptation, habituation, accommodation, familiarization, inurement,
naturalization, acclimation, acculturation.

acclimatize *verb acclimatize to tropical conditions*
adjust, adapt, accustom, get used, accommodate, accustom/habituate oneself, become seasoned, familiarize oneself, become inured,
become naturalized.

accommodate *verb* **1** *we can accommodate four
people* put up, house, cater for, board, lodge,
provide shelter for, shelter, provide with a
roof, harbour, billet. **2** *accommodate oneself to
new circumstances* | *accommodate our plans to suit
yours* adapt, adjust, modify, reconcile, fit, harmonize, conform. **3** *accommodate you with a
loan* provide, supply, furnish, serve, grant.
4 *accommodate them whenever possible* help,
assist, aid, lend a hand to, oblige, meet the
needs/wants of, do a favour to, favour, indulge.

accommodating *adjective an accommodating
person/attitude* obliging, cooperative, helpful,
adaptable, pliable, compliant, complaisant,
considerate, unselfish, willing, polite, kindly,
hospitable, kind, friendly, agreeable.

accommodation *noun* **1** *provide accommoda-
tion for four* | *do you have accommodation?* hous-
ing, lodging, board, shelter; place of residence,
house, billet; lodgings, quarters; *inf.* digs.
2 *the accommodation to new circumstances* | *accom-
modation of our plans to suit yours* adaptation,
adjustment, modification, reconciliation, fitting, harmonization. *See* ACCOMMODATE 2. **3** *the
accommodation of the firm with a loan* provision,
supply, supplying, furnishing, serving. *See*
ACCOMMODATE 3. **4** *the accommodation of the
younger members* help, assistance, aid, obliging,
favouring, indulgence. *See* ACCOMMODATE 4.

accompaniment *noun* **1** *the accompaniment of
speech with/by gestures* coexistence, coincidence,
concurrence, supplement. **2** *a musical accompaniment* backup, support, background, obbligato. **3** *salad as an accompaniment* supplement,
addition, adjunct, appendage, complement.

accompany *verb* **1** *accompany her to the dance*
escort, go with, go along with, keep company,

squire, attend on, usher, conduct, convoy,
chaperon. **2** *meat accompanied by vegetables* |
speech accompanied with gestures go with, go
along with, go together with, coexist/occur/
coincide with, supplement. **3** *accompany them
on the piano* play a musical accompaniment,
play with/for, back up, support.

accomplice *noun* confederate, accessory, collaborator, abettor, associate, partner, ally,
assistant, helper, aider, henchman, right hand,
right-hand man, fellow-conspirator, mate,
friend; *inf.* sidekick.

accomplish *verb* **1** *accomplish an aim* achieve,
carry out, fulfil, perform, attain, realize, succeed in, bring off, bring about, effect, execute,
effectuate. **2** *accomplish a task* finish, complete, carry through, do, perform, conclude,
effect, execute, consummate.
Opposites FAIL; give up (*see* GIVE).

accomplished *adjective* **1** *an accomplished
player* skilled, skilful, expert, gifted, talented,
proficient, adept, masterly, polished, practised,
capable, able, competent, experienced, professional, deft, consummate. **2** *an accomplished
aim* achieved, fulfilled, realized. *See* ACCOMPLISH
1. **3** *an accomplished task* finished, completed,
executed. *See* ACCOMPLISH 2.

accomplishment *noun* **1** *a woman of accom-
plishment* | *proud of her social accomplishments*
talent, ability, skill, gift, attainment, achievement, capability, proficiency. **2** *the army's
proud accomplishments* achievement, act, deed,
exploit, performance, attainment, feat, coup,
triumph. **3** *the accomplishment of aims* achievement, fulfilment, attainment, realization, success, effecting, execution. *See* ACCOMPLISH 1.
4 *the accomplishment of tasks* finishing, completion, performance, conclusion, execution, consummation. *See* ACCOMPLISH 2.

accord *verb* **1** *his statement does not accord with
hers* agree, concur, fit, correspond, tally,
match, conform, harmonize, suit, be in tune.
2 *accord them permission* | *accord a welcome* give,
grant, confer, bestow, tender, offer, present,
award, vouchsafe, concede.
Opposites DISAGREE; CONTRAST; WITHHOLD.

accord *noun accord between former enemies* | *in
accord with our plans* agreement, harmony, rapport, unison, concord, amity, sympathy, unanimity, accordance. **of one's own accord**
leaving of their own accord of one's own free will,
voluntarily, willingly, freely, unforced. **with
one accord** unanimously, in complete agreement, with one mind, of one voice, unitedly,
concertedly.

accordance *noun* **1** *the accordance of
permission* | *the accordance of a welcome* granting,
conferring, bestowal, tendering. *See* ACCORD
verb 2. **2** *accordance between opponents* accord,
agreement, harmony, concord, rapport. *See*
ACCORD *noun.* **3** *acting in accordance with their
wishes* agreement conformity, compliance.

according *adjective* **according to 1** *according
to the manager* as stated/maintained by, as
claimed by, on the authority of, on the report
of. **2** *acting according to their principles* in accordance with, in agreement with, in line with, in

keeping with, in compliance with, in harmony with, in conformity with, in obedience to, following, after. **3** *salary according to experience* in proportion to, commensurate with, in relation to.

accordingly *adverb* **1** *you know the truth and must act accordingly* appropriately, correspondingly, suitably, properly, fitly, consistently. **2** *they could not pay the rent and accordingly left* as a result, consequently, therefore, so, thus, as a consequence, in consequence, hence, *ergo*.

accost *verb* **1** *the police accosted him in the street* address, speak to, confront, approach, greet, hail, salute; *inf.* buttonhole. **2** *accosted by a prostitute* solicit, importune.

account *noun* **1** *a full account of the accident* statement, report, description, record, narration, narrative, story, recital, explanation, tale, chronicle, history, relation, version. **2** *pay their accounts on time* bill, invoice, reckoning, tally; charges, debts. **3** *accounts with several banks* bank account; current account, deposit account, savings account. **4** *the firm's accounts are in good order* ledger, balance sheet, financial statement; books. **5** *a person/matter of no account* importance, consequence, significance. **on account of** because of, owing to, on grounds of. **on no account** not under any circumstances, under no circumstances, certainly not, absolutely not, in any event.

account *verb* *they are accounted guilty | account her to be guilty* consider, regard, reckon, believe, think, look upon, view as, judge, count, deem. **account for** **1** *they must account for the delay* explain, explain away, give reasons for, show grounds for, justify, elucidate. **2** *oil accounts for most of their exports* be responsible for, make up, supply, provide, give. **3** *the army accounted for hundreds of terrorists* kill, destroy, put out of action, incapacitate.

accountability *noun* **1** *the accountability of the police for their actions* responsibility, answerability, liability. *See* ACCOUNTABLE 1. **2** *their accountability to the manager* responsibility, answerability, reporting, obedience. *See* ACCOUNTABLE 2. **3** *the accountability of his actions* explicability, comprehensibility, intelligibility.

accountable *adjective* **1** *accountable for one's actions* responsible, answerable, liable, chargeable. **2** *accountable to the manager* responsible, answerable, reporting to, under the charge of, obeying. **3** *his actions are not accountable* explicable, explainable, understandable, comprehensible, intelligible.

accoutrements *plural noun* equipment, gear, tackle, paraphernalia, apparatus, adornment, ornamentation; trappings, appurtenances, furnishings, appointments, fittings; *inf.* things, bits and pieces.

accredit *verb* **1** *accredited with the invention* credit with, have ascribed/attributed to, receive the credit for. **2** *accredited to Shakespeare* ascribe, attribute.

accredited *adjective* **1** *our accredited representative* official, authorized, legal, appointed, approved, recognized, certified, sanctioned. **2** *accredited theories* accepted, recognized,

believed, endorsed, orthodox. **3** *an accredited herd* certified, attested, licensed.

accrue *verb* **1** *bank interest accrued* accumulate, build/mount up, amass, collect, gather, grow, increase, augment. **2** *medical advances accrued from the new technology* arise, follow, ensue, result/emanate from.

accumulate *verb* **1** *dust accumulated over the weeks* gather, pile/build up, collect, amass, increase, augment, cumulate, accrue. **2** *accumulate money/books* amass, gather, collect, stockpile, pile/heap up, store, hoard, cumulate.

accumulation *noun* **1** *an accumulation of rubbish/money* stockpile, pile, heap, mass, collection, build-up, gathering, stock, store, hoard, stack, cumulation, accrual, aggregation. **2** *the accumulation of piles of dust | the accumulation of his collection of coins* gathering, collection, amassing, building up, stockpiling, cumulation, accrual. *See* ACCUMULATE.

accuracy *noun* **1** *the accuracy of the statistics* correctness, precision, exactness, rightness, validity. *See* ACCURATE 1. **2** *the accuracy of the description | say with any accuracy* correctness, exactness, closeness, faithfulness, truth, authenticity, veracity. *See* ACCURATE 2. **3** *the accuracy of the aim* precision, carefulness, meticulousness. *See* ACCURATE 3.

accurate *adjective* **1** *accurate statistics* correct, precise, exact, right, errorless, without error, valid; *inf.* spot on, bang on. **2** *an accurate description* correct, exact, close, faithful, true, truthful, authentic, factual, literal, veracious, strict. **3** *take accurate aim* precise, careful, meticulous, painstaking.
Opposites INACCURATE; INEXACT.

accursed *adjective* **1** *that accursed noise | those accursed money-lenders* hateful, detestable, despicable, horrible, foul, abominable, odious, obnoxious, execrable; *inf.* yucky. **2** *the witch and her accursed victims* under a curse, cursed, curse-laden, bewitched, bedevilled, damned, doomed, ill-fated, wretched, blighted.

accusation *noun* *deny the accusation* charge, allegation, attribution, incrimination, imputation, denouncement, indictment, arraignment, impeachment, citation, inculpation, blame.

accuse *verb* **1** *in court accused of murder* charge, indict, arraign, impeach, summon, cite, inculpate. **2** *accuse her of tearing the curtain* blame for, lay the blame on, hold responsible/accountable/answerable, impute blame to; *inf.* lay at the door of, stick on.
Opposites ABSOLVE; EXONERATE; DEFEND.

accustom *verb* *accustom herself to the new situation* adapt, adjust, acclimatize, get used to, make familiar/acquainted with, habituate.

accustomed *adjective* **1** *his accustomed style* usual, normal, customary, habitual, regular, routine, ordinary, fixed, set, typical, established, common, general. **2** *accustomed to public speaking | accustomed to the situation* used to, familiar/acquainted with, adapted, adjusted, habituated, inured.

ace *noun a tennis ace* expert, champion, master, star, winner, genius, virtuoso, adept; *inf.* wizard, dab hand, hotshot, whiz.

ace *adjective an ace player* expert, champion, brilliant, great, superb, outstanding, excellent, first-rate, fine, skilful, adept; *inf.* crack, A1, tiptop, hotshot.

acerbic *adjective* **1** *an acerbic wit/tone* harsh, sarcastic, sharp, biting, stinging, caustic, trenchant, bitter, astringent, vitriolic, virulent, mordant. **2** *an acerbic taste* sour, tart, bitter, acid, sharp, acrid, acidulous, pungent.

ache *noun* **1** *an ache in my back* pain, dull pain, soreness; pang, throb, twinge, smarting, gnawing, stabbing, spasm; suffering. **2** *an ache in my heart* suffering, sorrow, misery, distress, grief, anguish, affliction, woe, mourning. **3** *feel an ache for old times* longing, yearning, craving, desire, hunger, hungering, pining, hankering.

ache *verb* **1** *my head aches* hurt, be sore, be painful, be in pain, pain; throb, pound, twinge, smart, gnaw. **2** *my heart aches* grieve, be sorrowful, be distressed, be in distress, be miserable, mourn, agonize, suffer. **3** *she aches for sunshine* long for, yearn for, crave, desire, hunger for, pine for, hanker for/after, covet.

achieve *verb* **1** *achieve success* attain, reach, arrive at, gain, earn, realize, win, acquire, obtain, procure, get, wrest. **2** *achieve all the tasks begun* complete, finish, accomplish, carry through, fulfil, execute, conclude, perform, effect, consummate.

achievement *noun* **1** *the achievement of success/objectives* attainment, gaining, realization, acquiral, procurement. See ACHIEVE 1. **2** *the achievement of tasks begun* completion, finishing, accomplishment, fulfilment, execution, conclusion, consummation. See ACHIEVE 2. **3** *proud of their child's achievement* accomplishment, feat, performance, act, action, deed, effort, exploit.

acid *adjective* **1** *an acid taste/fruit* sour, tart, bitter, sharp, biting, acrid, pungent, acerbic, vinegary, vinegarish, acetic, acetous, acidulous. See ACERBIC 2. **2** *an acid wit/reply* acerbic, sarcastic, sharp, caustic, trenchant, vitriolic, mordant. See ACERBIC 1.

acid *noun.* See table.

TYPES OF ACID

amino acid	mineral acid
carboxylic acid	monobasic acid
dibasic acid	nucleic acid
fatty acid	organic acid
Lewis acid	tribasic acid

acknowledge *verb* **1** *acknowledge the need for reform* admit, grant, allow, recognize, accept, subscribe to, approve, agree to, acquiesce in, concede. **2** *acknowledge him with a wave* greet, salute, address, hail, recognize, notice. **3** *acknowledge a letter* answer, reply to, respond to, react to. **4** *acknowledge help* show appreciation for/of, express gratitude for, give thanks for, thank.

acknowledged *adjective the acknowledged leader* admitted, recognized, accepted, approved, accredited, declared, avowed.

acknowledgement *noun* **1** *the acknowledgement of the need for reform* admission, granting, recognition, acceptance, approval, agreement, acquiescence. See ACKNOWLEDGE 1. **2** *the acknowledgement of his presence with a wave* greeting, saluting, recognition, notice. See ACKNOWLEDGE 2. **3** *the acknowledgement of a letter | an acknowledgement* answering, answer, reply, response, reaction. See ACKNOWLEDGE 3. **4** *the/an acknowledgement of help* expression of appreciation/gratitude, thanks. See ACKNOWLEDGE 4.

acme *noun* peak, pinnacle, zenith, climax, culmination, height, high point, crown, summit, optimum, apex.
Opposites NADIR; BOTTOM.

acolyte *noun* assistant, helper, attendant, follower.

acquaint *verb acquaint oneself/you with the facts* familiarize, make familiar/conversant, make known to, make aware of, advise of, inform, apprise of, enlighten, let know.

acquaintance *noun* **1** *an acquaintance, not a close friend* associate, colleague, contact; *fml.* confrère. **2** *our acquaintance with them* association, relationship, contact, social contact, fellowship, companionship. **3** *have some acquaintance with his poetry* familiarity, knowledge, awareness, understanding, cognizance.

acquainted *adjective* **1** *acquainted with his poems* familiar with, conversant with, well versed in, knowledgeable in, cognizant in, apprised of, instructed in. **2** *acquainted with the mayor* known to, on friendly terms with, friendly with, on a sociable footing with.

acquiesce *verb* consent, agree, accept, concur, approve, assent, allow, comply, conform, concede, go along with, bow to, yield.

acquiescence *noun* consent, agreement, acceptance, concurrence, approval, assent, compliance, conforming, conceding, concession, yielding. See ACQUIESCE.

acquiescent *adjective* **1** *their response was acquiescent rather than disapproving* consenting, concurrent, compliant, concessionary. See ACQUIESCE. **2** *an acquiescent personality/attitude* submissive, servile, subservient, obsequious, ingratiating, toadying, Uriah Heepish, self-effacing; *inf.* bootlicking.

acquire *verb* obtain, come by, get, receive, gain, procure, earn, win, secure, take possession of, gather, collect, pick up, achieve, attain, appropriate, amass.

acquirement *noun* **1** *acquirements are as important as natural talent* attainment, achievement, accomplishment, skill, qualification. **2** *the acquirement of money* acquisition, obtaining, procurement, collecting, collection, achievement, attainment, appropriation. See ACQUIRE.

acquisition *noun* **1** *the library's/museum's recent acquisitions* gain, purchase, buy, possession, accession, addition; accretion, property. **2** *the acquisition of money* obtaining, procurement, collecting, attainment, appropriation. *See* ACQUIREMENT 2.

acquisitive *adjective* greedy, grasping, covetous, avaricious, predatory, avid, rapacious, mercenary.

acquisitiveness *noun* greed, covetousness, avarice, avidity, rapaciousness, rapacity. *See* ACQUISITIVE.

acquit *verb* **1** *acquit the accused of the offence* clear, absolve, exonerate, discharge, release, vindicate, liberate, free, deliver; *fml.* exculpate. **2** *they acquitted themselves well/badly* perform, act, behave, conduct oneself, comport oneself, bear oneself. **3** *acquit oneself of the task/duty* perform, discharge, execute, accomplish, carry out, effect.
Opposites CONVICT; find guilty; BLAME.

acquittal *noun* **1** *the acquittal of the accused* clearing, absolution, exoneration, discharge, release, vindication, liberation, deliverance; *fml.* exculpation. **2** *the acquittal of the task/duty* performance, discharge, execution, accomplishment. *See* ACQUIT 3.

acrid *adjective* **1** *an acrid taste/smell* pungent, sharp, sour, bitter, tart, harsh, acid, stinging, burning, irritating, vinegary, acerbic, acetic, acetous. **2** *an acrid wit/remark* acerbic, sarcastic, sharp, stinging, caustic, astringent, trenchant, vitriolic, virulent. *See* ACERBIC 1.

acrimonious *adjective* *an acrimonious attitude/remark* bitter, caustic, cutting, sarcastic, harsh, sharp, acid, acerbic, virulent, trenchant, stringent, spiteful, crabbed, vitriolic, venomous, irascible.

acrimony *noun* bitterness, causticity, sarcasm, harshness, sharpness, acidity, acerbicity, virulence, trenchancy, stringency, spitefulness, crabbedness, irascibility. *See* ACRIMONIOUS.

acrobatics *plural noun* **1** *acrobatics in the circus ring* gymnastics, gymnastic feats/skills; agility, skill. **2** *mental acrobatics* agility, skill, quick thinking.

act *noun* **1** *a daring/shameful act | acts of bravery/cowardice* deed, action, feat, performance, undertaking, operation, execution, exploit, enterprise, achievement, accomplishment. **2** *acts of parliament* bill, law, decree, statute, edict, dictum, enactment, resolution, ruling, judgement, ordinance, measure. **3** *an act of a play* division, part, section, segment. **4** *a music hall act* performance, turn, routine, show, sketch, skit. **5** *putting on an act | it's just an act* pretence, sham, fake, make-believe, show, feigning, affectation, counterfeit, front, posture, pose, dissimulation, dissemblance.

act *verb* **1** *you must act now | act wisely* take action, do, move, be active, perform, function, react, behave, be employed, be busy. **2** *the painkiller will act soon* work, take effect, operate, function, be efficacious. **3** *she's acting in a Shakespeare play* perform, play, play a part, be an actor/actress, be one of the cast; *inf.* tread the boards. **4** *he's acting the part of Lear* perform, play, portray, enact, represent, characterize, personify, stage. **5** *he's not ill but just acting* pretend, sham, fake, feign, put it on, dissemble, pose, dissimulate. **act for** *act for his sick father* represent, stand/fill in for, deputize/cover/substitute for, replace, take the place of, act in place of. **act on/upon** **1** *alcohol acts on the brain* affect, have an effect on, influence, alter, change, modify, transform. **2** *act on official instructions* act in accordance with, follow, obey, comply with, take heed/notice of, heed, conform to. **act up** *my car/child is acting up* misbehave, give/cause trouble, malfunction; *inf.* play up.

acting *noun* **1** *she wants to go in for acting* theatre, drama, the performing arts, dramatics, stagecraft, theatricals, performing, portraying. **2** *acting now will save trouble* taking action, moving, functioning, reacting. *See* ACT *verb* 1. **3** *the quick acting of the pills* action, working, taking effect. *See* ACT *verb* 2. **4** *the acting of the part of Lear* performance, playing, portrayal, enacting. *See* ACT *verb* 4. **5** *his acting is sometimes taken as real illness* pretending, pretence, play-acting, shamming, posturing, dissimulation. *See* ACT *verb* 5.

acting *adjective* *an acting head of department* deputy, substitute, temporary, interim, provisional, pro tem, *pro tempore*; *inf.* fill-in.

action *noun* **1** *their prompt action saved lives* act, deed, move, effort, operation, performance, undertaking, manoeuvre, endeavour, exertion, exploit. **2** *time for action | put ideas into action* acting, activity, doing, movement, motion, operating, operation, work, working, functioning, performance, effort, exertion. **3** *men of action* activity, energy, vitality, vigour, forcefulness, spirit, liveliness, vim; *inf.* get-up-and-go. **4** *the action of acid on metal* effect, influence, power, result, consequence. **5** *the action of the play is set in Spain* activity; events, happenings, incidents, episodes. **6** *a piece of the action | miss the action* activity, excitement, bustle; happenings, incidents; *inf.* goings-on. **7** *soldiers seeing action overseas* conflict, combat, warfare, fighting, battle. **8** *the military action at Ypres* battle, fighting, engagement, clash, encounter, skirmish, affray. **9** *raise an action* lawsuit, case, prosecution, litigation; legal proceedings.

actions *plural noun* *a man is judged by his actions, not his beliefs* behaviour, conduct, activity, comportment, deportment; ways.

activate *verb* **1** *activate the alarm system* switch on, turn on, start off, set going, trigger off, set in motion, actuate, energize. **2** *activated by envy* actuate, motivate, stimulate, move, drive, rouse, prompt. *See* ACTUATE 1.

active *adjective* **1** *an active member of the team | an active volcano* working, functioning, operating, operative, in action, in operation, in force, effective. **2** *active people | old people leading active lives* mobile, energetic, vigorous, vital, sprightly, lively, spry, busy, bustling, occupied, involved; *inf.* on the go/move; *Am. inf.* go-go. **3** *the active ingredients* effective, effectual, operational, powerful, potent, non-passive, non-inert.
Opposites INACTIVE; DORMANT; INERT.

activity *noun* **1** *markets are places of great activity* business, bustle, hustle and bustle, liveliness, movement, life, stir, animation, commotion, flurry, tumult; *inf.* toing and fro-ing, comings and goings. **2** *schoolwork and outside activities* interest, hobby, pastime, pursuit, occupation, venture, undertaking, enterprise, project, scheme. **3** *return to activity after being ill* functioning, mobility, effectiveness, vigour, strength, potency.

actor, actress *noun* performer, player, dramatic artist, Thespian; stage performer/player, play actor, film actor, film star, starlet, leading man/woman, trouper, tragedian. *See table. See also table at* FILM STAR.

actual *adjective* *her actual words | the actual cost* real, true, factual, genuine, authentic, verified, confirmed, veritable, existing.

actually *adverb* **1** *he's actually brilliant rather than stupid | actually, he's very clever* really, in fact, in point of fact, as a matter of fact, in reality, indeed, truly, in truth. **2** *she was actually expected to lie* literally, even, in reality.

actuate *verb* **1** *people actuated by greed* motivate, stimulate, move, drive, rouse, arouse, prompt, influence, impel, incite, spur on, urge, goad, animate, excite, kindle, awaken, activate. **2** *actuate an electrical device* activate, start off, trigger off. *See* ACTIVATE 2.

acumen *noun* *showing business acumen* astuteness, shrewdness, sharpness, cleverness, smartness, judgement, discernment, wisdom, perspicacity, ingenuity, insight, perspicuity, sagacity, penetration.

acute *adjective* **1** *an acute sense of hearing* sharp, keen, penetrating, discerning, sensitive, incisive. **2** *an acute mind/analysis* astute, shrewd, sharp, clever, smart, discerning, perceptive, perspicacious, penetrating, incisive, piercing, discriminating, sagacious, judicious. **3** *an acute shortage of food* severe, critical, crucial, grave, serious, urgent, pressing, vital, dangerous, precarious. **4** *an acute pain* sharp, shooting, piercing, keen, penetrating, stabbing, intense, excruciating, fierce, racking; *fml.*

exquisite. **5** *an acute illness* intense, severe, short and sharp, short-lasting.
Opposites DULL; CHRONIC.

acutely *adverb* *acutely conscious of his poverty* very, markedly, extremely, intensely, deeply, profoundly, keenly, sharply, painfully.

adage *noun* *as the old adage has it* saying, maxim, axiom, proverb, aphorism, saw, dictum, precept, truism, platitude; *fml.* apophthegm, gnome.

adamant *adjective* resolute, determined, firm, immovable, unshakable, uncompromising, unrelenting, unyielding, unbending, inflexible, obdurate, inexorable, intransigent.

adapt *verb* **1** *adapt a dress/novel | adapt one's way of life* adjust, tailor, convert, change, alter, modify, transform, remodel, reshape. **2** *you must adapt to the new environment* adjust, conform, acclimatize, accommodate, familiarize oneself with, habituate oneself.

adaptable *adjective* **1** *an adaptable dress | an adaptable way of life* adjustable, convertible, alterable, modifiable, variable, versatile. **2** *you must try to be adaptable* adjustable, flexible, pliant, compliant, malleable, versatile, resilient, easygoing, conformable.

adaptation *noun* **1** *the adaptation of a dress/novel* adjustment, tailoring, converting, alteration, changing, modification, remodelling. *See* ADAPT 1. **2** *the adaptation to a new environment* adjustment, conformity, acclimatization, accommodation, familiarization, habituation.

add *verb* **1** *he added an extra sentence* include, put on/in, attach, append, affix; *fml.* adjoin. **2** *add all the numbers* add up, add together, total, count, count up, compute; *inf.* tot up. **3** *"That's fine," he added* go on to say, state further; *inf.* tack on, tag on; *fml.* superimpose. **add to** *this added to their pain* increase, magnify, amplify, augment, intensify, aggravate, exacerbate. **add up 1** *add up the column of figures* add,

---

ACTORS AND ACTRESSES

Aldridge, Ira (1805–67; Am.)	Campbell, Mrs Patrick (1865–1940; Brit.)	Langtry, Lillie (1853–1929; Brit.)	Redgrave, Sir Michael (1908–85; Brit.)
Alleyn, Edward (1566–1626; Brit.)	Cibber, Colley (1671–1757; Brit.)	Lillie, Beatrice (1898–1989; Brit.)	Redgrave, Vanessa (b. 1937; Brit.)
Artaud, Antonin (1896–1948; Fr.)	Dench, Dame Judi (b. 1934; Brit.)	Lunt, Alfred (1892–1977; Am.)	Richardson, Ralph (1902–83; Brit.)
Ashcroft, Peggy (1907–91; Brit.)	Duse, Eleonora (1858–1924; It.)	McKellen, Sir Ian (b. 1939; Brit.)	Robeson, Paul (1898–1976; Am.)
Barrault, Jean-Louis (1910–94; Fr.)	Evans, Dame Edith (1888–1976; Brit.)	McKenna, Siobhán (1923–86; Ir.)	Roscius, Quintus (d. 62 B.C.; Rom.)
Barrymore, Lionel (1878–1954; Am.)	Garrick, David (1717–79; Brit.)	Mac Liammóir, Micheál (1899–1978; Ir.)	Smith, Dame Maggie (b. 1934; Brit.)
Bernhardt, Sarah (1844–1923; Fr.)	Gielgud, Sir John (b. 1904; Brit.)	Massey, Raymond (1896–1983; Can.)	Stanislavsky, Konstantin (1863–1938; Russ.)
Booth, Edwin (1833–93; Am.)	Guitry, Sacha (1885–1957; Fr.)	Olivier, Laurence, Baron (1907–89; Brit.)	Terry, Ellen (1847–1928; Brit.)
Branagh, Kenneth (b. 1960; Brit.)	Jordan, Dorothea (1762–1816; Ir.)	Plowright, Joan (b. 1929; Brit.)	Thorndike, Sybil (1882–1976; Brit.)
Burbage, Richard (c. 1567–1619; Brit.)	Jouvet, Louis (1887–1951; Fr.)	Rachel (Élisa Félix; 1820–58; Fr.)	Woffington, Peg (c. 1714–60; Ir.)
Burton, Richard (1925–84; Welsh)	Kean, Edmund (1787–1833; Brit.)		

add together, total, count, count up, compute; *inf.* tot up. **2** *it adds up to £100* amount to, come to. **3** *it all adds up to a disaster* amount to, constitute, comprise, signify; *inf.* spell, spell out. **4** *it doesn't add up* make sense, be/seem reasonable, be/seem plausible; *inf.* ring true, hold water, stand to reason. **Opposites** DEDUCT; REMOVE; SUBTRACT.

addendum *noun* addition, appendix, codicil, postscript, appendage, supplement, adjunct.

addict *noun* **1** *a drugs/heroin addict* abuser, user; *inf.* junkie, freak, head, fiend, tripper. **2** *a film addict* fan, enthusiast, devotee, follower, adherent; *inf.* buff, freak, nut.

addicted *adjective* **1** *addicted to drugs* dependent, dependent on; *inf.* hooked. **2** *addicted to the cinema* devoted, obsessed, dedicated; *inf.* hooked.

addiction *noun an addiction to drugs | addiction to the cinema* dependency, craving, devotion, obsession, dedication, enslavement, habit.

addition *noun* **1** *the addition of an extra sentence* inclusion, adding on, attachment, appendage. *See* ADD 1. **2** *the addition of a row of figures | check my addition* adding up, counting, totalling, computation, calculation; *inf.* totting up. *See* ADD 2. **3** *an addition to the family/library* increase, increment, extension, augmentation, gain, supplement, appendage. **in addition** *in addition, you may take three books | in addition to Jane* additionally, besides, as well, as well as.

additional *adjective* additional help extra, supplementary, further, more, other, over and above, fresh, supplemental.

additionally *adverb additionally he gave money* in addition, also, as well, besides, moreover, further, into the bargain, to boot.

additive *noun additives to food | chemical additives* supplement, addition, add-on; preservative, E number.

address *noun* **1** *the address on the envelope* inscription, label, superscription; directions. **2** *moved to a new address* house, home, location, place, residence, abode, domicile, dwelling, situation; whereabouts. **3** *an address to the crowd* speech, lecture, talk, dissertation, discourse, oration, sermon, harangue, diatribe, disquisition, philippic.

address *verb* **1** *address an envelope* direct, label, inscribe, superscribe. **2** *address the audience* talk to, speak to, give a talk to, make a speech to, lecture, give a discourse/dissertation/oration to, preach to, declaim to, harangue; *inf.* spout to. **3** *address someone across the street* greet, speak to, hail, salute. **4** *how to address the mayor* name, call, speak to, write, describe, designate; *fml.* denominate. **5** *address any remarks to the manager* direct, send, communicate, convey, forward, remit. **6** *address a ball* take aim at, aim at, face. **address onself to** apply oneself to, attend to, direct one's attention to, turn to, get down to, devote oneself to, take up, engage in, undertake, concentrate on.

adduce *verb* cite, put forward, mention, point out, quote, name, instance, present, offer, advance, propose, proffer.

adept *adjective adept at games | adept at growing roses* expert, clever, proficient, skilful, accomplished, brilliant, talented, first-rate, masterly; *inf.* top-notch, A1, wizard, ace.

adept *noun an adept at chess/tennis* expert, past master, genius, ace, virtuoso; *inf.* wizard, dab hand, hotshot.

adequacy *noun* **1** *dispute the adequacy of their salary* sufficiency, ampleness, reasonableness. *See* ADEQUATE 1. **2** *work noted for its adequacy rather than its excellence* passableness, tolerableness, acceptability, mediocrity, indifference. *See* ADEQUATE 2. **3** *not disputing his adequacy* capability, competence, suitability, ability, qualifications, fitness. *See* ADEQUATE 3.

adequate *adjective* **1** *adequate grounds for divorce | an adequate salary* sufficient, enough, ample, reasonable, satisfactory, requisite. **2** *your work is adequate but not good* passable, tolerable, acceptable, fair, middle-of-the-road, mediocre, unexceptional, indifferent, average, so-so, minimal; *inf.* nothing to write home about, no great shakes. **3** *he did not feel adequate to the task* up to, equal to, capable, competent, suited, suitable, able, qualified, fit. **Opposites** INADEQUATE; INSUFFICIENT.

adhere *verb* **1** *sticky tape adhering to the wall* stick, stick fast, cling, hold fast, cohere, be fixed, be pasted/glued. **2** *adhering to their principles* stick to, hold to, abide by, comply with, stand by, be faithful to, follow, obey, fulfil. **3** *adhere to the democratic party* be attached to, support, give support to, be connected with, be affiliated to, be a member of, follow.

adherent *noun* **1** *an adherent of communism* supporter, follower, upholder, advocate, disciple, votary, partisan, sectary, member; *inf.* hanger-on. **2** *an adherent of the cinema* fan, admirer, follower, enthusiast, devotee, lover, addict, aficionado; *inf.* buff, freak, fiend.

adherent *adjective an adherent surface* sticky, sticking, adhering, clinging, viscous, adhesive. *See* ADHESIVE *adjective*.

adhesive *adjective an adhesive substance* sticky, sticking, adhering, adherent, clinging, tacky, gluey, gummy, cohesive, viscous, viscid, glutinous; *fml.* mucilaginous.

adhesive *noun* glue, fixative, gum, paste, cement; *fml.* mucilage.

adieu *interjection/noun* goodbye, farewell. *See* GOODBYE.

adjacent *adjective* adjoining, neighbouring, next door, abutting, close, near, bordering, alongside, contiguous, proximate, attached, touching, conjoining.

adjoining *adjective an adjoining house* neighbouring, next door, adjacent, abutting, bordering, connected, connecting, contiguous, interconnecting, attached. *See* ADJACENT.

adjourn *verb* **1** *adjourn our meeting* break off, discontinue, interrupt, suspend, dissolve, postpone, put off, defer, delay, shelve, prorogue. **2** *the court adjourns for lunch* break off, discontinue, pause; *Am.* take a recess. **3** *the women adjourned to the drawing room* withdraw, retire, retreat; *fml.* repair.

adjournment noun **1** *the adjournment of our meeting* breaking-off, discontinuation, interruption, suspension, postponement, deferment, deferral, delay, shelving, prorogation. *See* ADJOURN 1. **2** *the court's adjournment* breaking-off, break, discontinuation, pause. **3** *the adjournment of the women to the drawing-room* withdrawing, retirement, retreat; *fml.* repairing.

adjudicate verb **1** *adjudicate at a musical competition* judge, arbitrate, referee, umpire. **2** *adjudicate a tribunal claim* judge, decide on, settle, determine, pronounce on, give a ruling on.

adjudication noun **1** *the adjudication at a competition* judging, arbitration, refereeing, umpiring. **2** *a tribunal adjudication* judgement, decision, pronouncement, ruling, settlement, determination, finding, verdict.

adjunct noun *a mere adjunct to the rest of the equipment* extra, addition, attachment, accessory, appendage, addendum, appurtenance, supplement.

adjust verb **1** *I cannot adjust to the new situation* adapt, become accustomed to, get used to, accommodate, acclimatize, reconcile oneself, habituate oneself, assimilate. **2** *adjust the dress* adapt, rearrange, alter, modify, change, remodel. **3** *adjust the brakes* regulate, modify, fix, repair, rectify, put in working order, set to rights, tune.

adjustable adjective **1** *adjustable seat-belts* alterable, adaptable, modifiable, movable. **2** *adjustable people* adaptable, accommodating, amenable, obliging, flexible, malleable, pliable, pliant, tractable.

adjustment noun **1** *the adjustment to a new situation* adaptation, accustoming, accommodation, acclimatization, reconciliation, habituation, assimilation. **2** *the adjustment of the dress* adaptation, alteration, modification. *See* ADJUST 2. **3** *the adjustment of the brakes* regulating, modifying, modification, fixing, repair. *See* ADJUST 3. **4** *make a small adjustment* adaptation, alteration, change, modification, rearrangement.

ad lib verb *the speaker cannot ad lib* extemporize, improvise, speak off the cuff, make an impromptu speech, speak impromptu.

ad lib adjective *an ad lib speech* off the cuff, impromptu, on the spot, extempore, improvised, unrehearsed, extemporaneous.

ad lib adverb *speak ad lib* off the cuff, impromptu, extempore, without preparation, without rehearsal, extemporaneously; *inf.* off the top of one's head.

administer verb **1** *administer the firm's financial affairs* manage, direct, control, conduct, run, govern, operate, superintend, supervise, oversee, preside over. **2** *administer justice/comfort* dispense, hand out, discharge, allot, deal, distribute, mete out, disburse, bestow, provide. **3** *administer a remedy/medicine* apply, give, dispense, provide, treat with.

administration noun **1** *he's in business/hospital administration* management, direction, control, conduct, execution, government, operation,

supervision. **2** *the Tory administration* government, ministry, regime, executive; term of office. **3** *the administration of justice* dispensation, discharge, allotment, dealing, distribution, disbursement, bestowal. *See* ADMINISTER 2. **4** *the administration of a remedy* application, dispensation, provision. *See* ADMINISTER 3.

administrative adjective *in an administrative role* managerial, management, directorial, executive, organizational, controlling, governmental, supervisory, regulatory.

administrator noun manager, director, executive, controller, head, chief, superintendent, supervisor.

admirable adjective **1** *admirable conduct in the circumstances* worthy, commendable, praiseworthy, laudable, good, estimable, honourable. **2** *an admirable musical performance* excellent, superb, brilliant, first-rate, first-class, supreme, great, fine, masterly, marvellous.

admiration noun **1** *filled with admiration for his courage* approval, regard, high regard, respect, approbation, appreciation, praise, esteem, veneration. **2** *she was the admiration of the whole village* object of admiration, pride, pride and joy, wonder, delight, marvel, sensation.

admire verb **1** *admire his courage* approve of, respect, think highly of, appreciate, applaud, praise, hold in high regard/esteem, venerate. **2** *she admired her hat* approve of, like, express admiration for, compliment, sing the praises of, be taken with. **3** *he admired her from afar* adore, love, be enamoured of, idolize; *inf.* carry a torch for.
Opposites DISAPPROVE; DESPISE.

admirer noun **1** *an admirer of modern art* enthusiast, fan, devotee, aficionado, supporter, adherent, follower, disciple, votary; *inf.* buff, freak. **2** *they teased her about her admirer* suitor, wooer, beau, sweetheart, lover, boyfriend, girlfriend.

admissible adjective *admissible evidence/behaviour* allowable, allowed, permissible, permitted, acceptable, passable, justifiable, tolerable.

admission noun **1** *admission to university | admission to the palace* admittance, entry, right of entry, entrance, access, entrée; *fml.* ingress. **2** *admission is £3* entrance fee, entry charge, ticket. **3** *an admission of guilt/failure* acknowledgement, confession, revelation, disclosure, divulgence, expression, declaration, utterance, avowal.

admit verb **1** *one ticket admits two people | the window admits little light* let in, allow/permit entry, give access to. **2** *the scheme does not admit non-shareholders* give admission to, allow, permit, accept, receive, let in. **3** *the room admits only 30 people* accommodate, cater for, hold. **4** *they admitted their guilt | admitting that they were wrong* acknowledge, confess, reveal, make known, disclose, divulge, declare, avow. **5** *admit that you may be right* concede, accept, grant, acknowledge, agree, allow, concur.
Opposites EXCLUDE; PROHIBIT; DENY.

admittance noun *no admittance to the palace* entry, right of entry, entrance, access. *See* ADMISSION 1.

admonish *verb* **1** *admonish the boys for smoking* reprimand, rebuke, scold, reprove, upbraid, chide, censure, berate; *inf.* tell off. **2** *she admonished us to seek help* advise, urge, caution, warn, counsel, exhort.

admonition *noun* **1** *deliver an admonition to the culprits* reprimand, rebuke, scolding; *inf.* telling-off. See ADMONISH 1. **2** *gave them an admonition to seek help* piece of advice, warning, exhortation; advice. See ADMONISH 2.

admonitory *adjective* **1** *admonitory remarks to the culprits* admonishing, reprimanding, rebuking, reproving, reproachful. See ADMONISH 1. **2** *admonitory suggestions to seek help* admonishing, advisory, cautioning, cautionary, counselling, exhortative. See ADMONISH 2.

ado *noun* *we set off without further ado* fuss, trouble, bother, commotion, upset, agitation, hubbub, confusion, disturbance, hurly-burly, flurry, to-do; *dial.* pother; *Am.* fuss and feathers.

adolescence *noun* *have acne during adolescence* teenage years, teens, youth, pubescence.

adolescent *adjective* **1** *adolescent problems* teenage, youthful, pubescent. **2** *despite her age she has a silly adolescent sense of humour* immature, juvenile, childish, puerile.

adolescent *noun* *adolescents are sometimes moody* teenager, youngster, young person, youth.

adopt *verb* **1** *adopt a child* take as one's own child, be adoptive parents to, take in, take care of. **2** *adopt eastern customs* assume, take on, take over, affect, embrace, espouse, appropriate, arrogate. **3** *adopt a candidate* select, choose, vote for. **4** *adopt the new measures* approve, endorse, accept, ratify, sanction, support, back.

adoption *noun* **1** *the adoption of a child* adopting, taking as one's own, taking in. See ADOPT 1. **2** *the adoption of eastern customs* assumption, taking on, affecting, affectation, espousal, appropriation, arrogation. See ADOPT 2. **3** *the adoption of the political candidate* selection, choosing, choice, voting for. See ADOPT 3. **4** *the adoption of the new measures by parliament* approval, endorsement, acceptance, ratification, sanctioning, support, backing. See ADOPT 4.

adorable *adjective* lovable, appealing, charming, sweet, enchanting, captivating, dear, darling, delightful, attractive, winsome, winning, fetching.

adoration *noun* **1** *the adoration of their children* love, loving, doting, devotion, idolization, worship. See ADORE 1. **2** *the adoration of God* worship, glorification, praising, praise, homage, exaltation, magnification, extolment, veneration. See ADORE 2. **3** *their adoration of travel* love, liking, enjoyment, great liking/enjoyment, relishing. See ADORE 3.

adore *verb* **1** *adore their children* love, be devoted to, dote on, cherish, hold dear, idolize, worship. **2** *let us adore God* worship, glorify, praise, revere, reverence, exalt, magnify, laud, extol, esteem, venerate. **3** *they adore ice cream* like, love, be fond of, enjoy, delight in, take

pleasure in, relish.
Opposites HATE; LOATHE; DETEST.

adorn *verb* *flowers adorn the room* decorate, embellish, add ornament to, ornament, trim, enhance, beautify, enrich, bedeck, deck, array, grace, emblazon.

adornment *noun* **1** *the adornment of the Christmas tree* decorating, decoration, embellishment, ornamentation, trimming, arraying, enhancement, beautification, enrichment. See ADORN. **2** *simply dressed with no adornment* ornamentation, ornament, embellishment, frippery, decoration; frills, accessories, trimmings.

adrift *adjective* **1** *a boat adrift on the sea* drifting, unmoored, unanchored. **2** *young people adrift in city streets* aimless, purposeless, without purpose/goal, directionless, unsettled, rootless. **3** *the tarpaulin on the load came adrift* unfastened, loose, untied, detached, unsecured. **4** *our plans have gone badly adrift* wrong, awry, amiss, astray, off course.

adroit *adjective* **1** *his adroit handling of the boat | adroit at tennis* skilful, skilled, expert, adept, dexterous, deft, clever, able, capable, competent, masterly, proficient. **2** *an adroit politician* skilful, expert, adept, clever, quickthinking, quick-witted, cunning, artful, resourceful, astute, shrewd.
Opposites CLUMSY; INEPT.

adroitness *noun* **1** *her adroitness at sailing* skill, skilfulness, expertise, adeptness, dexterity, deftness, cleverness, ability, capability, competence, proficiency. See ADROIT 1. **2** *his political adroitness* skill, skilfulness, expertise, adeptness, cleverness, quick-wittedness, cunning, artfulness, resourcefulness. See ADROIT 2.

adulation *noun* *adulation of pop stars* worship, hero-worship, idolization, adoration, glorification, praising, praise, flattery; blandishments.

adult *adjective* **1** *an adult women/tree* mature, grown-up, fully grown, full-grown, fully developed; *fml.* of age. **2** *adult magazines/videos* sexually explicit, obscene, pornographic; *inf.* full-frontal.

adulterate *verb* *adulterate the water/brandy* make impure, debase, degrade, spoil, contaminate, taint, doctor, water down, weaken, bastardize; *fml.* vitiate.

advance *verb* **1** *the army advanced* go/come/ move forward, proceed, go ahead, move along, press on, push forward, make progress, make headway, forge ahead, gain ground **2** *advance the date of publication | advance our lunch appointment* bring/put forward, make earlier. **3** *advance his promotion | advance the building schedule* speed up, accelerate, step up, hasten, expedite, hurry, quicken, forward. **4** *advance his chances of promotion* further, forward, help, assist, facilitate, promote, boost, improve, benefit, foster. **5** *her career advanced rapidly* go forward, go ahead, progress, develop, improve, thrive, flourish. **6** *advance a suggestion/theory* put forward, suggest, propose, submit, recommend, present, introduce, offer, proffer, adduce. **7** *the company advanced him £200* pay in advance, lend, supply on credit. **8** *prices are advancing rapidly* rise, increase, go up, mount

9 *war advanced prices* raise, increase, put up, inflate; *inf.* jack up, hike up.
Opposites RETREAT; POSTPONE; IMPEDE.

advance *noun* **1** *the advance of the army* going/coming/moving forward, movement forward, progress, headway. *See* ADVANCE *verb* 1. **2** *the advance of civilization* progress, development, advancement, movement forward, headway, improvement, betterment, furtherance. **3** *recent medical advances* development, discovery, breakthrough, finding, invention. **4** *an advance in the price of oil* rise, increase, mark-up. **5** *they paid me an advance of £20* down payment, deposit, retainer. **in advance** beforehand, ahead of time, earlier, previously.

advance *adjective* **1** *the advance party sent ahead*, leading, first. **2** *given advance warning* early, previous, prior, beforehand.

advanced *adjective* **1** *advanced technology* progressive, forward, highly developed, modern, ultra modern, avant-garde, ahead of the times. **2** *advanced studies* higher-level.

advancement *noun* **1** *furthering the advancement of knowledge* progress, development, improvement, furtherance. *See* ADVANCE *noun* 2, 3. **2** *a job offering advancement* promotion, improvement, progress, betterment, growth, rise, preferment.

advances *plural noun make friendly advances* approaches, overtures, moves, proposals, propositions.

advantage *noun* **1** *the main advantage is the size of the garden* benefit, asset, good point, boon, blessing. **2** *he had an advantage over her | the advantage of age* benefit, superiority, dominance, ascendancy, supremacy, power, mastery, upper hand, whiphand, trump card. **3** *little advantage in going | not to one's advantage* benefit, profit, gain, good.
Opposites DISADVANTAGE; HANDICAP; DETRIMENT.

advantageous *adjective* **1** *in an advantageous position* favourable, superior, dominant, powerful. **2** *advantageous to your career* beneficial, of benefit, helpful, of assistance, useful, valuable, of service, profitable.

advent *noun the advent of war | advent of modern techniques* arrival, coming, appearance, approach, occurrence.
Opposites DEPARTURE; DISAPPEARANCE.

adventitious *adjective* **1** *an adventitious encounter* accidental, unexpected, unplanned, chance, fortuitous, casual. **2** *adventitious influences* outside, external, extraneous, foreign, alien, extrinsic.

adventure *noun* **1** *a spirit of adventure | a life full of adventure* risk, hazard, danger, peril, gamble, gambling, uncertainty, precariousness. **2** *tales of the sailor's adventures* exploit, deed, feat, experience, incident.

adventurous *adjective* **1** *adventurous young men* daring, daredevil, bold, intrepid, audacious; *fml.* adventuresome, venturesome. **2** *an adventurous life* risky, dangerous, perilous, hazardous, precarious.

adversary *noun* opponent, opposer, antagonist, rival, enemy, foe, fellow contestant/competitor.

adverse *adjective* **1** *adverse circumstances | adverse weather conditions* unfavourable, unlucky, disadvantageous, inauspicious, unpropitious, unfortunate, untoward. **2** *adverse criticism* hostile, unfriendly, unfavourable, antagonistic, negative, opposing, inimical, antipathetic. **3** *adverse to health* harmful, dangerous, injurious, detrimental, disadvantageous, hurtful.
Opposites FAVOURABLE; AUSPICIOUS; BENEFICIAL.

adversity *noun* **1** *face adversity with courage* misfortune, ill luck, bad luck, trouble, hardship, distress, disaster, suffering, affliction, sorrow, misery, tribulation, woe; hard times. **2** *many adversities in their lives* misfortune, mishap, accident, shock, reverse, setback, disaster, catastrophe, tragedy, calamity, trial.

advertise *verb* **1** *advertise details of a meeting* make known/public, publicize, give publicity to, announce, broadcast, proclaim, call attention to. **2** *advertise a product* promote, publicize, give publicity to, call attention to, display, puff, give a puff to, tout, promulgate; *inf.* push, plug.

advertisement *noun* **1** *put an advertisement in the paper* notice, announcement, display; *inf.* advert, ad. **2** *a television advertisement | an advertisement for soap* promotion, display, commercial, puff, blurb; *inf.* advert, ad, push, plug. **3** *the advertisement of products* advertising, promotion, publicizing, touting; *inf.* plugging, pushing.

advice *noun* **1** *give advice to young people* guidance, counselling, counsel, help; recommendations, suggestions, hints, tips, ideas, opinions, views. **2** *an advice sent from the bank* notification, communication, information; data.

advisability *noun* desirability, wisdom, soundness, prudence, appropriateness, fitness, suitability, aptness, judiciousness, expediency.

advisable *adjective* desirable, best, wisest, sensible, sound, prudent, proper, appropriate, suitable, fitting, apt, judicious, recommended, suggested, expedient, politic.

advise *verb* **1** *cannot advise you on your affairs* give guidance, guide, counsel, give counsel, give recommendations, offer suggestions/opinions, give hints/tips, instruct. **2** *advise you of the facts* inform, notify, give notice, apprise, acquaint with, report on, warn. **3** *advise caution* suggest, commend, recommend, admonish, urge.

adviser, advisor *noun* counsellor, mentor, guide, consultant, confidant, confidante, coach, teacher, tutor, therapist.

advisory *adjective* advising, consultative, counselling, recommendatory, assisting.

advocacy *noun advocacy of political freedom* advising, recommending, support for, backing, arguing/argument for, promotion. *See* ADVOCATE *verb*.

advocate *verb advocate reducing expenditure* recommend, advise, favour, support, uphold, back, subscribe to, champion, speak for, campaign on behalf of, argue/plead/press for, urge, promote.

advocate noun **1** *an advocate of political freedom* supporter, upholder, backer, champion, spokesman, spokeswoman, spokesperson, speaker, campaigner, pleader, promoter, proponent, exponent, apostle, apologist. **2** barrister, counsel; *Am.* attorney.

aegis noun protection, guardianship, support, patronage, sponsorship, safeguarding, defence, championship, aid, guaranty; auspices.

aeon noun age, long period, eternity; ages.

aeroplane noun. *See table at* AIRCRAFT.

affability noun friendliness, amiability, geniality, congeniality, cordiality, pleasantness, agreeableness, good-humouredness, kindliness, courtesy, civility, approachability, sociability.

affable adjective friendly, amiable, genial, congenial, cordial, pleasant, agreeable, easygoing, good-humoured, good-natured, kindly, courteous, civil, approachable, sociable.

affair noun **1** *that's my own affair* concern, business, matter, responsibility. **2** *forget the sad affair* event, happening, occurrence, incident, episode, circumstance, adventure, case. **3** *an informal affair* party, function, reception, gathering; *inf.* get-together, do. **4** *an affair with a married man* love affair, relationship, romance, liaison, affair of the heart, intrigue, amour, affaire.

affairs plural noun *commercial/foreign affairs* concerns, matters, activities, transactions, undertakings, ventures, business.

affect[1] verb **1** *it affected his health | affected our attitude* have an effect on, influence, act on, work on, have an impact on, change, alter, transform. **2** *the disease affected his lungs* attack, strike at, infect, take hold of. **3** *the experience deeply affected us* move, touch, upset, disturb, trouble, perturb, agitate, stir, tug at the heartstrings.

affect[2] verb **1** *affect long words | affect bright clothes* assume, put on, adopt, like, have a liking for, espouse. **2** *affect a foreign accent | affect ignorance* pretend, feign, fake, counterfeit, sham, simulate.

affectation noun **1** *tired of her affectation | without affectation* pretence, pretension, pretensiousness, affectedness, artificiality, insincerity, posturing. **2** *her affectations annoy me* airs, airs and graces, pretensions; posing, posturing. **3** *an affectation of interest* façade, show, appearance, false display, pretence, feigning, shamming, simulation.

affected[1] adjective influenced, altered, changed. *See* AFFECT[1].

affected[2] adjective **1** *an affected style of writing* pretentious, artificial, unnatural, assumed, high-flown, ostentatious, contrived, studied, pompous, mannered. **2** *an affected politeness* put on, pretended, feigned, fake, counterfeit, sham, simulated.
Opposites NATURAL; UNPRETENTIOUS; GENUINE.

affecting adjective *an affecting scene* moving, touching, poignant, upsetting, pathetic, heart-rending. *See* AFFECT[1] 3.

affection noun *affection for her sister* love, liking, fondness, warmth, devotion, caring, attachment, friendship, amity; warm feelings.

affectionate adjective *an affectionate wife/hug* loving, fond, devoted, caring, tender, doting, friendly. *See* AFFECTION.

affianced adjective engaged, betrothed, contracted, pledged.

affiliate verb *they are affiliated to the union | the college is affiliated with the university* associate with, unite with, combine with, join with, ally with, amalgamate with, coalesce, form a federation/confederation, annex to, merge with, incorporate into.

affiliation noun **1** *the affiliation of the college to the university* uniting, combining, allying, amalgamation. *See* AFFILIATE. **2** *affiliations between clubs* connection, link, bond, tie, relationship; communication.

affinity noun **1** *the human's affinity with the ape* likeness, similarity, resemblance, correspondence, analogy, similitude. **2** *have an affinity for each other* liking, fondness, attraction, inclination, rapport, sympathy, partiality, penchant, predilection. **3** *the witness's affinity with the accused* relationship, kinship, connection, propinquity.

affirm verb state, assert, declare, aver, proclaim, pronounce, swear, attest; *fml.* asseverate.

affirmation noun statement, assertion, declaration, averment, proclamation, pronouncement, swearing, attestation; *fml.* asseveration.

affirmative adjective assenting, consenting, agreeing, concurring, corroborative, favourable, approving, positive.
Opposites dissenting; NEGATIVE.

affix verb **1** *affix a stamp to the envelope* attach, stick, fasten, fix, tack, glue, paste. **2** *affix a signature to a document* append, add, add on, attach.

afflict verb trouble, burden, distress, beset, harass, oppress, torment, plague, rack, smite.

affliction noun **1** *bearing affliction bravely* trouble, distress, pain, misery, suffering, wretchedness, hardship, misfortune, sorrow, torment, tribulation, woe. **2** *the afflictions of the old* trouble, disorder, disease, pain, suffering, trial, hardship, ordeal, scourge, plague, woe.

affluence noun wealth, prosperity, opulence, fortune, richness; riches, resources. *See* AFFLUENT.

affluent adjective rich, wealthy, prosperous, opulent, well off, moneyed, well-to-do, comfortable; *inf.* well-heeled, in the money, loaded.

afford verb **1** *cannot afford a new dress* pay for, meet the expense of, spare the price of. **2** *cannot afford the loss of staff* bear, sustain, stand. **3** *the tree affords shade* provide, supply, offer, give, impart, bestow, furnish, yield. **4** *the orchard affords a large crop* yield, produce, bear, supply, give.

affray noun fight, brawl, battle, quarrel, row, set-to, wrangle, fracas, altercation, disturbance, commotion, breach of the peace, mêlée, scrap, clash, scuffle, tussle; *inf.* free-for-all.

affront noun *sexist remarks are an affront to women* insult, offence, indignity, slight, snub, aspersion, provocation, injury, outrage; *inf.* slap in the face.

affront verb *he was affronted by her behaviour* insult, offend, outrage, provoke, slight, hurt, pique.

afoot adjective/adverb *trouble afoot | evil plans afoot* around, going on, abroad, circulating, current, stirring; *inf.* on the go; *lit.* astir.

aforesaid adjective aforementioned, aforenamed, previously described, foregoing, preceding, earlier, previous.

afraid adjective **1** *afraid of death | afraid to die* frightened, scared, terrified, apprehensive, fearful, nervous, alarmed at, intimidated by, terror-stricken. **2** *I'm afraid I can't help* sorry, regretful, apologetic, unhappy.

afresh adverb anew, again, over again, once again, once more.

after preposition **1** *leave after lunch* following, subsequent to, at the close/end of, later than. **2** *shut the door after you* behind, following, in the rear of. **3** *B comes after A* following, next to, nearest to, below. **4** *run after the thief | be after a job* in pursuit of, in search of, in quest of. **5** *after the way he acted she hates him* following, because of, as a result of, in view of, owing to, on account of. **6** *after all that she still loves him* despite, in spite of, regardless of, notwithstanding. **7** *enquire after her health* about, concerning, regarding, with reference to, apropos. **8** *they called their son after his grandfather* with the name of, the same as, in honour of, as a tribute to; *Am.* for. **9** *a painting after Rubens* in the style of, in the manner of, in imitation of, on the model of, following the pattern of.

after adverb **1** *the week after* later, following, afterwards, subsequently, thereafter. **2** *following on after* behind, in the rear, at the back. **Opposites** PREVIOUSLY; BEFORE.

after adjective *in after years* later, succeeding, subsequent, following.

afterlife noun *Christians believe in an afterlife* life after death, the hereafter, afterworld.

aftermath noun after-effects, effects, consequences, results; end result, outcome, upshot, issue, end.

afterwards adverb *afterwords they left* later, subsequently, then, thereupon, after, next.

again adverb **1** *start again* once more, afresh, anew, a second time, another time. **2** *again there is the question of money* moreover, besides, also, furthermore, further. **3** *he might come and again he might not* on the other hand, on the contrary, conversely. **4** *half as much again* in addition, over and above, also, too. **again and again** often, frequently, repeatedly, over and over, time and time again, continually, persistently.

against preposition **1** *people against the movement* opposed to, in opposition to, hostile to, at odds with, in disagreement with, versus, at cross-purposes with. **2** *rowing against the tide* in opposition to, counter to, resisting. **3** *leaning against the fence* touching, in contact with, close up to, up against, abutting. **4** *silhouetted against a black background* in contrast to, as a foil to. **5** *saving against a rainy day* in preparation for, in anticipation of, in expectation of, as provision for. **6** *his age is against him* disadvantageous to, unfavourable to, damaging to, detrimental to, prejudicial to. **7** *the exchange rate against the dollar* in exchange for, in return for, in compensation for.

age noun **1** *what age is the tree?* number of years, lifetime, duration, stage of life, generation; years. **2** *wisdom comes with age | age can bring infirmity* maturity, seniority, elderliness, oldness, old age; advancing years, declining years; *fml.* senescence. **3** *the Elizabethan/nuclear age* era, epoch, period, time. *See table. See also table at* ERA. **4** *we waited for an age | it took ages* a long time, an eternity; hours, days, months, years, aeons, hours/days/months on end.

GEOLOGICAL AGES

Cambrian period	Ordovician period
Carboniferous period	Palaeocene epoch
	Palaeozoic era
Cenozoic era	Permian period
Cretaceous period	Phanerozoic era
Devonian period	Pleistocene epoch
Eocene epoch	Pliocene epoch
Holocene epoch	Precambrian era
Jurassic period	Quaternary period
Mesozoic era	Silurian period
Miocene epoch	Tertiary period
Oligocene epoch	Triassic period

---

age verb *she has aged well* mature, ripen, grow up, come of age; grow old, decline, wither, fade, become obsolete.

aged adjective *a white-haired aged man* old, elderly, superannuated; *fml.* senescent; as old as the hills.

agency noun **1** *advertising agency* business, organization, company, firm, office, bureau, concern. **2** *through the agency of heat* activity, action, effect, influence, force, power, work. **3** *a young couple brought together through the agency of friends* good offices, mediation, intervention, intercession, instrumentality.

agenda noun programme, schedule, timetable, plan, list, scheme.

agent noun **1** *an insurance agent* representative, negotiator, emissary, envoy, factor, go-between; *inf.* rep. **2** *an enemy agent* spy; *inf.* mole; *Am. inf.* spook. **3** *our agents will be in touch* solicitor, lawyer; *Am.* attorney. **4** *the agent of his ruin* executor, author, performer, perpetrator, doer, operator, operative, mover. **5** *a cleansing agent* moving force, agency, cause, instrument, vehicle, means, power, force.

agglomeration *noun* collection, accumulation, mass, cluster, lump, clump, pile, heap, aggregate, miscellany, jumble, hotchpotch.

aggravate *verb* **1** *aggravate the situation/pain* worsen, make worse, exacerbate, inflame, intensify, increase, heighten, magnify. **2** *aggravate the teacher* annoy, irritate, anger, exasperate, provoke, irk, vex, get on one's nerves, rub up the wrong way; *inf.* needle. **Opposites** ALLEVIATE; IMPROVE; CALM; MOLLIFY.

aggravation *noun* **1** *the aggravation of the situation/pain* worsening, exacerbation, intensification, increase, magnification. *See* AGGRAVATE 1. **2** *the aggravation of the teacher* annoyance, irritation, angering, exasperation, provocation, vexation; *inf.* needling. *See* AGGRAVATE 2. **3** *just one more aggravation* irritant, nuisance, pest, grievance, thorn in the flesh; *inf.* headache.

aggregate *noun* **1** *the aggregate of goals* total, sum total, whole amount, totality, entirety, summation, gross. **2** *an aggregate of minerals* collection, accumulation, mass, cluster, clump, lump, pile, heap, concentration, assemblage, mixture, combination, agglomeration.

aggregate *adjective* **1** *the aggregate score* total, combined, whole, added. **2** *aggregate rock* composite, compound, combined, massed, clustered.

aggression *noun* **1** *an act of aggression* attack, assault, injury, encroachment, offence, invasion, infringement. **2** *a bloody aggression* attack, assault, onslaught, foray, raid, sortie, offensive, invasion.

aggressive *adjective* **1** *an aggressive person* quarrelsome, argumentative, belligerent, pugnacious, militant, warring. **2** *an aggressive act* hostile, belligerent, warring, combative, bellicose, invasive, intrusive. **3** *an aggressive salesman | aggressive sales promotion* assertive, forceful, insistent, vigorous, energetic, dynamic, bold, enterprising, go-ahead, zealous, pushing; *inf.* pushy. **Opposites** PEACEABLE; FRIENDLY; RETIRING.

aggressor *noun* attacker, assaulter, invader, assailant, provoker, instigator, initiator.

aggrieved *adjective* **1** *aggrieved at her treatment* resentful, angry, distressed, disturbed, piqued; *inf.* peeved. **2** *the aggrieved party* wronged, injured, abused, harmed, mistreated, ill-used.

aghast *adjective* horrified, appalled, astounded, amazed, thunderstruck, stunned, shocked, flabbergasted, awestruck; *inf.* floored.

agile *adjective* **1** *an agile body* active, nimble, spry, lithe, fit, supple, sprightly, in good condition, lively, quick-moving, limber. **2** *an agile mind* active, nimble, alert, sharp, acute, clever, quick-witted. **Opposites** INACTIVE; STIFF.

agility *noun* **1** *the agility of their bodies* activeness, nimbleness, litheness, fitness, suppleness. *See* AGILE 1. **2** *the agility of her mind* activeness, nimbleness, alertness. *See* AGILE 2.

agitate *verb* **1** *she was agitated by the delay* upset, work up, perturb, fluster, ruffle, disconcert, disquiet, flurry, trouble, worry. **2** *agitate the mixture* stir, whisk, beat, churn, shake, toss. **3** *agitate for tax reductions* campaign, argue, debate, dispute, wrangle.

agitation *noun* **1** *the agitation caused by delays* upset, perturbation, fluster, disconcertment, flurry, trouble, worry. *See* AGITATE 1. **2** *the agitation of the mixture* stirring, whisking, churning. *See* AGITATE 2. **3** *agitation for/against tax changes* campaigning, arguing, argument, wrangling. *See* AGITATE 3.

agitator *noun* troublemaker, instigator, *agent provocateur*, inciter, rabble-rouser, provoker, fomenter, firebrand, revolutionary, demagogue.

agnostic *noun* sceptic, unbeliever, disbeliever, doubter, questioner, doubting Thomas.

ago *adverb* in the past, in time gone by, since, formerly.

agog *adverb* eager, excited, impatient, in suspense, keen, curious, expectant, enthralled, enthusiastic, avid.

agonizing *adjective* excruciating, harrowing, racking, painful, acute, searing, insufferable, piercing, unendurable, torturous, tormenting; *lit.* exquisite.

agony *noun* suffering, pain, hurt, distress, torture, torment, anguish, misery, woe; pangs, throes.

agree *verb* **1** *agree with you | agree with your proposals* concur, be of the same mind/opinion, comply, see eye to eye, accord. **2** *agree to your proposals* consent to, accept, approve, acquiesce in, assent to, concede to, allow, admit, grant. **3** *the statements do not agree with each other* match, accord, correspond, conform, coincide, fit, tally, harmonize; *inf.* square. **4** *we agreed a time* settle on, arrange, arrive at, decide on. **5** *the warm climate agrees with me* suit, be good for. **Opposites** DISAGREE; REJECT; DIFFER.

agreeable *adjective* **1** *agreeable occasion* pleasant, pleasing, delightful, enjoyable, pleasurable, to one's liking. **2** *an agreeable youngster/manner* pleasant, likeable, charming, amiable, nice, friendly, good-natured. **3** *if you want us to go we are agreeable* willing, amenable, compliant, consenting, assenting, accommodating, tractable. **Opposites** DISAGREEABLE; UNPLEASANT; UNWILLING.

agreement *noun* **1** *we are in total agreement* accord, assent, concurrence, harmony, accordance, unity, concord. **2** *sign a business/international agreement* contract, compact, treaty, covenant, pact, bargain, settlement, proposal; *inf.* deal; *fml.* concordat. **3** *the agreement of the statements* matching, similarity, accordance, correspondence, conformity, coincidence, harmony. *See* AGREE 3.

agriculture *noun* farming, cultivation, tillage; agribusiness, agronomics, agronomy. *See table at* FARMING.

aground *adverb/adjective* beached, grounded, foundered, ashore, stuck, shipwrecked, on the ground/bottom.

ahead *adverb* **1** *they went ahead* in the front, at the head, in the lead, in the vanguard. **2** *the way ahead* forward, onwards, on. **ahead of**

AIRCRAFT

aerodyne	gyrodyne
Airbus™	helicopter
airliner	interceptor
amphibian	jet plane
autogiro	jumbo jet
biplane	jump jet
bomber	microlight
canard	multirole combat
Concorde	aircraft (MRCA)
convertiplane	multiplane
cyclogiro	night fighter
dive bomber	pusher
drone	seaplane
fighter	swing-wing
fighter-bomber	taxiplane
flying boat	triplane
freighter	turbofan
glider	turbojet
gyrocopter	turboprop

1 *straight ahead of us* in front of, towards the front of, before. **2** *ahead of time* in advance of, before, earlier than. **3** *he's ahead of us in maths* further on, more advanced, superior to, outdistancing, outstripping.
Opposites BEHIND; AFTER.

aid *verb* **1** *aid us in our effort | aid our effort* help, assist, support, lend a hand, succour, sustain, second. **2** *aid recovery/sleep* help, speed up, hasten, facilitate, expedite, encourage, promote.
Opposites HINDER; IMPEDE; DISCOURAGE.

aid *noun* **1** *give aid to a motorist* help, assistance, support, a helping hand, succour, encouragement. **2** *foreign aid* contribution, subsidy, gift, donation. **3** *a hospital aid* helper, assistant, girl/man Friday.
Opposites HINDRANCE; OBSTRUCTION.

ailing *adjective* ill, unwell, sick, sickly, poorly, weak, indisposed, under the weather.

ailment *noun* illness, disease, disorder, sickness, complaint, infection.

aim *verb* **1** *aim a gun* point, direct, take aim, train, sight, focus, position. **2** *aim at a scholarship* set one's sights on, try for, strive for, work towards, be after, seek, aspire to. **3** *aim to increase profits* plan, intend, resolve, propose, purpose, design.

aim *noun* **1** *the aim of a gun* pointing, directing, training; line of sight. *See* AIM *verb* 1.
2 *our aim is to win* goal, ambition, objective, object, end, target, intention, plan, purpose, aspiration, resolve, proposal, design, desire, wish.

aimless *adjective* **1** *an aimless life* purposeless, pointless, goalless, futile, undirected, objectless. **2** *aimless young people* goalless, unambitious, purposeless, undirected, drifting, wandering.
Opposites PURPOSEFUL; DETERMINED.

air *noun* **1** *the birds of the air | propelled through the air* atmosphere, sky, heavens, aerospace. *See table at* ATMOSPHERE. **2** *let's get some air* breeze, breath of air, puff of wind, whiff of wind, zephyr, draught. **3** *an air of peace* impression, appearance, look, atmosphere,

mood, quality, ambience, aura, manner, bearing, character, feeling, flavour, effect, tone.
4 *playing an old air* tune, melody, song, theme, strain.

air *verb* **1** *air the room/clothes* ventilate, aerate, freshen. **2** *air one's views/objections* make public, publicize, express, voice, publish, vent, disseminate, circulate, communicate, broadcast, reveal, proclaim, divulge.

aircraft *noun. See table.*

airily *adverb* "goodbye," *he said airily* lightly, light-heartedly, breezily, flippantly, gaily, blithely, jauntily, nonchalantly, cheerfully.

airing *noun* **1** *the airing of the room/clothes* ventilating, ventilation, aerating, freshening.
2 *take for an airing* outing, walk, stroll, excursion, jaunt; *fml.* promenade. **3** *the airing of one's views* publicizing, expression, voicing, publishing, venting, dissemination, circulation, communication, revelation, proclamation, divulgence. *See* AIR *verb* 2.

airless *adjective* stuffy, close, stifling, suffocating, unventilated, sultry, muggy, oppressive.

airport *noun. See table.*

INTERNATIONAL AIRPORTS

Airport	City
Arlanda	Stockholm
Barajas	Madrid
Benito Juarez	Mexico City
Charles De Gaulle	Paris
Cointrin	Geneva
Dorval	Montreal
Fiumicino	Rome
Frankfurt-Main	Frankfurt
Gatwick	London
Heathrow	London
J. F. Kennedy	New York
Kastrup	Copenhagen
La Guardia	New York
Linate	Milan
O'Hare	Chicago
Orly	Paris
Schiphol	Amsterdam
Sheremetyevo	Moscow

airs *plural noun* affectedness, posing, posturing; affectations, pretensions; *inf.* swank.

airtight *adjective* **1** *an airtight tin* closed, sealed, shut tight, impermeable. **2** *an airtight alibi* indisputable, incontrovertible, incontestable, irrefutable, unassailable.

airy *adjective* **1** *an airy day* breezy, windy, blowy, gusty. **2** *a light and airy office* well-ventilated, spacious, open. **3** *an airy being* delicate, insubstantial, ethereal, flimsy, wispy, incorporeal, vaporous. **4** *an airy promise/reply* light-hearted, breezy, flippant, blithe, gay, jaunty, nonchalant, insubstantial, cheerful.

aisle *noun* gangway, passageway, passage, corridor, path, lane, alley.

ajar *adjective/adverb* half open, slightly open, unfastened, unsecured, unlatched.

akin · alimony

20

akin *adjective akin to sailing/murder* related to, allied with, connected with, similar to, corresponding to.

alacrity *noun* readiness, promptness, willingness, eagerness, enthusiasm, haste, swiftness.

alarm *noun* **1** *have/hear a burglar/fire alarm* warning sound/device, alarm signal, alarm bell, danger/distress signal, siren, alert, tocsin. **2** *rumours causing alarm* fear, fright, terror, apprehension, panic, trepidation, nervousness, anxiety, unease, distress, consternation, disquiet, perturbation.

alarm *verb* **1** *crowds alarm her* frighten, scare, terrify, panic, startle, unnerve, distress, intimidate; *inf.* put the wind up. **2** *fire! you must alarm the neighbourhood* warn, alert, arouse, signal.

alarming *adjective* frightening, disturbing, terrifying, startling, shocking, distressing, dismaying, perturbing.

alarmist *noun* scaremonger, voice of doom, doomster, doom merchant.

alcohol *noun* strong drink, liquor, intoxicating liquor; spirits; *inf.* booze, tipple, the demon drink; *dial.* bevvy. *See table. See also tables at* BEER, MIXER, WHISKY, WINE.

ALCOHOLIC DRINKS	
absinthe	kvass
advocaat	liqueur
amaretto	Martini™
anisette	mead
aquavit	ouzo
arrack	pacharán
Bacardi™	pastis
Baileys™	Pernod™
Benedictine™	perry
blue curaçao	pisco
brandy	pombe
calvados	port
Campari™	poteen
chartreuse	raki
cider	Ricard™
Cinzano™	rum
Cointreau™	sake
crème de menthe	sambuca
Drambuie™	schnapps
Dubonnet™	sercial
framboise	sherry
Galliano™	Southern Comfort™
gin	Strega™
Grand Marnier™	tequila
Kahlua™	Tia Maria™
kirsch	vermouth
kummel	vodka

alcoholic *adjective alcoholic not soft drinks* intoxicating, inebriating, strong, hard, spirituous, vinous.

alcoholic *noun a confirmed alcoholic* alcohol addict, dipsomaniac, hard/heavy drinker, drunk, drunkard, tippler, sot, toper, inebriate, imbiber; *inf.* boozer, lush, alchy, dipso, soak, tosspot, wino, sponge.

alcove *noun* niche, recess, nook, opening, bay, hollow, cavity, corner.

alert *adjective* **1** *an alert mind/youngster* wideawake, sharp, bright, quick, keen, perceptive; *inf.* on the ball, on one's toes, quick off the mark. **2** *you must always be alert to danger* wideawake, on the look-out, aware, heedful, watchful, attentive, vigilant, observant, circumspect, wary, on one's guard; *fml.* on the qui vive.
Opposites SLOW; INATTENTIVE; OBLIVIOUS.

alias *adverb* also known as, also called, otherwise known as, otherwise; *inf.* a.k.a.

alias *noun* assumed name, false name, pseudonym, stage name, *nom de plume,* sobriquet; *fml. nom de guerre.*

alibi *noun* defence, plea, justification, explanation, reason, vindication, excuse, pretext.

alien *adjective* **1** *an alien culture* foreign, overseas, non-native, unnaturalized. **2** *an alien environment* strange, unfamiliar, unknown, outlandish, remote, exotic. **3** *behaviour alien to his principles* opposed, conflicting, contrary, adverse, incompatible, unacceptable, repugnant, hostile, antagonistic, inimical.

alien *noun* **1** *aliens deported in war-time* foreigner, outsider, stranger. **2** *aliens from Mars* extraterrestrial; *inf.* little green man.

alienate *verb* **1** *alienate his daughter from her mother* estrange, set against, turn away, make hostile, sever, divorce, separate, cut off, divide. **2** *alienate property* transfer, convey.

alienation *verb* **1** *alienation of his daughter* estrangement, severance, divorce, separation, cutting off. *See* ALIENATE 1. **2** *alienation of property* transfer, conveyance.

alight *adjective* **1** *set alight* on fire, ablaze, burning, lighted, lit, blazing, flaming, ignited. **2** *faces alight with joy* lit up, shining, bright, brilliant, illuminated.

alight *verb* **1** *alight from the bus* get off, dismount, disembark, descend. **2** *birds alighting on branches* land, come down, come to rest, touch down, settle, perch.
Opposites get on (*see* GET); BOARD; fly off (*see* FLY).

align *verb* **1** *align the books on the shelves* line up, range, arrange in line, rank, put in order, straighten. **2** *align with a political party* affiliate, ally, associate, join, cooperate, side, sympathize, agree.

alignment *noun* **1** *the alignment of the books* lining up, ranging, arrangement in line, straightening. *See* ALIGN 1. **2** *the alignment with a political party* affiliation, alliance, association, siding, sympathy. *See* ALIGN 2.

alike *adjective the sisters are so alike* like, similar, the same, indistinguishable, resembling, identical, interchangeable, corresponding.

alike *adverb think alike* similarly, the same, just the same, in the same way, identically, in like manner.

alimony *noun* maintenance, support, keep, sustenance, livelihood; *Scots* aliment.

alive *adjective* **1** *at least the captives are alive* living, live, breathing; *inf.* in the land of the living, alive and kicking; *fml.* animate. **2** *interest/debate is still very much alive* active, continuing, going on, existing, extant, prevalent, functioning, in the air/wind, in existence, in operation; *fml.* existent. **3** *seeming very much alive today* full of life, lively, active, energetic, alert, animated, vivacious, vigorous, spry, sprightly, vital, zestful, spirited. **4** *alive to the possibilities* alert to, awake to, aware/cognizant of. **5** *alive with vermin/crowds* overflowing, teeming, crowded, packed, bristling, swarming, thronged, bustling; *inf.* crawling, hopping, lousy; *Scots* hotching.
Opposites DEAD; EXTINCT; INACTIVE.

all *adjective* **1** *all animals are equal* each, each one of, every, every one of, every single. **2** *he worked all summer/buy all the wood* the whole of, every bit of, the complete, the entire, the totality of. **3** *in all earnestness* complete, entire, total, full, utter, greatest, perfect.

all *noun* **1** *all died* everyone, everybody, every/each person; *inf.* the whole lot. **2** *all were thrown away* everything, each thing; *inf.* the whole lot; lock, stock, and barrel. **3** *take all of it* everything, the whole/total amount, the entirety, the sum total, the aggregate.

all *adverb* *dressed all in black* completely, entirely, totally, wholly, altogether, fully, utterly.

allay *verb* *allay suffering/fears* lessen, diminish, reduce, relieve, calm, lull, alleviate, assuage, appease, quell, check, mitigate.

allegation *noun* claim, charge, accusation, professing, declaration, statement, assertion, averment, avowal, deposition, plea, affirmation; *fml.* asseveration.

allege *verb* claim, profess, declare, state, assert, aver, avow, affirm; *fml.* asseverate.

alleged *adjective* supposed, so-called, claimed, professed, declared, stated, designated. *See* ALLEGE.

allegiance *noun* loyalty, obedience, fidelity, faithfulness, duty, devotion, constancy, adherence, homage; *fml.* fealty.

allegorical *adjective* symbolic, metaphorical, figurative, emblematic, parabolic.

allegory *noun* **1** *Spenser's 'Faerie Queen' is an allegory* parable, fable, apologue. **2** *illustrate by allegory* symbolism, symbol, metaphor, analogy.

allergic *adjective* **1** *allergic to cow's milk* hypersensitive, sensitive, susceptible. **2** *allergic to work* averse, opposed, loath, hostile, antagonistic, disinclined.

allergy *noun* **1** *an allergy to cow's milk* hypersensitivity, sensitivity, susceptibility. **2** *an allergy to work* aversion, antipathy, opposition, hostility, antagonism, dislike.

alleviate *verb* *alleviate pain/poverty* reduce, lessen, diminish, relieve, ease, allay, abate, mitigate, assuage, palliate.

alley *noun* alleyway, lane, passage, passageway, path, pathway, corridor, backstreet.

alliance *noun* **1** *form an alliance/working in alliance with the French* union, association, coalition, league, confederation, federation, partnership, affiliation. **2** *the alliance between physics and maths* affinity, association, relationship.

allied *adjective* *a union of allied trades* associated, related, connected, linked, kindred.

allocate *verb* allot, assign, distribute, give out, share/mete/parcel out, dispense, apportion.

allocation *noun* **1** *spend our allocation for the year* allowance, quota, share, ration, portion, lot. **2** *the allocation of resources* allotment, assignment, distribution, giving out, apportionment. *See* ALLOCATE.

allot *verb* **1** *we allotted money for expenses* set aside, designate, earmark, assign, appropriate. **2** *allot portions to everyone* allocate, distribute, give out, dispense, apportion. *See* ALLOCATE.

allotment *noun* **1** *the allotment of money for expenses* setting aside, appropriation. *See* ALLOT 1. **2** *the allotment of portions* allocation, distribution, dispensing, apportionment. *See* ALLOT 2. **3** *your allotment for the year* allocation, allowance, quota. *See* ALLOCATION. **4** *digging his allotment* rented land, plot.

all-out *adjective* thorough, thoroughgoing, complete, total, exhaustive, vigorous, determined.

allow *verb* **1** *allow them to enter* permit, give permission to, let, authorize, sanction; *inf.* give the go-ahead to, give the green light to. **2** *allow £5 for expenses* allocate, allot, grant, give, assign, remit, spare. **3** *allow for wastage* plan for, take into consideration/account, make provision for, provide for. **4** *I allow that you won* admit, acknowledge, concede, grant, own, confess, agree.
Opposites PREVENT; FORBID; DENY.

allowable *adjective* *allowable expenses* permissible, admissible, authorized, sanctioned, justifiable, legitimate, lawful, legal; *inf.* legit.

allowance *noun* **1** *father gives her an allowance* remittance, payment, subsidy, grant, contribution. **2** *our book allowance* allocation, quota, share, ration, portion. **3** *tax/business allowances* rebate, discount, deduction, reduction, concession. **make allowances 1** *make allowances for his youth* take into consideration/account, bear in mind, have regard to. **2** *make allowances for him* make excuses, excuse, forgive, pardon.

alloy *noun* compound, mixture, amalgam, blend, combination, admixture, composite.

all right *adjective* **1** *the children are all right* safe, safe and sound, secure, unharmed, uninjured, well, fine; *inf.* OK. **2** *the coffee's all right?* satisfactory, acceptable, adequate, fine, passable; *inf.* OK.

all right *adverb* **1** *reached home all right* safely; *inf.* OK. **2** *worked out all right* satisfactorily, acceptably, fine; *inf.* OK.

all right *interjection* *all right! I'll go* right, yes, very well; *inf.* OK.

allude *verb* refer to, mention, touch upon, mention in passing/*en passant*, make an allusion to, cite.

allure *verb* attract, fascinate, entice, seduce, charm, enchant, bewitch, beguile, captivate, tempt, lure.

alluring *adjective* attractive, fascinating, charming, enchanting, captivating.

allusion *noun* reference, citation, mention, hint, intimation, suggestion.

ally *noun* confederate, partner, associate, accomplice, colleague, friend, helper, accessory, abettor.
Opposites ENEMY; OPPONENT; ADVERSARY.

ally *verb allied with France* unite, join, join forces, band together, go into partnership, combine, go into league, affiliate, form an alliance.

almanac *noun* yearbook, calendar, register, annual, annals.

almighty *adjective* **1** *Almighty God* supreme, all-powerful, omnipotent, most high. **2** *an almighty row* terrible, awful, dreadful, great.

almost *adverb* nearly, close to, just about, not quite, all but, not far from, approximately, practically, as good as, virtually, approaching, verging on, bordering on, well-nigh.

alone *adjective/adverb* **1** *be alone in the house* by oneself, solitary, unaccompanied, unattended, unescorted, companionless. **2** *succeed alone* by oneself, single-handed, unassisted, unaided. **3** *left all alone* solitary, lonely, deserted, abandoned, forsaken, forlorn, desolate, isolated. **4** *house standing alone* by itself, separate, detached, apart, unconnected. **5** *in his area the professor stands alone* unique, unparalleled, unequalled, unsurpassed, matchless, peerless. **6** *you alone can help* only, solely, just, exclusively, no one else, nothing but.

along *preposition* **1** *walk along the corridor/road* throughout the length of, from one end of to the other, through. **2** *grew along the verge* beside, by the side of, alongside, close by, on the edge of. **3** *somewhere along the way* in the course of, during, in the middle of.

along *adverb* **1** *move along* on, onwards, ahead, forwards. **2** *bring a friend along* in accompaniment, in company, as a partner. **along with** *poverty along with illness* together, in addition to, plus, coupled with, accompanying, accompanied by.

aloof *adverb stand aloof* at a distance, apart, separately, distanced, at arm's length.

aloof *adjective she's rather aloof* distant, detached, unresponsive, remote, unapproachable, standoffish, indifferent, unsympathetic, unsociable, unfriendly, cold, chilly.

aloud *adverb* out loud, audibly, clearly, distinctly, plainly, intelligibly.

alphabet *noun*. See table. See also table at PHONETIC ALPHABET.

already *adverb* **1** *known already* by this time, by now, before, before now, previously. **2** *young children reading already* as early as this, as soon as this, so soon, so early.

ALPHABETS				
Greek			**Hebrew**	
Α	α	alpha	א	aleph
Β	β	beta	ב	beth
Γ	γ	gamma	ג	gimel
Δ	δ	delta	ד	daleth
Ε	ε	epsilon	ה	he
Ζ	ζ	zeta	ו	waw
Η	η	eta	ז	zayin
Θ	θ	theta	ח	ḥeth
Ι	ι	iota	ט	ṭeth
Κ	κ	kappa	י	yodh
Λ	λ	lambda	כ	kaph
Μ	μ	mu	ל	lamedh
Ν	ν	nu	מ	mem
Ξ	ξ	xi	נ	nun
Ο	ο	omicron	ס	samekh
Π	π	pi	ע	'ayin
Ρ	ρ	rho	פ	pe
Σ	σ, ς	sigma	צ	ṣadhe
Τ	τ	tau	ק	qoph
Υ	υ	upsilon	ר	resh
Φ	φ	phi	ש	shin
Χ	χ	chi	ש	śin
Ψ	ψ	psi	ת	taw
Ω	ω	omega		

also *adverb* **1** *come along also* too, as well, besides, in addition, additionally, into the bargain, on top of that, to boot. **2** *also, he's ill* besides, furthermore, moreover, in addition, too, plus.

alter *verb* **1** *alter one's life style | alter a skirt* change, make different, adjust, adapt, modify, convert, reshape, remodel, vary, transform, transfigure, diversify, metamorphose. **2** *he's altered a lot* change, make different, metamorphose, suffer a sea change.

alteration *noun make an alteration* change, adjustment, adaptation, modification, conversion, variation, revision, amendment, transformation, transfiguration, metamorphosis.

altercation *noun* quarrel, row, argument, fight, wrangle, squabble, fracas; *inf.* set-to.

alternate *adjective* **1** *alternate weeks* every other, every second. **2** *alternate joy and sadness* in rotation, rotating, occurring in turns, interchanging, following in sequence, sequential. **3** *take an alternate route* alternative, different. See ALTERNATIVE *adjective* 1.

alternate *verb rain and sun alternated | rain alternated with sunshine* take turns, rotate, interchange, oscillate.

alternative *adjective* **1** *an alternative route* another, other, second, different. **2** *alternative medicine* non-standard.

alternative *noun* **1** *no alternative but to go* choice, option. **2** *have the alternative of going* choice, option, preference, election, substitute.

alternatively *adverb* alternatively, you can stay on the other hand, otherwise, instead, if not, or, as an alternative.

although *conjunction* though, even though, even if, even supposing, despite the fact that, while, whilst, albeit, notwithstanding the fact that.

altitude *noun* height, elevation; tallness, loftiness.

altogether *adverb* **1** *not altogether happy* completely, thoroughly, totally, entirely, absolutely, fully, utterly, perfectly, quite. **2** *altogether the day was fine* on the whole, all things considered, all in all, by and large, in general, in the main. **3** *nine of us altogether* in all, all told, *in toto*, taken together, in sum. *Opposites* PARTIALLY; RELATIVELY.

altruistic *adjective* unselfish, self-sacrificing, non-egotistical, public-spirited, philanthropic, humanitarian, charitable, open-handed. *Opposites* SELFISH.

always *adverb* **1** *he always comes early* every time, on every occasion, consistently, invariably, without exception, regularly, repeatedly, unfailingly. **2** *she's always complaining* continually, constantly, forever, repeatedly, perpetually, incessantly, eternally. **3** *you can always go by bus* whatever the circumstances, no matter what, in any event, in any case, come what may. **4** *he will love her always* forever and ever, evermore, eternally, ever, everlastingly, endlessly. *Opposites* SELDOM; NEVER; TEMPORARILY.

amalgamate *verb* combine, merge, unite, integrate, fuse, blend, mingle, intermingle, mix, intermix, incorporate; *lit.* commingle.

amass *verb* collect, gather, accumulate, pile/heap up, hoard, store up, assemble, garner; *inf.* stash away.

amateur *noun* non-professional, dilettante, layman, dabbler. *Opposites* PROFESSIONAL; EXPERT.

amateurish *adjective* unprofessional, unskilful, inexpert, incompetent, clumsy, crude, bungling.

amaze *verb* astonish, astound, surprise, dumbfound, flabbergast, daze, shock, stagger, stun, startle, bewilder, stupefy; *inf.* bowl over, strike dumb.

amazement *noun* astonishment, surprise, shock, bewilderment, stupefaction, wonder. *See* AMAZE.

ambassador *noun* diplomat, consul, envoy, emissary, legate, attaché, plenipotentiary, representative, deputy.

ambiguity *noun* **1** *the ambiguity of his remark* equivocacy, ambivalence, two-edgedness. **2** *the ambiguity of his meaning* doubtfulness, dubiety, obscurity, unclearness, vagueness, uncertainty, abstruseness. *See* AMBIGUOUS 2. **3** *full of ambiguities* equivocation, double-talk, obscurity, doubt, dubiety, uncertainty, puzzle, enigma, paradox.

ambiguous *adjective* **1** *we misunderstood because his remark was ambiguous* equivocal, ambivalent, two-edged. **2** *his meaning was ambiguous* cryptic, obscure, doubtful, dubious, unclear, vague, uncertain, indefinite, abstruse, puzzling, perplexing, enigmatic, paradoxical. *Opposites* CLEAR; UNEQUIVOCAL; DEFINITE.

ambition *noun* **1** *full of ambition to succeed* desire, aspiration, drive, striving, force, enterprise, eagerness, zeal, longing, yearning, hankering; *inf.* get-up-and-go, oomph. **2** *her ambition is to be boss* goal, aim, objective, purpose, intent, desire, wish, design, end, dream, hope.

ambitious *adjective* **1** *an ambitious man* aspiring, forceful, enterprising, go-ahead, zealous, purposeful, assertive, designing; *inf.* pushy, on the make. **2** *ambitious to be promoted* eager, enthusiastic, desirous of, striving, longing, avid, hankering after. **3** *an ambitious task* challenging, demanding, exacting, formidable, arduous, difficult, bold. *Opposites* AIMLESS; APATHETIC; EASY.

ambivalent *adjective* *an ambivalent attitude* equivocal, uncertain, doubtful, indecisive, inconclusive, irresolute, unresolved, hesitating, fluctuating, vacillating, mixed, opposing, conflicting, clashing. *Opposites* UNEQUIVOCAL; CERTAIN; CONCLUSIVE.

amble *verb* stroll, saunter, dawdle, wander, ramble; *inf.* mosey along.

ambush *noun* **1** *wait in ambush* hiding, concealment, cover, shelter, retreat, ambuscade. **2** *lay an ambush* trap, snare, pitfall, lure, ambuscade.

ambush *verb* *ambush the soldiers* waylay, lay a trap for, lie in wait for, trap, entrap, ensnare, decoy, ambuscade.

amenable *adjective* **1** *find her amenable to suggestion* tractable, agreeable, responsive, pliant, flexible, persuadable, adaptable, acquiescent, manageable, susceptible. **2** *amenable to the law* accountable, answerable, subject, liable, responsible. *Opposites* INFLEXIBLE; OBSTINATE.

amend *verb* **1** *amend a text* revise, alter, correct, modify, change, adjust. **2** *amend the situation* improve, remedy, ameliorate, better, fix, set right, repair, enhance.

amendment *noun* **1** *the amendment of the text* revision, alteration, modification, adjustment. *See* AMEND 1. **2** *the amendment of the situation* improvement, remedying, amelioration, betterment, fixing. *See* AMEND 2. **3** *amendments to the government bill* alteration, addendum, addition, adjunct, attachment, appendage.

amends *plural noun* *make amends for the mistake* compensation, recompense, reparation.

amenity *noun* **1** *amenities provided by the hotel* facility, service, convenience, resource, advantage. **2** *the amenity of his surroundings* pleasantness, agreeableness, pleasurableness, enjoyableness, niceness.

American Football *noun. See table at* FOOTBALL.

amiable *adjective* friendly, pleasant, agreeable, pleasing, charming, delightful, good-natured, sociable, genial, congenial. *Opposites* UNFRIENDLY; DISAGREEABLE.

amicable *adjective* *an amicable settlement* friendly, good-natured, civil, harmonious, cordial, non-hostile, peaceful. *Opposites* UNFRIENDLY; HOSTILE.

amid *preposition* in the midst of, amidst, in the middle/course of, among, amongst, in the thick of.

amiss *adjective something was amiss | flowers wouldn't seem amiss* wrong, awry, faulty, out of order, defective, unsatisfactory, incorrect, inappropriate.

ammunition *noun* **1** *running out of ammunition for the guns* projectiles; cartridges, gunpowder, powder. *See tables at* BULLET, EXPLOSIVE, MISSILE. **2** *run out of ammunition in an argument* information, data, input; pointers, points, advantages.

amnesty *noun* general pardon, pardon, pardoning, reprieve; absolution, forgiveness, dispensation, indulgence.

amok *adverb* frenziedly, in a frenzy, berserk, wildly, uncontrollably, maniacally, crazedly, insanely, violently, destructively.

among, amongst *preposition* **1** *live among trees/friends* in the midst of, amid, amidst, in the middle of, surrounded by, in the thick of. **2** *divide it among you* between, to each of. **3** *among us was a doctor* included in, out of, in the group of, in the number of, in the company of. **4** *decide among yourselves* by the joint action of, by all of, by the whole of, with one another, together, mutually, reciprocally.

amorous *adjective* loving, passionate, sexual, lustful, erotic, amatory.

amorphous *adjective* formless, unformed, shapeless, unshaped, structureless, unstructured, indeterminate, ill-organized, vague, nebulous; *fml.* inchoate.

amount *noun* **1** *a large amount of money/cloud/experience* quantity, measure, mass, volume, bulk, expanse, extent. **2** *the full amount* total, grand/sum total, aggregate; *inf.* whole caboodle, whole shebang.

amount *verb* **amount to 1** *the bill amounted to £50* add up to, total, come to, run to. **2** *their silence amounts to a confession* equal, add up to, be equivalent to, correspond to, approximate to. **3** *he never amounted to anything* become, grow/develop into, mature into, progress/advance to.

amphibian *noun. See table.*

AMPHIBIANS	
axolotl	natterjack toad
bullfrog	newt
caecilian	olm
clawed frog	platanna
Congo eel	poison-arrow
eft	frog
frog	salamander
Goliath frog	siren
hairy frog	spade-foot toad
hellbender	Suriname toad
midwife toad	toad
mud puppy	tree frog

ample *adjective* **1** *ample food to live on* enough, sufficient, adequate, plenty, more than enough, enough and to spare. **2** *an ample supply of wine* plentiful, abundant, copious, lavish, generous, liberal, profuse, bountiful, plenteous. **3** *of ample proportions | an ample bosom* large, big, substantial, extensive, wide, spacious, roomy, capacious, commodious. **Opposites** INSUFFICIENT; SCANTY; MEAGRE.

amplify *verb* **1** *amplify the sound/signal* increase, boost, magnify, intensify, heighten, augment, supplement. **2** *amplify your statement* expand, enlarge on, elaborate on, add to, develop, flesh out, go into detail about, expound on, expatiate on, explicate. **Opposites** REDUCE; CONDENSE.

amputate *verb* cut off, sever, remove, excise, lop, lop off, dismember.

amuse *verb* **1** *the clowns amused them* entertain, gladden, cheer, please, charm, delight, divert, beguile, enliven, regale with. **2** *amuse yourselves when I'm out* occupy, interest, entertain, divert, absorb, engross. **Opposites** BORE; DEPRESS.

amusement *noun* **1** *smiling with amusement* mirth, laughter, fun, merriment, gaiety, hilarity, enjoyment, pleasure, delight. **2** *provide a range of amusements* entertainment, diversion, interest, recreation, sport, pastime, hobby. **3** *the amusement of the children* entertaining, entertainment, diverting. *See* AMUSE 1.

amusing *adjective an amusing tale/story-teller* humorous, funny, comical, witty, entertaining, hilarious, facetious, droll, jocular. **Opposites** BORING; TEDIOUS; SOLEMN.

anaemic *adjective* **1** *anaemic and frail* weak, pale, wan, colourless, pallid, ashen; *inf.* bloodless. **2** *an anaemic effort/group* weak, feeble, powerless, impotent, vigourless, ineffective, ineffectual, enervated.

anaesthetic *noun give an anaesthetic to the patient* narcotic, opiate, soporific, stupefacient, painkiller, sedative, analgesic, anodyne; general anaesthetic, local anaesthetic.

anaesthetic *adjective an anaesthetic substance/effect* numbing, deadening, dulling, narcotic, opiate, soporific, stupefacient, painkilling, sedative, analgesic, anodyne.

analogous *adjective* similar, parallel, comparable, like, corresponding, related, kindred, matching, equivalent, homologous.

analogy *noun* similarity, parallel, correspondence, likeness, resemblance, correlation, relation, equivalence, similitude, homology.

analyse *verb* **1** *analyse the sample/structure* break down, dissect, separate out, fractionate, assay, decompose, examine; *fml.* anatomize. **2** *analyse the results of the match* study, examine, investigate, enquire into, dissect, review, evaluate, interpret.

analysis *noun* **1** *carry out analysis of the sample/structure* breakdown, dissection, fractionation, decomposition, assay, examination; *fml.* anatomization. **2** *the analysis of the match results* study, examination, investigation, enquiry, dissection, review, evaluation, interpretation.

analytical, analytic *adjective an analytical mind/approach* investigative, enquiring, dissecting, inquisitive, searching, critical, interpretative, diagnostic.

anarchic *adjective* lawless, ungoverned.

anarchist *noun* revolutionist, revolutionary, nihilist, rebel, insurgent, terrorist.

anarchy *noun* **1** *state of anarchy in the country* absence of government, nihilism, lawlessness, mobocracy, misgovernment, misrule, revolution. **2** *anarchy in the classroom* riot, disorder, chaos, rebellion, mutiny, tumult, mayhem, insurrection, disorganization.
Opposites LAW; ORDER; GOVERNMENT.

anathema *noun* **1** *racism is anathema to them* abomination, abhorrence, aversion, bane, bugbear, bête noir. **2** *following an anathema of the Church* excommunication, damnation, proscription, denunciation, curse, ban, malediction.

anatomy *noun* **1** *the anatomy of dogs* structure, make-up, composition, framework. **2** *undertake the anatomy of the animal/plant* dissection, cutting up, division, dismemberment, vivisection, zootomy. **3** *the anatomy of crime* analysis, examination, study, investigation, scrutiny, research, enquiry.

ancestor *noun* forebear, progenitor, forerunner, precursor, prototype.
Opposites DESCENDANT; SUCCESSOR.

ancestral *adjective* *ancestral home* inherited, hereditary, lineal.

ancestry *noun* **1** *of noble ancestry* lineage, descent, extraction, parentage, origin, derivation, genealogy, pedigree, blood, stock. **2** *research into one's ancestry* ancestors, antecedents, forefathers, forebears, progenitors; family tree.

anchor *noun* **1** *a ship's anchor* mooring, kedge, grapnel, killick, drogue. **2** *mother was the family's anchor* mainstay, support, protection; stability, security.

anchor *verb* **1** *anchor the boat* secure by anchor, secure, fasten. **2** *anchor the bush to a trellis* fasten, attach, connect, bind, affix.

ancient *adjective* **1** *in ancient times* earliest, early, of long ago, primeval, prehistoric, primordial. **2** *an ancient custom* age-old, timeworn, antique, long-lived, very old. **3** *positively ancient ideas* antiquated, old-fashioned, out of date, outmoded, archaic, bygone, obsolete, passé, superannuated, atavistic.
Opposites RECENT; MODERN; NEW.

ancillary *adjective* auxiliary, secondary, subsidiary, subordinate, accessory, contributory, supplementary, additional, extra, attendant.

and *conjunction* along with, with, together with, as well as, also, in addition to, including, plus.

anecdote *noun* story, tale, narrative, yarn, sketch, reminiscence.

anew *adverb* again, afresh, once more, once again, over again.

angel *noun* **1** *heavenly angels* messenger of god, heavenly messenger. *See table.* **2** *thanks! you're an angel* darling, dear, gem, saint, paragon.

3 *a play staged with an angel's help* backer, supporter, benefactor, promoter.

ORDERS OF ANGELS	
angels	principalities
archangels	seraphim
cherubim	thrones
dominations	virtues
powers	

angelic *adjective* **1** *angelic beings* seraphic, cherubic, celestial, heavenly, ethereal; *fml.* empyrean. **2** *an angelic child* virtuous, innocent, pure, good, saintly, beautiful, adorable.

anger *noun* *shout in anger* annoyance, rage, fury, indignation, temper, wrath, exasperation, irritation, vexation, ire, ill humour, irritability, outrage, pique, spleen; *lit.* choler.

anger *verb* *it angered him* annoy, infuriate, enrage, exasperate, irritate, incense, madden, vex, outrage, provoke, nettle, rile, pique, gall, fret.
Opposites PACIFY; PLACATE.

angle¹ *noun* **1** *a right angle | the angle of the walls* intersection, inclination; projection, corner, bend, fork, nook, niche, recess, elbow. **2** *take an angle on a news story* slant, approach, viewpoint, standpoint, point of view, position, opinion.

angle² *verb* **1** *angle the cam* slant, tilt, slope, turn. **2** *angle a news item* slant, skew, distort.

angle³ *verb* **1** *angle by the riverside* fish, cast, go fishing. **2** *angle for a compliment* seek, solicit, scheme, aim, try, fish; *inf.* be after.

angry *adjective* annoyed, furious, infuriated, indignant, enraged, irate, wrathful, exasperated, irritated, irascible, heated, incensed, maddened, ill-humoured, hot-tempered, outraged, vexed, provoked; *inf.* mad, hot under the collar; *fml.* choleric. *See* ANGER *verb.*
Opposites CALM; PLEASED.

angst *noun* anxiety, fear, apprehension, foreboding, disquiet.

anguish *noun* agony, suffering, torture, torment, pain, distress, misery, sorrow, grief, woe; pangs, throes.

angular *adjective* **1** *an angular shape* sharp-cornered, pointed, V-shaped, Y-shaped, forked, bifurcate. **2** *an angular woman* bony, gaunt, raw-boned, rangy, scrawny, spare, skinny, lean.

animal *noun* **1** *plants and animals* beast, creature, brute. *See tables. See also tables at* ARACHNID, BAT, BEAR, BIRD, CAT, CATTLE, DEER, DOG, DONKEY, FISH, FOWL, FOX, GAME, GOAT, HORSE, INSECT, LAIR, MARSUPIAL, MOLLUSC, MONKEY, PIG, RABBIT, RODENT, SEAL, SHEEP, SQUIRREL, WEASEL, WHALE, WOLF, WORM, YOUNG. **2** *the man was an animal* beast, brute, monster, barbarian, savage, fiend; *inf.* swine.

animal *adjective* **1** *animal as opposed to plant characteristics* animalistic, zooid, zooidal.

2 *animal passions* carnal, sensual, fleshly, bodily, physical, brutish, bestial.

animate *verb* **1** *a smile animated her face | music animated the group* give life to, enliven, liven up, cheer up, gladden, vitalize; *inf.* buck up, pep up. **2** *fresh hope animated them* encourage, hearten, inspire, excite, fire, rouse, stir, stimulate, incite, energize.

animate *adjective something animate* living, alive, live, breathing.

animated *adjective* **1** *an animated discussion* lively, energetic, active, vigorous, excited, enthusiastic, spirited, fiery, passionate, dynamic, forceful, vital, fervent, vivacious, buoyant. **2** *an animated cartoon* moving.
Opposites APATHETIC; INACTIVE; SLUGGISH.

animation *noun the animation of the discussion* liveliness, energy, vigour, excitement, enthusiasm, fieriness dynamism, passion, forcefulness, vitality, fervour, vivacity, buoyancy, verve, zest, sparkle; *inf.* zing.

annals *plural noun* archives, chronicles, records, accounts; register, history.

annex *verb* **1** *annex a garage to the house* add, attach, join, connect, append, adjoin, affix. **2** *annex a smaller country* take over, occupy, seize, conquer, appropriate, expropriate, arrogate.

annexe, annex *noun a school annexe* supplementary/additional building, extension, wing, ell.

annihilate *verb* destroy, wipe out, exterminate, decimate, eliminate, liquidate, abolish, obliterate, eradicate, extinguish, erase, root out, extirpate.
Opposites CREATE; BUILD; ESTABLISH.

anniversary *noun. See table at* WEDDING.

annotate *verb annotate a text* gloss, comment on, add notes/footnotes to, explain, interpret, elucidate, explicate.

annotation *noun* **1** *annotations in the margin* note, comment, gloss, commentary, footnote, explanation, interpretation, observation, eluci-

---

ANIMALS WITH MALE AND FEMALE FORMS

Animal	Male	Female	Animal	Male	Female	Animal	Male	Female
antelope	buck	doe	elephant	bull	cow	lion	lion	lioness
badger	boar	sow	ferret	jack	jill	lobster	cock	hen
bear	boar	sow	fish	cock	hen	moose	bull	cow
bobcat	tom	lioness	fox	fox	vixen	ox	bullock	cow
buffalo	bull	cow	giraffe	bull	cow	peacock	peacock	peahen
camel	bull	cow	goat	billygoat	nanny-goat	pheasant	cock	hen
caribou	stag	doe				pig	boar	sow
cat	tom	queen	goose	gander	goose	rhinoceros	bull	cow
cattle	bull	cow	hare	buck	doe	seal	bull	cow
chicken	cock	hen	hartebeest	bull	cow	sheep	ram	ewe
cougar	tom	lioness	horse	stallion	mare	swan	cob	pen
coyote	dog	bitch	impala	ram	ewe	tiger	tiger	tigress
deer	stag	doe	jackrabbit	buck	doe	weasel	boar	cow
dog	dog	bitch	kangaroo	buck	doe	whale	bull	cow
donkey	jackass	jennyass	leopard	leopard	leopardess	wolf	dog	bitch
duck	drake	duck				zebra	stallion	mare

ADJECTIVES RELATING TO ANIMALS AND BIRDS

Adjective	Creature	Adjective	Creature	Adjective	Creature
anguilliform	eel	corvine	crow	passerine	sparrow
anguine	snake	crustacean/		phocine	seal
anserine	goose	crustaceous	crab/lobster/	piscine	fish
apian	bee		shrimp	porcine	pig
aquiline	eagle	elephantine	elephant	psittacine	parrot
arachnoid	spider	equine	horse	saurian	lizard
asinine	donkey	feline	cat	sciurine	chipmunk/
avian	bird	gallinaceous	fowl		marmot/
batrachian	frog/toad	hircine	goat		squirrel
bovine	cow	hirundine	swallow	serpentine	snake
canine	dog	leonine	lion	simian	monkey
caprine	goat	leporine	hare	taurine	bull
cervid/cervine	deer	lupine	wolf	turdine	thrush
cetacean/		murine	mouse/rat	ursine	bear
cetaceous	dolphin/	musteline	ferret/	vermiform	worm
	porpoise/		skunk/	viperine/	
	whale		weasel	viperous	viper
chelonian	terrapin/tor-	ophidian	snake	viverrine	civet/
	toise/turtle	oscine	songbird		mongoose
colubrine	snake	otarid	sea lion/seal	vulpine	fox
columbine	dove	ovine	sheep		

dation, explication. **2** *the annotation of the text* glossing, commenting on, explaining, explanation. *See* ANNOTATE.

announce *verb* **1** *announce the results* make known/public, give out, declare, intimate, proclaim, report, disclose, reveal, divulge, publicize, broadcast, publish, advertise, promulgate. **2** *announce a guest* give the name of, name, herald, usher in. **3** *cigar smoke announcing his approach* signal, indicate, signify, give notice of, warn, foretell, herald, betoken, augur, portend, harbinger.

announcement *noun* **1** *the announcement of the results* declaration, intimation, proclamation, report, disclosure. *See* ANNOUNCE 1. **2** *make an announcement | give out an announcement* statement, report, intimation, bulletin, communiqué, message; information.

announcer *noun* commentator, presenter, newsreader, newscaster, broadcaster, reporter, anchorman, master of ceremonies, MC, herald.

annoy *verb* **1** *their behaviour annoyed her* irritate, exasperate, vex, ruffle, rile, irk, provoke, displease, anger, madden, rub one up the wrong way, get on one's nerves; *inf.* get to, bug. **2** *don't annoy her when she's reading* bother, disturb, pester, worry, harass, trouble, plague, harry.

annoyance *noun* **1** *to our annoyance* irritation, exasperation, displeasure, anger, vexation, ire. **2** *an annoyance to work late* nuisance, pest, bother, trial, irritant; *inf.* bind, bore, pain, pain in the neck, hassle.

annual *adjective* **1** *annual report* yearly, once a year. **2** *annual subscription* year-long.

annually *adverb* **1** *payable annually* yearly, by the year, once a year, per annum. **2** *visit annually* once a year, every year, each year.

annul *verb* nullify, declare null and void, quash, cancel, invalidate, rescind, revoke, repeal, abrogate, void, negate.

anodyne *noun* *an anodyne for the patient* analgesic, painkiller, pain-reliever, palliative.

anoint *verb* **1** *anoint the body* oil, apply ointment; spread over, smear, rub, embrocate. **2** *anoint the new king* consecrate, sanctify, bless, ordain, hallow.

anomalous *adjective* abnormal, atypical, irregular, deviant, deviating, aberrant, exceptional, rare, unusual, eccentric, odd, bizarre, peculiar, inconsistent.
Opposites NORMAL; REGULAR.

anomaly *noun* abnormality, irregularity, deviation, aberration, departure, rarity, eccentricity, oddity, peculiarity, inconsistency.

anon *adverb* soon, shortly, presently, in a short time, in a little while, by and by, before long, ere long.

anonymous *adjective* *an anonymous donor* unnamed, nameless, unidentified, unknown, unspecified, undesignated, unacknowledged, uncredited, unsigned, incognito; *fml.* innominate.

another *adjective* **1** *another chance* second, further, additional. **2** *it was another girl, not Jane* different, some other, not the same.

answer *noun* **1** *receive an answer* reply, response, acknowledgement, rejoinder, retort, riposte; *inf.* comeback. **2** *the answer to the clue* solution, explanation, resolution. **3** *his answer to the charge* defence, plea, refutation, rebuttal, vindication. **4** *his answer was to leave the room* reaction, response.
Opposites QUESTION; QUERY; PUZZLE.

answer *verb* **1** *answer a question/letter* reply to, respond to, acknowledge, come back to, make a rejoinder, retort, riposte. **2** *answer the bell/ phone* respond to, react to. **3** *answer to the description* fit, match, correspond to, be similar to, conform to, correlate to. **4** *answer our requirements* meet, satisfy, fulfil, fill, measure up to, serve. **answer back** talk back, be cheeky, be impertinent, contradict, argue with, disagree with. **answer for 1** *answer for her crimes* pay for, suffer for, be punished for, make amends for, make reparation for, atone for. **2** *cannot answer for my sister* vouch for, be responsible for, be accountable for, be liable for, take the blame for; *inf.* take the rap for.

answerable *adjective* *answerable to the manager | answerable for your safety* responsible, accountable, liable.

antagonism *noun* hostility, opposition, animosity, antipathy, enmity, rivalry, competition, dissension, friction, conflict.

antagonist *noun* adversary, enemy, foe, opponent, rival, competitor, contender.

antagonistic *adjective* hostile, ill-disposed, opposed, dissenting, adverse, antipathetic, inimical, at odds with.
Opposites FRIENDLY; SYMPATHETIC.

antagonize *verb* arouse hostility/enmity in, alienate, put against, estrange; *fml.* disaffect.

antecedents *plural noun* **1** *inherited from his antecedents* ancestors, forefathers, forebears, predecessors. **2** *check his antecedents* record, history, past, background.

antedate *verb* **1** *antedate a cheque* backdate, assign to an earlier date. **2** *antedate the civil war* precede, come/go before, anticipate.

antediluvian *adjective* **1** *in antediluvian times* prehistoric, primeval, primordial; *inf.* before the flood; *fml.* autochthonal. **2** *antediluvian attitudes* antiquated, old-fashioned, outmoded, out of date, archaic, obsolete; *inf.* out of the ark.

antelope *noun. See table at* DEER.

anteroom *noun* outer room, waiting-room, reception area, vestibule, lobby, foyer; *fml.* antechamber.

anthem *noun* **1** *church anthems* hymn, psalm, song of praise, plainsong, chorale, chant, canticle. **2** *a national anthem* song of praise, paean, state song.

anthology *noun* collection, compendium, treasury, compilation, miscellany, selection; *lit.* garland; *fml.* collectanea, ana, analects.

anticipate *verb* **1** *anticipate trouble | anticipate that trouble will occur* expect, foresee, predict, forecast; count on, look for, prepare for, await, contemplate. **2** *anticipating her birthday with pleasure* look forward to, await, look towards;

inf. lick one's lips over. **3** *anticipate his chess move* forestall, intercept, prevent, nullify; *inf.* beat one to it, beat to the draw. **4** *anticipate the invention of radio* antedate, come/go before, be earlier than.

anticipation *noun* **1** *in anticipation of success/ war* expectation, prediction, preparation, awaiting, contemplation. **2** *full of anticipation before the party* expectancy, hope, hopefulness.

anticlimax *noun* let-down, disappointment, comedown; disillusionment; *lit.* bathos.

antics *plural noun* pranks, capers, larks, tricks, romps, frolics; horseplay.

antidote *noun* **1** *an antidote to poison* antitoxin, countermeasure. **2** *an antidote to sadness* cure, remedy, corrective, countermeasure, counteragent.

antipathy *noun* aversion, hostility, dislike, enmity, opposition, antagonism, animosity, hatred, abhorrence, loathing, repugnance, animus.
Opposites LIKING; FRIENDSHIP; RAPPORT.

antiquated *adjective* *antiquated attitudes* out of date, old-fashioned, outmoded, passé, outworn, archaic, obsolete, antediluvian; *inf.* superannuated.

antique *adjective* **1** *antique furniture* antiquarian, old, vintage. **2** *antique customs* age-old, timeworn, early, earliest, prehistoric, primeval, primordial. **3** *antique attitudes* old-fashioned. *See* ANTIQUATED.

antique *noun* *the chair's an antique* heirloom, object of virtu, relic, curio.

antiseptic *adjective* **1** *an antiseptic substance* disinfectant, germicidal, bactericidal. **2** *an antiseptic surface* sterile, germ-free, uncontaminated, unpolluted, aseptic, sanitary, hygienic. **3** *antiseptic surroundings* clinical, characterless, undistinguished, unexciting.

antiseptic *noun* *swab with antiseptic* disinfectant, germicide, bactericide.

antisocial *adjective* **1** *dropping litter is antisocial* disruptive, disorderly, lawless, rebellious, asocial. **2** *feeling antisocial* unsociable, uncommunicative, reserved, unfriendly, withdrawn, retiring.

antithesis *noun* **1** *white is the antithesis of black* opposite, converse, reverse, inverse, other extreme. **2** *an attitude the antithesis of mine* opposite, contrast, contrariety, inverse, reversal.

anxiety *noun* **1** *anxiety about the future* worry, concern, uneasiness, apprehension, disquiet, nervousness, tenseness, misgiving, angst. **2** *full of anxiety to win* eagerness, desire, longing, yearning, avidity.

anxious *adjective* **1** *anxious about the future | anxious about her health* worried, concerned, uneasy, apprehensive, fearful, nervous, disturbed, tense. **2** *anxious to please* eager, keen, longing, yearning, avid.
Opposites CAREFREE; UNCONCERNED; NONCHALANT.

any *adjective* **1** *did you get any books/meat?* a, an, one, some, a single one, a single part. **2** *any book will do* any one, every, whatever, whichever; *inf.* any old.

any *pronoun* **1** *there are the thieves but do you recognize any?* anyone, anybody, somebody, someone. **2** *don't give him any* even one, even the smallest amount.

any *adverb* *is your father any better?* at all, in the least, to any extent, to some extent, somewhat, in any degree.

anyhow *adverb* **1** *go anyhow you like* in any way, anyway, in any manner, by any means. **2** *anyhow, you must go* in any case, in any event, at all events, no matter what. **3** *lying around anyhow* haphazardly, carelessly, heedlessly, negligently.

apart *adverb* **1** *with feet apart* separate, separately, separated, at a distance. **2** *a person/ house standing apart* to one side, aside, to the side, separately, alone, by oneself/itself, distant, isolated. **3** *a couple living apart* separate, separately, separated, divorced, not together. **4** *blow/break apart* to pieces, in pieces, to bits, asunder. **apart from** *no-one apart from him* except, but, other than, aside from, excluding, not counting, save.

apartment *noun* **1** *the royal/furnished apartments* accommodation, lodging, suite; living quarters, quarters, rooms. **2** *an appartment in New York* flat.

apathetic *adjective* uninterested, unmoved, unconcerned, unfeeling, unemotional, emotionless, unresponsive, indifferent, impassive, passive, listless, lethargic, languid, phlegmatic, torpid.

apathy *noun* lack of interest/concern/feeling/ emotion, unconcern, unresponsiveness, indifference, impassivity, passivity, dispassion, dispassionateness, listlessness, lethargy, languor, torpor.
Opposites ENTHUSIASM; EMOTION; PASSION.

ape *verb* imitate, mimic, copy, echo, mock, parody, parrot.

ape *noun.* *See table at* MONKEY.

aperture *noun* opening, gap, hole, orifice, window, crack, slit, space, chink, fissure, perforation, breach, eye, interstice.

apex *noun* top, summit, peak, pinnacle, tip, crest, vertex, acme, zenith, apogee.

aphrodisiac *noun* love potion, philtre, stimulant, stimulative.

apiece *adverb* each, for/from/to each, respectively, individually, separately.

aplomb *noun* poise, assurance, self-confidence, self-assurance, calmness, composure, collectedness, equanimity, equilibrity, level-headedness, sang-froid.

apocryphal *adjective* **1** *apocryphal evidence* unverified, unauthenticated, unsubstantiated, spurious, debatable, questionable, dubious, doubtful. **2** *apocryphal tales of his sexual prowess* mythical, fictitious, legendary, false, untrue, phony.

apologetic *adjective* sorry, regretful, contrite, remorseful, penitent, repentant, rueful.
Opposites UNREPENTANT; IMPENITENT.

apologize *verb* say one is sorry, say sorry, make an apology, express regret, ask forgiveness, ask for pardon, beg pardon; *inf.* eat humble pie.

apology *noun* **1** *deliver an apology* expression of regret; regrets. **2** *present my apologies for my absence* excuses. **3** *an/the apology for their beliefs* defence, vindication, justification, argument, apologia; plea, excuse. **4** *an apology for a man/ meal* travesty, poor excuse, excuse, mockery, caricature, imitation, substitute, makeshift, stopgap.

apostle *noun* **1** *Christian apostles* missionary, evangelical, evangelic, preacher, teacher, reformer, spreader of the faith/word; *fml.* proselytizer. *See table.* **2** *an apostle of acupuncture* advocate, supporter, crusader, campaigner, proponent, propagandist, pioneer.

THE APOSTLES OF JESUS CHRIST

Peter	James, son of
James, son of	Alphaeus
Zebedee	Judas/Thaddeus, son
John	of James
Andrew	Simon
Philip	Judas Iscariot
Bartholomew	Matthias (replaced
Matthew	Judas Iscariot)
Thomas	

---

appal *verb* shock, dismay, horrify, outrage, astound, alarm.

appalling *adjective* shocking, horrifying, frightful, outrageous, terrible, awful, dreadful, ghastly, hideous, harrowing, dire.

apparatus *noun* **1** *laboratory/gymnastic apparatus* equipment, gear, tackle, mechanism, outfit, plant; appliance, machine, device, contraption; instruments, tools. *See tables at* LABORATORY, TOOL. **2** *the apparatus of government* structure, system, organization, network, set-up, hierarchy.

apparel *noun* clothing, dress, attire, outfit, wear, costume, garb, habit; clothes, garments, robes, vestments, habiliments; *inf.* gear. *See tables at* DRESS, FOOTWEAR, HAT, SHIRT, SKIRT, TROUSERS.

apparent *adjective* **1** *problems apparent from the start* clear, plain, obvious, evident, discernible, perceivable, perceptible, manifest, patent. **2** *apparent calmness* seeming, ostensible, outward, superficial, specious, quasi.

apparently *adverb* apparently *he's ill* seemingly, it seems that, it appears that, on the face of it.

apparition *noun* **1** *frightened of the apparition* ghost, spectre, phantom, spirit, wraith; *inf.* spook; *fml./lit.* shade, revenant, visitant. **2** *the sudden apparition of the black figure* appearance, manifestation, materialization, emergence, visitation.

appeal *noun* **1** *an appeal for help* request, call, plea, entreaty, petition, supplication, solicitation, imploration. **2** *barrister asking for an appeal* reconsideration, re-examination, review, another opinion. **3** *hold little appeal* attraction, attractiveness, allure, charm, interest, fascination, temptation, enticement.

appeal *verb* **1** *appeal for money* ask for, request, put in a plea for, entreat, beg/beseech/ plead for, implore, solicit, petition for. **2** *appeal to a higher court* apply for an appeal. *See* APPEAL *noun* 2. **3** *appeals to her* attract, charm, interest, engage, fascinate, tempt, entice, allure, invite.

appear *verb* **1** *a messenger/solution appeared* come into view/sight, emerge, come forth, arrive, turn/show/crop up, materialize, surface, loom. **2** *he may appear at the meeting* attend, be present at, turn up at; *inf.* show up, show. **3** *she appeared sad* seem, look, have the appearance/air of being, give the impression of being. **4** *the new furniture range finally appeared | has his new book appeared?* come into being/existence, come out, become available, come on the market, be published/produced. **5** *she appears nightly* perform, play, act, take part, be on stage, come on.
Opposites DISAPPEAR; VANISH.

appearance *noun* **1** *the appearance of the messenger/solution* coming into view, emergence, arrival, advent, materialization, surfacing, looming. *See* APPEAR 1. **2** *his weekly appearance at meetings* attendance, presence, turning up. *See* APPEAR 2. **3** *having an appearance of sadness* look, air, expression, impression, manner, demeanour, bearing, aspect; *lit.* mien. **4** *poor but giving the appearance of being rich* semblance, guise, show, pretence, image, outward appearance, front, impression.

appease *verb* **1** *appease the enemy with gifts* placate, pacify, make peace with, conciliate, calm, tranquillize, soothe, quieten down, mollify, soften, propitiate. **2** *appease one's appetite/ curiosity* satisfy, assuage, take the edge off, blunt, relieve, quench, diminish.

appeasement *noun* **1** *policy of appeasement* conciliation, placation, concession, acquiescence, acceding, peace-offering, accommodation, propitiation. **2** *the appeasement of the enemy* placating, pacification, conciliation, calming. *See* APPEASE 1. **3** *the appeasement of one's appetite* satisfying, assuagement. *See* APPEASE 2.

append *verb* append *one's signature | append a clause* add, attach, affix, adjoin.

appendage *noun* **1** *an appendage to a will/family* addition, attachment, adjunct, addendum, appurtenance, accessory, affix. **2** *an animal's appendage* extremity, protuberance, projection, member, limb, tail.

appendix *noun* appendix *to a book* supplement, addendum, postscript, addition, extension, adjunct, codicil.

appertain *verb* **appertain to** belong to, relate to, be connected with, be part of, be relevant to, have relevance to, have to do with, be pertinent to, have reference to, have a bearing upon.

appetite *noun* **1** *an appetite for food* hunger, taste, palate, desire, relish. **2** *an appetite for adventure* hunger, thirst, need, liking, inclination, passion, longing, craving, yearning, hankering, zest, gusto, propensity, proclivity; *fml.* appetency.

appetizer *noun* starter, hors d'oeuvre, antipasto, canapé.

appetizing *adjective* **1** *an appetizing dish* mouth-watering, tasty, succulent, delicious, palatable. **2** *an appetizing prospect* tempting, inviting, enticing, appealing, alluring.

applaud *verb* **1** *the audience applauded* clap, cheer, whistle, give a standing ovation to, ask for an encore, put one's hands together; *inf.* give someone a big hand. **2** *applaud their courage* praise, express admiration/approval for, admire, compliment on, commend, acclaim, extol, laud.
Opposites HISS; CONDEMN; CENSURE.

applause *noun* **1** *the applause of the audience* clapping, handclapping, cheering, whistling, standing ovation; cheers, whistles, encores, bravos, curtain calls. **2** *won the applause of the neighbourhood* praise, admiration, approval, approbation, commendation, acclaim, acclamation, eulogy, extolment, laudation; compliments, accolades, plaudits.

appliance *noun* **1** *an electrical appliance* device, gadget, apparatus, implement, machine, instrument, tool, mechanism. **2** *the appliance of force* application, use. See APPLICATION 1.

applicable *adjective* **1** *rules applicable to everyone* relevant, appropriate, pertinent, apposite, apropos. **2** *an applicable remedy* fitting, suitable, useful.
Opposites INAPPLICABLE; IRRELEVANT.

applicant *noun* candidate, interviewee, competitor, enquirer, claimant, suppliant, supplicant, petitioner, suitor, postulant.

application *noun* **1** *the application of force* use, exercise, administration, employment, putting into operation/practice, practice. **2** *a remark having no application to the case* relevance, bearing, significance, pertinence, aptness, appositeness, germaneness. **3** *the application of ointment* putting on, rubbing in. See APPLY 3. **4** *students with application* industry, diligence, attentiveness, effort, hard work, assiduity, commitment, dedication, perseverance, persistence, sedulousness. **5** *an application for a job | application for a tax rebate* enquiry, request, claim, appeal, petition, entreaty, suit, solicitation, requisition, demand. **6** *a healing application* ointment, lotion, cream, rub, emollient, balm, poultice, unguent.

apply *verb* **1** *apply force/tact | apply the brakes* use, put to use, employ, utilize, administer, exercise, put into practice, bring into effect/play, bring to bear. **2** *the remark did not apply to the situation* be relevant/significant/pertinent, be apt/apposite/germane, have a bearing on. **3** *apply ointment* put on, rub in, cover with, spread, smear. **4** *apply for a job | apply for tax relief* make/put in an application, put in for, try for, enquire after, request, claim, seek, appeal, petition, make an entreaty, solicit, sue. **apply oneself** be industrious/diligent/assiduous, study, work hard, make an effort, pay attention, be attentive, commit/devote oneself, persevere, persist, put one's shoulder to the wheel; *inf.* buckle to.

appoint *verb* **1** *appoint him manager* name, designate, nominate, select, choose, elect, install as. **2** *appoint a time* set, fix, arrange, choose, establish, settle, determine, assign, designate, allot.

appointment *noun* **1** *cancel an appointment* meeting, engagement, date, interview, arrangement, rendezvous, assignation; *lit.* tryst. **2** *his new appointment as manager* job, post, position, situation, place, office, station. **3** *the appointment of him as boss* naming, nomination, selection. See APPOINT 1. **4** *the appointment of a time* setting, arrangement, establishment. See APPOINT 2.

apportion *verb* allocate, distribute, share out, divide out, hand/deal out, ration/mete/dole out, allot, dispense, assign.

apposite *adjective* appropriate, suitable, fitting, apt, relevant, to the point, pertinent, applicable, germane.

appraisal *noun* **1** *make an appraisal of the house* valuation, pricing, survey. **2** *an appraisal of their ability* assessment, evaluation, summing-up, estimation, estimate, judgement, sizing-up.

appraise *verb* **1** *appraise the property* value, survey, price, set a price on. **2** *appraise his ability* assess, evaluate, sum up, estimate, gauge, judge, review; *inf.* size up.

appreciable *adjective* *an appreciable amount* considerable, substantial, significant, sizeable, visible, goodly.

appreciate *verb* **1** *appreciate your help* be appreciative of, be thankful/grateful for, give thanks for, be indebted/beholden for. **2** *appreciate good staff/wine* value, hold in high regard, hold in esteem, prize, cherish, treasure, rate highly, respect, think highly of, think much of. **3** *appreciate the importance of* recognize, acknowledge, realize, know, be aware of, be conscious/cognizant of, be alive to, understand, comprehend, perceive, discern. **4** *the house appreciated in value* increase, gain, rise, mount, inflate, escalate.
Opposites DISPARAGE; IGNORE; DEPRECIATE.

appreciation *noun* **1** *express his appreciation for their help* gratitude, gratefulness, thankfulness, indebtedness, obligation; thanks. **2** *the appreciation of good staff/wine* valuing, esteem, regard, prizing, respect. See APPRECIATE 2. **3** *the appreciation of its importance* recognition, acknowledgement, realization, awareness, consciousness, cognizance, comprehension, perception, discernment. See APPRECIATE 3. **4** *the appreciation of house values* increase, rise, growth, gain, improvement, inflation, escalation. **5** *an appreciation of the poetry* review, critique, criticism, critical analysis, notice, commentary; praise, acclamation.

appreciative *adjective* **1** *most appreciative of your help* grateful, thankful, indebted, obliged, beholden; grateful for, thankful for. **2** *an appreciative audience* enthusiastic, responsive, supportive, encouraging, sympathetic, sensitive.

apprehend *verb* **1** *apprehend the criminal* arrest, catch, seize, capture, take prisoner, take into custody, haul in, detain; *inf.* collar, nab, nail, run in, nick, pinch, bust. **2** *apprehend the significance* understand, grasp, realize, recognize, appreciate, comprehend, discern, perceive; *inf.* twig, get the picture.

apprehension *noun* **1** *full of apprehension about the interview/future* anxiety, dread, alarm, worry, uneasiness, unease, nervousness, fear, misgiving, disquiet, concern, trepidation, perturbation, foreboding, presentiment, angst; nerves; *inf.* butterflies in the stomach, the willies, the heebie-jeebies. **2** *the apprehension of criminals* arrest, seizure, capture, detention; *inf.* collaring, nabbing, nailing. *See* APPREHEND 1. **3** *the apprehension of problems* understanding, realization, recognition, appreciation, comprehension, discernment, perception. *See* APPREHEND 2.

apprehensive *adjective* anxious, alarmed, worried, uneasy, nervous, frightened, fearful, mistrustful, concerned. *See* APPREHENSION 1.

apprentice *noun* trainee, learner, beginner, probationer, pupil, student, cub, greenhorn, tiro, novice, neophyte; *Am. inf.* rookie.

apprise *verb* inform, notify, tell, let know; *inf.* clue in, fill in.

approach *verb* **1** *someone's approaching the house* come/go/draw near/nearer, come/go/draw close/closer, move/edge near/nearer, draw nigh, catch up, gain on, near, advance, push forward, reach, arrive. **2** *don't approach strangers in the street* talk/speak to, make conversation with, engage in conversation, greet, address, salute, hail. **3** *approach them for a contribution* apply/appeal to, broach the matter to, make advances/overtures to, make a proposal to, sound out, proposition, solicit. **4** *approach the problem with care* set about, tackle, begin, start, commence, embark on, make a start on, undertake. **5** *a price approaching £600* come near/close to, approximate, be comparable/similar to, compare with.
Opposites LEAVE; AVOID.

approach *noun* **1** *the approach of footsteps* coming near/nearer, nearing, advance, advent, arrival. *See* APPROACH *verb* 1. **2** *the approach to the manor* driveway, drive, access road, road, avenue, street, passageway. **3** *make an approach to* | *make approaches* application, appeal, proposal, proposition; advances, overtures. **4** *the merest approach to a smile* approximation, likeness, semblance. **5** *a new approach to teaching* method, procedure, technique, style, way, manner, mode, *modus operandi*; means.

appropriate *adjective an appropriate time/remark* suitable, fitting, befitting, proper, seemly, right, apt, relevant, pertinent, apposite, applicable, congruous, opportune, felicitous, germane; *fml.* appurtenant.
Opposites INAPPROPRIATE; UNSUITABLE; IRRELEVANT.

appropriate *verb* **1** *appropriate a country/house* take possession of, take over, seize, commandeer, expropriate, annex, arrogate. **2** *appropriate money for education* set apart/aside, assign, allot, allocate, earmark, devote, apportion. **3** *appropriate company money* embezzle, misappropriate, steal, pilfer, filch, pocket, purloin; *inf.* pinch, nick, swipe; *fml.* peculate.

approval *noun* **1** *look on with approval* favour, liking, approbation, acceptance, admiration, appreciation, regard, esteem, respect, commendation, applause, acclaim, acclamation, praise. **2** *give approval to the minutes/application* acceptance, agreement, consent, assent, sanction, endorsement, blessing, permission, leave, confirmation, ratification, authorization, mandate, licence, validation, acquiescence, concurrence, imprimatur; *inf.* the go-ahead, the green light, the OK. **on approval** on trial, under probation; *inf.* on appro.

approve *verb* **1** *approve of their behaviour* think well of, like, look on with favour, give one's blessing to, be pleased with, admire, hold in regard/esteem, commend, favour, applaud, acclaim, praise. **2** *approve the minutes/application* accept, pass, agree to, sanction, consent/assent to, ratify, authorize, validate, accede to, acquiesce in, concur in, warrant; *inf.* give the go-ahead to, give the OK to, give the green light to, give the word to, buy.
Opposites CONDEMN; DISAPPROVE; REJECT.

approximate *adjective* **1** *the approximate price* rough, estimated, near, close, inexact; *inf.* guesstimate. **2** *your approximate neighbour* adjacent, next door, next, neighbouring, near, nearby, close by, adjoining, contiguous.

approximate *verb approximating to the truth* be close/near to, come close/near to, approach, border on, verge on, resemble, be similar to.

approximately *adverb approximately 40 miles* roughly, about, just about, around, *circa*, or so, more or less, in the neighbourhood of, in the region of, nearly, not far off, close to, near to, almost.

approximation *noun* **1** *200 is an approximation* guess, estimate, estimation, conjecture, rough calculation, rough idea; guesswork; *inf.* guesstimate. **2** *an approximation to the truth* semblance, similarity, likeness, correspondence. *See* APPROXIMATE *verb*.

appurtenances *plural noun* appendages, accoutrements, accessories, belongings, trappings; equipment, paraphernalia, impedimenta.

apron *noun* pinafore, overall; *inf.* pinny.

apropos *adjective* **1** *the remark was extremely apropos* appropriate, pertinent, relevant, apposite, apt, applicable, germane. **2** *apropos the meeting* | *apropos of that remark* with reference to, with regard/respect to, regarding, respecting, on the subject of, re.

apropos *adverb* **1** *talked apropos* appropriately, pertinently. **2** *apropos, we're not going by the way,* incidentally.

apt *adjective* **1** *an apt remark* suitable, fitting, appropriate, applicable, apposite, felicitous, apropos. **2** *apt to get angry* inclined, given, likely, liable, disposed, prone, ready, subject. **3** *an apt pupil* quick to learn, quick, bright, sharp, clever, smart, intelligent, able, gifted, talented, adept, competent, astute.
Opposites INAPPROPRIATE; UNLIKELY; SLOW.

aptitude *noun an aptitude for drawing* talent, gift, flair, bent, skill, knack; ability, proficiency, quickness, competence, capability, potential, capacity, faculty.

aptness noun **1** *the aptness of the remark* suitability, appropriateness, applicability. *See* APT 1. **2** *the aptness of the pupil* quickness, brightness, sharpness, cleverness, intelligence. *See* APT 3.

aquatic *adjective aquatic plants/sports* water, sea, river, marine, maritime, fluvial.

aqueduct noun channel, conduit, race, watercourse, waterway, bridge.

aquiline *adjective* eagle-like, hooked, curved.

arable *adjective* ploughable, tillable, cultivable, cultivatable, farmable; fertile, productive, fruitful, fecund.

arachnid noun. *See table.*

arbiter noun **1** *an arbiter of fashion* authority, judge, determiner, controller, director, governor, master, expert, pundit. **2** *the arbiter in the case* adjudicator. *See* ARBITRATOR.

arbitrary *adjective* **1** *a completely arbitrary decision* discretionary, discretional, personal, subjective, random, chance, whimsical, capricious, erratic, inconsistent, unreasoned, unreasonable, unsupported, irrational. **2** *an arbitrary ruler* despotic, tyrannical, tyrannous, absolute, autocratic, dictatorial, imperious, domineering, high-handed.
Opposites OBJECTIVE; RATIONAL; REASONED.

arbitrate *verb* adjudicate, judge, referee, umpire, adjudge, sit in judgement, pass judgement, settle, decide, determine.

arbitration noun adjudication, judgement, settlement, decision, determination; *fml.* arbitrament.

arbitrator noun adjudicator, judge, referee, umpire, arbiter.

arbour noun bower, alcove, grotto, recess, pergola, gazebo.

arc noun curve, bow, arch, bend, crescent, half-moon, semicircle, circular section/line; curvature.

arcade noun gallery, colonnade, cloister, loggia, piazza, portico, shopping mall/precinct.

ARACHNIDS	
bird-eating spider	red-back
black widow	red spider mite
camel spider	retiary spider
cardinal spider	scorpion
daddy longlegs *Am.*	scorpion spider
diadem spider	sheep tick
false scorpion	spider
funnel-web spider	spider mite
harvestman	sun spider
harvest mite	tarantula
hunting spider	tick
huntsman spider	trapdoor spider
itch mite	violin spider
jockey spider	water spider
katipo	whip scorpion
mite	white-tailed
money spider	spider
mygale	wind scorpion
orb weaver	wolf spider
raft spider	wood tick

arcane *adjective* secret, mysterious, hidden, concealed, recondite, covert, enigmatic, inscrutable, abstruse, esoteric, cryptic, occult.

arch noun **1** *a bridge with three arches* archway, vault, span. *See table at* VAULT. **2** *the arch of the rainbow* arc, bow, curve, semicircle; curvature, convexity.

arch *verb the cat arched its back* curve, bow, bend, arc; *fml.* embow.

arch *adjective an arch smile* playful, mischievous, roguish, saucy, artful, sly, knowing, frolicsome.

arch- *prefix archbishop | arch-enemy* chief, foremost, principal, leading, main, top, highest, greatest, pre-eminent.

archaeology noun. *See tables.*

archaic *adjective* old, obsolete, out of date, oldfashioned, outmoded, bygone, *passé*, antiquated, antique; *inf.* old hat.
Opposites NEW; MODERN; UP-TO-DATE.

arched *adjective* curved, vaulted, domed; *fml.* embowed.

archer noun bowman, toxophilite.

BRANCHES OF ARCHAEOLOGY			
Assyriology	palaeobotany	palaeoherpetology	palaeopathology
Egyptology	palaeoceanography	palaeohydrography	palaeophysiography
marine archaeology	palaeoclimatology	palaeolimnology	palaeophysiology
micropalaeontology	palaeodendrology	palaeology	palaeophytology
palaeobio-	palaeoecology	palaeometeorology	palaeornithology
geography	palaeogeography	palaeontography	palaeozoology
palaeobiology	palaeography	palaeontology	Sumerology

ARCHAEOLOGICAL DATING TECHNIQUES			
accelerator mass spectrometry	cross-dating	fission-track dating	rubidium-strontium dating
archaeomagnetic dating	dendro-chronology	potassium-argon dating	seriation
chronometric dating	electron spin resonance	radiocarbon dating	thermoluminescence

ARCHITECTURAL STYLES

Art Deco	classical	Egyptian	Islamic	Perpendicular
Art	colossal	Empire	mannerist	postmodernist
Nouveau	composite	Federation	medieval	quattrocento
baroque	Corinthian	flamboyant	Mesopotamian	Renaissance
Bauhaus	Cyclopean	functional	modernist	rococo
beaux-arts	Deconstruc-	Gothic	Moorish	Roman
brutalist	tionism	Gothic Revival	Moresque	Romanesque
Byzantine	De Stijl	Graeco-	Mozarabic	Saracen
Carolingian	Doric	Roman	Mudéjar	Saxon
Churriguer-	Early English	Grecian	neo-classical	transitional
esque	Early	Greek Revival	Norman	Tuscan
cinquecento	Renaissance	Ionic	Palladian	vernacular

ARCHITECTURAL TERMS

abacus	cavetto	ectype	frontis-	moulding	scotia
acanthus	chevron	egg and	piece	mullion	scroll
annulet	cinquefoil	anchor	gadroon	mutule	splay
anthemion	congé	egg and	gorgerin	neck-mould	stria
apophyge	copestone	dart	guilloche	ogee	stucco
architrave	cordon	egg and	gutta	ovolo	taenia
astragal	cornice	tongue	head mould	pendant	talon
atlas	corona	epistyle	headpiece	polychromy	terminal
baguette	coving	facet	helix	putto	torus
banderole	crocket	fascia	herm	quarter-	tracery
bas-relief	crown-	festoon	hood mould	round	transom
billet	piece	fillet	hypotra-	quatrefoil	trefoil
boss	cusp	finial	chelium	quirk	triglyph
calotte	cyma	flute	lierne	quoin	tympanum
canephorae	dancette	foil	listel	reed	vaulting
capstone	dentil	foliation	medallion	reglet	vignette
cartouche	dog-tooth	fret	metope	respond	volute
caryatid	echinus	frieze	modillion	rustication	zigzag

ARCHITECTS

Aalto, Alvar (1898–1976; Finn.)	Fischer von Erlach, Johann (1656–1723; Austrian)	Jones, Inigo (1573–1652; Brit.)	Palladio, Andrea (1508–80; It.)
Adam, Robert (1728–92; Scot.)	Foster, Sir Norman (b. 1935; Brit.)	Kahn, Louis I(sadore) (1901–74; Am.)	Piano, Renzo (b. 1937; It.)
Alberti, Leon Battista (1404–72; It.)	Fuller, Richard Buckminster (1895–1983; Am.)	Lasdun, Sir Denys (b. 1914; Brit.)	Pugin, Augustus (1812–52; Brit.)
Behrens, Peter (1868–1940; Ger.)	Gaudí, Antonio (1853–1926; Sp.)	Le Corbusier (1887–1965; Fr.)	Richardson, Henry (1838–86; Am.)
Bernini, Gian Lorenzo (1598–1680; It.)	Gropius, Walter (1883–1969; Ger.)	Lescot, Pierre (c. 1510–78; Fr.)	Rogers, Sir Richard (b. 1933; Brit.)
Borromini, Francesco (1599–1667; It.)	Hardouin-Mansart, Jules (1646–1708; Fr.)	Loos, Adolph (1870–1933; Austrian)	Spence, Sir Basil (1907–76; Scot.)
Bramante, Donato (1444–1514; It.)	Hawksmoor, Nicholas (1661–1736; Brit.)	Lutyens, Sir Edwin (1869–1944; Brit.)	Sullivan, Louis (1856–1924; Am.)
Brunelleschi, Filippo (1377–1446; It.)	Herrera, Juan de (c. 1530–97; Sp.)	Mackintosh, Charles Rennie (1868–1928; Scot.)	Tange, Kenzo (b. 1913; Jap.)
Callicrates (5th century B.C.; Gk)	Horta, Victor (1861–1947; Belg.)	Mansart, François (1598–1666; Fr.)	Vanbrugh, Sir John (1664–1726; Brit.)
Candela, Felix (b. 1910; Mex.)	Ictinus (5th century B.C.; Gk)	Mies van der Rohe, Ludwig (1886–1969; Ger.)	Venturi, Robert (b. 1925; Am.)
Costa, Lúcio (b. 1902; Brazilian)	Imhotep (c. 2600 B.C.; Egypt.)	Nervi, Pier Luigi (1891–1979; It.)	Vitruvius (1st century B.C.; Rom.)
de Churriguera, José (1650–1725; Sp.)	Jacobsen, Arne (1902–71; Da.)	Niemeyer, Oscar (b. 1907; Brazilian)	Wren, Sir Christopher (1632–1723; Brit.)
Delorme, Philibert (c. 1510–70; Fr.)			Yamasaki, Minoru (1912–86; Am.)

archetype *noun* prototype, original, pattern, model, standard, exemplar, mould, paradigm, ideal.

architect *noun* **1** *the architect of the house* designer, planner, building consultant, draughtsman. *See table.* **2** *the architect of the scheme* author, engineer, creator, originator, planner, deviser, instigator, founder, inventor, contriver, prime mover.

architecture *noun* **1** *studying architecture* design, planning, building, construction; *fml.* architectonics. **2** *eighteenth-century architecture* construction, style, design, structure, framework. *See tables. See also tables at* BUILDING, CHURCH, VAULT, WINDOW.

archives *plural noun* **1** *study the firm's archives* records, annals, chronicles, papers, documents, registers, rolls; history, documentation; *fml.* muniments. **2** *the archives are situated in the basement* records office, registry, museum, repository, chancery.

arctic *adjective* **1** *arctic regions* polar, far northern, northern; *fml.* boreal, hyperborean. **2** *arctic conditions* freezing, frigid, frozen, icy, glacial, frosty, chilly, cold; *fml.* gelid.

ardent *adjective* passionate, avid, impassioned, fervent, fervid, zealous, eager, earnest, enthusiastic, emotional, vehement, intense, fierce, fiery, profound, consuming.

ardour *noun* passion, avidity, fervour, zeal, eagerness, enthusiasm, earnestness, emotion, emotionalism, vehemence, intensity, fierceness, fire, fieriness, profundity.

arduous *adjective* taxing, difficult, hard, onerous, heavy, laborious, burdensome, exhausting, wearying, fatiguing, tiring, strenuous, gruelling, punishing, vigorous, tough, formidable, Herculean.
Opposites EASY; EFFORTLESS.

area *noun* **1** *the area around the city* region, district, zone, sector, territory, tract, stretch, quarter, locality, neighbourhood, domain, realm, sphere. **2** *the area of the room | the area of my knowledge* extent, size, expanse, scope, compass, range; measurements. **3** *specializing in the area of finance* field, sphere, discipline, realm, department, sector, province, domain, territory. **4** *the changing area* section, space, sector, part, portion. **5** *the area of a basement flat* yard, enclosure.

arena *noun* **1** *circus/boxing arena* ground, field, stadium, ring, stage, platform, amphitheatre, colosseum; *inf.* park; *Am.* bowl. **2** *the political arena* area/field of conflict, sphere of action/activity, battleground, battlefield, area, scene, sphere, realm, province, territory, domain, sector, theatre, lists.

argue *verb* **1** *the children are always arguing* disagree, quarrel, squabble, bicker, fight, wrangle, dispute, feud; *inf.* fall out, argy-bargy. **2** *argue that they are right* assert, declare, maintain, insist, hold, claim, contend, expostulate. **3** *argue the point/case* debate, dispute, discuss, controvert. **4** *argue him out of going | argue him into going* talk round, persuade, convince, prevail upon. **5** *the essay argued much research* point to, indicate, demonstrate, show, suggest, imply, exhibit, denote, be evidence of, display, evince.

argument *noun* **1** *the children had an argument* disagreement, quarrel, squabble, fight, row, difference of opinion, dispute, wrangle, clash, altercation, controversy, feud; *inf.* tiff, barney, falling out, set-to, dust-up. **2** *stick to the argument that they are right* assertion, declaration, claim, plea, contention, expostulation. **3** *the argument against capital punishment* line of reasoning, reasoning, logic, case, defence, evidence, argumentation, polemic; reasons, grounds. **4** *the argument of the biography* theme, topic, subject-matter, gist, outline, plot, storyline, summary, synopsis, abstract, précis.

argumentative *adjective* quarrelsome, belligerent, disputatious, contentious, combative, litigious, dissentient.

arid *adjective* **1** *arid areas* dry, dried up, desert, waterless, moistureless, parched, baked, scorched, dehydrated, desiccated, barren. **2** *arid surroundings/discussion* uninspiring, unstimulating, dull, dreary, drab, dry, colourless, flat, boring, uninteresting, monotonous, lifeless, tedious, vapid, jejune.
Opposites WET; FERTILE; INTERESTING.

aright *adverb* *hear aright* correctly, rightly, accurately, properly, exactly; *inf.* OK.

arise *verb* **1** *a difficulty arose* appear, come to light, make an appearance, crop/turn up, spring up, emerge, occur, ensue, set in, come into being/existence, begin. **2** *accidents arising from carelessness* result, be caused by, proceed, follow, stem, originate, emanate, ensue. **3** *arise and go* rise, stand up, get to one's feet, get up. **4** *birds arising* rise, ascend, go up, mount, climb, fly, soar.

aristocracy *noun* nobility, peerage, gentry, upper class, privileged/ruling class, élite, high society, patriciate; *inf.* upper crust; *lit.* haut monde.

aristocrat *noun* noble, nobleman, noblewoman, lord, lady, peer, peeress, patrician, grandee.

aristocratic *adjective* **1** *an aristocratic family* noble, titled, blue-blooded, high-born, upper-class, patrician, élite. **2** *aristocratic bearing/manners* well-bred, dignified, courtly, refined, elegant, stylish, gracious, fine, polite, haughty, proud.
Opposites PLEBEIAN; VULGAR.

arm *noun* **1** *arms and legs* limb, upper limb, forelimb, member, appendage. **2** *arm of the sea* inlet, estuary, channel, branch, strait, sound, firth. **3** *an arm of the civil service* branch, offshoot, section, department, division, sector, detachment, extension. **4** *the arm of the law* power, force, authority, strength, might, potency.

arm *verb* **1** *arm with guns/information* provide, supply, equip, furnish, issue with. **2** *arm oneself against criticism* prepare, forearm, make ready, brace, steel, fortify, gird one's loins.

armada *noun* fleet, flotilla, navy, squadron.

armaments *plural noun* arms, weapons, firearms, munitions; weaponry, ordnance, *matériel*.

armistice *noun* truce, ceasefire, peace, suspension of hostilities.

armour *noun* armour-plate, protective covering, covering, protection, sheathing, chain-armour, chain-mail; coat armour. *See table.*

PARTS OF A SUIT OF ARMOUR		
beaver	helmet	solleret
breast-plate	lance rest	taces
coutere	neck guard	tasset
cuirass	nose-piece	vambrace
cuisse	pauldron	ventail
gauntlet	poleyn	visor
gorget	rerebrace	
greave	sabaton	

armoury *noun* arms depot, ordnance depot, arsenal, magazine, ammunition dump.

arms *plural noun* **1** *carrying arms* weapons, firearms, guns, armaments; weaponry. *See tables at* GUN, MISSILE, WEAPON. **2** *the family arms* heraldic device, coat of arms, emblem, crest, insignia, escutcheon, shield, blazonry. *See table at* HERALDRY.

army *noun* **1** *the invading army* armed/military force, land force, soldiery, infantry; troops, soldiers, land forces; *Am.* military. *See table at* MILITARY. **2** *an army of tourists* horde, pack, host, multitude, mob, crowd, swarm, throng, array.

aroma *noun* smell, scent, odour, bouquet, fragrance, perfume, redolence.

aromatic *adjective* fragrant, sweet-smelling, scented, perfumed, balmy, piquant, spicy, savoury, pungent, odoriferous.

around *preposition* **1** *around the tree* about, on all sides of, on every side of, circling, encircling, surrounding, encompassing. **2** *thrown around the room* about, here and there, all over, everywhere, in all parts of. **3** *around 9 o'clock* | *around three miles* about, approximately, roughly, close to, near to, nearly, circa. **4** *turn around* in the opposite direction, in reverse, backwards, to the rear.

around *adverb* **1** *litter scattered around* about, here and there, all over, everywhere, in all directions, throughout. **2** *can't see anyone around* nearby, near, close by, close, at hand, at close range.

arouse *verb* **1** *arouse them at dawn* rouse, awaken, waken, wake, wake up. **2** *arouse panic* cause, induce, stir up, inspire, call forth, kindle, provoke, foster, whip up, sow the seeds of. **3** *arouse the crowd* rouse, incite, excite, provoke, goad, prompt, spur on, urge, encourage, egg on, animate, inflame, build a fire under. **4** *arouse sexually* excite, stimulate; *inf.* turn on.

arraign *verb* **1** *arraign for murder* accuse, charge, lay charges against, indict, impeach. **2** *arraign the assembled crowd* criticize, censure, find fault with, upbraid, reproach, rebuke, reprove, take to task.

arrange *verb* **1** *arrange the books/flowers* put in order, order, set out, group, sort, organize, tidy, position, dispose, marshal, range, align, line up, rank, file, classify, categorize, array, systematize. **2** *arrange to meet* | *arrange an appointment* settle on, decide, determine, agree, come to an agreement, settle on, come to terms about, plan, schedule, devise, contrive; *inf.* fix up. **3** *arrange for her to be met* make preparations, prepare, plan, organize. **4** *music arranged for the piano* score, adapt, orchestrate, instrument, harmonize.
Opposites DISARRANGE; DISTURB; CANCEL.

arrangement *noun* **1** *the arrangement of books/flowers* order, ordering, grouping, organization, positioning, system, disposition, marshalling, ranging, alignment, filing, classification, categorization, array. **2** *make an arrangement* | *make arrangements* preparations, plans, provisions; agreement, contract, compact. **3** *a musical arrangement* score, adaptation, orchestration, instrumentation, harmonization.

arrant *adjective* utter, downright, outright, absolute, out and out, rank, thorough, thoroughgoing, through and through, total, unmitigated, blatant, barefaced.

array *noun* **1** *an array of bottles/facts* collection, arrangement, assembling, assemblage, line-up, formation, ordering, disposition, marshalling, muster, amassing, show, display, agglomeration, aggregation. **2** *in silken array* attire, apparel, clothing, dress, garb, finery; garments.

array *verb* **1** *the books/troops are arrayed* assemble, arrange, draw up, group, order, range, rank, line up, place, position, dispose, marshal, muster, amass, agglomerate, aggregate. **2** *they were arrayed in silk* attire, clothe, dress, fit out, garb, deck, robe, apparel, accoutre.

arrears *plural noun* **1** *pay the arrears* outstanding payment, debt, balance, deficit. **2** *arrears of work* backlog, accumulation, pile-up. **in arrears** behind, behindhand, late, overdue, in the red, in default, in debt.

arrest *verb* **1** *arrest the thief* apprehend, take into custody, take prisoner, detain, seize, capture, catch, lay hold of, haul in; *inf.* nick, run in, nab, pinch, collar, bust, nail, pick up. **2** *arrest the spread of disease* stop, halt, end, bring to a standstill, check, block, hinder, delay, interrupt, prevent, obstruct, inhibit, slow down, retard, nip in the bud, stay. **3** *arrest their attention* attract, capture, catch, catch hold of, grip, engage, absorb, occupy, rivet, engross.

arrest *noun* **1** *the arrest of the thieves* apprehension, taking into custody, detention, seizure, capture; *inf.* nicking, running in. *See* ARREST *verb* 1. **2** *the arrest of the disease* stopping, stoppage, halt, ending, end, check, blocking, hindrance, delay, interruption, prevention, obstruction, retardation. *See* ARREST *verb* 2.

arresting *adjective* *an arresting face* striking, impressive, remarkable, extraordinary, unusual, noticeable, outstanding, conspicuous, stunning.

arrival noun **1** *the arrival of the guest/winter* coming, advent, appearance, entrance, entry, occurrence, approach. **2** *several recent arrivals* incomer, newcomer, visitor, visitant, guest, immigrant.

arrive verb **1** *the guests/winter arrived* come, appear, put in an appearance, come on the scene, enter, get here/there, happen, occur, present itself, turn/show up; *inf.* blow in. **2** *the actor's really arrived* succeed, make good, reach the top, prosper, flourish, get ahead, become famous, achieve recognition; *inf.* make it, make the grade, get somewhere.
Opposites DEPART; LEAVE.

arrogance noun haughtiness, pride, self-importance, conceit, egotism, snobbishness, snobbery, pomposity, superciliousness, high-handedness, condescension, disdain, imperiousness, lordliness, presumption, pretentiousness, swagger, bluster, bumptious-ness, insolence; *inf.* stuck-upness, uppitiness. *See* ARROGANT.

arrogant adjective haughty, proud, self-important, conceited, egotistic, snobbish, pompous, supercilious, overbearing, overween-ing, high-handed, condescending, disdainful, imperious, lordly, presumptuous, pretentious, swaggering, blustering, bumptious, insolent; *inf.* stuck-up, uppity, high and mighty.
Opposites MODEST; DIFFIDENT.

arrogate verb appropriate, assume, expropri-ate, seize, avail oneself of, commandeer.

arrow noun **1** *bow and arrow* shaft, bolt, dart, quarrel. **2** *follow the arrows* pointer, indicator, marker.

arsenal noun **1** *weapons in the arsenal* arms depot, magazine, armoury, ammunition dump, ordnance depot, repository. **2** *an ar-senal of sharp remarks* store, supply, stock, stock-pile, storehouse.

ART TECHNIQUES AND MEDIA

acrylic painting	encaustic	marquetry	sgraffito
action painting	engineering	metalwork	silk painting
airbrush painting	drawing	mezzotint	silk-screen printing
aquatint	engraving	miniature painting	sketching
batik	etching	montage	soft ground etching
brass rubbing	finger painting	mosaic	spray-can painting
calligraphy	fresco	mural painting	stained glass
cartooning	frottage	oil painting	tapestry
ceramics	gouache	painting	technical drawing
collage	grisaille	pastel	tempera
collotype	illumination	photography	trompe l'oeil
colour print	impasto	photogravure	painting
colour wash	intaglio	photomontage	watercolour
conté	lino cut	photoprint	wood carving
drawing	lithography	screen printing	woodcut
dry-point	lost wax	sculpture	wood engraving
enamelling	marbling	scumbling	zincography

ART SCHOOLS AND STYLES

abstract art	De Stijl	metaphysical paint-	Pre-Raphaelitism
abstract expression-	divisionism	ing	primitive art
ism	environmental art	minimalism	purism
action painting	expressionism	Minoan art	Rayonism
Aesthetic Movement	fauvism	Mogul art	realism
art brut	figurative art	mozarabic art	regionalism
art deco	Florentine school	naive art	Renaissance art
arte povera	folk art	naturalism	representational
art informel	futurism	neoclassicism	art
art nouveau	grand manner	neoexpressionism	rococo
Arts and Crafts	High Renaissance	neoimpressionism	romanticism
Movement	art	neoromanticism	Sienese school
avant-garde	impressionism	Neue Sachlichkeit	socialist realism
baroque	International	op art	social realism
Blaue Reiter	Gothic	orphism	suprematism
Byzantine art	intimisme	Ottoman art	surrealism
Camden School	Islamic art	performance art	symbolism
classicism	Jugendstil	photorealism	synchronism
cloisonnism	junk art	plein-air painting	synthetism
conceptual art	kinetic art	pointillism	tachism
concrete art	kitsch	pop art	transavant-garde
constructivism	land art	postimpressionism	Venetian school
cubism	magic realism	postmodernism	verism
Dada	mannerism	precisionism	vorticism

arson *noun* incendiarism, pyromania.

art *noun* **1** *studying art* painting, drawing, design; visual arts. *See tables. See also tables at* ARTIST, PAINTING. **2** *the art of writing/conversation* skill, craft, aptitude, talent, flair, gift, knack, facility; artistry, mastery, dexterity, expertness, skilfulness, adroitness, cleverness, ingenuity, virtuosity. **3** *use art to win* artfulness, cunning, deceit, deception, wiliness, slyness, craft, craftiness, guile, trickery, duplicity, artifice; wiles.

artery *noun* **1** *a blocked artery* blood vessel, aorta. *See table at* VEIN. **2** *crowded arteries* main road, high road, motorway, *autoroute, autobahn; Am.* throughway, highway.

artful *adjective* cunning, deceitful, wily, sly, crafty, duplicitous, scheming, designing, shrewd, politic, ingenious.

article *noun* **1** *three black articles* object, thing, item, commodity; *inf.* thingummy, thinguma-jig, thingumabob, what-d'ye-call-it. **2** *an article in the newspaper* item, piece, story, feature, report, account, write-up. **3** *an article in a legal document | articles of faith* clause, section, point, paragraph, division, part, passage.

articulate *adjective* **1** *an articulate speaker* eloquent, fluent, well-spoken, communicative, coherent, lucid, expressive, silver-tongued, vocal. **2** *an articulate speech* eloquent, clear, fluent, intelligible, comprehensible, understandable, lucid, coherent. **3** *articulate limbs* articulated, jointed, segmented.
Opposites INARTICULATE; HESITANT; UNINTELLIGIBLE.

articulate *verb* **1** *articulate words/ideas* enunciate, pronounce, voice, say, utter, express, vocalize. **2** *articulated parts* joint, hinge, connect, link, couple.

artifice *noun* **1** *an artifice to mislead* trick, stratagem, ruse, dodge, subterfuge, machination, manoeuvre, tactic, device, contrivance.

ARTISTS

Alma-Tadema, Sir Laurence (1836–1912; Brit., b. in the Netherlands)
Altdorfer, Albrecht (c. 1485–1538; Ger.)
Angelico, Fra (c. 1400–55; It.)
Apelles (4th century B.C.; Gk)
Arp, Jean (1887–1966; Fr.)
Bacon, Francis (1909–92; Ir.)
Bellini, Giovanni (c. 1429–1507; Venetian)
Blake, William (1757–1827; Brit., also poet)
Bonnard, Pierre (1867–1947; Fr.)
Bosch, Hieronymus (c. 1450–c. 1516; Du.)
Botticelli, Sandro (1445–1510; Florentine)
Boucher, François (1703–70; Fr.)
Boyd, Arthur (b. 1920; Austral.)
Braque, Georges (1882–1963; Fr.)
Bronzino, Il (Agnolo di Cosimo; 1503–72; Florentine)
Bruegel the Elder, Pieter (c. 1525–69; Flem.)

Burne-Jones, Sir Edward (1833–98; Brit.)
Canaletto (Antonio Canale; 1697–1768; Venetian)
Caravaggio (Michelangelo Merisi; 1573–1610; It.)
Carpaccio, Vittore (c. 1455–1525; It.)
Cassatt, Mary (1844–1926; Am.)
Cézanne, Paul (1839–1906; Fr.)
Chagall, Marc (1887–1985; Fr., b. in Russia)
Chirico, Giorgio de (1888–1978; It.)
Claude Lorraine (Claude Gellée; 1600–82; Fr.)
Constable, John (1776–1837; Brit.)
Corot, Camille (1796–1875; Fr.)
Cotman, John (1782–1842; Brit.)
Courbet, Gustave (1819–77; Fr.)
Cranach, Lucas (1472–1553; Ger.)
Dadd, Richard (1819–87; Brit.)
Dali, Salvador (1904–89; Sp.)
David, Jacques-Louis (1748–1825; Fr.)
Degas, Edgar (1834–1917; Fr.)

de Kooning, Willem (b. 1904; Am.)
Delacroix, Eugène (1798–1863; Fr.)
Delaunay, Robert (1885–1941; Fr.)
Delvaux, Paul (1897–94; Belg.)
Derain, André (1880–1954; Fr.)
Dobell, Sir William (1899–1970; Austral.)
Drysdale, Sir Russell (1912–81; Austral.)
Duccio (c. 1255–c. 1320; It.)
Dufy, Raoul (1877–1953; Fr.)
Dürer, Albrecht (1471–1528; Ger.)
El Greco (1541–1614; Sp., b. in Crete)
Ernst, Max (1891–1976; Ger.)
Exekias (6th century B.C.; Athenian, also potter)
Fragonard, Jean-Honoré (1732–1806; Fr.)
Freud, Lucian (b. 1922; Brit.)
Gainsborough, Thomas (1727–88; Brit.)
Gauguin, Paul (1848–1903; Fr.)
Gentile da Fabriano (c. 1370–1427; It.)
Géricault, Théodore (1791–1824; Fr.)

Ghirlandaio, Domenico (c. 1448–94; It.)
Giorgione (c. 1478–1510; It.)
Giotto (c. 1266–1337; It.)
Goes, Hugo van der (c. 1440–82; Flem.)
Goya (y Lucientes), Francisco de (1746–1828; Sp.)
Guarde, Francesco (1712–93; It.)
Hals, Frans (c. 1580–1666; Du.)
Hiroshige (Ando Tokitaro; 1797–1858; Jap. printmaker)
Hockney, David (b. 1937; Brit.)
Hogarth, William (1697–1764; Brit.)
Hokusai (1760–1849; Jap. printmaker)
Holbein the Younger, Hans (1497–1543; Ger.)
Homer, Winslow (1836–1910; Am.)
Hopper, Edward (1882–1967; Am.)
Hunt, William Holman (1827–1910; Brit.)
Ingres, Jean Auguste Dominique (1780–1867; Fr.)
John, Augustus (1878–1961; Brit.)
Johns, Jasper (b. 1930; Am.)

ARTISTS cont.

Kandinsky, Wassily (1866–1944; Russ.)	Moholy-Nagy, László (1895–1946; Hungarian)	Renoir, Pierre-Auguste (1841–1919; Fr.)	Sutherland, Graham (1903–80; Brit.)
Kauffmann, Angelica (1740–1807; Swiss)	Mondrian, Piet (1872–1944; Du.)	Reynolds, Sir Joshua (1723–92; Brit.)	Tiepolo, Giovanni Battista (1696–1770; It.)
Kitaj, R(onald) B(rooks) (b. 1932; Am.)	Monet, Claude (1840–1926; Fr.)	Ribera, José (c. 1591–1652; Sp.)	Tintoretto (1518–94; It.)
Klee, Paul (1879–1940; Swiss)	Morisot, Berthe (1841–95; Fr.)	Riley, Bridget (b. 1931; Brit.)	Titian (c. 1488–1576; Venetian)
Klimt, Gustav (1862–1918; Austrian)	Moses, Grandma (1860–1961; Am.)	Rivera, Diego (1886–1957; Mex.)	Toulouse-Lautrec, Henri de (1864–1901; Fr.)
Kokoschka, Oskar (1886–1980; Austrian)	Mucha, Alphonse (1860–1939; Cz.)	Roberts, Tom (1856–1931; Austral.)	Turner, J(oseph) M(allord) W(illiam) (1775–1851; Brit.)
Landseer, Sir Edwin (1802–73; Brit.)	Munch, Edvard (1863–1944; Norw.)	Rothko, Mark (1903–70; Am., b. in Latvia)	Uccello, Paolo (1397–1475; Florentine)
Léger, Fernand (1881–1955; Fr.)	Murillo, Bartolomé (c. 1618–82; Sp.)	Rousseau, Henri (1844–1910; Fr.)	Utamaro, Kitagawa (1753–1806; Jap.)
Lely, Sir Peter (1618–80; Du.)	Nash, Paul (1889–1946; Brit.)	Rubens, Peter Paul (1577–1640; Flem.)	Utrillo, Maurice (1883–1955; Fr.)
Leonardo da Vinci (1452–1519; It.)	Nicholson, Ben (1894–1982; Brit.)	Ruisdael, Jacob van (c. 1628–82; Du.)	Valadon, Suzanne (1867–1938; Fr.)
Lichtenstein, Roy (b. 1923; Am.)	Nolan, Sir Sidney (1917–93; Austral.)	Sargent, John Singer (1856–1925; Am.)	Van Dyck, Sir Anthony (1599–1641; Flem.)
Lippi, Fra Filippo (c. 1406–69; It.)	Nolde, Emil (1867–1956; Ger.)	Sarto, Andrea del (1486–1531; It.)	Van Eyck, Jan (c. 1370–1441; Flem.)
Lowry, L(awrence) S(tephen) (1887–1976; Brit.)	O'Keeffe, Georgia (1887–1986; Am.)	Schiele, Egon (1890–1918; Austrian)	Van Gogh, Vincent (1853–90; Du.)
Magritte, René (1898–1967; Belg.)	Palmer, Samuel (1805–81; Brit.)	Sesshu (1420–1506; Jap.)	Vasari, Giorgio (1511–74; It.)
Manet, Edouard (1832–83; Fr.)	Picasso, Pablo (1881–1973; Sp.)	Seurat, Georges (1859–91; Fr.)	Velázquez, Diego (1599–1660; Sp.)
Mantegna, Andrea (1431–1506; It.)	Piero della Francesca (c. 1420–92; It.)	Sickert, Walter (1860–1942; Brit.)	Vermeer, Jan (1632–75; Du.)
Martini, Simone (c. 1284–1344; It.)	Piper, John (1903–92; Brit.)	Signac, Paul (1863–1935; Fr.)	Veronese, Paolo (c. 1528–88; It.)
Masaccio (1401–28; Florentine)	Pissarro, Camille (1830–1903; Fr.)	Signorelli, Luca (c. 1441–1523; It.)	Vlaminck, Maurice de (1876–1958; Fr.)
Matisse, Henri (1869–1954; Fr.)	Pollock, Jackson (1912–56; Am.)	Siqueiros, David Alfaro (1896–1974; Mex.)	Vuillard, Edouard (1868–1940; Fr.)
Michelangelo (Buonarroti) (1475–1564; It.)	Poussin, Nicolas (1594–1665; Fr.)	Sisley, Alfred (1839–99; Fr.)	Warhol, Andy (c. 1928–87; Am.)
Millais, Sir John Everett (1829–96; Brit.)	Raeburn, Sir Henry (1756–1823; Scot.)	Soutine, Chaim (1893–1943; Fr.)	Watteau, Antoine (1684–1721; Fr.)
Miró, Joan (1893–1983; Sp.)	Raphael (1483–1520; It.)	Spencer, Sir Stanley (1891–1959; Brit.)	Whistler, James (1834–1903; Am.)
Modigliani, Amedeo (1884–1920; It.)	Rauschenberg, Robert (b. 1925; Am.)	Stella, Frank (b. 1936; Am.)	Zeuxis (5th century B.C.; Gk)
	Redon, Odilon (1840–1916; Fr.)	Stubbs, George (1724–1806; Brit.)	Zorn, Anders (1860–1920; Sw.)
	Rembrandt (Harmenszoon van Rijn) (1606–69; Du.)		

2 win by using *artifice* trickery, strategy, cunning, deceit, deception, craftiness, artfulness, wiliness, slyness, duplicity, guile, chicanery.

artificial *adjective* **1** *artificial silk/flowers* man-made, manufactured, synthetic, imitation, simulated, pseudo, ersatz, plastic, mock, sham, fake, bogus, counterfeit; *inf.* phoney. **2** *an artificial smile* feigned, false, affected, unnatural, assumed, pretended, insincere, contrived, forced, laboured, strained, hollow, spurious, meretricious; *inf.* phoney.
Opposites NATURAL; GENUINE; SINCERE.

artisan *noun* craftsman, craftswoman, skilled worker, journeyman, artificer, technician.

artist *noun* **1** *the artist's exhibition* painter, drawer, sculptor, old master. *See table. See also table at* SCULPTOR. **2** *furniture carved by an artist* craftsman, craftswoman, expert, adept, genius, past-master, maestro.

artistic *adjective* **1** *an artistic person* creative, talented, gifted, accomplished, imaginative, sensitive, cultivated. **2** *an artistic flower arrangement* decorative, beautiful, attractive, lovely, tasteful, graceful, stylish, elegant, exquisite, aesthetic, ornamental. **3** *the artistic temperament* temperamental, unconventional, bohemian, nonconformist.

artistry *noun* art, skill, ability, talent, genius, brilliance, expertness, flair, gift, creativity, proficiency, virtuosity, craftsmanship, workmanship.

artless *adjective an artless smile/remark* natural, simple, innocent, childlike, naive, ingenuous, guileless, sincere, frank, unpretentious.

as *conjunction* **1** *she came as we were leaving* just as, at the same time that, during the time that, at the time that, while, when. **2** *I must go home as it's late* since, because, seeing that, considering that, on account of. **3** *old as he is, he's healthy* although, though, even if. **4** *do as I say* in the manner that, in the way that. **5** *they live as their ancestors did* in the same manner that, in the same way that, like. **6** *the well-paid, as doctors, lawyers, and accountants* such as, like, for instance, for example, namely, viz. **7** *as you know, he's dead* a fact which, that which. **as for/to** on the subject of, as regards, with reference to, with regard to, with respect to. **as it were** so to speak, in a manner of speaking, in a way. **as yet** until now, up to now, up to the present time.

as *preposition* **1** *dressed as a policeman* in the guise of, with the appearance of, in the character of, so as to appear to be. **2** *as their employer I must sack them* in the role of, being, acting as, functioning as.

ascend *verb* climb, go/move up, mount, scale, rise, levitate, fly up, soar, slope upwards.

ascendancy, ascendency *noun* dominance, domination, control, power, authority, mastery, rule, command, supremacy, sway, sovereignty, the upper hand.

ascendant, ascendent *adjective* ascending, rising, going up, climbing, mounting, on the way up, on the rise, growing, increasing, flourishing, on the up and up, up-and-coming.

ascertain *verb* find out, get to know, ferret out, establish, discover, learn, determine, settle, identify, decide, verify, make certain, confirm; *inf.* pin down.

ascetic *noun an ascetic living alone in the forest* recluse, hermit, solitary, anchorite, self-denier, abstainer, celibate, nun, monk, stylite, fakir, dervish, yogi.

ascetic *adjective an ascetic way of life* austere, self-denying, abstinent, abstemious, self-disciplined, frugal, rigorous, strict, moderate, temperate, celibate, spartan, puritanical.

ascribe *verb* attribute, assign, accredit, credit, give credit to, put/set down to, chalk up to, impute, charge with, lay on, blame.

ashamed *adjective* **1** *ashamed of his conduct* humiliated, conscience-stricken, sorry, mortified, abashed, crestfallen, shamefaced, remorseful, discomfited, embarrassed, distressed, sheepish, red-faced, blushing, with one's tail between one's legs. **2** *ashamed to say* reluctant, unwilling, hesitant, restrained.
Opposites PROUD; SHAMELESS; PLEASED.

ashen *adjective* pale, pale-faced, pallid, wan, grey, grey-faced, white, colourless, anaemic, washed out, bleached, ghostly, deathlike, livid, leaden.

ashes *plural noun* **1** *ashes in the grate* cinders, embers; residue. **2** *the city was left in ashes* rubble, ruin; ruins. **3** *bury her ashes* remains.

ashore *adverb* to/on the shore, on land, on dry land, on the beach, shorewards, landwards.

aside *adverb* **1** *stand aside* to/on one side, to the side, alongside, apart, away, separately, detached, in isolation. **2** *joking aside* apart, notwithstanding.

aside *noun make an aside* whispered/confidential remark, casual remark, soliloquy, monologue.

asinine *adjective* stupid, silly, idiotic, foolish, brainless, nonsensical, senseless, halfwitted, fatuous, inane, imbecilic, moronic; *inf.* daft, dopey, balmy, batty, nutty, dumb, gormless.

ask *verb* **1** *ask her why|ask her about it* inquire, question, put a question to, query, interrogate, quiz, cross-examine, catechize; *inf.* grill, pump, give the third degree to. **2** *asked a favour|ask the boss for a rise* request, demand, appeal to, apply to, petition, call upon, entreat, beg, implore, beseech, plead, sue, supplicate. **3** *ask them to dine* invite, bid, summon.
Opposites ANSWER; REPLY.

askance *adverb* **1** *look askance at her neighbour* sideways, indirectly, obliquely, out of the corner of one's eye. **2** *look askance at their antics* disapprovingly, mistrustfully, suspiciously, with distrust/doubt.

askew *adverb/adjective* to one side, sideways, at an oblique angle, awry, out of line.

asleep *adjective/adverb* **1** *asleep in bed* sleeping, fast asleep, sound asleep, in a deep sleep, slumbering, napping, catnapping, dozing, resting, reposing, dormant, comatose; *inf.* snoozing, dead to the world, out like a light, kipping; *lit.* in the arms of Morpheus. **2** *my leg's asleep* numb, without feeling, deadened, benumbed.
Opposites AWAKE.

aspect *noun* **1** *look at every aspect of the problem* feature, facet, side, angle, slant, viewpoint, standpoint, light. **2** *a man with a fierce aspect* appearance, look, expression, air, countenance, demeanour, bearing; features; *fml.* mien. **3** *the southern aspect of the house* direction, situation, position, location, exposure, outlook. **4** *affording a pleasant aspect* outlook, view, scene, prospect.

asperity *noun* harshness, sharpness, roughness, severity, acerbity, bitterness, acrimony, sourness, astringency, virulence, sarcasm, irritability, irascibility, churlishness, crabbedness, peevishness, crossness.

aspersions *plural noun resent your aspersions| cast aspersions* disparaging/denigrating/malicious remarks, defamatory/slanderous remarks; disparagement, deprecation, denigration, defamation, slander.

asphyxiate *verb* choke, suffocate, smother, stifle, throttle, strangle, strangulate.

aspiration *noun aspirations to succeed* desire, longing, yearning, hankering, wish, ambition, hope, aim, objective, goal, object, dream, eagerness, enthusiasm, endeavour.

aspire *verb* desire, long to/for, yearn to/for, hanker after, be ambitious, hope to/for, wish to/for, dream of, hunger for, aim to/for, seek, pursue.

aspiring *adjective an aspiring leader* would-be, expectant, hopeful, ambitious, enterprising, optimistic, eager, striving, wishful.

ass *noun* **1** *riding on an ass* donkey; *inf.* moke. *See table at* DONKEY. **2** *a silly ass* fool, idiot, dolt, ninny, imbecile, nincompoop, blockhead, numskull, halfwit, dunce, simpleton, jackass; *inf.* twit, twerp, chump, nerd, nitwit, dimwit, dickhead, fathead.

assail *verb* **1** *assail the enemy with blows | a mind assailed by doubts* attack, assault, set about, lay into, beset, fall/set upon, accost, mug, charge; *inf.* jump. **2** *assailed with angry words/insults* bombard, berate, belabour, lash, abuse, criticize, harangue, revile, lambast, fulminate against; *inf.* sail into, tear into.

assailant *noun* attacker, mugger, aggressor, assaulter, accoster, assailer.

assassin *noun* murderer, killer, slayer, executioner, liquidator; *inf.* hit man, contract man.

assassinate *verb* murder, kill, slay, execute, liquidate, eliminate; *inf.* hit.

assassination *noun. See table.*

ASSASSINATIONS

Victim	Date
Julius Caesar	44 B.C.
Caligula	41 A.D.
Gobind Singh	1708
Abraham Lincoln	1865
Umberto I	1900
William McKinley	1901
Archduke Franz Ferdinand	1914
Grigori Rasputin	1916
Venustiano Carranza	1920
Michael Collins	1922
Leon Trotsky	1940
Mahatma Gandhi	1948
King Abdullah ibn Hussein	1951
Anastasio Somoza	1956
Solomon Bandaranaike	1959
Patrice Lumumba	1961
John F. Kennedy	1963
Lee Harvey Oswald	1963
Malcolm X	1965
Hendrik Verwoerd	1966
Martin Luther King Jr.	1968
Robert F. Kennedy	1968
Sheik Mujibur Rahman	1975
Aldo Moro	1978
Lord Mountbatten	1979
John Lennon	1980
Anwar Sadat	1981
Indira Gandhi	1984
Olof Palme	1986
Rajiv Gandhi	1991
Mohammed Boudiaf	1992

assault *noun* **1** *lead an army assault* attack, onslaught, onset, charge, offensive, act of aggression, storming. **2** *found guilty of assault* violent act, physical/verbal attack; sexual assault, sexual misconduct, molesting, sexual interference, rape.

assault *verb* **1** *assault the enemy forces* attack, make an onslaught/onset on, charge, undertake an offensive, storm. **2** *assault a policeman* attack, strike, hit, aim blows at. **3** *assault and murder a woman* sexually assault, molest, rape, interfere with.

assay *verb* **1** *assay metals* test, check, analyse, assess, evaluate, appraise, examine, inspect, investigate, scrutinize, probe. **2** *assay a reply* attempt, venture, try.

assay *noun metal assays* test, trial, check, analysis, assessment, evaluation, appraisal, examination, investigation, inspection, probe.

assemblage *noun an assemblage of old vases* collection, accumulation, conglomeration, cluster, medley, jumble.

assemble *verb* **1** *assemble the children/books/evidence* get together, bring/put together, gather, collect, round up, marshal, muster, summon, congregate, accumulate, amass, rally, convoke. **2** *the crowd assembled* gather, collect, come together, foregather, meet, congregate, convene, flock together. **3** *assemble the parts of the wardrobe* put together, piece/fit together, build, fabricate, construct, erect, manufacture, set up, connect, join.
Opposites DISPERSE; DEMOLISH.

assembly *noun* **1** *talking to a crowded assembly* gathering, meeting, group, body of people, crowd, throng, congregation, convention. **2** *the assembly of furniture/cars* putting/fitting together, building, fabrication, construction, erection, manufacture. *See* ASSEMBLE 3.

assent *noun give one's assent* agreement, concurrence, acceptance, approval, consent, acquiescence, compliance, approbation, permission, sanction, accord, accordance, accession.
Opposites DISSENT; REFUSAL.

assert *verb* **1** *assert that she is innocent* declare, state, announce, maintain, pronounce, proclaim, contend, aver, swear, avow, attest, affirm, allege, claim, postulate, asseverate. **2** *assert one's rights* uphold, press/push for, insist upon, stand up for, defend, vindicate.
assert oneself behave confidently, make one's presence felt, exert one's influence.

assertive *adjective an assertive personality* positive, confident, self-assured, dogmatic, aggressive, self-assertive, strong-willed, forceful, dominant, domineering; *inf.* pushy.
Opposites RETIRING; BASHFUL; TIMID.

assess *verb* **1** *assess the quality/value* evaluate, judge, gauge, rate, estimate, appraise, determine, weigh up, compute. **2** *assess taxation contributions* fix, evaluate, levy, impose, demand, rate.

assessment *noun* **1** *continuous assessment | the assessment of quality* evaluation, judgement, gauging, rating, estimation, appraisal. *See* ASSESS 1. **2** *tax assessment* evaluation, levy, charge, rate, toll, tariff, demand, fee.

asset *noun make the most of one's assets | an asset to the school* advantage, benefit, blessing, strong point, strength, boon, aid, help.
Opposites LIABILITY; HANDICAP.

assets *plural noun* property, estate, capital, wealth, money; resources, reserves, securities, holdings, possessions, effects, goods, valuables, belongings, chattels.

assiduous *adjective* diligent, industrious, hard-working, studious, persevering, persistent, laborious, unflagging, indefatigible, zealous, sedulous.

assign *verb* **1** *assign duties to all* allocate, allot, distribute, give out, dispense, apportion, consign. **2** *assign him to the post* appoint, select, install, designate, nominate, name, delegate, commission. **3** *assign Thursdays for trips* fix, appoint, decide on, determine, set aside/apart, stipulate, appropriate. **4** *assign her behaviour to jealousy* ascribe, put down to, attribute, accredit, chalk up to. **5** *assign her property* transfer, make over, convey, consign.

assignation *noun lovers making an assignation* rendezvous, tryst, date, appointment, meeting.

assignment *noun* **1** *carry out an assignment* task, job, duty, commission, charge, mission, responsibility, obligation. **2** *the assignment of duties* allocation, allotment, dispensation, apportionment, consignment. **3** *his assignment to the post* appointment, selection, installation, nomination. *See* ASSIGN 2. **4** *its assignment to jealousy* ascribing. *See* ASSIGN 4. **5** *the assignment of property* transfer, conveyance.

assimilate *verb* **1** *assimilate food/facts | assimilate people into a group* absorb, take in, incorporate, digest, ingest. **2** *assimilate your way of life to theirs* adapt, adjust, accustom, acclimatize, accommodate, become like/similar, blend in, fit, homogenize.

assist *verb* **1** *assist the old lady | assist the police* help, aid, lend a hand, succour, support, cooperate/collaborate with, abet, work with, play a part. **2** *he was only assisting his senior* be the assistant/subordinate to, help out, support, back, second. **3** *assist the factory's smooth operation* make easier, facilitate, expedite.
Opposites HINDER; IMPEDE.

assistance *noun* help, aid, succour, support, reinforcement, cooperation, collaboration; a helping hand.

assistant *noun* **1** *her assistant's in charge* subordinate, deputy, auxiliary, second in command, right hand man/woman, man/girl Friday, henchman. **2** *an assistant in the project* helper, colleague, associate, partner, confederate, accomplice, collaborator, accessory, abetter. **3** *an assistant in a department store* shop/sales assistant, salesperson, saleswoman, salesman, server, checkout girl/person/operator; *Am.* clerk.

associate *verb* **1** *associate wine with France* link, connect, relate, think of together, couple. **2** *they associate with criminals* mix, keep company, mingle, socialize, hobnob, fraternize; *inf.* run around, hang out, pal up. **3** *their clubs are associated* combine, join, connect, attach, affiliate, band together, ally, syndicate, incorporate, conjoin.

Association Football *noun. See table at* SOCCER.

assorted *adjective* mixed, varied, variegated, miscellaneous, diverse, diversified, motley, sundry, heterogeneous.
Opposites HOMOGENEOUS; SIMILAR; IDENTICAL.

assortment *noun* mixture, variety, miscellany, selection, medley, *mélange*, diversity, jumble, mishmash, hotchpotch, pot-pourri, farrago, salmagundi.

assuage *verb* **1** *assuage the pain* relieve, ease, alleviate, soothe, mitigate, lessen, allay, moderate, diminish, calm, palliate, abate, lull, temper, mollify. **2** *assuage their hunger/thirst* appease, satisfy, relieve, slake, quench, dull, blunt, allay, pacify, take the edge off.
Opposites AGGRAVATE; INTENSIFY.

assume *verb* **1** *assume he's coming* suppose, take for granted, presuppose, presume, imagine, think, believe, fancy, expect, accept, suspect, surmise, understand, gather; *Am.* guess. **2** *assume a thorough knowledge* feign, pretend, simulate, put on, counterfeit, sham. **3** *assume an air of authority | assume massive proportions* adopt, take on, acquire, come to have. **4** *assume a position of responsibility* undertake, enter upon, begin, set about, take on/up, embark on, take upon oneself, accept, shoulder. **5** *the invaders assumed power* seize, take, take over, appropriate, usurp, pre-empt, commandeer.

assumed *adjective an assumed name* false, fictitious, fake, feigned, pretended, made-up, bogus, sham, spurious, make-believe, counterfeit, pseudo; *inf.* phoney; *fml.* pseudonymous.

assumption *noun* **1** *on the assumption that you're right* supposition, presupposition, presumption, premise, belief, expectation, conjecture, surmise, guess, theory, hypothesis, suspicion, postulation. **2** *the assumption of a thorough knowledge* feigning, pretending, simulation. *See* ASSUME 2. **3** *the assumption of an air of authority* adoption, taking on. *See* ASSUME 3. **4** *the assumption of a position of responsibility* undertaking, entering upon, setting about, embarkation on. *See* ASSUME 4. **5** *the invaders' assumption of power* seizure, appropriation, usurping. *See* ASSUME 5. **6** *amazed at his assumption* arrogance, presumption, conceit, impertinence.

assurance *noun* **1** *shows remarkable assurance for her age* self-assurance, self-confidence, confidence, self-reliance, nerve, poise, positiveness. **2** *you have my assurance that I'll be there* word of honour, word, guarantee, promise, pledge, vow, oath, affirmation. **3** *no assurance of her success* certainty, guarantee. *See* ASSURE 3. **4** *life assurance* insurance.

assure *verb* **1** *I assure you that he's wrong* declare, affirm, give one's word, guarantee, promise, swear, certify, pledge, vow, attest. **2** *they assured him of their ability* convince, persuade, reassure, prove to. **3** *success is assured* ensure, make certain, make sure, secure, guarantee, seal, clinch, confirm. **4** *assure his life* insure.

ASTEROIDS		
Achilles	Chiron	Hygeia
Adonis	Eros	Icarus
Amor	Eunomia	Ida
Apollo	Euphrosyne	Iris
Astraea	Gaspra	Juno
Aten	Hebe	Pallas
Ceres	Hidalgo	Vesta

LAYERS OF THE EARTH'S ATMOSPHERE	
chemosphere	ozonosphere
exosphere	stratosphere
ionosphere	thermosphere
mesosphere	troposphere

assured *adjective* **1** *an assured manner* self-assured, self-confident, confident, self-reliant, poised, positive. **2** *an assured market* certain, sure, guaranteed, secure, reliable, dependable.

asteroid *noun. See table.*

astonish *verb* amaze, astound, dumbfound, stagger, surprise, stun, take aback, confound, take one's breath away; *inf.* flabbergast, floor.

astonishing *adjective* amazing, astounding, staggering, surprising, breathtaking, striking, impressive, bewildering, stunning.

astonishment *noun he failed to conceal his astonishment* surprise, amazement, wonder, disbelief; shock, numbness, bewilderment, confusion.

astound *verb* amaze, astonish, dumbfound, stagger, surprise. *See* ASTONISH.

astounding *adjective* amazing, astonishing, staggering, surprising. *See* ASTONISHING.

astray *adverb/adjective* **1** *go astray in the fog* off course, off the right track, adrift; lost. **2** *led astray by wicked men* into wrongdoing, into error/sin, to the bad.

astringent *adjective* **1** *an astringent lotion* contracting, constricting, constrictive, constringent, styptic. **2** *astringent criticism/conditions* severe, stern, harsh, rough, stringent, acerbic, austere, caustic, mordant, trenchant.

astrology *noun. See table at* ZODIAC.

astronaut *noun* spaceman, spacewoman, cosmonaut, space traveller. *See table at* PILOT.

astute *adjective* shrewd, sharp, acute, quick, quick-witted, clever, cunning, artful, ingenious, perceptive, discerning, crafty, wily, calculating, perspicacious, sagacious.
Opposites STUPID; DULL.

asunder *adverb* into pieces, to pieces, to bits, apart.

asylum *noun* **1** *seek an asylum in the church | political asylum* refuge, sanctuary, shelter, safety, safe keeping, protection; haven, retreat, harbour, port in a storm. **2** *shut away in an asylum* mental hospital, psychiatric hospital, institution; *derog.* madhouse, nuthouse, loony bin, funny farm.

asymmetrical *adjective* disproportionate, misproportioned, irregular, uneven, distorted, malformed, formless.

atavism *noun* reversion, throwback; recurrence, reappearance, resurgence.

atheism *noun* disbelief, nonbelief, unbelief, heresy, godlessness, scepticism, irreligion, heathenism, freethinking, apostasy, nihilism.

atheist *noun* non-believer, disbeliever, unbeliever, heretic, sceptic, heathen, freethinker, nihilist, infidel.

athlete *noun* sportsman, sportswoman, runner, player; gymnast, competitor, contestant; *inf.* keep-fit buff/freak. *See table at* SPORT.

athletic *adjective* **1** *an athletic person | of an athletic build* muscular, powerful, robust, able-bodied, sturdy, strong, strapping, vigorous, hardy, stalwart, well-built, brawny, thickset, Herculean; *inf.* husky. **2** *an athletic event* sports, sporting, games, gymnastics.

athletics *plural noun* sporting events, track and field events, sports, games, matches, contests, gymnastics. *See table.*

atmosphere *noun* **1** *the world's polluted atmosphere* air, aerosphere, aerospace, sky, heavens. *See table.* **2** *a friendly/unfriendly atmosphere* environment, milieu, medium, background, setting, air, ambience, aura, climate, mood, feeling, character, tone, tenor, spirit, quality, flavour; surroundings.

atom *noun* iota, jot, bit, whit, particle, scrap, shred, trace, speck, spot, dot, crumb, fragment, grain, morsel, mite.

ATHLETIC EVENTS			
biathlon	half-marathon	110m hurdles	triathlon
cross-country run	hammer throw	100m race	triple jump
decathlon	heptathlon	pole vault	tug-of-war
discus	high jump	relay race	20km walk
800m race	hurdling	shotput	200m race
fell run	javelin	1,600m relay	women's 100m
1,500m race	long-distance race	sprint	hurdles
50km walk	long jump	steeplechase	women's 3,000m
50m race	marathon	10,000m race	race
5,000m race	middle-distance	tetrathlon	women's 200m
400m hurdles	race	3,000m	hurdles
400m race	modern pentathlon	steeplechase	women's 80m
400m relay	one-mile race	tossing the caber	hurdles

atone *verb* make amends/reparation, compensate, pay the penalty, pay for, recompense, expiate, do penance.

atonement *noun* reparation, compensation, recompense, redress, indemnity, restitution, expiation, penance, redemption.

atrocious *adjective* **1** *atrocious crimes* brutal, barbaric, barbarous, savage, vicious, wicked, cruel, ruthless, merciless, villainous, murderous, heinous, nefarious, monstrous, inhuman, infernal, fiendish, diabolical, flagrant, outrageous. **2** *atrocious weather* very bad, unpleasant, appalling, dreadful, terrible, shocking.

atrocity *noun* **1** *atrocities committed in wartime* act of brutality/barbarity/savagery, crime, offence, injury; brutality, cruelty, barbarity. **2** *the atrocity of war* abomination, enormity, outrage, horror, evil, monstrosity, violation.

atrophy *verb* waste, waste away, wither, shrivel up, shrink, dry up, decay, wilt, decline, deteriorate, degenerate.

attach *verb* **1** *attach a label to the briefcase* fasten, fix, affix, join, connect, couple, link, secure, tie, stick, adhere, pin, hitch, bond, add, append, annex, subjoin. **2** *attach oneself to a group* affiliate with, join, join forces with, associate/combine with, ally/unite with, latch on to. **3** *attach no significance to it* ascribe, assign, attribute, accredit, apply, put, place, lay, impute, invest with. **4** *the state attaching criminals' property* seize, confiscate, appropriate; *Law* distrain. **5** *he is attached to the military unit* assign, second, allot, allocate, detail, appoint. *Opposites* DETACH; SEPARATE.

attached *adjective* **1** *is she attached?* married, engaged, having a partner, spoken for; *inf.* going steady. **2** *she is attached to her father* be fond of, full of regard for, devoted to.

attachment *noun* **1** *a strong attachment to one's aunt* fondness, love, liking, affection, devotion, loyalty, tenderness, bond, affinity. **2** *an electric drill and attachments* supplementary part, accessory, extension, fitting, extra, adjunct, addition, appurtenance, appendage, accoutrement. **3** *the cable attachment is loose* junction, connector, coupling, fastening, link, clamp. **4** *on attachment to the unit* assignment, secondment, detail, appointment. **5** *the attachment of a label* fastening, fixing, affixing. *See* ATTACH 1. **6** *my/the attachment of others to the group* affiliation, joining, association. *See* ATTACH 2. **7** *the attachment of criminals' property* seizure, confiscation, appropriation; *Law* distrainment.

attack *verb* **1** *attack the enemy | let us attack* assault, set/fall upon, strike at, rush, storm, charge, pounce upon, beset, besiege, beleaguer; strike, begin hostilities; *inf.* lay into, let one have it. **2** *an article attacking the writer* criticize, censure, berate, reprove, rebuke, impugn, harangue, find fault with, blame, revile, fulminate against, vilify; *inf.* slate, have a go at, knock, slam. **3** *attack a pile of work* set about, get/go to work on, get started on, undertake, embark on. **4** *a disease attacking the nervous system* affect, have an effect on, infect. *Opposites* DEFEND; PROTECT; PRAISE.

attack *noun* **1** *an attack on the enemy* assault, onslaught, offensive, onset, strike, storming, charge, foray, rush, incursion, inroad. *See* ATTACK *verb* 1. **2** *launch an attack on his writing* criticism, censure, berating, rebuke, reproval, impugnment, blame, revilement, vilification; *inf.* slating, knocking. *See* ATTACK *verb* 2. **3** *mount an attack on a pile of work* start, beginning, commencement, undertaking, onslaught. **4** *an asthmatic attack* fit, bout, seizure, spasm, convulsion, paroxysm, stroke; *fml.* access. *Opposites* DEFENCE.

attacker *noun* assailant, aggressor, assaulter, striker, mugger.

attain *verb* achieve, accomplish, obtain, gain, procure, secure, get, grasp, win, earn, acquire, reach, arrive at, realize, fulfil, succeed in, bring off, be successful.

attainable *adjective* achievable, obtainable, accessible, within reach, at hand, reachable, winnable, realizable, practicable, feasible, possible, potential, conceivable, imaginable.

attainment *noun* **1** *the attainment of his goal* achievement, accomplishment, gaining, procurement, acquiral, acquirement, acquisition, realization, fulfilment, completion, consummation, success. *See* ATTAIN. **2** *musical attainment* accomplishment, ability, art, skill, proficiency, mastery, talent, gift, capability, competence.

attempt *verb* **1** *attempt to explain* try, strive, aim, venture, endeavour, seek, undertake, set out, do one's best, take it upon oneself, essay; *inf.* give it a whirl. **2** *attempt an escape* try, venture, undertake, tackle, have a go/shot at, essay; *inf.* have a crack at.

attempt *noun* effort, try, endeavour, venture, trial, experiment, essay; *inf.* crack, go, shot.

attend *verb* **1** *attend a meeting | can you attend?* be present, be at, be here/there, appear, put in an appearance, turn up, visit, frequent, haunt; *inf.* show up, show. **2** *attend the sick* look after, take care of, care for, tend, nurse, mind, minister to. **3** *she was told but was not attending* pay attention, concentrate, listen, pay heed, heed, follow, take note, observe, notice, mark, watch. **4** *attend to this matter/customer* deal/cope with, see to, handle, take care of, give one's attention to, take charge of. **5** *the queen attended by her bodyguard* accompany, escort, guard, chaperon, squire, convoy. **6** *a plan attended with problems* accompanied by, be associated/connected with, go hand in hand with, occur/coexist with, result/arise from, follow upon, be a consequence of.

attendance *noun* **1** *attendance at church is not compulsory* presence, attending, appearance, being there; *inf.* showing up, showing. **2** *attendances vary* number present, turnout, crowd, audience, house, gate. **in attendance** present, giving assistance, supervising, monitoring, on guard.

attendant *noun* **1** *cloakroom attendant* assistant, helper, auxiliary, steward, waiter, servant, menial. **2** *the queen and her attendants* companion, escort, aide, guard, custodian, guide, usher, equerry, squire, lackey, flunkey.

attendant *adjective attendant circumstances* accompanying, concomitant, related, accessory, resultant, consequent.

attention *noun* **1** *wandering attention | give more attention to the problem* concentration, attentiveness, intentness, notice, observation, heed, heedfulness, regard, contemplation, deliberation, scrutiny; thought, thinking, studying. **2** *attract their attention* notice, awareness, observation, consciousness, heed, recognition, regard. **3** *for the personal attention of the manager* consideration, action, notice, investigation. **4** *medical attention* care, treatment, ministration, therapy. **5** *appreciate his attentions* civility, politeness, courtesy, respect, gallantry, urbanity, deference; compliments.

attentive *adjective* **1** *keen and attentive* alert, aware, awake, watchful, widewake, observant, noticing, concentrating, heeding, heedful, mindful, vigilant, on guard; *inf.* all ears; *fml.* on the qui vive. **2** *an attentive host* considerate, thoughtful, kind, polite, courteous, gracious, conscientious, civil, obliging, accommodating, gallant, chivalrous.
Opposites INATTENTIVE; HEEDLESS; DISCOURTEOUS.

attenuated *adjective* **1** *attenuated limbs | attenuated lengths of silk* thin, slender, threadlike, thinned down, stretched out, drawn out. **2** *attenuated force* weakened, reduced, lessened, decreased, diminished, impaired, enervated.

attest *verb* **1** *witnesses attest his account* affirm, aver, asseverate, confirm, testify to, vouch for, bear witness to, bear out, endorse, back up, support, corroborate, verify, authenticate. **2** *footsteps attested to his presence* prove, give proof of, provide evidence of, evidence, demonstrate, evince, display, exhibit, show, manifest, substantiate, confirm, verify, vouch for.

attic *noun* loft, garret, mansard.

attire *noun evening attire* clothing, dress, wear, outfit, apparel, garb, ensemble, costume, array, habit, wardrobe; clothes, garments, accoutrements; *inf.* gear, togs, glad rags, rig-out.

attire *verb attired in silk* dress, clothe, dress up, fit out, garb, robe, array, deck out, turn out, costume, accoutre; *inf.* doll up, rig out; *fml.* apparel.

attitude *noun* **1** *one's attitude to marriage* point of view, viewpoint, opinion, frame of mind, outlook, perspective, reaction, stance, position, approach; thoughts, ideas. **2** *bodies adopting different attitudes* position, stance, pose, stand; bearing, deportment, carriage.

attract *verb* **1** *magnets attract iron filings* draw, pull, magnetize. **2** *men attracted by small women | moths attracted to light* allure, entice, tempt, interest, fascinate, charm, engage, enchant, captivate, bewitch, seduce, inveigle.

attraction *noun* **1** *magnetic attraction* pull, draw, magnetism. **2** *the attraction of foreign travel* appeal, attractiveness, allure, pull, draw, enticement, temptation, inducement, interest, charm, fascination, glamour, enchantment, captivation, seduction; *inf.* come-on. **3** *one of*

the city attractions interest, feature, entertainment, activity, diversion.

attractive *adjective* **1** *an attractive proposal* appealing, agreeable, pleasing, inviting, tempting, interesting. **2** *an attractive woman/man* good-looking, striking, beautiful, handsome, pretty, stunning, gorgeous, prepossessing, fetching, comely, captivating, charming, fascinating, interesting, appealing, enchanting, alluring.
Opposites UNINVITING; UGLY; unattractive.

attribute *noun* **1** *kindness is one their attributes* quality, feature, characteristic, property, mark, trait, distinction, idiosyncrasy. **2** *the throne is an attribute of a king* symbol, indicator, mark, sign, trade mark, status symbol.

attribute *verb success attributed to hard work* ascribe, assign, accredit, put down to, lay at the door of, chalk up to.

attrition *noun* **1** *the smoothing of rock by attrition* abrasion, friction, rubbing, chafing, corroding, corrosion, erosion, eating away, grinding, scraping, wearing away, excoriation, detrition. **2** *defeat the enemy by a war of attrition* wearing down, weakening, debilitation, enfeebling, enervation, sapping, attenuation, harassment, harrying.

attune *verb* **1** *not yet attuned to the situation | attuned to their ideas* accustom, adjust, adapt, familiarize, acclimatize, assimilate, tailor, be fitted, be in tune/harmony/accord, homologize. **2** *attune an instrument* tune, regulate, modulate, harmonize.

auburn *adjective* reddish-brown, Titian, chestnut-coloured, copper-coloured, rust-coloured, hennaed. See table at COLOUR.

audacious *adjective* **1** *an audacious scheme/traveller* bold, daring, fearless, intrepid, brave, courageous, valiant, adventurous, plucky, daredevil, reckless; *inf.* gutsy, spunky. **2** *an audacious youth/remark* impudent, impertinent, insolent, presumptuous, cheeky, forward, rude, brazen, shameless, pert, saucy, defiant.

audacity *noun* **1** *the audacity of the scheme/man* boldness, daring, fearlessness, intrepidity, bravery, courage, valour, pluck, recklessness; *inf.* guts, spunk. **2** *the child had the audacity to swear* impudence, impertinence, insolence, presumption, cheek, forwardness, rudeness, brazenness, shamelessness, pertness, sauce, defiance.

audible *adjective* heard, hearable, clear, distinct, perceptible, discernible.
Opposites INAUDIBLE; FAINT; INDISTINCT.

audience *noun* **1** *a concert/TV audience* listeners, spectators, viewers, onlookers; assembly, gathering, crowd, assemblage, house, turnout, congregation, gallery. **2** *publications aimed at a wide audience* public, market, following; fans, devotees, aficionados; *inf.* buffs, freaks. **3** *an audience with the Pope* interview, meeting, hearing, consultation, discussion, reception.

audit *noun an audit of the firm's accounts* inspection, examination, scrutiny, investigation, review, check.

audit *verb audit the books* inspect, examine, go over/through, scrutinize, investigate, review, check.

augment *verb* **1** *augment one's income | augment the audience* increase, make larger/bigger/greater, boost, build up, enlarge, add to, expand, extend, amplify, raise, enhance, heighten, multiply, magnify, elevate, swell, inflate, escalate, intensify. **2** *his fortune augmented* increase, grow, build up, enlarge, expand, extend, rise, multiply, swell, inflate, escalate.
Opposites DECREASE; DIMINISH.

augur *verb it augurs well that they're talking* be a sign of, foretell, forecast, predict, prophesy, bode, foreshadow, promise, presage, portend, herald, betoken, harbinger.

augur *noun augurs foretelling disasters* seer, soothsayer, prophet, oracle.

august *adjective* dignified, solemn, majestic, stately, magnificent, noble, regal, imposing, impressive, exalted, lofty, grand, high-ranking, illustrious, distinguished, awe-inspiring.

aura *noun* ambience, atmosphere, air, quality, mood, character, spirit, feeling, tone, suggestión, emanation; vibrations; *inf.* vibes.

auspices *plural noun under the auspices of* patronage, guidance, influence, responsibility, control, protection.

auspicious *adjective* propitious, favourable, promising, bright, optimistic, hopeful, encouraging, opportune, timely, lucky, fortunate, providential, felicitous, rosy.

austere *adjective* **1** *an austere manner* harsh, stern, severe, strict, unfeeling, hard, rigorous, stringent, grim, cold, distant, formal, stiff, aloof, forbidding, grave, solemn, serious, unsmiling, unyielding, unbending, unrelenting, inflexible. **2** *monks leading an austere life* strict, self-denying, self-abnegating, ascetic, spartan, abstemious, abstinent, moral, upright, celibate, chaste, puritanical. **3** *decorated in an austere style* plain, simple, severe, unadorned, unornamented, unembellished, stark, subdued, sombre.
Opposites GENIAL; IMMODERATE; ELABORATE.

authentic *adjective* **1** *an authentic painting* genuine, true, bona fide, rightful, legitimate, lawful, legal, valid; *inf.* the real McCoy, kosher. **2** *an authentic statement* reliable, dependable, trustworthy, true, truthful, honest, faithful, credible; *inf.* straight from the horse's mouth.
Opposites FAKE; COUNTERFEIT; UNRELIABLE.

authenticate *verb* **1** *authenticate an agreement* validate, ratify, confirm, certify, seal, endorse, guarantee, warrant, underwrite. **2** *authenticate the work as being Shakespeare's* verify, substantiate, support, prove, evidence.

authenticity *noun* **1** *the authenticity of the painting* genuineness, rightfulness, legitimacy, legality, validity. **2** *the authenticity of the statement* reliability, dependability, trustworthiness, truth, honesty, faithfulness, credibility.

author *noun* **1** *the author of the book/article* writer, composer; novelist, dramatist, playwright, screenwriter, poet, essayist, biographer, librettist, lyricist, songwriter, journalist, columnist, reporter. *See tables at* PLAYWRIGHT, POET, WRITER. **2** *the author of their misfortune* cause, creator, originator, initiator, founder, planner, prime mover, designer.

authoritarian *noun the new headmaster is an authoritarian* disciplinarian, autocrat, despot, dictator, tyrant, absolutist.

authoritarian *adjective an authoritarian approach* disciplinarian, harsh, strict, autocratic, despotic, dictatorial, tyrannical, domineering, dogmatic, imperious, absolute, Draconian.

authoritative *adjective* **1** *an authoritative biography* official, approved, authorized, sanctioned, validated, authentic, genuine; *inf.* kosher. **2** *authoritative information* sound, dependable, reliable, trustworthy, authentic, valid, certified, attested, definitive, factual, accurate, scholarly. **3** *an authoritative manner* self-assured, confident, assertive, imposing, masterful, dogmatic, peremptory, arrogant, commanding, dominating, domineering, imperious, overbearing, authoritarian.

authorities *plural noun* administration, the establishment, government, officialdom, management, legislation, the police, bureaucracy, red tape; the powers that be.

authority *noun* **1** *have the authority to decide | a person of/in authority* authorization, right, power, might, sanction, influence, force, control, charge, prerogative, jurisdiction, rule, command, dominion, sovereignty, ascendancy, supremacy; *inf.* say-so. **2** *he is an authority on ecology* expert, specialist, professional, master, scholar, adept, pundit; *inf.* walking encyclopedia, bible. **3** *quoting authorities* used source, reference, documentation, bibliography, citation, quotation, quote, excerpt, passage. **4** *have his authority to act* permission, authorization, sanction, licence, warrant; *inf.* say-so. **5** *have on their authority that they were there* testimony, evidence, witness, attestation, sworn statement, declaration, word, avowal, deposition, profession.

authorize *verb* **1** *authorize them to represent us* give authority to, commission, empower, entitle, enable, accredit, license, certify, validate. **2** *authorize the sale* give authority/permission for, permit, allow, approve, give one's assent to, agree to, sanction, ratify, warrant, give leave for, countenance, accede to; *inf.* give the green light to, give the go-ahead for.

autobiography *noun* memoirs; life-story, diary, journal.

autocratic *adjective* despotic, dictatorial, tyrannical, domineering, imperious, omnipotent, all-powerful, absolute, Draconian, oppressive, high-handed; *inf.* bossy.

autograph *noun get an actor's autograph* signature, inscription, mark, cross, X.

autograph *verb autograph a programme* sign, attach one's signature, initial, countersign, mark, put one's cross/X.

automatic *adjective* **1** *an automatic washing machine* automated, mechanized, mechanical, push-button, robotic, self-activating, self-regulating, self-directing, self-propelling. **2** *an automatic reaction* instinctive, spontaneous, involuntary, unconscious, reflex, natural, mechanical. **3** *promotion is automatic* inevitable, routine, certain, assured, unavoidable, necessary.

autonomy *noun the people fought for autonomy | the region gained autonomy* independence, self-determination, autarchy; self-sufficiency, individualism.

available *adjective tickets are still available* unoccupied, free, untaken, vacant, usable, employable, ready; accessible, obtainable, at hand, convenient.

avarice *noun she turned to crime because of avarice* greed, acquisitiveness, covetousness, materialism; selfishness, self-interest, meanness, miserliness.

average *noun she calculated the average* mean, median, midpoint, centre; norm, standard, yardstick, rule.

average *adjective* **1** *the team played an average game | the house was an average size* ordinary, normal, typical, everyday; common, widespread, prevalent. **2** *she wrote average essays | his ability was no better than average* mediocre, moderate, unexceptional; second-rate, banal; pedestrian. **Opposites** OUTSTANDING; EXCEPTIONAL.

aversion *noun she had an aversion to spiders | his aversion to work became a problem* dislike, distaste, hatred, repugnance; avoidance, evasion, shunning, reluctance, unwillingness. **Opposites** LIKING; INCLINATION.

aviator *noun. See table at* PILOT.

avid *adjective she was an avid reader | he was an avid fan* keen, eager, enthusiastic, partial to, fond of, fervent, zealous, passionate about; *inf.*

crazy about, mad about. **Opposites** APATHETIC; INDIFFERENT.

avoid *verb he tried to avoid paying taxes | he avoided her in the street* shun, keep away from, eschew, steer clear of; evade, hide from, elude, shirk, dodge; abstain from, refrain from, hold back from. **Opposites** CONFRONT; FACE.

aware *adjective* **1** *he was aware of the problem | she was aware of hostility* conscious of, informed of, familiar with, sensitive to; *inf.* clued up on, in the know. **2** *he was aware of every movement | the watchmen were always aware* awake, watchful, vigilant, alert, cautious, paying attention. **Opposites** UNAWARE; IGNORANT; OBLIVIOUS.

awe *noun she gazed in awe | they were filled with awe* amazement, wonder, astonishment, stupefaction; reverence, honour, veneration; dread, fear.

awful *adjective* **1** *she had an awful cough | his new coat looked awful* nasty, unpleasant, distressing, troublesome, horrible; serious, severe; ugly, unattractive, foul, disgusting. **2** *the awful power of the gods | the awful presence of the high priestess* awe-inspiring, awesome, venerable, demanding respect, admirable, impressive, authoritative, daunting.

awkward *adjective* **1** *the appointment was at an awkward time* inconvenient, difficult, problematic; unhelpful, annoying, obstructive, vexatious, perverse. **2** *the gymnast had been an awkward child* clumsy, ungainly, inelegant, inept, gauche; lumbering, out of proportion, unwieldy. **Opposites** CONVENIENT; ADROIT.

awry *adjective the storm left the fence awry* lopsided, uneven, unequal, asymmetrical, askew, crooked.

Bb

babble verb **1** *babbling away unintelligibly* jabber, gibber, gabble, burble, chatter, mutter, mumble, prate, drivel, bleat, cackle; *inf.* rabbit, waffle, run on. **2** *he babbled the secret* blab, blurt out, reveal, divulge, let slip. **3** *the stream babbled quietly* murmur, whisper, gurgle.

babble noun *the babble of voices* jabbering, gabble, gabbling, gibberish, chatter, muttering, mumbling, clamour.

babe noun **1** *a new-born babe* baby, infant, child. **2** *just a babe in the world of business* innocent, ingénue, babe in arms, greenhorn, novice, tiro, beginner.

babel noun commotion, clamour, babble, hubbub, tumult, uproar, din.

baby noun **1** *holding a tiny baby* infant, newborn, child, babe, tiny tot; *inf.* sprog; *Scots* bairn; *Med.* neonate. **2** *the baby of the team* junior, youngest, subordinate.

baby verb *baby the children | baby his wife* pamper, spoil, cosset, indulge, pet, humour, coddle, mollycoddle, overindulge, spoonfeed, featherbed.

baby adjective *baby carrots* miniature, mini, diminutive, dwarf, tiny, minute, small, little, wee, midget.

babyish adjective childish, immature, infantile, juvenile, puerile, adolescent, jejune, pathetic, inane, namby-pamby.

back noun **1** *hurt one's back* spine, backbone, spinal column; human posterior; *Med.* dorsum. **2** *the back of the building* rear, rear end, far end, end, reverse, reverse side, other side; hind part, posterior, tail end, backside, hindquarters, stern. **behind one's back** secretly, deceitfully, slyly, sneakily, surreptitiously, covertly.
Opposites FRONT.

back adjective **1** *back garden/shed/teeth* rear, hind, end, hindmost, posterior. **2** *back copies* past, previous, earlier, former, bygone, expired, elapsed, obsolete.
Opposites FRONT; FOREMOST; FUTURE.

back adverb **1** *without looking back* backwards, behind, to the rear, rearwards. **2** *a few days back* earlier, previously, before, since, ago, heretofore. **3** *standing back from the road* to the rear, at a distance, remote from.

back verb **1** *back the proposal/candidate* support, endorse, approve, favour, advocate, help, assist, aid, promote, uphold, champion, encourage, second, abet. **2** *back the theatrical venture* sponsor, finance, subsidize, underwrite, subscribe to. **3** *back her statement* support, confirm, corroborate, substantiate, endorse, second, bolster, reinforce, stand by, side with, vouch for, attest to, sanction. **4** *back a horse/ runner* bet on, place a bet on, gamble on. **5** *the car backed out* go/move backwards, reverse.

back away withdraw, retire, retreat, fall back, recede, turn tail. **back down** yield, submit, surrender, give in, climb down, concede, concede defeat, backtrack, back-pedal, retract. **back out** go back on, withdraw from, cancel, renege on, abandon, retreat from, get cold feet, recant; *inf.* chicken out of. **back up** support, confirm. *See* BACK verb 3.
Opposites OPPOSE; HINDER; DENY.

backbiting noun slander, libel, defamation, abuse, scandalmongering, disparagement, denigration, detraction, malice, spite, spitefulness, cattiness, vilification, vituperation, calumny; slurs, aspersions; *inf.* bitching, knocking, slagging off, mud-slinging; *Am. inf.* bad-mouthing.

backbone noun **1** *an injured backbone* spine, spinal/vertebral column. *See table at* VERTEBRA. **2** *the backbone of the organization* framework, mainstay, support, basis, foundation, structure. **3** *lacking backbone* strength of character, firmness, determination, resolve, resolution, steadfastness, character, courage, grit, nerve, mettle, pluck, fortitude, tenacity, stamina, will-power; *inf.* bottle.

backer noun **1** *the theatre's backers* sponsor, patron, financier, benefactor, subsidizer, underwriter, well-wisher, Maecenas; *inf.* angel. **2** *backers of the plan/candidate* supporter, advocate, promoter, upholder, champion, seconder, second, abettor.

backfire verb **1** *the engine backfired* explode, detonate, discharge. **2** *the plan backfired* miscarry, rebound, recoil, boomerang, fail, disappoint; *inf.* flop.

background noun **1** *in the background of the painting* distance, rear, horizon. **2** *models posing against a white background* setting, backcloth, backdrop, scene, stage. **3** *check the employee's background* upbringing, rearing, education, history, environment, class, culture, experience; family circumstances, circumstances, qualifications, credentials. **4** *the political background* conditions, circumstances, environment, milieu, framework; factors, influences.
Opposites FOREGROUND; FRONT.

backhanded adjective indirect, oblique, ambiguous, equivocal, double-edged, two-edged, sarcastic, ironic, sardonic.

backing noun **1** *have the school's backing* support, approval, commendation, help, assistance, aid, helping hand, encouragement, cooperation, championship, promotion, advocacy, endorsement. **2** *set up with the backing of the directors* sponsorship, financing; finance, grant, subsidy; funds. **3** *the backing of the bank* security, surety, collateral, assurance, insurance, guarantee, warranty. **4** *musical backing* accompaniment, backup, harmony, obbligato.

backlash *noun* reaction, counteraction, repercussion, recoil, kickback, rebound, boomerang, retroaction, retaliation.

backlog *noun* accumulation, stockpile, heap, excess, hoard, stock, supply; arrears, reserves; *inf.* mountain.

back-pedal *verb* retract, take back, withdraw, retreat, reverse, backtrack, back down, renege, do an about-face, shift ground, tergiversate.

backslide *verb* relapse, lapse, regress, retrogress, revert, fall back, slip/fall from grace, stray, go astray, leave the straight and narrow, degenerate, deteriorate, turn one's back, tergiversate, apostatize.

backslider *noun* recidivist, turncoat, relapser, renegade, deserter, regressor, apostate, fallen angel, tergiversator.

backward *adjective* **1** *a backward look/somersault* rearward, towards the back/rear, reverse. **2** *a backward area* slow, behind, behindhand, underdeveloped, undeveloped, retarded, unprogressive, dull, sluggish, subnormal, unsophisticated. **3** *rather backward in a crowd* bashful, shy, retiring, diffident, hesitant, shrinking, timid, demure, chary, reluctant. **Opposites** FORWARD; ADVANCED; BOLD.

backwards *adverb* **1** *look backwards* rearwards, towards the back/rear, behind. **2** *running backwards* in reverse. **3** *a country going backwards* in reverse, worse, retrogressively, retrogradely.

backwash *noun* **1** *backwash of a ship* wash, backflow, wake, path, churning, disturbance. **2** *the backwash of the war* aftermath, result, effect; repercussions, reverberations, consequences, after-effects.

backwoods *plural noun* wilderness, no man's land; *Austral.* bush, outback; *inf.* back of beyond, middle of nowhere, the wilds, the sticks.

bacteria *plural noun* germs, microorganisms, microbes, parasites, bacilli; *inf.* bugs.

bad *adjective* **1** *bad workmanship | a bad driver* poor, unsatisfactory, inadequate, deficient, imperfect, defective, inferior, substandard, faulty, unacceptable, useless, worthless, inept, ineffectual; *inf.* duff, ropy. **2** *smoking is a bad habit | it's bad for you* harmful, hurtful, damaging, dangerous, injurious, detrimental, destructive, ruinous, deleterious, unhealthy, unwholesome, poisonous. **3** *a bad man | leading a bad life* immoral, wicked, wrong, evil, sinful, corrupt, base, reprobate, depraved, dishonest, dishonourable, crooked. **4** *a bad child* naughty, mischievous, disobedient, unruly, wayward, refractory. **5** *bad weather | having a bad time* disagreeable, unpleasant, unwelcome, uncomfortable, nasty, terrible, dreadful, adverse, grim, gloomy, unfortunate, unfavourable, unlucky, distressing. **6** *a bad time for house-buying* adverse, difficult, unfavourable, unfortunate, unsuitable, inappropriate, inapt. **7** *a bad mistake/accident* serious, severe, grave, disastrous, terrible, critical, acute. **8** *bad eggs | meat going bad* rotten, off, decayed, mouldy, putrid, tainted, spoiled, contaminated, putrescent, putrefacient. **9** *an invalid feeling bad* ill, unwell, sick, poorly, indisposed, ailing, weak, feeble, diseased; *inf.* under the weather, below par. **10** *feeling bad about their actions* sorry, apologetic, regretful, conscience-stricken, contrite, remorseful, guilty, penitent, rueful, sad, upset. **11** *a bad cheque* worthless, invalid, counterfeit, false, spurious, fraudulent, fake; *inf.* bogus, phoney. **not bad** all right, quite good, passable, tolerable, fair, average, moderate; *inf.* OK, so-so. **Opposites** GOOD; BENEFICIAL; VIRTUOUS; PLEASANT.

badge *noun* **1** *a badge on a cap/blazer* crest, emblem, insignia, device, shield, escutcheon, brand. **2** *showing the badge of servility* mark, sign, symbol, indication, indicator, signal, characteristic, trade mark.

badger *verb* pester, harass, plague, torment, bother, provoke, hound, nag, chivvy, goad, bully, importune, harry; *inf.* bug, hassle.

badinage *noun* banter, repartee, wordplay, raillery, chaff, drollery, waggery; pleasantries; *inf.* joshing, kidding, ribbing, ragging.

badly *adverb* **1** *do the job badly* poorly, wrongly, incorrectly, unsatisfactorily, inadequately, imperfectly, defectively, faultily, ineptly, inefficiently, shoddily, carelessly, ineffectually. **2** *work out badly* unsuccessfully, unfortunately, unhappily, unluckily, unfavourably. **3** *badly hurt/defeated* greatly, deeply, severely, seriously, extremely, intensely, exceedingly, gravely, acutely. **4** *behave badly* naughtily, wrongly, immorally, wickedly, improperly, evilly, criminally. **5** *want something badly* very much, greatly, exceedingly, extremely, enormously, tremendously, considerably. **Opposites** WELL.

baffle *verb* **1** *baffled by the problem* puzzle, perplex, mystify, nonplus, stump, flummox, confound, dumbfound, bamboozle, bewilder, confuse, amaze, stagger, stun. **2** *baffle their plans* thwart, frustrate, foil, balk, check, block, hinder, obstruct, bar, prevent, deflect, divert.

bag *noun* receptacle; handbag, shoulder bag, case, suitcase, briefcase, attaché case, grip, flight bag, backpack, rucksack, haversack, satchel, duffel bag.

bag *verb* **1** *bag three pheasants* catch, capture, shoot, kill, trap, snare, land. **2** *bag good seats* acquire, obtain, get, keep, come by, secure. **3** *the trousers bagged* sag, hang loosely, bulge, swell, balloon, fill out, inflate.

baggage *noun* luggage, gear, equipment, pack; belongings, things, suitcases, bags, effects, paraphernalia, trappings, impedimenta, accoutrements.

baggy *adjective* loose, slack, roomy, oversize, shapeless, ill-fitting, sagging, seated, bulging, ballooning, floppy.

bail *noun* *pay the prisoner's bail* surety, security, bond, guarantee, warranty, pledge, collateral.

bail *verb* **bail out, bale out** **1** *bail them out of their financial difficulties* help, assist, aid, rescue, relieve, give/lend a helping hand to. **2** *they bailed out before the crash* escape, get out, withdraw, retreat, beat a retreat, quit.

bait *noun* **1** *used as bait for the fish/mice* lure, decoy, troll, plug. **2** *low prices as bait for the consumer* attraction, lure, incentive, snare, temptation; allurement, enticement, incitement, inducement.

bait *verb* *bait the prisoner* torment, persecute, badger, plague, harry, harass, hound, provoke, tease, annoy, irritate; *inf.* hassle, needle, give a hard time to, wind up, nark.

bake *verb* **1** *bake the bread/meat* cook. **2** *earth baked by the sun* scorch, burn, sear, parch, dry, desiccate, fire.

balance *noun* **1** *weigh it on the balance* scales, weighing machine. **2** *maintain the balance of international power* equilibrium, evenness, symmetry, parity, equity, equipoise, correspondence, uniformity, equivalence. **3** *I tripped and lost my balance* steadiness, stability. **4** *people of ability and balance* composure, poise, equanimity, aplomb, stability, assurance, confidence, self-possession, coolness, level-headedness, sang-froid. **5** *her practicality acts as a balance to his genius* counterbalance, countercheck, counterweight, stabilizer, compensation, recompense, ballast, make-weight. **6** *pay the balance of the account | collect the balance of the order* remainder, rest, residue, difference, surplus, excess. **in the balance** uncertain, at a turning-point, critical, at a crisis. **on balance** taking everything into consideration, considering everything, all in all.
Opposites DIFFERENCE; INSTABILITY; UNCERTAINTY.

balance *verb* **1** *balancing the book on her head* steady, stabilize, poise. **2** *the weights must balance each other | advantages balancing disadvantages* counterbalance, counterweigh, counteract, offset, equalize, neutralize, compensate for, make up for, counterpoise. **3** *the profit and loss columns must balance | leisure and work time must balance* correspond, match, be level/parallel. **4** *balance the advantages and disadvantages* weigh, compare, evaluate, consider, deliberate, assess, appraise, estimate, review.

balcony *noun* **1** *the balcony of a villa* veranda, terrace, portico, loggia. **2** *the balcony of a theatre* gallery, upper circle; *inf.* the gods.

bald *adjective* **1** *a shining bald head* hairless, bald-headed, depilated, glabrous. **2** *a bald landscape* barren, treeless, bare, uncovered, stark, exposed, bleak, unsheltered. **3** *a concise bald statement* blunt, direct, forthright, straight, straightforward, downright, outright, plain, simple, unadorned, unvarnished, unembellished, stark, severe, austere.
Opposites HAIRY; FERTILE; embellished.

balderdash *noun* nonsense, rubbish, twaddle, drivel, foolishness, gibberish, bunkum, claptrap, stuff and nonsense; *inf.* bunk, piffle, hot air, bilge, bosh, cobblers, poppycock, rot, tommy-rot, bullshit, crap, guff, balls.

bale *noun* bundle, truss, pack, parcel, load.

bale *verb* **bale out** See BAIL *verb* bail out.

baleful *adjective* threatening, menacing, evil, wicked, malevolent, malignant, sinister, venomous, harmful, injurious, dangerous, deadly, noxious, pernicious.

balk *verb* **1** *balk at the high fence* refuse, demur, hesitate over, draw back from, flinch/shrink/shy from, jib, recoil, evade, shirk, dodge, resist, eschew. **2** *balk their advance* hinder, prevent, impede, obstruct, thwart, foil, check, stop, halt, bar, block, forestall, frustrate, baffle.
Opposites ACCEPT; ASSIST.

ball[1] *noun* **1** *a rubber ball | a ball of wool* sphere, globe, orb, globule, spheroid. *See table.* **2** *cannon ball* projectile; shot, grapeshot, bullet, pellet, slug.

BALL GAMES		
American football	fivepin bowling	rounders
Australian rules football	flat-green bowls	Rugby fives Rugby
boules	French	League
bowling	cricket	Rugby
baseball	Gaelic football	Union
basketball	golf	shinty
billiards	handball	short tennis
Canadian football	hockey	skittles
carom	hurley	snooker
billiards	ice hockey	soccer
cricket	korfball	softball
croquet	lacrosse	speedball
crown-green bowls	lawn tennis	squash
curling	netball	stoolball
	pelota	table tennis
	pool	tennis
	rackets	tenpin bowling
		volleyball

ball[2] *noun* **1** *a fancy-dress ball* dance, social gathering; *inf.* hop. **2** *they had a ball* great time; fun.

ballad *noun* folk-song, song, broadside, ditty.

ballast *noun* stabilizer, weight, counterweight; packing, filling.

ballet *noun*. See table.

BALLET STEPS AND POSITIONS		
arabesque	entrechat	piqué
attitude	fouetté	pirouette
balancé	glissade	plié
balloné	glissée	ronds de jambes à terre
batterie	grands battements	
bourrée	jeté	ronds de jambes en l'air
brisé volé	pas de basque	
cabriole	pas de chat	saut
chaîné	pas de cheval	sissonne
changement	pas de deux	soubresaut
chassé	petits battements	temps
contre-temps		tours en l'air
développé		
elevation		

balloon *noun* *travel in a balloon* hot-air balloon, airship, dirigible, Zeppelin, blimp, montgolfier.

balloon *verb* *skirts ballooning* swell out, puff out, fill out, billow, blow up, inflate, belly.

ballot *noun* vote, poll, election, referendum, plebiscite; voting, polling.

ballyhoo *noun* **1** *disturbed by the ballyhoo from the party* fuss, commotion. to-do, hullabaloo, racket. **2** *a lot of ballyhoo about the new film* publicity, propaganda, promotion, build-up; *inf.* hype.

balm *noun* **1** *apply balm to the burns* ointment, lotion, cream, salve, emollient, embrocation, liniment, unguent, balsam. **2** *balm for a troubled mind* remedy, curative, cure, restorative, palliative, anodyne, solace, consolation, comfort.

balmy *adjective* **1** *balmy breezes* mild, gentle, temperate, calm, tranquil, soothing, soft, fragrant, scented, perfumed. **2** *a balmy idea* foolish, stupid. *See* BARMY.

bamboozle *verb* **1** *bamboozled by their actions* puzzle, perplex, mystify, baffle, stump, bewilder, confuse, confound. **2** *bamboozle them into agreeing* trick, cheat, deceive, delude, hoodwink, mislead, hoax, fool, dupe, defraud, swindle; *inf.* gull, con.

ban *verb* *ban smoking* prohibit, forbid, veto, disallow, bar, debar, outlaw, proscribe, suppress, interdict, reject, restrict, banish.
Opposites ALLOW; SANCTION.

ban *noun* *impose a ban on smoking* prohibition, veto, bar, embargo, boycott, proscription, interdict, interdiction, suppression, stoppage, restriction, taboo; censorship, banishment.
Opposites PERMISSION; SANCTION.

banal *adjective* hackneyed, trite, clichéd, cliché-ridden, commonplace, platitudinous, humdrum, stock, stereotyped, pedestrian, unoriginal, unimaginative, stale, uninspired, prosaic, dull, everyday, ordinary, tired, inane, fatuous, jejune; *inf.* old hat.
Opposites ORIGINAL; IMAGINATIVE; FRESH.

banality *noun* **1** *the banality of his remarks* triteness, platitudinousness, pedestrianism, lack of originality, unimaginativeness, staleness, prosaicness, dullness, ordinariness, fatuity. *See* BANAL. **2** *talking in banalities* cliché, trite phrase, platitude, truism, bromide, triviality.

band¹ *noun* **1** *iron/rubber band* bond, binding, cord, strap, tie, connection, link, chain, thong, fetter, manacle, shackle, ligature, ring, hoop. **2** *a band round the waist/hair* belt, cord, braid, sash, girdle, ribbon, fillet, cincture; waistband, headband, hatband, wristband, sweatband. **3** *a band of white on the black* strip, stripe, streak, line, bar, striation.

band² *noun* **1** *a band of robbers* group, troop, company, gang, mob, pack, bunch, body, gathering, crowd, horde, throng, assembly, assemblage, association, society, club, clique, set, coterie. **2** *a singer with the band | a brass/jazz band* musical group, group, pop group, combo, ensemble, orchestra. *See table at* POPULAR MUSIC.

band³ *verb* *band together* join, group, unite, merge, combine, team up, gather, ally, affiliate, associate, federate, consolidate.

bandage *noun* dressing, gauze, compress, plaster, ligature; Elastoplast ™.

bandage *verb* bind, bind up, dress, cover, plaster.

bandit *noun* robber, brigand, outlaw, desperado, hijacker, plunderer, marauder, gangster, criminal, crook, thief, gunman, highwayman, footpad, pirate, racketeer.

bandy *adjective* *having bandy legs* bandy-legged, bowed, bow-legged, curved, crooked, bent, misshapen.

bandy *verb* **1** *bandy words* exchange, swap, trade, interchange, barter, reciprocate. **2** *bandy rumours about* circulate, spread, pass, toss about, disseminate.

bane *noun* ruin, death, ruination, destruction, scourge, torment, plague, affliction, calamity, despair, misery, woe, trouble, nuisance, trial, burden, blight, curse, nightmare, *bête noir*.

bang *noun* **1** *a loud bang* explosive noise, report, burst, boom, clash, clang, peal, clap, pop, slam, thud, thump. **2** *a bang on the head* blow, bump, hit, slap, punch, knock, stroke, smack, whack, rap, cuff, box, buffet; *inf.* wallop, bash, sock.

bang *verb* **1** *bang the table | banged her nose* hit, strike, beat, thump, hammer, knock, rap, pound, thud, pummel, whack; *inf.* bash. **2** *bang the door* slam, crash, clatter. **3** *the fireworks banged* explode, burst, blow up, detonate, pop, resound, echo.

bang *adverb* **1** *fell bang on the floor | bang went her hopes* noisily, violently, suddenly, abruptly. **2** *bang in the middle* precisely, right, exactly, absolutely, directly; *inf.* slap-bang, smack. **3** *bang up-to-date* completely, totally, right, absolutely.

bangle *noun* bracelet, wristlet, anklet, armlet.

banish *verb* **1** *banish from the country* exile, deport, expel, eject, drive away, expatriate, cast out, outlaw, transport, oust, evict, throw out, exclude, proscribe, excommunicate. **2** *banished from her presence | banish fear* dismiss, drive/send away, dispel, oust, cast/shut out, get rid of, ban, bar, exclude, eliminate, dislodge.
Opposites ADMIT; ACCEPT; WELCOME.

banishment *noun* exile, deportation, expulsion, expatriation, transportation, proscription. *See* BANISH 1.

banisters *plural noun* handrail, railing, rail, balustrade; balusters.

bank¹ *noun* **1** *a grassy bank* slope, rise, incline, gradient, mound, hillock, knoll. **2** *a river/canal bank* edge, side, shore, brink, margin, embankment.

bank² *verb* *bank an aircraft* tilt, slope, slant, incline, pitch. **bank up 1** *bank up the leaves | snow banked up* pile/heap up, stack up, gather, accumulate. **2** *bank up the fire/flames* damp down, stifle.

bank³ *noun* **1** *borrow from the bank* financial institution; commercial bank, high-street bank, clearing bank, merchant bank, savings bank, building society. **2** *empty the child's bank* piggy bank, cash-box, safe, strongbox, coffer. **3** *the card-game bank* kitty, pool, pot. **4** *a bank of information | blood bank* store, reserve, accumulation, stock, stockpile, reservoir, supply, fund, hoard, storehouse, repository, depository.

bank⁴ *verb* **1** *bank the money* deposit, save, save up, keep, lay by, put aside, put by for a rainy day; *inf.* salt away, stash away. **2** *bank with the national bank* deal with, do business with, invest with. **bank on/upon** rely on, count on, depend on, lean on, trust, believe in, have/place confidence in, pin one's hopes on.

bank⁵ *noun a bank of switches* row, line, tier, array, group, series, chain, course, progression, rank, succession.

bankrupt *adjective* **1** *bankrupt businessmen/businesses* insolvent, failed, ruined, penurious, impecunious, financially embarrassed, distressed, in the red; *inf.* on the rocks, broke, hard up, on one's uppers. **2** *bankrupt of funds/ideas* lacking, in need of, deficient in, wanting, without, deprived of, bereft of, exhausted of, depleted of.
Opposites SOLVENT.

bankrupt *verb* ruin, beggar, cripple, impoverish; *inf.* bust.

bankruptcy *noun* insolvency, liquidation, indebtedness, failure, ruin, ruination, disaster, penury; straitened circumstances.

banner *noun* **1** *the king's banner* flag, standard, pennant, pennon, gonfalon. **2** *the banners in the procession* placard, sign.

banquet *noun* dinner, dinner party, feast, meal, party, repast, treat, revel.

banter *noun* indulge in light-hearted banter repartee, *badinage*, chaff, teasing, joking, jesting, jocularity, raillery, wordplay, mockery, ridicule, persiflage; pleasantries; *inf.* kidding, ribbing, joshing.

banter *verb* bantering not insulting chaff, tease, joke, jest, mock, ridicule, make fun of, twit; *inf.* kid, rib, rag, josh.

baptism *noun* **1** *the baptism of the child* christening, naming, immersion, sprinkling; *fml.* aspersing. **2** *survive his baptism as a teacher* debut, initiation, introduction, inauguration, launch, beginning, commencement, rite of passage.

baptize *verb* **1** *baptize a baby* christen, name, immerse, sprinkle. **2** *baptize as a teacher* initiate, introduce, inaugurate, launch.

bar *noun* **1** *an iron bar | a window bar* rod, pole, stake, stick, batten, shaft, rail, pale, paling, spar, crosspiece. **2** *a bar of soap/gold* block, cake, wedge, lump. **3** *no bar to promotion | colour bar* obstacle, barrier, obstruction, hindrance, impediment, check, stop, deterrent, drawback, stumbling block, fly in the ointment. **4** *prisoner at the bar | the bar of the House of Commons* barrier, rail, railing, barricade. **5** *members of the Bar* barristers, advocates; counsel. **6** *bar of light* band, strip, line, belt, streak, stripe. **7** *a ship stuck on a bar* shoal, shallow, reef, sandbank, ridge, ledge, shelf. **8** *drinking in a bar* pub, public house, inn, tavern; saloon, snug, lounge. **9** *sandwich/breakfast bar* counter, table, buffet.

bar *verb* **1** *bar the door* bolt, lock, fasten, padlock, secure, latch. **2** *barred from entering |*

barred from the competition debar, prohibit, preclude, forbid, ban, exclude, keep out, block, impede; obstruct, hinder, restrain, check, stop, defer.
Opposites UNLOCK; ADMIT; ACCEPT.

bar *preposition* bar a few except, excepting, except for, with the exception of, apart from, besides, other than, excluding, barring, omitting, leaving out.

barb *noun* **1** *a barb in one's finger* thorn, needle, spike, prickle, bristle, prong, point, spicule. **2** *the barbs of his rival* insult, sneer, gibe, affront; scoffing, scorn, sarcasm, contumely; *inf.* dig.

barbarian *noun* **1** *knights defeating the barbarians* savage, brute, wild man/woman, troglodyte, monster. **2** *a classroom full of barbarians* ruffian, lout, vandal, hooligan, boor, ignoramus, philistine, yahoo.

barbarian *adjective* **1** *barbarian tribes* savage, uncivilized, primitive, brutish, wild, heathen. **2** *barbarian football supporters* loutish, hooligan, boorish, uncivilized, wild, rough, coarse, gross, uncouth, vulgar, philistine.

barbaric *adjective* **1** *barbaric tribes* savage, uncivilized, primitive. See BARBARIAN *adjective* 1. **2** *barbaric customs* brutal, savage, cruel, vicious, fierce, ferocious, bestial, barbarous, murderous, inhuman, ruthless, remorseless.

barbarism *noun* **1** *the barbarism of ancient tribes* savagery, uncivilizedness, primitiveness, brutishness, heathenism. **2** *the barbarism of the punishment* brutality, savagery, cruelty, barbarity. See BARBARITY 1. **3** *a speech full of barbarisms* misuse, misusage, misapplication, corruption, catachresis; error, slip, solecism.

barbarity *noun* **1** *the barbarity of the punishment* brutality, savagery, cruelty, viciousness, bestiality, inhumanity, ruthlessness. **2** *barbarities committed* atrocity, brutality, outrage, enormity.

barbarous *adjective* **1** *barbarous tribes* savage, uncivilized, barbarian. See BARBARIAN *adjective* 1. **2** *barbarous punishment* brutal, savage, cruel, barbaric. See BARBARIC *adjective* 2. **3** *barbarous tastes* unrefined, unsophisticated, uncultivated, uncultured, ignorant, vulgar, crude, uncouth, coarse.

barbecue *noun* hold a barbecue picnic, alfresco lunch/dinner, outdoor meal.

barbecue *verb* barbecue the steaks grill, charcoal, broil.

bare *adjective* **1** *sunbathing bare | a bare chest* naked, stark naked, nude, uncovered, exposed, unclothed, undressed, unclad, stripped, denuded. **2** *a bare room* empty, vacant, unfurnished, unadorned, uncovered, stark, austere, unembellished. **3** *a bare landscape* bleak, unsheltered, unprotected, unshielded, desolate, barren, treeless, without vegetation. **4** *the bare facts* simple, plain, bald, basic, essential, straightforward, stark, unvarnished, unembellished, cold, hard, sheer, literal. **5** *the bare minimum* mere, basic, meagre, scanty, inadequate. **6** *a cupboard bare of food* without, lacking, devoid of, wanting, destitute of.
Opposites clothed; embellished.

barefaced *adjective* blatant, flagrant, glaring, arrant, shameless, brazen, bold, impudent, insolent, audacious, brash, open, undisguised, unconcealed, transparent, patent, manifest, palpable.

barely *adverb* hardly, scarcely, only just, just, by the skin of one's teeth.
Opposites FULLY.

bargain *noun* **1** *make a bargain* agreement, contract, pact, transaction, deal, treaty, negotiation, arrangement, compact, covenant, concordant, understanding, pledge, promise, engagement. **2** *get a bargain* discount, reduction, good buy, sales article; *inf.* snip, steal, giveaway. **into the bargain** *into the bargain it rained* moreover, besides, also, over and above that, additionally, as well.

bargain *verb buyer and seller were bargaining* haggle, barter, deal, trade, traffic. **bargain for** *more than we bargained for* expect, anticipate, be prepared for, allow for, take into account/consideration, forsee, look for, contemplate, imagine. **bargain on** *bargaining on victory* rely on, depend on, count on, bank on, hope for, plan on, expect, anticipate.

barge *noun. See table at* SHIP.

barge *verb* **1** *barge in during prayers* burst in, break in, intrude, interrupt; *inf.* butt in, horn in. **2** *people barging into each other* bump, crash, collide, cannon, plough, smash. **3** *she was barging around* lurch, rush about.

bark[1] *noun the bark of a tree/shrub* covering, cortex, husk, coating, casing, crust, skin; hide, rind, shell, hull, sheath, integument.

bark[2] *verb bark one's shin* scrape, skin, abrade, rub, excoriate, strip, flay, shave.

bark[3] *verb* **1** *the dog barked* howl, woof, yelp, yap, bay, growl, snarl. **2** *the teacher barked at the pupils* shout, yell, bawl, thunder, scream, screech, shriek, snap, snarl, bluster.

barmy *adjective a barmy idea|a barmy old man* mad, foolish, stupid, idiotic, insane, silly, odd, queer, eccentric, peculiar, weird; *inf.* crazy, daft, batty, nutty, loony, loopy, crackpot, goofy, off one's head, round the bend/twist, out to lunch.
Opposites SANE; SENSIBLE.

barn *noun* outbuilding, shed, outhouse, shelter, byre; stables, mews.

baron *noun* **1** *the king and the barons* noble, nobleman, aristocrat, peer, lord. **2** *oil barons* tycoon, magnate, executive, industrialist, financier, captain of industry.

baroque *adjective* ornate, elaborate, decorated, embellished, flamboyant, ostentatious, extravagant, showy, fussy, florid, convoluted; rococo, grotesque.

barracks *plural noun* billet, garrison, camp, encampment, fort, cantonment, casern; quarters.

barrage *noun* **1** *soldiers killed by the enemy's barrage* gunfire, bombardment, shelling, battery, cannonade, volley, broadside, salvo, fusillade, wall/curtain/barrier of fire. **2** *a barrage of criticism* deluge, stream, storm, torrent, onslaught, flood, avalanche, hail, burst, mass, abundance, superabundance, plethora, profusion.

barrel *noun* cask, keg, butt, vat, tun, tub, tank, firkin, hogshead.

barren *adjective* **1** *a barren woman* infertile, sterile, childless; *fml.* infecund. **2** *barren land* infertile, unproductive, uncultivable, unfruitful, arid, desert, waste, desolate. **3** *barren discussion|barren way of life* uninteresting, boring, dull, uninspiring, stale, prosaic, futile, worthless, useless, valueless, unrewarding, purposeless, vapid, lacklustre.
Opposites FERTILE; FRUITFUL; PRODUCTIVE.

barricade *noun barricades keeping back the crowd* barrier, obstacle, blockade, bar, fence, obstruction, roadblock, bulwark, stockade, rampart, palisade.

barricade *verb barricade the door/house* blockade, obstruct, close up, bar, shut off/in, fence in, defend, fortify.

barrier *noun* **1** *the barrier in the car park* barricade, bar, fence, railing, obstacle, blockade, roadblock. **2** *a barrier to success|the language barrier* obstacle, hindrance, impediment, drawback, check, hurdle, restriction, stumblingblock, handicap, difficulty, restraint.

barrister *noun* professional pleader, counsel; *Scots* advocate; *Am.* attorney.

barter *noun an economy based on barter* trading, trade-off, exchange, swapping, bargaining, haggling, trafficking.

barter *verb barter his horse for food* trade, trade off, exchange, swap, bargain, traffic, haggle.

base *noun* **1** *the base of a column* foundation, support, prop, stay, stand, pedestal, rest, bottom, bed, foot, substructure, plinth. **2** *paints with an oil base* basis, core, essence, component, essential, fundamental, root, heart, principal, source, origin. **3** *mountaineers setting up a base* headquarters, centre, camp, site, station, settlement, post, starting-point.
Opposites TOP; APEX.

base *verb* **1** *based on historical facts* found, build, construct, form, establish, ground, rest, root, fasten, hinge, derive. **2** *based in London* locate, station, situate, post, place, install.

base *adjective* **1** *base motives* low, mean, sordid, bad, wrong, immoral, dishonourable, evil, wicked, debased, sinful, unprincipled, dissolute, disreputable, reprobate, corrupt, depraved, vile, shameful, scandalous, infamous, ignoble, vulgar, foul, despicable, contemptible. **2** *base servitude* menial, subservient, servile, lowly, mean, low, slavish, grovelling, snivelling, cowering, wretched, downtrodden, obsequious, sycophantic. **3** *base coin* debased, alloyed, impure, adulterated, spurious, counterfeit, pinchbeck. **4** *base metal* low-value, inferior, non-precious.
Opposites GOOD; ADMIRABLE; LOFTY.

baseball *noun. See table. See also tables at* SPORT.

baseless *adjective* groundless, unfounded, foundationless, unsupported, unsubstantiated, uncorroborated, unconfirmed, unjustifiable, unjustified.

BASEBALL TEAMS

Atlanta Braves	Minnesota Twins
Baltimore Orioles	New York Giants
Boston Red Sox	New York Mets
Brooklyn Dodgers	New York Yankees
California Angels	Oakland Athletics
Chicago Cubs	Philadelphia Phillies
Chicago White	Pittsburgh Pirates
Sox	St Louis Browns
Cincinnati Reds	St Louis Cardinals
Cleveland Indians	San Francisco Giants
Detroit Tigers	Texas Rangers
Kansas City Royals	Toronto Blue Jays
Los Angeles Dodgers	Washington
Milwaukee Braves	Senators

basement *noun* cellar, crypt, vault, garden flat; *inf.* below stairs.

bashful *adjective* shy, reserved, diffident, retiring, modest, self-conscious, coy, demure, reticent, self-effacing, hesitant, shrinking, backward, timid, timorous, abashed, blushing, embarrassed, shamefaced, sheepish.
Opposites BOLD; CONFIDENT; FORWARD.

bashfulness *noun* shyness, reserve, modesty, self-consciousness, coyness, demureness, reticence, self-effacement, hesitancy, timidity, timorousness, embrrassment. *See* BASHFUL.

basic *adjective* **1** *basic principles* fundamental, elementary, rudimentary, primary, radical, key, central, essential, vital, necessary, indispensable, intrinsic, underlying. **2** *basic salary* bottom, lowest-level, lowest, starting, ground, undermost, without commission. **3** *pretty basic accommodation* plain, simple, spartan, sparse, stark, unadorned, without frills.
Opposites SECONDARY; SUPPLEMENTARY; FANCY.

basically *adverb* fundamentally, at bottom, at heart, intrinsically, essentially, inherently, primarily, firstly, radically, mostly, for the most part, in the main, in substance.

basics *plural noun* fundamentals, essentials, facts, hard facts, rudiments, principles, practicalities, realities, the ABC; *inf.* nitty-gritty, brass tacks, nuts and bolts.

basin *noun* **1** *carry water in a basin* container, receptacle, vessel; bowl, dish, pan. **2** *the river basin* bed, channel.

basis *noun* **1** *no scientific basis for the statement* support, foundation, base, footing, reasoning, back-up; grounds. **2** *the statement will form the basis of the discussion* starting-point, premise,

fundamental point/principle, principal constituent, main ingredient; groundwork, core, essence. **3** *on a part-time basis* footing, procedure, condition, status, position.

bask *verb* **1** *bask in the sunshine* lie, laze, lounge, relax, loll, sunbathe, sun/warm oneself. **2** *bask in their admiration* luxuriate, revel, wallow, enjoy, delight, take pleasure in, rejoice in, relish, savour, indulge oneself in.

basket *noun* container, receptacle; hamper, creel, pannier, punnet.

bass *adjective* deep, deep-pitched, deep-toned, low, low-pitched, low-toned, resonant, sonorous.

bastard *noun* **1** *the King's bastard* illegitimate child, love child, natural son/daughter. **2** *a rotten bastard* scoundrel, cad, blackguard, villain, rascal.

bastard *adjective* **1** *bastard child* illegitimate, natural. **2** *a bastard language* adulterated, impure, hybrid, alloyed, inferior, imperfect, spurious, counterfeit, artificial, sham, false, fake.

bastardize *verb* *bastardize the language/coinage* debase, degrade, devalue, depreciate, corrupt, adulterate, defile, contaminate.

bastion *noun* **1** *the bastion of a fort* projection, bulwark, rampart, parapet. **2** *storm the enemy bastion* fort, fortress, citadel, keep, stronghold, garrison. **3** *the last bastion of privilege* protection, protector, defence, defender, support, supporter, prop, mainstay, stronghold.

bat *noun*. *See table.*

batch *noun* group, quantity, lot, bunch, accumulation, mass, cluster, set, collection, assemblage, pack, crowd, aggregate, conglomeration.

bath *noun* **1** *install a bath* bath-tub, tub, hip-bath, sitz-bath, whirlpool bath, sauna, steam bath. **2** *have a bath* wash, soak, dip, shower, douche, soaping.

bath *verb* *bath every day* have/take a bath, bathe, wash, soak, shower, douche, soap oneself.

bathe *verb* **1** *bathe the wound* clean, cleanse, wash, soak, steep, immerse, wet, moisten, rinse, suffuse. **2** *bathe in the sea* swim, take a dip. **3** *bathed in sunlight* envelope, suffuse.

bathe *noun* *a quick bathe in the sea* swim, dip.

bathing-costume *noun* bathing-suit, swimsuit, swimming-costume, swimming-trunks, trunks, bikini, monokini, one-piece swimsuit; *Austral. inf.* cossie, bathers.

BATS

barbastelle	fruit bat	long-eared bat	sheath-tailed bat
blossom bat	funnel-eared bat	mastiff bat	short-tailed bat
bulldog bat	ghost faced bat	mouse-tailed bat	slit-faced bat
butterfly bat	golden bat	moustached bat	smoky bat
disk-wing bat	hairless bat	naked-backed bat	spotted bat
epauletted fruit bat	hammer-headed bat	noctule	sucker-footed bat
false vampire	hog-nosed bat	painted bat	tomb-bat
flower bat	hollow-faced bat	pipistrelle	Trident bat
flying fox	horseshoe bat	roussette	tube-nosed bat
free-tailed bat	leaf-nosed bat	sac-winged bat	vampire bat

bathos noun anticlimax, let-down; sentimentality, mawkishness.

baton noun stick, bar, wand, rod, staff, club, truncheon, mace.

battalion noun **1** *military battalions* unit; troops, forces; garrison, division, regiment, brigade, squadron, company, platoon, section, detachment, contingent, legion. **2** *battalions of protesters* crowd, mob, throng, horde, multitude, herd, host.

batten[1] noun *a wooden batten* board, strip, bar, bolt, clamp.

batten[2] verb *batten down the hatches* fasten, fix, secure.

batten[3] verb *batten on the poor* thrive/flourish/prosper/fatten/increase/wax at the expense of, be a parasite on.

batter verb **1** *battering their children* hit, strike, beat, bash, assault, wallop, thump, thrash, lash, pound, deliver/rain blows on, pummel, buffet, belabour, abuse; *inf.* whack. **2** *countries battered by war* damage, injure, hurt, harm, bruise, wound, crush, shatter, smash, destroy, demolish, ruin, squash, impair, mar, spoil.

battered adjective *battered children* beaten, assaulted, thrashed, abused. *See* BATTER 1.

battery noun **1** *a battery of tests/units* series, sequence, set, cycle, chain, string, progression, succession. **2** *convicted of assault and battery* attack, mugging, grievous bodily harm, GBH, beating, striking, thumping, thrashing, bashing; aggression. **3** *the military battery* artillery, cannonry; guns, cannons.

battle noun **1** *battle between enemy forces* war, armed conflict, conflict, fight, clash, contest, struggle, skirmish, engagement, affray, encounter, confrontation, collision, meeting, campaign, crusade, tussle, scuffle, scrap, mêlée; fighting, warfare, combat, action; hostilities. *See table. See also table at* WAR. **2** *a battle of wills* clash, conflict, contest, competition, tournament, struggle, disagreement, argument, dispute, controversy, debate; dissension, altercation, strife.
Opposites TRUCE; PEACE.

battle verb **1** *battling against the elements* | *battle for a pay-rise* fight, struggle, strive, combat, contend, war, feud. **2** *battle one's way through*

the wind fight, struggle, labour, push. **3** *neighbours constantly battling* fight, war, feud, argue, quarrel, disagree, bicker, wrangle, cross swords, lock horns.

battleaxe noun *a battleaxe of a headmistress* dragon, harridan, tartar, martinet, termagant, virago, shrew, fury, stramullion.

battle-cry noun **1** *the battle-cry of the invaders* war cry, war whoop, rallying call. **2** *the battle-cry of the women's movement* slogan, motto, watchword, catchword, catchphrase, shibboleth.

battlefield noun battleground, front, battlefront, battle lines, field of operations, field of battle, combat zone, theatre/arena of war, battle stations.

battlement noun parapet, rampart, balustrade, wall, bulwark, barbican, bartizan; fortification, breastwork, crenellation, circumvallation, outwork.

battleship noun warship, man-of-war, ship of the line, gunboat, cruiser, battle cruiser, capital ship. *See table.*

BATTLESHIPS	
Ark Royal	King George V
Belgrano	New Jersey
Bismarck	Prince Albert
Constitution	Queen Elizabeth
Dreadnought	Royal Sovereign
Gloire	Victory
Invincible	Yamato

batty adjective mad, foolish, stupid, idiotic, insane, silly, odd, queer, eccentric; *inf.* crazy, daft, bats, barmy, bonkers, nutty, nuts, crackers, dotty, potty, loony, off one's head, round the bend, out to lunch.

bauble noun trinket, knick-knack, trifle, ornament, toy, plaything, gewgaw, gimcrack, bagatelle, kickshaw, bibelot.

bawd noun prostitute, whore, street-walker, woman of the streets; *inf.* hooker.

bawdy adjective pornographic, obscene, vulgar, indecent, blue, racy, titillating, crude, coarse, rude, gross, ribald, lewd, dirty, filthy, smutty,

BATTLES					
Battle of	**Date**	**Battle of**	**Date**	**Battle of**	**Date**
Actium	31 B.C.	El Mansûra	1250	Pharsalus	48 B.C.
Agincourt	1415	Erzurum	1877, 1916	Princeton	1777
Antietam	1862	Gettysburg	1863	River Plate	1939
Arbela	331 B.C.	Hastings	1066	Sadowa	1866
Atlantic	1940–3	Issus	333 B.C.	Salamis	480 B.C.
Ayacucho	1824	Jena	1806	Somme	1916
Balaclava	1854	Jutland	1916	Stalingrad	1942–3
Boyne	1690	Leyte Gulf	1944	Tannenberg	1914
Britain	1940	Marathon	490 B.C.	Trafalgar	1805
Bulge	1944–5	Marne	1914	Verdun	1916
Bunker Hill	1775	Megiddo	1469 B.C., 1918	Waterloo	1815
Cambrai	1917	Midway Islands	1942	Xuzhou	1949
Cerro Gordo	1847	Nile	1798	Ypres	1914, 1915,
Culloden	1746	Omdurman	1898		1917

off-colour, naughty, suggestive, indelicate, unseemly, indecorous, salacious, erotic, prurient, lascivious, licentious, risqué, scatological, Rabelaisian, near the bone, near the knuckle; *inf.* raunchy, nudge-nudge.
Opposites DECENT; SEEMLY; CLEAN.

bawl *verb* **1** *he bawled a reply|bawl to his brother* shout, call/cry out, yell, roar, bellow, screech, scream, howl, whoop, vociferate; *Am. inf.* holler. **2** *a child bawling* cry, sob, weep, wail, blubber, snivel, squall.

bay¹ *noun ships moored in the bay* cove, inlet, indentation, natural harbour, gulf, basin, sound, arm, bight, firth.

bay² *noun a table in the bay* alcove, recess, niche, opening, nook.

bay³ *noun the bay of the hounds* baying, howl, howling, bark, cry, ululation. *See* BAY⁴ *verb.*

bay⁴ *verb hounds baying* howl, bark, yelp, cry, growl, bellow, roar, clamour, ululate.

bayonet *noun. See table at* KNIFE.

bazaar *noun* **1** *an eastern bazaar* market, market-place, mart, exchange, souk. **2** *the church bazaar* fête, fair, sale, bring-and-buy.

be *verb* **1** *will there be many such people at the party?* exist, live, be alive, have life/being, breathe. **2** *the lamp is on the table|Mary is at the farm* be situated, be located, dwell, reside. **3** *the concert is tomorrow* take place, occur, come about, come to pass, arise, crop up, transpire, befall. **4** *she has been there all her life* remain, stay, last, continue, survive, endure, persist, prevail, obtain. **5** *he was at church* attend, be present, be at.

beach *noun sunbathing at/on the beach* seaside, coast; seashore, shore, water's edge, coastline, sands, sand, shingle, strand, plage, lido, margin; *fml.* littoral.

beachcomber *noun* **1** *beachcombers collecting wood* scavenger, forager, gatherer, collector, accumulator. **2** *beachcombers and other homeless* tramp, vagrant, hobo, wanderer, scrounger; *inf.* bum.

beached *adjective* aground, ashore, grounded, high and dry, stuck fast, marooned, stranded, wrecked, abandoned.

beacon *noun* warning fire/light, signal fire/light, bonfire, smoke signal, flare, beam, rocket, signal, danger signal; lighthouse, pharos, watchtower.

bead *noun* **1** *glass beads* ball, pellet, pill, globule, spheroid, oval. **2** *beads of sweat* drop, droplet, bubble, blob, dot, glob, dewdrop, teardrop.

beads *plural noun* **1** *wearing beads and earrings* string of beads. *See table at* JEWELLERY. **2** *telling one's beads* rosary, chaplet.

beak *noun* **1** *a bird's beak* bill, nib, mandible; *dial.* neb. **2** *the fellow's large beak* nose, snout, proboscis. **3** *a ship's beak* prow, bow, bowsprit, stem, rostrum, ram.

beam *noun* **1** *the roof beams* board, timber, plank, joist, rafter, girder, spar, support, lath, scantling. **2** *a beam of light* ray, shaft, stream, streak, flash, gleam, glow, glimmer, glint,

flare, bar; radiation, emission. **3** *a beam of happiness* smile, grin, bright look.

beam *verb* **1** *light beamed from the window* emit, radiate, shine. **2** *beam radio/television programmes* broadcast, transmit, direct, aim. **3** *beaming from ear to ear* smile, grin.

bean *noun. See table.*

BEANS AND PEAS		
adzuki bean	horse bean	runner bean
bean sprout	kidney	scarlet
black-eyed	bean	runner
bean	lentil	soya bean
broad bean	lima bean	split pea
butter-bean	mangetout	string bean
chickpea	mung bean	sugar pea
flageolet	pea-bean	sugar snap
French bean	petit pois	pea
garden pea	pinto bean	wax-pod
haricot bean	red bean	bean

bear *verb* **1** *bear gifts* carry, bring, transport, move, convey, take, fetch, haul; *inf.* tote. **2** *bear tales* spread, transmit, carry. **3** *bear a signature/inscription* carry, display, exhibit, show, be marked with. **4** *bear a crop* yield, produce, give forth, give, provide, supply, generate. **5** *bear a son* give birth to, breed, bring forth, beget, engender. **6** *bear the cost* carry, sustain, support, shoulder, uphold. **7** *cannot bear his attitude|can't bear the thought* stand, endorse, tolerate, put up with, abide, stomach, permit, allow, admit, brook; *Scots* thole. **8** *much pain to bear* suffer, endure, undergo, tolerate, put up with, experience, go through, support, weather. **9** *bear a grudge|bear evil thoughts* have, hold, harbour, possess, entertain, cherish. **10** *bear left* veer, curve, go, move, turn, fork, diverge, deviate, bend. **bear out** *bear out the facts* confirm, corroborate, substantiate, endorse, vindicate, give credence to, support, ratify, warrant, uphold, justify, prove, authenticate, verify. **bear up** *bearing up against disaster* cope, persevere, carry on, manage, endure, withstand, grin and bear it. **bear with** *bear with the delay* tolerate, put up with, endure, make allowances for, be patient with, show forbearance towards, suffer.
Opposites ABANDON; give up (*see* GIVE).

bear *noun. See table.*

BEARS		
American	giant panda	musquaw
black bear	grizzly bear	polar bear
Asiatic	Himalayan	sloth bear
black bear	black bear	red panda
brown bear	honey bear	spectacled
cinnamon	Kodiak	bear
bear	bear	sun bear

bearable *adjective* endurable, tolerable, supportable, sufferable, sustainable, admissible,

passable, manageable.
Opposites UNBEARABLE; INTOLERABLE; INSUFFERABLE.

beard noun *a man with a beard* facial hair, whiskers, bristle, stubble, designer stubble, five o'clock shadow; full beard, goatee, beaver, imperial, Vandyke, Abe Lincoln, side-whiskers, sideboards, sideburns, mutton-chops.

beard verb *beard the management* brave, confront, face, challenge, come face-to-face with, oppose, defy, stand up against, dare, throw down the gauntlet at.

bearded adjective unshaven, whiskered, bewhiskered, stubbly, bristly, hairy, hirsute, bushy, shaggy.

bearer noun **1** *a coffin/luggage bearer* carrier, porter, conveyor, transporter. **2** *a bearer of good news* messenger, agent, runner, courier. **3** *pay the bearer of the cheque* payee, consignee, beneficiary.

bearing noun **1** *having a distinguished bearing* deportment, posture, carriage, gait. **2** *her bearing throughout the trial* attitude, behaviour, manner, demeanour, air, aspect, mien. **3** *the bearing of a ship* course, direction. **4** *have a bearing on the case* relevance, pertinence, connection. **5** *lose one's bearings* orientation, location, position, situation, whereabouts, track, way.

beast noun **1** *a beast of the jungle* animal, creature, brute; mammal, quadruped. **2** *a cruel beast to his wife and children* brute, monster, savage, swine, pig, ogre, fiend, sadist, barbarian.

beastly adjective **1** *a beastly apparition* beast-like, bestial, animal, animal-like, brutal, theroid. **2** *a beastly cold* awful, terrible, horrible, rotten, nasty, foul, unpleasant, disagreeable, vile; inf. shitty.

beat verb **1** *beat the drum* bang, hit, strike, pound. **2** *he beats the dog/child* hit, strike, batter, thump, wallop, hammer, punch, knock, thrash, pound, pummel, slap, smack, flay, whip, lash, chastise, thwack, cuff, bruise, buffet, box, cudgel, club, birch, maul, pelt, drub; inf. belt, bash, whack, clout, slug, tan, biff, bop, lay into, do over, knock about, rough up, fill in. **3** *their hearts beating* throb, pound, thump, pulsate, pulse, palpitate, vibrate, tremble. **4** *the bird's wings beat* flap, flutter, quiver, tremble, vibrate. **5** *beat the eggs* mix, blend, whip, whisk, stir. **6** *waves beating against/on the shore* strike, dash, break against, lap, wash. **7** *beating metal into rods* hammer, forge, form, shape, work, stamp, fashion, model. **8** *beat a path* tread, tramp, trample, wear, track, groove. **9** *beat the opposition* defeat, conquer, vanquish, trounce, rout, overpower, overcome, overwhelm, overthrow, subdue, quash; inf. lick. **10** *beat the record* outdo, surpass, exceed, eclipse, transcend, top, outstrip. **beat up** assault, attack, mug, batter, thrash; inf. knock about/around, do over, work over, clobber, rough up, duff up, fill in.

beat noun **1** *the beat of the drum | three beats of the carpet* bang, banging, stroke, striking, blow, hit, punch, pound, pummel, slap, smack, thwack. **2** *the beat of his heart* throb, throbbing, pounding, pulsating, pulsing, beating,

thumping, palpitating, vibrating, vibration. **3** *musical/metrical beat* rhythm, stress, metre, time, measure, accent, cadence. **4** *policeman's beat* round, circuit, course, route, way, path, orbit.

beat adjective *dead beat after the walk* exhausted, tired, worn out, fatigued, wearied, spent.

beaten adjective **1** *the beaten contestant/army* defeated, vanquished, trounced, routed, overcome, overwhelmed, overpowered, bested, quashed; inf. licked. **2** *beaten metal* hammered, forged, formed, shaped, worked. See BEAT verb 7. **3** *beaten paths* trodden, well-trodden, much-trodden, well-used, much-travelled, trampled, worn, well-worn. **4** *the beaten eggs/cake mixture* mixed, blended, whipped, whisked, stirred, frothy, foamy.
Opposites VICTORIOUS; SUCCESSFUL.

beatific adjective **1** *a beatific existence* blessed, blissful, heavenly, celestial, paradisical. **2** *children with beatific smiles* rapturous, joyful, ecstatic, blissful, happy, glad.

beating noun **1** *the savage beating of the children* hitting, striking, battering, thrashing; corporal punishment, chastisement; inf. belting, bashing, pasting. See BEAT verb 2. **2** *recovering from their beating by the opposition* defeat, conquest, vanquishing, trouncing, overthrow, downfall. See BEAT verb 9. **3** *the beating of their hearts* throb, pulsating, pulse, pulsing, palpitating. See BEAT noun 2. **4** *the beating of the waves* striking, dashing, breaking. See BEAT verb 6.

beatitude noun blessedness, bliss, ecstasy, exaltation, supreme happiness, divine rapture, sainthood.

beau noun **1** *his sister's beau* boyfriend, sweetheart, lover, fiancé, partner, significant other, escort, admirer, suitor, follower; lit. swain. **2** *beaux of the eighteenth century* dandy, fop, coxcomb, gallant, cavalier, popinjay; inf. swell, toff.

beautiful adjective ravishing, gorgeous, stunning, alluring, lovely, attractive, pretty, handsome, good-looking, pleasing, comely, charming, delightful, glamorous, appealing, fair, fine, becoming, seemly, winsome, graceful, elegant, exquisite; fml. beauteous, pulchritudinous; Scots bonny.
Opposites UGLY; HIDEOUS.

beautify verb **1** *beautify the surroundings* adorn, embellish, enhance, decorate, ornament, garnish, gild, smarten, prettify, glamorize. **2** *beautify oneself* apply make-up/cosmetics, prettify, glamorize, prink, primp, preen; inf. do/doll oneself up.

beauty noun **1** *the beauty of the women/surroundings* loveliness, attractiveness, prettiness, handsomeness, allure, allurement, charm, glamour, grace, artistry, symmetry; fml. beauteousness, pulchritude. See BEAUTIFUL. **2** *the sisters were all great beauties* belle, charmer, enchantress, seductress, femme fatale, Venus, goddess; inf. good-looker, lovely, stunner, knockout, dish, cracker. **3** *the beauty of the scheme* attraction, good thing, advantage, benefit, asset, strong point, boon, blessing.

beaver verb **beaver away** work hard/assiduously/conscientiously, exert oneself, persevere, persist, hammer away; inf. slog, peg away, plug away, graft, get one's head down.

becalmed adjective motionless, at a halt, still, at a standstill, stranded, stuck, marooned.

because conjunction he left because he was ill since, as, in view of the fact that, owing to the fact that, seeing that. **because of** leaving because of ill health on account of, as a result of, owing to, by reason of, as a consequence of, thanks to, by virtue of.

beckon verb **1** beckon to the waiter signal, gesture, make a gesture, gesticulate, motion, wave, nod, call, summon, bid. **2** the sea beckons him draw, pull, call, invite, attract, tempt, entice, allure, coax, persuade, induce.

become verb **1** she became rich | become a scientist come to be, turn out to be, grow, grow into, mature into, evolve into, pass into, change into, turn into, alter into, transform into, be transformed into, be converted into, metamorphose into. **2** the dress becomes her suit, flatter, look good on, set off, enhance, embellish, ornament, grace. **3** it ill becomes you to behave like that befit, behove, suit, be suitable/fitting to. **4** what became of him? happen to, befell, be the fate/lot of.

becoming adjective **1** a becoming hat flattering, comely, attractive, lovely, pretty, handsome, stylish, elegant, chic, tasteful. **2** hardly becoming behaviour suitable, fitting, appropriate, apt, proper, right, decent, seemly, worthy, decorous, graceful, comme il faut. **3** behaviour becoming to a teacher befitting, suitable for, appropriate to, in keeping with, compatible with, consistent with, congruous with.
Opposites UNBECOMING; INAPPROPRIATE; IMPROPER.

bed noun **1** she liked to sleep in her own bed couch; inf. kip, sack. See table. **2** the importance of bed in relationships sexual intercourse, sex, lovemaking, physical relationship, intimacy, conjugality. **3** a flower bed plot, area, lot, patch, space, border, strip, row. **4** a bed of concrete base, basis, foundation, bottom, support, substructure, substratum; groundwork.

BEDS	
bassinet	futon
bed-settee	hammock
berth	king-size bed
bunk bed	litter
camp bed	pallet
canopied bed	palliasse
chair-bed	queen-size bed
chaise longue	single bed
cot	sofa bed
cradle	stretcher
crib	studio couch
daybed	sunbed
divan	tent-bed
double bed	truckle-bed
feather bed	twin bed
foldaway bed	waterbed
four-poster bed	Z-bed

bed verb **1** bricks bedded in concrete embed, set, fix into, insert, inlay, implant, bury, base, establish, found. **2** anxious to bed a woman go to bed with, have sex with, sleep with, seduce, spend the night with. **3** bed out the pansies plant, plant out, set in beds/soil. **bed down 1** bed down in the shed go to bed/sleep, retire, settle down, have a nap; inf. turn in, hit the sack/hay. **2** bed the children down put to bed, tuck in, settle down, say goodnight to.

bedclothes plural noun bedding, bedcovers, covers; blankets, duvets, quilts, eiderdowns, counterpanes, sheets, bed linen, linen.

bedeck verb deck, decorate, adorn, ornament, trim, festoon, array, embellish, garnish.

bedevil verb afflict, torment, beset, plague, harass, distress, trouble, worry, frustrate, annoy, vex, irritate, irk, pester, torture.

bedlam noun uproar, pandemonium, commotion, confusion, furore, hubbub, clamour, disorder, chaos, turmoil, tumult, noise, disarray; inf. madhouse.

bedraggled adjective muddy, muddied, wet, dirty, messy, sodden, soaking, soaking wet, soaked, drenched, saturated, dripping, soggy, splashed, soiled, stained, dishevelled, disordered, untidy, unkempt.

bedridden adjective confined to bed, housebound; inf. laid up, flat on one's back.

bedrock noun **1** the bedrock beneath the soil substratum, solid foundation, rock bed. **2** the finance is at bedrock lowest point/level, rock bottom, nadir. **3** the bedrock of their beliefs | get down to bedrock basis, core, nitty-gritty; basics, fundamentals, essentials.

beef noun **1** more noted for his beef than his brain brawn, muscle, muscularity, heftiness, burliness, bulk, physique, strength, powerfulness, robustness. See BEEFY 1. **2** tired of the beef about the traffic complaint, grumbling, grumble, criticism, objection, protestation, grievance; inf. griping, gripe, grousing, grouse, nit-picking.

beefy adjective **1** beefy wrestler brawny, muscular, hefty, burly, hulking, strapping, thickset, solid, strong, powerful, heavy, robust, sturdy, stocky. **2** a beefy young woman heavy, solid, fat, chubby, plump, overweight, stout, buxom, obese, fleshy, podgy, rotund, portly, corpulent, paunchy, dumpy.
Opposites SCRAWNY; PUNY.

beer noun. See table.

BEER		
ale	draught	pale ale
bitter	beer	porter
bottled beer	keg beer	real ale
	lager	shandy
brown ale	lite	stout
canned beer	mild	strong ale

beetle noun. See table at INSECT.

beetling adjective beetling brows/cliffs overhanging, projecting, protruding, sticking/jutting out.

befall *verb* happen, occur, take place, chance, crop up, arise, come about, come to pass, transpire, materialize, ensue, follow, result, fall, supervene.

befitting *adjective* fitting, fit, suitable, appropriate, apt, proper, right, seemly, decorous.

before *adverb* **1** *we've met before* previously, earlier, formerly, hitherto, in the past. **2** *they went on before* ahead, in front, in advance, in the lead.

before *preposition* **1** *before lunch | before the war | before going out* prior to, previous to, earlier than. **2** *B comes before C* in front of, ahead of, in advance of. **3** *said before witnesses* in the presence of, in the sight of, before the very eyes of, under the nose of. **4** *death before dishonour* in preference to, rather/sooner than. **Opposites** AFTER; BEHIND.

beforehand *adverb* before, before now, earlier, previously, in advance, in readiness, ahead of time, already, sooner.

befriend *verb* make friends with, make a friend of, look after, protect, keep an eye on, help, assist, aid, support, back, stand by, side with, encourage, sustain, uphold, succour, advise.

befuddled *adjective* **1** *befuddled old people* confused, dazed, groggy, muddled, bewildered, fuddled, stunned, numbed; *inf.* woozy. **2** *befuddled drunks* drunk, drunken, intoxicated, inebriated, stupefied, muddled, dazed, bewildered; *inf.* blotto, bombed, out of it, blitzed, legless, paralytic, smashed, wasted, wrecked, zonked.

beg *verb* **1** *beg in order to live* ask for money, solicit money, seek charity/alms, cadge, scrounge; *inf.* sponge, bum; *Am. inf.* mooch. **2** *beg for money/mercy* ask for, request, seek, look for, desire, crave, solicit, plead for, beseech, entreat, importune, plead with.

beget *verb* **1** *fathers begetting able sons* father, sire, procreate, generate, engender, spawn. **2** *differing opinion begetting strife* cause, give rise to, bring, bring about, create, produce, result in, occasion, effect, bring to pass, engender.

beggar *noun* **1** *accosted by a beggar* tramp, vagrant, mendicant, cadger, vagabond, pauper, down-and-out, derelict; *inf.* scrounger, sponger, bum; *Am. inf.* moocher, bag lady, hobo. **2** *what a lucky beggar!* fellow, person, bloke, individual, creature.

beggar *verb* *a nation beggared by war* impoverish, make poor, reduce to poverty, bankrupt, pauperize.

beggarly *adjective* **1** *a beggarly wage* inadequate, meagre, paltry, slight, miserly, pitiful, pathetic, stingy, niggardly, ungenerous, contemptible, despicable. **2** *beggarly accommodation* miserable, wretched, mean, base, vile, foul, sordid, shabby, shoddy, despicable. **3** *beggarly creatures* poor, poverty-stricken, impoverished, needy, penniless, destitute, indigent, impecunious.

beggary *noun* poverty, penury, destitution, indigence, impecuniousness, bankruptcy, insolvency, need, neediness, pauperism, pauperdom, mendicancy, vagrancy.

begin *verb* **1** *begin work* start, commence, set about, embark on, initiate, set in motion, institute, inaugurate, get ahead with. **2** *begin now!* start, commence, go ahead, get going; *inf.* fire away, kick off, get the show on the road, get to it, start the ball rolling, take the plunge. **3** *trouble began immediately* start, commence, arise, come into existence/being, happen, occur, spring up, crop up, emerge, dawn, appear, originate. **4** *rain began to fall* start, commence.
Opposites FINISH; END; STOP.

beginner *noun* novice, trainee, learner, apprentice, student, pupil, recruit, raw recruit, tiro, fledgling, neophyte, initiate, novitiate, tenderfoot, fresher; *inf.* greenhorn, rookie.
Opposites EXPERT; VETERAN.

beginning *noun* **1** *from the beginning of time | beginning of the match* start, starting-point, commencement, onset, outset, dawn, birth, inception, conception, emergence, rise; *inf.* kick-off. **2** *the beginning of the book* start, commencement, first part, opening, prelude, preface, introduction. **3** *philosophy having its beginnings in religion* origin, source, starting-point, fountainhead, spring, mainspring, embryo, germ; roots, seeds.

begrudge *verb* **1** *begrudge him his success* grudge, envy, resent, be jealous of. **2** *begrudge the time spent* grudge, resent, give unwillingly, be dissatisfied with.

beguile *verb* **1** *beguiled by her beauty* charm, attract, delight, please, enchant, bewitch, seduce. **2** *the comedian beguiling the audience* entertain, amuse, occupy, absorb, engage, distract, divert, engross. **3** *beguile the hours* pass, while away, spend.

beguiling *adjective* *a beguiling smile* charming, attractive, delightful, pleasing, enchanting, bewitching, seductive.

behalf *noun* **1** *acting on behalf of his client | on his client's behalf* for, representing, as a representative of, in the interests of, in the name of, in place of. **2** *collecting on behalf of the blind* in the interests of, for, for the benefit/good/sake of, to the advantage/profit of, on account of, in support of.

behave *verb* **1** *the children must behave themselves* act correctly/properly, conduct oneself well, act in a polite way, show good manners, mind one's manners. **2** *they behaved well/badly* act, perform, conduct oneself, acquit oneself, comport oneself. **3** *she behaves like a dictator | the engine behaved badly/well* act, perform, function, operate.

behaviour *noun* **1** *criticize his children's/opponent's behaviour* conduct, way of acting, response, comportment, deportment, bearing; actions, manners, ways. **2** *the erratic behaviour of the machine | study the behaviour of bees* action, performance, functioning, operation, reaction, response; actions, reactions, responses.

behead *verb* decapitate, guillotine.

behest *noun* order, command, decree, edict, rule, ruling, directive, direction, instruction, request, requirement, charge, bidding, wish, dictate, injunction, mandate, precept.

behind *preposition* **1** *behind the woodshed* at the back of, at the rear of, beyond, on the further side of, on the other side of; *Am.* in back of. **2** *running behind us* after, at the back of, to the rear of, following, in the wake of, close upon, hard on the heels of. **3** *trouble is behind us now* in the past of. **4** *behind the others in English* less advanced than, slower than, weaker than, inferior to. **5** *behind schedule* late in relation to, later than, after. **6** *he's behind the trouble* at the back of, at the bottom of, responsible for, causing, the cause/source of, giving rise to, instigating, initiating, urging. **7** *we're behind you all the way* backing, supporting, for, on the side of, in agreement with, financing.

behind *adverb* **1** *with the dog running behind* after, at the back, in the rear, in the wake. **2** *look behind* to/towards the back/rear, over one's shoulder. **3** *stay/leave behind* afterwards, remaining after departure. **4** *we're behind so don't stop* behindhand, behind schedule, late, slow. **5** *behind in payments* behindhand, in arrears, overdue, in debt.
Opposites in front (*see* FRONT); AHEAD.

behindhand *adverb* **1** *behindhand in paying* late, slow, dilatory, tardy, remiss. **2** *too behindhand for modern times* out of date, old-fashioned, behind the times/time, backward.

behold *verb* look at, see, observe, view, watch, survey, gaze at, stare at, scan, witness, regard, contemplate, inspect, take note of, mark, consider, pay heed to.

behold *interjection* look!, see!, lo!, ecce!

beholden *adjective* indebted, under obligation, obligated, bound, owing, thankful, grateful.

behove *verb* **1** *it behoves him to take over his father's business* be incumbent on, be obligatory for, be necessary for, be essential for, be expected of, be advisable for, be sensible for, be wise for. **2** *it ill behoves him to have an affair with his brother's fiancée* be fitting, befit, be suitable, be seemly, be proper, be decorous.

beige *adjective* buff, sand, oatmeal, neutral, biscuit, coffee, *café au lait. See table at* COLOUR.

being *noun* **1** *the purpose of our being* existence, living, life, animation, animateness, actuality, life blood, vital force, entity; *fml.* esse. **2** *shocked to the depths of her being* spirit, soul, nature, essence, substance, entity, quiddity. **3** *a sentient being* creature, person, human being, human, individual, mortal, living thing, man, animal.
Opposites NOTHINGNESS; OBLIVION.

belabour *verb* **1** *belabour the boy with blows* beat, hit, strike, batter, attack, flog, thrash, whip, lambaste, bombard, pelt. **2** *belabour the actor* criticize, attack, berate, censure, castigate, lay into, flay. **3** *belabour the point* overelaborate, discuss at length, go through with a fine-tooth comb; *inf.* flog to death.

belated *adjective* late, overdue, behindhand, behind time, delayed, tardy, unpunctual.

belch *verb* **1** *he belched after eating* eruct, eructate, hiccup, break wind, bring up wind, burp. **2** *factory chimneys belching smoke* give out, give off, pour out, discharge, emit, issue, vent, gush, eject, disgorge, spew out, vomit, cough up; *fml.* disembogue.

beleaguered *adjective* **1** *a beleaguered city* besieged, under siege, surrounded, blockaded, encircled, hemmed in, under attack. **2** *a film star beleaguered by fans* besieged, badgered, harassed, bothered, beset, pestered, plagued, tormented, vexed, set upon, persecuted.

belie *verb* **1** *her smile belied her anger* contradict, deny, give the lie to, disprove, refute, gainsay, confute. **2** *the official report belies the enormity of the disaster* misrepresent, falsify, distort, conceal, disguise. **3** *her performance belied our faith in her* fail to justify, be at odds with, not to live up to.

belief *noun* **1** *it is my belief that she is dead* opinion, feeling, impression, view, viewpoint, conviction, judgement, thinking, way of thinking, theory, notion. **2** *no belief in his powers* faith, credence, freedom from doubt, trust, reliance, confidence. **3** *Christian/political beliefs* doctrine, teaching, creed, dogma, ideology, principles, tenet, canon, credence, credo.
Opposites DISBELIEF; DOUBT; SCEPTICISM.

believable *adjective* credible, plausible, likely, creditable, probable, possible, acceptable, within the bounds of possibility, conceivable, imaginable.
Opposites UNBELIEVABLE; INCREDIBLE.

believe *verb* **1** *I don't believe you* consider honest/true, be convinced by, trust. **2** *don't believe his story* regard/accept as true, accept, credit, be convinced by, trust; *inf.* swallow, fall for, buy. **3** *I believe he's retired* | *believed the earth to be flat* think, be of the opinion that, understand, suppose, assume, presume, conjecture, surmise, reckon, guess, postulate/theorize that. **believe in 1** *believe in God/fairies* be convinced/sure/persuaded of the existence of. **2** *believe in alternative medicine* have faith in, trust, be convinced/persuaded by, set store by, value, swear by; *inf.* rate.
Opposites DISBELIEVE; DOUBT.

believer *noun* follower, adherent, supporter, disciple, upholder.
Opposites DISBELIEVER; SCEPTIC; AGNOSTIC.

belittle *verb* disparage, decry, deprecate, undervalue, underrate, underestimate, minimize, make light of, slight, detract from, downgrade, play down, depreciate, derogate, scoff at, sneer at.
Opposites PRAISE; EXAGGERATE; MAGNIFY.

belligerent *adjective* **1** *in a belligerent mood* | *a belligerent young woman quarrelling with everyone* aggressive, antagonistic, militant, pugnacious, quarrelsome, argumentative, disputatious, combative, quick-tempered, hot-tempered, irascible, captious. **2** *belligerent nations* at war, warring, battling, contending, militant, martial, warlike, warmongering.
Opposites FRIENDLY; PEACEABLE; PEACEFUL.

bellow *verb* roar, shout, bawl, yell, shriek, howl, scream, screech, call, cry out, whoop, ululate; *Am. inf.* holler.

belly *noun* **1** *a stabbing pain in the belly* stomach, abdomen, paunch; intestines, innards; *inf.* tummy, tum, insides, guts, corporation, pot, bread basket, pot belly, beer belly. **2** *the belly of the planes* underside, underpart, underbelly.

belly *verb the sail bellied out* swell, billow, bulge, fill out, balloon out, bag.

belong *verb* **1** *where does this book belong?* have a place/home, be classified, be categorized. **2** *they do not belong here* fit in, be suited to, have a rightful place, be part of; *inf.* go, click. **belong to 1** *the house belongs to them* be owned by, be the property of, be under the ownership of, be held by, be at the disposal of. **2** *she belongs to the sailing club/it belongs to the cat family* be a member of, be affiliated to, be allied to, be associated with, be connected to, be included in, be an adherent of. **3** *this lid belongs to that box* be part of, be an adjunct of, attach to, go with, relate to, be relevant to.

belongings *plural noun* possessions, personal possessions/effects, effects, goods, accoutrements, appurtenances; property, paraphernalia; *inf.* gear, things, stuff, junk.

beloved *adjective* **1** *my beloved children* dear, dearest, darling, adored, much loved, precious, cherished, sweet, treasured, prized, worshipped, idolized. **2** *beloved of everyone* loved, liked, adored, admired, respected, valued, esteemed, revered.

beloved *noun married her beloved* sweetheart, fiancé, fiancée, boyfriend, girlfriend, love, lover, betrothed; *fml.* paramour, inamorato, inamorata.

below *adverb* **1** *we could see it down below* further/lower down, in/to a lower position, underneath, beneath, downstairs. **2** *for further details see below* further on, at a later point/ place.

below *preposition* **1** *skirts below the knee | the valley below the village* further down than, lower than, under, underneath. **2** *prices/temperatures below average* less/lower than. **3** *ranking below him | work below standard* lower than, inferior to, subordinate to. **4** *that remark was below you* unworthy of, undignified for, degrading to, not befitting, unsuitable for, inappropriate for. *Opposites* ABOVE; OVER.

belt *noun* **1** *wearing a leather belt* girdle, sash, cummerbund, waistband, band, girth; *fml.* cincture, baldric, cestus. **2** *mechanics mending the machine's belt* band, conveyor belt, fan belt. **3** *America's corn belt* zone, region, area, district, tract, stretch, extent. **4** *a belt of white in the black* strip, band, stripe, bar, line, stria. **5** *a belt across the ears* blow, punch, smack, bang, thump; *inf.* clout, bash, wallop.

belt *verb* **1** *with her waist belted* encircle, gird, encompass, bind, tie, fasten. **2** *teachers can no longer belt children with a strap* strap, flog, whip, lash, cane, thrash, scourge, flail, birch, flagellate. **3** *belt the child with his fists* strike, hit, beat, punch, smack, thrash, thump, bang, batter, pound, pummel; *inf.* bash, sock, slog.

bemoan *verb* lament, mourn, deplore, regret, grieve for/over, express sorrow for, sorrow for, bewail, sigh over, weep over, repent, rue.

bemused *adjective a bemused look | bemused by the events* confused, bewildered, puzzled, perplexed, dazed, stunned, muddled, over-

whelmed, disconcerted, discomfited, astonished, astounded, stupefied, preoccupied, absent-minded, engrossed.

bench *noun* **1** *pupils sitting on a bench* form, long seat, seat, pew, stall, settle. **2** *carpenters at the bench* workbench, worktable, table, counter, trestle table, board. **3** *appear before the bench* court, bar, courtroom, tribunal. **4** *a member of the bench* judges, magistrates; judiciary, judicature.

benchmark *noun* standard, point of reference, gauge, criterion, norm, guideline, specification, model, pattern, touchstone, yardstick.

bend *verb* **1** *bend the iron bar | bend the little finger* make crooked/curved, curve, crook, flex, twist, bow, arch, warp, contort. **2** *the road bends to the right* curve, turn, twist, swerve, veer, incline, diverge, curl, deviate, deflect, coil, spiral, loop, divagate, incurvate. **3** *bend down over the sink* stoop, crouch, lean down/ over, bow, hunch. **4** *bend them to our will* mould, shape, direct, force, influence, compel, persuade, subdue, sway, subjugate. **5** *bend our steps homeward | bend our minds to the task* direct, point, aim, turn, train, steer, set. *Opposites* STRAIGHTEN.

bend *noun* curve, turn, corner, twist, angle, arc, swerve, veer, incline, divergence, crook, curling, deviation, deflection, coiling, spiral, loop, hook, incurvation; dogleg, hairpin bend, zigzag.

beneath *adverb upon the earth beneath* below, underneath, in/to a lower place. *Opposites* ABOVE; OVER.

beneath *preposition* **1** *sank beneath the waves* below, under, underneath, lower than. **2** *people beneath her socially* below, lower than, inferior to, secondary to, subservient to. **3** *beneath him to behave like that* below, unworthy of, undignified for, unbefitting, unbecoming.

benediction *noun* **1** *say a benediction* blessing, prayer, invocation; grace, thanksgiving; *lit.* orison. **2** *a state of benediction* blessedness, grace, beatitude, bliss, favour.

benefactor *noun* helper, patron, backer, sponsor, supporter, promoter, contributor, subscriber, subsidizer, donor, philanthropist, sympathizer, well-wisher; *inf.* angel, friend.

beneficial *adjective* advantageous, favourable, propitious, promising, helpful, accommodating, obliging, useful, serviceable, valuable, profitable, rewarding, gainful. *Opposites* DISADVANTAGEOUS; DETRIMENTAL.

beneficiary *noun* heir, inheritor, recipient, receiver, legatee, payee, assignee.

benefit *noun* **1** *for the benefit of all* advantage, good, gain, profit, help, aid, assistance, interest, welfare, well-being, betterment, asset, avail, use, service. **2** *enjoy the benefits of modern medicine* advantage, blessing, boon; good, usefulness; perquisites, perks, fringe benefits. **3** *living on government benefit* social security payment, insurance money, allowance, sick pay, unemployment benefit. *Opposites* DISADVANTAGE; DETRIMENT.

benefit verb **1** discoveries benefiting society do good to, be of service to, profit, serve, be of advantage to, advantage, help, aid, assist, contribute to, better, improve, advance, further. **2** criminals benefiting from their deeds profit, gain, reap benefits, make money; inf. cash in, make a killing.
Opposites DAMAGE; INJURE.

benevolence noun kindness, kind-heartedness, goodness, generosity, charity, altruism, goodwill, humanity, compassion, humanitarianism, philanthropism.

benevolent adjective **1** a benevolent attitude to others kind, kindly, kind-hearted, friendly, amiable, benign, generous, magnanimous, warm-hearted, considerate, thoughtful, well-meaning, altruistic, humane, compassionate, caring, sympathetic, obliging, helpful, humanitarian, philanthropic, bountiful, liberal, bounteous, beneficent. **2** a benevolent institution charitable, non-profit making, alms-giving, eleemosynary.
Opposites MALEVOLENT; UNKIND; UNSYMPATHETIC.

benighted adjective ignorant, unenlightened, backward, uncivilized, uncultured, uneducated, illiterate, crude.

benign adjective **1** with a benign smile/attitude kind, kindly, friendly, amiable, genial, gracious, cordial, generous, benevolent, gentle, sympathetic, obliging, accommodating, liberal. **2** a benign climate healthy, health-giving, wholesome, salubrious, temperate, pleasant, mild, balmy, agreeable, refreshing. **3** in benign circumstances favourable, advantageous, beneficial, propitious, auspicious, lucky, opportune, providential, encouraging, conducive, helpful, benevolent. **4** a benign tumour non-malignant, non-dangerous, harmless, innocent, curable, remediable, treatable.
Opposites UNFRIENDLY; HOSTILE; UNFAVOURABLE; MALIGNANT.

bent adjective **1** a bent iron rod curved, crooked, twisted, bowed, angled, warped, contorted. **2** bent backs bowed, arched, curved, stooped, hunched. **3** a bent policeman corrupt, dishonest, crooked, fraudulent, unprincipled, bribable. **4** her husband turned out to be bent homosexual, gay; inf. homo, queer. **bent on** bent on winning determined to, set on, insistent on, resolved to, fixed on, inclined to, disposed to, predisposed to.
Opposites STRAIGHT; UPRIGHT.

bent noun an artistic bent | a bent for design inclination, predisposition, disposition, leaning, tendency, penchant, bias, predilection, proclivity, propensity, talent, gift, flair, ability, knack, aptitude, facility, skill, capability, capacity, forte, genius.

bequeath verb **1** bequeath her estate to her son leave, will, make over, cede, endow on, bestow on, consign, commit, entrust, grant, transfer. **2** ideas bequeathed by previous inventors hand down/on, pass down/on, impart, transmit.

bequest noun **1** receive a bequest of £10,000 legacy, inheritance, endowment, estate, heritage, bestowal, bequeathal, gift, settlement. **2** the bequest of her collection to the museum bequeathing, leaving, willing, making over. See BEQUEATH 1.

berate verb scold, rebuke, reprimand, chide, reprove, upbraid, castigate, censure, criticize, rail at, harangue, lambaste, fulminate against, vituperate, read the riot act to; inf. tell off, give a dressing-down to, tear a strip off, bawl out.

bereave verb an accident bereaved him of his wife deprive, dispossess, rob, divest, strip.

bereavement noun **1** sympathize with her in her bereavement loss, deprivation, dispossession. See BEREAVE. **2** a series of family bereavements death, loss, passing, demise, decease, quietus.

bereft adjective **bereft of** deprived of, robbed of, cut off from, parted from, devoid of, wanting, lacking, destitute of, minus.

berry noun. See table at FRUIT.

berserk adjective frenzied, mad, insane, crazed, crazy, out of one's mind, hysterical, maniacal, manic, raving, wild, enraged, raging, uncontrollable, amok, unrestrainable; inf. off one's head, hyper, ape.

berth noun **1** book a berth in the train/ship bed, bunk, sleeping accommodation, billet, hammock, cot. **2** ships at their berths anchorage, mooring, docking site. **3** a cosy well-paid berth job, post, position, situation, place; employment, appointment, living.

berth verb **1** berth the ship moor, dock, anchor, land, tie up. **2** the ship berthed at dawn moor, dock, drop anchor, land. **3** the yacht berths four provide beds for, sleep, accommodate, put up, house, shelter, lodge.

beseech verb beg, implore, entreat, ask, plead with, pray, petition, call upon, appeal to, supplicate, invoke, adjure, crave.

beset verb **1** beset with fears | beset by anxieties attack, harass, assail, worry, plague, bother, trouble, perplex, torment, pester, hound, nag, bedevil, harry. **2** beset by enemy forces surround, besiege, encircle, ring round, enclose, encompass, hem in, shut/fence in.

besetting adjective his besetting sins habitual, persistent, inveterate, prevalent, troublesome, harassing, assailing.

beside preposition **1** walking beside him alongside, by/at the side of, abreast of, next to, with, by, adjacent to, cheek by jowl with, close to, near, nearby, neighbouring, next door to. **2** beside her work, his is poor compared with, in comparison with, next to, against, contrasted with, in contrast to/with. **beside oneself** berserk, frenzied, in a frenzy, mad, frantic, demented, insane, crazed, crazy, deranged, unbalanced, distraught, hysterical, uncontrolled, unrestrained, unhinged, out of one's mind. **beside the point** irrelevant, not applicable, immaterial.

besides adverb besides, it's too late also, in addition, additionally, moreover, furthermore, further, as well, too, what's more.

besides preposition three besides him apart from, in addition to, aside from, over and above, other than, not counting, excluding, not including, without.

besiege verb **1** *the castle besieged by the enemy* lay siege to, beleaguer, blockade, surround, encircle, encompass. *See table at* SIEGE. **2** *film stars besieged by reporters* surround, enclose, encircle, beleaguer, beset, shut in, hem in, fence in, hedge in. **3** *besieged with doubts* harass, assail, worry, plague, beset. *See* BESET 1.

besmirch verb *besmirch the firm's reputation* sully, slander, defame, tarnish, smear, stain, taint, damage.

besotted adjective **1** *besotted with his secretary* infatuated with, doting on, smitten, bewitched by, spellbound by, hypnotized by. **2** *besotted with drink* befuddled, drunk, intoxicated, stupefied, confused, muddled, dazed, bewildered; *inf.* blotto, bombed, out of it, smashed, zonked. *See* BEFUDDLED.

bespatter verb spatter, splatter, splash, bedaub, muddy, dirty, smear, besmirch, besprinkle, sully, begrime, befoul.

bespeak verb **1** *actions bespeaking a kind heart* give evidence of, indicate, demonstrate, exhibit, show, display, evince, manifest, reveal, betray, testify to, bear witness to. **2** *bespeak goods* order in advance, order prearranged, reserve, requisition.

best adjective **1** *the best player* foremost, finest, leading, top, chief, principal, highest, worthiest, supreme, superlative, unsurpassed, unexcelled, excellent, first-class, first-rate, outstanding, pre-eminent; *inf.* crack, ace. **2** *the best way to get there | the best solution* right, correct, most fitting, most suitable, most desirable, apt, advantageous.
Opposites WORST.

best adverb **1** *he played best* in the best way, superlatively, unsurpassedly, excellently, outstandingly. **2** *he likes tennis best* to the highest/greatest degree, greatly, extremely. **3** *her behaviour is best ignored* most sensibly, most wisely, most suitably, most fittingly, most advantageously.

best noun **1** *only the best may enter* finest, first class, top, cream, pick, flower, choice, élite. **2** *do your best* utmost, hardest, best endeavour; *inf.* damnedest. **3** *at his best in the morning* peak, prime, top form, height, apex. **4** *the best of having a car* most favourable/advantageous/pleasant aspect, advantage, asset, blessing, boon. **5** *dressed in her best* best clothes, finery, finest clothes; *inf.* Sunday best, best bib and tucker. **6** *give him my best* best wishes, regards, kindest regards, greetings, love.

best verb *best the opposition* defeat, beat, conquer, get the better of, trounce, thrash, triumph over, get the upper hand of, prevail over, outdo, outclass, surpass, outwit, outsmart, worst; *inf.* lick, make mincemeat of.

bestial adjective **1** *bestial treatment of prisoners* brutish, savage, brutal, inhuman, beastly, barbarous, barbaric, abominable, atrocious, cruel, primitive, wild, heathen. **2** *bestial sexual practices* depraved, vile, sordid, degenerate, degraded, gross, carnal, lustful, lecherous, prurient, lascivious, lewd, crude. **3** *bestial shapes* beastlike, animal, theroid, theriomorphic.

bestow noun give, present, confer on, grant, donate, endow with, hand over, allot, assign, consign, apportion, distribute, bequeath, impart, accord, award, honour with, entrust with, commit.

bestride verb **1** *bestriding the horse* straddle, bestraddle, sit/stand astride. **2** *a bridge bestriding the river* straddle, span, extend across, pass over, cross.

bet verb **1** *bet £100 that he wins* wager, gamble, stake, pledge, risk, venture, hazard, chance. **2** *he never bets* gamble, wager, speculate; *inf.* punt. **3** *you can bet they've gone* be certain/sure, state confidently, predict.

bet noun **1** *enter into a bet* wager, gamble, speculation, venture, game of chance, lottery, sweepstake, long shot. **2** *place a bet of £100* wager, stake, ante, pledge. **3** *my bet is that they'll go* prediction, forecast, opinion, belief, feeling, view, theory. **4** *they're/that's our best bet* choice, option, alternative, selection, possibility, course of action.

bête noire noun anathema, pet aversion, aversion, pet hate, bugbear, abomination.

betide verb happen, occur, take place, befall, supervene, transpire, come to pass, ensue, chance.

betoken verb **1** *white betokening chastity* indicate, denote, signify, suggest, evidence, typify, represent, show, demonstrate, manifest, bespeak. **2** *activities betokening war* augur, forebode, bode, portend, presage, foreshadow, prophesy, prognosticate, promise.

betray verb **1** *betray one's friends* inform on/against, be disloyal/unfaithful to, treat treacherously, break faith with, break one's promise to; *inf.* tell on, double-cross, stab in the back, sell down the river, sell out, blow the whistle on, squeal on. **2** *betray a secret | a smile betraying his feelings* reveal, disclose, divulge, give away, let slip, blurt out, blab, lay bare, bring to light, uncover, expose, exhibit, manifest, unmask. **3** *betrayed him into a wrong course of action* mislead, lead astray, delude, deceive, beguile, dupe, fool, hoodwink, cheat, trap, ensnare, gull, cozen. **4** *betrayed his mistress for another woman* abandon, desert, forsake, walk out on, jilt; *inf.* leave flat.
Opposites stand by (*see* STAND); CONCEAL.

betrayal noun **1** *the betrayal of his friends* informing on/against, being disloyal to, breaking faith with; *inf.* double-crossing. *See* BETRAY 1. **2** *the betrayal of a secret | betrayal of his feelings* revelation, disclosure, divulgence, giving away. *See* BETRAY 2. **3** *the betrayal into a wrong course of action* misleading, delusion, deception, duping, hoodwinking. *See* BETRAY 3. **4** *the betrayal of his mistress* abandonment, desertion, forsaking. *See* BETRAY 4. **5** *appalled by their betrayal* act of betrayal, breach of faith, bad faith, disloyalty, perfidy, treachery, duplicity, double-dealing, subversion, sedition, treason; *inf.* double-crossing, back-stabbing, sell out, whistle-blowing.

betroth verb engage, affiance, plight, contract, covenant; *lit.* espouse.

betrothal *noun* engagement, betrothment, marriage contract, plighting of one's troth, compact, covenant; *lit.* espousal.

better *adjective* **1** *the better players* finer, of higher quality, greater, superior, worthier, fitter. **2** *a better course of action* more fitting, more suitable, more appropriate, more desirable, more advantageous, more useful, more valuable. **3** *feeling better* healthier, fitter, less ill, stronger, well, cured, recovered, recovering, progressing, improving; *inf.* mending, on the mend.

better *adverb* **1** *he plays better now* in a better way, in a superior/finer way, to a higher standard. **2** *I understand him better* more, to a greater degree. **3** *her advice is better ignored* more sensibly, more wisely, more suitably, more fittingly, more advantageously.

better *verb* **1** *better the lot of the poor* make better, raise, improve, ameliorate, advance, promote, forward, further, amend, rectify, relieve, reform, enhance, enrich. **2** *better the previous record* improve on, beat, surpass, exceed, top, cap, outstrip, outdo, excel, go one better than. **Opposites** WORSEN.

betterment *noun* improvement, amelioration, furtherance, reform, enhancement, enrichment.

between *preposition* **1** *standing between them | sharing things between them* in the middle of, amidst, in the midst of, among. **2** *somewhere between the two cities* on the way along, on the course connecting, in the space separating. **3** *the bond between mother and baby* connecting, linking, joining, uniting, allying. **4** *the difference between them* separating, distinguishing, differentiating, discriminating.

bevel *noun* slope, slant, oblique, tilt, angle, cant, bezel, chamfer.

beverage *noun* drink, potation, potable; refreshment, liquid, liquor; *inf.* libation, bevvy. *See tables at* ALCOHOL, COFFEE, DRINK, TEA.

bevy *noun* **1** *a bevy of quails/birds* flock, flight. **2** *a bevy of beautiful girls* collection, gathering, assembly, array, galaxy, group, band, troupe, cluster; *inf.* bunch, gaggle.

bewail *verb* mourn, lament, grieve over, sorrow for/over, express woe/sorrow for, cry/weep over, wail/keen over, bemoan, regret, deplore, repent, rue, pine for.

beware *verb* *you must beware | beware of thieves* be careful/wary, be cautious, be on one's guard, take heed, watch out, look out, watch/look/mind out for, be on the lookout/alert for. **Opposites** IGNORE.

bewilder *verb* confuse, mix up, muddle, puzzle, perplex, baffle, mystify, nonplus, disconcert, confound, bemuse, daze, stupefy, befuddle, obfuscate; *inf.* stump, bamboozle.

bewildered *adjective* confused, muddled, puzzled, perplexed, nonplussed, uncertain, speechless, startled, taken aback, all at sea, thrown off balance. *See* BEWILDER.

bewitch *verb* **1** *the wizard bewitched the prince* put a spell on, cast a spell over, enchant, entrance, curse; *Am. inf.* hex. **2** *he was* bewitched by her beauty charm, enchant, beguile, captivate, entrance, fascinate, delight, allure, enrapture, spellbind, hypnotize, mesmerize, transfix.

bewitched *adjective* charmed, enchanted, beguiled, captivated, entranced, fascinated, enraptured, spellbound, hypnotized, mesmerized.

beyond *preposition* **1** *beyond the mountains* on the farther/far side of, on the other side of, further on than, past, after, over, behind. **2** *beyond midnight | beyond retirement age* after, past, later than, on the other side of. **3** *beyond our understanding/repair* outside the reach/range of, outside the limitations of, beyond the power/capacity of, surpassing. **4** *inflation beyond 10%* above, more than, greater than, exceeding, in excess of, over and above. **5** *notice nothing beyond his beard* other than, apart from, except.

beyond *adverb* *what lies beyond | the mountains beyond* yonder, further on, far off, far away, at a distance, afar. **Opposites** NEAR; CLOSE.

bias *noun* **1** *cut on the bias* slant, cross, diagonal, skew, angle, oblique, slope. **2** *have a bias in favour of/against socialism | have a musical bias* tendency, inclination, leaning, bent, partiality, penchant, predisposition, propensity, proclivity, proneness, predilection, prejudice, bigotry, intolerance, narrow-mindedness, one-sidedness. **Opposites** OBJECTIVITY; FAIRNESS; IMPARTIALITY.

bias *verb* **1** *bias the judges* prejudice, influence, sway, predispose. **2** *bias their decision* prejudice, influence, sway, distort, bend, twist, warp, weight, predispose.

biased *adjective* *a biased attitude* prejudiced, partial, one-sided, influenced, slanted, weighted, swayed, distorted, predisposed. **Opposites** UNBIASED; IMPARTIAL; FAIR.

Bible *noun* **1** *Christians studying the Bible* Holy Writ, the Holy Scriptures, the Good Book; New English Bible, Gideon Bible. *See table.* **2** *the gardener's bible* authority, handbook, manual, guide, textbook, primer, vade-mecum.

bibliography *noun* book list, list, catalogue, compilation, record.

bicker *verb* wrangle, quarrel, argue, squabble, have a row, fight, fall out, have a disagreement, disagree, dispute, spar; *inf.* row, scrap.

bicycle *noun* bike, cycle; tandem, unicycle, tricycle, racer, mountain bike; *inf.* push-bike, bone-shaker. *See table.*

bid *verb* **1** *bid £100 for the vase* offer, tender, proffer, propose, submit, put forward, advance. **2** *they bade him go* command, order, instruct, ask, tell, call for, direct, demand, enjoin, charge, summon, require, invite. **3** *bid them farewell* wish, greet, tell, call, say.

bid *noun* **1** *put in a bid of £3,000* offer, proposition, proffer, proposal, submission, tender, advance, ante, price, sum, amount. **2** *a bid for power* attempt, effort.

PARTS OF A BICYCLE

brake	drum	lights
brake block	brake	mudguard
brake	dynamo	pannier
caliper	fork	pedal
carrier	frame	reflector
chain	gear	roller
coaster	gearwheel	chain
brake	handlebars	saddle
crank	hub	spokes
crossbar	hub gear	sprocket
derailleur	inner	stabilizers
diamond	tube	toe clip
frame	kickstand	tyre

biddable *adjective* obedient, amenable, tractable, complaisant, cooperative, teachable, docile, meek.

bidding *noun* **1** *he left at his father's bidding* command, order, instruction, injunction, direction, demand, mandate, charge, summons, request, call, behest, invitation. **2** *present at the bidding* auction; making of bids, tendering; offers, tenders, proposals.

big *adjective* **1** *a big garden/car* large, sizeable, great, huge, enormous, immense, vast, massive, extensive, substantial, spacious, colossal, gigantic, mammoth, prodigious. **2** *a big man* large, tall, bulky, burly, hulking, huge, enormous, muscular, beefy, brawny, strapping, thickset, heavy, solid, corpulent, fat, obese, stout, gargantuan, elephantine, Brobdingnagian. **3** *a big boy now* | *a big sister* grown-up, adult, grown, mature, elder. **4** *a big decision/moment* important, significant, serious, momentous, salient, weighty, paramount. **5** *a big figure in the movement* important, influential, powerful, prominent, outstanding, leading, well-known, principal, foremost, noteworthy, notable, eminent, distinguished. **6** *big ideas/talk* arrogant, pretentious, ambitious, inflated, pompous, proud, haughty, conceited, boastful, bragging, bombastic. **7** *a big heart* generous, kindly, kind-hearted, benevolent, magnanimous, unselfish, altruistic, philanthropic, beneficient, humane.
Opposites SMALL; LITTLE; MINOR.

bigot *noun* fanatic, zealot, sectarian, dogmatist, chauvinist, jingoist, racist, sexist.

bigoted *adjective* prejudiced, intolerant, fanatical, narrow-minded, illiberal, biased, partial, one-sided, dogmatic, warped, twisted, jaundiced, chauvinistic, jingoistic, racist, sexist.
Opposites TOLERANT; LIBERAL.

bigotry *noun* prejudice, intolerance, fanaticism, narrow-mindedness, bias, partiality, dogmatism, discrimination, unfairness, injustice, chauvinism, jingoism, racism, sexism, provincialism. *See* BIGOTED.

bigwig *noun* VIP, dignitary, notable, notability, personage, celebrity, panjandrum; *inf.* somebody, heavyweight, big shot, big noise, big gun, big cheese, nob.

bilge *noun* *don't talk bilge* rubbish, nonsense, drivel, gibberish, balderdash, bunkum, hogwash, twaddle; *inf.* rot, codswallop, poppycock, claptrap, piffle, guff, tosh.

bilious *adjective* **1** *feeling bilious* liverish, out of sorts, queasy, nauseated, sick. **2** *of a bilious temperament* bad-tempered, ill-tempered, short-tempered, ill-humoured, cross, irritable, crotchety, grumpy, peevish, edgy, touchy, tetchy, crabby, cantankerous, testy, nasty; *inf.* grouchy, ratty. **3** *bilious colours* violent, garish, distasteful, nauseating.

bilk *verb* swindle, cheat, defraud, exploit, fleece, deceive, trick, bamboozle, rook, gull; *inf.* con, do, diddle.

bill¹ *noun* **1** *a bill for damages* | *a restaurant bill* account, invoice, statement, note/list of charges, reckoning, tally, score; *Am.* check; *Am. inf.* tab. **2** *post no bills* | *distribute bills* poster, advertisement, flier, notice, announcement, leaflet, circular, handout, handbill, brochure, placard, bulletin, broadsheet, broadside; *inf.* advert, ad. **3** *top of the bill* programme, playbill, list, listing, agenda, card, schedule, timetable, syllabus, roster, calendar, catalogue,

BOOKS OF THE BIBLE

Old	Job	Zephaniah	Thessalonians II	Additions to the
Testament	Psalms	Haggai	Timothy I	Book of Esther
Genesis	Proverbs	Zechariah	Timothy II	Wisdom of
Exodus	Ecclesiastes	Malachi	Titus	Solomon
Leviticus	Song of	**New**	Philemon	Ecclesias-
Numbers	Solomon	**Testament**	Hebrews	ticus
Deuteronomy	Isaiah	Matthew	James	Baruch
Joshua	Jeremiah	Mark	Peter I	Letter of
Judges	Lamentations	Luke	Peter II	Jeremiah
Ruth	Ezekiel	John	John I	Song of the
Samuel I	Daniel	Acts	John II	Three Holy
Samuel II	Hosea	Romans	John III	Children
Kings I	Joel	Corinthians I	Jude	Susanna
Kings II	Amos	Corinthians II	Revelation	Bel and the
Chronicles I	Obadiah	Galatians	**Apocrypha**	Dragon
Chronicles II	Jonah	Ephesians	Esdras I	Prayer of
Ezra	Micah	Philippians	Esdras II	Manasses
Nehemiah	Nahum	Colossians	Tobit	Maccabees I
Esther	Habakkuk	Thessalonians I	Judith	Maccabees II

inventory. **4** *a parliamentary bill* proposal, measure, projected/proposed law, piece of legislation.

bill² *verb* **1** *bill them for the goods* invoice, send an invoice to, charge for, debit, send a statement to, tabulate/list costs/expenditure. **2** *bill it all over the building* advertise, announce, post, give notice of, put up in lights. **3** *bill it for tomorrow* programme, schedule, enter on the timetable, timetable, put on the agenda.

bill³ *noun* *a bird's bill* beak; *dial.* neb.

billet *noun* **1** *billets for soldiers* quarters, living quarters, barracks, rooms; accommodation, lodging, housing, cantonment. **2** *an easy well-paid billet* job, post, situation, position, office, appointment, commission, assignment; employment.

billet *verb* *billet the soldiers in the town* accommodate, put up, lodge, house, quarter, station, shelter.

billow *noun* wave, surge, swell, tide, rush, deluge, flood, breaker, roller.

billow *verb* puff up, swell, fill out, balloon, belly, surge, roll.

billowy *adjective* wavelike, swelling, surging, undulating, rolling, tossing, rising, rising and falling, ebbing and flowing.

bin *noun* container, receptacle, box, can, crate.

bind *verb* **1** *bind the sheaves together | with their legs bound* tie, tie up, fasten, secure, attach, rope, strap, truss, lash, tether, fetter, chain, hitch, wrap. **2** *bind the wound* bandage, dress, tape, wrap, cover, swathe, encase. **3** *bind the surfaces together* stick, glue, cement, paste. **4** *bind the seams with gold* edge, trim, hem, border, finish. **5** *bound to answer/secrecy* compel, obligate, oblige, constrain, force, impel, engage, require, prescribe. **6** *bound by family ties* constrain, restrain, restrict, hamper, hinder, inhibit, yoke.
Opposites LOOSEN; SEPARATE.

bind *noun* **1** *waiting for them is a bind* nuisance, bore, irritation, inconvenience, vexation; *inf.* drag. **2** *we're in a bind over what to do* quandary, dilemma, predicament, difficulty, spot, tight spot.

binding *adjective* *the agreement is binding* irrevocable, unalterable, compulsory, obligatory, indissoluble, imperative, mandatory, necessary, conclusive.

binge *noun* spree, orgy, drinking/eating bout, fling; *inf.* bender, jag, blinder.

biochemist *noun. See table at* SCIENTIST.

biography *noun* life history, life, life story, memoir, profile, account; *inf.* bio.

biologist *noun. See table at* SCIENTIST.

bird *noun* songbird, songster, warbler, fowl, fledgling, feathered friend; bird of prey. *See table. See also tables at* COLLECTION, FOWL, GAME, YOUNG.

birth *noun* **1** *present at the child's birth* childbirth, delivery, parturition, confinement, nativity. **2** *the birth of jazz* origin, beginnings, start, source, emergence, commencement, fountainhead, genesis. **3** *of noble birth* origin,

descent, ancestry, lineage, line, extraction, derivation, family, parentage, house, blood, breeding, genealogy, pedigree, heritage, patrimony, stock, race, strain, background.
Opposites DEATH; DEMISE.

birthmark *noun* blemish, discoloration, naevus, patch, mole.

birthright *noun* right, due, privilege, heritage, patrimony, legacy.

birthstone *noun. See table.*

BIRTHSTONES	
Birthstone	**Month**
garnet	January
amethyst	February
bloodstone	March
diamond	April
emerald	May
pearl	June
ruby	July
sardonyx	August
sapphire	September
opal	October
topaz	November
turquoise	December

bisect *verb* cut in half, halve, cut/divide/split in two, split down the middle, cleave, separate into two, bifurcate, dichotomize.

bisexual *adjective* hermaphrodite, androgynous, epicene; *Tech.* monoclinous; *inf.* AC/DC, swinging both ways, kicking with both feet, ambidextrous, bi.

bit¹ *noun* **1** *bits of bread/cheese/sawdust* small piece, piece, section, part, segment, chunk, lump, hunk, portion, butt, stump, particle, fragment, atom, flake, sliver, chip, crumb, grain, speck, scrap, shred, trace, morsel, mouthful, iota, jot, tittle, whit, modicum, shard, hint, tinge, suggestion. **2** *see you in a bit* little, little while, short time, moment, minute, second, instant, short spell, short period, flash, blink of an eye; *inf.* jiffy, tick, before you know it, two shakes of a lamb's tail.

bit² *noun* *a horse's bit/a tool's bit* restraint, restrainer, check, curb, brake, snaffle.

bitch *noun* **1** *his wife's a real bitch* shrew, vixen, cat, virago, harpy, she-devil. **2** *this job's a real bitch* problem, difficulty, predicament, dilemma.

bitch *verb* **1** *stop bitching about your work* complain, grumble, moan, find fault, find fault with, carp, grouse, whine; *inf.* gripe, beef, bellyache. **2** *she's always bitching about her friends and relations* be spiteful about, blacken the name of, slander, decry, disparage, malign; *fml.* calumniate. **3** *that workman bitches up everything* botch, bungle, spoil, ruin, wreck, make a mess of; *inf.* mess up, screw up.

bitchy *adjective* nasty, mean, spiteful, malicious, catty, vindictive, rancorous, venomous, snide, shrewish, vixenish, cruel, backbiting.

bite *verb* **1** *bite into the food | bite one's nails* chew, munch, crunch, champ, masticate, eat;

nibble at, gnaw at. **2** *dogs biting people* sink one's teeth into, nip, snap at, tear at, wound. **3** *insects biting them* sting, prick, pierce, puncture, wound. **4** *biting on his pipe* clamp, grip, hold on to. **5** *acids biting into the metal* eat into, corrode, burn, eat away at, erode, dissolve, wear away. **6** *measures beginning to bite* take effect, work, have results. **7** *fish biting|new clients not biting* take the bait, be lured, be enticed, be tempted, be allured. **8** *what's biting you?* annoy, irritate, bother, displease, peeve, provoke, vex; *inf.* bug, get at, needle.

bite *noun* **1** *the dog gave her a playful bite* nip, snap. **2** *suffering from insect bites* sting, prick, puncture, wound, lesion, itch, smarting. **3** *a bite of the apple/food* mouthful, piece, morsel, bit. **4** *have a bite to eat* snack, light meal, refreshment. **5** *the sauce had a bite to it* sharpness, spiciness, piquancy, pungency, edge; *inf.* kick, punch.

biting *adjective* **1** *biting winds* sharp, freezing, cold, bitterly cold, harsh, nipping, stinging, piercing, penetrating. **2** *biting words* sharp, bitter, cutting, caustic, sarcastic, scathing, trenchant, mordant, stinging, withering, incisive, acid.

bitter *adjective* **1** *a bitter substance* acid, pungent, acrid, tart, sour, biting, harsh, unsweetened, vinegary, acetous, acerbic. **2** *a bitter old woman|feeling bitter* resentful, embittered, rancorous, acrimonious, piqued, ill-disposed, indignant, sullen, crabbed, sour, morose, begrudging, petulant, peevish, with a chip on one's shoulder. **3** *from bitter experience|bitter memories* painful, distressing, distressful, harrowing, heartbreaking, heart-rending, agonizing, unhappy, sad, poignant, grievous, tragic, galling, vexatious. **4** *bitter north winds* biting, sharp, intensely cold, freezing, harsh, stinging, piercing, penetrating, fierce. **5** *bitter quarrels/controversy* virulent, acrimonious, hostile, antagonistic, spiteful, vicious, rancorous, vindictive, malicious, malevolent, venomous. **Opposites** SWEET; PLEASANT; HAPPY.

bitterness *noun* **1** *the bitterness of the medicine* acidity, pungency, acridity, tartness, sourness, vinegariness, acerbity. *See* BITTER 1. **2** *the bitterness of the old woman* resentment, resentfulness,

---

BIRDS

accentor	budgerigar	crane	flamingo	hammer-	jacana
adjutant	bulbul	crested tit	flicker	head	jackdaw
bird	bullfinch	crocodile	flower-	harlequin	jay
albatross	bunting	bird	pecker	duck	junco
American	burrowing	crossbill	flycatcher	harpy eagle	kagu
eagle	owl	crow	francolin	harrier	kakapo
antbird	bush tit	cuckoo	friar-bird	Hawaiian	kea
Arctic tern	bush wren	cuckoo	frigate	goose	kestrel
auk	bustard	shrike	bird	hawfinch	killdeer
auklet	butcher-	curlew	frogmouth	hawk	kingbird
avadavat	bird	dabchick	fulmar	hawk-owl	kingfisher
avocet	buzzard	darter	gadwall	hedge spar-	kinglet
babbler	Canada	demoiselle	gallinule	row	kite
bald eagle	goose	crane	gannet	hen	kittiwake
Baltimore	canary	diamond-	garganey	heron	kiwi
oriole	canvas-back	bird	gnat-	herring	knot
barbet	caracara	dipper	catcher	gull	kooka-
barnacle	cardinal	diver	godwit	hoatzin	burra
goose	carrion	dove	goldcrest	hobby	lammer-
barn owl	crow	drongo	golden	honey-	geier
bateleur	cassowary	duck	eagle	creeper	lanner
bee-eater	catbird	dunlin	golden-eye	honeyeater	lapwing
bellbird	chaffinch	dunnock	goldfinch	honey-	lark
bird of	chat	eagle	goosander	guide	laughing
paradise	chickadee	eagle owl	goose	hooded	jackass
bittern	chicken	egret	goshawk	crow	laughing
blackbird	chiffchaff	eider duck	grackle	hoopoe	owl
blackcap	chipping	emperor	grassfinch	hoot owl	lily-trotter
black swan	sparrow	penguin	great tit	hornbill	linnet
blue-bill	chough	emu	grebe	horned	little owl
bluebird	coal tit	emu-wren	greenfinch	owl	long-tailed
blue tit	cockatiel	erne	greenshank	house mar-	tit
boat-bill	cockatoo	fairy	greylag	tin	lorikeet
bobolink	coly	penguin	goose	house spar-	lory
booby	condor	falcon	griffon	row	lovebird
bowerbird	coot	fantail	vulture	huia	lyre-bird
brambling	cormorant	fieldfare	grosbeak	humming-	macaw
brent-goose	corncrake	finch	grouse	bird	magpie
broad-bill	courser	finfoot	guillemot	ibis	mallard
brush	cowbird	firecrest	gull	jabiru	mallee
turkey	crake	fish owl	gyrfalcon	jacamar	bird

embitteredness, rancour, animosity, acrimony, grudge, sullenness, crabbedness, sourness. *See* BITTER 2. **3** *the bitterness of the experience/memories* pain, painfulness, distress, agony, unhappiness, sadness, poignancy, tragedy. *See* BITTER 3. **4** *the bitterness of the wind* sharpness, harshness, coldness, intensity, penetration. *See* BITTER 4. **5** *the bitterness of the quarrel/controversy* acrimony, hostility, antagonism, spitefulness, rancour, malice, malevolence, venom. *See* BITTER 5.

bizarre *adjective* strange, weird, peculiar, odd, unusual, uncommon, curious, abnormal, extraordinary, queer, freakish, offbeat, outlandish, unconventional, fantastic, *outré*, eccentric, grotesque, ludicrous, comical, ridiculous, droll, deviant, aberrant; *inf.* oddball, rum, wacky, way-out, off-the-wall.
Opposites ORDINARY; NORMAL.

blab *verb* **1** *blab a secret* blurt out, let slip, reveal, disclose, divulge, tell. **2** *they won't know unless he's blabbed* tell, inform, report, let the cat out of the bag, tattle; *inf.* squeal, sing. **3** *blabbing away at the bus-stop* gossip, chat, chatter, tittle-tattle, blabber.

black *adjective* **1** *black horses* dark, pitch-black, pitch-dark, pitch, jet-black, inky, coal-black, dusky, swarthy, blackish, nigrescent, stygian. *See table at* COLOUR. **2** *the Black races* Negro, Negroid, coloured, dark-skinned. **3** *black nights/skies* dark, starless, moonless, unlit, unlighted, unilluminated, gloomy, dusky, dim, overcast, crepuscular, tenebrous, Stygian, Cimmerian. **4** *children with black hands|black corners* dirty, grubby, filthy, grimy, unclean, muddy, sooty, soiled, stained, dingy. **5** *black news|a black day* sad, melancholy, depressing, dismal, distressing, gloomy, hopeless, sombre, doleful, mournful, lugubrious, funereal, pessimistic, ominous, foreboding. **6** *the crowd in a black mood* angry, threatening, menacing, hostile, furious, aggressive, belligerent, resentful, sullen. **7** *a black deed|black hearts* evil, wicked, sinful, bad, vile, villainous, criminal, iniquitous, nefarious, heinous, foul, ignoble, base, corrupt, depraved, devilish, diabolic. **8** *black humour* cynical, sick, macabre.
Opposites WHITE; CLEAR; LIGHT; CHEERFUL.

BIRDS cont.

manakin	oil-bird	raven	seagull	swan	waxbill
mandarin	oriole	razorbill	secretary	swiftlet	waxwing
duck	ortolan	redhead	bird	tailor-bird	weaver-
marabou	osprey	redpoll	seriema	takahe	bird
stork	ostrich	redshank	serin	tanager	weaver
marsh	ouzel	redstart	shag	tawny owl	finch
harrier	ovenbird	redwing	shearwater	teal	wheatear
martin	owl	reed-bird	sheathbill	tern	whimbrel
meadow-	owlet-	reedling	shelduck	thickhead	whinchat
lark	frogmouth	reed	shoebill	thornbill	whipbird
megapode	oxpecker	warbler	shoveler	thrasher	whippoor-
merganser	oyster-	rhea	duck	thrush	will
merlin	catcher	rhinoceros	shrike	tinamou	whistler
minivet	parakeet	bird	siskin	titlark	white-eye
mistle	parrot	rice-bird	skimmer	titmouse	white-
thrush	partridge	rifle bird	skua	toucan	throat
mocking-	peacock	ring-dove	skylark	towhee	whooping
bird	peafowl	ring-necked	smew	tragopan	crane
moorhen	peewee	pheasant	snake bird	treecreeper	whydah
Mother	peewit	ring ouzel	snipe	trogon	wigeon
Carey's	pelican	roadrunner	snow	tropic bird	willet
chicken	penguin	robin	bunting	trumpeter	willow
motmot	peregrine	rock-dove	snow goose	tui	warbler
mourning	falcon	roller	snowy owl	turaco	woodchat
dove	petrel	rook	song thrush	turkey	woodcock
mousebird	phalarope	rosella	sparrow	turkey	wood-
murre	pheasant	ruddy duck	sparrow-	vulture	creeper
Muscovy	phoebe	ruff	hawk	turnstone	wood-duck
duck	pigeon	sacred ibis	spoonbill	turtle-dove	woodpecker
mute swan	pigeon-	saddleback	starling	twite	wood
muttonbird	hawk	sanderling	stilt	tyrant fly-	pigeon
mynah bird	pintail	sand	stonechat	catcher	wren
nene	pipit	martin	stone	umbrella	wren-
nighthawk	plains-	sandpiper	curlew	bird	babbler
night heron	wanderer	sapsucker	stork	vulture	wrybill
nightingale	plover	scaup	storm	wagtail	wryneck
nightjar	pochard	scops owl	petrel	wall	yellow-
noddy	ptarmigan	screamer	sunbird	creeper	hammer
notornis	puffin	screech owl	sun	warbler	yellow
nutcracker	quetzal	scrub	bittern	wattle-	legs
nuthatch	rail	turkey	swallow	bird	zebra finch

black *verb* **1** *black the cargo | black the delivery firm* boycott, embargo, put an embargo on, blacklist, ban, bar. **2** *black his eye* blacken, make black, bruise, injure. **3** *black shoes* blacken, make black/blacker, polish.

black *noun* **in the black** solvent, in credit, in funds, without debt. **in black and white** **1** *wish to see the proposals in black and white* in print, written down, clearly/plainly/explicitly defined. **2** *see everything in black and white* in absolute terms, unequivocally, categorically, uncomprisingly, without shades of grey.

blackball *verb* vote against, blacklist, debar, bar, ban, exclude, shut out, expel, drum out, oust, cashier, ostracize, reject, repudiate, boycott, snub, shun, give the cold shoulder to.

blacken *verb* **1** *smoke blackening the walls* make black, darken, make dirty/sooty/smoky, begrime, besmudge, befoul. **2** *the sky blackened* grow/become black, darken, grow dim. **3** *they blackened his character* defame, speak ill/evil of, slander, libel, denigrate, disparage, slur, sully, decry, run down, vilify, malign, defile, impugn, smear, besmirch, tarnish, taint, stain, dishonour, drag through the mud, calumniate, traduce.

blackguard *noun* scoundrel, rogue, villain, wretch, cad, rascal, devil, miscreant; *inf.* jerk, rat, creep, louse, rotter, bounder, blighter, swine; *derog.* bastard; *inf.* scumbag.

blacklist *verb* debar, bar, ban, exclude, shut out, preclude, reject, repudiate, boycott, proscribe, blackball. *See* BLACKBALL.

blackmail *noun* *get the money by blackmail* extortion, exaction, extraction, intimidation, bribery, wresting, wringing, milking, bleeding, bloodsucking.

blackmail *verb* **1** *blackmail large sums of money from them* extort, exact, extract, bribe, wrest, force. *See* BLACKMAIL *noun*. **2** *blackmail people into paying* hold to ransom, threaten, coerce, force, compel.

blackout *noun* **1** *suffer a blackout* loss of consciousness, faint, coma, passing-out, period of oblivion, swoon; *inf.* flaking-out; *Med.* syncope. **2** *using candles during a sudden blackout* power cut, electricity failure. **3** *information blackout* cut-off, suppression, withholding, non-communication, censorship.

blame *verb* **1** *blame him for the accident* hold responsible/accountable, accuse, condemn, find guilty, assign/attribute fault/liability/guilt. **2** *blame the accident on him* ascribe, attribute, impute to, lay at the door of; *inf.* pin on, stick on. **3** *they're always blaming the child* find fault with, criticize, censure, reprimand, reproach, reprove, upbraid, scold, chide, berate, take to task.
Opposites FORGIVE; ABSOLVE; PRAISE.

blame *noun* **1** *put the blame for the accident on him* responsibility, guilt, accountability, liability, onus, culpability, fault; *inf.* rap. **2** *incur much blame for his behaviour* censure, criticism, incrimination, accusation, condemnation, reprimanding, reproach, recrimination, reproof, castigation, complaint, indictment, berating.

See BLAME *verb* 3.
Opposites INNOCENCE; ABSOLUTION; PRAISE.

blameless *adjective* innocent, not to blame, guiltless, above reproach/suspicion, in the clear, without fault, virtuous, moral, upright, irreproachable, unimpeachable, unoffending, sinless.
Opposites GUILTY; BLAMEWORTHY.

blameworthy *adjective* to blame, guilty, at fault, culpable, offending, wrong, erring, condemnable.
Opposites INNOCENT; BLAMELESS; PRAISEWORTHY.

blanch *verb* **1** *blanch in fear* go/become pale, pale, whiten, go white, become pallid. **2** *staying indoors had blanched her skin | sun blanching the carpet* made pale, whiten, made pallid, bleach, grey, wash out. **3** *blanch the almonds/peppers* scald, boil.

bland *adjective* **1** *bland food* tasteless, flavourless, mild, insipid. **2** *a bland speech* dull, middle-of-the-road, mediocre, nondescript, humdrum, boring, uninteresting, monotonous, unexciting, tedious, non-stimulating, uninspiring, weak, vapid. **3** *a bland manner* suave, urbane, smooth, affable, amiable, agreeable, gentle, gracious, courteous, congenial, unemotional, undemonstrative. **4** *bland breezes* mild, soft, calm, temperate, balmy, soothing, benign, mollifying, non-irritating, non-irritant.
Opposites SPICY; INTERESTING; STIMULATING.

blandishments *plural noun* flattery, cajolery, coaxing, wheedling, praise, fawning, toadying, ingratiating, inveiglement; compliments, soft words; *inf.* sweet talk, soft soap.

blank *adjective* **1** *a blank sheet of paper* void, empty, unfilled, unmarked, unwritten, clear, bare, clean, plain, spotless, white, vacant. **2** *a blank expression* expressionless, empty, vacant, deadpan, impassive, poker-faced, vacuous, lifeless, uninterested, emotionless, indifferent, uncomprehending. **3** *he looked blank | my mind went blank* uncomprehending, without ideas, at a loss, confused, puzzled, perplexed, bewildered, disconcerted, nonplussed, muddled, dumbfounded; *inf.* floored. **4** *a blank refusal* outright, absolute, unqualified, utter, complete, thorough, unalloyed.
Opposites FULL; EXPRESSIVE.

blank *noun* empty space, space, gap, emptiness, void, vacuum, vacancy, vacuity, nothingness.

blanket *noun* **1** *cover with a warm blanket* cover, covering, coverlet, bedcover, spread, rug, afghan; *Am.* throw. **2** *a blanket of snow/mist* covering, mass, layer, coat, coating, film, sheet, carpet, veneer, overlay, cloak, mantle, envelope, wrapping.

blanket *adjective* *a blanket agreement* across the board, overall, inclusive, all-inclusive, comprehensive, general, wide-ranging, sweeping.

blanket *verb* **1** *snow blanketing the earth | mist blanketing the hills* cover, overlay, coat, carpet, conceal, hide, mask, cloud, cloak, veil, shroud, envelop, surround. **2** *blanket out the television picture | shouting blanketing out his speech* obscure, suppress, extinguish.

blankness noun **1** *blankness of the paper/walls* voidness, emptiness, bareness, whiteness. *See* BLANK *adjective* 1. **2** *the blankness of her expression* expressionlessness, vacancy, lifelessness, emotionlessness, indifference, abstraction. *See* BLANK *adjective* 2. **3** *the blankness of her mind* lack of ideas, obliviousness, no recollection, lack of comprehension, confusion, perplexity, bewilderment. *See* BLANK *adjective* 3. **4** *the blankness of the refusal* outrightness, absoluteness, lack of qualification. *See* BLANK *adjective* 4.

blare verb **1** *car horns blaring* sound loudly, trumpet, blast, clamour, boom, roar, bellow, resound, honk, toot, peal, clang, screech. **2** *radios blaring out loud music* utter/give out loudly, blast out, boom out, screech out.

blarney noun smooth talk, flattery, cajolery, coaxing, wheedling; blandishments, soft/honeyed words, compliments; *inf.* sweet talk, soft soap.

blasé adjective indifferent, apathetic, uninterested, unexcited, nonchalant, uncaring, unmoved, emotionless, phlegmatic, lukewarm, unconcerned, offhand, bored, weary, world-weary, jaded, surfeited, glutted, cloyed, satiated.
Opposites ENTHUSIASTIC; EXCITED; RESPONSIVE.

blaspheme verb **1** *drunks blaspheming* swear, curse, utter oaths/profanities, damn, execrate, anathematize; *inf.* cuss. **2** *blaspheming Christ* profane, desecrate, revile, abuse.

blasphemous adjective profane, sacrilegious, irreligious, irreverent, impious, ungodly, godless, unholy.

blasphemy noun **1** *guilty of blasphemy* profaneness, profanity, sacrilege, irreligiousness, irreverence, impiety, impiousness, ungodliness, unholiness, desecration, execration. **2** *utter blasphemies* cursing, swearing, execration; curses, oaths, profanities.

blast noun **1** *a sudden blast of cold air* gust, rush, draught, blow, gale, squall, storm. **2** *a sudden blast of noise* blare, blaring, trumpeting, clamour, bellow, bellowing, boom, roar, clang, screech, wail, toot, honk, peal. **3** *people killed by the blast* explosion, detonation, discharge, blow-up, blowing-up, eruption, bang, burst. **4** *receive a blast from the teacher* outburst, attack, reprimand, rebuke, criticism, castigation, reproof.

blast verb **1** *car horns blasting away | blast the car horn* sound loudly, trumpet, blare, boom, roar. *See* BLARE 1. **2** *radios blasting out pop* utter/give out loudly, blare out, boom out, screech out. **3** *blast the building to bits* blow, demolish, blow to pieces, shatter, explode, break up, destroy, ruin, raze to the ground. **4** *frost blasted the plants* blight, kill, destroy, wither, shrivel. **5** *poverty blasting their hopes* kill, destroy, crush, dash, blight, wreck, ruin, spoil, mar, annihilate, disappoint, frustrate. **6** *blasting the pupils for being late* attack, reprimand, rebuke, criticize, upbraid, berate, castigate, reprove, rail at, flay. **7** *guns blasting* shoot, fire, blaze away, discharge, let fly. **blast off** *the rocket blasted off successfully* be launched, take off, lift off.

blasted adjective *blasted plants/hopes* blighted, destroyed, withered, shrivelled, ruined, devastated, spoiled, wasted.

blatant adjective flagrant, glaring, obtrusive, obvious, overt, manifest, conspicuous, prominent, pronounced, bare-faced, naked, sheer, outright, out and out, unmitigated, brazen, shameless, flaunting.
Opposites INCONSPICUOUS; SUBTLE.

blaze noun **1** *the house was destroyed in the blaze* fire, conflagration, holocaust; flames. **2** *a sudden blaze of light* beam, flash, flare, glare, streak, glitter; brightness, radiance, brilliance. **3** *left in a blaze of anger* outburst, burst, eruption, flare-up, explosion, outbreak, storm, torrent, blast, rush.

blaze verb **1** *the logs blazed up* burn, be ablaze, flame, burst into flames, catch fire. **2** *lights blazed in the street* shine, beam, flash, flare, glare, glitter. **3** *she blazed with fury* flare up, blow up, explode, seethe, fume, boil, smoulder; *inf.* see red, work oneself up, get steamed up. **4** *blaze away at the birds* shoot, fire, blast, discharge, let fly.

blazon verb *blazoned all over the newspapers* publicize, proclaim, broadcast, advertise, publish, make known, trumpet.

bleach verb **1** *the sun bleaching her hair/carpet* make white/whiter, make pale/paler, lighten, blanch, fade, wash out, decolour, decolorize, peroxide, etiolate. **2** *bones bleaching in the desert* grow white/whiter, grow pale/paler, lighten, blanch, fade.

bleached adjective lightened, blanched, faded, washed-out, decolorized, peroxided, stone-washed, etiolated.

bleak adjective **1** *a bleak landscape* bare, barren, desolate, exposed, unsheltered, open, windswept, windy, chilly, cold, waste, arid, desert, uncultivable, uncultivatable, unproductive. **2** *bleak surroundings/prospects* dreary, dismal, dark, gloomy, drab, sombre, wretched, depressing, grim, miserable, cheerless, joyless, uninviting, discouraging, disheartening, unpromising, hopeless.
Opposites SHELTERED; COSY; CHEERFUL.

bleary adjective **1** *bleary eyes* blurred, blurry, tired, watery, rheumy. **2** *bleary view* indistinct, dim, unclear, hazy, foggy, fogged, fuzzy, clouded, misty, murky.

bleed verb **1** *the wounded/wounds were bleeding badly* shed/lose blood, emit blood. **2** *doctors formerly bled patients* draw blood from, remove/take blood from; *fml.* phlebotomize. **3** *sap bleeding from a cut in the trunk* flow, run, ooze, seep, exude, trickle, weep, gush, spurt. **4** *bleeding money from the old man* extort, extract, squeeze, fleece, milk. **5** *bleeding their resources* drain, exhaust, sap, deplete, reduce. **6** *hearts are bleeding for them* ache, grieve, mourn, sorrow, suffer, agonize, anguish, sympathize, feel.

blemish noun **1** *a blemish on the fruit skin* mark, blotch, spot, patch, bruise, scar, speck, speckle, imperfection, discoloration, disfigurement, birthmark, naevus. **2** *a character blemish* defect, flaw, blot, taint, stain, smirch, dishon-

our, disgrace.
Opposites IMPROVEMENT; ENHANCEMENT.

blemish verb **1** *frost blemishing the fruit | her blemished skin* damage, mar, spoil, flaw, mark, spot, speckle, blotch, disfigure, discolour, deface. **2** *blemishing his reputation* sully, tarnish, blot, taint, stain, besmirch, injure, damage, impair, flaw.

blench verb flinch, start, shy, recoil, wince, quiver, shudder, tremble, quake, shrink, quail, cower.

blend verb **1** *blend the ingredients* mix, combine, intermix, admix, commix, mingle, commingle, amalgamate, coalesce, unite, merge, compound, alloy, fuse, synthesize, homogenize. **2** *colours blending with each other* harmonize, go with, go well with, complement, fit, suit.

blend noun *a blend of teas* mixture, mix, combination, admixture, mingling, commingling, amalgamation, amalgam, uniting, union, merging, compound, alloy, fusion, composite, concoction, synthesis, homogenization.

bless verb **1** *bless the altar* consecrate, sanctify, hallow, dedicate. **2** *bless God's name* glorify, praise, laud, exalt, magnify, extol. **3** *the priest blessed the children* ask God's favour/protection for, give a benediction for, invoke happiness on. **4** *I bless the day I met her | bless you for helping* give thanks for/to, thank. **5** *they were blessed with good looks | blessed with three children* endow, bestow, favour, provide, grace. **6** *the committee blessed the enterprise* sanction, approve, give approval for, be in favour of, endorse, support, give consent, smile upon.
Opposites CURSE; DAMN; BLIGHT.

blessed adjective **1** *a blessed place* consecrated, sanctified, hallowed, sacred, holy, divine, venerated, revered, beatified. **2** *the blessed Virgin* glorified, exalted, magnified, extolled. **3** *the blessed section of society* fortunate, lucky, favoured, endowed. **4** *blessed days of peace* happy, joyful, joyous, blissful, glad, cheerful, blithe, contented.

blessing noun **1** *utter a blessing* benediction, dedication, thanksgiving, consecration, invocation, commendation; grace. **2** *give the plan his blessing* approval, approbation, sanction, endorsement, support, backing, permission, leave, consent, assent, concurrence; good wishes. **3** *have the blessing of a quiet mind | what a blessing you're here* advantage, benefit, help, boon, godsend, favour, gift; luck, good fortune, gain, profit, bounty.
Opposites CURSE; DISADVANTAGE; BLIGHT.

blight noun **1** *plants killed by blight* disease, canker, infestation, pestilence, fungus, mildew. **2** *the blight which destroyed the city* affliction, plague, scourge, bane, woe, curse, misfortune, calamity, trouble, tribulation, evil, corruption, pollution, contamination.
Opposites BLESSING; FAVOUR.

blight verb **1** *trees blighted by frost* kill, destroy, wither, shrivel, blast, mildew. **2** *hopes blighted by war* kill, destroy, crush, dash, blast, wreck, ruin. See BLAST verb 5.

blind adjective **1** *guide dogs for blind people* unsighted, sightless, visually impaired, visionless, unseeing, stone-blind, partially sighted, half-blind, purblind, eyeless; inf. visually challenged. **2** *he must be blind not to know she loves him* imperceptive, slow, slow-witted, dim-witted, obtuse, dense, thick. **3** *blind to danger* unmindful of, careless of, heedless of, oblivious to, inattentive to, indifferent to, neglectful of, unaware of, unconscious of, unobservant of, ignorant of, insensitive of. **4** *blind loyalty* unreasoned, uncritical, unthinking, mindless, injudicious, undiscerning, indiscriminate, prejudiced, biased. **5** *in a blind rage* rash, impetuous, hasty, reckless, uncontrolled, uncontrollable, unrestrained, wild, frantic, violent, furious, irrational. **6** *a blind entrance* concealed, hidden, obscured, out of sight. **7** *a blind alley* dead-end, without exit, exitless, blocked, closed, barred, impassable. **8** *blind after the party* drunk, blind drunk, intoxicated; inf. smashed, paralytic, sloshed, plastered. See DRUNK adjective.
Opposites sighted; PERCEPTIVE; MINDFUL.

blind verb **1** *blinded in the accident* make blind, deprive of sight/vision, render unsighted/sightless, put one's eyes out, gouge out the eyes of. **2** *blinding the driver* obscure/block one's vision, get in one's line of vision, dazzle. **3** *blinded by love* deprive of judgement/reason/sense, deceive, delude, beguile, hoodwink. **4** *blind with science/facts* bewilder, confuse, overwhelm, overawe, swamp.

blind noun **1** *a window blind* screen, shade, curtain, shutter; venetian blind, roller blind. **2** *his job's a blind for his spying activities* camouflage, screen, smokescreen, front, façade, cover, disguise, cloak, pretext, masquerade, mask, feint.

blindly adverb **1** *feeling his way blindly* without sight, sightlessly, unseeingly. **2** *rushing on blindly* unmindfully, carelessly, heedlessly, rashly, impetuously, recklessly, uncontrolledly, wildly, frantically, irrationally. See BLIND adjective 3, 5. **3** *loving him blindly* uncritically, injudiciously, undiscerningly, indiscriminately. See BLIND adjective 4.

blink verb **1** *eyes blinking in the light* flutter, flicker, wink, bat, nictitate, nictate. **2** *people blinking in the sunlight* wink, peer, squint, screw up the eyes. **3** *city lights blinking* flicker, twinkle, waver, wink, glimmer, glitter, sparkle, shimmer, scintillate, flash, gleam, shine. **4** *teachers blinking at truancy* turn a blind eye to, take no notice of, disregard, overlook, ignore, condone, connive at.

bliss noun **1** *it's bliss to be on holiday* ecstasy, joy, elation, rapture, euphoria, happiness, delight, gladness, pleasure, heaven, paradise, seventh heaven, Eden, Utopia, Arcadia; halcyon days. **2** *in a state of bliss* blessedness, heavenly joy, divine happiness, beatitude.
Opposites MISERY; HELL.

blister noun **1** *blisters on the skin caused by burns* bleb, pustule, pimple, boil, cyst, abscess, carbuncle, ulcer, blain, papule, vesication, wen, furuncle. **2** *blisters on the paintwork* bubble, swelling, bulge, protuberance.

blistering *adjective* **1** *at blistering speed* | *in blistering heat* extreme, very great, greatest, intense, maximum, utmost. **2** *blistering criticism* scathing, fierce, severe, savage, sharp, biting, harsh, sarcastic, caustic, searing, mordant, trenchant.

blithe *adjective* **1** *in a blithe mood* happy, cheerful, cheery, light-hearted, jolly, merry, gay, joyful, carefree, buoyant, jaunty, animated, sprightly, vivacious, spirited, frisky, gladsome, mirthful. **2** *with a blithe disregard for others* casual, indifferent, careless, thoughtless, nonchalant, uncaring, unconcerned, heedless, untroubled, cool, blasé.
Opposites SAD; THOUGHTFUL.

blitz *noun* **1** *the blitz on London* bombardment, attack, assault, raid, offensive, onslaught, strike, blitzkrieg. **2** *a blitz on cleaning* attack, onslaught, all-out effort, onset, set-to, endeavour.

blizzard *noun* snowstorm, snow blast/squall.

bloat *verb* swell, puff up/out, blow up, distend, inflate, balloon, enlarge, expand, dilate.

blob *noun* **1** *a blob of cream* globule, glob, drop, droplet, bead, ball, bubble, pellet, pill. **2** *a blob of paint* spot, dab, splash, daub, blotch, blot, smudge, smear, mark.

bloc *noun* alliance, coalition, union, federation, league, ring, group, syndicate, combine, entente, party, wing, faction, cabal, clique, coterie.

block *noun* **1** *block of chocolate/soap* bar, cake, brick, chunk, hunk, lump, cube, ingot, wedge, mass, piece, wad. **2** *building a new science block* building, complex. **3** *block of seats/shares* group, batch, band, cluster, set, section, quantity. **4** *a block in the pipe* blockage, obstruction, stoppage. **5** *a block to progress* obstacle, bar, barrier, impediment, hindrance, deterrent, check, hurdle, stumbling-block, drawback, hitch.

block *verb* **1** *block the pipe* clog, stop up, choke, plug, close, obstruct; *inf.* bung up. **2** *block progress* hinder, obstruct, impede, halt, stop, bar, check, arrest, deter, thwart, frustrate, stand in the way of. **3** *block hats* shape, mould, form, fashion, frame, tailor.
Opposites CLEAR; FACILITATE.

blockade *noun* **1** *blockade of the city* siege, beleaguerment, investment, encirclement. **2** *a blockade at the border* | *a blockade to progress* barrier, barricade, obstacle, obstruction, block, hindrance, impediment, check, deterrent, hurdle, stoppage.

blockage *noun* **1** *a blockage in the pipes* obstruction, stoppage, block, occlusion, impediment. **2** *the blockage of the pipes* obstructing, blocking, stopping up, occluding.

blockhead *noun* dunce, numskull, dolt, fool, dullard, idiot, ignoramus, bonehead, nincompoop; *inf.* thickhead, dickhead, chump, pillock, wally, dork, geek; *Austral./Am. inf.* dingbat.

bloke *noun* man, boy, male, individual, body; *inf.* chap, fellow, guy, bod, punter, character, customer.

blond, blonde *adjective* fair, fair-haired, golden-haired, flaxen, tow-coloured, tow-headed; fair-skinned, fair-complexioned, light, light-coloured, light-toned, whitish.

blood *noun* **1** *a blood disease* | *blood was flowing* lifeblood, vital fluid, gore, whole blood; *lit.* ichor. *See table. See also table at* VEIN. **2** *of noble blood* ancestry, lineage, line, family, birth, extraction, descent, origin, genealogy, heritage, stock, race, pedigree, kinship, consanguinity. **3** *own flesh and blood* relations, kin, kindred; relationship, kinship. **4** *of hot blood* temperament, disposition, nature, humour, temper, spirit, feeling.

BLOOD CELLS	
basophil	monocyte
eosinophil	neutrophil
erythrocyte	platelet
granulocyte	red blood cell
leucocyte	white blood
lymphocyte	cell

blood-curdling *adjective* spine-chilling, chilling, terrifying, hair-raising, horrifying, horrific, horrendous, frightening, fearful, appalling, scaring.

bloodless *adjective* **1** *an invalid looking bloodless* anaemic, pale, wan, colourless, pallid, ashen, chalky, pasty, sallow, sickly, peaked, ghostlike, white as a sheet; *inf.* peaky. **2** *a bloodless young man* listless, languid, feeble, sluggish, languorous, apathetic, spiritless, passionless, phlegmatic, torpid, lackadaisical.

bloodshed *noun* killing, slaughter, slaying, carnage, butchery, massacre, murder, bloodletting, blood bath, gore, pogrom, decimation.

bloodthirsty *adjective* murderous, homicidal, savage, vicious, ruthless, barbarous, barbaric, brutal, bloody, sadistic, slaughterous, warlike, bellicose; *fml.* sanguinary.

bloody *adjective* **1** *a bloody nose* bleeding, unstaunched. **2** *a bloody cloth* blood-stained, blood-soaked, blood-marked, blood-spattered; *fml.* sanguinary. **3** *bloody actions/thoughts* bloodthirsty, murderous, homicidal, savage, vicious, slaughterous; *fml.* sanguinary. *See* BLOODTHIRSTY.

bloom *noun* **1** *perfect blooms* flower, blossom, floweret; flowering, blossoming, efflorescence. **2** *beauty losing its bloom* freshness, glow, lustre, sheen, radiance, flush, perfection, blush. **3** *genius no longer in full bloom* prime, perfection, heyday, vigour, flourishing, strength.

bloom *verb* **1** *plants blooming* flower, blossom, be in flower/blossom, come into flower/blossom, open, open out, bud, burgeon. **2** *they've bloomed since moving to the country* flourish, thrive, be in good health, get on well, prosper, succeed, progress.
Opposites WITHER; FADE; FAIL.

blossom *noun* apple *blossom* blooms, flowers, flowerets; blossoming, efflorescence.

blossom *verb* **1** *trees blossoming* be in flower, flower, bloom, burgeon. **2** *she blossomed in her new environment* | *the friendship blossomed* bloom, flourish, thrive, get on well, prosper, succeed, progress, develop, grow, mature.

blot noun **1** blots of ink/grease spot, blotch, splodge, smudge, patch, dot, mark, speck, smear. **2** a blot on his character stain, blemish, taint, flaw, fault, defect, tarnishing, imperfection, disgrace.

blot verb **1** paper blotted with ink-spots spot, blotch, smudge, dot, mark, speckle, smear, bespatter. **2** the event blotting his reputation stain, sully, tarnish, taint, besmirch, blacken. **3** blot up the grease soak up, absorb, dry up, dry out, take up. **blot out 1** typing fluid to blot out the print erase, obliterate, delete, rub out. **2** a tree blotting out the view hide, conceal, obscure, obliterate, darken, dim, shadow. **3** time blotting out memories wipe out, erase, efface, obliterate, expunge, destroy, exterminate.

blotch noun **1** a blotch of ink splodge, patch, smudge, dot, spot, speck, blot, stain, smear. **2** a blotch on the skin patch, blemish, mark, spot, eruption, birthmark, naevus.

blow¹ verb **1** the wind was blowing be in motion, puff, flurry, bluster, blast. **2** hair blowing in the breeze move, wave, flap, flutter, waft, stream, drift, whirl, undulate. **3** wind blowing the leaves/boats move, waft, toss, sweep, whisk, drive, buffet, whirl, transport, convey. **4** blow cigarette smoke breathe out, puff out, exhale, emit, expel. **5** he was blowing a bit breathe hard, puff, pant, wheeze, gasp, huff and puff. **6** blow the trumpet sound, play, toot, blare, blast. **7** blow £100 on a meal squander, fritter away, spend freely, lavish, dissipate. **8** blow one's chances spoil, ruin, bungle, make a mess of, muff; inf. botch, make a hash of, screw up. **9** blow about his big house boast, brag, crow; inf. talk big. **blow out 1** blow out the candle put out, extinguish, snuff, douse, stifle. **2** the walls suddenly blew out break open, burst, explode, blow up, shatter, rupture, crack. **blow over** pass away, pass, die down, be forgotten, sink into oblivion, come to an end, disappear, vanish, cease, subside, settle down, terminate. **blow up 1** the bombed building blew up explode, burst open, break open, shatter, rupture. **2** the bomb blew up explode, go off, detonate, erupt. **3** blow up the building bomb, detonate, explode, blast. **4** blow up the tyre/stomach inflate, pump up, fill up, swell, enlarge, distend, expand, puff up, balloon. **5** blow up the story exaggerate, overstate, embroider, colour, magnify, heighten, expand on. **6** he blew up at the news lose one's temper, become angry/enraged/furious, go into a rage/fury, erupt, go wild, rage; inf. hit the roof, go off the deep end, fly off the handle.

blow² noun **1** a bit of a blow today wind, breeze, gust, puff of wind, flurry, blast, gale, storm, tempest; turbulence. **2** a blow on the trumpet blast, blare, toot, sound.

blow³ noun **1** a blow on the head hit, knock, bang, punch, thump, smack, whack, thwack, buffet, stroke, rap; inf. bash, belt, clout, sock, wallop, battering, lick, slosh, bat. **2** her death was a blow shock, upset, calamity, catastrophe, disaster, misfortune, setback, disappointment, jolt, reversal.

blow-out noun **1** a blow-out at the minefield explosion, blast, detonation. **2** crash owing to a blow-out puncture, flat tyre, burst tyre, leak; inf. flat. **3** a birthday blow-out party, feast, celebration, binge, spree; inf. bash, knees-up, bean-feast, shindig, beano, rave, rave-up.

blowzy adjective **1** a dirty blowzy young woman dishevelled, slovenly, sluttish, slatternly, tousled, unkempt, untidy, sloppy, slipshod, messy, bedraggled. **2** a blowzy drunk coarse-looking, florid, ruddy-complexioned, red-faced.

bludgeon noun beaten with a bludgeon club, cudgel, stick, truncheon, heavy weapon.

bludgeon verb **1** bludgeoned to death club, cudgel, strike, hit, beat, beat up; inf. clobber. **2** bludgeoned into agreeing coerce, force, compel, browbeat, dragoon, bulldoze, bully, railroad, steamroller, pressurize, hector; inf. strong-arm.

blue adjective **1** a blue dress deep blue, navy blue. See table at COLOUR. **2** feeling blue depressed, gloomy, dejected, despondent, low, downcast, downhearted, unhappy, sad, melancholy, glum, morose, dismal; inf. down in the dumps. **3** blue jokes obscene, indecent, dirty, coarse, vulgar, bawdy, lewd, risqué, improper, smutty, offensive; inf. naughty, near the knuckle/bone, nudge-nudge.

blueprint noun plan, design, prototype, draft, outline, sketch, pattern, layout, representation.

blues plural noun a fit of the blues depression, gloominess, gloom, dejection, despondency, downheartedness, unhappiness, sadness, melancholy, glumness, moroseness, dismalness; low spirits, doldrums; inf. dumps, the hump.

bluff¹ verb **1** he's only bluffing pretend, sham, fake, feign, put it on, lie. **2** he's bluffing you deceive, delude, mislead, trick, hoodwink, hoax, take in, humbug, bamboozle, cozen; inf. put one over on.

bluff² noun it's just a bluff deception, deceit, pretence, sham, subterfuge, fake, show, false show, idle boast, feint, delusion, hoax, fraud; humbug, bluster.

bluff³ adjective **1** a bluff manner | a bluff old man frank, open, candid, outspoken, blunt, direct, plain-spoken, straightforward, downright, hearty, rough. **2** a bluff slope steep, sheer, vertical, precipitous, abrupt, sudden, acclivitous, perpendicular.
Opposites DIPLOMATIC; EVASIVE.

bluff⁴ noun cliff, headland, ridge, promontory, peak, crag, bank, slope, height, escarpment, scarp.

blunder noun mistake, error, inaccuracy, fault, slip, oversight, faux pas, gaffe; inf. slip-up, clanger, boob, boo-boo, howler, bloomer.

blunder verb **1** management blundered badly make a mistake, err; inf. slip up, screw up, blow it. **2** blundering about in the dark stumble, flounder, lurch, stagger, falter. **3** blunder the situation mismanage, botch, bungle, make a mess of.

blunt adjective **1** a blunt knife/blade not sharp, unsharpened, dull, dulled, edgeless. **2** a blunt

remark/manner/person frank, candid, outspoken, plain-spoken, straightforward, direct, bluff, to the point, brusque, abrupt, curt, short; *inf.* upfront.
Opposites SHARP; KEEN; SUBTLE.

blunt *verb* **1** *blunt the blade* make less sharp, make blunt/dull. **2** *blunt the appetite/enthusiasm* dull, take the edge off, deaden, dampen, numb, weaken, impair, appease.

blur *verb* **1** *blurring the view* make indistinct, make vague, obscure, dim, bedim, make hazy, befog, fog, cloud, becloud, mask, veil. **2** *blur the windscreen* smear, besmear, smudge, spot, blotch, blot, stain, besmirch. **3** *blur one's judgement/memory* dull, numb, make dim, make less sharp, deaden.

blur *noun* **1** *just a blur on the landscape | a blur in my memory* something hazy/indistinct/vague, haze; haziness, indistinctness, obscureness, obscurity, dimness, fogginess, cloudiness. **2** *a blur on the windscreen* smear, smudge, spot, blotch, blot, stain.

blurred *adjective* hazy, indistinct, faint, fuzzy, blurry, misty, foggy, unclear, vague, lacking definition, out of focus, nebulous.
Opposites CLEAR; DISTINCT; SHARP.

blurt *verb* **blurt out** call out, cry out, utter suddenly, exclaim, ejaculate, blab, disclose, divulge, reveal, let slip, babble, let the cat out of the bag, give the game away; *inf.* spill the beans, spout.

blush *verb* *blushing in embarrassment* redden, go pink/red, turn red/crimson/scarlet, flush, colour, crimson, burn up.

blush *noun* *hiding her blushes* flush; reddening, high colour, colour, rosiness, pinkness, ruddiness.

bluster *verb* **1** *wind blustering* blow fiercely, blast, gust, storm, roar. **2** *bullies blustering* rant, bully, domineer, hector, harangue, threaten, boast, brag, swagger, throw one's weight about, be overbearing, lord it, vaunt.

bluster *noun* **1** *the bluster of the wind* noise, roar, tumult, blasting, gusting, storming. **2** *the bullies' bluster* ranting, bravado, domineering, hectoring, bombast, boasting, bragging, swaggering, braggadocio; empty threats.

blustery *adjective* stormy, gusty, gusting, squally, wild, tempestuous; *inf.* blowy.

board *noun* **1** *a wooden board* plank, beam, panel, slat, length of timber, piece of wood. **2** *pay for one's board* food, sustenance; meals, daily meals, provisions, victuals; *inf.* grub, nosh. **3** *on the board of the firm* committee, council, panel, directorate, advisory group, advisorate, panel of trustees.

board *verb* **1** *board up the windows* cover up/over, close up, shut up, seal. **2** *they board with her* lodge, live, have rooms, room, be quartered, be housed. **3** *she boards three people* take in, put up, lodge, accommodate, house, feed. **4** *board the plane/train/bus* get on, enter, go on board, go aboard, step aboard, embark, mount; *fml.* emplane, entrain, embus.

BOARD GAMES	
backgammon	Monopoly™
checkers *Am.*	pachisi
chess	peggotty
Chinese chequers	Pictionary™
Chinese chess	race game
Cluedo™	Risk™
draughts	salta
fox and geese	Scrabble™
go	shogi
gobang	snakes and ladders
goose	solitaire
halma	steeplechase
kono	Trivial Pursuit™
ludo	uckers
mancala	wari
merrill	wei ch'i

board game *noun. See table.*

boast *verb* **1** *always boasting about his achievements* brag, crow, exaggerate, overstate, swagger, blow one's own trumpet, sing one's own praises, congratulate oneself, pat oneself on the back; *inf.* swank, talk big, blow hard. **2** *the town boasts two museums* possess, have, own, enjoy, pride oneself/itself on.
Opposites DEPRECATE; BELITTLE.

boast *noun* **1** *his boast is that he's best* brag, overstatement, self-praise, bluster, vaunt; bragging, crowing, blustering; *inf.* swank, swanking; *lit.* fanfaronade. *See* BOAST *verb* 1. **2** *the building is the boast of the town* pride, pride and joy, treasure, gem, pearl, valued object, source of satisfaction.

boastful *adjective* bragging, braggart, crowing, swaggering, cocky, conceited, arrogant, vain, egotistical, overbearing, blustering, overweening, vaunting; *fml.* vainglorious; *inf.* swanking, swanky, big-headed, swollen-headed.
Opposites MODEST; UNASSUMING.

boat *noun* vessel, craft. *See tables at* SAILING SHIP, SHIP.

bob *verb* **1** *bobbing in the water* move up and down, float, bounce, quiver, wobble. **2** *bobbed her head* nod, jerk, twitch, duck, waggle. **3** *bobbing on the dance floor* dance, bounce, skip, leap, jerk, weave.

bode *verb* augur, presage, portend, betoken, foretell, prophesy, predict, forebode, foreshadow, indicate, signify, purport.

bodily *adjective* *bodily functions/injuries* physical, corporeal, corporal, carnal, fleshly.

bodily *adverb* **1** *the audience rising bodily* as a body/group/mass, in a mass, as a whole, together, as one, collectively, en masse. **2** *threw him bodily into the river* wholly, completely, entirely, totally.

body *noun* **1** *well-formed bodies* frame, form, figure, shape, build, physique, framework, skeleton, trunk, torso. *See tables at* BONE, BRAIN, EAR, EYE, DIGESTION, GLAND, NERVE, TOOTH, VEIN, VERTEBRA. **2** *a body in the morgue* dead body, corpse, cadaver, carcass; remains, relics; *inf.* stiff. **3** *a lift accommodating six bodies* person, individual, being, human being, human, creature, mortal. **4** *the body of the plane* main part, principal part, hub, core. **5** *a body of water* mass, expanse, extent, aggregate. **6** *the body of political opinion* majority, preponderance, bulk, mass. **7** *the ruling body* group, party, band, association, company, confederation, bloc, congress, corporation, society. **8** *material with little body* substance, firmness, solidity, density, shape, structure.

bog *noun* marsh, marshland, swamp, mire, quagmire, morass, slough, fen; *dial.* sump.

bogged *verb* **bogged down** stuck, impeded, obstructed, halted, stopped, delayed, stalled, slowed down; trapped, entangled, ensnared.

bogey *noun* **1** *children imagining a bogey* bogeyman, evil spirit, bogle, ghost, apparition, spectre, phantom, hobgoblin, witch; *inf.* spook. **2** *always a bogey of mine* bugbear, pet hate, bane, anathema, bête noire, dread, bugaboo.

boggle *verb* **1** *boggled at paying so much* hesitate to, jib at, demur at, shrink/flinch from, hang back from, waver/falter at. **2** *they boggled at the sight* be surprised, take fright, start, be startled, be astounded/staggered, shy. **3** *the sight boggled my mind* startle, astound, astonish, amaze, overwhelm, shock, bowl over; *inf.* flabbergast.

bogus *adjective* fraudulent, counterfeit, fake, spurious, false, forged, sham, artificial, mock, make-believe, quasi, pseudo; *inf.* phoney, pseud.
Opposites GENUINE; AUTHENTIC.

bohemian *adjective* *a bohemian lifestyle* unconventional, unorthodox, nonconformist, offbeat, avant-garde, original, eccentric, alternative, artistic; *inf.* arty, arty-farty, way-out, off-the-wall, oddball.
Opposites CONVENTIONAL; CONSERVATIVE.

bohemian *noun* *bohemians of the 1960s* unconventional person, nonconformist, hippy, beatnik, drop-out, artistic person.

boil *verb* **1** *the soup is boiling* bubble, simmer, cook, seethe, heat, stew. **2** *boil the soup* bring to the boil, simmer, cook, heat. **3** *the sea was boiling* seethe, bubble, churn, froth, foam, fizz, effervesce, be agitated. **4** *the teacher was boiling* be/made angry/furious/indignant, rage, fume, seethe, rant, rave, storm, fulminate, bluster, explode, flare up; *inf.* blow one's top, fly off the handle, go off the deep end, hit the roof, go up the wall, blow a fuse.

boiling *adjective* **1** *boiling hot | boiling weather* very hot, scorching, roasting, baking, blistering, sweltering, searing, torrid. **2** *she was boiling at his insults* furious, incensed, fuming, enraged, infuriated, seething, indignant, irate, angry; *inf.* mad.

boisterous *adjective* **1** *boisterous children/parties* lively, active, bouncy, frisky, exuberant, spirited, noisy, loud, rowdy, unruly, wild, unrestrained, romping, rollicking, disorderly, rumbustious. **2** *boisterous winds* blustery, gusting, gusty, breezy, stormy, squally, rough, turbulent, raging, wild.
Opposites CALM; QUIET.

bold *adjective* **1** *a bold explorer | bold deeds* daring, intrepid, audacious, courageous, brave,

valiant, fearless, gallant, heroic, adventurous, enterprising, confident, undaunted, valorous. **2** *a bold young woman* brazen, shameless, forward, brash, impudent, audacious, cheeky, saucy, pert, immodest, unabashed, barefaced, bold as brass; *inf.* brassy. **3** *bold colours* striking, vivid, bright, eye-catching, conspicuous, distinct, pronounced, prominent, well-marked, showy, flashy.
Opposites TIMID; RETIRING; PALE.

bolshie *adjective* uncooperative, awkward, perverse, difficult, disobliging, stubborn, unhelpful, annoying; *inf.* bloody-minded.

bolster *noun* *laid his head on the bolster* pillow, cushion, pad, support.

bolster *verb* *bolster morale/bolster up the economy* strengthen, reinforce, support, boost, give a boost to, prop up, buoy up, shore up, hold up, maintain, buttress, aid, assist, help, revitalize, invigorate.

bolt *noun* **1** *window bolts* bar, catch, latch, lock, fastener, hasp. **2** *nuts and bolts* rivet, pin, peg. **3** *bolt of lightning* flash, shaft, streak, burst, discharge, flare. **4** *escape in one bolt |* *make a bolt for it* dash, dart, run, sprint, rush, bound, spring, leap, jump. **5** *firing bolts* arrow, dart, shaft, missile, projectile, thunderbolt, quarrel. **6** *a bolt of cloth* roll, quantity.

bolt *verb* **1** *bolt the door* bar, lock, fasten, latch. **2** *bolt the pieces together* rivet, pin, clamp, fasten, batten. **3** *they bolted from the room* dash, dart, run, sprint, hurtle, rush, bound, hurry, flee, fly, spring, leap, abscond, escape, make a break/run for it; *inf.* tear from. **4** *bolting his food* gulp, gobble, devour, wolf, guzzle, cram, stuff.

bolt *adverb* **bolt upright** straight up, very straight, rigid, stiff, completely upright.

bomb *noun* explosive, incendiary device, incendiary, blockbuster; missile, projectile, trajectile. *See tables at* EXPLOSIVE, MISSILE.

bomb *verb* bombard, blow up; shell, torpedo, blitz, strafe, cannonade.

bombard *verb* **1** *bombard military establishments* bomb, shell, torpedo, pound, blitz, strafe, pepper, cannonade, fusillade, fire at, attack, assault, raid. **2** *bombard with questions* assail, attack, besiege, beset, bother, subject to, hound, belabour.

bombardment *noun* **1** *the bombardment of London* bombing, shelling, strafing, torpedoing, blitz, blitzkrieg, air-raid, strafe, cannonade, fusillade, attack, assault. **2** *the bombardment of the film star with press questions* assailing, attack, besieging, barraging. *See* BOMBARD 2.

bombast *noun* pomposity, ranting, rant, bluster, turgidity, verbosity, pretentiousness, affectation, ostentation, grandiloquence, magniloquence, periphrasis, euphuism, fustian, braggadocio, rodomontade.

bona fide *adjective* genuine, authentic, real, true, actual, sterling, sound, legal, legitimate.

bonanza *noun* windfall, godsend, stroke/run of luck, boon, bonus.

bond *noun* **1** *the bond/bonds of friendship* tie, link, binding, connection, attachment, union, ligature, nexus. **2** *freed from his bonds* chains, fetters, shackles, manacles; rope, cord. **3** *enter into a bond*|*sign a bond* agreement, contract, pact, transaction, bargain, deal, covenant, compact, pledge, promise, treaty, concordat.

bond *verb* *bond the pieces of metal together* join, connect, fasten, stick, unite, attach, bind; glue, gum, fuse, weld.

bondage *noun* slavery, enslavement, captivity, servitude, thraldom, serfdom, oppression.

bone *noun*. *See table. See also table at* VERTEBRA.

bonus *noun* **1** *the pleasant environment was a bonus* extra, plus, gain, benefit, boon, perquisite, dividend, premium. **2** *a Christmas bonus* gratuity, tip, gift, perk, honorarium, reward, bounty, commission.
Opposites DISADVANTAGE; PENALTY.

bony *adjective* *a bony frame* angular, rawboned, gaunt, scraggy, scrawny, skinny, thin, emaciated, skeletal, cadaverous.

book *noun* **1** *read/publish a book* volume, tome, work, publication, title, opus, treatise, manual. *See tables at* LITERATURE, NOVEL. **2** *the exercise/rent book* booklet, pad, looseleaf notebook, notebook, jotter, ledger, log.

book *verb* **1** *book a room*|*book the seats/speaker* reserve, make reservations for, arrange in advance, engage, charter. **2** *book the meeting* arrange, programme, schedule, line up. **book in** *book in at the hotel*|*book in for the competition* register, enrol, enter, record/log one's arrival.

bookish *adjective* studious, scholarly, academic, literary, intellectual, brainy, highbrow, erudite, learned, pedantic, pedagoguish, bluestocking, impractical, ivory-towerish.

books *plural noun* *checking the books* accounts, records.

boom *verb* **1** *guns booming in the distance* resound, sound loudly, explode, bang, blast, blare, roar, bellow, rumble, reverberate, thunder. **2** *the teacher boomed* roar, bellow, shout, thunder. **3** *property market booming* burgeon, flourish, thrive, prosper, progress, do well, succeed, grow, develop, expand, increase, swell, intensify, mushroom, put on a spurt.

boom *noun* **1** *the boom of the guns* resounding, loud noise, explosion, banging, bang, blasting, blast, blare, roaring, roar, bellow, rumble, reverberation, thundering, thunder. **2** *the*

boom in private housing increase, upturn, upsurge, upswing, advance, growth, spurt, progress, development, expansion, improvement, boost, success.
Opposites DECLINE; SLUMP.

boomerang *verb* rebound, come back, spring back, return, recoil, reverse, ricochet, backfire.

boon *noun* benefit, advantage, gain, plus, bonus, good thing, blessing, godsend, windfall, perk, perquisite.
Opposites DISADVANTAGE; CURSE.

boon *adjective* *a boon companion* close, intimate, favourite, special, best, inseparable.

boor *noun* lout, oaf, rough, churl, philistine, vulgarian, yahoo, barbarian; *inf.* clodhopper, clod, peasant, yobbo, yob, plonker, casual.

boorish *adjective* rough, rude, coarse, ill-bred, ill-mannered, uncouth, churlish, gruff, uncivilized, unsophisticated, unrefined, crude, vulgar, gross, brutish, bearish, barbaric; *inf.* yobbish, clodhopping.
Opposites REFINED; CULTIVATED; SOPHISTICATED.

boost *verb* **1** *boost him up the tree* lift, raise, hoist, push, thrust, shove, heave, elevate, help, assist; *inf.* hoick. **2** *boost morale* raise, increase, improve, encourage, heighten, help, promote, foster, inspire, uplift. **3** *boost sales* increase, expand, raise, add to, improve, amplify, enlarge, inflate, promote, advance, develop, further, foster, facilitate, help, assist; *inf.* jack up, hike, hike up. **4** *boost their products* promote, advertise, publicize, praise, write up; *inf.* plug, give a plug to.
Opposites DECREASE; HINDER.

boost *noun* **1** *give him a boost into the tree* lift up, hoist up, push, thrust, shove, heave; *inf.* hoick up. **2** *give a boost to morale* uplift, shot in the arm; encouragement, help, inspiration, stimulus. **3** *a boost in sales* increase, expansion, rise, improvement, advance; *inf.* jacking up, hike. *See* BOOST *verb* 3. **4** *a boost for their products* promotion, advertisement, write-up; publicity, publicization; *inf.* plug, puff.

boot *noun* footwear; *inf.* welly, bovver boot. *See table at* FOOTWEAR.

boot *verb* **1** *boot the ball* kick, knock, punt. **2** *boot him out* throw out, kick out, dismiss, sack, expel, eject, oust. **3** *boot a computer* load, prepare, make ready.

HUMAN BONES

ankle-bone	femur	ischium	parietal	sesamoid	tarsal
anvil	fibula	jawbone	bone	bone	temporal
astragalus	floating rib	kneecap	patella	shin bone	bone
backbone	frontal bone	lunate bone	pelvis	shoulder	thigh
breastbone	funny bone	malleus	phalanx	blade	bone
calcaneus	hallux	mandible	pisiform	skull	tibia
carpal	hammer	maxilla	bone	sphenoid	ulna
cheekbone	heel bone	metacarpal	pubis	spinal	vertebra
clavicle	humerus	metatarsal	rachis	column	vertebral
collarbone	hyoid	nasal bone	radius	spine	column
costa	ilium	navicular	rib	stapes	vomer
cranium	incus	bone	sacrum	sternum	wrist-bone
cuboid	innominate	occipital	scaphoid	stirrup	zygomatic
ethmoid	bone	bone	scapula	talus	bone

booth noun **1** *market booth* stall, stand, counter. **2** *telephone booth* cubicle, compartment, enclosure, cupboard, carrel.

bootless adjective *bootless attempts* futile, vain, unsuccessful, useless, ineffective, ineffectual, abortive, unproductive, fruitless, unavailing; *lit.* Sisyphean.

booty noun spoil, loot, plunder, pillage, prize, haul; spoils, profits, pickings, takings, winnings; *inf.* swag, boodle, the goods.

bordello noun brothel, house of ill repute, house of prostitution, bawdy house, whorehouse, bagnio.

border noun **1** *the border of the lake/lawn* edge, verge, perimeter, boundary, margin, brink, skirt; fringes, bounds, limits, confines. **2** *passport checks at the border* frontier, boundary, march.

border verb **1** *woods bordering the fields* edge, skirt, bound. *See* BORDER *noun* 1. **2** *Portugal borders Spain* | *his garden borders on mine* adjoin, abut on, be adjacent to, be next to, neighbour, touch, join, connect, border on. **3** *border the skirt with lace* edge, fringe, hem, trim, bind, decorate, rim. **4** *border his territory* be/come close to, border on. **border on** *his reply is bordering on rudeness* | *bordering on the obscene* verge on, approximate to, approach, come close to, be near/similar to, resemble.

bore[1] verb *bore into the wood* | *bore a hole* pierce, perforate, puncture, penetrate, drill, tap, tunnel, burrow, mine, dig out, gouge out, sink.

bore[2] noun **1** *sink a bore to find oil* borehole, hole, shaft, tunnel. **2** *the bore of a rifle* calibre, diameter, gauge.

bore[3] verb *the talk/speaker bored her* weary, pall on, be tedious to, tire, fatigue, send to sleep, exhaust, wear out; bore to tears, bore to death, bore out of one's mind.
Opposites INTEREST; AMUSE; ENTERTAIN.

bore[4] noun tiresome person/thing, tedious person/thing, nuisance, bother, pest; *inf.* drag, pain, pain in the neck.

boredom noun tedium, tediousness, dullness, monotony, flatness, sameness, humdrum, dreariness, weariness, apathy, languor, ennui, world-weariness, malaise.
Opposites INTEREST; AMUSEMENT; ENTERTAINMENT.

boring adjective tedious, dull, monotonous, humdrum, repetitious, unvaried, uninteresting, unexciting, flat, dry-as-dust, weary, wearisome, tiring, tiresome; *inf.* samey.
Opposites INTERESTING; AMUSING; ENTERTAINING.

borrow verb **1** *borrow some money* ask for the loan of, receive/take as a loan, use/have temporarily; *inf.* cadge, mooch, scrounge, sponge, beg, bum. **2** *borrow another writer's plots* appropriate, commandeer, use as one's own, copy, plagiarize, pirate, take, adopt, purloin, steal, grab, filch, pinch, help oneself to, abstract, imitate, simulate. **3** *English borrowing words from French* adopt, appropriate, take in, take over, acquire, embrace.
Opposites LEND; LOAN.

bosom noun **1** *woman with a large bosom* breasts, bust, chest; *inf.* boobs, tits, knockers, bristols. **2** *bosom of the family/Church* heart, centre, core, midst, circle, protection, shelter, aegis. **3** *nurturing warm feelings in their bosoms* heart, soul, being; emotions, affections.

bosom adjective *bosom friends/companions* close, intimate, boon, confidential, dear, inseparable, faithful, thick as thieves.

boss noun *the boss of the factory* head, chief, manager, director, executive, administrator, leader, superintendent, supervisor, foreman, overseer, controller, employer, master, owner; *inf.* gaffer, governor; *Am. inf.* Mister Big, honcho, numero uno.

boss verb **1** *he's always bossing his brothers about* order about/around, give orders/commands to, bully, push around, domineer, dominate, ride roughshod over, control; throw one's weight about. **2** *he bosses the whole business* be in charge of, head, manage, run, administrate, direct, control, command, preside over, superintend, supervise, own.

bossy adjective domineering, dominating, overbearing, dictatorial, authoritarian, despotic, imperious, high-handed, autocratic.

botanist noun. *See table at* SCIENTIST.

botch verb *botch the situation/repair* bungle, do badly/clumsily, make a mess of, spoil, mar, muff, mismanage, mangle, fumble, throw a spanner in the works; *inf.* mess up, make a hash of, hash, foul up, screw up, blow, louse up, cock up, balls up.

both adjective/pronoun *both boys* | *both are here* the two, the two together.

bother verb **1** *don't bother your father* disturb, trouble, worry, pester, harass, annoy, upset, irritate, vex, inconvenience, provoke, plague, torment, nag, molest; *inf.* hassle, give someone a hard time, get in one's hair. **2** *don't bother yourself with that* | *don't bother* concern oneself, occupy/busy oneself, take the time, make the effort, trouble oneself, go to trouble, inconvenience oneself, worry oneself. **3** *it bothers me that I lost it* upset, trouble, worry, concern, distress, perturb, disconcert, fret.

bother noun **1** *don't go to any bother* trouble, effort, inconvenience, fuss, flurry, bustle, hustle and bustle, exertion, strain; pains; *inf.* hassle. **2** *what a bother we've missed it* nuisance, pest, annoyance, irritation, inconvenience, difficulty, problem, vexation. **3** *a bit of bother in the pub* trouble, disturbance, commotion, uproar, disorder, fighting, furore, brouhaha.

bottle noun **1** *a bottle of milk/wine* container; flask, carafe, decanter, pitcher, flagon, carboy, demijohn. *See table at* CHAMPAGNE. **2** *fond of the bottle* alcoholic drink, alcohol, drink, liquor; *inf.* booze. **3** *the bottle to fight* courage, bravery, nerve, boldness, confidence, daring, pluck; *inf.* guts, spunk.

bottle verb **bottle up** *bottle up feelings* keep back, suppress, restrain, keep in check, curb, contain, shut in, conceal.

bottleneck noun constriction, narrowing, obstruction, congestion, block, blockage, jam, hold-up.

bottom *noun* **1** *the bottom of the hill/pile* foot, lowest part/point, base. **2** *the bottom of the pillar* base, foundation, basis, support, pedestal, substructure, substratum, groundwork, underpinning. **3** *the bottom of the car* underside, lower side, underneath, undersurface, belly. **4** *the bottom of the sea* floor, bed, depths. **5** *the bottom of the garden* the furthest part, the farthest point, the far end. **6** *the bottom of the class* lowest level/position, least important/successful part, least honourable/valuable part. **7** *sitting on his bottom* hindquarters, buttocks; rear end, rear, seat, tail, posterior, rump; *inf.* backside, behind, bum, fundament, *derrière*, jacksy, arse; *Am. inf.* butt, ass. **8** *drinking too much was at the bottom of it* origin, cause, root, source, starting-point, core, centre, heart, base. **9** *get to the bottom of it* basis, foundation, reality, essence, nitty-gritty, substance; essentials.
Opposites TOP; APEX; SURFACE.

bottom *adjective on the bottom shelf* lowest, last, undermost, ground.
Opposites TOP; UPPER; HIGHEST.

bottomless *adjective* **1** *bottomless pit* deep, immeasurable, fathomless, unfathomable, unfathomed. **2** *bottomless reserves of energy* boundless, inexhaustible, infinite, unlimited, immeasurable.

bough *noun* branch, limb, twig.

boulder *noun* rock, stone.

boulevard *noun* avenue, drive, broad road, roadway, thoroughfare, promenade.

bounce *verb* **1** *the ball bounced* rebound, spring back, bob, recoil, ricochet, jounce. **2** *children bouncing about* leap, bound, jump, spring, bob, skip, prance, romp, caper, hurtle. **3** *bounce the troublemakers* throw out, eject, remove, expel, oust, get rid of, evict; *inf.* kick out, boot out.

bounce *noun* **1** *ball/material not having much bounce* spring, springiness, rebound, recoil, resilience, elasticity, give. **2** *losing bounce over the years* vitality, vigour, energy, vivacity, liveliness, life, animation, spiritedness, spirit, dynamism; *inf.* go, get-up-and-go, pep, oomph, pizazz, zing, zip. **3** *with a run and a bounce* leap, bound, jump, spring, bob, skip.

bouncing *adjective a bouncing young woman/baby | in bouncing health* robust, strong, vigorous, healthy, thriving, flourishing, blooming.

bound[1] *adjective* **1** *the bound prisoners* tied, tied up, secured, roped, tethered, fettered. *See* BIND *verb* 1. **2** *the bound sheets* fastened, secured, fixed, cased. **3** *she's bound to win* certain, sure, very likely, destined, predestined, fated. **4** *doctors bound by their professional code* obligated, obliged, duty-bound, constrained, pledged to, committed to, beholden to, compelled, required. **5** *a future bound up with hers* connected with, tied up with, allied to, attached to, dependent on. **6** *bound up in their own affairs* occupied with, busy with, preoccupied with, engrossed in, obsessed with.

bound[2] *verb bound over the fence | bound into the room* leap, jump, spring, bounce, hop, vault, hurdle, skip, bob, dance, prance, romp, caper, frisk, frolic, gambol, curvet.

bound[3] *noun reach the finishing-post in one bound | the bounds of the lambs* leap, jump, spring, bounce, hop, vault, hurdle; skip, bob, dance, prance, romp, caper, frisk, frolic, gambol, curvet.

bound[4] *verb* **1** *views bounded by prejudice* limit, confine, restrict, cramp, straiten, restrain, demarcate, delimit, circumscribe, define. **2** *estates bounded by walls* enclose, surround, wall in, encircle, hem in, circumscribe. **3** *Germany is bounded on the west by France | Germany bounds on France* border, adjoin, abut, be next/adjacent to, be contiguous with.

boundary *noun* **1** *the boundary between the countries* border, frontier, partition, dividing/bounding line. **2** *the boundary of the forest* bounds, border, periphery, perimeter; confines, limits, extremities, margins, edges. *See* BOUNDS 2. **3** *the boundary between sentiment and sentimentality* dividing line, borderline, demarcation line. **4** *pushing back the boundaries of knowledge* bounds, limits, outer limits, confines, extremities, barriers.

boundless *adjective* limitless, without limit, unlimited, illimitable, unbounded, endless, unending, never-ending, without end, inexhaustible, infinite, interminable, unceasing, everlasting, untold, immeasurable, measureless, incalculable, immense, vast, great.
Opposites LIMITED; RESTRICTED.

bounds *plural noun* **1** *within the bounds of possibility* limits, boundaries, confines, restrictions, limitations, demarcations. **2** *within the bounds of the estate* boundaries, borders, confines, limits, extremities, margins, edges, fringes, marches; periphery, perimeter, precinct, pale.

bountiful *adjective* **1** *a bountiful hostess* generous, magnanimous, liberal, kind, giving, open-handed, unstinting, unsparing, munificent, benevolent, beneficent, philanthropic; *fml.* eleemosynary. **2** *a bountiful supply of food* ample, abundant, bumper, superabundant, plentiful, copious, lavish, prolific, profuse, bounteous, princely, luxuriant, exuberant, plenteous.
Opposites MEAN; INHOSPITABLE; MEAGRE.

bounty *noun a bounty for finding the treasure* reward, recompense, remuneration, gratuity, tip, premium, bonus.

bouquet *noun* **1** *the bride carrying a bouquet* bunch/spray of flowers, spray, posy, wreath, garland, nosegay, boutonnière, chaplet, corsage, buttonhole. **2** *the wine's bouquet* aroma, smell, fragrance, perfume, scent, redolence, savour, odour; odiferousness. **3** *bouquets from the management* compliment, commendation, tribute, eulogy; praise; congratulations.

bourgeois *adjective* **1** *the bourgeois classes, not the nobility* middle-class, property-owning, propertied. **2** *bourgeois values* materialistic, capitalistic, non-Communist, money-oriented. **3** *bourgeois way of life* conventional, ordinary, uncultured, philistine, uncreative, unimaginative.

bout *noun* **1** *bouts of inactivity* spell, period, time, stretch, stint, turn, fit, run, session, round, season. **2** *a bout of flu* attack, fit, spell, paroxysm. **3** *defeated in the last bout* match, contest, round, competition, encounter, fight, struggle, set-to.

bovine *adjective* **1** *bovine creatures* cowlike, cattle-like. **2** *bovine people hating activity* lifeless, sluggish, stolid, inanimate, phlegmatic, torpid. **3** *too bovine to grasp the facts* stupid, thick, dense, slow, dim-witted, dull-witted, doltish.

bow¹ *verb* **1** *bow to the queen* incline the head/body, make obeisance, nod, curtsey, bob, genuflect, bend the knee, salaam, prostrate oneself. **2** *age had bowed his back* bend, stoop, curve, arch, crook. **3** *bow to the inevitable* give in, give way to, yield, submit, surrender, succumb, capitulate, accept, defer, acquiesce in, comply with, kowtow. **4** *enemy activities bowing down the tribes* subjugate, subdue, conquer, vanquish, overcome, crush, overpower, bring to one's knees, humble, humiliate. **5** *bowing them into the restaurant* usher, conduct, show, guide, direct, escort. **bow out** leave, resign, retire, withdraw, step down, give up, get out, quit, pull out, back out.

bow² *noun make a bow to the queen* inclination of the head/body, obeisance, nod, curtsey, bob, salaam; genuflection, prostration.

bow³ *noun the bow of a ship* prow, front, forepart, fore-end, stem, head, beak.

bowdlerize *verb* expurgate, censor, blue-pencil; *inf.* clean up.

bowel *noun* intestine, small intestine, large intestine, colon.

bowels *plural noun* **1** *an infection affecting the bowels* intestines, entrails, guts; *inf.* insides, innards; *fml.* viscera. **2** *the bowels of the earth/machine* interior, inside, core, belly, cavity; depths; *inf.* innards.

bower *noun* **1** *a bower in the garden* arbour, shady place, leafy shelter, alcove, pergola, grotto. **2** *taking tea in the bower* summerhouse, gazebo, conservatory. **3** *ladies' bowers* boudoir, chamber, bedroom.

bowl *noun* **1** *a bowl of fruit* dish, basin, vessel, container. **2** *the bowl of a tobacco pipe* hollow part, hollow, depression, dip. **3** *dust-bowl* hollow, crater, hole, depression, dip, valley. **4** *American football bowl* stadium, arena, amphitheatre, coliseum.

bowl *verb* **1** *bowl a fast ball* throw, pitch, hurl, fling, spin, send, deliver. **2** *bowl the balls in the skittles alley* roll, pitch. **3** *bowling along in their cars* trundle, move, travel, drive, go, proceed. **4** *bowl a wicket* strike, hit, knock. **bowl over 1** *bowled over by her beauty/news* overwhelm, astound, amaze, astonish, dumbfound, stagger, flabbergast, stun, surprise. **2** *bowl over an old woman* knock down, bring down, fell, floor.

box¹ *noun* **1** *a box of cigars/tea* container, receptacle, crate, case, carton, pack, package, chest, trunk, bin, coffer, casket. **2** *a theatre/telephone box* compartment, cubicle, enclosure, kiosk, cabin, hut.

box² *verb box the goods* package, pack, wrap, bundle up. **box in/up** enclose, shut in, hem in,

fence in, confine, restrain, constrain, cage in, coop up.

box³ *noun give him a box on the ears* thump, cuff, slap, punch. *See* BOX⁴ *verb* 2.

box⁴ *verb* **1** *he boxes professionally* fight, spar, grapple, take to fisticuffs. **2** *box him on the ears* strike, hit, thump, cuff, slap, punch, knock, wallop, batter, pummel, thwack, buffet; *inf.* belt, sock, clout, whack, slug, slam, whop.

boxer *noun* fighter, pugilist, prizefighter, sparring partner. *See table at* SPORT.

boxing *noun. See table.*

BOXING WEIGHT DIVISIONS

bantamweight	light heavyweight
cruiserweight	light middleweight
featherweight	lightweight
flyweight	light welter-
heavyweight	weight
junior lightweight	middleweight
light flyweight	welterweight

---

boy *noun* **1** *men and boys* youth, lad, youngster, young person, kid, schoolboy, junior, stripling, whippersnapper. **2** *send for the boy* page, servant, waiter, garçon, boots.

boycott *verb* **1** *boycott their company | the party* stay away from, ostracize, spurn, avoid, eschew, shun, reject, send to Coventry, blackball, blacklist. **2** *boycott their goods* ban, bar, black, blacklist, embargo, place an embargo on, prohibit, debar, outlaw, proscribe. ***Opposites*** WELCOME; SUPPORT; PROMOTE.

boyfriend *noun* sweetheart, young man, lover, man, suitor, admirer; *inf.* steady, date; *Am.* beau.

boyish *adjective* youthful, young, childlike, immature, adolescent, juvenile, childish, callow, green, puerile.

brace *noun* **1** *holding the pieces of metal in a brace* clamp, vice, fastener, coupling. **2** *the wall's brace* support, prop, beam, strut, stay, truss, reinforcement, buttress, shoring-up, stanchion. **3** *a brace of pheasants* two, couple, pair, duo. **4** *printing braces* bracket, parenthesis.

brace *verb* **1** *beams firmly braced* support, strengthen, reinforce, fortify, shore up, prop up, hold up, buttress. **2** *braced his foot against the wall* steady, secure, stabilize, make fast. **3** *brace oneself for the results* prepare, steady, strengthen, fortify, tense.

bracelet *noun. See table at* JEWELLERY.

bracing *adjective* invigorating, refreshing, stimulating, energizing, exhilarating, reviving, fortifying, strengthening, restorative, tonic, vitalizing, rousing, healthful, health-giving, fresh, brisk, crisp, cool. ***Opposites*** TIRING; TAXING.

bracket *noun* **1** *a wall bracket* support, prop, buttress. **2** *put the words in brackets* parenthesis, round bracket, square bracket, angle bracket, brace. **3** *in a different social/financial*

PARTS OF THE HUMAN BRAIN

amygdala	infundibulum
basal ganglia	insula
brainstem	medulla oblongata
Broca's area	meninges
central sulcus	mesencephalon
cerebellum	midbrain
cerebral aqueduct	neencephalon
cerebral cortex	optic chiasma
cerebrum	palaeencephalon
choroid plexus	pineal body
corpus callosum	pituitary gland
Deiters' nucleus	pons Varolii
diencephalon	prosencephalon
forebrain	putamen
fornix	rhombencephalon
globus pallidus	splenium
gyrus	telencephalon
hindbrain	thalamus
hypercolumn	ventricle
hypothalamus	vermis

bracket group, grouping, category, categorization, grade, grading, classification, class, set, section, division, order.

brackish *adjective* slightly salty/briny, saline, bitter, impure, undrinkable, unsavoury.

brag *verb* boast, crow, show off, bluster, blow one's own trumpet, sing one's own praises, pat oneself on the back; *inf.* talk big, blow hard, lay it on thick; *Am. inf.* shoot the bull, speak for Buncombe; *lit.* vaunt, roister, hyperbolize.

braggart *noun* boaster, brag, show-off, blusterer, trumpeter, braggadocio, fanfaronade, gasconader; *inf.* blow-hard, big-mouth, bag of wind, windbag, loud-mouth, gasbag, bullshitter, bull-shooter.

braid *verb* **1** *braid the thread/hair* weave, interweave, plait, entwine, twine, intertwine, interlace, twist, wind, interthread. **2** *braid the jacket* trim, decorate, edge, fringe, befrill.

braid *noun* **1** *trim it with braid* cord, thread, tape, twine, yarn. **2** *hair in braids* plait, pigtail.

brain *noun* **1** *studying the brain* cerebral matter; *fml.* encephalon. *See table.* **2** *have a good brain* mind, intellect, brainpower, intelligence, wit, head; powers of reasoning; *inf.* grey matter. **3** *one of the brains of our year* genius, intellectual, intellect, thinker, mind, scholar, mastermind, sage, pundit, polymath; *inf.* highbrow, egghead, Einstein.

brains *plural noun* not to have the brains to do it mind, intellect, intelligence, wit, head, sense, cleverness, brightness, understanding, shrewdness, sagacity, acumen, capacity, capability; *inf.* nous, savvy.

brainwashing *noun* indoctrination, inculcation, persuasion, conditioning, infixation.

brainy *adjective* clever, intelligent, bright, brilliant, smart, gifted.
Opposites STUPID; DULL.

brake *noun a brake on spending/enthusiasm* curb, check, damper, restraint, constraint, rein, control.

brake *verb brake approaching the junction* reduce speed, slow, slow down, decelerate, put on the brakes, hit the brake.

branch *noun* **1** *the branch of a tree* bough, limb, stem, twig, shoot, sprig, arm. **2** *the branch of the deer's antlers* offshoot, prong. **3** *the local branch of the bank* division, subdivision, section, subsection, department, part, wing, office. **4** *branches of the railway/stream* subdivision, subsidiary, tributary, feeder.

branch *verb* **1** *the road branches before the village | the road branched off* fork, divide, subdivide, furcate, bifurcate, divaricate; separate, diverge. **2** *they branched off from the motorway/topic* diverge from, deviate from, depart from, turn aside from, shoot off from, go off at a tangent to. **branch out** *the firm must branch out into new areas* extend, spread out, widen, broaden, diversify, open up, expand, enlarge, increase, proliferate, multiply.

brand *noun* **1** *a brand of canned soup* make, kind, type, sort, variety, line, label, trade name, trade mark, registered trade mark. **2** *her particular brand of humour* kind, type, sort, variety, style, stamp, cast. **3** *recognize the cow by its brand* identifying mark, identification, tag, marker, earmark. **4** *a brand on him for life* stigma, stain, blot, taint, slur.

brand *verb* **1** *identifying marks branded on cattle* burn, burn in, scorch, sear, stamp, mark. **2** *unhappy experiences branded on his mind* stamp, imprint, print, engrave, impress, fix. **3** *branded as a thief* stigmatize, mark, disgrace, discredit, denounce, besmirch, taint.

brandish *verb* wave, flourish, wield, raise, swing, shake, wag, display, flaunt, show off.

brash *adjective* **1** *a loud brash young man* bold, self-confident, self-assertive, audacious, aggressive, brazen, forward, cocky, impudent, insolent, impertinent, rude, cheeky. **2** *brash actions* hasty, rash, impetuous, impulsive, reckless, precipitate, careless, heedless, incautious. **3** *brash colours* loud, showy, garish, gaudy, ostentatious, vulgar, tasteless, tawdry.
Opposites RESERVED; CAUTIOUS; QUIET.

brass *noun*. See table.

brassy *adjective* **1** *a brassy blonde* loud, brazen, shameless, forward, bold, self-assertive, brash, pert, impudent, insolent, cheeky, flashy, vulgar, showy, garish; *inf.* pushy. **2** *brassy ornaments* brass, brazen, metallic. **3** *brassy music* blaring, loud, noisy, thundering, deafening, harsh, raucous, dissonant, cacophonous, jangling, grating, jarring, strident, piercing, shrill.

BRASS INSTRUMENTS

basset-horn	French horn	saxhorn
bass-horn	handhorn	slide
bombardon	helicon	trombone
bugle	horn	sousa-
cornet	mellophone	phone
cornopean	sackbut	trombone
euphonium	sarruso-	trumpet
flugelhorn	phone	tuba

brat noun imp, rascal, urchin, minx, whipper-snapper, spoiled brat.

bravado noun show of courage/confidence, swagger, swaggering, boldness, audacity, blustering, boasting, boastfulness, bragging, bombast, swashbuckling; *lit.* vaunting, braggadocio, fanfaronade.

brave adjective **1** *brave soldiers* courageous, valiant, intrepid, fearless, plucky, game, gallant, heroic, bold, daring, audacious, resolute, undaunted, dauntless, lion-hearted, valorous, doughty, mettlesome; *inf.* gutsy, spunky. **2** *a brave show* splendid, spectacular, fine, ostentatious, showy.
Opposites COWARDLY; FEARFUL; TIMID.

brave noun *Indian braves* warrior, soldier, fighter, fighting man.

brave verb *brave the weather* face, stand up to, endure, put up with, bear, suffer, withstand, defy, challenge, confront; bell the cat, beard the lion in his den, bite the bullet.

bravery noun courage, courageousness, valour, intrepidity, fearlessness, pluck, pluckiness, gameness, gallantry, heroism, boldness, daring, audacity, resolution, fortitude, grit, mettle, spirit, dauntlessness, doughtiness, hardihood; *inf.* guts, spunk.

bravo interjection well done!, take a bow!, encore!

brawl noun *a brawl in a public house* fight, affray, fracas, wrangle, mêlée, rumpus, scuffle, altercation, squabble, clash, quarrel, argument, disagreement, free-for-all, tussle, brouhaha, commotion, uproar, donnybrook; fisticuffs; *inf.* row, punch-up, scrap, ruckus.

brawl verb *brawling in the street* fight, wrangle, wrestle, scuffle, tussle, clash, battle, quarrel, argue, altercate; *inf.* row, scrap.

brawn noun brawniness, muscle, muscular strength, muscularity, burliness, heftiness, huskiness, physical strength, physique, robustness, might; *inf.* beefiness, beef.

brawny adjective muscular, burly, hefty, powerfully built, strong, robust, sturdy, powerful, strapping, husky, bulky, stalwart, mighty, sinewy, well-knit.
Opposites SCRAWNY; PUNY; WEAK.

bray verb whinny, neigh, hee-haw.

brazen adjective **1** *a brazen hussy* bold, audacious, defiant, forward, brash, presumptuous, pushing, impudent, insolent, impertinent, brassy, cheeky, pert, saucy, shameless, immodest, unashamed, unabashed; *inf.* pushy. **2** *brazen objects* brass, brassy, metallic.
Opposites RESERVED; MODEST; SHY.

brazen verb *brazen it out* be defiant, be unrepentant, be impenitent, be unashamed, be unabashed, stand one's ground, show a bold front, put a bold face on it.

breach noun **1** *a breach in the sea wall* break, rupture, split, crack, fissure, fracture, rent, rift, cleft, opening, gap, hole, aperture, chasm, gulf. **2** *a breach of the agreement | a breach of confidence* breaking, contravention, violation, infringement, non-observance, transgression, neglect, infraction; breach of promise, breach

of the peace. **3** *a breach in diplomatic relations | a breach between the two families* breaking-off, estrangement, separation, severance, parting, parting of the ways, division, rift, schism, disunion, alienation, disaffection, variance, difference, dissension, falling-out, quarrel, discord.

breach verb **1** *breach the enemy defences* break/burst through, rupture, split, make a gap in, open up. **2** *breach the contract/law* break, contravene, violate, infringe, defy, disobey, flaunt, transgress against, infract.

bread noun **1** *serve bread with the soup* white bread, brown bread. *See table.* **2** *earn the children's bread | our daily bread* food, nourishment, sustenance, subsistence, fare, nutriment, diet; provisions, victuals, viands; *fml.* aliment. **3** *spend the bread* money, cash, finance; funds; *inf.* dough, brass, dosh, the needful, the necessary, shekels, tin, dibs, spondulicks.

BREAD AND BREAD ROLLS

azyme	corn bread	pan loaf
bagel	crispbread	paratha
baguette	croissant	pikelet
bap	crumpet	pitta bread
bara brith	damper	platzel
barmbrack	dika bread	pone
barm cake	focaccia	poppadom
barracouta	French	pumper-
black bread	bread	nickel
breakfast	gluten	roti
roll	bread	rye bread
bridge roll	granary	schnecken
brioche	bread	scone
brownie	griddle	soda bread
Austral.	bread	sourdough
bun	manchet	split tin
challah	matzo	stollen
chapatti	muffin	stotty
ciabatta	nan bread	whole-grain
cob	panettone	bread

breadth noun **1** *the breadth of the room* width, broadness, wideness, thickness, span, spread. **2** *the breadth of her knowledge | the breadth of support* extent, extensiveness, scope, range, scale, degree, compass, spread, sweep, comprehensiveness, vastness, expanse, magnitude, measure, volume, immensity; dimensions. **3** *breadth of spirit* liberality, liberalness, broadmindedness, open-mindedness, freedom, latitude, magnanimity.

break verb **1** *break the cup/bag | broke his arm* smash, shatter, crack, fracture, split, burst, fragment, splinter, shiver, crash, snap, rend, tear, divide, sever, separate, part, demolish, disintegrate. **2** *the cup/bag/arm broke* smash, shatter, crack, fracture, split, burst, fragment, splinter, crash, snap, tear, sever, separate. **3** *the machine broke* become damaged, cease to operate/work/function, be unusable; *inf.* go kaput. **4** *the skin is not broken* pierce, puncture, perforate, penetrate, open up. **5** *break the law* contravene, violate, infringe, breach, commit a breach of, defy, disobey, flaunt, transgress against; *fml.* infract. **6** *break for tea* take a break, stop, pause, discontinue, rest, give up; *inf.* knock off, take five. **7** *break one's concentration/journey/sleep* interrupt, suspend, discontinue, cut, disturb, interfere with. **8** *break his resolve | it broke her morale* overcome, crush, overpower, overwhelm, subdue, defeat, cow, suppress, extinguish, weaken, impair, undermine, dispirit, demoralize, incapacitate, cripple, enfeeble. **9** *he broke under questioning* be overcome, crack, collapse, give in, yield, cave in, crumple, go to pieces. **10** *the recession/scandal broke him* ruin, crush, bring to one's knees, humble, degrade, reduce to nothing, bankrupt, make bankrupt, pauperize. **11** *break the news gently* tell, announce, impart, reveal, divulge, disclose, let out, make public, proclaim. **12** *break the record* beat, surpass, outdo, better, exceed, outstrip, top; *inf.* cap. **13** *break the code* decipher, decode, unravel, solve, figure out. **14** *the day/storm/scandal broke* begin, come into being, come forth, emerge, erupt, burst out, appear, occur. **15** *the weather broke* change, alter, vary, shift, metamorphose. **16** *break one's fall* cushion, soften, lessen, diminish, moderate. **17** *waves breaking against the sea wall* crash, hurl, dash, hit, collide with. **break away 1** *the prisoner broke away* run away, make a break for it, flee, make off, escape, decamp; *inf.* make a run for it, run for it, hook it, leg it. **2** *break away from the main political party* break with, detach oneself from, secede from, separate from, part company with, leave, form a splinter group. **break down 1** *the car broke down* stop working, cease to function, seize up, fail; *inf.* conk out, go kaput. **2** *the talks broke down | law and order broke down* fail, collapse, come to nothing, founder, fall through, come to grief, disintegrate; *inf.* fizzle out. **3** *he broke down and cried* lose control, collapse, cave in, crumble, be overcome, go to pieces, disintegrate, come apart at the seams; *inf.* lose one's cool, crack up. **4** *break down the resistance* overcome, crush, overpower, overwhelm, subdue, defeat, cow, suppress. See BREAK *verb* 8. **5** *break down and analyse the figures* separate/divide out, segregate, analyse, dissect, categorize, classify, itemize. **break in 1** *break in hurriedly* burst in, barge in, push/thrust one's way in. **2** *he broke in with his own comments* interrupt, butt in, intervene, cut in, intrude, interfere, put one's oar in. **3** *he broke in last night* break and enter, commit burglary, burgle, rob. **4** *break in the horse | break in the new recruits* train, tame, condition, prepare, initiate, show the ropes to. **5** *break in new shoes* begin to wear/use, become/get used to, accustom, habituate. **break into 1** *break into the conversation* interrupt, butt into, intervene in. **2** *break into a gallop/song* begin suddenly, commence, launch into, burst into, give way to. **3** *break into his savings* begin to use, use part of, open and use. **4** *break into the room hurriedly* burst/barge into, push/thrust one's way into. **5** *break into the house* burgle, rob. **break off 1** *break off a branch* pull off, snap off, detach, separate, sever. **2** *the handle broke off* come off, snap off, become detached, separate off, become separated/severed. **3** *break off diplomatic relations | broke off their engagement* end, bring to an end, terminate, stop, cease, finish, discontinue, call a halt to,

suspend, desist from. **break out 1** *break out of prison* escape, make one's escape, break loose, burst out, get free, free oneself, flee, abscond, bolt. **2** *war/fighting broke out* start/commence/occur suddenly, erupt, burst out, set in, arise. **3** *it's time she broke out and made her own decisions* become free/liberated, become emancipated, unshackle/unfetter oneself. **4** *break out in a rash* erupt, burst out. **5** *"Wait!" he broke out* exclaim, call out, cry, shout, utter, yell. **break up 1** *the meeting broke up at midnight | school breaks up tomorrow* adjourn, end, come to an end, stop, discontinue, terminate. **2** *the crowd broke up* disperse, scatter, disband, part, separate, go their separate ways, part company. **3** *the police broke up the crowd* disperse, scatter, disband, separate, put to rout, send off. **4** *the couple have broken up* separate, part, divorce, split up, dissolve a marriage/relationship, come to the parting of the ways. **5** *jealousy broke up their marriage* bring to an end, end, terminate, bring to a stop/halt, kill, destroy. **6** *breaking up at his jokes* laugh, burst out laughing, giggle, chuckle, chortle, guffaw, double up, split one's sides, hold one's sides; *inf.* fall about, be in stitches.

Opposites REPAIR; MEND; JOIN; ABIDE; OBEY.

break *noun* **1** *a break in the sea wall* crack, hole, gap, opening, gash, chink, fracture, split, fissure, tear, rent, rupture, rift, chasm, cleft. **2** *a break for tea* interval, stop, pause, halt, rest, respite, breathing-space, lull, interlude, intermission, recess; tea break, coffee break, supper break; *inf.* breather, breathing-spell, let-up, time out, down time. **3** *a weekend break* holiday, vacation, time off, recess. **4** *a break in their education* interruption, discontinuation, suspension, hiatus, lacuna. **5** *a break in the weather* change, alteration, variation. **6** *a break in diplomatic relations* rift, breach, split, rupture, discontinuation, schism, chasm, alienation, disaffection. **7** *although losing, we got a lucky break* stroke of luck, advantage, gain, opportunity, chance, opening.

breakable *adjective* fragile, frangible, frail, delicate, flimsy, insubstantial, brittle, crumbly, friable, not shatter-proof, destructible, gimcrack, jerry-built.

breakdown *noun* **1** *the car's/machine's breakdown* stopping, stoppage, seizing up, failure, malfunctioning; *inf.* conking-out. See BREAK *verb* break down 1. **2** *the breakdown of the talks* failure, collapse, foundering, falling-through; *inf.* fizzling-out. See BREAK *verb* break down 2. **3** *suffer a breakdown* collapse, nervous breakdown, loss of control, going to pieces, disintegration, caving-in; *inf.* crack-up. See BREAK *verb* break down 3. **4** *a breakdown of the figures* separation, division, segregation, itemization, analysis, dissection, categorization, classification.

breaker *noun children jumping over the breakers* wave, roller, comber, billow, surf; white horses.

break-in *noun break-ins in the neighbourhood* breaking and entering, house-breaking, burglary, forced/unlawful entry; robbery, theft. See BREAK *verb* break in 3.

breakneck *adjective* fast, rapid, speedy, swift, reckless, dangerous.

breakthrough *noun a breakthrough in cancer research* advance, step forward, leap, quantum leap, discovery, find, development, improvement; progress.

breakup *noun the breakup of their marriage/partnership* end, termination, cessation, dissolution, disintegration, splitting up, breakdown, failure, collapse, foundering. *See* BREAK *verb* break up 4, 5.

breakwater *noun* sea wall, jetty, embankment, barrier, mole, groyne.

breast *noun* **1** *her plump breasts* bust, bosom, chest, front, thorax; *inf.* boob, tit, knocker; *Tech.* mamma. **2** *warm feelings in their breasts* heart, soul, being, core, seat of the emotions/affections; feelings.

breath *noun* **1** *take a deep breath* gulp of air, inhalation, inspiration, exhalation, expiration, pant, gasp, wheeze; breathing, respiration. **2** *no breath left in him* breath of life, life, life force, animation, vital force. **3** *hardly a breath of air* breeze, puff, gust, waft, zephyr. **4** *a breath of spring* hint, suggestion, whiff, undertone, trace, touch, whisper, suspicion. **5** *stop for breath* break, interval, pause, lull, rest, respite, breathing-space; *inf* breather. **6** *all over in a breath* moment, instant, minute, second.

breathe *verb* **1** *she breathed deeply* respire, inhale, inspire, exhale, expire, puff, pant, gasp, wheeze, gulp. **2** *as long as he breathes* be alive, live, have life. **3** *breathe new life/courage into them* infuse, instil, inject, impart, imbue with, transfuse. **4** *breathe a message of love* whisper, murmur, sigh, say, utter, voice, articulate, express. **5** *her whole appearance breathed defiance* express, suggest, indicate, manifest, intimate, betoken, augur. **6** *the wind breathing through the trees* blow, whisper, murmur, sigh.

breather *noun* **1** *let's take a breather from work* break, interval, stop, pause, halt, rest, respite, lull, breathing-space, recess. *See* BREAK *noun* 2. **2** *I'm going out for a breather* breath of air, fresh air.

breathless *adjective* **1** *getting breathless climbing stairs* out of breath, wheezing, panting, puffing, gasping, choking, gulping, winded. **2** *breathless with excitement* agog, all agog, with bated breath, avid, eager, excited, on edge, on tenterhooks, in suspense, open-mouthed, anxious.

breathtaking *adjective* spectacular, impressive, magnificent, awesome, awe-inspiring, astounding, astonishing, amazing, thrilling, stunning, exciting.

breed *verb* **1** *lions breeding in captivity* reproduce, procreate, multiply, give birth, bring forth young, beget, propagate. **2** *breed horses* raise, rear, nurture. **3** *born and bred in the town* bring up, rear, raise, develop, educate, train, nurture. **4** *breed disease/discontent* cause, bring about, give rise to, create, produce, generate, arouse, stir up, induce, originate, occasion, make for.

breed *noun* **1** *a breed of cows* family, variety, type, kind, class, strain, stock, line. **2** *of European breed* stock, race, lineage, extraction, pedigree. **3** *a new breed of doctor* kind, type, variety, class, brand, strain.

breeding *noun* **1** *the season for breeding* reproducing, reproduction, generation, multiplying, propagation. *See* BREED *verb* 1. **2** *the breeding of horses/plants* raising, rearing, nurturing. **3** *a lady by breeding* upbringing, rearing, education, training, nurture. **4** *people of breeding* refinement, cultivation, culture, polish, civility, gentility, courtesy; manners.

breeze *noun* gentle wind, breath of wind, puff of air, zephyr, gust, flurry, waft, current of air, draught; sea breeze, land breeze, onshore breeze.

breeze *verb the family breezed along/in* stroll, sally, sail, sweep, glide, drift, flit.

breezy *adjective* **1** *a breezy day* windy, blowy, blustery, gusty, squally, airy, fresh. **2** *a breezy manner/individual* jaunty, cheerful, cheery, light-hearted, carefree, blithe, free and easy, easygoing, casual, airy, sprightly, lively, spirited, buoyant, sparkling, animated, vivacious, frisky, sunny; *inf.* bright-eyed and bushy-tailed.

brevity *noun* **1** *the brevity of the speech/report* shortness, briefness, conciseness, succinctness, compactness, terseness, economy of language, pithiness, crispness, concision, condensation, pointedness, curtness, compendiousness, brachylogy. **2** *the brevity of summer | the brevity of his life* shortness, briefness, transitoriness, transience, impermanence, ephemerality. *Opposites* VERBOSITY; LENGTH.

brew *verb* **1** *brew beer* make, ferment. **2** *brew tea* infuse, prepare. **3** *the tea is brewing* infuse, be in preparation; *dial.* mash. **4** *trouble is brewing* gather, gather force, form, loom, be in the offing, be imminent, be threatening, be impending, impend. **5** *brewing something evil* plot, scheme, hatch, plan, devise, invent, concoct, stir up, foment; *inf.* cook up.

brew *noun* **1** *favourite brew | home brew* drink, beverage, liquor, ale, beer, tea; infusion, preparation; witches' brew. **2** *a brew of sex, violence and horror* mixture, blend, concoction, potpourri, *mélange*, conglomeration.

bribe *noun give the minister a bribe to get the contract* inducement, enticement, lure, subornation, carrot, sop to Cerberus; *inf.* backhander, sweetener, graft, hush money, protection money, boodle, kickback; *Am. inf.* payola.

bribe *verb bribe the local mayor* buy off, corrupt, give an inducement to, suborn; *inf.* grease/oil the palm of, get at, pay off, give a backhander/sweetener to, fix, square.

bric-à-brac *noun* knick-knacks, trinkets, gewgaws, baubles, curios, ornaments, bibelots.

bridal *adjective* nuptial, marital, matrimonial, connubial, conjugal; *lit.* hymeneal, epithalamic.

bride *noun* newlywed, honeymooner, blushing bride; war bride, GI bride.

bridge *noun* **1** *a bridge over the river* arch, span, overpass, flyover, viaduct. *See table.* **2** *a bridge* *between the two families* bond, link, tie, connection, cord, binding.

bridge *verb* **1** *bridge the river* span, cross, cross over, go over, pass over, traverse, extend across, reach across, arch over. **2** *bridge our differences* join, unite, link, connect, tie, attach, bind, bridge the gap between.
Opposites DIVIDE; SEPARATE.

BRIDGES

Bridge	Location
Angostura Suspension Bridge	Venezuela
Bendorf Bridge	Germany
Bosporus Bridge	Turkey
Bridge of Sighs	Italy
Forth Bridge	U.K.
Gladesville Bridge	Australia
Golden Gate Bridge	U.S.A.
Hooghly River Bridge	India
Huang Ho Bridge	China
Humber Bridge	U.K.
Oland Island Bridge	Sweden
Pinang Bridge	Malaysia
Rio-Niteroi Bridge	Brazil
Second Narrows Bridge	Canada
Seven Mile Bridge	U.S.A.
Severn Bridge	U.K.
Sunshine Skyway	U.S.A.
Zarate-Brazo Largo	Argentina

---

bridle *noun* **1** *a horse's bridle* halter. *See table at* HARNESS. **2** *put a bridle on her tongue* curb, check, restraint, control.

bridle *verb* **1** *bridle your tongue/anger* curb, restrain, hold back, keep control of, keep in check, put a check on, check, govern, master, subdue. **2** *she bridled at his insults* bristle, get angry, become indignant, rear up, draw oneself up, feel one's hackles rise.

brief *adjective* **1** *a brief speech/report* short, concise, succinct, to the point, compact, terse, economic, pithy, crisp, condensed, compressed, pointed, curt, thumbnail, epigrammatic, sparing, compendious. **2** *brief summer days | a brief life* short, short-lived, fleeting, momentary, passing, fading, transitory, transient, temporary, impermanent, ephemeral, evanescent, fugacious. **3** *a brief skirt* short, scanty, skimpy. **4** *the boss was rather brief with him* short, abrupt, curt, sharp, brusque, blunt.
Opposites LONG; LENGTHY; LONG-DRAWN-OUT.

brief *noun* **1** *a brief of the proceedings* outline, summary, abstract, résumé, synopsis, précis, sketch, digest, epitome. **2** *the barrister's brief* argument, case, proof, data, defence, evidence, contention, demonstration. **3** *getting his brief for his new job* briefing, information, guidance, preparation, priming, data, intelligence; instructions, directions; *inf.* gen, run-down, low-down.

brief *verb* *brief the barrister/ambassador* instruct, inform, give instructions/information/directions, direct, guide, advise, prepare, prime; *inf.* give someone the gen/run-down/low-down, fill in, gen up, put someone in the picture.

briefing *noun* **1** *at a briefing to discuss the situation* conference, meeting, discussion, forum, seminar, symposium. **2** *recruits being given their briefing* brief, information, guidance, preparation; instructions, directions. *See* BRIEF *noun* 3.

briefly *adverb* **1** *he spoke briefly* concisely, succinctly, to the point, tersely, economically, sparingly. **2** *briefly, I want to say goodbye* in brief, concisely, succinctly, in a few words, in a nutshell. **3** *living briefly* fleetingly, momentarily, transitorily, transiently, temporarily, ephemerally.

brigade *noun* *fire brigade | the brigade of workers* group, band, team, squad, party, association, body, contingent, crew, force, outfit, section, organization.

brigand *noun* robber, bandit, outlaw, ruffian, desperado, plunderer, marauder, gangster, criminal, highwayman, pirate, freebooter.

bright *adjective* **1** *a bright light* shining, brilliant, vivid, intense, blazing, dazzling, beaming, sparkling, flashing, glittering, scintillating, gleaming, glowing, twinkling, glistening, shimmering; illuminated, luminous, lustrous, radiant, effulgent, incandescent, phosphorescent. **2** *a bright day* clear, cloudless, unclouded, fair, sunny, pleasant, clement. **3** *bright colours* vivid, brilliant, intense, glowing, bold, rich. **4** *bright children/minds* clever, intelligent, sharp, quick-witted, quick, smart, brainy, brilliant, astute, acute, ingenious, inventive, resourceful, proficient, accomplished. **5** *a bright smile/personality* happy, genial, cheerful, jolly, joyful, gay, merry, light-hearted, vivacious, lively, buoyant. **6** *a bright future* promising, optimistic, hopeful, favourable, propitious, auspicious, providential, encouraging, lucky, fortunate, good, excellent, golden.
Opposites DULL; DARK; STUPID

brighten *verb* **1** *lights brightening the room* make bright/brighter, light up, lighten, illuminate, illumine, irradiate. **2** *her mood brightening* cheer up, perk up. **3** *brightening her day/mood* cheer up, gladden, enliven, buoy up, animate; *inf.* buck up, pep up.

brilliance *noun* **1** *the brilliance of the lights* brightness, vividness, intensity, blaze, beam, dazzle, sparkle, flash, glitter, luminosity, lustre, radiance, effulgence, refulgence, resplendence. **2** *the brilliance of the spectacle* magnificence, splendour, splendidness, grandeur, glamour, pomp, lustre, resplendence, illustriousness, éclat.

brilliant *adjective* **1** *a brilliant light* bright, shining, vivid, intense, ablaze, radiant, beaming, gleaming, dazzling, luminous, lustrous, scintillating, resplendent, effulgent, refulgent, coruscating. **2** *brilliant children* bright, clever, intelligent, smart, brainy, intellectual, gifted, talented, accomplished, educated, scholarly, learned, erudite, cerebral, precocious. **3** *a brilliant course of action* clever, intelligent, smart, astute, cute, acute, masterly, resourceful, inventive, discerning. **4** *a brilliant display* magnificent, splendid, superb, impressive, remarkable, exceptional, glorious, illustrious.

5 *having a brilliant time | a brilliant film* excellent, superb, very good, outstanding, exceptional; *inf.* brill.
Opposites DARK; DIM; STUPID.

brim *noun* **1** *the brim of the cup | full to the brim* rim, lip, brink, edge. **2** *the brim of the hat/cap* projecting edge, visor, shield, shade.

brim *verb the cup was brimming | eyes brimming with tears* be full, be filled up, be filled to the top, be full to capacity, overflow, run/well over.

brimful *adjective* brimming, full, filled, over-full, running over, flush.

bring *verb* **1** *bring books/water* come conveying/carrying, carry, bear, take, fetch, convey, transport, send, deliver, lead, guide, conduct, usher, escort. **2** *war brought hardship* cause, create, produce, result in, wreak, effect, contribute to, engender, occasion. **3** *bring a legal action* put forward, prefer, propose, initiate, institute. **4** *his job brings him a huge wage* make, fetch, yield, net, gross, return, produce, command. **bring about 1** *bring about reforms* cause to happen/occur, cause, create, produce, give rise to, achieve, result in, effect, occasion, bring to pass, effectuate. **2** *bring a ship about* turn, turn round, reverse, reverse the direction of. **bring down 1** *bring down prices* cause to fall, lower, reduce, cut. **2** *bring down the government* cause to fall, overthrow, pull down, lay low. **3** *the bad news brought her down* depress, sadden, cast down, make desolate, weigh down. **bring forward** *bring forward points for discussion* raise, put forward, propose, suggest, table, adduce. **bring in** *his son/job brings in £3000* earn, yield, gross, net, return, fetch in, realize. **2** *bring in a new bill* introduce, launch, inaugurate, initiate, institute, usher in. **bring off** *bring off the attempt* pull off, carry off, achieve, succeed in, accomplish, bring about, carry out, execute, perform, discharge, complete. **bring up 1** *bring up the children* rear, raise, train, educate, care for, nurture, foster, develop. **2** *bring up the subject* raise, broach, introduce, mention, allude to, touch upon, propose, submit.

brink *noun* **1** *the brink of the cliff/lake* edge, verge, margin, rim, extremity, limit, border, boundary, fringe, skirt. **2** *on the brink of disaster* verge, edge, threshold, point.

brisk *adjective* **1** *at a brisk pace* quick, rapid, fast, swift, speedy, energetic, lively, vigorous, agile, nimble, spry, sprightly, spirited, alacritous. **2** *brisk weather* bracing, fresh, crisp, keen, biting, invigorating, refreshing, exhilarating, energizing; *inf.* nippy. **3** *a brisk manner | brisk speech* no-nonsense, brusque, abrupt, sharp, curt, crisp, snappy. **4** *business was brisk* rapid, busy, bustling, active, hectic.
Opposites SLUGGISH; QUIET.

bristle *noun* **1** *shave off his bristles* hair, stubble, designer stubble; whiskers. **2** *a hedgehog's bristles* prickle, spine, quill, thorn, barb.

bristle *verb* **1** *the dog's hair bristled* rise, stand up, stand on end, horripilate. **2** *she bristled at the insults* bridle, get angry/infuriated, become indignant, be irritated/defensive, rear up, draw oneself up. **3** *a place bristling with tourists* swarm, teem, crawl; *inf.* be thick, be alive.

bristly *adjective* hairy, stubbly, unshaven, whiskered, whiskery, bewhiskered, bearded, rough, prickly.

brittle *adjective* **1** *a brittle substance* breakable, splintery, shatterable, hard, crisp, fragile, frail, delicate, frangible. **2** *a brittle laugh* harsh, hard, sharp, strident, grating, rasping. **3** *a brittle young woman* edgy, on edge, nervous, nervy, tense, stiff; *inf.* uptight.

broach *verb* **1** *broach the subject* introduce, bring up, raise, mention, open, put forward, propound, propose, suggest, submit. **2** *broach a bottle* open, uncork, start; *inf.* crack. **3** *broach a barrel* pierce, puncture, tap, draw off.

broad *adjective* **1** *a broad street* wide, large. **2** *broad plains* extensive, vast, spacious, expansive, sweeping, boundless. **3** *offers a broad range of subjects* wide, wide-ranging, broad-ranging, general, comprehensive, inclusive, encyclopedic, all-embracing, universal, unlimited. **4** *the broad outline of the plan* general, undetailed, non-detailed, non-specific, unspecific, vague, loose. **5** *a broad hint* clear, obvious, direct, plain, explicit, straightforward, clear-cut, unmistakable, undisguised, unconcealed. **6** *broad daylight* full, complete, total, clear, open. **7** *a woman of broad views* broad-minded, liberal, open-minded, tolerant, unprejudiced, unbiased, fair, just, free-thinking, progressive. **8** *somewhat broad humour* coarse, vulgar, gross, unrefined, indelicate, indecent, improper, blue; *inf.* near the bone/knuckle.
Opposites NARROW; LIMITED; DETAILED.

broadcast *verb* **1** *broadcast programmes* transmit, relay, beam, send out, put on the air, radio, televise, telecast. **2** *broadcast the news of his downfall* make public, announce, report, publicize, publish, advertise, proclaim, air, spread, circulate, pass round, disseminate, promulgate, blazon. **3** *broadcast seed* scatter, sow, disperse, strew.

broadcast *noun appear on a radio/television broadcast* programme, radio/television show, show, transmission, telecast.

broaden *verb* **1** *broaden the road* make broader, widen, make wider. **2** *his shoulders broadened* become broader, widen, become wider, fill out. **3** *broaden his knowledge/experience/horizons* widen, expand, enlarge, extend, increase, augment, supplement, add to, amplify, fill out, develop, open up, swell.

broad-minded *adjective* open-minded, liberal, tolerant, forbearing, indulgent, impartial, unprejudiced, unbiased, unbigoted, undogmatic, catholic, flexible, dispassionate, just, fair, progressive, free-thinking.

broadside *noun* **1** *fire a broadside in war* volley, salvo, cannonade, barrage. **2** *receive broadsides from the press* attack, criticism, censure, assault, onslaught, abuse, battering, harangue, diatribe, philippic; *inf.* slating, flak, brickbats.

brochure *noun* booklet, leaflet, pamphlet, folder, handbill, hand-out, circular, notice, advertisement; *Am.* flyer.

broil *verb* **1** *broil meat* grill, barbecue, fry, toast. **2** *he was broiling in the sun* be hot, be roasting, be burning, be boiling.

broiling *adjective* *a broiling day* hot, scorching, roasting, boiling/burning hot, blistering, blistering/searing hot.

broke *adjective* penniless, moneyless, bankrupt, insolvent, poverty-stricken, impoverished, impecunious, penurious, indigent, destitute, ruined, without a penny to one's name, stony-broke, flat broke; *inf.* on one's uppers, cleaned out, strapped for cash, on one's beam ends, bust, skint.

broken *adjective* **1** *a broken cup/bag/arm* smashed, shattered, cracked, fractured, split, burst, fragmented, splintered, shivered, crushed, snapped, rent, torn, separated, severed, destroyed, demolished, disintegrated. **2** *the machine is broken* damaged, faulty, defective, out of order/commission, non-functioning, inoperative; kaput, bust. **3** *broken skin* pierced, punctured, perforated. **4** *broken laws* contravened, violated, infringed, disobeyed, disregarded, ignored, flaunted, transgressed, infracted. **5** *a broken sleep/journey | a broken chain of thought* interrupted, disturbed, disconnected, disrupted, discontinuous, fragmentary, incomplete, intermittent, spasmodic, erratic. **6** *a broken man/army* beaten, defeated, vanquished, overpowered, overwhelmed, subdued, crushed, humbled, dishonoured, ruined, crippled, demoralized, dispirited, discouraged. **7** *broken firms* ruined, crushed, bankrupt, bankrupted, pauperized, brought low, humbled. **8** *broken English* halting, hesitating, disjointed, faltering, stumbling, stammering, imperfect.

broken-down *adjective* **1** *a broken-down machine* broken, damaged, faulty, defective, out of order/commission, non-functioning, inoperative; *inf.* on the blink, kaput, bust, clapped out. **2** *a broken-down old cottage* dilapidated, in disrepair, ramshackle.

broken-hearted *adjective* heartbroken, grief-stricken, desolate, despairing, devastated, inconsolable, prostrated, miserable, overwhelmed, wretched, sorrowing, mourning, forlorn, woeful, bowed down, crestfallen.

broker *noun* agent, negotiator, middleman, intermediary, factor, dealer, broker-dealer, stockbroker, insurance broker.

bronze *adjective* bronze-coloured, copper-coloured, copper, reddish-brown, chestnut, metallic brown, rust-coloured, rust, henna.

brooch *noun* pin, clip, breast-pin, tie-pin, tie-clip.

brood *noun* **1** *the hen and her brood* young, offspring, progeny, family, hatch, clutch, nest, litter. **2** *Mrs Smith and her brood* children, offspring, family; youngsters; *inf.* kids.

brood *verb* **1** *brood over/about the problem* worry, fret, agonize, think, ponder, meditate, muse, mull, dwell upon, ruminate. **2** *hens brooding* sit on/hatch/incubate eggs, cover young.

brook *noun* *a mountain brook* stream, streamlet, burn, rivulet, rill, brooklet, runnel; *dial.* beck, gill.

brook *verb* *brook no delay* tolerate, stand, bear, allow.

brothel *noun* bordello, house of ill repute, house of prostitution, bawdy house, whorehouse, bagnio; *inf.* knocking-shop.

brother *noun* **1** *she has two brothers* sibling, sib, blood-brother; kinsman. **2** *brothers in crime* associate, colleague, companion, partner, comrade; *inf.* mate, pal, chum; *fml.* confrère, compeer. **3** *brothers praying* cleric, monk, friar, religious.

brotherhood *noun* **1** *ties of brotherhood* brotherliness, fraternalism, kinship. **2** *feelings of brotherhood* comradeship, fellowship, companionship, camaraderie, friendship, *esprit de corps*. **3** *a brotherhood of merchants* association, alliance, society, union, league, guild, coalition, affiliation, consortium, fraternity, club, lodge, sodality, clique, coterie.

brotherly *adjective* **1** *siblings ignoring brotherly ties* fraternal. **2** *the Bible tells us to practise brotherly love* friendly, affectionate, amicable, kind, kindly, cordial, sympathetic, benevolent, neighbourly, philanthropic, charitable, altruistic.

brow *noun* **1** *furrowing her brow* forehead, temple. **2** *plucking her brows* eyebrows. **3** *the brow of the hill* top, summit, peak, crown, apex, brink.

browbeat *verb* bully, force, coerce, compel, badger, dragoon, intimidate, tyrannize, hector, terrorize; *inf.* bulldoze.

brown *adjective* **1** *of a brown colour | brown hair/ horses* dark brown, blackish-brown, cocoa, fuscous, reddish-brown, copper-coloured, coppery, henna, walnut, brick, yellowish-brown, light brown, donkey brown, brunette; bay, sorrel, roan. *See table at* COLOUR. **2** *brown bodies in the sun* tanned, sunburnt, browned, bronze, bronzed.

brown *verb* *brown the meat* sear, seal, fry, grill, sauté.

browned off *adjective* fed up, discontented, disgruntled, discouraged, disheartened, bored, weary; *inf.* hacked off.

browse *verb* **1** *not reading in detail, just browsing* scan, skim, glance/look through, thumb/leaf/flip through, dip in. **2** *not buying anything, just browsing* look round, have a look, window-shop, peruse. **3** *cows browsing* graze, feed, eat, nibble, crop, pasture.

bruise *verb* **1** *bruise the skin* make black and blue, discolour, blacken, mark, blemish, contuse, injure, hurt. **2** *bruise the fruit* damage, mark, discolour, spoil, blemish. **3** *her feelings are easily bruised* hurt, upset, offend, insult, wound, displease, peeve, vex, distress.

bruise *noun* *a bruise on her face* black-and-blue mark, skin discoloration, blackening, mark, blemish, contusion, injury, swelling, oedema.

brunette *adjective* dark, dark-haired, brown-haired, black-haired, darkish.

brunt *noun* *bear the brunt of it* full force, force, impact, shock, burden, thrust, violence, pressure, strain, stress; repercussions, consequences.

brush noun **1** *sweep/clean/paint with a brush* broom, besom, whisk, sweeper, sweeping brush, hairbrush, clothes brush, scrubbing brush, toothbrush, paintbrush. **2** *with a brush of his arm* touch, stroke, hit; *inf.* swipe. **3** *a brush with the law/enemy* encounter, clash, conflict, confrontation, skirmish, tussle, fight, battle, engagement; *inf.* scrap, set-to. **4** *lost in the brush* brushwood, undergrowth, underwood, scrub, wood, thicket, copse; bushes.

brush verb **1** *brush the floor|brush one's clothes/teeth* sweep, groom, clean, buff. **2** *lips brushing her cheek* touch, flick, caress, kiss, glance, contact, stroke, sweep, scrape. **brush aside** *brush aside his objections* put aside, sweep aside, dismiss, shrug off, disregard, ignore, think no more of, forget about, have no time for. **brush off** *brush him off* cold-shoulder, rebuff, snub, cut, dismiss, ignore, spurn, slight, disregard, reject, repudiate, refuse, disown, deny, scorn, disdain. **brush up** **1** *brush up his French* revise, read up, polish up, go over, study, refresh one's memory of, relearn, cram; *inf.* rub up, bone up. **2** *brush yourself up* smarten, clean up.

brusque adjective abrupt, curt, blunt, short, sharp, terse, caustic, gruff, bluff, hasty, outspoken, plain-spoken, discourteous, impolite, rude, churlish.
Opposites POLITE; COURTEOUS.

brutal adjective **1** *a brutal attack/murderer* savage, cruel, bloodthirsty, vicious, ruthless, callous, heartless, merciless, pitiless, remorseless, uncivilized, inhuman, barbarous. **2** *brutal instincts* bestial, brutish, beastly, animal, coarse, carnal, sensual.
Opposites GENTLE; HUMANE; CIVILIZED.

brute noun **1** *jungle brutes* beast, wild beast, wild animal, animal, creature. **2** *a murderous brute|a brute to his wife and children* beast, monster, animal, swine, savage, sadist, barbarian, devil, fiend, ogre. **3** *that brute of a neighbour was rude* lout, oaf, boor, churl, dolt.

bubble noun **1** *blowing soap bubbles|bubbles in champagne* globule, glob, bead, blister, drop, droplet, vesicle, air cavity. **2** *the property bubble* illusion, delusion, fantasy, dream, chimera.

bubble verb **1** *champagne bubbling* fizz, effervesce, sparkle, foam, froth, spume. **2** *stew bubbling on the stove* boil, simmer, seethe, percolate. **3** *bubble with happiness* overflow, brim over, be filled.

bubbly adjective **1** *bubbly mineral water|bubbly detergent* fizzy, effervescent, carbonated, sparkling, foamy, frothy, sudsy. **2** *a bubbly personality* bubbling, vivacious, effervescent, sparkling, animated, ebullient, scintillating, bouncy, buoyant, excited, elated, lively, merry, happy.

buccaneer noun pirate, corsair, sea rover, freebooter, Viking.

buck verb **buck up** **1** *buck up or you'll be late* hurry, hurry/speed up, make haste, hasten, rush; *inf.* get a move on, step on it, shake a leg. **2** *buck up, don't be sad* cheer up, perk up, take heart, rally. **3** *a holiday will buck you up* cheer up, perk/brighten/buoy up, enliven, gladden, make happier.

bucket noun pail, scuttle, can, pitcher.

buckle noun **1** *the belt buckle* clasp, clip, catch, fastener, fastening, hasp. **2** *a buckle in the railway track* kink, warp, curve, distortion, wrinkle, bulge.

buckle verb **1** *buckling his trousers* fasten, hook, strap, tie, secure, clasp, catch, clip. **2** *the railway track buckled* become warped, become twisted, become curved, become distorted, become contorted, develop a kink/wrinkle/fold, bulge, crumple, cave in.

bucolic adjective rural, rustic, pastoral, country, agricultural.

bud noun *buds on the flowers/trees* shoot, sprout, burgeon, flowerlet, floret.

bud verb *flowers/trees were budding* sprout, send out shoots, form/develop buds, germinate, burgeon, pullulate.

Buddhism noun. *See table at* RELIGION.

budding adjective promising, potential, developing, beginning, fledgling, growing, burgeoning, incipient, embryonic, nascent.

budge verb **1** *the car won't budge* move, shift, stir, go, proceed. **2** *I can't budge the car* move, shift, remove, dislodge, get/set going. **3** *he's obstinate so he won't budge* change one's mind, give way, give in, yield, acquiesce. **4** *you won't budge him as he's determined* influence, sway, convince, persuade, bend.

budget noun **1** *draw up a budget for the year* financial plan/estimate/statement/blueprint. **2** *be over budget for the term* allowance, allocation, allotment, quota, ration.

budget verb **1** *budget her money/time* plan, schedule, allocate, ration, apportion. **2** *budget for a new car|we can budget £5000* plan, allow, save, set aside money, set aside.

buff adjective *buff envelopes* beige, straw-coloured, sandy, yellowish, yellowish-brown.

buff verb *buff one's nails|buff metal* polish, burnish, rub up, rub, smooth, polish, shine.

buff noun *a theatre buff* fan, enthusiast, devotee, aficionado, addict, admirer, expert; *inf.* freak.

buffer noun cushion, bulwark, guard, safeguard, shield, screen, intermediary.

buffet[1] noun **1** *the station buffet* café, cafeteria, snack bar, salad bar, refreshment stall/counter. **2** *a wedding buffet* cold table, cold meal, smorgasbord, self-service. **3** *buying a buffet for the dining room* sideboard, cabinet, china cabinet/cupboard.

buffet[2] noun **1** *a buffet on the head* blow, slap, smack, bang, box, cuff, thump, wallop, clout, whack, thwack, battering, knock, rap, poke, jab. **2** *the buffets of life* shock, jolt, jar.

buffet[3] verb **1** *winds buffeting the trees* batter, beat/knock against, strike, hit, bang, push against. **2** *robbers buffeted the old man* slap, smack, thump, wallop, clout, whack, thwack, cuff.

buffoon noun **1** *the buffoons in Shakespeare's plays* fool, clown, jester, comic, comedian, wit, wag, merry andrew, droll. **2** *he's just a buffoon* fool, dolt, idiot, nincompoop; *inf.* chump, numskull, dope, twit, nitwit, halfwit.

bug *noun* **1** *bitten by bugs* insect, flea, mite; *inf.* creepy-crawly. **2** *an illness caused by a bug* | *he's caught a bug* bacterium, germ, virus, microorganism; infection. **3** *he's caught the dancing bug* craze, fad, mania, obsession, passion, fixation. **4** *get rid of all the bugs in the machine* fault, flaw, defect, imperfection, failing, error, obstruction, gremlin; *inf.* snarl-up. **5** *place a bug in the phone* listening device, wire-tap, phone-tap, tap.

bug *verb* **1** *they've bugged his phone* tap, wire-tap, phone-tap. **2** *bugging his conversation* tap, listen in, eavesdrop on. **3** *he really bugs me* annoy, irritate, exasperate, anger, irk, vex, infuriate, inflame, provoke, try one's patience, get one's hackles up; *inf.* get one's back up, get on one's nerves, get in one's hair, be a thorn in one's flesh.

bugbear *noun* bane, anathema, abomination, pet hate, hate, bogey, nightmare, horror, dread, *bête noire*.

build *verb* **1** *build a house/road/car* construct, erect, put up, assemble, set up, raise, make, manufacture, fabricate, form. **2** *hopes built on false premises* found, base, establish. **3** *build a business from nothing* | *build a new career* establish, found, set up, originate, institute, start, begin, inaugurate, initiate, develop. **build up 1** *build up a business* establish, develop, expand. See BUILD *verb* 3. **2** *build up her morale* boost, strengthen, increase. **3** *build up the product* advertise, promote, publicize, puff; *inf.* plug, hype. **4** *important to build up his strength* develop, increase, improve, strengthen, augment, intensify, escalate. **5** *the wind is building up* strengthen, get stronger, increase, intensify, escalate.

Opposites DEMOLISH; DISMANTLE; DESTROY.

build *noun* *of a heavy build* body, frame, physique, figure, form, structure, shape.

building *noun* **1** *putting up new buildings* structure, construction, edifice, erection, pile. See table. **2** *the building of new houses* construction, erection, putting up, raising.

build-up *noun* **1** *the build-up of resources* expansion, increase, growth, enlargement, escalation, development, accumulation. **2** *the build-up of paperwork/traffic* accumulation, stockpile, accretion, mass, heap, store, stack, pile. **3** *tired of the play's/product's build-up* promotion, publicity, advertising, puff; *inf.* hype, plugging, plug, ballyhoo.

built-in *adjective* **1** *built-in wardrobes* integral, integrated, incorporated. **2** *built-in disadvantages* in-built, inherent, intrinsic, incorporated, inseparable, included, essential, implicit.

bulge *noun* **1** *a bulge in her pocket* | *body bulges* swelling, bump, lump, protuberance, protrusion, prominence, projection. **2** *a population bulge* boost, increase, rise, surge, intensification, augmentation.

bulge *verb* *with pockets/stomach bulging* swell, swell out, puff up/out, stick out, bag, belly, balloon, balloon up/out, project, protrude, jut out, distend, expand, dilate, enlarge, bloat.

bulk *noun* **1** *the sheer bulk of the rubbish/work* size, volume, bulkiness, quantity, weight, extent, mass, substance, magnitude, massiveness, hugeness, largeness, bigness, ampleness,

---

BUILDINGS

Building	Location	Building	Location
Alhambra	Granada, Spain	Pantheon	Rome
		Parliament House	Vienna
Blue Mosque	Istanbul	Parthenon	Athens
Buckingham Palace	London	Pennsylvania Station	New York
Casa Milá	Barcelona	Pompidou Centre	Paris
Chartres Cathedral	France	President's Palace	Brasília
Chrysler Building	New York	Pyramids	Egypt
Cologne Cathedral	Germany	Reims Cathedral	France
Colosseum	Rome	Sagrada Familia	Barcelona
Dome of the Rock	Jerusalem	St Basil's Cathedral	Moscow
Edinburgh Castle	U.K.	Ste-Chapelle	Paris
Eiffel Tower	Paris	St Mark's Cathedral	Venice
Empire State Building	New York	St Patrick's Cathedral	New York
Erechtheum	Athens	St Paul's Cathedral	London
Florence Cathedral	Italy	St Peter's	Rome
Galleria Vittorio Emanuele II	Milan	St Sophia	Istanbul
Guggenheim Museum	New York	Sears Tower	Chicago
Hall of Supreme Harmony	Beijing/Peking	Sun Temple	Konarak, India
Hermitage, the	St Petersburg	Sydney Opera House	Australia
Horyu-ji	Nara, Japan	Taj Mahal	Agra, India
Houses of Parliament	London	Transamerica Corporation building	San Francisco
Jefferson Memorial	Washington	Trans World Airways Terminal	New York
John Hancock Center	Chicago		
J. Paul Getty Museum	Malibu, California	U.S. Capitol	Washington
		Versailles	Paris
King's College Chapel	Cambridge, England	Westminster Abbey	London
Leaning Tower of Pisa	Italy	White House	Washington
Notre-Dame	Paris	World Trade Center	New York

amplitude; dimensions. **2** *the bulk of the applicants are women* majority, greater part/number, most, preponderance, major/main/better part, mass, body, generality, lion's share.

bulk *verb* *bulk the book out with pictures* make thicker, make bigger, make larger, expand, pad out, fill out, stretch out, augment. **bulk large** be important, be prominent, carry weight, dominate, preponderate, loom large.

bulky *adjective* **1** *bulky bags of rubbish* large, big, substantial, huge, enormous, massive, vast, immense, voluminous, colossal, hulking, heavy, weighty, ponderous. **2** *Mr. Smith's bulky body* stout, thickset, plump, fat, chubby, portly, tubby, obese. **3** *bulky items of furniture* awkward-shaped, awkward, unwieldy, cumbersome, unmanageable.
Opposites SMALL; SLIM; MANAGEABLE.

bulldoze *verb* **1** *bulldoze the area/buildings* demolish, flatten, level, raze. **2** *bulldoze his way through* | *bulldoze a path through the crowds* force, push, drive, shove, propel. **3** *they bulldozed him into going* bully, browbeat, coerce, intimidate, cow, bludgeon, dragoon, steamroller, railroad; *inf.* strong-arm.

bullet *noun. See table.*

BULLETS AND SHOT		
baton round	dumdum	rubber
buckshot	bullet	bullet
canister	grapeshot	shell
shot	pellet	slug
cannon ball	plastic	small shot
case-shot	bullet	soft-nosed
chain-shot	round shot	bullet

bulletin *noun* **1** *a television bulletin* news report, report, statement, announcement, newsflash, flash, account, message, communication, communiqué, dispatch, notification. **2** *an in-house bulletin* newspaper, newsletter, pamphlet, leaflet, broadsheet; listings.

bullish *adjective* **1** *bullish stock market* rising, improving, confident. **2** *feeling very bullish about the future* optimistic, hopeful, confident, positive, assured, cheerful, sanguine.

bully *noun* *the school bully* browbeater, intimidator, coercer, oppressor, persecutor, tyrant, tormentor, tough, bully-boy, ruffian, thug.

bully *verb* *bully the younger children* browbeat, intimidate, coerce, oppress, domineer, persecute, cow, tyrannize, pressurize, pressure, bulldoze; *inf.* push around, strong-arm, play the heavy with.

bully *adjective* *a bully performance* excellent, first-rate, very good, fine, admirable; *inf.* A1, wicked.

bulwark *noun* **1** *the castle's bulwarks* rampart, fortification, buttress, bastion, embankment, outwork, mole, breastwork, redoubt. **2** *a bulwark of classical education* support, mainstay, defence, guard, safeguard; defendant, protector.

bum¹ *noun* bottom, rear, rear end; buttocks; *inf.* sit-upon, BTM, arse; *Am. inf.* ass. *See* BOTTOM *noun* 7.

bum² *noun* **1** *a bum begging for money* tramp, vagrant, beggar, derelict, mendicant; *Am.* bag lady, hobo. **2** *just a lazy bum* loafer, idler, wastrel, good-for-nothing, ne'er-do-well, scrounger, cadger.

bum³ *verb* **1** *bum money from him* borrow, cadge, scrounge, sponge; *Am. inf.* mooch. **2** *bum around* loaf, lounge, idle, laze, wander.

bum⁴ *adjective* *bum personal stereos* useless, worthless, inferior, unsatisfactory, low-grade, poor, bad.

bumble *verb* **1** *the speaker was bumbling away* ramble, babble, mumble, mutter, stumble. **2** *drunks bumbling through the woods* stumble, lurch, blunder, muddle about, flounder about.

bumbling *adjective* *a bumbling idiot* clumsy, blundering, awkward, bungling, incompetent, inept, inefficient, muddled, stumbling, lumbering, botching, foolish.

bump *verb* **1** *the bus bumped the car* hit, bang, strike, knock, crash into, collide with; *inf.* slam. **2** *bump his head on the bar* hit, bang, strike, knock, hurt, injure, damage. **3** *the cart bumping along the road* bounce, jolt, jerk, rattle, shake, jounce. **4** *bump the car out of the mud* move, shift, budge, dislodge. **bump into 1** *the cars bumped into each other* collide with, crash/smash into, run into. **2** *we bumped into old schoolfriends* run into, come/run across, meet by chance, meet, meet up with, encounter, chance/happen upon, light upon. **bump off** *bump off his enemy* kill, murder, do away with, assassinate, eliminate, liquidate, dispatch.

bump *noun* **1** *hear a bump* thud, thump, bang, crash. **2** *land with a bump* collision, jolt, crash, smash, bang, thud, thump, knock, rap, impact. **3** *he has a bump on his head* lump, swelling, injury, contusion, nodule, node, tumescence, intumescence, protuberance. **4** *a bump on the road surface* bulge, hump, knob, knot, protuberance.

bumper *adjective* *a bumper crop* large, big, abundant, huge, massive, bountiful, exceptional, unusual, excellent; *inf.* whopping.

bumpkin *noun* country bumpkin, yokel, clodhopper, oaf, boor, lout, peasant, rustic; *Am. inf.* hill-billy, hick, hayseed, rube.

bumptious *adjective* self-important, conceited, arrogant, self-assertive, full of oneself, overbearing, puffed up, self-opinionated, cocky, presumptuous, pompous, forward; *inf.* pushy.

bumpy *adjective* **1** *a bumpy road* uneven, rough, potholed, rutted, pitted, lumpy, knobby. **2** *a bumpy flight* choppy, jolting, jolty, jerky, jarring, bouncy, rough.
Opposites EVEN; SMOOTH.

bunch *noun* **1** *a bunch of flowers* bouquet, spray, posy, sheaf, nosegay, corsage. **2** *a bunch of keys/bananas* cluster, assemblage, collection. **3** *a bunch of papers* batch, pile, stack, heap, bundle, mass, quantity, accumulation, agglomeration. **4** *a bunch of people* group, collection, gathering, band, gang, knot, cluster, party, crowd, flock, swarm, troop, mob, multitude.

bunch verb **1** *the crowd bunched together* cluster, huddle, gather, group, bundle, pack, herd, crowd, flock, mass, cram. **2** *cloth bunching up* gather, fold, pleat.

bundle noun **1** *a bundle of papers* collection, batch, pile, stack, heap, bunch, mass, quantity, accumulation, agglomeration. **2** *send off bundles of mail/clothes* package, pack, bale, parcel, packet. **3** *a bundle of sticks* bunch, bale, truss, faggot, fascicle.

bundle verb **1** *bundle the clothes into a bag* | *bundle them up* tie, tie up, tie together, package, parcel, wrap, bind, fasten together, bale, truss. **2** *bundle people inside/outside* | *bundled them off the road* hurry, hustle, rush, push, shove, thrust, throw. **3** *bundle children up in warm clothes* clothe, wrap, cover, muffle, swathe.

bungle verb botch, muff, spoil, make a mess of, mess up, mishandle, mismanage, fudge, mar, ruin; *inf.* louse up, screw up, foul up, cock up, bodge.

bungling adjective clumsy, incompetent, inept, unskilful, inexpert, botching, blundering, maladroit; *inf.* ham-fisted, ham-handed, cack-handed.

bunk[1] noun bed, berth, bunk-bed.

bunk[2] noun **do a bunk** run away, flee, bolt, fly, take flight, take off, clear out, take to one's heels, show a clean pair of heels, escape, make a run for it, abscond, decamp; *inf.* cut and run, do a runner, scarper, beat it, skedaddle, scram.

bunk[3] noun nonsense, bunkum.

bunkum noun nonsense, rubbish, balderdash, stuff and nonsense, twaddle, claptrap, humbug, tomfoolery; *inf.* rot, poppycock, baloney, piffle, bilge, bosh, hooey; *vulg.* bullshit; *Am.* hogwash.

buoy noun **1** *a harbour buoy* anchored float, marker; mooring, navigation mark, guide, beacon, signal. **2** *the buoy kept him afloat* lifebuoy, life-belt, life-jacket, life-preserver, Mae West.

buoy verb **buoy up 1** *buoying up the bereaved woman* cheer, cheer up, hearten, encourage, support, sustain; *inf.* keep afloat. **2** *buoying up her spirits* cheer up, raise, boost, uplift, lift, give a lift to.

buoyancy noun **1** *the buoyancy of the boat/water* floatability, lightness, levity, lifting effect, lift. **2** *the buoyancy of her mood/personality* cheerfulness, cheeriness, light-heartedness, carefreeness, joy, vivacity, animation, liveliness, high spirits, verve, sparkle, sprightliness, spiritedness, blitheness, jauntiness, breeziness, pep, happiness, merriment; *inf.* zing, zip.

buoyant adjective **1** *a buoyant substance* floatable, floating, afloat, light. **2** *a buoyant mood/personality* cheerful, cheery, light-hearted, bouncy, carefree, joyful, vivacious, animated, lively, high-spirited, sparkling, sprightly, blithe, jaunty, breezy, happy, merry; *inf.* peppy, zingy, zippy.
Opposites LEADEN; DEPRESSED.

burden noun **1** *the donkey's burden* load, cargo, weight, freight. **2** *the burden of parenthood* responsibility, onus, charge, duty, obligation, tax, trouble, care, worry, anxiety, tribulation, difficulty, strain, stress, weight, encumbrance, millstone, albatross; trials, tribulations.

burden verb **1** *donkeys burdened with heavy loads* load, be laden, weight, charge, weigh down, encumber, hamper. **2** *burdened with great sorrow* oppress, trouble, worry, distress, bother, afflict, torment, strain, stress, tax, overwhelm.

bureau noun **1** *a travel bureau* agency, office, service. **2** *a government bureau* department, division, branch. **3** *polish the bureau* writing-desk, desk, writing-table.

bureaucracy noun **1** *rule by bureaucracy* civil service, central administration, directorate; government officials, government ministries. **2** *cut through the bureaucracy to get a passport* red tape, officialdom, bumbledom; rules and regulations.

bureaucrat noun administrator, official, office-holder, civil servant, public servant, government servant, minister, functionary, mandarin, *apparatchik*, jack-in-office.

bureaucratic adjective official, administrative, governmental, ministerial, red-tape, by the book, rigid, inflexible.

burgeon verb **1** *flowers burgeoning* bud, sprout, put forth shoots, shoot, germinate, pullulate. **2** *a population burgeoning* grow, develop, flourish, thrive, mushroom, proliferate, snowball, increase, multiply, expand, escalate.

burglar noun housebreaker, cat burglar, thief, sneak-thief, robber, pilferer, filcher, picklock; *Am. inf.* second-story man/worker/thief.

burglary noun **1** *charged with burglary* housebreaking, breaking and entering, breaking in, forced entry, theft, robbery, larceny, pilfering, filching. **2** *suffered a burglary* break-in, theft, robbery.

burial noun **1** *the burial of the body* burying, interment, entombment, inhumation, sepulture. **2** *present at the burial* funeral, sepulture; obsequies, exequies.

burial-ground noun burial-place, cemetery, graveyard, churchyard, necropolis; *Am.* memorial park, potter's field; *lit.* golgotha, God's acre.

burlesque noun parody, caricature, travesty, farce, mockery, imitation, satire, lampoon; *inf.* send-up, take-off, spoof.

burly adjective thickset, brawny, powerfully built, well-built, muscular, strapping, big, hulking, hefty, beefy, bulky, sturdy, stocky, stout, strong-man.
Opposites SCRAWNY; PUNY; SLIGHT.

burn verb **1** *the house is burning* be on fire, be afire, be ablaze, blaze, go up, smoke, flame, be aflame, flare, flash, flicker, glow. **2** *he burned the papers* set on fire, set alight, ignite, put a match to, light, kindle, incinerate, reduce to ashes. **3** *burn the shirt with the iron* | *burn the bread* scorch, singe, sear, char. **4** *her forehead's burning* be hot, be warm, feel hot, be feverish, be fevered; *inf.* be on fire. **5** *his throat's burning* smart, sting, tingle, be sore, hurt, throb. **6** *the liquid burnt his throat* sting, bite, prickle, irritate, pain, hurt. **7** *burn with excitement/passion* be aroused, be emotional, simmer, smoulder, seethe. **8** *he was burning to get the prize* long, yearn, desire, be consumed with the desire, hunger after, lust, itch, pant, wish, want. **9** *burn energy* use, use up, consume, expend, eat up, exhaust.

burning *adjective* **1** *a burning house* blazing, aflaming, flaring, raging, ignited, glowing, flickering, smouldering, scorching. **2** *the burning meat* scorching, singeing, searing, charring. **3** *a burning forehead/day* hot, warm; *inf.* scorching, roasting, boiling, baking. **4** *a burning sensation* smarting, stinging, biting, prickling, irritating, caustic, searing, corroding, corrosive, painful. **5** *a burning desire* intense, fervent, fervid, ardent, passionate, eager. **6** *the burning issues of the day* important, crucial, significant, urgent, pressing, compelling, critical, vital, essential, acute, pivotal, climacteric.

burnish *verb* polish, shine, brighten, rub, buff, buff up, smooth.

burp *verb* belch, bring up wind, eruct, eructate; *dial.* rift.

burrow *noun rabbit burrows* tunnel, hole, hollow, excavation, lair, den, retreat.

burrow *verb* **1** *burrowing holes* dig, tunnel, excavate, hollow out, gouge out, scoop out. **2** *burrow one's way out* dig, tunnel. **3** *burrowing under the bedclothes* go under, hide, shelter, conceal oneself. **4** *burrow for matches/information* search for, look for, delve for, hunt for, ferret out.

burst *verb* **1** *the pipe has burst* split, split open, break open, rupture, crack, fracture, fragment, shatter, shiver, fly open. **2** *the cold weather burst the pipes* split, break open, tear apart, rupture, crack, fracture, fragment, shatter, shiver, rend asunder. **3** *the grenade burst* blow up, explode, detonate, fulminate. **4** *the water burst through the dam* break out, burst forth, pour forth, gush out, surge out, rush out. **5** *he burst into/from the room* barge, push/thrust/shove one's way. **6** *burst into tears/laughter* begin/start/commence suddenly, break out, erupt.

burst out **1** *"Coward!" she burst out* exclaim, cry out, call out, shout, yell. **2** *burst out crying* begin/start/commence suddenly. **3** *burst out of jail* break out, break loose, make one's escape, escape, get free. *See* BREAK *verb* break out 1.

bury *verb* **1** *bury the corpse* inter, lay to rest, consign to the grave, entomb, inhume, sepulchre; *lit.* inearth. **2** *bury her head in her hands* conceal, hide, cover with, put out of sight, submerge, sink, secrete, enshroud. **3** *bury the nail in the wood* drive in, embed, implant, sink, submerge. **4** *bury yourself in your work | be buried in a book* absorb oneself, immerse oneself, occupy oneself with, engross oneself, engage oneself, interest oneself.
Opposites EXHUME; UNEARTH; EXPOSE.

bush *noun* **1** *planting bushes in the garden | throw in the bushes* shrub, woody plant; thicket, undergrowth, shrubbery. *See table at* TREE. **2** *lost in the Australian bush* brush, scrub land, scrub, the wild; backwoods.

bushy *adjective* thick, shaggy, fuzzy, fluffy, luxuriant, unruly, rough.

business *noun* **1** *what business is he in* occupation, line, profession, career, trade, work, employment, job, pursuit, vocation, *métier*. **2** *do business with the French* trade, trading, commerce, trafficking, buying and selling, merchandizing, bargaining; dealings, transactions, proceedings. **3** *owning her own business* firm, company, concern, enterprise, organization, corporation, establishment, house, shop, venture, industry. **4** *that's none of your business* concern, affair, responsibility, duty, function, task, assignment, obligation, problem. **5** *the main business of the meeting* matter, subject, topic, point of discussion, theme, issue, question, problem, thesis. **6** *it was a peculiar business* affair, matter, thing, case, set of circumstances, issue.

businesslike *adjective* **1** *businesslike behaviour* professional, efficient, methodical, systematic, orderly, organized, well-ordered, practical, pragmatic, thorough, painstaking, meticulous, correct. **2** *a businesslike performance of the play* workaday, routine, prosaic, down-to-earth, conventional, unimaginative.

bust *noun* **1** *a woman with a large bust* chest, breasts, bosom, torso; *inf.* boobs, tits, knockers. **2** *a bust of Julius Caesar* sculptured/carved head and shoulders, head and shoulders.

bust *verb* **1** *they bust the machine* break, fracture, burst, rupture, crack. **2** *the crash will bust him* bankrupt, ruin, impoverish, pauperize, break. **3** *the police busted him* arrest, capture, catch, seize, raid; *inf.* collar, cop, nab.

bust *adjective* **go bust** become bankrupt, fail, be ruined, become insolvent, break.

bustle *verb* **1** *bustle about | bustle to and fro* hurry, rush, dash, scuttle, scurry, hasten, scamper, scramble, flutter, fuss; *inf.* tear. **2** *bustle the children out* hurry, rush, hasten, speed up, push.

bustle *noun the bustle of the market-place* activity, flurry, hurly-burly, stir, busyness, briskness, commotion, tumult, excitement, agitation, fuss; *inf.* to-do; *lit.* pother.

busy *adjective* **1** *the doctor's busy* occupied, engaged, working, at work, on duty, in a meeting, otherwise engaged. **2** *busy wrapping up goods* occupied in, engaged in, employed in, involved in, absorbed in, engrossed in, preoccupied with, working at, labouring at, toiling at, slaving at. **3** *a busy day* active, energetic, strenuous, full, hectic, exacting, bustling. **4** *busy as bees* active, energetic, industrious, lively, tireless, restless; *inf.* on the go. **5** *busy patterns* ornate, overelaborate, overdetailed, overdecorated, cluttered, fussy. **6** *a busy old woman* interfering, meddlesome, meddling, prying, inquisitive, snooping; *inf.* nosy, snoopy.
Opposites UNOCCUPIED; INACTIVE; QUIET; IDLE.

busy *verb busy himself in the garden* occupy, engage, employ, absorb, immerse, engross, involve, interest.

busybody *noun* meddler, interferer, snooper, pry, mischief-maker, troublemaker, gossip, scandalmonger, muckraker; *inf.* nosy parker.

but *conjunction* **1** *she's ill but she's going* nevertheless, yet, still, however. **2** *he went but she did not* on the other hand, on the contrary. **3** *cannot choose but to do it* other than, otherwise than, except.

but *preposition* **1** *everyone but him* except, with the exception of, excepting, other than, excluding, bar, barring, save. **2** *but for the rain he would have gone* without, except for, barring, notwithstanding.

but *adverb* *we can but try* only, just, simply, merely.

butch *adjective* mannish, masculine.

butcher *noun* **1** *buy steak from the butcher* meat merchant, meat seller, meat retailer. **2** *the general was a butcher* slaughterer, mass murderer, slayer, killer, serial killer, homicide, homicidal maniac, bloodshedder.

butcher *verb* **1** *butchering cattle* slaughter, cut up, carve up, joint, slice up, prepare, dress. **2** *butchering the enemy* slaughter, slay, massacre, murder, kill, put to death, exterminate, liquidate, assassinate, put to the sword, cut down, destroy. **3** *butcher the piano concerto | butcher the piece of joinery* botch, make a botch/mess of, wreck, ruin, spoil, bungle; *inf.* make a hash of, louse up, screw up, foul up.

butchery *noun* **1** *he's taken up butchery* meat selling, meat retailing, butchering. **2** *tribes noted for their butchery | the butchery of the enemy* slaughter, massacre, slaying, murdering, murder, mass murdering, homicide, blood shedding.

butt¹ *noun* **1** *the butt of a gun* handle, shaft, hilt, haft. **2** *the butt of a cigarette* stub, end, tail-end, remnant; *inf.* fag-end. **3** *sitting on his butt* bottom, buttocks.

butt² *noun* *the butt of his jokes* scapegoat, dupe, target, victim, laughing-stock, object, subject.

butt³ *noun* *a butt of ale* barrel, cask, pipe.

butt⁴ *verb* **1** *the ram butted her with his horns* push, thrust, shove, ram, bump, buffet, prod, poke, jab, knock, bunt. **2** *his land butts mine* abut, join, meet, conjoin. **3** *butt into a conversation | butt into a private matter* interrupt, intrude/interfere in, put one's oar into; *inf.* stick one's nose into.

butterfly *noun. See table.*

buttocks *noun* bottom, posterior, rump; hindquarters; *inf.* behind, bum, backside, sit-upon, BTM, arse; *Am. inf.* butt, ass.

button *noun* **1** *buttons on the sweater* fastener, stud, link. **2** *the button on the radio* disc, knob, switch.

buttonhole *verb* *buttonhole the MP* accost, waylay, take aside, importune, detain, grab, catch, talk at.

buttress *noun* **1** *a stone buttress* prop, support, abutment, strut, reinforcement, stanchion, pier. **2** *a buttress to the family* mainstay, upholder, sustainer, cornerstone, pillar.

buttress *verb* *buttress the economy | buttress your argument* strengthen, reinforce, prop up, support, shore up, underpin, brace, uphold, defend, back up.

buxom *adjective* plump, large-bosomed, big-bosomed, full-bosomed, shapely; *inf.* busty.

buy *verb* **1** *buy a house* purchase, make a purchase of, pay for, invest in, procure. **2** *he bought his way in* bribe, suborn, corrupt; *inf.* grease someone's palm, square, fix, rig. **3** *buy off the customers* pay off, drop charges.
Opposites SELL.

BUTTERFLIES AND MOTHS

Adonis blue	death's head hawk-	magpie moth	red admiral
angle shades	moth	marbled white	ringlet
apollo	drinker	meadow brown	satyrid
argus	eggar	merveille du jour	silk moth
atlas moth	emerald	milkweed	silkworm moth
bagworm moth	emperor moth	monarch	silver Y
birdwing	ermine	morpho	skipper
blue butterfly	fritillary	Mother Shipton	speckled wood
brimstone butterfly	fruit moth	mourning cloak	sulphur
brown butterfly	gatekeeper	noctuid	swallowtail
burnet	geometrid	nymphalid	butterfly
burnished brass	goat moth	oak eggar	swift moth
cabbage white	grayling	orange-tip	tiger moth
Camberwell	gypsy moth	owlet moth	tineid
Beauty	hairstreak	painted lady	tortoiseshell
cecropia moth	hawkmoth	papilionid	tortrix
cinnabar moth	heath	peacock butterfly	tussock moth
clearwing moth	io moth	peppered moth	underwing
clothes-moth	lackey	plume moth	vapourer
clouded yellow	lappet	prominent	wall brown
codling moth	large blue	pug	wax moth
comma	leopard moth	purple emperor	white admiral
copper	lobster moth	puss moth	winter moth
dagger	luna moth	pyralid	yellow-tail

buy *noun a good buy* purchase, acquisition, deal, bargain.

buzz *noun* **1** *the buzz of the bees* buzzing, hum, humming, murmur, drone, whirr, whirring, hiss, sibilation, whisper; *lit.* bombination, bombilation, susurration, susurrus. **2** *the buzz of the telephone/machines* ring, ringing, purr, purring. **3** *the buzz is he's gone* rumour, gossip, news, chitchat, report, whisper, scandal, hearsay.

buzz *verb* **1** *bees buzzing* hum, murmur, drone, whirr, hiss, whisper, sibilate; *lit.* bombinate, bombilate, susurrate. **2** *telephone/machines buzzing* ring, reverberate, purr. **3** *tongues buzzing* gossip, chatter, natter, tattle, spread rumours. **4** *people buzzing about* bustle, rush, dash, hurry. **5** *the place was buzzing* be active, be busy, be bustling.

by *preposition* **1** *the house by the school* next to, beside, alongside, near, close to. **2** *enter by the side door | come by the quiet roads* through, along, over, by way of, via. **3** *go by the building* past, in front of. **4** *be there by midday* no later than, at, before. **5** *arrested by the police | contact him by telephone* through the agency/means/instrumentality of, under the aegis of, through.

6 *meet by chance* through, because of, as a result of.

bygone *adjective* past, departed, dead, former, one-time, previous, forgotten, lost, of old, olden, ancient, antiquated, of yore, obsolete, extinct, out of date, outmoded, *passé*.

by-law, bye-law *noun* local regulation, rule, regulation, statute.

bypass *noun a bypass round the city* ring road, detour, circuitous route, roundabout way, alternative route.

bypass *verb* **1** *bypass the city* make a detour round, go round, pass round. **2** *bypass the difficulties* get round, circumvent, find a way round, avoid, evade. **3** *bypass the salesman and go the manager* ignore, pass over, miss out, circumvent, avoid, go over the head of; *inf.* short-circuit.

bystander *noun* onlooker, looker-on, observer, eyewitness, witness, spectator, watcher, viewer, beholder, gaper, passer-by; *inf.* gawper, rubberneck.

byword *noun* **1** *a byword for reliability* slogan, catchword, motto, example of, personification of, embodiment of. **2** *old bywords dying out* proverb, maxim, adage, aphorism, apophthegm.

Cc

cab *noun* **1** *order a cab* taxi, taxicab, minicab, hackney carriage, hackney. **2** *the driver's cab* cabin, compartment, quarters, cubicle, cubby-hole.

cabal *noun* **1** *a political plot laid by a cabal* clique, faction, coterie, league, confederacy, band, gang, party, set, ring, junta, junto. **2** *the cabal was discovered in time* intrigue, conspiracy, plot, scheme, plan, design.

cabaret *noun* **1** *watching the hotel's cabaret* entertainment, show, floorshow. **2** *employed as a singer in a cabaret* nightclub, club, nightspot, disco, discotheque.

cabbage *noun* **1** *cabbage and carrot salad* green cabbage, white cabbage, red cabbage, winter cabbage, savoy, Chinese cabbage. **2** *she's become a cabbage since her marriage* inactive/inert/apathetic/sluggish/vegetating/stagnating person, couch potato.

cabin *noun* **1** *a cabin by the lake* log cabin, hut, chalet, shack, shanty, shed; *Scots* bothy. **2** *a first-class cabin in the ship* stateroom, sleeping-quarters, berth, compartment, deck-house. **3** *an aircraft's cabin* compartment, passenger space, passenger accommodation. **4** *a driver's cabin* cab, compartment. *See* CAB 2.

cabinet *noun* **1** *a china cabinet* case, container. *See table at* CUPBOARD. **2** *the Prime Minister and the Cabinet* ministry, ministers, administration, council, counsellors, senate.

cable *noun* **1** *tied with cable* rope, cord, wire, line, cordage. **2** *send a cable* cablegram, telegram, telegraph, telemessage, wire.

cable *verb* *cable the news* telegraph, wire, radio.

cache *noun* **1** *secrete the treasure in a cache* hiding-place, hide-out, secret place, hole; *inf.* hidy-hole. **2** *find the cache of jewels* hoard, store, collection, fund, supply, hidden treasure, treasure, loot; *inf.* stash.

cachet *noun* prestige, distinction, stature, eminence, respect, admiration, approbation, approval, seal of approval, stamp of approval.

cackle *verb* **1** *hens cackling* cluck, clack, squawk. **2** *the audience cackling at his jokes* chuckle, chortle, laugh, giggle, titter, snigger, tee-hee. **3** *people cackling at the bus-stop* chatter, jabber, prattle, babble, gabble, clack, gibber, blather, clatter, blab; *inf.* spout away.

cacophony *noun* discord, dissonance, discordance, jarring, stridency, grating, rasping, caterwauling.

cad *noun* scoundrel, rat, rogue, rascal, double-crosser, knave; *inf.* bounder, rotter, heel.

cadaver *noun* corpse, dead body, remains, carcass; *inf.* stiff.

cadaverous *adjective* corpse-like, death-like, gaunt, haggard, drawn, emaciated, skeletal, thin, hollow-eyed, ashen, pale, wan, ghostly.

cadence *noun* **1** *musical/metrical cadence* rhythm, beat, pulse, rhythmical flow/pattern, measure, metre, tempo, swing, lilt, cadency. **2** *the cadence of her speech* intonation, inflection, accent, modulation.

café *noun* coffee bar, coffee shop, snack bar, tearoom, teashop, restaurant, cafeteria, wine bar, bistro.

cafeteria *noun* self-service restaurant, self-service canteen.

cage *noun* *cages in the zoo* enclosure, pen, pound, lock-up, coop; *Am.* corral; bird-cage, aviary, mew, hen coop.

cage *verb* **1** *cage the animals* confine, shut in, impound, pen, lock up, immure, incarcerate, imprison, coop, coop up, mew; *Am.* corral. **2** *don't cage him in - he likes freedom* confine, hem in, restrict, restrain.

cagey, cagy *adjective* guarded, secretive, non-committal, cautious, chary, wary, careful, shrewd, wily.

cajole *verb* wheedle, coax, beguile, flatter, seduce, humour, lure, entice, tempt, inveigle, manoeuvre, jolly; *inf.* sweet-talk, soft-soap, butter up.

cake *noun* **1** *cakes from the baker* bun, pastry. *See table.* **2** *a cake of chocolate/soap* block, bar, slab, lump, mass, cube, loaf, chunk.

cake *verb* **1** *blood caking on the bodies* solidify, harden, thicken, dry, bake, coagulate, consoli-

CAKES		
almond cake	fairy cake	pavlova
angel cake	flapjack	plum cake
baba	frangipane	pound cake
Bakewell	fruit cake	queen cake
tart	gateau	rock cake
baklava	Genoa cake	scone
bannock	gingerbread	seedcake
Battenburg	hoecake	shortcake
brownie	koeksister	simnel cake
cheesecake	kuchen	sponge cake
cruller	ladyfinger	strudel
cupcake	lardy-cake	Swiss roll
Danish	Madeira	teacake
pastry	cake	tipsy-cake
devil's food	madeleine	torte
cake	marble cake	upside-
doughnut	meringue	down cake
drop scone	millefeuille	Victoria
Dundee	muffin	sponge
cake	pancake	wedding
Eccles cake	pandowdy	cake
éclair	parkin	yule log

date, ossify; *lit.* inspissate. **2** *boots caked with mud* cover, coat, encrust, plaster.

calamitous *adjective* disastrous, catastrophic, cataclysmic, devastating, ruinous, dire, tragic, fatal, wretched, woeful.

calamity *noun* disaster, catastrophe, tragedy, misfortune, cataclysm, devastation, scourge, misadventure, mischance, mishap, ruin, tribulation, woe.

calculate *verb* **1** *calculate the sum* work out, compute, estimate, count up, figure out, reckon up, evaluate, enumerate, determine, gauge. **2** *she calculated her chances* estimate, gauge, judge, measure, weigh up, reckon, rate. **3** *the car was calculated to appeal to children* design, plan, aim, intend. **4** *we calculated on their early arrival* rely, depend, count, bank.

calculated *adjective* *a calculated crime/risk* considered, planned, premeditated, deliberate, intentional, intended, purposeful.
Opposites UNINTENTIONAL; SPONTANEOUS.

calculating *adjective* *a calculating young woman/killer* scheming, designing, contriving, devious, shrewd, manipulative, sharp, sly, crafty, Machiavellian.

calculation *noun* **1** *by their calculations it will cost £3000* computation, estimation, estimate, reckoning, figuring, forecast, gauging, judgement. *See* CALCULATE 1, 2. **2** *the calculation is wrong* result, answer. **3** *she got the job by sheer calculation* scheming, designing, contriving, deviousness, shrewdness, manipulation, slyness, craft, expedience, circumspection, deliberation.

calendar *noun. See table at* MONTH.

calibre *noun* **1** *the calibre of a gun* bore, diameter. **2** *statesmen of his calibre* quality, worth, distinction, stature, excellence, merit, ability, talent, capability, competence, capacity, endowments, gifts, strengths, scope.

call *verb* **1** *call out in pain* cry, cry out, shout, exclaim, yell, scream, shriek, roar. **2** *call him in the morning* awaken, waken, arouse, rouse. **3** *call her tomorrow* call up, ring, phone, phone up, telephone, give one a ring; *inf.* buzz, give one a buzz, give one a tinkle. **4** *call at the house* pay a call, pay a visit, pay a brief visit, stop by; *inf.* drop in, pop in. **5** *call a meeting* call together, convene, summon, order, convoke, assemble, announce, declare, proclaim, decree. **6** *call a doctor/taxi* send for, ask for, summon, contact, order, bid, fetch. **7** *they called the baby Jane | the flowers are called primulas* name, christen, style, designate, dub, entitle, denominate, describe as, label, term. **8** *I call it disgraceful* consider, think, regard, judge, estimate. **9** *called to the Bar | he was called to the Church* appoint, elect, ordain. **call for** **1** *this calls for a celebration | rudeness is not called for* need, require, be grounds for, justify, necessitate, demand, entail. **2** *call for the goods* collect, pick up, fetch, go for; *dial.* uplift. **call off** **1** *call off the dogs* order off, order away, stop, hold back, check, rein in. **2** *call off the date* cancel, postpone, countermand, rescind, revoke. **call on** **1** *call on his aunt* visit, pay a visit to, go and see; *inf.* look up, look in on,

drop in on. **2** *call on/upon them to help* appeal to, ask, request, entreat, urge, supplicate, invoke. **call up** **1** *call her up tomorrow* call, ring, telephone, phone. *See* CALL *verb* 3. **2** *it calls up painful memories* recall, bring/call to mind, summon up, evoke. **3** *call up all the young men* enlist, recruit, sign up; *Am.* draft.

call *noun* **1** *a call of pain* cry, shout, exclamation, yell, scream, shriek, roar. **2** *the calls of the bird* cry, song, chirp, chirping, tweet. **3** *have a prearranged call* signal, hail, whoop, cooee. **4** *give her a call tomorrow* telephone call, ring; *inf.* buzz, tinkle. **5** *make a call on her* visit, brief visit. **6** *first call for the plane | a call for unity* summons, invitation, request, plea, bidding, order, command, appeal, notice. **7** *there's no call to be rude* need, occasion, reason, cause, justification, grounds, excuse. **8** *there's no call for expensive wine here* demand, request, requirement, need, want, requisition. **9** *the call of the wild* attraction, lure, allurement, fascination, appeal, bewitchment.

call girl *noun* prostitute, whore, harlot, street walker, courtesan, woman of ill repute, fallen woman, loose woman, scarlet woman, woman of the night, woman of the town, *fille de joie*; *inf.* hooker, hustler.

calling *noun* vocation, occupation, career, profession, business, work, employment, job, trade, craft, line, line of work, pursuit, *métier*, walk of life, province, field.

callous *adjective* **1** *a callous jail warden* hard, hardened, tough, harsh, cold, insensitive, unfeeling, cold-hearted, hard-hearted, heartless, stony-hearted, hard-bitten, cruel, obdurate, case-hardened, indurate, indurated, inured, uncaring, unsympathetic, unresponsive, unsusceptible, indifferent, soulless. **2** *callous skin* hard, hardened, thickened, leathery.
Opposites KIND; COMPASSIONATE.

callow *adjective* immature, inexperienced, uninitiated, naive, unsophisticated, innocent, undeveloped, adolescent.
Opposites EXPERIENCED; SOPHISTICATED.

calm *adjective* **1** *a calm day* still, windless, mild, tranquil, balmy, halcyon, quiet, peaceful, pacific, undisturbed, restful. **2** *a calm sea* still, smooth, motionless, placid, waveless, unagitated, storm free. **3** *be/remain calm during the trouble* composed, collected, cool, cool-headed, controlled, self-controlled, self-possessed, quiet, tranquil, unruffled, relaxed, serene, unexcited, unexcitable, unflappable, undisturbed, unagitated, imperturbable, unemotional, unmoved, equable, stoical; *inf.* together.
Opposites STORMY; EXCITED; FRANTIC.

calm *noun* **1** *the calm before the storm | disturbing the day's calm* stillness, tranquillity, serenity, quietness, quietude, peace, peacefulness, harmony, restfulness, repose. **2** *nothing disturbs her calm* composure, coolness, self-control, tranquillity, serenity, equanimity, unflappability, imperturbability, equability, poise, sangfroid; *inf.* cool.

calm *verb* **1** *try to calm the child | calm her fears* soothe, quieten, pacify, hush, lull, tranquillize,

mollify, appease, allay, alleviate, assuage.
2 *the wind eventually calmed* quieten, still, settle, settle down, die down. **calm down** quieten; relax, settle.
Opposites AGITATE; STIR.

calumny *noun* slander, calumniation, defamation, libel, misrepresentation, false accusation, denigration, vilification, aspersions, mudslinging, backbiting, detraction, disparagement, deprecation, evil-speaking, insult, abuse, vituperation, obloquy, revilement, smear campaign.

camaraderie *noun* comradeship, companionship, brotherliness, fellowship, friendship, closeness, affinity, sociability.

camera *noun. See tables.*

CAMERAS

box	pinhole
camcorder	Polaroid™
disc	single-lens reflex
electronic	(SLR)
still	twin-lens reflex
instant	video camera
movie camera	view camera

PARTS OF A CAMERA

aperture	leaf shutter
automatic focusing	lens
system	light control
blimp	magazine
camera box	mirror
compound lens	mirror shutter
diaphragm	reflex viewer
exposure meter	registration pins
eyepiece	shutter
film gate	spool
film holder	take-up reel
fish-eye lens	telephoto lens
focal-plane	through-the-lens
shutter	metering system
focus control	viewfinder
focusing screen	wide-angle lens

---

camouflage *noun the soldiers' khaki uniforms were a camouflage | the polar bear's coat is a camouflage* disguise, protective colouring, mask, screen, cloak, cover, cover-up, false front, front, façade, masquerade, blind, concealment, subterfuge.

camouflage *verb camouflaged in white against the snow* disguise, hide, conceal, mask, screen, veil, cloak, cover, cover up, obscure.

camp[1] *noun* **1** *soldier's/Scout camp* encampment, camping ground, camp-site, tents, bivouac, cantonment. **2** *the right-wing camp* faction, party, group, clique, coterie, set, sect, cabal.

camp[2] *verb we camped in a field* pitch tents, pitch camp, set up camp, encamp, tent. **camp out 1** *we camped out in that field* sleep out, camp. **2** *we're camping out here till the house is decorated* live rough, live simply; *inf.* rough it, slum it, pig it.

camp[3] *verb* **camp it up** overdo it, overact, behave theatrically, posture, behave affectedly, ham it, lay it on, spread it on thick.

camp[4] *adjective* **1** *camp mannerisms* effeminate, affected, artificial, posturing, mannered, studied, homosexual, gay; *inf.* campy; *inf. derog* poncy, limp-wristed. **2** *camp humour* exaggerated, theatrical, flamboyant, overdone, extravagant, overdrawn, artificial; *inf.* over the top, camped up.

campaign *noun* **1** *Napoleon's Russian Campaign* war, battle, expedition, offensive, attack, crusade. **2** *an advertising campaign | a campaign against litter* course of action, operation, promotion, strategy, set of tactics, drive, push, crusade, movement, manoeuvre, battle plan.

campaign *verb campaigning for civil rights* fight, battle, work, push, crusade, strive, struggle, agitate.

can *noun a can of beans | a can of hot water* tin, container, receptacle.

can *verb can fruit* tin, preserve, bottle.

canal *noun* **1** *barges on the canal* channel, race, watercourse, waterway. *See table.* **2** *the alimentary canal* tube, duct, conduit, pipe.

cancel *verb* **1** *cancel a holiday/date* call off, stop, discontinue, give up, withdraw from, countermand, revoke, rescind. **2** *cancel an order* annul, declare void, declare null and void, nullify, quash, invalidate, set aside, retract, negate, revoke, rescind, repudiate, abrogate, repeal, abolish. **3** *cancel that last paragraph* delete, cross out, erase, strike out, rub out, blot out, expunge, obliterate, eradicate, efface. **4** *his friendliness cancels out her hostility* counterbalance, balance, offset, compensate, make up for, counteract, neutralize, redeem, countervail.
Opposites CONFIRM.

CANALS

Canal	Location	Canal	Location
All-American Canal	U.S.A.	Gulf Intracoastal Waterway	U.S.A.
Atlantic Intracoastal Waterway	U.S.A.	Manchester Ship Canal	U.K.
Cauvery Delta System	India	Moscow Canal	Russia
Corinth Canal	Greece	Panama Canal	Panama
Gezira Canals	Sudan	St Lawrence Seaway	Canada
Grand Canal	China	Suez Canal	Egypt
Grand Canal	Venice, Italy	Thal Canal	Pakistan
Grand Union Canal	U.K.	Western Yamuna Canal	India

cancer noun **1** *cancer of the breast* tumour, malignant tumour, malignancy, growth, malignant growth; *Med.* carcinoma, sarcoma, melanoma, metastasis. **2** *a cancer in our society* canker, blight, evil, corruption, rot, sickness, disease, pestilence, scourge, plague.

candid adjective **1** *she's always candid | candid remarks* frank, open, honest, truthful, sincere, forthright, direct, plain-spoken, outspoken, blunt, unequivocal, bluff, brusque; *inf.* straight from the shoulder. **2** *candid camera shots* unposed, spontaneous, impromptu, extemporary, uncontrived, informal, unstudied. **Opposites** SECRETIVE; GUARDED; EQUIVOCAL.

candidate noun **1** *two candidates for the post | parliamentary candidates* applicant, job applicant, office seeker, contender, nominee, contestant, aspirant, possibility; *inf.* runner. **2** *candidates for the final exams* examination-taker, entrant.

candle noun taper; tallow candle, wax candle, rush candle, Christmas candle, votary candle.

candour noun frankness, openness, honesty, truthfulness, sincerity, forthrightness, directness, plainspokenness, outspokenness, unequivocalness, bluntness, bluffness, brusqueness.

candy noun **1** *boil sugar to make candy* sugar-candy, toffee. **2** *American children asking for candy* sweets, sweetmeats, confectionery, bon-bons.

cane noun **1** *a walking cane | canes supporting plants* stick, staff, rod, stave; walking stick, alpenstock, shepherd's crook. **2** *sugar-cane* stem, stalk, shoot, reed.

cane verb **1** *cane the children* beat, strike, hit, flog, thrash, lash, strap, scourge; *inf.* tan one's hide. **2** *we really caned the opposition* trounce, thrash, vanquish, defeat, rout, put to rout.

canker noun **1** *a canker in the dog's ear* ulcer, ulceration, sore, running sore, lesion, blister, abscess. **2** *tree canker* fungus disease, blight, plant rot. **3** *a canker in society* cancer, blight, evil, corruption, rot, sickness, scourge. *See* CANCER 2.

cannibal noun anthropophagite, man-eater, people-eater; savage, barbarian, wild man.

cannon noun gun, field gun, mounted gun; *inf.* big gun.

cannonade noun barrage, bombardment, shelling, battery, pounding, attack, salvo, volley, broadside.

canny adjective **1** *canny savers* careful, cautious, prudent, thrifty. **2** *a canny business-woman* shrewd, sharp, astute, discerning, penetrating, perspicacious, clever, sensible, wise, judicious, sagacious, circumspect. **Opposites** CARELESS; FOOLISH.

canon[1] noun **1** *the canons of good taste* rule, ruling, principle, standard, criterion, test, measure, yardstick, benchmark, pattern, model, exemplar, precept, norm, formula, convention. **2** *a Church canon* law, rule, regulation, statute, decree, edict, dictate. **3** *a canon of saints | the canon of Shakespeare's plays* official list, list, catalogue, enumeration, litany, roll.

canon[2] noun prebendary. *See* ECCLESIASTIC noun.

canopy noun awning, shade, sunshade, cover, covering, tarpaulin, tester, baldachin; *lit.* cope.

cant[1] noun **1** *thieves' cant* slang, jargon, patter, lingo, terminology, argot. **2** *religious cant* hypocrisy, insincerity, sanctimony, sanctimoniousness, humbug, pseudo-piety, sham holiness, lip service, pretence.

cant[2] noun *the table is on a cant* slant, slope, tilt, angle, inclination.

cant[3] verb *the boat began to cant* tilt, tip, slope, slant, lean, incline, angle, overturn.

cantankerous adjective bad-tempered, short-tempered, ill-natured, crabbed, crabby, surly, irascible, irritable, grumpy, brusque, curt, abrupt, difficult, disagreeable, quarrelsome, touchy, perverse, testy, peevish, crusty, peppery, choleric, captious; *inf.* grouchy, crotchety, cranky.

canter noun amble, saunter, trot, jog, dogtrot, lope, gallop.

canvass verb **1** *canvassing during the general election* solicit votes, seek votes, campaign, electioneer, drum up support, persuade, convince. **2** *canvassing people's views | canvass buying habits* investigate, find out, enquire into, look into, examine, scrutinize, explore, study, analyse, sift, evaluate, survey, scan, poll. **3** *canvass an idea/suggestion/theory* discuss, debate, air, ventilate, argue, dispute.

canyon noun ravine, gully, valley, gorge, chasm, gulf, abyss.

cap noun **1** *doffing his cap* hat, bonnet, headgear; *inf.* lid. *See table at* HAT. **2** *replace the cap on the bottle* top, lid, stopper, cork, bung, plug. **3** *the cap of a wave | mountain caps* top, crest, peak, summit, apex, pinnacle.

cap verb **1** *mountains capped with snow* cover, top, crown, overlie, overspread, coat, blanket. **2** *cap his story | cap the ground record* beat, better, surpass, excel, outshine, transcend, eclipse, overshadow, outdo, outstrip, exceed. **3** *he's been capped for Wales* choose, select, pick, include. **4** *cap the price* limit, set a limit to, restrict, keep within bounds, curb. **cap it all** provide as a finishing touch, suffer as a final straw, suffer/find on top of everything else.

capability noun **1** *have the capability to do well | the capability of winning* ability, capacity, potential, aptitude, faculty, facility, power, competence, efficiency, effectiveness, proficiency, accomplishment, talent, adeptness, skill, skilfulness, experience, cleverness, intelligence, smartness. *See* CAPABLE. **2** *offer capabilities* talent, gifts, skill, aptitude, flair, knack, forte, strong point.

capable adjective *a very capable young woman* able, competent, adequate, efficient, effective, proficient, accomplished, talented, gifted, adept, skilful, masterly, experienced, practised, qualified, clever, intelligent, smart. **capable of 1** *capable of murder/lying* having the inclination/temperament to do, having a tendency/propensity to do, tending to, inclined to, predisposed to, prone to, liable to, likely to do. **2** *capable of improvement* needing, in need of,

requiring, wanting, susceptible to, admitting of, receptive of.
Opposites INCAPABLE; INCOMPETENT.

capacious *adjective* roomy, commodious, spacious, ample, large, voluminous, sizeable, substantial, vast, immense.
Opposites CRAMPED; NARROW; SMALL.

capacity *noun* **1** *the capacity to seat twenty* space, room, size, largeness, ampleness, amplitude, scope, magnitude, dimensions, proportions, extent. **2** *have the capacity to do the job* ability, capability, aptitude, potential, faculty, facility, power, competence, competency, proficiency, accomplishment, cleverness, intelligence, brains, head. See CAPABILITY. **3** *in his capacity as a teacher* position, post, job, office, function, role, appointment, province.

cape[1] *noun wearing a black cape* cloak. *See table at* COAT.

cape[2] *noun drowned off the cape* headland, head, point, promontory, neck, tongue, peninsula.

caper *verb goats/children capering about* frolic, frisk, romp, skip, gambol, cavort, prance, dance, leap, hop, jump, bound, spring, bounce.

caper *noun* **1** *the energetic capers of the children/goats* frolics, frisking, romping, skipping, gambols, gambolling, cavorting, prancing, dancing, leap. See CAPER *verb*. **2** *tired of their mischievous capers* prank, trick, practical joke, antic, lark, jest, jesting, jape, high jinks, mischief, escapade, stunt, game, sport, fun; *inf.* shenanigan; *Am. inf.* dido.

capital *adjective* **1** *our capital concern | take capital decisions* principal, chief, main, major, prime, paramount, foremost, predominant, overruling, leading, cardinal, central, key. **2** *make a capital error* grave, vital, important, serious, crucial, fatal. **3** *a capital show | a capital piece of work* splendid, excellent, first-rate, first-class, superb, fine, outstanding; *inf.* super, tiptop, A1, crack, top-notch.

capital *noun* **1** *Edinburgh is the capital of Scotland* first city, seat of government, centre of administration. *See table at* COUNTRY. **2** *write in capitals* capital letter, upper-case letter, majuscule, uncial, uncial letter; *inf.* cap. **3** *enough capital to buy the firm* money, finance, finances, funds, cash, hard cash, wherewithal, means, assets, liquid assets, wealth, resources, reserves, stock, principal; working capital, investment capital.

capitalism *noun* free enterprise, private enterprise, private ownership, privatized industries, *laissez-faire*.

capitalist *noun* financier, investor, banker, tycoon, moneyman; wealthy/rich person, plutocrat, nabob, bloated capitalist; *inf.* yuppie, loadsamoney.

capitalize *verb capitalize the firm* finance, back, provide backing for, fund, sponsor. **capitalize on** *capitalize on her rival's mistakes* take advantage of, put to advantage, profit from, turn to account, cash in on, make the most of, exploit.

capitulate *verb* surrender, yield, submit, give in, give up, come to terms, succumb, accede,

back down, cave in, relent, acquiesce; *inf.* throw in the towel/sponge.

caprice *noun* whim, whimsy, vagary, fancy, notion, fad, freak, humour, impulse, quirk, crotchet; changeableness, fickleness, volatility, inconstancy, fitfulness.

capricious *adjective* changeable, unpredictable, fickle, variable, inconstant, unstable, mercurial, volatile, impulsive, erratic, fanciful, faddish, freakish, irregular, fitful, whimsical, wayward, quirky.
Opposites STABLE; CONSISTENT; CONSTANT.

capsize *verb* overturn, turn over, upset, upend, knock over, tip over, invert, keel over, turn turtle.

capsule *noun* **1** *pain-relieving capsules* pill, tablet, lozenge, bolus, troche. **2** *plant capsules* seed case, pod, pericarp. **3** *remove the capsule from the wine bottle* seal, cap, cover. **4** *space capsule* craft, probe; detachable compartment, section.

captain *noun* **1** *the captain of the ship* commander, master, skipper; *inf.* old man. **2** *team captain* leader, head, skipper. **3** *captains of industry* chief, head, leader, boss, principal; *inf.* number one; *Am. inf.* honcho.

caption *noun* heading, title, wording, head, legend, inscription.

captious *adjective* carping, criticizing, critical, fault-finding, quibbling, cavilling; *inf.* nitpicking.

captivate *verb* charm, delight, enchant, bewitch, fascinate, beguile, enthral, entrance, enrapture, attract, allure, lure, win, infatuate, seduce, ravish, ensnare, dazzle, hypnotize, mesmerize.

captive *noun take captives | captives clamouring for freedom* prisoner, prisoner-of-war, hostage, slave, bondsman, convict, jailbird, detainee; *inf.* con.

captive *adjective captive animals* imprisoned, incarcerated, locked up, caged, interned, confined, penned up, detained, restrained; in captivity, in bondage.

captivity *noun* imprisonment, custody, detention, confinement, internment, incarceration, restraint, constraint, committal, bondage, slavery, servitude, enslavement, subjection, thraldom.

capture *verb* catch, arrest, apprehend, take prisoner, take captive, take into custody, seize, take, lay hold of, trap; *inf.* nab, collar, pinch, lift, nail, bag.
Opposites FREE; LIBERATE.

capture *noun* **1** *involved in the criminal's capture* arrest, apprehension, taking prisoner, taking captive, imprisonment, seizure, trapping; *inf.* nabbing, collaring, pinching. See CAPTURE *verb*. **2** *the captures of war* prize, trophy, gain; booty, pickings, pillage.

car *noun* **1** *hiring a car* motor car, motor, vehicle, motor vehicle, automobile, motorized vehicle, machine; *inf.* wheels, heap, crate, jalopy, limo; *Am. inf.* auto; company car, hired car; police car, patrol car, Panda car. *See tables.*

See also table at VEHICLE. **2** *railway car* coach, van; Pullman, cable car. *See table at* TRAIN.

carafe noun flask, decanter, jug, pitcher, flagon.

caravan noun **1** *holiday in a caravan* mobile home, camper, Dormobile; *Am.* trailer; *inf.* van. **2** *a gypsy caravan* wagon, covered cart, cart, van. **3** *merchant caravans in the desert* convoy, troop, band, company, group, cavalcade, procession.

carcass noun **1** *sheep carcasses* corpse, dead body, body; remains; *Med.* cadaver; *inf.* stiff. **2** *shift your carcass* body, person, self, oneself. **3** *the carcass of the building* frame, framework, skeleton, shell, hulk.

card noun **1** *use card to make the model* cardboard, pasteboard. **2** *send a card to her* postcard, greetings card, Christmas card, birthday card, good luck card, get well card, sympathy card. **3** *here's my card* identification; business card, calling card, ID card, identification card. **4** *deal the cards* playing cards, picture cards, face cards, tarot cards; pack of cards; cardgame. *See table. See also table at* POKER. **on the cards** *an election's on the cards* likely, possible, probable, liable, in the wind, in the air.

cardinal adjective **1** *cardinal sins/errors* main, chief, capital, principal, important, greatest, highest, vital, key, central, major, essential, foremost, leading, prime, paramount, pre-eminent, fundamental, basic, primary. **2** *painted cardinal red* red, scarlet, crimson, vermillion.

cardinal noun *cardinals in Rome* cardinal bishop, cardinal priest, high priest, archpriest. *See* ECCLESIASTIC *noun.*

care noun **1** *bowed down with care* worry, anxiety, trouble, disquiet, unease, distress, sorrow, anguish, grief, sadness, affliction, woe, hardship, tribulation, responsibility, stress, pressure, strain; burdens. **2** *no care for others* concern, regard, attention, interest, solicitude, looking after, sympathy. **3** *arrange the flowers with care* carefulness, attention, thought, regard, heed, forethought, mindfulness, conscientiousness, painstakingness, pains, accuracy, precision, meticulousness, punctiliousness, fastidiousness. **4** *cross the road with care* attention, caution, heedfulness, alertness, watchfulness, vigilance, wariness, awareness, circumspection, prudence. **5** *in the care of her uncle | in the care of the local authority* charge, protection, custody, keeping, safe keeping, control, management, ministration, supervision; guardianship, wardship.

Opposites HAPPINESS; NEGLECT; carelessness; INATTENTION.

TYPES OF CAR

armoured car	electric car	hot rod	rally car	station wagon
automatic	estate	Land Rover™	roadster	stock car
bubble car	four-wheel drive car	limousine	runabout	streetcar
cabriolet	hard top	Mini™	saloon	stretch
convertible	hatchback	off-roader	sedan *Am.*	limousine
coupé	hearse	open top	soft top	tourer
		racing car	sports car	

CAR PARTS

accelerator	clutch	gear	oil gauge	spark plug
alternator	connecting rod	gearbox	overrider	speedometer
anti-lock brake	cowl	gear lever	overrun brake	splashboard
anti-roll bar	crank	generator	piston	sprag
automatic choke	crankcase	grille	pneumatic tyre	starter
automatic transmission	cruise control	hazard warning light	power brakes	starter motor
axle	cylinder	headlight	power steering	steering column
bench seat	cylinder head	hood *Am.*	propeller shaft	steering gear
blinker	dashboard/dash	horn	rack-and-pinion	steering wheel
bodywork	differential gear	hydraulic brake	radial tyre	stick
bonnet	disc brake	hydraulic suspension	radiator	stick shift *Am.*
boot	distributor	hypoid gear	radius rod	stop light
brake	driving wheel	ignition	reach	suspension
brake drum	drum brake	ignition key	reflector	tachograph
brake light	fender *Am.*	indicator	reverse	tailpipe
bucket seat	filler cap	manifold	running board	tail wheel
bumper	fluid drive	mileometer	shaft	top gear
camshaft	flywheel	monocoque	shift *Am.*	tow bar
carburettor	four-wheel drive	muffler	shock absorber	track rod
catalytic converter	freewheel	number plate	sidelight	transmission
chassis	gate	odometer *Am.*	silencer	winker
	gauge		solenoid	wing

care verb *she doesn't care about her work | he didn't care what happened* be concerned, be interested, interest oneself, have regard, worry, trouble, mind; *inf.* give a damn, give a hoot, give a rap, give a hang. **care for** **1** *he cares for his wife deeply* love, be fond of, be in love with, cherish, hold dear, treasure. **2** *I don't care for her* like, be fond of, find congenial. **3** *would you care for some tea?* wish, want, desire, fancy, hanker after, long for; *inf.* have a yen for. **4** *care for the children* take care of, look after, mind, watch, tend, attend to, minister to, foster, nurse, provide for.

career noun **1** *choose a career* occupation, profession, vocation, calling, employment, job, métier. **2** *watch the career of the political party* course, progress, progression, procedure, passage, path. **3** *stop the horse in mid-career* rush, onrush, run, race, bolt, dash, gallop, impetus.

carefree adjective light-hearted, happy-go-lucky, cheerful, cheery, happy, merry, jolly, buoyant, breezy, easygoing, jaunty, frisky, blithe, airy, nonchalant, unworried, untroubled, insouciant; *inf.* upbeat.
Opposites ANXIOUS; WORRIED; MISERABLE.

careful adjective **1** *be careful crossing the road* cautious, heedful, alert, aware, attentive, watchful, vigilant, wary, on guard, chary, circumspect, prudent, mindful. **2** *be careful of your reputation* mindful, heedful, protective; *be careful about what you say* solicitous, thoughtful, attentive, concerned, having regard. **3** *a careful worker* attentive, conscientious, painstaking, meticulous, accurate, precise, scrupulous, punctilious, fastidious. **4** *a careful housekeeper | careful with her money* canny, cautious, thrifty, economical, economic.
Opposites CARELESS; INATTENTIVE; EXTRAVAGANT.

careless adjective **1** *a careless driver* inattentive, thoughtless, unthinking, forgetful, absent-minded, negligent, remiss, irresponsible, slapdash, slipshod, lax, slack; *inf.* sloppy. **2** *a careless piece of work* hasty, cursory, perfunctory, inaccurate, disorganized, slapdash, slipshod; *inf.* sloppy. **3** *a careless remark* unthinking, thoughtless, insensitive, indiscreet, unguarded. **4** *careless of her appearance* negligent, remiss, slapdash, slipshod, untidy, slovenly, slatternly; *inf.* sloppy, messy. **5** *careless rapture* carefree, light-hearted, happy-go-lucky, cheerful, merry, buoyant, blithe, nonchalant. See CAREFREE. **6** *careless elegance* unstudied, artless, casual, nonchalant, informal.
Opposites CAREFUL; METICULOUS.

caress noun *a loving caress* touch, stroke, fondle, fondling, pat, embrace, cuddle, hug, nuzzle, kiss.

caress verb *caress her* cuddle, fondle, pet, pat, embrace, hug, nuzzle, kiss; *caress her throat* kiss, touch/stroke lovingly.

caretaker noun superintendent, janitor, warden, porter, custodian, keeper, watchman, steward, curator, concierge. ,

cargo noun freight, freightage, load, lading, haul, consignment, contents, goods, merchandise, baggage; shipment, shipload, boatload, lorryload, truckload.

caricature noun cartoon, parody, burlesque, mimicry, travesty, distortion, satire, farce, lampoon, pasquinade; *inf.* send-up, take-off, spoof.

caricature verb parody, mimic, mock, ridicule, distort, satirize, lampoon, burlesque; *inf.* send up, take off.

carnage noun slaughter, wholesale slaughter, butchery, massacre, mass murder, mass destruction, indiscriminate bloodshed; blood bath, holocaust, pogrom; *inf.* shambles.

CARD GAMES

all fours	cribbage	Newmarket	rummy
auction bridge	Dom Pedro	noddy	Russian Bank
baccarat	duplicate bridge	old maid	Sancho Pedro
banker	écarté	ombre	scopa
basset	euchre	Pam	seven-up
beggar-my-neighbour	fan-tan	panguingue	sixty-six
belote	faro	patience	skat
bezique	five hundred	pedro	skin
blackjack	forty-five	Pelmanism	slapjack
Black Maria	gleek	penny ante	snap
blind poker	happy families	pinochle	snip-snap-snorum
Boston	hearts	piquet	solitaire *Am.*
brag	high-low	pitch	speculation
bridge	imperial	poker	spite and malice
California jack	klaberjass	pontoon	strip Jack naked
canasta	Klondike	Pope Joan	thirty-one
Canfield	lansquenet	primero	three-card monte
cassino	loo	quadrille	tredrille
cheat	lottery	quinze	twenty-five
chemin de fer	matrimony	red dog	vingt-et-un
cinch	Michigan	reverse	vint
coon-can	monte	rouge et noir	whipperginny
comet	muggins	rubber bridge	whist
	nap	ruff	

carnal *adjective* sexual, sensual, fleshly, erotic, lustful, lascivious, libidinous, lecherous, lewd, prurient, salacious, coarse, gross, lubricious.

carnival *noun* **1** *we are looking forward to the carnival* fiesta, festival, fête, gala, jamboree, holiday; revelry, revels, merrymaking, festivity, celebration; Mardi gras. **2** *the carnival has moved to another town* fair, amusement show, sideshows, circus.

carol *noun* Christmas song, nativity song, hymn, canticle; *inf.* noel.

carol *verb children carolling loudly* sing carols, go carolling, sing, chorus, warble, trill, chant.

carouse *verb* go on a spree, go on a drinking bout, go on a binge, binge, make merry, party, paint the town red, over-indulge, drink freely, roister, wassail, live it up, go on a bender, go on a pub-crawl.

carp *verb* complain, fault-find, find fault, criticize, cavil, pick on, quibble, censure, reproach, nag; *inf.* nit-pick.
Opposites APPLAUD; PRAISE.

carpenter *noun* joiner, cabinet-maker, woodworker.

carpet *noun* **1** *the lounge carpet* floor-covering, runner, matting, mat, rug; fitted carpet, magic carpet. *See table.* **2** *a carpet of leaves* covering, layer, expanse.

TYPES OF CARPET		
Axminster	ingrain	rag
Brussels	Kiddermin-	Turkish
chenille	ster	velvet
handwoven	Oriental	Wilton
hooked	Persian	

carriage *noun* **1** *carriages of former times* vehicle. *See table.* **2** *a railway carriage* compartment, car. *See table at* TRAIN. **3** *an elegant carriage* posture, bearing, stance, deportment, comportment, attitude, manner, presence, air, guise, demeanour, mien, behaviour, conduct. **4** *free carriage* transport, transportation, freight, freightage, conveyance, delivery, carrying.

carry *verb* **1** *carry a parcel* transport, convey, transfer, move, take, bring, bear, lug, haul, shift, fetch; conduct, pass on, transmit, relay.

2 *carry the weight of the column | carry responsibilities* support, sustain, bear, shoulder. **3** *carry the day/victory/motion* win, capture, gain, secure, effect, accomplish. **4** *a store carrying a brand* sell, stock, offer, have for sale, retail. **5** *carrying the latest news* communicate, give, release, publish, broadcast. **6** *carry the audience/crowd* influence, affect, have an effect on, motivate, stimulate, urge, spur on, impel, drive.

7 *women carrying themselves well* bear oneself, hold oneself, comport oneself, deport oneself, conduct oneself. **carry on 1** *carry on talking* go on, continue, keep, keep on, persist in, maintain, persevere in. **2** *carry on a business* run, operate, conduct, manage, administer, transact. **3** *he's carrying on with his secretary* have an affair, commit adultery; *inf.* have it off. **4** *children carrying on* misbehave, make mischief, be mischievous, cause a fuss/commotion; *inf.* create. **carry out 1** *carry out a promise/threat* fulfil, carry through, achieve, implement, realize, execute, effect, discharge. **2** *carry out an experiment/enquiry* conduct, perform, implement, execute.

cart *noun* **1** *collect garden rubbish in a cart* handcart, barrow, wheelbarrow, pushcart. **2** *horse-drawn carts* four-wheeled cart. *See table at* CARRIAGE.

cart *verb* **1** *cart away the rubbish* transport, convey, haul, transfer, move, shift. **2** *carting the luggage on holiday* lug, tote, carry; *dial.* humph.

carton *noun* box, package, cardboard box, container, case, pack, packet.

cartoon *noun* **1** *children's cartoons* comic strip; animated film, animated cartoon; animation. **2** *a political cartoon | newspaper cartoons* caricature, parody, lampoon, satire, burlesque, pasquinade; *inf.* take-off, send-up, spoof.

cartridge *noun* case, container, cylinder, capsule, cassette, magazine.

carve *verb* **1** *carve a figure out of stone* sculpt, sculpture, cut, chisel, hew, whittle, chip, form, shape, fashion, mould. **2** *carve initials on a tree* engrave, etch, notch, cut in, incise. **3** *carve meat* slice, cut up. **carve up** *carve up the territory* divide, partition, parcel out, apportion, dole out, subdivide, split up, separate out.

cascade *noun* waterfall, falls, fountain, water chute, shower, cataract, torrent, flood, deluge, outpouring, avalanche. *See table at* WATERFALL.

CARRIAGES AND CARTS				
barouche	chaise	droshky	jaunting car	sulky
brake	chariot	equipage	landau	surrey
break	clarence	fiacre	oxcart	tarantass
britzka	coach	fly	phaeton	tilbury
brougham	coach-and-four	four-in-hand	post-chaise	trap
buckboard	Conestoga	gharry	prairie	trishaw
buggy	wagon	gig	schooner	tumbril
cab	covered wagon	hackney	rickshaw	Victoria
calash	curricle	hansom	rig	vis-à-vis
Cape cart	dog cart	hay-cart	rockaway	wagon
carriole	drag	haywain	spider phaeton	wagonette
carry-all	dray	herdic	stagecoach	wain

cascade *verb* tumble, descend, pour, gush, surge, spill, overflow.

case[1] *noun* **1** *a cigarette case* container, box, receptacle, holder, canister. **2** *a case of wine* crate, box, carton, pack, bin, coffer, casket. **3** *bullet case | tape case* casing, covering, sheath, sheathing, wrapper, wrapping, cover, envelope, housing, jacket, capsule, folder, integument. **4** *checking in cases at the airport* suitcase, trunk, piece of luggage, item of baggage, briefcase; luggage, baggage. **5** *display case* cabinet, cupboard, chiffonier, bureau.

case[2] *noun* **1** *as has been the case previously stated* position, situation, circumstances, instance, occurrence, happening, occasion, conditions, plight, predicament, event, contingency, phenomenon. **2** *a case of cheating* instance, occurrence, occasion, example, illustration, specimen. **3** *the case comes up next week* lawsuit, suit, action, trial, proceedings, legal proceedings, legal process, legal cause, legal dispute. **4** *his case was that he was elsewhere* statement, plea, claim, alibi, postulation, explanation, exposition, thesis, testing, presentation. **5** *terminal cases* patient, sick person, invalid, sufferer, victim.

cash *noun* **1** *no cash with me* money, ready money, coinage, notes, bank notes, currency; *fml.* specie, legal tender. *See table at* CURRENCY. **2** *he has no cash of any kind* money, finance, wherewithal, resources, funds, capital, investment capital; *inf.* dough, bread, the ready.

cash *verb* *cash the cheque/bills* encash, realize, exchange, change, turn into cash/money.

cashier *noun* bank clerk, bank teller, teller, banker, treasurer, bursar, purser, accountant, controller, money man.

cashier *verb* dismiss, discharge, expel, drum out, throw out, cast out, discard, get rid of; *inf.* sack, give the boot to, boot out.

casino *noun* gambling club, gaming club, gambling house, gambling den.

cask *noun* barrel, keg, tun, vat, vessel, hogshead, firkin, pipe.

casket *noun* **1** *a jewel casket* box, case, container, receptacle, chest, coffer. **2** *funeral casket* coffin, pall, sarcophagus; *inf.* box; *sl* wooden overcoat.

cast *verb* **1** *cast a stone in the lake* throw, toss, fling, pitch, hurl, sling, heave, shy, lob, launch, let fly. **2** *cast their skins/coats* shed, discard, slough off, peel off, throw off, get rid of, let fall, let drop. **3** *cast a glance* shoot, direct, turn, throw, send out. **4** *cast a soft light* emit, give off, send out, shed, radiate, diffuse, spread out; *cast a shadow* form, create. **5** *cast doubt* throw, bestow, impart, confer, give, grant. **6** *cast one's vote* register, record, enter, vote. **7** *cast bronze | cast figures in bronze* shape, fashion, form, mould, model, sculpt. **8** *cast actors for the play* choose, select, pick, name, assign, appoint, allot. **9** *cast up the figures* add, total, reckon, sum. **10** *cast a fortune* predict, forecast, foretell, foresee, prophesy. **cast about** *cast about for his sock | cast about for an excuse* search, seek, look, grope about. **cast down** *the*

weather cast him down a bit depress, deject, dispirit, discourage, dishearten, desolate.

cast *noun* **1** *the cast of a dice* throw, toss, fling, pitch, hurl, shy, lob. *See* CAST *verb* 1. **2** *cast of features/mind* sort, kind, style, type, stamp, nature. **3** *plaster cast* figure, shape, mould, form. **4** *a cast in her eye* squint, twist, defect.

caste *noun* *a member of the upper caste* class, social class, order, social order, grade, grading, station, place, standing, position, status.

castigate *verb* punish, discipline, chastise, rebuke, reproach, scold, reprimand, censure, reprove, upbraid, berate, chide, admonish, criticize, chasten, take to task, dress down, give a dressing-down to, haul over the coals.

castle *noun* stronghold, fortress, keep, hold, citadel, fastness, peel, palace, chateau.

casual *adjective* **1** *a casual meeting* chance, accidental, unintentional, unexpected, unforeseen, unanticipated, fortuitous, serendipitous. **2** *a casual remark* offhand, random, impromptu, spontaneous, unpremeditated, unthinking. **3** *casual work* part-time, temporary, irregular. **4** *a casual read* cursory, perfunctory, superficial, desultory, hasty, hurried. **5** *a casual attitude to work* indifferent, apathetic, uncaring, uninterested, unconcerned, lackadaisical, blasé, nonchalant, lukewarm, insouciant, pococurante. **6** *casual clothes* informal, not formal, unceremonious, relaxed, leisure; *inf.* sporty. **7** *a casual acquaintance* slight, superficial, shallow.
Opposites INTENTIONAL; THOROUGH; FORMAL.

casualties *plural noun* *the casualties of the last war* dead, fatalities, losses, dead and wounded, wounded, injured, missing in action, missing.

casualty *noun* **1** *a war casualty* fatality, dead/wounded/injured person, victim. **2** *the firm was a casualty of the recession* victim, sufferer, loser, loss.

cat *noun* **1** *a cat by the fire* feline, domestic cat; *inf.* pussy, pussy cat, puss, moggy; *lit.* grimalkin; tabby, tomcat, tom, ginger tom, tortoiseshell, marmalade cat, kitten, mouser, wild cat, alley cat. *See table.* **2** *the cats of Africa* big cat. *See table.* **3** *spiteful cat* shrew, vixen, virago; *inf.* bitch.

catacombs *plural noun* underground tunnels/labyrinth/maze, tomb, underground cemetery, underground burial ground.

catalogue *noun* *a catalogue of library books* list, record, register, inventory, directory, index, roll, table, calendar, classification, guide, brochure.

catalogue *verb* list, classify, categorize, index, make an inventory of, inventory, record, register, file, alphabetize.

catapult *noun* *kill the creature with a catapult* sling; *Am.* slingshot. *See table at* MISSILE.

catapult *verb* *he was catapulted to freedom/success* launch/propel rapidly, hurtle, shoot, be flung.

cataract *noun* **1** *cataracts falling from the rocks* cascade, waterfall, falls, rapids, torrent, downpour. **2** *eye surgeons operate on cataracts* opacity, opaqueness.

catastrophe noun disaster, calamity, tragedy, blow, adversity, trouble, trials, mishap, misfortune, mischance, misadventure, failure, reverses, affliction, distress.

catcall noun whistle, boo, hiss, jeer; inf. the bird, a raspberry.

catch verb **1** catch the ball grasp, snatch, grab, seize, grip, clutch, clench, pluck, receive, acquire, come into the possession of, intercept. **2** catch the prisoner capture, seize, take captive, apprehend, take, arrest, lay hold of, trap, snare; inf. nab, collar. **3** catch what he said understand, follow, grasp, comprehend, make out, take in, fathom, discern, perceive, apprehend; inf. get the drift of, get the hang of, twig. **4** catch him unawares surprise, discover, come across, startle, detect. **5** catch pneumonia contract, get, become infected with, develop, succumb to, suffer from; inf. go/come down with. **6** catch his attention/fancy capture, attract, draw, captivate, bewitch. **7** catch a likeness capture, reproduce, represent, photograph, draw, paint. **catch on 1** sports catching on become popular, become fashionable, come into fashion/vogue; inf. become trendy, become all the rage. **2** eventually catch on to his intentions see through, find out, fathom, grasp, understand, comprehend, see the light about; inf. twig, latch on, figure out, get the picture about.
Opposites DROP; RELEASE; LOSE.

catch noun **1** the catch of the door/suitcase bolt, lock, fastener, fastening, clasp, hasp, hook, clip, latch, snib; Scots sneck. **2** what's the catch? snag, disadvantage, drawback, stumbling block, hitch, fly in the ointment, trap, trick, snare; inf. catch-22. **3** sell the catch at the market bag, hawl, net, take, yield. **4** he/she is quite a catch eligible man/woman/person, marriage prospect, suitable husband/wife/spouse.

catching adjective **1** a catching disease | is it catching? contagious, infectious, communicable, transmittable, transmissible. **2** a catching manner attractive, appealing, winning, captivating, charming, fetching, taking, fascinating, enchanting, bewitching, alluring.

catchword noun slogan, motto, password, watchword, byword, shibboleth, formula, refrain, saying.

catchy adjective memorable, popular, appealing, captivating, haunting, melodious, singable.

catechize verb interrogate, cross-examine, question, quiz, examine, grill, pump, give the third degree to, put through the third degree.

categorical adjective unqualified, unconditional, unequivocal, explicit, unambiguous, unreserved, absolute, direct, downright, emphatic, positive, express, conclusive.
Opposites QUALIFIED; EQUIVOCAL; TENTATIVE.

categorize verb classify, class, group, grade, order, arrange, sort, rank, break down, catalogue, list, tabulate.

category noun class, classification, group, grouping, head, heading, list, listing, designation, type, sort, kind, variety, grade, grading, order, rank, status, division, section, department.

cater verb **1** cater for all needs provide, furnish, supply, purvey. **2** cater for large parties provide food, feed, provision, victual.

caterwauling noun howl, howling, screech, screeching, shriek, shrieking, scream, screaming.

catharsis noun purging, purgation, purification, cleansing, depuration, lustration, release, emotional release; Tech. abreaction.

cathartic adjective puragative, purifying, cleansing, lustral, release-bringing.

catholic adjective **1** of catholic interest general, universal, widespread, global, world-wide, comprehensive, all-encompassing all-embracing, all-inclusive. **2** catholic tastes/views wide, broad, broad-based, eclectic, liberal, open-minded, tolerant, unbigoted, unsectarian, ecumenical.
Opposites LIMITED; NARROW.

cattle noun cows, bovines, beasts; stock, livestock. See table.

catty adjective catty female/remark spiteful, malicious, venomous, malevolent, nasty, ill-natured, mean.

caucus noun **1** attend a Senate caucus assembly, meeting, gathering, session, conference, convention, conclave. **2** a local parliamentary caucus group, party, bloc, faction, cabal, clique, coterie.

cause noun **1** the cause of the fire | the cause of her misfortune origin, root, source, beginning, genesis, occasion, mainspring, originator, author, creator, producer, agent, prime mover, maker. **2** no cause for alarm reason, grounds,

CATS					
Breeds of Domestic Cat	Cornish rex	Siamese	cheetah	jaguarundi	ocelot
	Devon rex	Somali	civet	jungle	ounce
	Exotic Short	Tiffanie	clouded	cat	pampas
Abyssinian	Hair	Tonkinese	leopard	leopard	cat
Angora	Maine Coon	Turkish Van	cougar	liger	panther
Asian/	Manx	**Wild Cats**	European	lion	puma
Burmilla	Oriental	African wild	wild cat	lynx	serval
Balinese	Short Hair	cat	eyra	margay	Temminck's
Birman	Persian	bobcat	Geoffroy's	mountain	golden cat
British	Long Hair	caracal	cat	cat	tiger
Short Hair	Russian	catamoun-	golden cat	mountain	tiger-cat
Burmese	Blue	tain	jaguar	lion	tigon

justification, call, basis, motive, motivation.
3 *devoted to the cause of human rights* principle,
ideal, belief, conviction, tenet, object, aim,
objective, purpose, *raison d'être*. **4** *plead his
cause* case, point of view, contention.
Opposites EFFECT; RESULT.

cause *verb cause trouble | cause the explosion* be
the cause of, make happen, bring about, give
rise to, begin, create, produce, originate, occasion, generate, effect, engender, lead to, result
in, precipitate, provoke.

caustic *adjective* **1** *caustic chemical substances*
corrosive, corroding, mordant, burning, acrid,
destructive. **2** *a caustic wit* sarcastic, cutting,
biting, mordant, stinging, sharp, scathing,
trenchant, virulent, acrimonious, astringent.

cauterize *verb* burn, sear, singe, disinfect, sterilize.

caution *noun* **1** *proceed with caution* alertness,
care, carefulness, attention, wariness, attentiveness, heed, heedfulness, watchfulness, vigilance, guardedness, circumspection, discretion, forethought, prudence, mindfulness.
2 *receive a caution from the police/headmaster*
warning, admonition, injunction, monition;
counsel. **3** *her uncle's a caution* comic, comedian, wit, humorist, wag, clown, joker, jester.

caution *verb* **1** *caution against driving fast | cau-
tion not to go* warn, advise, counsel, urge,
admonish. **2** *cautioned by the judge* give/deliver
a caution to, admonish, warn, give an injunction to.

cautious *adjective* careful, wary, watchful,
shrewd, prudent, circumspect, discreet,
guarded, chary, alert, heedful, attentive, vigilant, mindful; *inf.* cagey.
Opposites INCAUTIOUS; CARELESS; RECKLESS.

cavalcade *noun* procession, parade, march,
column, troop, file, train, caravan, cortège, retinue.

cavalier *noun* **1** *cavaliers dying for King Charles*
royalist, king's man. **2** *footsoldiers and cavaliers*
horseman, horse soldier, equestrian, knight,
chevalier. **3** *the lady and her latest cavalier | cava-
liers at the ball* escort, beau, gallant, gentleman,
courtier.

cavalier *adjective a cavalier attitude towards his
colleagues* offhand, condescending, haughty,
arrogant, lofty, lordly, disdainful, supercilious,
patronizing, scornful, contemptuous, discourteous, insolent.

cavalry *noun* **1** *infantry and cavalry* mounted
troops, horse soldiers, horsemen, horse, troop-
ers; light cavalry, heavy cavalry, dragoons,
lancers, hussars. **2** *the cavalry arrived just as we
were going bankrupt* timely/fortuitous help,
help, aid, white knight, saviour.

cave *noun* cavern, grotto, hollow, cavity, pothole, underground chamber, tunnel, cellar,
dugout, den.

caveat *noun* warning, caution, admonition,
monition; *inf.* red flag, alarm bells.

caveman *noun cavemen and their stone tools*
primitive man, prehistoric man. See table at
HUMAN.

caveman *adjective women resenting caveman tactics* primitive, uncivilized, crude, brutal, savage; masterful, domineering, autocratic.

cavern *noun* large cave, cave, grotto, hollow,
pothole. See CAVE.

cavernous *adjective cavernous depths/eyes* large,
huge, deep, hollow, sunken, yawning, unfathomable, dark.

cavil *verb* carp, find fault, quibble, complain,
criticize, censure, object, make objections; *inf.*
nit-pick.

cavity *noun* hole, hollow, crater, pit, orifice,
aperture, gap, dent.

cease *verb* **1** *cease working* stop, discontinue,
desist, desist from, end, finish, leave off, quit,
conclude, terminate, suspend, bring to a halt,

CATTLE

Breeds of Cattle			
Aberdeen Angus	Dexter	Meuse-Rhine-Ijssel	Texas
Africander	Droughtmaster	Miranda	Longhorn
Andalusian	Durham	Mongolian	Welsh Black
Australian Illawarra	Friesian	Murray Grey	West Highland
Shorthorn	Galician Blond	N'Dama	White
Ayrshire	Galloway	Pinzgauer	Galloway
Bangus	German Yellow	Polled Hereford	White Park
Barrosã	Guernsey	Polled Welsh	**Wild Cattle**
Beefalo	Hereford	Black	anoa
Beef Shorthorn	Highland	Red-and-White	banteng
Belgian Blue	Holstein-	Friesian	bison
Belted Galloway	Friesian	Red Poll	buffalo
Belted Welsh	Irish Moiled	Red Ruby Devon	gaur
Blonde d'Aquitaine	Jamaica Hope	Romagnola	gayal
Brahman	Jersey	Santa Gertrudis	kouprey
British White	Kerry	Shetland	musk ox
Brown Swiss	Kyloe	Shorthorn	ox
Charolais	Limousin	Simmental	sapi-utan
Chianina	Lincoln Red	South Devon	takin
Danish Red	Longhorn	Sussex	tsine
Devon	Luing	Swedish Red-and-	water buffalo
	Maine Anjou	White	yak

bring to an end, break off. **2** *the rain ceased* stop, halt, finish, come to a stop, come to an end, let up, die away, abate, terminate.
Opposites START; BEGIN; COMMENCE.

cease *adverb* **without cease** continuously, incessantly, unendingly, unremittingly, without cessation/stopping/let-up, without a pause/break, on and on, time without end. *See* CESSATION.

ceaseless *adjective* incessant, unceasing, unending, endless, never-ending, interminable, non-stop, constant, continuous, continual, uninterrupted, eternal, perpetual, unremitting, persistent.

cede *verb* yield, surrender, concede; abdicate, resign, hand over; relinquish, renounce, forsake, abandon, make over, turn over, transfer, deliver up, grant, give, bequeath.
Opposites RETAIN; KEEP.

ceiling *noun* **1** *the ceiling of the building* overhead, upper side, roof. **2** *a ceiling on prices* limit, upper limit, maximum, summit, pinnacle.

celebrate *verb* **1** *celebrate the poet's anniversary* commemorate, observe, honour, mark, keep, drink to, toast. **2** *celebrate after the exams* make merry, rejoice, enjoy oneself, party, paint the town; *inf.* go on a spree, go out on the town, whoop it up. **3** *celebrate his achievement* proclaim, make known, herald, announce, publicize, broadcast, advertise, promulgate. **4** *a poem celebrating the joys of love* praise, laud, extol, glorify, exalt, eulogize, reverence. **5** *celebrate a religious ceremony* perform, solemnize, ceremonialize.

celebrated *adjective* famous, famed, notable, noted, renowned, well-known, popular, prominent, distinguished, great, eminent, preeminent, outstanding, illustrious, acclaimed, revered, glorious, legendary, lionized.
Opposites UNKNOWN; OBSCURE; UNSUNG.

celebration *noun* **1** *the celebration of his birthday | anniversary celebrations* commemoration, observance, honouring, keeping, remembrance. **2** *having a celebration* party, carousal, festival, fête, carnival, gala; festivity, merrymaking, revelry, jollification, junketing; *inf.* spree, binge, beanfeast, bash. **3** *celebration of a religious ceremony* performance, solemnization.

celebrity *noun* **1** *celebrities at a charity ball* VIP, famous person, dignitary, big name, name, personality, star, superstar, lion, notable, luminary, personage; *inf.* bigwig, big shot, bit noise; *Am. inf.* big wheel. **2** *his celebrity spread far* fame, renown, notability, popularity, reputation, honour, prominence, prestige, distinction, eminence, pre-eminence, glory, illustriousness, stardom.
Opposites NONENTITY; OBSCURITY.

celestial *adjective* **1** *celestial beings* heavenly, divine, godly, godlike, ethereal, sublime, paradisical, elysian, spiritual, empyrean, immortal, angelic, seraphic, cherubic. **2** *celestial bodies/navigation* heavenly, astronomical, extraterrestrial, stellar, of the sky/heavens.

celibacy *noun* chastity, singleness, abstinence, self-denial, self-restraint, continence, abnega-

tion, asceticism, virginity, bachelorhood, spinsterhood, monkhood, nunhood, monasticism; *inf.* single blessedness.
Opposites MARRIAGE; PROMISCUITY.

cell *noun* **1** *a prison/monastic cell* cubicle, room, apartment, compartment, chamber, stall, enclosure, dungeon, lock-up. **2** *honeycomb cells* compartment, cavity, hole. **3** *a political cell* faction, caucus, nucleus, clique, coterie, group, party, unit.

cement *noun* adhesive, bonding, binder, glue, superglue, gum, paste.

cement *verb* bind, bond, stick, join, unite, attach, cohere, combine, affix, glue, gum, paste, solder, weld.

cemetery *noun* graveyard, burial ground, burial place, necropolis, churchyard, charnel house, golgotha.

censor *verb* *censor letters | censor the play* cut, delete, delete from, make cuts/changes to, blue-pencil, expurgate, bowdlerize.

censor *noun* *the film censor* examiner, inspector, expurgator, bowdlerizer.

censorious *adjective* fault-finding, critical, disapproving, condemnatory, reproachful, censuring, captious, carping, cavilling.

censure *verb* *censure him for his behaviour* criticize, condemn, blame, castigate, denounce, disapprove of, berate, upbraid, reprove, reproach, rebuke, reprimand, scold, chide, reprehend.
Opposites PRAISE; APPROVE; COMMEND.

censure *noun* *open to public censure | a vote of censure* criticism, condemnation, blame, castigation, denunciation, disapproval, berating, upbraiding, reproval, reproof, reproach, rebuke, reprimand, scolding, chiding, reprehension, obloquy.

central *adjective* **1** *a central position* middle, mid, median, medial, mesial, mean. **2** *central London/America* middle, mid, inner, interior. **3** *a central issue* main, chief, principal, foremost, fundamental, basic, key, essential, primary, pivotal, focal, core, cardinal.
Opposites OUTER; SUBORDINATE; MINOR.

centralize *verb* *centralize the administration* concentrate, centre, concentre, consolidate, amalgamate, condense, compact, unify, incorporate, streamline, focus, rationalize.

centre *noun* *the centre of the town* middle, middle point, midpoint, nucleus, heart, core, hub, kernel, focus, focal point, pivot.
Opposites EDGE; PERIPHERY; OUTSKIRTS.

centre *verb* *her interests centre on sport* concentrate, focus, pivot, converge, concentre, close in.

ceramics *plural noun. See table.*

cereal *noun* **1** *farmers growing cereals* grain. *See table.* **2** *she ate her cereal* breakfast food, cornflakes, porridge, muesli.

ceremonial *adjective* *ceremonial occasion/dress* formal, ritual, ritualistic, stately, solemn, dignified, celebratory, sacramental, liturgical.

CEREAL CROPS

barley	maize	rye
corn	millet	sorghum
durum	oats	wheat
emmer	rice	

ceremonial *noun the ceremonial of coronations* ceremony, rite, ritual, formality, custom, solemnity, sacrament, liturgy.

ceremonious *adjective* **1** *a ceremonious occasion* ceremonial, formal, ritual. *See* CEREMONIAL *adjective*. **2** *behave in a ceremonious manner* formal, punctilious, precise, scrupulous, stately, courtly, courteous, civil, deferential, stiff, rigid, affected; *inf.* starchy, just-so.

ceremony *noun* **1** *a wedding ceremony* rite, service, formality, observance, function, custom, sacrament, show. *See* CEREMONIAL *noun*. **2** *conducted with ceremony* formalities, niceties, pomp, protocol, decorum, etiquette, propriety, conventionality, punctilio, attention to detail; *inf.* fuss.

certain *adjective* **1** *I'm certain he's guilty* sure, positive, confident, convinced, assured, unwavering, unshaken, secure, satisfied, persuaded. **2** *her success/failure is certain* sure, assured, destined, fated, inevitable, reliable, inescapable, bound to happen, inexorable, ineluctable; *inf.* in the bag. **3** *it is certain that he will go* sure, definite, unquestionable, beyond question, indubitable, undeniable, irrefutable, incontrovertible, incontestable, obvious, evident, plain, clear, conclusive. **4** *no certain cure | a certain sign* sure, definite, assured, unfailing, unquestionable, undisputed, dependable, reliable, trustworthy, sound, foolproof; *inf.* sure-fire. **5** *there is no certain date yet* definite, decided, settled, fixed, established, determined. **6** *a certain lady/place that will remain anonymous* particular, specific, individual, special, especial, precise. **7** *to a certain extent* indeterminate, moderate, minimum.
Opposites UNCERTAIN; UNSURE; INDEFINITE.

certainly *adverb* **1** *he will certainly die* surely, definitely, assuredly, undoubtedly, undeniably, obviously, plainly, clearly. *See* CERTAIN 3. **2** *certainly, he'll be there* yes, of course, by all means.

certainty *noun* **1** *I cannot say with certainty* sureness, assuredness, positiveness, confidence, conviction, reliability, validity, conclusiveness, authoritativeness, truth, fact, factualness. **2** *it's a certainty that Britain will lose* inevitability, indubitability, inescapability, fact; *inf.* sure thing, cinch. **3** *that horse's a certainty* certain winner, certain happening; *inf.* sure-fire winner, cert, dead cert, cinch.
Opposites UNCERTAINTY; DOUBT.

certificate *noun* certification, document, authorization, credentials, testimonial, warrant, licence, voucher, diploma.

certify *verb* **1** *a document certifying their marriage* testify to, attest, corroborate, substantiate, verify, confirm, endorse, validate, vouch for, guarantee, authenticate, document, bear witness to, ratify, warrant; *certified dead* verified as, confirmed as, officially declared, vouched. **2** *she has been certified as a teacher* give a certificate/diploma to, recognize, accredit, license, authorize, qualify.

cessation *noun* end, termination, finish, conclusion, pause, break, respite, let-up; ceasing, stopping, halting, ending, finishing.

chafe *verb* **1** *chafe the child's feet* rub, warm, warm up. **2** *his neck chafed by his shirt* rub, abrade, graze, excoriate, scrape, scratch, rasp. **3** *material chafed by the rock* wear, wear away/ down, wear out, wear to shreds, fray, tatter, erode. **4** *the passengers were chafed by the delay* annoy, anger, irritate, exasperate, infuriate, enrage, incense, inflame, provoke, vex, worry, peeve, irk, ruffle. **5** *passengers chafing at the delay* be impatient, be angry/annoyed/irritated/ exasperated, fret, fume; *inf.* blow one's top, blow a fuse.

chaff *noun* **1** *chaff from the grain* husks, hulls, pods, shells, cases, casing. **2** *chaff for the cattle* straw, hay, fodder, silage. **3** *throw away the chaff | separate the chaff from the wheat* rubbish, refuse, waste, garbage, trash, dregs, remains, debris, junk, dross, detritus. **4** *the chaff of her classmates | the chaff of the comedian* banter, bantering, joking, jesting, badinage, raillery, teasing, joshing, waggishness, humour, wit, repartee, persiflage; *inf.* kidding, ragging, wisecracking, ribbing.

CERAMICS

agate-ware	Dresden china	Meissen ware	Seto ware
Arita ware	earthenware	mezza-maiolica	Sèvres
Berlin ware	eggshell china	Ming ware	soft-paste
bisque	faience	Nabeshima ware	porcelain
bone china	fine china	Nanking ware	Spode ware
Castleford ware	fired porcelain	Parian porcelain	stone china
Castor ware	flatware	porcelain	stoneware
champlevé	hard-paste	porcelain enamel	Staffordshire ware
Chantilly ware	hollowware	queen's ware	Sung ware
Chelsea porcelain	Imari ware	raku	Talavera ware
Ch'ing porcelain	ironstone	Rockingham ware	Tang ware
cloisonné	jasper ware	Royal Doulton	Ting ware
Coalport	Kakiemon ware	Royal Worcester	Toft ware
creamware	Kutani ware	salt-glaze	Vincennes ware
Crown Derby	Limoges	Satsuma porcelain	Wedgwood
Delft	maiolica/majolica	semi-porcelain	Worcester

chaff verb *chaffing his sister* banter, tease, josh; *inf.* kid, rag, rib.

chagrin noun *feeling chagrin at their treatment* annoyance, anger, irritation, vexation, displeasure, worry, dissatisfaction, resentment, rankling, smarting, discomposure, discomfiture, disquiet, fretfulness, spleen, embarrassment, mortification, humiliation, shame.

chagrin verb *chagrined by their treatment* annoy, anger, enrage, irritate, vex, displease, worry, peeve, irk, chafe, fret, dissatisfy, discompose, discomfit, disquiet, embarrass, mortify, humiliate, shame. *See* CHAGRIN *noun.*

chain noun **1** *a gold chain* series of links. **2** *a chain of events* series, succession, string, sequence, train, progression, course, set, cycle, line, row, concatenation. **3** *a chain of shops* group; firm, company. **4** *See* CHAINS.

chain verb *chain the dog to the wall* fasten, secure, tie, bind, tether, shackle, fetter, manacle, hitch, moor, handcuff, confine, restrain, trammel, gird, imprison.

chains plural noun *prisoners in chains* bonds, fetters, shackles, manacles, trammels.

chair noun **1** *tables and chairs* seat. *See table.* **2** *a university chair* professorship, professorate, headship. **3** *elected chair of the society* chairperson, chairman, chairwoman, president, spokesperson, spokesman, spokeswoman, MC, master/mistress of ceremonies. **4** *sent to the chair* electric chair; electrocution, execution; *inf.* hot seat.

chair verb *chair the meeting* preside over, lead, direct, manage, control, oversee, supervise.

chalk verb **chalk up 1** *chalk it up to experience* put down, ascribe, attribute, accredit, impute, charge. **2** *chalk up the score* record, register, enter, mark, log, score.

chalky adjective white, pale, wan, pallid, ashen, pasty, waxen, blanched, bleached, colourless.

challenge noun **1** *accept a sporting challenge* summons, call, invitation, bidding. **2** *a challenge to tradition* | *a challenge to the government* questioning, interrogation, opposition, stand, countercharge, defiance, confrontation, test, ultimatum. **3** *a new challenge in his life* difficult task/venture, hazard, risk, obstacle. **challenge to** questioning of, interrogation of, stand against, countercharge, ultimatum; opposition to, defiance, confrontation with.

CHAMPAGNE MEASURES		
magnum	=	2 bottles
jeroboam	=	2 magnums
rehoboam	=	3 magnums
methuselah	=	4 magnums
salmanazar	=	6 magnums
balthazar	=	8 magnums
nebuchadnezzar	=	10 magnums

challenge verb **1** *challenge someone to a competition* dare, summon, invite, bid, throw down the gauntlet to; defy to. **2** *challenge their authority* question, call into question, dispute, protest against, take exception to, object to, disagree with, demur against, be a dissenter of. **3** *the job really challenges him* test, tax, stimulate, arouse, inspire, excite, spur on.

chamber noun **1** *the judge's chambers* room, apartment, compartment, cubicle, hall. **2** *princess retiring to her chamber* room, bedroom, bedchamber, boudoir. **3** *the chambers in the caves/heart* compartment, cavity, hollow, cell. **4** *the upper chamber of the government* legislative body, legislature, assembly, council, house.

champagne noun. *See table.*

champion noun **1** *the champion of the competition* winner, title-holder, victor, conqueror, hero. **2** *the champion of the cause* defender, protector, upholder, supporter, advocate, backer, patron; *inf.* angel. **3** *ladies' champions taking part in a tournament* knight, man-at-arms, paladin, hero, warrior.

champion verb *champion the cause* defend, protect, uphold, support, stand up for, fight for, speak for, advocate, back, promote, espouse.

chance noun **1** *meet by chance* accident, coincidence, fortuity, serendipity, fate, destiny, fortune, luck, providence. **2** *a good chance that he'll win* prospect, possibility, probability, likelihood, likeliness, conceivability, odds. **3** *to get a second chance* opportunity, opening, occasion, turn, time; *inf.* shot. **4** *take a chance and run* risk, gamble, hazard, venture, speculation, long shot.
Opposites DESIGN; CERTAINTY.

chance verb **1** *it chanced that they arrived last* happen, occur, take place, come about, come to pass, befall, turn up, crop up. **2** *have to chance it* take a chance that, risk, hazard, gamble, venture, speculate, try one's luck, take a

CHAIRS AND STOOLS			
armchair	choir stall	milking stool	Sheraton chair
barrel chair	club chair	Morris chair	sofa
bar stool	couch	nursing chair	stall
bench	deckchair	panel-back chair	stool
bentwood chair	dining chair	pew	studio couch
box seat	divan	Queen-Anne	swivel chair
bucket seat	easy chair	chair	throne
camp chair	folding chair	recliner	wheel-back
cane chair	Grecian couch	rocking chair	chair
carver	high chair	settee	wheelchair
chaise longue	ladder-back chair	settle	Windsor chair
chesterfield	love seat	Shaker chair	wing chair

leap in the dark. **chance on/upon** *chance upon an old friend | chanced on the answer* come across, stumble on, come upon, meet, encounter; *inf.* bump into, run into.

chance *adjective a chance meeting/discovery* accidental, unexpected, unanticipated, unforeseen, unforeseeable, unlooked-for, unintended, unintentional, unpremeditated, unplanned, fortuitous, serendipitous.

chancy *adjective* risky, uncertain, hazardous, speculative, perilous, dangerous; *inf.* dicey, dodgy.

change *verb* **1** *change one's attitude/plans* alter, modify, transform, convert, vary, remodel, recast, restyle, reconstruct, reorder, reorganize, metamorphose, transmute, permutate, permute. **2** *she's changed | the world's changed* alter, be transformed, move on, evolve, metamorphose, fluctuate, diversify; *inf.* do an about-face, do a U-turn. **3** *change jobs/sides | change a pair of trousers* exchange, interchange, substitute, switch, replace, trade, barter; *inf.* swap.
Opposites RETAIN; STAY.

change *noun* **1** *a change in attitude/plan* difference, alteration, modification, transformation, conversion, variation, remodelling, reconstruction, reorganization, transition, innovation, metamorphosis, transfiguration, vicissitude, transmutation, mutation, permutation; *inf.* about-turn, U-turn. *See* CHANGE *verb* 1. **2** *a change of jobs* exchange, interchange, substitution, switch, trade, bartering; *inf.* swap. **3** *he's tired and needs a change* holiday, diversion, variation, variety; *inf.* break. **4** *have no change* coins, coinage, cash, silver, petty cash.

changeable *adjective* **1** *of changeable moods | changeable weather* changing, variable, varying, changeful, chameleon-like, chameleonic, protean, shifting, vacillating, volatile, mercurial, capricious, fluctuating, fluctuant, fluid, kaleidoscopic, fitful, wavering, unstable, unsteady, unsettled, irregular, erratic, unreliable, inconstant, fickle, mutable, unpredictable, many-faceted, chequered, vicissitudinous. **2** *changeable structures/laws* alterable, modifiable, convertible, mutable, permutable.
Opposites UNCHANGEABLE; CONSTANT; INVARIABLE.

channel *noun* **1** *the channel connecting the seas* passage, sea-passage, strait, neck, narrows, waterway, watercourse, fiord. **2** *the channel of the canal* bed, floor, bottom, depths. **3** *rainwater running through the channels* gutter, groove, furrow, conduit, duct, culvert, ditch. **4** *new channels for their energy* course, way, direction, path, route, approach. **5** *channels of communication* means, medium, agency, vehicle, route.

channel *verb* **1** *grooves channelling the rock* furrow, groove, flute, hollow out, cut. **2** *channelling water/energies* transmit, convey, transport, conduct, direct, guide.

chant *noun a religious chant | a victory chant* song, singing, chorus, melody, ditty, carol, psalm.

chant *verb* **1** *chant the liturgy* sing, recite, intone, cantillate. **2** *football fans chanting* shout, sing, chorus, carol.

chaos *noun* disorder, confusion, pandemonium, bedlam, tumult, upset, upheaval, disorganization, uproar, disruption, disarray, anarchy, lawlessness, riot.

chaotic *adjective* in chaos, disordered, confused, tumultuous, upset, disorganized, jumbled, topsy-turvy, askew, awry, disrupted, in disarray, anarchic, lawless, orderless.
Opposites ORDERLY; ordered.

chap *verb wind having chapped her hands* roughen, make raw, crack, make sore, redden, chafe.

chap *noun* man, fellow, male, boy; *inf.* bloke, guy, sort, cove, customer.

chaperon *noun the young lady's chaperon* companion, duenna, protectress, escort.

chaperon *verb chaperoning the girls to the ball* accompany, escort, attend, shepherd, watch over, take care of, keep an eye on, protect, guard, safeguard.

chapter *noun* **1** *the next chapter in the book* division, section, part, portion, episode. **2** *a tragic chapter in the club's history* period, time, phase, stage, episode. **3** *a chapter of accidents* series, sequence, succession, chain, progression, set. **4** *chapter of the cathedral* council, assembly, convocation, convention, synod, consistory. **5** *a chapter of the society* branch, section, division, wing, offshoot, lodge.

char *verb char the paper* scorch, singe, sear, toast, carbonize, cauterize.

character *noun* **1** *her character's changed | the character of the town has altered* personality, nature, disposition, temperament, temper; essential quality, ethos, individuality, complexion, constitution, make-up, cast, attributes, bent, genius. **2** *a person of character* moral strength/fibre, strength, honour, integrity, rectitude, uprightness, fortitude, backbone. **3** *damage his character* reputation, name, standing, position, status. **4** *he's one of the village's characters* eccentric, oddity, odd fellow, original, individual; *inf.* oddball, queer fish, odd fish, card. **5** *they're all friendly characters* person, individual, human being, fellow; *inf.* chap, bloke, guy, sort, type, customer. **6** *characters in Austen's novels* persona, person, portrayal, representation, role, part. **7** *in bold characters | Chinese characters* letter, sign, mark, symbol, type, cipher, hieroglyph, figure, device, rune, logo, emblem.

characteristic *noun one of her appealing/annoying characteristics* quality, essential quality, attribute, feature, trait, property, mannerism, mark, trade mark, idiosyncrasy, peculiarity, quirk.

characteristic *adjective their characteristic modesty* typical, distinguishing, distinctive, particular, special, individual, specific, peculiar, idiosyncratic, singular, representative, symbolic, symptomatic, diagnostic.
Opposites uncharacteristic; untypical; UNUSUAL.

characterize *verb* **1** *the landscape is characterized by hills and rivers* typify, distinguish, identify, specify, signalize, indicate, denote, designate, mark, stamp, brand, label. **2** *the* *playwright characterizing the heroine as hysterical* portray, depict, present, represent, describe.

charade *noun* pretence, travesty, fake, farce, parody, pantomime.

charge *verb* **1** *what do you charge for a room?* ask in payment, ask, fix a charge/price, expect, impose, levy. **2** *charge it to my account* debit, put down to, bill. **3** *charge him with murder* accuse of, indict, arraign, impeach, impute, blame, incriminate. **4** *charge the enemy* attack, storm, assault, rush, open fire on, fall on; *inf.* lay into, tear into. **5** *charged with the guardianship of the child* entrust, tax, weigh, weigh down, load, burden, encumber, hamper, saddle. **6** *charge a vessel/gun* fill, fill up, load, load up, pack, plug. **7** *charged with emotion* fill, load, imbue, suffuse, pervade, permeate, infuse, instil. **8** *I charge you to confess* order, command, bid, direct, exhort, instruct, enjoin, adjure, demand, require.
Opposites ABSOLVE; ACQUIT.

charge *noun* **1** *what is the charge for a room?* cost, price, fee, amount, rate, payment, expense, expenditure, outlay, dues, levy, toll. **2** *charges of murder* accusation, allegation, indictment, arraignment, impeachment, citation, imputation, blame, incrimination. **3** *the charge of the cavalry* attack, storming, assault, onrush, onslaught, onset, sortie, incursion. **4** *have charge of the children* responsibility, care, custody, guardianship, trust, protection, safekeeping, surveillance. **5** *your charge is to drive the car* duty, task, job, responsibility, office, obligation, assignment, business, burden. **6** *pay for his charge's education* ward, protégé, dependant, minor. **7** *the judge's charge to the jury* instruction, direction, order, command, dictate, injunction, exhortation, mandate.

charitable *adjective* **1** *be charitable towards the poor* philanthropic, giving, benevolent, generous, liberal, open-handed, kind, magnanimous, beneficent, bountiful, bounteous, munificent, big-hearted, humane, alms-giving, eleemosynary. **2** *a charitable interpretation of the situation* generous, liberal, tolerant, broad-minded, understanding, sympathetic, compassionate, lenient, indulgent, forgiving, kindly, favourable, gracious.
Opposites UNCHARITABLE; UNKIND.

charity *noun* **1** *relying on charity for survival* financial assistance, donations, contributions, hand-outs, gifts, funding, endowments, financial relief, alms-giving, philanthropy, benefaction. **2** *behave with charity towards fellow men* goodwill, compassion, humanity, humanitarianism, kindliness, love, sympathy, tolerance, indulgence, altruism, thoughtfulness, generosity, liberality, benevolence, benignity.

charlatan *noun* quack, mountebank, sham, fraud, fake, impostor, confidence trickster, confidence man, pretender, cheat, deceiver, swindler; *inf.* con man, phoney.

charm *noun* **1** *the charm of the resort/hostess* attractiveness, attraction, appeal, allure, allurement, fascination, captivation, pleasingness, desirability, engagingness, delightfulness. **2** *captivated by her charms* attractiveness, appeal, allure, beauty, wiles, blandishments.

LUCKY CHARMS		
amulet	ju-ju	rabbit's foot
ankh	mandala	St Christo-
churinga	mascot	pher medal
crucifix	medallion	scarab
fetish	mojo	shamrock
four-leaf	obeah	talisman
clover	periapt	tiki
horseshoe	phylactery	totem

3 *the sorcerer's charm* spell, magic formula, magic word, abracadabra; sorcery, magic. **4** *the charms on her bracelet* trinket, ornament, bauble, souvenir, *bijou*. **5** *wear/carry a lucky charm* good-luck charm. *See table.*

charm *verb charmed by the little girl | charmed by the music* delight, please, attract, win, win over, captivate, allure, lure, draw, fascinate, bewitch, beguile, enchant, enrapture, enamour, seduce, cajole, hypnotize, mesmerize.
Opposites REPEL; ALIENATE.

charming *adjective* delightful, pleasing, pleasant, appealing, attractive, winning, fetching, taking, captivating, winsome, engaging, lovely, agreeable, alluring, fascinating, bewitching, beguiling, enchanting, delectable, irresistible, seductive.
Opposites DISGUSTING; REPULSIVE.

chart *noun* *plot it out on a chart* graph, table, map, diagram, plan, blueprint, guide, scheme, tabulation.

chart *verb* **1** *chart the results* tabulate, map, map out, plot, graph, delineate, diagram, sketch, chart a course of, draft. **2** *chart their progress* follow, record, register, note.

charter *noun* **1** *privileges granted by royal charter* authority, authorization, sanction, warrant, document, covenant, deed, bond, permit, prerogative, privilege, right. **2** *the charter of the United Nations* constitution, code, canon, body of laws; principles, rules, laws. **3** *the charter of a boat* hiring, leasing, renting, engaging. **4** *have a charter to run a ferry* permit, licence, warrant, concession, franchise, indenture.

charts *plural noun* *pop charts* list, listing, league, catalogue, index.

chary *adjective* cautious, wary, leery, careful, circumspect, watchful, distrustful, apprehensive.
Opposites HEEDLESS; TRUSTFUL; unwary.

chase *verb* **1** *dogs chasing rabbits | police chasing after burglars* give chase to, pursue, run after, follow, hunt, hound, track, trail, tail. **2** *chase away the intruder* put to flight, drive, send, send packing. **3** *chase round doing the work* rush, hurry, make haste. **chase up** pester, harass.

chase *noun* *take part in the chase* pursuit, hunt, trail; hunting, coursing.

chasm *noun* **1** *a landscape full of chasms* gorge, abyss, canyon, ravine, pit, crater, crevasse, hole, hollow, opening, gap, fissure, crevice, cleft, rift, rent. **2** *a chasm between their points of view* schism, breach, gulf, rift; separation, alienation.

chassis *noun* framework, frame, skeleton, substructure, fuselage, bodywork, anatomy.

chaste *adjective* **1** *a chaste young woman | nuns leading a chaste life* virgin, virginal, vestal, celibate, abstinent, self-restrained, unmarried. **2** *chaste conduct/speech* virtuous, good, innocent, pure, decent, moral, decorous, modest, wholesome, righteous, upright, uncorrupted, incorrupt, uncontaminated, undefiled, unsullied. **3** *a chaste style* simple, plain, unadorned, unembellished, unaffected, unpretentious, austere, restrained.
Opposites PROMISCUOUS; IMMORAL.

chasten *verb* **1** *chastened by the experience* subdue, restrain, tame, curb, check, humble, cow, tone down. **2** *chasten the pupils* discipline, punish, penalize, castigate, scold, upbraid, reprimand, reprove, chide, take to task, haul over the coals.

chastise *verb* **1** *schoolmasters chastising children* punish, discipline, castigate, beat, thrash, smack, flog, whip, strap, cane, lash, birch, scourge; *inf.* wallop, thump, tan one's hide. **2** *the staff were chastised for arriving late* scold, upbraid, reprimand, reprove, chide, take to task, haul over the coals, chasten, castigate.
Opposites PRAISE; REWARD.

chastity *noun* **1** *nuns taking vows of chastity* chasteness, virginity, celibacy, abstinence, self-restraint, self-denial, continence, singleness, unmarried state; virtue, immaculateness. **2** *chastity of conduct/speech* virtue, goodness, innocence, purity, decency, morality, decorum, modesty, wholesomeness, righteousness. *See* CHASTE 2. **3** *chastity of style* simplicity, plainness, unpretentiousness, austerity. *See* CHASTE 3.
Opposites PROMISCUITY; IMMORALITY.

chat *verb* *chat with her colleagues* talk, gossip, chatter, have a conversation with, converse, tittle-tattle, prattle, clack, jabber, prate; *inf.* natter, gas, have a confab with, have a chinwag with, chin-wag, jaw, chew the rag/fat with. **chat up** flirt/trifle with.

chat *noun* *have a chat with* talk, gossip, conversation, chatter, heart-to-heart, tête-à-tête; *inf.* natter, confab, chin-wag.

chatter *verb* *children chattering in groups* chat, gossip, jabber, prattle, babble, tittle-tattle, tattle, blather; *inf.* natter, chin-wag. *See* CHAT *verb.*

chatter *noun* *tired of the children's/village chatter* talk, gossip, chit-chat, chitter-chatter, jabber, prattling, babbling, tittle-tattle, tattle, blathering, nattering, confab, chin-wag. *See* CHAT *noun.*

chatterbox *noun* gossiper, jabberer, babbler, tittle-tattler, blatherer; *inf.* natterer, windbag.

chatty *adjective* **1** *a chatty person* talkative, gossipy, gossiping, garrulous, loquacious, voluble, glib, effusive, gushing. **2** *a chatty style* informal, conversational, colloquial, gossipy, familiar, friendly, lively; *inf.* newsy.
Opposites TACITURN; FORMAL.

chauvinism *noun* jingoism, partisanship, excessive loyalty, prejudice, bias, machismo.

cheap *adjective* **1** *cheap prices/housing* inexpensive, low-priced, low-cost, economical, reasonable, moderately priced, keenly priced, keen, bargain, cut-price, economy, sale, reduced, marked-down, slashed, discounted; *inf.* bargain-basement. **2** *cheap and gaudy jewellery* poor-quality, inferior, shoddy, common, trashy, tawdry, tatty, paltry, worthless, second-rate, cheapjack, gimcrack; *inf.* tacky. **3** *a cheap joke* despicable, contemptible, low, base, unpleasant, mean, sordid, vulgar. **4** *she felt so cheap at her behaviour* ashamed, shameful, embarrassed, humiliated, mortified, debased, degraded, abashed, discomfited, disconcerted. **5** *he's a cheap operator* mean, stingy, parsimonious, tight-fisted, niggardly, money-grubbing, cheese-paring, penny-pinching, frugal, sparing, cheapskate.
Opposites EXPENSIVE; HIGH-CLASS; ADMIRABLE.

cheapen *verb* **1** *cheapen the cost of travel* lower, reduce, cut, mark down, slash, discount, depreciate. **2** *cheapening herself by working in that club* degrade, debase, demean, devalue, lower, belittle, denigrate, discredit, depreciate, derogate.

cheat *verb* **1** *cheat his partner | cheat into giving him money* deceive, trick, swindle, defraud, dupe, hoodwink, double-cross, gull; exploit, take advantage of, victimize; *inf.* do, con, diddle, bamboozle, finagle, bilk; rip off, fleece, take for a ride. **2** *cheat out of his inheritance* deprive of, deny, thwart, prevent from, preclude from, foil, frustrate, baulk, defeat. **3** *cheat the bad weather | cheat death* avoid, elude, evade, dodge, escape, steer clear of, shun, eschew. **4** *husbands and wives cheating on each other* be unfaithful to, commit adultery; *inf.* two-time.

cheat *noun* **1** *a cheat at sport | a cheat for a business partner* cheater, swindler, fraud, confidence trickster, confidence man/woman, trickster, deceiver, double-crosser, crook, rogue, shark, charlatan; *inf.* con man. **2** *win by a cheat* swindle, fraud, deception, deceit, trick, trickery, imposture, artifice; *inf.* con.

check *verb* **1** *luggage checked at the airport* examine, inspect, look at, look over, scrutinize, test, monitor, investigate, probe, enquire into, study; *inf.* give the once-over to. **2** *check the door's locked* confirm, make sure, verify, corroborate, validate, substantiate. **3** *check the vehicle's progress* stop, arrest, halt, bring to a standstill, slow down, brake, bar, obstruct, impede, block, retard, curb, delay. **4** *check one's laughter/tears* restrain, suppress, repress, contain, control, bridle, inhibit; *inf.* nip in the bud. **5** *check the children* scold, rebuke, reprimand, chide, reprove, berate, discipline, punish; *inf.* give a row to, tell off, read the riot act to. **6** *their stories don't check* correspond, agree, tally, dovetail, harmonize. **check up 1** *check up that he's telling the truth* check, investigate, confirm, ascertain, make sure, verify, corroborate, validate, substantiate. **2** *check up on his background* investigate, examine, inspect, research, scrutinize, probe, enquire into.
Opposites NEGLECT; IGNORE; START; RELEASE.

check *noun* **1** *a luggage check* examination, inspection, scrutiny, scrutinization, test, monitoring, investigation, probe, enquiry, study; *inf.* once-over. **2** *make a check that you have every-*

thing confirmation, verification, corroboration. See CHECK *verb* 2. **3** *a check in the production rate* stop, stopping, stoppage, arrest, halt, slowing-down, braking, obstruction, retardation, delay. See CHECK *verb* 3. **4** *act as a check to the riot/celebration* restraint, constraint, control, deterrent, hindrance, impediment, obstruction, inhibition, limitation, curb. **5** *the American asked for his check* bill, account, invoice, reckoning, tally; *Am.* tab.

checkmate *noun* **1** *the checkmate of the chess player's king* check, block, blockage, stop, stoppage, halt, arrest. **2** *the checkmate of the other army* defeat, beating, overthrow, rout, conquest, vanquishment, trouncing, drubbing.

checkmate *verb* **1** *checkmate his king* check, block, stop, halt, arrest. **2** *checkmate the opposing army* defeat, beat, overthrow, rout, vanquish, trounce, give a drubbing to.

check-up *noun* *a check-up from the doctor | giving the car a check-up* examination, inspection, appraisal, assessment, analysis, scrutinization, scrutiny, exploration, probe.

cheek *noun* **1** jowl, chop, gill. **2** *have the cheek to appear* impudence, audacity, temerity, brazenness, effrontery, nerve, impertinence, insolence; *inf.* gall, brass neck, sauce, lip. **3** *give the teacher cheek* impudence, impertinence, insolence, disrespect; *inf.* sauce, lip. **4** *the baby's inflamed cheeks* buttocks, bottom, rump; *inf.* behind, rear-end, arse. See BOTTOM *noun* 7.

cheeky *adjective* impudent, audacious, impertinent, insolent, forward, pert, disrespectful, insulting; *inf.* saucy; *Am. inf.* sassy.

cheep *verb* chirp, chirrup, twitter, tweet, warble, trill, chatter.

cheer *verb* **1** *crowds cheering the popstar/queen* hail, acclaim, hurrah, hurray, applaud, shout at, clap. **2** *his arrival cheered her* raise the spirits of, brighten, buoy up, perk up, enliven, animate, elate, exhilarate, hearten, uplift, give a lift to, gladden, encourage, incite, stimulate, arouse, comfort, solace, console, inspirit; *inf.* buck up. **cheer up 1** *his arrival cheered her up* raise the spirits of. See CHEER *verb* 2. **2** *she*

cheered up on his arrival brighten, perk up, liven up, rally; *inf.* buck up.

cheer *noun* **1** *the cheers of the crowd* acclaim, acclamation, hurrah, hurray, applause, ovation, plaudit, hailing, shout, shouting, clapping. **2** *Christmas is a time of cheer* cheerfulness, gladness, happiness, merriment, mirth, gaiety, joy, pleasure, blitheness, jubilation, high spirits, animation, buoyancy, light-heartedness, glee, optimism, hopefulness, merry-making, rejoicing, revelry, festivity. **3** *larders laden with Christmas cheer* fare, food, provisions, foodstuffs, drink; *inf.* eats.

cheerful *adjective* **1** *a cheerful mood/disposition* happy, bright, merry, glad, gladsome, gay, sunny, joyful, jolly, blithe, animated, buoyant, light-hearted, sparkling, gleeful, carefree, happy-go-lucky, breezy, cheery, sprightly, jaunty, smiling, laughing, bright-eyed and bushy-tailed, optimistic, hopeful, positive; in good spirits; *Am. inf.* peppy, chipper. **2** *a cheerful room/colour* bright, sunny, cheering, pleasant, agreeable, friendly, happy. **3** *his cheerful acceptance of the situation* willing, obliging, cooperative, compliant, complying, acquiescent, agreeing, assenting.
Opposites SAD; CHEERLESS; DULL; UNWILLING.

cheerio *interjection* goodbye, cheers, so long, farewell, adieu, *au revoir, ciao, auf Wiedersehen, adios*; *inf.* bye, bye-bye, see/catch you later, ta-ta, toodle-oo.

cheerless *adjective* gloomy, dreary, miserable, dull, depressing, dismal, bleak, drab, grim, austere, desolate, dark, dingy, sombre, uninviting, comfortless, forlorn.
Opposites CHEERFUL; HAPPY; BRIGHT.

cheers *interjection* **1** here's to you, good luck, here's health, *skol, slainte, prosit*; *inf.* here's mud in your eye, bottoms up, down the hatch. **2** goodbye, cheerio. See CHEERIO.

cheery *adjective* cheerful, happy, merry, glad; in good spirits. See CHEERFUL 1.

cheese *noun.* See table.

chef *noun* cook, cordon bleu cook, food preparer, baker, pastrycook, sous chef, commis chef, *chef de cuisine*; *Am. inf.* short-order cook.

CHEESES

Ami du Chambertin	Colby	Gorgonzola	Neufchâtel	Samsoe
Beaufort	cottage cheese	Gouda	Oka	Stilton
Bel Paese	cream cheese	grana	Parmesan	stracchino
blue brie	curd cheese	Gruyère	pecorino	Swiss
blue cheese	Danish blue	halloumi	Port Salut	cheese
blue vinney	Derby	Ilchester	provolone	taleggio
Boursin	Dolcelatte	Jarlesburg	quark	Tillamook
Brie	double	Lancashire	Reblochon	Tilsit
Caerphilly	Gloucester	Leicester	Red Leicester	Tomme de
Cambozola	Dunlop	Liederkranz	Reggiano	Savoie
Camembert	Edam	Limburger	ricotta	tvorog
Cantal	Emmental	Liptauer	Romano	vacherin
Chaumes	feta	Livarot	Roquefort	Vignotte
Cheddar	fromage frais	mascarpone	Sage Derby	Wensleydale
Cheshire	Gervais	Monterey	Saint Agur	Wiltshire
chèvre	gjetost	Monterey Jack	Sainte Honoré	Windsor
	Gloucester	mozzarella	Saint Nectaire	Windsor Red

chef-d'oeuvre *noun* masterpiece, magnum opus, masterwork, *pièce de résistance, tour de force*, jewel in the crown.

chemical *noun*. See table. See also tables at COM-POUND, ELEMENT.

chemist *noun*. See table at SCIENTIST.

chequered *adjective a chequered career* mixed, varied, diverse, diversified, eventful; full of ups and downs.

cherish *verb* **1** *cherish his loved one* care for, cosset, treasure, prize, hold dear, love, dote on, adore, idolize, revere, indulge. **2** *cherish the plants/orphans* care for, look after, tend, protect, preserve, shelter, support, nurture, foster. **3** *cherish hopes* have, entertain, harbour, cling to, foster, nurture.
Opposites ABANDON; NEGLECT.

cherub *noun* **1** *heavenly cherub* angel, seraph. **2** *cherubs in the baby contest* baby, babe, infant, innocent child, pretty child, lovable child, well-behaved child.

chest *noun* **1** *injured her chest* thorax, breast, sternum. **2** *pack his goods in chests* box, crate, case, trunk, container, coffer, casket.

chew *verb chew one's food* masticate, munch, champ, crunch, bite, gnaw, grind. **chew over** meditate on, ruminate on, mull over, consider, weigh up, ponder on, deliberate upon, reflect upon, muse upon, cogitate about.

chic *adjective* stylish, fashionable, smart, elegant, modish, voguish; *inf.* trendy, dressy, snazzy.
Opposites UNFASHIONABLE; INELEGANT.

chicanery *noun* misleading talk, fraud, fraudulence, deception, deceitfulness, duplicity, guile, cheating, duping, hoodwinking, dishonesty, subterfuge, craftiness, wiles, sophistry.

chide *verb* scold, upbraid, rebuke, reprimand, reproach, admonish, lecture, call to account, take to task, berate, castigate; *inf.* give a dressing-down to.

chief *noun* **1** *the chief of the tribe/village* head, headman, leader, chieftain, ruler, overlord, lord and master, commander, suzerain; *Am.* sachem. **2** *the chief of the firm* head, principal, leader, director, chairman, chairperson, chief executive, manager, superintendent, master, foreman; *inf.* boss, bossman, gaffer, kingpin, top dog, big cheese, Mr Big.

chief *adjective* **1** *chief priest* supreme, head, foremost, principal, highest, leading, grand, superior, premier, directing, governing. **2** *the chief point* main, principal, most important, uppermost, primary, prime, cardinal, central, key, vital, essential, predominant, pre-eminent.
Opposites MINOR; SUBORDINATE.

chiefly *adverb* mainly, in the main, principally, primarily, predominantly, especially, particu-

---

CHEMICALS

Common Name	Chemical Name	Common Name	Chemical Name
acetic acid	ethanoic acid	glycerine	glycerol
acetone	propanone	gypsum	calcium sulphate
acetylene	ethyne	hydrochloric acid	hydrogen chloride
alcohol	ethanol	hydrogen sulphide	
alumina	aluminium oxide	jeweller's rouge	ferric oxide
alum	potash alum	laughing gas	dinitrogen monoxide
ammonia		lithia	lithium hydroxide
baking soda	sodium bicarbonate	magnesia	magnesium oxide
benzene		malic acid	
bicarbonate of soda	sodium bicarbonate	marsh gas	methane
borax	sodium borate	nitric oxide	nitrogen monoxide
butane		oil of vitriol	sulphuric acid
calomel	mercurous chloride	peroxide	hydrogen peroxide
carbolic acid	phenol	plaster of Paris	calcium sulphate
carbon dioxide		potash	potassium carbonate
carbon monoxide		potassium chloride	
carbon tetrachloride	tetrachloromethane	potassium per-	
carborundum	silicon carbide	manganate	
caustic soda	sodium hydroxide	propane	
Chile saltpetre	sodium nitrate	quicklime	calcium oxide
chloroform	trichloroethane	red lead	lead oxide
cinnabar	mercuric sulphide	saltpetre	potassium nitrate
citric acid		silica	silicon dioxide
common salt	sodium chloride	silver nitrate	
corundum	aluminium oxide	soda	sodium carbonate
Epsom salts	magnesium sulphate	sodium bi-	
ether	diethyl ether	carbonate	
ethyl alcohol	ethanol	sugar	sucrose
firedamp	methane	sulphur dioxide	
folic acid	pteroylglutamic acid	tartaric acid	
formaldehyde	methanal	toluene	
formic acid	methanoic acid	washing soda	sodium carbonate
Glauber's salt	sodium sulphate	xylene	dimethylbenzene

larly, essentially, mostly, for the most part, on the whole, above all.

child noun **1** *two adults and a child* youngster, young person, young one, little one, boy, girl, baby, babe, infant, toddler, tot, tiny tot, adolescent, youth, juvenile, minor; *derog.* brat, chit; *inf.* kid, nipper, shaver, sprog; *Scots* bairn, wean. **2** *parents and their children* offspring, progeny, issue; descendant, scion; son, daughter, son and heir.

childbirth noun labour, confinement, parturition, delivery, *accouchement*, travail.

childhood noun youth, infancy, babyhood, preteens, minority, nonage, juniority, immaturity; boyhood, girlhood.

childish adjective **1** *the childish behaviour of the adults* immature, infantile, juvenile, puerile, silly, foolish, irresponsible, jejune. **2** *childish laughter* children's, childlike, youthful; boyish, girlish.
Opposites ADULT; MATURE.

childlike adjective **1** *childlike activities* children's, youthful. **2** *childlike reactions/innocence* ingenuous, innocent, artless, guileless, simple, naive, trusting, trustful, credulous, gullible.

chill noun **1** *a chill in the air* chilliness, coldness, coolness, iciness, crispness, rawness, sharpness, nip, bite, frigidity, gelidity. **2** *catch a chill* cold, flu, influenza, respiratory infection, virus. **3** *a chill in her manner* chilliness, coldness, coolness, aloofness, distance, unresponsiveness, lack of sympathy, frigidity, lack of welcome, hostility, unfriendliness. **4** *cast a chill over the proceedings* dread, fear, gloom, cloud, depression, damper, check to happiness, check to joy.

chill adjective **1** *a chill wind* chilly, cold, cool, icy, raw, biting. *See* CHILLY 1. **2** *a chill manner* chilly, cold, cool, aloof, distant, frigid, unresponsive, hostile. *See* CHILLY 3.

chill verb **1** *chilled by the wind* made cold, made colder, cool down. **2** *chill food* make colder, cool down, freeze, cook-chill, congeal. **3** *chill the enthusiasm/party spirit* lessen, reduce, dampen, depress, dispirit, discourage, dishearten.

chilly adjective **1** *a chilly breeze* cold, cool, icy, crisp, brisk, fresh, raw, sharp, biting, penetrating, freezing, frigid, chill; *inf.* nippy. **2** *feeling chilly* cold, cool, freezing, frozen to the marrow, shivery. **3** *a chilly manner* cold, cool, aloof, distant, unresponsive, unsympathetic, frigid, unwelcoming, hostile, unfriendly.
Opposites WARM; PASSIONATE.

chime verb **1** *bells chiming* ring, peal, toll, sound, ding, dong, clang, boom, tinkle, resound, reverberate. **2** *chime the bells* ring, peal, toll, strike, sound, tintinnabulate. **3** *bells/clock chiming 6 o'clock* indicate, mark, show. **chime in 1** *their ideas chime in with ours* harmonize, blend, correspond, be complementary, agree, be in agreement, accord, be in accordance. **2** *he's always chiming in when we're talking* interrupt, cut in, interpose; *inf.* chip in, butt in.

chimes plural noun bells, carillon, angelus, tocsin.

china noun **1** *ornaments made of china* pottery. *See table at* CERAMICS. **2** *set out the best china* dishes, tableware, dinner/tea service.

chink noun crack, fissure, crevice, cleft, cut, rift, split, slit, gap, opening, aperture, cavity, cranny.

chip noun **1** *chips on the sawmill's floor* shaving, paring, shard, flake, shred, sliver, splinter, fragment, snippet, scrap. **2** *the cup with a chip in it* nick, crack, notch, snick, fault, flaw, dent. **3** *gambling chips* counter, token, disc, man. **4** *steak and chips* potato straw, fried potato, game chip; *Am.* French fry.

chip verb **1** *chip a glass* nick, crack, snick, gash, damage. **2** *the paint chips easily* break off, crack, fragment, crumble. **3** *chipping away at a chunk of wood* whittle, chisel, hew. **chip in 1** *he's always chipping in with his suggestions* interrupt, cut in, interpose; *inf.* chime in, butt in. **2** *chip in to buy a present* contribute, make a contribution, subscribe, donate, make a donation, pay.

chirp verb chirrup, cheep, twitter, tweet, warble, trill, chatter.

chirpy adjective cheerful, cheery, happy, light-hearted, carefree, merry; in good spirits; *inf.* upbeat.

chit-chat noun chat, chatting, small talk, idle gossip, gossip, chatter, tittle-tattle.

chivalrous adjective **1** *behaving in a chivalrous way towards women* gallant, gentlemanly, courteous, gracious, mannerly, well-mannered, polite, thoughtful, protective, courtly. **2** *chivalrous followers of King Arthur* knightly, courtly, bold, courageous, brave, valiant, heroic, daring, intrepid, honourable, high-minded, just, fair, loyal, constant, true, gallant, magnanimous, protective.
Opposites RUDE; BOORISH; UNMANNERLY; COWARDLY.

chivalry noun **1** *his chivalry towards women* gallantry, gentlemanliness, courtesy, courteousness, graciousness, mannerliness, politeness, thoughtfulness, protectiveness, courtliness. **2** *chivalry at medieval courts* knightly code, knighthood, knight errantry; courtly manners. **3** *the chivalry of Arthur's followers* knightliness, courtliness, boldness, courage, bravery, valour, heroism, daring, intrepidity, honour, high-mindedness, integrity, justice, justness, fairness, loyalty, constancy, trueness, truthfulness, magnanimity, protectiveness.

chivvy verb prod, urge, goad, nag, pester, badger, hound, pressure, pressurize, harass, annoy; *inf.* hassle.

choice noun **1** *the questions are open to choice* not compulsory | *the choice of candidate* choosing, selection, picking, option, preference, election, adoption. **2** *no choice but to resign* alternative, option, possibility, solution, answer, way out. **3** *a wide choice of confectionery* selection, range, variety, supply, store, array, display. **4** *he was considered the right choice* selection, appointment, appointee, nominee, candidate.

choice adjective **1** *choice fruit* best, select, superior, first-class, first-rate, excellent, prime, prize, special, rare, exclusive, hand-picked.

113

choke · Christianity

2 *a few choice phrases* well-chosen, select, hand-picked, appropriate, apposite, apt.

choke verb **1** *choke her to death with his hands* strangle, strangulate, throttle. **2** *smoke choking him* asphyxiate, suffocate, smother, stifle, over-power. **3** *he choked on a fishbone* gag, gasp, retch, struggle for air, asphyxiate, suffocate. **4** *the drains are choked* clog, block, obstruct, occlude, plug, dam up, congest. **choke back** *choke back her tears* check, restrain contain, sup-press, control, repress, curb, bridle.

choose verb **1** *choose a book/career* select, pick, pick out, hand-pick, take, opt for, settle on, decide on, fix on, single out, adopt, designate, elect, espouse. **2** *do as you choose* prefer, like, wish, want, desire, fancy, favour.
Opposites REJECT; DECLINE.

choosy adjective fussy, finicky, pernickety, faddy, fastidious, particular, exacting, discrim-inating.

chop verb **1** *chop the trees* cut down, fell, hew, bring down, hack down, saw down. **2** *chop branches* cut off, lop, sever, hack off, saw off, cleave, sunder. **3** *chop services|the plans have been chopped* cut, reduce, decrease, decimate, axe, stop, halt. **4** *chop meat/vegetables* cut up, cube, dice, fragment, crumble. **chop down** cut, hew, fell, hack. *See* CHOP 1. **chop off** sever, cleave, sunder. *See* CHOP 2. **chop up** cut up, frag-ment. *See* CHOP 4.

choppy adjective rough, bumpy, turbulent, blustery, stormy, tempestuous, squally.

chore noun task, job, duty, errand, burden, routine; work, domestic work.

chortle verb chuckle, cackle, guffaw, laugh uproariously, roar/shake with laughter, split one's sides, be convulsed.

chorus noun **1** *singing in the festival chorus* choir, ensemble, choral group; choristers, singers, vocalists. **2** *girls of the chorus* dance troupe, corps de ballet; dancing girls. **3** *the chorus of the song* refrain, burden, strain, response. **in chorus** *give a reply in chorus* in unison, in concert, in harmony.

christen verb **1** *christen a child in church* bap-tize, give a name to, name, sprinkle, immerse. **2** *she was christened Sara* name, call, dub, style, term, designate, denominate. **3** *christen the glasses* begin using, break in.

Christianity noun. *See tables. See also table at* ECCLESIASTIC.

CHRISTIAN DENOMINATIONS, PAST AND PRESENT

Abode of Love *hist.*	Christian Brethren	Lollards *hist.*
Agapemone *hist.*	Christian Science	Low Church
Adventists	Church Army	Lutherans
African & Afro-Caribbean Churches	Churches of Christ	Maronites
	Churches of God	Mennonites
African Methodist Episcopal Church *Am.*	Church in Wales	Millenial Church
	Church of England	Moravian Church
African Methodist Episcopal Zion Church *Am.*	Church of Ireland	Nestorians
	Church of Scotland	New Testament Assembly
African Orthodox Church	Church of the New Jerusalem	Old Believers
American Baptist Churches	Congregationalists	Oriental Orthodox Church
American Orthodox Church	Conservative Baptists	Orthodox Church
Amish	Coptic Church	Paulicians *hist.*
Amish Mennonites	Countess of Huntingdon's Connexion *hist.*	Pentecostal Churches
Anabaptists *hist.*		Plymouth Brethren
Anglican Communion	Covenanters *hist.*	Presbyterians
Anglo-Catholics	Cumberland Presbyterian Church *Am.*	Primitive Methodists *hist.*
Apostolic Brethren		Protestants
Armenian Church	Disciples of Christ	Puritans *hist.*
Assemblies of God	Doukhobors *hist.*	Quakers
Assumptionists *hist.*	Dunkers *hist.*	Reformed Churches
Assyrian Church	Dutch Reformed Church	Religious Society of Friends
Baptists	Eastern Orthodox Church	River Brethren
Bogomils *hist.*	Episcopalians	Roman Catholics
Bohemian Brethren *hist.*	Evangelical Churches	Rosicrucians
Brethren (Dunkers) *hist.*	Free Church of Scotland	Russian Orthodox Church
Brethren in Christ	Free Presbyterian Church of Scotland	Salvation Army
Broad Church		Seventh-day Adventists
Buchanites *hist.*	Free Will Baptists	Shakers
Calvinistic Methodists	Gideons	Society of Friends
Cameronians *hist.*	Greek Orthodox Church	Swedenborgians
Camisards *hist.*	High Church	Syrian Orthodox Church
Catholic Apostolic Church	Huguenots *hist.*	Uniates
Catholics	Hussites *hist.*	Unitas Fratrum *hist.*
Celtic Church *hist.*	Hutterites	United Church of Christ
Chaldaean Christians	Independent Methodists	United Free Church
Cherubim & Seraphim Churches	Jehovah's Witnesses	Unitarians
	Jesus People	United Reformed Church
Christadelphians	Jumpers *hist.*	Wesleyans

chronic *adjective* **1** *a chronic illness* persistent, long-lasting, long-standing, constant, continual, continuous, incessant, lingering, unabating, deep-rooted, deep-seated, ingrained. **2** *a chronic liar* inveterate, confirmed, habitual, hardened. **3** *a chronic case of plagiarism* very bad, appalling, atrocious, dreadful, awful. **Opposites** ACUTE; TEMPORARY; MILD.

chronicle *noun a chronicle of historical events* register, record, annals, calendar, diary, journal, log, account, archive, history, story.

chronicle *verb chronicle events* record, put on record, set down, document, register, report, enter, note, relate, tell about.

chronological *adjective* sequential, consecutive, progressive, serial, ordered, historical; in order of time, in sequence.

chubby *adjective* plump, tubby, rotund, stout, portly, round, dumpy, fat, fleshy, flabby, paunchy. **Opposites** SKINNY; SLENDER.

chuck *verb* **1** *chuck it in the bucket* toss, fling, throw, cast, pitch, hurl, shy, heave, sling, let fly. **2** *chuck his job/girlfriend* abandon, give up, relinquish, quit, forsake; *inf.* drop, pack in.

chuckle *verb* laugh quietly, laugh to oneself, chortle, giggle, titter, cackle.

chum *noun* friend, bosom friend, companion, comrade, crony, *alter ego*; *inf.* pal, mate, buddy; *dial.* marrow.

chunk *noun* lump, hunk, block, slab, mass, square, wedge, dollop, piece, portion, part; *inf.* wodge.

church *noun* place of worship, the house of God, the Lord's house; cathedral, minster, chapel, temple, tabernacle, mosque, synagogue. *See table.*

PARTS OF A CHURCH	
aisles	flying buttress
ambulatory	font
apse	galilee
baptistery	narthex
blind-story	nave
buttress	rood-screen
chancel	sacristy
chevet	spire
choir	steeple
clerestory/clearstory	transept
conch	tribune gallery
crossing	triforium
crypt	vaulting
dome	vestry
flèche	westwork

churlish *adjective* boorish, oafish, loutish, ill-mannered, unmannerly, rude, impolite, discourteous, uncivil, surly, sullen, crabbed, ill-tempered, curt, brusque, rough. **Opposites** MANNERLY; POLITE.

CHRISTIAN DOCTRINAL MOVEMENTS AND HERESIES			
Abelianism	Biblicism	Hussitism	Moral Majority
Adoptionism	Brownism	Jansenism	Moral
Ambrosianism	Calvinism	Latitudianarianism	Rearmament
Antinomianism	Catharism	Liberation	Nestorianism
Antipaedobaptism	Charismatic	Theology	Oxford Group
Apollinarianism	Movement	Liturgical	Oxford Movement
Arianism	Chiliasm	Movement	Pentecostalism
Arminianism	Cursillo	Lullism	Pietism
Augustinianism	Evangelicalism	Mandeism	Protestantism
Barclayism	Fundamentalism	Manichaeism	Tractarianism
Basilidianism	Gnosticism	Montanism	Trinitarianism

MEMBERS OF CHRISTIAN RELIGIOUS ORDERS			
Antonians	Capuchins	Hospitallers	Praemonstraten-
Augustinian	Carmelites	Ignorantines	sians
Hermits	Carthusians	Jacobins	Salesians
Austin Friars	Christian	Jesuits	Servites
Barnabites	Brothers	Knights	Sisters of Charity
Benedictines	Cistercians	Templar	Sisters of the Love
Bernardines	Conceptionists	Marianists	of God
Black Friars	Conventuals	Marists	Sisters of the Sacred
Black Monks	Culdees	Minims	Cross
Blue Nuns	Doctrinarians	Minorites	Somascans
Bonhommes	Dominicans	Norbertines	Studites
Brethren of the	Franciscans	Oratorians	Sylvestrines
Common Life	Friars Minor	Passionists	Theatines
Brigittines	Friars Preachers	Paulines	Trappists
Brothers	Gilbertines	Piarists	Trinitarians
Hospitallers	Grey Friars	Poor Clares	Ursulines
Camaldolites	Grey Nuns	Poor Soldiers of	Visitandines
Canons Regular	Hieronymites	the Temple	White Friars

churn verb **1** *churn milk into butter* beat, whip up, agitate. **2** *churning the peaceful waters* agitate, disturb, stir up, shake up. **3** *water churning under the rocks* seethe, foam, froth, boil, swirl, toss, convulse.

cigarette noun filter-tip, king-size, menthol cigarette, cigar; *inf.* cig, ciggie, smoke, fag, gasper, cancer stick, coffin nail.

cinder noun ash, ember, clinker, charcoal.

cinema noun films, pictures, movies, motion pictures; *inf.* big screen, silver screen. *See table at* FILM STAR.

cipher noun **1** *written in cipher* code, secret writing; coded message, cryptograph. **2** *a row of ciphers* zero, nil, naught. **3** *Arabic ciphers* number, numeral, figure, digit, integer, character, symbol, sign. **4** *he's just a cipher in the firm* nobody, nonentity, nothing, nonperson.

circle noun **1** *draw a circle* round, ring, disc, loop, circumference, ball, globe, sphere, orb. **2** *move in different circles* area of activity, field of interest, scene, sphere, domain, province, realm, range, region, circuit, orbit, compass. **3** *her circle of friends* group, set, company, crowd, ring, coterie, clique, assembly, fellowship, class.

circle verb **1** *vultures circling above* move round, rotate, revolve, circulate, wheel, whirl, gyrate, pivot, swivel. **2** *circle the estate* surround, encircle, ring, ring round, enclose, envelop, hedge in, hem in, gird, belt, circumscribe; *circle the world* go round, orbit, circumnavigate.

circuit noun **1** *run a circuit of the track* round, lap, turn, beat, ambit, cycle, loop, compass, circumference. **2** *the circuit of the estate/field* border, boundary, bounding line, bounds, compass, limits, circumference. **3** *the judge's circuit* tour, journey, trip, excursion, travels, wanderings, peregrination, perambulation.

circuitous adjective roundabout, winding, meandering, tortuous, twisting, rambling, indirect, maze-like, labyrinthine.

circular adjective round, discoid, ring-shaped, annular, spherical, spheroid, globular.

circulate verb **1** *circulate the news* spread, spread around, disseminate, propagate, distribute, transmit, give out, issue, make known, make public, broadcast, publicize, advertise, publish, promulgate, pronounce. **2** *blood/air circulating* flow, move round, go round, rotate, revolve, whirl, gyrate.

circumference noun perimeter, periphery, border, boundary, bounds, limits, confines, outline, circuit, compass, extremity, edge, rim, verge, fringe, skirt.

circumlocution noun periphrasis, pleonasm, tautology, redundancy, convolution, discursiveness, circuitousness, verbosity, wordiness, prolixity, long-windedness, gobbledegook.

circumscribe verb **1** *circumscribe a circle* enclose, encircle, bound, encompass, gird, circumvent; define, delineate, outline, demarcate, delimit, mark off. **2** *activities circumscribed by poverty* restrict, limit, curb, confine, restrain, trammel, hamper.

circumspect adjective wary, cautious, careful, chary, watchful, alert, attentive, guarded, canny, vigilant, observant, suspicious, apprehensive, leery, prudent, judicious, politic, discerning, sagacious.

circumstances plural noun **1** *I know nothing of the circumstances | in the circumstances* situation, state of affairs, conditions, set of conditions, position, event, occurrence, background. **2** *living in poor circumstances* state, situation, conditions, times, financial position, plight, predicament, lot, fortune, means, resources, life style, station.

circumstantial adjective **1** *circumstantial evidence* based on circumstances, indirect, incidental, evidential, deduced, presumed, inferential, conjectural. **2** *a circumstantial account* detailed, precise, particular, exact, accurate, minute, explicit, pointed, to the point.

citadel noun fortress, fort, fortification, stronghold, keep, castle, tower, bastion, fastness, donjon.

citation noun **1** *citations from the Romantic poets* quotation, quote, extract, excerpt, reference, illustration, allusion, passage, source. **2** *a citation for gallantry* commendation, award, honour, mention. **3** *a citation from the courts* summons, subpoena, arraignment.

cite verb **1** *cite the statistics as evidence | cite extracts from the poem* quote, mention, name, enumerate, evidence, refer to, allude to, exemplify, excerpt, extract. **2** *cite him for his gallantry* commend, recommend, pay tribute to, mention. **3** *cited by the courts* summon, subpoena, arraign, serve with a writ.

citizen noun resident, inhabitant, dweller, denizen, townsman, townswoman, burgher, burgess, taxpayer, voter, freeman, subject.

city noun conurbation, metropolitan area, inner city, metropolis, municipality, town, burgh, megalopolis, urban sprawl, concrete jungle.

civic adjective municipal, public, community, local, communal, urban, metropolitan.

civil adjective **1** *civil war* interior, internal, domestic, home. **2** *civil responsibilities* civic, municipal, public, community, local. *See* CIVIC. **3** *civil government/rulers* civilian, lay, non-military, non-religious, secular. **4** *a civil young man | in a civil manner* polite, courteous, well-mannered, mannerly, well-bred, gentlemanly, ladylike, refined, urbane, polished, cultured, cultivated, civilized, cordial, genial, pleasant, affable, amiable.
Opposites MILITARY; RELIGIOUS; RUDE; UNCIVIL.

civilian noun *civilians called up* ordinary citizen, private citizen, non-military person, layperson.

civilian adjective *a civilian guard* civil, lay, non-military. *See* CIVILIAN *noun.*

civility noun **1** *treat even his opponents with civility* courtesy, courteousness, politeness, good manners, mannerliness, graciousness, cordiality, geniality, pleasantness, affability, amiability, urbanity, gallantry. **2** *observe the civilities* polite act, courtesy; etiquette, protocol, propriety, decorum.

civilization *noun* **1** *a threat to modern civilization* development, advancement, progress, enlightenment, culture, cultivation, edification, refinement, sophistication. **2** *ancient civilizations* society, community, nation, country, people, way of life. **3** *the civilization of the tribes* civilizing, enlightenment, socialization, humanizing, edification, education, improvement. *See* CIVILIZE.

civilize *verb* enlighten, socialize, humanize, edify, cultivate, educate, instruct, improve, culture, refine, polish, sophisticate.

civilized *adjective* **1** *civilized tribes* enlightened, socialized, educated. *See* CIVILIZE. **2** *she's very civilized but he's a boor* cultured, cultivated, sophisticated, educated, enlightened, urbane.
Opposites UNCIVILIZED; BARBAROUS; UNSOPHISTICATED.

clad *adjective* *clad in wool | warmly clad* clothed, dressed, attired, covered, apparelled.

claim *verb* **1** *claim the prize* lay claim to, ask as one's right, establish rights to, ask for, demand, request, requisition, require. **2** *claim that he's innocent* profess, maintain, assert, declare, protest, avow, aver, allege, postulate, affirm, hold. **3** *the fire claimed lives* take, cause, result in, involve.

claim *noun* **1** *a claim for damages* demand, request, application, petition, call. **2** *put forward his claim to the crown* right, rights, title, prerogative, privilege, heritage, inheritance, legacy. **3** *dispute his claims of innocence* profession, assertion, declaration, protestation, avowal, averment, allegation, postulation, affirmation.

claimant *noun* applicant, candidate, petitioner, supplicant, suppliant, suitor, postulant, pretender, plaintiff.

clairvoyance *noun* second sight, psychic powers, ESP, extrasensory perception, telepathy, sixth sense.

clamber *verb* scramble, climb, scale, ascend, mount, shin, shinny, scrabble, claw one's way.

clammy *adjective* moist, damp, humid, sweaty, sticky.

clamour *noun* **1** *the clamour of children's voices* uproar, noise, din, racket, shout, shouting, yelling, babel, blaring, commotion, brouhaha, hubbub, hullabaloo, outcry, vociferation. **2** *answer their clamours for more money* demand, call, petition, request, urging, protest, complaint, insistence, exigency.

clamp *noun* **1** *held tightly in a clamp* vice, press, brace, clasp, fastener, hasp. **2** *a clamp on the car* immobilizer, stop, check, block, obstruction, impediment, obstacle.

clamp *verb* **1** *a pipe clamped between his teeth* grip, hold, fix, clench, press, squeeze, secure, make fast, brace. **2** *clamp a curfew on the city* impose, inflict, lay on, set, charge, burden. **3** *clamp a car* put a clamp on, immobilize, impede, obstruct. *See* CLAMP *noun* 2. **clamp down on** *clamp down on spending/crime* limit,

restrain, restrict, confine, hold in check, crack down on, be severe with, suppress, prevent.

clamp-down *noun* *a clamp-down on spending/crime* limitation, restraint, restriction, holding in check, crack-down, severe treatment, suppression, prevention.

clan *noun* **1** *the Scottish clans* family, house, sept, tribe, gens, line. **2** *tired of the business clan* set, circle, crowd, in-crowd, gang, band, group, faction, clique, coterie, fraternity, brotherhood, community, society, sodality.

clandestine *adjective* secret, undercover, surreptitious, cloak-and-dagger, back-alley, furtive, concealed, hidden, hugger-mugger, underhand.
Opposites OPEN; ABOVE-BOARD.

clang *noun* *the clang of the bell | the clang of two gates closing* ringing, ring, resounding, reverberation, clank, clash, clangour, bong, chime, toll, clink, clunk, jangle.

clang *verb* *bells clanging | gates clanging shut* ring, resound, reverberate, clank, clash, bong, clink, chime, toll, peal.

clanger *noun* mistake, blunder, gaffe, bungle, muff, slip-up; *inf.* bloomer, howler, goof.

clank *noun* *the clank of chains* metallic sound, clang, clangour, clink, clunk, jangle.

clank *verb* *chains clanking* clang, clink, clunk, jangle.

clannish *adjective* cliquish, insular, exclusive, narrow, parochial, provincial.

clap *verb* **1** *clap on the back* strike, slap, smite, smack, bang, whack, wallop, clatter; *clap one's hands* strike/slap together. **2** *the audience clapping the cast/performance* applaud, cheer, acclaim; show one's appreciation, put one's hands together. **3** *clap him in jail/chains* cast, thrust, push, pitch, hurl, toss.

claptrap *noun* nonsense, drivel, rubbish, humbug, insincerity; *inf.* bunk, guff, flannel.

clarify *verb* **1** *clarify the situation* make clear, clear up, resolve, make plain, explain, elucidate, illuminate, throw light on, make simple, simplify. **2** *clarify butter* purify, refine.

clarity *noun* **1** *the clarity of his prose* clearness, lucidity, lucidness, plainness, simplicity, intelligibility, comprehensibility, obviousness, explicitness, unambiguity, precision. **2** *the clarity of the water* clearness, transparency, limpidity, translucence, pellucidity, glassiness.
Opposites OBSCURITY; DARKNESS.

clash *verb* **1** *clash the cymbals* strike, bang, clang, crash, clatter, clank, clink, rattle, jangle. **2** *the two sides clashed* be in conflict, war, fight, contend, do battle, come to blows, feud, grapple, wrangle, quarrel, cross swords, lock horns. **3** *the appointments clash* coincide, occur simultaneously, synchronize, conflict. **4** *the colours clash* be discordant, not match, lack harmony, jar, be incompatible; *inf.* scream.

clash *noun* **1** *the clash of cymbals* striking, bang, clang, crash, clatter, clank. *See* CLASH *verb* 1. **2** *the clash of the opposing sides* conflict, collision, confrontation, brush, warring, fighting, contending, feud, grappling, wrangling, quarrelling. **3** *the clash of the dates* coincidence, co-occurrence, concurrence, synchronization, conflict. **4** *the clash of the colours* discordance, discord, lack of harmony, incompatibility, jarring.

clasp *noun* **1** *the clasp of the necklace* catch, fastener, fastening, clip; hook, hook and eye, snap fastener, buckle, hasp. **2** *wearing a diamond clasp* pin, brooch. **3** *engage in a loving clasp* embrace, hug, cuddle, hold, grip, grasp.

class *noun* **1** *middle classes | professional class* social order, social division, stratum, rank, level, status, sphere, grade, group, grouping, set, classification, caste. **2** *in the highest class | degrees divided into three classes* category, classification, division, section, group, set, grade. **3** *a class of objects* category, group, set, kind, sort, type, collection, denomination, order, species, genre, genus. **4** *what class is the student/pupil in* study group, school group, seminar, tutorial. **5** *a player of class | a woman of class* quality, excellence, distinction, stylishness, elegance, chic.

class *verb books classed as textbooks* classify, categorize, group, grade, arrange, order, sort, codify, file, index, pigeon-hole.

classic *adjective* **1** *a classic performance* first-rate, first-class, excellent, brilliant, finest, outstanding, exemplary, masterly, consummate. **2** *a classic case/example* typical, standard, model, guiding, archetypal, stock, true-to-form, paradigmatic, prototypical. **3** *classic styles* simple, traditional, timeless, ageless, long-lasting, enduring, abiding, time-honoured, long-standing, long-established.

classic *noun* **1** *reading the classics* great work, established work, standard work, masterpiece. **2** *the match was a classic* masterpiece, excellent example. *See* CLASSIC *adjective* 1.

classical *adjective* **1** *a classical scholar | classical architecture* Greek, Grecian, Hellenic, Attic, Roman, Latin. **2** *classical music* serious, symphonic, concert, traditional, long-lasting. **3** *a classical style of design* simple, plain, restrained, pure, understated, harmonious, well-proportioned, balanced, symmetrical, elegant, aesthetic.

classification *noun the classification of books/ blood* classifying, categorizing, categorization, grouping, grading, arrangement, codifying, codification, taxonomy. *See* CLASSIFY.

classify *verb classify books/blood* categorize, class, group, grade, arrange, order, sort, type, rank, rate, designate, codify, catalogue, tabulate, file, index, assign, pigeon-hole, brand.

clatter *verb* rattle, clang, clank, clunk, bang.

clause *noun clause 9 of the document* section, paragraph, article, note, item, point, passage, part, heading, condition, provision, proviso, stipulation.

claw *noun a cat's/bird's/lobster's claws* nail, talon, unguis, pincer, nipper, chela.

claw *verb claw his face* scratch, tear, lacerate, scrape, graze, rip, dig into, maul.

clay *noun* **1** *clay used for pottery* argil, slip, kaolin, adobe, loam. **2** *buried beneath the clay* earth, ground, soil, sod.

clean *adjective* **1** *clean hands/clothes* unsoiled, spotless, unstained, unspotted, unsullied, unblemished, immaculate, speckless, hygienic, sanitary, washed, cleansed, laundered, scrubbed. **2** *clean air* pure, clear, natural, unpolluted, unadulterated, uncontaminated, untainted, unmixed. **3** *living clean lives* good, upright, honourable, respectable, virtuous, righteous, moral, reputable, upstanding, exemplary, innocent, guiltless, pure, decent, chaste, undefiled. **4** *a clean piece of paper* unused, unmarked, blank, vacant, void. **5** *the clean lines of the aeroplane* stream-lined, smooth, well-defined, definite, clean-cut, regular, symmetrical, simple, elegant, graceful, uncluttered, trim, shapely. **6** *a clean break to the marriage* complete, thorough, total, entire, conclusive, decisive, final. **7** *found to be clean after investigation* innocent, guiltless, guilt-free, crime-free.
Opposites DIRTY; FILTHY; IMMORAL.

clean *adverb a bullet clean through his shoulder | go clean out of my mind* completely, entirely, totally, fully, wholly, thoroughly, altogether, quite, utterly, absolutely.

clean *verb* **1** *clean one's hands/walls* wash, cleanse, wipe, sponge, scrub, scour, swab. **2** *clean one's clothes* dry-clean, launder. **3** *clean the room* tidy, set to rights; vacuum, hoover, dust, mop, sweep; *inf.* do.
Opposites DIRTY; SOIL; MESS.

cleanse *verb* **1** *cleanse the wound* clean, make clean, clean up, wash, bathe, rinse, disinfect. **2** *cleanse of his sins* purify, purge, absolve, lustrate.

clear *adjective* **1** *a clear day | clear weather* bright, cloudless, unclouded, fair, fine, light, undimmed, sunny, sunshiny. **2** *clear water/ glass* transparent, limpid, pellucid, translucent, crystalline, diaphanous, see-through. **3** *it was clear that he was guilty* obvious, evident, plain, apparent, sure, definite, unmistakable, manifest, indisputable, patent, incontrovertible, irrefutable, palpable, beyond doubt, beyond question. **4** *a clear account of the incident* understandable, comprehensible, intelligible, plain, explicit, lucid, coherent, distinct. **5** *a clear thinker* astute, keen, sharp, quick, perceptive, discerning, perspicacious, penetrating. **6** *a clear road/view* open, empty, free, unobstructed, unimpeded, unhindered, unlimited. **7** *a clear conscience* untroubled, undisturbed, peaceful, at peace, tranquil, serene, calm, innocent, guiltless, guilt-free, clean, sinless, stainless. **8** *four clear days* whole, full, entire, complete, total.
Opposites CLOUDY; OPAQUE; VAGUE; AMBIGUOUS.

clear *adverb* **1** *hear him loud and clear* clearly, distinctly, plainly, audibly. **2** *stand clear of the door* away from, at a distance from, apart from, out of contact with. **3** *got clear away* completely, entirely, thoroughly, fully, wholly, clear. *See* CLEAR *adjective* 8.

clear *verb* **1** *the weather cleared* clear up, brighten, lighten, break. **2** *clear the plates* remove, take away, tidy up/away. **3** *clear the drains* unblock, unclog, unstop. **4** *clear the room of objects* empty, vacate, evacuate, void, free, rid. **5** *clear the accused of charges* absolve, acquit, discharge, let go, exonerate, vindicate, excuse, pardon. **6** *clear the fence* jump, vault, leap, hop, pass over. **7** *clear £500 net,* make a profit of, realize a profit of, gain, earn, make, acquire, secure, bring, reap. **8** *clear goods | the ship was cleared* authorize, sanction, pass, approve, give consent to, permit/allow to pass, give one's seal of approval to; *inf.* give the go-ahead to, give the green light to. **clear out 1** *clear out the cupboard* empty, evacuate, tidy, tidy up. **2** *clear out the rubbish* get rid of, throw out, throw away, eject, eliminate. **3** *boys told to clear out* go away, get out, leave, depart, take oneself off, make oneself scarce, withdraw, retire, decamp. **clear up 1** *clear up the mystery/problem* solve, resolve, straighten out, find an answer to, unravel, untangle, explain, eluci-date; *inf.* crack. **2** *clear up the room/mess* tidy, tidy up, put in order, straighten up, clean up. **3** *the weather cleared up* improve, brighten. See CLEAR *verb* 1.

clearance *noun* **1** *slum clearance* clearing, removal, evacuation, eviction, emptying, depopulation, unpeopling, withdrawal, decant-ing. **2** *the clearance under the bridge* clearing, space, gap, allowance, margin, headroom, lee-way, room to spare. **3** *get clearance for their plans* authorization, consent, permission, sanc-tion, go-ahead, leave, endorsement; *inf.* green light.

clear-cut *adjective clear-cut proposals* definite, specific, precise, explicit, unambiguous, unequivocal.

clearly *adverb clearly he's ill | clearly a mistake* obviously, undoubtedly, without doubt, indu-bitably, plainly, undeniably, decidedly, surely, certainly, incontrovertibly, irrefutably, incon-testably, patently.

cleave[1] *verb* **1** *cleave the logs* split, split open, open, crack, lay open, divide, hew, hack, chop/slice up, sunder, sever, rend, rive. **2** *cleave a path* make, cut, plough, drive, bulldoze.

cleave[2] *verb* **cleave to** cling to, stick to, hold to, stand by, abide by, adhere to, be loyal/faith-ful to.

cleaver *noun* knife, chopper, hatchet, axe; butcher's knife, kitchen knife.

cleft *noun* split, crack, gap, fissure, crevice, rift, break, fracture.

clemency *noun* **1** *treat the prisoners with clemency* mercy, leniency, compassion, human-ity, pity, sympathy, kindness, magnanimity, fairness, temperance, moderation, indulgence. **2** *the clemency of the weather* mild-ness, balminess, warmness.

clench *verb* **1** *clench the teeth* close, shut, seal, fasten. **2** *clench the table edge* grip, grasp, clutch, hold, seize.

clergy *noun* clergymen, churchmen, clerics, ecclesiastics; ministry, priesthood, holy orders, the cloth, first estate. See table at ECCLESIASTIC.

clergyman *noun* churchman, churchwoman, man/woman of the cloth, man/woman of God, cleric, ecclesiastic, divine; father, padre, rev-erend; rabbi, imam. See tables at ECCLESIASTIC, PRIEST.

clerical *adjective* **1** *a clerical post in the office | clerical duties* secretarial, office, writing, typing, filing, bookkeeping; *inf.* pen-pushing. **2** *clerical clothes* ecclesiastical, churchly, priestly, pas-toral, sacerdotal, prelatic, apostolic, canonical.

clever *adjective* **1** *both stupid and clever people* intelligent, bright, sharp-witted, quick-witted, talented, gifted, smart, capable, able, compe-tent, apt, knowledgeable, educated, sagacious; *inf.* brainy. **2** *a clever move* shrewd, astute, adroit, canny, cunning, ingenious, artful, wily, inventive. **3** *clever with their hands* dexterous, skilful, adroit, nimble, deft, handy.
Opposites DULL; STUPID; AWKWARD.

cliché *noun* hackneyed phrase, platitude, com-monplace, banality, truism, saw, maxim, bro-mide; *inf.* old chestnut.

click *noun the click of the key in the lock* clink, clack, chink, snap, tick.

click *verb* **1** *the key clicked in the lock* clink, clack, chink, snap, tick. **2** *I see it's suddenly clicked* become clear, fall into place, come home to one, make sense. **3** *the two girls clicked immediately* get on, take to each other, hit it off, be compatible, be on the same wave-length, feel a rapport. **4** *the new toys clicked with the children* make a hit, prove popular, be successful, be a success, succeed, go down well.

client *noun* customer, patron, regular, habitué, buyer, purchaser, shopper, consumer, user, patient.

clientele *noun* clients, customers, patrons, reg-ulars; patronage, following, trade, business, market. See CLIENT.

cliff *noun* precipice, rock-face, face, crag, bluff, escarpment, scar, scarp, overhang, promon-tory, tor.

climate *noun* **1** *temperate climate* weather pat-tern, weather conditions, weather, tempera-ture. **2** *visit various climates* clime, country, place, region, area, zone. **3** *the political climate* atmosphere, mood, temper, spirit, feeling, feel, ambience, aura, ethos.

climax *noun* **1** *the climax of her campaign/career* culmination, height, peak, pinnacle, high point, summit, top, highlight, acme, zenith, apex, apogee, crowning point, ne plus ultra. **2** *reach climax* sexual climax, orgasm.
Opposites NADIR; ANTICLIMAX.

climax *verb* **1** *the campaign climaxed in victory* culminate, peak, come to a head, result, end. **2** *climax together* have an orgasm, orgasm; *inf.* come.

climb *verb* **1** *climb up the ladder | climb to the top* go up, ascend, mount, scale, clamber up, shin up. **2** *prices/temperatures are climbing* go up, rise, increase, shoot up, soar. **3** *the road climbs steeply* slope upward, incline, bank. **4** *climb up the ranks* make progress, get ahead, advance, work one's way up, make strides. **climb down 1** *climb down the ladder/tree* go down, descend, shin down. **2** *the government forced to climb down* back down, retract, retreat, eat one's words, eat humble pie.

clinch *verb* **1** *clinch the deal* settle, secure, seal, set the seal on, complete, confirm, conclude, assure, cap, close, wind up; *inf.* sew up. **2** *clinch a nail* fasten, make fast, secure, fix, clamp, bolt, rivet, pinion. **3** *boxers/lovers clinching* hug, embrace, cuddle, squeeze, clutch, grasp, grapple.

cling *verb the surfaces clung together* stick, adhere, hold, grip, clasp, clutch. **cling to** **1** *cling to the rope | clung to his friend* hold on to, hang on to, clutch, grip, grasp, clasp, cleave to, attach to, embrace. **2** *cling to one's beliefs* stick to, hold to, stand by, abide by, adhere to, be loyal/faithful to, remain true to, remain attached to; *inf.* stick with.

clinic *noun* medical centre, outpatients' clinic, polyclinic.

clinical *adjective* **1** *a clinical attitude to others' problems* objective, dispassionate, detached, uninvolved, cold, unsympathetic, unfeeling. **2** *clinical designs* plain, simple, unadorned, unornamented, stark, austere, severe, spartan.

clip¹ *verb* **1** *clip hair/fleece/hedges* cut, cut short, crop, snip, trim, shear, prune, pollard. **2** *clip him round the ear* hit, strike, box, cuff, smack, wallop, thump, punch, knock; *inf.* clout, whack; *Scots* skelp. **3** *the train was clipping along* speed, go fast, race, gallop, rush, dash, zoom, whip along, spank along, go like lightning.

clip² *noun* **1** *need a hair clip* cut, trim, shortening, shear, shearing, pruning. **2** *a clip round the ear* box, cuff, smack, wallop; *inf.* clout. *See* CLIP¹ *verb* 2. **3** *going at a clip* speed, fast rate, swift pace, velocity; *inf.* fair old rate. **4** *a clip from a film/newspaper* clipping, cutting, extract, excerpt, snippet, fragment.

clip³ *verb* clip *the papers together* pin, staple, fasten, fix, attach, hold.

clip⁴ *noun a paper-clip | bicycle clips* fastener, coupler, clasp.

clique *noun* coterie, circle, crowd, in-crowd, set, gang, group, clan, faction, pack, band, ring, fraternity, society, mob.

cloak *noun* **1** *wearing a black cloak* cape. *See table at* COAT. **2** *a cloak of darkness/secrecy* cover, screen, blind, mask, mantle, veil, shroud, shield, front, camouflage, pretext.

cloak *verb meetings cloaked in secrecy* hide, conceal, cover, cover up, screen, mask, veil, shroud, shield, cloud, camouflage, obscure, disguise.

clock *noun* timekeeper, timepiece, timer; chronometer, chronograph. *See table.*

clock *verb* **1** *clock the race* time, record the time; *inf.* stopwatch. **2** *she clocked a record time* register, record, achieve, attain; *inf.* do. **clock up** *we've clocked up 500 miles* register, record, attain, achieve; *inf.* do.

clog *noun* sabot, wooden shoe, wooden-soled shoe. *See table at* FOOTWEAR.

clog *verb* **1** *leaves clogging up the drains* block, obstruct, dam, congest, jam, occlude; stop up, dam up. **2** *clogging the system* obstruct, hinder, impede, hamper, shackle, burden.

CLOCKS	
alarm clock	hunter watch
analogue clock	journeyman clock
astronomical clock	long-case clock
atomic clock	marine chronom-
calendar clock	eter
carriage clock	pendulum clock
chronometer	pocket watch
clepsydra	quartz-crystal clock
clock radio	stem-winder *Am.*
cuckoo clock	stopwatch
digital watch/clock	sundial
egg-timer	travelling clock
grandfather clock	wall clock
half-hunter watch	water-clock
hourglass	wristwatch

cloister *noun* **1** *ecclesiastics in a cloister* convent, nunnery, monastery, abbey, priory, friary. **2** *walking in the cloisters* covered walk, walkway, corridor, aisle, arcade, gallery, piazza, ambulatory.

cloistered *adjective leading cloistered lives* secluded, sheltered, sequestered, shielded, shut-off, withdrawn, confined, restricted, insulated, reclusive, hermitic, cloistral.

close¹ *verb* **1** *close the door* shut, slam, fasten, secure, lock, bolt, bar, latch, padlock. **2** *close the bottle/opening* stop up, plug, seal, clog, choke, obstruct, occlude. **3** *close the meeting* bring to an end, end, conclude, finish, terminate, wind up, adjourn, discontinue. **4** *he closed by praying* come to an end, end, conclude, finish, cease, wind up, adjourn. **5** *close the bargain* complete, conclude, settle, clinch, seal, establish, fix, agree. **6** *the gap closed* narrow, lessen, grow smaller, dwindle, reduce. **7** *his arms closed around her | the boxers closed* come together, join, connect, come into contact, unite, clutch one another, grip, clench, grapple, couple. *Opposites* OPEN; CLEAR; START.

close² *noun at close of day/play* end, finish, conclusion, termination, cessation, completion, culmination, finale, wind-up.

close³ *noun city closes* courtyard, quadrangle, enclosure, piazza, cul-de-sac; *Scots* entry.

close⁴ *adjective* **1** *houses close to each other* near, adjacent, in close proximity, adjoining, neighbouring, hard by, abutting; *birthdays close together* near, occurring/falling near. **2** *a close resemblance | close in appearance* near, similar, like, alike, comparable, parallel, corresponding, akin. **3** *a close friend* intimate, dear, bosom, close-knit, inseparable, loving, devoted, attached, confidential; *inf.* matey, chummy, pally; *Am. inf.* buddy-buddy, palsy-walsy. **4** *close print | close formation* dense, condensed, compact, crowded, packed, solid, tight, cramped, congested, crushed, squeezed. **5** *a close game* evenly matched, well-matched, hard-fought, sharply contested, neck-and-neck, nose-to-nose; *inf.* fifty-fifty. **6** *a close description* accurate, true, faithful, literal, exact, precise, conscientious. **7** *pay close attention | on close examination* careful, concentrated, attentive,

assiduous, alert, vigilant, intent, dogged, painstaking, detailed, minute, intense, keen, thorough, rigorous, searching. **8** *under close arrest* strict, stringent, rigorous, thorough, tight. **9** *close weather* humid, muggy, airless, stuffy, fuggy, heavy, oppressive, stifling, suffocating, musty, unventilated. **10** *he's very close about his affairs* quiet, reticent, uncommunicative, reserved, private, unforthcoming, secretive, evasive. **11** *close with his money* mean, miserly, stingy, niggardly, parsimonious, penny-pinching, tight-fisted, tight, near; *inf.* mingy.
Opposites FAR; DISTANT; REMOTE; FRESH.

closet *noun a clothes closet* cupboard, wardrobe, cabinet, locker, storage room.

closet *adjective a closet homosexual/socialist* secret, unrevealed, undisclosed, hidden, concealed, furtive.

closet *verb closeted with the manager* shut away, sequester, seclude, cloister, confine, isolate.

closure *noun* closing down, shutting down, winding up, cessation of operations, cessation, termination, finish, conclusion.

clot *noun* **1** *a clot of blood* glob, lump, gob, clump, mass, obstruction, thrombus. **2** *a silly clot* fool, idiot, dolt, nitwit, half-wit; *inf.* dope, chump.

clot *verb blood clotting* coagulate, set, congeal, jell, thicken, cake, curdle.

cloth *noun silk cloth* fabric, material, stuff; textiles, dry goods, soft goods. *See table at* FABRIC.

clothe *verb* **1** *clothed in pure wool* dress, attire, rig, rig out, turn out, apparel, fit out, outfit, robe, garb, array, deck out, drape, accoutre, trap out, habit, invest; *inf.* doll up. **2** *hills clothed in cloud* cover, wrap, cloak, envelop, swathe, swaddle.
Opposites UNDRESS; UNCOVER.

clothes *plural noun put away one's clothes | wearing expensive clothes* garments, articles of clothing/dress; clothing, attire, outfits. *See* CLOTHING.

clothing *noun* clothes, garments; dress, attire, apparel, outfit, costume, garb, ensemble, vestments, raiment; *inf.* clobber, gear, rig-out, togs, get-up. *See tables at* COAT, DRESS, FOOTWEAR, HAT, SHIRT, SKIRT, TROUSERS.

cloud *noun* **1** *clouds in the sky* fleecy cloud, billowy cloud, billow; haze, cloudbank, mackerel sky. *See table.* **2** *a cloud of smoke* pall, shroud, mantle, cloak, screen, cover. **3** *a cloud on their happiness* shadow, threat; gloom, darkness. **4** *a cloud of insects* swarm, flock, mass, multitude, host, horde, throng.

cloudy *adjective* **1** *a cloudy sky* overcast, hazy, dark, grey, sombre, leaden, heavy, gloomy, dim, lowering, sunless, starless. **2** *cloudy recollections* blurred, vague, indistinct, hazy, indefinite, nebulous, obscure, confused, muddled. **3** *cloudy liquids* opaque, non-transparent, murky, muddy, milky, emulsified, opalescent, turbid.
Opposites BRIGHT; CLEAR.

clout *verb clout the child* hit, strike, smack, slap, cuff, box, thump, wallop; *inf.* whack, clobber, sock.

clout *noun* **1** *give him a clout* smack, slap, thump. *See* CLOUT *verb.* **2** *carry clout in the firm* influence, power, pull, weight, authority, prestige, standing.

clown *noun* **1** *circus clowns* jester, fool, buffoon, zany, harlequin, pierrot, merry andrew. **2** *he's sedate but his brother's a real clown* joker, comedian, comic, humorist, funnyman, wag, wit, prankster. **3** *the clown crashed my car* fool, idiot, dolt, nitwit, half-wit; *inf.* clot, dope.

clown *verb clown around* fool, act foolishly, jest, joke; *inf.* mess, muck, muck about.

cloy *verb* satiate, pall, surfeit, dull, sicken, nauseate.

cloying *adjective* sickly-sweet, sugary, saccharine, sickening, nauseating.

club *noun* **1** *hit him with a club* cudgel, bludgeon, cosh, stick, staff, truncheon, bat, baton; *Am.* blackjack. *See table at* WEAPON. **2** *a swimming/bridge club* society, group, association, organization, circle, set, clique, coterie, affiliation, league, union, federation, company, fraternity, brotherhood, sorority.

club *verb* hit, strike, beat, batter, bash, cudgel, bludgeon, cosh, truncheon, baste; *inf.* clout, clobber. **club together** join forces, pool resources, make a kitty, make a joint contribution, divide costs; *inf.* have a whip-round.

clue *noun* hint, indication, sign, evidence, information, intimation, pointer, guide, lead, tip, tip-off, inkling.

clump *noun* **1** *a clump of trees* group, cluster, bunch, collection, assembly, assemblage. **2** *clump of earth | clump of blood cells* mass, lump, clod, glob, agglutination.

clump *verb* **1** *houses clumped together* group, cluster, bunch, collect, assemble, congregate, mass, lump, bundle, pack. **2** *clump around in heavy boots* clomp, stamp, stump, stomp, thump, thud, bang, tramp, lumber, plod, trudge, stumble.

clumsy *adjective* **1** *clumsy and always breaking things* awkward, uncoordinated, ungainly, blundering, bungling, bumbling, inept, maladroit, inexpert, unhandy, unskilful, like a bull in a china shop; *inf.* cack-handed, ham-fisted, ham-handed, butter-fingered. **2** *a clumsy piece of furniture* awkward, unwieldy, hulking, heavy, solid, unmanoeuvrable. **3** *a clumsy apology* awkward, gauche, graceless, tactless, unpol-

CLOUD FORMATIONS	
altocumulus	lenticular cloud
altostratus	nimbostratus
anvil cloud	nimbus
cirrocumulus	noctilucent cloud
cirrostratus	rain cloud
cirrus	storm cloud
cumulonimbus	stratocumulus
cumulostratus	stratus
cumulus	thundercloud

ished, crude, uncouth, crass.
Opposites ADROIT; GRACEFUL.

cluster noun **1** *a cluster of berries/flowers* bunch, clump, collection, knot, group; *Tech.* raceme, panicle. **2** *cluster of people* gathering, group, collection, bunch, band, company, knot, body, assemblage, congregation.

cluster verb *people clustering round the church* gather, collect, assemble, congregate, group, come together, flock together, foregather.

clutch verb **1** *clutching her purse* grip, grasp, clasp, cling to, hang on to, clench. **2** *clutch at the branch* reach for, snatch at, grab, make a grab for, seize, catch at, claw at.

clutch noun *a clutch of eggs* set, setting, hatch, hatching, nest, incubation.

clutches plural noun *fall into the clutches of money-lenders* hands, power, control, hold, grip, grasp, claws, tyranny, possession, keeping, custody.

clutter noun **1** *a clutter of papers* mess, jumble, litter, heap, hotchpotch. **2** *his room in a clutter* mess, muddle, disorder, chaos, disarray, state of confusion/untidiness.

clutter verb *papers cluttering up the room* litter, make untidy, make a mess of, mess up, be strewn about, be scattered about.

coach[1] noun **1** *travel by express coach* bus, motorcoach, omnibus, charabanc. **2** *railway coaches* carriage, wagon; *Am.* car. *See table at* TRAIN. **3** *horses pulling a coach* carriage. *See table at* CARRIAGE.

coach[2] noun *tennis/maths coach* instructor, trainer, teacher, tutor, mentor.

coach[3] verb *coach in tennis/mathematics* instruct, train, teach, tutor, drill, prime, cram, put one through one's paces.

coagulate verb congeal, clot, gel, thicken, curdle.

coalesce verb unite, join together, combine, merge, amalgamate, integrate, affiliate, blend, fuse; *lit.* commingle.

coalition noun union, alliance, affiliation, league, association, federation, confederacy, bloc, compact, amalgamation, merger, conjunction, combination, fusion.

coarse adjective **1** *coarse material* rough, bristly, scratchy, prickly, hairy, shaggy. **2** *coarse features* heavy, rough, rugged, craggy, unrefined. **3** *coarse flour* crude, unrefined, unprocessed, unpurified. **4** *coarse behaviour/manners* rude, ill-mannered, uncivil, rough, boorish, loutish, churlish, uncouth, crass. **5** *coarse humour* bawdy, earthy, blue, ribald, vulgar, smutty, obscene, indelicate, indecent, offensive, lewd, pornographic, prurient; *inf.* raunchy.
Opposites FINE; REFINED; DECENT.

coarsen verb roughen, thicken, toughen, harden, harshen.

coast noun *a rugged coast* coastline, shore, seashore, shoreline, seacoast, beach, foreshore, strand, seaboard, water's edge, littoral.

coast verb *bicycles coasting downhill | coasting through life* freewheel, cruise, taxi, drift, glide, sail.

coat noun **1** *a winter coat* jacket, overcoat. *See table.* **2** *animals' coats* fur, hair, wool; fleece, hide, pelt, skin. **3** *a coat of paint* layer, covering, overlay, coating. **4** *a coat of dust* coating, layer, film. *See* COATING.

coating noun covering, layer, film, coat, dusting, blanket, sheet, glaze, skin, veneer, finish, lamination, patina, membrane.

coax verb wheedle, cajole, talk into, beguile, flatter, inveigle, entice, induce, persuade, prevail upon, win over; *inf.* sweet-talk, soft-soap.

cock noun *hens and cock* cockerel, chanticleer; *Am.* rooster.

cock verb **1** *a dog cocking its leg* raise, lift, lift up. **2** *cocked his hat* tilt, tip, slant, incline.

cocky adjective arrogant, conceited, egotistical, swollen-headed, vain, cocksure, swaggering, brash.

coddle verb pamper, cosset, mollycoddle, indulge, spoil, baby, humour, pet, feather-bed.

code noun **1** *a message in code* cipher, secret writing; coded message, cryptograph. *See table at* MORSE CODE. **2** *code of honour* ethics, morals, principles, maxims; morality, convention, etiquette, custom. **3** *highway code | legal code* laws, rules, regulations, system, canon.

COATS, CLOAKS, AND JACKETS

Afghan	duffel coat	lumber-jacket	pelisse	sports coat
anorak	Eisenhower	*Am.*	poncho	surcoat
Barbour™	jacket *Am.*	Mackinaw coat	raglan	tabard
blazer	frock coat	*Am.*	raincoat	topcoat
bolero	fur coat	mackintosh	reefer/reefing-	topper *Am.*
bomber jacket	gabardine	mantle	jacket	trench coat
Burberry™	coat	mess jacket	riding-jacket	tunic
cagoule	greatcoat	mink	sack coat *Am.*	ulster
cape	hacking jacket	monkey-jacket	shawl	vest *Am.*
capote	haik	Norfolk jacket	shell-jacket	waistcoat
cope	haori	oilskin	slicker *Am.*	waterproof
dolman jacket	hunting jacket	overcoat	smoking	windbreaker
domino	jerkin	parka	jacket	*Am.*
donkey jacket	kebaya	pea-jacket	sou'wester	windcheater
dreadnought	leather jacket	pelerine	spencer	wrap

coerce *verb* compel, force, pressure, pressurize, drive, impel, constrain, oblige; *inf.* twist one's arm, lean on, put the screws on, strongarm.

coffee *noun.* See table.

TYPES OF COFFEE	
cappuccino	Greek coffee
decaffeinated coffee	instant coffee
espresso	kahwa
filter coffee	Turkish coffee

coffer *noun* strongbox, moneybox, money chest, safe, chest, casket, box.

coffin *noun* casket, box, sarcophagus; *inf.* wooden overcoat.

cogent *adjective* convincing, forceful, forcible, effective, conclusive, persuasive, compelling, powerful, strong, potent, weighty, influential, authoritative, telling.
Opposites WEAK; unconvincing; INEFFECTIVE.

cogitate *verb* think, ponder, contemplate, consider, give consideration to, deliberate, meditate, reflect, mull over, muse, ruminate.

cognate *adjective* **1** *cognate words* related, kindred, akin, allied, congeneric, consanguine. **2** *cognate sciences* allied, affiliated, associated, similar, alike, connected, corresponding, correlated, analogous.

cognition *noun* perception, discernment, understanding, awareness, comprehension, apprehension, enlightenment, insight, intelligence, reason.

cognizant *adjective* aware, conscious, knowing, alive to, sensible of, familiar with, acquainted with, conversant with; *inf.* wise to.

cohabit *verb* live together, sleep with; *inf.* shack up with.

coherent *adjective* *a coherent argument* logical, rational, reasoned, lucid, articulate, systematic, orderly, organized, consistent, comprehensible, intelligible.
Opposites INCOHERENT; MUDDLED.

cohort *noun* troop, brigade, legion, squad, squadron, column, group, company, body, band.

coil *verb* wind, spiral, loop, curl, twist, twine, entwine, snake, wreathe, convolute.

coin *noun* **1** *gold coins* piece. See table at CURRENCY. **2** *pay in coin* coins, coinage, change, specie, silver, copper, gold.

coin *verb* **1** *coin a word* invent, create, make up, devise, conceive, originate, think up, dream up, formulate, fabricate. **2** *coin money* mint, mould, stamp out, die, monetize.

coincide *verb* **1** *dates coinciding* be concurrent, occur simultaneously, happen together, coexist, concur, synchronize. **2** *stories coinciding* accord, agree, correspond, concur, match, square, tally, harmonize.

coincidence *noun* **1** *arrive together by coincidence* accident, chance, fluke, luck, fortuity, serendipity. **2** *the coincidence of events/stories* coinciding. See COINCIDE.

coincidental *adjective* **1** *a coincidental meeting* accidental, chance, unplanned, unintentional, casual, lucky, fortuitous, serendipitous; *inf.* flukey. **2** *coincidental concerts* simultaneous, concurrent, synchronous, co-existent.

cold *adjective* **1** *a cold day* chilly, chill, cool, freezing, bitter, raw, icy, frigid, wintry, frosty, arctic, inclement, sunless, windy, glacial, polar, gelid, brumal; *inf.* nippy. **2** *feeling cold* chilly, chilled, cool, freezing, frozen, frozen stiff, frozen/chilled to the bone/marrow, shivery, numbed, benumbed. **3** *a cold woman/attitude* frigid, unresponsive, unfeeling, unemotional, phlegmatic, unexcitable, passionless, spiritless, unmoved, indifferent, lukewarm, apathetic, dispassionate, aloof, distant, reserved, remote, standoffish, insensitive, unsympathetic, uncaring, heartless, callous, cold-hearted, stony-hearted, unfriendly, inhospitable, glacial. **4** *the story is cold* dead, gone, extinguished, finished, defunct.
Opposites HOT; WARM; PASSIONATE.

cold-blooded *adjective* savage, inhuman, barbarous, heartless, ruthless, pitiless, merciless, stony-hearted.

collaborate *verb* **1** *collaborate on a book* cooperate, work together/jointly, join forces, join, unite, combine. **2** *collaborate with the enemy* conspire, fraternize, collude.

collaborator *noun* **1** *his collaborator on the book* co-worker, associate, colleague, partner, confederate. **2** *collaborators executed* conspirator, fraternizer, traitor, quisling, turncoat, colluder.

collapse *verb* **1** *the roof collapsed* fall in, cave in, give way, come apart, fall to pieces, crumple, subside. **2** *the onlooker collapsed* faint, pass out, lose consciousness, fall unconscious, keel over, fall prostrate, swoon. **3** *the business/talks collapsed* break down, fall through, fail, disintegrate, fold, founder, fall flat, miscarry, come to nothing; *inf.* flop. **4** *collapse in tears* break down, go to pieces; *inf.* crack up.

collapse *noun* **1** *the collapse of the roof* fall-in, cave-in, giving way, subsidence. See COLLAPSE *verb* 1. **2** *the collapse of the onlooker* fainting, faint, passing out, loss of consciousness, swooning, swoon. See COLLAPSE *verb* 2. **3** *the collapse of the talks/firm* breakdown, failure, disintegration, unsuccessfulness, foundering; *inf.* flop. See COLLAPSE *verb* 3. **4** *suffer a collapse* breakdown, nervous breakdown, attack, seizure, prostration; *inf.* crack-up.

collar *noun* *the shirt collar* neckband; ruff, ruche, wimple, bertha, rabato.

collar *verb* *collar the thief* catch, seize, grab, capture, arrest, apprehend.

collate *verb* **1** *collate a new edition with an older one* compare, contrast, set side by side, juxtapose, weigh against, differentiate, discriminate. **2** *collate pages/information* arrange, put in order, order, sort, categorize.

collateral *noun* *collateral for a bank loan* security, surety, guarantee, pledge.

colleague *noun* associate, partner, team-mate, workmate, fellow-worker, co-worker, collaborator, confederate, comrade, confrère.

collect *verb* **1** *collect jumble* gather, accumulate, assemble, amass, pile up, stockpile, save, store, hoard, heap up, aggregate. **2** *a crowd collected* gather, assemble, congregate, forgather, converge, cluster, flock together, mass, convene, rally. **3** *collect money for a present* gather, solicit, raise, secure, obtain, acquire. **4** *collect the dry-cleaning* call for, fetch, go and get. **5** *collect one's wits/strength* get together, muster, summon, assemble, rally.
Opposites DISPERSE; DISTRIBUTE.

collected *adjective calm and collected* cool, calm, serene, poised, controlled, composed, unperturbed, unruffled, unshaken.
Opposites EXCITED; HYSTERICAL.

collection *noun* **1** *a collection of jumble* accumulation, pile, stockpile, store, supply, stock, hoard, heap, mass, aggregation. **2** *a collection of people* gathering, assembly, assemblage, crowd, body, group, cluster, company, number, throng, congregation, flock, convocation. *See table.* **3** *a collection of stamps* set, series, array, assortment. **4** *a collection of essays* anthology, corpus, compilation, ana, collectanea, miscellanea, garland; collected works, analects, analecta. **5** *the amount of the collection for the present* subscription, donation, contribution, gift, alms. **6** *the church collection* offering, offertory, tithe.

collective *adjective collective action* joint, united, combined, shared, common, concerted, cooperative, corporate, collaborative, cumulative, aggregate.

college *noun* **1** *she went to college* educational establishment/institution; college of further education, CFE, polytechnic, poly, technical college, college of education, music college, PE college, university. **2** *the College of Heralds* association, fellowship, society, academy, union.

collide *verb* **1** *cars colliding* crash, crash head on, come into collision, smash, bump, bang. **2** *views collide* conflict, be in conflict, clash, differ, disagree, be at variance.

collision *noun* **1** *a motorway collision* crash, accident, smash, pile-up, bump, impact; *inf.* prang. **2** *a collision of views* conflict, clash, difference, disagreement, variance, opposition. **3** *take part in a military collision* confrontation, encounter, skirmish.

colloquial *adjective* conversational, informal, everyday, casual, familiar, chatty, idiomatic, vernacular, demotic.

collusion *noun* connivance, complicity, secret understanding, collaboration, intrigue, plotting; *inf.* cahoots.

colonize *verb* settle, people, populate, pioneer, open up, found.

colonnade *noun* peristyle, portico, arcade, covered walk, cloisters.

colony *noun* **1** *the king visited the colony* settlement, territory, province, dominion, protec-

COLLECTIVE NAMES FOR BIRDS AND ANIMALS

army of caterpillars	gang of elk	siege of herons
bale of turtles	herd of cattle/elephants	shoal of fish
band of gorillas	hive of bees	shrewdness of apes
bask of crocodiles	hover of trout	skein of geese in flight
bellowing of bullfinches	kennel of dogs	skulk of foxes
bevy of roe deer/quails/larks/	kindle of kittens	sloth of bears
pheasants	knot of toads	smack of jellyfish
bloat of hippopotami	labour of moles	span of mules
brood of chickens	leap/lepe of leopards	spring of teal
bury of rabbits	litter of kittens/pigs	stare of owls
busyness of ferrets	mob of kangaroos	string of horses
cete of badgers	murder of crows	stud of mares
charm of finches	murmuration of starlings	swarm of flies/bees
chattering of choughs	muster of peacocks/	tiding of magpies
cloud of gnats	penguins	trip of goats
clowder of cats	mute of hares	troop of baboons
congregation of plovers	obstinacy of buffalo	turmoil of porpoises
covey of partridges	pace of asses	turn of turtles
crash of rhinoceros	pack of hounds/grouse	unkindness of ravens
cry of hounds	paddling of ducks on water	watch of nightingales
descent of woodpeckers	pandemonium of parrots	yoke of oxen
desert of lapwings	parade of elephants	zeal of zebras
dout of wild cats	parcel of penguins	
down of hares	parliament of owls	
drift of swine	pod of seals	
drove of horses/bullocks	pride of lions	Many of these are fanciful or
erst of bees	rafter of turkeys	humorous terms which
exaltation of larks	rookery of rooks	probably never had any real
flock of sheep	safe of ducks	currency. They were taken up
fluther of jellyfish	sawt of lions	by Joseph Sturt in *Sports & Pas-*
gaggle of geese on land	school of whales/dolphins/	*times of England* (1801) and by
gam of whales	porpoises	other antiquarian writers.

torate, dependency, possession, satellite state. **2** *the Chinese colony in London* community, section, ghetto, district, quarter. **3** *a nudist colony* community, group, association, commune, settlement.

colossal *adjective* **1** *a colossal building* huge, gigantic, immense, enormous, massive, vast, gargantuan, mammoth, prodigious, mountainous, elephantine, Brobdingnagian. **2** *a colossal task* huge, enormous, immense, prodigious, Herculean, monumental, titanic.

colour *noun* **1** *a red colour* hue, shade, tint, tone, tinge. *See table.* **2** *paint in water-colours* paint, pigment, tint, colorant, coloration, dye. **3** *add colour to her cheeks* pinkness, rosiness, redness, ruddiness, blush, flush, glow, bloom. **4** *nations of different colours* skin-colour, skin-colouring, skin-tone, complexion, colouring, pigmentation. **5** *add colour to the description* vividness, life, animation, richness. **6** *under colour of friendship* outward appearance, false show, guise, show, front, façade, cloak, mask, semblance, pretence, pretext.

COLOURS

amber	ecru	powder blue
apricot	emerald	primrose
aquamarine	fawn	puce
auburn	fuchsia	purple
azure	ginger	raven
beige	gold	red
black	green	rose
blue	grey	royal blue
bottle green	hazel	ruby
bronze	indigo	russet
brown	iris	rust
buff	ivory	sable
burgundy	jade	saffron
burnt ochre	jet	salmon
burnt siena	khaki	sapphire
burnt	lavender	scarlet
umber	lemon	sea green
camel	lime green	sepia
caramel	magenta	silver
cerulean	mahogany	sky blue
cherry	maroon	tan
chestnut	mauve	tawny
chocolate	mushroom	Titian
cinnamon	mustard	topaz
claret	navy	turquoise
cobalt	ochre	ultra-
copper	olive	marine
coral	opal	umber
cream	orange	vermilion
crimson	peach	violet
cyan	pea green	viridian
dun	pearl	white
ebony	pink	yellow

colour *verb* **1** *colour the walls/fabric yellow* tint, paint, dye, stain, colourwash, tinge. **2** *she coloured* blush, flush, redden, go red, crimson, go crimson, burn. **3** *attitude coloured by childhood experiences* influence, affect, prejudice, distort, slant, taint, pervert, warp. **4** *colour the account* exaggerate, overstate, overdraw,

embroider, varnish, misrepresent, falsify, disguise, garble.

colourful *adjective* **1** *a colourful painting* bright-coloured, deep-coloured, bright, brilliant, intense, vivid, rich, vibrant, multicoloured, many-coloured, motley, variegated, psychedelic; *inf.* jazzy. **2** *a colourful description* vivid, graphic, interesting, lively, animated, rich.
Opposites COLOURLESS; DULL.

colourless *adjective* **1** *colourless fabric* uncoloured, achromatic, achromic, white, bleached, faded. **2** *colourless city girls* pale, wan, anaemic, washed-out, ashen, sickly. **3** *colourless accounts* uninteresting, dull, boring, tame, lifeless, dreary, lacklustre, characterless, insipid, vapid, vacuous. **colours** *plural noun* **1** *the King's colours* flag, standard, banner, ensign. **2** *a club's colours* badge, uniform, insignia, ribbon, rosette. **3** *see things in their true colours* nature, character, identity, aspect.

column *noun* **1** *marble columns* pillar, support, upright, post, shaft; pilaster, caryatid, obelisk, telamon. **2** *a column of people* line, file, row, queue, rank, string, procession, train, progression, cavalcade. **3** *a newspaper column* article, piece, item; editorial, leader, gossip column, agony column.

coma *noun* unconsciousness, insensibility, stupor, oblivion, black-out, torpor, trance, sopor.

comatose *adjective* **1** *comatose after the accident* in a coma, unconscious, insensible, out cold, blacked-out, torpid, insentient, soporose. **2** *feeling comatose after night shift* drowsy, sleepy, sluggish, lethargic, somnolent, torpid.

comb *noun* **1** *a brush and comb* hair comb, fine-tooth comb, curry-comb. **2** *a fowl's comb* coxcomb, crest, tuft, plume, caruncle.

comb *verb* **1** *comb one's hair* groom, untangle, curry, arrange, dress. **2** *comb wool* dress, card, tease, hackle, heckle, hatchel. **3** *comb the area for clues* search, scour, ransack, go over with a fine-tooth comb, rake, hunt, sift, rummage.

combat *noun* *engage in mortal combat* battle, fight, conflict, clash, skirmish, encounter, engagement, single combat, hand-to-hand combat; fighting, hostilities. *See tables at* BATTLE, WAR.

combat *verb* **1** *combat with the enemy* fight, do battle, wage war, clash with, enter into conflict, take up arms, grapple; *combat the enemy* fight with/against. **2** *combat disease* fight, battle against, oppose, strive against, make a stand against, resist, withstand, defy.

combatant *noun* **1** *several combatants injured* fighter, fighting man/woman, soldier, serviceman, servicewoman, warrior, battler, contender. **2** *the combatants in the dispute* adversary, antagonist, contender, opponent, enemy, foe, rival.

combatant *adjective* *combatant forces/parties* combating, fighting, warring, battling, opposing, conflicting, clashing, contending, belligerent.

combative *adjective* pugnacious, belligerent, aggressive, militant, bellicose, warlike, quarrelsome, argumentative, contentious, antagonistic, truculent.

combination *noun* **1** *in combination with the other forces* cooperation, association, union, alliance, partnership, coalition, league, consortium, syndication, federation. **2** *a combination of guilt and grief* mixture, mix, blend, amalgam, amalgamation, compound, alloy, composite.

combine *verb* **1** *combine to finish their work* join forces, get together, unite, team up, cooperate, associate, ally, pool resources, club together, amalgamate, merge, integrate. **2** *combine their efforts* join, put together, unite, pool, merge, integrate, fuse, marry, unify, synthesize. **3** *combine the ingredients* mix, blend, admix, amalgamate, bind, bond, compound, alloy, homogenize.
Opposites SEPARATE; PART.

combustible *adjective* inflammable, flammable, incendiary, explosive, conflagratory.
Opposites INCOMBUSTIBLE.

combustion *noun* burning, firing, fire, kindling, igniting, ignition.

come *verb* **1** *come to us* approach, advance, near, draw near, reach; move/travel towards, bear down on, close in on. **2** *they came last night* arrive, appear, put in an appearance, turn up, enter, materialize; *inf.* show up, fetch up, blow in. **3** *Easter came in March* occur, fall, take place, happen, transpire, come about, come to pass. **4** *the dress comes to her ankles* reach, extend, stretch. **5** *the car does not come in red* be available, be made, be produced, be on offer. **6** *come the fool* act, play, play the part of, behave like, imitate. **7** come climax, achieve orgasm, orgasm. **come about** happen, occur, take place, arise, come to pass, transpire, result, befall. **come across 1** *come across an old friend | come across an interesting fact* meet, encounter, run into, run across, chance upon, stumble upon, happen upon, light upon, hit upon, find, discover, unearth; *inf.* bump into. **2** *his message/sadness came across* be communicated, be understood, be clear, be perceived. **3** *come across with the money/information* give, hand over, deliver, produce, pay up; *inf.* come up with, fork out, cough up. **come along 1** *pupils/patients coming along well* progress, make progress, develop, improve, show improvement, make headway, get better, pick up, rally, recover, mend. **2** *come along there!* hurry, hurry up, make haste, speed up; *inf.* get a move on, move it, step on it, make it snappy. **come apart** break up, fall to pieces, disintegrate, come unstuck, crumble, separate, split, tear. **come by** get, obtain, acquire, procure, get possession of, get/lay hold of, get one's hands on, secure, win. **come clean** make a clean breast of it, own up, confess, admit to one's actions/crimes/sins. **come down** *the report came down against punishment | they came down in favour of an increase* decide, reach a decision, recommend, choose, opt. **come down on** rebuke, reprimand, reproach, criticize, berate; *inf.* jump on. **come down to** amount to, boil down to, end up as, result in. **come down with**

fall ill with, become sick with, catch, contract, take, fall victim to, be stricken with. **come forward** *helpers coming forward* step forward, volunteer, offer/offer one's services. **come into** *come into money* inherit, be left, be willed, succeed to, come in for, acquire, obtain. **come in for 1** *come in for some money* come into, inherit, acquire, obtain. See COME INTO. **2** *come in for criticism* get, receive, suffer, endure, bear the brunt of. **come off** *the attempt did not come off* succeed, be successful, be accomplished, work out, transpire, occur, happen, take place. **come on** *vegetables coming on nicely* progress, develop. See COME ALONG 1. **come out 1** *the newspaper comes out daily* be published, appear, be in print. **2** *the full story came out* become known, become common knowledge, be revealed, be divulged, be disclosed, be publicized, be released. **3** *flowers coming out* come into bloom, flower, appear. **4** *come out all right* end, finish, conclude, terminate. **5** *debutantes coming out* enter society, be presented, debut. **6** *come out* declare oneself a homosexual, come out of the closet. **come out with** *come out with an oath* utter, say, speak, let out, blurt out. **come round 1** *coming round annually* occur, take place, happen. **2** *come round after fainting* come to, regain consciousness, revive, wake up, recover. **3** *come round to one's way of thinking* be converted to, be persuaded by, give way to, yield to. **4** *come round in the evening* visit, call; *inf.* drop in, drop by, stop by, pop in. **come through 1** *come through the war* get through, survive, outlast, outlive. **2** *we have come through* get through, survive, remain alive, live on, endure. **come to 1** *the bill comes to £5* total, add up to, amount to. **2** *come to after fainting* come round, regain consciousness, awaken. See COME ROUND 2. **come up** *something came up* arise, occur, happen, crop up, turn up, spring up. **come up to 1** *she came up to his shoulder* come to, reach, extend to. **2** *come up to their standards* reach, measure up to, match up to, compare with, admit of comparison, bear comparison with, hold a candle to. **come up with** *come up with a plan* suggest, propose, submit, put forward, present, advance, put up, offer.
Opposites GO; LEAVE.

comeback *noun* **1** *the actor making a comeback* return, rally, resurgence, recovery, revival, rebound. **2** *children making cheeky comebacks* retort, reply, rejoinder, response, answer, retaliation, riposte.

comedian *noun* **1** *television comedian* comic, stand-up comic, funny man, funny woman, comedienne, comedy actor/actress, humorist. **2** *her uncle's a real comedian* comic, joker, wit, wag, jester, clown; *inf.* card, laugh.

comedown *noun* loss of status, loss of face, demotion, downgrading, degradation, humiliation, deflation, decline, reversal, anticlimax.

comedy *noun* **1** *theatres staging both comedy and tragedy* light entertainment, humorous play, farce, musical comedy, situation comedy, comedy of errors, burlesque, pantomime, slapstick, satire, vaudeville, comic opera; *inf.* sitcom. **2** *the comedy of the situation* humour, fun, funniness, wit, wittiness, joking, hilarity, levity,

facetiousness, farce, drollery.
Opposites TRAGEDY; GRAVITY.

comely adjective **1** *a comely young woman*
attractive, good-looking, pretty, beautiful,
beauteous, handsome, lovely, bonny, fair,
fetching, appealing, charming, winsome,
pleasing, engaging. **2** *not comely behaviour* fit,
fitting, suitable, proper, seemly, decent, decorous.
Opposites UGLY; IMPROPER.

come-on noun inducement, lure, enticement,
allurement, temptation, tantalization.

comeuppance noun deserved fate, just
deserts, deserts, due reward, retribution, punishment, recompense, requital.

comfort noun **1** *live in comfort* ease, easeful-
ness, freedom from hardship, serenity, repose,
tranquillity, contentment, content, well-being,
cosiness, plenty, sufficiency, luxury,
opulence. **2** *bring comfort to the bereaved* consolation, solace, condolence, sympathy, commiseration, help, support, succour, relief,
easement, alleviation, cheer, gladdening. **3** *a
comfort to her parents* solace, consolation, help,
aid, support.
Opposites DISCOMFORT; GRIEF; AGGRAVATION.

comfort verb **1** *comfort the bereaved* bring comfort to, console, solace, give condolences to,
give sympathy to, help, support, succour,
reassure, soothe, assuage, cheer, gladden.
2 *comforted by the fire* ease, soothe, refresh,
revive, hearten, cheer, invigorate, strengthen.
Opposites DISTRESS; DEPRESS.

comfortable adjective **1** *a comfortable room*
homelike, homely, cosy, snug. **2** *comfortable
clothes/shoes* well-fitting, loose-fitting, roomy.
3 *a comfortable lifestyle* pleasant, adequate, free
from hardship, well-off, well-to-do, affluent,
luxurious, opulent. **4** *feeling comfortable* at
ease, at one's ease, relaxed, serene, tranquil,
contented, cosy.
Opposites UNCOMFORTABLE; TIGHT; TENSE.

comforting adjective consoling, consolatory,
soothing, easing, cheering, reassuring, encouraging, assuaging.

comic adjective funny, humorous, amusing,
entertaining, diverting, droll, jocular, joking,
facetious, comical, witty, farcical, hilarious,
zany, side-splitting, priceless, waggish, whimsical.
Opposites SERIOUS; GRAVE.

comic noun **1** *a television comic* funny man/
woman. See COMEDIAN. **2** *he's a real comic* comedian, joker, wag. See COMEDIAN 2. **3** *reading a
comic* comic paper, funny magazine; *inf.* funny.

comical adjective **1** *a comical performance*
comic, funny, humorous, amusing. See COMIC
adjective. **2** *a comical hat* absurd, ridiculous,
silly, laughable, ludicrous, risible.

coming noun *the coming of Christ/summer* advent,
approach, nearing, arrival, appearance, accession.

coming adjective **1** *the coming appearance* | *the
coming storm* approaching, advancing, forthcoming, nearing, imminent, impending, close

at hand, in store, in the wind. **2** *the coming
actor* promising, aspiring.

command verb **1** *command you to go* order,
give orders to, direct, charge, instruct, bid,
enjoin, adjure, summon, prescribe, require.
2 *he commands the unit* be in command of, have
charge of, control, have control of, rule, govern, direct, preside over, head, lead, manage,
supervise, superintend.

command noun **1** *follow the commands* order,
decree, dictate, edict, instruction, directive,
direction, bidding, injunction, behest, mandate, fiat, precept, commandment, enjoining.
See COMMAND verb 1. **2** *under the command of the
French* charge, control, authority, power, mastery, ascendancy, government, direction, management, administration, supervision,
dominion, sway, domination.

commandeer verb seize, take possession of,
requisition, expropriate, appropriate, sequestrate, sequester, hijack, arrogate.

commander noun **1** *the commander of the expedition* leader, head, director, chief, boss; *inf.*
number one, top dog, kingpin, big cheese, big
white chief. **2** *naval commander* officer, captain. **3** *army commander* commander-in-chief,
C in C, commanding officer, CO.

commanding adjective **1** *a commanding posi-
tion/lead* controlling, directing, dominating,
dominant, superior, advantageous. **2** *a commanding manner/personality* authoritative, autocratic, masterful, assertive, peremptory,
imposing, impressive, august.

commemorate verb celebrate, pay tribute to,
pay homage to, remember, honour, salute,
mark, memorialize.

commemorative adjective memorial, celebratory, celebrative, remembering, honouring,
saluting, in honour of, in memory of, in
remembrance of, in tribute to.

commence verb **1** *ready to commence* begin,
start, make a beginning/start, go ahead, be off,
embark, set sail, set the ball rolling, get something off the ground; *inf.* get the show on the
road. **2** *commence the proceedings* begin, start,
open, enter/embark upon, inaugurate, initiate,
originate.
Opposites FINISH; END; CONCLUDE.

commend verb **1** *commend his work* praise,
applaud, speak highly of, approve, acclaim,
extol, laud, eulogize. **2** *commend action* recommend, approve, endorse, advocate. **3** *commend
her to your care* entrust, trust, deliver, commit,
hand over, give, consign, assign.
Opposites CRITICIZE; DISAPPROVE.

commendable adjective praiseworthy,
admirable, laudable, estimable, meritorious,
creditable, reputable, worthy, deserving.

commendation noun **1** *receive the judge's commendation* praise, applause, high opinion,
acclaim, acclamation, approval, approbation,
good opinion, credit, eulogies, extolment, laudation, encomium, panegyric. **2** *the commendation of his soul to God* entrust, trusting,
committal. See COMMEND 3.

commensurate *adjective* **1** *a commensurate amount of water to wine* equivalent, equal, corresponding, comparable, proportionate, proportional, commensurable. **2** *a salary commensurate with experience* in accordance with, according to, proportionate to, appropriate to, consistent with, corresponding to.

comment *verb* **1** *he commented unfavourably on her actions* remark, speak, make remarks, make a comment on, express an opinion on, say something about. **2** *"Good," he commented* say, remark, state, observe, interpose. **3** *comment on the text* write notes, annotate, explain, interpret, elucidate, clarify, shed light on.

comment *noun* **1** *pass comments on her appearance | arouse comment* remark, opinion, observation, view, statement, criticism. **2** *textual comment* annotation, note, footnote, gloss, marginalia, explanation, interpretation, elucidation, exposition.

commentary *noun* **1** *a television commentary* narration, description, account, review, analysis. **2** *textual commentary* annotation, notes, interpretation, analysis, exegesis, critique. *See* COMMENT *noun* 2.

commentator *noun* **1** *television commentator* reporter, commenter, broadcaster, narrator, correspondent; newscaster, sportscaster. **2** *text commentator* annotator, interpreter, expositor, critic, glossist, scholiast. **3** *commentator on society* commenter. *See* COMMENT *verb* 1, WRITER, AUTHOR, SPEAKER, LECTURER.

commerce *noun* **1** *work in commerce* business, trade, buying and selling, merchandizing, dealing, financial transaction, marketing, traffic. **2** *everyday social commerce* social relations, socializing, communication, dealings, traffic, intercourse.

commercial *adjective* **1** *commercial training* business, trade, marketing, merchandizing, sales, mercantile. **2** *not a commercial proposition* profitable, profit-making, business. **3** *town becoming too commercial* profit-orientated, money-orientated, mercantile, materialistic, mercenary.

commission *noun* **1** *get commission on the sale* percentage, brokerage, share, fee, compensation; *inf.* cut, rake-off. **2** *given the commission of designing the building* task, employment, piece of work, work, duty, charge, mission, responsibility. **3** *receive the commission to be official representative* authority, sanction, warrant, licence. **4** *set up a commission of enquiry* committee, board, board of commissioners, council, advisory body, delegation. **5** *the commission of a crime | sin of commission* committing, committal, execution, perpetration, performance.

commission *verb* **1** *commission an artist to paint a portrait* employ, engage, contract, appoint, book, authorize. **2** *commission a portrait* order, put in an order for, place an order for, contract for, pay for, authorize. **3** *commission the representatives* authorize, empower, accredit, sanction, invest.

commit *verb* **1** *commit a crime | commit suicide* perform, carry out, execute, enact, perpetrate, effect, do. **2** *commit to one's care* entrust, trust,

deliver, hand over, give, consign, assign. **3** *commit oneself to take part* pledge, promise, engage, bind oneself, covenant, obligate oneself, dedicate oneself. **4** *commit the thief to prison* imprison, jail, confine, lock up, custody, put away. **5** *commit the suicidal woman* hospitalize, institutionalize, confine.

commitment *noun* **1** *have too many commitments* undertaking, obligation, responsibility, duty, liability, tie, task, engagement. **2** *have no commitment to the job* dedication, devotion, involvement in, loyalty, allegiance, adherence. **3** *make a commitment to go* pledge, promise, vow, assurance, covenant.

commodious *adjective* roomy, spacious, capacious, large, extensive, ample.

commodity *noun* thing, item, article, product, article of merchandise.

common *adjective* **1** *the common people* ordinary, average, normal, typical, unexceptional, run-of-the-mill, plain, simple. **2** *a common style of writing* ordinary, unexceptional, undistinguished, run-of-the-mill, workaday, commonplace, common-or-garden, mediocre, pedestrian, hackneyed, trite, humdrum. **3** *a common occurrence* usual, ordinary, everyday, daily, regular, frequent, customary, habitual, routine, standard, repeated, recurrent, commonplace, run-of-the-mill. **4** *a common response* usual, ordinary, familiar, routine, stock, standard, conventional, traditional. **5** *a common belief* widespread, general, universal, popular, accepted, prevalent, prevailing. **6** *for the common good* communal, collective, community, public, popular. **7** *a common young woman* low, vulgar, coarse, uncouth, inferior, plebeian.
Opposites UNCOMMON; SPECIAL; RARE.

commonplace *adjective* **1** *a commonplace novel/youngster* ordinary, unexceptional, undistinguished, mediocre, pedestrian, dull, uninteresting, humdrum, hackneyed, trite. **2** *foreign holidays are commonplace | commonplace events* common, usual, ordinary, routine. *See* COMMON 2.

common sense *noun* good sense, sense, practicality, judgement, native wit/intelligence, level-headedness, prudence, discernment, astuteness, shrewdness, judiciousness, wisdom; *inf.* horse sense, gumption, nous.

commotion *noun* disturbance, racket, uproar, rumpus, tumult, clamour, riot, hubbub, hullabaloo, brouhaha, furore, hurly-burly, disorder, confusion, upheaval, disruption, agitation, excitement, fuss, disquiet, ferment, to-do, bustle, hustle and bustle.

communal *adjective* common, collective, shared, joint, general, public, community, cooperative, communalist.
Opposites INDIVIDUAL; EXCLUSIVE.

commune *verb* **1** *commune with close friends* converse, talk, communicate, speak, have a tête-à-tête, confer, confide. **2** *commune with nature* feel in close touch, feel at one, empathize, identify.

commune *noun* collective, cooperative, co-op, community, kibbutz.

communicable *adjective* infectious, contagious, catching, transmittable, transmissible, transferable; *inf.* taking.

communicate *verb* **1** *communicate information* transmit, pass on, transfer, impart, convey, relay, spread, disseminate, make known, publish, broadcast, announce, report, divulge, disclose, unfold, proclaim. **2** *not to communicate with him* be in touch, be in contact, have dealings, interface. **3** *you must be able to communicate* get one's ideas/message across, interface, be articulate, be fluent, be eloquent. **4** *communicate a disease* transmit, pass on, transfer, spread. **5** *her room communicates with his* connect, be connected to, adjoin, abut on.

communication *noun* **1** *communication is difficult* information transmission/transfer, transmission, dissemination, contact, getting in touch, radio/telephone link, connection, interface, social intercourse. **2** *received the communication* message, letter, report, statement, dispatch, news, information, data, intelligence, word.

communications *noun* **1** *all communications under enemy control* links, channels, routes, passages. **2** *studying communications* electronic communication, telecommunications, data communications, information technology, IT; *inf.* comms.

communicative *adjective* *not a very communicative person* expansive, forthcoming, talkative, loquacious, voluble, chatty, conversational, informative, frank, open, candid.
Opposites UNCOMMUNICATIVE; TACITURN; RESERVED.

communion *noun* **1** *a strange communion between each other | communion with nature* rapport, empathy, sympathy, accord, affinity, fellowship, togetherness, harmony, closeness, agreement, sharing, concord, unity, fusion, communication. **2** *Holy Communion* Eucharist.

communiqué *noun* official communication, bulletin, dispatch, report, news flash, announcement.

communism *noun* state ownership, collectivism, Sovietism, Bolshevism, Marxism, Leninism. *See table at* POLITICS.

community *noun* **1** *move to a new community* locality, district, neighbourhood. **2** *the community condemned her* residents, inhabitants; population, populace. **3** *work for the community* society, public, general public, body politic, nation, state. **4** *the Jewish community in Paris* group, section, body, company, set, ghetto. **5** *religious community* brotherhood, sisterhood, association. **6** *community of interests* similarity, likeness, agreement, affinity. **7** *community of property* shared possession, joint liability, common ownership, joint participation.

commute *verb* **1** *commute from Richmond to London* travel to and from, travel back and forth, shuttle. **2** *commute a sentence/penalty* lessen, reduce, shorten, curtail, mitigate, modify. **3** *commute an annuity to a lump sum* exchange, change, interchange, substitute, trade, barter, switch.

commuter *noun* daily traveller; *inf.* straphanger.

compact *adjective* **1** *a compact parcel* dense, packed close, pressed together, close, firm, solid, compressed, condensed. **2** *a compact car/flat/machine* small, economic of space, neat. **3** *a compact style* concise, succinct, terse, brief, condensed, pithy, to the point, epigrammatic, compendious.
Opposites LOOSE; LARGE; LENGTHY; RAMBLING.

compact *verb* *compact the sand* pack down, press down, compress, press together, condense, tamp.

compact *noun* *the two sides signed the compact* contract, agreement, covenant, pact, indenture, bond, treaty, alliance, bargain, deal, transaction, settlement, entente.

companion *noun* **1** *with an unknown companion | the girl and her companions* partner, escort, consort, friend, crony, comrade, colleague, associate, ally, confederate; *inf.* buddy, mate. **2** *the princess and her companion* attendant, aide, chaperon, duenna, squire. **3** *the companion of this book-end/volume* fellow, mate, twin, match, counterpart, complement. **4** *the Angler's Companion* guide, handbook, manual, reference book, *vade-mecum*.

companionship *noun* friendship, fellowship, company, society, togetherness, social intercourse, comradeship, camaraderie, association, brotherhood, sisterhood, intimacy, rapport.

company *noun* **1** *enjoy their company* companionship, friendship, fellowship. *See* COMPANIONSHIP. **2** *address the company* assembly, assemblage, gathering, meeting, audience, group, crowd, throng, congregation, convention. **3** *a company of actors/archers* group, band, party, body, association, society, fellowship, troupe, collection, circle, league, crew, guild. **4** *a retail company* business, firm, concern, corporation, house, establishment, conglomerate; *inf.* outfit. **5** *a company of soldiers* subdivision, unit, detachment. **6** *expecting company* guest(s), visitor(s), caller(s).

comparable *adjective* **1** *his acting is not comparable with his father's* as good as, equal, on a par, in the same class/league, on a level. **2** *comparable pay for comparable work* equivalent, commensurable, corresponding, proportional, proportionate, similar, like, parallel, analogous, related.

comparative *adjective* *living in comparative affluence* relative, in/by comparison, qualified, modified.

compare *verb* **1** *compare the two styles* contrast, juxtapose, weigh/balance/measure the differences between, collate, differentiate. **2** *the island has been compared to heaven* liken, equate, analogize. **3** *his work does not compare with Hardy's* bear comparison, be comparable, be the equal, be on a par, be in the same class, compete, match, approach, come up to, hold a candle. *See* COMPARABLE 1.

comparison *noun* **1** *make a comparison* contrast, juxtaposition, collation, differentiation. *See* COMPARE 1. **2** *no comparison between their works* comparability, analogy, resemblance, likeness, similarity, correlation.

compartment noun **1** *luggage/bomb compartment* section, part, partition, bay, chamber, niche. **2** *compartments of one's life* part, section, division, department, area. **3** *train compartment* carriage, coach; *Am.* car.

compass noun *within the compass of his power* scope, range, area, extent, reach, span, stretch, limits, bounds, field, sphere, zone, circumference.

compassion noun pity, tender-heartedness, soft-heartedness, tenderness, gentleness, mercy, leniency, fellow-feeling, understanding, sympathy, concern, consideration, humanity, kindness, kind-heartedness, charity, benevolence.

compassionate adjective soft-hearted, tender, gentle, merciful, lenient, understanding, sympathetic, pitying, humanitarian, humane, kindly, kind-hearted, charitable, benevolent.
Opposites CRUEL; UNKIND; UNSYMPATHETIC.

compatible adjective **1** *couples not compatible* well-suited, suited, like-minded, of the same mind, in agreement, in tune, in harmony, reconcilable, having affinity/rapport, accordant. **2** *views not compatible with actions* consistent, in keeping, reconcilable, consonant, congruous, congruent.
Opposites INCOMPATIBLE; INCONSISTENT.

compatriot noun fellow-countryman, fellow-countrywoman, countryman, countrywoman, fellow-citizen.

compel verb **1** *compel them to leave* force, make, coerce, drive, pressure, pressurize, dragoon, constrain, impel, oblige, necessitate, urge; *inf.* bulldoze, railroad, twist one's arm, strong-arm, put the screws on. **2** *compel obedience* force, enforce, exact, insist upon, necessitate, extort.

compelling adjective **1** *a compelling story* fascinating, gripping, enthralling, irresistible, hypnotic, mesmeric. **2** *compelling reasons* cogent, convincing, forceful, powerful, weighty, telling, conclusive, irrefutable.
Opposites BORING; WEAK.

compensate verb **1** *compensate for his evil deed* make amends, make restitution, make reparation, make up for, atone, expiate. **2** *compensate her for her loss* recompense, repay, reimburse, requite, indemnify. **3** *the cargo compensating for the light boat* counterbalance, counterpoise, counteract, balance, cancel out, neutralize, nullify.

compensation noun **1** *receive compensation for her loss* recompense, repayment, reimbursement, requital, indemnification, indemnity, damages. **2** *make compensation for his deed* amends, restitution, redress, atonement, expiation.

compete verb **1** *compete in the race* take part, enter, go in for, participate, be a contestant; *inf.* throw one's hat in the ring, be in the running. **2** *compete against/with his brother* contend, vie, strive, struggle, fight, pit oneself against.

competence noun **1** *the competence of the player* capability, ability, capacity, proficiency, adeptness, expertise, skill. **2** *the competence of*

the answer adequacy, appropriateness, suitability, pertinence, appositeness. **3** *competence to plead* fitness, qualification. **4** *a small competence* income, unearned income.

competent adjective **1** *a very competent player* capable, able, proficient, qualified, efficient, adept, accomplished, skilful. **2** *a competent answer* adequate, appropriate, suitable, pertinent, apposite. **3** *not competent to plead* fit, fitted, qualified.
Opposites INCOMPETENT; INEPT.

competition noun **1** *a chess competition* contest, match, game, tournament, event, meet, quiz. **2** *in competition with them* rivalry, vying, contest, opposition, struggle, contention, strife. **3** *the competition is poor* field, opposition; challengers, opponents, rivals.

competitive adjective **1** *a very competitive young man* competition-orientated, ambitious, vying, combative, aggressive. **2** *a competitive industry* aggressive, dog-eat-dog, cutthroat.

competitor noun **1** *competitors in the race* contestant, contender, challenger, participant, candidate, entrant. **2** *his business competitors* rival, opponent, adversary, antagonist; opposition.

compilation noun *a compilation of short stories* collection, anthology, album, corpus, garland, ana, collectanea.

compile verb gather, collect, accumulate, amass, assemble, put together, collate, marshal, organize, systematize, anthologize.

complacent adjective smug, self-satisfied, pleased with oneself, satisfied, contented, self-contented, pleased, gratified, placid, serene, bovine, self-righteous.
Opposites DISSATISFIED; DISCONTENTED.

complain verb **1** *complain about the service* lodge a complaint, criticize, find fault, carp, make a fuss; *inf.* kick up a fuss. **2** *always complaining* grumble, grouse, gripe, moan, grouch, whine, lament, bewail; *inf.* bellyache, beef, bitch.

complaint noun **1** *manager attending to complaints* criticism, grievance, charge, accusation, protest, remonstrance, statement of dissatisfaction; fault-finding; *Law* plaint. **2** *always full of complaint* grumbling, grumble, grousing, grouse. *See* COMPLAIN 2. **3** *a painful complaint* illness, disease, ailment, disorder, sickness, affliction, malady.

complement noun **1** *the perfect complement to the food* companion, addition, supplement, accessory, final/finishing touch. **2** *the school's full complement* amount, allowance, total, aggregate, load, capacity, quota.

complement verb *wine complementing the food* complete, round/set off, add to, go well with, be the perfect companion/addition to, add the final/finishing touch to, supplement.

complementary adjective complemental, completing, finishing, perfecting, culminative, consummative.

complete adjective **1** *the complete collection* entire, whole, full, total, intact, unbroken, undivided, uncut, unshortened, unabridged,

plenary. **2** *the task is complete* completed, finished, ended, concluded, accomplished, finalized. **3** *a complete fool* absolute, out-and-out, thoroughgoing, thorough, utter, total, perfect, consummate, unqualified, dyed-in-the-wool.
Opposites INCOMPLETE; PARTIAL.

complete *verb* **1** *complete the task* finish, end, conclude, finalize, realize, accomplish, achieve, fulfil, execute, effect, discharge, settle, clinch, do; *inf.* wrap up, polish off. **2** *complete the outfit* finish off, round off, make perfect, perfect, crown, cap, add the final/finishing touch.

completely *adverb completely exhausted* totally, utterly, absolutely, thoroughly, quite, wholly, altogether.

completion *noun* finish, ending, conclusion, close, finalization, realization, accomplishment, achievement, fulfilment, execution, consummation.

complex *adjective* **1** *a complex subject* complicated, difficult, involved, intricate, convoluted, knotty, perplexing, puzzling, cryptic, enigmatic. **2** *a complex structure* composite, compound, compounded, multiple, manifold, multiplex, heterogenous.
Opposites SIMPLE; EASY; ELEMENTARY.

complex *noun* **1** *building complex | complex of regulations* structure, scheme, composite, conglomerate, aggregation, network, system, organization, synthesis. **2** *a complex about her nose* obsession, phobia, fixation, preoccupation, *idée fixe.*

complexion *noun* **1** *a beautiful/sallow complexion* skin, skin colour, skin colouring, skin tone, colouring, pigmentation. **2** *put a new complexion on it* aspect, appearance, guise, look, light, countenance, angle. **3** *his brother is of a different complexion* character, nature, disposition, cast, stamp.

complexity *noun the complexities of the situation* complication, difficulty, intricacy, convolution, problem, puzzle, enigma, ramification, entanglement.

compliance *noun* **1** *compliance with the law* obedience, observance, abiding by, conforming, acquiescence, assent, agreement, accordance. **2** *noted for his compliance* yielding, submissiveness, submission, deference, passivity, subservience, servility.

complicate *verb* make difficult, make involved/intricate, confuse, muddle, jumble, snarl up, entangle.

complicated *adjective* difficult, involved, intricate, complex, convoluted, perplexing, puzzling, enigmatic, cryptic, entangled, Byzantine.
Opposites EASY; SIMPLE; STRAIGHTFORWARD.

complication *noun* **1** *meet complications* difficulty, problem, drawback, snag, obstacle, aggravation. **2** *a great deal of complication* difficulty, intricacy, complexity, confusion, muddle.

complicity *noun* collusion, conspiracy, collaboration, connivance, abetment.

compliment *noun receive compliments* flattering remark/comment, bouquet; praise, tribute, homage, admiration, flattery, commendation,

laudation, eulogy.
Opposites INSULT; CRITICISM.

compliment *verb* congratulate, felicitate, speak highly of, praise, sing the praises of, pay tribute/homage to, salute, admire, flatter, commend, honour, acclaim, laud, eulogize.
Opposites INSULT; CRITICIZE; CONDEMN.

complimentary *adjective* **1** *complimentary remarks* congratulatory, admiring, appreciative, approving, flattering, commendatory, laudatory, eulogizing, panegyrical. **2** *complimentary tickets* free of charge, given free.

compliments *plural noun the compliments of the season* greetings, good wishes, regards, respects, salutations.

comply *verb comply with the ruling* obey, observe, abide by, adhere to, conform to, acquiesce with, assent to, consent to, accord with, agree with, follow, respect, yield, submit.
Opposites IGNORE; DISOBEY; DISAGREE.

component *noun* part, piece, section, constituent, element, unit, module, item.

component *adjective* constituent, composing, integral, integrant, sectional, fractional.

compose *verb* **1** *compose a poem* write, make up, create, think up, devise, concoct, invent, compile, contrive, formulate, fashion, produce. **2** *compose one's dress/plans* put together, arrange, put in order, align, organize, assemble, collate, systematize. **3** *peoples composing a nation* make up, form, constitute, comprise. **4** *compose oneself* calm, calm down, quiet, collect, control, soothe, still, tranquillize, quell, pacify, assuage. **5** *compose a dispute* settle, resolve, reconcile, find a solution to.

composed *adjective feeling composed | a composed manner* calm, cool, collected, cool and collected, serene, tranquil, relaxed, poised, at ease, unruffled, self-controlled, untroubled, undisturbed, unperturbed, unworried, confident, self-possessed, level-headed; *inf.* together.
Opposites EXCITED; OVERWROUGHT.

composer *noun.* See table at MUSICIAN.

composite *adjective a composite structure* compound, complex, conglomerate, combined, blended, mixed, synthesized.

composite *noun a composite of various elements* compound, amalgam, blend, mixture, complex, combination, fusion, conglomerate, synthesis.

composition *noun* **1** *the composition of the soil* structure, constitution, make-up, conformation, configuration, organization, arrangement, lay-out, character. **2** *an adhesive composition* compound, amalgam, blend, mixture, mix, admixture. See COMPOUND *noun*. **3** *the composition of a poem* writing, making-up, creation, concoction, invention, compilation. See COMPOSE 1. **4** *a brilliant composition* work of art, creation, literary/musical/artistic work, poem, novel, opus, arrangement, symphony, picture. **5** *pupils writing a composition* essay, theme, piece of writing. **6** *admire the painting's composition* arrangement, proportions, harmony, balance, symmetry.

compost *noun* fertilizer, manure, humus, mulch.

composure *noun* aplomb, poise, self-possession, presence of mind, sang-froid, equanimity, equlibrium, self-control, self-command, calm, calmness, coolness, collectedness, serenity, tranquillity, imperturbability, inexcitability, placidity.

compound *noun a chemical/verbal compound* amalgam, blend, mixture, admixture, complex, combination, fusion, alloy, conglomerate, synthesis, medley, hybrid. *See table.*

TYPES OF CHEMICAL COMPOUNDS		
acetate	carbonate	ketone
acid	carboxylic	nitrate
alcohol	acid	nitride
aldehyde	chloride	nitro com-
alkaloid	chlorofluoro-	pound
alkane	carbon	oxide
alkene	(CFC)	paraffin
alkyne	cyanide	phosphate
amine	epoxide	salt
amino acid	ester	silicate
base	fluoride	silicone
bromide	hydro-	sulphate
carbide	carbon	sulphide
carbo-	hydroxide	
hydrate	iodide	

compound *adjective a compound substance* composite, complex, conglomerate, blended, not simple, fused. *See* COMPOUND *noun.*
Opposites SIMPLE.

compound *verb* **1** *compound the two ideas/substances* mix, blend, combine, put together, amalgamate, unite, coalesce, alloy, fuse, mingle, intermingle, synthesize. **2** *compound the sin/fear compounded with poverty* worsen, make worse, add to, augment, exacerbate, magnify, aggravate, intensify, heighten.

comprehend *verb* **1** *comprehend the facts* understand, grasp, take in, assimilate, fathom, perceive, discern, apprehend. **2** *cannot comprehend how he won* understand, conceive, imagine. *See* FATHOM 2. **3** *comprehend the whole school* include, take in, encompass, involve, embrace, contain, comprise.
Opposites MISUNDERSTAND; EXCLUDE.

comprehensible *adjective* intelligible, understandable, graspable, fathomable, discernible, conceivable, plain, clear, explicit, coherent, lucid.

comprehension *noun beyond one's comprehension* understanding, grasp, perception, ken, discernment, conception.

comprehensive *adjective* inclusive, all-inclusive, all-embracing, complete, full, encyclopedic, exhaustive, thorough, extensive, broad, widespread, far-reaching, blanket, umbrella, universal, catholic.

compress *verb* **1** *compress the pile of sand* pack down, press down, press together, squeeze together, squash, crush, condense, compact, cram, tamp, constrict. **2** *compress the text* abbreviate, shorten, abridge, contract, reduce.

comprise *verb* **1** *a board comprising only men* consist of, contain, include, be composed of, take in, embrace, encompass, comprehend. **2** *children comprising the audience* make up, form, constitute, compose.

compromise *verb* **1** *compromise on the wording* come to terms, come to an understanding, make a deal, make concessions, find a happy medium, find the middle grounds, strike a balance, meet halfway, give and take, take part in a trade-off. **2** *compromise him | compromise his reputation* discredit, dishonour, bring shame to, bring into disrepute, shame, embarrass, endanger, jeopardize, imperil. **3** *compromise his chances* prejudice, damage, injure, endanger, weaken.

compromise *noun reach a compromise* understanding, deal, happy medium, middle course, balance, trade-off, settlement by concession; terms; middle ground, give and take, adjustment.

compulsion *noun* **1** *under no compulsion to go* obligation, force, duress, constraint, coercion, pressure, oppression, enforcement. **2** *feel a compulsion to travel* urge, need, desire, motivation, necessity, preoccupation, obsession.

compulsive *adjective* **1** *compulsive viewing* fascinating, gripping, irresistible, compelling. *See* COMPELLING 1. **2** *a compulsive desire to wash* obsessive, uncontrollable, irresistible, compelling, driving, overwhelming, urgent, besetting. **3** *compulsive eating* addictive, obsessional, obsessive, uncontrollable, out of control, ungovernable. **4** *a compulsive gambler/drinker* addicted, addictive, obsessive, obsessional, dependent; *inf.* hooked.

compulsory *adjective* obligatory, mandatory, required, binding, forced, necessary, essential, de rigueur.

compunction *noun* remorse, regret, pangs of conscience, guilt, contrition, contriteness, penitence, repentance; scruples.

compute *verb* calculate, reckon, count, add up, total, figure out, work out, enumerate, sum, tally, cast up, measure, rate.

computer *noun. See tables. See also table at* PRINTER.

comrade *noun* companion, friend, colleague, partner, associate, co-worker, fellow-worker, mate, team-mate, ally, confederate, compatriot, compeer; *inf.* pal, buddy.

con *verb con the old lady* swindle, deceive, cheat, hoodwink, mislead, delude, bamboozle.

con *noun* con trick, confidence trick, swindle, deception, cheating; con man, confidence trickster, swindler, deceiver, cheater.

concave *adjective* curved in, incurved, incurvate, hollow, hollowed out, depressed, sunken, indented, scooped-out.

conceal *verb* **1** *conceal her face | conceal the letter* hide, cover, keep out of sight, keep hidden, screen, obscure, disguise, camouflage, mask, secrete, shelter, bury, tuck away. **2** *conceal his identity* hide, keep secret, keep dark, hush up, cover up, dissemble; *inf.* keep the lid on.
Opposites REVEAL; EXPOSE.

concealed *adjective a concealed entrance* hidden, obscured, unseen, invisible, screened, secreted, tucked away.

concealment *noun a place of concealment* hiding, hide-away, hide-out, retreat; secrecy, privacy, sheltering, secretion, camouflage.

concede *verb* **1** *concede defeat* acknowledge, admit, accept, own, allow, grant, accede, confess, recognize. **2** *concede some territory/goals* give up, yield, surrender, relinquish, cede, hand over.
Opposites DENY; DISPUTE; RETAIN.

conceit *noun* **1** *the winner full of conceit* pride, arrogance, vanity, self-admiration, self-love, self-importance, self-adulation, narcissism, *amour propre*, egotism, self-satisfaction, complacency, boasting, swagger, vainglory. **2** *conceits in the metaphysical poets* comparison, metaphor, simile, image; imagery, ornament, decoration. **3** *exchanging clever conceits* witticism, quip, *bon mot*, pleasantry, epigram. **4** *a mind occupied with conceits* fancy idea, notion, whim; fantasy, imagination, whimsy, vagary.

conceited *adjective* proud, arrogant, vain, self-important, cocky, haughty, supercilious, overweening, narcissistic, immodest, egotistical, puffed up, self-satisfied, complacent, boastful, swaggering, vainglorious; *inf.* big-headed, swollen-headed, swell-headed, stuck-up.
Opposites HUMBLE; MODEST.

conceivable *adjective not conceivable that he would lose* credible, believable, imaginable, thinkable, possible, understandable, comprehensible.

conceive *verb* **1** *women unable to conceive* become pregnant, become impregnated, become fertilized. **2** *conceive the idea | conceive a plan* think up, draw up, form, formulate, produce, develop, project, devise, contrive, conjure up, envisage. **3** *cannot conceive that/how he lost* imagine, think, believe, realize, appreciate, suppose, understand, comprehend, perceive, grasp, apprehend, envisage, visualize, fancy.

concentrate *verb* **1** *concentrate one's attention/ efforts on* focus, centre, converge, centralize, consolidate, bring to bear, congregate, cluster. **2** *concentrate on one's studies* be absorbed in, focus attention on, be engrossed in, give one's attention/mind to, put one's mind to, think about closely, consider closely, rack one's brains about/over. **3** *troops concentrating on the border | concentrate troops* collect, gather, congregate, accumulate, amass, cluster, rally, huddle. **4** *concentrate the liquid* condense, boil down, reduce, compress, distil.

concentrated *adjective a concentrated effort* intense, intense, consolidated, rigorous, vigorous; *inf.* all-out.

concentration *noun* **1** *lose one's concentration* close attention, absorption, application, engrossment, single-mindedness, heed. **2** *the concentration of one's attention/efforts* focusing, centralization, consolidation. *See* CONCENTRATE 1. **3** *the concentration of troops* collection, gathering, congregation. *See* CONCENTRATE 3.

concept *noun* idea, notion, abstraction, conceptualization, conception, hypothesis, theory, image, view.

PROGRAMMING LANGUAGES

Ada	BCPL	CORAL	Lisp	POP
Algol	C	CPL	Logo	Prolog
APL	C++	Forth	Modula	SIMULA
B	Cobol	Fortran	Pascal	Smalltalk
Basic	COMAL	JOVIAL	PL/I	SNOBOL

COMPUTER PARTS AND PERIPHERALS

acoustic coupler	dynamic memory	main memory	read only memory
arithmetic and logic	erasable program-	maths coprocessor	(ROM)
unit (ALU)	mable read-only	memory	removable disk
bar-code reader	memory (EPROM)	microfloppy	scanner
buffer	fax modem	microprocessor	secondary
bus	firmware	minidisk/mini-	memory
cache memory	fixed disk	diskette	semiconductor
cartridge	flash memory	modem	memory
cassette	flat-bed plotter	monitor	software
CD-ROM	flat-bed scanner	mouse	solid-state
console	floppy disk	non-volatile memory	memory
central processing	hard disk	optical disk	static RAM (SRAM)
unit (CPU)	hardware	plotter	tape streamer
control unit	input-output device	port	terminal
digitizer	input-output port	primary memory	trackerball
disk	joystick	printer	visual display unit
diskette	keyboard	processor	(VDU)
dynamic RAM	light-pen	random access	voice synthesizer
(DRAM)	magnetic-tape unit	memory (RAM)	wand
drum scanner	(MTU)	register	Winchester disk

conception *noun* **1** *when conception took place* conceiving, fertilization, impregnation, fecundation, inception of pregnancy. **2** *in at the conception of the project* inception, beginning, origination, origin, birth, initiation, formation, launching, invention, outset. **3** *a brilliant conception* plan, design, invention, creation, project, scheme, proposal. **4** *the conception of maths* idea, abstraction, concept. See CONCEPT. **5** *no conception of how to behave* idea, notion, perception, appreciation, understanding, clue, inkling, impression, picture.

concern *verb* **1** *affairs not concerning you* be the business of, affect, be relevant to, involve, apply to, pertain to, have a bearing on, bear on, be of interest to, touch. **2** *a report concerning cancer* be about, deal with, be connected with, relate to, have to do with, appertain to. **3** *concern herself in their affairs* interest/involve oneself in, be interested/involved in, take/have a hand in, busy oneself with, devote one's time to, be busy with. **4** *children's behaviour concerned teachers* worry, disturb, trouble, bother, perturb, make anxious, cause disquiet to, distress.

concern *noun* **1** *none of your concern* business, affair, interest, matter of interest, involvement, responsibility, charge, duty, job, task, occupation, mission, department, field, subject, discipline. **2** *news of concern to all of us* interest, importance, relevance, bearing, applicability. **3** *parents full of concern* worry, disturbance, anxiety, disquiet, perturbation, distress, apprehension. **4** *parents demonstrating their concern* care, caringness, solicitude, attentiveness, attention, consideration, regard. **5** *start a publishing concern* business, firm, company, enterprise, organization, corporation, establishment, house.

concerned *adjective* **1** *concerned parties* interested, involved, implicated, in on, party to. **2** *concerned parents going to the police* worried, disturbed, anxious, upset, uneasy, troubled, perturbed, distressed, bothered, exercised, apprehensive. **3** *both concerned and uncaring parents* caring, attentive, solicitous, responsible, considerate.

concerning *preposition* about, on the subject of, relating to, relevant to, regarding, as regards, with regard to, with reference to, referring to, with respect to, respecting, as to, touching on, in the matter of, re, apropos of.

concert *noun* **1** *a hall designed for concerts* musical entertainment, performance; symphony concert, variety concert, music hall, pop concert, rock concert. **2** *no concert in their actions* agreement, accordance, accord, unanimity, harmony, concord, concordance, unity, unison, consensus. **in concert** *act in concert* together, jointly, in combination, cooperatively, in cooperation, in collaboration, in league, in unison, shoulder to shoulder, side by side, concertedly.

concerted *adjective* *a concerted effort* jointly planned, combined, cooperative, joint, coordinated, united, collaborative, synchronized, interactive, synergetic.
Opposites SEPARATE.

concession *noun* **1** *the concession of defeat* acknowledgement, admission, acceptance, allowance, recognition. See CONCEDE 1. **2** *the concession of territory* yielding, surrender, relinquishment, ceding. See CONCEDE 2. **3** *make concessions | as a concession to their youth* allowance, adjustment, modification, compromise, indulgence, exception. **4** *price concessions* reduction, cut, discount, decrease. **5** *grant the concession* franchise, licence, permit, warrant, authorization.

conciliate *verb* placate, appease, pacify, propitiate, mollify, assuage, calm down, soothe, humour, reconcile, disarm, win over, restore harmony to.

conciliatory *adjective* placatory, appeasing, pacifying, pacificatory, propitiative, mollifying, assuaging, disarming, reconciliatory, peacemaking; *fml.* irenic.

concise *adjective* succinct, compact, terse, brief, short, condensed, compressed, crisp, pithy, to the point, epigrammatic, compendious, summary, synoptic.
Opposites LENGTHY; DISCURSIVE; WORDY.

conclave *noun* private meeting, secret meeting, conference, council, parley, session, assembly, congress, gathering, forgathering, congregation.

conclude *verb* **1** *the meeting concluded at 9 o'clock* end, finish, close, come/draw to an end, halt, cease, terminate, discontinue; *inf.* wind up. **2** *we concluded the meeting* end, finish, close, bring to an end. **3** *conclude an agreement* negotiate, come terms on, reach terms on, bring about, pull off, clinch, work out, accomplish, fix, effect, establish, engineer, settle, decide, determine, resolve. **4** *conclude that he had won* come to the conclusion, deduce, infer, decide, gather, reckon, judge, assume, presume, suppose, conjecture, surmise.
Opposites START; COMMENCE; EXTEND.

conclusion *noun* **1** *the conclusion of the meeting* end, finish, close, halting, cessation, termination, discontinuance; *inf.* wind-up. **2** *the conclusion of the agreement* negotiation, clinching, accomplishment, establishment, settling, resolution. See CONCLUDE 3. **3** *a predictable conclusion* outcome, result, upshot, issue, culmination, consequence. **4** *reach the conclusion that he was guilty* deduction, inference, decision, opinion, judgement, verdict, conviction, assumption, presumption. See CONCLUDE 4. **in conclusion** in closing, to sum up, finally, lastly, in winding up.

conclusive *adjective* decisive, clinching, definitive, definite, final, ultimate, categorical, incontestable, irrefutable, convincing, cogent.

concoct *verb* **1** *concoct a meal/stew* prepare, put together, make, cook, muster, mix, blend, brew; *inf.* rustle up. **2** *concoct an excuse* devise, invent, make up, think up, dream up, fabricate, form, formulate, hatch, plot, forge, scheme, design, fashion, brew; *inf.* cook up.

concoction *noun* **1** *a tasty concoction* preparation, mixture, blend, combination, brew, creation. **2** *don't believe that concoction* invention, fabrication, plot, scheme, designing.

concomitant *adjective* attendant, accompanying, associated, belonging, linked, affiliated, accessory, auxiliary.

concord *noun* agreement, harmony, accord, unity, oneness, consensus.
Opposites DISAGREEMENT; DISCORD.

concrete *adjective* **1** *concrete evidence* actual, real, factual, definite, genuine, substantial, material, tangible, unimaginary, specific. **2** *a concrete substance* solid, solidified, firm, consolidated, compact, dense, condensed, compressed, coalesced, petrified, calcified.
Opposites ABSTRACT; UNREAL.

concubine *noun* mistress, paramour, kept woman, courtesan, odalisque.

concupiscence *noun* sexual desire, desire, passion, sexual appetite, libido, lust, lustfulness, lechery, lasciviousness, libidinousness; *inf.* randiness, horniness.

concur *verb* **1** *they concur on/over the verdict* agree, be in accord, accord, be in harmony, acquiesce, assent, be in assent, be of the same mind, be in concord. **2** *the two events concurred* coincide, happen/occur together, be simultaneous, coexist, synchronize. **3** *they concurred in the attempt* cooperate, combine, unite, collaborate, join forces, act together, work together, pool resources.
Opposites DISAGREE.

concurrent *adjective* **1** *concurrent sentences* simultaneous, parallel, coexisting, coexistent, coincident, contemporaneous, synchronous, side-by-side. **2** *concurrent lines* converging, convergent, meeting, joining, uniting, intersecting. **3** *concurrent attitudes* agreeing, in agreement, in accord, in harmony, harmonious, assenting, in assent, of the same mind, like-minded, as one, at one, in rapport, compatible, consentient. **4** *concurrent action* cooperative, combined, united, joint, collaborative.

concussion *noun* **1** *suffer concussion in the accident* brain injury, brain incapacity, unconsciousness, loss of consciousness. **2** *damage caused by concussion* jarring, jar, jolting, jolt, shaking, shock, blow, bump, impact, clash, collision.

condemn *verb* **1** *condemn all violence | condemn him for his action* censure, denounce, deprecate, disapprove of, criticize, berate, upbraid, reprove, reproach, blame, reprehend, reprobate. **2** *condemn him to death* sentence, pass sentence on, convict. **3** *condemn the building* declare unfit, forbid the use of, proscribe, ban, bar. **4** *his action condemned him* declare guilty, prove one's guilt, accuse, incriminate, indict, inculpate, implicate. **5** *condemned to misery/poverty* doom, damn, force, compel, coerce, impel.
Opposites PRAISE; ACQUIT.

condemnatory *adjective* condemning, censuring, censorious, denunciatory, deprecatory, disapproving, critical, reproving, vituperative, reproachful.

condensation *noun* **1** *the condensation of the soup* concentration, concentrating, boiling down, reduction. See CONDENSE 1. **2** *the condensation of steam* liquefaction, liquidization, deliquescence, precipitation, distillation. **3** *the condensation of the report* shortening, abridgement, abbreviation, cutting, summarization. See CONDENSE 3. **4** *read the condensation* abridgement, summary, précis, digest, abstract, synopsis.

condense *verb* **1** *condense the soup by boiling* concentrate, thicken, boil down, reduce, solidify, coagulate. **2** *steam condensing on the mirror* liquefy, liquidize, deliquesce, precipitate. **3** *condense the report* shorten, abridge, abbreviate, cut, compress, contract, compact, curtail, summarize, précis, epitomize, encapsulate.
Opposites DILUTE; LENGTHEN; EXPAND.

condescend *verb* **1** *condescend to speak to him* lower oneself, deign, stoop, descend, unbend, humble/demean oneself, vouchsafe; *inf.* come down from one's high horse. **2** *condescend to younger people* treat condescendingly, patronize, talk down to, look down one's nose at.

condescending *adjective* patronizing, disdainful, supercilious, superior, snobbish, lofty, lordly; *inf.* snooty, snotty, toffee-nosed.

condition *noun* **1** *the human condition | the condition of slavery* state, state of existence, circumstance, situation, predicament. **2** *in a miserable condition* state, state of affairs, circumstance, situation, position, plight, predicament, quandary. **3** *athletes in good/poor condition* shape, form, order, fitness, physical fitness, health, state of health, fettle, kilter, trim, working order. **4** *a condition of the job* qualification, requirement, necessity, essential, demand, prerequisite, stipulation; terms. **5** *the conditions of the agreement | make certain conditions* restriction, rule, provision, proviso, contingency, stipulation, prerequisite, limitation, modification; terms, limits. **6** *a heart condition* disease, disorder, illness, complaint, problem, ailment, weakness, infirmity, malady. **7** *people of various conditions* social position, class, rank, status, station, stratum, grade, order, footing, caste, estate.

condition *verb* **1** *lotions conditioning the skin/leather* make healthy, improve, tone, tone up, prepare, make ready. **2** *cats conditioned to live in flats* train, teach, educate, coach, tutor, accustom, adapt, habituate, inure. **3** *childhood experiences conditioning later responses* influence, affect, govern, determine.

conditional *adjective* **1** *an offer conditional on references* dependent on, contingent on, subject to, based upon. **2** *given a conditional offer* qualified, having conditions, with reservations, restrictive, provisional, provisory, stipulatory.
Opposites UNCONDITIONAL; ABSOLUTE.

conditioned *adjective* *a conditioned response* learned, trained, taught, habituated.

conditions *plural noun* *live in pleasant conditions* circumstances, surroundings, environment, situation, milieu, way of life.

condolence *noun* commiseration, sympathy, fellow feeling, compassion, feeling, pity, solace, comfort.

condom *noun* contraceptive, barrier contraceptive, sheath, French letter; *inf.* rubber. See table at CONTRACEPTIVE.

condone verb overlook, disregard, let pass, turn a blind eye to, wink at, excuse, pardon, forgive, make allowances for, forget. *Opposites* CONDEMN; PUNISH.

conducive adjective *hardly conducive to study* contributing, contributory, helpful, instrumental, useful, favourable, advantageous.

conduct noun **1** *guilty of evil conduct* behaviour, way of behaving, comportment, bearing, deportment; actions, ways, habits, practices, manners. **2** *the conduct of the war* direction, running, management, administration, organization, control, guidance, supervision, leadership.

conduct verb **1** *conduct oneself well/badly* behave, act, comport, deport, acquit. **2** *conduct the proceedings* direct, run, be in charge of, manage, administer, organize, handle, be in control of, control, govern, regulate, supervise, lead, preside over. **3** *conduct us to our seats* show, guide, lead, escort, accompany, take.

conduit noun duct, pipe, tube, channel, canal, trough, passageway.

confectionery noun sweets, sweetmeats; Am. candy. *See table at* SWEET.

confederate noun *the villain had his confederates* accomplice, abettor, accessory, ally, associate, collaborator, colleague, partner.

confederate adjective *the confederate states* federal, federated, allied, in alliance, associated, united, combined, amalgamated.

confer verb **1** *confer a title/favour* bestow, present, grant, award, give, give out, hand out, accord. **2** *confer with her colleagues* have discussions, discuss, talk, consult, converse, exchange views, discourse, parley.

conference noun **1** *attend a conference* meeting, congress, convention, seminar, symposium, colloquium, forum, convocation. **2** *be in conference* discussion, consultation, conversation, deliberation, debate, communication, dialogue.

confess verb **1** *confess her guilt* admit, acknowledge, make a clean breast of, own up to, declare, make known, disclose, reveal, divulge, blurt out, expose. **2** *criminals forced to confess* own up, admit guilt, plead guilty, accept blame/responsibility, make a clean breast of it, unbosom oneself; *inf.* tell all, spill the beans, get something off one's chest. **3** *I must confess I don't know* admit, acknowledge, concede, grant, allow, own, say, declare, affirm, profess, assert. *Opposites* CONCEAL; DENY.

confession noun *listening to their confession* admission, owning-up, disclosure, revelation, divulgence, exposure, acknowledgement, avowal, unbosoming.

confidant, confidante noun close friend, bosom friend, friend, crony, intimate, familiar, *alter ego*, second self; *inf.* chum, pal, mate, buddy.

confide verb **1** *confide a secret to | confide that he was ill* disclose, reveal, divulge, impart, tell, intimate, confess, admit. **2** *confide in a friend* open one's heart to, unburden oneself to, unbosom oneself to, tell one's all to. **3** *confide a task* entrust, consign, hand over, make over, turn over, give over, commit, commend, assign.

confidence noun **1** *candidates full of confidence* self-confidence, self-assurance, assurance, self-reliance, self-possession, aplomb, poise, nerve, firmness, courage, boldness, mettle, fortitude. **2** *have no confidence in them* trust, reliance, faith, dependence, belief, credence. **3** *exchange confidences* secret, private affair, confidentiality, intimacy. *Opposites* DOUBT; UNCERTAINTY; DISTRUST.

confidential adjective **1** *confidential information* secret, private, classified, non-public, off-the-record, restricted, personal, intimate, privy; *inf.* hush-hush. **2** *a confidential friend* close, bosom, dear, intimate, familiar, trusted, trustworthy, trusty, faithful, reliable, dependable.

confidentially adverb *told confidentially* in confidence, in secret, in private, privately, between ourselves, behind closed doors, in camera, *sub rosa*.

confine verb **1** *birds confined in a cage* enclose, shut up, shut, cage, keep, coop up, pen, box up, lock up, imprison, intern, hold captive, incarcerate, impound, immure. **2** *remarks confined to the discussion | confined to bed* restrict, limit, keep within the limits of.

confinement noun **1** *keep in confinement* custody, imprisonment, detention, captivity, internment, incarceration. **2** *a difficult confinement* childbirth, labour, delivery, lying-in, travail, *accouchement*; Med. parturition.

confirm verb **1** *evidence confirming her statement | a letter confirming a booking* bear out, verify, corroborate, prove, endorse, validate, authenticate, substantiate, give credence to, evidence. **2** *confirm that he would appear* reassert, assert, give assurance, assure, affirm, pledge, promise, guarantee. **3** *confirm his appointment* ratify, endorse, approve, sanction, underwrite, authorize, warrant, accredit. **4** *confirm my doubts* strengthen, make firmer, reinforce, fortify. *Opposites* DENY; CONTRADICT.

confirmation noun **1** *confirmation of her statement/booking* verification, corroboration, proof, evidence, endorsement, validation, authentication, substantiation. **2** *confirmation of the appointment* ratification, endorsement, approval, sanction, authorization, accreditation.

confirmed adjective *a confirmed bachelor* long-established, established, dyed-in-the-wool, habitual, inveterate, through-and-through, seasoned, inured, settled, set, fixed, rooted.

confiscate verb seize, impound, take possession of, appropriate, commandeer, expropriate, sequestrate, sequester, arrogate.

conflagration noun blaze, raging fire, wall/sheet of flames, holocaust.

conflict noun **1** *the military conflict* battle, fight, war, warfare, clash, engagement, encounter, hostilities, contest, combat, collision, struggle, strife, tussle, scuffle, fracas,

scrap; *inf.* set-to. **2** *bitter conflict between the families* disagreement, dissension, hostility, feud, discord, friction, strife, antagonism, antipathy, ill will, bad blood, contention. **3** *the conflict between love and duty* clash, variance, divided loyalties, opposition, friction, schism.
Opposites HARMONY; AGREEMENT; PEACE.

conflict *verb* **1** *their opinions conflict* clash, differ, disagree, be at variance, be in opposition, be at odds, be incompatible, collide. **2** *conflict for victory* contend, contest, fight, combat, struggle, strive.

conflicting *adjective conflicting opinions/statements* clashing, differing, disagreeing, contradictory, contrary, opposing, incompatible, inconsistent, discordant, paradoxical, at odds, at variance.

conform *verb* **1** *refuse to conform* follow convention, be conventional, comply, obey the rules, adapt, adjust, follow the crowd, run with the pack, swim with the stream. **2** *conform to accepted standards* comply with, fall in with, follow, obey, adapt to, accommodate to, adjust, observe, yield. **3** *conform with my idea of an actor* fit, match, agree with, correspond to, tally with, square with, accord with, harmonize.
Opposites REBEL; CONTRADICT; DIFFER.

conformation *noun* **1** *a rocky conformation* structure, form, shape, formation, framework, build, configuration. **2** *conformation to accepted standards* compliance, adjustment, adaptation, accommodation.

conformist *noun* conventionalist, traditionalist, yes-man, stick-in-the-mud.

conformity *noun* **1** *noted for their conformity* conventionality, traditionalism, orthodoxy. *See* CONFORM 1. **2** *their conformity to accepted standards* compliance, obedience, observance, adaptation, adjustment, accommodation. *See* CONFORM 2. **3** *having a certain conformity* likeness, similarity, resemblance, correspondence, agreement, harmony, accord, affinity, compatibility, congruity, consonance.

confound *verb* **1** *confounded at the news* dumbfound, astound, amaze, astonish, stun, flabbergast, surprise, startle, disconcert, perplex, puzzle, mystify, baffle, nonplus, confuse, bewilder, dismay. **2** *confound the enemy* defeat, beat, overwhelm, overthrow, trounce. **3** *confound the argument* refute, contradict, demolish, annihilate, explode.

confront *verb* **1** *confronting the enemy* face, face up to, stand up to, resist, defy, oppose, challenge, attack, assault, accost, waylay. **2** *confront one's problems* face, tackle, come to grips with, meet head on. **3** *confront them with the proof* bring face to face, show, present. **4** *the problems confronting us* face, be in one's way, threat, trouble, harass, annoy, molest.
Opposites AVOID; DODGE.

confrontation *noun a confrontation with the government* conflict, clash, contest, collision, encounter; *inf.* set-to, showdown.

confuse *verb* **1** *confused by all the questions* bewilder, bemuse, perplex, baffle, puzzle, mystify, nonplus, befog. **2** *confuse the issue* muddle, mix up, jumble, throw into disorder, disorder, disarrange, tangle up; *inf.* snarl up. **3** *his talk confused with irrelevancies* obscure, make unclear, make indistinct. **4** *confuse the twins with each other* mistake, mix up. **5** *old age confused her mind* muddle, addle, befuddle, disorient, disorientate.

confused *adjective* **1** *a confused recollection* unclear, blurred, indistinct, hazy, foggy, obscure. **2** *a confused mess* muddled, jumbled, untidy, higgledy-piggledy, disordered, disorderly, disarranged, out of order, chaotic, disorganized, upset, topsy-turvy, at sixes and sevens. **3** *a confused old woman* muddled, addled, befuddled, bewildered, dazed, disoriented, disorientated, at sea, unbalanced, unhinged, demented; *inf.* discombobulated.
Opposites CLEAR; ORDERLY; PERCEPTIVE.

confusing *adjective confusing instructions* unclear, puzzling, baffling, complicated, difficult, ambiguous, misleading, inconsistent.

confusion *noun* **1** *people in a state of confusion* bewilderment, perplexity, bafflement, puzzlement, mystification, muddle, disorientation, befuddlement. **2** *the room in a state of confusion* muddle, jumble, jumbledness, untidiness, disorder, chaos, shambles, disorderliness, disarrangement, disorganization. **3** *frightened by the confusion at the airport* muddle, disorganization, bustle, commotion, upheaval, turmoil.

congeal *verb* solidify, harden, coagulate, thicken, set, concentrate, cake.

congenial *adjective* **1** *a congenial companion* genial, agreeable, friendly, pleasant, kindly, pleasing, amiable, nice, companionable, good-natured, sympathetic, compatible, like-minded, kindred. **2** *congenial work/places* agreeable, pleasant, pleasing, nice, suitable, well-suited, fit, favourable.
Opposites UNFRIENDLY; DISAGREEABLE; UNPLEASANT.

congenital *adjective* **1** *a congenital disease* inborn, inbred, innate, inherent, constitutional, inherited, hereditary, connate. **2** *a congenital liar | congenital dishonesty* inveterate, dyed-in-the-wool, thoroughgoing, thorough, utter, complete, established, rooted, ingrained, fixed, settled, set.

congested *adjective* **1** *congested roads* crowded, overcrowded, packed, jammed, blocked, obstructed, overflowing, teeming. **2** *congested lungs/noses* blocked, clogged, choked, plugged, stopped up, gorged.

congestion *noun* **1** *congestion on the roads* overcrowding, crowding, obstruction, jam, bottleneck; *inf.* snarl up. **2** *congestion of the lungs* blocking, clogging, choking, plugging.

conglomerate *noun* **1** *an international conglomerate* corporation, multinational, merger, joint concern, firm, company, trust, cartel. **2** *a rocky conglomerate* aggregate, agglomerate.

conglomerate *adjective a conglomerate mass* aggregate, agglomerate, amassed, gathered, clustered, combined.

congratulate *verb* wish joy to, felicitate, compliment, offer good wishes to.

congratulations *plural noun* felicitations, compliments, good wishes, best wishes, greetings.

congregate *verb* gather, assemble, group, flock together, convene, foregather, meet, amass, crowd, cluster, throng, rendezvous. *Opposites* DISPERSE; SCATTER.

congregation *noun* **1** *a congregation of people* gathering, assembly, group, flock, convention, meeting, crowd, conference, congress, mass, throng, conclave, convocation, conventicle. **2** *the minister's congregation* flock, parishioners, parish.

congress *noun* **1** *attend an international congress* assembly, meeting, gathering, conference, convention, convocation, council, synod, conventicle. **2** *join a professional congress* society, association, league, guild. **3** *vote for congress* legislative assembly, legislature, parliament, chamber of deputies, diet; representatives.

conic, conical *adjective* cone-shaped, conoid, pyramid-shaped, pyramidal, tapered, tapering, pointed, funnel-shaped, infundibular.

conjecture *verb* *conjecture that he would win* guess, surmise, speculate, infer, imagine, fancy, suspect, assume, suppose, believe, think, presume, presuppose, theorize, hypothesize.

conjecture *noun* *just a conjecture | open to conjecture* guess, guesstimate, inference, fancy, notion, suspicion, presumption, presupposition, theory, hypothesis; guessing, surmise, surmising, imagination, speculation, theorizing.

conjugal *adjective* connubial, matrimonial, nuptial, marital, married, wedded, spousal, bridal, hymeneal, epithalamic.

conjunction *noun* **1** *the conjunction of workers* association, union, uniting, affiliation, cooperation, combination, collaboration, coaction, alliance, federation. **2** *the conjunction of events* coincidence, co-occurence, simultaneousness, coexistence, contemporaneousness, concomitance.

conjure *verb* **1** *conjuring at the party* juggle, do tricks, do magic. **2** *conjure rabbits from a hat* summon, call up, invoke, rouse, raise up. **conjure up** *conjure up memories* recall, bring/call to mind, call up, evoke, recreate.

connect *verb* **1** *connect the hose to the tap* join, attach, fasten, affix, couple, clamp, secure, rivet, fuse, solder, weld. **2** *a road connecting the villages* join, link, unite, bridge. **3** *houses connecting with each other* adjoin, abut, touch, neighbour, lie next to, border, be adjacent to, impinge upon. **4** *she connects him with sadness* associate, link, relate to, identify, equate, bracket, draw a parallel with. *Opposites* DISCONNECT; SEVER; SEPARATE.

connection *noun* **1** *the connection has come loose* attachment, fastening, coupling, clamp, clasp, joint. **2** *the connection between the events* link, relationship, relation, relatedness, association, bond, tie-in, correspondence, parallel, analogy. **3** *in connection with this | in that connection* context, reference, frame of reference, relation. **4** *get a job through a connection* contact, friend, acquaintance, ally, associate, sponsor. **5** *dislike her husband's connection* relative, relation, kinsman, kinswoman; kin, kindred.

connive *verb* **1** *connive with others in the plot* conspire, collaborate, collude, be in collusion with, intrigue, plot, scheme, be a party to, abet, be an accessory to. **2** *connive at their behaviour* disregard, overlook, condone, turn a blind eye to, close/shut one's eyes to, let pass, ignore, look the other way, wink at, blink at, gloss over, pass over.

conniving *adjective* *a conniving rogue* scheming, colluding, nasty, unprincipled.

connoisseur *noun* gourmet, epicure, aesthete, arbiter of taste, expert, authority, specialist, pundit, cognoscente, one of the cognoscenti, devotee, aficionado, appreciator, fan, savant; *inf.* buff.

connotation *noun* undertone, undermeaning, nuance, hint, intimation, suggestion, implication, allusion, insinuation, reference.

conquer *verb* **1** *conquer the enemy* defeat, beat, overpower, overthrow, vanquish, subdue, rout, trounce, subjugate, triumph over, crush, quell. **2** *conquer the territory* seize, take possession of, occupy, invade, annex, appropriate, overrun, win. **3** *conquer one's fears* overcome, get the better of, vanquish, master, surmount, rise above, prevail over.

conqueror *noun* victor, winner, vanquisher, defeater, subjugator, champion, hero, lord, master, conquistador.

conquest *noun* **1** *the conquest of/over the enemy* conquering, victory, defeat, beating, overpowering, overthrow, vanquishment, rout, trouncing, subjugation, triumph, mastery, crushing, discomfiture. **2** *the conquest of the territory* seizing, possession, occupation, invasion, annexation, appropriation, overrunning, subjection. **3** *the conquest of the young ladies* captivation, enchantment, bewitching, seduction, enticement, enthralment. **4** *yet another of her conquests* captive, catch, acquisition, prize, admirer, fan, adherent, follower, supporter, worshipper; *inf.* push-over, walk-over.

conscience *noun* sense of right and wrong, moral sense, still small voice; morals, scruples, principles, ethics.

conscience-stricken *adjective* contrite, penitent, repentant, remorseful, sorry, regretful, guilty, guilt-ridden, troubled, ashamed.

conscientious *adjective* **1** *a conscientious person* diligent, careful, attentive, thorough, meticulous, punctilious, painstaking, hard-working, dedicated. **2** *a conscientious piece of work* careful, thorough, meticulous, precise, accurate, detailed. *Opposites* CARELESS; INATTENTIVE; LAX; SLAPDASH.

conscious *adjective* **1** *a conscious attempt at humour* deliberate, calculated, premeditated, on purpose, reasoned, knowing, studied, willed, volitional. **2** *in a conscious state* awake, aware, sentient, responsive, alert. **3** *conscious of the problem* aware, awake to, alert to, alive to, cognizant, sensible of, percipient; wise to. *Opposites* UNCONSCIOUS; UNAWARE.

consciousness noun **1** *regain consciousness* wakefulness, awakeness, awareness, sentience, responsiveness, alertness. **2** *lack of consciousness of the situation* awareness, realization, cognizance, perception, apprehension, recognition.

conscript verb *conscript recruits* enlist, recruit, call up, mobilize, levy.

consecrate verb **1** *consecrate the building* sanctify, bless, make holy, hallow, dedicate to God. **2** *a life consecrated to religion* dedicate, devote, pledge, commit, vow, set apart.

consecutive adjective successive, succeeding, following, in sequence, sequential, serial, in turn, progressive, step-by-step, continuous, uninterrupted, unbroken, chronological, seriate.

consensus noun agreement, consent, common consent, unanimity, harmony, concord, unity, concurrence.

consent verb *consent to their proposals* agree to, accept, approve, go along with, acquiesce in, accede to, concede to, yield to, give in to, submit to, comply with, abide by, concur with, conform to.
Opposites DISSENT; DISAGREE.

consent noun *give their assent* agreement, assent, acceptance, approval, permission, sanction, acquiescence, compliance, concurrence; *inf.* go-ahead, OK, green light.

consequence noun **1** *the consequence of the decision* result, effect, upshot, outcome, issue, event, end, aftermath, repercussion, reverberation. **2** *a matter of consequence* importance, note, significance, import, moment, weight, substance, portent. **3** *a person of consequence* importance, note, distinction, standing, status, prominence, prestige, eminence, repute, mark, esteem, rank.

consequent adjective resulting, resultant, ensuing, following, subsequent, successive, sequential.

consequently adverb as a result, therefore, thus, hence, subsequently, accordingly, *ergo*.

conservation noun preservation, protection, safeguarding, safekeeping, guarding, saving, care, charge, custody, husbandry, supervision, upkeep, maintenance.

conservative adjective **1** *politically conservative* right-wing, reactionary, traditionalist, Republican; *inf.* Tory. **2** *the young are more conservative than the old* conventional, traditional, reactionary, orthodox, cautious, prudent, careful, moderate, middle-of-the-road, temperate, stable, unchanging, old-fashioned, unprogressive, hide-bound, sober. **3** *a conservative attitude to the environment* conserving, preservative, protective, saving.
Opposites RADICAL; PROGRESSIVE.

conservatory noun **1** *plants in the conservatory* greenhouse, glasshouse, hot house. **2** *studying at the conservatory* conservatoire, music school, drama school, academy/institute of music/drama.

conserve verb preserve, save, keep, protect, take care of, hoard, store up, husband, use sparingly, reserve, nurse.
Opposites SQUANDER; WASTE.

consider verb **1** *consider your application* think about, weigh up, give thought to, examine, study, mull over, ponder, contemplate, deliberate over, cogitate about, chew over, meditate over, ruminate over, turn over in one's mind. **2** *consider the feelings of others* take into consideration, take into account, make allowances for, respect, bear in mind, have regard to, reckon with, remember. **3** *consider you suitable* think, believe, regard as, deem, hold to be, judge, rate. **4** *consider the horizon* contemplate, look at, observe, regard, survey, view, scrutinize, scan, examine, inspect.

considerable adjective **1** *a considerable amount* sizeable, substantial, appreciable, goodly, tolerable, fair, reasonable, tidy, ample, plentiful, abundant, marked, noticeable, comfortable, decent, great, large, lavish. **2** *in considerable pain* much, a lot of, a great deal of, great, a fair amount of. **3** *a considerable artist* distinguished, noteworthy, noted, important, significant, influential, illustrious, renowned.
Opposites LITTLE; NEGLIGIBLE; PALTRY; INSIGNIFICANT.

considerably adverb *considerably older* much, very much, a great deal, significantly, substantially, markedly, appreciably.

considerate adjective thoughtful, attentive, concerned, solicitous, mindful, heedful, kind, kindly, unselfish, compassionate, sympathetic, patient, charitable, generous, obliging, accommodating.

consideration noun **1** *give consideration to the proposal* thought, attention, heed, notice, regard, deliberation, discussion, reflection, contemplation, cogitation, rumination, examination, inspection, scrutiny, analysis, review. **2** *show consideration to their parents* considerateness, thoughtfulness, attentiveness, concern, solicitousness, solicitude, mindfulness, kindness, kindliness, unselfishness, compassion, sympathy, patience, charity, generosity, benevolence, friendliness. **3** *money a major consideration* issue, factor, point, concern, item, detail, aspect. **4** *for a small consideration* payment, fee, remuneration, compensation, recompense, emolument, perquisite. **5** *take age into consideration* account, reckoning, allowance.

considering preposition **1** *considering her age* taking into consideration, giving consideration to, bearing in mind, keeping in mind, in view of, in the light of. **2** *she's very well, considering* all things considered, considering everything, all in all.

consign verb **1** *consign her to his care* hand over, give over, deliver, assign, entrust, commend, remit, bequeath. **2** *consign to the dustbin | consign to misery* put away, deposit, commit. **3** *consign the package by air* send, dispatch, transmit, convey, post, mail.

consignment noun **1** *consignment to his care* handing over, assignment, entrusting, commendation. See CONSIGN 1. **2** *the consignment of parcels by air* sending, dispatch, conveyance. See CONSIGN 3. **3** *a consignment of coal* delivery, batch, shipment, containerload.

consist verb **1** *consist of flour and water* be composed of, be made up of, be formed of, comprise, contain, include, incorporate, embody, involve. **2** *her beauty consisting in her colouring* lie, reside, inhere, have its existence/being, be contained.

consistency noun **1** *mix to the right consistency* degree of thickness, degree of density, thickness, density, firmness, solidity, viscosity, cohesion. **2** *attitudes lacking consistency* steadiness, dependability, constancy, uniformity, lack of change, lack of deviation. **3** *the injuries showing consistency with stabbing* compatibility, conformity, congruity, agreement, accordance, consonance.

consistent adjective **1** *consistent attitudes* steady, dependable, constant, uniform, unchanging, undeviating, true to type. **2** *injuries consistent with stabbing | behaviour consistent with politeness* compatible, conforming to, congruous, agreeing, accordant, consonant. **Opposites** INCONSISTENT; IRREGULAR; INCOMPATIBLE.

consolation noun **1** *words of consolation* comfort, solace, sympathy, compassion, pity, commiseration, relief, help, support, cheer, encouragement, soothing, easement, succour, assuagement, alleviation. **2** *the baby is a consolation to her* comfort, solace, help, support.

console verb *console the loser* comfort, solace, sympathize with, express sympathy to, pity, commiserate with, help, cheer, encourage, ease, succour, alleviate, assuage. **Opposites** DISTRESS; UPSET.

consolidate verb **1** *consolidate his position* make stronger, strengthen, make secure, secure, make stable, stabilize, reinforce, fortify, cement. **2** *consolidate the territories | firms consolidating* combine, unite, merge, amalgamate, join, affiliate, fuse, federate. **3** *time for the business to consolidate* become stronger, become more secure, stabilize, strengthen one's position.

consonant adjective *behaviour consonant with status | consonant to wealth* compatible, consistent, in accordance, in harmony, suitable for, suited to, appropriate to.

consort noun *the queen and her consort* spouse, partner, companion, escort; husband, wife.

consort verb **consort with 1** *consort with criminals* associate with, keep company with, hang around with, go around with, mix with, spend time with, fraternize with, have dealings with. **2** *conduct consorting ill with his rank* go with, be in harmony with, be consistent with, accord with, be consonant with.

conspicuous adjective **1** *conspicuous changes* easily seen, clear, visible, obvious, evident, apparent, noticeable, observable, recognizable, discernible, perceptible, distinguishable, manifest, vivid. **2** *conspicuous colours | conspicuous modern buildings* striking, glaring, obtrusive, blatant, flagrant, showy, garish, bold, ostentatious. **3** *conspicuous members of the community* distinguished, outstanding, prominent, eminent, well-known, notable, famous, renowned, celebrated, illustrious. **Opposites** INCONSPICUOUS; UNOBTRUSIVE; OBSCURE.

conspiracy noun **1** *a conspiracy to overthrow the government* plot, scheme, stratagem, plan, machination, cabal; *inf.* frame-up. **2** *guilty of conspiracy* plotting, collusion, intrigue, connivance, collaboration, machination, treason.

conspirator noun conspirer, plotter, schemer, intriguer, colluder, collaborator, confederate, cabalist, traitor.

conspire verb **1** *conspire against the leader* form a conspiracy, plot, hatch a plot, scheme, intrigue, collude, collaborate, cabal, machinate; *inf.* be in cahoots with. **2** *events conspire against us* act together, work together, combine, join, unite, join forces, cooperate, coact, gang up on.

constancy noun **1** *her lover's constancy* faithfulness, fidelity, devotion, loyalty, staunchness, dependability, adherence, fealty. **2** *constancy of purpose* firmness, steadfastness, steadiness, resolution, resoluteness, fixedness, determination, perseverance, tenacity, application, doggedness. **3** *constancy of temperature* uniformity, evenness, regularity, stability, steadiness, invariableness, unchangingness, immutability.

constant adjective **1** *at a constant speed/temperature* uniform, even, regular, stable, steady, fixed, invariable, unvarying, unchanging, immutable. **2** *a constant stream of people* continuous, unbroken, uninterrupted. **3** *constant chattering* continual, never-ending, endless, unending, non-stop, incessant, unceasing, ceaseless, perpetual, persistent, interminable, unremitting, sustained, relentless, unrelenting. **4** *a constant lover* faithful, devoted, loyal, staunch, dependable, true, trustworthy, trusty. **5** *constant in his purpose* firm, steadfast, steady, resolute, determined, persevering, tenacious, dogged, unwavering, unflagging, unshaken. **Opposites** INCONSTANT; VARIABLE; FICKLE.

constantly adverb always, all the time, continually, continuously, endlessly, non-stop, incessantly, ceaselessly, perpetually, persistently, interminably, relentlessly.

constellation noun. See tables at STAR.

consternation noun surprise, amazement, astonishment, dismay, bewilderment, perturbation, mystification, confusion, anxiety, distress, alarm, panic, fear, fright, dread, horror, trepidation, shock, terror, awe.

constituent adjective *constituent parts* component, integral, elemental, basic, essential.

constituent noun **1** *analyse the constituents* component, component part, part, ingredient, element, integral part, unit, piece, fragment. **2** *talking to his constituents* voter, elector.

constitute verb **1** *the countries that constitute the European Union* form, make up, compose, comprise. **2** *a suggestion constituting a warning* be tantamount to, be the equivalent of, be regarded as, act as. **3** *constitute a committee* appoint, inaugurate, formally establish, authorize, commission, charter, induct, invest, empower, ordain. **4** *constitute a new school* establish, found, set up, institute, create.

constitution noun **1** *the British constitution | the society's constitution* body of law, system of laws/

rules, code, charter, canon; laws, rules, fundamental principles. **2** *the constitution of the committees varies* composition, make-up, structure, organization. **3** *the constitution of a new school* establishment, founding, foundation, setting up, institution, creation. **4** *people having a strong constitution* state of health, health, physique, physical condition, physical strength. **5** *people of a nervous constitution* mental make-up, disposition, temperament, temper, nature, character, mood.

constitutional *adjective* **1** *a constitutional body* constituted, legal, lawful, legitimate, authorized, statutory, chartered, vested. **2** *a constitutional weakness* inherent, inbred, intrinsic, congenital, organic, inborn, innate.

constitutional *noun* *go for a constitutional* walk, stroll, saunter, turn, airing.

constrain *verb* **1** *feel constrained to cooperate* force, compel, coerce, drive, impel, oblige, press, pressure, pressurize, urge, railroad, hustle. **2** *research constrained by lack of resources* hold back, restrict, hinder, impede, hamper, limit, curb, check, restrain. **3** *constrain political opponents* restrain, restrict, curb, confine, chain, shut in, lock up, imprison, incarcerate.

constrained *adjective* *a constrained manner* forced, uneasy, unnatural, inhibited, reserved, reticent, guarded.

constraint *noun* **1** *act under constraint* force, compulsion, coercion, obligation, pressure, impulsion. **2** *no constraints on their activities* restriction, hindrance, impediment, hampering, limitation, curb, check, restraint, damper. **3** *subject political opponents to constraint* restraint, restriction, confinement, imprisonment, incarceration. See CONSTRAIN 3. **4** *constraint of manner* forcedness, uneasiness, unnaturalness, inhibition, reservedness, reticence, guardedness, repression.

constrict *verb* **1** *constricted blood vessels* narrow, make smaller, tighten, compress, contract, squeeze, strangle, strangulate. **2** *constrict the flow of traffic* impede, obstruct, hinder, hamper, limit, restrict, check, curb, inhibit.

construct *verb* **1** *construct a housing estate | construct a bridge* build, erect, put up, set up, raise, elevate, establish, assemble, manufacture, fabricate, make. **2** *construct a plan/theory* form, formulate, put together, create, devise, design, invent, compose, fashion, mould, model, shape, frame, forge, engineer, fabricate, manufacture.

construction *noun* **1** *a bridge under construction* building, erection, elevation, establishment, assembly, manufacture, fabrication. See CONSTRUCT 1. **2** *an impressive construction* structure, building, edifice, assembly, framework. *See table at* BUILDING. **3** *the construction of a sentence* composition, formation, structure. **4** *put a different construction on her words* interpretation, reading, meaning, explanation, inference, explication.

constructive *adjective* *constructive suggestions* useful, helpful, productive, practical, positive,

valuable.
Opposites DESTRUCTIVE; NEGATIVE.

consul *noun* attaché, consul general; consulate, consulship.

consult *verb* **1** *consult an expert* ask, seek advice/information from, call in, turn to, take counsel from. **2** *consult a reference book* look up, refer to, turn to. **3** *consult with his colleagues* confer, discuss, talk, talk over, exchange views, deliberate, parley, powwow, palaver; *inf.* talk turkey. **4** *consult her feelings before acting* consider, take into consideration/account, have regard to, respect, have an eye to.

consultant *noun* **1** *a business consultant* adviser, expert, authority. **2** *a hospital consultant* senior doctor, specialist.

consultation *noun* **1** *have a consultation with one's adviser* meeting, talk, discussion, interview, session, audience, tête-à-tête, parley, powwow, colloquy. **2** *international consultations* conference, convention, symposium, forum, session, seminar.

consume *verb* **1** *consume cakes/lemonade* eat, eat up, drink, drink up, devour, ingest, swallow, gobble, gobble up, guzzle, snack on; *inf.* tuck into, scoff, down, put away, polish off, graze on. **2** *consumed by a desire* absorb, preoccupy, engross, eat up, devour, obsess, grip, monopolize, enthral. **3** *buildings consumed by fire* destroy, demolish, lay waste, wipe out, annihilate, devastate, raze, gut, ravage. **4** *cars consuming too much petrol* use, use up, utilize, expend, deplete, exhaust, waste, squander, drain, dissipate, fritter away.

consumer *noun* user, buyer, purchaser, customer, shopper, client, patron.

consuming *adjective* *a consuming passion* absorbing, compelling, pre-occupying, engrossing, devouring, obsessive, gripping, overwhelming.

consummate *adjective* complete, total, utter, absolute, perfect, superb, supreme, superior, ultimate, accomplished, expert, proficient, skilful, skilled, masterly, talented, gifted, polished, practised.

consummate *verb* *consummate his life's work* put the finishing touch to, perfect, complete, finish, accomplish, achieve, execute, carry out, perform, end, conclude, effectuate, crown, cap, set the seal on.

consumption *noun* **1** *unfit for human consumption* eating, drinking, devouring, ingestion. See CONSUME 1. **2** *consumption by fire* destruction, demolition, annihilation, devastation, razing, gutting. See CONSUME 3. **3** *the consumption of petrol* using, using up, utilization, expending, expenditure, depletion, exhaustion, waste, draining, dissipation. See CONSUME 4.

contact *noun* **1** *following contact with chemicals | on contact with an infected person* touch, touching, proximity, exposure, contiguity, junction, union, tangency. **2** *be in contact with* touch, communication, connection, correspondence, association. **3** *get a job through contacts* connection, acquaintance.

contact verb contact head office get/be in touch with, get hold of, communicate with, be in communication with; write to, write, notify, phone, call, ring up, speak to, reach.

contagious adjective catching, communicable, transmittable, transmissible, transferable, spreadable, infectious, epidemic, pandemic, pestilential, pestiferous, epizootic.

contain verb **1** the boat contained four people hold, have capacity for, carry, accommodate, seat. **2** the committee contains six members include, comprise, embrace, take in, incorporate, involve. **3** could not contain themselves | contain your mirth keep back, hold in, restrain, control, keep under control, keep in check, suppress, repress, curb, stifle.

container noun receptacle, vessel, holder, repository.

contaminate verb make impure, pollute, adulterate, defile, debase, corrupt, taint, infect, foul, spoil, soil, sully, tarnish, stain, befoul, vitiate, radioactivate.

contemplate verb **1** contemplate the portrait look at, view, regard, examine, inspect, observe, survey, scrutinize, scan, stare at, gaze at, eye. **2** contemplate the future think about, meditate over, consider, ponder, reflect over, mull over, muse on, dwell on, deliberate over, cogitate over, ruminate over, turn over in one's mind. **3** he is contemplating going think about, give thought to, consider, have in mind/view, envisage, intend, plan, propose, aim at, foresee, expect to.

contemplation noun **1** his contemplation of the painting viewing, examination, inspection, observation, survey, scrutiny, scanning, gazing at, eyeing. See CONTEMPLATE 1. **2** contemplation of the future meditation, consideration, pondering, reflection, rumination, deliberation, cogitation. See CONTEMPLATE 2. **3** lost in contemplation thought, meditation, reflection; inf. brown study.

contemplative adjective a contemplative mood/look thoughtful, pensive, reflective, meditative, musing, ruminative, introspective, intent, rapt, deep/lost in thought; inf. in a brown study.

contemporary adjective **1** Shakespeare and his contemporary writers contemporaneous, coexisting, coexistent, concurrent, coeval, synchronous; fml. coetaneous. **2** contemporary fashion modern, present-day, present, current, present-time, up-to-date, up-to-the-minute, fashionable, latest, recent, ultramodern, newfangled, à la mode; inf. with it.
Opposites OLD-FASHIONED; OUT OF DATE.

contemporary noun Yeats and his contemporaries peer, compeer, fellow.

contempt noun **1** feel/show contempt for the bully scorn, disdain, disrespect, condescension, derision, mockery, disgust, loathing, abhorrence, contumely. **2** fined for contempt of court disregard, disrespect, slighting, neglect, contumely.

contemptible adjective contemptible behaviour despicable, detestable, ignominious, lamentable, pitiful, low, mean, shameful, abject, unworthy, worthless, base, vile, shabby, cheap, sordid, degenerate.

contemptuous adjective with a contemptuous shrug scornful, disdainful, disrespectful, insulting, insolent, derisory, derisive, mocking, sneering, jeering, condescending, supercilious, arrogant, high and mighty; fml. contumelious.

contend verb **1** armies contending with each other | the contending teams compete, oppose, challenge, vie, contest, clash, strive, struggle, tussle, grapple, wrestle, scuffle, skirmish, battle, combat, fight, war, wage war, join battle, cross swords. **2** contending with problems cope with, face, grapple with, take on, pit oneself against. **3** contend that he's mad state, declare, assert, maintain, hold, claim, profess, allege, affirm, aver, pronounce.

content¹ noun **1** the content of the mixture component parts/elements. See CONTENTS 1. **2** the essay content is good, the style poor subject matter, subject, material, substance, matter, theme, ideas, burden, gist. **3** foods with a low sodium content amount, proportion, quantity. **4** the boiler's content volume, capacity, size.

content² adjective content with life contented, satisfied, pleased, happy, cheerful, glad, gratified, fulfilled, at ease, at peace, comfortable, serene, tranquil, unworried, untroubled, complacent.
Opposites DISCONTENTED; DISSATISFIED; UNHAPPY.

content³ noun filled with content contentment, contentedness, satisfaction, pleasure, happiness. See CONTENTMENT.

content⁴ verb **1** content oneself with a little make content, satisfy, be pleased/happy/glad, be fulfilled, be gratified. **2** sweets will content the child pacify, placate, soothe, appease, mollify.

contented adjective content, satisfied, pleased. See CONTENT² adjective.

contention noun **1** two groups in contention for the title competition, contest, rivalry, vying, opposition, striving, struggle, tussle, grappling, combat, battle, fighting, war. See CONTEND 1. **2** much contention between the families argument, disagreement, quarrelling, dispute, discord, feuding, hostility, enmity, strife, dissension. **3** it was her contention that she won argument, assertion, declaration, affirmation, allegation, claim, stand, position, opinion, view, belief, thesis.

contentious adjective **1** contentious people argumentative, quarrelsome, bickering, wrangling, disputatious, captious, factious, cavilling, litigious, competitive, combative, pugnacious, cross, perverse, querulous. **2** a contentious subject controversial, disputable, debatable, controvertible.

contentment noun content, contentedness, satisfaction, pleasure, happiness, cheerfulness, gladness, gratification, fulfilment, ease, comfort, peace, equanimity, serenity, tranquillity, repletion, complacency.

contents plural noun **1** the contents of the mixture/box constituents, components, ingredients, elements, items; content, load; inf. guts. **2** the

contest · contract

contents of the book text, subject matter, theme; sections, divisions, chapters.

contest *noun* **1** *take part in a sports/dancing contest* competition, match, game, event, tournament, meet, trial. **2** *a leadership contest* struggle, vying, conflict, battle, fight, combat, tussle, skirmish.

contest *verb* **1** *contest the seat* compete for, contend for, vie for, fight for, fight over, battle for, struggle for, tussle for. **2** *contest the decision* challenge, question, call into question, oppose, doubt, dispute, object to, litigate. **3** *contest the point* argue, debate, dispute, quarrel over, be in contention about.

contestant *noun* competitor, entrant, candidate, participant, player, contender, rival, opponent, adversary, antagonist, aspirant.

context *noun* **1** *in the present financial context* circumstances, conditions; situation, state of affairs, background, environment. **2** *take a statement out of its context* text, frame of reference, contextual relationship, subject, theme, topic.

contiguous *adjective* touching, in contact, meeting, joining, connecting, abutting, bordering, neighbouring, adjacent, near, nearby, close, vicinal.

continent *adjective* **1** *continent in one's drinking habits* self-restrained, abstemious, abstinent, sober, austere, ascetic, self-denying. **2** *sexually continent* chaste, celibate, pure, virtuous, self-restrained, virgin, virginal.

contingency *noun* chance event, event, eventuality, incident, happening, occurrence, juncture, accident, chance, possibility, fortuity, emergency, uncertainty.

contingent *adjective* **1** *help contingent upon resources* conditional on, dependent on, subject to, hinging on, controlled by. **2** *contingent effects* chance, incidental, accidental, possible, fortuitous, uncertain, random, haphazard.

contingent *noun* *an advance contingent* detachment, group, party, body, division, section, company, complement, deputation, mission; *inf.* bunch.

continual *adjective* **1** *continual complaints* frequent, repeated, constant, regular, persistent, habitual, recurrent, repetitive, oft-repeated. **2** *continual noise* continuous, perpetual, endless, constant, interminable. *See* CONTINUOUS.

continually *adverb* *continually interrupted* frequently, repeatedly, constantly, regularly, habitually, recurrently.

continuance *noun* continuation, persistence, staying power, endurance, survival, protraction.

continuation *noun* **1** *support the continuation of the search* continuance, carrying on, extension, furtherance, prolongation, perpetuation, continuity, progression. **2** *favour the continuation of the search in the morning* resumption, renewal, recommencement. **3** *appreciate the continuation of the story | the continuation of Godber's TV play* sequel, postscript, addition, supplement, appendix. **4** *the road is a continuation of the High Street* extension, prolongation.

continue *verb* **1** *the desert continues for miles* go on, extend, keep on, carry on, maintain course, drag on. **2** *the firm may continue* go on, carry on, last, remain, stay, endure, survive, live on, persist, subsist, abide. **3** *continue the session as long as possible* maintain, sustain, retain, prolong, protract, perpetuate, preserve. **4** *continue trying* go on, carry on, keep on, keep at, not stop, persist in, persevere in, prolong, pursue; *inf.* stick with/at. **5** *continue the search after a break* resume, renew, recommence, start again, carry on with, return to, take up. **6** *continue after lunch* go on, carry on, resume, recommence, proceed, pick up where one has left off.

Opposites STOP; DISCONTINUE; give up (*see* GIVE).

continuity *noun* **1** *ensure continuity of supplies* continuousness, uninterruptedness, flow, regular flow, progression. **2** *lack of continuity in the prose* cohesion, coherence, connection, interrelatedness, linkage, sequence.

continuous *adjective* *a continuous supply | continuous noise* uninterrupted, unbroken, consecutive, constant, without stopping, non-stop, perpetual, ceaseless, incessant, unceasing, unremitting, endless, everlasting, interminable, undivided.

Opposites INTERMITTENT; SPORADIC.

contort *verb* twist, wrench/bend out of shape, warp, deform, misshape.

contour *noun* outline, silhouette, profile, figure, shape, form; lines, curves.

contraband *noun* *accused of contraband* smuggling, illegal traffic, trafficking, black marketing, black marketeering, bootlegging, drug trafficking.

contraband *adjective* *contraband goods* illegal, illicit, unlawful, prohibited, banned, proscribed, taboo, interdicted, smuggled, black-market, bootleg, bootlegged.

contraceptive *noun* oral contraceptive, birth-control pill, barrier contraceptive; *Am.* prophylactic; *inf.* rubber, French letter. *See table.*

CONTRACEPTIVES	
cervical cap	female condom
coil/loop	Femidom™
combined pill	intrauterine device
condom/sheath	(IUD)
contraceptive ring	minipill
contraceptive	morning-after pill
sponge	pill
diaphragm	spermicide
Dutch cap	vaginal ring

contract *noun* agreement, compact, covenant, pact, settlement, arrangement, understanding, transaction, bargain, deal, treaty, concordat, convention, bond, commitment, entente, *entente cordiale.*

contract *verb* **1** *metals contracting* get smaller, become smaller, become shorter, shrink, reduce, shrivel. **2** *contracting metals* make smaller, make shorter, shrink. *See*

CONTRACTION. **3** *blood vessels contracting* | *muscles contracting* become narrower, narrow, tighten, become tighter, tense, draw in. **4** *contract your muscles* make narrower, narrow, constrict, tighten, make tighter, tense, draw in. **5** *contract a word/text* shorten, abbreviate, abridge, lessen, compress, condense, curtail, concentrate, précis, summarize, synopsize. **6** *contract with them to do the work* arrange, agree, reach an arrangement, establish, come to terms, negotiate, bargain, strike a bargain, close/clinch a deal, close, engage, settle, covenant. **7** *contract a disease* catch, get, come/go down with, develop, become infected with, be afflicted with. **8** *contract a debt* incur, acquire, fall into.
Opposites EXPAND; distend; LENGTHEN.

contraction noun **1** *the contraction of metals* getting smaller, shrinking. See CONTRACT *verb* 1, 2. **2** *the contraction of blood vessels* | *muscle contraction* narrowing, tightening, constricting, tensing. See CONTRACT *verb* 3, 4. **3** *pregnant women experiencing contractions* muscle-tightening/-tensing, womb-tightening, cramps. **4** *isn't is a contraction* shortened form, short form, shortening, elision, abridgement, abbreviation.

contradict verb **1** *contradict his father* say the opposite of, oppose, challenge, counter, be at variance with. **2** *contradict his father's statement* say the opposite of, oppose, deny, challenge, dispute, counter, refute, rebut, be at variance with, controvert, impugn, confute. **3** *the two set of facts contradict each other* be at variance with, disagree with, be in conflict with, clash, contravene, run counter to, be inconsistent with, dissent from, negate.
Opposites AGREE; CONFIRM; VERIFY.

contradiction noun **1** *the contradiction of his statement* denial, disputing, countering, refuting, rebuttal, controverting, impugning, confutation. **2** *the contradiction between the two statements* variance, variation, disagreement, conflict, clash, inconsistency, dissension, contravention, negation.

contradictory adjective **1** *hold a contradictory view* opposing, opposite, dissentient, dissenting, contrary, dissident; at variance, at odds. **2** *contradictory statements* contradicting, disagreeing, conflicting, clashing, contrasting, incompatible, irreconcilable, inconsistent, incongruous, contravening, negating, antithetical.

contraption noun device, machine, mechanism, gadget, contrivance, apparatus, invention, appliance; *inf.* thingumajig, thingumabob, whatsit, doodah, gismo.

contrary adjective **1** *holding contrary views* opposite, opposing, contradictory, clashing, conflicting, contrasting, incompatible, irreconcilable, inconsistent, incongruous, antithetical. **2** *a contrary young woman* perverse, awkward, wilful, wayward, obstinate, stubborn, headstrong, pigheaded, unaccommodating, intractable, recalcitrant, intransigent, refractory, cantankerous; *inf.* stroppy, cussed; Scots *inf.* thrawn.
Opposites COMPATIBLE; ACCOMMODATING.

contrary noun *the contrary is true* opposite, antithesis, reverse, contrariety. **on the contrary** quite the opposite, just the reverse, not at all, conversely, in contrast.

contrary adverb **contrary to** against, in opposition to, not in accord with.

contrast noun **1** *a marked contrast between them* difference, dissimilarity, distinction, disparity, dissimilitude, differentiation, distinguishment. **2** *he is a complete contrast to his brother* opposite, foil, antithesis. **3** *fair by contrast with his sister* comparison, differentiation, distinguishment.
Opposites SIMILARITY; SAMENESS.

contrast verb **1** *contrast the two writers* compare, juxtapose, set side by side, distinguish, differentiate, discriminate. **2** *theories and actions contrast sharply* form a contrast, contradict, be at variance, be contrary, diverge, differ.

contravene verb **1** *contravene a law* disobey, break, infringe, violate, transgress. **2** *evidence contravening the theory* contradict, be in conflict with, be in opposition to, clash with, be at variance with, run counter to, refute, rebut.

contretemps noun mishap, misadventure, unfortunate occurrence, accident, awkward moment.

contribute verb **1** *contribute money/help to the charity* give, donate, subscribe, give a donation/subscription, hand out, present, grant, endow, bestow, accord, confer, provide, supply, furnish; *inf.* chip in, pitch in. **2** *contributing articles to magazines* supply, provide. **3** *sensible eating contributing to good health* be conducive to, lead to, be instrumental in, have a hand in, bear a part in, add to, conduce to, help, promote, advance.

contribution noun **1** *contributions to the fund* donation, gift, subscription, offering, present, grant, bestowal, allowance, subsidy, endowment. **2** *accept contributions to the paper* article, piece, story, item. **3** *contribution to the discussion* input, participation; *inf.* one's pennyworth.

contributor noun **1** *the charity's contributors* giver, donor, subscriber, patron, supporter, backer, benefactor, subsidizer. **2** *newspaper contributors* correspondent, journalist, reporter, columnist, writer, critic, reviewer, freelance writer, freelance.

contrite adjective penitent, repentant, remorseful, regretful, sorry, chastened, conscience-stricken, guilt-ridden, in sackcloth and ashes.

contrivance noun **1** *a contrivance for ploughing* device, invention, gadget, contraption, appliance, apparatus, implement, tool, machine, mechanism, equipment, gear, tackle. **2** *fooled by a clever contrivance* stratagem, scheme, ruse, trick, plot, plan, dodge, intrigue, machination, expedient, fabrication, artifice. **3** *have to admire the contrivance of the plotter* inventiveness, ingenuity, creativity, originality.

contrive verb **1** *contrive a brilliant scheme* devise, concoct, engineer, invent, originate, create, construct, design, plan, work out, think/dream up, plot, fabricate. **2** *contrive to* *win* manage, find a way, engineer, manoeuvre, plot, plan, intrigue, scheme.

contrived *adjective* unnatural, artificial, forced, strained, laboured, overdone, elaborate, planned, invented, non-spontaneous.

control *verb* **1** *control the organization* be in control of, be in charge of, head, manage, direct, preside over, conduct, be in authority over, command, rule, govern, lead, supervise, superintend, oversee, dominate, master, reign over, be in the driver's seat of, be in the saddle of; *inf.* be the boss of. **2** *control prices | control the fire* keep in check, restrain, curb, contain, hold back, restrict, limit, regulate, constrain, subdue, bridle. **3** *control the traffic/machine* regulate, guide, monitor, steer, pilot.

control *noun* **1** *have control over the organization* charge, management, authority, power, command, direction, rule, government, jurisdiction, supervision, superintendence, guidance, dominance, mastery, reign, supremacy. **2** *get control of oneself* self-control, self-restraint, restraint, hold, check, curb, constraint. **3** *arms control | import controls* limitation, restriction, regulation, restraint, check, curb, brake. **4** *used as an experimental control* standard of comparison, standard, check. **5** *mission control* headquarters, base, centre of operations, command post.

controls *plural noun* **1** *import controls* means of limitation/restriction. See CONTROL *noun* 3. **2** *the machine's controls* instruments, levers, switches, dials, knobs; control panel, console, dashboard.

controversial *adjective* open to discussion/question, disputed, disputable, debatable, under discussion, at issue, contentious, contended, controvertible.

controversy *noun* dispute, argument, debate, disagreement, dissension, contention, altercation, wrangle, wrangling, quarrelling, squabbling, bickering, polemic.

contumely *noun* insult, scorn, derision, abuse, insolence, rudeness, churlishness, discourtesy.

contusion *noun* bruise, discoloration/blemish, injury, bump, lump.

conundrum *noun* **1** *children solving conundrums* riddle, puzzle, wordgame; *inf.* brain-teaser. **2** *a conundrum for the politicians* puzzle, problem, difficult question, enigma, mystery.

convalescence *noun* recovery, recuperation, improvement, getting better, rehabilitation, return to health, mending, restoration.

convene *verb* **1** *convene a meeting* call, call together, summon, convoke, round up, rally. **2** *the meeting convened* assemble, gather, collect, congregate, meet, foregather, muster.

convenience *noun* **1** *books arranged alphabetically for convenience* accessibility, handiness, availability. **2** *the convenience of the time* suitability, appropriateness, fitness, fittingness, favourableness, advantageousness, opportuneness, propitiousness, timeliness, expedience, usefulness, utility, serviceability. **3** *do it at your convenience* suitable opportunity, leisure, freedom, spare moment, spare time, free

time. **4** *for the convenience of all* service, use, benefit, advantage, accommodation, enjoyment, satisfaction, comfort, ease. **5** *few conveniences in the kitchen* gadget, labour-saving device, appliance, device, appurtenance, amenity, facility.

convenient *adjective* **1** *shops convenient for the houses* accessible, handy, at hand, close at hand, within reach, nearby, just round the corner, at one's fingertips, available, propinquant. **2** *choose a convenient time/setting* suitable, suited, appropriate, fit, fitting, favourable, advantageous, opportune, timely, well-timed, seasonable, expedient, useful, serviceable.
Opposites INCONVENIENT; INACCESSIBLE; UNSUITABLE.

convent *noun* nunnery, religious community, priory, motherhouse; convent school.

convention *noun* **1** *a medical convention* conference, congress, gathering, meeting, assembly, convocation, council of delegates/representatives, synod, conclave. **2** *follow convention | obey the conventions* conventionality, etiquette, formality, protocol, propriety, code, punctilio, custom, tradition, usage, practice. **3** *draw up a convention between countries* agreement, contract, pact, treaty, bargain, deal, compact, concordat.

conventional *adjective* **1** *conventional behaviour/attitudes* accepted, expected, customary, usual, standard, regular, normal, ordinary, correct, decorous, proper, orthodox, traditional, prevailing, prevalent, conformist, conservative, formal, ritual; *inf.* square, straitlaced. **2** *conventional works of art* run-of-the-mill, commonplace, common, ordinary, everyday, common-or-garden, prosaic, routine, stereotyped, pedestrian, hackneyed, unoriginal, clichéd, trite, platitudinous, bourgeois.
Opposites UNCONVENTIONAL; UNORTHODOX; ORIGINAL.

converge *verb* **1** *lines/opinions converging* meet, intersect, join, merge, unite, come together, become one, coincide, concur. **2** *crowds converging on the palace* approach, move towards, come closer to, close in on, centre on, focus on.
Opposites DIVIDE; SEPARATE; DIVERGE.

conversant *adjective* acquainted with, familiar with, knowledgeable about, well-versed in, informed about, well-informed about, apprised of, *au fait* with, experienced in, proficient in, practised in, skilled in; *inf.* well up on.

conversation *noun* **1** *deep in conversation* talk, discussion, chat, dialogue, discourse, communication, conference, gossip, colloquy, intercourse. **2** *having a conversation* talk, discussion, chat, dialogue, exchange, gossip, powwow, tête-à-tête; *inf.* chinwag, confab.

conversational *adjective* **1** *conversational English* informal, colloquial, chatty. **2** *a conversational person/talent* communicative, expansive, talkative, chatty, loquacious, garrulous, voluble.

converse¹ *verb* *converse with others* talk, speak, discuss, chat, have a talk/discussion with, communicate with.

converse² noun deep in converse conversation, talk, discussion. See CONVERSATION.

converse³ noun the converse is true opposite, contrary, reverse, antithesis, obverse, other side of the coin; inf. flip side.

converse⁴ adjective converse views opposite, opposing, contrary, reverse, counter, antithetical, obverse.

conversion noun **1** the conversion of coal/liquid to gas change, transformation, metamorphosis, transfiguration, transmutation, sea change; inf. transmogrification. **2** the conversion of the building alteration, adaptation, modification, reshaping, refashioning, remodelling, remaking, reconstruction, rebuilding. **3** religious conversion reformation, regeneration, proselytization. **4** the conversion of yards to metres | conversion of pounds to dollars change, turning, exchange, substitution, switch.

convert verb **1** convert coal/liquid to gas change, transform, metamorphose, transfigure, transmute; inf. transmogrify. **2** the sofa converts to a bed change into, make into, adapt to, transform into. **3** convert the building alter, adapt, modify, reshape, refashion, remodel, restyle, remake, reconstruct, rebuild, reorganize. **4** convert the heathens reform, regenerate, convince, cause to change beliefs, bring to God, baptize, proselytize, cause to be reborn. **5** convert yards to metres | convert pounds to dollars change, turn into; exchange for, substitute by, switch from.

convey verb **1** convey the goods transport, carry, bring, fetch, bear, move, shift, transfer, cart, lug. **2** pipes conveying water conduct, transmit, channel, guide. **3** convey information | convey the idea transmit, pass on, hand on, send, dispatch, communicate, make known, impart, relate, announce, tell, reveal, disclose. **4** convey property give the rights to, transfer, transmit, grant, cede, devolve, lease, bequeath, will; Law demise.

conveyance noun **1** by public conveyance transport, transportation, carriage, transfer, transference, transmission, movement, haulage, portage, cartage, shipment, freightage. **2** the conveyance broke down transport, vehicle; car, bus, coach, van, lorry. **3** the conveyance of information transmission, passing on, communication, imparting. See CONVEY 3. **4** conveyance of property transfer, granting, ceding, cession. See CONVEY 4.

convict verb convict him of the crime declare/find/pronounce/judge guilty, sentence, condemn.

convict noun ex-convicts getting jobs prisoner, jailbird, criminal, offender, law-breaker, felon; inf. crook, con, old lag.

conviction noun **1** she has previous convictions declaration/pronouncement of guilt, sentence, judgement, condemnation. **2** she spoke with conviction confidence, assurance, belief, certainty, certitude, persuasion, firmness, trust, earnestness. **3** my conviction is that he is dead belief, opinion, view, thought, idea, persuasion. **4** a person of conviction principle, belief, faith, creed.

convince verb **1** she convinced me that I was wrong make one certain, prove to, satisfy, assure, reassure. **2** convince him to vote for them persuade, prevail upon, sway, talk round, bring around, win over.

convincing adjective **1** a convincing argument cogent, powerful, persuasive, plausible, incontrovertible, conclusive. **2** a convincing person persuasive, plausible, credible. **3** a convincing victory impressive, decisive, conclusive.

convivial adjective genial, cordial, sociable, friendly, affable, amiable, congenial, agreeable, jolly, cheerful.

convocation noun assembly, gathering, meeting, congregation, conference, convention, congress, conclave, synod.

convolution noun **1** carvings with curves and convolutions twist, turn, coil, spiral, curl, twirl, kink, curlicue, whorl, sinuosity. **2** the convolutions of the plot complication, complexity, involvement, entanglement.

convoy noun **1** the convoy set off group, company, assemblage, line, fleet, cortège, caravan. **2** a fleet/company under convoy escort, protection, guard, bodyguard, defence, shield, guidance.

convoy verb **1** convoy a company of ships escort, accompany, attend, protect, guard, defend, guide, shepherd, flank. **2** convoy the children home escort, accompany, go along with, attend, chaperon.

convulse verb **1** audiences convulsed with laughter shake, churn up, discompose, unsettle. **2** a city convulsed with rioting shake, agitate, disturb, upset, disorder, unsettle, wrack. **3** the comedian convulsed the audience greatly amuse/entertain, divert; inf. slay, knock, knock them dead, crack up.

convulsion noun **1** the child went into convulsions fit, seizure, paroxysm, spasm, contractions, attack. **2** political convulsions in the city turmoil, tumult, commotion, upheaval, agitation, disturbance, disruption, unrest, upset, disorder, chaos. **3** have the audience in convulsions uncontrollable laughter, fit of laughter, paroxysm.

cook verb **1** cook a dish/meal prepare, put together, improvise. See table. **2** cook the books falsify, forge, alter. **3** what's cooking? happen, occur, take place. **cook up** concoct, make up, put together, devise, invent, create, contrive,

COOKING METHODS		
baking	fricasseeing	roasting
barbecuing	frying	sautéeing
boiling	grilling	scrambling
braising	marinating	simmering
broiling	oven-	smoking
casseroling	roasting	spit-
charbroiling	parboiling	roasting
coddling	pickling	steaming
curing	poaching	stewing
currying	pot-	stir-frying
deep-frying	roasting	toasting

fabricate, prepare, improvise, plot, plan, scheme.

cool *adjective* **1** *a cool drink | cool weather* fresh, refreshing, coldish, chilly, chilled, chilling, nippy, unheated, sunless, windy, breezy, draughty. **2** *keep cool in an emergency* calm, composed, collected, self-possessed, self-controlled, level-headed, unexcited, unperturbed, unmoved, unruffled, unemotional, relaxed, placid, serene; *inf.* together. **3** *a cool young woman* aloof, distant, reserved, standoffish, unfriendly, offhand, unwelcoming, uncommunicative, frigid, chilly, impassive, undemonstrative, unresponsive, apathetic, unenthusiastic, lukewarm, indifferent, unconcerned, uninterested, incurious. **4** *the cool way she stole* bold, audacious, brazen, presumptuous, overconfident, impudent, insolent, impertinent, forward, cheeky, shameless. **5** *a cool attempt at murder* calculated, premeditated, planned, deliberate, intentional, purposeful. **6** *thinks she's really cool* sophisticated, urbane, cosmopolitan, elegant; *inf.* streetwise. **7** *what a cool idea* marvellous, excellent, very good, splendid; *inf.* Al.
Opposites WARM; EXCITED; PASSIONATE.

cool *verb* **1** *cool the milk* cool down, make cold/colder, chill, refrigerate, freeze. **2** *the metal/milk cooled* cool down, become cold/colder, lose heat. **3** *cool his ardour* lessen, abate, moderate, temper, diminish, reduce, dampen, quiet, soothe, assuage, allay, mollify, settle. **4** *his ardour cooled* cool off, lessen, abate, moderate, diminish.

cool *noun* **1** *lose one's cool* self-control, control, calmness, composure, poise, self-possession, self-discipline. **2** *the cool of the evening* coolness, freshness, crispness, coldness, chill.

coop *noun chicken's coop* cage, pen, enclosure, hutch, pound, lock-up.

coop *verb coop up* *chickens/children cooped up* cage, cage/pen in, confine, enclose, hem in, shut/lock up, imprison, immure.

cooperate *verb* **1** *cooperate in the venture* work together, act/pull together, join forces, unite, act jointly, combine, collaborate, pool resources, conspire, connive, concur, coordinate, coact. **2** *he'll be released if he cooperates* be of assistance, assist, help, lend a hand, contribute, aid, abet, participate, go along; *inf.* pitch in, play ball.

cooperation *noun* **1** *the cooperation between the departments* combined effort, working together, joint action, unity, collaboration, connivance, concurrence, coordination, teamwork, give and take, synergy. **2** *thank you for your cooperation* assistance, help, aid, contribution, helping hand, participation, support, backing, good offices.

cooperative *adjective* **1** *a cooperative venture* joint, united, shared, unified, combined, concerted, collected, coordinated, collaborative, coactive. **2** *the public being cooperative* of assistance, assisting, helpful, helping, obliging, accommodating, aiding, contributing, participating, responsive.

coordinate *verb* **1** *coordinate the effort* arrange, organize, order, integrate, synchronize, correlate, harmonize, systematize. **2** *coordinating for the common good* cooperate, unite, combine, collaborate, coact, interrelate.

cope *verb single parents unable to cope* manage, succeed, survive, carry on, get through, get on, get along, get by, subsist, make the grade, come through, hold one's own; *inf.* make out. **cope with** *cope with the situation* handle, deal with, treat, weather, contend with, take care of, dispose of, grapple with, wrestle with, struggle with, tussle with.

copious *adjective* abundant, superabundant, plentiful, plenteous, ample, profuse, full, extensive, generous, lavish, rich, liberal, bounteous, bountiful, exuberant, luxuriant, overflowing, abounding.

copse *noun* thicket, grove, wood, coppice, boscage; *Am.* brush.

copy *noun* **1** *a copy of the document* facsimile, duplicate, duplication, carbon, carbon copy, photocopy, Xerox™, photostat™, transcript. **2** *a clever copy of the vase* imitation, reproduction, replica, replication, likeness, counterfeit, forgery, fake, sham. **3** *three copies of the paper* specimen, example, sample.

copy *verb* **1** *copy the document* duplicate, photocopy, xerox, photostat, transcribe. **2** *copy the vase/painting* reproduce, replicate, forge, counterfeit. **3** *copy his style* imitate, mimic, emulate, follow, echo, mirror, simulate, ape, parrot.

cord *noun* **1** string, rope, twine, cable, line, ligature. **2** *cords of friendship* bond, link, tie, connection.

cordial *adjective* **1** *a cordial welcome* friendly, warm, genial, affable, amiable, pleasant, gracious, warm-hearted, good-natured, welcoming, sincere, affectionate, hearty, wholehearted, heartfelt. **2** *cordial dislike* intense, acute, strong, fierce, keen, whole-hearted, heartfelt.
Opposites UNFRIENDLY; INSINCERE.

cordon *noun* **1** *a police/military cordon* barrier, line, chain, ring; picket line. **2** *wearing a cordon indicating rank* braid, cord, ribbon, riband, sash, decoration.

cordon *verb* **cordon off** *cordon off the area* close off, fence off, shut off, separate off, isolate, enclose, encircle, surround, picket.

core *noun* centre, heart, nucleus, nub, kernel, crux, heart of the matter, essence, quintessence, substance, gist, pith; *inf.* nitty-gritty.

cork *noun* stopper, stop, plug, bung.

corn *noun* **1** *corn used to make bread* cereal, cereal crop; Indian corn. See table at CEREAL. **2** *corn served as a first course* sweet corn, corn on the cob.

corner *noun* **1** *the corner of the road* angle, bend, curve, crook, turn. **2** *the corner where the roads meet* angle, projecting angle, intersection, junction, fork, convergence, juncture. **3** *hidden in odd corners* nook, cranny, niche, recess, crevice, cavity, hole, secret place, hideaway, hide-out; *inf.* hidey-hole. **4** *in a remote corner of*

England part, region, area, district, section, quarter; *inf.* neck of the woods. **5** *in a difficult corner* predicament, plight, tight spot; *inf.* pickle, hole. **6** *establish a corner of the property market* control, position of control, dominance, monopoly.

corner *verb* **1** *corner the enemy* drive into a corner, run to earth, block off, trap, bring to bay. **2** *corner the market* gain control/dominance of, control, dominate, monopolize; *inf.* hog.

corny *adjective* banal, trite, hackneyed, stale, commonplace, stereotyped, platitudinous, inane, fatuous, jejune, sentimental, mawkish, weak, feeble; *inf.* old hat.

corollary *noun* consequence, result, upshot, conclusion.

coronation *noun* crowning, enthronement, enthroning, accession to the throne, investiture, anointing, inauguration.

coronet *noun* crown, garland. *See table at* HAT.

corporal *adjective* bodily, fleshly, physical, corporeal, material, carnal, somatic.

corporate *adjective* combined, joint, united, communal, collective, shared, pooled, merged, allied, collaborative.

corporation *noun* **1** *a business corporation* company, firm, trust, partnership, combine, conglomerate. **2** *municipal corporation* council, town council, municipal authorities, civic authorities. **3** *a man with a huge corporation* paunch, pot-belly, pot, beer belly.

corps *noun* **1** *an army corps* unit, division, detachment, company, troop, contingent, squad, squadron. **2** *diplomatic/dancing corps* group, body, band, team, party, contingent, troupe, gang, pack, crew.

corpse *noun* dead body, body, cadaver, carcass, skeleton; remains; *inf.* stiff.

corpulent *adjective* fat, obese, plump, portly, stout, tubby, chubby, podgy, overweight, beefy, thickset, heavy, heavy-set, burly, bulky, well-padded, fleshy, rotund, roly-poly.

correct *adjective* **1** *the correct answer* right, accurate, true, actual, exact, precise, unerring, close, faithful, strict, faultless, flawless; *inf.* OK, on the mark, on the beam, spot on. **2** *correct behaviour* proper, suitable, fit, fitting, befitting, appropriate, apt, seemly, conventional, approved, accepted, standard, usual, customary, *comme il faut; inf.* OK.
Opposites INCORRECT; WRONG; IMPROPER.

correct *verb* **1** *correct the spelling errors* make/set right, rectify, right, amend, emend, remedy, redress, cure, improve, better, ameliorate, repair. **2** *correct an exam paper* indicate errors in, show mistakes in, point out faults in. **3** *correct a defect* rectify, counteract, offset, counterbalance, compensate for, make up for, neutralize. **4** *correct an instrument* adjust, regulate, fix, set, standardize, normalize, make conform. **5** *correct the children* scold, rebuke, chide, reprimand, reprove, admonish, lecture, berate, discipline, punish, chastise.

correction *noun* **1** *the correction of the text* amendment, emendation, rectifying, rectifica-

tion, improvement, modification, alteration, amelioration, repair. **2** *a house of correction* punishment, discipline, chastisement, castigation, admonition, reproof, reformation.

corrective *adjective* **1** *corrective surgery* remedial, therapeutic, restorative, curative, reparatory, reparative, rehabilitative. **2** *corrective training* punitive, disciplinarian, penal, castigatory, castigative, reformatory.

correctly *adverb* **1** *answer correctly* right, rightly, accurately, unerringly, precisely, faultlessly. **2** *dressed correctly* properly, suitably, fittingly, appropriately, aptly.

correlate *verb* **1** *subjects correlating with each other* correspond, tie in, equate, interact, relate, agree, coordinate. **2** *correlate the facts* bring together, compare, show a connection/relationship/association/correspondence, connect.

correlation *noun* correspondence, equivalence, reciprocity, mutual relationship, interrelationship, interdependence, interaction, mutuality, connection, relationship.

correspond *verb* **1** *accounts not corresponding* agree, be in agreement, accord, concur, coincide, conform, match, fit together, square, tally, dovetail, correlate. **2** *Congress corresponds to Parliament* be analogous, be similar, be comparable, be equivalent, be akin, compare with. **3** *correspond with a friend* exchange letters, write to, communicate, keep in touch/contact.

correspondence *noun* **1** *lack of correspondence between the accounts* agreement, accordance, accord, concurrence, coincidence, conformity, harmony, matching. **2** *the correspondence between Congress and Parliament* analogy, similarity, resemblance, comparability, correlation, relation. **3** *a backlog of correspondence* post, mail, communication; letters. **4** *enter into correspondence* letter-writing, writing, written communication.

correspondent *noun* **1** *her family are regular correspondents* letter-writer, pen-friend, pen-pal, communicator. **2** *newspaper correspondent* reporter, journalist, contributor, newspaperman, newspaperwoman; special correspondent, foreign correspondent; *inf.* stringer.

correspondent *adjective* *correspondent forms of legislature* analogous, similar, like, comparable, parallel, equivalent, akin, kindred.

corridor *noun* passage, passageway, aisle; hallway.

corroborate *verb* confirm, verify, bear out, authenticate, validate, certify, endorse, ratify, substantiate, back up, uphold, support, attest to, sustain, evidence.
Opposites DISPROVE; CONTRADICT.

corrode *verb* **1** *pipes corroded by rust* eat away, wear away, erode, gnaw, abrade, destroy, consume, rust, oxidize, oxidate. **2** *the metal has corroded* wear away, waste away, rust, disintegrate, crumble, fragment, be destroyed.

corrosive *adjective* *acid is corrosive* corroding, eroding, erosive, abrasive, biting, caustic, acrid, mordant, consumptive, destructive.

corrugated *adjective* furrowed, grooved, ridged, fluted, channelled, folded, crinkled, puckered, creased, wrinkled, crumpled, striate.

corrupt *adjective* **1** *corrupt officials* dishonest, bribable, crooked, fraudulent, dishonourable, unscrupulous, untrustworthy, venal; *inf.* bent, shady. **2** *a corrupt young man* | *corrupt acts* immoral, depraved, wicked, evil, sinful, degenerate, reprobate, perverted, dissolute, debauched, decadent, abandoned, lascivious, lewd, lecherous. **3** *a corrupt society/atmosphere* rotten, polluted, putrid, decayed, putrescent, tainted, infected, contaminated. **4** *a corrupt substance* adulterated, impure, alloyed, contaminated, tainted.
Opposites HONEST; ETHICAL; MORAL; PURE.

corrupt *verb* **1** *corrupt the new official* bribe, suborn, buy, buy off, induce, lure, entice; *inf.* pay off, grease the palm of. **2** *corrupt the young boy* deprave, pervert, warp, make degenerate, debauch. **3** *corrupt the atmosphere* make rotten, pollute, putrefy, taint, infect, contaminate, blight, mar. **4** *corrupt the substance* adulterate, alloy, contaminate, taint, defile, debase. **5** *corrupt the text* alter, tamper with, falsify, doctor.

corruption *noun* **1** *officials involved in corruption* bribery, bribing, subornation, extortion, jobbery, dishonesty, crookedness, fraud, fraudulence, unscrupulousness, shadiness, profiteering, criminality, villainy, venality; *inf.* graft. **2** *found guilty of moral corruption* immorality, depravity, vice, wickedness, evil, sin, iniquity, turpitude, degeneracy, perversion, dissolution, debauchery, decadence, lasciviousness, lewdness, lechery, impurity. **3** *corruption of the atmosphere* pollution, contamination. *See* CORRUPT *verb* 3. **4** *corruption of the substance* adulteration, debasement. *See* CORRUPT *verb* 4. **5** *text corruptions* alteration, falsification.

corsair *noun* pirate, buccaneer, marauder, raider, plunderer, freebooter.

corset *noun* girdle, panty girdle, belt, foundation garment, foundation, support garment, corselet, stays.

cortège *noun* **1** *a funeral cortège* procession, column, file, line, parade, cavalcade. **2** *the prince and his cortège* retinue, entourage, train; attendants.

cosmetic *noun* *apply cosmetics* beauty product, beauty aid, bit of make-up. *See* MAKE-UP 1.

cosmetic *adjective* **1** *a cosmetic product* make-up, beauty, beautifying. **2** *a purely cosmetic improvement* superficial, surface, touching-up. **3** *cosmetic surgery* beautifying, improving, non-essential, non-medical.

cosmic *adjective* **1** *cosmic laws* universal, worldwide. **2** *cosmic rays/dust* in/from space, occurring in space. **3** *disasters of cosmic proportion* vast, huge, immense, enormous, immeasurable, measureless, infinite, limitless.

cosmonaut *noun* astronaut, spaceman, spacewoman. *See table at* PILOT.

cosmopolitan *adjective* **1** *a cosmopolitan city/cosmopolitan influences* international, multiracial, universal, global, worldwide. **2** *a cosmopolitan attitude* liberal, broad-minded, unprejudiced, sophisticated, urbane, worldly, wordly-wise, well-travelled, jet-setting, globetrotting, unprovincial, cultivated, cultured.
Opposites PROVINCIAL; PAROCHIAL; UNSOPHISTICATED.

cost *verb* **1** *the book costs £30* be priced at, sell for, be valued at, fetch, come to, amount to; *inf.* set one back. **2** *valuers costing the goods* price, value, put a price on, estimate the cost/price of, evaluate. **3** *tragedy costing lives* | *work costing effort* involve, result in, lead to, involve the loss/expense/sacrifice of, necessitate. **4** *it cost them dear* do a disservice to, harm, hurt, injure, damage.

cost *noun* **1** *the cost of the house/holiday* price, asking price, selling price, charge, amount, value, valuation, quotation, rate, worth, payment, expenditure, expense, outlay; *inf.* damage. **2** *the cost in lives* | *work done at great cost* sacrifice, expense, loss, penalty, suffering, harm, hurt, injury, damage, deprivation, detriment.

costly *adjective* **1** *a costly house* expensive, dear, high-cost, high-priced, valuable, exorbitant, extortionate, extravagant; *inf.* steep. **2** *a costly victory* ruinous, catastrophic, disastrous, sacrificial, damaging, harmful, loss-making, deleterious, pyrrhic, Cadmean.
Opposites CHEAP; INEXPENSIVE.

costs *plural noun* expenses, outgoings; expenditure, money spent.

costume *noun* **1** *dressed in national costume* style of dress, dress, fashion, clothing, attire, apparel, garb, ensemble, outfit, uniform, livery, habit; clothes, garments, robes; *inf.* get-up, gear, togs. **2** *a woman in a green costume* suit, outfit, ensemble.

cosy *adjective* snug, comfortable, warm, homelike, homely, sheltered, secure, safe, at ease; *inf.* comfy, snug as a bug.
Opposites UNCOMFORTABLE.

coterie *noun* clique, set, crowd, circle, gang, club, community, league, alliance, faction, cabal.

cottage *noun* *a country cottage* | *a holiday cottage* cabin, chalet, shack; *Scots* but and ben.

couch *noun* *a couch and matching chairs* settee, settle, sofa, chaise longue; ottoman, day bed. *See table at* CHAIR.

couch *verb* *couched in loving terms* express, phrase, word, say, state, utter, set forth, frame, style.

cough *verb* *cough noisily* hack, hawk, clear one's throat, hem, bark.

cough *noun* *coughs and sneezes* hack, hawking, hem, bark; *inf.* frog/tickle in one's throat.

council *noun* **1** *the town council* local authority, governing body, parliament, cabinet, chamber, ministry. **2** *the design council* advisory body, board, board of directors, committee, assembly, panel, trustees, synod, diet, convocation. **3** *the committee is in council* conference, conclave, assembly, convocation; meeting, gathering.

counsel *noun* **1** *seek expert counsel* advice, guidance, direction, recommendation, information; opinion, suggestion, warning, admonition, caution. **2** *hold counsel with a friend* consultation, discussion, conference, deliberation, dialogue. **3** *counsel handling his case* barrister, advocate, attorney.

counsel *verb counsel him against going* advise, give guidance/direction, guide, direct, recommend, give one's opinion/suggestions, warn, admonish, caution.

counsellor *noun* adviser, guidance counsellor, director, mentor, confidant, guide.

count *verb* **1** *count the numbers* add up, total, sum up, calculate, tot up, compute, reckon up, enumerate, tally, cast up. **2** *count the people* keep a count of, count off, enumerate, tell, keep a tally of. **3** *counting everyone* include, take into account/consideration, number among, embrace, embody. **4** *count himself lucky* consider, think, regard, look upon, hold, judge, rate, deem, esteem. **5** *his presence does not count* matter, enter into consideration, be of account, signify, carry weight, weigh, mean anything, amount to anything, rate, tell; *inf.* cut any ice, have any clout. **count on/upon** rely on, depend on, lean on, bank on, trust, believe in, put/pin one's faith in, swear by, take for granted, take on trust. **count out** exclude, disregard, leave out, ignore, except, pass over, neglect.

count *noun* **1** *after the election count* counting, enumeration, calculation, computation, telling, tally, tallying, totting up, poll. **2** *the pollen count* total number, total, sum/grand total, amount, full amount, aggregate, whole, tally, reckoning.

countenance *noun* **1** *angry countenance* face, features, facial expression, expression, look, appearance, aspect, air, complexion, visage, physiognomy; *lit.* mien. **2** *not give countenance to the plan* support, backing, encouragement, endorsement, assistance, aid, approval, sanction, approbation, favour, acceptance, adoption, advocacy. **3** *lose countenance* composure, calmness, coolness, poise, self-possession, self-control, level-headedness, cool-headedness, equanimity, equilibrium; *inf.* one's cool.

countenance *verb* **1** *cannot countenance such behaviour* tolerate, approve, put up with, permit, allow, endure, brook; *inf.* stand for. **2** *countenance him in his project* encourage, support, back, help, aid, assist, champion, abet, take the side of, sanction, condone, endorse, warrant.

counter *noun* **1** *drinks on the counter* top, horizontal surface; worktop, working top, work surface, table, checkout, stand. **2** *game counters* token, disc, piece, man, marker, wafer.

counter *adverb* *run counter to expectation* against, in opposition to, contrary to, at variance with, in defiance of, in the reverse/wrong direction, against the tide, contrarily, contrariwise, conversely.

counter *adjective* *a counter-attack* opposing, opposed, opposite, contrary, adverse, conflicting, contradictory, contrasting, obverse.

counter *verb counter the attack* oppose, resist, rebut, combat, dispute, argue against, parry, hit back at, contradict, retaliate, ward off.

counteract *verb* **1** *counteract the attack* act against, act counter to, hinder, oppose, thwart, frustrate, foil, impede, check, restrain, resist, withstand, defeat. **2** *counteract the effects* counterbalance, offset, neutralize, annul, negate, invalidate, countervail, counterpoise.

counterbalance *verb* balance, equalize, compensate for, make up for, neutralize, offset, set off, undo, countervail, counterpoise.

counterfeit *adjective counterfeit money* fake, faked, copied, forged, imitation, feigned, simulated, fraudulent, sham, spurious, bogus, ersatz; *inf.* phoney, pseud, pseudo. **Opposites** GENUINE; AUTHENTIC.

counterfeit *noun not the original, a counterfeit* fake, copy, forgery, reproduction, imitation, fraud, sham; *inf.* phoney.

counterfeit *verb counterfeit money* fake, copy, reproduce, imitate, simulate, feign, falsify, sham.

countermand *verb* cancel, annul, revoke, rescind, reverse, repeal, retract, abrogate, quash, override, invalidate.

counterpart *noun* equivalent, equal, opposite number, parallel, complement, match, twin, mate, fellow, analogue, correlative, copy, duplicate.

countless *adjective* innumerable, incalculable, immeasurable, endless, limitless, without end/limit, boundless, infinite, inexhaustible, untold, legion, myriad, no end of/to.

country *noun* **1** *countries at war* nation, state, sovereign state, kingdom, realm, people, community, commonwealth. See table. **2** *his country right or wrong* native land, homeland, fatherland, motherland, mother country, land of one's birth; one's roots. **3** *driving through rough country* terrain, land, territory; region, area, district, part, neighbourhood; parts; *inf.* neck of the woods. **4** *voted in by the country* people, nation, public, population, populace, community, citizenry; inhabitants, residents, citizens, electors, voters, grass roots. **5** *live in the country, not the city* countryside, rural area/district, farmland, greenbelt, great outdoors; *Austral.* outback, bush; *derog.* provinces, backwoods, sticks, wilds, back of beyond, wilderness, middle of nowhere; *Am. inf.* boondocks.

country *adjective* rural, agrarian, agricultural, rustic, provincial, pastoral, Arcadian, bucolic; *lit.* georgic, sylvan.

countryman, countrywoman *noun* **1** *meet a fellow countryman abroad* compatriot, fellow citizen. **2** *countrymen and countrywomen at market* country dweller, farmer, farmhand, rustic, peasant, provincial; *derog.* yokel, bumpkin, bogtrotter; *dial.* hind; *Am. inf.* hayseed, hick.

countryside *noun* **1** *surrounded by beautiful countryside* landscape, scenery; scene, panorama, view, prospect, vista. **2** *living in the countryside* country, rural area/district, farmland. See COUNTRY *noun* 5.

county *noun the southern counties* shire, province, region, territory, administrative unit.

county *adjective county types* aristocratic, landowning, gentry, upper-class, tweedy; *inf.* upper

COUNTRIES OF THE WORLD

Country	Capital City	Country	Capital City
Afghanistan	Kabul	Guatemala	Guatemala City
Albania	Tirana	Guinea	Conakry
Algeria	Algiers	Guinea-Bissau	Bissau
Andorra	Andorra la Vella	Guyana	Georgetown
Angola	Luanda	Haiti	Port-au-Prince
Antigua and Barbuda	St John's	Honduras	Tegucigalpa
Argentina	Buenos Aires	Hungary	Budapest
Armenia	Yerevan	Iceland	Reykjavik
Aruba	Oranjestad	India	New Delhi
Australia	Canberra	Indonesia	Djakarta
Austria	Vienna	Iran	Tehran
Azerbaijan	Baku	Iraq	Baghdad
Bahamas, the	Nassau	Ireland	Dublin
Bahrain	Manama	Israel	Jerusalem
Bangladesh	Dhaka	Italy	Rome
Barbados	Bridgetown	Ivory Coast	Yamoussoukro
Belarus	Minsk	Jamaica	Kingston
Belgium	Brussels	Japan	Tokyo
Belize	Belmopan	Jordan	Amman
Benin	Porto Novo	Kazakhstan	Almaty (will transfer to Akmola in 2000)
Bhutan	Thimphu		
Bolivia	La Paz	Kenya	Nairobi
Bosnia-Herzegovina	Sarajevo	Kiribati	Bairiki
Botswana	Gaborone	Korea, North	Pyongyang
Brazil	Brasilia	Korea, South	Seoul
Brunei	Bandar Seri Begawan	Kuwait	Kuwait City
Bulgaria	Sofia	Kyrgyzstan	Bishkek
Burkina Faso	Ouagadougou	Laos	Vientiane
Burundi	Bujumbura	Latvia	Riga
Cambodia	Phnom Penh	Lebanon	Beirut
Cameroon	Yaoundé	Lesotho	Maseru
Canada	Ottawa	Liberia	Monrovia
Cape Verde Islands	Praia	Libya	Tripoli
Central African Republic	Bangui	Liechtenstein	Vaduz
Chad	N'Djamena	Lithuania	Vilnius
Chile	Santiago	Luxembourg	Luxembourg
China	Beijing/Peking	Macedonia, Former Yugoslav Republic of	Skopje
Colombia	Bogota	Madagascar	Antananarivo
Comoros	Moroni	Malawi	Lilongwe
Congo	Brazzaville	Malaysia	Kuala Lumpur
Costa Rica	San José	Maldives	Male
Croatia	Zagreb	Mali	Bamako
Cuba	Havana	Malta	Valletta
Cyprus	Nicosia	Marshall Islands	Majuro
Czech Republic	Prague	Mauritania	Nouakchott
Denmark	Copenhagen	Mauritius	Port Louis
Djibouti	Djibouti	Mexico	Mexico City
Dominica	Roseau	Micronesia	Kolonia
Dominican Republic	Santo Domingo	Moldova	Chişinău
Ecuador	Quito	Monaco	–
Egypt	Cairo	Mongolia	Ulan Bator
El Salvador	San Salvador	Montenegro	Podgorica
Equatorial Guinea	Malabo	Morocco	Rabat
Eritrea	Asmara	Mozambique	Maputo
Estonia	Tallinn	Myanmar	Rangoon/Yangon
Ethiopia	Addis Ababa	Namibia	Windhoek
Fiji	Suva	Nauru	–
Finland	Helsinki	Nepal	Kathmandu
France	Paris	Netherlands, the	Amsterdam
Gabon	Libreville	New Zealand	Wellington
Gambia, the	Banjul	Nicaragua	Managua
Georgia	Tbilisi	Niger	Niamey
Germany	Berlin	Nigeria	Abuja
Ghana	Accra	Norway	Oslo
Greece	Athens	Oman	Muscat
Grenada	St George's		

COUNTRIES OF THE WORLD *cont.*			
Country	**Capital City**	**Country**	**Capital City**
Pakistan	Islamabad	Swaziland	Mbabane
Palau	Koror	Sweden	Stockholm
Panama	Panama City	Switzerland	Berne
Papua New Guinea	Port Moresby	Syria	Damascus
Paraguay	Asunción	Taiwan	Taipei
Peru	Lima	Tajikistan	Dushanbe
Philippines	Manila	Tanzania	Dodoma
Poland	Warsaw	Thailand	Bangkok
Portugal	Lisbon	Togo	Lomé
Qatar	Doha	Tonga	Nuku'alofa
Romania	Bucharest	Trinidad and Tobago	Port of Spain
Russia	Moscow	Tunisia	Tunis
Rwanda	Kigali	Turkey	Ankara
St Kitts and Nevis	Basseterre	Turkmenistan	Ashgabat
St Lucia	Castries	Tuvalu	Funafuti
St Vincent and the		Uganda	Kampala
Grenadines	Kingstown	Ukraine	Kiev
San Marino	San Marino	United Arab Emirates	Abu Dhabi
São Tomé and Principe	São Tomé	U.K.	London
Saudi Arabia	Riyadh	U.S.A.	Washington D.C.
Senegal	Dakar	Uruguay	Montevideo
Serbia	Belgrade	Uzbekistan	Tashkent
Seychelles, the	Victoria	Vanuatu	Vila
Sierra Leone	Freetown	Vatican City	—
Singapore	Singapore	Venezuela	Caracas
Slovakia	Bratislava	Vietnam	Hanoi
Slovenia	Ljubljana	Western Samoa	Apia
Solomon Islands	Honiara	Yemen	Sana'a
Somalia	Mogadishu	Yugoslavia (see Serbia,	
South Africa	Pretoria	Montenegro, etc.)	
Spain	Madrid	Zaire	Kinshasa
Sri Lanka	Colombo	Zambia	Lusaka
Sudan	Khartoum	Zimbabwe	Harare
Suriname	Paramaribo		

crust, up-market, top-drawer, huntin',
shootin', fishin'.

coup *noun* **1** *pull off the coup of getting the pop
star to attend* successful action/act, feat, master-
stroke, deed, accomplishment, stroke, stroke
of genius, manoeuvre, stratagem, stunt, *tour de
force.* **2** *a coup in a South American country* overthrow, seizure of power, *coup d'état,* violent
change, revolt, revolution, rebellion, mutiny,
insurgence.

couple *noun* *an established couple* pair, duo, twosome, dyad, brace, span; partners, lovers, husband and wife, cohabitees. **a couple of 1** *a
couple of drinks* two, two or three, a few, a small
number of. **2** *a couple of men* two, a pair.

couple *verb* **1** *couple the joints* join, fasten,
attach, connect, unite, hitch together, fuse,
weld, bind, buckle, clasp, conjoin, marry.
2 *their names coupled together* join, link, associate, connect, ally. **3** *lovers coupling* copulate,
have sex/intercourse, have sexual relations,
make love, fornicate.

coupon *noun* **1** *petrol coupon* voucher, token,
ticket, slip, certificate, stub, detachable portion. **2** *fill in the coupon* form, entry/applica-
tion form.

courage *noun* bravery, valour, gallantry, heroism, fearlessness, intrepidity, lion-heartedness,
stout-heartedness, pluck, nerve, grit, boldness,
daring, audacity, dauntlessness, hardihood,
mettle, fortitude, firmness, resolution, tenacity, determination; *inf.* bottle, spunk, guts.
Opposites COWARDICE; FEAR.

courageous *adjective* brave, valiant, valorous,
gallant, heroic, fearless, intrepid, lion-hearted,
plucky, bold, daring, audacious, dauntless,
mettlesome, firm, resolute, tenacious, determined, indomitable.

courier *noun* **1** *send the parcel/information by
courier* messenger, special messenger, dispatch
rider, letter-carrier, mail-carrier, bearer, conveyor, envoy, emissary, harbinger, herald.
2 *the courier took them round the palace* guide,
tour guide/director, dragoman.

course *noun* **1** *the course of history* progression,
progress, advance, advancement, rise, march,
furtherance, proceeding, development, unfolding, flow, movement, continuity, sequence,
order, succession. **2** *go a bit off course* route,
way, track, direction, tack, path, line, lane,
road, passage, channel, trail, trajectory, orbit,
circuit, ambit. **3** *pursue a different course of
action* method, way, line of action, process,
procedure, manner, mode of behaviour/con-
duct, plan, system, policy, programme, regimen. **4** *in the course of an hour* duration,
passing, passage, lapse, period, term, span,
spell, sweep. **5** *taking an English course* course
of study, set of lectures, curriculum, programme, schedule; classes, lectures, studies.

6 *a course of treatment* sequence, series, system, regimen. **7** *a waterlogged course* racecourse, track, circuit, ground. **in due course** in time, at the appropriate time, in the course of time, when the time is ripe, sooner or later, in the end, eventually. **of course** naturally, obviously, certainly, definitely, undoubtedly, without a doubt, indubitably.

course *verb* **1** *blood coursing* flow, move, run, rush, surge, gush, race, hurry, speed, charge, dash. **2** *coursing hares* hunt, pursue, chase, follow, run after, track.

court *noun* **1** *appear in court* court of law, lawcourt, bench, bar, court of justice, justiciary, tribunal, forum, chancery, assizes. **2** *the queen's court* royal household, retinue, entourage, train, suite, cortège; attendants. **3** *situated near the queen's court* royal residence, palace, castle, manor, hall, chateau. **4** *monarch holding court* assembly, reception. **5** *paying court to the young lady* attention, homage, deference, suit, wooing, courtship; respects, addresses, blandishments. **6** *walking in the castle court* courtyard, quadrangle, square, cloister, esplanade, patio, piazza, plaza; *inf.* quad. **7** *tennis/squash court* playing area/enclosure, game area/enclosure, arena.

court *verb* **1** *he's courting her sister* pay court to, woo, pursue, chase, run after, set one's cap at, pay addresses to, pay suit to. **2** *the couple are courting* go out, go out together, go with each other, go steady, date, keep company. **3** *court the manager* curry favour with, cultivate, try to win over, pander to, fawn upon, toady to, wheedle; *inf.* soft-soap, butter up, bootlick. **4** *court fame* seek, solicit, ask for, crave. **5** *court disaster* invite, risk, provoke, lead to, cause, bring on, elicit.

courteous *adjective* polite, well-mannered, mannerly, civil, chivalrous, gallant, gracious, kind, considerate, pleasant, tactful, diplomatic, politic, cordial, genial, affable, respectful, deferential, well-bred, polished, refined, civilized, urbane.
Opposites DISCOURTEOUS; RUDE.

courtesan *noun* prostitute, harlot, whore, woman of ill repute, street-walker, call-girl, strumpet, lady of the night, *fille de joie.*

courtesy *noun* **1** *have the courtesy to wait* politeness, civility, courteousness, chivalry, gallantry, gallantness, good breeding, gentility, graciousness, kindness, consideration, tact, cordiality, respect, respectfulness, deference, decorousness, refinement, urbanity, courtliness, elegance; good manners, manners. **2** *the outing by courtesy of the firm* kindness, generosity, benevolence, indulgence, favour, consideration, consent, permission.

courtier *noun* attendant, henchman, follower; lady-in-waiting, page, squire, cup-bearer, trainbearer, liegeman.

courtly *adjective* polite, well-mannered, civil, courteous, chivalrous, gallant, gentlemanly, ladylike, aristocratic, well-bred, dignified, decorous, formal, ceremonious, stately, proper, polished, refined, cultivated, urbane, elegant, suave, debonair.

courtship *noun* **1** *his courtship of her* courting, wooing, pursuit, suit. See COURT *verb* 1. **2** *married after a long courtship* romance, affair, love affair, going steady, dating, keeping company.

courtyard *noun* quadrangle, square, cloister, esplanade, court. See COURT *noun* 6.

cove[1] *noun* *a sandy cove* bay, inlet, bight, creek, sound, anchorage; *Scots* firth, frith.

cove[2] *noun* *a funny cove* man, fellow; *inf.* chap, bloke, guy.

covenant *noun* *sign a covenant* contract, guarantee, agreement, bond, deed, warrant, pledge, promise, indenture, trust, commitment, compact, bargain, pact, arrangement, deal, treaty, concordat, convention.

covenant *verb* *covenant £100 to the school* pledge, promise, settle, contract, guarantee, engage, agree on, undertake.

cover *verb* **1** *a pile of earth covering potatoes* place over, place under cover, protect, shield, shelter, conceal, hide, house, secrete, bury. **2** *snow covering the fields* overlay, overspread, blanket, carpet, overlie, extend over, coat, layer, film, mantle, pave, submerge. **3** *girls covered in silk* clothe, attire, outfit, garb, robe, wrap, accoutre, swaddle, encase, sheathe. **4** *cover all the entrances* protect, defend, guard, shield, safeguard. **5** *cover several fields* include, deal with, contain, take in, comprise, involve, provide for, embrace, embody, incorporate, subsume, refer to, consider, examine, review, survey, take stock of. **6** *journalists covering the trial* report, write up, describe, tell of, give an account of, give details of, investigate. **7** *doctors covering for each other* relieve, act/double/substitute for, take over from, replace, stand/fill in for, take someone's place. **8** *the thief's sister covering for him* give an alibi to, provide with an alibi, alibi, shield, protect. **9** *money to cover expenses* be enough for, offset, balance, counterbalance, compensate for, make up for. **10** *cover against fire* insure, provide for, indemnify, protect. **11** *cover 30 miles | cover the ground rapidly* travel, travel/pass over, traverse, cross, range/tramp over. **cover up 1** *trying to cover up the mistake/scandal* conceal, hide, keep secret, hush up, keep dark, suppress, stonewall; *inf.* whitewash. **2** *cover up the potatoes* cover, place under cover, protect, shield, shelter. See COVER *verb* 1. **3** *cover yourself up* put on more clothes, dress, wrap up, swathe.
Opposites UNCOVER; EXPOSE; EXCLUDE.

cover *noun* **1** *take cover from the storm* covering, protection, shield, shelter, concealment, housing, refuge, sanctuary, haven, hiding-place. **2** *the jam-pot cover* lid, top, cap, covering. **3** *a cover of dust/snow* layer, coat, coating, film, blanket, overlay, carpet, mantle, canopy, crust. **4** *the business is a cover for spying* cover-up, disguise, front, camouflage, pretence, façade, pretext, false front, screen, smokescreen, mask, cloak, veil, window-dressing. **5** *the artillery providing cover for the infantry* protection, defence, guard, shield. **6** *provide cover for the doctor* relief, replacement, stand-in, substitute, locum. **7** *a policy giving cover against fire* insurance, protection, compensation, indemnification, indemnity. **8** *the covers of the* book jacket, dust jacket, wrapper, binding. **9** *under plain cover* envelope, wrapper, package; wrapping, packaging. **10** *gamebirds in cover* undergrowth, woods, shrubbery, thicket, copse. **11** *pull up the covers* bedclothes, sheets, blankets; bedcover, duvet, bedspread.

coverage *noun news coverage* reporting, reportage; reports, accounts, articles, pieces, stories.

covering *noun* **1** *provide covering for the children* cover, protection, shelter, housing. See COVER *noun* 1. **2** *a covering of dust/snow* layer, coat, coating, film, blanket, carpet. See COVER *noun* 3. **3** *the boiler covering* casing, case, wrapping, sheath, sheathing, jacket, housing.

covering *adjective a covering letter* accompanying, explanatory, introductory.

coverlet *noun* bedspread, bedcover, counterpane, eiderdown, quilt.

covert *adjective* secret, concealed, hidden, surreptitious, furtive, stealthy, private, underground.
Opposites OVERT; OPEN.

covet *verb* desire, want, wish for, long/yearn for, crave, hanker/lust after, thirst for, hunger after, set one's heart on, aspire to, aim after, envy, begrudge.

covetous *adjective covetous of her sister's house* desirous of, wanting, craving, yearning/longing for, greedy for, envious of. See COVET.

cow *noun* **1** *cows and pigs* bovine, heifer. See tables at CATTLE. **2** *what a cow!* bitch, minx, vixen, slut.

cow *verb teachers cowing the pupils* intimidate, overawe, awe, daunt, dismay, subdue, scare, frighten, petrify, terrorize, unnerve, browbeat, bully, domineer, bulldoze.

coward *noun* poltroon, craven, dastard, recreant, renegade; *inf.* chicken, scaredy-cat, funk, yellow-belly, sissy, big baby.

cowardly *adjective* lily-livered, faint-hearted, chicken-hearted, craven, base, spineless, timorous, timid, fearful, shrinking, pusillanimous, dastardly, afraid of one's shadow; *inf.* chicken, yellow, weak-kneed, gutless, yellow-bellied.
Opposites BRAVE; COURAGEOUS.

cowboy *noun* **1** *cowboys herding cattle* cowhand, cowman, cattleman, cowherd, herd, herdsman, drover, stockman, rancher, ranchero; *Am. inf.* cowpuncher, cowpoke, broncobuster; gaucho. **2** *the builders were cowboys* scoundrel, rogue, rascal, unscrupulous/irresponsible operator.

cower *verb* cringe, shrink, flinch, draw back, recoil, crouch, slink, wince, blench, quail, quake, tremble, quiver, grovel.

coy *adjective* arch, coquettish, flirtatious, kittenish, skittish, shy, modest, bashful, reticent, diffident, retiring, backward, self-effacing, shrinking, withdrawn, timid, demure, prudish, unconfident, lacking confidence, unsure.
Opposites BOLD; BRAZEN; IMPUDENT.

cozen *verb* cheat, deceive, beguile, trick, double-cross, swindle, take advantage of, play one false.

crabbed *adjective* **1** *a crabbed old man* crabby, bad-tempered, ill-tempered, ill-natured, ill-humoured, cross, cantankerous, crotchety, irritable, touchy, testy, grouchy, snappy, prickly, crusty, peevish, churlish, surly, sour, morose, acrimonious, captious, waspish, perverse, difficult, trying. **2** *crabbed handwriting* cramped, squeezed, scribbled, laboured, illegible, unreadable, indecipherable, hieroglyphical.

crabby *adjective* cross, bad-tempered, surly, grouchy, discontented. See CRABBED 1.

crack *verb* **1** *crack the cup* chip, fracture, fragment, break, chop, split, splinter, snap, cleave, craze. **2** *the rifle cracked* ring out, go bang, pop, snap, crackle, boom, explode, detonate. **3** *crack his head on a beam* hit, bang, bump, strike, knock, smack, whack, thump; *inf.* wallop, clout, clip. **4** *crack under questioning* give way, break down, collapse, go to pieces, lose control, yield, succumb, founder; *inf.* fall/come apart at the seams. **5** *crack the problem* solve, work out, get the answer to, find the solution to, fathom, decipher. **6** *crack a bottle* open, uncork, broach, drink. **crack up** break down, have a breakdown, collapse, go to pieces, lose control, go out of one's mind, go mad; *inf.* fall/come apart at the seams, go crazy, freak out.

crack *noun* **1** *a crack in the cup/wall* chip, fracture, break, split, crevice, fissure, chink, gap, cavity, breach, rift, rupture, cleft, slit, cranny, interstice. **2** *the crack of the gun* bang, report, pop, snap, crackle, boom, explosion, detonation. **3** *get a crack on the head* blow, hit, bang, bump, strike, knock, smack, whack, thump; *inf.* wallop, clout, clip. **4** *another crack at the competition* attempt, try, shot, opportunity; *inf.* go, stab. **5** *laugh at his cracks* joke, funny remark, quip, witticism, wisecrack, gag, jibe, satirical remark, insult; *inf.* dig.

crack *adjective a crack tennis-player/crack shot* expert, first-rate, first-class, excellent, brilliant, elite, choice, superior; *inf.* ace, A1.

cracked *adjective* **1** *cracked cups/walls* chipped, fractured, broken, split, splintered, damaged, defective, flawed, imperfect, crazed. **2** *he seems a bit cracked* mad, insane, out of one's mind, touched, crazed, crack-brained; *inf.* crazy, nuts, nutty, bats, batty, crackpot, off one's head/nut, round the bend/twist, loony, not the full shilling/pound.

crackle *verb* crack, crepitate, decrepitate, snap.

cradle *noun* **1** *babies sleeping in cradles* crib, bassinet, Moses' basket, cot, carry-cot. **2** *the cradle of democracy* birthplace, fount, fountainhead, source, place of origin, wellspring, beginning, breeding-place, nursery; origins, beginnings.

cradle *verb cradle the baby/cradle his head in her arms* hold, rock, nestle, shelter, support.

craft *noun* **1** *admire the artist's craft* skill, skilfulness, expertise, expertness, ability, mastery, artistry, art, technique, workmanship, aptitude, dexterity, talent, flair, knack, cleverness, genius; *inf.* know-how. **2** *use craft to get his way* craftiness, cunning, artfulness, artifice, scheming, guile, subterfuge, stratagem, slyness, wiliness, shrewdness, trickery, duplicity, deceit; wiles, ruses. **3** *take up a new craft* occupation, trade, vocation, calling, pursuit, business, line, work, employment. **4** *pilot a craft* vessel, ship, boat, aircraft, plane, spacecraft.

craftsman, craftswoman *noun* master, expert, skilled worker, dedicated/meticulous worker, artist, artificer, artisan, technician, maker, smith, wright.

craftsmanship *noun* workmanship, technique, artistry, expertise, skill, mastery.

crafty *adjective* cunning, artful, scheming, designing, calculating, wily, sly, devious, guileful, tricky, foxy, shrewd, astute, canny, sharp, duplicitous, deceitful, subtle, insidious, treacherous, crooked, fraudulent, underhand, underhanded.
Opposites NAIVE; HONEST; INGENUOUS.

crag *noun* cliff, bluff, escarpment, scarp, ridge, peak, pinnacle, tor.

cram *verb* **1** *cram clothes into the suitcase* stuff, push/shove/force into, pack in, ram down, press into, squeeze/jam/crush into, compress, compact, condense. **2** *cram the baskets | a bus crammed with people* stuff, overfill, fill, fill up, fill to overflowing, stuff to the gills, fill to the brim, overcrowd. **3** *cram for exams* study, revise, grind, grind away; *inf.* swot, swot/mug up.

cramp *verb* *cramp one's progress/style* restrict, limit, hamper, hinder, impede, hamstring, constrain, check, arrest, bridle, handicap, inhibit, thwart, stymie, obstruct, restrain, confine, shackle, encumber, clog.

cramp *noun* *suffer from cramp* muscular contraction, muscle spasm, pang, twinge, pain, shooting pain, ache, crick, stiffness, convulsion.

cramped *adjective* **1** *cramped accommodation* narrow, small, restricted, limited, confined, uncomfortable, closed in, hemmed in, tight, crowded, overfull, packed, squeezed, jammed in, congested. **2** *cramped handwriting* close, tightly packed, small, squeezed, crabbed, illegible, unreadable, indecipherable.

crane *noun* derrick, winch, hoist, davit, windlass, tackle.

cranium *noun* skull, head, crown; *inf.* brainpan, noddle, nut.

crank¹ *noun* *pedals attached to a crank* lever, arm, bar, shaft, spindle, crankshaft.

crank² *verb* **1** *crank an engine* start, turn over, get going, rev, rev up. **2** *crank up production* speed up, accelerate, hasten, hurry up, increase, improve.

crank³ *noun* *a fitness crank* eccentric, oddity, character, fanatic, zealot, maniac, enthusiast, devotee, fan, buff; *inf.* nut.

cranky *adjective* **1** *a cranky old man | a cranky diet* eccentric, unconventional, odd, peculiar, queer, strange, bizarre, idiosyncratic, quirky, freakish, freaky, obsessive, fanatical; *inf.* funny, wacky. **2** *a cranky teacher* bad-tempered, cross, crabby.

cranny *noun* chink, crack, crevice, slit, split, fissure, rift, cleft, opening, gap, cavity, hole, nook, interstice.

crash *verb* **1** *the sea crashed against the rocks | the glass crashed on the floor* smash, batter, dash, shatter, break, disintegrate, shiver, splinter, fracture, fragment. **2** *the cymbals crashed* clash, clang, clank, clatter, bang, smash, boom, thunder, explode. **3** *the trees crashed to the ground* fall, topple, tumble, overbalance, pitch, plunge, hurtle, lurch. **4** *the car crashed into the van* bump/run/drive/bang into, collide with, hit, hurtle/smash/plough into, jolt, jar. **5** *crash the car* smash, wreck, bump; *inf.* write off. **6** *the business crashed* collapse, fail, fold, fold up, go under, smash, founder, be ruined, cave in; *inf.* go broke/bust, come a cropper, go to the wall. **7** *crash the party* gatecrash, come uninvited to, intrude, sneak/slip into, invade; *inf.* horn in on.

crash *noun* **1** *the crash of crockery/cymbals* clash, clank, clang, clatter, bang, smash, clangour, racket, din, boom, thunder, explosion. **2** *involved in a crash* accident, smash, smash-up, collision, pile-up, bump, bang, thud; *inf.* prang. **3** *lost money in the crash* collapse, failure, bankruptcy, fold, smash, fall, ruin, ruination, downfall, depression, debacle.

crash *adjective* *a crash course/diet* intensive, concentrated, telescoped, rapid, urgent.

crass *adjective* **1** *don't be so crass* stupid, insensitive, blundering, dense, thick, doltish, oafish, boorish, asinine, coarse, gross, vulgar, crude, rude, uncouth, unsophisticated, unrefined. **2** *crass ignorance* gross, utter, downright, out-and-out, very great, complete, blatant, glaring, undisguised, naked.

crate *noun* box, case, packing case, tea chest, basket, hamper, container, receptacle.

crater *noun* hole, hollow, depression, dip, cavity, chasm.

crave *verb* **1** *crave a chocolate* long/yearn for, desire, want, wish for, hanker after, need, require, hunger/thirst for, be dying for, cry out for, lust after, pant for, be panting for, pine/sigh for; *inf.* fancy, have a yen for. **2** *crave pardon* ask for, plead/beg for, seek, entreat, beseech, implore, petition, pray for, solicit/sue for, supplicate.

craven *adjective* cowardly, chicken-hearted, lily-livered, faint-hearted, timorous, fearful, timid, base, pusillanimous, dastardly, recreant, poltroon; *inf.* chicken, yellow.

craving *noun* longing, yearning, desire, hankering, need, urge, hunger, thirst, lust, appetite, addiction, *cacoethes*; *inf.* yen.

crawl *verb* creep, go on all fours, move on hands and knees, inch, drag/pull oneself along, drag, trail, slither, squirm, wriggle, writhe, worm one's way, advance slowly/stealthily, sneak.

craze *noun* fad, vogue, trend, fashion, enthusiasm, passion, infatuation, obsession, mania, fixation, fancy, novelty, whim, fascination, preoccupation, rage; *inf.* thing, the latest.

crazed *adjective* insane, mad, wild, unbalanced, crazy. *See* CRAZY 1.

crazy *adjective* **1** *a crazy person* crazed, of unsound mind, insane, mad, mad as a hatter, mad as a March hare, lunatic, idiotic, wild, unbalanced, demented, deranged, berserk, unhinged, touched, maniacal, delirious, out of one's mind/head; *inf.* cracked, daft, bats, batty, loony, barmy, nuts, nutty, nutty as a fruit cake, cuckoo, bonkers, potty, mental, not all there, a bit lacking, round the bend/twist. **2** *a crazy idea* absurd, idiotic, stupid, silly, ridiculous, foolish, peculiar, odd, strange, queer, weird, eccentric, bizarre, fantastic, outrageous, wild, fatuous, inane, puerile, impracticable, senseless, unworkable, foolhardy, unrealistic, unwise, imprudent, ill-conceived, preposterous; *inf.* potty, cock-eyed, half-baked. **3** *crazy about opera* enthusiastic, mad, avid, keen, infatuated, passionate, smitten, fanatical, devoted to, fond/enamoured of, zealous, fervent, fervid, excited; *inf.* nuts on, gone on.

creak *verb* squeak, screech, squeal, groan, grate, grind, jar, rasp, scrape, scratch.

cream *noun* **1** *beauty/shoe/antiseptic cream* lotion, emulsion, emollient, paste; cosmetic, ointment, salve, unguent, liniment. **2** *the cream of the college* best/choice part, flower, elite, pick, prime, quintessence, *crème de la crème*.

cream *adjective* *a cream dress* cream-coloured, off-white, whitish, yellowish-white, buff. *See table at* COLOUR.

crease *noun* **1** *a trouser crease* ridge, furrow, groove, corrugation, fold, line, ruck, pleat, tuck. **2** *facial creases* wrinkle, line, crinkle, pucker, crow's feet.

crease *verb* **1** *the dress was creased in the journey* crumple, wrinkle, crinkle, rumple, pucker, ruck up. **2** *crease the trousers/paper* put a crease/fold in, ridge, furrow, groove, corrugate, pleat, tuck. **3** *jokes creasing them up* amuse greatly, amuse, entertain, make laugh; *inf.* make one fall about, have rolling in the aisles.

create *verb* **1** *create a new generation* bring into being/existence, give birth/life to, procreate, father, sire, beget, spawn. **2** *create a new environment* generate, originate, invent, initiate, engender, produce, design, devise, make, frame, fabricate, build, construct, erect, develop, shape, form, mould, forge, concoct, hatch. **3** *create a good impression* produce, make, result in, cause, be the cause of, bring about, give rise to, lead to. **4** *create new life peers | create a new system of government* invest, appoint, install, make, establish, found, institute, constitute, inaugurate, set up. *Opposites* DEMOLISH; DESTROY.

creation *noun* **1** *the creation of a new generation* birth, procreation, fathering, begetting, genesis, spawning. *See* CREATE 1. **2** *the creation of a new environment* generation, origination, invention, initiation, inception, design, devising, formation, production, fabrication, building, shaping, hatching. *See* CREATE 2. **3** *everything in creation* the world, the living/natural world, the universe, the cosmos, nature, life; all living things. **4** *the creation of new life peers* investing, investiture, appointment, installation, establishment, foundation, institution, inauguration. **5** *the poet's creation* work, work of art, achievement, production, opus, invention,

handiwork, masterpiece, *pièce de résistance*, *magnum opus*, *chef-d'oeuvre*. **6** *Paris creations* fashion, design, dress; clothes, hats.

creative *adjective* inventive, imaginative, original, artistic, inspired, visionary, talented, gifted, resourceful, ingenious, clever, productive, fertile.

creator *noun* **1** *praise their Creator* God, the Almighty. *See* GOD. **2** *the creator of the series* author, inventor, originator, initiator, maker, designer, producer, architect, prime mover, begetter, generator.

creature *noun* **1** *all God's creatures* living thing/entity, being. **2** *the creatures of the forest* animal, beast; *Am. inf.* critter. **3** *beautiful/poor creatures* person, human being, human, individual, character, fellow, soul, mortal; *inf.* body. **4** *the King's creature* minion, lackey, puppet, tool, hanger-on, parasite, dependant, toady, sycophant, hireling, retainer, vassal.

credence *noun* *place no credence in his statement* belief, faith, trust, confidence, reliance.

credentials *plural noun* testimonial, proof of identity/qualifications, certificate, diploma, document, warrant, licence, permit, card, voucher, passport, letter of introduction/recommendation, missive, deed, title; references; attestation, documentation.

credibility *noun* **1** *the credibility of the story* plausibility, tenability. *See* CREDIBLE 1. **2** *the government lacking credibility* acceptability, faith, trust, trustworthiness, reliability, dependability, integrity.

credible *adjective* **1** *a scarcely credible story* believable, conceivable, imaginable, plausible, tenable. **2** *the more credible party* acceptable, trustworthy, reliable, dependable. *Opposites* INCREDIBLE; UNBELIEVABLE; UNTRUSTWORTHY.

credit *verb* **1** *he couldn't credit it* believe, accept, put confidence in, trust, have faith in, rely on, depend on; *inf.* fall for, swallow, buy. **2** *credit him with the discovery* ascribe to, attribute to, assign to, accredit, give credit to, chalk up to, put down to, impute to.

credit *noun* **1** *receive credit for his performance* praise, acclaim, approval, commendation, acknowledgement, tribute, kudos, glory, recognition, regard, esteem, respect, merit, veneration, laudation; thanks. **2** *he gained credit in the city* name, reputation, repute, character, prestige, influence, standing, status, regard, esteem, estimation, acceptability, credibility; *inf.* clout. **3** *a credit to the town* source of honour/pride, feather in the cap, asset, proud boast, boast, glory, flower, gem. **4** *the story gaining credit* belief, believability, credence, faith, trust, reliability, reliance, confidence. **5** *his credit is good* financial standing/status, solvency. **on credit** *buy on credit* on hire purchase, on the HP, by instalments, by deferred payment, on account; *inf.* on tick, on the slate, on the never-never.

creditable *adjective* praiseworthy, commendable, laudable, meritorious, admirable, exemplary, worthy, up to the mark, respectable, reputable, estimable, honourable, deserving.

credulity noun credulousness, gullibility, gullibleness, naivety, naiveness, blind faith, greenness. See CREDULOUS.

credulous adjective over-trusting, over-trustful, gullible, naive, green, dupable, deceivable, unsuspicious, unsceptical, uncritical; inf. wet behind the ears.
Opposites INCREDULOUS; SCEPTICAL.

creed noun set of principles, system/statement of beliefs, profession of faith, teaching, doctrine, canon, dogma, tenet, catechism; beliefs, principles, rules, articles of faith, maxims.

creek noun boats sailing in the creek inlet, bay, cove, bight; Scots firth, frith.

creep verb 1 creeping along the ground crawl, go on all fours, move on hands and knees, inch, slither, squirm, wriggle, writhe, worm one's way, insinuate. See CRAWL. 2 creep up on them move stealthily, steal, sneak, tiptoe, approach unnoticed, slink, skulk. 3 employees creeping to the boss grovel, toady, kowtow, bow and scrape, fawn, cower, cringe, truckle; inf. suck up to, bootlick.

creep noun hate the little creep sycophant, toady, fawner, sneak; inf. bootlicker.

creeper noun trailing plant, trailer, climbing plant, climber, rambler.

creeps plural noun gave me the creeps feeling of horror/fear/terror/disgust/repulsion/revulsion.

creepy adjective a creepy film horrifying, horrific, horrible, frightening, scaring, terrifying, hair-raising, awful, disturbing, eerie, sinister, weird, nightmarish, macabre, menacing, ominous, threatening, disgusting, repellent, repulsive, revolting; inf. scary.

crescent noun shaped like a crescent half-moon, new moon, old moon, demilune, lunula, meniscus, sickle-shape.

crest noun 1 a cock's crest | the helmet crest cockscomb, comb, tuft, plume, topknot, tassel, mane, panache, aigrette; Tech. caruncle. 2 the crest of the hill summit, top, pinnacle, peak, crown, apex, ridge; heights. 3 the club crest

regalia, insignia, badge, emblem, device, coat of arms; Herald. bearing, charge.

crestfallen adjective downcast, dejected, depressed, glum, downhearted, disheartened, discouraged, dispirited, despondent, disappointed, disconsolate, in the doldrums, down in the dumps.

crevice noun fissure, cleft, chink, crack, cranny, split, rift, slit, gash, rent, fracture, opening, gap, hole, interstice.

crew noun 1 the ship's crew hands, sailors, seamen, mariners, ship's company, ship's complement. 2 the camera crew team, company, party, working party, gang, squad, force, corps, posse. 3 that peculiar crew over there crowd, lot, gang, mob, pack, horde, multitude, troop, swarm, herd, band, group, bunch, set.

crib noun 1 a baby's crib cradle, bassinet, cot, carry-cot. 2 a crib of animal fodder stall, manger, bin, box, rack, bunker, container. 3 a text crib key, translation, guide. 4 his answer is a crib of hers copy, plagiarism, plagiarization, reproduction, replica, duplication, piracy. 5 a country crib cottage, shack, hut, hovel, shanty; Scots bothy.

crib verb 1 crib someone's essay copy, plagiarize, reproduce, duplicate, pirate. 2 crib the animals enclose, shut in/up, confine, pen, coop, coop up, box in/up, hem in, fence in, rail in, corral, cage, imprison.

crick noun pain, cramp, twinge, spasm, pang; stiffness.

cricket noun. See table. See also table at SPORT.

crier noun town crier, announcer, proclaimer, herald.

crime noun 1 convicted of the crime offence, unlawful/illegal act, misdemeanour, misdeed, wrong, felony, violation, transgression, trespass, fault, injury; Law malfeasance, tort. 2 a crime against humanity sin, immoral act, evil, evil action, wrong, wrongdoing, vice, iniquity. 3 crime is on the increase lawbreaking, delinquency, wrongdoing, villainy, malefaction, ille-

CRICKETING TERMS AND EXPRESSIONS

all-rounder	crease	leg before	offside fielder	square leg
bail	cut	wicket (l.b.w.)	off spin	sticky dog
bat	daisy-cutter	leg bye	out-swinger	sticky
batsman/	deep square	leg glance	over	wicket
batswoman	leg	leg-side fielder	overthrow	stonewalling
batting crease	duck	leg slip	point	striker
beamer	fielder	leg spin	popping crease	stumped
body-line bowl-	fine leg	leg-theory	return crease	sweep
ing	flipper	bowling	reverse sweep	test match
bosie	googly	long hop	run	the covers
bouncer	golden duck	long leg	run out	the slips
boundary	gully	long off	scorer	third man
bowled	hat-trick	long on	seamer	ton
bowler	hit wicket	longstop	shooter	top-spinner
bye	hook	maiden	short leg	twelfth man
caught	how's that!/	mid-off	sight-screen	umpire
century	howzat!	mid-on	silly mid-off	wicket
chinaman	innings	mid-wicket	silly mid-on	wicketkeeper
cover	in-swinger	no-ball	silly point	wide
cow-shot	late cut	non-striker	square cut	yorker

gality, misconduct, felony, corruption, wickedness, evil; *Law* malfeasance.

criminal *adjective* **1** *a criminal act* unlawful, illegal, lawbreaking, illicit, lawless, felonious, indictable, delinquent, culpable, wrong, villainous, corrupt, evil, wicked, iniquitous, nefarious; *Law* malfeasant; *inf.* crooked, bent. **2** *a criminal waste of resources* deplorable, scandalous, preposterous, shameful, reprehensible, senseless, foolish, ridiculous, sinful, immoral. **Opposites** LAWFUL; LAW-ABIDING; COMMENDABLE.

criminal *noun* lawbreaker, offender, wrongdoer, felon, delinquent, miscreant, malefactor, culprit, villain, gangster, bandit, transgressor, sinner, trespasser; *Law* malfeasant; *inf.* crook, con, crim.

crimp *verb* **1** *crimp cloth/paper* flute, ruffle, pleat, corrugate, furrow, groove, ridge, crease, wrinkle, crinkle, crumple, pucker, gather, smock. **2** *crimp hair* wave, curl, frizz, frizzle.

cringe *verb* **1** *cringe in fear* cower, shrink, draw back, quail, flinch, recoil, start, shy, blench, dodge, duck, crouch, wince, tremble, quiver, shake. **2** *cringe to the boss* kowtow, grovel, toady/fawn to; *inf.* crawl, creep, bootlick.

crinkly *adjective* wrinkled, wrinkly, crinkled, creased, crimped, corrugated, fluted, furrowed, ridged, gathered, puckered, smocked. *See* CRIMP 1.

cripple *verb* **1** *the accident crippled him* make lame, disable, incapacitate, debilitate, impair, damage, hamstring, maim, weaken, enfeeble, paralyse. **2** *businesses crippled by the recession* damage, injure, ruin, destroy, weaken, impair, hamstring, hamper, impede, cramp, spoil, bring to a standstill, paralyse, enfeeble, vitiate.

crippled *adjective* lame, disabled, incapacitated, physically impaired/handicapped, deformed, housebound, bedridden; *inf.* laid up.

crisis *noun* **1** *the crisis of the fever | reaching a crisis* turning-point, critical/decisive point, crux, climax, climacteric, culmination, height, moment of truth, zero hour, Rubicon; *inf.* crunch. **2** *a financial crisis* emergency, disaster, catastrophe, calamity, extremity, predicament, plight, mess, trouble, difficulty, dilemma, quandary, exigency; dire straits; *inf.* fix, pickle, scrape.

crisp *adjective* **1** *crisp toast* brittle, crispy, crumbly, crunchy, breakable, friable. **2** *crisp lettuce* firm, fresh, unwilted, unwithered. **3** *crisp weather* brisk, bracing, fresh, refreshing, invigorating, dry, cool, chilly. **4** *a crisp account* brief, terse, succinct, concise, short, incisive, clear, pithy. **5** *a crisp manner* brisk, vigorous, decisive, brusque, curt, abrupt. **6** *a crisp appearance* clean-cut, neat, smart, spruce, trim, well-groomed; *inf.* snappy; *dial.* trig. **Opposites** SOFT; FLACCID; WORDY.

criterion *noun* measure, gauge, scale, yardstick, standard, norm, benchmark, touchstone, barometer, model, exemplar, classic example, rule, law, principle, canon.

critic *noun* **1** *theatre critics* reviewer, commentator, pundit, arbiter, evaluator, analyst, judge, expounder. **2** *answer his critics* fault-finder, attacker, censurer, detractor, carper, back-

biter, caviller, reviler, vilifier; *inf.* knocker, nitpicker.

critical *adjective* **1** *a critical point in history* crucial, deciding, decisive, climacteric, pivotal, important, momentous, high-priority, serious, vital, urgent, pressing, compelling, essential, exigent. **2** *in a critical condition* dangerous, grave, serious, risky, perilous, hazardous, touch-and-go, uncertain, precarious; *inf.* chancy. **3** *a critical attitude* fault-finding, captious, censorious, carping, cavilling, quibbling, niggling, disapproving, disparaging, judgemental, hypercritical, overcritical; *inf.* nit-picking. **4** *a critical essay* evaluative, analytic, interpretative, expository, commentative, explanatory, explicative, elucidative, annotative. **Opposites** UNIMPORTANT; SAFE; COMPLIMENTARY.

criticism *noun* **1** *actions receiving criticism* fault-finding, censure, reproof, condemnation, disapproval, disparagement, captiousness, carping, cavilling, animadversion; *inf.* nit-picking, brickbats, flak, bad press, bad notices, knocking, panning, slating, slamming. **2** *studying literary criticism* evaluation, comment, commentary, assessment, appreciation, appraisal, analysis, interpretation, explanation, explication, elucidation, annotation. **3** *read the criticism* review, notice, commentary, evaluation, critique, analysis, appraisal; *inf.* write-up.

criticize *verb* *criticize his behaviour* find fault with, censure, denounce, blame, condemn, pick holes in, disapprove of, disparage, carp at, cavil at, excoriate, animadvert on/upon; *inf.* nit-pick, hand out brickbats, give flak to, give a knocking/panning/slating/slamming to, knock, pan, slate, slam.

critique *noun* evaluation, analysis, assessment, appraisal; textual examination, commentary, critical essay, review.

croak *verb* **1** *"Who's there?" he croaked* speak/utter hoarsely/huskily/throatily/harshly, rasp, speak thickly, squawk, caw, grunt, wheeze. **2** *always croaking about something* grumble, complain, moan, grouse, whine, mutter, murmur. **3** *when the crook croaked* die, pass away, perish, expire; *inf.* kick the bucket. **4** *he croaked the cat* kill, butcher, murder.

crock *noun* **1** *a crock of salt* earthenware pot, pot, jar, vessel, container, pitcher, jug, ewer. **2** *a bit of a crock now* invalid, infirm person, broken-down person/thing, decrepit person/thing.

crockery *noun* dishes, pottery, china. *See table at* CERAMICS.

crony *noun* friend, companion, chum, mate, comrade, associate, confederate; *inf.* pal, buddy.

crook *noun* **1** *crooks imprisoned* criminal, villain, rogue, lawbreaker, thief, robber, swindler, cheat, racketeer; *inf.* crim, shark, con-man. **2** *the crook of one's arm | crook of the river* bend, curve, curvature, angle, bow, flexure.

crook *verb* *crook one's finger* bend, curve, angle, flex, hook, bow.

crooked *adjective* **1** *a crooked branch/road* bent, curved, twisted, contorted, warped, irregular, angled, bowed, hooked, flexed, winding, twisting, zigzag, meandering, deviating, sinuous, tortuous, serpentine, anfractuous. **2** *a crooked back* deformed, misshapen, out of shape, disfigured, crippled. **3** *the picture's crooked* not straight, tilted, at an angle, angled, slanted, aslant, slanting, sloping, askew, awry, to one side, off-centre, lopsided, uneven, unsymmetrical, asymmetric. **4** *a crooked fellow/deal* criminal, dishonest, corrupt, dishonourable, unscrupulous, unprincipled, fraudulent, illegal, unlawful, nefarious, crafty, deceitful, shifty, underhand, questionable, dubious; *inf.* shady, bent.
Opposites STRAIGHT; HONEST.

croon *verb* hum, sing softly, warble.

crop *noun* **1** *the apple crop* year's growth, harvest, yield, produce, vintage, gathering, reaping, gleaning, garnering, garner; fruits. **2** *the year's crop of students* batch, lot, collection, assortment, selection, supply. **3** *a bird's crop* craw, gullet, maw, throat.

crop *verb* **1** *crop the dog's tail/hair | crop the grass* cut, cut short, clip, trim, snip, shear, lop, curtail, reduce, mow, prune. **2** *sheep cropping* graze, nibble, browse. **3** *crop the fruits* harvest, pick, gather, collect, reap, garner, gather in, bring home. **crop up** *something cropped up* happen, occur, arise, turn up, spring up, emerge, appear, come to pass.

cross *noun* **1** *the sign of the cross* crucifix, rood. **2** *a cross to bear* trouble, worry, burden, trial, disaster; tribulation, affliction, misfortune, adversity, misery, woe, pain, suffering, calamity, catastrophe. **3** *a cross between two breeds/types* cross-breed, hybrid, hybridization, mixture, amalgam, blend, combination, mongrel, cur.

cross *verb* **1** *the bridge crossing the river* go across, span, extend/stretch across, pass over, bridge, ford. **2** *cross the road* go/travel across, cut across, traverse. **3** *the roads/lines crossed there* intersect, meet, join, converge, crisscross, interweave, intertwine, zigzag. **4** *hates being crossed* oppose, resist, thwart, frustrate, foil, obstruct, impede, hinder, hamper, block, check, deny, contradict. **5** *cross two species* cross-breed, interbreed, cross-fertilize, cross-pollinate, intercross, hybridize, mix, intermix, blend. **cross out** *cross out his name* delete, strike out, blue-pencil, cancel, eliminate, obliterate.

cross *adjective* **1** *she was cross at the children* angry, annoyed, irritated, in a bad mood, peeved, vexed, upset, piqued, out of humour, put out. **2** *a cross old woman* irritable, short-tempered, bad-tempered, ill-humoured, surly, churlish, disagreeable, irascible, touchy, snappy, snappish, impatient, peevish, petulant, fractious, crotchety, grouchy, grumpy, querulous, cantankerous, testy, captious, splenetic, waspish. **3** *cross ideas* contrary, opposing, opposite, adverse, unfavourable.
Opposites PLEASED; GOOD-HUMOURED; AGREEABLE.

cross-examine *verb* cross-question, question, interrogate, quiz, pump, catechize; *inf.* grill.

crossing *noun* **1** *a crash at the crossing* junction, crossroads, intersection. **2** *cross the street at the crossing* pedestrian crossing, street crossing, pelican crossing, underpass; *inf.* the green man.

crotch *noun* crutch, groin.

crotchet *noun* whim, whimsy, fancy, fad, vagary, notion, caprice, quirk, eccentricity.

crotchety *adjective* cross, bad-tempered, ill-natured, ill-humoured, crabbed, crabby, awkward, difficult, grumpy, grouchy, disagreeable, irritable, irascible, churlish, surly, touchy, testy, fractious, crusty, cantankerous, curmudgeonly.

crouch *verb* squat, bend, bend down, hunker, stoop, hunch over, cower, cringe.

crow *verb* *the winners were crowing over/about their victory* boast, brag, trumpet, gloat, show off, glory/exult in, vaunt, parade, swagger, bluster, strut; *inf.* blow one's own trumpet.

crowd *noun* **1** *crowds of people* throng, horde, mob, rabble, large number, mass, multitude, host, army, herd, flock, drove, swarm, troupe, pack, press, crush, flood, collection, company, gathering, assembly, assemblage, array, congregation, convention, concourse. **2** *he always follows the crowd and doesn't think for himself* majority, multitude, common people, populace, general public, mob, rank and file, the *hoi polloi*, proletariat, riff-raff; masses. **3** *the winebar crowd* group, set, lot, gang, bunch, circle, fraternity, clique, coterie. **4** *the pop group played to a capacity crowd* gate, house, turnout, audience, attendance; spectators, listeners, viewers.

crowd *verb* **1** *crowd round the teacher* gather, cluster, foregather, congregate, flock, swarm, throng, huddle, concentrate. **2** *people crowding into the hall* push, push one's way, shove, thrust forward, jostle, elbow, squeeze, pile in, pack. **3** *tourists crowding the streets | streets crowded with tourists* throng, pack, fill, overfill, congest. **4** *crowd people into the trains* pack, squeeze, cram, jam, bundle, stuff, pile. **5** *give him time! Don't crowd him* pressure, pressurize, harass, badger, pester, hound, nag, torment, plague; *inf.* hassle.

crowded *adjective* *crowded streets/buses* full, overfull, busy, overflowing, packed, jam-packed, crushed, cramped, congested, teeming, swarming, thronged, populous; *Am.* mobbed; *inf.* full to bursting.

crown *noun* **1** *the king's crown* coronal, wreath. *See table at* HAT. **2** *the champion winning the crown* laurel wreath, victor's garland, prize, trophy; honour, distinction, glory, kudos; laurels, bays. **3** *the power of the Crown* monarchy, monarch, sovereignty, sovereign, ruler, king, queen, emperor, empress, royalty; *inf.* royals. *See table at* ROYALTY. **4** *the crown of the hill* top, crest, summit, apex, head, tip, pinnacle. **5** *the crown of his achievements* climax, height, culmination, pinnacle, zenith, acme, ultimate, flower.

crown *verb* **1** *crown the queen* invest, inaugurate, induct, install. **2** *crown his career* cap, round off, be the culmination/climax of, put the finishing touch/touches to, consummate, top off, complete, perfect, conclude. **3** *the steeple crowning the church* top, surmount, over-top. **4** *he crowned his attacker* hit over the head, strike, box, bang, cuff, punch, buffet; *inf.* biff, wallop, bash.

crucial *adjective* **1** *a crucial moment in the talks* decisive, critical, determining, pivotal, central, testing, trying, searching. **2** *the matter is of crucial importance* very important, high-priority, essential, momentous, vital, urgent, pressing, compelling.

crucify *verb* **1** *crucify the wrongdoers* nail to a cross, execute/put to death on a cross. **2** *bullies crucifying the new pupils* persecute, torment, distress, harrow, torture. **3** *his play was crucified by the critics* tear apart, tear to pieces, criticize, attack, lampoon; *inf.* pan, slate.

crude *adjective* **1** *crude oil/flour* raw, unrefined, natural, coarse, unprocessed, unmilled, unpolished. **2** *a crude sculpture/dwelling* rudimentary, primitive, rough, rough-and-ready, rough-hewn, makeshift, unfinished, unpolished, unformed, undeveloped, rude. **3** *a crude sense of humour* coarse, vulgar, rude, uncouth, indelicate, earthy, indecent, dirty, bawdy, smutty, obscene, offensive, lewd, ribald, boorish, crass, tasteless; *inf.* blue, raunchy.
Opposites REFINED; SOPHISTICATED; DELICATE.

cruel *adjective* **1** *a cruel dictator/action* savage, brutal, inhuman, barbaric, barbarous, blood-thirsty, vicious, ferocious, fierce, evil, fiendish, callous, cold-blooded, sadistic, ruthless, merciless, pitiless, unrelenting, remorseless, unfeeling, heartless, inhumane, severe, harsh, stern, stony-hearted, hard-hearted, inclement, flinty. **2** *a cruel stroke of fate* unkind, painful, distressing, harrowing, harsh, grim, heartless.
Opposites KIND; MERCIFUL; COMPASSIONATE.

cruelty *noun* **1** *the cruelty of the dictator | cruelty of his actions* savageness, savagery, brutality, inhumanity, barbarism, barbarousness, viciousness, ferocity, fierceness, evil, fiendishness, callousness, sadism, ruthlessness, pitilessness, relentlessness, severity, harshness, inclemency. *See* CRUEL 1. **2** *the cruelty of the blow* unkindness, painfulness, harshness, grimness, heartlessness; pain, resulting distress.

cruise *verb* **1** *ships cruising* sail, voyage, journey. **2** *cars cruising along* coast, travel steadily, drift.

cruise *noun* go on a cruise sea/boat trip, voyage, sail.

crumb *noun* bit, fragment, morsel, particle, grain, atom, speck, scrap, shred, sliver, snippet, mite.

crumble *verb* **1** *crumble the biscuits* break up, crush, pulverize, pound, grind, powder, granulate, fragment, shiver, triturate, comminute. **2** *the empire was crumbling* disintegrate, fall to pieces, fall apart, collapse, break down/up, tumble down, decay, deteriorate, degenerate, fall into decay, go to rack and ruin, decompose, rot, rot away, moulder, perish, vanish, fade away, come to dust.

crumple *verb* **1** *crumple the dress* crush, crease, rumple, wrinkle, crinkle. **2** *the child's face*

crumpled pucker, screw up. **3** *resistance crumpling* collapse, fail, cave in, fall apart, give way, go to pieces, topple, shrivel.
Opposites IRON; STRAIGHTEN; SURVIVE.

crunch *verb* **1** *crunch biscuits* chew noisily, bite, munch, champ, chomp, gnaw, masticate, scrunch. **2** *crunch the snow* crush, grind, pulverize, pound, smash. **3** *crunch through the snow* move noisily, sound noisy/harsh, scrunch.

crunch *noun* crux, crisis, critical point, test, moment of truth/decision.

crusade *noun* **1** *knights/soldiers on a crusade* military campaign, holy war, jihad. **2** *a crusade against smoking* campaign, drive, push, struggle, cause, movement.

crusade *verb* *crusading for more resources* campaign, fight, work, do battle, take up arms, take up a cause.

crusader *noun* campaigner, fighter, battler, champion, advocate, reformer.

crush *verb* **1** *crush the grapes* squash, squeeze, mash, press, press down, compress, bruise. **2** *crush the material* crease, crumple, rumple, wrinkle, crinkle. **3** *crush the stones* break up, smash, shatter, pound, pulverize, grind, crumble, crunch, shiver, splinter, comminute. **4** *crush the rebellion | crush their opponents* put down, quell, quash, suppress, subdue, overcome, overwhelm, overpower, stamp out, defeat, conquer, vanish, extinguish. **5** *crushed by his criticism* mortify, humiliate, abash, quash, shame, chagrin; *inf.* put down. **6** *crush her in his arms* embrace, enfold, hug, squeeze, hold/press tight, clutch.

crush *noun* **1** *a crush at the cinema* crowd, jam, congestion, huddle. **2** *a crush on the teacher* infatuation, fancy, liking, love, passion; *inf.* pash. **3** *fruit crush* squash, fruit juice.

crust *noun* **1** *the crust of the bread/pie* outside, casing, shell, husk. *See* table. **2** *a crust of hard snow/skin* covering, cover, coating, caking, topping, layer, film, skin, blanket, mantle, incrustation, concretion, scab.

LAYERS OF THE EARTH'S CRUST

asthenosphere	oceanic crust
continental crust	sial
lithosphere	transition zone
lower mantle	upper mantle
Mohorovičić discontinuity	

---

crusty *adjective* **1** *crusty pastry* crisp, crispy, brittle, hard, well-baked, well-done, friable. **2** *a crusty old fellow | a crusty manner* brusque, surly, curt, gruff, cross, crabbed, crabby, grouchy, bad-tempered, short-tempered, irritable, irascible, ill-humoured, ill-natured, snappish, prickly, fretful, touchy, testy, snarling, cantankerous, choleric, splenetic, captious.

cry *verb* **1** *babies/women crying* shed tears, weep, sob, wail, snivel, blubber, whimper, whine, bawl, howl. **2** *he cried out her name | cried in terror* call out, exclaim, yell, scream, screech, bawl, shout, bellow, howl. **cry down**

cry down *his achievement* decry, run down, disparage, belittle, denigrate. **cry off** *cry off the appointment* cancel, withdraw, withdraw from, back out, back out of, beg off, excuse oneself.
Opposites LAUGH; WHISPER.

cry *noun* **1** *the baby's cries* weeping, sobbing, snivelling, blubbering, wailing, lamenting, lamentation, keening; sobs, wails, howls. **2** *cry of terror/pain* call, exclamation, scream, screech, yell, shout, bellow, howl.

crypt *noun* tomb, vault, undercroft, burial chamber, sepulchre.

cub *noun* **1** *lion and her cubs* young, offspring, whelp. **2** *newspaper cubs* trainee, learner, recruit, tenderfoot, youngster; *inf.* greenhorn.

cubbyhole *noun* **1** *put the letter in his cubbyhole* pigeon-hole, compartment, slot, recess, niche. **2** *the janitor in his cubbyhole* small room, den, snug.

cube *noun* six-sided body/shape, hexahedron, parallelepiped.

cuddle *verb* **1** *cuddling his wife* hug, embrace, enfold, clasp. **2** *couples cuddling in cars* embrace, make love, pet, fondle; *inf.* canoodle, neck, smooch. **3** *cuddle up in bed* snuggle, nestle, curl up.

cuddly *adjective* cuddlesome, huggable, warm, soft, buxom, plump, curvaceous.

cudgel *noun* *hit with a cudgel* club, bludgeon, stick, baton, truncheon, cosh, bat, bastinado; *Am.* blackjack; *dial.* shillelagh.

cudgel *verb* *the attacker cudgelled his victim* bludgeon, cosh, club, beat/strike with a stick, truncheon.

cue *noun* **1** *'away' is your cue* catchword, keyword, prompt, prompt-word, prompting, reminder. **2** *your cue to begin* signal, sign, indication, hint, suggestion, intimation.

cuff *verb* *cuff the child* slap, strike, hit, buffet. **off the cuff** impromptu, ad lib, extempore, extemporaneously, off the top of one's head, unrehearsed, improvised, offhand, on the spur of the moment, spontaneous, spontaneously.

cuisine *noun* cookery, cooking, *cordon bleu.*

cul-de-sac *noun* blind alley, dead end.

culminate *verb* come to a climax, peak, reach a pinnacle, come to a crescendo, come to an end, end, close, finish, conclude, terminate, come to a head; *inf.* wind up.

culmination *noun* high point, height, top, summit, climax, peak, pinnacle, crest, crown, crowning touch, zenith, acme, apex, high noon, consummation, completion, close, finish, conclusion, termination.

culpable *adjective* at fault, in the wrong, guilty, answerable, blameworthy, blamable, to blame, censurable, reproachable, reprovable, reprehensible, sinful; *fml.* peccant.
Opposites BLAMELESS; INNOCENT.

culprit *noun* person responsible, guilty party, wrongdoer, evildoer, lawbreaker, criminal, miscreant, delinquent, reprobate, transgressor, felon, sinner, malefactor; *inf.* baddie, bad guy.

cult *noun* **1** *belong to a strange religious cult* sect, religion, church, denomination, body, affiliation, faith, belief, persuasion, following, party, school, faction, clique. **2** *the modern pop-music cult* craze, fashion, fad; admiration, devotion, obsession, homage, worship, reverence, veneration, idolization.

cultivate *verb* **1** *cultivate the fields* till, farm, work, plough, dig, prepare, fertilize. **2** *cultivate a crop* plant, raise, tend, bring on, produce. **3** *cultivate the mind* culture, educate, train, civilize, enlighten, enrich, improve, better, develop, refine, polish, ameliorate, elevate. See CULTIVATED. **4** *cultivate people* seek the friendship/company of, run after, make advances to, ingratiate oneself with, curry favour with, woo, court, dance attendance on, associate/consort with; *inf.* butter up, suck up to. **5** *cultivate a friendship* pursue, devote oneself to, foster, promote, advance, further, forward, encourage, support, back, aid, help, assist, abet.

cultivated *adjective* *a cultivated young woman* cultured, educated, civilized, enlightened, refined, polished, sophisticated, discerning, discriminating, urbane.

cultural *adjective* **1** *cultural interests* artistic, educational, educative, enlightening, enriching, broadening, developmental, edifying, civilizing, elevating. **2** *cultural differences* lifestyle, ethnic, folk, racial.

culture *noun* **1** *a woman of culture* cultivation, education, enlightenment, accomplishment, edification, erudition, refinement, polish, sophistication, urbanity, discernment, discrimination, good taste, taste, breeding, politeness, gentility, savoir faire. **2** *seek culture* the arts, works of art, intellectual achievements; intellectual achievement, intellectual activity. **3** *belong to a different culture* civilization, way of life, lifestyle; customs, habits, ways, mores. **4** *cereal culture* cultivation, farming, agriculture, husbandry, agronomy.

cultured *adjective* cultivated, artistic, educated, enlightened, learned, knowledgeable, intellectual, highbrow, scholarly, well-informed, well-read, erudite, accomplished, well-versed, refined, genteel, polished, sophisticated, urbane.
Opposites IGNORANT; UNREFINED; UNSOPHISTICATED.

culvert *noun* channel, conduit, drain, gutter, watercourse.

cumbersome *adjective* **1** *cumbersome packages* awkward, unwieldy, bulky, weighty, heavy, hefty, clumsy, unmanageable, burdensome, cumbrous, inconvenient, incommodious. **2** *cumbersome procedures* slow, slow-moving, inefficient, unwieldy, cumbrous.
Opposites MANAGEABLE; CONVENIENT; EFFICIENT.

cumulative *adjective* accumulative, increasing, growing, enlarging, swelling, accruing, snowballing, collective, aggregate, amassed.

cunning *adjective* **1** *a cunning thief* crafty, devious, deceitful, wily, sly, shifty, artful, foxy, tricky, guileful, shrewd, astute, sharp, knowing, subtle, Machiavellian. **2** *a cunning device/artist* clever, ingenious, resourceful, inventive,

imaginative, skilful, deft, adroit, subtle, dexterous.
Opposites HONEST; GUILELESS; INGENUOUS.

cunning noun **1** the cunning of the thief craftiness, deviousness, deceitfulness, deceit, wiliness, slyness, artfulness, foxiness, trickery, trickiness, guile, shrewdness, astuteness, sharpness, subtlety. **2** admire the cunning of the process/artist cleverness, ingenuity, resourcefulness, inventiveness, imaginativeness, skill, skilfulness, deftness, adroitness, subtlety, finesse, dexterity, ability, capability.

cup noun **1** cups, saucers, and plates teacup, coffee cup, mug, beaker, demitasse. **2** win the cup trophy, chalice. **3** two cups of sugar cupful, teacupful, measuring cup. **4** a fruit/wine cup punch, drink, squash, draught, potion.

cupboard noun. See table.

Cupid noun **1** a statue of Cupid god of love, Eros, amoretto. **2** acting Cupid matchmaker, marriage broker.

cupidity noun greed, avarice, avariciousness, acquisitiveness, covetousness, rapacity, rapaciousness, voracity, voraciousness, desire, avidity.

cur noun **1** bitten by a cur mongrel, lurcher; inf. mutt. **2** married to a nasty cur scoundrel, cad, blackguard, wastrel, ne'er do well, villain; inf. rat, creep, louse, rotter, bounder, blighter.

curate noun assistant priest. See table at ECCLESIASTIC.

curative adjective curing, healing, therapeutic, medicinal, remedial, restorative, sanative.

curator noun keeper, custodian, conservator, guardian, caretaker, steward.

curb verb curb one's anger restrain, check, keep in check, control, constrain, contain, hold back, bite back, repress, suppress, moderate, dampen, put a brake on, impede, retard, subdue, bridle, muzzle.

curb noun curbs on expenditure restraint, check, control, constraint, deterrent, curtailment, limitation, limit, damper, brake, rein, suppressant, hindrance, retardant.

curdle verb turn, turn sour, congeal, coagulate, clot, solidify, thicken, condense.

cure noun a cure for cancer remedy, curative, medicine, cure-all, panacea, restorative, corrective, antidote, nostrum; treatment, therapy, healing, alleviation.

cure verb **1** cure the patient heal, restore, restore to health, make well/better, rehabilitate, treat. **2** cure the disease heal, remedy, doc-

tor, put/set right, fix, repair. **3** cure meat preserve, smoke, salt, dry, kipper, pickle.

curio noun trinket, knick-knack, bibelot, objet d'art.

curiosity noun **1** curiosity about what is happening inquisitiveness, spirit of inquiry, interest, investigativeness, researching, querying, asking questions, questioning, prying, snooping; inf. nosiness. **2** the object having curiosity value strangeness, oddness, peculiarity, eccentricity, idiosyncrasy, deviation, aberration. **3** he is a curiosity eccentric, individual, oddity, character, freak, original; inf. card, weirdo, oddball. **4** looking at the curiosities of the East novelty, oddity, phenomenon, rarity, wonder, marvel, sight, spectacle.

curious adjective **1** curious to know the facts inquisitive, inquiring, interested, investigating, searching, researching, querying, questioning, interrogative, puzzled, burning with curiosity. **2** curious about others' affairs inquisitive, prying, snooping, meddling, meddlesome, interfering, intrusive; inf. nosy, snoopy. **3** a curious site strange, unusual, rare, odd, peculiar, out of the ordinary, unexpected, extraordinary, remarkable, singular, novel, queer, bizarre, unconventional, unorthodox, phenomenal, weird, freakish, marvellous, wonderful, prodigious, exotic, mysterious, puzzling, quaint, unique; inf. rum, far out.
Opposites UNINTERESTED; INDIFFERENT; ORDINARY.

curl verb **1** the smoke/road curled upwards spiral, coil, twist, twist and turn, wind, curve, bend, loop, twirl, wreathe, meander, snake, corkscrew. **2** the heat curled the leaves up bend, twist, curve, coil, crisp. **3** curl the hair crimp, crinkle, kink, frizz, coil, wave, corkscrew.

curl noun **1** put curls in one's hair kink, ringlet, coil, wave, curlicue, corkscrew. **2** curls of smoke spiral, coil, twist, whorl, helix.

curly adjective **1** curly hair curling, curled, crimped, crinkly, kinked, wavy, waved, frizzy, permed, fuzzy, corkscrew. **2** a curly pattern spiralled, spiralling, coiling, coiled, curving, winding, corkscrew. See CURL verb 1.

currency noun **1** foreign currency money, medium of exchange, legal tender, cash, coinage, coin, specie, paper money; coins, bank notes, notes, bills. See table. **2** story gaining currency prevalence, acceptance, popularity, vogue, circulation, communication, transmission, dissemination, publicity, exposure.

current adjective **1** current fashions present, present-day, contemporary, ongoing, extant, existing, popular, modern, fashionable, in

CUPBOARDS AND CABINETS

armoire	chest	corner cupboard	lowboy
aumbry	chest of drawers	dresser	pantry
bookcase	chiffonier	drinks cabinet	sideboard
bookshelf	closet	highboy Am.	tallboy
cabinet	cocktail cabinet	hope chest Am.	wardrobe
canterbury	commode	larder	Welsh
cassone	Coolgardie safe	liquor cabinet Am.	dresser
cellaret	Austral.	locker	whatnot

CURRENCIES OF THE WORLD

Country	Currency	Country	Currency
Afghanistan	afghani of 100 puls	Equatorial Guinea	franc CFA*
Albania	lek of 100 qindarka	Eritrea	birr of 100 cents
Algeria	dinar of 100 centimes	Estonia	kroon of 100 sents
Andorra	franc of 100 cents and peseta of 100 céntimos	Ethiopia	birr of 100 cents
		Fiji	dollar of 100 cents
Angola	new kwanza of 100 lwei	Finland	markka of 100 penniä
		France	franc of 100 centimes
Anguilla	East Caribbean dollar of 100 cents	Gabon	franc CFA*
		Gambia, the	dalasi of 100 butut
Antigua and Barbuda	East Caribbean dollar of 100 cents	Germany	Deutschmark of 100 Pfennigs
Argentina	peso of 10,000 australes	Ghana	cedi of 100 pesewas
Armenia	dram of 100 couma	Greece	drachma of 100 leptae
Australia	dollar of 100 cents	Grenada	East Caribbean dollar of 100 cents
Austria	Schilling of 100 Groschen	Guatemala	quetzal of 100 centavos
Azerbaijan	manat of 100 gopik	Guinea	franc of 100 centimes
Bahamas, the	dollar of 100 cents	Guinea-Bissau	peso of 100 centavos
Bahrain	dinar of 1000 fils	Guyana	dollar of 100 cents
Bangladesh	taka of 100 poisha	Haiti	gourde of 100 centimes
Barbados	dollar of 100 cents	Honduras	lempira of 100 centavos
Belarus	rouble of 100 kopeks	Hungary	forint of 100 fillér
Belgium	franc/frank of 100 centimes/centiemen	Iceland	króna of 100 aurar
		India	rupee of 100 paisa
Belize	dollar of 100 cents	Indonesia	rupiah of 100 sen
Benin	franc CFA*	Iran	rial of 100 dinars
Bermuda	dollar of 100 cents	Iraq	dinar of 1000 fils
Bhutan	ngultrum of 100 chetrum	Ireland	punt of 100 pence
		Israel	shekel of 100 agora
Bolivia	boliviano of 100 centavos	Italy	lira
		Ivory Coast	franc CFA*
Bosnia-Herzegovina	dinar of 100 paras	Jamaica	dollar of 100 cents
Botswana	pula of 100 thebe	Japan	yen of 100 sen
Brazil	real of 100 centavos	Jordan	dinar of 1000 fils
Brunei	dollar of 100 sen	Kazakhstan	tenge
Bulgaria	lev of 100 stotinki	Kenya	shilling of 100 cents
Burkina Faso	franc CFA*	Kiribati	dollar of 100 cents
Burundi	franc of 100 centimes	Korea, North	won of 100 chon
Cambodia	riel of 100 sen	Korea, South	won of 100 chon
Cameroon	franc CFA*	Kuwait	dinar of 1000 fils
Canada	dollar of 100 cents	Kyrgyzstan	som
Cape Verde Islands	escudo Caboverdiano of 100 centavos	Laos	kip of 100 at
		Latvia	lats of 100 santimes
Central African Republic	franc CFA*	Lebanon	pound of 100 piastres
		Lesotho	loti of 100 lisente
Chad	franc CFA*	Liberia	dollar of 100 cents
Chile	peso of 100 centavos	Libya	dinar of 1000 dirhams
China	yuan of 10 jiao or 100 fen	Liechtenstein	franc of 100 rappen
		Lithuania	litas
Colombia	peso of 100 centavos	Luxembourg	franc of 100 centimes
Comoros	franc CFA*	Macedonia, Former	
Congo	franc CFA*	Yugoslav Republic of	dinar of 100 paras
Costa Rica	colón of 100 céntimos	Madagascar	Malagasy franc of 100 centimes
Croatia	kuna of 100 lipas		
Cuba	peso of 100 centavos	Malawi	kwacha of 100 tambala
Cyprus	pound of 100 cents	Malaysia	ringgit of 100 sen
Czech Republic	koruna of 100 haléřu	Maldives	rufiyaa of 100 laaris
Denmark	krone of 100 ore	Mali	franc CFA*
Djibouti	franc of 100 centimes	Malta	lira of 100 cents or 1000 mils
Dominica	East Caribbean dollar of 100 cents		
		Marshall Islands	dollar of 100 cents
Dominican Republic	peso of 100 centavos	Mauritania	ouguiya of 5 khoums
Ecuador	sucre of 100 centavos	Mauritius	rupee of 100 cents
Egypt	pound of 100 piastres or 1000 millièmes	Mexico	peso of 100 centavos
		Moldova	leu
El Salvador	colón of 100 centavos	Monaco	franc of 100 centimes

CURRENCIES OF THE WORLD *cont.*

Country	Currency	Country	Currency
Mongolia	tugrik of 100 möngö	Slovenia	tolar of 100 stotin
Montenegro	dinar of 100 paras	Solomon Islands	dollar of 100 cents
Morocco	dirham of 100 centimes	Somalia	shilling of 100 cents
Mozambique	metical of 100 centavos	South Africa	rand of 100 cents
Myanmar	kyat of 100 pyas	Spain	peseta of 100 céntimos
Namibia	dollar of 100 cents	Sri Lanka	rupee of 100 cents
Nauru	dollar of 100 cents	Sudan	dinar of 10 pounds
Nepal	rupee of 100 paisa	Suriname	guilder of 100 cents
Netherlands, the	guilder/florin of 100 cents	Swaziland	lilangeni of 100 cents
		Sweden	krona of 100 öre
New Zealand	dollar of 100 cents	Switzerland	franc of 100 rappen
Nicaragua	córdoba of 100 centavos	Syria	pound of 100 piastres
Niger	franc CFA*	Taiwan	dollar of 100 cents
Nigeria	naira of 100 kobo	Tajikistan	rouble of 100 kopeks
Norway	krone of 100 ore	Tanzania	shilling of 100 cents
Oman	rial Omani of 1000 baiza	Thailand	baht of 100 satang
		Togo	franc CFA*
Pakistan	rupee of 100 paisa	Tonga	pa'anga of 100 seniti
Palau	dollar of 100 cents	Trinidad and Tobago	dollar of 100 cents
Panama	balboa of 100 centésimos	Tunisia	dinar of 1000 millimes
		Turkey	lira of 100 kurus
Papua New Guinea	kina of 100 toea	Turkmenistan	manat
Paraguay	guaraní of 100 céntimos	Tuvalu	dollar of 100 cents
Peru	new sol of 100 cénts	Uganda	shilling of 100 cents
Philippines	peso of 100 centavos	Ukraine	karbovanets
Poland	zloty of 100 groszy	United Arab Emirates	dirham of 100 fils
Portugal	escudo of 100 centavos		
Qatar	riyal of 100 dirhams	U.K.	pound sterling of 100 pence
Romania	leu of 100 bani		
Russia	rouble of 100 kopeks	U.S.A.	dollar of 100 cents
Rwanda	franc of 100 centimes	Uruguay	peso of 100 centésimos
St Kitts and Nevis	East Caribbean dollar of 100 cents	Uzbekistan	sum
		Vanuatu	vatu of 100 centimes
St Lucia	East Caribbean dollar of 100 cents	Vatican City	Italian lira
		Venezuela	bolívar of 100 céntimos
St Vincent and the Grenadines	East Caribbean dollar of 100 cents	Vietnam	dông of 10 hào or 100 xu
		Western Samoa	tala of 100 sene
San Marino	Italian lira	Yemen	dinar of 1000 fils and riyal of 100 fils
São Tomé and Príncipe	dobra of 100 centavos	Yugoslavia (see Serbia, Montenegro, etc.)	
Saudi Arabia	riyal of 20 qursh or 100 halala	Zaire	zaire of 100 makuta
Senegal	franc CFA*	Zambia	kwacha of 100 ngwee
Serbia	dinar of 100 paras	Zimbabwe	dollar of 100 cents
Seychelles	rupee of 100 cents		
Singapore	dollar of 100 cents	*franc CFA = franc de la communauté financière africaine (franc of the African financial community)	
Slovakia	koruna of 100 haléřu		

fashion/vogue, up-to-date, up-to-the-minute; *inf.* trendy, now, in. **2** *ideas no longer current* prevalent, prevailing, accepted, in circulation, circulating, going around, making the rounds, talked of, common, general, popular, widespread, rife, on everyone's lips.
Opposites OUT OF DATE; OBSOLETE.

current *noun* **1** *current of air* steady flow, draught, up/down draught, wind, thermal. **2** *swimmers swept away by the current | a strong current* steady flow, stream, tide, channel. **3** *disturb the even current of village life* course, flow, progress, progression, tide. **4** *currents of opinion* trend, drift, tendency, tenor.

curse *noun* **1** *the witches'/priest's curse* malediction, evil eye, execration, imprecation, anath-

ema, damnation, excommunication; *inf.* jinx. **2** *angrily uttering curses* oath, swear-word, expletive, profanity, obscenity; swearing, blasphemy, bad/foul language. **3** *the curse of poverty* evil, affliction, burden, cross, bane, misfortune, misery, trouble, blight, harm, disaster, calamity, ordeal, tribulation, scourge, plague, torment.

curse *verb* **1** *the witch/priest cursed them* put a curse on, accurse, put the evil eye on, execrate, imprecate, anathematize, damn, excommunicate; *inf.* put a jinx on, jinx. **2** *curse at the policeman* utter oaths, swear, use bad/foul language, blaspheme, take God's/the Lord's name in vain, be foul-mouthed; *Am. inf.* cuss. **3** *poverty cursed his childhood* blight, afflict,

cursed · cut

cursed *adjective* **1** *that cursed table/ neighbour* accursed, annoying, confounded, unpleasant, hateful, detestable, odious, loathsome, foul, damnable, abominable, vile pestilential, infernal, devilish, fiendish, infamous, nefarious, pernicious. **2** *the cursed people died* accursed, under a curse, curse-laden, doomed, ill-fated, damned, execrated, anathematized; *inf.* jinxed. *See* CURSE *verb* 1.

cursory *adjective* hasty, rapid, hurried, quick, superficial, perfunctory, desultory, ephemeral, fleeting, passing, transient.
Opposites THOROUGH; LEISURELY.

curt *adjective* terse, abrupt, brusque, blunt, short-spoken, short, snappy, snappish, sharp, crisp, tart, gruff, offhand, summary, rude, impolite, unceremonious, ungracious, uncivil, brief, concise, succinct, compact, pithy.
Opposites POLITE; SUAVE; VERBOSE.

curtail *verb* reduce, cut short, cut, cut down/ back, decrease, lessen, diminish, retrench, slim down, tighten up, pare down, trim, dock, lop, truncate, shorten, abridge, abbreviate, contract, compress, shrink.
Opposites INCREASE; LENGTHEN; EXPAND.

curtain *noun* **1** *hang curtains* window hanging, screen, blind; *Am.* drape. **2** *a curtain of secrecy* screen, cover, shield, cloak, veil. **curtain off** shut off, separate off, screen off, isolate, hide, conceal, shield.

curtsy, curtsey *verb* drop a curtsy, bob, bow, genuflect, salaam.

curve *noun* bend, arch, turn, bow, loop, hook, half-moon; winding, camber, curvature. *See table.*

TYPES OF CURVE

arc	hyperbolic spiral
Archimedes spiral	hypocycloid
cardioid	involute
catenary	lemniscate
circle	logarithmic
cissoid	spiral
crescent	logistic curve
cycloid	oval
ellipse	parabola
epicycloid	roulette
equiangular spiral	sine curve
evolute	sinusoid
folium	spiral
helix	trochoid
hyperbola	witch of Agnesi

curve *verb* bend, arc, arch, bow, turn, inflect, incurve, swerve, twist, wind, hook, loop, spiral, coil.

curved *adjective* bent, arched, rounded, bowed, twisted, crooked, humped, sinuous. *See* CURVE *verb.*

cushion *noun* *resting on a cushion* pillow, bolster, pad, hassock, mat, squab, pillion, scatter cushion, floor cushion, beanbag.

cushion *verb* **1** *cushioning her head* pillow, bolster, cradle, support, prop up. **2** *cushion the blow* soften, lessen, diminish, mitigate, allay, deaden, muffle, stifle. **3** *cushion the child from reality* protect, shield, buttress.

custody *noun* **1** *in the custody of his mother | having custody of the children* guardianship, wardship, trusteeship, charge, care, keeping, keep, safe-keeping, protection, guidance, supervision, superintendence, surveillance, control, tutelage, aegis; auspices. **2** *suspects in custody* imprisonment, detention, confinement, incarceration, restraint, constraint, duress.

custom *noun* **1** *it was their custom to leave early* habit, practice, routine, way, wont, policy, rule. **2** *local customs* practice, convention, ritual, procedure, ceremony, form, formality, usage, observance, way, fashion, mode, style, praxis. **3** *thank them for their custom* trade, business, patronage, purchasing.

customarily *adverb* as a rule, usually, generally, in the ordinary way, ordinarily, normally, commonly, habitually, routinely, traditionally.

customary *adjective* *customary to tip | her customary practice* accustomed, usual, regular, common, habitual, traditional, routine, fixed, set, established, everyday, familiar, wonted, confirmed, normal, ordinary, favourite, popular, stock, well-worn.
Opposites UNUSUAL; EXCEPTIONAL; RARE.

customer *noun* patron, client, buyer, purchaser, shopper, consumer; clientele; *inf.* regular.

customs *plural noun* import taxes; duty, toll, levy, tariff.

cut *verb* **1** *cut his finger/throat* gash, slash, lacerate, slit, nick, notch, pierce, penetrate, wound, lance, incise, score. **2** *cut the logs/meat* cut up, chop, sever, divide, cleave, carve, slice. **3** *cut a key/gem* shape, fashion, form, mould, chisel, carve, sculpt, sculpture, chip away, whittle. **4** *cut a design* carve, engrave, incise, score. **5** *cut their hair | cut the hedge/the grass* trim, clip, snip, crop, prune, dock, shear, shave, pare, mow. **6** *cut some flowers* detach, gather, harvest, reap. **7** *cut expenditure* reduce, curtail, curb, retrench, cut back/down on, decrease, lessen, lower, diminish, contract, ease up on, prune, slash, slim down, rationalize, slenderize, economize on. **8** *cut the text* shorten, abridge, condense, abbreviate, contract, compact, précis, summarize, epitomize. **9** *cut the unsuitable parts* delete, edit out, blue-pencil, excise. **10** *his behaviour cut me* hurt, offend, wound, distress, grieve, pain, sting, trouble, discomfort. **11** *his old friend cut him* shun, ignore, snub, spurn, give the cold shoulder to, cold-shoulder, look right through, turn one's back on, slight, scorn, send to Coventry, insult; *inf.* freeze out. **12** *the lines cut here* intersect, bisect, cross, decussate. **13** *cut the engine | the engine suddenly cut* stop, come to a stop, halt, turn off, switch off, stop working, malfunction. **14** *cut a record/tape* record, make a recording on, put on disc/tape, make a tape of, tape-record. **cut across** *cut across national prejudices* transcend, go beyond, rise above. **cut back** *cut back on expenditure* economize, reduce.

See CUT verb 7. **cut down** **1** *cut down a tree* fell, saw down, hew, chop/hack down. **2** *cut down on expenditure* economize, reduce. See CUT verb 7. **3** *cut down in his prime* kill, slay, slaughter, massacre, mow down, dispatch. **cut in** *"Wait," he cut in|cut in on a conversation* interrupt, interpose, break in, intervene, intrude; *inf.* butt in. **cut off** **1** *cut off supplies/communication* break off, disconnect, interrupt, suspend, bring to an end, discontinue, halt, stop, intercept, obstruct, hinder, thwart. **2** *cut off from the town by snow* isolate, separate, sever. **3** *cut off without a penny* disinherit, disown, renounce. **4** *cut off in his prime* kill. See CUT DOWN 3. **cut out** **1** *cut out the bad part* remove, delete, excise, extract. **2** *cut out eating chocolate* give up, refrain from, stop, cease. **3** *cut out the middleman* leave out, omit, eliminate, exclude, do away with. **4** *cut out the competition* oust, supplant, displace, supersede. **5** *the engine cut out* stop, stop working. See CUT verb 13. **6** *not cut out for teaching* suit, equip/design for. **cut short** *cut short a holiday* interrupt, break off, leave unfinished, truncate, abort, bring to an untimely end. **cut up** *verb* **1** *cut up the meat* slice, carve, chop, dice, mince, grind, divide up. **2** *the mugger cut up the old man* slash, knife, stab, lacerate, wound, injure. **3** *the teacher really cut up his essay/friend* criticize, ridicule, find fault with, tear to pieces/shreds, take apart, give a hard time to; *inf.* pan, slate, knock.

cut *noun* **1** *a cut on his finger* gash, slash, laceration, incision, slit. **2** *a cut of meat* section, piece. **3** *go for a cut at the hairdresser* trim, clip, crop. **4** *a cut in expenditure/salary* cutback, decrease, reduction, lessening, curtailment, retrenchment, contraction. **5** *cut of her jacket* fashion, style. **6** *power cut* loss, temporary interruption. **7** *I want my cut* share, portion, proportion.

cut-price *adjective* reduced, cheap, bargain.

cutthroat *noun set upon by cutthroats* thug, killer, murderer, assassin, homicide, butcher, liquidator, slayer, executioner; *inf.* hit man.

cutthroat *adjective* **1** *a cutthroat attack* murderous, death-dealing, homicidal, savage, violent, bloody, bloodthirsty, fierce, ferocious, barbarous, cruel. **2** *a cutthroat business* ruthless, merciless, pitiless, unfeeling, relentless, dog-eat-dog, fiercely competitive.

cutting *adjective* **1** *a cutting wind* biting, bitter, piercing, raw, keen, penetrating, stinging, sharp, chill, chilling, icy. **2** *a cutting remark* hurtful, wounding, caustic, acid, barbed, acrimonious, trenchant, mordant, scathing, acerbic, sarcastic, sardonic, spiteful, vicious, malicious.

cutting *noun* **1** *collect cuttings about his famous mother* clipping, newspaper clip, clip. **2** *plant cuttings* slip, scion. **3** *a cutting from the length of material* piece, part, bit.

cycle *noun* **1** *occur in cycles* recurrent period, rotation, round, revolution. **2** *compare the completed cycles* series, sequence, succession, run. **3** *travel by cycle* bicycle, bike, tandem, tricycle, monocycle.

cyclone *noun* windstorm, storm, gale, squall, hurricane, whirlwind, tornado, typhoon.

cynic *noun* pessimist, doom merchant, doomster, doom and gloom merchant, sceptic, scoffer, doubter, misanthrope.

cynical *adjective* pessimistic, sceptical, scoffing, doubting, unbelieving, disbelieving, distrustful, suspicious, misanthropic, critical, sardonic.
Opposites OPTIMISTIC; CREDULOUS; TRUSTFUL.

cynicism *noun* pessimism, scepticism, scoffing, doubt, unbelief, disbelief, distrust, suspicion, misanthropy, criticism, sardonicism.

Dd

dab *verb dab one's eyes* | *dab paint on* pat, press, touch, blot, smudge, besmear, bedaub.

dab *noun* **1** *give one's eyes a quick dab* pat, press, touch, blot, smudge. **2** *add a dab of paint/butter* touch, bit, speck, spot, trace, drop, dash, soupçon, tinge, suggestion, hint, modicum.

dabble *verb* **1** *dabble in politics* toy with, dip into, scratch the surface of, flirt with, tinker with, potter about with, trifle with, play with, fiddle with, dally with, have a smattering of. **2** *dabble one's fingers/feet in water* dip, splash, paddle, wet, moisten, dampen, sprinkle, spray, spatter, slosh.

dabbler *noun a dabbler in art* dilettante, amateur, non-professional, layman, laywoman, tinkerer, potterer, trifler, dallier.

daft *adjective* **1** *a daft idea* silly, absurd, stupid, foolish, idiotic, insane, crazy, mad, lunatic, nonsensical, senseless, fatuous, ridiculous, ludicrous, asinine, witless; *inf.* dopey, cracked. **2** *the daft boy in the village* simple, simpleminded, feeble-minded, slow-witted, dim-witted, dull-witted, touched, deranged, unhinged, demented, out of one's mind, insane, mad; *inf.* not all there, not quite right, crazy, mental, nuts, nutty, dopey, crackers, cracked, potty, barmy, batty, cuckoo, bonkers, dotty, dippy. **3** *she's daft about him* besotted by, infatuated with, obsessed by, doting on, enthusiastic about; *inf.* crazy/nuts/nutty about, potty/dotty about, sweet/gone on.
Opposites SENSIBLE; INTELLIGENT.

dagger *noun* blade. *See table at* KNIFE.

daily *adjective* **1** *a daily newspaper* of/occurring each day, everyday, diurnal, quotidian, circadian. **2** *a daily occurrence* everyday, day-to-day, routine, ordinary, common, commonplace, usual, regular, habitual, customary, wonted.

daily *adverb visit her daily* every day, once a day, day after day, day by day, per diem.

dainty *adjective* **1** *dainty china figures* | *dainty little girls* petite, neat, delicate, exquisite, refined, tasteful, fine, elegant, graceful, trim, pretty. **2** *a dainty morsel* tasty, delicious, appetizing, choice, delectable, palatable, flavoursome, savoury, toothsome, luscious, juicy, succulent. **3** *a dainty eater* particular, discriminating, fastidious, fussy, choosy, finicky, finical, refined, nice, scrupulous, meticulous, squeamish.
Opposites CLUMSY; NASTY; UNCOUTH.

dainty *noun dainties with afternoon tea* titbit, delicacy, sweetmeat, confection, fancy, *bonne bouche*.

dais *noun* platform, stage, stand, podium, pulpit.

dale *noun* valley, vale, glen, dell, coomb; *Scots* strath.

dally *verb* **1** *dallying on the way home* dawdle, delay, loiter, linger, tarry, waste/kill time, take one's time, while away time; *inf.* dilly-dally. **2** *dally with his affections* | *dally with an idea* trifle, toy, flirt, tinker; *inf.* fool.
Opposites HURRY; HASTEN.

dam *noun a river dam* barricade, barrier, barrage, wall, embankment, obstruction, hindrance. *See table.*

DAMS	
Dam	**Location**
Akosombo	Ghana
Aswan High Dam	Egypt
Atatürk	Turkey
Bonneville	U.S.A.
Chicoasén	Mexico
Chivor	Colombia
El Cajón	Honduras
Fengman	China
Fort Peck	U.S.A.
Grand Coulee	U.S.A.
Grand Dixence	Switzerland
Guri	Venezuela
Hoover	U.S.A.
Iguri	Georgia
Itaipú	Paraguay
Kariba	Zambia/Zimbabwe
Mangla	Pakistan
Mauvoisin	Switzerland
Mica	Canada
Nurek	Tajikistan
Oroville	U.S.A.
Rogun	Tajikistan
Supung	Korea
Tarbela	Pakistan
Tucuruí	Brazil
Vaiont	Italy

damage *verb damage one's property/reputation* do damage to, harm, injure, hurt, impair, abuse, spoil, mar, deface, defile, vandalize, wreck, destroy, ruin, play havoc with, devastate, do mischief to, tamper with, mutilate.
Opposites REPAIR; IMPROVE.

damage *noun* **1** *damage to one's property/reputation* harm, injury, hurt, impairment, abuse, defilement, defacement, detriment, vandalism, destruction, ruin, havoc, devastation, mischief, outrage, accident, loss, suffering. **2** *what's the damage?* cost, expense, charge, bill, account, total.

damages *plural noun receive damages from the court* compensation, indemnity, reparation, reimbursement, restitution, satisfaction.

dame *noun* peeress, baroness, noblewoman, lady, dowager, aristocrat, *grande dame*.

damn verb **1** damned by the priest curse, doom, execrate, imprecate, excommunicate, anathematize, proscribe, interdict. **2** habitually damning curse, swear, blaspheme, maledict, use bad language. **3** damned by his neighbours condemn, censure, criticize, castigate, denounce, berate, reprimand, reprove, abuse, inveigh against, excoriate. **4** a play damned by the critics criticize, attack, flay; inf. pan, slam, slate, knock, blast, take to pieces, take apart.
Opposites BLESS; ACCLAIM; PRAISE.

damn noun not be worth a damn | not care a damn jot, whit, iota, hoot, two hoots; inf. tinker's damn, brass farthing.

damnable adjective **1** damnable cruelty accursed, cursed, diabolical, fiendish, infernal, abominable, atrocious, execrable, base, wicked, heinous, vile, despicable, detestable, hateful, horrible, hideous, obnoxious, revolting, repulsive, foul, repugnant. **2** damnable weather nasty, unpleasant, disagreeable, foul, objectionable.

damnation noun **1** suffer damnation sending to hell, eternal punishment, perdition, doom. **2** the damnation of/by the priest curse, execration, imprecation, excommunication, anathema, anathematization, proscription, interdict. **3** the damnation of his neighbours condemnation, censure, criticism, castigation, denunciation. See DAMN verb 3. **4** the damnation of the play criticism, attacking. See DAMN verb 4.

damned adjective **1** damned souls cursed, accursed, doomed, lost, condemned, execrated, excommunicated, anathematized. See DAMN verb 1. **2** this damned machine/weather annoying, confounded, uncooperative, nasty, hateful, detestable, odious.

damning adjective damning evidence incriminating, condemnatory, condemning, damnatory, implicating, implicatory, accusatorial.

damp adjective **1** damp clothes/grass wettish, moist, dank, soggy, dewy. **2** a damp day | damp weather wettish, rainy, drizzly, humid, clammy, muggy, misty, foggy, vaporous.
Opposites DRY; ARID.

damp noun **1** the damp in the house dampness, wetness, moisture, dankness. **2** the damp of the day dampness, wetness, raininess, humidity, clamminess, mugginess; rain, drizzle. See DAMPNESS 2. **3** act as a damp on our enjoyment damper, discouragement, check, curb, obstacle. See DAMPER.

damp verb **1** damp the clothes dampen, wet, moisten, humidify. **2** damp their enthusiasm | damp down his enjoyment dampen, discourage, dull, dispirit, depress, dash, cool, chill, check, curb, restrain, stifle, inhibit, deter, lessen, limit, diminish, allay, put a damper on, throw cold water on. **3** damp the noise | damp down the vibrations reduce, lessen, diminish, decrease, moderate. **4** damp the fire | damp down the furnace bank, smother, stifle, extinguish.

dampen verb **1** dampen the clothes/atmosphere wet, moisten, damp, humidify, vaporize. **2** dampen their enthusiasm damp, damp down, discourage, dull, dash, check, stifle, inhibit, put a damper on. See DAMP verb 2.

damper noun act as a damper on our enthusiasm discouragement, depression, chill, pall, gloom, cloud, check, curb, obstacle, hindrance, impediment, restraint, deterrent; inf. wet blanket.

dampness noun **1** dampness in the house damp, wetness, moisture, dankness. **2** the dampness of the weather damp, wetness, raininess, drizzliness, dankness, humidity, clamminess, mugginess; wet, mist, fog, vapour, rain, drizzle.

damsel noun young woman, girl, young lady, maid, maiden, lass.

dance verb **1** dance in the dancehall | dance with her move/sway to music, execute dance steps, twirl, pirouette; inf. shake a leg, hoof it; Am. inf. cut a rug. See table. See also table at BALLET. **2** children dancing about caper, skip, prance, hop, frolic, gambol, jump, jig, romp, bounce, whirl, spin. **3** dance a child on one's knee bounce, jiggle, dandle, ride.

dance noun **1** go to a dance ball, dancing party; inf. hop. **2** learn/perform a dance | study dance ballroom dance, folk dance, modern dance; ballet, eurythmics.

dandle verb dandle a child on one's knee dance, bounce, jiggle, ride.

dandy noun fop, coxcomb, popinjay, beau, blade, man about town, boulevardier, sharp dresser.

danger noun **1** an element of danger risk, peril, hazard, jeopardy, endangerment, imperilment, precariousness, insecurity, instability. **2** a danger to society menace, threat, peril, risk, minacity, imminence.

dangerous adjective **1** involved in a dangerous venture risky, perilous, hazardous, chancy, precarious, uncertain, insecure, unsound, unsafe, exposed, defenceless; inf. hairy. **2** a dangerous crook/omen menacing, threatening, alarming, ominous, nasty, ugly, treacherous, minacious.
Opposites SAFE; HARMLESS.

dangle verb **1** keys dangling from her waist hang, hang down, swing, sway, trail, droop, depend. **2** dangle the keys swing, sway, wave, brandish, flourish, flaunt. **3** he is always dangling after her follow, follow on the heels of, hang around, attach oneself to. **4** he dangled the temptation of a holiday hold out, entice someone with, lure someone with, tempt someone with.

dangling adjective hanging, drooping, swinging, swaying, trailing, unconnected, disconnected, loose.

dank adjective damp, wet, moist, humid, clammy, chilly.

dapper adjective **1** a dapper man dressed in black smartly dressed, smart, well-groomed, well-turned-out, neat, trim, spruce, out of a bandbox, stylish, chic; inf. natty. **2** dapper for his age active, agile, spry, sprightly, nimble, lively, brisk.

dapple verb dapple with paint | sunlight dappling the leaves dot, spot, fleck, bespeckle, mottle, stipple, bedaub.

dappled adjective dappled leaves | a dappled horse spotted, marked, mottled, flecked, blotched,

dare · dark

dare verb **1** *dare not go* have the courage to, pluck up courage to, take the risk to, be brave enough to, have the nerve to, risk, hazard, venture, make bold to. **2** *dare him to go* challenge, throw down the gauntlet, provoke, goad, taunt. **3** *dare his father's anger | dared the rapids* defy, brave, face, meet, meet head on, confront, stand up to.

dare noun *accept his dare* challenge, provocation, goad, taunt, ultimatum.

daredevil adjective *a daredevil attitude | daredevil actions* daring, adventurous, bold, audacious, courageous, intrepid, fearless, undaunted, dauntless, rash, heedless, madcap, harebrained, foolhardy, impetuous, imprudent, incautious, desperate.

daredevil noun *daredevils on the racing circuit* adventurer, desperado, stunt man, madcap, exhibitionist; *inf.* show-off.

daring adjective *a daring person/plan* bold, adventurous, brave, courageous, valiant, audacious, intrepid, fearless, undaunted, dauntless, unshrinking, rash, reckless, madcap, foolhardy, wild, daredevil, desperate. **Opposites** COWARDLY; CAUTIOUS.

daring noun *the daring of the explorers* boldness, adventurousness, bravery, courage, courageousness, valour, audacity, nerve, pluck, grit, intrepidity, fearlessness, rashness, recklessness, temerity, foolhardiness, wildness, desperation; *inf.* guts, spunk.

dark adjective **1** *a dark night* black, pitch-black, pitch-dark, inky, jet-black, unlit, unlighted, ill-lighted, poorly lit, dim, dingy, indistinct, shadowy, shady, murky, foggy, misty, cloudy, overcast, sunless. **2** *dark of hair* dark-haired, brunette, dark brown, jet-black, sable, ebony. **3** *dark of skin*, dark-skinned, swarthy, sallow, olive-skinned, dusky, black, ebony. **4** *dark thoughts* dismal, gloomy, sombre, cheerless, bleak, joyless, drab, dreary, depressed, dejected, melancholy, grim, grave, funereal, morose, mournful, doleful. **5** *in a dark mood* angry, moody, brooding, sullen, dour, glum, morose, sulky, frowning, scowling, glowering, forbidding, threatening, ominous. **6** *dark deeds* evil, wicked, sinful, villainous, iniquitous, vile, base, foul, horrible, atrocious, abominable, nefarious, barbaric, barbarous, sinister, damnable, fiendish, infernal, satanic, hellish, flagitious. **7** *the dark ages* unenlightened, ignorant, uneducated, unschooled, uncultivated, uncultured, unlettered, benighted. **8** *a dark meaning* abstruse, recondite, arcane, profound, deep, incomprehensible, obscure, unfathomable, puzzling, enigmatic, cryptic, complicated, complex, difficult, intricate. **9** *a dark secret | keep it dark* concealed, hidden, veiled, secret, mysterious, mystic, esoteric, occult. **Opposites** LIGHT; FAIR; CHEERFUL.

dark noun **1** *sitting in the dark* darkness, blackness, absence of light, gloom, gloominess, dim-

DANCES AND TYPES OF DANCING

allemande	eightsome reel	jive	ronde
Apache	fan dance	juba	round
ballet	fandango	Lambeth Walk	rumba
ballroom	farandole	lancers	Russian dance
barn dance	flamenco	limbo	samba
basse danse	fling	Lindy Hop	saraband
beguine	folk dance	Madison	sequence dance
belly dance	formation dancing	mambo	shag
black bottom	foxtrot	mashed potato	shake
bolero	frug	maypole dance	shimmy
boogie	galliard	mazurka	shuffle
bop	gallopade	merengue	slam dance
bossa nova	gavotte	Mexican hat	snake
Boston two-step	gigue	military two-step	soft-shoe
break-dance	habanera	minuet	shuffle
bunny hug	haka	morris dance	square dance
cachucha	[Helston] floral	old-time	stomp
cakewalk	dance	one-step	strathspey
cancan	[Helston] furry	palais glide	strut
carioca	Highland fling	paso doble	sword dance
cha-cha-cha	hoedown	Paul Jones	tango
charleston	hokey-cokey	pavane	tap dance
clog dance	hootchy-kootchy	polka	tarantella
conga	hornpipe	polonaise	torch
corroboree	hula-hula	quadrille	twist
Cossack dance	hully gully	quickstep	twosome reel
cotillion	hustle	rain dance	veleta
country dance	Irish jig	reel	vogueing
courante	Irish reel	rigadoon	volta
csardas	jazz dance	ring-shout	waltz
devil dance	jig	robotic dancing	war dance
disco	jitterbug	rock and roll	zapateado

ness, murk, murkiness, shadowiness, shade; *lit.* tenebrosity. **2** *when dark comes/falls* night, night-time, nightfall, dead of night, evening, twilight. **3** *in the dark about his motives* a state of ignorance/unenlightenment.

darken *verb* **1** *the sky darkened* grow dark/darker, blacken, cloud over, dim, grow dim. **2** *darken the room* make dark/darker, make dim, shade. **3** *darken one's skin* make dark/darker, tan, blacken, black, make opaque, begrime. **4** *his mood/face darkened* blacken, grow angry/annoyed, grow/become gloomy, become depressed/dispirited, grow troubled, sadden. **Opposites** LIGHTEN; BRIGHTEN.

darkness *noun* **1** *the darkness of the room | darkness fell* dark, blackness, gloom, dimness, murk, shadowiness; twilight, nightfall. *See* DARK *noun* 1, 2. **2** *the darkness of the middle ages* ignorance, lack of knowledge, unenlightenment. **3** *the darkness of her secret* mystery, concealment, secrecy, obscurity, veiledness. **Opposites** LIGHT; ENLIGHTENMENT.

darling *noun* **1** *goodbye, darling* dear, dearest, dear one, love, sweetheart, beloved, sweet, honey. **2** *the child's a little darling* charmer, pet, sweetheart, honey; *inf.* poppet, sweetie. **3** *the darling of the press* favourite, pet, apple of one's eye, toast; *inf.* blue-eyed boy; *Am. inf.* fair-haired boy.

darling *adjective* **1** *his darling wife* dear, dearest, loved, beloved, adored, cherished, treasured, precious, prized, valued. **2** *a darling little girl* adorable, sweet, lovely, attractive, charming, winsome, enchanting, engaging, captivating, bewitching, alluring; *inf.* cute.

darn *verb* *darn socks* mend, repair, sew up, stitch, patch.

darn *noun* *the darn is obvious* repair, mend, patch, reinforcement.

dart *noun* **1** *throwing a poisoned dart* arrow, barb, quarrel. **2** *make a sudden dart* dash, rush, run, bolt, bound, spring, leap, start.

dart *verb* **1** *dart into the bushes* dash, rush, bolt, fly, flash, sprint, tear, run, bound, shoot, spring, leap, start, scuttle; *inf.* scoot. **2** *dart an angry look* throw, cast, shoot, send, fling, toss, flash, hurl, sling, propel, project.

dash *noun* **1** *make a dash for freedom* rush, bolt, run, race, flight, dart, sprint, sortie, spurt; *inf.* scoot. **2** *a dash of water on his face* splash, sprinkle, spattering, plash. **3** *a dash of salt* little, bit, drop, pinch, sprinkling, grain, touch, trace, tinge, smack, suspicion, suggestion, soupçon. **4** *carry it off with dash* style, élan, verve, vigour, spirit, vivacity, liveliness, flair, panache, flourish, brio; *inf.* pizzazz.

dash *verb* **1** *dash into the road* rush, hurry, hasten, bolt, run, race, fly, dart, sprint, tear, speed; *inf.* scoot. **2** *waves dashing against the shore* strike, beat, break, crash, smash, batter, splinter, shatter. **3** *dash the plate to the floor* smash, crash, throw, hurl, fling, slam, sling, cast, pitch, catapult. **4** *dash her hopes* shatter, destroy, ruin, blight, spoil, frustrate, thwart, baulk, check. **5** *spirits dashed by the misfortune* depress, dispirit, deject, cast down, lower, sad-

den, dishearten, discourage, daunt, abash, dampen.

dashing *adjective* **1** *a dashing young officer* debonair, stylish, spirited, lively, buoyant, energetic, animated, dynamic, gallant, bold, daring, plucky, dazzling, swashbuckling; *inf.* peppy. **2** *dashing uniforms* smart, jaunty, sporty, stylish, elegant, fashionable, chic, dazzling, showy, flamboyant.

dastardly *adjective* cowardly, craven, fearful, faint-hearted, cowering, chicken-livered; *inf.* yellow.

data *plural noun* basic facts, facts, figures, statistics, details; information, material, input.

date *noun* **1** *on a certain date* day, point in time. **2** *artefacts from a previous date* time, age, period, era, century, decade, year, stage. **3** *we have a lunch date* appointment, engagement, meeting, rendezvous, assignation, tryst. **4** *who is his date?* partner, escort, girlfriend, boyfriend, beau; *inf.* steady. **to date** so far, as of now, up to now, up to the present, up to this point. **out of date** *out-of-date ideas/clothes* outdated, dated, old-fashioned, unfashionable, outmoded, obsolete, antiquated, archaic, passé; *inf.* old-hat. **up to date** *up-to-date ideas/clothes* modern, up-to-the-minute, current, contemporary, fashionable, à la mode; *inf.* trendy.

date *verb* **1** *the vase dates from the seventeenth century* originate in, come from, belong to, exist from, bear the date of. **2** *can you date this table?* assign a date to, put a date to, determine the date of, fix the period of. **3** *clothes beginning to date* become dated, become old-fashioned/outmoded/obsolete, show one's age, pass out of use, obsolesce. **4** *he's dating the girl next door* go out/around with, go with, take out; *inf.* go steady with.

dated *adjective* *dated fashions* out of date, outdated, old-fashioned, outmoded, antiquated, passé; *inf.* old-hat. **Opposites** FASHIONABLE; UP-TO-DATE.

daub *verb* **1** *daub paint on* smear, plaster, smudge, spatter, splatter, slap, slop. **2** *daub the walls with paint* smear, besmear, bedaub, plaster, spatter, splatter, cover, coat, deface.

daub *noun* *a daub of paint* smear, smudge, blot, spot, patch, blotch, splotch, splodge.

daunt *verb* intimidate, frighten, scare, alarm, overawe, dismay, disconcert, unnerve, take aback, abash, cow, unman, discourage, dishearten, dispirit, deter, put off. **Opposites** ENCOURAGE; HEARTEN.

dawdle *verb* go/walk slowly, move at a snail's pace, loiter, take one's time, dally, linger, delay, lag/trail behind, kill/waste time, fritter time away, idle, potter about; *inf.* dilly-dally. **Opposites** HURRY; HASTEN.

dawn *noun* **1** *get up at dawn* daybreak, break of day, sunrise, first light, early morning, crack of dawn, cock crow; *Am.* sun-up; *lit.* aurora, dayspring. **2** *the dawn of civilization* dawning, beginning, birth, start, rise, emergence, commencement, origin, inception, genesis, outset, onset, advent, appearance, arrival, unfolding, development. **Opposites** DUSK; END.

dawn verb **1** *day dawned* begin, break, grow light, lighten, brighten, gleam. **2** *civilization dawning* begin, be born, come into being/existence, start, rise, emerge, commence, originate, appear, arrive, unfold, develop. **3** *the truth suddenly dawned on them* occur to one, strike, hit, register, cross/enter one's mind, come into one's head, come to mind, pass through one's mind, flash across one's mind.

day noun **1** *when day dawns* daytime, daylight, daylight hours, broad daylight. **2** *work all day* twenty-four hours, full day, working day, solar day. **3** *in this modern day | in the days of Henry VIII* period, time, age, era, epoch, generation. **4** *the steam train has had its day* prime, heyday, full flowering, useful/productive lifetime, peak, zenith, ascendancy. **5** *set a day* date, set time, time, particular day, appointed day. **day after day** *raining day after day* continuously, relentlessly, persistently, without respite, continually, ceaselessly, regularly. **day by day** *grow bigger day by day* daily, gradually, steadily, progressively.

daybreak noun dawn, break of day, sunrise, first light. See DAWN noun 1.

daydream noun **1** *lost in a daydream* reverie, wool-gathering, musing, imagining, fantasy, vision, fancy, hallucination. **2** *their daydream never materialized* dream, pipedream, figment of the imagination; wishful thinking; fond hopes, wishes, castles in the air, castles in Spain.

daydream verb dream, muse, be lost in thought, stare into space, indulge in wool-gathering, fantasize, indulge in fancy, hallucinate.

daylight noun **1** *look at the colours in daylight* light of day, natural light, sunlight. **2** *children coming home in daylight* daytime, daylight hours; broad daylight. **3** *wake at daylight* dawn, daybreak, break of day, sunrise. See DAWN noun 1. **see daylight** **1** *after being confused she finally saw daylight* understand, comprehend, see the light, fathom, penetrate, discern; inf. get the idea, catch on, get the hang of it, twig, get the picture. **2** *his project never saw daylight* be completed/accomplished, see light of day, come to public attention.

daze verb **1** *dazed by the blow* stun, stupefy, shock, confuse, bewilder, befuddle, muddle, addle, numb, benumb, paralyse. **2** *dazed by the news* stun, shock, amaze, astonish, astound, dumbfound, stagger, startle, surprise, dismay, disconcert, take aback, bewilder, perplex, nonplus; inf. flabbergast, floor, take one's breath away.

daze noun *in a daze* stupor, state of shock, trancelike state, confused state; confusion, bewilderment, distraction, numbness.

dazzle verb **1** *dazzled by the car's headlights* blind temporarily, deprive of sight, bedazzle, daze, overpower. **2** *dazzled by her beauty/wit* overpower, overwhelm, overawe, awe, stagger, fascinate, hypnotize, strike dumb, dumbfound, strike, impress, amaze, astonish; inf. bowl over, take one's breath away.

dazzle noun **1** *overcome by the dazzle of the lights* brightness, brilliance, gleam, flash. **2** *fasci-*nated by the dazzle of the circus* brilliance, splendour, magnificence, glitter, sparkle, glory; inf. razzle-dazzle, razzmatazz, pizzazz.

dead adjective **1** *the dead man/flower* deceased, late, defunct, departed, lifeless, extinct, perished, gone, no more, passed on/away. **2** *dead matter* inanimate, lifeless, without life, exanimate. **3** *a dead issue/language* obsolete, outmoded, outdated, extinct, lapsed, passed, passé, discontinued, disused, fallen into disuse, stagnant, inactive, invalid, ineffective, inoperative, not working, barren, sterile. **4** *dead to my pleas* unresponsive, insensitive, indifferent, apathetic, dispassionate, unsympathetic, emotionless, unemotional, unfeeling, lukewarm, cold, frigid, wooden, inert. **5** *dead fingers* numb, numbed, benumbed, unfeeling, paralysed. **6** *dead eyes* emotionless, glazed, glassy, spiritless, impassive. **7** *dead desire* extinguished, finished, terminated, quenched, quashed, quelled, suppressed, smothered, stifled. **8** *a dead place to live | a dead time of day* dull, boring, uninteresting, tedious, tiresome, wearisome, uneventful, humdrum, flat, stale, insipid, vapid; inf. dead-and-alive. **9** *a dead loss/cert* complete, absolute, total, entire, outright, utter, downright, out-and-out, thorough, unqualified, unmitigated. **10** *come to a dead halt* abrupt, sudden, quick, rapid, swift, hurried, instantaneous, unexpected, unforeseen. **11** *a dead shot* accurate, exact, precise, unerring, unfailing, sure, correct, direct. **12** *feeling dead* tired, tired out, exhausted, worn out, fatigued, spent; inf. dead beat, played out, pooped.
Opposites LIVE; ALIVE; LIVING; LIVELY.

dead adverb *dead right/serious/tired* completely, absolutely, totally, entirely, exactly, utterly, thoroughly, categorically, without qualification.

deaden verb **1** *deaden the pain | deaden the effects of the blow* blunt, dull, muffle, weaken, diminish, reduce, subdue, suppress, moderate, soothe, assuage, abate, mitigate, alleviate, smother, stifle, damp, damp down, numb. **2** *deaden the sound* dull, muffle, reduce, moderate, stifle, damp down, mute. **3** *emotions deadened by grief* render/make insensitive, desensitize, numb, benumb, anaesthetize, impair, incapacitate, paralyse.

deadlock noun **1** *the talks ended in deadlock* stalemate, checkmate, impasse, standstill, halt, stop, stoppage, cessation, standoff. **2** *the game ended in deadlock* tie, draw, dead heat.

deadly adjective **1** *deadly poisons* fatal, lethal, mortal, death-dealing, dangerous, destructive, harmful, pernicious, noxious, malignant, venomous, toxic, poisonous, virulent. **2** *deadly enemies* mortal, hated, hostile, murderous, fierce, implacable, remorseless, unrelenting, grim, savage; inf. at each other's throats. **3** *deadly seriousness* intense, great, marked, extreme, excessive, immoderate, inordinate. **4** *deadly paleness* deathlike, deathly, ashen, ghostly, white, pallid, wan, pale, ghastly. **5** *a deadly aim* precise, accurate, unerring, unfailing, sure, true, on target, on the mark. **6** *a deadly speaker/speech* boring, dull, tedious, unin-

teresting, dry, monotonous, wearisome, humdrum, lacklustre.

deadly *adverb* completely, absolutely. *See* DEAD
adverb.

deaf *adjective* **1** *born deaf* with impaired hearing, unhearing, hard of hearing, stone deaf,
deaf as a post. **2** *deaf to their pleas* unmoved
by, indifferent to, oblivious to, heedless of,
unconcerned with, unmindful of.
Opposites HEEDFUL; ATTENTIVE.

deafen *verb the noise deafened us* make temporarily deaf, deprive of hearing, impair one's
hearing, burst one's eardrums.

deafening *adjective* very loud, ear-splitting,
ear-piercing, overpowering, overwhelming,
booming, thunderous, resounding, reverberating, ringing, dinning.

deal *verb* **1** *deal with a problem* attend to, see
to, take care of, cope with, handle, manage,
sort out, tackle, take measures. **2** *the book
deals with skin problems* be about, have to do
with, concern, concern itself with, discuss,
consider, treat of. **3** *deal honourably with the
prisoners* act, behave, conduct oneself. **4** *deal
in stocks and shares* trade, traffic, do business,
buy and sell, be concerned/engaged in, negotiate, bargain. **5** *deal cards* distribute, give out,
share out, divide out, hand out, dole out, mete
out, allocate, dispense, allot, assign, apportion,
bestow. **6** *deal a blow* deliver, administer, give,
direct, aim.

deal *noun* **1** *a deal of trouble* | *a great deal of
money* | *feel a good deal better* amount, quantity,
degree. **2** *finalize the deal* arrangement, transaction, agreement, negotiation, bargain, contract, pact, understanding, compact,
concordat. **3** *be given a fair deal* treatment,
handling, usage, procedure.

dealer *noun* **1** *a dealer in used cars* trader, salesman, saleswoman, salesperson, tradesman,
merchant, marketer, retailer, wholesaler, vendor, chandler, trafficker, pedlar. **2** *a dealer in
the stock market* jobber, broker.

dealing *noun a business noted for fair dealing*
business methods/practices, actions; treatment, policy, behaviour, conduct.

dealings *plural noun have dealings with the firm*
business, trade, commerce, trafficking, truck;
transactions, relations, negotiations.

dean *noun* **1** *dean of the arts faculty* faculty
head, head of department, university official,
provost. **2** *the cathedral dean* chapter head,
supervisor; rural dean. *See table at* ECCLESIASTIC.

dear *adjective* **1** *his dear wife* | *dear friends*
beloved, loved, darling, adored, cherished,
close, intimate, esteemed, respected. **2** *her
dearest possessions/possessions dear to him* precious, treasured, valued, prized, cherished,
favourite, favoured. **3** *what a dear child* sweet,
darling, endearing, lovable, attractive, winning, enchanting, winsome, angelic. **4** *a dear
brand of car* expensive, costly, highly priced,
high-priced, overpriced, exorbitant, valuable,
at a premium, up-market; *inf.* pricey, steep.
Opposites WORTHLESS; DISAGREEABLE; CHEAP.

dear *noun* **1** *goodbye, my dear* love, beloved,
darling, loved one, sweetheart, sweet, honey,
pet, precious, treasure. **2** *his mother's a dear*
lovable person, darling, sweetheart, pet, angel.

dear *adverb a victory costing dear* | *sell dear* at a
high price, at great cost, at a heavy cost,
much, with great loss/damage.

dearly *adverb* **1** *loving her dearly* very much,
greatly, deeply, extremely, profoundly. **2** *pay
dearly for mistakes* dear, at great cost, much,
with great loss/damage. *See* DEAR *adverb.*

dearth *noun* lack, scarcity, scarceness, want,
deficiency, shortage, shortness, insufficiency,
paucity, sparseness, meagreness, scantiness,
rareness, exiguity.
Opposites ABUNDANCE; SURFEIT.

death *noun* **1** *death by drowning* dying, decease,
demise, end, passing, passing away, passing
on, loss of life, expiration, quietus, departure
from life, final exit, eternal rest; *inf.* curtains.
See DIE 1. **2** *the death of his hopes* end, finish,
termination, cessation, ruin, ruination, extinction, destruction, extermination, eradication,
annihilation, obliteration, extirpation. **3** *death
came in the night* angel of death, grim reaper.
4 *their deaths were on his conscience* killing, slaying, murder, slaughter, fatality; bloodshed,
massacre, carnage.
Opposites LIFE; BIRTH.

deathless *adjective* immortal, undying, everlasting, eternal, unfading, perpetual, imperishable, timeless, memorable.

debacle *noun* fiasco, failure, downfall, collapse, disintegration, disaster, catastrophe,
tumult, turmoil, havoc, ruin, ruination, devastation, defeat, rout, overthrow.

debar *verb* **1** *debarred from the club* shut out,
exclude, bar, keep out, preclude. **2** *debarred
from voting* exclude, bar, prevent, prohibit, forbid, proscribe, disallow, veto.
Opposites ADMIT; ALLOW.

debase *verb* **1** *debase the sport* | *debase oneself*
degrade, devalue, demean, drag down, dis-
grace, dishonour, shame, bring shame to, discredit, lower/reduce the status of, cheapen,
humble, humiliate. **2** *debase coins* | *debase the
mixture* alloy, adulterate, depreciate, dilute,
contaminate, pollute, taint, corrupt, bastardize, vitiate.

debatable *adjective* arguable, disputable, questionable, open to question, controversial, contentious, doubtful, open to doubt, dubious,
uncertain, unsure, unsettled, undecided, borderline, moot.

debate *noun* **1** *a formal debate* | *open to debate*
discussion, argument, dispute, disputation,
difference of opinion, wrangle, altercation,
controversy, contention, war of words,
polemic. **2** *after some debate with himself* consideration, deliberation, reflection, contemplation, musing, meditation, cogitation.

debate *verb* **1** *debate the issue* discuss, argue,
argue the pros and cons of, dispute, wrangle,
bandy words, contend, contest, altercate, controvert, moot; *inf.* kick around. **2** *he debated
with himself* consider, think over, deliberate,
reflect, contemplate, muse, meditate, cogitate.

debauched *adjective* dissipated, dissolute, degenerate, corrupt, immoral, abandoned, profligate, intemperate, licentious, promiscuous, wanton.

debauchery *noun* dissipation, dissoluteness, degeneracy, corruption, immorality, profligacy, intemperance, licentiousness, promiscuity, wantonness, rakishness, libertinism, perversion.

debilitate *verb debilitated by his illness* weaken, make feeble, enfeeble, enervate, incapacitate, cripple, impair, sap, undermine, exhaust, wear out, prostrate, devitalize.

debility *noun* weakness, feebleness, frailty, infirmity, enfeeblement, enervation, incapacity, impairment, lack of energy, exhaustion, fatigue, lack of vitality, sickliness, decrepitude, malaise.

debonair *adjective* **1** *a debonair young man* suave, urbane, self-assured, elegant, refined, well-bred, genteel, smart, dashing, dapper, charming, courteous, mannerly, gallant, chivalrous; *inf.* smooth. **2** *debonair young people* carefree, jaunty, light-hearted, cheerful, cheery, merry, vivacious, buoyant, breezy, sprightly.

debris *noun* rubble, wreckage, detritus, rubbish, litter; remains, ruins, fragments.

debt *noun* **1** *pay my debts* money owing, bill, account, score, tally; dues, arrears, debits. **2** *acknowledge his debt to his family* indebtedness, obligation, liability. **3** *customers in debt | got himself into debt* a state of owing money, indebtedness; arrears; *inf.* the red.

debunk *noun* cut down to size, deflate, puncture, expose, show up, show in one's/its true light, mock, ridicule.

debut *noun* first appearance, first performance, first time, *première*, beginning, introduction, launching, coming-out, entrance.
Opposites FAREWELL; swansong; END; FINISH.

decadence *noun* **1** *the decadence of the empire* decay, degeneration, deterioration, decline, wane, ebb, debasement, degradation, retrogression. **2** *the decadence of the wealthy set* dissipation, dissoluteness, moral decay, debauchery, degeneracy, immorality, self-indulgence, licentiousness, hedonism, epicureanism, corruption, depravity.

decadent *adjective* **1** *a decadent empire* decaying, degenerating, deteriorating, declining, waning, ebbing, debased, degraded, falling off, on the wane. **2** *decadent behaviour/people* dissipated, dissolute, debauched, degenerate, immoral, self-indulgent, licentious, hedonistic, epicurean, corrupt, depraved.
Opposites PROSPEROUS; MORAL; VIRTUOUS.

decamp *verb* **1** *the manager decamped with the firm's takings* make off, run off/away, flee, take off, abscond, escape, cut and run; *inf.* skedaddle, hightail it, hotfoot it, vamoose, skip, do a moonlight flit. **2** *the soldiers decamped* break camp, strike tents, move on.

decant *verb* pour out, draw off, drain, tap.

decapitate *verb* behead, execute, guillotine, put on the block.

decay *verb* **1** *food/material decaying* rot, go bad, decompose, putrefy, spoil, perish, corrode. **2** *an empire decaying* degenerate, deteriorate, decline, fail, wane, ebb, dwindle, crumble, disintegrate, fall to pieces, sink, collapse, moulder, shrivel, wither, die, waste/wear away, atrophy.
Opposites THRIVE; FLOURISH; PROSPER.

decay *noun* **1** *the decay of the food/material* rotting, going bad, decomposition, putrefaction, putrescence, putridity, spoilage, perishing, corrosion. **2** *spot the decay in the food/teeth/flesh* rot, decomposition; caries, gangrene. **3** *the decay of the empire* degeneration, deterioration, decline, failure, waning, ebb, crumbling, disintegration, collapse, withering, death, atrophy. *See* DECAY *verb* 2.

decease *noun the decease of his wife* death, dying, demise, passing, passing away/on, expiration, quietus. *See* DEATH 1.

decease *verb he deceased before his wife* die, pass away/on, expire, perish, meet one's death.

deceased *adjective his deceased wife* late, dead, departed, defunct, lost, expired. *See* DEAD *adjective* 1.

deceit *noun* **1** *practise deceit* deceitfulness, deception, duplicity, double-dealing, fraud, fraudulence, cheating, trickery, duping, chicanery, underhandedness, cunning, craftiness, craft, wiliness, guile, dissimulation, dissembling, pretence, artifice, treachery; *inf.* hanky-panky. **2** *win by a deceit* deception, trick, stratagem, ruse, dodge, subterfuge, fraud, cheat, swindle, sham, imposture, hoax, pretence, fake, misrepresentation, blind, wile, artifice, shift, Trojan horse; *inf.* leg-pull.
Opposites HONESTY; CANDOUR; SINCERITY.

deceitful *adjective* **1** *don't believe that deceitful child* lying, untruthful, dishonest, mendacious, insincere, false, disingenuous, untrustworthy, two-faced, underhand, crafty, cunning, sly, guileful, hypocritical, perfidious. **2** *deceitful practices* deceptive, duplicitous, misleading, double-dealing, fraudulent, cheating, underhand, crooked, counterfeit, sham, bogus, dissembling, treacherous, perfidious, illusory, spurious, specious; *inf.* sneaky, tricky.

deceive *verb* **1** *his friendliness deceived us* take in, mislead, delude, fool, pull the wool over one's eyes, throw dust in the eyes of, misguide, lead on, trick, hoodwink, hoax, dupe, swindle, outwit, bamboozle, seduce, ensnare, entrap, beguile, double-cross, cozen, gull; *inf.* con, pull a fast one on, pull one's leg, take one for a ride. **2** *he's deceiving his wife* be unfaithful to, betray; *inf.* two-time; *Am. inf.* cheat on.

decelerate *verb* slow down, reduce speed, brake, put the brakes on, ease up.

decency *noun* propriety, decorum, seemliness, modesty, good taste, respectability, purity, correctness, good form, etiquette, delicacy, dignity, appropriateness, fitness, suitability.

decent *adjective* **1** *a scarcely decent exhibition* decorous, seemly, modest, proper, nice, tasteful, polite, respectable, pure, correct, dignified, delicate, appropriate, fitting, fit, suitable, becoming, *comme il faut*. **2** *decent kind of fellow*

obliging, helpful, accommodating, generous, kind, thoughtful, courteous, civil, honest, honourable, trustworthy, dependable, worthy, respectable, upright. **3** *earning quite a decent salary* acceptable, adequate, sufficient, ample, average, competent.
Opposites INDECENT; UNSUITABLE; DISHONEST.

deception *noun* **1** *practise deception* deceit, deceitfulness, double-dealing, duplicity, fraud, fraudulence, cheating, chicanery, trickery, underhandedness, cunning, dissimulation, pretence, artifice. *See* DECEIT 1. **2** *win by a deception* trick, stratagem, ruse, dodge, subterfuge, fraud, cheat, swindle, sham, pretence, blind. *See* DECEIT 2.

deceptive *adjective* **1** *appearances can be deceptive* deceiving, misleading, false, illusory, delusive, fallacious, ambiguous, specious, spurious, mock, pseudo. **2** *deceptive practices* deceitful, duplicitous, fraudulent, cheating, underhand, cunning, crafty, crooked, counterfeit, sham, bogus, dissembling; *inf.* sneaky, tricky.

decide *verb* **1** *to decide to go | I cannot decide* come to a decision, reach/make a decision, make up one's mind, resolve, come to a conclusion, commit oneself, choose. **2** *that decided the matter* settle, resolve, bring to a conclusion, determine, work out, clinch; *inf.* sew up. **3** *the judge will decide the case | the judge decided for/ against the defence* judge, adjudge, adjudicate, arbitrate, umpire, referee; make a judgement on, pass/pronounce judgement, give a verdict, make a ruling.

decided *adjective* **1** *a decided difference between them* distinct, clear, clear-cut, definite, certain, marked, pronounced, obvious, express, unmistakable, absolute, emphatic, categorical, unambiguous, undeniable, unequivocal, indisputable, undisputed, unquestionable. **2** *he's quite decided | a decided effort* determined, resolute, firm, strong-minded, dogged, purposeful, unhesitating, unwavering, unswerving, unfaltering, incisive, forceful, emphatic. **3** *the matter was decided* settled, resolved, concluded, determined, clinched; *inf.* sewn up. *See* DECIDE 2.
Opposites DOUBTFUL; INDECISIVE.

decidedly *adverb* decidedly *unwell* distinctly, clearly, definitely, certainly, positively, markedly, unmistakably, absolutely, downright, undeniably, unquestionably. *See* DECIDED 1.

deciding *adjective* **1** *the deciding factor* crucial, critical, decisive, determining, conclusive, most influential, significant, chief, principal, prime. **2** *the deciding vote* casting, determining, conclusive.

decipher *verb* **1** *decipher the coded message* decode, translate, interpret, construe, solve, work out, figure out, unravel, unfold, reveal; *inf.* crack. **2** *cannot decipher her handwriting* make out, read, understand, comprehend, deduce.

decision *noun* **1** *come to a decision* resolution, conclusion, determination, settling, settlement. **2** *the judge announced his decision* judgement, ruling, pronouncement, verdict, adjudgement, adjudication, arbitration; find-

ings. **3** *a man of decision* decisiveness, determination, resolution, resoluteness, resolve, firmness, strong-mindedness, doggedness, strength of mind/will, firmness of purpose, purpose, purposefulness.

decisive *adjective* **1** *a decisive person* determined, resolute, firm, dogged, purposeful, unhesitating, unwavering, unswerving, unfaltering, incisive, forceful, emphatic. **2** *a decisive factor* deciding, determining, determinate, definitive, conclusive, final, settling, critical, crucial, momentous, emphatic, absolute, categorical, significant, influential, important, definite, positive.
Opposites HESITANT; INDECISIVE; IRRESOLUTE; INSIGNIFICANT.

deck *verb* **1** *deck the rooms for Christmas* bedeck, decorate, adorn, ornament, trim, embellish, garnish, festoon, garland, trick out, beautify, prettify, enhance, grace, enrich. **2** *people all decked out in their Sunday best* dress up, clothe, attire, array, apparel, rig out, tog up, outfit; *inf.* be got up.

declaim *verb* **1** *ministers declaiming from the pulpit* make a speech, speak, hold forth, lecture, harangue, rant, rail, pronounce, sermonize, speechify, spout, make an oration, orate, perorate; *inf.* sound off, spiel. *See table at* ORATOR. **2** *the preacher declaiming against adultery* speak out, protest, rail, inveigh.

declamation *noun a passionate declamation* speech, address, oration, lecture, delivery, sermon, discourse, recitation, harangue, tirade; *Am. inf.* stump speech.

declamatory *adjective declamatory style* rhetorical, oratorical, theatrical, high-flown, bombastic, pompous, pretentious, orotund, fustian. *See table at* RHETORIC.

declaration *noun* **1** *the declaration of his interests | declaration of war* announcement, statement, proclamation, notification, pronouncement, publishing, broadcasting, promulgation, edict, manifesto, pronunciamento. **2** *his declaration that he was innocent* statement, assertion, maintaining, insistence, protestation, averment, affirmation, contention, profession, claim, allegation, avowal, swearing. **3** *his behaviour is a declaration of his innocence* acknowledgement, revelation, disclosure, manifestation, confirmation, proof, testimony, validation, certification, attestation.

declare *verb* **1** *declare one's interests | declare war* announce, make known, proclaim, pronounce, publish, broadcast, promulgate, trumpet, blazon. **2** *he declared that he was innocent* state, assert, maintain, aver, affirm, contend, profess, claim, allege, avow, swear. **3** *his behaviour declared his innocence* show, make known, reveal, disclose, manifest, confirm, prove, testify to, validate, certify, attest.

decline *verb* **1** *decline an invitation | we must decline | decline to comment* turn down, give the thumbs down to, rebuff, repudiate, forgo; refuse, say no, send one's regrets. **2** *his influence declined* get less, lessen, decrease, diminish, wane, dwindle, fade, ebb, fall/taper off, abate, flag. **3** *the empire is declining | his strength*

is *declining* deteriorate, degenerate, decay, fail, fall, wither, weaken, fade away, wane, ebb, sink. **4** *the terrain declines here* descend, slope/ slant down, dip, sink.
Opposites ACCEPT; FLOURISH; INCREASE.

decline noun **1** *the decline of his influence/ strength* lessening, decrease, downturn, downswing, diminishing, diminution, waning, dwindling, fading, ebb, falling-off, abatement, slump, plunge, nosedive. *See* DECLINE *verb* 2.
2 *the decline of the empire* deterioration, degeneration, decay, failure, fall, withering, enfeeblement, wane, ebb, atrophy. *See* DECLINE *verb* 3. **3** *hikers sighting a decline* slope, declivity, dip.

decompose verb **1** *corpses decomposing* decay, rot, go bad, putrefy, fester. **2** *the structure gradually decomposing* break up, fall apart, disintegrate, crumble. **3** *decompose the chemical substance* separate, break up/down, divide, disintegrate, dissect, analyse, atomize, dissolve, resolve.

decomposition noun **1** *the decomposition of the corpses* decay, rot, rotting, putrefaction, putrescence, putridity, cariosity, cariousness. **2** *the decomposition of the structure* disintegration, crumbling. *See* DECOMPOSE 2. **3** *the decomposition of the substance* separation, breakup, breakdown, division, disintegration, dissection, analysis, atomization, dissolution, resolution.

decor noun decoration, furnishing, furbishing, colour scheme, ornamentation.

decorate verb **1** *decorate the Christmas tree* adorn, ornament, trim, embellish, garnish, festoon, garland, trick out, beautify, prettify, enhance, grace, enrich. **2** *decorate the house* paint, wallpaper, paper, renovate, refurbish, furbish; *inf.* do up, spruce up. **3** *decorated for bravery* cite, honour, confer an award, give a medal to, pin a medal on.

decoration noun **1** *the decoration of the tree* adornment, ornamentation, trimming, embellishment, garnishing, beautification, prettification, enhancement. *See* DECORATE 1. **2** *admire the decoration* furnishing, colour scheme. *See* DECOR. **3** *buy tree decorations* ornament, trinket, bauble, spangle, knick-knack, gimcrack, doodah, gewgaw, fandangle; trimming, tinsel.
4 *a dress with many decorations* trimming, frill, flounce, furbelow, falderal, frippery, flourish, scroll, arabesque, curlicue. **5** *a decoration for bravery* award, medal, badge, star, ribbon, laurel, wreath; colours, insignia.

decorative adjective *decorative features* ornamental, fancy, adorning, embellishing, garnishing, beautifying, prettifying, enhancing, nonfunctional.

decorous adjective **1** *decorous behaviour* proper, seemly, decent, becoming, befitting, tasteful, in good taste, correct, *comme il faut*, appropriate, suitable, fitting, apt, apposite, polite, well-mannered, mannerly, well-behaved, genteel, refined, well-bred, dignified, respectable. **2** *decorous young ladies* modest, demure, reserved, sedate, staid.
Opposites INDECOROUS; UNSEEMLY; IMMODEST.

decorum noun **1** *behave with decorum* decorousness, propriety, properness, seemliness, decency, good taste, correctness, appropriateness, politeness, courtesy, refinement, breeding, deportment, dignity, respectability.
2 *observe decorum* etiquette, protocol, punctilio, customary behaviour, good form, politeness, politesse, conformity; *inf.* the thing to do.

decoy noun *a dead animal as a decoy | chocolates used as a decoy* lure, bait, enticement, inducement, temptation, attraction, allurement, ensnarement, entrapment, snare, trap, pitfall.

decoy verb *decoy the deer/child* lure, entice, induce, tempt, seduce, inveigle, ensnare, entrap, snare, trap.

decrease verb **1** *numbers/volume decreasing* lessen, grow less, diminish, reduce, drop, fall off, decline, dwindle, contract, shrink.
2 *decrease the numbers/amount* lessen, make fewer/less, lower, reduce, cut down/back, cut down/back on, curtail, contract, diminish.
3 *the wind/storm decreased* die down, abate, subside, let up, slacken, ebb, wane, taper off, peter out.
Opposites INCREASE.

decrease noun **1** *the decrease in numbers/ amount* lessening, lowering, reduction, drop, decline, falling-off, downturn, cut-back, curtailment, diminution, contraction, shrinkage.
2 *the decrease in the wind/storm* dying down, abatement, subsidence, letting-up, slackening, ebb, wane.
Opposites INCREASE.

decree noun **1** *the emperor's decree* edict, order, law, statute, act, ordinance, regulation, rule, injunction, enactment, command, mandate, proclamation, dictum, precept, manifesto, pronunciamento. **2** *the judge's decree* ruling, verdict, judgement, decision; findings.

decree verb *the emperor decreed it | fate decreed it* ordain, rule, order, command, dictate, lay down, prescribe, pronounce, proclaim, enact, adjudge, enjoin, direct, decide, determine.

decrepit adjective **1** *decrepit old men* feeble, enfeebled, infirm, weak, weakened, weakly, frail, wasted, debilitated, disabled, incapacitated, crippled, doddering, tottering, aged, old, elderly, senile, superannuated, effete, emasculated, senescent. **2** *decrepit old furniture/houses* dilapidated, rickety, broken-down, tumbledown, ramshackle, run-down, worn-out, battered, decayed, deteriorated, antiquated, superannuated, the worse for wear, on its last legs.
Opposites STRONG; FIT.

decry verb disparage, deprecate, belittle, cry down, discredit, depreciate, devalue, play down, derogate, detract, diminish, minimize, underestimate, underrate, undervalue, criticize, carp at, cavil at, censure, blame, condemn, denounce, run down, rail against, rap, traduce; *inf.* knock, do a hatchet job on.
Opposites PRAISE; OVERRATE.

dedicate verb **1** *dedicate her life to the Church* devote, give, give over, commit, pledge, surrender. **2** *dedicate the book to him* inscribe, address, name, assign, offer. **3** *dedicate a* *church* devote to God, bless, make holy, consecrate, sanctify, hallow.

dedicated *adjective a dedicated teacher* devoted, committed, wholehearted, single-minded, enthusiastic, zealous, sworn, pledged.
Opposites INDIFFERENT; APATHETIC.

dedication *noun* 1 *work with dedication* devotion, devotedness, commitment, wholeheartedness, single-mindedness, enthusiasm, zeal. 2 *her dedication to the Church* devotion, commitment, allegiance, loyalty, faithfulness, adherence. 3 *the dedication in the book* inscription, address, message. 4 *the dedication of the church* blessing, consecration, sanctification, hallowing.

deduce *verb* conclude, come to the conclusion that, infer, reason, gather, glean, come to understand, understand, assume, presume; *inf.* suss out.

deduct *verb* subtract, take away, take off, withdraw, abstract, remove, discount; *inf.* knock off.
Opposites ADD.

deduction *noun* 1 *the detectives' sound deduction* conclusion, inference, reasoning, assumption, presumption, corollary; results, findings. 2 *the deduction of tax* subtraction, taking-off, withdrawal, abstraction, removal. *See* DEDUCT.

deed *noun* 1 *brave deeds* act, action, feat, exploit, performance, achievement, accomplishment, undertaking, enterprise. 2 *in deed but not in name* fact, reality, truth. 3 *legal deeds* signed document, contract, legal agreement, indenture, instrument; title deed, deed of covenant.

deem *verb* think, believe, consider, judge, feel, imagine, conceive, regard, see, hold, estimate, calculate, suppose, reckon, account.

deep *adjective* 1 *a deep hole/wound* extending far down/in, cavernous, yawning, profound, bottomless, immeasurable, fathomless, unfathomable. 2 *a deep voice* low, low-pitched, full-toned, bass, rich, powerful, resonant, sonorous, rumbling, booming, resounding. 3 *a deep red colour* dark, intense, vivid, rich, strong. 4 *deep distrust* profound, extreme, intense, very great, great, grave, deep-seated, deep-rooted. 5 *a deep thinker/person* clever, intellectual, learned, wise, sagacious, sage, discerning, penetrating, perspicacious. 6 *deep affection* intense, heartfelt, deep-felt, fervent, ardent, impassioned, deep-seated, deep-rooted. 7 *a deep plot* cunning, crafty, artful, shrewd, astute, devious, scheming, designing, insidious, wily, ingenious. 8 *a deep mystery/secret* obscure, unclear, abstruse, mysterious, hidden, secret, unfathomable, recondite, esoteric, enigmatic, arcane. 9 *deep in thought* absorbed, engrossed, preoccupied, rapt, immersed, lost, intent, engaged.
Opposites HIGH; SHALLOW; LIGHT; SUPERFICIAL.

deep *adverb* 1 *dig deep* far down, far in. 2 *deep into the wood/night* far, long, late.

deep *noun* **the deep** 1 *ships wrecked on the deep* sea, ocean, main; high seas; *inf.* the briny. 2 *in the deep of the night* deepness, middle, midst, mid-point, central point.

deepen *verb* 1 *his distress/love deepened* grow, increase, intensify. 2 *deepen the hole* dig out, excavate, scoop out, hollow out. 3 *deepen his distress/love* increase, add to, intensify, magnify, strengthen, heighten, reinforce.

deeply *adverb* 1 *deeply impressed/hurt* very, greatly, extremely, profoundly, intensely, keenly, acutely. 2 *feel his death deeply* acutely, keenly, intensely, sharply, with feeling, feelingly, passionately, with distress.

deer *noun. See table.*

deface *verb* deface the book/wall with writing spoil, disfigure, mar, blemish, deform, ruin, sully, tarnish, damage, vandalize, injure, uglify.

de facto *adjective a de facto ruler* actual, existing, existent, real.

de facto *adverb* ruling de facto in fact, in reality, really, actually, in actuality, in effect.

defamation *noun* slander, libel, character assassination, aspersion, calumny, smear campaign, backbiting, vilification, traducement, defilement, obloquy, contumely, malicious gossip, scandal, abuse, malediction, disparage-

---

DEER AND ANTELOPES

addax	eland	mouse deer	rhebok
axis deer	elk	mule deer	roan antelope
barasingha	fallow deer	muntjac	roe deer
beisa	gazelle	musk deer	royal antelope
blackbuck	gemsbok	nilgai	sable antelope
blesbok	gerenuk	nyala	saiga
bongo	gnu	okapi	sambar
bontebok	goat-antelope	oribi	sasin
bushbuck	grysbok	oryx	sika
caribou	guemal	Père David's	sitatunga
chevrotain	hartebeest	deer	springbok
Chinese water	impala	pronghorn	steenbok
deer	klipspringer	antelope	swamp deer
Clark's gazelle	kob	pudu	tufted deer
dibatag	kudu	red deer	wapiti
dik-dik	marsh deer	reedbuck	water-buck
duiker	moose	reindeer	wildebeest

ment, denigration, detraction, derogation; smear, slur, insult; *inf.* mud-slinging.

defamatory *adjective* slanderous, libellous, calumnious, calumniatory, slurring, backbiting, vilifying, traducing, defiling, contumelious, malicious, abusive, injurious, maledictory, maledictive, disparaging, denigratory, detracting, derogatory, insulting; *inf.* mud-slinging.

defame *verb* slander, libel, cast aspersions on, asperse, blacken the name/character of, malign, smear, run down, speak evil of, backbite, vilify, traduce, besmirch, defile, stigmatize, disparage, denigrate, discredit, decry, insult; *inf.* do a hatchet job on, sling/fling/throw mud at, drag through the mud; *Am. inf.* bad-mouth.

default *noun* **1** *debtors guilty of default* non-payment, failure to pay, non-remittance; *inf.* welshing, bilking. **2** *lose the game by default | in default of evidence* absence, failure to appear, non-appearance, omission, lack, want, deficiency, neglect, negligence, delinquency, dereliction.

defaulter *noun* **1** *defaulters ordered to pay* non-payer, debt-dodger, levanter; *inf.* welsher, bilker. **2** *several defaulters in the competition* non-appearer, absentee.

defeat *verb* **1** *defeat their team/army* beat, conquer, win a victory over, get the better of, vanquish, rout, trounce, thrash, overcome, overpower, overthrow, overwhelm, crush, quash, quell, subjugate, subdue, repulse; *inf.* wipe the floor with, clobber, zap. **2** *your attitude defeats me | the problem defeats me* baffle, puzzle, perplex, confound, frustrate. **3** *defeat your own purpose* hinder, prevent, ruin, thwart, frustrate, foil, balk, hamper, obstruct, impede, discomfit; *inf.* put the kibosh on, nip in the bud. **4** *the motion was defeated* reject, overthrow, throw out, outvote.
Opposites LOSE; SURRENDER; ADVANCE.

defeat *noun* **1** *suffer defeat by the enemy* conquest, vanquishment, rout, beating, trouncing, thrashing, debacle, reverse, overpowering, overthrow, subjugation. *See* DEFEAT *verb* 1.
2 *the defeat of their plans* downfall, breakdown, collapse, failure, ruin, abortion, miscarriage; undoing, reverse, disappointment, setback, discomfiture, rejection, overthrow.
Opposites VICTORY; SUCCESS; TRIUMPH.

defeatist *noun* quitter, yielder, pessimist, prophet of doom, doomwatcher, reneger; *inf.* doomster.

defecate *verb* pass/discharge/excrete faeces, have a bowel movement, void excrement, have diarrhoea; *inf.* do number two, have a BM, do a pooh, do a woopsie.

defect *noun* **1** *a defect in the machine/writing* fault, flaw, imperfection, deficiency, weakness, weak spot/point, shortcoming, failing, snag, kink, deformity, blemish, crack, break, tear, scratch, spot, mistake, error; *inf.* bug. **2** *defects in the educational system* deficiency, shortage, shortfall, inadequacy, insufficiency, shortcoming, lack, want, omission, weakness, failing, fault, flaw, absence.

defect *verb* **1** *soldiers defected | party members defecting* go over to the enemy, desert, turn traitor, change sides/allegiances, *desert one's side/cause,* shift ground, break faith, tergiversate, be apostate, apostatize. **2** *defect from one's country/party* desert, abandon, forsake, renounce, repudiate, secede from, rebel against, revolt against; *inf.* rat on.

defection *noun* *soldiers guilty of defection* desertion, treason, betrayal, changing sides/allegiances, disloyalty, rebellion, mutiny, perfidy, tergiversation, apostasy, secession, dereliction, recreancy.

defective *adjective* **1** *a defective machine* faulty, flawed, imperfect, weak, deficient, deformed, incomplete, malfunctioning, in disrepair, cracked, torn, scratched. **2** *defective in character* lacking, wanting, deficient, inadequate, insufficient, short, low, scant. **3** *mentally defective* having learning difficulties, impaired, retarded, abnormal, subnormal.
Opposites PERFECT; INTACT; NORMAL.

defector *noun* deserter, turncoat, traitor, renegade, tergiversator, apostate, recreant; *inf.* rat.

defence *noun* **1** *built as a defence against the enemy* protection, shield, safeguard, guard, security, cover, shelter, screen, fortification, resistance, deterrent. **2** *build defences against the enemy* barricade, fortification, rampart, bulwark, buttress, fortress, fastness, keep, bastion. **3** *money spent on defence* military measures/resources, armaments, weapons. **4** *published a defence of his ideas* vindication, justification, apologia, apology, argument, plea, explanation, explication, excuse, extenuation, exoneration, palliation. **5** *the accused gave his defence* denial, rebuttal, plea, pleading, testimony, declaration, case, excuse, alibi.

defenceless *adjective* **1** *defenceless old people* helpless, vulnerable, weak, powerless, impotent. **2** *defenceless cities* undefended, unprotected, unguarded, unfortified, unarmed, vulnerable, open to attack, wide open, exposed, endangered.

defend *verb* **1** *defend the city* protect, guard, safeguard, watch over, keep from harm, preserve, secure, shield, shelter, screen, fortify, garrison, fight for. **2** *defend one's ideas* vindicate, justify, argue/speak for, speak on behalf of, give an apologia for, make a case for, plead for, explain, give reasons for, give the rationale behind, exonerate, palliate. **3** *the newspaper defended its journalist* support, back, stand by, stand/stick up for, argue for, champion, endorse, uphold, sustain, bolster.
Opposites ATTACK; CRITICIZE.

defendant *noun* accused, prisoner at the bar, appellant, litigant, respondent.

defender *noun* **1** *defenders of the city* protector, guard, bodyguard, guardian, preserver, keeper. **2** *defenders of the faith* supporter, backer, champion, upholder, endorser, sustainer, bolsterer.

defensible *adjective* **1** *a defensible position/attitude* defendable, justifiable, arguable, tenable, valid, maintainable, sustainable, plausible, permissible, excusable, pardonable, vindicable.

2 *defensible terrain* invulnerable, impregnable, impenetrable, secure, safe, unattackable, unassailable, fortified.

defensive *adjective* **1** *defensive enemy tactics* defending, protecting, protective, safeguarding, shielding, watchful, averting, withstanding, opposing. See DEFEND 1. **2** *the child's defensive attitude* self-defensive, over-sensitive, thin-skinned, prickly; *inf.* uptight.

defer[1] *verb defer the meeting* postpone, put off, adjourn, delay, hold over, shelve, put on ice, pigeon-hole, suspend, table, stay, hold in abeyance, prorogue.

defer[2] *verb defer to the expert | defer to your superior knowledge* yield, submit, bow, give way, give in, surrender, accede, capitulate, acquiesce, comply with, respect.

deference *noun* **1** *showing deference for the old* respect, regard, consideration, attentiveness, attention, thoughtfulness, esteem, courteousness, courtesy, politeness, civility, dutifulness, reverence, veneration, homage. **2** *his deference to the expert* yielding, submission, surrender, capitulation, accession, acquiescence, complaisance, obeisance.
Opposites DISRESPECT; DISCOURTESY.

deferential *adjective* **1** *a deferential regard for the old* respectful, considerate, thoughtful, attentive, courteous, polite, civil, reverent, reverential, dutiful, regardful. **2** *a deferential attitude to the experts* respectful, reverential, yielding, submissive, acquiescent, compliant, complaisant, tractable, obsequious, obeisant.

deferment *noun* **1** *the deferment of the meeting* postponement, deferral, putting off, adjournment, delay, shelving, suspension, tabling. **2** *be granted a deferment* postponement, respite, stay, moratorium, reprieve.

defiance *noun* **1** *treat the enemy with defiance* resistance, opposition, confrontation, non-compliance, disobedience, recalcitrance, rebelliousness, insubordination, contempt, disregard, scorn, insolence, contumacy. **2** *a spirit of defiance* challenge, provocation, daring, boldness, audacity, bravado, aggression, truculence; *lit.* derring-do.
Opposites SUBMISSION; OBEDIENCE.

defiant *adjective* **1** *defiant opposition* resistant, non-compliant, disobedient, recalcitrant, rebellious, insubordinate, mutinous, refractory, contemptuous, scornful, indifferent, insolent. **2** *with a defiant air* challenging, provocative, bold, audacious, aggressive, truculent.

deficiency *noun* **1** *vitamin deficiency* lack, want, shortage, dearth, insufficiency, inadequacy, scarcity, deficit, scantiness, paucity, absence. **2** *a deficiency in the system* defect, fault, flaw, imperfection, weakness, weak point/spot, failing, shortcoming, snag.

deficient *adjective* **1** *deficient in vitamins* lacking, wanting, short of, low on, defective. **2** *deficient quantities* insufficient, inadequate, scanty, meagre, skimpy, sketchy, exiguous. **3** *a deficient system* defective, faulty, flawed, imperfect, incomplete.

deficit *noun* **1** *the deficit is £100* shortfall, deficiency, shortage, slippage. **2** *we made a deficit*

loss, minus amount; indebtedness, debt.
Opposites SURPLUS; SURFEIT.

defile *verb* **1** *streets defiled by filth* pollute, foul, befoul, dirty, soil. **2** *defile young minds* corrupt, contaminate, taint, infect, tarnish, sully, pervert, vitiate. **3** *defile reputations* defame, sully, blacken, cast aspersions on, cast a slur on, denigrate, besmirch, stigmatize. **4** *defile the altar* desecrate, profane, treat sacrilegiously, make impure, contaminate, vitiate. **5** *defile young girls* ravish, rape, deflower, violate.

definable *adjective* determinable, ascertainable, fixable, fixed, definite, clear-cut, precise, exact, specific.

define *verb* **1** *define one's terms* give the meaning of, state precisely, spell out, describe, explain, expound, interpret, elucidate, clarify. **2** *define one's position* describe, determine, set out, outline, detail, specify, designate. **3** *define the boundary* mark out, fix, establish, settle, demarcate, bound, delimit, delineate, circumscribe. **4** *a tree defined against the light* outline, delineate, silhouette.

definite *adjective* **1** *definite plans* specific, particular, precise, exact, defined, well-defined, clear, clear-cut, explicit, express, determined, fixed, established, confirmed. **2** *it's definite that he's going* certain, sure, positive, guaranteed, settled, decided, assured, conclusive, final. **3** *definite boundaries* fixed, marked, demarcated, delimited, circumscribed.
Opposites INDEFINITE; UNCERTAIN; INDETERMINATE.

definitely *adverb definitely the best applicant* certainly, surely, for sure, without question, beyond any doubt, undoubtedly, indubitably, positively, absolutely, undeniably, unmistakably, plainly, clearly, obviously, categorically, decidedly, unequivocally, easily, far and away, without fail.

definition *noun* **1** *the definition of one's terms* meaning, statement of meaning, description, explanation, exposition, expounding, interpretation, elucidation, clarification. **2** *the definition of the boundaries* marking out, fixing, settling, establishment, determination, demarcation, bounding, delimiting, delimitation, delineation, circumscribing. **3** *the definition of the image* precision, sharpness, distinctness, clearness, clarity, contrast, visibility, focus.

definitive *adjective* **1** *the definitive answer* conclusive, final, ultimate, decisive, unconditional, unqualified, absolute, categorical. **2** *the definitive edition* authoritative, most reliable, most complete, exhaustive, most perfect.

deflate *verb* **1** *deflate the air-bed* let down, collapse, flatten, void, puncture. **2** *the air-bed deflated* collapse, empty of air, shrink, contract, flatten. **3** *deflate the pompous man* squash, humble, humiliate, mortify, chasten, subdue, dispirit; *inf.* put down, debunk. **4** *deflate a currency | deflate the economy* devalue, depreciate, depress, diminish, reduce.
Opposites INFLATE; blow up (*see* BLOW).

deflect *verb* **1** *cause the bullet to deflect* turn aside/away, turn, alter course, change course/direction, diverge, deviate, veer, swerve, slew, drift, bend, twist, curve, shy, ricochet, glance

off, divaricate, divagate. **2** *deflect the projectile |
deflect him from his purpose* turn aside/away,
turn, divert, switch, avert, sidetrack.

deflection *noun* deviation, divergence, diversion, declination, aberration, divarication,
divagation; turn, veer, swerve, drift, bend,
curve.

deform *verb* **1** *faces and bodies deformed by the
fire* disfigure, deface, misshape, mar, ruin,
spoil, uglify, damage, maim, injure, cripple,
mutilate, mangle. **2** *deform the pieces of metal*
misshape, distort, contort, buckle, twist, warp,
malform, gnarl.

deformed *adjective* **1** *deformed bodies* misshapen, malformed, distorted, contorted,
twisted, crooked, curved, gnarled, crippled,
maimed, humpbacked, hunchbacked, disfigured, ugly, unsightly, damaged, marred, muti-
lated, mangled. **2** *deformed minds* twisted,
warped, perverted, corrupted, depraved, vile,
gross.

deformity *noun* **1** *deformity of the body* malformation, misshapenness, misproportion, disfigurement, imperfection, abnormality,
irregularity, defacement, distortion, crookedness, ugliness, unsightliness; defect, flaw.
2 *deformity of minds* warpedness, perversion,
corruption, depravity, vileness, grossness.

defraud *verb* cheat, swindle, rob, fleece, rook,
bilk, trick, fool, take in, hoodwink, mislead,
delude, deceive, beguile, outwit; *lit.* cozen; *inf.*
gyp, con, do, diddle, rip off, take for a ride,
pull a fast one on, put one over on.

deft *adjective* dexterous, adroit, handy, nimble,
nimble-fingered, agile, skilful, skilled, proficient, adept, able, clever, expert, experienced.
Opposites CLUMSY; AWKWARD; MALADROIT.

defunct *adjective* **1** *defunct ancestors* dead,
deceased, departed, extinct, gone. **2** *defunct
practices/organizations* obsolete, expired, non-
existent, inoperative, invalid, non-functioning,
bygone, outmoded, old-fashioned, *passé.*
Opposites ALIVE; EXTANT.

defy *verb* **1** *defied their parents* disobey, disregard, ignore, slight, flout, fly in the face of,
thumb one's nose at, snap one's fingers at,
spurn, scoff at, deride, scorn. **2** *defy the enemy
forces* resist, withstand, brave, stand up to, confront, face, meet head-on, square up to, beard,
defeat, repulse, repel, thwart, frustrate, foil,
baffle. **3** *I defy you to stay* challenge, dare,
throw down the gauntlet.
Opposites OBEY; SURRENDER.

degeneracy *noun* corruption, decadence,
immorality, depravity, dissoluteness, debauchery, profligacy, wickedness, vileness, sinfulness, baseness, turpitude.

degenerate *adjective degenerate function/person*
degenerated, deteriorated, debased, declined,
degraded, corrupt, decadent, immoral,
depraved, dissolute, debauched, abandoned,
profligate, wicked, vile, sinful, vice-ridden, disreputable, despicable, base, sordid, low, mean,
ignoble.

degenerate *verb* deteriorate, decline, worsen,
decay, rot, fail, fall off, sink, slip, slide, go
downhill, regress, retrogress, lapse; *inf.* go to

pot, go to the dogs, hit the skids.
Opposites IMPROVE.

degenerate *noun* pervert, deviant, deviate,
fiend, wretch.

degeneration *noun* deterioration, debasement,
degradation, regression, retrogression; decay,
decline, descent, drop, sinking, slide, lapse. *See*
DEGENERATE *verb.*

degradation *noun* **1** *the degradation of his family* debasement, discrediting, demeaning, deprecation, shaming, disgracing, dishonouring,
humiliation, mortification. *See* DEGRADE 1. **2** *the
degradation of the officers* downgrading, demotion, reduction to the ranks, deposition. *See*
DEGRADE 2. **3** *witnessing a scene of degradation*
degeneracy, corruption, decadence, immorality, depravity, dissolution, debauchery, vice,
wickedness, sordidity, squalor.

degrade *verb* **1** *his family degraded by his behaviour* debase, discredit, cheapen, belittle,
demean, deprecate, deflate, devalue, lower,
reduce, shame, disgrace, dishonour, humble,
humiliate, mortify, abase, vitiate. **2** *officers
degraded* downgrade, demote, reduce/lower in
rank, reduce to the ranks, disrate, strip of
rank, cashier, depose, remove from office,
unseat, dethrone; *inf.* kick upstairs, drum out.
3 *degraded by her immoral associates* debase, corrupt, pervert, defile, sully, debauch.
Opposites DIGNIFY; UPGRADE; PROMOTE; IMPROVE.

degraded *adjective an immoral degraded crowd*
degenerate, debased, corrupt, decadent,
immoral, depraved, dissolute, debauched,
abandoned, profligate, despicable, sordid. *See*
DEGENERATE *adjective.*

degrading *adjective a degrading experience*
debasing, discrediting, cheapening, belittling,
demeaning, lowering, shaming, shameful,
humiliating, mortifying, disgraceful, dishonourable, undignified; *inf.* infra dig.

degree *noun* **1** *reach a high degree of
competence | third-degree burns* stage, level, grade,
step, gradation, rung, point, mark, measure,
notch, limit. **2** *to a marked degree* extent,
measure, magnitude, level, amount, quality,
intensity, strength, proportion, ratio. **3** *people
of higher degree* rank, class, standing, status,
station, position, grade, level, order, condition,
estate. **by degrees** gradually, slowly, by stages,
step by step, little by little, bit by bit, inch by
inch.

dehydrate *verb* **1** *they dehydrated the vegetables |
heat was dehydrating the walkers* dry, dry up/out,
sun-dry, desiccate, exsiccate, parch, sear.
2 *plants/bodies dehydrating* dry up, lose water,
become thirsty.

deify *verb* idolize, exalt, aggrandize, worship,
adore, venerate, revere, pay homage to.

deign *verb* condescend, stoop, lower oneself,
think/see fit, deem worthy, consent.

deity *noun* God, god, goddess, divine being,
celestial being, supreme being, divinity, demi-
urge; godhead. *See* GOD.

dejected *adjective* depressed, dispirited,
discouraged, disheartened, downhearted,
crestfallen, cast down, downcast, down, disap-

pointed, unhappy, sad, miserable, blue, wretched, despondent, woebegone, forlorn, sorrowful, disconsolate, doleful, glum, gloomy, melancholy, morose, low in spirits, low-spirited, long-faced; *inf.* down in the mouth/dumps.
Opposites CHEERFUL; LIGHT-HEARTED; HAPPY.

dejection *noun* depression, downheartedness, dispiritedness, discouragement, disappointment, unhappiness, sadness, misery, wretchedness, despondency, sorrowfulness, sorrow, disconsolateness, disconsolation, dolefulness, glumness, gloom, melancholy, despair; low spirits, blues; *inf.* the dumps.

delay *verb* **1** *delay our meeting* postpone, put off, adjourn, defer, hold over, shelve, suspend, table, stay, hold in abeyance, put on ice, put on the back burner. *See* DEFER [1]. **2** *visitors delayed by the traffic* hold up/back, detain, slow up, set back, hinder, obstruct, hamper, impede, bog down, check, hold in check, restrain, halt, stop, arrest. **3** *Hurry up! Don't delay!* linger, loiter, hold back, dawdle, dally, dilly-dally, lag/fall behind, not keep pace, procrastinate, stall, tarry.
Opposites ADVANCE; ACCELERATE.

delay *noun* **1** *the delay to the meeting* postponement, adjournment, deferment, suspension, tabling, stay. *See* DELAY *verb* 1. **2** *holiday traffic delays* hold-up, wait, set-back, detainment, detention, hindrance, obstruction, impediment, check, stoppage, halt, interruption. **3** *the delay between trains* wait, waiting period, interval, lull, interlude, intermission. **4** *her delay made us late* lingering, loitering, dawdling, dallying, dilly-dallying, procrastination, stalling, tarrying. *See* DELAY *verb* 3.

delectable *adjective* **1** *delectable food* delicious, appetizing, inviting, tasty, savoury, enjoyable, luscious, palatable, flavoursome, toothsome; *inf.* scrumptious, yummy, ambrosial. **2** *delectable girls/entertainment* delightful, charming, enchanting, adorable, captivating, winning, engaging, winsome, dainty, attractive, pleasing, agreeable, ravishing, exciting, titillating.
Opposites REVOLTING; NASTY.

delectation *noun* *for your delectation* delight, pleasure, enjoyment, entertainment, amusement, diversion, happiness, gratification, satisfaction, excitement, relish, titillation.

delegate *noun* *our country's/conference delegate* representative, deputy, agent, spokesman, spokeswoman, spokesperson, ambassador, envoy, legate, messenger, go-between, proxy, emissary, commissary.

delegate *verb* **1** *delegate tasks* pass on, hand over, transfer, give, commit, entrust, assign, relegate, consign, devolve. **2** *delegate him leader* appoint, designate, nominate, name, authorize, depute, commission, mandate, empower, choose, select, elect, ordain.

delegation *noun* **1** *our country's delegation* deputation, legation, contingent, mission, commission, embassy; delegates, envoys. **2** *the delegation of tasks* transference, committal, entrustment, assignment, relegation, consignment, devolution. *See* DELEGATE *verb* 1. **3** *his del-*

egation as leader appointment, designation, nomination, authorization, commissioning, selection, election. *See* DELEGATE *verb* 2.

delete *verb* cross/strike out, rub out, cut out, erase, cancel, blue-pencil, edit out, remove, take out, expunge, eradicate, obliterate, efface, wipe/blot out.

deleterious *adjective* harmful, injurious, hurtful, damaging, destructive, ruinous, bad, disadvantageous, noxious.

deliberate *adjective* **1** *a deliberate act* intentional, planned, considered, calculated, designed, studied, studious, painstaking, conscious, purposeful, wilful, premeditated, pre-planned, prearranged, preconceived, predetermined, aforethought. **2** *slow deliberate speech/steps* careful, unhurried, cautious, thoughtful, steady, regular, measured, unwavering, unhesitating, unfaltering, determined, resolute, ponderous, laborious.
Opposites ACCIDENTAL; UNINTENTIONAL; HASTY.

deliberate *verb* **1** *looking out of the window deliberating* think, ponder, muse, meditate, reflect, cogitate, ruminate, brood, excogitate, be in a brown study. **2** *deliberate the advantages* think over, consider, ponder, reflect on, mull over, review, weigh up, evaluate. **3** *deliberate with colleagues* discuss, debate, confer, consult.

deliberately *adverb* **1** *deliberately hurt her* intentionally, on purpose, purposefully, by design, knowingly, wittingly, consciously, premeditatedly, calculatedly, in cold blood. *See* DELIBERATE *adjective* 1. **2** *speak/walk very deliberately* carefully, unhurriedly, cautiously, steadily, measuredly, unwaveringly, unhesitatingly, determinedly, ponderously. *See* DELIBERATE *adjective* 2.

deliberation *noun* **1** *after his deliberation* thinking, thought, consideration, pondering, musing, mulling, meditation, reflection, cogitation, rumination, brooding, weighing up, excogitation. *See* DELIBERATE *verb* 1, 2. **2** *after deliberation with colleagues* discussion, debate, consultation, conferring, conference. **3** *speak with deliberation* care, carefulness, no hurry, caution, thoughtfulness, steadiness, determination, resoluteness, laboriousness. *See* DELIBERATE *adjective* 2.

delicacy *noun* **1** *the delicacy of the china/material* fineness, exquisiteness, fragility, slenderness, slightness, elegance, gracefulness, grace, daintiness, flimsiness, silkiness. *See* DELICATE 1. **2** *the delicacy of his health/wife* frailty, fragility, weakness, debilitation; sickliness, infirmity, poor/ill health. **3** *delicacy of the colours* paleness, mutedness, subtlety, softness, understatement. **4** *delicacy of the situation* difficulty, trickiness, sensitivity, ticklishness, precariousness. **5** *handle the matter with delicacy* care, consideration, sensitivity, sensibility, tact, discretion, finesse, diplomacy, politeness. **6** *the delicacy of her palate* discrimination, discernment, refinement, perceptiveness, criticalness, fastidiousness. *See* DELICATE 6. **7** *the delicacy of the mechanism* sensitivity, precision, accuracy, exactness. **8** *delicacy of touch* deftness, skill, expertise. **9** *buying some delicacies* gourmet food, titbit, dainty, treat, luxury, savoury, appetizer, *bonne bouche*.

delicate *adjective* **1** *delicate china/material* fine, exquisite, fragile, slender, slight, elegant, graceful, dainty, flimsy, silky, gauzy, gossamer, wispy. **2** *his wife is delicate* frail, sickly, weak, debilitated, infirm, ailing, in poor health, unwell. **3** *delicate colours* pastel, pale, muted, subtle, soft, subdued, understated, faint. **4** *a delicate matter/situation* difficult, tricky, sensitive, ticklish, critical, precarious, touchy; *inf.* sticky, dicey. **5** *require delicate handling* careful, considerate, sensitive, tactful, discreet, diplomatic, politic, kid-glove. **6** *a delicate palate* discriminating, discerning, refined, perceptive, critical, fastidious, finicky, pernickety, squeamish. **7** *a delicate mechanism* sensitive, precise, accurate, exact. **8** *a delicate touch* deft, skilled, skilful, expert. **9** *delicate food* dainty, choice, delicious. *See* DELICACY 9.
Opposites COARSE; ROBUST; STRONG; ROUGH.

delicious *adjective* **1** *delicious food* tasty, appetizing, mouth-watering, delectable, choice, dainty, savoury, flavoursome, flavourful, luscious, palatable, toothsome, ambrosial, ambrosian, nectareous, nectarean; *inf.* scrumptious, yummy. **2** *a delicious evening* delightful, enchanting, exquisite, enjoyable, pleasurable, entertaining, amusing, diverting, pleasant, agreeable, charming, nice.
Opposites REVOLTING; DISGUSTING; NASTY.

delight *noun filled with delight* pleasure, joy, happiness, gladness, gratification, bliss, rapture, ecstasy, elation, jubilation, excitement, entertainment, amusement; *transports*.

delight *verb* **1** *delighted by the news* please, gladden, cheer, gratify, thrill, excite, transport, enchant, captivate, entrance, charm, entertain, amuse, divert; *inf.* send. **2** *delight in reading* take/find pleasure, indulge, glory.
Opposites DISMAY; DISPLEASE; DISGUST.

delighted *adjective* pleased, joyful, happy, glad, gratified, overjoyed, blissful, enraptured, ecstatic, jubilant, thrilled, transported, excited, enchanted, captivated, entranced, charmed, entertained, amused, diverted; *inf.* sent.

delightful *adjective a delightful occasion/woman* pleasant, pleasing, agreeable, enjoyable, amusing, entertaining, diverting, pleasurable, pleasure-giving, gratifying, delectable, joyful, exciting, thrilling, rapturous, enchanting; captivating, fascinating, entrancing, ravishing, charming, attractive, beautiful, pretty, engaging, winning.

delineate *verb* **1** *delineate her features* trace, draw the lines of, outline, draw, sketch, draft, block in, contour. **2** *delineate the statistics* make a diagram of, make a chart of, chart, map, map out, diagram. **3** *delineate his achievements* describe, define, set forth, outline, depict, portray.

delinquency *noun* **1** *juvenile delinquency* wrongdoing, misdemeanour, misconduct, misbehaviour, mischievousness, transgression; offence, misdeed, crime. **2** *the soldier's delinquency* negligence, remissness, dereliction, omission, failure.

delinquent *noun damage done by delinquents* offender, wrongdoer, culprit, lawbreaker, criminal, hooligan, vandal, ruffian, hoodlum, miscreant, malefactor, transgressor; juvenile delinquent, young offender.

delinquent *adjective* **1** *delinquent young people* mischievous, culpable, transgressing, offending, criminal. **2** *delinquent policemen* negligent, neglectful, remiss, careless, slack, derelict.

delirious *adjective* **1** *delirious patients* raving, incoherent, babbling, light-headed, irrational, deranged, demented, unhinged, mad, insane, crazy, out of one's mind; *inf.* off one's head. **2** *delirious at the good news* ecstatic, euphoric, beside oneself, carried away, transported, hysterical, frenzied, wild with excitement, distracted, frantic, out of one's wits, feverish, Corybantic.
Opposites RATIONAL; COHERENT; DEPRESSED.

delirium *noun* **1** *affected by delirium* temporary madness/insanity, irrationality, light-headedness, raving, incoherence, babbling. **2** *happy delirium* ecstasy, euphoria, hysteria, frenzy, wild emotion, wildness, excitement, distraction, feverishness, fever, passion.

deliver *verb* **1** *deliver the mail/groceries* distribute, carry, bring, take, transport, convey, send, dispatch, remit. **2** *deliver the prisoners to the enemy* hand over, turn over, transfer, commit, grant, make over, give up, yield, surrender, relinquish, cede, resign. **3** *deliver them from enemies* set free, free, liberate, release, save, rescue, set loose, loose, extricate, discharge, ransom, emancipate, redeem, manumit. **4** *deliver a speech/sigh* utter, give voice to, voice, speak, give, give forth, express, pronounce, enunciate, proclaim, announce, declare, read, recite, broadcast, promulgate. **5** *deliver a blow | deliver a shot at* direct, aim, give, deal, administer, launch, inflict, throw, strike, hurl, pitch, discharge. **6** *deliver better sales figures* come up with, achieve, attain, provide, supply.
Opposites COLLECT; RECEIVE.

deliverance *noun* **1** *deliverance from prison/evil* liberation, release, rescue, escape, discharge, ransom, emancipation, salvation, redemption, manumission. **2** *deliverances from the pulpit* pronouncement, declaration, announcement, proclamation, report, lecture, sermon, speech.

delivery *noun* **1** *delivery is extra* distribution, carriage, transporting, transport, conveyance, dispatch. **2** *receive a delivery* consignment, load, batch. **3** *admire his clear delivery* manner of speaking, enunciation, articulation, intonation, elocution, utterance, presentation. **4** *a mother having a difficult delivery* confinement, labour, childbirth, parturition. **5** *delivery from the enemy* deliverance, liberation, release, rescue, escape. *See* DELIVERANCE 1. **6** *the delivery of a blow/ball* directing, aiming, launching, throwing, pitching. *See* DELIVER 5.

delude *verb* mislead, deceive, fool, take in, trick, dupe, cheat, hoodwink, beguile, outwit, misguide, lead on, bamboozle, defraud, swindle, double-cross; *lit.* cozen; *inf.* con, pull a fast one on, lead up the garden path, take for a ride, put one over on, two-time.

deluge noun **1** *houses swept away by the deluge* flood, spate, inundation, overflowing, flash flood, cataclysm. **2** *caught in the deluge without an umbrella* downpour, torrent, torrential rain, cloudburst. **3** *a deluge of correspondence* flood, rush, spate, torrent, avalanche, barrage, outpouring.

deluge verb **1** *towns deluged with polluted water* flood, inundate, swamp, engulf, submerge, drown, soak, drench, douse. **2** *deluged by correspondence* inundate, flood, overrun, overwhelm, engulf, swamp, overload.

delusion noun **1** *delusions of grandeur* false impression, false belief, misconception, misapprehension, misunderstanding, misbelief, mistake, self-deception, deception, error, fallacy, illusion, fancy, phantasm, fool's paradise. **2** *the delusion of the old lady* deluding, misleading, deception, fooling, tricking, duping. *See* DELUDE.

de luxe adjective luxurious, sumptuous, palatial, opulent, lavish, grand, rich, superior, exclusive, choice, select, elegant, splendid, costly, expensive; *inf.* plush, up-market.
Opposites BASIC; PLAIN; POOR.

delve verb **1** *delve into one's pockets/cupboards* search, rummage, ransack, dig into, ferret around, hunt through. **2** *delve into local history* research, investigate, look into, examine, probe, dig into, hunt through. **3** *animals delving* burrow, dig, excavate.

demagogue noun political agitator, agitator, soapbox orator, rabble-rouser, firebrand, haranguer, troublemaker. *See table at* ORATOR.

demand verb **1** *workers demanding a rise* ask/ call for, request, press for, insist on, urge, clamour for, make a claim for, lay claim to, claim. **2** *"What's that?" he demanded* ask, inquire, question, interrogate, challenge. **3** *work demanding care* require, need, necessitate, call for, take, involve, want, cry out for. **4** *parents demanding obedience | demand payment* expect, insist on, exact, impose, order, requisition.

demand noun **1** *give in to their demands* request, entreaty, claim, requisition; insistence, pressure, clamour. **2** *answer his demand* inquiry, question, interrogation, challenge. **3** *the demands of the job* requirement, need, necessity, want, claim, imposition, exigency. **in demand** requested, required, sought-after, popular, in vogue, fashionable; *inf.* trendy.

demanding adjective **1** *demanding children/ wives* nagging, harassing, clamorous, importunate, insistent, imperious. **2** *demanding jobs* challenging, taxing, exacting, exigent, tough, hard, difficult, tiring, wearing, exhausting.
Opposites EASYGOING; EASY; EFFORTLESS.

demarcation noun **1** *the demarcation of the areas* boundary, border, limit, bound, margin, frontier. **2** *the demarcation of the factory jobs* separation, division, distinction, differentiation, delimitation, marking off, definition.

demean verb lower, degrade, debase, devalue, demote, humble, abase, belittle, deprecate.

demeanour noun behaviour, conduct, bearing, air, appearance, mien, deportment, carriage, comportment.

demented adjective insane, mad, crazy, crazed, deranged, of unsound mind, out of one's mind, unhinged, unbalanced, touched, *non compos mentis*, maniacal, manic, frenzied, distraught, foolish, idiotic, crack-brained, lunatic; *inf.* daft, barmy, dotty, loopy, batty, potty, crackpot, dippy, wacky.
Opposites SANE; RATIONAL.

dementia noun madness; *senile dementia, Alzheimer's disease*, Alzheimer's.

demise noun death, decease, passing, expiration, end, termination, cessation, quietus.
Opposites BIRTH; START.

democracy noun representative government, constitutional government, popular government, self-government; republic, commonwealth. *See table at* POLITICS.

democratic adjective of the people, representative, popular, popularist, egalitarian, republican, self-governing, autonomous.

demolish verb **1** *demolish the building* knock down, pull/tear down, bring down, flatten, raze, level, bulldoze, dismantle, break up, pulverize. **2** *demolish the argument | demolish his self-confidence* destroy, put an end to, ruin, wreck, undo. **3** *demolish the opposition* defeat, conquer, vanquish, overthrow, overturn, quell, quash, suppress, destroy, annihilate, wipe out, finish off. **4** *demolish a plate of cakes* eat up, consume, devour, gobble up, put away.
Opposites BUILD; CONSTRUCT; CREATE.

demolition noun **1** *the demolition of the buildings* knocking down, pulling down, flattening, razing, levelling, bulldozing. *See* DEMOLISH 1. **2** *the demolition of the argument* destruction, ruin, ruination, wrecking, undoing. **3** *demolition of the opposition* defeat, conquest, vanquishing, overthrow, destruction, annihilation. *See* DEMOLISH 3.

demon noun **1** *the demons from hell* devil, evil/ malignant spirit, fiend, cacodemon. **2** *the dictator's a demon* devil, fiend, brute, monster, savage, beast, barbarian, villain. **3** *the demon of creativity* daimon, eudemon, genius, guardian/ ministering angel, familiar spirit, numen. **4** *he's a real demon for work* man/woman of action, hard worker, powerhouse, human dynamo, workaholic; *inf.* whizz kid, eager beaver, busy bee. **5** *a demon at sailing | a demon tennis player* master, wizard, addict, fanatic; *inf.* ace, freak.
Opposites ANGEL.

demonic, demoniac, demoniacal adjective **1** *demonic spirits* diabolic, diabolical, devilish, fiendish, satanic, hellish, infernal, evil, wicked, Mephistophelian, cacodemonic. **2** *demonic eyes/laughter* like one possessed, maniacal, manic, mad, crazed, frenzied, frantic, feverish, frenetic, hectic, furious, hysterical.

demonstrable adjective provable, verifiable, attestable, confirmable, evincible.

demonstrate verb **1** *demonstrate the proof of the proposition* show, indicate, determine, prove, validate, confirm, verify, establish. **2** *blushes* *demonstrating embarrassment* show, indicate, display, exhibit, express, manifest, evince, evidence. **3** *demonstrate putting on a bandage* show, illustrate, give an idea of, teach, describe, explain, make clear, explicate, expound. **4** *demonstrate against nuclear weapons* protest, march, parade, rally, sit in, picket.

demonstration noun **1** *demonstration of the proof of the proposition* indication, substantiation, confirmation, affirmation, verification, validation. *See* DEMONSTRATE 1. **2** *a demonstration of his embarrassment* indication, expression, manifestation, evincement; evidence. **3** *a demonstration of putting on a bandage* illustration, description, explanation, exposition, teach-in. **4** *a demonstration of the new product* exposition, presentation, exhibition; *inf.* expo. **5** *take part in a student demonstration* protest, protest march, march, parade, rally, mass rally/lobby, sit-in, picket; *inf.* demo.

demonstrative adjective **1** *a demonstrative person/reaction* emotional, unreserved, unrestrained, expressive, open, effusive, expansive, gushing, non-reticent, affectionate, loving, warm. **2** *demonstrative of their skill* indicative, illustrative, evincive, expository. **3** *demonstrative evidence* conclusive, convincing, telling, material, incontrovertible, irrefutable.
Opposites UNDEMONSTRATIVE; UNEMOTIONAL; RESERVED.

demoralize verb **1** *workers demoralized by the setbacks* discourage, dishearten, cast down, dispirit, deject, depress, daunt, unman, crush, sap, shake, undermine, devitalize, cripple, paralyse, weaken, enervate. **2** *brutes demoralizing the young* corrupt, deprave, debauch, pervert, debase, contaminate, defile, vitiate.
Opposites ENCOURAGE; HEARTEN.

demote verb downgrade, lower/reduce in rank, relegate, degrade, declass, strip of rank, reduce to the ranks, humble, disrate; *inf.* kick upstairs.
Opposites PROMOTE; UPGRADE.

demur verb raise objections, object, take exception, express reluctance/reservations/doubts, be unwilling, protest, lodge a protest, dispute, refuse, dissent, balk at, hesitate, cavil.

demur noun *go without demur* objection, protest, dispute, dissent, reluctance, reservation, unwillingness; doubts, qualms, misgivings.

demure adjective **1** *demure young girls* modest, unassuming, decorous, meek, reserved, quiet, shy, bashful, retiring, diffident, reticent, timid, timorous, shrinking, serious, grave, sedate, staid. **2** *demure young ladies* over-modest, coy, affected, mincing, prim, priggish, prissy, prudish, goody-goody, strait-laced, puritanical.
Opposites BRAZEN; SHAMELESS.

den noun **1** *the fox's den* lair, hole, hollow, shelter, hide-out; *inf.* hidey-hole. *See table at* LAIR. **2** *the bar's a real den | den of iniquity* place of crime/vice, site, haunt; *inf.* dive, joint. **3** *writing in his den* study, retreat, sanctum, *sanctum sanctorum*, sanctuary, hideaway, snuggery, cubbyhole.

denial noun **1** *a denial of the statement* contradiction, repudiation, disclaimer, retraction,

abjuration, disaffirmation; negation, dissent. **2** *the denial of the request* refusal, rejection, dismissal, rebuff, repulse, declination, veto, turndown; *inf.* thumbs down. **3** *the denial of Christ* renunciation, renouncement, disowning, repudiation, disavowal.
Opposites CONFESSION; ACCEPTANCE.

denigrate verb disparage, belittle, diminish, deprecate, detract from, decry, blacken one's character, defame, slander, libel, cast aspersions on, malign, vilify, calumniate, besmirch, run down, abuse, revile; *Am.* bad-mouth.
Opposites EXTOL; LAUD; ACCLAIM.

denizen noun inhabitant, habitant, dweller, resident, occupier, occupant.

denomination noun **1** *of various religious denominations* creed, faith, religious belief, Church, sect, religious group, persuasion, communion, order, fraternity, brotherhood, sisterhood, school. *See table at* CHRISTIANITY. **2** *coins/ weights of various denominations* value, unit, grade, size. **3** *creatures under various denominations* classification, class, category, grouping, group, type. **4** *things going under various denominations* name, title, term, designation, appellation, epithet, style, label, tag; *inf.* handle, moniker.

denote verb **1** *a smile denoting delight | the colour yellow denoting happiness* indicate, be a sign/ mark of, signify, betoken, symbolize, represent, stand for, typify. **2** *the word bankruptcy denotes financial ruin* mean, convey, designate, suggest, bring to mind, intimate, refer to, allude to, imply, connote.

denouement noun **1** *miss the denouement of the plan* resolution, solution, clarification, unravelling, final/last act, finale. **2** *the denouement of the argument* outcome, upshot, result, culmination, climax.

denounce verb **1** *denounce the council's policies* condemn, criticize, attack, censure, castigate, decry, rail/inveigh/fulminate against, declaim against, arraign, denunciate, revile. **2** *denounce his partner* accuse, inform against, incriminate, implicate, inculpate, charge, file charges, indict, impeach, take to court.

dense adjective **1** *a dense forest/crowd* close-packed, tightly packed, crowded, thickset, closely set, jammed together, crammed, compressed, compacted. **2** *a dense liquid/substance* of high density, heavy, concentrated, condensed. **3** *dense fog/smoke* thick, concentrated, opaque, impenetrable. **4** *too dense to understand* stupid, thick, slow-witted, slow, dull-witted, blockish, obtuse, bovine, lumpish, stolid; *inf.* dim.
Opposites SPARSE; THIN; LIGHT; CLEVER.

dentist noun. *See table at* DOCTOR.

deny verb **1** *deny the charge/statement* declare untrue, contradict, negate, nullify, dissent from, disagree with, repudiate, refute, controvert, disclaim, retract, take back, back-pedal, abjure, disaffirm, gainsay. **2** *deny the request* refuse, reject, turn down, dismiss, repulse, decline, veto; *inf.* give the thumbs down to, give the red light to. **3** *to deny Christ* renounce, disown, turn one's back on, repudiate,

discard, disavow.
Opposites ADMIT; ACCEPT.

deodorant noun **1** *body deodorant* antiperspirant. **2** *room deodorants* air-freshener, deodorizer, fumigant; *inf.* odour-eater.

depart verb **1** *they departed at midday* leave, go, go away/off, take one's leave/departure, take oneself off, withdraw, absent oneself, set off/out, start out, get going, get under way, quit, make an exit, exit, break camp, decamp, retreat, retire; *inf.* make tracks, shove off, split, cut out, vamoose, hightail it. **2** *depart from the norm* deviate, diverge, differ, vary, digress, veer, branch off, fork, swerve, turn aside.
Opposites ARRIVE; STAY.

departed adjective *departed loved ones* dead, deceased, late, gone, passed away/on, expired.

department noun **1** *the housing/books department* section, division, subdivision, unit, branch, segment, compartment, office, bureau, agency. **2** *that's the cook's department* area, area of responsibility, responsibility, area of interest, speciality, line, province, sphere, sphere of activity, domain, realm, jurisdiction, authority, function. **3** *the departments of France* administrative district, district, region, province, sector, division; territory, state, county, shire.

departure noun **1** *the hour of their departure* leaving, leave-taking, going, going away/off, withdrawal, setting off/out, starting out, exit, exodus, decamping, retreat, retiral. *See* DEPART 1. **2** *a departure from the norm* deviation, divergence, variation, digression, veering, branching off, swerving. *See* DEPART 2. **3** *the export market is a new departure for the firm* change of direction, change, difference of emphasis, shift, innovation, branching out, novelty.
Opposites ARRIVAL; RETURN.

depend verb **1** *success depends on hard work | it depends on how he proceeds* be dependent on, turn/hinge on, hang on, rest on, be contingent upon, be subject to, be controlled/determined by, be based on, revolve around, be influenced by, be resultant from, be subordinate to. **2** *depend on him for help* rely on, place reliance on, count/bank on, lean on, cling to, reckon/calculate on, trust in, put one's faith in, have confidence in, swear by, be sure of, be supported/sustained by.

dependable adjective reliable, trustworthy, trusty, faithful, responsible, steady, stable, sure, unfailing, true, steadfast.
Opposites UNRELIABLE; UNTRUSTWORTHY.

dependant noun minor, child, charge, protégé; minion, parasite, hanger-on, henchman.

dependence noun **1** *the venture's dependence on hard work* reliance, turning on, hingeing on, determination, bearing, relevancy, relationship, connection, interconnection, interdependence. *See* DEPEND 1. **2** *their dependence on their mother* reliance, trust, faith, confidence. *See* DEPEND 2. **3** *pity the children's dependence* helplessness, weakness, defencelessness, vulnerability, exposure. **4** *alcohol dependence* addiction, over-reliance, reliance, dependency; abuse.

dependency noun **1** *his dependency on his mother* dependence, reliance. *See* DEPEND 2. **2** *the children's utter dependency* dependence, helplessness, defencelessness. *See* DEPENDENCE 3. **3** *alcohol dependency* dependence, addiction, over-reliance, reliance. **4** *formerly a dependency of the US* colony, protectorate, province, fief. **5** *a dependency of the parent firm* subsidiary, adjunct, appendage, auxiliary, subject, attachment.

dependent adjective **1** *dependent on circumstances* depending on, conditional on, contingent on, determined by, subject to. **2** *dependent on their mother* relying on, reliant on, counting on, leaning on, supported by, sustained by. *See* DEPEND 2. **3** *dependent children* reliant, helpless, weak, defenceless, vulnerable, immature. **4** *dependent countries* subsidiary, subject, subservient.
Opposites INDEPENDENT.

depict verb **1** *a painting depicting him sitting* portray, represent, draw, paint, sketch, illustrate, delineate, outline, reproduce, render, limn, chart, map out. **2** *an account depicting his faults* describe, set forth/out, outline, sketch, detail, relate, narrate, recount, record, chronicle.

deplete verb exhaust, use up, consume, expend, spend, drain, empty, milk, evacuate, bankrupt, impoverish, reduce, decrease, diminish, lessen, lower, attenuate.
Opposites AUGMENT; INCREASE.

depletion noun exhaustion, using up, consumption, expenditure, draining, emptying, reduction, decrease, dwindling, diminution, lessening, lowering, attenuation.

deplorable adjective **1** *deplorable behaviour* disgraceful, shameful, dishonourable, blameworthy, disreputable, scandalous, reprehensible, despicable, abominable, base, sordid, vile, contemptible, execrable, opprobrious. **2** *in deplorable circumstances* lamentable, regrettable, unfortunate, wretched, dire, miserable, pitiable, pathetic, unhappy, sad, tragic, disastrous, distressing, grievous, calamitous.
Opposites HONOURABLE; ADMIRABLE; FORTUNATE.

deplore verb **1** *deplore his dreadful behaviour* be scandalized/shocked by, be offended by, disapprove of, condemn, censure, deprecate, denounce, decry, abhor. **2** *deplore the passing of the trams* regret, lament, mourn, rue, bemoan, grieve/sorrow over, bewail, pine for, shed tears for, weep over.

deploy verb **1** *deploy troops* arrange, position, dispose, spread out, extend, redistribute, station. **2** *deploy new arguments* use, utilize, set out/up, bring into play, have recourse to.

deport verb **1** *deport the refugees* banish, expel, exile, evict, transport, oust, expatriate, extradite. **2** *deport oneself badly* behave, conduct oneself, act, acquit oneself, comport oneself, bear/carry/hold oneself.

deportation noun *the deportation of refugees* banishment, expulsion, exile, eviction, ousting, transportation, extradition, expatriation.

deportment noun **1** *have lessons in deportment* carriage, bearing, posture, comportment, stance, attitude, demeanour, mien, air, appearance, aspect, style, manner. **2** *complain about the child's deportment* behaviour, conduct, etiquette; manners, actions.

depose *verb* **1** *depose the leader/king* remove from office, remove, unseat, dethrone, oust, displace, dismiss, discharge, cashier, strip of rank, demote; *inf.* sack, fire, give the push/boot to. **2** *depose that one saw the accused* make a deposition, swear, testify, attest to. *See* DEPOSITION 2.

deposit *verb* **1** *deposit the parcel on the floor* put, lay, set, set/put/lay down, drop, let fall. **2** *rivers depositing mud* let settle, set down, precipitate, dump. **3** *deposit money/jewels in the bank* bank, lodge, entrust, consign, save, store, hoard, stow, put away, lay in, squirrel away.

deposit *noun* **1** *leaving a chemical deposit* precipitation, sediment, sublimate, accumulation, deposition; dregs, lees; silt, alluvium. **2** *coal/iron deposits* bed, vein, lode, layer. **3** *put a deposit on the goods* down/part payment, instalment, security, retainer, pledge, stake. **4** *put the jewels in a deposit* depository, storehouse, warehouse. *See* DEPOSITORY.

deposition *noun* **1** *the deposition of the leader* removal, unseating, dethronement, ousting, displacement, dismissal, discharge, demotion. *See* DEPOSE 1. **2** *the witnesses' depositions* testimony, evidence, sworn statement/declaration, affidavit, attestation, affirmation.

depository *noun* repository, store, storehouse, warehouse, depot, reservoir, safe deposit, deposit, bank.

depot *noun* **1** *buses/trains returning to the depot* terminal, terminus; bus/railway station, garage. **2** *stored in the depot* storehouse, warehouse, repository, depository, magazine, cache, arsenal.

deprave *verb* corrupt, debauch, lead astray, pervert, seduce, debase, degrade, make degenerate, defile, pollute, contaminate, vitiate, brutalize, abuse.

depraved *adjective* corrupt, corrupted, immoral, unprincipled, reprobate, debauched, dissolute, abandoned, perverted, degenerate, profligate, debased, degraded, wicked, sinful, vile, base, iniquitous, criminal, vicious, brutal, lewd, licentious, lascivious, lecherous, prurient, obscene, indecent, libertine.
Opposites UPRIGHT; VIRTUOUS; PURE.

depravity *noun* corruption, corruptness, corruptedness, immorality, debauchery, dissoluteness, abandonment, perversion, degradation, degeneracy, profligacy, contamination, vitiation, wickedness, sinfulness, vileness, baseness, iniquity, criminality, viciousness, brutality, brutishness, lewdness, licentiousness, lasciviousness, lechery, prurience, obscenity, indecency, libertinism.

deprecate *verb* **1** *deprecate the committee's actions* disapprove of, criticize, deplore, frown upon, censure, condemn, protest against, inveigh/rail against, denounce; *inf.* slate, knock. **2** *deprecate his achievement* belittle, disparage, denigrate, decry, discredit, deflate,

diminish, depreciate. *See* DEPRECIATE 3.
Opposites PRAISE; EXTOL; EMPHASIZE.

deprecatory *adjective* **1** *make deprecatory remarks about the opposition* disapproving, critical, protesting, condemnatory, reproachful, upbraiding, castigatory, admonishing, denunciatory; *inf.* slating, knocking. *See* DEPRECATE 1. **2** *give a deprecatory smile at his mistake* apologetic, regretful, sorry, remorseful, contrite, penitent, repentant, rueful, compunctious, propitiatory. **3** *a deprecatory account of their achievement* belittling, disparaging, denigratory, derogatory, discrediting, deflating, diminishing, disdainful, derisive, snide, sneering, mocking, jibing.

depreciate *verb* **1** *the furniture has depreciated* decrease in value, lose value, decline in price. **2** *depreciate the value | depreciate the furniture* devalue, reduce, lower in value/price, mark down, cheapen, cut, slash. **3** *depreciate efforts to help* belittle, disparage, denigrate, decry, deprecate, make light of, discredit, underrate, undervalue, underestimate, deflate, detract from, derogate, diminish, minimize, run down, disdain, ridicule, deride, sneer at, mock, defame, traduce.
Opposites APPRECIATE; PRAISE; OVERRATE.

depreciation *noun* **1** *the depreciation of the furniture* devaluation, decrease/lowering/reduction in value, cheapening, mark-down. *See* DEPRECIATE 1, 2. **2** *the depreciation of their efforts* belittlement, disparagement, denigration, decrial, deprecation, discrediting, underrating, undervaluing. *See* DEPRECIATE 3.

depredation *noun* *the depredation of the town by the army/storm* plundering, pillaging, ravaging, despoliation, devastation, laying waste.

depress *verb* **1** *news that depressed her* make sad/unhappy, sadden, deject, cast down, make gloomy/despondent, dispirit, dishearten, discourage, dampen the spirits of, daunt, desolate, make desolate, weigh down, oppress. **2** *depress economic activity* slow down/up, weaken, lower, reduce, sap, enervate, debilitate, devitalize, impair, enfeeble, exhaust, drain. **3** *depress prices* reduce, lower, cut, cheapen, put/keep down, slash, depreciate, devalue, diminish, downgrade. **4** *depress the lever/grass* push down, press down, lower, level, flatten.
Opposites CHEER; ENCOURAGE; RAISE.

depressant *noun* sedative, tranquillizer, sleeping pill, soporific, opiate, hypnotic; *inf.* downer.

depressed *adjective* **1** *depressed at the news* sad, saddened, unhappy, gloomy, blue, glum, dejected, downhearted, cast down, downcast, down, crestfallen, despondent, dispirited, low, low in spirits, low-spirited, melancholy, disheartened, discouraged, fed up, daunted, desolate, moody, morose, pessimistic, weighed down, oppressed; *inf.* down in the dumps. **2** *a depressed section of land* sunken, hollow, concave, indented, dented, pushed in, recessed, set back. **3** *a depressed economy* weak, weakened, enervated, debilitated, devitalized, impaired. *See* DEPRESS 2. **4** *depressed prices* reduced, lowered, cut, cheapened, slashed,

devalued, marked-down, discounted. **5** *a depressed area* poverty-stricken, poor, destitute, disadvantaged, deprived, needy, distressed, run-down, down-at-heel.
Opposites CHEERFUL; STRONG; PROSPEROUS.

depressing *adjective depressing news* saddening, sad, unhappy, gloomy, dismal, bleak, black, sombre, grave, dreary, melancholy, dispiriting, disheartening, dejecting, discouraging, daunting, distressing, painful, heart-breaking.

depression *noun* **1** *patients suffering from depression* clinical depression, endogenous depression, reactive depression, melancholia. **2** *bad news caused her depression* sadness, unhappiness, despair, gloom, glumness, dejection, downheartedness, despondency, dispiritedness, melancholy, discouragement, desolation, dolefulness, moodiness, moroseness, pessimism, hopelessness; low spirits, blues; *inf.* the dumps. **3** *a depression in the landscape* hollow, indentation, dent, cavity, concavity, dip, valley, pit, hole, bowl, sink, sink-hole, excavation. **4** *an economic depression* slump, recession, decline, slowdown, standstill; paralysis, inactivity, stagnation; hard/bad times.

deprivation *verb* **1** *the deprivation of their rights* withholding, denial, withdrawal, removal, dispossession, taking away, stripping, expropriation, seizure, confiscation, robbing, appropriation, divestment, divestiture, wresting. **2** *areas of social deprivation* poverty, hardship, privation, destitution, disadvantage, need, neediness, want, distress, detriment.

deprive *verb deprive them of their rights* dispossess, strip, expropriate, divest, wrest, rob.

deprived *adjective the deprived section of the community* poor, destitute, disadvantaged, needy, in need, in want, lacking, distressed, forlorn.
Opposites FORTUNATE; WEALTHY.

depth *noun* **1** *measure the depth of the hole* deepness, distance downwards/inwards, drop, vertical extent, profundity. **2** *a person/thinker of depth* deepness, profoundness, profundity, wisdom, understanding, sagacity, discernment, insight, awareness, intuition, penetration, astuteness, acumen, shrewdness, acuity. **3** *an essay/issue of great depth* deepness, gravity, seriousness, weight, importance, moment, solemnity, complexity, intricacy, obtuseness, abstruseness, obscurity, reconditeness. **4** *the depth of the colour* deepness, intensity, richness, darkness, vividness, strength, brilliance. **5** *investigating the depths of the cave/sea* deepest part, remotest area, bottom, floor, bed, abyss, back, pit; bowels. **in depth** *investigate in depth* thoroughly, extensively, comprehensively, intensively.
Opposites HEIGHT; shallowness; TRIVIALITY.

deputation *noun* **1** *a deputation representing the homeless* delegation, legation, commission, embassy, committee; delegates, envoys, deputies. **2** *the deputation of the delegation* appointment, designation, nomination, commission, assignment, installation, investiture, induction, ordination.

depute *verb* **1** *depute a representative* appoint, designate, nominate, commission, assign,

install, invest, ordain. **2** *depute authority* delegate, transfer, assign, pass on, consign.

deputize *verb deputize for the chairman* take the place of, act for, stand in for, understudy, do a locum for.

deputy *noun act as the chairman's deputy* substitute, stand-in, representative, second in command, assistant, surrogate, proxy, delegate, agent, spokesperson, ambassador, lieutenant, legate, commissioner, envoy, go-between, mediator, nuncio, vice-regent, vice-president, vice-chancellor; *inf.* vice.

deputy *adjective a deputy manager* assistant, substitute, stand-in, representative, surrogate, proxy, subordinate.

deranged *adjective* mentally deranged, disturbed, unbalanced, unhinged, touched, insane, mad, crazy, crazed, demented, irrational, of unsound mind, *non compos mentis*, berserk, frenzied; *inf.* cracked, bonkers, potty, dotty, nuts, balmy, barmy, bats, batty, dippy, cuckoo, screwy, off one's trolley/rocker/chump, out to lunch.
Opposites SANE; RATIONAL.

derelict *adjective* **1** *derelict factories/ships* abandoned, forsaken, deserted, discarded, rejected, cast off, relinquished, ownerless. **2** *living in derelict properties* dilapidated, ramshackle, tumbledown, run-down, broken-down, in disrepair, crumbling, falling to pieces, rickety, neglected. **3** *derelict officers* negligent, neglectful, remiss, lax, careless, sloppy, slipshod, slack, irresponsible, delinquent.

derelict *noun derelicts begging in the street* down and out, vagrant, tramp, beggar, outcast, pariah, ne'er do well, good-for-nothing, wastrel; *inf.* dosser; *Am. inf.* hobo.

dereliction *noun* **1** *the dereliction of the factories/ ships* abandonment, forsaking, desertion, rejection, relinquishment, renunciation. *See* DERELICT *adjective 1.* **2** *accused of dereliction* negligence, neglect, neglectfulness, remissness, laxity, carelessness, sloppiness, slackness, irresponsibility, non-performance, delinquency, *laissez-faire*.

deride *verb* mock, ridicule, jeer at, scoff at, sneer at, make fun of, poke fun at, laugh at, scorn, pooh-pooh, flout at, lampoon, satirize, taunt, insult, torment, rag, tease, chaff, disdain, disparage, denigrate, slight, detract from, vilify; *fml.* contemn.

derision *noun* mockery, ridicule, jeering, scoffing, sneering, scorn, contempt, taunting, ragging, teasing, raillery, disdain, disrespect, disparagement, denigration, vilification, contumely; jeers, sneers, taunts, insults; satire, lampoon. *See* DERIDE.

derisive *adjective derisive shouts* mocking, ridiculing, jeering, scoffing, scornful, contemptuous, taunting, insulting, satirical, sarcastic, disdainful, disparaging, denigratory, derisory.

derisory *adjective* **1** *a derisory wage increase* laughable, ludicrous, ridiculous, insulting, contemptible, preposterous, outrageous, inadequate, tiny, minimal. **2** *derisory shouts* derisive, mocking, ridiculing, jeering, scoffing, scornful, contemptuous, taunting. *See* DERISIVE.

derivation noun **1** *the derivation of the word/custom* origin, source, root, etymology, fountainhead, wellspring, origination, beginning, foundation, basis, cause; ancestry, descent, genealogy, development, evolution. See DERIVE 1. **2** *undertake the derivation of the custom* tracing, following back. See DERIVE 2. **3** *the derivation of satisfaction from work* deriving, acquisition, extraction. See DERIVE 4. **4** *the derivation of facts* deriving, collecting, collection, gathering, gleaning, drawing out, eliciting, eduction, deduction, inference. See DERIVE 5.

derivative adjective **1** *derivative conclusions* derived, collected, elicited, educed, deduced, inferred. See DERIVE 5. **2** *derivative research* imitative, unoriginal, uninventive, non-innovative, copied, plagiaristic, plagiarized, second-hand, secondary, rehashed, warmed-up, thinly disguised.
Opposites ORIGINAL; INVENTIVE; innovative.

derivative noun **1** *a derivative of coal* by-product, spin-off, offshoot. **2** *a word and its derivatives* derived word, descendant.

derive verb **1** *derive from a Latin word* originate in, have one's/its origins in, have as a source, stem from, descend from, spring from, arise in. **2** *derive a word* trace back, follow back, etymologize. **3** *happiness deriving from marriage* originate in, stem from, proceed, flow, emanate, issue. **4** *derive satisfaction* acquire, obtain, get, gain, procure, extract. **5** *derive sufficient facts* collect, gather, glean, winnow, draw out, elicit, educe, deduce, infer.

derogate verb **1** *derogate their achievement/character* disparage, denigrate, belittle, diminish, deprecate, depreciate, downplay, detract from, deflate, decry, discredit, downgrade, defame, vilify. **2** *derogate from old standards* deviate, degenerate, deteriorate, decline, worsen, retrogress, retrograde.

derogatory adjective *a derogatory remark* disparaging, denigratory, belittling, diminishing, slighting, deprecatory, depreciatory, depreciative, detracting, deflating, discrediting, dishonouring, unfavourable, disapproving, uncomplimentary, unflattering, insulting, offensive, damaging, injurious, defamatory, vilifying.
Opposites COMPLIMENTARY; FLATTERING; LAUDATORY.

descend verb **1** *descend the hill/stairs* go down, come down, move down, climb down, pass down. **2** *the balloon descended* go down, come down, drop, fall, sink, subside, plummet, plunge, tumble, slump. **3** *descend from the train* get down, get off, alight, dismount, disembark; detrain, deplane. **4** *the hill descended to the valley* go down, slope, incline, dip, slant. **5** *will not descend to talk to servants* condescend, stoop, lower/abase oneself. **6** *descend in quality/values* degenerate, deteriorate, decline, sink, go downhill; inf. go to pot, go to the dogs. **7** *enemies/visitors descending on us* attack, assault, assail, pounce, raid, swoop, charge, come in force, arrive in hordes. **8** *a family descended from William the Conqueror* be a descendant of, derive/originate from, issue/spring from. **9** *houses descending from father to son* be handed/passed down, pass by heredity, be transferred by inheritance.
Opposites ASCEND; CLIMB.

descendants plural noun offspring, progeny, issue, family; scions.

descent noun **1** *the descent of the hill* going down, coming down. See DESCEND 1. **2** *the descent of the balloon* going down, drop, fall, sinking, subsiding, plummeting, plunge. See DESCEND 2. **3** *the descent from the train* getting down/off, alighting. See DESCEND 3. **4** *walk down the descent* slope, incline, dip, drop, gradient, declivity, declination, slant. **5** *descent in quality/values* degeneracy, deterioration, decline, debasement, degradation, sinking, decadence. See DESCEND 6. **6** *the descent of enemies/visitors* attack, assault, assailing, raid, charge, onslaught, incursion, foray, sortie. **7** *of noble descent* ancestry, parentage, lineage, extraction, genealogy, heredity, succession, stock, line, pedigree, blood, strain; origins.

describe verb **1** *describe the incident* give a description/account of, give details of, detail, tell, narrate, put into words, express, recount, relate, report, set out, chronicle, define, explain, elucidate, illustrate. **2** *he was described as brilliant* call, designate, pronounce, style, label, characterize, portray, depict. **3** *describe a circle* draw, delineate, mark out, outline, trace, sketch.

description noun **1** *give a description of the incident* account, detailed statement, report, setting out, chronicle, narration, recounting, relation, commentary, explanation, elucidation, illustration; details. **2** *the description of him as dishonest* calling, designation, pronouncement, styling, labelling, characterization, portrayal, depiction. **3** *the description of a circle* drawing, delineation, outline, tracing. See DESCRIBE 3. **4** *vegetables of some description* kind, sort, variety, type, brand, breed, category, class, designation, genre, ilk, kidney, grain, stamp, mould.

descriptive adjective detailed, explanatory, elucidatory, graphic, vivid, striking, expressive, illustrative, pictorial, depictive, picturesque, circumstantial.

descry verb catch sight of, see, make out, notice, discern, perceive, observe, detect, distinguish.

desecrate verb violate, defile, profane, treat sacrilegiously, blaspheme, pollute, contaminate, infect, befoul, debase, degrade, dishonour, vitiate.

desert verb **1** *desert one's wife/post* abandon, forsake, give up, cast off, leave, turn one's back on, leave high and dry, leave in the lurch, throw over, betray, jilt, strand, leave stranded, maroon, neglect, shun, relinquish, renounce; inf. walk/run out on, rat on. **2** *the soldier has deserted* abscond, defect, run away, make off, decamp, flee, fly, bolt, turn tail, go AWOL, take French leave, depart, quit, escape. **3** *desert a cause* abandon, forsake, turn one's back on, relinquish, renounce, betray, renege, apostatize.
Opposites MAINTAIN; STAY; stand by (see STAND).

desert *noun* **1** *lost in the African desert* wasteland, waste, wilderness, barrenness, solitude; wilds. *See table.* **2** *living in a cultural desert* uninteresting place/period, unproductive place/period, wasteland.

MAJOR DESERTS	
Desert	**Location**
Arabian	Egypt
Atacama	Chile
Chihuahuan	U.S.A./Mexico
Colorado	U.S.A.
Death Valley	U.S.A.
Gibson	Australia
Gobi	Mongolia/China
Great Basin	U.S.A.
Great Sandy	Australia
Great Victoria	Australia
Kalahari	South Africa/Namibia/ Botswana
Kara Kum	Turkmenistan
Kyzyl Kum	Kazakhstan/Uzbekistan
Libyan	Libya
Lut	Iran
Mojave	U.S.A.
Nafud	Saudi Arabia
Namib	Namibia
Negev	Israel
Nubian	Sudan
Painted	U.S.A.
Patagonian	Argentina
Rub' al Khali	Saudi Arabia/Oman/ Yemen/United Arab Emirates
Sahara	North Africa
Simpson	Australia
Sonoran	U.S.A./Mexico
Sturt	Australia
Syrian	Syria/Iraq/Jordan/Saudi Arabia
Taklimakan	China
Thar	India/Pakistan

desert *adjective* **1** *African desert regions* arid, dry, moistureless, parched, scorched, dried up, burnt, hot, burning, torrid. **2** *Arctic desert region* desolate, barren, bare, wild, empty, uninhabited, solitary, lonely, uncultivable, uncultivatable, infertile, unproductive, sterile, uncultivated, untilled.

deserted *adjective* **1** *a deserted wife* abandoned, forsaken, cast off, betrayed, jilted, stranded, marooned, neglected, shunned, relinquished, renounced, forlorn, bereft. **2** *deserted buildings* abandoned, forsaken, neglected, empty, vacant, uninhabited, unoccupied, untenanted, tenantless, unfrequented, secluded, isolated, desolate, lonely, solitary, godforsaken.
Opposites CROWDED; POPULOUS.

deserter *noun* **1** *army deserters* absconder, defector, runaway, fugitive, truant, escapee, derelict. **2** *deserters from the cause* defector, renegade, turncoat, traitor, betrayer, apostate, derelict; *inf.* rat.

desertion *noun* **1** *the desertion of his wife | sued for desertion* abandonment, forsaking, betrayal, relinquishment, renunciation. **2** *desertion from the army | disciplined for desertion* absconding, defection, decamping, flight, truancy, going AWOL, French leave, departure, escape, dereliction. **3** *desertion from/of the cause* defection, betrayal, apostasy.

deserve *verb* merit, be worthy of, warrant, rate, justify, earn, be entitled to, have a right to, have a claim on, be qualified for.

deserved *adjective* well-earned, merited, warranted, justified, justifiable, earned, rightful, due, right, just, fair, fitting, appropriate, suitable, proper, reasonable, condign.

deserving *adjective* worthy, meritorious, commendable, praiseworthy, laudable, admirable, estimable, creditable, virtuous, righteous, upright, good.

design *verb* **1** *draughtsmen designing the structure* plan, draw, draw plans of, sketch, outline, map out, plot, block out, delineate, draft, depict. **2** *designing clothes | designing schemes in his head* create, invent, originate, think up, conceive, fashion, fabricate, hatch, innovate; *inf.* dream up. **3** *words designed to hurt | a course designed for beginners* intend, aim, devise, contrive, purpose, plan, tailor, mean, destine.

design *noun* **1** *the design was left in the office* plan, blueprint, drawing, sketch, outline, map, plot, diagram, delineation, draft, depiction, scheme, model. **2** *admire the fabric designs* pattern, motif, style, arrangement, composition, make-up, constitution, configuration, organization, construction, shape, figure. **3** *a clever design to defeat the enemy* plan, enterprise, undertaking, scheme, plot, intrigue, expedient, stratagem, device, artifice. **4** *with the design of entering* intention, aim, purpose, plan, objective, goal, end, target, point, hope, desire, wish, dream, aspiration, ambition.

designate *verb* **1** *a new category designated helpers* call, name, entitle, term, christen, dub, style, label, denominate, nickname. **2** *designated ambassador* appoint, nominate, depute, delegate, select, choose, elect, assign, allot, ordain, induct. **3** *designate the place | at designated times* state, appoint, specify, define, stipulate, particularize, earmark, set aside, pinpoint. **4** *arrows designating direction* show, indicate, point out, mark, denote.

designation *noun* **1** *going under the designation of financial consultant* title, name, label, appellation, epithet, tag, style, denomination, nickname, sobriquet, cognomen; *inf.* moniker. **2** *opposing his designation as ambassador* appointment, nomination, selection, election, induction. *See* DESIGNATE 2. **3** *the designation of place and time* specification, defining, stipulation, earmarking. *See* DESIGNATE 3. **4** *the designation of direction by arrows* indication, marking, denotement, denoting. *See* DESIGNATE 4.

designer *noun* **1** *designer of bridges/buildings/ fabrics* creator, inventor, deviser, fashioner, originator, author, producer, artificer. *See tables at* ARCHITECT, ENGINEER, INVENTOR. **2** *dress designer* couturier, fashion designer, creator, fashioner. *See table at* FASHION. **3** *a troublemaking designer* plotter, schemer, intriguer, conniver, conspirator, machinator.

designing *adjective* scheming, plotting, intriguing, conspiring, conniving, calculating, Machiavellian, cunning, crafty, artful, wily, devious, shrewd, astute, sharp, insidious, treacherous, sly, underhand, deceitful, tricky; *inf.* crooked.

desirability *noun* **1** *the desirability of the property* attractiveness, allure, appeal, popularity, eligibility, agreeableness, excellence, worth. *See* DESIRABLE 1. **2** *the desirability of no one knowing* preferableness, advisability, advantageousness, advantage, benefit, merit, value, profit, expedience. **3** *the desirability of the young woman* sexual attractiveness/attraction, attractiveness, seductiveness, allurement, eroticism, fascination; *inf.* sexiness.

desirable *adjective* **1** *a desirable job* attractive, sought-after, in demand, popular, covetable, enviable, eligible, agreeable, appealing, pleasant, admirable, worthwhile, profitable, good, excellent. **2** *it is desirable that no one knows* preferable, advisable, recommendable, advantageous, beneficial, expedient, in everyone's interests. **3** *a desirable young woman* sexually attractive, attractive, seductive, alluring, erotic, fetching, fascinating, beguiling; *inf.* sexy.
Opposites UNDESIRABLE; INADVISABLE; UGLY.

desire *verb* **1** *desire happiness* wish for, want, long/yearn for, crave, set one's heart on, hanker after, have a fancy for, fancy, be bent on, covet, aspire to; *inf.* have a yen for. **2** *desire to go* wish, want, feel like, long, crave, have a fancy to. **3** *desire his/her body* lust after, burn for; *inf.* lech after, have the hots for. **4** *desire a cup of tea* request, ask for, want.

desire *noun* **1** *express a desire to go | her desire for success* wish, want, fancy, inclination, preference; wanting, longing, yearning, craving, eagerness, enthusiasm, hankering, predilection, aspiration, proclivity, predisposition. **2** *overcome by desire* sexual attraction, lust, lustfulness, sexual appetite, passion, carnal passion, concupiscence, libido, sensuality, sexuality, lasciviousness, lechery, salaciousness, libidinousness, prurience; *inf.* the hots.

desired *adjective* **1** *fitted to the desired length* required, necessary, proper, right, correct, exact, accurate, precise, specific, particular, appropriate, fitting, suitable, preferred, expected, express. **2** *the desired prize* wished for, longed for, yearned for, craved, coveted. *See* DESIRE *verb* 1.

desirous *adjective* **1** *desirous of success* desiring, wishing, wishful of, hopeful of, avid/eager/anxious for, craving, ambitious for. **2** *desirous to win* desiring, keen, avid, eager, ambitious, hoping, aspiring, anxious, willing, wishing, ready.
Opposites AVERSE; LOATH.

desist *verb* *they've been asked to desist | desist from laughing* stop, cease, discontinue, abstain, give up, forbear/refrain from, break/leave off.
Opposites CONTINUE; PERSIST.

desolate *adjective* **1** *desolate moors* bare, barren, bleak, dismal, desert, waste, wild. **2** *desolate farms* deserted, uninhabited, unoccupied, depopulated, forsaken, abandoned, unpeopled, untenanted, unfrequented, unvisited, solitary, lonely, isolated. **3** *desolate at the sad news* sad, unhappy, miserable, broken-hearted, wretched, downcast, cast down, dejected, downhearted, melancholy, gloomy, despondent, depressed, disconsolate, forlorn, cheerless, distressed, grieving, bereft.
Opposites FERTILE; POPULOUS; JOYFUL.

desolation *noun* **1** *the desolation of the remote landscape by war* destruction, laying waste, ruin, ruination, devastation, despoliation, havoc, ravaging. **2** *the desolation of the landscape* bareness, barrenness, bleakness, dismalness, wildness, isolation, solitude, solitariness, loneliness, remoteness; wasteland, wilderness, desert. **3** *her desolation at the news* sadness, unhappiness, misery, broken-heartedness, wretchedness, dejection, downheartedness, depression, melancholy, gloom, despondency, distress, grief.

despair *noun* **1** *unemployed and full of despair* hopelessness, dejection, depression, desperation, disheartenment, discouragement, despondency, disconsolateness, defeatism, pessimism, resignedness, melancholy, gloom, melancholia, misery, wretchedness, distress, anguish. **2** *the boy is the despair of the teacher* hopeless case, bane, burden, bother, scourge.
Opposites HOPE; JOY.

despair *verb* lose hope, give up hope, give up, lose heart, be discouraged, be despondent, be pessimistic, resign oneself, throw in the towel/sponge.

despairing *adjective* hopeless, dejected, depressed, desperate, suicidal, disheartened, discouraged, despondent, disconsolate, inconsolable, defeatist, pessimistic, resigned, melancholy, gloomy, downcast, forlorn, miserable, wretched, distressed, broken-hearted, heartbroken, grief-stricken, sorrowing, anguished.

despatch *verb, noun. See* DISPATCH *verb, noun.*

desperado *noun* criminal, lawbreaker, gangster, terrorist, outlaw, bandit, gunman, thug, ruffian, hooligan, villain, hoodlum, mugger.

desperate *adjective* **1** *a desperate criminal* reckless, rash, hasty, impetuous, foolhardy, audacious, daring, bold, madcap, wild, violent, frantic, mad, frenzied, lawless. **2** *a desperate act* reckless, rash, foolhardy, risky, hazardous, daring, precipitate, hare-brained, wild, imprudent, incautious, injudicious, indiscreet, ill-conceived. **3** *in desperate need* urgent, pressing, compelling, acute, critical, crucial, drastic, serious, grave, dire, extreme, great. **4** *desperate for money* in great need of, urgently requiring, in want of, lacking. **5** *the desperate state of the country* grave, very bad, appalling, outrageous, intolerable, deplorable, lamentable. **6** *trying to help desperate people* despairing, hopeless, wretched. *See* DESPAIRING. **7** *desperate measures* last-ditch, last-resort, do-or-die, futile.

desperately · destitute

desperately *adverb desperately ill/poor* seriously, gravely, severely, extremely, critically, acutely, dangerously, perilously.

desperation *noun* **1** *the desperation of the act* recklessness, rashness, impetuosity, foolhardiness, riskiness, audacity, boldness, wildness, imprudence, injudiciousness, violence, frenziedness, lawlessness. *See* DESPERATE 1, 2. **2** *the desperation of their state* urgency, criticalness, crucialness, seriousness, gravity, direness, extremity. **3** *the desperation of the homeless* hopelessness, despair, dejection, depression, despondency, disconsolateness, forlornness, melancholy, gloom, misery, wretchedness, distress, anguish, sorrow, pain. *See* DESPAIR *noun* 1.

despicable *adjective* contemptible, beyond contempt, reprehensible, vile, base, low, mean, scurvy, abominable, loathsome, hateful, detestable, odious, disreputable, infamous, villainous, ignoble, disgusting, sordid, distasteful, shameful, degrading, ignominious, cheap, shabby, miserable, wretched, sorry.
Opposites ADMIRABLE; NOBLE.

despise *verb* scorn, look down on, spurn, shun, disdain, slight, undervalue, deride, scoff/ jeer at, sneer at, mock, revile, hate, detest, loathe, abhor, abominate, execrate; *fml.* contemn.

despite *preposition* in spite of, notwithstanding, regardless of, in defiance of, in the face of.

despoil *verb* **1** *despoil the country* plunder, pillage, rob, ravage, harry, maraud, ravish, rape, depredate, raid, forage, ransack, loot, sack, rifle, devastate, lay waste, wreak havoc on, vandalize, destroy, ruin, wreck. **2** *despoil the city of its treasures* rob, dispossess, strip, deprive, denude, divest.

despondency *noun* hopelessness, disheartenment, discouragement, disconsolateness, dispiritedness, downheartedness, despair, defeatism, melancholy, gloom, melancholia, misery, wretchedness, distress, sorrow, sadness; low spirits, doldrums, blues.

despondent *adjective* hopeless, downcast, cast down, down, low, disheartened, discouraged, disconsolate, low-spirited, dispirited, downhearted, in despair, despairing, defeatist, blue, melancholy, gloomy, glum, morose, doleful, woebegone, miserable, wretched, distressed, sorrowful, sad.
Opposites HOPEFUL; CHEERFUL; HAPPY.

despot *noun* absolute ruler, autocrat, dictator, tyrant, oppressor, monocrat.

despotic *adjective* absolute, autocratic, dictatorial, tyrannical, oppressive, totalitarian, domineering, imperious, arrogant, high-handed, authoritarian, arbitrary, unconstitutional.

despotism *noun* absolutism, autocracy, dictatorship, tyranny, oppression, totalitarianism, monocracy, autarchy.

dessert *noun. See table.*

destination *noun London was our destination* journey's end, landing place, point of disembarkation, terminus, end of the line, end, station, stop, stopping-place, port of call.

destined *adjective* **1** *a plane destined for London* bound for, en route for, heading for/towards, directed/routed to, scheduled for. **2** *destined for the state* designed, intended, meant, set, set apart, designated, appointed, allotted. **3** *destined to die young* fated, ordained, preordained, foreordained, predestined, predetermined, doomed, foredoomed, certain, sure, bound, written in the cards.

destiny *noun* **1** *couldn't escape his destiny* fate, fortune, lot, portion, cup, due, future, doom. **2** *destiny drew them together* fate, divine decree, predestination, luck, fortune, chance, karma, kismet; the stars.

destitute *adjective* **1** *destitute refugees* poverty-stricken, indigent, impoverished, penurious, impecunious, penniless, insolvent, beggarly, beggared, down and out, poor, needy, hard up, badly off, on the breadline, hard-pressed, distressed, pauperized; *inf.* on one's uppers, up against it. **2** *destitute of ideas* devoid of, without, bereft of, deficient in, lacking, wanting,

---

DESSERTS

Apfelstrudel	crème caramel	kissel	steamed pudding
apple charlotte	crêpes Suzette	Knickerbocker	stewed fruit
apple pie	crumble	Glory	suet pudding
baked Alaska	custard	Mississippi mud	summer pudding
baklava	dairy ice cream	pie	sundae
banana split	egg custard	mousse	tapioca
banoffi pie	entremets	pandowdy	tipsy-cake
bavaroise	Eve's pudding	pavlova	tiramisu
Black Forest gateau	floating island	peach Melba	treacle tart
blancmange	fool	plum pudding	trifle
bread-and-butter	fresh fruit	rice pudding	upside-down
pudding	fruit cup	roly-poly	pudding
Brown Betty	fruit flan	semolina	Viennoise
cabinet pudding	fruit salad	shoofly pie *Am.*	[pudding]
cajeta	granita	sorbet	water ice
charlotte russe	ice cream	soufflé	whip (gooseberry
Christmas pudding	jam tart	sponge pudding	whip)
cobbler	jelly	spotted dick	yogurt
compote	junket	spumoni	zabaglione

deprived of, empty, drained.
Opposites PROSPEROUS; WEALTHY; RICH.

destitution noun **1** *the destitution of the refugees* dire poverty, poverty, indigence, penury, insolvency, privation, financial distress, pauperdom; impoverishment, impecuniousness, neediness. **2** *destitution of ideas* deficiency, dearth, lack, want, need, scarcity, meagreness, deprivation.

destroy verb **1** *destroy the bridge* demolish, knock down, pull down, tear down, level, raze, fell, dismantle, wreck, smash, shatter, crash, blow up, blow to bits, explode, annihilate, wipe out, bomb, torpedo. **2** *destroy the countryside* ruin, spoil, devastate, lay waste, ravage, wreak havoc on, ransack. **3** *destroy their confidence* terminate, quash, quell, crush, stifle, subdue, squash, extinguish, extirpate. **4** *destroy the herd/tribe* kill, kill off, slaughter, put to sleep, exterminate; slay, murder, assassinate, wipe out, massacre, liquidate, decimate.
5 *destroy the enemy/opponents* defeat, beat, conquer, vanquish, trounce, rout, drub; *inf.* lick, thrash.
Opposites BUILD; CONSTRUCT; CREATE.

destruction noun **1** *the destruction of the building* demolition, knocking down, pulling down, tearing down, levelling, razing, dismantling, wrecking, smashing, blowing up, wiping out, annihilation. See DESTROY 1. **2** *the destruction of the countryside* ruination, spoiling, devastation, laying waste, desolation, ravaging; ruin, havoc. See DESTROY 2. **3** *the destruction of their confidence* termination, quashing, quelling, crushing, stifling, subduing, extinguishing, extinction. See DESTROY 3. **4** *the destruction of the herd/tribe* killing, slaughter, slaying, murder, assassination, massacre. See DESTROY 4. **5** *the destruction of the enemy/opponents* defeat, beating, conquest, vanquishing, trouncing, rout. See DESTROY 5.

destructive adjective **1** *destructive winds/wars* ruinous, devastating, disastrous, catastrophic, calamitous, cataclysmic, ravaging, fatal, deadly, dangerous, lethal, damaging, pernicious, noxious, injurious, harmful, detrimental, deleterious, disadvantageous. **2** *destructive children* damaging, injurious, harmful, hurtful, mischievous, pernicious. **3** *destructive comments/criticism* non-constructive, negative, unfavourable, adverse, antagonistic, hostile, unfriendly, contrary, discrediting, invalidating, derogatory, denigrating, disparaging, disapproving, discouraging, undermining.

desultory adjective half-hearted, haphazard, random, aimless, rambling, erratic, irregular, unmethodical, unsystematic, chaotic, inconsistent, inconstant, fitful, capricious.
Opposites THOROUGH; METHODICAL; SYSTEMATIC.

detach verb **1** *detach the collar* unfasten, disconnect, unhitch, remove, separate, uncouple, loosen, free, sever, tear off, disengage, disjoin, disunite. **2** *detach oneself from the group* separate, move off, dissociate, segregate, isolate, cut off, disconnect, divide.
Opposites ATTACH; JOIN.

detached adjective **1** *a detached house* standing alone, separate, unconnected, not attached. **2** *a detached collar* unfastened, disconnected,

unhitched, separate, loosened, free, severed. See DETACH 1. **3** *observing in a detached way* dispassionate, aloof, indifferent, unconcerned, reserved, unemotional, impersonal, cool, remote. **4** *detached commentators* objective, disinterested, unbiased, unprejudiced, impartial, non-partisan, neutral, fair.
Opposites PASSIONATE; BIASED; INVOLVED.

detachment noun **1** *the detachment of the collar* unfastening, disconnection, unhitching, separation, uncoupling, loosening, severing, disengagement, disuniting. See DETACH 1. **2** *look on with detachment* dispassionateness, dispassion, aloofness, indifference, unconcern, lack of concern/emotion, reserve, coolness, remoteness. **3** *the detachment of the panel* objectivity, disinterest, lack of bias/prejudice, impartiality, nonpartisanship, neutrality, fairness. **4** *a detachment of soldiers* separate/specialized unit, task force, detail, patrol.

detail noun **1** *to the smallest detail* item, particular, fact, point, factor, element, circumstance, aspect, feature, respect, attribute, part, unit, component, member, accessory. **2** *don't bother with such a detail* unimportant point, insignificant item, trivial fact. **3** *fill in the details* particulars, fine points, niceties, minutiae, trivia. **4** *the detail of soldiers for fatigue duty* assignment, allotment, delegating, deputing. **5** *pass a detail of soldiers* detachment, task force, patrol. See DETACHMENT 4. **in detail** point by point, item by item, comprehensively, fully, thoroughly, exhaustively, blow by blow.

detail verb **1** *detail the arrangements* specify, set forth, set out, list, enumerate, tabulate, catalogue, spell out, delineate, relate, recount, narrate, recite, rehearse, describe, cite, point out, indicate, portray, depict, itemize, particularize, individualize. **2** *detail personnel for duty* appoint, assign, allocate, delegate, select, choose, name, nominate, elect, charge, commission, send.

detailed adjective **1** *a detailed bill/description* itemized, particularized, full, comprehensive, thorough, exhaustive, all-inclusive, circumstantial, precise, exact, specific, particular, meticulous. **2** *a detailed picture/story* complex, involved, elaborate, complicated, intricate, convoluted, entangled.

detain verb **1** *detained by business* hold/keep back, hold up, delay, keep, slow up/down, hinder, impede, check, retard, inhibit, stay.
2 *detain the accused* put/keep in custody, confine, imprison, lock up, incarcerate, impound, intern, restrain, hold, arrest; *inf.* collar.

detect verb **1** *detect hostility/smoke* notice, note, discern, perceive, make out, observe, spot, become aware of, recognize, distinguish, identify, catch, decry, sense, see, smell. **2** *accountants detected the theft* discover, find out, turn up, uncover, bring to light, expose, unearth, reveal, unmask, unveil. **3** *police detecting the crime* investigate, probe, track down, ferret out, sleuth.

detection noun **1** *the detection of hostility/smoke* noticing, discernment, perception, observation, awareness, recognition, distinguishing, identification. See DETECT 1. **2** *the early detection*

of the crime discovery, uncovering, exposure, exposé, revelation, unmasking. *See* DETECT 2.
3 *the police detection* investigating, probe, tracking down, sleuthing.

detective *noun* investigator; private investigator, CID man/woman, police officer; *inf.* sleuth, tec, dick, private eye, private dick, tail, shadow; *Am. inf.* gumshoe. *See* POLICEMAN.

detention *noun* **1** *unavoidable detention at work* holding up, delay, slowing up, hindrance, impediment, check, retardation. *See* DETAIN 1.
2 *kept in detention | boys with a detention after school* custody, confinement, imprisonment, incarceration, internment, restraint, detainment, duress, quarantine, arrest; keeping in, punishment. *See* DETAIN 2.

deter *verb* put off, prevent, stop, discourage, dissuade, talk out of, check, restrain, caution, frighten, intimidate, daunt, scare off, warn against, hold back, prohibit, hinder, impede, obstruct, block, inhibit.
Opposites ENCOURAGE; PERSUADE.

detergent *noun* cleaner, cleanser; soap powder/flakes, washing-up liquid.

detergent *adjective* cleaning, cleansing, abstergent.

deteriorate *verb* **1** *moral values deteriorating* get worse, worsen, decline, degenerate, sink, slip, go downhill, slide, lapse, fail, fall, drop, ebb, wane, retrograde, retrogress, slump, depreciate; *inf.* go to pot, go to the dogs.
2 *deteriorate their moral values* corrupt, debase, defile, impair. **3** *buildings/food deteriorating* disintegrate, become dilapidated, decline, degenerate, crumble, fall apart, fall to pieces, fall down, break up, decay, decompose, go bad.
Opposites IMPROVE; ameliorate.

deterioration *noun* **1** *the deterioration of morals* worsening, decline, degeneration, lapse, failure, downturn, ebb, waning, retrogression, slump, depreciation; corruption, debasement, defilement, contamination, pollution, vitiation, tainting, corrosion, impairment. *See* DETERIORATE 1, 2. **2** *the deterioration of buildings/food* disintegration, dilapidation, decline, degeneration, crumbling, falling apart, erosion, decay, decomposition. *See* DETERIORATE 3.

determination *noun* **1** *behave with determination* firmness, firmness of purpose, resoluteness, steadfastness, tenacity, single-mindedness, resolve, drive, push, thrust, fortitude, dedication, backbone, stamina, mettle, strong will, persistence, pertinacity, perseverance, conviction, doggedness, stubbornness, obduracy, intransigence. **2** *the committee's determination | the legal determination* decision, conclusion, judgement, verdict, opinion, decree, solution, result, arbitration, settlement, diagnosis, prognosis.

determine *verb* **1** *determine the place of meeting | determine who should go* settle, fix, decide, agree on, establish, judge, arbitrate, decree, ordain. **2** *determine the argument* settle, decide, resolve, conclude, end, terminate, finish. **3** *determine the room dimensions* find out, discover, learn, establish, calculate, work out, ascertain, check, verify, certify. **4** *determine to*

go alone make up one's mind, decide, resolve, choose, elect, fix on, purpose. **5** *what determined him to go?* made, prompt, impel, induce, influence, sway, lead. **6** *conditions determining the nature of the soil* affect, influence, act/work on, condition, regulate, decide, control, direct, rule, dictate, govern, form, shape, modify.

determined *adjective* **1** *a determined person/attitude* firm, resolute, steadfast, tenacious, purposeful, single-minded, dedicated, strong-willed, mettlesome, plucky, persistent, pertinacious, persevering, dogged, unflinching, unwavering, stubborn, obdurate, intransigent, indomitable, inflexible. **2** *determined to go | determined on going* bent on, intent on, set on.
Opposites IRRESOLUTE; HESITANT.

determining *adjective* *determining factors* deciding, conclusive, settling, decisive, definitive, crucial, critical, pivotal, important, essential.

deterrent *noun* curb, disincentive, discouragement, check, restraint, obstacle, hindrance, impediment, obstruction, block, barrier, inhibition.
Opposites INCITEMENT; INCENTIVE.

detest *verb* loathe, abhor, hate, despise, abominate, execrate, feel aversion/hostility/animosity towards, feel disgust/distaste for, recoil/shrink from, feel repugnance towards.
Opposites LOVE; ADORE.

detestable *adjective* loathsome, abhorrent, hateful, odious, despicable, contemptible, abominable, reprehensible, execrable, distasteful, disgusting, repugnant; *inf.* beastly.

detonate *verb* **1** *the bomb detonated* explode, go off, blow up, burst apart; bang, blast, boom. **2** *detonate the bomb* explode, set off, discharge, ignite, kindle, light, spark.

detour *noun* indirect course, roundabout/circuitous route, scenic/tourist route, diversion, digression, deviation, bypass, byway, bypath.

detract *verb* **1** *their conduct detracts from their achievement* take away from, diminish, reduce, lessen, lower, devalue, devaluate, depreciate. **2** *detract his attention* distract, divert, turn away, deflect, avert, shift.
Opposites INCREASE; ENHANCE; AUGMENT.

detractor *noun* *criticism from her detractors | detractors from his achievement/reputation* belittler, disparager, denigrator, deprecator, deflater, defamer, vilifier, backbiter, carper, caviller, scandalmonger, muckraker.

detriment *noun* injury, harm, damage, impairment, hurt, loss, disadvantage, disservice, ill, wrong, mischief.

detrimental *adjective* injurious, harmful, damaging, hurtful, deleterious, destructive, pernicious, disadvantageous, adverse, unfavourable, inimical, prejudicial.
Opposites ADVANTAGEOUS; BENEFICIAL; FAVOURABLE.

detritus *noun* debris, rubble, rubbish; remains, fragments, shards, ruins; flotsam and jetsam, grit, gravel, sand, powder, dust.

devastate *verb* **1** *devastate the cities* lay waste, leave desolate, destroy, ruin, demolish, wreck, raze, level, annihilate, ravage, ransack, sack, harry, despoil, spoil. **2** *devasted by the news* overcome, overwhelm, shock, traumatize, take aback, confound, bewilder, nonplus, disconcert, discompose, discomfit, perturb, chagrin; *inf.* floor.

devastating *adjective* **1** *devastating storms/criticism* destructive, ruinous, wrecking, deleterious, harmful, savage, annihilative. **2** *devastating news* overwhelming, shocking, traumatic, confounding, bewildering, disconcerting. See DEVASTATE 2. **3** *looking devastating in evening dress* stunning, glamorous, dazzling, ravishing, gorgeous, beautiful, lovely; *inf.* out of this world. **4** *devastating wit* effective, incisive, cutting, keen, mordant, biting, trenchant, satirical, sardonic, sarcastic, withering, savage.

devastation *noun* **1** *a scene of devastation* desolation, destruction, waste, ruin, wreckage; ruins, ravages. **2** *the devastation of the cities* laying waste, destruction, demolition, razing, annihilation, sacking, harrying. See DEVASTATE 1. **3** *her complete devastation* shock, traumatization, bewilderment, discomposure, discomfiture, perturbation. See DEVASTATE 2.

develop *verb* **1** *cities developing rapidly* grow, evolve, mature, expand, enlarge, spread, advance, progress, prosper, flourish, make headway. **2** *children developing into adults* grow, mature, turn. **3** *develop a plan* begin, commence, start, set in motion, originate, invent, form, establish, institute, fashion, generate. **4** *develop a new breed of pig/rose* generate, breed, propagate, rear, cultivate. **5** *develop a cough* begin to have, acquire, contract, pick up. **6** *develop a theme* elaborate, unfold, work out, enlarge on, expand, broaden, dilate on, amplify, add to, augment, magnify, supplement, reinforce. **7** *a row developed* begin, start, come about, follow, happen, result, ensue, break out.

development *noun* **1** *the development of cities* growth, evolution, maturing, expansion, spread, progress, headway. See DEVELOP 1. **2** *the development of a plan* originating, invention, forming, establishment, institution, generation. **3** *the development of a new breed* generation, breeding, propagation, rearing, cultivation. **4** *the development of themes* elaboration, unfolding, unravelling, enlarging, expansion, augmentation. See DEVELOP 6. **5** *new developments in the affair* event, turn of events, occurrence, happening, circumstance, incident, situation, issue, outcome, upshot. **6** *a housing development* complex, estate, structure, conglomeration.

deviant *adjective* *deviant behaviour* deviating, aberrant, divergent, digressive, abnormal, irregular, non-standard, anomalous, odd, freakish, peculiar, curious, queer, bizarre, eccentric, idiosyncratic, unorthodox, off-beat, wayward, perverse, devious, warped, twisted, perverted; *inf.* bent, kinky, quirky.
Opposites NORMAL; REGULAR; ORTHODOX.

deviant *noun* nonconformist, misfit, freak, rare bird, queer fellow, odd sort, pervert; *inf.* oddball, weirdo, dingbat.

deviate *verb* diverge, turn aside, step aside, depart from, digress, deflect, differ, vary, change, veer, swerve, bend, drift, stray, tack, slew.

deviation *noun* *deviation from the norm* divergence, turning aside, departure, digression, deflection, difference, variation, alteration, veering, straying, fluctuation, aberration, abnormality, irregularity, anomaly, inconsistency, discrepancy, variableness, oddness, freakishness; change, shift, veer, swerve, bend, drift.

device *noun* **1** *a handy device* appliance, gadget, implement, utensil, tool, piece of equipment/apparatus, apparatus, instrument, machine, contrivance, contraption, invention; *inf.* gizmo. **2** *win by a cunning device* design, plan, plot, scheme, ploy, project, stratagem, trick, artifice, ruse, dodge, stunt, gambit, shift, subterfuge, blind, manoeuvre, expedient, machination, strategy, improvisation, intrigue, conspiracy, fraud, wile, deception, imposture, sleight, humbug. **3** *the club device* emblem, symbol, insignia, crest, coat-of-arms, seal, badge, token, motif, design, mark, figure, motto, slogan, legend, logo, colophon, trade mark.

devil *noun* **1** *the Devil defeated by God* Satan. See table. **2** *tempted by devils* demon, fiend, evil spirit, cacodemon. **3** *the master was a devil* brute, savage, beast, monster, ogre, demon, fiend, terror, barbarian, blackguard, rogue, thug, scoundrel, villain, bully, knave. **4** *the child's a little devil* imp, scamp, rascal, rogue, mischief-maker, troublemaker. **5** *feel pity for the poor devils* wretch, unfortunate, beggar, creature, thing, sad case.

NAMES FOR THE DEVIL

Abbadon	Mephistopheles
Arch-fiend, the	Moloch
Auld Thief	Old Clootie
Beelzebub	old gentleman (in
Belial	black)
deil	Old Harry
Deuce	Old Hornie
dickens	Old Nick
Evil One, the	Old One
Foul Fiend	Old Scratchy
His Satanic Majesty	Prince of Darkness
Lord of the Flies	Satan
Lucifer	Tempter, the
Mephisto	Wicked One

devilish *adjective* **1** *devilish practices* diabolic, diabolical, demonic, demoniacal, fiendish, satanic, infernal, hellish. **2** *a devilish creature* wicked, evil, abominable, atrocious, detestable, execrable, villainous, sinister, accursed, damnable.

devilish *adverb* *devilish expensive* extremely, very, exceedingly, intensely, excessively, inordinately, fiendishly, hellishly.

devil-may-care *adjective* careless, reckless, heedless, rash, audacious, wanton, impetuous, impulsive, jaunty, swaggering, nonchalant, happy-go-lucky, easygoing, casual, flippant, indifferent, unconcerned, cavalier, insouciant.

devilry, deviltry *noun* **1** *enemy leaders full of devilry* evil, wickedness, vice, iniquity, sin, malevolence, maliciousness, malice, viciousness, nefariousness, cruelty, savagery, villainy. **2** *the devilry of the children* devilment, mischief-making, troublemaking, roguery, rascality, impishness; mischief; *inf.* monkey business. **3** *dealing in devilry* black magic, sorcery, witchcraft, black art, diablerie, diabolism.

devious *adjective* **1** *a devious merchant* underhand, cunning, crafty, sly, wily, artful, guileful, scheming, designing, calculating, dishonest, deceitful, double-dealing, treacherous, misleading, subtle, insidious, surreptitious, furtive, secretive; *inf.* crooked. **2** *go by a devious route* indirect, roundabout, deviating, circuitous, tortuous, rambling, wandering, erratic, digressive, excursive.
Opposites HONEST; CANDID; DIRECT.

devise *verb* concoct, contrive, work out, plan, form, formulate, plot, scheme, project, invent, originate, create, compose, construct, frame, think/dream up, conceive, imagine, fabricate, hatch, put together, arrange, prepare, order.

devoid *adjective* *devoid of water/people/interest* lacking, wanting, without, deficient in, empty/ vacant of, void/bare/barren of, bereft/denuded of, free from.

devolve *verb* **1** *power devolved to the regions* pass, hand over, transfer, delegate, consign, entrust. **2** *property devolving to a cousin* hand down, pass to, transfer, convey; *Law* alienate. **3** *the argument devolves on a belief in God* depend, be dependent, rely, turn, hinge.

devote *verb* assign, allot, allocate, set aside, set apart, reserve, commit, apply, consign, pledge, give, offer, dedicate, surrender.

devoted *adjective* **1** *a devoted follower* loyal, faithful, true, true blue, staunch, steadfast, constant, committed, dedicated, devout, fond, loving, admiring, affectionate, caring, attentive, warm, ardent. **2** *time devoted to the children* assigned, allotted, set aside, dedicated. *See* DEVOTE. **3** *buildings devoted to God* dedicated, consecrated, blessed, sanctified, hallowed.
Opposites DISLOYAL; UNFAITHFUL; INDIFFERENT.

devotee *noun* enthusiast, fan, admirer, addict, follower, adherent, disciple, supporter, champion, advocate, votary, fanatic, zealot; *inf.* buff, freak.

devotion *noun* **1** *the devotion of his followers* loyalty, faithfulness, fidelity, trueness, staunchness, steadfastness, constancy, commitment, adherence, allegiance, dedication, devoutness, fondness, love, admiration, affection, attentiveness, care, caring, warmness, closeness. **2** *churchmen full of devotion* devoutness, piety, religiousness, spirituality, godliness, holiness, sanctity, saintliness. **3** *look at her husband with devotion* ardour, idolization, love, fondness, affection, infatuation, passion, fervour, admiration, eagerness, yearning. **4** *morning devotions* religious worship, worship, religious observance; prayers, vespers, matins; prayer meeting, church service.
Opposites DISLOYALTY; INDIFFERENCE; HATRED.

devour *verb* **1** *devour the feast* eat greedily/hungrily, eat up, consume, swallow up, gulp down, gobble up, bolt, wolf down, guzzle, stuff down, cram in, gorge oneself on, feast on; *inf.* tuck into, pack away, dispatch, polish off, stuff one's face with, pig oneself on. **2** *flames devouring the house* consume, engulf, envelop, destroy, devastate, lay waste, demolish, wipe out, ruin, wreck, annihilate. **3** *hobbies devouring time/money* consume, use up, cost, spend, waste. **4** *children devouring books* be absorbed in, be engrossed in, take in, drink in/up, feast on, revel in, delight in, enjoy, relish, appreciate. **5** *devoured by anxiety/jealousy* consume, swallow up, engulf, swamp, overcome, overwhelm.

devout *adjective* **1** *a devout Christian* pious, religious, reverent, church-going, godly, saintly, holy, prayerful, orthodox, pure, righteous. **2** *devout hope* sincere, genuine, deep, profound, heartfelt, earnest, fervent, fervid, intense, ardent, vehement, passionate, zealous.
Opposites IMPIOUS; IRREVERENT; INSINCERE.

dexterity *noun* **1** *craftsmen showing dexterity* manual dexterity, deftness, adroitness, nimbleness of fingers, nimbleness, agility, skilfulness, skill, knack, adeptness, handiness, facility, proficiency, expertise, talent, artistry, craft, mastery, finesse, effortlessness, felicity. **2** *the firm's board showing dexterity* mental dexterity/ agility, cleverness, shrewdness, smartness, astuteness, cunning, craft, sagacity, sharp-wittedness, acuteness, ingenuity, resourcefulness, inventiveness.

dexterous *adjective* **1** *dexterous craftsmen* deft, adroit, nimble, agile, skilful, skilled, adept, handy, proficient, expert, talented, accomplished, artistic. *See* DEXTERITY 1. **2** *a dexterous businessman* clever, shrewd, smart, astute, cunning, crafty, wily, artful, sagacious, sharp-witted, acute, ingenious, resourceful, inventive. *See* DEXTERITY 2.

diabolic *adjective* **1** *diabolic forces* devilish, fiendish, demonic, demoniacal, satanic, infernal, hellish, cacodemonic. **2** *a diabolic slave master* fiendish, wicked, evil, sinful, savage, brutish, monstrous, barbaric, cruel, malevolent, malicious, black-hearted, nasty, abominable, hateful, execrable, damnable. **3** *a diabolic task* difficult, complicated, complex, tricky, nasty, unpleasant, dreadful, vile.

diabolical *adjective* **1** *See* DIABOLIC. **2** *diabolical taste/food* very bad, horrible, excruciating, appalling, shocking, outrageous, atrocious, vile. **3** *a diabolical liberty* very great, extreme, excessive, intolerable, unreasonable, undue, inordinate, uncalled-for.

diacritic *noun.* *See table at* ACCENT.

diadem *noun* crown, fillet. *See table at* HAT.

diagnose *verb* *diagnose measles* identify, determine, distinguish, recognize, detect, pinpoint, pronounce.

diagnosis *noun* **1** *a diagnosis of measles* identification, recognition, detection, pinpointing. *See* DIAGNOSE. **2** *consultants confirming the GP's*

diagnosis opinion, pronouncement, judgement, conclusion, interpretation.

diagonal *adjective* crossing, crossways, crosswise, slanting, slanted, sloping, oblique, angled, cornerways, cornerwise.

diagonally *adverb* crossways, crosswise, on the cross, on the slant, aslant, obliquely, at an angle, on the bias, cornerways, cornerwise.

diagram *noun* line drawing, drawing, sketch, draft, illustration, picture, representation, outline, delineation.

dial *verb* dial the number telephone, phone, ring, call.

dialect *noun* regional language, variety of language, vernacular, patois, non-standard language; regionalism, localism, provincialism; *inf.* local lingo.

dialectic *noun* discussion, debate, dialogue, disputation, argument, argumentation, contention, polemic, war of words, reasoning, ratiocination.

dialectic *adjective* dialectical, logical, analytical, disputatious, argumentative, contentious, polemic, rational, rationalistic.

dialogue *noun* **1** *the dialogue between friends| dialogue between the two sides* conversation, talk, tête-à-tête, chat, chit-chat, gossip, communication, debate, argument, exchange of views, discourse, discussion, conference, converse, colloquy, interlocution, duologue, confabulation, parley, palaver; *inf.* pow-wow, rap session. **2** *the dialogue of the novel/play* conversation, spoken part, script; lines.

diameter *noun* breadth, width, thickness, calibre.

diametrical *adjective* diametrical differences/ opposition direct, absolute, complete, exact, extreme, diametrically opposite, opposite, contrasting, conflicting, contrary, counter, antithetical, antipodal.

diaphanous *adjective* sheer, fine, delicate, light, thin, silken, chiffony, gossamer, gauzy, cobwebby, translucent, transparent, see-through.
Opposites THICK; COARSE; OPAQUE.

diarrhoea *noun* loose motions, looseness of the bowels; *inf.* the skitters, the runs, the trots, gippy tummy, holiday tummy, Delhi belly, Montezuma's revenge.

diary *noun* **1** *noted the meeting in her diary* appointment/engagement book, personal organizer; Filofax™. **2** *keep a diary of her holiday* day-by-day account, daily record, journal, chronicle, log, logbook, history, annal.

diatribe *noun* tirade, harangue, verbal onslaught, stream of abuse, denunciation, philippic, reproof, reprimand, rebuke, upbraiding; invective, vituperation, abuse, castigation, criticism, stricture; *inf.* tongue-lashing, slating, knocking.

dicey *adjective* uncertain, risky, chancy, difficult, tricky, dodgy, dangerous, ticklish; *inf.* hairy.

dicky *adjective* unsound, unsteady, unstable, unreliable, shaky, fluttery, weak, infirm, queer.

dictate *verb* **1** *dictate the letter* read out, read aloud, speak, say, utter, recite. **2** *dictate terms* prescribe, lay down, impose, set down, order, command, decree, ordain, direct, pronounce, enjoin, promulgate. **3** *always dictating to others* give orders, order about, lay down the law, impose one's will, boss about, domineer, act the tin god; *inf.* call the shots, throw one's weight around.

dictate *noun* **1** *at the commander's dictate* order, command, decree, edict, ordinance, dictum, direction, bidding, charge, behest, pronouncement, mandate, requirement, enjoining, injunction, ultimatum, promulgation. **2** *the dictates of conscience* code, guiding principle, law, rule, precept, dictum, axiom, maxim.

dictator *noun* absolute ruler, despot, autocrat, tyrant, oppressor.

dictatorial *adjective* **1** *dictatorial government* absolute, unlimited, unrestricted, arbitrary, omnipotent, all-powerful, autocratic, totalitarian, authoritarian, despotic, tyrannical, autarchic. **2** *dictatorial bosses* tyrannical, despotic, oppressive, iron-handed, imperious, overbearing, domineering, peremptory, high-handed, authoritarian, dogmatic, high and mighty; *inf.* bossy.
Opposites DEMOCRATIC; LIBERAL; LIMITED; SUBMISSIVE.

dictatorship *noun* **1** *living in dictatorships* autarchy, totalitarian state, absolute monarchy, reign of terror. **2** *revolting against dictatorship* absolute rule, despotism, autocracy, tyranny, authoritarianism, totalitarianism, absolutism.

diction *noun* **1** *learn diction at elocution lessons* enunciation, articulation, elocution, pronunciation, speech, intonation, inflection, delivery, fluency, rhetoric. **2** *impressed by the writer's diction* style, language, phraseology, phrasing, wording, usage, vocabulary, terminology, expression, idiom.

dictionary *noun* wordbook, vocabulary list, glossary, lexicon, concordance.

dictum *noun* **1** *the chairman's dictum* utterance, pronouncement, direction, injunction, assertion, statement, dictate, command, order, decree, edict. **2** *as the dictum has it* saying, maxim, axiom, proverb, adage, aphorism, saw, truism, platitude, cliché.

didactic *adjective* didactic prose instructive, instructional, educational, educative, informative, informational, edifying, preceptive, pedagogic, propaedeutic, pedantic, moralistic, homiletic.

die *verb* **1** *she died last night* pass away, pass on, lose one's life, depart this life, expire, decease, breathe one's last, meet one's end, lay down one's life, be no more, perish, go to one's last resting-place, cross the Styx; *inf.* give up the ghost, kick the bucket, push up the daisies, bite the dust, snuff it, croak, turn up one's toes, cash in one's chips, hop the twig. **2** *hope died* come to an end, end, vanish, disap-

pear, pass, fade, fall away, dwindle, melt away, dissolve, subside, decline, sink, lapse, ebb, wane, wilt, wither, evanesce. **3** *the engine died* stop, halt, fail, break down, peter out, fizzle out, run down, fade away, lose power. **4** *die of boredom/laughter* collapse with, be overcome with, be overwhelmed/overpowered by, succumb to. **5** *she's dying for water | dying to see you* be eager, be desperate, long.
Opposites LIVE; EXIST; START.

die-hard *adjective* ultraconservative, conservative, reactionary, dyed in the wool, intransigent, inflexible, immovable, unchanging, uncompromising, unyielding, indomitable, adamant, rigid.

diet¹ *noun* **1** *eat a healthy diet* selection of food, food and drink, food, fare; foodstuffs, provisions, victuals, comestibles, edibles, viands, rations, commons; nourishment, nutriment, sustenance, aliment. **2** *go on a diet* dietary regimen/regime, abstinence, period of fasting, fast; restricted diet, crash diet.

diet² *verb* *dieting to lose several pounds* follow a diet, be on a diet, eat sparingly/selectively, abstain, fast, slim, reduce, lose weight.
Opposites OVERINDULGE; GUZZLE.

diet³ *noun* **1** *elected to the diet* legislative assembly, congress, parliament, council, senate, synod. **2** *attend an international diet* conference, convention, assembly, convocation, conventicle, conclave, session.

differ *verb* **1** *tastes differ* be different, be unlike, be dissimilar, be distinguishable, vary, diverge. **2** *results differing from the norm* vary, diverge, deviate from, depart from, run counter to, contravene, contradict, contrast with. **3** *parties agreeing to differ* disagree, fail to agree, dissent, be at variance, be in dispute/opposition, oppose, take issue, conflict, clash, quarrel, argue, wrangle, quibble, squabble, altercate.
Opposites AGREE; COINCIDE.

difference *noun* **1** *the difference between/in their lifestyles* dissimilarity, unlikeness, dissimilitude, contrast, distinction, distinctness, differentiation, variance, variation, divergence, deviation, contrariety, antithesis, contradiction, contradistinction, nonconformity, disparity, imbalance, incongruity. **2** *spot the difference* distinction, peculiarity, oddity, idiosyncrasy, singularity, eccentricity, individuality. **3** *the two had a difference* difference of opinion, disagreement, dispute, disputation, argument, debate, misunderstanding, quarrel, row, wrangle, set-to, tiff, altercation, contretemps, clash, controversy, feud, vendetta. **4** *pay the difference* balance, remainder, rest, residue, residuum, excess.
Opposites SIMILARITY; LIKENESS; AFFINITY.

different *adjective* **1** *our lifestyles are different | tastes different from ours* unlike, dissimilar, non-identical, contrastive, contrasting, diverse, divergent, deviating, disparate, incompatible, inconsistent, opposed, at variance, at odds, clashing, conflicting, discrepant. **2** *looking completely different from last year* changed, altered, modified, transformed, metamorphosed, other. **3** *a different dress every day* sep-

arate, other, not the same, non-identical, distinct, individual, discrete. **4** *different people have commented | available in different colours* various, several, many, numerous, some, sundry, certain, assorted, varied, miscellaneous, diverse, manifold, multifarious, motley, variegated. **5** *looking for something different* unusual, out of the ordinary, uncommon, distinctive, rare, unique, novel, special, singular, remarkable, extraordinary, noteworthy, unconventional, atypical, odd, strange, bizarre; *inf.* something else.
Opposites SIMILAR; ALIKE; SAME; ORDINARY.

differential *adjective* *differential treatment/rates* distinctive, distinguishing, discriminating, discriminatory, different.

differential *noun* *maintain salary differentials* distinction, discrimination, difference; amount of difference, disparity, discrepancy.

differentiate *verb* **1** *differentiate between grades | can you differentiate the twins?* distinguish, discriminate, make a distinction, contrast, see/discern a difference; tell apart, set apart, separate, mark off. **2** *the yellow beak differentiates the male bird* make different, distinguish, set apart, contrast, identify. **3** *in time the species differentiated* modify, alter, change, become different, transform, adapt.

difficult *adjective* **1** *digging in this soil is difficult* hard, strenuous, arduous, laborious, demanding, formidable, tough, onerous, burdensome, exhausting, tiring, wearisome, back-breaking, painful, oppressive; *inf.* no picnic. **2** *a difficult problem* hard, complicated, complex, involved, intricate, puzzling, problematic, baffling, perplexing, knotty, thorny, ticklish, delicate, obscure, abstract, abstruse, recondite, enigmatic, profound, deep. **3** *a difficult child* troublesome, tiresome, demanding, unmanageable, intractable, perverse, recalcitrant, obstreperous, refractory, fractious, unaccommodating, uncooperative, uncompliant, unamenable. **4** *difficult people to choose presents for* hard to please/satisfy, fussy, particular, fastidious, perfectionist, critical, hypercritical, finicky, finical. **5** *arrive at a difficult time* inconvenient, ill-timed, disadvantageous, unfavourable. **6** *go through difficult times* hard, straitened, hard-pressed, bad, tough, grim, dark.
Opposites EASY; SIMPLE; ACCOMMODATING.

difficulty *noun* **1** *dig with difficulty* difficultness, hardness, strenuousness, arduousness, laboriousness, toughness, struggling, awkwardness; labour, strain, struggle. **2** *the difficulty of the problem* difficultness, hardness, complicatedness, complexity, intricacy, perplexity, knottiness, delicacy, obscurity, abstruseness. See DIFFICULT 2. **3** *encounter a difficulty* complication, problem, snag, hitch, hindrance, obstacle, pitfall, hurdle, impediment, obstruction, barrier. **4** *raise difficulties* protest, objection, complaint, gripe, demur, cavil. **5** *in difficulty | in financial difficulties* predicament, quandary, dilemma, plight, distress, embarrassment, trouble, hot/deep water; straits; *inf.* fix, jam, spot, scrape. **6** *the difficulty of the times* hardship, trial, tribulation, ordeal, exigency.

diffidence *noun* shyness, bashfulness, modesty, sheepishness, timidity, timidness, timorousness, apprehension, reserve, hesitancy, reluctance, constraint, doubt, insecurity, distrust, suspicion, unobtrusiveness, self-effacement, humility, meekness.

diffident *adjective* shy, bashful, modest, sheepish, unconfident, unassertive, timid, timorous, apprehensive, fearful, shrinking, reserved, withdrawn, hesitant, reluctant, doubtful, unsure, insecure, distrustful, suspicious, unobtrusive, self-effacing, unassuming, humble, meek.
Opposites BOLD; ASSERTIVE.

diffuse *adjective* **1** *diffuse light* diffused, spread out, scattered, dispersed, not concentrated. **2** *a diffuse style* verbose, wordy, prolix, long-winded, copious, profuse, discursive, rambling, wandering, meandering, maundering, digressive, circuitous, roundabout, circumlocutory, periphrastic, waffling, loose, vague.
Opposites CONCENTRATED; CONCISE; SUCCINCT.

diffuse *verb* spread around, send out, scatter, disperse, disseminate, dissipate, dispel, distribute, dispense, circulate, propagate, broadcast, promulgate, effuse.

diffusion *noun* **1** *the diffusion of light/knowledge* scattering, spreading, dispersal, dissemination, dispelling, distribution, dispensation, circulation, propagation, broadcasting, promulgation, effusion. **2** *writers given to diffusion* diffuseness, verbosity, verbiage, wordiness, prolixity, long-windedness, loquaciousness, loquacity, profuseness, discursiveness, rambling, wandering, digressiveness, circuitousness, circumlocution, periphrasis, waffling. *See* DIFFUSE *adjective* 2.

dig *verb* **1** *enjoy digging | dig the earth* break up soil/ground; work, break up, loosen up, turn over, spade, delve, till, cultivate, harrow, plough. **2** *dig a tunnel/hole* dig out, excavate, quarry, hollow out, scoop out, gouge, tunnel, burrow, mine, channel. **3** *dig someone in the ribs* poke, prod, jab, thrust, drive, push, punch. **4** *dig into the history* delve, search, probe, investigate, research. **5** *dig potatoes* unearth, dig up. **6** *dig the music* like, love, enjoy, appreciate. **7** *dig the statement* understand, comprehend, follow, grasp, make out; *inf.* get. **dig up 1** *dig up the corpse* exhume, bring to the surface, unearth. **2** *dig up new information* unearth, uncover, root out, extricate, bring to light, come up with, expose, discover, find, come across.

dig *noun* **1** *a dig in the ribs* poke, prod, jab, thrust, push, punch. **2** *tired of digs at his baldness* cutting remark, gibe, jeer, taunt, sneer, insult, slur, quip, insinuation; *inf.* wisecrack, crack.

digest *verb* **1** *digest food* assimilate, absorb, break down, dissolve, macerate. **2** *digest the facts* assimilate, absorb, take in, understand, comprehend, grasp, master, consider, think about, contemplate, mull over, weigh up, reflect on, ponder, meditate on, study. **3** *digest the leaflets* classify, catalogue, tabulate, codify, arrange, order, dispose, systematize, methodize. **4** *digest the information* shorten,

reduce, condense, abridge, compress, compact, summarize, précis.

digest *noun* *a digest of the week's news* summary, synopsis, abstract, précis, résumé, outline, abridgement, epitome, review, compendium.

digestion *noun* **1** *digestion of food* assimilation, absorption, breaking down, dissolution, maceration. *See table.* **2** *digestion of facts* assimilation, absorption, understanding, comprehension, mastery, consideration, contemplation. *See* DIGEST *verb* 2.

PARTS OF THE HUMAN DIGESTIVE SYSTEM	
anus	liver
buccal cavity/	oesophagus
mouth	pancreas
colon	rectum
duodenum	salivary
gall bladder	glands
ileum	stomach
intestine	teeth
jejunum	tongue

dignified *adjective* stately, noble, solemn, grave, formal, decorous, reserved, ceremonious, courtly, majestic, august, lofty, exalted, regal, lordly, imposing, impressive, grand.

dignify *verb* add dignity/distinction to, distinguish, honour, grace, adorn, exalt, enhance, ennoble, glorify, elevate, make lofty, aggrandize, upgrade.

dignitary *noun* public figure, notable, notability, worthy, personage, luminary, VIP, pillar of society, leading light, celebrity, big name, somebody, star, lion; *inf.* bigwig, top brass, big gun, big shot/noise, big wheel, celeb, lord/lady muck.

dignity *noun* **1** *the dignity of the occasion* stateliness, nobleness, nobility, solemnity, gravity, formality, decorum, propriety, reserve, ceremoniousness, courtliness, majesty, augustness, loftiness, exaltedness, regalness, regality, lordliness, impressiveness, grandeur. **2** *the dignity of work* worthiness, honourability, nobility, excellence, respectability; worth, merit, virtue. **3** *achieve dignity in the state/Church* high rank, high standing, high station, status, elevation, eminence, honour, glory, greatness, importance. **4** *conscious of their dignity* pride, self-esteem, self-conceit, self-regard, self-importance, self-respect, *amour propre*.
Opposites INFORMALITY; DISHONOUR; DEGRADATION; MODESTY.

digress *verb* get off the subject, stray from the point, deviate/deflect from the topic, go off at a tangent, diverge, turn aside, depart, drift, ramble, wander, meander, maunder.

digression *noun* **1** *his usual digression from the subject* straying, deviation, divergence, diversion, departure, drifting, rambling. *See* DIGRESS. **2** *an essay full of digressions* aside, deviation, deflection, detour, excursion, excursus, apostrophe, incidental remark, *obiter dictum*.

dilapidated *adjective* run-down, broken-down, tumbledown, ramshackle, in ruins, ruined, falling to pieces, falling apart, in disrepair, shabby, battered, rickety, shaky, crumbling, decayed, decaying, decrepit, worn-out, neglected, uncared-for.

dilate *verb* **1** *her pupils dilated* enlarge, widen, expand. **2** *dilate on the subject* expand, enlarge, expound, expatiate, elaborate.
Opposites NARROW; CONTRACT.

dilatory *adjective* slow, tardy, sluggish, snail-like, lazy, slack, indolent, delaying, dallying, dilly-dallying, loitering, lingering, dawdling, tarrying, procrastinating, postponing, deferring, putting off, tabling, shelving, temporizing, stalling, time-wasting, Fabian.
Opposites FAST; PROMPT.

dilemma *noun* difficult choice, Scylla and Charybdis, devil and the deep blue sea, Catch-22, vicious circle, quandary, predicament, plight, difficulty, tight corner/spot, problem, puzzle, mess, muddle; trouble, perplexity, confusion, embarrassment.

dilettante *noun* **1** *dilettantes not seriously interested* dabbler, potterer, trifler, dallier, amateur, non-professional. **2** *dilettantes always at the art gallery* art lover, lover of the arts, connoisseur, aesthete, member of the *cognoscenti*, arbiter elegantiae/elegantiarum.

diligence *noun* assiduity, assiduousness, application, concentration, industriousness, conscientiousness, attentiveness, heedfulness, constancy, intentness, earnestness, perseverance, sedulousness, persistence, tenacity, pertinacity, doggedness, laboriousness; care, attention, industry. See DILIGENT.

diligent *adjective* assiduous, industrious, conscientious, hard-working, painstaking, meticulous, thorough, careful, attentive, heedful, intent, earnest, studious, constant, persevering, sedulous, persistent, tenacious, pertinacious, zealous, active, busy, untiring, tireless, indefatigable, dogged, plodding, slogging, laborious.
Opposites LAZY; CARELESS; INDIFFERENT.

dilly-dally *verb* dally, dawdle, loiter, linger, take one's time, delay, waste time, tarry, hover, kill time, potter, trifle, procrastinate, dither, hesitate, falter, vacillate, waver, shilly-shally, hem and haw, fluctuate.

dilute *verb* **1** *dilute the solution* make weaker, weaken, make thinner, thin out, water down, cut, adulterate, mix. **2** *dilute the colourful details/dilute standards* make weaker, weaken, attenuate, reduce, diminish, decrease, lessen, mitigate, temper.
Opposites CONCENTRATE; THICKEN; INTENSIFY.

dim *adjective* **1** *a dim light* faint, weak, feeble, pale, dull, dingy, lustreless, muted. **2** *dim skies* dark, darkish, grey, overcast, leaden, gloomy, sombre, dusky, lowering, cloudy, hazy, misty, foggy, crepuscular, tenebrous. **3** *dim corridors* dark, darkened, gloomy, badly lit, poorly lit, dingy, dismal. **4** *a dim shape* vague, ill-defined, indistinct, unclear, shadowy, blurred, blurry, fuzzy, imperceptible, nebulous, obscured, bleared, bleary, obfuscated. **5** *a dim recollection* vague, indistinct, hazy, confused, blurred, shadowy, imperfect, obscure, remote. **6** *rather*

dim people stupid, thick, dense, slow-witted, slow, dull, doltish, limited, obtuse; *inf.* dumb, slow on the uptake. **7** *prospects are rather dim* gloomy, sombre, unpromising, unfavourable, discouraging, disheartening, depressing, dispiriting.
Opposites BRIGHT; DISTINCT; CLEVER.

dim *verb* **1** *dim the stage lights* turn down, lower, dip. **2** *the light dimmed* grow dim, fade, grow faint/feeble, dull, pale, blur. **3** *the skies dimmed* grow dark, darken, cloud over, grow leaden. See DIM *adjective* 2. **4** *memories/recollections dimming* grow dim, fade, blur, become blurred/confused.

dimension *noun* **1** *of huge dimension | the dimensions of the tank* measured extent, extent; length, width, breadth, depth, area, size, volume, capacity, bulk; proportions. **2** *underestimate the dimensions of the problem* size, extent, scope, measure, scale, range, magnitude, greatness, importance. **3** *add another dimension to entertainment* aspect, side, feature, facet, element.

diminish *verb* **1** *their power/strength diminished* lessen, grow less, decrease, reduce, shrink, contract, abate, grow weak/weaker. **2** *time diminished their power/strength* lessen, lower, decrease, reduce, curtail, cut, contract, narrow, constrict, truncate, retrench. **3** *the storm/empire diminished* subside, ebb, recede, wane, dwindle, slacken, die/fall away, fade, decline, die/peter out. **4** *try to diminish him | diminish his reputation* belittle, disparage, denigrate, depreciate, deprecate, derogate, devalue, demean, detract from, cheapen, defame, vilify.
Opposites INCREASE; GROW; BOOST.

diminution *noun* **1** lessening, lowering, decrease, reduction, contraction, abatement, weakening, curtailment, cut, cutback, constriction, truncating, retrenchment. See DIMINISH 1, 2. **2** *the diminution of the storm/empire* subsidence, ebb, receding, wane, slackening, dying away, failing, decline. See DIMINISH 3.

diminutive *adjective* small, little, tiny, petite, slight, elfin, minute, miniature, mini, small-scale, compact, microscopic, midget, undersized, dwarfish, pygmy, homuncular, Lilliputian; *inf.* wee, baby, half-pint.
Opposites ENORMOUS; GIGANTIC.

din *noun* loud noise, uproar, row, racket, commotion, hullabaloo, hubbub, tumult, clangour, outcry, brouhaha, crash, clatter, clash, shouting, yelling; clamour, noise, pandemonium, bedlam, babel.
Opposites SILENCE; HUSH.

din *verb* **1** *music dinning | loud voices dinning* blare, blast, clang, clatter, crash, clamour, shout, roar, yell, bellow, bawl. **2** *din the facts into pupils* drum, instil, hammer, inculcate, teach.

dine *verb* **1** *we dine at eight* have dinner/supper, eat, sup, feed, feast, banquet. See DINNER. **2** *dine on game* eat, consume, feed on.

dingy *adjective* dark, dull, dim, gloomy, drab, dismal, dreary, cheerless, dusky, sombre, murky, hazy, smoggy, smoky, sooty, dirty, discoloured, grimy, soiled, faded, shabby, worn,

dinky · direct

Opposites BRIGHT; well-lit; CLEAN.

dinky adjective a dinky little girl/car small, petite, dainty, neat, trim, cute, diminutive, mini, miniature.

dinner noun come to dinner | the firm's annual dinner evening meal, supper, main meal, lunch, repast, refection; feast, banquet, collation; inf. spread, blow-out.

dinosaur noun. See table. See also table at FOSSIL.

dint noun a dint on the car's roof dent, indentation, depression. **by dint of** by means of, by use of, by virtue of.

dip verb **1** dip the garment in dye immerse, submerge, plunge, duck, dunk, lower, sink, souse, douse, soak, drench, steep, bathe, rinse. **2** the sun dipping behind the horizon sink, set, go/drop down, descend, fade, disappear, subside. **3** profits dipping fall, go down, drop, drop/fall off, decrease, decline, slump. **4** the road dips slope down, slope, descend, go down, fall, sink, decline, slant down, droop, sag. **5** dip water scoop up, scoop, spoon, ladle. **dip into** **1** dip into a book skim, browse, look through, glance at, run through. **2** dip into art dabble in, scratch the surface of, play at, sample. **3** dip into one's purse | dip into the barrel reach into, put one's hand into, go into. **4** dip into one's savings draw on, use/spend part of.
Opposites RISE; ASCEND.

dip noun **1** give the garment/sheep a dip immersion, plunge, ducking, dunking, sousing, dousing, soaking, drenching. See DIP verb 1. **2** take a dip swim, bathe, dive, plunge, paddle. **3** a sheep dip liquid preparation/mixture, solution; disinfectant, preservative. **4** a cheese dip creamy preparation/mixture, concoction, sauce. **5** a dip in profits fall, falling-off, drop, dropping-off, decrease, decline, lowering, slump. **6** a dip in the terrain slope, incline, decline, slant, descent, hollow, concavity, depression, basin.

diplomacy noun **1** ministers skilled in diplomacy statesmanship, statecraft, international relations/politics; negotiations. **2** treating her parents' objections with diplomacy tactfulness, subtlety, discretion, judiciousness, prudence, delicacy, sensitivity, finesse, savoir faire, politeness, cleverness, artfulness, cunning, tact, care, skill.

diplomat noun **1** an international meeting of diplomats ambassador, envoy, emissary, legate, consul, attaché. **2** the diplomat of the firm tactful person, conciliator, reconciler, peacemaker, mediator, negotiator, tactician, arbitrator, intermediary, moderator, go-between, middleman, public relations officer.

diplomatic adjective **1** a diplomatic post ambassadorial, consular, foreign office. **2** diplomatic handling | a diplomatic young woman tactful, subtle, discreet, judicious, prudent, careful, delicate, sensitive, polite, politic, clever, skilful, artful.
Opposites INDISCREET; TACTLESS.

dire adjective **1** in dire straits | dire poverty terrible, dreadful, appalling, frightful, awful, horrible, atrocious, grim, cruel, grievous, disastrous, ruinous, miserable, wretched, woeful, calamitous, catastrophic, cataclysmic, distressing, harrowing, alarming, unspeakable, shocking, outrageous. **2** dire warnings ominous, sinister, portentous, gloomy, gloom-and-doom, grim, dreadful, dismal, unpropitious, inauspicious, unfavourable, pessimistic. **3** in dire need of money urgent, desperate, drastic, pressing, crying, vital, grave, critical, crucial, extreme, compelling, exigent.

direct verb **1** direct the operation administer, manage, be in charge/control/command of, lead, run, command, control, govern, conduct, handle, preside over, rule, supervise, superintend, oversee, guide, mastermind, regulate, orchestrate, engineer, dispose, dominate, domineer; inf. be the boss of, run the show, call the shots. **2** directed to work late command, order, give orders to, instruct, charge, bid, dictate, adjure, enjoin. **3** direct them to the station give directions to, show/point/indicate the way, guide, steer, lead, conduct, accompany, usher, escort, navigate, pilot. **4** remarks directed at parents aim at, address to, intend/mean for, destine for, focus on, point/level at, train, turn on, fix on. **5** direct the correspondence address, label, superscribe, post, send, mail.

direct adjective **1** a direct road straight, undeviating, unswerving, uncircuitous, shortest.

DINOSAURS

Alamosaurus	Coelophysis	Megalosaurus	Sauropelta
Albertosaurus	Coelosaurus	Melanosaurus	Scelidosaurus
Allosaurus	Compsognathus	Microvenator	Staurilcosaurus
Anchiceratops	Corythosaurus	Monoclonius	Stegosaurus
Anchisaurus	Deinocheirus	Nanosaurus	Stegoseras
Ankylosaurus	Deinocherus	Orthinomimus	Styracosaurus
Apatosaurus	Dilophosaurus	Orthitholestes	Syntarsus
Barosaurus	Diplodocus	Oviraptor	Tarbosaurus
Basilosaurus	Dryosaurus	Pentaceratops	Thescelosaurus
Brachiosaurus	Edmontosaurus	Pisanosaurus	Titanosaurus
Brontosaurus	Fabrosaurus	Plateosaurus	Torosaurus
Camarasaurus	Heterodontosaurus	Procompsognathus	Triceratops
Camptosaurus	Ichthyosaurus	Protoceratops	Troödon
Ceratosaurus	Iguanodon	Psittacosaurus	Tyrannosaurus
Cetiosaurus	Kentrosaurus	Riojasaurus	Velociraptor
Chasmosaurus	Leptoceratops	Saurolophus	

199

2 *a direct train/journey* straight through, through, non-stop, unbroken, uninterrupted. **3** *a direct approach* immediate, first-hand, personal, face-to-face, head-on, interventionist. **4** *a direct statement/manner* frank, blunt, straightforward, straight, straight to the point, explicit, clear, plain, unequivocal, unambiguous, honest, candid, open, sincere, plainspoken, outspoken, forthright, downright, point blank, matter-of-fact, categorical. **5** *the direct opposite* exact, absolute, complete, downright, thorough, diametrical. **6** *a direct quotation* exact, precise, word for word, verbatim, accurate, correct.
Opposites INDIRECT; EVASIVE; AMBIGUOUS.

direction *noun* **1** *the/his direction of the project* administration, management, government, supervision, superintendence, regulation, orchestration; control, command, conduct, handling, running, overseeing, masterminding, disposal; leadership, guidance. *See* DIRECT *verb* 1. **2** *ignore the teacher's direction* command, order, instruction, bidding, charge, dictate, enjoinment, prescription. *See* DIRECTIVE. **3** *which direction did they take?* way, route, course, path, track, road, line, run, bearing, orientation. **4** *the direction of their policy/statement* drift, aim, tack, scope, bent, bias, tendency, current, trend, tenor, inclination, leaning, proclivity, orientation. **5** *make out the direction on the parcel* address, label, mark, superscription.

directions *plural noun* instructions, guidelines, rules, regulations, recommendations, indications; guidance, briefing; plan.

directive *noun* direction, command, order, instruction, charge, bidding, injunction, ruling, regulation, dictate, decree, edict, notice, ordinance, enjoinment, prescription, mandate, fiat.

directly *adverb* **1** *travel directly* straight, in a straight line, as the crow flies, by the shortest route, without deviation. **2** *leave directly* immediately, at once, instantly, right/straight away, now, instantaneously, without delay/hesitation, quickly, speedily, promptly, soon, as soon as possible, shortly, in a little while; *inf.* pronto. **3** *speak directly* frankly, bluntly, straightforwardly, explicitly, clearly, plainly, unequivocally, unambiguously, sincerely, truthfully, outspokenly, forthrightly, pointblank, matter-of-factly, categorically, without prevarication. **4** *talk directly to the manager* at first hand, personally, face to face, head on. **5** *it's directly opposite* exactly, immediately, diametrically.

director *noun* administrator, controller, manager, executive, chairman, chairwoman, chairperson, chair, head, chief, principal, leader, governor, president, superintendent, supervisor, overseer, organizer, producer; *inf.* boss, kingpin, top dog, gaffer; *Am. inf.* honcho.

dirge *noun* elegy, lament, funeral song/chant, burial hymn, dead march, requiem, keen, threnody.

dirt *noun* **1** *clean the dirt from the room* grime, dust, soot, smut, muck, mud, filth, mire, sludge, slime, ooze, waste, dross, pollution; smudge, stain, tarnish; *inf.* crud, yuck, grot,

gunge. **2** *piles of dirt by the roadside* earth, soil, loam, clay, silt. **3** *disapprove of the dirt in modern novels* obscenity, indecency, smut, sordidness, coarseness, bawdiness, ribaldry, salaciousness, lewdness, pornography; *inf.* sleaze, sleaziness. *See* DIRTY *adjective* 2. **4** *spreading dirt about the neighbours* scandal, gossip, talk, rumour, slander, libel; revelations.

dirty *adjective* **1** *dirty rooms/clothes* unclean, soiled, grimy, begrimed, grubby, messy, dusty, sooty, mucky, muddy, filthy, bedraggled, slimy, polluted, sullied, foul, stained, spotted, smudged, tarnished, defiled, nasty; *inf.* cruddy, yucky, grotty, gungy. **2** *dirty jokes* blue, obscene, indecent, vulgar, smutty, coarse, bawdy, suggestive, ribald, salacious, risqué, prurient, lewd, lascivious, licentious, pornographic; *Am.* off colour; *inf.* sleazy. **3** *a dirty cheat* nasty, unpleasant, mean, base, low, vile, contemptible, despicable, cowardly, ignominious, sordid, beggarly, squalid. **4** *a dirty trick|dirty play* unsporting, unfair, dishonourable, unscrupulous, dishonest, crooked, illegal, deceitful, fraudulent, double-dealing, corrupt, treacherous. **5** *give a dirty look* full of dislike/hate, malevolent, smouldering, resentful, bitter, angry, indignant, annoyed, peeved, offended. **6** *dirty weather* unpleasant, nasty, foul, stormy, squally, gusty, rainy, misty, gloomy, murky, overcast, louring. **7** *a dirty shade of white* dingy, dull, muddy, dark, cloudy, not clear/pure. **8** *a dirty rumour* nasty, unkind, scandalous, defamatory, slanderous, libellous.
Opposites CLEAN; HONOURABLE; PLEASANT.

dirty *verb* *dirty clothes* soil, stain, muddy, begrime, blacken, mess up, spatter, smudge, smear, spot, splash, spoil, sully, pollute, foul, defile, besmirch.

dirty *adverb* *a dirty great jewel* very, extremely, exceedingly.

disability *noun* **1** *suffering from a physical disability* impairment, disablement, infirmity, defect, handicap, disorder, affliction, ailment, complaint, illness, malady. **2** *physical disability prevented him going* incapacity, infirmity, unfitness, weakness, powerlessness, impotence, incapability, inability, incompetence, ineptitude, disqualification.

disable *verb* **1** *the accident disabled him* incapacitate, impair, damage, put out of action, debilitate, indispose, weaken, enfeeble, make unfit, render infirm, cripple, lame, handicap, immobilize, hamstring, paralyse, prostrate. **2** *disable the machinery* render inoperative, make ineffective, paralyse, make harmless. **3** *disabled from voting* disqualify, invalidate, declare incapable, disenable.

disabled *adjective* physically challenged, incapacitated, impaired, handicapped, debilitated, unfit, out of action, infirm, weak, weakened, enfeebled, crippled, lame, immobilized, bedridden, paralysed.

disabuse *verb* undeceive, set right/straight, open the eyes of, wake someone up, disenchant.

disadvantage *noun* **1** *the advantages and disadvantages of the situation* drawback, snag, down-

side, weak spot/point, weakness, flaw, defect, fault, handicap, trouble, liability, nuisance, hindrance, obstacle, impediment; *inf.* minus, fly in the ointment. **2** *people suffering from financial disadvantage* deprivation, privation, hardship, lack, burden. **3** *to their disadvantage* disservice, detriment, prejudice, harm, damage; loss, injury, hurt, mischief.
Opposites ADVANTAGE; BENEFIT; GAIN.

disadvantaged *adjective* deprived, in need, in want, in distress, poor, poverty-stricken, discriminated against.

disadvantageous *adjective* unfavourable, adverse, unfortunate, unlucky, hapless, detrimental, prejudicial, deleterious, harmful, damaging, injurious, hurtful, destructive, inconvenient, inopportune, ill-timed, inexpedient, inadvisable.

disaffected *adjective* alienated, estranged, unfriendly, disunited; dissatisfied, disgruntled, discontented, disloyal, rebellious, mutinous, seditious, up in arms, hostile, antagonistic.

disagree *verb* **1** *the two sides disagreed* differ, fail to agree, dissent, stand opposed, be in dispute/contention, be at variance/odds, diverge, disaccord. **2** *the stories disagreed / stories disagreeing with each other* differ, be dissimilar, be unlike, be different, vary, conflict, clash, contrast, diverge, not correspond, not accord, be discordant. **3** *children constantly disagreeing* quarrel, argue, bicker, wrangle, squabble, spar, dispute, debate, take issue with, altercate; *inf.* fall out, have words. **4** *food disagreeing with him* be incompatible with, make ill/unwell, cause discomfort/distress, be injurious to.

disagreeable *adjective* **1** *a disagreeable experience* unpleasant, displeasing, nasty, horrible, dreadful, hateful, detestable, abominable, odious, objectionable, offensive, obnoxious, repugnant, repulsive, repellent, revolting, disgusting, distasteful, nauseating, unsavoury, unpalatable. **2** *a disagreeable old man* bad-tempered, ill-natured, unfriendly, unpleasant, difficult, nasty, cross, irritable, rude, surly, discourteous, impolite, churlish, peevish, brusque, abrupt, disobliging, contrary.

disagreement *noun* **1** *the disagreement of the two sides* lack of agreement, difference of opinion, dissent, dispute, variance, contention, disaccord, discord. **2** *the disagreement of/between the accounts* difference, dissimilarity, unlikeness, variation, variance, discrepancy, disparity, dissimilitude, incompatibility, incongruity, contradiction, conflict, clash, contrast, divergence, deviation, contravention, nonconformity, diversity. **3** *the disagreement between the children* quarrel, argument, wrangle, squabble, altercation, dispute, debate, disputation, discord, strife, conflict, war of words; bickering, sparring, contention, dissension, disharmony; *inf.* falling out.

disallow *verb* reject, say no to, refuse, dismiss, rebuff, repel, repulse, repudiate, ban, bar, debar, forbid, prohibit, veto, embargo, proscribe, negative, cancel, disclaim, disown, abjure, disavow.

disappear *verb* **1** *the sun disappearing behind the horizon* pass from sight, cease to be visible, vanish from sight, vanish, be lost to view/sight, recede, recede from view, fade, fade/melt away, withdraw, depart, retire, go, pass, flee, retreat, ebb, wane, dematerialize, evanesce, evaporate; *inf.* vamoose. **2** *customs/railways which have disappeared* die out, die, cease to be/exist, be no more, come to an end, end, vanish, pass away, expire, perish, become extinct, fade, melt away, leave no trace, pass into oblivion.

disappearance *noun* **1** *the disappearance of the sun* passing from sight, vanishing, receding from view, fading, melting away, withdrawal, departure, exit, retiral, passing, retreat, ebb, wane, eclipse, dematerialization, evanescence, evaporation. See DISAPPEAR 1. **2** *the disappearance of the customs/trams* dying out, death, vanishing, passing away, expiry, perishing, eclipse, extinction.

disappoint *verb* **1** *sorry to disappoint you / the news disappointed him* let down, fail, dishearten, depress, dispirit, upset, sadden, dash the hopes of, chagrin, dismay, disgruntle, disenchant, disillusion, dissatisfy, vex. **2** *disappoint their plans* thwart, frustrate, baulk, foil, defeat, baffle, hinder, obstruct, hamper, impede, interfere with.
Opposites CHEER; DELIGHT; FULFIL.

disappointed *adjective* **1** *disappointed children* upset, saddened, let down, disheartened, downhearted, cast down, downcast, depressed, dispirited, despondent, distressed, chagrined, disgruntled, disenchanted, disillusioned, discontented, dissatisfied, vexed. **2** *disappointed plans* thwarted, frustrated, baulked, foiled, defeated, failed, baffled. See DISAPPOINT 2.

disappointing *adjective* **1** *disappointing news* upsetting, saddening, disagreeable, disheartening, discouraging, depressing, dispiriting, distressing, disenchanting, dissatisfying, disconcerting, vexing. See DISAPPOINT 1. **2** *a disappointing effort* unsatisfactory, inadequate, insufficient, unworthy, inferior, second-rate, pathetic, lame.

disappointment *noun* **1** *hide one's disappointment* sadness, regret, depression, dispiritedness, despondency, distress, chagrin, disgruntlement, displeasure, disenchantment, disillusionment, discontent, dissatisfaction, vexation. **2** *the disappointment of their plans* thwarting, frustration, baulking, foiling; defeat, failure, non-success, ill-success, unfulfilment. **3** *the event was a disappointment* letdown, failure, fiasco, setback, blow, misfortune, disaster; *inf.* wash-out.

disapproval *noun* disapprobation, disfavour, displeasure, dislike, dissatisfaction, criticism, censure, blame, condemnation, denunciation, objection, exception, reproach, rebuke, reproof, remonstrance, disparagement, deprecation, animadversion.

disapprove *verb* **1** *disapprove of their behaviour* have/express a poor opinion of, dislike, find unacceptable, be against, be dissatisfied/displeased with, deplore, criticize, frown on, take a dim view of, look askance at, censure, blame, condemn, denounce, object to, take exception to, reproach, rebuke, reprove, remonstrate against, disparage, deprecate, animadvert; *inf.* look down one's nose at. **2** *disapprove the plans* turn down, reject, veto, disallow, set aside; *inf.* give the thumbs down to.

disarm *verb* **1** *disarm the terrorists/nation* unarm, deprive of arms, demilitarize, demobilize, render defenceless, make powerless. **2** *the country is disarming* lay down arms, demilitarize; *lit.* sheathe the sword, turn swords into ploughshares. **3** *disarmed by his smile* charm, win over, persuade, convert, mollify, appease, placate, conciliate, propitiate.

disarmament *noun* demilitarization, demobilization, arms reduction, weapons control, arms limitation; nuclear disarmament.

disarming *adjective* *a disarming smile* charming, winning, persuasive, irresistible, conciliatory. See DISARM 3.

disarrange *verb* bring/throw into disorder, order, make disorderly, disorder, untidy, make untidy, mess up, displace, disorganize, disturb, confuse, jumble, mix up, muddle, turn upside-down, upset, unsettle, throw into disarray, derange, discompose, scatter, shake up, dishevel, tousle, rumple; *inf.* turn topsy-turvy; *Am. inf.* muss up.

disarray *noun* **1** *troops in disarray* disorder, confusion, upset; disorderliness, disorganization, discomposure, unsettledness, disunity, indiscipline, unruliness. **2** *rooms/clothes in disarray* disorder, untidiness, confusion, chaos, dishevelment; mess, muddle, clutter, jumble, mix-up, tangle; shambles; *Scots* guddle.

disaster *noun* **1** *natural disasters* catastrophe, calamity, cataclysm, tragedy, act of God, accident, mishap, misadventure, mischance, stroke of ill-luck, setback, reverse of fortune, reversal, heavy blow, shock, buffet; adversity, trouble, misfortune, ruin, ruination. **2** *the play was a disaster* failure, fiasco; *inf.* flop, dud, wash-out.
Opposites BLESSING; GODSEND; SUCCESS.

disastrous *adjective* *disastrous events* catastrophic, calamitous, cataclysmic, tragic, adverse, devastating, ravaging, dire, terrible, shocking, appalling, dreadful, black, harmful, injurious, detrimental, ruinous, unfortunate, unlucky, hapless, ill-fated, ill-starred.

disavowal *noun* denial, contradiction, disclaimer, repudiation, renunciation, disowning, rejection.

disband *verb* **1** *the group disbanded* break up, disperse, dissolve, separate, go separate ways. **2** *disband the group* break up, dissolve, disperse, dismiss, demobilize.

disbelief *noun* unbelief, lack of belief, scepticism, incredulity, non-conviction, doubt, dubiety, discredit, distrust, mistrust, questioning, agnosticism, atheism, nihilism.

disbelieve *verb* not believe, not credit, give no credence to, be incredulous, be unconvinced, discredit, discount, not accept, reject, repudiate, distrust, mistrust, question, challenge, scoff at.

disbeliever *noun* unbeliever, sceptic, doubter, doubting Thomas, questioner, challenger, scoffer, agnostic, atheist, nihilist.

disburse *verb* pay out, lay out, spend, expend; *inf.* fork out, shell out, dish out.

discard *verb* throw away/out, get rid of, dispose of, toss out, jettison, scrap, dispense with, cast aside, reject, repudiate, abandon, relinquish, forsake, drop, have done with, shed; *inf.* dump, ditch.
Opposites KEEP; RETAIN.

discern *verb* see, notice, observe, perceive, make out, distinguish, detect, descry, recognize, determine, differentiate.
Opposites OVERLOOK; MISS.

discernible *adjective* visible, noticeable, observable, perceptible, perceivable, distinguishable, detectable, recognizable, apparent, obvious, clear, manifest, conspicuous, patent.

discerning *adjective* discriminating, astute, shrewd, ingenious, clever, intelligent, perceptive, sharp, quick, perspicacious, penetrating, critical, percipient, judicious, sensitive, subtle, prudent, sound, wise, aware, knowing, sagacious, sapient.

discharge *verb* **1** *discharge the prisoner* set free, free, let go, release, liberate, acquit, clear, absolve, pardon, exonerate, reprieve, exculpate, emancipate, manumit. **2** *discharge from employment* dismiss, remove, get rid of, discard, eject, oust, expel, cashier, deprive of office; *inf.* sack, fire, axe, send packing, give the boot to, boot out. **3** *discharge a weapon* fire, shoot, let/set off, explode, detonate. **4** *discharge pus/fumes* exude, ooze, excrete, give off, leak, dispense, emit, send out, send/pour forth, eject, release, gush, void, disembogue. **5** *discharge a duty* carry out, perform, do, accomplish, achieve, fulfil, execute, observe, abide by. **6** *discharge a load* unload, disburden, remove, unburden, off-load, relieve. **7** *discharge a debt/obligation* pay, settle, clear, honour, meet, liquidate, satisfy; *inf.* square.
Opposites IMPRISON; ENGAGE; NEGLECT.

discharge *noun* **1** *prisoners receiving a discharge* release, liberation, acquittal, clearance, absolution, pardon, exoneration, reprieve, exculpation, manumission. **2** *hear about his discharge from the firm* dismissal, removal, ejection, ousting, expulsion, cashiering, congé; *inf.* the sack, firing, axeing, the boot. See DISCHARGE *verb* 2. **3** *the/a discharge from a weapon* discharging, firing, shooting, explosion, detonation, blast, burst, pop, report, volley, salvo, fusillade. **4** *the discharge of pus/fumes* exuding, oozing, excretion, emission, ejection, release, emptying, voiding, voidance, disemboguement. **5** *exuding a watery discharge* excretion, exudate, emission, flow, secretion, ooze, suppuration, pus, seepage. **6** *discharge of one's duty* carrying out, performing, doing, accomplishment, achievement, fulfilment, execution, observance; performance. **7** *the discharge of a debt* payment, settlement, clearance, honouring, meeting. See DISCHARGE *verb* 7.

disciple *noun* apostle, follower, pupil, student, believer, adherent, devotee, votary, upholder, supporter, advocate, proponent, satellite, partisan. *See table at* APOSTLE.

disciplinarian *noun* martinet, authoritarian, hard taskmaster, stickler for order/punishment, formalist, tyrant, despot.

discipline *noun* **1** *school discipline* | *yoga is a useful discipline* training, drilling, exercise, regimen, routine, method; instruction, coaching, teaching, indoctrination, inculcation, systematization. **2** *discipline required for the exercise* control, self-control, self-restraint, strictness, orderliness, regulation, direction, government, restriction, limitation; restraint, check, curb. **3** *pupils in need of discipline* punishment, chastisement, castigation, correction; penalty, reprimand, rebuke, reproof. **4** *literature and other disciplines* field of study, field, branch of knowledge, course of study, course, area, subject, specialist subject, speciality, specialty.

discipline *verb* **1** *discipline the troops* train, drill, break in, exercise, instruct, coach, teach, educate, tutor, prepare, ground, indoctrinate, inculcate, inure, toughen. **2** *discipline oneself* control, restrain, regulate, govern, restrict, limit, check, curb. **3** *discipline the children* punish, chastise, castigate, correct, penalize, reprimand, rebuke, reprove.

disclaim *verb* deny, renounce, repudiate, reject, refuse, decline, disown, cast off, discard, abandon, wash one's hands of, turn one's back on, abjure, forswear, disavow, disaffirm.

disclaimer *noun* denial, renunciation, repudiation, rejection, abjuration, disavowal, disaffirmation.

disclose *verb* **1** *disclose confidential details* make known, reveal, divulge, tell, impart, communicate, make public, broadcast, publish, release, unveil, leak, let slip, blurt out, blab, admit, confess, avow; *inf.* spill the beans about, let the cat out of the bag about, blow the gaff, blow the lid off, squeal about. **2** *disclose the contents of the box* reveal, show, exhibit, expose, uncover, lay bare, unveil, bring to light.
Opposites CONCEAL; HIDE.

disclosure *noun* **1** *make disclosures of secret ceremonies* revelation, divulgence, exposé, communication, leak, admission, confession, avowal. **2** *the disclosure of vice by the newspaper* revealing, revelation, bringing to light, divulging, divulgence, broadcasting, publishing, uncovering, laying bare, unveiling; release, announcement, declaration, exposure.

discoloration *noun* stain, soiling, mark, streak, spot, blotch, tarnishing; blemish, flaw.

discolour *verb* stain, soil, mark, streak, spot, tarnish, fade, bleach, wash out.

discomfit *verb* **1** *discomfited by personal questions* embarrass, disconcert, make uncomfortable, take aback, nonplus, abash, confuse, ruffle, fluster, upset, disturb, perturb, discompose, discomfort; *inf.* faze, rattle, discombobulate. **2** *discomfit the enemy's plans* thwart, frustrate, foil, obstruct, hinder, hamper, check, upset.

discomfiture *noun* *the discomfiture of the interviewee* embarrassment, disconcertment, uneasi-

ness, unease, confusion, discomposure. *See* DISCOMFIT 1.

discomfort *noun* **1** *experience some discomfort in the injured leg* ache, pain, soreness, twinge, hurt, irritation, pang, throb, smart, malaise. **2** *lead the life of discomfort* lack of comfort/ease, trouble, unpleasantness, hardship, distress. **3** *blushing with discomfort* embarrassment, anxiety, disconcertment, unease, uneasiness, discomfiture, discomposure, disquietude. **4** *the discomforts of travel* inconvenience, difficulty, trouble, bother, nuisance, vexation, drawback, disadvantage, problem, trial, tribulation.

discomfort *verb* *discomforted by the hostile audience* make uncomfortable/uneasy, embarrass, disconcert, upset, ruffle, discompose, discomfit.

discomposure *noun* agitation, fluster, flurry, restlessness, nervousness, perturbation, disturbance, anxiety, uneasiness, unease, disquiet, disquietude, embarrassment, disconcertment, confusion, discomfiture, discomfort.

disconcert *verb* **1** *disconcerted by the silence in the room* unsettle, shake, disturb, perturb, daunt, take aback, abash, nonplus, confuse, bewilder, fluster, ruffle, upset, agitate, worry, embarrass, discomfit, discompose, perplex, confound, distract, throw off balance, put off one's stroke; *inf.* throw, faze, rattle. **2** *disconcerting their plans* thwart, frustrate, foil, obstruct, hinder, hamper, upset, undo.

disconcerting *adjective* *a disconcerting habit of grinning* unsettling, disturbing, perturbing, daunting, confusing, bewildering, upsetting, worrying, alarming, embarrassing, discomfiting, perplexing, bothering, bothersome, distracting, dismaying, awkward; *inf.* off-putting.

disconnect *verb* **1** *disconnect the electrical supply* undo, cut off, sever, uncouple, disengage, detach, unhook, unhitch, unlink, disjoin, disunite. **2** *cannot disconnect the two philosophies* separate, sever, divide, part, split up, dissociate, disentangle. **3** *our telephone conversation got disconnected* discontinue, interrupt, suspend, halt, stop.

disconnected *adjective* **1** *disconnected ideas* unconnected, separate, separated, unattached, dissociated. **2** *disconnected speech* disjointed, garbled, confused, jumbled, mixed-up, incoherent, unintelligible, rambling, wandering, disordered, illogical, irrational, uncoordinated.

disconsolate *adjective* sad, unhappy, miserable, despondent, wretched, heartbroken, forlorn, grief-stricken, inconsolable, woebegone, dejected, low, low-spirited, dispirited, down, depressed, downcast, gloomy, melancholy, blue; *inf.* down in the mouth/dumps.
Opposites HAPPY; JOYFUL.

discontent *noun* discontentment, dissatisfaction, restlessness, impatience, fretfulness, displeasure, unhappiness, misery, wretchedness, envy, regret, umbrage, disaffection, disquiet, vexation, exasperation, irritation, chagrin, pique.

discontented *adjective* dissatisfied, fed up, restless, impatient, fretful, complaining, displeased, disgruntled, querulous, unhappy, miserable, wretched, envious, regretful, disaffected, exasperated, irritated, chagrined, annoyed, peeved, piqued; *inf.* browned off, cheesed off, hacked off, brassed off, pissed off.

discontinue *verb* **1** *discontinue the service* stop, end, put an end/stop to, finish, bring to a halt, terminate, cease, abandon, give up, break off, cancel, drop, refrain from, quit, suspend, interrupt; *inf.* cut out. **2** *the road/conversation discontinued* stop, come to a stop/halt, terminate, leave off, pause.

discontinued *adjective* *a discontinued line/product* no longer available/produced, abandoned, given up, ended, finished, terminated, halted.

discord *noun* **1** *bitter discord between the deputy heads* disagreement, difference of opinion, dissension, dispute, argument, conflict, friction, contention, strife, opposition, hostility, wrangling, clashing, quarrelling, falling-out, war, division, incompatibility, variance, disunity, rupture. **2** *the discord of the instruments* lack of harmony, disharmony, dissonance, cacophony, harshness, jarring, jangling, din, racket.
Opposites ACCORD; CONCORD; HARMONY.

discordant *adjective* **1** *discordant attitudes* disagreeing, differing, contradictory, contrary, dissenting, disputatious, conflicting, at variance, at odds, contentious, opposing, hostile, clashing, divergent, incompatible, incongruous. **2** *discordant sounds* inharmonious, harsh, strident, shrill, grating, jarring, jangling, dissonant, cacophonous.
Opposites COMPATIBLE; HARMONIOUS; DULCET.

discount *verb* **1** *discount what he says* disregard, ignore, pass over, overlook, pay no attention to, take no notice of, brush off, gloss over. **2** *discount £5 from the price* deduct, take off, rebate; *inf.* knock off. **3** *discount the regular price* reduce, lower, lessen; *inf.* knock down. **4** *discount the products* mark down, reduce, put on sale.
Opposites NOTE; INCREASE; mark up (*see* MARK).

discount *noun* **1** *a good discount on the goods* mark down, deduction, price cut, cut, rebate, concession. **2** *goods at a discount* lower price, cut price, concessionary price, reduction.

discourage *verb* **1** *he was discouraged by lack of success* dishearten, dispirit, deject, cast down, depress, demoralize, disappoint, daunt, put off, intimidate, cow, unnerve, unman. **2** *discourage them from applying* put off, dissuade, deter, talk out of, advise against, urge against, caution against, restrain, inhibit, divert from, sidetrack from. **3** *discourage the idea* oppose, disapprove of, repress, deprecate, put a damper on, throw cold water on. **4** *a preparation discouraging damp* prevent, check, curb, hinder, obstruct, suppress, inhibit.
Opposites ENCOURAGE; PERSUADE.

discouraged *adjective* *discouraged job hunters* disheartened, dispirited, dejected, cast down, downcast, depressed, demoralized, disappointed, daunted, put off, crestfallen, glum; *inf.* down in the mouth/dumps. *See* DISCOURAGE 1.

discouragement *noun* **1** *experience discouragement* dispiritedness, downheartedness, dejec-

tion, depression, demoralization, disappointment, despondency, hopelessness, lack of confidence, pessimism, despair, gloom, melancholy; low spirits. **2** *ideas meeting with discouragement* opposition, disapproval, repression, deprecation. **3** *tired of discouragements to progress* deterrent, hindrance, obstacle, impediment, barrier, curb, check, damper, restraint, constraint, restriction, disincentive, setback, rebuff; *inf.* put-down.

discouraging *adjective* *discouraging news* disheartening, dispiriting, depressing, demoralizing, disappointing, off-putting, gloomy, unfavourable, unpropitious, inauspicious.

discourse *noun* **1** *engage in discourse* conversation, talk, dialogue, communication, discussion, conference, colloquy, converse, verbal exchange, chat, chit-chat, palaver, confabulation; *inf.* confab, rap. **2** *a discourse on art* address, speech, lecture, oration, sermon, homily, essay, treatise, dissertation, paper, study, disquisition.

discourse *verb* **1** *discourse with colleagues* converse, talk, discuss, debate, confer, speak, chat; *inf.* have a confab/chin-wag, chew the fat, rap. **2** *discourse on morals* give an address/talk, deliver a speech/lecture, lecture, sermonize, preach, hold forth, write learnedly, write at length, expatiate; *inf.* spout.

discourteous *adjective* rude, impolite, ill-mannered, bad-mannered, unmannerly, uncivil, curt, abrupt, brusque, short, gruff, boorish, churlish, ungracious, ungentlemanly, unladylike, ill-bred, uncouth, disrespectful, ungallant, insolent, impertinent, impudent.

discourtesy *noun* rudeness, impoliteness, lack of civility, incivility, ill-manneredness, unmannerliness, curtness, abruptness, brusqueness, ungraciousness, ill-breeding, uncouthness, disrespect, disrespectfulness, insolence. *See* DISCOURTEOUS.

discover *verb* **1** *discover a new holiday place | discover new talent* find, come across/upon, stumble upon, chance upon, light upon, locate, bring to light, uncover, unearth, turn up; *inf.* dig up. **2** *discover that he was lying* find out, come to know, learn, realize, detect, determine, ascertain, recognize, see, spot, notice, perceive, reveal, disclose; *inf.* twig, get wise to the fact. **3** *discover a new drug* invent, originate, devise, pioneer, design, contrive, conceive of. **4** *discover America* found, explore, pioneer.

discoverer *noun* **1** *the discoverer of America* founder, explorer, pioneer. **2** *the discoverer of penicillin* inventor, originator, pioneer, deviser, designer, initiator.

discovery *noun* **1** *the discovery of a quiet village | new talent* finding, locating, location, uncovering. *See* DISCOVER 1. **2** *the discovery that they lied* finding out, learning, realization, detection, determination, recognition, revelation, disclosure; *inf.* twigging. *See* DISCOVER 2. **3** *discovery of new drugs* invention, origination, devising, pioneering, introduction. **4** *recent discoveries* find, invention, breakthrough, innovation, lucky

discredit · diseased

strike, bonanza; findings. **5** *a voyage of discovery* exploration, pioneering, research.

discredit *verb* **1** *discredit their rivals* detract
from, bring into disrepute, defame, slur, slander, cast aspersions on, vilify, disparage, deprecate, denigrate, devalue, devaluate, degrade,
belittle, decry, dishonour, disgrace, censure.
2 *evidence to discredit the research* disprove, invalidate, refute, dispute, challenge, destroy the
credibility of, shake one's faith in, reject,
deny. **3** *the jury discredited the witness* disbelieve, give no credence to, discount, doubt, distrust, mistrust.

discredit *noun* **1** *bring discredit on the neighbourhood* disrepute, ill-repute, infamy, disgrace,
dishonour, shame, humiliation, ignominy,
stigma, harm, damage, censure, blame,
reproach, scandal, odium, opprobrium.
2 *regard the story with discredit* disbelief, lack of
credence, incredulity, question, doubt, distrust, mistrust, scepticism, suspicion.

discredited *adjective* brought into disrepute,
disproved, invalidated, refuted, rejected, discarded, denied, exploded, debunked.

discreet *adjective* careful, cautious, prudent,
judicious, circumspect, wary, guarded, chary,
tactful, reserved, diplomatic, considerate,
politic, strategic, wise, sensible, sagacious.
Opposites INDISCREET; RASH; TACTLESS.

discrepancy *noun* inconsistency, variance,
variation, disparity, deviation, divergence,
incongruity, difference, disagreement, dissimilarity, contrariety, conflict, discordance, gap,
lacuna.

discrete *adjective* separate, distinct, individual, detached, unattached, disconnected, discontinuous, disjunct.

discretion *noun* **1** *act with discretion* care, carefulness, caution, prudence, judiciousness,
judgement, circumspection, wariness, guardedness, chariness, tactfulness, tact, reserve,
diplomacy, consideration, strategy, discrimination, wisdom, sense, good sense, discernment,
sagacity, acumen, forethought, maturity. **2** *at
the discretion of the manager* choice, option, volition, will, preference, inclination, pleasure, liking, wish, desire, predilection, election,
disposition, mind.

discretionary *adjective* optional, elective,
open, open to choice, non-mandatory, unrestricted, voluntary, volitional.

discriminate *verb* **1** *discriminate between right
and wrong* distinguish, make/draw a distinction, differentiate, tell the difference, make a
difference, discern; separate, separate the
sheep from the goats, separate the wheat from
the chaff, segregate. **2** *discriminate against
women | discriminate in favour of Europeans* show
prejudice against/towards, be biased against/
towards, treat differently, treat as inferior/
superior, disfavour/favour, be intolerant/over-
tolerant towards.

discriminating *adjective* **1** *a discriminating
concert-goer* discerning, perceptive, astute,
shrewd, selective, particular, fastidious, critical, keen, tasteful, refined, sensitive, cultivated, cultured, artistic, aesthetic.

2 *discriminating rules* distinguishing, differentiating, prejudiced. See DISCRIMINATORY 1.

discrimination *noun* **1** *wine lovers of discrimination* discernment, perception, penetration,
perspicacity, acumen, astuteness, shrewdness,
selectivity, fastidiousness, judgement, keenness, taste, refinement, sensitivity, insight,
subtlety, cultivation, culture, artistry, aestheti-
cism. **2** *guilty of discrimination* prejudice, bias,
unfairness, inequity, intolerance, bigotry,
narrow-mindedness, favouritism, segregation;
positive discrimination.

discriminatory *adjective* **1** *discriminatory
employment rules* prejudiced, prejudicial, biased,
preferential, unfair, unjust, inequitable,
weighted, one-sided, partisan. **2** *a discriminatory drinker* discerning, critical. See DISCRIMIN-
ATING 1.

discursive *adjective* digressive, rambling, wandering, meandering, diffuse, episodic, circuitous, verbose, long-winded, wordy, prolix,
circumlocutory.
Opposites CONCISE; BRIEF.

discuss *verb* discuss the problem with colleagues*
talk over, talk/chat about, converse about, confer about, debate, exchange views on/about,
deliberate, consider, go into, thrash out, examine, review, study, scrutinize, analyse, weigh
up, sift, ventilate, argue, dispute; *inf.* kick
around.

discussion *noun* talk, conversation, dialogue,
chat, conference, debate, discourse, exchange
of views, symposium, seminar, consultation,
deliberation, parley, examination, review,
study, scrutiny, analysis, ventilation, argument, dispute; *inf.* confab.

disdain *noun* *look with disdain on pantomimes*
scorn, scornfulness, contempt, contemptuousness, derision, sneering, deprecation, disparagement, denigration, contumely,
opprobrium, arrogance, superciliousness,
haughtiness, hauteur, snobbishness, aloofness,
indifference, dislike, abhorrence.

disdain *verb* *disdain offers of help* scorn, show
contempt for, spurn, reject, refuse, rebuff, disregard, sneer at, pooh-pooh, deride, belittle,
undervalue, slight, despise, look down on, misprize; *inf.* look down one's nose at.

disdainful *adjective* scornful, contemptuous,
sneering, derisive, slighting, disparaging, arrogant, proud, supercilious, haughty, superior,
lordly, pompous, snobbish, insolent, aloof,
indifferent; *inf.* high and mighty, hoity-toity.

disease *noun* illness, sickness; disorder, complaint, malady, ailment, affliction, condition,
indisposition, upset, infirmity, disability,
abnormality; infectious disease, infection, contagious disease, contagion, viral disease, pestilence, plague, cancer, canker, blight; *inf.* bug,
virus. See table at ILLNESS.
Opposites HEALTH.

diseased *adjective* unhealthy, ill, ailing, sick,
sickly, unwell, unsound, unwholesome, infirm,
infected, abnormal, blighted, rotten, canker-
ous.

disembark verb land, arrive, get off, step off, alight, go ashore, dismount, deplane, detrain; *inf.* pile out.

disembodied *adjective* bodiless, incorporeal, discarnate, immaterial, intangible, insubstantial, impalpable, spiritual, ghostly, spectral, phantom, wraith-like.

disembowel verb eviscerate, exenterate, gut, draw.

disenchanted *adjective* disillusioned, disabused, undeceived, set straight, disappointed, let down, blasé, cynical, soured, jaundiced, sick, out of love, indifferent.

disenchantment *noun* disillusion, cynicism; disillusionment, disappointment, rude awakening.

disengage verb *disengage the clutch | disengage oneself from an embrace* release, loosen, loose, unfasten, detach, separate, disjoin, disunite, uncouple, undo, unhook, unloose, unhitch, unclasp, untie, free, set free, liberate, disentangle, disentwine, extricate.

disentangle verb **1** *disentangle the knotted wool* unravel, straighten, unwind, untwist, undo, unknot, untie, unsnarl, unkink, smooth out, comb, card. **2** *disentangle oneself* extricate, disentwine, release, loosen, detach, unfasten, unclasp, free, set free, liberate, disconnect.

disfavour *noun* **1** *look upon with disfavour* lack of favour, disapproval, disapprobation, dislike, displeasure, dissatisfaction, disregard, low opinion, low esteem. **2** *fall into disfavour* disapproval, unpopularity, discredit, disrepute, ill repute, ignominy, disgrace, shame, opprobrium. **3** *do someone a disfavour* disservice, bad turn, ill deed, discourtesy.

disfigure verb deface, deform, mutilate, blemish, flaw, scar, make ugly, uglify, spoil, mar, damage, injure, maim, vandalize, ruin, disfeature.
Opposites ADORN; ENHANCE.

disfigurement *noun* **1** *the disfigurement of the landscape* defacement, mutilation, scarring, spoiling, uglification, damaging, vandalizing, ruin. See DISFIGURE. **2** *an obvious disfigurement* blemish, flaw, blotch, imperfection, defect, scar, deformity, malformation, injury.

disgorge verb **1** *volcanoes disgorging lava | disgorging phlegm* spit out, spew out, belch, discharge, spout, vomit, regurgitate, throw up, eject, emit, expel, empty. **2** *disgorging their hold on the territory* give up, surrender, yield, cede, relinquish, hand over, renounce, resign, abandon.

disgrace *noun* **1** *the disgrace of being in prison* shame, humiliation, dishonour, scandal, degradation, ignominy, infamy, discredit, debasement, vitiation. **2** *be in disgrace | brought him disgrace* disfavour, discredit, disrepute, loss of face, disrespect, disapproval, disapprobation, disesteem, contempt, opprobrium, obloquy. **3** *his behaviour was a disgrace* blot, stain, blemish, black mark, scandal, smear, smirch, stigma, slur, dishonour, aspersion, defamation.

disgrace verb **1** *disgrace the family* bring disgrace to, bring shame upon, shame, humiliate, bring dishonour to, dishonour, discredit, degrade, debase, sully, besmirch, taint, stain, slur, stigmatize, brand, drag through the mud. **2** *the soldier was publicly disgraced* discredit, reproach, censure, blame, dishonour, disfavour, humiliate, mortify, disparage, demean, denigrate, belittle.
Opposites HONOUR; ESTEEM; FAVOUR.

disgraceful *adjective* **1** *disgraceful behaviour by the minister* scandalous, shocking, outrageous, shameful, shameless, dishonourable, disreputable, degrading, ignominious, blameworthy, culpable, contemptible, despicable, reprehensible, improper, unseemly, unworthy. **2** *your work is disgraceful* very bad, appalling, dreadful, terrible, shocking, intolerable, unworthy.

disgruntled *adjective* discontented, dissatisfied, displeased, unhappy, disappointed, annoyed, exasperated, vexed, irritated, peeved, put out, resentful, sulky, sullen, petulant, grumpy, churlish, testy; *inf.* fed up, cheesed off, hacked off.

disguise verb **1** *disguised as a policeman* camouflage, dress up, be under cover, be incognito, cover up, conceal, hide, mask, screen, shroud, veil, cloak. **2** *disguise the truth* cover up, misrepresent, falsify, give a false picture of, fake, fudge, feign, dissemble, dissimulate, gloss over, varnish.

disgust verb **1** *the slimy food disgusted me* sicken, nauseate, turn one's stomach, put off, revolt, repel, cause aversion; *inf.* turn off. **2** *her behaviour disgusted me* offend, outrage, shock, appal, scandalize, displease, dissatisfy, annoy, anger.

disgust *noun* **1** *look with disgust at the food* revulsion, repugnance, repulsion, aversion, nausea, distaste, disrelish, abhorrence, loathing, detestation. **2** *disgust at her behaviour* offence, outrage, shock, disapproval, displeasure, dissatisfaction, annoyance, anger.
Opposites PLEASURE; ADMIRATION; APPROVAL.

disgusting *adjective* **1** *disgusting food* sickening, nauseating, nauseous, revolting, repellent, off-putting, unpalatable, foul, nasty, unappetizing, distasteful, abhorrent, loathsome, detestable, obnoxious, odious; *inf.* grotty. **2** *disgusting behaviour* offensive, objectionable, outrageous, shocking, shameless, shameful, appalling, scandalous, vulgar, gross, vile, displeasing, annoying.

dish *noun* **1** *food in dishes* container, receptacle, bowl, plate, platter, salver. **2** *prepare a new dish* food, fare, recipe, dish of the day, *plat du jour*.

dish verb *dish one's plans* ruin, destroy, put an end to, spoil, wreck, torpedo. **dish out** distribute, hand out, deal out, allocate, dole out, mete out. **dish up** **1** *dish up the potatoes* serve, serve up, spoon, ladle, scoop. **2** *dish up the old material in new form* present, offer, produce, prepare.

dishearten verb discourage, cast down, dispirit, make dispirited/dejected, depress, crush, make crestfallen/downhearted, dash, dampen, put a damper on, daunt, disappoint, deter, sadden, weigh down.

dishevelled *adjective* untidy, tousled, rumpled, bedraggled, disordered, disarranged, messy, in a mess, unkempt, uncombed, slovenly, slatternly, blowsy, frowzy; *Am. inf.* mussed. **Opposites** TIDY; NEAT.

dishonest *adjective* fraudulent, cheating, untrustworthy, false, untruthful, dishonourable, unscrupulous, unprincipled, corrupt, swindling, deceitful, deceiving, deceptive, lying, crafty, cunning, designing, mendacious, double-dealing, underhand, treacherous, perfidious, unfair, unjust, disreputable, rascally, roguish, knavish; *inf.* crooked, shady, bent.

dishonesty *noun* fraud, fraudulence, cheating, chicanery, untrustworthiness, falseness, falsity, falsehood, untruthfulness, dishonour, unscrupulousness, corruption, criminality, sharp practice, deceit, deception, duplicity, lying, craft, cunning, trickery, wiliness, guile, double-dealing, underhandedness, treachery, perfidy, graft, unfairness, unjustness, improbity, rascality, knavishness; *inf.* crookedness, shadiness.

dishonour *noun* **1** *bring dishonour to the regiment* disgrace, shame, humiliation, scandal, discredit, degradation, ignominy, infamy, disrepute, ill-repute, loss of face, disfavour, debasement, abasement, odium, opprobrium, obloquy, vitiation. **2** *do him a dishonour* indignity, insult, affront, offence, abuse, outrage, slight, discourtesy. **3** *a dishonour to his profession* disgrace, blot, blemish, stigma. *See* DISGRACE *noun* 3.

dishonour *verb* **1** *dishonour the flag* disgrace, bring dishonour/shame to, shame, humiliate, discredit, degrade, debase, sully, stain, stigmatize. *See* DISGRACE *verb* 1. **2** *dishonour their hosts* insult, affront, abuse, slight, offend. **3** *dishonour the captives* rape, violate, ravish, defile, seduce, deflower.

dishonourable *adjective* **1** *a dishonourable act* disgraceful, shameful, shameless, shaming, disreputable, degrading, debasing, ignominious, ignoble, blameworthy, contemptible, despicable, reprehensible, base. **2** *a dishonourable man* unprincipled, blackguardly, unscrupulous, corrupt, untrustworthy, treacherous, perfidious, traitorous, disreputable, discreditable; *inf.* shady.

disillusion *verb* disabuse, disenchant, open the eyes of, shatter the illusions of, undeceive, set straight, enlighten, disappoint, make sadder and wiser.

disincentive *noun* discouragement, deterrent, damper, dissuasion, impediment, hindrance.

disinclination *noun* reluctance, lack of enthusiasm, hesitancy, hesitance, unwillingness, loathness, aversion, dislike, distaste, objection, demur, resistance, opposition, recalcitrance.

disinclined *adjective* reluctant, unenthusiastic, not in the mood, hesitant, unwilling, loath, averse, antipathetic, resistant, opposed, recalcitrant.

disinfect *verb* sterilize, sanitize, clean, cleanse, purify, fumigate, decontaminate.

disinfectant *noun* antiseptic, bactericide, germicide, sterilizer, sanitizer, cleansing agent, cleanser, fumigant, decontaminant.

disingenuous *adjective* insincere, feigned, deceitful, underhand, underhanded, duplicitous, double-dealing, two-faced, false, lying, untruthful, artful, cunning, crafty, wily, sly, shifty, scheming, calculating, designing, insidious.

disinherit *verb* cut off, cut off without a penny, dispossess, oust, disown, repudiate, renounce.

disintegrate *verb* fall apart, fall to pieces, break up, break apart, shatter, splinter, crumble, decompose, decay, rot, moulder, erode, dissolve, go to wrack and ruin.

disinterested *adjective* **1** *disinterested judges* unbiased, unprejudiced, impartial, detached, objective, uninvolved, dispassionate, impersonal, open-minded, neutral, outside, fair, just, equitable, even-handed, unselfish. **2** *disinterested in the lecture* uninterested, unconcerned, uninvolved, unresponsive, indifferent, bored, apathetic, blasé. **Opposites** BIASED; PARTIAL; INTERESTED.

disjointed *noun* **1** *a disjointed talk* incoherent, unconnected, disconnected, without unity, ununified, discontinous, rambling, wandering, disorganized, confused, disordered, fitful, spasmodic, aimless, directionless. **2** *disjointed limbs* dislocated, displaced, dismembered, disconnected, severed, separated, disarticulated, torn apart, disunited.

dislike *verb* have no liking for, have an aversion to, regard with distaste/animosity, feel hostility towards, be unable to tolerate/stomach, hold in disfavour, disfavour, have no taste for, object to, hate, detest, loathe, abominate, abhor, despise, scorn, shun, have a grudge against, execrate, disrelish, antipathize.

dislike *noun* aversion, disapproval, disapprobation, distaste, animosity, hostility, antipathy, antagonism, disinclination, disfavour, disesteem, hate, detestation, loathing, disgust, repugnance, enmity, abhorrence, disrelish, animus.

dislocate *verb* **1** *dislocate a bone* put out of joint, put out of place, displace, disjoint, disconnect, disengage; *Med.* luxate. **2** *dislocate plans | dislocate air services* disrupt, disturb, throw into disorder/disarray/confusion, confuse, disorganize, mess up, disorder, disarrange, turn topsy turvy.

dislodge *verb* remove, displace, force out, oust, eject, evict, unseat; *inf.* sack.

disloyal *adjective* unfaithful, faithless, false, false-hearted, untrue, inconstant, untrustworthy, treacherous, perfidious, traitorous, disaffected, subversive, seditious, unpatriotic, renegade, apostate, dissident, two-faced, double-dealing, deceitful.

disloyalty *noun* unfaithfulness, infidelity, faithlessness, breach of trust, breaking of faith, falseness, false-heartedness, falsity, inconstancy, untrustworthiness, treachery, perfidy, treason, disaffection, subversion, sedition, apostasy, dissidence, double dealing, Punic faith.

dismal *adjective* **1** *children looking dismal* gloomy, sad, unhappy, miserable, wretched, despondent, disconsolate, sorrowful, solemn, blue, melancholy, morose, woebegone, forlorn, lugubrious. **2** *dismal surroundings* gloomy, dreary, bleak, drab, dull, dark, dingy, cheerless, desolate, depressing, grim, funereal, comfortless, inhospitable, uninviting. **3** *a dismal piece of work* bad, poor, inept, bungling, disgraceful.
Opposites CHEERFUL; BRIGHT.

dismantle *verb* take apart, take to pieces, disassemble, pull apart, tear down, demolish, fell, destroy.
Opposites ASSEMBLE.

dismay *verb* **1** *dismayed by the appearance of the police* disconcert, take aback, startle, surprise, shock, disturb, perturb, upset, jolt, unsettle, unnerve, unman, alarm, frighten, scare. **2** *dismayed by their failure* discourage, put off, dishearten, dispirit, cast down, depress, disappoint, daunt, abash.

dismiss *verb* **1** *dismissed from the firm for theft* give notice to, discharge, expel, cashier, remove, oust, eject, lay off, make/declare redundant, deselect; *inf.* sack, give the sack to, fire, give one one's cards/books, give one one's marching orders, send packing, give the push/boot/heave-ho to, boot out. **2** *dismiss an assembly/army* disband, disperse, dissolve, discharge, send away, let go, release, free. **3** *dismiss foolish thoughts* put away, banish, think no more of, put out of one's mind, set/lay aside, abandon, have done with, reject, drop, disregard, repudiate, spurn, pooh-pooh.
Opposites ENGAGE; FORM; RETAIN.

dismissal *noun* **1** *his dismissal from the firm* notice, discharge, expulsion, removal, ejection; *inf.* the sack, sacking, firing, the push, the boot, the heave-ho. See DISMISS 1. **2** *the dismissal of the assembly* disbandment, dispersal, dissolution, discharge, permission to go/depart/leave, release, congé.

disobedience *noun* insubordination, unruliness, waywardness, indiscipline, rebellion, defiance, mutiny, revolt, recalcitrance, delinquency, non-compliance, infraction, perversity, naughtiness, mischievousness, mischief, contumacy. See DISOBEDIENT.

disobedient *adjective* insubordinate, unruly, wayward, undisciplined, rebellious, defiant, mutinous, recalcitrant, intractable, wilful, refractory, obstreperous, disorderly, delinquent, non-compliant, perverse, naughty, mischievous, contrary, contumacious.

disobey *verb* defy, not comply with, disregard, flout, contravene, infringe, overstep, resist, rebel against, fly in the face of, transgress, violate, set at naught.

disobliging *adjective* unhelpful, uncooperative, unaccommodating, unfriendly, unsympathetic, discourteous, uncivil.

disorder *noun* **1** *tidy up the disorder* untidiness, mess, chaos, muddle, clutter, jumble, confusion, disorderliness, disarray, disorganization; *inf.* shambles. **2** *police quelling the disorder* disturbance, disruption, tumult, riot, breach of

the peace, fracas, rumpus, brouhaha, mêlée, unrest. **3** *a disorder of the kidneys* disease, ailment, complaint, affliction, malady, sickness, illness.

disorderly *adjective* **1** *disorderly rooms* untidy, messy, chaotic, cluttered, jumbled, muddled, out of order, out of place, in disarray, disorganized, confused, deranged, upside-down, at sixes and sevens, unsystematic, irregular; *inf.* shambolic. **2** *disorderly crowds* unruly, boisterous, rough, rowdy, disobedient, undisciplined, lawless, wild, unmanageable, uncontrollable, ungovernable, obstreperous, refractory, rebellious, mutinous, turbulent, tumultuous, rioting.

disorganized *adjective* **1** *disorganized piles of books* disorderly, chaotic, jumbled, muddled, out of order, in disarray, confused, haphazard, random, unsystematic, irregular; *inf.* shambolic. **2** *a disorganized person* unorganized, unmethodical, unsystematic, haphazard, muddled, careless; *inf.* hit-or-miss.

disown *verb* repudiate, renounce, reject, cast off, abandon, forsake, turn one's back on, disclaim, deny, disallow, abnegate, disavow, disinherit.

disparage *verb* **1** *disparage their efforts* belittle, slight, decry, depreciate, devalue, devaluate, downgrade, demean, detract from, discredit, deprecate, denigrate, derogate, deflate, minimize, undervalue, underestimate, underrate, make light of, play down, disdain, dismiss, ridicule, deride, mock, scorn, lampoon. **2** *disparage their competitors* defame, run down, slander, libel, malign, speak ill/evil of, cast aspersions on, impugn, calumniate, vilify, traduce; *inf.* do a hatchet job on, rubbish; *Am. inf.* bad-mouth.
Opposites PRAISE; OVERRATE.

disparity *noun* discrepancy, inequality, unevenness, inconsistency, imbalance, incongruity, difference, dissimilarity, contrast, gap.

dispassionate *adjective* **1** *a dispassionate attitude to suffering* unemotional, emotionless, unmoved, unexcited, unexcitable, unflappable, unperturbed, nonchalant, unruffled, cool, collected, cool and collected, calm, composed, self-possessed, level-headed, self-controlled, temperate, sober, placid, equable, tranquil, serene; *inf.* laid-back, together. **2** *dispassionate judges* detached, impartial, objective, disinterested, indifferent, uninvolved, impersonal, unbiased, unprejudiced, neutral, fair, just, equitable, even-handed, square dealing, open-minded.

dispatch, despatch *verb* **1** *dispatch a parcel* send, send off, post, mail, forward, transmit, consign, remit, convey. **2** *dispatch the meeting in an hour/dispatch the task* finish, dispose of, conclude, settle, discharge, execute, perform, expedite, push through, accelerate, hasten, speed up, hurry on; *inf.* make short work of. **3** *enemy bullets dispatched the terrorists* kill, put to death, slay, do to death, put an end to, finish off, take the life of, slaughter, murder, assassinate, execute; *inf.* bump off, do in, knock off, eliminate, erase.

dispatch, despatch noun **1** *carried out with dispatch* promptness, promptitude, speed, alacrity, quickness, haste, hurry, swiftness, rapidity, expedition, expeditiousness. **2** *mentioned in military dispatches | a journalist's dispatch* communication, communiqué, bulletin, report, account, document, missive, letter, epistle, message, item, piece, article, news, instruction. **3** *guilty of the dispatch of the enemy* killing, death, slaying, slaughter, murder, assassination, execution. *See* DISPATCH *verb* 3.

dispel verb drive away, drive off, chase away, banish, rout, expel, disperse, scatter, dissipate, disseminate, dismiss, eliminate, allay.

dispensable adjective expendable, disposable, unnecessary, unessential, non-essential, needless, superfluous, uncalled-for.
Opposites INDISPENSABLE; ESSENTIAL.

dispensation noun **1** *dispensation of supplies* distribution, handing out, dealing out, dividing out, division, allocation, allotment, apportionment, assignment, bestowal, conferment, supplying, disbursement. *See* DISPENSE 1. **2** *receive a dispensation of food* quota, portion, share, part, award. **3** *the dispensation of justice* administration, discharge, execution, implementation, application, enforcement, effectuation, operation, direction. **4** *the political/religious dispensation* system, order, scheme, plan, arrangement, organization, management, disposal, regulation, stewardship. **5** *given dispensation from a duty | given a dispensation from attending* exemption, immunity, exception, indulgence; release, relief, reprieve, remission, relaxation, absolution; *inf.* letting off, let-off.

dispense verb **1** *dispense supplies* distribute, hand out, deal out, dole out, share out, divide out, parcel out, allocate, allot, apportion, assign, bestow, confer, supply, disburse. **2** *dispense justice* administer, discharge, carry out, execute, implement, apply, enforce, effectuate, operate, direct. **3** *dispense medicines* make up, prepare, mix, supply. **4** *dispense him from eating fish on Fridays* grant a dispensation to, exempt, excuse, except, release, relieve, reprieve, absolve; *inf.* let off. **dispense with 1** *dispense with formalities* waive, do without, omit, forgo, give up, relinquish, renounce, ignore, disregard, pass over, brush aside. **2** *dispense with their services* do away with, get rid of, dispose of, abolish, revoke, rescind, cancel, shake off, manage without.

disperse verb **1** *the crowd dispersed* break up, disband, separate, go separate ways, scatter, dissolve, leave, vanish, melt away. **2** *the wind dispersed the clouds* break up, scatter, dissipate, dispel, drive away, banish, dissolve. **3** *disperse seeds* scatter, scatter to the winds, disseminate, distribute, sow, sprinkle, spread, diffuse, strew, bestrew. **4** *disperse information* put into circulation, circulate, broadcast, publish, publicize, spread, diffuse.
Opposites GATHER; ASSEMBLE; COLLECT.

dispirit verb dishearten, discourage, cast down, make dejected, depress, crush, dash, dampen the spirits of, daunt, disappoint, deter, sadden; *inf.* throw cold water on.

displace verb **1** *displace the furniture* put out of place/order, disarrange, move, shift, relocate, transpose, derange, disorder, throw into disorder, dislocate. **2** *displace from office* remove, dismiss, discharge, depose, dislodge, eject, expel, force out, discard, cashier; *inf.* sack, fire, turf out. **3** *displaced the old headmaster* replace, take the place of, take over from, supplant, oust, supersede, succeed; *inf.* crowd out.

display verb **1** *display the goods* put on show, show, exhibit, put on view, expose to view, present, unveil, set forth, arrange, dispose, array, demonstrate, advertise, publicize. **2** *display their military power* show off, flaunt, parade, flourish, boast, vaunt; *inf.* flash. **3** *display emotion* show, evince, manifest, betray, show evidence of, reveal, disclose.
Opposites CONCEAL; HIDE.

display noun **1** *put on a display of sculpture* show, exhibition, exhibit, presentation, demonstration, spectacle, array. **2** *military display* show, spectacle, parade, pageant; pomp, flourish, ostentation. **3** *the display of emotion* showing, evincement, manifestation, betrayal, evidence, revelation, disclosure.

displease verb dissatisfy, put out, annoy, irritate, anger, irk, vex, provoke, offend, pique, peeve, gall, nettle, incense, exasperate, upset, perturb, disturb, discompose, disgust; *inf.* aggravate.

displeasure noun dissatisfaction, discontentment, disgruntlement, disfavour, disapproval, disapprobation, distaste, annoyance, irritation, anger, ire, wrath, pique, chagrin, offence, rancour, indignation, exasperation, perturbation, disturbance, disgust.

disposable adjective **1** *disposable plates* throwaway, non-returnable, paper, plastic, biodegradable. **2** *disposable assets* available, usable, accessible, obtainable.

disposal noun **1** *the disposal of rubbish* throwing away, clearance, discarding, jettisoning, ejection, scrapping, destruction; *inf.* dumping. **2** *the disposal of the business matters* settlement, determination, deciding, conclusion. *See* DISPOSE OF 2. **3** *the disposal of his estate* distribution, allotment, allocation, transfer, transference, making over, conveyance, bestowal, gift, bequest, sale. *See* DISPOSE OF 3. **4** *the disposal of the troops* arrangement, ordering, positioning, placement, lining-up, setting-up, organization, marshalling, grouping. *See* DISPOSE 1. **5** *at one's disposal* power, authority, control, direction, discretion, responsibility, management, government, determination, regulation.

dispose verb **1** *troops disposed in rows* arrange, order, place, put, position, array, range, line up, set up, organize, marshal, group, rank, categorize, systematize, adjust, fix, regulate. **2** *behaviour not disposing me to believe him* incline, make willing, predispose, make, move, prompt, lead, induce, tempt, actuate, motivate, bias, influence, condition, direct. **dispose of 1** *dispose of the rubbish* get rid of, throw away/out, clear out, discard, jettison, eject, unload, scrap, destroy; *inf.* dump. **2** *dispose of the business* deal with, settle, determine, decide,

finish, conclude, end. **3** *dispose of his estate* distribute, give out, allot, allocate, assign, part with, transfer, make over, give away, bestow, sell, auction. **4** *dispose of his enemy* kill, do away with, put to death, slay, murder, slaughter; *inf.* bump off, knock off. **5** *rapidly disposed of the food* consume, eat up, devour, finish off, put away; *inf.* polish off.
Opposites KEEP; RETAIN.

disposed *adjective* **1** *well-disposed to them* inclined, predisposed, minded. **2** *disposed to help them* inclined, willing, of a mind to, in the mood to, ready, prepared. **3** *disposed to black moods* inclined, given, prone, liable, apt.

disposition *noun* **1** *people of a calm disposition* nature, character, temperament, humour, make-up, constitution, spirit, temper, mood. **2** *a disposition to moodiness* inclination, tendency, proneness, propensity, leaning, proclivity, bias, bent, predilection, weakness, habit, readiness. **3** *the disposition of the troops* disposal, arrangement, ordering, positioning, placement, lining-up, setting-up, organization, marshalling, grouping. **4** *disposition of property* disposal, distribution, allocation, transfer, transference, bestowal. See DISPOSAL 3. **5** *have in one's disposition* disposal, power, authority, control, direction, management. See DISPOSAL 5.

dispossess *verb* **1** *dispossess them of their property* deprive, divest, strip, bereave. **2** *dispossess the tenants* dislodge, oust, eject, drive out, evict, turn out, dismiss.

disproportionate *adjective* *heads disproportionate to bodies | a reaction disproportionate to the danger* out of proportion, not in proportion, not commensurate, unbalanced, uneven, unequal, irregular, relatively too large/long/much, relatively too small/short/little, excessive, unreasonable.

disprove *verb* prove false, invalidate, refute, give the lie to, negate, rebut, confute, deny, contradict, controvert, discredit, expose.

disputable *adjective* debatable, open to discussion, arguable, contestable, controvertible, moot, open to question, questionable, doubtful.

disputation *noun* *a disputation ensued | open to disputation* debate, dispute; argumentation, altercation, dissension; polemics.

disputatious *adjective* disputative, argumentative, contentious, captious, quarrelsome, litigious, polemical.

dispute *verb* **1** *dispute with colleagues | dispute over what to do* debate, discuss, argue, disagree, have an altercation, altercate, clash, quarrel, wrangle, bicker, squabble. **2** *dispute his right to go* question, call into question, challenge, contest, deny, doubt, contradict, object to, oppose, controvert, impugn, gainsay.
Opposites AGREE; CONFIRM.

dispute *noun* **1** *open to dispute* debate, discussion, argument, controversy, contention, disagreement, altercation, dissension, conflict, friction, strife, discord, litigation. **2** *have a dispute over boundaries* argument, row, altercation, clash, quarrel, wrangle, squabble, feud, disturbance, fracas, brawl.

disqualify *verb* *disqualify the runner* declare ineligible, rule out, preclude, debar, prohibit, disentitle.

disquiet *noun* disquietude, inquietude, uneasiness, unease, unrest, anxiety, anxiousness, angst, nervousness, agitation, perturbation, upset, worry, concern, distress, trouble, alarm, fear, fretfulness, restlessness, dread, foreboding.

disquiet *verb* make uneasy/anxious/nervous, agitate, perturb, upset, disturb, unsettle, discompose, ruffle, worry, concern, distress, trouble, bother, alarm, frighten, make fretful/restless, vex.

disregard *verb* **1** *disregard the consequences* ignore, take no notice/account of, pay no attention/heed to, discount, set aside, neglect, forget, never mind, overlook, turn a blind eye to, pass over, gloss over, brush aside, laugh off, make light of; *inf.* play down. **2** *disregard the neighbours | disregard their achievement* slight, disparage, denigrate, disdain, despise, shun, cold shoulder, insult, affront; *inf.* turn one's nose up at.

disregard *noun* **1** *treat danger with disregard* lack of notice/attention/heed, inattention, heedlessness, carelessness, neglect, negligence, indifference. **2** *treat staff/achievements with disregard* scorn, contempt, disparagement, denigration, disdain, disrespect, disesteem.

disrepair *noun* dilapidation, deterioration, decay, collapse, shabbiness, ruin, ruination, decrepitude.

disreputable *adjective* **1** *disreputable dealer* of bad reputation, infamous, dishonourable, dishonest, unprincipled, villainous, notorious, ignominious, corrupt, unworthy, base, low, mean, questionable, unsavoury, unscrupulous, rascally, contemptible, reprehensible, despicable, discreditable, disgraceful, shameful, shocking, outrageous, scandalous; *inf.* crooked, shady. **2** *of disreputable appearance* shabby, slovenly, down-at-heel, seedy, dilapidated, threadbare, untidy, dishevelled, bedraggled; *inf.* scruffy.

disrepute *noun* *fall into disrepute* bad reputation, lack of respectability, notoriety, discredit, ill repute, unpopularity, disfavour, ill favour, disesteem, disgrace, shame, dishonour, infamy, ignominy, degradation, odium, opprobrium, obloquy.

disrespect *noun* lack of respect, discourtesy, lack of civility, incivility, impoliteness, unmannerliness, rudeness, ungraciousness, irreverence, lack of consideration, disregard, insolence, impudence, cheek, churlishness, scorn, contempt; ill manners.

disrespectful *adjective* discourteous, uncivil, impolite, unmannerly, ill-mannered, rude, irreverent, inconsiderate, insolent, impudent, impertinent, cheeky, churlish, scornful, contemptuous, insulting.

disrupt *verb* **1** *disrupt the meeting/traffic* throw into disorder/disarray, disorder, disorganize, cause confusion/turmoil in, disarrange, disturb, upset, interrupt, suspend, discontinue, interfere with, obstruct, impede, hamper; *inf.*

throw a spanner in the works. **2** *disrupt the capsule* break open/apart, shatter, split, sever, separate, cleave, split asunder, sunder, rive, rend.
Opposites ORGANIZE; ARRANGE.

disruption *noun the disruption of meetings/services* disorderliness, disorder, disorganization, confusion, turmoil, disarrangement, disarray, disturbance, upset, interruption, suspension, discontinuation, stoppage, interference, obstruction, impeding, hampering.

disruptive *adjective disruptive children* troublemaking, troublesome, divisive, unruly, disorderly, undisciplined, obstreperous, upsetting, disturbing, distracting, noisy.

dissatisfaction *noun* discontent, discontentment, disapproval, disapprobation, disappointment, frustration, unhappiness, regret, chagrin, dismay, vexation, annoyance, irritation, anger, exasperation, resentment, disquiet, restlessness, malaise, *Weltschmerz*.

dissatisfied *adjective* discontented, displeased, disgruntled, disapproving, unsatisfied, disappointed, unfulfilled, frustrated, unhappy, regretful, vexed, angry, resentful, restless. *See* DISSATISFACTION.

dissect *verb* **1** *dissect the corpse* cut up, cut/lay open, dismember, anatomize, vivisect. **2** *dissect the information* analyse, break down, examine, study, inspect, scrutinize, probe, explore, investigate.

dissection *noun* **1** *dissection of the corpse* cutting up, cutting open, dismemberment; anatomy, vivisection, autopsy, post-mortem, zootomy. **2** *the dissection of the information* analysis, breakdown, examination, study, inspection, scrutinization, probing, exploration, investigation.

disseminate *verb disseminate ideas/seeds* spread, circulate, broadcast, publish, publicize, proclaim, promulgate, propagate, dissipate, scatter, distribute, disperse, diffuse, bruit abroad.

dissension *noun* disagreement, difference of opinion, dispute, argument, dissent, nonconformity, variance, conflict, friction, strife, discord, contention, quarrelling, wrangling, bickering.

dissent *verb* **1** *dissent from official policy* express disagreement with, disagree with, differ from, be at variance with, decline/refuse, to support, not ratify, protest against, object to, dispute. **2** *dissent from the established Church practices* reject, repudiate, renounce, abjure, secede from, apostatize.
Opposites ASSENT; ACCEPT.

dissenter *noun* dissident, objector, protester, protestant, disputant, rebel, revolutionary, non-conformist, recusant, apostate, sectarian, heretic.

dissentient *adjective* dissenting, dissident, disagreeing, differing, protesting, objecting, opposing, non-conformist, non-compliant, recusant, apostate, schismatic, unorthodox, heterodox.

dissertation *noun* treatise, thesis, discourse, essay, critique, exposition, disquisition.

disservice *noun* bad/ill turn, dirty trick, disfavour, unkindness, injury, harm, hurt, damage, wrong, injustice; *inf.* kick in the teeth.

dissident *adjective dissident opinions in the organizations* dissentient, dissenting, disagreeing, differing, non-conformist, recusant, apostate, schismatic, heterodox. *See* DISSENTIENT.

dissident *noun expelling dissidents from the party* dissenter, rebel, objector, protester, nonconformist, recusant, apostate, heretic. *See* DISSENTER.

dissimilar *adjective* unlike, unalike, different, varying, variant, disparate, unrelated, divergent, deviating, diverse, various, contrasting, mismatched, distinct.

dissimilarity *noun* difference, unlikeness, dissimilitude, variance, disparity, unrelatedness, discrepancy, divergence, deviation, diversity, variation, non-uniformity, contrast, distinction, incomparability.

dissipate *verb* **1** *dissipate one's fears* disperse, scatter, drive away, dispel, dissolve. **2** *the crowd dissipated* break up, disperse, scatter, dissolve, disappear, vanish, melt away, melt into thin air, evaporate. **3** *dissipate their resources* squander, fritter, misspend, lavish, waste, exhaust, drain, deplete, spend, expend, burn up, use up, consume, run through.
Opposites ASSEMBLE; CONSERVE.

dissipated *adjective* **1** *a dissipated young man* dissolute, debauched, intemperate, profligate, abandoned, rakish, licentious, promiscuous, drunken, self-indulgent, wild, unrestrained, wanton, depraved, degenerate, corrupt. **2** *dissipated resources* squandered, frittered away, wasted, exhausted, depleted, consumed. *See* DISSIPATE 3.

dissociate *verb* **1** *dissociate his actions from his theories* separate, set apart, segregate, isolate, detach, disconnect, sever, divorce. **2** *dissociate the teams* disband, break up, dissolve, disperse, scatter, dismiss. **dissociate oneself from** sever connections with, break off relations with, withdraw from, part company with, quit, take one's leave of.

dissolute *adjective* debauched, dissipated, intemperate, profligate, abandoned, rakish, licentious, promiscuous, drunken, self-indulgent, wild, unrestrained, depraved, degenerate, corrupt. *See* DISSIPATED.

dissolution *noun* **1** *the dissolution of salt in water* dissolving, liquefaction, melting, deliquescence. **2** *the dissolution of the compound* breaking up, separation, resolution, decomposition, disintegration. **3** *the dissolution of the Roman empire* breaking up, disintegration, decay, collapse, death, demise, extinction, destruction, ruin, overthrow. **4** *the dissolution of hopes* disappearance, vanishing, evaporation, dwindling, dispersal, dissipation, evanescence. *See* DISSOLVE 3. **5** *the dissolution of the partnership/marriage* end, ending, finish, termination, conclusion, breakup, discontinuation, winding-up, disbanding, suspension. **6** *the dissolution of the societies/crowds* disbandment, separation, dispersal, scattering. *See* DISSOLVE 5. **7** *the dissolution of the rich young people* debauchery,

dissipation, intemperance, profligacy, abandonment, licentiousness, promiscuity, drunkenness, self-indulgence, wildness, lack of
restraint, depravity, degeneracy, corruption.

dissolve verb **1** *salt dissolves in water* go into
solution, liquefy, melt, deliquesce. **2** *dissolve
the salt in water* liquefy, melt, form into a solution, solvate. **3** *his hopes dissolved* disappear,
vanish, melt away, evaporate, dwindle, disperse, dissipate, disintegrate, crumble, decompose, perish, die, evanesce. **4** *dissolve a
partnership/society* bring to an end, end, terminate, break up, discontinue, wind up, disband,
dismiss, suspend, ruin. **5** *the societies/crowds
dissolved* break up, split up, disband, separate,
sever, disunite, disjoin, disperse, scatter, go
their separate ways. **6** *dissolve in tears/mirth*
break into, collapse into, be overcome with.

dissonance noun **1** *the dissonance of the music*
discordance, inharmoniousness, unmelodious-
ness, cacophony, harshness, stridency, grating,
jarring, jangle. **2** *the dissonance between their
actions and theories* disagreement, difference,
dissimilarity, variance, inconsistency, disparity, discrepancy, incongruity. **3** *the dissonance
between the families* discord, disagreement, difference of opinion, dissension, quarrelling,
wrangling, feuding.

dissuade verb persuade/advise against, per-
suade/advise/urge not to, put off, stop; talk out
of, discourage/deter from, divert, turn aside
from, disincline from.

distance noun **1** *the distance between the fields*
space, interval, span, gap, separation, stretch,
extent; length, width, depth. **2** *the distance of
the farm from the town* remoteness, farness.
3 *upset by her colleague's distance* aloofness,
reserve, remoteness, reticence, coolness, coldness, frigidity, stiffness, formality, restraint,
unresponsiveness. See DISTANT 6. **in the distance**
far away, far off, on the horizon, just in view,
afar, yonder.

distance verb **1** *distance oneself from the organization* place far-off, set apart, separate, dissociate, remove. **2** *distance the rest of the runners*
outdistance, outstrip, outrun, leave behind,
pass, outdo, surpass.

distant adjective **1** *a distant place* far, far-away,
far-off, remote, out of the way, outlying,
abroad, far-flung. **2** *a distant time* far-off, long
ago. **3** *three miles distant from each other* away,
off, apart, separated, dispersed, scattered. **4** *a
distant relative/likeness* not close, remote, indirect, slight. **5** *a distant memory* vague, faint,
indistinct, obscure, uncertain. **6** *a distant smile*
aloof, reserved, remote, uncommunicative,
unapproachable, stand-offish, withdrawn, reticent, restrained, cool, cold, frigid, stiff, formal,
ceremonious, unresponsive, unfriendly,
haughty, condescending.
Opposites NEAR; RECENT; FRIENDLY; approachable.

distaste noun dislike, displeasure, disfavour,
disinclination, dissatisfaction, disrelish, aversion, disgust, revulsion, repugnance, antipathy, loathing, detestation, horror.

distasteful adjective **1** *distasteful behaviour*
unpleasant, disagreeable, displeasing, undesir-

able, off-putting, uninviting, objectionable,
offensive, obnoxious, unsavoury, disgusting,
revolting, repugnant, abhorrent, loathsome,
detestable. **2** *distasteful food* unpalatable,
unsavoury, unappetizing, disgusting, sickening, nauseating, nauseous.

distended adjective enlarged, swollen, puffed-
up, puffy, inflated, ballooning, bloated, dilated,
stretched, expanded, extended, tumescent.

distil verb **1** *distil fresh water from sea water*
vaporize/evaporate and condense, sublime,
sublimate, fractionate. **2** *distil the essence from
a plant* extract, press out, squeeze out, express,
draw out. **3** *distil the chemical* separate, concentrate, purify, refine, rectify. **4** *distilling
beads of liquid* exude, give out, drip, leak, dribble.

distillation noun essence, extract, spirit, quintessence, elixir.

distinct adjective **1** *a distinct resemblance* clear,
clear-cut, well-defined, sharp, marked, decided,
definite, unmistakable, recognizable, obvious,
plain, plain as day, evident, apparent, manifest, patent, palpable, unambiguous, unequivocal. **2** *two distinct jobs* separate, individual,
different, unconnected, unassociated,
detached, discrete, dissimilar, unalike, disparate.
Opposites INDISTINCT; INDEFINITE; VAGUE.

distinction noun **1** *make the distinction between
right and wrong* differentiation, contradistinction, discrimination, division, separation,
dividing line, contrast. **2** *fail to notice the identifying distinctions* difference, dissimilarity, dissimilitude, contrast, differential, subtlety,
nicety, nuance. **3** *the distinctions of wealth and
rank* feature, characteristic, mark, individuality, peculiarity. **4** *pass the exam with distinction*
honour, credit, excellence, merit. **5** *people of
distinction* note, consequence, importance,
account, significance, greatness, prestige,
prominence, eminence, repute, reputation,
renown, fame, mark, celebrity, honour, merit,
worth, excellence, glory, name, rank, quality,
superiority.

distinctive adjective distinguishing, characteristic, typical, individual, particular, peculiar,
special, different, uncommon, unusual,
remarkable, singular, extraordinary, noteworthy, original, idiosyncratic.
Opposites ORDINARY; RUN-OF-THE-MILL.

distinctly adverb **1** *distinctly annoyed* clearly,
markedly, decidedly, definitely, unmistakably,
obviously, plainly, evidently, apparently, manifestly, patently, palpably. **2** *speak distinctly*
clearly, plainly, intelligibly, precisely.

distinguish verb **1** *distinguish one colour from
another* tell apart, differentiate, discriminate,
determine; tell the difference between, decide
between. **2** *his hair distinguishes him from the
others* make distinctive, set apart, separate, single out, mark off, characterize, individualize,
designate, categorize, classify. **3** *distinguish a
black shape* make out, see, discern, perceive,
observe, notice, detect, recognize, identify,
pick out, descry, apprehend, espy. **4** *distinguish himself in battle* make famous, bring fame/

honour to, bestow honour on, ennoble, dignify, glorify, win acclaim for, lionize, immortalize.

distinguishable *adjective no distinguishable difference* clear, plainly seen, obvious, evident, marked, well-defined, conspicuous, noticeable, discernible, perceptible, recognizable, manifest.

distinguished *adjective a distinguished scientist* famous, famed, eminent, renowned, prominent, well-known, noted, notable, esteemed, acclaimed, illustrious, celebrated, respected, legendary.
Opposites UNKNOWN; OBSCURE.

distinguishing *adjective a distinguishing mark* distinctive, differentiating, discriminating, determining, individualistic, peculiar, singular, characteristic, typical.

distort *verb* **1** *distort the metal | distort their features* twist, warp, contort, bend, buckle, deform, misshape, disfigure, mangle, wrench, wring, wrest. **2** *distort the facts* misrepresent, pervert, twist, falsify, garble, slant, bias, colour, tamper with, alter, change, torture.

distortion *noun* **1** *a distortion in the metal* twist, warp, contortion, bend, buckle, curvature, deformation, deformity, malformation, gnarl, knot; crookedness. **2** *a distortion of the truth* misrepresentation, perversion, twisting, falsification, garbling, colouring, alteration; slant, bias, change.

distract *verb* **1** *distract them from work* deflect, divert, sidetrack, turn aside, draw away. **2** *distract the children* amuse, entertain, divert, beguile, absorb, engage, occupy. **3** *bright lights distracting her* confuse, bewilder, perplex, puzzle, disturb, fluster, agitate, disconcert, discompose, confound, annoy, trouble, harass, worry, torment; *inf.* hassle. **4** *grief distracting her* make frantic, drive/make mad, madden, drive insane, make crazy, derange, throw into a frenzy.

distracted *adjective* **1** *rushing around in a distracted way* confused, bewildered, bemused, perplexed, agitated, flustered, troubled, harassed, worried; *inf.* hassled, in a flap. *See* DISTRACT 3. **2** *distracted women mourning their sons* grief-stricken, distraught, frantic, frenzied, raving, wild, hysterical, overwrought, mad, maddened, insane, crazed, deranged, out of one's mind.

distraction *noun* **1** *distraction from their work* diversion, interruption, disturbance, interference, obstruction. **2** *distractions laid on for the children* amusement, entertainment, diversion, pastime, recreation, hobby, game, occupation, divertissement. **3** *the distraction of the child at the crowds* confusion, bewilderment, befuddlement, perplexity, disturbance, agitation, perturbation, harassment. *See* DISTRACT 3. **4** *pity the distraction of the widow* frenzy, hysteria, mental distress, madness, insanity, crazedness, mania, derangement, delirium, alienation.

distress *noun* **1** *the lost child's distress* anguish, suffering, pain, agony, ache, affliction, torment, torture, misery, wretchedness, discomfort, heartache, heartbreak, sorrow, grief, woe,

sadness, desolation, trouble, worry, anxiety, perturbation, uneasiness, angst; tribulations, cries, wails. **2** *old people in distress* hardship, adversity, misfortune, trouble, calamity, need, want, poverty, lack, privation, destitution, indigence, impoverishment, penury, beggary; difficulties, dire straits.

distress *verb* **1** *the news distressed her* cause anguish/suffering, pain, upset, make miserable/wretched, grieve, sadden, trouble, worry, bother, arouse anxiety in, perturb, disturb, vex, harrow, torment. **2** *distress the furniture* damage, spoil, dent, scratch, simulate age/wear in.

distressing *adjective distressing news/sights* disturbing, worrying, upsetting, affecting, painful, sad, heartbreaking.

distribute *verb* **1** *distribute rations to the crowd* give out, hand out, allocate, allot, issue, dispense, administer, apportion, assign, deal out, share out, divide out, dole out, measure out, mete out, parcel out, dispose. **2** *distribute advertising leaflets* circulate, pass round, hand out, deliver, convey, transmit. **3** *distribute seeds evenly* disseminate, disperse, diffuse, scatter, spread, strew, sow. **4** *luggage distributed in categories* place, position, arrange, organize, dispose, group, class, classify, categorize, file, assort, compart, locate.

distribution *noun* **1** *distribution of rations* giving out, allocation, allotment, dispensation, administering, assignment, dealing out, division. *See* DISTRIBUTE 1. **2** *distribution of seeds* dissemination, dispersal, diffusion, scattering. *See* DISTRIBUTE 3. **3** *the distribution of luggage in categories* placement, position, arrangement, organization, disposition, grouping, classification, assortment, location. *See* DISTRIBUTE 4. **4** *in charge of sales and distribution* handling, delivery, transport, transportation, conveyance, mailing. **5** *an abnormal statistical distribution* frequency/probability of occurrence, prevalence, incidence.

district *noun* **1** *live in a pleasant district* area, region, place, locality, neighbourhood, quarter, sector, vicinity, territory, domain. **2** *an administrative district* administrative division, ward, parish, community, constituency, department, canton.

distrust *verb* mistrust, be suspicious of, be wary/chary of, be sceptical of, have doubts about, doubt, have misgivings about, wonder about, question, suspect, disbelieve, discredit; *inf.* be leery of.

distrust *noun* mistrust, lack of trust, no confidence, lack of faith, suspicion, wariness, chariness, scepticism, doubt, doubtfulness, dubiety, misgiving, questioning, qualms, disbelief, unbelief, incredulity, incredulousness, discredit; *inf.* leeriness.

disturb *verb* **1** *disturb them while they are working* interrupt, butt in on, distract, bother, trouble, pester, intrude on, interfere with, hinder, plague, harass, molest; *inf.* hassle. **2** *disturb papers on a desk* disarrange, muddle, disorganize, disorder, confuse, throw into disorder/confusion, derange, unsettle. **3** *the news disturbed* *them* concern, perturb, trouble, worry, upset, agitate, fluster, discomfit, disconcert, alarm, frighten, startle, dismay, distress, discompose, unsettle, ruffle, shake, confuse, bewilder, perplex, confound, excite. **4** *disturb the water* agitate, churn up, convulse, roil. **5** *don't disturb yourself* inconvenience, put out, put to trouble.

disturbance *noun* **1** *resent the disturbance to their work* interruption, distraction, intrusion, interference, hindrance, harassment. See DISTURB 1. **2** *the disturbance of papers* disarrangement, muddling, disorganization, confusing; muddle, disorder, confusion. **3** *causing emotional disturbance* concern, perturbation, trouble, worry, upset, agitation, discomfiture, alarm, distress, bewilderment. See DISTURB 3. **4** *the disturbance of the water* agitation, churning. See DISTURB 4. **5** *police called to a disturbance* uproar, commotion, row, rumpus, hullabaloo, tumult, turmoil, fracas, affray, brawl, riot; *inf.* ruction; *Am. inf.* ruckus.

disturbed *adjective* *emotionally disturbed* upset, troubled, unbalanced, disordered, maladjusted, neurotic, psychotic; *inf.* screwed up.

disturbing *adjective* *disturbing news* perturbing, troubling, worrying, upsetting, agitating, disconcerting, alarming, disquieting, startling, dismaying, frightening, distressing, unsettling, bewildering. See DISTURB 3.

disuse *noun* non-use, non-employment, lack of use, desuetude, neglect, abandonment, cessation, discontinuance, obsolescence.

disused *adjective* unused, neglected, abandoned, discontinued, obsolete.

ditch *noun* trench, channel, watercourse, dyke, canal, drain, gutter, gully, moat, furrow, rut.

ditch *verb* **1** *be engaged in digging and ditching* dig, trench, excavate, gouge, hollow out, drain. **2** *ditch the plan* abandon, throw out, discard, drop, scrap, jettison, get rid of, dispose of; *inf.* dump. **3** *ditch the police* evade, escape, elude, shake off, defeat, frustrate, baulk.

diurnal *adjective* **1** *a diurnal occurrence* daily, occurring every day, daytime, quotidian, circadian. **2** *a diurnal flower/animal* of the day, daytime, non-nocturnal.

divan *noun* day bed. See table at BED.

dive *verb* **1** *dive from the springboard* plunge/descend into water, go/jump into water, plummet, jump, leap, bound, spring, nosedive, fall, descend, submerge, drop, swoop, dip, pitch, bellyflop. **2** *dive out of sight* move quickly, leap, jump, lunge, rush, dart, dash, duck, dodge.

dive *noun* **1** *a dive from the springboard* plunge, plummet, jump, leap, spring, nosedive, fall, drop, swoop, bellyflop. **2** *a quick dive under the bed* leap, jump, lunge, rush, dart, dash, duck, dodge. **3** *drinking in dives* sleazy bar/nightclub; *inf.* drinking-joint, drinking-den, low joint, dump.

diverge *verb* **1** *the roads diverged* separate, divide, subdivide, split, part, disunite, fork, branch off, radiate, spread out, bifurcate, divaricate, ramify. **2** *opinions diverge* differ, disagree, be at variance/odds, conflict, clash.

3 *diverge from the norm* deviate, digress, depart, veer, stray, drift, turn aside, wander, divagate. **Opposites** JOIN; CONVERGE; AGREE; STAY.

divergence *noun* **1** *the divergence of the roads* separation, dividing, parting, forking, branching, bifurcation; fork, division. See DIVERGE 1. **2** *divergence of opinions* difference, disagreement, variance, varying, conflict. See DIVERGE 2. **3** *divergence from the norm* deviation, digression, departure, straying, deflection, divagation.

divergent *adjective* **1** *divergent opinions* differing, different, diverse, disagreeing, in disagreement, varying, conflicting, clashing, dissenting. **2** *divergent statistical results* deviating, digressing, abnormal, aberrant, divagating. **Opposites** SIMILAR; NORMAL.

divers *adjective* several, numerous, many, some; sundry, various, different, manifold.

diverse *adjective* various, miscellaneous, assorted, mixed, diversified, variegated, varied, varying, heterogeneous, different, differing, distinct, unlike, dissimilar, distinctive, contrasting, conflicting. **Opposites** IDENTICAL; SIMILAR; LIKE.

diversify *verb* **1** *diversify the range* vary, bring variety to, variegate, modify, assort, mix, alter, change, transform. **2** *firms must diversify* extend operations/products, expand, spread.

diversion *noun* **1** *the diversion of the stream* redirection, turning aside, deflection, digression, deviation, divergence. **2** *take the diversion* alternative route, detour. **3** *diversions provided for the children* amusement, entertainment, pastime, distraction, recreation, fun, relaxation, game, play, sport, hobby, pleasure, delight, enjoyment, beguilement, enchantment, divertissement.

diversity *noun* *diversity of opinion* diverseness, variety, miscellany, assortment, mixture, range, medley, multiplicity, variegation, heterogeneity, diversification, difference, unlikeness, dissimilarity, distinctiveness, dissimilitude, contrast, conflict.

divert *verb* **1** *divert the stream* turn aside, deflect, draw away, avert, switch/change the course of, redirect. **2** *divert him from his work* distract, detract, sidetrack, lead away, turn aside, deflect. **3** *clowns diverting the children* amuse, entertain, distract, delight, give pleasure to, beguile, enchant, interest, occupy, absorb, engross, recreate.

diverting *adjective* amusing, entertaining, humorous, fun, enjoyable, pleasurable, recreational, beguiling, interesting, absorbing.

divest *verb* **1** *divest them of their clothes | divested himself of his coat* unclothe, undress, disrobe, strip, denude; take off, remove, doff. **2** *divest them of power/property* deprive, strip, dispossess, relieve, bereave, despoil.

divide *verb* **1** *divide the rope in two | divide one group from another* cut up, sever, split, shear, bisect, halve, quarter, cleave, rend, sunder, rive; separate, part, segregate, partition, detach, disconnect, disjoin. **2** *the road divides here* diverge, branch, fork, split in two, divaricate. **3** *divide the food* share out, allocate, allot,

apportion, portion out, distribute, dispense, deal out, hand out, dole out, measure out, parcel out. **4** *politics divided them* estrange, alienate, break up, separate, spilt up, disunite, disaffect, set/pit against one another, cause disagreement between, sow dissension between, set at variance/odds, come between. **5** *divide into types* classify, sort, arrange, order, group, grade, rank, categorize, dispose, separate, segregate.
Opposites JOIN; UNITE; COMBINE.

dividend *noun* **1** *dividends paid to shareholders* share, portion, gain, surplus; *inf.* cut, divvy. **2** *dividends brought by hard work* bonus, extra, plus, benefit, fringe benefit, perquisite; *inf.* perk.

divine *adjective* **1** *a divine being* godly, godlike, heavenly, celestial, holy, angelic, seraphic, spiritual, saintly. **2** *divine worship* religious, holy, sacred, sanctified, consecrated, spiritual. **3** *divine music* supernatural, superhuman, mystical, exalted, beatific, blissful, ethereal, transcendental, transcendent, transmundane. **4** *looking divine | a divine evening* lovely, beautiful, charming, perfect, excellent, superlative, wonderful, glorious, marvellous, admirable; *inf.* super, stunning.
Opposites MORTAL; HELLISH; MUNDANE; UGLY.

divine *noun* theologian, clergyman, churchman, churchwoman, cleric, ecclesiastic. *See tables at* ECCLESIASTIC, PRIEST.

divine *verb* **1** *divine their plans | divine that they are going* guess, surmise, conjecture, speculate, suspect, suppose, assume, presume, deduce, infer, theorize, hypothesize. **2** *divine their need* intuit, discern, perceive, understand, grasp, apprehend, comprehend. **3** *divine the future* foretell, predict, foresee, forecast, presage, augur, portend, prognosticate, forebode. **4** *divine for water* dowse.

divinity *noun* **1** *the divinity of the being* divine nature, divineness, deity, godhead, godliness, holiness, sanctity. **2** *worship the divinity* deity, god, goddess, genius, spirit, guardian, angel, daemon. *See table at* GOD. **3** *study divinity* theology, religious studies, religion, scripture.

division *noun* **1** *the division of the rope/groups* dividing, cutting up, severance, splitting, bisection, cleaving; parting, separation, segregation, partitioning, disconnection, detachment. *See* DIVIDE 1. **2** *the division of rations* sharing out, allocation, allotment, apportionment, distribution. *See* DIVIDE 3. **3** *cross the division* dividing line, divide, boundary, boundary line, border, partition, line of demarcation. **4** *divisions of equal size* section, part, portion, piece, bit, segment, slice, fragment, chunk, component, share; compartment, category, class, group, grade, family. **5** *divisions of the firm* branch, department, section, sector, arm. **6** *a bitter division between the families* disagreement, difference of opinion, feud, breach, rupture, split; dissension, conflict, discord, variance, disunion, estrangement, alienation.

divisive *adjective* alienating, estranging, disruptive, troublemaking, troublesome, detrimental, damaging, injurious, pernicious, discordant, inharmonious.

divorce *noun* **1** *marriage ended in divorce* dissolution, disunion, breakup, split-up, annulment, official separation, separation, severance, breach, rupture. **2** *the divorce between their theories and their actions* separation, severance, division, split, partition.

divorce *verb* **1** *the couple divorced* annul/dissolve a marriage, split up, break up, separate, part. **2** *she divorced him* end a marriage with/to, have a marriage annulled/dissolved. **3** *views are divorced from reality* separate, disconnect, divide, dissociate, detach, disunite, sever, disjoin, split, sunder.
Opposites MARRY; CONNECT; JOIN.

divulge *verb* disclose, reveal, make known, tell, impart, communicate, publish, broadcast, proclaim, promulgate, declare, utter, expose, uncover, bring into the open, let slip, leak, let the cat out of the bag about, confess, betray; *inf.* spill the beans about.

dizzy *adjective* **1** *get dizzy on top of the ladder* giddy, light-headed, faint, vertiginous, weak at the knees, shaky, wobbly, off-balance, reeling, staggering; *inf.* woozy. **2** *feeling dizzy at the amount of information* dazed, bewildered, confused, muddled, bemused, befuddled, puzzled, perplexed; *inf.* woozy. **3** *dizzy heights/speeds* giddy-making, vertiginous, bewildering. **4** *dizzy young girls* giddy, scatterbrained, feather-brained, flighty, foolish, silly, light-headed, fickle, capricious, inconstant.

do *verb* **1** *do as you would be done by* act, behave, conduct oneself, comport oneself. **2** *do the job* perform, carry out, undertake, discharge, execute, accomplish, implement, achieve, complete, finish, conclude, bring about, effect, effectuate, realize, produce, engineer. **3** *this amount will do* be enough, be sufficient, be adequate, suffice, be satisfactory, be of use, fill/fit the bill, answer/serve the purpose, meet the needs, pass muster, measure up. **4** *do the meals* make, prepare, get ready, fix, produce, see to, arrange, organize, be responsible for, be in charge of, look after, take on. **5** *do a large picture* create, make, produce, originate, form, fashion, design, fabricate, manufacture. **6** *they're doing three plays* put on, perform, act, present, produce, give. **7** *do me a favour* render, afford, give, bestow, grant, pay. **8** *can't do this maths problem* solve, resolve, work out, puzzle out, figure out, decipher. **9** *what does he do?* work at, be employed at, have as a job/profession/occupation, earn a living at. **10** *how are you doing?* get on/along, progress, fare, make out, manage, continue. **11** *the play was done in Russian* translate, put, render, adapt, transform. **12** *the car was doing 90 mph* travel at, go/proceed at, be driven at. **13** *we did 50 miles* travel, journey, cover, traverse. **14** *they're doing Edinburgh today* sightsee, look at, visit, tour; *inf.* rubberneck. **15** *the crooked shopkeeper did us* cheat, defraud, swindle, fleece, bilk, trick, deceive, dupe, take advantage of, hoax, take one for a ride; *lit.* cozen. **16** *the journey did me in* tire out, exhaust, wear out, fatigue; *inf.* do in, fag out, shatter. **17** *the thieves did the pub last night* burgle, rob, break into. **do away with 1** *do away with the penalty* abolish, get rid of, discard, remove, discontinue, eliminate, repeal, revoke, rescind, cancel, annul, nullify. **2** *do away with his enemy* kill, put to death, slay, murder, slaughter, liquidate, assassinate, execute, dispatch; *inf.* do in, bump off, knock off, eliminate. **do in 1** *do in his enemy* kill, put to death, slay, murder, assassinate; *inf.* do away with, bump off. **2** *do in his business* ruin, reduce to nothing, wreck, destroy, smash, crush, wreak havoc on. **3** *the walk did me in* tire out, exhaust, wear out, fatigue, weary; *inf.* fag out, shatter, do. **do out of** prevent from having, deprive of, swindle/cheat/trick out of; *inf.* con/diddle out of. **do without** forgo, dispense with, abstain from, give up, refrain from, eschew.

do *noun* party, function, affair, event, occasion, fête, soirée; *inf.* beanfeast, bash, blow-out, rave-up, thrash, knees-up.

docile *adjective* manageable, controllable, tractable, malleable, manipulable, amenable, accommodating, compliant, pliant, obedient, biddable, dutiful, submissive, yielding, ductile. **Opposites** DISOBEDIENT; WILFUL; INTRACTABLE.

dock *noun tie up at the dock* pier, quay, wharf, jetty, marina, waterfront.

dock *verb* **1** *dock the dogs' tails* cut, cut short, shorten, crop, lop, truncate. **2** *dock money from wages* deduct, subtract, remove, take off. **3** *dock their wages* reduce, decrease, lessen, diminish.

docket *noun the docket with the package* document, documentation, paperwork, chit, chitty, certificate, counterfoil, label, tag, ticket, tab, bill, receipt.

docket *verb docket the package* document, label, tag, tab, mark, ticket.

doctor *noun* medical practitioner, physician, medical man/woman/person; general practitioner, GP, hospital doctor, consultant, house doctor, registrar, senior registrar; *inf.* doc, quack. *See table.*

doctor *verb* **1** *doctor the patients* treat, prescribe for, attend to, minister to, care for, cure, heal. **2** *doctor the machinery* patch up, repair, fix, mend, botch, cobble. **3** *doctor the drinks* adulterate, contaminate, dilute, water down, weaken, mix, cut, lace; *inf.* spike. **4** *doctor the evidence* tamper with, interfere with,

alter, change, falsify, disguise, fudge, pervert, misrepresent.

doctrinaire *adjective* **1** *doctrinaire teachers* dogmatic, authoritarian, rigid, inflexible, insistent, domineering, opinionated, intolerant, biased, prejudiced, fanatical. **2** *doctrinaire schemes* impractical, unpragmatic, unrealistic, theoretical, hypothetical, ideological, speculative, visionary.

doctrine *noun* creed, credo, dogma, belief, conviction, teaching; tenet, principle, precept, maxim; articles of faith, canons.

document *noun business documents* official paper, legal paper, paper, form, certificate, record, report, deed, voucher, instrument, charter; paperwork, documentation.

document *verb* **1** *document their statement* prove, back up, support, give weight to, corroborate, substantiate, authenticate, verify, validate, certify. **2** *the war was well documented in the press | his marriage is not documented* report, record, detail, tabulate, chart, register, cite, instance.

documentary *adjective* **1** *documentary evidence* documented, recorded, registered, tabulated, charted, written. **2** *a documentary film* factual, non-fictional, real-life, true to life, realistic.

dodder *verb* totter, teeter, stagger, shuffle, shamble, falter, shake, tremble, quiver.

doddering *adjective* doddery, tottering, tottery, staggering, shuffling, shambling, faltering, shaky, unsteady, trembling, trembly, quivering, infirm, decrepit, aged, in one's dotage, senile.

dodge *verb* **1** *dodge behind the door* dart, duck, dive, swerve, sidestep, veer, jump away, move aside. **2** *dodge the police* evade, elude, escape, fend off, avoid, stay/steer clear of, deceive, trick; *inf.* give the slip to. **3** *dodge awkward questions* evade, get out of, parry, fend off, fudge. **4** *dodge hard work* avoid, evade, shirk, shun, stay/steer clear of.

dodge *noun* **1** *a dodge to the right* dart, duck, dive, swerve, jump. **2** *a dodge to avoid work | a tax dodge* ruse, ploy, scheme, stratagem, subterfuge, trick, wile, deception, manoeuvre, device, machination, contrivance, artifice, expedient; sharp practice; *inf.* wheeze.

TYPES OF DOCTOR AND DENTIST

anaesthesiologist *Am.*	ENT (ear, nose, and throat) doctor	neurosurgeon	pathologist
anaesthetist	epidemiologist	nosologist	periodontist
aurist	exodontist	obstetrician	plastic
brain	forensic pathologist	oncologist	surgeon
surgeon	gastroenterologist	ophthalmologist	podiatrist
cardiologist	geriatrician	orthodondist	prosthodontist
chiropractor	gerontologist	orthopaedist	radiologist
chiropodist	gynaecologist	osteologist	radiotherapist
dentist	haematologist	otolaryngologist	rheumatologist
dermatologist	heart surgeon	otologist	serologist
diagnostician	immunologist	otorhino-	surgeon
endocrinologist	nephrologist	laryngologist	teratologist
endodontist	neurologist	paediatrician	urologist
		paedondontist	venereologist

doer · doing

doer *noun* **1** *the doer of the deed* performer, executor, accomplisher, effectuator. **2** *doers rather than thinkers* worker, organizer, achiever, high achiever, activist, hustler, entrepreneur; *inf.* busy bee, live wire, go-getter, whizz kid, powerhouse, wheeler-dealer.

doff *verb* **1** *doff their hats* raise, lift, remove, take off, touch, tip. **2** *doff their clothes* take off, remove, shed, strip off, throw off, cast off.

dog *noun* **1** *cats and dogs* canine, hound, mongrel, cur, tyke; bitch, male dog, pup, puppy, whelp; *inf.* doggy, pooch, mutt. *See table.* **2** *he's a dirty dog* scoundrel, blackguard, beast, cad, rogue, villain, cur, knave, heel, bastard. **3** *a lucky dog* person, fellow; *inf.* chap, guy. **4** *dogs related to the domesticated breeds* wild dog, wolf, fox. *See tables at* FOX, WOLF.

dog *verb* *dogged by ill luck* pursue, follow, track, trail, shadow, hound, plague, trouble, haunt; *inf* tail.

dogged *adjective* determined, resolute, obstinate, stubborn, tenacious, relentless, intent, single-minded, unshakable, unflagging, indefatigable, tireless, unfaltering, unwavering, persistent, persevering, pertinacious, unyielding, obdurate, firm, steadfast, steady, staunch. **Opposites** HESITANT; HALF-HEARTED.

doggedness *noun* determination, resolution, obstinacy, stubborness, tenacity, relentlessness, single-mindedness, tirelessness, persis-tence, perseverance, pertinacity, obdurance, endurance, steadfastness, steadiness. *See* DOGGED.

dogma *noun* **1** *Christian dogma* creed, credo, code of belief, conviction, teaching; belief, tenet, principle, precept, maxim; articles of faith, canons. **2** *tired of political dogma* unquestioned belief, unchallengeable conviction, arrogant conviction.

dogmatic *adjective* **1** *dogmatic papal statements* doctrinal, doctrinaire, canonical, authoritative, *ex cathedra*, oracular. **2** *dogmatic denial/attitude/youth* assertive, insistent, emphatic, categorical, downright, authoritarian, opinionated, peremptory, domineering, imperious, arrogant, overbearing, dictatorial, intolerant, biased, prejudiced; *inf.* pushy.

dogsbody *noun* skivvy, drudge, slave, menial, general factotum, man/maid of all work.

doing *noun* **1** *the doing of the deed* performance, carrying out, discharging, execution, accomplishment, implementation, achievement, effectuation, realization. **2** *famous for brave doings* deed, act, action, feat, exploit, work, enterprise, achievement; handiwork. **3** *take a lot of doing* effort, activity, exertion, work, application, struggle. **4** *get a doing from his father* beating, thrashing, thumping, battering, castigation, scolding.

BREEDS OF DOG

Aberdeen terrier	collie	Kerry blue terrier	Rhodesian ridgeback
affenpinscher	coonhound	King Charles spaniel	Rottweiler
Afghan hound	corgi	Komondor	St Bernard
Airedale terrier	dachshund	Kuvasz	saluki
akita	Dalmatian	Labrador retriever	Samoyed
Alaskan malamute	Dandie Dinmont	laika	schipperke
Alsatian	terrier	Lakeland terrier	schnauzer
Australian terrier	deerhound	Leonberg	Scottish
basenji	Doberman	Lhasa apso	deerhound
basset hound	pinscher	Malamute	Scottish terrier
beagle	elk-hound	Maltese dog/terrier	Sealyham terrier
Bedlington terrier	English setter	Manchester terrier	setter
Bernese mountain	field spaniel	mastiff	Shetland sheepdog
dog	Finnish spitz	Mexican hairless	shih-tzu
Blenheim spaniel	foxhound	Newfoundland	Skye terrier
bloodhound	fox terrier	Norfolk terrier	spaniel
Border collie	golden retriever	Norwich terrier	spitz
borzoi	Gordon setter	Old English sheep-	springer spaniel
Boston terrier	Great Dane	dog	Staffordshire bull
Bouvier des	greyhound	otter-hound	terrier
Flandres	griffon	papillon	staghound
boxer	Groenendael	Pekinese	terrier
Briard	harrier	Pharaoh hound	tosa
Brussels griffon	husky	pit bull terrier	vizsla
bulldog	Ibicencan hound	pointer	Weimaraner
bull mastiff	Ibizan hound	Pomeranian	Welsh corgi
bull terrier	Irish setter	poodle	Welsh hound
cairn terrier	Irish terrier	pug	Welsh terrier
Cavalier King	Irish wolfhound	puli	West Highland
Charles spaniel	Ivicene	Pyrenean mountain	terrier
chihuahua	Istrian pointer	dog	whippet
chow	Jack Russell terrier	Pyrenean sheepdog	wire-haired fox
Clumber spaniel	keeshond	Pyrenean wolfhound	terrier
cocker spaniel	kelpie	retriever	Yorkshire terrier

doings *plural noun* *have you got the doings for the repair?* necessary thing/part, relevant equipment, needful, doodah, thingumajig, thingummy, thingumabob, what's its name, what d'you call it; *inf.* doofer.

doldrums *plural noun* **1** *a fit of the doldrums* downheartedness, dejection, depression, melancholy, gloom, inertia, apathy, listlessness, malaise, boredom, tedium, ennui; blues, low spirits. **2** *a business in the doldrums* inactivity, inertia, flatness, stagnation, dullness, sluggishness, torpor.

dole *noun* **1** *redundant workers receiving the dole* unemployment benefit, benefit, social security, welfare; *Scots* buroo. **2** *dole given grudgingly to the poor* alms; charity, benefit; gift, donation, allowance, grant, portion, pittance, mite.

dole *verb* **dole out** deal out, allocate, allot, apportion, share out, mete out, distribute, divide up, dispense, hand out, give out, issue, assign, administer.

doleful *adjective* mournful, sorrowful, sad, dejected, disconsolate, depressed, gloomy, melancholy, blue, miserable, wretched; *inf.* down in the mouth/dumps.
Opposites CHEERFUL; JOYFUL; HAPPY.

doll *noun* figure, figurine, model, puppet, marionette, toy, plaything; *inf.* dolly.

dolphin *noun.* See table at WHALE.

dolour *noun* sorrow, grief, sadness, heartache, anguish, misery, distress, suffering.

dolt *noun* blockhead, dunderhead, thickhead, numskull, nitwit, dunce, fool, idiot, ass, simpleton, nincompoop, ignoramus, dullard, booby; *inf.* dope, chump, clot, dimwit, nerd; *Am. inf.* airhead, meatball.

domain *noun* **1** *the king's domain* realm, kingdom, empire, dominion, estate. See DOMINION 2. **2** *working in the scientific domain* area, field, region, province, sphere, section, discipline.

dome *noun* cupola, rotunda; hemisphere.

domestic *adjective* **1** *an unhappy domestic life | domestic water supply* home, family, household, domiciliary, private. **2** *preferring domestic people* domesticated, housewifely, stay-at-home, home-loving, homely. **3** *a domestic animal* domesticated, tame, pet, house-trained, trained, not wild. **4** *domestic markets* home, internal, not foreign, not export. **5** *domestic plants* native, indigenous, home-grown, home-bred, aboriginal, autochthonous.
Opposites PUBLIC; WILD; FOREIGN.

domestic *noun* employ a domestic domestic help, help, maid, domestic servant, servant, charwoman, daily help, daily, au pair, home help, menial, skivvy; *Am.* hired help.

domesticate *verb* **1** *domesticate an animal* tame, house-train, train, break in, gentle. **2** *domesticate a foreign tree* naturalize, acclimatize, habituate, accustom, familiarize, assimilate.

domesticated *adjective* **1** *domesticated animals* tame, tamed, pet, house-trained, broken-in. **2** *domesticated plants* naturalized, acclimatized, habituated. **3** *domesticated people* domestic,

housewifely; *inf.* house-trained. See DOMESTIC *adjective* 2.

domicile *noun* home, house, residence, residency, dwelling, dwelling-place, abode, habitation, lodging, accommodation.

domicile *verb* *they are domiciled in Switzerland* establish, settle, make one's home, take up one's abode, ensconce oneself.

dominant *adjective* **1** *the dominant member of the committee* ruling, governing, controlling, commanding, ascendant, presiding, supreme, authoritative, most influential, superior, most assertive, domineering. **2** *the dominant issue* predominant, most important, chief, main, principal, leading, primary, paramount, pre-eminent, outstanding, prominent, prevailing.
Opposites SUBMISSIVE; SUBSERVIENT.

dominate *verb* **1** *dominate the council* rule, govern, control, exercise control over, command, direct, preside over, have ascendancy/mastery over, master, domineer, tyrannize, intimidate, have the upper/whip hand over, ride roughshod over; have under one's thumb, be in the driver's seat, be in the saddle, wear the trousers; *inf.* boss, call the shouts. **2** *hostility/silence dominated* predominate, be paramount, be pre-eminent, prevail, be conspicuous, be most obvious, be most important. **3** *the hill dominates the town* overlook, tower above, stand over, project/jut over, hang/loom over, bestride.

domination *noun* *under foreign domination* rule, government, control, command, direction, authority, power, mastery, supremacy, sway, tyranny, intimidation, oppression, dictatorship.

domineer *verb* browbeat, bully, intimidate, hector, lord it over, tyrannize, be overbearing, ride roughshod over, trample on, have under one's thumb, rule with an iron hand, rule with a rod of iron, bend to one's will, subjugate; *inf.* boss around/about.

domineering *adjective* overbearing, imperious, authoritarian, high-handed, autocratic, peremptory, arrogant, haughty, dictatorial, masterful, forceful, coercive, tyrannical, despotic, oppressive, subjugating, iron-fisted, iron-handed; *inf.* bossy, pushy.
Opposites MEEK; SERVILE.

dominion *noun* **1** *have dominion over smaller states* supremacy, ascendancy, sway, mastery, rule, government, sovereignty, jurisdiction, control, command, direction, authority, power, domination, the upper/whip hand, overlordship, suzerainty. **2** *the king's dominions* realm, kingdom, empire, domain, country, province, territory, region, estate.

don *verb* put on, slip on, slip into, get into, pull on, dress/clothe/accoutre oneself in, rig oneself out in.
Opposites DOFF.

don *noun* university teacher/lecturer, college tutor, academic, scholar, pedagogue; *inf.* egghead.

donate *verb* give, contribute, make a contribution of, subscribe, make a gift of, gift, present, pledge, put oneself down for, bestow; *inf.* chip in; *Am. inf.* kick in.

donation *noun* contribution, subscription, gift, present, grant, offering, gratuity; alms; charity, benefaction, largesse.

done *adjective* **1** *the job is done* accomplished, complete, completed, executed, perfected, finished, ended, concluded, terminated, realized, consummated. **2** *the meat is done* cooked, ready. **3** *our store of logs is done* finished, used up, exhausted, depleted, spent. **4** *feeling done after the walk* worn out, exhausted, tired out, weary; *inf.* done in. *See* DONE *adjective* done in. **5** *such behaviour is not done* acceptable, proper, seemly, decorous, conventional, *de rigueur*. **6** *we were done by the shopkeeper* swindled, cheated, tricked, deceived, duped, hoodwinked; *inf.* conned, taken for a ride. **be done with** *See* DONE *adjective* have done with. **done for** finished, ruined, destroyed, broken, wrecked, undone, dashed, dead, doomed, lost, defeated, beaten, foiled, frustrated, thwarted; *inf.* washed-up. **done in** worn out, exhausted, tired out, weary, fatigued, played out, on one's last legs, fit to drop; *inf.* done, dog-tired, all in, dead beat, shattered, knackered, fagged out, bushed, pooped, worn to a frazzle. **have done with** be finished/through with, have no further dealings with, be no longer involved with/in, end relations with, give up, wash one's hands of.

done *interjection* *You're offering £10? Done!* agreed, settled, that's a bargain, accepted, right; *inf.* OK, you're on.

donkey *noun* **1** *an overloaded donkey* jackass, jack, jenny; *inf.* moke. *See table.* **2** *a silly donkey* fool, ass, idiot, nincompoop, nitwit, blockhead, dolt; *inf.* dope, chump, nerd.

ASSES AND DONKEYS		
burro	kulan	quagga
hinny	mule	zebra
kiang	onager	

donnish *adjective* scholarly, scholastic, pedagogic, erudite, bookish, pedantic.

donor *noun* giver, contributor, donator, grantor, benefactor, benefactress, supporter, backer, philanthropist; *inf.* angel.

doom *noun* **1** *what doom has in store* terrible/grim fate, destiny, fortune, lot, portion. **2** *companies/people facing doom* ruin, ruination, rack and ruin, downfall, destruction, catastrophe, disaster, extinction, annihilation, death, termination, quietus. **3** *the prisoner hearing his doom* condemnation, guilty verdict, sentence, judgement, pronouncement, decree, damnation. **4** *predicting doom* the Last Judgement, Judgement Day, doomsday, Armageddon, end of the world.

doom *verb* **1** *children doomed to be poor* fate, destine, predestine, ordain, preordain, foreordain, consign, condemn. **2** *prisoners doomed to die* condemn, sentence, judge, pronounce, decree, damn.

doomed *adjective* *doomed plans/lovers* ill-fated, star-crossed, foredoomed, unlucky, damned, bedevilled, ruined, crushed.

door *noun* **1** *wooden doors* doorway, portal, entrance, entry, exit, barrier; front door, back door, side door, cupboard door, sliding door, revolving door, trapdoor. **2** *doors to academic success* entrance, entry, access, opening, entrée, gateway, way, path, road, ingress. **out of doors** outside, outdoors, out, in/into the open air, alfresco.

dope *noun* **1** *smuggling dope* drugs, narcotics. *See* DRUG *noun* 2. **2** *a stupid dope* dolt, blockhead, dunderhead, thickhead, dunce, fool, idiot, nincompoop, nitwit; *inf.* chump, dimwit, nerd. **3** *give the dope on the situation* information, inside information, story, news; facts, data, details; *inf.* info, gen, low-down.

dope *verb* **1** *dope the hostage/horse* drug, administer drugs/narcotics/opiates to, knock out, anaesthetize, stupefy, sedate, narcotize. **2** *dope his drink* add drugs/narcotics/opiates to, doctor; *inf.* spike.

dormant *adjective* sleeping, asleep, slumbering, inactive, inert, latent, fallow, quiescent, inoperative, hibernating, comatose, stagnant, sluggish, lethargic, torpid, passive, motionless, immobile.
Opposites AWAKE; ACTIVE.

dose *noun* **1** *a dose of cough mixture* amount, quantity, measure, portion, draught. **2** *a dose of flu* bout, attack, spell.

dot *noun* spot, speck, fleck, point, mark, dab, particle, atom, iota, jot, mote, mite; full stop, decimal point. **on the dot** *3 o'clock on the dot | arrive on the dot* exactly, precisely, to the minute, on time, punctually, promptly; *inf.* on the button.

dot *verb* **1** *dotted with stains/ships* spot, fleck, bespeckle, mark, dab, stud, bestud, stipple, pock, freckle, sprinkle, scatter, pepper. **2** *dot the letters* mark with a dot, add a dot to, punctuate.

dotage *noun* senility, old age, caducity, second childhood, decrepitude, infirmity, feebleness; declining years.

dote *verb* *she dotes on/upon her grandchildren* idolize, adore, hold dear, love dearly, treasure, prize, make much of, lavish affection on, indulge, spoil, pamper.

doting *adjective* adoring, devoted, loving, fond, indulgent, pampering.

double *adjective* **1** *double yellow lines | a double eggcup* duplicate, twin, paired, in pairs, dual, coupled, twofold, binal, binate. **2** *a double portion* doubled, twice as much/many as usual, twofold, large. **3** *a double thickness* doubled, twofold, folded, folded in two, two-ply. **4** *a double meaning* dual, ambiguous, double-edged, two-edged, ambivalent, equivocal. **5** *a double life* dual, deceitful, false, dishonest, hypocritical, insincere, double-dealing, two-faced, treacherous, perfidious, Janus-faced.
Opposites SINGLE.

double *adverb* **1** *seeing double* two together, two at a time, in twos, by twos, two by two.

2 *pay double* twice, twice over, twice the amount.

double *verb* **1** *double the amount* multiply by two, increase twofold, enlarge, magnify. **2** *double as a bed and sofa* have/serve a dual purpose, have a dual role. **3** *he doubled for the main part | she doubles in the musical* be an understudy/subsitute, understudy; act two roles/ parts. **4** *double paper* fold, bend over.

double *noun the double of his cousin | the double of the other picture* look-alike, twin, clone, *doppelgänger*, duplicate, replica, copy, facsimile, counterpart, match, mate, fellow; *inf.* spitting image, dead spit/ringer, ringer. **at/on the double** at full speed, as fast as possible, very quickly, rapidly, briskly, with haste, in double-quick time, post-haste, right away, immediately, without delay, straight away; *inf.* p.d.q. (= pretty damn quick).

double-cross *verb* betray, cheat, defraud, trick, hoodwink, mislead, deceive, swindle; *inf.* two-time, take for a ride.

double-dealing *noun* duplicity, treachery, betrayal, double-crossing, bad faith, perfidy, breach of trust, fraud, fraudulence, underhandedness, cheating, dishonesty, untrustworthiness, mendacity, deception, trickery, deceit, two-facedness, hypocrisy; *inf.* crookedness.

double entendre *noun* ambiguity, double meaning, suggested meaning, innuendo, play on words, wordplay, pun.

doubt *verb* **1** *doubt his motives* have/entertain doubts about, be suspicious of, harbour suspicions about, suspect, distrust, mistrust, lack confidence in, have misgivings about, feel uneasy/apprehensive about, call in question, query, question. **2** *doubt that it is genuine* have doubts, be dubious, hesitate to believe, feel uncertain, be undecided, lack conviction, have scruples, query, question, challenge. **3** *still doubting last week* have doubts, be undecided, hesitate, waver, vacillate, demur.

doubt *noun* **1** *have doubts about his motives* distrust, mistrust, lack of confidence/faith, scepticism, uneasiness, apprehension; reservations, misgivings, suspicions, qualms. **2** *express doubt that it is genuine* dubiety, dubiousness, lack of certainty, uncertainty, indecision, lack of conviction, incredulity; queries, questions. **3** *full of doubts/doubt about his faith* uncertainty, indecision, hesitation; hesitancy, wavering, vacillation, irresolution, lack of conviction, demurral. **in doubt** *the issue is still in doubt | he is in doubt about it* doubtful, uncertain, undecided, unsettled, unresolved, confused, open to question, ambiguous, problematic; in a quandary/dilemma. **no doubt** *no doubt he will win* doubtless, certainly, of course, surely, assuredly, admittedly, probably, it is likely that.
Opposites TRUST; CONFIDENCE; CERTAINTY.

doubter *noun* sceptic, questioner, disbeliever, doubting Thomas, unbeliever, agnostic, scoffer, dissenter, pessimist, doomster.

doubtful *adjective* **1** *it is doubtful that he will come* in doubt, uncertain, unsure, unconfirmed, unsettled, improbable, unlikely.

2 *doubtful of/about his motives* suspicious, distrustful, mistrustful, sceptical, having reservations/misgivings, apprehensive, uneasy, questioning, unsure, incredulous. **3** *its genuineness is doubtful* uncertain, dubious, open to question, questionable, debatable, disputable, not definite, inconclusive, unresolved, unconfirmed, unsettled. **4** *the meaning of the word is doubtful* dubious, unclear, ambiguous, equivocal, obscure, vague, nebulous. **5** *doubtful about his religious convictions* uncertain, indecisive, hesitating, irresolute, wavering, vacillating. **6** *mixing with doubtful people* dubious, questionable, suspicious, suspect, under suspicion, unreliable, potentially disreputable.
Opposites CERTAIN; SURE; CLEAR.

doubtless *adverb* undoubtedly, without doubt, no doubt, of course, certainly, truly, assuredly, surely, positively, beyond a doubt, unquestionably, indisputably, clearly, obviously, very probably, very/most likely, presumably.

dour *adjective* unsmiling, sullen, morose, sour, gruff, churlish, uncommunicative, unfriendly, forbidding, grim, stern, severe, austere, harsh, dismal, dreary, gloomy.
Opposites CHEERFUL; FRIENDLY; SOCIABLE.

douse, dowse *verb* **1** *douse the walls with soapy water* drench, saturate, soak, souse, flood, deluge, wet, splash, hose down. **2** *douse the clothes in the tub* plunge, immerse, submerge, dip, dunk. **3** *douse the light* extinguish, put out, blow out, qench, snuff.

dovetail *verb* **1** *dovetail the pieces of wood* join, unite, fit, fit together, link, interlock, splice, mortise, tenon. **2** *our plans dovetailed with theirs* fit in, go together, coincide, go hand in glove, fall in, correspond, concur, agree, tally, accord, harmonize.

dowdy *adjective dowdy clothes/people* frumpish, frumpy, drab, dull, old-fashioned, unfashionable, not smart, inelegant, shabby, untidy, dingy, frowzy; *inf.* tacky.
Opposites CHIC; FASHIONABLE.

down¹ *adverb* **1** *the lift going down* to a lower point/part, to a low point, in a lower place/ position. **2** *fall down* to the ground, to the floor, below, beneath.

down² *preposition* **1** *walk down the street* to a lower part of, along, through. **2** *down the centuries* through, throughout.

down³ *adjective* **1** *feeling down* downcast, downhearted, dejected, depressed, sad, unhappy, miserable, wretched, low, blue, gloomy, melancholy; *inf.* down in the mouth/ dumps. **2** *the computer is down* not working, non-functioning, inoperative.

down⁴ *verb* **1** *down three of the enemy* knock/ throw/bring down, floor, fell, prostrate, tackle, trip up, overthrow, defeat, conquer, subdue. **2** *down three pints* drink, gulp down, swallow, drain, toss off, put away; *inf.* swill.

down⁵ *noun* having a down | ups and downs* fit/ period of depression, unpleasant time, reversal, setback, comedown. **have a down on** be against, be prejudiced against, be set against, bear a grudge towards, show antagonism to, be hostile to, show/feel ill-will towards.

down[6] *noun* fluff, fuzz, bloom, soft feathers, fine hair.

down-at-heel *adjective* shabby, shabbily-dressed, poorly-dresed, out-at-elbows, seedy, run-down, slovenly, slipshod.

downbeat *adjective* **1** *bored and downbeat down*, downcast, low, depressed, dejected, miserable, gloomy, pessimistic. **2** *talk in a down-beat manner* relaxed, nonchalant, casual, non-emphatic, insouciant, blasé; *inf.* laid-back.

downcast *adjective* *downcast at the news* disheartened, dispirited, downhearted, dejected, depressed, discouraged, daunted, dismayed, disappointed, disconsolate, crestfallen, despondent, sad, unhappy, miserable, wretched, down, low, blue, gloomy, glum, melancholy, sorrowful, doleful, mournful.

downfall *noun* **1** *the downfall of the leader* loss of power/prestige/wealth, fall, collapse, undoing, ruin, ruination, crash, destruction, debasement, degradation, disgrace, overthrow, defeat. **2** *soaked in a downfall* downpour, rainstorm, snowstorm, heavy rain/snow, deluge, cloudburst. *See* DOWNPOUR.
Opposites RISE; SUCCESS.

downgrade *verb* **1** *downgrade the office-bearers* demote, reduce in rank, remove from office, degrade, humble, debase; *inf.* take down a peg or two. **2** *downgrade their achievement* disparage, denigrate, detract from, run down, decry, belittle, make light of, minimize, defame; *Am. inf.* bad-mouth.

downhearted *adjective* disheartened, dispirited, downcast, dejected, depressed, discouraged, daunted, dismayed, disappointed, disconsolate, crestfallen, despondent. *See* DOWNCAST.

downpour *noun* rainstorm, snowstorm, deluge, torrential/pouring rain, cloudburst, downfall; torrents of rain.

downright *adjective* **1** *a downright lie* complete, total, absolute, out and out, outright, utter, sheer, thorough, thoroughgoing, categorical, unmitigated, unqualified, unconditional, positive, simple, wholesale, all out, arrant, rank. **2** *a very downright person* frank, forthright, straightforward, open, candid, plain-spoken, matter-of-fact, outspoken, blunt, bluff, brusque.

downright *adverb* *downright rude* completely, totally, absolutely, utterly, thoroughly, profoundly, categorically, positively.

down-to-earth *adjective* practical, sensible, realistic, matter-of-fact, no-nonsense, hard-headed, sane, mundane, unromantic, unidealistic.
Opposites ROMANTIC; IDEALISTIC; DREAMY.

downtrodden *adjective* oppressed, burdened, weighed down, overwhelmed, tyrannized, ground down, under the heel, helpless, powerless, prostrate, poor, miserable, wretched, distressed.

downward *adjective* going down, moving down, descending, sliding down, earthbound.

dowry *noun* marriage portion/settlement, *dot*; *Scots* tocher.

doze *verb* sleep lightly, nap, take a nap, catnap, slumber, take a siesta; *inf.* nod off, drift off, snooze, have a snooze, snatch forty winks, kip, get some kip/shut-eye, zizz, have a zizz.

drab *adjective* **1** *drab clothes/surroundings* dull, dull-coloured, colourless, mousy, dun-coloured, grey, greyish, dingy, dreary, dismal, cheerless, gloomy, sombre, depressing. **2** *a drab talk* uninteresting, boring, tedious, dry, dreary, lifeless, lacklustre, uninspired; *Scots inf.* dreich.
Opposites BRIGHT; GAUDY; CHEERFUL; INTERESTING.

draft *noun* **1** *a draft of the speech* preliminary version, rough sketch, outline, plan, skeleton, abstract. **2** *a draft of the new building* plan, sketch, drawing, line drawing, diagram, blueprint, delineation. **3** *a bank draft* money order, cheque, bill of exchange, postal order.

drag *verb* **1** *drag the body from the sea* haul, pull, draw, tug, yank, trail, tow, lug. **2** *time dragged* go/move slowly, creep/limp along, crawl, go at a snail's pace. **3** *the film dragged* | *his lecture dragged on* go on too long, go on and on, become tedious. **drag out** *drag out the lecture* protract, prolong, draw out, spin out, stretch out, lengthen, extend.

drag *noun* *the child/job is a drag* nuisance, source of annoyance, pest, trouble, bother, bore; *inf.* pain in the neck.

dragoon *noun* cavalryman, mounted soldier.

dragoon *verb* *dragoon them into helping* force, coerce, compel, drive, impel, constrain, browbeat, bully, tyrannize; *inf.* strong-arm, put the screws on.

drain *verb* **1** *drain the water from the tank* draw off, extract, withdraw, remove, pump off, milk, bleed, tap, filter. **2** *drain the tank* empty, void, evacuate. **3** *the liquid drained away* flow out, ooze, trickle, seep out, well out, leak, discharge, exude, effuse. **4** *legal costs draining resources* use up, exhaust, deplete, consume, expend, empty, sap, strain, tax, bleed. **5** *drain a drink* drink up, finish, gulp down, swallow, quaff; *inf.* down.

drain *noun* **1** *a sewage drain* channel, conduit, culvert, duct, gutter, sewer, trench, ditch, dyke, pipe, outlet. **2** *a drain on resources* exhaustion, depletion, consumption, expenditure, outflow, sapping, strain, tax.

drama *noun* **1** *studying drama* dramatic art, stagecraft, theatre, acting, dramaturgy, dramatics. *See table at* THEATRE. **2** *a Restoration drama* play, show; stage play, screenplay, radio play, television play, stage show, theatrical work, theatrical piece. *See table at* PLAY. **3** *the drama at the police station* exciting/emotional scene, thrilling/tense/sensational spectacle, excitement, crisis; dramatics, theatrics, histrionics.

dramatic *adjective* **1** *dramatic art* theatrical, stage, dramaturgic, Thespian. **2** *dramatic scenes in court* exciting, sensational, spectacular, startling, unexpected, thrilling, tense, suspenseful, electrifying, stirring, affecting. **3** *a dramatic view/description* striking, impressive, vivid, spectacular, breath-taking, moving, affecting, emotive, graphic, effective, powerful. **4** *a dramatic gesture* theatrical, artificial, exaggerated, overdone, stagy, histrionic.

dramatist *noun* playwright, scriptwriter, screenwriter, tragedy writer, comedy writer, dramaturgist, dramaturge. *See table at* PLAY-WRIGHT.

dramatize *verb* **1** *dramatize the novel* turn/adapt into a play, make a stage/screen play of, put into dramatic form. **2** *dramatize the incident* exaggerate, make a drama/performance of, overdo, overstate; *inf.* lay it on thick, ham up.

drape *verb* **1** *drape the walls in tapestry* cover, envelope, swathe, blanket, overlay, cloak, veil, shroud, decorate, adorn, array, deck, festoon. **2** *drape a shawl round her* hang, arrange, let fall in folds. **3** *drape an arm on the chair* hang, let fall, place loosely, lean, dangle, droop.

drastic *adjective* extreme, severe, desperate, dire, radical, harsh, sharp, forceful, rigorous, Draconian.
Opposites MILD; MODERATE.

draw *verb* **1** *draw a chair up | draw the table away* pull, haul, tow, trail, tug, yank, lug. **2** *draw alongside/level | drew to a close* move, go, come, proceed, approach. **3** *draw a sword/gun* pull out, take out, bring out, extract, withdraw, produce, unsheathe. **4** *draw curtains* shut, close, pull together. **5** *draw attention | draw large crowds* attract, allure, lure, entice, invite, engage, interest, win, catch the eye of, capture, captivate, fascinate, tempt, seduce. **6** *draw a breath* breathe in, inhale, suck in, inspire, respire. **7** *draw a salary* take, take in, receive, be in receipt of, get, procure, obtain, earn. **8** *draw a conclusion* deduce, infer, conclude, derive, gather, glean. **9** *draw liquid* drain, siphon off, pump off, tap, milk, bleed, filtrate. **10** *draw lots/straws* choose, pick, select, opt for, make a choice of, decide on, single out. **11** *draw a house | she loved to draw in the garden* make a drawing of, sketch, make a picture/diagram of, portray, delineate, represent, trace, map out, mark out, chart, paint, design; make drawings/pictures. **12** *draw a document* compose, formulate, write out. *See* DRAW *verb* draw up 2. **draw on** *draw on experience* make use of, use, have recourse to, exploit, employ, rely on, back on. **draw out 1** *draw out a gun* pull out. *See* DRAW *verb* 3. **2** *draw out the talk* prolong, protract, extend, lengthen, stretch out, drag out, spin out, make go on and on. **3** *draw the child out* induce to talk, persuade to speak, put at ease. **draw up 1** *draw up at the kerb* pull up, come to a halt/stop, halt, stop, rein in. **2** *draw up a document | draw up a set of rules* compose, formulate, frame, write out, put in writing, put down on paper, draft, prepare. **3** *troops drawn up for battle* arrange, put into position, order, marshal, range, rank.

draw *noun* **1** *the draw of the circus* attraction, lure, allure, pull, enticement, magnetism. **2** *there will be a draw at the dance* lottery, raffle, sweepstake. **3** *the match ended in a draw* tie, dead heat, stalemate.

drawback *noun* disadvantage, snag, catch, problem, difficulty, trouble, flaw, stumbling-block, hitch, handicap, hindrance, obstacle, impediment, hurdle, obstruction, barrier, curb, check, discouragement, deterrent, damper, inconvenience, nuisance, detriment, fault, weak spot, weakness, imperfection, defect; *inf.* fly in the ointment.
Opposites ADVANTAGE; BENEFIT.

drawing *noun* sketch, picture, illustration, representation, portrayal, delineation, depiction, composition, study, diagram, outline.

drawl *verb* speak slowly, draw out one's vowels/speech, twang, drone.

drawn *adjective* *pale and drawn* pinched, haggard, hollow-cheeked, strained, tense, taut, stressed, fraught, fatigued, tired, worn, drained, wan, sapped.

dread *verb* *dread the bully's arrival* fear, be afraid of, be terrified by, worry about, be anxious about, have forebodings about, tremble/shudder about, cringe/shrink from, quail/cower/flinch from; *inf.* have cold feet about, be in a blue funk about.

dread *noun* fear, fearfulness, fright, alarm, terror, apprehension, trepidation, horror, anxiety, concern, foreboding, dismay, perturbation, trembling, shuddering, flinching; *inf.* blue funk, heebie-jeebies. *See* DREAD *verb*.

dread *adjective* *the dread monster/exams* dreaded, feared, frightening, alarming, terrifying, frightful, terrible, horrible, dreadful, awful, dire, awesome.

dreadful *adjective* **1** *a dreadful sight/accident* terrible, frightful, horrible, grim, awful, dire, frightening, terrifying, alarming, distressing, shocking, appalling, harrowing, ghastly, fearful, hideous, horrendous, gruesome, tragic, calamitous, grievous. **2** *a dreadful man to deal with | dreadful weather spoiled the picnic* nasty, unpleasant, disagreeable, frightful, shocking, very bad, distasteful, repugnant, odious. **3** *a dreadful waste of time* shocking, outrageous, inordinate, great, tremendous.
Opposites PLEASANT; AGREEABLE.

dream *noun* **1** *saw his mother in a dream* dream sequence, nightmare; vision, fantasy, hallucination. *See* DREAM *verb* 1, 2. **2** *his dream to become rich* ambition, aspiration, goal, design, plan, aim, hope, yearning, desire, wish, notion, daydream, fantasy; castles in the air, castles in Spain. **3** *the bride was a dream* beauty, vision of loveliness, vision, delight, pleasure to behold, joy, marvel. **4** *go around in a dream* daydream, reverie, state of unreality, trance, daze, stupor; *Scots* dwam.

dream *verb* **1** *dream at night* have dreams/nightmares. **2** *he thought he saw a ghost but he was dreaming* hallucinate, have a vision, imagine things, fantasize. **3** *she was dreaming instead of working* daydream, be in a trance/reverie, be lost in thought, muse, be preoccupied, be abstracted. **4** *not dream of upsetting them | never dream that they would go* think, consider, visualize, conceive, suppose. **dream up** *dream up new schemes* conjure up, think up, invent, concoct, devise, create, hatch, fabricate; *inf.* cook up.

dreamer *noun* daydreamer, visionary, fantasist, fantasizer, fantast, romantic, romancer, idealist, impractical/unrealistic person, theorizer, Utopian, Don Quixote.

dreamland *noun* **1** *existing only in dreamland* land of make-believe, never-never land, fairy-. land, world of fantasy, cloudland, cloud-cuckoo-land. **2** *children in dreamland* sleep, slumber, land of Nod.

dreamy *adjective* **1** *a dreamy person* visionary, fanciful, fantasizing, romantic, idealistic, impractical, unrealistic, theorizing, daydreaming, quixotic. **2** *in a dreamy mood* daydreaming, thoughtful, lost in thought, pensive, speculative, preoccupied, abstracted, absent-minded, in a brown study, with one's head in the clouds. **3** *a dreamy recollection of the events* dreamlike, vague, dim, hazy, shadowy, misty, faint, indistinct, unclear. **4** *dreamy music* romantic, relaxing, soothing, calming, lulling, gentle, tranquil, peaceful. **5** *a dreamy young man | a dreamy dress* wonderful, marvellous, terrific, fabulous, heavenly; *inf.* fab, wicked.
Opposites PRACTICAL; DOWN-TO-EARTH.

dreary *adjective* **1** *a dreary day* gloomy, dismal, bleak, sombre, dull, dark, overcast, depressing. **2** *lead a dreary life* dull, drab, uninteresting, flat, dry, colourless, lifeless, tedious, wearisome, boring, humdrum, routine, monotonous, uneventful, run-of-the-mill, prosaic, commonplace, unvaried, repetitive. **3** *in a dreary frame of mind* gloomy, glum, sad, miserable, wretched, downcast, dejected, depressed, despondent, doleful, mournful, melancholic.
Opposites BRIGHT; INTERESTING; CHEERFUL.

dregs *plural noun* **1** *the dregs of the wine* sediment, deposit, residue, residuum, precipitate, sublimate, scum, debris, dross, detritus, refuse, draff; lees, grounds, scourings. **2** *the dregs of society* scum, riff-raff, rabble, refuse; down-and-outs, good-for-nothings, outcasts, dead-beats, tramps, vagrants.

drench *verb* soak, saturate, permeate, drown, inundate, flood, steep, douse, souse, wet, slosh.

dress *noun* **1** *wearing a black dress* frock, gown, garment, robe. *See table.* **2** *with her dress in disarray* clothes, garments; clothing, attire, apparel, costume, outfit, ensemble, garb; *inf.* gear, rig-out, get-up, togs, duds; *fml.* habiliment. **3** *birds/trees in their winter dress* covering, outer covering, plumage, feathers, pelt.

DRESSES		
backless dress	kimono	shamma
ballgown	little black dress	shirt-dress
cheongsam	maternity dress	shirt-waister
cocktail dress	maxidress	strapless dress
dinner gown	minidress	sundress
djellaba	muu-muu	tea gown
evening gown	overdress	tube dress
gymslip	pinafore dress	wedding dress
kaftan	sarong sari	yukata

dress *verb* **1** *she was dressed in black* clothe, attire, garb, fit out, turn out, array, apparel, robe, accoutre. **2** *she dressed quickly* put on clothes, don clothes, slip into clothes. **3** *dress for dinner* change, wear formal clothes, put on evening dress. **4** *dress the Christmas tree* decorate, adorn, ornament, trim, furbish, deck, bedeck, embellish, array, rig, drape; *inf.* trick out. **5** *dress poultry* prepare, get ready, clean. **6** *dress one's hair* comb, arrange, do, groom, put in order, straighten, adjust, preen; *inf.* fix. **7** *dress a wound* cover, bandage, bind up, put a plaster on. **8** *dress troops* line up, put in line, align, straighten, arrange, put into order, dispose, set out. **9** *dress land/soil* till, cultivate, work, dig, plough, fertilize, manure. **dress down** reprimand, scold, upbraid, rebuke, reprove, berate, castigate, haul over the coals; *inf.* tell off, carpet. **dress up 1** *dress up for the occasion* dress formally/smartly, wear evening dress; *inf.* doll oneself up, dress to the nines, put on one's glad rags. **2** *dress the child up* dress smartly; *inf.* doll up. **3** *dress up the plain garment | dress the room up* decorate, adorn, ornament, trim, embellish, titivate, beautify, prettify. **4** *dress up as Santa Claus | dress up for the fancy dress party* put on fancy dress, put on a disguise, disguise oneself, wear disguise.
Opposites UNDRESS; STRIP.

dressing *noun* **1** *a dressing for the salad/fish* relish, sauce, condiment; oil and vinegar, French dressing. **2** *put a dressing on the wound* covering, bandage, plaster, gauze; Elastoplast™. **3** *a top dressing on the soil* fertilizer, manure; dung.

dressmaker *noun* couturier, tailor, tailoress, modiste, seamstress, needlewoman.

dribble *verb* **1** *water dribbling from the tap* drip, trickle, fall in drops, drop, leak, ooze, exude, seep. **2** *the baby's dribbling* drool, slaver, slobber; *Scots* slabber.

dribble *noun* *a dribble of water* trickle, drip, small stream.

drift *verb* **1** *boats/leaves drifting along* be carried along/away, be borne, be wafted, float, go with the current, coast. **2** *people drifting about* wander aimlessly, wander, roam, rove, meander, coast, stray. **3** *snow drifting* pile up, bank up, accumulate, gather, form heaps, amass.

drift *noun* **1** *a drift to the right* movement, deviation, digression, variation. **2** *the drift of his argument* gist, essence, meaning, substance, core, significance, import, purport, tenor, vein, implication, direction, course, tendency, trend. **3** *a snow drift* pile, heap, bank, mound, mass, accumulation.

drill *verb* **1** *drill the new recruits* train, instruct, coach, teach, ground, inculcate, discipline, exercise, rehearse, put one through one's paces. **2** *drill the wood* bore/make a hole in, bore, pierce, puncture, penetrate, perforate.

drill *noun* **1** *military drill* training, instruction, coaching, teaching, grounding, indoctrination. *See* DRILL *verb* 1. **2** *children doing drill* exercises, physical exercises; strict training, workout. **3** *not to know the drill* procedure, routine, prac-

tice. **4** *an electric drill* boring/drilling tool,
revolving/rotary tool.

drink *verb* **1** *drink the water* swallow, gulp
down, drain, quaff, imbibe, partake of, swill,
toss off, guzzle, sup, sip; *inf.* swig. **2** *her husband drinks* take alcohol, be a serious/hard
drinker, tipple, indulge, be an alcoholic; *inf.*
take a drop, hit the bottle, booze, knock a few
back. **3** *drink one's health* drink to, toast, propose a toast to. **drink in** be absorbed/rapt/lost
in, be fascinated by, pay close attention to.
drink to toast, propose a toast to, wish success/
luck/health to, salute.

drink *noun* **1** *food and drink | water is the com-
monest drink* beverage, drinkable/potable liquid,
liquid refreshment; alcoholic drink, soft drink,
non-alcoholic drink, cold drink, hot drink,
thirst-quencher. *See table. See also tables at* COF-
FEE, TEA. **2** *no drink at the dance* alcoholic/strong
drink, alcohol, liquor, intoxicating liquor; spirits; *inf.* booze, hard stuff, hooch. *See tables at*
ALCOHOL, BEER, MIXER, WHISKY, WINE. **3** *take a drink
from the cup* swallow, gulp, sip, draught, swill;
inf. swig, slug. **4** *a drink of water* cup, glass,
mug, container. **5** *the plane ditched in the drink*
sea, ocean; *inf.* briny.

drinkable *adjective* fit to drink, potable.

drinker *noun* social drinker, heavy/hard
drinker, serious drinker, alcoholic, chronic
alcoholic, problem drinker, alcohol-abuser,
drunk, drunkard, dipsomaniac, tippler, toper,
sot, inebriate, imbiber; *inf.* boozer, soak, lush,
wino, alky, sponge, elbow-bender.

drip *verb* *water/blood/coffee is dripping* drop, dribble, trickle, splash, sprinkle, plop, leak, ooze,
exude, filter, percolate.

drip *noun* **1** *paint drips* drop, dribble, trickle,
splash, plop, leak. **2** *a boring drip* ineffective
person, weakling, ninny, milksop; *inf.* weed,
wet, wally.

drive *verb* **1** *drive a car* operate, steer, handle,
guide, direct, manage. **2** *we drove here* come/
go/travel by car, motor; *inf.* travel on wheels.
3 *he drove us here* chauffeur, run, give one a
lift. **4** *drive cattle to the barn* move, get going,
urge, press, push, impel, propel, herd, round-
up. **5** *driven to steal/despair* force, compel, constrain, impel, oblige, coerce, make, pressure,
goad, spur, prod. **6** *drove himself too hard* work,
overwork, tax, overtax, overburden. **7** *drive
the stake into the ground* hammer, ram, bang,
sink, plunge, thrust, stab. **drive at 1** *what are*

you driving at? mean, suggest, imply, infer, hint
at, refer to, allude to, intimate, indicate, have
in mind; *inf.* get at. **2** *she drove at the task* work
hard, hasten, rush.

drive *noun* **1** *go for a drive* run, trip, jaunt, outing, journey, excursion, tour, turn; *Scots* hurl;
inf. spin, joyride. **2** *the tree-lined drive* driveway,
road, roadway, avenue. **3** *a sales drive* effort,
push, sales push, campaign, publicity campaign, crusade, surge. **4** *a young man with drive*
energy, vigour, verve, ambition, push, enterprise, motivation, initiative, action, aggressiveness; *inf.* get-up-and-go, zip, pizazz, punch.

drivel *noun* **1** *speaking drivel* nonsense, twaddle, gibberish, balderdash, rubbish, stuff and
nonsense, bunkum, mumbo-jumbo; *inf.* rot,
tommy rot, poppycock, garbage, tripe, waffle,
bosh, bunk, blah, hogwash, crap. **2** *wipe away
the drivel* saliva, drool, drooling, dribble, slaver,
slobber.

drivel *verb* **1** *drivel about the rules* talk non-
sense/rubbish, babble, ramble, gibber, blather,
blether, prate, maunder; *inf.* waffle, witter on,
gab, gabble, talk through one's hat. **2** *babies
drivelling* drool, slaver, slobber, dribble; *Scots*
slabber.

driver *verb* **1** *passengers paying the driver | drivers
of heavy vehicles* chauffeur, taxi-driver, cab-
driver; operator; engine-driver, train-driver,
bus-driver, lorry-driver, truck-driver. **2** *drivers
charged with drink driving* car-driver, motorist.

drizzle *noun* *a drizzle falling* fine rain, Scotch
mist, sprinkle of rain, light shower; *dial.* miz-
zle.

droll *adjective* **1** funny, humorous, amusing,
comic, comical, clownish, farcical, zany, laughable, ridiculous, ludicrous, risible, jocular,
facetious, waggish, witty, whimsical, entertaining, diverting. **2** *a droll little girl* quaint,
odd, strange, queer, eccentric, outlandish,
bizarre, whimsical.

drone[1] *verb* **1** *aircraft droning overhead* make a
humming noise, hum, buzz, whirr, vibrate,
murmur, purr, whisper, sigh. **2** *drone on about
cutting costs* go on and on, speak monoton-
ously/boringly, talk interminably, intone.

drone[2] *noun the drone of aircraft* hum, buzz,
whirr, whirring, vibration, purr, whispering,
sigh.

drone[3] *noun the workers and the drones in the firm*
idler, loafer, layabout, lounger, do-nothing,

SOFT DRINKS

Water and Water-based Drinks			
barley water	sports drink	goat's milk	coconut milk
carbonated water	spring water	hot chocolate	cola
cordial	squash	ice milk *Am.*	cream soda
fizzy water	tonic water	lassi	fruit juice
ginger ale	**Milk and Milk Drinks**	malted milk	ginger beer
iced tea	camel's milk	milk shake	lemonade
kava	cocoa	soya milk	limeade
mineral water	condensed milk	**Other Soft Drinks**	orangeade
Perrier™	cream	atole	Pepsi™
soda water	evaporated milk	bitter lemon	root beer
	flavoured milk	cherryade	sarsaparilla
		Coca Cola™	sherbet

sluggard, laggard, parasite, leech, hanger-on; *inf.* lazybones, scrounger, sponger.

droop *verb* **1** *flowers drooping* hang, hang down, bend, bow, stoop, sag, sink, slump, fall down, drop. **2** *drooping after the news | spirits drooping* be despondent, lose heart, give up hope, become dispirited/dejected, flag, fade, languish, falter, weaken, wilt, shrivel, wither, decline, diminish, deteriorate.

drop *noun* **1** *a drop of water* droplet, globule, bead, bubble, blob, spheroid, oval. **2** *add just a drop* little, bit, dash, spot, dribble, driblet, splash, sprinkle, trickle, taste, trace, pinch, dab, speck, particle, modicum; *inf.* smidgen; *Am. inf.* tad. **3** *a drop in prices* decline, decrease, reduction, cut, cut-back, lowering, falling-off, fall-off, downturn, depreciation, devaluation, mark, slump. **4** *the path ended in a sudden drop* descent, incline, declivity, slope, plunge; abyss, chasm, precipice, cliff.

drop *verb* **1** *water dropping from the trees* fall in drops, fall, drip, dribble, trickle, plop, leak. **2** *the plane dropped out of the sky* drop down, fall, descend, plunge, plummet, dive, tumble. **3** *she dropped the parcel/ball* let fall/go, fail to hold. **4** *the girl dropped from exhaustion* fall/sink down, collapse, faint, swoon, drop/fall dead. **5** *prices dropped* fall, decrease, lessen, diminish, depreciate, go into decline, dwindle, sink, slacken off, plunge, plummet. **6** *drop singing lessons* give up, discontinue, end, stop, cease, terminate, finish with, withdraw/retire from, abandon, forgo, relinquish, dispense with, throw up. **7** *drop his girlfriend* desert, abandon, forsake, leave, throw over, jilt, discard, reject, repudiate, renounce, disown; *inf.* ditch, chuck, run out on, leave flat. **8** *drop half the workforce* dismiss, discharge, let go, declare/make redundant; *inf.* sack, fire, boot out. **9** *drop his aitches* omit, leave out, eliminate, elide, contract, slur.

drop off 1 *sales have dropped off* drop, fall, decrease, decline, plummet. *See* DROP *verb* 5. **2** *drop the goods/passengers off* deliver, deposit, set down, unload, leave, put off, allow to alight. **3** *people dropping off* fall asleep, doze, doze off, have a nap, catnap, drowse; *inf.* nod off, snooze, take forty winks, get some shut-eye. **drop out** *students dropping out of college* give up, abandon, renounce, leave, quit, forsake, back out, withdraw from, renege on, turn one's back on.

Opposites LIFT; RISE; take up (*see* TAKE); RETAIN.

drought *noun* dry spell/period, lack of rain; *Scots* drouth.

drove *noun* **1** *a drove of cattle/sheep/livestock* herd, flock, pack. **2** *droves of people going shopping* crowd, horde, swarm, multitude, mob, throng, host, collection, gathering, assembly, company, herd, crush, press, rabble.

drown *verb* **1** *engineers drowning the valley* flood, submerge, immerse, inundate, deluge, swamp, engulf, drench. **2** *outside noise drowning her speech* drown out, make inaudible, muffle, be louder than, deaden, stifle, overpower, overwhelm, overcome, engulf, swallow up. **3** *drowning his grief in work* suppress, deaden, stifle, quash, quench, extinguish, obliterate, wipe out, get rid of.

drowsy *adjective* **1** *feeling drowsy* sleepy, half-asleep, tired, weary, dozy, dozing, heavy, heavy-eyed, yawning, lethargic, sluggish, somnolent, slumberous, comatose, dazed, drugged; *inf.* dopey. **2** *drowsy weather* sleepy, sleep-inducing, soporific, lulling, soothing, dreamy, somniferous.

Opposites ALERT; LIVELY.

drubbing *noun* beating, thrashing, walloping, thumping, battering, trouncing, whipping, flogging, pounding, pummelling, bludgeoning; *inf.* hammering, licking, clobbering, work-over, working-over.

drudge *noun* *drudges working in the kitchen* menial, servant, slave, labourer, char, charwoman, hack, worker, toiler, maid/man of all work, general factotum; *inf.* skivvy, dogsbody.

drudge *verb* toil, labour, slave, plod on, grind/slog away, keep one's nose to the grindstone.

drudgery *noun* menial/hard work, donkey-work, toiling, toil, labour, hard/sweated labour, slavery, hack work, plodding; chores; *inf.* skivvying, grind, slog.

drug *noun* **1** *a new cancer drug* medical drug, medicine, medication, medicament, remedy, cure, cure-all, panacea, physic, magic bullet. *See table at* MEDICINE. **2** *addicted to drugs* addictive drug, recreational drug, illegal drug; *inf.* dope, downer, upper, speed, grass, hash, pot, horse, the big H, smack, coke, crack, E, acid. *See table.*

RECREATIONAL DRUGS		
alcohol	crack	mescaline
amphet-	Ecstasy	narcotics
amines	heroin	nicotine
barbitur-	lysergic acid	opium
ates	diethyl-	sedatives
caffeine	amide	stimulants
cannabis	(LSD)	tranquil-
cocaine	marijuana	lizers

drug *verb* **1** *drug the patient before the operation | drug the kidnapped child* anaesthetize, give an anaesthetic to, knock out, make/render unconscious, make/render insensible, stupefy, befuddle, narcotize; *inf.* dope. **2** *drug the patient rather than give counselling* give/administer drugs to, give medication/medicament to, medicate, dose, treat.

drugged *adjective* anaesthetized, knocked out, comatose, stupefied, insensible, befuddled, narcotized; *inf.* doped, stoned, dopey, on a trip, spaced out, zonked, high, high as a kite, turned on, flying, charged up.

drum *noun. See table at* PERCUSSION.

drum *verb* **1** *drum on the table | drum one's fingers* tap, beat, rap, knock, strike, tattoo, thrum. **2** *drum information into pupils* drive home, din, instil, hammer, inculcate. **drum out** *drum out of the club/regiment* expel from, dismiss/discharge from, throw out, oust from. **drum up** *drum up business/support* gather, collect, round up, summon, obtain, get, attract, canvass, solicit, petition, bid for.

drunk adjective drunk after hours in the pub drunken, drunk as a lord, blind drunk, dead drunk, intoxicated, inebriated, inebriate, the worse for drink, under the influence, tipsy, soused, befuddled, gin-soaked, maudlin, sottish, tippling, toping, bibulous, crapulent, crapulous; inf. tight, tiddly, squiffy, merry, happy, woozy, pie-eyed, half-seas-over, one over the eight, three sheets to the wind, under the table, out of it, legless, plastered, smashed, paralytic, sloshed, pissed, stoned, well-oiled, sozzled, blotto, blitzed, lit up, canned, bevvied, stewed, pickled, tanked-up, soaked, bombed, liquored up, tired and emotional, steaming; Scots inf fou.
Opposites SOBER.

drunk noun drunkard, inebriate, heavy/hard drinker, sot, toper, tippler, alcoholic, dipsomaniac, serious/problem drinker; inf. soak, boozer, lush, alky, wino, elbow-bender.

drunken adjective **1** drunken party-goers drunk, intoxicated, inebriated. See DRUNK adjective. **2** a drunken party debauched, dissipated, riotous, carousing, revelling, intemperate, roistering, orgiastic, bacchanalian, bacchic, wassailing, dionysian, saturnalian.

drunkenness noun intoxication, inebriation, inebriety, insobriety, tipsiness, intemperance, over-indulging, debauchery, hard drinking, serious drinking, alcoholism, alcohol abuse, dipsomania, sottishness, bibulousness, crapulence.

dry adjective **1** dry ground/regions arid, dried up/out, parched, scorched, dehydrated, desiccated, waterless, unwatered, moistureless, rainless, torrid, thirsty, droughty, barren, unproductive, sterile. **2** dry leaves withered, shrivelled, wilted, dehydrated, desiccated, wizened, sapless, juiceless. **3** dry cheese dried out, hard, hardened, stale. **4** a dry talk dull, uninteresting, boring, tedious, tiresome, wearisome, dreary, monotonous, flat, unimaginative, commonplace, prosaic, run-of-the-mill, humdrum, vapid; Scots inf dreich. **5** a dry wit subtle, low-key, deadpan, laconic, sly, sharp, ironic, sarcastic, satirical, cynical, droll, waggish. **6** a dry response/greeting unemotional, indifferent, cool, cold, aloof, remote, impersonal. **7** a dry state prohibitionist, teetotal, alcohol-free.
Opposites WET; FRESH; INTERESTING.

dry verb **1** the sun drying the earth make dry, dry out/up, parch, scorch, dehydrate, desiccate, dehumidify, sear. **2** the sun drying the leaves dry up, wither, shrivel, wilt, dehydrate, desiccate, wizen, mummify. **3** dry meat dehydrate, desiccate, preserve, cure. **4** dry the wet patch dry off, mop up, blot up, towel, drain. **dry up 1** dry up the ground parch, scorch, dehydrate. See DRY verb 1. **2** dry up leaves/skin wither, shrivel, wizen, mummify. See DRY verb 2. **3** inspiration dried up fail, become unproductive, grow barren/sterile, cease to yield. **4** actors drying up | she dried up at the sight stop speaking/talking, forget one's lines/words, shut up.

dual adjective double, twofold, duplicate, duplex, binary, twin, matched, paired, coupled.

dub verb **1** dubbed the greatest jazz singer call, name, christen, designate, term, entitle, style, label, denominate, nominate, tag, nickname. **2** queen dubbing a courtier knight, confer/bestow a knighthood on, invest with a knighthood.

dubiety noun doubtfulness, uncertainty, lack of certainty, unsureness, hesitancy, dubiosity, incertitude; doubt.

dubious adjective **1** dubious about going doubtful, uncertain, unsure, hesitant, undecided, wavering, vacillating, irresolute, on the horns of a dilemma, sceptical, suspicious; inf. iffy. **2** the outcome is dubious doubtful, undecided, unsure, unsettled, undetermined, indefinite, unresolved, up in the air, open, equivocal, debatable, questionable. **3** give a dubious reply equivocal, ambiguous, indeterminate, indefinite, unclear, vague, imprecise, hazy, puzzling, enigmatic, cryptic. **4** a dubious character questionable, suspicious, suspect, under suspicion, untrustworthy, unreliable, undependable; inf. shady, fishy.
Opposites CERTAIN; SURE; DEFINITE.

duck verb **1** duck behind the wall bend, bow down, bob down, stoop, crouch, squat, hunch down, hunker down. **2** duck one's head bow, lower, drop. **3** duck him in the pond immerse, submerge, plunge, dip, souse, douse, dunk. **4** duck the police/work dodge, evade, sidestep, avoid, steer clear of, elude, escape, shirk, shun.

duck noun. See table at FOWL.

duct noun pipe, tube, conduit, channel, passage, canal, culvert.

ductile adjective **1** a ductile substance pliable, pliant, flexible, plastic, malleable, tensile. **2** ductile people pliable, pliant, compliant, tractable, manipulable, docile, accommodating, cooperative, gullible.

dud noun the lightbulb/teacher is a dud failure, flop; inf. wash-out, lemon, loser.

dud adjective a dud lightbulb/teacher defective, broken, not working, not functioning, inoperative, ineffectual, failed, worthless; inf. bust, kaput, duff.

dudgeon noun in high dudgeon angry, annoyed, furious, in a temper, indignant, enraged, fuming, vexed, offended, resentful; inf. peeved.

due adjective **1** money/thanks due to them owing, owed, payable, payable now, receivable immediately, outstanding. **2** recognition due to a hero deserved by, merited by, earned by, justified by, appropriate to, fit for, fitting to, suitable for, right for. **3** treat with due respect proper, right and proper, correct, rightful, fitting, appropriate, apt, adequate, sufficient, enough, ample, satisfactory, requisite, apposite. **4** the essay is due tomorrow scheduled, expected, required, awaited, anticipated. **due to** due to uncertainty attributable to, ascribed to, ascribable to, caused by, assignable to, because of.

due adverb due north directly, straight, without deviating, undeviatingly, dead, exactly.

due noun receive only his due rightful treatment; rights, just deserts, deserts; inf. comeuppance.

duel *noun* **1** *challenge his rival to a duel* affair of honour; single combat. **2** *engage in a duel of wits* contest, competition, struggle, clash, battle, fight, encounter, engagement.

dues *plural noun pay one's dues to the club* fee, membership fee, subscription, charge, levy; charges.

duffer *noun* bungler, blunderer, oaf, fool, dunce, numskull, dunderhead, booby; *inf.* galoot, wally.

dulcet *adjective* sweet, melodious, musical, lyrical, silver-toned, euphonious, pleasant, agreeable, soothing, mellow.

dull *adjective* **1** *dull of wit* dull-witted, slow, slow-witted, unintelligent, stupid, dense, doltish, stolid, vacuous; *inf.* dim, dim-witted, thick, dumb, bird-brained. **2** *a dull reaction to others' pain* insensitive, unfeeling, unemotional, indifferent, unsympathetic, unresponsive, apathetic, blank, uncaring, passionless, callous. **3** *feeling dull in the winter* inactive, inert, slow, slow-moving, sleepy, drowsy, idle, sluggish, stagnant, lethargic, listless, languid, heavy, apathetic, torpid, phlegmatic, vegetative. **4** *trade is dull* slow, slack, sluggish, stagnant, depressed. **5** *a dull speech* dull as dishwater, uninteresting, boring, tedious, tiresome, wearisome, dry, monotonous, flat, bland, unimaginative, commonplace, prosaic, run-of-the-mill, humdrum, uneventful, vapid; *Scots inf* dreich. **6** *dull weather* overcast, cloudy, gloomy, dark, dim, dismal, dreary, bleak, sombre, leaden, murky, sunless, lowering. **7** *dull colours* drab, dreary, sombre, dark, subdued, muted, toned-down, lacklustre, lustreless, colourless, faded, washed-out; *fml.* subfusc. **8** *a dull sound* muffled, muted, indistinct, feeble. **9** *a dull edge* blunt, blunted, not sharp, unkeen, unsharpened, dulled, edgeless.
Opposites CLEVER; ACTIVE; INTERESTING; BRIGHT.

dull *verb* **1** *dull the appetite | dulled their grief* take the edge off, blunt, lessen, decrease, diminish, reduce, deaden, mute, tone down, allay, ease, soothe, assuage, alleviate, palliate. **2** *drugs dulling the senses* numb, benumb, stupefy, drug, sedate, tranquillize, narcotize. **3** *time dulling the colours* fade, bleach, wash out, decolourize, decolour. **4** *the sky dulled by clouds* darken, dim, bedim, obscure. **5** *spirits dulled by the bad news* dispirit, dishearten, depress, deject, sadden, discourage, cast down, dampen, put a damper on, cast a pall over.

duly *adverb* **1** *suggestions duly noted* in due manner, properly, correctly, rightly, fittingly, appropriately. **2** *he duly arrived* in due time, at the proper/right time, on time, punctually.

dumb *adjective* **1** *dumb from birth* without speech, mute. **2** *struck dumb at the sight* speechless, wordless, silent, mute, at a loss for words, voiceless, soundless, inarticulate, taciturn, uncommunicative, tongue-tied; *inf.* mum. **3** *dumb people and clever people* stupid, dull, dull-witted, slow, slow-witted, unintelligent, dense, foolish, doltish; *inf.* dim, dim-witted, thick.

dumbfound *verb* astound, astonish, amaze, startle, surprise, stun, take aback, stagger, overwhelm, confound, shock, confuse, bewilder, baffle, nonplus, perplex, disconcert; *inf.* flabbergast, throw, shake, knock for six, knock sideways.

dummy *noun* **1** *a tailor's/ventriloquist's dummy* lifelike model, mannequin, manikin, figure, lay figure. **2** *not a real book/shoe, just a dummy* representation, reproduction, sample, copy, imitation, counterfeit, sham, substitute. **3** *that dummy can't do anything* idiot, fool, dolt, dunce, blockhead, numskull, oaf, nincompoop, ninny, ass, donkey, dullard; *inf.* clot, nitwit, dim-wit, dope, chump, bonehead, jerk; *Am. inf.* airhead, schmuck.

dump *verb* **1** *dump the goods on the floor* place, put, put down, lay down, deposit, drop, let fall, throw down, fling down. **2** *dump the unwanted goods* dispose of, get rid of, throw away/out, scrap, jettison. **3** *the tanker dumped its load* discharge, empty out, pour out, tip out, unload, jettison. **4** *dump his wife* abandon, desert, leave, leave in the lurch, forsake, walk out on.

dump *noun* **1** *take the debris to the dump* refuse/rubbish dump, tip, rubbish tip, rubbish heap, junkyard, scrapyard; *Scots* midden. **2** *what a dump!* hovel, shack, slum, shanty, pigsty; *Scots* bothy; *inf.* hole, joint.

dumps *plural noun* **in the dumps** depressed, dejected, gloomy, despondent, downcast, disconsolate, melancholic; *inf.* blue.

dun *verb* *dun people for payment* press, importune, pressurize, solicit, plague, pester, nag, beset.

dun *adjective* *dun-coloured horses* greyish-brown, mud-coloured, muddy, khaki, umber.

dunce *noun* dolt, blockhead, dunderhead, thickhead, numskull, nincompoop, ninny, simpleton, halfwit, idiot, moron, ass, donkey, ignoramus, dullard; *inf.* dim-wit, dummy, bonehead, deadhead.

dungeon *noun* underground cell, cell, lock-up, black hole, oubliette; donjon, keep.

duplicate *adjective* *a duplicate set of keys* identical, twin, matching, matched, paired, corresponding, twofold.

duplicate *noun* **1** *a duplicate of the chair* copy, replica, facsimile, reproduction, exact/close likeness, twin, double, clone, match, mate, fellow, counterpart; *inf.* lookalike, spitting image, ringer, dead ringer. **2** *make a duplicate of the document* copy, carbon copy, carbon, photocopy, facsimile, fax; photostat™, Xerox™.

duplicate *verb* **1** *duplicate the documents* copy, make a carbon/facsimile of, photocopy, fax, reproduce, make a replica of, replicate, clone, photostat, xerox. **2** *duplicate the task* repeat, do over again, perform again, replicate.

duplicity *noun* deceitfulness, double-dealing, trickery, guile, chicanery, artifice, dishonesty, knavery, two-facedness.
Opposites HONESTY; CANDOUR.

durable *adjective* **1** *durable affection* lasting, long-lasting, enduring, persisting, persistent, abiding, continuing, constant, stable, fast, firm, fixed, permanent, unfading, changeless, unchanging, invariable, dependable, reliable.

2 *durable clothing/goods* long-lasting, hard-wearing, strong, sturdy, sound, tough, resistant, substantial, imperishable.
Opposites EPHEMERAL; FLIMSY.

duress *noun* **1** *sent away under duress* force, compulsion, coercion, pressure, pressurization, constraint, arm-twisting, enforcement, exaction. **2** *prisoners of war kept in duress* imprisonment, confinement, incarceration, detention, custody, captivity, restraint, constraint, bondage.

during *conjunction* throughout, through, throughout the time of, for the time of, in, within.

dusk *noun* twilight, evening, sunset, sundown, nightfall; dark, gloom, murk; *dial.* gloaming, eventide.

dusky *adjective* **1** *dusky maidens* dark, dark-skinned, dark-complexioned, dark-coloured, olive-skinned, swarthy. **2** *dusky light* shadowy, dim, dark, darkish, gloomy, murky, cloudy, misty, hazy, foggy, crepuscular, tenebrous.

dust *noun* **1** *dust on the furniture* fine powder, dirt, grime, smut, soot. **2** *kneel in the dust* ground, earth, soil, dirt, clay. **3** *kick up a dust* fuss, row, commotion, disturbance, uproar, fracas, rumpus, racket.

dust *verb* **1** *dust the furniture* wipe, brush, flick clean, clean, mop. **2** *dust with icing sugar* sprinkle, dredge, sift, scatter, powder, spray, cover, spread, strew.

dusty *adjective* **1** *a dusty room* dust-covered, dust-filled, undusted, dirty, grubby, grimy, unclean, sooty. **2** *a dusty substance* powdery, chalky, crumbly, friable. **3** *a dusty pink* greyish, muted, dull, pale. **4** *a dusty answer* curt, abrupt, terse, bad-tempered, unhelpful, rejecting.

dutiful *adjective* respectful, filial, deferential, reverent, reverential, conscientious, devoted, considerate, thoughtful, obedient, compliant, pliant, docile, submissive.
Opposites DISRESPECTFUL; REMISS.

duty *noun* **1** *a sense of duty to one's country/parents* responsibility, obligation, obedience, allegiance, loyalty, faithfulness, fidelity, respect, deference, reverence, homage. **2** *share out the duties* task, job, chore, assignment, commission, mission, function, office, charge, part, role, requirement, responsibility, obligation; work, burden, onus. **3** *pay duty* tax, levy, tariff, excise, toll, fee, impost; customs, dues. **off duty** not working, at leisure, on holiday, off, off work, free. **on duty** at work, working, busy, occupied, engaged, tied up; *inf.* on the job.

dwarf *verb* **1** *dwarfed by the effects of a drug* stunt, arrest/check growth, atrophy, bedwarf. **2** *a novelist dwarfing his contemporaries* tower above/over, overshadow, stand head and shoulders over, dominate, overtop. **3** *their efforts dwarfing his* overshadow, diminish, minimize.

dwarf *noun. See table.*

THE SEVEN DWARFS FROM SNOW WHITE

Bashful	Happy
Doc	Sleepy
Dopey	Sneezy
Grumpy	

---

dwell *verb* *dwell in Kensington* reside, live, be domiciled, lodge, stay, abide; *inf.* hang out. **dwell on/upon** *dwell on details/complaints* spend time on, linger over, harp on, discuss at length, expatiate on, elaborate on, expound on, keep talking/writing about, be preoccupied by, be obsessed by.

dwelling *noun* dwelling-place, residence, home, house, abode, domicile, establishment.

dwindle *verb* **1** *savings/hope dwindling* become/grow less, become/grow smaller, decrease, lessen, diminish, shrink, contract, fade, wane. **2** *the Roman empire dwindling* decline, fail, sink, ebb, wane, degenerate, deteriorate, decay, wither, rot, disappear, vanish, die out; *inf.* peter out.
Opposites INCREASE; GROW; FLOURISH.

dye *noun* **1** *dip the dress in a dye* colourant, colouring agent, colouring, pigment, tint, stain, wash. *See table.* **2** *of a green dye* colour, shade, hue, tint.

dye *verb* *dye a dress* colour, tint, pigment, shade, stain.

dyed-in-the-wool *adjective* entrenched, inveterate, established, deep-rooted, confirmed, complete, absolute, through and through, utter, thoroughgoing.

dying *adjective* **1** *a dying woman* terminally ill, at death's door, breathing one's last, on one's deathbed, in the jaws of death, having one foot in the grave, passing away, sinking fast,

---

DYES

alizarin	diazo com-	henna	Perkin's mauve	sappanwood
alkanet	pound	incarnadine	phthalocyanine	Saxon blue
aniline dye	eosin	indigo	dye	tartrazine
annatto	flavin	kermes	picric acid	turmeric
azo dye	fluorescein	litmus	Prussian blue	Tyrian purple
basic dye	fuchsine	madder	rhodamine	weld
cochineal	fustic	magenta	rhodamine dye	woad
copper	garancin	orchil	rosanaline	xanthene dye
sulphate	gentian violet	orpiment	saffron	zedoary

expiring, moribund, *in extremis*; *inf.* on one's/its last legs. **2** *dying customs* passing, fading, vanishing, failing, ebbing, waning. **3** *dying words* final, last.

dynamic *adjective* energetic, active, lively, alive, spirited, vital, vigorous, strong, forceful, powerful, potent, effective, effectual, high-powered, magnetic, aggressive, go-ahead, driving, electric; *inf.* go-getting, zippy, peppy.

dynasty *noun* line, succession, house, regime, rule, reign, dominion, empire; sovereignty, ascendancy, government, authority, administration, jurisdiction. *See table.*

DYNASTIES			
Abbasid	Ghaznavid	Merovingian	Seleucid
Achaemenid	Guelph	Ming	Seljuk
Anjou, House of	Gupta	Orange,	Shang
Attalid	Han	House of	Sui
Bharata	Jin	Plantagenet	Sung
Bourbon	Jagiellon	Qin	Tang
Braganza	Kajar	Qing	Tudor
Capetian	Lancaster,	Romanov	Valois
Carolingian	House of	Rurik	Yi
Egyptian (1–31)	Liao	Safavid	York, House of
Fatimid	Manchu	Sassanian	Yuan
Flavian	Mauryan	Saudi	Zhou

Ee

each *adjective each pupil received a book* every, every single.

each *pronoun each was nastier than the other* each one, every one, each and every one, one and all.

each *adverb give a pound each* apiece, per person, per capita, to each, for each, from each, individually.

eager *adjective* **1** *eager pupils* keen, enthusiastic, impatient, avid, fervent, earnest, diligent, zealous, passionate, wholehearted, ambitious, enterprising; *inf.*bright-eyed and bushy-tailed. **2** *eager to learn | eager for news* agog, anxious, intent, longing, yearning, itching, wishing, desirous, hopeful, thirsty, hungry, greedy; *inf.* hot.
Opposites INDIFFERENT; UNINTERESTED; APATHETIC.

eagerness *noun* keenness, enthusiasm, impatience, avidity, fervour, earnestness, diligence, zeal, passion, wholeheartedness, desire, longing, yearning, wishing, itch, hope, thirst, hunger, greed, ambition, enterprise. *See* EAGER.

ear *noun* **1** *an infection of the ear* inner ear, middle ear, external ear, outer ear. *See table.* **2** *have the ear of the king* attention, attentiveness, notice, heed, regard, consideration. **3** *an ear for a good song/musical* appreciation, discrimination, perception, musical taste.

PARTS OF THE HUMAN EAR

auditory canal	organ of Corti
auditory nerve	outer ear
auricle/pinna	perilymph
basilar membrane	pinna/auricle
cochlea	saccule
endolymph	semicircular canal
Eustachian tube	stapes/stirrup
hair cell	tectorial membrane
incus/anvil	tympanic mem-
inner ear	brane/eardrum
malleus/hammer	utricle
middle ear	vestibule

early *adverb* **1** *get up and set off early* early in the day, in the early morning, at dawn, at daybreak, at cock-crow, with the lark. **2** *guests should not arrive early* ahead of time, too soon, beforehand, before the usual/appointed time, prematurely. **3** *you should arrive early for the interview* in good time, before the appointed time, ahead of schedule.

early *adjective* **1** *an early crop/birth* advanced, forward, premature, precocious, untimely. **2** *an early reply* prompt, without delay, quick, speedy, rapid, fast, expeditious, timely. **3** *early man/settlements* primitive, primeval, primordial, prehistoric, autochthonous.
Opposites LATE; BELATED; OVERDUE.

earmark *verb earmark the money for a holiday* set/lay aside, keep back, allocate, reserve, designate, label, tag.

earn *verb* **1** *earn a good salary* make, get, receive, obtain, draw, clear, collect, bring in, take home, pull in, pocket, gross, net. **2** *earn their admiration* gain, win, rate, merit, attain, achieve, secure, obtain, deserve, be entitled to, be worthy of, have a right to, warrant.

earnest[1] *adjective* **1** *an earnest young man* serious, solemn, grave, intense, staid, studious, thoughtful, committed, dedicated, assiduous, keen, diligent, zealous, steady, hard-working. **2** *her earnest request/hope* sincere, fervent, fervid, ardent, passionate, warm, intense, heartfelt, wholehearted, profound, enthusiastic, zealous, urgent.
Opposites FRIVOLOUS; FLIPPANT; INSINCERE.

earnest[2] *noun* **in earnest** **1** *he was in earnest about the punishment* serious, not joking, unsmiling, sincere. **2** *they set to work in earnest* zealously, ardently, fervently, fervidly, passionately, wholeheartedly, with dedication/commitment, determinedly, resolutely.

earnest[3] *noun as earnest of my intent* guarantee, pledge, promise, security, token, deposit, down payment.

earnings *plural noun* income, salary, wage, pay, take-home pay, gross/net pay, remuneration, emolument, fee, stipend, honorarium, revenue, yield, profit, gain, return; wages, fringe benefits ; *inf.* perks.

earth *noun* **1** *earth, moon and stars* globe, world, planet, sphere, orb. **2** *dig up the earth* soil, loam, clay, dirt, sod, clod, turf, ground. **3** *between the earth and the sky* ground, dry ground, land.

earthenware *noun* pottery, crockery, stoneware; pots, crocks. *See table at* CERAMICS.

earthly *adjective* **1** *earthly beings* terrestrial, telluric, tellurian. **2** *earthly joys* worldly, temporal, secular, mortal, human, mundane, material, non-spiritual, materialistic, carnal, fleshly, physical, corporeal, gross, sensual, base, sordid, vile, profane. **3** *no earthly chance* feasible, possible, conceivable, imaginable, likely.
Opposites HEAVENLY; SPIRITUAL.

earthquake *noun. See table.*

earthy *adjective* **1** *earthy smell* soil-like, dirt-like. **2** *earthy peasants/pleasures* down-to-earth, unsophisticated, unrefined, homely, simple, plain, unpretentious, natural, uninhibited, rough, robust. **3** *an earthy sense of humour* bawdy, crude, coarse, rough, ribald, blue, indecent, indecorous, obscene.

MAJOR EARTHQUAKES		
City	Country	Date
Antioch	Syria	526 A.D.
Shaanxi	China	1556
Hokkaido	Japan	1730
Calcutta	India	1737
Messina	Italy	1908
Gansu	China	1920, 1932
Yokohama	Japan	1923
Chimbote	Peru	1970
Guatemala City	Guatemala	1976
Tangshan	China	1976
–	Iran	1978
Mexico City	Mexico	1985
–	Armenia	1988
San Francisco	U.S.A.	1906, 1989
–	India	1993
Los Angeles	U.S.A	1994
Kobe	Japan	1995

ease noun **1** *succeed with ease* no difficulty, no trouble/bother, facility, facileness, simplicity, effortlessness, deftness, adroitness, dexterity, proficiency, mastery. **2** *his ease of manner* naturalness, casualness, informality, unceremoniousness, lack of reserve/constraint, relaxedness, amiability, affability, unconcern, composure, aplomb, nonchalance, insouciance, urbanity, suaveness. **3** *ease of mind* peace, peacefulness, calmness, tranquillity, composure, serenity, repose, restfulness, quiet, contentment, security, comfort. **4** *a life of ease* comfort, contentment, content, enjoyment, affluence, wealth, prosperity, prosperousness, luxury, opulence; bed of roses.

ease verb **1** *ease the pain* mitigate, lessen, reduce, lighten, diminish, moderate, abate, ameliorate, relieve, assuage, allay, soothe, soften, palliate, mollify, appease. **2** *the storm/pain eased* lessen, grow less, moderate, abate, diminish, quieten, slacken off. **3** *ease her mind* comfort, give solace to, solace, console, soothe, calm, quieten, pacify. **4** *ease his promotion* make easy/easier, facilitate, expedite, speed up, assist, help, aid, advance, further, forward, smooth/clear the way for, simplify. **5** *ease it into position* guide, manoeuvre, inch, edge, steer, slide, slip, squeeze.
Opposites AGGRAVATE; INCREASE; HINDER.

easy adjective **1** *an easy task* not difficult, simple, effortless, uncomplicated, straightforward, undemanding, painless, trouble-free, facile, idiot-proof. **2** *an easy prey* compliant, exploitable, susceptible, accommodating, obliging, amenable, biddable, docile, gullible, manageable, manoeuvrable, tractable, pliant, yielding, trusting, acquiescent. **3** *an easy manner* natural, casual, informal, unceremonious, unreserved, unconstrained, unforced, easygoing, amiable, affable, unconcerned, composed, carefree, nonchalant, insouciant, urbane, suave; *inf.* laid-back. **4** *an easy mind* at ease, trouble-free, untroubled, unworried, at peace, calm, tranquil, composed, serene, quiet, contented, secure, relaxed, comfortable. **5** *go at an easy pace* even, steady, regular, comfortable, moderate, unexacting, undemanding,

leisured, unhurried.
Opposites DIFFICULT; DEMANDING; FORMAL; UNEASY.

easygoing adjective even-tempered, placid, happy-go-lucky, serene, relaxed, carefree, nonchalant, insouciant, tolerant, undemanding, amiable, patient, understanding, imperturbable; *inf.* laid-back, together.
Opposites INTOLERANT; TENSE.

eat verb **1** *eat chocolate* consume, devour, swallow, chew, munch, gulp down, bolt, wolf, ingest, tuck into; *inf.* put away, scoff. **2** *eat out | eat in the evening* have a meal, take food, feed, partake of food; breakfast, lunch, dine, banquet; *inf.* snack, graze. **3** *eat away material/ rock* erode, corrode, wear, gnaw away, crumble, dissolve, waste away, rot, decay, destroy.

eavesdrop verb listen in, snoop, spy; monitor, tap, wire-tap, overhear; *inf.* bug.

ebb verb **1** *the tide ebbed* go out, flow back, retreat, draw back, fall back, fall away, recede, abate, subside, retrocede. **2** *its popularity ebbed* decline, die/fade away, die out, lessen, wane, decrease, diminish, flag, dwindle, peter out, sink, weaken, deteriorate, decay, degenerate.

ebb noun **1** *the ebb of the tide* going out, flowing back, retreat, retreating, drawing back, receding, abating, subsiding, retrocession. See EBB verb 1. **2** *the ebb of popularity* decline, dying/fading away, lessening, waning, decrease, flagging, diminution, dwindling, petering out, sinking, deterioration, decay, degeneration. See EBB verb 2.

ebony adjective black, jet black, pitch black, coal black, black as night/pitch/hell, sable, inky, sooty.

ebullience noun exuberance, effervescence, buoyancy, exhilaration, elation, euphoria, high-spiritedness, jubilation, animation, sparkle, vivacity, enthusiasm, zest, irrepressibility; high spirits.

ebullient adjective exuberant, effervescent, buoyant, exhilarated, elated, euphoric, high-spirited, in high spirits, jubilant, animated, sparkling, vivacious, enthusiastic, irrepressible.

eccentric adjective odd, queer, strange, peculiar, weird, bizarre, outlandish, freakish, uncommon, irregular, abnormal, aberrant, anomalous, non-conformist, unconventional, singular, idiosyncratic, capricious, whimsical, quirky; *inf.* way-out, off-beat, dotty, nutty, screwy.
Opposites ORDINARY; CONVENTIONAL.

eccentric noun oddity, queer fish, freak, character, case, crank; *inf.* oddball, weirdo, nut, nutter, screwball.

eccentricity noun oddness, queerness, strangeness, weirdness, bizarreness, freakishness, unconventionality; peculiarity, irregularity, abnormality, anomaly, foible, idiosyncracy, caprice, whimsy, quirk; *inf.* way-outness, offbeatness. See ECCENTRIC adjective.

ecclesiastic noun clergyman, padre, churchman, churchwoman, man/woman of the cloth, preacher, reverend, cleric, holy man/woman,

CHRISTIAN ECCLESIASTICAL OFFICERS

acolyte	clerk in	patriarch
almoner	holy orders	pope
archbishop	confessor	precentor
beadle	curate	prelate
bishop	deacon	priest
canon	deaconess	primate
cantor	dean	rector
cardinal	elder	sexton
chapiain	father	succentor
church-	minister	thurifer
warden	Monsignor	verger
cleric	parson	vicar
	pastor	

abbé, divine, theologian. *See table. See also table at* PRIEST.

ecclesiastic *adjective* church, churchly, religious, spiritual, non-secular, non-temporal, pastoral, priestly, ministerial, holy, divine, clerical, sacerdotal; *inf.* churchy.

echelon *noun* level, grade, rank, step, rung, tier, degree.

echo *noun* **1** *the cave's echo | the echo of her call* reverberation, reverberating, resounding, ringing, repeating. **2** *the son an echo of his father* copy, imitation, reproduction, clone, duplicate, repeat, reflection, mirror image, parallel, parody. **3** *echoes of Picasso* suggestion, hint, trace, allusion, memory, reminder, remembrance, evocation, intimation; overtones, reminiscences.

echo *verb* **1** *echo round the room* reverberate, resound, reflect, ring, repeat. **2** *echo a statement | echo the main theme* copy, imitate, reproduce, repeat, reiterate, parrot, reflect, mirror, parallel, parody.

eclectic *adjective* **1** *eclectic interests* wideranging, broad, broad-based, comprehensive, general, varied, diverse, diversified, catholic, liberal, all-embracing, non-exclusive, many-sided, multifaceted, multifarious. **2** *eclectic philosophy* selective, selecting, choosing, picking and choosing.

eclipse *verb* **1** *eclipse the sun* blot out, block, cover, obscure, conceal, cast a shadow over, darken, shade, veil, shroud. **2** *eclipse his rival/success* outshine, overshadow, dwarf, put in the shade, surpass, excel, exceed, outstrip, transcend, outrival.

eclipse *noun* **1** *the eclipse of the sun* blotting out, blocking, covering, obscuring, concealing, veiling, shrouding, occultation, adumbration. *See* ECLIPSE *verb* 1. **2** *the eclipse of the empire* decline, fall, failure, deterioration, degeneration, weakening, ebb, waning. **3** *the eclipse of his rival/success* outshining, overshadowing, dwarfing, surpassing, excelling, outstripping, transcending. *See* ECLIPSE *verb* 2.

economic *adjective* **1** *the government's economic policy* financial, monetary, budgetary, fiscal, commercial, trade, mercantile. *See table.* **2** *an economic venture* profitable, profit-making, money-making, remunerative, viable, cost-effective, productive, solvent. **3** *an economic holiday* economical, cheap. *See* ECONOMICAL 2.

ECONOMIC TERMS AND THEORIES

added value	economic policy	M1/M2/M3/M4	private sector
aggregate demand	economic rent	macroeconomics	productivity
balanced budget	economies of scale	marginal efficiency	property
bear market	elasticity of demand	of capital	protection
boom/bust cycle	exchange value	marginalism	public sector
broad money	FIFO	market forces	put option
bull market	fiscal drag	Marxism	quantity theory of
capitalism	fiscal policy	materialism	money
centrally planned	five-year plan	means of production	recession
economy	free market	mercantilism	retail price index
colonialism	free trade	microeconomics	revisionism
command economy	fungible	mixed economy	slavery
competition	futures market	monetarism	slump
consumerism	gold standard	monetary policy	stagflation
corporate state	gross domestic	monopoly	statics
cost of production	product (GDP)	multiplier [effect]	supply and demand
deficit financing	gross national	narrow money	supply-side
demand curve	product (GNP)	national income	economics
demand economy	imperialism	neo-classicism	surplus
depression	inelastic	New Deal	surplus value
dialectical material-	inflationary gap	New Economics	syndicalism
ism	institutionalism	oligopoly	totalitarianism
diminishing returns	investment	options market	trade barrier
division of labour	Keynesianism	perfect competition	trade cycle
duopoly	labour theory of	physiocracy	Trotskyism
econometrics	value	positional goods	value added
economic classicism	laissez-faire	prices and incomes	velocity of money
economic	economics	policy	wage-price spiral
equilibrium	Leninism	principle of accelera-	welfare economics
economic growth	liquidity	tion	windfall profit

economical *adjective* **1** *economical with resources|economical with the salt* economizing, thrifty, sparing, careful, prudent, frugal, scrimping, mean, niggardly, stingy, penny-pinching, parsimonious, conservationist. **2** *an economical holiday* cheap, inexpensive, reasonable, low-cost, low-price, low-budget, budget.
Opposites EXTRAVAGANT; WASTEFUL; EXPENSIVE.

economist *noun. See table.*

economize *verb we must economize because we are short of money* cut back, retrench, budget, cut expenditure, be economical, be sparing/frugal, reduce/decrease wastage, scrimp, save, scrimp and save, cut corners, tighten one's belt, draw in one's horns.

economy *noun* **1** *the national economy* wealth, resources; financial state, financial management. **2** *practise economy|use with economy* thriftiness, sparingness, carefulness, prudence, frugalness, scrimping, meanness, niggardliness, stinginess, penny-pinching, parsimony, parsimoniousness; thrift, care, restraint, frugality, husbandry, conservation.

ecstasy *noun* bliss, rapture, elation, euphoria, joy, joyousness, jubilation, exultation, cloud nine, seventh heaven; transports, rhapsodies. *See* ECSTATIC.
Opposites MISERY; ANGUISH; TORMENT.

ecstatic *adjective* blissful, enraptured, rapturous, joyful, joyous, overjoyed, jumping for joy, jubilant, exultant, elated, in transports, rhapsodic, delirious with happiness/delight, in a frenzy of delight, orgasmic, on cloud nine, in seventh heaven.

eddy *noun* whirlpool, vortex, maelstrom, swirling, swirl, counter-current, counter-flow.

eddy *verb* swirl, swirl round, whirl.

edge *noun* **1** *the edge of the lake/plate* border, side, boundary, rim, margin, fringe, outer limit, extremity, verge, brink, lip, contour, perimeter, periphery, parameter, ambit. **2** *a voice with an edge* sting, bite; sharpness, severity, pointedness, acerbity, causticity, acidity, acrimony, virulence, trenchancy, pungency. **3** *have the edge on her* advantage, upper hand,

whip hand, lead, head start, dominance, superiority, ascendancy. **on edge** edgy, nervous, tense, uneasy. *See* EDGY.

edge *verb* **1** *edge the shears* put an edge on, sharpen, hone, whet, strop, file. **2** *edge with lace* trim, bind, hem, border, fringe, rim, verge. **3** *edge one's way through the crowd* inch, ease, elbow, worm, work, sidle, sidestep, gravitate. **4** *edge forward* inch, sidle, creep, steal.

edgy *adjective* on edge, nervous, tense, ill at ease, anxious, on tenterhooks, keyed up, restive, apprehensive, uneasy, irritable, irascible, touchy, tetchy; *inf.* nervy, twitchy, uptight, wired.

edible *adjective* fit/good to eat, consumable, digestible, palatable, comestible.
Opposites INEDIBLE.

edict *noun* decree, order, command, law, rule, ruling, regulation, act, enactment, statute, injunction, mandate, manifesto, proclamation, pronouncement, ordinance, dictate, dictum, fiat, pronunciamento, ukase.

edification *noun* instruction, education, tuition, teaching, schooling, tutoring, coaching, guidance, enlightenment, improvement, uplifting, elevation.

edifice *noun* building, structure, construction, erection; *inf.* pile. *See table at* BUILDING.

edify *verb* instruct, educate, teach, school, tutor, coach, guide, inform, enlighten, improve, uplift, elevate.

edit *verb* **1** *edit her book* copy-edit, revise, correct, emend, polish, check, modify, rewrite, rephrase, prepare/adapt/assemble for publication, redact; *inf.* clean up. **2** *he edits the paper* be the editor of, run, direct, be in charge of, be chief of, head, head up.

edition *noun* **1** *morning editions of the paper/programme* issue, number, printing, version. **2** *a first edition of the book* printing, impression, publication, issue.

educate *verb* instruct, teach, school, tutor, coach, train, drill, prime, inform, indoctrinate, inculcate, enlighten, edify, cultivate, develop, improve, prepare, rear, nurture, foster.

ECONOMISTS

Bagehot, Walter (1826–77; Brit.)	Friedman, Milton (b. 1912; Am.)	Kuznets, Simon (1901–85; Am.)	Passy, Frédéric (1822–1912; Fr.)
Baruch, Bernard (1870–1965; Am.)	Frisch, Ragnar (1895–1973; Norw.)	Lindale, Erik (1891–1960; Sw.)	Phillips, A. W. (1917–75; Brit.)
Beccaria, Cesare, Marchese di (1738–94; It.)	Galbraith, John Kenneth (b. 1908; Am.)	Malthus, Thomas (1766–1834; Brit.)	Quesnay, François (1694–1774; Fr.)
Beveridge, William, 1st Baron (1879–1963; Brit.)	George, Henry (1839–97; Am.)	Marx, Karl (1818–83; Ger.)	Schumpeter, Joseph (1883–1950; Am., b. in Austria)
Clark, John (1884–1963; Am.)	Hayek, Friedrich von (1899–1992; Austrian)	Meade, James (b. 1907; Brit.)	Smith, Adam (1723–90; Scot.)
Coase, Ronald (b. 1910; Brit.)	Heckscher, Eli (1879–1912; Sw.)	Monnet, Jean (1888–1979; Fr.)	Tinbergen, Jan (1903–94; Du.)
Edgeworth, Francis (1845–1926; Ir.)	Keynes, John Maynard, 1st Baron (1883–1946; Brit.)	Myrdal, Gunnar (1898–1987; Sw.)	Toynbee, Arnold (1852–83; Brit.)
Erhard, Ludwig (1897–1977; Ger.)		Pareto, Vilfredo (1848–1923; It.)	Veblen, Thorstein (1857–1929; Am.)

educated *adjective educated people* literate, schooled, well-read, informed, knowledgeable, enlightened, lettered, erudite, cultivated, cultured, refined; *inf.* highbrow.
Opposites ILLITERATE; IGNORANT.

education *noun* **1** *the education of the children* schooling, teaching, instruction, tuition, coaching, training, tutelage, drilling, disciplining, priming, informing, indoctrination, inculcation, enlightenment, edification, cultivation, development, improvement, preparation, rearing, nurturing, fostering. **2** *people of education* literacy, schooling, scholarship, knowledge, enlightenment, cultivation, culture, refinement; letters.

educational *adjective* **1** *an educational establishment* academic, learning, teaching, pedagogic. **2** *the film is educational* educative, instructive, informative, enlightening, edifying, improving, didactic, heuristic.

educator *noun* educationalist, teacher, schoolteacher, schoolmaster, schoolmistress, lecturer, tutor, coach, academic, pedagogue.

eerie *adjective* uncanny, unearthly, ghostly, spectral, mysterious, strange, unnatural, frightening, fearful, scaring, chilling, spine-chilling, blood-curdling; *Scots* eldritch; *inf.* spooky, scary, creepy.

efface *verb* **1** *efface the sketch/memory* remove, rub out, blot out, wipe out, blank out, obliterate, erase, delete, eradicate, expunge, eliminate, excise, annihilate, extirpate. **2** *efface oneself | be self-effacing* make inconspicuous, withdraw, keep out of the limelight, regard/treat as unimportant, be modest/diffident/retiring.

effect *noun* **1** *the effect of the changes* result, net result, outcome, upshot, consequence, conclusion, aftermath, issue; results, fruits. **2** *with effect from tomorrow* force, enforcement, operation, implementation, execution, action. **3** *speak to great effect | act with great effect* effectiveness, success, influence, efficacy, effectuality, weight, power, cogency. *See* EFFECTIVENESS. **4** *or words to that effect* sense, meaning, drift, tenor, significance, import, purport, essence. **in effect** effectively, actually, really, in actual fact, in reality, in truth, to all intents and purposes, for all practical purposes, essentially, in essence, virtually. **take effect** **1** *rules taking effect from tomorrow* come into being/force/operation, begin, become operative, become valid, become law. **2** *medicine taking effect* be effective, work, produce results, have the desired effect.

effect *verb* *effect a plan* effectuate, bring about, carry out, cause, make, produce, create, give rise to, perform, achieve, accomplish, complete, fulfil, implement, execute, actuate, initiate.

effective *adjective* **1** *effective administration* successful, productive, competent, capable, able, efficient, efficacious, effectual, useful, adequate, active, energetic. **2** *effective lighting* striking, impressive, exciting, attractive. **3** *effective arguments* powerful, forceful, forcible, cogent, compelling, potent, telling, persuasive,

convincing, moving. **4** *rules effective from tomorrow* valid, in force, in operation, operative, active, effectual.
Opposites INEFFECTIVE; INCOMPETENT; WEAK.

effectiveness *noun* **1** *the effectiveness of the administration* success, productiveness, competence, competency, capability, ability, efficiency, efficacy, effectuality, effectualness, usefulness, adequacy. *See* EFFECTIVE 1. **2** *the effectiveness of the argument* power, force, forcefulness, cogency, potency, persuasion, persuasiveness. *See* EFFECTIVE 3.

effects *plural noun* belongings, possessions, goods, goods and chattels, trappings, accoutrements, paraphernalia; property, luggage, baggage, bag and baggage, gear, equipment, tackle; *inf.* things, bits and pieces.

effectual *adjective* **1** *effectual actions/measures* effective, successful, efficacious, productive, efficient, powerful, potent, capable, competent, useful, functional, forcible. **2** *effectual documents* valid, legal, binding, lawful, in force, sound, licit.

effectuate *verb* effect, bring about, cause, make, produce, achieve, accomplish, implement, execute, actuate. *See* EFFECT *verb*.

effeminate *adjective* womanish, unmanly, effete, milksoppish; *inf.* wimpish, pansy-like, sissy.
Opposites VIRILE; MANLY.

effervesce *verb* **1** *wine effervescing* sparkle, bubble, fizz, froth, foam, ferment. **2** *the engaged couple effervescing* sparkle, be animated, be lively, be jubilant, be exuberant. *See* EFFERVESCENT 2.

effervescence *noun* **1** *the effervescence of the wine/water* bubbliness, sparkle, carbonation, fizziness, frothiness, foam, fermentation. **2** *the effervescence of the happy young people* vivacity, animation, liveliness, buoyancy, exuberance, exhilaration, ebullience, jubilation, sparkle, bubbliness, merriment, irrepressibility.

effervescent *adjective* **1** *effervescent wine* sparkling, carbonated, bubbly, bubbling, fizzy, fizzing, frothy, foamy, fermenting. **2** *effervescent holiday-makers* vivacious, animated, lively, buoyant, exuberant, exhilarated, ebullient, jubilant, sparkling, bubbly, merry, irrepressible.

effete *adjective* **1** *effete civilization* weakened, worn out, exhausted, finished, burnt out, played out, drained, spent, enfeebled, enervated, powerless. **2** *effete young men* effeminate, womanish, unmanly, milksoppish; *inf.* pansy-like, sissy, wimpish.

efficacious *adjective* effective, successful, efficient, effectual, productive, useful, competent, adequate, capable, able, potent, powerful.

efficacy *noun* effectiveness, success, successfulness, efficiency, effectuality, productiveness, usefulness, potency. *See* EFFICACIOUS.

efficiency *noun* **1** *admire her efficiency* capability, ability, competence, competency, effectiveness, productivity, skill, expertise, proficiency, adeptness, deftness, mastery, organization. *See*

EFFICIENT 1. **2** *the efficiency of the office* organization, well-orderedness, streamlinedness. *See* EFFICIENT 2.

efficient *adjective* **1** *an efficient person* capable, able, competent, effective, productive, skilful, expert, proficient, adept, deft, organized, workmanlike, businesslike. **2** *an efficient office* organized, well-organized, well-run, well-ordered, streamlined, labour-saving.
Opposites INEFFICIENT; INEPT; DISORGANIZED.

effigy *noun* likeness, image, model, dummy, representation, guy, carving, statue, bust.

effluent *noun* **1** *factory effluent* waste, sewage, pollutant, pollution, effluvium. **2** *the effluent of the dirty water* discharge, outflow, emission, emanation, exhalation.

effort *noun* **1** *put effort into it* exertion, force, power, energy, work, muscle, application, labour, striving, endeavour, toil, struggle, strain, stress; *lit.* travail; *inf.* elbow grease.
2 *win at the third effort* attempt, try, endeavour; *inf.* shot, go, crack, stab. **3** *admire his artistic efforts* achievement, accomplishment, attainment, result, creation, production, opus, feat, deed.

effortless *adjective* easy, simple, uncomplicated, undemanding, unexacting, painless, trouble-free, facile.
Opposites DIFFICULT; DEMANDING.

effrontery *noun* impertinence, insolence, impudence, cheek, audacity, temerity, presumption, gall, rashness, bumptiousness; *inf.* nerve, face, neck, brass neck.

effulgent *adjective* shining, bright, brilliant, dazzling, blazing, glowing, radiant, luminous, lustrous, incandescent, fluorescent, vivid, splendid; *lit.* refulgent, lucent.

effusion *noun* **1** *effusion of blood* gush, stream, outpouring, outflow, discharge, issue, efflux, spilling, shedding, voidance, extravasation.
2 *amazed at her passionate effusion* outburst, outpouring, stream of words, flow of speech, utterance, wordiness, speech, address, talk; words, writings.

effusive *adjective* gushing, unrestrained, unreserved, extravagant, fulsome, demonstrative, lavish, enthusiastic, rhapsodic, lyrical, exuberant, ebullient, expansive, wordy, verbose, long-winded, profuse; *inf.* over the top, OTT, smarmy.

egg *verb* **egg on** encourage, urge, push, drive, goad, spur on, prod, prompt, excite, exhort.

egghead *noun* intellectual, academic, scholar, brain, genius, blue-stocking, bookworm, pedagogue, pedant; *inf.* highbrow, Einstein, know-it-all, walking encyclopedia.

ego *noun* self, the self, oneself, identity; self-importance, self-esteem, self-conceit, self-image, *amour propre*, self-confidence.

egoism *noun* self-interest, self-centredness, selfishness, egocentricity, egomania, egotism, looking out for number one, self-seeking, self-absorption, self-love, narcissism, vanity, conceit, pride, self-esteem, self-importance.

egoist *noun* self-seeker, egocentric, egomaniac, egotist, narcissist.

egoistic *adjective* self-centred, selfish, egocentric, egotistic, self-seeking, self-absorbed, self-obsessed, self-loving, narcissistic, vain, conceited, proud, self-important.

egotism *noun* self-admiration, self-love, egomania, egocentricity, egoism, narcissism, self-conceit, conceit, vanity, pride, arrogance, self-esteem, self-importance, self-glorification, superiority, self-praise, boastfulness, bragging, braggadocio, fanfaronade; *inf.* blowing one's own trumpet.

egotist *noun* self-admirer, egomaniac, egocentric, egoist, boaster, bragger; *inf.* blowhard, bighead.

egotistic *adjective* self-admiring, egocentric, egoistic, narcissistic, conceited, vain, proud, arrogant, self-important, superior, boastful, bragging.

egregious *adjective* glaring, flagrant, blatant, gross, outrageous, monstrous, rank, enormous, shocking, scandalous, appalling, heinous, intolerable, infamous, notorious, grievous, arrant.

egress *noun* **1** *seek a means of egress* exit, way out, door/gate out, out-passage, out-lane, escape route, outlet, vent. **2** *the egress of the crowd* leaving, departure, exit, withdrawal, exodus, issue, emergence, flowing out, escape, emanation, debouchment.

ejaculate *verb* **1** *ejaculate fluid/semen/vomit* emit, eject, discharge, release, expel, spurt.
2 *men unable to ejaculate* emit/discharge semen, climax, have an orgasm, orgasm; *inf.* come.
3 *ejaculate a cry* utter, call out, voice, vocalize.
4 *"Watch out!" he ejaculated* cry out, call out, exclaim, shout out, blurt out, yell.

ejaculation *noun* **1** *the ejaculation of fluid/semen/vomit* emission, ejection, discharge, release. *See* EJACULATE 1. **2** *his premature ejaculation* emission/discharge of semen, climax, orgasm; *inf.* coming. **3** *they heard an ejaculation* cry, call, exclamation, shout, yell, utterance.

eject *verb* **1** *eject sewage/smoke/semen* emit, discharge, exude, excrete, expel, cast out, release, spew out, disgorge, spout, vomit, ejaculate.
2 *he was ejected from the plane/vehicle* propel, thrust out, throw out, expel. **3** *eject the intruder from the building | eject him from his house | ejected from the country* throw out, turn out, put out, cast out, remove, evict, expel, oust, put out in the street, dispossess, banish, deport, exile; *inf.* chuck out, kick out, turf out, boot out, heave out, bounce. **4** *eject her from a senior job* sack, dismiss, discharge, oust, dislodge, get rid of, send packing; *inf.* fire, axe, hand someone his/her cards, chuck out, kick out, boot out, give the boot to.

ejection *noun* **1** *ejection of sewage/smoke/semen* emission, discharge, exudation, excretion, expulsion, ejaculation, release. *See* EJECT 1.
2 *his ejection from the plane* propulsion, expulsion. *See* EJECT 2. **3** *ejection from the building/house/country* throwing out, removal, eviction, expulsion, ousting, dispossessing, banishment, deportation, exile; *inf.* chucking out, turfing out, bouncing. *See* EJECT 3. **4** *her ejection from the senior job* sacking, dismissal, discharge,

ousting, dislodgement; *inf.* firing, axing, chucking out, turfing out, the boot, heave-ho. *See* EJECT 4.

eke *verb* **eke out** **1** *eke out a living* scrape, scrimp, scrimp. **2** *you must eke out the butter ration* be economical with, economize on, be frugal/sparing with, husband; *inf.* go easy with. **3** *eke out the meat with vegetables* stretch out, add to, increase, supplement, augment, enlarge.

elaborate *adjective* **1** *elaborate plans* complicated, detailed, complex, involved, intricate, studied, painstaking, careful. **2** *elaborate patterns* detailed, complex, ornate, fancy, showy, fussy, ostentatious, extravagant, baroque, rococo, precious; *inf.* flash.
Opposites SIMPLE; PLAIN.

elaborate *verb* **1** *elaborate on a plan* expand on, enlarge on, amplify, flesh out, add flesh to, add detail to, expatiate on. **2** *elaborate the plan* develop, work out, improve, refine, polish, perfect, embellish, enhance, ornament, embroider.

élan *noun* style, flair, flourish, dash, verve, panache, spirit, vivacity, vitality, zest, brio, *esprit; inf.* oomph, pizazz.

elapse *verb* pass, go by, go on, slip away, slip by, roll by, slide by, steal by.

elastic *adjective* **1** *elastic material* stretchy, stretchable, springy, flexible, pliant, pliable, supple, yielding, rubbery, plastic, rebounding, recoiling, resilient. **2** *elastic plans/attitudes* flexible, adaptable, fluid, adjustable, accommodating, variable, yielding; *inf.* easy.
Opposites RIGID; INFLEXIBLE.

elasticity *noun* **1** *elasticity of the fibre* stretchiness, springiness, flexibility, pliancy, suppleness, rubberiness, plasticity, resilience; *inf.* give. **2** *elasticity of plans/attitude* flexibility, adaptability, adjustability, fluidity, variability.

elated *adjective elated at the news | an elated smile* overjoyed, ecstatic, blissful, joyful, jubilant, euphoric, exultant, rhapsodic, transported, exhilarated, ebullient, delighted, cheered, excited, animated, roused, gleeful, over the moon, in seventh heaven. *See* ECSTATIC.
Opposites MISERABLE; DEJECTED.

elation *noun* ecstasy, bliss, euphoria, rapture, joy, jubilation, exhilaration, rhapsody, transport, ebullience, delight, glee, excitement, animation.

elbow *noun* **1** *leaning on one's elbow* arm-joint, bend of the arm. **2** *elbow of the pipe* bend, joint, turning, corner, right angle, crook, flexure.

elbow *verb elbow out of the way | elbow one's way through the crowd* push, jostle, nudge, shoulder, knock, bump, crowd, bulldoze.

elbow-room *noun* space, room, breathing-space, scope, freedom, latitude, leeway, *Lebensraum.*

elder *adjective* older, senior, first-born.

elderly *adjective* oldish, advanced in years, ageing, aged, old, grey-haired, ancient, superannuated, past one's prime, senescent; *inf.* over the

hill, long in the tooth.
Opposites YOUNG; YOUTHFUL.

elderly *plural noun* **the elderly** elderly people, older people, senior citizens, pensioners, old-age pensioners, OAPs, retired people; *inf.* golden oldies, wrinklies, woopies (= well-off older people).

elect *verb elect an MP | elect a team captain* vote for, cast one's vote for, choose by ballot, choose, pick, select, appoint, opt for, decide on, plump for, designate, determine.

elect *plural noun* **the elect** the chosen, the selected, the preferred, the appointed, the designated, the élite.

election *noun* **1** *vote in an election* ballot, poll; hustings; general election, local election. **2** *the election of the MP | the election for team captain* voting, choosing, picking, selection, choice, appointment; vote, ballot. *See* ELECT *verb.*

elector *noun* voter, member of the electorate, constituent, selector, chooser.

electric *adjective* **1** *electric power* generated by electricity, galvanic, voltaic. **2** *electric kettles* electric-powered, electrically operated/powered, mains-operated, battery-operated, electrically charged. **3** *an electric moment | the effect was electric* tense, charged, exciting, dynamic, thrilling, startling, stimulating, rousing, stirring, moving, jolting, shocking, galvanizing.

electrify *verb* excite, thrill, startle, shock, arouse, rouse, move, stimulate, stir, animate, fire, charge, invigorate, jolt, galvanize.

elegance *noun* style, gracefulness, grace, taste, tastefulness, fashion, culture, beauty, charm, polish, refinement, exquisiteness, finesse, discernment, dignity, distinction, propriety, luxury, sumptuousness, opulence, *haute couture.*

elegant *adjective* stylish, graceful, tasteful, artistic, fashionable, cultured, beautiful, lovely, charming, exquisite, polished, cultivated, refined, aesthetic, suave, debonair, modish, dignified, luxurious, sumptuous, opulent.
Opposites INELEGANT; UNFASHIONABLE; GAUCHE.

elegiac *adjective* funereal, lamenting, doleful, mournful, dirgelike, melancholic, plaintive, keening, sad, nostalgic, valedictory; *fml.* threnodic.

elegy *noun* funeral poem/song, lament, dirge, plaint, requiem, keening; *fml.* threnody, threnode.

element *noun* **1** *an element of truth | a stable element of the group* basis, ingredient, factor, feature, detail, trace, component, constituent, part, section, portion, piece, segment, member, unit, module, subdivision, integrand. **2** *in his natural element* environment, habitat, medium, milieu, sphere, field, domain, realm, circle, resort, haunt. **3** *scientists discovered a new element* chemical element. *See* table.

elemental *adjective* **1** *elemental truth* basic, fundamental, rudimentary, embryonic, primitive, radical, essential, elementary. **2** *elemental influences* natural, atmospheric, meteorological, environmental.

elementary *adjective* **1** *elementary puzzle* easy, simple, straightforward, uncomplicated, rudimentary, facile, simplistic. **2** *elementary maths* basic, fundamental, rudimentary, primary, preparatory, introductory. **Opposites** COMPLICATED; ADVANCED; SENIOR.

elements *plural noun* **1** *exposed to the elements* weather, climate, atmospheric conditions/forces, environment; *lit.* clime. **2** *the elements of good manners* basics, essentials, principles, foundations, fundamentals, rudiments.

elephantine *adjective* huge, massive, enormous, immense, hulking, bulky, mammoth, gargantuan, heavy, weighty, ponderous, lumbering, clumsy, laborious.

elevate *verb* **1** *elevate the load* raise, lift, hoist, hike up, raise up/aloft. **2** *elevate to management* promote, give promotion, upgrade, improve the position/status of, advance, give advancement, exalt, prefer, aggrandize; *inf.* kick upstairs. **3** *elevate her spirits* | *she felt elevated* cheer, gladden, brighten, perk up, give a lift/boost to, lighten; cheer up, animate, exhilarate, elate, boost, buoy up, uplift.

elevated *adjective* **1** *elevated banners* raised, lifted up, hoisted, high up, aloft, upraised, uplifted. **2** *an elevated position* high, higher, high/higher up, great, grand, lofty, dignified, noble, exalted, magnificent, sublime, inflated, pompous, bombastic, orotund, fustian. **3** *elevated spirits/state* cheerful, cheered up, glad, joyful, happy, overjoyed, gleeful, excited, animated, elated, exhilarated, in high spirits, blithe. **4** *elevated literary style* lofty, exalted, inflated, pompous, bombastic, orotund, fustian.

elevation *noun* **1** *elevation of the building* height, altitude, tallness. **2** *the elevation behind the town* height, rise, raised/rising ground, hill, mountain, hillock, mound, mount, eminence; *fml.* acclivity. **3** *elevation to the board* promotion, upgrading, advancement, preferment, aggrandizement, step up the ladder; *inf.* kick upstairs. **4** *elevation of thought* grandeur, greatness, nobility, magnificence, loftiness, majesty, grandioseness, sublimity.

elf *noun* fairy, pixie, sprite, dwarf, gnome, goblin, hobgoblin, imp, brownie, leprechaun, puck, troll, banshee, kobold, nix, nixie.

elfin *adjective* **1** *elfin features/child* elflike, elfish, elvish, pixie-like, puckish, small, little, tiny, dainty, diminutive, wee, pint-sized, Lilliputian. **2** *elfin mischief* mischievous, impish, puckish, playful, arch.

elicit *verb* obtain, bring out, draw out, extract, extort, exact, wrest, evoke, derive, call forth, educe.

eligible *adjective* **1** *an eligible candidate* suitable, appropriate, fitting, acceptable; worthy, qualified. **2** *an eligible bachelor* available, single, unmarried. **Opposites** INELIGIBLE; UNSUITABLE; UNQUALIFIED.

élite *noun* **the élite 1** *the élite among the students* the best, the pick, the cream, *crème de la crème*, the elect, meritocracy. **2** *the élite of society* aristocracy, nobility, gentry, establishment, high society, jet set, beautiful people, beau

CHEMICAL ELEMENTS

Element	Symbol	Element	Symbol	Element	Symbol	Element	Symbol
actinium	Ac	fluorine	F	nickel	Ni	scandium	Sc
aluminium	Al	francium	Fr	niobium	Nb	seaborgium	—
americium	Am	gadolinium	Gd	nitrogen	N	selenium	Se
antimony	Sb	gallium	Ga	nobelium	Nb	silicon	Si
argon	Ar	germanium	Ge	osmium	Os	silver	Ag
arsenic	As	gold	Au	oxygen	O	sodium	Na
astatine	At	hafnium	Hf	palladium	Pd	strontium	Sr
barium	Ba	hahnium	Ha	phosphorus	P	sulphur	S
berkelium	Bk	helium	He	platinum	Pt	tantalum	Ta
beryllium	Be	holmium	Ho	plutonium	Pu	technetium	Tc
bismuth	Bi	hydrogen	H	polonium	Po	tellurium	Te
boron	B	indium	In	potassium	K	terbium	Tb
bromine	Br	iodine	I	praseo-		thallium	Tl
cadmium	Cd	iridium	Ir	dymium	Pr	thorium	Th
caesium	Cs	iron	Fe	prometh-		thulium	Tm
calcium	Ca	krypton	Kr	ium	Pm	tin	Sn
californium	Cf	lanthanum	La	protactin-		titanium	Ti
carbon	C	lawrencium	Lr	ium	Pa	tungsten/	
cerium	Ce	lead	Pb	radium	Ra	wolfram	W
chlorine	Cl	lithium	Li	radon	Rn	uranium	U
chromium	Cr	lutetium	Lu	rhenium	Re	vanadium	V
cobalt	Co	magnesium	Mg	rhodium	Rh	xenon	Xe
copper	Cu	manganese	Mn	rubidium	Rb	ytterbium	Yb
curium	Cm	mendelevium	Md	ruthenium	Ru	yttrium	Y
dysprosium	Dy	mercury	Hg	rutherford-		zinc	Zn
einsteinium	Es	molybdenum	Mo	ium	Rf		zirconium	Zr
erbium	Er	neodymium	Nd	kurchatov-			
europium	Eu	neon	Ne	ium	Ku		
fermium	Fm	neptunium	Np	samarium	Sm		

monde, *haut monde.*
Opposites RIFF-RAFF; RABBLE.

elixir *noun* **1** *an elixir for all ills* panacea, cure-all, universal/sovereign remedy, wonder drug, magic bullet, nostrum. **2** *elixir of eucalyptus* extract, essence, concentrate, quintessence, pith, mixture, solution, potion, tincture.

elliptical *adjective* **1** *an elliptical shape* oval, egg-shaped, ovate, ovoid. **2** *an elliptical style of writing* terse, concise, succinct, compact, economic. **3** *elliptical prose/speech* abstruse, cryptic, ambiguous, obscure, recondite.

elocution *noun* diction, speech, enunciation, articulation, voice production, pronunciation, phrasing, delivery, utterance, speech-making, public speaking, oratory, declamation. *See table at* RHETORIC.

elongate *verb* lengthen, stretch out, make longer, extend, draw out, prolong, protract.

elope *verb* **1** *elope to Gretna Green* run off/away together, run off/away with a lover, run away to marry, slip away, sneak off, steal away. **2** *elope from the camp* escape, make one's escape, flee, abscond, bolt, decamp.

eloquence *noun* **1** *the eloquence of the speaker/argument/speech* expressiveness, articulacy, articulateness, fluency, facility, diction, enunciation, command of language, power of speech, oratory, rhetoric, persuasiveness, forcefulness; *inf.* gift of the gab. **2** *the eloquence of the glance* expressiveness, significance, meaningfulness, suggestiveness, revelation, pregnancy.

eloquent *adjective* **1** *an eloquent speaker/argument/speech* expressive, well-spoken, articulate, fluent, graceful, silver-tongued, smooth-tongued, well-expressed, vivid, effective, graphic, pithy, persuasive, glib, forceful. **2** *an eloquent look* expressive, significant, meaningful, suggestive, revealing, telling, pregnant.
Opposites INARTICULATE; TONGUE-TIED.

elsewhere *adverb* somewhere else, in/to another place, in/to a different place, not here, not present, absent, away, abroad, hence.

elucidate *verb* *please elucidate! | elucidate the meaning* explain; make clear/plain, interpret, illuminate, throw light on, comment on, annotate, gloss, spell out; *fml.* explicate.

elucidation *noun* explanation, clarification, interpretation, illumination, comment, commentary, annotation, gloss, explication, exposition.

elude *verb* *the fox eluded the hunter* avoid, get away from, dodge, evade, escape, lose, duck, shake off, give the slip to, throw off the scent, flee, circumvent, bilk; *inf.* ditch.

elusive *adjective* **1** *an elusive person* difficult to catch/find, evasive, slippery, shifty, cagey. **2** *an elusive perfume* indefinable, subtle, unanalysable, intangible, impalpable, fleeting, transient, transitory, fugitive. **3** *an elusive answer* ambiguous, baffling, puzzling, misleading, evasive, equivocal, deceitful, deceptive, fallacious, fraudulent, elusory.

Elysium *noun* heaven, paradise, eternity, kingdom come.

emaciated *adjective* thin as a rake, wasted, gaunt, skeletal, anorexic, scrawny, cadaverous, shrivelled, shrunken, withered, haggard, drawn, pinched, wizened, attenuated, atrophied.

emaciation *noun* gauntness, scrawniness, cadaverousness, haggardness. *See* EMACIATED.

emanate *verb* **1** *desire emanating from jealousy* arise, originate, stem, derive, emerge, proceed, come forth, issue. **2** *emanating fumes* give off, give out, send out, send forth, discharge, emit, exhale, radiate.

emanation *noun* **1** *emanation of hostility from rivalry* arising, origination, derivation, emergence. **2** *a foul-smelling emanation* discharge, emission, effluent, exhalation, radiation, effusion, efflux.

emancipate *verb* **1** *emancipate slaves* free, set free, liberate, release, let loose, deliver, discharge, unchain, unfetter, unshackle, untie, unyoke, manumit. **2** *emancipate women* allow to vote, give voting rights to, enfranchise, affranchise; free from restriction/restraint.

emancipation *noun* **1** *emancipation of slaves* setting free, liberation, release, deliverance, discharge, unfettering, unshackling, manumission; freedom, liberty. *See* EMANCIPATE 1. **2** *the emancipation of women* enfranchisement, affranchisement; right to vote.

emasculate *verb* **1** *emasculate a bull* castrate, neuter, geld, spay, desex, unman. **2** *emasculate the power of the state* weaken, debilitate, make feeble/feebler, enfeeble, enervate, impoverish, remove the sting from, pull the teeth of.

embalm *verb* **1** *embalm a corpse* preserve, anoint, mummify, lay out. **2** *embalm memories* remember, keep in mind, look back on, reminisce about, cherish, treasure, conserve, store, consecrate, immortalize, enshrine. **3** *flowers embalming the air* perfume, make fragrant, scent, aromatize.

embargo *noun* ban, bar, prohibition, stoppage, interdict, proscription; restriction, restraint, blockage, check, barrier, impediment, obstruction, hindrance.

embargo *verb* ban, bar, prohibit, stop, interdict, debar, proscribe; restrict, restrain, block, check, impede, obstruct, hinder.

embark *verb* **1** *passengers embarking* board ship, enplane, go on board, go aboard, take ship; set sail, put to sea, weigh anchor, take off. **2** *embark on an adventure* begin, start, commence, undertake, set about, enter on, go into, take up, venture into, launch into, turn one's hand to, engage in, broach, institute, initiate; *inf.* have a go at.
Opposites DISEMBARK; LAND; END.

embarrass *verb* make uncomfortable/awkward, make self-conscious, upset, disconcert, discomfit, discompose, confuse, fluster, agitate, nonplus, discountenance, distress, chagrin, shame, humiliate, abash, mortify.

embarrassed *adjective* uncomfortable, awkward, self-conscious, disconcerted, upset, discomfited, discomposed, confused, flustered, agitated, nonplussed, discountenanced, distressed, chagrined, shamed, humiliated, abashed, mortified; *inf.* with egg on one's face.

embarrassing *adjective* **1** *embarrassing remark* disconcerting, discomfiting, discomposing, upsetting, confusing, flustering, agitating, discountenancing, distressing, shaming, humiliating, mortifying. **2** *embarrassing moment* awkward, compromising, tricky.

embarrassment *noun* **1** *overcome with embarrassment* discomfort, awkwardness, self-consciousness, bashfulness, discomfiture, discomposure, confusion, agitation, distress, chagrin, shame, humiliation, mortification. **2** *financial embarrassment* difficulty, predicament, plight, mess, dilemma, entanglement, imbroglio; *inf.* bind, pickle, fix, scrape, quandary. **3** *embarrassment of riches* excess, surplus, abundance, over-abundance, profusion, glut, surfeit, superfluity, avalanche, deluge, *embarras de choix.*

embassy *noun* **1** *the British embassy* consulate, legation, ministry. **2** *the archbishop's embassy* envoy, representative, legate; delegation, deputation.

embed, imbed *verb* insert, implant, plant, set/ fix in, root, drive in, hammer in, ram in, sink.

embellish *verb* *embellish a ceiling* | *embellish the truth* decorate, adorn, ornament, dress, dress up, beautify, enhance, trim, garnish, gild, varnish, embroider, enrich, deck, bedeck, festoon, emblazon, bespangle, elaborate, exaggerate.

embellishment *noun* *the embellishment of a ceiling/story* decoration, ornamentation, adornment, beautification, enhancement, trimming, garnishing, gilding, varnishing, embroidery, enrichment, bedecking, festooning, emblazoning, elaboration, exaggeration.

embezzle *verb* steal, rob, thieve, pilfer, appropriate, misappropriate, purloin, filch, abstract, put one's hand in the till, dip into the public purse, peculate, defalcate; *inf.* nick, rip off.

embezzlement *noun* thieving, stealing, robbing, fraud, larceny, pilfering, appropriation, misappropriation, purloining, filching, abstraction, peculation, defalcation; theft, robbery, misuse of funds; *inf.* nicking, ripping off.

embitter *verb* **1** *embittered by her divorce* make bitter, make resentful, sour, anger, disillusion, poison, disaffect, envenom. **2** *embitter the situation* aggravate, worsen, exacerbate, exaggerate.

emblazon *verb* **1** *emblazoning a shield* decorate, adorn, ornament, embellish, illuminate, colour, paint. **2** *emblazoned on the screen* proclaim, publicize, publish, trumpet, glorify, extol, praise, laud.

emblem *noun* crest, badge, symbol, device, representation, token, image, figure, mark, sign; insignia.

embodiment *noun* **1** *the embodiment of new design features in the car* incorporation, combination, bringing together, collecting, inclusion, consolidation, assimilation, integration, organization, systemization. *See* EMBODY 1. **2** *he is the embodiment of good manners* | *the embodiment of renaissance man* personification, representa-

tion, incarnation, incorporation, symbol, symbolization, type, exemplification, example, exemplar, realization, manifestation, expression, reification. *See* EMBODY 2.

embody *verb* **1** *a vehicle embodying technological advances* incorporate, combine, bring together, comprise, collect, include, contain, constitute, take in, consolidate, encompass, assimilate, integrate, concentrate, organize, systematize. **2** *he embodies good manners* | *embodying renaissance man* personify, represent, symbolize, stand for, typify, exemplify, incorporate, realize, manifest, express, incarnate, concretize, reify.

embolden *verb* give courage to, make brave/ braver, encourage, hearten, strengthen, rouse, stir, stimulate, cheer, fire, inflame, animate, invigorate, vitalize, inspirit.

embrace *verb* **1** *embrace his wife* take/hold in one's arms, hold, hug, cuddle, clasp, squeeze, clutch, seize, grab, nuzzle, enfold, enclasp, encircle; *inf.* canoodle with, neck with. **2** *embrace the new philosophy* welcome, accept, receive enthusiastically/wholeheartedly, take up, adopt; *fml.* espouse. **3** *embrace the whole area* cover, include, take in, deal with, involve, take into account, contain, comprise, incorporate, encompass, embody, subsume, comprehend, enfold.

embrace *noun* hug, bear hug, cuddle, squeeze, clasp, hold, clutch, clinch, nuzzle; *inf.* necking session.

embroider *verb* **1** *embroider a design/tablecloth* sew, decorate with needlework. **2** *embroider the story/truth* touch up, dress up, embellish, elaborate, colour, enlarge on, exaggerate, paint, gild, invent, fabricate.

embroidery *noun* **1** *thread for embroidery* needlework, needlepoint, sewing, tatting; tapestry, sampler. *See table at* SEWING. **2** *embroidery of the story/truth* touching up, dressing up, embellishment, adornment, ornamentation, elaboration, colouring, exaggeration, gilding; invention, fabrication, tall story, fisherman's tale, angler's tale.

embryonic *adjective* just beginning, early, undeveloped, unformed, rudimentary, immature, incipient, primary, elementary, seminal, germinal, inchoate.

emend *verb* edit, correct, revise, alter, rewrite, rectify, improve, polish, refine, expurgate, censor, bowdlerize, redact.

emendation *noun* editing, correction, revision, alteration, rewriting, rectification, improving, improvement, polishing, refinement, expurgation, censoring, bowdlerization, redaction.

emerge *verb* **1** *emerge from a building* | *emerge from a state of depression* come out, come into view, appear, come up, become visible, surface, spring up, crop up, materialize, arise, proceed, issue, come forth, emanate. **2** *facts emerging* become known, become common knowledge, come out, come to light, get around, become apparent, transpire, come to the fore.

Opposites ENTER; DISAPPEAR; FADE.

emergence noun **1** *his emergence from the building* coming out, appearance, arrival, arising, surfacing, springing up, materializing, materialization, issue, emanation. **2** *emergence of the facts* becoming known, coming to light, disclosure, exposure, unfolding, publication, publicizing, publishing, broadcasting.

emergency noun *supplies for an emergency* urgent situation, crisis, danger, accident, difficulty, plight, predicament, quandary, dilemma, crunch, scrape, extremity, exigency, necessity; unforeseen circumstances, dire/desperate straits; *inf.* pickle.

emergency adjective *emergency exit/supplies* urgent, accident, danger; reserve, back-up, substitute, alternative, spare, extra.

emergent adjective emerging, developing, beginning, coming out, budding, arising, dawning, embryonic.

emigrate verb move abroad, leave one's country, migrate, relocate, resettle, defect, trek.

emigration noun moving abroad, migration, departure, relocation, resettling, expatriation, exodus, defection, trekking.

eminence noun **1** *eminence of the statesman* importance, greatness, prestige, reputation, fame, distinction, renown, pre-eminence, celebrity, prominence, illustriousness, notability, rank, standing, station, note, dignity. **2** *church built on an eminence* elevation, rise, rising/raised ground, height.

eminent adjective important, great, distinguished, well-known, celebrated, famous, renowned, noted, prominent, esteemed, noteworthy, pre-eminent, superior, outstanding, high-ranking, exalted, revered, elevated, august, paramount.
Opposites UNIMPORTANT; UNKNOWN.

eminently adverb *eminently suitable* very, well, greatly, highly, exceedingly, extremely, exceptionally, remarkably, outstandingly, strikingly, notably, prominently, surpassingly, signally.

emissary noun ambassador, envoy, agent, delegate, representative, deputy, go-between, attaché, legate, courier, herald, scout, spy.

emission noun **1** *the emission of fumes/light* discharge, outpouring, issue, oozing, leaking, excretion, secretion, ejection, emanation, radiation, exhalation, exudation, effusion, ejaculation, disgorgement, issuance. **2** *a deafening emission* utterance, declaration, expression, pronouncement, vocalization.

emit verb **1** *emit fumes/light* discharge, pour out, give out/off, issue, send forth, throw out, ooze, leak, excrete, secrete, eject, emanate, radiate, exhale, ejaculate, exude. **2** *emit a terrified scream* utter, express, voice, pronounce, declare, articulate, vocalize.

emolument noun payment, pay, salary, income, fee, stipend, revenue, return, profit, gain, reward, compensation, recompense, honorarium; wages, earnings, fees, profits, proceeds.

emotion noun feeling, sentiment, passion, reaction, response, sensation; warmth, ardour,

fervour, vehemence, joy, sorrow, pity, fear, horror.

emotional adjective **1** *emotional person* feeling, passionate, hot-blooded, warm, responsive, demonstrative, tender, loving, sentimental, ardent, fervent, sensitive, excitable, temperamental, melodramatic. **2** *an emotional farewell* moving, touching, affecting, poignant, emotive, pathetic, tear-jerking, heart-rending, soul-stirring, impassioned.
Opposites UNEMOTIONAL; APATHETIC; COLD.

emotionless adjective *emotionless person/response/stave* unemotional, unfeeling, undemonstrative, cold, cold-blooded, impassive, indifferent, detached, remote, imperturbable, frigid, phlegmatic, glacial, blank, toneless.

emotive adjective *an emotive issue* sensitive, delicate, controversial, touchy, awkward.

empathize verb identify with, be in tune with, be on the same wavelength as, talk the same language as; sympathize, understand.

emperor noun ruler, sovereign, king; tsar, kaiser, imperator, khan, mikado.

emphasis noun **1** *putting the emphasis on the first syllable* stress, accent, accentuation, weight. **2** *putting the emphasis on talent* importance, stress, attention, priority, weight, urgency, force, accent, accentuation, insistence, significance, prominence, underlining, intensity, import, mark, power, moment, pre-eminence, underscoring.

emphasize verb **1** *emphasize the first word* put the stress/accent/force on, stress, accentuate. **2** *emphasize the problems* put/lay stress on, give an emphasis to, stress, accent, accentuate, underline, call attention to, highlight, give prominence to, point up, spotlight, play up, feature, intensify, strengthen, heighten, deepen, italicize, underscore, insist on.
Opposites UNDERSTATE; play down (*see* PLAY); MINIMIZE.

emphatic adjective **1** *emphatic improvement* marked, pronounced, decided, positive, definite, distinctive, unmistakable, important, significant, strong, striking, powerful, resounding, telling, momentous. **2** *he was emphatic | an emphatic denial* definite, decided, certain, determined, absolute, direct, forceful, forcible, earnest, energetic, vigorous, categorical, unequivocal.
Opposites INSIGNIFICANT; HESITANT; TENTATIVE.

empire noun **1** *Napoleon guarding his empire* kingdom, realm, domain, territory, jurisdiction, province, commonwealth. *See table.* **2** *hold empire over* command, rule, control, authority, power, supremacy, government, sovereignty, sway, dominion.

empirical, empiric adjective practical, observed, pragmatic, seen, experimental, experiental, heuristic.

employ verb **1** *employ three people* hire, have in employment, engage, take on, take into employment, sign up, put on the payroll, enrol, commission, enlist, retain, indenture, apprentice. **2** *employed in polishing the floor* occupy, engage, keep busy. **3** *employ all his* *waking hours* occupy, take up, use up, put to use, make use of, fill, spend. **4** *employ cunning* use, apply, make use of, exercise, exert, utilize, ply, bring to bear.

employed *adjective* **1** *no longer employed in work,* working, in employment, in a job. **2** *employed in gazing out of the window* occupied, busy, engaged, preoccupied.
Opposites UNEMPLOYED; JOBLESS; UNOCCUPIED.

employee *noun* worker, blue-collar worker, white-collar worker, workman, member of staff, wage-earner, hand, hired hand, assistant, labourer, hireling.

employer *noun* boss, manager, owner, proprietor, patron, contractor, director, head man/woman, top man/woman; firm of employment, organization; *inf.* skipper, gaffer, governor; *Am. inf.* honcho.

employment *noun* **1** *the employment of new staff* hiring, hire, engagement, taking on, signing up, enrolment, commissioning, enlisting, apprenticing. **2** *employment as a teacher* job, work, business, line, occupation, profession, trade, calling, vocation, craft, *métier*, employ, service, pursuit. **3** *employment of resources/cunning* use, application, exercise, utilization, exertion.

emporium *noun* **1** *traders in the emporium* bazaar, market place, market, fair, mart, shopping quarter. **2** *an old-fashioned emporium replaced by a supermarket* shop, store, department store, establishment.

empower *verb* **1** *empowered to arrest you* authorize, license, certify, accredit, qualify, sanction, warrant, commission, delegate. **2** *resources empowering him to act* allow, enable, give power/means/strength to, equip.

emptiness *noun* **1** *an emptiness in her life* vacuum, void, hiatus. **2** *the emptiness of the place/house/page* vacantness, hollowness, voidness, desolation, bareness, barrenness, lack of contents/adornment, blankness, clearness. **3** *the emptiness of the threats/gestures* meaninglessness, futility, ineffectiveness, ineffectuality, uselessness, worthlessness, fruitlessness, insubstantiality, idleness. **4** *the emptiness of her existence* aimlessness, purposelessness, meaninglessness, worthlessness, hollowness, barrenness, senselessness, silliness, banality, frivolity, inanity, triviality. **5** *the emptiness of the expression/stare* blankness, expressionlessness, vacantness, vacuousness, unintelligence.

empty *adjective* **1** *empty bowl/house/page* containing nothing, without contents, unfilled,

vacant, hollow, void, unoccupied, uninhabited, desolate, bare, unadorned, barren, blank, clear. **2** *empty threats/gestures* meaningless, futile, ineffective, ineffectual, useless, worthless, idle, insubstantial, fruitless. **3** *empty existence* aimless, purposeless, meaningless, hollow, barren, senseless, unsatisfactory, silly, banal, inane, frivolous, trivial, worthless, valueless, profitless. **4** *empty expression/stare* blank, expressionless, vacant, unintelligent, deadpan, vacuous, absent. **5** *thirsty and empty* hungry, starving, famished, ravenous, unfed.
Opposites FULL; OCCUPIED; MEANINGFUL; WORTHWHILE.

empty *verb* **1** *empty the room/lorry* make vacant, vacate, clear, evacuate, void, unload, unburden. **2** *empty the liquid* drain, pour out, exhaust, use up, deplete, sap. **3** *the room emptied* clear, become vacant/empty. **4** *the liquid emptied* flow out, pour out, drain, discharge, issue, emit, exude, ooze.

empty-headed *adjective* stupid, silly, brainless, hare-brained, scatterbrained, featherbrained, scatty, giddy, skittish, flighty, frivolous, dizzy, vacuous; *inf.* dopey, batty, dotty.

enable *verb* **1** *enable you to vote* allow, permit, authorize, entitle, qualify, fit, license, sanction, warrant, accredit, validate, commission, delegate, legalize, empower. **2** *enable you to cross the river* allow, permit, give the means/resources to, equip, prepare, facilitate, capacitate.

enact *verb* **1** *enact Hamlet | enact the role of Hamlet* act, act out, play, perform, stage, appear as, portray, depict, represent, impersonate, personify; *fml.* personate. **2** *a bill enacted by Parliament* command, order, decree, ordain, legislate, rule, make law, pass, pronounce, approve, ratify, sanction.

enactment *noun* **1** *the enactment of scene 3 | enactments of King Lear* acting, playing, performing, staging, performance, appearance, portrayal, depiction, representation, personification; *fml.* personation. **2** *the enactment of the new law* passing, decreeing, ordaining, legislating, approval, ratification, sanction. **3** *enactments of Parliament* law, bill, act, order, decree, regulation, statute, edict, measure, motion, proclamation, command, commandment, pronouncement, ordinance, dictate, ratification; legislation.

enamoured *adjective* in love, loving, infatuated, captivated, charmed, enchanted, fasci-

---

EMPIRES

Almoravid	Carthaginian	Inca	Parthian
Asokan	Central African	Islamic	Phoenician
Assyrian	Eastern (Roman)	Khmer	Portuguese
Athenian	Empire	Macedonian	Roman
Austrian	Frankish	Mali	Russian
Austro-Hungarian	French	Mayan	Spanish
Aztec	Fulani	Median	Spanish American
Babylonian	German	Mogul	Venetian
British	Hittite	Mongol	Western (Roman)
Byzantine	Holy Roman	Ottoman	Empire

nated, bewitched, enthralled, entranced, enraptured; *inf.* smitten, mad, crazy, nuts, wild.

encampment *noun* camp, military camp, bivouac, camp-site, camping ground.

encapsulate *verb* **1** *encapsulate the views of the committee* sum up, summarize, condense, abridge, précis, compress, digest, epitomize. **2** *encapsulate all the main points* include, contain, embrace, capture.

enchant *verb* bewitch, make spellbound, fascinate, charm, captivate, entrance, enthrall, beguile, hypnotize, mesmerize, enrapture, delight, enamour.

enchanter *noun* wizard, witch, sorcerer, warlock, necromancer, magician, spell-binder, magus, conjuror, hypnotist, mesmerist, witch doctor, medicine man, soothsayer, seer.

enchanting *adjective* bewitching, charming, delightful, attractive, appealing, captivating, irresistible, fascinating, engaging, endearing, entrancing, alluring, winsome, ravishing.

enchantment *noun* **1** *witches with powers of enchantment* magic, witchcraft, sorcery, wizardry, necromancy, conjuration, hypnotism, mesmerism, charm, incantation. **2** *a time of enchantment* bliss, ecstasy, heaven, rapture, joy; transports. **3** *the enchantment of the view/dancing* charm, delight, attractiveness, appeal, captivation, irresistibility, fascination, entrancement, allure, allurement, glamour.

enchantress *noun* witch, sorceress, fairy, fairy godmother, siren, Circe, hex. *See also* ENCHANTER.

encircle *verb* **1** *enemy troops encircling the town* | *encircle the error* surround, enclose, circle, ring, encompass, circumscribe. **2** *trees encircling the lake* close in, shut in, fence in, wall in, hem in, confine.

enclose *verb* **1** *enclosing the garden* surround, circle, ring, close in, shut in, fence/wall/hedge in, hem in, confine, encompass, encircle, circumscribe, encase; *fml.* gird. **2** *enclose a cheque* include, send with, put in, insert, enfold.

enclosure *noun* **1** *spectators/cattle in the enclosure* special/assigned area, arena; compound, ring, yard, pen, pound, fold, paddock, stockade, sty, corrall, krall, court, cloister, close; precincts; *fml.* pale, enceinte, circumvallation. **2** *the enclosure of a cheque* inclusion, insertion, enfolding. **3** *an enclosure with the letter* insertion, thing enclosed.

encompass *verb* **1** *encompass the castle* surround, enclose, ring, encircle, close in, shut in, fence/wall/hedge in, hem in, confine. **2** *encompassing all disciplines* include, cover, embrace, take in, contain, envelop, deal with, comprise, incorporate, embody.

encore *noun* *play/take an encore* repeat, repeat/extra performance, replay; curtain call.

encounter *verb* **1** *encounter an old friend* meet, meet by chance, run into, run across, come upon, stumble across, chance/happen upon; *inf.* bump into. **2** *encounter problems* be faced with, confront, contend with, tussle with. **3** *encounter the enemy* accost, confront; fight, do battle with, clash with, come into conflict with, engage with, struggle with, contend with, combat, skirmish with, tussle with.

encounter *noun* **1** *an encounter with an old friend* meeting, chance meeting. *See* ENCOUNTER *verb* 1. **2** *an encounter with the enemy* fight, battle, clash, conflict, contest, dispute, combat, collision, confrontation, engagement, skirmish, scuffle, tussle, brawl; *inf.* run-in, set-to, brush.

encourage *verb* **1** *encourage the losers* cheer, rally, stimulate, motivate, inspire, stir, incite, animate, hearten, invigorate, embolden, inspirit; *inf.* buck up. **2** *encourage him to try again* urge, persuade, egg on, prompt, influence, exhort, sway, spur, goad. **3** *encourage exports* help, assist, aid, support, back, advocate, abet, boost, favour, promote, further, advance, forward, foster, strengthen.
Opposites DISCOURAGE; DISSUADE; HINDER.

encouragement *noun* **1** *the encouragement of the losers* rallying, stimulation, motivation, inspiration, incitement, animation, heartening, invigorating, emboldening, inspiriting. **2** *encouragement to go ahead* urging, persuasion, egging on, prompting, exhortation; spur, goad. **3** *encouragement of exports* help, assistance, support, promotion, furtherance, advocacy, backing, boosting, favouring, furthering, advancing, forwarding, fostering, strengthening.

encroach *verb* trespass, intrude, invade, infringe, impinge, infiltrate, overrun, usurp, appropriate, tread on someone's toes; *inf.* muscle in on, invade someone's space.

encroachment *noun* trespassing, intrusion, invasion, infringement, impingeing, infiltration, incursion, overrunning, usurping, appropriation.

encumber *verb* **1** *injury encumbered his efforts* | *encumbered with two small children* hinder, hamper, obstruct, impede, inconvenience, handicap, retard, check, cramp, constrain, restrain. **2** *a room encumbered with old furniture* block up, fill up, stuff, clog, congest. **3** *encumbered with taxes* burden, load, weigh down, tax, overtax, saddle, trammel, stress, strain.

encumbrance *noun* **1** *the encumbrance of heavy luggage* hindrance, hampering, obstruction, impediment, inconvenience, handicap, restraint, constraint. **2** *the encumbrance of a room with old furniture* blocking up, filling, stuffing, clogging, congestion. **3** *debts are an encumbrance* burden, weight, load, responsibility, obligation, stress, strain, tax, onus, trammel.

encyclopedic *adjective* comprehensive, complete, wide-ranging, all-inclusive, thorough, exhaustive, all-embracing, universal, all-encompassing, vast, compendious.

end *noun* **1** *the end of the table* | *the north end* edge, border, boundary, extremity, limit, margin, furthermost part, point, tip, extent. **2** *the end of the affair/novel* ending, finish, close, conclusion, termination, completion, resolution, climax, finale, culmination, denouement, epilogue; *inf.* wind-up. **3** *a cigarette end* | *the end of a pencil* remnant, remainder, fragment, vestige;

leftovers. **4** *her end in life* aim, goal, purpose, intention, intent, objective, object, design, motive, aspiration, *raison d'être*. **5** *the commercial end of the business* side, section, area, field, part, share, portion, segment, province; responsibility, burden, load. **6** *a peaceful/sad end* death, dying, demise, doom, extinction, annihilation, extermination; ruin, ruination, destruction, dissolution; death-blow, *coup de grâce*, finishing stroke; curtains. **7** *the end was that he shot himself* result, consequence, outcome, upshot, issue.
Opposites BEGINNING; START; BIRTH.

end *verb* **1** *the show/book ended* come to an end, finish, close, stop, cease, conclude, terminate, discontinue, break off, fade away, peter out; *inf.* wind up. **2** *to end a relationship/book* bring to an end, finish, close, stop, cease, conclude, terminate, break off, discontinue, complete, dissolve, resolve; *inf.* wind up. **3** *end his life/hopes* put an end to, destroy, annihilate, extinguish.
Opposites BEGIN; START.

endanger *verb* *endangering the species* threaten, put in danger, expose to danger, put at risk, expose, risk, jeopardize, imperil, hazard, compromise.

endearing *adjective* charming, attractive, adorable, lovable, sweet, engaging, winning, captivating, enchanting, winsome.

endearment *noun* **1** *affectionate endearments* sweet talk, sweet nothings, soft words, blandishments. **2** *words of endearment* love, affection, fondness, liking, attachment.

endeavour *verb* *endeavour to win* try, attempt, strive, work at, try one's hand at, do one's best, venture, aspire, undertake, struggle, labour, essay; *inf.* have a go/shot/stab at.

endeavour *noun* *make an endeavour to win* | *his best endeavour* try, attempt, trial, effort, striving, venture, undertaking, aspiration, enterprise, struggle, labouring, essay; *inf.* go, crack, shot, stab.

ending *noun* end, finish, close, conclusion, stopping, cessation, termination, expiration, resolution, completion.
Opposites BEGINNING; START.

endless *adjective* **1** *endless patience* unending, without end, unlimited, infinite, limitless, boundless, continual, everlasting, unceasing, interminable, incessant, measureless, untold, incalculable. **2** *an endless chain* continuous, uninterrupted, unbroken, whole, entire, never-ending. **3** *endless love* unending, without end, constant, everlasting, unfading, perpetual, immortal, deathless. **4** *endless talk/travelling* non-stop, interminable, monotonous, over-long, unremitting, boring.
Opposites FINITE; LIMITED; TRANSIENT.

endorse *verb* **1** *endorse a cheque* countersign, sign, autograph, underwrite, superscribe, validate. **2** *endorse the course of action* approve, support, back, favour, recommend, advocate, champion, subscribe to, uphold, authorize, ratify, sanction, warrant, affirm, confirm, vouch for, corroborate.

endorsement *noun* **1** *the endorsement on the document/cheque* | *endorsement of the signature* countersignature, autograph, underwriting, validation. **2** *the endorsement of their actions* approval, support, backing, recommendation, advocacy, championship, authorization, ratification, warrant, affirmation, corroboration. *See* ENDORSE 2.

endow *verb* **1** *endow with talent* provide, give, present, gift, confer, bestow, enrich, supply, furnish, award, invest; *fml.* endue. **2** *endow a foundation* | *endow a hospital bed* bequeath money for, bestow, will, donate money for, leave money for, make over to, settle on; pay for, finance, fund.

endowment *noun* **1** *an endowment of money* | *endowment of a scholarship* gift, present, bestowal, grant, donation, award, proffering, bequeathing, settlement, legacy, provision; largesse, finance, funding, revenue, income. **2** *natural endowments* ability, gift, talent, flair, aptitude, genius, attribute, power, strength, capability, capacity, facility, faculty, qualification, characteristic, quality, feature.

endurance *noun* **1** *endurance of his love/Christianity* lasting power, durability, stability, permanence, continuance, continuity, changelessness, immutability, longevity, everlastingness, immortality. **2** *beyond endurance* toleration, sufferance, fortitude, forbearance, perseverance, acceptance, patience, resignation. **3** *sports which are tests of endurance* stamina, staying power, fortitude, perseverance, tenacity; *inf.* guts.

endure *verb* **1** *love endures* last, live on, continue, persist, remain, stay, hold on, survive, wear well; *lit.* abide, bide, tarry. **2** *endure the difficult situation* | *can't endure the new manager* put up with, stand, bear, tolerate, suffer, abide, submit to, countenance, brook; *inf.* stick, stomach, swallow. **3** *endure poverty/pain* experience, undergo, go through, meet, encounter; bear, tolerate, cope with, suffer, brave, withstand, sustain, weather; *Scots* thole.
Opposites DIE; FADE.

enduring *adjective* lasting, long-lasting, durable, permanent; stable, steady, steadfast, imperishable, continuing, remaining, persisting, prevailing, abiding, eternal, immortal, perennial, unwavering, unfaltering.
Opposites SHORT-LIVED; TRANSIENT.

enemy *noun* foe, opponent, rival, adversary, antagonist, hostile party; opposition, competition.

energetic *adjective* **1** *energetic exercises/person* active, lively, vigorous, strenuous, brisk, dynamic, spirited, animated, vital, vibrant, sprightly, tireless, indefatigable, peppy, zippy; bright-eyed and bushy-tailed. **2** *energetic approach* forceful, forcible, determined, emphatic, aggressive, high-powered, driving, effective, effectual, powerful, potent.
Opposites LAZY; INACTIVE; WEAK.

energize *verb* **1** *energize him to get up* activate, stimulate, arouse, rouse, motivate, stir, goad, spur on, prompt. **2** *music might energize the party* enliven, liven up, animate, invigorate, pep up, electrify, vitalize. **3** *energize the device* activate, start up, switch on, turn on, get going.

energy *noun* **1** *she was full of energy* vigour, strength, stamina, forcefulness, power, might, potency, effectiveness, efficiency, efficacy, cogency, drive, push, exertion, enterprise, enthusiasm, animation, life, liveliness, pep, vivacity, vitality, spirit, spiritedness, fire, zest, verve, dash, *élan*, sparkle, buoyancy, effervescence, exuberance, *brio*, ardour, zeal, passion; *inf.* vim, zip, zing. **2** *power stations producing energy* power. *See table.*

enervate *verb* weaken, make feeble, exhaust, tire, fatigue, wear out, strain, wash out, debilitate, enfeeble, sap, incapacitate, devitalize, prostrate.

enfold *verb* **1** *mist enfolded the valley* enclose, fold, envelop, encircle, swathe, shroud, swaddle. **2** *enfolded in his arms* clasp, embrace, hug, hold, wrap.

enforce *verb* **1** *enforce the law* apply, carry out, administer, implement, bring to bear, impose, discharge, fulfil, execute, prosecute, put through. **2** *enforce silence* force, compel, insist on, require, necessitate, oblige, urge, exact, coerce, pressure, pressurize, dragoon, bulldoze, constrain, extort.

enforced *adjective enforced silence* forced, compelled, required, prescribed, imposed, necessitated, obliged, urged, exacted, coerced, pressured, pressurized, dragooned, bulldozed, constrained, extorted; unwilling, involuntary, unwarranted.
Opposites VOLUNTARY; OPTIONAL.

enforcement *noun* **1** *enforcement of the law* application, carrying out, administering, implementation, imposition, discharge, fulfilment, execution, prosecution. **2** *enforcement of silence* coercement, exactment, coercing, exacting, requiring, pressurizing, dragooning, bulldozing.

enfranchise *verb enfranchise women* give the vote to, give voting rights to, give/grant suffrage to, give/grant franchise to, naturalize, give citizenship to.

engage *verb* **1** *engage a housekeeper* employ, hire, take on, appoint, put on the payroll, enlist, enrol, commission. **2** *engage a boat/room* rent, hire, book, reserve, charter, lease, prearrange, bespeak. **3** *engage one's interest| engaged in a book* occupy, fill, employ, hold, grip, secure; preoccupy, absorb, engross. **4** *engage one's attention/affection* catch, attract, draw, gain, win, capture, captivate, arrest. **5** *engage in a project| engage in many sports* enter

into, become involved in, undertake, occupy oneself with, embark on, set about, take part in, join in, participate in, partake in/of, launch into, throw oneself into, tackle **6** *engage in a contract| engage to marry* contract, promise, agree, guarantee, undertake, pledge, oblige, obligate, vouch, vow, commit oneself, bind oneself, covenant. **7** *engaging at dawn| engage in battle* join battle, do battle with, fight with, wage war with, attack, enter into combat, clash with, encounter, take on, set to, skirmish with, grapple with, wrest with, take the field. **8** *engage gear* fit together, join together, join, interconnect, mesh, intermesh.
Opposites DISMISS; DISCHARGE; give up (*see* GIVE).

engaged *adjective* **1** *the manager is engaged* busy, occupied, in conference, unavailable; *inf.* tied up. **2** *the toilet/room is engaged* occupied, in use, unavailable, reserved, booked. **3** *engaged couples* betrothed, affianced, plighted, espoused; *inf.* spoken for.
Opposites FREE; UNOCCUPIED; UNATTACHED.

engagement *noun* **1** *her engagement as housekeeper* employment, appointment, work, job, post, situation, hire, business, stint. **2** *the engagement of a boat/room* rent, hire, booking, reservation, charter, lease, prearrangement. **3** *enter into a contractual engagement* contract, agreement, bond, pact, compact, promise, obligation, stipulation. **4** *they broke off their engagement* betrothal, marriage pledge. **5** *total engagement in the subject* absorption, preoccupation. **6** *a previous engagement* appointment, date, commitment, arrangement, meeting, interview, assignation, rendezvous, tryst. **7** *an engagement at sea* fight, battle, clash, conflict, struggle, attack, assault, confrontation, encounter, offensive; warfare, action, combat, strife; hostilities.

engaging *adjective* attractive, charming, appealing, pleasing, pleasant, agreeable, delightful, likeable, lovable, sweet, winning, taking, captivating, fetching, enchanting, winsome, fascinating.

engender *verb* **1** *engender feelings of hostility| engender hostility* cause, produce, create, give rise to, bring about, lead to, arouse, rouse, excite, provoke, incite, induce, instigate, generate, hatch, effect, occasion, effectuate, foment. **2** *engender sons* give birth to, father, breed, create, conceive, procreate, reproduce, bring forth, propagate, spawn, sire, beget.

engine *noun* **1** *the engine of the car* motor, mechanism, machine, power source, generator. *See table.* **2** *engines of war* instrument, implement, device, appliance; machinery, apparatus, means.

TYPES AND SOURCES OF ENERGY

alternative energy	fission energy	kinetic energy	potential energy
biomass energy	fossil fuel	light	renewable energy
chemical energy	fusion energy	lignite	solar energy
coal	gas	natural gas	tidal power
electrical energy	geothermal energy	nuclear power	wave power
electromagnetic energy	heat	oil	whale oil
	hydroelectric power	photosynthesis	wind power

TYPES OF ENGINE	
Diesel engine	jet engine
dynamo	petrol engine
gas turbine	ramjet engine
heat engine	rocket engine
internal-combustion engine	steam engine
	turbine
ion engine	Wankel engine

engineer noun **1** *the engineer who designed the bridge* planner, designer, builder, architect; inventor, originator, deviser, contriver. *See table. See also tables at* ARCHITECT, INVENTOR. **2** *ship's engineer* operator, controller, handler, director, driver.

engineer verb bring about, cause, plan, plot, scheme, contrive, devise, manoeuvre, manipulate, orchestrate, mastermind, originate, manage, control, superintend, direct, conduct, handle, concoct; *inf.* wangle.

engineering noun. See table.

engrave verb **1** *engrave the silver cup | engrave her initials* carve, etch, inscribe, cut, chisel, imprint, impress, print, mark, chase. **2** *word's engraved on my heart* fix, set, imprint, stamp, brand, impress, embed, ingrain, lodge.

engraving noun **1** *the engraving of the stone* carving, etching, sculpting, inscribing, inscription, cutting, chiselling, chasing, lithography, photoengraving, dry-point. **2** *we bought three engravings* carving, etching, print, lithograph, impression, block, plate, dry-point, cut, woodcut.

engross verb **1** *engross my attention* occupy, preoccupy, absorb, engage, rivet, grip, hold, interest, catch, captivate, arrest, immerse, involve, envelop, engulf, fixate. **2** *engross the market* corner, monopolize, capture, sew up.

ENGINEERS			
Armstrong, Edwin (1890–1954; Am.)	Cockerell, Sir Christopher (b. 1910; Brit.)	Junkers, Hugo (1859–1935; Ger.)	Roebling, John (1806–69; Am.)
Armstrong, William (1810–1900; Brit.)	Curtiss, Glenn (1878–1930; Am.)	Kennelly, Arthur (1861–1939; Am.)	Savery, Thomas (c. 1650–1715; Brit.)
Austin, Herbert (1866–1941; Brit.)	Daimler, Gottlieb (1834–1900; Ger.)	Kilby, Jack (b. 1923; Am.)	Siemens, Ernst Werner von (1816–92; Ger.)
Baird, John Logie (1888–1946; Scot.)	Dalén, Nils (1869–1937; Sw.)	Lilienthal, Otto (1848–96; Ger.)	Siemens, Sir William (1823–93; Brit., b. in Germany)
Baker, Sir Benjamin (1840–1907; Brit.)	De Forest, Lee (1873–1961; Am.)	Marconi, Guglielmo (1874–1937; It.)	Sikorsky, Igor (1889–1972; Am.)
Bardeen, John (1908–91; Am.)	Diesel, Rudolf (1858–1913; Ger.)	Mauchly, John (1907–80; Am.)	Sinclair, Sir Clive (b. 1940; Brit.)
Bazalgette, Sir Joseph (1819–91; Brit.)	Eckert, John Presper (b. 1919; Am.)	Maudslay, Henry (1771–1831; Brit.)	Steinmetz, Charles (1865–1923; Am.)
Benz, Karl (1844–1929; Ger.)	Eiffel, Alexandre (1832–1923; Fr.)	Messerschmitt, Willy (1898–1978; Ger.)	Stephenson, George (1781–1848; Brit.)
Bessemer, Sir Henry (1813–98; Brit.)	Evans, Oliver (1755–1819; Am.)	Mitchell, R(eginald) J(oseph) (1895–1937; Brit.)	Stephenson, Robert (1803–59; Brit.)
Blériot, Louis (1872–1936; Fr.)	Ferranti, Sebastian (1864–1930; Brit.)	Nasmyth, James (1808–90; Brit.)	Taylor, Frederick (1856–1915; Am.)
Boulton, Matthew (1728–1814; Brit.)	Fleming, Sir John (1849–1945; Brit.)	Nervi, Pier (1891–1979; It.)	Telford, Thomas (1757–1834; Scot.)
Bramah, Joseph (1748–1814; Brit.)	Fokker, Anthony (1890–1939; Du.)	Newcomen, Thomas (1663–1729; Brit.)	Tesla, Nikola (1856–1943; Am., b. in Croatia)
Braun, Wernher von (1912–77; Am., b. in Germany)	Froude, William (1810–79; Brit.)	Nobel, Alfred (1833–96; Sw.)	Trevithick, Richard (1771–1833; Brit.)
Brindley, James (1716–72; Brit.)	Fulton, Robert (1765–1815; Am.)	Nobile, Umberto (1885–1978; It.)	Tsiolkovski, Konstantin (1857–1935; Russ.)
Brunel, Isambard Kingdom (1806–59; Brit.)	Gabor, Dennis (1900–79; Brit.)	Olsen, Kenneth (b. 1926; Am.)	Vauban, Sébastien Le Prestre de (1633–1707; Fr.)
Brunel, Sir Marc Isambard Kingdom (1769–1849; Brit., b. in France)	Goddard, Robert (1882–1945; Am.)	Otto, Nikolaus (1832–91; Ger.)	Vitruvius (1st century B.C.; Rom.)
	Heinkel, Ernst (1888–1958; Ger.)	Parsons, Sir Charles (1854–1931; Brit.)	Wallis, Sir Barnes (1887–1979; Brit.)
Carnot, Lazare (1753–1823; Fr.)	Hero of Alexandria (1st century A.D.; Gk)	Piccard, Jean (1884–1963; Am., b. in Switzerland)	Watt, James (1736–1819; Scot.)
Cayley, Sir George (1773–1857; Brit.)	Ilyushin, Sergei (1894–1977; Russ.)	Porsche, Ferdinand (1875–1951; Austrian)	Whittle, Sir Frank (b. 1907; Brit.)
	Jansky, Karl (1905–50; Am.)	Rennie, John (1761–1821; Brit.)	

BRANCHES OF ENGINEERING

aerodynamics	electronics
aeronautical	engineering
engineering	environmental
aerospace	engineering
engineering	ergonomics
agricultural	fluid dynamics
engineering	hydraulics
astronautics	mechanical
automotive	engineering
engineering	mining
chemical engineering	engineering
civil engineering	naval engineering
cosmonautics	nuclear engineering
electrical	production
engineering	engineering

3 *engross a legal document* reproduce, copy, type; rewrite/reproduce in larger form.

engrossed *adjective looking completely engrossed* preoccupied, absorbed, engaged, riveted, gripped, caught up, captivated, immersed, intent, rapt, involved, enveloped, engulfed.

engrossing *adjective an engrossing article* absorbing, riveting, gripping, captivating, arresting, interesting, fascinating, intriguing, compelling, enthralling.

engulf *verb* consume, overwhelm, flood, deluge, swamp, swallow up, submerge, bury, immerse, inundate, envelop, encompass.

enhance *verb* **1** *enhance her beauty/reputation* add to, increase, heighten, stress, emphasize, strengthen, improve, augment, boost, intensify, reinforce, magnify, amplify, enrich, complement. **2** *enhance property prices* raise, lift, increase, escalate, elevate, augment, swell, exalt, aggrandize; *inf.* jack up, hike.

enhancement *noun* **1** *enhancement of beauty* heightening, emphasis, stress, strengthening, augmenting, intensification, reinforcement, magnification, amplification, enrichment. **2** *enhancement of property prices* rise, increase, increment, escalation, elevation, augmentation, swelling, exaltation, aggrandizement; *inf.* jacking-up, hike.

enigma *noun* mystery, puzzle, riddle, conundrum, paradox, problem, quandary, dilemma, labyrinth, maze, a closed book; *inf.* poser, teaser, brain-teaser.

enigmatic *adjective* mysterious, puzzling, baffling, obscure, perplexing, mystifying, cryptic, unfathomable, incomprehensible, inexplicable, inscrutable, Sphinx-like, recondite, esoteric, arcane, secret; ambiguous, equivocal, paradoxical, doubtful.

enjoin *verb* **1** *enjoin people to stay indoors* direct, order, command, urge, bid, demand, instruct, decree, ordain, warn, require, call upon, charge, advise, counsel. **2** *enjoin late-night opening* ban, bar, prohibit, forbid, disallow, embargo, interdict, place an injunction on, proscribe, preclude, obstruct, restrain.

enjoy *verb* **1** *enjoy music* like, love, be entertained/amused by, find/take pleasure in, delight in, appreciate, rejoice in, relish, revel in, savour, luxuriate in; *inf.* fancy. **2** *enjoy good health/facilities | enjoy a good standard of living* have, possess, own, benefit from, have the benefit/advantage/use of, avail oneself of, be blessed/favoured with. **enjoy oneself** have fun, have a good time, have the time of one's life, party, make merry; *inf.* have a ball, let one's hair down.
Opposites DISLIKE; HATE.

enjoyable *adjective* entertaining, amusing, delightful, nice, pleasant, lovely, fine, good, great, agreeable, pleasurable, delicious, delectable, diverting, satisfying, gratifying.
Opposites UNPLEASANT; DISAGREEABLE; HATEFUL.

enjoyment *noun* **1** *find enjoyment in reading | eat with enjoyment* amusement, entertainment, diversion, recreation, pleasure, delight, happiness, gladness, joy, fun, gaiety, jollity, satisfaction, gratification, delectation, zeal, relish, gusto. **2** *the enjoyment of good health/facilities* possession, use, ownership, benefit, advantage, blessing, favour, exercise.

enlarge *verb* **1** *enlarge the living area* make larger/bigger, expand, extend, add to, stretch, amplify, augment, supplement, magnify, multiply; widen, broaden, lengthen, elongate, deepen, thicken; *inf.* jumboize. **2** *his spleen is enlarged* distend, dilate, swell, blow up, inflate, bloat, bulge, tumefy, protuberate. **3** *enlarge a photograph* make larger/bigger, blow up.
4 *enlarge on the topic* elaborate, expatiate.
Opposites REDUCE; DIMINISH; LESSEN.

enlargement *noun* **1** *enlargement of the living area* increase, expansion, extension, magnification, amplification, augmentation, supplementation, supplement, multiplication, broadening, lengthening, elongation, deepening, thickening. **2** *enlargement of the spleen* distension, dilation, swelling, bloating, intumescence, tumefaction, protuberation; bulge, protuberance. **3** *photographic enlargement* magnification, blow-up, large print.

enlighten *verb* inform, make aware, instruct, teach, educate, tutor, indoctrinate, illuminate, apprise, edify, civilize, cultivate, counsel, advise.

enlightened *adjective* informed, aware, educated, knowledgeable, learned, wise, literate, intellectual, tutored, indoctrinated, illuminated, apprised; civilised, refined, cultured, cultivated, sophisticated, liberal, open-minded, broad-minded.
Opposites IGNORANT; ILLITERATE; NARROW-MINDED.

enlightenment *noun* awareness, understanding, insight, education, learning, knowledge, erudition, wisdom, instruction, teaching, indoctrination, illumination, edification, awakening; culture, refinement, cultivation, civilization, sophistication, liberalism, open-mindedness, broad-mindedness.

enlist *verb* **1** *enlist soldiers/staff | enlist her help* enrol, sign up, recruit, hire, employ, register, take on, engage, obtain, procure, secure, gather, muster. **2** *enlist in the army/venture* join, join up, enrol/register in, sign on/up for, enter into, volunteer for.

enliven *verb* brighten up, cheer up, wake up, give a lift/boost to, ginger up, buoy up, hearten, gladden, excite, stimulate, rouse, refresh, exhilarate, invigorate, revitalize, vitalize, light a fire under; *inf.* perk up, jazz up.

enmity *noun* hostility, ill-will, hate, hatred, antagonism, antipathy, aversion, animosity, bitterness, spite, malice, venom, rancour, malevolence, animus.
Opposites FRIENDSHIP; LOVE; GOODWILL.

en masse *adverb* as a group, in a body, as one, as a whole, in a mass.

ennoble *verb* *ennobled by grief | ennobling the author* make noble/great, dignify, exalt, elevate, raise, enhance, magnify, aggrandize, nobilitate, honour, glorify, lionize.

ennui *noun* boredom, tedium, listlessness, lethargy, lassitude, languor, sluggishness, dissatisfaction, melancholy.

enormity *noun* **1** *the enormity of the crime/act/ suggestion* outrageousness, wickedness, evilness, vileness, monstrousness, hideousness, dreadfulness, heinousness, atrocity, cruelty, brutality, depravity, nefariousness. **2** *commit enormities in wartime* outrage, horror, evil, crime, atrocity, abomination, violation, villainy, transgression, disgrace.

enormous *adjective* huge, immense, massive, vast, gigantic, colossal, astronomic, mammoth, mountainous, gargantuan, prodigious, tremendous, stupendous, excessive, titanic, Herculean, Brobdingnagian; *inf.* jumbo.
Opposites MINUTE; TINY.

enormously *adverb* *enormously wealthy* to a very large/great extent, tremendously, markedly, hugely, massively.

enormousness *noun* *enormousness of the head* hugeness, massiveness, vastness, immenseness, magnitude, greatness, largeness.

enough *adjective* *enough food/time* sufficient, adequate, ample, abundant.
Opposites INSUFFICIENT; INADEQUATE.

enough *noun* *we've had enough* sufficient/adequate amount, sufficiency, adequacy, ample supply, abundance, amplitude; plenty, full measure; *inf.* plenitude.

enough *adverb* *not warm enough | paints well enough* sufficiently, adequately, amply, satisfactorily, passably, tolerably, reasonably, fairly.

en passant *adverb* in passing, by the way, talking of, while on the subject, that reminds me, apropos.

enquire *verb.* See INQUIRE.

enquiry *noun.* See INQUIRY.

enrage *verb* annoy, anger, infuriate, irritate, madden, exasperate, provoke, incense, irk, agitate, inflame, incite, make one's hackles rise, make one's blood boil; *inf.* wind up, get one's back/dander up.

enraged *adjective* angry, angered, furious, annoyed, irate, livid, raging, fuming, irritated, maddened, exasperated, incensed, provoked, irked, agitated, inflamed; *inf.* mad, wild, wound-up.

enrapture *verb* delight, thrill, charm, captivate, fascinate, enchant, bewitch, entrance, enthrall, beguile, transport, ravish; *inf.* blow one's mind, turn on.

enrich *verb* **1** *a nation enriched by oil* make rich/ richer, feather the nest of. **2** *enrich the soil | enrich one's quality of life* make richer, improve, enhance, add to, augment, supplement, upgrade, refine, polish, ameliorate, aggrandize. **3** *enrich the fabric* decorate, adorn, ornament, embellish, beautify, garnish, gild, grace.

enrol *verb* **1** *enrol three new pupils* register, sign on/up, take on, enlist, recruit, enter, engage, admit, accept. **2** *he enrolled for military service | enrolling for a new course* sign on, volunteer, register, matriculate. **3** *enrol the statistics* record, enter, put down, note.

enrolment *noun* **1** *the enrolment of pupils/soldiers* registration, signing on/up, joining up, enlisting, recruitment, engagement, admission, acceptance. **2** *the enrolment of statistics* record, register, list, note, catalogue.

en route *adverb* on the way, in transit, along/ on the road.

ensconce *verb* settle, install, establish, nestle, curl up, snuggle up.

ensemble *noun* **1** *the parts forming a pleasing ensemble* whole, whole thing, collection, set, combination, accumulation, sum, total, totality, entirety, assemblage, aggregate, composite; *inf.* whole caboodle. **2** *a green ensemble* outfit, costume, suit, coordinates, matching separates; *inf.* get-up, gear, rig-out. **3** *a jazz ensemble* group, band, company, troupe, cast, chorus, circle, association; trio, quartet, quintet.

enshrine *verb* **1** *enshrine the saint's relic* sanctify, dedicate, consecrate, hallow, deify, exalt. **2** *enshrine it in his heart* preserve, cherish, revere, hold sacred, treasure, venerate, immortalize.

enshroud *verb* shroud, cloak, cloud, veil, enfold, enwrap, cover, obscure, bury, conceal, hide, pall, mask.

ensign *noun* **1** *ensign of the ship* flag, banner, standard, pennant, streamer. **2** *ensign of the family* badge, shield, crest, escutcheon; coat of arms, armorial bearings.

ensnare *verb* catch, capture, trap, net, snare, entangle, embroil, enmesh, entrap.

ensue *verb* follow, come next/after, result, occur, happen, turn up, arise, come to pass, transpire, befall, proceed, succeed, issue, derive, stem, supervene.

ensure *verb* **1** *ensure success | ensure that he will win* make certain, make sure, guarantee, secure, effect, warrant, certify, confirm. **2** *ensure his inheritance* make safe, protect, guard, safeguard, secure.

entail *verb* *entails hard work* involve, require, call for, necessitate, demand, impose; cause, bring about, produce, result in, lead to, give rise to, occasion.

entangle *verb* **1** *entangle wool* tangle, twist, ravel, knot, intertwine, jumble, snarl up, mat. **2** *entangle in a net* catch, trap, snare, ensnare,

entrap, enmesh. **3** *entangled business affairs* complicate, confuse, muddle, jumble, mix up. **4** *entangle them in his affairs* involve, implicate, embroil, incriminate, inculpate.
Opposites DISENTANGLE; UNRAVEL; RELEASE.

entanglement *noun* **1** *the entanglement of his business affairs* complication, involvement, confusion, muddle, jumble, tangle, mix-up, mess. **2** *his entanglement with his secretary* affair, liaison, amour, intrigue.

enter *verb* **1** *enter a room | a river entering the sea | a bullet entering the chest* come in/into, go in/into, pass into, move into, flow into, penetrate, pierce, puncture. **2** *enter the army | enter the teaching profession* become a member of, join, enrol in, enlist in, sign up for, take up, become connected/associated with, commit oneself to. **3** *enter a competition | entered for the marathon/school* take part in, become a competitor in, participate in, put one's name down for, go in for, obtain/gain entrance to. **4** *enter the date of birth* record, register, put down, set/take down, note, mark down, catalogue, document, list, log, file, index. **5** *enter a protest* put forward, offer, present, proffer, submit, register, tender. **6** *enter another term of office | enter into negotiations* begin, start, commence, embark on, engage in, undertake, venture on. **7** *enter into details/conversation* become involved with/in, concern oneself with, participate in, engage in, join in.
Opposites LEAVE; DEPART; WITHDRAW.

enterprise *noun* **1** *the festival is a challenging enterprise* venture, undertaking, project, operation, endeavour, effort, task, plan, scheme, campaign. **2** *a young person with enterprise* resourcefulness, resource, initiative, drive, gumption, imagination, imaginativeness, spirit, spiritedness, enthusiasm, zest, dash, ambition, energy, vigour, vitality, boldness, daring, spirit of adventure, audacity, courage, intrepidity; *inf.* get-up-and-go, go, push, oomph, zip, vim. **3** *a thriving enterprise | private enterprise* business, industry, firm, commercial concern/operation, corporation, establishment, house.

enterprising *adjective* resourceful, go-ahead, entrepreneurial, imaginative, spirited, enthusiastic, eager, keen, zealous, ambitious, energetic, active, vigorous, vital, bold, daring, adventurous, audacious, courageous, intrepid; *inf.* peppy, pushy, up-and-coming.
Opposites UNIMAGINATIVE; unadventurous.

entertain *verb* **1** *entertain the guests with music* amuse, divert, delight, please, charm, cheer, beguile, interest, engage, occupy. **2** *entertain at home* play host/hostess, have/receive guests, provide hospitality, have people round, have company, hold/throw a party, keep open house, have a dinner/lunch party. **3** *entertain colleagues at home* play host/hostess to, show hospitality to, invite to a meal/party, wine and dine, treat, welcome, fête. **4** *entertain evil intentions* harbour, nurture, foster, cherish, hold, have, possess, hide, conceal. **5** *entertain the idea/proposal* consider, give consideration to, take into consideration, give some thought to, think about/over, contemplate, weigh up, pon-

der, muse over, cogitate, bear in mind, heed, pay attention to.
Opposites BORE; DEPRESS; REJECT.

entertainer *noun* performer, artiste, actor, actress, comedian, comedienne, singer, dancer, comic, impressionist, mime artist, acrobat, conjuror, magician.

entertaining *adjective* *an entertaining recital/comic* amusing, diverting, recreational, delightful, pleasurable, pleasing, charming, enchanting, cheering, beguiling, engaging, interesting, funny, humorous, witty, comical, hilarious.
Opposites BORING; UNINTERESTING.

entertainment *noun* **1** *play the piano for entertainment* amusement, fun, enjoyment, diversion, recreation, distraction; pastime, hobby, leisure activity/pursuit, sport. **2** *a one-woman entertainment* show, performance, concert, play, cabaret, presentation, spectacle, pageant.

enthrall *verb* **1** *enthralled by the performance* hold spellbound, captivate, enchant, beguile, entrance, fascinate, bewitch, grip, rivet, charm, delight, enrapture, transport, carry away, intrigue, mesmerize, hypnotize. **2** *conquerors enthralling the villagers* enslave, subjugate, subdue, vanquish, conquer.

enthralling *adjective* spellbinding, captivating, enchanting, fascinating, bewitching, gripping, riveting, charming, delightful, intriguing, mesmerizing, hypnotic.

enthuse *verb* **1** *enthuse about astronomy* be enthusiastic, rave, praise to the skies, gush, wax lyrical, bubble over, effervesce; *inf.* get all worked up, go over the top. **2** *her excitement enthused the others* make enthusiastic. See ENTHUSIASTIC.

enthusiasm *noun* **1** *greet with enthusiasm* eagerness, keenness, ardour, fervour, warmth, passion, zeal, zest, vehemence, fire, excitement, exuberance, ebullience, avidity, wholeheartedness, commitment, devotion, devotedness, fanaticism, earnestness. **2** *stamp-collecting, is one of the child's enthusiasms* hobby, pastime, interest, recreation, passion, fad, craze, mania.

enthusiast *noun* fan, supporter, follower, devotee, lover, admirer, fanatic, zealot, aficionado; *inf.* buff, freak.

enthusiastic *adjective* eager, keen, ardent, fervent, warm, passionate, zealous, vehement, excited, exuberant, ebullient, spirited, avid, hearty, wholehearted, committed, devoted, fanatical, earnest.
Opposites APATHETIC; UNINTERESTED; INDIFFERENT.

entice *verb* lure, tempt, seduce, inveigle, lead astray/on, beguile, coax, cajole, wheedle, decoy, bait.

enticement *noun* **1** *enticements such as high salaries* lure, temptation, allure, attraction, bait, decoy; *inf.* come-on. **2** *the enticement of the child* luring, tempting, seduction, inveiglement, beguilement, coaxing, cajoling, decoying.

entire *adjective* **1** *one's entire life* whole, complete, total, full, continuous, unbroken. **2** *not an entire success* absolute, total, outright,

unqualified, thorough, unreserved, unmitigated, unmodified, unrestricted. **3** *emerge entire from the accident | an entire unblemished peach* sound, intact, undamaged, unmarked, unharmed, perfect, unbroken, unimpaired, unblemished, unflawed, unspoiled, unmutilated.
Opposites PARTIAL; INCOMPLETE; QUALIFIED.

entirely *adverb* **1** *not entirely correct* absolutely, completely, totally, fully, wholly, altogether, utterly, in every respect, unreservedly, without reservation, without exception, thoroughly, perfectly. **2** *entirely yours* only, solely, exclusively.
Opposites PARTLY; PARTIALLY; SLIGHTLY.

entirety *noun* **1** *the population in its entirety* totality, wholeness, completeness, fullness, unity, undividedness. **2** *the entirety of the firm's outgoings* sum, total, aggregate.

entitle *verb* **1** *entitle you to claim the estate* give the right to, qualify, make eligible, authorize, sanction, allow, permit, enable, empower, warrant, accredit, enfranchise, capacitate. **2** *they entitled the book 'Doom'* call, name, give the title of.

entity *noun* **1** *a living entity* body, being, person, creature, individual, organism, object, article, thing, real thing, substance, quantity, existence, ens. **2** *the organization's very entity* being, inner being, existence, life, substance, essence, essential nature, quintessence, quiddity.

entourage *noun* **1** retinue, escort, attendant, company, cortege, train, suite, bodyguard; attendants, companions, members of court, followers, camp followers, associates; *inf.* groupies. **2** *a pleasant entourage* surroundings, environs, circumstances; environment, milieu, element, ambience.

entrails *plural noun* intestines, internal organs, bowels, vital organs, viscera; *inf.* guts, insides, innards.

entrance *verb* **1** *they entranced us with their dancing/beauty* hold spellbound, captivate, enchant, bewitch, beguile, enthrall, enrapture, ravish, send into transports/raptures, charm, delight. **2** *children entranced by a wizard* put under a spell, put in a trance, bewitch, hypnotize, mesmerize.

entrance *noun* **1** *the entrance to the building* way in, entry, means of entry/access, access, approach, door, doorway, gate, gateway, drive, driveway, passageway, gangway, entrance hall, foyer, lobby, porch, portal, threshold. **2** *the entrance of the gladiators | the hero making an entrance* coming/going in, entry, appearance, arrival, introduction, ingress. **3** *refused entrance to the club* entry, admission, admittance, permission to enter, right of entry, access, ingress, *entrée*.
Opposites EXIT; DEPARTURE.

entrant *noun* **1** *entrants to the college* new member, beginner, newcomer, fresher, freshman, new arrival, probationer, trainee, novice, tiro, initiate, neophyte, proselyte, cub, greenhorn; *inf.* rookie. **2** *the entrants for javelin throwing*

competitor, contestant, participant, player, candidate, applicant, rival, opponent.

entrap *verb* **1** *entrap his prey* trap, snare, catch, net, enmesh, bag. **2** *entrap him into marriage* lure, trick, inveigle, seduce, lead on, entice, bait, decoy.

entreat *verb* beg, implore, beseech, plead with, appeal to, petition, solicit, pray, crave, exhort, enjoin, importune, supplicate.

entreaty *noun* appeal, plea, beseeching, pleading, petition, solicitation, prayer, importuning, supplication, suit. *See* ENTREAT.

entrée *noun* *entrée to high society* entry, entrance, means of entry, access, admission, admittance, right of entry, permission to enter.

entrench, intrench *verb* **1** *the army entrenched across the river | the party entrenched on the opposition benches* install, settle, establish, ensconce, lodge, set, root, plant, embed, anchor, seat; *inf.* dig in. **2** *entrench on their neighbour's territory* encroach on, trespass on, infringe on, impinge on, intrude on, infiltrate, invade, interlope.

entrenched, intrenched *adjective entrenched political bias* deep-seated, deep-rooted, rooted, well-established, fixed, set firm, firm, ingrained, unshakable, irremovable, indelible, dyed in the wool.

entrepreneur *noun* businessman, businesswoman, business person, business executive; commercial intermediary, intermediary, enterpriser, middleman, promotor; *inf.* whiz-kid.

entrust *verb* **1** *entrust his children to her* give custody of, hand over, make over, commit, assign, consign, deliver. **2** *entrusted with the task | entrust the responsibility to him* give into the charge/care/custody of, charge, invest, commit; turn over, hand over, consign, delegate, depute, commend; put into the hands of.

entry *noun* **1** *the main entry to the building* way in, entrance, means of access, access, approach, door, doorway, gate, gateway, driveway, passageway, entrance hall, foyer, lobby, porch, portal, threshold. *See* ENTRANCE *noun* 1. **2** *the entry of the soldiers/actors* coming/going in, entrance, appearance, arrival, introduction, ingress. **3** *refuse entry to the gatecrashers* entrance, admission, admittance, permission to enter, access. *See* ENTRANCE *noun* 3. **4** *an entry in a profit and loss account | an entry in his diary* item, statement, listing, record, note, jotting, memo, account, description. **5** *fifty entries in the competition* entrant, competitor, contestant, participant, player, candidate. *See* ENTRANT 2. **6** *you can submit four entries* attempt, try, effort, turn, submission; entry form; *inf.* go.
Opposites EXIT; DEPARTURE.

entwine *verb* wind round, twist round, intertwine, interlink, interlace, interweave, twine, link, lace, braid, plait, knit, criss-cross, entangle.

enumerate *verb* **1** *enumerate the qualities required* list, itemize, specify, spell out, name, give, cite, detail, recite, quote, relate, recount. **2** *enumerate the sums of money involved* count, calculate, add up, total, compute, tally, sum up, reckon, number.

enunciate *verb* **1** *enunciate her words with clarity* pronounce, articulate, sound, speak, say, utter, voice, vocalize, enounce. **2** *enunciate his controversial opinions* give voice to, express, utter, state, declare, pronounce, assert, affirm, put forward, propound, proclaim, promulgate, publish, broadcast.

envelop *verb* *the coat/fog enveloped him* enfold, cover, wrap, enwrap, swathe, swaddle, cloak, blanket, surround, engulf, encircle, encompass, conceal, hide, obscure.

envelope *noun* *put the letter in an envelope* wrapper, wrapping, wrap, cover, covering, casing, case, jacket, shell, sheath, skin, coating, capsule, holder, container.

enviable *adjective* exciting envy, desirable, worth having, covetable, tempting, excellent, fortunate, lucky, favoured.

envious *adjective* jealous, covetous, desirous, green with envy, green, green-eyed, grudging, begrudging, resentful, jaundiced.

environment *noun* surroundings, conditions, circumstances; habitat, territory, domain, milieu, medium, element, situation, location, locale, background, setting, scene, context, ambience, atmosphere, mood.

environmentalist *noun* conservationist, preservationist, ecologist, green, eco-activist; *inf.* econut, ecofreak.

environs *plural noun* *London and its environs* surrounding area, neighbourhood, vicinity, locality; precincts, outskirts, suburbs, purlieus.

envisage *verb* **1** *envisage the future/consequences* foresee, predict, imagine, visualize, picture, anticipate, envision. **2** *cannot envisage failure* imagine, contemplate, conceive of, think of, visualize, accept.

envoy *noun* **1** *envoys living in the embassy* legate, consul, attaché, chargé d'affaires, plenipotentiary. **2** *the Archbishop of Canterbury's envoy* emissary, accredited messenger, courier, representative, intermediary, delegate, deputy, agent, mediator, go-between.

envy *noun* **1** *envy of her beautiful hair | envy of his rich neighbour* enviousness, covetousness, jealousy, desire; resentment, resentfulness, discontent, spite. **2** *it was the envy of the town* object/source of envy.

envy *verb* *envy him his large house* be envious of, be jealous of, be covetous of, covet, begrudge, grudge.

ephemeral *adjective* fleeting, short-lived, transitory, momentary, transient, brief, short, temporary, passing, impermanent, evanescent, fugitive, fugacious.

epic *noun* *epics by Homer | direct an epic* long poem, long film, long story, heroic poem, saga, history, legend. *See* EPIC *adjective.*

epic *adjective* **1** *an epic poem* heroic, grand, long. **2** *of epic proportions | an epic journey* very great, very large, huge, very long, grand, extraordinary, ambitious.

epicene *adjective* **1** *epicene individuals* bisexual, hermaphrodite, androgynous. **2** *epicene creatures* neuter, sexless, asexual. **3** *epicene men* effeminate, womanish, unmanly, effete, weak.

epicure *noun* **1** *a restaurant guide for epicures* gourmet, *bon viveur, bon vivant,* gastronome, connoisseur; *inf.* foodie. **2** *epicures interested only in sensual pleasures* hedonist, sensualist, sybarite, voluptuary, libertine, glutton, gourmand.

epicurean *adjective* **1** *epicurean banqueters* pleasure-seeking, hedonistic, sensualist, self-indulgent, sybaritic, libertine, gluttonous, gourmandizing. **2** *epicurean attitude to food* gourmet, gastronomic.

epidemic *noun* **1** *many people died in the epidemic* widespread illness/disease, outbreak, plague, scourge. **2** *an epidemic of burglaries* outbreak, wave, upsurge, upswing, upturn, increase, growth, rise, mushrooming.

epidemic *adjective* *reaching epidemic proportions* rife, rampant, wide-ranging, extensive, widespread, sweeping, prevalent, predominant.

epigram *noun* **1** *puns and epigrams* witticism, quip, *bon mot,* pun, *double entendre, jeu d'esprit,* Atticism. **2** *proverbs and epigrams* saying, proverb, maxim, adage, axiom, aphorism, saw; words of wisdom.

epigrammatic *adjective* succinct, concise, terse, compact, crisp, short, brief, tight, pointed, to the point, witty, pithy, sharp, pungent, well-tuned.

epilogue *noun* conclusion; concluding speech, concluding programme, swan song, postscript, PS, afterword, coda, codicil, appendix, tailpiece, postlude.

episode *noun* **1** *the second episode of the story* instalment, part, section, chapter, passage, scene. **2** *an episode in his life* incident, occurrence, event, happening, experience, adventure, occasion, matter, affair, business, interlude, circumstance.

episodic *adjective* intermittent, irregular, sporadic, occasional, rambling, disconnected, digressive, discursive, wandering, anecdotal, picaresque.

epistle *noun* letter, missive, communication, correspondence, message, bulletin, note, line.

epitaph *noun* inscription, commemoration, elegy.

epithet *noun* **1** *'blessed' was an epithet often applied to her | his epithet was 'the Iron Duke'* description, descriptive word/expression/phrase, appellation, designation, label, tag; nickname, name, pet name, title. **2** *shouting epithets at the policeman* term of abuse, oath, curse, swear-word, obscenity, expletive, four-letter word.

epitome *noun* **1** *the epitome of politeness* personification, embodiment, essence, quintessence, archetype, representation, model, typification, type, example, exemplar, prototype. **2** *an epitome of his written works* summary, précis, résumé, outline, synopsis, abstract, digest, abridgement, abbreviation, condensation, conspectus, compendium.

epitomize *verb* **1** *epitomize the spirit of the age* personify, embody, exemplify, typify, represent, be representative of, symbolize, illustrate, incarnate. **2** *epitomize his works* summarize, précis, make a

résumé/outline of, abridge, condense, shorten, reduce.

epoch *noun* era, age, period, time, date. *See table at* AGE.

eponym *noun. See table.*

equable *adjective* **1** *an equable disposition* eventempered, easygoing, calm, composed, col-

EPONYMS			
Eponym	**Originator of Eponym**	**Eponym**	**Originator of Eponym**
America	Vespucci, Amerigo (1454–1512)	mauser	Mauser, Peter Paul (1838–1914)
bailey bridge	Bailey, Sir Donald (1901–85)	mausoleum	Mausolus (d. 353 B.C.)
biro	Biro, László (1900–85)	maverick	Maverick, Samuel (1803–70)
bloomers	Bloomer, Amelia (1818–94)	mesmerism	Mesmer, Franz (1734–1815)
boycott	Boycott, Charles Cunningham (1832–97)	molotov cocktail	Molotov, Vyacheslav (1890–1986)
bunsen burner	Bunsen, Robert (1811–99)	morse code	Morse, Samuel (1791–1872)
cardigan	Brudenell, James, 7th Earl of Cardigan (1797–1868)	mount Everest	Everest, Sir George (1790–1866)
casanova	Casanova, Giovanni (1725–98)	nicotine	Nicot, Jean (c. 1530–1600)
cicerone	Cicero, Marcus Tullius (106–43 B.C.)	nissen hut	Nissen, Lt. Col. Peter (1871–1930)
clerihew	Bentley, Edmund Clerihew (1875–1956)	orrery	Boyle, Charles, 4th Earl of Orrery (1676–1731)
colt 45	Colt, Samuel (1814–62)	pasteurize	Pasteur, Louis (1822–95)
cyrillic script	St Cyril (827–69 A.D.)	Pavlova	Pavlova, Anna (1881–1931)
daguerreotype	Daguerre, Louis (1787–1851)	peach melba	Melba, Dame Nellie (1861–1931)
derby	Stanley, Edward, 12th Earl of Derby (1752–1834)	pinchbeck	Pinchbeck, Christopher (1670–1732)
diesel	Diesel, Rudolf (1858–1913)	plimsoll line	Plimsoll, Samuel (1824–98)
Dow-Jones index	Dow, Charles (1851–1902) and Jones, Edward (1856–1920)	Pulitzer prize	Pulitzer, Joseph (1847–1911)
		pullman	Pullman, George (1831–97)
draconian	Draco (7th century B.C.)	pyrrhic victory	Pyrrhus (319–272 B.C.)
epicure	Epicurus (341–270 B.C.)	Queensbury rules	Douglas, John, 8th Marquis of Queensbury (1844–1900)
fosbury flop	Fosbury, Richard (b. 1947)	quisling	Quisling, Vidkun (1887–1945)
galvanize	Galvani, Luigi (1737–98)	rachmanism	Rachman, Peter (1920–62)
garibaldi biscuit	Garibaldi, Giuseppe (1807–82)	rastafarianism	Selassie, Emperor Haile, (Ras Tafari Makonnen; 1892–1975)
gat, gatling gun	Gatling, Richard (1818–1903)		
geiger counter	Geiger, Hans (1882–1945)	Rubik cube	Rubik, Ernö (b. 1944)
gerrymander	Gerry, Elbridge (1744–1814)	sadism	Sade, Marquis de (1740–1814)
granny Smith apple	Smith, Maria (d. 1870)	sandwich	Montague, John, 4th Earl of Sandwich (1718–92)
greengage	Gage, Sir William (1777–1864)	saxophone	Sax, Antoine-Joseph (1814–94)
guillotine	Guillotin, Joseph (1738–1814)	shrapnel	Shrapnel, Henry (1761–1842)
guppy	Guppy, Robert (1836–1916)	sideburns	Burnside, Ambrose (1824–81)
Hobson's Choice	Hobson, Thomas (c. 1544–1631)	silhouette	Silhouette, Etienne de (1709–67)
hoover	Hoover, William H. (1849–1932)	sousaphone	Sousa, John (1854–1932)
		stakhanovite	Stakhanov, Alexei (1906–77)
jacuzzi	Jacuzzi, Candido (1903–86)	tarmac	McAdam, John (1756–1836)
kalashnikov	Kalashnikov, Mikhail (b. 1919)	teddy bear	Roosevelt, Theodore (1858–1919)
leotard	Léotard, Jules (1842–70)		
loganberry	Logan, James (1841–1928)	thespian	Thespis (6th century B.C.)
machiavellian	Machiavelli, Niccolò (1469–1527)	tommy gun	Thompson, John (1860–1940)
		Vandyke	Van Dyck, Sir Anthony (1599–1641)
masochism	Sacher-Masoch, Leopold von (1836–95)	wellingtons	Wellesley, Arthur, 1st Duke of Wellington (1769–1852)
Mason and Dixon line	Mason, Charles (1730–87) and Dixon, Jeremiah (d. 1777)	Winchester rifle	Winchester, Oliver (1810–80)
		Yale lock	Yale, Linus (1821–68)
		zeppelin	Zeppelin, Ferdinand von (1838–1917)

lected, cool, calm and collected, serene, tranquil, placid, level-headed, imperturbable, unexcitable, unflappable, unruffled; *inf.* unfazed. **2** *equable temperatures* uniform, even, constant, steady, stable, regular, unvarying, consistent, unchanging. **3** *an equable climate* uniform, moderate, non-extreme.
Opposites TEMPERAMENTAL; EXCITABLE; UNEVEN; EXTREME.

equal *adjective* **1** *of equal height* the same, one and the same, identical, alike, like, comparable, commensurate. **2** *a sum equal to the previous sum* the same as, identical to, equivalent to, commensurate with, proportionate to, tantamount to, on a par with. **3** *an equal contest* even, evenly matched, evenly balanced, balanced, level, evenly proportioned; *inf.* fifty-fifty, level pegging, neck and neck. **4** *equal to the task* capable of, fit for, up to, strong/good enough for, adequate for, sufficient for, suitable for, suited, ready for. **5** *receive equal treatment* the same, identical, like, uniform, unbiased, impartial, non-partisan, fair, just, even-handed, egalitarian. **6** *keep it at an equal temperature* even, constant, uniform, steady, stable, level, unchanging, unvarying, unfluctuating.
Opposites UNEQUAL; DIFFERENT; UNEVEN.

equal *noun* *treat their staff as equals | they are equals in strength* equivalent, peer, compeer, coequal, mate, twin, alter ego, counterpart, match, parallel.

equal *verb* **1** *four plus five equals nine* be equal to, be equivalent to, come to, amount to, add up to, make, total, correspond to. **2** *she equals him in strength* be equal/even/level with, be equivalent to, match, parallel, correspond to, come up to, measure up to, equate with, be tantamount to, vie with, rival, emulate. **3** *equal the previous record* match, be level with, reach, parallel, come up to, measure up to, achieve.

equality *noun* sameness, identicalness, identity, equitability, parity, likeness, similarity, uniformity, evenness, levelness, balance, correspondence, parallelism, comparability, fairness, justness, impartiality, egalitarianism, equal opportunity.
Opposites INEQUALITY; DIFFERENCE; unevenness.

equalize *verb* **1** *equalize the score* make equal, make even, even up, make level, level up, balance, square, match. **2** *equalize the irregularities* level, level off, smooth, even off, balance, make uniform, regularize.

equanimity *noun* composure, presence of mind, self-possession, self-control, level-headedness, even-temperedness, equilibrium, poise, aplomb, sang-froid, calmness, calm, coolness, cool-headedness, serenity, placidity, tranquillity, phlegm, imperturbability, unexcitability; *inf.* cool, unflappability.

equate *verb* **1** *equate disagreement with disloyalty* regard as the same, regard as identical, liken, compare, bracket together, associate, think of together, connect, link, ally. **2** *the two sides of the accounts do not equate* be equal, be alike, balance, correspond, agree, be commensurate, square, tally, compare, match, be equivalent, be parallel.

equation *noun* equality, equalization, likeness, identity, balance, balancing, correspondence, equivalence, agreement, comparison, matching, equating, paralleling.

equatorial *adjective* tropical, torrid, sultry, humid, steamy, sweltering, jungle-like.

equestrian *adjective* *an equestrian event/statue* on horseback, mounted, in the saddle.

equestrian *noun* horseman, horsewoman, rider; mounted soldier, mounted policeman, cavalryman, Horse Guard, trooper, hussar, cossack, cowboy.

equilibrium *noun* **1** *a state of equilibrium between the physical forces* balance, stability, steadiness, evenness, symmetry, equipoise, counterpoise, equipollence. **2** *losing her equilibrium and shouting* equanimity, composure, calmness, coolness, sang-froid, tranquillity, collectedness, serenity, poise, self-possession, imperturbability, steadiness, stability; *inf.* cool, unflappability.

equip *verb* *equipped for the sea crossing | not equipped for academic life* fit out, kit out, rig out, prepare, provide, supply, stock, arm, array, attire, dress, outfit, accoutre; suit, endow.

equipment *noun* gear, tools, tackle, stuff, apparatus, baggage, luggage, outfit, furniture, *matériel*; things, supplies, paraphernalia, accoutrements, furnishings; *inf.* box of tricks. *See tables at* LABORATORY, TOOL.

equipoise *noun* **1** *physical forces in equipoise* equilibrium, balance, stability, steadiness. *See* EQUILIBRIUM 1. **2** *scales using an equipoise counterweight, counterbalance, counterpoise, ballast, stabilizer, makeweight; compensation.

equitable *adjective* fair, fair-minded, just, even-handed, right, rightful, proper, reasonable, honest, impartial, unbiased, unprejudiced, non-discriminatory, disinterested, dispassionate, open-minded.
Opposites INEQUITABLE; UNFAIR; UNJUST.

equity *noun* equitableness, fairness, fair-mindedness, fair play, justness, justice, even-handedness, rightness, rightfulness, rectitude, righteousness, properness, reasonableness, honesty, integrity, uprightness, impartiality, lack of discrimination/bias/prejudice, disinterest, disinterestedness, open-mindedness.

equivalence *noun* equalness, equality, sameness, identicalness, identity, similarity, likeness, comparability, interchangeability, correspondence, commensurateness. *See* EQUIVALENT *noun.*

equivalent *adjective* *a job with equivalent status* equal, the same, much the same, identical, similar, like, alike, interchangeable, comparable, corresponding, correspondent, commensurate, matching, on a par, tantamount, synonymous, homologous.
Opposites DIFFERENT; DISSIMILAR.

equivalent *noun* *an ambassador or his equivalent* equal, counterpart, parallel, alternative, match, double, twin, peer, opposite number.

equivocal *adjective* **1** *an equivocal reply* ambiguous, ambivalent, two-edged, indefinite, vague, obscure, unclear, uncertain, hazy, indeterminate, roundabout, oblique, circuitous, misleading, evasive, duplicitous, paradoxical. **2** *equivocal character* doubtful, dubious, questionable, suspicious, suspect.
Opposites UNEQUIVOCAL; DEFINITE.

equivocate *verb* prevaricate, evade/dodge the issue, beat about the bush, sit on the fence, hedge, hedge one's bets, quibble, fence, parry questions, fudge the issue, vacillate, shilly-shally, hesitate, hum and haw, shuffle about, tergiversate; *inf.* pussyfoot around, waffle, flannel.

equivocation *noun* prevarication, evasion, dodging, hedging, quibbling, quibble, fencing, parrying, fudging, vacillation, shilly-shallying, hesitation, humming and hawing, shuffling, qualification, tergiversation; *inf.* pussyfooting, waffle, flannel, weasel words. *See* EQUIVOCATE.

era *noun* age, epoch, aeon, period, time, generation, stage, cycle, season; times, days. *See table. See also table at* AGE.

ERAS	
Eras	**Year of Era in 1995**
Byzantine	7504
Jewish	5756
Roman (ab urbe condita)	2748
Babylonian (Nabonassar)	2744
Japanese	2655
Greek (Seleucid)	2307
Indian (Saka)	1917
Diocletian	1712
Mohammedan (Hegira)	1416

eradicate *verb* get rid of, root out, uproot, remove, extirpate, wipe out, weed out, eliminate, do away with, abolish, stamp out, annihilate, extinguish, excise, erase, obliterate, efface, expunge, destroy, kill, deracinate.

eradication *noun* removal, extirpation, elimination, abolition, annihilation, extinguishing, excision, erasure, obliteration, effacement, expunging, expunction, destruction, killing, deracination.

erase *verb* remove, rub out, wipe out, wipe off, blot out, scrape off, obliterate, efface, expunge, excise, cross out, strike out, delete, cancel, blue-pencil.

erect *verb* **1** *erect a building* build, construct, put up, assemble, put together. **2** *erect a flagpole* put up, raise, elevate, mount. **3** *erect a tent* put up, set up, set upright, assemble. **4** *erect a theory/institution* establish, form, set up, found, institute, initiate, create, organize.
Opposites DEMOLISH; DISMANTLE; DESTROY.

erect *adjective* **1** *stand erect|erect rows of soldiers* upright, straight, vertical. **2** *erect flagpoles* raised, elevated. **3** *an erect penis* hard, rigid, stiff, firm.
Opposites BENT; HORIZONTAL; FLACCID.

erection *noun* **1** *the erection of the building* building, construction, putting up, assembly. *See* ERECT *verb* 1. **2** *the erection of a flagpole* raising, elevation. *See* ERECT *verb* 2. **3** *the erection of a theory/institution* establishment, formation, setting up, foundation, institution, initiation, creation, organization. **4** *an ugly brick erection* building, structure, edifice, construction; *inf.* pile. **5** *unable to achieve an erection* tumescence, tumidity, turgescence.

erode *verb* *wind eroded the rocks|envy eroded the friendship* wear, wear away/down, eat, eat away at, corrode, abrade, gnaw, gnaw away at, grind down, excoriate, consume, devour, spoil, disintegrate, deteriorate, destroy.

erosion *noun* wearing away, corrosion, abrasion, excoriation, consumption, disintegration, deterioration, attrition, destruction.

erotic *adjective* titillating, sexually stimulating, sexually exciting/arousing, erogenous, aphrodisiac, seductive, sensual, carnal, amatory, salacious, suggestive, pornographic; *inf.* sexy, steamy.

err *verb* **1** *err in thinking them guilty* be in error, be wrong, be incorrect, be inaccurate, make a mistake, be mistaken, mistake, make a blunder, blunder, misjudge, miscalculate, misunderstand, misapprehend, misconstrue, get things/it wrong, bark up the wrong tree, get the wrong end of the stick, be wide of the mark; *inf.* slip up, boob, make a bloomer/boo-boo. **2** *to err is human* do wrong, go wrong, go astray, sin, behave badly, misbehave, transgress, trespass, fall from grace, lapse, degenerate.

errand *noun* message, task, job, commission, chore, assignment, undertaking, charge, mission.

errant *adjective* **1** *errant knights of old* itinerant, peripatetic, roaming, roving, wandering, journeying, travelling, nomadic. **2** *errant schoolboys* erring, mischievous, badly behaved, misbehaving, lawless, criminal, delinquent, sinning, offending, transgressing, aberrant, deviant.

erratic *adjective* **1** *erratic conduct* inconsistent, variable, varying, irregular, unstable, unreliable, unpredictable, capricious, whimsical, fitful, wayward, abnormal, eccentric, aberrant, deviant. **2** *steer an erratic course* wandering, meandering, wavering, directionless.
Opposites CONSISTENT; PREDICTABLE.

erring *adjective* errant, mischievous, badly behaved, misbehaving, lawless, criminal, delinquent, sinning. *See* ERRANT 2.

erroneous *adjective* wrong, incorrect, inaccurate, inexact, untrue, false, mistaken, fallacious, unfounded, without foundation, spurious, invalid, faulty, flawed, unsound, specious.
Opposites RIGHT; CORRECT.

error *noun* **1** *detect an error in the arithmetic| errors in his report* mistake, inaccuracy, miscalculation, misreckoning, blunder, fault, flaw, oversight, misprint, literal, erratum, misinterpretation, misreading, fallacy, misconception, delusion; *inf.* slip-up, bloomer, boob, booboo, howler, boner. **2** *done in error* mistake, erroneousness, oversight, misjudgement, miscalculation, misconception. **3** *see the error of his ways* wrongdoing, mischief, mischievousness, misbehaviour, misconduct, lawlessness, criminality, delinquency, sin, sinfulness, evil, evildoing.

ersatz *adjective* artificial, imitation, fake, simulated, synthetic, substitute, man-made, plastic, sham, counterfeit, pretended, pretend, bogus, spurious; *inf.* phoney, pseudo, pseud.

erudite *adjective* learned, educated, well-read, well-educated, scholarly, intellectual, knowledgeable, literate, lettered, cultivated, cultured; *inf.* brainy, highbrow.
Opposites ILLITERATE; IGNORANT.

erudition *noun* learning, scholarship, education, intellect, knowledge, literacy, cultivation, culture; letters.

erupt *verb* **1** *lava erupted from the volcano | the volcano erupted* belch/pour forth, gush, vent, spew, boil over; become active, flare up, eject/vent material, eruct, eructate. **2** *violence erupted* break out, flare up, blow up, burst forth, explode, go off. **3** *spots erupted on her face* break out, flare up, appear suddenly, burst forth, make an appearance, pop up, emerge, become visible.

eruption *noun* **1** *an eruption of violence | volcanic eruptions* outbreak, outburst, flare-up, explosion, flaring, venting. **2** *a skin eruption* outbreak, rash, inflammation.

escalate *verb* **1** *the war effort escalated | the war escalated* grow/develop rapidly, mushroom, increase, be increased, be stepped up, heighten, intensify, accelerate, be extended, be enlarged, be magnified, be amplified. **2** *prices will escalate* go up, mount, soar, climb, spiral; *inf.* be jacked/hiked up, go through the roof/ceiling.
Opposites DECREASE; DIMINISH; LESSEN.

escapade *noun* adventure, act of recklessness, stunt, prank, trick, caper, romp, frolic, fling, spree; antics; *inf.* lark, skylarking, scrape, fooling around, shennanigans.

escape *verb* **1** *the prisoners escaped* make one's escape, get away, run away, run off, break out, break free, make a break for it, flee, make one's getaway, bolt, abscond, decamp, fly, slip away, steal away; *inf.* do a bunk, vamoose, skedaddle, hightail it, do a runner, fly the coop; *Am. inf.* take a powder. **2** *escape punishment* avoid, evade, dodge, elude, sidestep, circumvent, shake off, give the slip to, keep out of the way of, shun, steer clear of, shirk; *inf.* duck, bilk; *Scots inf* body-swerve. **3** *gas escaping* leak, seep, pour out/forth, gush, spurt, issue, flow, discharge, emanate, drain.

escape *noun* **1** *the escape from jail | an escape route* running away, breakout, flight, getaway, bolting, absconding, decamping, fleeing. *See* ESCAPE *verb* 1. **2** *an escape from punishment/death* avoidance, evasion, dodging, eluding, elusion, circumvention; *inf.* ducking, bilking, body-swerve. *See* ESCAPE *verb* 2. **3** *a gas/water escape*

leak, leakage, seepage, gush, spirt, issue, flow, discharge, outflow, outpouring, emanation, efflux. **4** *write as a means of escape* escapism, fantasy, fantasizing, wool-gathering, non-realism, getting away from it all. *See* ESCAPISM.

escapism *noun* fantasy, fantasizing, dreaming, daydreaming, wool-gathering, wishful thinking.

eschew *verb* avoid, abstain from, give up, refrain from, forgo, shun, renounce, forswear, swear off, abjure, steer clear of, have nothing to do with, give a wide berth to, fight shy of; *inf.* kick, pack in, jack in.

escort *noun* **1** *the royal party and its escort | the ship's escort* entourage, retinue, train, cortège, attendant company, protection, bodyguard, defence, convoy, contingent; attendant, guide, chaperon, guard, protector, safeguard, defender. **2** *her escort for the evening | an escort agency* partner, companion, beau, attendant, gigolo, call-girl, prostitute, rent-boy; *inf.* date.

escort *verb* **1** *escort the royal party | escort the ship/ambulance* accompany, guide, conduct, lead, usher, shepherd, guard, protect, safeguard, defend, convoy. *See* ESCORT *noun* 1. **2** *escort her to the dance* partner, accompany, take out, go out with, attend on.

esoteric *adjective* abstruse, obscure, cryptic, recondite, arcane, abstract, inscrutable, mysterious, hidden, secret, private, mystic, magical, occult, cabbalistic.

especial *adjective* **1** *people of especial talent* special, exceptional, extraordinary, out of the ordinary, uncommon, unusual, outstanding, striking, remarkable, marked, notable, noteworthy, signal, superior, eminent, distinguished. **2** *her own especial brand of charm* special, individual, particular, distinctive, peculiar, personal, own, unique, singular, exclusive, specific, private.

especially *adverb* **1** *especially talented* exceptionally, extraordinarily, uncommonly, unusually, outstandingly, strikingly, remarkably, markedly, notably, signally, eminently. **2** *especially in the summer* particularly, above all, mainly, chiefly, principally. **3** *bought especially for you* specially, specifically, with someone in mind, exclusively, expressly, particularly, uniquely.

espionage *noun* spying, intelligence, undercover work, surveillance, infiltration, reconnaissance, counter-espionage, counter-intelligence; *inf.* bugging, wire-tapping.

espousal *noun* *the espousal of Christianity/socialism* embracing, adoption, taking up, support, backing, championship, promotion, advocacy, defence. *See* ESPOUSE.

espouse *verb* *espouse Christian/socialist principles* embrace, adopt, take up, take to one's heart, side with, be on the side of, support, back, champion, promote, advocate, defend, stand up for.

espy *verb* catch sight of, glimpse, spot, see, notice, observe, make out, spy, sight, discern, behold, perceive, descry.

essay · etch

essay noun

essay *noun* **1** *write an essay* composition, dissertation, paper, article, thesis, discourse, treatise, tract, disquisition; *inf.* piece. **2** *make a final essay* attempt, try, effort, endeavour, venture, undertaking; *inf.* shot, go, crack, stab, bash.

essay *verb* *essay the higher ascent* attempt, make an attempt at, try, try one's hand at, venture, undertake, take on; *inf.* have a shot/go/crack/stab at.

essence *noun* **1** *the essence of truth* essential part/constituent, fundamental nature/quality, innermost being/entity, quintessence, substance, sum and substance, nature, crux, heart, soul, life, lifeblood, kernel, marrow, pith, quiddity, *esse*, reality, actuality. **2** *essence of peppermint* extract, concentrate, concentration, distillate, tincture, elixir, abstraction; scent, perfume. **in essence** basically, fundamentally, to all intents and purposes, essentially, in effect, substantially, in the main, materially, at heart, virtually. **of the essence** essential, necessary, indispensable, vital, crucial, of the greatest/utmost importance.

essential *adjective* **1** *cost-cutting is essential* necessary, indispensable, vital, crucial, requisite, important, needed. **2** *the essential theme of the play* basic, fundamental, inherent, intrinsic, innate, elemental, characteristic, indigenous, principal, cardinal. **3** *the essential gentleman* absolute, complete, perfect, ideal, quintessential. **Opposites** NON-ESSENTIAL; DISPENSABLE; SECONDARY.

essential *noun* *experience is an essential* necessity, prerequisite, requisite, basic, fundamental, *sine qua non*, rudiment; *inf.* must.

establish *verb* **1** *establish a new firm/colony* set up, form, found, institute, start, begin, bring into being, create, inaugurate, organize, build, construct, install, plant. **2** *establish his guilt | establish that he is guilty* prove, show to be true, show, demonstrate, attest to, certify, confirm, verify, evidence, substantiate, corroborate, validate, authenticate, ratify. **Opposites** DEMOLISH; DESTROY; DISPROVE.

established *adjective* accepted, official, conventional, traditional, proven, settled, fixed, entrenched, dyed in the wool, inveterate.

establishment *noun* **1** *the establishment of the firm/colony* setting up, formation, founding, foundation, inception, creation, inauguration, organization, building, construction, installation. *See* ESTABLISH 1. **2** *a gentleman's establishment* residence, house, household, home, dwelling, abode, domicile, estate. **3** *clients patronizing his establishment* firm, business, place of business, company, shop, store, office, factory, emporium, commercial concern, concern, organization, enterprise, corporation, conglomerate. **the Establishment** the authorities, the powers that be, the system, bureaucracy, officialdom; *inf.* Big Brother.

estate *noun* **1** *a large country estate* property, piece of land, landholding, manor, domain; lands. **2** *an industrial/housing estate* area, piece of land, land, region, tract; development. **3** *his estate on death amounted to £300,000* assets, resources, effects, possessions, belongings; wealth, fortune, property. **4** *the three estates* social/political group, level, order, stratum, grade, class, rank, standing, status, caste. **5** *the estate of matrimony* state, condition, situation, circumstance, lot, position.

estate agent *noun* property agent, property dealer; *Am.* realtor, real-estate agent.

esteem *noun* hold in high esteem estimation, good opinion, regard, respect, admiration, honour, reverence, deference, veneration, appreciation, approval, approbation, favour, credit.

esteem *verb* **1** *esteem it a favour* consider, regard as, think, deem, hold, view as, judge, adjudge, rate, reckon, account, believe; *lit.* opine. **2** *highly esteemed by the community* regard, respect, value, admire, honour, look up to, think highly of, revere, venerate, appreciate, approve of, favour, like, love, cherish, prize, treasure.

estimate *verb* **1** *estimate the cost* make an estimate, calculate roughly/approximately, work out, assess, compute, gauge, reckon, evaluate, judge, appraise, guess; *inf.* guesstimate. **2** *I estimate him to be honest* consider, believe, think, regard as, judge, rate, view as, reckon, guess, conjecture, surmise; *lit.* opine.

estimate *noun* **1** *the joiner's estimate* estimated price/cost/value, price, costing, valuation, evaluation, assessment, appraisal. **2** *make an estimate of the cost* estimation, approximate/rough calculation, educated/informed guess, rough guess; *inf.* guesstimate. **3** *in my estimate he is dishonest* estimation, opinion, judgement, consideration, mind, thinking, way of thinking, view, point of view, viewpoint, feeling, conviction, deduction, conclusion, guess, conjecture, surmise.

estimation *noun* **1** *in my estimation he is the better candidate* estimate, opinion, judgement, consideration, mind, way of thinking, view, feeling, deduction, conclusion, surmise. *See* ESTIMATE *noun* 3. **2** *go down in one's estimation* esteem, good opinion, favourable opinion, regard, respect, admiration, deference, veneration, appreciation, approval, approbation, favour. *See* ESTEEM *noun*.

estrange *verb* *circumstances estranged him from his wife* alienate, drive apart, set apart, part, separate, divorce, sever, disunite, make hostile/unfriendly towards, antagonize, cause antagonism between, set against, set at odds, destroy the affections of, disaffect.

estrangement *noun* alienation, parting, separation, divorce, breakup, split, breach, severance, disunity, division, hostility, antagonism, antipathy, embitteredness, disaffection.

estuary *noun* inlet, river mouth, cove, bay, creek, arm of the sea; *Scots* firth.

et cetera, etcetera *adverb* and so on, and so forth, and the rest, and/or the like, and/or more of the same, et al., etc.; *inf.* and what have you.

etch *verb* engrave, carve, cut, furrow, burn into, eat into, imprint, impress, stamp, inscribe, ingrain, infix.

etching *noun* engraving, carving, cut, print, imprint, impression, stamp, inscription.

eternal *adjective* **1** *life eternal* everlasting, without end, endless, never-ending, immortal, infinite, enduring, deathless, permanent, immutable, indestructible, imperishable. **2** *stop that eternal row* | *those eternal questions* endless, never-ending, without end, ceaseless, incessant, non-stop, constant, continuous, continual, unbroken, without respite, interminable, unremitting, relentless, persistent, perpetual.
Opposites TRANSIENT; INTERMITTENT.

eternally *adverb* **1** *eternally in hell* | *eternally yours* everlastingly, forever, for always, evermore, for all time, till the end of time, world without end. **2** *eternally on the phone* constantly, continuously, morning noon and night, day and night, perpetually, incessantly, unceasingly, interminably, persistently.

eternity *noun* **1** *believe in eternity* immortality, everlasting life, afterlife, the hereafter, world without end, world hereafter, next world, heaven, paradise, nirvana. **2** *on the phone for an eternity* long time, age, seemingly forever, the duration; ages, ages and ages.

ethereal *adjective* **1** *ethereal beauty/fabric* delicate, fairy-like, fragile, exquisite, dainty, fine, gossamer-like, gossamery, wispy, diaphanous, insubstantial, airy, shadowy, subtle, tenuous. **2** *ethereal regions/music* heavenly, celestial, unearthly, other-worldly, paradisical, Elysian, sublime, divine.
Opposites SUBSTANTIAL; SOLID; EARTHLY.

ethical *adjective* moral, honourable, upright, righteous, good, virtuous, high-minded, decent, principled, honest, just, fair, right, correct, proper, fitting, seemly, decorous.
Opposites UNETHICAL; IMMORAL; UNPRINCIPLED.

ethics *plural noun* moral code, morality; morals, moral principles, moral values, principles, rules of conduct, standards, virtues, dictates of conscience.

ethnic *adjective* racial, cultural, national, tribal, native, indigenous, aboriginal, autochthonous, traditional, folk.

ethos *noun* spirit, character, tenor, flavour, disposition, rationale, code, morality, moral code; attitudes, beliefs, principles, standards, ethics.

etiolated *adjective* blenched, bleached, whitened, white, colourless, pale, chalky, chalk-white, faded, washed-out, wan, ghostly.

etiquette *noun* rules of conduct/behaviour, good manners, manners; code of behaviour/conduct, code of practice, proper/good conduct, accepted behaviour, protocol, good form, form, courtesy, politeness, civility, propriety, decorum, convention, custom, usage, politesse.

eugenics *plural noun* racial improvement, controlled/selective breeding, planned evolution.

eulogize *verb* praise highly, praise to the skies, sing the praises of, wax lyrical about, extol, laud, acclaim, pay tribute to, applaud, magnify, exalt, glorify, panegyrize, commend, compliment, pay compliments to, offer bouquets to; *inf.* rave about.

eulogy *noun* praise, accolade, extolment, lauding, acclamation, acclaim, paean, panegyric, tribute, applause, magnification, exaltation, glorification, encomium, commendation; praises, plaudits, compliments, bouquets; *inf.* raving. *See* EULOGIZE.
Opposites CRITICISM; CENSURE.

euphemism *noun* understatement, softening, substitute, polite term, politeness, genteelism, hypocorism.

euphemistic *adjective* understated, softened, indirect, vague, inoffensive, polite, genteel.

euphonious *adjective* harmonious, melodious, melodic, musical, pleasant-sounding, sweet-sounding, mellow, mellifluous, tuneful, dulcet, lyrical, rhythmical, symphonious, canorous.

euphoria *noun* elation, joy, joyousness, jubilation, ecstasy, rapture, bliss, exhilaration, exaltation, glee, excitement, buoyancy, intoxication, merriment; high spirits.

euphoric *adjective* elated, joyful, jubilant, ecstatic, enraptured, rapturous, blissful, exhilarated, exalted, high-spirited, gleeful, excited, buoyant, intoxicated, merry, on cloud nine, in seventh heaven, over the moon; *inf.* on a high.

euphuism *noun* high-flown language, purple pose, grandiloquence, floweriness, ornateness, floridity, bombast, periphrasis, circumlocution.

euthanasia *noun* mercy-killing, merciful release, quietus.

evacuate *verb* **1** *people evacuated the bombed town* leave, vacate, abandon, move out of, quit, withdraw from, retreat from, flee, depart from, go away from, retire from, decamp from, desert, forsake; *inf.* pull out of. **2** *firemen evacuated the room* empty, make empty, clear. **3** *evacuate waste matter* | *evacuate the bowels* excrete, expel, eject, discharge, eliminate, void, purge, empty out, drain, defecate.

evacuation *noun* **1** *the people's evacuation of the town* leaving, vacating, abandonment, withdrawal, retreat, exodus, departure, flight, desertion, forsaking. *See* EVACUATE 1. **2** *evacuation of waste products* | *bodily evacuations* excretion, expulsion, ejection, discharge, elimination, voiding, voidance, purging, emptying, draining, defecation; bowel movement/motion, stool, excrement, urination, urine; faeces, egesta.

evade *verb* **1** *evade the enemy* | *evade one's share of the work* avoid, dodge, escape from, elude, sidestep, circumvent, shake off, give the slip to, keep out of the way of, keep one's distance from, steer clear of, shun, shirk; *inf.* duck, bilk; *Scots inf* body-swerve. **2** *evade the question/issue* avoid, quibble about, be equivocal/evasive about, dodge, hedge, fence, fend off, parry, skirt round, fudge, not give a straight answer to; *inf.* duck, cop out of.
Opposites FACE; CONFRONT.

evaluate *verb* assess, put a value/price on, appraise, size up, weigh up, gauge, judge, rate, rank, estimate, calculate, reckon, measure, determine.

evaluation noun assessment, appraisal, assay, weighing up, gauging, ranking, estimation, reckoning. See EVALUATE.

evanesce verb vanish, vanish into thin air, fade, disappear, evaporate, melt away, peter out, disperse, dissolve.

evanescent adjective **1** evanescent summer days vanishing, fading, evaporating. See EVANESCE. **2** evanescent youth ephemeral, fleeting, short-lived, transient, transitory, fugitive, fugacious, momentary, temporary, brief.

evangelical adjective **1** evangelical beliefs according to the Gospel, scriptural, biblical, canonical, textual, orthodox. **2** evangelical spirit evangelistic, missionary, converting. See EVANGELISTIC.

evangelist noun missionary, preacher, revivalist, reformer, converter, crusader, propagandist, campaigner, gospeller, proselytizer.

evangelistic adjective missionary, preaching, revivalist, reforming, converting, crusading, propagandist, campaigning, evangelical, proselytizing.

evangelize verb spread the faith/word, act as a missionary, preach, reform, convert, crusade, campaign, spread propaganda, proselytize.

evaporate verb **1** water evaporates in heat become vapour, vaporize, volatilize. **2** the hot sun evaporated the puddles vaporize, dry, dry up, dry out, remove moisture from, dehydrate, desiccate, sear, parch. **3** the vision evaporated vanish, fade, disappear, melt away, dissolve, disperse, dissipate, dematerialize, evanesce.

evaporation noun **1** the evaporation of water vaporizing, volatilization. **2** the evaporation of the vision vanishing, fading, disappearance, dispersal, evanescence. See EVAPORATE 3.

evasion noun **1** the evasion of the enemy | evasion of one's share of the work avoidance, dodging, escape, eluding, elusion, sidestepping, circumvention, shunning, shirking; inf. ducking, the go-by. See EVADE 1. **2** skilled at evasion subterfuge, deception, trickery, cunning, prevarication, quibbling, equivocation, dodging, hedging, fencing, fending, parrying, skirting round, fudging; inf. ducking, flannel, waffle.

evasive adjective **1** evasive tactics avoiding, dodging, escaping, eluding, sidestepping, shunning, shirking. See EVADE 1. **2** evasive replies prevaricating, quibbling, equivocating, equivocal, parrying, fudging, indirect, roundabout, circuitous, oblique, cunning, artful, casuistic; inf. flannelling, waffling, cagey. **Opposites** FRANK; DIRECT.

eve noun **1** on the eve of the election evening before, night before, day before, period before. **2** a summer eve evening, night.

even adjective **1** an even surface level, flat, plane, smooth, uniform, flush, true. **2** an even temperature/colour/breathing uniform, constant, steady, stable, consistent, unvarying, unchanging, unwavering, unfluctuating, regular. **3** even amounts | even chances of success equal, the same, much the same, identical, like, alike, similar, to the same degree, comparable, commensurate, corresponding, parallel, on a par,

on an equal footing, evenly matched; inf. even steven. **4** the players/scores are even all square, drawn, tied, level, level pegging, neck and neck, nip and tuck, neck and crop; inf. even steven. **5** of an even disposition even-tempered, equable, placid, serene, well-balanced, composed, calm, tranquil, cool, unperturbable, unexcitable, unruffled, unflappable, peaceful. **get even** have/take one's revenge, be revenged, revenge oneself, even the score, settle accounts, get one's own back, give as good as one gets, return tit for tat, pay someone back, reciprocate. **get even with** have/take one's revenge on, be revenged on, revenge oneself on, get one's own back on one, repay. **Opposites** UNEVEN; BUMPY; UNEQUAL; VARIABLE.

even adverb **1** even colder yet, still, more so, all the more, all the greater, to a greater extent. **2** even a kid can do it | even the teacher laughed unexpectedly, paradoxically, surprisingly. **3** she was attractive, beautiful even indeed, to be sure, you could say, possibly, more precisely, veritably. **4** I could not even get up at all, not quite, so much as, hardly, barely, scarcely, no more than. **even as** even as we speak at the very time/moment that, just as, as, exactly when, while, whilst, during the time that. **even so** even so I shall attend nevertheless, nonetheless, all the same, despite that, in spite of the fact, be that as it may, still, yet, notwithstanding.

even verb **1** even out the bumps/imperfections smooth, level, flatten, make flush, plane. **2** even up the differences in wages make equal, make the same, make uniform, make comparable, balance up, standardize, regularize, equalize.

even-handed adjective fair, just, impartial, unbiased, unprejudiced, non-partisan, non-discriminatory, disinterested, dispassionate, equitable.

evening noun **1** go out in the evening late afternoon, night, close of day, twilight, dusk, nightfall, sunset, sundown; lit. eve, even, eventide. **2** the evening of her life | the evening of the Renaissance close, end, declining years, last/latter part, epilogue.

event noun **1** sudden death is a sad event | the garden party was a successful event occasion, affair, business, matter, happening, occurrence, episode, experience, circumstance, fact, eventuality, phenomenon. **2** track events | the javelin event competition, contest, game, tournament, round, bout, race. **3** in the event he won end, conclusion, outcome, result, upshot, consequence, issue, termination, effect, aftermath. **at all events** in any event, at any rate, in any case, anyhow, anyway, whatever happens, come what may, regardless, regardless of what happens, willy-nilly.

eventful adjective busy, event-filled, action-packed, full, lively, active, important, noteworthy, memorable, notable, remarkable, outstanding, fateful, momentous, significant, crucial, critical, historic, consequential, decisive. **Opposites** UNEVENTFUL; DULL; INSIGNIFICANT.

eventual *adjective* final, end, closing, concluding, last, ultimate, later, resulting, ensuing, consequent, subsequent.

eventuality *noun* event, occurrence, happening, case, contigency, chance, likelihood, possibility, probability.

eventually *adverb* in the end, at the end of the day, ultimately, in the long run, finally, when all is said and done, one day, some day, sooner or later, sometime.

eventuate *verb* **1** *the election eventuated in a change of government* end in, result in, have as a result/consequence. **2** *after the war famine eventuated* be the result, be a consequence, follow, ensue, come about, happen, occur, take place.

ever *adverb* **1** *'twas ever thus* always, at all times, forever, eternally, everlastingly, until the end of time; *inf.* until the twelfth of never, until the cows come home. **2** *will he ever go?* at any point, at any time, on any occasion, in any circumstances. **3** *grew ever larger | ever present | ever changing* always, at all times, constantly, continually, endlessly, unendingly, everlastingly, incessantly, unceasingly, perpetually, repeatedly, habitually, recurrently, unremittingly. **4** *ever so easy* very, to the greatest extent/degree, very much so. **5** *when will she ever learn?* at all, in any way, on earth. **6** *as beautiful as ever* up till now, until now, before.

everlasting *adjective* **1** *everlasting life* never-ending, endless, without end, eternal, perpetual, undying, immortal, deathless, indestructible, abiding, enduring, infinite, boundless, timeless. **2** *their everlasting complaints* endless, interminable, never-ending, non-stop, incessant, ceaseless, constant, continual, continuous, unremitting, relentless, uninterrupted, recurrent, monotonous, tedious, wearisome, tiresome, boring.
Opposites TRANSIENT; OCCASIONAL.

evermore *adverb* forever, always, for always, for all time, until the end of time, until death, until death do us part, endlessly, without end, ceaselessly, unceasingly, constantly.

every *adjective* **1** *every house/child* each, every single. **2** *there is every chance of recovery* as much/great/likely as possible, all possible, all probable.

everyday *adjective* **1** *an everyday occurrence* daily, diurnal, circadian, quotidian. **2** *everyday wear* ordinary, common, usual, regular, customary, habitual, accustomed, familiar, frequent, routine, run-of-the-mill, stock, conventional, plain, workaday, mundane, unimaginative, prosaic, dull.
Opposites UNUSUAL; EXTRAORDINARY.

everyone *pronoun* everybody, each one, every person, each person, each and every one, all, one and all, all and sundry, the whole world, every mother's son, every Tom, Dick, and Harry, every man jack.

everything *pronoun* each thing, each item/article, every single thing, all, the lot, the whole lot, the entirety, the total, the aggregate; *inf.* the whole caboodle, the whole shooting match, the whole shebang, everything but the kitchen sink.

everywhere *adverb* all around, all over, in all places, in every place/spot/part, in each place, far and wide, near and far, high and low, throughout the land, the world over, ubiquitously.

evict *verb* turn out, put out, throw out, throw out on the streets, throw out on one's ear, eject, expel, oust, remove, dispossess, dislodge, drum out, show the door to; *inf.* chuck out, kick out, turf out, boot out, heave out, give the heave-ho to, bounce, give the bum's rush to.

eviction *noun* ejection, expulsion, removal, dispossession, dislodgement, clearance. *See* EVICT.

evidence *noun* **1** *produce evidence of guilt* proof, confirmation, verification, substantiation, corroboration, affirmation, authentication, support; grounds. **2** *give evidence in court* testimony, sworn statement, attestation, deposition, declaration, allegation, affidavit. **3** *evidence of a struggle* sign, indication, mark, manifestation, token; signs. **in evidence** *with police very much in evidence* obvious, noticeable, conspicuous, visible, on view, on display.

evidence *verb* *blushes evidencing guilt* indicate, show, be evidence of, reveal, display, exhibit, manifest, denote, evince, signify, testify to.

evident *adjective* obvious, clear, apparent, plain, plain as daylight, plain as the nose on your face, unmistakable, noticeable, conspicuous, perceptible, visible, discernible, transparent, manifest, patent, palpable, tangible, indisputable, undoubted, incontrovertible, incontestable.
Opposites OBSCURE; DUBIOUS.

evidently *adjective* **1** *evidently he disagrees* it seems, it would seem, it appears, apparently, seemingly, so it seems, as far as one can tell/judge, from all appearances, outwardly, ostensibly. **2** *quite evidently furious* obviously, clearly, plainly, unmistakably, perceptibly, indisputably, undoubtedly, without question. *See* EVIDENT.

evil *adjective* **1** *evil deeds* wicked, bad, wrong, morally wrong, immoral, sinful, vile, base, corrupt, iniquitous, depraved, heinous, villainous, nefarious, reprobate, sinister, atrocious, vicious, malicious, malevolent, demonic, devilish, diabolic. **2** *evil influence* bad, harmful, hurtful, injurious, destructive, detrimental, deleterious, mischievous, pernicious, malignant, venomous, noxious. **3** *evil weather/temper* unpleasant, nasty, disagreeable, horrible, foul, vile. **4** *fall on evil times* unlucky, unfortunate, unfavourable, adverse, unhappy, disastrous, catastrophic, ruinous, calamitous, unpropitious, inauspicious, dire, woeful.
Opposites VIRTUOUS; GOOD; PLEASANT.

evil *noun* **1** *more evil in the world than good* wickedness, bad, badness, wrong, wrongdoing, sin, sinfulness, immorality, vice, iniquity, vileness, baseness, corruption, depravity, villainy, atrocity, malevolence, devilishness. *See* EVIL *adjective* 1. **2** *the evils of war* harm, pain, hurt, misery, sorrow, suffering, disaster, misfortune, catastrophe, ruin, calamity, affliction, woe; ills.
Opposites VIRTUE; GOODNESS; BENEFIT.

evince *verb* indicate, show, reveal, display, exhibit, make clear/plain, manifest, demonstrate, signify, evidence.

evocative *adjective* reminiscent, suggestive, reawakening, rekindling.

evoke *verb* **1** *evoke a response* cause, bring about, bring forth, induce, arouse, excite, awaken, give rise to, stir up, kindle, stimulate, elicit, educe. **2** *evoke memories/spirits* summon, summon up, call forth, conjure up, invoke, raise, recall.

evolution *noun* evolvement, development, unfolding, unrolling, growth, progress, progression, working out, expansion; natural selection, Darwinism. *See* EVOLVE 1.

evolve *verb* **1** *the subject evolved* develop, unfold, unroll, grow, progress, open out, work out, mature, expand, elaborate, disclose. **2** *gases were evolved* emit, yield, give off.

exacerbate *verb* aggravate, make worse, worsen, intensify, exasperate, add fuel to the fire, put salt on the wound.

exact *adjective* **1** *an exact description* precise, accurate, correct, unerring, faithful, close, true, just, veracious, literal, strict, errorless; *inf.* on the nail, spot on. **2** *an exact person* precise, careful, meticulous, painstaking, methodical, punctilious, conscientious, rigorous, scrupulous, exacting.
Opposites INEXACT; INACCURATE; CARELESS.

exact *verb* **1** *exact obedience* demand, require, insist on, compel, command, call for, impose, request. **2** *exact a ransom* demand, extort, extract, force, wring, wrest, squeeze; *inf.* bleed.

exacting *adjective* **1** *an exacting task* demanding, difficult, hard, arduous, tough, laborious, tiring, taxing, troublesome, stringent, onerous. **2** *an exacting person* demanding, strict, stern, firm, rigorous, harsh, rigid, unyielding, unsparing, imperious.

exactly *adverb* **1** *exactly right | exactly as I expected* precisely, absolutely, just, quite, in every respect; *inf.* on the nail, bang on, spot on. **2** *work the prices out exactly* precisely, accurately, correctly, without error. **3** *repeat my words exactly* word for word, literally, to the letter, closely, faithfully. **not exactly** *not exactly pleased to see us* not at all, by no means, not by any means, in no way, certainly not; not really.

exactly *interjection* precisely, just so, quite so, quite, indeed, absolutely, truly, certainly, definitely, assuredly, undoubtedly.

exactness *noun* **1** *the exactness of the description* precision, accuracy, accurateness, correctness, veracity. *See* EXACT *adjective* 1. **2** *the exactness of our teacher* precision, care, meticulousness, punctiliousness, conscientiousness, rigour. *See* EXACT *adjective* 2.
Opposites INACCURACY; NEGLIGENCE.

exaggerate *verb* **1** *exaggerate the difficulties | exaggerate how difficult it was* overstate, overemphasize, overstress, overestimate, overvalue, magnify, amplify, aggrandize. **2** *he's not that tall—you're exaggerating* overstate, embellish, amplify, embroider, colour, add colour, over-elaborate, overdraw, make a mountain out of a molehill, hyperbolize; *inf.* lay it on thick, lay it on with a trowel.
Opposites UNDERSTATE; play down (*see* PLAY); MINIMIZE.

exaggerated *adjective* **1** *an exaggerated account* overstated, overemphasized, extravagant, inflated, highly coloured, excessive, hyperbolic; *inf.* tall. **2** *an exaggerated frown | exaggerated make-up* overdone, extravagant, theatrical.

exaggeration *noun* **1** *say without exaggeration* overstatement, overemphasis, magnification, amplification, embroidery, embellishment, extravagance, excessiveness, excess, pretentiousness, hyperbole; *inf.* purple prose, puffery. **2** *the exaggeration of their ability* overstatement, overestimation, overvaluation, aggrandizement.

exalt *verb* **1** *exalt to the highest rank* elevate, promote, raise, advance, upgrade, ennoble, aggrandize. **2** *exalt the composer* praise, extol, glorify, acclaim, pay homage/tribute to, laud, reverence, worship, revere, lionize, magnify. **3** *exalt one's spirits* excite, stimulate, animate, enliven, exhilarate, uplift, elevate, inspire.

exaltation *noun* **1** *exaltation to high rank* promotion, advancement, raising, ennoblement, aggrandizement; rise, elevation. **2** *the exaltation of royalty* high rank, eminence, grandeur, dignity, honour, loftiness, prestige, fame. **3** *greet with exaltation* praise, extolment, glorification, acclamation, applause, homage, tribute, reverence, worship; plaudits. **4** *exaltation of the spirits* stimulation, animation, exhilaration, elevation, inspiration. **5** *full of exaltation* elation, exultation, joy, rapture, rhapsody, ecstasy, bliss, transport, happiness, delight.

exalted *adjective* **1** *from his exalted position in the firm* high, high-ranking, lofty, grand, eminent, prestigious, elevated, august. **2** *exalted aims* high-minded, lofty, elevated, noble, intellectual, ideal, sublime, inflated, pretentious. **3** *in an exalted mood* elated, exultant, jubilant, joyful, triumphant, rapturous, rhapsodic, ecstatic, blissful, transported.

exam *noun* *an English exam* examination, test, set of questions/exercises; paper, question paper, oral, viva.

examination *noun* **1** *the examination of the facts* study, inspection, scrutiny, investigation, analysis, review, research, observation, exploration, consideration, appraisal. *See* EXAMINE 1. **2** *the physical examination of a patient* check-up, inspection, assessment, observation, scrutiny. **3** *examination of witnesses* questioning, interrogation, cross-examination, cross-questioning, third degree. *See* EXAMINE 3. **4** *sit the examination* exam, test. *See* EXAM.

examine *verb* **1** *examine the facts* look at, look into, study, inspect, survey, scrutinize, investigate, analyse, review, scan, observe, research, sift, explore, probe, check out, consider, appraise, weigh, weigh up, vet. **2** *examine a patient* look at, inspect, check over, give a check-up to, assess, observe, scrutinize. **3** *examine the candidates/witnesses* put/address questions to, question, test, quiz, interrogate, cross-examine, cross-question, catechize, give the third degree to; *inf.* grill, pump.

example *noun* **1** *an example of cave painting* sample, specimen, instance, representative case, case in point, illustration. **2** *follow someone else's example* model, pattern, precedent, paradigm, standard, parallel case, criterion. **3** *the hero is an example to everyone* model, ideal, pattern, standard, paradigm, paragon. **4** *someone as an example to other prisoners* warning, caution, lesson, admonition. **for example** for instance, e.g., to give an example/instance, by way of illustration, as an illustration, to illustrate.

exasperate *verb* **1** *exasperate the teacher* anger, annoy, infuriate, irritate, incense, madden, enrage, provoke, irk, vex, gall, pique, try the patience of, get on the nerves of, make one's blood boil; *inf.* bug, needle, get to, rile. **2** *exasperate a difficult situation* aggravate, make worse, worsen, exacerbate. *See* EXACERBATE.

exasperation *noun* **1** *show exasperation at their behaviour* anger, annoyance, fury, irritation, rage, vexation, pique. *See* EXASPERATE 1. **2** *the exasperation of the difficulties* aggravation, exacerbation. *See* EXASPERATE 2.

excavate *verb* **1** *excavate a trench* dig, dig out, hollow out, scoop out, gouge, cut out, quarry, mine. **2** *excavate an ancient city/vase* unearth, dig up, uncover, bring to the surface, reveal, disinter, exhume.

excavation *noun* **1** *the excavation of the site* digging, hollowing, quarrying. *See* EXCAVATE 1. **2** *mining/archaeological excavations* hole, hollow, cavity, pit, crater, cutting, trench, trough; burrow, quarry, mine, colliery.

exceed *verb* **1** *if the price exceeds £10* be greater/more than, go beyond, pass, top. **2** *her abilities far exceed his* be greater than, surpass, be superior to, better, pass, beat, outdo, outstrip, outshine, transcend, top, cap, overshadow, eclipse. **3** *exceed the speed limit* | *exceed one's responsibility* go beyond, go over, do more than, overstep, go for the burn, out-Herod Herod, go over the top.

exceedingly *adverb* extremely, exceptionally, extraordinarily, tremendously, enormously, vastly, greatly, highly, hugely, supremely, inordinately, surpassingly, superlatively, especially, unusually, very.

excel *verb* **1** *excel at tennis* be pre-eminent/outstanding, be skilful/talented, be proficient, shine, be master, wear the crown. **2** *her cousin excels her at games* be better than, be superior to, surpass, outshine, eclipse, overshadow, outdo, outrival, outclass, outstrip, beat hollow, top, pass, transcend.

excellence *noun* merit, eminence, pre-eminence, distinction, greatness, fineness, quality, superiority, supremacy, transcendence, value, worth, skill.

excellent *adjective* very good, of high quality, of a high standard, first-rate, first-class, great, fine, distinguished, superior, superb, outstanding, marvellous, brilliant, noted, notable, eminent, pre-eminent, supreme, superlative,

admirable, worthy, sterling, prime, select; *inf.* A1, ace, brill, capital, top-notch, tip-top, champion; *Austral. inf.* beaut.
Opposites POOR; INFERIOR.

except *preposition* *except you* | *except for me* with the exception of, excepting, excluding, leaving out, but, besides, barring, bar, other than, omitting, with the omission/exclusion of, exclusive of, saving, save.

except *verb* *I except present company* exclude, leave out, omit, rule out, pass over, bar.

exception *noun* **1** *with the exception of you* exclusion, omission, non-inclusion. *See* EXCEPT *verb*. **2** *the case being an exception* special case, departure, deviation, anomaly, irregularity, inconsistency, quirk, peculiarity, oddity, freak. **take exception** object, be offended, take offence, raise an objection, resent, take umbrage, demur, disagree, cavil.

exceptionable *adjective* *rude and exceptionable behaviour* objectionable, offensive, disagreeable, obnoxious, repugnant. *See* OBJECTIONABLE.

exceptional *adjective* **1** *this noise is exceptional* unusual, uncommon, abnormal, out of the ordinary, atypical, rare, odd, anomalous, singular, peculiar, inconsistent, deviant, divergent, aberrant. **2** *a person of exceptional ability* unusually good, excellent, extraordinary, remarkable, outstanding, special, especial, phenomenal, prodigious.
Opposites USUAL; NORMAL; AVERAGE.

excerpt *noun* extract, citation, quotation, quote, passage, selection, part, section, fragment, piece, portion, pericope.

excess *noun* **1** *an excess of fat/enthusiasm* surplus, surfeit, overabundance, superabundance, superfluity, plethora, glut, overkill, oversufficiency; too much, more than enough, enough and to spare. **2** *throw out the excess* remainder, residue, overload, overflow; leftovers. **3** *a life of excess* immoderation, lack of restraint, overindulgence, prodigality, intemperance, debauchery, dissipation, dissoluteness.
Opposites DEARTH; SHORTAGE; MODERATION.

excess *adjective* *excess baggage/food* extra, additional, too much, surplus, superfluous, spare, redundant.

excessive *adjective* too much, to too great a degree, superfluous, immoderate, extravagant, lavish, superabundant, unreasonable, undue, uncalled-for, extreme, inordinate, unwarranted, unnecessary, needless, disproportionate, exorbitant, enormous, outrageous, intemperate, unconscionable; *inf.* over the top, OTT.

excessively *adverb* to too great a degree, unduly, immoderately, unreasonably. *See* EXCESSIVE.

exchange *verb* *exchange compliments* trade, swap, barter, interchange, reciprocate, bandy.

exchange *noun* **1** *the exchange of information* interchange, trade, trade-off, swapping, barter, giving and taking, bandying, traffic, reciprocity, tit for tat; dealings. **2** *the floor of the exchange* stock exchange, money market, bourse.

excise verb **1** *surgeons excised the spleen* cut out, cut off, remove, eradicate, extirpate; *Tech.* resect. **2** *excise the offending passage* remove, delete, cut out, cut, cross/strike out, erase, blue-pencil, expunge, eliminate, expurgate, bowdlerize.

excise noun duty, tariff, toll, levy; customs.

excitable adjective temperamental, emotional, highly strung, nervous, edgy, mercurial, volatile, tempestuous, hot-tempered, quick-tempered, hot-headed, passionate, fiery, irascible, testy, moody, choleric.

excite verb **1** *excite the children too much* stimulate, rouse, arouse, animate, move, thrill, discompose, inflame, titillate; *inf.* turn on, wind up. **2** *excite feelings of love* cause, bring about, rouse, arouse, awaken, incite, provoke, stimulate, kindle, evoke, stir up, elicit. **3** *excite a rebellion* cause, incite, bring about, stir up, instigate, foment.

excited adjective *excited children* stimulated, aroused, animated, thrilled, agitated, overwrought, feverish, wild; *inf.* high, wound up, turned on. See EXCITE 1.
Opposites INDIFFERENT; APATHETIC.

excitement noun **1** *jumping up and down with excitement* agitation, animation, emotion, anticipation, exhilaration, elation, enthusiasm, feverishness, discomposure, perturbation, ferment, tumult. **2** *one of the excitements of travel* adventure, thrill, pleasure, stimulation; *inf.* kick. **3** *the excitement of feelings* arousal, awakening, stimulation, evocation, kindling. See EXCITE 2.

exciting adjective *an exciting event* thrilling, stirring, stimulating, exhilarating, intoxicating, rousing, electrifying, invigorating, moving, inspiring, titillating, provocative, sensational; *inf.* sexy.
Opposites BORING; UNINTERESTING; FLAT.

exclaim verb call, cry, call/cry out, shout, yell, roar, bellow, shriek, ejaculate, utter, proclaim; *fml.* vociferate.

exclamation noun call, cry, shout, yell, roar, bellow, shriek, ejaculation, interjection, utterance, expletive.

exclude verb **1** *exclude women from membership* debar, bar, keep out, shut out, prohibit, forbid, prevent, disallow, refuse, ban, blackball, veto, stand in the way of, proscribe, interdict. **2** *exclude the possibility* eliminate, rule out, preclude, count out, reject, set aside, except, repudiate, omit, pass over, leave out, ignore. **3** *the price excludes drinks* be exclusive of, not include, not be inclusive of, omit, leave out. **4** *exclude from a building* throw out, turn out, eject, remove, evict, expel, oust, ban; *inf.* bounce, chuck out, kick/boot out.
Opposites INCLUDE; ACCEPT; ADMIT.

exclusion noun **1** *the exclusion of women* debarment, barring, keeping out, prevention, refusal, proscription. See EXCLUDE 1. **2** *the exclusion of robbery as a motive* elimination, ruling out, precluding, rejection, omission. See EXCLUDE 2. **3** *the exclusion of meals from the price* non-inclusion, omission, leaving out. See EXCLUDE 3. **4** *the exclusion of drunks* throwing

out, ejection, removal, eviction, expulsion. See EXCLUDE 4.

exclusive adjective **1** *an exclusive club* select, selective, choice, restrictive, restricted, closed, private, limited, discriminative, cliquish, clannish, snobbish, fashionable, chic, elegant, luxurious, high-class, aristocratic, top-people's; *inf.* posh, ritzy, classy, swish, up-market. **2** *my exclusive attention* complete, undivided, full, absolute, entire, whole, total, all of, unshared. **3** *the exclusive means of travel* sole, only, unique, individual, single, one-off. **4** *exclusive of drinks* not including, excluding, leaving out, omitting, excepting, with the exception of, except for, not counting, barring. **5** *mutually exclusive* incompatible, inimical, antithetical.
Opposites OPEN; PARTIAL; INCLUSIVE.

excommunicate verb exclude, expel, cast out, banish, eject, remove, bar, debar, proscribe, interdict, repudiate; *fml.* anathematize, unchurch.

excoriate verb **1** *excoriate skin* abrade, scrape, scratch, flay, strip, peel, skin, decorticate. **2** *excoriate the wrongdoers* denounce, censure, condemn, criticize, blame, accuse, berate, upbraid, rebuke, reprimand, reprove, scold, chide, read someone the riot act, chastise, castigate, inveigh/rail against, let fly at, abuse, attack, revile, vilify; *inf.* carpet, lambaste, bawl out, give someone a rocket, tear someone off a strip, tear into, give someone what for.

excrement noun waste matter, ordure, dung, manure; excreta, faeces, stools, droppings.

excrescence noun **1** *excrescence on the body/tree* growth, lump, swelling, protuberance, outgrowth, eruption; cancer, boil, carbuncle, pustule. **2** *excrescence on the landscape* something ugly, eyesore, monstrosity, disfigurement; *inf.* sight.

excrete verb *excrete faeces/urine* pass, void, discharge, eject, evacuate, expel, eliminate, exude, emit, egest; defecate, urinate.

excruciating adjective *an excruciating pain* agonizing, racking, torturous, insufferable, unbearable, severe, intense, extreme, harrowing, searing, piercing, acute; *fml.* exquisite.

excursion noun **1** *an excursion to the seaside | a shopping excursion* trip, day trip, expedition, jaunt, outing, journey, tour. **2** *an excursion from the main topic* digression, deviation, detour, wandering, rambling.

excusable adjective forgivable, pardonable, defensible, justifiable, understandable, condonable, venial.
Opposites INEXCUSABLE; UNFORGIVABLE.

excuse verb **1** *excuse the wrongdoer* forgive, pardon, exonerate, absolve, acquit, make allowances for, bear with, tolerate, indulge; *fml.* exculpate. **2** *excuse their behaviour* forgive, pardon, condone, justify, defend, vindicate, mitigate, explain. **3** *excuse them from heavy work* let off, exempt, spare, absolve, release, relieve, free, liberate.
Opposites PUNISH; CONDEMN; OBLIGE.

excuse noun **1** *their excuse for being late* defence, justification, reason, explanation,

261

apology, vindication, mitigation; grounds, mitigating circumstances. **2** *his illness was just an excuse for his absence* pretext, ostensible reason, pretence, front, cover-up, subterfuge, fabrication, evasion, escape; *inf.* cop-out. **3** *an excuse for a man/car* apology, travesty, poor specimen, pitiful example, mockery, poor substitute.

execrable *adjective* abominable, abhorrent, loathsome, odious, heinous, hateful, detestable, despicable, foul, vile, deplorable, invidious, atrocious, offensive, disgusting, repulsive, obnoxious, nauseous, damnable.

execrate *verb* **1** *execrate violence* abhor, abominate, loathe, hate, detest, despise, deplore, be repelled by, have an aversion to, feel hostility to, not be able to stand. **2** *execrate and blaspheme* curse, swear at, revile, imprecate, inveigh, fulminate, vituperate, condemn, damn, censure, denounce, excoriate.

execute *verb* **1** *execute a murderer* put to death, carry out a sentence of death, kill; hang, send to the gibbet, behead, guillotine, decapitate, electrocute, send to the electric chair, send to the chair, shoot, put before a firing squad, send to the gas chamber, crucify, stone to death; *inf.* string up. **2** *execute a plan of action* carry out, accomplish, perform, implement, effect, bring off, achieve, complete, fulfil, enact, enforce, put into effect, do, discharge, prosecute, engineer, administer, attain, realize, render. **3** *execute a dance | execute a piece of music* perform, present, stage, render.
Opposites NEGLECT.

execution *noun* **1** *the execution of a murderer* putting to death, capital punishment; death sentence. See EXECUTE 1. **2** *the execution of a plan* carrying out, accomplishment, performance, implementation, effecting, bringing off, achievement, completion, fulfilment, enactment, enforcement, discharge, prosecution, engineering, administering, attainment, realization, rendering. **3** *execution of a piece of music | her superb execution of the dance* performance, presentation, staging, rendition, delivery, technique, style, mode.

executioner *noun* **1** *public executioner* hangman, headsman, firing squad, Jack Ketch. **2** *the executioner of a member of a rival gang* assassin, killer, murderer; *inf.* hit man, slayer.

executive *noun* **1** *a bank executive* administrator, official, director, manager, VIP; *inf.* boss, bigwig, big wheel, big Daddy/Chief; *Am. inf.* honcho. **2** *the executive has increased in number* administration, leadership, management, hierarchy; *inf.* top brass.

executive *adjective* *executive powers* administrative, decision-making, directing, controlling, managerial; law-making.

exegesis *noun* *exegesis of a scriptural text* explanation, explication, interpretation, exposition, elucidation, clarification, annotation.

exemplar *noun* **1** *an exemplar of morality* model, ideal, standard of perfection/excellence, epitome, paradigm, paragon, pattern, criterion, benchmark. **2** *an exemplar of birds of prey* example, specimen, exemplification, type, illustration, prototype, instance.

exemplary *adjective* **1** *exhibiting exemplary behaviour* ideal, model, perfect, excellent, admirable, commendable, faultless, laudable, praiseworthy, meritorious, honourable. **2** *exemplary jail sentences* warning, cautionary, admonitory, monitory, example-setting, lesson-teaching. **3** *exemplary member of the species* typical, representative, illustrative, characteristic, epitomic.

exemplify *verb* **1** *exemplify Impressionist painting* typify, epitomize, represent, personify, embody, illustrate. **2** *exemplify the talk with slides* illustrate, give an example/instance of, demonstrate, instance, depict.

exempt *verb* *exempt from taxation* free from, release from, make an exception of/for, exclude from, excuse from, let off, give/grant immunity from, absolve/except from, liberate from, spare, exonerate from, relieve of, discharge from, dismiss from; *inf.* let off.
Opposites LIABLE; SUBJECT.

exempt *adjective* *declared exempt from taxation* free from, excused from, immune to, not subject/liable to, absolved/excepted from, spared, released from, discharged from, dismissed from. See EXEMPT *verb.*

exemption *noun* *be granted exemption from military service* immunity, indemnity, dispensation, freedom, exclusion, release, absolution, exception, exoneration, relief, discharge, special treatment, privilege, favouritism.

exercise *noun* **1** *physical exercise* activity, exertion, effort, action, work, movement, training, physical training, drill, drilling, discipline; work-out, warm-up, limbering-up; gymnastics, sports, aerobics, callisthenics, keep fit. **2** *the exercise of patience* employment, use, application, utilization, implementation, practice, operation, exertion, discharge, accomplishment. **3** *an English exercise* problem, task, piece of work; practice, schooling, drilling.

exercise *verb* **1** *exercise in order to lose weight* do exercises, work out, train, exert oneself, drill. See EXERCISE *noun* 1. **2** *exercise patience* employ, use, make use of, utilize, apply, implement, practise, exert. **3** *a problem exercising the mind* worry, disturb, trouble, perplex, distress, preoccupy, annoy, make uneasy, perturb, vex, gall, peeve, stir up, afflict, pain, burden.

exert *verb* **1** *exert pressure* exercise, employ, use, make use of, utilize, apply, wield, bring into play, bring to bear, set in motion, expend, spend. **2** *exert yourself and you will be able to do it* apply oneself, put oneself out, make an effort, spare no effort, try hard, do one's best, give one's all, strive, endeavour, struggle, labour, toil, strain, work, push, drive, go all out; *inf.* put one's back into it.

exertion *noun* **1** *physical exertion* effort, exercise, work, struggle, strain, stress, endeavour, toil, labour, action, industry, assiduity; pains. **2** *the exertion of pressure* exercise, employment, use, utilization, expenditure, application.

exhaust *verb* **1** *the climb exhausted them* tire, tire out, wear out, fatigue, drain, weary, sap, enervate, tax, overtax, debilitate, prostrate, enfeeble, disable; *inf.* take it out of, knacker, poop, fag out, knock out, burn out. **2** *exhaust the supply of fuel* use up, consume, finish, deplete, expend, spend, run through, dissipate, waste, squander, fritter away; *inf.* blow. **3** *exhaust a well of its water* empty, drain, void, evacuate, deplete. **4** *exhaust the subject* say all there is to say about, treat in detail, treat thoroughly, develop completely, expound in detail about, study in great detail, research completely, go over with a fine-toothed comb. **Opposites** INVIGORATE; REPLENISH.

exhausted *adjective* **1** *cold and exhausted* tired out, worn out, fatigued, weary, sapped, enervated, weak, faint, debilitated, prostrate, enfeebled, spent; *inf.* all in, done in, dead beat, dead tired, dog-tired, knackered, ready to drop, dead on one's feet, burnt out, played out. **2** *exhausted supplies* used up, at an end, consumed, finished, depleted. *See* EXHAUST 2. **3** *an exhausted well* empty, drained, depleted, dry, void. *See* EXHAUST 3.

exhausting *adjective* tiring, fatiguing, wearing, gruelling, punishing, strenuous, arduous, back-breaking, taxing, laborious, enervating, sapping, debilitating. *See* EXHAUST 1.

exhaustion *noun* **1** *fail to go on because of exhaustion* fatigue, great tiredness, weakness, debility, collapse, weariness, faintness, prostration, enervation, lassitude; *Med.* asthenia. **2** *the exhaustion of resources* using up, consumption, depletion, dissipation. *See* EXHAUST 2.

exhaustive *adjective* all-inclusive, comprehensive, intensive, all-out, in-depth, total, all-embracing, encyclopedic, thorough, complete, full, thoroughgoing, extensive, profound, far-reaching, sweeping. **Opposites** PERFUNCTORY; SKETCHY.

exhibit *verb* **1** *exhibit products* put on display/show/view, display, show, demonstrate, set out/forth, present, model, expose, air, unveil, array, flaunt, parade. **2** *exhibit signs of sadness* show, express, indicate, reveal, display, demonstrate, make clear/plain, betray, give away, disclose, manifest, evince, evidence.

exhibit *noun* *a furniture exhibit* display, show, showing, demonstration, presentation, exhibition, viewing.

exhibition *noun* **1** *a book exhibition* display, show, fair, demonstration, presentation, exhibit, exposition, mounting, spectacle. *See* EXHIBIT verb 1. **2** *an exhibition of bad temper* display, show, expression, indication, revelation, demonstration, betrayal, disclosure, manifestation.

exhilarate *verb* make happy/cheerful, cheer up, enliven, elate, gladden, delight, brighten, excite, thrill, animate, invigorate, lift, stimulate, raise the spirits of, revitalize, exalt, inspirit; *inf.* perk/pep up.

exhilaration *noun* elation, joy, happiness, gladness, delight, excitement, gaiety, merriment, mirth, hilarity, glee, animation, vivacity, invigoration, stimulation, revitalization, exaltation; high spirits.

exhort *verb* urge, persuade, press, encourage, sway, prompt, advise, counsel, incite, goad, stimulate, push, beseech, entreat, bid, enjoin, admonish, warn.

exhortation *noun* urging, persuasion, pressing, insistence, encouragement, prompting, advice, recommendation, counselling, incitement, pushing, beseeching; entreaty, enjoinder, admonition, warning, instruction, injunction, lecture, harangue. *See* EXHORT.

exhume *verb* *exhume a corpse* | *exhume old memories* dig up, unearth, disinter, disentomb, unbury, resurrect, reincarnate.

exigency *noun* **1** *a situation of exigency* urgency, emergency, crisis, criticalness, necessity, imperativeness, stress, extremity, difficulty, trouble, pressure. **2** *the exigencies of war* need, demand, requirement, necessity, want, essential, requisite.

exiguous *adjective* scant, scanty, meagre, sparse, bare, slim, slight, slender, paltry, skimpy, negligible, mere, trifling, diminutive.

exile *verb* *be exiled from one's native country* banish, expatriate, deport, expel, drive out, eject, oust, proscribe, outlaw, bar, ban, ostracize, uproot, separate, excommunicate.

exile *noun* **1** *sent into exile* banishment, expatriation, deportation, expulsion; uprooting, separation. *See* EXILE verb. **2** *exiles from their homeland* expatriate, deportee, displaced person, refugee, outlaw, outcast, pariah; *inf.* DP, expat.

exist *verb* **1** *querying that ghosts exist* be, have being, have existence, live, have life, be living, subsist, breathe, draw breath, be extant, be viable. **2** *cannot exist in a cold climate* live, survive, subsist, occur, remain, continue, last, endure, prevail. **3** *enough money barely to exist on* survive, live, stay alive, eke out a living, subsist. **Opposites** DIE; FADE.

existence *noun* **1** *come into existence* | *the existence of ghosts* being, existing, actuality, reality, fact, living, subsistence, survival, *esse.* **2** *a poverty-stricken existence* way of life, life style, manner of living/survival, mode of being. **3** *alien existences* being, entity, creation.

existent *adjective* existing, in existence, living, extant, surviving, remaining, abiding, enduring, prevailing, present, current.

exit *noun* **1** *theatre/motorway exit* way out, door, gate, door/gate out, passage out, out-lane, outlet, vent, egress. **2** *his exit from politics* departure, leaving, withdrawal, retirement, going, retreat, leave-taking, flight, exodus, farewell, adieu. **Opposites** ENTRANCE; ENTRY; ARRIVAL.

exodus *noun* mass departure, flight, withdrawal, exit, leaving, escape, fleeing, evacuation, migration, emigration, retreat, retirement, hegira.

exonerate *verb* **1** *exonerate from any responsibility* absolve, acquit, clear, discharge, vindicate, exculpate, declare innocent, dismiss, let off, excuse, pardon, justify. **2** *exonerate from duty* excuse, exempt, except, release, relieve, free,

let off, liberate, discharge.
Opposites CHARGE; IMPLICATE; INCRIMINATE.

exoneration noun **1** *exoneration from responsibility* acquittal, absolution, discharge, vindication, exculpation, dismissal, excusing, pardon, amnesty, justification. **2** *exoneration from duty* excusing, exemption, release, liberation, freedom, discharge, indemnity, immunity, dispensation.

exorbitant adjective excessive, extortionate, extreme, unreasonable, immoderate, inordinate, outrageous, preposterous, monstrous, unwarranted, undue, unconscionable.
Opposites CHEAP; MODERATE.

exorcise verb **1** *exorcise the evil spirit* drive out, cast out, expel. **2** *exorcise a place of evil spirits* deliver, free, purify, rid, disenchant.

exorcism noun **1** *exorcism of evil spirits* driving out, casting out, expulsion. **2** *exorcism of a place of evil spirits* deliverance, freeing, purification, ridding, disenchantment.

exordium noun introduction, opening, beginning, preface, prelude, foreword, preamble, prologue, proem, prolegomenon.

exotic adjective **1** *exotic fruits* foreign, non-native, tropical, imported, introduced, novel, alien, external, extraneous, extrinsic. **2** *exotic clothing* striking, outrageous, colourful, extraordinary, extravagant, sensational, unusual, remarkable, astonishing, strange, outlandish, bizarre, peculiar, impressive, glamorous, fascinating, mysterious, curious, different, unfamiliar. **3** *exotic dancing* erotic, go-go, striptease, titillating, risqué, sexy.

expand verb **1** *metals expand when heated | the company is expanding* become/grow larger, enlarge, increase, increase in size/scope, swell, inflate, magnify, amplify, distend, lengthen, stretch, extend, multiply. **2** *expand the territory/business* make larger/greater/bigger, increase, magnify, amplify, add to, extend, multiply. **3** *petals expanding in the sunshine | faces expanding in smiles* open out, spread out, unfold, unfurl, unroll, unravel. **4** *expand one's account of the accident* elaborate on, add detail to, amplify, embellish, enlarge on, flesh out, expatiate on, develop, expound, pad out.
5 *guests losing their reserve and expanding* become relaxed, relax, grow friendlier, become less shy/reserved, become sociable; *inf.* loosen up.
Opposites CONTRACT; CONDENSE.

expanse noun *an expanse of green/water* area, stretch, region, tract, breadth, extent, sweep, space, plain, field, extension, vastness.

expansion noun **1** *expansion of metals/business* enlargement, increase, magnification, amplification, stretching, distension, protraction, extension, multiplication. **2** *flowers expanding in the sun* opening out, unfolding, unfurling, unrolling, unravelling. **3** *an expansion of one's account* elaboration, amplification, embellishment, fleshing out, expatiation, development, expounding, padding out.

expansive adjective **1** *the expansive qualities of metal when heated* expandable, expanding, extendable, extending; extensive, wide. **2** *on an expansive scale* extensive, wide-ranging,

broad, wide, widespread, all-embracing, comprehensive, thorough, universal. **3** *guests growing expansive* sociable, friendly, outgoing, affable, unreserved, talkative, communicative, uninhibited, frank, open, genial, garrulous, loquacious, extrovert.

expatiate verb *expatiate on the plans* expand on, enlarge on, elaborate on, amplify, embellish, expound, go into detail about, discourse on, dwell on, dissertate on.

expatriate verb *expatriate criminals* deport, exile, banish, expel, cast out, proscribe, outlaw.

expatriate noun *expatriates working abroad* emigrant, émigré, exile, displaced person, refugee, outcast, *Gastarbeiter*; *inf.* expat, DP.

expatriate adjective emigrant, living abroad, exiled, banished, cast out, deported.

expect verb **1** *don't expect that he will come* think, believe, assume, suppose, imagine, presume, conjecture, calculate, surmise, reckon. **2** *expect a letter | expect a large crowd* anticipate, await, envisage, look for, look forward to, watch for, hope for, contemplate, bargain for, have in prospect, predict, forecast. **3** *teachers expect complete obedience* insist on, require, demand, exact, count on, call for, rely on, look for, wish, want, hope for.

expectancy noun **1** *in a state of excited expectancy* anticipation, expectation, eagerness, hope, waiting, suspense, conjecture, anxiety. **2** *life expectancy* prospect, outlook, likelihood, probability.

expectant adjective **1** *children's expectant faces* anticipating, anticipatory, expecting, awaiting, eager, hopeful, in suspense, ready, watchful, anxious, on tenterhooks. **2** *expectant mothers* pregnant, expecting, expecting a child, in the family way; *Tech.* gravid.

expectation noun **1** *in expectation of the arrival of Father Christmas* anticipation, expectancy, readiness, hope. See EXPECTANCY 1. **2** *an expectation that she will win* assumption, belief, supposition, presumption, assurance, conjecture, surmise, reckoning, calculation; confidence. **3** *future expectations* prospects, hopes; outlook, speculation, good fortune.

expecting adjective pregnant, expectant. See EXPECTANT 2.

expediency, expedience noun *interested only in the expediency of the plan, not in moral principles* convenience, advantageousness, advantage, usefulness, benefit, profitability, profit, gain, gainfulness, practicality, utilitarianism, utility, pragmatism, desirability, suitability, advisability, appropriateness, aptness, fitness, effectiveness, helpfulness, judiciousness, timeliness, opportunism, propitiousness.

expedient adjective *expedient to tell a white lie | an expedient rather than moral course of action* convenient, advantageous, useful, beneficial, profitable, gainful, practical, pragmatic, desirable, suitable, advisable, appropriate, apt, fit, effective, helpful, politic, judicious, timely, opportune, propitious.

expedient *noun an expedient to achieve an end* means, measure, method, resource, scheme, plan, plot, stratagem, manoeuvre, machination, agency, trick, ruse, artifice, device, tool, contrivance, invention, shift, stopgap.

expedite *verb* **1** *expedite the procedure of obtaining planning permission* accelerate, speed up, hurry, hasten, step up, precipitate, quicken, urge on, forward, advance, facilitate, further, promote, press. **2** *expedite the task* finish/ accomplish/achieve quickly, dispatch; *inf.* dash off, make short work of.
Opposites DECELERATE; OBSTRUCT; HINDER.

expedition *noun* **1** *an expedition to find a lost tribe* organized journey/voyage, undertaking, enterprise, mission, project, quest, exploration, safari, trek. **2** *a shopping expedition* trip, excursion, outing, journey, jaunt. **3** *three members of the expedition died* group, team, party, company, crew, band, troop, crowd. **4** *carry out orders with maximum expedition* speed, haste, promptness, swiftness, alacrity, quickness, rapidity, velocity, celerity, readiness, dispatch.

expeditious *adjective an expeditious response* speedy, immediate, instant, prompt, swift, quick, rapid, fast, punctual, ready, brisk, nimble, hasty, summary.

expel *verb* **1** *expel them from the country* banish, exile, evict, oust, drive out, throw out, cast out, expatriate, deport, proscribe, outlaw; *inf.* chuck out, kick/boot out, turf out, heave out, give the bum's rush to, send packing. **2** *expel someone from a club* bar, ban, debar, blackball, throw out, drum out, oust, reject, dismiss, ostracize. **3** *expel cooking smells* discharge, eject, eliminate, excrete, evacuate, belch, void, spew out.
Opposites ADMIT; WELCOME.

expend *verb* **1** *expend time and money on acquiring luxuries* spend, lay out, pay out, disburse, lavish, squander, waste, fritter, dissipate; *inf.* fork out, shell out, dish out. **2** *expend all one's ammunition/energy* use up, consume, exhaust, deplete, drain, sap, empty, finish off.

expendable *adjective workers considered expendable* dispensable, able/likely to be sacrificed, replaceable, non-essential, inessential, unimportant.

expenditure *noun* **1** *limit expenditure and save money* spending, outlay/outgoings, costs, expenses, payments. **2** *the expenditure of money on defence* spending, outlay, disbursement, lavishing, squandering. *See* EXPEND 1. **3** *the expenditure of one's ammunition* using up, consumption, exhaustion, depletion, draining, sapping.
Opposites INCOME; CONSERVATION.

expense *noun* **1** *the expense of private schooling* cost, price, charge, outlay, fee, amount, rate, figure, quotation. **2** *the expense of time, energy and money* spending, outlay, laying out, paying out, disbursement, lavishing, squandering. *See* EXPEND 1. **3** *victory at the expense of lives* cost, sacrifice.

expensive *adjective expensive clothes/tastes* dear, costly, high-priced, exorbitant, extortionate, overpriced, lavish, extravagant; *inf.* steep.
Opposites CHEAP; ECONOMICAL.

experience *noun* **1** *experience of teaching* | *experience of prison life* involvement in, practice, participation in, contact with, familiarity with, acquaintance with, exposure to, observation of, understanding of, impression of. **2** *a frightening/wonderful experience* event, incident, occurrence, happening, affair, episode, adventure, encounter, circumstance, case, test, trial, ordeal. **3** *experience more valuable than a university degree* skill, practical knowledge, practice, training, learning, understanding, wisdom, savoir faire, maturity; *inf.* know-how.

experience *verb experience hardship* | *experience great happiness* have experience of, undergo, encounter, meet, feel, know, become familiar with, come into contact with, face, participate in, live/go through, sustain, suffer.

experienced *adjective* **1** *experienced workers* having experience, practised, accomplished, skilful, proficient, seasoned, trained, expert, adept, competent, capable, knowledgeable, qualified, well-versed, professional, mature, master, veteran. **2** *experienced woman, not an innocent girl* worldly wise, sophisticated, knowing, mature, worldly, initiated; *inf.* having been around.

experiment *noun* **1** *medical experiments with rats* test, investigation, trial, trial run, try-out, examination, observation, enquiry, questioning, pilot study, demonstration, venture. **2** *results obtained by experiment* research, experimentation, observation, trial and error, try-out, analysis, testing.

experiment *verb experiment on animals* | *experiment with new methods* conduct experiments, carry out trials/tests, conduct research; test, investigate, examine, explore, observe.

experimental *adjective experimental basis/stage* trial, test, trial and error, exploratory, empirical, investigational, observational, pilot, tentative, speculative, preliminary, probationary, at the trial stage, under review, under the microscope, on the drawing-board.

expert *noun an expert on ancient Rome* | *experts at playing golf* authority, past master, specialist, professional, adept, pundit, maestro, virtuoso, wizard, connoisseur; *cognoscenti; inf.* old hand, dab hand, ace, buff, pro.

expert *adjective an expert tennis player* skilful, experienced, practised, qualified, knowledgeable, specialist, professional, proficient, adept, master, masterly, brilliant, accomplished, able, deft, dexterous, adroit, apt, capable, competent, clever, well-versed, *au fait; inf.* wizard, ace, crack, top-notch.
Opposites INEXPERT; AMATEUR.

expertise *noun* skill, skilfulness, mastery, masterliness, proficiency, knowledge, command, professionalism, deftness, dexterity, facility, ability, knack, capability, competence, cleverness; *inf.* know-how.

expiate *verb expiate his wrongdoing* atone for, make amends for, make up for, do penance for, pay for, redress, make redress/reparation for, make recompense for.

expiation *noun* atonement, redemption, penance, redress, reparation, recompense, purgation; amends.

expire *verb* **1** *your bus ticket has expired | your period of contract expires in May* be no longer valid, run out, finish, end, come to an end, terminate, conclude, discontinue, stop, cease, lapse. **2** *the old lady expired at midnight* die, pass away/on, decease, depart this life, perish, breathe one's last, meet one's Maker, give up the ghost, go to the great beyond, cross the great divide; *inf.* kick the bucket. **3** *expire slowly while the X-ray is being taken* breathe out, exhale.

expiry *noun* **1** *the expiry of the contract period | expiry of the lease* finish, end, termination, conclusion, discontinuation, cessation, lapse, expiration, invalidity. **2** *the expiry of the patient* death, passing away/on, decease, demise. *See* EXPIRE 2.

explain *verb* **1** *explain the procedure* give an explanation of, describe, define, make clear/plain/intelligible, spell out, interpret, unfold, clarify, throw light on, clear up, decipher, decode, elucidate, expound, explicate, delineate, demonstrate, teach, illustrate, expose, resolve, solve. **2** *explain their actions* give an explanation for, account for, give a reason/justification for, justify, give an excuse/alibi/apologia for, defend, vindicate, mitigate.

explanation *noun* **1** *the explanation of the procedure* description, definition, interpretation, clarification, deciphering, decoding, elucidation, expounding, explication, demonstration, illustration, exposure, resolution, solution. **2** *an explanation of their motives* account, justification, reason, excuse, defence, vindication, mitigation, apologia.

explanatory *adjective* by way of explanation, descriptive, illustrative, interpretive, demonstrative, illuminative, elucidative, elucidatory, explicative, expository, justificatory, exegetic.

expletive *noun* swear-word, oath, curse, obscenity, epithet, exclamation; *inf.* dirty word, four-letter word; *Am. inf.* cuss-word.

explicable *adjective* explainable, accountable, definable, understandable, interpretable, intelligible, ascertainable, resolvable, soluble, justificatory.

explicate *verb* **1** *explicate a literary text* explain, explain in detail, make explicit, clarify, make plain/clear, spell out, interpret, elucidate, illuminate, expound, unfold, untangle, put into plain English. **2** *explicate an idea* develop, evolve, work out, construct, formulate, devise, build, concoct, assemble.

explicit *adjective* **1** *explicit instructions* clearly expressed, easily understandable, detailed, clear, crystal-clear, direct, plain, obvious, precise, exact, straightforward, definite, distinct, categorical, specific, positive, unequivocal, unambiguous. **2** *explicit criticism | explicit sexual description* outspoken, unrestrained, unreserved, uninhibited, open, candid, frank, forth-

EXPLORERS AND NAVIGATORS

Amundsen, Roald (1872–1928; Norw.)	Cabot, John (c. 1450–c. 99; It.)	Frobisher, Sir Martin (1535–94; Engl.)	Peary, Robert (1856–1920; Am.)
Baffin, William (c. 1584–1622; Brit. navigator)	Cartier, Jacques (1491–1557; Fr. navigator)	Fuchs, Sir Vivian (b. 1908; Brit.)	Pizarro, Francisco (c. 1475–1541; Sp. conquistador)
Banks, Sir Joseph (1743–1820; Brit.)	Cousteau, Jacques (b. 1910; Fr. underwater explorer)	Gama, Vasco de (c. 1469–1524; Port. navigator)	Ponce de León, Juan (1460–1521; Sp.)
Barth, Heinrich (1821–65; Ger.)	Covilhã, Pêro da (c. 1460–c. 1526 Port.)	Hillary, Sir Edmund (b. 1919; NZ)	Raleigh, Sir Walter (1554–1618; Brit.)
Bass, George (1771–1803; Brit. navigator)	Dias, Bartolomeu (c. 1450–1500; Port. navigator)	Hume, Hamilton (1797–1873; Austral.)	Rasmussen, Knud (1879–1933; Da.)
Bellingshausen, Fabian, Baron von (1778–1852; Russ.)	Diemen, Anthony van (1593–1645; Du.)	Iberville, Pierre le Moyne, Sieur d' (1661–1706; Fr.-Can.)	Ross, Sir James (1800–62; Brit.)
Bering, Vitus (1681–1741; Da.)	Eric the Red (late 10th century; Norw.)	Leif Eriksson (11th century; Icel.)	Scott, Robert (1868–1912; Brit.) Shackleton, Sir
Boone, Daniel (1734–1820; Am. pioneer)	Eyre, Edward John (1815–1901; Brit.)	Livingstone, David (1813–73; Scot.)	Ernest (1874–1922; Brit.)
Brazza, Pierre Savorgnan de (1852–1905; Fr.)	Flaherty, Robert (1884–1951; Am. also filmmaker)	Magellan, Ferdinand (c. 1480–1521; Port.)	Soto, Hernando de (c. 1496–1542; Sp.) Stanley, Sir Henry Morton (1841–1904;
Burke, Robert O'Hara (1820–61; Ir.)	Flinders, Matthew (1774–1814; Brit. navigator)	Nansen, Fridtjof (1861–1930; Norw.)	Brit.) Vespucci, Amerigo (1454–1512; It. navigator)
Burton, Sir Richard (1821–90; Brit.)	Frémont, John (1813–90; Am.)	Orellana, Francisco de (c. 1490–1546; Sp.)	Wilkins, Sir George (1888–1958; Brit., b. in Australia)
Byrd, Richard (1888–1957; Am.)		Park, Mungo (1771–c. 1806; Scot.)	Wrangel, Ferdinand, Baron von (1794–1870; Russ.)

explode · exposé

right, direct, plain-spoken, point-blank, full-frontal, no holds barred.
Opposites VAGUE; IMPLICIT; INDIRECT.

explode verb **1** *the firework/boiler exploded* blow up, detonate, burst, fly apart, fly into pieces, go off, erupt; *inf.* go bang. **2** *explode the firework* detonate, set off, let off, fire off, let fly. **3** *explode in anger* give vent to, blow up, rage, rant and rave, storm, bluster; *inf.* fly off the handle, hit the roof, blow one's cool/top, blow a fuse, flip one's lid, freak out. **4** *explode a myth* disprove, invalidate, refute, repudiate, discredit, debunk, belie, give the lie to, ridicule, blow up, blow sky-high, knock the bottom from. **5** *world population exploding* increase suddenly/rapidly/dramatically, mushroom, escalate, burgeon, rocket, accelerate, heighten.

exploit noun feat, deed, adventure, stunt, achievement, accomplishment, attainment.

exploit verb **1** *exploit natural resources* make use of, put to use, utilize, use, use to good advantage, turn/put to good use, turn to account, profit from/by, make capital out of, capitalize on; *inf.* cash in on, milk. **2** *exploit the workers | exploit his good nature* make use of, take advantage of, abuse, impose upon, play upon, misuse; *inf.* walk all over, walk over, take for a ride, put one over on.

exploration noun **1** *the exploration of space | a voyage of exploration* investigation, study, survey, research, inspection, probe, examination, scrutiny, observation, search, inquiry, analysis. **2** *conduct an exploration into the interior of the continent* expedition, trip, tour, survey, reconnaissance; travels.

exploratory adjective investigative, probing, fact-finding, analytic, experimental, trial, searching.

explore verb **1** *explore the Antarctic* travel, traverse, tour, range over, survey, take a look at, inspect, scout, reconnoitre, prospect. **2** *explore several possible solutions* investigate, look into, enquire into, consider, examine, research, survey, scrutinize, study, review, take stock of.

explorer noun traveller, discoverer, tourer, surveyor, scout, reconnoitrer, prospector. *See table.*

explosion noun **1** *a loud explosion* bang, blast, boom, rumble, crash, crack, report, thunder, roll, clap, detonation, discharge, eruption. **2** *an angry explosion* outburst, flare-up, fit, out-

break, paroxysm, eruption. **3** *an explosion of population* sudden/rapid/dramatic increase, mushrooming, escalation, burgeoning, rocketing, acceleration, speeding-up, heightening.

explosive adjective **1** *explosive substance* inflammable, volatile, eruptive, unstable. *See table.* **2** *explosive temperament* fiery, angry, touchy, stormy, violent, vehement, volatile, volcanic. **3** *an explosive situation* tense, charged, critical, serious, inflammable, volcanic, dangerous, perilous, hazardous, ugly, overwrought.

exponent noun **1** *an exponent of traditional teaching methods* advocate, supporter, upholder, backer, defender, champion, spokesperson, promoter, propagandist, proponent. **2** *an exponent lecturing on modern art* interpreter, commentator, expounder, explainer, expositor, elucidator, illustrator, demonstrator. **3** *a famous exponent of mime* practioner, performer, player, interpreter, executant, presenter. **4** *the finest extant exponent of cave painting* example, illustration, specimen, sample, type, exemplar, instance, model, representation.

export verb **1** *export goods* sell overseas/abroad, market overseas/abroad, send overseas/abroad. **2** *export ideas* transmit, spread.
Opposites IMPORT.

expose verb **1** *expose the skin to sunlight* uncover, lay bare, bare, leave unprotected, strip, reveal, denude. **2** *expose to danger/abuse* lay open to, leave unprotected from, put at risk of, put in jeopardy of, make vulnerable to, make subject to, subject to; endanger, risk, hazard. **3** *expose one's ignorance* reveal, uncover, show, display, make obvious, exhibit, disclose, manifest, unveil. **4** *expose a crime/criminal* bring to light, disclose, uncover, reveal, make known, let out, divulge, denounce, unearth, unmask, detect, betray, smoke out; *inf.* spill the beans on, blow the whistle on, pull the plug on. **5** *expose to new ideas* bring into contact with, introduce to, present with, make familiar/conversant/acquainted with, familiarize/acquaint with, make aware of. **expose oneself** display/reveal/show the genitalia; *inf.* flash.
Opposites COVER; PROTECT; CONCEAL.

exposé noun exposure, disclosure, uncovering, revelation, divulgence.

BOMBS AND EXPLOSIVES

A-bomb	firebomb	landmine	petard
acoustic mine	flying bomb	letter bomb	petrol bomb
atom bomb	fragmentation	limpet mine	plastic explosive
blockbuster	bomb	lyddite	RDX
bombshell	gelignite	magnetic mine	Semtex
car bomb	grenade	Mills bomb	shell
cluster bomb	gun cotton	mine	smoke bomb
cordite	gunpowder	molotov cocktail	time bomb
depth charge	hand grenade	napalm	trinitrotoluene
dynamite	H-bomb	neutron bomb	(TNT)
enhanced radiation	hydrogen bomb	nitroglycerine	torpedo
bomb	incendiary bomb	nuclear bomb	

exposed *adjective an exposed hillside* open, unprotected, without shelter/protection, unsheltered, open to the elements/weather.

exposition *noun* **1** *the exposition of modern educational theories* explanation, interpretation, description, elucidation, explication, illustration; *fml.* exegesis. **2** *give an exposition of the advantages of nuclear power* explanation, account, description, commentary, study, treatise, discourse, dissertation, critique. **3** *a trade exposition* exhibition, fair, display, show, presentation, demonstration; *inf.* expo, demo.

expository *adjective an expository statement of the theory* explanatory, interpretative, descriptive, elucidatory, explicatory, explicative, illustrative; *fml.* exegetic, hermeneutic.

expostulate *verb expostulate with an opponent* remonstrate with, argue with, reason with, make a protest to, raise an objection with.

exposure *noun* **1** *the exposure of the skin to sunlight* uncovering, baring, stripping, revelation, denudation. **2** *exposure to danger/abuse* subjection/submission to, laying open to. *See* EXPOSE 2. **3** *exposure of one's ignorance* revelation, uncovering, showing, display, exhibition, disclosure, manifestation, unveiling. **4** *exposure of a crime/criminal* disclosure, uncovering, revelation, divulgence, denunciation, unmasking, detection, betrayal. *See* EXPOSE 4. **5** *exposure to new ideas* contact with, introduction/presentation to. *See* EXPOSE 5. **6** *resent the exposure given to the affair* publicity, publicizing, advertising, broadcasting, airing. **7** *a sunny exposure* position, setting, location, aspect, view, outlook, frontage.

expound *verb* **1** *expound one's views on education* explain, detail, spell out, set forth, describe, discuss. **2** *expound the Scriptures* interpret, explain, give a commentary on, annotate, illustrate, explicate.

express *verb* **1** *express one's feelings in a speech* put into words, state, voice, give voice to, enunciate, communicate, utter, pronounce, articulate, verbalize, give vent to, word, couch, proclaim, assert, point out, speak, say. **2** *express appreciation with a gift* show, indicate, demonstrate, convey, communicate, intimate, denote, exhibit, illustrate, manifest, make manifest, reveal, evince, symbolize, embody. **3** *express juice from fruit* press out, squeeze, extract, force out. **express onself** communicate one's thoughts/opinions/views, put thoughts into words, speak one's mind, say one's piece.

express *adjective* **1** *express service* rapid, swift, fast, quick, speedy, prompt, high-speed, brisk, expeditious, direct, non-stop. **2** *express instructions* explicit, clear, plain, distinct, unambiguous, precise, specific, well-defined, unmistakable, unequivocal, pointed, exact, outright. **3** *done with the express purpose of embarrassing them* particular, sole, purposeful, special, especial, specific, singular.

expression *noun* **1** *public expression of grievances* statement, voicing, uttering, utterance, pronouncement, articulation, verbalization, venting, wording, proclamation, assertion.

2 *send flowers as an expression of appreciation* indication, demonstration, show, conveyance, communication, intimation, exhibition, illustration, manifestation, revelation, embodiment. **3** *a particularly apt expression* word, phrase, term, choice of words, turn of phrase, wording, language, phrasing, phraseology, speech, diction, idiom, style, delivery, intonation, execution; *fml.* locution. **4** *a sad expression on her face* look, appearance, air, countenance, aspect; *fml.* mien. **5** *playing the piano with expression* feeling, emotion, passion, intensity, poignancy, artistry, depth, spirit, vividness, ardour, power, force, imagination.

expressionless *adjective* **1** *expressionless reading of poetry* dull, dry, boring, wooden, undemonstrative, apathetic, unimpassioned, weak, devoid of feeling/emotion. *See* EXPRESSION 5. **2** *a totally expressionless face* blank, deadpan; *inf.* poker-faced, inscrutable, emotionless, vacuous.

expressive *adjective* **1** *an expressive face/gesture* full of emotion/feeling, indicating emotion/feeling, emotional, eloquent, telling, demonstrative, suggestive, vivid. **2** *an expressive piece of music* emotional, eloquent, passionate, intense, poignant, moving, striking, evocative, sympathetic, artistic, vivid, graphic, ardent, powerful, imaginative. **3** *expressive of their contempt* showing, indicative, demonstrating, demonstrative, suggesting, revealing, underlining.
Opposites EXPRESSIONLESS; INEXPRESSIVE; UNEMOTIONAL.

expressly *adverb* **1** *expressly forbidden* absolutely, explicitly, clearly, plainly, distinctly, precisely, specifically, unequivocally. **2** *laws expressly made to stop vandalism* purposefully, particularly, solely, specially, especially, specifically, singularly.

expropriate *verb* seize, take away, take over, take, appropriate, take possession of, misappropriate, requisition, commandeer, impound, confiscate, usurp, assume, arrogate.

expulsion *noun* **1** *expulsion from school* removal, eviction, ejection, banishment, debarment, dismissal, discharge; *inf.* sacking, drumming out. **2** *the expulsion of waste materials* ejection, discharge, elimination, excretion, voiding, voidance, evacuation.

expunge *verb* erase, remove, rub out, wipe out, cross out, strike out, delete, eradicate, cancel, blot out, efface, destroy, obliterate, annul, extinguish, abolish, annihilate.

expurgate *verb* bowdlerize, censor, blue-pencil, clean up, purge, purify, sanitize, emasculate.

exquisite *adjective* **1** *exquisite skin/grace* beautiful, lovely, delicate, fragile, elegant, fine, subtle, ethereal. **2** *exquisite taste* discriminating, discerning, sensitive, selective, refined, cultivated, cultured, appreciative, educated, fastidious, impeccable, polished, consummate. **3** *exquisite pain* intense, acute, keen, piercing, sharp, excruciating, poignant.

extant *adjective* still existing, in existence, living, alive, surviving, remaining, undestroyed,

subsisting, present, existent.
Opposites EXTINCT; DEAD.

extemporaneous, extemporary *adjective an extemporaneous vote of thanks* extempore, impromptu, spontaneous, ad lib, improvised, unrehearsed, unplanned, unprepared, unpremeditated; *inf.* off the cuff; *fml.* improvisatory.

extempore *adjective an extempore speech* impromptu, spontaneous, ad lib, improvised, unrehearsed, unplanned, unprepared, extemporaneous. *inf.* off the cuff, off the top of one's head.

extempore *adverb he spoke extempore* ad lib, spontaneously, extemporaneously; *inf.* off the cuff.

extemporize *verb* improvise, ad lib, play it by ear, think on one's feet. *See* EXTEMPORE *adjective.*

extend *verb* **1** *extend the territory/spring* expand, increase, enlarge; lengthen, widen, broaden, stretch, stretch out, draw out, elongate. **2** *extend the scope of the law* widen, increase, add to, expand, broaden, enlarge, augment, amplify, supplement, enhance, develop. **3** *extend the period of credit* prolong, increase, lengthen, stretch out, protract, spin out, drag out. **4** *extend one's arms* stretch out, reach out, spread out, straighten out, unroll, unfurl. **5** *extend a welcome* offer, give, grant, proffer, present, confer, hold out, advance, impart, put forth, reach out. **6** *the road extends for many miles* continue, stretch, stretch out, carry on, run on, last, unroll, unfurl, range.
Opposites DECREASE; CONTRACT; NARROW; CURTAIL.

extended *adjective* **1** *extended credit facilities | extended hours* longer lasting, prolonged, increased, lengthened, elongated, protracted. **2** *extended family* widened, enlarged, expanded, far-reaching, comprehensive, broad.

extension *noun* **1** *the extension of the territory/spring* expansion, increase, enlargement; elongation. *See* EXTEND 1. **2** *the extension of a period of credit* prolongation, increase, lengthening, protraction. *See* EXTEND 3. **3** *an extension to the house/collection* annexe, wing; addition, add-on, adjunct, addendum, augmentation, supplement, appendage. **4** *ask for an extension to complete an essay* more/extra time, increased time, additional time, a longer period.

extensive *adjective* **1** *extensive grounds around the house* large, large-scale, sizeable, substantial, spacious, considerable, capacious, commodious, vast, immense. **2** *an extensive knowledge of the subject* comprehensive, thorough, complete, broad, wide, wide-ranging, all-inclusive, all-embracing, wholesale, universal, boundless, catholic.
Opposites SMALL; LIMITED.

extent *noun* **1** *the full extent of the track/parklands* length, area, expanse, stretch, range, scope. **2** *the extent of her knowledge* coverage, breadth, range, scope, degree, comprehensiveness, thoroughness, completeness, all-inclusiveness.

extenuating *adjective extenuating circumstances* mitigating, palliating, palliative, justifying, moderating, qualifying.

exterior *noun the exterior of the building* outside, outside surface, outer/external surface, outward appearance/aspect, façade, covering, shell.
Opposites INTERIOR; INSIDE.

exterior *adjective the exterior layer* outer, outside, outermost, outward, external, surface, superficial.

exterminate *verb* kill, destroy, eradicate, annihilate, eliminate, abolish, extirpate; *inf.* bump off.

external *adjective* **1** *an external wall* outer, outside, outward, exterior, surface, superficial, extraneous, extrinsic. **2** *an external student* extramural; outside, visiting, non-resident.

extinct *adjective* **1** *an extinct species* died out, defunct, no longer existing, vanished, wiped out, gone, lost. **2** *an extinct volcano/fire* inactive, no longer active; extinguished, burnt out, quenched, put out, doused. **3** *extinct beliefs/passions* dead, defunct, ended, terminated, obsolete, outmoded, out of date, antiquated, passé.
Opposites EXTANT; ALIVE.

extinction *noun* dying out, death, vanishing, extinguishing, quenching, ending, termination. *See* EXTINCT.

extinguish *verb* **1** *extinguish the light/fire* put out, blow out, quench, smother, douse, snuff out, stifle, dampen down, choke. **2** *extinguish passion* destroy, kill, end, remove, annihilate, wipe out, eliminate, abolish, eradicate, erase, expunge, exterminate, extirpate, obscure, suppress.
Opposites LIGHT; KINDLE.

extol *verb* praise, praise highly, praise to the skies, sing the praises of, applaud, acclaim, pay tribute to, laud, eulogize about, exalt, commend, congratulate, celebrate, compliment, glorify, panegyrize, magnify; *inf.* cry up.
Opposites CONDEMN; CRITICIZE.

extort *verb extort money | extort a confession* extract, force, exact, coerce, wring, wrest, squeeze, milk, obtain by blackmail; *inf.* put the screws on to obtain; *Austral. inf.* put the bite on to obtain.

extortion *noun obtain money by extortion* force, coercion, compulsion, exaction, oppression, blackmail. *See* EXTORT.

extortionate *adjective* **1** *extortionate prices* exorbitant, excessive, outrageous, preposterous, immoderate, unreasonable, inordinate, inflated, sky-high. **2** *extortionate methods* exacting, grasping, blood-sucking, avaricious, rapacious, usurious, harsh, severe, rigorous, hard, oppressive.

extortionist, extortioner *noun* blackmailer, blood-sucker, exacter, rack-renter.

extra *adjective* **1** *extra money required* more, additional, further, supplementary, supplemental, added, auxiliary, ancillary, subsidiary, other, accessory. **2** *we always have extra food left after lunch* spare, surplus, left over, excess, superfluous, redundant, reserve, unused.

extra *adverb* **1** *try extra hard* especially, exceptionally, extremely, unusually, particularly, extraordinarily, uncommonly, remarkably; *inf.* with all the stops out. **2** *charge postage and package extra* in addition, as well, besides, over and above, on top, into the bargain, to boot.

extra *noun* **1** *an optional extra* addition, supplement, adjunct, addendum. **2** *film extras* extra person/actor, supernumerary, walking on part, walk-on, spear-carrier.
Opposites NECESSITY; ESSENTIAL.

extract *verb* **1** *extract a tooth* draw out, pull out, remove, take out, pluck out, prize out, wrench out, tear out, uproot, withdraw, extirpate; *fml.* deracinate. **2** *extract money* extort, force, exact, elicit, coerce, wrest, wring, squeeze. **3** *extract juice* squeeze, press, express, distil, separate, take out. **4** *extract a section from a chapter* abstract, select, choose, reproduce, copy, quote, cite, cull. **5** *extract a principle* deduce, educe, derive, elicit, develop, evolve.

extract *noun* **1** *extract of malt* concentrate, essence, distillate, juice, solution, decoction. **2** *extracts from newspapers* excerpt, passage, abstract, citation, selection, quotation, cutting, clipping, fragment; analects.

extraction *noun* **1** *the extraction of a tooth* removal, drawing out, pulling out, uprooting, extirpation; *fml.* deracination. *See* EXTRACT *verb* 1. **2** *extraction of money* extortion, exacting, wresting. *See* EXTRACT *verb* 2. **3** *extraction of juice* squeezing, expressing, distillation, separation. *See* EXTRACT *verb* 3. **4** *Irish by extraction* descent, ancestry, parentage, lineage, blood, derivation, origin, race.

extradite *verb* *extradite a criminal* deport, expel, banish, exile, outlaw.

extradition *noun* deportation, expulsion, banishment, exile, outlawing.

extraneous *adjective* **1** *extraneous forces* external, outside, exterior, extrinsic, alien, foreign. **2** *extraneous material* irrelevant, immaterial, inapplicable, inapt, inappropriate, inapposite, unrelated, unconnected, off the subject, peripheral, beside the point, wide of the mark, not pertinent, not germane.

extraordinary *adjective* **1** *extraordinary talent* exceptional, unusual, uncommon, rare, unique, singular, signal, peculiar, unprecedented, outstanding, striking, remarkable, phenomenal, marvellous, wonderful; *inf.* fabulous. **2** *how extraordinary that we met* amazing, surprising, strange, unusual, remarkable, astounding, curious. **3** *an extraordinary colour combination* odd, weird, strange, curious, bizarre, unconventional.
Opposites ORDINARY; COMMONPLACE.

extravagance *noun* **1** *extravagance leading to debt* spendthrift behaviour/ways, squandering, overspending, profligacy, prodigality, wastefulness, lavishness, recklessness, excess. **2** *the extravagance of his compliments* excessiveness, exaggeration, exaggeratedness, unreservedness, outrageousness, immoderation, preposterousness, absurdity, irrationality, recklessness, wildness; excess, overkill, lack of restraint/reserve. **3** *extravagance of the prices/clothes* exorbitance, excessiveness, expensive-

ness, unreasonableness, immoderation; costliness; *inf.* steepness.

extravagant *adjective* **1** *extravagant way of life* spendthrift, squandering, thriftless, profligate, prodigal, improvident, wasteful, lavish, reckless, imprudent, excessive. **2** *extravagant compliments* excessive, exaggerated, unrestrained, unreserved, outrageous, immoderate, preposterous, absurd, irrational, reckless, wild; *inf.* over-the-top, OTT. **3** *extravagant prices/clothes* exorbitant, excessive, extortionate, unreasonable, immoderate, inordinate; expensive, dear, costly, overpriced; *inf.* steep.
Opposites THRIFTY; RESTRAINED; CHEAP.

extravaganza *noun* spectacle, pageant, spectacular/impressive show/display.

extreme *adjective* **1** *in extreme danger | extreme cold* utmost, uttermost, maximum, supreme, greatest, great, acute, intense, severe, highest, high, ultimate, exceptional, extraordinary. **2** *extreme punitive measures* harsh, severe, Draconian, stringent, stern, strict, drastic, unrelenting, relentless, unbending, unyielding, uncompromising, unmitigated, radical, overzealous. **3** *a person of extreme views | an extreme radical* immoderate, intemperate, fanatical, exaggerated, excessive, overzealous, outrageous, inordinate, unreasonable; *inf.* over-the-top, OTT. **4** *on the extreme edge | in the extreme south* outermost, farthest, most remote, remotest, most distant, outlying, far-off, faraway, ultimate, last, endmost, final, terminal, apogean.
Opposites MODERATE; MILD; NEAR.

extreme *noun* **1** *the extremes of heat/wrath* highest/greatest degree, maximum, height, ultimate, zenith, pinnacle, climax, acme, apex, *ne plus ultra*. **2** *the extremes of bliss and despair* opposite, pole, contrary, counter, contradiction, antonym. **in the extreme** *generous in the extreme* extremely, exceedingly, exceptionally, excessively, extravagantly, inordinately.

extremely *adverb* very, exceedingly, exceptionally, intensely, greatly, acutely, utterly, excessively, inordinately, extraordinarily, markedly, uncommonly, severely; *inf.* awfully, terribly.

extremist *noun* radical, fanatic, zealot, diehard, ultra.

extremity *noun* **1** *the extremities of the territory* limit, outer limit, farthest point, end, boundary, bound, border, frontier, edge, margin, termination, periphery, verge, brink, horizon; *fml.* ambit. **2** *frostbite of the extremities* limb, appendage, digit; arm, leg, hand, foot, finger, toe. **3** *the extremity of the heat* the greatest/highest degree, extreme, maximum degree, intensity, acuteness, excess, zenith, pinnacle, top, acme, apex; *fml.* apogee. **4** *help the poor in their extremity* hardship, adversity, trouble, misfortune, plight, destitution, indigence, exigency; crisis, emergency, setback; dire straits, hard times.

extricate *verb* *extricate oneself/someone from a difficult situation* extract, free, release, disentangle, get out, remove, withdraw, let loose, detach, disengage, liberate, rescue, save, disencumber, deliver; *inf.* get off the hook.

extrinsic *adjective* **1** *extrinsic influence* extraneous, external, exterior, outside, outward, alien, foreign, not intrinsic. **2** *extrinsic information* extraneous, irrelevant, immaterial, inapplicable, inapt, inappropriate, inapposite, unrelated, unconnected, off the subject, peripheral, beside the point, wide of the mark, not pertinent, not germane.

extrovert, extroverted *adjective* outgoing, outwardly directed, sociable, socializing, social, friendly, people-oriented, lively, cheerful, effervescent, exuberant.
Opposites INTROVERTED; INTROSPECTIVE.

extrovert *noun* outgoing person, socializer, mixer, mingler, life and soul of the party.

extrude *verb* **1** *extrude glue from a tube* force out, thrust out, press out, squeeze out, eject, expel. **2** *a branch extruding from the tree* protrude, project, jut out, stick out, poke out, extend, hang out, beetle.

exuberant *adjective* **1** *exuberant with joy at winning* elated, animated, exhilarated, lively, high-spirited, spirited, buoyant, cheerful, sparkling, full of life, effervescent, vivacious, excited, ebullient, exultant, enthusiastic, irrepressible, energetic, vigorous, zestful; *inf.* bouncy, upbeat. **2** *exuberant expressions of thanks* effusive, lavish, fulsome, exaggerated, unreserved, unrestrained, unlimited, wholehearted, generous, excessive, superfluous, prodigal. **3** *exuberant foliage* profuse, luxuriant, lush, thriving, abundant, superabundant, prolific, teeming, lavish, copious, rich, plentiful, abounding, overflowing, rank.
Opposites DEPRESSED; RESTRAINED; MEAGRE.

exude *verb* **1** *sweat exuding through the pores* ooze, seep, filter, filtrate, leak, discharge, trickle, drip, issue. **2** *exuding beads of sweat* ooze, secrete, excrete, discharge, emit, issue, emanate, give out, pour out, gush, jet. **3** *exuding confidence* ooze, give out, give forth, send out, issue, emit, emanate, display.

exult *verb* **1** *exult at/in his sister's success* rejoice, be overjoyed, be joyful, be jubilant, be elated, be delighted, be ecstatic, jump for joy, revel, be in ecstasy, be over the moon, be on cloud nine, be in seventh heaven. **2** *exulting over their opponents* triumph, gloat, crow, glory.

exultant *adjective* exulting, rejoicing, overjoyed, joyful, jubilant, elated, triumphant, delighted, ecstatic, cock-a-hoop, gleeful, enraptured, transported.

exultation *noun* rejoicing, joy, jubilation, elation, exhilaration, delight, ecstasy, glee, rapture, triumph, glory; transports.

eye *noun* **1** *injury to the eye* organ of sight, eyeball; *inf.* peeper; *lit.* orb. *See table.* **2** *have sharp eyes* eyesight, vision, sight, observation; powers of observation. **3** *an eye for art* appreciation, perception, discernment, discrimination, taste, judgement, recognition, awareness, sensitivity. **4** *keep an eye on|under her mother's eagle eye* watch, observance, lookout; observation, surveillance, vigilance, view, notice. **5** *to my eye/in my eyes they are guilty* estimation, opinion, view, point of view, judgement, belief, viewpoint, mind. **6** *eye of the needle* hole, aperture, perforation, eyelet. **7** *the eye of a daisy* centre, middle, heart, kernel, hub. **see eye to eye** agree, be in agreement/accord, concur, be on the same wavelength, get on, get along. **up to one's eyes** fully occupied, very busy, engrossed, engaged, overwhelmed, inundated, caught up, wrapped up; *inf.* up to here.

eye *verb* **1** *eye with longing* look at, gaze at, stare at, contemplate, study, survey, view, inspect, scrutinize, scan, glance at, regard, behold; *inf.* clock; *Am. inf.* eyeball. **2** *eye the girls* ogle, leer at, make eyes at; *inf.* give the glad eye to.

eye-catching *adjective* striking, arresting, spectacular, captivating, attractive, showy.

eyeful *noun* **1** *get an eyeful of that* look, good look, stare, gaze, view; *inf.* shufti, gander, butcher's, load. **2** *the model is quite an eyeful* vision, dream, beauty, dazzler; *inf.* stunner, good-looker, knockout, sight for sore eyes, bobby-dazzler.

eyesight *noun* sight, vision, range of vision, observation, perception.

eyesore *noun* blemish, blot, scar, blight, disfigurement, defacement, defect, monstrosity, carbuncle, atrocity, disgrace, ugliness; *inf.* sight.

eyewitness *noun* witness, observer, onlooker, looker-on, bystander, spectator, watcher, viewer, beholder, passer-by; *inf.* rubberneck.

PARTS OF THE HUMAN EYE

aqueous humour	extrinsic muscle	lens	sclera
blind spot	eyeball	limbus	stroma
choroid	eyelash/cilium	optic foramen	suspensory ligament
ciliary body	eyelid/blepharon/	optic nerve	tarsal plate
cone	palpebra	orbit	tear glands (lacrimal
conjunctiva	fovea	retina	glands)
cornea	iris	rod	vitreous humour

fable *noun* **1** *a fable about a fox* moral tale, parable, apologue; bestiary. **2** *heroes in Norse fables* story, legend, myth, traditional story, saga, epic, lay. **3** *children telling fables* lie, untruth, falsehood, white lite, fib, piece of fiction, fabrication, invention, story, fairy story, cock and bull story, figment of the imagination, fantasy; *inf.* tall story, yarn, terminological inexactitude.

fabric *noun* **1** *made of a silky fabric* cloth, material, textile, stuff, web. *See table.* **2** *the fabric of the building | the fabric of society* framework, frame, structure, make-up, constitution, essence.

fabricate *verb* **1** *fabricate the furniture from components* assemble, construct, build, erect, put together, make, form, frame, fashion, shape, manufacture, produce. **2** *fabricate a reason for lateness* make up, invent, think up, concoct, hatch, trump up, devise, formulate, coin. **3** *fabricate a document* forge, falsify, fake, counterfeit.

fabulous *adjective* **1** *of fabulous wealth* incredible, unbelievable, inconceivable, unimaginable, astounding, amazing, astonishing, breath-taking, prodigious, phenomenal, remarkable, extraordinary, tremendous; *inf.* legendary. **2** *a fabulous time at the party* marvellous, wonderful, great, superb, spectacular; *inf.* fab, fantastic, super, super-duper, out of this world. **3** *fabulous creatures* mythical, imaginary, legendary, fantastical, fictitious, fictional, made-up, invented, unreal, hypothetical, apocryphal. *See table at* MONSTER.

façade *noun* **1** *the façade of the building* front, frontage, face, exterior, outside. **2** *a façade of friendliness* show, appearance, guise, semblance, mask, veneer, masquerade, camouflage, pretence, illusion.

face *noun* **1** *a beautiful face* countenance, visage, physiognomy; features, lineaments; *inf.* mug, dial, phizog, phiz, kisser, clock. **2** *with a furious face* expression, look, air, demeanour, aspect. **3** *what a face! | make a face* scowl, grimace, frown, pout, moue. **4** *the face of the building* front, frontage, façade. *See* FAÇADE 1. **5** *the face of the countryside* outward appearance, appearance, aspect, air. **6** *put a brave/bold face on it* appearance, façade, display, show, exterior, guise, mask, veneer, camouflage, pretence. **7** *lose face* prestige, standing, status, dignity, honour, respect, image. **8** *have the face to turn up* audacity, effrontery, impudence, impertinence, cheek, boldness, presumption, temerity, bumptiousness; *inf.* nerve, gall, brass neck, neck, sauce. **face to face** facing, con-

---

FABRICS AND FIBRES

acetate	cord	gunny	mohair	sharkskin
acrylic	corduroy	haircloth	moire	sheer
alpaca	cotton	Harris tweed	moleskin	shoddy
angora	crepe	hemp	mousseline	silk
astrakhan	crepe-back	herringbone	muslin	stammel
baize	satin	hessian	nankeen	stockinet
brocade	crepe de	hopsack	netting	suede
brocatelle	Chine	horsehair	nylon	swansdown
buckram	crimplene™	huckaback	oiled silk	tabaret
bunting	crinoline	jacquard	organdie	tabby
burlap	Dacron™	jean	organza	tapestry
calico	damask	jersey	Orlon™	tarpaulin
cambric	denim	jute	Paisley	Terylene™
camel hair	doeskin	lamé	panne velvet	ticking
Canton crepe	Donegal	leatherette™	piqué	toile
canvas	tweed	linen	plaid	towelling
cashmere	drill	linsey-	plush	tricot
challis	duffel	woolsey	polyester	Tricotine
chambray	dungaree	long cloth	poplin	tulle
cheesecloth	faille	Lycra™	polyvinyl	tweed
chenille	felt	Mackinaw *Am.*	chloride (PVC)	twill
cheviot	flannel	mackintosh	rayon	velour
chiffon	flannelette	madras	sackcloth	velvet
chinchilla	gabardine	Malines	sailcloth	velveteen
chino	gauze	marocain	sarsenet	vicuña
chintz	Georgette crepe	Marseilles	sateen	viscose
coconut	gingham	matting	satin	webbing
matting	gossamer	melton	say	wool
coir	grenadine	microfibre	serge	worsted

fronting, opposing, conflicting; *inf.* eyeball to eyeball. **on the face of it** from appearances, to all appearances, so it appears/seems, so it would appear/seem, apparently, seemingly.

face *verb* **1** *buildings facing the sea* front onto, look towards, look onto, overlook, give onto, be opposite to. **2** *the problems facing us* confront, present itself, meet, be in the way, stand in the way. **3** *face rejection* encounter, meet, come across, be confronted by, come up against, experience. **4** *face facts* face up to, come to terms with, accept, confront, meet head-on, cope with, deal with, get to grips with, brazen out. **5** *face criticism/danger* encounter, meet, face out, meet head-on, confront, dare, brave, defy, oppose, resist, withstand. **6** *face the collar of the coat* put a facing on, cover, line. **7** *face stone* dress, finish, polish, smooth, level, coat, cover, surface, clad, veneer. **face up to** face, come to terms with, accept, confront, cope with. *See* FACE *verb* 4.
Opposites EVADE; DODGE.

facet *noun* **1** *one facet of the problem* aspect, angle, side, slant, feature, characteristic, factor, element, point, part, phase. **2** *facet of a gem* side, plane, surface, face.

facetious *adjective* jocular, flippant, playful, frivolous, light-hearted, non-serious, funny, amusing, humorous, comical, comic, joking, jesting, witty, droll, whimsical, tongue-in-cheek, waggish, jocose.
Opposites SERIOUS; GRAVE.

facile *adjective* **1** *facile speeches/charm* superficial, shallow, glib, slick, urbane, suave, bland. **2** *facile tasks* easy, simple, uncomplicated, unchallenging, like falling off a log; *inf.* easy-peasy.

facilitate *verb* make easy/easier, ease, make smooth/smoother, smooth, smooth the path of, assist, help, aid, expedite, speed up, accelerate, forward, advance, promote, further, encourage.
Opposites HINDER; OBSTRUCT.

facility *noun* **1** *perform the task with facility* ease, effortlessness, smoothness, absence/lack of difficulty. **2** *facility of expression* ease, smoothness, fluency, eloquence, articulateness, slickness, glibness. **3** *a facility for wood-carving* skill, skilfulness, dexterity, adroitness, adeptness, deftness, aptitude, ability, gift, talent, expertise, expertness, knack, proficiency, bent, readiness. **4** *leisure facilities* amenity, resource, appliance, aid, opportunity, advantage, convenience, benefit; means, equipment.

facing *noun* **1** *the facing of a jacket lapel* covering, lining, interfacing, reinforcement. **2** *the facing of the building* façade, front, surface, fronting, false front, coating, covering, cladding, veneer, prótective/decorative layer, overlay, stucco, revetment.

facsimile *noun* copy, replica, reproduction, duplicate, carbon, carbon copy, photocopy, Xerox™, photostat™, Mimeograph, transcript, reprint, clone, image, fax.

fact *noun* **1** *a fact not a rumour* actuality, reality, certainty, factuality, certitude; truth, naked truth, gospel. **2** *do not omit a single fact* detail, particular, point, item, piece of information/data, factor, feature, element, component, circumstance, specific. *See* FACTS. **3** *charged with being an accessory after the fact* happening, occurrence, incident, event, act, deed. **in fact** *in fact he's gone already* actually, in point of fact, indeed, in truth, in reality.
Opposites UNTRUTH; FALSEHOOD; FICTION.

faction *noun* **1** *the younger faction | a more radical faction* sector, section, group, side, party, band, set, ring, division, contingent, lobby, camp, bloc, clique, coalition, confederacy, coterie, caucus, cabal, junta, ginger group, splinter group, pressure group, minority group; *inf.* gang, crew. **2** *a club full of faction* infighting, dissension, discord, strife, contention, conflict, friction, argument, difference of opinion, disagreement, controversy, quarrelling, division, divisiveness, clashing, disharmony, disunity, variance, rupture, tumult, turbulence, upheaval, dissidence, rebellion, insurrection, sedition, mutiny, schism.

factious *adjective* dissenting, contentious, discordant, conflicting, argumentative, disagreeing, disputatious, quarrelling, quarrelsome, divisive, clashing, warring, at variance, at loggerheads, at odds, disharmonious, tumultuous, turbulent, dissident, rebellious, insurrectionary, seditious, mutinous, schismatic, sectarian, partisan.

factor *noun* **1** *the financial factor* element, part, component, ingredient, constituent, point, detail, item, facet, aspect, feature, characteristic, consideration, influence, circumstance, thing, determinant. **2** *a business factor* agent, representative, deputy, middleman, intermediary, go-between; *Scots* land-agent, estate manager, land steward, reeve.

factory *noun* manufacturing building/complex, plant; works; workshop, mill, foundry.

factotum *noun* general employee, odd-job man, general handyman, man/maid of all work, Jack of all trades, man Friday, girl Friday; *inf.* Mr Fix-it.

facts *plural noun* *the police just want the facts* information, itemized information, whole story; details, data; *inf.* info, gen, low-down, score, dope.

factual *adjective* *a factual account* fact-based, realistic, real, true to life, circumstantial, true, truthful, accurate, authentic, genuine, sure, veritable, exact, precise, strict, honest, faithful, literal, matter-of-fact, verbatim, word for word, unbiased, objective, unprejudiced, unvarnished, unadorned, unadulterated, unexaggerated.
Opposites UNTRUE; FICTITIOUS; UNREAL.

faculties *plural noun* *old people in possession of all their faculties* powers, capabilities, senses, wits; reason, intelligence.

faculty *noun* **1** *the faculty of speech* power, capability, capacity, attribute, property. **2** *a faculty for learning languages* aptitude, ability, facility, flair, gift, talent, bent, knack, disposition, proficiency, readiness, skill, dexterity, adroitness. **3** *the arts faculty* department, university/college department, division, section. **4** *the whole fac-*

ulty *approved of the decision* members of a profession, profession, discipline. **5** *the Church conferring the faculty to conduct marriage services* authorization, licence, power, right, prerogative, privilege, permission, sanction.

fad *noun* craze, mania, rage, enthusiasm, fancy, passing fancy, whim, vogue, fashion, trend, mode.

faddy *adjective* faddish, fussy, finicky, hard to please, fastidious, particular, over-particular; *inf.* choosy, picky, pernickety.

fade *verb* **1** *the curtains/colour faded* lose colour, become pale/paler, grow pale, pale, become bleached, become washed out, dull, dim, grow dull/dim, lose lustre. **2** *time had faded the colours* pale, bleach, whiten, wash out, dull, discolour, decolorize, dim, etiolate. **3** *flowers fading* wither, wilt, die, droop, shrivel, decay, etiolate. **4** *light/hope fading* grow less, dim, die away, dwindle, grow faint, fail, wane, disappear, vanish, die, decline, dissolve, peter out, melt away, evanesce. **5** *the Roman empire was fading* die out, diminish, decline, fail, deteriorate, degenerate. *See* FAIL *verb* 9.
Opposites THRIVE; INCREASE.

faeces *plural noun* excrement, bodily waste, waste matter, ordure, dung, manure; excreta, stools, droppings.

fail *verb* **1** *their attempt failed* not succeed, be unsuccessful, lack success, fall through, fall flat, break down, abort, miscarry, be defeated, suffer defeat, be in vain, be frustrated, collapse, founder, misfire, not come up to scratch, meet with disaster, come to grief, come to nothing/naught, fizzle out, miss the mark, run aground, go astray; *inf.* flop, come a cropper, bite the dust. **2** *fail the exam / failed twice* not pass, be unsuccessful, be found wanting/deficient/defective, not make the grade, not pass muster, not come up to scratch, be rejected; *inf.* flunk. **3** *fail to understand/attend* be unable, omit, neglect, forget. **4** *fail them in their hour of need* let down, neglect, desert, forsake, abandon, disappoint. **5** *the crops failed* be insufficient, be inadequate, be deficient, be wanting, be lacking, fall short. **6** *the light/hope failing* fade, grow less, dim, die away, dwindle, wane, disappear, vanish, peter out, dissolve. *See* FADE 4. **7** *the engine failed* break down, stop working, cease to function, cut out; *inf.* conk out, become kaput. **8** *the old man is failing* grow weak/weaker, become feeble, lose strength, flag, become ill, sink. **9** *her health failed / the empire failed* decline, go into decline, fade, diminish, dwindle, wane, ebb, deteriorate, sink, collapse, pass, decay, crumble, degenerate. **10** *his business failed* collapse, crash, smash, go under, go to the wall, go bankrupt, become insolvent, go into receivership, cease trading, be closed, close down; *inf.* fold, flop, go bust/broke.
Opposites SUCCEED; INCREASE; THRIVE.

fail *noun* failure, non-success. *See* FAILURE 1. **without fail** for certain, certainly, with certainty, definitely, whatever happens.

failing *noun* unpunctuality *is his failing* fault, shortcoming, weakness, weak spot, imperfection, defect, flaw, blemish, frailty, foible, draw-

back.
Opposites STRENGTH; FORTE; ASSET.

failing *preposition failing some disaster we shall come in* the absence of, in default of, lacking, notwithstanding.

failure *noun* **1** *the failure of their attempt* non-success, lack of success, non-fulfilment, abortion, miscarriage, defeat, frustration, collapse, foundering, misfiring, coming to nothing, fizzling out. *See* FAIL *verb* 1. **2** *their plan was a failure* vain attempt, abortion, defeat, fiasco, debacle, botch, blunder; *inf.* flop, wash-out. **3** *he feels a failure since losing his job* incompetent, loser, non-achiever, ne'er-do-well, disappointment; *inf.* flop, dud, no-hoper, non-starter, wash-out. **4** *failure to attend / failure in the line of duty* omission, neglect; negligence, remissness, non-observance, non-performance, dereliction, delinquency. **5** *the failure of the crops* insufficiency, inadequacy, deficiency, lack, dearth, scarcity, shortfall. **6** *the failure of the light* fading, lessening, dimming, waning, vanishing. *See* FAIL *verb* 6. **7** *the failure of the engine* breaking down, non-function, cutting out; *inf.* conking out. **8** *the failure of his health / failure of the empire* failing, decline, fading, dwindling, waning, sinking, deterioration, collapse, breakdown, loss, decay, crumbling, degeneration. **9** *the failure of his business* collapse, crashing, going under, bankruptcy, close-down, ruin; *inf.* folding, flop.
Opposites SUCCESS; TRIUMPH.

faint *adjective* **1** *a faint mark / faint traces* indistinct, unclear, dim, obscure, pale, faded, bleached. **2** *a faint noise* indistinct, scarcely audible/perceptible, vague, low, soft, muted, muffled, stifled, subdued, weak, feeble, whispered. **3** *a faint chance of success* slight, small, remote, vague, minimal. **4** *a faint response / faint praise* weak, feeble, unenthusiastic, half-hearted, low-key. **5** *feeling faint* giddy, dizzy, light-headed, weak-headed, muzzy, weak, vertiginous; *inf.* woozy.
Opposites CLEAR; LOUD; GREAT; STRONG.

faint *verb faint from loss of blood* lose consciousness, black out, pass out, collapse; *inf.* flake out, keel over, conk out; *lit.* swoon.

faint *noun fall over in a faint* loss of consciousness, blackout, collapse, fainting fit; *lit.* swoon; *Med.* syncope.

faint-hearted *adjective* timid, timorous, fearful, spiritless, weak, cowardly, unmanly, lily-livered; *inf.* chicken-hearted, yellow.

faintly *adverb* **1** *not faintly amusing* slightly, remotely, vaguely, somewhat, a little, in the least. **2** *call faintly* indistinctly, softly, weakly, feebly, in a whisper, in subdued tones.

fair *adjective* **1** *a fair trial* just, impartial, unbiased, unprejudiced, objective, even-handed, dispassionate, disinterested, detached, equitable, above-board, lawful, legal, legitimate, proper, square; *inf.* on the level. **2** *a fair person* fair-minded, just, impartial, unbiased, unprejudiced, open-minded, honest, upright, honourable, trustworthy, above-board. **3** *fair weather* fine, dry, bright, clear, sunny, cloudless, unclouded. **4** *fair winds* favourable,

advantageous, helpful, beneficial. **5** *fair hair* |
fair and dark children blond/blonde, yellow,
flaxen, light brown, strawberry blonde, fair-
haired, light-haired, flaxen-haired, tow-
headed. **6** *fair skin* pale, light-coloured, white,
cream-coloured, creamy, peaches and cream,
chalky. **7** *fair maidens* beautiful, pretty, lovely,
attractive, good-looking, bonny, comely, well-
favoured; *lit.* beauteous. **8** *a fair number of peo-
ple* | *a fair chance of winning* reasonable, passable,
tolerable, satisfactory, respectable, decent, all
right, goodish, pretty good, not bad, moderate,
so-so, average, middling, ample, adequate, sufficient. **9** *a fair copy of the essay* clean, clear,
unblemished.
Opposites UNFAIR; DARK; UGLY.

fair *noun* **1** *a trade fair* exhibition, display,
show, exhibit, exposition; *inf.* expo. **2** *the
county fair* fête, gala, festival, carnival. **3** *an
agricultural fair* market, open-air market, mart,
exchange.

fairly *adverb* **1** *treated fairly* justly, equitably,
impartially, without prejudice, objectively,
even-handedly, properly, lawfully, legally, legit-
imately. **2** *fairly good* quite, reasonably, passably, tolerably, satisfactorily, moderately,
rather, somewhat, adequately; *inf.* pretty.
3 *children fairly shrieking with laughter* positively,
really, absolutely, decidedly, veritably.

fair-minded *adjective* fair, just, impartial,
unprejudiced, open-minded, honest, honourable. *See* FAIR *adjective* 2.

fairness *noun* **1** *treat everyone with fairness*
justness, impartiality, objectivity, even-
handedness, disinterest, equitability, equity,
legality, properness. *See* FAIR *adjective* 1. **2** *the
fairness of the judge* fair-mindedness, justness,
impartiality, open-mindedness, honesty,
integrity, probity, rectitude, trustworthiness.
See FAIR *adjective* 2. **3** *the fairness of the maidens*
beauty, prettiness, loveliness, attractiveness,
comeliness.

fairy *noun* pixie, elf, sprite, imp, brownie, leprechaun, kelpie, dwarf, gnome, goblin, hobgoblin, nix, peri, puck.

fairy tale *noun* **1** *read the child a fairy tale* fairy
story, folk tale, legend, romance. **2** *the child's
telling fairy tales* lie, white lie, untruth, tall
story, fairy story, fabrication, invention, piece
of fiction; *inf.* cock-and-bull story, terminological inexactitude.

faith *noun* **1** *have faith in the cure/doctor* trust,
belief, confidence, conviction, credence, credit,
reliance, dependence, optimism, hopefulness.
2 *of what faith are they?* religion, church, persuasion, belief, creed, teaching, dogma, doctrine, sect, denomination. **3** *keep/break faith*
loyalty, allegiance, faithfulness, fidelity, fealty,
constancy, devotion, obedience, commitment.
Opposites DISBELIEF; DISTRUST; DISLOYALTY.

faithful *adjective* **1** *faithful followers* loyal, constant, devoted, dependable, reliable, true, true-
blue, trusty, trustworthy, staunch,
unswerving, unwavering, steadfast, obedient,
dutiful, dedicated, committed. **2** *a faithful copy*
accurate, true, exact, precise, close, strict,
without error, unerring, just so; *inf.* spot on,

on the button.
Opposites DISLOYAL; UNFAITHFUL; TREACHEROUS;
IMPRECISE.

faithful *noun* **the faithful** believers, loyal members, adherents, followers, communicants;
congregation, brethren.

faithfulness *noun* **1** *the faithfulness of the followers* fidelity, loyalty, constancy, devotion,
dependability, reliability, trustworthiness,
staunchness, steadfastness, obedience, duty,
dedication, commitment, allegiance, adher-
ence, fealty. **2** *the faithfulness of the description*
accuracy, truth, exactness, precision, closeness, strictness, justness.

faithless *adjective* **1** *faithless followers* unfaithful, disloyal, false, false-hearted, untrue,
untrustworthy, traitorous, treacherous, perfidious, inconstant, fickle, unreliable, undependable, deceitful, two-faced. **2** *faithless heathens*
unbelieving, disbelieving, doubting, sceptical,
agnostic, atheistic, irreligious.

faithlessness *noun* unfaithfulness, infidelity,
disloyalty, falseness, false-heartedness,
betrayal, untrustworthiness, traitorousness,
treachery, perfidy, inconstancy, fickleness,
unreliability, undependability, deceit, deceitfulness, two-facedness.

fake *adjective* **1** *a fake five pound note* counterfeit, forged, sham, imitation, fraudulent, false,
bogus, spurious, pseudo; *inf.* phoney. **2** *fake
furs/pearls* sham, imitation, artificial, synthetic,
mock, simulated, reproduction, ersatz. **3** *a
fake accent* affected, put-on, assumed, feigned,
pseudo, insincere; *inf.* phoney, pseud.
Opposites GENUINE; AUTHENTIC; SINCERE.

fake *noun* **1** *the note is a fake* counterfeit,
forgery, copy, sham, imitation, fraud, reproduction, hoax; *inf.* phoney. **2** *the doctor is a fake*
charlatan, impostor, mountebank, quack; *inf.*
phoney.

fall *verb* **1** *leaves/rain falling* come/go down,
descend, drop, drop down, sink, gravitate, cascade, plop, plummet. **2** *the child fell* fall down,
fall over, trip, trip over, stumble, slip, slide,
tumble, topple over, keel over, go head over
heels, collapse, fall in a heap, take a spill.
3 *ground falling* fall away, slope, slope down,
incline/slant downwards. **4** *water levels falling*
sink, sink lower, subside, recede, abate,
settle. **5** *demand/prices fell* fall off, drop off, go
down, decline, decrease, grow less, diminish,
dwindle, depreciate, plummet, slump, deteriorate. **6** *empires falling* die, fade, fail, decline,
deteriorate, flag, wane, ebb, degenerate, go
downhill; *inf.* go to the dogs. **7** *soldiers falling
in war* die, be killed/slain, be a casualty/fatality,
be lost, drop dead, perish, meet one's end.
8 *towns falling to the enemy* | *fall to temptation* sur-
render, yield, submit, give in, give up, give
way, capitulate, succumb, resign oneself; be
overthrown by, be taken by, be defeated by, be
conquered by, lose one's position to, pass into
the hands of. **9** *Christmas falls on a Saturday* |
darkness fell take place, occur, happen, come
about, come to pass. **10** *it so fell that she died*
occur, happen, come about, come to pass,
befall, chance, arise, result, fall out. **11** *the
horse fell lame* | *she fell asleep* | *falling in love*

become, grow, pass into. **12** *God punishing angels for falling* sin, do wrong, transgress, err, go astray, yield to temptation, commit an offence, lapse, fall from grace, backslide, trespass. **fall apart** *the wardrobe/system fell apart* fall/come to pieces, fall/come to bits, disintegrate, break up, crumble, dissolve. **fall back** retreat, withdraw, draw back, retire. **fall back on** resort to, call upon, call into play/action, call/press into service, have recourse to, make use of, use, employ, rely on, depend on. **fall behind** **1** *fall behind in the race* be/get left behind, fall/drop back, lose one's place, lag, trail, not keep up. **2** *fall behind with the rent* get into arrears/debt, not keep up with. **fall down** **1** *the child fell down* fall, fall over, trip. *See* FALL *verb* 2. **2** *fall down on the task* fail, be unsuccessful, not succeed, not make the grade, not come up to expectations, fall short, disappoint. **fall for** **1** *fall for his friend's sister* fall in love with, become infatuated with, desire, be attracted/smitten by, lose one's heart to; *inf.* fancy. **2** *fall for an old trick* be taken in by, be fooled/deceived/duped by, accept; *inf.* swallow. **fall in** *the roof fell in* cave in, collapse, sink inwards, come down about one's ears, crash in, crumble. **fall in with** **1** *fall in with bad company* meet, encounter, get involved with, take up with. **2** *fall in with their plans* agree to/with, accept, assent to, concur with, go along with, support, back, give one's backing to, cooperate with. **fall off** *demand fell off* drop off, go down, decrease, decline, slump, deteriorate. *See* FALL *verb* 5. **fall out** **1** *husband and wife falling out* quarrel, argue, squabble, fight, bicker, have a difference of opinion, differ, have a disagreement, disagree, clash, wrangle, get into conflict, get into a dispute. **2** *it fell out that we lost* happen, occur, come about, take place, turn out, chance, arise, befall, result. **fall short** *the charity appeal fell short* | *fall short of perfection* be deficient, be/prove inadequate, disappoint; fail to meet/reach, fail to live up to, miss. **fall through** come to nothing, fail, fail to happen, miscarry, abort, go awry; *inf.* fizzle out. **fall to** *fall to and eat/work* set to, begin, start, commence, set/go about, get to work, set the ball rolling, put one's shoulder to the wheel, get moving, get the show on the road.
Opposites RISE; THRIVE; SURVIVE.

fall *noun* **1** *the child had a fall* trip, tumble, spill, stumble, slipping, slip, slide, topple, keeling over, nosedive, collapse. **2** *a fall in demand/prices* fall-off, drop, dropping off, decline, decrease, cut, lessening, lowering, dip, diminishing, dwindling, reduction, depreciation, plummeting, slump, deterioration. **3** *the fall of the Roman empire* death, demise, downfall, ruin, collapse, failure, decline, deterioration, wane, ebb, degeneration, destruction, overthrow. **4** *the fall of the city to the enemy* surrender, yielding, submission, giving in, capitulation, succumbing, resignation, defeat. **5** *the fall of the land* slope, downward slope/slant/incline, declivity, descent, downgrade. **6** *the fall of Lucifer* sin, wrongdoing, transgression, error, yielding to temptation, offence, lapse, fall from grace, backsliding; original sin, the Fall.

fallacious *adjective* false, erroneous, untrue, wrong, incorrect, faulty, flawed, inaccurate, inexact, imprecise, mistaken, misleading, fictitious, spurious, counterfeit, deceptive, fraudulent, delusive, delusory, illusory, sophistic; *inf.* bogus, phoney.
Opposites TRUE; CORRECT; AUTHENTIC.

fallacy *noun* mistaken belief, misbelief, misconception, false notion, misapprehension, misjudgement, miscalculation, error, mistake, untruth, inconsistency, illusion, delusion, deceit, deception, sophism; sophistry, casuistry.

fallen *adjective* **1** *fallen women* immoral, loose, shamed, disgraced, dishonoured, ruined, sinful, unchaste. **2** *fallen soldiers* dead, killed, slain, lost, perished, slaughtered.

fallible *adjective* liable/prone/open to error, error-prone, erring, errant, imperfect, flawed, frail, weak, mortal.
Opposites INFALLIBLE; PERFECT.

fallow *adjective* *fallow land* | *fields/ideas lying fallow* uncultivated, unploughed, untilled, unplanted, unsown, unseeded, unused, undeveloped, dormant, resting, inactive, idle, inert, empty, neglected, barren, unproductive.

false *adjective* **1** *a false interpretation/account* untrue, incorrect, wrong, erroneous, faulty, invalid, unfounded; untruthful, fictitious, concocted, fabricated, invented, inaccurate, inexact, imprecise, flawed, unreal, counterfeit, forged, fraudulent, spurious, misleading. **2** *a false friend* false-hearted, unfaithful, faithless, treacherous, disloyal, traitorous, perfidious, two-faced, double-dealing, untrustworthy, untrue, deceitful, deceiving, deceptive, dishonourable, dishonest, duplicitous, hypocritical, unreliable, unsound, untruthful, lying, mendacious. **3** *false furs/pearls* fake, artificial, imitation, synthetic, simulated, sham, mock, bogus, ersatz, spurious, counterfeit, feigned, forged, make-believe, pseudo; *inf.* phoney.
Opposites TRUE; LOYAL; FAITHFUL; GENUINE.

falsehood *noun* **1** *telling falsehoods* lie, fib, untruth, false statement, falsification, perjury, fabrication, invention, piece of fiction, fiction, story, fairy story/tale, exaggeration; *inf.* terminological inexactitude. **2** *guilty of falsehood* deceit, deception, deceitfulness, two-facedness, double-dealing, dissimulation, prevarication, equivocation, mendacity, untruthfulness, perjury, perfidy, treachery, treason, casuistry.
Opposites TRUTH.

falsetto *noun* high voice, high-pitched tone, squeak, squeal.

falsify *verb* **1** *falsify a document* alter, counterfeit, forge, fake, doctor, tamper with, distort, adulterate, pervert. **2** *falsify their statement* disprove, show to be false, prove unsound, refute, confute, rebut, contradict, oppose; misrepresent, garble, misstate, misquote.

falter *verb* **1** *falter before proceeding* hesitate, waver, oscillate, fluctuate, delay, vacillate, be undecided, blow hot and cold, shilly-shally, hum and haw, drag one's feet, sit on the fence. **2** *falter over her words* stammer, stutter, stumble, speak haltingly.

fame *noun* renown, celebrity, eminence, notability, note, distinction, mark, prominence, esteem, importance, greatness, account, preeminence, glory, honour, illustriousness, stardom, reputation, repute; notoriety, infamy.
Opposites OBSCURITY; DISGRACE; DISREPUTE.

familiar *adjective* **1** *familiar face/task/excuse* well-known, known, recognized, customary, accustomed, common, everyday, ordinary, commonplace, frequent, habitual, usual, repeated, routine, stock, mundane, run-of-the-mill, conventional, household, domestic; *inf.* common or garden. **2** *a familiar atmosphere* informal, casual, relaxed, comfortable, easy, free, free-and-easy, at ease, at home, friendly, unceremonious, unrestrained, unconstrained, unreserved, open, natural, simple. **3** *familiar acquaintances* close, intimate, dear, near, confidential, bosom, friendly, neighbourly, sociable, amicable, hail fellow well met; *inf.* pally, chummy, buddy-buddy, thick, thick as thieves. **4** *object to him being familiar with the staff* over-familiar, over-free, presumptuous, disrespectful, forward, bold, impudent, impertinent, intrusive; *inf.* pushy. **familiar with** *familiar with the system* acquainted with, conversant with, versed in, well up in, with knowledge of, knowledgeable about, instructed in, *au fait* with, at home with, no stranger to, *au courant* with.
Opposites UNFAMILIAR; STRANGE; FORMAL.

familiarity *noun* **1** *his familiarity with the technique* acquaintance with, acquaintanceship with, knowledge of, grasp of, mastery of, understanding of, comprehension of, experience of, skill with. **2** *the familiarity of the atmosphere* informality, casualness, ease, comfortableness, friendliness, lack of ceremony/restraint/reserve, naturalness, simplicity. *See* FAMILIAR 2. **3** *the familiarity of their relationship* closeness, intimacy, nearness, friendliness; *inf.* chumminess. *See* FAMILIAR 3. **4** *object to his familiarity* overfamiliarity, presumption, presumptuousness, disrespect, forwardness, boldness, impudence, impertinence, intrusiveness; liberties.

familiarize *verb* **1** *familiarize the pupils with the system* make familiar with, make conversant with, acquaint with, accustom to, habituate to, instruct in, coach in, train in, teach in, school in, prime in, indoctrinate in, initiate into. **2** *naturalists/broadcasters familiarizing exotic plants* make known, bring to notice, bring to public attention, make familiar.

family *noun* **1** *two families living together* parent/parents and child/children, household, *ménage*, clan, tribe; nuclear family, extended family. **2** *she wants a family* children, offspring, little ones, progeny, descendants, issue, scions; brood; *inf.* kids. **3** *the old man had no family* relatives, relations, people, kin, next of kin, kinsfolk, kinsmen, one's own flesh and blood, folk. **4** *of a noble family* ancestry, extraction, parentage, birth, pedigree, genealogy, background, family tree, descent, lineage, line, bloodline, blood, race, strain, stock, breed, stirps; dynasty, house; forebears, forefathers, antecedents, roots. **5** *a family of plants* class,

genus, species, kind, type, group, taxonomic group.

famine *noun* **1** *famine striking the village* scarcity of food, food shortage. **2** *water famine* scarcity, lack, dearth, want, deficiency, shortage, insufficiency, paucity, exiguity, drought. **3** *dying of famine* starvation, hunger, food-deprivation, lack of food, anorexia, inanition.

famished *adjective* starving, starving to death, starved, ravenous, hungry, undernourished.

famous *adjective* well-known, renowned, celebrated, famed, prominent, noted, notable, great, eminent, pre-eminent, distinguished, esteemed, respected, venerable, illustrious, acclaimed, honoured, exalted, glorious, remarkable, signal, popular, legendary, lionized, much-publicized.
Opposites UNKNOWN; OBSCURE.

fan[1] *noun* install a fan air-cooler, air-conditioner, ventilator, blower, aerator, flabellum, punkah.

fan[2] *verb* **1** *fan the atmosphere | fanning her face* cool, ventilate, air, aerate, blow, freshen, refresh. **2** *fan the flames/passion* intensify, increase, arouse, excite, agitate, ignite, kindle, stimulate, stir up, work up, whip up, incite, instigate, provoke. **3** *people/flags fanning out* spread, spread out, open out, open up, unfurl, unfold, outspread, stretch out.

fan[3] *noun* a fan of the local pop group admirer, lover, enthusiast, devotee, addict, aficionado, zealot, follower, disciple, adherent, supporter, backer, champion, votary; *inf.* buff, fiend, freak, nut, groupie.

fanatic *noun* a religious fanatic zealot, extremist, radical, activist, militant, sectarian, bigot, partisan, devotee, addict, enthusiast, visionary.

fanatical *adjective* **1** *a fanatical religious sect* extremist, extreme, zealous, radical, activist, militant, sectarian, bigoted, dogmatic, prejudiced, intolerant, narrow-minded, partisan, rabid. **2** *a fanatical film-goer* enthusiastic, eager, keen, fervent, passionate, over-enthusiastic, obsessive, immoderate, frenzied, frenetic; *inf.* wild, gung-ho.

fanciful *adjective* **1** *fanciful notions/beings* imaginary, fancied, fantastic, romantic, mythical, fabulous, legendary, unreal, illusory, visionary, made-up, make-believe, fairy-tale, extravagant. **2** *a fanciful child* imaginative, inventive, impractical, whimsical, capricious, visionary, chimerical. **3** *fanciful decoration* imaginative, creative, curious, extravagant, fantastic, bizarre, strange, eccentric.

fancy *noun* **1** *a child subject to fancy* caprice, whimsy, sudden impulse, vagary, eccentricity, peculiarity; whim, quirk, notion, kink. **2** *have a fancy for an icecream* desire, urge, wish, want, yearning, longing, inclination, bent, hankering, impulse; fondness, liking, love, partiality, preference, predilection, taste, relish, humour, penchant; *inf.* yen, itch. **3** *the poet's fancy* imagination, imaginative power, creativity, conception; images, mental images, visualizations. **4** *the spaceship was only a fancy* figment of the imagination, hallucination, illusion, delusion, fantasy, vision, dream, reverie, daydream. **5** *I* *have a fancy it will rain* idea, vague idea, guess, thought, notion, supposition, opinion.

fancy *verb* **1** *we fancy it will rain* have an idea, guess, think, think it likely/conceivable, believe, suppose, surmise, suspect, conjecture, reckon. **2** *he fancies a drink* would like, wish for, want, desire, long for, yearn for, crave, have a yearning/craving for, hanker after, covet; *inf.* have a yen for. **3** *he fancies the new girl* find attractive, be attracted/captivated/infatuated by, take to, desire, lust after, burn for; *inf.* have taken a shine to, have a crush on, be wild/mad about, go for, lech after.

fancy *adjective* **1** *fancy decorations* ornate, elaborate, ornamented, ornamental, decorated, decorative, adorned, embellished, intricate, lavish, ostentatious, showy, luxurious, sumptuous, baroque, rococo; *inf.* jazzy, ritzy, snazzy, posh, classy. **2** *fancy notions* fanciful, imaginary, fantastic, romantic, make-believe, farfetched, illusory, delusive, extravagant, flighty, whimsical, capricious, chimerical; *inf.* far-out.

fanfare *noun* **1** *the queen greeted by a fanfare* flourish, trumpet call, blast of trumpets, fanfaronade. **2** *the new store opened with much fanfare* show, showiness, display, ostentation, commotion, fuss, publicity, sensationalism, ballyhoo; *inf.* to-do, hype, pizazz.

fantastic *adjective* **1** *fantastic notions* fanciful, imaginary, romantic, unreal, illusory, make-believe, irrational, extravagant, wild, mad, absurd, incredible, strange, eccentric, whimsical, capricious. **2** *fantastic shapes* strange, weird, queer, peculiar, outlandish, eccentric, bizarre, grotesque, freakish, whimsical, fanciful, quaint, imaginative, exotic, unreal, extravagant, elaborate, ornate, intricate, rococo, baroque, phantasmagoric, Kafkaesque. **3** *a fantastic amount of work* tremendous, enormous, huge, very great, terrific, impressive, overwhelming. **4** *the film was fantastic* marvellous, wonderful, sensational, superb, excellent, brilliant, first-class, top-notch; *inf.* ace, brill, magic.
Opposites REAL; ORDINARY; POOR.

fantasy, phantasy *noun* **1** *novels full of fantasy* fancy, imagination, creativity, invention, originality, vision, myth, romance. **2** *indulge in fantasy* fancy, speculation, daydreaming, reverie; flight of fancy, fanciful notion, dream, daydream, pipe-dream. **3** *seeing fantasies* apparition, phantom, spectre, ghost, figment of the imagination, hallucination, vision, illusion, mirage.

far *adverb* **1** *it's not far to the house | far away | far into the night* a long way, a great distance, any great distance, a good way, afar. **2** *far the best | far too soon* to a great extent/degree, very much, much, by much, by a great amount, considerably, by a long way, markedly, immeasurably, decidedly, by far. **by far, by far and away** to a great extent/degree, very much, much, by a great amount/deal, by a long way/chalk/shot, considerably, immeasurably, decidedly, markedly, positively, easily, beyond the shadow of a doubt. **far and wide** *search far and wide* everywhere, in all places, extensively, here, there and everywhere, widely, broadly,

worldwide. **far out** *her clothes/ideas are far out* weird, bizarre, outlandish, unorthodox, unconventional, radical, extreme, esoteric; *inf.* way out, kinky. **go far** *the young man will go far* get on, get on in the world, be successful, succeed, make one's way in the world, make headway/progress, gain advancement, make a name for oneself, climb the ladder of success, rise in the world, set the Thames/world/heather on fire, cut a swath; *inf.* go places. **so far** *the play's OK so far* up till/to now, until now, up to this point, to date.

far *adjective* *visit far places* far-away, far-off, distant, remote, out of the way, far-flung, far-removed, outlying, inaccessible, back of beyond, God-forsaken.
Opposites NEAR; NEIGHBOURING.

farce *noun* **1** *starring in a bedroom farce* slapstick, slapstick comedy, burlesque, satire, parody, travesty, buffoonery, absurdity, ridiculousness. **2** *the interviews were just a farce* mockery, absurdity, sham, pretence, piece of futility, joke.

farcical *adjective* **1** *a farcical situation* ridiculous, ludicrous, absurd, laughable, risible, preposterous, facetious, silly, foolish, nonsensical, asinine. **2** *a farcical play* comic, slapstick, custard-pie, humorous, amusing.

fare *noun* **1** *how much is the bus fare?* ticket price, transport cost, price, cost, charge, fee. **2** *pick up three fares* passenger, traveller, fare payer, ticket payer; *inf.* pick-up. **3** *the canteen serving plain fare* food, menu, diet, table, nourishment, nutriment; meals, eatables, rations, provisions, commons, victuals, viands; *inf.* eats, nosh.

fare *verb* **1** *how did you fare?* get on, proceed, get along, progress, make out, do, manage, succeed, prosper. **2** *it fared badly with him* turn out, go, happen, proceed, progress.

farewell *interjection* goodbye, so long, cheerio, adieu, ciao, *adios, Auf Wiedersehen; inf.* see you, see you later.

farewell *noun* *farewells are sad* goodbye, adieu, leave-taking, parting, send-off, departure, departing, going away.

far-fetched *adjective* improbable, unlikely, remote, implausible, incredible, scarcely credible, unbelievable, difficult to believe, dubious, doubtful, unconvincing, strained, laboured, strange, fantastic, fanciful, unrealistic; *inf.* hard to swallow/take.

farm *noun* farmland, land; smallholding, holding, farmstead, steading, homestead, grange, plantation; *Scots* croft; *Am.* ranch; *Austral.* station.

farm *verb* **1** *farm the land* cultivate, bring under cultivation, till, work, plough, plant. **2** *her husband farms* be a farmer, practise farming, cultivate/till/work the land, rear livestock, do agricultural work. **3** *farm her former neighbour's children* foster, care for, have in care, mind, babysit. **farm out** **1** *farm out his work* contract out, subcontract, delegate, assign to others. **2** *farm out a franchise* rent, rent out, lease, let. **3** *farm out the child* have fostered, have cared for, send to a childminder, put in care.

farmer noun agriculturalist, agronomist, smallholder, yeoman; Scots crofter; Am: rancher.

farming noun agriculture, agronomy, tilling, tillage, cultivation, agribusiness. See table.

TYPES OF FARMING	
arboriculture	intensive farming
arable farming	livestock farming
dairy farming	market gardening
extensive farming	mixed farming
factory farming	organic farming
fish farming	sharecropping
floriculture	share farming
forestry	silviculture
horticulture	subsistence
husbandry	farming
hydroponics	viticulture

far-sighted adjective **1** not near-sighted, but far-sighted long-sighted, hyperopic, hypermetropic. **2** far-sighted in his choice having foresight, prudent, prescient, discerning, judicious, shrewd, provident, politic, canny, cautious, careful, watchful, wise, sagacious.

farther adjective the farther boat is almost out of sight more distant/advanced. See FURTHER adjective 2.

farther adverb she stopped and would come no farther to a more advanced point. See FURTHER adverb 2.

farthest adjective most distant. See FURTHEST.

fascinate verb captivate, enchant, beguile, bewitch, enthral, infatuate, enrapture, entrance, hold spellbound, transfix, rivet, mesmerize, hypnotize, allure, lure, tempt, entice, draw, tantalize, charm, attract, intrigue, delight, absorb, engross.
Opposites BORE; REPEL; turn off (see TURN).

fascinating adjective captivating, enchanting, beguiling, bewitching, enthralling, ravishing, entrancing, compelling, spellbinding, riveting, gripping, alluring, tempting, enticing, irresistible, seductive, charming, attractive, intriguing, delightful, absorbing.
Opposites BORING; DULL.

fascination noun captivation, enchantment, allure, lure, allurement, attraction, attractiveness, appeal, charm, magnetism, pull, draw, spell, sorcery, magic, glamour.

fashion noun **1** the fashion in clothes/behaviour current/latest style, style, vogue, trend, latest thing, latest taste, mode, craze, rage, fad, general tendency, convention, custom, practice. **2** she works in fashion clothes, clothes industry, clothes design, couture; inf. rag trade. See table. **3** people of fashion fashionable society, high society, society, social elite, the beautiful people, beau monde; inf. jet set. **4** working in an untidy fashion manner, way, style, method, mode, system, approach. **5** they built a boat of some fashion kind, type, sort, make, design, description. **after a fashion** he put the tent up after a fashion somehow or other, somehow, in a way, in a rough way, in an approximate manner, to a certain extent, in a manner of speaking.

fashion verb fashion a boat out of logs make, construct, build, manufacture, create, devise, shape, form, mould, forge, hew, carve.

fashionable adjective **1** fashionable clothes in fashion, stylish, up-to-date, up-to-the-minute, modern, voguish, in vogue, modish, popular, all the rage, trendsetting, latest, smart, chic, elegant, natty; inf. trendy, with it, ritzy. **2** fashionable areas/restaurants high-class, hightoned; inf. classy, swank.
Opposites UNFASHIONABLE; OLD-FASHIONED; DATED.

fast adjective **1** at a fast pace quick, rapid, swift, speedy, brisk, fleet-footed, hasty, hurried, accelerated, express, flying. **2** remain fast friends loyal, devoted, faithful, firm, steadfast, staunch, constant, lasting, unchanging, unwavering, enduring. **3** the door is fast fastened, closed, shut, secured, secure, firmly fixed. **4** fast women promiscuous, licentious, dissolute, loose, wanton. **5** lead fast lives wild, dissipated, dissolute, debauched, promiscuous, intemperate, immoderate, rakish, unrestrained, reckless, profligate, self-indulgent, extravagant.
Opposites SLOW; DISLOYAL; VIRTUOUS.

fast adverb **1** run fast quickly, rapidly, swiftly, speedily, briskly, hastily, with all haste, in haste, hurriedly, in a hurry, post-haste, expeditiously, with dispatch, like the wind, like a shot/flash, hell for leather, like a bat out of hell; inf. lickety-split. **2** stuck fast firmly, tightly, securely, immovably, fixedly. **3** fast asleep sound, deeply, completely. **4** live fast

FASHION DESIGNERS			
Armani, Giorgio (b. 1936; It.)	Dior, Christian (1905–57; Fr.)	Kenzo (b. 1940; Jap.)	Oldfield, Bruce (b. 1950; Brit.)
Balenciaga, Cristóbal (1895–1972; Sp.)	Erté (1892–1990; Fr.)	Klein, Calvin (b. 1942; Am.)	Quant, Mary (b. 1934; Brit.)
Cardin, Pierre (b. 1922; Fr.)	Gaultier, Jean-Paul (b. 1952; Fr.)	Lacroix, Christian (b. 1951; Fr.)	Saint-Laurent, Yves (b. 1936; Fr.)
Chanel, Coco (1883–1971; Fr.)	Hamnett, Katharine (b. 1952; Brit.)	Lagerfeld, Karl-Otto (b. 1938; Ger.)	Versace, Gianni (b. 1946; It.)
Conran, Jasper (b. 1959; Brit.)	Hartnell, Norman (1901–78; Brit.)	Lauren, Ralph (b. 1939; Am.)	Westwood, Vivienne (b. 1941; Brit.)
Courrèges, André (b. 1923; Fr.)	Karan, Donna (b. 1948; Am.)	Miyake, Issey (b. 1939; Jap.)	Yamamoto, Kansai (b. 1944; Jap.)

wildly, dissipatedly, intemperately, rakishly, recklessly. See FAST *adjective* 5.

fast *verb fasting during Lent* abstain from food, refrain from eating, deny oneself food, go without food, go hungry, eat nothing, starve oneself, go on hunger strike.
Opposites EAT; FEAST.

fasten *verb* **1** *fasten a brooch to the dress* attach, fix, affix, clip, pin, tack. **2** *fasten the door* bolt, lock, secure, make secure/fast, chain, seal. **3** *fasten the links of the chain* join, connect, couple, unite, link. **4** *fasten the goat to the tree* attach, tie, bind, tether, hitch, anchor. **5** *fasten his gaze on her* direct, aim, point, focus, fix, rivet, concentrate, zero in. **6** *the dress fastens at the back* become closed, close; button, zip. **7** *the gang fastening on the younger boys* take hold of, seize, catch/grab hold of, grab, snatch.
Opposites UNFASTEN; OPEN; UNLOCK.

fastidious *adjective* hard to please, critical, overcritical, hypercritical, fussy, finicky, overparticular; *inf.* choosy, picky, pernickety.
Opposites EASYGOING; SLOPPY.

fat *adjective* **1** *fat old men* plump, stout, overweight, obese, heavy, large, solid, corpulent, chubby, tubby, portly, rotund, podgy, flabby, gross, pot-bellied, paunchy; *inf.* beefy, roly-poly, elephantine. **2** *fat substances* fatty, greasy, oily, oleaginous, adipose, unctuous, sebaceous. **3** *fat land* fertile, productive, fruitful, rich, lush, flourishing, thriving. **4** *a fat part in a play* substantial, large, sizeable, major, important, significant, considerable. **5** *a fat income* large, substantial, profitable, remunerative, lucrative. **6** *a fat book* thick, big, substantial, broad, extended. **7** *fat chance* very little, not much, minimal, hardly any.
Opposites THIN; LEAN; MINOR.

fat *noun* **1** *too much fat in the meat* fatty tissue, fat cells, adipose tissue. **2** *he'll have to get rid of his fat* excessive weight, fatness, plumpness, stoutness, obesity, chubbiness, tubbiness, flabbiness, corpulence, bulk; *inf.* flab, blubber, beef. See FAT *adjective* 1. **3** *add fat to the cake* animal/vegetable fat; lard, suet, butter, margarine.

fatal *adjective* **1** *a fatal blow/illness* causing death, mortal, deadly, lethal, death dealing, killing, terminal, final, incurable. **2** *fatal to our plans* ruinous, destructive, disastrous, catastrophic, calamitous, cataclysmic. **3** *the fatal moment* fateful, critical, crucial, decisive, determining, pivotal, momentous, important.
Opposites HARMLESS; BENEFICIAL.

fatalism *noun* stoicism, resignation, passive acceptance, acceptance; predeterminism, predestinarianism, necessitarianism.

fatality *noun* **1** *three fatalities in the accident* dead person, death, casualty, mortality, loss; dead. **2** *the fatality of the blow* deadliness, lethalness. **3** *a road noted for its fatalities* fatal accident, disaster, catastrophe.

fate *noun* **1** *fate meant them to meet* destiny, providence, God's will, nemesis, kismet, predestination, predetermination, chance, astral influence, one's lot in life; the stars. **2** *courts deciding our fate* future, outcome, issue, upshot,

end. **3** *met his fate in battle* death, end, destruction, ruin, doom, catastrophe, downfall, disaster, collapse, defeat.

fated *adjective a fated meeting|fated to meet* predestined, preordained, foreordained, destined, inevitable, inescapable, sure, ineluctable, doomed.

fateful *adjective* **1** *a fateful meeting* critical, crucial, decisive, determining, pivotal, momentous, important, fated. **2** *a fateful course of action* disastrous, ruinous, destructive, fatal, lethal, deadly.

Fates *plural noun.* See table.

THE THREE FATES

Lachesis (assigns a person's destiny)
Clotho (spins the thread of life)
Atropos (cuts the thread of life)

---

father *noun* **1** male parent, begetter, paterfamilias, patriarch; adoptive father, stepfather; *inf.* dad, daddy, pop, poppa, pa, old boy, old man, governor, gaffer, pater. **2** *investigate the history of his fathers* forefather, ancestor, forebear, progenitor, primogenitor, predecessor, forerunner, precursor. **3** *the father of modern history* founder, originator, initiator, prime mover, architect, inventor, creator, maker, author. **4** *the city fathers* leader, elder, patriarch, senator. **5** *God bless you, Father* priest, pastor, padre, parson, clergyman, father confessor, abbé, curé. **6** *Father in heaven* God, our Lord, the Lord God, the Deity.

father *verb* **1** *he fathered three sons* sire, beget, procreate, engender, bring into being, give life to. **2** *father the project* found, establish, institute, originate, initiate, invent, create, generate, conceive.

fatherland *noun* native land/country, native soil/heath, homeland, home, one's mother country, motherland, land of one's birth/fathers, the old country.

fatherly *adjective* paternal, kindly, kind, affectionate, tender, caring, benevolent, sympathetic, understanding, indulgent, protective, supportive, patriarchal.

fathom *verb* **1** *fathom the depth of the water* sound, plumb, measure, estimate, gauge, probe. **2** *fathom their motives* understand, comprehend, grasp, perceive, penetrate, divine, search out, get to the bottom of, ferret out.

fatigue *verb it fatigues him to walk* tire, tire out, overtire, make weary, weary, exhaust, wear out, drain, prostrate, enervate; *inf.* take it out of, do in, fag out, whack, poop.

fatigue *noun suffering from fatigue* tiredness, overtiredness, weariness, exhaustion, prostration, lassitude, debility, enervation, lethargy, listlessness.
Opposites ENERGY; VIGOUR.

fatness *noun* plumpness, stoutness, obesity, heaviness, largeness, corpulence, portliness, chubbiness, tubbiness, rotundity, podginess, flabbiness, grossness; *inf.* beefiness.

fatten verb **1** *fatten the cattle for market* make fat/fatter, feed up, feed, build up, overfeed, bloat. **2** *children fattening up on good food* grow fat/fatter, get fat, put on weight, gain weight, get heavier, thicken, widen, broaden, expand, spread out. **3** *fatten the land* feed, fertilize, nourish, nurture, enrich.

fatty adjective fat, greasy, oily, oleaginous, adipose, unctuous, sebaceous.

fatuous adjective silly, foolish, stupid, inane, pointless, senseless, nonsensical, childish, puerile, idiotic, brainless, mindless, vacuous, asinine, moronic, witless, ridiculous, ludicrous, laughable, risible.

fault noun **1** *a fault in the material* defect, flaw, imperfection, blemish, snag. **2** *a fault in her character* defect, flaw, failing, shortcoming, weakness, weak point, infirmity, lack, deficiency. **3** *a fault in the calculation* error, mistake, inaccuracy, blunder, oversight; *inf.* slip-up, boob. **4** *blame one child for another's faults* misdeed, wrongdoing, offence, misdemeanour, misconduct, sin, vice, lapse, indiscretion, peccadillo, transgression, trespass. **5** *whose fault was the accident?* culpability, blameworthiness, responsibility, accountability, answerability. **at fault** *which driver was at fault?* to blame, blameworthy, blamable, in the wrong, culpable, responsible, accountable, answerable. **to a fault** *generous to a fault* excessively, unduly, in the extreme, immoderately, out of all proportion, overmuch, needlessly; *Scots* overly; *inf.* over the top, OTT.
Opposites MERIT; STRENGTH; ASSET.

fault verb **1** *cannot fault his behaviour* find fault with, criticize, complain about, quibble about, find lacking, censure, impugn, pick holes in. **2** *the judge failed to fault him* hold responsible/accountable/blameworthy/culpable, hold to blame, call to account.

fault-finding noun criticism, carping, complaining, captiousness, cavilling, quibbling, niggling, hair-splitting; *inf.* nit-picking.

fault-finding adjective critical, overcritical, hypercritical, censorious, carping, captious, cavilling, quibbling, niggling, hair-splitting, pettifogging; *inf.* nit-picking.

faultless adjective **1** *a faultless piece of work* without fault, perfect, flawless, without blemish, unblemished, impeccable, accurate, correct, exemplary, model. **2** *the wife of the prisoner was faultless* innocent, without guilt, guiltless, blameless, above reproach, irreproachable, sinless, pure, unsullied.
Opposites IMPERFECT; GUILTY.

faulty adjective **1** *a faulty lock* broken, not working, malfunctioning, out of order, damaged, defective, unsound; *inf.* on the blink, kaput. **2** *faulty reasoning* defective, flawed, unsound, wrong, inaccurate, incorrect, erroneous, imprecise, fallacious, impaired, weak, invalid.
Opposites PERFECT; WORKING; CORRECT.

faux pas noun blunder, gaffe, mistake, slip-up, indiscretion, impropriety, lapse of etiquette, solecism, peccadillo; *inf.* boob, boo-boo.

favour noun **1** *do me a favour* good turn, service, kind act, good deed, kindness, courtesy, benefit, boon. **2** *look on him with favour* approval, approbation, esteem, goodwill, kindness, benevolence, friendliness. **3** *owe his job to favour rather than merit* favouritism, bias, partiality, prejudice, partisanship. **4** *enjoy the favour of the King* patronage, backing, support, aid, assistance, championship, aegis; auspices. **5** *wear political favours* ribbons, rosette, badge, token. **in favour of** *in favour of hanging* on the side of, for, pro, giving support/backing to, right behind; all for.
Opposites DISFAVOUR; DISAPPROVAL; DISSERVICE.

favour verb **1** *he favours returning* advocate, approve of, recommend, support, back, endorse, sanction. **2** *the young man favoured blondes* prefer, go in for, go for, choose, opt for, select, pick, plump for, single out, fancy, like, incline towards. **3** *the father favours his son* show favouritism towards, have a bias towards, treat with partiality, indulge, pamper, spoil. **4** *the wind favoured the other team* be to the advantage of, be advantageous to, benefit, help, assist, aid, advance, abet, succour. **5** *favour us with a smile* do a favour/service to, do a good turn to, oblige, serve, accommodate.
Opposites OPPOSE; DISLIKE; HINDER.

favourable adjective **1** *a favourable report* good, approving, commendatory, praising, well-disposed, enthusiastic. **2** *the circumstances are favourable* in one's favour, advantageous, beneficial, on one's side, helpful, good, hopeful, promising, fair, auspicious, propitious, opportune, timely, encouraging, conducive, convenient, suitable, fit, appropriate. **3** *a favourable reply* affirmative, in the affirmative, positive, encouraging. **4** *make a favourable impression* good, pleasing, agreeable, successful, positive.
Opposites UNFAVOURABLE; CRITICAL; DISADVANTAGEOUS.

favourite adjective *my favourite book* best-loved, most-liked, pet, favoured, dearest, preferred, chosen, choice, treasured, ideal.

favourite noun **1** *the daughter is the father's favourite* preference, first choice, choice, pick, pet, beloved, darling, idol, god, goddess, jewel, jewel in the crown; *inf.* blue-eyed boy, teacher's pet. **2** *the favourite won* expected/probable winner, front-runner.
Opposites BÊTE NOIRE.

favouritism noun guilty of favouritism bias, partiality, prejudice, unfair preference, partisanship, one-sidedness, nepotism, inequality, unfairness, inequity.

fawn adjective *fawn trousers* yellowish-brown, greyish-brown, buff, beige, greige, neutral. *See table at* COLOUR.

fawn verb *fawning on the manager* kowtow to, toady to, truckle to, bow and scrape to, grovel before, be obsequious/servile to, curry favour with, pay court to, ingratiate oneself with, dance attendance on, lick the boots of; *inf.* butter up.

fawning adjective obsequious, servile, sycophantic, toadyish, slavish, bowing and scraping, grovelling, abject, crawling, creeping, cringing, prostrate, flattering, ingratiating, over-deferential; *inf.* bootlicking.

fear noun **1** *filled with fear at the danger* fright, fearfulness, terror, alarm, panic, trepidation, apprehensiveness, dread, nervousness, fear and trembling, timidity, disquiet, trembling, quaking, quivering, consternation, dismay; shivers, butterflies, tremors; *inf.* funk, blue funk. **2** *all her fears were removed* phobia, aversion, dread, bête noire, bugbear, bogey, nightmare, horror, terror; *inf.* the creeps. *See table at* PHOBIA. **3** *express fear that he would die* anxiety, worry, unease, uneasiness, apprehension, nervousness, agitation, concern, disquiet, disquietude, foreboding, misgiving, doubt, suspicion, angst. **4** *filled with fear at the sight of the angel* awe, wonder, amazement, reverence, veneration. **5** *there is little fear of her leaving* likelihood, probability, possibility, chance, prospect.

fear verb **1** *they fear their father* be afraid/fearful/apprehensive of, be scared of, dread, live in fear/dread of, go in terror of. **2** *she fears spiders* be afraid of, dread, have a horror/dread of, have a phobia about, shudder at, take fright at; *inf.* have brown trousers at. **3** *fear to go out* be too afraid/scared/apprehensive to, dare not, hesitate to; *inf.* have cold feet about. **4** *I fear for her health* worry about, feel anxious/concerned about, have anxieties/qualms about, feel disquiet for, be solicitous for. **5** *they fear God* stand in awe of, revere, reverence, venerate. **6** *I fear that you may be right* be afraid, suspect, have a suspicion, expect, anticipate, foresee, have a foreboding, apprehend.

fearful adjective **1** *fearful of making a noise* afraid, frightened, scared, terrified, alarmed, apprehensive, uneasy, nervous, tense, nervy, panicky, timid, timorous, faint-hearted, diffident, intimidated, hesitant, disquieted, trembling, quaking, quivering, shrinking, cowering, cowardly, pusillanimous; *inf.* jittery, jumpy. **2** *a fearful accident* terrible, dreadful, appalling, frightful, ghastly, horrific, horrible, horrendous, shocking, awful, atrocious, hideous, monstrous, dire, grim, unspeakable, gruesome, distressing, harrowing, alarming. **3** *a fearful cold/mess* terrible, appalling, very bad, extremely bad, very great. **4** *the angels were a fearful sight* awesome, awe-inspiring, imposing, impressive, venerable.
Opposites INTREPID; BOLD.

fearfully adverb **1** *crawl forward fearfully* apprehensively, in fear and trembling, uneasily, nervously, timidly, timorously, diffidently, hesitantly, with one's heart in one's mouth. **2** *she's fearfully polite* extremely, exceedingly, remarkably; *inf.* tremendously, awfully, terribly, frightfully.

fearless adjective unafraid, brave, courageous, valiant, intrepid, valorous, gallant, plucky, lion-hearted, stout-hearted, heroic, bold, daring, confident, undaunted, indomitable, doughty, undaunted, unflinching, unshrinking, unblenching, unabashed; *inf.* game, gutsy, spunky.
Opposites COWARDLY; CRAVEN.

fearsome adjective *a fearsome sight* frightening, alarming, unnerving, daunting, horrifying,

horrendous, dismaying, awe-inspiring, awesome.

feasibility noun practicability, possibility, workability, viability, suitability, expedience. *See* FEASIBLE.

feasible adjective practicable, possible, likely, workable, doable, achievable, attainable, accomplishable, realizable, reasonable, viable, realistic, within reason, useful, suitable, expedient.
Opposites IMPRACTICAL; IMPOSSIBLE.

feast noun **1** *everyone enjoyed the feast last night* banquet, celebration meal, lavish dinner, repast, treat, entertainment, jollification, junket, orgy; revels, festivities; *inf.* beanfeast, blow-out, spread, beano, bash, thrash. **2** *the feast of St Stephen* celebration, festival, religious festival, feast day, saint's day, holy day, holiday, fête, gala day, festivity. *See table at* FESTIVAL, SAINT. **3** *a feast for the eyes* pleasure, gratification, delight, treat, joy.
Opposites FAST; FAMINE.

feast verb **1** *feast on venison and claret* wine and dine, banquet, gorge oneself on, eat one's fill of, partake of, indulge in, overindulge in, gormandize, stuff one's face with, stuff oneself with. **2** *feast the visiting King* throw a feast for, hold a banquet for, wine and dine, regale, entertain, treat. **3** *feast our eyes on the beauty* delight, please, give pleasure to, gratify, gladden, treat, thrill.

feat noun deed, act, action, exploit, performance, accomplishment, achievement, attainment, manoeuvre, move, stunt.

feather noun **1** *a bird's feather* plume, quill, pinion, plumule, pinna. **2** *the bird's feathers* plumage, down, hackles; crest, tuft.

feathery adjective **1** *feathery chicks* feathered, downy, fluffy, fleecy, plumed, plumy, plumose, plumate. **2** *feathery material* light, feather-like, light as a feather, gossamer-like, wispy, unsubstantial, ethereal.

feature noun **1** *one feature of life in the country* aspect, characteristic, facet, side, point, attribute, quality, property, trait, mark, hallmark, trade mark, peculiarity, idiosyncracy. **2** *make a feature of the tombola at the fair* special attraction, attraction, highlight, focal point, focus, draw; *inf.* crowd-puller. **3** *read the features in the magazine section* main item/article, article, piece, item, report, story, column.

feature verb **1** *the festival features a new opera* present, give prominence to, promote, star, spotlight, highlight, emphasize, play up, accentuate. **2** *do women feature in his life?* have prominence, play a part, have a place.

features plural noun face, countenance, visage, physiognomy; lineaments; *inf.* mug, kisser.

fecund adjective fruitful, productive, fertile, potent, prolific, proliferating, propagative.

federal adjective federated, federative, confederate, allied, in alliance, in league, united, linked, banded together.

federation noun confederation, confederacy, federacy, league, alliance, coalition, union, syndicate, association, amalgamation, combination, combine, entente, society, fraternity, Bund.

fee noun charge, price, cost, payment, remuneration, emolument.

feeble adjective **1** *old people grown feeble* weak, weakly, weakened, frail, infirm, delicate, slight, sickly, puny, failing, ailing, helpless, powerless, debilitated, decrepit, doddering, tottering, enervated, enfeebled, effete, etiolated; *Scots* shilpit. **2** *a feeble attempt at humour* ineffective, ineffectual, unsuccessful, inadequate, unconvincing, futile, poor, weak, tame, paltry, slight. **3** *he's too feeble to stand up to his boss* weak, ineffective, ineffectual, inefficient, incompetent, inadequate, indecisive, wishy-washy. **4** *a feeble light* dim, indistinct, faint, unclear, vague.
Opposites STRONG; ROBUST; EFFECTIVE; FORCEFUL.

feeble-minded adjective **1** *the child was declared feeble-minded* mentally defective, retarded, simple, slow-witted. **2** *he must be feeble-minded to believe that* stupid, idiotic, foolish, half-witted, vacant, slow on the uptake; *inf.* bone-headed, dumb, soft in the head, not the full shilling, off one's trolley, out to lunch.

feed verb **1** *feed the baby* give food/nourishment to, nurture; suckle, breast-feed, bottle-feed. **2** *feed the family/guests* give food to, nourish, sustain, cater for, provide for, wine and dine. **3** *the baby is feeding* eat, take nourishment, partake of food, consume, devour food. **4** *cattle feeding* graze, browse, crop. **5** *feed on grass* live on, exist on, subsist on. **6** *feed his self-esteem* gratify, bolster up, strengthen, augment, add to, encourage, minister to, add fuel to. **7** *feed information to the troops* supply, provide, give, furnish.

feed noun **1** *cattle feed* food, fodder, provender, forage, pasturage, silage. **2** *have a good feed* feast, meal, dinner, repast, banquet; *inf.* nosh, nosh-up, spread, tuck-in.

feel verb **1** *feel her face* touch, stroke, caress, fondle, finger, thumb, handle, manipulate, paw, maul. **2** *feel the ship's motion* be aware/conscious of, notice, observe, perceive, be sensible of, have a sensation of. **3** *feel pain* experience, know, have, undergo, go through, bear, endure, suffer. **4** *feel one's way* grope, fumble, poke, explore. **5** *feel the temperature of the water* sense, try, try out, test, sound out. **6** *he feels that he should go* think, believe, consider it right, consider, be of the opinion, hold, judge, deem. **7** *I feel that he's hiding something* have a feeling, sense, get the impression, feel in one's bones, have a hunch, have a funny feeling, just know, intuit. **8** *the air feels damp* seem, appear, strike one as. **feel for** *feel for the poor* sympathize with, be sorry for, pity, feel sympathy/compassion for, be moved by, weep for, grieve for, one's heart bleeds for, commiserate with, condole with, empathize with. **feel like** *feel like a holiday* would like, want, wish, desire, fancy, feel in need of; *inf.* have a yen for.

feel noun **1** *you can tell by feel* touch, sense of touch, tactile sense. **2** *the material has a nice feel* texture, surface, finish. **3** *I don't like the feel of the place* atmosphere, ambience, aura, mood, air, impression; *inf.* vibrations, vibes. **4** *have a*

feel for that kind of work knack, aptitude, flair, talent, gift, art, trick, faculty.

feeler noun **1** *the creature's feeler* antenna, tentacle, whisker. **2** *put out feelers to get people's opinions* probe, trial balloon, tentative proposal/suggestion, advance, leak; overtures.

feeling noun **1** *tell what it is by feeling* feel, touch, sense of touch, tactile sense. **2** *a feeling of pain* awareness, consciousness, sensation, sense, perception. **3** *I had a feeling that you would be there* idea, vague idea, funny feeling, impression, suspicion, sneaking suspicion, notion, inkling, hunch, apprehension, presentiment, premonition, foreboding. **4** *look at him with feeling* emotion, affection, fondness, warmth, love, sentiment, passion, ardour, fervour, intensity, heat, fire, vehemence. **5** *show feeling for others* sympathy, pity, compassion, understanding, concern, sensitivity, tender-heartedness, grief, commiseration, condolence, empathy, fellow-feeling. **6** *my feeling is that will go* instinct, opinion, intuition, impression, point of view, thought, way of thinking, theory, hunch. **7** *a feeling of neglect about the place* feel, atmosphere, ambience, aura, mood, air, impression; *inf.* vibrations, vibes.

feeling adjective **1** *a feeling person* sensitive, warm, tender, caring, soft-hearted, sympathetic, compassionate, responsive, sentient, sensible, emotional, demonstrative. **2** *a feeling letter* emotional, passionate, impassioned, ardent, intense, fervent, fervid.

feelings plural noun *hurt their feelings | strong feelings* sensibilities, sensitivities, self-esteem, ego; emotions, passions, sentiments.

feign verb **1** *feign sleep* fake, simulate, sham, affect, give the appearance of. **2** *he's only feigning* pretend, fake, make believe, sham, put it on, act, play-act, malinger.

felicitations plural noun congratulations, good wishes, best wishes, blessings, greetings, salutations, compliments.

felicitous adjective **1** *a felicitous expression* apt, well-chosen, well-expressed, well-put, fitting, suitable, appropriate, apposite, pertinent, germane, to the point. **2** *a felicitous event* happy, joyful, harmonious, fortunate, lucky, successful, prosperous.

feline adjective catlike, leonine, graceful, sinuous, slinky, sensual, stealthy, insidious.

fell verb **1** *fell a tree/building* cut down, hew, level, raze, raze to the ground, demolish, knock down. **2** *fell him with one blow* knock down/over, strike down, flatten, ground, floor, prostrate, overthrow, kill.

fellow noun **1** *that fellow over there* man, male, boy, person, individual; *inf.* chap, bloke, guy, codger, character, customer. **2** *the drunk and his fellows were thrown out* friend, companion, crony, mate, associate, colleague, comrade, partner, co-worker; *inf.* chum, pal, buddy. **3** *wish to impress his fellows* peer, compeer, equal, contemporary, confrère. **4** *the fellow of the shoe* counterpart, mate, partner, match, twin, brother, double.

fellowship noun **1** *join the club for fellowship* companionship, companionability, sociability, comradeship, fraternization, camaraderie, friendship, amiability, amity, affability, geniality, kindliness, cordiality, intimacy, social intercourse; *inf.* chumminess, palliness, clubbiness. **2** *the church fellowship* association, society, club, league, union, guild, affiliation, order, fraternity, brotherhood, sorority, sodality, amalgamation, consortium, corporation.

female *noun* **1** *two males and a female* woman, lady, girl, lass; *inf.* bird, chick, dame. **2** *animals which are female* cow, duck, bitch, ewe, mare, sow, nanny goat, hen, doe, vixen.

female *adjective* feminine, womanly, womanlike, ladylike.
Opposites MALE.

feminine *adjective* **1** *a very feminine young woman* soft, delicate, gentle, tender, graceful, womanly, ladylike, girlish, refined, modest. **2** *a feminine man* effeminate, womanish, effete, unmanly, unmasculine, weak; *inf.* sissy, sissyish, limp-wristed.
Opposites MASCULINE; MANNISH; MANLY.

fence *noun* **1** *a fence round the field/town* enclosure, barrier, paling, railing, rail, wall, hedge; barricade, rampart, stockade, palisade, circumvallation. **2** *stolen goods from the fence* receiver, dealer. **on the fence** uncommitted, uncertain, undecided, vacillating, irresolute, neutral, impartial.

fence *verb* **1** *fence the garden* | *fence off the field* enclose, surround, circumscribe, encircle, encompass. **2** *fence in the cows* shut in, confine, pen, separate off, secure, imprison. **3** *he fences as a hobby* go fencing, engage in swordplay/ swordsmanship. **4** *fence when asked questions* hedge, be evasive, beat about the bush, dodge the issue, parry questions, prevaricate, equivocate, fudge the issue, shilly-shally, vacillate, tergiversate.

fencing *noun. See table.*

FENCING TERMS		
blade	en garde		mask
corps à	on guard	parry
corps	épée	piste
counter-	feint	remise
attack	flèche	riposte
counter-	foil	running
riposte	foil button	attack
coupé	foil grip	sabre
cutover	foil guard	supination
electrical	guard	touch
foil	lunge	touché

fend *verb fend off their blows* | *fend off questions* ward off, keep off, turn aside, stave off, divert, deflect, avert, defend oneself against, guard against, parry, forestall. **fend for oneself** provide/shift for oneself, take care of oneself, get by.

ferment *noun* **1** *use a ferment in the beer* fermenting substance, fermentation agent, yeast, mould, bacteria, leaven, leavening. **2** *children in a ferment of excitement* stir, fever, furore, frenzy, brouhaha, confusion, fuss, stew, hub-

bub, hurly-burly, racket, imbroglio; tumult, commotion, uproar, turmoil, agitation, disruption, turbulence.

ferment *verb* **1** *beer/yeast mixtures fermenting* undergo fermentation, foam, froth, bubble, effervesce, seethe, boil, rise, work. **2** *ferment the beer/yeast mixture* subject to fermentation, cause to effervesce. **3** *his words fermenting the crowd* excite, agitate, inflame, incite. **4** *ferment trouble* cause, incite, excite, provoke, arouse, stir up, foment. **5** *the crowd fermenting with excitement* seethe, smoulder, boil, be agitated.

ferocious *adjective* **1** *a ferocious animal* fierce, savage, wild, feral, untamed, predatory, rapacious. **2** *ferocious troops* fierce, savage, ruthless, brutal, brutish, cruel, pitiless, merciless, vicious, violent, inexorable, barbarous, barbaric, inhuman, bloodthirsty, murderous, tigerish, wolfish. **3** *ferocious heat* fierce, very great, intense, extreme, acute.
Opposites TAME; GENTLE; MILD.

ferret *verb* **1** *ferreting in her handbag* rummage, search about, scrabble around, rifle through, forage around, sift through. **2** *ferret out the facts* search out, unearth, discover, disclose, elicit, bring to light, get at, run to earth, track down, dig up, root out, hunt out, drive out, fish out, nose out, sniff out, smell out.

ferry *noun the ferry runs hourly* ferryboat, shuttle, packet boat, packet.

ferry *verb* **1** *the boat ferries across everyday* go back and forth, come and go, run, shuttle. **2** *ferry the passengers across the water* carry, transport, convey, run, ship, shuttle, chauffeur.

fertile *adjective* **1** *fertile soil* fruitful, productive, fecund, rich. **2** *fertile young people* potent, virile, child-producing, fecund, generative, reproductive, propagative. **3** *fertile imaginations* inventive, creative, original, ingenious, resourceful, visionary, constructive, productive.
Opposites INFERTILE; BARREN; UNIMAGINATIVE.

fertilize *verb* **1** *fertilize the soil* add fertilizer to, feed, enrich, mulch, compost, dress, top-dress. **2** *fertilize the egg/cow* impregnate, inseminate, fecundate, make pregnant. **3** *fertilize the plant* pollinate, make fruitful, fructify.

fertilizer *noun* plant food, manure, dung, compost, dressing, top-dressing; bone-meal, guano, marl.

fervent *adjective* passionate, ardent, impassioned, intense, vehement, heartfelt, fervid, emotional, emotive, warm, devout, sincere, eager, earnest, zealous, enthusiastic, excited, animated, spirited; *lit.* perfervid.
Opposites APATHETIC; COLD; UNEMOTIONAL.

fervid *adjective* fervent, passionate, ardent, impassioned, intense. *See* FERVOUR.

fervour *noun* fervency, passion, ardour, impassionedness, intensity, vehemency, fervidness, emotion, warmth, devoutness, sincerity, eagerness, earnestness, zeal, enthusiasm, excitement, animation, spirit; *inf.* perfervidness.
Opposites APATHY; INDIFFERENCE.

fester verb **1** a wound festering suppurate, matter, come to a head, gather, maturate, run, discharge. **2** animal corpses festering rot, decay, go bad, go off, decompose, disintegrate. **3** resentment festering in their minds rankle, chafe, gnaw, cause bitterness/resentment/vexation.

festival noun **1** a church festival saint's day, holy day, feast day, holiday, anniversary, commemoration, rite, ritual, day of observance. See table. See also table at SAINT. **2** the Edinburgh festival festival of music and drama, musical festival, festival of music, arts festival, science festival. **3** take part in the town's annual festival fête, gala day, carnival; celebrations, festivities; Welsh eisteddfod.

festive adjective festive occasions joyous, joyful, happy, jolly, merry, gay, jovial, light-hearted, cheerful, cheery, jubilant, convivial, good-time, gleeful, mirthful, uproarious, rollicking, backslapping, celebratory, gala, holiday, carnival, sportive, festal.

festivity noun **1** the festivity of the occasion joyfulness, jollity, merriment, pleasure, amusement, gaiety, cheerfulness, jubilance, convivialness, cheeriness, gleefulness, glee, mirthfulness, mirth, revelry, sportiveness. **2** enjoy the festivities festive event, celebration, festival, entertainment, party, jollification, revelry, carousal, sport; fun and games, celebrations, festive proceedings.

festoon noun a festoon of flowers garland, wreath, chaplet, lei, swathe, swag.

festoon verb be festooned with flowers garland, wreathe, hang, drape, decorate, adorn, ornament, array, deck, bedeck, swathe, beribbon.

fetch verb **1** fetch the milk/doctor go and get, get, go for, bring, carry, deliver, convey, transport, escort, conduct, lead, usher in. **2** the vase fetched £40 sell for, go for, bring in, realize, yield, earn, cost, afford.

fetching adjective attractive, charming, enchanting, sweet, winsome, taking, captivating, fascinating, alluring.

fête noun gala, fair, garden party, sale of work.

fetish noun **1** a foot/leather fetish fixation, sexual fixation, compulsion, obsession, mania, idée fixe; inf. thing. **2** carry a fetish talisman, charm, amulet. See table at CHARM.

fetter verb **1** fetter the prisoners chain, chain up, shackles, bind, tie, tie up, hobble. **2** fettered by petty restrictions restrict, hinder, impede, obstruct, constrain, confine, restrain.

fetters plural noun chains, shackles, bond, irons, manacles, trammels; restraint, check.

fettle noun condition, shape, form, state, order, way; inf. kilter.

feud noun **1** a state of feud between the families vendetta, rivalry, hostility, enmity, conflict, strife, discord, bad blood, animosity, antagonism, unfriendliness, grudge, estrangement, schism. **2** start a feud vendetta, quarrel, conflict, argument, bickering, falling-out, broil.

fever noun **1** the child's fever subsided feverishness, febricity; Med. pyrexia; inf. temperature, temp. **2** in a fever of excitement ferment, frenzy, furore; turmoil, agitation, excitement, restlessness, unrest, passion, intensity.

feverish adjective **1** the child is feverish fevered, febrile, burning, hot. **2** look feverish flushed,

RELIGIOUS FESTIVALS					
Festival	Religion	Month	Festival	Religion	Month
Epiphany	Christian	January	Raksha Bandhan	Hindu	August
New Year	Chinese	January/	Lammas	Pagan	August
		February	Janmashtami	Hindu	August/
Shrove Tuesday	Christian	February/March			September
Ash Wednesday	Christian	February/March	Moon Festival	Chinese	September
Purim	Jewish	February/March	Rosh Hashana	Jewish	September/
Mahashivaratri	Hindu	February/March			October
Holi	Hindu	February/March	Yom Kippur	Jewish	September/
Easter	Christian	March/April			October
Passover	Jewish	March/April	Succoth	Jewish	September/
Holi Mohalla	Sikh	March/April			October
Rama Naumi	Hindu	March/April	Dusshera	Hindu	October
Ching Ming	Chinese	March/April	Samhain	Pagan	October
Baisakhi	Sikh	April	Diwali	Hindu/Sikh	October/
Beltane	Pagan	April			November
Lailat ul-Isra			Guru Nanak's		
wal Mi'raj	Islamic	April/May	Birthday	Sikh	November
Lailat ul-Bara'h	Islamic	April/May	Bodhi Day	Buddhist	November
Vesak	Buddhist	April/May	Christmas	Christian	December
Shavuoth	Jewish	May/June	Hanukkah	Jewish	December
Lailat ul-Qadr	Islamic	May/June	Winter Festival	Chinese	December
Eid ul-Fitr	Islamic	May/June	Birthday of Guru		
Martyrdom of			Gobind Singh	Sikh	December/
Guru Arjan	Sikh	May/June			January
Dragon Boat			Martyrdom of		
Festival	Chinese	June	Guru Tegh		
Dhammacakka	Buddhist	July	Bahadur	Sikh	December/
Eid ul-Adha	Islamic	July			January

red-faced, red. **3** *feverish excitement* frenzied, frenetic, agitated, excited, restless, nervous, worked up, overwrought, frantic, distracted, flustered, impatient; *inf.* in a tizzy.

few *adjective* **1** *few people were there* not many, hardly any, scarcely any, one or two, a handful of, a sprinkling of; *inf.* a couple of. **2** *very few buses* few and far between, infrequent, sporadic, irregular. **3** *opportunities are few* scarce, rare, negligible, scant, thin on the ground. *Opposites* MANY; FREQUENT; PLENTIFUL.

few *noun a few were there* a small number, one or two, a handful, a sprinkling.

fiancé, fiancée *noun* husband-to-be, wife-to-be, bride-to-be, future husband/wife, prospective husband/wife, prospective spouse, betrothed; *inf.* intended.

fiasco *noun* failure, disaster, catastrophe, mess, ruination, debacle, abortion; *inf.* flop, wash-out.

fib *noun tell a fib* lie, white lie, untruth, falsehood, fabrication, piece of fiction, fiction, fairy story, tall tale; *inf.* terminological inexactitude, whopper.

fibre *noun* **1** *the fibres of the carpet* thread, strand, tendril, filament, fibril. **2** *made of a coarse fibre* material, substance, cloth, stuff. *See table at* FABRIC. **3** *a person of a different fibre* character, nature, make-up, spirit, disposition, temperament. *See* MORAL FIBRE.

fickle *adjective* capricious, changeable, variable, unpredictable, volatile, mercurial, inconstant, unstable, vacillating, unsteady, unfaithful, faithless, irresolute, flighty, giddy, erratic, fitful, irregular, mutable. *Opposites* CONSTANT; STABLE.

fickleness *noun* capriciousness, unpredictableness, volatility, inconstancy, instability, vacillation, unfaithfulness, fitfulness, mutability. *See* FICKLE.

fiction *noun* **1** *a work of fiction* story telling, story narration, romance, fable, fantasy, legend. **2** *guilty of a polite fiction* piece of fiction, fabrication, invention, concoction, lie, fib, untruth, falsehood, fairy tale/story, tall story, improvisation, prevarication; *inf.* cock and bull story, whopper, angler's tale. *Opposites* FACT; TRUTH.

fictional *adjective a fictional character* fictitious, made up, invented, imaginary, unreal, non-existent. *Opposites* REAL; ACTUAL.

fictitious *adjective* **1** *a fictitious character* made up, imaginary. *See* FICTIONAL. **2** *a fictitious address* false, untrue, bogus, sham, counterfeit, fake, fabricated. **3** *a fictitious name* false, assumed, invented, made up, concocted, spurious, improvised. **4** *his account is fictitious* made up, untrue, false, imagined, imaginary, apocryphal. *Opposites* FACTUAL; REAL; GENUINE.

fiddle *noun* **1** *play the fiddle* violin, viola, cello, double bass. **2** *the new appointment was a fiddle* fraud, fix, swindle, wangle, racket, bit of sharp practice.

fiddle *verb* **1** *stop fiddling with your pencil* | *he's fiddling about* fidget with, play with, fuss with, toy with, finger, mess about with, fool around with; waste time, act aimlessly. **2** *he's fiddling with the engine* tinker with, play about with, tamper with, interfere with; *inf.* monkey around with. **3** *fiddle one's tax return* falsify; *inf.* cook. **4** *someone in the accounts department has been fiddling* cheat, swindle; *inf.* diddle, finagle, cook the books.

fiddling *adjective a fiddling amount* trifling, insignificant, trivial, petty, small; *inf.* piddling.

fidelity *noun* **1** *his fidelity to his wife/king* faithfulness, loyalty, devotedness, devotion, allegiance, commitment, constancy, true-heartedness, trustworthiness, dependability, reliability, staunchness, obedience. **2** *the fidelity of the copy* accuracy, exactness, exactitude, precision, preciseness, strictness, closeness, faithfulness, correspondence, conformity, authenticity. *Opposites* DISLOYALTY; TREACHERY; PERFIDY.

fidget *verb* **1** *children fidgeting* move restlessly, wriggle, squirm, twitch, jiggle; *inf.* have ants in one's pants. **2** *fidget with one's pencil* fiddle with, play with, fuss with. *See* FIDDLE *verb* 1. **3** *his silence fidgeted her* worry, make uneasy, agitate, bother, upset, ruffle.

fidgety *adjective* restless, restive, on edge, jumpy, uneasy, nervous, nervy, twitchy; *inf.* jittery, like a cat on hot bricks.

field *noun* **1** *cows in the field* pasture, meadow; grassland; *lit.* glebe, lea, mead, sward, greensward. **2** *specializing in the field of electronics* area, area of activity, sphere, regime, discipline, province, department, line, speciality, métier. **3** *in his field of vision* range, scope, purview; limits, confines. **4** *the field for the race/job is high quality* applicants, candidates, entrants, competitors, runners, possibles, possibilities; competition.

field *verb* **1** *field the ball* catch, stop, retrieve, return, throw back. **2** *field questions deftly* deal with, handle, cope with, deflect, turn aside.

fiend *noun* **1** *fiends of hell* devil, demon, evil spirit, cacodemon. **2** *the slavemaster was a fiend* brute, savage, beast, barbarian, monster, ogre, sadist, blackguard. **3** *a drugs fiend* addict, abuser, user. **4** *a cinema fiend* addict, fanatic, maniac, enthusiast, devotee, fan, aficionado; *inf.* buff, freak, nut.

fiendish *adjective* **1** *a fiendish stepfather* wicked, cruel, brutal, brutish, savage, barbaric, barbarous, inhuman, murderous, vicious, bloodthirsty, ferocious, ruthless, heartless, pitiless, merciless, black-hearted, unfeeling, malevolent, malicious, villainous, odious, base, malignant, devilish, diabolical, hellish, demonic, satanic, ungodly. **2** *a fiendish plan to leave early* cunning, clever, ingenious. **3** *a fiendish problem* difficult, complex, complicated, intricate.

fierce *adjective* **1** *a fierce animal/enemy* ferocious, savage, wild, vicious, feral, untamed, bloodthirsty, dangerous, cruel, brutal, murderous, slaughterous, menacing, threatening, terrible, grim, tigerish, wolfish. **2** *a fierce love*

intense, ardent, passionate, impassioned, fervent, fervid, fiery, uncontrolled. **3** *a fierce wind* violent, strong, stormy, blustery, gusty, boisterous, tempestuous, raging, furious, turbulent, tumultuous, cyclonic, typhonic. **4** *suffer from fierce headaches* very bad, severe, intense, grave, awful, dreadful. **5** *fierce competition* competitive, keen, intense, strong, relentless, cut-throat.
Opposites TAME; GENTLE; MILD.

fight verb **1** *the armies fought* battle, do battle, give battle, war, wage war, go to war, make war, attack, mount an attack, take up arms, combat, engage, meet, come to blows, exchange blows, close, clash, skirmish, struggle, contend, grapple, wrestle, scuffle, tussle, collide, spar, joust, tilt. **2** *the two men fought* come to blows, exchange blows, attack/assault each other, hit/punch each other, box, brawl; *inf.* scrap. **3** *the two families have been fighting for years* feud, quarrel, argue, bicker, squabble, wrangle, dispute, be at odds, disagree, battle, altercate; *inf.* fall out. **4** *we fought the council's decision* contest, take a stand against, oppose, dispute, object to, withstand, resist, defy, strive/struggle against, take issue with. **5** *fight a battle* wage, carry on, conduct, engage in, wage, prosecute. **fight back 1** *children told to fight back* defend oneself, put up a fight, retaliate, counter-attack, give tit for tat, reply. **2** *fight back the tears* suppress, repress, check, curb, restrain, contain, bottle up. **fight off** ward off, beat off, stave off, repel, repulse, hold at bay, resist.

fight noun **1** *the army lost the last fight* battle, engagement, action, clash, conflict, combat, contest, encounter, skirmish, scuffle, tussle, brush, exchange. *See table at* BATTLE. **2** *a fight outside the pub* brawl, row, affray, fracas, mêlée, sparring match, exchange, free-for-all, struggle, disturbance; fisticuffs; *inf.* set-to, scrap, punch-up. **3** *the two families have had a fight* quarrel, disagreement, difference of opinion, dispute, argument, altercation, feud. **4** *lose all the fight in him* spirit, will to win, gameness, pluck, aggression, belligerence, militancy, resistance, power to resist.

fighter noun **1** *the military fighters* fighting man/woman, soldier, man-at-arms, warrior; armed aircraft. *See table at* MILITARY. **2** *place bets on the younger fighter* boxer, pugilist, wrestler; prizefighter, champion wrestler; *inf.* champ, bruiser. **3** *fighters for the title* contestant, contender, competitor, rival.

figurative adjective non-literal, metaphorical, allegorical, representative, emblematic, symbolic, imagistic.

figure noun **1** *illegible figures | add up the figures* number, whole number, numeral, digit, integer, cipher, numerical symbol. **2** *be unable to put a figure on the work involved* cost, price, amount, value, total, sum, aggregate. **3** *figures unrecognizable in the mist* shape, form, outline, silhouette. **4** *have a well-developed figure* body, physique, build, frame, torso; proportions; *inf.* vital statistics, chassis. **5** *see figure 20* diagram, illustration, picture, drawing, sketch, chart, plan, map. **6** *artists good at drawing figures* human representation, likeness, image of a person. **7** *the lily is a figure of purity* symbol, emblem, sign, representative. **8** *the figures on the wood* pattern, design, motif, device, depiction. **9** *one of the figures of the town council* dignitary, notable, notability, personage, somebody, worthy, celebrity, leader, force, personality, presence, character; *inf.* big shot, big noise, bigwig, big Daddy, Mr Big.

figure verb **1** *figure up the row of numbers* count, calculate, add up, tot up, work out, total, sum, tally, reckon, compute. **2** *she figures in his autobiography* appear, feature, be featured/mentioned, be referred to, play a part/role, be conspicuous. **3** *we figure that they'll go* think, consider, conclude. **4** *that figures* be likely/probable, be understandable, make sense. **figure out 1** *figure out the cost* work out, calculate, compute, reckon, assess. **2** *figure out why they came* understand, comprehend, work out, make out, fathom, see, reason, imagine, decipher, resolve; *inf.* make head or tail of, twig.

figurehead noun **1** *the king is just a figurehead* titular head, nominal leader, cipher, token, mouthpiece, puppet, man of straw. **2** *figurehead on the ship's prow* carving, bust, sculpture, image, statue.

figure of speech noun. *See table at* RHETORIC.

figures plural noun *good at figures* arithmetic, counting; calculations, statistics.

filament noun fibre, fibril, thread, strand, string, tendril, wire, cable, cord.

filch verb steal, thieve, pilfer, rob, take, purloin, abstract, misappropriate, embezzle, shoplift; *inf.* walk off with, nick, swipe, snaffle, lift, snitch, knock off.

file¹ noun **1** *put documents/data in a file* folder, box, portfolio, document case, filing cabinet; card file, computer file, data file. **2** *get out your file* dossier, information; documents, records, data, particulars, case notes. **3** *a file of people* line, column, row, string, chain, queue.

file² verb **1** *file the information* categorize, classify, organize, put in place, put in order, pigeon-hole, put on record, record, enter, store. **2** *file for divorce* apply for, put in for, register for, sign up for. **3** *people filing in* walk/march in a line, march, parade, troop, pass in formation.

file³ verb *file one's nails* smooth, shape, buff, rub, rub down, polish, burnish, furbish, refine, scrape, abrade, rasp, sandpaper, pumice.

filigree noun wirework, fretwork, fret, latticework, lattice, grillwork, scrollwork.

fill verb **1** *fill the cup | the pond slowly filled* make/become full, fill up, fill to the brim, fill to overflowing. **2** *people filled the room* occupy all of, crowd, overcrowd, congest, cram, pervade. **3** *fill the shelves* stock, pack, load, supply, furnish, provide, replenish, restock, refill. **4** *fill the children* feed fully, satisfy, stuff, cram, satiate, sate, surfeit, glut. **5** *perfume/hostility filled the air* pervade, spread throughout, permeate, suffuse, imbue, charge, saturate. **6** *fill the hole* stop, stop up, block up, bung up, plug, seal, close, clog. **7** *he filled the post of manager* occupy, hold, take up. **8** *fill the order/commission* carry out, execute, perform, complete, fulfil. **fill in 1** *fill in the form* complete, answer, fill up; *Am.* fill out. **2** *fill in for the manager* deputize, substitute, stand in, take over. **3** *fill me in on the events* inform, advise, tell, notify, acquaint, apprise, up date; *inf.* put wise, put in the picture. **fill out 1** *the children have filled out*

grow fatter, become plumper/rounder. **2** *fill out the story* round out, expand.
Opposites EMPTY; VACATE.

fill *noun* **one's fill** *eat one's fill | have had one's fill of her* all one wants, as much as one can take, enough, more than enough, plenty, ample, sufficient.

fillip *noun* stimulus, incentive, encouragement, inducement, motivation, spur, goad, prod, push.

FILM STARS

Allen, Woody (b. 1935; Am. also director)	Davis, Bette (1908–89; Am.)	Hepburn, Katharine (b. 1909; Am.)	Peck, Gregory (b. 1916; Am.)
Astaire, Fred (1899–1987; Am. also dancer)	Dean, James (1931–55; Am.)	Hepburn, Audrey (1929–93; Am., b. in Belgium)	Pickford, Mary (1893–1979; Am., b. in Canada)
Attenborough, Richard, Baron (b. 1923; Brit. also director)	Deneuve, Catherine (b. 1943; Fr.) De Niro, Robert (b. 1943; Am.)	Hoffman, Dustin (b. 1937; Am.) Hopkins, Sir Anthony (b. 1937; Welsh)	Poitier, Sidney (b. 1924; Am., b. in the Bahamas) Quinn, Anthony (b. 1915; Am., b. in Mexico)
Bacall, Lauren (b. 1924; Am.)	Depardieu, Gérard (b. 1948; Fr.) Dietrich, Marlene	Kapoor, Raj (1924–88; Ind.)	Reagan, Ronald (b. 1911; Am.)
Bankhead, Tallulah (1903–68; Am.)	(1901–92; Am., b. in Germany)	Karloff, Boris (1887–1969; Brit.)	Redford, Robert (b. 1936; Am.)
Bardot, Brigitte (b. 1934; Fr.)	Eastwood, Clint (b. 1930; Am. also director)	Keaton, Buster (1895–1966; Am.)	Robinson, Edward G. (1893–1972; Am., b. in Romania)
Bergman, Ingrid (1915–82; Am., b. in Sweden)	Fairbanks, Douglas (1883–1939; Am.) Fields, W. C.	Kelly, Gene (b. 1912; Am. also dancer) Kelly, Grace	Rogers, Ginger (1911–95; Am. also dancer)
Bogarde, Sir Dirk (b. 1921; Brit.)	(1880–1946; Am.) Flynn, Errol	(1929–82; Am.) Laughton, Charles	Schwarzenegger, Arnold (b. 1942; Am., b. in Austria)
Bogart, Humphrey (1899–1957; Am.)	(1909–59; Am., b. in Australia)	(1899–1962; Am., b. in Britain)	Sellers, Peter (1925–80; Brit.)
Bow, Clara (1905–65; Am.)	Fonda, Henry (1905–82; Am.)	Lee, Bruce (1940–73; Am.)	Stallone, Sylvester (b. 1946; Am.)
Boyer, Charles (1897–1978; Fr.)	Fonda, Jane (b. 1937; Am.)	Leigh, Vivien (1913–67; Brit., b. in India)	Stewart, James (b. 1908; Am.)
Brando, Marlon (b. 1924; Am.)	Ford, Harrison (b. 1942; Am.)	Lemmon, Jack (b. 1925; Am.)	Streep, Meryl (b. 1949; Am.)
Brooks, Mel (b. 1926; Am.)	Foster, Jodie (b. 1962; Am.)	Loren, Sophia (b. 1934; Fr., b. in Italy)	Swanson, Gloria (1899–1983; Am.)
Burton, Richard (1925–84; Welsh)	Gable, Clark (1901–60; Am.)	Maclaine, Shirley (b. 1934; Am.)	Tati, Jacques (1908–82; Fr.)
Cagney, James (1899–1986; Am.)	Garbo, Greta (1905–90; Am., b. in Sweden)	McQueen, Steve (1930–80; Am.) Mason, James	Taylor, Elizabeth (b. 1932; Am., b. in Britain)
Caine, Sir Michael (b. 1933; Brit.)	Garland, Judy (1922–69; Am.)	(1909–84; Brit.) Mastroianni, Marcello (b. 1924; It.)	Tracy, Spencer (1900–67; Am.)
Chan, Jackie (b. 1954; Hong Kong also director)	Gibson, Mel (b. 1956; Austral., b. in America, also director)	Mercouri, Melina (1925–94; Gk)	Valentino, Rudolf (1895–1926; Am., b. in Italy)
Chaplin, Charlie (1889–1977; Am., b. in Britain)	Gish, Lillian (1893–1993; Am.)	Mifune, Toshiro (b. 1920; Jap.)	Wayne, John (1907–79; Am.)
Close, Glenn (b. 1947; Am.)	Goldberg, Whoopi (b. 1949; Am.)	Mills, Sir John (b. 1908; Brit.)	Weaver, Sigourney (b. 1949; Am.)
Connery, Sean (b. 1930; Scot.)	Grant, Cary (1904–86; Am., b. in Britain)	Monroe, Marilyn (1926–62; Am.)	Welles, Orson (1915–85; Am. also director)
Cooper, Gary (1901–61; Am.)	Guinness, Sir Alec (b. 1914; Brit.)	Newman, Paul (b. 1925; Am.)	West, Mae (1892–1980; Am.)
Costner, Kevin (b. 1955; Am. also director)	Harlow, Jean (1911–37; Am.)	Nicholson, Jack (b. 1937; Am.)	
Crawford, Joan (1908–77; Am.)	Hayworth, Rita (1918–87; Am.)	Pacino, Al (b. 1939; Am.)	

film noun **1** *a film of dust* layer, coat, coating, covering, cover, dusting, sheet, blanket, skin, tissue, membrane, pellicle. **2** *see the mountain through a film* haze, mist, cloud, blur, veil; murkiness. **3** *see a recent film* movie, picture; *Am.* motion picture; *inf.* flick.

film verb **1** *film the wedding* photograph, record on film, take pictures of, shoot, make a film of, televise, video. **2** *her eyes filmed over* become blurred, blur, cloud over, mist over, dull, blear.

film star noun. *See table. See also table at* ACTOR.

filmy adjective diaphanous, transparent, see-through, translucent, sheer, gauzelike, gauzy, gossamer, gossamery, cobwebby, delicate, fine, light, thin, airy, floaty, fragile, flimsy, unsubstantial.

filter noun *strain the coffee through a filter* strainer, sieve, sifter, riddle, colander, gauze, netting, cheesecloth.

filter verb **1** *filter the coffee* strain, sieve, sift, riddle, filtrate; clarify, purify, clear, refine. **2** *liquid filtering through* trickle, ooze, seep, leak, dribble, percolate, flow out, drain, well, exude, escape, leach.

filth noun **1** *the floors covered in filth | the filth of the house* dirt, muck, grime, mud, mire, sludge, slime, squalor, foul matter, excrement, dung, manure, ordure, sewage, rubbish, refuse, garbage, trash, pollution, contamination, defilement, rotting material, decay, putrefaction, putrescence; filthiness, uncleanness, foulness, nastiness; *inf.* crud. **2** *objecting to filth in magazines* pornography, obscenity, indecency, smut, corruption, vulgarity, vileness; *inf.* porn, hard porn, raunchiness.

filthy adjective **1** *filthy canals* dirty, mucky, muddy, murky, slimy, squalid, unclean, foul, nasty, feculent, polluted, contaminated, rotten, decaying, smelly, fetid, putrid, faecal. **2** *filthy faces/clothes* unwashed, unclean, dirty, dirt-encrusted, grubby, muddy, mucky, black, blackened, begrimed. **3** *a filthy liar* low, despicable, contemptible, base, mean, vile, nasty, sordid. **4** *filthy magazines* pornographic, obscene, indecent, smutty, corrupt, coarse, bawdy, vulgar, lewd, licentious, vile, depraved, foul, dirty, impure; *inf.* blue, raunchy. **Opposites** SPOTLESS; CLEAN; PURE.

final adjective **1** *the final act* last, closing, concluding, finishing, end, ending, terminating, terminal, ultimate, eventual, endmost. **2** *their decision is final* absolute, conclusive, irrevocable, unalterable, irrefutable, incontrovertible, indisputable, unappealable, decisive, definitive, definite, settled, determinate. **Opposites** FIRST; INTRODUCTORY.

finale noun end, finish, close, conclusion, climax, culmination, denouement, last act, final scene, final curtain, epilogue; *inf.* wind-up.

finality noun conclusiveness, decisiveness, definiteness, definitiveness, completeness, absoluteness, irrevocableness, irrefutability, inevitability, unavoidableness.

finalize verb complete, conclude, settle, decide, agree on, work out, tie up, wrap up, put the finishing touches to; *inf.* sew up, clinch.

finally adverb **1** *we finally won* in the end, at last, at long last, ultimately, eventually, at the last minute, at the very last minute, at length, in the long run, when all was said and done. **2** *"finally, I declare the meeting over"* to conclude, in conclusion, lastly. **3** *they have separated finally* absolutely, conclusively, irrevocably, decisively, definitively, definitely, for ever, for good, for all time, once and for all, permanently, inexorably.

finance noun **1** *she lectures/works in finance* financial affairs, money matters, pecuniary/fiscal matters, economics; money management, commerce, business, investment, banking, accounting. *See table. See also table at* ECONOMICS. **2** *finances are low* funds, assets, resources; money, capital, cash, wealth, wherewithal, revenue, stock; financial condition/state.

FINANCIAL TERMS

agio	Income Bonds
agiotage	inflation
arbitrage	inflationary spiral
bank rate	interest rate
bill of exchange	managed currency
bimetallism	minimum lending
capital-expenditure	rate
budget	money market
deflation	par
depreciation	parity
devaluation	PEP
disinflation	rallying
effective rate	reflation
equalization fund	revolving fund
exchange premium	shares
exchange rate	sinking fund
financial year	snake
floating currency	stagflation
foreign exchange	strong currency
market	TESSA
gilt-edged	unit trust
securities	valuta
gold standard	venture capital

---

finance verb pay for, fund, back, subsidize, underwrite, capitalize, guarantee, provide capital/security for, furnish credit for.

financial adjective money, monetary, pecuniary, fiscal, economic, budgetary.

find verb **1** *find a gold watch* come across, chance upon, light upon, happen upon, stumble on. **2** *find a cure/answer/hotel* discover, come up with, hit upon, turn up, bring to light, uncover, unearth, ferret out, locate, lay one's hands on, encounter. **3** *we found the missing glove* get back, recover, retrieve, regain, repossess, recoup. **4** *find the money | find happiness* get, obtain, acquire, procure, gain, earn, achieve, attain, win. **5** *find it pays to be honest | found that everyone had gone* discover, become aware, realize, learn, conclude, detect, observe, notice, note, perceive. **6** *find the cheese too strong* consider, regard as, think, judge, deem, gauge, rate. **7** *the arrow found its mark* reach, attain, arrive at, gain, achieve. **find out 1** *we found out they were lying* discover, become aware

that, realize, learn. *See* FIND *verb* 5.   **2** *find out the truth* discover, detect, bring to light, reveal, expose, unearth, disclose, unmask, ferret out, lay bare.
Opposites LOSE; MISLAY.

find *noun the vase is quite a find* asset, acquisition, lucky discovery, catch, bargain, good buy, godsend, boon, windfall.

finding *noun the finding of the committee | the findings of the court* decision, verdict, conclusion, pronouncement, judgement, decree, order, recommendation.

fine *adjective* **1** *that's fine with me* all right, satisfactory, acceptable, agreeable, convenient, suitable, good; *inf.* OK, tickety-boo.   **2** *I'm fine, thanks* all right, in good health, quite well; *inf.* OK.   **3** *a fine painting/performance/wine* excellent, first-class, first-rate, great, exceptional, outstanding, admirable, quality, superior, splendid, magnificent, beautiful, exquisite, choice, select, prime, supreme, rare; *inf.* A1, splendiferous, top-notch, top-hole.   **4** *a fine day* fair, dry, bright, clear, cloudless, sunny, balmy, clement.   **5** *fine china/bones* fragile, delicate, frail, dainty, slight.   **6** *fine material* sheer, light, lightweight, chiffony, diaphanous, filmy, gossamer, gossamery, gauzelike, gauzy, cobwebby, transparent, translucent, airy, ethereal, thin, flimsy.   **7** *a fine sand/powder* fine-grained, powdery, powdered, ground, crushed, pulverized, comminuted, triturated.   **8** *fine clothes* expensive, elegant, stylish, smart, chic, fashionable, modish, high-fashion, lavish.   **9** *fine gold* refined, pure, sterling, solid, unadulterated, unalloyed, unpolluted, one hundred per cent.   **10** *a fine distinction* subtle, fine-drawn, tenuous, hair-splitting, precise, minute, elusive, abstruse, nice, over-nice.   **11** *a fine taste in art* discriminating, discerning, tasteful, fastidious, critical, sensitive, refined, intelligent.   **12** *a fine mind* keen, acute, sharp, quick, perspicacious, clever, intelligent, brilliant, finely honed/tuned.   **13** *a fine young man/woman* good-looking, attractive, handsome, lovely, pretty, striking, well-favoured, bonny, smart-looking, comely, fair, seemly.
Opposites POOR; DULL; COARSE.

fine *noun get a fine for illegal parking* penalty, financial penalty, punishment, forfeit, forfeiture, mulct; damages.

fine *verb fine for stealing* impose a fine on, exact a penalty, penalize, punish by fining, mulct.

finery *noun* Sunday best, frippery, adornment, splendour, showiness, gaudiness, trumpery; elaborate/best clothes, trappings, decorations, gewgaws; *inf.* glad rags, best gear, best bib and tucker.

finesse *noun* **1** *handle the problem with finesse* tact, discretion, diplomacy, delicacy, refinement, grace, elegance, sophistication, subtlety, polish, savoir faire, skill, expertise, wisdom, worldly wisdom, craft; tactfulness, adroitness, adeptness, skilfulness, cleverness, artfulness.   **2** *win by a clever finesse* trick, stratagem, ruse, manoeuvre, scheme, artifice, machination, bluff, wile; *inf.* dodge.

finger *verb finger the fruit/material* touch, feel, handle, toy with, play about with, fiddle with, stroke, caress, maul, meddle with; *inf.* paw.

finicky *adjective* fussy, over-particular, fastidious, pernickety, hard to please, overcritical, difficult; *inf.* picky, choosy.

finish *verb* **1** *finish the task* complete, accomplish, execute, discharge, carry out, deal with, do, get done, fulfil, achieve, attain, end, conclude, close, bring to a conclusion/end/close, finalize, stop, cease, terminate, round off, put the finishing touches to; *inf.* wind up, wrap up, sew up, polish off, knock off.   **2** *finish working* stop, cease, discontinue, give up, have done with, suspend.   **3** *finish the milk | finish up/off the food* use, use up, consume, eat, devour, drink, exhaust, empty, deplete, drain, expend, dispatch, dispose of.   **4** *the job finished her | finish off the enemy* overcome, defeat, overpower, conquer, overwhelm, get the better of, best, worst, rout, bring down, put an end to, do away with, dispose of, get rid of, destroy, annihilate, kill, exterminate, liquidate, drive to the wall; *inf.* wipe out, do in.   **5** *finish her education* perfect, polish, refine, put the final/finishing touches to, crown.   **6** *finish the surface of the table/vase* put a finish on, varnish, lacquer, stain, coat, veneer, wax, gild, glaze, give a shine to, polish, burnish, smooth off.
Opposites START; BEGIN.

finish *noun* **1** *at the finish of the task/race* completion, accomplishment, execution, fulfilment, achievement, consummation, end, conclusion, close, closing, cessation, final act, finale, denouement; last stages; *inf.* winding-up.   **2** *the finish of the enemy* defeat, overpowering, destruction, rout, bringing down, end, annihilation, death, extermination, liquidation, ruination; *inf.* ruin, curtains.   **3** *people of finish* cultivation, culture, refinement, polish, style, sophistication, suaveness, urbanity, education.   **4** *a table/material with a beautiful finish* surface, texture, grain, veneer, coating, lacquer, glaze, lustre, gloss, polish, shine, patina, smoothness.

finished *adjective* **1** *finished tasks* completed, accomplished, executed, over and done with, over, in the past; *inf.* wrapped up, sewn up. *See* FINISH *verb* 1.   **2** *the finished milk bottle* empty, drained, used up, exhausted, spent.   **3** *a finished performance* accomplished, expert, proficient, masterly, polished, impeccable, classic, consummate, flawless, skilful, skilled, dexterous, adroit, professional, talented, gifted, elegant, graceful.   **4** *finished hopes | firms which are finished* at an end, gone, gone to the wall, over with, doomed, lost, ruined, bankrupt, wrecked; *inf.* washed up.

finite *adjective* not infinite, bounded, limited, subject to limitations, restricted, delimited, demarcated, terminable.

fire *noun* **1** *killed in a fire* blaze, conflagration, inferno, holocaust; flames.   **2** *hit by enemy fire* gunfire, sniping, flak, bombardment, shelling; volley, barrage, fusillade, salvo.   **3** *people of fire* energy, spirit, life, liveliness, animation, vigour, verve, vivacity, sparkle, scintillation, dash, vim, gusto, *élan*, enthusiasm, fervour, fervency, eagerness, impetuosity, force, potency, driving power, vehemence, ardour, passion, intensity, zeal; *inf.* pep. **4** *writings with fire* passion, ardour, intensity, inspiration, imagination, creativity, inventiveness, flair. **on fire 1** *houses on fire* burning, ablaze, blazing, aflame, in flames, flaming, alight, fiery. **2** *on fire with passion* passionate, ardent, fervent, intense, excited, eager, enthusiastic.

fire *verb* **1** *fire the haystacks* set fire to, set on fire, set alight, set ablaze, put a match to, light, ignite, kindle, enkindle. **2** *fire the guns* shoot, let off, discharge, trigger, set off. **3** *fire a missile* launch, hurl, discharge, eject. **4** *fire the explosives* explode, detonate, touch off. **5** *they fired him with enthusiasm* arouse, rouse, stir up, excite, enliven, inflame, put/breathe life into, animate, inspire, motivate, stimulate, incite, galvanize, electrify, impassion. **6** *fire the assistant* dismiss, discharge, declare redundant, give someone his/her marching orders, get rid of, show someone the door, oust, depose, cashier; *inf.* sack, give the sack to, axe.

firebrand *noun* troublemaker, agitator, rabble-rouser, demagogue, tub-thumper, soapbox orator.

fire-proof *adjective* non-flammable, non-inflammable, incombustible, unburnable, fire-resistant, flame-resistant, flame-retardant.

fireworks *plural noun* **1** *a fireworks display on Guy Fawkes night* pyrotechnics, *feu d'artifice*. See table. **2** *there were fireworks when she heard the news* tantrums, hysterics, paroxysms, pyrotechnics; outburst, fit, frenzy, uproar, row.

FIREWORKS	
banger	maroon
Bengal light	petard
Catherine wheel	pin-wheel
fizgig	rocket
fountain	Roman candle
girandole	serpent
golden rain	sparkler
indoor firework	squib
jumping jack	whizz-bang

firm *adjective* **1** *a firm surface* hard, hardened, stiff, rigid, inflexible, inelastic, unyielding, resistant, solid, solidified, compacted, compressed, condensed, dense, close-grained, congealed, frozen, set, jelled, stony, steely, adamantine. **2** *the poles were firm in the ground* fixed, fast, secure, secured, stable, set, established, tight, immovable, irremovable, unshakable, stationary, motionless, taut, anchored, rooted, embedded; riveted, braced, cemented, nailed, tied. **3** *firm plans* fixed, settled, decided, definite, established, unalterable, unchangeable. **4** *a firm handshake* strong, vigorous, sturdy. **5** *a firm friendship* constant, unchanging, enduring, abiding, durable, deep-rooted, long-standing, long-lasting, steady, stable, staunch. **6** *firm about not going* resolute, determined, decided, resolved, unfaltering, unwavering, unflinching, unswerving, unyielding, unbending, inflexible, obdurate, obstinate,

stubborn, hard line, strict, intransigent, unmalleable.
Opposites SOFT; FLABBY; UNSTABLE; INDEFINITE.

firm *noun a manufacturing firm* company, business, concern, house, establishment, organization, corporation, conglomerate, partnership, cooperative; *inf.* outfit.

firmament *noun* sky, heaven, blue sky, the blue, vault of heaven, vault, celestial sphere; heavens, skies; *lit.* empyrean, welkin.

firmness *noun* **1** *the firmness of the surface* hardness, stiffness, rigidity, inflexibility, inelasticity, resistance, solidity. See FIRM *adjective* 1. **2** *the firmness of the handshake* strength, vigour, sturdiness. **3** *the firmness of the friendship* constancy, endurance, durability, steadiness, stability, staunchness. See FIRM *adjective* 5. **4** *the firmness of the refusal/teacher* resolution, determination, resolve, strength/fixity of purpose, obduracy, inflexibility, stubbornness, strictness, intransigence. See FIRM *adjective* 6.

first *adjective* **1** *the first stages of man* earliest, initial, opening, introductory, original, premier, primitive, primeval, primordial, pristine. **2** *first principles* primary, beginning, basic, fundamental, key, rudimentary, cardinal. **3** *the first people in the land* leading, foremost, principal, highest, ruling, chief, head, main, major, greatest, pre-eminent, supreme.
Opposites LAST; SUBSIDIARY; LOWLY.

first *adverb* **1** *first he said he was a doctor* at first, to begin with, at the beginning/start, at the outset, initially. **2** *first we must wash our hands* before anything/all else, first and foremost. **3** *first, I don't want it, second...* in the first place, firstly. **4** *I'd die first* sooner, rather, in preference, more willingly.

first *noun from the first* beginning, very beginning, start, outset, commencement; *inf.* the word go.

firsthand *adverb/adjective learn firsthand* direct, directly, from the original source, straight from the horse's mouth.

first-rate *adjective* first-class, second to none, top, premier, superlative, prime, excellent, superb, outstanding, exceptional, tip-top, admirable; *inf.* top-notch, ace, A1, crack.

fiscal *adjective* financial, economic, monetary, money, pecuniary, capital.

fish *verb* **1** *boys fishing in the stream* go fishing, angle, cast. **2** *fish for keys* look for, search for, hunt for, grope for, delve for, cast about for. **fish out** pull out, haul out, extricate, extract, retrieve, produce.

fish *noun.* See table.

fisher *noun* fisherman, angler, piscator, piscatorian.

fishy *adjective* **1** *a fishy smell* fishlike, piscatorial, piscine. **2** *fishy eyes* expressionless, inexpressive, vacant, deadpan, wooden, dull, lacklustre, glassy, glass-eyed. **3** *something fishy about it* questionable, dubious, doubtful, suspect, suspicious, odd, queer, peculiar, strange, not quite right; *inf.* funny, shady, not kosher.

FISH

albacore	cod	half-beak	pike	smelt
alewife	coelacanth	halibut	pikeperch	smooth hound
allis shad	conger eel	hammerhead	pilchard	snake mackerel
amberjack	cornetfish	shark	pilot fish	snapper
anchovy	crappie	hatchetfish	pipefish	snipe fish
anemone fish	croaker	herring	piranha	snook
angelfish	crucian carp	hogfish	plaice	sockeye salmon
angel shark	cusk	horse mackerel	pollack	sole
angler fish	cutlass fish	houting	pollan	sparling
arapaima	dab	humpback	pomfret	spadefish
archer fish	dace	salmon	pompano	spearfish
argentine	damselfish	ice fish	pope	sprat
bandfish	danio	ide	porbeagle	stargazer
barbel	darter	jack	porcupine fish	sterlet
barracuda	dealfish	jewfish	porgy	stickleback
barramundí	devil ray	John Dory	pout	stingray
basking shark	discus	killifish	powan	stone bass
bass	dogfish	kingfish	puffer fish	stonefish
batfish	Dolly Varden	knifefish	pumpkinseed	sturgeon
beluga	dolphin-fish	koi carp	rabbitfish	sucker
bib	dorado	labyrinth fish	rainbow trout	sunfish
bichir	dory	lake trout	ratfish	surgeon fish
billfish	dragonet	lamprey	ray	swordfish
bitterling	dragonfish	lancetfish	redfin	swordtail
blackfish	drum	lantern fish	redfish	tarpon
bleak	eagle ray	leatherjacket	remora	tautog
blenny	eel	lemon sole	requiem shark	tench
blindfish	eelpout	ling	ribbonfish	tetra
blowfish	electric eel	livebearer	roach	thornback
bluefish	electric ray	lizardfish	rockling	threadfin
blue shark	elephant-snout	loach	roughy	thresher
boarfish	fish	lumpsucker	rudd	shark
Bombay duck	fighting fish	lungfish	ruffe	tigerfish
bonefish	filefish	mackerel	sailfish	tiger shark
bonito	firefish	madtom	saithe	toadfish
bonnethead	flatfish	mako	salmon	tomcod
bonnetmouth	flat-head	manta	sand eel	tommy ruff
bowfin	flounder	marlin	sandfish	toothcarp
boxfish	fluke	menhaden	sardine	tope
bream	flying fish	midshipman	sargassum fish	topminnow
brill	flying gurnard	miller's thumb	sauger	torpedo ray
brisling	four-eyed fish	minnow	saury	trevally
buffalo fish	frogfish	molly	sawfish	triggerfish
bullhead	garfish	monkfish	scad	trout
bummalo	garpike	moonfish	scat	trunkfish
burbot	glassfish	Moorish idol	scorpion fish	tuna
butterfish	globe-fish	moray eel	sculpin	turbot
butterfly fish	goatfish	mosquitofish	scup	twaite shad
butterfly ray	goby	mudfish	sea bass	vendace
candiru	goldfish	mudminnow	sea bream	viperfish
candlefish	goose-fish	mudskipper	sea horse	wahoo
capelin	gourami	mullet	sea perch	weakfish
carp	grayling	mummichog	searobin	weatherfish
carpet shark	grenadier	Murray cod	sea trout	weever
catfish	grouper	muskellunge	sergeant-fish	wels
cavefish	grunion	needlefish	shad	whale shark
char	grunt	nurse shark	shanny	whitebait
characin	gudgeon	oarfish	shark	whitefish
chimaera	guitarfish	oilfish	sharksucker	white shark
chub	gulper eel	old wife	sheepshead	whiting
chum salmon	gunnel	opah	shovelhead	wolf-fish
cichlid	gunnard	orfe	shovelnose	wrasse
cisco	gurnard	paddlefish	shubunkin	wreckfish
climbing perch	gwyniad	parrotfish	silverside	x-ray fish
clingfish	haddock	pearlfish	skate	yellowtail
coalfish	hagfish	perch	skipjack tuna	zander
cobia	hake	pickerel	skipper	zebra fish ·

fission noun splitting, parting, division, cleaving, rupture, breaking, severance, disjuncture, scission.

fissure noun opening, crack, crevice, cleft, chink, cranny, groove, slit, gash, gap, hole, breach, break, fracture, fault, rift, rupture, split, rent, interstice, scission.

fit adjective **1** *feeling fit* well, healthy, in good health, in shape, in good shape, in good trim, in trim, in good condition, strong, robust, hale and hearty, sturdy, hardy, stalwart, vigorous. **2** *fit to drive* able, capable, competent, adequate, good enough, satisfactory, ready, prepared, qualified, trained, equipped, eligible, worthy; *inf.* up to scratch. **3** *a fit occasion|fit behaviour* fitting, proper, due, seemly, decorous, decent, right, correct, apt, appropriate, *comme il faut*, suitable, convenient, apposite, relevant, pertinent.
Opposites UNHEALTHY; UNFIT; INAPPROPRIATE.

fit verb **1** *the shoes don't fit* be the right/correct size, be big/small enough, be the right shape. **2** *facts fitting our theory* agree with, be in agreement with, accord with, concur with, correspond with, match, dovetail with, tally with, suit, go with, be congruent with, conform to, be consonant with. **3** *fit the parts together* join, connect, put together. **4** *fit the carpet* put in place/position, position, lay, fix, insert, arrange, adjust, shape. **5** *fit your expenditure to your income* adjust, adapt, modify, alter, regulate, accommodate. **6** *the training will fit him for many jobs* make suitable, qualify, prepare, make ready, prime, condition, train. **7** *fit the kitchen with units* fit out, equip, provide, supply, furnish. **fit in** belong to, match, square with; accord, agree, concur, conform. **fit out/up** *fit out the caravan/army* equip, provide, supply, furnish, kit/rig out, outfit, accoutre.

fit noun **1** *an epileptic fit* convulsion, spasm, paroxysm, seizure, attack; *Med.* ictus. **2** *a fit of coughing* attack, bout, spell. **3** *a fit of the giggles* bout, burst, outburst, outbreak. **4** *she'll have a fit* fit of temper, tantrum, outburst of anger/rage. **5** *when the fit was on him* mood, whim, fancy, impulse, caprice. **by fits and starts** on and off, off and on, spasmodically, intermittently, sporadically, erratically, irregularly, interruptedly, fitfully.

fitful adjective *fitful sleep* broken, disturbed, irregular, uneven, intermittent, sporadic, spasmodic, disconnected, unsteady, variable.

fitness noun **1** *improve your fitness* physical fitness, health, good health, condition, shape, good condition/shape, strength, robustness, sturdiness, vigour. **2** *his fitness to drive* ability, capability, competency, preparedness, qualification, eligibility, worthiness. *See* FIT *adjective* 2. **3** *the fitness of the occasion* properness, propriety, seemliness, correctness, aptness, suitability, convenience, relevance, pertinence. *See* FIT *adjective* 3.

fitted adjective **1** *not fitted to the life* suited, suitable, right, equipped, cut out for. **2** *fitted wardrobes* built-in, fixed, permanent. **3** *fitted sheets* fitting tightly/well, shaped.

fitting adjective *a fitting occasion|not fitting to go early* fit, proper, due, right, suitable, appropriate, *comme il faut*. *See* FIT *adjective* 3.

fitting noun **1** *an electrical fitting* part, piece, component, attachment, accessory. **2** *kitchen fittings* furnishings, units, fixtures, appointments, accoutrements, appurtenances; furniture, equipment.

fix verb **1** *fix the shelf to the wall* fasten, secure, make fast, attach, connect, join, couple; stick, glue, cement, pin, nail, screw, bolt, clamp, bind, tie, pinion. **2** *fix the post in the ground* plant, implant, install, anchor, embed, establish, position, station, situate. **3** *fix a date/price* decide on, settle, set, agree on, arrive at, arrange, determine, establish, define, name, specify. **4** *fix the car* repair, mend, sort, see to, patch up, put right, put to rights, restore, remedy, rectify, adjust. **5** *fix her gaze on them* direct, focus, level at, rivet. **6** *fix the colour/dye* make fast, set, make permanent. **7** *has the glue fixed?* set, solidify, congeal, harden, stiffen. **8** *fix one's hair* arrange, put in order, adjust, dress. **9** *fix something to eat* prepare, make, make ready, put together, cook. **10** *I'll fix him for that* get even with, revenge oneself on, get one's revenge on, wreak vengeance on, take retribution on, give someone his/her just deserts, punish, deal with; *inf.* get one's own back, pay someone back, sort someone out, settle someone's hash, cook someone's goose. **11** *fix the outcome of the race* rig, manipulate, manoeuvre, arrange fraudulently; *inf.* fiddle. **12** *fix the judges* bribe, influence, influence unduly. **fix up 1** *fix up a meeting* fix, arrange, organize, plan, agree on, settle on, decide on. **2** *fix you up a room|fix you up with a bed* provide with, supply with, furnish with, accommodate with, lay on.
Opposites BREAK; CANCEL; CHANGE.

fix noun *in a bit of a fix* predicament, plight, quandary, dilemma, difficulty, spot of trouble, bit of bother, muddle, mess, corner, ticklish/tricky situation, tight spot; *inf.* pickle, jam, hole, spot, scrape, bind.

fixation noun obsession, preoccupation, complex, compulsion, mania, monomania, *idée fixe*, phobia; *inf.* hang-up, thing.

fixture noun **1** *kitchen fixtures* fixed appliance, attachment, fixity. **2** *a Sunday fixture* sporting event, match, game, competition, contest, meet, race.

fizz verb **1** *wine fizzing* bubble, effervesce, sparkle, froth, foam. **2** *the solution fizzing* hiss, sputter, fizzle, sibilate.

fizzle verb **fizzle out** peter out, come to nothing, fall through, come to grief, end in failure, fail, miscarry, abort, collapse; *inf.* flop, fold.

fizzy adjective bubbly, bubbling, sparkling, effervescent, carbonated, gassy.
Opposites STILL.

flabbergast verb astound, amaze, dumbfound, strike dumb, render speechless, stun, stagger, confound, daze, overcome, overwhelm, nonplus, disconcert; *inf.* bowl over.

flabby adjective flaccid, unfirm, out of tone, drooping, pendulous, limp; *inf.* out of shape.
Opposites FIRM; TAUT; STRONG.

flaccid *adjective* flabby, unfirm, drooping, limp. *See* FLABBY.
Opposites FIRM; TAUT; STRONG.

flag[1] *noun* standard, ensign, banner, banderole, pennant, pennon, gonfalon, streamer; bunting; colours.

flag[2] *verb* **1** *flag the places on the map* indicate, mark, mark out, label, tab, docket. **2** *the police flagged him down* wave down, signal to stop, signal, hail, gesture/motion to stop.

flag[3] *verb* **1** *I'm flagging* tire, become fatigued, grow tired/weary, weaken, grow weak, lose one's strength. **2** *his strength/interest is flagging* fade, fail, decline, wane, ebb, diminish, decrease, taper off. **3** *flowers flagging* droop, sag, hang down, wilt.

flagon *noun* bottle, decanter, carafe, flask, jug, ewer, pitcher, crock.

flagrant *adjective* glaring, obvious, blatant, outrageous, scandalous, shocking, disgraceful, shameless, dreadful, terrible, gross, enormous, heinous, atrocious, monstrous, wicked, iniquitous, villainous.
Opposites UNOBTRUSIVE; SLIGHT.

flagstone *noun* paving stone, stone block/slab, slab, flag.

flail *verb* **1** *with arms flailing* swing wildly, wave helplessly, thrash about, move erratically. **2** *flail the corn/enemy* thresh, thrash, beat, strike, batter, drub.

flair *noun* **1** *have a flair for languages* natural ability, ability, aptitude, capability, facility, skill, talent, gift, knack, bent, feel, genius. **2** *all the women of the family had flair* style, panache, elegance, dash, élan, taste, good taste, discernment, discrimination.

flake *noun* *a flake of paint/snow* chip, shaving, peeling, scale, sliver, wafer, fragment, bit, particle.

flake *verb* *paint/skin flaking* chip, peel, peel off, scale off, blister; *Tech.* desquamate, exfoliate.
flake out faint, pass out, collapse, drop, keel over; *lit.* swoon.

flamboyant *adjective* **1** *flamboyant gestures* extravagant, theatrical, showy, ostentatious, dashing, swashbuckling. **2** *flamboyant clothes/colours* colourful, brilliantly coloured, bright, exciting, dazzling, glamorous, splendid, resplendent, showy, gaudy, flashy. **3** *flamboyant architecture* elaborate, ornate, fancy, baroque, rococo, arabesque.
Opposites NATURAL; DULL; SIMPLE.

flame *noun* **1** *see the flames in the distance* fire, blaze, conflagration. **2** *burn with a flame* brilliant light, brightness, glow, gleam. **3** *flame is a bright colour* red, reddish-orange. **4** *the flame of love* passion, passionateness, warmth, ardour, fervour, fervency, fire, excitement, intensity, keenness, eagerness, enthusiasm. **5** *an old flame* boyfriend, girlfriend, sweetheart, lover, partner, beloved, beau, inamorato, inamorata.

flame *verb* **1** *the wood flamed* burn, blaze, burst into flame, catch fire. **2** *the light flamed* glow, shine, flash, beam, glare, sparkle.

flame-proof *adjective* non-flammable, non-inflammable, flame-resistant, fire-resistant, incombustible.

flaming *adjective* **1** *a flaming bonfire* blazing, ablaze, burning, on fire, afire, in flames, aflame, ignited, fiery, red-hot, raging, glowing. **2** *a flaming mood* furious, enraged, fuming, incensed, infuriated, mad, angry, raging, wrathful; *inf.* livid. **3** *a flaming row* angry, furious, violent, vehement, frenzied, incensed, passionate, raging. **4** *flaming colours* bright, brilliant, vivid, flamboyant, red, reddish-orange, scarlet. **5** *a flaming idiot* utter, absolute, damned, damnable.

flank *noun* **1** *the animal's flank* side, haunch, loin, quarter, thigh. **2** *the flank of the enemy/mountain* side, wing.

flank *verb* *lawns flank the house* be situated along, border, edge, bound, fringe, skirt.

flannel *noun* *talk a lot of flannel* nonsense, rubbish, prevarication, hedging, equivocation, evasion, flattery, blarney; *inf.* baloney, rot, waffle, soft soap, sweet talk.

flannel *verb* prevaricate, hedge, equivocate, be evasive, talk blarney, use flattery, flatter; *inf.* waffle, soft-soap, sweet-talk, butter up.

flap *verb* **1** *flap one's wings/arms* move up and down, flutter, beat, thresh, thrash, wave, agitate, vibrate, wag, waggle, shake, swing, oscillate. **2** *with wings/arms flapping* move up and down, beat, flail. **3** *curtains flapping at the window* flutter, swing, sway. **4** *the hostess is flapping* panic, go into a panic, become flustered, be agitated, fuss; *inf.* press the panic button, be in a state, be in a tizzy/dither/twitter.

flap *noun* **1** *the flap of wings* flutter, beat, fluttering, beating, waving, shaking, flailing. *See* FLAP *verb* 1, 2. **2** *a flap of material* fold, overlap, overhang, covering, tab, apron, lappet. **3** *the hostess is in a flap* panic, fluster, state of panic/agitation; *inf.* state, dither, twitter, tizzy, blue funk, stew.

flare *verb* **1** *the fire flared* flare up, blaze, flame, burn unsteadily. **2** *lights flared on the shore* flash, gleam, glow, sparkle, glitter, flicker. **3** *his nostrils flared* spread outwards, broaden, widen, widen at the bottom, splay. **flare up 1** *the fire flared up* blaze, burn violently. *See* FLARE *verb* 1. **2** *trouble/disease flared up* broke out, burst out, recur. **3** *the two women flared up* lose one's temper, lose control, become blazing mad, explode, fly into a temper/passion, boil over, boil over with rage, fire up, go berserk, throw a tantrum; *inf.* blow one's top, fly off the handle, lose one's cool.

flare *noun* **1** *burn with a flare* unsteady flame, blaze, burst, flash, flicker, glimmer, shimmer, dazzle, glare, gleam. **2** *flares for ships* signal, distress-signal, rocket, beacon, light, flashlight. **3** *a skirt with a flare* gradual widening, outward spread.

flash *verb* **1** *lights flashed* light up, shine out, flare, blaze, glare, beam, gleam, glint, sparkle, flicker, shimmer, twinkle, glimmer, glisten, scintillate, coruscate, fulgurate. **2** *the runners/cars/time flashed past* dart, dash, tear, shoot, zoom, streak, fly, whistle, rush, bolt, race, bound, speed, career; *inf.* scoot, skedaddle. **3** *flash her new ring* show off, flaunt, flourish, display, exhibit. **4** *the peculiar man flashed at the girls* expose oneself, show one's genitals.

flash *noun* **1** *a flash of light* blaze, burst, glare, flare, shaft, ray, streak, gleam, glint, sparkle, flicker, shimmer, twinkle, glimmer. *See* FLASH *verb* 1. **2** *he came in a flash* instant, moment, second, split second, minute, trice, twinkling, twinkling of an eye, twinkle, wink of an eye, two shakes, two shakes of a lamb's tail; *inf.* jiffy, bat of an eye. **3** *a flash of enthusiasm/wit* sudden show, outburst, burst, outbreak, brief display/exhibition. **4** *flashes on animals/uniforms* patch, bright patch, streak, stripe; emblem, insignia.

flash *adjective flash clothes* ostentatious, showy, vulgar, tasteless, cheap, tawdry; *inf.* tacky. *See* FLASHY.

flashy *adjective flashy clothes/cars* ostentatious, showy, in bad/poor taste, tasteless, pretentious, cheap, cheap and nasty, tawdry, garish, loud, flamboyant, gawdy, meretricious; *inf.* tacky, snazzy, jazzy, glitzy, ritzy.

flask *noun* bottle, flagon, decanter, carafe, pitcher, jug, ewer.

flat *adjective* **1** *a flat surface* level, horizontal, levelled, even, smooth, unbroken, plane. **2** *lying flat on the ground* stretched out, spread-eagled, prone, supine, prostrate, recumbent. **3** *a flat dish* shallow, not deep. **4** *a flat tyre* deflated, collapsed, blown out, burst, punctured, ruptured. **5** *a flat denial* outright, direct, out and out, downright, straight, plain, explicit, absolute, definite, positive, firm, final, conclusive, complete, utter, categorical, unqualified, unconditional, unquestionable, unequivocal. **6** *in a flat voice|flat jokes* monotonous, boring, dull, tedious, uninteresting, lifeless, lacklustre, dead, vapid, bland, insipid, prosaic. **7** *feeling rather flat* depressed, dejected, dispirited, low, down, without energy, enervated. **8** *the market is flat* slow, inactive, sluggish, slack, not busy.
Opposites UNEVEN; VERTICAL; INFLATED; EXCITING.

flat *adverb she told him flat that she was going* outright, directly, straight, plainly, explicitly, absolutely, definitely, conclusively, categorically. *See* FLAT *adjective* 5. **flat out** at full speed, all out, as fast as possible, post-haste, at full tilt, full steam ahead; *inf.* hell for leather.

flat *noun* apartment, set of rooms; rooms; *inf.* pad.

flatten *verb* **1** *flatten the surface* make flat, level, level out/off, make even, even out, smooth, smooth out/off, plane. **2** *children flattening the grass* compress, trample, press down, crush, squash, compact. **3** *flatten the old buildings* demolish, tear down, knock down, raze, raze to the ground. **4** *flatten his opponent* knock down, knock to the ground, floor, knock off one's feet, fell, prostrate. **5** *even sarcasm fails to flatten him* crush, quash, squash, deflate, snub, humiliate; *inf.* put down.

flatter *verb* **1** *courtiers flattering the queen* compliment, praise, sing the praises of, praise to excess, praise to the skies, eulogize, puff up,

pay court to, pay blandishments to, blandish, fawn upon, cajole, humour, flannel, wheedle; *inf.* sweet-talk, soft-soap, butter up, lay it on thick, lay it on with a trowel, play up to. **2** *that dress flatters her colouring* suit, become, set off, show to advantage, enhance; *inf.* do something for.

flattering *adjective* **1** *flattering words* complimentary, fulsome, adulatory, praising, blandishing, laudatory, honeyed, sugary, ingratiating, cajoling; *inf.* sweet-talking, soft-soaping. *See* FLATTER 1. **2** *a flattering dress* becoming, enhancing.
Opposites UNFLATTERING; CONDEMNATORY; UNBECOMING.

flattery *noun* praise, adulation, overpraise, false praise, eulogy, puffery, laudation, blarney, fulsomeness, fawning, cajolery, wheedling; compliments, blandishments, honeyed words; *inf.* sweet talk, soft soap, buttering-up, flannel.

flatulence *noun* wind, intestinal gas; belching; *inf.* farting.

flaunt *verb* show off, parade, display ostentatiously, exhibit, draw attention to, make a show of, wave, dangle, brandish.

flavour *noun* **1** *dislike the flavour of the herb* taste, savour, tang, relish. **2** *add some flavour to the sauce* flavouring, seasoning, tastiness, tang, relish, piquancy, spiciness, zest; *inf.* zing. **3** *capture the flavour of the poem/place* spirit, essence, soul, nature, character, quality, feel, feeling, ambience, tone, style, stamp, property.

flavour *verb* **1** *flavour the stew* add flavour/flavouring to, season, add seasoning/herbs/spices to, spice, add piquancy to, ginger up. **2** *flavour the punch with cinnamon* season, lace, imbue, infuse.

flavouring *noun* **1** *add flavouring to the stew* flavour, seasoning. *See* FLAVOUR *noun* 2. **2** *vanilla flavouring* essence, extract, tincture.

flaw *noun* **1** *a flaw in his character* fault, defect, imperfection, blemish, failing, foible, shortcoming, weakness, weak spot. **2** *a flaw in the china/material* fault, defect, crack, chip, fracture, break, crevice, fissure, rent, split, tear.
Opposites ASSET; STRENGTH.

flawless *adjective* **1** *a flawless performance* faultless, perfect, impeccable. **2** *a flawless complexion* perfect, blemish-free, unflawed, unimpaired, unmarred. **3** *a flawless piece of china* perfect, whole, intact, sound, unbroken, undamaged.
Opposites IMPERFECT; DEFECTIVE.

fleck *noun a fleck of white in the black cloth* spot, mark, speck, speckle, freckle.

fleck *verb black material flecked with white* spot, mark, speckle, dot, sprinkle, spatter, stipple, mottle, streak, freckle.

flee *verb* **1** *she fled from the blaze|the burglar fled when disturbed* run, run away, run off, bolt, rush, speed, take flight, take to flight, make off, fly, abscond, retreat, beat a retreat, beat a hasty retreat, depart hastily/abuptly, make a quick exit, run for it, make a run for it, take off, take to one's heels, decamp, escape, make one's escape/getaway, show a clean pair of heels, do a disappearing act, vanish; *inf.* cut and run, make oneself scarce, scarper, beat it, do a bunk, skedaddle, split, scram, light out. **2** *they fled the country* run away from, leave hastily/abruptly, fly, escape from; *inf.* skip.

fleece *noun* *a sheep's fleece* wool, coat.

fleece *verb* **1** *fleece the sheep* shear, clip. **2** *fleece the old lady of her savings* swindle, defraud, cheat, rob, strip, mulct, bilk, overcharge; *inf.* con, take for a ride, diddle, rip off, sting, bleed, take to the cleaners, soak.

fleecy *adjective* woolly, downy, fluffy, shaggy, soft, smooth; fleecelike, lanate, lanose.

fleet *noun* *the fleet set sail* flotilla, naval force, squadron, armada; *lit.* navy, argosy.

fleet *adjective* swift, fast, rapid, quick, speedy, expeditious, nimble, fleet of foot, nimble-footed, swift-footed, like the wind.

fleeting *adjective* rapid, swift, brief, short-lived, short, momentary, transient, transitory, ephemeral, fugitive, evanescent, fugacious, vanishing, flying, passing, flitting, here today and gone tomorrow, temporary, impermanent. **Opposites** PERMANENT; ENDURING.

fleetness *noun* swiftness, fastness, rapidity, quickness, speed, speediness, velocity, celerity, nimbleness, nimble-footedness, swift-footedness.

flesh *noun* **1** *flesh and bones* muscle, tissue, muscle tissue, brawn. **2** *carry too much flesh* fat; fatness, obesity, corpulence. **3** *not much flesh in the essay* substance, pith, matter, body. **4** *the spirit is willing but the flesh is weak | the pleasure of the flesh* body, human body, human nature, physical nature, physicality, corporeality, carnality, animality, sensuality, sensualism. **5** *all flesh would perish in such conditions* mankind, man, humankind, people, human race/species, humanity, *Homo sapiens*; animate life, the living; human beings, living creatures. **flesh and blood** *ignored their own flesh and blood* family, kin, kinsfolk; relatives, relations, blood relations; *inf.* folk. **in the flesh** *saw the actor in the flesh* in person, before one's eyes, in front of one, in one's presence.

flesh *verb* **flesh out** **1** *the children have fleshed out a bit* put on weight, grow fatter, fatten up. **2** *flesh out the material* fill out, expand, make more substantial, add substance/detail to.

flex *noun* *electric flex* cable, wire; *Am.* cord.

flex *verb* **1** *flex one's muscles* contract, tighten, make taught. **2** *flex one's arm* bend, curve, crook, angle.

flexible *adjective* **1** *flexible materials* bendable, pliant, pliable, elastic, springy, plastic, mouldable. **2** *flexible young bodies* supple, agile, limber, lithe, lissom, double-jointed. **3** *my arrangements are flexible* adaptable, adjustable, open-ended, open, open to change, changeable, variable. **4** *the young man is too flexible* tractable, malleable, compliant, manageable, amenable, biddable, docile, submissive, yielding. **Opposites** RIGID; STIFF; INFLEXIBLE; SET.

flick *verb* **1** *flick the horse with a whip* strike, hit, rap, tap, touch. **2** *flick on the switch* click, snap, flip, tap. **3** *cows' tails flicking* swish, wag, waggle. **flick through** skim, flip over, glance over/through, browse through, thumb through, skip over.

flicker *verb* **1** *lights flickering* twinkle, sparkle, blink, flash, shimmer, glitter, glimmer, glint, flare. **2** *with eyelids flickering* flutter, quiver, vibrate, bat, open and shut.

flight¹ *noun* **1** *watching the flight of the eagle* flying, soaring, mounting. **2** *a flight of geese/birds* flying group, flock; skein, bevy, covey; migration. **3** *a flight of bees* swarm, cloud. **4** *a history of flight* aviation, flying, air transport, aerial navigation; aeronautics. **5** *have a good flight* airline trip, journey, shuttle; *inf.* plane trip. **6** *climb two flights* flight of stairs, staircase, set of steps/stairs.

flight² *noun* *the flight of the beaten army* fleeing, running away, absconding, retreat, departure, hasty departure, exit, exodus, decamping, escape, get away, disappearance, vanishing. *See* FLEE. **put to flight** chase, chase off, drive off, scare off, rout, scatter, scatter to the four winds, disperse, stampede. **take flight** flee, run away, bolt, make off, fly, abscond, beat a hasty retreat, take off, decamp.

flighty *adjective* frivolous, giddy, scatter-brained, hare-brained, fickle, changeable, inconstant, unsteady, whimsical, capricious, skittish.

flimsy *adjective* **1** *a flimsy box* insubstantial, unsubstantial, slight, makeshift, jerry-built, gimcrack, rickety, ramshackle, shaky, fragile, frail. **2** *made of a flimsy material* thin, light, lightweight, delicate, sheer, filmy, diaphanous, transparent, translucent, see-through, chiffony, gossamer, gauzy, cobwebby. **3** *a flimsy excuse* feeble, weak, poor, inadequate, thin, transparent, unconvincing, implausible, unsatisfactory, paltry, trifling, trivial, shallow. **Opposites** STURDY; THICK; SOLID.

flinch *verb* **1** *did not flinch when being caned* draw back, pull back, start back, recoil, withdraw, shrink back, shy away, cringe, cower, crouch, quail, wince, blench. **2** *flinch from his duty* shrink from, shy away from, shirk, turn away from, swerve from, dodge, avoid, duck, baulk at.

fling *verb* *fling the clothes in the river* throw, toss, hurl, cast, pitch, sling, heave, fire, shy, launch, propel, catapult, send flying, let fly; *inf.* lob, chuck.

fling *noun* **1** *with one fling of the javelin* throw, toss, hurl, cast, pitch, shot, heave; *inf.* lob, chuck. *See* FLING *verb.* **2** *have a last fling before marriage* binge, spree, good time, bit of fun, night on the town. **3** *have a fling at winning the match* try, attempt, go, shot, stab, venture; *inf.* crack, bash, whirl.

flip *verb* **1** *flip a coin* flick, toss, throw, pitch, cast, spin, twist. **2** *flip a switch* flick, click, snap, tap. **flip through** skim, glance through. *See* FLICK THROUGH.

flippant *adjective* *a flippant remark* frivolous, superficial, shallow, glib, thoughtless, carefree,

irresponsible, insouciant, offhand, disrespectful, impertinent, impudent, irreverent, cheeky, pert, saucy; *inf.* flip.
Opposites SERIOUS; RESPONSIBLE.

flirt *verb* **1** *she's always flirting with the boys* toy with, trifle with, make eyes at, ogle, lead on; philander with, dally with; *inf.* chat up. **2** *flirt with the idea of going | flirt with antiques* toy with, trifle with, play with, entertain the idea/possibility of, consider, give thought to, dabble in.

flirt *noun* *the new girl's a flirt* coquette, tease, vamp, heartbreaker, trifler, philanderer, wanton; *inf.* cockteaser.

flirtatious *adjective* coquettish, provocative, teasing, amorous, philandering, dallying, come-hither.

float *verb* **1** *things light enough to float on water* stay afloat, be buoyant, be buoyed up. **2** *craft floating along* bob, glide, sail, slip, slide, drift. **3** *not working, just floating about* move aimlessly, drift, wander, meander; *inf.* bum around. **4** *float a company* launch, get going, get off the ground, establish, set up, instigate, initiate, promote.
Opposites SINK; SUBMERGE; TERMINATE.

floating *adjective* **1** *floating substances* buoyant, buoyed up, non-submerged, afloat; suspended, drifting. **2** *floating craft* gliding, sailing. *See* FLOAT 2. **3** *floating voters* uncommitted, unattached, fluctuating, variable. **4** *a floating population* not fixed, moving, unsettled, wandering, migratory. **5** *floating currencies* fluctuating, variable, not fixed.

flock *verb* collect, gather, foregather, come together, assemble, group, bunch, congregate, converge, crowd, herd, troop, throng, swarm, mill, huddle.

flock *noun* **1** *a flock of sheep* fold, drove, herd. **2** *a flock of birds/geese* flight, bevy, skein, gaggle. *See table at* COLLECTION. **3** *a flock of people* crowd, gathering, assembly, company, collection, congregation, group, throng, mass, host, multitude, troop, herd, convoy.

flog *verb* **1** *slave-drivers flogging slaves* whip, horsewhip, lash, flay, flagellate, birch, scourge, belt, cane, strap, thrash, beat, whack, wallop, chastise, trounce; *inf.* lambaste, tan the hide of. **2** *flog oneself to finish in time* drive, push, strain, punish, tax, overtax, make every effort, overexert, overwork; *inf.* kill oneself, pull out all the stops. **3** *flog the goods cheaply* sell, put on sale, offer for sale.

flogging *noun* whipping, horsewhipping, lashing, flaying, flagellation, birching, belting, caning, beating; *inf.* lambasting, hiding. *See* FLOG 1.

flood *noun* **1** *houses damaged in the flood* deluge, inundation, torrent, spate, overflow, flash flood, freshet. **2** *a flood of rain* downpour, torrent, cloudburst. **3** *a flood of mail* profusion, overabundance, superabundance, plethora, superfluity, glut; *inf.* tons, heaps. **4** *a flood of tears* outpouring, rush, stream, flow.

flood *verb* **1** *rivers flooding* overflow, break the banks, brim over, swell, surge, pour forth, disembogue. **2** *flood the town* inundate, deluge, pour over, immerse, submerge, swamp, drown, engulf. **3** *mail flooding in | relief flooded* through her pour, flow, surge. **4** *flood the market with fruit* overfill, oversupply, saturate, glut, overwhelm.

floor *noun* *on the second floor* storey, level, tier, deck.

floor *verb* **1** *floor him with one blow* knock down, ground, fell, prostrate. **2** *this problem/attitude floors me* defeat, beat, baffle, stump, perplex, puzzle, nonplus, confound, dumbfound, confuse, discomfit, disconcert; *inf.* throw.

flop *verb* **1** *flop into a chair* collapse, slump, drop, fall, tumble. **2** *the old man's head flopped to the side* dangle, droop, sag, hang limply. **3** *the play flopped* fail, fall flat, founder, close, be unsuccessful, be a disaster, miss the mark, go down like a lead balloon; *inf.* bomb.
Opposites SUCCEED; FLOURISH.

flop *noun* *the play was a flop* failure, fiasco, loser, disaster, debacle; *inf.* no-hoper, no-go, washout, dud, lemon.

floral *adjective* *a floral dress* flower-patterned, flowery.

florid *adjective* **1** *a florid complexion* ruddy, red-faced, red, reddish, high-coloured, flushed, blushing, blowsy, rubicund, rubescent, erubescent. **2** *florid decorations* ornate, flamboyant, overelaborate, embellished, busy, fussy, baroque. **3** *florid prose* high-flown, flowery, verbose, overelaborate, grandiloquent, purple, euphuistic. *See* FLOWERY 2.
Opposites PALE; PLAIN.

flotsam *noun* **1** *flotsam floating from the ship* wreckage, floating remains. **2** *clear up the flotsam and jetsam in the yard* rubbish, junk, odds and ends, debris, detritus.

flounder *verb* **1** *floundering about in the mud/dark* thrash, struggle, stumble, blunder, fumble, grope. **2** *he's floundering when it comes to maths* struggle, find difficulties, be confused, be in the dark, be out of one's depth. **3** *flounder his way through the speech* stumble, falter, blunder, muddle, bungle.

flourish *verb* **1** *flourish the sword/prize* brandish, wave, twirl, wield, swing, swish, shake, wag, hold aloft, display, exhibit, flaunt, parade, vaunt; *inf.* show off. **2** *the plants are flourishing* thrive, grow, grow/do well, develop, burgeon, bloom, blossom, bear fruit, burst forth. **3** *we are all flourishing* be well, be in good health, be strong, be vigorous, bloom, thrive, get on/ahead, get on well, prosper, be successful, succeed, make progress/headway; *inf.* be in the pink, be fine and dandy, go great guns.
Opposites FAIL; WITHER; DECLINE.

flout *verb* *flout convention | flout the rules* defy, scorn, disdain, show contempt for, spurn, scoff at, mock, laugh at, deride, ridicule, sneer at, jeer at, gibe at, insult, poke fun at, make a fool of; *inf.* cock a snook at.
Opposites OBEY; OBSERVE.

flow *verb* **1** *blood/rivers flowing* move, go along, course, run, circulate, proceed, glide, stream, ripple, swirl, surge, sweep, roll, rush, whirl, drift, slide, trickle, gurgle, babble. **2** *blood flowing from the wound* gush, stream, well, spurt, spout, squirt, spew, jet, spill, leak, seep, ooze, drip. **3** *springs flowing from the mountains | ideas flowing from her pen* arise, issue, spring, originate, derive, emanate, emerge, pour, proceed. **4** *the lands flowed with milk and honey* overflow with, be abundant in, abound in, teem with, be rich in, be full of.

flow *noun* **1** *the flow of the water* course, current, drift, stream, spate, tide. **2** *stem the flow of blood* gush, stream, welling, spurting, spouting, outpouring, outflow. *See* FLOW *verb* 2. **3** *a*

flow of words/complaints flood, deluge, outpouring, outflow, abundance, superabundance, plethora, excess, effusion, succession, train.

flower *noun* **1** *pick/plant several flowers* bloom, blossom, floweret, floret; annual, perennial. *See tables.* **2** *in the flower of their youth* prime, peak, zenith, acme, height, heyday, springtime; salad days. **3** *the flower of the nation died in battle* finest, best, pick, choice, choicest, most select, élite, cream, *crème de la crème*.

FLOWERING PLANTS

acacia	chickweed	gillyflower	mayweed	shamrock
acanthus	Chinese	gladiolus	meadow	slipperwort
aconite	lantern	globe thistle	saffron	snakeroot
African violet	chrysan-	golden rod	meadowsweet	snapdragon
agrimony	themum	goosefoot	mignonette	snowdrop
alkanet	cinquefoil	groundsel	milkwort	soapwort
alyssum	clematis	harebell	mimosa	Solomon's seal
amaryllis	clove pink	hawkweed	mint	sorrel
anemone	clover	heather	mistletoe	speedwell
arrowroot	coltsfoot	hellebore	moccasin	spider plant
arum lily	columbine	helleborine	flower	spikenard
asphodel	comfrey	hemlock	mock orange	spurge
aspidistra	coneflower	henbane	monkshood	stitchwort
aster	convolvulus	herb	montbretia	St John's wort
aubrietia	cornflower	Christopher	moonflower	stock
avens	cotoneaster	herb Gerard	morning glory	stonecrop
azalea	cow parsley	herb Paris	motherwort	sundew
balsam	cowpea	herb Robert	mullein	sunflower
bedstraw	cowslip	hibiscus	narcissus	sweet pea
begonia	cranesbill	hogweed	nasturtium	sweet william
belladonna	crocus	hollyhock	nettle	tansy
bellflower	crowfoot	honesty	nightshade	teasel
bindweed	cuckoo pint	honeysuckle	oleander	thistle
bittersweet	cyclamen	hop	orchid	thorn apple
black-eyed	daffodil	houseleek	oxlip	thyme
Susan	dahlia	hyacinth	pansy	tiger lily
bladderwort	daisy	hydrangea	pasque flower	toadflax
bleeding heart	dandelion	iris	passion flower	touch-me-not
bluebell	deadly night-	japonica	pennyroyal	tradescantia
borage	shade	jasmine	peony	traveller's joy
bougainvillea	dead nettle	jonquil	peppermint	trefoil
bramble	delphinium	kingcup	petunia	tulip
broom	dock	knapweed	phlox	twayblade
bryony	dropwort	knotgrass	pimpernel	valerian
buddleia	duckweed	laburnum	pink	Venus flytrap
bugle	edelweiss	lady's finger	pitcher plant	verbena
bugloss	eglantine	lady's slipper	plantain	veronica
burdock	evening prim-	lady's smock	poinsettia	vervain
burnet	rose	lady's tresses	polyanthus	vetch
busy Lizzie	eyebright	larkspur	poppy	violet
buttercup	figwort	lavender	primrose	wallflower
butterwort	firethorn	lemon balm	primula	water lily
cactus	flax	lilac	pyracantha	willowherb
camellia	fleabane	lily	ragged robin	wintergreen
camomile	forget-me-not	lily of the valley	ragwort	wisteria
campion	forsythia	lobelia	rhododendron	witchweed
candytuft	foxglove	loosestrife	rock rose	wolfbane
cardinal flower	frangipani	lords and ladies	rose	wood sorrel
carnation	freesia	lotus	rosebay	wormwood
carrion flower	fritillary	lupin	rue	woundwort
catchfly	fuchsia	magnolia	sage	yarrow
catmint	furze/gorse	mallow	salvia	yellow
catnip	gardenia	marigold	samphire	archangel
celandine	gentian	may-apple	saxifrage	yucca
cheese plant	geranium	mayflower	scabious	zinnia

INFLORESCENCES		
bract	involucel	rhachis
bractede	involucre	spadix
capitulum	monocha-	spathe
catkin	sium	spike
corymb	panicle	spikelet
cyathium	pedicel	umbel
cyme	peduncle	
floret	raceme	

PARTS OF A FLOWER		
androecium	ladicule	pollen
anther	lemma	pollen grain
calyx	lip	pollinium
carpel	nectary	receptacle
carpophore	nucellus	sepal
corolla	ovary	spur
filament	ovule	stamen
glume	palea	stigma
gynoecium	petal	style
hypanthium	placenta	tepal

flowery *adjective* **1** *flowery patterns* floral, flower-covered, flower-patterned. **2** *flowery language* high-flown, ornate, fancy, elaborate, overelaborate, highly figurative, verbose, grandiloquent, purple, rhetorical, euphuistic, bombastic, baroque, pleonastic.

flowing *adjective* **1** *flowing streams* coursing, gliding, rippling, swirling, drifting, trickling. See FLOW *verb* 1. **2** *lands flowing with milk and honey* overflowing with, abounding in, teeming with, rich in, full of. **3** *flowing prose* fluent, free-flowing, effortless, smooth, unbroken, uninterrupted, continuous, graceful, elegant. **4** *flowing hair* loose, hanging loose/free, unconfined.

fluctuate *verb* **1** *prices fluctuating* rise and fall, go up and down, see-saw, yo-yo, be unstable, be unsteady, vary, shift, change, alter, swing, oscillate, undulate, ebb and flow. **2** *she fluctuates between going and not going* waver, vacillate, hesitate, change one's mind, alternate, veer, shilly-shally, hem and haw, teeter, totter, see-saw, yo-yo, blow hot and cold.

fluctuation *noun* **1** *fluctuation in prices/results* rise and fall, rising and falling, see-sawing, yo-yoing, instability, unsteadiness, variation, shift, change, alteration, swing, oscillation, undulation, ebb and flow. **2** *the fluctuation of her opinion* wavering, vacillation, hesitation, alternation, shilly-shallying, inconstancy, fickleness. See FLUCTUATE 2.

flue *noun* duct, passage, channel, shaft, air passage, airway, vent.

fluency *noun* **1** *fluency as a speaker* articulacy, articulateness, eloquence, volubility. **2** *the fluency of the prose* smoothness, flowingness, fluidity, gracefulness, effortlessness, naturalness. See FLUENT 2. **3** *her fluency in German* command, facility, articulacy.

fluent *adjective* **1** *a fluent after-dinner speaker* articulate, eloquent, smooth-spoken, silver-tongued, voluble. **2** *fluent prose* smooth, flow-

ing, fluid, graceful, effortless, natural, easy, elegant, smooth-sounding, mellifluous, euphonious. **3** *fluent in French* having a command of, articulate in.
Opposites HESITANT; INARTICULATE.

fluff *noun* **1** *fluff off the blankets* down, fuzz, lint, nap, pile, dust, dustball, fuzzball; *Scots* oose. **2** *the fluff of the chicks* down, downiness, fuzz, soft fur. **3** *not notice the actor's fluff* mistake, error, bungle, forgetfulness; *inf.* foul-up, screw-up, cock-up.

fluff *verb* **1** *actors fluffing their lines* forget, deliver badly, bungle, muddle up, make a mess of; *inf.* mess up, foul up, screw up, cock up. **2** *the cricketer fluffing a catch* miss, bungle.

fluid *noun* flowing substance; liquid, gas, solution.

fluid *adjective* **1** *a fluid substance moving along the pipe* gaseous, gassy, liquid, liquefied, melted, molten, uncongealed, running, flowing, fluxional. **2** *a fluid prose style | a fluid movement* fluent, smooth, smooth-flowing, flowing, graceful, elegant, effortless, easy, natural. **3** *our plans are fluid* flexible, open to change, adaptable, adjustable, not fixed, not settled, variable, mutable. **4** *the situation is fluid* subject/likely to change, unstable, unsteady, ever-shifting, fluctuating, mobile, mercurial, protean.
Opposites SOLID; FIRM; STILTED.

fluke *noun* *win by a fluke* lucky stroke, stroke of luck, stroke of good fortune, piece of good luck, lucky chance/shot/break.

flunkey *noun* **1** *Queen Elizabeth I and her flunkeys* manservant, footman, valet, liveried servant, lackey, page. **2** *the politician and his flunkeys* lackey, toady, minion, yes-man, sycophant, hanger-on, camp-follower, tool, puppet, cat's paw; *inf.* bootlicker.

flurry *noun* **1** *a flurry of snow/rain* squall, gust, shower. **2** *a sudden flurry of activity* burst, spurt, outbreak, spell, bout. **3** *the hostess in a flurry of excitement* fluster, fuss, bustle, whirl, stir, ferment, hubbub, commotion, hustle, flap, tumult, hurry, pother, agitation, disturbance, furore, excitement, perturbation; *inf.* to-do.

flurry *verb* *the unexpected guests flurried her* fluster, upset, disconcert, ruffle, unsettle, put off one's stroke, put on edge, unnerve, bother, agitate, disturb, confuse, bewilder, muddle, hustle; *inf.* rattle, hassle.

flush *verb* **1** *she flushed in embarrassment* blush, turn red, go red/rosy, redden, crimson, colour, colour up, burn up, flame up, glow, suffuse with colour, mantle. **2** *flush the toilet* wash out, rinse out, cleanse, hose down, swab. **3** *flush away the waste* eject, expel. **4** *rivers flushing the meadows* flood, overflow, overrun, swamp. See FLOOD *verb* 1, 2.

flush *noun* **1** *embarrassed flushes* blush, high colour, colouring up. See FLUSH *verb* 1. **2** *the first flush of youth* bloom, glow, freshness, radiance, vigour.

flushed *adjective* **1** *flushed faces* blushing, red, reddened, crimson, ruddy, rosy, rubicund, burning, fiery, flaming, glowing, feverish.

2 *flushed with success* elated, delighted, thrilled, exhilarated, excited, worked up, animated, aroused, inflamed, impassioned, intoxicated; *inf.* high.

fluster *verb unexpected guests fluster her* make nervous, agitate, ruffle, flurry, unsettle, upset, bother, put on edge, discompose, panic, perturb, disconcert, confuse, throw off balance, confound, nonplus; *inf.* hassle, rattle, faze, put into a flap, throw into a tizz.

fluster *noun unexpected guests putting her into a fluster | causing fluster* nervous state, state of agitation, flurry, bustle, flutter, panic, upset; discomposure, agitation, perturbation, confusion, turmoil, commotion; *inf.* dither, flap, state, tizz.

flutter *verb* **1** *a bird fluttering its wings* flap, beat, quiver, agitate, vibrate, ruffle. **2** *flutter one's eyelashes* flicker, bat. **3** *butterflies fluttering in the air* flit, hover, flitter. **4** *flags fluttering in the breeze* flap, wave, flop, ripple, quiver, shiver, tremble. **5** *with hearts fluttering* beat rapidly, pulsate, palpitate.

flutter *noun* **1** *the flutter of the birds' wings* flapping, beating, quivering. *See* FLUTTER *verb* 1. **2** *the flutter of her eyelashes* flickering, batting. **3** *the flutter of the flags* flapping, waving, flopping, rippling. *See* FLUTTER *verb* 4. **4** *in a flutter at the unexpected news* fluster, flurry, bustle, panic; *inf.* dither, state, flap, tizz. *See* FLUSTER *noun.* **5** *have a flutter on a horse* bet, gamble, wager.

fly *verb* **1** *birds flying overhead* flutter, flit, hover, soar, wing, wing its way, take wing, take to the air, mount. **2** *flying to Paris* go by aeroplane, travel/go by air; *inf.* plane it. **3** *fly the plane* pilot, operate, control, manoeuvre. **4** *ships flying the British flag* display, show, wave. **5** *flags flying* flap, wave, flutter, toss. **6** *time flew past* go quickly, pass swiftly, slip past, race, rush/tear past. **7** *the runners flew by* race, dash, shoot, rush, tear, bolt, zoom, scoot, dart, speed, hasten, hurry, scamper, career, go like the wind; *inf.* be off like a shot, hare off. **8** *the beaten army plan to fly* flee, run, run away, bolt, take flight, make off, abscond, beat a retreat, run for it, take to one's heels, decamp, make one's escape; *inf.* cut and run, scarper, do a bunk, skedaddle. *See* FLEE. **fly at** attack, assault, strike, strike out at, hit, lay into, pitch into, light into, rush at, charge, fall upon, pounce upon; *inf.* have a go at, get stuck into. **2** *she just let fly at him* lose one's temper, explode, erupt with anger, let someone have it, give free reign to one's emotions, keep nothing back, give vent to one's emotions, lash out at.

fly *noun. See table at* INSECT.

flying *adjective* **1** *flying creatures* airborne, fluttering, flitting, hovering, soaring, winging. *See* FLY 1. **2** *a flying visit* brief, short, short-lived, hurried, hasty, rushed, fleeting, transitory, transient, fugacious. **3** *her flying footsteps* fast, rapid, swift, quick, speedy, fleet; *lit.* winged.

foal *noun* young horse, colt, filly, pony.

foam *noun the foam on the beer | washing-up foam* froth, bubbles, fizz, effervescence, head, spume, lather, suds.

foam *verb* froth, froth up, cream, bubble, fizz, effervesce, spume, lather.

focus *noun* **1** *the focus of attention/activity* focal point, centre, central point, centre of attention, core, hub, pivot, magnet, cynosure. **2** *the focus of the light* focal point, point of convergence.

focus *verb* **1** *focus the camera on her* turn, converge, bring into focus, bring to a focus. **2** *focus our attention on budgets* concentrate, fix, bring to bear, centre, pinpoint, rivet; *inf.* zero/zoom in on.

foe *noun* enemy, opponent, adversary, rival, antagonist, combatant, fellow-contestant.

foetus *noun* embryo, fertilized egg, unborn baby.

fog *noun* **1** *fog decreasing visibility* mist, mistiness, smog, murk, murkiness, haze, brume, gloom; *inf.* pea-souper. **2** *go around in a mental fog* haze, daze, stupor, trance; bewilderment, confusion, perplexity, bafflement, vagueness, stupefaction, disorientation.

fog *verb* **1** *windscreens fogging over/up* mist over, become misty, cloud over, steam up. **2** *alcohol fogging their minds/judgement* befuddle, becloud, bedim, bewilder, confuse, muddle, perplex, baffle, blind, darken, obscure, daze, stupefy, obfuscate.

foggy *adjective* **1** *a foggy day* misty, smoggy, dark, dim, grey, overcast, murky, hazy, gloomy; *inf.* soupy. **2** *have only a foggy recollection of the event* vague, indistinct, dim, hazy, shadowy, cloudy, clouded, dark, obscure, unclear, befuddled, confused, bewildered, muddled, dazed, stupefied.

foible *noun* weakness, weak point, failing, shortcoming, flaw, blemish, defect, frailty, infirmity, quirk, idiosyncrasy; *inf.* hang-up. *Opposites* STRENGTH; ASSET.

foil *noun the perfect foil for her blonde beauty* contrast, striking difference, antithesis, complement.

foil *verb foil the attempt* thwart, frustrate, put a stop to, stop, baffle, defeat, check, checkmate, circumvent, counter, baulk, disappoint, impede, obstruct, hamper, hinder, cripple, nip in the bud; *inf.* mess up, screw up.

foist *verb* **1** *foist his ideas on everyone | foist the vase off as antique* force upon, impose upon, thrust upon, unload upon; palm off, pass off, fob off, get rid of. **2** *foist an illegal clause into the document* sneak, insinuate, interpolate, insert, introduce, stick, squeeze, edge.

fold¹ *noun* **1** *a sheep fold* enclosure, pen. **2** *welcome them into the fold of the church* congregation, assembly, body, church membership, brethren; parishioners, churchgoers; *inf.* flock.

fold² *noun* **1** *a fold in the cloth* folded portion, double thickness, overlap, layer, pleat, turn, gather, crease, knife-edge. **2** *a fold in the skin* wrinkle, pucker, furrow, crinkle; crow's foot.

fold³ *verb* **1** *fold the paper* double, double over, double up, crease, turn under, turn up, bend,

folder · fool

overlap, tuck, gather, pleat, crimp, crumple, dog-ear. **2** *fold her in his arms* enfold, wrap, wrap up, enclose, envelop, clasp, embrace, hug, squeeze. **3** *the firm folded* fail, collapse, go out of business, close, shut down, go bankrupt, crash, go to the wall; *inf.* go bust, go under, flop.

folder *noun* file, binder, portfolio, envelope.

foliage *noun* leaves; leafage, frondescence, vegetation.

folk *noun* **1** *country folk* people, citizenry, populace, population, general public, public, race, clan, tribe, ethnic group. **2** *has she no folk of her own?* relatives, relations, family, kinsfolk, kinsmen, kin, kindred, flesh and blood.

folklore *noun* legend, myth, mythology, lore, oral history, tradition, folk tradition; legends, fables, myths, old wives' tales.

follow *verb* **1** *children following after each other* go behind/after, come behind/after, walk behind, tread on the heels of. **2** *he followed his father as mayor* come after, succeed, replace, take the place of, step into the shoes of, supersede, supplant. **3** *he objects to his sister following him around* come/go after, go with, escort, accompany, attend, trail; *inf.* tag. **4** *dogs following rabbits* | *detectives following criminals* chase, pursue, run after, trail, shadow, hunt, stalk, track, dog, hound, course; *inf.* tail. **5** *follow the rules* | *follow etiquette* obey, observe, comply with, conform to, heed, pay attention to, note, have regard to, mind, be guided by, accept, yield to. **6** *his conclusion follows from your theory* | *the conclusion follows logically* result from, be consequent on, arise from, develop from, ensue from, emanate from, issue from, proceed from, spring from, flow from; result, arise, ensue, supervene. **7** *cannot follow your argument* understand, comprehend, take in, grasp, fathom, get, catch on to, appreciate, keep up with, see; *inf.* latch on to. **8** *he followed the poetic style of Shelley* | *he follows Shelley* copy, imitate, emulate, take as a pattern/example; pattern oneself on, adopt the style of, style oneself on. **9** *he follows fantasy fiction* be a follower of, be a fan/admirer/devotee of, be devoted to, be interested in, cultivate an interest in, be a supporter of, support, keep abreast of, keep up to date with. **follow through** *follow through a project* continue to the end, complete, bring to completion, bring to a finish, see something through. **follow up** *follow up the findings* research, investigate, find out about, look into, check out, make enquiries into, pursue. *Opposites* LEAD; MISUNDERSTAND; FLOUT.

follower *noun* **1** *the new prime minister and his followers* companion, escort, attendant, henchman, retainer, minion, lackey, toady, servant, page, squire; *inf.* hanger-on, sidekick. **2** *Picasso and his followers* imitator, emulator, copier; *inf.* copycat. **3** *followers of Christ* apostle, disciple, adherent, supporter, believer, worshipper, votary, pupil. **4** *followers of the Beatles* supporter, enthusiast, fan, admirer, devotee; *inf.* groupie, camp-follower, rooter.

following *adjective* **1** *the following day* next, ensuing, succeeding, subsequent, successive. **2** *will the following people leave* about to be men-

tioned/specified. **3** *there was a quarrel and a following fight* resulting, ensuing, consequent, consequential. *Opposites* PRECEDING; FOREGOING.

following *noun* *the new ideas/leaders have quite a following* body of support, backing, clientele, public, audience, circle, coterie, retinue, train; supporters, backers, admirers, fans, adherents, devotees, advocates, patrons.

folly *noun* foolishness, absurdity, absurdness, stupidity, silliness, nonsense, nonsensicalness, senselessness, illogicality, inanity, madness, craziness, idiocy, imbecility, lunacy, ridiculousness, ludicrousness, fatuousness, fatuity, rashness, recklessness, imprudence, indiscretion, irrationality; *inf.* daftness. *Opposites* WISDOM; SENSE.

foment *verb* instigate, incite, provoke, agitate, excite, stir up, arouse, encourage, urge, actuate, initiate.

fond *adjective* **1** *fond of music* having a liking/love for, having a taste/fancy for, partial to, keen on, attached to, in love with, enamoured of, having a soft spot for, addicted to; *inf.* hooked on. **2** *his fond wife* adoring, devoted, loving, affectionate, caring, warm, tender, amorous, doting, indulgent, overindulgent, overfond; uxorious. **3** *fond hopes of success* foolish, naive, overoptimistic, deluded, delusory, credulous, absurd, empty, vain, Panglossian. *Opposites* HOSTILE; INDIFFERENT; SENSIBLE.

fondle *verb* caress, stroke, pat, pet, cuddle, hug, nuzzle, dandle.

fondness *noun* **1** *look upon his brother with fondness* affection, love, warmth, tenderness, kindness, devotion, care, attachment, excessive devotion, dotingness; uxoriousness. **2** *have a fondness for chocolate* liking, love, taste, partiality, preference, weakness, soft spot, penchant, predilection, fancy, susceptibility. *Opposites* HATRED; DISLIKE.

food *noun* **1** *give food to the children* nourishment, sustenance, nutriment, subsistence, aliment, fare, diet, menu, table, bread, daily bread, board, provender, cooking, cuisine; foodstuffs, refreshments, edibles, meals, provisions, rations, stores, viands, victuals, commons, comestibles; solids; *inf.* eats, eatables, nosh, grub, chow, scoff. *See tables at* BEAN, BREAD, CAKE, CEREAL, CHEESE, COOKING, DESSERT, FRUIT, HERB, JOINT, MEAT, NUT, PASTA, PASTRY, SAUCE, SPICE, SWEET, VEGETABLE, VITAMIN. **2** *food for the cattle* fodder, feed, provender, forage. **3** *food for thought* stimulus, mental nourishment, something to think about, pabulum.

fool *noun* **1** *don't try to explain—he's a fool* idiot, ass, nitwit, halfwit, numskull, nincompoop, ninny, blockhead, dunce, dunderhead, dolt, ignoramus, dullard, illiterate, moron, simpleton, silly, dooby, jackass, loon, mooncalf; *inf.* dope, clot, chump, bonehead, fathead, birdbrain, twit, zombie, twerp, nerd; *Am. inf.* airhead. **2** *she always makes him look like a fool* | *make a fool of him* dupe, butt, laughing-stock, gull, pushover, easy mark, tool, cat's-paw; *inf.* stooge, sucker, sap, mug, fall guy. **3** *the fools of Shakespeare's day* jester, clown, buffoon, comic, jokester, zany, Merry Andrew, Harlequin, motley, Pierrot, Punchinello.

fool *verb* **1** *they certainly fooled the teacher* deceive, trick, play a trick on, hoax, make a fool of, dupe, take in, mislead, hoodwink, bluff, delude, beguile, bamboozle, cozen, gull; *inf.* con, kid, put one over on, have on. **2** *we thought he was dead but he was only fooling* pretend, make believe, feign, put on an act, act, sham, fake, counterfeit; *inf.* kid. **3** *the boys are always fooling* play the fool, jest, joke, play tricks, clown around, caper, cavort; *inf.* mess about. **4** *fool around with their cutlery* fiddle, play, fiddle/play around, toy, trifle, meddle, tamper, mess, interfere, monkey, monkey around. **5** *fool with someone else's wife* have an affair, philander, flirt, commit adultery.

foolery *noun* fooling, clowning, tomfoolery, hoaxing, horseplay, mischief, buffoonery, silliness, larking about; antics, capers, practical jokes, pranks, shenanigans, monkey tricks, larks.

foolhardy *adjective* reckless, rash, daredevil, devil-may-care, impulsive, hot-headed, impetuous, madcap, heedless, precipitate, daring, bold, adventurous, venturous, venturesome, incautious, imprudent, irresponsible, injudicious, desperate; *lit.* temerarious.

foolish *adjective* **1** *a foolish plan/idea* silly, absurd, senseless, nonsensical, unintelligent, inane, pointless, fatuous, ridiculous, laughable, derisible, risible, imprudent, incautious, irresponsible, injudicious, indiscreet, unwise, unreasonable, ill-advised, ill-considered, impolitic; *inf.* damfool, dotty, crack-brained, nutty, for the birds. **2** *a foolish fellow* stupid, silly, idiotic, simple, unintelligent, halfwitted, brainless, doltish, dull, dull-witted, dense, ignorant, illiterate, moronic, witless, weakminded, mad, crazy; *inf.* dumb, dopey, daft, potty, dotty, barmy, batty, dippy, cuckoo, screwy, wacky.
Opposites SENSIBLE; WISE; SOUND.

foolishness *noun* **1** *the foolishness of their actions* folly, stupidity, silliness, imprudence, lack of caution/foresight, indiscretion, irresponsibility, foolhardiness, senselessness, absurdity, inanity, madness, craziness, lunacy. **2** *talking foolishness* nonsense, rubbish, bunkum, gobbledegook, humbug, balderdash, claptrap, hogwash, rigmarole; *inf.* rot, tommy rot, bunk, tosh, poppycock, piffle, hooey, garbage, crap.

foolproof *adjective* infallible, never-failing, unfailing, certain, sure, guaranteed, safe, dependable, trustworthy.

foot *noun* **1** *an animal's foot* paw, hoof, trotter, pad. **2** *the foot of the structure* base, bottom, foundation, substructure, understructure. **3** *the foot of the road* bottom, end, edge, boundary, extremity, limit, border.

football *noun. See table. See also table at* SOCCER.

footing *noun* **1** *lose one's footing* foothold, secure position, grip, toehold, support. **2** *his business was on a secure footing* basis, foundation, groundwork, establishment. **3** *on a friendly*

AMERICAN FOOTBALL TEAMS	
Atlanta Falcons	New England
Buffalo Bills	Patriots
Chicago Bears	New Orleans Saints
Cleveland Browns	New York Giants
Dallas Cowboys	New York Jets
Denver Broncos	Philadelphia Eagles
Detroit Lions	Phoenix Cardinals
Green Bay Packers	Pittsburgh Steelers
Houston Oilers	San Diego Chargers
Indianapolis Colts	San Francisco 49ers
Kansas City Chiefs	Seattle Seahawks
Los Angeles Raiders	Tampa Bay
Los Angeles Rams	Buccaneers
Miami Dolphins	Washington
Minnesota Vikings	Redskins

footing relationship, standing, state, condition, position, basis, foundation; relations, terms.

footling *adjective* trivial, trifling, petty, insignificant, unimportant, minor, silly, pointless, immaterial, irrelevant, time-wasting, fiddling; *inf.* piddling, piffling.

footstep *noun* **1** *I hear her footsteps* footfall, step, tread. **2** *see footsteps in the snow* footprint, footmark, trace, track.

footwear *noun. See table.*

BOOTS AND SHOES		
babouche	getas	running
ballet shoes	gumboots	shoes
brogues	hobnail	sabots
buskins	boots	sandals
chappals	jackboots	scuffs
chukka	lace-ups	ski boots
boots	loafers *Am.*	slingbacks
climbing	moccasins	slip-ons
boots	moon boots	slippers
clogs	mukluks	sneakers *Am.*
combat	mules	snowshoes
boots	open-toed	stilettos
court shoes	sandals	stogies *Am.*
cowboy	overshoes	thigh boots
boots	Oxfords	thongs *Am.*
crepe-soled	paratrooper	top-boots
shoes	boots	trainers
Cuban heels	pattens	waders
desert boots	platforms	walking
Doc Martens	plimsolls	boots
(DMs)™	pumps	wedgies *Am.*
espadrilles	riding boots	Wellington
flip-flops	rubbers *Am.*	boots
football	rubber-soled	winkle-
boots	shoes	pickers
galoshes	rugby boots	zoris

fop *noun* dandy, coxcomb, popinjay, beau, poseur; *inf.* peacock, swell, toff.

forage *noun* **1** *forage for cattle* fodder, feed, food, foodstuff, provender, herbage, pasturage. **2** *an enemy forage into the castle* raid, foray, assault, invasion, incursion, plundering, ravaging, looting.

forage *verb* **1** *forage about for food | forage for her keys* search for, seek; look around for, hunt for, cast about for, rummage around for, scratch around for, scour for; *inf.* go on the scrounge for, scrounge for. **2** *the enemy forces foraged the village* raid, assault, invade, plunder, ravage, loot.

forbear *verb* refrain from, abstain from, desist from, keep from, restrain oneself from, hold back from, resist the temptation to, stop oneself from, withhold from, eschew, avoid, shun, decline, cease, give up, leave off, break off.

forbearance *noun* **1** *teachers showing great forbearance* tolerance, toleration, patience, resignation, endurance, long-sufferingness, self-control, restraint, leniency, lenity, clemency, moderation, temperance, indulgence. **2** *his forbearance from speaking* refraining, abstinence, desisting, resistance, withholding, avoidance. *See* FORBEAR.

forbid *verb* *dog fighting is forbidden* prohibit, ban, bar, debar, outlaw, veto, proscribe, disallow, interdict, preclude, exclude, rule out, stop, declare taboo.
Opposites ALLOW; AUTHORIZE; PERMIT.

forbidden *adjective forbidden territory* prohibited, out of bounds, banned, debarred, outlawed, vetoed, proscribed, interdicted, taboo, verboten.

forbidding *adjective* **1** *a forbidding manner* stern, harsh, grim, hard, tough, hostile, unfriendly, disagreeable, nasty, mean, abhorrent, repellent; *inf.* off-putting. **2** *a forbidding landscape* frightening, threatening, ominous, menacing, sinister, daunting, foreboding.

force *noun* **1** *requiring a lot of force* strength, power, potency, vigour, energy, might, muscle, stamina, effort, exertion, impact, pressure, life, vitality, stimulus, dynamism; *inf.* punch. **2** *use force to persuade them* compulsion, coercion, duress, pressure, pressurization, constraint, enforcement, violence; *inf.* arm twisting. **3** *arguments with force* persuasiveness, cogency, validity, weight, effectiveness, efficacy, efficaciousness, influence, power, strength, vehemence, significance; *inf.* bite, punch. **4** *from force of habit* agency, effect, influence. **5** *speaking with great force* vehemence, intensity, vigour, drive, fierceness, feeling, passion, vividness. **6** *a task force/a military force* body of people, corps, detachment, unit, squad, squadron, battalion, division, patrol, regiment, army. **in force 1** *rules no longer in force* in operation, operative, valid, on the statute book, current, effective, binding. **2** *the fans were out in force* in full strength, in great numbers, in great quantities, in hordes.

force *verb* **1** *force them to go* exert/use use force on, compel, coerce, make, use duress on, bring pressure to bear on, pressurize, pressure, press-gang, constrain, impel, drive, oblige, necessitate, urge by force; *inf.* put the squeeze/bite on, use strong-arm tactics on. **2** *force the door/safe* force open, break open, burst open, blast, prise open, crack. **3** *the wind forced them back* drive, propel, push, thrust, shove, press. **4** *force a confession from them* wrest, extract, wring, extort, drag.

forced *adjective* **1** *a forced confession* enforced, compulsory, compelled, obligatory, mandatory, involuntary, unwilling. **2** *a forced laugh* strained, unnatural, artificial, false, feigned, overdone, affected, contrived, stilted, laboured, wooden, self-conscious.

forceful *noun forceful speakers/arguments* vigorous, powerful, potent, strong, weighty, dynamic, energetic, assertive, effective, cogent, telling, persuasive, convincing, compelling, moving, impressive, valid.
Opposites WEAK; FEEBLE.

forcible *adjective* **1** *forcible entry* by force, using force, forced, violent. **2** *forcible conscription* compulsory, obligatory, imposed, required, binding. **3** *forcible arguments* forceful, vigorous, powerful, potent. *See* FORCEFUL.

forcibly *adverb* **1** *thrown out forcibly* compulsorily, under compulsion, by force, under coercion, against one's will, under protest, of necessity, willy-nilly. **2** *speak forcibly* forcefully, vigorously, powerfully, potently, dynamically, energetically, assertively, effectively, cogently, tellingly, persuasively, convincingly, movingly, impressively.

forebear *noun* forefather, ancestor, forerunner, progenitor, primogenitor, predecessor, father.

forebode *verb* augur, presage, portend, foreshadow, foreshow, foretoken, betoken, prefigure, presignify, signify, mean, indicate, point to, foretell, forecast, predict, prophesy, forewarn, warn of, prognosticate.

foreboding *noun* **1** *a foreboding that the car would crash* presentiment, premonition, intuition, sixth sense, feeling, vague feeling, misgiving, suspicion, anxiety, apprehension, apprehensiveness, fear, dread. **2** *listening to the forebodings of the soothsayer* augury, prophecy, prediction, presage, prognostication, forecast, warning, omen, portent, sign, foretoken, token.

forecast *verb* *he forecast that they would be late* predict, foretell, foresee, prophesy, forewarn, prognosticate, augur, divine, guess, hazard a guess, conjecture, speculate, estimate, calculate.

forecast *noun* *his forecast proved wrong* prediction, prophecy, forewarning, prognostication, augury, guess, conjecture, speculation, prognosis, projection; *inf.* guesstimate.

forefather *noun* forebear, ancestor, forerunner. *See* FOREBEAR.

forefront *noun* **1** *in the forefront of my mind* front, forward/foremost position, fore, foreground. **2** *in the forefront of the party* lead, leading position, head, position of prominence, van, vanguard, spearhead.
Opposites BACK; BACKGROUND.

forego *See* FORGO.

foregoing *adjective* preceding, precedent, prior, previous, former, above, aforesaid, aforementioned, antecedent, anterior.

foregone *adjective* **1** *in foregone days* past, former, earlier, previous, prior. **2** *foregone conclusions* predetermined, predecided, preordained, predestined, fixed, cut-and-dried, inevitable.

foreground noun **1** in the foreground of the picture front, fore, forefront. **2** in the foreground forefront, lead, position of prominence, vanguard. See FOREFRONT 2.

foreign adjective **1** from foreign parts overseas, alien, distant, remote. **2** foreign objects strange, unfamiliar, unknown, exotic, outlandish, odd, peculiar, curious. **3** matters foreign to the discussion irrelevant, not pertinent, unrelated, unconnected, inappropriate, inapposite, extraneous, extrinsic, outside.
Opposites HOME; NATIVE; FAMILIAR; RELEVANT.

foreigner noun non-native, alien, immigrant, incomer, newcomer, stranger, outsider.

foreman noun chargehand, overseer, supervisor, manager, superintendent; inf. boss, gaffer; Am. inf. honcho.

foremost adjective leading, principal, premier, prime, top, first, primary, front, advanced, paramount, chief, main, most important, supreme, highest, pre-eminent.

forerunner noun predecessor, precursor, ancestor, antecedent, forefather, herald, harbinger, usher, advance guard.

foresee verb foreknow, anticipate, envisage, predict, foretell, forecast, prophesy, divine, prognosticate, forebode, augur.

foreshadow verb forebode, bode, presage, augur, portend, omen, foretoken, betoken, foreshow, indicate, signify, mean, point to, suggest, signal, prefigure, promise.

foresight noun forethought, discernment, far-sightedness, circumspection, prudence, presence of mind, judiciousness, discrimination, perspicacity, care, caution, precaution, readiness, preparedness, anticipation, provision, prescience.

forest noun wood, woodland, tree plantation, plantation; woods, trees. See table.

TYPES OF FOREST AND WOOD

boreal forest	mixed forest
broadleaf forest	monsoon forest
chaparral	montane rainforest
cloud forest	rainforest
coniferous forest	scrub
deciduous forest	subtropical forest
dry tropical forest	taiga
dry tropical scrub	temperate
evergreen forest	rainforest
garigue	thorn forest
jungle	tropical deciduous
maquis	forest
Mediterranean scrub	tropical rainforest

---

forestall verb pre-empt, intercept, anticipate, be beforehand, get ahead of, steal a march on, thwart, frustrate, stave off, ward off, fend off, avert, prevent, hinder, impede, obstruct, sidetrack.

forestry noun forest management, forest planting, tree growing, arboriculture, silviculture, dendrology.

foretell verb **1** she foretold his death predict, forecast, foresee, prophesy, forewarn, prognos-

ticate, augur, divine. **2** the first match foretold the final result forebode, augur, presage, portend, foreshadow, foreshow, foretoken, betoken, prefigure, point to, indicate.

forethought noun foresight, far-sightedness, circumspection, prudence, judiciousness, care, precaution, anticipation, provision. See FORESIGHT.

forever adverb **1** loving each other forever always, ever, evermore, for all time, till the end of time, till the cows come home, till hell freezes over, till Doomsday, eternally, undyingly, world without end, perpetually, in perpetuity; inf. for keeps, for good and all. **2** he's forever playing loud music all the time, incessantly, continually, constantly, perpetually, endlessly, unremittingly, interminably, everlastingly.

forewarn verb prewarn, warn, give advance/fair warning to, put on one's guard, tip off, put on the qui vive, alert, caution, advise, apprise, precaution, premonish.

foreword noun introduction, preface, preamble, preliminary/front matter, prologue, prolegomenon.

forfeit noun pay/suffer a forfeit as a punishment forfeiture, fine, penalty, mulct; damages; confiscation, loss, relinquishment, amercement; Law sequestration.

forfeit verb children having to forfeit their sweets/treats relinquish, hand over, give up, surrender, renounce, be stripped/deprived of; Law escheat.

forge[1] verb **1** blacksmiths forging horseshoes hammer out, beat into shape, shape, form, fashion, mould, found, cast, make, manufacture, frame, construct, create. **2** forge an excuse invent, make up, devise, coin, fabricate, put together. **3** forge handwriting/banknotes copy, copy fraudulently, imitate, fake, falsify, counterfeit.

forge[2] verb soldiers forging on advance steadily/gradually, press on, push on, plod along. **forge ahead** advance rapidly, progress quickly, make swift progress, increase speed, put a spurt on.

forger noun counterfeiter, falsifier, faker, copyist, coiner.

forgery noun **1** accused of forgery of signatures/coins fraudulent copying/imitation, falsification, faking, counterfeiting, coining. **2** the vase is a forgery fake, counterfeit, sham, fraud, imitation, reproduction; inf. phoney.

forget verb **1** forget her phone number fail to remember/recall, fail to think of, let slip. **2** it's best to forget unhappy times cease to remember, put out of one's mind, disregard, ignore, let bygones be bygones. **3** I forgot my gloves leave behind, omit to take, overlook. **forget oneself** misbehave, behave improperly.
Opposites REMEMBER; RECOLLECT; TAKE.

forgetful adjective **1** old people growing forgetful apt to forget, absent-minded, amnesic, amnesiac, abstracted, vague. **2** forgetful of one's duties neglectful, negligent, heedless, careless, unmindful, inattentive, oblivious, lax, remiss, disregardful.

forgetfulness *noun* **1** *suffering from forgetfulness* absent-mindedness, amnesia, poor memory, lapse of memory, abstraction, vagueness, wool-gathering. **2** *guilty of forgetfulness of their duty* negligence, heedlessness, carelessness, inattention, obliviousness, laxness, remissness, disregard.

forgive *verb* pardon, excuse, exonerate, absolve, acquit, let off, let bygones be bygones, bear no malice, harbour no grudge, bury the hatchet; *inf.* let someone off the hook.
Opposites BLAME; CONDEMN; CONVICT.

forgiveness *noun* pardon, amnesty, exoneration, absolution, acquittal, remission, absence of malice/grudges, mercy.

forgiving *adjective* *a forgiving nature* lenient, merciful, compassionate, magnanimous, humane, clement, mild, soft-hearted, forbearing, tolerant, placable.

forgo, forego *verb* do/go without, waive, renounce, relinquish, sacrifice, forswear, surrender, abjure, abandon, cede, yield, abstain from, refrain from, eschew.

forgotten *adjective* unremembered, out of mind, past recollection, beyond/past recall, consigned to oblivion, obliterated, blotted out, buried, left behind, bygone, past, gone, lost, irrecoverable.

fork *verb* *our road forks left | the road forks* branch, branch off, diverge, bifurcate, divaricate, divide, split, separate, go in different directions, go separate ways.

forked *adjective* branching, branched, diverging, bifurcate, divaricate, Y-shaped, V-shaped, pronged, divided, split, separated.

forlorn *adjective* **1** *children looking forlorn* unhappy, sad, miserable, wretched, pathetic, woebegone, lonely, disconsolate, desolate, cheerless, pitiable, pitiful, uncared-for. **2** *a forlorn farmhouse* abandoned, forsaken, deserted, forgotten, neglected. **3** *a forlorn attempt* hopeless, desperate, despairing, in despair.
Opposites HAPPY; HOPEFUL.

form *verb* **1** *form shapes* make, fashion, shape, model, mould, forge, found, construct, build, assemble, put together, set up, erect, create, produce, concoct, devise. **2** *form plans* formulate, devise, think up, plan, draw up, frame, forge, hatch, develop, organize; *inf.* dream up. **3** *form an alliance* set up, bring about, devise, establish, found, organize, institute, inaugurate. **4** *shapes began to form* take shape, materialize, appear, show up, become visible, come into being/existence. **5** *form bad habits* acquire, develop, get, pick up, contract, grow into; *inf.* get into. **6** *form the children into lines* arrange, draw up, line up, assemble, organize, order, range, dispose, rank, grade. **7** *these books form the complete series* make, make up, comprise, constitute, compose. **8** *this plank will form the bridge* constitute, serve as, be a component/element/part of. **9** *forming young children's minds* develop, train, teach, instruct, educate, school, drill, discipline.

form *noun* **1** *observe the form of the crystals* shape, configuration, formation, conforma-

tion, structure, construction, arrangement, disposition, outward form/appearance, exterior. **2** *of a well-built form* body, physique, figure, shape, build, frame, anatomy, silhouette, contour. **3** *help in the form of the postman* shape, appearance, manifestation, semblance, guise, character, description. **4** *a form of punishment* type, kind, sort, variety, species, genus, genre, stamp, kidney. **5** *admire the form of the painting | his literary work lacks form* structure, framework, format, organization, planning, order, orderliness, symmetry, proportion. **6** *put the mixture into a form* mould, cast, shape, matrix, pattern. **7** *the form of the athletes matters most* fitness, condition, good condition, health, shape, trim, fettle. **8** *not good form to yawn* manners; polite behaviour, acceptable conduct, etiquette, convention, protocol; *inf.* done thing. **9** *know the form for organizing the garden party* manner, method, mode, style, system, formula, set formula, procedure, correct/usual way, convention, custom, ritual, protocol, etiquette; rules. **10** *fill in the forms* document, application form, application, sheet of paper, paper. **11** *what form is your daughter in?* class, year; *Am.* grade.

formal *adjective* **1** *formal documents/procedures* official, set, fixed, conventional, standard, regular, customary, approved, prescribed, pro forma, legal, lawful, ceremonial, ritual. **2** *a formal dinner* ceremonial, ceremonious, ritualistic, elaborate. **3** *a very formal person | have a formal manner* reserved, aloof, remote, correct, proper, conventional, precise, exact, punctilious, stiff, unbending, inflexible, standoffish, prim, stuffy, strait-laced. **4** *a formal garden* symmetrical, regular, orderly, arranged, methodical.
Opposites INFORMAL; CASUAL; UNOFFICIAL.

formality *noun* **1** *dislike the formality of the occasion* conventionality, ceremoniousness, ritual, red tape, decorum, etiquette, protocol. **2** *obey the formalities* rule, convention, custom, matter of form, official procedure, formal gesture; form, punctilio.

formation *noun* **1** *planes flying in formation* configuration, format, structure, organization, order, arrangement, pattern, design, disposition, grouping, layout. **2** *the formation of the new buildings is nearly complete* manufacture, making, construction, building, erecting, fashioning, shaping. See FORM *verb* 1. **3** *the formation of a new government* setting up, establishment, founding, institution, creation, inauguration. **4** *dislike the formation of the committee* composition, make-up, constitution, organization. **5** *the formation of the national character* genesis, development, evolution, emergence.

formative *adjective* **1** *in a child's formative years* developing, developmental, growing, mouldable, malleable, impressionable, susceptible, educable, teachable. **2** *a formative influence on the child* forming, shaping, moulding, determinative, influential.

former *adjective* **1** *the former ruler* ex-, previous, prior, preceding, precedent, foregoing, earlier, one-time, quondam, erstwhile, antecedent, anterior, *ci-devant*, late, sometime. **2** *in former times* earlier, past, long past, bygone, long ago, long departed, long gone, old, ancient, of yore. **3** *the former person* first-mentioned, first.

formerly *adverb* previously, at an earlier time, in earlier times, at one time, once, once upon a time, in times past, heretofore.

formidable *adjective* **1** *of a formidable appearance* intimidating, redoubtable, daunting, alarming, frightening, terrifying, petrifying, horrifying, dreadful, awesome, fearsome, menacing, threatening, dangerous; *inf.* scary. **2** *a formidable task* arduous, onerous, difficult, tough, colossal, mammoth, challenging, overwhelming, staggering, huge, tremendous; *inf.* mind-boggling, mind-blowing. **3** *a formidable opponent* strong, powerful, mighty, impressive, terrific, tremendous, great, redoubtable, indomitable, invincible.
Opposites PLEASANT; EASY; WEAK.

formula *noun* **1** *a legal/mathematical formula* formulary, established form of words, set of words/symbols, set expression, code. **2** *the formula for writing a successful novel* recipe, prescription, rubric, blueprint, method, procedure, convention, ritual, *modus operandi*; principles, rules, precepts.

formulate *verb* **1** *formulate one's thoughts in plain English* express/state clearly, define, articulate, set down, frame, give form to, specify, particularize, itemize, detail, designate, systematize, indicate. **2** *formulate our plans* draw up, work out, map out, plan, prepare, compose, devise, think up, conceive, create, invent, originate, coin, design.

fornication *noun* sexual intercourse, sex, coitus, copulation.

forsake *verb* **1** *forsake his wife and children* desert, abandon, leave, leave in the lurch, quit, throw over, jilt, cast off, discard, repudiate, reject, disown; *inf.* leave flat; *Am. inf.* give someone the air. **2** *forsake her life of luxury* give up, renounce, relinquish, forgo, turn one's back on, repudiate, have done with, discard, set aside.
Opposites RETURN; KEEP; RETAIN.

forsaken *adjective* **1** *forsaken wives* deserted, abandoned, cast off, discarded, jilted, rejected. **2** *what a forsaken place* godforsaken, remote, isolated, marooned, lonely, solitary, deserted, derelict, desolate, dreary, forlorn.

forswear *verb* *forswear drinking* give up, renounce, abjure, reject, relinquish, forgo, quit, do without; *inf.* cut out.

fort *noun* fortress, stronghold, citadel, fastness, garrison, castle, tower, donjon, keep, turret, fortification, redoubt, battlement.

forte *noun* strong point, strength, *métier*, speciality, talent, skill, gift, bent; *inf.* bag, thing.

forth *adverb* **1** *from that day forth* onward, onwards, forward, forwards. **2** *go forth from the tent* out, outside, away, off, away from home, abroad.

forthcoming *adjective* **1** *forthcoming events* future, coming, approaching, expected,

prospective, imminent, impending. **2** *no reply was forthcoming* made available, available, ready, at hand, accessible, obtainable, at one's disposal; *inf.* on tap. **3** *the children are not very forthcoming* communicative, informative, talkative, expansive, voluble, chatty, conversational, loquacious, open, unreserved.
Opposites PAST; RETICENT.

forthright *adjective* *a forthright person* direct, frank, candid, blunt, outspoken, plain-speaking, plain-spoken, downright, straightforward, open, honest.
Opposites SECRETIVE; RETICENT; DISHONEST.

forthwith *adverb* right away, immediately, at once, instantly, this instant, directly, straightaway, without delay, quickly.

fortification *noun* **1** *the fortification of the walls* strengthening, reinforcement, bracing. **2** *soldiers manning the fortifications* battlement, rampart, bastion, bulwark, parapet, blockhouse, barricade, buttress, stronghold, palisade, stockade, outwork.

fortify *verb* **1** *fortify the town* build defences round, garrison, embattle, guard, cover, protect, secure. **2** *fortify the walls* strengthen, reinforce, shore up, brace, buttress. **3** *fortify himself with a drink* strengthen, invigorate, energize, revive, embolden, give courage to, encourage, cheer, hearten, buoy up, reassure, make confident, brace, sustain. **4** *fortify wine* add spirits/alcohol to. **5** *fortify food* add vitamins/minerals to.

fortitude *noun* strength, strength of mind, moral strength, firmness of purpose, backbone, grit, mettle, courage, nerve, pluck, bravery, fearlessness, valour, intrepidity, stout-heartedness, endurance, patience, long-sufferingness, forbearance, tenacity, pertinacity, perseverance, resolution, resoluteness, determination.

fortress *noun* fort, stronghold, citadel, fastness. *See* FORT.

fortuitous *adjective* chance, unexpected, unanticipated, unforeseen, unlooked-for, serendipitous, casual, haphazard, random, accidental, unintentional, unplanned, unpremeditated, incidental; lucky, fortunate, felicitous; *inf.* fluky.

fortunate *adjective* **1** *a fortunate person* lucky, in luck, favoured, blessed, born with a silver spoon in one's mouth, born under a lucky star, having a charmed life, happy, felicitous, prosperous, well-off, successful, flourishing; *inf.* sitting pretty, jammy. **2** *in a fortunate position* advantageous, favourable, helpful, providential, auspicious, propitious, promising, encouraging, opportune, felicitous, profitable, fortuitous, timely, well-timed, convenient.

fortune *noun* **1** *a merchant of great fortune* wealth, treasure, affluence, opulence, opulency, prosperity, substance, property; riches, assets, means, possessions, estates. **2** *the ring cost a fortune* huge amount, mint, king's ransom; *inf.* packet, bundle, bomb, pile. **3** *by good fortune he won* chance, mere chance, accident, coincidence, contingency, happy chance, fortuity, serendipity, luck, providence. **4** *tell one's* *fortune* destiny, fate, lot, cup, portion, kismet; stars. **5** *fortune smiled on him* Lady Luck, Dame Fortune, fate. **6** *the fortunes of the club* state of affairs, condition, position; circumstances.

fortune-teller *noun* seer, soothsayer, prophet, prophetess, augur, diviner, sibyl, oracle, astrologer, clairvoyant.

forum *noun* **1** *a forum for discussion about the new road* meeting, assembly, symposium, round table conference, debate, discussion place, discussion medium. **2** *awarded damages by the forum* court, tribunal. **3** *Caesar and Brutus meeting in the forum* public meeting place, public square, market place.

forward *adjective* **1** *a forward movement* moving forwards/ahead, onward, advancing, progressing, progressive. **2** *the plants are forward this year* advanced, well-advanced, early, premature, precocious. **3** *the forward force* front, at the front/fore, fore, frontal, foremost, head, leading, advance. **4** *a forward young woman* bold, brash, brazen, brazen-faced, barefaced, audacious, presumptuous, presuming, assuming, familiar, overfamiliar, overassertive, overconfident, overweening, aggressive, thrusting, pert, impudent, impertinent, cheeky, insolent, unabashed; *inf.* pushy, cocky, brass-necked, fresh. **5** *forward planning* future, for the future, prospective.
Opposites BACKWARD; LATE; SHY.

forward *adverb* **1** *move forward* towards the front, frontwards, onward, onwards, on, ahead, forth. **2** *step forward for the prize* out, forth, into view, into the open, into public notice, into prominence. **3** *from today forward* on, onward, hence.

forward *verb* **1** *forward the letter/parcel* send on, send, pass on, dispatch, transmit, post, mail, ship, freight, deliver. **2** *his help forwarded our plans* advance, further, speed up, hasten, hurry along, expedite, accelerate, step up, aid, assist, help, foster, encourage, promote, favour, support, back, give backing to.

forward-looking *adjective* progressive, go-ahead, modern, enterprising, reforming, radical, liberal; *inf.* go-getting.

forwardness *noun* *the forwardness of the young woman* boldness, brashness, brazenness, audacity, presumption, overfamiliarity, overconfidence, aggressiveness, pertness, impudence, impertinence, cheek, cheekiness, insolence; *inf.* pushiness, cockiness.

forwards *adverb* towards the front, frontwards. See FORWARD *adverb* 1.

fossil *noun* remains, reliquae, petrified remains; surviving trace/impression, remnant, relic. See table. See also table at DINOSAUR.

foster *verb* **1** *foster freedom of thought* encourage, promote, further, stimulate, boost, advance, forward, cultivate, foment, help, aid, assist, support, uphold, back, give backing to, facilitate. **2** *foster a child* bring up, rear, raise, care for, take care of, mother, parent. **3** *foster hopes of being rich* cherish, harbour, entertain, nurse, nourish, nurture, hold, sustain.

foul *adjective* **1** *that food looks foul* disgusting, revolting, repulsive, nauseating, sickening, loathsome, abominable, odious, offensive, nasty. **2** *that cheese smells foul* foul-smelling, evil-smelling, ill-smelling, stinking, high, fetid, rank, mephitic; *lit.* noisome. **3** *foul water* contaminated, polluted, adulterated, infected,

---

FOSSILS

acanthodian	creodont	ground sloth	multi-	Quetzalcoatlus
Aegypto-	Cro-Magnon	Gryphaea	tuberculate	Ramapithecus
pithecus	Man	Hesperornis	Neanderthal	Rhampho-
Aepyornis	Cryptoclidus	Hyracotherium	Man	rhynchus
amber	Cygnognathus	Ichthyornis	nothosaur	rugose coral
ammonite	cynodont	ichthyosaur	nummulite	sabretooth
anoplothere	Deinotherium	Ichthyostega	osteostracan	Seymouria
anthracothere	Diatryma	Java man	ostracoderm	Sivapithecus
Archaeopteryx	Dicynodon	labyrinthodont	pantodont	Sivatherium
Archelon	Dimetrodon	Lepidodendron	Paranthropus	Smilodon
Arsinoitherium	Dimorphodon	lepidosaur	Parapithecus	stromatolite
arthrodire	dinocephalian	lepospondyl	pareiasaur	symmetro-
Australo-	Dinornis	Lucy	Peking Man	dont
pithecus	Diprotodon	Lycaenops	pelycosaur	synapsid
Baluchitherium	dire wolf	mammoth	Phororhacos	temnospondyl
Barylambda	Dryopithecus	mastodon	phytosaur	thecodont
belemnite	elasmosaur	Megaloceros	placoderm	therapsid
Brontops	elephant-bird	Megatherium	placodont	Thylacosmilus
brontothere	eohippus	Merychippus	Plesiadapis	titanothere
caenolestid	Eryops	Mesohippus	plesiosaur	Toxodon
calamite	eurypterid	mesosaur	Pliopithecus	trilobite
cave bear	giant elk	miacid	pliosaur	Uintatherium
cave lion	Giganto-	microsaur	Proconsul	woolly
cephalaspid	pithecus	Moeritherium	Propliopithecus	mammoth
chalicothere	Glyptodon	Morganucodon	Psilophyton	woolly
condylarth	Gompho-	Moropus	pteranodon	rhinoceros
coprolite	therium	mosasaur	pterodactyl	Zeuglodon
corallite	graptolite	Moschops	pterosaur	Zinjanthropus

tainted, defiled, impure, filthy, dirty, unclean.
4 *foul carcasses* rotten, rotting, decayed, decomposed, putrid, putrescent, putrefactive, carious. **5** *use foul language* foul-mouthed, blasphemous, profane, obscene, vulgar, gross, coarse, filthy, dirty, indecent, indelicate, suggestive, smutty, blue, off-colour, low, lewd, ribald, salacious, scatological, offensive, abusive.
6 *he's a foul creature* horrible, detestable, abhorrent, loathsome, hateful, despicable, contemptible, abominable, offensive, odious, disgusting, revolting, dishonourable, disgraceful, base, low, mean, sordid, vile, wicked, vicious, heinous, execrable, iniquitous, nefarious, notorious, infamous, scandalous, egregious, flagitious. **7** *foul play by their competitors* unfair, unjust, dishonourable, dishonest, underhand, unsportsmanlike, unsporting, unscrupulous, unprincipled, immoral, crooked, fraudulent, dirty; *inf.* shady. **8** *foul*

clothes dirty, filthy, unwashed, soiled, grimy, grubby, stained, dirt-encrusted, muddied, begrimed, feculent. **9** *foul weather* dirty, nasty, disagreeable, bad, rough, wild, stormy, rainy, wet, blustery, squally, misty, foggy, murky, gloomy.
Opposites ATTRACTIVE; FRAGRANT; PURE; FAIR.

foul verb **1** *foul the pavement/water* dirty, soil, stain, blacken, muddy, begrime, splash, spatter, smear, besmear, besmirch, defile, pollute, contaminate, taint, sully. **2** *foul up the fishing line* snarl, entangle, twist, tangle, muddle. **3** *foul the traffic/drains* clog, choke, block, jam.

found verb **1** *found a new company* establish, set up, institute, originate, initiate, bring into being, create, start, inaugurate, constitute, endow, organize, develop. **2** *found the building* lay the foundations of, build, construct, erect,

BREEDS OF FOWL

Breed	Type of Fowl	Breed	Type of Fowl
Ancona	chicken	Modern Langshan	chicken
Andalusian	chicken	Muscovy	duck
Australorp	chicken	Nankin	bantam
Aylesbury	duck	Narragansett	turkey
Black East Indian	duck	New Hampshire Red	chicken
Black Norfolk	turkey	Nicholas	turkey
Booted	bantam	Norfolk Grey	chicken
Bourbon Red	turkey	North Holland Blue	chicken
Brahma	chicken	Old English Game	bantam
Brecon Buff	goose	Old English Pheasant Fowl	chicken
Bresse	chicken	Orloff	chicken
Broad-Breasted Bronze	turkey	Orpington	chicken
Broad-Breasted White	turkey	Orpington	duck
Cambridge Bronze	turkey	Pearl Grey	guinea fowl
Campine	chicken	Phoenix	chicken
Cayuga	duck	Pilgrim	goose
Chinese	goose	Plymouth Rock	chicken
Cochin	chicken	Poland	chicken
Crested	duck	Redcap	chicken
Crèvecour	chicken	Rhode Island Red	chicken
Croad Langshan	chicken	Roman	goose
Dorking	chicken	Rosecomb	bantam
Embden	goose	Rouen	duck
Faverolle	chicken	Rumpless	bantam
Frizzles	bantam	Scots Dumpy	chicken
Hamburgh	chicken	Scots Grey	chicken
Houdan	chicken	Sebastopol	goose
Indian Game	chicken	Sebright	bantam
Indian Runner	duck	Sicilian Buttercup	chicken
Ixworth	chicken	Silkie	chicken
Jersey Giant	chicken	Spanish	chicken
Jubilee Indian Game	chicken	Sultan	chicken
Khaki Campbell	duck	Sumatra Game	chicken
La Fleche	chicken	Sussex	chicken
Lakenfelder	chicken	Toulouse	goose
Lavender	guinea fowl	Transylvanian Naked	
Leghorn	chicken	Necks	chicken
Magpie	duck	Welsh Harlequin	duck
Malay	chicken	Welsummer	chicken
Malines	chicken	Whalesbury	duck
Mammoth Bronze	turkey	White	guinea fowl
Marans	chicken	White Austrian	turkey
Marsh Daisy	chicken	White Holland	turkey
Minorca	chicken	Wyandotte	chicken
Modern Game	chicken	Yokohama	chicken

put up, elevate. **3** *found his story on fact* base, ground, root.

foundation *noun* **1** *the foundation of the building* base, bottom, bedrock, substructure, substratum, understructure, underpinning. **2** *lay the foundations of maths* basis, groundwork; principles, fundamentals, rudiments. **3** *the foundation of the company* founding, establishing, setting up, institution, initiation, inauguration, constitution, endowment. *See* FOUND 1. **4** *set up an educational foundation* endowed institution, institution.

founder *noun* builder, constructor, maker, establisher, institutor, initiator, beginner, inventor, discoverer, framer, designer, architect, creator, author, originator, organizer, developer, generator, prime mover, father, patriarch.

founder *verb* **1** *ships foundered* sink, submerge, go to the bottom, go down, be lost at sea, capsize, run aground, be swamped; *inf.* go to Davy Jones's locker. **2** *plans foundered* fail, not succeed, fall through, break down, go wrong/awry, misfire, come to grief/nothing, miscarry, abort, flounder, collapse; *inf.* come a cropper. **3** *the horse foundered* stumble, trip, stagger, lurch, fall, topple, sprawl, go lame, collapse.

foundling *noun* abandoned infant, orphan, waif, stray, outcast.

fountain *noun* **1** *fountains built in the square* water fountain, jet, spray, spout, spurt, well, fount. **2** *fountains welling up from the mountain* spring, stream, source, well, fountainhead. **3** *the fountain of knowledge* fount, fountainhead, source, rise, well-head, well-spring, well, beginning, commencement, origin, cause, birth, genesis, root, mainspring, derivation, inception, inspiration, *fons et origo*.

fowl *noun* domestic fowl; chicken, hen, cock, bantam, duck, turkey, goose; poultry. *See table.*

fox *noun*. *See table.*

FOXES	
African sand fox	cross fox
Arctic/white/polar fox	fennec
	grey fox
Azara's fox	hoary fox
bat-eared fox	kit/steppe fox
Bengal/Indian fox	red fox
Blanford's fox	pale fox
blue fox	Ruppell's sand fox
Brant fox	Samson fox
Cape fox	silver fox
Chama fox	small-eared fox
chiloé fox	South American
Colpeo fox	foxes (Dusicyon –
common fox (v.	not true foxes)
vulpes)	swift fox
Corsac fox	Tibetan sand fox
crab-eating fox	

foyer *noun* entrance hall, reception area, hall, vestibule, lobby, anteroom, antechamber.

fracas *noun* disturbance, quarrel, altercation, fight, brawl, affray, row, rumpus, scuffle, tussle, skirmish, free-for-all, brouhaha, mêlée, donnybrook, riot, uproar, commotion; trouble, tumult, turmoil, pandemonium; *Scots* stushie.

fraction *noun* **1** *a fraction of the population* part, subdivision. **2** *cost a fraction of what you paid* | *move a fraction closer* small part, tiny piece, minute amount, bit, mite, scrap, trifle.

fractious *adjective* **1** *fractious children* cross, irritable, fretful, bad-tempered, crabbed, peevish, petulant, ill-humoured, ill-natured, querulous, testy, snappish, touchy, irascible, sulky, sullen, morose. **2** *the fractious element on the committee* unruly, rebellious, insubordinate, stubborn, obstinate, contrary, refractory, recalcitrant, unmanageable, intractable.

fracture *noun* **1** *the fracture of a bone* breaking, breakage, splitting, cleavage, rupture. **2** *a fracture in the bone* break, breakage, crack, split. *See table.* **3** *a fracture in the rock* split, crack, fissure, cleft, rift, slit, rent, chink, crevice, gap, opening, aperture.

TYPES OF HUMAN BONE FRACTURE	
Colles' fracture	impacted fracture
comminuted fracture	march fracture
	open fracture
compound fracture	Pott's fracture
green-stick fracture	simple fracture

fracture *verb* *the bone/material fractured* break, crack, split, splinter, rupture.

fragile *adjective* **1** *fragile pottery* easily broken, breakable, brittle, frangible, smashable, splintery, flimsy, frail, insubstantial, delicate, dainty, fine. **2** *feeling fragile after the party* ill, unwell, ailing, sickly, delicate, weak, infirm, unsound.
Opposites DURABLE; TOUGH; STRONG.

fragment *noun* **1** *fragments of glass from the bowl* piece, part, particle, chip, chink, shard, sliver, splinter, smithereen. **2** *a fragment of cloth* scrap, bit, snip, snippet, wisp, tatter. **3** *find the fragments of a book* remnant, remainder, fraction; remains, shreds.

fragmentary, fragmental *adjective* *fragmentary evidence* incomplete, disconnected, disjointed, broken, discontinuous, uneven, piecemeal, incoherent, scrappy, bitty, sketchy, unsystematic.

fragrance *noun* **1** *the fragrance of the roses* fragrancy, scent, perfume, bouquet, aroma, smell, sweet smell, redolence, balm, balminess. **2** *a bottle of fragrance* scent, perfume, toilet water; cologne, eau-de-Cologne.

fragrant *adjective* *fragrant flowers* scented, perfumed, aromatic, sweet smelling, redolent, balmy, odorous, odiferous.
Opposites SMELLY; FOUL.

frail *adjective* **1** *frail china* fragile, easily broken, breakable, frangible, delicate. *See* FRAGILE 1. **2** *frail old ladies* infirm, weak, delicate, slight, slender, puny, unsound, ill, ailing, unwell, sickly. **3** *frail creatures* weak, easily led/tempted, susceptible, impressionable, mal-

leable, vulnerable, fallible.
Opposites TOUGH; ROBUST; STRONG.

frailty noun **1** *the frailty of the china* fragility, brittleness, frangibility, flimsiness, insubstantiality, delicacy, daintiness, fineness. **2** *the frailty of the old* infirmness, infirmity, weakness, delicacy, slightness, puniness, illness. See FRAIL 2. **3** *the frailty of human nature* weakness, susceptibility, impressionability, vulnerability, fallibility. See FRAIL 3. **4** *excuse their frailties* foible, weakness, weak point, flaw, blemish, defect, failing, fault, shortcoming, deficiency, peccadillo.

frame noun **1** *built on a frame of steel* framework, substructure, structure, shell, casing, support, skeleton, scaffolding, foundation, body, chassis. **2** *the man had a huge frame* body, physique, build, figure, shape, size, skeleton, carcass. **3** *a photograph frame* mount, mounting, setting. **4** *alter the frame of society* order, organization, scheme, system, plan, fabric, form, constitution. **5** *a sad frame of mind* state, condition; mood, humour, temper, spirit, attitude.

frame verb **1** *frame the structure* assemble, put together, put/set up, build, construct, erect, elevate, make, fabricate, manufacture, fashion, mould, shape, forge. **2** *frame a policy* put together, formulate, draw up, plan, draft, map/plot/sketch out, shape, compose, form, devise, create, establish, conceive, think up, hatch; *inf.* dream up, cook up. **3** *frame a picture* | *hair framing his face* enclose, encase, surround. **4** *to frame a colleague* incriminate, fabricate charges/evidence against; *inf.* fit up.

frame-up noun false charge, trumped-up charge, plot, conspiracy, collusion; *inf.* put-up job, fit-up.

framework noun **1** *the framework of the building* frame, substructure, shell, skeleton. See FRAME noun 1. **2** *the framework of society* frame, order, organization, scheme, fabric. See FRAME noun 4.

franchise noun **1** *women given the franchise* right to vote, the vote, suffrage, enfranchisement. **2** *grant him a fast-food franchise* | *the corporation was given a franchise* warrant, warranty, charter, licence; permission, leave, consent, privilege, prerogative.

frank adjective **1** *a frank person/reply* candid, direct, forthright, plain, plain-spoken, straight, straight from the shoulder, downright, explicit, outspoken, blunt, bluff, open, sincere, honest, truthful, undissembling, guileless, artless. **2** *show frank admiration* open, obvious, transparent, patent, manifest, undisguised, unconcealed, unmistakable, evident, noticeable, visible.
Opposites RETICENT; EVASIVE; INSINCERE.

frank verb *frank a letter* stamp, postmark, mark, imprint.

frankly adverb **1** *frankly, I think he is lying* to be frank/honest, candidly, honestly, truthfully. See FRANK adjective 1. **2** *he spoke frankly* candidly, directly, plainly, explicitly, bluntly, openly, honestly, truthfully, without dissembling.

frantic adjective panic-stricken, panic-struck, panicky, beside oneself, at one's wits' end,

frenzied, wild, hysterical, frenetic, berserk, distraught, overwrought, worked up, distracted, agitated, distressed, out of control, uncontrolled, unhinged, mad, crazed, out of one's mind, maniacal; *inf.* fraught.

fraternity noun **1** *a strong bond of fraternity in the family* brotherhood, kinship. **2** *the teaching fraternity* profession, band of workers. **3** *join a university fraternity* club, society, association, guild, set, circle.

fraternize verb associate, mix, go around with, keep company with, hobnob with, socialize, mingle, consort; *inf.* hang around/out with.

fraud noun **1** *found guilty of fraud* fraudulence, sharp practice, cheating, swindling, trickery, deceit, double-dealing, duplicity, treachery, chicanery, skulduggery, imposture, embezzlement, crookedness; *inf.* monkey business. **2** *perpetrate a fraud* ruse, trick, hoax, deception, subterfuge, stratagem, wile, artifice, swindle; *inf.* con, rip-off. **3** *the man is a fraud* impostor, fake, sham, cheat, cheater, swindler, double-dealer, trickster, confidence trickster, pretender, charlatan, quack, mountebank; *inf.* phoney, con man. **4** *the vase/banknote is a fraud* fake, sham, counterfeit, forgery; *inf.* phoney.

fraudulent adjective dishonest, cheating, swindling, criminal, deceitful, double-dealing, duplicitous, dishonourable, unscrupulous; *inf.* crooked, sharp, shady.

fraught adjective **1** *fraught with danger* full of, filled with, teeming with, attended by, accompanied by. **2** *the fraught young mother* anxious, overwrought, distraught, worked up, distracted, agitated, distressed.

fray verb **1** *the cloth is fraying* unravel, wear, wear thin, wear out/away, become threadbare, become tattered/ragged. **2** *tempers/nerves were frayed by the experience* strain, tax, overtax, irritate, put on edge, make edgy/tense.

freak noun **1** *that animal is a freak* freak of nature, aberration, abnormality, irregularity, oddity, monster, monstrosity, malformation, mutant, *rara avis*. **2** *the neighbours think he's a bit of a freak* oddity, peculiar person; *inf.* queer fish, odd bod, oddball, weirdo, weirdie, wayout person, nutcase, nut. **3** *they are film freaks* enthusiast, fan, fanatic, addict, aficionado, devotee; *inf.* buff, fiend, nut. **4** *she is full of freaks* whim, caprice, vagary, fad, fancy, quirk, crotchet. **5** *by a freak he discovered the answer* anomaly, unusual occurrence, peculiar turn of events, quirk, quirk/twist of fate; chance; *inf.* fluke.

freak adjective *a freak storm* abnormal, unusual, atypical, aberrant, exceptional, unaccountable, unpredictable, unforeseeable, bizarre, queer, odd, unparalleled; *inf.* fluky.

free adjective **1** *a free booklet* free of charge, for nothing, complimentary, gratis, without charge, at no cost; *inf.* for free, on the house. **2** *free of responsibilities* without, devoid of, lacking in, exempt from, not liable to, safe from, immune to, unaffected by, clear of, unencumbered by, relieved of, released from, rid of; *inf.* sans. **3** *he is not free today* unoccupied, available, not at work, not busy, not tied up, idle,

at leisure, with time on one's hands, with time to spare. **4** *is this place free?* empty, vacant, available, spare, unoccupied, untaken, uninhabited, tenantless. **5** *a free nation* independent, self-governing, self-governed, self-ruling, self-directing, sovereign, autonomous, democratic, emancipated, enfranchised, manumitted. **6** *the animals are free* at liberty, at large, loose, on the loose, unconfined, unbound, untied, unchained, unshackled, unfettered, unrestrained, wild. **7** *free to choose* able, allowed, permitted, unrestricted. **8** *a free flow of water | is the way forward free?* unobstructed, unimpeded, unhampered, clear, unblocked. **9** *the free end of the rope* not fixed, unattached, unfastened, loose. **10** *free with their money* generous, lavish, liberal, open-handed, unstinting, giving, munificent, bountiful, bounteous, charitable, extravagant, prodigal. **11** *a free natural manner* free and easy, easygoing, natural, open, frank, relaxed, casual, informal, unceremonious, unforced, spontaneous, uninhibited, artless, ingenuous; *inf.* laid-back. **12** *he's a bit too free in his manner for my liking* familiar, overfamiliar, presumptuous, forward, bold, assertive, aggressive, impudent; *inf.* cheeky, cocky. **free and easy** easygoing, natural, relaxed, casual, informal, tolerant. See FREE *adjective* 11.
Opposites OCCUPIED; BUSY; DEPENDENT; CAPTIVE.

free *verb* **1** *free the prisoners/animals* set free, release, let go, set at liberty, liberate, set/let/turn loose, untie, unchain, unfetter, unshackle, unmanacle, uncage, unleash, deliver. **2** *free the accident victims from the car* get free, rescue, release, get loose, extricate, disentangle, disengage, disencumber. **3** *freed from paying tax* exempt, make exempt, except, excuse, relieve.

freedom *noun* **1** *colonies seeking their freedom* independence, self-government, sovereignty, autonomy, democracy, emancipation, manumission, enfranchisement, home rule. **2** *prisoners/animals enjoying their freedom* liberty, release, deliverance, non-confinement. **3** *freedom from tax* exemption, immunity, impunity. **4** *freedom of speech* right, privilege, prerogative. **5** *freedom to move around | freedom to operate* scope, latitude, elbow room, wide margin, flexibility, facility, free rein, licence. **6** *admire her freedom of manner* naturalness, openness, lack of reserve/inhibition, casualness, informality, lack of ceremony, spontaneity, artlessness, ingenuousness. **7** *he treats her with too much freedom* familiarity, overfamiliarity, presumption, forwardness, impudence; *inf.* cheek. See FREE *adjective* 12.
Opposites DEPENDENCE; CAPTIVITY; RESPECT.

freely *adverb* **1** *speaking freely, I do not like them* frankly, openly, candidly, plainly, bluntly, unreservedly, without constraint. **2** *prisoners not allowed to speak freely* of one's own volition/accord, voluntarily, of one's own free will.

freeze *verb* **1** *the lake has frozen* ice over/up, glaciate, solidify, harden. **2** *freeze to death | I'm freezing* get chilled, get chilled to the bone/marrow, go numb with cold, turn blue with cold, shiver, shiver with cold, feel Jack Frost's fingers. **3** *freeze the vegetables* deep-freeze. **4** *he*

froze as he saw the gun stop dead, stop in one's tracks, stop, stand still, stand stock still, go rigid, become motionless. **5** *freeze prices* fix, hold, peg, suspend.

freezing *adjective* **1** *freezing winds* bitterly cold, chill, chilling, frosty, glacial, arctic, wintry, raw, biting, piercing, penetrating, cutting, stinging, numbing, Siberian. **2** *freezing children/toes* chilled through, chilled to the bone/marrow, numb with cold, frostbitten.

freight *noun* **1** *a separate charge for the freight* transportation, conveyance, freightage, carriage, portage, haulage. **2** *unload the freight* cargo, load, lading, consignment, merchandise; goods.

frenzied *adjective* frantic, frenetic, panic-stricken, panic-struck, beside oneself, at one's wits' end, wild, hysterical, distraught, distracted, overwrought, agitated, mad, crazed, out of one's mind, maniacal; *inf.* fraught. See FRANTIC.

frenzy *noun* **1** *go into a frenzy at the news* mental derangement, madness, mania, insanity, wild excitement, wildness, hysteria, distraction, agitation; fit, seizure, paroxysm. **2** *a frenzy of activity* bout, outburst, fit, spasm.

frequency *noun* **1** *the frequency of accidents on that road* frequentness, recurrence, repetition, persistence. **2** *infant mortality has decreased in frequency* rate of occurrence, rate of repetition, commonness.

frequent *adjective* **1** *frequent accidents* occurring often, recurrent, repeated, persistent, continuing, many, numerous, quite a few/lot, several. **2** *a frequent caller* regular, habitual, customary, common, usual, familiar, everyday, continual, constant, incessant.
Opposites INFREQUENT; FEW; RARE.

frequent *verb* visit, visit often, go to regularly/repeatedly, attend, attend frequently, haunt, patronize; *inf.* hang out at.

frequenter *noun* regular visitor, regular customer, regular, habitué, haunter.

frequently *adverb* often, very often, many times, many a time, again and again, over and over again, on several occasions, repeatedly, recurrently, habitually, continually, constantly.

fresh *adjective* **1** *is the fruit fresh?* garden-fresh, newly harvested, crisp, unwilted, unfaded, not stale. **2** *fresh, not tinned fruit* raw, natural, unprocessed, unpreserved, undried, uncured, crude. **3** *fresh ideas* new, brand-new, recent, latest, up-to-date, modern, modernistic, ultramodern, new fangled, different, innovative, original, novel, unusual, unconventional, unorthodox. **4** *feeling very fresh on holiday* energetic, vigorous, invigorated, vital, lively, vibrant, spry, sprightly, bright, alert, bouncing, refreshed, rested, restored, revived, like a new person, fresh as a daisy; *inf.* full of vim/beans, rarin' to go, bright-eyed and bushy-tailed; *Am. inf.* chipper. **5** *a fresh complexion* healthy-looking, healthy, clear, bright, youthful-looking, wholesome, blooming, glowing, fair, rosy, pink, reddish, ruddy. **6** *curtains looking fresh* bright, clean, spick and span, unfaded. **7** *fresh*

supplies more, other, additional, further, extra, supplementary, auxiliary. **8** *a fresh morning* | *fresh air* bright, clear, cool, crispy, crisp, sparkling; pure, unpolluted, clean, refreshing. **9** *fresh winds* cool, chilly, brisk, bracing, invigorating. **10** *fresh recruits* young, youthful, new, newly arrived, untrained, unqualified, inexperienced, untried, raw, callow, green, immature, artless, ingenuous, naive; *inf.* wet behind the ears. **11** *a fresh young man* familiar, overfamiliar, presumptuous, forward, bold, audacious, brazen, impudent, impertinent, insolent, disrespectful, pert, saucy; *inf.* cheeky, cocky, brass-necked.
Opposites STALE; TIRED; DULL.

freshen *verb* **1** *a walk will freshen you* | *the swim freshened her up* refresh, rouse, stimulate, revitalize, restore, revive, liven up. **2** *freshen the room* air, ventilate, deodorize, purify. **3** *freshen a drink* top up, refill. **4** *I must freshen up* wash oneself, tidy oneself, tidy/spruce oneself up, titivate oneself.

fret *verb* **1** *fretting about her mother's absence* be distressed, be upset, feel unhappy, be anxious, worry, agonize, anguish, pine, brood, mope, fuss, make a fuss, complain, grumble, whine; *inf.* feel peeved. **2** *the loud noise frets him* irritate, annoy, infuriate, exasperate, anger, rile, provoke, vex, irk, gall, pique, rankle with, nettle, ruffle, harass, torment, bother, trouble, disturb; *inf.* peeve.

fretful *adjective* distressed, upset, miserable, cross, crabbed, fractious, peevish, petulant, tetchy, out of sorts, irritable, bad-tempered, ill-natured, edgy, irascible, grumpy, crotchety, touchy, captious, testy, querulous, complaining, grumbling, whining; *Am.* cranky.

friction *noun* **1** *ropes worn by friction* rubbing, abrading, abrasion, attrition, chafing, fretting, gnawing, grating, rasping, scraping, excoriation. **2** *cause friction in the family* dissension, dissent, disagreement, discord, strife, conflict, clashing, contention, dispute, disputation, arguing, argument, quarrelling, bickering, squabbling, wrangling, fighting, hostility, rivalry, animosity, antagonism, resentment, bad feeling, ill feeling, bad blood, disharmony.

friend *noun* **1** *on holiday with friends* companion, boon companion, crony, mate, bosom friend, comrade, playmate, soul mate, intimate, confidante, confidant, familiar, *alter ego*, shadow, ally, associate; *inf.* pal, chum, china; *Am. inf.* buddy. **2** *friends of the local theatre* patron, backer, supporter, benefactor, well-wisher; *inf.* angel. **3** *their brother/sister and his/her friend* girl friend, boy friend, partner, lover; *inf.* live-in; *Scots inf.* bidie-in.
Opposites ENEMY; FOE.

friendless *adjective* companionless, alone, all alone, by oneself, lone, lonely, lonesome, with no one to turn to, solitary, with no ties, unattached, single, forlorn, unpopular, unbefriended.

friendliness *noun* affability, amiability, warmth, geniality, affection, companionability, cordiality, conviviality, sociability, comradeship, neighbourliness, approachability, com-

municativeness, good-naturedness, amenability, benevolence. See FRIENDLY 1.

friendly *adjective* **1** *a friendly person* affable, amiable, warm, genial, agreeable, affectionate, companionable, cordial, convivial, sociable, hospitable, comradely, neighbourly, outgoing, approachable, accessible, communicative, open, unreserved, easygoing, good-natured, kindly, benign, amenable, well-disposed, sympathetic, benevolent; *inf.* matey, chummy; *Am. inf.* clubby, buddy-buddy. **2** *on friendly terms* amicable, congenial, cordial, close, intimate, familiar, peaceable, peaceful, conciliatory, non-hostile, unwarlike; *inf.* thick with. **3** *a friendly wind swept the boat to the shore* helpful, favourable, advantageous, benevolent, well-disposed.
Opposites UNFRIENDLY; UNSOCIABLE; HOSTILE.

friendship *noun* **1** *their friendship lasted years* companionship, friendly/close relationship, intimacy, amity, mutual affection, affinity, rapport, mutual understanding, harmony, comradeship, fellowship, attachment, alliance; cordial relations. **2** *she always shows friendship to new people* friendliness, affability, amiability, warmth, geniality, cordiality, neighbourliness, good-naturedness, kindliness. See FRIENDLINESS.

fright *noun* **1** *start back in fright* fear, fear and trembling, terror, alarm, horror, dread, fearfulness, apprehension, trepidation, consternation, dismay, perturbation, disquiet, panic, nervousness, jitteriness; *inf.* blue funk, jitters, heebie-jeebies, willies. **2** *give them a fright* scare, shock; shivers; *inf.* jitters, a fit of the heebie-jeebies. **3** *woke up looking a fright* ugly/horrible/grotesque sight, eyesore; *inf.* mess, sight.

frighten *verb* scare, alarm, startle, terrify, terrorize, petrify, give a shock to, shock, appal, panic, throw into panic, unnerve, unman, intimidate, cow, daunt, dismay, make one's blood run cold, freeze one's blood; *inf.* scare the living daylights out of, scare stiff, scare out of one's wits, scare witless, make one's hair stand on end, make one's hair curl, put the wind up, throw into a blue funk, make someone jump out of his/her skin, spook.
Opposites REASSURE; COMFORT; ENCOURAGE.

frightful *adjective* **1** *the corpse was a frightful sight* dreadful, terrible, horrible, horrid, hideous, ghastly, grisly, gruesome, macabre, grim, dire, abhorrent, revolting, repulsive, loathsome, odious, fearful, fearsome, terrifying, alarming, shocking, harrowing, appalling, daunting, unnerving. **2** *a frightful woman* unpleasant, disagreeable, dreadful, horrible, terrible, awful, appalling, ghastly, insufferable, unbearable, annoying, irritating. **3** *have a frightful cold* very bad, terrible, dreadful, awful, ghastly, nasty.

frigid *adjective* **1** *frigid conditions* very cold, bitterly cold, bitter, freezing, frozen, icy, frosty, chilly, wintry, arctic, glacial, Siberian, polar, gelid, Hyperborean. **2** *a frigid look/welcome* cold, icy, austere, distant, aloof, remote, unapproachable, forbidding, stiff, formal, unbending, cool, unfeeling, unemotional, unfriendly, hostile, unenthusiastic. **3** *a frigid woman* sexually unresponsive, cold, passionless, passive,

inorgasmic.
Opposites HOT; PASSIONATE.

frill noun flounce, ruffle, ruff, furbelow, ruche, ruching, gather, tuck, fringe, purfle.

frills plural noun a plain meal with no frills ornamentation, decoration, embellishment, fanciness, ostentation, fuss; trimmings, falderals, affectations, extras, additions, superfluities, bits and pieces; inf. jazz, flash, fandangle.

fringe noun 1 a skirt with a fringe border, trimming, frill, edging; tassels. 2 on the fringe of the wood | the fringe of society outer edge, edge, borderline, perimeter, periphery, margin, rim; limits, borders, outskirts, verges, marches.

fringe adjective fringe theatre experimental, unconventional, unorthodox.

fringe verb 1 fringe a skirt trim, edge, befringe. 2 trees fringe the lake edge, border, skirt, surround, enclose.

frisk verb 1 lambs frisking frolic, gambol, cavort, caper, cut capers, skip, dance, leap, romp, trip, prance, hop, jump, bounce, rollick, sport, curvet. 2 frisked at the airport search, check, inspect; Am. inf. shake down.

frisky adjective lively, bouncy, active, frolicsome, coltish, playful, romping, rollicking, sportive, spirited, in high spirits, high-spirited, exuberant, joyful; inf. high, full of beans.

fritter verb 1 fritter away money squander, waste, overspend, misspend, spend like water, dissipate, run through, get through. 2 fritter away time waste, squander, misuse, idle away, while away, dally away.

frivolity noun 1 the serious student needs a little frivolity light-heartedness, levity, gaiety, fun, silliness, foolishness. 2 the frivolity of the girls frivolousness, giddiness, flightiness, dizziness, flippancy, silliness, zaniness, empty-headedness. See FRIVOLOUS 1. 3 the frivolity of the remark frivolousness, flippancy, superficiality, shallowness. See FRIVOLOUS 2.

frivolous adjective 1 frivolous young girls lacking seriousness, non-serious, lacking in sense, senseless, flippant, giddy, flighty, dizzy, silly, foolish, facetious, zany, light-hearted, merry, superficial, shallow, empty-headed, feather-brained; inf. flip. 2 a frivolous remark non-serious, flippant, ill-considered, superficial, shallow, inane, facetious; inf. flip. 3 frivolous clothes impractical, flimsy, frothy. 4 frivolous details trivial, trifling, minor, petty, insignificant, unimportant, paltry, niggling, peripheral.

frog noun. See table at AMPHIBIAN.

frolic verb frisk, gambol, cavort, caper, skip. See FRISK 1.

frolic noun 1 enjoy a frolic in the garden game, romp, lark, antic, caper, escapade, prank, revel, spree. 2 the children's frolic fun, fun and games, gaiety, merriment, mirth, amusement, laughter, jollity; inf. skylarking, high jinks.

front noun 1 towards the front of the building fore, forepart, foremost part, forefront, foreground, anterior. 2 paint the front of the building frontage, face, facing, façade. 3 at the front in the battle front line, vanguard, van, first line, firing line. 4 at the front of the queue beginning,

head, top, lead. 5 put a brave front on it look, appearance, face, exterior, air, manner, expression, show, countenance, demeanour, bearing, mien, aspect. 6 his shop is a front for his drug dealing cover, cover-up, blind, façade, disguise, pretext, mask. **in front** 1 the runners in front in the lead, to the fore, ahead, in the van, in advance. 2 in front of her in the queue ahead of, before, preceding.
Opposites BACK; REAR.

front adjective the front runners first, foremost, leading, lead.

front verb the house fronts on the lake face towards, look out on, overlook, lie opposite to.

frontier noun border, boundary, bound, limit, edge, rim; confines, marches.

frost noun 1 there was a frost last night freeze, freeze-up; inf. Jack Frost. 2 frost on the trees white frost, hoar-frost, rime. 3 frost in her greeting coldness, coolness, iciness, glaciality, frigidity, hostility, unfriendliness.

frosty adjective 1 a frosty morning freezing, frozen, rimy, frigid, glacial, arctic, icy, wintry, bitterly cold, bitter, cold; inf. nippy. 2 a frosty welcome cold, cool, icy, glacial, frigid, unfriendly, unwelcoming, unenthusiastic.

froth noun a froth on the liquid foam, spume, fizz, effervescence, scum, lather; head; bubbles, suds.

froth verb beer frothing in the glass | soap suds frothing foam, spume, cream, bubble, fizz, effervesce, lather.

frothy adjective 1 frothy lemonade foaming, foamy, foam-like, spumy, spumous, spumescent, bubbling, bubbly, fizzy, effervescent, sparkling. 2 a frothy dress frilly, flouncy, insubstantial. 3 a frothy novel light, lightweight, insubstantial, lacking substance, trivial, trifling, petty, paltry, insignificant, worthless, trite, hackneyed.

frown verb 1 the teacher frowning at the pupils scowl, glower, glare, lower, look daggers at, give black looks to; inf. give a dirty look to. 2 frowning in thought knit one's brows. 3 the club frowned at/on scruffy clothes disapprove of, show/indicate disapproval of, view with dislike/disfavour, dislike, discourage, look askance at, not take kindly to, not think much of, take a dim view of.

frozen adjective 1 frozen ground ice-covered, icy, icebound, frosted, hard, hard as iron. 2 frozen conditions frosty, icy, bitterly cold, glacial, frigid, arctic, Siberian, polar. 3 children are frozen freezing, very cold, chilled, chilled to the bone/marrow, numb with cold, shivering; inf. frozen to death.

frugal adjective 1 a frugal old man thrifty, sparing, economical, saving, careful, prudent, provident, unwasteful, abstemious, scrimping, niggardly, cheese-paring, penny-pinching, miserly, parsimonious, stingy. 2 a frugal amount of food meagre, scanty, paltry, insufficient.
Opposites EXTRAVAGANT; SPENDTHRIFT; LAVISH.

fruit noun. See table.

fruitful *adjective* **1** *fruitful trees* fruit-bearing, fructiferous, fruiting. **2** *a fruitful family* fertile, fecund, potent, fructuous, generative, progenitive. **3** *fruitful discussions* useful, worthwhile, productive, well-spent, profitable, advantageous, beneficial, rewarding, gainful, successful, effective.
Opposites BARREN; FUTILE; FRUITLESS.

fruition *noun* fulfilment, realization, materialization, actualization, achievement, attainment, success, completion, consummation, perfection, maturity, maturation, ripening.

fruitless *adjective* futile, vain, in vain, useless, abortive, to no avail, worthless, pointless, to no effect, idle, ineffectual, ineffective, inefficacious, unproductive, unrewarding, profitless, unsuccessful, unavailing.
Opposites PRODUCTIVE; PROFITABLE; FRUITFUL.

fruits *plural noun the fruits of our labours* results, consequences, effects, advantages; outcome, upshot, benefit, profit, reward.

fruity *adjective* **1** *a fruity chuckle* rich, deep, resonant, full. **2** *a fruity story* bawdy, blue, smutty, racy, risqué, juicy, indecent, indelicate, vulgar, coarse, off-colour, suggestive, titillating, salacious, sexy; *inf.* near the knuckle, spicy.

frustrate *verb* **1** *frustrate their attempts* defeat, thwart, check, block, counter, foil, baulk, disappoint, forestall, baffle, stymie, stop, spoil, cripple, nullify, obstruct, impede, hamper, hinder, circumvent. **2** *lack of success frustrated him* discourage, dishearten, dispirit, depress, dissatisfy, make discontented, anger, annoy, vex, irk, irritate, embitter.
Opposites FACILITATE; ENCOURAGE.

frustration *noun* **1** *the frustration of their plans* defeat, lack of success, non-success, non fulfilment, thwarting, foiling, baulking, forestalling, hampering, circumvention. *See* FRUSTRATE 1. **2** *full of frustration at their failure* dissatisfaction, disappointment, discontentment, anger, annoyance, irritation, vexation, resentment, bitterness.

fuddled *adjective* **1** *a fuddled mind* confused, muddled, bewildered, muzzy, stupefied, addled; *inf.* woozy, woolly-minded. **2** *fuddled people from the pub* drunk, inebriated, intoxicated, tipsy, tight; *inf.* legless, loaded, bevied. *See* DRUNK.

fuddy-duddy *noun* old fogy, museum piece, conservative; *inf.* stick-in-the-mud, square, stuffed shirt.

fudge *verb* **1** *fudge the issue* evade, dodge, skirt, shift ground about, avoid. **2** *fudge the accounts* falsify, fake; *inf.* cook. **3** *fudge his way through the speech* waffle, equivocate, hedge, hem and haw, shuffle.

fuel *noun* **1** *fuel for the heating/car* heat/power source; coal, wood, oil, petrol, diesel oil, paraffin, kerosene. *See table at* ENERGY. **2** *need fuel on cold mornings* nourishment, food, sustenance, fodder. **3** *his answer was fuel to her anger* incitement, provocation, goading, stimulus, incentive, encouragement, ammunition.

fuel *verb* **1** *fuel the steam engine* supply with fuel, fire, stoke up, charge, power. **2** *fuel her anger* fan, inflame, incite, provoke, goad, stimulate, encourage.

fugitive *noun* escapee, runaway, deserter, refugee.

fugitive *adjective* **1** *a fugitive prisoner* escaping, runaway, fleeing, deserting; *inf.* AWOL, on the run. **2** *fugitive happiness* transient, transitory, fleeting, ephemeral, evanescent, fugacious, flitting, momentary, short-lived, short, brief, passing, impermanent.

fulfil *verb* **1** *fulfil his task* carry out, accomplish, achieve, execute, perform, discharge, implement, complete, bring to completion, finish, conclude, effect, effectuate, perfect. **2** *fulfil his*

FRUITS

ackee	capulin	genipap	mandarin	pineapple	sour plum
alligator	carambola	gooseberry	mango	pippin	soursop
pear	carob	gourd	mangosteen	plantain	spice-berry
ananas	cherimoya	granadilla	manzanilla	plum	star-apple
apple	cherry	grape	medlar	pomegran-	star fruit
apricot	chinaberry	grapefruit	melon	ate	strawberry
avocado	chokeberry	greengage	minneola	pomelo	sweetsop
babaco	citron	guava	mombin	prickly pear	tamarillo
bael	clementine	hackberry	mulberry	quandong	tamarind
bakeapple	coconut	huckleberry	muscat	quince	tangelo
banana	costard	jaboticaba	musk	rambutan	tangerine
barberry	crab apple	jackfruit	melon	raspberry	tayberry
bayberry	cranberry	jujube	myrobalan	redcurrant	tomato
bearberry	crowberry	kaki	nectarine	salmonberry	tree tomato
bergamot	currant	kiwi fruit	nipa	sapodilla	Ugli fruit™
bilberry	damson	kumquat	olive	satsuma	watermelon
blackberry	date	lemon	orange	service-	white
black-	dewberry	lime	passion	berry	currant
currant	durian	lingonberry	fruit	sharon fruit	whortle-
blueberry	elderberry	loganberry	pawpaw	sloe	berry
boysenberry	feijoa	longan	peach	sour cherry	winter
breadfruit	fig	loquat	pear	sour gourd	cherry
bullace	geebung	lychee	persimmon	sour orange	youngberry

desire satisfy, realize, attain, consummate.
3 *fulfil the job requirements* fill, answer, meet, obey, comply with, satisfy, conform to, observe.
Opposites FAIL; NEGLECT.

fulfilled *adjective she doesn't feel fulfilled* satisfied, content, happy.

full *adjective* **1** *the cup is full* filled, filled up, filled to the brim, brimful, brimming, filled to capacity. **2** *the shop was full* crowded, packed, crammed, solid with people, chock-a-block, chock-full; *inf.* jam-packed, wall-to-wall. **3** *the seats/rooms are full* occupied, taken, in use.
4 *full supermarket shelves* filled, loaded, well-stocked. **5** *children feeling full* replete, satisfied, sated, gorged, glutted, cloyed. **6** *a full list of names* complete, entire, whole, comprehensive, thorough, exhaustive, detailed, all-inclusive, all-encompassing, extensive, unabridged. **7** *a full programme of events | give full details* abundant, plentiful, copious, ample, sufficient, broad-ranging, satisfying, complete. **8** *full of energy/smiles/mistakes* filled with, abounding in, brimful of. **9** *a full figure* well-rounded, rounded, plump, buxom, shapely, curvaceous, voluptuous; *inf.* busty. **10** *a full skirt* loose-fitting, baggy, voluminous, capacious. **11** *a full voice* rich, deep, resonant, loud, strong; *inf.* fruity.
Opposites EMPTY; INCOMPLETE; LIMITED.

full *noun* **in full** *give me the account in full* in its entirety, in total, *in toto*, without omission/abridgement. **to the full** *live life to the full* fully, thoroughly, completely, to the utmost, to capacity.

full *adverb* *hit him full in the face* directly, right, straight, squarely; *inf.* smack, smack bang.

full-grown *adjective* fully grown, mature, adult, grown-up, of age, fully developed, fully fledged, in full bloom, ripe, in one's prime.

fullness *noun* **1** *the fullness of the list* completeness, comprehensiveness, thoroughness, exhaustiveness, extensiveness. *See* FULL *adjective* 6. **2** *the fullness of her figure* roundedness, plumpness, buxomness, shapeliness, curvaceousness. *See* FULL *adjective* 9. **3** *the fullness of his voice* richness, resonance, loudness, strength; *inf.* fruitiness. **4** *the doctors detected a fullness in her stomach* swelling, enlargement, distension, dilation, tumescence. **in the fullness of time** in due course, when the time is ripe, eventually.

full-scale *adjective* **1** *a full-scale search/reorganization* thorough, comprehensive, extensive, exhaustive, all-out, all-encompassing, all-inclusive, thoroughgoing, wide-ranging, sweeping, major, in-depth. **2** *a full-scale drawing* full-size, unreduced.

fully *adverb* **1** *fully covered by the insurance* completely, entirely, wholly, totally, thoroughly, in all respects, utterly. **2** *fully staffed* completely, amply, sufficiently, satisfactorily, enough.
3 *he's fully 80 years old* quite, at least, without exaggeration.

fully-fledged *adjective* mature, fully developed, trained, qualified, proficient, experienced, time-served.

fulminate *verb* **1** *fulminate against the government* protest against, rail against, declaim against, inveigh against, denounce, decry, disparage, condemn, criticize, censure, arraign. **2** *chemicals fulminating* explode, detonate, blow up.

fulmination *noun* *his fulmination against the government* denunciation, violent protest, railing, decrying, condemnation, invective, tirade, diatribe, philippic, obloquy.

fulsome *adjective* *fulsome compliments* excessive, extravagant, overdone, immoderate, inordinate, overappreciative, insincere, ingratiating, fawning, sycophantic, adulatory, cloying, nauseating, sickening, saccharine, unctuous; *inf.* over-the-top, OTT, smarmy.

fumble *verb* **1** *fumble for his keys* grope, feel about, search blindly, scrabble around. **2** *fumble around in the dark* feel/grope one's way, stumble, blunder, flounder. **3** *fumble her speech* bungle, botch, mismanage, mishandle, muff, spoil; *inf.* make a mess/hash of, fluff, screw up, foul up; *Am. inf.* flub. **4** *fumble a ball* fail to catch, miss, drop, mishandle, misfield.

fume *verb* *the teacher is fuming* be enraged, seethe, boil, be livid, rage, rant and rave, be furious, be incensed, flare up; *inf.* be up in arms, get hot under the collar, fly off the handle, be at boiling point, foam at the mouth, get all steamed up, raise the roof, flip one's lid, blow one's top.

fumes *plural noun* **1** *fumes from the exhaust* vapour, gas, smoke, exhalation, exhaust, pollution. **2** *the petrol fumes sickened her* smell, stink, reek, stench.

fumigate *verb* disinfect, purify, sterilize, sanitize, sanitate, cleanse, clean out.

fun *noun* **1** *what do you do for fun?* amusement, entertainment, relaxation, recreation, enjoyment, pleasure, diversion, distraction, play, good time, jollification, junketing, merry-making; *inf.* living it up. **2** *she's full of fun* merriment, gaiety, mirth, laughter, hilarity, glee, gladness, cheerfulness, joy, jollity, zest; high spirits. **3** *a figure of fun* joking, jest, teasing, banter, badinage. **fun and games** play, playfulness, horseplay, clowning/fooling around, tomfoolery, buffoonery; *inf.* skylarking. **in fun** jokingly, as a joke, in jest, to tease, teasingly, for a laugh. **make fun of** ridicule, rag, deride, mock, scoff at, sneer at, taunt, jeer at, parody, lampoon; *inf.* rib, send up, take off.
Opposites WORK; MISERY.

fun *adjective* **1** *a fun time* amusing, entertaining, enjoyable, diverting, pleasurable. **2** *a fun person* amusing, witty, entertaining, lively, convivial.

function *noun* **1** *his function in the firm* role, capacity, responsibility, duty, task, chore, job, post, situation, office, occupation, employment, business, charge, concern, province, part, activity, operation, line, mission, *raison d'être*; *inf.* thing, bag, line of country. **2** *what is that machine's function?* use, purpose, task.
3 *invited to a function* social event/occasion, affair, gathering, reception, party; *inf.* do, beanfeast.

function *verb* **1** *is the machine functioning?* work, go, run, be in working/running order, operate. **2** *he functions as her butler | the sofa functions as a bed* serve, act, perform, operate, officiate, do duty, have/do the job of, play the role of, act the part of.

functional *adjective* **1** *functional clothes* practical, useful, serviceable, utilitarian, utility, working, work-a-day, hard-wearing. **2** *is the machine functional?* working, in working order, going, running, operative, in operation, in commission.

functionary *noun* official, office-bearer, office-holder, public servant, civil servant, bureaucrat, red tapist.

fund *noun* **1** *the church preservation fund* reserve, pool, collection, kitty, endowment, foundation, grant, investment, capital; savings. **2** *a fund of knowledge* stock, store, accumulation, mass, mine, reservoir, supply, storehouse, treasury, treasure-house, hoard, repository.

fund *verb fund the project* finance, back, pay for, capitalize, provide finance/capital for, subsidize, stake, endow, support, float.

fundamental *adjective fundamental principles* basic, basal, foundational, rudimentary, elemental, underlying, primary, cardinal, initial, original, prime, first, principal, chief, key, central, structural, organic, constitutional, inherent, intrinsic, vital, essential, important, indispensable, necessary.

fundamentally *adjective fundamentally he is an honest man* basically, at heart, at bottom, deep down, essentially, intrinsically.

fundamentals *plural noun get down to fundamentals* basics, first/basic principles, essentials, rudiments; crux, crux of the matter, *sine qua non*; *inf.* nuts and bolts, nitty-gritty.

funds *plural noun totally out of funds* money, ready money, cash, hard cash, capital, the wherewithal; means, assets, resources, savings; *inf.* dough, bread, the ready, folding money.

funeral *noun* burial, burying, interment, inhumation, entombment, cremation; funeral rites, obsequies, exequies.

funereal *adjective* **1** *funereal colours* black, dark, drab. **2** *a funereal atmosphere | wearing a funereal expression* gloomy, dismal, dreary, depressing, sombre, grave, solemn, sad, melancholy, lugubrious.

fungus *noun* parasite, saprophyte; mushroom, toadstool, mould, mildew, rust. *See table.*

funny *adjective* **1** *a funny story/situation* amusing, comic, comical, humorous, hilarious, entertaining, diverting, laughable, hysterical,

FUNGI			
agaric	cramp balls	horn of plenty	sac fungus
amanita	dead men's fingers	horsehair toadstool/	saffron milkcap
amethyst deceiver	death cap	mushroom	scarlet elf-cup
anise cap	deceiver	horse mushroom	scarlet hood
artist's fungus	destroying angel	ink cap	shaggy inkcap
bay bolete	devil's bolete	jelly babies	shaggy parasol
beefsteak fungus	dog stinkhorn	jelly fungus	sickener
bird's-nest fungus	dryad's saddle	jelly tongue	slippery jack
black bulgar	ear fungus	jew's ear	spike cap
blewit	ear pick fungus	King Alfred's cakes	spring amanita
blusher	earth ball	lawyer's wig	stag's-horn fungus
blushing bracket	earth fan	mushroom	St George's
bolete	earthstar	liberty cap	mushroom
boletus	earth tongue	lorchel	stinkhorn
bonnet	elf-cup	meadow mushroom	stinking parasol
bootlace fungus	ergot	milk cap	sulphur fungus
bracket fungus	fairy button	milk drop	sulphur tuft
brain fungus	fairy cakes	miller	tawny grisette
bulgar	fairy club	morel	toadstool
butter cap	fairy-ring	old man of the	tough shank
Caesar's mushroom	mushroom	woods	truffle
cage fungus	false chanterelle	orange-peel fungus	tuckahoe
candle snuff fungus	false death cap	oyster mushroom	velvet cap
caterpillar fungus	false morel	panther cap	velvet foot
cauliflower fungus	field mushroom	parasol mushroom	velvet shank
cep	fire fungus	parrot toadstool	wax cap
champignon	flame fungus	penny bun	weeping widow
chanterelle	fly agaric	plums and custard	witches' butter
chicken of the	funnel cap	poached egg fungus	wood blewit
woods	ghost fungus	poison pie	wood hedgehog
clouded agaric	giant puffball	polypore	wood mushroom
club foot	grisette	porcelain fungus	wood witch
club fungus	hedgehog fungus/	prince	wood woollyfoot
coral fungus	mushroom	puffball	yellow-staining
coral-spot	herald of the winter	russet shank	mushroom	yellow
cow-pat toadstool	honey fungus	russula	stainer

riotous, side-splitting, droll, absurd, rich, ridiculous, ludicrous, risible, farcical, silly, slapstick; *inf.* killing. **2** *he can be very funny* amusing, humorous, entertaining, droll, witty, waggish, facetious, jolly, jocular. **3** *what a funny hat* strange, peculiar, odd, queer, weird, bizarre, curious. **4** *he's a funny character* strange, peculiar, odd, mysterious, suspicious, dubious; *inf.* shady.
Opposites SERIOUS; SAD; NORMAL.

furious *adjective* **1** *furious parents* enraged, raging, infuriated, fuming, boiling, incensed, inflamed, frenzied, very angry, indignant, mad, raving mad, maddened, wrathful, beside oneself, in high dudgeon; *inf.* livid, hot under the collar, up in arms, foaming at the mouth. **2** *a furious storm/struggle* violent, fierce, wild, intense, vehement, unrestrained, tumultuous, turbulent, tempestuous, stormy, boisterous.

furnish *verb* **1** *furnish a room* provide with furniture, fit out, rig out, appoint, outfit. **2** *furnish you with what you require* supply, equip, provide, provision, give, grant, present, offer, bestow, endow.

furniture *noun* furnishings, house fittings, appointments, effects, movables, chattels; *inf.* stuff, things. *See table. See also tables at* BED, CHAIR, CUPBOARD, TABLE.

TYPES AND STYLES OF FURNITURE

Bauhaus	Louis Quatorze
bentwood	Louis Quinze
bombé	Louis Seize
boulle	Louis Treize
cabriole	Queen Anne
Chippendale	Regency
Duncan Phyfe	reproduction
Empire	rustic
Gothic Revival	Scandinavian
Hepplewhite	Shaker
inlaid	Sheraton
Jacobean	

---

furore *noun* **1** *a furore when they found out* commotion, uproar, disturbance, hullabaloo, turmoil, tempest, tumult, brouhaha, stir, excitement, to-do, outburst, outcry. **2** *in a furore* rage, madness, frenzy, fit. **3** *a furore for old films* craze, enthusiasm, mania, fad, obsession.

furrow *noun* **1** groove, trench, channel, rut, trough, hollow, ditch, seam. **2** *furrows on her brow/skin* crease, line, wrinkle, corrugation, crinkle, crow's foot.

further *adjective* **1** *further supplies* additional, more, extra, supplementary, other, new, fresh. **2** *the further boat is almost out of sight* more distant/advanced/remote, remoter, further away/off, farther.

further *adverb* **1** *further, you will go now* furthermore, moreover, what's more, also, besides, additionally, as well, to boot, on top of that, over and above that, by the same token. **2** *she stopped and would come no further* to a more advanced point, more forward/onward, farther.

further *verb* *further our plans* advance, forward, facilitate, aid, assist, help, lend a hand to, abet, expedite, hasten, speed up, push, give a push to, promote, back, contribute to, encourage, foster, champion.

furtherance *noun* **1** *furtherance in the firm* advancement, promotion, elevation, preferment; *inf.* step-up. **2** *the furtherance of our plans* furthering, advancement, forwarding, facilitating, aiding, assisting, pushing, promotion, backing. *See* FURTHER *verb.*

furthermore *adverb* moreover, what's more, also, besides, additionally, as well, further. *See* FURTHER *adverb* 1.

furthest *adjective* furthest away, farthest, furthermost, most distant, most remote, outermost, outmost, extreme, uttermost, ultimate.

furtive *adjective* secret, secretive, stealthy, surreptitious, sneaky, sneaking, skulking, slinking, clandestine, hidden, covert, cloaked, conspiratorial, sly, underhand, under the table, wily.
Opposites OPEN; ABOVE-BOARD.

fury *noun* **1** *the fury of the parents* great anger, rage, ire, wrath, madness, passion, frenzy, furore. **2** *the fury of the storm* fierceness, ferocity, violence, turbulence, tempestuousness, severity, intensity, vehemence, force, great force, power, potency. **3** *she is a real fury* virago, hell-cat, termagant, spitfire, vixen, shrew, hag.

fuse *verb* **1** *fuse the ingredients* combine, amalgamate, put together, unite, blend, intermix, intermingle, merge, meld, coalesce, compound, agglutinate, join, integrate, weld, solder. **2** *fuse the solid* melt, melt down, smelt, dissolve, liquefy.
Opposites SEPARATE; DISCONNECT.

fuss *noun* **1** *the fuss over the preparations* fluster, flurry, bustle, to-do, ado, agitation, excitement, bother, stir, commotion, confusion, tumult, uproar, upset, worry, over-anxiety, pother, palaver, storm in a teacup, much ado about nothing; *inf.* flap, tizzy, stew. **2** *a fuss in the pub last night* row, altercation, squabble, argument, quarrel, dispute, upset; trouble, bother, unrest; *inf.* dust-up, barney, hassle. **3** *make a fuss about the service* complaint, objection; *inf.* grouse, gripe.

fuss *verb* **1** *organizers fussing around the place* | *fuss over details* bustle, bustle about, dash about, rush about, tear around, buzz around; worry, be agitated/worried, make a big thing-gout of nothing, make a mountain out of a molehill; *inf.* get worked up over nothing, be in a flap, flap, be in a tizzy, be in a stew. **2** *fuss about the service* kick up a fuss, make a fuss, complain, raise an objection; *inf.* grouse, gripe. **3** *the baby is fussing* be upset, fret, cry, be cross, be crabbed; *inf.* take on. **4** *fuss their mother* irritate, annoy, vex, bother, pester, disturb, nag.

fussy *adjective* **1** *a fussy eater* particular, over-particular, finicky, pernickety, faddish, faddy, fastidious, hard to please, difficult, exacting, demanding, discriminating, selective, dainty; *inf.* choosy, picky, nit-picking. **2** *fussy rooms/*

paintings busy, cluttered, overdecorated, over-embellished, over-elaborate, over-ornate, rococo.

futile *adjective* **1** *a futile search* vain, in vain, to no avail, unavailing, useless, ineffectual, ineffective, inefficacious, unsuccessful, fruitless, abortive, unproductive, impotent, barren, unprofitable, hollow. **2** *a futile statement* trivial, unimportant, petty, trifling, valueless, worthless, inconsequential, idle.
Opposites USEFUL; FRUITFUL; SIGNIFICANT.

futility *noun* **1** *the futility of the search* uselessness, ineffectiveness, fruitlessness, abortiveness. *See* FUTILE 1. **2** *the futility of the statement* triviality, unimportance, pettiness, worthlessness. *See* FUTILE 2.

future *noun* **1** *things might improve in the future* time to come, time ahead, hereafter; coming times. **2** *no future in the firm* prospects, expectations; anticipation, outlook, likely success/advancement/improvement.

fuzzy *adjective* **1** *masses of fuzzy hair* | *a fuzzy-skinned peach* frizzy, downy, down-covered, woolly, linty, napped. **2** *everything's gone all fuzzy* out of focus, unfocused, blurred, blurry, bleary, misty, indistinct, unclear, distorted, ill-defined, indefinite. **3** *fuzzy recollection* confused, muddled, fuddled, befuddled, foggy, misty, shadowy, blurred.

Gg

gabble *verb old women gabbling away* jabber, babble, chatter, chitter-chatter, prattle, rattle, blabber, gaggle, gibber, cackle, drivel, blab, gossip, splutter; *inf.* blah, blah-blah.

gabble *noun tired of their gabble* jabbering, babbling, chattering, gibbering, babble, chatter, gibberish, drivel, gossip, twaddle; *inf.* flannel, waffle, blah. *See* GABBLE *verb.*

gad *verb he's always gadding about* gallivant, roam, wander, travel around, rove, ramble, run around, range, flit about, meander, stray; *inf.* traipse; *Scots* stravaig.

gadabout *noun* gallivanter, rambler, rover, wanderer, traveller, nomad, globe-trotter.

gadget *noun* appliance, apparatus, instrument, implement, tool, contrivance, device, mechanism, invention, thing; *inf.* contraption, widget, gismo.

gaffe *noun* mistake, blunder, slip, indiscretion, solecism, *faux pas*, gaucherie; *inf.* clanger, bloomer, howler, boob, boo-boo.

gaffer *noun* **1** *old gaffers sitting in the square* old man, old fellow; *inf.* old bloke, old boy, old guy, grandad, old geezer; *Am.* old-timer. **2** *he's the gaffer of the factory* foreman, ganger, overseer, supervisor, manager, superintendent; *inf.* boss; *Am.* honcho.

gag *noun his gags amused her* joke, jest, witticism, quip, funny remark, hoax, prank; *inf.* wisecrack, crack.

gag *verb* **1** *gag her mouth* put a gag on, stop up, block, plug, clog, stifle, smother, muffle. **2** *the press have been gagged* silence, muzzle, curb, check, restrain, suppress, repress. **3** *he gagged when he saw the corpse* choke, retch, gasp, struggle for breath, convulse, almost vomit, keck, heave.

gaiety *noun* **1** *appreciating the gaiety of the children* gayness, cheerfulness, light-heartedness, merriment, glee, blitheness, gladness, happiness, high spirits, good spirits, delight, pleasure, joy, joyfulness, joyousness, exuberance, elation, jollity, hilarity, mirth, joviality, liveliness, vivacity, animation, effervescence, buoyancy, sprightliness, exultation, *joie de vivre*. **2** *join in the gaiety of the fair* fun, festivity, merrymaking, revelry, revels, jollification, celebration, gala, frolics. **3** *the gaiety of the dresses* colourfulness, brightness, brilliance, sparkle, glitter, gaudiness, showiness, show, garishness.
Opposites GLOOM; MISERY.

gain *verb* **1** *gain an advantage* obtain, get, acquire, procure, secure, attain, build up, achieve, arrive at, come to have, win, capture, net, pick up, reap, gather. **2** *gain experience/weight* get more of, increase in, add on. **3** *gain a wage* earn, bring in, make, get, clear, gross, net, realize, produce. **4** *the police were gaining on the escaped prisoner* catch up with, catch up on, narrow the gap between, get nearer to, close in on, overtake, come up to, approach. **5** *the escaped prisoner was gaining on the police* widen the gap between, get further ahead of, leave behind, draw away from, outdistance, do better than. **6** *the ship gained the shore* reach, arrive at, get to, come to, attain. **gain time** stall, procrastinate, delay, use delaying tactics, temporize, use Fabian tactics, dally, use dilatory tactics; *inf.* put on the back burner.
Opposites LOSE.

gain *noun* **1** *his gain from the deal was negligible* profit, earnings, income, advantage, benefit, reward, emolument, yield, return, winnings, proceeds, dividend, interest; *inf.* pickings. **2** *a gain in experience/weight* more of, increase, augmentation, addition, rise, increment, accretion, accumulation. **3** *their gain against the enemy* advance, advancement, progress, forward movement, headway, improvement, step forward. **4** *show off his latest gains* acquisition, acquirement, achievement.
Opposites LOSS; DECREASE.

gainful *adjective* profitable, remunerative, paying, financially rewarding, rewarding, lucrative, money-making, productive, beneficial, advantageous, worthwhile, useful.

gainsay *verb there's no gainsaying his honesty* deny, dispute, disagree with, disbelieve, contradict, contravene, challenge, oppose, controvert, disaffirm.

gait *noun* walk, step, stride, pace, tread, manner of walking, bearing, carriage.

gala *noun children having a gala* festival, fête, festivities, carnival, pageant, jamboree, party, celebration.

gala *adjective a gala occasion* festive, holiday, carnival, celebratory, merry, gay, joyous, joyful, jovial, diverting, entertaining, spectacular, showy, ceremonial, ceremonious.

galaxy *noun* **1** *look at a galaxy through a telescope* constellation, stars, the heavens. *See table. See also tables at* STAR. **2** *a galaxy of stars* dazzling assemblage, host, brilliant gathering, illustrious group.

GALAXIES	
Andromeda Galaxy	Small Magellanic
Black-eye Galaxy	Cloud | Nubecular
Cartwheel Galaxy	Minor
Helix Galaxy	Sombrero Galaxy
Large Magellanic	Spindle Galaxy
Cloud | Nubecular	Sunflower Galaxy
Major	Triangulum
Milky Way Galaxy	Galaxy
Pinwheel Galaxy	Whirlpool Galaxy

gale *noun* **1** *lost at sea in a gale* storm, tempest, squall, hurricane, tornado, cyclone, typhoon, mistral, sirocco. *See tables at* WIND. **2** *gales of laughter* outburst, peal, ring, shriek, shout, roar, scream, howl, fit, eruption.

gall¹ *noun* **1** *have the gall to answer back* impudence, insolence, impertinence, cheek, nerve, face, audacity, brashness, effrontery, temerity, sauciness; *inf.* brass, brass neck, sauce, chutzpah. **2** *words full of gall* bitterness, resentment, rancour, acrimony, malice, spite, malignity, venom, malevolence, virulence, sourness, acerbity, asperity, animosity, antipathy, hostility, enmity, bad blood, ill feeling, animus, bile, spleen.

gall² *noun* **1** *a gall on the horse's skin* sore, abrasion, scrape, scratch, graze, canker, ulceration. **2** *the children are a gall to him* source of vexation/irritation/annoyance, vexation, irritation, irritant, annoyance, pest, nuisance, provocation, bother, torment, plague; *inf.* botheration, aggravation.

gall³ *verb* **1** *gall the skin* abrade, chafe, rub, rub raw, scrape, graze, skin, scratch, excoriate, fret, rasp, bark. **2** *her attitude galls him* vex, irritate, infuriate, irk, annoy, rub up the wrong way, provoke, exasperate, pique, rile, nettle, bother, ruffle, fret, pester, torment, harass, rankle, embitter; *inf.* aggravate, peeve.

gallant *adjective* **1** *gallant soldiers* brave, courageous, valiant, valorous, bold, plucky, daring, fearless, intrepid, manly, manful, dashing, heroic, heroical, lion-hearted, stout-hearted, doughty, mettlesome, great-spirited, honourable, noble. **2** *a gallant courtier|gallant to the ladies* chivalrous, gentlemanly, courtly, courteous, mannerly, polite, attentive, gracious, considerate, thoughtful, obliging, deferential. **3** *a gallant ship* fine, great, dignified, stately, noble, splendid, elegant, magnificent, majestic, imposing, glorious, regal, august. **Opposites** COWARDLY; DISCOURTEOUS; RUDE.

gallant *noun* **1** *the gallants of the court of King Arthur* knight, champion, hero, paladin, valiant, adventurer, cavalier, chevalier, *preux chevalier*. **2** *young gallants at a ball* man about town, man of fashion, man of the world, ladies' man, lady-killer, dandy, fop, beau. **3** *a young lady and her gallant* beau, escort, partner, suitor, wooer, admirer, lover, boyfriend, paramour.

gallantry *noun* **1** *the gallantry of the troops* bravery, braveness, courage, courageousness, valour, boldness, pluck, daring, fearlessness, intrepidity, manliness, heroism, doughtiness. *See* GALLANT *adjective* 1. **2** *the gallantry of the courtiers* chivalry, chivalrousness, gentlemanliness, courtliness, courteousness, politeness, mannerliness, attentiveness, graciousness, consideration, thoughtfulness. *See* GALLANT *adjective* 2.

galling *adjective* *a galling experience* vexing, vexatious, irritating, infuriating, irksome, annoying, provoking, exasperating, troublesome, bothering, harassing, rankling, embittering, bitter. *See* GALL³ *verb* 2.

gallivant *verb* gad about, roam, wander, travel around, rove, ramble. *See* GAD.

gallop *verb* **1** *the horse galloped* go at full speed, canter, lope, prance, frisk. **2** *the children galloped home* race, rush, dash, tear, sprint, bolt, fly, run, shoot, dart, hurry, hasten, speed, career, scamper, scurry, scud, zoom.

gallows *noun* gibbet, scaffold.

galore *adverb* *have books/food/friends galore* in abundance, in profusion, in great quantity, in plenty, aplenty, in huge numbers, to spare, everywhere, all over the place.

galvanize *verb* *galvanize them into action* electrify, shock, startle, jolt, stir, excite, rouse, arouse, awaken, spur, prod, urge, stimulate, give a stimulus to, invigorate, fire, animate, vitalize, energize, exhilarate, thrill, dynamize, inspire.

gambit *noun* stratagem, manoeuvre, machination, move, play, ruse, trick, ploy, artifice.

gamble *verb* **1** *he loves to gamble* bet, wager, place a bet, lay a wager/bet, back the horses, game, stake, try one's luck on the horses; *inf.* punt, play the ponies, have a flutter. **2** *he gambled when he invested in that firm* take a chance, take a risk, take a leap in the dark, leave things to chance, speculate, venture, buy a pig in a poke; *inf.* stick one's neck out, go out on a limb; *Am.* take a flier. **3** *gamble on his parents being absent* act in the hope that, trust that, chance that, take a chance that, bank on.

gamble *noun* **1** *have a gamble on the horses* bet, wager, punt; *inf.* flutter. **2** *it was a gamble but they decided to go* risk, hazard, chance, lottery, speculation, venture, random shot, leap in the dark, pig in a poke, pot luck, blind bargain.

gambol *verb* frolic, frisk, cavort, caper, cut capers, skip, dance, leap, romp, trip, prance, hop, jump, spring, bounce, rollick, curvet.

game *noun* **1** *children playing a game* pastime, diversion, entertainment, amusement, recreation, play, sport, distraction, frolic, romp, fun, merriment. *See table. See also tables at* BOARD, CARD. **2** *we were only playing a game on him* joke, practical joke, prank, jest, trick, hoax; *inf.* lark. **3** *there's a game tomorrow* match, contest, tournament, meeting, sports meeting, event, athletic event, round, bout. *See tables at* ATHLETICS, OLYMPICS, SPORT. **4** *he's in the oil game* business, line, occupation, trade, profession, industry, enterprise, activity, calling; *inf.* line of country. **5** *what's his game?* scheme, trick, plot, ploy, stratagem, strategy, cunning plan, crafty designs, tactics, artifice, device, manoeuvre. **6** *they went shooting game* wild animals, wild fowl, quarry, prey, big game. *See table.* **make game of** make fun of, make a fool of, poke fun at, ridicule, deride, make a laughing-stock of, mock, scoff at, jeer at, make sport of, make the butt of one's jokes, taunt; *inf.* rib, rag, send up. **play the game** play by the rules, play fair, be a good sport.

game *verb* gamble, bet, wager. *See* GAMBLE *verb* 1.

game *adjective* **1** *who's game enough to knock at her door?* plucky, brave, courageous, valiant, unafraid, fearless, gallant, bold, intrepid,

GAME BIRDS		
black grouse	grouse	red grouse
bobwhite	guinea fowl	ruffed grouse
capercaillie	moorfowl	sage grouse
duck	partridge	turkey
golden pheasant	peafowl	waterfowl
goose	pheasant	wildfowl
	ptarmigan	woodcock
	quail	

stout-hearted, lion-hearted, dauntless, undaunted, daring, dashing, spirited, unblenching, unflinching. **2** *I'm game to go abroad if you are* willing, favourably inclined, desirous, eager, interested, enthusiastic, ready, prepared, disposed.

gamut *noun* entire range, whole spectrum, complete scale, complete sequence, whole series, full sweep, full compass, entire scope, entire area, full catalogue.

gang *noun* **1** *a gang of people gathered* group, band, crowd, company, gathering, pack, horde, mob, herd. **2** *the young man and his gang* clique, circle, social set, coterie, lot, ring, club; fraternity, sorority; *inf.* crew. **3** *gang of labourers/roadmen* squad, team, troop, shift, detachment, posse, troupe.

gangling, gangly *adjective gangling lad of sixteen* lanky, rangy, spindly, spindling, loosely built, loosely jointed, stringy, skinny, angular, awkward, awkwardly tall.

gangster *noun* gang-member, racketeer, bandit, brigand, robber, ruffian, thug, hoodlum, tough, desperado, Mafioso, terrorist; *inf.* crook; *Am. inf.* mobster, hood.

gap *noun* **1** *a gap in the wall* opening, cavity, hole, aperture, space, breach, orifice, break, fracture, rift, rent, fissure, cleft, chink, crack, crevice, cranny, divide, discontinuity, interstice. **2** *gaps in the musical programme for refreshment* pause, intermission, interval, inter-

lude, break; *Am.* recess. **3** *gaps in his account* omission, blank, lacuna, hiatus, void, vacuity. **4** *the gap between the old and the young* breach, difference, divergence, disparity.

gape *verb* **1** *gaping at the procession* stare, stare in wonder, goggle, gaze, ogle; *inf.* gawk, rubberneck. **2** *the chasm gaped before them* open wide, become open wide, open up, yawn, part, crack, split.

garb *noun* **1** *admire the fine garb* clothes, clothing, garments, dress, attire, apparel, costume, outfit, wear, habit, uniform, array, habiliment, vestments, livery, trappings; *inf.* gear, get-up, togs, rig-out, duds. **2** *dressed in the garb of a soldier* clothes, attire, uniform, kit, style, fashion, look. **3** *wearing the garb of sanity* outward appearance, appearance, guise, outward form, exterior, aspect, semblance, look.

garb *verb garbed in black* clothe, dress, attire, apparel, array, robe, cover, outfit, fit, rig out, kit out.

garbage *noun* **1** *put the garbage out* waste material, waste, domestic rubbish, rubbish, refuse, debris, litter, junk, filth, discarded matter; swill, detritus; scraps, scourings, leftovers, remains, slops; *inf.* muck; *Am.* trash. **2** *talking a lot of garbage* nonsense, rubbish, twaddle, drivel, foolishness, balderdash; *inf.* hogwash, poppycock, rot, tommy-rot, tosh, bosh, piffle.

garble *verb* **1** *the child accidentally garbled the message* mix up, get mixed up, jumble, confuse. **2** *the enemy deliberately garbled the message* change around, distort, twist, twist around, warp, slant, mutilate, tamper with, doctor, falsify, pervert, corrupt, adulterate, misstate, misquote, misreport, misrender, misrepresent, mistranslate, misinterpret, misunderstand.

gargantuan *adjective* extremely big/large, gigantic, giant, enormous, monstrous, huge, colossal, vast, immense, tremendous, massive, hulking, towering, mammoth, prodigious, ele-

GAMES			
Aunt Sally	dumb crambo	kickean	poker dice
bagatelle	fan-tan	leapfrog	postman's knock
beetle	fivestones	liar dice	prison base
bingo	follow-my-leader	lotto	quoits
blind man's buff	forfeits	mah-jong	roulette
bumble-puppy	fox and geese	marbles	sardines
catch	grandmother's	murder in the dark	shove-halfpenny
cat's cradle	footsteps	musical chairs	shovelboard
charades	hangman	nim	Simon Says
Chinese whispers	hazard	noughts and	spillikins
conkers	hide-and-seek	crosses	spin the bottle
consequences	hoopla	pachinko	swy
cowboys and	hopscotch	paintball	tag
Indians	hunt the slipper	pall-mall	taw
crambo	hunt the thimble	pass the parcel	tick-tack-toe
craps	I spy	piggy	tiddlywinks
curling	it	pig in the middle	tig
darts	jacks	pinball	tipcat
diabolo	jackstraws	pin the tail on the	trap-ball
dominoes	jukskei	donkey	twenty questions
ducks and drakes	keno	pitch-and-toss	two-up

phantine, mountainous, monumental, titanic, Brobdingnagian; *inf.* whopping.

garish *adjective garish colours | wearing a garish shirt* flashy, loud, showy, gaudy, glaring, flaunting, bold-coloured, glittering, tinselly, brassy, tawdry, raffish, tasteless, in bad taste, vulgar, meretricious, cheap, Brummagem; *inf.* flash.
Opposites DRAB; SOBER; TASTEFUL.

garland *noun wear a garland of flowers* wreath, festoon, lei, loop of flowers, laurel, laurels, bays, coronet, crown, coronal, chaplet, fillet, headband.

garland *verb garland in flowers* wreathe, festoon, adorn, decorate, deck, crown.

garment *noun* 1 *wearing a white garment* piece of clothing, article of clothing, item of dress, cover, covering. 2 *wearing strange garments* clothes, clothing, dress, attire, apparel, costume, outfit, garb. *See* GARB *noun* 1.

garner *verb squirrels garnering nuts* gather, collect, accumulate, heap, pile up, amass, assemble, stack up, store, lay up/by, put/stow away, hoard, stockpile, deposit, husband, reserve, save, preserve, save for a rainy day.

garner *noun* granary, store, storehouse, depository, vault, treasure-house.

garnish *verb garnish the dish with parsley* decorate, adorn, trim, ornament, embellish, deck, deck out, bedeck, festoon, enhance, grace, beautify, prettify, set off, add the finishing touch to.

garnish *noun a parsley garnish for the meat* decoration, adornment, trim, trimming, garniture, ornament, ornamentation, embellishment, enhancement, beautification, finishing touch.

garret *noun* attic, loft, cock-loft, roof-space.

garrison *noun* 1 *the garrison arrived at the fort* armed force, military detachment/unit, platoon, brigade, squadron; troops, militia, soldiers. 2 *the garrison was under siege* fort, fortress, fortification, stronghold, blockhouse, citadel, camp, encampment, command post, base, station; barracks.

garrison *verb* 1 *the town was garrisoned by the allied forces* defend, guard, protect, preserve, fortify, man, occupy, supply with troops. 2 *troops garrisoned in the town* station, post, put on duty, assign, position, billet; send in.

garrulity *noun* 1 *the garrulity of the old man* garrulousness, talkativeness, chattiness, loquacity, gift of the gab, volubility, verbosity,

long-windedness, prating, prattling; *inf.* mouthiness, gabbiness. *See* GARRULOUS 1. 2 *the garrulity of the account* wordiness, long-windedness, verbosity, prolixity, diffuseness, prosiness. *See* GARRULOUS 2.

garrulous *adjective* 1 *a garrulous old man* talkative, chatty, chattering, gossiping, loquacious, voluble, verbose, long-winded, babbling, prattling, prating, blathering, jabbering, gushing, effusive; *inf.* mouthy, gabby. 2 *a garrulous account* long-winded, wordy, verbose, rambling, prolix, diffuse, prosy, gossipy, chatty; *inf.* windy, gassy.
Opposites TACITURN; RETICENT.

gas *noun*. See table.

gash *noun a gash in his hand* cut, slash, wound, tear, laceration, gouge, incision, slit, split, rent, nick, cleft.

gash *verb gash his hand* cut, slash, wound, tear, lacerate, gouge, incise, slit, split, rend, nick, cleave.

gasp *verb gasping as he climbed the hill* pant, puff, pant and puff, puff and blow, blow, catch one's breath, draw in one's breath, gulp, choke, fight for breath, wheeze.

gasp *noun* 1 *she gave a gasp of surprise* exclamation, ejaculation, gulp, drawing-in of breath. 2 *his final gasps* breath, pant, puff, blowing, gulp, choke.

gastric *adjective* stomach, stomachical, abdominal, intestinal, coeliac.

gate *noun* 1 *build a gate* barrier, door, portal; wicket, postern, lich-/lych-gate, five-barred gate. 2 *crowds blocking the gates to the match* gateway, doorway, access, entrance, exit, egress, opening, passage.

gather *verb* 1 *people gathered in the square* come together, collect, assemble, congregate, meet, group, cluster together, crowd, mass, flock together, foregather, convene, muster, converge, accumulate. 2 *gather the school together* call together, summon, get together, assemble, collect, congregate, convene, round up, muster, marshal. 3 *gather stocks of food | gather the facts* get/put together, collect, accumulate, amass, assemble, garner, store, stockpile, heap up, pile up, stack up, hoard; *inf.* stash away. 4 *the event gathered a huge audience* attract, draw, draw together/in, pull, pull in, collect, pick up. 5 *we gather that he is dead* understand, be given to understand, believe, be led to believe, hear, learn, infer, draw the inference, deduce, conclude, come to the conclusion,

GASES				
acetylene	carbon	fluorine	neon	producer gas
afterdamp	dioxide	helium	nerve gas	propane
ammonia	carbon	hydrogen	nitrogen	radon
argon	monoxide	krypton	nitrogen	sarin
arsine	chlorine	laughing gas	dioxide	sulphur
biogas	coal gas	lewisite	nitrous	dioxide
butadiene	CS gas	marsh gas	oxide	tabun
butane	cyanogen	methane	oxygen	tear gas
butene	ethane	mustard gas	phosgene	town gas
Calor™	ethylene	natural gas	phosphine	xenon

assume, surmise. **6** *gather to one's bosom* embrace, clasp, enfold, hold, hug, cuddle. **7** *gather in the harvest* harvest, collect, pick, pluck, cull, garner, crop, reap, glean. **8** *gather in strength/force* increase, grow, rise, build, expand, enlarge, swell, extend, wax, intensify, deepen, heighten, thicken. **9** *gather the waist of the dress* ruffle, shirr, pleat, pucker, tuck, fold. **10** *the boil has gathered* come to a head, swell up, suppurate, fester.
Opposites SCATTER; DISPERSE; SEPARATE.

gathering noun **1** *a gathering of people* assembly, assemblage, collection, company, congregation, group, party, band, knot, crowd, flock, throng, mass, mob, horde, meeting, meet, convention, conclave, rally, turn-out, congress, convocation, concourse, muster; *inf.* get-together. **2** *his gathering of coins* collection, accumulation, assemblage, aggregation, aggregate, mass, store, stock, stockpile, heap, pile, cluster, agglomeration, conglomeration, concentration. **3** *the gathering of stores/facts* collecting, accumulation, assembly, assembling, garnering. See GATHER 3. **4** *a gathering on the back of his neck* boil, abscess, carbuncle, pustule, pimple, spot, sore, ulcer, tumour; *inf.* zit.

gauche adjective *a gauche manner/person/remark* awkward, clumsy, gawky, ungainly, bumbling, lumbering, maladroit, socially inept, lacking in social graces, inelegant, graceless, unpolished, unsophisticated, uncultured, uncultivated.
Opposites SOPHISTICATED; ELEGANT; ADROIT.

gaudy adjective *wearing a very gaudy shirt* bold-coloured, over-bright, garish, loud, glaring, bright, brilliant, flashy, showy, ostentatious, tawdry, raffish, tasteless, in bad taste, vulgar, meretricious, cheap, Brummagem; *inf.* flash.
Opposites DRAB; SOBER; TASTEFUL.

gauge verb **1** *gauge the thickness of the metal* measure, calculate, compute, determine, count, weigh, check, ascertain. **2** *you must gauge his aptitude* evaluate, appraise, assess, place a value on, estimate, guess, judge, adjudge, rate, reckon, determine; *inf.* guesstimate.

gauge noun **1** *find a gauge of his abilities* measure, basis, standard, guide, guideline, touchstone, yardstick, benchmark, criterion, rule, norm, example, model, pattern, exemplar, sample, test, indicator. **2** *the gauge of a barrel/gun/wire/railway* extent, degree, scope, area, size, measure, capacity, magnitude, depth, height, width, thickness, span, bore.

gaunt adjective **1** *a gaunt old woman* haggard, drawn, cadaverous, skeletal, emaciated, skin-and-bones, skinny, spindly, stalky, over-thin, spare, bony, angular, lank, lean, raw-boned, pinched, hollow-cheeked, starved-looking, scrawny, scraggy, shrivelled, wasted, withered; *inf.* looking like death warmed up. **2** *gaunt landscape* bleak, barren, bare, desolate, dreary, dismal, forlorn, grim, stern, harsh, forbidding.
Opposites OBESE; FAT; LUSH.

gawk verb stare, gape, goggle, gaze, ogle; *inf.* rubberneck.

gawky adjective *a shy gawky teenager* ungainly, lanky, clumsy, lumbering, blundering, gauche,

maladroit, oafish, loutish, doltish, clodhopping, lumpish.
Opposites GRACEFUL; ADROIT.

gay adjective **1** *feeling gay* merry, jolly, light-hearted, cheerful, mirthful, jovial, glad, happy, bright, in good spirits, in high spirits, joyful, elated, exuberant, cock-a-hoop, animated, lively, sprightly, vivacious, buoyant, effervescent, playful, frolicsome. **2** *have a gay time* merry, festive, amusing, enjoyable, entertaining, convivial, hilarious. **3** *gay colours | wearing a very gay shirt* bright, brightly coloured, vivid, brilliant, richly coloured, many-coloured, multicoloured, flamboyant, gaudy. **4** *gay men/women* homosexual, lesbian, homoerotic; *derog. inf.* bent, queer, camp, poofy, limp-wristed, butch.
Opposites GLOOMY; DULL; DRAB.

gay noun homosexual, lesbian; *derog. inf.* queer, poof, homo, dyke.

gaze verb *gaze at the scene* stare, look fixedly, gape, goggle, stand agog, watch in wonder, ogle, eye, take a good look, contemplate; *inf.* gawk, rubberneck, give the once-over.

gaze noun *fix his gaze on her* stare, fixed look, intent look, gape.

gazette noun newspaper, journal, periodical, paper, news-sheet, newsletter, organ; *derog.* rag.

gear noun **1** *the car's gear* gearwheel, tooth-wheel, cog, cogwheel. **2** *the steering gear of a boat* gears, mechanism, machinery, works. **3** *the workman's gear* equipment, apparatus, tools, kit, implements, tackle, appliances, contrivances, utensils, supplies, accoutrements, trappings, accessories, paraphernalia; *inf.* stuff. **4** *teenagers like modern gear* clothes, clothing, garments, dress, attire, apparel, garb, outfit, wear, costume, array, habit, vestments; *inf.* get-up, togs, rig-out, duds. **5** *their daughter and all her gear* belongings, things, luggage, baggage, kit, effects, goods and chattels, chattels, paraphernalia, accoutrements, personal possessions, trappings, impedimenta; *inf.* stuff.

gelatinous adjective jelly-like, glutinous, viscid, viscous, gummy, sticky, gluey, mucilaginous, slimy; *inf.* gooey.

geld verb castrate, neuter, emasculate, asexualize.

gelid adjective freezing, frozen, icy, ice-cold, arctic, glacial, polar, frosty, wintry, snowy, bitterly cold, chilly, Siberian, hyperborean, hyperboreal; *Med.* algid.

gem noun **1** *a ring set with gems* jewel, precious stone, semiprecious stone, stone, solitaire, brilliant, *bijou*. See table. **2** *the gem of his collection of books* jewel, jewel in the crown, pick, flower, cream, *crème de la crème*, wonder, prize, treasure, pearl, masterpiece, *chef-d'oeuvre*.

genealogy noun pedigree, family tree, ancestry, line, lineage, descent, parentage, birth, derivation, extraction, family, dynasty, house, race, strain, stock, breed, blood-line, stemma, stirps, heritage, history, roots.

general adjective **1** *the general practice is to apply in writing* usual, customary, common,

GEMSTONES		
agate	corundum	moss agate
almandine	diamond	onyx
amber	emerald	opal
amethyst	fire-opal	plasma
aquamarine	garnet	ruby
bloodstone	greenstone	sapphire
cairngorm	hawk's-eye	sardonyx
carbuncle	hyacinth	topaz
carnelian	jade	tourmaline
cat's-eye	jasper	turquoise
chalcedony	lapis lazuli	zircon

ordinary, normal, standard, regular, typical, conventional, everyday, habitual, run-of-the-mill. **2** *in general use | the general feeling* common, extensive, widespread, broad, wide, accepted, prevalent, prevailing, universal, popular, public, generic. **3** *a general pay-rise/rule* across-the-board, blanket, universal, sweeping, broad, broad-ranging, comprehensive, all-inclusive, encyclopedic, indiscriminate, catholic. **4** *a general store | his general knowledge* mixed, assorted, miscellaneous, variegated, diversified, composite, heterogeneous. **5** *a general account* non-detailed, undetailed, broad, loose, approximate, non-specific, unspecific, vague, ill-defined, indefinite, inexact, imprecise, rough. **6** *a general view* panoramic, sweeping, extended, bird's-eye.
Opposites UNUSUAL; SPECIFIC; DETAILED.

generality noun **1** *talking in generalities* generalization, general statement, general principle, non-specific statement, loose/vague statement, indefinite statement, sweeping statement. **2** *a situation not conforming to the generality* general principle/rule/law. **3** *the generality of people are kind* majority, greater part, bulk, mass, body. **4** *the generality of its use* commonness, widespread nature, broadness, prevalence, universality, popularity. See GENERAL 2. **5** *the generality of the board* universality, broadness, comprehensiveness, all-inclusiveness, catholicity. See GENERAL 3. **6** *the generality of the statement* lack of detail, broadness, looseness, approximation, lack of specification, vagueness, indefiniteness, inexactitude, imprecision, roughness. See GENERAL 5.

generally adverb **1** *it generally rains there in the spring* in general, usually, as a rule, normally, ordinarily, almost always, customarily, habitually, typically, regularly, for the most part, mainly, by and large, on average, on the whole, in most cases. **2** *not generally known* commonly, widely, extensively, comprehensively, universally. See GENERAL 2. **3** *speaking generally* in a general sense, without detail, loosely, approximately, broadly, in non-specific terms. See GENERAL 5. **4** *they are generally liked* mostly, for the most part, mainly, in the main, largely, chiefly, predominantly, on the whole.
Opposites UNUSUALLY; PARTICULARLY; RARELY.

generate verb **1** *generate electricity* bring into being, cause to exist, produce. **2** *generating children* beget, procreate, engender, sire, father, breed, spawn, produce, propagate. **3** *generate argument* cause, give rise to, create, produce,

initiate, originate, occasion, sow the seeds of, arouse, whip up, propagate.

generation noun **1** *the generation of the human race* begetting, procreation, engendering, genesis, reproduction, siring, propagation. **2** *the generation of ideas* causing, creation, production, initiation, origination, inception, occasioning, propagation. **3** *people of the same generation* age, age group, peer group. **4** *a generation ago* life span, lifetime. **5** *generations ago* age, era, epoch, times, days.

generic adjective **1** *alcoholic drink, a generic name for beer, wines and spirits* non-specific, general, common, collective, inclusive, all-inclusive, all-encompassing, comprehensive, blanket, sweeping, universal. **2** *goods having a trade mark rather than generic goods* non-exclusive, non-trade-marked, non-registered.

generosity noun **1** *the generosity of our host* liberalness, liberality, kindness, magnanimity, benevolence, beneficence, bounteousness, bounty, munificence, hospitality, charitableness, charity, open-handedness, lavishness. See GENEROUS 1. **2** *the generosity of his spirit* nobility, nobleness, magnanimity, loftiness, high-mindedness, honourableness, honour, goodness, unselfishness, altruism, lack of prejudice, disinterest.

generous adjective **1** *generous with money | a generous host* liberal, kind, magnanimous, benevolent, beneficent, bountiful, bounteous, munificent, hospitable, charitable, open-handed, lavish, ungrudging, unstinting, free-handed, princely. **2** *a generous spirit* noble, magnanimous, lofty, high-minded, honourable, good, unselfish, altruistic, unprejudiced, disinterested. **3** *a generous supply of cakes* liberal, abundant, plentiful, lavish, ample, copious, rich, superabundant, overflowing.
Opposites MEAN; SELFISH; MEAGRE.

genesis noun beginning, commencement, start, outset, birth, origin, source, root, creation, engendering, inception, generation, propagation.

genial adjective *genial person/manner/smile* amiable, affable, good-humoured, good-natured, warm, warm-natured, pleasant, agreeable, cordial, well-disposed, amenable, cheerful, cheery, friendly, congenial, amicable, sociable, convivial, kind, kindly, benign, happy, sunny, jovial, easygoing, sympathetic.
Opposites UNFRIENDLY; UNKIND; MOROSE.

geniality noun amiability, affability, good humour, warmth, pleasantness, agreeableness, cordiality, cheerfulness, cheeriness, friendliness, congeniality, amicableness, sociability, conviviality, kindness, happiness, joviality.

genius noun **1** *the boy is a genius* brilliant person, virtuoso, prodigy, master, mastermind, master-hand, maestro, mental giant, gifted child, intellectual, intellect, expert, adept; *inf.* brains, Einstein. **2** *a person of genius* brilliance, great intelligence/intellect, remarkable cleverness, brains, fine mind, creative power. **3** *a genius for carpentry/cooking* gift, talent, flair, bent, turn, knack, aptitude, forte, faculty, abil-

ity, capability, capacity, endowment, propensity, inclination.
Opposites DOLT; DUNCE; STUPIDITY.

genre *noun* genus, species, kind, sort, type, variety, style.

genteel *adjective* **1** *living in genteel poverty* well-born, aristocratic, noble, blue-blooded, patrician, well-bred, respectable, refined, ladylike, gentlemanly. **2** *genteel behaviour* well-mannered, mannerly, courteous, civil, decorous, gracious, courtly, polished, cultivated, stylish, elegant. **3** *the old lady is very genteel* over-polite, mannered, with affected manners, affected, exaggeratedly well-mannered, affectedly refined, ultra-refined.
Opposites PLEBEIAN; RUDE; COARSE.

gentility *noun* **1** *proud of her gentility* nobility, noble birth, blue blood, good breeding, respectability, refinement, ladylikeness, gentlemanliness. **2** *the gentility of their behaviour* politeness, good manners, mannerliness, courteousness, civility, decorum, propriety, graciousness, courtliness, polish, cultivation, stylishness, elegance. **3** *the gentility of the old lady* over-politeness, affectation, ultra-refinement.

gentle *adjective* **1** *a gentle person* kind, kindly, tender, benign, humane, lenient, merciful, clement, compassionate, tender-hearted, sweet-tempered, placid, serene, mild, soft, quiet, still, tranquil, peaceful, pacific, reposeful, meek, dove-like. **2** *a gentle wind* mild, moderate, light, temperate, balmy, soft, zephyr-like. **3** *her gentle touches* soft, light, smooth, soothing. **4** *a gentle animal* tame, placid, docile, biddable, manageable, tractable, meek, easily handled, trained, schooled, broken. **5** *a gentle slope* gradual, slight, easy, imperceptible. **6** *of gentle birth* genteel, aristocratic, noble, well-born, well-bred, blue-blooded, patrician, upper-class, high-born, respectable, refined, cultured, elegant, polished, polite, ladylike, gentlemanly.
Opposites CRUEL; HARSH; ROUGH; FIERCE.

gentlemanly *adjective* gentlemanlike, well-mannered, mannerly, well-bred, well-behaved, civil, courteous, polite, chivalrous, considerate, obliging, accommodating, honourable, gallant, noble, cultivated, cultured, civilized, polished, refined, suave, urbane.

genuine *adjective* **1** *a genuine diamond* real, authentic, true, pure, actual, bona fide, veritable, sound, sterling, pukka, legitimate, lawful, legal, valid, non-counterfeit, non-fake, original, unadulterated, unalloyed; *inf.* the real McCoy, honest-to-goodness, kosher. **2** *she's a very genuine person* sincere, truthful, honest, frank, candid, open, undeceitful, natural, unaffected, artless, ingenuous; *inf.* up-front.
Opposites FAKE; BOGUS; INSINCERE.

genus *noun* **1** *a botanical genus* subdivision, subfamily. **2** *a genus of table* kind, sort, type, variety, class, species, category, genre.

geometry *noun. See tables at* MATHEMATICS, SHAPE, TRIANGLE.

germ *noun* **1** *illness caused by a germ* microbe, micro-organism, bacillus, bacterium, virus; *inf.*

bug. **2** *the germ of an idea* beginning, start, commencement, inception, seed, embryo, bud, root, rudiment, origin, source, fountain, fountain head. **3** *a fertilized germ* egg, ovum, ovule, embryo, nucleus, seed, bud.

germane *adjective* relevant, pertinent, material, applicable, related, connected, akin, allied, analogous, a propos, apposite, appropriate, apt, fitting, suited, felicitous, proper, to the point, to the purpose.

germinate *verb* **1** *plants germinating* sprout, burgeon, bud, develop, grow, shoot, shoot up, spring up, swell, vegetate, pullulate. **2** *an idea germinating in his mind* originate, grow, begin, start, commence, take root, develop.

gestation *noun* development, incubation, maturation, ripening, pregnancy, gravidity, parturiency.

gesticulate *verb* gesture, make a sign, sign, signal, motion, wave, indicate.

gesture *noun* **1** *make a gesture for them to sit down* sign, signal, motion, motioning, wave, indication, gesticulation. **2** *a political/friendly gesture* action, deed, act.

gesture *verb* gesticulate, make a sign, signal, motion, wave, indicate.

get *verb* **1** *get a new book | where did you get that hat from?* acquire, obtain, come by, come into possession of, procure, secure, buy, purchase. **2** *get a letter from her father* receive, be sent, be given. **3** *go and get that book | she got her hat from the hall* go for, fetch, bring, collect, carry, transport, convey. **4** *get what you want* gain, acquire, achieve, attain, reach, win, find; *inf.* bag. **5** *get £200 per week* earn, be paid, bring in, make, clear, gross, net, pocket; *inf.* pull in, take home. **6** *the police got the thief* capture, seize, grab, lay hold of, grasp, collar, take captive, arrest, apprehend, take, trap, entrap; *inf.* nab, bag. **7** *get flu/measles* catch, become infected by, contract, be smitten by, come/go down with, be afflicted by, take. **8** *try to get him on the phone/radio* telephone, call, phone, ring, radio, reach, communicate with, contact, get in touch with. **9** *I didn't get what he said* hear, catch, take in, perceive. **10** *don't you get what he means?* understand, grasp, comprehend, see, fathom, follow, work out, apprehend, make head or tail of; *inf.* catch on, get the hang of. **11** *we got home/there early* arrive, reach, come; *inf.* make it. **12** *we got her to go* persuade, induce, coax, wheedle into, talk into, prevail upon, influence, sway, convince, win over. **13** *get to see the new film* manage, succeed, fix, arrange, organize, contrive. **14** *get fat/wet/old* become, grow, come to be, turn, turn into, wax. **15** *get a meal* prepare, make preparations for, get ready, cook; *Am. inf.* fix. **16** *that music gets me* affect, have an effect on, move, touch, touch to the quick, stir, arouse, stimulate, excite, grip, impress, leave an impression on; *inf.* send, turn on. **17** *I'll get him for that* avenge oneself on, take vengeance on, get even with, pay someone back, return like for like, give tit for tat, settle the score with, demand an eye for an eye and a tooth for a tooth; *inf.* get back at, get one's own back on. **18** *you've got me there, I don't know* baffle,

puzzle, stump, mystify, confound, nonplus.
19 *she really gets me | her nagging is beginning to
get to me* irritate, get on someone's nerves,
annoy, vex, provoke, anger, exasperate, infuriate, rile, get someone's back up, rub someone
up the wrong way, upset, bother, nettle, pique;
inf. bug, get someone's goat. **get about** *can he
get about yet?* move about, move around, travel.
get across *get across the message* communicate,
get over, put over, make understood/clear,
impart, convey, transmit. **get ahead** *young man
getting ahead* make good, do well, succeed, be
successful, progress, advance, prosper, flourish, rise in the world; *inf.* go places, get somewhere. **get along 1** *I don't get along with his
mother* get on, be on friendly terms, be
friendly, be in harmony, be compatible, agree,
see eye to eye; *inf.* hit it off. **2** *how are you getting along?* get on, fare, manage, progress,
advance, cope; *inf.* get by, make out. **get
around 1** *get around his objections* circumvent,
bypass, outmanoeuvre, outwit; *inf.* outsmart.
2 *get around his father* persuade, induce, prevail
upon, talk round, wheedle, coax, win over,
convert, sway. **3** *she certainly gets around* travel,
visit, circulate, socialize. **get at 1** *always getting at the pupil* pick on, find fault with, carp,
criticize, nag, taunt. **2** *what are you getting at?*
suggest, hint, imply, intend, lead up to,
mean. **3** *the jockey was got at* bribe, buy off,
influence, corrupt, suborn. **get away** *the prisoners got away* escape, make good one's escape,
flee, break free, break out, decamp, depart. **get
back 1** *get back at dawn* return, come home,
come back, arrive home, arrive back. **2** *get
back her lost gloves* recover, retrieve, regain,
repossess, recoup. **3** *get back at his torturer*
take vengeance on, avenge oneself on, get
even with, get. See GET 17. **get by** *get by on little
money* cope, manage, subsist, survive, exist,
fare, get along, contrive to get along, make
both ends meet, keep the wolf from the door;
inf. keep one's head above water, make out.
get off *get off the bus* alight from, climb off, dismount from, leave; descend from, disembark,
exit. **get on 1** *get on the bus* board, climb on;
mount, ascend, embark. **2** *how are you getting
on?* get along, fare, manage, cope; *inf.* make
out. See GET ALONG 2. **3** *husband and wife do
not get on* get along, be on friendly terms, be in
harmony. See GET ALONG 1. **get out 1** *let's
get out now* leave, depart, go away, be off, withdraw; *inf.* vamoose, clear out. **2** *prisoners getting out* escape, break free, break out, free
oneself, extricate oneself, abscond, decamp.
3 *the news has got out* be made public, become
known, be revealed, be publicized, be disclosed, leak, be leaked, spread, circulate, be
noised abroad. **get out of** *get out of digging the
garden* avoid, dodge, evade, escape, shirk. **get
over 1** *get over flu* recover from, recuperate
from, get better after, pull through, survive.
2 *get over a lover | she hasn't got over her love affair*
forget, think no more of, write off, come
round from. **3** *get the message over* communicate, get across, make understood, impart. See
GET ACROSS. **4** *get over one's fear of dogs* overcome, master, get the better of, shake off,
defeat, win a battle over. **get round.** See GET
AROUND. **get together 1** *get together the evidence*

collect, gather, assemble, accumulate, compile,
amass. **2** *we must get together soon* meet, meet
up, have a meeting, see each other, socialize,
foregather, congregate; *inf.* party.
Opposites LOSE; MISUNDERSTAND; LEAVE.

getaway *noun* escape, flight, break-out, break,
abscondment, decampment.

get-together *noun* meeting, party, social gathering, gathering; *inf.* do, beanfeast, bash,
thrash.

get-up *noun* outfit, clothes, clothing, dress,
garb, apparel, garments; *inf.* rig-out.

get-up-and-go *noun* go, energy, vigour, vitality, dynamism, vim, enthusiasm, eagerness,
drive, push, initiative, ambition; *inf.* bounce.

ghastly *adjective* **1** *a ghastly murder/accident*
terrible, horrible, frightful, dreadful, awful,
horrid, horrendous, hideous, shocking, grim,
grisly, gruesome, gory, terrifying, frightening.
2 *feel ghastly* ill, unwell, sick; *inf.* awful, terrible, dreadful. **3** *feels ghastly about losing her
temper* bad, ashamed, shameful; *inf.* awful, terrible, dreadful. **4** *a ghastly mistake* very bad,
serious, grave, critical, unforgivable; *inf.* awful,
terrible, dreadful. **5** *what a ghastly man* odious,
loathsome, nasty, foul, contemptible, low,
mean, base; *inf.* horrible, dreadful, abominable, appalling. **6** *her ghastly appearance*
death-like, deathly pale, pale, pallid, wan,
ashen, colourless, white, white as a sheet, haggard, drawn, ghostlike, ghostly, spectral,
cadaverous.
Opposites PLEASANT; CHARMING; HEALTHY.

ghost *noun* **1** *haunted by a ghost* spectre,
apparition, phantom, spirit, wraith, revenant,
phantasm, soul, manes, lemures; *lit.* shade; *inf.*
spook. **2** *the ghost of a smile* suggestion, hint,
trace, glimmer, semblance, shadow, impression, faint appearance.

ghostly *adjective* *a ghostly figure* ghostlike, spectral, phantom-like, phantom, wraithlike, phantasmal, phantasmic, unearthly, supernatural,
other-worldly, insubstantial, illusory, shadowy,
eerie, weird, uncanny; *inf.* spooky.

giant *noun* giants in legend colossus, man mountain, behemoth. See tables. See also table at MON-
STER.

RACES OF GIANTS	
Brobdingnagians	Jotuns
Cyclops	Titans

GIANTS	
Antaeus	Goliath
Atlas	King Kong
Blunderbore	Magog
Briareus	Mimas
Fafner	Orion
Fenrir	Pantagruel
Gargantua	Polyphemus
Gog	Ymir

giant *adjective a giant insect* gigantic, enormous, colossal, huge, immense, vast, mammoth, monumental, monstrous, gargantuan, titanic, elephantine, prodigious, stupendous, very large, Brobdingnagian; *inf.* jumbo, industrial-size.

gibberish *noun* meaningless talk, babble, gabble, jabbering, nonsense, rubbish, twaddle, drivel, balderdash, mumbo-jumbo, blather, double-talk, prattle; *inf.* poppycock, gobbledegook, rot, tommy-rot, bosh, piffle.

gibe, jibe *verb the students gibed at the politician* jeer, mock, sneer at, scoff at, taunt, scorn, deride, ridicule, hold up to ridicule, laugh at, poke fun at, make fun of, tease, twit; *inf.* rib, rag.

gibe, jibe *noun the gibes of the crowd* taunt, sneer, jeer; mocking, sneering, scoffing, taunts, scorn, derision, ridicule, teasing, sarcasm; *inf.* dig.

giddy *adjective* **1** *get giddy climbing ladders* dizzy, light-headed, faint, reeling, unsteady, vertiginous; *inf.* woozy. **2** *a giddy girl* flighty, silly, frivolous, skittish, irresponsible, flippant, whimsical, capricious, light-minded, feather-brained, scatterbrained, fickle, erratic, changeable, inconstant, irresolute, mercurial, volatile, unsteady, unstable, unbalanced, impulsive, reckless, wild, careless, thoughtless, heedless, carefree, insouciant.

gift *noun* **1** *receive a birthday/leaving gift | gift shop/token* present, offering, bounty, largesse, donation, contribution, boon, grant, bonus, gratuity, benefaction, bequest, legacy, inheritance, endowment. **2** *the gift of a car* giving, presentation, bestowal, conferment, donation, contribution, grant, endowment. **3** *a gift for foreign languages* talent, flair, aptitude, facility, knack, bent, turn, aptness, ability, faculty, capacity, capability, attribute, skill, expertise, genius; mind for.

gift *verb gift a cup to the school* present, give, bestow, confer, proffer, donate, contribute, endow, bequeath, leave, will.

gifted *adjective gifted child | gifted at singing/dancing* talented, brilliant, intelligent, clever, bright, smart, sharp, ingenious, able, accomplished, capable, masterly, skilled, adroit, proficient, expert.
Opposites STUPID; UNSKILLED; INEPT.

gigantic *adjective* giant, enormous, colossal, huge, immense, vast, mammoth, gargantuan, Brobdingnagian; *inf.* jumbo. See GIANT *adjective.*
Opposites DIMINUTIVE; TINY.

giggle *verb* titter, snigger, snicker, chuckle, chortle, laugh, cackle; *inf.* tee-hee, ha-ha.

gigolo *noun* **1** *hire a gigolo for the evening* male escort, male companion, dancing partner. **2** *a gigolo who hangs round rich women* male prostitute, ladies' man, lady-killer; *inf.* toy boy.

gild *verb* **1** *gild the table top* make golden/gilt/aureate, aurify, inlay with gold, cover with gold, paint/lacquer gold. **2** *gild the lily* adorn, decorate, embellish, ornament, bedeck, deck, garnish, array, enrich, enhance, brighten up, dress up, prettify, beautify, grace. **3** *gild the truth* dress up, embroider, sugar-coat, window-dress, camouflage, disguise.

gimcrack *adjective* shoddy, cheap, tawdry, kitsch, flimsy, badly made, jerry-built; *inf.* tacky, tatty.

gimmick *noun* publicity, device, contrivance, eye-catching novelty, stunt, scheme, trick, dodge, ploy, stratagem.

gingerly *adverb* cautiously, with caution, warily, charily, cannily, carefully, attentively, heedfully, vigilantly, watchfully, guardedly, prudently, circumspectly, judiciously, suspiciously, hesitantly, reluctantly, timidly, timorously.

gird *verb* **1** *gird on his sword* belt, bind, fasten. **2** *trees girded the lake* surround, circle, encircle, ring, enclose, encompass, compass, confine, hem in, pen, enfold, engird, girdle. **3** *gird oneself for battle* prepare, make ready, get ready, ready, brace, fortify, steel, buttress.

girdle *noun* **1** *wearing a red girdle round the dress* sash, belt, cummerbund, band, braid, obi, fillet; *lit.* cincture. **2** *a light-support girdle* corset, corselet, foundation garment, panti-girdle; *Med.* truss.

girdle *verb trees girdling the lake* surround, circle, encircle, ring, enclose, encompass, gird. See GIRD 2.

girl *noun* **1** *a teenage girl | he has a boy and a girl* female child, daughter, miss, lass, young woman, young lady, young unmarried woman; *Scots* lassie; *inf.* bird; *derog. inf* tart; *Am. inf.* babe, chick. **2** *he and his girl* girlfriend, sweetheart, fiancée, lover, lady-love, mistress, inamorata.

girth *noun* circumference, size, bulk, measure, perimeter.

gist *noun* substance, essence, quintessence, drift, sense, general sense, significance, idea, import, core, nucleus, nub, kernel, pith, marrow, burden, crux, important point.

give *verb* **1** *gave him the book | give a donation to the hospital* hand, present, donate, bestow, contribute, confer, hand over, turn over, award, grant, accord, leave, will, bequeath, make over, entrust, consign, vouchsafe. **2** *give out the prizes* distribute, allocate, allot, mete out, hand out, disperse, apportion, dole out, assign; *inf.* dish out. **3** *give the impression* show, display, demonstrate, set forth, indicate, manifest, evidence. **4** *give them time* allow, permit, grant, accord, offer. **5** *give a reprimand* administer, deliver, deal. **6** *give advice* provide, supply, furnish, proffer, offer. **7** *give no trouble* cause, be a source of, make, create. **8** *give news of the battle* impart, communicate, announce, transmit, convey, transfer, send, purvey. **9** *land giving a good crop | giving good results* produce, yield, afford, result in. **10** *the car gave a jolt* perform, execute, make, do. **11** *give a shout* yell, let out, utter, issue, emit. **12** *give his life for his country* give up, sacrifice, relinquish, devote. **13** *give place to others* surrender, concede, yield, give up, cede. **14** *she gave me to believe* lead, make, cause, force. **15** *the chair gave* give way, collapse, break, break down, fall apart, come apart; bend, buckle. **give away** **1** *give away secrets* reveal, disclose, divulge, let slip, leak, let out, expose, uncover. **2** *give his*

friend *away* betray, inform on; *inf.* grass on, rat on, blow the whistle on. **give in** give up, surrender, admit defeat, concede defeat, concede, yield, capitulate, submit, comply, succumb, quit, retreat; *inf.* throw in the sponge/towel. **give off** emit, send out, pour out, throw out, discharge, exude, exhale, release, vent, produce. **give out 1** *give out fumes* give off, emit, send out, discharge, exude. *See* GIVE OFF. **2** *give out that he is leaving* announce, declare, make known, communicate, impart, broadcast, publish, disseminate. **3** *supplies were giving out* run out, be used up, be consumed, be exhausted, be depleted, come to an end, fail. **give up 1** *give up smoking* stop, cease, quit, desist from, leave off, swear off, renounce, forswear, abandon, discontinue; *inf.* chuck, cut out. **2** *give up in the face of the enemy* give in, surrender, concede defeat, yield, capitulate. *See* GIVE IN. **3** *she's just given up* despair, lose heart, abandon hope, give up hope.
Opposites ACCEPT; RECEIVE; TAKE; WITHDRAW.

giver *noun* donor, donator, contributor, granter, grantor, benefactor, backer, fairy godmother; *inf.* angel.

glacial *adjective glacial conditions* freezing, frozen, icy, icy-cold, frigid, bitterly cold, wintry, arctic, polar, gelid, Siberian; *Med.* algid.

glad *adjective* **1** *glad you're here* happy, pleased, pleased as Punch, well-pleased, delighted, gratified, thrilled, overjoyed, elated, over the moon, satisfied, contented, grateful; *inf.* chuffed, tickled pink. **2** *glad to help* willing, more than willing, eager, ready, prepared, happy, pleased, delighted. **3** *hear the glad news* happy, joyful, delightful, welcome, cheering, cheerful, pleasing, gratifying. **4** *the children's glad laughter* merry, gay, jolly, cheerful, cheery, joyful, joyous, gleeful, mirthful, happy, animated.
Opposites UNHAPPY; SAD; RELUCTANT.

gladden *verb* make happy, delight, cheer, cheer up, hearten, brighten up, raise the spirits of, please, elate, buoy up, give a lift to; *inf.* buck up.

gladly *adverb I'll gladly help* with pleasure, happily, willingly, cheerfully, eagerly, ungrudgingly.

glamorous *adjective* **1** *a glamorous woman* alluring, dazzling, glittering, well-dressed, smart, elegant, beautiful, lovely, attractive, charming, fascinating, exciting, beguiling, bewitching, enchanting, entrancing, irresistible, tantalizing; *inf.* glitzy, ritzy. **2** *a glamorous career* exciting, fascinating, stimulating,

thrilling, high-profile, dazzling, glossy, glittering; *inf.* ritzy, glitzy.
Opposites DOWDY; DULL; BORING.

glamour *noun* **1** *women with glamour* beauty, loveliness, attractiveness, allure, attraction, elegance, charm, fascination; *inf.* glitz, pizzazz. *See* GLAMOROUS 1. **2** *the glamour of foreign travel* allure, attraction, charm, fascination, excitement, enchantment, captivation, magic, spell.

glance *verb* **1** *glance at the stranger* look quickly/briefly at, take a quick look at, cast a brief look at, look hurriedly at, glimpse, catch a glimpse of, peek at, peep at; *inf.* sneak a look at. **2** *glance through the paper|glance over his work* skim through, leaf through, flick through, flip through, thumb through, scan, dip into. **3** *lights glancing on water* flash, gleam, glitter, glisten, glint, glimmer, shimmer, flicker, sparkle, twinkle, reflect, coruscate. **4** *the arrow glanced off the tree* ricochet, rebound, be deflected; bounce/fly off. **5** *the car glanced the wall* graze, skim, touch, brush. **6** *glance at/over the subject of money* touch upon, mention in passing, give a mention to, mention, refer to, allude to, make an allusion to, skim over.
Opposites STUDY; SCRUTINIZE.

glance *noun* **1** *take a glance at* brief look, quick look, rapid look, glimpse, peek, peep; *inf.* gander, once-over. **2** *the glance of the sun on the water* flash, gleam, glitter, glittering, glint, glimmer, shimmer, flicker, sparkle, twinkle. *See* GLANCE *verb* 3.

gland *noun. See table.*

glare *verb* **1** *teachers glaring at pupils* stare angrily, glower, scowl, frown, lour, give someone black looks, look threateningly/menacingly at, give someone dirty looks, look daggers. **2** *lights glaring* blaze, flare, flame, beam, dazzle.

glare *noun* **1** *give a glare at his enemy* angry stare, glower, scowl, frown, lour, black look, threatening/menacing look, dirty look. **2** *the glare of lights* blaze, flare, flame, harsh beam, dazzle.

glaring *adjective* **1** *glaring lights* blazing, dazzling. *See* GLARE *verb* 2. **2** *a glaring error* conspicuous, obvious, overt, manifest, patent, visible, unconcealed, flagrant, blatant, egregious, outrageous, gross.
Opposites DIM; INCONSPICUOUS.

glass *noun* **1** *a glass of water* tumbler, flute, schooner, balloon, beaker, goblet, chalice;

HUMAN GLANDS

Endocrine Glands	testis	gastric gland	parotid gland
adrenal gland	thyroid gland	lacrimal gland	preputial gland
corpus luteum	**Exocrine Glands**	Lieberkühn's	prostate gland
islets of	Bartholin's gland	gland	salivary gland
Langerhans	breast	liver	sebaceous gland
ovary	Brunner's gland	mammary gland	sublingual gland
parathyroid gland	buccal gland	meibomian/tarsal	submandibular/sub-
pineal gland	Cowper's/bulbo-	gland	maxillary gland
pituitary gland	urethral gland	pancreas	sweat gland

wineglass, sherry-glass, brandy-glass. **2** *windows made of glass* glass plate. *See table.*

TYPES OF GLASS

bottle glass	lead crystal
bulletproof glass	opal glass
clear glass	plate glass
crown glass	quartz glass
crystal	reinforced
cut glass	glass
fibreglass	safety glass
flint glass	sheet glass
frosted glass	stained glass
laminated glass	toughened glass

---

glasses *plural noun put on his glasses* spectacles, eyeglasses, bifocals, sun-glasses, lorgnette, monocle, pince-nez, field-glasses, binoculars, opera-glasses.

glassy *adjective* **1** *a glassy surface on the table* glasslike, shiny, glossy, highly-polished, smooth. **2** *the sea is glassy* glasslike, mirror-like, smooth, clear, crystal-clear, transparent, translucent, limpid, pellucid. **3** *the pavements are glassy* slippery, icy, ice-covered. **4** *a glassy stare* expressionless, glazed, blank, empty, vacant, vacuous, deadpan, fixed, unmoving, motionless, lifeless.

glaze *verb* **1** *glaze china* enamel, lacquer, varnish, coat, polish, burnish, gloss. **2** *glaze the cake/pie/apples* coat, cover, ice, frost. **3** *his eyes glazed over* become glassy, grow expressionless, go blank, be motionless. *See* GLASSY 4.

glaze *noun* **1** *add a glaze to the china* enamel, lacquer, gloss, lustre, finish. *See* GLAZE *verb* 1. **2** *put a glaze on the cake/pie* coating, icing, frosting.

gleam *noun* **1** *a gleam of light* beam, flash, glow, shaft, ray, flare, glint. *See* GLEAM *verb.* **2** *the gleam of the polished brass* glow, lustre, gloss, shine, sheen, brightness, brilliance, flash, coruscation. **3** *a gleam of hope* glimmer, flicker, ray, trace, suggestion, hint, inkling, grain.

gleam *verb lights gleaming* shine, radiate, flash, glow, flare, glint, glisten, glitter, beam, shimmer, glimmer, glance, sparkle, twinkle, scintillate.

glee *noun* merriment, gaiety, mirth, mirthfulness, delight, joy, joyfulness, joyousness, gladness, happiness, pleasure, jollity, hilarity, jocularity, joviality, exhilaration, high spirits, blitheness, cheerfulness, exaltation, elation, exuberance, verve, liveliness, triumph.

gleeful *adjective* merry, gay, delighted, mirthful, joyful, overjoyed, joyous, glad, happy, pleased, jolly, jovial, exhilarated, high-spirited, blithe, cheerful, elated, exuberant, cock-a-hoop, triumphant.

glib *adjective* slick, smooth, smooth-talking, smooth-spoken, fast-talking, plausible, quick/ready of tongue, fluent, suave, talkative, voluble, loquacious, having kissed the Blarney Stone, unctuous; *inf.* sweet-talking, having the

gift of the gab.
Opposites TONGUE-TIED; INARTICULATE.

glide *verb* **1** *skaters/ships gliding along* slide, move smoothly, slip, skim, sail, skate, float, drift, flow, coast. **2** *time glided by* pass, slip, elapse, steal away, roll on.

glimmer *noun* **1** *a glimmer of light* gleam, flash, flicker, glint, shimmer, blink, twinkle, sparkle, glow, ray. **2** *a glimmer of hope* gleam, flicker, ray, trace. *See* GLEAM *noun* 3.

glimmer *verb lights glimmering* gleam, flash, flicker, shimmer, blink, twinkle, sparkle, glow.

glimpse *noun* glance, brief look, quick look, peek, peep. *See* GLANCE *noun* 1.

glimpse *verb* catch a glimpse of, catch sight of, catch a quick sight of, spot, spy, espy, descry.

glint *verb diamonds glinting* shine, sparkle, flash, twinkle, glitter, glimmer, blink, wink, shimmer, glisten, dazzle, gleam, scintillate.

glint *noun the glint of diamonds* sparkle, flash, twinkle, glitter, glimmer, blink, gleam. *See* GLINT *verb.*

glisten *verb face glistened with tears/sweat* shine, shimmer, sparkle, twinkle, flicker, blink, wink, glint, glance, gleam, flash, scintillate, coruscate.

glitter *verb stars glittering* sparkle, twinkle, flicker, blink, wink, shimmer, glimmer, glint, gleam, flash, scintillate, coruscate.

glitter *noun* **1** *the glitter of stars* sparkle, twinkle, flicker, blink, winking. *See* GLITTER *verb.* **2** *the glitter of show business* showiness, flashiness, ostentation, glamour, pageantry, fanfare, splendour; *inf.* razzle-dazzle, glitz, ritziness, pizzazz.

gloat *verb* relish, take pleasure in, delight in, revel in, rejoice in, glory in, exult in, triumph over, crow about; *inf.* rub it in.

global *adjective* **1** *global recession* worldwide, world, universal, international, planetary. **2** *a global rule* general, comprehensive, all-inclusive, all-encompassing, all-out, encyclopedic, exhaustive, thorough, total, across-the-board, with no exceptions.

globe *noun* **1** *everywhere in the globe* world, universe, earth, planet. **2** *in the shape of a globe* sphere, orb, ball, round.

globule *noun* bead, ball, drop, droplet, pearl, particle.

gloom *noun* **1** *the gloom of the night/room* gloominess, dimness, darkness, dark, blackness, murkiness, murk, shadowiness, shadow, shade, shadiness, cloud, cloudiness, dullness, obscurity, dusk, twilight. **2** *a state of gloom* low spirits, melancholy, sadness, unhappiness, sorrow, grief, woe, despondency, misery, dejection, downheartedness, dispiritedness, glumness, desolation, depression, the blues, despair, pessimism, hopelessness.
Opposites LIGHT; GAIETY; CHEER.

gloomy *adjective* **1** *a gloomy day* dark, cloudy, overcast, sunless, dull, dim, shadowy, dismal, dreary. **2** *a gloomy room* dark, black, unlit, murky, shadowy, sombre, dingy, dismal, dreary, crepuscular; *lit.* tenebrous, Stygian.

3 *gloomy news* bad, black, sad, saddening, distressing, sombre, melancholy, depressing, dispiriting, disheartening, disappointing, cheerless, comfortless, pessimistic, hopeless. **4** *feeling gloomy* in low spirits, melancholy, sad, unhappy, sorrowful, woebegone, despondent, disconsolate, miserable, dejected, downcast, downhearted, dispirited, glum, desolate, depressed, blue, despairing, pessimistic, morose; *inf.* down in the mouth.
Opposites BRIGHT; HAPPY; CHEERFUL.

glorify *verb* **1** *glorify God* worship, adore, exalt, extol, pay homage to, pay tribute to, honour, revere, reverence, venerate. **2** *wars glorified the position of the king* add lustre to, aggrandize, ennoble, exalt, elevate, raise, lift up, magnify, add dignity to, dignify, augment, increase, advance, boost, promote. **3** *glorify the conqueror* praise, sing/sound the praises of, extol, laud, eulogize, magnify, panegyrize, acclaim, applaud, cheer, hail, celebrate, lionize, cry up.

glorious *adjective* **1** *our glorious monarch* illustrious, noble, celebrated, famous, famed, renowned, distinguished, honoured, eminent, excellent, magnificent, majestic, splendid, supreme, sublime, triumphant, victorious. **2** *a glorious day* beautiful, bright, brilliant, sunny, perfect. **3** *have a glorious time* splendid, marvellous, wonderful, delightful, enjoyable, pleasurable, excellent, fine; *inf.* terrific, great, fab.
Opposites UNKNOWN; DULL; MISERABLE.

glory *noun* **1** *to the glory of God* worship, adoration, exaltation, extolment, honour, reverence, veneration, thanksgiving. **2** *win glory in battle* renown, fame, prestige, honour, distinction, illustriousness, acclaim, credit, accolade, recognition, laudation, extolment; *inf.* kudos. **3** *the glory of Versailles* splendour, resplendence, magnificence, grandeur, majesty, pomp, pageantry, beauty.
Opposites BLASPHEMY; SHAME; DISGRACE; ugliness.

glory *verb* *glory in their success* exult in, rejoice in, take pleasure in, take pride in, preen oneself on, be proud of, delight in, revel in, triumph over, boast about, crow about, gloat about.

gloss¹ *noun* **1** *the gloss of the furniture* shine, sheen, lustre, gleam, brightness, brilliance, sparkle, shimmer, polish, burnish. **2** *a gloss of respectability* façade, front, camouflage, disguise, mask, false appearance, semblance, show, deceptive show, veneer, surface.

gloss² *verb* **1** *gloss the furniture* make glossy, shine, give a shine to, polish, burnish. **2** *gloss the china* glaze, varnish, lacquer, enamel, japan. **3** *gloss over the truth* deal rapidly with, evade, avoid, smooth over, conceal, hide, cover up, camouflage, disguise, mask, veil, draw/pull a veil over, whitewash.

gloss³ *noun* *add glosses to the text* explanation, explication, interpretation, elucidation, annotation, commentary, comment, note, footnote, scholium, translation.

gloss⁴ *verb* *gloss the text* give an explanation/explication of, explain, interpret, elucidate, annotate, add a commentary to, comment on, add notes/footnotes to, translate, construe.

glossy *adjective* **1** *glossy furniture* shining, shiny, glassy, gleaming, bright, brilliant, sparkling, shimmering, polished, burnished, glazed. **2** *glossy hair* shining, gleaming, sleek, smooth, silky, silken.
Opposites DULL; LUSTRELESS.

glow *noun* **1** *the glow from the light* subdued light, gleam, glimmer, incandescence, luminosity, phosphorescence, lambency. **2** *the glow of the garden flowers* brightness, vividness, brilliance, colourfulness, richness, radiance, splendour. **3** *the glow of her complexion* blush, flush, rosiness, pinkness, redness, crimson, scarlet, reddening, bloom. **4** *induce a warm glow* warmth, happiness, contentment, satisfaction. **5** *the glow of his love* passion, ardour, fervour, vehemence, intensity, earnestness, impetuosity.

glow *verb* **1** *the light glowed* shed a glow, gleam, glimmer, shine. **2** *the fire glowed* burn without flames, smoulder. **3** *she glowed with pleasure* blush, flush, redden, grow pink, crimson, go scarlet, colour, be suffused with colour. **4** *glow with pride* radiate, thrill, tingle.

glower *verb* *glower at his enemy* scowl, stare angrily, glare, frown, lour, give someone black/dirty looks, look daggers.
Opposites SMILE; GRIN.

glower *noun* *give a glower* scowl, angry stare, glare, frown, lour, black look, dirty look.

glowing *adjective* **1** *glowing coals* aglow, smouldering, incandescent, candescent, luminous, phosphorescent, lambent. **2** *a glowing complexion* rosy, pink, reddish, red, ruddy, florid. **3** *glowing colours* bright, vivid, brilliant, colourful, rich, radiant. **4** *a glowing report* complimentary, highly favourable, enthusiastic, ecstatic, rhapsodic, eulogistic, laudatory, acclamatory, panegyrical, adulatory; *inf.* rave.

glue *noun* *stick pictures on with glue* adhesive, fixative, gum, paste, cement, mucilage, epoxy resin.

glue *verb* *glue the pages together* stick, gum, paste, affix, fix, cement, agglutinate, conglutinate.

glum *adjective* in low spirits, gloomy, melancholy, sad, despondent, miserable, dejected, downcast, downhearted, dispirited, depressed; *inf.* down in the mouth. *See* GLOOMY 4.
Opposites CHEERFUL; MERRY.

glut *noun* *a glut of apples* surplus, excess, surfeit, superfluity, overabundance, superabundance, oversupply, overprofusion, saturation.
Opposites DEARTH; SCARCITY.

glut *verb* **1** *glut the market* saturate, supersaturate, overload, oversupply, flood, inundate, deluge. **2** *glut the children* cram full, stuff, gorge, satiate, overfeed, fill up. **3** *glut the passage* clog, choke up, obstruct, stop up, dam up.

glutinous *adjective* glue-like, sticky, gummy, adhesive, viscid, mucilaginous, viscous, pasty, tacky, mucous.

glutton noun gourmand, gormandizer, gorger, gobbler, guzzler; inf. pig, greedy pig, gannet, greedy guts.

gluttonous adjective greedy, gormandizing, gourmand, insatiable, voracious, edacious; inf. piggish, hoggish, gutsy.

gluttony noun greed, greediness, gourmandism, gormandizing, insatiability, voraciousness, voracity, edaciousness, edacity; inf. piggishness, hoggishness, gutsiness.

gnarled adjective **1** a gnarled tree knotty, knotted, lumpy, bumpy, nodular, knurled, rough, twisted, crooked, distorted, contorted. **2** gnarled hands knotty, lumpy, knurled, rough, twisted, arthritic, leathery, wrinkled, rugged, weather-beaten. **3** a gnarled disposition cantankerous, crabbed, crabby, crotchety, grumpy, snappish, peevish, disagreeable; inf. grouchy; Am. cranky.

gnash verb grind, strike together, grit, rasp, grate.

gnaw verb **1** dogs gnawing the bone chew, munch, crunch, masticate, bite, nibble, worry. **2** rust gnawing away the metal erode, corrode, wear away, wear down, eat away, fret, consume, devour. **3** worry gnawing at her prey on someone's mind, nag, torment, plague, harry, harass, fret, distress, trouble, worry.

go verb **1** go forward/backward/up move, proceed, progress, pass, walk, travel, journey, repair. **2** time to go go away, leave, depart, withdraw, set off, set out, decamp; inf. beat it, scram. **3** does the machine go? work, be in working order, function, operate, be operative, run, perform. **4** go grey/peculiar/bad become, grow, get, come to be, wax. **5** go bang/"moo" | the bell went make/emit a sound, sound, sound out, resound. **6** this road goes all the way to the sea extend to, stretch to, reach, spread to, give access to, lead to. **7** as time went by pass, pass by, elapse, lapse, slip away, tick away, fly. **8** where does this book go? belong, have a place, fit in, be located, be situated, be found, lie, stand. **9** her headache has gone stop, cease, disappear, vanish, be no more, fade away, melt away. **10** all my money has gone be finished, be spent, be used up, be exhausted, be consumed. **11** the old lady has gone die, be dead, pass away, decease, expire, perish; inf. give up the ghost, kick the bucket. **12** these clothes will have to go be discarded, be thrown away, be disposed of. **13** some of the staff will have to go be dismissed, be made redundant; inf. be sacked, be axed, get the axe/chop. **14** the money will go to charity be assigned to, be allotted to, be applied to, be devoted to, be awarded to, be granted/given to, be ceded to. **15** how did your interview go? turn out, work out, fare, progress, develop, result, end, end up, eventuate. **16** the carpet and curtains don't go go together, go with each other, match, harmonize, blend, suit each other, be suited, complement each other, be in accord, accord, be compatible. **17** his behaviour does not go with his theories fit, fit in with, conform to, comply with, be in line with. **18** this goes to prove his theory serve, contribute, help, incline, tend. **19** the bridge went break, give way, collapse, fall down, cave in, crumble, disintegrate, fall to pieces. **go about 1** a rumour going about circulate, pass around; be passed around, be spread, be broadcast. **2** how do you go about buying a house? set about, begin, approach, tackle, undertake. **go ahead** work is going ahead go, progress, make progress, proceed, advance. **go along with 1** we went along with our neighbours go with, accompany, escort. **2** I'll go along with your plans comply with, cooperate with, acquiesce in, follow, agree with, assent to, concur with. **go around.** See GO verb go about 1. **go back on** go back on one's word renege on, repudiate, retract. **go by 1** as time goes by pass, elapse, move on, proceed, flow. **2** go by the rules follow, obey, observe, be guided by, take as a guide, heed. **go down 1** the ship went down in a storm sink, be submerged, founder, go under. **2** prices are going down decrease, drop, fall, become lower, be reduced, decline, plummet. **3** the champion is going down in the first round be beaten, be defeated, suffer defeat, lose, fail, collapse. **4** his name will go down in history be commemorated, be remembered, be recalled, be immortalized. **go far** a young man bound to go far do well, do well for oneself, be successful, succeed, make progress, get on, get on in the world, get ahead, make a name for oneself, advance oneself, set the world/ Thames/heather on fire. **go for 1** go for the newspapers go and get, fetch. **2** the dog went for him attack, assault, assail, launch oneself at, set upon, spring at/upon, rush at. **3** he doesn't go for clever women be attracted to, be fond of, admire, favour, like, prefer, choose, hold with. **go in for** go in for sport engage in, take part in, participate in, practise, pursue, take up, espouse, adopt, embrace. **go into 1** go into everything wholeheartedly participate in, take part in, undertake, enter. **2** the police are going into the evidence thoroughly investigate, research, inquire into, look into, examine, study, review, check, scrutinize, analyse, delve into, dig into, pursue, probe. **go off 1** the bomb went off explode, detonate, blow up, burst, erupt; inf. go bang. **2** we went off at dawn leave, go away, depart, set out, set off, decamp, move out. **3** the cheese has gone off go bad, go stale, go sour, be rotten, be past the sell-by date. **go on 1** how long did the talk go on? last, continue, proceed, endure, persist, stay, remain, happen, occur. **2** she does go on a bit ramble on, talk on and on, carry on talking, chatter, prattle, blether; inf. waffle, witter on. **go out 1** he has gone out of the office leave, exit, depart from. **2** the lights/passion went out be extinguished, be turned off, be doused, be quenched, fade, die out. **3** a boy and girl going out together go with each other, court; inf. go steady, date. See GO verb go together 2. **go over** go over the accounts read over, look over, inspect, examine, study, scan, run over; inf. give the once-over. **go through 1** go through torture undergo, be subjected to, suffer, experience, bear, stand, tolerate, endure, weather, brook, brave. **2** go through money spend, use up, run through, consume, exhaust. **3** go through someone's pockets look through, search, hunt through, check, inspect, examine; inf. frisk. **go together 1** the carpets and curtains do not go together go, match,

harmonize, blend, suit each other. *See* GO *verb* 16. **2** *they have been going together for months* go out, go out together, go with each other, see each other, court, keep company, woo; *inf.* go steady, date. **go under 1** *the ship went under in a storm* go down, sink, be submerged. *See* GO *verb* go down 1. **2** *the firm has gone under* fail, founder, go bankrupt, go into receivership, go to the wall; *inf.* go bust, fold, flop. **go with 1** *we'll go with you* go along with, accompany, escort. **2** *the carpets do not go with the curtains* match, complement, harmonize/blend/accord with. **3** *his sister is going with her brother* go out with, see; *inf.* go steady with, date. *See* GO *verb* go together 2. **go without 1** *go without chocolate* do without, abstain from, deny oneself, be denied, lack, want. **2** *she went without to feed her children* go short, be in need, be in want.
Opposites COME; ARRIVE; break down (*see* BREAK).

go *noun* **1** *have a go at hang-gliding* try, attempt, effort, bid, essay, endeavour; *inf.* shot, stab, crack, whirl, whack. **2** *people with a lot of go* energy, vigour, dynamism, force, verve, vim, vitality, spirit, animation, vivacity, drive, push, determination, enterprise; *inf.* get-up-and-go, pep, oomph.

goad *noun* **1** *a goad to spur cattle* spiked stick, stick, spike, prod, staff, crook, pole, rod. **2** *a goad to action* stimulus, incentive, incitement, instigation, inducement, stimulation, impetus, motivation, pressure, spur, prick, jolt, poke.

go-ahead *noun* *get the go-ahead for the scheme* permission, assent, consent, authorization, sanction, leave, warranty, confirmation, imprimatur; *inf.* green light, OK, okay, thumbs up.

go-ahead *adjective* *a go-ahead firm | a very go-ahead young man* enterprising, ambitious, progressive, pioneering; *inf.* up-and-coming, go-getting.

goal *noun* *the goals of the organization* aim, objective, object, end, purpose, target, ambition, design, intention, intent, aspiration, ideal.

goat *noun* **1** *farmers keeping goats* billy-goat, billy, nanny-goat, nanny, kid. *See table.* **2** *he's a silly goat* fool, idiot, nincompoop, ninny, dolt, ass; *inf.* nitwit, halfwit, twit, chump, nerd; *Am.*

GOATS	
Breeds of Goat	Toggenbury
Anglo-Nubian	Valais Blackneck
Angora	**Wild Goats**
Apulian	bezoar
Bagot	ibex
Chamois	markhor
Coloured	Spanish ibex
Dutch White	tahr
French Alpine	tur
Grisons Striped	**Goat-Antelopes**
Kashmiri	chamois
Murcian	goral
Saanen	mountain goat
Somali	musk ox
Soviet Mohair	serow
Syrian Mountain	takin
Telemark	

inf. dingbat. **3** *an old goat chasing young girls* lecher, lascivious man; *inf.* dirty old man, DOM.

gobble *verb* gulp, swallow hurriedly, wolf, bolt, guzzle, devour, stuff down, gluttonize, gormandize; *inf.* scoff, shovel.

gobbledegook *noun* jargon, obscure language, unintelligible language, pretentious language, verbosity, prolixity, verbiage, circumlocution, periphrasis; *inf.* gibberish.

go-between *noun* intermediary, mediator, middleman, medium, agent, broker, dealer, factor, liaison, contact, contact person, pander, panderer.

goblet *noun* wineglass, chalice, beaker, tumbler, cup; *Scots* tass.

goblin *noun* hobgoblin, gnome, dwarf, imp, elf, sprite.

God *noun* Christian God; Jewish God, YHWH/Yahweh; Muslim God, Allah. *See table.*

NAMES OF GOD	
Allah	Holy Ghost, the
Almighty, the	Holy One, the
Almighty God	Holy Spirit
Alpha and Omega	Holy Trinity, the
Creator, the	Jah
Deity, the	Jehovah
Divine Being	King of Kings
Eternal, the	Lord, the
Everlasting	Lord of Lords
Father	Maker, the
Father, Son, and	Our Father
Holy Ghost	Our Maker
Father, the	Prime Mover, the
First Cause	primum mobile
God Almighty	Spirit of God
Godhead, the	Supreme Being, the
God the Father	Trinity, the
God the Son	Yahweh

god *noun* **1** *tribal gods* deity, divine being, divinity, spirit, genius, numen. *See table.* **2** *false gods* idol, graven image, icon, golden calf.

God-forsaken *adjective* *a God-forsaken place* desolate, dismal, dreary, bleak, wretched, miserable, gloomy, deserted, abandoned, forlorn, neglected, remote, in the back of beyond, backward.

godless *adjective* **1** *churchgoers pitying godless people* atheistic, agnostic, sceptical, faithless, nullifidian. **2** *missionaries converting godless people* heathen, pagan, ungodly, impious, irreligious, unrighteous, unprincipled, sinful, wicked, evil, depraved.

godlike *adjective* **1** *godlike forgiveness* godly, divine, celestial, heavenly, sacred, holy, saintly. **2** *a godlike beauty* divine, deific, deiform, transcendent, superhuman.

godly *adjective* God-fearing, devout, pious, religious, pietistic, believing, righteous, moral, virtuous, good, holy, saintly.

GODS AND GODDESSES

Greek
Aphrodite
Apollo
Ares
Artemis
Asclepius
Athene
Cronus
Cybele
Demeter
Dionysus
Eos
Eros
Gaia
Glaucus
Hades
Hebe
Hecate
Helios
Hephaestus
Hera
Hermes
Hestia
Hyperion
Hypnos
Iris
Leto
Leucothea
Moros
Nemesis
Nereus
Nike
Pan
Persephone
Pollux
Pontus
Poseidon
Proteus
Rhea
Thetis
Uranus
Zeus
Roman
Aesculapius
Apollo
Aurora
Bacchus
Bellona
Ceres
Cupid
Cybele
Diana
Flora
Janus
Juno
Jupiter
Juventas
Maia
Mars
Mercury
Minerva
Morpheus
Mors
Neptune
Pluto
Priapus
Proserpina

Quirinus
Saturn
Sol
Somnus
Terminus
Uranus
Venus
Vesta
Vulcan
Norse
Aegir
Aesir, the
Balder
Bragi
Freya
Frigga
Gerda
Heimdall
Hel
Hermod
Höd
Hoenir
Idun
Lofri
Loki
Mimir
Nerthus
Njorth
Odin
Sif
Skuld
Surt
Thor
Tyr
Ull
Urd
Vali
Vanir, the
Verdandi
Vidar
Celtic
Anu
Boann
Boanna, the
Bran
Brigit
Cernunnos
Dagda, the
Danu
Dian Cecht
Epona
Gobniu
Ludd/Nudd
Lug
Macha
Manannan
Nuada
Ogma
Pwyll
Rhiannon
Egyptian
Ament
Ammon
Anhur
Anquet
Anubis
Aten

Atum
Bast
Behdety
Bes
Buto
Geb
Hapi
Harakhtes
Harmakhis
Haroeris
Harsaphes
Harsiesis
Hathor
Heket
Horus
Imhotep
Isis
Khensu
Khepera
Khnum
Maat
Mertseger
Meskhent
Min
Mont
Mut
Nefertum
Neheh
Nekhebit
Nephthys
Nun
Nut
Osiris
Ptah
Ra
Renenet
Renpet
Sati
Sebek
Seker
Sekhmet
Selket
Sesheta
Seth
Shai
Shu
Taueret
Tefnut
Thoth
Upuaut
**Middle
   Eastern**
Adad
Anu
Ashtart
Ashur
Attis
Baal
Baalat
Belili
Cybele
Ea
Enlil
Ishtar
Marduk
Mot
Ninurta

Shamash
Sin
Hindu
Aditi
Agni
Bhairavi
Brahma
Devi
Durga
Ganesha
Hanuman
Indra
Jagannatha/
   Juggernaut
Kali
Kama
Kartikeya
Krishna
Lakshmi
Maruts, the
Mitra
Parvati
Prajapati
Puchan
Radha
Rama
Rudra
Sakti
Sarasvati
Savitar
Siva/Shiva
Skanda
Soma
Surya
Tvashtar
Uma
Ushas
Varuna
Vata
Vishnu
Yama
African
Asia
Asia-Bussu
Bumba
Cagn
Evua
Fa
Famien
Guruhi
Juok
Kaka-Guia
Legba
Libanza
Mahou
Massim Biambe
Mebeli
Minepa
Muluku
Nampa
Ndriananahery
Nenaunir
Nyamia
Nzame
Pan
Phebele
Rabefihaza

Rock-Sene
Sakarabru
Tilo
Unkulunkulu
Aztec
Camaxtli
Chalchiuht-
   licue
Chicomecoatl
Cihuatcoatl
Coatlicue
Huitzilo-
   pochtli
Meztli
Mictlancihuatl
Mictlante-
   cuhtli
Quetzalcoatl
Tenochtitlan
Tezcatlipoca
Tlahuizcalpan-
   tecuhtli
Tlaloc
Tlazolteotl
Tonatiuh
Tzinteotl
Xilonen
Xiuhtecuhtli
Xochipili
Xochiquetzal
Xolotl
Yacatecuhtli
Mayan
Acat
Akua
Bacab
Backlum-
   Chaam
Chin
Cukulcan
Echua
Hapikern
Hunab Ku
Itzamna
Ixazaluoh
Kinebahan
Nohochacyum
Usukun
Uyitzin
Xamaniqinqu
Yantho
Yuncemil
Inca
Apu-Punchau
Catequil
Chasca
Choun
Cuycha
Inti
Mama-Cocha
Mama-Cuna
Mama-Quilla
Manco-Capac
Nina
Pachacamac
Pachamama
Viracocha

godsend *noun* boon, blessing, benediction, benison, stroke of luck, piece of good fortune, windfall, bonanza.

goggle *verb* stare, gape, gaze, ogle; *inf.* gawk, rubberneck.

goings-on *plural noun strange goings-on at the bank* misconduct, misbehaviour, conduct, behaviour, mischief, pranks; *inf.* funny business, monkey business, hanky-panky.

golf *noun. See table.*

gold *noun* **1** *gold is more precious than silver* gold pieces, gold nugget, bullion, gold ingot, gold bar. **2** *misers counting their gold* money, wealth, treasure, fortune, riches.

golden *adjective* **1** *golden hair* gold-coloured, blond, blonde, yellow, yellowish, fair, flaxen, tow-coloured, bright, gleaming, resplendent, brilliant, shining. **2** *a golden future* successful, prosperous, flourishing, thriving, rosy, bright, brilliant, rich. **3** *golden memories* happy, joyful, delightful, glorious, precious, treasured. **4** *golden opportunities* fine, superb, excellent, favourable, opportune, promising, rosy, advantageous, profitable, fortunate, providential, auspicious, propitious. **5** *the golden boy of athletics* talented, gifted, special, favourite, favoured, cherished, beloved, pet, acclaimed, applauded, praised, lauded; *inf.* blue-eyed. **Opposites** DARK; UNFAVOURABLE.

good *adjective* **1** *a good person* virtuous, moral, ethical, righteous, right-minded, right-thinking, honourable, honest, upright, high-minded, noble, worthy, admirable, estimable, exemplary. **2** *a good child* well-behaved, obedient, well-mannered, manageable, tractable, malleable. **3** *that's good* satisfactory, acceptable, good enough, passable, tolerable, adequate, fine, excellent; *inf.* great, OK, hunky-dory. **4** *a good thing to do* right, correct, proper, fitting, suitable, appropriate, decorous, seemly. **5** *a good driver* competent, capable, able, accomplished, efficient, skilful, adept, proficient, dexterous, expert, excellent, first-class, first-rate; *inf.* A1, tiptop, top-notch. **6** *good brakes/friends* reliable, dependable, trustworthy. **7** *in good condition* fine, healthy, sound, robust, strong, vigorous. **8** *a good party* enjoyable, pleasant, agreeable, pleasing, pleasurable, amusing, cheerful, convivial, congenial, sociable, satisfying, gratifying, to one's liking. **9** *good of you to come* kind, kindly, kind-hearted, good-hearted, friendly, obliging, well-

disposed, charitable, gracious, sympathetic, benevolent, benign, altruistic. **10** *come at a good time* convenient, fitting, suitable, favourable, advantageous, fortunate, lucky, propitious, auspicious. **11** *milk is good for you* wholesome, health-giving, healthful, nutritional, beneficial, salubrious, salutary. **12** *is this cheese still good?* fit to eat, eatable, edible, untainted, fresh. **13** *the food is good here* delicious, tasty, appetizing; *inf.* scrumptious, yummy. **14** *a good reason for going* valid, genuine, authentic, legitimate, sound, bona fide. **15** *wait a good hour* full, entire, whole, complete, solid, not less than. **16** *a good number came* considerable, substantial, goodly, sizeable, large, sufficient, ample; *inf.* tidy. **17** *good friends* close, intimate, bosom, fast, dear, valued, treasured. **18** *wear her good clothes* best, finest, newest, nicest, smartest, special, party, Sunday. **19** *good weather* fine, fair, mild, clear, bright, cloudless, sunshiny, sunny, calm, balmy, tranquil, clement, halcyon. **make good** **1** *make good the damage* compensate for, make recompense for, make amends for, make restitution for, pay for, reimburse for. **2** *make good a promise* fulfil, carry out, effect, discharge, live up to. **3** *make good a statement* substantiate, back up, demonstrate the truth of, confirm, prove, validate, authenticate. **4** *he made good in America* be successful, succeed, do well, get ahead, reach the top, set the world/Thames/heather on fire. **Opposites** BAD; INADEQUATE; POOR.

good *noun* **1** *for your own good* benefit, advantage, behalf, gain, profit, interest, well-being, welfare, usefulness, avail, service. **2** *tell good from bad* virtue, goodness, morality, ethics, righteousness, rightness, rectitude, honour, honesty, uprightness, integrity, probity, worth, merit. **for good** for always, for ever, permanently, never to return, *sine die.*

good *interjection* fine, very well, all right; *inf.* okay, OK, okey-dokey.

goodbye *interjection* farewell, au revoir, adieu; *inf.* bye, cheerio, cheers, see you later, see you, so long, toodle-oo, ciao; *inf.* bye-bye, ta-ta.

good-for-nothing *adjective a good-for-nothing son* useless, of no use, no-good, lazy, idle, slothful, feckless.

good-for-nothing *noun a real good-for-nothing* ne'er-do-well, waster, wastrel, black sheep, layabout, idler, loafer, sluggard.

GOLFING TERMS				
ace	bye	flagstick	mashie iron	rub of the
addressing the	caddie	follow-through	midiron	green
ball	dead ball	fore!	niblick	sand shot
albatross	divot	forecaddie	nineteenth	sclaff
backswing	dog-leg hole	green	hole	spot putting
baff	dormy	handicap	par	tee
birdie	downswing	hanging ball	pin	tee off
bisque	driver	hole-high	pitch and putt	trap
blaster	driving iron	ball	putter	upswing
bogey	dubbed shot	hole in one	recovery	water hazard
brassie	eagle	iron	shot	wedge
bunker	fairway	lofted shot	rough	wood shot

good-humoured *adjective* amiable, affable, easygoing, genial, cheerful, cheery, happy, pleasant, good-tempered.

good-looking *adjective* attractive, handsome, pretty, lovely, beautiful, personable, comely, well-favoured, fair.

goodly *adjective a goodly amount* considerable, substantial, sizeable, significant, large, great, ample, sufficient; *inf.* tidy.

good-natured *adjective* kind, kindly, kind-hearted, warm-hearted, generous, benevolent, charitable, friendly, helpful, accommodating, amiable, tolerant.

goodness *noun* **1** *the goodness of the saint* virtue, virtuousness, morality, righteousness, rectitude, honour, honesty, uprightness, integrity, probity, nobility, worthiness, merit. **2** *she had the goodness to stay* kindness, kindliness, kind-heartedness, warm-heartedness, generosity, obligingness, benevolence, beneficence, friendliness, goodwill, compassion, graciousness, charitableness, unselfishness. **3** *the goodness in the food* nourishment, nutritional value, nutrition, wholesomeness. *See* GOOD *adjective* 11.
Opposites BADNESS; MEANNESS; HARM.

goods *plural noun all her goods and chattels* belongings, possessions, property, effects, gear, things, paraphernalia, chattels, movables, appurtenances, trappings, accoutrements; *inf.* stuff.

goodwill *noun full of goodwill* friendliness, friendship, kindness, kindliness, benevolence, compassion, amity.
Opposites ILL WILL; HOSTILITY; ENMITY.

gorge *noun the stream at the foot of the gorge* chasm, canyon, ravine, abyss, defile, pass, cleft, crevice, rift, fissure.

gorge *verb* **1** *gorge oneself on ice-cream* stuff, cram, fill, glut, satiate, surfeit, overeat. **2** *gorge the food* bolt, gobble, guzzle, gulp down, wolf, devour, stuff down, gormandize, raven; *inf.* shovel.

gorgeous *adjective* **1** *a gorgeous sight* magnificent, splendid, superb, grand, resplendent, stately, impressive, imposing, sumptuous, luxurious, elegant, opulent, dazzling, brilliant, glittering, breath-taking. **2** *we had a gorgeous time* wonderful, marvellous, first-rate, delightful, enjoyable, entertaining, excellent; *inf.* glorious, terrific. **3** *a gorgeous blonde* attractive, beautiful, lovely, good-looking, sexy; *inf.* stunning.
Opposites DULL; MISERABLE; UGLY.

gory *adjective* **1** *a gory film* bloody, bloodthirsty, sanguinary, violent, murderous, brutal, savage, horror-filled, horrific; *inf.* blood-and-thunder, blood-and-guts. **2** *a gory garment* bloody, blood-stained, blood-soaked.

gospel *noun* **1** *studying the Gospel* Christian doctrine, Christ's teaching, the New Testament, the writings of the evangelists. *See table at* BIBLE. **2** *believing in the gospel of hard work* principle, tenet, doctrine, ethic, belief, creed, credo. **3** *she's gone and that's gospel* the truth, the whole truth, a certainty, a fact, actual fact, verity.

gossamer *noun* cobweb, spider's web, silky substance, gauze, tissue, chiffon, thistledown, feather.

gossamer *adjective a scarf of gossamer material* gossamery, cobwebby, silky, gauzy, chiffony, feathery, light, fine, delicate, frail, flimsy, insubstantial, airy, diaphanous, sheer, transparent, see-through, translucent.

gossip *noun* **1** *have you heard the gossip about her?* rumours, scandal, tittle-tattle, tattle, idle talk, hearsay, smear campaign, whispering campaign; *inf.* mud-slinging, dirt. **2** *have a gossip with the neighbours* chat, blather, blether, conversation, talk, prattle; *inf.* chit-chat, chin-wag, jaw, yackety-yack. **3** *he's just a gossip* gossip-monger, scandalmonger, busybody, blether, blatherskite, tittle-tattler, babbler, chatterer, prattler.

gossip *verb* **1** *gossiping about her colleagues* spread gossip/rumours, circulate rumours, spread stories. **2** *spend too much time gossiping* chat, chit-chat, blather, blether, talk, tattle, babble, gabble, prattle, prate; *inf.* chin-wag, jaw, yack.

govern *verb* **1** *govern the country* rule, reign over, be in power over, exercise control over, hold sway over, preside over, administer, lead, be in charge of, control, command, direct, order, guide, manage, conduct, oversee, supervise, superintend, steer, pilot. **2** *govern one's passions* control, restrain, keep in check, check, curb, hold back, keep back, bridle, rein in, subdue, constrain, contain, arrest. **3** *the weather will govern our decision* determine, decide, sway, rule, influence, have an influence on, be a factor in.

government *noun* **1** *the country's government is weak* administration, regime, parliament, congress, ministry, council, executive, the powers that be. *See table. See also table at* POLITICS. **2** *their government of the country has been criticized* rule, administration, leadership, command, direction, control, guidance, management, conduct, supervision, superintendence. **3** *the government of one's emotions* control, restraint, checking, curbing, bridling, constraint, discipline.

gown *noun* dress, frock, garment, costume, garb, habit; evening gown, ball-gown, dinner-gown. *See table at* DRESS.

grab *verb* **1** *grab his collar* grasp, clutch, grip, clasp, lay hold of, catch hold of, take hold of, fasten upon, collar. **2** *grab the money from him* seize, snatch, pluck, snap up, appropriate, capture; *inf.* bag, nab.

grab *noun* clutch, grasp, firm hold; hug, embrace. **up for grabs** available, accessible, obtainable, to be had, up for sale.

grace *noun* **1** *the grace of the ballerina* gracefulness, suppleness, fluidity of movement, smoothness, ease, elegance, agility; *inf.* poetry in motion. **2** *admire the grace of the women* elegance, refinement, finesse, culture, cultivation, polish, suaveness, good taste, taste, tastefulness, charm, attractiveness, beauty, loveliness, comeliness. **3** *have the grace to apologize* manners, mannerliness, courtesy, courteousness, decency, consideration, tact, tactfulness, breeding, decorum, propriety, etiquette. **4** *fall from grace* favour, goodwill, preferment. **5** *acquire a house by grace of the king* favour, good will, generosity, kindness, kindliness, benefaction, beneficence, indulgence. **6** *beg the king's grace* mercy, mercifulness, compassion, pardon, reprieve, forgiveness, leniency, lenity, clemency, indulgence, charity, quarter. **7** *ask for a year's grace* delay, postponement, deferment, deferral. **8** *say grace* blessing, benediction, thanks, thanksgiving, prayer.

grace *verb* **1** *paintings gracing the room* adorn, decorate, ornament, embellish, enhance, beautify, prettify, set off, deck, enrich, garnish. **2** *grace the gathering with his presence* dignify, distinguish, add distinction to, honour, favour, glorify, elevate.

graceful *adjective* **1** *graceful ballerinas* supple, fluid, flowing, smooth, easy, elegant, agile, nimble. **2** *graceful women* elegant, refined, cultured, cultivated, polished, suave, having good taste, charming, appealing, attractive, beautiful, lovely, comely.
Opposites INELEGANT; UNGAINLY.

gracious *adjective* **1** *a gracious lady* kind, kindly, kind-hearted, warm-hearted, benevolent, friendly, amiable, affable, pleasant, cordial, courteous, considerate, polite, civil, chivalrous, well-mannered, charitable, indulgent, obliging, accommodating, beneficent, benign. **2** *a gracious room | gracious way of life* elegant, tasteful, comfortable, luxurious. **3** *gracious God* merciful, compassionate, gentle, mild, lenient, humane, clement.
Opposites DISCOURTEOUS; ungracious; INELEGANT; CRUEL.

grade *noun* **1** *what grade did he reach?* degree of proficiency/quality/merit, level, stage, echelon, rank, standing, station, position, order, class. **2** *all belonging to the same grade* category, class, classification, type, brand. **3** *progress one grade at a time* stage, step, rung, notch. **4** *a steep grade* gradient, slope, incline, hill, rise, bank, acclivity, declivity. **make the grade** pass, pass muster, measure up, measure up to expectation, come up to standard, come up to scratch, succeed, be successful, come through with flying colours, win through, qualify, get through.

grade *verb* *grade the vegetables* classify, class, categorize, sort, group, order, brand, size, rank, evaluate, rate, value, range, graduate.

gradient *noun* slope, incline, hill, rise, rising ground, bank, acclivity, declivity, grade.

gradual *adjective* **1** *a gradual improvement* step-by-step, degree-by-degree, progressive, successive, continuous, systematic, regular, steady, even, moderate, slow, measured, unhurried.

GOVERNMENTS

Country	Government	Upper Chamber	Lower Chamber
Afghanistan	Parliament	National Assembly	Senate
Andorra	Valleys of Andorra General Council	—	—
Australia	Federal Parliament	Senate	House of Representatives
Brazil	National Congress	Senate	Chamber of Deputies
Canada	Parliament	Senate	House of Commons
China	National People's Congress	—	—
Denmark	Folketing	—	—
Egypt	People's Assembly	—	—
Finland	Eduskunta	—	—
France	Parliament	Senate	National Assembly
Germany	Parliament	Bundesrat	Bundestag
Iceland	Althing	—	—
India	Parliament	Rajya Sabha	Lok Sabha
Indonesia	People's Consultative Congress	House of People's Representatives	—
Iran	Parliament	Senate	Majlis
Ireland	Oireachtas	Seanad	Dáil Eireann
Israel	Knesset	—	—
Japan	Diet	House of Councillors	House of Representatives
Jordan	National Assembly	Council of Ministers	House of Representatives
Kenya	National Assembly	—	—
Laos	Parliament	Council of Ministers	National Assembly
Malaysia	Parliament	Senate	House of Representatives
Mexico	Congress	Senate	Chamber of Deputies
Morocco	Chamber of Representatives	—	—
New Zealand	House of Representatives	—	—
Norway	Storting	Lagting	Odelsting
Pakistan	National Assembly	—	—
Russia	Federal Assembly	Federation Council	State Duma
Spain	Cortes Generales	Senate	Congress of Deputies
Sweden	Riksdag	—	—
Tunisia	National Assembly	—	—
U.K.	Parliament	House of Lords	House of Commons
U.S.A.	Congress	Senate	House of Representatives

2 *a gradual slope* gentle, not steep, moderate. **Opposites** SUDDEN; ABRUPT.

gradually *adverb gradually improve* bit by bit, little by little, by degrees, step by step, inch by inch, piece by piece, drop by drop, slowly, progressively, successively, continuously, constantly, regularly, at a regular pace, steadily, evenly, moderately.

graduate *verb* **1** *graduated last summer* take an academic degree, receive one's degree, become a graduate. **2** *graduate a scale* mark off, measure off, divide into degrees, grade, calibrate. **3** *graduate income tax bands* arrange in order, order, group, classify, class, categorize, rank. **4** *graduate to a more senior post* move up, progress, advance, gain promotion, be promoted.

graft¹ *noun* **1** *a plant graft* shoot, bud, scion, slip, new growth, sprout, splice. **2** *a skin graft* transplant, implantation, implant. **3** *succeed by sheer graft* hard work, work, toil, effort, labour, industry, the sweat of one's brow.

graft² *verb* **1** *graft a shoot on to a stock* insert, engraft, affix, slip, join. **2** *graft skin* transplant, implant.

graft³ *noun get ahead in business by graft* bribery, illegal means, unlawful practices, underhand means, payola; *inf.* palm-greasing.

grain *noun* **1** *farmers growing grain* cereal, cereal crops. *See table at* CEREAL. **2** *a grain of corn* kernel, seed, grist. **3** *grains of sand* particle, granule, bit, piece, scrap, crumb, fragment, morsel, mote, speck, mite, iota, molecule, atom. **4** *not a grain of truth in it* iota, trace, hint, suggestion, suspicion, soupçon, spark, scintilla. **5** *the grain of wood/cloth* texture, intertexture, surface, fabric, weave, nap, fibre, pattern. **6** *a man of a different grain* disposition, character, nature, make-up, humour, temperament, temper, inclination.

grammar *noun. See table.*

grand *adjective* **1** *grand houses* impressive, magnificent, imposing, splendid, striking, superb, palatial, stately, large, monumental, majestic. **2** *a grand feast* splendid, luxurious, sumptuous, lavish, magnificent, glorious, opulent, princely. **3** *bow down before the grand people in the land* great, noble, aristocratic, distinguished, august, illustrious, eminent, esteemed, elevated, exalted, celebrated, pre-eminent, prominent, leading, notable, renowned, famous. **4** *make a grand gesture* ostentatious, showy, pretentious, lordly, ambitious, imperious. **5** *the grand total* complete, comprehensive, total, all-inclusive, inclusive, exhaustive, final. **6** *the grand hall/master* principal, main, chief, leading, head, supreme. **7** *have a grand time* very good, excellent, wonderful, marvellous, splendid, first-class, first-rate, outstanding, fine, enjoyable, admirable; *inf.* superb, terrific, great, super, smashing. **Opposites** INFERIOR; unimpressive; LOWLY.

grandeur *noun* **1** *the grandeur of the houses* impressiveness, magnificence, splendour, splendidness, superbness, stateliness, largeness, majesty. **2** *the grandeur of the feast* splendour, luxuriousness, luxury, sumptuousness,

GRAMMATICAL TERMS

ablative	defective verb	indeclinable	object	proper noun
ablative absolute	definite article	indefinite article	objective case	reciprocal
accusative	deictic	indicative	oblique case	reflexive
active voice	deixis	indirect object	optative	relative clause
adjective	demonstrative	infinitive	paratactic	relative pronoun
adjunct	deponent	infix	parataxis	sandhi
adverb	determiner	inflect	participle	sentence
affix	diminutive	inflection	particle	singular
anaphora	direct object	instrumental	partitive	strong verb
antecedent	disjunct	intensifier	passive voice	subject
aorist	distributive	interjection	past tense	subjective case
aspect	dual	interrogative	perfective	subjunct
auxiliary verb	enclitic	intransitive verb	perfect tense	subjunctive
binding	ergative	irregular verb	periphrastic	substantive
case	feminine	iterative	person	suffix
causative	final clause	jussive	personal pronoun	superlative
clause	finite verb	locative	phrasal verb	tense
cognate	frequentative	main clause	phrase	tmesis
collective noun	future perfect	masculine	pluperfect	transitive verb
comparative	future tense	mass noun	plural	uncountable noun
complement	gender	middle voice	possessive	verb
conditional	genitive	modal verb	postpositive	vocative
conjugation	gerund	modifier	predeterminer	voice
conjunct	gerundive	mood	predicate	weak verb
conjunction	govern	negative	prefix	
copula	government	neuter	preposition	
countable	imperative	nominative	present tense	
dative	imperfect	noun	preterite	
declension	impersonal verb	number	proclitic	
			pronoun	

lavishness, magnificence, opulence. **3** *the grandeur of the ruling classes* greatness, nobility, illustriousness, eminence, elevation, exaltation, prominence, pre-eminence, renown, fame.

grandfather *noun* **1** *a little girl playing with her grandfather* inf. grandad, grandpa, grandpop; Am. inf. gramps, grand daddy. **2** *writing the history of their grandfathers* forefather, ancestor, forebear, progenitor, father.

grandiloquent *adjective grandiloquent speech/ writing* pompous, pretentious, ostentatious, high-flown, wordy, bombastic, magniloquent, euphuistic, periphrastic, orotund, fustian.

grandiose *adjective* **1** *grandiose plans* ambitious, over-ambitious, extravagant, high-flown, high-sounding, pompous, pretentious, flamboyant; inf. over-the-top, OTT. **2** *grandiose buildings* grand, impressive, magnificent, imposing, splendid, striking, superb, stately, majestic.
Opposites MODEST; HUMBLE.

grandmother *noun* inf. grandma, granny, gran, nan.

grant *verb* **1** *grant them an interview* agree to, consent to, give one's assent to, assent to, accede to, permit, give one's permission for, allow, concede, accord, vouchsafe. **2** *grant them an award* bestow, confer, give, impart, award, present, donate, contribute, provide, endow, furnish, supply, allocate, allot, assign. **3** *I grant you that you may be right* admit, acknowledge, concede, go along with, yield, cede. **4** *grant property to his heirs* transfer, convey, transmit, pass on, hand on, assign, bequeath.

grant *noun a grant for studying* award, endowment, donation, contribution, allowance, subsidy, allocation, allotment, bursary, gift, present.

granule *noun* grain, particle, crumb, fragment, bit, scrap, mite, molecule, atom, iota, jot.

graph *noun* grid, chart, diagram, histogram, bar chart.

graphic *adjective* **1** *a graphic description of the events* vivid, striking, expressive, descriptive, illustrative, lively, forcible, detailed, well-defined, well-delineated, well-drawn, telling, effective, cogent, clear, lucid, explicit. **2** *a graphic representation* diagrammatic, representational, pictorial, illustrative, drawn, delineative.
Opposites DULL; VAGUE.

grapple *verb* **1** *grapple with the enemy* wrestle with, fight with, struggle with, tussle with, clash with, close with, engage with, combat with, battle with, brawl with. **2** *grapple with a problem* tackle, face, cope with, deal with, confront, address oneself to, attack, get down to, come to grips with. **3** *grapple the thief* seize, grab, lay hold of, take hold of, grip, clench, hold, grasp, clasp. **4** *grapple the boat* secure, fasten, make fast, hook, pin.

grasp *verb* **1** *grasp his hand* grip, clutch, clasp, hold, clench, take/latch on to, lay hold of, catch, seize, grab, snatch, catch at, grapple. **2** *grasp the point* understand, comprehend, follow, see, take in, realize, perceive, apprehend; inf. get, get the picture, get the drift, catch on.

grasp *noun* **1** *take a firm grasp of the rail* grip, hold, clutch, clasp, clench. **2** *beyond the grasp of her enemy* clutches, power, control, command, mastery, dominion, rule. **3** *well within your grasp* capacity, reach, scope, limits, range, compass. **4** *have a good grasp of the subject* understanding, comprehension, perception, apprehension, awareness, grip, realization, knowledge, ken, mastery.

grass *noun. See table.*

grasping *adjective a grasping old miser* avaricious, greedy, acquisitive, rapacious, grabbing, covetous, mean, miserly, parsimonious, niggardly, stingy, tight-fisted, penny-pinching,

---

GRASSES, SEDGES, AND RUSHES

bamboo	darnel	melick	spartina
barley	dog's-tail	millet	spear grass
beach grass	durra	oat	spelt
beard grass	elephant grass	oat-grass	spinifex
bent	esparto	orchard grass	squirrel-tail grass
Bermuda grass	feather grass	paddy	star grass
bluegrass	fescue	pampas grass	sugar cane
bristle grass	finger grass	panic	switch grass
brome	fiorin	papyrus	sword grass
broomcorn	fog	quack grass	tef
buffalo grass	foxtail	quaking grass	teosinte
bulrush	gama grass	quitch	timothy grass
bunch grass	hair-grass	redtop	tussock grass
canary grass	herd's-grass	reed	twitch grass
China grass	Indian corn	reed grass	vernal grass
cocksfoot	Indian rice	reed mace	wheat
cordgrass	Kentucky bluegrass	rice	wild oat
corn	lemon grass	rush	wild rice
cotton grass	lyme grass	rye	wire grass
couch grass	maize	ryegrass	woodrush
crabgrass	marram grass	sedge	Yorkshire fog
cutgrass	meadow grass	sorghum	zoysia

hoarding, selfish, possessive; *inf.* grabby.
Opposites GENEROUS; ALTRUISTIC.

grate *verb* **1** *grate cheese/onions* shred, rub into
pieces, pulverize, mince, grind, granulate, triturate. **2** *the knife grated against the metal surface*
rasp, scrape, jar, scratch, grind, creak, rub,
grit. **3** *his voice/behaviour grates on me* irritate,
set someone's teeth on edge, rub someone up
the wrong way, jar on, irk, annoy, vex, gall,
nettle, peeve, rankle with, anger, rile, exasperate, chafe, fret, get someone down; *inf.* get on
someone's nerves, aggravate.

grateful *adjective* **1** *grateful to you* thankful,
filled with gratitude, indebted, obliged, obligated, under obligation, beholden. **2** *a grateful
letter* thankful, appreciative. **3** *a grateful rest*
pleasant, agreeable, pleasing, pleasurable, satisfying, gratifying, cheering, refreshing, welcome, acceptable, nice.
Opposites UNGRATEFUL.

gratify *verb* **1** *their appreciation gratified her*
please, give pleasure to, make happy, make
content, delight, make someone feel good,
gladden, satisfy, warm the cockles of the
heart, thrill. **2** *gratify their desires* fulfil,
indulge, humour, comply with, pander to,
cater to, pacify, appease, give in to.

grating *adjective* **1** *a grating noise* rasping,
scraping, jarring, scratching, grinding, creaking. **2** *a grating voice* harsh, raucous, strident,
screeching, piercing, shrill, squawking,
squawky, squeaky, discordant, hoarse,
croaky. **3** *a grating personality* irritating, jarring, annoying, vexatious, irksome, galling,
exasperating, offensive, disagreeable, unpleasant.

gratis *adverb* free of charge, free, without
charge, for nothing, at no cost, without paying, without payment, on the house, freely,
gratuitously; *inf.* for free.

gratitude *noun* gratefulness, thankfulness,
thanks, thanksgiving, appreciation, indebtedness, recognition, acknowledgement, sense of
obligation.
Opposites INGRATITUDE.

gratuitous *adjective* **1** *gratuitous work* free,
gratis, complimentary, voluntary, unpaid,
unrewarded, unasked-for, free of charge, without charge, for nothing, at no cost, without
payment, on the house; *inf.* for free. **2** *gratuitous insults/violence* unjustified, unprovoked,
groundless, ungrounded, causeless, without
cause, without reason, unfounded, baseless,
uncalled-for, unwarranted, unmerited, needless, unnecessary, superfluous.

gratuity *noun* tip, perquisite, fringe benefit,
bonus, gift, present, donation, reward, recompense, largesse, benefaction, boon, *pourboire,
douceur,* baksheesh; *inf.* perk.

grave *noun* burying place, tomb, sepulchre,
vault, burial chamber, burial pit, mausoleum,
crypt, last home, last resting place, long home.

grave *adjective* **1** *a grave expression/mood*
solemn, earnest, serious, sober, sombre,
severe, unsmiling, long-faced, stone-faced,
grim-faced, grim, gloomy, preoccupied,
thoughtful, pensive, subdued, muted, quiet,
sedate, dignified, staid, dour. **2** *grave matters*
serious, important, all-important, significant,
momentous, weighty, urgent, pressing, of
great consequence, vital, crucial, critical,
acute, pivotal, life-and-death, exigent, perilous,
hazardous, dangerous, threatening, menacing.
Opposites CAREFREE; FRIVOLOUS; TRIVIAL.

graveyard *noun* cemetery, burial ground,
churchyard, memorial park, necropolis, charnel house; *inf.* boneyard; *Am.* potter's field; *lit.*
God's acre, golgotha.

gravitate *verb* **1** *gravitate to the bottom of the
sea* sink, fall, drop, descend, precipitate, be pre-
cipitated, settle. **2** *gravitate towards the attractive girl* move towards, head towards, be drawn
to, be pulled towards, be attracted to, drift
towards, lean towards, incline towards.

gravity *noun* **1** *the gravity of her expression/mood*
solemnity, earnestness, seriousness, sobriety,
sombreness, severity, grimness, thoughtfulness, pensiveness, sedateness, dignity, staidness, dourness. *See* GRAVE *adjective* 1. **2** *the
gravity of the situation* seriousness, importance,
significance, momentousness, moment,
weightiness, consequence, vitalness, crucialness, criticalness, acuteness, exigence, perilousness, peril, hazard, danger. *See* GRAVE
adjective 2.

graze¹ *verb* *sheep grazing* feed, crop, browse,
ruminate.

graze² *verb* **1** *the car grazed the wall* brush,
brush against, touch, touch lightly, rub lightly,
shave, glance off, skim, kiss. **2** *graze his knee*
scrape, abrade, skin, scratch, chafe, bark,
bruise, contuse.

graze³ *noun* *he has a graze on his knee* scrape,
abrasion, scratch, bruise, contusion.

greasy *adjective* **1** *greasy food* fatty, fat, oily,
buttery, oleaginous, adipose, sebaceous.
2 *greasy roads* slippery, slippy, slimy. **3** *a
greasy fellow* unctuous, oily, slimy, smooth-
tongued, smooth, glib, suave, slick, fawning,
ingratiating, grovelling, sycophantic, toadying,
flattering, gushing; *inf.* smarmy.

great *adjective* **1** *a great expanse of forest* large,
big, extensive, vast, immense, unlimited,
boundless, spacious, huge, enormous, gigantic,
colossal, mammoth, monstrous, prodigious,
tremendous, stupendous. **2** *describe in great
detail* considerable, substantial, pronounced,
exceptional, inordinate, sizeable. **3** *the great
thing is to keep your temper* important, salient,
essential, significant, crucial, critical, vital,
momentous, weighty, dominant, consequen-
tial. **4** *the great cities of the world* major, main,
most important, leading, chief, principal, capital, paramount, primary. **5** *a great occasion*
grand, impressive, magnificent, imposing,
splendid, majestic, glorious, sumptuous. **6** *the
great people of the land* prominent, eminent, pre-
eminent, distinguished, august, illustrious, celebrated, noted, notable, noteworthy, famous,
famed, renowned, leading, top, high, high-
ranking, noble. **7** *a great thinker* gifted, talented, outstanding, remarkable, exceptional,
first-rate, incomparable. **8** *a great tennis player*
expert, skilful, skilled, able, masterly, adept,

adroit, proficient, good; *inf.* crack, ace, A1. **9** *a great film-goer* enthusiastic, eager, keen, zealous, devoted, active. **10** *we had a great time* enjoyable, excellent, marvellous, wonderful, first-class, first-rate, admirable, fine, very good; *inf.* terrific, tremendous, fantastic, fabulous, fab. **11** *he's a great fool* absolute, utter, out-and-out, downright, thoroughgoing, total, complete, perfect, positive, arrant, unmitigated, unqualified, consummate, egregious; *inf.* thundering.
Opposites SMALL; UNIMPORTANT; ORDINARY.

greatly *adverb greatly admired/superior* very much, much, by a considerable amount, considerably, to a great extent, extremely, exceedingly, enormously, vastly, immensely, tremendously, hugely, markedly, mightily, remarkably, abundantly.

greatness *noun* **1** *the greatness of the forest* largeness, bigness, boundlessness, extensiveness, vastness, immensity, hugeness, enormity, spaciousness, prodigiousness, magnitude, size, bulk, mass, length. **2** *the greatness of the occasion* grandness, grandeur, impressiveness, magnificence, pomp, splendour, gloriousness, sumptuousness, majesty. **3** *the greatness of the leaders* eminence, distinction, lustre, illustriousness, celebrity, noteworthiness, fame, renown, nobility. **4** *admire the greatness of the players* talent, expertness, expertise, skill, skilfulness, adeptness, proficiency.

greed, greediness *noun* **1** *appalled at the greed of the eaters* gluttony, gormandizing, gourmandism, voraciousness, voracity, ravenousness, insatiability, omnivorousness, edaciousness, edacity; *inf.* hoggishness, piggishness, gutsiness, swinishness; *lit.* esurience. **2** *the greed of the miser* avarice, acquisitiveness, graspingness, rapacity, covetousness, cupidity, miserliness, tight-fistedness, parsimony. **3** *greed for knowledge* avidity, eagerness, desire, hunger, craving, longing, enthusiasm, impatience.

greedy *adjective* **1** *a fat, greedy man* gluttonous, gormandizing, gourmand, voracious, ravenous, ravening, insatiable, insatiate, omnivorous, gannet-like, edacious; *inf.* hoggish, piggish, gutsy, swinish; *lit.* esurient. **2** *a greedy miser* avaricious, acquisitive, grasping, rapacious, grabbing, covetous, cupidinous, hoarding, miserly, niggardly, tight-fisted, close-fisted, parsimonious; *inf.* grabby, money-grubbing. **3** *greedy for knowledge* avid, eager, hungry, desirous, craving, longing, enthusiastic, anxious, impatient.
Opposites GENEROUS; ALTRUISTIC; APATHETIC.

green *adjective* **1** *green clothes* greenish, viridescent, virescent, glaucous; sea-green, aquamarine, aqua, eau-de-Nil, olive-green, pea-green, emerald-green, sage-green, acid-green. *See table at* COLOUR. **2** *green land* verdant, grass-covered, grassy, leafy, verdurous. **3** *green plums* unripe, not ripe, immature. **4** *green wood* unseasoned, not aged, unfinished, pliable, supple. **5** *green tobacco/tea/bacon* raw, fresh, undried, unfermented, unsmoked. **6** *a green old age* flourishing, vigorous, strong, sturdy, sound, healthy. **7** *keep memories of her*

green fresh, flourishing, remembered, unforgotten. **8** *a green apprentice* inexperienced, untrained, inexpert, unqualified, ignorant, unversed, new, raw, immature, simple, unsophisticated, unpolished, naive, innocent, ingenuous, callow, credulous, gullible, wet behind the ears. **9** *feel green on seeing his new bike* envious, jealous, covetous, grudging, resentful. **10** *look/go green* greenish, pale, wan, pallid, ashen, ill, sick, sickly, unhealthy, nauseous. **11** *green issues | Green politicians* environmentalist, conservationist, preservationist; environmentally sound/friendly, ecologically sound.

green *noun cows grazing on the green* village green, common, grassy area, grass, lawn, greensward, sward, turf.

greenhouse *noun* hothouse, glasshouse, conservatory.

green light *noun give the plans the green light* permission, approval, assent, consent, authorization, sanction, leave, warranty, confirmation, imprimatur, blessing; *inf.* OK, okay, go-ahead, thumbs up.

greens *plural noun* **1** *eat up your greens* vegetables, leaf vegetables; *inf.* veg, veggies. *See table at* VEGETABLE. **2** *the greens/Greens won more votes* environmentalists, conservationists, preservationists, ecologists.

greet *verb* **1** *greet his neighbour in the street* say hello to, address, salute, hail, nod to, wave to, raise one's hat to, acknowledge the presence of, accost. **2** *the hostess greeted the guests at the door* receive, meet, welcome.

greeting *noun* **1** *return his neighbour's greeting* hello, hallo, salute, salutation, address, nod, wave, acknowledgement. **2** *receive a birthday greeting* message, tidings.

greetings *plural noun send birthday greetings* good wishes, best wishes, regards, kind regards, congratulations, compliments, respects.

gregarious *adjective* sociable, social, company-loving, companionable, convivial, outgoing, friendly, affable, cordial, hospitable, hail-fellow-well-met.
Opposites UNSOCIABLE; RESERVED.

grey *adjective* **1** *a grey dress* greyish, silvery; silver-grey, pearl-grey, pearly, gun-metal grey, smoke-grey. *See table at* COLOUR. **2** *invalids looking grey* ashen, wan, pale, pallid, colourless, bloodless, anaemic, livid. **3** *a grey day* cloudy, overcast, dull, dark, sunless, gloomy, dim, dreary, dismal, drab, cheerless, depressing, misty, foggy, murky. **4** *grey people* characterless, colourless, dull, uninteresting, neutral, anonymous. **5** *a grey area* doubtful, unclear, uncertain, indistinct, mixed. **6** *the grey vote* grey-haired, elderly, old, aged, ancient, hoary, venerable.

grief *noun grief at his death* sorrow, mourning, mournfulness, bereavement, lamentation, misery, sadness, anguish, pain, distress, agony, affliction, suffering, heartache, heartbreak, broken-heartedness, heaviness of heart, trouble, woe, tribulation, trial, desolation, despondency, dejection, despair, remorse, regret.

come to grief fail, miscarry, meet with failure, meet with disaster; *inf.* come unstuck, come a cropper, go phut.
Opposites JOY; DELIGHT; CELEBRATION.

grievance *noun* **1** *answer the workers' grievances* complaint, charge, protest, moan, axe to grind, bone to pick; *lit.* plaint; *inf.* grouse, gripe, beef; *Am. inf.* crow to pluck. **2** *workers claiming a grievance* wrong, injustice, unjust act, unfairness, injury, damage, hardship, offence, affront, insult.

grieve *verb* **1** *the widow is still grieving | grieving for/over/about his dead wife* mourn, lament, be sorrowful, sorrow, be sad, weep and wail, cry, sob, suffer, ache, be in anguish, be distressed, eat one's heart out; bewail, bemoan. **2** *his behaviour grieved her* hurt, wound, pain, sadden, break someone's heart, upset, distress, cause suffering to, crush. **3** *grieve the loss of her dog* bewail, bemoan, regret, rue, deplore, take to heart.
Opposites REJOICE; CHEER.

grievous *adjective* **1** *a grievous injury* painful, agonizing, hurtful, afflicting, wounding, damaging, injurious, severe, sharp, acute. **2** *grievous news* calamitous, disastrous, distressing, sorrowful, mournful, sad, crushing. **3** *grievous sins/crimes* heinous, flagrant, glaring, outrageous, shocking, appalling, atrocious, gross, dire, iniquitous, nefarious, grave, deplorable, shameful, lamentable, dreadful, egregious, flagitious. **4** *a grievous sound* grief-stricken, anguished, agonized, mournful, sorrowful, tragic, pitiful, heart-rending.

grim *adjective* **1** *teachers looking grim* stern, forbidding, formidable, fierce, ferocious, threatening, menacing, harsh, sombre, cross, churlish, crabbed, morose, surly, sour, ill-tempered, implacable, cruel, ruthless, merciless. **2** *grim determination* resolute, determined, firm, decided, obstinate, adamant, unyielding, unwavering, unfaltering, unshakeable, obdurate, inflexible, unrelenting, relentless, inexorable, strong-willed, dead set. **3** *a grim sight/accident* dreadful, dire, ghastly, horrible, horrendous, horrid, terrible, awful, appalling, frightful, shocking, unspeakable, harrowing, grisly, gruesome, hideous, macabre.
Opposites GENTLE; AMIABLE; PLEASANT.

grimace *verb* *grimace behind her back* make a face, make faces, pull a face, scowl, frown, mouth, sneer, pout.

grimace *noun* *make a grimace* scowl, frown, sneer, face, wry face, distorted expression, pout, mouth, moue.

grime *noun* dirt, smut, soot, dust, mud, filth; *inf.* muck, gunge, yuck, crud.

grimy *adjective* begrimed, dirty, dirt-encrusted, grubby, soiled, stained, smutty, sooty, dusty, muddy, muddied, filthy, besmirched, besmeared; *inf.* mucky, gungy, yucky, cruddy.

grin *verb* *she grinned at him | grin like a Cheshire cat* smile broadly, smile/grin from ear to ear.
Opposites FROWN; GLOWER.

grind *verb* **1** *grind coffee beans/nuts* crush, pound, pulverize, mill, powder, granulate, grate, crumble, mash, smash, comminute, triturate, kibble, levigate. **2** *grind knives* sharpen, file, whet, smooth, polish, sand. **3** *grind one's teeth* gnash, grit, grate, scrape, rasp. **4** *grind down the poor* oppress, persecute, tyrannize, afflict, maltreat, ill-treat, scourge, torture, torment, molest, harass, harry. **5** *grind away at the task* labour, toil, slog, slave, drudge, plod, sweat; *inf.* plug.

grind *noun* *he regards his job as a grind* drudgery, chore, slog, travail, toil, hard work, labour, slavery, forced labour, exertion; *inf.* fag, sweat.

grip *noun* **1** *lose his grip of the railing* hold, grasp, clutch, clasp, clench. **2** *have a firm grip* handgrip, handshake, hand-clasp, clasp. **3** *have her in a grip* hold, hug, embrace; *inf.* clinch. **4** *have a grip of the problem* grasp, understanding, comprehension, perception, awareness, apprehension. See GRASP *noun* 4. **5** *in the grip of an addiction | the tyrant's grip* clutches, control, domination, dominion, command, power, mastery, influence, hold, possession, rule. **6** *pack a grip* bag, holdall, overnight bag, travelling bag, flight bag, kit-bag, Gladstone bag, valise. **come/get to grips with** *come to grips with his opponent | must get to grips with the problem* face, face up to, meet head on, confront, encounter, deal with, cope with, handle, tackle, grasp, undertake, take on, grapple with, close with, contend with.

grip *verb* **1** *grip the railing* grasp, clutch, clasp, clench, hold, grasp/take/lay hold of, latch on to, grab, seize, catch, catch at. **2** *the actor/ speech gripped the audience* absorb, engross, rivet, spellbind, hold spellbound, entrance, fascinate, enthrall, hold, catch, compel, mesmerize.

gripe *verb* *griping about money* complain, grumble, moan, groan, protest, whine; *inf.* grouse, bellyache, beef, bitch, grouch, whinge.

gripe *noun* *listen to their gripes* complaint, grumble, moan, groan, grievance, objection, protest, whine; *inf.* grouse, bellyaching, beefing, beef, bitching, grouching, whinging.

gripping *adjective* *a gripping story* riveting, spellbinding, compulsive, compelling, absorbing, engrossing, entrancing, fascinating, enthralling, thrilling, exciting; *inf.* unputdownable.

grisly *adjective* *a grisly sight/story* gruesome, ghastly, frightful, horrid, horrifying, horrible, horrendous, grim, awful, dreadful, terrible, fearful, hideous, disgusting, repulsive, repugnant, revolting, repellent, macabre, spine-chilling, sickening, shocking, appalling, abominable, loathsome, abhorrent, odious.
Opposites PLEASANT; ATTRACTIVE.

grit *noun* **1** *put grit on icy roads* gravel, pebbles, sand, dust, dirt. **2** *he has no grit* pluck, mettle, mettlesomeness, backbone, spirit, strength of character, nerve, gameness, courage, bravery, valour, fortitude, stamina, toughness, hardiness, determination, resolution, doggedness, tenacity, perseverance, endurance; *inf.* gumption, guts, spunk, bottle.

grit *verb* *grit one's teeth* grate, grind, gnash, scrape, rasp.

gritty adjective **1** a gritty substance sandy, grainy, granular, gravelly, pebbly, powdery, dusty. **2** a gritty fighter plucky, mettlesome, spirited, game, courageous, brave, hardy, tough, determined, resolute, dogged, tenacious, enduring; inf. gutsy, spunky.

groan noun **1** a groan of pain moan, cry, sigh, murmur, whine, whimper. **2** make a list of their groans complaint, grumble, objection, protest, grievance, moan; inf. grouse, gripe, beefing, bellyaching, bitching. **3** the groan of the gate creak, grating, squeak, screech.

groan verb **1** groan in pain moan, cry, call out, sigh, murmur, whine, whimper. **2** groaning about working conditions complain, grumble, object, moan, lament; inf. grouse, gripe, beef, bellyache, bitch. **3** the gate groaned creak, grate, squeak, screech.

groggy adjective dazed, stunned, stupefied, in a stupor, muzzy, dizzy, faint, befuddled, muddled, confused, bewildered, punch-drunk, shaky, staggering, reeling, unsteady, wobbly; inf. woozy, woolly-headed.

groom noun **1** the groom brushing the horse stable boy/stable girl, stable hand/lad, equerry. **2** her groom was late bridegroom, husband-to-be, newly-married man, newly-wed.

groom verb **1** groom one's hair | groom oneself arrange, fix, adjust, do, dress, put in order, tidy, make tidy, brush, comb, smooth, spruce up, smarten up, preen, primp, freshen up. **2** groom the horses curry, brush, rub, rub down, clean. **3** groom the pupils for university train, coach, prepare, prime, make ready, ready, instruct, tutor, drill, teach, educate, school.

groove noun **1** a groove in the ground furrow, channel, trench, trough, canal, gouge, hollow, indentation, rut, gutter, cutting, cut, score, rabbet, rebate. **2** they were tired of being in a groove rut, routine, habit, treadmill; inf. daily grind.

grope verb **1** grope one's way feel, fumble, pick, move blindly. **2** grope for one's keys fumble for, fish for, scrabble for, cast about for, search for, hunt for, look for, grabble for.

gross adjective **1** he's grown gross obese, massive, immense, huge, colossal, corpulent, overweight, bloated, bulky, hulking, fat, big, large, lumpish, cumbersome, unwieldy. **2** gross jokes coarse, crude, vulgar, obscene, rude, ribald, lewd, bawdy, dirty, filthy, earthy, smutty, blue, risqué, indecent, indelicate, improper, impure, unseemly, offensive, sensual, sexual, pornographic. **3** her brother is gross boorish, loutish, oafish, coarse, crass, vulgar, ignorant, unrefined, unsophisticated, uncultured, uncultivated, undiscriminating, tasteless, insensitive, unfeeling, imperceptive, callous; inf. yobbish. **4** a gross error flagrant, blatant, glaring, outrageous, shocking, serious, egregious, manifest, obvious, plain, apparent. **5** gross income total, whole, entire, aggregate, before deductions, before tax.
Opposites SLENDER; PURE; REFINED; NET.

gross verb he grosses £20,000 per annum earn, make, bring in, take; inf. rake in.

grotesque adjective **1** a grotesque costume/sight bizarre, weird, outlandish, freakish, strange, odd, peculiar, unnatural, fantastic, fanciful, whimsical, ridiculous, ludicrous, absurd, incongruous, preposterous, extravagant. **2** a grotesque shape misshapen, distorted, twisted, deformed, malformed, misproportioned.

ground noun **1** fall to the ground earth, terra firma, floor; inf. deck. **2** the ground is wet earth, soil, dirt, land, terrain, clay, loam, turf, clod, mould, sod, dust. **3** players going to the ground stadium, pitch, field, arena, park. See GROUNDS.

ground verb **1** ground his suspicions on her behaviour base, found, establish, set, settle. **2** ground the pupil in maths teach, instruct, coach, tutor, train, drill, educate, school, prepare, initiate, familiarize with, acquaint with, inform.

groundless adjective groundless fears without basis, baseless, without foundation, unfounded, unsupported, imaginary, illusory, false, unsubstantiated, unwarranted, unjustified, unjustifiable, uncalled-for, unprovoked, without cause/reason/justification, unreasonable, irrational, illogical, empty, idle, chimerical.

grounds plural noun **1** a house set in large grounds surroundings, land, property, estate, acres, tract of land, lawns, gardens, park, parkland, area, domain, holding, territory. **2** grounds for concern reason, cause, basis, base, foundation, call, justification, rationale, argument, premise, occasion, factor, excuse, pretext, motive, inducement. **3** coffee grounds dregs, lees, deposit, sediment, precipitate, settlings, grouts.

groundwork noun foundation, base, basis, cornerstone, footing, underpinning, fundamentals, basics, ABC, elements, essentials, preliminaries, preparations, spadework.

group noun **1** divide the books into groups category, classification, class, set, lot, batch, family, species, genus, bracket. **2** a group of people band, company, party, body, gathering, congregation, assembly, collection, cluster, crowd, flock, pack, troop, gang, batch; inf. bunch. **3** belong to the radical group on the committee clique, coterie, faction, circle, set. **4** she joined a sewing group society, association, league, guild, circle, club, work party. **5** a group of trees clump, cluster.

group verb **1** group pupils according to ability classify, class, categorize, sort, grade, rank, bracket. **2** group the children for a photograph assemble, collect, gather together, arrange, organize, marshal, range, line up, dispose. **3** the police grouped round the prisoner collect, gather, assemble, cluster. **4** they grouped together to form a club get together, band together, associate, consort.

grouse verb grouse about the weather complain, grumble, moan, groan, protest; inf. gripe, bellyache, beef, bitch, grouch, whinge.

grouse noun tired of their grouses complaint, grumble, moan, groan, grievance, objection, protest; *inf.* gripe, bellyaching, beefing, beef, bitching, grouching, whinging.

grovel *verb* **1** *grovel to the boss* abase oneself, humble oneself, kowtow, bow and scrape, toady, fawn, fawn upon, lick someone's boots, curry favour, curry favour with, flatter; *inf.* crawl, butter someone up, be all over someone, suck up to, bootlick. **2** *grovel before the tyrant* crawl, creep, slither, kneel, fall on one's knees, prostrate oneself, throw oneself at someone's feet.

grow *verb* **1** *the child/pile grew* get taller, get bigger, get larger, stretch, heighten, lengthen, enlarge, extend, expand, spread, thicken, widen, fill out, swell, increase, multiply. **2** *the plants are growing* shoot up, spring up, develop, sprout, burgeon, bud, germinate, pullulate, flourish, thrive. **3** *her fear grows from her insecurity* arise, originate, stem, spring, issue. **4** *the business is growing* flourish, thrive, prosper, succeed, progress, make progress, make headway, advance, improve, expand. **5** *grow prettier* become, come to be, get to be, get, turn, wax. **6** *grow corn* cultivate, produce, farm, propagate, raise.
Opposites SHRINK; DECREASE; FAIL.

growl *verb* snarl, howl, yelp, bark.

grown-up *noun* adult, grown man, man, grown woman, woman, mature man, mature woman.

grown-up *adjective* adult, mature, of age, fully-grown, full-grown, fully-developed.

growth *noun* **1** *the growth in population | the growth of the town* augmentation, increase, proliferation, multiplication, enlargement, expansion, extension, development, evolution, aggrandizement, magnification, amplification, growing, deepening, heightening, widening, thickening, broadening, swelling. **2** *the growth of the plants* development, maturation, germination, shooting up, springing up, burgeoning, pullulation, sprouting, blooming, vegetation. **3** *the growth of the industry* expansion, rise, progress, success, advance, advancement, improvement, headway. **4** *find a growth on her body* tumour, lump, excrescence, intumescence, tumefaction.
Opposites DECREASE; DECLINE; FAILURE.

grub *verb* **1** *grub up plants/hedgerows* dig up, unearth, disinter, root out, uproot, root up, deracinate, pull out, tear out. **2** *grub in the ground* dig, spade, delve, excavate, burrow. **3** *grub out information* search out, ferret out, root out, uncover, unearth, disinter. **4** *grub among the old papers* search, hunt, rummage, scour, probe, root around; *inf.* rootle around. **5** *grub away at the task* grind, labour, toil, drudge, slog, slave, plod, sweat; *inf.* plug.

grub *noun* **1** *grubs developing* larva, caterpillar, maggot. **2** *cheap grub* food, meals, sustenance, victuals, rations; *inf.* eats, nosh.

grubby *adjective* dirty, unwashed, grimy, begrimed, filthy, messy, soiled, smutty, besmeared, scruffy, shabby, untidy, unkempt, slovenly, slatternly, sordid, squalid; *inf.* mucky, gungy, cruddy.
Opposites CLEAN; SPOTLESS.

grudge *noun* *nurse a grudge* resentment, spite, malice, bitterness, ill-will, pique, umbrage, grievance, hard feelings, rancour, malevolence, venom, hate, hatred, dislike, aversion, animosity, antipathy, antagonism, enmity, animus.

grudge *verb* **1** *grudge her a piece of the cake* begrudge, give unwillingly, give reluctantly, give stintingly. **2** *grudge her her success* resent, mind, take ill, begrudge, envy, be jealous of.

gruelling *adjective* *a gruelling five-hour walk* exhausting, tiring, fatiguing, wearying, taxing, demanding, trying, arduous, laborious, backbreaking, strenuous, punishing, crushing, draining, difficult, hard, harsh, severe, stiff, grinding, brutal, relentless, unsparing, inexorable.

gruesome *adjective* *gruesome details of the murder | gruesome sight* grisly, ghastly, frightful, horrid, horrible, horrifying, horrendous, awful, grim, dreadful, terrible, fearful, hideous, disgusting, repulsive, repugnant, revolting, repellent, macabre, spine-chilling, sickening, shocking, appalling, abominable, loathsome, abhorrent, odious.

gruff *adjective* **1** *a gruff voice* hoarse, harsh, rough, throaty, husky, croaking, rasping, low, thick, guttural. **2** *a gruff old man* surly, churlish, brusque, curt, blunt, abrupt, grumpy, crotchety, crabby, crabbed, cross, bad-tempered, ill-natured, crusty, tetchy, bearish, sullen, sour, uncivil, rude, unmannerly, impolite, discourteous, ungracious; *inf.* grouchy.
Opposites SOFT; COURTEOUS; GRACIOUS.

grumble *verb* **1** *always grumbling about the weather* complain, moan, groan, protest, object, find fault with, carp, whine; *inf.* grouse, gripe, bellyache, beef, bitch, grouch, whinge. **2** *stomach was grumbling* rumble, gurgle, murmur, growl, mutter, roar.

grumble *noun* **1** *listen to their grumbles* complaint, moan, groan, protest, grievance, objection, whine; *inf.* grouse, gripe, bellyaching, beefing, beef, bitching, grouching, whinging. **2** *the grumble of his stomach* rumble, gurgle, murmur, growl, muttering, roar.

grumpy *adjective* *grumpy first thing in the morning* bad-tempered, surly, churlish, crotchety, crabby, tetchy, crusty, bearish, ill-natured; *inf.* grouchy.

guarantee *noun* **1** *get a guarantee that the goods are perfect* warranty, warrant, contract, covenant, bond, guaranty. **2** *give his guarantee that he will return* pledge, promise, assurance, word, word of honour, oath, bond. **3** *the house acts as a guarantee for a loan* collateral, security, surety, earnest, guaranty. **4** *her father is the guarantee of the loan* guarantor, warrantor, underwriter, voucher, sponsor, supporter, backer; *Law* bondsman.

guarantee *verb* **1** *guarantee a loan* put up collateral for, give earnest money for, provide surety for, provide security for, underwrite, sponsor, vouch for, support, back. *See* GUARANTEE *noun* 3, 4. **2** *I guarantee that I shall return* promise, pledge, give a pledge, give an assurance, give assurances, give one's word, swear, swear to the fact.

guarantor *noun* guarantee, warrantor, underwriter. *See* GUARANTEE *noun* 4.

guard *verb* **1** *guard the town* stand guard over, protect, watch over, cover, patrol, police, defend, shield, safeguard, preserve, save, conserve, secure, screen, shelter. **2** *guard the prisoners* keep under guard, keep under surveillance, keep watch over, mind, supervise, restrain. **3** *guard against losing your bag | guard against thieves* beware, keep watch, be alert, take care, keep an eye out, be on the alert, be on the qui vive, be on the lookout; *inf.* keep one's eyes peeled/skinned.

guard *noun* **1** *volunteer as castle guards* protector, defender, guardian, guarder, bodyguard, custodian, sentinel, sentry, watchman, nightwatchman, scout, lookout, watch, picket, garrison. **2** *prison guards* warder, jailer, keeper; *inf.* screw. **3** *act as a guard for the precious load* escort, convoy, patrol. **4** *soldiers on guard* watch, close watch, watchfulness, vigilance, caution, heed, attention, care, wariness. **5** *a guard for a machine* safety guard, safety device, safeguard, protective device, shield, bulwark, screen, fence, fender, bumper, buffer, cushion, pad. **off one's guard, off guard** *the question/enemy caught him off his guard* unprepared, unready, unalert, unwatchful, napping, with one's defences down. **on one's guard** *keep on your guard* on the alert, vigilant, wary, watchful, cautious, careful, heedful, circumspect, on the lookout, on the qui vive, prepared, ready.

guarded *adjective* *a guarded reply* careful, cautious, circumspect, wary, chary, reluctant, noncommittal, reticent, restrained, reserved, discreet, prudent; *inf.* cagey.

guardian *noun* *the guardian of the castle | guardians of public morals* guard, protector, defender, preserver, champion, custodian, warden, keeper, curator, caretaker, steward, trustee.

guerrilla *noun* freedom fighter, underground fighter, terrorist, member of the resistance, partisan, irregular soldier, irregular.

guess *verb* **1** *guess the weight* make a guess at, conjecture, surmise, estimate, reckon, fathom, hypothesize, postulate, predict, speculate; *inf.* guesstimate. **2** *I guess that you're right* conjecture, surmise, reckon, hazard a guess, suppose, believe, think, imagine, judge, consider, feel, suspect, dare say, fancy, divine, deem.

guess *noun* *my guess was wrong* conjecture, surmise, estimate, guesswork, hypothesis, theory, reckoning, judgement, supposition, feeling, assumption, inference, prediction, speculation, notion; *inf.* guesstimate.

guesswork *noun* guessing, conjecture, surmise, estimate, supposition, hypothesis, theory, presupposition, assumption, presumption, prediction, suspicion, speculation; *inf.* guesstimate.

guest *noun* **1** *the hostess welcoming guests* visitor, caller, company, visitant. **2** *a guest in the hotel* boarder, lodger.
Opposites HOST; LANDLADY, LANDLORD.

guidance *noun* **1** *under the guidance of the headmaster* direction, leadership, auspices, management, control, handling, conduct, government, charge, rule, teaching, instruction. **2** *career guidance* counselling, counsel, advice, direction, recommendation, suggestion, tip, hint, pointer, intelligence, information, instruction.

guide *verb* **1** *guide them to their seats* lead, lead the way to, conduct, show, usher, shepherd, direct, show the way to, pilot, steer, escort, accompany, convoy, attend. **2** *guide the firm through its problems* control, direct, steer, manage, command, be in charge of, govern, rule, preside over, superintend, supervise, handle, regulate, manipulate, manoeuvre. **3** *guide young school leavers* give counselling to, counsel, give advice to, advise, give direction to, make recommendations to, make suggestions to, give someone tips/hints/pointers, inform, give information/intelligence to, instruct.

guide *noun* **1** *a tourist guide* leader, conductor, director, courier, pilot, usher, escort, attendant, convoy, chaperon, cicerone. **2** *act as a career guide* counsellor, adviser, mentor, confidant, tutor, teacher, guru, therapist. **3** *a light as a guide to shipping* marker, indicator, pointer, mark, landmark, guiding light, sign, signal, beacon, lodestar, signpost, key, clue. **4** *use that essay as a guide* model, pattern, example, exemplar, standard, criterion, touchstone, measure, benchmark, yardstick, gauge, norm, archetype, prototype, paradigm, ideal, precedent, guiding principle. **5** *read a guide to Paris* guidebook, tourist guide, travelogue, directory, handbook, manual, ABC, instructions, key, catalogue, vade-mecum.

guideline *noun* guiding principle, criterion, measure, standard, gauge, yardstick, benchmark, touchstone, rule, regulation.

guild *noun* association, society, club, union, league, federation, organization, company, fellowship, order, lodge, brotherhood, fraternity, sisterhood, sorority, alliance, combine, corporation, consortium, syndicate, trust.

guile *noun* cunning, duplicity, craftiness, craft, artfulness, art, artifice, wiliness, wiles, foxiness, slyness, deception, deceit, underhandedness, double-dealing, trickery, trickiness, sharp practice, treachery, chicanery, skulduggery, fraud, gamesmanship, knavery.
Opposites HONESTY; CANDOUR.

guileless *adjective* ingenuous, artless, open, sincere, genuine, naive, simple, innocent, unsophisticated, unworldly, trustful, trusting, honourable, frank, candid.

guilt *noun* **1** *prove/admitted his guilt* guiltiness, culpability, blame, blameworthiness, censurableness, wrongdoing, wrong, wrongfulness, criminality, unlawfulness, misconduct, delinquency, sin, sinfulness, iniquity. **2** *haunted by guilt* guiltiness, feelings of guilt, guilty conscience, bad conscience, remorse, regret, contrition, contriteness, repentance, penitence, compunction, conscience, self-accusation, self-reproach, self-condemnation, shame, disgrace, dishonour, stigma.
Opposites INNOCENCE; shamelessness.

guiltless *adjective* free from guilt, innocent, blameless, free from blame, unblamable, uncensurable, unimpeachable, inculpable, irreproachable, above reproach, clear, pure, sinless, faultless, spotless, stainless, immaculate, unsullied, uncorrupted, undefiled, untainted, unblemished, untarnished, impeccable.

guilty *adjective* **1** *found guilty of the crime* to blame, blameworthy, blamable, culpable, at fault, responsible, censurable, criminal, convicted; reproachable, condemnable, erring, errant, wrong, delinquent, offending, sinful, wicked, evil, unlawful, illegal, illicit, reprehensible, felonious, iniquitous. **2** *feel guilty* conscience-stricken, remorseful, ashamed, shamefaced, regretful, contrite, compunctious, repentant, penitent, rueful, sheepish, hangdog.
Opposites INNOCENT; BLAMELESS; UNREPENTANT.

guise *noun* **1** *in the guise of a witch* external appearance, likeness, costume, clothes, outfit, dress, habit, style. **2** *under the guise of friendship* pretence, disguise, show, external appearance, outward form, screen, cover, blind.

gulf *noun* **1** *ships sailing into the gulf* bay, cove, inlet, bight. **2** *a gulf opened up by an earthquake* chasm, abyss, hollow, pit, hole, opening, rift, cleft, fissure, split, crevice, gully, canyon, gorge, ravine. **3** *a gulf has developed between husband and wife* chasm, abyss, rift, split, wide difference, area of difference, division, gap, separation.

gullet *noun* oesophagus, throat, pharynx, crop, craw.

gullible *adjective* credulous, trustful, overtrustful, easily deceived, easily taken in, unsuspecting, unsuspicious, ingenuous, naive, innocent, simple, inexperienced, green, foolish, silly, wet behind the ears.
Opposites CYNICAL; SUSPICIOUS.

gully *noun* ravine, canyon, gorge, valley, gulf, chasm, abyss; *Am.* gulch. See GULF 2.

gulp *verb* **1** *gulp a drink* swallow, quaff, swill, toss off; drain one's glass; *inf.* swig, knock back. **2** *gulp one's food* bolt, wolf, gobble, guzzle, devour; *inf.* tuck into. **3** *gulp back the tears* fight back, suppress, stifle, smother, choke back, strangle.

gulp *noun* *take a gulp of the water* swallow, mouthful, draught; *inf.* swig.

gum *noun* *stick the page/wood together with gum* glue, adhesive, fixative, paste, cement, mucilage, resin, synthetic/epoxy resin.

gum *verb* *gum the pieces together* stick, glue, paste, affix, cement. **gum up** **1** *gum up the mechanism* clog, choke up, stop up, obstruct. **2** *gum up the works* obstruct, impede, hinder, interfere with, bring to a halt.

gumption *noun* *hasn't got much gumption* initiative, resourcefulness, enterprise, cleverness, astuteness, shrewdness, acumen, common sense, wit, mother wit, discernment, sagacity, native ability, spirit, forcefulness, backbone, pluck, mettle, nerve, courage; *inf.* get-up-and-go, grit, spunk, nous, savvy, horse sense.

gun *noun* *inf.* shooter, piece. *See table. See also tables at* BULLET, MISSILE, WEAPON.

gunman *noun* hold-up man, armed robber, sniper, gangster, terrorist, assassin, murderer, liquidator, bandit; *inf.* gunslinger, hitman, gun, hired gun, trigger man, stick-up man, hatchet man, hood, mobster. *Am.* gunfighter, shootist.

gurgle *verb* **1** *water gurgling* bubble, ripple, murmur, babble, burble, tinkle, lap, splash, plash, purl. **2** *babies gurgling* crow, burble, babble, chuckle, laugh.

gurgle *noun* **1** *the gurgle of water* bubbling, ripple, babble, tinkle. *See* GURGLE *verb* 1. **2** *the gurgle of babies* crowing, burbling, chuckle. *See* GURGLE *verb* 2.

guru *noun* teacher, spiritual teacher, tutor, sage, swami, maharishi, guiding light, mentor, leader, master, authority.

gush *verb* **1** *water gushing from the pipe* stream, rush forth, spout, spurt, surge, jet, well out, pour forth, burst forth, cascade, flood, flow, run, issue, emanate. **2** *she gushed about the beautiful room* be effusive, effuse, overenthuse, enthuse, wax enthusiastic, wax lyrical, effervesce, bubble over, get carried away, fuss, babble, prattle, jabber, gabble, blather, chatter, make too much, overstate the case.

GUNS			
airgun	Colt™	Kalashnikov	revolver
AK-47	double-barrelled	Lewis gun	rifle
anti-aircraft gun	gun	light machine-gun	sawn-off shotgun
arquebus	duelling pistol	M-1 rifle	semi-automatic
assault gun	elephant gun	M-60 machine-gun	shotgun
automatic	Enfield rifle	machine-gun	siege gun
bazooka	falconet	magazine rifle	single-barrelled
Big Bertha	field gun	matchlock	gun
blunderbuss	flintlock	Maxim gun	six-shooter
Bofors gun	fowling piece	mine-thrower	smoothbore
brass cannon	fusil	mortar	Sten gun
breech-loader	Garand rifle	musket	subgun
Bren gun	Gatling gun	muzzle-loader	sub-machine gun
Brown Bess	hackbut	pistol	swivel
cannon	handgun	pistolet	tommy-gun
cannon royal	heavy gun	pom-pom	Uzi
carbine	howitzer	repeating rifle	Winchester™

gush *noun a gush of water* stream, outpouring, spurt, jet, spout, burst, rush, surge, cascade, flood, torrent, spate, freshet.

gust *noun* **1** *a gust of wind blew the hat away* blast, flurry, puff, blow, rush, squall, breeze, gale. **2** *a gust of laughter/temper* outburst, burst, outbreak, eruption, explosion, gale, fit, paroxysm, storm, surge.

gust *verb wind gusting* blast, blow, puff, rush, squall.

gusto *noun perform/eat with gusto* relish, zest, enthusiasm, zeal, fervour, verve, enjoyment, delight, exhilaration, pleasure, appreciation, liking, fondness, appetite, savour, taste.
Opposites APATHY; INDIFFERENCE; DISTASTE.

gut *noun* **1** *a sore gut* stomach, belly, abdomen, bowels, colon; *inf.* insides, innards; *Med.* solar plexus. **2** *remove the guts from the animal* intestines, entrails, vital organs, vital parts, viscera; *inf.* insides, innards.

gut *verb* **1** *gut the fish/rabbit* eviscerate, disembowel, draw, dress, clean, exenterate. **2** *thieves/fire gutted the empty house* ransack, strip, empty, plunder, loot, rob, rifle, ravage, sack, clear out, destroy, devastate, lay waste.

gut *adjective a gut reaction* instinctive, intuitive, involuntary, spontaneous, unthinking, natural, basic, emotional, heartfelt, deep-seated.

guts *plural noun* courage, bravery, valour, backbone, nerve, fortitude, pluck, mettle, mettlesomeness, gameness, spirit, boldness, audacity, daring, hardiness, toughness, forcefulness, stamina, will-power, tenacity; *inf.* grit, gumption, spunk, bottle.

gutter *noun water running in the gutter* drain, sewer, sluice, culvert, conduit, pipe, duct, channel, trough, trench, ditch, furrow, cloaca.

guttersnipe *noun* street urchin, street Arab, ragamuffin, waif, gamin, mudlark.

guttural *adjective guttural voice/accent* throaty, husky, gruff, gravelly, croaking, harsh, rasping, deep, low, rough, thick.

guy *noun* **1** *who is that guy?* man, male, fellow, lad; *inf.* chap, bloke, customer. **2** *burn a guy* effigy, figure, representation.

guy *verb guy the poor old man* ridicule, make fun of, poke fun at, make game/sport of, mock, sneer at, caricature; *inf.* send up, rib, rag, take off.

guzzle *verb* **1** *guzzle food* gulp, gobble, bolt, wolf, devour; cram oneself, stuff oneself, gormandize; *inf.* tuck into, scoff, put away. **2** *guzzle beer* gulp down, swallow greedily, quaff, swill, toss off; *inf.* knock back, swig.

gymnastics *noun.* See table.

GYMNASTIC EVENTS	
asymmetric bars	rhythmic
beam	gymnastics
floor exercises	rings
high bar	side horse vault
horse vault	sports aerobics
parallel bars	trampolining
pommel horse	tumbling

gypsy *noun* Romany, tzigane, didicoi, traveller, rover, roamer, wanderer, rambler; *derog.* transient, vagrant, vagabond, tinker.

gyrate *verb* rotate, revolve, wheel round, turn round, circle, whirl, pirouette, twirl, swirl, spin, swivel.

gyration *noun* rotation, circumrotation, revolution, wheeling, turning around, circling, convolution, circumconvolution, whirling, pirouetting, twirling, swirling, spinning, swivelling.

habit noun **1** *it was his habit to go for a morning walk* custom, practice, procedure, wont, way, routine, matter of course, style, pattern, convention, policy, mode, rule. **2** *he had a habit of peering* tendency, propensity, predisposition, proclivity, penchant, leaning, bent, inclination, custom, practice, quirk. **3** *a cheerful habit of mind* disposition, temper, temperament, nature, character, make-up, constitution, humour, frame of mind. **4** *get into the habit of smoking* addiction, dependence, weakness, fixation, obsession. **5** *a riding habit | his old-fashioned habit* costume, dress, garb, attire, apparel, clothes, clothing, garments, livery, uniform; *inf.* gear, togs, rig-out, rags.

habitable adjective inhabitable, livable-in, fit to live in, fit to occupy, tenantable, fit to lodge/reside in.

habitat noun **1** *the animal's natural habitat* environment, natural environment, natural setting/background/element, home, abode. **2** *the habitat of students* home, abode, residence, residency, dwelling, dwelling-place, habitation, location, situation, address.

habitation noun **1** *fit for habitation* occupancy, occupation, tenancy, residence, residency, living, dwelling, housing, inhabitance, inhabitancy, inhabitation, lodging, lodgement, domiciliation, billeting, quartering. **2** *settled into a new habitation* home, house, residence, residency, dwelling, dwelling-place, abode, domicile, lodging, lodging-place, quarters, living quarters, rooms, apartment, flat, accommodation, housing, roof over one's head; *inf.* pad, digs. **3** *the habitation of the flat* occupancy, occupation, inhabitance, inhabiting, tenancy, tenure.

habitual adjective **1** *taking his habitual route/place* customary, accustomed, regular, usual, normal, set, fixed, established, routine, wonted, common, ordinary, familiar, traditional. **2** *their habitual grumbling* persistent, constant, continual, recurrent, repeated, perpetual, non-stop, continuous, frequent. **3** *a habitual smoker* by habit, confirmed, addicted, chronic, inveterate, hardened, ingrained.
Opposites UNACCUSTOMED; INFREQUENT; OCCASIONAL.

habituate verb *habituate oneself to a hot climate* accustom, make used to, adapt, acclimatize, condition, break in, inure, harden, season, train, school, discipline, familiarize, make familiar with.

habitué noun frequenter, frequent visitor, regular visitor, regular customer, regular patron/client, constant visitor, familiar face.

hack verb **1** *hack down the tree* cut down, chop down, fell, hew, saw down. **2** *hack one's way through the jungle* cut, hew, slash, clear. **3** *hack the carcass* gash, cut, chop, mangle, mutilate, lacerate, shatter, fracture. **4** *children hacking away* cough, rasp, choke; *inf.* bark.

hack noun **1** *a farmer with just an old hack horse* horse, hired horse, tired-out horse, worn-out horse, jade; *inf.* nag, crock. **2** *no specialist staff, just hacks* drudge, labourer, menial, slave, factotum, toiler, plodder; *inf.* skivvy. **3** *newspapers just employing hacks* literary drudge, penny-a-liner, scribbler, Grub Street writer.

hack adjective *using hack phrases* banal, trite, overused, tired, worn-out, stale, stereotyped. *See* HACKNEYED.

hackle noun **make someone's hackles rise** anger, annoy, enrage, vex; *inf.* make someone see red, get someone's dander up, rile.

hackneyed adjective *using hackneyed phrases* hack, banal, trite, overused, overworked, tired, worn-out, time-worn, stale, stereotyped, clichéd, platitudinous, unoriginal, unimaginative, commonplace, common, pedestrian, prosaic, run-of-the-mill, stock, conventional; *inf.* played-out, corny, old-hat.
Opposites FRESH; ORIGINAL.

hag noun crone, witch, gorgon, harridan, fury, ogress, hellcat, harpy, shrew, virago, vixen, termagant; *inf.* battleaxe, old bat.

haggard adjective drawn, gaunt, pinched, hollow-cheeked, hollow-eyed, ghastly, ghost-like, deathlike, wan, pallid, cadaverous, peaked, drained, careworn, emaciated, wasted, thin.
Opposites SLEEK; PLUMP; HALE.

haggle verb **1** *haggle over the price* bargain, drive a hard bargain, beat down, chaffer, higgle, patter; *Am.* dicker. **2** *children haggling* wrangle, squabble, bicker, quarrel, argue, dispute.

hail[1] verb **1** *hail a friend* salute, greet, say hello to, nod to, wave to, smile at, lift one's hat to, acknowledge. **2** *hail a taxi* signal, make a sign to, flag, flag down, wave down, call, shout to, sing out to, halloo, accost. **3** *hail the king* acclaim, applaud, cheer, praise, sound the praises of, laud, extol, pay tribute to, pay homage to, exalt, glorify. **4** *hail from England* come from, be a native of, be born in, originate in, have one's roots in.

hail[2] noun *give a hail* call, cry, shout, signal, greeting, salutation, salute, hello, acknowledgement.

hail[3] noun **1** *hail falling* hailstones, sleet, frozen rain. **2** *a hail of bullets/protest* shower, rain, storm, volley, barrage, bombardment, pelting.

hail[4] verb *hail stones/curses down on them | stones hailed down on him* shower, rain, rain down, pelt, pepper, batter, bombard, volley; beat down upon.

hair *noun* **1** *she has beautiful hair* head of hair, locks, tresses, shock, mop. **2** *animal's hair* coat, fur, pelt, hide, wool, fleece, mane. **by a hair, by a hair's breadth** by the narrowest of margins, by a narrow margin, by the skin of one's teeth, by a split second; *inf.* by a whisker. **let one's hair down** throw off one's inhibitions, relax, be informal; *inf.* hang loose, let it all hang out; *Am. inf.* chill out. **not turn a hair** remain calm; *inf.* keep one's cool, keep one's hair on, not bat an eyelid. **split hairs** quibble, argue over nothing, fuss over trifles, niggle, cavil, pettifog; *inf.* nit-pick.

hair-raising *adjective* spine-chilling, blood-curdling, terrifying, petrifying, horrifying, frightening, alarming, shocking, exciting, thrilling; *inf.* scary, creepy.

hairy *adjective* hair-covered, hirsute, woolly, shaggy, bushy, furry, fleecy, fuzzy, bearded, unshaven, bewhiskered, stubbly; *Tech.* pilose, pileous, pappose.

halcyon *adjective* **1** *halcyon weather* mild, calm, still, tranquil, quiet, serene, pleasant, moderate, temperate, gentle, placid, peaceful, windless, stormless. **2** *halcyon days of youth* carefree, happy, blissful, golden, joyful, joyous, contented, flourishing, thriving, prosperous, palmy.

hale *adjective* healthy, in good health, well, fit, bursting with good health, flourishing, blooming, in excellent shape, in fine fettle, strong, robust, vigorous, hardy, sturdy, hearty, full of vim, able-bodied, lusty; *inf.* in the pink, fit as a fiddle, in tip-top condition.

half *noun* *take a half* equal part/portion/section/division, fifty per cent, hemisphere, semi-sphere. **by half** *too smart by half* excessively, far, to too great an extent, by an excessive amount, considerably, very much. **by halves** *do something by halves* inadequately, insufficiently, incompletely, imperfectly, scrappily, skimpily.

half *adjective* **1** *half orange* halved, divided in two, in two equal parts, bisected, hemispherical. **2** *half measures | a half smile* partial, incomplete, limited, moderate, slight, inadequate, insufficient.

half *adverb* **1** *half-cooked | she half smiled* partly, partially, in part, part, incompletely, inadequately, insufficiently, slightly, barely. **2** *half inclined to agree* nearly, very nearly, to a certain extent, to a considerable extent, all but, almost. **not half 1** *not half good enough | not half bad* not at all, not in any way, not nearly. **2** *he didn't half lose his temper* to a great extent, to a considerable extent, certainly, indeed.

half-baked *adjective* **1** *half-baked plans* ill-conceived, poorly-planned, unplanned, not thought through, premature, undeveloped, unformed, ill-judged, short-sighted, injudicious, impractical; *inf.* crackpot. **2** *a half-baked young man* foolish, stupid, silly, brainless, senseless, ignorant, inexperienced, immature, callow, green, credulous, wet behind the ears; *inf.* half-witted, dim-witted, dopey.

half-hearted *adjective* *plan received a half-hearted welcome* lukewarm, unenthusiastic, apathetic, indifferent, uninterested, unconcerned, cool, listless, lacklustre, dispassionate, unemotional, cursory, perfunctory, superficial, passive, neutral.

halfway *adverb* **1** *go halfway* midway, to/in the middle, to/at the midpoint. **2** *halfway finished* almost, nearly, just about, in part, partly, part, to a certain degree/extent, in some measure. **meet someone halfway** reach a compromise with, come to terms with, strike a balance with, find a happy medium with, establish a middle ground with, give and take with; *inf.* go fifty-fifty with.

halfway *adjective* *the halfway point* midway, equidistant, mid, middle, intermediate, central, mean, medial, median.

halfwit *noun* simpleton, idiot, dolt, blockhead, dunderhead, dullard, dunce, fool, numbskull; *inf.* nitwit, moron, dim-wit, imbecile, crackpot, nut.

halfwitted *adjective* *you halfwitted fool! | halfwitted plans* simple-minded, feeble-minded, simple, stupid, idiotic, doltish, dull-witted, foolish, silly, half-baked; *inf.* dim-witted, crazy, moronic, barmy, batty, nutty, cracked, nit-witted, crackpot.

hall *noun* **1** *concerts held in the main hall* auditorium, assembly room, chamber; assembly hall, conference hall, concert hall, church hall, town hall. **2** *hostesses greeting their guests in the hall* entrance hall, vestibule, hallway, entry, lobby, foyer, passageway, passage.

hallmark *noun* **1** *the hallmark on silver* assay mark, stamp of authenticity, authentication seal, endorsement of authentication. **2** *good craftsmanship is his hallmark* mark, trade mark, stamp, sign, sure sign, telltale sign, badge, device, symbol, indicator, indication, index.

hallucinate *verb* *certain drugs can make you hallucinate* have/experience hallucinations, see visions, have a vision, fantasize, imagine things, dream, be delirious; *inf.* see things, be on a trip.

hallucination *noun* *this drug causes hallucinations* illusion, figment of the imagination, imagining, vision, mirage, false conception, fantasy, apparition, dream, delirium, phantasmagoria; *inf.* trip.

halo *noun* nimbus, aureole, aureola, aura, gloriole, ring of light, crown of light, radiance, corona, halation.

halt¹ *verb* **1** *halt at the traffic lights* come to a halt, stop, come to a stop, come to a standstill, pull up, draw up, wait. **2** *halt for the day* stop, finish, cease, break off, call it a day, down tools, desist, discontinue, rest; *inf.* knock off. **3** *work has halted* stop, finish, cease, come to an end, be at an end, draw to a close, run its course. **4** *halt progress* bring to a halt/stop, arrest, check, block, curb, stem, terminate, end, put an end to, put a stop to, bring an end to, crush, nip in the bud, frustrate, baulk, obstruct, impede, hold back.
Opposites GO; BEGIN; FURTHER.

halt² *noun* **1** *a halt in the work* stop, stopping, stoppage, cessation, close, end, desistance, discontinuation, discontinuance, standstill, pause, interval, interlude, intermission, break, hiatus, rest, respite, breathing-space, time out; *inf.* breather. **2** *come/draw/grind to a halt* stop, standstill.

halt³ *verb* **1** *keep halting when speaking* falter, hesitate, stammer, stutter, stumble, flounder, fumble for words. **2** *halting between going and staying* hesitate, waver, vacillate, dither, be unsure, be undecided, be in doubt, have qualms/misgivings; *Scots* swither.

halter *noun* bridle, harness; *Am.* headstall. *See table at* HARNESS.

halting *adjective* **1** *walk with a halting gait* limping, hobbling, stumbling, unsteady, awkward. **2** *speak in halting tones* faltering, hesitating, stammering, stuttering, stumbling, laboured.

halve *verb* *halved the orange with a knife | try to halve imports* cut in half, divide into two equal parts, divide in two, divide equally, split in two, sever in two, share equally, dichotomize, reduce by fifty per cent.

halves *plural noun* **by halves** *See* HALF *noun* by halves.

hammer *noun* *workmen using hammers* claw-hammer, sledgehammer, mallet, beetle, gavel. *See table at* TOOL.

hammer *verb* **1** *hammer out a horseshoe | hammer it on the anvil* beat out, shape, form, mould, forge, fashion, make, fabricate. **2** *a bully hammering little boys* beat, batter, pound, pummel, hit, strike, slap, cudgel, bludgeon, club; *inf.* wallop, clobber. **3** *hammer the opposition* trounce, defeat utterly, inflict heavy damage on, bring someone to their knees, beat, thrash, worst, drub, give a drubbing to; *inf.* clobber, beat hollow. **4** *hammer facts into the pupils* drum into, din into, drive into, teach over and over again, drub into. **5** *hammer away at the problem* persevere, persist; work, pound away, keep on, plod/slog away, labour, grind away, drudge, peg away; *inf.* stick, beaver away, plug away. **6** *hammer out a solution | still hammering out the detail* thrash out, work out, resolve, form a resolution about, sort out, settle, negotiate, bring about, bring to a satisfactory conclusion, bring to a finish, come to a decision on, complete, accomplish, produce, carry through, effect.

hamper *verb* *hamper progress* hinder, obstruct, impede, hold back, inhibit, retard, slow down, hold up, restrain, block, check, frustrate, baulk, thwart, foil, curb, interfere with, cramp, restrict, bridle, handicap, stymie, hamstring, shackle, fetter, encumber, cumber, trammel; *inf.* throw a spanner in the works.
Opposites AID; EXPEDITE; FACILITATE.

hamper *noun* *a picnic/Christmas hamper* basket, creel, pannier, wickerwork box, box, container, holder.

hamstring *verb* **1** *hamstring the athlete* cripple, lame, injure, disable, hock. **2** *hamstring the opposition's plans* frustrate, thwart, baulk, foil, check, curb, hamper, ruin, prevent, stop. *See* HAMPER *verb.*

hand *noun* **1** *large hands* palm, fist; *inf.* paw, mitt, duke; *Scots* nieve. **2** *the hand of a clock* dial pointer, indicator, needle. **3** *give the workers a*

hand *helping hand, help, assistance, aid, support, succour, relief.* **4** *sack a number of hands* worker, workman, work person, employee, operative, hired hand, hired man, hired person, hired help, labourer, artisan, crewman, crew. **5** *have a neat hand* writing, handwriting, penmanship, script, calligraphy, chirography. **6** *try your hand at baking* ability, skill, art, artistry, craftsmanship. **7** *give a big hand to the singer* applause, round of applause, clapping of hands, clap, handclap, ovation. **at hand, to hand 1** *help is at hand | keep the book to hand* readily available, available, at one's disposal, handy, ready, within reach, accessible, close, close at hand, near, nearby; *inf.* on tap. **2** *your big moment is at hand* close at hand, imminent, approaching, coming, about to happen, impending. **by hand** *make it by hand* manually, with one's hands, using one's hands. **from hand to mouth** *live from hand to mouth* in poverty, meagrely, scantily, skimpily, precariously, uncertainly, insecurely, improvidently; *inf.* on the breadline. **hand in glove** *working hand in glove with the enemy* in partnership, in league, in close association, in collusion; *inf.* in cahoots. **hand in hand 1** *walking hand in hand* holding hands, clasping hands, with hands clasped. **2** *working hand in hand together*, closely, side by side, in close association, in partnership, conjointly, concurrently. **in hand 1** *the matter is in hand* receiving attention, being dealt with, under control, under way. **2** *have money in hand* ready, available, available for use, in reserve, put by. **to hand** *See* HAND *noun* at hand. **try one's hand** try, make an attempt, attempt, essay; *inf.* have/take a shot, have a go.

hand *verb* **1** *hand the book to her* give, pass, pass over, hand over, deliver, present. *See* HAND *verb* hand over. **2** *hand her out of the car | hand an old lady across the road* help, assist, aid, give someone a helping hand, guide, convey, lead. **hand down/on** *hand down/on the family jewels* pass down, pass on, give, transfer, transmit, bequeath, will. **hand out** *hand out food supplies* distribute, give out, pass out, deal out, dole out, mete out, dispense, apportion, disseminate, disburse; *inf.* dish out. **hand over** *hand over the money* give, give up, pass, pass over, present, turn over, deliver, surrender, yield, release; *inf.* fork out.

handbag *noun* bag, shoulder-bag, clutch bag, evening bag, flight bag, travelling bag; *Am.* purse.

handbill *noun* circular, advertisement, notice, pamphlet, leaflet, brochure, bulletin; *inf.* junk mail; *Am.* flyer.

handbook *noun* guide, guidebook, travel guide, tourist guide, manual, instruction manual, instructions, book of directions, directory, vade-mecum, Baedeker, ABC.

handcuff *verb* put handcuffs on, manacle, fetter, shackle.

handcuffs *plural noun* manacles, fetters, shackles; *inf.* cuffs, bracelets, darbies.

handful *noun* **1** *a handful of people* few, small number, small amount, small quantity, sprinkling. **2** *the child is a handful* nuisance, pest, bother, irritant, source of annoyance, thorn in the flesh, bugbear; *inf.* pain, pain in the neck.

handicap *noun* **1** *pupils suffering from a handicap* physical/mental disability, physical/mental disadvantage, physical/mental abnormality, impairment. **2** *her poverty was a handicap in her career* disadvantage, impediment, hindrance, obstruction, obstacle, encumbrance, check, block, curb, trammel, barrier, stumbling block, constraint, restriction, limitation, drawback, shortcoming.
Opposites ADVANTAGE; BENEFIT.

handicap *verb handicapped by his slight build* put at a disadvantage, disadvantage, impede, hinder, impair, hamper, obstruct, check, block, encumber, curb, trammel, bridle, hold back, constrain, restrict, limit.

handicraft *noun go to handicraft classes* craft, handiwork, craftsmanship, workmanship, artisanship, art, skill.

handiwork *noun* **1** *admire the handiwork at the crafts exhibition* handicraft, craft, craftsmanship. *See* HANDICRAFT. **2** *this is the handiwork of a maniac* action, achievement, work, doing, creation, design, product, production, result.

handle *noun held the handle of the tool/sword* shaft, grip, handgrip, hilt, haft, knob, stock, helve.

handle *verb* **1** *handle the goods* touch, feel, finger, hold, grasp, grip, pick up, lift, pat, caress, stroke, fondle, poke, maul; *inf.* paw. **2** *handle difficult pupils* cope with, deal with, treat, manage, control. **3** *handle their business affairs* be in charge of, control, manage, administer, direct, guide, conduct, supervise, take care of. **4** *handle a car* drive, steer, operate, manoeuvre. **5** *his paper handled the story well* deal with, treat, discuss, discourse on. **6** *dealers handling grain* deal in, traffic in, trade in, market, sell, stock, carry.

handout *noun* **1** *beggars waiting for handouts* alms, charity, gifts of food/money/clothes, dole. **2** *read the handout* press release, circular, advertising leaflet, brochure, pamphlet, bulletin, notice, literature. **3** *accept the handouts from reps* free sample; *inf.* freebie.

hand-picked *adjective hand-picked team of negotiators* select, specially-selected, élite, choice, specially-chosen, elect.

hands *plural noun in the hands of the enemy* possession, keeping, clutches, grasp, charge, care, power, authority, command, management, control, custody, guardianship, supervision, disposal, jurisdiction. **hands down** *win hands down* easily, with no trouble, effortlessly, without effort; *inf.* no sweat.

handsome *adjective* **1** *a handsome man* good-looking, attractive, personable; *inf.* dishy. **2** *a handsome woman* good-looking, attractive, personable, elegant, fine, well-formed, well-proportioned, stately, dignified. **3** *a handsome gift* generous, magnanimous, liberal, lavish, bounteous, considerable, sizeable, large, ample, abundant, plentiful.
Opposites UGLY; PLAIN; MEAGRE.

handwriting *noun* writing, hand, penmanship, script, calligraphy, chirography; *inf.* scrawl, scribble, fist.

handy *adjective* **1** *is the book handy?* to hand, at hand, available, within reach, accessible, near, nearby, close, at one's fingertips, convenient; *inf.* on tap. **2** *a handy instrument* useful, helpful, practicable, practical, serviceable, functional, expedient, easy-to-use, neat, convenient. **3** *a handy person* dexterous, deft, nimble-fingered, adroit, adept, proficient, skilful, skilled, expert, clever/good with one's hands.
Opposites INCONVENIENT; USELESS; INEPT.

hang *verb* **1** *mobiles hanging from the ceiling* hang down, be suspended, dangle, swing, sway, be pendent. **2** *hang the picture* suspend, put up, put on a hook. **3** *hang the prisoner* send to the gallows, put the noose on, send to the gibbet, gibbet, execute; *inf.* string up. **4** *hang wallpaper* stick on, attach, fix, fasten on, append, paste, glue, cement. **5** *a hall hung with tapestries* decorate, adorn, ornament, deck, drape, cover, furnish. **6** *hawks hanging in the air* hover, float, be poised, flutter, flit, drift, remain static. **hang about/around** **1** *hang about, he won't be long* hold on, wait, wait a minute, linger, loiter, tarry, dally, waste time; *inf.* hang on. **2** *hang about bars* frequent, be a regular visitor to, be a regular client of, haunt; *inf.* hang out in. **3** *hang about with thugs* associate with, keep company with, be a friend/companion of; *inf.* hang out with. **hang back** *hang back when volunteers were asked for* hold back, stay back, stay in the background, be reluctant, hesitate, demur, recoil, shrink back. **hang down** *with her skirt hanging down* droop, trail, sag. **hang fire** *they're hanging fire until prices rise* delay, hang back, hold back, procrastinate, stall, adopt Fabian tactics. **hang on** **1** *hang on to her mother's hand* hold, hold fast to, cling to, cling on to, grip, clutch, grasp, cleave to. **2** *everything hangs on the financial position* depend, be dependent on, turn on, hinge on, rest on, be conditional on, be contingent upon, be determined by, be conditioned by. **3** *hang on his every word* listen closely to, be very attentive to, concentrate hard on, be rapt by, give ear to; be all ears for. **4** *hang on till things improve* hold out, hold on, persevere, persist, go on, carry on, continue, remain, endure. **5** *hang on, I'll get him* hold on, wait, wait a minute, stop, stay, remain, hold the line. **hang over** **1** *trees hanging over the fence* lean over, bend over, bend downwards, bend forwards, bow, droop. **2** *the threat of redundancy is hanging over them* loom, be imminent, impend, menace, threaten, approach, draw near; *inf.* be just around the corner.

hang *noun* **get the hang of** get the knack of, acquire the technique of, catch on, grasp, comprehend, understand.

hangdog *adjective looked at him with a hangdog expression* shamefaced, ashamed, embarrassed, guilty-looking, sheepish, abashed, abject, cowed, cringing, downcast, crestfallen, browbeaten, defeated, intimidated, wretched.

hanger-on noun follower, henchman, retainer, appendage, dependant, parasite, minion, lackey, vassal, flunkey, camp-follower, sycophant, fawner, sponger, leech; *inf.* groupie, freeloader.

hangover noun after-effects, effects of alcohol, crapulence, crapulousness; *inf.* morning after feeling.

hang-up noun **1** *a hang-up about French films* preoccupation, fixation, obsession, phobia, bee in one's bonnet, *idée fixe; inf.* thing. **2** *she has a hang-up about maths* mental block, psychological block, block, inhibition, difficulty, problem; *inf.* thing.

hank noun *hanks of coloured wool* skein, coil, loop, twist, length, roll, piece.

hanker verb *hanker after/for a holiday abroad* long for, have a longing for, yearn for, crave, desire, hunger for, thirst for, be bent on, covet, want, wish for, set one's heart on, pine for, be itching for, lust after; *inf.* be dying for, have a yen for.

hankering noun longing, yearning, craving, desire, hunger, thirst, want, wish, urge, itch, lust; *inf.* yen.

haphazard adjective unplanned, random, unsystematic, unorganized, unmethodical, orderless, aimless, indiscriminate, undirected, irregular, slapdash, thrown together, careless, casual, hit-or-miss.
Opposites METHODICAL; SYSTEMATIC; REGULAR.

hapless adjective *the hapless child began to cry* unlucky, luckless, out of luck, unfortunate, ill-starred, forlorn, wretched, woebegone, unhappy; *inf.* down on one's luck.

happen verb **1** *the accident happened at dawn* take place, occur, come about, come to pass, present itself, arise, materialize, appear, come into being, chance, arrive, transpire, crop up, develop, supervene, eventuate; *inf.* come off. **2** *what happened to her?* become of, befall, betide. **3** *I happened to meet her* chance, have the good/bad fortune to, be someone's fortune/misfortune to. **4** *happen upon hidden treasure* chance upon, stumble on, discover unexpectedly, find, meet by chance, encounter.

happening noun occurrence, event, incident, occasion, affair, circumstance, action, case, phenomenon, eventuality, episode, experience, adventure, scene, proceedings, chance.

happily adverb **1** *I shall happily go* with pleasure, gladly, delightedly, willingly, freely, contentedly, enthusiastically, with all one's heart and soul. **2** *children playing happily* cheerfully, merrily, gaily, light-heartedly, joyfully, blithely. *See* HAPPY 1. **3** *happily, it turned out all right* luckily, fortunately, as luck would have it, providentially.

happiness noun cheerfulness, cheeriness, merriness, gaiety, good spirits, high spirits, light-heartedness, joy, joyfulness, joviality, glee, blitheness, carefreeness, enjoyment, gladness, delight, exuberance, elation, ecstasy, bliss, blissfulness, euphoria, transports. *See* HAPPY 1.

happy adjective **1** *happy children* cheerful, cheery, merry, gay, in good spirits, in high spirits, light-hearted, joyful, joyous, jovial, gleeful, buoyant, blithe, blithesome, carefree, untroubled, smiling, glad, delighted, exuberant, elated, ecstatic, blissful, euphoric, overjoyed, thrilled, in seventh heaven, over the moon, floating/walking on air; *inf.* on cloud nine, on top of the world. **2** *happy to see you* glad, pleased, delighted, contented, satisfied, gratified, thrilled. **3** *by a happy chance* lucky, fortunate, favourable, advantageous, beneficial, helpful, opportune, timely, convenient, propitious, auspicious. **4** *a happy choice* apt, appropriate, fitting, fit, good, right, proper, seemly.
Opposites SAD; DISPLEASED; UNFORTUNATE.

happy-go-lucky adjective *he's always so happy-go-lucky | has such a happy-go-lucky manner* carefree, light-hearted, devil-may-care, blithe, free and easy, easygoing, nonchalant, casual, untroubled, unworried, unconcerned, insouciant, heedless, irresponsible, improvident.

harangue noun lecture, tirade, diatribe, speech, talk, sermon, exhortation, declamation, oration, address, homily, peroration; *inf.* spiel.

harass verb **1** *children harassing their mother* bother, pester, annoy, exasperate, worry, fret, disturb, agitate, provoke, badger, hound, torment, plague, persecute, harry, tease, bait, nag, molest, bedevil; *inf.* hassle, give someone a hard time, drive someone up the wall. **2** *troops harassing the enemy* harry, attack repeatedly, raid, beleaguer, press hard, oppress.

harassed adjective *harassed parents* distraught, under pressure, stressed, under stress, strained, worried, careworn, troubled, vexed, agitated, fretting; *inf.* hassled.

harbinger noun herald, forerunner, precursor, usher, announcer, *avant-courier*, sign, portent, omen, augury.

harbour noun **1** *ships in harbour* port, anchorage, haven, dock, harbourage, marina. **2** *a safe harbour for refugees* place of safety, refuge, shelter, haven, sanctuary, retreat, asylum, sanctum, covert.

harbour verb **1** *harbour criminals* give shelter to, shelter, house, lodge, put up, take in, billet, provide refuge for, shield, protect, conceal, hide, secrete. **2** *harbour resentment* nurse, nurture, maintain, hold on to, cherish, cling to, retain, entertain, brood over.

hard adjective **1** *hard ground* firm, solid, solidified, compact, compacted, condensed, close-packed, compressed, dense, rigid, stiff, unyielding, resistant, unmalleable, inflexible, unpliable, tough, strong, stony, rock-like. **2** *hard physical work* arduous, strenuous, heavy, tiring, fatiguing, exhausting, back-breaking, laborious, rigorous, exacting, formidable, tough, difficult, uphill, toilsome, Herculean. **3** *a hard problem* difficult, complicated, complex, involved, intricate, puzzling, perplexing, baffling, knotty, thorny, bewildering, enigmatic, insoluble, insolvable, unfathomable, incomprehensible. **4** *a hard master* harsh, hard-hearted, severe, stern, cold, cold-hearted,

unfeeling, unsympathetic, grim, ruthless, oppressive, tyrannical, pitiless, merciless, unrelenting, unsparing, lacking compassion, callous, cruel, vicious, implacable, obdurate, unyielding, unjust, unfair. **5** *hard living conditions* difficult, grim, harsh, unpleasant, disagreeable, uncomfortable, intolerable, unendurable, unbearable, insupportable, distressing, painful, disastrous, calamitous. **6** *a hard blow/knock* forceful, violent, heavy, strong, powerful, sharp, fierce, harsh. **7** *a hard worker* hard-working, energetic, industrious, diligent, assiduous, conscientious, sedulous, keen, enthusiastic, zealous, earnest, persevering, persistent, unflagging, untiring, indefatigable. **8** *hard words | no hard feelings* angry, acrimonious, bitter, antagonistic, hostile, resentful, rancorous. **9** *the hard facts* actual, definite, undeniable, indisputable, verifiable, plain, cold, bare, bold, harsh, unvarnished, unembellished. **10** *hard liquor* alcoholic, strong, spirituous. **11** *hard drugs* addictive, habit-forming, harmful, noxious, injurious.
Opposites SOFT; EASY; GENTLE.

hard *adverb* **1** *push hard* strenuously, energetically, powerfully, heavily, with all one's might, with might and main, heartily, vigorously, with vigour, forcefully, with force, forcibly, with great effort, fiercely, intensely. **2** *work hard* energetically, industriously, diligently, assiduously, conscientiously, enthusiastically, sedulously, with application, earnestly, with perseverance, persistently, indefatigably; *inf.* like billy-oh. See HARD *adjective* 7. **3** *our victory was hard won* with difficulty, with effort, laboriously, after a struggle, painfully. **4** *her death hit him hard* badly, intensely, violently, forcefully, harshly, distressingly, painfully, agonizingly. **5** *it was raining hard* heavily, steadily, cats and dogs, buckets. **6** *look hard at* keenly, sharply, carefully, closely, painstakingly. **7** *they followed hard on his heels* close, near. **hard by** *living hard by the motorway* right by, beside, near to, nearby, close to, close by, not far from, a step away from, within a stone's throw of. **hard up** poor, short of money/cash, in financial difficulties, penniless, impoverished, impecunious, bankrupt, in the red, without means of support, on one's beam-ends; *inf.* broke, stony-broke, cleaned out, bust, strapped, on one's uppers, skint. **hard-and-fast** *adjective hard-and-fast rules* binding, set, strict, stringent, inflexible, rigorous, immutable, unalterable, uncompromising, incontestable, incontrovertible.

hard-bitten *adjective hard-bitten journalists* hardened, case-hardened, hardened, inured, toughened by experience, tough, cynical, down-to-earth.

hard-boiled *adjective hard-boiled young women* cynical, unsentimental, lacking sentiment, tough, down-to-earth, world-weary.

hard-core *adjective* **1** *hard-core socialists* die-hard, dyed-in-the-wool, staunch, steadfast, dedicated, intransigent, uncompromising, obstinate, stubborn, extreme. **2** *hard-core*

pornography explicit, blatant, obscene; *inf.* full-frontal.

harden *verb* **1** *the cement hardened* become hard, solidify, set, stiffen, bake, anneal, cake, freeze, congeal, clot, coagulate. See HARD *adjective* 1. **2** *harden one's heart* toughen, make insensitive/unfeeling, deaden, numb, benumb. **3** *life had hardened him* make tough, toughen, case-harden, make unfeeling, brutalize, make callous, indurate. **4** *harden to cold* accustom, habituate, acclimatize, inure. **5** *harden one's defences* strengthen, fortify, reinforce, buttress, brace, gird.

hardened *adjective a hardened criminal* habitual, accustomed, chronic, inured, seasoned, inveterate, incorrigible, irredeemable, reprobate, impenitent, unregenerate, shameless.

hard-headed *adjective hard-headed businessmen* shrewd, astute, sharp, sharp-witted, tough, unsentimental, hard-bitten, practical, pragmatic, realistic, level-headed, cool-headed, sensible, rational, with one's feet on the ground.

hard-hearted *adjective mother could be so hard-hearted* hard, heartless, unfeeling, unsympathetic, uncompassionate, lacking compassion, without sentiment, cold, cold-hearted, uncaring, unconcerned, indifferent, unmoved, unkind, cruel, callous, inhuman, merciless, pitiless, stony-hearted, stony. See HARD *adjective* 4.

hard-hitting *adjective a hard-hitting report* tough, uncompromising, unsparing, strongly worded, vigorous, pulling no punches, straight-talking, blunt, frank, critical.

hardihood *noun* **1** *the hardihood of the soldiers* bravery, courage, valour, boldness, intrepidity, heroism. See HARDY 2. **2** *the hardihood of the children in defying the teacher* audacity, rashness, foolhardiness, impudence. See HARDY 3.

hardiness *noun the hardiness of the children* healthiness, strength, robustness, sturdiness, toughness, ruggedness, vigour. See HARDY 1.

hard-line *adjective hard-line members of the party* extreme, tough, uncompromising, inflexible, unyielding, intransigent, not giving an inch.

hardly *adverb hardly able to walk | can hardly see | hardly alive* scarcely, barely, only just, just, almost not, with difficulty, with effort.
Opposites FULLY; UNDOUBTEDLY.

hard-pressed *adjective* **1** *the retreating army was hard-pressed* closely pursued, hotly pursued, harried, hounded, under attack, in a tight corner. **2** *hard-pressed workers* overloaded, over-burdened, overworked, overtaxed, under pressure, harassed, in difficulties, with one's back to the wall; *inf.* pushed, up against it.

hardship *noun suffer great hardship* adversity, deprivation, privation, want, need, destitution, poverty, austerity, desolation, misfortune, distress, suffering, affliction, pain, misery, wretchedness, tribulation, trials, trials and tribulation, burdens, calamity, catastrophe, disaster, ruin, ruination, oppression, persecution, torment, torture, travail.
Opposites PROSPERITY; EASE; COMFORT.

hard-wearing *adjective hard-wearing shoes/carpet* durable, strong, tough, stout, rugged, made to last, resilient, well-made.

hard-working *adjective many hard-working pupils* diligent, industrious, conscientious, assiduous, sedulous, energetic, keen, enthusiastic, zealous, busy, with one's shoulder to the wheel.
Opposites LAZY; IDLE.

hardy *adjective* **1** *hardy children* healthy, fit, strong, robust, sturdy, tough, rugged, vigorous, lusty, stalwart, hale and hearty, sound in body and limb, fit as a fiddle, in fine fettle, in good kilter, in good condition. **2** *hardy men defying death* brave, courageous, valiant, bold, valorous, intrepid, fearless, heroic, stout-hearted, daring, plucky, mettlesome. **3** *hardy children defying the teacher* audacious, rash, reckless, foolhardy, impetuous, daredevil, brazen, impudent.
Opposites DELICATE; WEAK; COWARDLY.

hare-brained *adjective* **1** *a hare-brained scheme* foolish, foolhardy, rash, reckless, madcap, wild, ridiculous, half-baked, ill-thought-out, ill-conceived; *inf.* crackpot. **2** *a hare-brained young girl* foolish, silly, empty-headed, scatter-brained, feather-brained, brainless, giddy, dizzy, whimsical, capricious, flighty; *inf.* half-witted.

hark *verb hark! the birds are singing* harken, listen, pay attention, pay heed, give ear. **hark back** *hark back to subjects previously discussed* go back, turn back, look back, think back, revert, regress, retrovert, remember, recall, recollect.

harlequin *noun dressed as a harlequin* jester, fool, buffoon, zany.

harlequin *adjective a harlequin pattern* chequered, variegated, varicoloured, parti-coloured, multicoloured, many-coloured, motley.

harlot *noun* whore, prostitute, call-girl, streetwalker, loose woman, fallen woman, woman of the night, *fille de joie*, madam, procuress, bawd; *inf.* tart, pick-up girl, pro, tramp, scrubber, hooker; *lit.* strumpet.

harm *noun* **1** *inflict harm on* hurt, injury, pain, suffering, trauma, adversity, disservice, abuse, damage, mischief, detriment, defacement, defilement, impairment, destruction, loss, ruin, havoc. **2** *men full of harm* badness, evil, wrongdoing, wrong, wickedness, vice, iniquity, sin, sinfulness, immorality, nefariousness.
Opposites GOOD; BENEFIT.

harm *verb harm the child/building | try not to harm their relationship* hurt, injure, wound, inflict pain/suffering/trauma on, abuse, maltreat, ill-treat, ill-use, molest, do violence to, damage, do mischief to, deface, defile, impair, spoil, mar, blemish, destroy.

harmful *adjective* **1** *harmful effects* hurtful, injurious, wounding, abusive, detrimental, deleterious, disadvantageous, destructive, dangerous, pernicious, noxious, baneful, toxic. **2** *a harmful influence* bad, evil, malign, wicked, corrupting, subversive.
Opposites HARMLESS; BENEFICIAL; GOOD.

harmless *adjective* **1** *a harmless substance* innocuous, innoxious, safe, non-dangerous, non-toxic, non-irritant, mild. **2** *a harmless old man* innocuous, inoffensive, unoffending, innocent, blameless, gentle.

harmonious *adjective* **1** *a harmonious musical piece* melodious, tuneful, musical, harmonizing, sweet-sounding, mellifluous, dulcet, euphonious, symphonious, rhythmic, consonant. **2** *a harmonious atmosphere/relationship* peaceful, peaceable, friendly, amicable, cordial, amiable, agreeable, congenial, united, in harmony, in rapport, in tune, attuned, in accord, compatible, sympathetic. **3** *a harmonious collection of colours/buildings* compatible, congruous, coordinated, concordant, well-matched, matching.
Opposites DISCORDANT; HOSTILE; INCONGRUOUS.

harmonize *verb* **1** *the colours harmonize well* be harmonious, go together, fit together, be compatible, blend, mix well, be congruous, be consonant, be well-coordinated, match. **2** *their stories/thoughts harmonize* be in accord, agree, be in assent, correspond, coincide, tally, be in unison, be congruent, be of one mind. **3** *harmonize relations* restore harmony to, settle differences, reconcile, patch up, make peaceful, negotiate peace between, heal the breach, pour oil on troubled waters.

harmony *noun* **1** *working in harmony* agreement, assent, accord, accordance, concordance, concurrence, cooperation, unanimity, unity, unison, oneness, amity, amicability, good will, affinity, rapport, sympathy, like-mindedness, friendship, fellowship, comradeship, peace, peacefulness. **2** *the harmony of the colours* compatibility, congruity, consonance, concord, coordination, blending, balance, symmetry, suitability. **3** *enjoy the harmony at the concert* tune, melody, tunefulness, melodiousness, mellifluousness, euphony, euphoniousness.
Opposites DISAGREEMENT; INCONGRUITY; DISSONANCE.

harness *noun horse's harness* tackle, tack, equipage, equipment, gear, accoutrement, trappings, yoke, bridle. *See table.* **in harness** working, at work, employed, in occupation, in action, active, busy.

PARTS OF A HARNESS FOR A HORSE

backband	crupper
bellyband	girth
bit	hackamore *Am.*
blinders *Am.*	halter
blinkers	hames
breastband	headstall *Am.*
breeching	reins
bridle	saddlepad
collar	traces

---

harness *verb* **1** *harness the horses* put in harness, saddle, yoke, bridle, hitch up, couple. **2** *harness the sun's rays | must harness her energies* control, utilize, put to use, render useful, make productive, turn to good account, apply, exploit, channel, mobilize, capitalize on.

harp *noun playing the harp* lyre; aeolian/wind harp, jew's harp, Celtic harp, clarsach. *See table at* STRING. **harp on** *harp on his untidiness* dwell on, persist in talking about, repeat complaints about, nag about, press/labour the point about; *inf.* go on and on about.

harridan *noun* shrew, harpy, virago, termagant, vixen, scold, nag, fishwife, witch, hellcat, tartar, spitfire, fury, hag, gorgon; *inf.* old bag, battleaxe.

harrowing *adjective harrowing cries/sight/experience* distressing, agonizing, excruciating, traumatic, heart-breaking, heart-rending, painful, racking, afflicting, chilling, disturbing, vexing, alarming, perturbing, unnerving, horrifying, terrifying.

harry *verb* **1** *invaders harrying the villagers* plunder, rob, raid, sack, pillage, devastate, ravage, despoil, lay waste to. **2** *children harrying their mother* harass, annoy, bother, pester, disturb, worry, badger, chivvy, plague, vex, torment, tease, molest, persecute, bedevil; *inf.* hassle, drive someone up the wall.

harsh *adjective* **1** *a harsh noise* grating, jarring, grinding, rasping, strident, jangling, raucous, ear-piercing, discordant, dissonant, unharmonious. **2** *a harsh voice* rough, coarse, guttural, hoarse, croaking, raucous, strident, gravelly, gruff. **3** *harsh colours* gaudy, garish, glaring, over-bold, bold, loud, flashy, showy, crass, crude, vulgar. **4** *harsh conditions/countryside* grim, severe, desolate, stark, austere, barren, rough, bleak, bitter, wild, inhospitable, comfortless, spartan. **5** *a harsh winter* severe, hard, bitter, bitterly cold, freezing, arctic, Siberian. **6** *a harsh reply* abrupt, brusque, blunt, curt, gruff, short, surly, concise, clipped, impolite, discourteous, uncivil, ungracious. **7** *a harsh ruler* cruel, brutal, savage, barbarous, hard-hearted, despotic, tyrannical, ruthless, uncompassionate, unfeeling, merciless, pitiless, relentless, unrelenting, inhuman. **8** *harsh rules/measure* stern, severe, grim, stringent, austere, uncompromising, inflexible, punitive, Draconian.
Opposites MELLIFLUOUS; SOFT; GENTLE; LENIENT.

harum-scarum *adjective* reckless, rash, wild, impetuous, daredevil, madcap, hare-brained, foolhardy, thoughtless, careless, heedless, frivolous.

harvest *noun* **1** *celebrate the end of the harvest* harvest time, harvest tide, harvesting, reaping, ingathering, harvest home. **2** *a good harvest of wheat/apples* crop, yield, produce, vintage. **3** *the squirrels have a harvest of nuts* store, supply, stock, stockpile, hoard, cache, accumulation. **4** *The harvest of hard work* product, fruits, return, effect, result, consequence.

harvest *verb* **1** *harvest the crop* gather in, gather, reap, glean, pick, pluck, collect. **2** *squirrels harvesting nuts* collect, amass, accumulate, hoard, garner. **3** *harvest benefits from his experience* acquire, gain, obtain, get, derive, procure, secure, net.

hash¹ *noun* **make a hash of** make a mess of, botch, bungle, mishandle, mismanage, muddle up, mix up, get into a jumble; *inf.* screw up.

hash² *noun* hashish, marijuana, marihuana, cannabis, ganja, hemp; *inf.* grass, pot.

hassle *noun* **1** *tired of all the hassle* inconvenience, trouble, bother, annoyance, nuisance, trials and tribulation, harassment, badgering, difficulty, problem, struggle. **2** *a hassle at the pub last night* fight, quarrel, squabble, argument, disagreement, dispute, altercation, wrangle, tussle, struggle; *inf.* set-to, barney, fisticuffs, argy-bargy.

hassle *verb* *stop hassling him* annoy, badger, harass, hound, pester, bother, trouble, worry, torment, plague; *inf.* give someone a hard time.

haste *noun* **1** *fulfil the order with haste* speed, swiftness, rapidity, rapidness, quickness, fastness, alacrity, promptness, promptitude, dispatch, expeditiousness, expedition, celerity, fleetness, briskness, immediateness, urgency. **2** *haste causes carelessness* hastiness, hurriedness, hurry, rushing, hustling, impetuosity, recklessness, rashness, foolhardiness, precipitateness, impulsiveness, heedlessness, carelessness.
Opposites DELAY; CARE.

hasten *verb* **1** *you must hasten to get there on time* make haste, hurry, hurry up, go fast, move faster, go quickly, dash, rush, speed up, run, race, sprint, fly, tear along, bolt, scurry, scamper, scuttle; *inf.* get a move on, step on it, hotfoot it, hightail it. **2** *hasten the growth/work* speed up, accelerate, hurry on, quicken, advance, push forward, urge on, facilitate, precipitate, aid, assist, help, boost, increase, step up.
Opposites SLOW; DAWDLE; DECELERATE; DELAY.

hasty *adjective* **1** *with hasty steps* swift, rapid, quick, fast, speedy, hurried, hurrying, running, prompt, expeditious, fleet, brisk, urgent. **2** *a hasty visit/glance* quick, short, rapid, brief, rushed, short-lived, fleeting, transitory, cursory, perfunctory, superficial, slight. **3** *a hasty decision* hurried, rushed, impetuous, reckless, rash, foolhardy, precipitate, impulsive, headlong, heedless, thoughtless, careless, ill-conceived. **4** *a hasty temper/nature* hot-headed, quick-tempered, irascible, irritable, impatient, fiery, excitable, volatile, choleric, snappish, snappy, brusque.
Opposites SLOW; LEISURELY; CAUTIOUS.

hat *noun* soft hat, straw hat. *See table.*

hatch *verb* **1** *hatch eggs* incubate, brood, sit on, cover. **2** *hatch chicks* bring forth. **3** *hatch a scheme* devise, concoct, contrive, plan, scheme, design, invent, formulate, originate, conceive, dream up, think up; *inf.* cook up.

hatchet *noun* axe, cleaver, pickaxe, poleaxe, chopper, mattock, machete, tomahawk. *See tables at* TOOL, WEAPON.

hate *verb* **1** *hate his rival/job* loathe, detest, abhor, dislike, abominate, despise, execrate, have an aversion to, feel hostile towards, be unable to abide/bear/stand, view with dislike, be sick of, be tired of, shudder at, be repelled

by, recoil from. **2** *I hate to upset her* be reluctant, be loath, be unwilling, feel disinclined, be sorry, dislike, not have the heart, shy away from, flinch from, shrink from.
Opposites LOVE; LIKE; RELISH.

hate noun. See HATRED.

hateful adjective loathsome, detestable, abhorrent, abominable, despicable, execrable, odious, revolting, repugnant, repellent, disgusting, obnoxious, offensive, insufferable, horrible, unpleasant, nasty, disagreeable, foul, vile, heinous.
Opposites ADMIRABLE; LOVABLE; GOOD.

hatred noun hate, loathing, detestation, abhorrence, dislike, abomination, execration, aversion, hostility, ill-will, enmity, animosity, antagonism, antipathy, animus, revulsion, repugnance, odium, rancour, grudge.

haughty adjective *she is so haughty | had a haughty expression* proud, arrogant, conceited, self-important, egotistical, vain, swollen-headed, overweening, overbearing, presumptuous, supercilious, condescending, lofty, patronizing, snobbish, scornful, imperious, lordly, high-handed; *inf.* on one's high horse, snooty, high and mighty, stuck-up, hoity-toity, uppity, uppish.
Opposites MODEST; HUMBLE.

haul verb **1** *haul the body out of the water* drag, draw, pull, tug, heave, trail, lug, tow, take in tow, hale. **2** *haul merchandise* transport, convey, move, cart, carry, convoy, ship.

haunt verb **1** *ghosts haunting the castle* walk, roam, visit; *inf.* spook. **2** *haunt bars* frequent, be a regular client of, visit regularly, spend all one's time in; *inf.* hang out in, hang about/around. **3** *thoughts of guilt haunted him* obsess, prey on the mind of, prey on, torment, plague, beset, harry, disturb, trouble, worry, oppress, burden, weigh on, recur to, come back to, stay with.

haunt noun *the local pub was one of his haunts* stamping-ground, frequented place, favourite spot, resort, rendezvous, meeting-place; *inf.* hang-out, local, watering-hole.

haunting adjective **1** *haunting music* evocative, poignant, atmospheric, wistful, disturbing, nostalgic. **2** *haunting memories* persistent, recurring, recurrent, indelible, unforgettable.

have verb **1** *we have two cars* own, possess, keep, keep for one's use, use, hold, retain, occupy. **2** *we had three cups of tea* get, be given, receive, accept, obtain, acquire, procure, secure, gain. **3** *the flat has five rooms* contain, include, comprise, embrace, embody, comprehend, take in, incorporate. **4** *she had a lot of trouble with him* experience, undergo, go through, encounter, meet, find, be subjected to, submit to, suffer from, endure, tolerate, put up with. **5** *have a good time* experience, enjoy. **6** *have doubts/misgivings* feel, entertain, have/keep/bear in mind, harbour, foster, nurse, cherish. **7** *have the impudence to answer back* show, display, exhibit, demonstrate, manifest, express. **8** *they had her doing all their work* make, cause, oblige, require, force, coerce, induce, prevail upon, talk into, persuade. **9** *I'll have the engineer repair the telephone* ask, request, bid, tell, give orders to, order, command, direct, enjoin. **10** *she won't have such behaviour* permit, allow, put up with, tolerate, stand, brook, support, endure, abide. **11** *she had a baby daughter* give birth to, bear, deliver, be delivered of, bring into the world, bring forth, beget. **12** *they certainly had you* fool, trick, take in, dupe, outwit, deceive, cheat, swindle; *inf.* do, diddle. **13** *he boasted that he had had all the woman there* have sexual intercourse with, have sex with, make love to/with, copulate with, have carnal knowledge of; *inf.* bed, lay. **have had it 1** *he won't win now, he's had it* have no chance, have no chance of success, have no hope, be finished, be out, be defeated, have lost. **2** *you've had it when your mother finds you* be about to be punished, be going to be chastised, be in for a scolding; *inf.* be for it. **have on 1** *she had on a blue dress* wear, be wearing, be dressed in, be clothed in. **2** *I have something on today* have planned, have arranged, be committed to, have on the agenda. **3** *have someone on* tease, joke with, play a joke on, trick, play a trick on, pull someone's leg; *inf.* kid. **4** *the police have something on him* have information about, have evidence against, know something bad/incriminating about. **have to** *have to clean the floor* must, have got to, be bound to, be obliged to, be under an obligation to, be forced to, be compelled to.

HATS AND HEADGEAR

balaclava	cocked hat	hard hat	panama	tam-o'shanter
baseball cap	coif	headband	peaked cap	tarboosh
beany	coonskin hat	headscarf	pillbox hat	ten-gallon
beret	coronet	helmet	pork-pie hat	hat
boater	cowl	high hat	puggaree	tiara
bobble hat	cockscomb	homburg	rebozo	top hat
bonnet	crash helmet	hood	shako	topi
bowler	crown	jester's cap	skullcap	toque
busby	deerstalker	jockey cap	snood	tricorn
calash	derby	keffiyeh	sombrero	trilby
cap	diadem	kepi	sou'wester	turban
chaplet	dunce's cap	mantilla	stetson	veil
circlet	fedora	mitre	stovepipe hat	wimple
cloche	fez	mob cap	sun-bonnet	wreath
cloth cap	flat cap	mortarboard	tammy	yarmulke

haven noun **1** *ships entering a haven* harbour, harbourage, port, anchorage, moorage, dock, cove, bay. **2** *refugees seeking a safe haven* refuge, shelter, sanctuary, asylum, retreat, sanctum, sanctum sanctorum, covert.

haversack noun knapsack, rucksack, backpack, satchel, kitbag.

havoc noun **1** *forest fires causing/wreaking havoc* devastation, destruction, damage, ruination, ruin, rack and ruin, despoliation, ravaging, waste, wreckage, gutting, desolation, extermination, disaster, catastrophe, cataclysm. **2** *the havoc in the room when the children left* chaos, disorder, confusion, disruption, disorganization, mayhem; *inf.* shambles.

hawk verb peddle, sell, market, vend, doorstep, cry, tout; *Am.* bark.

hawker noun pedlar, door-to-door salesman, travelling salesman, barrow boy, huckster, vendor, crier, colporteur.

hay noun straw, pasturage, fodder, forage, feed. **make hay while the sun shines** make the most of an opportunity, capitalize on an advantageous situation, exploit an opportune occasion, strike while the iron is hot, *carpe diem*, seize the day.

haywire adjective **go haywire** go wrong, go out of control, become disorganized, cease to function properly.

hazard noun **1** *face hazards on the journey* danger, peril, risk, jeopardy, threat, menace. **2** *a game of hazard* chance, accident, luck, contingency, fortuity, fortuitousness.

hazard verb **1** *hazard a guess* venture, put forward, proffer, offer, submit, advance, volunteer. **2** *hazard his life* risk, put at risk, endanger, expose to danger, imperil, put in jeopardy, jeopardize.

hazardous adjective **1** *a hazardous journey* dangerous, danger-filled, risky, perilous, fraught with danger/risk/peril, precarious, unsafe, insecure, threatening, menacing; *lit.* parlous; *inf.* dicey, hairy. **2** *a hazardous venture* open to chance, chancy, risky, uncertain, unpredictable, precarious, speculative. **Opposites** SAFE; SURE.

haze noun **1** *a haze covered the town* mist, film of mist, mistiness, fog, cloud, cloudiness, smog, vapour. **2** *her mind is in a state of haze* vagueness, confusion, muddle, befuddlement, bewilderment, obscurity, dimness, indistinctness.

hazy adjective **1** *a hazy day* misty, foggy, cloudy, smoggy, overcast. **2** *hazy memories* vague, indefinite, blurred, fuzzy, muzzy, faint, confused, muddled, unclear, obscure, dim, indistinct, ill-defined. **Opposites** CLEAR.

head noun **1** *hurt his head* skull, cranium, poll, sconce; *inf.* pate, nut, noddle, conk, bonce. **2** *he has a good head* | *use your head* mind, intellect, intelligence, brain, brains, mentality, wit, wits, wisdom, sense, reasoning, rationality, understanding; *inf.* loaf, upper storey, grey matter. **3** *a head for business* mind, brain, aptitude, ability, capacity, flair, talent, faculty.

4 *the head of the organization/team/school/nation* leader, chief, commander, director, chairman, managing director, manager, superintendent, controller, administrator, supervisor, captain, principal, headmaster, headmistress, head teacher, governor, president, premier, prime minister, headman. **5** *at the head of the firm* top, command, control, controls, charge, leadership, headship, directorship. **6** *at the head of the hill* top, summit, peak, crest, crown, tip, brow, apex, vertex. **7** *at the head of the queue* front, fore, forefront, van, vanguard. **8** *matters coming to a head* climax, culmination, crisis, critical point, turning-point, crossroads. **9** *at the head of the stream* origin, source, fountainhead, fount, well-head, well-spring, headwater. **10** *a head on the beer* froth, foam, lather, suds. **11** *standing on the head looking out to sea* headland, promontory, point, cape, foreland. **12** *the material is listed under various heads* heading, category, class, classification. *See* HEADING 1. **13** *rushed to the head to be sick* toilet, lavatory, WC, bathroom, water-closet, latrine; *inf.* loo, bog; *Am. inf.* john, can. **go to one's head 1** *the wine has gone to my head* make intoxicated, intoxicate, make dizzy, make someone's head spin; *inf.* make woozy. **2** *their praise went to her head* make conceited/arrogant/boastful, puff up. **head first 1** *fall head first downstairs* on one's head, head foremost, headlong, head on, diving, plunging. **2** *rush into things head first* without thinking, rashly, recklessly, precipitately, carelessly, heedlessly. *See* HEADLONG 2. **head over heels** *head over heels in love* utterly, completely, thoroughly, full, wholeheartedly, intensely, passionately, fervently, fervidly, uncontrollably; *inf.* madly. **keep one's head** *keep one's head in a crisis* keep calm, keep cool, remain unruffled, maintain one's equilibrium, keep control of oneself; *inf.* keep one's cool. **lose one's head** panic, lose control of oneself, lose control of the situation, get flustered/confused, get angry, get excited, get hysterical; *inf.* lose one's cool, blow one's top, freak out, fly off the handle.

head adjective *the head gardener/teacher/priest* chief, leading, main, principal, first, prime, premier, foremost, topmost, supreme, cardinal.

head verb **1** *head the expedition* be at the head/front of, lead, be the leader of, lead the way for, go/be first, precede. **2** *head the firm* be at the head of, be in charge of, be in command of, command, be in control of, control, run, lead, be the leader of, manage, direct, administer, supervise, rule, govern, guide. **3** *a tower headed by a spire* crown, top, surmount, cap, tip. **4** *head for town* make for, go to, go in the direction of, direct one's steps towards, point oneself towards, aim for, set out for, start out for, go/turn towards, steer towards, make a beeline for. **head off 1** *head off the charging bull* divert, deflect, turn aside, intercept, stop in mid-course, block off, cut off. **2** *head off disaster* ward off, fend off, forestall, avert, prevent, parry, baulk, check, stop.

headache noun **1** *she is susceptible to headaches* sore head, pain in the head, migraine; *Med.* cephalgia. **2** *her nephew is nothing but a* *headache to her* nuisance, bother, pest, trouble, vexation, bane, bugbear, worry, inconvenience; *inf.* pain, pain in the neck.

heading *noun* **1** *materials listed under various headings* head, category, class, classification, subject, topic, division, section, branch, department. **2** *put the headings on the illustrations/articles* title, caption, headline, name, rubric, banner headline.

headlong *adverb* **1** *fall headlong into the bushes* head first, on one's head, head foremost, head on. *See* HEAD *noun* head first. **2** *rush headlong into a decision* hastily, in haste, hurriedly, impetuously, impulsively, unrestrainedly, impatiently, without thinking, rashly, recklessly, wildly, prematurely, precipitately, carelessly, heedlessly.

head-on *adjective* **1** *a head-on collision* direct, front-to-front. **2** *a head-on confrontation* direct, directly opposing/opposite, straight-on, face-to-face; *inf.* eyeball-to-eyeball, full-frontal.

headquarters *plural noun* HQ, main office, head office, main branch, centre of operations, home base, command post.

headstone *noun* gravestone, tombstone, stone, monument, memorial.

headstrong *adjective* stubborn, stubborn as a mule, obstinate, obdurate, mulish, inflexible, intransigent, intractable, pigheaded, unyielding, self-willed, refractory, recalcitrant, ungovernable, wayward, contrary, wilful, perverse, unruly, wild, reckless, heedless, rash.

headway *noun* **make headway** make progress, make way, progress, advance, get ahead, get on, proceed, develop, gain ground, go forward by leaps and bounds, make strides.

heady *adjective* **1** *a heady drink* intoxicating, inebriating, inebriant, potent, strong, spirituous. **2** *she was heady with success* exhilarated, excited, overjoyed, thrilled, overwhelmed, euphoric, ecstatic, overpowered, in seventh heaven, over the moon; *inf.* on cloud nine. **3** *the heady days of youth* exhilarating, exciting, stimulating, rousing, arousing, invigorating, thrilling, galvanizing, electrifying. **4** *a heady person/action* impetuous, rash, reckless, wild, foolhardy, thoughtless, heedless, imprudent, incautious, impulsive, precipitate.

heal *verb* **1** *heal the wound* cure, make well, make better, remedy, treat, mend, restore, regenerate. **2** *the skin began to heal* get better, get well, be cured, mend, be on the mend, be restored, improve, show improvement. **3** *heal the breach* conciliate, reconcile, patch up, settle, set right, put right, make good, harmonize. **4** *heal the sorrow* alleviate, appease, mitigate, ameliorate, assuage, allay, palliate, soften.

health *noun* **1** *full of health* healthiness, fitness, well-being, good condition, good trim, good shape, fine fettle, soundness, robustness, strength, vigour, salubrity, good kilter. **2** *his health is not good* state of health, constitution, physical state, physical health, physical shape, condition, form, tone.

healthy *adjective* **1** *a healthy young man* in good health, fit, physically fit, in good condition/trim/shape/kilter, in fine fettle, in fine/top form, robust, strong, vigorous, hardy, flourishing, hale and hearty, hale, hearty, bursting with health, blooming, active; *inf.* in the pink. **2** *a healthy climate* health-giving, salubrious, invigorating, bracing, stimulating, refreshing, tonic. **3** *a healthy diet* health-giving, healthful, good for one, nutritious, nourishing, wholesome, beneficial.
Opposites UNHEALTHY; ILL; ADVERSE.

heap *noun* **1** *a heap of rubbish* pile, stack, mass, mound, mountain, stockpile, accumulation, collection, lot, assemblage, amassment, aggregation, agglomeration, conglomeration, hoard, store, stock, supply. **2** *a heap of trouble* a lot, lots, a great deal, an abundance, plenty, a superabundance; *inf.* loads, tons. **3** *lost a heap of money | earn heaps of money* a lot, lots, a great deal, abundance, considerable quantities, huge quantities, plenty, a mint; *inf.* oodles, loads, tons, pots, stacks, lashings.

heap *verb* **1** *heap up leaves/money* pile up, stack, amass, stockpile, mound, accumulate, collect, assemble, hoard, store, store up, stock up, set aside, lay by. **2** *heap praise/insults on him* bestow, confer, shower, give, grant, assign, load, burden.

hear *verb* **1** *he does not hear* have the sense of hearing, perceive sound, have the faculty of hearing, have the auditory faculty. **2** *I listened but I didn't hear what he said* catch, take in, overhear; *inf.* get, latch on to. **3** *we heard that he was dead | how did you hear of his appointment?* be informed, be told, be made aware, receive information, find out, discover, learn, gather, pick up, be given to understand, hear tell, get wind. **4** *the chief judge heard the case* try, judge, pass judgement on, ajudicate, examine, investigate, inquire into, consider.

hearing *noun* **1** *his hearing is poor* power of hearing, faculty/sense of hearing, ability to hear, aural faculty, auditory perception. **2** *give someone a hearing* chance to speak, opportunity to express one's point of view, opportunity to be heard, chance to put one's side of the story, interview, audience. **3** *they were within hearing* earshot, hearing distance/range, reach, carrying range, range of one's voice, auditory range. **4** *present at the hearing* inquiry, trial, inquest, investigation, inquisition, review, examination.

hearsay *noun* *according to hearsay, he is a thief* rumour, gossip, tittle-tattle, tattle, common talk, common knowledge, idle talk, mere talk, report, talk of the town, word of mouth, *on dit*; *inf.* buzz, grapevine.

heart *noun* **1** *his heart isn't right* *inf.* ticker. **2** *love her with all his heart* passion, love, affection, emotions, feelings. **3** *he has no heart* tender feelings, tenderness, warm emotions, compassion, sympathy, empathy, responsiveness to others, humanity, fellow feeling, concern for others, pathos, goodwill, humanitarianism, benevolence, kindness, kindliness, brotherly love. **4** *I don't have the heart to go on holiday* spirit, enthusiasm, keenness, eagerness, liveliness. **5** *heroes with great heart* courage, bravery, valour, intrepidity, fearlessness, heroism, stout-heartedness, boldness, pluck, mettle, backbone, nerve, fortitude, purpose, resolution, determination; *inf.* guts, spunk, gumption. **6** *the heart of the matter/universe* centre, central part, core, nucleus, middle, kernel, essential part, hub, quintessence, essence, crux, marrow, pith, substance, sum and substance. **after one's own heart** *a person/holiday after my own heart* of the kind that one likes, to one's liking, attractive to one, favoured by one, desirable. **at heart** *at heart he is a kind man* basically, fundamentally, at bottom, in essence, essentially, intrinsically, innately, in reality, really, in fact, actually, truly, in truth. **by heart** *learn by heart* off by heart, by rote, word for word, pat, off pat, by memory, parrot-fashion. **do one's heart good** do someone good, give someone pleasure, please, gladden, make happy, cheer, delight, gratify, satisfy. **eat one's heart out** *jilted lovers eating their hearts out* sorrow, grieve, mourn, ache, suffer, agonize, pine, mope, fret, regret, brood, repine, be filled with envy. **from the bottom of one's heart** *apologize from the bottom of my heart* with all one's heart, profoundly, deeply, sincerely, devoutly, heartily, fervently, passionately. **have a change of heart** *they had a change of heart about moving* change one's mind, change one's tune, have a rethink. **have a heart** *have a heart and let them off* be kind, be merciful, be lenient, be compassionate, be sympathetic, be considerate. **have one's heart set on** *the little girl had her heart set on the doll* long for, yearn for, desire, be desirous of, wish for, want badly, crave. **heart and soul** *devote oneself heart and soul to the project* enthusiastically, eagerly, zealously, wholeheartedly, gladly, with open arms, thoroughly, completely, entirely, absolutely. **lose one's heart to** *she lost her heart to a soldier* fall in love with, fall for, take a liking/fancy to, become infatuated with. **take heart** *take heart from the fact that you did better than many others* cheer up, brighten up, be heartened, be encouraged, be comforted, perk up, revive, derive comfort/satisfaction from; *inf.* buck up. **with one's heart in one's mouth** *she looked into the dark space with her heart in her mouth* in fear, fearfully, with apprehension, apprehensively, with fear and trembling, with alarm, with trepidation, with bated breath.

heartache *noun* sorrow, grief, sadness, anguish, pain, hurt, agony, suffering, misery, wretchedness, despair, desolation, despondency, woe; *lit.* dolour.

heartbreaking *adjective* *heartbreaking cries/tale* heart-rending, sad, pitiful, poignant, tragic, painful, agonizing, distressing, desolating, affecting, grievous, bitter, cruel, harsh, harrowing, tear-jerking, excruciating.

heartbroken *adjective* broken-hearted, heartsick, miserable, sorrowful, sad, anguished, suffering, grieving, grieved, dejected, dispirited, disheartened, downcast, disconsolate, crestfallen, disappointed, crushed, desolate, despondent, in low spirits.

heartburn *noun* dyspepsia, indigestion, brash; *Med.* pyrosis.

hearten *verb* cheer, cheer up, raise the spirits of, invigorate, revitalize, energize, animate, revivify, exhilarate, uplift, elate, comfort, encourage, buoy up, pep up; *inf.* buck up, give a shot in the arm to.
Opposites DISCOURAGE; DEPRESS; DISHEARTEN.

heartfelt *adjective* *sends his heartfelt sympathy* deeply, deeply felt, deep, profound, wholehearted, sincere, honest, devout, genuine, unfeigned, earnest, ardent, fervent, passionate, kindly, warm, cordial, enthusiastic, eager.

heartily *adverb* **1** *thanked/welcomed them heartily* warmly, cordially, feelingly, from the bottom of one's heart, deeply, profoundly, wholeheartedly, sincerely, genuinely, unfeignedly. **2** *eat heartily* with eagerness, eagerly, with enthusiasm, enthusiastically, zealously, earnestly, vigorously, energetically, resolutely. **3** *dislike him heartily* | *am heartily sick of this weather* very much, completely, totally, absolutely, thoroughly.

heartless *adjective* unfeeling, unsympathetic, uncompassionate, unkind, uncaring, unmoved, untouched, cold, cold-hearted, cold-blooded, hard-hearted, cruel, harsh, stern, hard, brutal, merciless, pitiless, ruthless.
Opposites COMPASSIONATE; KIND; MERCIFUL.

heart-rending *adjective* heartbreaking, sad, pitiful, painful, distressing, affecting, harrowing, tear-jerking. *See* HEARTBREAKING.

heartsick *adjective* sick at heart, heavy-hearted, heartsore, dejected, downcast, dispirited, depressed, despondent, disappointed.

heart-to-heart *adjective* *a-heart-to-heart talk* intimate, personal, unreserved, candid, frank, open.

heart-to-heart *noun* *have a heart-to-heart* tête-à-tête, cosy chat.

heart-warming *adjective* **1** *a heart-warming story* touching, moving, affecting, warming, cheering, cheerful, gladdening, encouraging, uplifting. **2** *a heart-warming job* gratifying, satisfying, rewarding, pleasing.

hearty *adjective* **1** *a hearty welcome* enthusiastic, eager, warm-hearted, warm, cordial, jovial, friendly, affable, unreserved, ebullient, exuberant, effusive. **2** *a hearty dislike* wholehearted, complete, total, absolute, thorough, genuine, unfeigned. **3** *a hearty young/old man* strong, robust, hardy, vigorous, stalwart, healthy, sound, sturdy, active, energetic, hale, hale and hearty. **4** *a hearty meal* substantial, solid, abundant, ample, sizeable, filling, nutritious, nourishing.
Opposites COOL; SLIGHT; WEAK.

heat *noun* **1** *the heat melted the ice* hotness, warmth, warmness, calefaction, torridness. **2** *the heat of summer* hotness, warmth, sultriness, torridness, torridity, swelter, heatwave, hot spell, dog days. **3** *the heat of the child frightened her* high temperature, fever, feverishness, febrility, febricity, flush; *Med.* pyrexia. **4** *speak with heat* warmth, passion, vehemence, intensity, ardour, fervour, fervency, fervidness, zeal, eagerness, enthusiasm, animation, earnestness, excitement, agitation.
Opposites COLD; APATHY.

heat verb **1** *heat up the milk* warm, warm up, make hot, make warm, reheat, cook; *inf.* hot, hot up. **2** *the day heated up* grow hot, grow warm, become hotter/warmer, get hotter/warmer. **3** *the argument heated up* grew passionate/vehement/fierce/angry. See HEATED 1. **4** *the subject seemed to have heated him* arouse, rouse, excite, inflame, stimulate, stir, animate, anger, make angry, enrage.

heated adjective **1** *a heated argument* passionate, vehement, fierce, angry, furious, stormy, tempestuous, frenzied, raging, intense, impassioned, violent. **2** *both parties were rather heated* excited, roused, animated, inflamed, angry, furious, enraged.

heater noun electric heater, gas heater, convector heater, fan heater, storage heater, radiator, brazier; car heater, water heater, immersion heater.

heathen noun **1** *missionaries converting heathens* unbeliever, infidel, pagan, idolater/idolatress, atheist, disbeliever, agnostic, sceptic, heretic. **2** *lands invaded by heathens* barbarian, savage.

heathen adjective **1** *converting a heathen tribe* heathenish, infidel, pagan, godless, irreligious, idolatrous, atheistic, agnostic, heretical. **2** *invaded by heathen tribes* barbarian, barbarous, savage, uncivilized, brutish.

heave verb **1** *heaving heavy weights* lift, haul, pull, tug, raise, hoist, upheave. **2** *heave the hammer in the games* throw, cast, toss, fling, hurl, let fly, pitch, send; *inf.* sling, chuck. **3** *heave a sigh* give, utter, let out, pant, gasp, blow, puff, breathe, sigh, sob. **4** *people heaving as the ship sailed* vomit, be sick, spew, retch, gag; *inf.* throw up.

heaven noun **1** *children were told their granny was in heaven* abode of God, abode of the angels, Kingdom of God, paradise, bliss, next life, life to come, next world, the hereafter, Abraham's bosom, Zion, nirvana, Valhalla, Elysium, Elysian Fields, empyrean, Avalon, the Isles of the Blessed, happy hunting-ground. **2** *she was in heaven when she heard the news* ecstasy, bliss, sheer bliss, transports, rapture, supreme happiness, supreme joy, perfect contentment, seventh heaven, paradise, Eden, utopia, dreamland, fairyland. **3** *the heavens opened* sky, skies, firmament, ether, empyrean, aerosphere, vault of heaven, the blue; *lit.* welkin.

heavenly adjective **1** *heavenly concerns* cosmic, extraterrestrial, unearthly, extramundane, not of this world, other-worldly, celestial, paradisical, empyrean, empyreal, Elysian. **2** *heavenly beings* celestial, divine, angelic, seraphic, cherubic, blessed, blest, beatific, beatified, holy, godlike, immortal, superhuman, paradisical. **3** *a heavenly party* delightful, pleasurable, enjoyable, marvellous, gratifying, wonderful, blissful, rapturous, sublime; *inf.* glorious, divine. **4** *a heavenly dress* beautiful, exquisite, perfect, superb, ravishing, alluring, enchanting, entrancing, ideal; *inf.* divine.
Opposites HELLISH; DREADFUL; UGLY.

heavily adverb **1** *walking heavily* with difficulty, slowly, laboriously, painfully, awk-wardly, clumsily, ponderously. **2** *heavily defeated* utterly, completely, thoroughly, absolutely, decisively, roundly, soundly. **3** *drink heavily* excessively, to too great an extent, to a great extent, too much, very much, a great deal, copiously. **4** *ground heavily packed* compactly, densely, closely, hard, thick, thickly.

heavy adjective **1** *a heavy log/load* weighty, bulky, hefty, big, large, substantial, massive, enormous, mighty, colossal, ponderous, unwieldy, cumbersome, burdensome, awkward, unmanageable. **2** *a heavy responsibility* onerous, burdensome, difficult, oppressive, unbearable, intolerable. **3** *a heavy task* hard, difficult, arduous, laborious, demanding, exacting, irksome, troublesome, trying. **4** *a heavy blow* hard, forceful, strong, severe, grievous, harsh, intense, sharp, stinging, penetrating, overwhelming. **5** *a heavy man* large, bulky, hulking, stout, overweight, fat, obese, corpulent, portly, tubby, paunchy, lumbering. **6** *a heavy mist* dense, thick, solid. **7** *heavy ground* difficult, muddy, sticky, considerable, miry, boggy, clayey, clogged. **8** *heavy traffic/losses/crop* very much/great, large, considerable, considerable quantities of, abundant, copious, profuse, superabundant, huge numbers of. **9** *heavy fighting* severe, intense, serious, grave. **10** *heavy newspapers* serious, grave, deep, sombre, profound. **11** *heavy reading* difficult, dull, over-serious, tedious, boring, uninteresting, dry, wearisome, dry as dust. **12** *feeling heavy after dinner* sleepy, drowsy, sluggish, inactive, indolent, inept, idle, apathetic, listless, torpid. **13** *heavy of heart* sad, sorrowful, downcast, dejected, disconsolate, disheartened, despondent, downhearted, depressed, crestfallen, disappointed, grieving, gloomy, melancholy. **14** *heavy with child* burdened, encumbered, weighted down, laden, loaded, oppressed. **15** *heavy seas/waves* rough, wild, stormy, tempestuous, turbulent, squally, boisterous, violent. **16** *heavy day/skies* cloudy, overcast, grey, dark, dull, gloomy, dreary, leaden, louring. **17** *heavy features* coarse, ungraceful, broad, wide, jowly. **heavy on** *heavy on the petrol/butter* using a lot of, using too much, over-using, extravagant with, lavish with.
Opposites LIGHT; SLIGHT; HAPPY.

heavy-handed adjective **1** *heavy-handed and always breaking things* clumsy, awkward, maladroit, bungling, blundering, unhandy, inept, unskilful, inexpert, graceless, ungraceful, like a bull in a china shop; *inf.* ham-handed, ham-fisted. **2** *too heavy-handed to deal with the bereaved* insensitive, tactless, thoughtless, inept. **3** *a heavy-handed father* harsh, hard, stern, severe, oppressive, domineering, overbearing, tyrannical, despotic, autocratic, ruthless, merciless.

heckle verb shout down, shout at, interrupt, disrupt, barrack, jeer, taunt, badger, bait, harass, give trouble to, pester; *inf.* give someone a hard time.

hectic adjective *a hectic day/life* very busy, very active, frantic, frenetic, frenzied, bustling, flustering, flurried, fast and furious, turbulent,

tumultuous, confused, exciting, excited, wild.
Opposites QUIET; CALM; LEISURELY.

hector verb bully, torment, intimidate, ride
roughshod over, browbeat, cow, coerce, bulldoze, steamroller, strong-arm, badger, bait,
harass, plague, provoke, threaten, menace; inf.
bulldoze, ballyrag.

hedge noun 1 planted a hedge round the garden
hedgerow, row of bushes, quickset. 2 grow a
hedge against the wind barrier, screen, protection, wind-break. 3 a hedge against inflation
safeguard, guard, protection, shield, cover,
insurance, insurance cover.

hedge verb 1 the trees hedge in the garden surround, enclose, encircle, circle, border, edge,
skirt. 2 hedged in by petty restrictions hem in,
confine, restrict, limit, hinder, obstruct,
impede. 3 she hedged when questioned equivocate, prevaricate, be vague/ambivalent, be non-
committal, dodge the question/issue, sidestep
the issue, hum and haw, beat about the bush,
pussyfoot around, temporize, quibble; inf. beg/
duck the question, waffle. 4 hedge yourself
against inflation safeguard, guard, protect,
cover, shield, take out insurance, take out
insurance cover, insure oneself.

heed noun pay no heed heedfulness, attention,
attentiveness, notice, note, regard, regardful-
ness, mindfulness, mind, respect, consideration, thought, care, caution, watchfulness,
wariness, chariness.

heed verb heed what they say pay heed to, be
heedful of, pay attention to, attend to, take
notice of, take note of, notice, note, pay regard
to, bear in mind, be mindful of, mind, mark,
consider, take into account/consideration, be
guided by, follow, obey, adhere to, observe,
take to heart, be on guard for, be alert to, be
cautious of, watch out for.

heedful adjective heedful of advice attentive,
careful, mindful, cautious, prudent, circumspect, wary, chary, observant, watchful, vigilant, alert, on guard, on the alert, on one's
toes, on the qui vive.

heedless adjective unheeding, inattentive,
careless, incautious, unmindful, disregardful,
regardless, unnoticing, unthinking, thoughtless, improvident, unwary, oblivious, unobservant, unwatchful, unvigilant, negligent,
neglectful, rash, reckless, foolhardy, precipitate.
Opposites HEEDFUL; ATTENTIVE; MINDFUL.

heel noun 1 the heel of a shoe heelpiece, wedge,
wedge heel, stiletto, stiletto heel, platform
heel. 2 the heel of the loaf crust, end, remnant,
remainder, tail-end, stump, butt, rump. 3 he's
an utter heel scoundrel, cad, blackguard; inf. rat,
swine, rotter, bounder. **Achilles' heel** weak
spot, weakness, vulnerable spot, soft underbelly, downfall, undoing. **down at heel** shabby,
shabbily-dressed, poorly-dressed, out-at-
elbows, seedy, run-down, slovenly, slipshod.
take to one's heels run away, run off, take
flight, flee, escape; inf. show a clean pair of
heels, skedaddle, hightail it, hotfoot it, split,
vamoose.

heel verb ships heeling over cant, tilt, list, tip,
lean, lean over, keel over, incline, careen.

heft verb heft the load lift, lift up, raise, raise up,
hoist, hike up, heave, throw up, boost, boost
up.

hefty adjective 1 hefty young man heavy, bulky,
hulking, big, large, stout, massive, huge, muscular, brawny, strapping, solidly-built, powerfully-built, sturdy, rugged, stalwart, beefy. 2 a
hefty blow hard, forceful, heavy, powerful, vigorous, mighty. 3 a hefty load heavy, weighty,
big, large, massive, tremendous, immense,
bulky, awkward, unwieldy, cumbersome, ponderous. 4 a hefty price/bill substantial, sizeable,
expensive, huge, colossal, overpriced.
Opposites SLIGHT; LIGHT; SMALL.

height noun 1 measure the height highness, altitude, loftiness, elevation, distance/extent
upwards. 2 3 metres in height tallness, highness, stature. 3 on the mountain height top,
mountain-top, hilltop, summit, crest, crown,
pinnacle, peak, apex, vertex, apogee. 4 at the
height of his powers culmination, crowning
point, high point, peak, zenith, climax, consummation, perfection, apex. 5 the height of
fashion/rudeness utmost degree, uttermost, ultimate, acme, ne plus ultra, very limit, limit,
extremity, maximum, ceiling. 6 afraid of
heights | the heights above the town high ground,
high places, rising ground, hill, mountain,
cliff, precipice, summit.

heighten verb 1 heighten the ceiling make
higher, raise, lift, elevate. 2 heighten their status magnify, ennoble, exalt, enhance.
3 heighten the tension make greater, intensify,
raise, increase, add to, augment, build up,
boost, strengthen, amplify, magnify, aggravate, enhance, improve.

heinous adjective heinous crimes/criminal atrocious, abominable, abhorrent, odious,
detestable, loathsome, hateful, execrable,
wicked, monstrous, horrible, ghastly, shocking, flagrant, contemptible, reprehensible,
despicable.

heir, heiress noun beneficiary, legatee, inheritor, inheritress, inheritrix, successor, next in
line, scion.

helix noun spiral, screw, corkscrew, whorl,
twist, coil, loop, volute, curl, curlicue.

hell noun 1 wicked spirits in hell infernal
regions, inferno, hellfire, eternal fire, fire and
brimstone, nether world, lower world, abode
of evil spirits, abode of the damned, perdition,
abyss, bottomless pit, Hades, Acheron, Tar-
tarus, Erebus, Gehenna. 2 it was hell in the
battle purgatory, torment, torture, misery, suffering, affliction, anguish, agony, ordeal,
wretchedness, nightmare, woe, tribulation, trials and tribulations. 3 get hell from the teacher
upbraiding, scolding, castigation, vituperation,
reprimand, censure, criticism, disapprobation;
inf. what for. **hell for leather** as fast/quickly/
rapidly/speedily/swiftly as possible, very fast/
quickly/rapidly/speedily/swiftly/hurriedly, pell-
mell, post-haste, at the double, helter-skelter,
headlong, full tilt, hotfoot; inf. like a bat out of
hell. **raise hell** 1 partygoers raising hell party,

carouse, revel, make a noise, cause a disturbance, cause a commotion, be loud and noisy,
raise the roof, raise Cain. **2** *his father raised hell*
be very angry, be furious, be enraged, protest,
expostulate, complain, object, remonstrate,
raise the roof, raise Cain.

hellish *adjective* **1** *hellish spirits* diabolical,
demonic, demoniac, demoniacal, devilish,
fiendish, satanic, infernal, hell-born. **2** *a hellish slavemaster* brutal, brutish, barbarous, barbaric, savage, murderous, bloodthirsty, cruel,
wicked, inhuman, ferocious, vicious, ruthless,
relentless, detestable, abominable, accursed,
execrable, nefarious. **3** *a hellish day* unpleasant, nasty, disagreeable; *inf.* horrible, horrid,
awful.

hellish *adverb* *hellish cold/expensive* very, to a
great extent, extremely, excessively; *inf.*
awfully, jolly, ever so.

helm *noun* *the captain of the ship at the helm*
wheel, tiller, rudder, steering gear, automatic
pilot. **at the helm** *the managing director at the
helm of the firm* in charge, in command, in control, directing, in authority, in the seat of
authority, at the wheel, in the driving seat, in
the saddle.

help *verb* **1** *help the old lady off the bus* assist,
aid, lend a helping hand, lend a hand, guide,
be of service to, be useful to, succour,
befriend. **2** *help the charity* assist, aid, contribute to, support, back, promote, boost, give
a boost to, uphold. **3** *help the pain/situation*
soothe, relieve, ameliorate, alleviate, mitigate,
assuage, remedy, cure, heal, improve, ease,
facilitate, restore. **4** *can I help you?* serve, be of
assistance/help, give help. **5** *he helped himself to
my books* take, appropriate, take possession of,
commandeer, steal, make free with; *inf.* pinch,
walk off with, nick. **cannot help** *he cannot help
it/snoring* be unable to prevent/stop/cease/halt/
avoid/abstain from/refrain from/keep from/for-
bear from/break the habit of.

help *noun* **1** *give the old lady some help* assistance, aid, helping hand, service, use, guidance, benefit, advantage, avail, support,
backing, succour. **2** *no help for the condition*
relief, amelioration, alleviation, mitigation,
assuagement, remedy, cure, healing, improvement, ease, restorative, corrective, balm,
salve. **3** *ask the help for assistance* helper, assistant, employee, worker, hired help, maid,
domestic help, servant, daily.

helper *noun* **1** *the jumble sale helpers gathered
together* assistant, aider, aid worker. **2** *the chief
and his helper* assistant, subsidiary, aide, adjutant, deputy, second, second-in-command, auxiliary, right-hand man/woman, henchman,
girl/man Friday; *inf.* sidekick. **3** *the author and
his helpers* colleague, associate, co-worker, helpmate, helpmeet, partner, ally, collaborator.

helpful *adjective* **1** *a helpful suggestion* useful,
of use, of service, beneficial, advantageous,
valuable, profitable, instrumental, constructive, practical, productive. **2** *helpful people* supportive, friendly, kind, obliging,
accommodating, cooperative, sympathetic,
considerate, caring, neighbourly, charitable,
benevolent.
Opposites USELESS; UNSYMPATHETIC.

helping *noun* *a second helping of potatoes* serving,
portion, ration, piece, plateful, bowlful, spoonful.

helpless *adjective* **1** *a helpless invalid* weak,
feeble, disabled, impotent, incapable, infirm,
debilitated, powerless, dependent, unfit,
invalid, bedridden, paralysed; *inf.* laid-up.
2 *troops left helpless in the wilderness* defenceless,
unprotected, vulnerable, exposed, abandoned,
forlorn, destitute, desolate.
Opposites FIT; CAPABLE.

helpmate *noun* associate, partner, companion,
helper, helpmeet.

helter-skelter *adverb* *run helter-skelter* hastily,
hurriedly, as fast/quickly/rapidly/speedily as
possible, pell-mell, headlong, rashly, recklessly,
precipitately, impetuously, impulsively, carelessly, heedlessly, wildly.

hem *noun* *the decorative hem on a skirt* border,
edge, edging, trim, trimming, fringe, frill,
flounce, valance.

HERALDIC TERMS

accrued	brisure	gorged	potent
allusive arms	cabré	guardant	proper
amethyst	canton	gules	purpure
annulated cross	chaplet	honour point	quadrate
argent	charge	impaled	quartered
armed	chevron	lined	rampant
aversant	chief	lodged	rayoné
azure	cordon	lozenge	regardent
bar	couchant	main	reversed
barrulet	courant	moline	rustre
baton sinister	crest	mullet	sable
bearing	delf	naissant	saltire
bend	dexter	or	sanguine
bendlet	ecartelé	ordinary	shield
bevel	entire	orle	sinister
bezant	ermine	passant	tawney
billet	etoile	pheon	tincture
blazon	fess point	pile	vair
bordure	fimbriated	point	vert

hem verb **1** hem the dress put a hem on, bind, edge, trim, fringe. **2** trees hemming the lake border, edge, skirt, surround, encircle, circle, enclose, encompass. **3** feel hemmed in by trees/restrictions close in, shut in, hedge in, pen in, keep within bounds, confine, constrain, restrain, restrict, limit, trap.

hence adverb hence my decision not to go therefore, thus, on that account, because of that, for this reason, consequently, ergo.

henceforth adverb henceforth you will arrive on time from now on, from this day/time on, from this day forth/forward, hereafter, in future, in the future, hence, henceforward, hereinafter, subsequently, in time to come, after this.

henchman noun assistant, aide, supporter, follower, right-hand man/woman, girl/man Friday, adjutant, subordinate, underling, lackey, flunkey, toady, hired killer/assassin; inf. sidekick, hit man, hatchet man, hood.

henpecked adjective henpecked husbands bullied, dominated, browbeaten, nagged, subjugated, led by the nose, without a mind of one's own, cringing, cowering, meek, timid, docile; inf. under the thumb.

herald noun **1** news announced by the court herald messenger, crier, announcer, bearer of tidings, courier. **2** a herald of things to come forerunner, precursor, harbinger, usher, sign, omen, portent, indication, augury.

herald verb **1** companies heralding their new products announce, make public, make known, proclaim, broadcast, publicize, advertise, promote, promulgate, trumpet, beat the drum about. **2** prototypes heralding major new inventions usher in, pave the way for, show in, harbinger, precede, be the forerunner/precursor of, portend, indicate, augur, presage, promise, foreshadow, forebode, foretoken.

heraldry noun. See table.

herb noun. See table. See also table at SPICE.

HERBS	
angelica	marjoram
anise	mint
basil	oregano
bay leaf	parsley
bergamot	peppermint
borage	pot-herb
camomile	rosemary
chervil	rue
chicory	saffron
chives	sage
comfrey	savory
dill	sesame
fennel	sorrel
fenugreek	spearmint
lavender	sweet cicely
lemon mint	tarragon
lovage	thyme

Herculean adjective a Herculean task arduous, laborious, back-breaking, onerous, strenuous, difficult, hard, tough, formidable, huge, massive, uphill.

herd noun **1** a herd of cattle drove, collection, assemblage, flock, pack, cluster. See table at COLLECTION. **2** flocks tended by a herd shepherd, cowherd, cattle-man, cowman, herdsman, herder, drover. **3** a herd of people crowd, horde, multitude, mob, mass, host, throng, swarm, press. **4** ignore the tastes of the herd the masses, the mob, the populace, the rabble, the riff-raff, the hoi polloi, peasants; inf. plebs, proles, the great unwashed.

herd verb **1** herd the sheep into the pens drive, round up, shepherd, guide, lead, force, urge, goad. **2** people herding together in the hall assemble, gather, collect, congregate, flock, rally, muster, huddle, get together. **3** shepherds herding the sheep look after, take care of, watch, stand guard over, guard, tend.

here adverb **1** bring it here | he died here to/at/in this place/spot/location, hither, to here. **2** here I must pause now, at this point, at this point in time, at this time, at this juncture.

hereafter adverb hereafter to be called the author after this, from now on, from this day/time on, from this day forth/forward, in future, in the future, hence, henceforth, henceforward. See HENCEFORTH.

hereafter noun believe in the hereafter life after death, the after-life, life to come, the after-world, next world, the beyond, immortality, heaven, paradise.

hereditary adjective **1** hereditary characteristics genetic, genetical, congenital, innate, inborn, inherent, inbred, family, transmissible, transferrable. **2** hereditary property inherited, handed down, obtained by inheritance, bequeathed, willed, transferred, transmitted, family, ancestral.

heredity noun this disorder is the result of heredity passing on of genetic characteristics; genetics, genetic make-up, genes, congenital characteristics/traits.

heresy noun apostasy, dissent, dissension, dissidence, unbelief, scepticism, agnosticism, atheism, nonconformity, unorthodoxy, separatism, sectarianism, free thinking, heterodoxy, recusancy, schism, revisionism, idolatry, paganism.

heretic noun apostate, dissenter, dissident, unbeliever, sceptic, agnostic, atheist, nonconformist, separatist, sectarian, free thinker, renegade, recusant, schismatic, revisionist, idolater, pagan.

heretical adjective heretical beliefs/views dissident, sceptical, agnostic, atheistical, nonconformist, separatist, sectarian, free-thinking, heterodox, unorthodox, renegade, recusant, schismatic, revisionist, idolatrous, pagan.

heritage noun **1** proud of his country's heritage history, tradition, background. **2** proud of his family heritage ancestry, lineage, descent, extraction, family, dynasty, bloodline, heredity, birth. **3** receive a heritage from his father inheritance, legacy, bequest, endowment, estate, patrimony, portion, birthright, lot.

hermit noun recluse, solitary, anchorite/anchoress, ancress, eremite, stylite, pillarist, pillar-saint, ascetic.

hermitage *noun* retreat, refuge, haven, shelter, sanctuary, sanctum, sanctum sanctorum, asylum, hideaway.

hero *noun* **1** *the hero of the battle/hour* champion, conquering hero, victor, conqueror, brave man, man of courage, great man, man of the hour, celebrity, lion, cavalier, paragon, shining example, exemplar, paladin, knight, *beau idéal*. **2** *the teacher was the girl's hero* idol, ideal, ideal man/woman, popular figure; *inf.* heart-throb. **3** *the hero of the play/opera* principal male character/role, lead actor, leading man, male lead, male star/superstar, male protagonist.
Opposites COWARD; VILLAIN.

heroic *adjective* **1** *heroic soldier/deeds* brave, courageous, valiant, valorous, intrepid, fearless, gallant, stout-hearted, lion-hearted, bold, daring, undaunted, dauntless, doughty, manly, virile, chivalrous. **2** *read tales of heroic characters/myths* classic, classical, Homeric, mythological, legendary, fabulous. **3** *heroic language* epic, epical, Homeric, grandiloquent, high-flown, high-sounding, extravagant, grandiose, bombastic, rhetorical, pretentious, turgid, magniloquent, orotund, elevated.
Opposites COWARDLY; TIMID; SIMPLE.

heroine *noun* **1** *declared a heroine for saving the child* brave woman, woman of courage, great woman, woman of the hour, celebrity, paragon, shining example. **2** *the heroine of the play/opera* principal female character/role, lead actress, leading lady, female lead, female star/superstar, prima donna, diva, female protagonist.

heroism *noun* bravery, courage, courageousness, valour, valiance, intrepidity, fearlessness, gallantry, stout-heartedness, lion-heartedness, boldness, daring, dauntlessness, doughtiness, manliness, virility, mettle, spirit, fortitude, chivalry.

hero worship *noun* idolization, putting on a pedestal, adulation, worship, adoration, glorification, exaltation, idealization, admiration, high esteem, veneration.

hesitancy *noun* **1** *hesitancy when making decisions* uncertainty, unsureness, doubt, doubtfulness, scepticism, irresolution, indecision, indecisiveness, vacillation, oscillation, shilly-shallying, stalling, cunctation. **2** *show hesitancy about interfering* reluctance, unwillingness, disinclination, demurral, scruples, misgivings, qualms.

hesitant *adjective* **1** *hesitant when making decisions* hesitating, uncertain, unsure, doubtful, dubious, sceptical, irresolute, indecisive, vacillating, wavering, oscillating, shilly-shallying, hanging back, stalling, delaying, cunctatory, disinclined, unwilling, half-hearted, lacking confidence, diffident, timid, shy. **2** *hesitant about giving advice* reluctant, unwilling, disinclined, diffident, having scruples/misgivings/qualms about.
Opposites DETERMINED; FIRM; CONFIDENT.

hesitate *verb* **1** *always hesitate before making a decision* pause, delay, hang back, wait, be uncertain, be unsure, be doubtful, be indeci-

sive, vacillate, oscillate, waver, dither, shilly-shally, dally, stall, temporize; *inf.* dilly-dally; *Scots* swither. **2** *she hesitates to interfere* be reluctant, be unwilling, be disinclined, shrink from, hang back from, think twice about, baulk at, demur from, scruple to, have misgivings/qualms about, be diffident about. **3** *he hesitates a lot when giving a speech* stammer, stumble, stutter, falter, hum and haw, fumble for words, be halting, halt.

hesitation *noun* **1** *they never acted without some hesitation* pause, delay, cunctation, hanging back, waiting, waiting period, uncertainty, unsureness, doubt, doubtfulness, dubiousness, scepticism, irresolution, indecisiveness, vacillation, wavering, oscillation, shilly-shallying, stalling, temporizing; *inf.* dilly-dallying; *Scots* swithering. **2** *feel some hesitation about interfering* reluctance, unwillingness, disinclination, demurral, scruples, misgivings, qualms. **3** *complain about his hesitation when speaking publicly* stammering, stumbling, stuttering, faltering, humming and hawing, fumbling for words, haltingness.

hew *verb* **1** *hew down a tree* chop, chop down, hack, hack down, axe, cut/saw down, fell. **2** *hew off branches* lop, cut off, chop off, sever, trim, prune. **3** *hew a piece of wood into a figure* carve, sculpt, sculpture, shape, fashion, form, model, whittle, chip, hammer, chisel, rough-hew.

heyday *noun* prime, prime of life, bloom, full flowering, flowering, peak, peak of perfection, pinnacle, culmination, crowning point, salad days.

hiatus *noun* **1** *a hiatus in the manuscript* gap, break, lacuna, blank, discontinuity, interruption. **2** *an anatomical hiatus* opening, aperture, cavity, hole, fissure, cleft, foramen, breach. **3** *a hiatus in the programme* interval, intermission, pause, lull, rest, break, suspension, abeyance.

hibernate *verb* sleep, winter, overwinter, lie dormant, be idle, lie low, stagnate, vegetate; *inf.* hole up.

hidden *adjective* **1** *hidden treasure* concealed, unrevealed, secret, unseen, out of sight, not visible, not on view, covered, masked, shrouded. **2** *a hidden meaning/motive* secret, concealed, obscure, indistinct, indefinite, unclear, vague, cryptic, mysterious, covert, under wraps, abstruse, arcane, recondite, clandestine, ulterior, unfathomable, inexplicable, occult, mystical.

hide *verb* **1** *prisoners hiding from the police* go into hiding, conceal oneself, take cover, find a hiding-place, lie low, keep out of sight, secrete oneself, go to ground, go underground, cover one's tracks; *inf.* hole up. **2** *hide the jewels* secrete, conceal, put in a hiding-place, store away, stow away, stash, lock up. **3** *clouds hiding the sun* obscure, cloud, darken, block, eclipse, obstruct. **4** *hide one's motives* keep secret, conceal, keep dark, withhold, suppress, hush up, mask, veil, shroud, camouflage, dissemble, disguise; *inf.* keep mum, keep under one's hat.
Opposites REVEAL; DISCLOSE.

hide *noun an animal's hide* skin, pelt, coat, fur, fleece.

hideaway *noun* hiding-place, den, lair, retreat, shelter, refuge, hermitage, cache; *inf.* hide-out, hidey-hole.

hidebound *adjective hidebound officials/ideas* narrow-minded, narrow, intolerant, conventional, fixed in one's views, set in one's opinions/ways, intractable, uncompromising, rigid, prejudiced, bigoted, conservative, ultra-conservative, reactionary, orthodox, fundamentalist, strait-laced.

hideous *adjective* **1** *a hideous sight* ugly, unsightly, grotesque, monstrous, repulsive, repellent, revolting, gruesome, disgusting, grim, ghastly, macabre. **2** *a hideous crime* horrible, horrific, horrendous, horrifying, frightful, shocking, dreadful, outrageous, monstrous, appalling, terrible, terrifying, heinous, abominable, foul, vile, odious, loathsome, contemptible, execrable.
Opposites BEAUTIFUL; PLEASANT.

hide-out *noun* hiding-place, hideaway, retreat, shelter. *See* HIDEAWAY.

hiding *noun got a good hiding from his father* beating, thrashing, whipping, caning, spanking, flogging, drubbing, thumping, battering; *inf.* walloping, licking, tanning, whaling, lathering, larruping.

hie *verb* hurry, hasten, go quickly, speed, rush, run, dash, scamper, scuttle, dart, tear.

hierarchy *noun* ranking, grading, social order, class system, pecking order.

hieroglyphics *plural noun* code, cipher, cryptogram, cryptograph, shorthand; *inf.* scribble, scrawl.

high *adjective* **1** *a high building* tall, lofty, elevated, soaring, towering, steep. **2** *a high official* high-ranking, leading, top, ruling, powerful, important, principal, chief, main, prominent, eminent, influential, distinguished, notable, exalted, illustrious. **3** *high ideals* high-minded, noble, virtuous, moral, lofty. **4** *a high wind* intense, extreme, strong, forceful, vigorous, powerful, potent, sharp, violent. **5** *high prices* dear, top, excessive, stiff, inflated, exorbitant, extortionate, high-priced, expensive, costly; *inf.* steep. **6** *a high lifestyle* high-living, extravagant, luxurious, lavish, rich, grand, prodigal, sybaritic. **7** *have a high opinion of them* good, favourable, approving, admiring, flattering. **8** *the children are high before the holidays* overexcited, excited, boisterous, in high spirits, high-spirited, ebullient, bouncy, elated, ecstatic, euphoric, exhilarated, joyful, merry, happy, cheerful, jolly; *inf.* high as a kite. **9** *high on drugs* drugged, drug-affected, intoxicated, inebriated, delirious, hallucinating; *inf.* stoned, turned on, on a trip, tripping, hyped up, freaked out, spaced out. **10** *high voice/notes* high-pitched, acute, high-frequency, soprano, treble, piping, shrill, sharp-toned, piercing, penetrating. **11** *the meat/cheese is high* going bad, going off, rotting, smelling, tainted; *inf.* ponging, niffy, whiffy.
high and dry *ships/wives left high and dry* stranded, marooned, abandoned, helpless, des-

titute, bereft. **high and mighty** *high and mighty people looking down on the poor* haughty, arrogant, self-important, proud, conceited, egotistic, overweening, overbearing, snobbish, condescending, disdainful, supercilious, imperious; *inf.* stuck-up, uppity, highfalutin. **in high dudgeon** in indignation, indignant, in anger, angrily, angry, with resentment, resentful, offended, vexed, in a huff; *inf.* peeved.
Opposites LOW; LOWLY; DEEP.

high *adverb flying high in the sky* high up, far up, way up, at a great height, at altitude, aloft. **high and low** *look high and low* everywhere, all over, far and near, far and wide, in every nook and cranny, extensively, exhaustively.

high *noun* **1** *profits/temperatures reached a new high* high level, height, record, record level, peak, summit, top, zenith, apex. **2** *he's on a high with drugs* intoxication, delirium, ecstasy, euphoria, transports; *inf.* trip, freak-out.

high-born *adjective* noble, noble-born, of noble birth, well-born, aristocratic, patrician, blue-blooded.

highbrow *noun* intellectual, scholar, savant, mastermind, genius; *inf.* egghead, brain, brainbox, bookworm; *Am.* Brahmin.

highbrow *adjective highbrow person/programme/pursuits* intellectual, scholarly, bookish, cultured, cultivated, educated, sophisticated; *inf.* brainy.

high-class *adjective* superior, luxurious, de luxe, select, choice, élite, top-flight, first-rate, elegant, posh, upper-class, up-market; *inf.* tip-top, A1, super, super-duper, classy.

highfalutin *adjective* pompous, pretentious, affected, supercilious, condescending, grandiose, lofty, magniloquent, bombastic; *inf.* swanky.

high-flown *adjective uses very high-flown language* high-sounding, bombastic, grandiloquent, magniloquent, overdone, overdrawn, ornate, exaggerated, elaborate, extravagant, flowery, florid, pretentious, overblown.

high-handed *adjective high-handed person/manner* arbitrary, autocratic, dictatorial, despotic, tyrannical, domineering, oppressive, peremptory, imperious, overbearing, arrogant, haughty, lordly; *inf.* bossy.

highland *noun* plateau, tableland, ridge, heights, hill, hilly country, mountain, mountainous region, uplands.

highlight *noun this is the highlight of the day/show/tour* outstanding feature, main feature, feature, high point, high spot, best part, climax, peak, memorable part, focal point, focus, centre of interest, cynosure.

highlight *verb a programme highlighting famine* give prominence to, call attention to, bring to the fore, focus attention on, feature, place emphasis on, give emphasis to, emphasize, accentuate, accent, stress, underline, spotlight, bring home, point up.

highly *adverb* **1** *highly entertaining/inflammable* very, very much, to a great extent, greatly, extremely, decidedly, certainly, exceptionally, tremendously, vastly, immensely, eminently, supremely, extraordinarily. **2** *speak highly of* approvingly, favourably, well, warmly, appreciatively, admiringly, with approbation, enthusiastically.

highly strung *adjective highly strung artist/racehorse* nervous, nervy, easily upset/agitated, on edge, edgy, excitable, tense, taut, stressed, temperamental, neurotic, irritable, overwrought, restless, wound up.

high-minded *adjective high-minded intellectuals/ ideals* noble-minded, moral, virtuous, ethical, upright, righteous, principled, honourable, good, fair, pure, lofty, elevated.

high-powered *adjective high-powered executives* dynamic, aggressive, assertive, energetic, driving, ambitious, go-ahead, effective, enterprising, vigorous, forceful; *inf.* go-getting.

high-pressure *adjective high-pressure salesmen | used high-pressure sales techniques* aggressive, insistent, persistent, intensive, forceful, high-powered, importunate, bludgeoning, coercive, compelling, persuasive, not taking no for an answer; *inf.* pushy.

high-priced *adjective* expensive, dear, costly, exorbitant, extortionate, excessive, stiff; *inf.* pricey, steep.

high-sounding *adjective high-sounding language/ phrases* high-flown, bombastic, grandiloquent, magniloquent, elaborate, pretentious. *See* HIGH-FLOWN.

high-spirited *adjective* spirited, lively, full of life, animated, vibrant, vital, dynamic, active, energetic, full of vim, vigorous, boisterous, bouncy, frolicsome, effervescent, buoyant, cheerful, exuberant, ebullient, exhilarated, vivacious, joyful, full of fun.

high spirits *plural noun* liveliness, animation, vitality, dynamism, boisterousness, bounciness, cheerfulness, exuberance, vivacity, joy, *joie de vivre. See* HIGH-SPIRITED.

hijack *verb* commandeer, seize, expropriate, take over, skyjack.

hike *verb* **1** *hike over the hills* walk, march, tramp, trek, trudge, plod, ramble, wander, backpack; *inf.* hoof it, leg it, take shanks's pony. **2** *he hiked up his trousers/load* hitch up, pull up, jack up, lift, raise. **3** *they've hiked up the prices* raise, increase, put up, add to; *inf.* jack up.

hike *noun go on a hike* walk, march, tramp, trek, ramble, trudge, wander.

hilarious *adjective* **1** *a hilarious play/story* very funny, extremely amusing, humorous, entertaining, comical, uproarious, side-splitting. **2** *a hilarious party* amusing, entertaining, uproarious, merry, jolly, mirthful, animated, vivacious, sparkling, exuberant, boisterous, noisy, rowdy.
Opposites SAD; SERIOUS.

hilarity *noun the joke provoked great hilarity* amusement, comedy, mirth, laughter, merriment, levity, glee, high spirits.

hill *noun* **1** *the hills behind the town* elevation, heights, high land, hillock, hilltop, knoll, hummock, mound, rising ground, tor, mount, fell, ridge; *Scots* brae. *See table at* RANGE. **2** *cars going* slowly up the hill slope, rise, incline, gradient, acclivity; *Scots* brae. **3** *a hill of rubbish* mountain, heap, pile, mound, stack, drift.

hillock *noun* knoll, barrow, knob, hummock, monticule; *dial.* knap.

hilt *noun* handle, haft, handgrip, grip, shaft, hold, helve. **to the hilt** *back the leader to the hilt* completely, fully, wholly, entirely, totally, to the maximum extent, all the way.

hind *adjective horse's hind legs* rear, back, hinder, posterior, caudal.

hinder *verb hinder their efforts/progress* hamper, impede, hold back, interfere with, delay, hold up, slow down, retard, obstruct, inhibit, handicap, hamstring, block, interrupt, check, trammel, forestall, curb, baulk, thwart, frustrate, foil, baffle, stymie, stop, bring to a halt, arrest, abort, defer, prevent, debar.
Opposites AID; FACILITATE; EXPEDITE.

hindmost *adjective hindmost wagon in the train* last, furthest behind, furthest back, rearmost, rear, nearest the rear, endmost, most remote.

hindrance *noun prove a hindrance to their plans* impediment, obstacle, interference, obstruction, handicap, block, restraint, interruption, check, bar, barrier, drawback, snag, difficulty, stumbling-block, encumbrance, curb, stoppage, trammel, deterrent, prevention, debarment.
Opposites AID; HELP; ADVANTAGE.

hinge *verb plans hinge on finance* depend on, turn on, be contingent on, hang on, pivot on, revolve around, rest on, centre on.

hint *noun* **1** *give a hint that he was leaving* inkling, clue, suggestion, innuendo, tip-off, insinuation, implication, indication, mention, allusion, intimation, whisper, a word to the wise. **2** *write gardening hints* tip, pointer, advice, help, suggestion; *inf.* wrinkle. **3** *just a hint of garlic* suspicion, suggestion, trace, touch, dash, soupçon, speck, sprinkling, tinge, whiff, breath, taste, scent.

hint *verb he hinted that he was leaving* give a clue, suggest, give someone a tip-off, insinuate, imply, indicate, mention, allude to the fact, make an allusion, intimate, let it be known, signal, make a reference to the fact, refer to the fact.

hippy *noun* beatnik, flower person/child, bohemian; *inf.* drop-out.

hire *verb* **1** *hire a boat/car/dress* rent, lease, charter, engage. **2** *hire staff* appoint, sign on, take on, engage, employ, secure the services of, enlist, contract with.

hire *noun* **1** *worthy of their hire* pay, salary, wage, earnings, remuneration, fee, charge, stipend, price. **2** *the hire will cost £100* rent, rental, lease.

hiss *noun* **1** *the hiss of the snake/kettle* hissing, sibilation, sibilance, buzz, whistle, wheeze. **2** *the hisses of the audience* boo, jeer, shout of derision, catcall, hoot, whistle, clamour, scoffing; *inf.* raspberry.

hiss *verb* **1** *snake/kettle was hissing* sibilate, buzz, whistle, wheeze. **2** *the audience is hissing* boo, jeer, cry/howl down, shout one's disapproval, deride, catcall, utter catcalls, hoot, scoff at, scorn, mock, taunt, decry, ridicule, revile; *inf.* blow raspberries.

historian *noun* chronicler, annalist, archivist, recorder, historiographer, palaeographer, biographer, antiquarian. *See table.*

historic *adjective historic event/house* famous, famed, notable, celebrated, renowned, momentous, significant, important, consequential, red-letter, memorable, remarkable, outstanding, extraordinary, epoch-making.

historical *adjective* **1** *a historical rather than a legendary account* factual, recorded, documented, chronicled, archival, authentic, actual, attested, verified, confirmed. **2** *in historical times* old, past, former, prior, bygone, ancient; *lit.* of yore.

history *noun* **1** *the history of the times* annals, chronicles, records, public records, account, study, story, tale, saga, narrative, recital, reports, memoirs, biography, autobiography. **2** *what is the young man's history?* life story, background, antecedents, experiences, adventures, fortunes. **3** *that is history now* the past, former times, bygone days, yesterday, the old days, the good old days, days of old, time gone by, antiquity; *lit.* days of yore, olden days/ times, yesteryear.

hit *verb* **1** *his father hit him* strike, slap, smack, buffet, punch, box, cuff, beat, thump, batter, pound, pummel, thrash, hammer, bang, knock, swat; *inf.* whack, wallop, bash, belt, clout, clip, clobber, sock, biff, swipe. **2** *the car hit the lorry* run into, bang into, smash into, crash into, knock into, bump, collide with, meet head-on. **3** *her death hit him hard* affect, have an effect on, make an impression on, influence, make an impact on, leave a mark on, impinge on, move, touch, overwhelm, devastate, damage, hurt; *inf.* knock back, knock for six. **4** *hit the right tone in his speech | hit the bull's-eye* achieve, accomplish, reach, attain, arrive at, gain, secure, touch, strike. **hit home** *his remarks hit home* have the intended effect, reach the target, strike home, hit the mark. **hit it off** *the children hit it off right away* get on, get on well, be/get on good terms with, become friends, take to each other, warm to each other, find things in common; *inf.* be on the same wavelength. **hit on/upon** *hit on the solution* stumble on, chance on, light on, come upon, blunder on, discover, uncover, arrive at, think of, come up with. **hit out at** *hit out at his*

HISTORIANS

Acton, John, 1st Baron (1834–1902; Brit.)	Einhard (c. 770–840 A.D.; Frankish)	Michelet, Jules (1798–1874; Fr.)	Si ma Qian (c. 145–c. 85 B.C.; Chin.)
Adams, Henry (1838–1918; Am.)	Firdausi (c. 935–c. 1020; Pers.)	Mommsen, Theodor (1817–1903; Ger.)	Suetonius (c. 69–c. 140 A.D.; Rom.)
Anchieta, José de (1534–97; Port.)	Froissart, Jean (c. 1333–1401; Fr.)	Namier, Sir Lewis (1888–1960; Brit.)	Tabari, Muhammad ibn Jarir al-
Anna Comnena (1083–c. 1148 A.D.; Byzantine)	Gibbon, Edward (1737–94; Brit.)	Nennius (9th century A.D.; Welsh)	(838–923 A.D.; Arab.)
Arrian (2nd century A.D.; Rom.)	Gregory of Tours, St (c. 538–94 A.D.; Fr.)	Nevins, Allan (1890–1971; Am.)	Tacitus, Cornelius (c. 55–c. 120 A.D.; Rom.)
Ban Gu (32–92 A.D.; Chin.)	Guicciardini, Francesco (1483–1540; Floren-	Niebuhr, Barthold (1776–1831; Ger.)	Taylor, A. J. P. (1906–90; Brit.)
Beaglehole, John (1901–71; NZ)	tine)	Opitz (von Bober- feld), Martin (1597–1639; Ger.	Thiers, Louis Adolphe (1797–1877; Fr.)
Bede, St (c. 673–735 A.D.; Engl.)	Guizot, François (1787–1874; Fr.)	historiographer)	Toynbee, Arnold (1889–1975; Brit.)
Carlyle, Thomas (1795–1881; Scot.)	Herodotus (c. 484–c. 425 B.C.; Gk)	Otto of Freising (c. 1111–58; Ger.)	Trevelyan, George Macaulay (1876–1962; Brit.)
Cato the Elder (234–149 B.C.; Rom.)	Huizinga, Johan (1872–1945; Du.)	Pachymeres, Georgius (1242–c. 1310;	Trevor-Roper, Hugh, Lord Dacre (b. 1914;
Dilthey, Wilhelm (1833–1911; Ger. historiographer)	Ibn Khaldun (1332–1406; Arab.)	Byzantine)	Brit.)
Dio Cassius (c. 150–235 A.D.; Rom.)	Josephus, Flavius (c. 38–c. 100 A.D.; Jewish)	Parkman, Francis (1823–93; Am.)	von Ranke, Leopold (1795–1886; Ger.)
Diodorus Siculus (1st century B.C.; Gk)	Krochmal, Nachman (1785–1840; Jewish)	Polybius (c. 200–c. 120 B.C.; Gk)	Wedgwood, Dame Cicely (b. 1910; Brit.)
Dionysius of Halicar- nassus (1st century B.C.; Gk)	Livy (59 B.C.–17 A.D.; Rom.)	Prescott, William (1796–1859; Am.)	William of Malmes- bury (c. 1090–c. 1143;
Du Cange, Charles (1610–88; Fr.)	Macaulay, Thomas, 1st Baron (1800–59; Brit.)	Procopius (6th century A.D.; Byzan- tine)	Engl.)
	Madariaga y Rojo, Salvador de (1886–1978; Sp.)	Sallust (c. 86–c. 34 B.C.; Rom.)	William of Tyre (c. 1130–85; Fr.)
		Saxo Grammaticus (c. 1150–c. 1206; Da.)	Xenophon (c. 430–c. 354 B.C.; Gk)

enemies lash out at, attack, assail, strike out at, rail against, inveigh against, denounce, revile, condemn, castigate, censure, vilify.

hit *noun* **1** *the hit from his father* blow, slap, smack, buffet, punch, box, cuff, beating, thump, thumping, battering, bang; *inf.* whack, wallop, bashing, belting, clout, clobbering, swipe. See HIT *verb* 1. **2** *a nasty hit at her hair* gibe, taunt, jeer, piece of sarcasm; *inf.* dig.

hitch *verb* **1** *hitch the trailer to the car* fasten, connect, attach, join, couple, unite, tie, tether, bind, harness, yoke. **2** *hitching up their skirts/socks* pull up, hike up, jerk up; *inf.* yank up. **3** *hitching in France* hitch-hike, hitch a lift, thumb a lift.

hitch *noun* *what's the hitch?* hindrance, hold-up, delay, impediment, obstacle, obstruction, barrier, stoppage, stumbling-block, block, check, snag, catch, difficulty, problem, trouble.

hither *adverb* *he came hither* here, to here, over here, to this place, near, nearer, close, closer.

hitherto *adverb* *hitherto he was unemployed* until now, up until now, till now, up to now, so far, previously, thus far, heretofore, before, beforehand.

hit-or-miss *adjective* *a hit-or-miss attempt/method* haphazard, random, aimless, undirected, disorganized, indiscriminate, careless, casual, offhand, cursory, perfunctory.

hoar *noun* hoar-frost, frost, rime, rime frost, verglas, Jack Frost.

hoard *noun* *a hoard of food/money* store, stockpile, supply, reserve, reservoir, fund, cache, accumulation, heap, pile, mass, amassment, aggregation, conglomeration, treasure house, treasure trove; *inf.* stash.

hoard *verb* *hoard food/money* store, store up, stock up, stockpile, put by, put away, lay by, lay in, set aside, pile up, stack up, stow away, husband, save, buy up, accumulate, amass, heap up, collect, gather, garner, squirrel away; *inf.* stash away.

hoarder *noun* collector, saver, miser, niggard, magpie, squirrel.

hoarse *adjective* *a hoarse voice* croaking, croaky, throaty, harsh, rough, gruff, husky, gravelly, grating, rasping, guttural, raucous, discordant, cracked.
Opposites MELLOW; SMOOTH; SOFT.

hoary *adjective* **1** *hoary hair/head* grey, greyhaired, white, white-haired, silvery, silveryhaired, grizzled, grizzly. **2** *hoary gentleman* old, elderly, aged, at an advanced age, venerable, time-honoured. **3** *hoary jokes* old, antiquated, ancient, antique, old as the hills, hackneyed, trite.

hoax *noun* *the telephone call was a hoax* practical joke, joke, jest, prank, trick, ruse, deception, fraud, imposture, cheat, swindle; *inf.* con, fast one, spoof, scam.

hoax *verb* *hoax the old woman* play a practical joke on, play a joke/jest on, play a prank on, trick, fool, deceive, bluff, hoodwink, delude, dupe, take in, cheat, swindle, defraud, pull the wool over someone's eyes, gull; *inf.* con, pull a

fast one on, take someone for a ride, put one over on someone, spoof; *lit.* cozen.

hobble *verb* walk with difficulty, limp, walk with a limp, walk lamely, walk haltingly, falter, move unsteadily, shuffle, totter, stagger, reel; *Scots* hirple.

hobby *noun* leisure activity, leisure pursuit, leisure interest, pastime, diversion, recreation, relaxation, divertissement, sideline, entertainment, amusement, sport, game.

hobgoblin *noun* goblin, imp, elf, gnome, dwarf, bogey, bogeyman, evil spirit.

hobnob *verb* *hobnobbing with journalists* fraternize, associate, socialize, mingle, mix, keep company, go around, consort; *inf.* hang around, hang out.

hocus-pocus *noun* **1** *accuse the salesman of hocus-pocus* trickery, chicanery, deception, deceit, artifice, stratagem, sleight of hand, legerdemain, ruse, hoax, sham, delusion, pretence, imposture. **2** *the hocus-pocus spoken by the magician* spell, mumbo-jumbo, abracadabra, magic words, magic formula, incantation, chant, invocation, charm.

hodgepodge *noun*. See HOTCHPOTCH.

hog *noun* **1** *farmer raising hogs* pig, boar, swine, porker, grunter. **2** *hogs at the table* glutton, gourmand, gormandizer, cormorant, wolf, big eater, trencherman, trencherwoman; *inf.* pig, gannet.

hogwash *noun* *talking hogwash* nonsense, rubbish, gibberish, twaddle, drivel, balderdash, humbug, bunkum, trash; *inf.* gobbledook, piffle, bunk, bosh, tosh, bilge, tripe, rot, tommyrot, crap, hooey.

hoi polloi *noun* the common people, the populace, the masses, the many, the proletariat, the peasants, the commons, the commonality, the lower orders, the third estate, the rabble, the riffraff, the herd, the common herd, the mob, ragtag and bobtail; *inf.* plebs, proles, the great unwashed.

hoist *verb* *hoist the load on to the lorry* lift, raise, upraise, heave, jack up, hike up, elevate, erect.

hoist *noun* *need a hoist for the heavy load* crane, winch, tackle, capstan, pulley, jack, elevator, lift.

hold *verb* **1** *hold his hand* hold on to, clasp, clutch, grasp, grip, seize, clench, cling to; *lit.* cleave to. **2** *hold his sweetheart in his arms* embrace, hug, enfold, clasp, cradle, fondle. **3** *hold the relevant documents* have, possess, own, retain, keep. **4** *hold pleasant memories* cherish, harbour, treasure, retain. **5** *will it hold his weight* bear, carry, take, support, hold up, keep up, sustain, prop up, buttress, brace, suspend. **6** *police are holding the suspect* detain, confine, hold in custody, impound, constrain, keep under constraint, lock up, imprison, put behind bars, incarcerate. **7** *you cannot hold him from going* hold back, restrain, impede, check, bar, curb, stop, retard, delay, prevent. **8** *hold the interest of the audience* keep, maintain, occupy, engage, involve, absorb, engross, immerse, monopolize, arrest, catch, spellbind, fascinate, rivet. **9** *he holds a well-paid post* hold down, be in, occupy, fill, maintain, continue in, enjoy, boast. **10** *the bottle holds one litre* | *the hall holds 400 people* contain, have a capacity for, accommodate, take, comprise. **11** *we hold that he is guilty* maintain, think, believe, consider, regard, deem, judge, assume, presume, reckon, suppose, esteem. **12** *will the good weather hold?* go on, carry on, remain, continue, stay, persist, last, endure, keep up, persevere. **13** *the old rule still holds* hold good, stand, apply, be in force, be in operation, operate, remain valid, remain, exist, be the case. **14** *hold you responsible* make, think, consider, regard as, view, treat as. **15** *hold a meeting* call, convene, assemble, conduct, run, preside over, officiate at. **hold back 1** *hold back a laugh* keep back, suppress, repress, stifle, smother. **2** *hold back progress* prevent, impede, obstruct, hinder, check, curb, inhibit, restrain, control. **3** *hold back from hitting him* keep, desist, forbear, stop oneself, restrain oneself. **4** *hold back information* withhold, not disclose, suppress, refuse to disclose. **hold down 1** *hold down the people* oppress, repress, tyrannize, dominate. **2** *hold down prices* keep low, keep down, keep at a low level. **3** *hold down a job* hold, be in, occupy, fill, continue in. *See* HOLD *verb* 9. **hold forth 1** *hold forth about politics* speak at length, speak, talk, declaim, discourse, lecture, harangue, preach, orate, speechify, sermonize, perorate; *inf.* spout, spiel. **2** *hold forth the hand of friendship* hold out, extend, proffer, offer. *See* HOLD *verb* hold out. **hold off 1** *the storm held off* not occur, not happen, be delayed. **2** *hold off the attack* keep off, keep at bay, fend off, stave off, ward off, repel, repulse, rebuff. **3** *hold off making a decision* delay, postpone, put off, defer, keep from, refrain from, avoid. **hold on 1** *hold on to his hand* clasp, clutch, grasp. *See* HOLD *verb* 1. **2** *if the survivors can hold on* survive, last, carry on, keep going, continue; *inf.* hang on. **3** *hold on to the house* keep, keep/retain possession of, retain ownership of, not sell/give away, keep for oneself. **hold one's own 1** *they held their own in the battle* stand firm, stand fast, stand one's ground, maintain one's position, stay put, not be defeated. **2** *the patient is holding his own* survive, be still alive, not lose strength, do well. **hold out 1** *hold out the hand of friendship* extend, proffer, offer, present, hold forth. **2** *hold out against the attack* stand fast, stand firm, resist, withstand, endure, carry on, persist, persevere, fight to the end, fight to the last man; *inf.* hang on. **3** *as long as supplies hold out* last, continue, remain. **hold over** *hold the matter over until the next meeting* put off, postpone, defer, delay, defer, adjourn, suspend, waive. **hold up 1** *hold up progress* delay, hinder, impede, obstruct, retard, slow, slow down, set back, stop, bring to a halt, prevent. **2** *hold up his weight* hold, bear, carry, support, sustain. *See* HOLD *verb* 5. **3** *hold up the flag* | *she held up her father as an example* display, exhibit, show, put on show, present, flaunt, brandish. **4** *hold up a bank/train* | *they held up travellers* rob, commit armed robbery on, hold to ransom, waylay, mug; *inf.* stick up. **5** *will his story hold up* survive investigation, be convincing, bear examination, be verifiable, be provable, hold

water. **hold with** *he doesn't hold with modern education trends* approve of, agree with, be in favour of, support, give support to, subscribe to, countenance, take kindly to.
Opposites give up (*see* GIVE); hand over (*see* HAND); RELEASE.

hold *noun* **1** *keep a firm hold of the child's hand* grasp, grip, clutch, clasp. **2** *lose his hold on the cliff* foothold, footing, toe-hold, anchorage, purchase, leverage, prop, stay. **3** *government tightened its hold on the country* grip, power, control, dominion, authority, ascendancy. **4** *he has a hold over the younger boy* influence, mastery, dominance, sway; *inf.* pull, clout. **5** *put it on hold* pause, delay, postponement, deferment.

holder *noun* **1** *ticket-holder* | *the present holder of the title* owner, possessor, bearer, proprietor, keeper, custodian, purchaser, incumbent, occupant. **2** *cigarette-holder* container, case, casing, receptacle, stand, cover, covering, housing, sheath.

hold-up *noun* **1** *a hold-up on the motorway* delay, wait, stoppage, obstruction, bottleneck, traffic jam, hitch, snag, set-back, trouble, problem. **2** *a bank hold-up* robbery, theft, burglary, mugging; *inf.* stick-up.

hole *noun* **1** *a hole in the wall/material* opening, aperture, orifice, gap, space, breach, break, fissure, crack, rift, puncture, perforation, cut, incision, split, gash, rent, slit, vent, notch. **2** *a hole in the ground* excavation, pit, crater, shaft, mine, dug-out, cave, cavern, pothole, cavity, chamber, hollow, scoop, pocket, depression, dent, dint, dip. **3** *an animal's hole* burrow, lair, den, covert, earth, set, nest, retreat, shelter, recess. **4** *they took us to a real hole for a meal* slum, hovel; *inf.* dump, dive, joint. **5** *the captives were thrown into a black hole* dungeon, prison, cell, oubliette. **6** *spot the hole in their argument* flaw, fault, defect, loophole, crack, inconsistency, discrepancy, error, fallacy. **7** *they are in a financial hole* predicament, mess, plight, difficulty, trouble, corner, tight corner, spot, tight spot, quandary, dilemma, muddle, tangle, imbroglio; *inf.* fix, jam, scrape, pickle, hot water. **pick holes in** find fault with, criticize, pull to pieces, run down, cavil at, carp at, disparage, denigrate; *inf.* slag off, slate.

hole *verb* *rocks holed the ship* make a hole in, puncture, perforate, pierce, spike, stab, lacerate, gash, split, rent. **hole up 1** *the animals have holed up for the winter* hibernate, retire, go to sleep, lie dormant. **2** *the thieves have holed up somewhere* hide, hide out, lie low, conceal oneself, go underground.

hole-and-corner *adjective* *hole-and-corner affair/method* secret, secretive, in secret, furtive, stealthy, surreptitious, underhand, clandestine, backstair; *inf.* sneaky.

holiday *noun* **1** *go on holiday* | *take a holiday* vacation, break, time off, leave, leave of absence, furlough, sabbatical, day/week/month off, breathing-space. **2** *celebrate a holiday* festival day, saint's day, feast day, holy day, day of observance, festival, festivity, fête, gala day, carnival day, celebration, anniversary, public holiday, bank holiday. *See tables at* FESTIVAL, SAINT.

holier-than-thou · homogeneous

holier-than-thou *adjective* sanctimonious, self-righteous, unctuous, pietistic, pietistical, religiose, pharisaic, priggish, smug, self-satisfied; *inf.* goody-goody; *Scots* unco guid.

holiness *noun* sanctity, sanctitude, saintliness, sacredness, divineness, divinity, godliness, blessedness, spirituality, religiousness, piety, righteousness, goodness, virtue, virtuousness, purity.

hollow *adjective* **1** *a hollow vessel* empty, unfilled, vacant, void, not solid, hollowed out. **2** *hollow cheeks/marks* sunken, deep-set, dented, indented, depressed, concave, caved-in, incurvate, cavernous. **3** *a hollow sound* muffled, muted, low, dull, deep, rumbling, flat, toneless, dead, sepulchral. **4** *a hollow victory/triumph* valueless, worthless, useless, of no use, of no avail, unavailing, empty, fruitless, profitless, unprofitable, pointless, meaningless, insignificant, specious, pyrrhic. **5** *hollow compliments/condolences* insincere, hypocritical, feigned, artificial, false, dissembling, deceitful, sham, counterfeit, spurious, untrue, unsound, flimsy, faithless, treacherous, two-faced. **6** *feeling hollow* empty, hungry, famished, starving, starved, half-starved, ravenous. **beat someone hollow** trounce, thrash, rout, worst, defeat soundly, beat, overcome, overwhelm, outdo, surpass; *inf.* hammer.
Opposites SOLID; FULL; MEANINGFUL.

hollow *noun* **1** *hollows in the ground* depression, indentation, concavity, dent, dint, dip, dimple, hole, crater, cavern, pit, cavity, well, trough, basin, cup, bowl, niche, nook, cranny, recess. **2** *picnic in the hollow* valley, dell, dingle, dale, glen, gorge, ravine.

hollow *verb* *river banks hollowed out by water* scoop out, gouge out, dig out, excavate, furrow, groove, channel, indent, dent.

holocaust *noun* fire, inferno, conflagration, destruction, devastation, demolition, ravaging, annihilation; massacre, mass murder, carnage, slaughter, butchery, extermination, genocide, ethnic cleansing.

holy *adjective* **1** *a holy person* God-fearing, godly, pious, pietistic, devout, spiritual, religious, righteous, good, virtuous, moral, saintly, saintlike, sinless. **2** *a holy place* blessed, blest, sanctified, consecrated, hallowed, sacred, sacrosanct, dedicated, venerated, divine, religious.
Opposites SACRILEGIOUS; IMPIOUS.

home *noun* **1** *where is his home?* house, abode, domicile, residence, dwelling, dwelling-place, habitation. **2** *live a long way from home* home town, birthplace, homeland, native land, fatherland, motherland, mother country, country of origin. **3** *she comes from a good home* family, family background, family circle, household. **4** *estate agents advertising homes* house, flat, apartment, bungalow, terraced house, semi-detached house, detached house, cottage, accommodation; *inf.* pad, semi. **5** *private home for the elderly* residential home, institution, shelter, refuge, hostel, hospice, retirement home, nursing home, convalescent home/hospital, children's home, old people's home. **6** *the home of the buffalo | ancient tribes*

had their home here abode, habitat, natural habitat, environment, natural element, natural territory, original habitation, home ground, stamping-ground, haunt, domain. **at home 1** *is Jane at home?* in, present, available. **2** *at home in the academic world* familiar with, used to, comfortable, at ease, relaxed, in one's element, on familiar territory, on home ground. **3** *at home with computers* familiar with, proficient in, conversant with, skilled in, competent at, well-versed in; *inf.* well up in, up on. **4** *Lady Travers is at home* entertaining, receiving guests, giving a party. **bring home** *the programme brought home the tragedy of famine | bring home to her the risk she is taking* drive home, press home, make someone aware of, make someone conscious of, emphasize, stress, impress upon someone, underline, highlight. **nothing to write home about** nothing important, nothing worth mentioning, nothing to comment on, nothing out of the ordinary.

home *adjective* **1** *home issues, as opposed to international* domestic, internal, interior, local, national, native. **2** *home produce* home-grown, home-made, home-bred.

home *verb* **home in on** *home in on the main issue* aim at, focus on, focus attention on, concentrate on, pinpoint, zero in on, zoom in on.

homeland *noun* native land, country of origin, fatherland, motherland, mother country.

homeless *adjective* of no fixed abode, down-and-out, destitute, derelict, without a roof over one's head, vagrant; *inf.* dossing.

homelike *adjective* homely, homey, homy, comfortable, cosy, snug, cheerful, welcoming, friendly, congenial, hospitable, informal, relaxed, intimate; *inf.* comfy; *Am.* down-home, homestyle.

homely *adjective* **1** *homely atmosphere/place* homelike, comfortable, cosy, snug, welcoming, informal, relaxed. *See* HOMELIKE. **2** *a homely but friendly place* plain, simple, modest, unsophisticated, natural, everyday, ordinary, unaffected, unassuming, unpretentious. **3** *a homely girl* plain, plain-featured, plain-looking, unattractive, ill-favoured, ugly; *inf.* not much to look at, short on looks.
Opposites ELEGANT; GRAND; ELABORATE; BEAUTIFUL.

homespun *adjective* *homespun advice/philosophy* plain, simple, homely, modest, natural, artless, unsophisticated, unpolished, unrefined, inelegant, coarse, rough, rude, rustic.

homicidal *adjective* *homicidal maniac | has homicidal tendencies* murderous, death-dealing, mortal, deadly, lethal, violent, maniacal, berserk.

homicide *noun* **1** *found guilty of homicide* murder, manslaughter, killing, slaying, slaughter, assassination, patricide, matricide, infanticide. *See table at* ASSASSINATION. **2** *a convicted homicide* murderer, killer, slayer, assassin, patricide, matricide, infanticide; *inf.* hitman.

homily *noun* *gave a short homily on forgiveness* sermon, preaching, lecture, discourse, lesson, talk, speech, address, oration.

homogeneous *adjective* **1** *consisting of homogeneous parts* identical, alike, all alike, of the same kind, all the same, the same, all one, all of a piece, uniform, unvaried, unvarying, consistent. **2** *homogeneous substances* similar, kindred, akin, comparable, analogous, corresponding, parallel, correlative, cognate. **Opposites** DIFFERENT; DISSIMILAR; heterogeneous.

homogenize *verb* make uniform, combine, coalesce, fuse, merge, blend, emulsify.

homogenous *adjective.* See HOMOGENEOUS.

homosexual *adjective* **1** *homosexual men* gay, homoerotic, homophile; *inf. derog* bent, queer, camp, poofy. **2** *homosexual women* gay, lesbian, homoerotic, homophile; *inf. derog* butch.

homosexual *noun* **1** *he's a homosexual* gay, homophile; *inf. derog* queer, poof, queen; *Am. inf. derog* faggot, fag. **2** *she's a homosexual* gay, lesbian, homophile; *inf. derog* butch, dyke.

honest *adjective* **1** *honest people* upright, honourable, moral, ethical, principled, righteous, right-minded, virtuous, good, worthy, decent, law-abiding, high-minded, upstanding, just, fair, incorruptible, truthful, true, veracious, trustworthy, trusty, reliable, conscientious, scrupulous, reputable, dependable, loyal, faithful. **2** *an honest reply* truthful, sincere, candid, frank, direct, forthright, straightforward, open, genuine, plain-speaking, matter-of-fact, outspoken, blunt, undisguised, unfeigned, unequivocal. **3** *an honest mistake* real, true, genuine, authentic, actual, above-board, bona fide, proper, straight, fair and square; *inf.* on the level, honest-to-goodness. **4** *an honest judgement* fair, just, equitable, even-handed, impartial, objective, balanced, unprejudiced, disinterested, unbiased.
Opposites DISHONEST; INSINCERE; UNFAIR.

honestly *adverb* **1** *earn his living honestly* fairly, by fair means, by just means, lawfully, legally, legitimately, honourably, decently, ethically, morally, without corruption; *inf.* on the level. **2** *honestly, I tell you he's not going | she told me honestly she was leaving* to be honest, speaking truthfully, truthfully, speaking frankly, in all sincerity, candidly, frankly, openly, plainly, in plain language, to someone's face, straight out, without dissembling, without shilly-shallying; *inf.* straight up, Scouts' honour.

honesty *noun* **1** uprightness, honourableness, honour, integrity, morals, morality, ethics, principle, high principles, righteousness, rectitude, virtue, goodness, probity, worthiness, justness, fairness, incorruptibility, truthfulness, truth, veracity, trustworthiness, reliability, conscientiousness, reputability, loyalty, faithfulness, fidelity. See HONEST 1. **2** *the honesty of his reply* truthfulness, truth, sincerity, candour, frankness, forthrightness, openness, genuineness, bluntness. See HONEST 2. **3** *the honesty of his judgement* fairness, justness, justice, equitability, even-handedness, impartiality, objectiveness, lack of prejudice, lack of bias, balance.

honorarium *noun* remuneration, recompense, fee, salary, pay, emolument, reward.

honorary *adjective* *made an honorary member* nominal, in name/title only, titular, unofficial, *ex officio*, complimentary, unpaid.

honour *noun* **1** *a man of honour* honesty, uprightness, integrity, ethics, morals, high principles, righteousness, rectitude, virtue, goodness, decency, probity, worthiness, worth, fairness, justness, justice, truthfulness, trustworthiness, reliability, dependability, faithfulness, fidelity. **2** *the honour of winning the battle* fame, renown, glory, prestige, illustriousness, noble reputation, esteem, distinction, notability, credit; *inf.* kudos. **3** *his honour is at stake* reputation, good name, name. **4** *protecting a lady's honour* chastity, virginity, virtue, purity, innocence, modesty. **5** *treat the hero with honour* acclaim, acclamation, applause, accolades, tributes, homage, praise, compliments, lauding, eulogy, paeans, adoration, reverence, veneration, adulation, exaltation, glorification. **6** *it was an honour to serve him* privilege, source of pleasure/pride/satisfaction, pleasure, joy, compliment, favour.
Opposites DISHONOUR; DISGRACE; CONDEMNATION.

honour *verb* **1** *all his pupils honour him* hold in honour, have a high regard for, hold in esteem, esteem, respect, admire, defer to, reverence, revere, venerate, worship, idolize, value, prize. **2** *the crowd honoured the victor* acclaim, applaud, give accolades to, pay homage to, pay tribute to, lionize, praise, cheer, compliment, laud, eulogize, sing paeans to, panegyrize. **3** *honour the agreement/guarantee* fulfil, discharge, carry out, observe, keep, be true to, be faithful to, live up to. **4** *honour the cheque* cash, pay out money for, clear, accept, take, pass.

honourable *adjective* **1** *honourable men* honest, upright, ethical, moral, principled, high-principled, upstanding, righteous, right-minded, virtuous, good, decent, worthy, fair, just, true, truthful, trustworthy, trusty, reliable, dependable, faithful. **2** *an honourable victory* famous, renowned, glorious, prestigious, distinguished, esteemed, notable, noted, great, eminent, noble, illustrious, creditable. **3** *an honourable member of the community* worthy, respected, respectable, reputable, decent, venerable.

honours *plural noun* *honours given to the victor* rewards, awards, prizes, decorations, titles, distinctions, laurels, laurel wreaths, bays.

hood *noun* head covering, cowl, head scarf. See table at HAT.

hoodlum *noun* **1** *hoodlums vandalizing telephone kiosks* ruffian, hooligan, thug, rowdy, delinquent, vandal, mugger; *inf.* tough, rough, yob, yobbo. **2** *hoodlums killing policemen* gangster, mobster, gunman, murderer, assassin, terrorist; *inf.* hit man, hatchet man; *Am. inf.* hood.

hoodwink *verb* deceive, delude, dupe, outwit, fool, befool, trick, get the better of, cheat, take in, hoax, mislead, defraud, swindle, gull, pull the wool over someone's eyes; *inf.* con, bamboozle, lead up the garden path, pull a fast one on, put one over on, take for a ride, make a sucker of; *lit.* cozen.

hook *noun* **1** *a harvest hook* billhook, scythe, sickle, falchion, scimitar, sabre, cutlass. **2** *hang your coat on the hook* peg, holder. **3** *the hook of the dress is broken* hook-and-eye, fastener, catch, clasp, clip, link. **4** *animals caught in hooks* snare, trap, noose, springe. **5** *a hook in the river* crook, angle, loop, curve, bend, bow, arc, dog-leg, horseshoe bend, oxbow, hairpin turn/bend. **by hook or by crook** by any means whatsoever, by any means, by fair means or foul, no matter how, somehow or other, somehow, in one way or another. **hook, line, and sinker** *believe the story hook, line, and sinker* completely, entirely, thoroughly, wholly, totally, utterly, through and through. **off the hook** **1** *her evidence got him off the hook* acquitted, cleared of the charge, exonerated, in the clear, let off, vindicated. **2** *her brother's taking his mother to the airport - she's off the hook* under no obligation, uncommitted, not bound, free.

hook *verb* **1** *hook the dress/necklace* fasten, secure, fix, close the clasp. **2** *hook the animals* snare, ensnare, trap, entrap, enmesh.

hooked *adjective* **1** *a hooked nose* hook-shaped, hooklike, aquiline, curved, bent, bowed, angular; *Med.* falcate, falciform. **2** *been hooked for years* | *they're hooked on drugs/television/gambling* dependent, addicted, addicted to, devoted to, given to.

hooligan *noun* ruffian, thug, rowdy, delinquent, vandal, mugger, hoodlum; *inf.* tough, rough, yob, yobbo.

hoop *noun* ring, band, circle, circlet, loop, wheel, girdle.

hoot *noun* **1** *the owl's hoot* call, screech, whoop, cry, tu-whit, tu-whoo. **2** *the hoots of the audience* boo, hiss, jeer, catcall, yell, shout of derision, whistle; *inf.* raspberry. **3** *the woman/story is a hoot* somebody/something very funny; *inf.* scream, laugh, card, caution.

hoot *verb* **1** *the owls hooted* call, screech, whoop, tu-whit-tu-whoo, tu-whoo. **2** *the audience hooted at the comedian* boo, hiss, jeer, catcall, cry/howl down, deride, mock, taunt, decry, ridicule, condemn, shout, yell; *inf.* blow raspberries.

hop *verb frogs hopping* jump, leap, bound, spring, vault, bounce, skip, caper, dance, frisk.

hop *noun* **1** *get there in one hop* jump, leap, bound, spring, vault, bounce, skip. **2** *a quick hop over the Channel* flight, short flight, plane trip, trip, quick trip, jaunt. **3** *a hop in the local hall* dance, disco, party, social.

hope *noun full of hope that we shall win* hopefulness, expectation, expectancy, anticipation, desire, longing, wish, wishing, craving, yearning, aspiration, ambition, dream, belief, assurance, assumption, confidence, conviction, faith, trust, optimism.
Opposites DESPAIR; PESSIMISM.

hope *verb hope to win* | *hope for a victory* be hopeful of, expect, anticipate, look forward to, await, contemplate, foresee, desire, long, wish, crave, yearn, aspire, be ambitious, dream, believe, feel assured, assume, have confidence, be convinced, rely on, count on, trust in.

hopeful *adjective* **1** *hopeful candidates* | *hopeful of winning* full of hope, expectant, anticipating, anticipative, looking forward to, optimistic, confident, assured, buoyant, sanguine. **2** *hopeful news/signs* promising, encouraging, heartening, gladdening, optimistic, reassuring, auspicious, favourable, propitious, cheerful, bright, pleasant, rosy.
Opposites HOPELESS; PESSIMISTIC; DISCOURAGING.

hopefully *adverb* **1** *travelling hopefully* with hope, full of hope, expectantly, with anticipation, optimistically, confidently, with assurance, buoyantly, sanguinely. **2** *hopefully he will win* it is to be hoped that, with luck, all being well, if all goes well, if everything turns out all right, probably, conceivably, feasibly.

hopeless *adjective* **1** *feeling hopeless* without hope, despairing, in despair, desperate, pessimistic, defeatist, dejected, downhearted, despondent, demoralized, disconsolate, downcast, wretched, woebegone, forlorn, suicidal. **2** *a hopeless case* beyond hope, despaired of, lost, beyond remedy, irremediable, remediless, beyond recovery, past cure, incurable, beyond repair, irreparable, irreversible, incorrigible, serious, grave, fatal, deadly. **3** *a hopeless task/situation* impossible, impracticable, futile, useless, vain, pointless, worthless, forlorn, no-win, unattainable, unachievable. **4** *she's hopeless at maths* poor, incompetent, ineffective, ineffectual, inadequate, inferior; *inf.* no good, useless.
Opposites HOPEFUL; OPTIMISTIC; ACCOMPLISHED.

horde *noun hordes of people/penguins on the beach* crowd, mob, throng, mass, large group, multitude, host, army, pack, gang, troop, drove, crew, band, flock, swarm, gathering, assemblage, press.

horizon *noun* **1** *disappearing over the horizon* skyline, range of vision, field of view, view, vista. **2** *broaden the child's horizon* scope, range of experience, area of knowledge, perspective, perception, prospect, outlook, compass, sphere, purview.

horizontal *adjective* flat, flat as a pancake, plumb, level, supine, prone, flush.
Opposites VERTICAL; ERECT.

horoscope *noun.* See table at ZODIAC.

horrendous *adjective* **1** *a horrendous sight* dreadful, awful, horrid. See HORRIBLE 1. **2** *a horrendous child* nasty, disagreeable, unpleasant. See HORRIBLE 2.

horrible *adjective* **1** *a horrible sight/accident* dreadful, awful, horrid, terrible, horrifying, terrifying, frightful, fearful, horrendous, shocking, appalling, hideous, grim, ghastly, harrowing, gruesome, disgusting, revolting, repulsive, loathsome, abhorrent, detestable, hateful, abominable. **2** *horrible child/weather/food/picture/mess* nasty, disagreeable, unpleasant, mean, unkind, obnoxious, odious; *inf.* horrid, awful, dreadful, terrible, beastly, ghastly, frightful, fearful, horrendous, shocking, appalling, hideous, revolting, abominable.
Opposites PLEASANT; AGREEABLE.

horrid *adjective* **1** *a horrid sight* dreadful, awful, horrifying, terrible, frightful, hideous, grim, ghastly, revolting, abhorrent, abominable. See HORRIBLE 1. **2** *a horrid child* horrible, nasty, disagreeable, unpleasant, mean, unkind, obnoxious. See HORRIBLE 2.

horrify *verb* **1** *the apparition horrified the children* terrify, terrorize, intimidate, frighten, frighten out of one's wits, alarm, scare, scare to death, startle, panic, throw into a panic, make someone's blood run cold; *inf.* make someone's hair stand on end, make someone's hair curl, scare stiff, scare the living daylights out of. **2** *his attitude horrifies me* shock, appal, outrage, scandalize, disgust, revolt, repel, nauseate, sicken, offend, dismay; *inf.* turn off.

horror *noun* **1** *full of horror at the sight of the ghost* terror, fear, fear and trembling, fearfulness, fright, alarm, dread, awe, panic, trepidation, apprehensiveness, uneasiness, nervousness, dismay, consternation. **2** *view his attitude with horror* abhorrence, abomina-

tion, loathing, hate, detestation, repulsion, revulsion, disgust, distaste, aversion, hostility, antipathy, animosity.

horse *noun* mount, steed, hack, pony, Shetland pony, cob, palfrey, nag, racehorse, filly, jade, draught-horse, cart-horse, packhorse, hunter, bay, sorrel, pinto, piebald; foal, colt, stallion, mare; *inf.* gee-gee. *See tables. See also table at* HARNESS.

horseman, horsewoman *noun* rider, equestrian, horse-soldier, cavalier, dragoon, jockey; cavalryman, cowboy/cowgirl.

horseplay *noun* clowning, fooling, fooling around, tomfoolery, buffoonery, pranks, prac-

HORSE SPORTS

Arab racing	eventing	one-day eventing	showing
competitive trail	gymkhana	point-to-point	showjumping
riding	harness-racing	polo	steeplechasing
cross-country	horse-racing	puissance	three-day
dressage	hunting	rodeo	eventing
endurance riding	marathon driving	scurry	trotting

POINTS OF A HORSE

cannon bone	ergot	hind quarters	poll
cheek	feathers	hock	ribs
chest	fetlock	hoof	shank
chestnut	fetlock joint	knee	sheath
chin groove	flank	loin	shoulder
coffin bone	forearm	mane	splint bone
coronet	forelock	navicular bone	stifle
crest	frog	pastern	tail
croup	gaskin	pedal bone	tendon
dock	gullet	point of hip	windpipe
elbow	heel	point of shoulder	withers

BREEDS OF HORSE AND PONY

Andalusian	Galloway	Missouri fox-trotting	Saddlebred
Anglo-Arab	Gelderlander	horse	Salerno
Appaloosa	Gotland	Morgan	Sandalwood pony
Arab	Hackney	mustang	Schleswig
Barb	Haflinger	New Forest pony	Shetland pony
Basuto pony	Hanoverian	Nonius	Shire horse
Breton	Highland pony	Noriker	Standardbred
brumby	Holstein	Norwegian racing	Suffolk Punch
Camargue	Huçul	trotter	Swedish
Caspian	Hunter	Oldenburger	warmblood
Cleveland Bay	Iceland pony	Orlov trotter	Tartar pony
Clydesdale	Irish draught	Palomino	Tennessee walking
Comtois	Irish hunter	Paso Fino	horse
Conestoga	Jutland	Percheron	Tersky
Connemara pony	Kabardin	Pinto	thoroughbred
criollo	Karabakh	Pinzgauer	Timor
Dales pony	Kathiawari	Plateau Persian	Trakehner
Dartmoor pony	Kazakh	polo pony	trotter
Dutch draught	Lippizaner	pony of the Amer-	Viatka
Dutch warmblood	Lokai	icas	Waler
Exmoor pony	Lundy Island	Quarter Horse	warmblood
Falabella	Mangalarga	Russ	Welsh cob
Fell pony	Manipur pony	Russian heavy	Welsh Mountain
Fjord	Mérens pony	draught	pony
Friesian	miniature	Russian warmblood	Yorkshire coach
Galiceño	Shetland	Sable Island	horse

tical jokes, antics, capers, high jinks, rough-and-tumble, romping, skylarking; *inf.* rough-housing, shenanigans, monkey business.

horse sense *noun* common sense, sense one is born with, mother wit, judgement, soundness of judgement, practicality; *inf.* nous, gumption, savvy.

horticulture *noun* cultivation of gardens, gardening, floriculture, arboriculture. *See table at* FARMING.

hosanna *noun* shout of praise, alleluia, song of praise, paean, laudation, glorification, hurrah, huzzah, cheer.

hose *noun* **1** *a rubber hose* tube, tubing, pipe, siphon, conduit, channel, outlet. **2** *wearing red hose* socks, stockings, tights, hosiery.

hosiery *noun* leg-covering, hose, socks, stockings, tights, knee socks, ankle socks, leggings.

hospitable *adjective* welcoming, sociable, convivial, generous, liberal, bountiful, open-handed, congenial, friendly, neighbourly, warm, warm-hearted, cordial, kind, kindly, kind-hearted, amicable, well-disposed, amenable, helpful.
Opposites INHOSPITABLE; UNFRIENDLY; MEAN.

hospital *noun* medical centre, clinic, infirmary, sanatorium.

hospitality *noun* hospitableness, welcome, sociability, conviviality, generosity, liberality, bountifulness, open-handedness, friendliness, neighbourliness, warmth, warm-heartedness, cordiality, kindness, kind-heartedness, amicability, amenability, helpfulness.

host¹ *noun* **1** *the host of the pub* proprietor, proprietress, landlord, landlady, innkeeper, hotel-keeper, hotelier. **2** *the host greeting his guests* party-giver, entertainer. **3** *the host of the radio/TV show* presenter, compère, master of ceremonies, MC, anchorman, anchorwoman; *inf.* emcee.
Opposites GUEST.

host² *verb* **1** *host a party* to be the host/hostess of, give. **2** *host a radio/TV show* present, introduce, compère; *inf.* emcee.

host³ *noun a host of people gathered for the march* multitude, crowd, throng, horde, mob, army, legion, crush, herd, pack, flock, swarm, troop, band, mass, assemblage, assembly, array, myriad.

hostage *noun* pawn, gage, security, surety, pledge, captive, prisoner.

hostile *adjective* **1** *hostile to the idea* antagonistic, opposed, averse, opposite, ill-disposed, against, inimical; *inf.* anti. **2** *hostile weather conditions* adverse, unfavourable, unpropitious, disadvantageous, inauspicious. **3** *a hostile crowd* belligerent, bellicose, aggressive, warlike, warring, militant, antagonistic, unfriendly, unkind, unsympathetic, malevolent, malicious, spiteful, wrathful, angry.
Opposites FRIENDLY; FAVOURABLE; PEACEFUL.

hostilities *plural noun* war, warfare, fighting, conflict, militancy, strife, action, battles.

hostility *noun* **1** *their hostility to the idea* antagonism, opposition, aversion, animosity, ill-will, enmity, inimicalness. **2** *the hostility of the crowd* belligerence, bellicosity, aggression, warlikeness, militancy, antagonism, unfriendliness, unkindness, malevolence, malice, spite, wrath, anger.

hot *adjective* **1** *hot food straight from the oven* heated, very warm, boiling, boiling hot, piping, piping hot, scalding, red-hot, sizzling, steaming, scorching, roasting, searing. **2** *a hot day* very warm, boiling hot, boiling, blazing hot, sweltering, parching, scorching, roasting, searing, blistering, baking, oven-like, torrid, sultry. **3** *the curry is very hot* peppery, spicy, pungent, piquant, fiery, sharp, biting, acrid. **4** *the child is hot* feverish, fevered, febrile, flushed, red, pyretic. **5** *hot on the idea of free speech* ardent, eager, enthusiastic, keen, fervent, fervid, zealous, vehement, passionate, animated, excited. **6** *hot with anger* inflamed, furious, infuriated, seething, raging, fuming, wrathful, angry, indignant. **7** *hot young men* randy, sexually excited, sex-hungry, lustful, lascivious, lecherous, libidinous; *inf.* horny. **8** *a hot temper/argument* heated, violent, furious, fierce, ferocious, stormy, tempestuous, savage. **9** *hot from the presses/warehouses* new, fresh, recent, late, brand-new, just out, just released, just issued. **10** *this brand of trainers is hot with children* popular, in vogue, in demand, sought-after, in favour, well-liked, well-loved. **11** *hot on their heels* close, following closely, near. **12** *hot goods* stolen, illegally obtained, smuggled, wanted.
Opposites COLD; MILD.

hot air *noun* empty talk, nonsense, bombast, verbiage, wind, blather, blether, claptrap; *inf.* gas, bunkum, guff, bosh.

hotbed *noun the place is a hotbed of vice/crime* breeding-ground, forcing-house, seed-bed, nursery, cradle, nest, womb.

hot-blooded *adjective* **1** *hot-blooded young lovers* passionate, impassioned, ardent, sensual, sex-hungry, lustful, libidinous, randy; *inf.* horny. **2** *hot-blooded people quarrelling* excitable, temperamental, fiery, spirited, impulsive, rash, wild, quixotic.

hotchpotch *noun* hodgepodge, mixture, jumble, mishmash, miscellany, medley, *mélange*, mess, clutter, odds and ends, pot-pourri, farrago, gallimaufry, olio, olla podrida.

hotel *noun* inn, tavern, pub, hostelry, motel, boarding-house, guest-house.

hotfoot *adverb ran hotfoot to the river* post-haste, pell-mell, helter-skelter, hurriedly, hastily, speedily, quickly, fast, rapidly, swiftly.

hotheaded *adjective* hot-tempered, short-tempered, quick-tempered, fiery, hasty, excitable, volatile, rash, impetuous, impulsive, reckless, foolhardy, wild, unruly.

hothouse *noun* greenhouse, glasshouse, conservatory.

hothouse *adjective hothouse children* over-protected, pampered, coddled, over-indulged, spoiled, spoonfed, sheltered, shielded, delicate, frail, fragile, sensitive, dainty.

hound *noun* **1** *she breeds hounds* bloodhound, foxhound, wolfhound, greyhound, dog, hunting dog. *See table at* DOG. **2** *he's a mean hound* scoundrel, cad, blackguard, rascal, rogue, villain, miscreant, knave, scallywag; *inf.* rotter, bounder, wrong'un.

hound *verb* **1** *police hounding the criminal* chase, give chase to, pursue, follow, hunt, hunt down, stalk, track, trail, follow on the heels of, shadow; *inf.* tail. **2** *hound him to do as they wished* nag, bully, browbeat, pester, harass, harry, keep after, urge, badger, goad, prod, provoke, impel, force, pressure, pressurize.

house *noun* **1** *new estate of 200 houses | his house is over there* abode, residence, domicile, home, habitation; bungalow, cottage; *inf.* semi. **2** *how many are in the house?* household, family, family circle, home, ménage. **3** *the House of Stewart* family, clan, family tree, line, lineage, dynasty, ancestry, ancestors, kindred, blood, race, strain, tribe. **4** *a publishing house* firm, business, company, concern, corporation, enterprise, organization; *inf.* outfit. **5** *the lower House* legislative body, legislative assembly, parliament, congress, chamber. **6** *a large house for the event* audience, gathering, assembly, congregation, listeners, spectators. **7** *a house owned by the brewery* inn, pub, public house, tavern, hotel, hostelry. **on the house** free, for nothing, gratis, without payment.

house *verb* **1** *the building houses 20 people* accommodate, lodge, put up, take in, have room for, have space/capacity for, sleep, shelter, harbour. **2** *the box houses the machinery* cover, sheathe, protect, shelter, guard, contain, keep.

household *noun how many are in the household?* family, family circle, house, home, ménage.

household *adjective household articles/bleach* domestic, family, ordinary, everyday, common, usual, run-of-the-mill.

householder *noun* home-owner, resident, occupant, occupier, tenant.

housekeeping *noun* household management, home economics, housecraft, domestic science, housewifery.

housing *noun* **1** *a shortage of housing* accommodation, houses, dwellings, homes, shelter, habitations. **2** *housing for machinery* case, casing, cover, covering, sheath, container, enclosure, jacket, capsule, holder.

hovel *noun* shack, shanty, hut; *inf.* dump, hole; *Scots* bothy.

hover *verb* **1** *kites hovering in the air* be suspended, hang, fly, flutter, float, drift, be wafted. **2** *students hovering by the notice-board* linger, hang about, wait near, stay near. **3** *hovering between going and staying* waver, vacillate, fluctuate, oscillate, alternate, seesaw; *Scots* swither.

however *adverb however, you will have to go* nevertheless, be that as it may, nonetheless, notwithstanding, anyway, anyhow, regardless, despite that, still, yet, just the same, though.

however *conjunction however he approached the problem* whatever way, regardless of how.

howl *verb* **1** *dogs howling* bay, yowl, yelp, ululate, quest. **2** *children howling* yell, wail, bawl, scream, shriek, bellow, roar, shout, caterwaul,

yelp, cry, weep, ululate; *Am. inf.* holler. **3** *howling at the clown's antics* laugh loudly, roar with laughter, split one's sides; *inf.* fall about.

howl *noun* **1** *the howls of the dogs* bay, yowl, yelp, ululation, questing. **2** *children's howls* yell, wail, bawl, bellow, roar, caterwauling, crying. *See* HOWL *verb* 2.

howler *noun* mistake, error, blunder, gaffe, malapropism; *inf.* bloomer, boo-boo, clanger.

hub *noun* **1** *the hub of a wheel* pivot, axis, nave. **2** *the hub of the firm* centre, centre of activity, middle, core, heart, nerve centre, focus, focal point.

huddle *verb* **1** *huddle into the hall* crowd, press, throng, flock, pack, cram, herd, squeeze, bunch up, cluster, gather, congregate. **2** *huddle up under her coat* curl up, snuggle, cuddle, nestle, hunch up.

huddle *noun* **1** *a huddle of people* crowd, throng, press, pack, cluster, gathering. **2** *a huddle of objects* heap, jumble, confusion, muddle, tangle, mess. **3** *people going into a huddle* conference, discussion, consultation, meeting, powwow; *inf.* confab.

hue[1] *noun* **1** *a blue hue* colour, tone, shade, tint, tinge, dye. **2** *political opinions of every hue* complexion, cast, aspect, light.

hue[2] *noun* **hue and cry** outcry, uproar, commotion, racket, clamour, furore, brouhaha, hullabaloo, much ado. *See* HULLABALOO.

huff *noun* **in a huff** in a bad mood, sulky, having a sulk, having a fit of the sulks, peeved; *inf.* miffed.

hug *verb* **1** *hug his wife* embrace, cuddle, take in one's arms, hold close, enfold in one's arms, clasp/press to one's bosom, squeeze. **2** *hug the shore* keep close to, stay near to, follow closely, follow the course of. **3** *hug his memories* cling to, hold onto, cherish, harbour, nurse, keep close.

hug *noun give the child a hug* embrace, cuddle, squeeze, hold, clasp, bear-hug; *inf.* clinch.

huge *adjective* enormous, immense, great, massive, colossal, vast, prodigious, gigantic, giant, gargantuan, mammoth, monumental, monstrous, elephantine, extensive, bulky, mountainous, titanic, Herculean, Brobdingnagian; *inf.* jumbo.
Opposites TINY; DIMINUTIVE.

hulk *noun* **1** *the hulk of a ship* wreck, shipwreck, derelict, ruin, shell, skeleton, hull, frame. **2** *a clumsy great hulk* oaf, lout, lump, lubber, bull in a china shop; *inf.* lummox; *Am.* klutz.

hulking *adjective* **1** *a hulking great wardrobe* cumbersome, unwieldy, bulky, weighty, massive, ponderous. **2** *a hulking boy* clumsy, awkward, ungainly, lumbering, lumpish, loutish, large, overgrown.

hull *noun* **1** *the hull of a ship* body, framework, frame, skeleton, structure, casing, covering. **2** *the hull of fruit* rind, skin, peel, shell, husk, pod, shuck, capsule, integument, pericarp.

hull *verb hull fruit* peel, pare, skin, trim, shell, husk, shuck.

hullabaloo *noun* uproar, commotion, roar, racket, din, noise, clamour, disturbance, hubbub, outcry, furore, brouhaha, hue and cry, pandemonium, tumult, turmoil, fuss, to-do, much ado, bedlam, babel, hurly-burly; *inf.* rumpus, ruction; *Am.* ruckus.

hum *verb* **1** *bees/machines humming* drone, murmur, vibrate, throb, thrum, buzz, whirr, purr. **2** *humming a tune* sing, croon, whisper, mumble. **3** *things are humming* be busy, be active, bustle, move quickly, vibrate, pulsate, buzz.

hum *noun* *the hum of bees/machines* drone, murmur, vibration, throb, thrum, buzz, whirr, purr.

human *adjective* **1** *a human creature* anthropoid, mortal. **2** *human frailty/weaknesses* mortal, physical, bodily, fleshly, carnal, corporal. **3** *a very human person* kind, kindly, considerate, understanding, sympathetic, compassionate, approachable, accessible, humane. *See* HUMANE. **4** *they're only human* mortal, flesh and blood, fallible, weak, frail, vulnerable, erring. *Opposites* ANIMAL; SPIRITUAL; INHUMAN.

human *noun* *animals and humans* human being, mortal, member of the human race, individual, living soul, soul; man, woman, child; *inf.* body. *See table.*

EARLY HUMANS

Australopithecus	Kabwe man
Cro-Magnon man	Neanderthal
Heidelberg man	man
Homo erectus	Peking man
Homo habilis	Pithecanthropus
Homo sapiens	Ramapithecus
Java man	Solo man

---

humane *adjective* *a humane ruler | humane to animals* kind, kindly, kind-hearted, good, good-natured, compassionate, considerate, understanding, sympathetic, forgiving, merciful, lenient, forbearing, gentle, tender, mild, clement, benign, benevolent, charitable, generous, magnanimous, approachable, accessible. *Opposites* CRUEL; BRUTAL; INHUMANE.

humanitarian *adjective* **1** *humanitarian enemy soldiers* humane, kind, good, compassionate, sympathetic, merciful, lenient, gentle, magnanimous. *See* HUMANE. **2** *interested in humanitarian issues* philanthropic, altruistic, welfare, charitable.

humanitarian *noun* philanthropist, altruist, benefactor, good Samaritan, social reformer, do-gooder.

humanities *plural noun* classics, classical studies, classical languages, classical literature, liberal arts, literae humaniores.

humanity *noun* **1** *bombs bringing the end of humanity* humankind, human race, the human species, mankind, man, people, mortals, *Homo sapiens*. **2** *err because of their humanity* humanness, human nature, mortality, flesh and blood. **3** *monks noted for their humanity* kindness, kind-heartedness, goodness, good-heartedness, benevolence, compassion,

sympathy, understanding, pity, mercy, mercifulness, gentleness, tenderness, leniency, tolerance, goodwill, brotherly love, fellow-feeling, generosity, magnanimity, charity, philanthropy.

humble *adjective* **1** *brilliant but humble* modest, unassuming, self-effacing, unassertive, unpretentious, unostentatious, meek. **2** *the villagers are humble people* plain, common, ordinary, simple, poor, of low birth, low-born, of low rank, low-ranking, low, lowly, inferior, plebeian, proletarian, base, mean, unrefined, vulgar, unimportant, insignificant, inconsequential, undistinguished, ignoble. **3** *hate his humble attitude to the boss* servile, submissive, obsequious, subservient, deferential, over-respectful, slavish, sycophantic. *Opposites* ARROGANT; PROUD; IMPORTANT.

humble *verb* **1** *humble them by his criticism* humiliate, mortify, bring down, bring low, subdue, chasten, shame, put to shame, abash, abase, degrade, make someone eat humble pie, take down a peg or two. *See* HUMILIATE. **2** *feel humbled in the presence of the great man* belittle, demean, deflate, depreciate, disparage. **3** *humble the enemy* crush, trounce, rout, break, conquer, vanquish, defeat, utterly overwhelm, smash, bring to one's knees.

humbug *noun* **1** *taken in by the humbug* hoax, trick, trickery, cheat, cheating, bluff, ruse, wile, stratagem, fraud, swindle, deceit, deception, imposture, pretence, sham, delusion; *inf.* con. **2** *the salesman's a humbug* charlatan, imposter, fake, sham, fraud, cheat, trickster, swindler, mountebank, quack, deceiver, dissembler; *inf.* con-man, phoney. **3** *he talks a lot of humbug* nonsense, rubbish, balderdash, twaddle, bunkum; *inf.* rot, tommy-rot, bunk, boloney, bosh, tosh, hogwash, crap.

humdrum *adjective* *humdrum life/routine* commonplace, run-of-the-mill, routine, unvaried, unvarying, ordinary, everyday, mundane, uneventful, monotonous, repetitious, dull, uninteresting, banal, boring, tedious, tiresome, wearisome. *Opposites* REMARKABLE; EXCITING.

humid *adjective* *humid atmosphere/day* muggy, sticky, steamy, clammy, close, sultry, damp, moist, dank, wet, wettish, soggy, misty. *Opposites* DRY; ARID.

humidity *noun* humidness, mugginess, stickiness, steaminess, clamminess, closeness, sultriness, dampness, damp, moistness, dankness, moisture, wetness, sogginess.

humiliate *verb* mortify, humble, shame, bring low, put to shame, make ashamed, disgrace, embarrass, discomfit, chasten, subdue, abash, abase, debase, degrade, crush, make someone eat humble pie, take down a peg or two; *inf.* put down; *Am. inf.* make someone eat crow.

humiliation *noun* mortification, humbling, loss of pride, shame, disgrace, loss of face, dishonour, indignity, discredit, ignoring, embarrassment, discomfiture, affront, abasement, debasement, degradation, submission, humble pie; *inf.* put-down.

humility noun **1** *the winner showed humility* lack of pride, humbleness, modesty, modestness, meekness, self-effacement, unpretentiousness, unobtrusiveness, diffidence. **2** *dislike his humility towards the boss* servility, submissiveness, obsequiousness, subservience, deference, sycophancy.
Opposites ARROGANCE; PRIDE.

humorist noun comic writer, writer of comedy, cartoonist, caricaturist, comic, comedian, comedienne, joker, jokester, clown, jester, wag, wit, funny man.

humorous adjective **1** *a humorous story* funny, comic, comical, witty, jocular, amusing, laughable, hilarious, side-splitting, rib-tickling, facetious, farcical, ridiculous, ludicrous, absurd, droll. **2** *a humorous person* funny, amusing, entertaining, witty, jocular, facetious, waggish, whimsical.
Opposites SERIOUS; SOLEMN.

humour noun **1** *not to see the humour of the situation* funny side, funniness, comic side, comical aspect, comedy, laughableness, facetiousness, farcicalness, farce, jocularity, hilarity, ludicrousness, absurdness, absurdity, drollness. **2** *entertain them with his humour* comedy, jokes, joking, jests, jesting, gags, wit, wittiness, witticisms, waggishness, pleasantries, buffoonery; *inf.* wisecracks. **3** *what humour is she in today?* mood, temper, temperament, frame of mind, state of mind, disposition, spirits. **4** *change one's actions according to his humours* whim, caprice, fancy, whimsy, propensity, inclination, bent, vagary, quirk, kink, idiosyncrasy, eccentricity, crotchet.
Opposites GRAVITY; SOLEMNITY.

humour verb **1** *humour the child* indulge, pamper, spoil, cosset, coddle, mollify, soothe, placate, gratify, satisfy, pander to, go along with, accommodate. **2** *humour their fantasies* adapt to, make provision for, give in to, yield to, go along with, acquiesce in, indulge, pander to, tolerate, permit, allow, suffer.

hump noun *a hump on his back | hump in the tree* protuberance, protrusion, projection, bulge, swelling, lump, bump, knob, hunch, mass, nodule, node, intumescence, tumefaction. **give someone the hump** depress, bring low, give someone the blues; *inf.* bring down. **over the hump** *we were doing badly but we're over the hump* over the worst part, over the worst of it, out of the woods, in the clear, on the road to recovery, getting better, on the way up, making progress.

hump verb **1** *stop humping your back* hunch, arch, curve, crook, curl up. **2** *hump the luggage to the train* lug, heave, carry, lift, shoulder, hoist; *Scots* humph.

hunch noun **1** *a hunch on his back* hump, protuberance, protrusion, bulge, swelling, bump, intumescence. *See* HUMP *noun*. **2** *have a hunch that she will win* feeling, presentiment, premonition, intuition, sixth sense, suspicion, inkling, impression, idea.

hunch verb **1** *hunching his back* hump, arch, curve. *See* HUMP *verb* 1. **2** *hunch oneself up over one's books* crouch, stoop, bend, huddle, squat.

hunger noun **1** *suffering from hunger* hungriness, need for food, lack of food, emptiness, ravenousness, famishment, starvation, famine, voracity, greed, greediness, edacity, esurience. **2** *a hunger for knowledge/travel* craving, longing, yearning, desire, want, need, thirst, appetite, appetence, pining, itch, lust, hankering; *inf.* yen.

hunger verb **1** *hungering for/after knowledge* crave, have a craving for, long for, yearn for, have a yearning for, desire, want, need, thirst for, have an appetite for, pine for, lust after, itch for, hanker after; *inf.* have a yen for. **2** *hunger for food* be hungry, feel hunger, be ravenous, be famished, be starving.

hungry adjective **1** *hungry children | the people are hungry* in need of food, empty, hollow, ravenous, famished, famishing, starving, starved, half-starved, sharp-set, greedy, voracious; *inf.* peckish. **2** *hungry for knowledge* craving, in need/want of, eager/keen for, desirous of, covetous of, longing/yearning/pining for. *See* HUNGER *verb* 1.
Opposites FULL; REPLETE.

hunk noun **1** *a hunk of cheese* large piece, block, chunk, lump, mass, slab, wedge, square, gobbet, dollop, portion; *inf.* wodge; *Scots* dod. **2** *the film star is a hunk* he-man, muscle-man, Adonis.

hunt verb **1** *hunt stags/criminals* chase, give chase, pursue, stalk, track, trail, follow, shadow, hunt down, hound; *inf.* tail. **2** *hunt for her keys* search for, look for, look high and low for, seek, try to find, scour for, forage for, fish for, rummage for, scrabble for, ferret for.

hunt noun **1** *the hunt for foxes/hares/stags/criminals* chase, pursuit, course, coursing, stalking, tracking, trailing, shadowing; *inf.* tailing. **2** *the hunt for her keys* search, quest, rummage; seeking, foraging, scrabbling, ransacking. *See* HUNT *verb* 2.

hurdle noun **1** *runners clearing hurdles* fence, railing, rail, wall, hedge, hedgerow, bar, barrier, barricade. **2** *a hurdle in the way of their plans* barrier, obstacle, hindrance, impediment, obstruction, stumbling-block, snag, complication, difficulty, handicap.

hurl verb *hurl stones/insults* throw, fling, pitch, cast, toss, heave, fire, launch, let fly, shy, propel, project, dart, catapult; *inf.* sling, chuck.

hurly-burly noun commotion, hubbub, bustle, tumult, turmoil, turbulence, pandemonium, bedlam, furore, uproar, upheaval, disorder, confusion, chaos, unrest, agitation, disruption, trouble.

hurricane noun typhoon, cyclone, tornado, windstorm, storm, gale, tempest, squall, whirlwind; *Am. inf.* twister. *See tables at* WIND.

hurried adjective **1** *with hurried steps* quick, fast, swift, rapid, speedy, hasty, breakneck, post-haste. **2** *a hurried glance* hasty, quick, swift, rapid, rushed, cursory, superficial, perfunctory, offhand, passing, fleeting, transitory.
Opposites SLOW; LEISURELY; THOROUGH.

hurry verb **1** *hurry or we'll be late* hurry up, move quickly, be quick, make haste, hasten, speed, speed up, lose no time, press on, push on, run, dash, rush, go hell for leather; *inf.* get a move on, put one's foot down, step on it, get cracking, shake a leg, fly, race, scurry, scamper, put a spurt on, go like a bat out of hell, hightail it, hotfoot it. **2** *hurry them on* speed up, quicken, hasten, accelerate, expedite, urge on, drive on, push on, goad, prod, hustle. **Opposites** DAWDLE; DELAY.

hurry *noun* **1** *surprised at the hurry of the crowd* speed, quickness, fastness, swiftness, rapidity, haste, celerity, expedition, dispatch, promptitude. **2** *what's all the hurry?* haste, urgency, rush, flurry, bustle, hubbub, hurry-scurry, turmoil, agitation, confusion, commotion.

hurt *verb* **1** *my foot hurts* be sore, be painful, cause pain, ache, smart, nip, sting, throb, tingle, burn. **2** *he has hurt his leg* injure, cause injury to, wound, cause pain to, bruise, cut, scratch, lacerate, maim, mutilate, damage, disable, incapacitate, debilitate, impair. **3** *his cruel words hurt her* upset, sadden, cause sorrow, cause suffering, grieve, wound, distress, pain, cut to the quick, sting, cause anguish, offend, give offence, discompose. **4** *that will not have hurt his reputation* harm, damage, spoil, mar, blight, blemish, impair.
Opposites HEAL; CHEER; SOOTHE; IMPROVE.

hurt *noun* **1** *the hurt in his hand was acute* pain, soreness, ache, smarting, stinging, throbbing, suffering, pangs, discomfort. **2** *a hurt on his leg* sore, wound, injury, bruise, cut, scratch, laceration. **3** *the hurt he caused her* upset, sadness, sorrow, suffering, grief, distress, pain, misery, anguish, affliction. **4** *the hurt caused to his reputation* harm, damage, injury, detriment, blight, loss, disadvantage, mischief.

hurt *adjective* **1** *a hurt leg* wounded, injured, bruised, cut, lacerated, sore, painful, aching, smarting, throbbing. *See* HURT *verb* 1, 2. **2** *a hurt child/expression* upset, sad, sorrowful, grieving, grief-stricken, aggrieved, distressed, anguished, offended, piqued. *See* HURT *verb* 3.

hurtful *adjective* **1** *hurtful remarks* upsetting, wounding, injurious, distressing, unkind, nasty, mean, malicious, spiteful, cutting, cruel, mischievous, offensive. **2** *actions hurtful to his career* harmful, damaging, injurious, detrimental, disadvantageous, deleterious, destructive, prejudicial, ruinous, inimical.

husband *noun* spouse, consort, partner, groom, bridegroom; *inf.* hubby, old man, the other half; *dial.* man.

husband *verb* *husband resources* conserve, preserve, save, save for a rainy day, put aside, put by, reserve, store, hoard, use sparingly, use economically, manage thriftily, budget.

husbandry *noun* **1** *men engaged in husbandry* farming, agriculture, farm management, land management, agronomy, agronomics, agribusiness, cultivation, tillage; animal husbandry. **2** *practise husbandry with the available resources* budgeting, economy, good housekeeping, careful management, thrift, frugality, sparingness, saving.

hush *verb* **1** *hush the children* silence, quieten, quieten down, shush; *inf.* shut up. **2** *they suddenly hushed* fall silent, become silent, quieten,

quieten down; *inf.* pipe down, shut up. **3** *hush their fears* still, quieten, calm, soothe, allay, assuage, pacify, mollify, compose. **hush up** *hush up the scandal* suppress, conceal, cover up, keep secret, keep dark, smother, stifle, squash.

hush *noun* *a hush fell over the room* quiet, quietness, silence, stillness, still, soundlessness, peacefulness, peace, calm, tranquillity.

hush-hush *adjective* *hush-hush information* top secret, secret, confidential, classified, restricted.

husk *noun* hull, shell, covering, pod, shuck, rind, skin, peel, integument, pericarp.

husky *adjective* **1** *a husky voice* throaty, gruff, deep, gravelly, hoarse, coarse, croaking, croaky, rough, thick, guttural, harsh, rasping. **2** *a husky young man* brawny, well-built, strapping, muscular, big and strong, rugged, burly, sturdy, powerfully-built, thickset; *inf.* beefy.

hussy *noun* minx, seductress, trollop, slut, loose woman, jade; *inf.* vamp, tramp, floozy, tart, scrubber; *lit.* wanton, strumpet.

hustle *verb* **1** *hustle them out of the way* push, shove, thrust, crowd, jostle, elbow, nudge, shoulder. **2** *hustle them into making a decision* force, coerce, impel, pressure, badger, pester, prompt, urge, goad, prod, spur, propel, egg on. **3** *have to hustle to get there on time* hurry, be quick, hasten, make haste, move quickly, dash, rush, fly; *inf.* get a move on, put one's foot down, step on it.

hustle *noun* *tired of the hustle of life* activity, hurry, rushing, hurry-scurry, haste, flurry, hurly-burly, bustle, hubbub, tumult, fuss.

hut *noun* shed, lean-to, shack, cabin, shanty, hovel; *Scots* bothy.

hybrid *noun* cross-breed, cross, mixed-breed, half-breed, half-blood, mixture, conglomerate, composite, compound, amalgam.

hygiene *noun* cleanliness, personal hygiene, personal cleanliness, public health, environmental health, sanitation, sanitary measures.

hygienic *adjective* *kitchens must be hygienic* sanitary, clean, germ-free, disinfected, sterilized, aseptic, sterile, unpolluted, uncontaminated, healthy, pure.
Opposites DIRTY; FILTHY; INSANITARY.

hymn *noun* psalm, anthem, carol, religious song, paean, song of praise, chant, plainsong, spiritual.

hype *noun* *a lot of hype for the new film* publicity, promotion, advertising, puff, puffery, ballyhoo; *inf.* plug, plugging, razzmatazz.

hyperbole *noun* exaggeration, overstatement, excess, overkill.

hypercritical *adjective* overcritical, captious, fault-finding, carping, cavilling, over-exacting, over-censorious, hair-splitting, niggling, quibbling, pedantic, over-rigorous, over-strict; *inf.* nit-picking.

hypnosis *noun* hypnotic suggestion, autosuggestion, mesmerism.

hypnotic *adjective* *hypnotic drugs/effect* mesmeric, mesmerizing, sleep-inducing, sleep-producing, soporific, somniferous, somnific, numbing, sedative, stupefactive.

hypnotize verb **1** *hypnotize the patient* put under, put out, send into a trance, mesmerize, put to sleep. **2** *they were hypnotized by her beauty* fascinate, bewitch, entrance, beguile, spellbind, magnetize.

hypochondria noun valetudinarianism, imagined ill-health, hypochondriasis, health obsession.

hypochondriac adjective hypochondriacal, valetudinarian, malingering, obsessed with one's health, preoccupied with ill-health.

hypocrisy noun sanctimoniousness, sanctimony, pietism, false goodness, Pharisaism, insincerity, falseness, falsity, deceptiveness, deceit, deceitfulness, deception, dishonesty, dissembling, duplicity, imposture, cant, two-facedness, double-dealing, pretence, speciousness; *inf.* phoniness.
Opposites HONESTY; SINCERITY.

hypocrite noun Pharisee, pietist, canter, tartuffe, Holy Willie, whited sepulchre, deceiver, dissembler, impostor, pretender, charlatan, mountebank, quack; *inf.* phoney, creeping Jesus.

hypocritical adjective sanctimonious, pietistic, Pharisaical, canting, unctuous, insincere, false, fraudulent, deceitful, deceptive, dishonest, untruthful, lying, dissembling, duplicitous, two-faced, double-dealing, untrustworthy, perfidious, specious, spurious; *inf.* phoney.

hypothesis noun **1** *a working hypothesis* theorem, thesis, proposition, theory, postulate, axiom, premise. **2** *impossible to deduce anything from his hypothesis* supposition, assumption, presumption, conjecture, speculation.

hypothetical adjective *to take a hypothetical case* supposed, assumed, presumed, putative, theoretical, conjectured, imagined, speculative, notional, academic.

hysteria noun hysterics, loss of control, frenzy, outburst/fit of agitation, panic attack, loss of reason, fit of madness, delirium; *inf.* the screaming habdabs.

hysterical adjective **1** *hysterical at the news of his death* frenzied, in a frenzy, frantic, out of control, berserk, beside oneself, distracted, distraught, overwrought, agitated, in a panic, mad, crazed, delirious, out of one's mind/wits, raving. **2** *hysterical play/game* very funny, wildly amusing, hilarious, uproarious, side-splitting, comical, farcical, screamingly funny.
Opposites CALM; COMPOSED; SERIOUS.

Ii

ice noun **1** *ships encountering ice* frozen water; frost, rime, icicle, iceberg, glacier. **2** *ice in a drink* ice cubes, crushed ice; *inf.* rocks. **3** *an ice for dessert* ice-cream, sorbet, water ice, sherbet. **4** *you could feel the ice in her greeting* coldness, coolness, frigidity, stiffness, aloofness, distance, unresponsiveness, reserve, reticence, constraint, restraint. **on ice** *our project is on ice for the moment* in abeyance, in reserve, awaiting attention, pending.

ice verb **1** *the lake has iced over* freeze, freeze over, harden, solidify. **2** *ice drinks* add ice to, cool, chill, refrigerate. **3** *ice the cake* cover with icing, frost, add frosting, glaze.

icing noun *icing on the birthday cake* frosting, glaze, sugar paste; royal icing, butter icing, glacé icing, fondant icing.

icon noun image, idol, likeness, representation, figure, statue.

icy adjective **1** *icy winds/weather* freezing, frigid, chill, chilly, chilling, frosty, biting, bitter, raw, arctic, glacial, Siberian, polar, gelid. **2** *icy roads* frozen over, ice-bound, frosty, rimy, glassy, like a sheet of glass, slippery; *inf.* slippy. **3** *an icy welcome* cold, cool, frigid, frosty, stiff, aloof, distant, unfriendly, unwelcoming, unresponsive, uncommunicative, reserved, reticent, constrained, restrained. **Opposites** BOILING; HOT; WARM.

idea noun **1** *the idea of death scares her* concept, conception, conceptualization, thought, image, abstraction, perception, notion. **2** *tell him your ideas on the subject* thought, theory, view, viewpoint, opinion, feeling, outlook, belief, judgement, conclusion. **3** *I had an idea that he was dead* thought, understanding, belief, impression, feeling, notion, suspicion, fancy, inkling. **4** *could you give me some idea of the cost?* estimation, approximation, guess, surmise; *inf.* guesstimate. **5** *our idea is to open a new shop* plan, design, scheme, aim, intention, objective, object, purpose, end, goal, target. **6** *she's not my idea of a good mother* notion, vision, archetype, ideal example, exemplar, pattern.

ideal noun **1** *she never married; she had her mind set on an ideal* standard of perfection/excellence, epitome, peak of perfection, paragon, nonpareil. **2** *an ideal at which we can aim* archetype, prototype, model, pattern, exemplar, example, paradigm, criterion, yardstick. **3** *a man of high ideals* principle, standard, moral value; morals, ethics.

ideal adjective **1** *ideal beauty* perfect, consummate, supreme, absolute, complete, flawless, exemplary, classic, archetypal, model, quintessential. **2** *confusing ideal and concrete matters* abstract, conceptual, intellectual, mental, philosophical, theoretical, hypothetical. **3** *she dreams of an ideal world* unattainable, Utopian,

unreal, impracticable, ivory-towered, imaginary, romantic, visionary, fanciful.

idealist noun **1** *an idealist who does not accept second-best* perfectionist. **2** *idealist dreaming of a perfect world* Utopian, visionary, romanticist.

idealistic adjective Utopian, perfectionist, visionary, romantic, quixotic, unrealistic, impracticable, castle-building. **Opposites** PRACTICAL; REALISTIC; DOWN-TO-EARTH.

ideally adverb *ideally, everyone should have enough to live on* in a perfect world, in a Utopia, all things being equal, theoretically, hypothetically, in theory.

identical adjective **1** *that is the identical dress that she wore last night* the same, the very same, one and the same, selfsame. **2** *they have identical personalities* alike, like, similar, much the same, indistinguishable, corresponding, matching, twin. **Opposites** DIFFERENT; UNLIKE.

identification noun **1** *witnesses helping in the identification of the criminal* recognition, singling out, spotting, pointing, pinpointing, naming; *Am. inf.* fingering. See IDENTIFY 1. **2** *the identification of the best method* establishment, finding out, ascertainment, diagnosis, selection, choice. **3** *show the doorman his identification* ID card, ID, badge, letter of introduction; papers, credentials. **4** *her identification with her fellow patient* empathy, rapport, fellow feeling, bond of sympathy, sympathetic cord, sympathy; *inf.* good vibes.

identify verb **1** *identify the criminal* recognize, single out, pick out, spot, point out, pinpoint, discern, distinguish, name; *inf.* put the finger on; *Am. inf.* finger. **2** *identify the problem* establish, find out, ascertain, diagnose, select, choose. **3** *I identify her with my youth* associate, connect, think of in connection with. **4** *she identifies with all struggling artists* empathize, have a rapport with, relate to, respond to. See IDENTIFICATION 4.

identity noun **1** *the identity of the criminal has not been established* name, specification. **2** *felt that he lost his identity on emigrating* personality, self, selfhood, ego, individuality, distinctiveness, singularity, uniqueness, differentness. **3** *a case of mistaken identity* identification, recognition, naming. See IDENTIFICATION 1. **4** *the identity of their interests* identicalness, sameness, selfsameness, indistinguishability, interchangeability, likeness, alikeness, similarity, closeness, accordance.

ideology noun doctrine, creed, credo, teaching, dogma, theory, thesis; tenets, beliefs, opinions.

idiocy noun **1** *the idiocy of their actions* stupidity, stupidness, foolishness, senselessness, inanity, absurdity, fatuity, fatuousness, asinity, lack of intelligence, lunacy, craziness, insanity;

inf. dumbness, daftness. **2** *tired by their idiocies* stupid actions, inane remarks; foolish talk, absurdity. **3** *the idiocy of the youngest child* feeble-mindedness, weak-mindedness, imbecility.
Opposites WISDOM; SENSE.

idiom *noun* **1** *unable to think of a clever idiom* turn of phrase, set phrase, fixed expression, phrase, expression, locution. **2** *adopt the modern idiom* language, mode of expression, phraseology, style of speech, speech, talk, usage, parlance, vernacular, jargon, patois; *inf.* lingo.

idiosyncrasy *noun* peculiarity, individual/personal trait, singularity, oddity, eccentricity, mannerism, quirk, habit, characteristic, speciality, quality, feature.

idiot *noun* **1** *the idiots stole the car* blockhead, nitwit, dunderhead, dolt, dunce, halfwit, fool, ass, booby, nincompoop, ninny, ignoramus, cretin, moron; *inf.* numskull, dim-wit. **2** *the village idiot* mentally handicapped/retarded person, retardate, moron, halfwit, imbecile.

idiotic *adjective* an idiotic idea/action stupid, foolish, senseless, inane, absurd, fatuous, asinine, unintelligent, halfwitted, hare-brained, lunatic, crazy, insane, moronic; *inf.* dumb, daft.

idle *adjective* **1** *an idle fellow* lazy, indolent, slothful, shiftless, sluggish, loafing, do-nothing, dronish. **2** *machines lying idle* not in operation, not operating, inoperative, not working, inactive, out of action, unused, not in use, mothballed. **3** *the building workers are idle just now* not working, unemployed, out of work, jobless, out of a job, redundant; *inf.* on the dole. **4** *pass away the idle hours* unoccupied, empty, vacant, unfilled. **5** *idle rumours* groundless, without grounds, baseless, foundationless, lacking foundation. **6** *idle remarks* unimportant, trivial, trifling, shallow, foolish, insignificant, superficial, without depth, inane, fatuous, senseless, meaningless, purposeless, unnecessary. **7** *idle threats* useless, in vain, vain, worthless, futile, ineffective, ineffectual, inefficacious, unproductive, fruitless, pointless, meaningless. **8** *idle pleasures* frivolous, trivial, trifling, shallow, insubstantial, worthless, nugatory.
Opposites INDUSTRIOUS; ACTIVE; BUSY; MEANINGFUL.

idle *verb* **1** *idle away the hours* while, laze, loaf, lounge, loiter, dawdle, dally, fritter, potter, waste, fool away. **2** *stop idling and work* do nothing, sit back and do nothing, laze, loaf, be inactive, mark time, shirk, slack, vegetate; *inf.* take it easy, rest on one's oars. **3** *idle down to the shops* saunter, stroll, dawdle, potter, drift, move slowly. **4** *the engine idling* tick over.

idol *noun* **1** *pagans worshipping idols* icon, god, false god, effigy, image, graven image, fetish, likeness. **2** *the singer is the idol of teenagers* hero, heroine, favourite, darling, beloved, pet, apple of one's eye, blue-eyed boy/girl, star, superstar; *inf.* pin-up.

idolatrous *adjective* **1** *idolatrous tribes of old* idol-worshipping, idolistic, icon-worshipping, fetishistic, pagan, heathen, heretical. **2** *idolatrous fans of the singer* hero-worshipping, idoliz-

ing, worshipping, worshipful, adulatory, adoring, lionizing, reverential, glorifying.

idolatry *noun* **1** *the idolatry of non-Christian tribes* idolism, idolization, idolatrism, idol-worship, fetishism, iconolatry, icon-worship, paganism, heathenism. **2** *the idolatry of the singer's fans* idolization, idolizing, worshipping, hero-worshipping, adulation, adoring, loving, admiring, doting, lionization, lionizing, reverence, glorification.

idolize *verb* **1** *idolize false gods* worship, bow down before, glorify, exalt, revere, deify. **2** *idolize the pop singer* hero-worship, worship, adulate, adore, love, look up to, admire, dote upon, lionize, reverence, revere, venerate.

idyll *noun* **1** *poets writing idylls* pastoral, eclogue, georgic, rural poem. **2** *enjoying an idyll* wonderful/perfect/romantic time, moment of bliss, honeymoon, paradise, heaven on earth, Garden of Eden, Shangri-La.

if *conjunction* **1** *if you go he will go* on condition that, provided, providing, supposing, assuming, on the assumption that, allowing. **2** *I don't know if he will come* whether, whether or not. **3** *a boring if well-paid job* although, even, though, however, yet.

if *noun* *the situation is full of ifs* doubt, uncertainty, hesitation, condition, stipulation.

iffy *adjective* **1** *the situation is a bit iffy* doubtful, uncertain, unsure, undecided, unsettled, indeterminate, unresolved; *inf.* up in the air. **2** *I'm a bit iffy about going* doubtful, dubious, unsure, uncertain, undecided, hesitant, tentative.

ignite *verb* **1** *ignite the fire* light, set fire to, set on fire, set alight, fire, kindle, inflame, touch off; *inf.* set/put a match to. **2** *the fire ignited* catch/take fire, catch, burst into flames, burn up, burn, flame up, kindle.
Opposites EXTINGUISH; DOUSE; go out (*see* GO).

ignominious *adjective* **1** *an ignominious defeat* shameful, dishonourable, disgraceful, humiliating, mortifying, discreditable, disreputable, undignified, infamous, ignoble, inglorious, scandalous, abject, sorry, base. **2** *his ignominious behaviour* contemptible, despicable, offensive, revolting, wicked, vile, base, low.
Opposites HONOURABLE; GLORIOUS; ADMIRABLE.

ignominy *noun* **1** *the ignominy of defeat* shame, dishonour, disgrace, humiliation, mortification, discredit, stigma, disrepute, infamy, ignobleness, scandal, opprobrium, obloquy, abjectness. **2** *behave with ignominy* contemptibleness, dishonour, wickedness, baseness, vileness, dishonesty, treachery.
Opposites HONOUR.

ignorance *noun* **1** *ignorance of the law* unawareness, unfamiliarity, unconsciousness, lack of enlightenment, lack of knowledge/information, inexperience, greenness, innocence; *lit.* nescience. **2** *appalled at the ignorance of the pupils* lack of education/knowledge, illiteracy, lack of intelligence, unintelligence, stupidity, thickness, denseness, unenlightenment, benightedness.
Opposites KNOWLEDGE; EDUCATION; ENLIGHTENMENT.

ignorant *adjective* **1** *ignorant of legal procedure* unaware of, unfamiliar with, unconversant with, unacquainted with, unconscious of, uninformed about, unenlightened about, inexperienced in, blind to, uninitiated in, unschooled in, naive about, innocent about; *inf.* in the dark about; *lit.* nescient of. **2** *ignorant pupils* unscholarly, uneducated, untaught, unschooled, untutored, untrained, illiterate, unlettered, unlearned, unread, uninformed, unknowledgeable, unintelligent, stupid, unenlightened, benighted; *inf.* thick, dense, dumb. **3** *ill-mannered, ignorant louts* rude, crude, coarse, vulgar, gross, insensitive.

ignore *verb* **1** *ignore their nasty remarks* disregard, pay no attention/heed to, take no notice of, brush aside, pass over, shrug off, push aside, shut one's eyes to, be oblivious to, turn a blind eye to, turn a deaf ear to. **2** *ignore her former friend* slight, spurn, cold-shoulder, look right through, look past, turn one's back on, send to Coventry; *inf.* give someone the brush-off, pass up, cut dead, cut. **3** *just ignore the first question* set aside, pay no attention to, take no account of, omit, leave out, overlook, neglect; *inf.* skip.

ill *adjective* **1** *the patient has been ill for some time | feeling rather ill* not well, unwell, ailing, poorly, sick, sickly, on the sick list, infirm, off-colour, afflicted, indisposed, out of sorts, diseased, bedridden, invalided, weak, feeble, valetudinarian; *inf.* under the weather, laid up, seedy, dicky, queasy, queer, funny. **2** *the ill feeling/will in the firm* hostile, antagonistic, acrimonious, belligerent, bellicose, unfriendly, unkind, spiteful, rancorous, resentful, malicious, malevolent, bitter. **3** *his ill temper* fractious, irritable, irascible, cross, cantakerous, crabbed, surly, snappish, gruff, sullen. **4** *an ill wind | suffering ill luck* adverse, unfavourable, unadvantageous, unlucky, unfortunate, unpropitious, inauspicious, unpromising, ominous, infelicitous. **5** *the ill-effects of the medicine/accident* harmful, detrimental, deleterious, hurtful, damaging, pernicious, destructive, ruinous. **6** *a person of ill repute* bad, infamous, low, wicked, nefarious, vile, evil, foul, sinful, iniquitous, sinister, corrupt, depraved, degenerate. **7** *ill manners* rude, unmannerly, impolite, objectionable, boorish. **8** *ill management* unsatisfactory, unacceptable, inadequate, deficient, faulty, poor, unskilful, inexpert. **ill at ease** *adjective* uncomfortable, uneasy, awkward, embarrassed, self-conscious, out of place, strange, unsure, uncertain, unsettled, hesitant, faltering, restless, unrelaxed, disquieted, unquiet, disturbed, discomfited, troubled, anxious, on edge, edgy, nervous, tense, on tenterhooks, apprehensive, distrustful; *inf.* on pins and needles.
Opposites HEALTHY; WELL; FRIENDLY; FAVOURABLE.

ill *noun* **1** *she meant him no ill* harm, hurt, injury, mischief, pain, trouble, unpleasantness, misfortune. **2** *the ills of life* pain, misfortune, suffering, misery, woe, affliction, damage, disaster, tribulation; troubles, problems, trials. **3** *bodily ills* illness, ill/poor health; ailment, disorder, complaint, sickness, disease, malady, infirmity, indisposition, infection, contagion.

ill *adverb* **1** *speak ill of them* badly, unfavourably, with disfavour, with disapproval, with hostility, hostilely, unkindly, maliciously, spitefully. **2** *it went ill with them* badly, hard, adversely, unsuccessfully, unfortunately, unluckily, inauspiciously. **3** *we could ill afford it* barely, scarcely, hardly, with difficulty. **4** *ill-adapted to country life* badly, poorly, insufficiently, inadequately, unsatisfactorily, faultily.

ill-advised *adjective* unwise, ill-considered, imprudent, incautious, injudicious, ill-judged, impolitic, misguided, foolish, wrong-headed, foolhardy, rash, hasty, overhasty, short-sighted, uncircumspect, thoughtless, careless, reckless.
Opposites WISE; SENSIBLE.

ill-assorted *adjective* mismatched, incongruous, unsuited, incompatible, inharmonious, uncongenial.

ill-bred *adjective* ill-mannered, bad-mannered, unmannerly, rude, impolite, discourteous, uncivil, ungentlemanly, unladylike, boorish, churlish, loutish, vulgar, coarse, crass, uncouth, crude, unrefined, uncivilized, ungallant, indelicate, indecorous, unseemly.

ill-defined *adjective* indistinct, unclear, blurred, fuzzy, vague, nebulous, shadowy, dim.

ill-disposed *adjective* hostile, opposing, opposed, antagonistic, unfriendly, unsympathetic, averse, contrary, antipathetic, inimical; *inf.* anti, down on.

illegal *adjective* unlawful, illegitimate, illicit, lawless, criminal, actionable, felonious, unlicensed, unauthorized, unsanctioned, unwarranted, unofficial, outlawed, banned, forbidden, barred, prohibited, interdicted, proscribed, contraband, black-market, under the counter, bootleg.
Opposites LEGAL; LAWFUL.

illegible *adjective* unreadable, hard to read, indecipherable, unintelligible, scrawled, scribbled, hieroglyphic, squiggly, crabbed, faint, obscure; *inf.* clear as mud.
Opposites LEGIBLE; CLEAR.

illegitimate *adjective* **1** *illegitimate use of property* illegal, unlawful, illicit, lawless, criminal, unlicensed, unauthorized, unsanctioned. *See* ILLEGAL. **2** *an illegitimate child* natural, love, born out of wedlock, born on the wrong side of the blanket, fatherless, bastard. **3** *an illegitimate deduction* illogical, wrongly inferred/deduced, unsound, spurious, incorrect, invalid. **4** *illegitimate language usage* irregular, non-standard, substandard, ungrammatical, dialectal, colloquial, informal.
Opposites LAWFUL; LEGAL; LEGITIMATE.

ill-fated *adjective* unlucky, luckless, unfortunate, hapless, unhappy, doomed, blighted, star-crossed, ill-starred, ill-omened.

ill-favoured *adjective* plain, ugly, ugly looking, hideous, unsightly, unlovely, unattractive; *Am.* homely.

ill feeling *noun* ill will, bad blood, hostility, enmity, hatred, no love lost, antipathy, aversion, dislike, antagonism, acrimony, animus, indignation, anger, wrath, unfriendliness,

unkindness, spite, spitefulness, rancour, grudge, resentment, bitterness, dissatisfaction, malice, malevolence, belligerence, bellicosity; hard feelings.
Opposites FRIENDSHIP; GOODWILL.

ill-founded *adjective* baseless, groundless, without foundation, foundationless, unjustified, unsupported, unsubstantiated, unproven, unverified, unauthenticated, unreliable.

ill humour *noun* ill temper, bad temper, temper, bad mood, huff, pet, fit of pique, rage; moodiness, irritability, irascibility, peevishness, crossness, crabbedness, testiness.

illicit *adjective* illegal, unlawful, illegitimate, lawless, criminal, unlicensed, unauthorized, unsanctioned, unofficial, outlawed, banned, forbidden, prohibited. See ILLEGAL.
Opposites LICIT; LEGAL; LAWFUL.

illiteracy *noun* illiterateness, inability to read; lack of education, ignorance, unenlightenment, benightedness; *lit.* nescience.

illiterate *adjective* unable to read; uneducated, untaught, unschooled, untutored, uninstructed, unlearned, unlettered, ignorant; *lit.* nescient.

ill-judged *adjective* ill-advised, ill-considered, unwise, imprudent, injudicious, misguided, foolish, foolhardy, rash, hasty, short-sighted. See ILL-ADVISED.

ill-mannered *adjective* unmannerly, mannerless, rude, impolite, discourteous, uncivil, insolent, impertinent, badly behaved, ill-behaved, boorish, loutish, oafish, uncouth, coarse, gross, ill-bred.

ill-natured *adjective* ill-tempered, bad-tempered, ill-humoured, moody, irritable, irascible, surly, peevish, petulant, cross, crabbed, testy, grouchy, disagreeable, perverse, mean, nasty, disobliging, spiteful, malicious.

illness *noun* ailment, sickness, disorder, complaint, malady, disease, affliction, attack, disability, indisposition, infection, contagion; ill health, poor health. See table.
Opposites HEALTH; FITNESS.

illogical *adjective* unsound, unreasonable, unreasoned, irrational, faulty, spurious, fallacious, fallible, unproved, untenable, specious, unscientific, sophistic, casuistic, inconclusive, inconsistent, incorrect, invalid, wrong, absurd, preposterous, meaningless, senseless.

ILLNESSES AND MEDICAL CONDITIONS

acromegaly	decompression	leprosy	Raynaud's disease
Addison's disease	sickness	leptospirosis	rheumatic fever
AIDS	dengue	leukaemia	rheumatoid
Alzheimer's disease	dermatitis	listeriosis	arthritis
anaemia	diabetes	lupus	rickets
angina	diphtheria	Lyme disease	ringworm
anorexia nervosa	dysentery	malaria	rubella
appendicitis	Ebola fever	measles	St Vitus's dance
arthritis	eczema	Ménière's disease	salmonella
asbestosis	elephantiasis	meningitis	scarlet fever
Asperger's	emphysema	motor neurone	schizophrenia
syndrome	encephalitis	disease	scurvy
asthma	epilepsy	mountain sickness	shingles
autism	food poisoning	multiple sclerosis	sickle-cell anaemia
avitaminosis	gastroenteritis	mumps	silicosis
beriberi	German measles	Munchausen's syn-	sinusitis
bilharzia	glandular fever	drome (by proxy)	sleeping sickness
Bright's disease	glaucoma	muscular dystrophy	sleepy sickness
bronchitis	goitre	myalgic encephalitis	smallpox
brucellosis	gonorrhoea	myasthenia gravis	spina bifida
bulimia nervosa	gout	narcolepsy	sweating-sickness
cancer	Graves' disease	nephritis	Sydenham's chorea
candidiasis	haemophilia	osteoporosis	syphilis
Chagas' disease	hepatitis	Paget's disease	tetanus
chickenpox	herpes	Parkinson's disease	thalassaemia
cholera	Hodgkin's disease	pellagra	tonsillitis
cirrhosis	Huntington's chorea	peritonitis	toxic shock
clinical depression	hyperthyroidism	pernicious anaemia	syndrome
coeliac disease	impetigo	phenylketonuria	toxoplasmosis
colitis	influenza	plague	trachoma
common cold	jaundice	pneumoconiosis	tuberculosis
coronary heart	kala-azar	pneumonia	typhoid fever
disease	Kaposi's sarcoma	poliomyelitis	typhus
Crohn's disease	Kawasaki disease	porphyria	venereal disease
Cushing's disease	kwashiorkor	psittacosis	Weil's disease
cyanosis	laryngitis	psoriasis	whooping cough
cystic fibrosis	Lassa fever	psychosis	yaws
cystitis	legionnaires' disease	rabies	yellow fever

ill-starred *adjective* ill-fated, unlucky, unfortunate, hapless, doomed, blighted, ill-omened. *See* ILL-FATED.

ill-tempered *adjective* ill-humoured, cross, bad-tempered, irritable, irascible, peevish, crabbed, choleric, cantankerous, grumpy, grouchy, crusty, splenetic.

ill-timed *adjective* inopportune, inconvenient, awkward, inappropriate, untimely, mistimed, badly timed, unwelcome, unfavourable, unfortunate, inept.
Opposites OPPORTUNE; TIMELY.

ill-treat *verb* treat badly, abuse, harm, injure, damage, handle roughly, mishandle, ill-use, maltreat, misuse; *inf.* knock about.
Opposites PAMPER; cosset; SPOIL.

illuminate *verb* **1** *lights illuminating the hall* light, light up, throw/cast light upon, brighten, shine on, irradiate; *lit.* illumine. **2** *illuminate the problem* clarify, make clear, clear up, shed/cast light on, elucidate, explain, make explicit, explicate, expound. **3** *illuminate a manuscript* adorn, decorate, ornament, embellish, enhance, illustrate.
Opposites DARKEN; CONFUSE.

illuminating *adjective an illuminating talk* instructive, informative, enlightening, explanatory, revealing, helpful.

illumination *noun* **1** *the illumination of the hall* lighting, lighting up, brightening, irradiation. *See* ILLUMINATE 1. **2** *see the illumination in the dark* light, beam/ray/shaft of light, radiance, gleam, glitter, effulgence; lights. **3** *the illumination of the problem* clarification, elucidation, explanation, explication. *See* ILLUMINATE 2. **4** *illumination coming to savage tribes* enlightenment, understanding, awareness, insight, learning, education, instruction, information, knowledge, revelation.

illusion *noun* **1** *create the illusion of depth* false/deceptive appearance, deception, faulty perception, misperception. **2** *under the illusion that he was her first love* delusion, misapprehension, misconception, deception, false/mistaken impression, fallacy, error, misjudgement, fancy. **3** *see an illusion* hallucination, figment of the imagination, phantom, spectre, mirage, phantasm, fantasy, will-o'-the-wisp, ignis fatuus.
Opposites REALITY; TRUTH.

illusive, illusory *adjective* deceptive, delusory, delusional, delusive, illusionary, false, fallacious, mistaken, erroneous, misleading, untrue, specious, unreal, imagined, imaginary, fancied, non-existent, fanciful, notional, chimerical, dreamlike.

illustrate *verb* **1** *illustrate the story* add pictures/drawings/sketches to, provide artwork for, adorn, decorate, ornament, embellish. **2** *illustrate his point* exemplify, demonstrate, point up, show, instance, make plain/clear, clarify, bring home, emphasize, interpret.

illustration *noun* **1** *the illustration in the child's book* picture, drawing, sketch, plate, figure; artwork, adornment, decoration, ornamentation, embellishment. **2** *interesting illustrations explaining his theory* example, typical case, case in point, instance, specimen, sample, exemplar, analogy. **3** *appreciate the illustration of his theory* exemplification, demonstration, pointing up, showing, instancing, clarification, emphasis, interpretation.

illustrative *adjective* exemplifying, explanatory, elucidative, explicative, expository, interpretative, interpretive.

illustrious *adjective* renowned, famous, famed, well-known, celebrated, acclaimed, noted, notable, distinguished, esteemed, honoured, prominent, pre-eminent, splendid, brilliant, remarkable, great, noble, glorious, exalted, venerable.
Opposites UNKNOWN; OBSCURE.

ill will *noun* ill feeling, bad blood, hostility, enmity, hatred, antipathy, antagonism, acrimony, animus, unfriendliness, spite, rancour, resentment, malice; hard feelings. *See* ILL FEELING.

image *noun* **1** *images of the saints* likeness, representation, resemblance, effigy, figure, figurine, doll, statue, statuette, sculpture, bust, idol, icon, fetish, graven image, false god, painting, picture, portrait. **2** *the image formed by the camera/telescope* reproduction, optical representation, reflection; picture, facsimile, photograph, snapshot, photo. **3** *an image of what the new country would be like* mental picture/representation, vision, concept, conception, idea, perception, impression, fancy, thought. **4** *he is the image of his father* double, living image, replica, clone, copy, reproduction, counterpart, similitude, doppelganger; *inf.* very spit, spitting image, chip off the old block, ringer, dead ringer. **5** *politicians trying to improve their images* public impression/perception/conception. **6** *he is the image of goodness* emblem, symbol, archetype, perfect example, embodiment, incarnation. **7** *the use of images in poetry* figure of speech, conceit, trope, figurative expression.

imaginable *adjective* thinkable, conceivable, supposable, believable, credible, comprehensible, possible, within the bounds of possibility, probable, likely, plausible, feasible.

imaginary *adjective* fanciful, fancied, fantastic, unreal, non-existent, illusory, illusive, visionary, dreamy, dreamlike, shadowy, unsubstantial, chimerical, figmental, notional, assumed, supposed, suppositious, fictitious, fictional, legendary, mythical, mythological, made-up, invented, hallucinatory, phantasmal, phantasmic, spectral, ghostly, ideal, idealistic, Utopian, romantic.
Opposites REAL; ACTUAL.

imagination *noun* **1** *the poem shows imagination | handling the project needs imagination* imaginative faculty, creative power, creativity, vision, inspiration, power of fancy, fancifulness, insight, inventiveness, originality, invention, innovation, resourcefulness, ingenuity, enterprise, cleverness, wit. **2** *I thought I saw her but it was only my imagination* mental image, illusion, fancy, figment of the imagination, vision, dream, chimera, shadow, phantom, conceptualization, unreality.

imaginative *adjective an imaginative writer/cook/ planner* creative, visionary, inspired, fanciful, inventive, original, innovative, resourceful, ingenious, enterprising, clever, whimsical. **Opposites** UNIMAGINATIVE; RUN-OF-THE-MILL; PEDESTRIAN.

imagine *verb* **1** *he imagines a bright future for himself* picture, see in the mind's eye, visualize, envisage, envision, conjure up, dream about, dream up, fantasize about, conceptualize, think up, conceive, think of, plan, project, scheme. **2** *I imagine he'll be late* assume, presume, suppose, think, believe, be of the opinion that, take it, gather, fancy, judge, deem, infer, deduce, conjecture, surmise, guess, reckon, suspect, realize.

imbecile *noun* **1** *imbeciles unable to look after themselves* mental defective, retardate, halfwit, idiot. **2** *that child is an imbecile* fool, idiot, dolt, halfwit, nitwit, dunce, dunderhead, dullard, simpleton; *inf.* thickhead, dim-wit, dope.

imbecile *adjective* **1** *an imbecile patient* mentally defective/retarded, feeble-minded, simple. **2** *that imbecile child has got the wrong key* stupid, foolish, idiotic, doltish, halfwitted, witless, dull; *inf.* dense, thickheaded, dimwitted, dopey. **3** *what an imbecile thing to do* foolish, stupid, silly, idiotic, senseless, absurd, crazy, mad, fatuous, inane, asinine.

imbed *verb. See* EMBED *verb.*

imbibe *verb* **1** *imbibe some water* drink, quaff, swallow, consume; *inf.* swig, knock back, sink. **2** *he doesn't imbibe any more* drink, drink alcohol, take strong drink. **3** *imbibe the fresh air* drink in, breathe in, inhale. **4** *imbibe ideas* assimilate, absorb, take in, digest, learn, acquire, gain, pick up. **5** *imbibe moisture* absorb, soak up, blot up, sop up, suck up, draw up, take up.

imbroglio *noun* **1** *cannot sort out the imbroglio in the office* complicated situation, complication, complexity, problem, difficulty, trouble, entanglement, confusion, muddle, mess, quandary. **2** *an imbroglio of papers* confused heap, jumble, muddle, mess. **3** *people involved in an imbroglio in the bar* disagreement, conflict, altercation, argument, quarrel, fight, row, commotion, disturbance, turmoil, fracas.

imbue *verb he imbues his sermons with topicality* fill, impregnate, inject, inculcate, instil, ingrain, inspire, permeate, charge.

imitate *verb* **1** *imitate the language of Shakespeare | imitate his elder brother in everything* copy, emulate, take as a model/pattern, follow the example of, follow as an example, take after, follow, follow suit, take a page from someone's book, tread in the steps of, walk in the footsteps of, echo. **2** *cruel children imitating the crippled man* mimic, ape, impersonate, do an impression of, parody, mock, caricature, burlesque, travesty; *inf.* send up, take off, spoof, do; *Am. inf.* make like. **3** *the stage set imitated a street market* look like, simulate, echo, mirror. **4** *imitate the portrait* copy, reproduce, replicate, duplicate, counterfeit, forge, fake.

imitation *noun* **1** *the house was built in imitation of Robert Adam* emulation, resemblance. *See* IMI-TATE 1. **2** *the cruel imitation of the crippled man* mimicking, mimicry, aping, impersonation, impression, parody, mocking, mockery, caricature, burlesque, travesty; *inf.* send-up, take-off, spoof. **3** *a bad imitation of the portrait* copy, reproduction, counterfeit, forgery, fake.

imitation *adjective imitation leather/antiques* artificial, synthetic, simulated, man-made, ersatz, mock, sham, fake, reproduction, repro; *inf.* pseudo, phoney. **Opposites** REAL; GENUINE.

imitative *adjective* **1** *an imitative style | a style imitative of Dickens* in imitation of, copying, copied, emulating, emulated, derivative, unoriginal, mimicking, mimetic, echoic, parrotlike, plagiarized, second-hand; *inf.* copycat. **2** *an imitative word* onomatopoeic, echoic.

imitator *noun* copier, copyist, emulator, follower, mimic, echo, impersonator, epigone, plagiarist, counterfeiter, forger, ape, parrot.

immaculate *adjective* **1** *immaculate white sheets | immaculate rooms* clean, spotless, unsoiled, unstained, snowy-white, whiter than white, speckless, spick and span, neat, neat as a new pin, spruce, trim. **2** *of immaculate character* flawless, faultless, stainless, unblemished, spotless, pure, perfect, above reproach, innocent, virtuous, incorrupt, guiltless, sinless, unsullied, undefiled, untarnished, uncontaminated, unpolluted. **Opposites** FILTHY; DIRTY; BLAMEWORTHY.

immaterial *adjective* **1** *it's immaterial what he thinks* unimportant, inconsequential, of no matter/moment, of little account, irrelevant, insignificant, trivial, petty, slight, inappreciable. **2** *immaterial as ghosts* not material, incorporeal, bodiless, unembodied, disembodied, discarnate, intangible, impalpable, ethereal, unsubstantial, airy, aerial, spiritual, ghostly, transcendental, unearthly, supernatural. **Opposites** IMPORTANT; SIGNIFICANT; TANGIBLE.

immature *adjective* **1** *immature fruit/plans* unripe, undeveloped, unformed, imperfect, unfinished, incomplete, half-grown, crude, raw, green, unmellowed, unfledged, untimely. **2** *an immature young man* adolescent, childish, babyish, infantile, juvenile, puerile, jejune, callow, inexperienced, green, unsophisticated; *inf.* wet behind the ears. **Opposites** RIPE; MATURE.

immaturity *noun* **1** *the immaturity of the fruit/ plans* unripeness, imperfection, lack of completion, crudeness, crudity, rawness, greenness. *See* IMMATURE 1. **2** *the immaturity of the young men* adolescence, childishness, babyishness, infantileness, juvenility, puerility, lack of experience, inexperience. *See* IMMATURE 2 .

immeasurable *adjective* not measurable, measureless, limitless, boundless, unbounded, illimitable, infinite, incalculable, unfathomable, fathomless, undeterminable, indeterminate, inestimable, extensive, vast, innumerable, countless, numberless, endless, neverending, interminable, inexhaustible, bottomless.

immediate *adjective* **1** *an immediate reaction* instant, instantaneous, on the spot, prompt, swift, speedy, sudden, abrupt. **2** *his immediate neighbour* near, nearest, next, next door, close, closest, adjacent, adjoining, abutting, contiguous, proximate. **3** *the immediate cause of his failure* direct, primary. **4** *in the immediate past* recent. **5** *our immediate plans* present, current, existing, existent, actual, extant, urgent, pressing. **6** *get immediate experience* direct, firsthand, hands on, in service, in the field, on the job.

immediately *adverb* **1** *he went away immediately* right away, right now, straight away, at once, instantly, now, this/that very minute, this/that instant, directly, promptly, forthwith, without delay, without hesitation, unhesitatingly, *tout de suite*; *inf.* before you can/could say Jack Robinson, pronto. **2** *he was immediately behind us* right, directly, closely, at close quarters. **3** *I heard the news immediately from the victim* directly, at first hand, without intermediary.

immemorial *adjective* ancient, age-old, timeless, dateless, archaic, of yore, rooted in the past, long-standing, time-honoured, ancestral, traditional.

immense *adjective* huge, vast, massive, enormous, gigantic, colossal, giant, great, very large, extensive, infinite, immeasurable, illimitable, monumental, tremendous, prodigious, elephantine, monstrous, titanic, Brobdingnagian; *inf.* ginormous, mega.
Opposites TINY; MINUTE.

immerse *verb* **1** *immerse the cloth in the dye* submerge, plunge, dip, dunk, duck, sink, douse, souse, soak, drench, imbue, saturate. **2** *immerse the Christian converts* baptise, christen, purify, lustrate. **3** *immerse oneself in one's work* absorb, engross, occupy, engage, preoccupy, involve, engulf; *inf.* lose oneself in.

immigrant *noun* non-native, settler, incomer, newcomer, new arrival, migrant, naturalized citizen, expatriate.

imminent *adjective* impending, at hand, fast-approaching, close, near, approaching, coming, forthcoming, on the way, about to happen, upon us, in the offing, on the horizon, in the air, brewing, threatening, menacing, looming.
Opposites DISTANT; REMOTE.

immobile *adjective* immobilized, without moving, unmoving, motionless, unable to move, immovable, still, static, at rest, stationary, at a standstill, stock-still, dormant, rooted, fixed to the spot, rigid, frozen, stiff, riveted, like a statue, as if turned to stone, immotile, immovtive.

immobilize *verb* bring to a standstill/halt, halt, stop, put out of action, render inactive, inactivate, paralyse, make inoperative, freeze, transfix, disable, cripple.

immoderate *adjective* excessive, extreme, intemperate, lavish, undue, inordinate, extravagant, unreasonable, unjustified, unwarranted, uncalled-for, outrageous, egregious, unrestrained, unrestricted, uncontrolled, unlimited, unbridled, uncurbed, self-indulgent,

overindulgent, prodigal, profligate, wanton, dissipative.

immoderation *noun* excess, excessiveness, intemperateness, inordinateness, lavishness, lack of restraint, self-indulgence, overindulgence, profligacy, wantonness, dissipation. *See* IMMODERATE.

immodest *adjective* forward, bold, brazen, impudent, unblushing, shameless, wanton, indecorous, improper, indecent; *inf.* fresh, cheeky.

immoral *adjective* bad, wrongdoing, unprincipled, dishonest, unethical, wicked, evil, sinful, impure, iniquitous, corrupt, depraved, vile, base, degenerate, debauched, abandoned, dissolute, villainous, nefarious, miscreant, reprobate, perverted, indecent, lewd, licentious, pornographic, unchaste, of easy virtue, bawdy.

immorality *noun* badness, dishonesty, unethicalness, wickedness, evil, impurity, sinfulness, sin, iniquity, corruption, depravity, vileness, vice, turpitude, degeneracy, debauchery, dissolution, perversion, indecency, lewdness, licentiousness, bawdiness. *See* IMMORAL.

immortal *adjective* **1** *immortal beings/love* never dying, undying, deathless, eternal, ever living, everlasting, never-ending, endless, imperishable, perdurable, timeless, indestructible, unfading, undecaying, perennial, evergreen, perpetual, lasting, enduring, constant, abiding, immutable, indissoluble; *lit.* sempiternal. **2** *immortal poets* famous, celebrated, remembered, commemorated, honoured, lauded, glorified.
Opposites MORTAL; EPHEMERAL; TRANSITORY.

immortal *noun* **1** *mythological immortals* god, goddess, Olympian. *See table at* GOD. **2** *the immortals of poetry* great, hero, genius, celebrity.

immortality *noun* **1** *angels blessed with immortality* eternal life, deathlessness, everlastingness, endlessness, imperishability, timelessness, unfadingness, evergreenness, perpetuality, constancy. *See* IMMORTAL *adjective* 1. **2** *the immortality of the poet* fame, renown, repute, celebrity, commemoration, honour, glory.

immortalize *verb* commemorate, memorialize, eternalize, eternize, perpetuate, exalt, laud, glorify.

immovable *adjective* **1** *immovable concrete pillars* set firm/fast, fast, firm, fixed, secure, stable, rooted, riveted, moored, anchored, stuck, jammed, stiff, unbudgeable. **2** *the spectators stood immovable* motionless, unmoving, stationary, still, stock-still, at a standstill, dead still, statue-like. **3** *the planning committee were immovable* adamant, firm, steadfast, unwavering, unswerving, resolute, determined, tenacious, stubborn, dogged, obdurate, inflexible, unyielding, unbending, uncompromising, unshakeable, inexorable.

immune *adjective* not subject to, not liable to, protected from, safe from, unsusceptible to, secure against, exempt from, clear of, free from, freed from, absolved from, released from, excused from, relieved of, spared from,

excepted from, exempted from, unaffected by, resistant to, proof against; *inf.* let off.
Opposites LIABLE; SUSCEPTIBLE; PRONE.

immunity *noun* **1** *immunity from the disease* non-susceptibility to, resistance to, protection from, immunization/inoculation against. **2** *immunity from tax* non-liability (for), exemption, exception, freedom, release. **3** *diplomatic immunity* indemnity, privilege, prerogative, special treatment, right, charter, liberty, licence, permission. **4** *immunity from religious observance* indemnity, dispensation, absolution, exoneration, excusal.

immunize *verb* inoculate, vaccinate, protect, shield, safeguard; *inf.* give a jab to.

imp *noun* **1** *devils and imps* little devil, demon, hobgoblin, goblin, elf, sprite, puck, gnome, dwarf. **2** *the child's a little imp* scamp, rogue, rascal, minx, mischief-maker, trouble-maker, prankster, brat, gamin, urchin, tearaway.

impact *noun* **1** *the impact of the two cars* collision, contact, crash, smash, striking, clash, bump, bang, knock, jolt, thump, whack, thwack, slam, smack, slap. **2** *the impact of his talk* influence, effect, impression; results, consequences, repercussions. **3** *he took the full impact of the blow* force, full force, shock, brunt, impetus, pressure.

impair *verb* weaken, lessen, decrease, reduce, blunt, diminish, deteriorate, enfeeble, debilitate, enervate, damage, mar, spoil, injure, harm, hinder, disable, cripple, impede, undermine, vitiate.
Opposites INCREASE; IMPROVE; ENHANCE.

impale *verb* transfix, pierce, stab, prick, stick, spear, spike, run through, disembowel.

impalpable *adjective* **1** *if there is a lump in the abdomen it is impalpable* intangible, imperceptible to the touch. **2** *find his conclusions impalpable* abstruse, obscure, unclear, indiscernible, tenuous, esoteric, recondite.

impart *verb* **1** *impart the good news* pass on, convey, communicate, transmit, relate, tell, make known, report, disclose, reveal, divulge, proclaim, broadcast. **2** *his age imparts wisdom to his words* bestow, confer, give, grant, lend, accord, afford, assign, offer, yield, contribute, dispense.

impartial *adjective* unbiased, unprejudiced, disinterested, detached, objective, neutral, equitable, even-handed, fair, fair-minded, just, open-minded, without favouritism, free from discrimination, non-partisan, with no axe to grind, without fear or favour.

impartiality *noun* lack of bias/prejudice, disinterest, detachment, objectivity, neutrality, even-handedness, fairness, justness, open-mindedness. *See* IMPARTIAL.

impassable *adjective* **1** *impassable roads* unnavigable, untraversable, impenetrable, closed, blocked, obstructed, pathless, trackless. **2** *impassable obstacles* insurmountable, insuperable, unconquerable.

impasse *noun* deadlock, dead end, stalemate, checkmate, standstill, full/dead stop; *Am.* stand-off.

impassioned *adjective* passionate, amorous, ardent, fervent, fervid, perfervid, vehement, intense, violent, fiery, burning, inflamed, emotional, emotive, zealous, eager, enthusiastic, animated, excited, aroused, feverish, frantic.

impatience *noun* **1** *wait with impatience for the doors to open* restlessness, restiveness, impetuosity, eagerness, avidity, excitability, anxiety, agitation, nervousness, edginess, fretfulness, jitteriness, fluster, disquiet, disquietude. **2** *answer with impatience* abruptness, brusqueness, shortness, curtness, irascibility, irritability, testiness, snappiness, querulousness, peevishness, intolerance.

impatient *adjective* **1** *an impatient crowd* restless, restive, impetuous, eager, excitable, anxious, agitated, nervous, edgy. **2** *an impatient answer* abrupt, brusque, terse, short, short-tempered, quick-tempered, curt, irritated, angry, testy, snappy, querulous, peevish, intolerant. **3** *impatient to see her boyfriend* anxious, eager, keen, avid, desirous, yearning, longing.

impeach *verb* **1** *impeach his neighbour for breaking his fence* charge, accuse, bring a case/charge against, indict, inculpate, implicate, blame, censure, hold accountable for, denounce, arraign. **2** *they impeached his honour* challenge, question, call into question, cast doubt on, impugn, attack, assail, revile, discredit, deprecate, cast slurs/aspersions on, malign, slander.

impeccable *adjective* **1** *impeccable behaviour | speak impeccable French* perfect, faultless, flawless, unblemished, exemplary, correct, exact, precise, ideal. **2** *an impeccable young woman* virtuous, innocent, chaste, pure, pure as the driven snow, sinless, upright, irreproachable, unimpeachable, blameless, above suspicion, incorrupt.
Opposites IMPERFECT; SINFUL.

impecunious *adjective* penniless, insolvent, poor, poor as a church mouse, without a penny, without a sou, hard up, impoverished, poverty-stricken, destitute, unable to make ends meet, needy, indigent, penurious; *inf.* broke, flat/stony broke, strapped for cash, cleaned out; skint.
Opposites WEALTHY; AFFLUENT.

impede *verb* hinder, obstruct, hamper, handicap, block, check, bar, curb, hold back, hold up, delay, interfere with, disrupt, retard, slow, slow down, brake, restrain, thwart, frustrate, baulk, stop; *inf.* put a spanner in the works.
Opposites ASSIST; ADVANCE; FACILITATE.

impediment *noun* **1** *an impediment to our plans* hindrance, obstruction, obstacle, handicap, block, stumbling-block, check, encumbrance, bar, barrier, curb, brake, restraint, drawback, difficulty, snag, set-back, clog. **2** *she has an impediment so has to speak slowly* stammer, stutter, speech defect, hesitancy, faltering.

impedimenta *plural noun* equipment, gear, baggage, luggage; effects, possessions, belongings, goods, movables, traps, accoutrements, odds and ends, things; *inf.* stuff.

impel *verb* **1** *impel him to go* urge, press, exhort, force, oblige, constrain, necessitate, require, demand, make, apply pressure, pressure, pressurize, spur, prod, goad, incite, prompt, chivvy, persuade, inspire. **2** *impel the vehicle* actuate, set in motion, get going, get moving, propel.

impending *adjective* imminent, at hand, approaching, coming, forthcoming, close, near, nearing, on the way, about to happen, upon us, in the offing, on the horizon, in the air/wind, brewing, looming, threatening, menacing.

impenetrable *adjective* **1** *impenetrable containers* impervious, impermeable, solid, dense, thick, hard, closed, sealed, hermetically sealed, resistant, waterproof, puncture-proof, tight, unpierceable. **2** *impenetrable forests* impassable, unpassable, inaccessible, thick, dense, overgrown, jungly, pathless, trackless, untrodden. **3** *impenetrable jargon* incomprehensible, unintelligible, indiscernible, baffling, puzzling, abstruse, obscure, hidden, inexplicable, unfathomable, recondite, inscrutable, enigmatic. **4** *impenetrable ignorance* stupid, senseless, obtuse, gross, prejudiced, bigoted, biased, narrow-minded.

impenitent *adjective* unrepentant, unrepenting, uncontrite, remorseless, obdurate, unfeeling, uncaring, abandoned.

imperative *adjective* **1** *it is imperative that you stay* important, vital, essential, of the essence, crucial, critical, necessary, indispensable, required, mandatory, obligatory, exigent, pressing, urgent. **2** *an imperative tone of voice* imperious, authoritative, peremptory, commanding, lordly, masterful, autocratic, dictatorial, domineering, overbearing, magisterial.
Opposites UNIMPORTANT; OPTIONAL; SUBMISSIVE.

imperceptible *adjective* unnoticeable, unobtrusive, unapparent, slight, small, gradual, subtle, faint, fine, inappreciable, inconsequential, tiny, minute, miniscule, microscopic, infinitesimal, undetectable, indistinguishable, indiscernible, invisible, indistinct, unclear, obscure, vague, indefinite, shadowy, inaudible, muffled, impalpable.
Opposites OBVIOUS; NOTICEABLE.

imperceptibly *adverb* unnoticeably, unobtrusively, unseen, gradually, slowly, subtly, inappreciably, undetectably, infinitesimally, little by little, bit by bit.

imperfect *adjective* **1** *imperfect goods sold cheaply* faulty, flawed, defective, blemished, damaged, impaired, broken. **2** *an imperfect set of books* incomplete, not whole/entire, deficient, broken, partial. **3** *imperfect knowledge of the subject* deficient, inadequate, insufficient, lacking, rudimentary, limited, patchy, sketchy. **4** *imperfect plants* undeveloped, immature, premature.

imperfection *noun* **1** *an imperfection in the vase* fault, flaw, defect, deformity, blemish; crack, break, scratch, cut, tear, stain, spot. **2** *the imperfection of the set* incompleteness, deficiency, partialness. **3** *an imperfection in his character* failing, flaw, foible, deficiency, weakness, weak point, shortcoming, fallibility, frailty, infirmity, peccadillo.

imperial *adjective* **1** *his/her imperial majesty* royal, sovereign, regal, monarchal, kingly, queenly, princely, majestic, imperatorial. **2** *he has an imperial carriage* majestic, magnificent, grand, great, lofty, imposing, august, stately, splendid, glorious, exalted. **3** *the imperial ruler of the region* supreme, absolute, dominant, predominant, paramount, chief. **4** *very imperial in her manner* commanding, lordly, masterful, authoritative, imperious, peremptory, domineering. *See* IMPERIOUS.

imperil *verb* endanger, expose to danger, put in danger/jeopardy, put at risk, risk, jeopardize, hazard, gamble with, take a chance with.

imperious *adjective* peremptory, overbearing, overweening, domineering, high-handed, assertive, authoritative, commanding, lordly, masterful, dictatorial.

impermanent *adjective* non-permanent, not permanent, temporary, transient, transitory, passing, fleeting, momentary, short-lived, ephemeral, evanescent, volatile.

impersonal *adjective* **1** *an impersonal assessment of the candidates* detached, objective, disinterested, dispassionate, neutral, unbiased, unprejudiced, unswayed, fair, equitable, even-handed. **2** *an impersonal manner* cold, cool, frigid, aloof, formal, stiff, rigid, wooden, starchy, stilted, stuffy, matter-of-fact, businesslike, bureaucratic.
Opposites BIASED; FRIENDLY; WARM.

impersonate *verb* imitate, mimic, personate, mock, ape, parody, caricature, burlesque, masquerade as, pose as, pass oneself off as; *inf.* take off, do.

impersonation *noun* imitation, mimicry, impression, personation, mockery, parody, caricature, burlesque, travesty; *inf.* take-off.

impertinence *noun* **1** *the impertinence of the young woman* insolence, impudence, cheek, rudeness, impoliteness, unmannerliness, lack of civility, discourtesy, boldness, brazenness, audacity, effrontery, presumptuousness, brashness; *inf.* brass neck, nerve, sauce, lip, gall. *See* IMPERTINENT 1. **2** *impertinence of the information* irrelevance, inapplicability, inappositeness, unrelatedness. *See* IMPERTINENT 2.

impertinent *adjective* **1** *an impertinent youth/act* insolent, impudent, cheeky, rude, impolite, unmannerly, ill-mannered, uncivil, coarse, crude, uncouth, discourteous, disrespectful, bold, brazen, audacious, presumptuous, forward, pert, brash, shameless; *inf.* brass-necked, saucy, fresh, flip. **2** *this document is impertinent to the case* irrelevant, inapplicable, inapposite, immaterial, unrelated, unconnected, not germane; beside the point.
Opposites MANNERLY; POLITE; PERTINENT.

imperturbable *adjective* self-possessed, composed, collected, calm, cool, calm and collected, tranquil, serene, inexcitable, unflappable, even-tempered, easygoing, unperturbed, at ease, unruffled, untroubled, undismayed, unmoved, nonchalant.
Opposites NERVOUS; EDGY; EXCITABLE.

impervious *adjective* **1** *impervious to arguments* unmoved by, unaffected by, proof against,

immune to, invulnerable to, unreceptive to, untouched by, unswayable by, closed to.
2 *impervious containers* impenetrable, impermeable, sealed, hermetically closed. *See* IMPENETRABLE 1.

impetuous *adjective* **1** *an impetuous action* hasty, precipitate, headlong, impulsive, spontaneous, impromptu, spur-of-the-moment, unthinking, unplanned, unthought out, ill-conceived, ill-considered, unreasoned, reckless, rash, foolhardy, heedless. **2** *an impetuous person* impulsive, hasty, spontaneous, eager, enthusiastic, impatient, excitable, ardent, passionate, zealous, headstrong, rash, reckless, foolhardy, wild, uncontrolled. **3** *an impetuous wind* violent, forceful, powerful, vigorous, vehement, raging, rampant, unrestrained, uncontrolled, unbridled.
Opposites CAUTIOUS; WARY.

impetus *noun* **1** *the car lost impetus on the steep slope* momentum, propulsion, impelling force, continuing motion, energy, force, power.
2 *the student needs some impetus to start studying* stimulus, instigation, actuation, moving force, motivation, incentive, inducement, inspiration, encouragement, influence, push, urging, pressing, spur, goading, goad.

impiety *noun* **1** *churchgoers offended at his impiety* godlessness, ungodliness, unholiness, irreligion, sinfulness, unrighteousness, sacrilege, irreverence, disrespect, profaneness, scoffing, derision, apostasy, atheism, agnosticism, paganism, heathenism. **2** *appalled at their impieties* sin, vice, wrongdoing, evildoing, transgression, desecration, profanity, blasphemy.

impinge *verb* **impinge on** **1** *impinge on other people's rights* encroach on, infringe, intrude on, invade, trespass on, obtrude into, make inroads into, violate, usurp. **2** *impinge on her consciousness* affect, have an effect/bearing on, impress, touch, exert influence on, bear upon. **3** *the rain impinging on the roof* strike, hit, dash/crash/smash against, collide with.

impious *adjective* godless, ungodly, unholy, irreligious, sinful, unrighteous, sacrilegious, profane, blasphemous, irreverent, disrespectful, apostatic, atheistic, agnostic, pagan, heathen.

impish *adjective* **1** *impish little boys* mischievous, mischief-making, full of mischief, rascally, roguish, prankish, unruly, troublemaking, devilish, sportive. **2** *an impish smile* elfin, pixyish, puckish, mischievous, roguish.

implacable *adjective* unplacatable, unappeasable, unpacifiable, not to be appeased/pacified, unmollifiable, rancorous, grudge-holding, unforgiving, inexorable, adamant, unyielding, uncompromising, unrelenting, relentless, ruthless, remorseless, merciless, pitiless, heartless, cruel, hard.

implant *verb* **1** *implant radical ideas in her head* inculcate, instil, insinuate, inject, inseminate, sow, infuse, introduce. **2** *implant the posts in the ground* embed, fix firmly, fix, place, plant, root, set. **3** *implant hormone pellets under the skin* insert, place, put in place. **4** *implant skin tissue from a different part of the body* graft, engraft.

implausible *adjective* not likely, unlikely, improbable, hard to believe, incredible, unbelievable, unimaginable, inconceivable, debatable, questionable, doubtful.

implement *noun* **1** *garden/kitchen implements* tool, utensil, appliance, instrument, device, apparatus, contrivance, gadget; *inf.* gismo. **2** *use her faith as an implement of peace* agent, medium, channel, expedient; means.

implement *verb* *implement their instructions* fulfil, carry out, execute, perform, discharge, accomplish, achieve, realize, put into effect/action, bring about, effect, enforce.
Opposites IMPEDE; NEGLECT.

implementation *noun* *the implementation of their instructions* fulfilment, execution, discharge, accomplishment, realization, effecting, enforcement. *See* IMPLEMENT *verb.*

implicate *verb* **1** *try to implicate his friend when he was accused* incriminate, compromise, inculpate, accuse, charge, blame, impeach, involve, entangle. **2** *he was not implicated in the events* involve, concern, include, associate, connect, embroil, entangle; be a part of, tie up with.
Opposites ABSOLVE; DISSOCIATE.

implication *noun* **1** *resent the implication that he was lying* suggestion, inference, insinuation, innuendo, hint, allusion, reference, assumption, presumption. **2** *the implication of his friend in the charge* incrimination, inculpation, blame. *See* IMPLICATE 1. **3** *their implication in the events* involvement, concern, association, connection, entanglement. *See* IMPLICATE 2.

implicit *adjective* **1** *there was implicit criticism in his voice* implied, indirect, inferred, deducible, unspoken, unexpressed, undeclared, unstated, tacit, understood, hinted, suggested. **2** *implicit in the argument was a lack of confidence in management* implied, inherent, latent, taken for granted. **3** *have implicit trust in the doctor* absolute, complete, entire, total, wholehearted, perfect, sheer, utter, unqualified, unconditional, unreserved, positive, unshaken, unshakable, unhesitating, unquestioning, firm, steadfast, constant.
Opposites DIRECT; EXPLICIT; OBVIOUS; LIMITED.

implicitly *adverb* *trust the doctor implicitly* absolutely, completely, totally, wholeheartedly, utterly, unconditionally, unreservedly, without reservation, positively, unhesitatingly, unquestioningly, firmly. *See* IMPLICIT 3.

implied *adjective* *their implied criticism* implicit, indirect, inferred, deducible, unspoken, unexpressed, tacit, hinted, suggested. *See* IMPLICIT 1.

implore *verb* *implored her to come | implore forgiveness* appeal to, beg, entreat, plead with, beseech, pray, ask, request, solicit, supplicate, importune, press; crave, plead for, appeal for.

imply *verb* **1** *he implied that all was not well* insinuate, say indirectly, hint, suggest, infer, intimate, give to understand, signal, indicate. **2** *being a civil servant implies discretion* involve, entail, presuppose, presume, assume. **3** *war* *implies bloodshed* signify, mean, indicate, denote, connote, betoken, point to.

impolite *adjective* unmannerly, ill-mannered, bad-mannered, rude, discourteous, uncivil, ill-bred, ungentlemanly, unladylike, ungracious, ungallant, disrespectful, inconsiderate, boorish, churlish, loutish, rough, crude, unrefined, indelicate, indecorous, insolent, impudent, impertinent.

impolitic *adjective* injudicious, ill-judged, undiplomatic, unwise, imprudent, ill-advised, misguided, ill-considered, short-sighted, uncircumspect, indiscreet, incautious, maladroit, inexpedient, untimely.

import *noun* **1** *exports and imports* imported commodity/service, foreign commodity, non-domestic commodity. **2** *did you get the import of what he said?* gist, drift, sense, essence, meaning, purport, message, thrust, implication, pith, core, sum and substance. **3** *men of import in the town* importance, significance, consequence, moment, magnitude, substance, weight.

importance *noun* **1** *the importance of the talks* significance, momentousness, seriousness, graveness, urgency, gravity, weightiness, value. *See* IMPORTANT 1. **2** *people of importance* prominence, eminence, pre-eminence, note, notability, noteworthiness, influence, power, high rank, status, prestige, standing, mark.

important *adjective* **1** *important talks* of import, consequential, significant, of great import/consequence, far-reaching, critical, crucial, pivotal, momentous, of great moment, serious, grave, urgent, substantial, weighty, valuable. **2** *the important points to remember* significant, salient, chief, main, principal, major. **3** *it is important to the project that he is there* of concern, of interest, relevant, of value, valuable, necessary, essential. **4** *the important people in the town* prominent, eminent, pre-eminent, leading, foremost, outstanding, distinguished, esteemed, notable, noteworthy, of note, of import, influential, of influence, powerful, power-wielding, high-ranking, high-level, top-level, prestigious.
Opposites UNIMPORTANT; INSIGNIFICANT; MINOR.

importunate *adjective* persistent, insistent, pertinacious, dogged, earnest, unremitting, continuous, pressing, urgent, demanding, exigent, exacting, clamorous, entreating, solicitous, suppliant, imploratory, imprecatory.

importune *verb* **1** *importune him for money* beg, beseech, entreat, implore, plead with, appeal to, call upon, supplicate, solicit, petition, harass, beset, press, dun. **2** *importune men in the street* solicit, make sexual advances towards.

impose *verb* **1** *impose a tax* enforce, apply, exact, levy, charge, put on, lay on, set, establish, fix, decree, ordain, institute, introduce, promulgate. **2** *impose her views on the group* force, foist, inflict, thrust, obtrude. **3** *impose a new leader on them* appoint, superimpose, superpose; *inf.* saddle with. **4** *impose herself on the company* force/foist/thrust oneself, intrude, break in, obtrude, interlope, trespass; *inf.* gatecrash, crash, butt in, horn in. **5** *not wishing to*

impose on your good nature take advantage of, abuse, exploit, play on, be a burden on. **6** *impose fake antiques on the public* palm off, foist, pass off, fob off.

imposing *adjective* impressive, striking, splendid, grand, majestic, august, lofty, stately, dignified.
Opposites MODEST; MEAN; UNIMPOSING.

imposition *noun* **1** *the imposition of new taxes* enforcement, application, exacting, levying, fixing, decreeing, institution. *See* IMPOSE 1. **2** *new impositions on tax payers* tax, levy, charge, tariff, toll, tithe. **3** *unfair impositions on the poor* burden, load, charge, onus, encumbrance. **4** *the imposition of her on the company* intrusion, obtrusion, interlopement, trespassing; *inf.* gatecrashing, butting in, horning in. *See* IMPOSE 4.

impossible *adjective* **1** *an impossible task* not possible, beyond the bounds of possibility, out of the question, unthinkable, unimaginable, inconceivable, beyond the realm of reason, impracticable, unattainable, unachievable, unobtainable, beyond one, hopeless. **2** *an impossible story* unbelievable, incredible, absurd, ludicrous, ridiculous, preposterous, outlandish, outrageous. **3** *an impossible child* unmanageable, intractable, recalcitrant, wayward, objectionable, intolerable, unbearable. **4** *life became impossible for the homeless* unbearable, intolerable, unendurable, hopeless.
Opposites POSSIBLE; PLAUSIBLE; TOLERABLE.

imposter, impostor *noun* masquerader, pretender, deceiver, fake, fraud, sham, charlatan, quack, mountebank, hoodwinker, bluffer, trickster, deluder, duper, cheat, cheater, swindler, defrauder, exploiter, confidence man/woman, rogue; *inf.* phoney, con man, con artist.

imposture *noun* misrepresentation, pretence, deceit, fraudulence, deception, fraud, charlatanry, quackery, trickery, duping, cheating, swindling.

impotence *noun* **1** *helpers angry at their impotence* powerlessness, lack of power, helplessness, inability, incapability, incapacity, incompetence. **2** *the impotence of the defeated army* powerlessness, helplessness, weakness, feebleness, exhaustion, enervation, debilitation. *See* IMPOTENT 2. **3** *the impotence of their attempts* ineffectiveness, ineffectualness, inefficiency, inadequacy, uselessness, futility, unsuccessfulness. *See* IMPOTENT 3.

impotent *adjective* **1** *impotent to help* powerless, helpless, unable, incapable, incapacitated, incompetent. **2** *the defeated general and his impotent forces* powerless, helpless, enfeebled, weak, feeble, frail, worn out, exhausted, spent, enervated, debilitated, prostrate, crippled, paralysed, infirm. **3** *make impotent attempts to help* ineffective, ineffectual, inefficient, inadequate, inept, useless, worthless, vain, futile, unavailing, unsuccessful, profitless.
Opposites POWERFUL; STRONG; EFFECTIVE.

impound *verb* **1** *impound stray animals* shut up/in, pen up/in, fence in, coop up, hem in, tie up, cage, enclose, confine, imprison, incarcerate, immure. **2** *impound legal documents* appropriate, take possession of, seize, commandeer, expropriate; *Law* distrain; *Scots* poind.

impoverished *adjective* **1** *impoverished homeless people* poverty-stricken, destitute, penurious, beggared, indigent, impecunious, penniless, poor, needy, in distressed/reduced/straitened circumstances, down and out, bankrupt, insolvent, ruined; *inf.* broke, flat/stony broke, on one's uppers. **2** *impoverished soil* exhausted, depleted, diminished, weakened, drained, used up, spent, played out. **3** *impoverished region/landscape* barren, bare, arid, desolate, empty, dead, waste, denuded.
Opposites WEALTHY; AFFLUENT.

impracticable *adjective an impracticable plan* not feasible, impossible, out of the question, unworkable, unachievable, unattainable, unrealizable, unsuitable.
Opposites POSSIBLE; FEASIBLE.

impractical *adjective* **1** *an impractical solution* unworkable, useless, ineffective, ineffectual, inefficacious, unrealistic, impossible, nonviable, inoperable, inoperative, unserviceable. **2** *his work is too impractical for a civil engineer* theoretical, abstract, academic, speculative. **3** *an impractical young woman* unrealistic, unbusinesslike, idealistic, romantic, starry-eyed, visionary, quixotic.
Opposites PRACTICAL; FEASIBLE; REALISTIC.

imprecation *noun* **1** *under an imprecation* curse, malediction, execration. **2** *embarrassed by his imprecations* swearing, cursing, blaspheming, blasphemy, foul language.

imprecise *adjective* **1** *an imprecise estimate of the cost* inexact, approximate, estimated, rough, inaccurate, incorrect. **2** *an imprecise account of the incident* vague, loose, indefinite, inexplicit, hazy, blurred, indistinct, woolly, confused, ambiguous, equivocal.

impregnable *adjective* **1** *an impregnable castle* impenetrable, unattackable, unassailable, inviolable, secure, strong, stout, invulnerable, invincible, unconquerable, unbeatable, indestructible. **2** *an impregnable argument* irrefutable, indisputable, incontestable, unquestionable, flawless, faultless.

impregnate *verb* **1** *impregnate the cloth with dye* permeate, suffuse, imbue, penetrate, pervade, fill, infuse, soak, steep, saturate, drench, inundate. **2** *impregnate the young woman* make pregnant, inseminate; *inf.* put in the family way, put in the club. **3** *impregnate the ovum* fertilize, fecundate.

impresario *noun* organizer, manager, producer; director, conductor, maestro, precentor, ballet master.

impress *verb* **1** *impress the crowd with his speech* make an impression/impact on, move, sway, bend, influence, affect, affect deeply, stir, rouse, excite, inspire, galvanize; *inf.* grab. **2** *impress upon them the need for speed* emphasize, stress, bring home, establish, fix deeply, instil, inculcate, urge. **3** *impress one's name on a metal strip* stamp, imprint, print, mark, engrave, emboss. **4** *she's always trying to impress* make an impression, draw attention to

oneself, show off, cut a good figure, cut a dash.

impression *noun* **1** *make an impression on the crowd* effect, influence, sway, impact, hold, power, control. **2** *the impression where his head lay* | *the impression made by the ring* mark, indentation, dent, hollow, outline, stamp, stamping, imprint, impress. **3** *I have the impression that he is bored* feeling, vague feeling, sense, sensation, awareness, perception, notion, idea, thought, belief, opinion, conviction, fancy, suspicion, inkling, intuition, hunch; *inf.* funny feeling. **4** *his impression of the politician* impersonation, imitation, mimicry, parody, caricature, burlesque, travesty; *inf.* send-up, take-off. **5** *the impression sold out* print run, printing, imprinting, issue, edition.

impressionable *adjective* susceptible, suggestible, persuadable, receptive, responsive, sensitive, open, gullible, ingenuous, pliable, malleable, mouldable.

impressive *adjective* **1** *an impressive building* imposing, magnificent, splendid. **2** *an impressive musical performance* moving, affecting, touching, stirring, rousing, exciting, powerful, inspiring.
Opposites ORDINARY; UNEXCITING.

imprint *noun the imprint of his feet* impression, print, mark, indentation, stamp, sign.

imprint *verb* **1** *imprint a seal on wax* stamp, print, impress, mark, engrave, emboss. **2** *imprint the details on his mind* fix, establish, stamp, impress, etch.

imprison *verb* put in prison, send to prison, jail, lock up, take into custody, put under lock and key, put away, incarcerate, intern, confine, detain, constrain, immure; *inf.* send down.
Opposites FREE; LIBERATE; RELEASE.

imprisonment *noun* custody, incarceration, internment, confinement, detention, duress; *inf.* porridge.

improbable *adjective* unlikely, highly unlikely, doubtful, dubious, questionable, implausible, far-fetched, unconvincing, unbelievable, incredible, ridiculous.

impromptu *adjective an impromptu speech* ad lib, unrehearsed, unprepared, extempore, extemporized, extemporaneous, spontaneous, improvised, unscripted, unstudied, unpremeditated; *inf.* off the cuff.

impromptu *adverb she spoke impromptu* ad lib, without preparation/rehearsal, extempore, spontaneously, on the spur of the moment; *inf.* off the cuff, off the top of one's head.

improper *adjective* **1** *improper behaviour* unseemly, indecorous, unbecoming, unfitting, unladylike, ungentlemanly, impolite, indiscreet, injudicious. **2** *an improper remark* indecent, risqué, off-colour, indelicate, suggestive, blue, smutty, obscene, lewd, pornographic. **3** *draw an improper inference* inaccurate, incorrect, wrong, erroneous, false. **4** *an improper tool for the job* inappropriate, unsuitable, unsuited, unfitting, inapt, inapplicable, incongruous.

impropriety noun **1** *guilty of impropriety* incorrectness, indecorum, indecorousness, unseemliness, indiscretion, bad taste, immodesty, indecency. **2** *appalled at her improprieties* improper act, improper remark. *See* IMPROPER 1, 2.

improve verb **1** *try to improve conditions* make better, better, ameliorate, amend, mend, reform, rehabilitate, set/put right, correct, rectify, help, advance, upgrade, revamp, modernize, gentrify; *inf.* give a face-lift to. **2** *things are improving* get/grow better, make headway, advance, come along, develop, progress, make progress, pick up, rally, perk up; *inf.* look up, take a turn for the better, take on a new lease of life. **3** *she was ill but she's improving now* recover, get better/well, recuperate, convalesce, gain strength; *inf.* be on the mend, turn the corner. **4** *can you improve on your offer* increase, make larger, raise, put up; *inf.* jack up.
Opposites WORSEN; DETERIORATE; IMPAIR; REDUCE.

improvement noun **1** *the improvement of conditions* betterment, amelioration, reform, rehabilitation, rectifying, rectification, advance, upgrading, revamp, gentrification; *inf.* face-lift. *See* IMPROVE 1. **2** *there has been an improvement in the economy* betterment, change for the better, advance, development, rally, recovery, upswing, comeback; progress, growth.

improvident adjective **1** *improvident people left penniless in old age* thriftless, unthrifty, spendthrift, wasteful, prodigal, extravagant, squandering, unfrugal, uneconomical, shiftless. **2** *improvident troops* incautious, unobservant, unwatchful, unwary, unvigilant, unalert, heedless, careless, inattentive; *inf.* asleep on the job, asleep at the wheel.
Opposites THRIFTY; CAUTIOUS.

improvise verb **1** *if you haven't prepared anything you'll have to improvise* ad lib, extemporize, make it up as you go along; *inf.* speak off the cuff, play it by ear. **2** *you'll have to improvise a shelter* throw/put together, devise, contrive, concoct, rig, jury rig.

improvised adjective **1** *improvised entertainment* impromptu, ad lib, unrehearsed, extempore, spontaneous; *inf.* off the cuff. *See* IMPROMPTU adjective. **2** *an improvised shelter* thrown together, makeshift, devised, rigged, jury-rigged.

imprudent adjective indiscreet, ill-considered, thoughtless, unthinking, incautious, unwary, improvident, irresponsible, foolish, injudicious, ill-judged, unwise, ill-advised, impolitic, careless, hasty, overhasty, rash, reckless, heedless, foolhardy.

impudence noun impertinence, insolence, cheek, boldness, effrontery, audacity, brazenness, pertness, sauciness, presumption, bumptiousness, rudeness, shamelessness; bad/ill manners; *inf.* brass neck, face, nerve, lip, sauce. *See* IMPUDENT.

impudent adjective impertinent, insolent, cheeky, bold, audacious, brazen, brazen-faced, pert, saucy, presumptuous, forward, bumptious, impolite, rude, disrespectful, ill-mannered, bad-mannered, unmannerly, ill-bred, shameless, immodest; *inf.* fresh, cocky, brass-necked.
Opposites POLITE; respectful; MODEST.

impugn verb *impugn his motives* challenge, call into question, question, dispute, query, cast aspersions on, look askance at, attack, assail, berate, criticize, denounce, censure.

impulse noun **1** *the impulse driving the machine* impetus, propulsion, impulsion, momentum, force, thrust, push, surge. **2** *the literary impulse* stimulus, inspiration, stimulation, incitement, incentive, inducement, motivation, urge. **3** *buy the coat on impulse* sudden desire/fancy, spur of the moment, notion, whim, caprice. **4** *suppress sexual impulse* drive, urge, instinct, appetite, proclivity.

impulsive adjective **1** *an impulsive action* hasty, impromptu, snap, spontaneous, extemporaneous, sudden, quick, precipitate, impetuous, ill-considered, unplanned, unpremeditated, thoughtless, rash, reckless. **2** *an impulsive person* hasty, spontaneous, impetuous, instinctive, intuitive, passionate, emotional, rash, reckless, madcap, devil-may-care, foolhardy.
Opposites DELIBERATE; PREMEDITATED; CAUTIOUS.

impunity noun *played truant with impunity* exemption/freedom from punishment/retribution/harm, immunity, indemnity, excusal, non-liability, licence, dispensation, pardon, reprieve, stay of execution.

impure adjective **1** *impure chemicals* adulterated, alloyed, mixed, admixed, combined, blended, debased. **2** *impure water* contaminated, polluted, tainted, infected, foul, dirty, filthy, unclean, feculent, sullied, defiled, unwholesome, poisoned. **3** *impure women* unchaste, unvirginal, immoral, loose, promiscuous, wanton, immodest, shameless, corrupt, dissolute, depraved, licentious, lascivious, prurient, lustful, lecherous, lewd. **4** *impure thoughts* lewd, lustful, lecherous, obscene, dirty, indecent, ribald, risqué, smutty, pornographic, improper, crude, vulgar, coarse, gross.

impurity noun **1** *the impurity of the chemical* adulteration, admixture, debasement. *See* IMPURE 1. **2** *the impurity of the water* contamination, pollution, foulness, filthiness, unwholesomeness. *See* IMPURE 2. **3** *impurities in the chemicals/water* foreign body, contaminant, pollutant, adulterant; dross, dirt, filth, grime, scum; bits. **4** *the impurity of the women* unchasteness, unchastity, immorality, looseness, promiscuity, wantonness, immodesty, lasciviousness, lust, lechery, lewdness. *See* IMPURE 3. **5** *the impurity of their thoughts* lewdness, lustfulness, obscenity, ribaldry, smut, smuttiness, impropriety, crudity, vulgarity. *See* IMPURE 4.

impute verb *impute the crime to him* ascribe, attribute, assign, credit, accredit; connect with, associate with.

in adjective **1** *short skirts were in then* fashionable, in fashion, in vogue, voguish, stylish, in style; *inf.* trendy, all the rage. **2** *she seems to be in with the teacher* in favour, favoured, liked; *inf.* in someone's good books.

in noun **ins and outs** the ins and outs of the situation intricacies, particulars, facts, details, features, characteristics, traits, particularities, peculiarities, idiosyncrasies.

inability noun incapability, incapableness, incapacity, incompetence, ineptitude, inaptitude, unfitness, ineffectiveness, powerlessness, uselessness, inefficacy, ineligibility, unqualifiedness.

inaccessible adjective houses inaccessible in the winter unreachable, out of reach, beyond reach, unapproachable, impenetrable, unattainable, out of the way, remote, back of beyond, God-forsaken; inf. unget-at-able.

inaccuracy noun **1** the inaccuracy of the results incorrectness, erroneousness, wrongness, mistakenness, fallaciousness, faultiness, inexactness, inexactitude, imprecision. **2** the accounts were full of inaccuracies error, mistake, miscalculation, erratum, corrigendum, slip, fault, blunder, defect; inf. slip-up, howler, bloomer, boo-boo. **3** a document full of inaccuracies error, mistake, slip, slip of the pen, printer's error, literal; inf. typo.

inaccurate adjective **1** your calculation is inaccurate incorrect, wrong, erroneous, faulty, inexact, imprecise, out. **2** the report is inaccurate incorrect, wrong, erroneous, fallacious, false, not true, not right, imperfect, flawed, defective, unsound, unreliable, wide of the mark; inf. full of holes.

inactive adjective **1** he hates to be inactive but he has to stay in bed immobile, motionless, inert, stationary. **2** all the machines lying inactive idle, inoperative, non-functioning, not working, out of service, unused, out of use, not in use, unoccupied, unemployed, inert, mothballed. **3** a former sportsman now completely inactive idle, inert, slow, sluggish, indolent, lazy, lifeless, slothful, lethargic, stagnant, vegetating, vegetant, dilatory, torpid; inf. low-key. **4** an inactive volcano dormant, quiescent, latent, passive.

inadequacy noun **1** the inadequacy of the food supply inadequateness, insufficiency, dearth, deficiency, meagreness, scantness, scarcity, paucity. See INADEQUATE 1. **2** war brought food inadequacies shortage, deficit, lack, dearth, scarcity. **3** the inadequacy of the present staff incompetence, incapability, unfitness, ineffectiveness, ineffectuality, inefficiency, inefficacy, inexpertness, lack of skill/proficiency, inaptness, ineptness. **4** show up his inadequacies as a manager shortcoming, fault, failing, flaw, defect, imperfection, weakness, foible.

inadequate adjective **1** inadequate food supplies insufficient, not enough, too little, too few, lacking, found wanting, deficient, short, in short supply, meagre, scanty, scant, niggardly, scarce, sparse, skimpy, scrimpy, sketchy, incomplete. **2** an inadequate teacher incompetent, incapable, not able, unfit, ineffective, ineffectual, inefficient, inefficacious, unskilful, inexpert, unproficient, inapt, inept; inf. not up to scratch.
Opposites ADEQUATE; SUFFICIENT; COMPETENT.

inadmissible adjective inadmissible evidence not allowable, unallowable, prohibited, precluded,

unacceptable, improper, inappropriate, inapposite, irrelevant, immaterial, impertinent, not germane, beside the point.

inadvertent adjective **1** an inadvertent omission accidental, unintentional, chance, unpremeditated, unplanned, uncalculated, unconscious, unwitting, involuntary. **2** an inadvertent driver inattentive, careless, negligent, thoughtless, heedless, unheeding, unmindful, unobservant.
Opposites DELIBERATE; INTENTIONAL; CAREFUL.

inadvisable adjective ill-advised, unwise, injudicious, ill-judged, imprudent, impolitic, inexpedient, foolish.

inalienable adjective inalienable rights untransferable, unforfeitable, inherent, unchallengeable, inviolable, sacrosanct.

inane adjective silly, foolish, stupid, idiotic, absurd, ridiculous, ludicrous, fatuous, trifling, frivolous, senseless, nonsensical, unintelligent, mindless, puerile, asinine, futile, worthless, vacuous, vapid; inf. daft.

inanimate adjective **1** inanimate objects lifeless, without life, exanimate, dead, inert, insentient, insensate, extinct, defunct. **2** inanimate people spiritless, apathetic, lazy, inactive, phlegmatic, listless, lethargic, sluggish, torpid.

inapplicable adjective rules inapplicable to the situation irrelevant, immaterial, not germane, inapposite, not pertinent, impertinent, inappropriate, unrelated, unconnected, beside the point.

inapposite adjective irrelevant, immaterial, not germane, not pertinent, impertinent, inapplicable. See INAPPLICABLE.

inappreciable adjective imperceptible, microscopic, infinitesimal, miniscule, minute, tiny, slight, small, insignificant, negligible, petty, trivial, trifling, paltry; inf. piddling.

inappropriate adjective **1** inappropriate behaviour unsuitable, unfitting, unseemly, unbecoming, indecorous, improper, ungentlemanly, unladylike, ungenteel. **2** inappropriate dress unsuitable, inapposite, incongruous, out of place/keeping. **3** it would be inappropriate to comment unsuitable, inexpedient, inadvisable, injudicious, infelicitous, untimely.

inapt adjective **1** an inapt remark inappropriate, unsuitable, unsuited, unfitting, out of place, inapposite, inapplicable, not pertinent, impertinent, not germane, incongruous, out of keeping, unrelated, unconnected. **2** an inapt tradesman inept, incompetent, unadept, incapable, unskilful, inexpert, clumsy, awkward, maladroit, undexterous, heavy-handed; inf. cack-handed.

inarticulate adjective **1** inarticulate cries/sounds unintelligible, incomprehensible, incoherent, unclear, indistinct, blurred, muffled, mumbled, muttered. **2** inarticulate children uneloquent, poorly spoken, non-fluent, faltering, hesitating, halting, stumbling, stuttering, stammering. **3** inarticulate emotion unspoken, unuttered, unexpressed, unvoiced, wordless, silent, mute, dumb, speechless, voiceless, soundless, taciturn, tongue-tied.

inattention noun **1** *pupils guilty of inattention* inattentiveness, distraction, preoccupation, absent-mindedness, daydreaming, reverie, wool-gathering, mental wandering, lack of concentration/application, staring into space; brown study. **2** *inattention to duty* neglect, negligence, remissness, forgetfulness, carelessness, thoughtlessness, heedlessness, disregard, indifference, unconcern, inconsideration.

inattentive adjective **1** *inattentive pupils* distracted, *distrait*, preoccupied, absent-minded, daydreaming, wool-gathering, lost in thought, off in a world of one's own, lacking concentration/application, in a brown study, with one's head in the clouds; *inf.* miles away. **2** *inattentive to duty | inattentive guards* neglectful, negligent, remiss, forgetful, careless, thoughtless, heedless, disregarding, indifferent, unconcerned, inconsiderate.

inaudible adjective not heard, hard to hear, hard to make out, indistinct, imperceptible, out of earshot, faint, muted, soft, low, muffled, stifled, dull, whispered, muttered, murmured, mumbled.

inaugural adjective first, initial, introductory, opening, maiden, dedicatory.

inaugurate verb **1** *inaugurate the conference proceedings* initiate, begin, start, commence, launch, start off, set in motion, get going, get under way, ring up the curtain on, get off the ground. **2** *inaugurate the new chancellor of the university* install, instate, induct, invest, ordain. **3** *inaugurate the new building* open, open officially, dedicate.
Opposites TERMINATE; wind up (*see* WIND).

inauspicious adjective unpropitious, unpromising, unlucky, unfortunate, infelicitous, unhappy, unfavourable, ill-omened, ominous, ill-fated, ill-starred, untoward, untimely.

inborn adjective innate, inherent, inherited, congenital, hereditary, in the family, in the blood/genes, inbred, connate, ingrained, constitutional, structural.

inbred adjective inherent, innate, ingrained, deep-seated.

incalculable adjective **1** *the distance/number is incalculable* immeasurable, measureless, inestimable, uncountable, incomputable, not to be reckoned, endless, without end, infinite, boundless, limitless, fathomless, bottomless, innumerable, countless, without number, numberless, multitudinous, enormous, immense, vast. **2** *an incalculable risk* unpredictable, indeterminable, unforeseeable.

incandescent adjective white-hot, intensely hot, red-hot, bright, brilliant, dazzling, shining, gleaming, glowing, aglow.

incantation noun chant, chanting, invocation, conjuration, spell, magic formula/word; abracadabra, open sesame.

incapable adjective **1** *tired of employing incapable people* lacking ability, incompetent, ineffective, ineffectual, inefficacious, inadequate, unfit, unfitted, unqualified, inept, inapt, unable, useless, feeble; *inf.* not up to scratch. **2** *fell down incapable* helpless, powerless, impotent. **3** *incapable of doing good* unable to, not

capable of, lacking experience to, lacking the ability to. **4** *problems incapable of solution* not admitting, not open to, impervious to, resistant to, not susceptible to.

incapacitated adjective *incapacitated and unable to play football* disabled, debilitated, unfit, immobilized, crippled, indisposed, *hors de combat*; *inf.* laid up, out of action.
Opposites FIT; ABLE.

incapacity noun **1** *his incapacity to do a job well* inability, incapability, incompetence, incompetency, inadequacy, unfitness, ineffectiveness, ineffectuality, inefficiency, powerlessness, impotence. **2** *legal incapacity* lack of entitlement, lack of legal ability, inability, disqualification.

incarcerate verb imprison, jail, put in prison/jail, throw in prison/jail, lock up, put under lock and key, intern, impound, take captive, put into detention, detain, clap in irons, confine, shut away, shut in, coop up, immure, restrain, restrict; *inf.* send down.

incarceration noun imprisonment, internment, captivity, detention, bondage, confinement, restraint.

incarnate adjective **1** *the devil incarnate* in bodily/human form, in the flesh, made manifest, embodied, corporeal, fleshly. **2** *tactlessness incarnate* embodied, personified, typified.

incarnation noun **1** *in another incarnation* life, bodily form, manifestation, embodiment. **2** *she is the incarnation of motherliness* embodiment, personification, exemplification, type, avatar.

incautious adjective **1** *incautious guards not spotting the enemy* unwary, unchary, unwatchful, unvigilant, unalert, off-guard, inattentive, unobservant, inadvertent; *inf.* asleep on the job, asleep at the wheel. **2** *incautious of him to trust her* unwise, imprudent, ill-advised, ill-judged, injudicious, uncircumspect, improvident, thoughtless, careless, impetuous, hasty, precipitate, rash, reckless, foolhardy.

incendiary adjective **1** *an incendiary bomb* combustible, flammable, fire-producing, fire-raising. **2** *an incendiary speech* inflammatory, incensing, inciting, instigating, arousing, stirring, provocative, rabble-rousing, seditious, subversive.

incendiary noun **1** *buildings deliberately set alight by incendiaries* fire-raiser, fire-setter, arsonist, pyromaniac; *inf.* firebug. **2** *crowds driven to rioting by incendiaries* demagogue, agitator, *agent provocateur*, rabble-rouser, instigator, inciter, insurgent, firebrand, revolutionary.

incense verb *the naughty children incensed the teacher* anger, enrage, infuriate, exasperate, irritate, madden, provoke, rile, inflame, agitate, nettle, vex, irk, get one's hackles up; *inf.* make one's blood boil, make one see red, get in one's hair, get one's dander up.

incense noun *sweet-smelling incense* perfume, fragrance, scent, aroma, bouquet, redolence, balm.

incentive *noun* inducement, incitement, stimulus, stimulant, impetus, encouragement, motivation, inspiration, impulse, goad, spur, lure, bait; *inf.* carrot.
Opposites DETERRENT; DISCOURAGEMENT.

inception *noun* beginning, commencement, start, starting point, outset, opening, debut, inauguration, initiation, institution, birth, dawn, origin, rise; *inf.* kick-off.

incessant *adjective* ceaseless, unceasing, nonstop, endless, unending, never-ending, everlasting, eternal, constant, continual, perpetual, continuous, uninterrupted, unbroken, ongoing, unremitting, persistent, recurrent.
Opposites INTERMITTENT.

incidence *noun* rate, frequency, prevalence, occurrence, amount, degree, extent.

incident *noun* **1** *unhappy incidents in her life* event, happening, occurrence, episode, adventure, experience, proceeding, occasion, circumstance, fact, matter. **2** *the police were called to an incident in the bar* disturbance, commotion, row, scene, fracas, contretemps, skirmish, clash, conflict, confrontation, brush.

incidental *adjective* **1** *her part in the event was incidental* accidental, by chance, chance, fortuitous, random. **2** *travel incidental to her job* related (to), connected (with), associated (with), accompanying, attendant, concomitant, contingent, by the way. **3** *her social engagements are incidental upon her job* ancillary (to), subordinate (to), subsidiary (to), secondary (to). **4** *incidental expenses* minor, trivial, trifling, petty, small, meagre.
Opposites DELIBERATE; ESSENTIAL; MAJOR.

incidentally *adverb* **1** *incidentally, I'm leaving tomorrow* by the way, by the by, in passing, *en passant*, speaking of, on the subject of, apropos of. **2** *she helped quite incidentally* accidentally, by chance, fortuitously, by a fluke, as luck would have it.

incinerate *verb* burn, burn up, reduce to ashes, carbonize, cremate.

incipient *adjective* beginning, commencing, starting, inceptive, initial, inchoative, original, inaugural, nascent, newborn, embryonic, embryonal, germinal, rudimentary, developing.
Opposites FINAL; MATURE.

incise *verb* **1** *incise the skin* cut, cut into, make an incision in, slit, slit open, gash, slash, notch, nick, furrow. **2** *incise the stone* engrave, etch, sculpt, sculpture, carve.

incision *noun* cut, opening, slit, gash, slash, notch, nick.

incisive *adjective* **1** *an incisive mind* keen, acute, sharp, penetrating, astute, shrewd, perspicacious, clever, smart, quick. **2** *an incisive turn of phrase* caustic, acid, sharp, biting, cutting, stinging, tart, trenchant, mordant, sarcastic, sardonic.
Opposites VAGUE; DULL; MILD.

incite *verb* **1** *incite a rebellion* instigate, provoke, foment, whip up, stir up, prompt. **2** *incite them to rebel* egg on, encourage, urge, goad, spur on, prod, stimulate, drive on, excite, arouse, agitate, inflame, stir up, provoke.
Opposites DISCOURAGE; DETER.

incitement *noun* *incitement to action* encouragement, urging, goading, spurring, prodding, stimulation, agitation, provocation, instigation; spur, impetus.

incivility *noun* bad/ill manners; unmannerliness, impoliteness, discourtesy, discourteousness, rudeness, disrespect, boorishness.

inclement *adjective* **1** *inclement weather* rough, stormy, squally, blustery, severe, bitter, raw, foul, nasty, harsh. **2** *inclement judges* harsh, unmerciful, pitiless, unpitying, ruthless, remorseless, hard-hearted, hard, cruel, inexorable, unrelenting, callous, severe, rigorous, Draconian.
Opposites FINE; MILD.

inclination *noun* **1** *he has an inclination to overeat* | *an inclination towards overeating* tendency, leaning, propensity, proclivity, proneness, liableness, disposition, predisposition, subjectability, weakness. **2** *an inclination for blondes* penchant, predilection, predisposition, partiality, preference, affinity, attraction, fancy, liking, fondness, affection, love. **3** *an inclination of the head* bow, bowing, bend, bending, nod, lowering, stooping. **4** *an inclination in the terrain* slope, slant, gradient, bank, ramp, lift, tilt, acclivity, rise, ascent, declivity, descent, drop, dip, sag, cant, bevel, angle.
Opposites AVERSION; DISLIKE; DISINCLINATION.

incline *verb* **1** *the land inclines towards the shore* curve, bend, slope, slant, bank, cant, bevel, tilt, lean, tip, list, deviate. **2** *he inclines towards the left in politics* tend, lean, swing, veer, have a preference/penchant for, be attracted to, have an affinity for. **3** *that inclines me to believe you* | *I'm inclined to believe you* predispose, dispose, influence, bias, prejudice, sway, make willing, persuade, bend. **4** *the door is inclined to bang* have a tendency, be liable/likely. **5** *incline the head* bow, bend, nod, lower, stoop, cast down.

include *verb* **1** *the group includes representatives from all countries* contain, hold, take in, admit, incorporate, embrace, encompass, comprise, embody, comprehend, subsume. **2** *remember to include them on the invitation list* allow for, add, insert, put in, enter, introduce, count in, take account of, build in, number, incorporate.
Opposites EXCLUDE; OMIT.

including *preposition* *everyone is going including me* counting, inclusive of.

inclusion *noun* *the inclusion of new material* addition, insertion, incorporation, introduction.

inclusive *adjective* **1** *an inclusive price* all-in, all-embracing, comprehensive, with everything included, *in toto*. **2** *the total inclusive of VAT* including, taking into account/consideration, counting, taking account/cognizance of. **3** *from Monday to Friday inclusive* including the limits stated, encompassed.

incognito *adjective/adverb* under an assumed name, with one's identity concealed, in disguise, disguised, in masquerade, camouflaged, unrecognized, unidentified, sailing under false colours.

incognizant *adjective* unaware, unconscious, ignorant, unknowing, unsuspecting, unknowledgeable, unenlightened.

incoherent *adjective incoherent speech* unconnected, disconnected, disjointed, disordered, confused, mixed-up, muddled, jumbled, scrambled, rambling, wandering, discursive, illogical, unintelligible, inarticulate, mumbled, muttered, stuttered, stammered.

incombustible *adjective* noncombustible, uninflammable, non-flammable, flameproof, fireproof, unburnable, unignitable, flame-retardant, flame-resistant.
Opposites flammable; INFLAMMABLE.

income *noun* salary, pay, remuneration, revenue; earnings, wages, receipts, takings, profits, gains, proceeds, means.

incoming *adjective* **1** *the incoming tide/train* coming, coming in, approaching, entering, arriving. **2** *the incoming president* new, succeeding.
Opposites OUTGOING.

incomparable *adjective* beyond compare, inimitable, unequalled, without equal, matchless, nonpareil, paramount, unrivalled, peerless, unparalleled, unsurpassed, transcendent, superior, superlative, supreme.

incomparably *adverb* beyond compare, by far, far and away, easily, immeasurably.

incompatible *adjective* **1** *he and his wife are incompatible* inharmonious, unsuited, mismatched, ill-assorted, uncongenial, incongruous, like day and night, uncomplementary, conflicting, antagonistic, antipathetic, dissentient, disagreeing, discordant, like cat and dog. **2** *incompatible colours* inharmonious, discordant, clashing, jarring, uncomplementary. **3** *views incompatible with his behaviour* differing from, contrary to, at odds with, inconsistent with, in opposition to, diametrically opposed to. *See* INCONGRUOUS 1.
Opposites COMPATIBLE; HARMONIOUS; CONSISTENT.

incompetent *adjective* **1** *incompetent to do the task* unable, incapable, unfitted, unfit, unsuitable, unqualified, inapt, inept, inefficient, ineffectual, ineffective, inadequate, deficient, insufficient, useless. **2** *an incompetent performance* unskilful, inexpert, inept, bungling, botched, awkward, maladroit, clumsy, gauche, floundering.

incomplete *adjective* **1** *an incomplete task* unfinished, unaccomplished, partial, undone, unexecuted, unperformed, undeveloped. **2** *an incomplete set of books* deficient, lacking, wanting, defective, imperfect, not entire, not total, broken. **3** *an incomplete text* deficient, shortened, curtailed, abridged, expurgated, bowdlerized.

incomprehensible *adjective* **1** *incomprehensible writing* illegible, unintelligible, indecipherable, unreadable. **2** *an incomprehensible theory* unintelligible, inapprehensible, too difficult, too hard, complicated, complex, involved, intricate; *inf.* over one's head, tough. **3** *his motives are incomprehensible* beyond comprehension, unfathomable, impenetrable, profound, deep, inexplicable, puzzling, enigmatic, mysterious, abstruse, recondite.

inconceivable *adjective* unimaginable, unthinkable, incomprehensible, incredible, unbelievable, implausible, impossible, out of the question, preposterous, ridiculous, ludicrous.

inconclusive *adjective* indefinite, indecisive, indeterminate, undetermined, still open to question, open to doubt, vague, unestablished, unsettled, ambiguous; *inf.* up in the air.

incongruity *noun* incompatibility, inconsistency, inappropriateness, unsuitability, inaptness, inharmoniousness, discordancy, disparity, discrepancy.

incongruous *adjective* **1** *behaviour incongruous with his principles* incompatible with, inconsistent with, out of keeping/place with, differing from, contrary to, inappropriate to, unsuited to, at odds with, in opposition to, diametrically opposed to, conflicting with, irreconcilable with. **2** *modern furniture seeming incongruous in the old-fashioned setting* out of place/keeping, strange, odd, absurd, unsuitable, inappropriate, incompatible, inharmonious, discordant, clashing, jarring.
Opposites APPROPRIATE; CONSISTENT; SUITABLE.

inconsequential *adjective* *his influence is inconsequential* insignificant, negligible, inappreciable, unimportant, of minor importance, of little/no account, trivial, trifling, petty; *inf.* piddling.

inconsiderable *adjective* *a not inconsiderable sum of money* insignificant, negligible, trifling, petty, small, slight, niggling, minor, inappreciable; *inf.* piddling.

inconsiderate *adjective* thoughtless, unthinking, unthoughtful, uncaring, heedless, unmindful, regardless, undiscerning, insensitive, unsolicitous, tactless, uncharitable, unkind, unbenevolent, ungracious, selfish, self-centred, egotistic.

inconsistent *adjective* **1** *actions inconsistent with his politics* incompatible with, out of keeping with, out of place with, differing from, contrary to, at odds with, at variance with, in opposition to, conflicting with, in conflict with, irreconcilable, discordant with, discrepant with. **2** *inconsistent character/actions* inconstant, unstable, unsteady, changeable, variable, erratic, irregular, unpredictable, capricious, fickle, whimsical, mercurial, volatile.

inconsolable *adjective* grief-stricken, brokenhearted, heartbroken, sick at heart, bowed down, miserable, wretched, woebegone, disconsolate, desolate, despairing, forlorn, unhappy, sad, upset.

inconspicuous *adjective* **1** *an inconspicuous house* unnoticeable, unobtrusive, indistinct, ordinary, plain, run-of-the-mill, unremarkable, undistinguished, unostentatious, unimposing, hidden, camouflaged. **2** *try to be as inconspicuous as possible* unnoticeable, unobtrusive, insignificant, unostentatious, quiet, retiring, in the background; *inf.* low-key.

inconstant *adjective* **1** *inconstant quantities* not constant, changeable, variable, mutable, unstable, unsteady, unsettled, unfixed. **2** *inconstant friends* changeable, fickle, capricious, volatile, mercurial, faithless, unfaithful.

incontestable *adjective* indisputable, incontrovertible, undeniable, irrefutable, unquestionable, beyond dispute/question/doubt, indubitable, unshakable, beyond a shadow of a doubt, conclusive, decisive, definite, established, sure, certain, positive.

incontinent *adjective* **1** *incontinent desires* unrestrained, unbridled, unchecked, uncurbed, ungoverned, uncontrolled, uncontrollable. **2** *incontinent young men* licentious, lascivious, lustful, lecherous, lewd, libidinous, promiscuous, randy, debauched, dissolute, dissipated, loose, degenerate, wanton. **3** *incontinent old people* lacking bladder/bowel control.

incontrovertible *adjective* incontestable, indisputable, undeniable, irrefutable, unquestionable, beyond question/doubt, indubitable, conclusive, decisive, positive. *See* INCONTESTABLE.

inconvenience *noun* **1** *not wishing to cause you any inconvenience* trouble, bother, disruption, disturbance, vexation, worry, annoyance, disadvantage, difficulty, embarrassment. **2** *their arrival was an inconvenience* trouble, bother, source of disruption/vexation/annoyance, nuisance, burden, hindrance; *inf.* pain, drag, bore. **3** *the inconvenience of the furniture* awkwardness, unwieldiness, cumbersomeness, unhandiness.

inconvenience *verb* disturb, bother, trouble, worry, disrupt, put out, impose upon, burden, distract, annoy, discommode.

inconvenient *adjective* **1** *call at an inconvenient time* awkward, unsuitable, inappropriate, inopportune, inexpedient, disadvantageous, disturbing, troublesome, bothersome, tiresome, vexatious, annoying, embarrassing, ill-timed, untimely, unseasonable. **2** *an inconvenient size of wardrobe* awkward, unwieldy, cumbersome, unmanageable, unhandy, difficult.

incorporate *verb* **1** *incorporate the various ingredients to form a whole* merge, coalesce, fuse, blend, mix, amalgamate, combine, unite, integrate, unify, compact. **2** *the document incorporates all our thoughts* embody, include, comprise, embrace, absorb, subsume, assimilate.

incorrect *adjective* **1** *incorrect answers* not right, wrong, inaccurate, erroneous, wide of the mark. **2** *an incorrect account of what happened* not right, inaccurate, mistaken, faulty, inexact, untrue, fallacious, non-factual, flawed; *inf.* full of holes. **3** *incorrect behaviour* improper, lacking in propriety, unbecoming, unseemly, indecorous, unsuitable, inappropriate, unladylike, ungentlemanly.

incorrigible *adjective* *an incorrigible criminal* hardened, incurable, inveterate, unreformable, irreformable, unreformative, irredeemable, hopeless, beyond hope/redemption, impenitent, uncontrite, unrepentant.

incorruptible *adjective* **1** *incorruptible members of society* virtuous, upright, high-principled, honourable, honest, moral, ethical, trustworthy, straight, unbribable, untemptable. **2** *incorruptible materials* imperishable, indestructible, non-biodegradable, not decaying, indissoluble, indissolvable, everlasting.

increase *verb* **1** *demand has increased* grow, grow greater/larger/bigger, expand, extend, multiply, intensify, heighten, mount, escalate, snowball, mushroom, swell, wax. **2** *increase the demand* add to, boost, enhance, build up, augment, enlarge, expand, extend, spread, heighten, raise, intensify, strengthen, magnify, proliferate, inflate; *inf.* step up.
Opposites DECREASE; REDUCE.

increase *noun* *the increase in size/demand* growth, rise, enlargement, expansion, extension, increment, addition, development, intensification, heightening, escalation, snowballing, mushrooming, boost, augmentation, strengthening, magnification, inflation; *inf.* stepping-up, step-up. *See* INCREASE *verb.*

increasingly *adverb* *he is increasingly annoying* more and more, progressively.

incredible *adjective* **1** *find his story incredible* unbelievable, hard to believe, beyond belief, far-fetched, inconceivable, unimaginable, unthinkable, impossible, implausible, highly unlikely, quite improbable, absurd, preposterous, questionable, dubious, doubtful, fictitious, mythical. **2** *an incredible athletic performance* extraordinary, supreme, great, wonderful, marvellous, tremendous, prodigious, astounding, amazing, astonishing, awe-inspiring, awesome, superhuman; *inf.* magic, fab, fantastic.

incredulity *noun* *view his story with incredulity* incredulousness, disbelief, unbelief, scepticism, distrust, mistrust, doubt, dubiousness, dubiety, suspicion.

incredulous *adjective* *incredulous listeners to his tale* disbelieving, unbelieving, sceptical, cynical, distrusting, distrustful, mistrusting, mistrustful, doubtful, doubting, dubious, unconvinced, suspicious.

increment *noun* **1** *an increment in salary* increase, gain, addition, augmentation, supplement, addendum, adjunct, accretion, accrual, accrument, profit. **2** *appalled by the increment in quantities/prices* enlargement, expansion, extension, escalation, mushrooming; *inf.* step-up. *See* INCREASE *noun.*

incriminate *verb* charge, accuse, indict, impeach, arraign, blame, implicate, inculpate, involve, inform against, blacken the name of, stigmatize; *inf.* point the finger at, stick/pin the blame on, grass on, rat on.

inculcate *verb* *inculcate Latin into schoolchildren* instil, implant, fix, ingrain, infuse, imbue, impress, imprint, indoctrinate, teach, hammer, din.

inculpate *verb* charge, accuse, indict, impeach, arraign, incriminate, blame. *See* INCRIMINATE.

incumbent *adjective* **1** *incumbent on you to be present* binding, obligatory, mandatory, necessary, compulsory, compelling. **2** *the invalid incumbent on the couch* lying, reclining, reposing, resting, lounging.

incumbent *noun the incumbent of the office* office-holder, official, functionary, occupier.

incur *verb incur his wrath | incurred huge debts* bring upon oneself, expose oneself to, lay oneself open to, provoke, be liable/subject to, contract, meet with, experience.

incurable *adjective* **1** *an incurable illness* beyond cure, cureless, unhealable, terminal, fatal, untreatable, inoperable, irremediable. **2** *an incurable romantic* inveterate, dyed in the wool, incorrigible, hopeless, beyond hope.

incursion *noun the enemy's midnight incursion* raid, foray, sortie, attack, assault, onslaught, invasion, onset, sally.

indebted *adjective indebted to you for your help* in someone's debt, beholden, under an obligation, obliged, obligated, grateful, thankful, appreciative.

indecency *noun* **1** *the indecency of the remark* suggestiveness, indelicacy, improperness, impurity, risquéness, ribaldry, bawdiness, foulness, vulgarity, grossness, crudity, dirtiness, smuttiness, smut, coarseness, obscenity, blueness, lewdness. *See* INDECENT 1. **2** *the indecency of the haste* impropriety, unseemliness, indecorum, indecorousness, unsuitableness, inappropriateness, bad taste, tastelessness, unacceptability, offensiveness. *See* INDECENT 2.

indecent *adjective* **1** *an indecent suggestion/joke* suggestive, indelicate, improper, impure, risqué, off-colour, ribald, bawdy, foul, vulgar, gross, crude, dirty, smutty, coarse, obscene, blue, lewd, lascivious, licentious, salacious, pornographic, scatological; *inf.* raunchy. **2** *marry with indecent haste after the funeral* improper, unseemly, indecorous, unbecoming, unsuitable, inappropriate, unfitting, unbefitting, in bad taste, tasteless, unacceptable, offensive, outrageous.
Opposites DELICATE; PROPER; SEEMLY.

indecipherable *adjective* illegible, unreadable, unclear, indistinct, unintelligible, cramped, crabbed.

indecision *noun his indecision lost him the job* indecisiveness, irresolution, irresoluteness, vacillation, fluctuation, hesitancy, hesitation, tentativeness, ambivalence, doubt, shilly-shallying, uncertainty. *See* INDECISIVE 1.

indecisive *adjective* **1** *an indecisive person* irresolute, vacillating, wavering, fluctuating, hesitant, tentative, faltering, ambivalent, doubtful, in two minds, shilly-shallying, undecided, indefinite, uncertain, unresolved, undetermined, sitting on the fence; *inf.* blowing hot and cold. **2** *an indecisive ballot* inconclusive, open, indeterminate, undecided, unsettled, indefinite, unclear; *inf.* up in the air.

indecorous *adjective* unbecoming, unseemly, improper, unsuitable, inappropriate, impolite, unladylike, ungentlemanly, ill-bred, ill-mannered, in bad taste, crude.

indecorum *noun* unbecomingness, unseemliness, impropriety, improperness, unsuitability, inappropriateness, impoliteness, bad taste, crudeness. *See* INDECOROUS.

indeed *adverb* **1** *he is indeed her brother* in fact, in point of fact, in truth, truly, actually, really, in reality, certainly, surely, for sure, to be sure, positively, absolutely, doubtlessly, undoubtedly, without doubt, undeniably, veritably. **2** *indeed I shall come | very pleased indeed* yes, certainly, emphatically.

indefatigable *adjective indefatigable workers* tireless, untiring, never-tiring, unwearied, unflagging, persistent, tenacious, dogged, assiduous, industrious, indomitable, relentless, unremitting.

indefensible *adjective* **1** *indefensible behaviour* inexcusable, unjustifiable, unpardonable, unforgivable, inexpiable. **2** *an indefensible theory* untenable, unarguable, insupportable, unmaintainable, unwarrantable, flawed, faulty, specious, implausible. **3** *indefensible buildings* defenceless, vulnerable, exposed, pregnable, unfortified, unguarded, unprotected, unshielded, unarmed.

indefinable *adjective an indefinable atmosphere in the room* indescribable, inexpressible, nameless, obscure, unanalysable.

indefinite *adjective* **1** *the venue for the meeting is as yet indefinite* undecided, unfixed, undetermined, unsettled, inconclusive, undefined, unknown, uncertain, unspecific, unexplicit, imprecise, inexact, vague, doubtful. **2** *an indefinite shape in the distance* ill-defined, indistinct, blurred, fuzzy, hazy, dim, vague, obscure. **3** *an indefinite answer* vague, unclear, imprecise, inexact, ambiguous, ambivalent, equivocal, confused, evasive, abstruse. **4** *she's a bit indefinite about whether she's going or not* undecided, indecisive, irresolute, vacillating, wavering, hesitant, tentative, uncertain. *See* INDECISIVE 1. **5** *an indefinite number/amount* indeterminate, unspecified, unlimited, limitless, infinite, immeasurable, boundless.

indefinitely *adverb suspended indefinitely* for an unspecified time/period, for an unlimited time/period, without a fixed limit, *sine die.*

indelible *adjective indelible marks/memories* inerasable, ineradicable, unobliterable, ineffaceable, unexpungeable, indestructible, permanent, lasting, enduring, inextirpable, ingrained, unfading, imperishable.

indelicate *adjective* **1** *indelicate manners/behaviour* vulgar, coarse, rough, unrefined, uncultivated, tasteless, unmannerly, unseemly, unbecoming, indecorous, immodest, boorish, churlish, loutish, offensive. **2** *indelicate jokes* indecent, impure, risqué, ribald, bawdy, vulgar, gross, crude, dirty, smutty, obscene, blue, lewd. *See* INDECENT 1.

indemnify *verb* **1** *indemnify them for their loss* reimburse, compensate, make restitution/amends to, recompense, repay, pay, pay back, remunerate. **2** *indemnify travellers against transport problems* insure, underwrite, guarantee, protect, secure, make secure, give security to, endorse.

indemnity *noun* **1** *receive indemnity for losses sustained* reimbursement, compensation, restitution, reparation, redress, requital, atonement, payment, repayment, remuneration, recompense; amends. **2** *take out indemnity against lost luggage* insurance, assurance, protection, security, endorsement; guarantee, safeguard. **3** *receive diplomatic indemnity for his crimes* legal exemption, immunity, diplomatic immunity, privilege, prerogative, impunity.

indent¹ *verb indent for a new uniform* ask for, request, order, requisition.

indent² *verb* **1** *the sea had indented the coastline* notch, nick, make notches/nicks in, scallop, serrate, pink. **2** *indent the line* move right, move further from the margin/edge.

indenture *noun* contract, written agreement, compact, covenant, certificate, deed, document, lease, warranty, bond, written commitment.

independence *noun* **1** *states seeking independence* self-government, self-rule, home rule, self-legislation, self-determination, sovereignty, autonomy, non-alignment, freedom, separation, autarchy. **2** *financial independence* self-sufficiency, self-reliance. **3** *independence of spirit* individualism, boldness, liberation, unconstraint, unrestraint, lack of constraint/restraint. *See* INDEPENDENT 5.

independent *adjective* **1** *an independent state* self-governing, self-ruling, self-legislating, self-determining, sovereign, autonomous, autonomic, free, absolute, non-aligned, autarchic. **2** *two independent units make up the desk* separate, individual, free-standing, self-contained. **3** *the two firms are quite independent of each other* separate, unconnected, unrelated, unattached, distinct, individual. **4** *independent people not requiring financial help* self-sufficient, self-supporting, self-reliant; *inf.* standing on one's own feet. **5** *an independent spirit* free-thinking, individualistic, unconventional, bold, liberated, unconstrained, unrestrained, unfettered, untrammelled.
Opposites DEPENDENT; SUBSERVIENT.

indescribable *adjective* undescribable, inexpressible, undefinable, beyond words/description, surpassing/beggaring description, incommunicable, ineffable, unutterable, incredible, extraordinary, remarkable, prodigious.

indestructible *adjective* durable, enduring, unbreakable, infrangible, imperishable, inextinguishable, undecaying, perennial, deathless, undying, immortal, endless, everlasting.

indeterminate *adjective* **1** *an indeterminate number of people are expected* undetermined, unfixed, indefinite, unspecified, unstipulated, unknown, uncertain, unpredictable, uncounted, uncalculated. **2** *an indeterminate reply* vague, hazy, unclear, obscure, ambiguous, ambivalent, equivocal, inconclusive, inexact, imprecise, inexplicit, ill-defined.

index *noun* **1** *an index to the information* guide, key, directory, catalogue; table of contents, thumb index, card index. **2** *his untidy appearance was an index to his disorderly mind* mark, token, sign, symptom, indication, clue, hint. **3** *the index on the compass* pointer, indicator, needle, hand. **4** *injure his index* index finger, forefinger, first finger.

indicate *verb* **1** *his lack of concentration indicates his distress* point to, show, evince, manifest, reveal, be a sign/symptom of, be symptomatic of, mark, signal, denote, bespeak, betoken, connote, suggest, imply. **2** *he indicated the right direction* point to/out, designate, specify. **3** *he indicated his displeasure* show, demonstrate, exhibit, display, manifest, evince, express, make known, tell, state, reveal, disclose, register, record.

indication *noun* **1** *his tiredness is an indication of his overwork* sign, symptom, mark, manifestation, signal, omen, augury, portent, warning, hint. **2** *the indication of the right direction* pointing out, designation, specification. **3** *he frowned as an indication of his displeasure* show, demonstration, exhibition, display, manifestation, evincement, revelation, disclosure, register, record.

indicative *adjective his behaviour is indicative of his attitude* indicatory, demonstrative, suggestive, symptomatic, typical, characteristic, symbolic, emblematic. *See* INDICATE 1.

indicator *noun* **1** *the indicator on the dial* pointer, needle, marker, index. **2** *a temperature indicator* gauge, meter, display. **3** *an economic indicator* index, guide, mark, sign, signal, signpost, symbol.

indict *verb* accuse, charge, arraign, impeach, prosecute, bring to trial, put on trial, cite, summons, incriminate, inculpate.

indictment *noun* accusation, charge, arraignment, impeachment, prosecution, citation, summons, incrimination, inculpation.

indifference *noun* **1** *the indifference of the spectators* apathy, lack of concern, unconcernedness, heedlessness, disregard, lack of interest, aloofness, detachment, coldness, coolness, impassivity, lack of passion/emotion/feeling. *See* INDIFFERENT 1. **2** *the indifference of the players* mediocrity, adequacy, averageness, ordinariness, lack of distinction. *See* INDIFFERENT 2. **3** *the indifference of the issues* unimportance, insignificance, inconsequence, triviality, slightness, pettiness, irrelevance. *See* INDIFFERENT 3. **4** *the indifference of the judges* impartiality, disinterest, lack/absence of bias, non-partisanship, neutrality, objectivity, dispassionateness, dispassion, detachment, justness, justice, equitability, even-handedness, fairness, fair-mindedness.

indifferent *adjective* **1** *totally indifferent spectators | kidnappers totally indifferent to the pain of their victims* apathetic, unconcerned, careless, heedless, regardless, uncaring, uninterested, unimpressed, aloof, detached, distant, cold, cool, impassive, dispassionate, unresponsive, passionless, unemotional, emotionless, unmoved, unexcited, unfeeling, unsympathetic, uncompassionate, callous. **2** *an indifferent player* mediocre, middling, moderate, medium, fair, not bad, passable, adequate, barely adequate, average, ordinary, commonplace, undistinguished, uninspired; *inf.* OK, so-so. **3** *an indifferent issue* unimportant, insignificant, inconsequential, of no importance/consequence, minor, trivial, trifling, slight, of no matter, petty, irrelevant, immaterial. **4** *an indifferent judge* impartial, disinter-

ested, unbiased, non-discriminatory, neutral, unprejudiced, non-partisan, uninvolved, objective, dispassionate, detached, just, equitable, even-handed, fair, fair-minded.
Opposites ENTHUSIASTIC; BRILLIANT; BIASED.

indigenous *adjective* native, original, aboriginal, autochthonous, autochthonal.

indigent *adjective* poverty-stricken, impoverished, penniless, penurious, impecunious, poor, beggared, destitute, in want, in need, needy, in distress, in financial/dire straits, down and out; *inf.* broke, stony broke, hard up, on one's uppers, strapped for cash, skint.
Opposites WEALTHY; AFFLUENT.

indigestion *noun* dyspepsia, dyspepsy, hyperacidity, acidity, heartburn, waterbrash, pyrosis; upset stomach, gastric upset.

indignant *adjective* angry, angered, irate, incensed, furious, infuriated, annoyed, wrathful, enraged, exasperated, heated, riled, in a temper, in high dudgeon, provoked, piqued, disgruntled, in a huff; *inf.* fuming, livid, aggravated, mad, seeing red, up in arms, peeved, huffy, miffed, narked.

indignation *noun* anger, fury, rage, wrath, exasperation, pique, disgruntlement, umbrage, offence, resentment, ire. *See* INDIGNANT.

indignity *noun* affront, insult, abuse, mistreatment, injury, offence, outrage, slight, snub; humiliation, aspersion, disrespect, discourtesy, dishonour, obloquy; *inf.* slap in the face.

indirect *adjective* **1** *an indirect route* roundabout, circuitous, deviant, divergent, wandering, meandering, winding, curving, tortuous, zigzag. **2** *an indirect way of giving the news* oblique, discursive, digressive, long-drawn-out, rambling, circumlocutory, periphrastic, allusive. **3** *an indirect insult* backhanded, lefthanded, devious, insidious, deceitful, underhand, surreptitious; *inf.* sneaky. **4** *an indirect result of the talks* incidental, accidental, unintended, secondary, subordinate, ancillary, collateral, contingent.

indirectly *adverb* **1** *hear the information indirectly* second-hand, in a roundabout way. **2** *tell them the news indirectly* by implication, obliquely, circumlocutorily, periphrastically.

indiscernible *adjective* **1** *an indiscernible difference in attitude* imperceptible, imperceivable, unnoticeable, unapparent, hidden, indistinguishable, inappreciable, impalpable, subtle, minute, minuscule, microscopic. **2** *indiscernible to the naked eye* invisible, imperceivable, undetectable, indistinct, indefinite, obscure, shadowy, unclear, dim.

indiscreet *adjective* **1** *an indiscreet course of action | an indiscreet remark* unwise, imprudent, injudicious, impolitic, ill-advised, ill-thought-out, ill-considered, ill-judged, ill-gauged, foolish, incautious, careless, unwary, hasty, rash, reckless, impulsive, precipitate, foolhardy, tactless, untactful, insensitive, undiplomatic. **2** *indiscreet behaviour* immodest, indelicate, indecorous, unseemly, indecent, shameless, brazen, bold.

indiscretion *noun* **1** *guilty of indiscretion* imprudence, injudiciousness, foolishness, folly,

lack of caution, carelessness, hastiness, rashness, tactlessness, lack of diplomacy. *See* INDISCREET 1. **2** *embarrassed by her indiscretions* gaffe, *faux pas*, breach of etiquette, slip, blunder, lapse, mistake, error; *inf.* slip-up, bloomer. **3** *the indiscretion of her behaviour* immodesty, indelicacy, indecorum, indecorousness, unseemliness, indecency, shamelessness, brazenness, boldness.

indiscriminate *adjective* **1** *indiscriminate reading habits | indiscriminate choice of clothes* undiscriminating, unselective, unparticular, uncritical, undifferentiating, aimless, careless, haphazard, random, unsystematic, unmethodical, broad-based, wholesale, general, sweeping; *inf.* hit-or-miss. **2** *an indiscriminate collection of furniture* jumbled, mixed, haphazard, motley, miscellaneous, diverse, varied, mongrel, confused, chaotic, thrown together; *inf.* higgledy-piggledy.
Opposites SELECTIVE; SYSTEMATIC.

indispensable *adjective* essential, of the essence, vital, crucial, imperative, key, necessary, requisite, required, needed, needful, important, of the utmost importance, urgent, pressing, high-priority, fundamental.
Opposites DISPENSABLE; SUPERFLUOUS; NON-ESSENTIAL.

indisposed *adjective* **1** *indisposed and so unable to be present* ill, unwell, sick, ailing, confined to bed, incapacitated; *inf.* on the sick list, under the weather, poorly, out of sorts/commission, laid up. **2** *indisposed to believe him* unwilling, disinclined, reluctant, hesitant, loath, averse, not in favour of.

indisposition *noun* **1** *absent owing to indisposition* illness, sickness, ill health; ailment, complaint, disorder, malady, disease. **2** *his indisposition towards modernizing the factory* unwillingness, disinclination, reluctance, hesitation, hesitancy, loathness, aversion, dislike, distaste.

indisputable *adjective* incontestable, incontrovertible, undeniable, irrefutable, unquestionable, indubitable, beyond dispute/question/doubt, beyond the shadow of a doubt, unassailable, certain, sure, positive, definite, absolute, final, conclusive.

indistinct *adjective* **1** *indistinct figures in the distance* blurred, fuzzy, out of focus, bleary, hazy, misty, shadowy, dim, obscure, indefinite, indistinguishable, barely perceptible, undefined. **2** *indistinct writing* indecipherable, illegible, unreadable, unintelligible, pale, faded. **3** *indistinct noises* muffled, low, muted, muttered, mumbled.

indistinguishable *adjective* **1** *the twins/views are indistinguishable* identical, alike, very similar; *inf.* as like as two peas in a pod. **2** *his identity was indistinguishable in the dark* indiscernible, imperceptible, hard to make out, indefinite, unnoticeable, obscure, camouflaged, invisible.

individual *adjective* **1** *each individual flower/house* single, separate, sole, lone, solitary, distinct, distinctive, particular, specific, peculiar, detached, isolated. **2** *an individual style* charac-

399

teristic, distinctive, particular, peculiar, typical, personal, personalized, own, private, special, especial, singular, original, unique, exclusive, idiosyncratic.
Opposites COLLECTIVE; ORDINARY.

individual noun **1** *several individuals arrived late | a most unpleasant individual* person, personage, human being, creature, mortal, living soul, body, character, type. **2** *she's very much an individual* individualist, free spirit, nonconformist, original, eccentric, bohemian, maverick, egocentric, *rara avis*, rare bird, rarity, loner, lone wolf.

individualist noun individual, free spirit, nonconformist, eccentric, egocentric. See INDIVIDUAL noun 2.

individualistic adjective *an individualistic way of dealing with things* free-thinking, independent, nonconformist, unorthodox, unconventional, original, eccentric, bohemian, maverick, strange, odd, egocentric.

individuality noun *works of individuality* distinctiveness, distinction, originality, uniqueness, singularity, peculiarity, personality, character.

individually adverb *tutor each student individually* one at a time, one by one, singly, separately, independently, apart; personally; *lit.* severally.

indoctrinate verb *indoctrinate the pupils with his political ideas* instruct, teach, drill, ground, initiate, inculcate, impress on, instil in, imbue, impregnate, brainwash, propagandize, proselytize.

indolent adjective lazy, idle, slothful, do-nothing, sluggish, lethargic, slow, slow-moving, slack, shiftless, languid, lackadaisical, apathetic, listless, impassive, inactive, inert, torpid, fainéant.
Opposites INDUSTRIOUS; ACTIVE.

indomitable adjective invincible, unconquerable, undefeatable, unbeatable, unassailable, impregnable, unyielding, unsubmissive, stalwart, stout-hearted, lion-hearted, staunch, resolute, firm, steadfast, determined, intransigent, inflexible, adamant, unflinching, courageous, brave, valiant, heroic, intrepid, fearless.
Opposites SUBMISSIVE; COWARDLY.

indubitable adjective beyond doubt, beyond the shadow of a doubt, indisputable, unarguable, beyond dispute/question, unquestionable, undeniable, irrefutable, incontestable, incontrovertible, certain, sure, positive, definite, absolute, conclusive.

induce verb **1** *induce them to go* persuade, talk into, get, prevail upon, prompt, move, inspire, instigate, influence, exert influence on, press, urge, incite, encourage, impel, actuate, motivate, inveigle, coax, wheedle. **2** *induce a reaction* bring about, bring on, cause, produce, effect, create, give rise to, generate, originate, engender, occasion, set in motion, develop, lead to.
Opposites DISSUADE; HINDER; DETER.

inducement noun **1** *offer a salary increase as an inducement* incentive, attraction, encouragement, bait, lure, reward, incitement, stimulus, influence, spur, goad, impetus, motive, provo-

cation; *inf.* carrot, come-on. **2** *gave in to their inducement to go* persuasion, prompting, urging, incitement, encouragement, inveigling. See INDUCE 1.

indulge verb **1** *indulge one's appetites* give way to, yield to, pander to, cater to, satisfy, gratify, fulfil, satiate, appease. **2** *indulge in a bout of self-pity* give oneself up to, give rein to, give free rein to, wallow in, luxuriate in, revel in. **3** *indulge the child* pamper, spoil, coddle, mollycoddle, cosset, pander to, humour, go along with, baby, pet. **indulge oneself** treat oneself, give oneself a treat, splurge; *inf.* have a spree, paint the town red, go on the town.

indulgence noun **1** *the indulgence of one's appetites* satisfaction, gratification, fulfilment, satiation, appeasement. **2** *lead a life of indulgence* self-gratification, dissipation, dissoluteness, intemperance, immoderation, immoderateness, debauchery, excess, lack of restraint, unrestraint, prodigality, extravagance. **3** *travelling is his only indulgence* extravagance, luxury, treat. **4** *I was allowed the indulgence of going on board ship* privilege, courtesy, favour, treat. **5** *treat the prisoners with indulgence* tolerance, forbearance, compassion, humanity, kindness, understanding, sympathy, liberalness, liberality, forgiveness, leniency, mercy, clemency. **6** *dislike indulgence of the children* pampering, spoiling, coddling, mollycoddling, cosseting, humouring, partiality. See INDULGE 3.

indulgent adjective **1** *indulgent judges* tolerant, forbearing, compassionate, humane, kind, kindly, understanding, sympathetic, liberal, forgiving, lenient, merciful, clement. **2** *indulgent parents* permissive, easygoing, compliant, fond, doting, pampering, spoiling, mollycoddling, cosseting, humouring.
Opposites INTOLERANT; STERN; STRICT.

industrial adjective manufacturing.

industrialist noun manufacturer, producer, captain of industry, magnate, tycoon, business/manufacturing baron, capitalist, financier.

industrious adjective hard-working, diligent, assiduous, sedulous, conscientious, steady, laborious, busy, busy as a bee, active, bustling, energetic, on the go, vigorous, determined, dynamic, indefatigable, tireless, persistent, pertinacious, zealous, productive.
Opposites IDLE; INDOLENT; LAZY.

industry noun **1** *involved in heavy industry* manufacturing, production, fabrication, construction. **2** *employed in the publishing industry* business, trade, commercial enterprise, field, line, craft, métier. **3** *work with industry* industriousness, diligence, assiduity, application, sedulousness, sedulity, conscientiousness, concentration, intentness, steadiness, laboriousness, busyness, activity, energy, vigour, effort, determination, dynamism, tirelessness, persistence, pertinacity, zeal, productiveness.

inebriated adjective intoxicated, inebriate, drunk, drunken, blind drunk, drunk as a lord, the worse for drink, in one's cups, tipsy, merry, befuddled; *inf.* tight, one over the eight,

under the influence, half-cut, half-seas-over, three sheets to the wind, plastered, stoned, loaded, blotto, pickled, paralytic, out of it, under the table, legless, pie-eyed, smashed, sloshed, well-oiled, well-lubricated, stewed to the gills, tanked up, bevvied, pissed, pissed as a newt; *Scots* stotious, fou.
Opposites SOBER; ABSTEMIOUS.

inedible *adjective* unedible, uneatable, not fit to eat, unconsumable, unwholesome, off, rotten, bad, putrid, poisonous.

ineffable *adjective* **1** *ineffable joy/cheek* inexpressible, unutterable, beyond words, indescribable, undefinable. **2** *the ineffable name of Jehovah* not to be uttered, unutterable, not to be spoken, unmentionable, taboo.

ineffective *adjective* **1** *ineffective attempts to hold back the water* ineffectual, vain, to no avail, unavailing, useless, worthless, unsuccessful, futile, fruitless, unproductive, profitless, abortive, inadequate, inefficient, inefficacious, powerless, impotent, idle, feeble, weak, incompetent, inept, lame, barren, sterile. **2** *ineffective people* ineffectual, unproductive, inadequate, inefficient, inefficacious, powerless, impotent, incompetent, inept, feeble, weak.

ineffectual *adjective* **1** *ineffectual efforts* ineffective, vain, unavailing, useless, worthless, futile, fruitless, unproductive, abortive, inadequate, inefficient, inefficacious, lame, inept. *See* INEFFECTIVE 1. **2** *ineffectual people* ineffective, inadequate, inefficient, inefficacious, powerless, impotent, inept. *See* INEFFECTIVE 2.

inefficient *adjective* **1** *inefficient people* ineffective, badly organized, disorganized, incompetent, inept, incapable, unprepared, ineffectual, inefficacious. **2** *an inefficient method of procedure* incompetent, unskilful, inexpert, wasteful, uneconomical, negligent, lax, slipshod, sloppy, slack.

inelegant *adjective* **1** *inelegant manners* unrefined, uncultured, uncultivated, unpolished, unsophisticated, unfinished, gauche, crude, uncouth, ill-bred, coarse, vulgar. **2** *sit in an inelegant position* awkward, clumsy, ungainly, ungraceful, graceless.

ineligible *adjective* **1** *ineligible candidates* unqualified, unfitted, unfit, unequipped, unsuitable, unacceptable, undesirable, ruled out, legally disqualified; *Law* incompetent. **2** *ineligible suitors* unmarriageable, unsuitable, undesirable, unacceptable.

inept *adjective* **1** *an inept tradesman* incompetent, unadept, incapable, unskilful, unskilled, inexpert, clumsy, awkward, maladroit, undexterous, heavy-handed; *inf.* cack-handed. **2** *an inept attempt* incompetent, unadept, unskilful, inadequate, bungling, awkward, maladroit, unproductive, unsuccessful, ineffectual; *inf.* cack-handed. **3** *an inept remark in the circumstances* out of place, badly timed, inapt, inappropriate, unsuitable, infelicitous. **4** *always doing inept things* absurd, foolish, silly, stupid, inane, nonsensical, senseless, farcical, ridiculous, ludicrous, asinine, crazy; *inf.* screwy.
Opposites COMPETENT; APPROPRIATE; SENSIBLE.

inequality *noun* **1** *inequality of salaries/opportunity* unequalness, disparity, imparity, imbalance, lack of balance, unevenness, disproportion, discrepancy, nonconformity, variation, variability, difference, dissimilarity, contrast. **2** *treat women with inequality* bias, prejudice, discrimination, preferentiality. **3** *the inequality of the surface* unevenness, irregularity, roughness.

inequitable *adjective* unjust, unfair, partial, prejudiced, biased, partisan, discriminatory, preferential, one-sided, intolerant, bigoted.

inequity *noun* the inequity of the sentence/treatment unfairness, injustice, unjustness, partisanship, partiality, bias, preferentialism, discrimination.

inert *adjective* **1** *inert bodies lying around* inactive, unmoving, motionless, immobile, still, stock-still, stationary, static, lifeless, inanimate, unconscious, passive, out cold, comatose, dormant, dead. **2** *inert members of the company* inactive, idle, indolent, slack, lazy, slothful, dull, sluggish, lethargic, stagnant, languid, lackadaisical, listless, torpid, otiose, fainéant.
Opposites ACTIVE; ENERGETIC.

inertia *noun* inertness, inactivity, inaction, inactiveness, motionlessness, immobility, unemployment, stagnation, stasis, passivity, idleness, indolence, laziness, sloth, slothfulness, dullness, sluggishness, lethargy, languor, listlessness, torpor, fainéance.
Opposites ACTION; ACTIVITY; ENERGY.

inescapable *adjective* unavoidable, inevitable, unpreventable, inexorable, assured, certain, bound/sure to happen, ineludible, ineluctable.

inestimable *adjective* of inestimable value immeasurable, measureless, incalculable, priceless, beyond price, precious, invaluable, worth its weight in gold, worth a king's ransom, unparalleled, supreme, superlative.

inevitable *adjective* unavoidable, unpreventable, inexorable, inescapable, fixed, settled, irrevocable, fated, destined, predestined, ordained, decreed, out of one's hands, assured, certain, sure, bound/sure to happen, for sure, necessary, ineluctable.
Opposites avoidable; UNCERTAIN.

inexact *adjective* not accurate, not exact, imprecise, approximate, incorrect, erroneous, wrong, false, fallacious, wide of the mark.

inexcusable *adjective* unexcusable, unpardonable, unforgivable, unatonable, inexpiable, unjustifiable, unwarrantable, indefensible, blameworthy, censurable, reprehensible, outrageous.

inexhaustible *adjective* **1** *a seemingly inexhaustible supply of ammunition* unlimited, limitless, illimitable, infinite, boundless, endless, never-ending, unrestricted, bottomless, measureless, copious, abundant. **2** *inexhaustible workers* indefatigable, tireless, untiring, unwearying, weariless, unfaltering, unfailing, unflagging, unwavering, unremitting, persevering, persistent, dogged.

inexorable *adjective* **1** *the inexorable march of progress* relentless, unavoidable, inescapable, inevitable, unpreventable, irrevocable, fated, destined, certain. *See* INEVITABLE. **2** *inexorable tyrants* adamant, obdurate, unbending, unyielding, immovable, intransigent, implacable, unappeasable, unforgiving, uncompromising, inflexible, strict, severe, iron-handed, stringent, harsh, exacting, rigorous, Draconian, cruel, ruthless, relentless, pitiless, merciless, remorseless.

inexpedient *adjective* impolitic, ill-advised, unadvisable, injudicious, ill-judged, unwise, imprudent, ill-considered, thoughtless, wrongheaded, foolish, detrimental, harmful.

inexpensive *adjective* low-cost, low-price, low-priced, reasonably priced, reasonable, economical, cheap, budget, reduced, sale-price, half-price, marked-down, discount, discounted, cut-rate, bargain, bargain-basement.

inexperienced *adjective* lacking experience, untrained, untutored, undrilled, unqualified, unpractised, amateur, unskilled, uninitiated, uninformed, ignorant, unacquainted, unversed, naive, unsophisticated, unfledged, untried, unseasoned, new, callow, immature, fresh, green, raw; *inf.* wet behind the ears.

inexpert *adjective* unskilled, unskilful, amateur, amateurish, unprofessional, untrained, unpractised, unqualified, incompetent, maladroit, inept, clumsy, awkward, bungling, bumbling, blundering; *inf.* cack-handed.

inexplicable *adjective* unexplainable, inexplainable, unaccountable, incomprehensible, beyond comprehension/understanding, unintelligible, unfathomable, baffling, puzzling, perplexing, mystifying, insoluble, bewildering, mysterious, strange, weird, abstruse, enigmatic, inscrutable.

inexpressible *adjective* indescribable, undescribable, beyond words/description, unutterable, undefinable, unspeakable, incommunicable, ineffable.

inexpressive *adjective* expressionless, blank, vacant, empty, deadpan, dead, lifeless, poker-faced, inscrutable, emotionless, impassive, inanimate, bland, cold, stony.

inextinguishable *adjective* unquenchable, ever-burning, unsuppressible, irrepressible, indestructible, imperishable, undying, enduring, lasting, eternal.

inextricable *adjective* **1** *an inextricable situation* inescapable. **2** *the two family histories are inextricable* entangled, tangled, ravelled, inseparable, mixed up, confused. **3** *an inextricable problem* complicated, knotty, convoluted, intricate, involved, complex, perplexing, puzzling, baffling, labyrinthine, mazelike.

infallible *adjective* **1** *an infallible remedy* unfailing, without failure, foolproof, dependable, trustworthy, reliable, sure, certain; *inf.* surefire. **2** *an infallible memory* error-free, unerring, unfailing, faultless, flawless, impeccable, unimpeachable, perfect.

infamous *adjective* **1** *an infamous robber* notorious, disreputable, ill-famed, of ill-repute, iniquitous, ignominious, dishonourable, discreditable, villainous, bad, wicked, vile, odious, nefarious. **2** *guilty of infamous conduct* abom-

inable, outrageous, shocking, monstrous, disgraceful, dishonourable, shameful, atrocious, heinous, detestable, loathsome, hateful, wicked, vile, base, iniquitous, criminal, odious, nefarious, scandalous, egregious, flagitious. *Opposites* HONOURABLE; REPUTABLE.

infancy *noun* **1** *die in infancy* babyhood, early childhood. **2** *the infancy of space science* start, commencement, beginning, origin, rise, emergence, outset, onset, dawn, birth, cradle, conception, genesis; beginnings, early stages.

infant *noun* **1** *die when an infant* babe, baby, little child, tot, little one, neonate; *Scots* bairn, wean. **2** *an infant in the publishing industry* beginner, novice, newcomer, learner, apprentice, trainee, new recruit, tiro, new boy/girl, initiate, novitiate, neophyte, *ingénue*, innocent, child, mere child, babe in arms; *inf.* greenhorn, rookie, fresher.

infant *adjective* *an infant industry* emergent, developing, dawning, nascent.

infantile *adjective* babyish, childish, puerile, immature, juvenile.

infantry *noun* infantrymen, foot soldiers, ranks; rank and file, cannon fodder; *inf.* Tommies; *Am.* GIs.

infatuated *adjective* *they're infatuated | he's infatuated with her* in love, head over heels in love, hopelessly in love; enamoured, besotted, captivated, bewitched, beguiled, spellbound, fascinated, enraptured, carried away, obsessed, swept off one's feet; taken with, under the spell of; *inf.* smitten, sweet on, keen on, mad about, wild about, crazy about, nuts about, stuck on, turned on by.

infatuation *noun* passing fancy, fancy, passion, obsession, fixation, craze, mania; *inf.* puppy/calf love, crush, thing, hang-up, pash.

infect *verb* **1** *infect the wound* cause infection/disease in, make septic, contaminate, poison, ulcerate. **2** *infect the others with the germs* pass/transmit infection to, pass on to, spread to. **3** *infect the air/water* contaminate, pollute, taint, make foul, blight, spoil, mar, impair. **4** *infect others with his wickedness* influence, corrupt, pervert, debauch, debase, degrade, vitiate. **5** *infect others with his enthusiasm/laughter* influence, affect, imbue, infuse, excite, inspire, stimulate, animate.

infection *noun* **1** *an infection in the wound* septicity, septicaemia, contamination, poison, ulceration; germs, bacteria. **2** *the infection of the air/water* contamination, pollution, tainting, fouling, spoiling, blighting. *See* INFECT 3. **3** *catch an infection of the lungs* disease, disorder, virus, contagion; *inf.* bug.

infectious *adjective* **1** *an infectious disease* infective, communicable, transmittable, transmissible, catching, spreading; contagious. **2** *infectious material* germ-laden, contaminating, polluting, pestilential, septic, toxic, noxious, virulent, poisonous. **3** *her laughter/enthusiasm is infectious* catching, spreading, contagious, communicable, irresistible, compelling.

infer *verb* **1** *from the evidence they inferred that he was guilty* deduce, reason, conclude, gather, understand, presume, conjecture, surmise, read between the lines, theorize, hypothesize; *inf.* figure, suss, guesstimate. **2** *his conduct inferred a guilty conscience* indicate, point to, signal, signify, demonstrate, show, bespeak, evidence. **3** *she inferred in her speech that he was a coward* imply, insinuate, hint, suggest, intimate.

inference *noun* **1** *dispute the inference from the evidence* deduction, conclusion, ratiocination, presumption, conjecture, surmise, reasoning, theorizing. See INFER 1. **2** *resent her inference that he was a coward* implication, insinuation, suggestion, intimation.

inferior *adjective* **1** *in an inferior position* lower, lesser, subordinate, junior, secondary, subsidiary, ancillary, second-class, second-fiddle, minor, subservient, lowly, humble, servile, menial. **2** *inferior goods* imperfect, faulty, defective, substandard, low-quality, low-grade, shoddy, cheap, reject, gimcrack; *inf.* grotty. **3** *an inferior teacher* second-rate, indifferent, mediocre, incompetent, poor, bad, awful.
Opposites SUPERIOR; SENIOR; EXCELLENT.

inferior *noun* *despise his inferiors* subordinate, junior, underling, menial.

inferiority *noun* **1** *the inferiority of the goods* imperfection, faultiness, deficiency, shoddiness, cheapness; *inf.* grottiness. See INFERIOR *adjective* 2. **2** *the inferiority of the teaching* second-rateness, indifference, mediocrity, incompetence, poorness. See INFERIOR *adjective* 3. **3** *conscious of his inferiority* inferior status/position, lowliness, subordination, subservience.

infernal *adjective* **1** *the infernal regions* lower, nether, hellish, Hadean, Plutonic, Plutonian, Stygian, Styxian, Acherontal, Tartarean, Avernal, chthonic. **2** *infernal wickedness/crimes* hellish, diabolical, devilish, demonic, demoniac, fiendish, satanic, malevolent, malicious, heinous, vile, atrocious, execrable, unspeakable, outrageous. **3** *the infernal car won't start* damned, damnable, accursed, cursed, pestiential, wretched.

infertile *adjective* **1** *infertile soil* barren, unfruitful, unfructuous, sterile, unproductive, non-productive, arid. **2** *infertile women* barren, sterile, infecund, childless, unprolific.

infest *verb* overrun, spread through, take over, overspread, pervade, permeate, penetrate, infiltrate, invade, swarm over, crawl over, beset, pester, plague.

infidel *noun* unbeliever, disbeliever, heathen, heretic, pagan, agnostic, atheist, irreligionist.

infidelity *noun* **1** *discovering the spouse's infidelity* unfaithfulness, adultery, cuckoldry; affair, liaison, intrigue, amour; *inf.* fooling/playing around, cheating, hanky-panky. **2** *the servant's infidelity to his master* breach of trust, faithlessness, unfaithfulness, treachery, perfidy, perfidiousness, disloyalty, falseness, traitorousness, treason, double-dealing, duplicity.
Opposites FIDELITY; FAITHFULNESS.

infiltrate *verb* **1** *water infiltrated the roof* pervade, penetrate, filter through, percolate, seep into/through, soak into. **2** *they infiltrated the enemy's meeting* slip into, sneak into, creep into,

insinuate oneself into, worm one's way into, invade, intrude on.

infinite *adjective* **1** *infinite space* boundless, unbounded, unlimited, limitless, without limit/end, extensive, vast. **2** *infinite numbers of insects* countless, without number, numberless, innumerable, immeasurable, incalculable, untold, uncountable, inestimable, indeterminable, vast, enormous, stupendous, prodigious. **3** *infinite depths* limitless, boundless, measureless, immeasurable, fathomless, bottomless. **4** *infinite patience* unlimited, boundless, endless, unending, no end of, never-ending, inexhaustible, interminable, absolute, total.

infinitesimal *adjective* minute, tiny, microscopic, minuscule, very small, teeny, wee, Lilliputian, inappreciable, insignificant, inconsiderable, trifling; *inf.* piddling.
Opposites HUGE; ENORMOUS; SUBSTANTIAL.

infinity *noun* *the infinity of space | stare into infinity* boundlessness, limitlessness, unlimitedness, endlessness, infinitude, infiniteness; infinite distance, space.

infirm *adjective* **1** *infirm old people* feeble, enfeebled, weak, frail, debilitated, decrepit, disabled, in poor/declining health, failing, ailing, doddering, doddery, tottering, wobbly, lame, crippled. **2** *of infirm judgement* indecisive, irresolute, wavering, vacillating, fluctuating, faltering. **3** *infirm furniture* rickety, unsteady, shaky, wobbly, unsound, flimsy, tumbledown, jerry-built, on its last legs, decayed.
Opposites HEALTHY; FIT; STABLE.

infirmity *noun* **1** *suffering from an infirmity* ailment, illness, malady, disease, disorder, sickness. **2** *moral infirmities* fault, failing, defect, flaw, weakness, imperfection, foible. **3** *the infirmity of the old people* feebleness, weakness, frailty, debilitation, impairment, decrepitude, disability, dodderiness. See INFIRM 1. **4** *the infirmity of his judgement* indecision, irresoluteness, irresolution, vacillation. See INFIRM 2. **5** *the infirmity of the furniture* ricketiness, wobbliness, unsoundness, flimsiness. See INFIRM 3.

inflame *verb* **1** *inflame the passions of the crowd* incite, excite, arouse, rouse, stir up, work up, whip up, agitate, fire, ignite, kindle, foment, impassion, provoke, stimulate, actuate.
2 *inflame the onlookers with his cruelty to the child* enrage, incense, infuriate, exasperate, anger, madden, provoke, rile. **3** *inflame the feud* aggravate, intensify, make worse, exacerbate, fan, fuel. **4** *her face inflamed with anger* redden, flush, suffuse, make glow, make hot.

inflamed *adjective* **1** *an inflamed arm* red, hot, angry-looking, swollen, sore, infected, festered, septic. **2** *inflamed passions* excited, aroused, roused, stirred, kindled, impassioned. See INFLAME 1.

inflammable *adjective* flammable, burnable, combustible, ignitable, ignitible, incendiary, deflagrable.
Opposites INCOMBUSTIBLE; non-flammable.

inflammation *noun* *treat the inflammation on his leg* redness, hotness, heat, swelling, soreness,

403

sore, painfulness, tenderness, infection, festering, eruption, suppuration, septicity.

inflammatory *adjective* **1** *an inflammatory reaction to the drug* red, hot, swollen, sore, painful, tender, eruptive, allergic. *See* INFLAMMATION. **2** *an inflammatory speech* inflaming, inciting, arousing, rousing, stirring, fiery, passionate, impassioned, provocative, provoking, instigative, actuating, fomenting, rabble-rousing, demagogic, rebellious, revolutionary, insurgent, seditious, mutinous, anarchic. *See* INFLAME 1.

inflate *verb* **1** *inflate the rubber dinghy | inflate one's cheeks* blow up, pump up, aerate, puff up, puff out, dilate, distend, swell. **2** *his cheeks inflated* puff up, puff out, dilate, distend, swell. **3** *every time he tells the story he inflates the element of danger* increase, extend, amplify, augment, expand, intensify, exaggerate. **4** *please do not inflate his self-importance* add to, boost, augment, intensify, magnify, escalate, aggrandize. **5** *inflate prices* increase, boost, raise, escalate, step up.
Opposites DEFLATE; COLLAPSE; play down (*see* PLAY *verb*); DECREASE.

inflated *adjective* **1** *inflated rubber toys* blown up, pumped up, dilated. **2** *inflated prices* increased, raised, escalated, stepped up. **3** *an inflated sense of his own importance* exaggerated, magnified, aggrandized. **4** *inflated prose style* high-flown, extravagant, pretentious, pompous, rhetorical, grandiloquent, bombastic, orotund.

inflection *noun* **1** *the inflection of the line* curving, curvature, bending, turning; curve, bend, turn, bow, crook, angle, arc, arch. **2** *the inflection of his voice* change of pitch/tone/timbre, flow, modulation, accentuation, emphasis, stress, cadence, rhythm. **3** *a language with inflections* conjugation, declension.

inflexible *adjective* **1** *an inflexible substance* non-flexible, rigid, stiff, unbendable, unyielding, taut, hard, firm, inelastic, unmalleable. **2** *inflexible rules* unalterable, unchangeable, immutable, unvarying, firm, fixed, hard and fast, unbendable, uncompromising, stringent, rigorous, inexorable. **3** *inflexible people/attitudes* adamant, firm, immovable, unadaptable, dyed in the wool, unaccommodating, uncompliant, stubborn, obdurate, obstinate, intractable, unbending, intolerant, relentless, merciless, pitiless, uncompromising, inexorable, steely, iron-willed.

inflict *verb* administer, deal out, mete out, serve out, deliver, apply, lay on, impose, levy, exact, wreak.

infliction *noun* **1** *the infliction of punishment* administering, administration, dealing out, meting out, delivering, application, imposition, levying, exaction, wreaking. **2** *recovering from his infliction* trouble, worry, suffering, affliction, hurt, torture, torment, tribulation, punishment, penalty.

influence *noun* **1** *have a good/bad influence on them* effect, impact; control, sway, ascendancy, power, mastery, agency, guidance, domination, rule, supremacy, leadership, direction,

pressure. **2** *under the influence of drugs* effect, control, hold, sway, power. **3** *he has influence on the board* power, authority, sway, prestige, standing, footing; good offices, connections; *inf.* clout, pull.

influence *verb* **1** *his illness influenced his behaviour* affect, have an effect on, impact on, sway, bias, incline, motivate, actuate, determine, guide, control, change, alter, transform. **2** *he tried to influence the jury* affect, sway, bias, bring pressure to bear on; *inf.* pull strings with, pull rank on. **3** *he influenced her not to go* persuade, induce, impel, incite, manipulate, prompt.

influential *adjective* **1** *an influential member of the board* powerful, important, leading, authoritative, controlling, dominant, predominant, prestigious. **2** *money was an influential issue in his decision to go* instrumental, guiding, significant, important, persuasive, telling, meaningful.
Opposites UNIMPORTANT; IMPOTENT; INSIGNIFICANT.

influx *noun* inrush, rush, inflow, inundation, flood, invasion, intrusion, incursion, ingress, convergence.

inform *verb* **1** *inform him of the facts* tell, let know, apprise, advise, notify, announce to, impart to, relate to, communicate to, acquaint, brief, instruct, enlighten, make conversant, make knowledgeable, send word to; *inf.* put in the picture, fill in, clue in/up, put wise, spill the beans to, tip off, tip the wink to, give the low-down to, give the inside story to. **2** *inform on his accomplices* betray, denounce, incriminate, inculpate, blab on; *inf.* grass on, rat on, squeal on, tell tales about, tell on, blow the whistle on, spill the beans about, put the finger on, sell down the river, nark, snitch on, peach; *Scots inf.* clype on. **3** *optimism informs her writing* characterize, typify, pervade, permeate, suffuse, infuse, imbue, instil. **4** *her love of God informed her* inspire, animate, arouse, fire, kindle.

informal *adjective* **1** *an informal party | informal dress* non-formal, casual, unceremonious, unofficial, simple, unpretentious, everyday, relaxed, easy. **2** *informal language* colloquial, vernacular, non-literary, simple, natural, everyday, unofficial, unpretentious; *inf.* slangy.

informality *noun* non-formality, casualness, lack of ceremony, unceremoniousness, unofficialness, simplicity, naturalness, unpretentiousness, ease, relaxedness.

information *noun* **1** *the information has been recorded* data, facts. **2** *what information do you have? | has she sent any information?* knowledge, intelligence, news, notice, word, advice, counsel, instruction, enlightenment; tidings; message, report, communiqué, communication; *inf.* info, gen, low-down, dope, inside story, bumf, dirt.

informative *adjective* instructive, illuminating, enlightening, edifying, educational, revealing, telling, communicative, chatty, newsy, gossipy.

informed *adjective* knowledgeable, well-briefed, abreast of the facts, well-posted, primed, well-versed, up-to-date, *au courant, au fait.*

informer *noun* informant, betrayer, traitor, Judas; *inf.* grass, rat, squealer, snout, stool pigeon, tell-tale, whistle-blower, canary, nark, snitch, peacher; *Scots inf.* clype.

infraction *noun* breach, violation, transgression, contravention, infringement, intrusion, encroachment, invasion.

infrequent *adjective* few and far between, rare, occasional, sporadic, irregular, uncommon, unusual, exceptional.

infringe *verb* **1** *infringe the law* break, disobey, violate, contravene, transgress, breach, infract, disregard, take no notice of. **2** *infringe on his neighbour's land* encroach, impinge, intrude, trespass.

infringement *noun* **1** *an infringement of the rules* breaking, violation, contravention, breach, transgression, infraction, non-observance, non-compliance. **2** *an infringement on his property* encroachment, impingement, intrusion, trespass.

infuriate *verb* enrage, incense, inflame, madden, exasperate, anger, provoke, rile, make one's blood boil, make one's hackles rise, annoy, irritate, vex, pique; *inf.* aggravate, make one see red, get one's back up, get one's goat, bug, get one.

infuriating *adjective* maddening, exasperating, provoking, annoying, irritating, vexing, vexatious, galling; *inf.* aggravating.

ingenious *adjective* *an ingenious person | an ingenious course of action* clever, shrewd, astute, smart, sharp, bright, brilliant, talented, masterly, resourceful, inventive, creative, original, subtle, crafty, wily, cunning, skilful, adroit, deft, capable; *inf.* on the ball.
Opposites STUPID; UNIMAGINATIVE.

ingenuous *adjective* *too ingenuous to lie* open, sincere, honest, frank, candid, direct, forthright, artless, guileless, simple, naive, innocent, genuine, undeceitful, undeceptive, undissembling, undissimulating, above-board, trustful, truthful, unsuspicious; *inf.* on the level.
Opposites INSINCERE; ARTFUL.

inglorious *adjective* disgraceful, shameful, dishonourable, ignominious, discreditable, disreputable, humiliating, mortifying, unheroic, ignoble, blameworthy, culpable.

ingrained *adjective* **1** *ingrained dirt* fixed, infixed, planted, implanted, rooted, deep-rooted, permanent, built-in. **2** *ingrained stupidity* inbred, inherent, intrinsic, hereditary, inherited, in the blood/family.

ingratiate *verb* **ingratiate oneself** *ingratiate herself with the director* seek the favour of, curry favour with, toady to, crawl to, grovel to, fawn over, play up to, be a yes man/woman to, be a sycophant to; *inf.* suck up to, rub up the right way, lick the boots of.

ingratiating *adjective* sycophantic, toadying, fawning, unctuous, obsequious, servile, over-humble, crawling, flattering, wheedling, cajoling; *inf.* bootlicking.

ingratitude *noun* ungratefulness, thanklessness, unthankfulness, lack of appreciation, unappreciativeness, non-recognition.

ingredient *adjective* constituent, component, element, part, unit, item, feature.

ingress *noun* **1** *find the ingress to the castle* way in, entrance, entry, approach. **2** *that ticket gives you ingress to the concert* admission, admittance, access, right of entry.

inhabit *verb* live in, dwell in, reside in, occupy, tenant, lodge in, make one's home in, settle in, settle, people, populate.

inhabitant *noun* resident, resider, dweller, occupant, occupier, habitant, settler.

inhale *verb* breathe in, draw in, suck in, sniff in, gasp, gulp, inspire.
Opposites exhale; EXPIRE.

inharmonious *adjective* **1** *inharmonious sounds* unharmonious, unmelodious, unmusical, tuneless, discordant, dissonant, harsh, jarring, jangling, raucous, strident. **2** *holding inharmonious views* conflicting, incompatible, contradictory, irreconcilable, antagonistic, antipathetic, dissentient. **3** *an inharmonious relationship* quarrelsome, argumentative, disputatious.

inherent *adjective* **1** *an inherent tendency to high blood pressure* inborn, inbred, innate, hereditary, inherited, in the blood/family, congenital, familial. **2** *an inherent part of the boat's design* intrinsic, innate, built-in, inseparable, essential, basic, fundamental, ingrained.

inherit *verb* **1** *inherit a fortune/estate* become/fall heir to, be bequeathed, be left, be willed, come into/by. **2** *inherit the title* succeed to, accede to, assume, take over, be elevated to.

inheritance *noun* **1** *value their inheritance* legacy, bequest, endowment, birthright, heritage, patrimony. **2** *his inheritance of the title* accession, succession, assumption, elevation. See INHERIT 2.

inhibit *verb* **1** *inhibit progress* hold back, impede, hinder, hamper, interfere with, obstruct, curb, check, restrict, restrain, constrain, bridle, rein in, baulk, frustrate, arrest, prevent, stop. **2** *inhibit them from going* forbid, prohibit, ban, bar, debar, vet, interdict, proscribe.

inhibited *adjective* *feel inhibited in the presence of parents* shy, reticent, self-conscious, reserved, constrained, repressed, embarrassed, tongue-tied, subdued, withdrawn; *inf.* uptight.
Opposites UNINHIBITED; OUTGOING; EXTROVERT.

inhibition *noun* **1** *regret the inhibition of progress* holding back, impediment, hindrance, hampering, interference, obstruction, curb, check, restriction, restraint, constraint, bridling, baulking, frustration, arrest, prevention, stopping. **2** *suffer from inhibition in the presence of parents* shyness, reticence, reserve, self-consciousness, constraint, repression, embarrassment, subduedness, withdrawnness.

inhospitable *adjective* **1** *an inhospitable host/welcome* unwelcoming, unsociable, unsocial, antisocial, unfriendly, uncivil, discourteous, ungracious, uncongenial, ungenerous, cool, cold, chilly, aloof, unkind, unsympathetic, ill-disposed, hostile, inimical, xenophobic. **2** *an inhospitable landscape* uninviting, unwelcoming, barren, bleak, bare, uninhabitable, sterile, desolate, lonely, empty, forbidding, hostile, inimical.

inhuman *adjective* **1** *an inhuman cry* nonhuman, non-mortal, animal, ghostly. **2** *inhuman people* unkind, unkindly, inconsiderate, uncompassionate, unsympathetic, unapproachable, inhumane. *See* INHUMANE.

inhumane *adjective* unkind, unkindly, inconsiderate, uncompassionate, unfeeling, unsympathetic, unforgiving, cold-blooded, heartless, hard-hearted, pitiless, merciless, ruthless, remorseless, brutal, cruel, harsh, savage, vicious, barbaric, barbarous, bestial, fiendish, diabolical.

inhumanity *noun* unkindness, lack of compassion/feeling/sympathy, cold-bloodedness, heartlessness, hard-heartedness, pitilessness, mercilessness, ruthlessness, remorselessness, brutality, cruelty, harshness, savagery, viciousness, barbarity, bestiality, fiendishness.

inimical *adjective* **1** *an inimical atmosphere* hostile, unfriendly, unkind, inhospitable, unwelcoming, unfavourable, cold, unsociable, adverse, opposed, antagonistic, contrary, antipathetic, ill-disposed. **2** *inimical to their survival* harmful, injurious, detrimental, deleterious, hurtful, damaging, dangerous, pernicious, destructive, noxious, toxic, virulent. *Opposites* FRIENDLY; WARM; ADVANTAGEOUS.

inimitable *adjective* matchless, unmatched, incomparable, unparalleled, unrivalled, unsurpassed, unsurpassable, unique, superlative, supreme, model, faultless, perfect, consummate, ideal, unexampled, nonpareil, peerless.

iniquitous *adjective* **1** *an iniquitous action* wicked, sinful, evil, immoral, villainous, criminal, heinous, vile, foul, base, odious, abominable, execrable, atrocious, malicious, outrageous, monstrous, shocking, scandalous, reprehensible, unjust. **2** *an iniquitous robber* wicked, èvil, criminal, lawless, crooked, dishonourable, unprincipled, blackguardly, degenerate, corrupt, reprobate, immoral, dissolute.

iniquity *noun* **1** *his falling into iniquity* wickedness, sin, sinfulness, vice, evil, ungodliness, godlessness, wrong, wrongdoing, badness, villainy, knavery, lawlessness, crime, baseness, heinousness. **2** *appalled at his iniquities* sin, vice, offence, crime, transgression, injury, violation, atrocity, outrage. *Opposites* VIRTUE; RIGHT.

initial *adjective* *the initial stages of the enterprise* first, beginning, commencing, starting, opening, early, prime, primary, elementary, foundational, introductory, inaugural, inceptive, incipient, inchoate. *Opposites* FINAL.

initial *verb* *initial the document* put one's initials on, sign, undersign, countersign; endorse.

initially *adverb* in/at the beginning, at first, at the start/outset, to begin/start with, originally, in the early stages.

initiate *verb* **1** *initiate the proceedings* begin, start off, commence, open, institute, inaugurate, get under way, set in motion, lay the foundations of, lay the first stone of, launch, actuate, instigate, trigger off, originate, pioneer, sow the seeds of; start the ball rolling. **2** *initiate the pupil in science* teach, instruct, coach, tutor, school, train, drill, prime, familiarize, indoctrinate, inculcate. **3** *initiate the new member into the organization* admit, introduce, induct, install, instate, incorporate, ordain, invest, enlist, enrol, sign up. *Opposites* END; CLOSE.

initiate *noun* **1** *train the initiates in the organization* beginner, new boy/girl, newcomer, learner, trainee, apprentice, probationer, new/raw recruit, greenhorn, novice, tiro, novitiate, neophyte; *inf.* rookie. **2** *long-standing initiate of the organization* member, card-carrier, enlistee, enrolee.

initiation *noun* **1** *the initiation of the proceedings* beginning, starting, commencement, opening, institution, inauguration, launch, actuation, instigation. *See* INITIATE *verb* 1. **2** *an initiation ceremony* admission, admittance, introduction, induction, installation, ordination, investment, enlistment, enrolment, baptism.

initiative *noun* **1** *take the initiative* first step, first move, first blow, lead, gambit, opening move/gambit, beginning, start, commencement. **2** *promotion for those with initiative* enterprise, inventiveness, resourcefulness, resource, originality, creativity, drive, dynamism, ambition, ambitiousness, verve, dash, leadership; *inf.* get-up-and-go, zing, push, pep, zip.

inject *verb* **1** *inject the child/arm* syringe, inoculate, vaccinate; *inf.* jab. **2** *inject fluid into the patient | inject heroin* introduce, intromit, insert, syringe; *inf.* shoot, shoot up, mainline. **3** *inject some enthusiasm into the class* introduce, instil, bring in, infuse, imbue.

injection *noun* **1** *a tetanus injection* inoculation, vaccination, vaccine, shot, booster; *inf.* jab; *inf.* fix, hit. **2** *the injection of some enthusiasm* introduction, instilment, instilling, infusion, imbuing.

injudicious *adjective* imprudent, unwise, inadvisable, ill-considered, ill-judged, ill-advised, impolitic, inexpedient, unrecommendable, misguided, incautious, undesirable, indiscreet, inappropriate, unsuitable, wrong-headed, wrong, hare-brained, foolish, hasty, rash; *inf.* dumb.

injunction *noun* command, instruction, order, ruling, direction, directive, dictum, dictate, mandate, ordainment, enjoinment, admonition, precept, ultimatum.

injure *verb* **1** *injure his foot* hurt, harm, damage, wound, maim, cripple, lame, disable, mutilate, deform, mangle. **2** *injure his health* harm, damage, impair, weaken, enfeeble. **3** *injure his reputation by his conduct* ruin, spoil, mar, damage, blight, blemish, besmirch, tarnish, undermine. **4** *guilty of injuring his fellow citizens* do an injury to, wrong, do an injustice to, offend against, abuse, maltreat, defame, vilify, malign; *inf.* do the dirty on.

injured *adjective* **1** *his injured leg* hurt, wounded, broken, fractured, sore, maimed, crippled, lame. *See* INJURE 1. **2** *the injured party* wronged, offended, abused, maltreated, ill-treated, defamed, vilified, maligned. **3** *give him an injured look* reproachful, hurt, wounded, upset, cut to the quick, put out, unhappy, disgruntled, displeased, condemnatory, censorious.

injurious *adjective injurious to health* harmful, hurtful, damaging, deleterious, detrimental, disadvantageous, unfavourable, destructive, pernicious, ruinous, disastrous, calamitous, malignant.
Opposites INNOCUOUS; ADVANTAGEOUS; FAVOURABLE.

injury *noun* **1** *dangerous machines bound to cause injury* harm, hurt, wounding, damage, impairment, affliction. **2** *his injuries taking long to heal* wound, sore, bruise, cut, gash, laceration, abrasion, lesion, contusion, trauma. **3** *do an injury to his neighbours by his conduct* injustice, wrong, ill, offence, disservice, grievance, evil.

injustice *noun* **1** *the injustice of the verdict* unjustness, unfairness, inequitableness, inequity, bias, prejudice, favouritism, partiality, one-sidedness, discrimination, partisanship. **2** *infamous for his injustices done to others* unfairness, unjustness, inequity, wrong, injury, offence, evil, villainy, iniquity.

inkling *noun* **1** *they gave no inkling of their intentions* hint, clue, intimation, suggestion, indication, whisper, suspicion, insinuation, innuendo. **2** *have no inkling of how best to proceed* idea, vague idea, notion, glimmering; knowledge, slight knowledge; *inf.* foggiest idea, the foggiest.

inky *adjective inky nights* black, pitch-black, coal-black, jet-black, sable, ebony, dark.

inlaid *adjective* inset; veneered, enamelled, ornamented, enchased, tessellated, mosaic, studded, lined, tiled.

inland *adjective inland towns* interior, inshore, internal, up-country.

inlet *noun* cove, bay, arm/armlet of the sea, bight, creek, fjord, sound; *Scots* firth, sea loch.

inmate *noun* **1** *hospital inmates* patient, hospital case. **2** *prison inmates* prisoner, convict, captive, jailbird.

inmost *See* INNERMOST.

inn *noun* public house, pub, tavern, bar, hotel.

innate *adjective* **1** *an innate tendency* inborn, inbred, connate, congenital, hereditary, inherited, in the blood/family, inherent, intrinsic, ingrained, natural, native, indigenous. **2** *an innate part of the plan* essential, basic, fundamental, quintessential, organic, radical. **3** *an innate capacity* instinctive, intuitive, spontaneous, unlearned, untaught.

inner *adjective* **1** *the inner rooms* interior, inside, central, middle, further in. **2** *the inner political circle* restricted, privileged, confidential, intimate, private, exclusive, secret. **3** *the inner meaning* unapparent, veiled, obscure, esoteric, hidden, secret, unrevealed. **4** *man's inner life* spiritual, emotional, mental,

psychological, psychic.
Opposites OUTER; EXTERIOR; OUTSIDE.

innermost, inmost *adjective* **1** *the innermost section* furthest in, deepest within, central, middle. **2** *innermost beliefs* intimate, private, personal, deep, deepest, profound, secret, hidden.

innkeeper *noun* publican, landlady, landlord, mine host, bar-keeper, hotelier.

innocence *noun* **1** *the innocence of the prisoners* guiltlessness, blamelessness, freedom from guilt/blame, unblameworthiness, inculpability, unimpeachability, irreproachability, clean hands. **2** *the innocence of their play* harmlessness, innocuousness, safety, lack of danger/ malice, inoffensiveness, innoxiousness. *See* INNOCENT *adjective* 2. **3** *the innocence of the young girls* virtuousness, virtue, purity, lack of sin, sinlessness, morality, decency, righteousness, chastity, virginity, immaculateness, impeccability, spotlessness. *See* INNOCENT *adjective* 3. **4** *the innocence of the new army recruits* simpleness, ingenuousness, naivety, lack of sophistication, artlessness, guilelessness, frankness, openness, credulity, inexperience, gullibility. *See* INNOCENT *adjective* 5.
Opposites GUILT; SIN.

innocent *adjective* **1** *innocent prisoners* not guilty, guiltless, blameless, clear, in the clear, above suspicion, unblameworthy, inculpable, unimpeachable, irreproachable, clean-handed. **2** *innocent fun* harmless, innocuous, safe, non-injurious, unmalicious, unobjectionable, inoffensive, innoxious, playful. **3** *innocent young girls* virtuous, pure, sinless, moral, decent, righteous, upright, chaste, virginal, virgin, immaculate, impeccable, pristine, spotless, stainless, unblemished, unsullied, incorrupt, uncorrupted. **4** *innocent of guile* free from, without, lacking, empty of, clear of, unacquainted with, ignorant of, unaware of, unfamiliar with, nescient of, untouched by. **5** *too innocent for the world of business* simple, ingenuous, naive, unsophisticated, artless, guileless, childlike, frank, open, unsuspicious, trustful, trusting, credulous, inexperienced, unworldly, green, gullible; *inf.* wet behind the ears. **6** *innocent tumours* benign, non-cancerous, non-malignant.
Opposites GUILTY; SINFUL.

innocent *noun an innocent in the business world* child, babe, babe in arms, *ingénue*, novice, greenhorn.

innocuous *adjective* **1** *an innocuous substance* harmless, unhurtful, uninjurious, safe, danger-free, non-poisonous. **2** *an innocuous person* harmless, inoffensive, unobjectionable, unexceptionable, unoffending, mild, peaceful, bland, commonplace, run-of-the-mill, insipid.
Opposites HARMFUL; DANGEROUS; INJURIOUS.

innovation *noun* new method/device/measure, introduction, modernism, modernization, novelty, change, alteration, variation, transformation, metamorphosis, renovation, restyling, recasting, remodelling, coining, neology, neologism.

innuendo *noun* insinuation, implication, suggestion, hint, overtone, allusion, inkling, imputation, aspersion.

innumerable *adjective* very many, numerous, countless, untold, incalculable, numberless, unnumbered, beyond number, infinite, myriad; *inf.* umpteen, masses, oodles.
Opposites FEW; FINITE.

inoculate *verb* immunize, vaccinate; *inf.* give shots/jabs.

inoculation *noun* immunization, vaccination, injection, shot; *inf.* jab.

inoffensive *adjective* **1** *an inoffensive substance* harmless, innocuous, unhurtful, safe, danger-free. See INNOCUOUS 1. **2** *an inoffensive person* harmless, innocuous, unobjectionable, unexceptionable, mild, peaceful.

inoperative *adjective* **1** *inoperative machines* not operative, not in operation, not working, out of order, out of service/commission/action, non-active, broken, broken-down, defective, faulty; *inf.* kaput, knackered. **2** *an inoperative system* useless, ineffectual, ineffective, inefficient, inadequate, worthless, valueless, futile, unproductive, abortive.

inopportune *adjective* inconvenient, ill-timed, badly timed, mistimed, untimely, unseasonable, inappropriate, unsuitable, inapt, ill-chosen, infelicitous, unfavourable, unfortunate, unpropitious, inauspicious.

inordinate *adjective* excessive, immoderate, overabundant, extravagant, unrestrained, unrestricted, unlimited, unwarranted, uncalled-for, undue, unreasonable, disproportionate, exorbitant, extreme, outrageous, preposterous, unconscionable.
Opposites MODERATE; LIMITED.

inquest *noun* inquiry, investigation, inquisition, probe.

inquire *verb* **1** *inquire into the cause of the fire* make inquiries, conduct an inquiry, question, query, investigate, research, look into, examine, explore, probe, scan, search, scrutinize, study, inspect, reconnoitre. **2** *inquire about the weather | inquire his name* ask, make inquiries about; quiz, interrogate; *inf.* grill.

inquiring *adjective* *an inquiring mind* questioning, investigative, curious, interested, analytical, probing, exploring, searching, scrutinizing, inquisitive.

inquiry *noun* **1** *conduct an inquiry into the murder* investigation, examination, exploration, sounding, probe, search, scrutiny, scrutinization, study, inspection, reconnoitring, interrogation. **2** *reply to her inquiry* question, query.

inquisition *noun subject the suspects to an inquisition* interrogation, cross-examination, examination, investigation, quizzing, questioning, inquiry, inquest; *inf.* grilling, third degree.

inquisitive *adjective* *inquisitive neighbours* inquiring, questioning, probing, scrutinizing, curious, burning with curiosity, interested, over-interested, intrusive, meddlesome, prying, snooping, snoopy, peering, spying; *inf.* nosy, nosy-parker.
Opposites INDIFFERENT; APATHETIC; UNINTERESTED.

inroad *noun* **1** *enemy inroads* invasion, raid, foray, attack, assault, onslaught, charge, offensive, sally, sortie. **2** *object to the inroads on her time* encroachment, intrusion, incursion, infringement, trespassing.

insane *adjective* **1** *insane people in hospital* mad, severely mentally disordered, of unsound mind, deranged, demented, *non compos mentis*, out of one's mind, unhinged, crazed, crazy. **2** *he's insane to take that job* extremely foolish, mad, mad as a hatter, raving mad, out of one's/mind, unhinged, not all there, crazy; *inf.* bonkers, cracked, crackers, barmy, batty, bats, cuckoo, loony, loopy, nuts, nutty, screwy, bananas, off one's rocker/head/chump/nut, out of one's head, round the bend/twist, off one's trolley. **3** *an insane idea* very foolish, mad, crazy, idiotic, stupid, senseless, nonsensical, irrational, impracticable, pointless, absurd, ridiculous, ludicrous, bizarre, fatuous; *inf.* daft.

insanitary *adjective* unsanitary, unsanitized, unhygienic, impure, unclean, dirty, dirtied, filthy, contaminated, polluted, foul, feculent, infected, septic, infested, disease-ridden, germy, unhealthy, insalubrious, noxious.

insanity *noun* **1** *patients suffering from insanity* madness, severe mental disorder, mental derangement, dementia, frenzy, delirium. **2** *the insanity of the idea* folly, foolishness, madness, craziness, idiocy, stupidity, senselessness, irrationality, absurdity. See INSANE 3.

insatiable *adjective* insatiate, unappeasable, unquenchable, greedy, hungry, craving, voracious, ravening, gluttonous, omnivorous, avid, desirous, eager.

inscribe *verb* **1** *inscribe one's name on the book/ stone* imprint, write, stamp, impress, mark, brand, engrave, etch, carve, cut. **2** *inscribe the candidates in the book* enter, register, record, write, list, enrol, enlist, engross. **3** *inscribe his novel to his son* dedicate, address.

inscription *noun* **1** *read the inscription on the gravestone* engraving, writing, etching, lettering, legend, epitaph, epigraph; words. **2** *the inscription on the book* dedication, address, message.

inscrutable *adjective* **1** *an inscrutable expression* enigmatic, unreadable, impenetrable, cryptic, deadpan, sphinxlike; *inf.* poker-faced. **2** *an inscrutable situation* mysterious, inexplicable, unexplainable, incomprehensible, beyond comprehension/understanding, unintelligible, puzzling, baffling, unfathomable, arcane.
Opposites OPEN; EXPRESSIVE; TRANSPARENT.

insect *noun.* See table. See also table at BUTTERFLY.

insecticide *noun* insect spray, insect powder, fly-spray, pesticide, insect killer.

insecure *adjective* **1** *insecure children* unconfident, lacking confidence, diffident, timid, uncertain, unsure, doubtful, hesitant, anxious, fearful, apprehensive, worried. **2** *insecure fortresses* vulnerable, open to attack, defenceless, unprotected, ill-protected, unguarded, unshielded, exposed, in danger, dangerous, perilous, hazardous. **3** *insecure fitments* loose, flimsy, frail, fragile, infirm, weak, unsubstantial, jerry-built, rickety, wobbly, shaky, unsteady, unstable, unsound, decrepit.

insecurity noun **1** *the insecurity of the children* lack of confidence/security, diffidence, timidity, uncertainty, anxiety, apprehension, worry. *See* INSECURE 1. **2** *the insecurity of the fortresses* vulnerability, defencelessness, lack of protection, unguardedness, danger, peril, perilousness. *See* INSECURE 2. **3** *the insecurity of the fitments* looseness, flimsiness, frailty, fragility, infirmity, ricketiness, wobbliness, shakiness, unsteadiness, instability, decrepitude. *See* INSECURE 3.

insensible adjective **1** *try to rouse the insensible man* unconscious, insensate, senseless, insentient, anaesthetized, comatose, knocked out, inert, stupefied; *inf.* out, out cold, out for the count, zonked. **2** *insensible fingers and toes* numb, benumbed, numbed, lacking feeling/sensation. **3** *insensible of their danger* unaware of, ignorant of, without knowledge of, unconscious of, unmindful of, oblivious to. **4** *insensible to their suffering* indifferent to, impervious to, deaf to, unmoved by, untouched by, unaffected by, unresponsive to, inured to. **5** *a passionate person among insensible people* apathetic, dispassionate, cool, passionless, emotionless,

detached, indifferent, aloof, hard, hard-hearted, tough, cruel, callous. **6** *an insensible difference in their views* imperceptible, unnoticeable, indiscernible, indistinguishable, negligible, slight, minute, minuscule.
Opposites CONSCIOUS; AWARE; RESPONSIVE.

insensitive adjective **1** *insensitive to pain/cold* impervious to, immune to, proof against, insusceptible to, unaffected by, nonreactive to, unreactive to. **2** *insensitive to the demands of the public* unresponsive to, impervious to, indifferent to, unaffected by, unmoved by, oblivious to, unappreciative of. **3** *insensitive people laughing at the funeral* heartless, unfeeling, callous, tactless, thick-skinned, uncaring, unconcerned, uncompassionate, unsympathetic.

insentient adjective inanimate, lifeless, inert, vegetative, insensate, numb, anaesthetized, comatose.

inseparable adjective **1** *inseparable parts* unseparable, inseverable, indivisible, undividable, indissoluble. **2** *inseparable companions* constant, devoted, close, intimate, bosom.

insert verb **1** *insert a nail in the wall* put in/into, place in, press in, push in, stick in, thrust in, drive in, work in, slide in, slip in, tuck in; *inf.*

INSECTS

alder fly	burying	devil's	harlequin	mole cricket	spider
amazon	beetle	coach-	bug	mosquito	wasp
ant	bush cricket	horse	head louse	moth	spittlebug
ambrosia	butterfly	digger wasp	Hercules	oil beetle	springtail
beetle	cabbage	diving	beetle	phylloxera	squash bug
ant	root fly	beetle	honey ant	plant bug	stag beetle
ant-lion	caddis-fly	dobsonfly	honey bee	plant	stick
aphid	capsid bug	dor-beetle	hornet	hopper	insect
army ant	carpenter	dragonfly	horntail	pond-skater	stink bug
army worm	bee	driver ant	horsefly	potato	stonefly
assassin	carpet	drosophila	housefly	beetle	stylops
bug	beetle	dung-beetle	hoverfly	potter wasp	termite
back-	chafer	earwig	ichneumon	praying	thrips
swimmer	chigger	elm bark	June bug	mantis	tiger beetle
bark beetle	chinch bug	beetle	katydid	red ant	tortoise
bedbug	cicada	fire ant	ked	red bug	beetle
bee	click beetle	firebrat	kissing bug	rhinoceros	tree hopper
bee fly	cockchafer	firefly	lacewing	beetle	tsetse fly
beetle	cockroach	flea	lac insect	robber fly	warble fly
black beetle	Colorado	flea beetle	ladybird	rove beetle	wasp
blackfly	potato	fly	lantern-fly	sandfly	water
blister	beetle	froghopper	leaf beetle	sawfly	beetle
beetle	corn borer	fruit fly	leafcutter	scale insect	water-
bloodworm	cotton	gadfly	ant	scarab	boatman
blowfly	stainer	gall midge	leafcutter	scorpion fly	water bug
bluebottle	crab louse	gall wasp	bee	screw-worm	water
body louse	crane-fly	giant water	leafhopper	sexton	scorpion
boll-weevil	cricket	bug	leaf insect	beetle	water
bombardier	croton bug	glow-worm	leather-	sheep ked	strider
beetle	cuckoo-spit	Goliath	jacket	shield bug	webspinner
booklouse	insect	beetle	locust	silverfish	weevil
bookworm	cutworm	grain weevil	louse	slave-	whirligig
borer	damselfly	grasshopper	mason bee	making	white ant
bot fly	darkling	greenbottle	May-bug	ant	whitefly
bristletail	beetle	greenfly	mayfly	snakefly	wireworm
buffalo gnat	death-watch	ground	mealworm	soldier	wood borer
bug	beetle	beetle	mealy bug	beetle	woodwasp
bumble-bee	deer fly	ground bug	midge	Spanish fly	woodworm

pop in. **2** *insert a sentence into the paragraph* put in, introduce, enter, interpolate, inset, interpose, interject, implant, infix.
Opposites EXTRACT; WITHDRAW.

insert *noun an insert in the magazine* insertion, inset, supplement, circular, advertisement; *inf.* ad.

inside *noun* **1** *the inside of the book* interior, inner part/side/surface; contents. **2** *a sore inside | sore insides* stomach, abdomen, gut; internal organs, intestines, viscera, entrails, bowels, bodily/vital organs; *inf.* belly, tummy, guts, bread basket.

inside *adverb* **1** *go/stand inside* indoors; in/into the interior, in/into the house, in/into the building, within. **2** *inside she felt frightened* emotionally, in her thoughts/feelings, intuitively, instinctively.

inside *adjective* **1** *the inside part* interior, inner, internal, inward, on/in the inside, inmost, innermost, intramural. **2** *have inside information* confidential, classified, restricted, reserved, privileged, private, internal, privy, secret, exclusive, esoteric.

insidious *adjective* stealthy, subtle, surreptitious, sneaky, sneaking, cunning, crafty, designing, intriguing, Machiavellian, artful, guileful, sly, wily, tricky, slick, deceitful, deceptive, underhand, double-dealing, duplicitous, dishonest, insincere, disingenuous, treacherous, perfidious; *inf.* crooked.
Opposites STRAIGHTFORWARD; ARTLESS; HONEST.

insight *noun* **1** *a person of insight* intuition, perception, awareness, discernment, understanding, penetration, acumen, perspicacity, perspicaciousness, discrimination, judgement, shrewdness, sharpness, acuteness, flair, vision. **2** *give an insight into country life* awareness, understanding, realization, revelation, observance; *inf.* eye-opener.

insignia *noun/plural noun* **1** *insignia of office* badge, decoration, medallion, ribbon, crest, emblem, symbol, sign, mark, seal, signet. **2** *politeness is meant to be the insignia of the firm* mark of distinction, trade mark, label, trait, characteristic.

insignificant *adjective* **1** *insignificant details* unimportant, of minor/no importance, of little importance/import, trivial, trifling, negligible, inconsequential, of no consequence/account, of no moment/matter, inconsiderable, not worth mentioning, nugatory, meagre, paltry, scanty, petty, insubstantial, unsubstantial, flimsy, irrelevant, immaterial; *Am. inf.* dinky. **2** *insignificant members of the government* unimportant, uninfluential, powerless, small-fry.

insincere *adjective* lacking sincerity, not candid, not frank, disingenuous, dissembling, dissimulating, pretended, devious, hypocritical, deceitful, deceptive, duplicitous, dishonest, underhand, double-dealing, false, faithless, disloyal, treacherous, two-faced, lying, untruthful, mendacious, evasive, shifty, slippery.

insinuate *verb* **1** *he insinuated that she was dishonest* imply, hint, whisper, suggest, indicate, convey the impression, intimate, mention. **2** *insinuate doubts into their minds* infiltrate,

implant, instil, introduce, inculcate, infuse, inject. **insinuate oneself** *insinuate herself into his affections* worm oneself into, work one's way into, ingratiate oneself with, curry favour with; *inf.* get in with.

insinuation *noun* **1** *resent the insinuation that he was dishonest* implication, suggestion, hint, innuendo, intimation, mention, reference, allusion, aspersion, slur. **2** *the insinuation of doubts* infiltration, implanting, instilling, instillation, introduction. *See* INSINUATE 2. **3** *their insinuation into her affections* worming, ingratiation. *See* INSINUATE ONESELF.

insipid *adjective* **1** *an insipid person* lacking personality, colourless, anaemic, drab, inanimate, spiritless, jejune, vapid, dull, uninteresting, boring, unentertaining. **2** *insipid prose* unimaginative, characterless, flat, bland, vapid, uninteresting, dull, prosaic, boring, monotonous, tedious, wearisome, dry, dry as dust, humdrum, run-of-the-mill, trite, banal, hackneyed, stale. **3** *insipid soup* tasteless, flavourless, savourless, bland, thin, watery, watered-down, unappetizing, unpalatable; *Scots* wersh.
Opposites INTERESTING; IMAGINATIVE; TASTY.

insist *verb* **1** *if they refuse you must insist* stand firm, be firm, stand one's ground, make a stand, be resolute, be determined, be emphatic, not take no for an answer, brook no refusal. **2** *insist that they go* demand, require, command, importune, entreat, urge, exhort. **3** *she insists that she is innocent* maintain, assert, declare, hold, contend, pronounce, proclaim, aver, propound, avow, vow, swear, be emphatic, emphasize, stress, repeat, reiterate.

insistence *noun* **1** *her insistence that they go* requirement, command, importuning, entreaty, urging, exhortation; demands. **2** *her insistence that she is innocent* maintenance, assertion, declaration, contention, avowal, emphasis, stress. *See* INSIST 3. **3** *the insistence of the demands* persistence, doggedness, incessantness, urgency, coercion, exigency. *See* INSISTENT 2. **4** *the insistence of the call of the birds* constancy, incessantness, repetition, recurrence. *See* INSISTENT 3.

insistent *adjective* **1** *she is insistent that you go* emphatic, determined, resolute, tenacious, importunate, persistent, unyielding, obstinate, dogged, unrelenting, inexorable. **2** *insistent demands for payment* persistent, determined, dogged, incessant, urgent, pressing, compelling, high-pressure, pressurizing, coercive, demanding, exigent. **3** *the insistent call of the bird* constant, incessant, iterative, repeated, repetitive, recurrent.

insolence *noun* impertinence, impudence, cheek, cheekiness, ill-manneredness, rudeness, disrespect, incivility, insubordination, contempt, abuse, offensiveness, contumely, audacity, boldness, brazenness, brashness, pertness, forwardness, effrontery; insults; *inf.* gall, back-chat, sauce; *Am. inf.* chutzpah.

insolent *adjective* impertinent, impudent, cheeky, rude, ill-mannered, disrespectful, insubordinate, contemptuous, insulting, abusive, offensive, audacious, bold, brazen, brash,

pert, forward; *inf.* fresh.
Opposites POLITE; respectful; MODEST.

insoluble *adjective* **1** *an insoluble substance* not soluble, indissoluble, indissolvable, undissolvable. **2** *insoluble problems/puzzles/situations* insolvable, unsolvable, baffling, unfathomable, indecipherable, complicated, perplexing, intricate, involved, impenetrable, inscrutable, enigmatic, obscure, mystifying, inexplicable, incomprehensible, mysterious.

insolvency *noun* bankruptcy, indebtedness, liquidation, financial ruin, default, pennilessness, impoverishedness, penury, impecuniousness, beggary.

insolvent *adjective* bankrupt, indebted, in debt, liquidated, ruined, defaulting, in the hands of the receivers, penniless, impoverished, penurious, impecunious; *inf.* gone bust, gone to the wall, on the rocks, in the red, in queer street, broke, hard up, strapped for cash.

insomnia *noun* sleeplessness, wakefulness, insomnolence, restlessness.

insouciant *adjective* carefree, nonchalant, untroubled, unworried, unconcerned, heedless, casual, easygoing, free and easy, happy-go-lucky, indifferent, frivolous, capricious.

inspect *verb* examine, check, go over, look over, survey, scrutinize, vet, audit, study, pore over, view, scan, observe, investigate, assess, appraise; *inf.* give the once-over.

inspection *noun* examination, check, checkup, look-over, survey, scrutiny, vetting, view, scan, observation, investigation, probe, assessment, appraisal; *inf.* once-over, going-over, look-see. *See* INSPECT.

inspector *noun* examiner, checker, scrutinizer, scrutineer, vetter, auditor, surveyor, scanner, observer, investigator, overseer, supervisor, assessor, appraiser, critic.

inspiration *noun* **1** *acts as an inspiration to his work* stimulus, stimulation, motivation, fillip, encouragement, influence, muse, goad, spur, incitement, arousal, rousing, stirring. **2** *his pictures lack inspiration* creativity, originality, inventiveness, genius, insight, vision, afflatus. **3** *have a sudden inspiration* bright idea, brilliant/timely thought, revelation; illumination, enlightenment.

inspire *verb* **1** *inspire the artist | inspire the artist's work* stimulate, motivate, encourage, influence, inspirit, animate, fire the imagination of. **2** *ambition inspired him to work* rouse, stir, spur, goad, energize, galvanize. **3** *her beauty inspired love in many men* arouse, excite, quicken, inflame, touch off, spark off, ignite, kindle, give rise to, produce, bring about, prompt, instigate.
Opposites DISCOURAGE; DISPIRIT; EXTINGUISH.

inspired *adjective* **1** *an inspired operatic performance* brilliant, outstanding, supreme, superlative, dazzling, exciting, thrilling, enthralling, wonderful, marvellous, memorable; *inf.* out of this world. **2** *an inspired guess* intuitive, instinctive.

instability *noun* **1** *instability of human relationships* impermanence, unendurability, tempor-

ariness, transience, inconstancy. **2** *the instability of his physical condition* unsteadiness, uncertainty, precariousness, fluidity, fluctuation. **3** *the instability of the furniture* unsteadiness, unsoundness, shakiness, ricketiness, wobbliness, frailty, flimsiness, unsubstantiality. **4** *children leading lives of instability* insecurity, precariousness, unpredictability, unreliability, uncertainty; *inf.* chanciness. **5** *upset by her instability* changeableness, variability, capriciousness, volatility, flightiness, vacillation, wavering, fitfulness, oscillation.

install *verb* **1** *install kitchen units* put in, insert, put in place, position, place, emplace, fix, locate, situate, station, lodge. **2** *install him as rector* induct, instate, institute, inaugurate, invest, ordain, introduce, initiate, establish. **3** *install themselves in the best seats* ensconce, position, settle.
Opposites REMOVE; EXTRACT.

installation *noun* **1** *the installation of kitchen units* putting in, insertion, positioning, placing, fixing, situating. *See* INSTALL 1. **2** *the installation of the rector* induction, instatement, inauguration, investiture, ordination, initiation. *See* INSTALL 2. **3** *factory installations* machinery, plant, equipment. **4** *military installations* base, camp, station, post, establishment.

instalment *noun* **1** *pay for goods by instalment* part/partial payment, hire purchase, HP. **2** *issue the novel in instalments* part, portion, section, segment, chapter, division, episode.

instance *noun* **1** *an instance of his insolence* case, case in point, example, illustration, exemplification, occasion, occurrence. **2** *in the first instance* stage, step. **3** *they went away at his instance* behest, instigation, urging, demand, insistence, request, prompting, solicitation, entreaty, importuning, pressure.

instance *verb* *the teacher instanced several examples* give, cite, mention, name, specify, quote, adduce.

instant *noun* **1** *gone in an instant* moment, minute, second, split second, trice, twinkling, twinkling of an eye, flash, flash of lightning; *inf.* jiffy, shake, two shakes of a lamb's tail. **2** *at this instant I am not sure* moment, time, present time, this minute, this very minute, particular/specific time, moment in time, juncture, point. **on the instant** now, right away, immediately, instantly, forthwith, without delay.

instant *adjective* **1** *instant recognition* instantaneous, immediate, on-the-spot, prompt, rapid, sudden, abrupt. **2** *instant whip/coffee/potato* pre-prepared, ready-prepared, ready-mixed, pre-cooked, fast, easy/quick to prepare, easy/quick to make. **3** *at his instant request* urgent, pressing, earnest, importunate, exigent, imperative.

instantaneous *adjective* *death was instantaneous* instant, immediate, on the spot, direct, prompt, expeditious, rapid, sudden, abrupt.

instantaneously *adverb* right away, straight away, immediately, at once, now, instantly, on the instant, forthwith, then and there, quick as lightning, in a trice, in less than no time, in a fraction of a second, in the twinkling of an eye, before you can say Jack Robinson, before you can turn around; *inf.* in a jiffy.

instate *verb* install, induct, inaugurate, invest, ordain, initiate.

instead *adverb I'll have a chocolate ice cream instead* as an alternative/substitute/replacement, for preference. **instead of** *I'll have chocolate instead of strawberry ice cream* as an alternative to, as a substitute/replacement for, in place/lieu of, in preference to, rather than.

instigate *verb* **1** *instigate legal proceedings | instigate a rebellion* bring about, start, initiate, actuate, generate, incite, provoke, inspire, foment, kindle, stir up, whip up. **2** *instigate them to rebel* incite, encourage, egg on, urge, prompt, goad, prod, induce, impel, constrain, press, persuade, prevail upon, sway, entice. **Opposites** HALT; DISCOURAGE.

instigation *noun the proceedings/rebellions were at his instigation* initiation, actuation, incitement, encouragement, urging, inducement, persuasion, enticement. See INSTIGATE.

instigator *noun* prime mover, inciter, motivator, agitator, fomenter, troublemaker, *agent provocateur*, ringleader, leader.

instil *verb* **1** *instil water into the substance* add gradually, introduce, infuse, inject. **2** *instil common sense into the children* introduce, insinuate, infuse, inculcate, implant, teach, drill, arouse. **3** *instil the children with common sense* infuse, imbue, permeate, inculcate.

instinct *noun* **1** *birds migrate by instinct | she found the way here by instinct* inborn/inherent tendency, natural feeling, innate inclination, intuition, sixth sense, inner prompting. **2** *he has an instinct for poetry* talent, gift, ability, capacity, faculty, aptitude, knack, bent, trait, characteristic.

instinctive *adjective* **1** *birds' instinctive behaviour pattern* inborn, inherent, innate, inbred, natural, intuitive, intuitional, involuntary, untaught, unlearned. **2** *his instinctive reaction was to hide* automatic, reflex, mechanical, spontaneous, involuntary, impulsive, intuitive, unthinking, unpremeditated.

institute *verb* **1** *institute legal proceedings* begin, start, commence, set in motion, put into operation, initiate. **2** *institute new organizations | institute reforms* found, establish, start, launch, bring into being, bring about, constitute, set up, organize, develop, create, originate, pioneer. **3** *institute the new rector* install, instate, induct, invest, ordain, introduce, initiate, appoint. **Opposites** HALT; END.

institute *noun* **1** *start an educational institute* institution, organization, foundation, society, association, league, guild, consortium. **2** *build an institute for research* foundation, institution, academy, school, college, conservatory, seminary, seat of learning. **3** *legal/local institutes* law, rule, regulation, decree, tenet, principle, precedent, institution, custom, tradition, convention, practice.

institution *noun* **1** *the institution of legal proceedings* starting, commencement, initiation. See INSTITUTE *verb* 1. **2** *the institution of new orga-*

nizations foundation, establishment, setting up, creation, origination, pioneering. See INSTITUTE *verb* 2. **3** *the institution of the new rector* installation, instatement, induction, investiture. See INSTITUTE *verb* 3. **4** *start educational institutions* institute, organization, society, association. See INSTITUTE *noun* 1. **5** *a research institution* institute, foundation, academy, college. See INSTITUTE *noun* 2. **6** *in an institution for life* hospital, mental hospital, children's home, prison, reformatory, detention centre. **7** *local institutions* institute, law, rule, custom, tradition, convention, practice. See INSTITUTE *noun* 3. **8** *the old man was an institution in the village* regular/prominent feature, familiar sight.

institutional *adjective* **1** *institutional methods* organized, established, bureaucratic, accepted, orthodox, conventional, customary, formal, systematic, methodical, orderly; *inf.* establishment. **2** *institutional food* uniform, same, unvarying, unvaried, unchanging, regimented, monotonous, bland, dull, insipid. **3** *an institutional atmosphere in the building* cold, cheerless, clinical, dreary, drab, unwelcoming, uninviting, impersonal, formal, forbidding.

instruct *verb* **1** *instruct the messenger to take a reply* tell, direct, order, command, bid, charge, enjoin, demand, require. **2** *instruct the pupils in science* teach, educate, tutor, coach, train, school, drill, ground, prime, prepare, guide, inform, enlighten, edify, discipline. **3** *instruct them that I shall be late* inform, tell, notify, acquaint, make known to, advise, apprise. **4** *instruct one's lawyer* give the facts to, give information to, brief.

instruction *noun* **1** *get good instruction in the arts* teaching, education, tutoring, tutelage, coaching, training, schooling, drilling, grounding, priming, preparation, guidance, information, enlightenment, edification, discipline; lessons, classes, lectures. **2** *his instruction was to leave at once* direction, directive, briefing, order, command, charge, injunction, requirement, ruling, mandate.

instructions *plural noun* **1** *his instructions are to leave now* directions, orders, commands, requirements. See INSTRUCTION 2. **2** *read the instructions to find out* directions; key, book of rules, guide.

instructive *adjective* instructional, informative, informational, educational, educative, enlightening, illuminating, useful, helpful, edifying, cultural, uplifting, academic, didactic, doctrinal.

instructor *noun* teacher, schoolteacher, schoolmaster, schoolmistress, educator, lecturer, professor, pedagogue, tutor, coach, trainer, adviser, counsellor, guide, mentor, demonstrator.

instrument *noun* **1** *surgical instruments* implement, tool, appliance, apparatus, mechanism, utensil, gadget, contrivance, device, aid; *inf.* contraption. *See table. See also table at* TOOL. **2** *musicians tuning their instruments* musical instrument. *See tables at* BRASS, KEYBOARD, PERCUSSION, STRING, WOODWIND. **3** *the ship's instruments* measuring device, gauge, meter. **4** *her information was the instrument which led to his arrest |*

the instrument of his downfall agency, agent, prime mover, catalyst, cause, factor, channel, medium, force, mechanism, instrumentality, vehicle, organ; means. **5** he was just the king's instrument pawn, puppet, tool, cat's-paw, dupe, minion, creature, flunkey; inf. stooge.

SURGICAL INSTRUMENTS

curette	raspatory
depressor	retractor
dilator/dilater/	scalpel
dilatator	scarificator
elevator	scoop
forceps	snare
guillotine	tenaculum
haemostat/	trepan
hemostat *Am.*	trephine
osteoclast	trocar
osteotome	xyster
protractor	

---

instrumental adjective she was instrumental in catching the thief helpful, of help/assistance, useful, of use/service, contributory, active, involved, influential, significant, important.

insubordinate adjective rebellious, mutinous, insurgent, seditious, insurrectional, riotous, disobedient, non-compliant, defiant, refractory, recalcitrant, contumacious, undisciplined, ungovernable, uncontrollable, unmanageable, unruly, disorderly.

insubordination noun rebelliousness, rebellion, mutinousness, mutiny, insurgence, sedition, insurrection, riotousness, rioting, defiance, non-compliance, disobedience, refractoriness, recalcitrance, contumacy, ungovernability, unruliness. See INSUBORDINATE.

insubstantial adjective **1** insubstantial buildings/furniture flimsy, fragile, frail, weak, feeble, jerry-built. **2** an insubstantial argument weak, feeble, thin, slight, tenuous, insignificant, inconsequential. **3** insubstantial shapes unsubstantial, unreal, illusory, illusive, delusive, hallucinatory, phantom, phantasmal, spectral, ghostlike, intangible, impalpable, incorporeal, visionary, imaginary, imagined, fanciful, chimerical, airy, vaporous.

insufferable adjective intolerable, unbearable, unendurable, insupportable, not to be borne, past bearing, too much to bear, impossible, too much, more than one can stand, more than flesh and blood can stand, enough to try the patience of Job, enough to test the patience of a saint, unspeakable, dreadful, excruciating, grim, outrageous.

insufficient adjective inadequate, deficient, in short supply, scarce, meagre, scant, scanty, too small/little/few, not enough, lacking, wanting, at a premium.

insular adjective **1** country people leading insular lives isolated, detached, separate, segregated, solitary, insulated, self-sufficient. **2** have insular ideas narrow, narrow-minded, illiberal, prejudiced, biased, bigoted, provincial, parochial, parish-pump, blinkered, inward-looking, lim-

ited, restricted.
Opposites LIBERAL; OPEN-MINDED; COSMOPOLITAN.

insulate verb **1** insulate pipes/wires/walls make non-conducting; heatproof, soundproof, make shockproof, cover, wrap, enwrap, encase, envelop, pad, cushion, seal. **2** long-term hospital patients are insulated from the world segregate, separate, isolate, detach, cut off, keep/set apart, sequester, exclude, protect, shield.

insult verb insult him by calling him lazy | insult his honour offend, give/cause offence to, affront, slight, hurt the feelings of, hurt, abuse, injure, wound, mortify, humiliate, disparage, discredit, depreciate, impugn, slur, revile.
Opposites COMPLIMENT; FLATTER.

insult noun upset by their insults about his character affront, slight, gibe, snub, barb, slur; abuse, disparagement, depreciation, impugnment, revilement, insolence, rudeness, contumely; aspersions; inf. dig.

insulting adjective insulting behaviour offensive, affronting, slighting, abusive, injurious, wounding, mortifying, humiliating, disparaging, discrediting, depreciating, deprecatory, impugning, reviling, scurrilous, snubbing, insolent, rude, contumacious.

insuperable adjective insuperable difficulties insurmountable, impassable, overwhelming, invincible, unconquerable, unassailable.

insupportable adjective **1** insupportable pain insufferable, intolerable, unbearable, unendurable, more than flesh and blood can stand. See INSUFFERABLE. **2** insupportable claims unjustifiable, indefensible, untenable, unmaintainable, implausible, specious.

insurance noun **1** take out travel insurance assurance, financial protection, indemnity, indemnification, surety, security, cover, coverage, guarantee, warranty, warrant, provision. **2** he took an umbrella as an insurance against it raining safeguard, precaution, protection, provision, preventive measure.

insure verb **1** insure her life/jewels protect against death/loss/damage, assure, indemnify, cover, underwrite, guarantee, warrant. **2** insured against fire/theft take out insurance, protect, guarantee.

insurgent noun insurgents rising against the king rebel, revolutionary, revolutionist, revolter, mutineer, rioter, insurrectionist, insurrectionary, seditionist, malcontent.

insurgent adjective insurgent forces fighting the king rebellious, revolutionary, revolting, mutinying, mutinous, rioting, lawless, insurrectionist, insurrectionary, seditious, factious, subversive, insubordinate, disobedient.

insurmountable adjective insuperable, invincible, unconquerable, impassable, overwhelming, unassailable, hopeless, impossible.

insurrection noun rebellion, revolt, revolution, uprising, rising, riot, mutiny, sedition, coup, coup d'état, putsch; insurgency, insurgence.

intact adjective whole, complete, entire, perfect, all in one piece, sound, unbroken, unsevered, undamaged, unscathed, uninjured, unharmed, unmutilated, inviolate, unviolated,

413

intangible · intensify

undefiled, unblemished, unsullied, faultless, flawless.
Opposites BROKEN; damaged.

intangible adjective **1** intangible things impalpable, untouchable, not perceptible by touch, incorporeal, phantom, spectral, ghostly. **2** an intangible air of sadness indefinable, indescribable, vague, subtle, unclear, obscure, mysterious.

integral adjective **1** an integral part of the organization essential, necessary, indispensable, requisite, basic, fundamental, inherent, intrinsic, innate. **2** integral parts of the machine constituent, component, integrant. **3** an integral design/concept entire, complete, whole, total, full, intact, unified, integrated, undivided.

integrate verb **1** integrate the various parts unite, join, combine, amalgamate, consolidate, blend, incorporate, coalesce, fuse, merge, intermix, mingle, commingle, assimilate, homogenize, harmonize, mesh, concatenate. **2** integrate school districts desegregate, open up.

integrated adjective **1** integrated parts united, joined, amalgamated, consolidated, assimilated, concatenated. See INTEGRATE 1. **2** integrated schools desegregated, non-segregated, unsegregated, racially mixed, racially balanced.

integration noun the integration of the parts into a whole unification, amalgamation, consolidation, incorporation, coalescing, fusing, assimilation, homogenizing, homogenization, concatenation.

integrity noun **1** doubt the integrity of the council uprightness, honesty, rectitude, righteousness, virtue, probity, morality, honour, goodness, decency, truthfulness, fairness, sincerity, candour; principles, ethics. **2** challenge the integrity of the empire unity, unification, wholeness, entirety, completeness, totality, cohesion.
Opposites DISHONESTY.

intellect noun **1** a person of little intellect intelligence, reason, understanding, comprehension, mind, brain, thought, sense, judgement. **2** leave the decisions to the intellects intellectual, genius, thinker, mastermind; inf. brain, mind, egghead, Einstein.

intellectual adjective **1** an intellectual exercise mental, cerebral, academic. **2** an intellectual family intelligent, academic, well-educated, well-read, erudite, learned, bookish, donnish, highbrow, scholarly, studious. **3** using only intellectual considerations mental, cerebral, rational, logical, clinical, unemotional, nonemotional.
Opposites PHYSICAL; ILLITERATE; STUPID.

intellectual noun **1** one of the great intellectuals of our time intellect, genius, thinker, mastermind; inf. egghead. See INTELLECT 2. **2** disapprove of the intellectuals in the club academic, academician, man of letters, don, bluestocking, pundit, highbrow, bookworm, pedant; inf. egghead, walking encyclopedia.

intelligence noun **1** people of great intelligence intellect, mind, brain, brain-power, mental capacity/aptitude, reason, understanding, comprehension, acumen, wit, cleverness, bright-

ness, brilliance, sharpness, quickness of mind, alertness, discernment, perception, perspicacity, penetration, sense, sagacity; brains; inf. grey matter, nous. **2** the intelligence came too late to save him information, news, notification, notice, account, knowledge, advice, rumour; facts, data, reports, tidings; inf. gen, low-down, dope. **3** he's in military intelligence information collection, enemy investigation, surveillance, observation, spying.

intelligent adjective **1** intelligent children clever, bright, brilliant, sharp, quick, quick-witted, smart, apt, discerning, thinking, perceptive, perspicacious, penetrating, sensible, sagacious, well-informed, educated, enlightened, knowledgeable; inf. brainy. **2** is there intelligent life on the planet? rational, reasoning, higher-order.
Opposites STUPID; SLOW.

intelligentsia plural noun intellectuals, academics, literati, cognoscenti, illuminati, highbrows, pedants; the enlightened. See INTELLECTUAL noun 2.

intelligible adjective a scarcely intelligible message understandable, comprehensible, clear, lucid, plain, explicit, unambiguous, legible, decipherable.
Opposites UNINTELLIGIBLE; INCOHERENT; INCOMPREHENSIBLE.

intemperate adjective **1** an intemperate indulgence of the appetites immoderate, self-indulgent, excessive, inordinate, extreme, extravagant, unreasonable, outrageous. **2** intemperate drinkers immoderate, excessive, drunken, drunk, intoxicated, inebriated, alcoholic, sottish; inf. boozy. **3** intemperate rages uncontrolled, unrestrained, uncurbed, unbridled, ungoverned, tempestuous, violent. **4** lead an intemperate life immoderate, dissolute, dissipated, debauched, profligate, prodigal, loose, wild, wanton, licentious, libertine.

intend verb **1** he intends to go mean, plan, have in mind/view, propose, aim, resolve, be resolved, be determined, expect, purpose; contemplate, think of. **2** they intended the bullet for the leader mean, aim, destine, purpose, plan, scheme, devise.

intense adjective **1** intense heat/cold acute, fierce, severe, extreme, harsh, strong, powerful, potent, vigorous, great, profound, deep, concentrated, consuming. **2** an intense desire to learn earnest, eager, ardent, keen, enthusiastic, zealous, excited, impassioned, passionate, fervent, fervid, burning, consuming, vehement, fanatical. **3** an intense person nervous, nervy, tense, fraught, overwrought, highly strung, emotional.
Opposites MILD; CALM.

intensify verb **1** her indifference intensified his love heighten, deepen, strengthen, increase, reinforce, magnify, enhance, fan, whet. **2** intensify the quarrel aggravate, exacerbate, worsen, inflame; inf. add fuel to the flames. **3** intensify their efforts to find the child increase, extend, augment, boost, escalate, step up.
Opposites DECREASE; DIMINISH; RELAX.

intensity noun **1** *the intensity of the heat* acuteness, fierceness, severity, extremeness, extremity, harshness, strength, power, powerfulness, potency, vigour, greatness, concentration. *See* INTENSE 1. **2** *the intensity of their desire* ardour, keenness, enthusiasm, zeal, excitement, passion, fervour, fervency, vehemence, fanaticism. **3** *her intensity frightens people* nervousness, tenseness, fraughtness, emotionalism, emotion. *See* INTENSE 3.

intensive *adjective an intensive search | intensive revision* in-depth, concentrated, exhaustive, all-out, thorough, thoroughgoing, total, all-absorbing.

intent *adjective* **1** *an intent expression* concentrated, concentrating, fixed, steady, steadfast, absorbed, attentive, engrossed, occupied, preoccupied, rapt, enrapt, wrapped up, focused, observant, watchful, alert, earnest, committed, intense. **2** *intent on getting their own way* set on, bent on, committed to, firm about; determined to, resolved to; *inf.* hell-bent on.

intent *noun it was their intent to win* intention, purpose, aim, objective, goal, end, plan. *See* INTENTION 1. **to all intents and purposes** virtually, in practical terms, practically, as good as.

intention *noun* **1** *it is his intention to be leader* aim, purpose, intent, goal, objective, end, end in view, target, aspiration, ambition, wish, plan, design, resolve, resolution, determination. **2** *he assaulted the old man without intention* premeditation, preconception, design, plan, calculation.

intentional *adjective an intentional crime* intended, deliberate, meant, done on purpose, wilful, purposeful, purposed, planned, calculated, designed, premeditated, preconceived, predetermined, prearranged, preconcerted, considered, weighed up, studied.
Opposites ACCIDENTAL; INADVERTENT.

intentionally *adverb she damaged the toy intentionally* deliberately, on purpose, purposefully, by design, wilfully.

inter *verb* bury, consign to the grave, entomb, lay to rest, inhume, inearth, inurn, ensepulchre, sepulchre.

intercede *verb intercede in the strike | intercede for the child with her parents* mediate, negotiate, arbitrate, intervene, interpose, step in, plead for, petition for.

intercept *verb* **1** *intercept the ball* stop, cut off, deflect, head off, seize, expropriate, commandeer, catch. **2** *intercept the train* check, arrest, block, obstruct, impede, cut off, deflect, head off.

intercession *noun* mediation, negotiation, arbitration, mediatorship, intervention, interposition, pleading, petition, entreaty, supplication; good offices. *See* INTERCEDE.

interchange *verb* **1** *interchange ideas* exchange, trade, trade off, swap, barter, bandy, reciprocate. **2** *interchange the simpleton with the young prince* substitute, change, cause to change places, switch, replace, supplant.

interchange *noun* **1** *the interchange of ideas* exchange, trading, trade, trade-off, swap, barter, bandying, give and take, reciprocation, reciprocity, interplay, crossfire. **2** *the interchange of babies* substitution, change, switch, replacement, supplanting. **3** *a car crash at the interchange* junction, intersection. *See* INTERSECTION 2.

interchangeable *adjective* exchangeable, transposable, equivalent, corresponding, correlative, reciprocal, comparable.

intercourse *noun* **1** *business intercourse* dealings; trade, traffic, commerce, communication, intercommunication, association, connection, contact, correspondence, communion, congress. **2** *have intercourse with a minor* sex, sexual intercourse, sexual relations, coitus, coition, copulation, carnal knowledge, intimacy, love-making, sexual congress, congress.

interdict *noun under an interdict preventing him from visiting* prohibition, ban, injunction, restraining order, embargo, veto, proscription, preclusion, exclusion order.

interdict *verb interdict him from going* prohibit, forbid, ban, embargo, veto, proscribe, disallow, preclude, exclude, prevent.

interest *noun* **1** *look with interest at the new product* attentiveness, attention, undivided attention, absorption, engrossment, heed, regard, notice, scrutiny, curiosity, inquisitiveness. **2** *an object of interest* curiosity, attraction, appeal, fascination, charm, allure. **3** *a matter of interest to all of us* concern, importance, import, consequence, moment, significance, note, relevance, seriousness, weight, gravity, priority, urgency. **4** *his interests include reading and music* leisure activity, pastime, hobby, diversion, amusement, pursuit, relaxation; *inf.* thing, scene. **5** *have an interest in the business* share, stake, portion, claim, investment, involvement, participation; stock, equity. **6** *you must declare your interest in the case* involvement, partiality, partisanship, preference, one-sidedness, favouritism, bias, prejudice, discrimination. **7** *his commercial interests are in trouble* concern, business, matter, care; affairs. **8** *earn interest on investments* dividend, profit, return, percentage, gain. **9** *it is in their interests to go* benefit, advantage, good, profit, gain. **in the interests of** for the sake/benefit of, to the advantage of, in the furtherance of.
Opposites BOREDOM; TEDIUM; IMPARTIALITY.

interest *verb* **1** *the book interests her* attract/hold/engage the attention of, attract, absorb, engross, fascinate, rivet, grip, captivate, amuse, intrigue, arouse curiosity in. **2** *the outcome of the war interests us all* affect, have an effect/bearing on, concern, involve. **3** *can I interest you in this computer?* arouse one's interest, persuade to buy, sell.

interested *adjective* **1** *the interested children* attentive, intent, absorbed, engrossed, curious, fascinated, riveted, gripped, captivated, intrigued. **2** *interested parties waiting in the lawyer's office* concerned, involved, implicated. **3** *no interested person can judge the contest* involved, partial, partisan, one-sided, biased, prejudiced, discriminative, discriminating.
Opposites APATHETIC; INDIFFERENT; DISINTERESTED.

interesting *adjective* absorbing, engrossing, fascinating, riveting, gripping, compelling, compulsive, spell-binding, captivating, appealing, engaging, amusing, entertaining, stimulating, thought-provoking, diverting, exciting, intriguing.

interfere *verb* **1** *emotional problems interfering with his work* hinder, inhibit, impede, obstruct, get in the way of, check, block, hamper, handicap, cramp, trammel, frustrate, thwart, baulk. **2** *interfere in other people's business* meddle with, butt into, pry into, tamper with, intrude into, intervene in, get involved in, intercede in; *inf.* poke one's nose in, horn in, stick one's oar in; *Am. inf.* kibitz on.

interference *noun* **1** *his work suffered from the interference of his emotional problems* hindrance, impediment, obstruction, handicap, baulk. **2** *resent her interference in their affairs* meddling, meddlesomeness, prying, intrusion, unwelcome intervention, intercession.

interim *adjective* *an interim appointment | interim measures* temporary, provisional, pro tem, stopgap, caretaker, acting, intervening, makeshift, improvised.

interim *noun* *in the interim we shall choose a new leader* meantime, meanwhile, intervening time, interval, interregnum.

interior *adjective* **1** *the interior part of the building* inner, inside, on the inside, internal, inward. **2** *the interior parts of the country* inland, non-coastal, central, up-country, remote. **3** *the country's interior affairs* home, domestic, civil, local. **4** *his interior motivation* instinctive, intuitive, impulsive, involuntary, spontaneous; *inf.* gut. **5** *his interior self* inner, spiritual, mental, psychological, emotional, private, personal, intimate, secret, hidden.

interior *noun* **1** *the interior of the building* inside, inner part/side/surface, centre, middle, nucleus, core, heart. **2** *The interior of the country* centre, heartland, hinterland.
Opposites EXTERIOR; OUTSIDE.

interject *verb interject light-hearted remarks into a serious conversation* throw in, insert, introduce, interpolate, interpose, insinuate, add, mingle, intersperse.

interjection *noun* **1** *the interjection of jokes into the script* insertion, introduction, interpolation, interposition, insinuation, intermixing, intermingling, interspersion. **2** *he gave an interjection of pain* cry, exclamation, ejaculation, utterance.

interloper *noun* unwanted visitor/guest, trespasser, invader, intruder, encroacher, gatecrasher.

interlude *noun* interval, intermission, break, recess, pause, respite, rest, breathing-space, halt, stop, stoppage, hiatus, delay, wait.

intermediary *noun* mediator, go-between, broker, agent, middleman, negotiator, arbitrator.

intermediate *adjective* in-between, halfway, in the middle, middle, mid, midway, medial, median, intermediary, intervening, interposed, transitional.

interment *noun* burial, burying, entombment, inhumation, sepulture, funeral; funeral rites, exequies.

interminable *adjective* **1** *an interminable road* seemingly endless, never-ending, without end, everlasting, ceaseless, incessant. **2** *an interminable talk* seemingly endless, never-ending, uninterrupted, monotonous, tedious, wearisome, boring, long-winded, wordy, loquacious, prolix, verbose, rambling. **3** *interminable supplies of food from his benefactor* seemingly endless, unlimited, boundless, infinite, countless, untold, numberless, innumerable, unmeasured, incalculable, indeterminable.

intermingle *verb* mingle, mix, commingle, intermix, commix, blend, fuse, amalgamate, merge, combine, compound, interweave.

intermission *noun* interval, interlude, interim, entr'acte, break, recess, rest, pause, respite, lull, stop, stoppage, halt, cessation, suspension; *inf.* let-up, breather, time out.

intermittent *adjective* fitful, spasmodic, irregular, sporadic, occasional, periodic, cyclic, recurrent, recurring, broken, discontinuous, on again and off again, on and off.
Opposites CONTINUOUS; STEADY.

intern *verb* confine, hold in custody, imprison, impound, detain.

internal *adjective* **1** *internal wall* interior, inside, inner, inward. **2** *the country's/firm's internal affairs* home, domestic, civil, interior, in-house, in-company. **3** *his internal opinion* mental, psychological, emotional, subjective, private, intimate.

international *adjective* cosmopolitan, global, universal, worldwide, intercontinental.

interpolate *verb* insert, interject, intercalate, interpose, introduce, insinuate, add, inject, put in, work in.

interpolation *noun* insert, insertion, interjection, intercalation, introduction, addition, injection.

interpose *verb* **1** *interpose a barrier between the speaker and the audience* place between, put between. **2** *interpose a few jokes in the script* insert, interject, introduce, insinuate, add. **3** *interpose in the quarrel* intervene, intercede, step in, mediate, arbitrate, interfere, intrude, obtrude, butt in, meddle; *inf.* barge in, horn in, muscle in.

interpret *verb* **1** *interpret the difficult text for the pupils* explain, elucidate, expound, explicate, clarify, make clear, illuminate, shed light on, gloss, simplify, spell out. **2** *interpreted her silence as consent* understand, understand by, construe, take, take to mean, read. **3** *interpret the hieroglyphics* decode, decipher, crack, solve, untangle, unravel. **4** *interpret for the foreign ambassador* translate, transcribe, transliterate, paraphrase. **5** *dancers interpreting the ballet* portray, depict, present, perform, execute, enact.

interpretation *noun* **1** *the interpretation of the difficult text* explanation, elucidation, expounding, explication, clarification, exegesis. *See* INTERPRET 1. **2** *his interpretation of her silence as consent* understanding, construal, reading.

3 *the interpretation of the coded message* decoding, deciphering. See INTERPRET 3. **4** *the scientist's interpretation of the results* analysis, reading, diagnosis. **5** *her instant interpretation of the foreign ambassador's speech* translation, transcription, transliteration; paraphrase. **6** *the dancer's interpretation of the ballet* portrayal, depiction, presentation, performance, execution, rendering, rendition, enactment.

interpreter *noun* **1** *foreign language interpreter* translator, transcriber. **2** *a skilful interpreter of the dance* portrayer, performer, exponent. **3** *an interpreter of the world situation* commentator, annotator, scholiast.

interrogate *verb* question, put/pose questions to, inquire of, examine, cross-examine, cross-question, quiz, pump, grill, give the third degree to, probe, catechize; *inf.* put the screws on.

interrogation *noun* **1** *give way under interrogation* | *a long interrogation* questioning, quizzing, investigation, examination, cross-examination, cross-questioning, pumping, grilling, third degree, probing, inquisition, catechization; inquiry, catechism. **2** *complain about the policeman's interrogations* question, query, enquiry, poser.

interrogative *adjective* questioning, quizzing, quizzical, inquiring, curious, inquisitive, investigative, grilling, third-degree, inquisitorial, probing, catechistic.

interrupt *verb* **1** *interrupt his speech* | *she continuously interrupted* cut in (on), break in (on), barge in (on), intrude (on), disturb, heckle, interfere (with); *inf.* butt in (on), chip in (on), chime in (on), horn in (on), muscle in (on). **2** *interrupt the talks for a time* suspend, discontinue, break the continuity of, break, break off, hold up, delay, lay aside, leave off, postpone, stop, put a stop to, halt, bring to a halt/standstill, cease, end, cancel, sever. **3** *only a few trees interrupted the flatness of the landscape* break, break up, punctuate. **4** *the huge office block interrupts our view* obstruct, impede, block, interfere with, cut off.

interruption *noun* **1** *resent his interruption* cutting in, interference, disturbance, intrusion, obtrusion; *inf.* butting in, horning in. See INTERRUPT 1. **2** *the interruption of the talks* suspension, discontinuance, breaking off, delay, postponement, stopping, halt, cessation. See INTERRUPT 2. **3** *there was an interruption of half an hour in the talks* intermission, interval, interlude, break, pause, recess, gap, hiatus.

intersect *verb* **1** *the motorway would intersect an agricultural area* cut across/through, cut in two/half, divide, bisect. **2** *the lines intersect* cross, criss-cross, meet, connect.

intersection *noun* **1** *the intersection of the lines* crossing, criss-crossing, meeting. **2** *a car crash at the intersection* road junction, junction, interchange, crossroads, roundabout; *inf.* spaghetti junction.

intersperse *verb* **1** *intersperse flowers among the trees* scatter, distribute, disperse, spread, strew, dot, sprinkle, pepper. **2** *intersperse drawings in the text* insert, interpose, interpolate, incorpor-

ate, intercalate. **3** *intersperse the text with illustrations* vary, diversify, variegate.

intertwine *verb* entwine, interwind, interweave, interlace, twist together, coil, twirl, convolute.

interval *noun* **1** *in the interval before the next meeting* interim, interlude, intervening time, time, period, meantime, meanwhile, wait, space. **2** *drinks served in the theatre during the interval* intermission, break, half-time, pause, lull, respite, breather, breathing-space, gap, hiatus, delay. **3** *the intervals between the trees* distance, space, gap, interspace. **4** *children in the playground during the interval* break, recess, playtime.

intervene *verb* **1** *in the years that intervened* come/occur between, come to pass, occur, befall, happen, arise, take place, ensue, supervene, succeed. **2** *intervene in the dispute* intercede, mediate, arbitrate, negotiate, step in, involve oneself, come into, interpose, interfere, intrude.

intervention *noun* *his intervention in the dispute* intercession, mediation, arbitration, negotiation, agency, involvement, interposing, interposition, interference, intrusion.

interview *noun* **1** *candidates nervous at the interview* conference, discussion, meeting, talk, dialogue, evaluation. **2** *the prime minister giving an interview to the press* audience, question and answer session, exchange, dialogue, colloquy, interlocution.

interview *verb* talk to, have a discussion/dialogue with, hold a meeting with, confer with, question, put questions to, sound out, examine, interrogate, cross-examine, evaluate.

interviewer *noun* **1** *the interviewer of candidates* evaluator, assessor, examiner, questioner, interrogator. **2** *the television interviewer* questioner, reporter, correspondent.

interweave *verb* **1** *interweave strands of various fabrics* weave, intertwine, twine, twist, interlace, braid, plait. **2** *their financial affairs are interwoven* intermingle, mingle, interlink, intermix, mix, blend, fuse, interlock, knit, connect, associate.

intestinal *adjective* abdominal, enteric, visceral, coeliac, stomachic, gastric, duodenal.

intestines *plural noun* entrails, viscera; small intestine, large intestine, bowel, colon, gut; *inf.* guts, insides, innards.

intimacy *noun* **1** *an intimacy between them* closeness, close association/relationship, familiarity, confidentiality, close friendship, comradeship, amity, affection, warmth, understanding. **2** *guilty of intimacy with a minor* sex, intercourse, sexual intercourse/relations, coition, coitus, carnal knowledge, love-making.

intimate *adjective* **1** *intimate friends* close, near, dear, nearest and dearest, cherished, bosom, familiar, confidential, warm, friendly, comradely, amicable; *inf.* thick; *Am. inf.* buddy-buddy. **2** *in an intimate atmosphere* informal, warm, cosy, friendly, comfortable, snug, tête-à-tête; *inf.* comfy. **3** *a diary giving intimate details*

personal, private, confidential, secret, privy.
4 *his intimate views* private, innermost, inmost,
inner, inward, intrinsic, deep-seated,
inherent. **5** *an intimate knowledge of the law*
experienced, deep, in-depth, profound,
detailed, thorough, exhaustive, personal, firsthand, direct, immediate. **6** *have intimate relations with a minor* sexual, carnal, fornicatory,
unchaste.
Opposites DISTANT; COLD; FORMAL; PUBLIC.

intimate *noun* close/best/bosom friend, constant companion, confidant, confidante, close
associate, mate, crony, *alter ego*, Achates; *inf.*
chum, pal, buddy, mucker.

intimate *verb* **1** *intimate to the crowd that they
should go* announce, make known, state, tell,
inform, communicate, impart. **2** *in his speech
he intimated that he would like to be chairman*
imply, suggest, let it be known, hint, insinuate, give an inkling that, indicate, signal; *inf.*
tip someone the wink that.

intimation *noun* **1** *receive the intimation of his
resignation* announcement, statement, information, communication, notice. **2** *the intimation
that he wished the chairmanship* implication, suggestion, hint, insinuation, inkling, indication,
signal, reference, allusion.

intimidate *verb* frighten, terrify, scare, alarm,
terrorize, overawe, awe, cow, subdue, daunt,
domineer, browbeat, bully, tyrannize, coerce,
compel, bulldoze, pressure, pressurize,
threaten; *inf.* push around, lean on, twist
someone's arm.

intimidation *noun* **1** *the intimidation of shopkeepers by gangs* frightening, terrorization, subduing, domineering, bullying, tyrannization,
coercion, threatening; *inf.* arm-twisting. *See*
INTIMIDATE. **2** *leave his premises out of intimidation*
fear, terror, alarm, awe, trepidation.

intolerable *adjective* unbearable, unendurable,
beyond endurance, insufferable, insupportable, not to be borne, more than one can
stand, impossible, painful, excruciating, agonizing.

intolerance *noun* **1** *the intolerance of the village
inhabitants* bigotry, illiberalism, narrow-
mindedness, parochialism, provincialism, insu-
larity, prejudice, bias, partisanship,
one-sidedness; chauvinism, jingoism, racism,
xenophobia, sexism, ageism, homophobia. *See*
INTOLERANT 1. **2** *his intolerance to/of the sun* sensitivity, hypersensitivity, allergy.

intolerant *adjective* **1** *intolerant citizens objecting to incomers* bigoted, illiberal, narrow-
minded, narrow, parochial, provincial, insular,
small-minded, prejudiced, biased, partial, partisan, one-sided, warped, twisted, fanatical;
chauvinistic, jingoistic, racist, xenophobic, sexist, ageist, homophobic. **2** *intolerant of sun* sensitive to, hypersensitive to, allergic to.

intonation *noun* **1** *a characteristic northern intonation* pitch, tone, timbre, cadence, lilt, inflection, accentuation, emphasis, stress. **2** *listen to
the intonation of the monks* chant, chanting,
incantation, invocation.

intone *verb* **1** *the choir intoned a psalm* chant/
sing/recite in a monotone. **2** *the headmaster*

intoned his speech slowly and with emphasis utter,
speak, say, articulate, voice, enunciate, pronounce, deliver.

intoxicate *verb* **1** *the cocktails intoxicated them*
inebriate, make drunk, befuddle, fuddle, stupefy. *See* INTOXICATED. **2** *the sunny weather intoxicated them* exhilarate, elate, thrill, invigorate,
animate, enliven, excite, arouse, inflame,
enrapture.

intoxicated *adjective* inebriated, inebriate,
drunk, drunken, drunk as a lord, blind/dead
drunk, the worse for drink, under the influence, tipsy, merry, befuddled, stupefied, staggering; *inf.* one over the eight, half-seas-over,
three sheets to/in the wind, tight, pickled,
soused, under the table, sloshed, plastered,
stewed, well-oiled, canned, loaded, stoned,
bombed out of one's mind, lit up, tanked up,
smashed, paralytic; *Scots inf.* stotious, fou.
Opposites SOBER.

intoxicating *adjective* **1** *intoxicating drinks*
intoxicant, alcoholic, strong, spiritous, inebriant. **2** *intoxicating news* exhilarating, heady,
elating, thrilling, animating, exciting.

intoxication *noun* **1** *suffering from the effects of
intoxication* drunkenness, inebriation, inebriety, insobriety, alcoholism, dipsomania, tipsiness, befuddledment, stupefaction; *inf.*
tightness. **2** *intoxication following the good news*
exhilaration, elation, ecstasy, euphoria, thrill,
invigoration, animation, excitement, rapture,
delirium.

intractable *adjective* unmanageable,
ungovernable, uncontrollable, uncompliant,
stubborn, obstinate, obdurate, perverse, disobedient, unsubmissive, indomitable, refractory, recalcitrant, insubordinate, rebellious,
wild, unruly, rowdy.
Opposites MANAGEABLE; SUBMISSIVE; OBEDIENT.

intransigent *adjective* uncompromising, irreconcilable, implacable, relentless, unrelenting,
inexorable, unbending, unyielding, hard-line,
die-hard, immovable, inveterate, rigid, tough,
tenacious, stubborn, obdurate.
Opposites COMPLIANT; FLEXIBLE.

intrench *See* ENTRENCH.

intrenched *See* ENTRENCHED.

intrepid *adjective* fearless, unafraid,
undaunted, dauntless, undismayed,
unalarmed, unflinching, bold, daring, audacious, adventurous, dashing, rash, reckless,
brave, courageous, valiant, valorous, stout-
hearted, lion-hearted, gallant, manly, stalwart,
plucky, game, spirited, mettlesome, doughty;
inf. gutsy, spunky.
Opposites TIMID; COWARDLY.

intricate *adjective* **1** *intricate patterns* tangled,
entangled, ravelled, twisted, knotty, convo-
luted, involute, mazelike, labyrinthine, winding, serpentine, circuitous, sinuous,
roundabout, fancy, elaborate, ornate, Byzantine, rococo. **2** *intricate problems* complex,
complicated, difficult, involved, perplexing,
puzzling, thorny, mystifying, enigmatic,
obscure.
Opposites PLAIN; SIMPLE; STRAIGHTFORWARD.

intrigue verb **1** *your behaviour intrigues me* | *intrigued by the new play* interest, absorb, arouse one's curiosity, attract, draw, pull, rivet one's attention, rivet, fascinate, charm, captivate, divert, pique, titillate. **2** *they are intriguing to kill the king* plot, conspire, scheme, connive, complot, manoeuvre, machinate, devise. **3** *intriguing without her husband's knowledge* have an affair, philander, commit adultery; *inf.* carry on.

intrigue noun **1** *involved in an intrigue to kill the king* plot, conspiracy, collusion, complot, conniving, cabal, scheme, ruse, stratagem, wile, dodge, artifice, manoeuvre, machination, trickery, sharp practice, double-dealing. **2** *her husband found out about the intrigue* love affair, affair, liaison, amour; adultery; *inf.* carrying on.

intriguer noun plotter, conspirator, conniver, collaborator, machinator, Machiavelli.

intriguing adjective *intriguing news* | *an intriguing play* interesting, absorbing, compelling, attractive, appealing, riveting, fascinating, captivating, diverting, titillating, tantalizing.

intrinsic adjective inherent, inborn, inbred, congenital, natural, native, indigenous, constitutional, built-in, ingrained, implanted, basic, fundamental, elemental, essential, true, genuine, real, authentic.
Opposites EXTRINSIC; EXTRANEOUS.

introduce verb **1** *introduce his friends to each other* present, present formally, make known, acquaint, make acquainted. **2** *introduce the speaker* present, announce, give an introduction to. **3** *introduce his talk with a short biography* preface, precede, lead into, commence, start off, begin. **4** *introduce a new method of teaching* bring in, bring into being, originate, launch, inaugurate, institute, initiate, establish, found, set in motion, organize, develop, start, begin, commence, usher in, pioneer. **5** *introduce his ideas* propose, put forward, suggest, broach, advance, bring up, set forth, submit, moot, air, ventilate. **6** *introduce a note of solemnity to the party* insert, inject, interject, interpose, interpolate, intercalate, add, bring, infuse, instil.

introduction noun **1** *the introduction of friends/speakers* presentation, formal presentation. **2** *an informative introduction to the book* foreword, preface, front matter, preamble, prologue, prelude, prolegomenon, proem, exordium, lead-in; *inf.* intro, prelims. **3** *the introduction of new teaching methods* origination, launch, inauguration, institution, establishment, development, start, commencement, pioneering. *See* INTRODUCE 4. **4** *his introduction to a new way of life* baptism, initiation, inauguration, debut, first acquaintanceship. **5** *the course provides an introduction to the subject* basics, rudiments, fundamentals; groundwork. **6** *the introduction of a serious note to the party* insertion, injection, interjection, interposition, interpolation, intercalation, addition, infusion. *See* INTRODUCE 6.

introductory adjective **1** *the speaker's introductory remarks* | *the introductory section of the book* prefatory, preliminary, precursory, lead-in, initiatory, opening, initial, starting, commencing. **2** *an introductory course* preparatory, elementary, basic, basal, rudimentary, fundamental, initiatory.
Opposites FINAL; closing; LAST.

introspective adjective inward-looking, inner-directed, introverted, self-analysing, self-examining, subjective, contemplative, reflective, meditative, musing, pensive, brooding, preoccupied.

introverted adjective inward-looking, inner-directed, introspective, self-absorbed, contemplative, withdrawn, shy, reserved.

intrude verb **1** *not wish to intrude* interrupt, push/thrust oneself in, gatecrash, barge in, encroach, butt in, interfere, obtrude. **2** *intrude on their grief* encroach on, invade, impinge on, infringe on, trespass on, obtrude on, violate.

intruder noun **1** *police found an intruder in the house/grounds* burglar, housebreaker, thief, raider, invader, prowler, trespasser. **2** *the strangers were regarded as intruders at the party* unwelcome guest/visitor, gatecrasher, interloper, infiltrator.

intrusion noun *resent the intrusion* interruption, gatecrashing, interference, encroachment, invasion, infringement, trespass, obtrusion, violation.

intrusive adjective **1** *intrusive neighbours* intruding, interrupting, interfering, invasive, obtrusive, trespassing, meddlesome, inquisitive; *inf.* pushy, nosy. **2** *intrusive music* interrupting, invasive, disturbing, annoying, irritating, irksome, unwanted.

intuition noun **1** *knew by intuition where the child was* instinct, sixth sense, divination, presentiment, clairvoyance, second sight, extrasensory perception, ESP. **2** *I had an intuition that the child was there* feeling, feeling in one's bones, hunch, inkling, presentiment, foreboding.

intuitive adjective intuitional, instinctive, instinctual, innate, inborn, inherent, untaught, unlearned, involuntary, spontaneous, automatic.

intumescence noun swelling, distension, bloating, dilatation, tumefaction, turgescence, turgidity.

inundate verb **1** *the river inundating the town* flood, deluge, overflow, overrun, swamp, submerge, engulf, drown, cover, saturate, soak. **2** *inundated with correspondence* overwhelm, overpower, overburden, swamp, bog down, glut.

inundation noun **1** *people lost in the inundation* flood, deluge, torrent, overflow, tidal wave, flash flood, spate. **2** *not coping with the inundation of work* flood, deluge, overabundance, superabundance, plethora, excess, superfluity, surplus; *inf.* tons, heaps.

inure verb harden, toughen, indurate, season, temper, habituate, familiarize, accustom, naturalize, acclimatize.

invade verb **1** *the enemy invaded the city* march into, overrun, occupy, storm, take over, descend upon, make inroads on, attack, assail, assault, raid, plunder. **2** *invade their privacy* interrupt, intrude on, obtrude on, encroach on, infringe on, trespass on, burst in on, violate. **3** *doubts invaded his mind* assail, permeate, pervade, fill, spread over.

invader *noun* **1** *enemy invaders of the town* attacker, assailant, assaulter, raider, plunderer. **2** *invaders of their privacy* interrupter, intruder, obtruder, encroacher, infringer, trespasser, violator.

invalid[1] *adjective his invalid mother* ill, sick, ailing, unwell, infirm, bedridden, valetudinarian, disabled, frail, feeble, weak, debilitated; *inf.* poorly.

invalid[2] *noun doctors visiting invalids* ill/infirm person, valetudinarian, sufferer, patient, convalescent.

invalid[3] *adjective* **1** *the bye-law is now invalid* inoperative, legally void, null, null and void, void, not binding, nullified, revoked, rescinded, abolished. **2** *an invalid assumption/ argument* baseless, unfounded, groundless, unjustified, unsubstantiated, unwarranted, untenable, illogical, irrational, unscientific, false, faulty, fallacious, spurious, unacceptable, inadequate, unconvincing, ineffectual, unsound, weak, useless, worthless.

invalidate *verb* **1** *invalidate the contract* render invalid, void, nullify, annul, cancel, quash, veto, negate, revoke, rescind, abolish, terminate, repeal, repudiate. **2** *invalidate the argument* weaken, undermine, disprove, refute, rebut, negate, discredit, debase.

invaluable *adjective* priceless, beyond price, inestimable, precious, costly, worth its weight in gold, worth a king's ransom.

invariable *adjective* unchanging, changeless, unchangeable, constant, unvarying, unvaried, invariant, unalterable, immutable, fixed, stable, set, steady, unwavering, static, uniform, regular, consistent.

invariably *adverb he invariably arrives last* always, every/each time, on every occasion, at all times, without fail/exception, regularly, consistently, repeatedly, habitually, unfailingly, infallibly, inevitably.

invasion *noun* **1** *the invasion of the city* overrunning, occupation, incursion, offensive, attack, assailing, assault, raid, foray, onslaught, plundering. **2** *the invasion of privacy* interruption, intrusion, obtrusion, encroachment, infringement, breach, infraction, trespass, violation.

invective *noun* vituperation, railing, fulmination, berating, upbraiding, castigation, reproval, admonition, denunciation, disparagement, censure, recrimination, abuse, contumely, obloquy; tirade, diatribe, philippic, harangue, tongue-lashing, reprimand, reproach, rebuke, billingsgate.

inveigh *verb inveigh against the decision* rail, protest, complain vehemently, fulminate, harangue; denounce, censure, condemn, criticize, disparage, denigrate, revile, abuse, vilify, impugn.

inveigle *verb* ensnare, delude, persuade, talk into, cajole, wheedle, coax, sweet-talk, beguile,

tempt, decoy, lure, allure, entice, seduce, deceive.

invent *verb* **1** *invent a new machine/word* originate, create, innovate, discover, design, devise, contrive, formulate, think up, conceive, come up with, hit upon, compose, frame, coin. **2** *he invented that story* make up, fabricate, concoct, hatch, trump up, forge; *inf.* cook up.

invention *noun* **1** *the invention of the zip | invention of new words* origination, creation, innovation, discovery, design, devising, contriving, coining, coinage. See INVENT 1. **2** *his most famous invention* origination, creation, innovation, discovery, design, contrivance, construction, coinage; *inf.* brainchild. **3** *an artist of great invention* inventiveness, originality, creativity, creativeness, imagination, artistry, inspiration, ingenuity, resourcefulness, genius, skill. **4** *his account of the event was pure invention* fabrication, concoction, fiction, falsification, forgery, fake, deceit, myth, fantasy, romance, illusion, sham. **5** *they refused to believe his obvious invention* fabrication, lie, untruth, falsehood, fib, piece of fiction, figment of one's imagination, yarn, story; *inf.* tall story.

inventive *adjective an inventive artist* original, creative, innovational, imaginative, artistic, inspired, ingenious, resourceful, innovative, gifted, talented, skilful, clever.
Opposites UNIMAGINATIVE; PEDESTRIAN.

inventor *noun* originator, creator, innovator, discoverer, author, architect, designer, deviser, developer, initiator, coiner, father, prime mover, maker, framer, producer. *See table. See also tables at* ARCHITECT, ENGINEER.

inventory *noun* list, listing, checklist, catalogue, record, register, tally, account, description, statement.

inverse *adjective the inverse side* opposite, converse, contrary, reverse, counter, reversed, inverted, transposed, retroverted.

inverse *noun look at the inverse of the coin* opposite side, converse side, obverse side, other side; *inf.* flip side.

inversion *noun* **1** *the inversion of the boat* overturn, overturning, upturning, capsizing. *See* INVERT 1, 2. **2** *the inversion of their previous relationship* reverse, turning about, transposal, transposition, contrary, antithesis, converse.

invert *verb* **1** *invert the eggcup/pullover* turn upside down, upturn, turn inside out. **2** *the boat inverted* turn upside down, overturn, upturn, turn turtle, capsize, upset. **3** *invert the printed picture* reverse, interpose, retrovert. **4** *their previous relationship of bully and victim has been inverted* reverse, transpose, turn about/ around.

invest *verb* **1** *invest in the business* put/sink money into, lay out money on, provide capital for, fund, subsidize. **2** *invest money/energy in the venture* spend, expend, lay out, put in, use up, devote, contribute, donate, give. **3** *invest power in the king's eldest son* vest, endow, confer, bestow, grant, entrust; give, place. **4** *the rector/ king will be invested tomorrow* install, induct, inaugurate, instate, ordain, initiate, swear in, consecrate, crown, enthrone. **5** *he invested his*

INVENTORS

Inventor	Principal inventions
Archimedes (c. 287–212 B.C.)	Archimedes' screw (according to tradition)
Arkwright, Sir Richard (1732–92)	mechanical cotton-spinning frame
Armstrong, Edwin (1890–1954)	FM radio
Auer, Karl (1858–1929)	incandescent gas mantle
Babbage, Charles (1792–1871)	calculating machine
Baekeland, Leo (1863–1944)	Bakelite
Baird, John Logie (1888–1946)	240-line mechanically scanned television system
Bardeen, John (1908–91)	transistor
Bell, Alexander Graham (1847–1922)	telephone
Berliner, Emile (1851–1929)	flat phonograph disk
Bessemer, Sir Henry (1813–98)	Bessemer process
Bodmer, Johann (1786–1864)	machine tools
Braille, Louis (1809–52)	Braille raised writing system
Brattain, Walter (1902–87)	transistor
Braun, Karl (1850–1918)	crystal diode
Bunsen, Robert (1811–99)	Bunsen burner
Cartwright, Edmund (1743–1823)	power loom
Cayley, Sir George (1773–1857)	caterpillar tractor
Cockerell, Sir Christopher (b. 1910)	hovercraft
Crompton, Samuel (1753–1827)	spinning mule
Daguerre, Louis-Jacques-Mandé (1789–1851)	first practical photographic process
Davy, Sir Humphry (1778–1829)	Davy lamp
Deere, John (1804–86)	first cast steel plough
Deforest, Lee (1873–1961)	triode valve
Dewar, Sir James (1842–1923)	vacuum flask
Du Mont, Allen (1901–65)	cathode-ray tube
Dunlop, John (1840–1921)	pneumatic tyre
Edison, Thomas (1847–1931)	phonograph and carbon filament lamp
Elion, Gertrude B. (b. 1918)	DNA-blocking drugs
Fahrenheit, Gabriel (1686–1736)	mercury thermometer
Foucault, Jean (1819–68)	gyroscope
Friese-Greene, William (1855–1921)	motion-picture camera
Fulton, Robert (1765–1815)	steamship
Gabor, Dennis (1900–79)	holography
Ginsburg, Charles (b. 1920)	videotape recorder
Goodyear, Charles (1800–60)	vulcanized rubber
Guericke, Otto von (1602–86)	air pump
Gutenberg, Johann (1398–1468)	printing with movable type
Hargreaves, James (d. 1778)	spinning jenny
Helmholtz, Baron Hermann (1821–94)	ophthalmoscope
Hero of Alexandria (1st century A.D.)	aeolipyle
Hooke, Robert (1635–1703)	balance spring for watches
Howe, Elias (1819–67)	sewing machine
Ives, Frederick (1856–1937)	halftone photography
Jacquard, Joseph-Marie (1752–1834)	Jacquard loom
Laënnec, René (1781–1826)	stethoscope
Land, Edwin (1909–91)	Polaroid camera
Leonardo da Vinci (c. 1495–97)	armoured tank
Lumière, Auguste (1862–1954)	cinematograph
Lumière, Louis (1864–1948)	cinematograph
McAdam, John (1756–1836)	macadamization of roads
McCormick, Cyrus (1809–84)	reaping machine
Maxim, Sir Hiram (1840–1916)	Maxim machine gun
Montgolfier, Jacques-Étienne (1745–99)	hot-air balloon
Montgolfier, Joseph-Michel (1740–1810)	hot-air balloon
Morse, Samuel Finley (1791–1872)	telegraph and morse code
Niepce, Joseph-Nicéphore (1765–1833)	photographic images
Otis, Elisha (1811–61)	first elevator with a safety device
Parsons, Sir Charles (1854–1931)	steam turbine
Remington, Eliphalet (1793–1861)	typewriter
Senefelder, (Johan Nepomuk Franz) Aloys (1771–1834)	lithography
Shockley, William (1910–89)	transistor
Sholes, Christopher (1819–90)	typewriter
Shrapnel, Henry (1761–1842)	shrapnel shell

INVENTORS *cont.*	
Inventor	**Principal inventions**
Siemens, Sir William (1823–83)	open-hearth steel process
Singer, Isaac (1811–75)	first commercially successful sewing machine
Stephenson, George (1781–1848)	steam locomotive
Su Sung (1020–1101)	an astronomical water clock
Tesla, Nikola (1857–1943)	transformer
Townes, Charles (b. 1915)	maser
Tull, Jethro (1674–1741)	seed drill
Volta, Count Alessandro (1745–1827)	voltaic pile
Watt, James (1736–1819)	improved steam engine
Whitney, Eli (1765–1825)	mechanical cotton-gin
Whittle, Sir Frank (b. 1907)	jet aircraft engine

bride in silk clothe, attire, dress, garb, robe, gown, drape, swathe, adorn, deck. **6** *the enemy army invested the city* besiege, lay siege to, beleaguer, beset, surround, enclose.

investigate *verb* research, probe, explore, inquire into, make inquiries about, go/look into, search, scrutinize, study, examine, inspect, consider, sift, analyse; *inf.* check out, suss out.

investigation *noun* research, probe, exploration, inquiry, fact-finding, search, scrutinization, scrutiny, study, survey, review, examination, inspection, consideration, sifting, analysis, inquest, hearing, questioning, inquisition.

investigator *noun* **1** *the investigator of the complaints* researcher, prober, explorer, inquirer, fact-finder, searcher, scrutinizer, scrutineer, reviewer, examiner, inspector, analyser, questioner, inquisitor. **2** *hire a private investigator to find the criminal* detective, private eye; *inf.* dick, sleuth, Sherlock; *Am. inf.* gumshoe.

investiture *noun* *the investiture of the rector/king* investment, installation, inauguration, instatement, ordination, induction, initiation, swearing in, consecration, crowning, enthroning.

investment *noun* **1** *his business is not a safe investment* venture, speculation, risk. **2** *his investment amounts to £3,000* stake, money/capital; *inf.* ante. **3** *the investment of the rector* installation, inauguration, instatement, ordination. *See* INVESTITURE.

inveterate *adjective* **1** *an inveterate conservative/drinker* confirmed, habitual, inured, hardened, chronic, die-hard, deep-dyed, dyed-in-the-wool, long-standing, addicted, hard-core, incorrigible. **2** *an inveterate habit* ingrained, deep-seated, deep-rooted, deep-set, entrenched, long-established, ineradicable, incurable.

invidious *adjective* **1** *make invidious comparisons* discriminatory, unfair, prejudicial, slighting, offensive, objectionable, deleterious, detrimental. **2** *it put her in an invidious position* unpleasant, awkward, unpopular, repugnant, hateful.
Opposites FAIR; DESIRABLE; PLEASANT.

invigorate *verb* revitalize, energize, fortify, strengthen, put new strength/life/heart in, brace, refresh, rejuvenate, enliven, liven up, animate, exhilarate, pep up, perk up, stimulate, motivate, rouse, excite, wake up, galvanize, electrify.

invincible *adjective* **1** *an invincible opponent* unconquerable, undefeatable, unbeatable, unassailable, invulnerable, indestructible, impregnable, indomitable, unyielding, unflinching, dauntless. **2** *an invincible hurdle* insuperable, unsurmountable, overwhelming, overpowering.
Opposites VULNERABLE; DEFENCELESS; WEAK.

inviolable *adjective* *inviolable rights/oaths* inalienable, untouchable, unalterable, sacrosanct, sacred, holy, hallowed.

inviolate *adjective* *a treaty still inviolate | purity still inviolate* intact, unbroken, whole, entire, complete, untouched, undamaged, unhurt, unharmed, unscathed, unmarred, unspoiled, unsullied, unstained, undefiled, unpolluted, pure, virgin.

invisible *adjective* **1** *invisible to the passers-by* unseeable, out of sight, undetectable, imperceivable, indiscernible, indistinguishable, unseen, unnoticed, unobserved, hidden, concealed. **2** *invisible hairnets* inconspicuous, unnoticeable, imperceptible.

invitation *noun* **1** *reject their invitation to lunch* asking, bidding, call; *inf.* invite. **2** *accept their invitation to apply for the post* request, call, appeal, petition, solicitation, supplication, summons. **3** *he regarded her friendliness as a sexual invitation* welcome, encouragement, provocation, overture, attraction, draw, allurement, lure, bait, enticement, temptation, tantalization; *inf.* come-on, glad eye.

invite *verb* **1** *they invited him to dinner* ask, bid, summon; request someone's company/presence at. **2** *invite applications* ask for, request, call for, solicit, look for, seek, appeal for, petition, summon. **3** *invite disaster* cause, bring on, bring upon oneself, draw, make happen, induce, provoke. **4** *she invited his advances* welcome, encourage, foster, attract, draw, allure, entice, tempt, court, lead on.

inviting *adjective* *an inviting prospect* attractive, appealing, pleasant, agreeable, delightful, engaging, tempting, enticing, alluring, winning, beguiling, fascinating, enchanting, entrancing, bewitching, captivating, intri-

guing, irresistible, ravishing, seductive.
Opposites REPELLENT; REPULSIVE; OFFENSIVE.

invocation noun an invocation for God's help call, prayer, request, supplication, entreaty, solicitation, beseeching, imploring, importuning, petition, appeal.

invoice noun receive the invoice for building alterations bill, account, statement of charges, itemization.

invoke verb 1 invoke God's help call for, call up, pray for, request, supplicate, entreat, solicit, beseech, beg, implore, importune, call on, petition, appeal to. 2 invoke the amendment to the constitution apply, implement, call into use, put into effect/use, resort to, use, have recourse to, initiate.

involuntary adjective 1 an involuntary reaction reflexive, reflex, automatic, mechanical, unconditioned, spontaneous, instinctive, instinctual, unconscious, unthinking, unintentional, uncontrolled. 2 their cooperation was involuntary unwilling, against one's will/wishes, reluctant, unconsenting, grudging, disinclined, forced, coerced, coercive, compelled, compulsory, obligatory.
Opposites VOLUNTARY; WILLING.

involve verb 1 his new job involves total discretion entail, imply, mean, denote, betoken, connote, require, necessitate, presuppose. 2 try to involve everyone in the party preparations include, count in, cover, embrace, take in, number, incorporate, encompass, comprise, contain, comprehend. 3 the criminal tried to involve others in the crime implicate, incriminate, inculpate, associate, connect, concern. 4 try to introduce the pupils to something that involves them interest, be of interest to, absorb, engage, engage/hold/rivet the attention of, rivet, grip, occupy, preoccupy, engross. 5 the situation was further involved by the police activity complicate, perplex, confuse, mix up, confound, entangle, tangle, embroil, enmesh.

involved adjective 1 very involved situation/problem/politics complicated, difficult, intricate, complex, elaborate, confused, confusing, mixed up, jumbled, tangled, entangled, convoluted, knotty, tortuous, labyrinthine, Byzantine. 2 involved parties should declare themselves implicated, incriminated, inculpated, associated, concerned, participating, taking part.
Opposites SIMPLE; DISINTERESTED.

invulnerable adjective 1 she seemed invulnerable against emotional or physical abuse unwoundable by, unhurtable by, proof against, insensitive to, insusceptible to, indestructible by. 2 invulnerable fortresses impenetrable, impregnable, unassailable, unattackable, inviolable, invincible, undefeatable, secure, safe, safe and sound.
Opposites VULNERABLE; DEFENCELESS.

inward, inwards adverb proceed inward inside, towards the inside, within.

inward adjective 1 the inward section interior, inside, internal, inner, innermost. 2 his inward thoughts private, personal, intimate, hidden, secret, confidential, privy.
Opposites OUTWARD; EXTERIOR; OUTSIDE.

inwardly adverb he smiled, but inwardly he hated her at heart, deep down/within, in one's heart, inside, privately, secretly.

inwards See INWARD adverb.

iota noun bit, mite, speck, atom, jot, whit, particle, fraction, morsel, grain; inf. smidgen.

irascible adjective irritable, quick-tempered, short-tempered, thin-skinned, snappy, snappish, testy, touchy, edgy, surly, cross, crusty, crabbed, grouchy, crotchety, cantankerous, querulous, captious, fractious.

irate adjective angry, very angry, wrathful, infuriated, furious, indignant, annoyed, irritated, vexed, incensed, enraged, raging, fuming, ireful, ranting, raving, mad, in a frenzy; inf. foaming at the mouth.

ire noun anger, wrath, rage, fury, indignation, annoyance, exasperation, irritation, hot temper,.resentment, choler, spleen.

iridescent adjective shimmering, shimmery, glittering, sparkling, dazzling, kaleidoscopic, multicoloured, rainbow-like, variegated, shot.

irk verb irritate, annoy, provoke, vex, pique, peeve, nettle, exasperate, ruffle, discountenance, anger, infuriate, incense, try one's patience; inf. get one's goat, get one's back up.

irksome adjective irritating, annoying, vexing, vexatious, exasperating, infuriating, tiresome, wearisome, tedious, trying, troublesome, boring, uninteresting, disagreeable.

iron verb iron their shirts press, smooth. **iron out** 1 iron out the problems straighten out, sort out, clear up, settle, solve, resolve, unravel. 2 iron out their differences get rid of, eliminate, eradicate, erase, harmonize, reconcile, smooth over.

ironic adjective 1 an ironic remark/wit satirical, mocking, scoffing, ridiculing, derisory, derisive, scornful, sneering, sardonic, wry, double-edged, sarcastic. 2 ironic that he died immediately after he won the money paradoxical, incongruous.

irons plural noun fetters, chains, shackles, bonds, manacles.

irony noun 1 the irony of his wit|use irony satire, mockery, ridicule, derision, scorn, wryness, sarcasm. 2 it was an irony that he died soon after winning money paradox, incongruity, incongruousness.

irradiate verb 1 beacons irradiating the coastline illuminate, light up, light, brighten, cast light upon, illumine. 2 irradiate young minds enlighten, inform, instruct, teach, tutor, give insight to, illumine, edify, inspire. 3 irradiate tumours/food treat with radiation, expose to radiation, X-ray.

irrational adjective 1 irrational fears illogical, unreasonable, groundless, invalid, unsound, implausible, absurd, ridiculous, silly, foolish, senseless, nonsensical, ludicrous, preposterous, crazy. 2 an irrational person illogical, unthinking, unintelligent, stupid, brainless, mindless, senseless, muddled, muddle-headed, confused, demented, insane, crazy, unstable.

irreconcilable adjective 1 irreconcilable points of view incompatible, at odds, at variance, opposite, contrary, incongruous, opposing, conflicting, clashing, discordant. **2** *irreconcilable enemies* implacable, unappeasable, uncompromising, inexorable, intransigent, hard line, inflexible.

irrecoverable *adjective* unrecoverable, unregainable, unreclaimable, irretrievable, irredeemable, unsavable, unsalvageable, irreparable, lost, lost and gone, gone for ever.

irrefutable *adjective* incontrovertible, incontestable, indisputable, undeniable, unquestionable, beyond question, indubitable, beyond doubt, conclusive, decisive, definite, certain, sure, positive, definitive, fixed, final, irrefragable, apodictic.

irregular *adjective* **1** *an irregular coastline* asymmetric, unsymmetric, without uniformity, non-uniform, uneven, broken, jagged, ragged, serrated, crooked, curving, craggy. **2** *an irregular road surface* uneven, unlevel, rough, bumpy, lumpy, knotty, pitted. **3** *an irregular pulse* uneven, unsteady, shaky, fitful, variable, erratic, spasmodic, wavering, fluctuating, aperiodic. **4** *an irregular attender at meetings* inconsistent, erratic, sporadic, variable, inconstant, desultory, haphazard, intermittent, occasional, unpunctual, unsystematic, capricious, unmethodical. **5** *irregular periods of employment* disconnected, sporadic, fragmentary, haphazard, patchy, intermittent, occasional, random, fluctuating, coming and going. **6** *his appointment was most irregular* out of order, contrary, perverse, against the rules, unofficial, unorthodox, unconventional, abnormal. **7** *an irregular result* anomalous, aberrant, deviant, abnormal, unusual, uncommon, freak, extraordinary, exceptional, odd, peculiar, strange, eccentric, bizarre, queer. **8** *lead an irregular life* immoral, dissolute, dissipated, intemperate, immoderate, lascivious, licentious, degenerate, wanton, improper, indecent, lawless, wild, unruly, disorderly. **9** *an irregular army* guerrilla, underground, resistance, mercenary.

irregular *noun irregulars shot dead by the army* guerrilla, underground/resistance fighter, mercenary.

irregularity *noun* **1** *the irregularity of the coastline* lack of symmetry, asymmetry, unsymmetricalness, non-uniformity, unevenness, jaggedness. See IRREGULAR *adjective* 1. **2** *the irregularity of the road surface* unevenness, unlevelness, roughness, bumpiness, pittedness. See IRREGULAR *adjective* 2. **3** *the irregularities on the surface* roughness, bump, lump, pit, hole. **4** *the irregularity of the pulse* unevenness, unsteadiness, shakiness, fitfulness, fluctuation. See IRREGULAR *adjective* 3. **5** *the irregularity of their attendance* inconsistency, inconstancy, desultoriness, haphazardness, intermittence, patchiness. See IRREGULAR *adjective* 4, 5. **6** *the irregularity of his appointment* unorthodoxy, unconventionality. See IRREGULAR *adjective* 6. **7** *the irregularity of the result* anomaly, anomalousness, aberrance, aberrancy, deviation, abnormality, unusualness, freakishness. See IRREGULAR *adjective* 7. **8** *spot the irregularities in the result* anomaly, aberration, deviation,

abnormality. **9** *the irregularity of his life* immorality, dissoluteness, dissipation, intemperance, immoderation, degeneracy, lawlessness, wildness, unruliness. See IRREGULAR *adjective* 8.

irrelevant *adjective* inapposite, inapt, inapplicable, impertinent, non-germane, immaterial, unrelated, unconnected, inappropriate, extraneous, beside the point, not to the point, out of place, nothing to do with it, neither here nor there.

irreligious *adjective* **1** *make irreligious remarks* impious, irreverent, heretical, sacrilegious, ungodly, blasphemous, profane. **2** *trying to preach the gospel to irreligious people* atheistic, unbelieving, non-believing, agnostic, sceptical, infidel, heathen, pagan, unenlightened.

irreparable *adjective irreparable damage to his reputation* beyond repair, past mending, irreversible, irrevocable, irretrievable, irrecoverable, irremediable, incurable, ruinous.

irreplaceable *adjective* priceless, invaluable, inestimably precious, unique, worth its weight in gold, rare.

irrepressible *adjective* **1** *irrepressible optimism* unrestrainable, uncontainable, insuppressible, uncontrollable, unstoppable, unquenchable, unreserved, unchecked, unbridled. **2** *irrepressible children playing* bubbling over, buoyant, effervescent, ebullient, vivacious, animated, spirited, lively.

irreproachable *adjective* beyond reproach, blameless, unblameworthy, unblamable, faultless, flawless, guiltless, sinless, innocent, unimpeachable, inculpable, irreprehensible, impeccable, immaculate, unblemished, stainless, pure.

irresistible *adjective* **1** *an irresistible impulse* overwhelming, overpowering, compelling, insuppressible, irrepressible, forceful, potent, imperative, urgent. **2** *an irresistible fate* unavoidable, inevitable, inescapable, unpreventable, ineluctable, inexorable, relentless. **3** *an irresistible beauty/gateau* fascinating, alluring, enticing, seductive, captivating, enchanting, ravishing, tempting, tantalizing.

irresolute *adjective* uncertain, unsure, doubtful, dubious, undecided, undecisive, unresolved, undetermined, unsettled, vacillating, wavering, hesitant, hesitating, tentative, in two minds, oscillating.

irrespective *adjective* **irrespective of** regardless of, without regard/reference to, setting aside, discounting, ignoring, notwithstanding.

irresponsible *adjective* **1** *irresponsible people* undependable, unreliable, untrustworthy, careless, reckless, rash, flighty, giddy, scatterbrained, erratic, hare-brained, feather-brained, immature; *inf.* harum-scarum. **2** *irresponsible actions* thoughtless, ill-considered, unwise, injudicious, careless, reckless, immature.

irretrievable *adjective* irrecoverable, unregainable, unsalvageable, unsavable, irreclaimable, irredeemable, irreparable, lost, hopeless.

irreverent *adjective* **1** *children irreverent to their parents* disrespectful, unrespectful, impertinent, insolent, impudent, rude, cheeky, discourteous, impolite, uncivil; *inf.* flip. **2** *irreverent remarks about God* impious, irreligious, heretical, sacrilegious, ungodly, blasphemous, profane.

irreversible *adjective irreversible damage/decisions* unalterable, irreparable, unrectifiable, irrevocable, unrepealable, final.

irrevocable *adjective irrevocable decisions/fate* unalterable, unchangeable, irreversible, unreversible, fixed, settled, fated, immutable, predetermined, predestined.

irrigation *noun* watering, wetting, spraying, sprinkling, moistening, soaking, flooding, inundating.

irritable *adjective* bad-tempered, ill-tempered, ill-humoured, irascible, cross, snappish, snappy, edgy, testy, touchy, crabbed, peevish, petulant, cantankerous, grumpy, grouchy, crusty, dyspeptic, choleric, splenetic.
Opposites GOOD-HUMOURED; CHEERFUL; IMPERTURBABLE.

irritate *verb* **1** *the children irritate the old man* annoy, vex, provoke, irk, nettle, peeve, get on one's nerves, exasperate, infuriate, anger, enrage, incense, make one's hackles rise, ruffle, disturb, put out, bother, pester, try one's patience; *inf.* aggravate, rub up the wrong way, get one's goat, get one's back up, get up one's nose, drive up the wall, drive one bananas. **2** *the rough cloth irritated her skin* chafe, fret, rub, pain, hurt, inflame, aggravate.

irritating *adjective irritating habits/people* annoying, vexing, provoking, irksome, exasperating, infuriating, maddening, disturbing, bothersome, troublesome, pestering; *inf.* aggravating. *See* IRRITATE 1.

irritation *noun* **1** *snap in irritation* irritability, annoyance, impatience, vexation, exasperation, indignation, crossness, ill-temper, anger, fury, rage, wrath, displeasure, ire; *inf.* aggravation. **2** *the child is an irritation to her* source of annoyance, annoyance, irritant, pest, nuisance, tease, thorn in the flesh; *inf.* pain in the neck, pain.

island *noun* isle, islet. *See table.*

isolate *verb* set apart, segregate, cut off, separate, detach, abstract, quarantine, keep in solitude, sequester, insulate.

isolated *adjective* **1** *feeling isolated far from her friends* alone, solitary, lonely, separated, segre-

---

LARGEST ISLANDS IN THE WORLD

Greenland	Denmark
New Guinea	Indonesia/Papua New Guinea
Borneo	Indonesia/Malaysia/Brunei
Madagascar	
Baffin	Canada
Sumatra	Indonesia
Honshu	Japan
Victoria	Canada
Great Britain	U.K.
Ellesmere	Canada

(Australia is classified as a continent)

---

gated, exiled, forsaken, forlorn. **2** *an isolated place* remote, out of the way, off the beaten track, outlying, secluded, hidden, unfrequented, lonely, desolate, God-forsaken. **3** *an isolated example | an isolated case of polio* single, solitary, unique, random, unrelated, unusual, uncommon, exceptional, abnormal, atypical, untypical, anomalous, freak.

isolation *noun* **1** *the isolation of the patients was necessary* segregation, separation, detachment, abstraction, quarantine, sequestration, insulation. *See* ISOLATE. **2** *the country girl's isolation in the city* lack of contact, separation, segregation, exile, forlornness, aloneness, solitariness, loneliness. **3** *the isolation of the village depressed her* remoteness, seclusion, loneliness, desolation. *See* ISOLATED 2.

issue *noun* **1** *debate the issue for hours* matter, matter in question, point at issue, question, subject, topic, affair, problem, bone of contention, controversy, argument. **2** *the issue is still in doubt* result, outcome, decision, upshot, end, conclusion, consequence, termination, effect, denouement. **3** *the next issue of the magazine* edition, number, printing, print run, impression, copy, instalment, version. **4** *the issue of the new stamps/paper/shares* issuing, issuance, publication, circulation, distribution, supplying, supply, dissemination, sending out, delivery. **5** *Abraham and his issue* offspring, progeny, children; heirs, scions, descendants; *inf.* brood. **6** *the issue of the stream* outflow, effusion, discharge, debouchment, emanation.
at issue *the matters at issue* to be discussed, under discussion, for debate, in dispute, to be decided, unsettled. **take issue** *take issue with management over pay* disagree with, dispute with, raise an objection with/about, make a protest about, challenge, oppose.

issue *verb* **1** *issue new stamps | issue a news statement* put out, give out, deal out, send out, distribute, circulate, release; disseminate, announce, proclaim, broadcast. **2** *smoke issuing from the chimney | liquid issuing from the machine* emit, exude, discharge, emanate, gush, pour forth, seep, ooze. **3** *people issued from the building* emerge, come out, come forth, appear; leave. **4** *his knowledge issues from a love of books* derive, arise, stem, proceed, spring, originate, result; be a result/consequence of.
Opposites WITHDRAW; ENTER.

itch *verb* **1** *her head itches* be itchy, tingle, prickle, tickle, be irritated. **2** *itch for a new car* long, have a longing, yearn, hanker, pine, ache, burn, hunger, thirst, lust, pant, desire greatly, crave.

itch *noun* **1** *have an itch in the head* itchiness, tingling, prickling, tickling, irritation, burning; *Med.* formication, paraesthesia. **2** *have an itch for a new car* great desire, longing, yearning, craving, hankering, ache, burning, hunger, thirst, lust; *inf.* yen.

itching *adjective* **1** *an itching head* itchy, tingling, prickling. *See* ITCH *noun* 1. **2** *itching to go/know* longing, yearning, craving, aching, burning, avid, agog, keen, eager, impatient, raring, dying.

itchy *adjective* itching, tingling, prickling. *See* ITCH *noun* 1.

item *noun* **1** *three items for sale* article, thing, piece of merchandise; goods. **2** *several items to be discussed* point, detail, matter, consideration, particular, feature, circumstance, aspect, component, element, ingredient. **3** *items in an account* entry, record. **4** *a news item* piece of news/information, piece, story, bulletin, article, account, report, feature, dispatch. **5** *Jim and Jane are an item now* couple, recognized couple; partners.

itemize *verb itemize the house contents* list, inventory, record, set out, document, register, tabulate, detail, particularize, specify, instance, enumerate, number.

iterate *verb* repeat, restate, dwell on, hammer away at, harp on about, press one's point about, emphasize, stress, underscore.

itinerant *adjective* travelling, peripatetic, journeying, wandering, roaming, roving, rambling, wayfaring, unsettled, nomadic, migratory, vagabond, vagrant, gypsy.

itinerary *noun* **1** *his itinerary takes him through France* route, planned route, travel plan, course of travel, journey. **2** *the travel agent gave her her itinerary* travel plan/schedule, schedule, timetable, programme; travel arrangements. **3** *keep an itinerary of foreign journeys* diary, journal, logbook, daybook, log, record. **4** *a considerable number of itineraries are in publication* guidebook, travel guide/book, guide.

Jj

jab *verb* jab in the ribs/nose poke, prod, dig, nudge, elbow, thrust, stab, bump, tap, punch, box; *inf.* sock, biff.

jab *noun* a jab in the ribs/nose poke, prod, dig, nudge, stab, punch. *See* JAB *verb*.

jabber *verb* chatter, gibber, prattle, babble, gabble, prate, blather, clack, rattle, ramble.

jack *verb* **jack up** **1** jack up the car lift, lift up, hoist, raise, elevate, uprear, hike up, haul up. **2** shopkeepers jacking up prices raise, put up, push up, make higher, increase, boost, inflate, escalate.

jacket *noun* **1** wearing a jacket and matching trousers short coat, blazer, cardigan; *inf.* cardi. *See table at* COAT. **2** a jacket for a machine | a jacket for a hot-water tank casing, case, encasement, sheath, sheathing, envelope, cover, covering, wrapping, wrapper, wrap.

jackpot *noun* kitty, pool, pot, bank, first prize, main prize, prize, winnings, reward, bonanza. **hit the jackpot** win a large prize, win a lot of money, strike it rich/lucky, have a great success, be very successful; *inf.* make a killing.

jaded *adjective* **1** a jaded appetite satiated, sated, allayed, surfeited, glutted, cloyed, gorged, dulled, blunted. **2** feel jaded after the week's work tired, wearied, weary, fatigued, worn out, exhausted, spent; *inf.* played out, done, done in, bushed, pooped, fagged out.

jagged *adjective* the jagged edge of the broken window serrated, toothed, notched, indented, denticulate, nicked, pointed, snaggy, spiked, barbed, uneven, rough, ridged, ragged, craggy, broken, cleft.

jail, gaol *noun* sent to jail for theft prison, lockup, detention centre; *inf.* nick, clink, inside, stir, slammer, cooler, jug, quod, choky, can; *Am.* jailhouse, penitentiary; *Am. inf.* pen.

jail, gaol *verb* they jailed him for life send to prison, imprison, clap in prison, send down, lock up, put away, incarcerate, confine, detain, intern, impound, immure.

jailer, gaoler *noun* prison warder, warder, prison warden, warden, guard, keeper, captor; *inf.* screw.

jam¹ *verb* **1** jam something in the door to keep it closed wedge, sandwich, insert, force, ram, thrust, push, stick, press, cram, stuff. **2** the ushers jammed too many people into the hall cram, pack, crowd, squeeze, crush. **3** the broken-down vehicles jammed the roads obstruct, block, clog, close off, congest. **4** the machine has jammed become stuck, stick, stall, halt, stop.

jam² *noun* **1** a jam of people crowd, throng, mass, multitude, horde, herd, swarm, mob, pack, crush, press. **2** caught in a jam on the motorway traffic jam, hold-up, obstruction, congestion, bottleneck, stoppage; *Am.* gridlock.

3 in a financial jam predicament, plight, straits, trouble, quandary; *inf.* fix, pickle, spot of bother, hole, spot, tight spot, scrape.

jam³ *noun* spread jam on bread preserve, preserves, conserve, jelly, marmalade, confiture.

jamb *noun* doorjamb, doorpost, upright, post, pillar.

jamboree *noun* gathering, rally, party, get-together, celebration, festivity, festival, fête, carnival, jubilee, revelry, merrymaking, carouse, spree; *inf.* do, beanfeast, shindig, blow-out, bash, rave-up.

jangle *verb* **1** the chains jangled clank, clink, clang, clash, clatter, rattle, vibrate, chime. **2** the noise jangled his nerves jar on, grate on, irritate, disturb.

jangle *noun* the jangle of chains clank, clink, clang, clangour, clash, clatter, rattle, cacophony, din, dissonance, stridor, reverberation, jarring.

janitor *noun* caretaker, concierge, doorkeeper, doorman, custodian; *Scots* school caretaker.

jar *noun* store rice in a jar glass container, container, receptacle, vessel, carafe, flagon, flask, pitcher, jug, vase, urn, pot; jamjar.

jar *verb* **1** the knife jarred against the metal surface grate, rasp, scratch, squeak, screech. **2** he jarred his neck in the crash jolt, jerk, shake, vibrate. **3** the sound jarred his nerves | her manner jarred on him grate (on), jangle, irritate, disturb, upset, discompose, irk, annoy, nettle, vex. **4** his views jarred with hers clash, conflict, be inharmonious, be in opposition, be at variance, be at odds.

jargon *noun* **1** the jargon of street traders cant, slang, argot, idiom, usage, vernacular, dialect, patois; *inf.* lingo. **2** technical jargon specialized language; computerese, legalese, bureaucratese, journalese, buzz word, gobbledegook, psychobabble.

jaundiced *adjective* **1** jaundiced skin | his jaundiced face yellow, yellowish, yellow-tinged, yellow-skinned, sallow. **2** a jaundiced view of life cynical, pessimistic, sceptical, distrustful, suspicious, misanthropic, bitter, resentful, jealous, envious, narrow-minded, bigoted, prejudiced.
Opposites OPTIMISTIC; NAIVE.

jaunt *noun* went on a jaunt to the seaside trip, outing, short drive, short excursion, short expedition, short tour, mini-holiday, short break, airing, stroll, ramble.

jaunty *adjective* **1** in a jaunty mood sprightly, bouncy, buoyant, lively, breezy, perky, frisky, merry, blithe, carefree, joyful. **2** a jaunty outfit smart, stylish, spruce, trim, dapper, fancy, flashy; *inf.* natty.
Opposites DEPRESSED; SERIOUS; SEDATE.

javelin *noun* spear, shaft, bolt, pike, assegai, dart. *See table at* MISSILE.

jaw *noun* **1** *break one's jaw* jawbone, mandible, maxilla. **2** *have a jaw about old times* chat, gossip, conversation, talk, blether, blather; *inf.* natter, chinwag.

jaw *verb* *jaw about old times | the speaker jawed on* chat, chatter, gossip, talk, converse, babble, lecture, drone; *inf.* natter.

jaws *noun pl* *the jaws of the cave | the jaws of Hell* mouth, maw, opening, entrance, entry, ingress, orifice, aperture, abyss.

jazz *noun* **1** *listen to jazz* jazz music. *See tables.* **2** *her performance needs a bit of jazz* liveliness, animation, vivacity, spark, spirit, zest; *inf.* pizazz. **3** *can't be bothered with formal invitations and all that jazz* things like that, stuff, rigmarole, paraphernalia. **jazz up** *verb jazz up her performance | jazz up the living room* brighten up, liven up, enliven, put some spirit into, put some animation into, add some colour to, enhance.

jazzy *adjective* *jazzy car/clothes* flashy, fancy, stylish, smart, gaudy; *inf.* flash, snazzy.

jealous *adjective* **1** *jealous of her beauty* begrudging, grudging, resentful, envious, green with envy, green-eyed, covetous, desirous, emulous. **2** *a jealous lover* suspicious, distrustful, mistrustful, doubting, insecure, apprehensive of rivals, possessive. **3** *jealous of*

TYPES OF JAZZ

acid jazz	boogie-	free-form	hot jazz	ragtime	swing
Afro-Cuban	woogie	fusion	jive	razz-	third
avant-	bop	Harlem	mainstream	matazz	stream
garde	cool	honky-	modern	rooty-toot	trad jazz
bebop	Dixieland	tonk	progressive	skiffle	west coast

JAZZ MUSICIANS AND SINGERS

Armstrong, Louis (1900–71; Am. trumpeter/singer/bandleader)

Baker, Chet (1929–88; Am. trumpeter/singer)

Basie, Count (1904–84; Am. pianist/bandleader)

Bechet, Sidney (1897–1959; Am. soprano saxophonist)

Beiderbecke, Bix (1903–31; Am. cornettist/pianist)

Blakey, Art (1919–90; Am. drummer/bandleader)

Bolden, Buddy (1868–1931; Am. cornettist)

Brubeck, Dave (b. 1920; Am. pianist)

Charles, Ray (b. 1930; Am. pianist/singer)

Christian, Charlie (1916–42; Am. guitarist)

Coleman, Ornette (b. 1930; Am. saxophonist)

Coltrane, John (1926–67; Am. saxophonist)

Dankworth, John (b. 1927; Brit. saxophonist)

Davis, Miles (1926–91; Am. trumpeter)

Dolphy, Eric (1928–64; Am. saxophonist)

Domino, Fats (b. 1928; Am. pianist/singer)

Ellington, Duke (1899–1974; Am. bandleader/pianist)

Evans, Bill (1929–80; Am. pianist)

Evans, Gil (1912–88; Can. pianist)

Fitzgerald, Ella (b. 1918; Am. singer)

Getz, Stan (1927–91; Am. saxophonist)

Gillespie, Dizzy (1917–93; Am. trumpeter/bandleader)

Goodman, Benny (1909–86; Am. clarinettist/bandleader)

Grappelli, Stephane (b. 1908; Fr. violinist)

Hampton, Lionel (b. 1913; Am. vibraphonist/bandleader)

Hancock, Herbie (b. 1940; Am. pianist)

Hawkins, Coleman (1904–69; Am. saxophonist)

Herman, Woody (1913–87; Am. clarinettist/saxophonist/singer)

Hines, Earl (1905–83; Am. pianist)

Holiday, Billie (1915–59; Am. singer)

Lyttelton, Humphrey (b. 1921; Brit. trumpeter)

Marsalis, Wynton (b. 1962; Am. trumpeter)

Miller, Glenn (1904–44; Am. trombonist/bandleader)

Mingus, Charles (1922–79; Am. bass player)

Monk, Thelonius (1917–82; Am. pianist)

Morton, Jelly Roll (1885–1941; Am. pianist)

Mulligan, Gerry (b. 1927; Am. saxophonist)

Oliver, Joe "King" (1885–1938; Am. cornettist)

Parker, Charlie "Bird" (1920–55; Am. saxophonist)

Pepper, Art (1925–82; Am. saxophonist)

Peterson, Oscar (b. 1925; Can. pianist)

Powell, Bud (1924–66; Am. pianist)

Rainey, Gertrude "Ma" (1886–1939; Am. singer)

Reinhardt, Django (1910–53; Belg. guitarist)

Roach, Max (b. 1924; Am. drummer)

Rollins, Sonny (b. 1930; Am. saxophonist)

Schuller, Gunther (b. 1925; Am. French horn player)

Shaw, Artie (b. 1910; Am. clarinettist)

Shorter, Wayne (b. 1933; Am. saxophonist)

Smith, Bessie (1894–1937; Am. singer)

Tatum, Art (1910–56; Am. pianist)

Teagarden, Jack (1905–64; Am. trombonist)

Vaughan, Sarah (1924–90; Am. singer)

Waller, Fats (1904–43; Am. pianist)

Young, Lester (1909–59; Am. saxophonist)

her *chastity* protective, vigilant, watchful, heedful, mindful, careful, solicitous, on guard, wary.

jealousy noun **1** *show jealousy at her rival's success* grudgingness, resentment, resentfulness, ill-will, bitterness, spite, envy, covetousness; green-eyed monster. **2** *the jealousy of her husband* suspicion, suspiciousness, distrust, mistrust, doubt, insecurity, apprehension about rivals, possessiveness. **3** *guard his honour with jealousy* vigilance, watchfulness, heedfulness, attentiveness, care.
Opposites ADMIRATION; TRUST.

jeans plural noun blue jeans, denims; Levis™.

jeer verb *crowds jeering the politician | he jeered at authority* mock, ridicule, deride, taunt, gibe, scorn, contemn, flout, cry down, tease, hector, barrack, boo, hiss; scoff at, laugh at, sneer at; *inf.* knock.
Opposites CHEER; APPLAUD.

jeer noun *the jeers of the crowd* mockery, ridicule, derision; banter, scoffing, teasing, hectoring, barracking; sneer, taunt, gibe, boo, hiss, catcall, abuse; *inf.* knocking.

jejune adjective **1** *a jejune person* naive, simple, unsophisticated, immature, inexperienced, ignorant, uninformed; *inf.* wet behind the ears. **2** *jejune behaviour* childish, immature, juvenile, puerile, silly, senseless, inane. **3** *jejune prose* insipid, uninteresting, dull, vapid, arid, dry, trite, banal, boring, tedious.
Opposites SOPHISTICATED; MATURE; INSPIRED.

jell verb **1** *let the dessert jell* set, stiffen, solidify, harden, thicken, congeal, coagulate. **2** *ideas beginning to jell* take shape, take form, form, crystallize, come together.

jeopardize verb put in jeopardy, put at risk, risk, expose to risk, expose to danger, lay open to danger, endanger, imperil, threaten, menace, take a chance with, gamble with.

jeopardy noun risk, danger, endangerment, peril, hazard, precariousness, insecurity, vulnerability, threat, menace.
Opposites SAFETY; SECURITY.

jerk verb **1** *jerk him inside by the arm* pull, yank, tug, wrench, tweak, pluck. **2** *the car jerked along* jolt, lurch, bump, jump, bounce, jounce. **3** *his arm was jerking* twitch, shake, tremble, be in convulsion. **4** *jerk a reply | 'yes,' he jerked* snap, say curtly, utter brusquely.

jerk noun **1** *pull it out with a jerk* pull, yank, tug, wrench, tweak. **2** *the car stopped with a jerk* jolt, lurch, bump, start, jar. **3** *he's a complete jerk* fool, idiot, rogue, scoundrel; *inf.* nerd, twit, dimwit, dope, creep, heel.

jerky adjective **1** *a jerky movement of the limbs* spasmodic, fitful, convulsive, twitchy, shaking, shaky, tremulous, uncontrolled. **2** *the jerky motion of the car* jolting, lurching, jumpy, bumpy, bouncy, jouncing, rough.
Opposites SMOOTH.

jerry-built adjective *the sports centre is jerry-built* badly built, carelessly built, thrown together, gimcrack, improvised, insubstantial, flimsy, unstable, rickety, ramshackle, defective, faulty,
flawed, cheap, cheapjack, shoddy.
Opposites STURDY; SOLID; SUBSTANTIAL.

jersey noun sweater, pullover, jumper, top; *inf.* woolly.

jest noun **1** *tell jests* joke, witticism, gag, quip, sally, *bon mot*; *inf.* crack, wisecrack, funny. **2** *play a jest on someone* joke, prank, hoax, practical joke, trick, jape; *inf.* leg-pull, lark. **3** *they did it in jest* fun, sport, play, banter. **4** *they made a jest of him* laughing stock, butt, fool, Aunt Sally; *inf.* stooge, fall guy.

jest verb **1** *they joked and jested all evening* joke, tell jokes, crack jokes, quip, banter; *inf.* wisecrack. **2** *she took them seriously but they were jesting* fool, fool around, tease, play a prank, play a practical joke, hoax, play a hoax, pull someone's leg; *inf.* kid, have someone on.

jester noun **1** *her uncle's a jester* joker, comic, comedian, humorist, wag, wit, quipster, prankster, hoaxer. **2** *the jesters in Shakespeare's plays* fool, court fool, clown, zany, buffoon, merry-andrew, harlequin, pantaloon, wearer of the motley.

jet noun **1** *a jet of water* stream, gush, spurt, spout, spray, rush, fountain, spring. **2** *put a jet on the hose* nozzle, spout, nose, sprinkler, sprinkler head, spray, rose, atomizer. **3** *travel in a jet* jetplane, jetliner, turbojet, ramjet, jumbo jet. *See table at* AIRCRAFT.

jet verb **1** *water jetted out of the hose* shoot, gush, spurt, spout, well, rush, spray, squirt, spew, stream, surge, flow, issue. **2** *jet off to Spain* fly, travel by plane, zoom.

jet adjective *a jet cat* jet-black, black, pitch-black, pitch, ebony, ink-black, ink, sooty, coal-black, sable, raven, sloe-black. *See table at* COLOUR.

jettison verb **1** *jettison heavy goods from a ship* throw overboard, throw over the side, unload, eject. **2** *jettison unwanted clothes* throw out, throw away, discard, get rid of, toss out, scrap, dump.
Opposites KEEP; RETAIN.

jetty noun *tie the boat to the jetty* pier, wharf, quay, harbour, dock, breakwater, mole, groyne.

jewel noun **1** *a crown set with priceless jewels* gem, gemstone, precious stone, stone, brilliant, *bijou*; *inf.* sparkler, rock. *See table at* GEM. **2** *she wore a jewel on her dress* piece of jewellery, trinket, ornament. **3** *the jewel of his collection* choicest example, pearl, flower, pride, pride and joy, cream, *crème de la crème*, plum, boast. **4** *his wife is an absolute jewel* treasure, one in a million, saint, paragon; *inf.* one of a kind.

jeweller noun lapidary, gemmologist.

jewellery noun jewels, gems, precious stones, treasure, regalia, trinkets, ornaments; costume jewellery. *See table. See also table at* GEM.

Jezebel noun loose woman, wanton, scarlet woman, *femme fatale*, temptress, vamp, woman of easy virtue, whore, prostitute, harlot, strumpet, jade, hussy, trollop; *inf.* tart, scrubber.

jib verb **1** *jib at taking his money* balk at, recoil from, shrink from, stop short of, refuse. **2** *the*

JEWELLERY	
anklet	hatpin
armlet	locket
bangle	marquise
beads	medallion
bracelet	necklace
brooch	necklet
chain	nose stud
charm bracelet	nosering
choker	pendant
circlet	pin
clip	ring
cuff link	rivière
diadem	seal ring
dress watch	signet ring
ear stud	slave-bangle
earring	sleeper
eternity ring	stud
fibula	tiara
friendship	tiepin
ring	torc
hair slide	wristlet

horse jibbed at the fence balk at, stop short at, retreat from, refuse.

jiffy *noun* moment, second, split second, minute, instant, flash, trice, twinkling of an eye; *inf.* two shakes of a lamb's tail.

jig *verb children jigging up and down* bob up and down, bounce, jump about, leap up and down, skip, hop, prance, caper, jounce.

jilt *verb* reject, cast aside, discard, throw over, drop, leave, forsake; *inf.* ditch, dump, give the brush-off, give the heave-ho, give the elbow.

jingle *verb* **1** *money jingling* clink, chink, jangle, rattle, clank. **2** *the bell jingled* tinkle, ding, go ding-dong, go ting-a-ling, ring, chime, tintinnabulate.

jingle *noun* **1** *the jingle of money* clink, chink. See JINGLE *verb* 1. **2** *the jingle of the bell* tinkle, tinkling, ding, ding-dong, ting-a-ling, ringing, tintinnabulation, chime. **3** *sing a little jingle* ditty, chorus, refrain, short song, limerick, piece of doggerel, carol, melody, tune, catchy tune.

jingoism *noun* patriotism, excessive patriotism, blind patriotism, nationalism, chauvinism, flag-waving.

jinx *noun* curse, malediction, spell, plague, affliction; black magic, voodoo, evil eye, bad luck, evil fortune; *Am.* hex.

jinx *verb* curse, cast a spell on, put a voodoo spell on, bewitch; *Am.* hex.

jitter *verb she's jittering* be jittery, be nervous, be nervy, be uneasy, be anxious, be agitated, be on edge, be jumpy, tremble, shake, fidget. **the jitters** *noun it gives me the jitters* nervousness, nerves, fit of the nerves, uneasiness, anxiety, agitation, trembling, shaking, fidgeting, jumpiness; *inf.* the willies, the heebie-jeebies.

jittery *adjective* nervous, nervy, uneasy, anxious, agitated, trembling, quivering, shaking, shaky, fidgety, jumpy.
Opposites CALM; LAID-BACK.

job *noun* **1** *this job will take hours* work, piece of work, task, undertaking, chore, assignment, venture, enterprise, activity, business, affair. **2** *what is his job?* occupation, profession, trade, employment, vocation, calling, career, field of work, means of livelihood, métier, pursuit, position, post, situation, appointment. **3** *it is his job to open the mail* duty, task, chore, errand, responsibility, concern, function, role, charge, office, commission, capacity, contribution. **4** *we must get this job off to the distributors* work, product, batch, lot, consignment. **5** *I had a job to get here* difficult task, problem, trouble, bother, hard time, trial, tribulation. **6** *the police arrested him for the job* crime, felony, burglary, break-in, theft.

jobber *noun* broker, dealer, agent, middleman.

jobless *adjective* unemployed, without paid employment, out of work, without work, workless, idle, inactive, unoccupied.

jockey *noun* rider, horse-race rider, horseman/horsewoman, equestrian. *See table at* SPORT.

jockey *verb* **1** *jockey for position* | *jockey oneself into position* | *jockey him into lending money* manoeuvre, manipulate, engineer, elbow, insinuate, ingratiate, wheedle, coax, cajole; *inf.* finagle. **2** *jockey the old lady* cheat, swindle, dupe, hoodwink, trick, deceive, take in, exploit, bamboozle, delude, hoax; *inf.* con.

jocular *adjective a jocular mood* | *a jocular person* humorous, funny, witty, comic, comical, facetious, joking, jesting, playful, roguish, waggish, whimsical, droll, jocose, teasing, sportive, amusing, entertaining, diverting, hilarious; farcical, laughable.
Opposites SOLEMN; SERIOUS; EARNEST.

jocund *adjective* cheerful, cheery, merry, happy, gay, blithe, light-hearted, carefree, buoyant, jolly, jovial, in high spirits, smiling, laughing.

jog *verb* **1** *she jogs for exercise* go jogging, run slowly, dogtrot, jogtrot, trot, canter, lope. **2** *they know they won't win but they are jogging along* trudge, plod, tramp, lumber, stump, pad. **3** *she jogged him in the ribs* nudge, prod, poke, push, elbow, tap. **4** *the sight jogged her memory* stimulate, activate, stir, arouse, prompt. **5** *his backpack jogged up and down on his back* bounce, bob, joggle, jiggle, jounce, jolt, jerk, shake.

join *verb* **1** *join the pieces of string/wood/metal together* fasten, attach, tie, bind, couple, connect, unite, link, splice, yoke, knit, glue, cement, fuse, weld, solder. **2** *the two clubs have joined together* join forces, amalgamate, merge, combine, unify, ally, league, federate. **3** *we joined them in their venture* join forces with, team up with, band together with, cooperate with, collaborate with, affiliate with. **4** *join the army* | *join a sports club* enlist, sign up, enrol; become a member of, enlist in, sign up for, enrol in. **5** *join the search party* join in, participate in, take part in, partake in, contribute to, lend a hand with. **6** *his land joins ours* adjoin, conjoin, abut on, border, border on, touch, meet, verge on, reach to, extend to.
Opposites DETACH; SEPARATE; LEAVE.

joint *noun* **1** *reinforce the pipes at the joint* join, junction, juncture, intersection, nexus, knot, seam, coupling; coupler. **2** *cut the Sunday joint* joint of meat. *See table.* **3** *drinking in some joint* club, nightclub, bar. **4** *what a filthy joint* place, dwelling, house, establishment; *inf.* hole. **5** *smoke a joint* marijuana cigarette; *inf.* reefer, stick.

JOINTS OF MEAT	
Lamb	tenderloin
best end of neck	trotter
breast	**Beef**
chump	brisket
chump chops	chuck
leg	fillet steak
loin	flank
loin chop *Am.*	fore rib
neck slice *Am.*	leg
rib *Am.*	neck
riblets *Am.*	porterhouse steak
scrag-end	*Am.*
shoulder	rib
Pork	rolled ribs
back rib *Am.*	round *Am.*
belly	round steak *Am.*
blade	rump
hand	shin
hock	short loin *Am.*
leg	silverside
leg fillet	sirloin
loin	T-bone
shoulder	tenderloin *Am.*
side *Am.*	topside
spare rib	undercut steak

joint *adjective a joint interest* common, shared, joined, mutual, combined, collective, cooperative, allied, united, concerted, consolidated.

joint *verb joint a carcass* cut, carve, cleave, chop, hew, hack, sever, segment, divide, dismember, disjoint.

jointly *adverb decide jointly* together, in combination, in conjunction, as one, mutually, in partnership, cooperatively, in cooperation, in league, in collusion; *inf.* in cahoots.

joke *noun* **1** *tell a joke* jest, witticism, quip, gag, yarn, pun, sally; *inf.* wisecrack, crack, funny. **2** *play a joke on him* practical joke, prank, trick, hoax, jape; *inf.* leg-pull, lark. **3** *we did it for a joke* fun, sport, play, banter, whimsy. **4** *he is the joke of the class* laughing-stock, butt, figure of fun, target, fair game, jest, Aunt Sally.

joke *verb* **1** *they joked and jested all evening* tell jokes, crack jokes, jest, banter, quip; *inf.* wise-crack. **2** *she took them seriously but they were joking* fool, fool around, tease, pull someone's leg; *inf.* kid, have someone on.

joker *noun* **1** *her uncle's a joker* comic, stand-up comic, comedian, humorist, funny man/ woman, jester, wag, wit, quipster, banterer, prankster, practical joker, hoaxer, trickster; *inf.* kidder, wisecracker. **2** *take no account of jokers that might spoil the plan* unexpected fac-

tor, catch, hitch, drawback, pitfall, trap, snare, hindrance, impediment. **3** *who's that joker?* person, man/woman, fellow; *inf.* chap, guy, bloke.

jolly *adjective* merry, gay, joyful, joyous, jovial, happy, glad, mirthful, gleeful, cheerful, cheery, carefree, buoyant, lively, bright, light-hearted, blithe, jocund, sprightly, elated, exuberant, exhilarated, jubilant, high-spirited, sportive, playful.
Opposites MISERABLE; LUGUBRIOUS.

jolt *verb* **1** *people in the crowd jolting each other* bump against, knock against, bump into, bang into, collide with, jostle, push, shove, elbow, nudge, jar. **2** *the car jolted along* bump, bounce, jounce, start, jerk, lurch, jar. **3** *the accident jolted him* upset, disturb, perturb, shake, shake up, shock, stun, disconcert, discompose, disquiet, startle, surprise, astonish, amaze, stagger.

jolt *noun* **1** *one of the crowd gave him a jolt* bump, knock, bang, hit, push, shove, nudge, jar. **2** *the car moved in jolts* bump, bounce, jounce, shake, jerk, lurch, start, jar. **3** *her death came as a jolt* shock, bombshell, blow, upset, setback, surprise, bolt from the blue, thunderbolt.

jostle *verb* **1** *people jostling each other* bump against, knock against, bump into, bang into, collide with, jolt, push, shove, elbow. **2** *jostle her way through* push, thrust, shove, press, squeeze, elbow, force.

jot *noun not care a jot* iota, whit, little bit, bit, scrap, fraction, atom, grain, particle, morsel, mite, speck, trace, trifle, tinge; *inf.* smidgen, tad.

jot *verb jot down the details* write down, note, note down, make a note of, take down, put down, mark down, list, make a list of, register, record, chronicle.

journal *noun* **1** *keep a journal on his travels* diary, daybook, notebook, commonplace-book, log, logbook, chronicle, record, register. **2** *publish medical journals* periodical, magazine, trade magazine, review, publication, professional organ. **3** *the proprietor of several national journals* newspaper, paper, daily newspaper, daily, weekly newspaper, weekly, gazette.

journalism *noun* **1** *have a job in journalism* the press, the newspaper business, the newspaper world, print media, the fourth estate, Fleet Street; radio journalism, television journalism. **2** *do not admire their style of journalism* reporting, newspaper writing, feature writing, news coverage, broadcasting.

journalist *noun* reporter, newspaperman/news-paperwoman, newsman/newswoman, news-hound, pressman/presswoman, feature writer, columnist, correspondent, contributor, commentator, reviewer, editor, sub-editor; broadcaster; *inf.* stringer, sub.

journey *noun go on a long/short journey* trip, expedition, excursion, travels, tour, trek, voyage, cruise, safari, peregrination, roaming, roving, globe-trotting, odyssey, pilgrimage, outing, jaunt.

journey verb *journey to India* go, travel, go on a trip, go on an expedition, go on an excursion, tour, voyage, sail, cruise, fly, hike, trek, roam, rove, ramble, wander, meander, peregrinate, globe-trot.

jovial adjective *jovial person/comment/mood/gathering* jolly, jocular, jocose, jocund, happy, cheerful, cheery, glad, in good spirits, merry, gay, mirthful, blithe, buoyant, animated, convivial, sociable, cordial.
Opposites MISERABLE; MOROSE.

joy noun **1** *receive the gift with joy* delight, pleasure, gladness, enjoyment, gratification, happiness, rapture, glee, bliss, ecstasy, elation, rejoicing, exultation, jubilation, euphoria, ravishment, transport, felicity. **2** *their daughter is a joy* source of joy, treasure, prize, gem, jewel, pride and joy, delight. **3** *it is a joy to see you* pleasure, delight, treat, thrill. **4** *we had no joy from the bank* success, satisfaction, good fortune, luck, achievement.

joyful adjective **1** *joyful at the news* overjoyed, elated, beside oneself with joy, thrilled, delighted, pleased, gratified, happy, glad, blithe, gleeful, jubilant, ecstatic, exultant, euphoric, enraptured, over the moon, in seventh heaven, on cloud nine; *inf.* tickled pink. **2** *we heard the joyful news* glad, happy, good, pleasing, cheering, gratifying, heartwarming. **3** *a joyful occasion/song* joyous, happy, cheerful, merry, gay, festive, celebratory.
Opposites DEPRESSED; MISERABLE; SAD.

joyless adjective **1** *a joyless existence/place* gloomy, dreary, drab, dismal, bleak, depressing, cheerless, grim, desolate, comfortless. **2** *joyless children* unhappy, sad, miserable, wretched, downcast, dejected, depressed, despondent, melancholy, mournful.

joyous adjective joyful, happy, cheerful, merry. See JOYFUL 1, 3.

jubilant adjective *his jubilant family welcomed him home* rejoicing, overjoyed, exultant, triumphant, elated, thrilled, euphoric, ecstatic, enraptured, rhapsodic, transported, exuberant, on top of the world, walking on air, over the moon, in seventh heaven, on cloud nine; *inf.* tickled pink.
Opposites DOWNCAST; DESPONDENT.

jubilation noun exultation, triumph, elation, joy, euphoria, ecstasy, rapture, transport, exuberance.

jubilee noun celebration, commemoration, anniversary, holiday, feast day, festival, gala, carnival, fête, festivity, revelry. See tables at FESTIVAL, WEDDING.

judge verb **1** *judge the murder case* try, hear evidence, sit in judgement, give a verdict, pronounce a verdict, pass sentence, pronounce sentence, sentence, decree. **2** *judge the contest* adjudicate, adjudge, umpire, referee, arbitrate, mediate. **3** *judge the entries | judge his conduct for yourself* assess, appraise, evaluate, weigh up, size up, gauge, examine, review, criticize, diagnose. **4** *judge the distance to be three miles* estimate, assess, reckon, guess, surmise; *inf.* guesstimate. **5** *I judge that he is not honest |*

judge him to be dishonest consider, believe, think, form the opinion, deduce, gather, conclude.

judge noun **1** *the judge pronounced sentence* magistrate, sheriff, his/her honour; *inf.* beak, m'lud; high-court judge. **2** *the flower-show judge* appraiser, assessor, evaluator, critic, expert. **3** *the contest judge* adjudicator, umpire, referee, arbiter, arbitrator, mediator.

judgement noun **1** *he has no judgement* discernment, acumen, shrewdness, common sense, good sense, sense, perception, perspicacity, percipience, penetration, discrimination, wisdom, judiciousness, prudence, sagacity, understanding, intelligence, powers of reasoning. **2** *the adjudicator/magistrate gave his judgement* verdict, decision, adjudication, ruling, finding, opinion, conclusion, decree, sentence. **3** *in my judgement he is dishonest* opinion, view, belief, conviction, estimation, evaluation, assessment, appraisal. **4** *the Day of Judgement | Judgement Day* damnation, doom, fate, punishment, retribution, sentence.

judicial adjective **1** *judicial process/review* judiciary, juridical, judicatory, legal. **2** *a judicial mind* judgelike, impartial, unbiased, critical, analytical, discriminating, discerning, perceptive.

judicious adjective *a judicious course of action* wise, prudent, politic, sagacious, shrewd, astute, sensible, common-sense, sound, well-advised, well-considered, well-judged, considered, thoughtful, expedient, practical, discerning, discriminating, informed, intelligent, smart, clever, enlightened, logical, rational, discreet, careful, cautious, circumspect, diplomatic.
Opposites INJUDICIOUS; FOOLISH; ILL-ADVISED.

jug noun pitcher, ewer, crock, carafe, decanter, jar, urn, vessel, receptacle, container.

juggle verb *juggle the figures* change around, alter, tamper with, falsify, fake, manipulate, manoeuvre, rig, massage; *inf.* fix, doctor, cook.

juice noun extract, sap, secretion, liquid, liquor, fluid, serum; orange juice, meat juice.

juicy adjective **1** *juicy fruit* succulent, moist, lush, sappy, watery, wet, flowing. **2** *a juicy tale* racy, risqué, spicy, sensational, thrilling, fascinating, colourful, exciting, vivid.
Opposites DRY; UNEXCITING.

jumble verb *jumble up the toys* disarrange, disorganize, disorder, dishevel, muddle, confuse, tangle, shuffle, mix, mix up, mingle, put in disarray, make a shambles of, throw into chaos.

jumble noun *a jumble of toys* clutter, muddle, confusion, litter, mess, hodgepodge, hotchpotch, mishmash, confused heap, miscellany, motley collection, mixture, medley, gallimaufry, farrago.

jumbo adjective *jumbo packet/sausages* giant, gigantic, immense, huge, extra-large, oversized.

jump verb **1** *jump around* spring, leap, bound, hop, bounce, skip, caper, gambol, frolic, frisk, cavort. **2** *jump over the rope* high-jump, leap over, vault, pole-vault, hurdle, clear, go over,

sail over. **3** *she jumped when she heard the noise*
start, flinch, jerk, recoil, twitch, quiver, shake,
wince; *inf.* jump out of one's skin. **4** *jump a
piece of text* skip, miss, omit, leave out, cut out,
pass over, overlook, disregard, ignore. **5** *jump
the traffic lights* overshoot, drive through, disregard, ignore. **6** *prices jumped* rise, go up, leap
up, increase, mount, escalate, surge. **7** *retail-
ers jumping prices* raise, put up, up, increase,
escalate, hike up, advance, boost, elevate, augment; *inf.* jack up. **8** *youths jumped the old man*
pounce on, set upon, fall on, swoop down on,
attack, assault; *inf.* mug. **jump at** *jump at the
opportunity* grab, snatch, accept eagerly, go for
enthusiastically, show enthusiasm for. **jump
the gun** *jump the gun by applying for a job not yet
advertised* act prematurely, be too soon, act too
soon, be previous, be ahead of time, anticipate.

jump *noun* **1** *with one jump* spring, leap, vault,
bound, hop, bounce, skip. **2** *the jumps in the
race* hurdle, fence, rail, hedge, obstacle, barrier, gate. **3** *a jump in the sequence* gap, break,
hiatus, interruption, space, lacuna, breach,
interval. **4** *she gave a jump at the sight* start,
flinch, jerk, twitch, quiver, shake, wince. **5** *the
car started with a jump* start, jolt, jerk, lurch,
bump, jounce, jar. **6** *a jump in prices* rise,
increase, upturn, upsurge, escalation, hike,
boost, advance, elevation, augmentation.

jumper *noun* sweater, pullover, jersey, top; *inf.*
woolly.

jumpy *adjective* **1** *feeling jumpy waiting for news*
nervous, nervy, edgy, on edge, jittery, agitated,
fidgety, anxious, uneasy, restive, tense,
alarmed, apprehensive, panicky. **2** *the jumpy
movements of the car* jolting, fitful, convulsive,
jerky, lurching, bumpy, jouncing, jarring.
Opposites CALM; LAID-BACK.

junction *noun* **1** *reinforcement at the junction of
the pipes* join, joint, juncture, link, bond, connection, seam; joining, coupling, linking, weld-
ing, union. **2** *cars stop at the junction*
crossroads, crossing, intersection, interchange;
motorway junction, railway junction.

juncture *noun* **1** *at this juncture we should vote*
point, point in time, time, stage, period, critical point, crucial moment, moment of truth,
turning-point, crisis, crux, extremity. **2** *reinforcement at the juncture of the pipes* junction,
join, joint, coupling, union. See JUNCTION 1.

jungle *noun* **1** *wild animals in the thick jungle*
forest, tropical forest, rain forest, wilderness,
wilds, the bush. **2** *a jungle of paperwork/facts*
jumble, tangle, disarray, confusion, hotchpotch, hodgepodge, heap, mass, mess, mishmash, motley selection, gallimaufry, farrago.
law of the jungle survival of the fittest, each
man for himself, dog-eat-dog, cutthroat competition.

junior *adjective* **1** *the junior member* younger.
2 *the junior position* subordinate, lesser, lower,
minor, secondary, inferior.

junk *noun* *clear up all this junk* rubbish, refuse,
litter, scrap, waste, garbage, trash, debris, leavings, leftovers, remnants, cast-offs, rejects,
odds and ends, bric-à-brac, oddments.

junk *verb* *junk unwanted things* throw out, throw
away, discard, get rid of, dispose of, scrap; *inf.*
dump.

junket *noun* *have a junket on his birthday* feast,
festivity, revelry, party, picnic, celebration,
spree, excursion; *inf.* do, bash, thrash, beanfeast.

junket *verb* *junketing to celebrate victory* feast,
eat, drink, and be merry, throw a party, entertain, party, picnic, celebrate, go on a spree, go
on an excursion.

jurisdiction *noun* **1** *under the governor's jurisdiction* authority, control, administration, command, leadership, power, dominion,
sovereignty, rule, mastery, sway, say, influence. **2** *living in adjoining jurisdictions* territory,
district, province, domain, principality, realm,
area, zone. **3** *the jurisdiction of his authority*
extent, range, scope, bounds, compass, sphere,
area, field, orbit.

just *adjective* **1** *a just judge* fair, fair-minded,
equitable, even-handed, impartial, unbiased,
objective, neutral, disinterested, unprejudiced,
open-minded. **2** *a just man* upright, honourable, upstanding, honest, righteous, ethical, moral, virtuous, principled, good, decent,
straight, truthful, sincere. **3** *just criticism*
valid, sound, well-founded, well-grounded, justified, justifiable, warrantable, defensible, reasonable. **4** *just deserts* deserved, well-deserved,
merited, earned, rightful, due, proper, fitting,
appropriate, apt, suitable, condign. **5** *the just
heir* lawful, legitimate, legal, licit, rightful, genuine; *inf.* kosher. **6** *a just account of the events*
true, truthful, accurate, correct, factual, exact,
precise, close, faithful, strict.
Opposites UNJUST; BIASED; DISHONEST; undeserved.

just *adverb* **1** *I just saw him* only now, a
moment ago, a second ago, a short time ago,
recently, lately, not long ago. **2** *the house is just
right* exactly, precisely, absolutely, completely,
totally, entirely, perfectly. **3** *we just made it*
only just, barely, scarcely, hardly, by a narrow
margin, by a hair's breadth; *inf.* by the skin of
one's teeth. **4** *she's just a child* only, merely,
simply, but, nothing but, no more than. **5** *I
just told him what I thought of him* really, indeed,
truly, actually, certainly. **just about 1** *I've got
just about every one of his books* all but, almost,
nearly, practically, well-nigh, not quite. **2** *we
lost it just about here* near, around, close to, in
the vicinity of.

justice *noun* **1** *expect justice from the courts*
justness, fairness, fair play, fair-mindedness,
equitableness, equity, even-handedness, impartiality, impartialness, lack of bias, objectivity,
neutrality, disinterestedness, lack of prejudice,
open-mindedness. See JUST *adjective* 1. **2** *a man
of justice* justness, uprightness, integrity, honour, honesty, righteousness, ethics, morals,
virtue, principle, decency, propriety. See JUST
adjective 2. **3** *see the justice of his criticism* validity, justification, soundness, reasonableness.
See JUST *adjective* 3. **4** *the justice of his heirdom*
lawfulness, legitimacy, legality, licitness. See
JUST *adjective* 5. **5** *demand justice* amends, recompense, redress, compensation, reparation,

requital, retribution, penalty, punishment.
6 *the justice was passing sentence* judge, magistrate, sheriff.
Opposites INJUSTICE; BIAS; DISHONESTY.

justifiable *adjective* valid, sound, well-founded, lawful, legitimate, legal, tenable, right, defensible, supportable, sustainable, warrantable, vindicable, reasonable, within reason, sensible, acceptable, plausible.
Opposites UNJUSTIFIABLE; INDEFENSIBLE.

justification *noun* **1** *give as the justification of his behaviour* grounds, reason, just cause, basis, explanation, rationalization, defence. *See* JUSTIFY 1. **2** *the justification of his crime* substantiation, proof, establishment, verification, legalization. *See* JUSTIFY 2. **3** *outline the justification for our fears* warranty, substantiation, reasonableness, confirmation. *See* JUSTIFY 3. **4** *the justification of the accused* acquittal, absolution, exoneration, exculpation, pardon, excusing. *See* JUSTIFY 4.

justify *verb* **1** *justify his behaviour* give grounds for, give reasons for, show just cause for, explain, give an explanation for, rationalize, defend, stand up for, uphold, sustain. **2** *he had to justify his claim* substantiate, prove,

establish, verify, certify, vindicate, legalize, legitimize. **3** *his conduct justified our worries* warrant, substantiate, bear out, show to be reasonable, prove to be right, confirm. **4** *the accused was finally justified* declare innocent, pronounce not guilty, acquit, clear, absolve, exculpate, exonerate, pardon, excuse.

justly *adverb* **1** *justly proud* justifiably, rightfully, with reason, with good reason. **2** *behave justly* fairly, equitably, impartially, without bias, objectively, without prejudice, disinterestedly. **3** *describe the incident justly* accurately, correctly, truthfully, faithfully.

jut *verb* stick out, project, protrude, poke out, bulge out, overhang, beetle.

juvenile *adjective* **1** *juvenile entrants* young, junior, minor. **2** *a juvenile attitude* childish, puerile, infantile, jejune, immature, inexperienced, callow, green, unsophisticated, naive; *inf.* wet behind the ears.
Opposites ADULT; MATURE.

juxtapose *verb* place/set side by side, place parallel, put adjacent, compare.

Kk

kaleidoscopic adjective **1** *a kaleidoscopic pattern* many-coloured, variegated, motley, rainbowlike, many-splendoured, psychedelic. **2** *a kaleidoscopic scene* changeable, ever-changing, variable, varying, mutable, protean, ever-moving, fluid, mobile, unstable, unsteady, labile. **3** *a kaleidoscopic set of facts* complex, complicated, intricate, convoluted, confused, disordered, disarranged, jumbled, muddled, chaotic.

keel noun **1** *the keel of a boat* bottom, bottom side, underside. *See table at* SHIP. **2** *admiring the keels sailing on the sea* boat, ship, vessel, craft.

keel verb *the boat suddenly keeled* keel over, turn over, overturn, turn upside down, turn turtle, capsize, topple over, upset. **keel over 1** *the boat keeled over* turn over, overturn, capsize. **2** *a member of the crowd keeled over* faint, fall down in a faint, collapse, lose consciousness, pass out, black out.

keen adjective **1** *a keen edge to the blade* sharp, sharp-edged, sharpened, fine-edged, razor-sharp. **2** *a keen sense of smell* sharp, acute, discerning, perceptive, sensitive, discriminating. **3** *a keen mind* sharp, astute, quick-witted, sharp-witted, shrewd, perceptive, penetrating, perspicacious, clever, bright, smart, intelligent, brilliant, wise, canny, sagacious, sapient; *inf.* brainy. **4** *be the butt of her keen wit* acerbic, acid, biting, caustic, tart, pointed, mordant, trenchant, incisive, razor-like, razor-sharp, finely honed, cutting, stinging, scathing, sardonic, satirical. **5** *keen pupils* willing, eager, enthusiastic, avid, earnest, intent, diligent, assiduous, conscientious, zealous, fervent, fervid, impatient. **6** *keen on learning/girls* fond of, devoted to, eager for, hungry for, thirsty for. **7** *keen to learn* eager to, longing to, yearning to, impatient to, itching to; *inf.* rarin' to. *See* KEEN *adjective* 5.
Opposites BLUNT; DULL; APATHETIC.

keen verb *keen over the dead body* wail, lament, weep, sob, cry, ululate, howl, moan, groan, mourn, sorrow, grieve.

keenness noun **1** *the keenness of the blade* sharpness, razor-sharpness. *See* KEEN *adjective* 1. **2** *the keenness of her sense of smell* sharpness, acuteness, perceptiveness, sensitivity. *See* KEEN *adjective* 2. **3** *the keenness of his mind* sharpness, astuteness, quick-wittedness, sharp-wittedness, perspicacity, shrewdness, cleverness, brightness, intelligence, canniness. *See* KEEN *adjective* 3. **4** *the keenness of her wit* acerbity, acidity, causticity, tartness, mordancy, trenchancy, incisiveness, sardonicism, satire. *See* KEEN *adjective* 4. **5** *the keenness of the pupils* willingness, eagerness, enthusiasm, avidity, intentness, diligence, assiduity, zeal, fervour, devotion, impatience. *See* KEEN *adjective* 5, 6, *and* 7.

keep verb **1** *keep going* carry on, continue, maintain, persist, persevere. **2** *he kept the ring which she gave him* hold on to, keep hold of, retain, retain in one's possession; *inf.* hang on to. **3** *he keeps all his old newspapers* save up, accumulate, store, hoard, amass, pile up, collect, garner. **4** *keep the memory of her* preserve, conserve, keep alive, keep fresh. **5** *does the grocer keep string?* sell, stock, have in stock, carry, deal in, trade in. **6** *he is responsible for keeping the estate* look after, keep in good order, tend, mind, maintain, keep up, manage, superintend. **7** *the boy keeps the sheep* tend, care for, look after, mind, guard, safeguard, protect, watch over, shield, shelter. **8** *he could not keep a wife and children on his salary* provide for, support, maintain, sustain, subsidize, feed, nurture, provide board for. **9** *keep it from her* keep secret, keep hidden, hide, conceal, keep dark, withhold, hush, hush up, not breathe a word of, suppress, censor. **10** *keep one's promise/word* keep to, abide by, comply with, fulfil, carry out, effectuate, keep faith with, stand by, honour, obey, observe. **11** *keep the Sabbath* observe, hold, celebrate, commemorate, respect, ritualize, solemnize, ceremonialize. **12** *what kept you?* keep back, hold back, hold up, delay, detain, retard, hinder, obstruct, impede, hamper, constrain, check, block, hamstring, prevent. **keep at 1** *we'll finish in time if we keep at it* persist, persevere, be persistent, be pertinacious, carry on, keep going, continue, work away, see it through; *inf.* stick at it, stay the distance, hang on in there, slave away, peg away. **2** *the teacher kept at us to work* keep on at, keep after, go on at, chivvy, badger, harp on at, nag, harass. **keep back 1** *what kept you back?* hold, back, hold up, delay, detain. *See* KEEN verb 12. **2** *keep back information* withhold, keep secret, keep hidden, hide, conceal, suppress. *See* KEEP verb 9. **keep from 1** *keep myself from falling* prevent, stop, restrain, check, halt. **2** *keep him from harm* keep safe, preserve, protect, guard, safeguard, shield, shelter. **keep off 1** *keep off his property* keep away from, stay away from, stay off, remain at a distance from, not go near, not approach, not stand on, not walk on, not touch, not trespass on. **2** *keep off the subject* avoid, steer clear of, not mention, not refer to, not allude to, abstain from, evade, dodge, shun, eschew. **3** *keep off chocolate/wine/cigarettes* refrain from, abstain from, give up, quit, renounce, turn aside from; *inf.* swear off. **4** *the rain kept off* stay away, not start, not begin. **keep on 1** *keep on going* go on, carry on, continue, persist, persevere. **2** *the boss decided to keep the man on* continue to employ, keep employing, retain the services of, not to dismiss; *inf.* not to sack. **3** *keep on about his faults* keep talking, go on, go on and on, refer to again and again, dwell on, repeat oneself,

ramble on, rant on; *inf.* witter on.   **4** *keep on at* keep at, keep after, go on at, chivvy, badger, nag. *See* KEEP *verb* keep at 2. **keep to 1** *keep to his word* keep, abide by, comply with, stand by, honour. *See* KEEP *verb* 10.   **2** *keep to the path/subject* not stray from, not wander from, stay with; *inf.* stick with. **keep under** *the poor were kept under by the authorities* suppress, oppress, tyrannize, tyrannize over, keep in submission, keep down, keep under one's thumb, quell, squelch. **keep up 1** *keep up the payments/progress* maintain, continue with, go on with, carry on with, keep going.   **2** *try to keep up in the race* keep pace, keep abreast, not fall behind, not lag behind.   **3** *keep up with the rest* keep pace with, keep abreast of, compete with, vie with, rival.   **4** *keep up with latest developments* keep pace with, keep abreast of, keep informed about, learn about, retain an interest in.   **5** *keep up with old friends* stay in touch with, keep in contact with, remain in correspondence with, be in communication with, keep alive one's friendship with, remain acquainted with.
Opposites give up (*see* GIVE); DISCARD; ABANDON.

keep *noun* **1** *pay for their/its keep* maintenance, support, board, board and lodging, subsistence, sustenance, food, nourishment, living, livelihood, upkeep.   **2** *enemies storming the keep* donjon, dungeon, tower, stronghold, fastness, citadel, fortress, fort, castle. **for keeps** forever, for always, for good, once and for all.

keeper *noun* **1** *prisoners escaping their keeper* jailer, gaoler, warder, warden, guard, custodian, sentry; *inf.* screw.   **2** *a museum/lighthouse keeper* curator, conservator, attendant, caretaker, steward, superintendent, overseer, administrator.   **3** *his brother's keeper* guardian, escort, bodyguard, chaperon, chaperone, nursemaid, nurse.

keeping *noun* **1** *children/property in the keeping of the grandfather* keep, guardianship, protection, protectorship, trusteeship, trust, safe keeping, safeguard, care, charge, custody, possession, auspices, aegis, patronage.   **2** *behaviour in keeping with their beliefs* agreement, harmony, accordance, accord, concurrence, conformity, consistency, correspondence, congruity, compliance, proportion.

keepsake *noun* memento, souvenir, remembrance, reminder, token of remembrance, relic, favour.

keg *noun* *don't like keg beer* barrel, cask, vat, tun, butt, drum, hogshead, firkin, container, vessel.

kernel *noun* **1** *grown from a kernel* grain, seed, germ, stone, nut.   **2** *the kernel of the problem* nub, nucleus, core, centre, heart, marrow, pith, substance, essence, essential part, gist, quintessence; *inf.* nitty-gritty, nuts and bolts, brass tacks.

key *noun* **1** *key in the lock* latchkey, passkey, master-key, skeleton key.   **2** *the key to the problem* answer, solution, explanation, guide, clue, cue, pointer, gloss, interpretation, explication, annotation, clarification, exposition, translation.   **3** *musical key* tone, pitch, timbre, tonal-

ity, tone colour.   **4** *a poem in a mournful key* mood, humour, vein, style, character, spirit.

keyboard *noun*. See table.

KEYBOARD INSTRUMENTS		
accordion	harmonium	pianino
calliope	harpsichord	piano
celest	melodeon	pianoforte
clavichord	Moog™	pianola
clavicythera	Novachord	spinet
dulcitone	Ondes	synthesizer
forte-piano	Martenot	virginal
grand piano	organ	Wurlitzer™

keynote *noun* **1** *musical keynote* tonic, leading note.   **2** *the keynote of the speech* theme, gist, salient point, substance, essence, pith, centre, heart, core, nucleus, marrow, policy line.

keystone *noun* **1** *the keystone of the pillar* central stone, cornerstone, quoin.   **2** *the keystone of the theory* principle, basis, foundation, linchpin.

kibosh *verb* **put the kibosh on** stop, bring to an end, put an end to, put a stop to, check, curb, nip in the bud, quell, quash, suppress, crack down on.

kick *verb* **1** *kick the ball* boot, put one's boot to, punt.   **2** *the gun kicked* recoil, spring back.   **3** *kick against the rules* protest against, resist, oppose, rebel against, spurn, object to, complain about, grumble about; *inf.* gripe about, grouse about, beef about, bitch about.   **4** *kick the habit* give up, stop, abandon, quit, leave off, desist from. **kick around 1** *kick around the poor people* abuse, mistreat, maltreat, push around.   **2** *kick around ideas* discuss, talk over, debate, thrash out, argue the pros and cons. **kick off** *kick off the proceedings* start, begin, commence, open, get under way, get going, start the ball rolling, initiate. **kick out** throw out, eject, expel, get rid of, force out, turn out, oust, evict, dismiss, discharge, give someone his marching orders; *inf.* send packing, show the door to, sack, fire, give the boot to, boot out, give the axe to, throw out on one's ear, give the bum's rush to.

kick *noun* **1** *gave the ball a kick* boot, punt.   **2** *she steals for kicks* thrill, excitement, stimulation, fun, pleasure, enjoyment, amusement, gratification; *inf.* buzz.   **3** *the drink has quite a kick* strength, potency, tang, zip, alcoholic effect; *inf.* punch, zing.   **4** *there's no kick left in the firm* vigour, force, forcefulness, energy, vitality, vivacity, liveliness, verve, animation, enthusiasm, zest, zip; *inf.* punch, zing.

kick-off *noun* start, beginning, commencement, outset, opening, initiation.

kid *noun* *an adult and three kids* child, young one, young person, youngster, little one, baby, toddler, tot, infant, boy/girl, adolescent, juvenile, teenager, youth; *inf.* kiddie; *Scots* bairn.

kid *verb* **1** *he was only kidding* tease, joke, jest, fool, fool around, pull someone's leg, chaff, be facetious; *inf.* have someone on.   **2** *don't kid yourself you won't win* deceive, delude, fool, trick, cozen, gull, hoodwink, hoax, beguile, bamboozle.

kidnap *verb* abduct, seize, snatch, capture, hold to ransom, take as hostage.

kill *verb* **1** *he killed three people* take someone's life, slay, murder, do away with, do to death, slaughter, butcher, massacre, assassinate, liquidate, wipe out, destroy, erase, eradicate, exterminate, dispatch, put to death, execute, hang, behead, guillotine, send to the electric chair; *inf.* bump off, do in, knock off, top. **2** *kill all his hopes* destroy, put an end to, ruin, extinguish, scotch, quell. **3** *kill time* pass, spend, expend, while away, fill up, occupy, use up. **4** *the walk will kill you* exhaust, overtire, tire out, fatigue, wear out, fag out, debilitate, enervate, prostrate, tax, overtax, strain. **5** *these shoes are killing me | my feet were killing me* hurt, cause pain, cause discomfort, be uncomfortable, be painful. **6** *kill the information in the file* cancel, delete, remove, erase, cut out, eradicate, expunge, obliterate; *inf.* zap. **7** *kill the parliamentary bill* defeat, veto, vote down, reject, overrule. **8** *wall-linings killing the noise* deaden, muffle, dull, dampen, smother, stifle. **9** *kill the bottle of wine* consume, drink up, drain, empty, finish; *inf.* knock back. **10** *his jokes kill me* overwhelm with laughter, amuse greatly, make someone laugh; *inf.* have people rolling in the aisles, make someone crack up.

killer *noun* slayer, murderer, slaughterer, butcher, assassin, liquidator, destroyer, exterminator, executioner, gunman, homicide, patricide, matricide, infanticide, fratricide, sororicide, regicide; *inf.* hit man.

killing *noun* **1** *guilty of killing* slaying, murder, manslaughter, homicide, slaughter, butchery, massacre, bloodshed, carnage, liquidation, destruction, extermination, execution, patricide, matricide, infanticide. *See* KILL 1 *and* KILLER. *See table at* ASSASSINATION. **2** *make a killing on the stock market | she made a killing in the sales* financial success, bonanza, fortune, windfall, gain, profit, booty, piece of good luck, coup; *inf.* bomb, clean-up.

killing *adjective* **1** *a killing blow* deadly, fatal, lethal, mortal, death-dealing, murderous, homicidal. **2** *a killing walk/task* exhausting, tiring, fatiguing, debilitating, enervating, prostrating, taxing, punishing. **3** *a killing joke* hilarious, uproarious, rib-tickling, comical, amusing, laughable, absurd, ludicrous, outrageous; *inf.* screamingly funny.

killjoy *noun* spoilsport, dampener, damper; *inf.* wet blanket, party-pooper.

kilter *noun* condition, state, shape, fettle, trim, fitness, repair, order, working order.

kin *noun* *no kin living in the area* relatives, relations, family, connections, folks, people, kindred, kith and kin, kinsfolk, kinsmen/ kinswomen.

kind *adjective* *kind people/invitation* kindhearted, kindly, generous, charitable, giving, benevolent, bounteous, magnanimous, big-hearted, warm-hearted, altruistic, philanthropic, humanitarian, humane, tenderhearted, soft-hearted, gentle, mild, lenient,

merciful, clement, pitying, forbearing, patient, tolerant, sympathetic, compassionate, understanding, considerate, helpful, thoughtful, good, nice, decent, pleasant, benign, friendly, genial, congenial, amiable, amicable, cordial, courteous, gracious, good-natured, warm, affectionate, loving, indulgent, obliging, accommodating, neighbourly.
Opposites UNKIND; MEAN; NASTY.

kind *noun* **1** *different kinds of paper/creatures* sort, type, variety, brand, class, category. **2** *different kinds of plant* genus, species, family, strain. **3** *human kind* race, species. **4** *a difference in kind rather than degree* nature, character, manner, aspect, disposition, humour, style, stamp, mould.

kindle *verb* **1** *kindle a fire* light, set alight, set on fire, set fire to, ignite, start, torch. **2** *kindle interest* stimulate, rouse, arouse, excite, stir, awaken, inspire, inflame, incite, induce, provoke, actuate, activate, touch off.

kindly *adjective* **1** *a kindly old lady | a kindly expression on her face* kind, kind-hearted, generous, charitable, magnanimous, warm-hearted, humane, gentle, sympathetic, compassionate, understanding, considerate, helpful, thoughtful, good, nice, decent, polite, friendly, genial, pleasant, amiable, amicable, cordial. **2** *a kindly climate* pleasant, agreeable, mild, gentle, benign, favourable, beneficial, advantageous.
Opposites UNKIND; MEAN; DISAGREEABLE.

kindness *noun* **1** *the kindness of the people* kindheartedness, kindliness, generosity, charitableness, charity, good will, benevolence, magnanimity, hospitality, philanthropy, warm-heartedness, altruism, humanitarianism, humaneness, tender-heartedness, gentleness, mildness, leniency, clemency, patience, tolerance, sympathy, compassion, fellow-feeling, understanding, considerateness, consideration, helpfulness, thoughtfulness, goodness, niceness, decency, pleasantness, friendliness, geniality, congeniality, amiability, cordiality, graciousness, warmth, affection, lovingness, love, indulgence, neighbourliness. *See* KIND *adjective.* **2** *do the neighbours a kindness* kind act, good deed, good turn, favour, help, service, aid.

kindred *noun* **1** *have no living kindred* kin, relatives, relations, family, people. *See* KIN. **2** *he did not know of the kindred between them* kinship, relationship, blood ties, family ties, consanguinity. *See* KINSHIP 1. **3** *there is a definite kindred between them* kinship, affinity, similarity, likeness, correspondence. *See* KINSHIP 2.

kindred *adjective* **1** *kindred members of the wedding party* related, connected, of the same blood, of the same family, consanguineous, cognate. **2** *kindred spirits enjoying the same things* like, similar, resembling, corresponding, matching, congenial, allied.

king *noun* **1** *crowned king of Sweden* monarch, sovereign, ruler, crowned head, majesty, royal personage, emperor, overlord, prince. *See table at* ROYALTY. **2** *king of jazz* leading light, luminary, star, superstar, kingpin; *inf.* big wheel, mogul.

kingdom noun **1** the ruler's kingdom realm, empire, domain, country, land, nation, state, province, territory. **2** the plant kingdom division, grouping, group, classification, class, category, family, genus, kind. **3** the headmaster's kingdom stops at the school gates sphere/field of influence, area of power, dominion, province, territory.

kink noun **1** a kink in the rope twist, bend, coil, corkscrew, curl, twirl, knot, tangle, entanglement. **2** a kink in one's hair curl, wave, crimp, frizz, crinkle. **3** a kink in the neck crick, spasm, twinge, tweak, stab of pain. **4** a few kinks in the plan flaw, defect, imperfection, hitch, snag, difficulty, complication. **5** a person full of kinks quirk, whim, whimsy, caprice, vagary, eccentricity, foible, idiosyncrasy, crotchet, fetish, deviation.

kinky adjective **1** a kinky rope twisted, bent, coiled, curled. See KINK 1. **2** kinky hair curly, wavy, crimped, frizzy, frizzed, crinkled. **3** kinky ideas quirky, peculiar, odd, strange, queer, bizarre, eccentric, idiosyncratic, weird, outlandish, unconventional, unorthodox, whimsical, capricious, fanciful; inf. way-out, far out. **4** kinky sexual habits perverted, warped, deviant, deviative, unnatural, abnormal, depraved, degenerate, lascivious, licentious, lewd, sadistic, masochistic.

kinsfolk noun kin, relatives, relations, family, kindred. See KIN.

kinship noun **1** kinship was thought more of than friendship blood relationship, relationship, blood ties, family ties, consanguinity, common ancestry, common lineage, kindred. **2** a kinship between the friends | kinship between their interests affinity, similarity, likeness, correspondence, kindred, concordance, alliance, association, equivalence, parallelism, symmetry.

kiosk noun booth, stand, news-stand, stall, bookstall; telephone kiosk, refreshments kiosk.

kismet noun destiny, fate, fortune, providence, portion, lot, one's lot in life, what is to come, what is written in the stars, the writing on the wall, God's will, predestination, preordination, predetermination, doom.

kiss verb **1** friends/lovers kissing | she kissed him | he kissed her hand salute/greet with the lips, brush the lips against, blow a kiss to, osculate; inf. peck, give a peck to, give a smacker to, smooch, canoodle, neck, snog. **2** the branches kissed the lake caress, brush lightly against, brush against, touch gently, graze, glance off.

kiss noun **1** exchange kisses salutations/greetings with the lips, hand kiss, osculation; inf. peck, smacker, smooch, snog. **2** the kiss of the flowers against her cheeks light/gentle touch, brush, graze, glance.

kit noun **1** a plumber's kit | bicycle repair kit equipment, apparatus, set of tools, tools, implements, instruments, utensils, gear, tackle, supplies, paraphernalia, accoutrements, effects, stuff, trappings, appurtenances; inf. things, the necessary. **2** football kit outfit, clothing, dress, uniform, colours; inf. rig-out,

gear, strip. **3** build furniture from a kit set of parts, set of components; DIY kit, do-it-yourself kit.

kit verb **kit out** kit out the children with sports equipment equip, supply, provide, fit out, fix up, furnish, outfit, deck out, rig out, arm, accoutre.

kitchen noun kitchenette, galley, cookhouse, bakehouse, scullery.

kittenish adjective playful, frolicsome, frisky, cute, coquettish, coy.

knack noun talent, aptitude, aptness, gift, flair, bent, forte, ability, capability, capacity, expertise, expertness, skill, skilfulness, genius, facility, propensity, dexterity, adroitness, readiness, quickness, ingenuity, proficiency, competence, handiness.
Opposites INABILITY; blind spot.

knave noun scoundrel, blackguard, villain, rogue, reprobate, miscreant, cheat, swindler, rascal, wrongdoer, evildoer, wretch, cur, louse, devil, dastard; inf. rotter, bounder.

knavery noun knavishness, villainy, baseness, roguery, unscrupulousness, cheating, swindling, duplicity, double-dealing, chicanery, deceit, deception, fraud, trickery, rascality, wrongdoing, evildoing, corruption.

knead verb knead the dough | the masseur kneaded his body work, manipulate, press, squeeze, massage, rub, form, shape.

kneel verb knelt before the altar get down on one's knees, fall to one's knees, genuflect, bow, bow down, stoop, make obeisance, kowtow.

knell noun **1** hear the knell of the church bells toll, tolling, ring, ringing, peal, chime, sound, resounding, death-knell. **2** the knell of their way of life death-knell, end, beginning of the end, presage of the end.

knell verb **1** funeral bells knelling toll, ring, peal, chime, sound, resound. **2** the drawing of the curtains knelled the end of the day herald, announce, proclaim, augur.

knickers plural noun pants, panties, briefs, bikini briefs, underpants, drawers, bloomers, underwear, lingerie, Directoire knickers, camiknickers; inf. smalls.

knick-knack noun showy ornament, piece of bric-à-brac, trifle, trinket, bauble, gewgaw, gimcrack, bagatelle, kickshaw, bibelot, plaything.

knife noun stab the victim with a knife blade, cutting tool. See table.

knife verb knife the victim to death stab, pierce, run through, impale, bayonet, transfix, cut, slash, lacerate, wound.

knight noun knights went off to the Crusades horseman, equestrian, cavalryman, gallant, knight errant, Sir Galahad, lord.

knit verb **1** knit wool into a sweater loop, weave, interweave, crochet. See table. See also table at WEAVE. **2** knit one's brows wrinkle, crease, furrow, gather, draw in, contract. **3** the tragedy knitted the community together join, link, bind,

KNIVES		
bayonet	hunting-	poniard
bowie knife	knife	scalpel
bread-knife	jackknife	sheath knife
bush knife	kitchen	skean-dhu
carving	knife	skiver
knife	kris	Stanley
clasp-knife	kukri	knife™
cleaver	machete	steak knife
craft knife	panga	stiletto
dagger	parang	Swiss Army
dirk	paring-knife	knife™
fish-knife	penknife	switchblade
flick knife	pocket knife	table knife

KNITTING STITCHES	
cable stitch	ribbing
garter stitch	shell-stitch
moss stitch	slip-stitch
plain stitch	stocking stitch
purl stitch	trellis stitch

unite, draw together, ally. **4** *the wound is knitting* draw together, heal, mend, become whole.

knit *noun wearing a brightly coloured knit* sweater, jumper, pullover, jersey, cardigan; *inf.* cardi, woolly.

knob *noun* **1** *turn the knob on the door/machine* doorknob, handle, door-handle, switch, on/off switch. **2** *iron knobs on the saddle* stud, boss, protuberance, knop. **3** *knobs on the tree* knot, knar, knur, knurl, gnarl, excrescence, protuberance. **4** *knobs on the backs of her hands* bump, bulge, swelling, lump, knot, node, nodule, pustule, growth, tumour, protuberance, tumescence. **5** *a knob of coal* lump, nub, nubble.

knock *verb* **1** *knock on/at the door* tap, rap, bang, pound, hammer. **2** *knock his head with her fist* strike, hit, slap, smack, box, punch, cuff, buffet, thump, thwack, batter, pummel; *inf.* clip, clout, wallop. **3** *knock against the sideboard* knock into, bang into, bump into, collide with, run into, crash into, crash against, smash into, dash against, jolt. **4** *knock the play* criticize, find fault with, take apart, take to pieces, pick holes in, run down, shoot down, carp at, cavil at, deprecate, belittle, disparage, minimize, censure, condemn; *inf.* slam, lambaste, pan. **knock about/around 1** *men knocking their wives around* strike, hit, beat, beat up, batter, maul, punch, mistreat, maltreat, illtreat, abuse, manhandle, hurt, cause injury to, injure, bruise, wound, damage. **2** *knock about the countryside for a while* travel, wander, roam, ramble, rove, range, saunter, stroll, jaunt, gallivant, traipse, gad. **knock down 1** *knock down the buildings* demolish, pull down, level, raze. **2** *knock down the trees* fell, cut down, hew. **3** *knock down his opponent* knock to the floor, floor, throw to the ground. **4** *knock down the prices/goods* lower, bring down, put down, decrease, reduce, slash. **knock into 1** *knock into his car* knock against, bang into, bump into, collide with, run into, crash into, crash against, smash into, dash against, jolt. **2** *I knocked into her yesterday* run into, meet by chance, come across, encounter, chance upon, happen upon, stumble upon; *inf.* bump into. **knock off 1** *they knock off at 5 o'clock* stop work, finish work, finish working, finish the working day, clock off, close shop, shut down; *inf.* call it a day. **2** *knock off smoking | knock it off!* stop, finish, give up, terminate, conclude,

bring to an end. **3** *knock off his rival* kill, slay, murder, assassinate, do away with, get rid of, dispose of, finish off; *inf.* do in, bump off, top. **4** *knock off goods from the lorry* steal, rob, thieve, filch, pilfer, purloin; *inf.* pinch, nick, lift. **knock out 1** *knock him out with the blow* render unconscious, floor, prostrate; *inf.* KO, kayo, knock cold, put out cold. **2** *knock out his opponent in the first round* eliminate, defeat, beat, vanquish, overthrow. **3** *the storm knocked out the electrical supply* make inoperative, put out of order, destroy, damage. **4** *walking that far knocked her out* knock up, exhaust, wear out, tire out, tire, overtire, fatigue, weary, enervate, fag out, debilitate, make ill; *inf.* do in, poop. **5** *they were knocked out by her performance* overwhelm, dazzle, amaze, astound, impress, affect deeply; *inf.* bowl over. **knock up 1** *knock up some food/shelves* put together quickly, prepare hastily, build rapidly, improvise, devise, jerrybuild. **2** *the hard work knocked him up* knock out, exhaust, wear out, tire out, fatigue, enervate, debilitate. See KNOCK *verb* knock out 4. **3** *we knocked up 1000 miles on the journey* achieve, reach, make, attain; *inf.* clock up. **4** *the housekeeper knocked up the maids in the morning* wake up, call, awaken, rouse, get up, get out of bed. **5** *he was accused of knocking up the young girl* make pregnant, impregnate, get with child, inseminate; *inf.* get in the club, put up the spout/stick/duff, put one in the oven of. **6** *they're knocking up before the tennis match* practise, have a practice game, warm up, hit a ball around.

knock *noun* **1** *a knock at the door* tap, rap, rat-tat, rat-tat-tat, bang. See KNOCK *verb* 1. **2** *a knock on the ear* slap, smack, blow, box, punch, cuff, buffet, thump, thwack; *inf.* clip, clout, wallop. See KNOCK *verb* 2. **3** *the knock damaged the car* collision, crash, bang, bump, smash, thud, jolt. See KNOCK *verb* 3. **4** *the knocks of the reviewers* criticism, strictures, fault-finding, carping, cavilling, deprecation, disparagement, censure, condemnation; *inf.* slamming, lambasting, panning. See KNOCK *verb* 4. **5** *receive many knocks in her life* set-back, reversal, rebuff, rejection, misfortune, bad luck, defeat, failure.

knockout *noun* **1** *win the boxing match by a knockout* finishing blow, coup de grâce; *inf.* KO, kayo. See KNOCK *verb* knock out 1. **2** *take part in a knockout elimination contest/competition.* See KNOCK *verb* knock out 2. **3** *her outfit/performance was a knockout* sensation, hit, smash hit, success, triumph, winner, attraction, coup, master stroke.

knoll *noun* hillock, hill, hummock, elevation, mound, hump, knob, barrow.

knot *noun* **1** *a knot in the string/tie* loop, twist, bend, intertwinement, interlacement, ligature, joint. *See table.* **2** *a knot in the wood* lump, knob, node, nodule, protuberance, knur, knurl, knar, gnarl. **3** *a knot of trees* clump, cluster. **4** *a knot of people* group, cluster, bunch, band, circle, ring, gathering, company, throng, crowd, flock, gang, assemblage, mob, pack.

KNOTS	
bend	mesh knot
Blackwall hitch	overhand knot
bow	prusik
bowknot	reef knot
bowline	rolling hitch
bowline on the bight	round turn and two
carrick bend	half hitches
cat's-paw	running bowline
clove hitch	running knot
diamond knot	sailor's knot
Englishman's tie	sheepshank
figure-of-eight	sheet bend
knot	shroud-knot
fisherman's bend	slip-knot
fisherman's knot	square knot
granny knot	surgeon's knot
half hitch	thumb knot
hangman's knot	timber hitch
harness hitch	true-love knot
hawser-bend	Turk's head
Hercules knot	wall-knot
hitch	wale-knot
loop-knot	water-knot
love-knot	weaver's knot
Matthew Walker	Windsor knot

knot *verb* *knot the rope to the pier* tie, loop, bind, secure, tether, lash, leash.

knotty *adjective* **1** *a knotty problem* difficult, complicated, intricate, complex, Byzantine, thorny, perplexing, baffling, mystifying, obscure, unfathomable. **2** *a knotty piece of wood* knotted, gnarled, knurled, lumpy, bumpy, nodose, nodular, rough, coarse. **3** *a knotty piece of thread* knotted, tangled, entangled, twisted, ravelled.

know *verb* **1** *know what they are saying* be aware of, notice, perceive, realize, be conscious of, be cognizant of, sense, recognize; *inf.* latch on to. **2** *know the rules* have knowledge of, understand, comprehend, apprehend, be conversant with, be familiar with, be acquainted with, have memorized, have learned by heart. **3** *have known tragedy* be familiar with, be acquainted with, experience, undergo, go through. **4** *do you know her husband?* | *get to know one's neighbours* have met, be acquainted with, have dealings with, associate with, be friends with, socialize with, fraternize with, be intimate with, be close to, be on good terms with; *inf.* be thick with; *Scots* ken. **5** *know one brand from another* distinguish, differentiate, tell, tell which is which, identify, make out, discern.
Opposites IGNORE; MISUNDERSTAND.

know-how *noun* knowledge, savoir faire, expertise, expertness, skill, skilfulness, proficiency, adeptness, dexterity, adroitness, aptitude, ability, capability, competence, faculty, knack, talent, gift, flair, bent, ingenuity.
Opposites INABILITY; IGNORANCE.

knowing *adjective* **1** *give a knowing look* astute, shrewd, perceptive, meaningful, well-informed, significant, eloquent, expressive. **2** *a knowing little girl* aware, astute, shrewd, perceptive, sophisticated, worldly, worldly-wise. **3** *a knowing infringement of rules* conscious, intentional, intended, deliberate, wilful, purposeful, calculated, on purpose, by design.
Opposites INGENUOUS; INNOCENT; ACCIDENTAL.

knowingly *adverb* *would not knowingly hurt them* consciously, willingly, intentionally, deliberately, wilfully, purposefully, on purpose, by design, calculatedly.

knowledge *noun* **1** *be taught by people of knowledge* learning, erudition, scholarship, letters, education, enlightenment, wisdom. **2** *his knowledge of the subject* understanding, grasp, comprehension, apprehension, cognition, adeptness, skill, expertise, proficiency, know-how, savoir faire. **3** *his knowledge of the area* acquaintanceship, familiarity, conversance. **4** *where do you acquire the knowledge?* information, facts, intelligence, data, news, reports, rumours.
Opposites IGNORANCE; ILLITERACY.

knowledgeable *adjective* **1** *knowledgeable people* well-informed, informed, educated, learned, erudite, scholarly, well-read, cultured, cultivated, enlightened. **2** *knowledgeable about the workings of the machine* having a knowledge of, acquainted with, familiar with, experienced in, expert in, conversant with, having an understanding of.

known *adjective* *a known fact* recognized, acknowledged, admitted, declared, proclaimed, avowed, confessed, published, revealed.
Opposites UNKNOWN; SECRET.

kowtow *verb* **1** *slaves kowtowing to their masters* bow, kneel, genuflect, prostrate oneself, throw oneself at the feet of, humble oneself to. **2** *he's always kowtowing to management* grovel, fawn, pay court, curry favour, bow and scrape, toady; *inf.* suck up to, lick the boots of.

kudos *noun* prestige, glory, acclaim, acclamation, praise, extolment, approbation, tribute, honour.
Opposites infamy; DISHONOUR.

Ll

label noun **1** *put a label on the luggage/goods* identification tag, ID tag, tag, ticket, tab, sticker, marker, docket. **2** *he resented his label of "four eyes"* epithet, name, nickname, title, sobriquet, designation, denomination, description, characterization. **3** *goods sold under the label of a famous department store* brand, brand name, tradename, trade mark, proprietary name, logo.

label verb **1** *label the specimens* attach labels to, tag, tab, ticket, stamp, mark, put stickers on, docket. **2** *label him a liar* describe, designate, identify, classify, class, categorize, brand, call, name, term, dub.

laboratory noun. See table.

LABORATORY EQUIPMENT

alembic	filter funnel
aludel	fume cupboard
aspirator	gas jar
balance	graduated flask
Beckmann ther-	Kipp's apparatus
mometer	Leibig condenser
Bunsen burner	measuring cylinder
burette	pipette
capillary tube	pneumatic trough
centrifuge	reagent bottle
condenser	receiver
crucible	reflux condenser
deflagrating spoon	spatula
Erlenmeyer flask	thermometer
evaporating dish	U-tube

laborious adjective **1** *a laborious task* hard, heavy, difficult, arduous, strenuous, fatiguing, tiring, wearying, wearisome, tedious. **2** *laborious students* painstaking, careful, meticulous, diligent, assiduous, industrious, hard-working, scrupulous, persevering, pertinacious, zealous. **3** *the laborious style of the writer* laboured, strained, forced. See LABOURED 2.
Opposites EASY; SIMPLE; EFFORTLESS; NATURAL.

labour noun **1** *paid well for his labour* work, employment, job, toil, exertion, effort, industry, industriousness, hard work, hard labour, travail, drudgery, slog, donkey-work, sweat of one's brow, menial work; *inf.* grind, sweat. **2** *the labours of Hercules* task, job, chore, undertaking, commission, assignment, charge, venture. See table. **3** *a lack of labour in the area* potential employees, employees, workers, workmen, workforce, working people, hands, labourers. **4** *in labour for many hours having the child* childbirth, birth, parturition, child delivery, delivery, birth contractions, contractions, labour pains, labour pangs, labour throes, travail.

labour verb **1** *labour for little reward* work hard, work away, toil, slave away, drudge, grub away, plod on/away, grind/sweat/away, struggle, strive, drudge away, exert oneself, overwork, travail, work like a slave, work one's fingers to the bone, work like a Trojan; *inf.* kill oneself, plug away. **2** *labour the point* belabour, overemphasize, lay too much emphasis on, overdo, strain, overelaborate, dwell on, expound on, expand. **3** *labour to finish on time/labour for victory* strive, struggle, endeavour, work, make every effort, do one's best, do one's utmost. **4** *labour under universal disapproval | labouring under a delusion* suffer from, be a victim of, be burdened by, be overburdened by, be disadvantaged by. **5** *ships labouring on heavy seas* roll, pitch, heave, toss, turn.

laboured adjective **1** *laboured breathing* difficult, strained, forced, heavy, awkward. **2** *a laboured style of writing* contrived, affected, studied, stiff, strained, stilted, forced, unnatural, artificial, overdone, overworked, heavy, ponderous, ornate, elaborate, overelaborate, intricate, convoluted, complex, laborious.
Opposites EASY; NATURAL.

labourer noun worker, workman, navvy, working man, hand, manual worker, unskilled worker, blue-collar worker, drudge, menial.

labyrinth noun **1** *a labyrinth in the grounds | the office is a labyrinth of passages* maze, warren, network, circuitous course, winding, coil, convolution, twisting and turning, meander, meandering, entanglement. **2** *the plot of the book was a labyrinth* entanglement, tangle, jungle, snarl, intricacy, confusion, perplexity, complication, puzzle, riddle, enigma, problem.

labyrinthine adjective **1** *labyrinthine paths* maze-like, meandering, winding, wandering, twisting, circuitous, tangled. **2** *labyrinthine plots* intricate, complicated, complex, involved, tortuous, convoluted, tangled, entangled, confusing, puzzling, perplexing, mystifying, bewildering, baffling.

lace noun **1** *a covering made of lace* filigree, meshwork, openwork, tatting, netting. **2** *fasten the shoes/bodice with laces* shoelace, bootlace, lacing, string, cord, thong, twine, tie.

THE LABOURS OF HERCULES

Nemean lion	Cretan Bull
Lernaean Hydra	Horses of Diomedes
Wild Boar of Ery-	Girdle of Hippolyte
manthus	Cattle of Geryon
Hind of Ceryneia	Cerberus
Stymphalian Birds	Golden Apples of
Augean Stables	Hesperides

lace verb **1** *lace the shoes/bodice* lace up, do up, fasten, secure, close, bind, tie, twine, thread, string. **2** *lace their fingers* interweave, twine, intertwine. **3** *lace her into a corset* compress, confine, constrict, squeeze. **4** *the sunset lacing the sky with colour* streak, stripe, striate, band. **5** *lace the coffee with brandy* mix, blend, flavour, fortify, strengthen, stiffen; *inf.* spike. **lace into 1** *lace into the members of the other gang* set about, set upon, fall upon, attack, assault, assail, beat, strike, thrash, thresh, tear into; *inf.* lay into, sail into, belt. **2** *lace into the child for unpunctuality* scold, chide, berate, upbraid, castigate, condemn, harangue, rant at, rave at; *inf.* pitch into, lambaste.

lacerate verb **1** *lacerate her hand on barbed wire* tear, gash, slash, cut, cut open, rip, rend, mangle, mutilate, hurt, wound, injure, maim. **2** *the parting lacerated her feelings* hurt, wound, distress, harrow, torture, torment, afflict, crucify.

laceration noun **1** *the laceration of her hand* tearing, gashing, slashing. *See* LACERATE 1. **2** *a bleeding laceration on the animal's back* tear, gash, slash, cut, rip, rent, mutilation, wound, injury.

lachrymose adjective tearful, weeping, crying, sobbing, with tears in the eyes, close to tears, on the verge of tears, sad, mournful, woeful, lugubrious, dolorous; *inf.* weepy.

lack noun *a lack of food/talent* absence, want, need, deprivation, deficiency, privation, dearth, insufficiency, shortage, shortness, scarcity, scarceness, paucity. **Opposites** ABUNDANCE; EXCESS; SUFFICIENCY.

lack verb *they lack food* be lacking, be without, have need of, need, stand in need of, require, want, feel the want of, be short of, be deficient in, miss.

lackadaisical adjective apathetic, listless, languid, languorous, lethargic, limp, sluggish, enervated, spiritless, unanimated, indifferent, half-hearted, lukewarm, uninterested, unenthusiastic, idle, lazy, indolent, inert. **Opposites** ENTHUSIASTIC; EXCITED.

lackey noun **1** *rich men and their lackeys* toady, sycophant, flatterer, fawner, flunkey, minion, doormat, stooge, hanger-on, parasite, camp-follower, tool, puppet, instrument, pawn, creature, cat's-paw; *inf.* yes-man, bootlicker. **2** *tales of the emperor and his lackeys* flunkey, footman, manservant, valet, liveried servant, steward, equerry.

lacklustre adjective **1** *lacklustre prose* bland, insipid, vapid, dull, flat, dry, prosaic, run-of-the-mill, commonplace, matter-of-fact, unimaginative, uninspired, uninteresting, boring, tedious, wearisome. **2** *lacklustre people* dull, uninteresting, boring, unimaginative, apathetic, spiritless, unanimated, dull-witted, vacuous.

laconic adjective **1** *a laconic reply* brief, concise, terse, succinct, short, economical, elliptical, crisp, pithy, to the point, incisive, abrupt, blunt, curt. **2** *a laconic person* of few words, untalkative, uncommunicative, reticent, reserved, taciturn, quiet, silent. **Opposites** VERBOSE; GARRULOUS; LONG-WINDED.

lad noun **1** *when he was just a lad* boy, schoolboy, youth, juvenile, youngster, stripling, young man; *inf.* kid, little shaver; *Scots* laddie. **2** *who's that lad over there?* boy, man, fellow; *inf.* chap, guy, bloke.

ladder noun **1** *climb the ladder to the loft* stepladder, set of steps; kitchen steps, loft ladder, folding ladder, rope ladder, Jacob's ladder. **2** *the social/career ladder* hierarchy, scale, set of stages, stratification, pecking order.

laden adjective *women laden with shopping* loaded, burdened, heavily-laden, weighed down, weighted, fully charged, encumbered, hampered, oppressed, taxed.

ladle noun *a soup ladle* spoon, scoop, dipper, bailer.

ladle verb *ladle out the soup/water* spoon out, scoop out, dish up/out, bail out.

lady noun **1** *give that lady your seat* woman, female; young woman, old woman. **2** *the lady and her servants* noblewoman, gentlewoman, duchess, countess, peeress, viscountess, baroness.

ladylike adjective genteel, refined, well-bred, cultivated, polished, decorous, proper, correct, respectable, well-mannered, courteous, polite, civil, gracious.

lag verb **1** *lag behind in the race* fall behind, fall back, trail, not keep pace, bring up the rear. **2** *stop lagging and keep up* loiter, linger, dally, straggle, dawdle, hang back, delay, move slowly, drag one's feet; *inf.* dilly-dally. **3** *their efforts were lagging* flag, wane, ebb, fall off, diminish, decrease, ease up, let up, slacken, abate, fail, falter, grow faint.

laggard noun loiterer, lingerer, dawdler, straggler, sluggard, snail, delayer, idler, slowcoach, loafer, lounger; *inf.* lazybones.

lagoon noun pool, pond, lake, reservoir, tarn; *Scots* loch; *Am.* bayou.

laid-back adjective relaxed, at ease, easy, leisurely, unhurried, casual, easygoing, free and easy, informal, nonchalant, unexcitable, imperturbable; *inf.* unflappable. **Opposites** NERVOUS; TENSE; EDGY.

laid up adjective *mother's been laid up for ten days* bedridden, ill in bed, housebound, immobilized, incapacitated, disabled, ill, sick, ailing, on the sick-list, out of action.

lair noun **1** *the animal's lair* tunnel, dugout, hollow, cave, haunt. *See table.* **2** *retreat to his lair in the house* retreat, hideaway, refuge, sanctuary, sanctum, sanctum sanctorum, study, den, snug; *inf.* hide-out.

laissez-faire noun *believe in laissez-faire* free enterprise, private enterprise, individualism, free trade, non-intervention, non-interference, non-involvement, indifference.

laissez-faire adjective *a laissez-faire attitude* non-interventional, non-interfering, non-restrictive, uninvolved, indifferent, lax, loose, permissive, live-and-let-live.

lake noun pond, tarn, pool, reservoir, lagoon; *Scots* loch; *dial.* lough; *Am.* bayou. *See table.*

LAIRS AND HOMES OF ANIMALS

Lair	Animal	Lair	Animal
anthill	ant	earth	fox
aquarium	fish	eyrie	eagle
aviary	bird	fold	sheep
beehive	bee	form	hare
burrow	rabbit/	hole	fox
	fox	holt	otter
byre	cow	kennel	dog
coop	chicken	sett	badger
covert	game	stable	horse
den	lion	sty	pig
dovecote	dove	warren	rabbit
drey	squirrel		

lambaste *verb* **1** *cruel masters lambasting the slaves* beat, thrash, flog, lash, drub, strike, thump, thwack, batter, hammer, pummel; *inf.* wallop, clout, paste, lace into. **2** *lambaste the children for being late* scold, reprimand, rebuke, chide, reprove, admonish, berate, upbraid, rail at, rant at; *inf.* lace into, pitch into.

lame *adjective* **1** *a lame man/leg* limping, hobbling, halting, crippled, game, disabled, incapacitated, defective; *inf.* gammy. **2** *a lame excuse* weak, feeble, thin, flimsy, unconvincing, unsatisfactory, inadequate, insufficient, deficient, defective, ineffectual.

lament *verb* **1** *widows lamenting* mourn, grieve, sorrow, wail, moan, groan, weep, cry, sob, complain, keen, ululate, howl, beat one's breast. **2** *lamenting the lack of sports facilities* complain about, bemoan, bewail, deplore.

lament *noun* **1** *the laments of the bereaved* wail, wailing, lamentation, moan, moaning, groan, weeping, crying, sob, sobbing, complaint, keening, ululation, howl. **2** *play/recite a lament* dirge, requiem, elegy, monody, threnody; *Scots* coronach.

lamentable *adjective* **1** *a lamentable state of affairs* deplorable, regrettable, tragic, terrible, wretched, woeful, sorrowful, distressing, grievous. **2** *a lamentable salary* miserable, pitiful, poor, meagre, low, unsatisfactory, inadequate; *inf.* measly.

lamentation *noun* lament, wail, wailing, moaning, weeping, keening. See LAMENT *noun* 1.

lamp *noun* **1** *all the lamps were lit* light, lantern; table lamp, standard lamp, night-light, foglamp, oil-lamp, gas lamp, light-bulb. **2** *see the lamps of a car* headlight, headlamp, sidelight, fog light, fog-lamp, tail-light, brake light.

lampoon *noun* satire, burlesque, travesty, parody, skit, caricature, pasquinade, squib, take-off; *inf.* send-up.

lampoon *verb* satirize, parody, caricature, ridicule, mock, make fun of, burlesque, pasquinade, take off, do a take-off of; *inf.* send up.

lance *noun* **1** *a knight's lance* spear, pike, javelin. **2** *a doctor's lance* scalpel, knife, lancet.

lance *verb* *lance the boil* cut, cut open, slit, incise, puncture, prick, stab.

land *noun* **1** *glad to be back on land* dry land, ground, solid ground, earth, terra firma. **2** *the land is fertile there* soil, earth, loam, dirt. **3** *prefer working on the land to working in town* farmland, agricultural land, country, countryside, rural areas. **4** *houses with plenty of land around them* ground, fields, open space, open area, expanse, stretch, tract, unbuilt land, green area, green belt. **5** *he owns all the land here* property, ground, acres, estate, realty, real property. **6** *born in a far land* country, nation, fatherland, motherland, state, realm, province, territory, district, region, area, domain.

land *verb* **1** *the plane landed* touch down, alight, make a landing, come in to land. **2** *the pilot landed the plane* make a landing, bring down, put down, take down. **3** *the ship landed at Dover* berth, dock, reach the shore. **4** *we landed at Dover* berth, dock, reach the shore, go ashore, disembark, debark. **5** *how did we land up here?* arrive, get, reach, find oneself, end up, turn up; *inf.* wind up. **6** *his behaviour landed him in jail* bring, lead, cause to go to, cause to arrive in. **7** *land a good job* get, acquire, obtain, procure, secure, gain, net, win, carry off. **8** *land a blow* deal, deliver, deposit, give, catch; *inf.* fetch.

landlady, landlord *noun* **1** *the landlord of the pub* publican, pub-owner, innkeeper, hotel-keeper, hotelier, host, mine host. **2** *the landlord of the rented flats* owner, proprietor, lessor, householder, freeholder.

landmark *noun* **1** *one of the landmarks of the town* distinctive feature, prominent feature, feature, monument. **2** *a landmark in the town's history* milestone, watershed, turning-point, turning, critical point, crisis, historic event. **3** *landmarks dividing the two estates* marker, demarcator, boundary line, boundary fence, pale, picket. **4** *landmarks indicating the distance* milepost, milestone, guidepost, cairn.

NATURAL LAKES

Lake	Location
Baikal	Russia
Balkhash	Kazakhstan
Bangweulu	Zambia
Erie	Canada/U.S.A.
Eyre	Australia
Great Bear	Canada
Great Slave	Canada
Huron	U.S.A./Canada
Ladoga	Russia
Maracaibo	Venezuela
Michigan	U.S.A.
Nicaragua	Nicaragua
Nyasa	Malawi/Tanzania/ Mozambique
Onega	Russia
Ontario	Canada/U.S.A.
Superior	U.S.A./Canada
Tanganyika	Zaïre/Burundi/Tanzania/ Zambia
Titicaca	Peru/Bolivia
Victoria	Uganda/Tanzania/Kenya
Winnipeg	Canada

landscape noun countryside, scene, scenery, outlook, view, aspect, prospect, vista, panorama, perspective.

landslide noun **1** killed in a landslide avalanche, landslip, rockfall. **2** win an election by a landslide decisive victory, runaway victory, overwhelming majority.

lane noun **1** travel through the lanes narrow road, narrow way, passageway, passage, alley, path, pathway, footpath, track. **2** traffic lanes track, course, road-division.

language noun **1** children acquiring language speech, speaking, talking, words, vocabulary, utterance, verbal expression, verbalization, vocalization, communication, conversation, converse, discourse, interchange. **2** the French language tongue, speech, parlance, mother tongue, native tongue; inf. lingo. See tables. See also table at NORTH AMERICAN INDIAN. **3** various forms of language found throughout the country/world speech, dialect, vernacular, regionalism, provincialism, localism, rhyming slang, patois, lingua franca, barbarism, vulgarism, colloquialism, informal language, slang, idiom, idiolect, jargon, patter, cant, legalese, medicalese, journalese, newspeak, bureaucratese, pidgin English; inf. lingo, gobbledegook. **4** admire the language of the speaker/writer vocabulary, terminology, wording, phrasing, phraseology, style, diction, expression, manner of writing/speaking, rhetoric.

languid adjective **1** a languid young woman languishing, listless, languorous, lackadaisical, spiritless, vigourless, lacking energy, lethargic, torpid, idle, inactive, inert, indolent, lazy, sluggish, slow-moving, unenthusiastic, apathetic, indifferent. **2** feeling languid after her illness weak, weakly, sickly, faint, feeble, frail, limp, flagging, drooping, fatigued, enervated, debilitated. **3** a languid response apathetic, lukewarm, half-hearted, unenthusiastic, bored, passive. **Opposites** ENERGETIC; VIGOROUS.

languish verb **1** she languished after his departure droop, flag, wilt, wither, fade, fail, weaken, decline, go into a decline, waste away; inf. go downhill. **2** people languishing away in institutions waste away, rot, decay, wither away, be abandoned, be neglected, be forgotten, be disregarded. **3** languish for her lover pine for, yearn for, long for, sigh for, hunger for, desire, want, mope for, repine for, grieve for, mourn for.

languor noun **1** feeling full of languor in the heat listlessness, lethargy, torpor, idleness, inactivity, inertia, indolence, laziness, sluggishness, sleepiness, drowsiness, somnolence, dreaminess, relaxation. **2** disturb the languor of the atmosphere stillness, tranquillity, calm, calmness, lull, silence, windlessness.

lank adjective **1** lank hair lifeless, lustreless, limp, straggling, straight, long. **2** lank youths tall, thin, lean, lanky, skinny, spindly, gangling, gangly, scrawny, scraggy, angular, bony, gaunt, raw-boned, gawky, rangy; inf. weedy.

lap[1] noun **1** sit on mother's lap knee, knees. **2** live in the lap of luxury security, secureness, safety, protection, refuge, comfort. **3** the arrangements are in your lap responsibility, charge, task, job, obligation.

lap[2] noun **1** three laps of the stadium circuit, circle, loop, orbit, round, compass, ambit. **2** the last lap of the journey round, tour, section, stage.

lap[3] verb **1** lap blankets around her wrap, wind, fold, twist. **2** lap her in blankets wrap, swathe, cover, envelop, enfold, encase, wind, swaddle.

lap[4] verb **1** water lapping against the shore wash, splash, beat, swish, slap, plash, slosh. **2** cats lapping milk drink up, drink, lick up, sip, sup.

lapse noun **1** forgive his occasional lapse slip, error, mistake, blunder, failing, fault, failure, omission, oversight, negligence, dereliction; inf. slip-up. **2** after a lapse of time interval, gap, pause, intermission, interlude, lull, hiatus, break, passage. **3** a lapse in standards decline,

LANGUAGE GROUPS AND FAMILIES

Afro-Asiatic	Brythonic/Brittonic	Gur	Lenapi	Penutian	Slavonic/Slavic
Algonquian	Bushman	Hamitic	Malayo-Polynesian	Permic	Sudanic
Altaic	Caddoan	Hamito-Semitic	Mande	Piman	Tagalic
Anatolian	Canaanitic	Hellenic	Mayan	Polynesian	Teutonic
Araucanian	Carib	Indic	Melanesian	Rhaeto-Romance	Thraco-Phrygian
Arawakan	Caucasian	Indo-European	Micronesian	Romance	Tibeto-Burman
Aryan	Celtiberian	Indo-Germanic	Mongolic	Salish	Tungusic
Athapaskan	Celtic	Indo-Hittite	Mon-Khmer	Samoyed	Tupi-Guarani
Australian	Chadic	Indo-Iranian	Mosan	Sanskritic	Turanian
Austro-Asiatic	Chari-Nile	Indonesian	Munda	Scandinavian	Turkic
Austro-nesian	Chibchan	Indo-Pacific	Muskogean	Semi-Bantu	Ugric
Aymara	Chinese	Iranian	Na-Dene	Semitic	Ural-Altaic
Baltic	Cushitic	Iroquoian	Nahuatlan	Semito-Hamitic	Uralic
Balto-Slavonic	Dardic	Italic	Niger-Congo	Shona	Uto-Aztecan
Bantu	Dravidian	Kanuri	Nilo-Saharan	Sinitic	Voltaic
Benue-Congo	Ethiopic	Keresan	Nilotic	Sino-Tibetan	Wakashan
Berber	Finnic	Khoisan	Nootkan	Siouan	Yuman
	Finno-Ugric	Kordofanian	Panoan		
	Germanic	Kwa	Papuan		
	Goidelic				
	Guaycuru				

LANGUAGES

Abkhazian	Creole	Ibanag	Laotian/Lao	Norwegian	San
Achinese	Croatian	Ibibio	Lapp/	Nuba	Sandawe
Afrikaans	Czech	Ibo	Lappish	Nuer	Sango
Ainu	Danakil	Icelandic	Latin	Nupe	Sanskrit
Akkadian	Dani	Ido	Latvian	Nyanja	Santali
Akan	Danish	Igbo	Laz	Nyamwezi	Sardinian
Albanian	Dinka	Ijo	Lepcha	Nyasa	Sasak
Aleut	Divehi	Ila	Lesghian	Nyoro	Sauk
Amharic	Duala	Ingush	Limbu	Occitan	Scythian
Andaman	Dusun	Inuktitut	Lingala	Oraon	Sebei
Anglo-	Dutch	Irish	Lithuanian	Oriya	Senoi
Saxon	Dyak	Italian	Livonian	Osmanli	Sepik
Annamese	Dyula	Japanese	Loma	Ossetian	Serbian
Arabic	Dzongkha	Javanese	Lozi	Ostyak	Serbo-
Aramaic	Edo	Jivaro	Luba	Otomi	Croat
Aranda	Efik	Kabardian	Luganda	Ovambo	Sesotho
Armenian	Egyptian	Kachin	Lugbara	Pahari	Setswana
Assamese	Elamite	Kalmuck/	Lunda	Pahlavi	Shan
Assyrian	English	Kalmyk	Luo	Palauan	Shelta
Avar	Estonian	Kamba	Lusatian	Palaung	Sherbro
Aymara	Etruscan	Kanarese	Lushai	Pali	Shilha
Azerbaijani	Ewe	Kannada	Lycaonian	Pampangan	Shilluk
Aztec	Faeroese	Kara-Kalpak	Lycian	Pangasinan	Shina
Babylonian	Fan	Karamojong	Macedonian	Panjabi/	Siamese
Bahasa	Fante	Karelian	Madurese	Punjabi	Sidamo
Indonesia	Farsi	Karen	Magyar	Pano	Sindebele
Bajau	Fijian	Kashmiri	Malagasy	Pashto	Sindhi
Balinese	Finnish	Kashubian	Malay	Peguan	Sinhalese
Baluchi	Flemish	Kawi	Malayalam	Persian	Slovak
Barotse	Fon	Kazakh	Malinke	Phoenician	Slovene
Bashkir	Formosan	Khalkha	Maltese	Phrygian	Sogdian
Basque	French	Khasi	Manchu	Pictish	Somali
Batak	Frisian	Khmer	Mandarin	Pintupi	Songhai
Beach-la-	Fulah	Kikongo	Manganja	Police Motu	Sorbian
mar	Fulani	Kikuyu	Manipuri	Polish	Sotho
Beja	Fulfulde	Kingwana	Manx	Portuguese	Spanish
Belorussian	Ga	Kirundi	Maori	Prakrit	Suk
Bemba	Gaelic	Kissi	Marathi	Provençal	Sukuma
Bengali	Galibi	Kiswahili	Marquesan	Prussian	Sulu
Bihari	Galician	Kolami	Marshallese	Punic	Sumerian
Bokmål	Galla	Komi	Masai	Quechua	Sundanese
Brahui	Garo	Kond	Mende	Quiché	Susu
Breton	Gaulish	Kongo	Messapic	Rai	Swahili
Bugis	Ge'ez	Konkani	Miao	Rajasthani	Swazi
Bulgarian	Georgian	Kono	Mingrelian	Rajmahali	Swedish
Burmese	German	Koranko	Mixtec	Rarotongan	Syriac
Buryat/	Gilbertese	Korean	Modoc	Rawang	Tagalog
Buriat	Gond	Korwa	Mon	Rejang	Tahitian
Cantonese	Gothic	Koryak	Mongol/	Rhaetian	Taino
Catalan	Greek	Krio	Mongolian	Riff	Taita
Chagatai	Guarani	Kru	Mordvin	Riksmål	Tajik
Chagga	Guaycuru	Kuki	Mossi	Romaic	Tamang
Chaldee/	Gujarati	Kumyk	Motu	Romanes	Tamashek
Chaldean	Gurkhali	Kurdish	Mysian	Romanian	Tamil
Chechen	Gurung	Kurukh	Naga	Romansch	Tatar
Cheremiss	Hausa	Kyrgyz/	Nama	Romany	Tehuelche
Chichewa	Hawaiian	Kirghiz	Ndebele	Ronga	Telugu
Chin	Hebrew	Ladino	Nenets	Russian	Temne
Chinese	Herero	Lai	Nepali	Ruthenian	Teso
Chinook	Himyaritic	Lahnda	Newari	Rwanda	Thai
Jargon	Hindi	Lamba	Ngbandi	Sabaean	Thracian
Chukchi	Hindustani	Lamut	Nguni	Sahaptin	Tibetan
Chuvash	Hittite	Langobardic	Nicobarese	Saharan	Ticuna
Circassian	Hmong	langue	Niuean	Sakai	Tigré
Congolese	Ho	d'oc	Nogay	Samal	Tigrinya
Coptic	Hottentot	langue	Norn	Samburu	Tiv
Cornish	Hungarian	d'oïl	Norse	Samoan	Tocharian

LANGUAGES *cont.*					
Toda	Tumbuka	Uduk	Venetic	Warao	Yao
Tolai	Tungus	Ugaritic	Veps	Warlpiri	Yenisei
Tonga	Tupi	Uigur	Vietnam-	Welsh	Yiddish
Tongan	Turkish	Ukrainian	ese	Wendish	Yoruba
Tshiluba	Turkmen	Urdu	Vogul	Wolof	Yupik
Tsonga	Tuva	Uzbek	Volapük	Xhosa	Zande
Tswana	Twi	Vai	Wa	Yaghnobi	Zulu
Tulu	Udmurt	Venda	Wapishana	Yakut	Zyrian

downturn, fall, falling, falling-away, slipping, drop, deterioration, worsening, degeneration, backsliding. **4** *the lapse of her season ticket* expiry, voiding, invalidity, termination. **5** *lapse of faith* abandonment, forsaking, relinquishment, defection, renunciation, repudiation, rejection, disavowal, denial, abjuration, apostasy.

lapse *verb* **1** *standards have lapsed* decline, fall, fall off, drop, deteriorate, worsen, degenerate; *inf.* go downhill, go to pot. **2** *our friendship lapsed when we left school* cease, end, come to an end, stop, terminate. **3** *the season ticket has lapsed* become void, become invalid, expire, run out, terminate, become obsolete. **4** *lapse into silence/sleep* slide, slip, drift, sink, subside, submerge. **5** *time has lapsed* elapse, pass, go by, go on, roll on, glide by, run its course.

lapsed *adjective* **1** *lapsed season tickets* void, invalid, expired, run out, out of date, terminated. **2** *lapsed traditions* obsolete, old, former, past, bygone, forgotten, extinct, outworn, abandoned. **3** *lapsed Christians* non-practising, lacking faith, backsliding, recidivist, apostate.

larceny *noun* theft, stealing, robbery, pilfering, purloining, burglary, misappropriation; *inf.* filching, nicking.

larder *noun* pantry, storage room, storeroom, store, still-room, cooler, scullery. *See table at* CUPBOARD.

large *adjective* **1** *large buildings/sums* big, great, of considerable size, sizeable, substantial, goodly, tall, high, huge, immense, enormous, colossal, massive, mammoth, vast, prodigious, gigantic, giant, monumental, stupendous, gargantuan, man-size, king-size, giant-size, outsize, considerable; *inf.* jumbo, whopping. **2** *a large man/woman* big, burly, heavy, bulky, thickset, powerfully built, heavyset, chunky, strapping, hulking, hefty, ample, fat, obese, corpulent. **3** *a large supply* abundant, copious, plentiful, ample, liberal, generous. **4** *take the large view*|*officials with large powers* wide, wide-ranging, large-scale, broad, extensive, far-reaching, sweeping, comprehensive, exhaustive. **at large 1** *wild animals are at large*|*some prisoners at large* at liberty, free, unconfined, unrestrained, roaming, on the loose, on the run, fugitive. **2** *society at large* as a whole, as a body, generally, in general, in the main. **3** *a report given at large* in detail, with full details, exhaustively, at length. **by and large** *by and large we are better off* on the whole, generally, in general, all things considered, taking everything into consideration, for

the most part, in the main, as a rule. *Opposites* SMALL; SLIGHT; MEAGRE.

largely *adverb* *he is largely to blame* to a large extent, to a great degree, chiefly, for the most part, mostly, mainly, in the main, principally, in great measure.

large-scale *adjective* **1** *a large-scale police search* extensive, wide-reaching, wide-ranging, sweeping, wholesale, global. **2** *large-scale prints* enlarged, blown-up, magnified.

largesse *noun* **1** *known for her largesse* generosity, kindness, liberality, open-handedness, munificence, bounty, bountifulness, beneficence, benefaction, altruism, charity, philanthropy, alms-giving. **2** *distributing largesse* gift, present, contribution, donation, handout, endowment, grant, aid, alms.

lark¹ *noun* *larks singing* skylark, meadowlark, songbird.

lark² *noun* *tired of the children's larks* prank, horseplay, trick, fooling, antic, mischief, escapade, fun, cavorting, caper, play, game, romp, frolic, sport, rollicking, gambol, jape, fling, skylark.

lark³ *verb* *children larking about* play pranks, indulge in horseplay, play tricks, fool about, make mischief, have fun, cavort, caper, play, romp, frolic, sport, rollick, gambol, disport, skylark.

lascivious *adjective* **1** *lascivious old men leering at girls* lewd, lecherous, lustful, licentious, promiscuous, libidinous, prurient, salacious, lubricious, concupiscent, debauched, depraved, degenerate, dissolute, dissipated. **2** *lascivious magazines/talk* lewd, blue, obscene, smutty, gross, bawdy, dirty, salacious; *inf.* raunchy.

lash *noun* **1** *produce a lash to beat the slaves* whip, horsewhip, bullwhip, scourge, flagellum, cat-o'-nine-tails, cat. **2** *six lashes with a whip*| *with one lash of his fist* stroke, stripe, blow, hit, strike, bang, thwack, thump; *inf.* swipe, wallop, whack.

lash *verb* **1** *lash the children with a whip/belt* whip, horsewhip, scourge, birch, switch, flog, flail, flagellate, thrash, beat, strike, batter, hammer; *inf.* wallop, whack, lam, lambaste. **2** *waves lashing the ship* buffet, pound, batter, beat against, dash against, smack against, strike, knock. **3** *lash him for his behaviour* berate, upbraid, castigate, scold, rebuke, chide, reprove, reproach, harangue, rant at, fulminate against, attack, censure, criticize, condemn, flay; *inf.* bawl out, pitch into, lambaste. **4** *lions lashing their tails* flick, wag, wave, whip, switch. **5** *lash the crowd to a frenzy* provoke, incite, arouse, excite, agitate, stir up, whip up, work up, egg on, goad. **6** *lash the boat to the side of the ship* fasten, bind, tie, tether, hitch, attach, join, rope, strap, leash, make fast, secure. **lash out 1** *lash out at his critics* speak out against, burst into angry speech at, shout at, lose one's temper at, attack verbally, attack physically, denounce, harangue, rant at, fulminate against, criticize, condemn, censure; *inf.* pitch/lace into. **2** *lash out on a new dress* spend lavishly, be extravagant, spend a lot of money; *inf.* push the boat out, go on a spending spree, go on a shopping binge.

lass *noun* girl, young woman, young lady, schoolgirl, maid, maiden, miss; *inf.* bird; *Scots* lassie; *Ir.* colleen.

last¹ *adjective* **1** *the last runner arrived* hindmost, rearmost, at the end, at the back, final, aftermost. **2** *his last words* final, closing, concluding, ending, finishing, terminating, ultimate, terminal. **3** *our last chance* final, only remaining, only one left. **4** *the last thing she would want* least likely, most unlikely, least suitable, least wanted, least favourite. **5** *last Thursday* latest, most recent. **the last word 1** *that is the chairman's last word on the subject* final statement, summation, ultimatum, final decision, definitive statement. **2** *have the last word in an argument* final remark, final say, closing statement, concluding remark. **3** *the last word in sports cars* most fashionable, most up-to-date, latest, newest, peak, best, epitome, quintessence, acme of perfection, cream, *crème de la crème, ne plus ultra, dernier cri.*
Opposites FIRST; INITIAL.

last² *adverb* *come last* at the end, at the rear, in the rear, behind, after.

last³ *noun* *stay to the last* end, ending, finish, close, conclusion, completion, finale, termination, the bitter end. **at last** in the end, finally, eventually, at length, ultimately, in conclusion.

last⁴ *verb* **1** *how long will the symptoms last?* continue, go on, carry on, remain, persist, keep on. **2** *how long will the climbers last in the snow?* survive, exist, live, subsist, hold on, hold out. **3** *those shoes won't last* last long, wear well, stand up to wear, keep, endure. **4** *the heartache won't last* be permanent, be constant, last long.

last⁵ *noun* *shoemaker's last* mould, model, pattern, form, matrix.

last-ditch *adjective* *a last-ditch attempt* desperate, frantic, frenzied, wild, struggling, straining, final, last-chance, last-minute, last-gasp, all-out.

lasting *adjective* *a lasting peace* long-lasting, enduring, long-lived, lifelong, abiding, continuing, long-term, surviving, persisting, permanent, deep-rooted, durable, constant, eternal, undying, everlasting, perennial, perpetual, unending, never-ending, immortal, ceaseless, unceasing, interminable, imperishable, indestructible.
Opposites SHORT-LIVED; EPHEMERAL.

lastly *adverb* *lastly I want to thank you all* finally, in conclusion, to conclude, to sum up, in drawing things to a close.

latch *noun* *the latch on the door* catch, fastening, hasp, hook, bar, bolt, lock; *Scots* sneck, snib.

latch *verb* *latch the door* fasten, secure, make fast, bar, bolt, lock; *Scots* sneck, snib.

late *adjective* **1** *she's always late* unpunctual, behind time, behind schedule, behind, behindhand, not on time, tardy, overdue, delayed, dilatory, slow. **2** *her late husband* deceased, dead, departed, defunct, non-extant. **3** *the late government* former, previous, preceding, past, prior. **4** *some late news* recent, fresh, new, last-minute, up-to-date, up-to-the-minute.
Opposites PUNCTUAL; EARLY; ALIVE; EXISTING.

late *adverb* **1** *he arrived late* unpunctually, behind time, behindhand, belatedly, tardily, at the last minute, at the tail end, dilatorily, slowly. **2** *we worked late yesterday* past the usual finishing/stopping/closing time, after hours. **3** *get home late from the dance* late at night, in the early hours of the morning; *inf.* in the wee small hours. **of late** lately, recently, latterly, in the past few days, in the last couple of weeks, in recent times.

lately *adverb* of late, recently. See LATE *adverb* of late.

latent *adjective* *latent talent* dormant, quiescent, inactive, passive, hidden, unrevealed, concealed, unapparent, indiscernible, imperceptible, invisible, covert, undeveloped, unrealized, potential, possible.
Opposites OBVIOUS; EVIDENT; CONSPICUOUS.

later *adjective* *the later bus* subsequent, next, following, succeeding, successive, sequential.

later *adverb* **1** *I can't come today but I'll come later* later on, at a later time, at a later date, at a future time/date, at some point in the future, in the future, in time to come. **2** *he arrived and she came later* later on, after, afterwards, subsequently, by and by, in a while, after a bit.

lateral *adjective* sidewise, sideways, sidelong, sideward, edgewise, edgeways, indirect, oblique, slanting, askance.

latest *adjective* *the latest news/style* most recent, newest, up-to-date, up-to-the-minute, current, modern, fashionable, in fashion, in vogue, in; *inf.* with-it.

lather *noun* **1** *soap not producing much lather* suds, soapsuds, foam, froth, bubbles. **2** *horses covered in lather* sweat, perspiration. **3** *getting in a lather over the exams* nervous state, state of agitation, state of anxiety, fluster, flutter, fret, fuss, frenzy, fever, pother; *inf.* flap, sweat, tizzy, dither, twitter, state, stew.

latitude *noun* **1** *on the same latitude as Moscow* parallel, meridian, grid line. **2** *give his staff a great deal of latitude in decision-making | children given too much latitude* scope, scope for initiative, freedom of action, freedom from restriction, freedom, unrestrictedness, liberty, free play, *carte blanche*, leeway, elbow-room, licence, indulgence, laxity.

latter *adjective* **1** *the latter is the better* last-mentioned, second-mentioned, second of the two, second. **2** *the latter part of the year/process* later, hindmost, closing, end, concluding, final. **3** *the technology of latter times* recent, latest, modern.
Opposites FORMER.

latter-day *adjective latter-day missionaries* modern, present-day, present-time, current, contemporary.

latterly *adverb* **1** *the old man was in a coma latterly* towards the end, at the end, finally. **2** *latterly management has been more reasonable* recently, lately, of late.

lattice *noun* lattice-work, fretwork, open framework, openwork, trellis, network, mesh, web, tracery, reticulation, grating, grid, grille.

laud *verb* **1** *laud their efforts* praise, sing the praises of, extol, hail, applaud, acclaim, commend, admire, approve of, make much of, cheer, celebrate, eulogize, panegyrize. **2** *laud the Creator* glorify, worship, magnify, exalt, pay tribute to, pay homage to, honour, adore, revere, venerate.

laudable *adjective laudable behaviour/actions* praiseworthy, commendable, admirable, worthy of admiration, meritorious, deserving, creditable, worthy, estimable, of note, noteworthy, exemplary, excellent.
Opposites BLAMEWORTHY; CONTEMPTIBLE.

laudation *noun* extolment, applause, praise, acclaim, acclamation, commendation, admiration, approval, approbation, eulogy, panegyric, paean, encomium.

laudatory *adjective* praising, extolling, acclamatory, commendatory, admiring, approving, approbatory, complimentary, adulatory, celebratory, eulogizing, eulogistic, panegyric, panegyrical, encomiastical.

laugh *verb* chuckle, chortle, guffaw, giggle, titter, snigger, ha-ha, tee-hee, burst out laughing, roar/hoot with laughter, shake with laughter, be convulsed with laughter, split one's sides, be rolling in the aisles, be doubled up; *inf.* be in stitches, die laughing, be creased up, fall about, crack up, break up. **laugh at 1** *laugh at the beggar* mock, ridicule, deride, scoff at, jeer at, sneer at, make fun of, poke fun at, make a fool of, make one's butt, lampoon, satirize, taunt, tease; *inf.* send up, take the mickey out of. **2** *laugh at danger* laugh off, belittle, make light of, close one's eyes to, refuse to acknowledge, discount, rule out, ignore, dismiss, disregard, reject the possibility of, shrug off, brush aside, scoff at, pooh-pooh. **laugh off** *laugh off danger* laugh at, belittle, make light of, discount, shrug off. *See* LAUGH *verb* laugh at 2. **laugh on the other side of one's face** *you'll be laughing on the other side of your face when the police catch up with you* show sudden disappointment, be dejected, be disheartened, be downcast, eat one's words, get a taste of one's own medicine; *inf.* get one's comeuppance.

laugh *noun* **1** *give a laugh* chuckle, chortle, guffaw, giggle, titter, snigger, roar/hoot of laughter, peal of laughter, belly-laugh. **2** *her uncle's such a laugh* comedian, comic, joker, humorist, wag, wit, entertainer, clown; *inf.* card, case, caution, hoot, scream. **3** *we didn't mean to hurt her, it was just a laugh* joke, jest, prank, lark, trick, piece of fun, bit of mischief.

laughable *adjective* **1** *a laughable business proposition* ludicrous, ridiculous, absurd, derisory, derisive, risible, preposterous, outrageous. **2** *children finding the entertainment laughable* amusing, funny, humorous, hilarious, uproarious, comical, comic, entertaining, diverting, farcical, droll, mirthful, side-splitting.
Opposites SERIOUS; GRAVE.

laughing stock *noun* figure of fun, dupe, butt, fool, everybody's fool, stooge, fair game, everybody's target, victim, Aunt Sally; *inf.* fall guy.

laughter *noun* **1** *hear the laughter* laughing, chuckling, chortling, guffawing, giggling, tittering, sniggering, cachinnation; *inf.* hooting. **2** *a source of laughter* amusement, entertainment, humour, mirth, merriment, gaiety, hilarity, glee, light-heartedness, blitheness.

launch *verb* **1** *launch the ship* set afloat, float. **2** *launch a rocket/missile* fire, discharge, propel, project, send forth, throw, cast, hurl, let fly. **3** *launch a search/project* set in motion, get going, begin, start, commence, embark upon, initiate, instigate, institute, inaugurate, establish, set up, organize, introduce, usher in, start the ball rolling. **4** *launch out into criticism* burst into, start, begin.

launder *verb sheets were freshly laundered* wash, wash and iron, wash and press, clean, dry-clean.

laundry *noun* **1** *put the laundry into the washing machine* washing, dirty washing, wash, dirty clothes, clothes to be cleaned. **2** *take the washing to a laundry* launderette, dry cleaner's, laundry room, public wash-house, Chinese laundry; *Am.* laundromat.

laurels *plural noun* honours, awards, trophies, prizes, rewards, tributes, bays, praises, laudation, acclaim, acclamation, commendation, credit, glory, honour, distinction, fame, renown, prestige, recognition; *inf.* kudos.

lavatory *noun* toilet, WC, water-closet, bathroom, public convenience, ladies, gents, cloakroom, powder room, privy, latrine; *inf.* loo, bog; *Am.* washroom, rest room; *Am. inf.* can, john, head; *humorous* little girls' room, little boys' room.

lavish *adjective* **1** *a lavish supply* copious, abundant, superabundant, plentiful, profuse, prolific, unlimited. **2** *too lavish in her catering* extravagant, excessive, immoderate, wasteful, squandering, profligate, prodigal, thriftless, improvident, intemperate, unrestrained, dissolute, wild. **3** *a lavish hostess* generous, liberal, bountiful, open-handed, unstinting, free, munificent, overgenerous, extravagant. **4** *a lavish display of flowers* luxuriant, lush, gorgeous, sumptuous, costly, opulent, pretentious, showy.
Opposites MEAGRE; FRUGAL.

lavish *verb lavish presents/praises on his children* heap, shower, pour, deluge, give freely, give generously, give unstintingly, bestow freely, waste, squander, dissipate.

law noun **1** *the law of the land* system of laws, body of laws, constitution, code, legal code, charter, rules and regulations, jurisprudence. **2** *parliament issuing laws* rule, regulation, statute, enactment, act, decree, edict, command, order, ordinance, commandment, directive, pronouncement, covenant. **3** *obey the laws of the game* rule, regulation, principle, direction, instruction, guideline. **4** *moral laws* rule, principle, precept, standard, criterion, formula, tenet, doctrine, canon. **5** *law of nature* generalization, general truth, axiom, maxim, truism. **6** *go to law* litigation, legal action, legal proceedings, lawsuit. **7** *a career in the law* legal profession, bar. **8** *the law has arrived* police, officers of the law; *inf.* fuzz, the Old Bill, pigs, bobbies, boys in blue.

law-abiding adjective lawful, righteous, honest, honourable, upright, upstanding, good, virtuous, orderly, peaceable, peace-keeping, peaceful, dutiful, duteous, obedient, compliant, complying.

lawbreaker noun criminal, felon, wrongdoer, miscreant, offender, delinquent, culprit, transgressor, violator, convict, jailbird; *inf.* crook, baddy.

lawful adjective **1** *lawful actions* legal, legitimate, licit, just, valid, permissible, allowable, rightful, proper, constitutional, legalized, sanctioned, authorized, warranted, approved, recognized. **2** *a lawful person* law-abiding, righteous, honourable, orderly. *See* LAW-ABIDING. *Opposites* UNLAWFUL; ILLEGAL.

lawless adjective **1** *a lawless country* without law and order, anarchic, disorderly, ungoverned, unruly, insurrectionary, insurgent, revolutionary, rebellious, insubordinate, riotous, mutinous, seditious, terrorist. **2** *lawless actions* unlawful, illegal, law-breaking, illicit, illegitimate, criminal, felonious, wrongdoing, miscreant, transgressing, violating. **3** *lawless rage* unbridled, unrestrained, unchecked, uncontrolled, immoderate, intemperate, wild. *Opposites* LAW-ABIDING; ORDERLY; RESTRAINED.

lawsuit noun suit, case, legal action, action, legal proceedings, proceedings, litigation, trial, bringing to book, bringing of charges, indictment.

lawyer noun solicitor, legal practitioner, legal adviser, criminal lawyer, civil lawyer, barrister, advocate, counsel, Queen's Counsel, QC, defending counsel, prosecuting counsel; *inf.* brief; *Am.* attorney.

lax adjective **1** *lax about discipline in the school* slack, slipshod, negligent, neglectful, remiss, careless, heedless, unmindful, inattentive, casual, easygoing, lenient, permissive, indulgent, overindulgent, complaisant, overtolerant. **2** *a lax description* loose, inexact, inaccurate, imprecise, unrigorous, vague, indefinite, non-specific, broad, general. **3** *lax flesh* slack, flabby, flaccid, limp, yielding, sagging, drooping, droopy, hanging. *Opposites* CONSCIENTIOUS; CAREFUL.

laxative noun purgative, aperient, cathartic, senna, ipecacuanha, castor oil.

lay verb **1** *lay the parcel on the table* put, place, set, deposit, plant, settle, posit. **2** *lay the carpet* position, set out, arrange, dispose. **3** *lay charges* put forward, bring forward, advance, submit, present, prefer, offer, lodge. **4** *lay the blame at his door* attribute, assign, ascribe, allocate, allot, impute. **5** *lay bets* wager, bet, gamble, stake, give odds, hazard, risk, chance. **6** *lay plans* devise, arrange, contrive, make, prepare, work out, hatch, concoct, design, plan, plot. **7** *lay the burden on him* impose, inflict, encumber, saddle, tax, charge, burden, apply. **8** *lay eggs* deposit, produce, bear, oviposit. **9** *lay him with a blow* lay low, lay out, floor, fell, knock down, prostrate. **10** *lay their fears* allay, assuage, soothe, calm, still, quiet, relieve, ease, alleviate, mitigate, palliate, suppress. **11** *lay his unruly hair* flatten, smooth, level. **12** *lay the woman/man* have sex with, have intercourse with, have sexual relations with, copulate with, go to bed with, sleep with; *inf.* bed. **lay aside 1** *lay aside the dress for the customer* put aside, put to one side, keep, save, store. **2** *lay aside one's studies* abandon, cast aside, forsake, reject, renounce, repudiate, discard. **3** *lay aside evil thoughts* set aside, put aside, dismiss, disregard, put out of one's mind, ignore, forget, shelve. **lay bare** *lay bare one's secret thoughts* reveal, make known, disclose, divulge, show, expose, exhibit, uncover, unveil, unmask. **lay down 1** *lay down their weapons* surrender, relinquish, give up, yield, cede, turn over. **2** *it is laid down that candidates must be interviewed* set down, stipulate, formulate, prescribe, order, command, ordain, postulate, demand, proclaim, assert, maintain. **3** *lay down wine* store, put into store, keep for future use, keep, save. **lay hands on 1** *if I ever lay hands on the thief* lay hold of, get hold of, catch, seize. *See* LAY verb lay hold of. **2** *I just can't lay hands on that book* find, locate, unearth, bring to light, run to earth, discover, acquire, turn up. **3** *priests laying hands on members of the congregation* bless, consecrate, confirm, ordain. **lay hold of** *lay hold of the thief* get hold of, get one's hands on, catch, seize, grab, snatch, clutch, grip, grasp, lay hands on. **lay in** *lay in a supply of logs* stock up with/on, stockpile, store, accumulate, amass, heap up, hoard, collect. **lay into 1** *lay into their attackers* set about, set upon, assail, attack, hit out at, strike out at, let fly at; *inf.* lace/sail/pitch into, lambaste. **2** *lay into the child for being late* scold, rebuke, chide, berate, upbraid, reproach, reprove, castigate, punish, criticize, censure, condemn, rant at, rave at, harangue; *inf.* pitch into, lambaste. **lay it on** *he's laying it on to charm his mother-in-law* exaggerate, stretch the truth, overdo it, flatter, pay extravagant compliments, give fulsome praise, overpraise, soft-soap; *inf.* pile it on, lay it on thick, lay it on with a trowel, sweet-talk. **lay off 1** *lay off half of the workforce* let go, make redundant, dismiss, discharge, pay off; *inf.* sack, fire. **2** *lay off hitting him* stop, cease, desist from, refrain from, give up, discontinue, leave off, finish; *inf.* give over; *Am.* quit. **3** *lay off alcohol* desist from, refrain from, give up, leave alone, leave off, not touch. **lay on** *lay on refreshments* provide, supply, furnish, give. **lay out 1** *lay out the plans* spread out, set out, arrange, display, exhibit. **2** *lay out a garden* set out, arrange, plan, design. **3** *lay out a lot of money* spend, expend, pay, disburse, contribute, give, invest; *inf.* shell out, fork out. **4** *lay out his opponent* knock out, knock unconscious, knock down, fell, floor, flatten, prostrate; *inf.* KO, kayo, knock for six.

lay *adjective* **1** *a lay preacher* laic, laical, secular, non-clerical, non-ordained. **2** *a lay member of the club* non-professional, amateur, non-specialist, dilettante.

layabout *noun* good-for-nothing, ne'er-do-well, do-nothing, idler, loafer, lounger, shirker, wastrel, fainéant, sluggard, laggard; *inf.* skiver, waster.

layman, lay person *noun he's a dealer; I'm just an interested layman* amateur, non-professional, dilettante.

lay-off *noun many lay-offs at the factory* redundancy, dismissal, discharge; *inf.* sacking, firing.

layout *noun* **1** *the layout of the house* arrangement, geography, plan. **2** *the magazine's layout* arrangement, design, format, formation.

lay person *noun.* See LAYMAN.

laze *verb lazing all day in the garden* idle, do nothing, loaf, lounge, lounge about, loll around, waste time, fritter away time.

laziness *noun* idleness, indolence, slothfulness, sloth, inactivity, inertia, lethargy, languor, remissness, laxity. See LAZY.

lazy *adjective* idle, indolent, slothful, work-shy, inactive, inert, sluggish, lethargic, languorous, listless, torpid, slow-moving, remiss, negligent, lax.
Opposites ACTIVE; INDUSTRIOUS; ENERGETIC.

lead¹ *verb* **1** *lead him to the right spot* guide, show someone the way, conduct, lead the way, usher, escort, steer, pilot. **2** *the evidence led him to believe he was guilty* cause, induce, prompt, move, incline, dispose, predispose, persuade, sway, influence, prevail, bring round. **3** *his action led to disaster* cause, result in, bring on, call forth, provoke, contribute to. **4** *lead the procession* be at the head of, be at the front of, head. **5** *lead the country/discussion* command, direct, govern, rule, manage, be in charge of, regulate, preside over, head, supervise, superintend, oversee; *inf.* head up. **6** *he was leading after the first lap* be in the lead, be in front, be out in front, be ahead, be first, come first, precede. **7** *leading the field* be at the front of, be ahead of, outdistance, outrun, outstrip, leave behind, outdo, excel, exceed, surpass, outrival, outshine, eclipse, transcend. **8** *lead a happy life* have, live, pass, spend, experience, undergo. **lead off** *lead off the dance* begin, start, start off, commence, open; *inf.* kick off. **lead on** *he won't marry her; he's just leading her on* deceive, mislead, delude, hoodwink, dupe, trick, beguile, tempt, entice, lure, tantalize, inveigle, seduce; *inf.* string along. **lead the way 1** *he led the way to the spot* guide, conduct, show the way. **2** *the scientist led the way in space development* initiate things, take the first step, make a start, break

ground, blaze a trail, lay the foundation, lay the first stone. **lead up to** *lead up to asking them for money* prepare the way for, pave the way for, open the way for, do the groundwork for, work round/up to, make overtures about, make advances about, hint at, approach the subject of, introduce the subject of.
Opposites FOLLOW; TRAIL.

lead² *noun* **1** *the runner in the lead* leading position/place, first place, advance position, van, vanguard. **2** *take the lead in the market* first position, head place, forefront, primacy, pre-eminence, supremacy, advantage, edge, precedence. **3** *a lead of half a lap* margin, gap, interval. **4** *prefects should act as a lead to others* example, model, pattern, standard of excellence. **5** *she's in the lead in the new play* leading role, star/starring role, star part, title role, principal part. **6** *she's/he's the lead in the play* star, principal character, male lead, female lead, leading man, leading lady, hero, heroine. **7** *a dog's lead* leash, tether, rein, cord, rope, chain. **8** *we have no leads in the murder hunt* clue, pointer, guide, hint, tip, suggestion, indication, intimation, tip-off.

lead³ *adjective in the lead position* leading, first, top, foremost, front, head, chief, principal, main, most important, premier, paramount, prime, primary.
Opposites LAST.

lead⁴ *noun* **1** *sink a lead to test the depth* weight, sinker, plummet, plumb, bob. **2** *remove the lead from the wound* lead pellet, shot, ammunition.

leaden *adjective* **1** *leaden limbs* heavy, weighty, burdensome, cumbersome, inactive, inert. **2** *leaden steps* heavy, laboured, lumbering, plodding, sluggish. **3** *leaden prose* heavy, unimaginative, uninspired, uninteresting, dull, boring, tedious, monotonous, insipid, vapid. **4** *leaden skies* grey, greyish, grey-coloured, cloudy, gloomy, overcast, louring, oppressive, dark, dreary, dismal, bleak.

leader *noun* **1** *the leader of the country/committee/team* ruler, head, chief, commander, director, governor, principal, captain, skipper, manager, superintendent, supervisor, overseer, foreman, kingpin; *inf.* boss, number one; *Am. inf.* honcho. **2** *a leader of fashion* pace-setter, pacemaker, trend-setter, front runner. **3** *a leader in the field of genetics* front runner, innovator, pioneer, trail-blazer, pathfinder, groundbreaker, originator.

leadership *noun* **1** *under the leadership of a responsible person* rule, command, headship, directorship, direction, governorship, administration, captaincy, management, supervision, control, guidance, authority, superintendency. **2** *he is competent but has no leadership qualities* authority, control, direction, guidance, initiative, influence.

leading *adjective* **1** *play the leading role* chief, main, most important, principal, foremost, supreme, paramount, dominant, superior, ruling, directing, guiding, controlling; *inf.* number-one. **2** *one of the leading writers* chief, most important, foremost, greatest, best, outstanding, pre-eminent, supreme, principal, top-rank, of the first rank, first-rate. **3** *the leading runner* front, first, in first place.

leaf *noun* **1** *a leaf from the tree/plant* frond, flag, needle, pine needle, pad, lily-pad. *See table.* **2** *a leaf missing from the book* page, sheet, folio, flyleaf. **turn over a new leaf** *she turned over a new leaf after she was punished* reform, improve, mend one's ways, become a new person, change completely, make a fresh start.

TYPES OF LEAF		
acicular	feather-	pinnatifid
acuminate	veined	pinnati-
amphi-	geminate	partite
stomatic	hastate	pinnatisect
bipinnate	isobilateral	plicate
bipinna-	laciniate	prophyll
tifid	lanceolate	reticulate
biserrate	linear	revolute
biternate	lingulate	rhombic
bract	multifid	rhomboid
cataphyll	multifoliate	runcinate
complicate	oblong	sagittate
compound	obovate	scutate
conjugate	odd-pinnate	serrate
cordate	orbicular	simple
cotyledon/	oval	spathulate
seed leaf	ovate	ternate
crenate	palmate	triangular
decom-	panduri-	trifoliate
pound	form	tripinnate
decurrent	pedate	trullate
elliptic	pedatifid	umbilicate
ensiform	peltate	unifolio-
entire	perfoliate	late
equitant	pinnate	unijugate

leaf *verb* **1** *leafing through a book* flick, skim, browse, glance. **2** *trees leafing* bud, put out leaves, burst into leaves, turn green, foliate.

leaflet *noun* pamphlet, booklet, brochure, handbill, bill, circular; *inf.* advert; *Am.* flyer.

league *noun* **1** *a league of nations* alliance, confederation, confederacy, federation, union, association, coalition, combine, consortium, affiliation, guild, corporation, conglomerate, cooperative, partnership, fellowship, syndicate, band, group. **2** *sign a league* pact, compact, covenant, treaty, concordat, contract, agreement, settlement. **3** *a football league* group, band, association. **4** *he is not in the same league as his brother* ability group, level of ability, level, class, category. **in league with** *he was in league with the other crook* in alliance with, allied with, cooperating with, collaborating with, leagued with, linked with, hand in glove with, in collusion with; *inf.* in cahoots with.

league *verb* *they leagued together to promote their interests* ally, join forces, unite, form an association, band together, combine, amalgamate, form a federation, confederate, collaborate.

leak *noun* **1** *see a leak in the bucket* hole, opening, crack, crevice, chink, fissure, puncture, cut, gash, slit, rent, break, rift. **2** *a water/gas leak* drip, leaking, leakage, escape, seeping, seepage, oozing, percolation, discharge. **3** *a leak of secret information to a newspaper* disclosure, divulgence, revelation, uncovering.

leak *verb* **1** *water/gas leaking* escape, drip, seep out/through, ooze out, exude, discharge, issue, gush out. **2** *leak information to the press* disclose, divulge, reveal, make known, make public, tell, impart, pass on, relate, give away, let slip, let the cat out of the bag; *inf.* spill the beans about, take the lid off.

lean *verb* **1** *the ladder leaning against the wall | his wife leaning on his arm* rest, be supported, be propped up, recline, repose. **2** *the pole/ship is leaning* incline, bend, slant, tilt, be at an angle, slope, bank, list, heel, careen. **3** *she leans towards anarchy* incline towards, tend towards, have a tendency towards, have a propensity for, have a proclivity for, have a preference for, be attracted to, have a liking for, gravitate towards, have an affinity with. **4** *she leans on her husband* depend on, be dependent on, rely on, count on, pin one's faith on, have faith in, trust, have every confidence in.

lean *adjective* **1** *lean and hungry people/animals* thin, slender, slim, spare, lank, skinny, scrawny, scraggy, bony, gaunt, emaciated, skin and bones, raw-boned, rangy, gangling. **2** *lean meat* non-fat, low-fat, unfatty. **3** *a lean harvest* meagre, scanty, sparse, poor, inadequate, insufficient. **4** *lean years for art* unproductive, unfruitful, arid, barren, bare, non-fertile. *Opposites* FAT; ABUNDANT.

leaning *noun* *a leaning towards anarchy* tendency, inclination, bent, proclivity, propensity, penchant, predisposition, predilection, proneness, partiality, preference, bias, attraction, liking, fondness, taste.

leap *verb* **1** *children leaping around* jump, bound, bounce, hop, skip, romp, caper, spring, frolic, frisk, cavort, gambol, dance. **2** *leap to one's feet* jump, jump up, spring. **3** *leap the obstacle* jump, jump over, high-jump, vault over, vault, spring over, bound over, hurdle, clear, cross over, sail over. **4** *leap to help* jump, hurry, hasten, rush, hurtle. **5** *leap to conclusions* arrive at hastily, reach hurriedly, come to overhastily, form hastily. **6** *prices have leapt* increase rapidly, soar, rocket, sky-rocket, shoot up, escalate, mount. **7** *leap to stardom* rocket, sky-rocket, advance/mount/ascend rapidly, climb the ladder. **leap at** *leap at the chance* accept eagerly, grasp, grasp with both hands, grab, take advantage of.

leap *noun* **1** *clear the obstacle at the first leap* jump, vault, spring, bound, hop, skip. **2** *a leap in the number of jobless* rapid increase, sudden rise, escalation, soaring, surge, upsurge, upswing. **by leaps and bounds** *progress by leaps and bounds* rapidly, swiftly, quickly, speedily, at an amazing rate.

learn *verb* **1** *learn French* acquire a knowledge of, gain an understanding of, acquire skill in, become competent in, grasp, master, take in, absorb, assimilate, pick up. **2** *learn the poem* learn by heart, get by heart, memorize, commit to memory, become word-perfect in, get off pat. **3** *we learned that he had gone* discover, find out, detect, become aware of, gather, hear, be informed, have it brought to one's attention, understand, ascertain, discern, perceive. **4** *learn of his departure* find out about, hear of, get word of, be informed of, have brought to one's attention, get wind of.

learned *adjective* *learned professors/journals* erudite, scholarly, well-educated, knowledgeable, well-read, widely read, well-versed, well-informed, lettered, cultured, intellectual, academic, literary, bookish, studious, pedantic, sage, wise; *inf.* highbrow.
Opposites IGNORANT; ILLITERATE.

learner *noun* beginner, trainee, apprentice, pupil, student, novice, tiro, neophyte, initiate, greenhorn, learner driver.

learning *noun* **1** *a man of learning* erudition, scholarship, knowledge, education, letters, culture, intellect, academic attainment, book-learning, information, pedantry, sageness, wisdom. **2** *happy to leave learning behind* study, studying, education, schooling, tuition, teaching, instruction.

lease *verb* **1** *lease a house/car from an agency* rent, hire, charter. **2** *lease their house to visitors from Canada* rent, rent out, let, let out, hire, hire out, sublet.

lease *noun* sign a lease for the house/car rental agreement, hire agreement, charter, contract.

leash *noun* **1** *a dog's leash* lead, rein, tether, rope, cord, chain. **2** *keep a tight leash on his anger* rein, curb, control, check, restraint, hold.
straining at the leash straining at the leash to get out in the sunshine impatient, eager, anxious, enthusiastic, itching, dying.

leash *verb* **1** *leash the dog* put the leash/lead on, fasten, hitch up, tether, tie up, secure. **2** *leash one's anger* curb, control, keep under control, check, restrain, hold back, suppress.

leather *noun* jackets made of leather | leather gloves skin, hide, kid, doeskin, pigskin, suede, imitation leather, leatherette.

leather *verb* leather the guilty child strap, belt, beat, thrash, flog, whip, lash, scourge; *inf.* wallop, lather.

leathery *adjective* **1** *leathery skin* wrinkled, wizened, weather-beaten, rough, rugged, coriaceous. **2** *leathery meat* tough, hard, hardened, coriaceous.

leave *verb* **1** *leave hurriedly* depart, go away, go, withdraw, retire, take oneself off, exit, take one's leave, make off, pull out, quit, be gone, decamp, disappear, say one's farewells/goodbyes; *inf.* push off, shove off, cut, do a bunk, split, vamoose. **2** *leave for France* set off, set sail. **3** *leave his wife* abandon, desert, forsake, discard, turn one's back on, leave in the lurch. **4** *has left his job* give up, quit, abandon, move from. **5** *leave his gloves at the hotel* leave behind, forget, mislay. **6** *leave the job to them* assign, allot, consign, hand over, give over, refer, commit, entrust. **7** *he left the estate to his nephew* bequeath, will, endow, hand down, transfer, convey; *fml.* demise, devise. **8** *the quarrel left feelings of resentment* leave behind, cause, produce, generate, result in. **leave in the lurch** leave the firm in the lurch by walking out let down, leave in trouble, leave helpless, leave stranded, leave high and dry, abandon, desert,

forsake. **leave off** *leave off talking* stop, cease, finish, halt, end, desist from, break off, give up, discontinue, refrain from; *inf.* give over, knock off; *Am.* quit. **leave out** **1** *leave out a sentence* miss out, omit, omit by accident, fail to include, overlook. **2** *please leave him out of the invitation list* exclude, omit, except, eliminate, count out, disregard, ignore, reject, repudiate.
Opposites COME; ARRIVE; STAY.

leave *noun* **1** *get leave to be absent* permission, consent, authorization, sanction, warrant, dispensation, concession, indulgence. **2** *going on leave for three weeks* holiday, vacation, break, time off, furlough, sabbatical, leave of absence; *inf.* hols, vac. **3** *they took their leave* leaving, leave-taking, departure, parting, withdrawal, exit, farewell, goodbye, adieu.

leaven *noun* **1** *add leaven to the dough* leavening, ferment, barm, raising agent, yeast, baking powder. **2** *the children added some leaven to the solemn occasion* transformer, modifier, catalyst, enlivening influence, lightening effect.

leaven *verb* **1** *leaven the dough* raise, make rise, ferment, work, lighten. **2** *leaven the atmosphere of formality* permeate, infuse, pervade, penetrate, imbue, suffuse, transform, modify, lighten, enliven, stimulate.

leavings *plural noun* residue, remainder, remains, remnants, leftovers, scraps, oddments, odds and ends, fragments, junk, waste, dregs, refuse, rubbish, debris, sweepings.

lecher *noun* libertine, womanizer, lady-killer, seducer, adulterer, fornicator, pervert, debauchee, rake, roué, Don Juan, Casanova, Lothario; *inf.* dirty old man, DOM, lech, flasher.

lecherous *adjective* lustful, promiscuous, randy, carnal, sensual, licentious, lascivious, lewd, salacious, libertine, libidinous, lubricious, concupiscent, debauched, dissolute, wanton, intemperate, dissipated, degenerate, depraved; *inf.* horny, raunchy.

lechery *noun* lust, lustfulness, promiscuity, randiness, carnality, sensualness, sensuality, licentiousness, lasciviousness, lewdness, salaciousness, salacity, libertinism, libidinousness, lubricity, concupiscence, debauchery, dissoluteness, wantonness, intemperance, dissipation, degeneracy, depravity; *inf.* horniness, raunchiness.

lecture *noun* **1** *attend a lecture on the environment* talk, speech, address, discourse, disquisition, lesson, sermon, homily, harangue. **2** *children given a lecture for being late* scolding, chiding, reprimand, rebuke, reproof, reproach, remonstration, upbraiding, berating, tirade, diatribe; *inf.* dressing-down, telling-off, talking-to.

lecture *verb* **1** *lectured on local politics* give a lecture, give a talk, talk, give a speech, make a speech, speak, give an address, address, discourse, expound, hold forth, give a sermon, sermonize, harangue; *inf.* spout, jaw. **2** *he lectures in philosophy* teach, tutor in, instruct in, give instruction in, give lessons in. **3** *lecture the children for being late* scold, chide, reprimand, rebuke, reprove, reproach, remonstrate with, upbraid, berate, castigate, haul over the coals, give a tirade to, give a diatribe to; *inf.* lambaste, give a dressing-down to, give a talking-to to, tell off.

lecturer *noun* **1** *the lecturer gave a talk on villages* speaker, public speaker, speech-maker, orator, preacher. **2** *he is a lecturer in French* university teacher, college teacher, tutor, reader, instructor, academic, academician.

ledge *noun* shelf, sill, mantel, mantelpiece, mantelshelf, projection, protrusion, overhang, ridge, step.

ledger *noun* account book, record book, register, registry, log.

lee *noun in the lee of the hill* shelter, protection, cover, refuge.

leech *noun I can't get rid of her; she's such a leech* clinger, hanger-on, parasite, barnacle, constant appendage, sycophant, toady, bloodsucker, extortioner, sponger; *inf.* scrounger, freeloader.

leer *verb* ogle, look lasciviously at, look suggestively at, give sly looks to, eye, wink at, watch, stare, goggle, sneer, smirk, grin; *inf.* give someone the glad eye, give someone the once-over.

leer *noun* lascivious look, lecherous glance, suggestive look, sly glance, wink, stare, sneer, smirk, grin; *inf.* the glad eye, the once-over.

leery *adjective* wary, chary, cautious, careful, guarded, on one's guard, suspicious, distrustful, mistrusting.

lees *plural noun emptied the lees from a wine glass* dregs, sediment, deposit, grounds, settlings, residue, remains; *Tech.* precipitate, sublimate.

leeway *noun the tight budget leaves little leeway for design costs* room to manoeuvre, room to operate, scope, latitude, elbow-room, slack, space, margin, play.

left *adjective* **1** *the left side* left-hand, sinistral, sinister, sinistrous; port, starboard. **2** *a left politician* left-wing, leftist, socialist, radical, progressive, liberal, communist, communistic. **Opposites** RIGHT.

left-handed *adjective* **1** *left-handed writers* sinistral; *inf.* cack-handed, southpaw. **2** *a left-handed compliment* back-handed, ambiguous, equivocal, double-meaning, double-edged, dubious, indirect, enigmatic, cryptic, paradoxical, ironic, sardonic. **3** *a left-handed attempt at putting things right* awkward, clumsy, fumbling, unskilful, gauche, maladroit; *inf.* cack-handed.

leftover *noun a leftover from a bygone age* survivor, residue, legacy.

leftover *adjective leftover food* remaining, excess, surplus, extra, uneaten, unused, unwanted.

leftovers *plural noun give the leftovers to the dogs* remainder, excess, surplus, leavings, uneaten food, unused supplies, scraps, odds and ends. *See* LEAVINGS.

leg *noun* **1** *her injured leg* lower limb, limb, member, shank; *inf.* stump, peg, pin. **2** *the legs of the tripod | chair legs* support, upright, prop, brace, underpinning. **3** *the final leg of the journey* part, portion, segment, section, bit, stretch, stage, lap. **give someone a leg up to** *give him a leg up onto the wall | give her a leg up in*

her career act as someone's support to, support, help up, help, give someone assistance, assist, lend someone a helping hand, come to someone's aid, aid, give someone a boost, boost, advance. **not have a leg to stand on** *after his accomplice confessed, he did not have a leg to stand on* have nothing to support one's story/opinion etc., lack support, lack validity, lack credence, be vulnerable, be defenceless. **on its last legs 1** *this furniture is on its last legs* about to break, about to collapse, dilapidated, worn out, rickety. **2** *the firm's on its last legs* about to fail, about to go bankrupt, failing, near to ruin, going to the wall; *inf.* going bust. **on one's last legs** *she's on her last legs after the long journey* exhausted, worn out, fatigued, fagged out, about to collapse, about to break down, about to die, dying, at death's door; *inf.* all in, done in, shattered. **pull someone's leg** *we didn't mean to upset her; we were just pulling her leg* tease, chaff, rag, make fun of, trick, hoax, fool, deceive; *inf.* kid, have on, rib; *Am. inf.* put on. **stretch one's legs** *stop the car and stretch one's legs* go for a walk, take a walk, go for a stroll, move about, promenade, get some exercise, get some air, take the air.

leg *verb* **leg it** *having missed the bus we had to leg it | let's leg it out of here* walk, go on foot, hurry; *inf.* hightail it, go on Shanks's pony, hotfoot it.

legacy *noun* **1** *willed a legacy of several thousand pounds* bequest, inheritance, heritage, bequeathal, endowment, gift, patrimony, heirloom; *fml.* devise. **2** *a legacy of Celtic culture | this is the legacy of unemployment* inheritance, heritage, tradition, hand-me-down, residue.

legal *adjective* **1** *legal behaviour* lawful, legitimate, licit, legalized, valid, right, proper, sound, permissible, permitted, allowable, allowed, above-board, admissible, acceptable, authorized, sanctioned, warranted, licensed; *inf.* legit. **2** *legal processes/adviser* judicial, juridical, jurisdictive, forensic. **Opposites** ILLEGAL; UNLAWFUL; CRIMINAL.

legality *noun dispute the legality of their actions* lawfulness, legitimacy, legitimateness, validity, rightness, rightfulness, soundness, permissibility, admissibility.

legalize *verb legalize soft drugs* make legal, decriminalize, legitimize, legitimatize, legitimate, validate, ratify, permit, allow, admit, accept, authorize, sanction, warrant, license.

legate *noun a papal legate* envoy, emissary, agent, ambassador, representative, commissioner, nuncio, messenger.

legatee *noun the chief legatees mentioned in the will* beneficiary, recipient, inheritor, heir, heiress.

legation *noun* **1** *part of the French legation in Britain* mission, diplomatic mission, embassy, consulate, ministry, delegation, deputation, representation, envoys. **2** *the address of the British legation* embassy, consulate, diplomatic establishment, ministry.

legend *noun* **1** *a book of Scandinavian legends* myth, saga, epic, folk-tale, folk-story, traditional story, tale, story, narrative, fable, romance. **2** *Greta Garbo became a legend* famous person, celebrity, star, superstar, luminary. **3** *the legends under the photographs* | *legends on coins* caption, inscription, dedication, motto, device. **4** *the legends accompanying the tables* key, code, cipher, explanation, table of symbols.

legendary *adjective* **1** *legendary figures in Icelandic saga* mythical, heroic, traditional, fabled, fictitious, fictional, story-book, romantic, fanciful, fantastical, fabulous. **2** *a legendary actor* celebrated, acclaimed, illustrious, famous, famed, renowned, well-known, popular, remembered, immortal.
Opposites FACTUAL; HISTORICAL; UNKNOWN.

legerdemain *noun* **1** *stage magicians practising legerdemain* sleight of hand, juggling, conjuring, prestidigitation, trickery, hocus-pocus, thaumaturgy. **2** *a politician noted for his legerdemain* trickery, cunning, artfulness, craftiness, craft, wiles, deceit, deception, dissimulation, double-dealing, artful argument, specious reasoning, sophistry.

legibility *noun* readability, readableness, ease of reading, decipherability, clearness, clarity, plainness, neatness.

legible *adjective* easily read, easy to read, readable, decipherable, clear, distinct, plain, carefully written, neat.
Opposites ILLEGIBLE; INDECIPHERABLE.

legion *noun* **1** *legions of soldiers* army, brigade, regiment, battalion, company, troop, division, unit, force. **2** *legions of people arrived for the festival* horde, host, throng, multitude, crowd, drove, mass, mob, gang, swarm, flock, herd.

legislate *verb* **1** *it is parliament's task to legislate* make laws, pass laws, enact laws, formulate laws, establish laws, codify laws. **2** *they must legislate for more council houses* pass laws, decree, order, ordain, prescribe, authorize, make provision for.

legislation *noun* **1** *his office is in charge of legislation* law-making, law enactment, law formulation, codification, prescription. **2** *dislike the new legislation* law, body of laws, constitution, rules, regulations, acts, bills, statutes, enactments, charters, ordinances, measures, canon, code.

legislative *adjective* *legislative assembly/powers* law-making, law-giving, judicial, juridical, jurisdictive, parliamentary, congressional, senatorial.

legislator *noun* law-maker, law-giver, parliamentarian, congressman, senator, politician.

legitimate *adjective* **1** *legitimate actions* legal, lawful, licit, within the law, going by the rules; *inf.* legit. **2** *the legitimate heir* lawful, rightful, genuine, authentic, real, true, proper, correct, authorized, sanctioned, warranted, acknowledged, recognized, approved; *inf.* legit, kosher. **3** *a legitimate reason for being late* valid, sound, admissible, acceptable, well-founded, justifiable, reasonable, plausible, credible, believable, reliable, logical, rational.
Opposites ILLEGAL; ILLEGITIMATE; INVALID.

legitimize *verb* legitimate, legalize, pronounce lawful, declare legal, decriminalize, validate,

permit, warrant, authorize, sanction, license, give the stamp of approval to.

leisure *noun* *seek a hobby for periods of leisure* | *leisure pursuits* free time, spare time, spare moments, time to spare, idle hours, inactivity, time off, relaxation, recreation, freedom, holiday, vacation, breathing space, breathing spell, respite; *inf.* time to kill. **at one's leisure** *you can do this work at your leisure* at one's convenience, when it suits one, in one's own good time, when one can fit it in, without need for haste, without haste, unhurriedly, without hurry, when one gets round to it.
Opposites WORK; OCCUPATION.

leisurely *adjective* *at a leisurely pace* unhurried, relaxed, easy, easygoing, gentle, comfortable, restful, slow, lazy, lingering; *inf.* laid-back.
Opposites BRISK; HURRIED; FAST.

lend *verb* **1** *lend him a book* loan, give someone the loan of, let someone have the use of, advance. **2** *the flowers lend beauty to the room* impart, add, give, bestow, confer, provide, supply, furnish. **3** *lend his professional skill to the venture* give, contribute, donate, grant. **lend an ear** *lend an ear to what the teacher is saying* listen, pay attention to, take notice of, heed, pay heed to, give ear to. **lend a hand** *lend a hand with the preparations* help, help out, give a helping hand, assist, give assistance, aid, make a contribution; *inf.* pitch in. **lend itself to** *the house does not lend itself to being divided* be suitable for, be suited to, be appropriate for, be adaptable to, have the right characteristics for.
Opposites BORROW; DETRACT.

length *noun* **1** *what length is the cloth?* distance lengthwise, distance, extent lengthwise, extent, linear measure, span, reach. **2** *he's been here for quite a length of time* period, stretch, duration, term, span. **3** *a length of cloth* piece, portion, section, measure, segment, swatch. **4** *a speech noted for its length* longness, lengthiness, extensiveness, protractedness, elongation, prolixity, prolixness, wordiness, verbosity, verboseness, long-windedness, tediousness, tedium. **at length** **1** *speak at length* for a long time, for ages, for hours, on and on, interminably, endlessly. **2** *deal at length with the problem* fully, to the fullest extent, in detail, in depth, thoroughly, exhaustively, completely. **3** *at length he agreed to accept* after a long time, after a considerable time, finally, at last, at long last, eventually, in the end, ultimately, in time. **go to any length(s)** *she would go to any lengths to save her child* do absolutely anything, go to any extreme, go to any limits, observe no limits.

lengthen *verb* **1** *lengthen a skirt* make longer, elongate, let down. **2** *the days are lengthening* grow longer, get longer, draw out, stretch. **3** *lengthen the time taken* | *lengthened his speech* make longer, prolong, increase, extend, expand, protract, stretch out, draw out.
Opposites SHORTEN; CURTAIL; DECREASE.

lengthy *adjective* **1** *a lengthy affair* long, very long, long-lasting, prolonged, extended, protracted, long-drawn-out. **2** *a lengthy speech* long, very long, over-long, protracted, long-drawn-out, diffuse, discursive, verbose, wordy,

lenience · lethargic

prolix, long-winded, tedious.
Opposites SHORT; BRIEF; CONCISE.

lenience, leniency *noun* **1** *the leniency of the judge* mercy, mercifulness, clemency, lenity, humanity, tolerance, compassion, indulgence, gentleness. *See* LENIENT 1. **2** *the leniency of the sentence* mildness, mercifulness, lenity, moderateness, lack of severity.

lenient *adjective* **1** *a lenient judge* merciful, clement, sparing, moderate, compassionate, humane, forbearing, tolerant, liberal, magnanimous, indulgent, kind, gentle, easygoing. **2** *a lenient sentence* mild, merciful, moderate, non-severe.
Opposites MERCILESS; SEVERE; HARSH.

lens *noun. See table.*

SHAPES OF LENSES	
biconcave	convex
biconvex	planoconcave
concave	planoconvex

leper *noun a social leper* social outcast, outcast, pariah, untouchable, *persona non grata*.

leprechaun *noun* elf, sprite, fairy, gnome; little people.

lesbian *noun* homosexual, gay, homoerotic, Sapphic, tribade; *derog. inf.* lezzy, butch; dyke.

lesbian *adjective* homosexual, gay, homoerotic, Sapphic, tribadic; *inf.* queer.

lesion *noun lesions on her face after the accident* wound, injury, sore, abrasion, scratch, scrape, cut, gash, laceration, trauma.

less *adjective of less importance* smaller, slighter, not so much, not so great.

less *pronoun have less than they have* smaller amount, not so much.

less *adverb she reads less now* to a lesser degree, to a smaller extent, not so much.

less *preposition £100 less the deposit* minus, subtracting, excepting, without.

lessen *verb* **1** *the wind/pain lessened* grow less, abate, decrease, diminish, subside, moderate, slacken, die down, let up, ease off, tail off, ebb, wane. **2** *the tablets lessened the pain* relieve, soothe, allay, assuage, alleviate, palliate, ease, dull, deaden, blunt, take the edge off. **3** *his behaviour lessened him in their eyes* diminish, lower, reduce, minimize, degrade, discredit, devalue, belittle, humble.
Opposites INCREASE; MAGNIFY.

lesser *adjective* **1** *one of his lesser works* less important, minor, slighter, secondary, inferior. **2** *lesser people had to stand* subordinate, minor, inferior.

lesson *noun* **1** *have a music lesson* class, period of instruction/teaching/coaching/tutoring/schooling. **2** *children doing lessons* exercise, schoolwork, homework, assignment, school task. **3** *reading the lesson in church* Bible passage, Bible reading, scripture, text. **4** *punished as a lesson to others* example, warning, deterrent, message, moral, precept. **5** *hardship*

taught him valuable lessons knowledge, wisdom, enlightenment, experience, truths.

lest *conjunction lest we forget* in case, in order to avoid, for fear that.

let *verb* **1** *let them play there* allow, permit, give permission to, give leave to, authorize, sanction, grant, warrant, license, assent to, consent to, agree to, give the go-ahead to, give the thumbs up to; *inf.* give the green light to. **2** *let the people through* allow to go, permit to pass. **3** *let it be known* cause, make, enable. **4** *he let his house* let out, rent, rent out, lease, hire, hire out, sublet. **let down** **1** *they felt he had let them down* fail to support, fail, fall short of expectation, disappoint, disillusion, forsake, abandon, desert, leave stranded, leave in the lurch, betray. **2** *let down the skirt* lengthen, make longer. **let fly** **1** *let fly a large stone* hurl, fling, throw, propel, pitch, lob, toss, heave, launch, shoot; *inf.* chuck. **2** *she just let fly at him* lose one's temper, explode, erupt with anger, let someone have it, give free reign to one's emotions, keep nothing back, give vent to one's emotions, lash out at. **let in** *let the dog in* allow to enter, admit, open the door to, grant entrance to, give access to, give right of entry to, receive, welcome, greet. **let in for** *let them in for a lot of expense* involve, draw into, implicate. **let in on** *let them in on the deal* include, count in, admit, allow to share in, let participate in, take in. **let off** **1** *let off the firework* explode, detonate. **2** *letting off fumes* give off, discharge, emit, release, exude, leak. **3** *let the guilty man off* acquit, release, discharge, reprieve, absolve, exonerate, pardon, forgive, exempt, spare. **let on** **1** *don't let on that you know him* reveal, make known, tell, disclose, divulge, let out, give away, leak. **2** *he let on that he was deaf* pretend, feign, affect, make out, make believe, simulate, fake. **let out** **1** *let the animals out of the cage* allow to leave, open the door for, grant exit to, let go, free, set free, release, liberate. **2** *she let out a scream* emit, utter, give vent to, produce. **3** *she let out that she knew him* reveal, make known, tell, disclose. *See* LET ON 1. **let up** **1** *the thunderstorm finally let up* lessen, abate, decrease, diminish, subside, moderate, slacken, die down, ease off, tail off, ebb, wane. **2** *if you don't let up you'll have a breakdown* do less, relax one's efforts, relax, stop. **3** *please let up on the child* treat less severely, be more lenient with, be kinder to; *inf.* go easy on.

let-down *noun the match was a let-down* disappointment, disillusionment, non-success, fiasco, anticlimax; *inf.* wash-out.

lethal *adjective a lethal blow/dose | potentially lethal set of circumstances* fatal, deadly, mortal, death-dealing, murderous, poisonous, toxic, dangerous, virulent, noxious, destructive, disastrous, calamitous, ruinous.
Opposites HARMLESS; SAFE.

lethargic *adjective* sluggish, inactive, slow, slothful, torpid, phlegmatic, listless, languid, apathetic, passive, weary, enervated, fatigued, sleepy, narcotic. *See* LETHARGY.
Opposites ACTIVE; ENERGETIC.

lethargy *noun* sluggishness, inertia, inactivity, slowness, sloth, idleness, torpor, torpidity, lifelessness, dullness, listlessness, languor, languidness, phlegm, apathy, passivity, weariness, lassitude, fatigue, sleepiness, drowsiness, somnolence, narcosis.

letter *noun* **1** *written in bold letters | letter of the alphabet* character, alphabetical character, sign, symbol. **2** *send a letter* written message, message, written communication, communication, note, line, business letter, missive, epistle, dispatch, love-letter, billet-doux, fan letter, letter of thanks, thank-you letter, bread-and-butter letter, reply, acknowledgement; *inf.* Dear John letter. **to the letter** *follow our instructions to the letter* with strict attention to detail, strictly, precisely, exactly, accurately, literally, word for word, verbatim. **the letter of the law** *interpret agreements according to the letter of the law* exact wording, literal interpretation, form of words.

lettered *adjective* *a lettered person* learned, erudite, academic, well-educated, educated, wellread, widely read, cultured, cultivated, scholarly, literary; *inf.* highbrow.

letters *plural noun* *a man of letters* learning, scholarship, erudition, education, culture, cultivation, literature, humanities, belles-lettres.

let-up *noun* *no let-up in the hostilities* lessening, abatement, decrease, diminishing, diminution, subsidence, moderation, slackening, dying down, easing off, tailing off, ebbing, waning.

level *adjective* **1** *a level surface* flat, smooth, even, uniform, plane, flush, horizontal. **2** *keep the temperature level* even, uniform, regular, consistent, constant, stable, steady, unchanging, unvarying, unfluctuating. **3** *the two teams are level* equal, on a level, in a position of equality, close together, neck and neck, level-pegging, side by side, on a par, with nothing to choose between them; *inf.* even-Steven. **4** *hang the pictures level with each other* on the same level, on a level, at the same height, aligned, in line, balanced. **5** *have a level temper* even, even-tempered, equable, steady, stable, calm, serene, tranquil, composed, unruffled. *Opposites* UNEVEN; BUMPY; VERTICAL; VARIABLE.

level *noun* **1** *at eye-level* height, highness, altitude, elevation, distance upward. **2** *what level is he in the firm?* level of achievement, position, rank, standing, status, station, degree, grade, stage, standard. **3** *what level of expense have you in mind?* extent, amount, quantity, measure, degree, volume, size. **4** *glad to be back on the level after mountaineering* flat surface, flat, horizontal, plane, plain. **5** *levels of rock* layer, stratum, bed. **6** *what level do you live on?* floor, storey. **on the level** *are you sure your partner's on the level?* honest, above-board, straight, fair, genuine, true, sincere, open, straightforward; *inf.* upfront, kosher.

level *verb* **1** *level the surface* level out, make level, even off, even out, make flat, flatten, smooth, smooth out, plane. **2** *level the buildings* raze, raze to the ground, pull down, knock down, tear down, demolish, flatten, bulldoze, lay waste, destroy. **3** *level the trees* fell, cut down, chop down, hew down. **4** *level his opponent* knock down, knock to the ground, throw to the ground, lay out, prostrate, flatten, floor, fell, knock out; *inf.* KO, kayo. **5** *his goal levelled the score* make level, equalize, make equal, even, even up. **6** *level his gun at the target* aim, point, direct, train, sight, focus, beam, zero in on, draw a bead on. **7** *he's not levelling with you* be honest, be above-board, tell the truth, tell all, be frank, be open, hide nothing, keep nothing back, be straightforward, put all one's cards on the table; *inf.* be upfront.

level-headed *adjective* sensible, full of common sense, prudent, circumspect, shrewd, wise, reasonable, rational, sane, composed, calm, cool, collected; cool, calm, and collected; cool-headed, balanced, self-possessed, unruffled, even-tempered, imperturbable; *inf.* unflappable, together.

lever *noun* **1** *use a lever to prise the lid off* bar, crowbar, handspike, jemmy. **2** *release the lever to operate the machine* handle, grip, pull, switch.

lever *verb* *lever the lid open | lever the load up* prise, force, move, jemmy, raise, lift, hoist, purchase; *Am.* pry.

leverage *noun* **1** *not enough leverage to move the load* purchase, force, strength. **2** *not have the leverage to win over the committee* power, influence, authority, weight, ascendancy, rank; *inf.* pull, clout.

levitate *noun* *people claiming to be able to levitate* rise into the air, float, hover, be suspended, glide, fly.

levity *noun* **1** *showing levity at a solemn occasion* light-heartedness, carefreeness, light-mindedness, humour, facetiousness, fun, jocularity, hilarity, frivolity, flippancy, triviality, silliness, giddiness, skittishness. **2** *the levity of her nature* fickleness, inconstancy, instability, unsteadiness, variability, changeability, unreliability, undependability, inconsistency, flightiness.
Opposites GRAVITY; CONSTANCY.

levy *noun* **1** *the levy of taxes* collection, gathering, raising, imposition, exaction, assessment. See LEVY *verb* 1. **2** *unable to pay the levy* tax, taxation, tariff, toll, excise, customs, duty, dues, imposition, impost, assessment. **3** *inspect the levy* conscripts, troops, forces, armed forces, army, militia, guard.

levy *verb* **1** *levy taxes* collect, gather, raise, impose, exact, demand, charge, tax. **2** *levy troops* conscript, call up, enlist, muster, mobilize, rally, press; *Am.* draft.

lewd *adjective* **1** *a lewd old man* lecherous, lustful, licentious, lascivious, promiscuous, carnal, sensual, randy, prurient, salacious, lubricious, libidinous, concupiscent, debauched, dissipated, dissolute, profligate, unchaste, wanton. **2** *lewd literature* obscene, pornographic, blue, bawdy, salacious, suggestive, ribald, indecent, vulgar, crude, smutty, dirty, coarse, gross, foul, vile; *inf.* raunchy.

lewdness *noun* **1** *the lewdness of the old man* lechery, lust, lustfulness, licentiousness, lasciviousness, promiscuity, carnality, sensuality, randiness, prurience, pruriency, salaciousness, salacity, lubricity, libidinousness, concupiscence, debauchery, dissipation, dissoluteness, profligacy, unchasteness, wantonness. **2** *the lewdness of the literature* obscenity, blueness, bawdiness, salaciousness, salacity, suggestiveness, ribaldry, indecency, vulgarity, crudeness, smut, smuttiness, dirtiness, coarseness, grossness, foulness, vileness; *inf.* raunchiness.

liability *noun* **1** *admit liability for the lost goods* responsibility, legal responsibility, accountability, answerability, blame, blameworthiness, culpability, amenableness. **2** *meet his financial liabilities* obligation, financial obligation, debt, indebtedness, debit, arrears, dues. **3** *don't take her brother with you - he will just be a liability* hindrance, encumbrance, burden, impediment, handicap, nuisance, inconvenience, drawback, drag, disadvantage, millstone round one's neck, stumbling-block, cross to bear. **4** *dislike her liability to burst into tears* aptness, likelihood, inclination, tendency, disposition, predisposition, proneness.

liable *adjective* **1** *husbands liable for their wives' debts | hotels are not liable for customers' lost property* responsible, legally responsible, accountable, answerable, chargeable, blameworthy, at fault, censurable, amenable. **2** *liable to injury* exposed, open, subject, susceptible, vulnerable, in danger of, at risk of, pregnable. **3** *liable to burst into tears* apt, likely, inclined, tending, disposed, predisposed, prone.
Opposites UNACCOUNTABLE; SAFE; UNLIKELY.

liaison *noun* **1** *no liaison between the departments* communication, contact, connection, interchange, link, linkage, tie-up. **2** *he acts as liaison between the departments* intermediary, contact man/woman/person, linkman, linkwoman, linkperson, go-between. **3** *his wife found out about his liaison* affair, love affair, relationship, romance, intrigue, amour, amorous/ romantic entanglement, entanglement, flirtation; *inf.* hanky-panky.

liar *noun* teller of lies, teller of untruths, fibber, fibster, perjurer, falsifier, false witness, fabricator, equivocator, prevaricator, deceiver, spinner of yarns; *inf.* storyteller.

libation *noun* **1** *offer a libation to the gods* liquid offering, offering, tribute, oblation, sacrifice. **2** *in need of a libation after the long walk* drink, liquid refreshment, beverage, alcoholic drink, dram, bracer; *inf.* tincture.

libel *noun* *a writer found guilty of libel* defamation of character, defamation, denigration, vilification, disparagement, derogation, aspersions, calumny, slander, false report, traducement, obloquy, abuse, slur, smear, smear campaign.

libel *verb* *his biographer libelled him* defame, vilify, give someone a bad name, blacken someone's name, denigrate, disparage, derogate, cast aspersions on, asperse, calumniate, slander, write false reports about, traduce, abuse, revile, malign, slur, smear, fling mud at, drag someone's name through the mud/mire.

libellous *adjective* *published libellous remarks* defamatory, denigratory, vilifying, disparaging, derogatory, aspersive, calumnious, calumniatory, slanderous, false, misrepresentative, traducing, abusive, reviling, malicious,

maligning, scurrilous, slurring, smearing, muckraking.

liberal *adjective* **1** *a liberal supply of food* abundant, copious, ample, plentiful, lavish, profuse, munificent, bountiful, rich, handsome, generous. **2** *hosts liberal with their hospitality* generous, magnanimous, open-handed, unsparing, unstinting, ungrudging, lavish, munificent, bountiful, bounteous, beneficent, big-hearted, kind-hearted, kind, philanthropic, charitable, altruistic, unselfish. **3** *people of liberal ideas who are against discrimination of any kind* tolerant, unprejudiced, unbiased, unbigoted, impartial, non-partisan, disinterested, broad-minded, enlightened, catholic, indulgent, permissive. **4** *a liberal interpretation of the law* broad, loose, flexible, non-restrictive, free, general, non-literal, not strict, not close, inexact, imprecise. **5** *liberal in his politics* advanced, forward-looking, progressive, reformist, radical, latitudinarian. **6** *a liberal education* wide-ranging, broad-based, general, humanistic.
Opposites MISERLY; NARROW-MINDED; CONSERVATIVE; REACTIONARY.

liberate *verb* *liberate prisoners | liberate the occupied country* set free, free, release, let out, let go, discharge, set loose, unshackle, unfetter, unchain, deliver, rescue, emancipate, manumit, unyoke.
Opposites CONFINE; IMPRISON.

liberation *noun* **1** *the liberation of the prisoners* freeing, release, discharge, unshackling, deliverance, emancipation, manumission. See LIBERATE. **2** *women seeking liberation* freedom, equality, equal rights, non-discrimination, emancipation, enfranchisement.

liberator *noun* rescuer, saviour, deliverer, freer, emancipator, manumitter.

libertine *adjective* *disapprove of their libertine ways* licentious, lustful, lecherous, lascivious, dissolute, dissipated, debauched, immoral, wanton, decadent, depraved, profligate, rakish, sensual, promiscuous, unchaste, impure, sinful, intemperate, abandoned, corrupt.

libertine *noun* *seduced by a libertine* lecher, seducer, debauchee, profligate, rake, roué, wanton, loose liver, sensualist, reprobate, womanizer, adulterer, Don Juan, Lothario, Casanova; *inf.* lech.

liberty *noun* **1** *countries which have always had liberty* freedom, independence, autonomy, sovereignty, self-government, self-rule. **2** *prisoners gaining their liberty* freedom, liberation, release, discharge, deliverance, emancipation, manumission. **3** *have the liberty to choose* freedom, free will, volition, latitude, option, choice, non-compulsion, non-coercion. **4** *given the liberty to leave the grounds* right, prerogative, privilege, permission, sanction, authorization, licence, *carte blanche*, dispensation, exemption. **5** *sacked because of the liberties he took | was guilty of taking liberties* overfamiliarity, familiarity, disrespect, impropriety, indecorum, breach of etiquette, impertinence, insolence, impudence, presumptuousness, presumption, forwardness, audacity. **at liberty 1** *the thief/animal is still at liberty* free, loose, on the loose, at large, unconfined.

2 *you are at liberty to do as you wish* free, permitted, allowed, entitled.
Opposites DEPENDENCE; CAPTIVITY; CONSTRAINT.

libidinous *adjective* lustful, lecherous, lascivious, lewd, carnal, sensual, salacious, prurient, concupiscent, lubricious, dissolute, debauched, degenerate, decadent, wanton, immoral, unchaste, impure, intemperate, randy; *inf.* horny.

libido *noun has a high/low libido* sexual desire, sex drive, sexual appetite, sexiness, sexual passion, lust, lustfulness, randiness; *inf.* horniness.

licence *noun* **1** *be given licence to sell their wares* permission, leave, liberty, freedom, consent, authority, authorization, sanction, approval, warranty, certification, accreditation, entitlement, privilege, prerogative, right, dispensation, exemption. **2** *they have the licence to do as they please* freedom, liberty, free will, latitude, choice, option, independence, self-determination. **3** *have a driving licence* permit, certificate, credential, document, documentation, pass. **4** *appalled at the licence at the all-night party* licentiousness, dissoluteness, dissipation, debauchery, immorality, decadence, profligacy, immoderation, intemperateness, indulgence, self-indulgence, excess, excessiveness, lack of restraint, lack of control, irresponsibility, abandon, disorderliness, unruliness, lawlessness, anarchy.

license *verb* **1** *license them to sell alcohol* grant a licence to, give a licence to, give a permit to, authorize, give authorization to, grant the right to, warrant, certify, accredit, charter, franchise. **2** *license them to ride the horses at weekends* give permission to, permit, allow, grant leave to, entitle, give the freedom to, sanction, give one's approval to, empower.
Opposites BAN; FORBID.

licentious *adjective* dissolute, lustful, lecherous, lascivious, dissipated, debauched, immoral, wanton, decadent, depraved, profligate, sensual, promiscuous, unchaste, impure, intemperate, abandoned.
Opposites MORAL; VIRTUOUS.

licit *adjective declared a licit action* legal, lawful, legitimate, permissible, admissible, allowable, acceptable.

lick *verb* **1** *lick the ice-cream* pass the tongue over, touch with the tongue, tongue, taste, lap. **2** *flames licking the walls* touch, play over, flick over, dart over, ripple over. **3** *lick the opponents* defeat, beat, conquer, trounce, thrash, rout, vanquish, overcome, overwhelm, overpower, drub; *inf.* wipe the floor with. **4** *lick his son* beat, thrash, flog, whip, strike, hit, thwack, slap, spank; *inf.* wallop, whack, lambaste. **5** *lick the problem* get the better of, overcome, solve, find an answer to, find a solution to.

licking *noun* **1** *the team gave their opponents a good licking* defeat, beating, trouncing, thrashing, drubbing. **2** *the boy received a licking from his father* beating, thrashing, flogging, whipping, slapping, spanking; *inf.* walloping, hiding, tanning.

lid *noun* cover, top, cap, cork, stopper, plug. **put the lid on** *when the teacher found out it put the lid on their plans* be the end of, put an end to, put a stop to, ruin, put paid to, destroy. **take the lid off** *take the lid off the scandal* expose, reveal, bring to light, make known, make public, bring into the open.

lie¹ *noun witness found to be telling lies* untruth, falsehood, barefaced lie, fib, white lie, little white lie, fabrication, made-up story, trumped-up story, invention, piece of fiction, fiction, falsification, falsity, fairy story, cock-and-bull story, dissimulation, prevarication, departure from the truth; *inf.* terminological inexactitude, tall tale, whopper. **give the lie to** *the historical evidence gave the lie to his theory* disprove, contradict, negate, deny, refute, rebut, challenge, gainsay.
Opposites TRUTH; FACT.

lie² *verb the witness was lying* tell a lie, tell an untruth, tell a falsehood, perjure oneself, fib, tell a white lie, fabricate, invent/make up a story, falsify, dissemble, dissimulate, prevaricate, depart from the truth, be economical with the truth, bear false witness; *inf.* tell a terminological inexactitude.

lie³ *verb* **1** *he was lying not sitting* recline, be recumbent, be prostrate, be supine, be prone, be stretched out, sprawl, rest, repose, relax, lounge, loll. **2** *the town lies on the other side of the hill* be, be situated, be located, be placed, be positioned, be found. **3** *two poets lie there* be buried, be interred. **4** *lie dormant* remain, continue, stay, be. **5** *his guilt lies heavily on him* press down, weigh down, be a great weight on, be a burden to, oppress. **lie in** *their strength lies in their faith* consist, be inherent, inhere, be present, exist, reside. **lie low** *they lay low during the police search* hide, go into hiding, hide out, conceal oneself, keep out of sight, keep a low profile, take cover, go to earth, go to ground, go underground; *inf.* hole up.

liege *noun* liege lord, lord, feudal lord, overlord, suzerain, master, chief, chieftain, superior.

lieutenant *noun the gang-leader and his lieutenant* assistant, aide, deputy, second-in-command, right-hand man/woman, henchman, henchwoman, subordinate; *inf.* sidekick.

life *noun* **1** *is there life in the body?* existence, being, animation, aliveness, viability. **2** *is there life on Mars?|no sign of life* living things, living beings, living creatures, human/animal/plant life, fauna, flora, human activity. **3** *many lives were lost in the war* person, human being, individual, mortal, soul. **4** *worked hard all her life* lifetime, days, duration of life, course of life, life-span, time on earth, existence, career; *inf.* one's born days. **5** *the life of a battery* duration, active life, functioning period, period of effectiveness, period of usefulness. **6** *modern conveniences make life easier* course of life, living, activities, conduct, behaviour. **7** *he should really have won but that's life* the human condition, the way of the world, the world, the times we live in, the usual state of affairs. **8** *he leads/has a very affluent life* way of life, way

of living, manner of living, lifestyle, situation, position. **9** *he wrote a life of the poet | she is writing her life* biography, autobiography, life story, memoirs, history, career, diary, journal, confessions. **10** *children full of life | put some life in the party* animation, vivacity, liveliness, vitality, verve, high spirits, sparkle, exuberance, buoyancy, effervescence, enthusiasm, energy, vigour, dynamism, go, brio; *inf.* oomph, pizazz, pep, zing. **11** *he was the life of the firm* life force, vital spirit, spirit, vital spark, animating spirit, moving force, lifeblood, very essence, essence, heart, core, soul. **come to life 1** *the town comes to life at night* become active, come alive, become lively, wake up, awaken, show signs of life. **2** *toys come to life in the play* become animate, come alive, become a living creature. **for dear life, for dear life's sake** *they ran for dear life | they banged the door for dear life's sake* as fast/hard etc. as possible, for all one is worth, in desperation, with urgency, urgently, with as much vigour as possible, like the devil. **give one's life 1** *he gave his life for his friend* die for, sacrifice oneself for, die to save. **2** *give one's life to teaching* dedicate oneself, devote oneself, give oneself, pledge oneself, surrender oneself.
Opposites DEATH; DEMISE.

life-and-death *adjective a life-and-death decision* vital, of vital importance, crucial, critical, urgent, momentous, important, serious.

lifeblood *noun manufacturing is the lifeblood of the economy* life, life-force, animating spirit, moving force, driving force, vital spark, inspiration, animus, essence, heart, core.

life-giving *adjective* vitalizing, animating, vivifying, energizing, invigorating, enlivening, stimulating.

lifeless *adjective* **1** *the boy was lifeless on being pulled from the water* dead, deceased, gone, cold, defunct. **2** *prefer lifeless statues to people* inanimate, without life, abiotic. **3** *lifeless stretches of country* barren, sterile, bare, desolate, stark, arid, unproductive, uncultivated, empty, uninhabited, unoccupied. **4** *a lifeless performance* spiritless, lacking vitality, unspirited, lacklustre, apathetic, uninspired, colourless, dull, flat, stiff, wooden, tedious, uninspiring.
Opposites ALIVE; ANIMATE; LIVELY.

lifelike *adjective a lifelike portrait* true-to-life, realistic, photographic, speaking, faithful, authentic, exact, vivid, graphic, natural.

lifelong *adjective a lifelong commitment* for all one's life, lifetime's, lasting, constant, enduring, abiding, permanent.

lifestyle *noun an affluent lifestyle* way of life, way of living, manner of living, life.

lifetime *noun* **1** *many technological advances in his lifetime* life, life-span, existence. *See* LIFE 4. **2** *what is the lifetime of the average battery?* life, duration, functioning period. *See* LIFE 5. **3** *wait a lifetime for him to change his ways* all one's life, a very long time; *inf.* ages, an age.

lift *verb* **1** *lift the sack* pick up, uplift, hoist, upheave, raise, raise up, upraise, heft. **2** *lift the flag* raise high, hold up, bear aloft. **3** *your visit lifted his spirits* raise, buoy up, boost, ele-

vate. **4** *the new player lifted their game* improve, boost, enhance, make better, ameliorate, upgrade. **5** *the mist lifted* rise, disperse, dissipate, disappear, vanish, be dispelled. **6** *lift the ban* raise, remove, withdraw, revoke, rescind, cancel, annul, void, countermand, relax, end, stop, terminate. **7** *lift the potatoes* dig up, pick, pull up, take up. **8** *lift food to the famine region* airlift, transport by air, transport, move, transfer. **9** *lift one's voice* raise, make louder, louden, amplify. **10** *lift the passage from a critic* plagiarize, pirate, copy, abstract; *inf.* crib. **11** *someone's lifted my purse* steal, thieve, rob, pilfer, purloin, filch, pocket, take, appropriate; *inf.* pinch, nick, swipe.
Opposites DROP; LOWER; PLACE.

lift *noun* **1** *give the child a lift up* hoist, heave, push, thrust, shove, help, a helping hand. **2** *the visitors gave the patient a lift* boost, fillip, pick-me-up, stimulus; *inf.* shot in the arm. **3** *the new player gave their game a lift* boost, improvement, enhancement, upgrading, amelioration. **4** *give the children a lift to school* car ride, ride, run, drive, transportation. **5** *go up in the lift | goods lift* elevator, hoist.

light¹ *noun* **1** *see by the light of the sun/fire* illumination, luminescence, luminosity, shining, gleaming, brightness, brilliance, glowing, blaze, glare, incandescence, effulgence, refulgence, lambency, radiance, lustre, sunlight, moonlight, starlight, lamplight, firelight, electric light, gaslight, ray of light, shaft of light, beam of light. **2** *bring the light over here* lamp, torch, flashlight, lantern, candle, taper, beacon. **3** *strike a light* flame, spark, match, lighter. **4** *we like to travel in the light, not the dark* daylight, daylight hours, daytime, day, hours of sunlight. **5** *we shall leave at light* first light, dawn, crack of dawn, daybreak, sunrise, cock-crow, morning. **6** *see things in a different light | things appeared in a new light* aspect, angle, slant, approach, viewpoint, point of view. **7** *light finally dawned and I solved the problem* enlightenment, illumination, understanding, comprehension, awareness, knowledge, elucidation, explanation. **8** *he was one of the lights in the theatre group* leading lights, luminary, star, guiding light, expert, authority. **9** *he did his best; he acted according to his lights | by her own lights* she knew mental powers, intelligence, intellect, knowledge, understanding, talent. **bring to light** *the search brought to light new evidence* reveal, disclose, expose, uncover, show up, unearth, bring to notice. **come to light** *new evidence came to light* be discovered, be uncovered, be unearthed, appear, come out, turn up, transpire. **in the light of** *in the light of his previous convictions* taking into consideration, considering, taking into account, bearing in mind, keeping in mind, mindful of, taking note of, in view of. **shed/throw light on** *can you shed any light on this matter?* elucidate, clarify, clear up, explain, offer an explanation for.
Opposites DARK; DARKNESS; IGNORANCE.

light² *adjective* **1** *a light room* full of light, bright, well-lit, well-lighted, well-illuminated, sunny. **2** *wearing light clothes* light-coloured, light-toned, pale, pale-coloured, pastel, pastel-coloured, whitish, faded, bleached. **3** *she had*

light hair light-coloured, fair, blond.
Opposites DARK.

light³ *verb* **1** *light the fire* set burning, set fire to, set a match to, ignite, kindle. **2** *fireworks lit up the sky* illuminate, brighten, lighten, irradiate, flood with light, floodlight; *lit.* illumine. **3** *a smile lit up her face* irradiate, brighten, animate, make cheerful, cheer up, enliven. **4** *light them to their seats* direct, guide, usher, escort.

light⁴ *adjective* **1** *the suitcases are light* non-heavy, easy to carry, portable. **2** *small, light children* slight, thin, slender, skinny, underweight, small, tiny. **3** *wearing light clothes* lightweight, thin, flimsy, insubstantial, delicate, floaty, gossamer. **4** *a light tap on the shoulder | heard a light knock* gentle, slight, delicate, soft, weak, faint, indistinct. **5** *light tasks* moderate, easy, simple, undemanding, untaxing, unexacting, effortless, facile; *inf.* cushy. **6** *light music/reading/entertainment* non-serious, readily-understood, light-hearted, entertaining, diverting, recreative, pleasing, amusing, humorous, funny, frivolous, superficial, trivial, trifling. **7** *a light attack of flu | a light sentence* non-severe, mild, moderate, slight. **8** *this is no light matter* unimportant, insignificant, trivial, trifling, petty, inconsequential. **9** *a light meal* non-heavy, non-rich, non-large, easily digested, small, modest, scanty, skimpy, frugal. **10** *with light heart* light-hearted, carefree, cheerful, cheery, happy, gay, merry, blithe, sunny, untroubled. **11** *with light fingers | was light of foot* nimble, deft, agile, supple, lithe, spry, sprightly, graceful, light-footed. **12** *feeling light in the head* light-headed, giddy, dizzy, vertiginous, faint, unsteady; *inf.* woozy. **13** *light in character* frivolous, giddy, skittish, flighty, fickle, erratic, mercurial, volatile, capricious. **14** *of light morals* non-chaste, loose, promiscuous, licentious, dissolute, dissipated, wanton. **15** *light soil* non-dense, porous, crumbly, friable.
Opposites HEAVY; WEIGHTY; SERIOUS; SEVERE.

light⁵ *verb* **light into** *light into their attackers* attack, assault, set upon, fall upon, strike, beat, tear into; *inf.* lay into, let someone have it, lambaste, lace into. **light upon** *light upon treasure | lit upon the truth* come across, chance upon, happen upon, stumble upon, hit upon, find, discover, encounter.

lighten¹ *verb* **1** *the sky lightened* become lighter, grow brighter, brighten. **2** *the flames lightened* blaze, glow, gleam, flicker, sparkle. **3** *it was lightening this morning* emit lightning, flash lightning, fulgurate. **4** *the larger windows lightened the room* make lighter, make brighter, brighten, light up, illuminate, shed light on, cast light on, irradiate. **5** *the sun had lightened the colours* whiten, bleach, pale.
Opposites DARKEN.

lighten² *verb* **1** *lighten the horse's load* make lighter, lessen, reduce, ease. **2** *lighten his burden of pain* lessen, reduce, ease, alleviate, mitigate, allay, relieve, assuage, ameliorate. **3** *the good news lightened his mood* brighten, cheer up, gladden, hearten, buoy up, perk up, lift, uplift,

enliven, elate, inspire, revive, restore.
Opposites INCREASE; INTENSIFY; DEPRESS.

light-fingered *adjective* *shopkeepers on the watch for light-fingered people* thieving, thievish, stealing, pilfering, filching, shop-lifting, pocket-picking, dishonest; *inf.* crooked.

light-footed *adjective* light of foot, spry, sprightly, light on one's feet, graceful, nimble, agile, lithe.

light-headed *adjective* **1** *feeling light-headed at the top of the ladder* giddy, dizzy, vertiginous, faint, unsteady, light in the head; *inf.* woozy. **2** *light-headed young girls* giddy, scatterbrained, feather-brained, hare-brained, flighty, dizzy, frivolous, superficial, empty-headed, vacuous, flippant, shallow, light-minded, silly, inane; *inf.* birdbrained.

light-hearted *adjective* carefree, cheerful, cheery, happy, glad, gay, merry, playful, jolly, joyful, jovial, gleeful, frolicsome, effervescent, in good spirits, blithe, sunny, untroubled; *inf.* chirpy, upbeat.
Opposites MISERABLE; GLOOMY.

lighthouse *noun* light-tower, warning light, guiding light, beacon, suitor's landmark, pharos.

lightly *adverb* **1** *snow falling lightly* slightly, thinly, softly, gently. **2** *salt the food lightly* sparingly, sparsely, slightly. **3** *get off lightly* easily, without severe punishment, leniently. **4** *jump lightly over the fence* easily, nimbly, agilely, lithely, spryly, gracefully. **5** *dismiss the subject lightly* airily, carelessly, heedlessly, uncaringly, indifferently, thoughtlessly, flippantly, frivolously, slightingly; *inf.* breezily.

lightweight *adjective* **1** *lightweight clothes* light, thin, flimsy. *See* LIGHT⁴ *adjective* 3. **2** *lightweight prose | he's a lightweight writer* insignificant, of no account, unimportant, of no consequence, inconsequential, insubstantial, trivial, trifling, paltry, petty, of no merit, of no value, valueless, worthless.
Opposites HEAVY; WEIGHTY; heavyweight; SIGNIFICANT.

likable *adjective. See* LIKEABLE.

like *adjective* *like people are attracted to each other | houses of like design* similar, much the same, more or less the same, not unlike, comparable, corresponding, resembling, analogous, parallel, equivalent, of a kind, identical, matching, akin.
Opposites UNLIKE; DISSIMILAR; DIFFERENT.

like *preposition* **1** *he paints like Picasso* in the same way as, in the manner of, in a similar way to, after the fashion of, along the lines of. **2** *it was like him to be generous* typical of, characteristic of, in character with.

like *noun* *not see his like again* equal, match, counterpart, fellow, twin, mate, parallel, peer, compeer.

like *verb* **1** *they like each other* be fond of, have a liking for, be attracted to, be keen on, love, adore, have a soft spot for. **2** *he likes swimming* enjoy, be keen on, find/take pleasure in, love, adore, find agreeable, delight in, relish, revel in; *inf.* get a kick from. **3** *we should like you to*

go wish, want, desire, prefer, had sooner, had
rather. **4** *how would you like it if it happened to
you?* feel about, regard, think about, appreciate.
Opposites DISLIKE; HATE.

likeable, likable *adjective* pleasant, nice,
friendly, agreeable, amiable, genial, charming,
engaging, pleasing, appealing, winning, attractive, winsome, lovable, adorable.

likelihood *noun very little likelihood of his winning*
likeliness, probability, good chance, chance,
prospect, good prospect, reasonable prospect,
possibility, distinct possibility, strong possibility.

likely *adjective* **1** *it is likely that he will go* probable, distinctly possible, to be expected, on the
cards, odds-on, possible. **2** *it is likely to rain at
this time of year* apt, inclined, tending, disposed,
liable, prone. **3** *he gave a likely enough reason*
reasonable, plausible, feasible, acceptable,
believable, credible, tenable, conceivable.
4 *that's a likely story! who would believe that?*
unlikely, implausible, unacceptable, unbelievable, incredible, untenable, inconceivable. **5** *a
likely place for a picnic* suitable, appropriate, fit,
fitting, acceptable, proper, right, qualified, relevant, reasonable. **6** *the most likely young people
in the firm* likely-to-succeed, promising, talented, gifted; *inf.* up-and-coming.
Opposites UNLIKELY; IMPROBABLE; INCREDIBLE.

likely *adverb* *he'll very likely refuse* probably, in
all probability, no doubt, doubtlessly; *inf.* like
enough, like as not.

liken *verb* *liken his work to that of Picasso* show
the resemblance/similarity between, compare,
equate, analogize, draw an analogy between,
draw a parallel between, parallel, correlate,
link, associate.

likeness *noun* **1** *there is a distinct likeness in the
faces of the two friends* alikeness, resemblance,
similarity, sameness, similitude, correspondence, analogy, parallelism. **2** *appear in the
likeness of Santa Claus* guise, semblance, appearance, outward form, form, shape, character.
3 *he will draw a likeness of your child* picture,
drawing, sketch, painting, portrait, photograph, study, representation, image, bust,
statue, statuette, sculpture, icon.

likewise *adverb* **1** *she left early and he did likewise* in like manner, in the same way, similarly, in similar fashion, the same. **2** *we
enjoyed the food and likewise the company* in addition, also, too, besides, moreover, furthermore,
into the bargain, as well.

liking *noun* fondness, love, affection, desire,
preference, partiality, penchant, bias, weakness, weak spot, soft spot, appreciation, taste,
predilection, fancy, inclination, bent, leaning,
affinity, proclivity, propensity, proneness, tendency.
Opposites DISLIKE; AVERSION; HATRED.

lilt *noun* *a lilt in her voice* rise and fall, cadence,
inflection, upswing, rhythm.

limb *noun* **1** *injure a limb* arm, leg, wing, member, extremity, appendage. **2** *cut down limbs
from the tree* branch, bough. **3** *a limb of a mountain* spur, projection. **4** *the society is a limb of an
international organization* branch, section, member, offshoot. **out on a limb 1** *he put himself out
on a limb when he voted against the bill* isolated,
stranded, segregated, set apart, separate, solitary, sequestered. **2** *you will be out on a limb if
you challenge the headmaster's authority* in a precarious position, vulnerable, in a risky situation.

limber *verb* **limber up** warm up, loosen up,
stretch, exercise, get ready.

limbo *noun* **1** *souls in limbo* abode of unbap-
tized infants. **2** *slaves sentenced to limbo* imprisonment, incarceration, confinement,
internment, detention, captivity, bondage,
prison. **in limbo** *the proposals are in limbo* in
abeyance, suspended, in a state of suspension,
in a state of uncertainty, in a state of neglect,
up in the air, hanging fire, awaiting action; *inf.*
on the back burner.

limelight *noun* *people in the limelight | those seek-
ing the limelight* focus of attention, public attention, public notice, public eye, public
recognition, publicity, glare of publicity, fame,
renown, celebrity, stardom, notability, eminence, prominence, spotlight.

limit *noun* **1** *outside the 200-mile fishing limit*
boundary, boundary line, bound, bounding
line, partition line, demarcation line, end-
point, cut-off point, termination. **2** *push his
patience to the limit* extremity, utmost, greatest
extent, ultimate, breaking-point, end-point,
the bitter end. **3** *cross the limits of his land*
boundary, border, bound, frontier, edge,
perimeter, confines, periphery. **4** *impose a
speed/spending limit* maximum, ceiling, limitation, restriction, curb, check, restraint. **the
limit** *his latest action is the limit* the last straw,
the straw that broke the camel's back, enough,
more than enough; *inf.* the end, it.

limit *verb* **1** *limit their expenditure* place a limit
on, restrict, curb, check, keep within bounds,
hold in check, restrain, confine, control,
ration, reduce. **2** *the long skirt limited her freedom to move freely* restrict, curb, restrain, constrain, hinder, impede, hamper, check,
trammel. **3** *the extent of their land is limited by
high fencing* demarcate, define, delimit, delimitate, mark off, stake out, encircle, encompass,
bound, circumscribe.

limitation *noun* **1** *the new rules imposed a limitation on their freedom* restriction, curb, restraint,
constraint, qualification, control, check, hindrance, impediment, obstacle, obstruction,
bar, barrier, block, deterrent. **2** *you must recognize your own limitations* inability, incapability,
incapacity, defect, frailty, weakness. **3** *the new
plan has its limitations* weak point, weakness,
drawback, snag, defect.

limited *adjective* **1** *committees having only limited powers* restricted, curbed, checked, controlled, restrained, constrained. **2** *provide
limited accommodation* restricted, scanty, sparse,
cramped, basic, minimal, inadequate. **3** *of limited experience* restricted, little, narrow, scanty,
basic, minimal, inadequate, insufficient.
4 *he's a hard worker but he's a bit limited* unintelligent, slow, slow-witted, not very bright, dull-
witted, stupid, dense, unimaginative, stolid.

Opposites UNLIMITED; LIMITLESS; ABSOLUTE; BOUND-
LESS.

limitless *adjective* **1** *a limitless expanse of forest*
infinite, endless, never-ending, interminable,
immense, vast, extensive, measureless. **2** *limitless optimism/enthusiasm* unlimited, boundless,
unbounded, illimitable, infinite, endless,
never-ending, unceasing, interminable, inexhaustible, constant, perpetual.

limp *verb* **1** *he still limps after the injury* walk
with a limp, walk with a jerk, hobble, shuffle,
shamble. **2** *the damaged ship limped into harbour* move slowly, crawl, drag.

limp *noun walk with a pronounced limp* lameness,
hobble, jerk, uneven gait, shuffle.

limp *adjective* **1** *limp leaves/flesh* lacking firmness, floppy, drooping, droopy, soft, flaccid,
flabby, loose, slack. **2** *feeling limp after the long
illness* without energy, tired, fatigued, weary,
exhausted, worn-out, lethargic, enervated, feeble, frail, puny, debilitated. **3** *he's rather a limp
character* weak, characterless, ineffectual,
insipid, wishy-washy, vapid, jejune; *inf.* wet.
Opposites FIRM; STIFF; ENERGETIC; STRONG.

limpid *adjective* **1** *limpid water/eyes* clear,
crystal-clear, transparent, glassy, glass-like,
translucent. **2** *limpid prose* lucid, clear, plain,
understandable, intelligible, comprehensible,
coherent, explicit, unambiguous. **3** *limpid
seas/days* calm, still, serene, tranquil, placid,
peaceful, unruffled, unperturbed.

line¹ *noun* **1** *draw lines* rule, bar, score, underline, underscore, stroke, slash. **2** *lines of white
through the black material* band, stripe, strip,
belt, seam. **3** *lines on her face* furrow, wrinkle,
crease, crow's-foot, groove, scar. **4** *admire the
lines of the sculpture | the line of her dress/figure* out-
line, contour, configuration, shape, figure,
delineation, silhouette, profile, cameo. **5** *the
ball went over the line | the state line* boundary,
boundary line, limit, border, borderline, frontier, demarcation line, edge, margin, perime-
ter, periphery. **6** *the line of the march | our line of
flight* course, route, track, channel, path, way,
road, lane, trajectory. **7** *his line of thought*
direction, course, drift, tack, tendency, trend,
bias, tenor. **8** *taking a tough line | the line of least
resistance* course of action, course, procedure,
technique, way, system, method, *modus
operandi*, policy, practice, scheme, approach,
avenue, position. **9** *what line is he in?* line of
work, line of business, business, field, area,
trade, occupation, employment, profession,
work, job, calling, career, pursuit, activity,
province, specialty, forte; *inf.* line of country,
game. **10** *he is stocking a new line of cosmetics*
brand, kind, sort, type, variety. **11** *a line of figures* row, column, series, sequence, succession,
progression. **12** *a line of people* row, queue,
procession, column, file, string, chain, array;
inf. crocodile. **13** *behind enemy lines* formation,
position, disposition, front, front line, firing-
line. **14** *he comes from a noble line* lineage,
descent, ancestry, parentage, family, extraction, heritage, stock, strain, race, breed.
15 *hang the washing on the line | a clothes-line | a
fishing-line* rope, string, cord, cable, wire,
thread, twine, strand, filament. **16** *drop her*

mother a line note, letter, card, postcard, message, word, communication. **17** *give his usual
line about having no money* spiel, story, patter,
piece of fiction, fabrication. **draw the line** *draw
the line at lending him money* stop short of, bar,
proscribe, set a limit at; *inf.* put one's foot
down about. **in line 1** *stand in line to be served*
in a row, in a queue, in a column, in a file.
2 *are the two pipes in line?* in alignment, aligned,
straight, plumb, true. **3** *their views are very
much in line* in agreement, in accord, in harmony, in step, in conformity, in rapport.
4 *keep the junior staff in line* under control, in
order, in check, obedient, conforming with the
rules. **in line for** *in line for the post of manager* a
candidate for, in the running for, on the short
list for, being considered for, next in succession for. **lay it on the line** *lay it on the line to him
that he would be sacked if he was late again* speak
frankly, state openly, be direct with, speak
honestly, pull no punches; *inf.* give it to someone straight. **lay/put on the line** *put his job on
the line* risk, put at risk, set at risk, put in danger, endanger, imperil. **toe the line** *pupils who
do not toe the line are asked to leave* conform,
obey the rules, comply with the rules, observe
the rules, abide by the rules, submit, yield.

line² *verb* **1** *grief had lined her face* mark with
lines, cover with lines, furrow, wrinkle,
crease. **2** *trees lined the driveway* border, edge,
fringe, bound, skirt, hem, rim, verge. **line up**
1 *line the children up* arrange in a line, arrange
in lines, put in rows, arrange in columns,
group, marshal. **2** *the children lined up* form a
line, form lines, get into rows/columns, file,
form a queue, queue up, group together, fall
in; *inf.* form a crocodile. **3** *line up entertainment
for the party* get together, organize, prepare,
assemble, lay on, get, obtain, procure, secure,
produce, come up with.

line³ *verb line a skirt | have lined the drawers with
paper* put a lining in, back, interline, face,
panel, inlay, paper.

lineage *noun* line, descent, ancestry, family,
extraction. See LINE¹ *noun* 14.

lineament *noun* distinctive feature, feature,
features, distinguishing characteristic, outline,
line, contour, configuration, physiognomy,
profile, face, countenance, visage.

lined *adjective* **1** *lined paper* ruled, feint. **2** *a
lined face* furrowed, wrinkled, creased. **3** *lined
skirt/drawers* interlined, faced. See LINE³.

liner *noun* **1** *travel to Australia by liner* ocean
liner, ship, boat, passenger vessel, aeroplane,
aircraft, airliner; *inf.* plane. **2** *eye-shadow and
liner* eye-liner, eyebrow pencil, eye pencil, lip-
liner.

lines *plural noun forget her lines* words, speech,
script, part.

line-up *noun* **1** *the line-up for tonight's show/game*
list of performers/players, list, team, selection,
array. **2** *the line-up for the inspection parade* line,
row, queue.

linger *verb* **1** *linger after the others went* stay,
remain, wait around, hang around, delay, daw-
dle, loiter, dally, take one's time, tarry; *inf.*
dilly-dally. **2** *the infection lingered* persist, con-

tinue, remain, stay, hang around, be pro-
tracted, endure. **3** *dying man is lingering* | *customs which linger on* die slowly, stay alive, survive, last, stay around, continue.
Opposites LEAVE; VANISH; DIE.

lingerie *noun* underwear, underclothes, underclothing, undergarments, nightwear, nightclothes; *inf.* undies, smalls, frillies.

lingering *adjective* **1** *lingering doubts* remaining, surviving, persistent. **2** *a lingering illness* persistent, protracted, long-drawn-out.

lingo *noun* language, tongue, speech, jargon, terminology, phraseology, idiom, dialect, patter, vernacular, lingua franca.

linguistic *adjective* semantic, lingual, semasiological. *See tables at* GRAMMAR, LANGUAGES.

lining *noun* *a skirt/drawer lining* backing, interlining, facing, inlay.

link *noun* **1** *a link in the metal chain* ring, loop, connection, connective, coupling, joint, knot. **2** *one of the links in the organization* component, constituent, element, part, piece, member, division. **3** *a link between smoking and cancer* connection, relationship, relatedness, association, tie-up. **4** *strong family links* bond, tie, attachment, connection, relationship, association, affiliation, mutual interest.

link *verb* **1** *the joint linking the two pieces* join, connect, fasten together, attach, bind, unite, couple, yoke. **2** *the press linking their names together* join, connect, associate, relate, bracket.
Opposites DETACH; SEPARATE.

lion *noun* **1** *lions with their cubs* big cat, lioness. *See table at* CAT. **2** *a lion in the battle* lion-heart, lion-hearted man/woman/person, hero, heroine, man/woman/person of courage, brave man/woman/person, conqueror, champion, warrior, knight. **3** *photographing the lions at the party* celebrity, person of note, dignitary, notable, VIP, public figure, luminary, star, superstar, big name, leading light, idol; *inf.* big shot, bigwig, big noise, somebody. **beard the lion in his den** defy danger, face up to danger, brave danger, confront danger, court destruction, tempt providence.

lion-hearted *adjective* brave, courageous, valiant, gallant, intrepid, valorous, fearless, bold, daring, dauntless, stout-hearted, stalwart, heroic.

lionize *verb* *team captain was lionized wherever he went* make much of, treat as a celebrity, glorify, exalt, magnify, acclaim, sing the praises of, praise, extol, laud, eulogize, fête, pay tribute to, put on a pedestal, hero-worship, worship, idolize, adulate, aggrandize.

lip *noun* **1** *the lip of a cup/crater* edge, rim, brim, margin, border, verge, brink. **2** *punish the child for lip* cheek, impertinence, impudence, insolence, rudeness, audacity, effrontery; *inf.* sauce, backchat. **keep a stiff upper lip** keep control of oneself, not show emotion, appear unaffected, bite one's lip; *inf.* keep one's cool. **lick one's lips** show enjoyment, show pleasure/anticipation, drool, slaver.

liquid *noun* fluid, liquor, solution, juice, sap.

liquid *adjective* **1** *liquid substances* fluid, flowing, running, runny, watery, aqueous, liquefied, melted, molten, dissolved, hydrous. **2** *liquid eyes* clear, transparent, limpid, unclouded, bright, shining, brilliant, glowing, gleaming. **3** *liquid notes* clear, pure, smooth, flowing, fluent, fluid, mellifluent, mellifluous, dulcet, sweet, soft, melodious. **4** *liquid assets* convertible, negotiable.
Opposites SOLID; CLOUDY.

liquidate *verb* **1** *liquidate debts* pay, pay in full, pay off, settle, clear, discharge, square, make good, honour. **2** *liquidate a firm/partnership* close down, wind up, dissolve, break up, disband, terminate, annul. **3** *liquidate assets* convert to cash, convert, cash, cash in, sell off, sell up, realize. **4** *liquidate an enemy* kill, murder, put to death, do away with, assassinate, put an end to, eliminate, get rid of, dispatch, finish off, destroy, annihilate, obliterate; *inf.* do in, bump off, rub out, wipe out.

liquidize *verb* blend, crush, purée, pulverize, process.

liquor *noun* **1** *addicted to liquor* spirits, alcohol, alcoholic drink, strong drink, drink, intoxicant, inebriant; *inf.* booze, hard stuff, juice, grog; *Am. inf.* the sauce, hooch. *See table at* ALCOHOL. **2** *cooking liquor* liquid, stock, broth, bouillon, juice, gravy, infusion, extract, concentrate.

list[1] *noun* *a list of purchases/films* catalogue, inventory, record, register, roll, file, index, directory, listing, enumeration, table, tabulation, schedule, syllabus, calendar, programme, series.

list[2] *verb* *list the purchases* make a list of, note down, write down, record, register, set down, enter, itemize, enumerate, catalogue, file, tabulate, schedule, chronicle, classify, alphabetize.

list[3] *verb* *vessels listing* lean, lean over, tilt, tip, heel, heel over, careen, cant, incline, slant, slope.

listen *verb* **1** *listen to the speaker/speech* pay attention to, be attentive to, attend, hark, concentrate on hearing, give ear to, lend an ear to; hang on someone's words, keep one's ears open, prick up one's ears; *inf.* be all ears, pin back one's ears. **2** *if you'd listened to your teacher you would have passed* pay attention, take heed, heed, give heed, take notice, mind, obey, do as one is told by, believe. **listen in** *listen in to someone's conversation* eavesdrop, overhear, tap, wiretap; *inf.* bug.
Opposites IGNORE.

listless *adjective* languid, lethargic, languishing, enervated, lackadaisical, spiritless, unenergetic, lifeless, inactive, inert, indolent, apathetic, passive, dull, heavy, sluggish, slothful, limp, languorous, torpid, supine, indifferent, uninterested, impassive.
Opposites ENERGETIC; LIVELY.

litany *noun* **1** *church litany* prayer, invocation, petition, supplication, devotion; *lit.* orison. **2** *a litany of complaints* recital, recitation, catalogue, list, listing, enumeration.

literacy *noun* reading ability, reading proficiency, learning, book learning, education, culture, knowledge, scholarship, erudition, learnedness, enlightenment, articulateness, articulacy.

literal *adjective* **1** *a literal translation* word-for-word, verbatim, line-for-line, letter-for-letter, exact, precise, faithful, close, strict, undeviating, true, accurate. **2** *a literal account* true, accurate, genuine, authentic, veritable, plain, simple, unexaggerated, unvarnished, unembellished, undistorted. **3** *rather a literal person* literal-minded, down-to-earth, prosaic, factual, matter-of-fact, unimaginative, colourless, commonplace, tedious, boring, dull, uninspiring, prosy.
Opposites LOOSE; VAGUE; INACCURATE.

literally *adverb* **1** *translated literally* word for word, verbatim, line for line, letter for letter, exactly, precisely, faithfully, closely, strictly, strictly speaking, to the letter, accurately. **2** *literally thousands of people* actually, really, truly, honestly, certainly, surely, positively, absolutely.

literary *adjective* **1** *literary works* written, published, printed, in print. **2** *a literary man* well-read, widely read, educated, well-educated, scholarly, learned, intellectual, cultured, erudite, bookish, studious, lettered; *inf.* highbrow. **3** *a literary word* formal, poetic.

literate *adjective* **1** *scarcely literate* able to read and write, educated, schooled. **2** *book-buying literate people* educated, well-educated, well-read, scholarly, learned, intellectual, erudite, cultured, cultivated, knowledgeable, well-informed. **3** *literate prose* well-written, stylish, polished, articulate, lucid, eloquent.

literature *noun* **1** *study English literature* written works, writings, printed works, published works, letters, belles-lettres. *See table. See also tables at* NOVEL, PLAY, PLAYWRIGHT, POEM, POET, THEATRE, WRITER. **2** *receive literature about the course* printed matter, brochure, leaflet, pamphlet, circular, information, data, facts; *inf.* bumf.

lithe *adjective* agile, flexible, supple, limber, loose-limbed, pliant, pliable, lissome.

litigant *noun* litigator, opponent in law, opponent, contestant, contender, disputant, plaintiff, claimant, complainant, petitioner.

litigation *noun* lawsuit, legal case, case, legal dispute, legal contest, legal action, legal proceedings, suit, suit at law.

litigious *adjective* *litigious neighbours* argumentative, disputatious, quarrelsome, contentious, belligerent, aggressive, pugnacious, combative.

litter *noun* **1** *litter lying on the grass* rubbish, debris, refuse, junk, odds and ends, fragments, detritus, flotsam; *Am.* trash. **2** *a litter of books everywhere* disorder, untidiness, clutter, jumble, confusion, mess, disarray, disorganization, disarrangement; *inf.* shambles. **3** *a litter of pups/piglets* brood, young, offspring, progeny, family, issue. **4** *invalids carried in litters* stretcher, portable bed/couch, palanquin. **5** *strew litter in the barn* animal bedding, bedding, straw, floor covering.

litter *verb* **1** *litter the place up with rubbish* make untidy, mess up, make a mess of, clutter up, throw into disorder, disarrange; *inf.* make a

shambles of. **2** *litter papers about* scatter, strew, throw around.

little *adjective* **1** *a little man* small, short, slight, petite, tiny, wee, miniature, mini, diminutive, minute, infinitesimal, microscopic, minuscule, dwarf, midget, pygmy, bantam; *inf.* teeny, teeny-weeny, pint-sized. **2** *she died when he was little* small, young, junior. **3** *after a little period* short, brief, fleeting, short-lived, momentary, transitory, ephemeral. **4** *exaggerate little difficulties* unimportant, insignificant, minor, trivial, trifling, petty, paltry, inconsequential, negligible, nugatory. **5** *gain little advantage* hardly any, small, scant, meagre, skimpy, sparse, insufficient, exiguous; *inf.* piddling. **6** *nasty little minds* mean, narrow, narrow-minded, small-minded, base, cheap, shallow, petty, illiberal, provincial, parochial, insular. **7** *pretty little rooms* pleasingly small, sweet, nice, dear, cute, appealing; *inf.* dinky.
Opposites BIG; LARGE; LONG; CONSIDERABLE.

little *adverb* **1** *little known as an artist* hardly, barely, scarcely, not much, only slightly, only just. **2** *little seen around* hardly ever, hardly, scarcely ever, scarcely, not much, rarely, seldom, infrequently. **little by little** gradually, slowly, bit by bit, by degrees, step by step, progressively.

little *noun* **1** *add just a little* small amount, bit, touch, trace, hint, soupçon, trifle, dash, taste, pinch, dab, spot, sprinkling, speck, modicum, grain, fragment, snippet. **2** *he'll go in a little* short time, little while, minute, moment, second, bit, before you can say Jack Robinson.

liturgy *noun* ritual, worship, service, ceremony, rite, observance, celebration, office, sacrament.

live *verb* **1** *when dinosaurs lived* be alive, have life, be, have being, breathe, draw breath, exist, walk the earth. **2** *invalids/customs not*

LITERARY SCHOOLS	
absurdism	modernism
acmeism	Movement, the
aestheticism	naturalism
Augustans	neoclassicism
beat generation	neorealism
Bloomsbury group	occultism
classicism	Pléiade, la
Dadaism	postmodernism
Euphuism	post-structuralism
existentialism	pre-Raphaelitism
expressionism	pre-Romanticism
futurism	primitivism
Georgian poets	realism
Gongorism	Renaissance
Gothicism	humanism
Harlem Renaissance	romanticism
hermeticism	Russian formalism
imagism	social realism
Lake poets	socialist realism
Liverpool poets	structuralism
magic realism	Sturm und Drang
mannerism	surrealism
medievalism	symbolism
metaphysical	transcendentalism
poets	verismo
minimalism	vorticism

expected to live remain/stay alive, survive, last, endure, persist, abide, continue, stay around. **3** *live quietly* pass/spend one's life, have a life/lifestyle, conduct oneself, lead one's life, behave, comport oneself. **4** *he lives by begging* keep alive, survive, make a living, earn one's living, subsist, support oneself, maintain oneself, make ends meet, keep body and soul together. **5** *live on vegetables* live off, subsist, feed, rely for nourishment on, thrive. **6** *live in the city* dwell, reside, have one's home, have one's residence, inhabit, lodge, be settled; *inf.* hang out, hang one's hat; *Scots* stay. **7** *he really lived when he was young* enjoy life, enjoy oneself, have fun, be happy, make the most of life, flourish, prosper, thrive. **live it up** live extravagantly, live in clover, live in the lap of luxury; *inf.* go on a spree, push the boat out, paint the town red, have a ball, make whoopee.

live *adjective* **1** *live bodies* alive, living, having life, breathing, animate, vital, existing, existent; *inf.* in the land of the living. **2** *a real live tiger* actual, in the flesh, not imaginary, true-to-life, genuine, authentic. **3** *a live show* unpre-recorded, unedited, with an audience. **4** *live coals* glowing, aglow, burning, alight, flaming, aflame, blazing, hot, smouldering. **5** *live electric wires* charged, connected, active, switched on. **6** *live bombs* unexploded, explodable, explosive. **7** *a live issue* current, topical, active, prevalent, important, of interest, lively, vital, pressing, burning, pertinent, controversial, debatable, unsettled. **live wire** person of energy, self-starter, self-motivator; *inf.* ball of fire, human dynamo, life and soul of the party, go-getter, whiz-kid, mover and shaker, hustler. **Opposites** DEAD; INACTIVE.

livelihood *noun* **1** *earn a livelihood* living, subsistence, means of support, income, keep, maintenance, sustenance, upkeep. **2** *a poorly paid livelihood* job, work, employment, occupation, trade, profession, career.

livelong *adjective the livelong day* whole, entire, total, complete, full, unbroken, undivided.

lively *adjective* **1** *lively young people* full of life, active, animated, energetic, alive, vigorous, alert, spirited, high-spirited, vivacious, enthusiastic, keen, cheerful, buoyant, sparkling, bouncy, perky, sprightly, spry, frisky, agile, nimble; *inf.* chirpy, go-go, chipper, peppy. **2** *maintain a lively pace* brisk, quick, rapid, swift, speedy, vigorous. **3** *a lively discussion* animated, spirited, stimulating, heated, enthusiastic, forceful, interesting, eventful. **4** *a lively scene at the beach* busy, crowded, bustling, hectic, swarming, teeming, astir, buzzing, thronging. **5** *lively writing/decoration* vivid, colourful, bright, striking, graphic, stimulating, exciting, effective, imaginative. **6** *things got lively in the war area* eventful, exciting, busy, dangerous; *inf.* hairy. **Opposites** LISTLESS; LIFELESS; SLOW; APATHETIC.

liven *verb* **1** *liven the party up* enliven, put some life into, brighten up, cheer up, perk up, put some spark into, add some zest to, give a boost to, animate, vitalize, vivify; *inf.* pep up, hot up. **2** *do liven up* cheer up, brighten up, waken up, perk up; *inf.* buck up.

livery *noun* uniform, regalia, costume, dress, attire, habit, garb, clothes, clothing, suit, garments, apparel, ensemble, vestments; *inf.* get-up, gear, togs.

livid *adjective* **1** *a livid patch on his forehead* discoloured, bruised, black-and-blue, purplish, bluish, greyish-blue. **2** *the livid faces of the dying* ashen, deathly pale, pale, pallid, white, greyish, bloodless, ghastly. **3** *livid with his son* furious, infuriated, fuming, seething, beside oneself, incensed, enraged, exasperated, angry, indignant, wrathful, ireful; *inf.* mad, boiling.

living *adjective* **1** *living creatures* alive, live, having life, breathing, animate, vital, existing, existent; *inf.* in the land of the living. **2** *living languages* current, in use, extant, existing, existent, contemporary, operating, active, ongoing, continuing, surviving, persisting. **3** *a living likeness* exact, close, faithful, true-to-life, authentic, genuine.
Opposites DEAD; EXTINCT; OBSOLETE.

living *noun* **1** *earn a living* livelihood, subsistence, means of support, income, keep, maintenance, sustenance, upkeep. **2** *lose his living* job, work, employment, occupation, trade, profession, career. **3** *high living* way of life, lifestyle, manner/way/mode of living, life, conduct, behaviour.

living-room *noun* sitting-room, drawing-room, lounge, parlour, family room.

load *noun* **1** *the lorry's/aircraft's load* cargo, freight, charge, burden, lading, contents, consignment, shipment, lorryload, shipload, containerload, busload. **2** *the heavy load of single parents* burden, onus, weight, responsibility, duty, charge, obligation, tax, strain, trouble, worry, encumbrance, affliction, oppression, handicap, trial, tribulation, cross, millstone, albatross, incubus.

load *verb* **1** *load the lorry/cart* fill, fill up, lade, freight, charge, pack, pile, heap, stack, stuff, cram. **2** *load the staff with responsibility* burden, weigh down, weight, saddle, charge, tax, strain, encumber, hamper, handicap, overburden, overwhelm, oppress, trouble, worry. **3** *load a gun* prime, charge, fill. **4** *load a dice* weight, add weight to, bias, rig.

loaded *adjective* **1** *a loaded lorry/basket* full, filled, laden, freighted, charged, packed, stacked. *See* LOAD *verb* 1. **2** *a loaded gun/camera* primed, charged, filled, containing ammunition, ready to fire, ready for use. **3** *loaded dice* weighted, biased, rigged. **4** *loaded questions* manipulative, cunning, insidious, artful, crafty, tricky, trapping. **5** *loaded tourists* rich, wealthy, well off, well-to-do, affluent, moneyed; *inf.* well-heeled, rolling in it, flush, on easy street. **6** *loaded when leaving the pub* drunk, intoxicated, inebriated; *inf.* sozzled, plastered, stoned, smashed, legless. *See* DRUNK *adjective*.

loaf *noun* **1** *sugar loaf | two sliced loaves* block, cake, slab, brick, lump, hunk. **2** *use your loaf* head, mind, common sense, sense, brains; *inf.* chump, gumption.

loaf *verb loafing around at home* laze, lounge, do nothing, idle, lie around, hang about, waste time, fritter away time, take things easy, twiddle one's thumbs, sit on one's hands.

loan noun *a loan from the bank* lending, moneylending, advancing; advance, credit, mortgage.

loan verb *loan money* | *loaned a painting* lend, advance, give credit, give on loan, let out.

loath adjective *loath to go* reluctant, unwilling, disinclined, not in the mood, against, averse, opposed, resisting.
Opposites EAGER; ENTHUSIASTIC.

loathe verb *asked why he loathes her so* hate, detest, abhor, despise, abominate, have an aversion to, not be able to bear, dislike, shrink from, recoil from, feel repugnance towards, be unable to stomach, execrate.
Opposites LOVE; LIKE.

loathing noun hatred, hate, detestation, abhorrence, aversion, abomination, repugnance, disgust, revulsion, odium, antipathy, dislike, ill will, enmity, execration.

loathsome adjective hateful, detestable, abhorrent, odious, repugnant, disgusting, repulsive, revolting, nauseating, abominable, vile, nasty, obnoxious, horrible, offensive, disagreeable, despicable, contemptible, reprehensible, execrable; *inf.* horrid, yucky.
Opposites LOVABLE; DELIGHTFUL.

lob verb *lobbed the sack over the wall* throw, toss, fling, pitch, shy, hurl, loft, heave, flip; *inf.* chuck.

lobby noun **1** *a pram in the lobby* porch, hall, hallway, entrance-hall, entrance, vestibule, foyer, corridor, passage, passageway, anteroom, antechamber. **2** *the animal rights lobby* pressure group, interest group, ginger group, lobbyists, supporters.

lobby verb **1** *lobby MPs* seek to influence, try to persuade, bring pressure to bear on, urge, press, pressure, solicit. **2** *lobby for animal rights* press for, campaign for, push for, promote, drum up support for; *inf.* pull strings for.

local adjective **1** *local politics* community, district, neighbourhood, regional, city, town, municipal, provincial, village, parish, parishpump. **2** *our local store* in the area, nearby, near, at hand, close by, neighbourhood. **3** *the pain being local* | *administer a local anaesthetic* confined, restricted, contained, limited, circumscribed, delimited, specific.
Opposites NATIONAL; GENERAL.

local noun **1** *locals disliking change* local person, native, inhabitant, resident, parishioner; *derog. inf.* local yokel. **2** *drinking in his local* pub, public house, bar, inn, tavern; *inf.* boozer, watering-hole.

locale noun *a suitable locale for the conference* place, site, spot, position, location, venue, area, neighbourhood, locality, setting, scene.

locality noun **1** *the murderer was still in the locality of the crime* vicinity, surrounding area, area, neighbourhood, district, region, environs, locale; *fml.* locus. **2** *identify the locality of the car* location, position, place, whereabouts, bearings; *fml.* locus. *See* LOCATION 1.

localize verb *succeed in localizing the infection* confine, restrict, contain, limit, circumscribe, delimit, delimitate.

locate verb **1** *locate the source of infection* find, find out, discover, identify, pinpoint, detect, uncover, track down, run to earth, unearth, hit upon, come across, reveal, pin down, define. **2** *factories located near the sea* situate, site, position, place, put, build, establish, station, set, fix, settle.

location noun **1** *identify the location of the ship* position, place, situation, whereabouts, bearings, site, spot, point; *fml.* locus. **2** *a pleasant location for a house* position, place, situation, site, spot, scene, setting, venue, locale.

lock[1] verb **1** *lock the door* bolt, fasten, bar, secure, make secure, padlock. **2** *pieces of the puzzle locking together* interlock, engage, mesh, join, link, unite. **3** *wheels locked* jam, become immovable, become rigid. **4** *locked in each other's arms* | *locked in combat* clasp, clench, entangle, entwine, embrace, hug, squeeze. **lock in** *a town locked in by hills* enclose, encircle, surround, shut in, hem in. **lock out** *lock out late arrivals* keep out, shut out, refuse entrance to, deny admittance to, exclude, bar, debar, ban, ostracize. **lock up** *lock up prisoners* shut up, shut in, confine, imprison, jail, incarcerate, put behind bars, put under lock and key, cage, coop up, fence in, pen in, wall in.
Opposites UNLOCK; OPEN; SEPARATE.

lock[2] noun *force the lock* bolt, catch, fastener, clasp, bar, hasp. *See table.*

LOCKS	
barrel	snap-lock
Chubb lock™	spring lock
combination	stock-lock
cylinder	time lock
lever-tumbler	twist-lock
mortise lock	warded
padlock	Yale lock™
radial pin-tumbler	

lock[3] noun *a lock of hair* strand, tuft, tress, curl, ringlet, kiss-curl, lovelock.

locker noun cupboard, compartment, cabinet, cubicle, storeroom, storage room. *See table at* CUPBOARD.

lock-up noun **1** *prisoners in the lock-up* prison, jail, cell, police cell; *inf.* cooler, slammer, jug, can, stir, clink, quod, choky. **2** *hire a lock-up* garage, store, storeroom, storage/space.

locomotion noun movement, motion, moving, action, travel, travelling, walking, perambulation, progress, progression, headway.

lodestar noun *his father's career was a lodestar to him* guiding star, guide, guiding principle, standard, model, pattern.

lodge noun **1** *retired nanny living at the lodge* gatehouse. **2** *a shooting/ski lodge* house, cottage, cabin, chalet. **3** *the Masonic lodge* branch, chapter, section, association, society, club, group, fraternity, sorority. **4** *an animal's lodge* lair, den, hole, retreat, haunt, shelter.

lodge *verb* **1** *he's lodging at the Smiths'* stay, board, have lodgings, put up, reside, dwell, sojourn, stop; *inf.* have digs; *Am.* room. **2** *the Smiths can lodge all of the children* house, provide accommodation for, accommodate, put up, billet, shelter, harbour, entertain. **3** *lodge money* deposit, put in, bank, reposit. **4** *lodge a complaint* register, submit, put forward, place, file, lay, put on record, record. **5** *the bullet lodged in his brain* become fixed, become embedded, become implanted, stick, become caught, come to rest. **6** *lodge power in the governor* place, put, lay, vest, entrust, transfer, consign, deliver.

lodger *noun* boarder, paying guest, PG, guest, tenant; *Am.* roomer.

lodging *noun* **1** *gave them lodging for the night* accommodation, shelter, board, housing, a roof over one's head. **2** *move to new lodgings* accommodation, rooms, place, residence, dwelling, abode, habitation; *inf.* digs.

lofty *adjective* **1** *lofty peaks* towering, soaring, tall, high, elevated, sky-high, sky-scraping. **2** *lofty contempt* arrogant, haughty, proud, self-important, conceited, overweening, disdainful, supercilious, condescending, patronizing, lordly, snobbish, scornful, contemptuous, insulting, cavalier; *inf.* high-and-mighty, stuck-up, snooty, toffee-nosed, uppity. **3** *lofty thoughts/ideals* noble, exalted, grand, sublime, imposing, esoteric. **4** *lofty members of the community* eminent, leading, noted, notable, well-known, distinguished, famous, renowned, illustrious, esteemed, celebrated, noble, aristocratic.
Opposites LOW; MODEST; LOWLY.

log *noun* **1** *logs of wood* block, piece, chunk, billet, stump, trunk, branch, bole. **2** *a ship's log* logbook, record, register, journal, diary, day-book, chart, account, tally.

log *verb* **1** *log details of the voyage* set down, make a note of, note/write down, jot down, register, record, book down, file, chart, tabulate, catalogue. **2** *log 50 miles a day* achieve, attain, make, do, go, cover, travel, traverse.

loggerheads *plural noun* **at loggerheads** in conflict, at war, quarrelling, at daggers drawn, fighting, wrangling, feuding, in disagreement, at odds, at variance, in opposition, estranged; *inf.* at each other's throats.

logic *noun* **1** *studying logic* science of reasoning, science of deduction, science of thought, dialectics, argumentation, ratiocination. *See table at* PHILOSOPHY. **2** *her logic was flawed* line of reasoning, chain of reasoning, process of reasoning, reasoning, argument, argumentation. **3** *no logic in her actions* reason, sound judgement, judgement, wisdom, sense, good sense, common sense, rationale, relevance, coherence; *inf.* horse sense.

logical *adjective* **1** *a logical argument* reasoned, well-reasoned, rational, sound, cogent, coherent, well-organized, clear, consistent, relevant. **2** *the logical thing to do* rational, reasonable, sensible, intelligent, wise, judicious. **3** *the logical outcome* most likely, likeliest, plausible, obvious. **4** *not a logical person* reasoning, thinking, straight-thinking, rational, consistent.
Opposites ILLOGICAL; IRRATIONAL; UNLIKELY.

logistics *plural noun the logistics of combining two schools* organization, strategy, tactics, planning, plans, management, masterminding, direction, orchestration, engineering, coordination, execution, handling.

logo *noun* trade mark, emblem, company emblem, device, symbol, design, seal, stamp, logotype.

loiter *verb* **1** *loiter at street corners* hang around, hang about, linger, wait, skulk, loaf, lounge, idle, waste time; *lit.* tarry. **2** *loiter along the road* dawdle, go slowly, take one's time, go at a snail's pace, dally, stroll, saunter, delay, loll; *inf.* dilly-dally.

loll *verb* **1** *lolling on the sofa* lounge, slump, flop, sprawl, relax, recline, rest, lie around, lean against, repose on. **2** *loll around the house* lounge, loaf, idle, loiter, hang about/around, vegetate, languish. **3** *with his tongue lolling* hang down, hang, hang out, hang loosely, dangle, droop, sag, flap, flop.

lone *adjective* **1** *a lone yachtsman* by oneself, alone, single, solitary, sole, unaccompanied, without companions, companionless, lonely. **2** *a lone parent* single, unmarried, separated, divorced, unattached, without a partner/husband/wife, partnerless, husbandless, wifeless. **3** *a lone landscape* lonely, desolate, barren, isolated, remote, deserted, uninhabited. *See* LONELY 3.

loneliness *noun* **1** *the loneliness of people living alone* friendlessness, lonesomeness, forlornness, isolation, sadness, despondency. *See* LONELY 1. **2** *the loneliness of his existence* aloneness, solitariness. *See* LONELY 2. **3** *the loneliness of the landscape* desolation, isolation, remoteness, seclusion, desertedness. *See* LONELY 3.

lonely *adjective* **1** *lonely people at Christmas/feeling lonely* friendless, companionless, lonesome, forlorn, forsaken, abandoned, rejected, isolated, outcast, sad, unhappy, despondent. **2** *lead a lonely existence* lone, by oneself, alone, single, solitary, sole, companionless. *See* LONE 1. **3** *a lonely landscape* desolate, barren, isolated, out-of-the-way, remote, secluded, off the beaten track, deserted, uninhabited, unfrequented, unpopulated, God-forsaken, lone.
Opposites POPULAR; SOCIABLE; POPULOUS.

loner *noun* lone wolf, recluse, hermit, solitary, anchorite, eremite.

lonesome *adjective* lonely, friendless, forlorn, isolated, sad. *See* LONELY 1.

long *adjective* **1** *three metres long* in length, lengthways, lengthwise. **2** *a long road/way/time* lengthy, extended, extensive, stretched out, spread out. **3** *a long speech | ten long years* lengthy, prolonged, protracted, over-long, extended, long-drawn-out, long-drawn, spun out, dragged out, seemingly endless, interminable, long-winded, verbose, prolix, tedious.
before long soon, shortly, in a short time, in a minute, in a moment, before you know it, any

467

minute now.
Opposites SHORT; BRIEF.

long verb long for peace wish for, desire, want,
yearn for, crave, hunger for, thirst for, itch for,
covet, lust after, hope for, dream of, pine for,
eat one's heart out over, have a fancy for, hanker for/after; inf. have a yen for.

long-drawn-out adjective lengthy, prolonged,
protracted, over-long, long-drawn, interminable, tedious. See LONG adjective 3.

longing noun a longing for peace wish, desire,
wanting, yearning, craving, hunger, thirst,
itch, covetousness, lust, hope, dream, aspiration, pining, fancy, urge, hankering; inf. yen.

longing adjective a longing look wishful,
desirous, yearning, craving, covetous, hopeful,
wistful, avid.

long-lasting adjective long-lasting friendship
long-lived, long-running, long-established,
long-standing, abiding, enduring, established.

long-lived adjective long-lasting, enduring,
durable, old; fml longevous.

long-standing adjective long-standing invitation/
arrangement long-established, well-established,
established, fixed, time-honoured, time-
hallowed, abiding, enduring.

long-suffering adjective his long-suffering wife
patient, having the patience of Job, forbearing,
tolerant, uncomplaining, stoical, resigned,
easygoing, indulgent, charitable, forgiving.

long-winded adjective long-winded speaker/speech
verbose, wordy, garrulous, prolix, discursive,
diffuse, rambling, repetitious, lengthy, over-
long, prolonged, protracted, long-drawn-out,
tedious.

look verb 1 look over there! see, take a look,
glance, fix one's gaze, focus, observe, view,
regard, eye, take in, watch, examine, study,
inspect, scan, scrutinize, survey, check, contemplate, consider, pay attention to, run the
eyes over, peep, peek, glimpse, gaze, stare,
gape, ogle; inf. take a dekko, take a butcher's,
take a gander, give someone/something the
once-over, take a shufti, take a squint, gawp,
rubberneck; Am. inf. eyeball. 2 she looks ill | he
looked a fool seem, seem to be, appear, appear
to be, give every appearance/indication of
being, look to be, present as being, strike
someone as being. 3 the room looks east | the
house looks onto the sea face, overlook, front,
front on, give onto. **look after** take care of,
care for, attend to, tend, mind, keep an eye on,
watch, sit with, nurse, take charge of, supervise, protect, guard. **look at** take a look at,
observe, view, eye, watch, examine, study,
inspect, scan, scrutinize, survey, check, contemplate, consider, pay attention to, run one's
eyes over. See LOOK verb 1. **look back** look back
on/over her life reflect on, think about, recall,
bring to mind, muse on, brood on, ponder on,
reminisce about. **look down on** regard with
contempt, treat with contempt, scorn, disdain,
hold in disdain, sneer at, spurn, disparage,
pooh-pooh, despise; inf. look down one's nose
at, turn up one's nose at. **look for** 1 look for
the lost glove search for, hunt for, seek, look
around for, cast about for, forage for. 2 look

for some improvement anticipate, expect, await,
count on, reckon on, hope for, look forward to.
look forward to anticipate, await with pleasure, wait for, be unable to wait for, count the
days until, long for, hope for. **look into** investigate, explore, research, probe, search into, go
into, inquire about, make inquiries about, ask
questions about, ask about, delve into, dig
into, examine, study, scrutinize, check, follow
up, check up on; Am. check out. **look like**
resemble, bear a resemblance to, have a look
of, have the appearance of, put someone in
mind of, make someone think of, take after,
be the image of; inf. be the spitting image of,
be the spit of, be a dead ringer for, favour.
look on with a crowd looking on watch, observe,
spectate, be a spectator, view, witness. **look
on/upon** look on it as a favour | look upon him as a
brother regard, consider, think of, deem, judge,
see, take, reckon. **look out** you'll drop it if you
don't look out watch out, beware, be on guard,
be alert, be wary, be vigilant, be careful, pay
attention, take heed, keep one's eyes open,
keep one's eyes peeled/skinned, keep an eye
out, be on the qui vive. **look over** look
through, inspect, examine, check, monitor,
read through, scan, run through, cast an eye
over, flick through, give something/someone
the once-over, take stock of, view, peruse; inf.
take a dekko at; Am. check out; Am. inf. eyeball.
look to 1 look to the future consider, give
thought to, think about, turn one's thoughts
to, take heed of, pay attention to. 2 look to the
family for support turn to, resort to, have
recourse to, fall back on, avail oneself of, make
use of. **look up** 1 look up the information search
for, seek out, research, hunt for, track down,
find, locate. 2 look up a reference book consult,
refer to, turn to. 3 look them up in London visit,
pay a visit to, call on, go to see, look in on; inf.
drop in on. 4 things are looking up get better,
improve, show improvement, pick up, come
along/on, make progress, make headway,
shape up, perk up, ameliorate. **look up to** look
up to his brother admire, hold in admiration,
have a high opinion of, think highly of, hold in
high regard, regard highly, respect, hold in
esteem, esteem, revere, idolize, worship, hero-
worship, put on a pedestal, lionize.

look noun 1 one look at the evidence | gave him a
worried look sight, glance, observation, view,
examination, study, inspection, scan, survey,
peep, peek, glimpse, gaze, stare, gape, ogle; inf.
eyeful, dekko, butcher's, gander, look-see,
once-over, squint, shufti. 2 an angry look
expression, face, countenance, features,
mien. 3 houses having a dilapidated/Scandinavian
look | she has a depressed look about her appear-
ance, air, aspect, bearing, cast, demeanour,
features, semblance, guise, façade, impression,
effect. 4 miniskirts are the look this year fashion,
style, latest style, vogue, trend, fad, craze,
rage.

look-alike noun double, twin, exact likeness,
image, living image, exact match, replica,
clone, duplicate, doppelganger; inf. spitting
image, spit, spit and image, ringer, dead
ringer.

lookout *noun* **1** *on the lookout for danger* watch, guard, vigil, alertness, qui vive. **2** *lookouts located along the coast* observation post, lookout point, lookout station, lookout tower, watch-tower, tower, coastguard station. **3** *the lookout was killed* guard, sentry, sentinel, watchman, vedette. **4** *it's a poor lookout* prospect, future, outlook, view of the future, chances. **5** *it's your own lookout if you're penniless* business, concern, affair, responsibility, worry; *inf.* pigeon, funeral.

loom *verb* **1** *a shape loomed out of the darkness* appear, emerge, become visible, take shape, materialize, reveal itself, appear indistinctly, take on a threatening shape. **2** *cliffs loomed above them* tower, soar, rise, rise up, mount, overhang, hang over, dominate. **3** *exams are looming* be imminent, impend, be close, be ominously close, threaten, menace.

loop *noun* **1** *loops of ribbon* coil, hoop, noose, circle, ring, oval, spiral, curl, twirl, whorl, twist, convolution. **2** *a loop in the road* bend, curve, kink, arc.

loop *verb* **1** *loop the string* coil, form a hoop with, form hoops with, make a circle with, make circles with, bend into spirals/whorls. **2** *the estate loops around the castle* encircle, form a ring round, surround, encompass. **3** *loop the sections together* fasten, tie, join, connect. **4** *the creature looped along the path | the aircraft looped upwards* coil, wind, circle, twist, spiral, bend, curl, curve, turn.

loophole *noun* **1** *a loophole in the law* let-out, let-out clause, means of evasion/avoidance, means of escape, escape clause, escape route, ambiguity, omission. **2** *a loophole in the wall* hole, gap, opening, slot, aperture.

loose *adjective* **1** *cows loose in the street* at large, at liberty, free, on the loose, unconfined, untied, unchained, untethered, unsecured, unshackled, unfastened, unrestricted, unbound, freed, let go, liberated, released, set loose. **2** *the handle is loose* wobbly, not secure, insecure, rickety, unsteady, movable. **3** *loose hair* untied, unpinned, unbound, hanging free, flowing, floppy. **4** *loose clothes* loose-fitting, easy-fitting, generously cut, slack, baggy, bagging, sagging, sloppy. **5** *a loose translation* inexact, imprecise, vague, indefinite, ill-defined, broad, general, non-specific, diffuse, unrigorous, unmeticulous. **6** *loose women/morals* immoral, disreputable, dissolute, corrupt, fast, promiscuous, debauched, dissipated, degenerate, wanton, whorish, unchaste, licentious, lascivious, lustful, libertine, abandoned, profligate, reprobate, careless, thoughtless, negligent, rash, heedless, unmindful. **7** *be/hang loose* relaxed, informal, uninhibited, unreserved, frank, open, unceremonious, unconstrained. **at a loose end** with nothing to do, unoccupied, at leisure, idle, twiddling one's thumbs. **break loose** escape, make one's escape, run off, run away, flee, take to one's heels, make off. **let loose 1** *let the cows loose* set free, unloose, turn loose, set loose, loose, untie, unchain, untether, unfasten, detach, unleash, let go, release, free, liberate. **2** *let loose a cry of pain* give, emit, burst out with, give forth, send forth, shout, yell, bellow. **on the loose** *cows on the loose* at liberty, free, at large, unconfined.
Opposites SECURE; TIGHT; LITERAL.

loose *verb* **1** *loose the dogs* let loose, set free, unloose, turn loose, set loose, untie, unchain, untether, unleash, detach, let go, release. *See* LET LOOSE 1 (LOOSE). **2** *loose her grip | persuade them to loose their control* loosen, relax, slacken, weaken, lessen, reduce, diminish, moderate, soften. **3** *loose a missile* discharge, shoot, loose off, fire off, eject, catapult.
Opposites CONFINE; TIGHTEN.

loose-limbed *adjective* supple, agile, limber, lithe, lissom, flexible, pliant, pliable.

loosen *verb* **1** *loosen a nut* slacken, slack, unstick. **2** *the nut loosened* become loose, work loose, work free. **3** *loosen a belt | loosened his trousers* slacken, let out, undo, unfasten, unhook. **4** *loosen her grip | try to loosen government control* loose, relax, slacken, weaken, lessen, moderate. *See* LOOSE *verb* 2. **5** *don't be so tense—loosen up* relax, ease up/off; *inf.* let up, hang loose, lighten up.
Opposites TIGHTEN.

loot *noun* booty, spoils, spoil, plunder, haul, stolen goods, pillage, prize; *inf.* swag, the goods, hot goods, boodle.

loot *verb* *looting unoccupied property* plunder, pillage, rob, burgle, steal from, ransack, sack, maraud, ravage, despoil, spoliate.

lop *verb* **1** *lop off several branches* cut off, chop, chop off, hack off, prune, sever, clip, dock, crop, remove, detach. **2** *lop hundreds of pounds from the costs* cut, cut back, slash, axe, remove, take off, trim, prune, dock, eliminate.

lope *verb* bound, stride, spring, gallop, canter, lollop, leap, jump.

lopsided *adjective* asymmetrical, unsymmetrical, unevenly balanced, uneven, unbalanced, off-balance, unequal, askew, squint, tilting, crooked, out of true, out of line, awry.

loquacious *adjective* talkative, overtalkative, garrulous, voluble, long-winded, wordy, verbose, effusive, chatty, gossipy, chattering, babbling, blathering, gibbering; *inf.* having the gift of the gab, yacking, big-mouthed, gabby, gassy.
Opposites RETICENT; TACITURN.

loquacity *noun* talkativeness, overtalkativeness, garrulousness, garrulity, volubility, long-windedness, wordiness, verbosity, effusiveness, logorrhoea, chattiness, gossipiness, chattering, babble, blathering, gibbering; *inf.* gift of the gab, yackety-yack, yacking, big mouth, blah-blah, gabbiness, gassiness.

lord *noun* **1** *swear allegiance to their lord | lord of all he surveys* master, lord and master, ruler, leader, chief, monarch, sovereign, king, emperor, prince, governor, commander, captain, overlord, suzerain, baron, potentate, liege. **2** *the lords in disagreement with the king* noble, nobleman, peer, aristocrat, feudal lord, landowner, lord of the manor, seigneur; duke, earl, viscount. **3** *believe in the Lord* God, Jesus, Jesus Christ, Christ, Christ the Lord, the Redeemer, the Saviour. *See table at* GOD.

lord *verb* **lord it** **1** *arrogant people lording it* put on airs, be overbearing, swagger around, play the lord; *inf.* act big. **2** *lord it over the juniors* order about/around, domineer, dictate to, pull rank on, tyrannize; *inf.* boss about/around.

lordly *adjective* **1** *a lordly disregard for others* imperious, arrogant, haughty, high-handed, overbearing, overweening, overconfident, dictatorial, authoritarian, peremptory, autocratic, tyrannical, supercilious, disdainful, condescending, patronizing; *inf.* high-and-mighty, bossy, stuck-up, snooty, uppity, hoity-toity, toffee-nosed. **2** *lordly beings/splendour* noble, aristocratic, lofty, exalted, majestic, grand, regal, princely, kingly, masterful, imperial, stately, dignified, magnificent, grandiose.

lore *noun* **1** *researching Gypsy lore* traditions, folklore, beliefs, superstitions, legends. **2** *bird lore* knowledge, learning, wisdom, know-how, skill.

lorry *noun* truck, wagon, juggernaut, pick-up, van. *See table at* VEHICLE.

lose *verb* **1** *has lost his keys* mislay, misplace, fail to keep/retain, fail to keep sight of, drop, forget. **2** *losing a lot of blood* be deprived of, suffer the loss of. **3** *trying to lose their pursuers* leave behind, outdistance, outstrip, outrun. **4** *lose the police in the crowd* escape from, evade, elude, dodge, give someone the slip, shake off, throw off, throw off the scent, duck, get rid of. **5** *lose the way | lose track of* stray from, wander from, fail to keep to, fail to keep in sight. **6** *lose the opportunity* fail to grasp/take, fail to take advantage of, let pass, miss, forfeit, neglect; *inf.* pass up, lose out on. **7** *hope to win but expect to lose | lost the contest/battle* suffer defeat, be defeated, be the loser, be worsted, get/have the worst of it, be beaten, be conquered, be vanquished, be trounced, come off second-best, fail, come to grief, meet one's Waterloo; *inf.* lose out, come a cropper. **8** *lose time/effort* waste, squander, dissipate, spend, expend, consume, deplete, exhaust, use up. **lose out** **1** *the poor lose out | he lost out on the profits* be unsuccessful, be defeated, be the loser, be disadvantaged, fail to take advantage of, fail to benefit from; *inf.* miss out on. **2** *lose out to a more experienced applicant* be defeated by, be beaten by, be beaten into second place by, be replaced by.

loser *noun* runner-up, also-ran, the defeated, the vanquished, failure, born loser; *inf.* flop, dud, non-starter, no-hoper, wash-out, lemon, two-time loser.

loss *noun* **1** *report the loss of the keys* mislaying, misplacement, dropping, forgetting. **2** *loss of blood/life/prestige/money* losing, deprivation, privation, forfeiture, bereavement, disappearance, waste, squandering, dissipation. **3** *families/firms suffering loss* deprivation, privation, detriment, disadvantage, damage, injury, impairment, harm, hurt, ruin, destruction, undoing, incapacitation, disablement. **4** *regret the civilian losses* casualty, fatality, dead, death toll, number killed/dead/wounded. **5** *firms making a loss | the company has made significant losses* deficit, debit, debt, lack of profit, deficiency, losing, depletion, minus sum of money.

at a loss *we are at a loss to understand his motives* baffled, nonplussed, mystified, stumped, stuck, puzzled, perplexed, bewildered, ignorant, lost, at one's wit's ends, confused; *inf.* clueless.

lost *adjective* **1** *lost children/books* missing, strayed, gone missing/astray, mislaid, misplaced, vanished, disappeared, forgotten. **2** *lost travellers/ships* stray, astray, off-course, off-track, disorientated, having lost one's bearings, adrift, going round in circles, at sea. **3** *lost opportunities* missed, passed, forfeited, neglected, wasted, squandered, dissipated, frittered, gone by the board; *inf.* down the drain. **4** *lost tribes/traditions* extinct, dead, bygone, lost and gone, lost in time, past, vanished, forgotten, unremembered, unrecalled, consigned to oblivion. **5** *lost ships/towns/armies* destroyed, ruined, wiped out, wrecked, finished, perished, demolished, obliterated, effaced, exterminated, eradicated, annihilated, extirpated. **6** *lost souls* damned, fallen, irredeemable, irreclaimable, irretrievable, past hope, hopeless, past praying for. **7** *lost to all shame* impervious, immune, closed, unreceptive, unaffected by, unmoved by, untouched by. **8** *lost in thought | she was lost in a book* engrossed in, absorbed in, preoccupied by, taken up by, spellbound by, distracted by, entranced by, rapt, abstracted, dreamy, distrait, absent-minded, somewhere else, not there, not with us. **9** *we are lost to understand the motive* at a loss, baffled, nonplussed, mystified, puzzled, perplexed, ignorant. *See* AT A LOSS (LOSS).

lot *noun* **1** *a lot of people | lots of books* many, a great many, a good/great deal, a deal, a great quantity, quantities, a considerable number, numerous, a large amount, an abundance, plenty, masses, scores; *inf.* loads, loadsa, heaps, piles, oodles, stacks, scads, reams, wads, oceans, miles; *Am. inf.* gobs. **2** *smile a lot* much, a good/great deal, to a great extent, often, frequently, many times. **3** *draw lots* slip of paper, number, straw, counter, die, pebble. **4** *decided by lot* chance, luck, lottery, drawing lots, gamble, hazard, accident, serendipity, fortuity. **5** *his lot in life* fate, destiny, fortune, doom, situation, circumstances, portion, plight. **6** *the brothers' lots* share, portion, quota, ration, allowance, percentage, part, piece; *inf.* cut. **7** *sold as a lot* set, batch, collection, load, group, bundle, consignment, quantity, assortment, parcel. **8** *a lot of land | parking lots* allotment, piece of ground, plot, patch of ground, tract of land, building lot. **draw lots** toss a coin, toss, throw a dice, draw straws, cut straws, decide on the toss of a coin, decide on the throw of a dice, decide on the drawing of straws. **throw in one's lot with** join forces with, join up with, form an alliance with, ally with, align oneself with, link up with, go into league with, combine with, join fortunes with, make common cause with.
Opposites FEW; LITTLE.

lotion *noun* cream, salve, ointment, moisturizer, balm, emollient, lubricant, unguent, liniment, embrocation, pomade, hand lotion, body lotion.

lottery noun **1** *take part in a lottery* draw, raffle, sweepstake, game of chance, gamble, drawing of lots, bingo, tombola. **2** *life is a lottery* gamble, game of chance, risk, hazard, venture.

loud adjective **1** *loud music/noises* blaring, booming, noisy, deafening, resounding, reverberant, sonorous, stentorian, roaring, thunderous, tumultuous, clamorous, head-splitting, ear-splitting, ear-piercing, piercing, strident, harsh, raucous. **2** *loud behaviour* noisy, rowdy, boisterous, rough, rollicking. **3** *loud young women* brash, brazen, bold, loud-mouthed, vociferous, raucous, aggressive, coarse, crude, rough, crass, vulgar, brassy; *inf.* pushy. **4** *loud demands* vociferous, clamorous, insistent, vehement, emphatic, urgent, importunate, demanding. **5** *loud colours/wallpaper* garish, gaudy, flashy, flamboyant, lurid, glaring, showy, obtrusive, vulgar, tawdry, tasteless, meretricious; *inf.* flash, naff, kitsch, camp, tacky.
Opposites QUIET; SOFT; GENTLE; RESTRAINED.

loudly adverb **1** *speak/play loudly* at full/top volume, at the top of one's voice, boomingly, noisily, deafeningly, tumultuously, clamorously, piercingly, raucously. See LOUD 1. **2** *behave loudly* noisily, rowdily, boisterously, roughly, brashly, aggressively, coarsely, crassly. See LOUD 2, 3.

loud-mouth noun **1** *loud-mouths showing off* braggart, brag, boaster, blusterer, swaggerer, braggadocio; *inf.* windbag, big-mouth, blowhard, gasbag. **2** *loud-mouths discussing neighbours' affairs* blabbermouth, blabber, gossip, gossipmonger, scandalmonger, busybody, chatterer, prattler; *inf.* gasbag.

loud-mouthed adjective **1** *disturbed by loud-mouthed spectators* noisy, vociferous, bragging, boasting, swaggering; *inf.* big-mouthed. **2** *upset by loud-mouthed neighbours* blabbing, tactless, gossiping, indiscreet, undiplomatic.

loudspeaker noun speaker, speaker unit, speaker system, public address system, PA system, loud hailer, megaphone, microphone; *inf.* mike.

lounge verb **1** *lounge around on deckchairs* laze, lie, lie around, recline, relax, take it easy, sprawl, slump, loll, repose. **2** *lounge around at street corners* loaf, idle, loiter, hang about, linger, skulk, waste time; *inf.* hang out.

lounge noun **1** *have tea in the lounge* sitting-room, drawing-room, living-room, parlour. **2** *the lounge of a hotel* public room, sitting-room, cocktail lounge.

lour, lower verb **1** *an old man louring at the children* scowl, frown, look sullen, glower, glare, give someone black looks, look daggers; *inf.* give someone dirty looks. **2** *skies louring* cloud over, look black, darken, blacken, become overcast, be gloomy, appear threatening/menacing.

lousy adjective **1** *a lousy player/parent* very bad, poor, incompetent, inadequate, unsatisfactory, inferior, careless, second-rate, terrible, miserable; *inf.* rotten, no-good, duff, poxy. **2** *a lousy trick to play* dirty, low, mean, base, despicable,

contemptible, low-down, hateful, detestable, loathsome, vile, wicked, vicious; *inf.* rotten. **3** *lousy bedclothes* lice-infested, lice-ridden, lice-infected, pedicular. **lousy with** *places lousy with tourists* full of, covered in, well-supplied with, crowded with, overrun by, swarming with, teeming with, alive with, crawling with.

lout noun boor, oaf, dolt, churl, bumpkin, yahoo, gawk, lubber, barbarian; *inf.* yob, yobbo, slob, clodhopper, clod; *Am. inf.* lummox.

loutish adjective boorish, oafish, doltish, churlish, awkward, inept, blundering, maladroit, gawky, lubberly; *inf.* yobbish, slobbish, clodhopping.

lovable adjective adorable, dear, sweet, cute, charming, lovely, likeable, attractive, delightful, captivating, enchanting, engaging, bewitching, pleasing, appealing, winsome, winning, taking, endearing, affectionate, warm-hearted, cuddly.
Opposites HATEFUL; LOATHSOME.

love verb **1** *he loves her* care for, be in love with, be fond of, feel affection for, be attracted to, be attached to, hold dear, adore, think the world of, dote on, worship, idolize, treasure, prize, cherish, be devoted to, desire, want, be infatuated with, lust after, long for, yearn for, adulate; *inf.* fancy, have a crush on, have a pash on, lech after, have the hots for, be soft on. **2** *she loves chocolate* like, have a liking for, have a weakness for, be partial to, have a soft spot for, be addicted to, enjoy, find enjoyment in, relish, savour, appreciate, take pleasure in, delight in; *inf.* get a kick out of, have a thing about. **3** *couples loving each other on the grass* embrace, cuddle, hug, caress, fondle, pet, make love, kiss; *inf.* neck, canoodle, smooch.
Opposites HATE; LOATHE; DETEST.

love noun **1** *the couple's love for each other* affection, fondness, care, concern, attachment, regard, warmth, intimacy, devotion, adoration, passion, ardour, desire, lust, yearning, infatuation, adulation. **2** *her love of chocolate* liking for, weakness for, partiality for, enjoyment of, appreciation of, delight in, relish, passion for. **3** *love for one's fellow men* care, caring, regard, solicitude, sympathy, warmth, friendliness, friendship, rapport, brotherhood, kindness, charity. **4** *be brave, my love* beloved, loved one, true love, love of one's life, dear, dearest, dear one, darling, sweetheart, sweet, sweet one, angel, lover, inamorato/inamorata. **5** *their love was short-lived* love affair, affair, romance, relationship, liaison. See LOVE AFFAIR. **fall in love with** become sexually attracted to, form an attachment to, develop a fondness for, become infatuated with, become smitten with; *inf.* develop a crush on. **in love with** attracted to, sexually attracted to, infatuated with, enamoured of, smitten by, besotted with, devoted to, having a passion for, consumed with desire for, lusting after; *inf.* leching after, having the hots for.

love affair noun affair, romance, relationship, meaningful relationship, liaison, amour, intrigue, affair of the heart, *affaire de coeur*.

lovelorn adjective lovesick, unrequited in love, crossed in love, spurned, jilted, ill-starred, miserable, unhappy, pining, moping.

lovely *adjective* **1** *a lovely girl* beautiful, pretty, attractive, good-looking, glamorous, comely, handsome, sweet, fair, charming, adorable, enchanting, engaging, bewitching, winsome, seductive, ravishing. **2** *a lovely surprise* delightful, pleasant, nice, agreeable, pleasing, marvellous, wonderful; *inf.* terrific, fabulous, fab.
Opposites UGLY; HORRIBLE; DISAGREEABLE.

lovemaking *noun* sexual intercourse, intercourse, act of love, sexual relations, intimate relations, intimacy, copulation, coitus, coition, sexual union/congress, congress, carnal knowledge, mating; *inf.* sex, it, the other, nooky, rumpy-pumpy, humping.

lover *noun* **1** *left her husband for her lover* boyfriend, girlfriend, man friend, woman friend, mistress, lady-love, paramour, other man, other woman, beau, loved one, beloved, sweetheart, inamorato/inamorata; *inf.* bit on the side, bit of fluff, toy boy, fancy man, fancy woman. See table. **2** *a lover of antiques/Italy* admirer, devotee, fan, enthusiast, aficionado; *inf.* buff, freak.

loving *adjective* *a loving daughter/kiss* affectionate, fond, devoted, caring, adoring, doting, solicitous, demonstrative, tender, warm, warm-hearted, friendly, kind, sympathetic, charitable, cordial, amiable, amorous, ardent, passionate.

low *adjective* **1** *a low table* short, small, little, squat, stubby, stunted, truncated, dwarfish, knee-high. **2** *low land* low-lying, ground-level, sea-level, flat, sunken, depressed, subsided, nether. **3** *of low birth | low members of society* lowly, humble, low-born, low-bred, low-ranking, plebeian, peasant, poor, common, ordinary, simple, plain, unpretentious, inferior, subordinate, obscure. **4** *supplies are low* sparse, meagre, scarce, scanty, scant, few, little, deficient, inadequate, paltry, measly, trifling, reduced, depleted, diminished. **5** *a low hum* soft, quiet, muted, subdued, muffled, hushed, quietened, whispered, murmured, gentle, dulcet, indistinct, inaudible. **6** *feeling low* low-spirited, down, depressed, dejected, despondent, disheartened, down-hearted, downcast, gloomy, glum, unhappy, sad, miserable, blue, fed up, morose, moody, heavy-hearted, forlorn; *inf.* down in the mouth, down in the dumps, brassed off, cheesed off. **7** *in a low state of health | invalids getting low* weak, weakly, feeble, enfeebled, debilitated, frail, delicate, fragile, infirm, ill, ailing, unhealthy, poorly, helpless, powerless, stricken, prostrate, failing, declining, sinking, fading, dying. **8** *of low intelligence* low-grade, inferior, substandard, below par, second-rate, deficient, defective, wanting, lacking, inadequate, mediocre, unacceptable, worthless. **9** *low expectations* lowly, simple, plain, ordinary, commonplace, run-of-the-mill, modest, unambitious, unpretentious, unaspiring. **10** *have a low opinion of them* unfavourable, poor, bad, adverse, hostile, negative. **11** *a low thing to do* mean, nasty, foul, bad, wicked, evil, vile, vicious, despicable, contemptible, heinous, villainous, base, dishonourable, unprincipled, dastardly, ignoble, sordid. **12** *low creatures* mean, nasty, foul, vile, despicable, contemptible, base, villainous, hateful, loathsome, reprehensible, depraved, debased, wretched, miserable, sorry. **13** *low comedy/humour* vulgar, crude, coarse, obscene, indecent, gross, ribald, smutty, bawdy, pornographic, blue, rude, rough, unrefined, indelicate, improper, offensive. **14** *low prices/wages* cheap, inexpensive, moderate, reasonable, modest, bargain-basement.
Opposites HIGH; CHEERFUL; ADMIRABLE.

low *verb* cattle lowing moo, bellow.

low-down *noun* information, data, facts, facts and figures, intelligence, inside information; *inf.* info, gen, dope.

lower¹ *adjective* **1** *of lower status* lesser, lower-level, lower-grade, subordinate, junior, inferior, minor, secondary. **2** *her lower lip* under, underneath, nether. **3** *lower prices/wages* cheaper, reduced, decreased, lessened, cut, slashed, curtailed, pruned.

lower² *verb* **1** *lower the flag/weight* let down, take down, haul down, drop, let fall, let sink.

LOVERS OF FACT AND FICTION

Anna Karenina and Alexei Vronski	Gertrude Stein and Alice B. Toklas	Paris and Helen
Antony and Cleopatra	Harlequin and Columbine	Petrarch and Laura
Beatrice and Benedick	Heathcliff and Cathy	Porgy and Bess
Bonnie and Clyde	Heloise and Abelard	Pyramus and Thisbe
Byron and Lady Caroline Lamb	Henry Miller and Anaïs Nin	Richard Burton and Elizabeth Taylor
Charles II and Nell Gwyn	Hero and Leander	Rimbaud and Verlaine
Chopin and George Sand	Horatio Nelson and Lady Emma Hamilton	Romeo and Juliet
Dante and Beatrice	Humphrey Bogart and Lauren Bacall	Rosalind and Orlando
Daphnis and Chloe		Samson and Delilah
Darby and Joan	Jane Eyre and Edward Rochester	Scarlett O'Hara and Rhett Butler
David and Bathsheba	Lady Chatterley and Mellors	Tristan and Isolde
Dido and Aeneas	Lancelot and Guinevere	Troilus and Cressida
Edward VIII and Wallis Simpson	Napoleon and Josephine	Virginia Woolf and Vita Sackville-West
Elizabeth Barrett and Robert Browning	Oscar Wilde and Lord Alfred Douglas	W. B. Yeats and Maud Gonne
Eros and Psyche	Paolo and Francesca	W. H. Auden and Christopher Isherwood

2 *lower one's voice* | *lower the volume* modulate, soften, quieten, hush, tone down, muffle, turn down, mute. **3** *will only lower him in her eyes* degrade, debase, demean, downgrade, discredit, devalue, dishonour, disgrace, belittle, humble, humiliate, disparage. **4** *lower the temperature/prices* reduce, bring down, decrease, lessen, cut, slash, curtail, prune. **5** *the winds lowered* abate, die down, subside, let up, moderate, slacken, dwindle, lessen, ebb, fade away, wane, taper off, lull.
Opposites RAISE; INCREASE; BOOST.

lower³ *verb. See* LOUR.

low-grade *adjective* poor-quality, inferior, substandard, below standard, not up to scratch, second-rate, bargain-basement, poor, bad; *Am. inf.* two-bit.

low-key *adjective* restrained, muted, subtle, quiet, understated, played down, toned down, relaxed, downbeat, easygoing, modulated, softened; *inf.* laid-back.

lowly *adjective* **1** *of lowly birth* | *lowly members of society* low, humble, low-born, low-ranking, plebeian, peasant, poor, common, ordinary, inferior, subordinate. *See* LOW *adjective* 3. **2** *feeling lowly before God* humble, meek, submissive, dutiful, docile, mild, gentle, modest, unassuming. **3** *lowly ambitions* low, simple, plain, ordinary, commonplace, run-of-the-mill, modest, unambitious, unpretentious, unaspiring.
Opposites NOBLE; ARISTOCRATIC; ARROGANT; AMBITIOUS.

low-spirited *adjective* low, down, depressed, dejected, despondent, gloomy, unhappy, miserable, blue; *inf.* down in the mouth, down in the dumps. *See* LOW *adjective* 6.

loyal *adjective* faithful, true, true-hearted, tried and true, trusted, trustworthy, trusty, true-blue, steadfast, staunch, dependable, reliable, devoted, dutiful, patriotic, constant, unchanging, unwavering, unswerving, firm, stable.
Opposites DISLOYAL; TREACHEROUS.

loyalty *noun* faithfulness, fidelity, fealty, allegiance, trueness, true-heartedness, trustiness, trustworthiness, steadfastness, staunchness, dependability, reliability, devotion, duty, patriotism, constancy, stability. *See* LOYAL.
Opposites DISLOYALTY; TREACHERY.

lozenge *noun* tablet, pastille, cough sweet, cough drop, gum, gumdrop, jujube; *Med.* troche.

lubber *noun* oaf, dolt, boor, gawk; *inf.* yob, yobbo, slob; *Am. inf.* lummox.

lubberly *adjective* awkward, clumsy, blundering, bumbling, lumbering, inept, maladroit, ungainly, gawky, oafish, doltish, boorish, lumpish, lumpen, like a bull in a china shop, all fingers and thumbs, heavy-handed; *inf.* yobbish, slobbish, clodhopping, butter-fingered.

lubricant *noun* lubricator, oil, grease, emollient, lard, fat, moisturizer, lotion, unguent.

lubricate *verb* **1** *lubricate the machinery* oil, grease, make slippery, moisturize. **2** *lubricate the planning process* make smooth, smooth the way for, oil the wheels for.

lucid *adjective* **1** *a lucid description* clear, clear-cut, crystal-clear, comprehensible, intelligible, understandable, plain, simple, direct, straightforward, graphic, explicit, obvious, evident, apparent, distinct, transparent, overt, cogent. **2** *an old man who is scarcely lucid* sane, rational, in one's right mind, in possession of one's faculties, of sound mind, *compos mentis*, sensible, clear-headed; *inf.* all there, with all one's marbles. **3** *lucid pools* clear, crystal-clear, transparent, limpid, translucent, glassy, pellucid. **4** *lucid stars* bright, shining, gleaming, luminous, radiant, lustrous.
Opposites CONFUSED; MUDDLED; CLOUDY.

luck *noun* **1** *as luck would have it* fate, fortune, destiny, predestination, the stars, chance, fortuity, accident, hazard, serendipity. **2** *wishing you luck* good luck, good fortune, success, successfulness, prosperity, advantage, advantageousness, felicity; *inf.* lucky break. **in luck** lucky, fortunate, blessed with good luck, favoured, born under a lucky star, advantaged, successful, prosperous, happy. **out of luck** unlucky, unfortunate, luckless, cursed with ill-luck, unsuccessful, disadvantaged, miserable.

luckily *adverb* luckily he survived fortunately, by good luck, by good fortune, happily, providentially, as luck would have it, propitiously.

luckless *adjective* luckless competitors unlucky, unfortunate, unsuccessful, out of luck, down on one's luck, jinxed, hapless, ill-starred, ill-fated, unhappy, miserable, wretched, forlorn, star-crossed.

lucky *adjective* **1** *lucky people* fortunate, blessed with good luck, favoured, born under a lucky star, charmed; successful, prosperous, happy; advantaged, born with a silver spoon in one's mouth. **2** *a lucky guess* fortunate, fortuitous, providential, advantageous, timely, opportune, expedient, auspicious, propitious. *See table at* CHARM.
Opposites UNLUCKY; UNFORTUNATE; UNFAVOURABLE.

lucrative *adjective* profitable, profit-making, moneymaking, paying, high-income, well-paid, high-paying, gainful, remunerative, productive, fat, fruitful, rewarding, worthwhile.

lucre *noun* money, cash, profit, profits, gain, proceeds, winnings, pay, remuneration, earnings, income, yield, revenue; *inf.* dosh, dough, bread, the ready.

ludicrous *adjective* absurd, ridiculous, laughable, risible, derisible, comic, comical, farcical, silly, funny, humorous, droll, amusing, diverting, hilarious, crazy, zany, nonsensical, odd, outlandish, eccentric, incongruous, preposterous.
Opposites SENSIBLE; SERIOUS; SOLEMN.

lug *verb* **1** *lugging a heavy suitcase* carry, bear, tote, transport; *inf.* hump; *Scots* humph. **2** *lugging a handcart behind him* haul, drag, heave, trail, tug, tow.

luggage *noun* bags, baggage, bag and baggage, cases, suitcases, trunks, things, gear, belongings, kit, effects, goods and chattels, impedimenta, paraphernalia, accoutrements.

lugubrious *adjective* mournful, doleful, melancholy, dismal, gloomy, sombre, funereal, sor-

rowful, morose, miserable, joyless, woebegone, woeful, dirgelike, elegaic.
Opposites CHEERFUL; JOYFUL.

lukewarm *adjective* **1** *lukewarm water* tepid, warm, blood-hot, blood-warm, at room temperature, at skin temperature. **2** *lukewarm about going to the party* indifferent, cool, cold, half-hearted, apathetic, unenthusiastic, uninterested, unconcerned, impassive, dispassionate, unresponsive, sluggish, phlegmatic, Laodicean.

lull *verb* **1** *lull the child to sleep* rock to sleep, lullaby, soothe, quiet, hush. **2** *lull their fears* soothe, quiet, silence, calm, hush, still, quell, assuage, allay, ease, alleviate, pacify, mitigate. **3** *the storm lulled* abate, die down, subside, let up, moderate, slacken, lessen, dwindle, decrease, diminish, ebb, fade away, wane, taper off, lower.

lull *noun* **1** *a lull in the proceedings* pause, respite, interval, break, hiatus; *inf.* let-up. **2** *the lull before the storm* calm, calmness, stillness, quiet, quietness, tranquillity, silence, hush.

lullaby *noun* cradle-song, *berceuse*.

lumber¹ *noun* *lumber in the attic* jumble, clutter, junk, rubbish, odds and ends, cast-offs, rejects, trash, refuse, white elephants.

lumber² *verb* *lumber him with her jobs* burden, load, saddle, encumber, impose upon; *inf.* land.

lumber³ *verb* *heard him lumbering around upstairs* clump, stump, plod, trudge, stamp, shuffle, shamble, stumble, waddle, lump along.

lumbering *adjective* awkward, clumsy, heavy-footed, blundering, bumbling, inept, maladroit, ungainly, like a bull in a china shop, ungraceful, lumpish, hulking, ponderous, stolid, lubberly; *inf.* clodhopping.

luminary *noun* *a luminary of the council* leading light, guiding light, star, superstar, megastar, leader, notable, dignitary, VIP, celebrity, big name, household name, somebody, name, important personage, lion; *inf.* bigwig, big shot, big cheese, biggie, celeb.

luminous *adjective* **1** *luminous stars/colours* lighted, lit, illuminated, shining, bright, brilliant, radiant, dazzling, glowing, effulgent, luminescent, phosphorescent, vivid, resplendent. **2** *a luminous account* lucid, clear, crystal-clear, comprehensible, intelligible, plain, simple, direct, straightforward, graphic, obvious, distinct, apparent. See LUCID 1.

lump¹ *noun* **1** *a lump of putty* chunk, wedge, hunk, piece, mass, cake, nugget, ball, dab, pat, clod, gob, gobbet, wad, clump, cluster, mound. **2** *a lump on his head* bump, swelling, bruise, bulge, protuberance, protrusion, growth, carbuncle, hump, tumour, tumescence, node.

lump² *verb* *often lump together* put together, combine, group, unite, pool, mix together, blend, merge, mass, fuse, conglomerate, coalesce, consolidate.

lump³ *verb* *like it or lump it | you'll have to lump the situation* put up with, bear, endure, take, stand, tolerate, suffer, brook; *Scots* thole.

lumpish *adjective* **1** *a lumpish young woman* heavy, stolid, lumbering, ponderous, elephantine, awkward, clumsy, ungainly, gawky, hulking, lethargic, bovine, vegetable-like, pudding-like. **2** *lumpish children* stupid, dull-witted, slow-witted, slow, doltish, oafish; *inf.* thick, dumb, dopey.

lumpy *adjective* **1** *a lumpy mattress* bumpy, knobbly, bulging, uneven. **2** *lumpy custard* curdled, clotted, granular, grainy.

lunacy *noun* **1** *suffering from lunacy* insanity, insaneness, madness, mental illness/derangement, dementia, dementedness, loss of reason, unsoundness of mind, mania, frenzy, psychosis; *inf.* craziness. **2** *the sheer lunacy of the decision* madness, insanity, foolishness, folly, foolhardiness, stupidity, idiocy, irrationality, illogicality, senselessness, absurdity, absurdness, silliness, inanity, ludicrousness; *inf.* craziness, daftness.
Opposites SANITY; SENSE; PRUDENCE.

lunatic *noun* *driving like a lunatic* maniac, madman, madwoman, imbecile, idiot, psychopath; *inf.* loony, nut, nutter, nutcase, head case, basket case, headbanger, screwball, psycho.

lunatic *adjective* *a lunatic idea | it was a lunatic thing to do* mad, insane, foolish, stupid, foolhardy, idiotic, crack-brained, irrational, unreasonable, illogical, senseless, nonsensical, absurd, silly, inane, asinine, ludicrous, imprudent, preposterous; *inf.* crazy, daft.

lunch *noun* luncheon, midday meal, brunch; *dial.* dinner.

lunge *noun* **1** *make a lunge towards the open door* spring, jump, leap, bound, dash, charge, pounce, dive. **2** *take a lunge at his attacker* stab, jab, poke, thrust, swing, pass, cut, feint; *inf.* swipe.

lunge *verb* **1** *lunge towards the door* spring, jump, leap, bound, dash, charge, pounce, dive. **2** *lunge at his attacker* stab, jab, poke, thrust at, pitch into, lash out at, take a swing at, aim a blow at; *inf.* take a swipe at.

lurch *verb* **1** *drunks lurching home* stagger, sway, reel, weave, stumble, totter. **2** *ships lurching in the storm* list, roll, pitch, toss, sway, veer, swerve.

lure *verb* *lure them into a trap | lured by greed* entice, attract, induce, inveigle, decoy, draw, lead, allure, tempt, seduce, beguile, ensnare, magnetize, cajole.

lure *noun* *use sweets as a lure to the children* enticement, attraction, inducement, decoy, draw, allurement, temptation, bait, magnet, drawing card, carrot; *inf.* come-on.

lurid *adjective* **1** *lurid colours/sunsets* overbright, brilliant, glaring, flaming, dazzling, glowing, intense, vivid, showy, gaudy, fiery, blood-red, burning. **2** *lurid descriptions of their affair* sensational, melodramatic, exaggerated, extravagant, graphic, explicit, unrestrained, shocking, startling; *inf.* full-frontal. **3** *lurid details of the murder* gruesome, gory, grisly, macabre, repugnant, revolting, disgusting, ghastly. **4** *lurid complexions* pale, pallid, ashen, colourless, chalk-white, white, wan, sallow, ghostly,

lurk · lyrics

ghastly.
Opposites MUTED; RESTRAINED; SUBTLE.

lurk verb skulk, lie in wait, lie low, hide, conceal oneself, take cover, crouch, sneak, slink, prowl, steal, tiptoe.

luscious adjective **1** luscious fruit delicious, juicy, sweet, succulent, mouth-watering, tasty, appetizing, delectable, palatable, toothsome, nectar-like; inf. scrumptious, yummy. **2** luscious blondes voluptuous, sensuous, sexy, gorgeous, beautiful, attractive.

lush adjective **1** lush vegetation luxuriant, abundant, profuse, exuberant, dense, thick, riotous, overgrown, prolific, rank, teeming, jungle-like, flourishing, verdant, green. **2** lush fruits juicy, succulent, fleshy, pulpy, ripe, soft, tender, fresh. **3** lush drawing-rooms luxurious, sumptuous, grand, palatial, opulent, lavish, elaborate, extravagant; inf. plush, ritzy.
Opposites BARREN; MEAGRE; DRY.

lush noun alcoholic, heavy/hard drinker, problem drinker, drinker, drunk, drunkard, toper, sot, dipsomaniac; inf. alky, boozer, dipso, tosspot, soak.

lust noun **1** satisfy his lust sexual desire, sexual appetite, sexual longing, sexual passion, libido, sex drive, sexuality, biological urge, randiness. **2** guilty of lust lechery, lecherousness, lasciviousness, lewdness, carnality, licentiousness, salaciousness, salacity, prurience, concupiscence, wantonness, randiness; inf. horniness, raunchiness, the hots. **3** a lust for gold greed, greediness, desire, craving, covetousness, avidness, avidity, cupidity, longing, yearning, hunger, thirst, appetite, passion.

lust verb lust after girls | lusting for power/revenge be consumed with desire for, desire, crave, covet, want, need, long for, yearn for, hunger for, thirst for, ache for; inf. have the hots for, lech after.

lustful adjective lecherous, lascivious, lewd, libidinous, licentious, salacious, prurient, concupiscent, wanton, unchaste, hot-blooded, passionate, sensual, sexy, randy; inf. horny, raunchy.

lustily adverb children crying lustily loudly, vigorously, heartily, at the top of one's voice, with might and main, powerfully, forcefully.

lustre noun **1** admire the lustre of the table sheen, gloss, shine, burnish, glow, gleam, sparkle, shimmer. **2** the lustre of the stars brilliance, brightness, dazzle, luminousness, radiance, refulgence, lambency. **3** bring lustre to the school honour, glory, credit, merit, prestige, renown, fame, distinction, notability.

lustreless adjective dull, flat, matt, unburnished, unpolished, tarnished, dingy, dim, dark, drab, gloomy, colourless, washed out, faded.

lustrous adjective shiny, shining, glossy, gleaming, glowing, bright, burnished, polished, dazzling, sparkling, glistening, twinkling, shimmering, luminous.

lusty adjective **1** lusty young men healthy, strong, vigorous, robust, hale and hearty, hearty, energetic, lively, blooming, rugged, sturdy, tough, stalwart, brawny, hefty, husky, burly, solidly built, powerful, virile, red-blooded. **2** a lusty cry loud, vigorous, hearty, powerful, forceful.

luxuriant adjective **1** luxuriant vegetation lush, abundant, profuse, exuberant, dense, thick, riotous, overgrown, prolific, teeming, verdant. See LUSH adjective 1. **2** luxuriant prose florid, flowery, ornate, elaborate, fancy, adorned, decorated, embellished, embroidered, extravagant, flamboyant, ostentatious, showy, high-flown, baroque, rococo.
Opposites BARREN; MEAGRE; PLAIN.

luxuriate verb **1** luxuriate in a hot bath bask in, revel in, delight in, enjoy, wallow in, savour, appreciate; inf. get a kick out of, get a charge from. **2** plants luxuriating thrive, flourish, bloom, prosper, do well, burgeon, spring up, sprout, shoot up, mushroom. **3** luxuriating after a life of poverty live in luxury, live in the lap of luxury, live off the fat of the land, be in clover, take it easy, relax, have the time of one's life, lead the life of Riley.

luxurious adjective **1** luxurious surroundings opulent, affluent, sumptuous, expensive, rich, costly, de luxe, lush, grand, splendid, magnificent, lavish, well-appointed, comfortable, extravagant, ornate, fancy; inf. plush, posh, ritzy, swanky. **2** luxurious habits self-indulgent, sensual, pleasure-loving, comfort-seeking, epicurean, hedonistic, sybaritic.
Opposites POOR; AUSTERE; SPARTAN.

luxury noun **1** live in luxury luxuriousness, opulence, affluence, sumptuousness, richness, grandeur, splendour, magnificence, lavishness, lap of luxury, bed of roses. **2** the luxury of independence boon, benefit, advantage, delight, bliss, comfort. **3** one of life's luxuries extra, non-essential, frill, extravagance, indulgence, treat, refinement.

lying noun accused of lying untruthfulness, fabrication, fibbing, perjury, white lies, little white lies, falseness, falsity, dishonesty, mendacity, lack of veracity, story-telling, dissimulation, dissembling, prevarication, deceit, guile, crookedness, double-dealing.

lying adjective lying witnesses untruthful, fabricating, false, dishonest, mendacious, dissimulating, dissembling, prevaricating, deceitful, guileful, crooked, double-dealing, two-faced.
Opposites TRUTHFUL; HONEST.

lynch verb put to death, execute, hang, kill, murder, slay; inf. string up.

lyric adjective **1** lyric poetry songlike, musical, melodic, melodious, expressive, deep-felt, personal, subjective, passionate, lyrical. **2** lyric voices light, silvery, clear, lilting, flowing, dulcet, sweet, mellifluous, mellow, lyrical.

lyrical adjective **1** lyrical verse lyric, songlike, musical, melodic, expressive, personal. See LYRIC 1. **2** lyrical voices light, silvery, clear, flowing, sweet. See LYRIC 2. **3** lyrical about her success enthusiastic, rhapsodic, effusive, rapturous, ecstatic, euphoric, carried away, emotional, impassioned.

lyrics plural noun the lyrics of the song words, libretto, book, text.

macabre *adjective* gruesome, grisly, grim, gory, morbid, grim, ghastly, hideous, horrific, horrible, horrifying, horrid, horrendous, terrifying, frightening, frightful, fearsome, shocking, dreadful, appalling, loathsome, repugnant, repulsive, sickening.

mace *noun* staff, club, cudgel, bludgeon, bastinado. *See table at* WEAPON.

macerate *verb* pulp, mash, squash, soften, liquefy, soak, steep.

machete *noun* knife, cutlass, cleaver, kukri. *See table at* KNIFE.

machiavellian *adjective* devious, cunning, crafty, artful, wily, sly, scheming, designing, conniving, opportunistic, insidious, treacherous, perfidious, two-faced, double-dealing, unscrupulous, deceitful, dishonest.

machinations *plural noun* schemes, plot, intrigues, conspiracies, complots, designs, plans, devices, ploys, ruses, trick, wiles, stratagems, tactics, manoeuvres, contrivances, expedients.

machine *noun* **1** *the cutting machine broke down* appliance, apparatus, instrument, tool, device, contraption, gadget, mechanism, engine, motor. **2** *the competitor's machine* vehicle, car, bicycle, motor cycle, aeroplane; *inf.* bike, motor bike, plane. **3** *machines took over from men* robot, automaton, mechanical man, zombie, puppet. **4** *the party machine* organization, system, structure, agency, machinery, council, cabal, clique; *inf.* set-up.

machinery *noun* **1** *factory machinery* equipment, apparatus, mechanism, gear, tackle, instruments, gadgetry. **2** *the machinery of local government* workings, organization, system, structure, agency, channel, vehicle; *inf.* set-up, nuts and bolts, brass tacks, nitty-gritty.

machinist *noun* machine-operator, operator, operative, worker.

machismo *noun* masculinity, manliness, virility, toughness, chauvinism, male chauvinism, sexism.

macrocosm *noun* **1** *exploration of the macrocosm* universe, cosmos, world, wide world, globe, creation, solar system. **2** *society and other macrocosms* complete system, system, total structure, structure, totality, entirety.

mad *adjective* **1** *gone mad with grief* stark mad, insane, deranged, demented, of unsound mind, crazed, lunatic, *non compos mentis*, unbalanced, unhinged, unstable, distracted, manic, frenzied, raving, distraught, frantic, hysterical, delirious, psychotic, not quite right, mad as a hatter, mad as a March hare, foaming at the mouth; *inf.* crazy, off one's head, out of one's mind, off one's nut, nuts, nutty, off one's rocker, round the bend, round the twist, raving mad, barmy, batty, bonkers, crackers, crackpot, cuckoo, loopy, loony, bananas, loco, dippy, screwy, with a screw loose, out of one's tree, off one's trolley, off the wall, not all there, not the full shilling, not the full pound note, not right upstairs. **2** *mothers mad at their children* flaming mad, blazing mad, angry, furious, infuriated, irate, raging, enraged, fuming, blazing, in a towering rage, incensed, wrathful, seeing red, cross, indignant, exasperated, irritated, berserk, out of control, beside oneself; *inf.* livid, wild, ape, in a wax, with guns blazing. **3** *a mad scheme/idea* insane, foolish, stupid, lunatic, foolhardy, idiotic, crackbrained, irrational, unreasonable, illogical, senseless, nonsensical, absurd, impractical, silly, inane, asinine, ludicrous, wild, unwise, imprudent, preposterous; *inf.* crazy, daft. **4** *mad about jazz* wildly enthusiastic, passionate, impassioned, avid, eager, keen on, ardent, zealous, fervent, fanatical, devoted to, infatuated with, in love with; *inf.* crazy, nuts, dotty, hooked on, wild, gone on. **5** *mad, passionate love* wild, unrestrained, uncontrolled, abandoned, excited, frenzied, frantic, frenetic, ebullient, energetic, boisterous. **like mad 1** *run like mad* furiously, as fast as possible, as fast as one's legs can carry one, fast, hurriedly, quickly, rapidly, speedily, hastily, energetically; *inf.* billy-oh. **2** *love her like mad* madly, enthusiastically, unrestrainedly, wildly, passionately, intensely, ardently, fervently, to distraction, devotedly.
Opposites SANE; CALM; SENSIBLE; APATHETIC.

madcap *adjective* daredevil, impulsive, wild, reckless, rash, hotheaded, daring, adventurous, heedless, thoughtless, incautious, imprudent, indiscreet, ill-advised, hasty, foolhardy, foolish, senseless, impractical, hare-brained, crack-brained; *inf.* crazy, crackpot.

madcap *noun* daredevil, hothead, tearaway, adventurer/adventuress, wild man/woman.

madden *verb* **1** *maddened by their behaviour* anger, infuriate, send into a rage, enrage, incense, exasperate, irritate, inflame, annoy, provoke, upset, agitate, vex, irk, pique, gall, make one's hackles rise, raise one's hackles, make one's blood boil, make one see red, get one's back up; *inf.* aggravate, get up one's nose, nark, bug, make one livid. **2** *in a mental hospital maddened by grief* drive mad/insane, derange, unhinge, unbalance; *inf.* drive off one's head, send round the bend. *See* MAD 1.

maddening *adjective* infuriating, exasperating, irritating, annoying, provoking, upsetting, vexing, irksome, unsettling, disturbing, troublesome, vexatious, galling.

made-up *adjective* **1** *a made-up story* invented, fabricated, trumped-up, concocted, devised, manufactured, fictional, false, untrue, unreal, sham, specious, spurious, imaginary, mythical. **2** *made-up young women* painted, done up, powdered, rouged. **3** *cabinets already made up* put together, built, constructed, finished, ready, prepared, fixed.

madhouse noun **1** *certified and in a madhouse* mental hospital, mental institution, psychiatric hospital, asylum, lunatic asylum; *inf.* nuthouse, funny farm, loony bin. **2** *it was a madhouse with the wedding preparations* bedlam, babel, chaos, pandemonium, uproar, turmoil, wild disarray, scene of confusion, disorder, three-ring circus.

madly adverb **1** *behaving madly* insanely, dementedly, distractedly, frenziedly, maniacally, frantically, hysterically, deliriously, wildly; *inf.* crazily. **2** *rushing around madly like mad*, furiously, fast, hurriedly, quickly, speedily, hastily, energetically. See LIKE MAD 1 (MAD). **3** *love her madly* enthusiastically, unrestrainedly, wildly, intensely, fervently, to distraction. See LIKE MAD 2 (MAD). **4** *madly expensive* extremely, very, exceedingly, excessively, absurdly, ridiculously.

madman noun maniac, lunatic, imbecile, psychopath; *inf.* loony, nut, nutter, nutcase, head case, basket case, headbanger, screwball, psycho.

madness noun **1** *madness caused by grief* insanity, insaneness, dementia, mental illness/derangement, dementedness, instability of mind, unsoundness of mind, lunacy, distraction, mania, frenzy, psychosis; *inf.* craziness. **2** *concealing her madness at the children's behaviour* anger, fury, rage, infuriation, irateness, wrath, ire, crossness, indignation, exasperation, irritation; *inf.* lividness, wildness. **3** *amazed at the madness of the decision* insanity, folly, foolishness, stupidity, lunacy, foolhardiness, idiocy, irrationality, unreasonableness, illogicality, senselessness, nonsense, nonsensicalness, absurdness, absurdity, silliness, inanity, ludicrousness, wildness, imprudence, preposterousness; *inf.* craziness, daftness. See MAD 3. **4** *known for her madness about jazz* enthusiasm, passion, impassionedness, avidness, eagerness, keenness, ardour, zeal, fervour, fanaticism, infatuation. See MAD 4.

maelstrom noun **1** *ships destroyed in a maelstrom* whirlpool, vortex, eddy, swirl, Charybdis. **2** *the maelstrom of war* turbulence, tumult, uproar, commotion, disorder, disarray, chaos, confusion, upheaval, pandemonium, bedlam.

maestro noun master, expert, virtuoso, genius; *inf.* ace, whiz.

magazine noun periodical, journal, publication, supplement, colour supplement; *inf.* glossy, book.

magenta adjective fuchsia, reddish-purple, purplish-red, crimson, mauvish-crimson, carmine. See table at COLOUR.

magic noun **1** *believers in magic* sorcery, witchcraft, wizardry, enchantment, spell-working, necromancy, the supernatural, occultism, the occult, black magic, black art, voodoo, hoodoo, sortilege, thaumaturgy. **2** *the magic of the conjuror* sleight of hand, legerdemain, conjuring,

illusion, prestidigitation, deception, trickery, juggling; *inf.* jiggery-pokery. **3** *the magic of the stage* allure, allurement, enchantment, entrancement, fascination, charm, glamour, magnetism, enticement.

magic adjective **1** *a magic place* magical, enchanting, entrancing, spellbinding, fascinating, captivating, charming, glamorous, magnetic, irresistible, hypnotic. **2** *the tennis game was magic* marvellous, wonderful, excellent; *inf.* brilliant, terrific, brill, fabulous, fab.

magician noun **1** *frightened by the magician in the story* sorcerer, sorceress, witch, wizard, warlock, enchanter, enchantress, spell-worker, spell-caster, necromancer, thaumaturge. **2** *the magician at the children's party* illusionist, conjuror, legerdemainist, prestidigitator, juggler. **3** *he is a magician at the piano* genius, master, virtuoso, expert, marvel, wizard, maestro; *inf.* ace, whiz.

magisterial adjective imperious, peremptory, authoritative, masterful, lordly, domineering, dictatorial, autocratic, overbearing, overweening, high-handed, arrogant, haughty, supercilious, patronizing; *inf.* bossy.

magnanimity noun generosity, charitableness, charity, benevolence, beneficence, openhandedness, big-heartedness, kindness, munificence, bountifulness, largesse, altruism, philanthropy, unselfishness, selflessness, self-sacrifice, mercy, leniency. See MAGNANIMOUS.

magnanimous adjective generous, generous to a fault, charitable, benevolent, beneficent, open-handed, big-hearted, great-hearted, kind, kindly, munificent, bountiful, liberal, altruistic, philanthropic, noble, unselfish, selfless, self-sacrificing, ungrudging, unstinting, forgiving, merciful, lenient, indulgent.
Opposites MEAN; SELFISH; PETTY; VINDICTIVE.

magnate noun *a business magnate* tycoon, captain of industry, baron, industrialist, entrepreneur, financier, top executive, chief, leader, VIP, notable, nabob, grandee; *inf.* big shot, bigwig, big wheel, fat cat, mogul.

magnet noun **1** *a magnet attracting iron filings* lodestone, magnetite, field magnet, bar magnet, electromagnet, solenoid. **2** *the refreshment tent was the magnet at the fair* focus, focal point, centre of attraction, cynosure. **3** *her beauty was a magnet to all* lure, allurement, attraction, fascination, captivation, enticement, draw, appeal, charm, temptation.

magnetic adjective alluring, attractive, fascinating, captivating, entrancing, enchanting, enthralling, appealing, charming, engaging, tempting, tantalizing, seductive, inviting, irresistible, magic, bewitching, charismatic, hypnotic, mesmeric.

magnetism noun *the leader has great magnetism* allure, attraction, fascination, captivation, enchantment, appeal, draw, drawing power, pull, charm, temptation, seductiveness, magic, spell, charisma, hypnotism, mesmerism.

magnification noun **1** *the magnification of the specimen* increase, augmentation, enlargement, extension, expansion, intensification, heightening, enhancement, aggrandizement. See MAG-

NIFY 1. **2** *the magnification of their troubles* exaggeration, overstatement, overemphasis, overplaying, dramatization, embroidery, embellishment, enhancement. See MAGNIFY 2.

magnificence *noun* splendour, splendidness, resplendence, grandeur, impressiveness, imposingness, glory, majesty, nobility, pomp, pomp and circumstance, stateliness, sumptuousness, opulence, luxuriousness, luxury, lavishness, richness, brilliance, radiance, elegance, gorgeousness, éclat; *inf.* ritziness, poshness. See MAGNIFICENT 1.

magnificent *adjective* **1** *magnificent processions/apartments* splendid, resplendent, grand, grandiose, impressive, imposing, striking, glorious, superb, majestic, august, noble, stately, exalted, awe-inspiring, royal, regal, kingly, princely, sumptuous, opulent, luxurious, lavish, rich, brilliant, radiant, elegant, gorgeous; *inf.* splendiferous, ritzy, posh. **2** *a magnificent performance/game* excellent, masterly, skilful, virtuoso, splendid, impressive, fine, marvellous, wonderful; *inf.* terrific, glorious, superb, brilliant, out of this world. **Opposites** MODEST; POOR.

magnify *verb* **1** *bacteria visible when magnified* increase, augment, enlarge, extend, expand, amplify, intensify, heighten, deepen, broaden, widen, dilate, boost, enhance, aggrandize. **2** *magnifying their troubles* exaggerate, overstate, overdo, overemphasize, overplay, dramatize, colour, embroider, embellish, enhance, inflate, make a mountain out of a molehill, draw the long bow; *inf.* make a big thing out of, blow up, blow up out of all proportion. **Opposites** REDUCE; UNDERSTATE; play down (*see* PLAY).

magniloquence *noun* grandiloquence, loftiness, grandiosity, pompousness, pretentiousness, bombast, rhetoric, orotundity, fustian, boastfulness, braggadocio. See MAGNILOQUENT.

magniloquent *adjective* grandiloquent, high-sounding, high-flown, lofty, grandiose, pompous, pretentious, bombastic, rhetorical, declamatory, sonorous, orotund, fustian, stilted, turgid, boastful, bragging, braggart; *inf.* highfalutin.

magnitude *noun* **1** *estimate the magnitude of the explosion* size, extent, measure, proportions, dimensions, volume, weight, quantity, mass, bulk, amplitude, capacity. **2** *amazed at the magnitude of the epidemic* size, extent, greatness, largeness, bigness, immensity, vastness, hugeness, enormity, enormousness, expanse. **3** *underestimate the magnitude of his problem/rank* importance, significance, weight, moment, consequence, mark, notability, note, greatness, distinction, eminence, fame, renown. **of the first magnitude** of the utmost importance, of the greatest significance, very important, of importance, of significance, of note, of moment, of consequence. **Opposites** TRIVIALITY; smallness.

maid *noun* **1** *employ a maid* maidservant, housemaid, serving maid, lady's maid, chambermaid, maid-of-all-work, servant, domestic, girl, au pair. **2** *two lads and a maid* maiden, girl, young lady, lass, miss, nymph, slip of a girl, wench; *lit.* damsel; *Scots* lassie. **3** *no longer a maid* virgin, vestal virgin. See MAIDEN *noun* 2.

maiden *noun* **1** *lads and maidens* maid, girl, lass; *lit.* damsel. See MAID 2. **2** *no longer a maiden* virgin, chaste girl, unmarried girl, celibate, vestal virgin.

maiden *adjective* **1** *maiden aunt* unmarried, spinster, unwed, unwedded, single, husbandless, spouseless, celibate. **2** *maiden voyage/speech* first, initial, inaugural, introductory, initiatory. **3** *maiden territory* virgin, intact, undefiled, untrodden, untapped, unused, untried, untested, fresh, new.

maidenhood *noun* virginity, maidenhead, celibacy.

maidenly *adjective* maidenlike, virginal, chaste, pure, undefiled, virtuous, unsullied, vestal, demure, reserved, retiring, decorous, seemly, decent, gentle.

mail¹ *noun* **1** *collect the mail* post, letters, packages, parcels, correspondence, communications, airmail, registered mail. **2** *criticizing the mail* post, postal system, postal service, post office.

mail² *verb* *mail the letter/package* post, send by mail/post, send, dispatch, airmail.

mail³ *noun* *knights wearing mail* armour, coat of mail, chain-mail, chain-armour, plate armour.

maim *verb* wound, injure, hurt, cripple, disable, put out of action, lame, incapacitate, impair, mar, mutilate, disfigure, mangle.

main *adjective* **1** *the main office/road/issue* head, chief, principal, leading, foremost, most important, central, prime, premier, primary, supreme, predominant, pre-eminent, paramount, cardinal, crucial, vital, critical, pivotal, urgent. **2** *by main force* sheer, pure, utter, downright, mere, plain, brute, stark, absolute, out-and-out, direct. **Opposites** SUBSIDIARY; MINOR.

main *noun* **in the main** for the most part, on the whole, mainly, mostly, by and large, all in all, effectively.

mainly *adverb* *the people are mainly visitors* for the most part, mostly, in the main, on the whole, largely, by and large, to a large extent, to a great degree, predominantly, chiefly, principally, substantially, overall, in general, generally, usually, commonly, as a rule.

mainspring *noun* *jealousy was the mainspring of the crime* motive, motivation, driving force, incentive, impulse, cause, prime mover, reason, origin, root, generator, basis.

mainstay *noun* *the mainstay of the family | she is the mainstay of the theatre company* chief support, prop, linchpin, pillar, pillar of strength, bulwark, buttress, backbone, anchor, foundation, base.

maintain *verb* **1** *maintain friendly relations | must maintain efficiency* continue, keep going, keep up, keep alive, keep in existence, carry on, preserve, conserve, prolong, perpetuate, sustain. **2** *maintain the houses/roads* keep in good condition, keep in repair, keep up, conserve, preserve, keep intact, care for, take good care of, look after. **3** *maintain a family* support, pro-

vide for, keep, finance, feed, nurture, nourish, sustain. **4** *maintain his innocence | he maintains that he is innocent* insist on, hold to, declare, assert, state, announce, affirm, aver, avow, profess, claim, allege, contend, asseverate. **5** *maintain a position* uphold, defend, fight for, stand by, take up the cudgels for, argue for, champion, support, back, advocate.
Opposites break off (*see* BREAK); NEGLECT; DENY.

maintenance *noun* **1** *the maintenance of friendly relations* continuation, continuance, keeping up, carrying on, preservation, conservation, prolongation, perpetuation. *See* MAINTAIN 1. **2** *pay for the maintenance of the property* upkeep, repairs, preservation, conservation, care. *See* MAINTAIN 2. **3** *the maintenance of a family is costly* supporting, keeping, upkeep, financing, feeding, nurture. *See* MAINTAIN 3. **4** *pay maintenance to his children* aliment, alimony, support, allowance, keep, upkeep, subsistence.

majestic *adjective* regal, royal, kingly, queenly, princely, imperial, noble, lordly, august, exalted, awesome, elevated, lofty, stately, dignified, distinguished, magnificent, grand, splendid, resplendent, glorious, impressive, imposing, marvellous, superb, proud.

majesty *noun* **1** *the majesty of the procession* regalness, royalty, royalness, kingliness, queenliness, nobility, nobleness, augustness, exaltation, awesomeness, awe, loftiness, stateliness, dignity, magnificence, grandeur, grandness, splendour, resplendence, glory, impressiveness, superbness, pride. *See* MAJESTIC. **2** *the majesty invested in him* sovereignty, authority, power, dominion, supremacy.

major *adjective* **1** *the major part is complete* larger, bigger, greater, main. **2** *one of our major poets* greatest, best, most important, leading, foremost, chief, main, outstanding, first-rate, notable, eminent, pre-eminent, supreme. **3** *a major issue | a matter of major importance* important, significant, crucial, vital, great, weighty, paramount, utmost, prime. **4** *major surgery* serious, radical, complicated.
Opposites MINOR; UNIMPORTANT; TRIVIAL.

majority *noun* **1** *the majority of the people/audience* larger part/number, greater part/number, most, more than half, bulk, mass, main body, preponderance, lion's share. **2** *their majority was halved* winning margin, winning difference, superiority of numbers/votes. **3** *young people reaching their majority* legal age, coming-of-age, seniority, adulthood, manhood, womanhood, maturity, age of consent.
Opposites MINORITY.

make *verb* **1** *make sandcastles/furniture* build, construct, assemble, put together, put up, erect, manufacture, produce, fabricate, create, form, fashion, model, mould, shape, forge. **2** *make them pay* force to, compel to, coerce into, press into, drive into, pressure into, pressurize into, oblige to, require to, prevail upon to, dragoon into, impel to, constrain to, urge to; *inf.* railroad into, put the heat on, put the screws on, use strong-arm tactics on. **3** *make a noise/scene* cause, create, give rise to, produce, bring about, generate, engender, occasion,

effect. **4** *make a bow* perform, execute, do, accomplish, carry out, effect, practise, engage in, prosecute. **5** *make him chairman* create, appoint, designate, name, nominate, select, elect, vote in, install, invest, ordain, assign. **6** *make a will/film* compose, put together, frame, formulate, prepare, write, direct. **7** *make money | he's making a profit | can't make a good wage* gain, acquire, obtain, get, realize, secure, win, earn, net, gross, clear, bring in, take home, pocket. **8** *make tea* prepare, get ready, make arrangements for, put together, concoct, cook; *inf.* whip up; *Am. inf.* fix. **9** *make laws* draw up, frame, form, formulate, enact, lay down, establish, institute, found, originate. **10** *that makes £100* come to, add up to, total, amount to. **11** *what do you make the total?* estimate, calculate, compute, gauge, reckon. **12** *what do you make of him?* look upon, view, regard, consider, think of, judge, deem, evaluate, adjudge. **13** *make a decision* come to, settle on, determine on, conclude, establish, seal. **14** *make a speech* give, deliver, utter, give voice to, enunciate, recite, pronounce. **15** *make a great leader | the sofa makes a good bed* be, act as, serve as, constitute, perform the function of, play the part of, represent, embody. **16** *make the first eleven* achieve, attain, get into, gain access to, gain a place in. **17** *make the bus/party* catch, arrive in time for, arrive at, reach, get to, succeed in attending. **18** *boasting about making girls* seduce, have sexual intercourse with, make love to, go to bed with, sleep with; *inf.* have sex with.
make as if/though *make as if to run away | made as if he was mad* act as if/though, pretend, feign, give the impression, make a show of, affect, feint; *inf.* put it on. **make away with 1** *make away with his bags/money/wife* make off with, run away with, abscond with, steal, purloin, kidnap, abduct; *inf.* nick, swipe, nab. *See* MAKE *verb* make off with. **2** *make away with the evidence* do away with, destroy, dispose of, get rid of, eliminate; *inf.* dump. **3** *make away with his enemy* do away with, kill, murder, assassinate, put to death, slaughter, execute, eliminate; *inf.* bump off, do in. **make believe** pretend, fantasize, indulge in fantasy, daydream, build castles in the air, build castles in Spain, dream, imagine, romance, play-act, act, enact. **make do 1** *we have very little but we make do* get by on few resources, get by, get along, scrape by, manage, cope, survive, muddle through, make the best of a bad job. **2** *make do with what you have* get by with/on, make the best of, put to the best use, make the most of, improvise. **make for 1** *make for a safe place* go towards, head for, aim for, make one's way towards, proceed towards, direct one's footsteps towards, steer a course towards, be bound for. **2** *this will make for a good relationship* contribute to, be conducive to, promote, facilitate, further, advance, forward, favour. **make off** *on seeing the police they made off* run away/off, take to one's heels, leave, take off, beat a hasty retreat, flee, bolt, fly, make a getaway, make one's getaway, make a quick exit, abscond, decamp; *inf.* clear off, beat it, make tracks, split, cut and run, do a runner, leg it, skedaddle, vamoose, hightail it. **make off with** *make*

off with his bags/money/wife make away with, run off/away with, abscond with, steal, purloin, appropriate, kidnap, abduct; *inf.* nick, swipe, nab, waltz off with, filch. **make out 1** *make out a figure in the distance* discern, see, distinguish, espy, behold, perceive, descry, notice, observe, recognize, pick out, detect, discover. **2** *unable to make out what she says* understand, comprehend, follow, grasp, fathom, work out, figure out, interpret. **3** *unable to make out the handwriting* decipher, work out, figure out, understand, interpret. **4** *they made out that he was violent* assert, declare, affirm, aver, allege, claim, suggest, imply, pretend. **5** *how did you make out?* get on, get along, fare, do, get by, proceed, go, progress, manage, survive. **6** *how do you make that out?* prove, show to be true, establish, demonstrate, substantiate, verify, validate, authenticate, corroborate. **7** *make out an application form* fill out, fill in, complete, write out, inscribe. **make over 1** *make over his property to his son* transfer, sign over, turn over, hand over, transmit, assign, convey. **2** *make over the old house* renovate, remodel, redo, restore, redecorate, brighten up, improve, upgrade, gentrify; *inf.* do up. **make up 1** *the children's statements make up the case for the prosecution* comprise, form, compose, constitute. **2** *make up the balance* supply, furnish, provide. **3** *extra people required to make up the full complement* complete, round off, meet, finish. **4** *children making up for their previous rudeness* make amends for, atone for, compensate for, make recompense for, make reparation for, make redress for, offset. **5** *kiss and make up* be friends again, bury the hatchet, declare a truce, make peace, forgive and forget, shake hands, become reconciled, settle differences, mend fences, call it quits. **6** *make up a medicine/prescription* prepare, mix, concoct, put together. **7** *make up an excuse* invent, fabricate, concoct, hatch, coin, trump up, dream up, think up, devise, manufacture, formulate, frame, construct; *inf.* cook up. **8** *make up a short story* compose, write, create, originate, devise. **9** *make up her face* use make-up on, apply cosmetics to, powder, rouge; *inf.* put on one's face, do one's face, paint one's face, tart oneself up, do oneself up, apply one's warpaint. **make up one's mind** come to a decision, make/reach a decision, decide, determine, resolve, settle on a plan of action, choose/determine/resolve/settle one's course of action, reach a conclusion. **make up to 1** *making up to their boss* curry favour with, fawn on, toady to, lick someone's boots, truckle to, flatter; *inf.* butter up, play up to, be all over. **2** *making up to her friend's husband* flirt with, make romantic advances to, court, woo; *inf.* chat up, make eyes at, make sheep's eyes at, give the come-on to. **make way** *make way for the king* clear the way for, make a space for, make room for, stand back for, allow to pass, allow through.
Opposites DEMOLISH; DESTROY.

make *noun* **1** *different makes of car/buy the store's own make* brand, label, trade mark, sort, type, variety, style, mark, marque. **2** *a burly make of dog/a clumsy make of machine* build,

form, frame, structure, construction, shape. **3** *a man of a different make from his brother* character, nature, temperament, temper, disposition, humour. *See* MAKE-UP 3.

make-believe *noun* pretence, fantasy, daydreaming, dreaming, imagination, romancing, fabrication, play-acting, charade, masquerade. *See* MAKE BELIEVE.

make-believe *adjective* *a make-believe world/friend* pretended, feigned, made-up, fantasy, fantasized, dream, imagined, imaginary, unreal, fictitious, mock, sham; *inf.* pretend.
Opposites REAL; ACTUAL.

maker *noun* *the maker of the machines/clockmakers* manufacturer, builder, constructor, producer, creator, fabricator, author, architect, framer.

Maker *noun* God. *See table at* GOD.

makeshift *adjective* stopgap, make-do, provisional, temporary, rough and ready, substitute, improvised, stand-by, jerry-built, thrown-together.

make-up *noun* **1** *girls putting on their make-up/actors applying make-up* cosmetics, greasepaint, maquillage, foundation, powder, blusher, rouge, eye make-up, eye-liner, eye-shadow, eyebrow pencil, lipstick, lip gloss; *inf.* warpaint, face paint. **2** *the make-up of the machines varies* structure, composition, constitution, formation, form, format, configuration, construction, assembly, arrangement, organization. **3** *family backgrounds which contribute to the make-up of individuals* character, nature, temperament, temper, personality, disposition, humour, make, stamp, mould, kidney, cast of mind, frame of mind; *inf.* what makes someone tick.

making *noun* *the making of the cars/image-making* manufacture, manufacturing, building, construction, production, creation, fabrication, forming, moulding, forging. **in the making** budding, burgeoning, coming, emergent, growing, developing, nascent.

makings *plural noun* **1** *have the makings of a leader* potential, potentiality, promise, capacity, capability, qualities, characteristics, ingredients, materials, essentials, beginnings, basics. **2** *his makings are less than his outgoings* income, earnings, pay, wages, salary, returns, takings, proceeds, profits, revenue.

maladjusted *adjective* disturbed, unstable, ill-adjusted, neurotic, alienated from society, muddled, confused; *inf.* mixed-up, screwed-up, untogether.

maladroit *adjective* awkward, clumsy, inept, bungling, bumbling, incompetent, unskilful, unhandy, ungainly, inelegant, graceless, gauche, all fingers and thumbs, like a bull in a china shop; *inf.* butter-fingered, ham-fisted, cack-handed.
Opposites ADROIT; GRACEFUL; ELEGANT; SKILFUL.

malady *noun* disease, disorder, illness, sickness, ailment, affliction, complaint, infection, indisposition, infirmity. *See table at* ILLNESS.

malaise *noun* lassitude, listlessness, languour, enervation, weakness, feebleness, infirmity, illness, sickness, unease, discomfort, anxiety, *angst*, disquiet, melancholy, depression, despondency, dejection, weariness, ennui.

malapropism *noun* wrong word, misuse, misusage, misapplication, infelicity.

malcontent *noun young malcontents resenting the adults* grumbler, complainer, moaner, faultfinder, carper, agitator, troublemaker, mischief-maker, rebel, dissentient; *inf.* grouser, griper, nit-picker, bellyacher, beefer, stirrer.

malcontent *adjective a malcontent mood in the crowd* discontented, dissatisfied, disgruntled, disaffected, restive, unhappy, grumbling, complaining, fault-finding, carping, resentful, troublemaking, rebellious, dissentious, factious; *inf.* nit-picking, bellyaching. *See* MALCONTENT *noun.*

male *adjective male bird/plant/characteristics* masculine, manlike, manly, virile.
Opposites FEMALE.

male *noun* **1** *two males and a female* man, gentleman, boy, lad, youth; *inf.* chap, fellow, bloke, guy. **2** *animals which are males | male has brighter plummage* dog, tomcat, bull, ram, stallion, buck, stag, boar, billy-goat, cock, gander, drake.

malediction *noun* curse, imprecation, execration, anathema, voodoo; damning, damnation.

malefactor *noun* criminal, lawbreaker, felon, convict, offender, wrongdoer, evildoer, villain, miscreant, delinquent, sinner, reprobate, transgressor, outlaw, trespasser; *inf.* crook.

malevolence *noun* malignance, malignity, malice, maleficence, ill nature, ill will, animosity, hostility, hatred, hate, spite, spitefulness, vindictiveness, rancour, revengefulness, viciousness. *See* MALEVOLENT.

malevolent *adjective* malign, malignant, malicious, maleficent, evil-intentioned, evilminded, ill-natured, hostile, unfriendly, spiteful, baleful, vindictive, revengeful, rancorous, vicious, pernicious, cruel, fierce.
Opposites BENEVOLENT; FRIENDLY; KIND.

malformation *noun* deformity, distortion, crookedness, misshapenness, disfigurement, misproportion.

malformed *adjective* deformed, distorted, crooked, twisted, misshapen, disfigured, misproportioned.

malfunction *verb the computer is malfunctioning* develop a fault, go wrong, break down, break, fail, cease to function/work, stop working; *inf.* conk out, go kaput.

malfunction *noun* **1** *detect a malfunction in the machine* fault, defect, flaw, impairment; *inf.* glitch. **2** *complain about the malfunction of the machine* breakdown, failure, collapse; *inf.* conking out.

malice *noun* malevolence, maliciousness, malignity, malignance, evil intentions, ill will, ill feeling, animosity, animus, hostility, enmity, bad blood, hatred, hate, spite, spitefulness, vindictiveness, rancour, bitterness, grudge, venom, spleen, harm, destruction, defamation; *inf.* bitchiness, cattiness.

malicious *adjective* malevolent, malign, malignant, evil, evil-intentioned, ill-natured, hostile, spiteful, baleful, vindictive, rancorous, bitter, venomous, pernicious, harmful, hurtful, destructive, defamatory; *inf.* bitchy, catty.
Opposites BENEVOLENT; KINDLY; FRIENDLY.

malign *verb* slander, libel, defame, smear, run a smear campaign against, blacken someone's name/character, calumniate, vilify, speak ill of, spread lies about, accuse falsely, cast aspersions on, misrepresent, traduce, denigrate, disparage, slur, derogate; *inf.* bad-mouth, run down, drag through the mud.
Opposites PRAISE; EXTOL.

malignant *noun* **1** *a malignant old woman | has malignant intentions* malevolent, malign, malicious, evil, evil-intentioned, hostile, spiteful, vindictive, rancorous, venomous, pernicious, harmful, hurtful, destructive. **2** *a malignant growth* cancerous, non-benign. **3** *a malignant disease* dangerous, virulent, uncontrollable, deadly, fatal, life-threatening, lethal.
Opposites BENEVOLENT; KINDLY; BENIGN.

malinger *verb* feign/fake illness, pretend to be ill, pretend to be an invalid, have a fake illness, shirk, pretend; *inf.* put it on, skive.

mall *noun* shopping centre, shopping plaza, shopping precinct, shopping complex.

malleable *adjective* **1** *malleable substances* workable, shapable, mouldable, plastic, pliant, ductile, tractile. **2** *malleable people being bullied* pliable, compliant, easily influenced, accommodating, adaptable, impressionable, susceptible, amenable, biddable, tractable, manageable, governable.

malnutrition *noun* undernourishment, poor diet, inadequate diet, unhealthy diet, lack of food, starvation, famine, anorexia.

malodorous *adjective* foul-smelling, evilsmelling, fetid, smelly, stinking, reeking, rank, noisome, mephitic; *inf.* niffing, niffy, pongy, stinking to high heaven.

malpractice *noun doctors guilty of malpractice* unprofessional conduct, unprofessionalism, dereliction, negligence, carelessness, breach of ethics, unethical behaviour, misconduct, wrongdoing.

maltreat *verb* treat badly, ill-treat, ill-use, mistreat, misuse, abuse, handle/treat roughly, mishandle, manhandle, maul, bully, injure, harm, hurt, molest; *inf.* beat up, rough up, do over.

maltreatment *noun* ill-treatment, ill use, mistreatment, abuse, rough handling, mishandling, manhandling, bullying, injury, harm. *See* MALTREAT.

mammoth *adjective* huge, enormous, giant, gigantic, vast, immense, mighty, colossal, massive, gargantuan, prodigious, monumental, stupendous, mountainous, elephantine, kingsize, Brobdingnagian; *inf.* whopping, ginormous, humongous.

man *noun* **1** *three men and a woman* male, adult male, gentleman; *inf.* chap, fellow, bloke, guy. **2** *no man is perfect* human being, human, mortal, person, individual, one, personage. **3** *Man*

is *more intelligent than animals* Homo sapiens, mankind, the human race, the human species, humankind, human beings, humans, people. **4** *employ a man to do the garden* workman, worker, labourer, helper, hand. **5** *the nobleman and his man* valet, manservant, gentleman's gentleman, batman, attender, retainer, page, footman, flunkey, Jeeves. **6** *his sister and her man* husband, spouse, boyfriend, partner, lover, common-law husband, escort, beau, live-in lover, significant other, cohabitee; *inf.* toy boy. **to a man** with no exceptions, without exception, bar none, one and all, everyone, each and everyone, unanimously, as one.
Opposites WOMAN.

man *verb* **1** *man the bar/fort* supply with men/people/staff, furnish with men/people/staff, staff, crew. **2** *man the pumps* work, operate, use, utilize, service.

manacles *plural noun* handcuffs, chains, irons, hand shackles/fetters; *inf.* cuffs, bracelets, darbies.

manage *verb* **1** *manage the team/organization* be in charge of, run, be head of, head, direct, control, preside over, lead, govern, rule, command, superintend, supervise, oversee, administer, organize, conduct, handle, guide, be at the helm of; *inf.* head up. **2** *manage to survive* succeed in, contrive, engineer, bring about/off, achieve, accomplish, effect. **3** *will you manage?* cope, deal with the situation, get along/on, carry on, survive, make do, be/fare all right, weather the storm; *inf.* make out, get by. **4** *can you manage the dog/children?* cope with, deal with, handle, control, master, influence. **5** *manage a weapon* wield, use, operate, work, ply, handle, manipulate, brandish, flourish.
Opposites MISMANAGE; FAIL.

manageable *adjective* **1** *manageable tasks* easy, doable, practicable, possible, feasible, attainable, viable. **2** *manageable children/people* controllable, governable, tamable, tractable, pliant, compliant, docile, accommodating, amenable, yielding, submissive. **3** *manageable tools* handy, easy, user-friendly.
Opposites DIFFICULT; UNMANAGEABLE; IMPRACTICABLE; INTRACTABLE.

management *noun* **1** *the workers' dispute with management* managers, employers, owners, proprietors, directors, board of directors, board, directorate, executives, administration; *inf.* bosses, top brass. **2** *responsible for the management of the firm* running, charge, care, direction, leadership, control, governing, ruling, command, superintendence, supervision, overseeing, administration, organization, conduct, handling, guidance.

manager *noun* **1** *managers and workers* employer, director, executive, head of department, administrator, superintendent, supervisor; *inf.* boss, gaffer. **2** *the team's manager* organizer, controller, comptroller.

mandate *noun* *by mandate of the electorate/king* authority, bidding, direction, instruction, authorization, sanction, warrant, order, command, directive, ruling, decree, edict, dictate,

charge, injunction, statute, law, ordinance, fiat, ukase.

mandatory *adjective* obligatory, compulsory, binding, required, requisite, essential, imperative, necessary.
Opposites VOLUNTARY; OPTIONAL; DISCRETIONARY.

manful *adjective* manly, brave, courageous, gallant, heroic, intrepid, valiant, bold, stout, stout-hearted. *See* MANLY 1.
Opposites COWARDLY; TIMOROUS.

manfully *adverb* bravely, courageously, gallantly, heroically, intrepidly, valiantly, boldly, stoutly, stout-heartedly, stalwartly, hard, strongly, vigorously, with might and main, like a Trojan, with all one's strength, to the best of one's abilities, as best one can, determinedly, resolutely, desperately, with desperation, with all the stops out.

mange *noun* scabies, scab, itch, rash, eruption, skin infection.

manger *noun* trough, feeding trough, fodder rack.

mangle *verb* **1** *mangle the captured animals | had mangled the enemy* mutilate, hack, cut about, lacerate, maul, tear at, rend, butcher, disfigure, deform. **2** *mangle the piece of music* spoil, ruin, mar, bungle, mess up, make a mess of; *inf.* murder.

mangy *adjective* **1** *mangy animals* scabby, scaly, diseased. **2** *mangy carpets/flats* shabby, scruffy, moth-eaten, worn, shoddy, dirty, mean, squalid, filthy, seedy; *inf.* grotty. **3** *he's a mangy individual* contemptible, despicable, hateful, odious, nasty, mean, base, low.

manhandle *verb* **1** *accused of manhandling prisoners* handle roughly, push, pull, shove, maul, mistreat, ill-treat, abuse, injure, damage, beat, batter; *inf.* knock about, beat up, rough up. **2** *having to manhandle the huge parcels* move/carry/lift manually, heave, haul, push, shove, pull, tug, manoeuvre; *inf.* hump.

manhood *noun* **1** *reach manhood* adult maleness, maturity, sexual maturity, puberty. **2** *insult his manhood* maleness, masculinity, masculineness, manliness, virility, machismo. **3** *soldiers demonstrating their manhood* manliness, bravery, courage, heroism, intrepidity, valour, boldness, mettle, spirit, fortitude. *See* MANLINESS 1.

mania *noun* **1** *the mania phase of the manic depressive illness | suffering from mania* frenzy, franticness, violence, wildness, hysteria, raving, derangement, dementia. **2** *a mania for collecting old china* obsession, compulsion, fixation, fetish, fascination, preoccupation, passion, enthusiasm, desire, urge, craving, craze, fad; *inf.* thing.

maniac *noun* *murder committed by a maniac* madman, madwoman, mad person, deranged person, psychopath, lunatic; *inf.* loony, nutcase, nut, nutter, psycho, screwball.

manifest *verb* **1** *manifest strange symptoms* display, show, exhibit, demonstrate, present, evince, express, reveal, indicate, make plain, declare. **2** *manifest his guilt* prove, be evidence of, establish, show, evidence, substantiate, cor-

roborate, verify, confirm, settle.
Opposites HIDE; MASK; DENY.

manifest *adjective a manifest disinterest in the proceedings* obvious, clear, plain, apparent, patent, noticeable, perceptible, visible, transparent, conspicuous, unmistakable, distinct, blatant, glaring.

manifestation *noun* **1** *a manifestation of solidarity* display, show, exhibition, demonstration, presentation, exposition, illustration, exemplification, indication, declaration, expression, profession. **2** *produce manifestations of their presence* evidence, proof, testimony, substantiation, sign, indication, mark, symbol, token, symptom.

manifesto *noun* proclamation, pronouncement, declaration, declaration of political policies, announcement, statement, publication, notification.

manifold *adjective* multifarious, multiple, multifold, numerous, many, several, multitudinous, various, varied, diverse, assorted, sundry, copious, abundant.

manikin *noun* dwarf, midget, little man, homunculus, pygmy, Tom Thumb.

manipulate *verb* **1** *manipulate the tool/weapon* handle, wield, ply, work, operate, use, employ, utilize, exercise. **2** *manipulate his colleagues | has manipulated the situation* influence, control, use to one's advantage, exploit, manoeuvre, engineer, steer, direct, guide, pull the strings. **3** *manipulate the figures* juggle, massage, falsify, doctor, tamper with, fiddle with, tinker with; *inf.* cook.

manipulator *noun* **1** *the manipulator of the tools* handler, wielder, operator. See MANIPULATE 1. **2** *don't trust him—he is a manipulator* exploiter, manoeuvrer, conniver, intriguer, puller of strings, puppet-master. See MANIPULATE 2.

mankind *noun* man, *Homo sapiens*, the human race, the human species, humankind, human beings, humans, people.

manliness *noun* **1** *show their manliness in battle* manhood, bravery, braveness, courage, courageousness, heroism, intrepidity, valour, boldness, fearlessness, stout-heartedness, dauntlessness, mettle, spirit, fortitude. *See* MANLY 1. **2** *his thinness contrasting with his brother's manliness* masculinity, virility, strength, robustness, muscularity, powerfulness, ruggedness, toughness. See MANLY 2.

manly *adjective* **1** *exhibiting manly characteristics* manful, brave, courageous, gallant, heroic, intrepid, valiant, valorous, bold, fearless, stout, stout-hearted, dauntless; *inf.* macho, Ramboesque. **2** *a manly figure* masculine, all-male, virile, strong, robust, vigorous, muscular, powerful, well-built, strapping, sturdy, rugged, tough; *inf.* macho.
Opposites COWARDLY; UNMANLY; EFFEMINATE.

man-made *adjective* manufactured, synthetic, artificial, imitation, ersatz, plastic.

manner *noun* **1** *do the work in an efficient manner* way, means, method, system, approach, technique, procedure, process, methodology, routine, practice, fashion, mode, style, habit, custom. **2** *have an unfriendly manner* look, air, appearance, demeanour, aspect, mien, bearing, cast, deportment, behaviour, conduct. **3** *what manner of person is he?* kind, sort, type, variety, form, nature, breed, brand, stamp, class, category.

mannered *adjective* affected, unnatural, artificial, stilted, theatrical, posed, stagy, pretentious, put-on; *inf.* pseudo.

mannerism *noun* habit, characteristic, characteristic gesture, trait, idiosyncrasy, quirk, foible, peculiarity.

mannerly *adjective* well-mannered, well-behaved, polite, courteous, civil, gentlemanly, ladylike, genteel, decorous, respectful, well-bred, refined, polished, civilized, cultivated, gracious, chivalrous.
Opposites RUDE; IMPOLITE.

manners *plural noun* **1** *it is bad manners to stare* social behaviour, behaviour, conduct, way of behaving, social habit. **2** *it is manners to remain seated* correct behaviour, etiquette, good form, protocol, politeness, decorum, propriety, social graces, formalities, *politesse*; *inf.* the done thing.

mannish *adjective* masculine, manlike, unfeminine, unwomanly, unladylike, Amazonian; *inf.* butch, dyke.

manoeuvre *noun* **1** *manoeuvre of troops* movement, deployment, operation, exercise. **2** *park the vehicle in one manoeuvre* skilful movement/move, movement, move, clever stroke, stroke, skilful measure/handling. **3** *get the promotion by a series of manoeuvres* trick, stratagem, tactic, machination, manipulation, artifice, subterfuge, device, dodge, ploy, ruse, scheme, plan, plot, intrigue; *inf.* wangle.

manoeuvre *verb* **1** *manoeuvre the car* move, work, negotiate, steer, guide, direct, manipulate. **2** *manoeuvres things to suit himself* manage, manipulate, contrive, engineer, devise, plan, plot; *inf.* wangle. **3** *he is manoeuvring for the leadership* scheme, intrigue, plot, use trickery/artifice, machinate, pull strings.

manse *noun* vicarage, parsonage, rectory, deanery.

mansion *noun* imposing residence, manor-house, manor, hall, stately home, house, abode, seat.

manslaughter *noun* killing, slaying, murder, homicide, patricide, matricide, fratricide, infanticide, regicide.

mantle *noun* **1** *ladies wearing mantles of red* cloak, cape, shawl, wrap, poncho, pelisse. **2** *a mantle of snow/darkness* covering, cover, blanket, curtain, canopy, cloud, pall, envelope, veil, cloak, shroud, screen, mask.

mantle *verb* *fields mantled in snow | houses mantled in darkness* cover, blanket, curtain, envelop, veil, cloak, wrap, shroud, cloud, conceal, hide, disguise, mask.

manual *adjective* **1** *manual work* with one's hands, labouring, physical. **2** *manual gearchange* hand-operated, done by hand, by hand, non-automatic.
Opposites AUTOMATIC; MECHANICAL.

manual *noun an instruction manual* handbook, set of instructions, instructions, guidebook, guide; *inf.* bible, book of words.

manufacture *verb* **1** *manufacture cars* make, produce, mass-produce, build, construct, assemble, put together, create, fabricate, turn out, process, form, fashion, model, mould, shape, forge. **2** *manufacture an excuse* make up, invent, fabricate, concoct, hatch, coin, trump up, dream up, think up, devise, formulate, frame, construct; *inf.* cook up.

manufacture *noun the manufacture of cars* making, production, mass-production, construction, assembly, creation, fabrication, processing. *See* MANUFACTURE *verb* 1.

manufacturer *noun* maker, producer, builder, constructor, creator, fabricator, factory-owner, industrialist, captain/baron of industry.

manure *noun* farmyard manure, dung, animal excrement, muck, guano, droppings, ordure, fertilizer.

many *adjective many people/books/times* numerous, innumerable, a large/great number of, countless, scores of, myriad, great quantities of, multitudinous, multiple, copious, abundant, various, sundry, diverse, several, frequent; *inf.* a lot of, umpteen, lots of, masses of, scads of, heaps of, piles of, bags of, tons of, oodles of, an army of, zillions of.

many *noun many were killed | so many have been thrown out* many people, many things, scores, large numbers, great quantities, a large number, a host, a horde, a crowd, a multitude, a mass, an accumulation, an abundance, a profusion, plenty; *inf.* lots, a lot, umpteen, armies, scads, heaps, piles, bags, tons, masses, oodles, a thousand and one, zillions. **the many** *have to listen to the wishes of the many* the majority, the people, the masses, the multitude, the rank and file, the crowd, the hoi polloi.
Opposites FEW.

map *noun* chart, plan, plot, guide, street guide, town plan, road-map, atlas, gazetteer.

map *verb map the surface of the moon* chart, plot, delineate, depict, portray. **map out** *map out the conference programme* set out, lay out, detail, draw up, sketch out, plan, plot out.

mar *verb marred her beauty/career/happiness* spoil, detract from, impair, damage, ruin, wreck, disfigure, blemish, scar, deface, harm, hurt, injure, deform, mutilate, maim, mangle, tarnish, taint, contaminate, pollute, sully, stain, blot, debase, vitiate; *inf.* foul up.
Opposites IMPROVE; ADORN.

maraud *verb* **1** *maraud around the countryside* foray, raid, go on forays/raids, forage, plunder, go looting, pirate, freeboot; *Scots* reive. **2** *tribes marauding the neighbouring villages* raid, plunder, loot, pillage, foray, ransack, forage, ravage, harry, sack, despoil.

marauder *noun* raider, plunderer, pillager, looter, ravager, robber, pirate, freebooter, buccaneer, corsair, rover, bandit, brigand, rustler, highwayman; *Scots* reiver, cateran.

march *verb* **1** *armies marching* walk, step, pace, tread, stride, footslog, tramp, hike, trudge,

stalk, strut, parade, file. **2** *time marches on* move forward, advance, progress, forge ahead, make headway, go on, continue on, roll on, develop, evolve.

march *noun* **1** *soldiers/scouts on a march* route march, walk, footslog, tramp, trek, hike, parade. **2** *a quick/slow march* step, pace, stride, gait. **3** *a march against pit closures* demonstration, parade, procession; *inf.* demo. **4** *the march of time/progress* advance, progress, progression, passage, headway, continuance, development, evolution.

marches *plural noun lives in the Welsh marches* boundary, border, borderland, frontier, limits, confines.

margin *noun* **1** *the margin of the lake* edge, side, verge, border, perimeter, boundary, limits, periphery, brink, brim. **2** *the margin between the countries* border, borderland, boundary, boundary line, frontier, bounding line, demarcation line. **3** *little margin for error* leeway, latitude, scope, room, room for manoeuvre, space, allowance, extra, surplus. **4** *win by a narrow margin | a margin of one vote* measure of difference, degree of difference, difference, amount.

marginal *adjective* **1** *marginal areas* border, boundary, on the edge, peripheral. **2** *the difference is marginal* slight, small, tiny, minute, low, minor, insignificant, minimal, negligible.

marijuana *noun* cannabis, hashish, bhang, hemp, kef, kif, charas, ganja, sinsemilla; *inf.* drugs, dope, hash, grass, pot, stuff, mary jane, tea, the weed.

marinade *verb* marinate, soak, steep, immerse.

marine *adjective* **1** *marine life* sea, aquatic, salt-water, sea-water, oceanic, pelagic, thalassic. **2** *marine careers* maritime, nautical, naval, seafaring, seagoing.

mariner *noun* sailor, seaman, seafarer, seafaring man, sea dog, salt, Jack tar, bluejacket; *inf.* tar, limey, matelot.

marital *adjective marital vows/bliss* matrimonial, marriage, wedding, conjugal, connubial, nuptial, spousal, married, wedded.

maritime *adjective* **1** *maritime careers* naval, marine, nautical, seafaring, seagoing. **2** *maritime areas* coastal, seaside, littoral.

mark *noun* **1** *marks left on the table* stain, blemish, blot, smear, trace, spot, speck, dot, blotch, smudge, splotch, bruise, scratch, scar, dent, pit, pock, chip, notch, nick, line, score, cut, incision, gash. **2** *the marks on a horse/cow* marking, blaze, spot, speckle, stripe, brand, earmark. **3** *question mark | proofreader's marks* exclamation mark, symbol, sign, character, question mark, quotation marks. **4** *marks showing the way* marker, guide, pointer, landmark, direction post, signpost, milestone, waymark. **5** *mark of respect* sign, symbol, indication, symptom, feature, token, badge, emblem, evidence, proof, clue, hint. **6** *recognize the king's/firm's mark* seal, stamp, signet, symbol, emblem, device, badge, motto, monogram, hallmark, trade mark, logo, watermark, label, tag, flag. **7** *put one's mark on the document* cross, X, scribble, squiggle, signature, autograph, initials, imprint. **8** *marks left by the thief* print, fingerprint, thumbprint, footprint, imprint, track, trail, trace, vestige. **9** *war left its mark on him* impression, imprint, traces, vestiges, remains, effect, impact, influence. **10** *have the mark of an honest man* characteristic, feature, trait, attribute, quality, stamp, peculiarity. **11** *the bullet/insult missed its mark* target, goal, aim, bull's-eye, objective, object, end, purpose, intent, intention. **12** *work falling below the mark* standard, required standard, norm, par, level, criterion, gauge, yardstick, rule, measure, scale. **13** *a person of mark* distinction, importance, consequence, eminence, pre-eminence, prominence, note, notability, fame, repute, greatness, prestige, celebrity, glory, standing, rank. **14** *nothing of mark occurred* note, noteworthiness, importance, consequence. **make one's mark** *by 30 he had made his mark in the financial world* be successful, gain success, be a success, succeed, prosper, get on, make good, achieve recognition; *inf.* make it. **wide of the mark 1** *his observations were wide of the mark* irrelevant, inapplicable, inapposite, inappropriate, not to the point, beside the point. **2** *his answers were wide of the mark* inaccurate, incorrect, wrong, erroneous, inexact, off-target, fallacious.

mark *verb* **1** *mark the table* stain, smear, smudge, scratch, scar, dent, chip, notch, score, cut, gash. See MARK *noun* 1. **2** *mark your property* put one's name on, name, initial, put one's seal on, label, tag, stamp, flag, hallmark, watermark, brand, earmark. **3** *mark the places on a map* name, indicate, write down, tag, label, flag. **4** *mark essays* correct, assess, evaluate, appraise; *Am.* grade. **5** *mark the goods at £10* price, put a price-tag on, cost. **6** *the children marked his displeasure* see, notice, observe, take note of, discern, descry, spot, recognize; *inf.* get a load of. **7** *you should mark his words* take heed of, pay heed to, heed, take notice of, pay attention to, attend to, note, mind, bear in mind, give a thought to, take into consideration. **8** *a day marked by misfortune* characterize, distinguish, identify, denote, brand, signalize. **9** *mark his birthday* celebrate, commemorate, honour, observe, recognize, acknowledge, solemnize. **10** *marked for greatness* designate, choose, select, nominate. **mark down 1** *mark down the prices* reduce, decrease, lower, cut, put down, take down, slash. **2** *mark down the goods* reduce, lower the price of, make cheaper, sell at a give-away price; *Am.* put on sale. **mark out 1** *mark out the football pitch* mark off, mark the boundaries/limits of, measure out, demarcate, delimit. **2** *his honesty marked him out from the rest of the gang* set apart, separate, single out, differentiate, distinguish. **mark up 1** *mark up the price* raise, increase, put up, up, hike up, escalate; *inf.* jack up. **2** *mark up the goods* increase/raise the price of.

marked *adjective* pronounced, decided, striking, clear, glaring, blatant, unmistakable, remarkable, prominent, signal, conspicuous, noticeable, noted, distinct, pointed, salient, recognizable, identifiable, distinguishable, obvious, apparent, evident, manifest, open, patent, written all over one.
Opposites IMPERCEPTIBLE; INCONSPICUOUS.

markedly *adverb* decidedly, strikingly, remarkably, unmistakably, conspicuously, noticeably, pointedly, distinctly, recognizably, obviously, clearly, plainly, apparently, evidently, manifestly, to a marked extent, to a great extent. See MARKED.

market *noun* **1** *shopping at the market* marketplace, mart, shopping centre, bazaar, souk, retail outlet. **2** *no market for such expensive goods* demand, call, want, desire, need. **3** *the market is sluggish* trade, business, commerce, buying and selling, dealing. **in the market for** wishing to buy, in need of, wanting, lacking, wishing for, desiring. **on the market** on sale, up for sale, for sale, purchasable, available, obtainable.

market *verb* *market furniture* sell, retail, offer for sale, put up for sale, vend, peddle, hawk.

marksman, markswoman *noun* sharpshooter, good shot; *inf.* crack shot, dead shot.

maroon *verb* abandon, forsake, leave behind, leave, desert, strand, leave stranded, turn one's back on, leave isolated.

marriage *noun* **1** *their marriage lasted 20 years | join in marriage* married state, matrimony, holy matrimony, wedlock, conjugal bond, union, match. **2** *invited to their marriage* marriage ceremony, wedding, wedding ceremony, nuptials. **3** *the marriage of their skills* alliance, union, merger, unification, amalgamation, combination, affiliation, association, connection, coupling; *inf.* hook-up.

married *adjective* **1** *married couple* wedded, wed, joined in marriage, united in wedlock; *inf.* spliced, hitched. **2** *married bliss* marital, matrimonial, connubial, conjugal, nuptial, spousal.
Opposites UNMARRIED; SINGLE.

marrow *noun* *marrow of his statement* core, kernel, nucleus, pith, heart, centre, soul, spirit, essence, quintessence, gist, substance, sum and substance, meat, stuff; *inf.* nitty-gritty, nuts and bolts.

marry *verb* **1** *the couple married last year* be married, wed, be wed, become man and wife, become espoused; *inf.* tie the knot, walk down the aisle, take the plunge, get spliced, get hitched, get yoked. **2** *he married her | she married him* wed, take to wife/husband, espouse. **3** *marry their skills* join, join together, unite, ally, merge, unify, amalgamate, combine, affiliate, associate, link, connect, fuse, weld, couple.

marsh *noun* marshland, bog, peatbog, swamp, swampland, morass, mire, quagmire, quag, slough, fen, fenland, bayou.

marshal *verb* **1** *marshal the pupils | tried to marshal his thoughts* gather together, assemble, collect, muster, draw up, line up, align, set/put in order, arrange deploy, dispose, rank. **2** *marshal the guests to their seats* usher, guide, escort, conduct, lead, shepherd, take.

marshy *adjective* boggy, swampy, muddy, squelchy, miry, quaggy, fenny, paludal.

marsupial *noun.* See table.

MARSUPIALS		
antechinus	marsupial	potoroo
bandicoot	mole	quokka
bettong	marsupial	quoll
bilby	mouse	ringtail
cuscus	marsupial	smin-
dasyure	rat	thopsis
dibbler	numbat	Tasmanian
dunnart	opossum	devil
glider	pademelon	thylacine
kangaroo	phalanger	wallaby
koala	phascogale	wallaroo
marsupial	planigale	wombat
cat	possum	yapok

MARTIAL ARTS AND COMBAT SPORTS		
aikido	kung fu	t'ai chi
boxing	ninjutsu	chu'an
judo	pa-kua	tang soo
ju-jitsu	Silat	do
karate	sumo	Thai
kendo	wrestling	boxing
kick-boxing	tae kwon do	wrestling

martial adjective **1** martial exploits military, soldierly, army. **2** martial arts militant, warlike, combative, belligerent, bellicose, aggressive, pugnacious.

martial arts plural noun. See table.

martinet noun disciplinarian, stickler for discipline, hard taskmaster.

martyr noun sufferer, victim, Christian martyr, early martyr.

martyr verb **1** martyr them for their beliefs make a martyr of, martyrize, put to death, burn at the stake, immolate, throw to the lions, crucify. **2** the invading army martyred the villagers persecute, torture, inflict agony on.

martyrdom noun persecution, ordeal, torture, torment, suffering, agony, anguish.

marvel verb marvel at their exploits be amazed by, be filled with amazement at, be awed by, be full of wonder at, wonder at, stare at, gape at, goggle at, not believe one's eyes/ears at.

marvel noun his desserts are a marvel wonder, wonderful thing, amazing thing, prodigy, sensation, spectacle, phenomenon, miracle; inf. something else, something to shout about, something to write home about, eye-opener.

marvellous adjective **1** his solo climb was marvellous amazing, astounding, astonishing, awesome, breathtaking, sensational, remarkable, spectacular, stupendous, phenomenal, wondrous, prodigious, miraculous, extraordinary. **2** he's a marvellous singer excellent, splendid, wonderful; inf. magnificent, superb, glorious, super, great, smashing, fantastic, terrific, fabulous, fab, brill, awesome, ace, mean, bad, wicked; Am. inf. boffo.
Opposites ORDINARY; RUN-OF-THE-MILL; DREADFUL.

masculine adjective **1** that's a masculine trait male, manly, manlike, virile, of men, man's, men's, male-oriented. **2** she likes masculine men manly, all-male, virile, robust, vigorous, muscular, strapping, rugged; inf. macho. See MANLY 2. **3** he has all the masculine virtues manful, brave, courageous, gallant, heroic, valiant, bold, fearless, stout-hearted; inf. Ramboesque, macho. See MANLY 1. **4** masculine woman mannish, manlike, unfeminine, unwomanly, Amazonian; inf. butch, dyke.
Opposites FEMININE; EFFEMINATE.

masculinity noun **1** admire the masculinity of his physique manliness, virility, robustness, vigour, muscularity, ruggedness. See MANLINESS 2. **2** show their masculinity in battle manliness, manhood, bravery, courage, courageousness, heroism, intrepidity, mettle, fortitude. See MANLINESS 1.

mash verb mash the potatoes crush, pulp, purée, smash, squash, pound, beat.

mash noun feed the mash to the dogs pulp, mush, paste, purée, slush, pap.

mask noun **1** wearing masks to the party false face, domino, visor. **2** wearing masks for protection protective mask, swimming mask, snorkel mask, gas mask, safety goggles, fencing mask, skier's mask, surgical mask, visor. **3** under the mask of being a tourist disguise, guise, concealment, cover, cover-up, cloak, camouflage, veil, screen, front, false front, façade, blind, semblance, false colours, pretence.

mask verb mask her identity/feelings disguise, hide, conceal, cover up, obscure, cloak, camouflage, veil, screen.

mass noun **1** a mass of wood/cloud concretion, lump, block, chunk, hunk, piece; inf. wodge. **2** gathered in a mass | a mass of fibres concentration, conglomeration, aggregation, amassment, assemblage, collection. **3** men in the mass total, totality, whole, entirety, aggregate. **4** a mass of people | masses of people/toys many, a large number, an abundance, a profusion, numerous, countless, myriad, a multitude, group, crowd, mob, horde, throng, host, troop; inf. a lot, lots, scads, piles, heaps, bags, tons. See MANY adjective, noun. **5** the mass of people voted against majority, greater part, major part, most, bulk, main body, preponderance, almost all, lion's share. **6** measure the mass of the body size, magnitude, bulk, dimension, capacity, greatness, bigness.

mass adjective mass hysteria/suicide | the mass media wholesale, universal, widespread, general, large-scale, extensive, pandemic, popular.

mass verb **1** clouds massing amass, accumulate, assemble, gather, collect, draw together, join together. **2** generals massing their troops assemble, gather together, marshal, muster, rally, round up, mobilize.

massacre noun mass slaughter, wholesale slaughter, slaughter, wholesale/indiscriminate killing, mass murder, mass homicide, mass slaying, mass execution, mass destruction, carnage, butchery, blood bath, annihilation, extermination, liquidation, decimation, pogrom, genocide, ethnic cleansing, holocaust.

massacre verb slaughter, butcher, slay, murder, kill, annihilate, exterminate, liquidate, decimate, eliminate, kill off, wipe out, mow down, cut down, cut to pieces.

massage *noun have a massage to relieve aches and pains* rub, rub-down, rubbing, kneading, pummelling, palpation, manipulation; reflexology, acupressure, shiatsu, aromatherapy.

massage *verb massage stiff limbs* rub, rub down, knead, pummel, palpate, manipulate.

masses *plural noun the common people, the* populace, the proletariat, the multitude, the commonality, the crowd, the mob, the rabble, the *hoi polloi*, the *canaille*; *inf.* the great unwashed.

massive *adjective* huge, immense, enormous, vast, mighty, extensive, gigantic, colossal, mammoth, monumental, elephantine, mountainous, gargantuan, king-size, monstrous, prodigious, titanic, hulking, bulky, weighty, hefty, solid, substantial, big, large, great; *inf.* ginormous, whopping, humongous.
Opposites TINY; MINUTE.

mast *noun* **1** *a ship's mast* spar, boom, yard, gaff, foremast, mainmast, topmast, mizzen-mast, mizzen. *See table at* RIGGING. **2** *the mast on top of the building* flagpole, flagstaff, pole, post, support, upright.

master *noun* **1** *master of the household/hunt | the dog's master* lord and master, lord, overlord, ruler, overseer, superintendent, director, manager, controller, governor, commander, captain, chief, head, headman, principal, owner, employer; *inf.* boss, top dog, big cheese; *Am. inf.* honcho. **2** *master of the ship* captain, skipper, commander. **3** *pupils being taught by the master* schoolmaster, headmaster, teacher, schoolteacher, tutor, instructor, pedagogue, preceptor. **4** *a master of innuendo | a tennis master* expert, adept, professional, authority, pundit, genius, master-hand, maestro, virtuoso, prodigy, pastmaster, grand master, wizard; *inf.* ace, pro, dab hand; *Am. inf.* maven. **5** *students/followers sitting at the feet of the master* guru, teacher, spiritual leader, guide, swami, Roshi.

master *adjective* **1** *master craftsmen* masterly, expert, adept, proficient, skilled, skilful, deft, dexterous, practised, experienced; *inf.* crack. **2** *master spirit/plan* controlling, ruling, directing, commanding, dominating. **3** *master bedroom* chief, main, principal, leading, prime, predominant, foremost, great, most important.

master *verb* **1** *master one's horse/emotions* conquer, vanquish, defeat, overcome, overpower, triumph over, subdue, subjugate, govern, quell, quash, suppress, control, curb, check, bridle, tame. **2** *master the technique* learn, learn thoroughly, become proficient in, acquire skill in, grasp; *inf.* get the hang of, get clued up about.

masterful *adjective* **1** *masterful men marrying meek women* dominating, authoritative, powerful, controlling, domineering, tyrannical, despotic, dictatorial, overbearing, overweening, imperious, peremptory, high-handed, arrogant, haughty. **2** *masterful handling of the situation* masterly, expert, consummate, clever, adept, adroit, skilful, skilled, proficient, deft,

dexterous, accomplished, polished, excellent, superlative, first-rate, fine, talented, gifted; *inf.* crack, ace.
Opposites WEAK; INEPT.

masterly *adjective masterly handling of the situation* masterful, expert, consummate, adept, skilful, deft, dexterous, accomplished, polished, excellent, superlative, first-rate, talented, gifted; *inf.* crack, ace. *See* MASTERFUL 2.

mastermind *verb mastermind the project* direct, manage, plan, organize, arrange, engineer, conceive, devise, forge, originate, initiate, think up, come up with, have the bright idea of; *inf.* be the brains behind.

mastermind *noun the mastermind behind the plan* genius, intellect, author, architect, engineer, director, planner, organizer, deviser, originator, manager, prime mover; *inf.* brain, brains, brainbox.

masterpiece *noun magnum opus*, master-work, *chef-d'oeuvre*, work of art, creation, *pièce de résistance*.

master-stroke *noun* stroke of genius, *tour de force*, *coup de maître*, successful manoeuvre, feat of triumph, triumph, victory, complete success.

mastery *noun* **1** *gain mastery over the enemy | mastery over his emotions* control, domination, command, ascendancy, supremacy, superiority, triumph, victory, the upper hand, the whip hand, rule, government, power, authority, jurisdiction, dominion, sovereignty. **2** *admire his mastery of the language* command, grasp, knowledge, familiarity with, understanding, comprehension, expertise, skill, prowess, proficiency, ability, capability; *inf.* know-how.

masticate *verb* chew, munch, champ, chomp, crunch, eat.

masturbation *noun* auto-eroticism, onanism, self-abuse, self-gratification; *inf.* playing with oneself.

mat *noun* **1** *wipe one's feet on the mat* doormat, welcome mat, rug, carpet. **2** *a mat of hair* mass, tangle, knot, mesh.

mat *verb the blood had matted her hair* tangle, entangle, knot, ravel.

match *noun* **1** *a tennis/boxing match* contest, competition, game, tournament, bout, event, test, trial, meet. **2** *she's no match for the champion* equal, equivalent, peer, counterpart, rival, competitor. **3** *this glove is a match for that one* mate, fellow, companion, twin, counterpart, pair, complement. **4** *the new one is an exact match for the previous one* look-alike, double, twin, duplicate, copy, replica; *inf.* spitting image, spit and image, spit, dead spit, ringer, dead ringer. **5** *make a good match* marriage, union, partnership, pairing, alliance, affiliation, combination.

match *verb* **1** *curtains which match the walls | their stories match each other* complement, blend with, harmonize with, go with, tone with, coordinate with, team with, tally with, correspond to, accord with. **2** *these socks don't match* be a pair, be a set, be the same. **3** *her strength matches his* be equal to, be a match for measure up to, rival, vie with, compete with, compare with, parallel, be in the same category as, keep pace with, keep up with. **4** *match him with one of her friends* | *match the socks* marry, pair up, mate, couple, unite, join, combine, link, ally; *inf.* hitch up, yoke.

matching *adjective* corresponding, equivalent, complementing, parallel, analogous, complementary, harmonizing, blending, toning, coordinating, the same, paired, twin, coupled, double, duplicate, identical, like.
Opposites UNLIKE; DIFFERENT; DISSIMILAR.

matchless *adjective* unmatched, incomparable, beyond compare, unequalled, without equal, unrivalled, unparalleled, unsurpassed, inimitable, peerless, unique, consummate, perfect, transcendent.

matchmaker *noun* marriage broker, go-between, marriage bureau, dating agency.

mate *noun* **1** *his mates gave him a leaving present* workmate, fellow worker, co-worker, associate, colleague, companion, compeer. **2** *he goes out with his mates on Saturdays* friend, companion, comrade, crony; *inf.* pal, chum, buddy; *dial.* marrow. **3** *he/she is looking for a mate* husband, wife, spouse, partner, companion, helpmate, live-in lover; *inf.* significant other, POSSLQ (= person of the opposite sex sharing living quarters), other half, better half. **4** *where's the mate of this sock?* fellow, twin, match, companion, pair, one of a pair, other half, equivalent. **5** *a plumber's mate* assistant, helper, apprentice, subordinate.

mate *verb* **1** *animals mating* breed, copulate, couple. **2** *mate the animals* bring together, pair, couple, join.

material *noun* **1** *organic/nuclear material* matter, substance, stuff, medium, constituent elements. *See table at* ELEMENT. **2** *clothes of strong material* fabric, cloth, stuff, textile. *See table at* FABRIC. **3** *enough material for a book* data, information, facts, facts and figures, evidence, details, notes; *inf.* info, gen.

material *adjective* **1** *the material, rather than the spiritual, world* corporeal, physical, bodily, fleshly, tangible, substantial, concrete. **2** *material pleasures* non-spiritual, physical, bodily, fleshly, worldly, earthly, temporal. **3** *material facts* important, of consequence, consequential, momentous, weighty, vital, essential, indispensable, key, significant, meaningful. **4** *material evidence* relevant, applicable, pertinent, apposite, germane, apropos.

materialize *verb* **1** *our plans did not materialize* come into being, happen, occur, come about, come to pass, take place; *inf.* shape up. **2** *the guests did not materialize* appear, turn up, become visible, come into view, come into sight, show oneself/itself, present oneself/itself, reveal oneself/itself, come to light, emerge.

materially *adverb* *not materially affected by the plans* significantly, much, greatly, to a great extent, considerably, substantially, essentially, fundamentally, seriously, gravely.

maternal *adjective* **1** *maternal feelings* motherly, protective. *See* MOTHERLY. **2** *his maternal grandparents* on one's mother's side, on the distaff side.

maternity *noun* motherhood, motherliness.

mathematical *adjective* **1** *mathematical problems* arithmetical, numerical, statistical, algebraic, geometrical, trigonometrical. *See table.* **2** *with mathematical care* precise, exact, rigorous, unerring, correct, strict, meticulous, scrupulous, careful.

mathematician *noun. See table.*

matrimonial *adjective* *matrimonial home/dispute* marital, marriage, wedding, conjugal, connubial, nuptial, spousal, married, wedded.

matrimony *noun* holy matrimony, marriage, wedlock, union.

matted *adjective* tangled, entangled, knotted, tousled, dishevelled, uncombed.

matter *noun* **1** *organic/waste matter* material, substance, stuff, medium. **2** *concentrate on the matter, not the style* content, subject matter, text, argument, substance, sense, thesis. **3** *no laughing matter* affair, business, proceeding, situation, circumstance, event, happening, occurrence, incident, episode, occasion, experience. **4** *discuss important matters* subject, topic, issue, question, point, case, concern, theme. **5** *issues of little matter* importance, consequence, significance, note, import, moment, weight. **6** *wounds full of matter* pus, suppuration, purulence, discharge; *tech.* sanies. **as a matter of fact** actually, in actual fact, in fact, in point of fact, really, in truth, to tell the truth, truly. **no matter** it does not matter, it makes no difference/odds, it is unimportant, never mind, don't worry about it. **the matter** *is anything the matter?* | *what is the matter?* | *there is nothing the matter* trouble, upset, distress, worry, problem, difficulty, complication.

matter *verb* *your lateness/wealth doesn't matter* be of importance, be of consequence, make a difference, make any difference, signify, be relevant, carry weight, count.

matter-of-fact *adjective* factual, literal, prosaic, down-to-earth, straightforward, plain, mundane, unembellished, unvarnished, unimaginative, uncreative, unemotional, unsentimental, deadpan, flat, dull, dry, pedestrian, lifeless, humdrum.

mature *adjective* **1** *mature human beings* adult, grown-up, grown, fully grown, full-grown, of age. **2** *young people becoming very mature* sensible, responsible, wise, discriminating, shrewd, practical, sagacious. **3** *mature fruits/cheese* ripe, ripened, mellow, ready, seasoned. **4** *our plans are now mature* complete, finished, finalized, developed, prepared, ready.
Opposites IMMATURE; CHILDISH; GREEN.

mature *verb* **1** *when the children have matured* grow up, develop fully, become adult, reach adulthood, be fully grown, be full-grown, come of age. **2** *when the young people have matured* become sensible/responsible/wise/discriminating. *See* MATURE *adjective* 2. **3** *when the fruit/cheese has matured* ripen, grow ripe, become

488

MATHEMATICAL TERMS

abscissa
addition
algebra
algorithm
aliquot part
analysis
antilogarithm
Apollonius' theorem
Argand diagram
arithmetic mean
arithmetic progres-
 sion
array
associative law
asymptote
Banach space
base
Bayes' theorem
Bernoulli numbers
Bessel functions
binomial
binomial theorem
Boolean algebra
Briggsian
 logarithms
calculus
Cantor set
cardinal number
Cartesian coordin-
 ates
catastrophe theory
Cauchy sequence
chaos theory
Chinese remainder
 theorem
coefficient
common denomina-
 tor
commutative law
complex number
conjugate
coordinate geometry
cosecant
cosine
cotangent
cube
cube root
decimal point
definite integral
de Moivre's
 formula
denominator
derivative
determinant
difference
differential
 calculus
differential
 equation
differentiation
digit
Diophantine
 equation
Dirichlet series
distributive law
division
divisor

eigenfunction
eigenvalue
eigenvector
equation
Eratosthenes, sieve
 of
Euclidean geometry
Euclid's axioms
Euler's constant
Euler's formula
expansion
exponent
exponential func-
 tion
extrapolation
factor
factorial
Fermat's last
 theorem
Fibonacci numbers
field
formula
four-colour theorem
Fourier analysis
Fourier series
fractal
fractal set
fraction
function
fuzzy set
Galois group
game theory
Gaussian distribu-
 tion
Gauss's theorem
geometric mean
geometric progres-
 sion
Gödel numbers
googol
googolplex
gradient
Green's theorem
group
group theory
harmonic progres-
 sion
Hermitian matrix
highest common
 factor
Hilbert space
Hilbert's problems
hyperbolic cosine
hyperbolic sine
hyperbolic
 tangent
identity
imaginary number
improper fraction
indefinite integral
inequality
infinitesimal
 calculus
integer
integral calculus
integrand
integration

intercept
interpolation
inverse
irrational number
iteration
Julia set
Klein bottle
Lagrange's theorem
Laplace operator
least squares
 method
Legendre poly-
 nomials
Leibniz's theorem
L'Hôpital's rule
Lie group
limit
linear equation
Lobachevskian
 geometry
locus
logarithm
long division
lowest common
 denominator
lowest common
 multiple
Maclaurin series
magic square
Mandelbrot set
Markov chain
matrix
mean
median
Mersenne numbers
midpoint theorem
Möbius strip
modulus
Monte Carlo
 method
multiple
multiplicand
multiplication
multiplier
Napierian
 logarithm
natural logarithm
natural numbers
Newton method
node
null hypothesis
number theory
numerator
operator
ordinal number
origin
parameter
partial derivative
Pascal's triangle
percentile
perfect number
perfect square
permutation
point of inflection
Poisson
 distribution
polar coordinates

polynomial
power
power series
prime number
product
proof
proper fraction
Pythagoras'
 theorem
quaternion
queuing theory
quotient
ratio
rational number
real number
reciprocal
recurring decimal
recursion
remainder
remainder theorem
repeating decimal
Riemannian
 geometry
ring
root
root-mean-square
Russell's paradox
scalar
secant
series
set
set theory
significant figure
Simpson's rule
simultaneous
 equations
sine
solution
square
square number
square root
stationary point
Stirling's approxi-
 mation
Stokes' theorem
sub-group
subset
substitution
subtraction
sum
surd
tangent
Taylor series
tensor
transcendental
 function
transfinite number
transform
trigonometric func-
 tion
unity
unknown
variable
vector
Venn diagram
vulgar fraction
whole number

ripe, become mellow, mellow, maturate. **4** *our plans gradually matured* be complete, be finished, be fully developed, maturate. *See* MATURE *adjective* 4.

maturity *noun* **1** *children reaching maturity* matureness, adulthood, manhood/womanhood, puberty, full growth, majority, coming-of-age. **2** *the maturity of the young people* matureness, sensibleness, sense of responsibility, responsibleness, wisdom, discrimination, shrewdness, practicality, sagacity. **3** *the maturity of the fruit/cheese* matureness, ripeness, mellowness. **4** *the maturity of our plans* matureness, completion, finalization, developed state, preparedness, readiness.

maudlin *adjective* mawkish, sentimental, oversentimental, sickeningly sentimental, tearful, lachrymose; *inf.* weepy, soppy, mushy, slushy, schmaltzy.

maul *verb* **1** *mauled by a lion* tear to pieces, claw, lacerate, mutilate, mangle. **2** *mauling the women present* handle roughly, handle clumsily, manhandle, paw, molest. **3** *fathers mauling children* beat, batter, thrash, ill-treat; *inf.* belt, wallop, clobber, rough up, kick about. **4** *his book was mauled by the critics* censure, condemn, find fault with, give a bad press to, take

to pieces; *inf.* knock, slate, slam, pan, lambaste.

mausoleum *noun* tomb, sepulchre, crypt, charnel-house.

maverick *noun* nonconformist, rebel, dissenter, dissident, individualist, bohemian, eccentric; *inf.* trend-setter.

mawkish *adjective* maudlin, oversentimental, sickeningly sentimental, lachrymose; *inf.* mushy, slushy, schmaltzy. *See* MAUDLIN.

maxim *noun* aphorism, proverb, adage, saw, saying, axiom, precept, epigram, gnome.

maximum *noun reach its maximum* most, utmost, uttermost, extremity, upper limit, height, ceiling, top, summit, peak, pinnacle, crest, apex, vertex, apogee, acme, zenith.

maximum *adjective the maximum amount* highest, greatest, biggest, largest, topmost, most, utmost, supreme, maximal.
Opposites MINIMUM; LEAST.

maybe *adverb* perhaps, it could be that, possibly; *dial.* happen; *lit.* peradventure.

mayhem *noun* havoc, disorder, confusion, chaos, bedlam, destruction, violence, trouble,

MATHEMATICIANS

Abel, Niels (1802–29; Norw.)	Chu Shih-Chieh (c. 1300; Chin.)	Hypatia (c. 370–415 A.D.; Gk)	Minkowski, Hermann (1864–1909; Ger., b. in Russia)
Abu al-Wafa (940–98 A.D.; Pers.)	d'Alembert, Jean le Rond (1717–83; Fr.)	Jacobi, Karl Gustav Jacob (1804–51; Ger.)	Napier, John (1550–1617; Scot.)
Agnesi, Maria (1718–99; It.)	Dedekind, Richard (1831–1916; Ger.)	Jeans, Sir James (1877–1946; Brit.)	Neumann, John von (1903–57; Am.)
al-Khwarizmi, Muhammed ibn Musa (c. 780–c. 850 A.D.; Arab.)	Diophantus of Alexandria (3rd century A.D.; Gk)	Jordan, Camille (1838–1922; Fr.)	Pappus of Alexandria (4th century A.D.; Gk)
Apollonius of Perga (c. 261–c. 190 B.C.; Gk)	Euclid (c. 300 B.C.; Gk)	Kolmogorov, Andrei (1903–87; Russ.)	Pascal, Blaise (1623–62; Fr.)
Babbage, Charles (1791–1871; Brit.)	Eudoxus of Cnidus (c. 408–c. 355 B.C.; Gk)	Kovalevskaya, Sofya (1850–91; Russ.)	Poincaré, Jules (1854–1912; Fr.)
Bhaskhara II (1114–c. 85; Ind.)	Euler, Leonhard (1707–83; Swiss)	Lagrange, Joseph, Comte de (1736–1813; Fr.)	Poisson, Siméon (1781–1840; Fr.)
Bolyai, János (1802–60; Hungarian)	Fermat, Pierre de (1601–65; Fr.)	Lambert, Johann (1728–77; Ger.)	Ptolemy (2nd century A.D.; Egypt.)
Boole, George (1815–64; Brit.)	Fibonacci, Leonardo (c. 1170–c. 1230; It.)	Laplace, Pierre, Marquis de (1749–1827; Fr.)	Pythagoras (c. 580–500 B.C.; Gk)
Brahmagupta (c. 598–c. 665 A.D.; Ind.)	Fourier, Jean, Baron (1768–1830; Fr.)	Legendre, Adrien (1752–1833; Fr.)	Ramanujan, Srinivara (1887–1920; Ind.)
Briggs, Henry (1561–1630; Brit.)	Frege, Gottlob (1848–1925; Ger.)	Liouville, Joseph (1809–82; Fr.)	Rheticus (Georg von Lauchen; 1514–76; Ger.)
Cantor, Georg (1845–1918; Russ.)	Galois, Évariste (1811–32; Fr.)	Lobachevski, Nikolai (1792–1856; Russ.)	Riemann, Georg (1826–66; Ger.)
Cardano, Girolamo (1501–76; It.)	Gauss, Karl (1777–1855; Ger.)	Lovelace, Countess of (Ada King; 1815–52; Brit.)	Stirling, James (1692–1770; Scot.)
Cauchy, Augustin, Baron (1789–1857; Fr.)	Germain, Sophie (1776–1831; Fr.)	Mandelbrot, Benoit (b. 1924; Am., b. in Poland)	Stokes, Sir George (1819–1903; Brit.)
Cayley, Arthur (1821–95; Brit.)	Gödel, Kurt (1906–78; Am.)	Markov, Andrei (1856–1922; Russ.)	Taylor, Brook (1685–1731; Brit.)
	Gregory, James (1638–75; Scot.)	Maupertuis, Pierre de (1698–1759; Fr.)	Turing, Alan (1912–54; Brit.)
	Hermite, Charles (1822–1901; Fr.)		Wiener, Norbert (1894–1964; Am.)
	Hilbert, David (1862–1943; Ger.)		

maze · meanness

disturbance, commotion, tumult, pandemonium.

maze noun **1** *a maze in the castle grounds* labyrinth, network of paths. **2** *a maze of regulations* network, mesh, web, jungle, tangle, confusion, snarl, imbroglio.

meadow noun field, grassland, pasture, paddock, lea.

meagre adjective **1** *meagre supplies* paltry, sparse, scant, scanty, spare, inadequate, insufficient, insubstantial, exiguous, short, little, small, slight, slender, poor, puny, skimpy, scrimpy, miserly, niggardly, stingy, pathetic; *inf.* measly, as scarce as hens' teeth. **2** *meagre bodies* thin, lean, emaciated, skinny, spare, scrawny, scraggy, bony, gaunt, starved, underfed.
Opposites ABUNDANT; COPIOUS; OBESE.

meagreness noun paltriness, sparseness, scarcity, scantiness, inadequacy, insufficiency, exiguity, shortness, slightness, skimpiness, miserliness, stinginess; *inf.* measliness. *See* MEAGRE.

meal noun repast, collation, banquet, feast, picnic, barbecue, buffet; *inf.* blow-out.

mean¹ verb **1** *what do the words mean?* indicate, signify, betoken, express, convey, denote, designate, spell out, show, stand for, represent, symbolize, portend, connote, imply, purport, suggest, allude to, intimate, hint at, insinuate, drive at. **2** *not mean to break it* intend, have in mind, have in view, contemplate, think of, purpose, plan, have plans, set out, aim, aspire, desire, want, wish. **3** *meant to be used | not meant for the army* intend, made, design, destine, predestine, fate. **4** *this will mean war* involve, entail, lead to, result in, give rise to, bring about cause, engender, produce. **5** *this means a lot to her* have importance, have significance, matter. **6** *dark clouds meaning rain* presage, portend, foretell, augur, promise, foreshadow.

mean² adjective **1** *a mean old man* miserly, niggardly, parsimonious, tight-fisted, close-fisted, penny-pinching, penurious, grasping, greedy, avaricious, ungenerous, illiberal, close, near; *inf.* stingy, tight, mingy, cheap. **2** *a mean creature* base, dishonourable, ignoble, disreputable, vile, sordid, foul, nasty, despicable, contemptible, abominable, odious, hateful, horrible. **3** *of mean understanding/intellect* inferior, poor, limited, restricted, meagre, scant. **4** *a mean hovel* shabby, poor, wretched, dismal, miserable, squalid, sordid, seedy, mangy, broken-down, run-down, dilapidated, down-at-heel; *inf.* scruffy, grungy. **5** *a mean act | a mean old woman* nasty, disagreeable, unpleasant, unfriendly, offensive, obnoxious, cross, ill-natured, bad-tempered, irritable, churlish, surly, cantankerous, crotchety, crabbed, crabby, grumpy; *inf.* grouchy. **6** *of mean birth | mean peasants* low, lowly, low-born, humble, modest, common, ordinary, base, proletarian, plebeian, obscure, undistinguished, ignoble.
Opposites GENEROUS; HONOURABLE; LUXURIOUS.

mean³ noun *find a mean between frankness and rudeness* mid-point, middle, median, norm, average, middle course, middle way, happy medium, golden mean.

mean⁴ adjective *the mean temperature* middle, median, medial, average, normal, standard, medium, middling.

meander verb **1** *meander about in the sunshine* wander, roam, ramble, rove, stroll, amble, drift; *inf.* mosey/tootle along. **2** *rivers meandering through the country* wind, zigzag, snake, curve, turn, bend.

meandering adjective **1** *meandering crowds* wandering, roaming, rambling. *See* MEANDER 1. **2** *meandering streams* winding, zigzag, snaking, serpentine, tortuous. **3** *meandering prose* rambling, tortuous, circuitous, indirect, roundabout, convoluted, anfractuous.

meaning noun **1** *understand the meaning of what he said* signification, sense, message, import, drift, gist, essence, substance, purport, connotation, denotation, implication, significance, thrust. **2** *what is the meaning of the word?* definition, explanation, interpretation, elucidation, explication. **3** *it was not our meaning to delay him* intention, purpose, plan, aim, goal, end, object, objective, aspiration, desire, want, wish. **4** *his life has no meaning* significance, point, value, worth, consequence, account. **5** *a glance full of meaning* significance, implication, allusion, intimation, insinuation, eloquence, expression.

meaning adjective meaningful, significant, pointed, eloquent. *See* MEANINGFUL 3.

meaningful adjective **1** *a meaningful statement/remark* significant, important, relevant, material, valid, worthwhile. **2** *a meaningful relationship* significant, important, serious, sincere, in earnest. **3** *a meaningful glance* significant, pointed, suggestive, eloquent, expressive, pregnant.
Opposites MEANINGLESS; UNIMPORTANT; TRIVIAL.

meaningless adjective **1** *meaningless babble* senseless, unintelligible, incomprehensible, incoherent. **2** *a meaningless act of violence* senseless, pointless, purposeless, motiveless, irrational, inane. **3** *lead meaningless lives* empty, futile, pointless, aimless, valueless, worthless, trivial, insignificant, inconsequential.

meanness noun **1** *the meanness of the old man* miserliness, niggardliness, parsimony, parsimoniousness, tight-fistedness, penny-pinching, penury; *inf.* stinginess, cheapness, tightness, minginess. *See* MEAN² 1. **2** *the meanness of the creature* baseness, vileness, sordidness, foulness, nastiness, contemptibility, abominableness, odiousness. *See* MEAN² adjective 2. **3** *the meanness of his intellect* poorness, limitations, meagreness. *See* MEAN² 3. **4** *the meanness of the hovel* shabbiness, wretchedness, dismalness, misery, squalor, sordidness, seediness, dilapidation; *inf.* grunginess. *See* MEAN² 4. **5** *an act of such meanness | the meanness of the old woman* nastiness, disagreeableness, unpleasantness, unfriendliness, crossness, bad temper, irritability, surliness, cantankerousness. *See* MEAN² 5. **6** *the meanness of her birth* lowness, lowliness, humbleness, commonness, baseness, obscurity, ignobility. See MEAN² 6.

means *plural noun* **1** *a means of getting there* way, method, expedient, process, mode, manner, agency, medium, instrument, channel, avenue, course. **2** *a man of means* money, capital, wealth, riches, affluence, substance, fortune, property. **3** *haven't the means to buy it* money, resources, capital, finance, funds, wherewithal; *inf.* dough, bread, lolly. **by all means** of course, certainly, definitely, surely, absolutely. **by means of** *get the money by means of borrowing* through, by dint of, with the help of, with the aid of. **by no means** *by no means poor* in no way, not at all, not in the least, not in the slightest, not the least bit.

meantime *adverb* **1** meanwhile, in the meantime, for the time being, for now. See MEANWHILE 1. **2** *meantime back at the ranch* at the same time. See MEANWHILE 2.

meanwhile *adverb* **1** *meanwhile I shall wait* meantime, in the meantime, for the time being, for now, for the moment, in the intervening period, in the interim, in the interval, in the meanwhile. **2** *meanwhile back at the ranch* at the same time, simultaneously, concurrently, coincidentally.

measurable *adjective* **1** *a measurable quantity of sand* assessable, gaugeable, estimable, appraisable, computable, quantifiable, fathomable. **2** *a measurable improvement* significant, appreciable, noticeable, visible, perceptible, obvious, striking, material.

measure *noun* **1** *find the measure of the material* size, dimension, proportions, magnitude, amplitude, mass, bulk, volume, capacity, quantity, weight, extent, expanse, area, range. See MEASUREMENT 2. **2** *use a linear measure* system, standard, units, scale. **3** *use a measure to check the size* rule, ruler, tape-measure, gauge, meter, scale, level, yardstick. **4** *receive a measure of her father's estate* share, portion, division, allotment, part, piece, quota, lot, ration, percentage; *inf.* rake-off. **5** *have a measure of wit* quantity, amount, certain amount, degree. **6** *sales are the measure of the company's success* yardstick, test, standard, touchstone, criterion, benchmark. **7** *take drastic measures* action, act, course, course of action, deed, proceeding, procedure, step, means, expedient, manoeuvre. **8** *announce measures to control crime* statute, act, bill, law, resolution. **9** *do what you like within measure* moderation, limit, limitation, bounds, control, restraint. **10** *poetic measure* metre, cadence, rhythm. **beyond measure** immeasurably, incalculably, infinitely, limitlessly, immensely, extremely, vastly, excessively. **for good measure** as a bonus, as an extra, into the bargain, to boot, in addition, besides, as well.

measure *verb* **1** *measure the material/quantity* calculate, compute, estimate, quantify, weigh, size, evaluate, rate, assess, appraise, gauge, measure out, determine, judge, survey. **2** *measure one's words* choose carefully, select with care, consider, think carefully about, plan, calculate. **3** *measure one's work to one's time* adapt, adjust, fit, tailor. **4** *measure his strength against his brother's* pit, set, match, test, put into com-

petition with. **measure out** mete out, measure, deal out, dole out, share out, divide out, parcel out, allocate, allot, apportion, assign, distribute, administer, dispense, issue. **measure up** **1** *measure up the windows for curtains* measure, take the measurements of, estimate the size of. **2** *he was sacked because he didn't measure up* come up to standard, fulfil expectations, fit/fill the bill, pass muster, be adequate, be capable, be suitable; *inf.* come up to scratch, make the grade, cut the mustard, be up to snuff. **3** *didn't measure up to the requirements* meet, come up to, be equal to, match, be on a level with.

measured *adjective* **1** *measured amounts* measured out, calculated, computed, quantified. See MEASURE *verb* 1. **2** *measured tread* regular, steady, even, rhythmical, slow, dignified, stately, sedate, leisurely, unhurried. **3** *measured words* carefully chosen, selected with care, well-thought-out, studied, calculated, planned, premeditated, considered, deliberate, reasoned.

measurement *noun* **1** *the measurement of the quantity* calculation, computation, estimation, quantification, quantifying, weighing, sizing, evaluation, assessment, appraisal, gauging. See MEASURE *verb* 1. **2** *take the first measurement at noon | the measurements of the carpet are wrong* size, dimension, proportions, magnitude, amplitude, mass, bulk, volume, capacity, extent, expanse, amount, quantity, area, length, height, depth, weight, width, range. See table at UNIT.

meat *noun* **1** *vegetarians don't eat meat* flesh, animal flesh. See table. See also table at JOINT. **2** *meat and drink* food, nourishment, sustenance, provisions, rations, fare, viands, victuals, comestibles, provender, feed; *inf.* grub, eats, chow, nosh, scoff. **3** *the meat of the matter* substance, pith, marrow, heart, kernel, core, nucleus, nub, essence, essentials, gist, fundamentals, basics; *inf.* nitty-gritty, nuts and bolts.

TYPES OF MEAT			
Meat	**Animal**	**Meat**	**Animal**
beef	cow	pork	pig
huss	dogfish	veal	calf
lamb	lamb	venison	deer
mutton	sheep		

meaty *adjective* **1** *a meaty stew* meat-filled, fleshy. **2** *a meaty discussion/book* giving food for thought, substantial, pithy, meaningful, profound, deep, involved, interesting, significant.

mechanical *adjective* **1** *a mechanical device* automated, automatic, machine-driven, motor-driven, power-driven. **2** *mechanical gestures* automatic, machine-like, unthinking, unconscious, unfeeling, unemotional, cold, involuntary, instinctive, routine, habitual, perfunctory, cursory, lacklustre, lifeless, unanimated, dead, casual, careless, inattentive, negligent.
Opposites MANUAL; CONSCIOUS; EMOTIONAL.

mechanism *noun* **1** *a mechanism for folding paper* machine, apparatus, appliance, tool, device, instrument, contraption, contrivance, gadget, structure, system. **2** *the mechanism of the car* motor, workings, works, gears, components; *inf.* innards, guts. **3** *the mechanism for complaints* process, procedure, system, operation, method, technique, workings, means, medium, agency, channel.

meddle *verb* interfere, butt in, intrude, intervene, interlope, pry, nose; *inf.* stick one's nose in, horn in, snoop.

meddlesome *adjective* meddling, interfering, intrusive, prying; *inf.* snooping, nosy. *See* MEDDLE.

mediate *verb* **1** *mediate between the warring factions* act as mediator/go-between/middleman/ intermediary, arbitrate, negotiate, conciliate, intervene, intercede, interpose, moderate, umpire, referee, act as peacemaker, reconcile differences, restore harmony, make peace, bring to terms, step in. **2** *mediate a difference of opinion* settle, arbitrate, umpire, reconcile, resolve, mend, clear up, patch up. **3** *mediate a peace settlement* bring about, effect, effectuate, make happen, negotiate.

mediation *noun* arbitration, negotiation, intervention, intercession, interposition, good offices, conciliation, reconciliation.

mediator *noun* arbitrator, arbiter, negotiator, go-between, middle-man, intermediary, honest broker, peacemaker, intervenor, interceder, moderator, umpire, referee, judge, conciliator, reconciler.

medicinal *adjective medicinal herbs | for medicinal purposes* medical, therapeutic, curative, healing, remedial, restorative, health-giving, analeptic.

medicine *noun* **1** *given medicine* medication, medicament, drug, remedy, cure, physic. *See table.* **2** *study medicine* medical science, practice of medicine, healing art. **take one's medicine** accept one's punishment, take the consequences of one's actions; *inf.* get what is

coming to one, take the rap, take it on the chin.

medieval *adjective* **1** *medieval history* of the Middle/Dark Ages, Middle-Age, Dark-Age, Gothic. **2** *his attitude is medieval* antiquated, archaic, antique, obsolete, antediluvian, primitive, outmoded, outdated, old-fashioned, *passé*, unenlightened; *inf.* out of the ark.

mediocre *adjective* **1** *her work is mediocre* indifferent, average, middle-of-the-road, middling, ordinary, commonplace, pedestrian, run-of-the-mill, tolerable, passable, adequate, uninspired, undistinguished, unexceptional; *inf.* so-so, fair-to-middling, nothing to write home about, no great shakes. **2** *mediocre goods/actors* inferior, second-rate, second-class, low-grade, poor, shabby, minor.

mediocrity *noun* **1** *the mediocrity of her work* mediocreness, indifference, ordinariness, commonplaceness, passableness, lack of inspiration, unexceptionalness. *See* MEDIOCRE 1. **2** *the mediocrity of the goods* inferiority, second-rateness, poorness, shabbiness. *See* MEDIOCRE 2. **3** *they are mediocrities* nonentity, nobody, nothing, lightweight, cipher, second-rater; *inf.* no-hoper.

meditate *verb* **1** *he's meditating on/upon the past* engage in contemplation about, be in a thoughtful state about, contemplate, think about/over, muse on/about, ponder on/over, consider, concentrate on, reflect on, deliberate about/on, ruminate about/on/over, brood over, mull over, be in a brown study over; *inf.* put on one's thinking cap about. **2** *he's meditating leaving/revenge* think about, consider, have in mind, intend, plan, project, design, devise, scheme, plot.

meditation *noun* contemplation, thought, musing, pondering, consideration, reflection, deliberation, rumination, brooding, mulling over, reverie, brown study, concentration.

medium *noun* **1** *find the medium between two extremes* mean, median, mid-point, middle, centre point, average, norm, standard, middle way, middle course, middle ground, compromise, happy medium, golden mean. **2** *through the medium of television | want to use wood as an artistic medium* means of communication, means/mode of expression, means, agency, channel, avenue, vehicle, organ, instrument, instrumentality. **3** *organisms growing in their natural medium* habitat, element, environment, surroundings, milieu, setting, conditions, atmosphere. **4** *visit a medium to contact the dead* spiritualist, spiritist, necromancer.

medium *adjective* **1** *in the medium position* middle, mean, medial, median, midway, mid-point, intermediate. **2** *of medium height* average, middling.

medley *noun* assortment, miscellany, mixture, *mélange*, variety, collection, motley collection, pot-pourri, conglomeration, jumble, confusion, mishmash, hotchpotch, hodgepodge, pastiche, patchwork, farrago, gallimaufry, olio, salmagundi, mixed bag, mix; *inf.* omnium gatherum.

meek *adjective* **1** *meek, Christian people* patient, long-suffering, forbearing, resigned, gentle,

TYPES OF MEDICATION

anaesthetic	appetite suppressant
analgesic	beta blocker
antacid	bronchodilator
anthelmintic	decongestant
antibiotic	depressant
antibacterial	diuretic
anticoagulant	emetic
anticonvulsant	expectorant
antidepressant	fungicide
antidote	immuno-
antiemetic	suppressive
antiepileptic	laxative
antifungal	muscle relaxant
antihistamine	sedative
anti-	steroid
inflammatory	stimulant
antipsychotic	tonic
antipyretic	tranquillizer
antiseptic	vasoconstrictor
antitussive	vasodilator

peaceful, docile, modest, humble, unassuming, unpretentious. **2** *meek people being bullied by the strong* submissive, yielding, unresisting, compliant, acquiescent, deferential, weak, timid, frightened, spineless, spiritless; *inf.* weak-kneed.
Opposites IMPATIENT; ASSERTIVE; OVERBEARING.

meekness *noun* **1** *Christian meekness* patience, forbearance, resignation, gentleness, peacefulness, docility, modesty, humility, humbleness. *See* MEEK 1. **2** *the meekness of the pupils faced by bullies* submissiveness, lack of resistance, compliance, acquiescence, deference, weakness, timidity, fearfulness, spinelessness, lack of spirit.

meet *verb* **1** *meet friends for tea | met an old friend on the train* encounter, come face to face with, make contact with, run into, run across, come across, come upon, chance upon, happen upon, light upon; *inf.* bump into. **2** *where the land and sea meet* come together, abut, adjoin, join, link up, unite, connect, touch, converge, intersect. **3** *the committee met on Saturday* gather, assemble, come together, foregather, congregate, convene, convoke, muster, rally. **4** *meet the proposal with hostility* deal with, handle, treat, cope with, approach, answer. **5** *meet the demands of the job* satisfy, fulfil, measure up to, come up to, comply with. **6** *meet one's responsibilities* carry out, perform, execute, discharge, take care of. **7** *meet the cost* pay, settle, honour, square. **8** *meet death bravely* face, encounter, undergo, experience, go through, bear, suffer, endure. **9** *meet the enemy at dawn* encounter, confront, engage, engage in battle with, join battle with, clash with, fight with.
Opposites AVOID; SEPARATE; DISPERSE.

meeting *noun* **1** *the meeting of the two friends/ lovers* encounter, contact, assignation, rendezvous, tryst. **2** *address the meeting* gathering, assembly, conference, congregation, convention, convocation, conclave; *inf.* get-together. **3** *the meeting of land and sea* abutment, junction, conjunction, union, convergence, confluence, concourse, intersection. **4** *crowds flocking to the meeting* meet, race-meeting, athletics meeting, sports meeting.

melancholic, melancholy *adjective* despondent, dejected, depressed, down, downhearted, downcast, disconsolate, glum, gloomy, sunk in gloom, miserable, dismal, dispirited, low, in low spirits, in the doldrums, blue, mournful, lugubrious, woeful, woebegone, doleful, sorrowful, unhappy, heavyhearted, low-spirited, sombre, pensive, defeatist, pessimistic; *inf.* down in the dumps, down in the mouth.
Opposites CHEERFUL; JOYFUL; MERRY.

melancholy *noun* despondency, dejection, depression, gloom, gloominess, misery, low spirits, doldrums, blues, woe, sadness, sorrow, unhappiness, pensiveness, defeatism, pessimism, melancholia; *inf.* dumps.

mélange *noun* assortment, miscellany, mixture, medley, variety, motley collection, conglomeration, jumble, mishmash, hotchpotch, hodgepodge, farrago, mixed bag. *See* MEDLEY.

mêlée *noun* fight, quarrel, fracas, affray, fray, rumpus, commotion, tumult, brawl, scuffle, struggle, skirmish, free-for-all, tussle; *inf.* setto, shindy, shindig.

mellifluous *adjective* *speak in mellifluous tones* sweet, sweet-sounding/toned, dulcet, honeyed, mellow, soft, soothing, smooth, silvery, euphonious, musical.

mellow *adjective* **1** *mellow fruit* ripe, mature, well-matured, soft, juicy, tender, luscious, sweet, full-flavoured, flavoursome. **2** *a mellow, tuned voice* dulcet, sweet, sweet-sounding, tuneful, euphonious, melodious, mellifluous, smooth, full, rich, well-rounded. **3** *a mellow old man* gentle, easy-going, pleasant, kindly, kind-hearted, amicable, amiable, good-natured, affable, gracious. **4** *in a mellow mood* genial, jovial, jolly, cheerful, happy, merry. **5** *feeling mellow after two glasses of wine* tipsy; *inf.* happy, merry.
Opposites GREEN; unripe; HARSH; NASTY.

melodious *adjective* melodic, musical, tuneful, harmonious, lyrical, dulcet, sweet, sweet-sounding, sweet-toned, silvery, silvery-toned, euphonious.
Opposites DISCORDANT; HARSH; GRATING.

melodramatic *adjective* theatrical, stagy, over-dramatic, histrionic, oversensational, extravagant, overdone, over-emotional; *inf.* actressy, camp, hammy.

melody *noun* **1** *composing melodies* tune, air, strain, music, refrain, theme, song. **2** *not much melody in this music* melodiousness, tunefulness, musicality, harmony, lyricism, sweetness, euphony.

melt *verb* **1** *solids melting* liquefy, dissolve, deliquesce, thaw, unfreeze, defrost, soften, fuse. **2** *the crowd melted away* disperse, vanish, vanish into thin air, fade away, disappear, dissolve, evaporate, evanesce. **3** *her charm melted the old lady | her charm melted the old lady's heart* soften, touch, disarm, mollify.

member *noun* **1** *a member of the club* card-carrying member, adherent, associate, fellow. **2** *many victims had injured members* part of the body, organ, limb, appendage, extremity, arm, leg. **3** *a member of the mathematical set* element, constituent, component, part, portion.

membrane *noun* sheet, layer, film, skin, tissue, pellicle, integument.

memento *noun* souvenir, keepsake, reminder, remembrance, token, memorial, trophy, relic, vestige.

memoir *noun* *write a memoir on World War II* account, historical account, monograph, record, chronicle, essay, narrative.

memoirs *plural noun* *write one's memoirs* autobiography, life story, life, memories, recollections, personal recollections, reminiscences, experiences, journal, diary.

memorable *adjective* **1** *a memorable event/person* unforgettable, not to be forgotten, signal, momentous, significant, historic, notable, noteworthy, important, consequential, remarkable, outstanding, extraordinary, striking, impressive, distinctive, distinguished,

famous, celebrated, illustrious. **2** *a memorable tune* unforgettable, catchy, striking.
Opposites RUN-OF-THE-MILL; COMMONPLACE; forgettable.

memorandum *noun* reminder, note, message, minute, aide-mémoire; *inf.* memo.

memorial *noun* **1** *install a memorial to him* monument, statue, plaque, cairn, shrine, tombstone. **2** *this will serve as a memorial of him* remembrance, memento, souvenir.

memorial *adjective* *memorial service* remembrance, commemorative, commemorating, monumental.

memorize *verb* commit to memory, remember, learn by heart, get by heart, learn off, learn, learn by rote.

memory *noun* **1** *my memory of the events is faint* | *her memory is poor* remembrance, recollection, powers of recall, recall, reminiscence, powers of retention, retention. **2** *build a statue in memory of him* remembrance, commemoration, honour, tribute. **3** *a computer's memory* memory bank, storage bank, store, information store.

menace *noun* **1** *an atmosphere full of menace* threat, ominousness, intimidation, warning, ill-omen, commination. **2** *he/it is a menace to the residents* threat, danger, peril, risk, hazard, jeopardy, source of apprehension/dread/fright/fear/terror. **3** *the child next door is a menace* nuisance, pest, source of annoyance, annoyance, plague, torment, troublemaker, mischief-maker.

menace *verb* **1** *older boys menacing the young* threaten, intimidate, issue threats to, frighten, scare, alarm, terrify, bully, browbeat, cow, terrorize. **2** *bad weather menacing* loom, impend, lour, be in the air, be in the offing.

menacing *adjective* **1** *a menacing look/silence* threatening, ominous, intimidating, frightening, terrifying, alarming, forbidding, minatory, minacious. **2** *a menacing storm* looming, louring, impending.
Opposites FRIENDLY; AUSPICIOUS.

mend *verb* **1** *mend the furniture* repair, fix, put back together, patch up, restore, rehabilitate, renew, renovate, make whole, make well, cure, heal. **2** *mend socks* | *mend a hole in the sweater* sew, stitch, darn, patch. **3** *the invalid will soon mend* get better, recover, recuperate, improve, be well, be cured, be all right. **4** *try to mend matters/the situation* put right, set straight, rectify, put in order, correct, amend, emend, improve, make better, better, ameliorate, reform.
Opposites BREAK; TEAR; WORSEN.

mendacious *adjective* **1** *mendacious people* lying, untruthful, dishonest, deceitful, dissembling, insincere, disingenuous, hypocritical, fraudulent, unveracious, economical with the truth. **2** *mendacious tales* lying, untrue, false, fraudulent, fictitious, falsified, fabricated, invented, made up.

mendicant *adjective* begging, cadging; *inf.* scrounging, sponging; *Am. inf.* mooching.

mendicant *noun* beggar, beggarman/woman, tramp, vagrant, vagabond, cadger; *inf.* scrounger, sponger; *Am.* hobo; *Am. inf.* moocher, bum.

menial *adjective* *menial duties/jobs* lowly, humble, low-grade, low-status, unskilled, routine, humdrum, boring, dull.
Opposites NOBLE; ELEVATED; ARISTOCRATIC; SKILLED.

menial *noun* servant, domestic servant, domestic, drudge, maid of all work, labourer, slave, underling, vassal, lackey, flunkey; *inf.* dogsbody, skivvy, gofer.

menstruation *noun* period, menses, menstrual cycle, monthly flow; *inf.* the curse, monthlies, the usual.

mental *adjective* **1** *mental work* intellectual, cerebral, brain. **2** *mental hospital/nurse* psychiatric. **3** *he's completely mental* mad, insane, deranged, disturbed, mentally unbalanced, mentally ill, mentally unstable, psychotic, lunatic; *inf.* crazy, off one's head, off one's trolley, out to lunch.
Opposites PHYSICAL; SANE.

mentality *noun* **1** *of a slightly twisted mentality* cast of mind, frame of mind, turn of mind, way of thinking, way one's mind works, mind, psychology, mental attitude, outlook, character, disposition, make-up. **2** *of low-grade mentality* intellect, intellectual capabilities, intelligence, IQ (= intelligence quotient), brainpower, brains, mind, comprehension, understanding, wit, rationality, powers of reasoning; *inf.* grey matter.

mentally *adverb* in the mind, in the brain, in the head, intellectually, psychologically.

mention *verb* **1** *he only mentioned it* allude to, refer to, touch on, speak briefly of, hint at. **2** *he mentioned your name* say, state, name, cite, quote, call attention to, adduce. **3** *don't mention this to anyone* tell, speak about/of, utter, communicate, let someone know, disclose, divulge, reveal, intimate, whisper, breathe a word of; *inf.* let on about. **don't mention it** don't apologize, it doesn't matter, don't worry. **not to mention** not counting, not including, to say nothing of, aside from, as well as, besides, in addition to.

mention *noun* **1** *made no mention of your request* | *a mention in the book* reference, allusion, observation, remark, statement, announcement, indication. **2** *a mention in dispatches* honourable mention, acknowledgement, citation, recognition, tribute.

mentor *noun* guide, advisor, counsellor, therapist, guru, spiritual leader, confidant, teacher, tutor, coach, instructor.

menu *noun* bill of fare, tariff, *carte du jour*; *inf.* what's on.

mercantile *adjective* commercial, trade, trading, marketable.

mercenary *adjective* **1** *mercenary people interested only in money* money-oriented, grasping, greedy, acquisitive, avaricious, covetous, bribable, venal; *inf.* money-grubbing. **2** *mercenary soldiers* hired, paid, bought, professional, venal.
Opposites ALTRUISTIC; PHILANTHROPIC; GENEROUS.

495

mercenary *noun* professional soldier, hired soldier, soldier of fortune; free lance, *condottiere*, galloglass.

merchandise *noun* damaged merchandise goods, wares, stock, commodities, produce, vendibles.

merchandise *verb* **1** *merchandise a wide range of goods* market, sell, retail, buy and sell, distribute, deal in, trade in, traffic in, do business in, vend. **2** *merchandise the new range* promote, advertize, publicize, push, puff, give a puff to, beat the drum for; *inf.* hype, plug.

merchant *noun* **1** *a fruit merchant* trader, dealer, trafficker, wholesaler, broker, seller, salesman/woman/person, vendor, retailer, shopkeeper, distributor. **2** *speed merchants* enthusiast, fan; *inf.* freak, buff.

merciful *adjective* lenient, clement, compassionate, pitying, forgiving, forbearing, sparing, humane, mild, soft-hearted, tender-hearted, kind, sympathetic, liberal, tolerant, generous, beneficent, benignant.
Opposites MERCILESS; CRUEL.

merciless *adjective* unmerciful, ruthless, relentless, inexorable, harsh, pitiless, uncompassionate, unforgiving, unsparing, unpitying, implacable, barbarous, inhumane, inhuman, hard-hearted, heartless, callous, cruel, unsympathetic, unfeeling, illiberal, intolerant, rigid, severe, stern.
Opposites MERCIFUL; COMPASSIONATE.

mercurial *adjective* mecurial child/temperament volatile, capricious, temperamental, fickle, changeable, unpredictable, variable, erratic, quicksilver, inconstant, unstable, unsteady, fluctuating, wavering, vacillating, flighty, impulsive.
Opposites STABLE; STEADY; CONSTANT.

mercy *noun* **1** *the mercy of the judge* leniency, clemency, compassion, compassionateness, pity, charity, forgiveness, forbearance, quarter, humanity, humaneness, mildness, soft-heartedness, tender-heartedness, kindness, sympathy, liberality, tolerance, generosity, beneficence, benignancy. **2** *thankful for small mercies* boon, favour, piece of luck, blessing, godsend. **at the mercy of** **1** *at the mercy of the tyrant* in the power of, under/in the control of, in the clutches of. **2** *at the mercy of the storm* threatened by, prey to, open to, exposed to, defenceless against, unprotected against, vulnerable to.
Opposites SEVERITY; CRUELTY; INHUMANITY.

mere *adjective* a mere child nothing more than, no better than, no more important than, just a, only a, pure and simple.

merge *verb* **1** *the two firms merged* join together, join forces, amalgamate, unite, combine, incorporate, coalesce, team up. **2** *merge the firms* join, amalgamate, unite, combine, incorporate, coalesce. **3** *the colours merged* blend, fuse, mingle, mix, intermix, homogenize. **4** *caused her personality to merge into his* run into, melt into, become assimilated into/in, become lost in, be swallowed up by, be buried in, be submerged in.
Opposites DIVERGE; SPLIT; SEPARATE.

merger *noun* amalgamation, combination, union, fusion, coalition, alliance, incorporation.

merit *noun* **1** *the merit of his work* excellence, goodness, quality, high quality, worth, worthiness, value. **2** *the merits of the scheme* good point, strong point, advantage, asset, plus. **3** *receive his merits* what one deserves, desert, just deserts, due, right, reward, recompense.
Opposites INFERIORITY; FAULT; DISADVANTAGE.

merit *verb* merit a prize deserve, be deserving of, earn, be worthy of, be worth, be entitled to, have a right to, have a claim to, warrant, rate, incur.

meritorious *adjective* praiseworthy, laudable, commendable, admirable, estimable, creditable, excellent, exemplary, good, worthy, deserving.
Opposites WORTHLESS; discreditable.

merriment *noun* cheerfulness, gaiety, high-spiritedness, high spirits, blitheness, buoyancy, carefreeness, levity, frolicsomeness, sportiveness, joy, joyfulness, joyousness, jolliness, jollity, rejoicing, jocundity, conviviality, festivity, merry-making, revelry, mirth, mirthfulness, glee, gleefulness, laughter, hilarity, amusement, fun.

merry *adjective* **1** *merry children playing* cheerful, cheery, gay, in good spirits, high-spirited, blithe, blithesome, light-hearted, buoyant, carefree, frolicsome, sportive, joyful, joyous, rejoicing, jolly, jocund, convivial, festive, mirthful, gleeful, happy, glad, laughing. **2** *a merry tale* comical, comic, amusing, funny, humorous, facetious, hilarious. **3** *slightly merry after the party* tipsy, mellow; *inf.* happy, tiddly, squiffy. **make merry** have fun, have a good time, enjoy oneself, have a party, party, celebrate, carouse, revel, rejoice; *inf.* have a ball, make whoopee.
Opposites MISERABLE; SAD; GLOOMY.

mesh *noun* **1** *wire mesh | purse made of fine silk mesh* network, netting, net, tracery, web, lattice, latticework, lacework, trellis, reticulation, plexus. **2** *caught in the mesh of political intrigue* net, tangle, entanglement, web, snare, trap.

mesh *verb* **1** *gears meshing* be engaged, connect, interlock. **2** *our ideas do not mesh* harmonize, fit together, go together, coordinate, match, be on the same wavelength, dovetail. **3** *mesh the prey* net, snare, ensnare, entangle, enmesh, trap, catch.

mesmerize *verb* **1** *hypnotists mesmerizing people* hypnotize, put into a trance, put under. **2** *he was mesmerized by her beauty* hold spellbound, spellbind, entrance, enthral, bewitch, captivate, enchant, fascinate, grip, magnetize, hypnotize.

mess *noun* **1** *clear up the mess in the kitchen* disorder, untidiness, disarray, dirtiness, filthiness, clutter, shambles, litter, jumble, muddle, chaos, confusion, disorganization, turmoil. **2** *have to get out of this mess* plight, predicament, tight spot, tight corner, difficulty, trouble, quandary, dilemma, muddle, mix-up, confusion, imbroglio, fine kettle of fish; *inf.* jam, fix, pickle, stew, hole. **3** *what a mess he made of the* *project* muddle, botch, bungle; *inf.* hash, muck, foul-up, screw-up, cock-up. **4** *cat's mess* dirt, excrement, faeces, excreta.

mess *verb* **1** *mess up the kitchen* dirty, befoul, litter, besmirch, pollute, clutter up, disarrange, throw into disorder, dishevel. **2** *mess up the project* botch, bungle, muff, make a mess of, mar, spoil, ruin; *inf.* make a hash of, make a muck of, muck up, foul up, screw up, cock up. **3** *mess with the cutlery* fiddle, play, tinker, toy. **mess about, mess around** potter about, amuse oneself, pass the time, do nothing very much, fiddle about, play about, fool about; *inf.* muck about.

message *noun* **1** *leave a message | there's a telephone message for you* communication, piece of information, news, word, tidings, note, memorandum, letter, missive, bulletin, communiqué, dispatch; *inf.* memo. **2** *the message of the sermon* meaning, import, idea, point, purport, intimation, theme, moral. **3** *be sent on a message* errand, task, job, commission, mission. **get the message** get the point, get the drift, understand, comprehend, take the hint; *inf.* understand what's what, catch on, get it, get the picture.

messenger *noun* message-bearer, message-carrier, courier, errand-boy/girl, runner, envoy, emissary, agent, go-between, herald, harbinger.

messy *adjective* untidy, disordered, dirty, filthy, grubby, slovenly, cluttered, littered, muddled, in a muddle, chaotic, confused, disorganized, in disarray, disarranged, dishevelled, unkempt; *inf.* sloppy, shambolic.
Opposites TIDY; CLEAN; ORDERLY.

metal *noun. See tables.*

TYPES OF METAL

actinide	coinage metal
alkali metal	lanthanide
alkaline-earth metal	rare-earth metal
alloy	transition metal
amalgam	

COMMON METALS AND ALLOYS

aluminium	German	silver
antimony	silver	sodium
babbitt	gold	solder
metal	gunmetal	stainless
barium	iron	steel
bell metal	lead	steel
beryllium	lithium	strontium
bismuth	magnesium	tantalum
brass	manganese	thallium
Britannia	mercury	thorium
metal	molyb-	tin
bronze	denum	titanium
cadmium	nickel	tungsten
calcium	niobium	uranium
cast iron	ormolu	vanadium
chromium	pewter	white
cobalt	pinchbeck	metal
copper	platinum	zinc
cupro-nickel	potassium	zirconium

metallic *adjective* **1** *metallic goods* metal, made of metal, metal-like, iron, steel, stainless-steel. **2** *metallic sounds* grating, harsh, jarring, jangling, dissonant, raucous. **3** *metallic colours/paint* shiny, gleaming, lustrous, polished, burnished.

metamorphosis *noun* transformation, transfiguration, change, alteration, conversion, change-over, mutation, transmutation, sea change; *inf.* transmogrification.

metaphor *noun* figure of speech, image, trope, allegory, analogy, symbol, emblem. *See table at* RHETORIC.

metaphorical *adjective* non-literal, figurative, allegorical, symbolic, emblematic, emblematical.

mete *verb* **mete out** deal out, dole out, measure out, divide out, allocate, allot, apportion, assign, distribute, administer, dispense, issue. *See* MEASURE *verb* measure out.

meteor *noun. See table.*

meteoric *adjective* *meteoric rise to fame* lightning, rapid, swift, fast, quick, speedy, overnight, sudden, dazzling, brilliant, spectacular, flashing, momentary, fleeting, transient, ephemeral, evanescent, brief, short-lived.
Opposites SLOW; GRADUAL; LONG-DRAWN-OUT.

method *noun* **1** *use old-fashioned methods* procedure, technique, system, practice, *modus operandi*, process, approach, way, course of action, scheme, plan, rule, arrangement, form, style, manner, mode. **2** *method in his madness* order, orderliness, sense of order, organization, arrangement, structure, form, system, planning, plan, design, purpose, pattern, regularity.

methodical *adjective* **1** *a methodical approach* orderly, well-ordered, organized, systematic, structured, logical, well-regulated, planned, efficient, businesslike. **2** *a methodical person* organized, systematic, efficient, businesslike, meticulous, punctilious.
Opposites DISORGANIZED; CHAOTIC; INEFFICIENT.

meticulous *adjective* **1** *a meticulous proofreader* conscientious, careful, ultra-careful, scrupulous, punctilious, painstaking, demanding, exacting, thorough, perfectionist, fastidious, particular. **2** *a meticulous report* careful, exact, precise, detailed, thorough, rigorous, painstaking.
Opposites CARELESS; SLOPPY; SLAPDASH.

metropolis *noun* capital, city, chief town. *See table at* COUNTRY.

mettle *noun* **1** *men of a different mettle* calibre, character, disposition, nature, temperament, temper, personality, make-up, stamp, kind, sort, variety, mould, kidney. **2** *soldiers of mettle* courage, courageousness, bravery, gallantry, valour, intrepidity, fearlessness, boldness, daring, hardihood, grit, pluck, nerve, gameness, backbone, spirit, fortitude, indomitability; *inf.* guts, bottle, spunk.

microscopic *adjective* invisible to the naked eye, scarcely perceptible, infinitesimal, minuscule, tiny, minute.
Opposites MASSIVE; ENORMOUS; GIGANTIC.

midday *noun* noon, twelve noon, twelve midday, twelve o'clock, high noon, noontide, noontime, noonday, twelve hundred, twelve hundred hours, one-two-double-O.

middle *adjective* **1** *the middle point between two extremes* mid, mean, medium, medial, median, midway, halfway, central, equidistant. **2** *the middle ranks* intermediate, intermediary, intermedial.

middle *noun* **1** *the middle of the line/scale* mean, median, mid-point, halfway point, centre, dead centre. **2** *in the middle of the crowd* midst, heart, centre, thick. **3** *have a thickening middle* midriff, waist, waistline.

middleman *noun* intermediary, go-between, broker, distributor.

middling *adjective* average, medium, ordinary, fair, moderate, adequate, passable, tolerable, mediocre, indifferent, run-of-the-mill, unexceptional, unremarkable; *inf.* fair-to-middling, so-so.

midget *noun* *midgets in circuses* dwarf, homunculus, manikin, gnome, pygmy, Tom Thumb; *inf.* shrimp.

midget *adjective* **1** *midget species of plants* dwarf, miniature, baby. **2** *midget beings/dogs* tiny, minute, very small, pocket, toy, pygmy.

midnight *noun* twelve o'clock, twelve midnight, twelve at night, dead of night, the middle of the night, the witching hour.
Opposites MIDDAY; NOON.

midst *noun* middle, centre, heart, bosom, core, kernel, nucleus, nub, interior, depths, thick.

midway *adverb* halfway, in the middle, at the mid-point, in the centre, betwixt and between.

mien *noun* look, appearance, aspect, aura, expression, countenance, demeanour, air, manner, bearing, carriage, deportment.

miffed *adjective* annoyed, displeased, offended, aggrieved, piqued, nettled, vexed, irked, upset, hurt, put out, resentful, in a huff; *inf.* narked.

might *noun* force, power, strength, mightiness, powerfulness, forcefulness, potency, toughness, robustness, sturdiness, muscularity, vigour, energy, stamina, stoutness. **with might and main** with all one's strength, with everything one has got, as hard as one can, as hard as possible, with maximum force, full force, full blast, forcefully, powerfully, strongly, vigorously.

mighty *adjective* **1** *a mighty figure of a man | struck a mighty blow* forceful, powerful, strong, lusty, manful, potent, tough, robust, sturdy, muscular, strapping, vigorous, energetic, stout. **2** *a mighty structure/mountain* huge, massive, vast, enormous, colossal, giant, gigantic, prodigious, monumental, mountainous, towering, titanic.
Opposites PUNY; FEEBLE; TINY.

migrant *adjective* migrating, migratory, travelling, roving, roaming, wandering, drifting, nomadic, itinerant, peripatetic, vagrant, gypsy, transient, unsettled, on the move.

migrant *noun* vagrant, nomad, itinerant, traveller, gypsy, transient, rover, wanderer, drifter.

migrate *verb* **1** *migrate to another place* emigrate, move, resettle, relocate, go abroad, go overseas. **2** *tramps migrating* travel, voyage, journey, trek, hike, rove, roam, wander, drift.

migratory *adjective* migrant, migrating, travelling, roving, wandering, nomadic, itinerant, vagrant, transient, unsettled. *See* MIGRANT *adjective.*

mild *adjective* **1** *of a mild disposition* tender, gentle, soft, soft-hearted, tender-hearted, sensitive, sympathetic, warm, warm-hearted, compassionate, humane, forgiving, conciliatory, forbearing, merciful, lenient, clement, placid, meek, docile, calm, tranquil, serene, peaceful, peaceable, pacific, good-natured, amiable, affable, genial, easy, easygoing, mellow. **2** *mild winds* gentle, soft, moderate, warm, balmy. **3** *mild food* bland, spiceless, non-spicy, insipid, tasteless.
Opposites CRUEL; HARSH; STRONG; SPICY.

mildness *noun* **1** *the mildness of her disposition* tenderness, gentleness, softness, sensitivity, warmness, compassion, meekness, docility, calmness, tranquillity, placidity, serenity, amiability, affability, geniality, mellowness. *See* MILD 1. **2** *the mildness of the winds* softness, moderation. *See* MILD 2. **3** *mildness of the food* blandness, lack of spiciness, insipidness, tastelessness.

milieu *noun* environment, surroundings, background, setting, scene, location, sphere, element.

militant *adjective* **1** *militant members of the organization* aggressive, assertive, vigorous, active, ultra-active, combative, pugnacious; *inf.* pushy. **2** *militant groups/armies* fighting, warring, combating, contending, in conflict, clash-

---

METEOR SHOWERS		
Meteor Shower	**Normal Date**	**(Peak date)**
April Lyrids	April 19 – 25	(April 22)
Delta Aquarids	July 15 – August 20	(July 29)
Eta Aquarids	April 24 – May 20	(May 5)
Geminids	December 7 – 16	(December 14)
June Lyrids	June 11 – 21	(June 16)
Leonids	November 15 – 20	(November 17)
Orionids	October 16 – 27	(October 22)
Perseids	July 23 – August 20	(August 12)
Quadrantids	January 1 – 6	(January 3)
Taurids	October 30 – November 30	(November 4)
Ursids	December 17 – 25	(December 23)

militant · milky

ing, embattled, in arms, belligerent, bellicose.
Opposites RETIRING; PACIFIC; PEACEFUL.

militant noun **1** *militants in the party* activist, partisan. **2** *militants meeting on the battlefield* fighter, fighting man, soldier, warrior, combatant, belligerent, aggressor.

military adjective *military forces* army, service, soldierly, soldierlike, armed, martial. *See tables.*

military noun army, forces, armed forces, services, militia, soldiery, navy, air force, marines.

militate verb **militate against** *his attitude will militate against him* operate against, go against, count against, tell against, weigh against, be

detrimental to, be disadvantageous to, be to the disfavour of, be counter to the interests of, conflict with the interests of.

milk verb **1** *milk sap from a tree* | *milk money from shopkeepers* draw, draw off, express, siphon, tap, drain, extract. **2** *milk the poor people* exploit, take advantage of, impose on, bleed, suck dry.

milksop noun coward, weakling, namby-pamby; *inf.* mummy's boy, sissy, pansy, wimp, scaredy-cat; *Am. inf.* fraidy-cat.

milky adjective *milky skin* white, milk-white, snow-white, whitish, creamy, pearly, nacreous, ivory, alabaster, off-white, clouded, cloudy.

MILITARY LEADERS AND WARRIORS

Achilles (legendary Gk warrior)

Agricola, Gnaeus Julius (40–93 A.D.; Rom. general)

Alanbrooke, Alan Francis Brooke, 1st Viscount, (1883–1963; Brit. soldier)

Albuquerque, Alfonso de (1453–1515; Port. soldier)

Alcibiades (c. 450–04 B.C.; Athenian general/statesman)

Alexander the Great (356–23 B.C.; King of Macedon)

Alexander, Harold (1891–1969; Brit. field marshal/statesman)

Allen, Ethan (1739–89; Am. soldier)

Allenby, Edmund, 1st Viscount, (1861–1936; Brit. soldier)

Amr ibn al-As (d. 663 A.D.; Arab. soldier)

Antony, Mark (c. 83–30 B.C.; Rom. general/triumvir)

Aristides the Just (5th century B.C.; Athenian general/statesman)

Artemisia (5th century B.C.; Pers. warrior)

Atatürk, Kemal (1881–1938; Turk. general/statesman)

Bar Kokhba (d. 135 A.D.; Jewish freedom fighter)

Beatty, David (1871–1936; Brit. admiral)

Bolívar, Simón (1738–1830; S. Am. soldier/statesman)

Boudicca/Boadicea (d. 62 A.D.; Queen of the Iceni)

Brutus, Marcus Junius (c. 85–42 B.C.; Rom. soldier)

Caesar, Julius (100–44 B.C.; Rom. soldier/statesman)

Calles, Plutarco (1877–1945; Mex. soldier/political leader)

Carranza, Venustiano (1859–1920; Mex. soldier/political leader)

Chiang Kai-shek (1887–1975; Chin. soldier/statesman)

Clausewitz, Karl von (1780–1831; Prussian general/military theorist)

Clive of Plassey, Robert, Baron (1725–74; Brit. general/colonial administrator)

Clovis (c. 466–51 A.D.; King of the Franks)

Coriolanus, Gaius (5th century B.C.; Rom. general)

Cromwell, Oliver (1599–1658; Engl. general/statesman)

Dayan, Moshe (1915–81; Israeli general/statesman)

de Gaulle, Charles (1890–1970; Fr. general/statesman)

de Wet, Christiaan (1854–1922; Afk. general)

Díaz, Porfirio (1830–1915; Mex. general/statesman)

Drake, Sir Francis (c. 1540–96; Engl. sailor)

Dundee, Viscount (John Graham of Claverhouse; c. 1649–89; Scot. soldier)

Eisenhower, Dwight (1890–1970; Am. general/statesman)

El Cid (Rodrigo Diáz de Vivar; c. 1043–99; Sp. soldier)

Enver Pasha (1881–1922; Turk. military/political leader)

Ershad, Hussain (b. 1930; Bangladeshi soldier/politician)

Fabius, Quintus (d. 203 B.C.; Rom. general/statesman)

Fairfax, Thomas, 3rd Baron Fairfax (1612–71; Engl. general)

Foch, Ferdinand (1851–71; Fr. general)

Genghis Khan (1162–1227; Mongol commander)

Geronimo (1829–1909; Apache chief)

Giap, Vo Nguyen (b. 1912; Vietnamese military/political leader)

Gordon, Charles George (1833–85; Brit. general)

Grant, Ulysses S. (1822–85; Am. general)

Gustavus Adolphus (1594–1632; King of Sweden)

Haig, Douglas (1861–1928; Brit. field marshal)

Hannibal (247–182 B.C.; Carthaginian general)

Hector (legendary Trojan warrior)

Hindenburg, Paul Ludwig von Beneckendorff und von (1847–1934; Ger. field marshal/statesman)

Hideyoshi, Toyotomi (1536–98; Jap. commander)

Itúrbide, Agustín de (1783–1824; Mex. soldier/emperor)

Jackson, Andrew (1767–1845; Am. general/statesman)

Jackson, Thomas "Stonewall" (1824–63; Am. general)

Jellicoe, John Rushworth, 1st Earl (1859–1935; Brit. admiral)

Jervis, John, Earl St Vincent (1735–1823; Brit. admiral)

Joffre, Joseph Jacques Césaire (1852–1931; Fr. marshal)

John of Austria, Don (1545–78; Sp. soldier)

Jugurtha (d. 104 B.C.; King of Numidia)

499

mill · mimic

mill noun workers employed at the mill factory, plant, foundry, works, workshop, shop, industrial centre.

mill verb mill coffee/grain grind, pulverize, pound, crush, powder, crunch, granulate, comminute, triturate. **mill around** people milling around everywhere move around, wander around, amble, meander, crowd, swarm, throng.

millstone noun a millstone round our necks load, burden, weight, dead weight, onus, duty, tax, obligation, responsibility, trouble, misfortune, affliction, cross to bear, cross, albatross round one's neck.

mime noun take part in a mime dumb show, mummery, pantomime.

mime verb mime his intentions use gestures to indicate, gesture, indicate by dumb show, indicate by sign language.

mimic verb **1** mimic his friend impersonate, give an impersonation of, imitate, copy, ape, caricature, parody; inf. take off. **2** the monkey's actions mimicked those of man resemble, look like, have/take on the appearance of, echo, mirror, simulate.

mimic noun mimicker, impersonator, impressionist, imitator, parodist, copyist, parrot, ape.

MILITARY LEADERS AND WARRIORS cont.

Kitchener, Herbert (1850–1916; Brit. soldier/statesman)
Kosciusko, Thaddeus (1746–1817; Pol. soldier)
Kusunoki Masashige (1294–1336; Jap. samurai warrior)
Kutuzov, Mikhail Ilarionovich, prince (1745–1813; Russ. field marshal)
Lafayette, Marie Joseph, Marquis de (1757–1834; Fr. soldier/statesman)
Lawrence, T(homas) E(dward) "Lawrence of Arabia" (1888–1935; Brit. soldier)
Lee, Robert E. (1807–70; Am. general)
Leonidas (d. c. 480 B.C.; King of Sparta)
Lin Biao (1908–71; Chin. soldier/politician)
Ludendorff, Erich (1865–1937; Ger. general)
Lysander (d. 396 B.C.; Spartan general)
MacArthur, Douglas (1880–1964; Am. general)
Marius, Gaius (c. 157–86 B.C.; Rom. general/politician)
Marlborough, 1st Duke of (John Churchill; 1650–1722; Brit. general)
Minamoto Yoritomo (1147–99; Jap. soldier)

Moltke, Helmuth, Count von (1800–91; Prussian soldier)
Montcalm, Louis Josèph de Montcalm-Gozon, Marquis de (1712–59; Fr. general)
Montgomery, Bernard Law "Monty" (1887–1976; Brit. field marshal)
Montrose, James Graham, 1st Marquis of (1612–50; Scot. general)
Moore, Sir John (1761–1809; Brit. general)
Mountbatten, Louis (1900–79; Brit. admiral)
Mzilikazi (c. 1790–1868; Zulu warrior-king)
Napoleon I (Napoleon Bonaparte; 1769–1821; Fr. emperor)
Nelson, Horatio (1758–1805; Brit. admiral)
Ney, Michel (1768–1815; Fr. marshal)
O'Higgins, Bernardo (c. 1778–1842; Chilean revolutionary/statesman)
Patton, George Smith (1885–1945; Am. soldier)
Pershing, John Joseph (1860–1948; Am. general)
Pétain, Philippe (1856–1951; Fr. general/statesman)

Pompey the Great (106–48 B.C.; Rom. general/statesman)
Rommel, Erwin the "Desert Fox" (1891–1944; Ger. field marshal)
Rupert, Prince (1619–82; Engl. general)
Saladin (c. 1137–93; sultan of Egypt and Syria)
Santa Anna, Antonio López de (1794–1876; Mex. soldier/statesman)
Schlieffen, Alfred, Graf von (1833–1913; Prussian field marshal)
Schwarzkopf, H. Norman (b. 1935; Am. general)
Scipio Africanus (c. 185–129 B.C.; Rom. general/politician)
Sebuktigin (d. 995 A.D.; Turk. soldier)
Shaka (c. 1787–1828; Zulu military leader)
Sheridan, Philip (1831–88; Am. soldier)
Sherman, William Tecumseh (1820–91; Am. general)
Shovel, Sir Cloudesley (1650–1707; Engl. naval commander)
Smuts, Jan Christiaan (1870–1950; S. Afr. soldier/statesman)
Suleiman the Magnificent (c. 1494–1566; Ottoman emperor)

Sulla (138–78 B.C.; Rom. general/politician)
Tamerlane (Timur Lenk; c. 1336–1405; Mongol ruler)
Tokugawa, Ieyasu (1542–1616; Jap. shogun)
Tuchachevsky, - Mikhail (1893–1937; Russ. soldier/politician)
Villa, Pancho (1878–1923; Mex. revolutionary)
Wallenstein, Albrecht von (1583–1634; Austrian soldier)
Washington, George (1732–99; Am. general/statesman)
Wellington, 1st Duke of, "the Iron Duke", (Arthur Wellesley; 1769–1852; Brit. soldier/statesman)
William the Conqueror (c. 1027–87; King of England)
Wolfe, James (1727–59; Brit. general)
Xenophon (c. 430–354 B.C.; Gk military leader/writer)
Xerxes I (5th century B.C.; King of Persia)
Yamamoto, Isoroku (1884–1943; Jap admiral)
Zapata, Emiliano (1879–1919; Mex. revolutionary)
Zhukov, Georgi (1896–1974; Soviet military leader)

mince verb **1** *finely minced beef* chop/cut into tiny pieces, grind, crumble, hash. **2** *she minces along, head in the air* walk affectedly, take tiny/baby steps, strike a pose, attitudinize, pose, posture, put on airs, be affected.

mincing adjective affected, pretentious, over-done, over-dainty, effeminate, niminy-piminy, foppish, precious; *inf.* sissy, la-di-da.

mind noun **1** *be all in the mind* brain, head, seat of intellect, psyche, ego, subconscious. **2** *have an active mind* brainpower, powers of thought, intellect, intellectual capabilities, mentality, intelligence, powers of reasoning, brain, brains, wits, understanding, comprehension, sense, ratiocination; *inf.* grey matter, brain-box. **3** *my mind was wandering* thoughts, thinking, concentration, attention, application, absorption. **4** *bring thoughts of him to mind* memory, recollection, remembrance. **5** *be of the same mind* opinion, way of thinking, thoughts, outlook, view, viewpoint, point of view, belief, judgement, attitude, feeling, sentiment. **6** *have a mind to go home* inclination, desire, wish, urge, will, notion, fancy, intention, intent, aim, purpose, design. **7** *of unsound mind* mental balance, sanity, senses, ~its, reason, reasoning, judgement. **8** *one of ~e great minds* genius, intellect, intellectual, ~hinker; *inf.* brain, egghead. **be in two minds** ~e undecided, be uncertain, be unsure, be hesi-~ant, hesitate, waver, vacillate, dither, shilly-shally; be on the horns of a dilemma. **bear/keep in mind** remember, be mindful of, do not forget, take into consideration, consider, take cognizance of, take note of. **cross one's mind** occur to one, come to one, enter one's mind/head, come into one's consciousness. **keep in mind** *see* MIND *noun* bear in mind. **put in mind** remind, call up, conjure up, suggest. **to one's mind** in one's opinion, according to one's way of thinking, to one's way of thinking, from one's standpoint, in one's estimation, in one's judgement.
Opposites BODY; DISINCLINATION.

mind verb **1** *didn't seem to mind their rudeness/smoking* be offended by, take offence at, object to, care about, be bothered by, be upset by, be affronted by, resent, dislike, disapprove of, look askance at. **2** *mind what the teacher says* take heed of, heed, pay heed to, be heedful of, pay attention to, attend to, concentrate on, listen to, note, take notice of, mark, observe, have regard for, respect, obey, follow, comply with, adhere to. **3** *mind your own business* attend to, pay attention to, concentrate on, apply oneself to, have regard for. **4** *mind the step | mind you don't cut yourself* be careful of, be cautious of, beware of, be on one's guard for, be wary of, be watchful of, watch out for, look out for, keep one's eyes open for, take care. **5** *mind you go* make sure, be sure, ensure that, take care, take care that; remember to, be sure to. **6** *mind the house/shop/baby* look after, take care of, attend to, tend, have charge of, keep an eye on, watch. **mind out** be careful, be cautious, beware, be on one's guard, be wary, be watchful, watch out, look out, keep one's eyes open, take care. **never mind** *never mind about the cost* do not bother about, pay no attention to, do not worry about, disregard, forget, do not take into consideration, do not give a second thought to.

mindful adjective *mindful of her feelings* paying attention to, heedful of, watchful of, careful of, wary of, chary of, regardful of, taking into account, cognizant of, aware of, conscious of, alert to, alive to, sensible of.
Opposites HEEDLESS; OBLIVIOUS.

mindless adjective **1** *a mindless idiot* stupid, foolish, brainless, senseless, witless, empty-

AMERICAN MILITARY RANKS		
Army and Air Force	Captain	Rear Admiral
Chief of Staff	First Lieutenant	Captain
General	Second Lieutenant	Commander
Lieutenant General	**Navy**	Lieutenant Commander
Major General	Chief of Naval	Lieutenant
Brigadier General	Operations	Lieutenant junior
Colonel	Fleet Admiral	grade (j.g.)
Lieutenant Colonel	Admiral	Ensign
Major	Vice Admiral	Midshipman

BRITISH MILITARY RANKS		
Army	**Royal Navy**	**Royal Air Force**
Field Marshal	Admiral of the Fleet	Marshal of the Royal Air Force
General	Admiral	Air Chief Marshal
Lieutenant General	Vice Admiral	Air Marshal
Major General	Rear Admiral	Air Vice-Marshal
Brigadier	Commodore	Air Commodore
Colonel	Captain	Group Captain
Lieutenant Colonel	Commander	Wing Commander
Major	Lieutenant Commander	Squadron Leader
Captain	Lieutenant	Flight Lieutenant
Lieutenant	Sub lieutenant	Flying Officer
Second Lieutenant	Midshipman	Pilot Officer

headed, unintelligent, dull, slow-witted, obtuse, weak-minded, feather-brained; *inf.* birdbrained, dumb, dopey, moronic. **2** *mindless actions/violence* unthinking, thoughtless, careless, ill-advised, negligent, neglectful, brutish, barbarous, barbaric, gratuitous. **3** *mindless tasks* mechanical, automatic, routine.
Opposites INTELLIGENT; THOUGHTFUL; INTERESTING.

mine *noun* **1** *work in a mine* colliery, pit, excavation, well, quarry, lode, vein, deposit, coalmine, gold-mine, diamond-mine. **2** *the librarian/book is a mine of information* source, reservoir, quarry, repository, store, storehouse, abundant supply, wealth, mint; *inf.* goldmine. **3** *blown up by a mine* explosive, land-mine, depth charge. **4** *mines built under fortifications* tunnel, trench, sap.

mine *verb* **1** *mine coal* excavate, quarry for, dig for, dig up, extract, unearth. **2** *armies mining* lay mines. **3** *mine a fortification* dig a mine/tunnel/trench/sap under, undermine, weaken.

miner *noun* coalminer, collier, pitman, gold-miner.

mineral *noun. See table. See also table at* ROCK.

NECESSARY DIETARY MINERALS

calcium	chlorine
fluorine	chromium
iodine	copper
iron	manganese
magnesium	molybdenum
phosphorus	selenium
zinc	silicon
Trace Elements	sulphur
boron	vanadium

mingle *verb* **1** *mingle the water and wine* | *mingle the two colours* mix, blend, combine, compound, homogenize, merge, unite, join, amalgamate, fuse. **2** *the colours mingle* intermingle, mix, intermix, coalesce, blend, fuse, merge, unite, commingle. **3** *guests mingling at the party* circulate, socialize, hobnob, fraternize, associate with others, meet people.
Opposites SEPARATE; PART.

miniature *adjective* small-scale, scaled-down, mini, midget, baby, toy, pocket, dwarf, Lilliputian, reduced, diminished, small, tiny, wee, minute, minuscule, microscopic; *inf.* pint-sized.
Opposites GIANT; GIGANTIC; ENORMOUS.

minimal *adjective* minimum, least, least possible, smallest, littlest, slightest, nominal, token.
Opposites MAXIMUM; MOST.

minimize *verb* **1** *minimize the costs/work* keep at/to a minimum, reduce, decrease, curtail, cut back on, prune, slash. **2** *minimize the size* reduce, decrease, diminish, abbreviate, attenuate, shrink, miniaturize. **3** *minimize his achievement* belittle, make light of, decry, discount, play down, deprecate, depreciate, underestimate, underrate.
Opposites maximize; INCREASE; EXAGGERATE.

minimum *noun* *reduce to the minimum* lowest level, bottom level, bottom, depth, nadir, least, lowest, slightest.

minimum *adjective* *the minimum amount* minimal, lowest, smallest, littlest, least, least possible, slightest.
Opposites MAXIMUM; MOST.

minion *noun* **1** *the nobleman and his minions* lackey, flunkey, henchman, creature, toady, sycophant, flatterer, fawner, lickspittle, underling, hireling, servant, dependant, hanger-on, parasite, leech; *inf.* yes-man, bootlicker. **2** *the queen's minion* favourite, pet, darling, jewel, apple of one's eye.

minister *noun* **1** *government ministers* cabinet member, secretary, department chief. **2** *ministers saying prayers* minister of religion, clergyman, cleric, ecclesiastic, churchman, preacher, padre. *See table at* ECCLESIASTIC. **3** *the British minister in Egypt* ambassador, diplomat, consul, plenipotentiary, envoy, emissary, legate, delegate, representative, chargé d'affaires, chargé.

minister *verb* *minister to the patient* | *he ministered to their needs* administer to, attend to, tend, look after, take care of, see to, cater to, serve, accommodate, be solicitous of, pander to.

ministration *noun* aid, help, assistance, succour, relief, support, backing, cooperation, service.

ministry *noun* **1** *work for the ministry* government, cabinet, administration. **2** *go in for the ministry* the Church, the priesthood, holy orders, the pulpit. **3** *the ministry for foreign affairs* department, office, bureau.

minor *adjective* **1** *a minor poet* little-known, unknown, lesser, insignificant, unimportant, inconsequential, inferior, lightweight, subordinate. **2** *suffer minor discomfort* slight, small, insignificant, unimportant, inconsequential, trivial, negligible, trifling. **3** *Smith minor* junior, younger.
Opposites MAJOR; SIGNIFICANT; CONSIDERABLE.

minstrel *noun* musician, singer, bard, troubadour; *lit.* jongleur.

mint *noun* **1** *earn a mint* fortune, small fortune, vast sum of money, millions, king's ransom; *inf.* pile, stack, heap, packet, bundle, bomb. **2** *he is a mint of ideas* mine, source, reservoir, storehouse, wealth, gold-mine. *See* MINE *noun* 2.

mint *adjective* *in mint condition* brand-new, as new, unused, perfect, unblemished, undamaged, unmarred, untarnished, fresh, first-class; *inf.* spanking new.

mint *verb* **1** *mint coins* stamp, stamp out, punch, die, cast, strike, coin, monetize, make, manufacture, produce. **2** *mint new words* coin, invent, make up, fabricate, think up, dream up, hatch up, devise, fashion, forge, produce.

minute *noun* **1** *I'll only be a minute* | *please wait a minute* moment, short time, second, instant; *inf.* tick, jiffy. **2** *the minute he appeared* moment, instant, point, point in time, time, juncture, stage. **in a minute** in a short time, shortly, very soon, in a moment/second/trice/ flash, in an instant, in the twinkling of an eye;

inf. in a tick/jiffy, in two shakes, in two shakes of a lamb's tail. **up to the minute** up-to-date, ultra-modern, modern, fashionable, modish, stylish, in vogue, voguish, chic, in, all the rage; *inf.* bang up-to-date, trendy, with it, now.

minute *adjective* **1** *a minute creature* tiny, minuscule, microscopic, miniature, diminutive, Lilliputian, little, small; *inf.* knee-high to a grasshopper. **2** *a minute difference* infinitesimal, negligible, trifling, trivial, paltry, petty, insignificant, inconsequential, unimportant, slight, minimal. **3** *in minute detail* detailed, exhaustive, meticulous, punctilious, painstaking, close, strict, exact, precise, accurate. **Opposites** GIGANTIC; HUGE; SUPERFICIAL.

minutely *adverb minutely dissected/discussed* in detail, exhaustively, meticulously, punctiliously, painstakingly, closely; *inf.* with a fine tooth comb.

minutes *plural noun* record, proceedings, transactions, notes, transcript.

minutiae *plural noun* subtleties, niceties, finer points, particulars, minute detail, minor details, trivia, trifles, non-essentials.

miracle *noun* wonder, marvel, prodigy, phenomenon, act of thaumaturgy.

miraculous *adjective* **1** *Jesus performing miraculous feats* inexplicable, unaccountable, preternatural, superhuman, supernatural, fantastic, magical, thaumaturgic, phenomenal, prodigious, wonderful, wondrous, remarkable. **2** *it is miraculous that you have finished* amazing, astounding, remarkable, extraordinary, incredible, unbelievable; *inf.* fantastic.

mirage *noun* optical illusion, illusion, hallucination, phantasmagoria, phantasm.

mire *noun* **1** *stuck in a mire* marsh, marshland, bog, peatbog, swamp, swampland, morass, quagmire, quag, slough, fen, fenland, bayou. **2** *mire all over their shoes* mud, slime, dirt, filth; *inf.* muck. **in the mire** *in the mire over money* in difficulties, in trouble, having problems, in dire straits, in a mess; *inf.* in a fix/hole.

mire *verb* **1** *cars mired in the swamp* sink, sink down, bog down, stick in the mud. **2** *they are mired in financial problems* entangle, catch up, involve, bog down. **3** *children mired from playing outside* make muddy/dirty, cake with dirt/soil, begrime, besmirch.

mirror *noun* **1** *the mirror on the wall* looking-glass, glass, reflector, reflecting surface; cheval-glass, rear-view mirror, wing mirror. **2** *he is a mirror of his father* reflection, twin, double, exact likeness, image, replica, copy, clone, match; *inf.* spitting image, spit, dead ringer for.

mirror *verb children mirroring his actions/statements* reflect, imitate, emulate, simulate, copy, follow, mimic, echo, ape, parrot, impersonate.

mirth *noun* gaiety, merriment, high spirits, cheerfulness, cheeriness, hilarity, glee, laughter, jocularity, levity, buoyancy, blitheness, light-heartedness, joviality, joyousness, fun, enjoyment, amusement, pleasure, merry-making, jollity, festivity, revelry, frolics, sport.

mirthful *adjective* gay, high-spirited, cheerful, cheery, hilarious, gleeful, laughter-filled, jocular, buoyant, carefree, blithe, light-hearted, jovial, joyous, fun-filled, enjoyable, amusing, pleasurable, merry, jolly, festive, frolicsome, sportive, playful.
Opposites DEPRESSED; MISERABLE; DEJECTED.

misadventure *noun* **1** *lost it through misadventure* accident, misfortune, bad luck, ill fortune, ill luck, poor/hard luck, mischance. **2** *be involved in a misadventure* accident, mishap, setback, disaster, tragedy, calamity, catastrophe, contretemps, debacle.

misanthropist *noun* misanthrope, hater of mankind, recluse, hermit.

misapprehend *verb* misunderstand, be mistaken, misinterpret, misconstrue, misread, miscalculate, get the wrong idea, get it wrong, receive a false impression, be under a delusion, get the wrong end of the stick, be barking up the wrong tree.

misapprehension *noun* misunderstanding, mistake, error, mix-up, misinterpretation, misconstruction, misreading, misjudgement, misconception, misbelief, miscalculation, the wrong idea, a false impression, delusion.

misappropriate *verb* **1** *misappropriate the firm's money* embezzle, steal, thieve, swindle, pocket, peculate, help oneself to; *inf.* nick, pinch, lift. **2** *misappropriate the tools* misuse, misapply, misemploy, put to a wrong use.

misbegotten *adjective* **1** *the king's misbegotten child* illegitimate, bastard, natural, born out of wedlock, born on the wrong side of the blanket. **2** *a misbegotten scoundrel* contemptible, disreputable, dishonourable, dishonest, base, wretched. **3** *their misbegotten plans* abortive, ill-conceived, ill-advised, ill-made, badly planned, badly thought-out, hare-brained.

misbehave *verb* behave badly, be bad, be naughty, be disobedient, be up to mischief, misconduct oneself, be guilty of misconduct, be bad-mannered, show bad/poor manners, be rude, fool around; *inf.* carry on, act up.

misbehaviour *noun* misconduct, bad behaviour, disorderly conduct, badness, naughtiness, disobedience, mischief, mischievousness, delinquency, misdeed, misdemeanour, bad/poor manners, rudeness, fooling around; *inf.* carrying on, acting up, shenanigans.

misbelief *noun* **1** *religious misbelief* false belief, unorthodoxy, heresy. **2** *guilty of misbelief* wrong belief, delusion, illusion, fallacy, error, mistake, misconception, misapprehension.

miscalculate *verb the answer is wrong—you have miscalculated* calculate wrongly, make a mistake, go wrong, err, blunder, be wide of the mark; *inf.* slip up, make a booboo, boob.

miscarriage *noun* **1** *the woman had a miscarriage* spontaneous abortion. **2** *the miscarriage of our plans* unsuccessfulness, failure, aborting, foundering, ruination, non-fulfilment, misfiring. *See* MISCARRY 2. **3** *miscarriage of justice* failure, breakdown, mismanagement, perversion, thwarting, frustration.

miscarry verb **1** *the woman miscarried* have a miscarriage, abort, have a spontaneous abortion, lose the baby. **2** *our plan miscarried* go wrong, go awry, go amiss, be unsuccessful, fail, misfire, abort, be abortive, founder, come to nothing, come to grief, meet with disaster, fall through, be ruined, fall flat; *inf.* bite the dust, go up in smoke, go phut.

miscellaneous adjective varied, assorted, mixed, diverse, sundry, variegated, diversified, motley, multifarious, jumbled, confused, indiscriminate, heterogeneous, farraginous.

miscellany noun assortment, mixture, *mélange*, variety, collection, motley collection, medley, pot-pourri, conglomeration, jumble, confusion, mix, mishmash, hotchpotch, hodgepodge, pastiche, patchwork, farrago, gallimaufry, olio, salmagundi, mixed bag; *inf.* omnium gatherum.

mischance noun **1** *we lost it by mischance* accident, misfortune, bad luck, ill fortune, ill luck, poor luck, misadventure. **2** *a life full of mischances* misfortune, mishap, misadventure, setback, failure, disaster, tragedy, calamity, catastrophe, contretemps, debacle.

mischief noun **1** *children getting up to mischief* mischievousness, naughtiness, badness, bad behaviour, misbehaviour, misconduct, pranks, wrongdoing, delinquency; *inf.* monkey tricks, monkey business, shenanigans, goings-on. **2** *with mischief in her eyes* impishness, roguishness, rascality, devilment. **3** *do mischief to them | did mischief to their property* harm, hurt, injury, impairment, damage, detriment, disruption, trouble.

mischievous adjective **1** *mischievous child* full of mischief, naughty, bad, badly behaved, misbehaving, disobedient, troublesome, vexatious, playful, frolicsome, rascally, roguish, delinquent. **2** *a mischievous smile* playful, teasing, impish, roguish, waggish, arch. **3** *mischievous gossip* malicious, spiteful, malignant, vicious, wicked, evil. **4** *with mischievous intent* hurtful, harmful, injurious, damaging, detrimental, deleterious, destructive, pernicious. **Opposites** GOOD; well-behaved; HARMLESS.

misconception noun misapprehension, misunderstanding, mistake, error, misinterpretation, the wrong idea, a false impression, delusion. *See* MISAPPREHENSION.

misconduct noun **1** *children guilty of misconduct* misbehaviour, bad behaviour, disorderly conduct, badness, mischief, naughtiness, misdeed, misdemeanour, wrongdoing, delinquency, rudeness. *See* MISBEHAVIOUR. **2** *doctors guilty of misconduct* professional misconduct, unprofessional behaviour, unethical behaviour, malpractice, impropriety, immorality. **3** *the misconduct of the affair* mismanagement, mishandling, misgovernment, misdirection.

misconstrue verb misinterpret, put a wrong interpretation on, misunderstand, misapprehend, misread, misjudge, get it wrong, get the wrong idea, receive a false impression, take the wrong way, get the wrong end of the stick.

miscreant noun villain, wrongdoer, criminal, evildoer, sinner, scoundrel, wretch, reprobate, blackguard, rogue, rascal.

misdeed noun wrongdoing, evil deed, crime, criminal act, misdemeanour, offence, error, peccadillo, transgression, sin.

misdemeanour noun misdeed, wrongdoing, crime, offence, error, transgression. *See* MISDEED.

miser noun skinflint, penny-pincher, niggard, cheese-parer, Scrooge; *inf.* money-grubber, cheapskate, tightwad. **Opposites** SPENDTHRIFT; PHILANTHROPIST.

miserable adjective **1** *feeling miserable* unhappy, sorrowful, dejected, depressed, downcast, down-hearted, down, despondent, disconsolate, desolate, wretched, glum, gloomy, dismal, blue, melancholy, low-spirited, mournful, woeful, woebegone, sad, doleful, forlorn, crestfallen; *inf.* down in the mouth, down in the dumps. **2** *a miserable hovel* wretched, mean, poor, shabby, squalid, filthy, foul, sordid, seedy, dilapidated. **3** *miserable wretches* poverty-stricken, needy, penniless, impoverished, beggarly, destitute, indigent, down at heel, out at elbow. **4** *miserable scoundrels* contemptible, despicable, base, mean, low, vile, sordid, scurvy. **5** *miserable salaries/supplies* meagre, paltry, scanty, low, poor, niggardly, pathetic. **6** *miserable weather/ conditions* unpleasant, disagreeable, displeasing, uncomfortable, wet, rainy, stormy. **Opposites** HAPPY; CHEERFUL; LUXURIOUS; RESPECTABLE.

miserly adjective mean, niggardly, parsimonious, tight-fisted, close-fisted, penny-pinching, cheese-paring, penurious, grasping, greedy, avaricious, ungenerous, illiberal, close, near; *inf.* stingy, mingy, tight, money-grabbing; *Am.* cheap. **Opposites** GENEROUS; LAVISH; EXTRAVAGANT; SPEND-THRIFT.

misery noun **1** *suffer/undergo misery* distress, wretchedness, hardship, suffering, affliction, anguish, torment, torture, agony, pain, discomfort, deprivation, poverty, grief, sorrow, heartbreak, heart-brokenness, despair, depression, dejection, desolation, gloom, melancholy, woe, sadness, unhappiness. **2** *endure untold miseries* trouble, misfortune, adversity, affliction, ordeal, pain, sorrow, burden, load, blow, trial, tribulation woe, torment, catastrophe, calamity, disaster. **3** *he's a real old misery* killjoy, spoilsport, pessimist, prophet of doom, complainer, moaner; *inf.* sourpuss, grouch, wet blanket, doom-merchant. **Opposites** COMFORT; PLEASURE; JOY.

misfire verb miscarry, go wrong, go awry, go amiss, fail, fall through; *inf.* bite the dust, go up in smoke, go phut. *See* MISCARRY 2.

misfit noun fish out of water, square peg in a round hole, nonconformist, eccentric, maverick; *inf.* oddball, weirdo.

misfortune noun **1** *by misfortune we got lost* bad luck, ill luck, ill fortune, poor/hard luck, accident, misadventure, mischance. **2** *endure many misfortunes* trouble, setback, reverse, adversity, reverse of fortune, misadventure, mishap, stroke of bad luck, blow, failure, accident, disaster, tragedy, affliction, sorrow, misery, woe, trial, tribulation, catastrophe, calamity.

misgiving noun qualm, doubt, reservation, second thoughts, suspicion, distrust, anxiety, apprehension, unease, uncertainty, hesitation.

misguided adjective **1** their action was misguided mistaken, deluded, erroneous, fallacious, wrong, unwarranted, uncalled-for, misplaced, ill-advised, unwise, injudicious, imprudent, foolish. **2** misguided people believed him misled, misdirected, misinformed, labouring under a delusion/misapprehension, deluded, ill-advised, foolish.

mishandle verb **1** mishandle the project mismanage, misdirect, misgovern, misconduct, maladminister, bungle, botch, muff, make a mess of; inf. make a hash of, make a pig's ear of, foul up, screw up. **2** mishandle the prisoners handle roughly, treat roughly, mistreat, maltreat, manhandle; inf. rough up. See MALTREAT.

mishap noun **1** without further mishap misfortune, ill luck, ill fortune, bad luck, poor/hard luck, accident, misadventure, mischance. **2** after a series of mishaps accident, trouble, setback, reverse, adversity, misadventure, misfortune, stroke of bad luck, blow, disaster, trial, tribulation, catastrophe, calamity.

mishmash noun hotchpotch, hodgepodge, jumble, scramble, tangle, confusion, miscellany, mixture, medley, assortment, mélange, variety, collection, pot-pourri, pastiche, farrago, gallimaufry, olio, salmagundi, mixed bag; inf. omnium gatherum.

misinform verb give someone wrong information, mislead, misdirect, misguide, put on the wrong track; inf. give someone a bum steer.

misinterpret verb put a wrong interpretation on, misconstrue, misunderstand, misapprehend, misread, get something wrong, inf. get the wrong end of the stick. See MISCONSTRUE.

misjudge verb have a wrong opinion about, be wrong about, get the wrong idea about, get the wrong end of the stick about.

mislay verb lose, misplace, put in the wrong place, lose track of, miss, be unable to find, be unable to lay one's hands on, forget the whereabouts of, forget where one has put something.
Opposites FIND; LOCATE.

mislead verb misinform, misguide, misdirect, delude, take in, deceive, fool, hoodwink, lead astray, throw off the scent, send on a wild-goose chase, pull the wool over someone's eyes; inf. lead up the garden path, take for a ride.

misleading adjective confusing, deceptive, deceiving, delusive, evasive, equivocal, ambiguous, fallacious, spurious, illusory, casuistic, sophistical.

mismanage verb misdirect, mishandle, misgovern, misconduct, maladminister, bungle, botch, muff, make a mess of; inf. make a hash

of, make a pig's ear of, mess up, foul up, screw up.

misogynist noun woman-hater, anti-feminist, male chauvinist, chauvinist; inf. male chauvinist pig, MCP.

misplace verb put in the wrong place, mislay, lose, be unable to find, be unable to lay one's hands on. See MISLAY.

misprint noun printing error, typographical error, typing error, mistake, literal, corrigendum, erratum; inf. typo.

misquote verb misquoted the president/speech/figures misstate, misreport, misrepresent, distort, twist, falsify, garble, muddle.

misrepresent verb give a false account of, give a false idea of, misstate, misreport, misquote, misinterpret, falsify, distort, garble.

misrule noun **1** accuse the government of misrule bad government, misgovernment, mismanagement, misdirection, maladministration, negligence. **2** misrule descended on the country lawlessness, disorder, chaos, anarchy.

miss[1] verb **1** miss a shot let go, bungle, botch, muff, fail to achieve. **2** miss the bus fail to catch/get, be too late for. **3** miss the meeting fail to attend, be too late for, absent oneself from, be absent from, play truant from, take French leave from; inf. skip. **4** miss an opportunity fail to seize/grasp, let slip, let go, pass up, overlook, disregard. **5** I'm sorry, I missed what you said fail to hear/catch, fail to take in, mishear, misunderstand. **6** did they miss their father regret the absence/loss of, feel the loss of, feel nostalgic for, long to see, long for, pine for, yearn for, ache for. **7** we did not miss the children until darkness fell notice the absence of, find missing. **8** try to miss the traffic avoid, evade, escape, dodge, sidestep, steer clear of, give a wide berth to.
Opposites CATCH; GET; ATTEND.

miss[2] noun one hit and three misses failure, omission, slip, blunder, error, mistake, fiasco; inf. flop.

miss[3] noun girl, schoolgirl, young lady, lass, maiden, maid, damsel.

misshapen adjective out of shape, deformed, malformed, ill-proportioned, misproportioned, twisted, distorted, contorted, warped, curved, crooked, wry, bent, hunch-backed.

missile noun projectile, weapon for throwing. See table. See also table at WEAPON.

missing adjective lost, mislaid, misplaced, nowhere to be found, absent, not present, gone, gone astray, unaccounted for.

mission noun **1** accomplish his mission assignment, commission, task, job, errand, work, chore, business, undertaking, operation, duty, charge, trust, goal, aim, purpose. **2** her mission in life is to heal the sick vocation, calling, pursuit, quest, undertaking. **3** a trade mission delegation, deputation, task force, legation.

missionary noun evangelist, converter, apostle, proselytizer, preacher, minister, priest.

missive noun communication, message, letter, note, memorandum, bulletin, communiqué, report, dispatch; inf. memo.

505   misspent · mix

misspent *adjective* dissipated, wasted, squandered, thrown away, prodigal.

mist *noun* haze, fog, smog, cloud, vapour, condensation, steam, film; *dial.* haar; *inf.* pea-souper.

mist *verb* **mist over, mist up** become cloudy, cloud, cloud over, become hazy, haze over, become foggy, fog over, fog up, become blurred; steam up.

mistake *noun* error, fault, inaccuracy, slip, blunder, miscalculation, misunderstanding, oversight, gaffe, *faux pas*, solecism, misapprehension, misreading; *inf.* slip-up, bloomer, boob, booboo, howler, clanger.

mistake *verb* **1** *mistake his meaning* get wrong, misunderstand, misapprehend, misinterpret, misconstrue, misread. **2** *mistake him for his brother* take someone for, mix someone up with, confuse someone with, misinterpret something as. **be mistaken** *you are mistaken* be wrong, be in error, be at fault, be under a misapprehension, be misinformed, be misguided, be wide of the mark, be barking up the wrong tree, get the wrong end of the stick.

mistaken *adjective* *mistaken impressions/idea* wrong, erroneous, inaccurate, incorrect, false, fallacious, unsound, unfounded, misguided, misinformed, wide of the mark.
Opposites CORRECT; RIGHT; ACCURATE.

mistakenly *adverb* by mistake, wrongly, in error, erroneously, incorrectly, falsely, fallaciously, misguidedly.

mistreat *verb* maltreat, treat badly, ill-treat, ill-use, misuse, abuse, mishandle, harm, hurt, molest; *inf.* beat up, rough up. See MALTREAT.

mistress *noun* lover, live-in lover, girlfriend, partner, lady-love, paramour, kept women, concubine, inamorata.

mistrust *verb* **1** *mistrust him | I mistrust his motives* feel mistrustful of, distrust, feel distrustful of, have doubts about, be suspicious of, suspect, have reservations about, have misgivings about, be wary of. **2** *mistrust his ability* have no confidence in, question, doubt, lack faith in.

mistrustful *adjective* distrustful, doubtful, dubious, suspicious, chary, wary, uncertain, cautious, hesitant, sceptical; *inf.* leery.

misty *adjective* **1** *misty weather* hazy, foggy, cloudy. **2** *a misty shape* hazy, blurred, fuzzy, dim, indistinct, vague. **3** *a misty idea of what it is like* hazy, vague, obscure, nebulous.
Opposites CLEAR; DISTINCT.

misunderstand *verb* misapprehend, misinterpret, misconstrue, misread, get the wrong idea, receive a false impression, get the wrong end of the stick, be barking up the wrong tree. See MISUNDERSTANDING.

misunderstanding *noun* **1** *his misunderstanding of the statement* misapprehension, mistake, error, mix-up, misinterpretation, misconstruction, misreading, misconception, misbelief, the wrong idea, a false impression; *inf.* the wrong end of the stick. See MISAPPREHENSION. **2** *the friends have had a misunderstanding* disagreement, difference, difference of opinion, clash of views, dispute, quarrel, argument, tiff, squabble, conflict; *inf.* falling-out, spat, scrap.

misuse *verb* **1** *misuse their talents/money* put to wrong use, misapply, misemploy, abuse, squander, waste, dissipate. **2** *misuse the children* maltreat, mistreat, treat badly, ill-treat, ill-use, abuse, mishandle, manhandle, harm, hurt, bully, molest; *inf.* beat up, rough up. See MALTREAT.

misuse *noun* **1** *the misuse of their talents/money* wrong use, misapplication, misemployment, abuse, squandering, waste, dissipation. **2** *this misuse of the verb* misusage, malapropism, barbarism, catachresis. **3** *misuse of the children* maltreatment, mistreatment, ill-treatment, ill use, abuse, rough handling, mishandling, manhandling, bullying, injury, harm, molesting.

mitigate *verb* alleviate, reduce, diminish, lessen, weaken, attenuate, allay, assuage, palliate, appease, soothe, relieve, ease, soften, temper, mollify, lighten, still, quieten, quiet, tone down, moderate, modify, extenuate, calm, lull, pacify, placate, tranquillize.
Opposites AGGRAVATE; INCREASE; INTENSIFY.

mitigating *adjective* extenuating, exonerative, justificatory, justifying, vindicatory, vindicating, exculpatory, palliative, qualifying, modifying, tempering.

mix *verb* **1** *mix cement | mix the water and the wine* admix, blend, put together, combine,

---

MISSILES AND MISSILE WEAPONS

air-to-air missile	bullet	longbow	sling
anti-ballistic-missile	catapult	mangonel	spear
anti-missile missile	crossbow	Minuteman	star shell
anti-tank weapon	cruise missile	MIRV (multiple inde-	surface-to-air missile
arbalest	dart	pendently-targeted	surface-to-surface
arrow	Exocet™	re-entry vehicle)	missile
assegai	flare	mortar	throw-stick
ballista	fléchette	Patriot™	torpedo
ballistic missile	gas shell	pellet	trebuchet
bazooka	guided missile	Polaris	Trident
blowpipe	gun	rocket	V-1
bolas	harpoon	Scud missile	V-2
bolt	intercontinental	shell	whiz-bang
boomerang	ballistic missile	shrapnel	woomera
bow	javelin	sidewinder	woomerang

mingle, compound, homogenize, alloy, merge, unite, join, amalgamate, fuse, coalesce, interweave. **2** *the two of them together just don't mix* be compatible, get along/on, be in harmony, be like-minded, be of the same mind; *inf.* be on the same wavelength. **3** *he doesn't mix* socialize, mingle, associate with others, meet people. **4** *she mixes with all sorts* associate, mingle, have dealings, fraternize, hobnob. **mix up 1** *mix up the medicine* mix, blend, combine. **2** *mix up the dates* confuse, get confused, muddle, muddle up, get muddled up, get jumbled up, scramble, mistake. **3** *hush or you'll mix me up* confuse, throw into confusion, muddle, muddle up, fluster, upset, disturb. **4** *he is mixed up in the crime* involve, implicate, entangle, embroil, draw into, incriminate.
Opposites SEPARATE; DIVIDE.

mix *noun* mixture, blend, combination, compound, alloy, merger, union, amalgamation, fusion, coalition.

mixed *adjective* **1** *a mixed collection* assorted, varied, miscellaneous, diverse, diversified, motley, heterogeneous. **2** *of mixed breed* hybrid, cross-bred, interbred, mongrel. **3** *have mixed reactions* ambivalent, equivocal, unsure, uncertain.

mixed-up *adjective* *a mixed-up kid* maladjusted, ill-adjusted, disturbed, confused, muddled; *inf.* screwed-up, untogether.

mixer *noun* **1** *put it in the mixer* blender, food processor, liquidizer. **2** *she's shy but he's a mixer* socializer, mingler, social butterfly; *inf.* life and soul of the party, party person. **3** *the host had to buy more mixers* drink for mixing, drink for cocktails. *See table.*

mixture *noun* **1** *pour out the mixture* compound, blend, mix, brew, combination, concoction, alloy. **2** *a mixture of objects* assortment, variety, *mélange*, collection, motley collection, medley, pot-pourri, conglomeration, jumble, mix, mishmash, hotchpotch, pastiche, farrago, mixed bag. *See* MISCELLANY. **3** *the dog is a mixture* cross, cross-breed, mongrel, hybrid.

mix-up *noun* confusion, muddle, jumble, misunderstanding, mistake.

moan *noun* **1** *the moans of the injured man* groan, lament, lamentation, wail, whimper,

whine. **2** *the moan of the wind* groan, sigh, sough, murmur, whisper. **3** *tired of his moans* moans and groans, complaint, complaining, whine, whining, carping; *inf.* grouse, grousing, gripe, griping, grouch, grouching, whinge, whingeing. beef, beefing.

moan *verb* **1** *the injured man moans* groan, wail, whimper, whine. **2** *the wind moaning* groan, sigh, sough, murmur, whisper. **3** *always moaning about the weather* complain, whine, carp; *inf.* grouse, gripe, grouch, whinge, beef.

mob *noun* **1** *police tried to move the mob of spectators on* crowd, horde, multitude, rabble, mass, body, throng, host, pack, press, gang, drove, herd, flock, gathering, assemblage. **2** *despising the mob* the common people, the masses, the populace, the multitude, the commonality, the proletariat, the crowd, the rabble, the *hoi polloi*, the *canaille*; *inf.* the great unwashed. **3** *those gatecrashers left but another mob arrived* lot, group, set, troop, company; *inf.* gang.

mob *verb* **1** *mob the royal car | fans mobbed the football team* crowd around, swarm around, surround, besiege, jostle. **2** *mob the theatre* crowd into, cram full, fill to overflowing, fill, pack, throng. **3** *prisoners mobbing the murderer* set upon, attack, harass, fall upon, assault.

mobile *adjective* **1** *the patient is mobile* able to move, able to move around, moving, walking, motile, ambulatory. **2** *a mobile face* expressive, animated, ever-changing, changeable. **3** *mobile shops | set up a mobile missile launcher* movable, transportable, portable, travelling, peripatetic, locomotive. **4** *socially mobile* moving, on the move, flexible, adaptable, adjustable.
Opposites IMMOBILE; EXPRESSIONLESS; STATIONARY.

mobilize *verb* **1** *mobilize the troops* call up, call to arms, muster, marshal, rally, assemble, organize, make ready, prepare, ready. **2** *mobilize for action* get ready, prepare, ready oneself.

mock *verb* **1** *rich children mocking the peasants* ridicule, jeer at, sneer at, deride, treat with contempt, treat contemptuously, scorn, make fun of, poke fun at, laugh at, laugh to scorn, tease, taunt, twit, chaff, gibe at, insult, flout; *inf.* rag, kid, rib, take the mickey out of. **2** *children mocking the crippled woman | they mocked*

MIXED DRINKS AND MIXERS

Angostura Bitters	gin and tonic	pink gin	snowball
bitter lemon	gin sling	pink lady	soda
black velvet	glögg	prairie oyster	spritzer
Bloody Mary	Harvey wallbanger	punch	St Clements
brandy Alexander	highball	rattlesnake	swizzle
brandy and soda	John Collins	red-eye	Tabasco™
Bronx	Kir	Rob Roy	tequila sunrise
Buck's Fizz	Manhattan	rum and black	Tom-and-Jerry
champagne cocktail	margarita	sangria	Tom Collins
cobbler	martini	Sazarac	tonic
daiquiri	mimosa	screwdriver	vodka and tonic
dry ginger	mint julep	sea breeze	whisky and soda
Gibson	Moscow mule	Shirley Temple	whisky mac
gimlet	old-fashioned	side-car	whisky sour
gin and it	Pimm's™	Singapore sling	White Lady
	pina colada	snake-bite	Worcester sauce

their teacher's mannerisms imitate, mimic, parody, ape, caricature, satirize, lampoon, burlesque; *inf.* take off, send up. **3** *the wind mocked their attempts to proceed* defy, set at naught, thwart, frustrate, foil, disappoint.

mock *adjective mock leather/money* imitation, artificial, simulated, synthetic, ersatz, so-called, fake, sham, false, spurious, bogus, counterfeit, forged, pseudo, pretended; *inf.* pretend.

mockery *noun* **1** *a note of mockery in his voice* ridicule, jeering, sneer, derision, contempt, scorn, disdain, teasing, taunting, gibe, insult, contumely; *inf.* ribbing. **2** *the trial was a mockery* laughing-stock, farce, parody, travesty, caricature, lampoon, burlesque; *inf.* take-off, send-up, spoof. **3** *his attempt to run was a mockery* travesty, inanity, act of stupidity, futile act, joke, laugh, apology, poor specimen.

mocking *adjective a mocking smile* sneering, derisive, derisory, contemptuous, scornful, disdainful, sardonic, insulting, satirical.

mocks *plural noun* mock examinations/exams, trial examinations/exams, preliminary exams; *inf.* prelims.

model *noun* **1** *a model of a train* replica, representation, mock-up, copy, dummy, imitation, facsimile, image. **2** *this is the model of the projected sculpture/building* prototype, protoplast, archetype, type, mould, original, pattern, design, paradigm, sample, example, exemplar. **3** *this is the model of car I want* style, design, mode, form, mark, version, type, variety, kind, sort. **4** *she was a model as a teacher/a model of tact* ideal, paragon, perfect example, perfect specimen, exemplar, the epitome of something, *beau idéal*, nonpareil, acme, *crème de la crème*; *inf.* pick of the bunch. **5** *he used his wife as a model* artist's model, photographic model, sitter, poser, subject. **6** *she is a model in Paris* fashion model, mannequin; *inf.* clothes-horse. **7** *this dress is a model* original design, original.

model *adjective* **1** *the model building* prototypical, prototypal, archetypal, illustrative. **2** *a model teacher* ideal, perfect. *See* MODEL *noun* 4. **Opposites** DEFICIENT; IMPERFECT.

moderate *adjective* **1** *moderate views* non-extreme, middle-of-the-road, non-radical, non-reactionary. **2** *moderate demands* non-excessive, reasonable, within reason, within due limits, fair, just. **3** *moderate behaviour* not given to excesses, restrained, controlled, temperate, sober, steady. **4** *moderate winds* temperate, calm, equable, mild. **5** *moderate work/success* average, middle-of-the-road, middling, ordinary, fair, fairish, modest, tolerable, passable, adequate, indifferent, mediocre, run-of-the-mill; *inf.* so-so, fair-to-middling. **6** *moderate amount/prices* reasonable, within reason, acceptable, average, fair, fairish, modest, lowish. **Opposites** IMMODERATE; EXTREME; UNREASONABLE.

moderate *verb* **1** *the wind has moderated* die down, abate, let up, calm down, lessen, decrease, diminish, slacken. **2** *moderate the force/pain* lessen, decrease, diminish, mitigate, alleviate, allay, appease, assuage, ease, palliate, soothe, soften, calm, modulate, pacify. **3** *moderate his anger* curb, check, keep in check, keep in control, temper, regulate, restrain, subdue, repress, tame. **4** *moderating the assembly* arbitrate, mediate, referee, judge, chair, take the chair of, preside over.

moderately *adverb* **1** *moderately expensive* quite, rather, somewhat, fairly, reasonably, to a certain degree, to some extent, within reason, within limits. **2** *the work is moderately good/she did moderately well in the test* fairly, tolerably, passably.

moderation *noun* **1** *the moderation of their behaviour/moderation in all things* moderateness, restraint, self-restraint, control, self-control, temperateness, temperance, non-indulgence. *See* MODERATE *adjective* 1-5. **2** *the moderation of the force/pain* lessening, decrease, mitigation, allaying, appeasement, assuagement, soothing, calming, modulation, pacification. *See* MODERATE *verb* 1-3. **3** *the moderation of the assembly* arbitration, mediation, refereeing, chairing, presiding over. *See* MODERATE *verb* 4. **in moderation** moderately, within reason, within due limits.

modern *adjective* **1** *in modern times* contemporary, present-day, present-time, present, current, twentieth-century, existing, existent. **2** *her clothes/ideas are very modern* up-to-date, up-to-the-minute, fashionable, in fashion, in, in style, in vogue, voguish, modish, the latest, new, newfangled, fresh, modernistic, ultra-modern, advanced, progressive; *inf.* trendy, with-it. **Opposites** PAST; OUT OF DATE; OLD-FASHIONED.

modernize *verb* **1** *modernize the methods/machinery* make modern, update, bring up to date, bring into the twentieth century, renovate, remodel, remake, redo, refresh, revamp, rejuvenate; *inf.* do over. **2** *the industry must modernize* get up to date, move with the times; *inf.* get in the swim, drag oneself into the twentieth century, get on the ball, get with it.

modest *adjective* **1** *he was modest about his achievements* self-effacing, self-deprecating, humble, unpretentious, unassuming, free from vanity, keeping one's light under a bushel. **2** *children too modest to speak* shy, bashful, self-conscious, diffident, reserved, retiring, reticent, quiet, coy, embarrassed, blushing, timid, fearful, meek. **3** *modest behaviour/clothes* decorous, decent, seemly, demure, proper, discreet, delicate, chaste, virtuous. **4** *modest demands/improvement* moderate, fair, tolerable, passable, adequate, satisfactory, acceptable, unexceptional, small, limited. **5** *a modest gift/house* unpretentious, simple, plain, humble, inexpensive, low-cost. **Opposites** BOASTFUL; CONCEITED; IMMODEST; EXPENSIVE.

modesty *noun* **1** *admire his modesty* lack of vanity, humility, self-effacement, lack of pretension, unpretentiousness. *See* MODEST 1. **2** *her modesty prevented her speaking* shyness, bashfulness, self-consciousness, reserve, reticence, timidity, meekness. *See* MODEST 2. **3** *modesty of her behaviour/clothes* decorum, decorousness, seemliness, demureness, propriety, chasteness.

See MODEST 3. **4** *the modesty of their demands* moderation, fairness, passableness, adequacy, satisfactoriness, acceptability, smallness. *See* MODEST 4. **5** *the modesty of the gift/house* lack of pretension, unpretentiousness, simplicity, plainness, inexpensiveness, lack of extravagance. *See* MODEST 5.

modicum *noun* small amount, little, little bit, bit, particle, iota, jot, atom, whit, grain, speck, scrap, crumb, fragment, shred, mite, dash, drop, dab, pinch, ounce, inch, touch, tinge, trifle; *inf.* teeny bit.

modification *noun* **1** *the modification of the punishment* lessening, reduction, decrease, abatement, mitigation, restriction. *See* MODIFY 1. **2** *the modification of the design* altering, alteration, adjusting, adjustment, adaptation, refashioning, refining, refinement. *See* MODIFY 2. **3** *the modifications made to the plans* alteration, change, adjustment, adaptation, variation, revision, refinement, transformation.

modify *verb* **1** *modify the punishment* lessen, reduce, decrease, diminish, lower, abate, soften, mitigate, restrict, limit, moderate, temper, blunt, dull, tone down, qualify. **2** *modify the design* alter, make alterations to, change, adjust, make adjustments to, adapt, vary, revise, recast, reform, reshape, refashion, rework, remould, redo, revamp, reorganize, refine, transform.

modulate *verb* **1** *modulate the proportions* regulate, adjust, moderate, temper. **2** *modulate one's voice* adjust/vary/adapt/modify the tone of.

mogul *noun* notable, VIP, magnate, tycoon, baron, captain, lord; *inf.* bigwig, big noise, big shot, big cheese, big gun, big wheel.

moist *adjective* **1** *moist weather* wet, wettish, damp, dampish, clammy, humid, dank, rainy, drizzly, drizzling, dewy, dripping, soggy. **2** *a moist cake* succulent, juicy, soft, spongy.

moisten *verb* make wet/wettish, wet, dampen, damp, water, soak, bedew, humidify, irrigate.

moisture *noun* water, liquid, wetness, wet, dampness, damp, humidity, dankness, wateriness, rain, dew, drizzle, perspiration, sweat.

moisturize *verb* *moisturize the skin* apply lotion/cream to, keep supple.

mole *noun* spot, blemish, mark, blotch, discoloration, freckle.

molecule *noun* *not a molecule of politeness* particle, iota, jot, atom, whit, grain, speck, scrap, crumb, shred, ounce, modicum. *See* MODICUM. *See table at* PARTICLE.

molest *verb* **1** *children molesting their mother* pester, annoy, nag, chivvy, plague, torment, harass, badger, harry, persecute, bother, worry, trouble, needle, provoke, vex, agitate, disturb, upset, fluster, ruffle, irritate, exasperate, tease; *inf.* bug, hassle. **2** *accused of molesting children* abuse, sexually abuse, interfere with, sexually assault, rape, ravish, assault, attack, injure, hurt, harm, mistreat, maltreat, ill-treat, manhandle.

mollify *verb* *mollify his mother* | *tried to mollify her anger* calm, calm down, pacify, placate, appease, soothe, still, quiet, tranquillize.

MOLLUSCS	
abalone	periwinkle
argonaut	piddock
bivalve	pteropod
cephalopod	quahog
chiton	ram's-horn snail
clam	round clam
cockle	scallop
cuttlefish	scaphopod
edible snail	sea butterfly
gaper	sea hare
gastropod	sea lemon
hard clam	sea slug
mussel	shipworm
nautilus	slug
nudibranch	snail
octopus	soft-shell clam
ormer	squid
oyster	swan mussel
paper nautilus	teredo
paua	whelk
pearly nautilus	winkle

mollusc *noun. See table.*

mollycoddle *verb* pamper, coddle, cosset, spoil, overindulge, indulge, baby, feather-bed, wait on hand and foot, nanny.

moment *noun* **1** *only lasted a moment* minute, short time, second, instant; *inf.* tick, jiffy. **2** *the very moment he came* minute, instant, point, point in time, time, juncture, stage. **3** *matters of no great moment* importance, import, significance, value, consequence, prominence, eminence, note, weight, mark, concern, interest, gravity, seriousness. **in a moment** in a short time, shortly, very soon, in a minute/second/trice/flash, in an instant, in the twinkling of an eye; *inf.* in a tick/jiffy, in two shakes, in two shakes of a lamb's tail.

momentarily *adverb* briefly, temporarily, just for a moment/second/instant/minute, for a short time.

momentary *adjective* brief, short, short-lived, fleeting, passing, transient, transitory, ephemeral, evanescent, fugitive, temporary, impermanent.
Opposites LENGTHY; PERMANENT.

momentous *adjective* crucial, critical, vital, decisive, pivotal, serious, grave, weighty, important, significant, consequential, of moment, of importance, of consequence, fateful, historic; *inf.* earth-shaking, earth-shattering.
Opposites UNIMPORTANT; TRIVIAL; INSIGNIFICANT.

momentum *noun* impetus, impulse, propulsion, thrust, push, driving-power, drive, power, energy, force.

monarch *noun* sovereign, ruler, crowned head, potentate, king, queen, emperor, empress. *See table at* ROYALTY.

monarchy *noun* **1** *abolish the monarchy* absolutism, absolute power, autocracy, monocracy, kingship, royalism, sovereignty, despotism. **2** *the country is a monarchy* kingdom, sovereign state, realm, principality, empire.

509

monastery *noun* religious house, religious community; friary, abbey, convent, nunnery, priory.

monastic *adjective* monastical, cloistered, cloistral, monachal, coenobitic, conventual, canonical, ascetic, celibate, contemplative, meditative, sequestered, secluded, withdrawn, reclusive, recluse, eremitic, hermit-like, anchoritic.

monetary *adjective* money, cash, financial, capital, pecuniary, fiscal, budgetary.

money *noun* **1** *not enough money to buy the business* cash, hard cash, ready money, finance, capital, funds, banknotes, currency, coin, coinage, silver, copper, legal tender, specie; *inf.* wherewithal, dough, lolly, bread, dosh, brass, loot, the necessary, the needful, the ready, readies, shekels, spondulicks, tin, dibs, gelt, mazuma, moolah, rhino, filthy lucre, pelf; *Am. inf.* the green stuff. *See table at* CURRENCY. **2** *he is a man of money* affluence, wealth, riches, prosperity. **in the money** moneyed, well-to-do, well-off, affluent, rich, wealthy, prosperous, in clover; *inf.* rolling in it, loaded, stinking rich, well-heeled, flush, made of money, on Easy Street.

moneyed *adjective* well-to-do, well-off, affluent, rich, wealthy, prosperous; *inf.* in the money, rolling in it, loaded, well-heeled. *See* MONEY, IN THE MONEY.

money-making *adjective* profitable, lucrative, gainful, paying, remunerative, successful, thriving, going.

mongrel *noun* *the dog is a mongrel* cross-breed, cross, half-breed, mixed breed, hybrid, cur.

mongrel *adjective* *a mongrel bitch* cross-bred, of mixed breed, hybrid.

monitor *noun* **1** *monitors watching shoppers/workers* detector, scanner, recorder, security system, security camera, observer, watchdog, overseer, supervisor, invigilator. **2** *elected class monitor* prefect, head girl/boy, head pupil.

monitor *verb* *monitor his movements/condition* observe, scan, record, survey, follow, keep an eye on, keep track of, check, oversee, supervise, invigilate.

monk *noun* brother, monastic, religious, friar, abbot, prior.

monkey *noun* **1** *monkeys in the jungle* primate, simian. *See table.* **2** *the child is a little monkey* rascal, scamp, imp, rogue, mischief-maker, devil. **make a monkey of** make a fool of, make someone look a fool, make someone look foolish, make a laughing-stock of, ridicule, deride, make fun of.

monkey *verb* **monkey about, monkey around** fool about/around, play about/around, potter about; *inf.* muck about, mess about. **monkey with** fiddle with, play with, tinker with, tamper with, interfere with, meddle with, fool with, trifle with, mess with.

monkey business *noun* **1** *children up to monkey business* mischief, naughtiness, pranks, clowning, skylarking; *inf.* monkey tricks, carrying-on, shenanigans, goings-on. **2** *there's been some monkey business in the accounts department* dishonesty, trickery, misconduct, misdemeanour, chicanery, skulduggery; *inf.* funny business, hanky-panky.

monkey tricks *plural noun* mischief, pranks; *inf.* monkey business. *See* MONKEY BUSINESS 1.

monologue *noun* soliloquy, speech, address, lecture, oration, sermon.

monopolize *verb* **1** *monopolize the market* exercise a monopoly of, corner, control, take over, have sole rights in. **2** *monopolize the conversation* dominate, take over, not let anyone else take part in, not let anyone else get a word in edgeways. **3** *monopolize his wife* keep to oneself, take up all the attention of, not allow to associate with others.

monotonous *adjective* **1** *a monotonous job* unvarying, lacking/without variety, unchanging, repetitious, all the same, uniform, routine, humdrum, run-of-the-mill, commonplace, mechanical, uninteresting, unexciting, prosaic, wearisome, dull, boring, tedious, tiresome; *inf.* samey. **2** *a monotonous voice* flat, unvarying, toneless, uninflected, droning, soporific. *Opposites* VARIED; INTERESTING; EXCITING.

monotony *noun* **1** *the monotony of the job* lack of variety, lack of variation, repetition, repetitiveness, sameness, uniformity, routine, routineness, humdrumness, lack of interest, lack of excitement, prosaicness, wearisomeness, dullness, boredom, tedium, tiresomeness; *inf.* sameyness. **2** *the monotony of her voice* flatness, tonelessness, lack of inflection, drone.

monster *noun* **1** *frightened by the monster in the myth* fabulous creature, mythical creature, sea-monster. *See table.* **2** *the step-parents are monsters* fiend, beast, brute, barbarian, savage, villain, ogre, devil, demon. **3** *the foetus was a monster* monstrosity, miscreation, malformation, abortion, freak, freak of nature, mutant,

MONKEYS AND APES

baboon	grass monkey	mona monkey	saki
Barbary ape	green monkey	New World	siamang
bonobo	guenon	monkey	spider monkey
capuchin monkey	hanuman langur	night monkey	squirrel-monkey
chimpanzee	howler monkey	Old World	tamarin
colobus	langur	monkey	titi
diana monkey	leaf monkey	orang-utan	uakari
douroucouli	macaque	patas monkey	vervet
gelada	mandrill	proboscis	woolly monkey
gibbon	mangabey	monkey	woolly spider
gorilla	marmoset	rhesus monkey	monkey

MONSTERS AND DEMONS	
Abominable	harpy
Snowman	hippogriff
afreet	hobgoblin
basilisk	Hydra
behemoth	incubus
Bigfoot/Sasquatch	King Kong
bogey	kraken
bunyip	lamia
Caliban	leviathan
centaur	Lilith
Cerberus	Loch Ness monster
Charybdis	manticore
chimera	Medusa
cockatrice	Minotaur
dragon	orc
fire-drake	Ravana
Frankenstein's	Scylla
monster	sphinx
ghoul	succubus
gnome	taniwha
goblin	troll
Godzilla	vampire
golem	werewolf
Gorgon	wyvern
Grendel	yeti
griffin	zombie

teratism, *lusus naturae.* **4** *a monster of a man/ building* giant, mammoth, leviathan. *See table at* GIANT.

monster *adjective a monster lorry/tower* huge, enormous, massive, vast, immense, colossal, gigantic, monstrous, stupendous, prodigious, tremendous, giant, mammoth, gargantuan, titanic, Brobdingnagian; *inf.* jumbo, whopping, ginormous.

monstrosity *noun* **1** *a monstrosity of a building* enormity, horror, eyesore, carbuncle. **2** *the monstrosity of the attack* monstrousness, outrageousness, scandalousness, atrocity, heinousness, horror, hideousness, foulness, vileness, odiousness, viciousness, cruelty, savagery, brutishness, fiendishness, devilishness. *See* MONSTROUS 3. **3** *the foetus is a monstrosity* monster, miscreation, abortion, freak, mutant. *See* MONSTER *noun* 3.

monstrous *adjective* **1** *monstrous creatures being born* miscreated, malformed, unnatural, abnormal, grotesque, gruesome, repellent, freakish, mutant, teratoid. **2** *monstrous lorries* huge, enormous, massive, vast, immense, colossal, gigantic, tremendous, giant. *See* MONSTER *adjective*. **3** *it was a monstrous thing to do* outrageous, shocking, disgraceful, scandalous, atrocious, heinous, evil, abominable, terrible, horrible, dreadful, hideous, foul, vile, nasty, ghastly, odious, loathsome, intolerable, contemptible, despicable, vicious, cruel, savage, brutish, bestial, barbaric, inhuman, fiendish, devilish, diabolical, satanic.
Opposites NORMAL; TINY; ADMIRABLE.

month *noun. See table.*

monument *noun* **1** *build a monument to the dead soldiers* memorial, statue, shrine, reliquary, sepulchre, mausoleum, cairn, pillar, column, obelisk, dolmen, cromlech, megalith. **2** *place a monument on the grave* gravestone, headstone, tombstone. **3** *travel scholarships as a monument to his talent* memorial, commemoration, remembrance, reminder, testament, witness, token.

monumental *adjective* **1** *a monumental effort* great, huge, enormous, immense, vast, exceptional, extraordinary, tremendous, stupendous, prodigious, staggering. **2** *a monumental*

MONTHS OF THE YEAR		
Gregorian	Li Qui	**Islamic**
January	Chu Shu	Muharram
February	Bai Lu	Safar
March	Qui Fen	Rabi I
April	Han Lu	Rabi II
May	Shuang Jiang	Jumada I
June	Li Dong	Jumada II
July	Xiao Xue	Rajab
August	Da Xue	Shaban
September	Dong Zhi	Ramadan
October	Xiao Han	Shawwal
November	Da Han	Dhu al-Qadah
December	**Jewish**	Dhu al-Hijjah
Chinese Agricultural	Nisan	**French Revolutionary**
Li Chun	Iyyar	Vendemiaire (wine harvest)
Yu Shui	Sivan	Brumaire (fog)
Jing Zhe	Thammuz	Frimaire (frost)
Chun Fen	Ab	Nivose (snow)
Qing Ming	Elul	Pluviose (rain)
Gu Yu	Tishri	Ventose (wind)
Li Xia	Hesvan	Germinal (seed)
Xiao Man	Kislev	Floreal (flower)
Mang Zhong	Tebet	Prairial (meadow)
Xia Zhi	Sebat	Messidor (harvest)
Xiao Shu	Adar	Thermidor (heat)
Da Shu	First Adar (leap years only)	Fructidor (fruit)

error huge, enormous, terrible, colossal, egregious, catastrophic, staggering, unforgivable, indefensible; *inf.* whopping. **3** *a monumental work of art* massive, impressive, striking, remarkable, magnificent, awe-inspiring, marvellous, majestic, stupendous, prodigious, historic, epoch-making, classic, memorable, unforgettable, enduring, permanent, immortal. **4** *monumental tributes* commemorative, celebratory, in memory, recalling to mind.

mood *noun* **1** *in a happy mood* humour, temper, disposition, frame of mind, state of mind, spirit, tenor, vein. **2** *he's in a mood* bad mood, bad temper, fit of bad/ill temper, fit of irritability, fit of pique, low spirits, fit of melancholy, depression, sulk, the sulks, bout of moping, doldrums, blues; *inf.* the dumps. **in the mood for/to** *in the mood for dancing* | *in the mood to dance* feeling like, inclined to, disposed towards, minded to, interested in, keen on/to, eager to, having enthusiasm for, willing to.

moody *adjective* **1** *teenagers are often moody* temperamental, changeable, unpredictable, volatile, mercurial, unstable, unsteady, erratic, fitful, impulsive, capricious. **2** *don't say anything—he's moody today* in a mood, in a bad mood, bad-tempered, ill-tempered, ill-humoured, short-tempered, irritable, irascible, crabbed, crabby, cantankerous, cross, crotchety, crusty, testy, touchy, petulant, in a pique, sullen, sulky, moping, gloomy, glum, depressed, dejected, despondent, melancholic, doleful, lugubrious, introspective, in a huff, huffed, huffy; *inf.* down in the dumps, down in the mouth.
Opposites STABLE; AMIABLE; HAPPY.

moon *noun* satellite. *See table. See also table at* PLANET. **many moons ago** a long time ago, ages ago; *inf.* yonks ago. **once in a blue moon** hardly ever, almost never, rarely, very seldom. **over the moon** ecstatic, euphoric, elated, rapturous, thrilled, jubilant, overjoyed, transported, in seventh heaven; *inf.* on cloud nine.

moon *verb* languish, idle, mope, daydream, be in a reverie, be in a brown study; *inf.* mooch.

moor *noun* moorland, heath, grouse-moor, fell.

moor *verb* *moored the boat at the quayside* secure, fix firmly, fasten, make fast, tie up, lash, anchor, berth.

moot *adjective* *a moot point* debatable, open to debate, open to discussion, questionable, open to question, open, doubtful, disputable, arguable, contestable, controversial, unresolved, undecided.

moot *verb* *moot the question of money* broach, bring up, mention, introduce, put forward, propose, suggest, propound.

mop *noun* **1** *clean the floor with a kitchen mop* swab, squeegee, sponge. **2** *a mop of hair* shock, thatch, mane, tangle, mass, mat.

mop *verb* **1** *mop the floor* clean, wipe, wash, swab, sponge. **2** *mop one's face* wipe, clean, dry. **mop up 1** *mop up the spilt water* soak up, absorb, sponge, clean, wipe. **2** *mop up all the profits* absorb, use up, exhaust, consume, swallow up. **3** *mop up the last bits of work* finish off, make an end of, clear up, eliminate, dispatch.

LUNAR SEAS	
Lunar Sea	**Latin name**
Bay of Dew	Sinus Roris
Bay of Heats	Sinus Aestuum
Bay of Rainbows	Sinus Iridum
Border Sea	Mare Marginis
Central Bay	Sinus Medii
Eastern Sea	Mare Orientale
Foaming Sea	Mare Spumans
Humboldt's Sea	Mare Humboldtianum
Lake of Death	Lacus Mortis
Lake of Dreams	Lacus Somniorum
Marsh of Decay	Palus Putredinis
Marsh of Epidemics	Palus Epidemiarum
Marsh of Mists	Palus Nebularum
Marsh of Sleep	Palus Somnii
Ocean of Storms	Oceanus Procellarum
Sea of Clouds	Mare Nubium
Sea of Cold	Mare Frigoris
Sea of Crises	Mare Crisium
Sea of Fertility	Mare Fecunditatis
Sea of Humours	Mare Humorum
Sea of Ingenuity	Mare Ingenii
Sea of Knowledge	Mare Cognitum
Sea of Moscow	Mare Moscoviense
Sea of Nectar	Mare Nectaris
Sea of Rains	Mare Imbrium
Sea of Serenity	Mare Serenitatis
Sea of Tranquillity	Mare Tranquillitatis
Sea of Vapours	Mare Vaporum
Sea of Waves	Mare Undarum
Southern Sea	Mare Australe
Smyth's Sea	Mare Smythii

4 *mop up the enemy territory* complete the occupation of, take over, secure. **5** *mop up resisting soldiers* kill off, eliminate, dispose of, make away with.

mope *verb* **1** *she's moping because her friend's gone* be miserable, be sad, be despondent, pine, fret, grieve, brood, sulk. **2** *mope about the place* wander, idle, languish, droop, moon; *inf.* mooch.

moral *adjective* **1** *moral issues* ethical. **2** *a moral man/woman* ethical, good, virtuous, righteous, upright, upstanding, high-minded, principled, honourable, honest, just, decent, chaste, pure, blameless. **3** *moral act/behaviour* good, virtuous, honourable, right, proper, fit, decent, decorous. **4** *moral support* psychological, emotional, mental.
Opposites IMMORAL; BAD; DISHONOURABLE.

moral *noun* *the moral of the story* lesson, teaching, message, meaning, significance, point.

morale *noun* self-confidence, confidence, heart, spirit, hope, hopefulness, optimism, determination, zeal.

moral fibre *noun* strength of character, firmness of purpose, resolution, toughness of spirit.

morality *noun* **1** *the morality of abortion* ethics, rights and wrongs. **2** *a man/woman of morality* ethics, goodness, virtue, righteousness, rectitude, uprightness, integrity, principles, honour, honesty, justness, decency, chasteness, chastity, purity, blamelessness. **3** *discuss*

morality morals, moral code, moral standards, ethics, principles of right and wrong, standards/principles of behaviour.

morals *plural noun* ethics, moral code, principles of right and wrong, principles, moral behaviour/conduct, standards/principles of behaviour, standards, morality, sense of morality, scruples, mores.

morass *noun* **1** *in a morass of detail* confusion, muddle, tangle, entanglement, mix-up, jumble, clutter. **2** *get stuck in a morass* marsh, marshland, bog, peatbog, swamp, quagmire, slough, fen.

moratorium *noun* suspension, postponement, stay, halt, freeze, embargo, ban, standstill, respite.

morbid *adjective* **1** *morbid thoughts/details* gruesome, grisly, macabre, hideous, dreadful, horrible, unwholesome. **2** *a morbid person* death-orientated, death-obsessed, death-fixated. **3** *don't be so morbid* gloomy, glum, dejected, melancholy, lugubrious, pessimistic, given to looking on the black side. **4** *a morbid condition* diseased, infected, sickly, ailing. **5** *a morbid growth* malignant, deadly, pathological.

mordant *adjective* **1** *mordant wit/remarks* acid, caustic, trenchant, cutting, incisive, stinging, biting, acerbic, stringent, bitter, sarcastic, virulent, vitriolic, venomous, waspish. **2** *a mordant solution* acid, acidic, caustic, corrosive, vitriolic.

more *adjective* *require more space* additional, supplementary, further, added, extra, increased, spare, fresh, new.

more *adverb* *concentrate more* to a greater extent, further, longer, some more.

more *pronoun* *need more* additional amount/number, greater quantity/part, addition, supplement, extra, increase, incrementation.

moreover *adverb* besides, furthermore, further, more than that, what is more, in addition, also, as well, to boot.

morgue *noun* mortuary, charnel-house, funeral parlour; *Am.* funeral home.

moribund *adjective* **1** *moribund old men* dying, on one's deathbed, near death, near the end, breathing one's last, fading fast, failing rapidly, having one foot in the grave, on one's last legs, *in extremis*. **2** *moribund customs* dying, declining, on the decline, waning, on the way out, obsolescent, on its last legs.

morning *noun* forenoon, a.m., early part of the day, dawn, daybreak, sunrise; *lit.* morn.

moron *noun* *he's a complete moron* fool, dolt, dunce, dullard, blockhead, dunderhead, ignoramus, numskull, nincompoop; *inf.* idiot, imbecile, nitwit, halfwit, dope, dimwit, dummy; *Am. inf.* schmuck.

morose *adjective* sullen, gloomy, glum, sombre, sober, saturnine, lugubrious, mournful, depressed, dour, melancholy, melancholic, doleful, blue, down, low, moody, taciturn, pessimistic, sour, scowling, sulky, surly, churlish, crabbed, crabby, cross.
Opposites CHEERFUL; JOYFUL; MERRY.

morse code *noun. See table.*

MORSE CODE			
Letter	**Code**	**Letter**	**Code**
A	.−	O	−−−
B	−...		·· *Am.*
C	−.−.	P	.−−.
	··· *Am.*		···· *Am.*
D	−..	Q	−−.−
E	.		···−· *Am.*
F	..−.	R	.−.
	.−· *Am.*		··· *Am.*
G	−−.	S	...
H	....	T	−
I	..	U	..−
J	.−−−	V	...−
	−..−· *Am.*	W	.−−
K	−.−	X	−..−
L	.−..		···−· *Am.*
	— *Am.*	Y	−.−−
M	−−		··· *Am.*
N	−.	Z	−−..
			···· *Am.*

morsel *noun* mouthful, bite, nibble, bit, crumb, grain, particle, fragment, piece, scrap, segment, soupçon, taste.

mortal *adjective* **1** *mortal beings | the mortal world* temporal, transient, ephemeral, passing, impermanent, perishable, human, earthly, worldly, corporeal, fleshly. **2** *a mortal blow* death-dealing, deadly, fatal, lethal, killing, murderous, terminal, destructive. **3** *mortal enemies* deadly, to the death, sworn, out-and-out, irreconcilable, bitter, implacable, unrelenting, remorseless. **4** *mortal pain/fear* terrible, awful, intense, extreme, severe, grave, dire, very great, great, unbearable, agonizing. **5** *of no mortal use* conceivable, imaginable, perceivable, possible.

mortal *noun* *mortals must die* human being, human, earthling, person, man/woman, being, body, individual.

mortality *noun* **1** *humans subject to mortality* temporality, transience, ephemerality, impermanence, perishability, humanity, earthliness, worldliness. *See* MORTAL *adjective* 1. **2** *appalled at the wartime mortality* bloodshed, death, loss of life, fatalities, killing, slaying, carnage, slaughter.

mortification *noun* **1** *their mortification at their failure* humiliation, disgrace, shame, dishonour, abasement, discomfiture, embarrassment. *See* MORTIFY 1. **2** *her mortification at their remarks* hurt, affront, offence, annoyance, displeasure, vexation, discomfiture, embarrassment. *See* MORTIFY 2. **3** *the mortification of the flesh* subduing, control, controlling, restraint, suppression, disciplining, chastening. **4** *the mortification of flesh* gangrene, festering, necrosis, putrefaction.

mortify *verb* **1** *they were mortified by their failure* humiliate, humble, cause to eat humble pie, bring low, disgrace, shame, dishonour, abash, fill with shame, put to shame, chasten, degrade, abase, deflate, crush, discomfit, embarrass, take down a peg or two. **2** *their remarks mortified her* hurt, wound, affront,

offend, annoy, displease, vex, embarrass.
3 *mortify the flesh | mortify such fleshly pleasures* subdue, get under control, control, restrain, suppress, discipline, chasten. **4** *flesh mortifying* become gangrenous, fester, necrose, putrefy.

mortuary *noun* morgue, charnel-house. *See* MORGUE.

most *noun* *most did not vote* majority, greatest number/quantity/part, nearly all, almost all, bulk, mass.
Opposites MINORITY.

mostly *adverb* **1** *they were mostly young* for the most part, on the whole, in the main, largely, mainly, chiefly, predominantly. **2** *mostly we eat at home* for the most part, usually, generally, in general, as a general rule, as a rule, ordinarily, normally, commonly.

mot *noun* **bon mot**, witticism, quip, pun, epigram, aphorism, maxim, saw, saying, proverb, adage, axiom.

moth *noun*. *See table at* BUTTERFLY.

mother *noun* female parent, materfamilias, matriarch, earth mother, foster mother, biological mother, birth mother, adoptive mother, surrogate mother; *inf.* mum, mummy, mumsy, ma, mam, mamma, mammy, mater, old lady; *Am. inf.* mom.

mother *adjective* inborn, innate, connate, native, natural.

mother *verb* **1** *mother the orphans* look after, care for, tend, raise, rear, foster, cherish, fuss over, indulge, spoil. **2** *she mothered twins | countries which have mothered geniuses* be the mother of, give birth to, bear, produce, bring forth.

motherly *adjective* maternal, protective, comforting, caring, loving, affectionate, fond, warm, tender, gentle, kind, kindly.

motion *noun* **1** *the motion made her sick | vehicles in motion* motility, mobility, locomotion, movement, moving, changing place/position, travel, travelling, going, progress, passing, passage, flow, action, activity, course. **2** *a motion with her hand* movement, gesture, gesticulation, signal, sign, wave, nod. **in motion** *trains in motion* moving, going, travelling, not at rest, on the move, under way. **set/put in motion** *set the process in motion* get going, get under way, get in operation, get working/functioning, start, begin, commence.

motion *verb* *motioned to me to step forward* gesture, gesticulate, signal, sign, wave, nod.

motionless *adjective* unmoving, still, stock-still, at a standstill, stationary, immobile, immovable, static, at rest, halted, stopped, paralysed, transfixed, frozen, inert, lifeless.
Opposites MOVING; MOBILE; ACTIVE.

motivate *verb* **1** *that motivated him to write* move, cause, lead, persuade, prompt, actuate, drive, impel, spur, induce, provoke, incite, inspire. **2** *trying to motivate the pupils/children* give incentive to, stimulate, inspire, arouse, excite, stir, spur, goad.

motivation *noun* **1** *he has no motivation* ambition, drive, inspiration. **2** *you must give the children some motivation to succeed* incentive,

stimulus, inspiration, inducement, incitement, spur, goad, motive.

motive *noun* motivation, reason, rationale, thinking, grounds, cause, basis, occasion, incentive, inducement, incitement, influence, lure, attraction, inspiration, persuasion, stimulus, spur, goad, pressure; *inf.* what makes one tick.

motley *adjective* **1** *motley collection of old clothes* assorted, varied, miscellaneous, mixed, diverse, diversified, variegated, heterogeneous. **2** *a motley coat* many-coloured, multicoloured, particoloured, many-hued, variegated, kaleidoscopic, prismatic.
Opposites HOMOGENEOUS; UNIFORM.

motorcycle *noun*. *See table at* VEHICLE.

mottled *adjective* blotched, blotchy, splotchy, speckled, spotted, streaked, marbled, flecked, freckled, dappled, stippled, variegated, piebald, pied, brindled, tabby.

motto *noun* **1** *'waste not, want not' should be your motto* maxim, aphorism, adage, saying, saw, axiom, truism, precept, epigram, proverb, byword, gnome. **2** *the club's motto* slogan, watchword, cry. **3** *cracker mottoes* joke.

mould¹ *noun* **1** *set the mixture in a mould* cast, die, form, matrix, shape. **2** *the mould of history* shape, form, figure, cast, outline, line, configuration, formation, format, structure, frame, construction, build, cut, style, model, pattern, type, kind, brand, make. **3** *objects constructed on a mould* frame, framework, template. **4** *people of heroic mould* character, nature, calibre, kind, sort, stamp, type, kidney.

mould² *verb* **1** *mould plastic into pipes* cast. **2** *mould the model from clay* shape, form, fashion, model, construct, frame, make, create, design, carve, sculpt, chisel, forge. **3** *mould children's minds* influence, affect, direct, shape, form, make.

mould³ *noun* *mould covered the woodwork* mouldiness, fungus, mildew, blight, must, mustiness, dry rot, wet rot.

mouldy *adjective* mildewed, blighted, musty, fusty, decaying, rotting, rotten, bad, spoiled.

mound *noun* **1** *a mound of leaves* heap, pile, stack. **2** *flat country broken by mounds* hillock, hill, knoll, rise, hummock, tump, embankment, bank, dune. **3** *Pictish mounds* barrow, tumulus.

mount *verb* **1** *mount the stairs* ascend, go up, climb up, clamber up, make one's way up, scale. **2** *mount the bus* get on to, climb on to, jump on to. **3** *he mounted the horse* get on to, get astride, get on the back of. **4** *costs mounting up* accumulate, accrue, pile up, grow, multiply. **5** *prices/fear mounting* increase, grow, escalate, intensify. **6** *mount a picture* frame, set, dispose. **7** *mount an exhibition* stage, put on, install, prepare, organize, arrange, set in motion; *inf.* get up.
Opposites DESCEND; ALIGHT; DECREASE.

mount *noun* **1** *choose a quiet mount* horse, steed. **2** *a plain mount for the gem/picture* setting, fixture, frame, support, stand, base, backing, foil.

mountain noun **1** *rocky mountains* peak, height, elevation, eminence, pinnacle, fell, alp, Munro; *Scots* ben; *lit.* mount. *See table. See also table at* RANGE. **2** *mountains of clothes* heap, pile, mound, stack, abundance; *inf.* ton. **3** *a butter mountain* surplus, surfeit, excess, overabundance.

mountainous adjective **1** *mountainous regions* hilly, high, highland, high-reaching, steep, lofty, towering, soaring, alpine, rocky. **2** *mountainous athletes* huge, enormous, immense, massive, vast, gigantic, mammoth, hulking, mighty, monumental, colossal, ponderous, prodigious, Brobdingnagian. *Opposites* FLAT; LEVEL; PUNY.

mourn verb **1** *the widow is still mourning* grieve, sorrow, keen, lament, wail, wear mourning, wear black, wear widow's weeds. **2** *mourn for her dead husband* grieve for, sorrow over, weep for, regret/deplore the loss of, bewail, bemoan. *Opposites* REJOICE.

mournful adjective **1** *mournful music* sad, sorrowful, doleful, gloomy, sombre, melancholy, lugubrious, funereal, elegaic. **2** *had such a mournful expression | looked so mournful* sad, doleful, dejected, depressed, downcast, disconsolate, melancholy, gloomy, miserable, lugubrious, woeful, unhappy, heavy-hearted, sombre. *Opposites* JOYFUL; HAPPY; MERRY.

mourning noun **1** *the mourning of the bereaved* grief, grieving, sorrowing, lamentation, keening, wailing, weeping, moaning. **2** *wear mourning* black clothes, black, widow's weeds, weeds, sackcloth and ashes.

mouse noun. *See table at* RODENT.

mousy adjective **1** *a mousy person* timid, fearful, timorous, self-effacing, unobtrusive, unassertive, withdrawn, shy. **2** *mousy hair/ colours* brownish-grey, greyish, grey, duncoloured, colourless, neutral, drab, dull, lacklustre.

mouth noun **1** *open their mouths* lips, jaws, maw, muzzle; *inf.* gob, trap, chops, kisser. **2** *mouth of the cave/trumpet* opening, entrance, entry, inlet, door, doorway, gateway, portal, hatch, aperture, orifice, vent, cavity, crevice, rim, lips. **3** *the mouth of the river* river mouth, estuary, outlet, embouchure. **4** *he's all mouth and no action* empty talk, idle talk, babble, claptrap, boasting, bragging, braggadocio; *inf.* hot air, gas. **5** *don't take any mouth from her* impudence, cheek, insolence, impertinence, rudeness, incivility, effrontery, audacity; *inf.* lip, backchat, neck. **down in the mouth** down, down-hearted, dejected, downcast, low in spirits, depressed, dispirited, discouraged, disheartened, disconsolate, crestfallen, miserable, unhappy; *inf.* down in the dumps.

mouthful noun bite, swallow, spoonful, forkful, nibble, sip, sup, taste, drop, bit, piece, morsel, sample.

mouthpiece noun **1** *he is his company's mouthpiece* spokesman, spokeswoman, spokesperson, negotiator, intermediary, mediator, agent, representative. **2** *he publishes the mouthpiece of the union* organ, journal, periodical, publication.

movable adjective mobile, transportable, transferable, portable, portative.

move verb **1** *men moving slowly* go, walk, march, proceed, progress, advance. **2** *move objects* carry, transport, transfer, transpose, change over, shift, switch. **3** *time moves fast* progress, advance, pass. **4** *the government must move soon* take action, act, do something, get moving. **5** *our neighbours are moving* move house, relocate, change house, change jobs, move away, leave, go away. **6** *she was moved by the performance* affect, touch, impress, upset, disturb, disquiet, agitate; make an impression on, have an impact on, tug on someone's heartstrings. **7** *the sight moved her to tears* provoke, incite, actuate, rouse, excite, urge, incline, stimulate, motivate, influence, persuade, lead, prompt, cause, impel, induce. **8** *as the spirit moves him | she was moved to act*

MOUNTAINS			
Mountain	**Location**	**Mountain**	**Location**
Aconcagua	Argentina	Kilimanjaro	Tanzania
Annapurna	Nepal	Kinabalu	Malaysia
Ararat	Turkey	Logan	Canada
Bonete	Argentina	McKinley	U.S.A.
Chimborazo	Ecuador	Makalu I	Nepal/Tibet/China
Citlaltépetl	Mexico	Margherita	Zaire/Rwanda
Communism Peak	Tajikistan	Matterhorn	Switzerland/Italy
Cotopaxi	Ecuador	Mont Blanc	France/Italy
Damavand	Iran	Muztag	China
Dufourspitze	Switzerland	Nanga Parbat	Pakistan
Dykh-Tau	Russia	Ojos del Salado	Argentina/Chile
Elbrus	Russia	Pissis	Argentina
Etna	Italy	Pobedy	Kyrgyzstan
Everest	Nepal/Tibet	Popocatépetl	Mexico
Fujiyama	Japan	Ras Dashen	Ethiopia
Huascarán	Peru	St Elias	U.S.A./Canada
Jaya	Indonesia	Tirich Mir	Pakistan
K2 | Godwin-Austen	India	Tupungato	Argentina/Chile
Kanchenjunga	Nepal/India	Weisshorn	Switzerland
Kenya	Kenya		

activate, get going, propel, drive, push, shift, motivate. **9** *nothing can move him on that | she will not move on this issue* change, budge, change someone's mind; *inf.* do an about-turn, do a U-turn. **10** *move that he be sacked* propose, put forward, advocate, recommend, urge, suggest. **11** *the goods are not moving* sell, be sold, move from the shelf, retail, be marketed.
Opposites STAND; STAY; DETER.

move *noun* **1** *birds frightened by the man's slightest move* movement, motion, moving, action, activity, gesture, gesticulation. **2** *arrange our move* removal, change of house/address/job, relocation, transfer; *Scots* flit, flitting. **3** *plan our next move* action, act, deed, measure, step, tack, manoeuvre, tactic, stratagem, ploy, ruse, trick. **4** *it's your move in the game* turn, go; *inf.* shot. **get a move on** hurry up, make haste, speed up, move faster, get moving; *inf.* get cracking, make it snappy, step on it, shake a leg. **make a move** take action, act, do something. **on the move** **1** *cars/birds on the move* moving, in motion, going, travelling, journeying, under way, on the wing. **2** *things are on the move* progressing, making progress, advancing, moving/going forward.

movement *noun* **1** *the movement of the furniture* moving, carrying, transportation, transferral, shifting. **2** *make a sudden movement* moving, move, motion, action, activity, gesture, gesticulation. **3** *the movement of time* progress, progression, advance, passing, passage. **4** *the clock's movement* mechanism, machinery, works, workings, action, wheels; *inf.* innards, guts. **5** *form a peace movement* group, party, organization, faction, wing, coalition, front. **6** *mount a peace movement* campaign, crusade, drive. **7** *play the first movement* part, section, passage. **8** *a movement towards better government* trend, tendency, drift, swing, current. **9** *no movement in the stock market* rise/fall, change, variation, fluctuation. **10** *some movement has been made in the situation* progress, advance, improvement, step forward, breakthrough.

moving *adjective* **1** *a moving story* affecting, touching, emotive, emotional, poignant, pathetic, stirring, arousing, upsetting, disturbing. **2** *moving parts* movable, mobile, motile, unfixed. **3** *the moving force behind the scheme* driving, dynamic, impelling, motivating, stimulating, inspirational.
Opposites UNEMOTIONAL; IMMOBILE; INERT.

mow *verb* cut, trim, crop, clip, scythe, shear.
mow down *armies mowing down the townspeople* slaughter, massacre, butcher, cut to pieces, cut down, decimate.

much *adjective* *not much time | too much trouble* a great/large amount of, a great number of, a great deal of, plenty of, ample, copious, abundant; *inf.* a lot of, lots of.
Opposites LITTLE.

much *adverb* **1** *I much regret it* greatly, to a great extent/degree, exceedingly, considerably, decidedly, indeed; *inf.* a lot. **2** *he's not here much often*, frequently; *inf.* a lot. **much of a muchness** much the same, more or less the same, very similar, almost alike, practically identical, practically indistinguishable.

much *noun* *he doesn't know much* a good deal, a great deal; *inf.* a lot, lots.

muck *noun* **1** *clear the muck from the barn* dung, manure, ordure, excrement, guano, droppings, faeces. **2** *clean the muck from the car* dirt, grime, filth, mud, slime, sludge, scum, mire; *inf.* gunk, gunge. **make a muck of** botch, bungle, muff, make a mess of, mess up, mar, spoil, ruin; *inf.* make a hash of, foul up, screw up.

muck *verb* **muck up** See MAKE A MUCK OF.

mud *noun* sludge, clay, silt, mire, dirt, soil.

muddle *verb* **1** *muddle the dates | he's muddled up the situation* confuse, get confused, mix up, jumble, jumble up, scramble, disarrange, disorganize, throw into disorder, get into a tangle, make a mess of, mess up. **2** *numbers muddle her* confuse, disorientate, bewilder, befuddle, daze, perplex, puzzle, baffle, nonplus, confound.

muddle *noun* **1** *files in a muddle* chaos, disorder, disarray, confusion, disorganization, jumble, mix-up, mess, clutter, tangle. **2** *she's in such a muddle | her mind's in a muddle* state of confusion, disorientation, bewilderment, perplexity, puzzlement, bafflement.

muddled *adjective* **1** *muddled files* chaotic, in disorder, in disarray, disorganized, jumbled, mixed-up, scrambled, tangled; *inf.* higgledy-piggledy. **2** *muddled people trying to cope* confused, disorientated, at sea, befuddled, bewildered, dazed, perplexed. See MUDDLE *verb* 2. **3** *muddled thinking/logic* confused, jumbled, incoherent, unclear, woolly, muddied, loose.
Opposites ORDERLY; CLEAR; LUCID.

muddy *adjective* **1** *a muddy substance* mucky, miry, oozy, slushy, slimy. **2** *muddy ground/field* marshy, boggy, swampy. **3** *muddy shoes* mud-caked, dirty, filthy, grubby, grimy. **4** *muddy stream/liquid/colours* cloudy, murky, smoky, dingy, dull, turbid, opaque, brownish-green. **5** *muddy thinking* confused, jumbled, incoherent, woolly. See MUDDLED 3.

muddy *verb* **1** *muddy the waters | muddied his hands* dirty, begrime, soil. **2** *muddy the issue* make unclear, cloud, confuse, mix up, jumble, scramble, get into a tangle.

muffle *verb* **1** *muffle oneself up against the cold* wrap up, cover up, swathe, swaddle, envelop, cloak. **2** *muffle the sound* deaden, dull, dampen, stifle, smother, suppress, soften, quieten, hush, mute, silence.

muffled *adjective* *muffled sound* faint, indistinct, unclear, dull, muted, dampened, stifled, smothered, suppressed.

mug *noun* **1** *a mug of cocoa | beer mug* beaker, cup, tankard, pot, glass, toby jug. **2** *he's a mug to believe her* fool, simpleton, innocent; *inf.* sucker, muggins, soft touch. **3** *he has an ugly mug* face, countenance, visage, features; *inf.* clock, phiz, phizog.

mug *verb* assault, attack, beat up, knock down, rob; *inf.* rough up, do over.

muggy *adjective* close, stuffy, sultry, oppressive, airless, humid, clammy, sticky.
Opposites FRESH; AIRY.

mull verb **mull over** think over, think about, consider, ponder, reflect on, contemplate, meditate on, deliberate about/on, muse on, ruminate over/on, weigh up, have one's mind on, examine, study, review.

multifarious adjective many, multiple, numerous, legion, sundry, diverse, diversified, varied, variegated, manifold, different, miscellaneous, assorted.

multiple adjective several, many, numerous, various, collective, manifold.

multiply verb **1** people multiplying in great numbers breed, reproduce. **2** troubles are multiplying increase, grow, accumulate, augment, proliferate, spread.

multitude noun **1** a multitude of people came crowd, assembly, throng, host, horde, mass, mob, legion, army; inf. a lot, lots. **2** he despises the multitude the common people, the masses, the populace, the commonality, the proletariat, the mob, the crowd, the rabble, the hoi polloi, the canaille; inf. the great unwashed.

munch verb chew, champ, chomp, masticate, crunch, eat.

mundane adjective **1** mundane issues/prose common, ordinary, everyday, workaday, usual, prosaic, pedestrian, routine, customary, regular, normal, typical, commonplace, banal, hackneyed, trite, stale, platitudinous. **2** mundane not spiritual matters worldly, earthly, terrestrial, secular, temporal, fleshly, carnal, sensual.
Opposites EXTRAORDINARY; IMAGINATIVE; SPIRITUAL.

municipal adjective civic, civil, city, metropolitan, urban, town, borough, community, public.

munificence noun **1** the munificence of the host bounty, bountifulness, bounteousness, liberality, generosity, charity, charitableness, magnanimity, magnanimousness, largesse. See MUNIFICENT 1. **2** the munifence of the supplies abundance, copiousness, profusion. See MUNIFICENT 2.

munificent adjective **1** he is a munificent provider bountiful, bounteous, liberal, generous, free, open-handed, charitable, hospitable, big-hearted, beneficent, benevolent, ungrudging, magnanimous, philanthropic. **2** munificent supplies of food plentiful, ample, abundant, copious, lavish, profuse, princely.
Opposites MEAN; MISERLY; MEAGRE.

murder noun **1** commit murder | guilty of murder killing, slaying, manslaughter, homicide, slaughter, assassination, butchery, carnage, massacre. See table at ASSASSINATION. **2** driving there was murder an ordeal, a trial, a frustrating/unpleasant/difficult/dangerous experience, a misery, agony; inf. hell, hell on earth.

murder verb **1** murder his brother kill, slay, put to death, do to death, take the life of, shed the blood of, slaughter, assassinate, butcher, cut to pieces, massacre; inf. bump off, do in, eliminate, hit, rub out, blow away. **2** murder the song mangle, mutilate, ruin, make a mess of, spoil, mar, destroy. **3** they murdered our team trounce, beat soundly, beat decisively, thrash, defeat utterly, give a drubbing to; inf. slaughter, hammer, make mincemeat of.

murderer noun killer, slayer, homicide, slaughterer, cutthroat, assassin, butcher, patricide, matricide, fratricide. See MURDER noun 1.

murderous adjective **1** a murderous blow fatal, lethal, deadly, mortal, death-dealing, homicidal, savage, barbarous, brutal, bloodthirsty, bloody. **2** a murderous climb arduous, difficult, strenuous, exhausting, formidable, harrowing, dangerous; inf. killing, hellish.

murky adjective **1** murky streets/shadows dark, dim, gloomy. **2** murky weather foggy, misty, cloudy, louring, overcast, dull, grey, dismal, dreary, cheerless. **3** murky pools dirty, muddy, dingy, dull, cloudy, turbid, opaque. **4** a murky past dark, questionable, doubtful, obscure, enigmatic, nebulous, mysterious, hidden, secret.
Opposites BRIGHT; CLEAR; BLAMELESS.

murmur noun **1** the murmur of the stream babble, burble, whisper, purl, rustle, buzzing, drone, sigh; inf. whoosh. **2** tell him in a murmur whisper, undertone, mutter, mumble. **3** have heard murmurs against his presidency mutter, grumble, moan, complaint, carping, whisper; inf. grouse, gripe, beef, bitch.

murmur verb **1** streams murmuring babble, burble, whisper, purl, rustle, buzz, drone, sigh; inf. whoosh. **2** murmured that she wished to leave whisper, speak in an undertone, speak sotto voce, mutter, mumble. **3** murmur against the king mutter, grumble, moan, complain, carp; inf. grouse, gripe, beef, bitch.
Opposites SHOUT; YELL.

muscle noun **1** strain a muscle muscular tissue, sinew, tendon, ligament, thew. See table. **2** she likes a man with muscle muscularity, brawn; inf. beef. **3** the new chairman has no muscle power, potency, force, forcefulness, might, strength, weight, influence; inf. clout, pull.

HUMAN MUSCLES	
abdominal muscle	quadriceps
biceps	rhomboideus
deltoid	sartorius
gastrocnemius	scalenus
gluteus	soleus
pectoral muscle	splenius
peroneal muscle	trapezius
psoas	triceps

muscle verb **muscle in on** trust him to muscle in on our trip push/force one's way into, elbow one's way into, impose oneself on, invite oneself to; inf. butt in on.

muscular adjective **1** muscular tissue/pain sinewy, fibrous. **2** muscular men doing weightlifting brawny, strapping, powerfully built, solidly built, hefty, stalwart, sturdy, rugged, burly; inf. beefy, husky. **3** a muscular character/attempt vigorous, potent, powerful, strong, energetic, active, dynamic, aggressive, determined, resolute.
Opposites WEAK; PUNY; FEEBLE.

muse verb **1** stand and muse think, meditate, be lost in contemplation/thought, be in a brown study, reflect, deliberate, day dream, be in a reverie. **2** *muse over the situation* think over, think about, consider, ponder, reflect on, contemplate, meditate on, deliberate about/on, mull over, ruminate over/on, weigh up, have one's mind on, examine, study, review. **3** *"I wonder," he mused* say thoughtfully/reflectively/meditatively.

muse *noun the poetic muse is silent* inspiration, afflatus, creative influence, stimulus, stimulation. *See table.*

THE NINE MUSES	
Muse	**Muse of**
Calliope	epic poetry
Clio	history
Erato	lyric poetry and hymns
Euterpe	flute playing
Melpomene	tragedy
Polyhymnia	mime
Terpsichore	lyric poetry and dance
Thalia	comedy
Urania	astronomy

mushroom *noun gather/cook mushrooms* fungus; field mushroom, chanterelle, morel, ink-cap, Chinese mushroom. *See table at* FUNGI.

mushroom *verb new towns mushrooming* spring up, shoot up, sprout, burgeon, burst forth, grow/develop rapidly, boom, thrive, flourish, prosper.

music *noun* melody, tune, air, rhythm, harmonization, orchestration. *See tables. See also tables at* JAZZ, OPERA, ORCHESTRA, POPULAR MUSIC, SCALE.

musical *adjective* tuneful, melodic, melodious, harmonious, lyrical, sweet-sounding, mellifluous, dulcet, euphonious. *See table.*
Opposites DISCORDANT; HARSH; GRATING.

musical instrument *noun. See tables at* BRASS, KEYBOARD, ORCHESTRA, PERCUSSION, STRING, WOODWIND.

musician *noun. See table.*

musing *noun* thinking, meditation, contemplation, deliberation, pondering, reflection, rumination, day dreaming, reverie, brown study, wool-gathering.

muss *verb* dissarrange, misarrange, put out of place, make untidy, make a mess of, mess up, rumple, dishevel, tousle.

must[1] *noun the new show is a must* something not to be missed, essential, necessity, necessary thing, imperative, requirement, requisite, prerequisite.

must[2] *noun a smell of must* mould, mustiness, mouldiness, mildew, fungus.

muster *verb* **1** *muster the soldiers* assemble, bring together, call/gather together, call up, summon, rally, mobilize, round up, marshal, collect, convoke. **2** *we must muster at dawn* assemble, gather together, come together, meet, congregate, convene. **3** *muster one's courage* call up, gather together, summon, rally, screw up.

muster *noun soldiers present for the muster* assembly, assemblage, rally, mobilization, call-up, round-up, convocation, meeting, congregation, convention. **pass muster** measure up, come up to scratch, be acceptable, qualify; *inf.* make the grade, fill/fit the bill.

musty *adjective* **1** *musty books/food/rooms* mouldy, mildewed, mildewy, fusty, decaying, stale, stuffy, airless, damp, dank. **2** *musty ideas* antiquated, obsolete, ancient, antediluvian, out-of-date, outdated, old-fashioned, out-of-fashion, out-of-style, behind the times, passé, hoary, moth-eaten, worn-out, threadbare, hackneyed, trite, clichéd.
Opposites FRESH; MODERN.

mutable *adjective* changeable, variable, alterable, convertible, adaptable, modifiable, transformable, transmutable, inconstant, unsteady, unstable, vacillating, wavering, unsettled, inconsistent, volatile, capricious.

mutation *noun* **1** *undergo genetic mutation* change, variation, alteration, modification, transformation, metamorphosis, evolution, transmutation, transfiguration. **2** *the creature is a genetic mutation* mutant, deviant, anomaly, freak.

mute *adjective* **1** *mute with surprise* silent, speechless, wordless, unspeaking, taciturn, uncommunicative; *inf.* mum. **2** *animals born mute* dumb, voiceless, speechless, aphasic, aphonic. **3** *a mute appeal* silent, dumb, wordless, unexpressed, unspoken.
Opposites VOLUBLE; SPOKEN.

mute *verb* **1** *mute the sound* deaden, dull, dampen, muffle, stifle, smother, suppress, soften, quieten, soft-pedal, turn down. **2** *mute the colour scheme* soften, subdue, tone down, make less intense.

muted *adjective muted colours* soft, softened, subdued, subtle, discreet, toned down, quiet, understated.

mutilate *verb* **1** *mutilate the bodies* dismember, tear limb from limb, amputate limbs from, cut to pieces, lacerate, hack up, butcher, mangle, cripple, maim, lame, disable, disfigure. **2** *mutilate a limb* cut off, chop off, hack off, lop off, tear off, pull off, damage, injure, impair. **3** *mutilate a text* mar, spoil, ruin, damage, butcher, mangle, distort, cut, hack, censor, bowdlerize, expurgate.

mutinous *adjective* rebellious, insurgent, insurrectionary, revolutionary, anarchistic, subversive, seditious, traitorous, insubordinate, disobedient, riotous, rioting, unruly, disorderly, restive, contumacious, refractory, out of control, uncontrollable, ungovernable, unmanageable; *inf.* bolshie.

mutiny *noun* rebellion, revolt, insurrection, insurgence, insurgency, uprising, rising, riot, revolution, resistance, disobedience, defiance, insubordination, protest, strike.

mutiny *verb* rebel, revolt, take part in an insurrection/insurgence/uprising, riot, rise up, resist/oppose authority, defy authority, be insubordinate, protest, strike.

mutter *verb* **1** *going along muttering* talk under one's breath, talk to oneself, whisper, speak in an undertone, speak *sotto voce*, mumble, murmur. **2** *mutter against the king* murmur, grumble, moan, complain, carp; *inf.* grouse, gripe, beef, bitch.

muzzle *noun* **1** *the dog's muzzle is wet with blood* mouth, jaw, maw. **2** *the dog pushed its muzzle into the bucket* nose, snout. **3** *put a muzzle on the dangerous dog* gag, guard, restraint, bridle.

muzzle *verb* **1** *muzzle the dog* put a muzzle on, gag, bridle. **2** *attempts to muzzle the press* silence, impose silence on, censor, suppress, stifle, inhibit, restrain, check, fetter.

myopic *adjective* **1** *myopic guests peering across the table* short-sighted, near-sighted, purblind. **2** *a board full of myopic people* narrow, narrow-minded, short-sighted, insular, parochial, provincial, limited, prejudiced, unimaginative, uncreative.

myriad *noun* *a myriad of butterflies in the sky* a great number/quantity, scores, multitude, host, horde, army, legion, mass, throng, swarm, sea; *inf.* millions, thousands, oodles, zillions, a lot.

myriad *adjective* *myriad colours* innumerable, countless, incalculable, immeasurable, numerous, multitudinous, multifarious, manifold, multiple, several, many, various, sundry, diverse.

mysterious *adjective* **1** *God moves in mysterious ways* enigmatic, inscrutable, impenetrable,

---

MUSICAL DIRECTIONS

Term	Translation	Term	Translation
a battuta	return to strict time	marcia	march
a cappella	unaccompanied	meno mosso	slower pace
accelerando	accelerating	mezza voce	at half strength
adagietto	fairly slowly	mezzo	half
adagio	slowly	mezzoforte/mf	fairly loudly
ad libitum	at will	moderato	moderately
affettuoso	tenderly	molto	very
agitato	agitated	morendo	dying away
al fine	to the end	mosso	fast
allargando	broadening	moto	motion
allegretto	fairly lively	nobilmente	nobly
allegro	lively	non troppo	not too much
al segno	as far as the sign	obbligato	not to be omitted
amoroso	tenderly	ped	pedal
andante	moderately slow	pesante	heavily
andantino	slightly faster than andante	pianissimo/pp	very soft
animato	spirited	p(iano)	soft
assai	very	più	more
a tempo	in the original tempo	pizz(icato)	plucked
attacca	continue without stopping	poco	a little
bis	repeat	portamento	carrying one note into the next
calando	becoming quieter and slower	prestissimo	as fast as possible
cantabile	in a singing manner	presto	very fast
capriccioso	freely	rall(entando)	slowing down
coda	final part of a movement	ravvivando	quickening
col legno	with stick of the bow	rinforzando/rfz	accentuated
con amore	tenderly	rit(ardando)	slowing down
con brio	with vigour	ritenuto	more slowly
con fuoco	fiery	scherzando	playfully
con sordino	with a mute	segno	sign
cresc(endo)	becoming louder	semplice	simply
da capo	from the beginning	sempre	always/throughout
dal segno	from the sign	senza	without
decrescendo	becoming quieter	sf(orzando)/sfz	strongly accented
dim(inuendo)	becoming quieter	sordino	mute
dolente	sorrowfully	sostenuto	sustained
doppio	double	sotto voce	in an undertone
f(orte)	loudly	staccato	detached
fortissimo/ff	very loudly	stretto	in quicker time
giocoso	playfully	stringendo	intensifying
glissando	sliding	subito	immediately
in modo di	in the manner of	tacet	instrument remains silent
larghetto	fairly slowly	tempo	speed/beat
largo	very slowly	ten(uto)	held
legato	tied/smoothly	tutti	whole orchestra
leggiero	lightly	vivace	lively
lento	slowly	vif	lively
maestoso	majestically	vivement	lively
marcato	accented	zoppa	syncopated

TYPES OF MUSIC

acid house	dhrupad	heavy metal	opera	rockabilly
ballet music	disco	high life	opera buffa	rock and roll
bebop	dodecaphonic	hip hop	orchestral	salsa
bhangra	music	house	music	serialism
bluegrass	easy listening	indie	Palm Court	sijo
blues	electro	jazz	popular music	ska
calypso	flamenco	klezmer	psychobilly	skiffle
chamber music	folk	kwela	punk	soca
choral music	funk	liturgical music	qawwali	soul
church music	fusion	marabi	ragamuffin	spiritual music
classical music	gagaku	mbaqanga	ragga	swing
contrapuntal	gangsta rap	minimalist	ragtime	symphonic
music	garage	music	rap	music
country and	go-go	motet	reggae	techno
western	gospel	Motown	rhythm and	thrash metal
country	grand opera	musique	blues |	zouk
dancehall	grunge	concrète	R and B	zydeco

MUSICAL FORMS

air	concerto	mass	ricercar
anthem	concerto grosso	motet	rondo
aria	descant	movement	round
arietta	duet	octet	scherzo
aubade	entr'acte	opera	septet
bagatelle	entrée	operetta	serenade
ballad	étude	oratorio	sextet
ballet	fantasia	overture	sinfonia
barcarole	fantasy	part-song	sinfonia concertante
canon	finale	passacaglia	solo
canticle	fugue	polonaise	sonata
canzone	humoresque	prelude	sonatina
capriccio	hymn	psalm	song
carol	impromptu	quartet	spiritual
cavatina	interlude	quintet	suite
chaconne	intermezzo	recitative	symphony
chorale	lullaby	refrain	toccata
chorus	madrigal	requiem	trio
concertino	march	rhapsody	variation

MUSICALS

Musical	Date	Composer/librettist	Musical	Date	Composer/librettist
A Chorus Line	1975	Hamlish/Kleban	My Fair Lady	1956	Loewe/Lerner
Boy Friend, The	1953	Wilson	No, No, Nanette	1925	Youmans/Harbach
Broadway Melody	1929	Brown			
Cabaret	1966	Kander/Ebb	Oklahoma!	1943	Rodgers/Hammerstein
Carousel	1945	Rodgers/Hammerstein	Oliver	1960	Bart
Cats	1981	Lloyd Webber	Show Boat	1927	Kern/Hammerstein
Evita	1978	Lloyd Webber			
Grease	1972	Jacobs/Casey	Sound of Music, The	1959	Rodgers/Hammerstein
Guys and Dolls	1950	Loesser			
Hair	1967	MacDermot/Ragni/Rado	South Pacific	1949	Rodgers/Hammerstein
Jazz Singer, The	1927	Cohn/Raphaelson	Student Prince, The	1924	Romberg
Jesus Christ, Superstar	1971	Lloyd Webber/Rice	Sweeney Todd	1979	Sondheim
Joseph and the Amazing Technicolour Dreamcoat	1968	Lloyd Webber/Rice	West Side Story	1957	Bernstein/Sondheim
Les Misérables	1980	Schönberg/Boublil/Kretzmer	Wizard of Oz, The	1903	Sloane and Tietjens/Baum

MUSICIANS AND COMPOSERS

Albinoni, Tomaso (1671–1751; It. composer)

Arne, Thomas (1710–78; Engl. composer)

Babbitt, Milton (b. 1916; Am. composer)

Bach, Johann Sebastian (1685–1750; Ger. composer/keyboard player)

Barber, Samuel (1910–81; Am. composer)

Barenboim, Daniel (b. 1942; Israeli composer/pianist)

Bartók, Béla (1881–1945; Hungarian composer)

Bax, Sir Arnold (1883–1953; Engl. composer)

Beethoven, Ludwig van (1770–1827; Ger. composer)

Bellini, Vincenzo (1801–35; It. composer)

Berg, Alban (1885–1935; Austrian composer)

Berlioz, Hector (1803–69; Fr. composer/conductor)

Bernstein, Leonard (1918–90; Am. composer/conductor/pianist)

Bizet, Georges (1838–75; Fr. composer)

Borodin, Aleksandr (1833–87; Russ. composer)

Boulanger, Nadia (1887–1979; Fr. composer)

Boulez, Pierre (b. 1925; Fr. composer)

Brahms, Johannes (1833–97; Ger. composer)

Britten, Benjamin (1913–76; Engl. composer/pianist/conductor)

Bruckner, Anton (1824–96; Austrian composer/organist)

Byrd, William (1543–1623; Engl. composer)

Cage, John (1912–92; Am. composer)

Campion, Thomas (1567–1620; Engl. composer)

Carrillo, Julián (1875–1965; Mex. composer)

Casals, Pablo (1876–1973; Sp. cellist)

Chopin, Frédéric (1810–49; Pol. composer)

Copland, Aaron (1900–90; Am. composer)

Corelli, Arcangelo (1653–1713; It. composer/violinist)

Couperin, François (1668–1733; Fr. composer)

Debussy, Claude (1862–1918; Fr. composer)

Delius, Frederick (1862–1934; Brit. composer)

Dohnányi, Ernö (1877–1960; Hungarian composer/pianist)

Dolmetsch, Arnold (1858–1940; Brit. instrument maker, b. in France)

Donizetti, Gaetano (1797–1848; It. composer)

du Pré, Jacqueline (1945–87; Engl. cellist)

Duruflé, Maurice (1902–86; Fr. composer)

Dvořák, Antonín (1841–1904; Cz. composer)

Elgar, Sir Edward (1857–1934; Brit. composer)

Falla, Manuel de (1876–1946; Sp. composer/pianist)

Fauré, Gabriel (1845–1924; Fr. composer/organist)

Franck, César (1822–90; Fr. composer, b. in Belgium)

Gershwin, George (1898–1937; Am. composer)

Glass, Philip (b. 1937; Am. composer)

Gluck, Christoph (1714–87; Ger. composer)

Gould, Glenn (1932–82; Can. composer/pianist)

Grainger, Percy (1882–1961; Am. composer/pianist, b. in Australia)

Grieg, Edvard (1843–1907; Norw. composer)

Hallé, Sir Charles (1819–95; Ger. conductor/pianist)

Handel, George Frederick (1685–1759; Ger. composer)

Haydn, Franz Joseph (1732–1809; Austrian composer)

Henze, Hans Werner (b. 1926; Ger. composer)

Hindemith, Paul (1895–1963; Ger. composer)

Holst, Gustav (1874–1934; Brit. composer)

Honegger, Arthur (1892–1955; Fr. composer)

Humperdinck, Engelbert (1854–1921; Ger. composer)

Ives, Charles (1874–1954; Am. composer)

Janáček, Leoš (1854–1928; Cz. composer)

Khachaturian, Aram (1903–78; Soviet composer)

Klemperer, Otto (1885–1973; Israeli composer/conductor, b. in Germany)

Kodály, Zoltán (1882–1967; Hungarian composer)

Ligeti, György Sándor (b. 1923; Hungarian composer)

Liszt, Franz (1811–86; Hungarian composer/pianist)

Mahler, Gustav (1860–1911; Austrian composer/conductor)

Mendelssohn, Felix (1809–47; Ger. composer)

Menuhin, Yehudi, Baron (b. 1916; Brit. violinist)

Messiaen, Olivier (1908–92; Fr. composer/organist)

Meyerbeer, Giacomo (1791–1864; Ger. composer)

Milhaud, Darius (1892–1974; Fr. composer)

Monteverdi, Claudio (1567–1643; It. composer)

Mozart, Wolfgang Amadeus (1756–91; Austrian composer)

Mussorgsky, Modest (1839–81; Russ. composer)

Nielsen, Carl August (1865–1931; Da. composer)

Offenbach, Jacques (1819–80; Ger. composer)

Orff, Carl (1895–1982; Ger. composer/conductor)

Paderewski, Ignacy (1860–1941; Pol. composer/pianist)

Paganini, Niccolò (1782–1840; It. composer/violinist)

Palestrina, Giovanni Pierluigi da (c. 1525–94; It. composer)

Poulenc, Francis (1899–1963; Fr. composer)

Previn, André (b. 1929; Am. composer/conductor/pianist, b. in Germany)

Prokofiev, Sergei (1891–1953; Russ. composer)

Puccini, Giacomo (1858–1924; It. composer)

Purcell, Henry (1659–95; Brit. composer/organist)

Rachmaninov, Sergei (1873–1943; Russ. composer/pianist/conductor)

Rameau, Jean-Philippe (1683–1764; Fr. composer/organist)

MUSICIANS AND COMPOSERS *cont.*

Ravel, Maurice (1875–1937; Fr. composer)	composer, b. in Austria)	Stockhausen, Karlheinz (b. 1928; Ger. composer)	Tortelier, Paul (1914–90; Fr. cellist)
Reich, Steve (b. 1936; Am. composer)	Schubert, Franz (1797–1828; Austrian composer)	Stradivari, Antonio (c. 1644–1737; It. violin-maker)	Toscanini, Arturo (1867–1957; It. conductor)
Rimsky-Korsakov, Nikolai (1844–1908; Russ. composer)	Schumann, Robert (1810–56; Ger. composer)	Strauss, Richard (1864–1949; Ger. composer/conductor)	Vaughan Williams, Ralph (1872–1958; Brit. composer)
Rossini, Gioacchino (1792–1868; It. composer)	Scriabin, Aleksandr (1872–1915; Russ. composer/pianist)	Strauss the Younger, Johann (1825–99; Austrian composer/violinist/conductor)	Verdi, Giuseppe (1813–1901; It. composer)
Rubinstein, Anton (1829–94; Russ. composer/pianist)	Segovia, Andrés (1893–1987; Sp. composer/guitarist)		Villa-Lobos, Heitor (1887–1959; Brazilian composer)
Rubinstein, Artur (1888–1982; Am. pianist, b. in Poland)	Shostakovich, Dmitri (1906–75; Russ. composer)	Stravinsky, Igor (1882–1971; Am. composer, b. in Russia)	Vivaldi, Antonio (1678–1741; It. composer/violinist)
Saint-Saëns, Camille (1835–1921; Fr. composer/conductor/keyboard player)	Sibelius, Jean (1865–1957; Finn. composer)	Sullivan, Sir Arthur (1842–1900; Engl. composer)	Wagner, Richard (1813–83; Ger. composer)
Salieri, Antonio (1750–1825; It. composer)	Smetana, Bedřich (1824–84; Cz. composer)	Tallis, Thomas (c. 1505–85; Engl. composer)	Walton, Sir William (1902–83; Engl. composer)
Satie, Erik (1866–1925; Fr. composer)	Solti, Sir Georg (b. 1912; Brit. conductor, b. in Hungary)	Tchaikovsky, Pyotr (1840–93; Russ. composer)	Weber, Carl Maria von (1786–1826; Ger. composer)
Scarlatti, Domenico (1685–1757; It. composer/keyboard player)	Sousa, John (1854–1932; Am. composer/bandleader)	Telemann, Georg Philipp (1681–1767; Ger. composer/organist)	Webern, Anton von (1883–1945; Austrian composer)
Schoenberg, Arnold (1874–1951; Am.	Stern, Isaac (b. 1920; Am. violinist, b. in Russia)	Tippett, Sir Michael (b. 1905; Brit. composer)	Weill, Kurt (1900–50; Ger. composer) Wolf, Hugo (1860–1903; Austrian composer)

incomprehensible, inexplicable, unexplainable, unfathomable, unaccountable, insoluble, obscure, arcane, abstruse, cryptic, unknown, recondite, secret, preternatural, supernatural, uncanny, mystical, peculiar, strange, weird, curious, bizarre, undisclosed, mystifying, baffling, puzzling, perplexing, bewildering, confounding. **2** *he was being very mysterious about his whereabouts* secretive, reticent, noncommittal, discreet, evasive, furtive, surreptitious.
Opposites OBVIOUS; STRAIGHTFORWARD; OPEN.

mystery noun **1** *his death remains a mystery* enigma, puzzle, secret, unsolved problem, problem, riddle, conundrum, question, question mark, closed book, unexplored ground, *terra incognita.* **2** *his whereabouts are clothed in mystery* secrecy, concealment, obscurity, obscuration, vagueness, nebulousness, inscrutability, inexplicability.

mystic, mystical adjective **1** *a mystic experience* spiritual, paranormal, transcendental, other-worldly, supernatural, preternatural, non-rational, occult, metaphysical. **2** *mystic rites* symbolic, representational, allegorical,

metaphorical, emblematic, emblematical, non-literal. **3** *mystical events* obscure, cryptic, enigmatic, abstruse, arcane, recondite, inscrutable, inexplicable, unfathomable, mysterious.

mystify verb confuse, bewilder, confound, perplex, baffle, nonplus, puzzle, elude, escape; *inf.* stump, beat, bamboozle.

myth noun **1** *read ancient myths* legend, saga, tale, story, fable, folk tale, allegory, parable, fairy story/tale, bestiary. **2** *her having a rich father was just a myth* fantasy, delusion, figment of the imagination, invention, fabrication, untruth, lie; *inf.* story, fairy story/tale, tall story.

mythical adjective **1** *a mythical creature* legendary, mythological, fabled, chimerical, imaginary, imagined, fabulous, fantastical, fairy-tale, story-book, fictitious, allegorical. **2** *a mythical rich uncle* fantasy, imagined, imaginary, pretended, make-believe, unreal, fictitious, invented, fabricated, made-up, untrue; *inf.* pretend.
Opposites REAL; ACTUAL.

mythology noun body of myths, myths, legend, lore, folklore, folk tales, stories.

Nn

nadir *noun* the lowest point, the lowest level, the bottom, rock-bottom, the depths, all-time low, as low as one can get, zero; *inf.* the pits.
Opposites ZENITH; ACME; CLIMAX.

nag¹ *verb* **1** *parents nagging children* scold, carp, pick on, keep on at, harp on at, be on someone's back, henpeck, bully, upbraid, berate, chivvy, criticize, find fault with, complain to, grumble to; *inf.* go on at. **2** *children nagging mothers about buying toys* badger, pester, plague, torment, harry, goad, worry, vex, harass, irritate; *inf.* hassle, drive up the wall.

nag² *noun his nag of a wife* shrew, scold, harpy, termagant, fault-finder, carper, caviller, complainer, grumbler; *inf.* grouser.

nag³ *noun ride an old nag* broken-down old horse, jade, hack, Rosinante; *inf.* bag of bones, plug.

nagging *adjective* **1** *a nagging wife* scolding, carping, cavilling, criticizing, fault-finding, complaining, grumbling. *See* NAG¹ *verb* 1. **2** *a nagging pain* persistent, continuous, aching, painful, distressing.

naiad *noun* water nymph. *See table at* NYMPH.

nail *noun* **1** *drive a nail into the wood* pin, brad, tack, sprig, rivet. **2** *cut one's nails|the animal's nails* fingernail, toenail, claw, talon, nipper, pincer.

nail *verb* **1** *nail the pieces together* pin, tack, hammer, fix, fasten, secure, join, attach. **2** *nail the headmaster at the meeting* get hold of, grab, get the attention of, make someone commit himself/herself, pin down. **3** *nail his lies|nailed the myth* expose, reveal, detect, uncover, unmask, bare, unearth, dig out. **4** *nail the thief* catch, seize, capture, apprehend, arrest, take into custody; *inf.* collar, nab, pinch.

naive *adjective* **1** *naive young girls* innocent, artless, childlike, simple, ingenuous, guileless, trusting, unsophisticated, unworldly, jejune, natural, unaffected, unpretentious, frank, open, candid. **2** *unbelievably naive employees* gullible, overtrusting, overtrustful, credulous, unsuspicious, unsuspecting, deceivable, dupable, callow, raw, green, immature, inexperienced; *inf.* wet behind the ears.
Opposites DISINGENUOUS; EXPERIENCED; WORLDLY.

naiveté, naivety *noun* **1** *the young girl's naiveté* innocence, artlessness, childlikeness, simplicity, ingenuousness, guilelessness, lack of guile, unsophistication, lack of sophistication, unworldliness, naturalness, candour. *See* NAIVE 1. **2** *their unbelievable naiveté* gullibility, credulousness, credulity, overtrustfulness, lack of suspicion, callowness, greenness, immaturity. *See* NAIVE 2.

naked *adjective* **1** *naked bodies/men* stark naked, nude, in the nude, bare, stripped, exposed, unclothed, undressed, uncovered, undraped, disrobed, *au naturel*; *inf.* without a stitch on, starkers, in one's birthday suit, in the raw, in the altogether, in the buff, naked as the day one was born, mother naked; *Am. inf.* buck naked. **2** *naked landscapes/rooms* bare, barren, stark, uncovered, denuded, stripped, treeless, grassless, unfurnished. **3** *the naked truth* undisguised, unqualified, unadorned, stark, bald, unvarnished, unveiled, unmitigated, unexaggerated, plain, simple, open, patent, evident, apparent, obvious, manifest, overt, unmistakable, blatant, glaring, flagrant. **4** *naked flames/sword* exposed, unprotected, unguarded, uncovered, unsheathed, unwrapped. **5** *feeling naked in an alien country* defenceless, unprotected, vulnerable, exposed, helpless, weak, powerless.
Opposites clothed; embellished.

nakedness *noun* **1** *embarrassed at his nakedness* nudity, bareness, undress, state of undress. *See* NAKED 1. **2** *the nakedness of the landscape* bareness, barrenness, starkness. *See* NAKED 2. **3** *her feeling of nakedness in the alien country* defencelessness, vulnerability, exposure, helplessness. *See* NAKED 5.
Opposites DRESS; PROTECTION.

namby-pamby *adjective* over-sentimental, sentimental, mawkish, maudlin, insipid, colourless, anaemic, feeble, weak, vapid, spineless, effeminate, womanish, effete, prim, prissy, mincing, simpering; *inf.* wet, wishy-washy, wimpish, weedy.

name *noun* **1** *the name of the person/family/plant/tree/book* appellation, designation, cognomen, denomination, sobriquet, title, style, label, tag, epithet, first/second name, Christian/given name, surname, family name, maiden name, nickname, pet name, stage name, pseudonym, alias, *nom de guerre, nom de plume*; *inf.* moniker, handle. **2** *he's a name in the theatre* big name, celebrity, luminary, star, dignitary, VIP, lion; *inf.* celeb, megastar, big noise/shot, bigwig. **3** *make his name in films* reputation, fame, renown, repute, note, distinction, eminence, prominence, honour, esteem, prestige.

name *verb* **1** *name the child/plant* baptize, christen, give a name to, call, entitle, label, style, term, title, dub, denominate. **2** *name the criminal|name the most suitable day* identify, specify, mention, cite, give. **3** *name his successor* appoint, choose, select, pick, nominate, designate.

named *adjective* **1** *a girl named Anne* called, by the name of, under the name of, baptized, christened, entitled, styled. *See* NAME *verb* 1. **2** *named individuals/articles* identified, specified, mentioned, cited, given.

nameless *adjective* **1** *nameless graves* unnamed, untitled, unlabelled, untagged, innominate. **2** *nameless poets/benefactors* unnamed, anonymous, unidentified, undesignated, unspecified. **3** *nameless fears/vices* unspeakable, unutterable, inexpressible, unmentionable, indescribable, abominable, horrible, horrific.

namely *adverb* viz, that is to say, i.e., to wit, specifically.

nap¹ *verb children napping in the afternoon* take a nap, catnap, doze, sleep lightly, rest, lie down, drowse; *inf.* drop off, nod off, snooze, snatch forty winks, get some shut-eye, have a kip, zizz, get some zizz.

nap² *noun have a nap* catnap, doze, light sleep, rest, lie-down; *inf.* snooze, forty winks, shut-eye, kip, zizz.

nap³ *noun the nap on velvet/carpets* pile, down, surface, shag, weave, grain, fibre.

narcissism *noun* self-admiration, self-love, conceit, self-conceit, vanity, egotism.

narcissistic *adjective* self-admiring, self-loving, in love with oneself, conceited, vain, egotistic.

narcotic *adjective narcotic substances* opiate, sleep-inducing, soporific, somnolent, hypnotic, anaesthetic, stupefying, stupefacient, painkilling, pain-dulling, analgesic, anodyne, numbing, calming, tranquillizing, sedative.

narcotic *noun* drug, opiate, sleeping-pill, anaesthetic, painkiller, analgesic, anodyne, tranquillizer, sedative, soporific. *See tables at* DRUG, MEDICINE.

narrate *verb* tell, relate, recount, recite, unfold, give an account of, give a report of, set forth, chronicle, describe, detail, portray, sketch out, rehearse, repeat.

narration *noun* **1** *a fascinating narration* account, story, story-telling, tale, telling, relation, recital, reciting, report, chronicling, chronicle, description, portrayal, sketch, rehearsal, repetition. **2** *do the narration for the film* voice-over, voice, spoken part.

narrative *noun* account, statement, report, chronicle, history, story, tale.

narrator *noun* **1** *spellbound by the narrator* recounter, relater, reporter, describer, chronicler, annalist, storyteller, taleteller, teller of tales, raconteur, anecdotist, author, writer. **2** *the film's narrator* voice-over.

narrow *adjective* **1** *narrow roads/waists* not wide, not broad, narrow-gauged, slender, thin, slim, slight, spare, attenuated, tapering. **2** *narrow spaces* confined, confining, constricted, tight, cramped, close, restricted, limited, incommodious, pinched, straitened, squeezed, meagre, scant, scanty, spare, scrimped, exiguous. **3** *a narrow range* limited, restricted, select, exclusive. **4** *a narrow interpretation* literal, exact, precise, close, faithful. **5** *a narrow old woman* narrow-minded, intolerant, illiberal, prejudiced, bigoted, parochial, provincial, insular, small-minded. *See* NARROW-MINDED.
Opposites WIDE; BROAD; BROAD-MINDED.

narrowly *adverb* **1** *narrowly escaped with his life* barely, scarcely, just, only just, just and no more, by a hair's breadth; *inf.* by a whisker.

2 *look at her opponent narrowly* closely, carefully, scrutinizingly, attentively.

narrow-minded *adjective* intolerant, illiberal, unliberal, over-conservative, conservative, hidebound, dyed-in-the-wool, reactionary, close-minded, unreasonable, prejudiced, bigoted, biased, discriminatory, warped, twisted, jaundiced, parochial, provincial, insular, small-minded, petty-minded, petty, mean-spirited, prudish, strait-laced.

narrows *plural noun* strait, sound, channel, passage.

nascent *adjective* beginning, budding, embryonic, incipient, young, growing, developing, evolving, burgeoning, forming.

nastiness *noun* **1** *appalled by the nastiness of the sight/mess/taste/smell* unpleasantness, disagreeableness, vileness, foulness, loathsomeness, ugliness, offensiveness, squalor, filthiness, filth, pollution, unsavouriness, smelliness, stink; *inf.* yuckiness, yukkiness, yuck, grottiness. *See* NASTY 1. **2** *the nastiness of the situation* dangerousness, danger, seriousness. *See* NASTY 2. **3** *the nastiness of his temper* ill temper, ill nature, ill humour, bad-temperedness, crossness, unpleasantness, viciousness, spitefulness; *inf.* grouchiness. *See* NASTY 3. **4** *the nastiness of the weather* disagreeableness, foulness, wetness. *See* NASTY 4. **5** *the nastiness of the videos* obscenity, pornography, indecency, foulness, smuttiness, vulgarity, lewdness. *See* NASTY 5.

nasty *adjective* **1** *a nasty sight/mess/taste/smell* unpleasant, disagreeable, distasteful, horrible, vile, foul, hateful, loathsome, revolting, disgusting, odious, obnoxious, repellent, repugnant, ugly, offensive, objectionable, noisome, squalid, dirty, filthy, impure, polluted, tainted, unpalatable, unsavoury, unappetizing, evil-smelling, foul-smelling, smelly, stinking, rank, fetid, malodorous, mephitic; *inf.* yucky, yukky, grotty, niffing. **2** *a nasty illness/situation* dangerous, serious, critical, crucial, severe, alarming, threatening. **3** *a nasty old man | was so nasty to his mother* ill-tempered, ill-natured, ill-humoured, bad-tempered, cross, surly, unpleasant, disagreeable, vicious, spiteful, malicious, mean; *inf.* grouchy. **4** *nasty weather* unpleasant, disagreeable, foul, wet, rainy, stormy, foggy. **5** *nasty jokes/videos* obscene, pornographic, indecent, foul, vile, blue, off colour, smutty, bawdy, vulgar, ribald, risqué, lewd, lascivious, licentious.
Opposites DELIGHTFUL; PLEASANT; AGREEABLE.

nation *noun* country, land, state, kingdom, empire, realm, republic, confederation, union of states, commonwealth, people, race, tribe, society, community, population. *See table at* COUNTRY.

national *adjective* **1** *national not local issues* state, public, federal, governmental, civic, civil. **2** *national as opposed to international problems* domestic, internal, indigenous, native. **3** *a national strike/search* nationwide, country-wide, state, coast-to-coast, widespread, overall, comprehensive, general.
Opposites LOCAL; INTERNATIONAL; DOMESTIC.

national *noun a national of this country* citizen, subject, native, resident, inhabitant.

nationalism *noun* patriotism, allegiance/loyalty/fealty to one's country, chauvinism, jingoism, xenophobia.

nationalistic *adjective* patriotic, loyal to one's country, pro one's country, chauvinistic, jingoistic, xenophobic.

nationality *noun* nation, race, ethnic group, tribe. *See table. See also table at* PEOPLE.

nationwide *adjective* national, country-wide, state, coast-to-coast, widespread, overall, comprehensive, all-embracing, general, extensive.

native *adjective* **1** *native instinct* inborn, inherent, innate, connate, built-in, intrinsic, instinc-tive, intuitive, natural, natural-born, congenital, hereditary, inherited, in the blood, in the family, inbred, ingrained. **2** *native/plants/produce* indigenous, original, home-grown, home-made, domestic, local. **3** *native tongue* mother, vernacular. **4** *native peoples* original, indigenous, aboriginal, autochthonous.

native *noun a native of France | natives of other continents* inhabitant, dweller, resident, citizen, national, aborigine, autochthon.

nativity *noun* birth, childbirth, delivery, parturition.

natter *verb nattering away to her neighbour* chat, chatter, gossip, talk idly, prattle, blather, blether, prate, gabble, jabber, palaver; *inf.* rabbit on, witter on, jaw.

NATIONALITIES

Africa	Austrians	Cambodians	Niueans
Algerians	Azerbaijanis	Chinese	Palauans
Angolans	Belgians	Filipinos	Papuans
Botswanans	Belorussians/	Indians	Rarotongans
Cameroonians	Belarussians	Indonesians	Samoans
Chadians	Bosnians	Iranians	Tahitians
Congolese	Bulgarians	Iraqis	Tongan
Egyptians	Croats/Croatians	Israelis	Trobrianders
Eritreans	Cypriots	Japanese	**North American**
Ethiopians	Czechs	Jordanians	Americans
Gabonese	Danes	Kazakhs	Canadians
Gambians	Dutch	Khmer	Mexicans
Ghanaians	Estonians	Koreans (North and	**South and Central American**
Guineans	Finns	South)	**and Caribbean**
Ivorians	French	Kuwaitis	Antiguans
Kenyans	Georgians	Kyrgyz/Kirghiz	Argentinians
Liberians	Germans	Laotians	Bahamians
Libyans	Greeks	Lebanese	Barbadians/Bajans
Madagascans	Hellenes	Malaysians	Barbudans
Malagasy	Hungarians	Maldivians	Belizeans
Malawians	Icelanders	Mauritians	Bermudans
Malians	Irish	Mongolians	Bolivians
Mauritanians/	Italians	Nepalese	Brazilians
Mauretanians	Latvians	Omanis	Chileans
Moroccans	Lithuanians	Pakistanis	Colombians
Mozambicans	Luxembourgeois	Qataris	Costa Ricans
Namibians	Macedonians	Saudis	Cubans
Nigerians	Maltese	Sikkimese	Dominicans
Rwandans	Moldavians/	Singaporeans	Ecuadorians
Senegalese	Moldovans	Sri Lankans	Grenadians
Senegambians	Monegasques	Syrians	Guatemalans
Sierra Leoneans	Netherlanders	Taiwanese	Guayanans
Somalis	Norwegians	Tajiks	Haitians
South Africans	Poles	Thais	Hondurans
Sudanese	Portuguese	Tibetans	Jamaicans
Swazis	Romanians	Turks	Kittitians
Tanzanians	Russians	Turkmen	Martiniquans
Tigreans	Serbs	Uzbeks	Nicaraguans
Togolese	Slovaks	Vietnamese	Panamanians
Tunisians	Slovenes	Yemenis	Paraguayans
Ugandans	Spaniards	**Australasian and**	Peruvians
Voltaic	Swedes	**Oceanic**	Puerto Ricans
Zaireans	Swiss	Australians	Salvadoreans
Zambians	Ukrainians	Fijians	Surinamese
Zimbabweans	**Asia**	Gilbertese	Trinidadians
Europe	Afghans	Marquesans	Uruguayans
Albanians	Bangladeshis	Marshallese	Venezuelans
Andorrans	Bhutanese	Nauruans	West Indians
Armenians	Burmese	New Zealanders	

natter *noun having a natter with her friend* chat, gossip, talk, conversation, tête-à-tête, blather, blether, palaver; *inf.* chin-wag, jaw.

natty *adjective* dapper, trim, spruce, well-turned-out, well-dressed, smart, stylish, fashionable, chic, elegant; *inf.* snazzy, trendy.

natural *adjective* **1** *in the natural course of events* usual, normal, regular, common, ordinary, everyday, typical, routine, run-of-the-mill. **2** *her natural instincts* native, native-born, in-born, inherent, innate, connate, built-in, intrinsic, instinctive, intuitive, natural, natural-born, congenital, hereditary, inherited, ingrained. **3** *natural charm* artless, ingenuous, candid, open, frank, genuine, real, authentic, simple, unsophisticated, unaffected, unpretentious, spontaneous, relaxed, unstudied. **4** *natural produce* organic, pure, unrefined, unpolished, unbleached, unmixed, whole, plain, real, chemical-free, additive-free. **Opposites** ABNORMAL; UNNATURAL; ARTIFICIAL; REFINED.

naturalist *noun* botanist, biologist, zoologist, ecologist, natural historian. *See table at* SCIENTIST.

naturalistic *adjective* realistic, real-life, true-to-life, lifelike, factual, graphic, representational; *inf.* kitchen-sink, warts and all.

naturalize *verb* **1** *people wishing to be naturalized* endow with rights of citizenship, confer citizenship on, enfranchise. **2** *plants becoming naturalized* introduce, acclimatize, domesticate; *Am.* acclimate. **3** *new words having been naturalized* adopt, accept, take in, assimilate, absorb, incorporate, homogenize.

naturally *adverb* **1** *behave naturally* artlessly, ingenuously, candidly, unaffectedly, unpretentiously, spontaneously. *See* NATURAL 3. **2** *naturally, he is going* of course, certainly, as might be expected, as you/one would expect, as was anticipated.

naturalness *noun* **1** *the naturalness of her charm* artlessness, ingenuousness, openness, genuineness, simplicity, unsophistication, lack of sophistication, lack of affectation, unpretentiousness, spontaneity. *See* NATURAL 3. **2** *the naturalness of the produce* purity, pureness, wholeness, lack of chemicals, lack of additives.

nature *noun* **1** *it is in the nature of man* character, characteristic, essence, essential qualities/attributes/features/traits, constitution, make-up, complexion, stamp, personality, identity. **2** *communing with nature* Mother Nature, natural forces, creation, the environment, the earth, mother earth, the world, the universe, the cosmos; landscape, scenery. **3** *things of this nature* kind, sort, type, variety, description, category, class, classification, species, style. **4** *he has a pleasant nature* temperament, temper, personality, disposition, humour, mood, outlook.

naught *noun* nothing, nought, nil, zero, love, nothingness; *inf.* zilch.

naughty *adjective* **1** *a naughty child* bad, mischievous, badly behaved, misbehaving, disobedient, defiant, unruly, roguish, wayward, delinquent, undisciplined, unmanageable, ungovernable, fractious, refractory, perverse,

errant, sinful, wicked, evil. **2** *naughty films* blue, risqué, smutty, off-colour, indecent, improper, vulgar, bawdy, ribald, lewd, licentious. **Opposites** GOOD; well-behaved; OBEDIENT; DECENT.

nausea *noun* **1** *travellers overcome by nausea* sickness, vomiting, retching, gagging, biliousness, queasiness, faintness, seasickness, car-sickness, airsickness, motion sickness, morning sickness; *inf.* throwing-up. **2** *horror films causing feelings of nausea* disgust, revulsion, repugnance, distaste, aversion, loathing, abhorrence, detestation, odium.

nauseate *verb* make sick, sicken, make one's gorge rise, turn one's stomach, revolt, disgust, repel, repulse, offend; *inf.* make someone want to throw up; *Am. inf.* gross out.

nauseous *adjective* **1** *nauseous food* nauseating, sickening, sickly, disgusting, revolting; *inf.* sick-making. **2** *a nauseous sight* disgusting, revolting, repulsive, repellent, repugnant, offensive, loathsome, abhorrent, odious. **3** *feeling nauseous* nauseated, sick, queasy, green, unwell, off colour, indisposed, seasick, carsick, airsick; *inf.* green about the gills, under the weather, below par.

nautical *adjective* maritime, naval, marine, seagoing, seafaring, yachting, boating, sailing.

navel *noun* **1** *the baby's navel* umbilicus; *lit.* omphalos; *inf.* belly-button, tummy-button. **2** *the navel of the organization* central point, centre, middle, hub.

navigable *adjective* **1** *navigable rivers* negotiable, passable, traversable, clear, unobstructed. **2** *navigable vessels* steerable, sailable, seaworthy, watertight.

navigate *verb* **1** *the captain/passenger navigated* direct the course, plan/plot the course, give directions, map-read. **2** *navigate the craft* steer, pilot, manoeuvre, guide, direct, handle, drive, skipper. **3** *navigate the Atlantic* sail, sail across, cross, traverse, cruise, journey, voyage.

navigation *noun* **1** *the navigation of the craft* steering, pilotage, manoeuvring, guidance, directing. *See* NAVIGATE 2, 3. **2** *study navigation* seamanship, pilotage, helmsmanship, chart-reading, map-reading.

navigator *noun* pilot, helmsman, seaman, mariner. *See tables at* EXPLORER, PILOT.

navvy *noun* labourer, manual worker, workman.

navy *noun* *watch the arrival of the navy* fleet, flotilla, armada.

nay *adverb* impressive, nay, magnificent and indeed, or rather, and even, and more than that.

near *adjective* **1** *the shop's very near* close, close by, nearby, alongside, at close range/quarters, accessible, within reach, close/near at hand, at hand, handy, not far off/away, a stone's throw away, neighbouring, adjacent, adjoining, bordering, contiguous, proximate; *inf.* within spitting distance. **2** *the time is near | the near future* close/near at hand, next, approaching, coming, imminent, forthcoming, in the offing, impending, looming, proximate, immediate. **3** *near relatives* closely related, related, connected, akin, allied, close, intimate, familiar, dear. **4** *a near escape* close, narrow, by a hair's breadth; *inf.* by a whisker. **5** *the old man's so near* mean, close, miserly, tight-fisted, close-fisted, niggardly, parsimonious, ungenerous, grasping; *inf.* tight; *Am.* cheap. **near miss** near thing, narrow escape; *inf.* close shave. **Opposites** FAR; DISTANT; REMOTE.

near *adverb they live near* close, nearby, close by, alongside, close/near at hand, at hand, within reach, within close range, within earshot, within sight, not far off/away, a stone's throw away; *inf.* within spitting distance.

near *preposition near the house* close to, close by, in the neighbourhood of, next to, adjacent to, alongside, bordering on, contiguous to, adjoining, within reach of, a stone's throw away from; *inf.* within spitting distance of.

near *verb we are nearing our destination* get near to, draw near to, get close to, approach, come close to, come towards, move towards, lean towards.

nearly *adverb nearly all gone* almost, all but, as good as, virtually, next to, close to, well-nigh, about, just about, practically, roughly, approximately, not quite; *inf.* pretty nearly/much/well.

nearness *noun* **1** *the nearness of the shops* closeness, accessibility, handiness, proximity, propinquity. *See* NEAR *adjective* 1. **2** *the nearness of the wedding day* closeness, imminence, immediacy. *See* NEAR *adjective* 2. **3** *the nearness of the relatives* closeness, intimacy, familiarity. *See* NEAR *adjective* 3. **4** *the nearness of the old man* meanness, miserliness, tight-fistedness, niggardliness, parsimony, parsimoniousness. *See* NEAR *adjective* 5.

near-sighted *adjective* short-sighted, myopic, purblind.

neat *adjective* **1** *a neat house* neat and tidy, neat as a new pin, tidy, orderly, well-ordered, straight, in good order, shipshape and Bristol fashion, in apple-pie order, spick and span. **2** *a neat person/dresser* tidy, spruce, trim, smart, dapper, well-groomed, well-turned-out, dainty, fastidious, organized, well-organized, methodical, systematic; *inf.* natty. **3** *wearing neat clothes* simple, plain, unadorned, unornamented, unpretentious, unassuming. **4** *a neat saying* elegant, well-put, well-expressed, well-turned, clever, witty, pithy, apt, felicitous. **5** *neat footwork/movements* adroit, skilful, expert, practised, dexterous, deft, accurate, precise, nimble, agile, graceful, stylish, effortless, easy. **6** *neat drinks* straight, undiluted, unmixed, pure. **Opposites** DISORDERLY; UNTIDY; CLUMSY.

neatly *adverb* **1** *neatly dressed* tidily, smartly, simply, plainly. *See* NEAT 2, 3. **2** *neatly put* aptly, cleverly, wittily, pithily. *See* NEAT 4. **3** *neatly executed steps* adroitly, skilfully, expertly, deftly, precisely, nimbly, agilely, gracefully, effortlessly. *See* NEAT 5.

neatness *noun* **1** *the neatness of the room* tidiness, orderliness, straightness. *See* NEAT 1. **2** *the neatness of her dress* tidiness, spruceness,

trimness, smartness, fastidiousness, simplicity, plainness. *See* NEAT 2, 3. **3** *the neatness of the remark* elegance, cleverness, wit, pithiness, aptness, felicity. **4** *the neatness of her movements* adroitness, deftness, precision, nimbleness, grace, gracefulness, ease, effortlessness. *See* NEAT 5.

nebulous *adjective* **1** *nebulous figures in the distance* shapeless, unformed, amorphous, shadowy, dim, indistinct, indefinite, vague, unclear, obscure, misty, cloudy, hazy, fuzzy. **2** *nebulous ideas about his future career* uncertain, indefinite, indeterminate, imprecise, vague, hazy, unformed, abstract, muddled, confused, ambiguous.

necessarily *adverb* **1** *plans which are necessarily vague* of necessity, by force of circumstance, willy-nilly, like it or not, perforce. **2** *he won't necessarily have to go* certainly, definitely, undoubtedly, inevitably, unavoidably, inescapably, automatically, incontrovertibly, inexorably.

necessary *adjective* **1** *a necessary reduction in expenditure* needed, needful, essential, required, requisite, vital, indispensable, imperative, mandatory, obligatory, compulsory, *de rigueur*. **2** *a necessary evil* certain, sure, inevitable, unavoidable, inescapable, inexorable, ineluctable, fated, preordained. **Opposites** UNNECESSARY; NON-ESSENTIAL; DISPENSABLE.

necessitate *verb* require, make necessary, demand, call for, entail, involve, exact, oblige, compel, impel, force, leave no choice but to.

necessities *plural noun food and clothing are basic necessities* needs, essentials, requisites, requirements, indispensables, fundamentals, necessaries, exigencies.

necessitous *adjective* needy, in need, in want, poor, badly off, impoverished, poverty-stricken, penniless, impecunious, penurious, destitute, indigent, disadvantaged, underprivileged, unable to make ends meet, in straitened circumstances.

necessity *noun* **1** *silence is a necessity* essential, requisite, requirement, prerequisite, necessary, fundamental, *sine qua non*, desideratum. **2** *she left out of necessity* need, needfulness, call, force/pressure of circumstance, exigency, obligation. **3** *necessity made them steal* need, neediness, want, poverty, deprivation, privation, penury, destitution, indigence. **4** *a logical necessity that night follows day* certainty, inevitability, inescapability, inexorability, ineluctability, fate, destiny.

necromancer *noun* spiritualist, spiritist, medium, magician, wizard, warlock, witch, sorcerer/sorceress, enchanter/enchantress, wonder-worker, thaumaturgist.

necromancy *noun* spiritualism, magic, black magic, black art, wizardry, witchcraft, witchery, sorcery, enchantment, spell-casting, spell-weaving, wonder-working, thaumaturgy, demonology, voodooism.

necropolis *noun* cemetery, graveyard, churchyard, burial-ground, burial place, garden of remembrance, memorial park, God's Acre.

née *adjective* born, formerly, previously, heretofore.

need *verb* **1** *it needs work on it* have need of, require, necessitate, demand, call for, have occasion for, want, lack, be without. **2** *he needs her* miss, desire, yearn for, pine for, crave for. **3** *I didn't need to go* have to, be under an obligation to, be obliged to, be compelled to, be under a compulsion to.

need *noun* **1** *their needs are few* requirement, want, wish, demand, prerequisite, requisite, essential, desideratum. **2** *he has need of a coat* want, lack, shortage, requirement. **3** *no need to be frightened | there is no need to go* necessity, call, force of circumstance, exigency, obligation. **4** *people in need* neediness, want, poverty, deprivation, privation, penury, destitution, indigence. **5** *in one's hour of need* crisis, emergency, urgency, distress, trouble, extremity, exigency.

needful *adjective* *do what is needful* needed, requisite, required, stipulated, necessary, essential, vital, indispensable.

needle *noun* **1** *sharp-pointed steel needles* sewing needle, darner, bodkin, knitting-needle; hypodermic needle. **2** *the needle on the dial* arrow, pointer, indicator. **3** *pricked by a needle in the wood* pine needle, thorn, prickle, bramble, briar, bristle, spine.

needle *verb* **1** *needle them into action* goad, spur, prod, prick, sting, press, nag, persuade. **2** *the boys were deliberately needling the teacher* provoke, bait, harass, annoy, anger, irritate, vex, irk, nettle, ruffle, taunt, pester; *inf.* aggravate, rile, niggle, get to.

needless *adjective* unnecessary, uncalled-for, gratuitous, undesired, unwanted, pointless, useless, dispensable, expendable, inessential. *Opposites* NECESSARY; USEFUL.

needlework *noun* needlecraft, sewing, stitching, embroidery, tapestry, crocheting. *See tables at* SEWING, STITCH.

needy *adjective* necessitous, poor, poverty-stricken, deprived, disadvantaged, penurious, impecunious, impoverished, penniless, destitute, indigent, on the breadline, in straitened circumstances. *Opposites* WEALTHY; AFFLUENT.

ne'er-do-well *noun* good-for-nothing, wastrel, black sheep, loafer, idler, layabout, shirker, sluggard, drone; *inf.* skiver, waster.

nefarious *adjective* wicked, evil, sinful, iniquitous, villainous, criminal, heinous, atrocious, vile, foul, base, abominable, odious, horrible, horrendous, dreadful, terrible, detestable, loathsome, execrable, depraved, shameful, scandalous, monstrous, outrageous, flagitious.

negate *verb* **1** *facts negating your theory* nullify, render null and void, annul, void, invalidate, cancel, revoke, rescind, abrogate, repeal, retract, countermand, disestablish, reject, disprove, explode, overrule. **2** *try to negate the existence of God* deny, dispute, call in/into question, gainsay, contradict, disprove, refute, discredit, disclaim, repudiate, renounce, oppose. *Opposites* CONFIRM; RATIFY.

negation *noun* **1** *the negation of the theory* nullification, voiding, cancellation, revocation, rescinding, abrogation, repeal, retraction. *See* NEGATE 1. **2** *the attempted negation of the existence of God* denial, contradiction, disproval, disclaiming, repudiation. *See* NEGATE 2. **3** *anarchy is the negation of government* opposite, reverse, antithesis, contrary, converse, want, lack, absence, deficiency. **4** *a life full of negation* nothingness, nothing, nullity, blankness, void, non-existence, vacuity, nonentity.

negative *adjective* **1** *negative replies* in the negative, saying 'no', rejecting, refusing, dissenting, contradictory, contradicting, contrary, opposing, opposite, opposed, denying, gainsaying. **2** *rather a negative young man* unenthusiastic, uninterested, lackadaisical, colourless, anaemic, insipid, vapid, weak, spineless, purposeless. **3** *a negative reaction* pessimistic, defeatist, gloomy, gloom-laden, cynical, jaundiced, critical, fault-finding, complaining, unhelpful, unconstructive, uncooperative. *Opposites* POSITIVE; AFFIRMATIVE; ENTHUSIASTIC; OPTIMISTIC.

negative *noun* *reply in the negative* rejection, refusal, dissension, opposite, denial, contradiction.

negative *verb* **1** *negative a request/application* turn down, refuse, assent to, reject, veto, forbid, prohibit, give the thumbs down to, give the red light to, nullify, negate. **2** *negative his theory/statement* disprove, give the lie to, belie, show to be false, invalidate, refute, contradict, deny, negate, gainsay, discredit, explode, squash. **3** *negative the effect* neutralize, counteract, cancel out, offset, balance, equalize.

neglect *verb* **1** *neglect their children* fail to look after, fail to provide for, abandon, forsake, leave alone. **2** *neglect his work* let slide, skimp on, shirk, be remiss about, be lax about, pay little/no attention to, not attend to, leave undone, procrastinate about. **3** *neglect to lock the door* omit, fail, forget, not remember. **4** *neglect his warning* disregard, ignore, pay no attention/heed to, overlook, disdain, scorn, slight, spurn, rebuff. *Opposites* care for (*see* CARE); attend to (*see* ATTEND); HEED.

neglect *noun* **1** *parents/workers guilty of neglect* negligence, neglectfulness, lack of proper care and attention, remissness, carelessness, heedlessness, lack of concern, unconcern, slackness, laxity, laxness, failure to act, dereliction, default. **2** *his neglect of her warning* disregard, ignoring, inattention to, heedlessness, indifference to, disdain, scorn, slight, spurning, rebuff. *Opposites* CARE; ATTENTION.

neglected *adjective* **1** *neglected children* uncared for, unkempt, mistreated, abandoned, forsaken. **2** *neglected gardens* untended, derelict, overgrown. **3** *neglected opportunities/warnings* disregarded, ignored, spurned, unappreciated, underestimated.

neglectful *adjective* negligent, remiss, lax, careless, inattentive, heedless, thoughtless, unmindful, forgetful, indifferent, uncaring.

negligence *noun* neglect, lack of proper care and attention, remissness, laxity, laxness, dereliction, dereliction of duty, carelessness, inattention, inattentiveness, heedlessness, thoughtlessness, unmindfulness, forgetfulness, inadvertence, oversight, omission, failure, disregard, default, shortcoming, indifference, slackness, sloppiness, slipshodness, procrastination.

negligent *adjective* neglectful, remiss, lax, careless, inattentive, heedless, thoughtless, neglectful, unmindful, uncaring, forgetful, disregardful, indifferent, offhand, cursory, slack, sloppy, slapdash, slipshod, procrastinating, dilatory. *Opposites* CAREFUL; ATTENTIVE; CONSCIENTIOUS.

negligible *adjective* *a negligible amount* trivial, trifling, insignificant, of no account, not worth bothering about, paltry, petty, tiny, minute, small, minor, inconsequential, inappreciable, imperceptible. *Opposites* SIGNIFICANT; CONSIDERABLE.

negotiable *adjective* **1** *pay is negotiable* open to discussion, discussable, debatable, subject to bargaining, transactional. **2** *negotiable cheques* transferable. **3** *negotiable roads* passable, navigable, crossable, traversable, penetrable, unblocked, unobstructed.

negotiate *verb* **1** *negotiate a deal/settlement* work out, thrash out, arrange, reach an agreement on, agree on, settle, come to terms about, conclude, pull off, bring off, contract, complete, transact, execute, fulfil, orchestrate, engineer. **2** *unions and managements negotiate* bargain, drive a bargain, hold talks, confer, debate, discuss, discuss terms, discuss a settlement, consult together, parley, haggle, wheel and deal, dicker. **3** *negotiate the hurdles | careful negotiating the icy roads* clear, get over, get through, pass over, make it over, cross, get past, get round, surmount.

negotiation *noun* **1** *the negotiations went on all day* bargaining, conference, debate, talks, discussion, consultation, parleying, haggling, wheeling and dealing, dickering. **2** *the negotiation of the settlement* working out, thrashing out, discussing the terms of, settlement, pulling off, transaction. See NEGOTIATE 1, 2.

negotiator *noun* bargainer, parleyer, haggler, wheeler-dealer, dickerer.

neighbourhood *noun* **1** *move to a different neighbourhood* district, area, region, locality, part, quarter, precinct, community; *inf.* neck of the woods, stamping-ground. **2** *he doesn't live here but somewhere in the neighbourhood* vicinity, surrounding district, environs, proximity, purlieus. **in the neighbourhood of** *in the neigh-*

bourhood of £5000 around, about, approximately, roughly, nearly, almost, close to, just about.

neighbouring *adjective* *neighbouring village/families* adjacent, adjoining, bordering, abutting, contiguous, next, nearby, nearest, closest, near, very near, close/near at hand, not far away, in the vicinity.

neighbourly *adjective* friendly, cordial, kind, helpful, obliging, generous, hospitable, companionable, sociable, amiable, affable, genial, well-disposed, civil, easy to get along with. *Opposites* UNFRIENDLY; UNKIND.

neither *adjective* *neither sister* not either, not the one nor the other.

nemesis *noun* **1** *nemesis won the day* fate, destiny, retribution, vengeance. **2** *meet his nemesis* downfall, undoing, ruin, destruction, Waterloo.

neologism *noun* neology, new word, new term, new phrase, new expression, coinage, newly coined word, made-up word, nonce-word, portmanteau word, vogue word; *inf.* buzz-word.

neophyte *noun* **1** *neophytes in the religious community* novice, noviciate, convert, proselyte, catechumen. **2** *introducing the neophytes to the club* beginner, newcomer, new member, new entrant, new recruit, raw recruit, initiate, novice, noviciate, tiro, greenhorn, learner, trainee, apprentice, probationer, pupil, student; *inf.* rookie.

ne plus ultra *noun* the ultimate, the last word, acme, culmination, perfection, the uttermost degree.

nepotism *noun* favouritism, patronage, partisanship, partiality, preferential treatment; *inf.* the old boy network.

nerve *noun* **1** *rock-climbing requires nerve* courage, courageousness, bravery, valour, intrepidity, fearlessness, daring, coolness, cool-headedness, boldness, pluck, gameness, hardihood, mettle, spirit, backbone, fortitude, endurance, firmness of purpose, resolution, stout-heartedness, determination, tenacity, steadfastness; *inf.* grit, guts, spunk, bottle. **2** *she had the nerve to ask for more* temerity, impudence, impertinence, effrontery, cheek, insolence, audacity, boldness, presumption, gall, brazenness; *inf.* neck, face, brass neck, brass, sauce, chutzpah. **3** *he damaged a nerve in his hand* nerve fibre. See table.

nerve *verb* soldiers nerved by his presence embolden, encourage, hearten, steel, fortify. **nerve oneself** *nerve oneself to climb up* brace oneself, steel oneself, summon/gather/screw up one's courage; *inf.* psych oneself up.

HUMAN NERVOUS SYSTEM

autonomic nervous system	optic nerve	sensory nerves
brain	parasympathetic nervous	solar plexus
central nervous system	system	spinal cord
cranial nerves	peripheral nervous system	spinal nerves
femoral nerve	peroneal nerve	sympathetic nervous system
motor nerves	radial nerve	tibial nerve
nerve cell/neurone	sciatic nerve	ulnar nerve

nerve-racking *adjective* stressful, worrying, anxious, disquieting, tense, harrowing, frightening, distressing, difficult, trying, harassing; *inf.* nail-biting.

nerves *plural noun* nervousness, strain, nervous tension, tenseness, tension, stress, anxiety, worry, apprehensiveness, apprehension; *inf.* butterflies in the stomach, collywobbles, the jitters, the willies.

nervous *adjective* **1** *a nervous person | she is of a nervous disposition* easily frightened, timid, timorous, fearful, apprehensive, anxious, edgy, highly-strung, tense, strained, excitable, jumpy, hysterical; *inf.* nervy. **2** *feeling nervous about the interview* on edge, edgy, tense, strained, anxious, agitated, worried, fretful, uneasy, disquieted, restless, impatient, excitable, jumpy, on tenterhooks, fidgety, ruffled, flustered, apprehensive, perturbed, fearful, frightened, scared, with one's heart in one's mouth, quaking, trembling, shaking, shaking in one's shoes, shaky; *inf.* nervy, with butterflies in one's stomach, jittery, twitchy, in a state, uptight, wired.
Opposites BOLD; CALM; LAID-BACK.

nervous breakdown *noun* breakdown, mental breakdown, nervous collapse, personal crisis, clinical depression; *inf.* crack-up.

nervousness *noun* **1** *given to nervousness* timidity, timorousness, fearfulness, anxiety, tenseness. *See* NERVOUS 1. **2** *a feeling of nervousness about the interview* edginess, tension, nervous tension, tenseness, strain, stress, anxiety, agitation, worry, uneasiness, disquiet, restlessness, impatience, jumpiness, apprehensiveness, apprehension, perturbation, fearfulness, trembling; *inf.* nerviness, jitteriness, twitchiness. *See* NERVOUS 2.

nervy *adjective* **1** *a nervy kind of person* nervous, timid, timorous, fearful, anxious, highly-strung, tense, excitable. *See* NERVOUS 1. **2** *feeling nervy about the outcome* edgy, on edge, tense, anxious, worried, fretful, uneasy, restless, impatient, on tenterhooks, apprehensive, shaky, jumpy; *inf.* jittery, uptight. *See* NERVOUS 2.

nescient *adjective* ignorant, unaware, unconscious, unenlightened, benighted, uneducated, illiterate, unschooled, unknowledgeable.

nest *noun* **1** *birds/creatures building nests* bird's nest, eyrie, wasps' nest, ants' nest, lair, den, drey, lodge, burrow, set, form. **2** *a love-nest | a thieves' nest* retreat, hideaway, hiding-place, shelter, refuge, snuggery, resort, den, haunt; *inf.* hide-out, hidey-hole. **3** *a nest of tables* set, cluster, assemblage, group, series.

nest egg *noun* life savings, savings, reserve funds, reserve, money/something for a rainy day, cache.

nestle *verb* snuggle, curl up, huddle together, cuddle up, nuzzle.

net¹ *noun* **1** *trim a dress with net | net curtains | ball hit the net* netting, tulle, fishnet, meshwork, mesh, latticework, lattice, openwork, webbing, tracery, reticulum. **2** *fishermen casting their nets* fishing net, drag, drag-net, drift, drift-net, seine, seine-net. **3** *fall into the enemy's net* trap, booby trap, snare, mesh, pitfall, stratagem.

net² *verb* *net the animal/runaway* catch, take captive, trap, snare, ensnare, entangle, enmesh, bag; *inf.* nab, collar.

net³, nett *adjective* **1** *their net salary* take-home, after-tax, after-deductions, bottom-line, clear. **2** *the net result* final, ultimate, concluding, conclusive, closing, actual.

net⁴, nett *verb* *was netting £200 per week* take home, clear, earn, make, bring in, get, pocket, receive, gain, obtain, realize; *inf.* pull in.

nether *adjective* **1** *in the nether part of the store* lower, low, low-level, bottom, under, basement, underground. **2** *myths about the nether regions* infernal, hellish, underworld, Hadean, Plutonian, Stygian, Avernal.
Opposites UPPER.

nettle *verb* irritate, provoke, ruffle, try someone's patience, annoy, incense, exasperate, irk, vex, pique, bother, pester, harass, torment, plague; *inf.* aggravate, rile, peeve, rub up the wrong way, get under someone's skin, get in someone's hair, get someone's goat, get to.

nettled *adjective* irritated, irritable, provoked, ruffled, annoyed, incensed, irked, vexed, piqued, harassed; *inf.* riled, peeved. *See* NETTLE.

network *noun* **1** *a pattern consisting of a network of lines* meshwork, latticework, openwork, mesh, lattice, webbing, tracery, filigree, fretwork. **2** *a network of old friends | the old boy network* interconnection, nexus, system, complex, organization, structure, arrangement, formulation. **3** *a network of roads | the electricity network* interconnection, grid, circuitry, plexus.

neurosis *noun* mental illness, mental disorder, psychological disorder, mental disturbance, mental derangement, mental/emotional instability, psychological maladjustment, psychoneurosis, psychopathy, obsession, phobia, fixation.

neurotic *adjective* **1** *treating neurotic patients* mentally ill, mentally disturbed, mentally deranged, unstable, maladjusted, psychopathic, obsessive, phobic. **2** *his wife is completely neurotic* suffering from nerves, over-anxious, obsessive, phobic, fixated, compulsive, over-sensitive, hysterical, irrational.
Opposites STABLE; WELL-BALANCED; CALM; LAID-BACK.

neuter *adjective* *neuter organisms* asexual, sexless, unsexed.

neuter *verb* **1** *neuter a tom-cat/bull* castrate, geld, emasculate, dress; *inf.* cut, fix, doctor. **2** *neuter a bitch* spay, dress; *inf.* fix, doctor.

neutral *adjective* **1** *referees must be neutral* impartial, unbiased, unprejudiced, open-minded, non-partisan, without favouritism, even-handed, disinterested, non-aligned, dispassionate, objective, detached, uninvolved, uncommitted. **2** *neutral countries during the war* non-combatant, non-combative, non-fighting, non-participating, non-aligned, unallied, uninvolved, non-interventionist. **3** *he's rather a neutral character* indefinite, indeterminate, unremarkable, ordinary, commonplace, average, run-of-the-mill, everyday, bland, uninter-

esting, colourless, insipid, dull. **4** *curtains of a neutral colour* beige, greige, stone-coloured, stone, pale, colourless, uncoloured, achromatic, achromic.
Opposites BIASED; PARTISAN; COMBATANT; DEFINITE.

neutrality *noun* **1** *challenge the neutrality of the referee* impartiality, lack/absence of bias/prejudice, open-mindedness, objectivity, even-handedness, disinterestedness, detachment. See NEUTRAL 1. **2** *the neutrality of the countries* non-combativeness, non-alignment, non-participation, non-involvement, non-intervention, non-interventionism.

neutralize *verb* **1** *neutralize the poison* counteract, cancel, nullify, negate, annul, undo, invalidate, frustrate, be an antidote to. **2** *her warmth neutralizing their hostility* offset, counterbalance, counteract, compensate for, make up for, cancel out, negate.

never *adverb* not ever, at no time, not at any time, not once, not at all, certainly not, not in any circumstances, under no circumstances, on no account; *lit.* ne'er; *inf.* no way, not on your life, not in a million years, not on your nelly.
Opposites ALWAYS; FOREVER.

never-ending *adjective* **1** *a seemingly never-ending saga* endless, unending, without end, perpetual, everlasting, interminable, without ceasing, ceaseless, unceasing, incessant, non-stop, continuous, continual, uninterrupted, unbroken, unremitting, relentless, persistent; *inf.* eternal. **2** *a never-ending supply of books* endless, infinite, limitless, boundless. **3** *their never-ending love* endless, without end, perpetual, everlasting, infinite, eternal, lasting, enduring, abiding, constant, unchanging, unwavering, unfaltering.

never-never *noun* hire-purchase, HP, instalment system.

nevertheless *adverb* none the less, even so, however, still, yet, be that as it may, for all that, just the same, though, in any event, notwithstanding, regardless.

new *adjective* **1** *new techniques* modern, recent, advanced, state-of-the-art, present-day, contemporary, current, latest, up-to-date, up-to-the-minute, new-fashioned, modish, brand new, newly arrived, modernist, ultra-modern, avant-garde, futuristic, newfangled; *inf.* way-out, far-out. **2** *in need of new ideas* modern, state-of-the-art, up-to-date, new-fashioned, novel, original, fresh, unhackneyed, imaginative, creative, experimental. **3** *a new rather than a second-hand book* pristine, fresh, mint, in mint condition, virgin, unused. **4** *new people next door | starting a new job* unfamiliar, unknown, strange, different, unaccustomed, untried. **5** *a new bit on the house* additional, added, extra, supplementary, further, another. **6** *feel like a new person* refreshed, renewed, improved, restored, reinvigorated, regenerated, reborn, remodelled.
Opposites OLD; OBSOLETE; SECOND-HAND.

newborn *adjective* just born, new-fledged, neonatal.

newcomer *noun* **1** *newcomers to the town* new arrival, arrival, incomer, immigrant, settler, stranger, outsider, foreigner, alien, intruder, interloper; *inf.* johnny-come-lately. **2** *a newcomer to the game* beginner, novice, learner, trainee, probationer, new recruit, raw recruit, tiro, greenhorn, initiate, neophyte.

newfangled *adjective* *dislike newfangled methods/machines* modern, ultra-modern, state-of-the-art, contemporary, fashionable, new-fashioned, gimmicky.

newly *adverb* just, just recently, lately, of late.

news *noun* information, facts, data, report, story, news item, news flash, account, statement, announcement, press release, communication, communiqué, message, bulletin, dispatch, disclosure, revelation, word, talk, the latest, gossip, tittle-tattle, rumour, scandal, exposé; *inf.* gen, info.

newspaper *noun* paper, gazette, journal, tabloid, broadsheet, daily paper, daily, evening paper, weekly paper, weekly, scandal sheet; *inf.* rag.

New Testament *noun. See table at* BIBLE.

next *adjective* **1** *the next patient/day* following, succeeding, successive, subsequent, later, ensuing. **2** *the next house* neighbouring, adjacent, adjoining, bordering, contiguous, closest, nearest, proximate.

next *adverb* *next we went to the zoo* then, later, at a later time, after, afterwards, thereafter, subsequently, at a subsequent time, after this/that, after that time.

nibble *verb* take small bites from, bite, gnaw, peck at, pick at, pick over, eat, munch, eat between meals; *inf.* snack on.

nibble *noun* **1** *have a nibble of the cheese* bite, gnaw, peck, munch, taste, crumb, piece, morsel, soupçon. **2** *party nibbles* snack, titbit, canapé, hors-d'oeuvre.

nice *adjective* **1** *have a nice time* good, pleasant, enjoyable, pleasurable, agreeable, delightful, amusing, satisfying, gratifying, marvellous. **2** *a nice lady/friend* pleasant, agreeable, likable, charming, delightful, amiable, friendly, kindly, genial, gracious, sympathetic, understanding, compassionate, good. **3** *nice manners/behaviour* polite, courteous, civil, refined, cultivated, polished, genteel, elegant, seemly, decorous, proper, fitting, suitable, appropriate, respectable, good, virtuous. **4** *a nice distinction* fine, ultra-fine, subtle, minute, precise, exact, accurate, strict, close, careful, meticulous, rigorous. **5** *it's a nice day* fine, dry, sunny, warm, pleasant, agreeable. **6** *she is too nice to eat with her fingers* fastidious, delicate, refined, dainty, particular, discriminating, over-refined, over-particular, fussy, finicky; *inf.* pernickety.
Opposites UNPLEASANT; NASTY; UNREFINED; ROUGH.

nicely *adverb* **1** *children behaving nicely* well, politely, courteously, decorously, properly, fittingly, suitably, respectably, virtuously. See NICE 3. **2** *distinguish nicely between possibilities* finely, subtly, precisely, exactly, strictly, closely, carefully, meticulously, rigorously. See NICE 4.

niceness noun **1** *appreciate their neighbour's niceness* pleasantness, agreeableness, friendliness, geniality. **2** *the niceness of the children's behaviour* politeness, courtesy, refinement, civility, gentility, respectability. **3** *they laugh at the niceness of her table manners* fastidiousness, delicacy, over-refinement, fussiness, finickiness, pernicketiness.

nicety noun **1** *the niceties of meaning* finer point, subtlety, nuance, detail. **2** *the nicety of the judgement* precision, accuracy, exactness, meticulousness, rigour.

niche noun **1** *vases placed in a niche in the wall* alcove, recess, nook, cranny, cubbyhole. **2** *his niche in life* calling, vocation, place, position, job; *inf.* slot.

nickname noun pet name, family name, familiar name, diminutive; *inf.* moniker, handle.

nifty adjective **1** *a nifty piece of footwork* agile, nimble, deft, adroit, skilful, neat. **2** *wearing rather nifty clothes* smart, stylish, elegant, chic; *inf.* natty.

niggardly adjective **1** *a niggardly old man* mean, miserly, stingy, tight-fisted, parsimonious, penny-pinching, cheese-paring, avaricious; *Am. inf.* tight-assed. **2** *a niggardly supply of food* meagre, paltry, skimpy, scanty, measly, inadequate, insubstantial, miserable; *inf.* piddling.
Opposites GENEROUS; LAVISH; ABUNDANT.

niggle verb **1** *he was always niggling about money* fuss, nag, carp, criticize, cavil; *inf.* nit-pick. **2** *many doubts were niggling him* irritate, annoy, worry, trouble, rankle.

night noun night-time, darkness, dark, hours of darkness. **night and day** all the time, around the clock, ceaselessly, incessantly, continuously.
Opposites DAY; LIGHT.

nightfall noun sunset, sundown, dusk, evening, twilight; *lit.* eventide, crepuscule, gloaming.

nightly adjective at night, night-time, nocturnal.

nightmare noun **1** *I have had nightmares since the accident* bad dream, incubus, phantasmagoria. **2** *the interview was a nightmare* ordeal, horror, torment, torture.

nihilism noun **1** *former believers are turning to nihilism* rejection, repudiation, renunciation, denial, abnegation; disbelief, scepticism; negativism, cynicism, pessimism. **2** *they lapsed into political nihilism* anarchy, lawlessness, disorder, chaos. **3** *he felt himself to be in a state of nihilism* nihility, nothingness, non-existence, void.

nil noun nought, zero, love, duck; nothing, naught, none; `inf.` zilch.

nimble adjective **1** *nimble gymnasts/movements* agile, lithe, sprightly, spry, lively, quick, quick-moving, graceful, skilful, deft. **2** *nimble of wit* quick-thinking, clever, bright, quick, quick-witted, alert.
Opposites STIFF; CLUMSY; DULL.

nip verb **1** *nip his arm* pinch, tweak, squeeze, grip, bite, nibble. **2** *nip off the withered shoots* snip, cut off, lop, dock. **3** *frost nipping her cheeks* sting, bite, hurt. **4** *I'm nipping off to the shops* dart, hurry, rush, scurry, scamper. **nip in the bud** *her plans were nipped in the bud* stop, quash, quell, check, thwart, frustrate.

nipple noun teat, udder, dug, mamilla, papilla; *dial.* pap.

nippy adjective icy, chilly, bitter, raw, piercing, stinging.

nirvana noun enlightenment, oblivion; paradise, heaven; bliss, joy, peace, serenity, tranquillity.

nit-picking adjective captious, hair-splitting, quibbling, fault-finding, ultra-critical, critical, cavilling, pedantic.

nitty-gritty noun crux, gist, substance, essence, quintessence; core, heart, centre, kernel, nucleus; essentials, basics, facts; *inf.* brass-tacks, nuts and bolts.

nitwit noun fool, ninny, idiot, nincompoop, dolt, dunce, ignoramus, noodle, donkey; *inf.* dope, chump, twit, dimwit, wally, nerd, jerk, pillock.

no adverb no indeed, absolutely not, under no circumstances, by no means, never; *inf.* not on your life, no way; *Am. inf.* nope, no siree.
Opposites YES.

nobble verb **1** *nobble the jury* influence, bribe, win over, secure the support of; *inf.* get at. **2** *nobble the racehorse* tamper with, interfere with, disable, incapacitate, weaken. **3** *nobble the firm's profits* steal, rob, embezzle; *inf.* pinch, nick, swipe. **4** *nobble the thief* grab, seize, capture; *inf.* nab, collar.

Nobel Prize noun. *See table.*

nobility noun **1** *the nobility are not always wealthy* lords, peers, peers of the realm, aristocracy, high society, the élite, the upper class; *inf.* nobs. **2** *the nobility of his deed* magnanimity, generosity, selflessness, honour, integrity, bravery. **3** *the nobility of his thoughts* loftiness, grandness. *See* NOBLE *adjective* 3. **4** *he admired the nobility of the setting* impressiveness, splendour, magnificence, stateliness, grandeur. **5** *the nobility of the breed* excellence, prime quality.

noble noun nobleman, noblewoman, lord, lady, peer, peer of the realm, aristocrat.

noble adjective **1** *the noble people of the land* aristocratic, patrician, blue-blooded, titled, landed, born with a silver spoon in one's mouth. **2** *noble deeds* noble-minded, magnanimous, generous, self-sacrificing, honourable, virtuous, brave. **3** *noble thoughts* lofty, grand, exalted, elevated. **4** *of noble appearance* impressive, magnificent, striking, awesome, stately, grand, dignified. **5** *horses of a noble strain* first-rate, prime, choice, prize, quality; *inf.* A1, top-notch.
Opposites HUMBLE; DISHONOURABLE; ignoble; BASE.

nod verb **1** *nod one's head* incline, bob, bow, dip, duck. **2** *nod a greeting* signal, gesture, motion, sign, indicate. **3** *the audience began to nod* doze off, drop off, fall asleep, nap, slumber. **4** *even Homer nods* make a mistake, err, blunder, slip up.

node *noun* protuberance, swelling, lump, growth, excrescence, knob, knot, nodule, bump, bulge.

noise *noun* sound, loud sound, din, hubbub, clamour, racket, row, uproar, tumult, commotion, rumpus, pandemonium.

noisome *adjective* disgusting, repugnant, revolting, repulsive, obnoxious; offensive, nauseating; unpleasant, disagreeable, horrible, detestable, loathsome.

noisy *adjective* **1** *noisy neighbours* rowdy, clamorous, boisterous, obstreperous, turbulent; *inf.* rackety. **2** *noisy music* loud, blaring, blasting, deafening, ear-splitting.
Opposites QUIET; SOFT.

nomad *noun* itinerant, traveller, migrant, wanderer, roamer, rover; transient, vagabond, vagrant, tramp.

nominal *adjective* **1** *the nominal head* in name only, titular, formal; theoretical, self-styled; purported, supposed. **2** *a nominal sum* token, symbolic; minimal, trivial, insignificant.

nominate *verb* **1** *they nominated several candidates* name, propose, put forward, submit, present, recommend; *inf.* put up. **2** *he nominated his successor* name, designate, appoint, assign, select, choose.

non-aligned *adjective* neutral, uncommitted, impartial, uninvolved, unallied.

non-believer *noun* atheist, agnostic, sceptic, doubter, doubting Thomas, unbeliever, disbeliever, cynic, infidel, pagan, heathen.

nonce *noun* **for the nonce** for the present, for the moment, for the present moment, for the time being, for now, for just now.

nonchalance *noun* composure, self-possession, sang-froid, equanimity, imperturbability, calm, coolness, unconcern, indifference, dispassionateness, detachment, detachedness, apathy, casualness, carefreeness, insouciance, carelessness; *inf.* cool.

nonchalant *adjective* composed, self-possessed, imperturbable, unexcitable, calm, cool, collected, cool calm and collected, cool as a cucumber, unconcerned, indifferent, unemotional, blasé, dispassionate, detached, apathetic, casual, offhand, carefree, insouciant, easygoing, careless; *inf.* laid-back.
Opposites ANXIOUS; CONCERNED; EXCITED.

non-combatant *adjective* non-combative, non-fighting, non-belligerent, pacifist, civilian, neutral, non-aligned, non-participating.

non-committal *adjective* cautious, guarded, circumspect, wary, careful, discreet, politic, tactful, diplomatic, prudent, playing one's

---

RECENT NOBEL PRIZEWINNERS

Physics			
1985	Klaus Von Klitzing	1990	Elias Corey
1986	Ernst Ruska	1991	Richard Ernst
	Gerd Binnig	1992	Rudolph Marcus
	Heinrich Rohrer	1993	Michael Smith
1987	Alex Müller		Kary Mullis
	Georg Bednorz	1994	George Olah
1988	Leon Lederman		
	Melvin Schwartz		
	Jack Steinberger		
1989	Hans Dehmelt		
	Wolfgang Paul		
	Norman Ramsey		
1990	Jerome Friedman		
	Henry Kendall		
	Richard Taylor		
1991	Pierre Gilles De Gennes		
1992	Georges Charpak		
1993	Joseph Taylor		
	Russell Hulse		
1994	Bertram N. Brockhouse		
	Clifford G. Shull		

Physiology or Medicine
1985 Joseph Goldstein / Michael Brown
1986 Stanley Cohen / Rita Levi-Montalcini
1987 Susumu Tonegawa
1988 James Black / Gertrude Evans / George Hitchins
1989 Michael Bishop / Harold Varmus
1990 Joseph Murray / E. Donnall Thomas
1991 Erwin Neher / Bert Sakmann
1992 Edmond Fischer / Edwin Krebs
1993 Phillip Sharp / Richard Roberts
1994 Alfred G. Gilman / Martin Rodbell

Chemistry
1985 Herbert Hauptman / Jerome Karle
1986 Dudley Hersbach / Yuan Tseh Lee / John Polanyi
1987 Donald Cram / Jean-Marie Lehn / Charles Pedersen
1988 Johann Deisenhofer / Robert Huber / Hartmut Michel
1989 Sidney Altman / Thomas Cech

Literature
1985 Claude Simon
1986 Wole Soyinka
1987 Joseph Brodsky
1988 Naguib Mahfouz
1989 Camilo José Cela
1990 Octavio Paz
1991 Nadine Gordimer
1992 Derek Walcott
1993 Toni Morrison
1994 Kenzaburo Oë

Peace
1985 International Physicians for the Prevention of Nuclear War
1986 Elie Wiesel
1987 Oscar Arias Sánchez
1988 United Nations Peacekeeping Forces
1989 Dalai Lama
1990 Mikhail Gorbachev
1991 Aung San Suu Kyi
1992 Rigoberta Menchú
1993 Nelson Mandela / F. W. de Klerk
1994 Yasser Arafat / Shimon Peres / Yitzhak Rabin

Economic Sciences
1985 Franco Modigliani
1986 James Buchanan
1987 Robert M. Solow
1988 Maurice Allais
1989 Trygve Haavelmo
1990 Harry M. Markowitz / William F. Sharpe / Merton Miller
1991 Ronald Coase
1992 Gary Becker
1993 Robet Fogel / Douglass North
1994 John Harsanyi / John Nash / Reinhard Selten

cards close to one's chest, giving nothing away, sitting on the fence, unrevealing, temporizing, evasive, equivocal, vague, reserved. *Opposites* CARELESS; INDISCREET; revealing.

non compos mentis *adjective* of unsound mind, mentally deranged, mentally unbalanced, mentally ill, insane, mad; *inf.* crazy.

nonconformist *noun the nonconformists of society* radical, dissenter, dissentient, protester, rebel, seceder, maverick, individualist, deviant, misfit, fish out of water, eccentric, iconoclast, outsider; *inf.* drop-out, hippie, freak, oddball.

nondescript *adjective* indefinite, indeterminate, unclassifiable, indescribable, indistinguishable, vague, blending into the background, unremarkable, featureless, undistinguished, ordinary, commonplace, average, mediocre, unexceptional, unmemorable, uninteresting, uninspiring, dull, colourless, anaemic, insipid, bland; *inf.* common-or-garden. *Opposites* DISTINCTIVE; EXTRAORDINARY.

none *pronoun* **1** *we expected several people but none came* no one, nobody, not one, not a one, never a one, not a soul, not a single person. **2** *she expected presents but none came* nothing, nothing at all, not a thing, not a single thing, not a one, nil, zero. **3** *none of this concerns me* not any, not a part, not a bit. *Opposites* MANY.

none *adverb none the wiser* not at all, not a bit, in no way, to no extent.

nonentity *noun* nobody, person of no account, person of no importance, cipher, non-person; *inf.* nothing, small beer, small fry, lightweight.

non-essential *adjective* inessential, unessential, unnecessary, needless, unneeded, unrequired, superfluous, redundant, dispensable, expendable, peripheral, unimportant, insignificant, inconsequential, irrelevant, inapplicable, inapposite, extraneous.

nonetheless *adverb* nevertheless, even so, however, still, yet, be that as it may, for all that, just the same, though, in any event, notwithstanding, regardless.

non-existent *adjective* unreal, hypothetical, suppositional, fictional, fictitious, imagined, imaginary, fancied, fanciful, mythical, legendary, fantasy, illusory, delusive, illusionary, hallucinatory, insubstantial, inexistent, missing, unreal.

non-intervention *noun laissez-faire*, neutrality, non-participation, non-interference, non-involvement, inaction, passivity.

non-observance *noun non-observance of the rules* ignoring, non-compliance, disobedience, unruliness, infringement, violation.

nonpareil *adjective his artistic work is nonpareil* | *as a writer he is nonpareil* unparalleled, unrivalled, without rival, incomparable, peerless, matchless, unmatched, without equal, unequalled, unsurpassed, unique, unbeatable, supreme.

nonpareil *noun the nonpareils of the art world* nonesuch, *crème de la crème*, élite, jewel, jewel in the crown, gem, paragon.

nonplus *verb* take aback, stun, dumbfound, confound, astound, astonish, amaze, surprise, disconcert, discomfit, dismay, make one halt in one's tracks, puzzle, perplex, baffle, mystify, stump, confuse, bewilder, embarrass, fluster; *inf.* faze, flummox, floor.

nonsense *noun* **1** *talk nonsense* rubbish, balderdash, drivel, gibberish, twaddle, blather, stuff and nonsense; *inf.* tommy-rot, bunkum, trash, tripe, tosh, bosh, double Dutch, gobbledegook, mumbo-jumbo, poppycock, flannel, waffle, claptrap, bilge, bull. **2** *tired of their nonsense* foolishness, folly, silliness, senselessness, stupidity, ridiculousness, ludicrousness, inanity, fatuity, joking, jesting, clowning, buffoonery, drollery. *Opposites* SENSE; WISDOM.

nonsensical *adjective* **1** *nonsensical remarks* meaningless, incomprehensible, unintelligible, senseless, incongruous. **2** *a nonsensical scheme* foolish, absurd, silly, inane, senseless, stupid, ridiculous, ludicrous, preposterous, harebrained, irrational, idiotic, insane; *inf.* crazy, crackpot, nutty, wacky.

non-stop *adjective non-stop commentaries/nagging* incessant, unceasing, ceaseless, constant, continuous, continual, without interruption, unbroken, unfaltering, steady, unremitting, relentless, persistent, endless, never-ending, unending, interminable; *inf.* eternal.

non-stop *adverb talk non-stop* incessantly, unceasingly, constantly, continuously, continually, steadily, unremittingly, relentlessly, persistently, endlessly. *See* NON-STOP *adjective*.

nook *noun* **1** *a room full of nooks and crannies* corner, cranny, recess, alcove, niche, opening, cavity, crevice, gap, cubbyhole, inglenook. **2** *find a quiet nook to be alone* hideaway, retreat, refuge, shelter, den; *inf.* hide-out, hidey-hole.

noon *noun* midday, twelve noon, twelve midday, twelve o'clock, high noon, noontime, noontide, noonday, twelve hundred, twelve hundred hours, one-two-double-O.

no one *pronoun* nobody, not a one, not anyone, not a person, not a single person, never a one, not a soul.

norm *noun* **1** *measured against the norm* standard, criterion, measure, gauge, yardstick, benchmark, touchstone, scale, rule, pattern, model, type. **2** *six hours a day is the norm* average, mean, normal rate, the usual, the rule.

normal *adjective* **1** *the normal temperature/method* usual, standard, average, common, ordinary, natural, general, commonplace, conventional, typical, regular, routine, run-of-the-mill, everyday, accustomed, habitual, prevailing, popular, accepted, acknowledged; *inf.* common-or-garden. **2** *of normal size* average, medium, middling, standard, mean. **3** *the patient isn't normal* well-adjusted, well-balanced, rational, compos mentis, sane. *Opposites* ABNORMAL; UNUSUAL; IRRATIONAL.

normality *noun* **1** *return to normality* | *the normality of his surroundings* usualness, commonness, ordinariness, naturalness, commonplaceness, conventionality, regularity, routine, accustomedness, habitualness. *See*

NORMAL 1. **2** *question the normality of the patient* balance, rationality, sanity.

normally *adverb* **1** *behave normally* as usual, ordinarily, naturally, conventionally, routinely, typically, regularly. **2** *normally, we eat late* usually, ordinarily, as a rule, as a general rule, generally, in general, mostly, commonly, habitually.

north *adjective north winds* northern, northerly, northwardly, Arctic, polar, boreal.

north *adverb go north* northwards, northward, northwardly.

North American Indian *noun. See table.*

nose *noun* **1** *have a large nose* proboscis, bird's bill/beak, elephant's trunk; animal's snout/muzzle, *inf.* beak, snout, conk, snoot, schnozzle, hooter, snitch; *dial.* neb. **2** *have a good nose* sense of smell, olfactory sense. **3** *a nose for a good story* instinct, sixth sense, intuition, insight, perception, gift for discovering/detecting. **4** *admire the wine's nose* bouquet, aroma, fragrance, perfume, scent, smell. **by a nose** win *by a nose* by a hair's breadth, by the narrowest of margins, by a narrow margin, narrowly, by the skin of one's teeth; *inf.* by a whisker. **on the nose** *£200 on the nose | arrive at 6 pm on the nose* exactly, precisely, promptly, prompt, on time, on target; *inf.* on the dot, spot on, on the button.

nose *verb* **1** *dogs nosing out the thieves* smell out, sniff out, follow the scent of, scent out, search for, detect, run to earth/ground. **2** *dogs were nosing his arm* nudge, push, nuzzle. **3** *nose around the room* pry, search, peer, prowl, have a good look; *inf.* snoop. **4** *nose into someone's business* pry into, interfere in, meddle in, inquire into; *inf.* poke one's nose into. **5** *nose the car forward* ease, inch, move, run.

nosedive *noun* **1** *the plane/parachutist took a nosedive* dive, plunge, swoop. **2** *the nosedive taken by prices* fall, drop, plunge, decline.

nosedive *verb* **1** *the plane nosedived out of the sky* dive, plunge, swoop, drop, plummet. **2** *the prices situation nosedived after the news* fall, drop, plunge, plummet, go down, decline, worsen, get worse.

nosegay *noun* bouquet, posy, spray, bunch of flowers.

nosh *noun* food, fare, sustenance, meal, repast, snack, victuals, viands, comestibles, provisions, aliment; *inf.* grub, scoff, chow.

nostalgia *noun* longing/yearning/pining for the past, regret, regretfulness, reminiscence, remembrance, recollection, wistfulness, homesickness.

nostalgic *adjective* longing/yearning/pining for the past, regretful, reminiscing, remembering, recollecting, wistful, sentimental, emotional about the past, maudlin, homesick.

nostrum *noun* **1** *prescribing nostrums for patients* patent medicine, medicine, medication, drug, potion, pill, quack remedy, elixir, remedy, cure, panacea, sovereign remedy, magic bullet. **2** *claiming to have a nostrum for the country's problems* remedy, cure, cure-all, panacea, solution, perfect solution, answer, magic bullet, magic formula, recipe, recipe for success.

nosy *adjective* prying, inquisitive, quizzing, probing, eavesdropping, curious, interfering, meddlesome, intrusive; *inf.* snooping, snoopy.

notability *noun* **1** *the notability of his achievements* noteworthiness, importance, significance, momentousness, memorability, impressiveness, extraordinariness. See NOTABLE *adjective* 1. **2** *the notability of the members of council* eminence, pre-eminence, distinction, illustriousness, greatness, prestige, fame, renown, reputation, acclaim, consequence. See NOTABLE *adjective* 2. **3** *the notabilities of the university/theatre* dignitary, notable, celebrity, luminary star, superstar, VIP, personage, worthy, lion; *inf.* somebody, celeb, megastar, big shot, big gun.

notable *adjective* **1** *a notable achievement* noteworthy, remarkable, outstanding, important,

NORTH AMERICAN INDIAN PEOPLES

Algonquin	Crow	Kwakiutl	Ottawa	Tiwa
Apache	Dakota	Lummi	Paiute	Tlingit
Arapaho	Delaware	Malecite	Papago	Tsimshian
Arikara	Fox	Mandan	Passama-	Tunica
Assiniboine	Haida	Menominee	quoddy	Tuscarora
Athapaskan	Hidatsa	Miccosukee	Pawnee	Twana
Bannock	Hopi	Micmac	Peigan	Tzotzil
Blackfoot	Hupa	Mohawk	Penobscot	Umatilla
Caddo	Huron	Mohican	Pequot	Ute
Cayuga	Illinois	Mojave	Pima	Walapai
Cherokee	Iowa	Narragansett	Potawatomi	Wallawalla
Cheyenne	Iroquois	Natchez	Powhatan	Washoe
Chickasaw	Karankawa	Navajo	Pueblo	Wichita
Chinook	Karok	Nez Percé	Quinault	Winnebago
Chippewa	Kekchi	Nootka	Seminole	Wyandot
Chitimacha	Keres	Ojibwa	Seneca	Yakima
Choctaw	Kickapoo	Omaha	Shawnee	Yana
Comanche	Kiowa	Oneida	Shoshone	Yavapai
Cree	Klamath	Onondaga	Sioux	Yurok
Creek	Kutenai	Osage	Spokane	Zuñi

significant, momentous, memorable, unforgettable, pronounced, marked, striking, impressive, uncommon, unusual, particular, special, extraordinary, conspicuous, rare, signal. **2** *notable people in the town* noted, of note, distinguished, eminent, pre-eminent, well-known, prominent, illustrious, great, famous, famed, renowned, celebrated, acclaimed. **Opposites** INSIGNIFICANT; unremarkable; UNHEARD-OF; OBSCURE.

notable *noun the notables of the university* notability, dignitary, celebrity, luminary, star, VIP; *inf.* celeb, megastar. *See* NOTABILITY 3.

notably *adverb notably successful* remarkably, outstandingly, significantly, markedly, strikingly, impressively, uncommonly, unusually, particularly, especially, extraordinarily, conspicuously, signally.

notation *noun* system of symbols, symbols, signs, code, cipher, hieroglyphics, shorthand, musical notation.

notch *noun* **1** *make a notch in the wood* indentation, dent, nick, groove, gouge, cut, mark, incision, score, scratch, gash, slit, cleft. **2** *her singing is several notches up from the rest of the choir* degree, grade, gradation, level, step, stage, rung.

notch *verb notch the wood* indent, make an indentation in, dent, nick, gouge, cut, mark, score, scratch, gash, slit. *See* NOTCH *noun* 1.
notch up *notch up another success* score, achieve, attain, gain, make, register, record.

note *noun* **1** *always kept a note of her purchases* record, account. **2** *there is a note in the register* entry, item, notation, record, comment, jotting, inscription. **3** *leave him a note* letter, message, memorandum; *inf.* memo. **4** *drop them a note* letter, epistle, missive, communication, thank-you note, bread-and-butter letter. **5** *read the notes in the book* footnote, annotation, commentary, gloss, marginalia, explanation, explication, exposition, exegesis. **6** *exchange notes for coins* banknote, bill, paper money; *inf.* fiver, tenner. **7** *worthy of note* notice, attention, attentiveness, heed, observation, consideration, thought, regard, care, mindfulness. **8** *people of note* distinction, eminence, pre-eminence, illustriousness, greatness, prestige, fame, renown, reputation, acclaim, consequence. **9** *a note of amusement in her voice* tone, intonation, inflection, sound, indication, hint, element.

note *verb* **1** *note the date in your diary* write down, put down, jot down, mark down, enter, mark, record, register. **2** *note his comments in your report* mention, make mention of, refer to, allude to, touch on, indicate, point out, make known, state. **3** *he noted their concern* take note of, take notice of, see, observe, perceive, behold, detect, take in.

notebook *noun* notepad, memorandum book, exercise book, jotter, scratch pad, register, logbook, log, diary, journal, commonplace book, record book, personal organizer; Filofax™; *inf.* memo pad.

noted *adjective a noted artist* of note, notable, distinguished, eminent, pre-eminent, well-

known, prominent, illustrious, great, famous, famed, renowned, celebrated, acclaimed.
Opposites UNKNOWN; UNHEARD-OF; OBSCURE.

notes *plural noun make/take notes on the conference | his notes for the screenplay* jottings, record, report, commentary, chronicle, transcript, minutes, observations, impressions, synopsis, précis, sketch, outline.

noteworthy *adjective a noteworthy achievement* notable, remarkable, outstanding, important, significant, marked, striking, impressive, unusual, conspicuous, rare, signal. *See* NOTABLE *adjective* 1.
Opposites INSIGNIFICANT; ORDINARY.

nothing *noun* **1** *nothing to declare* not anything, nothing at all, nought, naught, nil, not a thing, not a single thing; *inf.* zilch, sweet Fanny Adams. **2** *write nothing in the right-hand column* nought, zero, cipher, 0. **3** *the wound is a mere nothing* trifling matter, piece of trivia, matter of no importance/consequence, bagatelle; *inf.* no big deal. **4** *they treat her like a nothing* nobody, person of no account, nonentity, cipher; *inf.* small beer, lightweight. **5** *pass into nothing* nothingness, non-existence, non-being, nullity. *See* NOTHINGNESS 1. **for nothing 1** *work for nothing* free, for free, gratis, without charge, without payment, gratuitously. **2** *do all that studying for nothing* in vain, to no avail, to no purpose, futilely, needlessly. **nothing but** *nothing but a miracle can save us* only, solely, simply, purely, merely.
Opposites SOMETHING; CELEBRITY; BEING.

nothingness *noun* **1** *pass into nothingness* nothing, non-existence, non-life, non-being, nihility, nullity, oblivion, void, vacuum, blankness. **2** *aware of the nothingness of his work* insignificance, unimportance, triviality, worthlessness, valuelessness, pointlessness, uselessness, meagreness.

notice *noun* **1** *escape my notice* attention, attentiveness, heed, note, observation, cognizance, regard, consideration, interest, thought, mindfulness, watchfulness, vigilance. **2** *see the notice on the board* information sheet, bulletin, poster, handbill, bill, circular, leaflet, pamphlet, advertisement. **3** *receive notice of the planning request* notification, apprisal, announcement, intimation, information, intelligence, news, communication, advice, instruction, order, warning. **4** *workers have received their notice* notice to quit, redundancy notice, dismissal; *inf.* marching orders, the sack, the boot. **5** *plays receiving poor notices* review, write-up, critique.

notice *verb* see, note, take note of, observe, perceive, discern, detect, behold, descry, spot, distinguish, make out, take heed of, heed, pay attention to, take notice of, mark, regard.
Opposites OVERLOOK; IGNORE; DISREGARD.

noticeable *adjective no noticeable improvement | was it noticeable?* observable, visible, discernible, perceptible, detectable, distinguishable, distinct, evident, obvious, apparent, manifest, patent, plain, clear, conspicuous, unmistakable, pronounced, striking, blatant.
Opposites IMPERCEPTIBLE; UNOBTRUSIVE.

notification noun **1** the notification of the tenants informing, telling, warning, alerting. See NOTIFY 1. **2** the notification of his intentions disclosure, divulgence, announcement, declaration, publishing. See NOTIFY 2. **3** receive a notification notice, announcement, statement, declaration, communication, message, information, advice.

notify verb **1** notify the tenants inform, tell, advise, acquaint, apprise, warn, alert, caution. **2** notify his intentions to the tenants make known, disclose, reveal, divulge, announce, declare, broadcast, publish, communicate.

notion noun **1** have strange notions about children idea, belief, opinion, thought, impression, view, conviction, concept, conception, conceptualization, assumption, presumption, hypothesis, theory, postulation, abstraction, apprehension, understanding. **2** a notion to go to the sea impulse, inclination, fancy, whim, wish, desire, caprice.

notional adjective hypothetical, theoretical, suppositional, speculative, conceptual, abstract, imaginary, fanciful, fancied, unreal, illusory, unsubstantiated, ideal.
Opposites ACTUAL; REAL.

notoriety noun infamy, ill/evil repute, bad reputation/name, disrepute, dishonour, scandal, opprobrium, obloquy.

notorious adjective **1** a notorious murderer/liar infamous, of ill repute, having a bad reputation/name, ill-famed, disreputable, dishonourable. **2** a notorious murder | in a notorious accident black spot well-known, infamous, prominent, scandalous, opprobrious, obloquial, legendary.

notwithstanding adverb notwithstanding, we must go nevertheless, nonetheless, even so, however, still, yet, be that as it may, for all that, just the same, through, in any event, regardless.

notwithstanding preposition notwithstanding the delay despite, in spite of, regardless of.

nought noun nothing, naught, nil, zero, love, nothingness; inf. zilch.

nourish verb **1** nourish the children feed, nurture, provide for, care for, take care of, tend, attend to, bring up, rear. **2** nourish growth encourage, promote, foster, stimulate, boost, further, advance, forward, contribute to, be conducive to, assist, help, aid. **3** nourish hopes of success cherish, entertain, harbour, foster, hold, have.

nourishing adjective nutritious, nutritive, wholesome, healthy, health-giving, healthful, beneficial, good for one.
Opposites UNHEALTHY; unwholesome.

nourishment noun food, nutriment, nutrition, sustenance, subsistence, aliment, provisions, provender, meat, fare, viands, victuals, daily bread; inf. grub, scoff, chow.

nouveau riche noun new-rich, parvenu, arriviste, arrivé, upstart.

novel adjective new, fresh, different, original, unusual, uncommon, unfamiliar, rare, unique, singular, imaginative, unhackneyed, unconventional, creative, innovative, groundbreaking, trail-blazing, modern, ultra-modern, advanced, futuristic.
Opposites OLD; RUN-OF-THE-MILL; HACKNEYED; UNIMAGINATIVE.

novel noun book, story, tale, narrative, work of fiction. See table.

TYPES OF NOVEL	
Aga saga	photonovel
antinovel	picaresque novel
Bildungsroman	roman-à-clef
bodice-ripper	romantic novel
dime novel	roman-fleuve
epistolary novel	saga
Gothic novel	stream of conscious-
graphic novel	ness
historical novel	sword and sorcery
nouveau roman	techno-thriller
novelette	thriller
novelization	western
novella	whodunnit

novelist noun novel writer, author/authoress, writer, writer of fiction, fiction-writer, creative writer, fictionist. See table at WRITER.

novelty noun **1** the novelty of the idea/approach newness, freshness, difference, originality, unusualness, uniqueness, rareness, imaginativeness, creativity. See NOVEL adjective. **2** a stall selling novelties memento, souvenir, knickknack, trinket, bauble, trifle, gimmick, curiosity, gimcrack.

novice noun **1** novices to the work beginner, newcomer, apprentice, trainee, learner, probationer, student, pupil, new recruit, raw recruit, tiro, initiate, novitiate, neophyte, greenhorn; inf. rookie. **2** welcoming the novices to the convent novitiate, postulant, neophyte.
Opposites EXPERT; PROFESSIONAL.

noviciate noun **1** undertaking their noviciate apprenticeship, traineeship, training, probation, trial period, test period, initiation, indoctrination. **2** noviciates in the convent novice, postulant, neophyte.

now adverb **1** we do not have any now just now, right now, at present, at the present time, at this time, at the moment, at this moment in time, for the time being, currently; Am. presently. **2** you must go now right away, right now, immediately, at once, straight away, instantly, promptly, without delay. **now and again/then** occasionally, on occasions, sometimes, from time to time, at times, once in a while, every once in a while, at intervals, periodically.
Opposites THEN.

nowadays adverb **1** nowadays there is unemployment at the present time, in these times, in this day and age, today, just now, now, at the moment, at present. **2** I never see her nowadays these days, any more, now.

noxious adjective noxious fumes/chemical nocuous, noisome, harmful, hurtful, injurious, damaging, destructive, ruinous, pernicious, malignant, detrimental, deleterious, prejudicial, menacing, threatening, unwholesome, unhealthy, insalubrious, poisonous, toxic. **Opposites** INNOCUOUS; SAFE.

nuance *noun nuances of colour/meaning* shade, shading, gradation, subtlety, fine distinction, nicety, refinement, degree.

nuclear weapon *noun. See tables at* MISSILE, WEAPON.

nucleus *noun* core, kernel, centre, heart, nub, basis, pith, meat, marrow, focus, pivot.

nude *adjective in the nude*, naked, stark naked, bare, stripped, exposed, unclothed, undressed, uncovered, *au naturel*; *inf*. without a stitch on, starkers, in one's birthday suit, in the raw, in the altogether, in the buff, naked as the day one was born, mother naked; *Am. inf*. buck naked.

nudge *verb* poke, jab, prod, dig, jog, elbow, bump, touch, push, shove.

nudge *noun* poke, jab, prod, dig, jog, dig in the ribs, elbow, bump, touch, push, shove.

nudity *noun* nakedness, bareness, bare skin, undress, state of undress. **Opposites** DRESS.

nugget *noun* chunk, lump, piece, mass, clump, wad, hunk; *inf*. wodge; *Scots* dod.

nuisance *noun* pest, bother, plague, irritant, source of annoyance, annoyance, vexation, trouble, burden, weight, problem, difficulty, worry, affliction, trial, tribulation, bore, inconvenience, disadvantage, handicap, thorn in the side/flesh; *inf*. drag. **Opposites** HELP; BLESSING; ADVANTAGE.

null *adjective* **1** *render the ruling null* null and void, void, invalid, annulled, nullified, cancelled, abolished, revoked, rescinded, repealed. **2** *the null effects of the trade embargo* ineffectual, useless, in vain, worthless, futile, powerless, unproductive, non-existent, negative. **3** *null expressions | such null young people* blank, expressionless, vacuous, characterless, colourless, insipid, vapid, inane, senseless, foolish.

nullify *verb* render null and void, declare null and void, annul, disannul, void, invalidate, cancel, abolish, set aside, revoke, rescind, repeal, reverse, abrogate, discontinue, retract, withdraw, renounce, repudiate, countermand, veto, negate, terminate, dissolve, cast aside, do away with, bring to an end, obliterate. **Opposites** RATIFY; VALIDATE; CONFIRM.

nullity *noun* **1** *the nullity of the document* invalidity, non-validity, illegality. **2** *the nullity of their attempts* ineffectualness, uselessness, worthlessness, futility, powerlessness, nonexistence. **3** *the nullity of the expressions/people* blankness, expressionlessness, vacuity, characterlessness, insipidity, vapidity, inanity.

numb *adjective numb fingers | she was feeling numb with grief/cold* benumbed, dead, without feeling, sensationless, deadened, insensible, insensate, torpid, dull, anaesthetized, drugged, dazed, stunned, stupefied, in shock, paralysed, immobilized, frozen, chilled. **Opposites** SENSITIVE; RESPONSIVE.

numb *verb cold numbing her fingers | grief numbing her* benumb, deaden, dull, anaesthetize, drug, daze, stun, stupefy, paralyse, immobilize, freeze, chill.

number *noun* **1** *add up the numbers* figure, digit, numeral, cipher, character, symbol, unit, integer, whole number, cardinal number, ordinal number, Roman number, Arabic number. *See table at* NUMERAL. **2** *the number of accidents has increased* total, aggregate, score, tally, count, sum, summation. **3** *a large number of people* quantity, amount, group, collection, company, crowd. **4** *the latest number of the magazine* edition, issue, printing, imprint, copy.

number *verb* **1** *number the items/reasons* enumerate, count, add up, total, calculate, compute, reckon, tell, estimate, assess, take stock of. **2** *number the accounts* assign a number to, categorize by number, specify by number. **3** *number them among my friends* count, include, reckon. **4** *his days are numbered* limit, limit in number, restrict, fix.

numberless *adjective on numberless occasions* innumerable, countless, multitudinous, myriad, numerous, many, untold, infinite, more than one can count, immeasurable, abundant, copious.

numbing *adjective* benumbing, deadening, dulling, anaesthetizing, dazing, paralysing, freezing. *See* NUMB *verb*.

numbness *noun* lack of feeling, lack of sensation, deadness, insensibility, torpor, dullness, stupefaction, paralysis, immobility, chill.

numeral *noun* number, figure, digit, cipher, character, symbol, unit, integer. *See table*.

ROMAN NUMERALS			
Roman	**Arabic**	**Roman**	**Arabic**
I	1	XVI	16
II	2	XVII	17
III	3	XVIII	18
IV	4	XIX	19
V	5	XX	20
VI	6	L	50
VII	7	C	100
VIII	8	D	500
IX	9	M	1000
X	10	$\bar{V}$	5000
XI	11	$\bar{X}$	10 000
XII	12	$\bar{L}$	50 000
XIII	13	$\bar{C}$	100 000
XIV	14	$\bar{D}$	500 000
XV	15	$\bar{M}$	1 000 000

numerous *adjective* many, very many, innumerable, myriad, multitudinous, several, quite a few, various, diverse; *inf*. a lot of, lots of. **Opposites** FEW.

nuncio *noun* envoy, legate, messenger, ambassador.

nuptial *adjective* matrimonial, marriage, marital, wedding, conjugal, connubial, bridal, spousal, hymeneal, married, wedded.

nuptials *plural noun* wedding, wedding ceremony, marriage ceremony, marriage.

nurse verb **1** *nurse the patient* take care of, care for, look after, tend, attend to, minister to, treat, doctor. **2** *a mother nursing her baby* suckle, breast-feed, feed, wet-nurse. **3** *nurse her career* nurture, encourage, promote, boost, further, advance, contribute to, assist, help. *See* NOURISH 2. **4** *nurse feelings of resentment* harbour, have, hold, entertain, foster, cherish, nourish.
Opposites NEGLECT; HINDER.

nurture verb **1** *nurture the children* feed, nourish, provide for, care for, take care of, tend, attend to, bring up, rear. **2** *nurture the pupils* educate, school, train, tutor, coach. **3** *nurture growth | nurtured her career* encourage, promote, foster, stimulate, develop, cultivate, boost, further, advance, forward, contribute to, be conducive to, assist, help, aid.
Opposites NEGLECT; HINDER.

nurture noun **1** *provide nurture* food, nutrition, nutriment, sustenance, subsistence. **2** *the nurture of the children* feeding, tending, rearing. *See* NURTURE verb 1. **3** *the nurture of the pupils* education, schooling, training, discipline. *See* NURTURE verb 2. **4** *the nurture of her career/hopes* encouragement, promotion, fostering, development, cultivation, boosting, furtherance, advancement, assistance. *See* NURTURE verb 3.

nut noun **1** *squirrels eating nuts* kernel, store, seed, stone. *See table.* **2** *a cinema nut* fan, enthusiast, aficionado, devotee, follower; *inf.* buff, freak, fiend. **3** *he was attacked by a nut* madman, lunatic, psychopath; *inf.* maniac, nutcase, loony, weirdo, oddball, crackpot, screwball.

nutrition noun nourishment, nutriment, food, sustenance, subsistence, aliment, provisions, provender, victuals, daily bread; *inf.* grub, scoff, chow. *See* NOURISHMENT.

nutritious adjective nourishing, nutritive, wholesome, health-giving, healthy, healthful, beneficial, good for one.
Opposites UNHEALTHY.

nuts adjective mad, insane, deranged, demented, irrational, non compos mentis, lunatic, psychopathic; *inf.* nutty, crazy, bananas, loony, loopy, batty, barmy, out of one's mind, off one's head, not the full shilling/pound, with a screw loose, out to lunch.

nuts and bolts plural noun fundamentals, basics, practicalities, essentials; *inf.* nitty-gritty.

nuzzle verb **1** *dogs nuzzling their masters nose* nudge, prod, push. **2** *nuzzle up to her mother* snuggle, cuddle, nestle, lie close to, curl up.

nymph noun **1** *the nymphs of legend* wood nymph, water nymph. *See table.* **2** *nymphs dancing with the boys* girl, lass, damsel, maiden, maid.

NYMPHS		
dryad	nereid	sprite
hamadryad	Oceanid	sylph
naiad	oread	undine

NUTS				
acorn	candlenut	double	hognut	pine nut
almond	cashew	coconut	horse chestnut	pistachio
areca nut	chestnut	dwarf	ivory-nut	quandong
beechnut	chincapin	chestnut	litchi nut	Queensland
betel-nut	cob-nut	earth-nut	macadamia nut	nut
bitternut	coco-de-mer	filbert	mockernut	sal nut
Brazil nut	coconut	groundnut	monkey-nut	saouari nut
breadnut	coffee nut	grugru nut	palm nut	sweet chestnut
burrawang	cola nut	gum nut	peanut	walnut
nut	conker	hazelnut	pecan	water chestnut
butternut	coquilla nut	hickory nut	pignut	white walnut

Oo

oaf *noun* **1** *that oaf tripped me up* lout, gawk, lubber, blunderer, bungler, boor, churl, bumpkin, yokel, brute, gorilla, bull in a china shop: *inf.* clodhopper, lummox, galoot. **2** *the oaf doesn't understand* fool, dolt, blockhead, numskull, dunderhead, dunce, dullard, nincompoop, ninny, simpleton, booby; *inf.* idiot, moron, imbecile, sap, dummy, bonehead, thickie, thickhead, nitwit, dim-wit, halfwit, chump, clod, clot, goon, zombie; *Am. inf.* schmuck.

oafish *adjective* **1** *oafish boys trying to dance* clumsy, awkward, loutish, gawkish, gawky, lumbering, lubberly, blundering, heavy, bungling, boorish, churlish, brutish; *inf.* clodhopping. **2** *oafish children looking blank* dull, stupid, blockish, doltish, blockheaded, dunderheaded, slow-witted, obtuse; *inf.* dim, dense, thick, moronic, dim-witted, halfwitted, dumb, slow on the uptake, boneheaded, thickheaded.

oasis *noun* **1** *an oasis in the desert* watering-hole, fertile spot. **2** *an oasis among all the noise* refuge, haven, retreat, sanctuary, sanctum, hiding-place, hideaway; *inf.* hideout.

oath *noun* **1** *take an oath to tell the truth | on my oath* sworn statement, vow, promise, pledge, avowal, affirmation, attestation, bond, word of honour, word, troth. **2** *oaths uttered by the man* curse, swear-word, expletive, blasphemy, profanity, imprecation, malediction, obscenity, bad/foul language, strong language, epithet, four-letter word, dirty word, bad word, naughty word; *inf.* cuss.

obdurate *adjective* **1** *obdurate children | he was obdurate about not going* stubborn, obstinate, headstrong, wilful, adamant, firm, fixed, dogged, unyielding, unbending, inflexible, unshakeable, unmalleable, intractable, unimpressible, pigheaded, mulish, iron-willed, hard-hearted. **2** *obdurate criminals* hardened, case-hardened, cold-blooded, tough, unresponsive, unfeeling, insensitive, impenitent, unrepenting, uncontrite, shameless. *Opposites* AMENABLE; COMPLIANT; MALLEABLE; PENITENT.

obedience *noun* dutifulness, duteousness, duty, sense of duty, observance of the law/rules, conformity, conformability, deference, respect, compliance, acquiescence, tractability, amenability, malleability, yielding, submission, docility, meekness. *See* OBEDIENT.

obedient *adjective* biddable, dutiful, duteous, law-abiding, rule-abiding, conforming, deferential, respectful, compliant, acquiescent, tractable, amenable, malleable, governable, under control, well-trained, yielding, submissive, docile, meek, subservient, obsequious, servile. *Opposites* DISOBEDIENT; INTRACTABLE; UNRULY.

obeisance *noun* **1** *make obeisance to the emperor* bow, curtsy, bob, genuflection, stoop, salaam, kowtow. **2** *pay obeisance to the emperor* homage, worship, adoration, reverence, respect, veneration, honour, submission.

obelisk *noun* monolith, column, pillar, shaft, needle, monument.

obese *adjective* overweight, fat, plump, stout, ample, chubby, tubby, portly, rotund, corpulent, podgy, paunchy, fleshy, big, heavy, on the heavy side, large, bulky, chunky, outsize, massive, gross, Falstaffian. *Opposites* THIN; SKINNY.

obesity *noun* fatness, corpulence, plumpness, stoutness, rotundness, rotundity, portliness, chubbiness, tubbiness, podginess, fleshiness, bigness, largeness, bulk, grossness, weight problem, *embonpoint*.

obey *verb* **1** *obey the rules* abide by, comply with, adhere to, observe, conform to, respect, acquiesce in, consent to, agree to, follow. **2** *obey orders* perform, carry out, execute, put into effect, fulfil, act upon. **3** *you must obey your mother* be dutiful to, do as/what someone says, follow the orders of, carry out the orders of, heed, be regulated by, be governed by. *Opposites* DISOBEY; IGNORE; DEFY.

obfuscate *verb* **1** *obfuscate the issue* confuse, obscure, blur, muddle, jumble, complicate, make abstruse/unclear, garble, scramble, muddy, cloud, conceal, hide, veil. **2** *the brightest of people obfuscated by the problem* puzzle, perplex, baffle, confound, bemuse, bewilder, mystify, nonplus; *inf.* stump, beat, bamboozle.

obituary *noun* death notice; *inf.* obit.

object *noun* **1** *wooden objects* thing, something, anything, body, entity, phenomenon, article, item, device, gadget; *inf.* thingumajig, thingumabob, doodad, whatsit, what's-its-name, what-d'you-call-it, thingy. **2** *the object of our discussion* subject, subject matter, substance, issue, concern. **3** *the object of their affection/abuse* focus, target, recipient, butt, victim. **4** *our object is to win* objective, aim, goal, target, end, end in view, ambition, purpose, design, intent, intention, idea, point. *See* OBJECTIVE *noun.*

object *verb* **1** *they were successful but many people objected* raise objections, protest, lodge a protest, demur, beg to differ, be in opposition, remonstrate, expostulate, take exception. **2** *object to the plan* raise objections to, protest against, lodge a protest against, argue against, oppose, be in opposition to, remonstrate against, expostulate about, take exception to, complain about. *Opposites* APPROVE; ACCEPT.

objection *noun* **1** *their objection to the plan is understandable* protest, protestation, demurral,

opposition, remonstration, remonstrance,
expostulation, complaining about, dissatisfaction with, disapproval of. **2** *lodge/name their objections* argument, counter-argument, demurral, opposition, remonstration, remonstration, expostulation, doubt, complaint, grievance, scruple, qualm; *inf.* niggle.
Opposites APPROVAL; ACCEPTANCE.

objectionable *adjective objectionable people/ behaviour/smells* offensive, obnoxious, unpleasant, disagreeable, unacceptable, nasty, disgusting, repulsive, repellent, abhorrent, repugnant, revolting, loathsome, nauseating, hateful, detestable, reprehensible, deplorable, insufferable, intolerable, despicable, contemptible, odious, vile, obscene, foul, horrible, horrid, noxious.
Opposites PLEASANT; AGREEABLE; ACCEPTABLE.

objective *adjective referees must be objective* unbiased, bias-free, unprejudiced, prejudice-free, impartial, neutral, uninvolved, non-partisan, disinterested, detached, dispassionate, unswayed, even-handed, equitable, fair, just, open-minded.
Opposites BIASED; PARTIAL; SUBJECTIVE.

objective *noun our objective is to win* object, aim, goal, target, end, end in view, ambition, aspiration, intent, intention, purpose, idea, point, desire, hope, design, plan, scheme, plot.

objectively *adverb look at the issue objectively* with objectivity, without bias, without prejudice, impartially, disinterestedly, with detachment, dispassionately, equitably, even-handedly, fairly, justly, open-mindedly, with an open mind, without fear or favour.

objectivity *noun* absence of bias/prejudice, impartiality, disinterest, detachment, dispassion; dispassionateness, equitability, even-handedness, fairness, justness, justice, open-mindedness.

obligate *verb we felt obligated to attend* oblige, compel, require, necessitate, impel, force, constrain, press, pressure, pressurize.

obligation *noun* **1** *the obligations specified by the contract* requirement, pre-requisite, demand, necessity, command, order, constraint, compulsion; *inf.* must. **2** *fulfil/discharge one's obligations* duty, function, chore, task, job, assignment, commission, business, burden, charge, onus, trust, liability, responsibility, accountability, indebtedness, debt, engagement. **3** *we attended only from a sense of obligation* duty, compulsion, necessity, enforcement, duress, pressure. **4** *the obligation is still binding* contract, agreement, deed, covenant, compact, bond, treaty, deal, pact, understanding, transaction. **under an obligation** *under an obligation to them* obliged to, beholden to, owing someone a favour, indebted to, in someone's debt, owing someone a debt of gratitude, duty-bound to, honour-bound to, be grateful to, owing someone thanks.

obligatory *adjective* **1** *the agreement is obligatory* binding, valid, legal, in force, effective. **2** *maths/attendance is obligatory* compulsory, enforced, prescriptive, mandatory, necessary, essential, required, requisite, imperative, *de rigueur*, unavoidable, unescapable.
Opposites VOLUNTARY; OPTIONAL.

oblige *verb* **1** *ties of friendship oblige me to go* put under an obligation, leave someone no option, require, necessitate, obligate, compel, call for, force, constrain, press, pressure, pressurize, impel. **2** *will you oblige me by going?* do someone a favour, do someone a kindness, do someone a service, serve, accommodate, meet the wants/needs of, help, accommodate, put oneself out for, indulge, gratify the wishes of, help, assist.

obliging *adjective* helpful, eager to help/please, accommodating, willing, complaisant, indulgent, friendly, kind, generous, considerate, cooperative, neighbourly, agreeable, pleasant, good-natured, amiable, civil, courteous, polite.
Opposites DISOBLIGING; OBSTRUCTIVE; DISCOURTEOUS.

oblique *adjective* **1** *an oblique line* slanting, slanted, sloping, sloped, inclined, at an angle, angled, tilted, listing, diagonal; *Am.* cater-cornered. **2** *an oblique compliment | oblique references to the crime* indirect, implied, roundabout, circuitous, circumlocutory, ambagious, evasive, backhanded.
Opposites STRAIGHT; DIRECT.

oblique *noun words separated by an oblique* oblique line/stroke, solidus, slanting line, slant, slash, back slash.

obliquely *adverb* **1** *the line runs obliquely* at an angle, slantwise, aslant, diagonally. **2** *refer obliquely to the matter* indirectly, in a roundabout way, not in so many words, not outright, circuitously, evasively.

obliterate *verb* **1** *obliterate all traces of blood | had obliterated all memories of her* erase, eradicate, efface, blot out, rub out, wipe out, expunge, sponge out, delete, cross out, strike out, blue-pencil, remove, cancel. **2** *the army/village was obliterated* destroy, exterminate, annihilate, wipe out, eliminate, eradicate, extirpate, decimate, liquidate, demolish.
Opposites CREATE; ESTABLISH.

obliteration *noun* **1** *the obliteration of the stains/memories* erasing, eradication, effacement, rubbing out, blotting out, expunging, deletion, striking out, removal, cancellation. *See* OBLITERATE 1. **2** *the obliteration of the army/village* destruction, extermination, annihilation, wiping out, elimination, eradication, extirpation, decimation, liquidation, demolition.

oblivion *noun* **1** *sitting in a state of oblivion as people shouted* obliviousness, heedlessness, unmindfulness, unawareness, unconsciousness, insensibility, inattentiveness, disregard, disregardfulness, forgetfulness, absent-mindedness, amnesia, unconcern, abstraction, preoccupation, absorption. *See* OBLIVIOUS. **2** *the old traditions have sunk into oblivion* neglect, disuse, non-existence, abeyance, suspension. **3** *oblivion came when he hit his head* blackness, darkness, blankness, unconsciousness, insensibility, senselessness, stupor, coma.
Opposites CONSCIOUSNESS; awareness; EXISTENCE.

oblivious *adjective he was completely oblivious of/ to his surroundings | she is oblivious to danger* unheeding, heedless of, unmindful of,

unaware of, unconscious of, insensible of, ignorant of, blind to, unobservant of, deaf to, inattentive to, disregardful of, neglectful of, forgetful of, absent-minded, careless of, unconcerned with, abstracted, *distrait*, preoccupied, absorbed, far away.
Opposites AWARE; CONSCIOUS; ATTENTIVE.

obloquy noun **1** *bring obloquy on the family* discredit, shame, dishonour, disgrace, humiliation, loss of face, ignominy, disfavour, disrepute, ill repute, infamy, scandal, odium. **2** *undergo the obloquy of the crowd* abuse, attack, opprobrium, censure, criticism, condemnation, denunciation, reproach, castigation, reproof, upbraiding, invective, railing, tirade, defamation, denigration, vilification, slander, libel, insult, aspersions, calumny, contumely.
Opposites HONOUR; PRAISE.

obnoxious adjective *obnoxious man/behaviour/smell* offensive, objectionable, unpleasant, disagreeable, unacceptable, nasty, disgusting, repulsive, repellent, abhorrent, repugnant, revolting, loathsome, nauseating, sickening, hateful, detestable, reprehensible, deplorable, insufferable, intolerable, despicable, contemptible, odious, vile, obscene, foul, horrible, horrid, noxious.
Opposites DELIGHTFUL; PLEASANT; AGREEABLE.

obscene adjective **1** *obscene publications/jokes* indecent, pornographic, blue, off-colour, risqué, lewd, salacious, smutty, lecherous, lascivious, licentious, prurient, lubricious, ribald, scatological, scabrous, bawdy, suggestive, vulgar, dirty, filthy, foul, coarse, gross, vile, nasty, offensive, immoral, impure, immodest, shameless, unchaste, improper, unwholesome, erotic, carnal, sexy; *inf.* raunchy. **2** *the murder was an obscene act* atrocious, heinous, vile, foul, outrageous, shocking, repugnant, repulsive, revolting, nauseating, sickening, wicked, evil, odious.
Opposites DECENT; PURE; PROPER.

obscenity noun **1** *the obscenity of the publication* indecency, lewdness, salaciousness, smuttiness, lechery, lasciviousness, licentiousness, prurience, lubricity, ribaldry, scatalogy, scabrousness, bawdiness, suggestiveness, vulgarity, dirt, dirtiness, filth, filthiness, foulness, coarseness, grossness, vileness, nastiness, immorality, impurity, immodesty, shamelessness, unchasteness, impropriety, unwholesomeness, eroticism, carnality, sexiness. **2** *the obscenity of the crime* atrocity, heinousness, vileness, foulness, repugnance, wickedness, evil. *See* OBSCENE 2. **3** *a stream of obscenities came from him* curse, oath, swear-word, expletive, imprecation, blasphemy, bad/foul language, strong language, epithet, profanity, four-letter word, dirty word, bad word, naughty word; *inf.* cuss.

obscure adjective **1** *obscure references* unclear, indeterminate, opaque, abstruse, recondite, unexplained, concealed, hidden, arcane, enigmatic, deep, cryptic, mysterious, puzzling, perplexing, confusing, intricate, involved, unfathomable, incomprehensible, impenetrable, vague, indefinite, hazy, uncertain, doubtful, dubious, ambiguous, equivocal. **2** *obscure shapes looming out of the mist* indistinct, vague, shadowy, hazy, blurred, fuzzy, cloudy. **3** *obscure parts of the forest* dark, dim, black, unlit, murky, sombre, gloomy, shady, shadowy. **4** *obscure villages* unknown, unheard-of, out-of-the-way, off the beaten track, remote, hidden, secluded, God-forsaken. **5** *obscure poets* little-known, unknown, unheard-of, undistinguished, insignificant, inconspicuous, minor, unimportant, unrenowned, unrecognized, unhonoured, unsung, inglorious.
Opposites CLEAR; PLAIN; DISTINCT; FAMOUS.

obscure verb **1** *obscure the main issue* confuse, blur, muddle, complicate, make abstruse, obfuscate, garble, cloud, muddy, conceal, hide, veil. **2** *clouds obscure the sun* hide, conceal, cover, veil, screen, mask, cloak, shroud, block, block out, eclipse, adumbrate. **3** *clouds obscured the sky* darken, blacken, dim, bedim.
Opposites CLARIFY; REVEAL; BRIGHTEN.

obscurity noun **1** *the obscurity of the reference* lack of clarity, unclearness, opaqueness, reconditeness, arcaneness, enigma, deepness, abstruseness, mystery, puzzle, confusion, intricacy, involvement, incomprehensibility, impenetrability, vagueness, uncertainty, doubtfulness, ambiguity, equivocalness. *See* OBSCURE adjective 1. **2** *the obscurity of the village* remoteness, seclusion. *See* OBSCURE adjective 4. **3** *the obscurity of the poet* insignificance, inconspicuousness, unimportance, lack of fame/renown/honour/recognition, ingloriousness. **4** *a text full of obscurities* difficulty, problem, complication, intricacy, opacity, enigma, puzzle, perplexity, mystery, ambiguity.
Opposites CLARITY; FAME.

obsequies plural noun funeral rites, funeral service, funeral, burial ceremony, burial, last offices, exequies.

obsequious adjective servile, subservient, submissive, slavish, menial, abject, fawning, grovelling, cringing, toadying, truckling, sycophantic, ingratiating, unctuous, oily, Uriah Heepish; *inf.* bootlicking.
Opposites PROUD; ARROGANT.

observable adjective noticeable, visible, perceptible, perceivable, detectable, discernible, recognizable, obvious, evident, apparent, manifest, patent, clear, distinct, plain, unmistakable, appreciable.

observance noun **1** *the observance of laws* observation of, keeping of, obeying, obedience to, adherence to, abiding by, compliance with, heeding. **2** *observance of duty/rites* carrying out, performance, execution, discharge, fulfilment, honouring. **3** *religious observances* rite, ritual, ceremony, ceremonial, celebration, festival, practice, tradition, custom, formality, form, service, office.
Opposites DISREGARD; NEGLECT.

observant adjective **1** *an observant boy spotted the thief* alert, sharp-eyed, sharp, eagle-eyed, attentive, vigilant, wide-awake, watchful, heedful, on the qui vive, on the lookout, on guard, mindful, intent, aware, conscious, with one's eyes peeled/skinned; *inf.* not missing a thing/trick, on the ball. **2** *observant members of the community/faith* dutiful, obedient, conforming, law-abiding, orthodox, practising.

Opposites INATTENTIVE; DREAMY; unobservant;
NEGLIGENT.

observation *noun* **1** *our observation of the man
upset him* seeing, noticing, watching, viewing,
eyeing, witnessing. *See* OBSERVE 1. **2** *keep the
thief/patient under observation* scrutiny, scrutinization, watch, watching, monitoring, surveillance, inspection, attention, consideration,
study, review, examination. **3** *record your
observations on the experiment* findings, results,
information, data, remarks, comments, notes,
annotation, report, description, opinion,
thoughts, reflections. **4** *make a sarcastic observation* remark, comment, statement, utterance,
pronouncement, declaration. **5** *observation of
the law/rules/customs* observance of, keeping of,
obedience to, adherence to, compliance with,
heeding. *See* OBSERVANCE 1.

observe *verb* **1** *we observe him go into the bank*
see, catch sight of, notice, note, perceive, discern, detect, espy, behold, watch, view, spot,
witness; *inf.* get a load of. **2** *police observe the
house* keep under observation, watch, keep
watch on, look at, keep under surveillance,
keep in sight, keep in view, spy upon, monitor,
reconnoitre, scan; *inf.* keep an eye on, keep
tabs on. **3** *doctors observe the patient* keep under
observation, keep under scrutiny, scrutinize,
watch, monitor, keep under surveillance,
inspect, study, review, examine, check. **4** *"A
good try," he observed* say, remark, comment,
state, utter, enunciate, exclaim, announce,
declare, pronounce. **5** *observe the rules* keep,
obey, adhere to, abide by, heed, follow, comply
with, conform to, acquiesce in, consent to,
accept, respect, defer to. **6** *observe one's duty*
carry out, perform, execute, discharge, fulfil.
7 *observe Christmas* celebrate, keep, recognize,
commemorate, mark, remember, solemnize.
Opposites OVERLOOK; IGNORE; DISOBEY.

observer *noun* watcher, looker-on, onlooker,
witness, eyewitness, spectator, bystander,
beholder, viewer, commentator, reporter,
sightseer, spotter; *inf.* rubberneck.

obsess *verb* *her memory obsesses him* | *memories
which obsess his mind* preoccupy, haunt, monopolize, have a hold on, possess, consume,
engross, have a grip on, grip, dominate, rule,
control, be on one's mind, be uppermost in
one's mind, prey on, plague, torment, hound,
bedevil. **be obsessed by** be preoccupied with,
be haunted by, be possessed by, be beset by, be
consumed with, be gripped by, be dominated
by, be plagued by, be bedevilled by; *inf.* have a
bee in one's bonnet about, have a thing about,
be hung up on.

obsession *noun* preoccupation, fixation, *idée
fixe*, ruling/consuming passion, mania, enthusiasm, infatuation, compulsion, phobia, complex, fetish, craze; *inf.* bee in one's bonnet,
hang-up, thing.
Opposites INDIFFERENCE.

obsessive *adjective* *an obsessive concern for
hygiene* excessive, overdone, consuming, compulsive, besetting, gripping, haunting.

obsolescent *adjective* going out of use, going
out of fashion, dying out, on the decline,
declining, waning, on the wane, disappearing,

past its prime, ageing, moribund; *inf.* on the
way out.

obsolete *adjective* *obsolete machinery/words* no
longer in use, in disuse, disused, outworn, discarded, discontinued, extinct, bygone, outmoded, *démodé*, *passé*, antiquated, out of date,
outdated, out, superannuated, old-fashioned,
out of fashion, out of style, behind the times,
old, dated, antique, archaic, ancient, antediluvian, time-worn, past its prime, having seen
better days; *inf.* old-hat, out of the ark.
Opposites CURRENT; MODERN; UP-TO-DATE.

obstacle *noun* bar, barrier, obstruction,
impediment, hindrance, hurdle, barricade,
blockade, stumbling-block, block, blockage,
curb, check, stop, stoppage, deterrent, baulk,
snag, difficulty, catch, drawback, hitch, interference, interruption, fly in the ointment.
Opposites HELP; ADVANTAGE; ENCOURAGEMENT.

obstinacy *noun* stubbornness, mulishness, pig-
headedness, wilfulness, perversity, refractoriness, recalcitrance, contumaciousness,
firmness, steadfastness, inflexibility, immov-
ability, intransigence, intractability, persistence, pertinacity, tenacity, doggedness,
single-mindedness, relentlessness.
Opposites COMPLIANCE.

obstinate *adjective* *obstinate woman/resistance*
stubborn, stubborn as a mule, mulish, pig-
headed, headstrong, wilful, self-willed, strong-
minded, perverse, refractory, recalcitrant,
contumacious, unmanageable, firm, steadfast,
unyielding, inflexible, unbending, immovable,
intransigent, intractable, uncompromising,
persistent, persevering, pertinacious, tenacious, dogged, single-minded, relentless, unrelenting.
Opposites COMPLIANT; AMENABLE; FLEXIBLE;
TRACTABLE.

obstreperous *adjective* *obstreperous person/
behaviour* unruly, disorderly, turbulent, rowdy,
boisterous, rough, riotous, out of control,
uncontrolled, out of hand, wild, rampaging,
undisciplined, unrestrained, unbridled,
ungoverned, unmanageable, noisy, loud, clamorous, raucous, vociferous; *inf.* stroppy, bolshie.
Opposites ORDERLY; QUIET; RESTRAINED.

obstruct *verb* **1** *logs obstruct the road/river*
block, barricade, bar, cut off, shut off, choke,
clog, dam up. **2** *floods obstructing traffic* hold
up, bring to a standstill, stop, halt, block, prohibit. **3** *obstructing our efforts/progress* hinder,
impede, hamper, block, interfere with, interrupt, hold up, frustrate, thwart, baulk, inhibit,
curb, brake, bridle, hamstring, encumber,
restrain, slow, retard, delay, arrest, check,
stop, halt, restrict, limit.
Opposites CLEAR; ADVANCE; FACILITATE; HELP.

obstruction *noun* obstacle, impediment, hindrance, bar, barrier, barricade, hurdle, block,
blockage, stumbling-block, blockade, curb,
check, stop, stoppage, deterrent, baulk, snag,
difficulty, catch, drawback, restriction, hitch,
fly in the ointment.
Opposites AID; HELP; ENCOURAGEMENT.

obstructive *adjective* **1** *obstructive measures/tactics* blocking, delaying, hindering, stalling, inhibiting, interrupting, restrictive, preventative, preventive. **2** *obstructive people* unhelpful, uncooperative, awkward.
Opposites HELPFUL; SUPPORTIVE; COOPERATIVE.

obtain *verb* **1** *obtain tickets/promotion* get, get hold of, acquire, come by, procure, secure, gain, earn, achieve, attain, take possession of, get one's hands on, seize, grab, pick up. **2** *new rules obtain* be in force, be in use, be effective, exist, stand, prevail, hold, be the case, reign, rule, hold sway.
Opposites LOSE; give up (*see* GIVE); RELINQUISH.

obtainable *adjective* *no tickets obtainable* available, to be had, procurable, achievable, attainable, at hand, ready; *inf.* on tap.

obtrusive *adjective* **1** *obtrusive colours/music* noticeable, conspicuous, obvious, unmistakable, blatant, flagrant, bold, audacious, intrusive. **2** *obtrusive behaviour* forward, interfering, meddling, prying, intrusive, officious, importunate; *inf.* pushy, nosy.
Opposites UNOBTRUSIVE; RESTRAINED; RETIRING.

obtuse *adjective* *too obtuse to understand* stupid, dull, dull-witted, slow-witted, slow, uncomprehending, unintelligent, imperceptive, bovine, stolid, insensitive, thick-skinned; *inf.* dim, dense, thick, dim-witted, slow on the uptake, boneheaded, dumb, dopey.
Opposites BRIGHT; CLEVER.

obvious *adjective* clear, clear-cut, crystal-clear, plain, visible, noticeable, perceptible, discernible, detectable, recognizable, evident, apparent, manifest, distinct, palpable, patent, conspicuous, unconcealed, overt, pronounced, transparent, prominent, unmistakable, indisputable, undeniable, as plain as a pikestaff, as plain as the nose on one's face, staring someone in the face; *inf.* sticking out like a sore thumb, sticking out a mile.
Opposites IMPERCEPTIBLE; INCONSPICUOUS; OBSCURE.

obviously *adjective* **1** *obviously pregnant* clearly, plainly, visibly, noticeably, discernibly, evidently, manifestly, distinctly, patently, unmistakably, undeniably. *See* OBVIOUS. **2** *obviously, we must go* of course, certainly, undoubtedly, clearly.

occasion *noun* **1** *we met on one or two occasions* time, juncture, point, situation, instance, case, circumstance. **2** *it was a sad occasion* event, incident, occurrence, happening, episode, affair, experience. **3** *we met at a college occasion* function, party, affair, celebration; *inf.* get-together, do. **4** *if the occasion arises* opportunity, golden opportunity, chance, opening, contingency. **5** *have occasion to believe* reason, cause, grounds, justification, call, excuse, inducement.

occasion *verb* *occasion much grief* cause, give rise to, bring about, result in, lead to, prompt, provoke, produce, create, generate, engender, originate, effect.

occasional *adjective* *an occasional meeting/letter* infrequent, intermittent, irregular, sporadic, odd, rare, casual, incidental.
Opposites REGULAR; HABITUAL.

occasionally *adverb* now and then, now and again, from time to time, sometimes, at times, every so often, once in a while, on occasion, periodically, at intervals, irregularly, sporadically, infrequently, intermittently, on and off, off and on.

occult *adjective* supernatural, magic, magical, mystical, mystic, preternatural, transcendental, unrevealed, secret, hidden, concealed, invisible, obscure, recondite, arcane, abstruse, esoteric, inexplicable, unfathomable, mysterious, cryptic, enigmatic.

occult *noun* **the occult** the supernatural, magic, black magic, witchcraft, sorcery, wizardry, the black arts, diabolism, devil worship, supernaturalism, mysticism.

occupancy *noun* occupation, tenancy, tenure, residence, residency, inhabitancy, inhabitance, inhabitation, habitation, habitancy, living, possession, possessorship, holding, owner-occupancy.

occupant *noun* occupier, owner-occupier, tenant, renter, lease-holder, lessee, inhabitant, resident, dweller, householder, addressee, incumbent, inmate.

occupation *noun* **1** *what is his occupation?* job, work, profession, business, employment, employ, career, calling, métier, vocation, trade, craft, line, field, province, area. **2** *occupation of the house* occupancy, tenancy, tenure, residence, inhabitancy, habitation, possession, holding. *See* OCCUPANCY. **3** *suffer the occupation of their land* possession, foreign rule, invasion, seizure, take-over, conquest, capture, overthrow, subjugation, subjection.

occupational *adjective* employment, work, professional, business, career, vocational.

occupied *adjective* **1** *everyone is occupied just now* busy, engaged, working, at work, employed; *inf.* tied up, hard at it. **2** *all the rooms are occupied* full, engaged, taken, in use, unavailable. **3** *the houses are all occupied* inhabited, lived-in, tenanted, settled.
Opposites FREE; VACANT; EMPTY.

occupy *verb* **1** *occupy the lower flat* live in, inhabit, reside in, dwell in, be the tenant of, tenant, have one's residence/abode in, make one's home in; *Scots* stay in. **2** *occupy her time | will occupy too much space* fill, fill up, take up, use up, utilize, cover. **3** *occupy a top post* hold, be in, fill, have; *inf.* hold down. **4** *occupy oneself* engage, employ, absorb, engross, preoccupy, immerse, interest, involve, entertain, divert, amuse, beguile. **5** *the invading army occupied their country* take possession of, invade, overrun, seize, take over, capture, garrison.
Opposites LEAVE; ABANDON; QUIT.

occur *verb* **1** *the accident/promotion occurred last year* happen, take place, come about, come to pass, materialize, transpire, arise, crop up, turn up, befall, eventuate. **2** *the disease occurs in the tropics* be found, be met with, be present, exist, have its being, appear, present itself, show itself, manifest itself, arise, spring up. **3** *an idea occurs to me | didn't it occur to you to telephone?* come to mind, spring to mind, come to one, enter one's head, cross one's mind, strike one, hit one, dawn on, suggest itself.

occurrence noun **1** *robbery is an everyday occurrence* happening, event, incident, circumstance, affair, episode, proceedings, adventure. **2** *the occurrence of the disease is nationwide* existence, appearance, manifestation, materialization, springing up.

ocean noun. *See table.*

odd adjective **1** *an odd woman | she's becoming odd* strange, eccentric, queer, peculiar, idiosyncratic, unconventional, outlandish, droll, weird, bizarre, offbeat, freakish, whimsical; *inf.* wacky, freaky, kinky, off-the-wall. **2** *rather an odd happening* unusual, uncommon, irregular, strange, peculiar, funny, curious, queer, abnormal, atypical, different, out-of-the-ordinary, exceptional, rare, extraordinary, remarkable, singular, deviant, aberrant, freak, freakish, bizarre, weird. **3** *do odd jobs* occasional, casual, temporary, part-time, seasonal, periodic, irregular, miscellaneous, various, varied. **4** *at odd moments* occasional, random, irregular, periodic, haphazard, chance, fortuitous, fragmentary, various, sundry. **5** *an odd sock* unmatched, unpaired, left-over, spare, remaining, surplus, superfluous, lone, single, solitary, sole. **odd man out** exception, outsider, nonconformist, misfit, maverick, individualist, fish out of water; *inf.* freak.
Opposites ORDINARY; USUAL; REGULAR.

oddity noun **1** *comment on the oddity of his behaviour* strangeness, eccentricity, queerness, peculiarness, peculiarity, weirdness, freakishness; *inf.* wackiness. *See* ODD 1. **2** *the oddity of the happening* unusualness, uncommonness, peculiarness, peculiarity, abnormality, rarity, rareness, bizarreness. *See* ODD 2. **3** *the house is an oddity | this is a grammatical oddity* curiosity, rarity, anomaly, aberration, irregularity, phenomenon. **4** *he is an oddity* eccentric, crank, original, misfit, fish out of water, *rara avis*; *inf.* character, card, oddball, weirdo, crackpot, nut, screwball, freak, odd/queer fish. **5** *her character oddities* peculiarity, idiosyncrasy, eccentricity, mannerism, quirk, twist, kink, crotchet.

oddment noun **1** *oddments of material* scrap, remnant, leftover, fragment, snippet, offcut, bit, piece, end, shred, sliver, stub, tail-end; *inf.* fag-end. **2** *shops selling oddments* miscellanea, odds and ends, sundry, knick-knack, notion, novelty, souvenir, keepsake, memento.

odds plural noun **1** *the odds are in his favour* advantage, lead, edge, superiority, supremacy, ascendancy. **2** *the odds are that he will win* likelihood, probability, chances, balance. **3** *against heavy odds* difference, disparity, unevenness, inequality, discrepancy, variation, dissimilarity. **at odds 1** *at odds with each other* in conflict, in disagreement, on bad terms, at daggers drawn, at loggerheads. **2** *at odds with his principles* out of keeping, not in keeping, in opposition to, at variance. **odds and ends** bits and pieces, bits, pieces, oddments, fragments, remnants, scraps, offcuts, cuttings, snippets, miscellanea, leftovers, leavings, debris.

odious adjective abhorrent, repugnant, disgusting, repulsive, repellent, revolting, foul, vile, unpleasant, disagreeable, loathsome, detestable, hateful, despicable, contemptible, objectionable, offensive, horrible, horrid, abominable, heinous, atrocious, execrable.
Opposites DELIGHTFUL; PLEASANT; AGREEABLE.

odium noun abhorrence, repugnance, disgust, revulsion, loathing, detestation, hatred, dislike, disapproval, antipathy, contempt.

odour noun **1** *the odour of baking | a strong odour of bad drains* aroma, smell, scent, perfume, fragrance, bouquet, redolence, essence, stench, stink; *inf.* niff, pong. **2** *an odour of ill will about the place* atmosphere, air, ambience, aura, spirit, quality, flavour, emanation.

odyssey noun journey, voyage, trek, quest, peregrination, crusade, pilgrimage, journeying.

off adjective **1** *the teacher is taking a day off* away, absent. **2** *the match is off* cancelled, postponed, shelved. **3** *chips are off* unavailable, unobtainable, finished. **4** *these answers are off* incorrect, inaccurate, wrong, in error, erroneous. **5** *the food/milk is off* bad, rotten, decomposed, mouldy, high, sour, rancid, turned.
Opposites PRESENT; ON; AVAILABLE.

off adverb *feeling rather off* ill, unwell, sick, poorly; *inf.* under the weather, below par. **off and on** on and off, sporadically, irregularly, intermittently, at intervals, periodically, once in a while, every so often, now and then, now and again, from time to time, occasionally.

offbeat adjective eccentric, unconventional, unorthodox, idiosyncratic, unusual, strange, bizarre, weird, freakish, outlandish, *outré*, Bohemian, hippie, freaky; *inf.* kinky, way-out, far-out, off-the-wall.

OCEANS AND SEAS

Adriatic Sea	Barents Sea	Indian Ocean	North Sea
Aegean Sea	Beaufort Sea	Inland Sea	Okhotsk, Sea of
Andaman Sea	Bering Sea	Ionian Sea	Pacific Ocean
Antarctic Ocean	Black Sea	Irish Sea	Red Sea
Arabian Sea	Caribbean Sea	Japan, Sea of	Ross Sea
Arafura Sea	Caspian Sea	Java Sea	Sargasso Sea
Aral Sea	China Sea	Kara Sea	Savu Sea
Arctic Ocean	Coral Sea	Laptev Sea	South China Sea
Atlantic Ocean	Dead Sea	Ligurian Sea	Tasman Sea
Azov, Sea of	East China Sea	Marmara, Sea of	Weddell Sea
Baltic Sea	Galilee, Sea of	Mediterranean	White Sea
Banda Sea	Greenland Sea	Sea	Yellow Sea

Opposites ORDINARY; CONVENTIONAL; RUN-OF-THE-MILL.

off-colour *adjective* **1** *feeling off-colour* ill, unwell, sick, queasy, poorly, out of sorts, not oneself, run-down, peaky, washed out; *inf.* not up to par, below par, under the weather. **2** *off-colour jokes* risqué, racy, blue, vulgar, indecent, smutty, dirty, ribald, obscene, bawdy, pornographic; *inf.* raunchy.

offence *noun* **1** *commit an offence* crime, illegal act, breaking of the law, breach/violation/infraction of the law, wrongdoing, wrong, misdemeanour, act of misconduct, misdeed, peccadillo, sin, transgression, act of dereliction, shortcoming, fault, lapse; *Law* malfeasance. **2** *an offence against society* affront, injury, hurt, source of harm, outrage, atrocity, insult, injustice, indignity, slight, snub. **3** *her behaviour causes offence* annoyance, anger, indignation, exasperation, wrath, ire, displeasure, disapproval, dislike, animosity, resentment, pique, vexation, umbrage, antipathy, aversion, opposition, enmity. **4** *the enemy's offence* attack, assault, act of aggression, aggression, onslaught, offensive, thrust, charge, sortie, sally, invasion, incursion. **take offence** *take offence at his remarks* be offended at/by, be affronted at/by, take umbrage at, feel upset at/by, get annoyed at, get angry at, feel piqued at/by, feel resentment at, resent, get/go into a huff; *inf.* be miffed.

offend *verb* **1** *his behaviour offended them* give offence to, hurt the feelings of, wound, be an affront to, affront, upset, displease, annoy, anger, incense, exasperate, vex, pique, put out, gall, irritate, provoke, ruffle, disgruntle, rankle with, outrage, insult, slight, humiliate; *inf.* rile, miff, rattle, put someone's back up, tread on someone's corns/toes. **2** *offend his ear | will offend her sense of taste | guaranteed to offend art-lovers* cause offence to, be offensive to, displease, upset, be disagreeable to, put someone off, be distasteful to, repel, disgust, revolt, nauseate; *inf.* turn someone off. **3** *apologize for having offended* commit a crime, break the law, do wrong, sin, go astray, fall from grace, err, transgress.
Opposites PLEASE; DELIGHT.

offended *adjective* hurt, wounded, affronted, upset, displeased, annoyed, angered, incensed, exasperated, vexed, piqued, put out, irritated, ruffled, disgruntled, resentful, outraged, insulted, in a huff, huffy; *inf.* riled, miffed, rattled. See OFFEND 1.

offender *noun* wrongdoer, culprit, criminal, lawbreaker, miscreant, delinquent, sinner, transgressor, malefactor.

offensive *adjective* **1** *an offensive remark/person* hurtful, wounding, abusive, affronting, displeasing, annoying, exasperating, vexing, galling, irritating, provocative, provoking, objectionable, outrageous, insulting, humiliating, rude, discourteous, uncivil, impolite, unmannerly, impertinent, insolent, disrespectful. **2** *an offensive smell/sight* disagreeable, unpleasant, nasty, foul, vile, objectionable, odious, abominable, detestable, loathsome, repugnant, disgusting, obnoxious, repulsive,

repellent, nauseating, sickening, unpalatable, distasteful, unsavoury, noisome; *inf.* horrid, yucky. **3** *the offensive army* attacking, on the attack, assaulting, invading, invasive, aggressive, combative, martial, warlike, belligerent, bellicose, hostile; *inf.* on the warpath.
Opposites COMPLIMENTARY; PLEASANT; DEFENSIVE.

offensive *noun* *many killed in the offensive* attack, assault, onslaught, drive, invasion, push, thrust, charge, sortie, sally, act of war, incursion. **be on the offensive** attack, begin to attack, attack first, be aggressive, strike the first blow, start a war/battle/quarrel; *inf.* be on the warpath.

offer *verb* **1** *offer a suggestion* put forward, propose, advance, submit, propound, suggest, recommend, make a motion of, put to the motion, move. **2** *offer to help* volunteer one's services, volunteer, offer one's service, offer assistance/help, be at someone's service, be at someone's disposal, make oneself available, show readiness/willingness to help. **3** *the job offers good career prospects* afford, provide, supply, give, furnish, make available, present, give an opportunity for. **4** *offer the house for sale at £100,000* put up for sale, put on the market, put under the hammer, ask for bids for. **5** *he has offered for the house* put in an offer for, bid for, put in a bid for, offer to buy, tender for. **6** *offer his son to the gods | a goat was offered to the goddess* offer up, offer as a sacrifice, sacrifice. **7** *as opportunities offer* arrive, appear, happen, occur, come on the scene, present itself, show itself. **8** *offer violence/resistance* attempt, try, essay, show, give.
Opposites WITHDRAW; REFUSE; WITHHOLD.

offer *noun* **1** *offers of help* proposal, proposition, suggestion, submission, approach, overture. **2** *accept the highest offer* bid, bidding price. **3** *counteract their offers of resistance* attempt, endeavour, essay.

offering *noun* **1** *collecting offerings from the members* contribution, donation, subscription, gift, present, alms, charity, hand-out. **2** *offerings to the gods* sacrifice, oblation, immolation.

offhand *adjective* *an offhand manner | her behaviour was very offhand* casual, unceremonious, cavalier, careless, indifferent, perfunctory, cursory, uninterested, unconcerned, blasé, curt, abrupt, terse, brusque, discourteous, uncivil, impolite, rude; *inf.* off, couldn't-care-less, take-it-or-leave-it.
Opposites CAREFUL; THOROUGH.

offhand *adverb* **1** *always acts very offhand* casually, unceremoniously, cavalierly, perfunctorily, cursorily, unconcernedly, curtly, abruptly, discourteously, rudely. See OFFHAND *adjective*. **2** *I cannot say offhand* extempore, impromptu, ad lib, extemporaneously, without preparation, without consideration, without rehearsal, spontaneously; *inf.* off the cuff, off the top of one's head, just like that.

office *noun* **1** *his office is near his home* place of business, base, workplace, workroom, room. **2** *he has the office of treasurer* post, position, appointment, role, place, situation, station. **3** *the office of administrator is demanding | to hold high office* work, employment, business, duty, function, responsibility, obligation, charge, tenure. **4** *perform their domestic offices* job, work, task, chore, duty, assignment, commission, routine.

officer *noun* **1** *an officer in charge of the men* military officer, army officer, naval officer, air force officer, commissioned officer, non-commissioned officer. **2** *the officer in charge of the investigation* police officer, policeman/policewoman, PC/WPC, officer of the law/peace, constable, detective; *inf.* copper, cop, bobby, pig, dick, gumshoe. **3** *the officers of the society* office-holder, office-bearer, official, committee member, board member, administrator, executive, functionary, bureaucrat. **4** *courts sending out officers* representative, agent, deputy, messenger, envoy.

offices *plural noun through the good offices of* assistance, help, aid, support, backing, patronage, aegis, auspices, intervention, intercession, mediation, advocacy, recommendation, word.

official *adjective* **1** *official permission | his appointment is now official* authorized, accredited, approved, validated, authenticated, certified, endorsed, sanctioned, licensed, recognized, accepted, legitimate, legal, lawful, bona fide, proper, *ex cathedra; inf.* kosher. **2** *an official function* formal, ceremonial, solemn, conventional, ritualistic, pompous; *inf.* stuffed-shirt.
Opposites UNOFFICIAL; UNAUTHORIZED; INFORMAL.

official *noun* **1** *club/party officials* officer, office-holder, office-bearer, administrator, executive. *See* OFFICER 3. **2** *officials of the court* officer, representative, agent. *See* OFFICER 4.

officiate *verb* **1** *who will officiate in the absence of the chairman?* take charge, be in charge, preside, take the chair. **2** *officiate at the service/proceedings* be in charge of, be responsible for, chair, preside over, manage, oversee, superintend, conduct, run, operate.

officious *adjective officious bureaucrats/behaviour* over-zealous, over-busy, bustling, interfering, intrusive, meddlesome, meddling, prying, inquisitive, importunate, forward, obtrusive, self-important, opinionated, dictatorial, domineering; *inf.* pushy, nosy.
Opposites INDIFFERENT; DETACHED; RETIRING.

offing *noun* **in the offing** *a salary increase is in the offing* on the way, coming soon, coming up, close at hand, near, imminent, in prospect, on the horizon, on the cards, in the wings.

offload *verb offload the cargo/responsibility* unload, unburden, disburden, jettison, get rid of, discharge, transfer, shift; *inf.* dump.

off-putting *adjective had a rather off-putting manner* discouraging, disheartening, dispiriting, daunting, disconcerting, discomfiting, dismaying, upsetting, unsettling, unnerving, intimidating, frightening, fearsome, formidable.

offset *verb weights offsetting each other | this year's profits offset last year's loss* counterbalance, counterpoise, counteract, countervail, balance, balance out, cancel out, neutralize, compensate for, make up for, make good, indemnify.

offshoot *noun* **1** *plant offshoots* side-shoot, shoot, offset, branch, bough, limb, sucker, tendril, runner, scion. **2** *he is an offshoot of a noble family* descendant, scion, relation, relative, kin. **3** *his business is an offshoot of the family firm* branch, subsidiary, adjunct, appendage. **4** *his attitude is an offshoot of his war experiences* result, outcome, aftermath, consequence, upshot, product, by-product, spin-off, ramification.

offspring *noun* **1** *the couple have no offspring* children, family, progeny, young, issue, descendants, heirs, successors, spawn; *inf.* kids. *See table at* YOUNG. **2** *he/she is the offspring of the headmaster* child, son, daughter, descendant, heir, successor; *inf.* kid.
Opposites PARENT; ANCESTOR; FOREBEAR.

often *adverb* frequently, many a time, on many occasions, repeatedly, again and again, time and again, time and time again, time after time, over and over, over and over again, day in day out; *lit.* oft, oft-times; *inf.* a lot.
Opposites SELDOM; NEVER.

ogle *verb ogle the girl at the next table* stare at, gaze at, eye amorously, look flirtatiously at, leer at, make eyes at, make sheep's eyes at; *inf.* give someone the glad eye, give someone the once-over, eye up, undress with one's eyes, give someone the come-on.

ogre/ogress *noun* **1** *frightened of the ogre* monster, giant/giantess, troll, bogeyman, bogey, bugbear, demon, devil. **2** *the teacher's an ogre* frightening person, monster, harridan, shrew, termagant, harpy, tartar, fury, gorgon; *inf.* battleaxe.

oil *noun* **1** *use oil to lubricate the surface/skin* lubricant, grease, petroleum jelly, penetrating oil, baby oil, bath oil; Vaseline™. **2** *fry in oil not lard* cooking oil, vegetable oil; sunflower oil, corn oil, olive oil, peanut oil, rape-seed oil, walnut oil.

oil *verb oil the surface/lock* lubricate, grease, smear with oil, make slippery/smooth, anoint.

oily *adjective* **1** *oily fish* oil-containing, oleaginous. **2** *oily food* greasy, fatty, buttery, swimming in oil/fat. **3** *oily charm/remarks* smooth, over-smooth, smooth-talking, honey-tongued, flattering, fulsome, glib, suave, urbane, unctuous, subservient, servile, oleaginous.

ointment *noun* medicated cream/lotion, emollient, salve, balm, liniment, embrocation, unguent, gel.

OK, okay *interjection okay, I'll go* yes, all right, right, very well, very good; *inf.* right you are, righto.

OK, okay *noun give the OK to* agreement, consent, assent, permission, authorization, endorsement, sanction, approval, seal of approval, approbation, the thumbs up, the go-ahead; *inf.* the green light, say-so.
Opposites REFUSAL; DENIAL.

OK, okay *adjective an okay bloke/job | the film was OK* all right, reasonable, acceptable, tolerable, passable, satisfactory, adequate, middling; *inf.* not bad, so-so, fair-to-middling.

OK, okay *verb OK the project* give one's consent to, consent to, say yes to, agree to, give one's

approval to, approve, pass, authorize, sanction, give something the thumbs up, give something the go-ahead, give something the nod, rubber-stamp; *inf.* give something the green light, give something one's say-so.
Opposites REFUSE; FORBID; VETO.

old *adjective* **1** *old people* older, mature, elderly, aged, advanced in years, up in years, getting on, grey-haired, grizzled, hoary, past one's prime, ancient, decrepit, senescent, senile, venerable, senior; *inf.* past it, over the hill, long in the tooth.**2** *old clothes* worn, worn-out, cast-off, shabby, torn, tattered, ragged, old-fashioned, out-of-date, outmoded, *démodé.* **3** *old farm buildings* dilapidated, broken-down, run-down, tumbledown, ramshackle, decaying, crumbling, disintegrating. **4** *old ideas* out-of-date, outdated, old-fashioned, outmoded, *passé,* archaic, obsolete, extinct, antiquated, antediluvian, superannuated; *inf.* old-hat, out of the ark. **5** *in the old days* of old, olden, bygone, past, early, earlier, earliest, primeval, primordial, prehistoric. **6** *old customs* age-old, long-standing, long-lived, long-established, time-honoured, enduring, lasting. **7** *old cars* antique, veteran, vintage. **8** *old for her years* | *he's an old hand* mature, wise, sensible, experienced, knowledgeable, well-versed, practised, skilled, skilful, adept. **9** *an old girlfriend* ex-, former, previous, one-time, sometime, erstwhile; *lit.* quondam. **old age** oldness, elderliness, age, agedness, declining years, advanced years, winter/autumn of one's life, senescence, senility, dotage. **old man** elderly man, senior citizen, old-age pensioner, OAP, grandfather, old fogy; *lit.* greybeard; *inf.* gaffer, oldie, wrinkly, oldster, old codger, old boy, old geezer, old-stager, old-timer.
Opposites YOUNG; NEW; MODERN.

older *adjective the older child* | *she's older than me* elder, more advanced in years, senior.

old-fashioned *adjective* old, former, out of fashion, outmoded, *démodé,* unfashionable, out of style, out-of-date, outdated, dated, out, dead, old-time, behind the times, past, bygone, *passé,* archaic, obsolescent, obsolete, ancient, antiquated, superannuated, antediluvian, old-fogyish, old-fangled; *inf.* old-hat, not with it.
Opposites MODERN; UP-TO-DATE; FASHIONABLE.

Old Testament *noun. See table at* BIBLE.

old-time *adjective old-time customs/dancing* old, former, past, bygone, old-fashioned, archaic, ancient.

old-world *adjective* **1** *old-world charm* old, archaic, old-fashioned, quaint, traditional, ceremonious, chivalrous, gallant, courtly. **2** *old-world cottages* old, old-fashioned, traditional, quaint, picturesque.

Olympic Games *noun. See table.*

omen *noun* portent, sign, token, foretoken, harbinger, premonition, forewarning, warning, foreshadowing, prediction, forecast, prophesy, augury, straw in the wind, writing on the wall, auspice, presage, presentiment, feeling, vague feeling, foreboding, misgiving; *inf.* funny feeling, feeling in one's bones.

ominous *adjective* **1** *ominous clouds* | *the future was looking ominous* threatening, menacing, minatory, black, dark, gloomy, heavy, sinister, bad, unpromising, unpropitious, pessimistic, inauspicious, unfavourable, unlucky, ill-fated. **2** *ancients believing in ominous signs* oracular, augural, divinatory, prophetic, premonitory, prognostic, sibyllic.
Opposites PROMISING; AUSPICIOUS; PROPITIOUS.

omission *noun* **1** *the omission of his name from the list* leaving out, exclusion, exception, non-inclusion, deletion, erasure, elimination, expunction. **2** *guilty of a sin of omission* neglect, neglectfulness, negligence, dereliction, forgetfulness, oversight, disregard, non-fulfilment, default, failure. **3** *note several omissions from the list* exclusion, oversight, gap, lacuna.
Opposites ADDITION; INCLUSION.

omit *verb* **1** *omit his name from the list* leave out, exclude, except, miss out, miss, fail to mention, pass over, drop, delete, erase, eliminate, expunge, rub out, cross out; *inf.* give something a miss. **2** *omit to close the door* forget to, neglect to, fail to, leave undone, overlook, skip.
Opposites ADD; INCLUDE.

omnipotence *noun* all-powerfulness, almightiness, supremacy, pre-eminence, invincibility, supreme power, absolute/unlimited power, undisputed sway, divine right.

omnipotent *adjective* all-powerful, almighty, supreme, pre-eminent, invincible.

HOSTS OF THE OLYMPIC GAMES

Year	City	Country	Year	City	Country
1896	Athens	Greece	1956	Melbourne	Australia
1900	Paris	France	1960	Rome	Italy
1904	St Louis	U.S.A.	1964	Tokyo	Japan
1908	London	U.K.	1968	Mexico City	Mexico
1912	Stockholm	Sweden	1972	Munich	West Germany
1920	Antwerp	Belgium	1976	Montreal	Canada
1924	Paris	France	1980	Moscow	Soviet Union
1928	Amsterdam	Netherlands	1984	Los Angeles	U.S.A.
1932	Los Angeles	U.S.A.	1988	Seoul	South Korea
1936	Berlin	Germany	1992	Barcelona	Spain
1948	London	U.K.	1996	Atlanta	U.S.A.
1952	Helsinki	Finland	2000	Sydney	Australia

omnipresent · open

omnipresent *adjective* all-present, present everywhere, ubiquitous, all-pervasive, infinite, boundless.

omniscient *adjective* all-knowing, all-wise, all-seeing, all-perceiving.

omnivorous *adjective* all-devouring, eating anything, pantophagous, indiscriminate.

on *adverb* **on and off** *came on and off for three years* off and on, sporadically, irregularly, intermittently, at intervals, periodically, every so often, now and then. *See* OFF *adverb,* OFF AND ON. **on and on** *talked/rambled on and on* at great length, incessantly, constantly, continuously, endlessly, interminably, unremittingly, relentlessly.

once *adverb* **1** *they were friends once* at one time, once upon a time, previously, formerly, in the past, in times gone by, in times past, in the old days, long ago. **2** *I saw him only once* on one occasion, one time, one single time. **3** *he did not once help* ever, at any time, on any occasion. **at once** **1** *you must leave at once* immediately, right away, right now, this moment, now, straight away, instantly, directly, forthwith, without delay; *inf.* before you can say Jack Robinson. **2** *they both arrived at once* at the same time, at one and the same time, at the same instant/moment, together, simultaneously. **once and for all** **1** *you must decide once and for all* decisively, conclusively, finally, positively, determinedly. **2** *he has gone once and for all* for always, for good, forever, permanently, finally. **once in a while** every now and again/then, now and again/then, occasionally, on the odd occasion, on occasion, at times, from time to time; *inf.* once in a blue moon.
Opposites NOW; OFTEN.

once *conjunction* *he'll be all right once she's gone* as soon as, when, after, the minute.

oncoming *adjective* *oncoming traffic* approaching, advancing, nearing, onrushing, forthcoming, imminent.

one *adjective* **1** *one person* a single, a solitary, a sole, a lone. **2** *one day they'll come* some. **3** *they are now one* united, allied, joined, unified, bound, wedded, married.

onerous *adjective* burdensome, heavy, crushing, back-breaking, oppressive, weighty, arduous, strenuous, difficult, hard, formidable, laborious, exhausting, tiring, exigent, taxing, demanding, exacting, wearing, wearisome, fatiguing.
Opposites EASY; EFFORTLESS.

oneself *pronoun* the id, the self, ego; *inf.* number one, numero uno. **by oneself** **1** *stay by oneself* alone, all alone, on one's own, in a solitary state, unaccompanied, companionless, unattended; *inf.* on one's tod. **2** *do the work by oneself* alone, all alone, on one's own, by one's own efforts, unaided, without help, without assistance, independently.

one-sided *adjective* **1** *one-sided opinions* biased, prejudiced, partisan, partial, discriminatory, coloured, inequitable, unfair, unjust, narrow-minded, bigoted. **2** *a one-sided game/discussion* uneven, unequal, unbalanced, lopsided.

one-time *adjective* *one-time journalist* ex-, former, previous, sometime, erstwhile; *lit.* quondam.

ongoing *adjective* **1** *ongoing projects* in progress, current, extant, progressing, advancing, successful, developing, evolving, growing. **2** *the work in the factory is ongoing* continuous, continual, uninterrupted, unbroken, non-stop, incessant, unending, constant.

onlooker *noun* looker-on, eyewitness, witness, observer, spectator, watcher, viewer, bystander, sightseer; *inf.* rubberneck.

only *adverb* **1** *only enough for two* just, at most, not more than, barely, scarcely. **2** *he's only saying that* just, merely, simply, purely.

only *adjective* **1** *their only son* single, one and only, solitary, sole, lone. **2** *the only place to eat* only possible, individual, unique, exclusive.

onomatopoeic *adjective* imitative, echoic.

onset *noun* **1** *the onset of the invading army* onslaught, assault, attack, charge, onrush. *See* ONSLAUGHT. **2** *the onset of trouble* start, beginning, commencement, inception, outbreak; *inf.* kick-off.
Opposites RETREAT; END.

onslaught *noun* assault, attack, charge, onrush, onset, storming, sortie, sally, raid, foray, push, thrust, drive, blitz.

onus *noun* burden, weight, load, responsibility, liability, obligation, duty, charge, encumbrance, cross to bear, millstone round one's neck, albatross.

ooze *verb* **1** *pus oozing from the wound* flow, discharge, exude, seep, trickle, drip, dribble, filter, filtrate, percolate, excrete, escape, leak, drain, bleed, sweat. **2** *she was positively oozing charm* exude, pour forth, send out, let loose, display, exhibit, manifest.

ooze *noun* **1** *the ooze of pus* flow, discharge, exudation, seeping, trickling, leak. *See* OOZE *verb.* **2** *the ooze at the bottom of the river* deposit, alluvium, silt, mude, slime, mire, muck.

opacity *noun* **1** *the opacity of the glass* non-transparency, non-translucence. **2** *the opacity of the windscreen* cloudiness, filminess, haziness, dirtiness, muddiness, griminess. *See* OPAQUE 2. **3** *the opacity of the text* abstruseness, obscurity, unclearness, lack of clarity, enigma, unintelligibility, incomprehensibility. *See* OPAQUE 3.

opalescent *adjective* multicoloured, many-hued, prismatic, rainbow-like, kaleidoscopic, iridescent, opaline, milky, pearly, nacreous.

opaque *adjective* **1** *opaque glass* non-transparent, non-translucent, non-see-through. **2** *opaque windscreens* cloudy, filmy, blurred, smeared, hazy, misty, dirty, dingy, muddy, muddied, grimy; *inf.* smeary. **3** *a piece of opaque prose* abstruse, obscure, unclear, cryptic, enigmatic, unfathomable, unintelligible, incomprehensible, baffling, perplexing.
Opposites TRANSPARENT; CLEAR; LUCID.

open *adjective* **1** *open doors* not shut, not closed, unlocked, unbolted, unlatched, unbarred, unfastened, unsecured, ajar, wide open, agape, gaping, yawning. **2** *open boxes/drains* uncovered, coverless, unlidded, topless,

unsealed. **3** *open spaces/countryside* unenclosed, unfenced, exposed, unsheltered, wide, wide open, extensive, broad, spacious, sweeping, airy, uncrowded, uncluttered, undeveloped, unbuilt-up. **4** *open roads* unobstructed, unblocked, clear, passable, navigable. **5** *maps open on the table* spread out, unfolded, unfurled, unrolled, straightened out, extended, stretched out. **6** *open material/fabric* openwork, holey, full of holes, honeycombed, lacy, filigree, airy, cellular, porous, spongy. **7** *quite open about her dislike* frank, candid, honest, forthright, direct, blunt, plain-spoken, downright. **8** *the shop/theatre is open* open to the public, open for business, admitting customers/visitors. **9** *an open meeting/competition* public, general, non-exclusive, accessible, non-restrictive, unrestricted, non-discriminatory. **10** *the job is still open* vacant, available, unfilled, unoccupied, free. **11** *open hostility* obvious, clear, noticeable, visible, apparent, evident, manifest, overt, conspicuous, patent, unconcealed, unhidden, undisguised, blatant, flagrant. **12** *three courses open to us* available, on hand, obtainable, accessible. **13** *the system is open to abuse* wide open to, allowing of, permitting, vulnerable to, exposed to, susceptible to, liable to, at the mercy of, an easy target for. **14** *the subject is still open* open to debate, open for discussion, yet to be decided, undecided, unresolved, unsettled, arguable, debatable, moot. **15** *keep an open mind* unbiased, prejudice-free, unprejudiced, non-partisan, impartial, non-discriminatory, objective, disinterested, dispassionate, detached. **16** *have an open disposition* frank, honest, artless, natural, simple, guileless, ingenuous, innocent. **17** *open hosts* open-handed, generous, liberal, bountiful, munificent.
Opposites SHUT; closed; SECRETIVE; BIASED.

open *verb* **1** *open the door* throw open, unlock, unbolt, unlatch, unbar, unfasten. **2** *open the parcel* unwrap, undo, untie, unseal. **3** *open the bottle* uncork, broach, crack. **4** *open out the map* spread out, unfold, unfurl, unroll, straighten out, extend, stretch out. **5** *the crack opened* open up, come apart, split, separate, rupture. **6** *we open tomorrow* open for business, be ready for customers/visitors, admit customers, begin business, set up shop, put up one's plate, have a launch, start, begin, commence, start the ball rolling; *inf.* kick off. **7** *open his heart* lay bare, bare, uncover, expose, exhibit, disclose, divulge, pour out.
Opposites CLOSE; SHUT; WRAP.

open-air *adjective* outdoor, out-of-doors, outside, alfresco.

open-handed *adjective* generous, liberal, lavish, free, bountiful, bounteous, munificent; benevolent, charitable, magnanimous.

opening *noun* **1** *an opening in the fence/wall* gap, aperture, space, hole, orifice, vent, slot, break, breach, crack, split, fissure, cleft, crevice, chink, interstice, rent, rupture. **2** *an opening in the new office* vacancy, position, job, opportunity, chance; *inf.* break, lucky break. **3** *the opening of the match* beginning, start, commencement, outset, inception, launch, birth,

dawn; *inf.* kick-off. **4** *present at the gallery's opening* opening ceremony, official opening, launch.
Opposites CLOSURE; CLOSE; END; TERMINATION.

openly *adverb* **1** *she told him quite openly* frankly, candidly, honestly, forthrightly, directly, bluntly, unreservedly, straight from the shoulder, with no holds barred. **2** *conduct their affair openly* publicly, in public, in full view of people, blatantly, flagrantly, brazenly, with no attempt at concealment, overtly, unashamedly, shamelessly, unabashed, wantonly, immodestly.

open-minded *adjective* **1** *open-minded judges* unbiased, unprejudiced, prejudice-free, non-partisan, impartial, non-discriminatory, objective, disinterested, dispassionate, detached, tolerant, liberal, broad-minded, undogmatic. **2** *writers should be open-minded* receptive, open to suggestions, open to new ideas, amenable.

opera *noun.* See tables.

operate *verb* **1** *the machine ceased to operate* work, function, go, run, perform, act, be in action. **2** *he can operate the machine* work, make go, run, use, utilize, employ, handle, manipulate, manoeuvre, ply, manage, be in charge of. **3** *operate on the accident victim* perform an operation, perform surgery; *inf.* put under the knife.
Opposites break down (see BREAK); FAIL.

operation *noun* **1** *the operation of the machine is crucial* working, functioning, running, performance. See OPERATE 1. **2** *his operation of the machine* working, using, handling, manipulation. See OPERATE 2. **3** *when the building was evacuated the operation went smoothly* activity, exercise, affair, business, undertaking, enterprise, task, job. **4** *operations on the stock exchange* transaction, business, deal, proceedings. **5** *military operations* manoeuvre, exercise, campaign, assault. **6** *an operation to remove the appendix* surgery, major surgery, minor surgery. See table. **in operation** *rules/machines not yet in operation* operative, in force, effective, in use, functioning, working, valid. See OPERATIVE *adjective* 1, 2.

operational *adjective* *machines now operational* operative, workable, in operation, working, in working order, functioning, functional, going, in use, usable, in action, ready for action.
Opposites BROKEN; out of order.

operative *adjective* **1** *the rules are operative now* in operation, in force, effective, valid. **2** *the machines are now operative* operational, workable, working, functioning, functional, usable. See OPERATIONAL. **3** *"might" is the operative word* key, relevant, significant, crucial, vital, important, essential.
Opposites INVALID; out of order; IRRELEVANT.

operative *noun* **1** *factory operatives* worker, workman, machinist, operator, mechanic, factory hand/employee. **2** *a foreign power's operatives* agent, secret agent, undercover agent, spy, double agent; *inf.* spook, mole. **3** *employ a private operative* detective, private detective, private investigator, sleuth; *inf.* private eye, dick, gumshoe.

operator *noun* **1** *machine operators* operative, machinist, machine-handler, mechanic, practitioner. **2** *transport operators* driver, bus-driver, taxi-driver, lorry-driver, truck-driver, haulier, hauler; *inf.* cabby, trucker. **3** *a smart operator* manoeuvrer, manipulator, machinator, mover, wheeler-dealer; *inf.* punter.

opiate *noun* drug, narcotic, sedative, tranquillizer, depressant, bromide, soporific, morphine, opium, laudanum; *inf.* downer. *See table at* DRUG.

opinion *noun* point of view, view, viewpoint, belief, thought, thinking, way of thinking, standpoint, theory, judgement, estimation, feeling, sentiment, impression, notion, assumption, conception, conviction, persuasion, creed, dogma. **a matter of opinion** *how he should be punished is a matter of opinion* open to/for discussion, open to debate, debatable, a debatable point, open to question, a moot point, up to the individual.

OPERA SINGERS

Baker, Dame Janet (b. 1933; Brit. mezzo-soprano)
Bumbry, Grace (b. 1937; Am. mezzo-soprano)
Butt, Dame Clara (1872–1936; Brit. contralto)
Callas, Maria (1923–77; Am. soprano of Gk parentage)
Carreras, José (b. 1946; Sp. tenor)
Caruso, Enrico (1873–1921; It. tenor)
Chaliapin, Fyodor (Ivanovich) (1873–1938; Russ. bass)

Christoff, Boris (1919–93; Bulg. bass)
de los Ángeles, Victoria (b. 1923; Sp. soprano)
Domingo, Placido (b. 1941; Sp. tenor)
Evans, Sir Geraint (Llewellyn) (1922–92; Welsh baritone)
Ferrier, Kathleen (1912–53; Brit. contralto)
Fischer-Dieskau, Dietrich (b. 1925; Ger. baritone)
Flagstad, Kirsten (1895–1962; Norw. soprano)

Gigli, Beniamino (1890–1957; It. tenor)
Gobbi, Tito (1915–84; It. baritone)
Lehmann, Lilli (1848–1929; Ger. soprano)
Lehmann, Lotte (1885–1976; Am. soprano, b. in Germany)
Lind, Jenny (1820–87; Sw. soprano)
Melba, Dame Nellie (1861–1931; Austral. soprano)
Nilsson, Birgit (b. 1918; Sw. soprano)

Norman, Jessye (b. 1945; Am. soprano)
Pavarotti, Luciano (b. 1935; It. tenor)
Price, Leontyne (b. 1927; Am. soprano)
Schwarzkopf, Dame Elisabeth (b. 1915; Ger. soprano)
Sutherland, Dame Joan (b. 1926; Austral. soprano)
Tebaldi, Renata (b. 1922; It. soprano)
Tetrazzini, Luisa (1871–1940; It. soprano)
Te Kanawa, Dame Kiri (b. 1944; NZ soprano)

OPERAS

Opera	First Performed	Composer	Opera	First Performed	Composer
Aida	1871	Verdi	Otello	1887	Verdi
Barber of			Parsifal	1882	Wagner
Seville, the	1816	Rossini	Pelléas et		
Bartered Bride, the	1866	Smetana	Mélisande	1902	Debussy
Boris Godunov	1874	Mussorgsky	Peter Grimes	1945	Britten
Carmen	1875	Bizet	Prince Igor	1890	Borodin
Cavalleria			Rake's Progress, the	1951	Stravinsky
Rusticana	1890	Mascagni	Rhine Gold, the	1869	Wagner
Così fan tutte	1790	Mozart	Rigoletto	1851	Verdi
Der Rosenkavalier	1911	R. Strauss	Ring of the		
Dido and Aeneas	1689	Purcell	Nibelungs, the	1876	Wagner
Don Giovanni	1787	Mozart	Salome	1905	R. Strauss
Eugene Onegin	1879	Tchaikovsky	Siegfried	1876	Wagner
Fidelio	1805	Beethoven	Tales of		
I Pagliacci	1892	Leoncavallo	Hoffman, the	1881	Offenbach
La Bohème	1896	Puccini	Tannhäuser	1845	Wagner
La Traviata	1853	Verdi	Threepenny		
Madame Butterfly	1904	Puccini	Opera, the	1927	Weill
Magic Flute, the	1791	Mozart	Tosca	1900	Puccini
Marriage of			Tristan and		
Figaro, the	1786	Mozart	Isolde	1865	Wagner
Merry Widow, the	1905	Lehar	Turandot	1926	Puccini
Orfeo	1607	Monteverdi	Twilight of		
Orpheus and			the Gods, the	1876	Wagner
Eurydice	1762	Gluck	Valkyrie, the	1870	Wagner

551

opinionated *adjective* dogmatic, of fixed views, of preconceived ideas, pontifical, doctrinaire, dictatorial, self-assertive, positive, confident, assured, cocksure, pompous, self-important, adamant, obstinate, stubborn, pigheaded, headstrong, wilful, single-minded, inflexible, uncompromising, bigoted.

opponent *noun the two opponents shook hands | an opponent of the government* opposer, the opposition, rival, adversary, fellow-contestant, fellow-competitor, enemy, foe, antagonist, contender, dissenter, disputant.
Opposites ALLY; PARTNER; COLLEAGUE.

opportune *adjective wait for an opportune moment* advantageous, favourable, auspicious, propitious, good, lucky, happy, timely, well-timed, fortunate, providential, felicitous, convenient, expedient, suitable, apt, fitting, relevant, applicable, pertinent.
Opposites DISADVANTAGEOUS; UNFAVOURABLE; INCONVENIENT.

opportunism *noun* exploitation, expediency, taking advantage, unscrupulousness, exploitation, striking while the iron is hot, making hay while the sun shines, making the best of a bad job.

SURGICAL OPERATIONS

Technical Name	Operation	Technical Name	Operation
adenoidectomy	removal of adenoids	neurectomy	removal of nerve
angioplasty	repair of blood vessel	neurotomy	incision of nerve
appendicectomy/		oesophagectomy	opening of oesophagus
appendectomy	removal of appendix	oophorectomy	removal of ovary
arteriotomy	incision of artery	orchidectomy	removal of testis
cheiloplasty	repair of lips	orchidotomy	incision of testis
cholecystectomy	removal of gall bladder	ostectomy	removal of bone
cholecystotomy	incision of gall bladder	osteotomy	incision of bone
colectomy	removal of colon	ovariectomy	removal of ovary
colostomy	opening of colon	ovariotomy	incision of ovary
craniotomy	incision of skull	palatoplasty	repair of cleft palate
cystectomy	removal of bladder	pancreatectomy	removal of pancreas
cystoplasty	repair of bladder	pericardiectomy/	
cystostomy	opening of bladder	pericardectomy	removal of all or part of
cystotomy	incision of bladder		membrane around heart
dermatoplasty	repair of skin	pericardiotomy	incision of membrane
embolectomy	removal of blood clot		around heart
enterostomy	opening of small intestine	perineoplasty	repair of vaginal opening
enterotomy	incision of intestine	phalloplasty	repair of penis
episiotomy	incision of vaginal opening	pharyngectomy	removal of pharynx
		phlebotomy	incision of vein
gastrectomy	removal of whole or part of stomach	pleurotomy	incision of pleural membrane
gastroplasty	repair of stomach	pneumonectomy	removal of lung
gastrostomy	opening of stomach	polypectomy	removal of polyp
gastrotomy	incision of stomach	prostatectomy	removal of prostate gland
glossectomy	removal of all or part of tongue	rhinoplasty	repair of nose
		salpingectomy	removal of fallopian tube
haemorrhoid-ectomy	removal of haemorrhoids	salpingostomy	opening of fallopian tube
hepatectomy	removal of all or part of liver	splenectomy	removal of spleen
		tenotomy	incision of tendon
hepaticostomy	opening of bile duct	thoracoplasty	repair of thorax
hysterectomy	removal of womb	thoracotomy	incision of chest cavity
hysterotomy	incision of womb	thrombectomy	removal of blood clot
laparotomy	incision of abdomen	thymectomy	removal of thymus gland
laryngectomy	removal of larynx	thyroidectomy	removal of all or part of thyroid gland
laryngotomy	incision of larynx		
lithotomy	removal of kidney stone	tonsillectomy	removal of tonsils
lobectomy	removal of lobe of an organ	tonsillotomy	incision of tonsil
		tracheostomy	opening of windpipe
lobotomy	incision of nerve fibres from frontal lobe of brain	tracheotomy	incision of windpipe
		ureterectomy	removal of ureter
		ureterostomy	opening of ureter
		ureterotomy	incision of ureter
lumpectomy	removal of breast tumour	urethroplasty	repair of urethra
mammaplasty	reshaping of breast	urethrotomy	incision of urethra
mastectomy	removal of breast	vagotomy	incision of vagus nerve
myotomy	incision of muscle	valvotomy	incision of heart valve
nephrectomy	removal of kidney	varicotomy	excision of varicose veins
nephrostomy	opening of kidney	vasectomy	removal of all or part of vas deferens
nephrotomy	incision of kidney		

opportunity noun lucky chance, chance, good time, golden opportunity, favourable time/occasion/moment, right set of circumstances, appropriate time/moment; inf. break.

oppose verb 1 oppose the proposals dislike, disapprove of, be hostile to, take a stand against, be/stand against, stand up to, stand up and be counted against, take issue with, take on, contradict, counter, argue against, counterattack, confront, resist, withstand, defy, fight, put up a fight against, combat, fly in the face of. 2 oppose memory and imagination compare, contrast, juxtapose, offset, balance, counterbalance, set against, pit against, parallel. **be opposed to** be opposed to the plans | am opposed to going to war be against, be in opposition to, dislike, be in disagreement with, disagree with, be averse to, be hostile to, be antagonistic to, be inimical to; inf. be anti.
Opposites SUPPORT; DEFEND; PROMOTE.

opposing adjective 1 hold opposing opinions opposite, differing, different, contrary, contradictory, conflicting, clashing, incompatible, at variance, irreconcilable. See OPPOSITE adjective 2. 2 on opposing sides opposite, rival, competitive, enemy, warring, fighting, contending, combatant.

opposite adjective 1 people/houses opposite each other facing, face-to-face with; inf. eyeball to eyeball with. 2 hold opposite opinions diametrically opposite, opposing, differing, different, unlike, contrary, reverse, contradictory, conflicting, clashing, discordant, dissident, at variance, incompatible, irreconcilable, antipathetical, poles apart. 3 on opposite sides opposing, rival, competitive, enemy, warring, fighting, contending, combatant.
Opposites SAME; IDENTICAL; LIKE.

opposite noun reverse, contrary, antithesis, converse, inverse, contradiction, the other extreme, the other side of the coin.

opposition noun 1 express their opposition to the plans dislike, disapproval, hostility, resistance, defiance. See ÓPPOSE 1. 2 back the opposition opponent, opposing side, other side, other team, rival, adversary, competition, antagonist, enemy, foe.

oppress verb 1 the invading army oppressed the people overwhelm, overpower, subjugate, enslave, suppress, crush, subdue, quash, quell, bring someone to his/her knees. 2 the tyrant oppressed the citizens tyrannize, crush, suppress, repress, abuse, maltreat, persecute, rule with a rod of iron, trample on, trample underfoot, ride roughshod over. 3 oppressed by grief weigh down, lie heavy on, weigh heavy on, burden, crush, depress, dispirit, dishearten, take the heart out of, discourage, sadden, make despondent, deject, desolate.

oppressed adjective 1 the oppressed citizens/children tyrannized, subjugated, enslaved, crushed, subdued, repressed, persecuted, abused, maltreated, misused, browbeaten, downtrodden, disadvantaged, underprivileged. 2 oppressed, grief-stricken widows weighed down, depressed, dispirited, despondent, dejected, desolate. See OPPRESS 3.

oppression noun 1 the oppression of the people by the invading army overwhelming, subjugation, subduing. See OPPRESS 1. 2 the tyrant's oppression of the people tyranny, suppression, abuse, persecution. See OPPRESS 2. 3 people suffering from oppression for generations tyranny, despotism, abuse, maltreatment, persecution, cruelty, brutality, injustice, ruthlessness, harshness, hardship, misery, suffering, wretchedness. 4 oppression brought on by grief depression, despondency, dejection, desolation. See OPPRESS 3.

oppressive adjective 1 an oppressive regime tyrannical, despotic, Draconian, iron-fisted, high-handed, repressive, domineering, harsh, crushing, cruel, brutal, ruthless, relentless, merciless, pitiless, inexorable, unjust, undemocratic. 2 oppressive weather muggy, close, airless, stuffy, stifling, suffocating, sultry, torrid.
Opposites LENIENT; HUMANE; FRESH.

oppressor noun tyrant, despot, autocrat, subjugator, persecutor, bully, iron hand, slave-

ORATORS			
Churchill, Sir Winston (1874–1965; Brit. orator)	Dion Chrysostom (c. 40–c. 112 A.D.; Gk orator)	Henry, Patrick (1736–99; Am. orator)	Lucian (c. 120–c.180 A.D.; Gk rhetorician)
Cicero, Marcus Tullius (106–43 B.C.; Rom. orator)	Flood, Henry (1732–91; Ir. orator)	Ibárruri, Dolores "La Pasionara" (1895–1989; Sp. orator)	Lysias (c. 445–c. 380 B.C.; Gk orator)
Cleon (d. c. 422 B.C.) Athenian demagogue)	Gandhi, Mahatma (1869–1948; Ind. orator)	Isocrates (436–338 B.C.; Athenian rhetorician)	Malcolm X (1925–65; Am. civil-rights leader)
Danton, Georges (Jacques) (1759–94; Fr. revolutionary orator)	Garvey, Marcus (1897–1940; Jamaican orator)	King, Jr, Martin Luther (1929–68; Am. civil-rights leader)	Pericles (c. 495–429 B.C.; Athenian orator)
Demosthenes (384–322 B.C.; Athenian orator)	Grattan, Henry (1746–1820; Ir. orator)	Longinus Dionysus (1st century A.D.; Gk rhetorician)	Quintilian (c. 35–c. 96 A.D.; Rom. rhetorician)
Desmoulins, Camille (1760–94; Fr. revolutionary orator)	Hébert, Jacques-René (1757–94; Fr. demagogue)		Sheridan, Richard Brinsley (1751–1816; Ir. orator)

driver, hard taskmaster, scourge, dictator, tormentor, torturer.

opprobrium *noun bring opprobrium on his family* disgrace, shame, dishonour, ignominy, discredit, loss of face, disrepute, ill repute, infamy, notoriety, odium, obloquy.

opt *verb* **opt for** *opt for a red one* choose, select, pick, decide on, settle on, plump for, prefer; *inf.* go for.

optimistic *adjective* **1** *an optimistic person* disposed to look on the bright side, always expecting the best, inclined to look through rose-coloured spectacles, hopeful, full of hope, Pollyannaish, Panglossian. **2** *feeling optimistic about the future | was in optimistic mood* positive, sanguine, hopeful, confident, bullish, cheerful, buoyant; *inf.* upbeat.
Opposites PESSIMISTIC; GLOOMY.

optimum *adjective* **1** *the optimum time to choose* most favourable, best, most advantageous, most appropriate, ideal, perfect. **2** *plants in optimum condition* peak, top, best, perfect, ideal, flawless, superlative, optimal; *inf.* tiptop, A1.

option *noun* **1** *have little option* choice, freedom of choice, power to choose, right to choose. **2** *have no other option* choice, alternative, other possibility, preference.

optional *adjective attendance/tipping is optional* non-compulsory, not required, voluntary, up to the individual, discretionary, at one's discretion, elective.
Opposites COMPULSORY; OBLIGATORY; MANDATORY.

opulence *noun* **1** *the opulence of the family* affluence, wealth, richness, riches, money, fortune, prosperity. **2** *the opulence of the house/furnishings* luxury, luxuriousness, sumptuousness, lavishness; *inf.* plushiness, ritziness. **3** *the opulence of the vegetation* abundance, superabundance, copiousness, plentifulness, profuseness, prolificness, luxuriance, cornucopia.

opulent *adjective* **1** *opulent families* affluent, wealthy, rich, well-off, well-to-do, moneyed, prosperous; *inf.* well-heeled, rolling in it. **2** *opulent houses* luxurious, sumptuous, lavishly appointed; *inf.* plush, plushy, ritzy. **3** *opulent vegetation* abundant, superabundant, copious, plentiful, profuse, prolific, luxuriant.
Opposites PENNILESS; POOR; SPARSE.

opus *noun* work, composition, *oeuvre*, piece, creation, production.

oracle *noun* **1** *the oracles of classical times* prophet/prophetess, seer, soothsayer, sibyl, augur, wise man/woman, sage. **2** *he regards*

himself as an oracle on architecture authority, expert, mastermind, specialist, connoisseur, pundit, guru, mentor, adviser.

oracular *adjective* **1** *his statement proved oracular* prophetic, prescient, augural, divinatory, mantic. **2** *his answers are always rather oracular* ambiguous, equivocal, two-edged, obscure, enigmatic, cryptic, abstruse, arcane, puzzling, perplexing, baffling.

oral *adjective* spoken, verbal, vocal, uttered, said.

oral *noun* oral examination, interview, viva voce; *inf.* viva.

oration *noun delivered an oration* speech, lecture, address, homily, sermon, discourse, declamation, harangue, tirade; *inf.* spiel.

orator *noun* speaker, public speaker, speechmaker, lecturer, declaimer, haranguer, rhetorician, Cicero. *See table.*

oratorical *adjective oratorical style* rhetorical, grandiloquent, magniloquent, high-flown, high-sounding, bombastic, grandiose, orotund, declamatory, Ciceronian.

orb *noun* sphere, globe, ball, round, circle, ring.

orbit *noun* **1** *the planet's orbit* revolution, circle, circuit, cycle, rotation, circumgyration, path, course, track, trajectory. **2** *subjects within his orbit of responsibility* sphere, sphere of influence, range, reach, scope, ambit, sweep, domain.

orbit *verb orbit the earth* revolve round, circle round, go/sail/fly round, encircle, circumnavigate.

orchestra *noun. See table.*

orchestrate *verb* **1** *orchestrate the piece of music* arrange, score. **2** *orchestrate the event* organize, arrange, put together, set up, manage, stage-manage, mastermind, coordinate, integrate.

ordain *verb* **1** *ordain a new priest* appoint, confer holy orders on, frock, induct, install, invest, anoint, consecrate. **2** *his lack of success seems to have been ordained* fate, predestine, predetermine, preordain. **3** *parliament ordained that taxes be increased* decree, legislate, rule, order, command, enjoin, dictate, prescribe, pronounce. **4** *ordain new laws* decree, enact, lay down, establish, set out.

ordeal *noun* trial, test, tribulation, painful/disturbing experience, suffering, affliction, distress, agony, anguish, torture, torment, calamity, trouble, nightmare.
Opposites BLISS; PLEASURE.

INSTRUMENTS IN A FULL SYMPHONY ORCHESTRA

Instrument	Number	Instrument	Number	Instrument	Number
bass clarinet	1	double basses	9	timpani	4
bass drum	1	flutes	3	triangle	1
bassoons	3	French horns	5	trombones	4
celesta	1	glockenspiel	1	trumpets	4
cellos	11	harp	1	tuba	1
clarinets	3	oboes	3	violas	12
contrabassoon	1	piano	1	violins, first	18
cor anglais	1	piccolo	1	violins, second	17
cymbals	1 pair	snare drum	1		

order noun **1** *restore order to the room* orderliness, neatness, tidiness, trimness, harmony, apple-pie order. **2** *no sense of order in the filing system* method, organization, system, plan, uniformity, regularity, symmetry, pattern. **3** *everything is in good/working order* condition, state, shape, situation. **4** *arrange in alphabetical/numerical order* arrangement, grouping, system, systemization, organization, form, structure, disposition, classification, categorization, codification, series, sequence, progression, succession, layout, set-up. **5** *give orders to fire | must obey the king's orders* command, direction, directive, instruction, behest, decree, edict, injunction, law, rule, regulation, mandate, ordinance, stipulation, dictate, say-so. **6** *lack of order in the land* law, lawfulness, law and order, discipline, control, peace, calm, quiet, quietness, peace and quiet, tranquillity. **7** *place an order for bread/tickets* request, call, requirement, requisition, demand, booking, reservation, commission, notification, application. **8** *the lower orders of society* rank, class, caste, grade, level, degree, position, station. **9** *the social order* grouping, grading, ranking, system, class system, caste system, hierarchy, pecking order. **10** *work of a high order* kind, sort, type, variety, genre, nature. **11** *botanical/biological orders* taxonomic group, class, subclass, family, species, breed. **12** *a religious order* brotherhood, sisterhood, community. **13** *they all belong to some order* lodge, society, secret society, guild, club, association, league, union, fellowship, fraternity, confraternity, sorority, brotherhood, sisterhood, sodality. **14** *raise a point of order* procedure, correct procedure, standard procedure, ruling. **in order 1** *the library books are in order* in sequence, in series, in alphabetical order, in numerical order, in order of merit, in order of seniority, classified, categorized. **2** *the room is in order* orderly, tidy, neat, trim, shipshape, shipshape and Bristol fashion, in apple-pie order. **3** *is it in order for her to attend?* acceptable, all right, fitting, suitable, appropriate, right, correct; *inf.* OK. **out of order** *the machine is out of order* broken, broken-down, not working, unserviceable, not in working order, not functioning, nonfunctional, inoperative, in disrepair, out of commission; *inf.* bust, kaput, gone phut, on the blink, wonky, gone haywire; *Am. inf.* on the fritz.
Opposites DISORDER; CHAOS; DISARRAY.

order verb **1** *order them to fire* give the order to, command, give the command to, instruct, direct, bid, enjoin. **2** *the king has ordered that tomorrow be a holiday* decree, ordain, rule, legislate, enjoin, prescribe, pronounce. **3** *order bread/tickets* put in an order for, place an order for, request, call for, requisition, make one's requirements/demands known, book, reserve, contract for, apply for, send away for. **4** *order the files better | thought it was time to order his life* put in order, set in order, organize, systematize, methodize, arrange, dispose, lay out, marshal, group, classify, catalogue, codify, tabulate, put/set to rights, sort out, tidy up, regulate.

orderly adjective **1** *an orderly room* in order, neat, tidy, trim, shipshape, shipshape and Bristol fashion, in apple-pie order. **2** *an orderly business/person* organized, well-organized, well-regulated, methodical, systematic, systematized, efficient, businesslike. **3** *an orderly class of pupils* well-behaved, law-abiding, nonviolent, disciplined, quiet, peaceful, controlled, restrained.
Opposites DISORDERLY; UNTIDY; UNRULY.

ordinarily adverb *ordinarily he is well-behaved* as a rule, generally, as a general rule, in general, in the general run of things, usually, normally, habitually, customarily, commonly.

ordinary adjective **1** *our ordinary procedure* usual, normal, standard, typical, stock, common, customary, habitual, accustomed, wonted, everyday, quotidian, regular, routine, established, settled, fixed, prevailing, humdrum. **2** *we lead very ordinary lives | ordinary houses* run-of-the-mill, common, conventional, standard, typical, average, commonplace, workaday, humdrum, unremarkable, unexceptional, unmemorable, pedestrian, prosaic, unpretentious, modest, plain, simple, humble; *inf.* common or garden. **3** *a very ordinary piece of writing | the dress is too ordinary* average, run-of-the-mill, pedestrian, prosaic, uninteresting, dull, uninspired, unimaginative, hackneyed, stale, undistinguished, unexceptional, unremarkable, mediocre, indifferent, second-rate.
Opposites UNUSUAL; EXTRAORDINARY; UNIQUE.

ordinary noun **out of the ordinary** *want something out of the ordinary* unusual, uncommon, atypical, non-standard, exceptional, extraordinary, rare, unique, remarkable, striking, noteworthy, memorable, distinguished, impressive, outstanding, special, exciting, imaginative, creative, inspired.

organ noun **1** *he plays the organ* pipe-organ, reed-organ, electric organ, electronic organ, barrel-organ, hand-organ, mouth-organ, harmonica; *inf.* hurdy-gurdy. **2** *vital organs* biological structure, part, part of the body, component, constituent, element. **3** *the organ of the trade union* newspaper, paper, journal, periodical, magazine, newsletter, gazette, bulletin, publication, means of communication, mouthpiece, voice, forum.

organic adjective **1** *organic ingredients* natural, non-chemical, pesticide-free, chemical-free, additive-free. **2** *organic matter* living, live, animate, biotic, biological. **3** *the music in the play is organic not incidental* fundamental, basic, structural, integral, inherent, innate, intrinsic, vital, essential, indispensable. **4** *society is an organic whole* structured, organized, systematic, systematized, ordered, methodical, methodized.

organism noun **1** living entity, living thing, living structure, being, something, creature, animal, plant. **2** *the computer company is a complex organism* structure, system, organization, set-up.

organization noun **1** *the organization of the firm/files/party* establishment, development, assembly, arrangement, regulation, coordination, systematization, methodization, categorization, administration, running, management. See ORGANIZE. **2** *the human body is a complex organization* structure, system, whole, unity, organism, set-up. **3** *he is now head of the organization* company, firm, concern, operation, corporation, institution, group, consortium, conglomerate, combine, syndicate, federation, confederation, association, body.

organize *verb* establish, set up, form, lay the foundations of, found, institute, create, originate, begin, start, develop, build, frame, construct, assemble, structure, shape, mould, put together, arrange, dispose, regulate, marshal, put in order, put straight, coordinate, systematize, methodize, standardize, collocate, group, sort, sort out, classify, categorize, catalogue, codify, tabulate, be responsible for, be in charge of, take care of, administrate, run, manage, lick/knock into shape, see to. **Opposites** DESTROY; JUMBLE; disorganize.

orgy *noun* **1** *a drunken orgy* drunken bout, drunken party, wild party, carousal, debauch, revel, revels, revelry, bacchanalia, saturnalia; *inf.* spree, binge, jag, bender, love-in; *Am. inf.* toot. **2** *a spending orgy | go on an orgy of killing* bout, overindulgence, excess, surfeit; *inf.* spree, splurge, binge.

orientate *verb* **1** *difficult to orientate oneself in the fog* get/find one's bearings, get the lie of the land, establish one's location. **2** *orientate himself to his new life* adapt, adjust, accommodate, familiarize, acclimatize, find one's feet. **3** *orientate students towards science subjects* direct, guide, lead, point someone in the direction of, turn. **4** *orientate the course towards beginners* aim, direct, slant, angle, intend for, design for.

orientation *noun* **1** *orientation is difficult in the dark* getting one's bearings. See ORIENTATE 1. **2** *his orientation to his new way of life* adaptation, adjustment, accommodation, familiarization, acclimatization. **3** *establish one's orientation* bearings, location, position, direction. **4** *the orientation of students* directing, direction, guiding. See ORIENTATE 3. **5** *the orientation of the course towards beginners* aiming, directing, designing. See ORIENTATE 4.

orifice *noun* opening, hole, vent, aperture, gap, space, breach, break, rent, slot, slit, cleft, cranny, fissure, crevice, rift, crack, chink.

origin *noun* **1** *the origin of the word* source, derivation, root, roots, provenance, etymology, genesis, aetiology. **2** *the origins of life* source, basis, base, well-spring, spring, well-head, fountain-head, fountain, genesis, *fons et origo*. **3** *the origin of the age of steam* birth, dawn, dawning, beginning, start, commencement, emergence, inception, launch, creation, early stages, inauguration, foundation. **4** *explore the family's origin(s)* descent, ancestry, pedigree, lineage, heritage, parentage, extraction, beginnings. **Opposites** END; DEATH; DEMISE.

original *adjective* **1** *the original inhabitants* aboriginal, indigenous, early, earliest, first, initial, primary, primordial, primal, primeval, primitive, autochthonal, authochthonous. **2** *his work is original* innovative, innovatory, inventive, new, novel, fresh, creative, imaginative,

resourceful, individual, ingenious, unusual, unconventional, unorthodox, unprecedented, ground-breaking. **3** *this painting is original* not copied, genuine, authentic, archetypal, prototypical, master. **Opposites** LAST; UNORIGINAL; DERIVATIVE.

original *noun* **1** *this is the original, not a copy* original work/painting, archetype, prototype, master. **2** *he really is an original* eccentric, oddity, crank, nonconformist; *inf.* oddball, queer fish, nut, character, card, case, screwball, weirdo; *Am. inf.* wacko.

originality *noun* *admire the originality of his work* innovativeness, innovation, inventiveness, newness, novelty, break with tradition, freshness, creativity, imaginativeness, resourcefulness, individuality, unusualness, unconventionality, unprecedentedness.

originally *adverb* *originally he was unwilling* at first, in the beginning, to begin with, at the start, at the outset, initially.

originate *verb* **1** *the spring originates in the mountains* arise, rise, flow from, emanate from, issue from. **2** *the quarrel originated from a misunderstanding* have its origin in, arise, stem, spring, result, derive, start, begin, commence. **3** *he originated the idea* give birth to, be the father/mother of, set in motion, set up, invent, dream up, conceive, discover, initiate, create, formulate, inaugurate, pioneer, introduce, establish, found, evolve, develop, generate. **Opposites** TERMINATE; DESTROY.

originator *noun* father/mother, inventor, discoverer, initiator, architect, author, prime mover, founder, pioneer, establisher, developer. See ORIGINATE 3.

ornament *noun* **1** *a house full of ornaments* knick-knack, trinket, bauble, gewgaw, accessory, decoration, frill, furbelow, whatnot, doodah. **2** *the beautiful house/dress needs little ornament* decoration, adornment, embellishment, trimming, garnish, garnishing. **3** *the ornament of the company's range* jewel, jewel in the crown, gem, treasure, pride, flower, leading light, *crème de la crème*.

ornamental *adjective* *ornamental pool/plates* decorative, decorating, adorning, embellishing, ornamenting, embroidering.

ornate *adjective* **1** *ornate furnishings* elaborate, overelaborate, decorated, embellished, adorned, ornamented, fancy, fussy, busy, ostentatious, showy, baroque, rococo; *inf.* flash. **2** *ornate prose/speeches* elaborate, overelaborate, flowery, florid, flamboyant, laboured, strained, stilted, pretentious, high-flown, high-sounding, grandiose, pompous, orotund, magniloquent, grandiloquent, oratorical, bombastic; *inf.* highfalutin. **Opposites** PLAIN; AUSTERE; SIMPLE.

orotund *adjective* **1** *orotund voices* strong, powerful, full, rich, deep, sonorous, resonant, ringing, reverberating, booming. **2** *orotund speeches* ornate, overelaborate, laboured, strained, pretentious, high-flown, grandiose, pompous, magniloquent, bombastic; *inf.* highfalutin. See ORNATE 2.

orthodox adjective **1** hold orthodox religious beliefs | an orthodox Jew conformist, doctrinal, of the faith, of the true faith, sound, conservative, correct, faithful, true, true-blue, devoted, strict, devout. **2** orthodox behaviour conventional, accepted, approved, correct, proper, conformist, established, traditional, prevailing, customary, usual, regular, standard, comme il faut, de rigueur.
Opposites UNORTHODOX; NONCONFORMIST; UNCONVENTIONAL.

orthodoxy noun **1** the orthodoxy of his religious beliefs conformism, conformity, doctrinalism, conservatism, soundness, correctness, faithfulness, devotion, devoutness, strictness. **2** the orthodoxy of his behaviour conventionality, conventionalism, correctness, properness, propriety, traditionalism. See ORTHODOX 2.

oscillate verb **1** the pendulum oscillating swing, move back and forth, move backwards and forwards, move to and fro; inf. wigwag. **2** oscillate between feeling hot and cold swing, sway, fluctuate, see-saw, waver, vacillate, vary, hesitate, yo-yo.

oscillation noun **1** the oscillation of the pendulum swing, swinging, moving backwards and forwards. See OSCILLATE 1. **2** his oscillation between courses of action fluctuation, wavering, vacillation, yo-yoing. See OSCILLATE 2.

ossify verb **1** material ossifying with age harden, solidify, stiffen, become rigid, fossilize, petrify. **2** beliefs have ossified into rigid dogma become rigid, become unyielding/obdurate, become inflexible, grow unprogressive, become unreceptive, harden, solidify.

ostensible adjective outward, apparent, seeming, professed, alleged, claimed, purported, pretended, feigned, specious, supposed.

ostensibly adverb apparently, allegedly, supposedly. See OSTENSIBLE.

ostentation noun showiness, show, conspicuousness, obtrusiveness, loudness, extravagance, flamboyance, gaudiness, flashiness, pretentiousness, affectation, flaunting, exhibitionism, vulgarity, bad taste; inf. showing-off, flashness, swank. See OSTENTATIOUS.

ostentatious adjective ostentatious jewellery/manner showy, conspicuous, obtrusive, loud, extravagant, flamboyant, gaudy, flashy, pretentious, affected, overdone, overelaborate, vulgar, kitsch; inf. flash, over-the-top, OTT, swanky.
Opposites PLAIN; UNOBTRUSIVE; SUBDUED.

ostracism noun the cold shoulder, exclusion, barring, shunning, avoidance, boycotting, repudiation, rejection, banishment, exile. See OSTRACIZE.

ostracize verb cold-shoulder, give someone the cold shoulder, send to Coventry, exclude, shut out, bar, keep at arm's length, shun, spurn, avoid, boycott, repudiate, cast out, reject, blackball, blacklist, black, banish, exile, expel, excommunicate, debar, leave out in the cold; inf. hand someone the frozen mitt.
Opposites WELCOME; ACCEPT; FRATERNIZE.

other adjective **1** use other means different, unlike, variant, dissimilar, disparate, distinct, separate, alternative. **2** need a few other examples more, additional, further, extra, supplementary.

otherwise adverb **1** hurry, otherwise we'll be late or else, or, if not. **2** he's too young, otherwise he's fine in other respects, in other ways, apart from that. **3** he could not have acted otherwise in any other way, differently.

ounce noun not to have an ounce of courage iota, whit, trace, particle, atom, speck, scrap, shred, crumb, grain, drop.

oust verb ousted from his post drive out, force out, thrust out, expel, eject, put out, evict, throw out, dispossess, dismiss, dislodge, displace, depose, unseat, topple, disinherit; inf. fire, sack.

out adverb **1** the manager's out just now not in, not here, not at home, gone away, away, elsewhere, absent, away from one's desk. **2** the children have gone out outside, outdoors, out of doors. **3** tire them out completely, thoroughly, entirely, wholly. **4** the fire is out not burning, extinguished, quenched, doused, dead. **5** the boxer is completely out out cold, unconscious, knocked out, senseless; inf. KO'd, flaked out. **6** your secret is out revealed, disclosed, divulged, in the open, out in the open, known, exposed, common knowledge, public knowledge. **7** the flowers are out open, in bloom, in full bloom, blooming. **8** long hair is out this year unfashionable, out-of-fashion, dated, out-of-date, not in, behind the times, démodé, passé; inf. old-hat. **9** that idea is out inappropriate, unsuitable, irrelevant, not worth considering.
Opposites IN; INSIDE; FASHIONABLE.

out-and-out adjective absolute, complete, utter, downright, thorough, thoroughgoing, total, perfect, unmitigated, unqualified, consummate, inveterate, dyed-in-the-wool, true-blue.

outbreak noun outbreak of disease eruption, flare-up, upsurge, outburst, sudden appearance, start, rash.

outburst noun an outburst of anger/laughter burst, explosion, eruption, outbreak, flare-up, access, attack, fit, spasm, paroxysm.

outcast noun social outcast pariah, persona non grata, leper, untouchable, castaway, exile, displaced person, refugee, evictee, evacuee.

outclass verb surpass, be superior to, be better than, outshine, eclipse, overshadow, outdistance, outstrip, outdo, outplay, outrank, outrival, trounce, beat, defeat; inf. be a cut above, be head and shoulders above, run rings round, leave standing, outfox.

outcome noun consequence, result, end result, sequel, upshot, issue, product, conclusion, after-effect, aftermath, wake; inf. pay-off.

outcry noun clamour, howls of protest, protest, complaints, objections, fuss, outburst, commotion, uproar, tumult, hue and cry, hullaballoo, ballyhoo, racket.

outdated adjective out of date, out of style, out of fashion, old-fashioned, unfashionable, outmoded, dated, démodé, passé, behind the times,

antiquated, archaic; *inf.* old-hat, not with it.
Opposites CURRENT; MODERN; FASHIONABLE.

outdistance *verb* outstrip, outrun, outpace, leave behind, overtake, pass, shake off, lose; *inf.* leave standing.

outdo *verb* surpass, top, exceed, excel, get the better of, outstrip, outshine, eclipse, overshadow, transcend, outclass, outdistance, overcome, beat, defeat, outsmart, outmanoeuvre; *inf.* be a cut above, be head and shoulders above, run rings round, outfox.

outdoor *adjective* out-of-doors, outside, open-air, alfresco.
Opposites INSIDE.

outer *adjective* **1** *pierce the outer layer* outside, outermost, outward, exterior, external, surface, superficial. **2** *the outer areas of the estate* outlying, distant, remote, far-away, peripheral, fringe, perimeter.
Opposites INNER; INSIDE; INTERIOR.

outfit *noun* **1** *wearing a smart outfit* clothes, dress, ensemble, suit, costume, garb, kit, accoutrements, trappings; *inf.* rig-out, get-up, gear, togs. **2** *a car repair outfit* kit, equipment, tools, tackle, apparatus, paraphernalia. **3** *a small publishing outfit* organization, set-up, company, firm, business, unit, group, team, coterie, clique.

outfit *verb* equip, kit out, fit out, rig out, supply, furnish with, provide with, stock with, provision, accoutre, attire.

outfitter *noun* clothier, tailor, dressmaker, couturier, costumier, modiste; *Am.* haberdasher.

outflow *noun* outflowing, outpouring, outrush, rush, discharge, issue, spurt, jet, gush, leakage, drainage, outflux, effluence, efflux.

outgoing *adjective* **1** *outgoing people* extrovert, unreserved, demonstrative, affectionate, warm, friendly, genial, cordial, affable, hail-fellow-well-met, sociable, communicative, open, expansive, talkative, gregarious, approachable, easygoing, easy. **2** *the outgoing president* retiring, departing, leaving, withdrawing, ex-, former, past, late.
Opposites RESERVED; INTROVERTED; WITHDRAWN; INCOMING.

outgoings *plural noun* costs, expenses, expenditure, outlay, overheads.

outing *noun* trip, excursion, jaunt, expedition, pleasure trip, tour, mystery tour, airing; *inf.* spin.

outlandish *adjective* strange, unfamiliar, unknown, unheard-of, odd, unusual, extraordinary, peculiar, queer, curious, singular, eccentric, quaint, bizarre, grotesque, preposterous, fantastic, *outré*, weird; *inf.* freaky, wacky, far-out, off-the-wall.
Opposites ORDINARY; COMMONPLACE; CONVENTIONAL.

outlaw *noun* fugitive, outcast, exile, pariah, bandit, desperado, brigand, criminal, robber; *inf.* villain.

outlaw *verb* **1** *outlaw the thief* banish, exile, cast out, expel, send away, repudiate, put a price on someone's head. **2** *outlaw the sale of liquor* ban, bar, prohibit, forbid, embargo, make illegal, disallow, proscribe, interdict.

outlay *noun* expenditure, expenses, spending, outgoings, money spent, cost, price, charge, payment, disbursement.

outlet *noun* **1** *water outlets* way out, exit, vent, vent-hole, outfall, valve, safety-valve, duct, blow-hole, channel, trench, culvert, cut, conduit. **2** *an outlet for her emotion/creativity* means of expression, release, means of release, release mechanism, safety-valve. **3** *an outlet for their farm produce* retail outlet, market, market-place, selling-place, shop, store.

outline *noun* **1** *an outline of our plans* draft, rough draft, rough, sketch, tracing, skeleton, framework, layout, diagram, plan, design, schema. **2** *give an outline of what happened* thumbnail sketch, rough idea, quick run-down, abbreviated version, summary, synopsis, résumé, précis, main points, bones, bare bones. **3** *draw an outline of the building* contour, silhouette, profile, lineaments, delineation, configuration, perimeter, circumference.

outline *verb* **1** *outline the shape* sketch, delineate, trace, silhouette. **2** *outline your ideas* sketch out, give a thumbnail sketch of, give a rough idea of, give a quick run-down on, summarize, précis.

outlook *noun* **1** *a gloomy outlook on life* view, point of view, viewpoint, perspective, attitude, frame of mind, standpoint, slant, angle, interpretation, opinion. **2** *the house has a pleasant outlook* view, vista, prospect, panorama, aspect.

outlying *adjective* outer, outermost, out-of-the-way, remote, distant, far-away, far-flung, peripheral, isolated, inaccessible, off the beaten track, backwoods. *See* OUT OF THE WAY 1.

outmoded *adjective* old-fashioned, unfashionable, out of fashion, out of style, outdated, out of date, dated, *passé*, *démodé*, behind the times, antiquated, archaic, obsolete; *inf.* old-hat.
Opposites FASHIONABLE; MODERN.

out of date *adjective* **1** *out-of-date clothes* outdated, dated, old-fashioned, out of fashion, behind the times, archaic, obsolete. *See* OUTMODED. **2** *the licence is out of date* expired, lapsed, elapsed, invalid, void, null and void.
Opposites CURRENT; MODERN; FASHIONABLE.

out of the way *adjective* **1** *out-of-the-way places* outlying, outer, outermost, remote, distant, far-away, far-flung, peripheral, isolated, lonely, inaccessible, obscure, off the beaten track, unfrequented, backwoods. **2** *I don't find his methods out of the way* uncommon, unusual, odd, peculiar, abnormal, strange, curious, extraordinary, out of the ordinary, outlandish.
Opposites ACCESSIBLE; NEAR; HANDY; RUN-OF-THE-MILL.

out of work *adjective* *an out-of-work actor* | *he is out of work* unemployed, jobless, out of a job, redundant, laid off, idle; *inf.* on the dole, signing on.

outpouring *noun* outflow, effluence, efflux, flux, outflux, debouchment, cascade, deluge, spate, stream, spurt, jet, torrent.

output *noun* production, product, amount/quantity produced, productivity, yield, harvest, achievement, accomplishment.

outrage noun **1** *outrages committed by the soldiers* atrocity, act of violence, evil, act of wickedness, crime, horror, enormity, brutality, barbarism, inhumane act. **2** *the sacking of the men was an outrage | the building is an outrage* offence, affront, insult, injury, abuse, indignity, scandal, desecration, violation. **3** *arouse outrage in the citizens* anger, fury, rage, indignation, wrath, annoyance, shock, resentment, horror, amazement.

outrage verb **1** *outrage the community* anger, infuriate, enrage, incense, madden, annoy, shock, horrify, amaze, scandalize, offend. **2** *outrage the churches/women* abuse, maltreat, misuse, injure, desecrate, defile, profane, rape, ravage, ravish, violate.

outrageous adjective **1** *his outrageous behaviour when drunk* intolerable, insufferable, insupportable, unendurable, unbearable, impossible, exasperating, offensive, provocative, maddening, distressing. **2** *commit outrageous acts* atrocious, heinous, abominable, wicked, vile, foul, monstrous, horrible, horrid, dreadful, terrible, horrendous, hideous, ghastly, unspeakable, gruesome. **3** *outrageous prices* immoderate, excessive, exorbitant, unreasonable, preposterous, scandalous, shocking; *inf.* steep, over the top, OTT.
Opposites ACCEPTABLE; MILD; MODERATE.

outré adjective unconventional, eccentric, odd, outlandish, strange, extraordinary, unusual, bizarre, freakish, freaky, queer, weird; *inf.* rum, offbeat, off-the-wall, wacky, way-out, far-out.

outright adjective **1** *an outright fool* out-and-out, absolute, complete, downright, utter, thorough, thoroughgoing, perfect, total, unmitigated. *See* OUT-AND-OUT. **2** *the outright winner* definite, unequivocal, unqualified, incontestable, undeniable, unmistakable.

outright adverb **1** *reject the proposal outright* completely, entirely, wholly, totally, categorically, absolutely. **2** *killed outright* instantly, instantaneously, immediately, at once, straight away, there and then, on the spot. **3** *tell her outright* openly, candidly, frankly, honestly, forthrightly, directly, plainly, explicitly, unreservedly.

outset noun start, starting point, beginning, commencement, dawn, birth, inception, opening, launch, inauguration; *inf.* kick-off.
Opposites CONCLUSION; END; FINISH.

outshine verb surpass, eclipse, put in the shade, overshadow, be superior to, be better than, outclass, outstrip, outdistance, outdo, top, tower above, dwarf, transcend, upstage; *inf.* be head and shoulders above, be a cut above, leave standing.

outside adjective **1** *outside layers* outer, outermost, outward, exterior, external. **2** *outside furniture/toilet* outdoor, out-of-doors. **3** *an outside chance* unlikely, improbable, slight, slender, slim, small, faint, negligible, marginal, remote, distant, vague.
Opposites INSIDE; INNER; INTERIOR.

outside adverb go outside outdoors, out of doors, out of the house.

outside noun **1** *brown on the outside* outer side, exterior, surface, outer surface, case, skin, shell, sheath. **2** *the outside of the building* exterior, front, face, façade.

outsider noun odd man out, alien, stranger, foreigner, outlander, immigrant, emigrant, émigré, incomer, newcomer, parvenu, *arriviste*, interloper, intruder, gatecrasher, outcast, misfit.

outskirts plural noun vicinity, neighbourhood, environs, edges, outlying districts, fringes, margin, periphery, borders, boundary, suburbs, suburbia, purlieus, *faubourgs*.

outsmart verb get the better of, outwit, outmanoeuvre, outperform, outplay, be cleverer than, steal a march on, trick, dupe, make a fool of; *inf.* outfox, put one over on, pull a fast one on, give someone the run-around, run rings round.

outspoken adjective candid, frank, forthright, direct, straightforward, straight-from-the-shoulder, plain, plain-spoken, explicit, blunt, brusque, unequivocal, unreserved, unceremonious.
Opposites DIPLOMATIC; RETICENT; EVASIVE.

outstanding adjective **1** *an outstanding painter* pre-eminent, eminent, well-known, notable, noteworthy, distinguished, important, famous, famed, renowned, celebrated, great, excellent, remarkable, exceptional, superlative. **2** *the painting is outstanding* striking, impressive, eye-catching, arresting, memorable, remarkable. **3** *outstanding debts* unpaid, unsettled, owing, due. **4** *work outstanding* to be done, unfinished, remaining, pending, ongoing.
Opposites UNEXCEPTIONAL; MEDIOCRE; COMPLETE.

outward adjective **1** *outward layers* outer, outside, outermost, exterior, external, surface, superficial. **2** *no outward sign of his grief* external, superficial, visible, observable, noticeable, perceptible, discernible, apparent, evident, obvious.
Opposites INWARD; INNER; INTERNAL.

outwardly adverb **1** *outwardly visible* externally, on the outside. **2** *outwardly he seems all right* on the surface, superficially, on the face of it, to all appearances, to the eye, as far as one can see, to all intents and purposes, apparently, evidently.

outweigh verb be greater than, exceed, be superior to, take precedence over, have the edge on/over, preponderate.

outwit verb get the better of, be cleverer than, outsmart, outmanoeuvre, steal a march on, trick, dupe, make a fool of; *inf.* outfox, put one over on, pull a fast one on. *See* OUTSMART.

outworn adjective *outworn ideas/traditions* outdated, out of date, old-fashioned, out of fashion, outmoded, behind the times, ancient, archaic, antiquated, obsolescent, obsolete, disused, abandoned, cast out, rejected, discredited, tired, exhausted, stale, hackneyed, superannuated; *inf.* old-hat, out of the ark.
Opposites UP-TO-DATE; FRESH; ORIGINAL.

oval adjective egg-shaped, ovoid, ovate, oviform, elliptical, ellipsoidal.

ovation noun applause, hand-clapping, clapping, cheering, cheers, acclaim, acclamation, praise, plaudits, laurels, tribute, accolade, laudation, extolment; *inf.* bouquets.

oven noun stove, kitchen stove, microwave oven, haybox, kiln.

over adverb **1** *fly over* overhead, above, on high, aloft. **2** *the relationship is over* ended, at an end, finished, concluded, terminated, no more, extinct, gone, dead, a thing of the past, ancient history. **3** *have food over* left over, left, remaining, unused, surplus, superfluous, in excess, extra, in addition. **over and over** again and again, over and over again, repeatedly, time and again, time and time again, ad nauseam.

over preposition **1** *earn over £20,000* more than, above, in excess of, exceeding. **2** *he has three people over him* above, superior to, higher up than, more powerful than. **3** *all over the world/place* throughout, all through, throughout the extent of, everywhere in, in all parts of, around. **over and above** *over and above the sum mentioned* in addition to, on top of, plus, as well as, besides, not to mention, let alone. *Opposites* UNDER; BELOW.

overact verb exaggerate; *inf.* ham, camp it up, pile it on, lay it on.

overall adjective *an overall plan/improvement* comprehensive, universal, all-embracing, inclusive, all-inclusive, general, sweeping, complete, blanket, umbrella, global.

overall adverb *overall, things have improved* on the whole, in general, generally speaking.

overawe verb intimidate, daunt, disconcert, abash, dismay, frighten, alarm, scare, terrify, terrorize.

overbalance verb lose one's balance, lose one's footing, fall over, topple over, tip over, keel over, capsize, overturn, turn turtle.

overbearing adjective domineering, autocratic, tyrannical, despotic, oppressive, high-handed, lordly, officious, dogmatic, dictatorial, pompous, peremptory, arrogant, haughty, cocksure, proud, over-proud, overweening, presumptuous, supercilious, disdainful, contemptuous; *inf.* bossy, throwing one's weight about, cocky.

overblown adjective **1** *an overblown piece of writing* overwritten, extravagant, florid, pompous, overelaborate, over-flowery, pretentious, high-flown, turgid, bombastic, grandiloquent, magniloquent, euphuistic, fustian, aureate; *inf.* over the top, OTT. **2** *overblown roses/beauty* past its/one's prime, past its/one's best, fading.

overcast adjective cloudy, clouded, clouded over, overclouded, sunless, darkened, dark, murky, misty, hazy, foggy, grey, leaden, louring, threatening, heavy, promising rain, dismal, dreary. *Opposites* BRIGHT; CLEAR.

overcharge verb **1** *overcharge the customers* charge too much, cheat, swindle, fleece, short change; *inf.* rip off, sting, diddle, do, rook, clip. **2** *overcharge the description* overwrite, overdraw, overdo, overstate, exaggerate, hyperbolize, overcolour, overembroider, embroider, embellish; *inf.* pile it on, lay it on thick, lay it on with a trowel.

overcoat noun winter coat. *See table at* COAT.

overcome verb **1** *overcome the enemy | must overcome her resistance* conquer, defeat, vanquish, beat, be victorious over, gain a victory over, prevail over, get the better of, triumph over, best, worst, trounce, rout, gain mastery over, master, overpower, overwhelm, overthrow, subdue, subjugate, quell, quash, crush; *inf.* lick, clobber, whip, wipe the floor with, tank, blow out of the water. **2** *overcome one's disability* conquer, get the better of, triumph over, master, surmount, rise above.

overcome adjective *too overcome to react* overwhelmed, emotional, moved, affected, speechless, at a loss for words; *inf.* bowled over.

overconfident adjective cocksure, swaggering, blustering, self-assured, self-assertive, brash, overbearing, overweening, presumptuous, egotistic, riding/heading for a fall; *inf.* cocky.

overcritical adjective hypercritical, fault-finding, captious, carping, cavilling, quibbling, hair-splitting, niggling, hard to please, over-particular, fussy, finicky, over-exacting; *inf.* nit-picking, pernickety.

overcrowded adjective overfull, full to overflowing, crammed full, packed as tight as sardines, congested, overloaded, overpopulated, overpeopled, overrun, thronged, swarming, teeming; *inf.* full to the gunwales, jam-packed, like the Black Hole of Calcutta. *Opposites* DESERTED; EMPTY; VACANT.

overdo verb **1** *overdo the comic scenes* overact, overplay, exaggerate, do to death; *inf.* ham up, camp up, go overboard over. **2** *overdo the sympathy* do to excess, carry too far, carry to extremes, exaggerate, belabour, stretch/strain a point over, overstate, overemphasize, hyperbolize, not know when to stop, do to death; *inf.* pile on, lay on thick, lay on with a trowel, make a production of, make a big deal out of. **3** *overdo the meat* overcook, overbake, burn, burn to a crisp; *inf.* burn to a frazzle. **overdo it** do too much, overwork, work too hard, strain oneself, do too much, overtax oneself, overtax one's strength, overburden oneself, overload oneself, drive oneself too hard, push oneself too far/hard, wear oneself out, burn the candle at both ends, have too many irons in the fire, have too many balls in the air, burn oneself out, bite off more than one can chew; *inf.* knock oneself out, work/run oneself into the ground. *Opposites* UNDERSTATE; play down (*see* PLAY).

overdone adjective **1** *the flattery/sympathy was overdone* excessive, too much, undue, immoderate, inordinate, disproportionate, beyond the pale, extravagant, overenthusiastic, effusive, over-effusive, gushing, fulsome; *inf.* a bit much, over the top, OTT, hyped up, laid on with a trowel. **2** *overdone food* overcooked, overbaked, dried out, burnt, burnt to a cinder/crisp; *inf.* burnt to a frazzle.

overdue *adjective* **1** *our arrival/visit is overdue* late, not on time, behind schedule, behind-hand, delayed, belated, tardy, unpunctual. **2** *overdue bills* unpaid, owed, owing, outstanding, unsettled, in arrears.

overeat *verb* eat too much, eat like a horse, gorge oneself, stuff oneself, overindulge, overindulge oneself, surfeit, guzzle, gormandize; *inf.* binge, stuff one's face, pack it away, make a pig of oneself, pig out.

overemphasize *verb* place/put too much emphasis on, overstress, put/lay too much stress on, exaggerate, attach too much importance/weight to, make too much of, overdo, overdramatize, make something out of nothing, make a mountain out of a molehill, belabour the point; *inf.* blow up out of all proportion.
Opposites UNDERSTATE; play down (*see* PLAY).

overflow *verb* **1** *the water was overflowing* flow over, run over, spill over, brim over, well over, pour forth, stream forth, discharge, surge, debouch. **2** *water overflowed the land* flood, deluge, inundate, submerge, cover, swamp, engulf, drown, soak, drench, saturate. **overflowing with** **1** *overflowing with people* full of, crowded with, thronged with, swarming with, teeming with, abounding in. **2** *hearts overflowing with kindness* full of, very full of, filled with, filled to the brim with, brimful of, abounding in.

overflow *noun* **1** *the overflow from the cistern* excess water, overspill, spill, spillage, flood, flooding, inundation. **2** *the overflow of the meeting* surplus, additional people/things, extra people/things.

overhang *verb* stand out, stick out, extend, project, protrude, jut, jut out, beetle, bulge out, loom, cantilever.

overhaul *verb* **1** *overhaul the engine* check, check out, check over, give something a check-up, investigate, inspect, examine, service, repair, mend, recondition, renovate, revamp, fix up, patch up. **2** *overhaul the other runners* overtake, pass, get ahead of, outdistance, outstrip, gain on, catch up with, draw level with.

overhead *adverb* *clouds overhead | bird flew overhead* above, up above, high up, up in the sky, on high, aloft.

overheads *plural noun* expenses, expenditure, outlay, disbursement, running costs, operating costs.

overindulge *verb* **1** *overindulge and have a hangover* drink/eat too much, be immoderate, be intemperate, overdo it, drink/eat/go to excess, not know when to stop; *inf.* binge, go on a binge, paint the town red, push the boat out, go overboard, live it up, make a pig of oneself. **2** *overindulge the children* give in to, spoil, cosset, pamper, mollycoddle, feather-bed; *inf.* spoil rotten.

overjoyed *adjective* full of joy, joyful, elated, jubilant, thrilled, delighted, euphoric, ecstatic, in raptures, rapturous, enraptured, in transports, transported, delirious with happiness, on top of the world; *inf.* tickled pink, over the moon, on cloud nine, in seventh heaven.
Opposites DEJECTED; DEPRESSED.

overlay *verb* **1** *overlay the floor with carpet* cover, overspread, carpet, blanket. **2** *overlay the table with gold* inlay, laminate, veneer, varnish, gild, decorate, ornament.

overload *verb* overburden, weigh down, encumber, overcharge, overtax, oppress, impose strain on, strain; *inf.* saddle with.

overlook *verb* **1** *he overlooked a mistake on the first page* fail to notice/observe/spot, miss, leave, neglect to notice, leave unnoticed; *inf.* slip up on. **2** *overlook tasks* leave undone, ignore, disregard, omit, neglect, forget. **3** *decide to overlook his crime* deliberately to ignore, not to take into consideration, disregard, take no notice of, let something pass, turn a blind eye to, wink at, blink at, excuse, pardon, forgive, condone, let someone off with; *inf.* let something ride. **4** *the house overlooks the sea* look over, look onto, front onto, give over, open out over, have a view of, afford a view of, command a view of.
Opposites SPOT; NOTE; PUNISH.

overly *adverb* *not overly concerned* too, to too great an extent/degree, unduly, excessively, inordinately, immoderately.

overpower *verb* **1** *overpower the enemy* gain control over, overwhelm, overcome, get the upper hand over, gain mastery over, master, best, worst, conquer, defeat, vanquish, trounce, rout, subjugate, quell, quash, crush; *inf.* whip. **2** *his charm overpowered her* overcome, overwhelm, move, stir, affect, touch, impress, take aback; *inf.* bowl over, knock/hit for six, get to.

overpowering *adjective* **1** *overpowering grief* overwhelming, burdensome, weighty, unbearable, unendurable, intolerable, shattering; *inf.* mind-blowing. **2** *an overpowering smell* over-strong, suffocating, stifling, nauseating. **3** *overpowering evidence* compelling, forceful, telling, irrefutable, undeniable, unquestionable, indisputable, incontestable, incontrovertible.
Opposites MILD; SLIGHT.

overrate *verb* *overrated him | overrate his chances* overestimate, overvalue, overprize, exaggerate the worth of, think too much of, attach too much importance to, expect too much of.
Opposites UNDERRATE; UNDERESTIMATE.

overreach *verb* *overreach the enemy* get the better of, outsmart, outwit; *inf.* outfox, steal a march on, trick, make a fool of, pull a fast one on. *See* OUTSMART. **overreach oneself** overestimate one's ability, try to do too much, go too far, try to be too clever/smart, defeat one's own ends, have one's scheme backfire on one, be hoist with one's own petard, bite off more than one can chew.

overreact *verb* get overexcited, get upset over nothing, act irrationally, lose one's sense of proportion, make something out of nothing, make a mountain out of a molehill; *inf.* go over the top, press the panic button.

override *verb* **1** *his career overrides all other considerations* be more important than, take prior-

561

ity over, take precedence over, supersede, out-weigh. **2** *override her objections* trample on, ride roughshod over, set aside, ignore, disregard, discount, pay no heed to, take no account of, close one's mind to, turn a deaf ear to.

overriding *adjective the overriding consideration* most important, predominant, principal, primary, paramount, chief, main, major, foremost, central, focal, pivotal; *inf.* number one. **Opposites** INSIGNIFICANT; IRRELEVANT.

overrule *verb overrule their objections* rule against, disallow, override, veto, set aside, overturn, cancel, reverse, rescind, repeal, revoke, repudiate, annul, nullify, declare null and void, invalidate, void, abrogate.

overrun *verb* **1** *the enemy army was overrunning their country* invade, march into, penetrate, occupy, beseige, storm, attack, assail. **2** *rats overrunning the warehouses* swarm over, surge over, inundate, overwhelm, permeate, infest. **3** *weeds overrunning the garden* spread over, spread like wildfire over, grow over, cover, choke, clog; *inf.* run riot over. **4** *the lecture overran* exceed the allotted time, go/run over the allotted time, be too long.

overseer *noun* supervisor, superintendent, foreman, manager/manageress, master, boss; *inf.* gaffer, super; *Am. inf.* honcho.

overshadow *verb* **1** *that runner overshadows the others | the achievement of the others is overshadowed* outshine, eclipse, put in the shade, surpass, be superior to, outclass, outstrip, outdo, top, transcend, tower above, dwarf, upstage; *inf.* be head and shoulders above, be a cut above. **2** *his death overshadowed the family gathering* cast gloom over, blight, take the pleasure out of, bring a note of sadness to, take the edge off, mar, spoil, ruin. **3** *clouds overshadowing the sun | many trees overshadowed the garden* cloud, darken, bedim, dim, conceal, obscure, eclipse, screen, shroud, veil.

oversight *noun* **1** *done in oversight* carelessness, inattention, neglect, inadvertence, laxity, dereliction, omission. **2** mistake, error, blunder, gaffe, fault, omission, slip, lapse; *inf.* slip-up, bloomer, goof, boob, booboo. **3** *have oversight of the workforce* supervision, surveillance, superintendence, charge, care, administration, management, direction, control, handling.

overt *adjective overt hostility* obvious, noticeable, observable, visible, undisguised, unconcealed, apparent, plain, plainly seen, plain to see, manifest, patent, open, public, blatant, conspicuous. **Opposites** HIDDEN; SURREPTITIOUS; COVERT.

overtake *verb* **1** *cars/runners overtaking each other* pass, get past, go past, go by, overhaul, leave behind, outdistance, outstrip, go faster than. **2** *misfortune overtook them* befall, happen to, come upon, hit, strike, fall upon, overwhelm, engulf, take by surprise, surprise, catch unawares, catch unprepared, catch off guard.

overthrow *verb* **1** *overthrow the government* cause the downfall of, remove from office, overturn, depose, oust, unseat, dethrone, dis-establish. **2** *overthrow the army of occupation* conquer, vanquish, defeat, beat, rout, trounce, best, worst, subjugate, crush, quash, quell, overcome, overwhelm, overturn, overpower. **3** *kids overthrowing cars* throw over, turn over, overturn, tip over, topple over, upset, capsize, knock over, upturn, upend, invert.

overthrow *noun* **1** *the overthrow of the government* downfall, deposition, ousting. *See* OVERTHROW *verb* 1. **2** *the overthrow of the army* defeat, vanquishing, rout, subjugation, crushing, overwhelming, overturning. *See* OVERTHROW *verb* 2.

overtone *noun* hidden meaning, secondary meaning, implication, innuendo, hint, suggestion, insinuation, association, connotation, undercurrent, nuance, flavour, colouring, vein.

overture *noun* **1** *miss the overture* musical introduction/opening, prelude. **2** *the enemy making peace overtures* advances, move, opening move, conciliatory move, approach, proposal, proposition, offer, suggestion, motion.

overturn *verb* **1** *the boat overturned* capsize, keel over, overbalance, tip over, topple over. **2** *boys overturning cars* upturn, turn over, throw over, overthrow, tip over, topple over, upset, knock over, upend, invert. **3** *overturn the previous decision* overrule, override, veto, set aside, cancel, reverse, rescind, repeal, revoke, repudiate, annul, nullify, invalidate, void, abrogate. **4** *overturn the government* overthrow, cause the downfall of, depose, oust, unseat. *See* OVERTHROW *verb* 1. **5** *overturn the army of occupation* conquer, vanquish, defeat, trounce, worst, subjugate, crush, quell, overcome. *See* OVERTHROW *verb* 2.

overweening *adjective* arrogant, haughty, proud, vain, vainglorious, conceited, self-important, egotistical, high-handed, domineering, presumptuous, lordly, peremptory, pompous, officious, blustering, self-confident, cocksure, self-assertive, opinionated, bold, forward, insolent, supercilious, disdainful, patronizing; *inf.* cocky, high and mighty, throwing one's weight about/around. **Opposites** MODEST; DIFFIDENT; UNASSUMING.

overweight *adjective* obese, fat, plump, stout, ample, chubby, tubby, corpulent, rotund, portly, podgy, paunchy, heavy, on the heavy side, big, hefty large, bulky, chunky, outsize, massive, gross, Falstaffian; *inf.* well-padded, well-upholstered, roly-poly. **Opposites** SKINNY; SCRAWNY; THIN.

overwhelm *verb* **1** *the generous present overwhelmed her* overcome, move, make emotional, daze, dumbfound, shake, take aback, leave speechless, stagger; *inf.* bowl over, knock for six, blow one's mind, flabbergast. **2** *they were overwhelmed with work/mail* inundate, flood, deluge, engulf, submerge, swamp, bury, overload, overburden, snow under. **3** *overwhelm the army of occupation* overcome, overpower, conquer, vanquish, defeat, subjugate, quell, quash, crush. *See* OVERCOME *verb* 1.

overwhelming *adjective* **1** *an overwhelming desire to laugh* uncontrollable, irrepressible, irresistible, overpowering. **2** *an overwhelming amount of mail* profuse, enormous, immense, inordinate, massive, huge, stupendous, prodigious, staggering, shattering; *inf.* mind-boggling, mind-blowing. **3** *the overwhelming majority* vast, massive, great, large.

overwork *verb* **1** *the staff are all overworking* work too hard, do too much, overdo it, work like a Trojan, work like a horse/slave, work day and night, burn the midnight oil, drive/push oneself too hard, overtax oneself, sweat, work one's fingers to the bone; *inf.* work one's tail off, work/run oneself into the ground. **2** *the factory owner overworks the men* exploit, sweat, be a hard taskmaster, overburden, oppress, be a slave driver; *inf.* drive into the ground. **3** *overwork certain words* overuse, overemploy.

overworked *adjective overworked employees* stressed, under stress, stress-ridden, strained, overtaxed, overburdened, exhausted, fatigued, worn-out.

overwrought *adjective* **1** *overwrought mothers* tense, agitated, nervous, on edge, edgy, keyed-up, highly strung, overexcited beside oneself, distracted, jumpy, frantic, frenzied, hysterical; *inf.* nervy, in a state, in a tizzy, uptight, twitchy, strung-up, wound-up. **2** *overwrought decoration/designs* overornate, overelaborate, overembellished, overblown, overcharged, florid, busy, fussy, strained, contrived, overworked, baroque, rococo.
Opposites CALM; LAID-BACK; PLAIN.

owe *verb* be in debt to, be indebted to, be in arrears to, be under an obligation to, be obligated to, be beholden to.

owing *adjective* owed, outstanding, unpaid, payable, due, overdue, in arrears. **owing to** because of, as a result of, on account of.

own *adjective* personal, individual, particular, private.

own *noun* **hold one's own** **1** *she can hold her own against the men in the firm* maintain/keep one's position, stick up for oneself, look after one's interests; *inf.* fight one's corner. **2** *the patient is holding his own* be in a stable condition, be stable, be surviving, have a chance of survival. **on one's own** **1** *live/go on one's own* alone, all alone, by oneself, unaccompanied; *inf.* on one's tod. **2** *be on one's own* single, unmarried, unattached, footloose and fancy-free. **3** *build the business on her own* all by herself, independently, unaided, unassisted, by one's own efforts, standing on one's own two feet, off one's own bat.

own *verb* **1** *they own three cars* possess, have in one's possession, have, keep, retain, maintain, hold, enjoy. **2** *I own that he is right* admit, allow, concede, grant, accept, acknowledge, recognize, agree. **own up** *won't own up | own up to the crime* confess to, confess everything, admit to, acknowledge that, tell the truth about, make a clean breast of it; *inf.* come clean.

owner *noun* **1** *the owner of the car* possessor, holder, keeper. **2** *the owner of the hotel* proprietor/proprietress/proprietrix, landlord, landlady. **3** *the dog's owner* master/mistress, keeper.

ownership *noun* possession, right of possession, proprietorship, proprietary rights, title.

ox *noun* bull, bullock, steer. *See table at* CATTLE.

Pp

pace *noun* **1** *take one pace towards her* step, stride. **2** *walk with an ambling pace* gait, walk, tread. **3** *runners unable to keep up with the pace of the race* speed, swiftness, fastness, quickness, rapidity, velocity, tempo; *inf.* clip, lick. **4** *the fast/slow pace of life there* rate of progress, tempo, momentum, measure.

pacific *adjective* **1** *make pacific overtures* peace-making, placatory, placating, conciliatory, propitiatory, appeasing, mollifying, calming, mediatory, mediating, diplomatic, irenic. **2** *a pacific nation* peace-loving, peaceable, pacifist, non-violent, non-aggressive, non-belligerent, non-combative, mild, gentle, dovelike, dovish. **3** *pacific waters* calm, still, motionless, smooth, tranquil, peaceful, at peace, placid, unruffled, undisturbed.
Opposites HOSTILE; AGGRESSIVE; STORMY.

pacifist *noun* conscientious objector, passive resister, peace-lover, peacemaker, peace-monger, dove, satyagrahi; *inf.* conchie.

pacify *verb* *pacify the angry woman* calm, calm down, placate, conciliate, propitiate, appease, mollify, sooth, tranquillize, quieten.

pack *noun* **1** *carry his goods in a pack* bundle, parcel, bale, truss; *lit.* fardel. **2** *carry a pack on his back* bag, backpack, rucksack, knapsack, kitbag. **3** *buy a pack of cigarettes* packet, container, package, carton. **4** *a pack of animals* herd, drove, flock, troop. **5** *a pack of thieves* gang, crowd, mob, group, band, company, troop, set, clique; *inf.* crew, bunch. **6** *a pack of lies* great deal, collection, parcel, assortment, mass, assemblage, bunch; *inf.* load, heap.

pack *verb* **1** *pack a suitcase* fill, load, bundle, stuff, cram. **2** *pack clothes in a suitcase* put, place, store, stow. **3** *pack the glass in straw* package, parcel, wrap, wrap up, box, bale, cover, protect. **4** *young people packing the stadium* fill, crowd, throng, mob, cram, jam, press into, squeeze into. **5** *snow packed by the wind against the wall* compact, compress, press, tamp, ram. **pack in 1** *also* **pack into** *everyone was packing into the small car* crowd, cram, jam, squeeze, press. **2** *a show that has been packing them in for years* draw in, pull in, attract, fill the theatre etc. with. **3** *pack in one's job* resign, leave, give up, abandon; *inf.* chuck, jack in. **pack off** *pack the children off to bed* send off, dispatch, dismiss, put away, bundle off; *inf.* send packing. **pack up 1** *pack up one's equipment for the night* put away, tidy up/away, clear up, store. **2** *decided to pack up for the day* finish, leave off, halt, stop, cease; *inf.* call it a day, pack/jack it in. **3** *his car packed up on the motorway* break down, stop working, cease to function, fail, give out, stall, come to a halt; *inf.* conk out, go kaput.
Opposites unpack; EMPTY.

package *noun* **1** *a Christmas package | sweets in a brightly-coloured package* parcel, packet, container, box, carton. **2** *you cannot select individual sections of the deal you must go for the whole package* package deal, whole, unit, lot, entity, combination.

package *verb* *package the gift and send it* pack, pack up, parcel, parcel up, wrap, wrap up, gift-wrap, box.

packaging *noun* *low-cost goods in expensive packaging* wrapping, wrappers, packing, covering, container, packet, presentation.

packed *adjective* *theatre groups playing to packed halls* full, filled, filled to capacity, crowded, thronged, mobbed, crammed, jammed, packed like sardines, overfull, overloaded, brimful, chock-full, chock-a-block, full to the gunwales; *inf.* jam-packed.

packet *noun* **1** *buy a packet of cigarettes/sweets* pack, carton, box, container, package, bag. **2** *received a packet by post* parcel, package, container, padded bag.

pact *noun* *sign a pact with the opposing side* agreement, treaty, deal, contract, settlement, bargain, compact, covenant, bond, concordat, entente, protocol.

pad *noun* **1** *a pad to prevent friction* padding, wadding, wad, stuffing, buffer. **2** *a pad to rest one's head on* cushion, pillow, bolster. **3** *a pad to absorb the blood* gauze pad, piece/wad of cotton wool, dressing, compress. **4** *write one's notes in a pad* note-pad, writing-pad, notebook, jotter; *inf.* memo-pad. **5** *the animal's injured pad* paw, foot, sole.

pad *verb* *pad the package with tissue paper/cotton wool* pack, stuff, line, cushion, protect. **pad out** *pad out a few facts with a lot of detail* fill out, expand, augment, amplify, increase, add to, stretch out, eke out, flesh out, lengthen, spin out, protract, elaborate.

padding *noun* **1** *use padding to prevent the china being damaged* packing, stuffing, filling, filler, wadding, cushioning, lining, wrapping. **2** *an essay with few facts and too much padding* filling-out, wordiness, verbiage, verbosity, verboseness, prolixity, prolixness; *inf.* waffle, hot air.

paddle¹ *noun* *use the paddles to row ashore* oar, scull, sweep.

paddle² *verb* *paddle one's way to the shore* row, pull, oar, scull, pole, punt.

paddle³ *verb* **1** *paddle one's hands/feet in cold water* dabble, splash, plunge, plash. **2** *children paddling at the seaside* wade, splash about.

paddock *noun* *horses grazing in the paddock* field, meadow, enclosure, yard, pen, pound, corral.

padlock *noun* *renew the padlock on the gate* lock, catch, latch, fastening, fastener.

padre · painter

padre noun soldiers asking the padre for advice minister, priest, parson, vicar, pastor, rector, reverend, chaplain, clergyman, cleric, man of God, man of the cloth.

paean noun **1** paeans to God song of praise, praise, hymn, psalm, anthem, exaltation, glorification, magnification. **2** the retiring chairman had received paeans from the board-members | films receiving paeans of praise praise, eulogy, encomium, panegyric, compliment, bouquet.

pagan noun missionaries trying to convert pagans unbeliever, non-believer, disbeliever, heathen, infidel, idolater, pantheist, atheist, polytheist.

pagan adjective missionaries trying to cope with pagan beliefs paganistic, paganish, heathen, heathenish, heathenistic, infidel, idolatrous, pantheistic, atheistic, polytheistic.
Opposites RELIGIOUS; GODLY.

page¹ noun **1** a report 20 pages long sheet, side, leaf, folio, recto, verso. **2** his bravery will be recorded in the pages of history report, account, anecdote, book, volume, writing. **3** one of the glorious pages of British history | a glorious page in this distinguished writer's life chapter, event, episode, incident, time, period, stage, phase, epoch, era, point.

page² verb page the report/book number, give a number to, paginate, foliate.

page³ noun **1** employed by the hotel as a page page-boy, messenger-boy; Am. bellboy, bellhop; inf. buttons. **2** the king's pages page-boy, servant boy, serving boy, attendant, train-bearer, squire.

page⁴ verb page a hotel guest call, ask for, summon, send for.

pageant noun a pageant was part of the centenary festival display, spectacle, extravaganza, show, parade, scene, representation, tableau, tableau vivant.

pageantry noun all the pageantry of a coronation pageant, display, spectacle, magnificence, pomp, splendour, grandeur, glamour, flourish, glitter, theatricality, show, showiness; inf. pizazz.

pain noun **1** a pain in her leg soreness, hurt, ache, aching, throb, throbbing, smarting, twinge, pang, spasm, cramp, discomfort, irritation, tenderness. **2** invalids enduring pain all their lives suffering, physical suffering, agony, affliction, torture, torment. **3** the pain of losing a loved one suffering, mental suffering, emotional suffering, hurt, sorrow, grief, heartache, broken-heartedness, sadness, unhappiness, distress, misery, wretchedness, anguish, affliction, woe, agony, torment, torture. **4** that child is a pain nuisance, pest, bother, vexation, source of irritation, worry, source of aggravation; inf. pain in the neck, drag. See PAINS.

pain verb **1** her foot is still paining cause pain, be painful, hurt, be sore, ache, throb, smart, twinge, cause discomfort, be tender. **2** the memory of the event still pains her hurt, grieve, sadden, distress, make miserable/wretched, cause anguish to, afflict, torment, torture. **3** it pained her to tell him to go worry, distress, trouble, hurt, vex, embarrass.

pained adjective wear a pained expression hurt, aggrieved, reproachful, offended, insulted, vexed, piqued, upset, unhappy, distressed, wounded; inf. miffed.

painful adjective **1** a painful arm sore, hurting, aching, throbbing, smarting, cramped, tender, inflamed, irritating, agonizing, excruciating. **2** endure a painful experience disagreeable, unpleasant, nasty, distressing, disquieting, disturbing, miserable, wretched, agonizing, harrowing. **3** a painful climb arduous, laborious, strenuous, rigorous, demanding, exacting, trying, hard, tough, difficult. **4** it was painful to watch him work so slowly irksome, tedious, annoying, vexatious.
Opposites PAINLESS; PLEASANT; AGREEABLE.

painfully adverb **1** a leg that is painfully swollen achingly, agonizingly, excruciatingly. **2** become painfully thin distressingly, alarmingly, worryingly, excessively; inf. terribly, dreadfully. **3** it was painfully obvious that he was incompetent embarrassingly, uncomfortably, disconcertingly, markedly, woefully.

painkiller noun take painkillers for headaches analgesic, anodyne, palliative, lenitive.

painless adjective **1** a painless medical procedure pain-free, without pain. **2** getting rid of him proved painless easy, simple, trouble-free, effortless, plain sailing; inf. as easy as pie, as easy as falling off a log, as easy as ABC, a piece of cake, child's play, a cinch.

pains plural noun childbirth pains contractions, labour, birth-pangs. **be at pains** they were at pains to put him at ease try hard, make every effort, take care, put oneself out.

painstaking adjective **1** a painstaking investigation careful, thorough, assiduous, conscientious, meticulous, punctilious, sedulous, scrupulous, searching. **2** a painstaking student careful, thorough, assiduous, attentive, diligent, industrious, hard-working, conscientious, meticulous, punctilious, sedulous, scrupulous, persevering, pertinacious.
Opposites CARELESS; NEGLIGENT; SLAPDASH.

paint noun **1** buy paint for the walls colouring, colourant, tint, dye, stain, pigment, emulsion, emulsion paint, gloss, gloss paint, distemper, wash, whitewash. **2** the paint required for his picture colourant, tint, pigment, water-colour, oil, oil-paint, oil-colour. **3** apply paint to her face make-up, cosmetic, greasepaint, maquillage; inf. warpaint.

paint verb **1** paint the walls apply paint to, decorate, colour, tint, dye, stain, distemper, whitewash. **2** paint slogans on the walls daub, smear, plaster, spray-paint. **3** paint his mother | painted the scene from her window portray, depict, delineate, draw, sketch, represent, catch a likeness of. **4** paint a story of great happiness/misery tell, recount, narrate, unfold, describe, depict, portray, evoke, conjure up. **paint the town red** paint the town red at the end of the exams celebrate; inf. go out on the town, whoop it up, make whoopee, have a night on the tiles; Am. step out.

painter noun. See table at ARTIST.

painting noun picture, illustration, portrayal, depiction, delineation, representation, likeness, drawing, sketch, portrait, oil-painting, water-colour; *inf.* oil. *See table.*

TYPES OF PAINTING	
action painting	landscape
animal painting	narrative painting
annunciation	nativity
architectural	nocturne
painting	nude
battle scene	panorama
cloudscape	pastoral
commemorative	pietà
painting	portrait
crucifixion	riverscape
equestrian painting	seascape
exterior	skyscape
historical painting	still life
interior	townscape

pair noun **1** *the pair walked down the road* twosome, two, two people, couple, duo. **2** *a pair of pheasants* brace, two, couple. **3** *a pair of gloves* matched set, matching set. **4** *a coach and pair* team, yoke, span, two horses. **5** *the happy pair after their wedding* married couple, couple, man and wife, husband and wife, partners, lovers.

pair verb **pair off** *pair off the children for games* arrange/group in pairs, pair up, put together. **pair up** *we paired up to go on holiday | if you pair up to do the work* get together, join up, link up, team up, unite, form a partnership.

pal noun *they're best pals* friend, mate, companion, crony, comrade; *inf.* chum, buddy.

palace noun *the king's summer palace* royal residence, castle, château. *See table at* BUILDING.

palatable adjective **1** *chefs providing palatable dishes* tasty, appetizing, pleasant-tasting, flavourful, flavoursome, delicious, delectable, mouth-watering, savoury, luscious, toothsome; *inf.* scrumptious, yummy, moreish. **2** *unlikely to find the truth palatable* agreeable, pleasant, pleasing, pleasurable, nice, attractive, acceptable, satisfactory.
Opposites UNPALATABLE; TASTELESS; INSIPID; UNPLEASANT.

palate noun **1** *a sore palate* roof of the mouth, hard palate, soft palate. **2** *have no palate for food after witnessing the accident* appetite, stomach, **3** *have a good palate | dry wines that suit her palate* sense of taste, taste, taste buds. **4** *have no palate for that style of prose* taste, liking, appreciation, enjoyment, relish, enthusiasm.

palatial adjective *palatial residences* luxurious, de luxe, imposing, splendid, grand, magnificent, stately, majestic, opulent, sumptuous, plush; *inf.* plushy, posh.
Opposites HUMBLE; MODEST; CRAMPED.

palaver noun **1** *always a lot of palaver when guests come to stay* fuss, fuss and bother, commotion, fluster, flurry, agitation, stir. **2** *a palaver in the boardroom* conference, discussion,

meeting, talks, colloquy; *inf.* confab, pow-wow, gassing.

pale adjective **1** *a pale complexion | pale with fear* white, whitish, white-faced, colourless, anaemic, wan, drained, pallid, pasty, peaky, ashen, ashy, waxen, green, as white as a sheet/ ghost, deathly pale. **2** *pale colours/shades* light, light-coloured, pastel, muted, low-key, restrained, faded, bleached, whitish, washedout, etoliated. **3** *the pale light of dawn* dim, faint, weak, feeble, thin.
Opposites FLUSHED; DARK; BRIGHT.

pale verb **1** *she paled at the gruesome sight* grow pale, become pale, go/turn white, blanch, lose colour. **2** *other problems paled beside their financial difficulties* pale into insignificance, fade, dim, diminish, lessen, decrease in importance, lose significance.

pale noun **beyond the pale** *his behaviour at the party was considered beyond the pale* unacceptable, unseemly, improper, indiscreet, unsuitable, irregular, unreasonable, out-of-line.

pall verb *the pleasures of sunbathing began to pall* lost its/their etc. interest, lose attraction, cloy, become tedious, become boring, grow tedious, grow tiresome.

pall noun **1** *the pall over the coffin* funeral cloth, coffin covering. **2** *a pall of smoke/darkness* dark covering, shroud, mantle, cloak. **3** *the news cast a pall over the gathering* cloud, shadow, gloom, depression, melancholy, sombreness, gravity.

palliate verb **1** *palliate the pain* relieve, ease, soothe, alleviate, mitigate, assuage, abate, allay, dull, take the edge off, blunt. **2** *palliate an offence* extenuate, minimize, make light of, tone down, play down, downplay, make allowances for, excuse, whitewash.

pallid adjective **1** *pallid faces | invalids looking pallid* pale, white, whitish, white-faced, colourless, anaemic, wan, drained, pasty, peaky, ashen, ashy, waxen, sickly, ghostly, ghastly, lurid, green, as white as a sheet/ghost, deathly pale, like death; *inf.* like death warmed up. **2** *a pallid performance* colourless, uninteresting, dull, boring, tedious, unimaginative, lifeless, uninspired, spiritless, bloodless, bland, vapid.
Opposites FLUSHED; VIVID.

pallor noun *the pallor of the invalid* paleness, whiteness, colourlessness, wanness, pallidness, pastiness, peakiness, ashenness, sickliness, ghastliness, luridness.

palm¹ verb **palm off** *palm off a broken-down car on him* foist, fob, pass off, offload, thrust, get rid of; *inf.* unload. **grease someone's palm** bribe, buy off, give money to, corrupt, suborn; *inf.* give a backhander to, give a sweetener to, square. **have in the palm of one's hand** have control over, have power over, have at one's mercy, have in one's clutches.

palm² noun *win the palm* victory, triumph, success, honour, glory, fame, prize, trophy, award, crown, wealth, laurels, bays.

palmist noun *get my future told by a palmist* palm-reader, fortune-teller, clairvoyant.

palmy *adjective in the palmy days of the firm* prosperous, thriving, flourishing, golden, glorious, happy, halcyon.

palpable *adjective* **1** *a palpable swelling* tangible, feelable, touchable, solid, concrete. **2** *a palpable error* obvious, apparent, clear, plain, evident, manifest, visible, conspicuous, patent, blatant, glaring, definite, unmistakable. **Opposites** INTANGIBLE; UNOBTRUSIVE.

palpitate *verb* **1** *with her heart palpitating* beat rapidly, pulsate, pulse, throb, flutter, quiver, vibrate, pound, thud, thump, pump. **2** *she was palpitating with fear* tremble, quiver, quake, quaver, shake.

paltry *adjective* **1** *a paltry sum of money* small, meagre, trifling, minor, insignificant, trivial, derisory; *inf.* piddling. **2** *a paltry excuse/trick* mean, low, base, worthless, despicable, contemptible, miserable, wretched, sorry, puny. **Opposites** CONSIDERABLE; SUBSTANTIAL; IMPRESSIVE.

pamper *verb pamper oneself | does pamper her husband* spoil, cosset, indulge, overindulge, humour, coddle, mollycoddle, baby, wait on someone hand and foot, cater to someone's every whim, feather-bed.

pamphlet *noun a pamphlet giving advice on Aids* leaflet, booklet, brochure, circular.

pan¹ *noun* **1** *pans simmering on the stove* saucepan, pot, frying-pan, preserving pan, fish-kettle, pressure-cooker, casserole, wok; *Am.* skillet. **2** *bedpan/dustpan* container, vessel, receptacle. **3** *salt-pans* depression, dip, indentation, hollow, crater, cavity.

pan² *verb* **1** *pan for gold* search for, look for, sift for. **2** *critics panning the play* criticize, censure, find fault with, flay, roast, take to pieces; *inf.* slate, slam, knock, rubbish. **pan out** *see how things pan out* work out, turn out, come out, fall out.

pan³ *verb cameras panning the strikers' march* scan, sweep, follow, track, traverse.

panacea *noun a panacea for the economic ills* cure-all, cure for all ills, universal cure, universal remedy, elixir, nostrum.

panache *noun open the village fête with panache | dress with panache* dash, flourish, flamboyance, élan, style, verve, zest, brio, éclat; *inf.* pizazz.

pancake *noun* crêpe, drop scone, blini, tortilla.

pandemic *adjective diseases pandemic in the African continent* widespread, universal, global, extensive, prevalent, wholesale, rife, rampant.

pandemonium *noun pandemonium reigned when the pop concert was cancelled* uproar, tumult, turmoil, commotion, clamour, din, hullaballoo, hubbub, hue and cry, chaos, confusion, disorder, bedlam. **Opposites** SILENCE; PEACE.

pander *verb pander to her every whim | pander to the taste of the majority* give in to, gratify, indulge, humour, please, satisfy, cater for.

panegyric *noun* **1** *a panegyric on the hero's achievements* eulogy, paean, encomium, extolment, laudation, accolade, testimonial, tribute, exaltation, glorification. **2** *a talk full of panegyric* eulogy, praise, adulation, acclamation,

extolment, laudation, exaltation, glorification. **Opposites** CRITICISM; CENSURE.

pang *noun* **1** *hunger pang* pain, sharp pain, shooting pain, twinge, spasm, ache. **2** *feel a pang of remorse* twinge, qualm, misgiving, scruple, regret, feeling of uneasiness.

panic *noun feel panic at the sight of the smoke* alarm, fright, fear, terror, horror, trepidation, nervousness, agitation, hysteria, perturbation, dismay, disquiet.

panic *verb* **1** *panic at the sight of the smoke* be alarmed, take fright, be filled with fear, be scared, be terrified/horrified, be nervous, be agitated, be hysterical, lose one's nerve, overreact, be perturbed, be filled with dismay, go to pieces; *inf.* lose one's cool, get the jitters, get into a tizzy/tiz-woz, get the wind up, run around like a headless chicken. **2** *be panicked into jumping from the window* alarm, frighten, scare, terrify, petrify, startle, agitate, unnerve; *inf.* put the wind up someone.

panic-stricken *adjective* panicky, alarmed, frightened, scared, terrified, terror-stricken, petrified, horror-stricken, horrified, aghast, nervous, agitated, hysterical, perturbed, dismayed, disquietened; *inf.* in a tizzy, in a tiz-woz.

panoply *noun the full panoply of a royal wedding* array, trappings, display, show, splendour.

panorama *noun* **1** *the panorama from the top of the tower* wide view, aerial view, bird's-eye view, view, vista, spectacle. **2** *present a panorama of the political events of the decade* survey, overview, perspective, appraisal.

panoramic *adjective* **1** *a panoramic view from the tower* wide, extensive, sweeping, bird's-eye. **2** *a panoramic presentation of the events of the decade* wide, wide-ranging, extensive, comprehensive.

pant *verb* **1** *panting after climbing the hill* breathe heavily, puff, huff and puff, blow, gasp, wheeze. **2** *panting for a drink | she was panting for some new clothes* long for, yearn for, crave, pine for, ache for, hunger for, thirst for, lust after, burn for, sigh for; *inf.* have a yen for. **3** *with his heart panting* throb, palpitate, pulsate, pulse, pound, thump, beat rapidly.

pant *noun disturbed by the pants from the dog* puff, gasp, wheeze.

pantry *noun pies stolen from the pantry* larder, cold-room, still-room, buttery, storeroom.

pants *plural noun* **1** *he wears brightly-patterned pants* underpants, briefs, boxer shorts, Y-fronts. **2** *she wears frilly pants* knickers, briefs, panties; *Am.* underpants. **3** *wear old pants for gardening* trousers, slacks, jeans; *inf.* strides.

pap *noun* **1** *prepare pap for the baby/invalid* baby food, soft food, mush, pulp; *inf.* goo. **2** *prefer pap to serious novels* trivia, drivel, rubbish, trash, pulp.

paper *noun* **1** *go for the morning paper* newspaper, magazine, journal, gazette, broadsheet, tabloid, scandal sheet, daily, weekly; *inf.* rag. **2** *lose the papers relating to the house ownership* legal paper, document, certificate, record, deeds, instrument, assignment. **3** *write a* *paper on child development* essay, article, work, dissertation, treatise, thesis, monograph, study, report, analysis. **4** *put striped paper on the bedroom walls* wallpaper, wall-covering, anaglypta, lining paper. **5** *use a larger sheet of paper* writing paper. *See table.* **on paper 1** *put your objections on paper* in writing, written down, in black and white. **2** *on paper the scheme looked fine but in practice it was a disaster* in theory, theoretically, hypothetically, in the abstract.

PAPER SIZES			
A Series			
A0	1149	×	841 mm
A1	841	×	594 mm
A2	594	×	420 mm
A3	420	×	297 mm
A4	297	×	210 mm
A5	210	×	148 mm
A6	148	×	105 mm
A7	105	×	74 mm
A8	74	×	52 mm
A9	52	×	37 mm
A10	37	×	26 mm
B Series			
B0	1414	×	1000 mm
B1	1000	×	707 mm
B2	707	×	500 mm
B3	500	×	353 mm
B4	353	×	250 mm
B5	250	×	176 mm
B6	176	×	125 mm
B7	125	×	88 mm
B8	88	×	62 mm
B9	62	×	44 mm
B10	44	×	31 mm
C Series			
C4	324	×	229 mm
C5	229	×	162 mm
C6	162	×	114 mm
Imperial			
foolscap	17	× 13½ inches	(330 × 200 mm)
crown	20	× 15 inches	(504 × 384 mm)
demy	22½	× 17½ inches	(564 × 444 mm)
royal	25	× 20 inches	(620 × 500 mm)
elephant	28	× 23 inches	(711 × 584 mm)
imperial	30	× 22 inches	(762 × 559 mm)

paper *verb paper the walls* wallpaper, line, hang wallpaper on, decorate. **paper over** *paper over the firm's difficulties* hide, conceal, draw a veil over, disguise, camouflage, cover up, gloss over, whitewash.

papers *plural noun* **1** *sign the adoption papers* legal paper, document, certificate. *See* PAPER *noun* 2. **2** *escape using forged papers* identification papers, identification documents, identity card, ID. **3** *go through her papers after her death* personal papers, personal documents, letters, records, files.

papery *adjective papery clothes/walls* paper-thin, ultra-thin, flimsy, insubstantial, fragile, frail.

par *noun up to par* average, mean, standard, normal, norm. **below par 1** *work that is below par* below average, substandard, inferior, lack-

ing, wanting, second-rate, poor; *inf.* not up to scratch, not up to snuff. **2** *feeling below par since having flu* slightly unwell/unhealthy, unfit, off colour, poorly, indisposed, out of sorts; *inf.* not oneself, under the weather. **on a par with** *modern novels which are on a par with those of the great classical writers* equal to, a match for, on a level with, on an equal footing with, of the same standard as, as good as. **par for the course** *his behaviour does not surprise me - it's par for the course* usual, normal, standard, typical, predictable, what one would expect. **up to par** *work no longer up to par* up to the mark, satisfactory, acceptable, good enough, adequate, passable; *inf.* up to scratch, up to snuff.

parable *noun the parable of/about the prodigal son* allegory, moral story, moral tale, story with a moral, fable.

parade *noun* **1** *watch the parade of the soldiers| parade of children in fancy dress* march, procession, progression, cavalcade, spectacle, pageant, array. **2** *make a parade of their wealth* display, exhibition, show, spectacle, flaunting, ostentation, demonstration; *inf.* showing-off.

parade *verb* **1** *soldiers/children parading during the centenary celebrations* march, process, go in columns, file by. **2** *parade their wealth/knowledge* display, exhibit, show, demonstrate, air, make a show of, flaunt; *inf.* show off. **3** *parade up and down in her new hat* strut, swagger; *inf.* swank.

paradigm *noun a paradigm for others to copy* example, pattern, model, standard, gauge, criterion, archetype, prototype, paragon, exemplar.

paradise *noun* **1** *believe in paradise after death* heaven, heavenly kingdom, kingdom of heaven, abode of the saints, Elysium, the Elysian Fields. **2** *Adam and Eve in paradise* the Garden of Eden, Eden. **3** *think the holiday island a paradise* Eden, fairyland, utopia, Shangri-La. **4** *thinking it was paradise in her arms* heaven, bliss, ecstasy, supreme joy, seventh heaven.
Opposites HELL.

paradox *noun a paradox that there is so much poverty in such a rich country* contradiction, self-contradiction, inconsistency, incongruity, anomaly, enigma, puzzle, absurdity, oxymoron.

paradoxical *adjective it is paradoxical that there is so much poverty in such a rich country* contradictory, self-contradictory, inconsistent, incongruous, anomalous, enigmatic, puzzling, absurd.

paragon *noun a paragon of good behaviour* perfect example, good example, ideal, model, pattern, exemplar, nonpareil, paradigm, standard, criterion, archetype, prototype, quintessence, epitome, apotheosis, acme, jewel, flower.

paragraph *noun* **1** *the essay should be divided into paragraphs* section, subdivision, segment. **2** *a paragraph in the local paper about the death* article, item, piece, notice, note.

parallel *adjective* **1** *parallel lines* side by side, equidistant, collateral. **2** *the judge considering a parallel case| cases parallel to each other* similar, like, resembling, analogous, comparable,

parallel equivalent, corresponding, matching, duplicate. **3** *parallel processes* concurrent, coexistent, coexisting.
Opposites DIFFERENT; DIVERGENT.

parallel noun **1** *find a parallel for the case* analogue, counterpart, equivalent, correspondent, match, duplicate, equal. **2** *draw a parallel between the two cases* similarity, likeness, resemblance, analogy, correspondence, comparison, equivalence, symmetry.

parallel verb **1** *the case parallels the murder of her neighbour* be similar to, be like, resemble, bear a resemblance to, be analogous to, be an analogy with, correspond to, compare with, be comparable/equivalent to. **2** *his account of the incident parallels the policeman's* match, correspond to, agree with, be in harmony with, conform to. **3** *his rowing feat has never been paralleled* match, equal, rival, emulate.

paralyse verb **1** *paralysed legs* immobilize, render/make powerless, numb, deaden, dull, obtund, incapacitate, debilitate, disable, cripple. **2** *he was paralysed in the accident* immobilize, incapacitate, debilitate, disable, cripple. **3** *paralyse the transport system* immobilize, bring to a halt, bring to a complete stop, bring to a grinding halt, bring to a standstill, freeze, put out of order/commission. **4** *paralysed with fear at the sight* immobilize, render motionless, freeze, unnerve, terrify, shock, stun, stagger.

paralysis noun **1** *suffer from paralysis of the legs* immobility, powerlessness, lack of feeling, numbness, palsy, incapacity, debilitation; *Med.* paresis. **2** *lead to paralysis of the rail network* immobilization, breakdown, shut-down, stopping, stoppage, halt, standstill.

paralytic adjective **1** *paralytic limbs* immobile, immobilized, powerless, numb, dead, palsied, incapacitated, debilitated, disabled, crippled. **2** *completely paralytic after the party* drunk, inebriated, intoxicated; *inf.* legless, sloshed, smashed, stoned, plastered, pie-eyed, steaming, stewed.

parameter noun *within the parameters of the budget* limit, limitation, limiting factor, restriction, constant, specification, guidelines, framework.

paramount adjective *financial considerations are paramount* most important, of greatest importance, of prime importance, of supreme importance, of greatest significance, uppermost, supreme, predominant, foremost, first and foremost, pre-eminent, outstanding.

paramour noun **1** *his wife found out about his paramour* mistress, lover, girlfriend, kept woman, inamorata; *inf.* fancy woman, bit on the side. **2** *preferring her paramour to her husband* lover, boyfriend, inamorato; *inf.* fancy man, toy boy, bit on the side.

paranoid adjective *paranoid about what everyone was saying about her* suspicious, mistrustful, distrustful, fearful, insecure.

parapet noun **1** *the parapet of a balcony* wall, railing, handrail, fence, barrier. **2** *soldiers sheltering behind the parapet* fortification, barricade, rampart, bulwark, bank, embankment.

paraphernalia plural noun **1** *all the artist's paraphernalia* equipment, gear, stuff, apparatus, implements, tools, materials, accoutrements, trappings, appurtenances, appointments. **2** *loaded with her suitcase and all her paraphernalia* baggage, bags and baggage, luggage, personal belongings, belongings, possessions, things, impedimenta; *inf.* clobber.

paraphrase verb *paraphrase the complicated instructions* reword, put in other words, rephrase, restate, rehash, interpret, gloss.

paraphrase noun *a simple paraphrase of the instructions* rewording, rephrasing, restatement, restating, rehash, interpretation, gloss.

parasite noun *a parasite on society | a parasite totally dependent on others* hanger-on, sponger, cadger, leech, bloodsucker, passenger, drone; *inf.* scrounger, freeloader.

parcel noun **1** *tie the parcel with string* package, packet, pack, bundle. **2** *a parcel of land* plot, tract, piece, lot, patch. **3** *a parcel of thieves* band, pack, gang, group, company, collection, crowd, mob, troop; *inf.* crew, bunch. **4** *a parcel of lies* pack, great deal, collection, assortment, mass, assemblage, bunch; *inf.* heap, load.

parcel verb *parcel up the goods* pack, pack up, package, wrap, wrap up, gift-wrap, tie up, do up, box, bundle up. **parcel out** *parcel out the food to the needy* distribute, divide out, share out, hand out, deal out, dole out, dispense, allocate, allot, portion out, apportion, mete out, carve up; *inf.* divvy up.

parched adjective **1** *parched ground/grass* dried up, dried out, dry, baked, burned, scorched, seared, desiccated, dehydrated, withered, shrivelled. **2** *parched from walking in the heat* thirsty, dehydrated; *inf.* dry.
Opposites WET; SOAKING.

pardon noun **1** *seek their pardon* forgiveness, forbearance, indulgence, condonation, clemency, lenience, leniency, mercy. **2** *the accused received a pardon* free pardon, reprieve, release, acquittal, absolution, amnesty, exoneration, exculpation.

pardon verb **1** *begged her to pardon him | pardon me | could never pardon such an offence* forgive, excuse, condone, let off. **2** *the accused man was pardoned* reprieve, release, acquit, absolve, exonerate, exculpate.
Opposites BLAME; PUNISH.

pardonable adjective *a pardonable error* forgivable, excusable, allowable, condonable, understandable, minor, slight, venial.

parent noun **1** *resemble one of his parents* mother/father; *inf.* old man/old woman, old lady. **2** *the parent of all his misfortune* source, root, origin, originator, well-spring, fountain, cause, author, architect.

parent verb *parent three sons* be the parent of, bring into the world, produce, procreate, look after, rear, bring up, raise.

parentage noun *a successful man of humble parentage* family, birth, origins, extraction, ancestry, lineage, descent, heritage, pedigree.

pariah noun *a social pariah* outcast, leper, persona non grata, untouchable, undesirable.

parish noun **1** *local administrators of the parish* community, district, commune, canton. **2** *the parish choosing a new minister* parishioners, churchgoers, congregation, flock, fold.

parity noun *workers having parity of status/salary* equality, levelness, identity, sameness, unity, uniformity, evenness, equivalence, parallelism, correspondence.

park noun **1** *children playing in the park* public park, public garden, recreation ground, playground, play area. **2** *park surrounding the mansion-house* parkland, grassland, lawns, grounds. **3** *few players left on the park* field, playing-field, stadium, arena.

park verb **1** *park the car on a yellow line* stop, pull up, leave, station. **2** *park the baby in his pram* put, place, set, seat, leave, plonk.

parlance noun *fail to understand the parlance of the young* speech, language, talk, vocabulary, phraseology, idiom, vernacular, jargon, patter, argot, patois; *inf.* lingo.

parliament noun *the parliaments of different countries* legislative assembly, lawmaking body, congress, senate, chamber, house, convocation, diet. *See table at* GOVERNMENT.

Parliament noun *the Queen recalling Parliament* the Houses of Parliament, the House of Commons/Lords, the Commons, the Lords, the House, the Lower/Upper House, Westminster.

parliamentary adjective **1** *parliamentary assemblies* legislative, legislatorial, lawmaking, lawgiving, governmental, congressional, senatorial, democratic, representative. **2** *parliamentary behaviour/language* orderly, proper, seemly, by the rules, according to the rule book.

parlour noun **1** *have tea in the parlour* sitting-room, front-room, best room, drawing-room, lounge. **2** *a beauty parlour* salon, shop, establishment, store.

parochial adjective *a parochial attitude to life* provincial, small-town, parish-pump, insular, inward-looking, narrow, narrow-minded, petty, small-minded, limited, restricted. *Opposites* COSMOPOLITAN; LIBERAL.

parody noun **1** *a parody of a gothic novel* burlesque, lampoon, satire, pastiche, caricature, mimicry, take-off; *inf.* spoof, send-up. **2** *trial was a parody of justice* travesty, poor imitation, misrepresentation, perversion, corruption.

parody verb *parody an operatic aria* burlesque, lampoon, satirize, caricature, mimic, take off; *inf.* send up.

paroxysm noun *a paroxysm of coughing/rage* fit, attack, convulsion, spasm, seizure, outburst, outbreak, eruption.

parrot verb *children parroting the teacher's words* repeat, echo, copy, imitate, mimic, ape, take off.

parry verb **1** *parry a blow* ward off, fend off, stave off, turn aside, avert, deflect, block, rebuff, repel, repulse, hold at bay. **2** *parry awkward questions* avoid, dodge, evade, elude, steer clear of, sidestep, circumvent, fight shy of; *inf.* duck.

parsimonious adjective mean, miserly, niggardly, tight-fisted, close-fisted, close, near, grasping, money-grubbing, Scrooge-like, scrimping, skimping, penny-pinching, cheese-paring, penurious, ungenerous; *inf.* stingy, tight, mingy. *Opposites* EXTRAVAGANT; GENEROUS; LAVISH.

parsimony noun meanness, miserliness, niggardliness, closeness, tight-fistedness, close-fistedness; *inf.* stinginess, tightness. *See* PARSIMONIOUS.

parson noun priest, reverend, clergyman, cleric, chaplain, churchman, man of the cloth, man of God, preacher, divine. *See table at* ECCLESIASTIC.

part noun **1** *the early part of her life | part of an orange* portion, division, section, segment, bit, piece, fragment, scrap, slice, fraction, chunk, wedge. **2** *spare parts* component, bit, constituent, element, module. **3** *body parts | parts of the body* organ, member, limb. **4** *an unknown part of the country* section, area, region, sector, quarter, territory, neighbourhood. **5** *a book/play in several parts* volume, book, section, episode. **6** *his part in the project* function, role, job, task, work, chore, responsibility, capacity, participation, duty, charge. **7** *play the part of Hamlet* role, character. **8** *learn his part* lines, words. **9** *a man of many parts* talent, gift, ability, capability, capacity, skill, attribute. **for the most part** *for the most part they are reliable* on the whole, in the main, by and large, all in all, generally, to all intents and purposes, mostly. **in good part** *take the teasing in good part* good-naturedly, good-humouredly, without offence, cheerfully, well. **in part** *success due in part to good luck* partly, partially, to a certain extent/degree, to some extent/degree, somewhat, in some measure. **on the part of** *an error on the part of the headmaster | on his part* made by, done by, carried out by, caused by, by. **take part in** *take part in the protest* participate in, join in, engage in, play a part in, contribute to, be associated with, associate oneself with, be involved in, share in, have a hand in, have something to do with, partake in. **take someone's part, take the part of** *take his mother's part in the quarrel | take the part of weaker candidates* take the side of, side with, support, back, back up, abet, aid and abet. *Opposites* WHOLE; ENTIRETY.

part verb **1** *the crowd parted to let the police through* divide, divide in two, separate, split, split in two, break up, sever, disjoin. **2** *the police parting the crowd* divide, separate, split up, break up, sever, cleave. **3** *couples deciding to part* separate, seek/get a separation, split up, break up, part company, go their etc. separate ways, divorce, get divorced, seek/get a divorce. **4** *exchange kisses before parting* take one's departure, take one's leave, leave, go, go away, say goodbye/farewell/adieu, say one's goodbyes, separate; *inf.* split, push off, hit the road. **part with** *part with her last few pounds* give up, relinquish, forgo, surrender, let go of, renounce, sacrifice, yield, cede. *Opposites* GATHER; JOIN; MARRY; ARRIVE.

part · partly

part *adjective* **1** *in part payment* partial, half. **2** *a part-conversion of the building* partial, half, semi-, demi-.

partake *verb* **1** *partake in the protest* take part in, participate in, join in, engage in, play a part in, contribute to, be associated with, associate oneself with, be involved in, share in, have a hand in, have something to do with. **2** *partake of Christmas cheer* consume, eat, take, receive, drink, share in. **3** *their manner partook of insolence* suggest, have the qualities/attributes of, hint at, evidence, demonstrate, exhibit, show.

partial *adjective* **1** *a partial solution/eclipse* part, in part, limited, incomplete, imperfect, fragmentary. **2** *a partial judgement/judge* biased, prejudiced, partisan, coloured, one-sided, discriminatory, preferential, interested, unjust, unfair, inequitable. **be partial to** *be partial to dark chocolate | always been partial to holidays in the sun* have a liking for, like, love, have a fondness for, be fond of, be keen on, have a weakness/taste for, have a soft spot for, be taken with, care for, have a predilection/proclivity/penchant for.
Opposites COMPLETE; WHOLE; UNBIASED; IMPARTIAL.

partiality *noun* **1** *condemn the partiality of the judge* bias, prejudice, partisanship, discrimination, preference, favouritism, unjustness, unfairness, inequity. **2** *their partiality for chocolate | has always had a partiality for holidays in the sun* liking, love, fondness, keenness, taste, weakness, soft spot, inclination, predilection, proclivity, penchant.

partially *adverb* *partially paralysed* partly, in part, not wholly, not fully, half, somewhat, to a certain extent/degree, to some extent/degree, in some measure, fractionally, slightly.

participant *noun* *participants in the protest/concert* participator, member, contributor, associate, sharer, partaker.

participate *verb* *participate in the protest* take part in, join in, engage in, play a part in, contribute to, be associated with, associate oneself with, be involved in, share in, have a hand in, have something to do with, partake in.

participation *noun* *their participation in the protest/concert* part, contribution, association, involvement, partaking. *See* PARTICIPATE.

particle *noun* **1** *particles of dust* tiny bit, tiny piece, speck, spot, atom, molecule. *See table.* **2** *not a particle of common sense* iota, jot, whit, grain, bit, scrap, shred, morsel, mite, atom, hint, touch, trace, suggestion, tittle.

SUBATOMIC PARTICLES

anti-	gluon	neutron
electron	hadron	nucleon
antineutron	kaon	photon
antiproton	lambda	pion
antiquark	particle	positron
baryon	lepton	proton
boson	meson	psi particle
electron	muon	quark
fermion	neutrino	tau particle

particular *adjective* **1** *in this particular case* specific, individual, single, distinct, precise. **2** *take particular care | a matter of particular importance* special, especial, singular, peculiar, exceptional, unusual, uncommon, notable, noteworthy, remarkable, outstanding. **3** *particular about hygiene | he is so particular about what he eats* fastidious, discriminating, selective, fussy, painstaking, meticulous, punctilious, nice, exacting, demanding, critical, over-particular, over-fastidious, finicky; *inf.* pernickety, choosy, picky. **4** *require a particular account of the incident* detailed, exact, precise, faithful, close, thorough, blow-by-blow, itemized, circumstantial, painstaking, meticulous, punctilious, minute.
Opposites GENERAL; ORDINARY; CARELESS.

particular *noun* **in particular** **1** *have someone in particular* in mind specific, special, distinct, precise. **2** *the desserts in particular were delicious* particularly, specifically, especially, specially.

particularize *verb* *particularize your reasons for leaving* specify, be specific about, detail, itemize, list, enumerate, spell out, cite.

particularly *adverb* **1** *a film that is particularly good* especially, specially, singularly, peculiarly, distinctly, markedly, exceptionally, unusually, uncommonly, notably, remarkably, outstandingly, surprisingly. **2** *ask for him particularly* in particular, specifically, explicitly, expressly, specially, especially.

parting *noun* **1** *the parting of the crowd* division, dividing, separation, separating, splitting, breaking up, severance, disjoining, detachment, partition. **2** *sad at the parting of his parents* separation, splitting up, breakup, breaking up, divorce, split, rift, rupture. **3** *partings taking place at the railway station* departure, leave-taking, goodbye, farewell, adieu, valediction.

parting *adjective* *a parting handshake* departing, leaving, goodbye, farewell, valedictory, last, final.

partisan *noun* **1** *a partisan of the breakaway party* supporter, adherent, devotee, backer, champion, upholder, follower, disciple, fan, votary. **2** *partisans fighting against the ruling power* guerrilla, resistance fighter, underground fighter.

partisan *adjective* *a partisan attitude to the legal dispute* biased, prejudiced, coloured, one-sided, discriminatory, preferential, partial, interested, unjust, unfair, inequitable.
Opposites IMPARTIAL; UNBIASED.

partition *noun* **1** *the partition of India* division, dividing, subdivision, separation, segregation, splitting-up, breaking-up, break-up, severance. **2** *erect a partition to divide the room* room-divider, divider, dividing wall, separator, screen, barrier, wall, fence.

partition *verb* **1** *partition India* divide up, separate, segregate, split up, break up, sever. **2** *partition the room to make two sleeping areas* divide, divide up, subdivide, separate, separate off, screen off, wall off, fence off.

partly *adverb* *partly responsible for the mistake* in part, partially, not wholly, not fully, half, somewhat, to a certain extent/degree, to some extent/degree, in some measure, fractionally, slightly.

partner noun **1** *his partner in business* associate, colleague, co-worker, team-mate, co-operator, collaborator, ally, comrade, companion, consociate. **2** *his partner in crime* accomplice, confederate, accessory, collaborator, fellow-conspirator; *inf.* sidekick. **3** *invite workers and partners to the party* wife/husband, spouse, mate, girlfriend/boyfriend, consort, helpmate, helpmeet.

partnership noun **1** *work in partnership with his brother* association, cooperation, collaboration, alliance, union, fellowship, companionship, consociation. **2** *a partnership in crime* collaboration, collusion, connivance, conspiracy. **3** *the partnership formed by the brothers was bought out* company, firm, corporation, cooperative, conglomerate, combine, syndicate.

parturition noun childbirth, labour.

party noun **1** *invite guests to a party* social gathering, social function, gathering, function, reception, celebration, festivity, at-home, soirée, orgy, bacchanal; *inf.* get-together, do, bash, shindig, knees-up, rave-up. **2** *a shooting/search party* group, band, company, body, squad, team, crew, contingent, detachment, unit; *inf.* bunch. **3** *belong to a left-wing party* political party, alliance, affiliation, association. **4** *both parties declared they were right* side, grouping, faction, camp, set, caucus. **5** *a certain party who shall be nameless* person, individual, human being, somebody, someone; *inf.* character. **6** *the judge speaking to both parties* litigant, plaintiff, defendant.

parvenu noun *villagers suspicious of parvenus* arrivé, arriviste, nouveau riche, intruder, upstart.

pass¹ verb **1** *traffic passing along the road* go, move, proceed, progress, drive, run, travel, roll, flow, course. **2** *pass her hand over her forehead* move, cross. **3** *cars passing us/other runners passing them* go past, move past, go ahead of, get ahead of, go by, overtake, outstrip, outdistance. **4** *pass the frontier/barrier* go over, go across, get across, get through, cross, traverse. **5** *pass the butter* hand over, reach, let someone have, give, transfer. **6** *the title passes to his eldest son* be passed on, be transferred, be made over, be turned over, be signed over, go, devolve. **7** *time passed slowly* go by, proceed, progress, advance, roll by, slip by, glide by, flow by, elapse. **8** *how to pass the time* spend, occupy, fill, take up, use, employ, while away, beguile. **9** *pass all understanding* exceed, surpass, transcend. **10** *let the matter pass* go, go unheeded, go unnoticed, go unremarked, go undisputed, go uncensored. **11** *students passing their exams* gain a pass in, get through, be successful in, succeed in, meet the requirements of, pass muster in; *inf.* come up to scratch in, come up to snuff in. **12** *the examiners passed everyone/all the material was passed* let through, declare acceptable/adequate/satisfactory, declare successful, accept, approve. **13** *pass the bill/motion* vote for, accept, approve, adopt, authorize, ratify, sanction, validate, legalize. **14** *pass judgement/sentence* pronounce, utter, express, deliver, declare. **15** *after all that*

has *passed* happen, occur, take place, come about, befall, supervene. **16** *the storm/anger passed* blow over, run its course, ebb, die out, fade, fade away, evaporate, draw to a close, disappear, finish, end, terminate. **17** *pass urine | was passing blood in the faeces* discharge, excrete, eliminate, evacuate, expel, emit. **come to pass** *it came to pass that the old man died* come about, happen, occur, befall, arise. **pass for** *she could pass for 30 | pass for a much younger woman* be taken for, be regarded as, be accepted as, be mistaken for. **pass off 1** *the demonstration passed off without incident* take place, happen, occur, be completed, be brought to a conclusion. **2** *the pain gradually passed off* pass, fade, fade away, disappear, vanish, die down, ebb, come to an end. **3** *pass him off as her husband* present as genuine, present with intent to deceive, give a false identity, have accepted as genuine. **pass out 1** *old ladies passing out in the heat* faint, collapse, lose consciousness, black out, keel over, swoon; *inf.* flake out. **2** *pass out the exam papers* hand out, distribute, give out, deal out, dole out, allot, allocate. **pass over 1** *pass over the interruption and proceed* ignore, disregard, overlook, forget, pay no attention to, gloss over, take no notice of, close one's eyes to, turn a deaf ear to, turn a blind eye to. **2** *he was passed over for promotion* overlook, ignore, disregard, forget, neglect, not take into consideration, omit. **pass up** *pass up an opportunity for promotion* fail to take advantage of, waive, reject, refuse, decline, neglect, let slip, ignore, brush aside, forgo.
Opposites HALT; STOP; FAIL; REJECT.

pass² noun **1** *gain a pass in the French exam* success, victory. **2** *soldiers requiring a pass to go out for the evening* warrant, permit, authorization, licence, passport, visa, safe conduct, exeat. **3** *old-age pensioners receiving a bus pass | a press pass* warrant, permit, free ticket, free admission, complimentary ticket, reduced ticket; *inf.* freebie. **4** *object to his passes* sexual advance, advance, sexual overture, sexual approach/suggestion; *inf.* proposition. **come to a pretty pass** *things have come to a pretty pass when they had to sell the house* reach a critical state, reach a crucial juncture, come to a difficult state of affairs, be in a worrying predicament, be in a sad plight, be in troubled circumstances, be in dire straits; *inf.* be in a pickle/hole. **make a pass at** *make a pass at his friend's wife* make sexual advances to, make sexual overtures to, make a sexual approach/suggestion to; *inf.* make a play for, make a proposition to, proposition.

pass³ noun *a mountain pass* narrow road, gap, gorge, defile, col, canyon.

passable adjective **1** *work that is passable | a passable knowledge of the subject* adequate, all right, tolerable, fair, acceptable, satisfactory, mediocre, middling, ordinary, average, run-of-the-mill, moderately good, not too bad, unexceptional, indifferent; *inf.* so-so, OK, nothing to write home about. **2** *roads scarcely passable in the snow* crossable, traversable, navigable, unblocked, unobstructed, open, clear.

passage noun **1** *the passage of time* passing, progress, advance, process, flow, course. **2** *our passage through life* | *their passage through foreign lands* journey, voyage, transit, trek, crossing, trip, tour. **3** *denied passage to the country* access, entry, admission, leave to travel in, permission to pass through, safe conduct, warrant, passport, visa. **4** *his passage from boyhood to manhood* | *the passage from liquid to solid* change, change-over, transformation, transition, conversion, shift, switch. **5** *a passage through the mountains* | *underground passages* road, route, path, way, track, trail, lane, channel, course, conduit. **6** *bicycles left in the passage* passageway, corridor, hall, hallway, entrance hall, entrance, vestibule, lobby. **7** *read aloud passages from the novel* extract, excerpt, brief, quotation, citation, section, verse. **8** *the passage of the bill by Parliament* acceptance, approval, adoption, authorization, ratification, sanction, validation, enactment, legalization.

passé adjective *ideas that are passé* out of date, outdated, dated, outmoded, outworn, old-fashioned, out of fashion, out of style, obsolete, obsolescent, archaic, antiquated, antediluvian; *inf.* old-hat, fuddy-duddy.
Opposites MODERN; UP-TO-DATE; FASHIONABLE.

passenger noun **1** *bus/train passengers* rider, fare-payer, traveller, fare. **2** *just a passenger in the firm* drone, idler, parasite, hanger-on; *inf.* freeloader.

passer-by noun *passers-by helped the accident victim* bystanders, onlooker, witness, spectator; *inf.* rubberneck.

passing noun **1** *the passing of time* passage, progress, advance, process, flow, course. **2** *regret the passing of old customs* | *mourn his aunt's passing* disappearance, fading, demise, death, end, termination, expiry, loss. **3** *the passing of the bill by Parliament* acceptance, approval, adoption, enactment. See PASSAGE 8. **in passing** *mention in passing that he was leaving* incidentally, by the by, by the way, *en passant*, parenthetically, in the course of conversation.

passing adjective **1** *a passing interest in local history* fleeting, transient, transitory, ephemeral, brief, short-lived, short, temporary, momentary. **2** *a passing glance told her everything* brief, quick, hasty, hurried, cursory, superficial, casual.
Opposites PERMANENT; CAREFUL.

passion noun **1** *do everything with great passion* intensity, fervour, fervidness, ardour, zeal, vehemence, fire, emotion, feeling, zest, enthusiasm, eagerness, excitement, animation. **2** *fly into a passion* rage, blind rage, fit of rage, fit of anger, fit of temper, temper, towering rage, outburst of anger, tantrum, fury, frenzy, paroxysm. **3** *his passion for her* love, sexual love, desire, sexual desire, lust, concupiscence, ardour, infatuation, adoration. **4** *his passion for motor bikes* enthusiasm, fascination, keen interest, obsession, fixation, craze, mania. **5** *one of the passions of his life* idol, hero/heroine, heart's desire, obsession, preoccupation, hobby-horse.

passionate adjective **1** *a passionate entreaty/performance* impassioned, intense, fervent, fervid, ardent, zealous, vehement, fiery, emotional, heartfelt, zestful, enthusiastic, eager, excited, animated. **2** *a passionate lover* ardent, aroused, desirous, hot, sexy, amorous, sensual, erotic, lustful; *inf.* turned-on. **3** *a very passionate person* intense, emotional, ardent, vehement, fiery. **4** *break the vase in a passionate fit* enraged, furious, angry, hot-tempered, frenzied, violent, wild, tempestuous.
Opposites APATHETIC; FRIGID.

passionless adjective **1** *a passionless creature* cold, emotionless, frigid, passive, unfeeling, unresponsive, undemonstrative, unfeeling, withdrawn, unapproachable, aloof, detached, distant, dispassionate, remote. **2** *a passionless performance* emotionless, spiritless, lifeless, flat, zestless, insipid, lacklustre, colourless, anaemic, vapid.

passive adjective **1** *play a passive role in the marriage/firm* inactive, non-active, inert, non-participating, uninvolved. **2** *a passive attitude to their invaders* unresisting, non-resistant, unassertive, yielding, submissive, compliant, pliant, acquiescent, quiescent, resigned, obedient, tractable, malleable. **3** *look on with a passive expression* | *rather a passive person* impassive, emotionless, unmoved, unresponsive, undemonstrative, dispassionate, detached, distant, remote, aloof, indifferent.
Opposites ACTIVE; ASSERTIVE; EMOTIONAL.

passport noun **1** *show passports at the border* travel document, travel papers, papers, travel permit, visa, identity card, ID. **2** *his passport to happiness* means of access, avenue, access, entry, entrée, admission, admittance, open sesame.

password noun *give the password to gain entry* watchword, key word, word of identification, signal, word, open sesame, shibboleth.

past adjective **1** *in times past* gone by, gone, bygone, elapsed, over, over and done with, ended, former, long ago. **2** *the past few months* recent, preceding, last, latter, foregone. **3** *past achievements/chairmen* former, previous, prior, foregoing, late, erstwhile, one-time, sometime, ex-.
Opposites PRESENT; FUTURE.

past noun **in the past** *we used to go there in the past* in days gone by, in bygone days, in former times, formerly, previously, before.

past preposition **1** *walk past the shop* in front of, by, beyond. **2** *past retirement age* beyond the limits of, beyond, in excess of.

past adverb *drive/hurried past* by, on, further on.

pasta noun. See table.

paste noun **1** *stick cuttings on the page/wall with paste* adhesive, glue, gum, cement. **2** *mix to a paste* mixture, blend, compound, pulp, mush, pap; *inf.* goo. **3** *fish paste* spread, pâté, purée.

paste verb *paste cuttings into a book* stick, fasten, glue, gum, cement.

pastel adjective *pastel colours* pale, soft, delicate, muted, subdued, faint, low-key.
Opposites DARK; BRIGHT; RICH; VIVID.

pastiche noun *a work that is a pastiche of various styles* medley, mélange, miscellany, blend, mix-

573

pastille · pathetic

TYPES OF PASTA

agnolotti	noodles
annellini	orecchiette
bigoli	paglia e fieno
bucatini	pappardelle
cannelloni	penne
capelli	pipe
cappelletti	ravioli
conchiglie	rigatoni
cravattine	risoni
ditali	rotelle
ditalini	rotini
ditaloni	spaghetti
farfalle	spaghettini
farfalline	spaghettone
fettucce	stelline
fettuccine	tagliatelle
fidelini	tagliolini
fusilli	taglioni
gramigna	tortellini
lasagne	tortelloni
linguine	tortiglioni
lumache	trenette
macaroni	tuffoloni
manicotti	vermicelli

ture, pot-pourri, mosaic, patchwork, hotch-potch, hodgepodge, jumble, mishmash, galli-maufry, farrago.

pastille noun suck a pastille lozenge, sweet, drop, gum, gumdrop, jujube, tablet, pill, troche.

pastime noun take up snooker as a pastime hobby, leisure activity, sport, game, recreation, diversion, amusement, entertainment, distraction, relaxation.

past master noun a past master at disguise expert, virtuoso, wizard, genius, artist, old hand; inf. dab hand.

pastor noun listen to the pastor preaching priest, reverend, clergyman, churchman, cleric, divine. See table at ECCLESIASTIC.

pastoral adjective **1** a pastoral scene rural, country, rustic, simple, idyllic, innocent, Arcadian, agricultural, bucolic, georgic. **2** his pastoral duties ministerial, vicarial, parsonical, priestly, rectorial, ecclesiastical, clerical.

pastry noun **1** buy pastries for tea tart, tartlet, pie, pasty, patty, vol-au-vent, quiche, Danish pastry; inf. Danish. **2** bake some pastry pie-crust. See table.

TYPES OF PASTRY

cheese pastry	pie pastry
choux pastry	puff pastry
filo pastry	rough puff pastry
flaky pastry	short pastry
flan pastry	shortcrust pastry
Greek cheese pastry	strudel pastry
hot-water crust pastry	suetcrust pastry
	sweet pastry

pasture noun cows in the pasture pasturage, pasture land, grassland, grass, field, grazing land, grazing, meadow.

pat verb **1** pat the child on the head|pat the dog stroke, clap, caress, fondle, pet. **2** pat the mixture tap, slap, dab. **pat oneself on the back, pat someone on the back** pat himself on the back for bringing off the deal congratulate, praise, commend, compliment, applaud, throw bouquets at.

pat noun **1** a pat on the cheek light blow, stroke, clap, caress. **2** flatten the mixture with a pat light blow, tap, slap, dab. **3** a pat of butter dab, lump, cake, portion. **give oneself a pat on the back, give someone a pat on the back** see PAT verb.

patch noun **1** put a patch over the hole piece of cloth, piece of material. **2** a patch over the eye cover, covering, pad, shield. **3** a cabbage patch|patch of ground plot, area, piece, ground, land, lot, tract, parcel. **4** encounter a bad patch period, time, spell, stretch, interval, term.

patch verb **1** patch the trousers put a patch on, cover, mend, repair, sew, sew up, stitch, stitch up. **2** patch the roof repair/fix hastily, do a makeshift repair on, repair/fix clumsily, repair/fix temporarily. **patch up 1** patch up the roof repair/fix hastily. **2** patch up the quarrel make up, settle, resolve, set right.

patchwork noun work that was a patchwork of different styles hotchpotch, hodgepodge, mishmash, jumble, medley, mélange, miscellany, pot-pourri, mosaic, blend, mixture. See PASTICHE.

patchy adjective a patchy knowledge of the subject sketchy, bitty, uneven, varying, variable, erratic, random.
Opposites COMPLETE; COMPREHENSIVE; UNIFORM; CONSTANT.

patent noun take out a patent for his invention licence, copyright, registered trade mark.

patent adjective **1** it was patent to everyone that she was lying|her patent dislike of him obvious, clear, plain, evident, apparent, manifest, transparent, conspicuous, blatant, glaringly obvious, unmistakable, unconcealed. **2** patent medicine patented, proprietary, licensed, branded, brand-name.
Opposites UNOBTRUSIVE; INCONSPICUOUS.

paternal adjective **1** take a paternal interest in the boy fatherly, fatherlike, patriarchal, protective, concerned, solicitous, kindly, benevolent. **2** his paternal grandfather patrilineal, patrimonial, on the father's side.

paternity noun **1** dispute paternity fatherhood. **2** of unknown paternity descent, extraction, lineage, parentage, family.

path noun **1** a path through the forest pathway, footpath, footway, track, jogging track, trail, tow-path, walk. **2** the moon's path round the earth course, route, circuit, track, orbit, trajectory. **3** unable to predict the path he will take course of action, route, procedure, direction, approach, method, system, strategy. **4** the path to success way, road, avenue, route.

pathetic adjective **1** children in rags were a pathetic sight pitiful, pitiable, piteous, to be pitied, moving, touching, poignant, affecting, distressing, heartbreaking, heart-rending, sad, wretched, mournful, woeful. **2** a pathetic

attempt/performance pitiful, lamentable, deplorable, miserable, wretched, feeble, woeful, sorry, poor, contemptible, inadequate, unsatisfactory, worthless.
Opposites COMICAL; CHEERFUL; ADMIRABLE; EXCELLENT.

pathological *adjective* **1** *a pathological condition* morbid, diseased. **2** *a pathological liar* irrational, compulsive, obsessive, unreasonable, illogical.

pathos *noun the pathos in the dying girl's speech* poignancy, pitifulness, pitiableness, piteousness, sadness, plaintiveness.

patience *noun* **1** *wait in the long queue with patience* calmness, composure, even temper, even-temperedness, equanimity, equilibrium, serenity, tranquillity, restraint, self-restraint, imperturbability, inexcitability, tolerance, long-suffering, indulgence, forbearance, endurance, resignation, stoicism, fortitude; *inf.* unflappability, cool. **2** *a task requiring patience* perseverance, persistence, endurance, tenacity, assiduity, diligence, staying power, indefatigability, doggedness, singleness of purpose.
Opposites IMPATIENCE; AGITATION; EXASPERATION.

patient *adjective children told to be patient when waiting for Christmas | have to be patient about delayed flights* uncomplaining, serene, calm, composed, even-tempered, tranquil, restrained, imperturbable, inexcitable, tolerant, accommodating, long-suffering, forbearing, indulgent, resigned, stoical; *inf.* unflappable, cool.

patient *noun doctors examining patients* sick person, invalid, case, sufferer.

patio *noun deck-chairs on the patio* terrace, courtyard, veranda; *Am.* deck, piazza.

patois *noun visitors unable to understand the local patois* local speech, vernacular, dialect, local parlance; *inf.* lingo.

patrician *noun Roman patricians | patricians looking down on the peasants* aristocrat, noble, nobleman, lord; *inf.* nob.

patrician *adjective a patrician family* aristocratic, noble, well-born, high-born, blue-blooded.

patriot *noun patriots dying for their country* nationalist, loyalist, chauvinist, flag-waver, jingoist, jingo.

patriotic *adjective patriotic people singing the national anthem* nationalist, nationalistic, loyalist, loyal, chauvinistic, flag-waving, jingoistic.

patrol *verb soldiers patrolling the border area* make the rounds of, perform sentry-duty on, walk the beat of, pound the beat of, range, police, keep watch on, guard, keep guard on, keep a vigil on, monitor.

patrol *noun* **1** *make regular patrols of the border area* patrolling, round, sentry-duty, beat-pounding, policing, watch, guard, vigil, monitoring. **2** *report the matter to the patrol* patrolman/patrolwoman, sentinel, sentry, garrison, guard, watchman, watch, security man, night-watchman, policeman/policewoman.

patron *noun* **1** *a patron of the theatre/arts* sponsor, backer, benefactor/benefactress, promoter, friend, helper, supporter, upholder, champion, protector; *inf.* angel. **2** *regular patrons of the salon | car park for patrons only* customer, client, frequenter, shopper, buyer, purchaser; *inf.* regular.

patronage *noun* **1** *customers taking their patronage elsewhere* trade, custom, business, commerce, trafficking, shopping, buying, purchasing. **2** *their patronage of the arts | a festival under the patronage of local firms* sponsorship, backing, funding, financing, promotion, help, aid, assistance, support, encouragement, championship, protection. **3** *a post under the patronage of the Queen* power of appointment, right of appointment. **4** *treat his staff with patronage* patronizing, condescension, disdain, scorn, contempt, snobbery, snobbishness.

patronize *verb* **1** *patronize those less well-off than she is* look down on, talk down to, condescend to, treat condescendingly, treat with condescension, treat like a child, treat as inferior, treat with disdain, treat scornfully/contemptuously, be snobbish to. **2** *patronize the new salon* be a customer of, be a client of, frequent, shop at, buy from, do business with, deal with, trade with. **3** *patronize the arts | wants to patronize the new theatre* be a patron of, sponsor, back, fund, finance, promote, help, aid, assist, support, encourage, champion, protect.

patronizing *adjective a patronizing attitude to younger people* condescending, supercilious, superior, haughty, lofty, lordly, disdainful, scornful, contemptuous, snobbish; *inf.* uppity, snooty, toffee-nosed.

patter¹ *verb* **1** *mice pattering across the attic floor* scurry, scuttle, trip. **2** *rain pattering on the window* pitter-patter, tap, drum, beat, pound, pelt, rat-a-tat, go pit-a-pat, pit-a-pat.

patter² *noun* **1** *the patter of mice on the floor above* pattering, scurrying, scuttling, tripping. **2** *the patter of rain on the window* pitter-patter, pattering, tap, tapping, drumming, beat, beating, pounding, pelting, rat-a-tat, pit-a-pat.

patter³ *noun* **1** *the salesman's patter* spiel, glib talk, monologue, harangue; *inf.* sales pitch, line. **2** *can't understand the young people's patter* speech, language, jargon; *inf.* lingo. *See* PARLANCE.

pattern *noun* **1** *the pattern on the wallpaper* design, decoration, motif, marking, ornament, ornamentation, device, figure. **2** *study the rats' behaviour pattern* system, order, arrangement, method, sequence. **3** *a knitting pattern* design, guide, blueprint, model, plan, template, stencil, instructions. **4** *a pattern of elegance* model, ideal, exemplar, paradigm, example, archetype, prototype, paragon, criterion, standard, gauge, norm, guide, yardstick, touchstone, benchmark. **5** *a book of textile patterns* sample, swatch, specimen.

pattern *verb pattern himself on his father* model/mould/style/form/shape oneself on.

patterned *adjective patterned carpets/china* decorated, ornamented, figure.

paucity noun *a paucity of evidence* scarcity, sparseness, sparsity, dearth, shortage, insufficiency, deficiency, lack, want, meagreness, paltriness.
Opposites ABUNDANCE.

paunch noun **1** *developing quite a paunch* fat/protruding stomach/belly/abdomen, pot-belly, pot; *inf.* beer-belly, corporation. **2** *a belt round his paunch* stomach, belly, abdomen.

pauper noun *once a rich person, now a pauper* poor person, penniless person, bankrupt person, bankrupt, insolvent person, beggar, mendicant, down-and-out, homeless person.

pause noun *a pause in the fighting* break, halt, cessation, stoppage, interruption, lull, respite, stay, discontinuation, gap, interlude, intermission, interval, rest, delay, hesitation; *inf.* let-up, breather.

pause verb *pause for thought* stop, halt, cease, discontinue, break, take a break, desist, rest, hold back, delay, hesitate, waver; *inf.* let up, take a breather.
Opposites CONTINUE; PROCEED.

pave verb *pave the front path* concrete, asphalt, flag, tile, tar, macadamize, floor. **pave the way for** *pave the way for radical change* prepare for, prepare the way for, clear the way for, make preparations for, make provision for, get ready for, lay the foundations/groundwork for, put things in order for, set the scene for.

pavement noun *a car mounting the pavement* footpath, paved path, pedestrian way, walkway; *Am.* sidewalk.

paw noun *an animal's paw* foot, pad, forepaw, hind paw.

paw verb *accused of pawing the female staff* molest, maul; *inf.* touch up, goose.

pawn verb *pawn her necklace to pay the rent* deposit with a pawnbroker, put in pawn, give as security, pledge, mortgage; *inf.* pop; *inf. esp Amer* hock, put in hock.

pawn noun *members of staff who were pawns in the struggle for power in the firm* tool, cat's-paw, instrument, puppet, dupe; *inf.* stooge.

pay verb **1** *pay him for work done* give payment to, settle up with, remunerate, reimburse, recompense, reward, indemnify, requite. **2** *pay hundreds of pounds for his services* pay out, spend, expend, lay out, part with, disburse, hand over, remit, render; *inf.* dish out, shell out, fork out, cough up. **3** *pay his debts* pay off, pay in full, settle, discharge, meet, clear, square, honour, liquidate. **4** *pay the bill* settle, foot, defray, square, discharge. **5** *the business/work does not pay* make money, be profitable, make a profit, be remunerative, make a return. **6** *investments paying large sums of money* pay out, yield, return, produce, bring in; *inf.* rake in. **7** *it would pay you to listen to his advice* repay, be advantageous to, be of advantage to, be of benefit to, be beneficial to, be profitable to, be worthwhile to. **8** *pay compliments* give, bestow, extend, offer, proffer, render. **9** *pay him for what he did* pay back, punish, avenge oneself on, get revenge on. **pay back 1** *pay back the loan* repay, pay off, give back, return, reimburse. **2** *pay her back for her treatment of him*

pay, repay, punish, avenge oneself on, get revenge on, retaliate against, settle a score with, get even with. **pay for 1** *pay for their services/meal* foot the bill for, settle up for, defray the cost of; *inf.* shell out for, fork out for, cough up for. **2** *make him pay for his mistakes* be punished for, pay a penalty for, suffer for, atone for, make atonement for, pay the price for, get one's deserts for, take one's medicine for; *inf.* get one's comeuppance for. **pay off 1** *pay off his debts* pay, pay in full, settle, discharge, meet, clear, square, honour, liquidate. **2** *pay off some workers* make/declare redundant, dismiss, discharge, lay off, let go; *inf.* sack, fire. **3** *his hard work paid off* meet with success, be successful, be effective, work, get results, be profitable. **pay out** *pay out a lot of money on the mortgage* pay, spend, expend, lay out, part with, hand over, remit; *inf.* dish out, shell out, fork out, cough up. **pay up** *pay up or be sued* pay, make payment, settle up, pay in full, meet one's obligations.
Opposites OWE; WITHHOLD.

pay noun *get one's pay at the end of the month* payment, salary, wages, earnings, fee, remuneration, recompense, reimbursement, reward, stipend, emoluments.

payable adjective *a bill that is payable now* due, to be paid, owed, owing, outstanding, unpaid.

payment noun **1** *receive payment for his services* pay, salary, wages, earnings, fee, remuneration, recompense. See PAY *noun.* **2** *in payment of the account* settlement, discharge, clearance, squaring, liquidation. **3** *make twelve monthly payments* instalment, premium, amount, remittance.

pea noun. See table at BEAN.

peace noun **1** *the peace of the countryside* peace and quiet, peacefulness, tranquillity, restfulness, calm, calmness, quiet, quietness, stillness, still. **2** *a mind seeking peace* peacefulness, tranquillity, serenity, calm, calmness, composure, placidity, rest, repose, contentment. **3** *hope for peace between the countries* peacefulness, peaceableness, harmony, harmoniousness, accord, concord, amity, amicableness, goodwill, friendship, cordiality, non-aggression, non-violence, cease-fire. **4** *sign the peace | the Peace of Versailles* treaty, truce, agreement, armistice, cessation of hostilities.
Opposites NOISE; AGITATION; CONFLICT; WAR.

peaceable adjective **1** *a peaceable person/temperament* unwarlike, peace-loving, non-aggressive, non-belligerent, non-violent, non-combative, easygoing, placid, gentle, mild, good-natured, even-tempered, amiable, amicable, pacific, pacifist, pacifistic, dovelike, dovish, irenic. **2** *a peaceable set of negotiations* peaceful, strife-free, harmonious, amicable, amiable, friendly, cordial.
Opposites AGGRESSIVE; BELLIGERENT; WARLIKE.

peaceful adjective **1** *in a peaceful setting* tranquil, restful, quiet, calm, still, undisturbed. **2** *a peaceful mind* at peace, tranquil, serene, calm, composed, placid, at rest, in repose, reposeful, undisturbed, untroubled, unworried, anxiety-free. **3** *peaceful conditions between the two countries* peaceable, at peace, on good

terms, strife-free, harmonious, amicable, friendly, cordial, non-violent, unwarlike.
Opposites NOISY; agitated; HOSTILE; WARRING.

peacemaker *noun call in a third party as a peacemaker* conciliator, mediator, arbitrator, pacifier, appeaser, peacemonger.

peak *noun* **1** *snow on the mountain peaks* top, summit, crest, pinnacle. **2** *climb several peaks* mountain, hill, height, alp. **3** *the peak of a cap* brim, visor, projection. **4** *at the peak of his career as a singer* height, high point, climax, culmination, zenith, acme, meridian, apogee, prime, heyday, *ne plus ultra*.
Opposites BOTTOM; NADIR; trough.

peak *verb* **1** *prices peaking just before Christmas* reach its/their etc. height, reach the highest point. **2** *the political party's popularity peaked too soon* reach its/their etc. height, reach the highest point, culminate, reach the high point, reach a climax, reach the zenith.

peaky *adjective looking rather peaky this morning* peaked, pale, wan, drained, drawn, pallid, pasty, white, whitish, anaemic, whey-faced, ill-looking, sickly-looking.

peal *noun* **1** *hear the peal of the church bells* ring, ringing, chime, clang, resounding, reverberation, tintinnabulation. **2** *bell-ringers ringing a peal* carillon, chime. **3** *the peal of laughter* ring, ringing, tinkle, roar, boom, resounding, reverberation. **4** *the peal of thunder* roar, boom, rumble, crash, clap, resounding, reverberation.

peal *verb* **1** *bells pealing* ring, ring out, chime, clang, resound, reverberate. **2** *thunder pealed around us* roar, boom, rumble, crash, resound, reverberate.

peasant *noun* **1** *peasants driving cows to market* small farmer, agricultural worker, rustic, son of the soil. **2** *refusing to sit with people he called peasants* lout, boor, churl, yokel, provincial.

peccadillo *noun treat his peccadilloes as major crimes* misdemeanour, minor offence, petty offence, indiscretion, lapse, misdeed, error, infraction; *inf.* slip-up.

peck *verb* **1** *birds pecking the wood* bite, strike, hit, tap, rap, jab. **2** *peck her on the cheek* kiss, plant a kiss on, give someone a peck. **3** *hens pecking at the corn* pick at, pick up, eat. **4** *children pecking at their food* nibble, pick at, eat sparingly of.

peculiar *adjective* **1** *a peculiar smell* strange, odd, queer, funny, curious, unusual, abnormal. **2** *peculiar clothes/appearance* strange, odd, queer, funny, curious, unusual, abnormal, eccentric, unconventional, bizarre, weird, quaint, outlandish, out-of-the-way, grotesque, freakish, offbeat, droll, comical; *inf.* far-out, way-out. **3** *have a peculiar walk* characteristic, distinctive, distinct, individual, individualistic, distinguishing, special, unique, idiosyncratic, conspicuous, notable, remarkable. **4** *feel rather peculiar* unwell, poorly, ill, below par, strange, indisposed; *inf.* funny, under the weather.
peculiar to *peculiar to that period of history* belonging to, characteristic of, typical of, representative of, indicative of, exclusive to.
Opposites NORMAL; ORDINARY.

peculiarity *noun* **1** *the peculiarity of the smell* peculiarness, strangeness, oddness, queerness, abnormality. See PECULIAR 1. **2** *the peculiarity of her clothes/appearance* peculiarness, strangeness, oddness, queerness, eccentricity, unconventionality, bizarreness, weirdness, outlandishness, grotesqueness, freakishness, drollness. See PECULIAR 2. **3** *a geographical peculiarity of the region | a peculiarity of the breed* characteristic, feature, quality, property, trait, attribute, mark, stamp, hallmark. **4** *peculiarities of dress/behaviour* abnormality, eccentricity, oddity, idiosyncrasy, quirk, foible.

pecuniary *adjective of no pecuniary advantage* financial, monetary, fiscal.

pedagogic *adjective pedagogic considerations* educational, teaching, academic, scholastic.

pedagogue *noun* **1** *children taking notes from a pedagogue* teacher, schoolmaster/schoolmistress, tutor, lecturer, instructor, educator, educationalist. **2** *a pedagogue without inspiration* dogmatist, pedant.

pedant *noun* **1** *pedants insisting on the rules being interpreted literally* precisionist, perfectionist, formalist, dogmatist, literalist, quibbler, hair-splitter, casuist, sophist, pettifogger; *inf.* nit-picker. **2** *pedants displaying their knowledge* intellectual, academic, pedagogue, highbrow, bluestocking; *inf.* egghead.

pedantic *adjective* **1** *a pedantic interpretation of the rules* precise, precisionist, exact, scrupulous, overscrupulous, punctilious, meticulous, over-nice, perfectionist, formalist, dogmatic, literalist, literalistic, quibbling, hair-splitting, casuistic, casuistical, sophistic, sophistical, pettifogging; *inf.* nit-picking. **2** *a pedantic display of knowledge* intellectual, academic, scholastic, didactic, bookish, pedagogic, donnish, highbrow, pretentious, pompous; *inf.* egghead. **3** *a pedantic account of the incident* formal, stilted, stiff, stuffy, unimaginative, uninspired, rhetorical, bombastic, grandiloquent, high-flown, euphuistic; *inf.* highfalutin.

pedantry *noun* **1** *his pedantry in interpreting the rules* precision, precisionism, exactness, scrupulousness, punctiliousness, meticulousness, over-niceness, over-nicety, perfectionism, formalism, dogmatism, literalism, quibbling, hair-splitting, casuistry, sophistry, pettifogging; *inf.* nit-picking. **2** *an audience tired of the speaker's pedantry* intellectualism, scholasticism, didacticism, bookishness, pedagogism, donnishness, pretentiousness, pomposity, pompousness. **3** *the pedantry of his prose* formality, stiltedness, stiffness, stuffiness, unimaginativeness, lack of inspiration, rhetoric, bombast, grandiloquence, euphuism.

peddle *verb* **1** *peddle goods round the doors* hawk, sell, sell from door to door, tout, market, vend; *inf.* flog, push. **2** *peddle his political views to his workmates* present, offer, introduce, spread, promote, advocate, recommend.

pedestal *noun a bust of Shakespeare on a pedestal* base, support, stand, foundation, pillar, column, plinth. **put on a pedestal** *put his father on a pedestal* idealize, exalt, glorify, adulate, worship, deify.

pedestrian noun *areas for pedestrians only* person on foot, walker, foot-traveller, hiker, foot-slogger.
Opposites DRIVER.

pedestrian adjective **1** *pedestrian traffic* on foot, walking. **2** *pedestrian precincts in the city* pedestrianized, for pedestrians, for pedestrians only. **3** *piece of pedestrian prose* plodding, unimaginative, uninspired, unexciting, dull, flat, prosaic, turgid, stodgy, mundane, humdrum, banal, run-of-the-mill, commonplace, ordinary, mediocre; inf. nothing to write home about.
Opposites IMAGINATIVE; INSPIRED; EXCITING.

pedigree noun **1** *proud of his aristocratic pedigree* ancestry, descent, lineage, line, extraction, heritage, parentage, birth, family, strain, stock, blood, stirps. **2** *draw up the son's/dog's pedigree* genealogy, family tree, ancestral record, line of descent.

pedigree adjective *a pedigree spaniel* pedigreed, pure-bred, thoroughbred, pure-blooded, full-blooded.

peek verb *peek into the Christmas package before Christmas* take a secret look, take a sly/stealthy look, peep, glance, cast a brief look, look hurriedly, look; inf. sneak a look, take a gander, have a look-see.

peek noun *take a peek into the Christmas package before Christmas* secret look, sly look, stealthy look, sneaky look, peep, glance, glimpse, brief/hurried look, look; inf. gander, look-see.

peel verb **1** *peel the skin from the fruit* pare, strip, remove, take off. **2** *peel the fruit* pare, skin, decorticate. **3** *skin peeling after getting sunburnt* flake, scale off, come off in layers, desquamate. **4** *peel off his wet clothes* strip off, cast off, remove, doff. **keep one's eyes peeled** *keep one's eyes peeled for the lost kitten* keep one's eyes skinned, keep a sharp look-out, be on the look-out, look out, watch closely, be alert, be on guard.

peel noun *the peel of the fruit* rind, skin, covering, zest, shell, husk, epicarp.

peep[1] verb **1** *peep through the keyhole* take a secret look, take a sly look, peek; inf. sneak a look. See PEEK verb. **2** *snowdrops peeping through the hard winter ground* appear, show, come into view, become visible, emerge, spring up, pop up.

peep[2] noun *take a peep at the secret document* secret look, sly look, stealthy look, sneaky look, peek, glance. See PEEK noun.

peep[3] verb *fledglings peeping in the nest* cheep, chirp, chirrup, tweet, twitter, pipe, squeak.

peep[4] noun **1** *the peep of a fledgling from the nest* cheep, chirp, chirrup, tweet, twitter, piping, squeak. **2** *not a peep out of the children* sound, noise, cry, utterance, word; inf. cheep. **3** *we expected a protest but there was not a peep out of the opposition* complaint, grumble, moan, groan, word; inf. gripe, grouse.

peep-hole noun *look through the peep-hole in the door to see who's there* aperture, opening, spyhole, judas, slit, crack, clink, crevice, fissure.

peer verb *peer at the faded handwriting* | *peer through the mist* look closely, try to see, look through narrowed eyes, narrow one's eyes, screw up one's eyes, squint.

peer noun **1** *one of the peers of the realm* | *a life peer* noble, nobleman, aristocrat, lord, titled man, patrician. **2** *look older than his peers* | *be a cleverer child than his peers* compeer, fellow, equal, match, like, co-equal, confrère.

peerage noun **1** *elevated to the peerage* nobility, aristocracy. **2** *the peerage voted on the bill* nobility, aristocracy, peers and peeresses, lords and ladies, upper classes, the House of Lords, the Lords.

peerless adjective *a peerless performance* incomparable, beyond compare, matchless, unmatched, unrivalled, unsurpassed, unequalled, without equal, unparalleled, superlative, second to none, nonpareil.

peeve verb *his behaviour really peeved her* irritate, annoy, anger, vex, provoke, upset, exasperate, irk, pique, nettle, get on someone's nerves, rub up the wrong way; inf. aggravate, miff, rile, get under someone's skin, get in someone's hair.

peevish adjective *the children were tired and peevish* | *peevish old men* irritable, fractious, fretful, cross, crabbed, crabby, petulant, complaining, querulous, sulky, moody, in a bad mood, grumpy, ill-tempered, ill-natured, ill-humoured, surly, churlish, touchy, testy, snappish, snappy, crusty, splenetic; inf. ratty, whingeing.
Opposites AFFABLE; EASYGOING.

peg noun *fasten the pieces of wood with a peg* pin, nail, dowel, spike, skewer, brad, screw, bolt, post, clothes-peg. **take down a peg or two** *feel like taking the conceited young fool down a peg or two* humble, humiliate, mortify, bring down, bring low; inf. settle someone's hash.

peg verb **1** *peg the clothes to the line* | *peg a tent to the ground* pin, attach, fasten, fix, secure, make fast. **2** *peg prices at last year's level* fix, set, control, freeze, limit. **peg away at** *peg away at their studies* apply oneself to, work hard at, work away at, persevere at, persist in, keep at, hammer away at; inf. beaver away at, plug away at, stick at, stick with.

pejorative adjective *always making pejorative remarks* derogatory, disparaging, deprecatory, slighting.
Opposites COMPLIMENTARY; LAUDATORY; approbatory.

pellet noun **1** *a paper pellet* | *a pellet of bread* ball, little ball. **2** *firing pellets at birds* bullet, shot, lead shot, buckshot. **3** *take pellets for indigestion* pill, tablet, capsule, lozenge, bolus.

pell-mell adverb **1** *children rushing pell-mell from the school* helter-skelter, headlong, impetuously, recklessly, hurriedly, hastily. **2** *books lying pell-mell around the room* in disorder, in confusion, in a muddle, in disarray, untidily, in a mess, anyhow.

pellucid adjective **1** *pellucid water* transparent, translucent, clear, crystal-clear, glassy, limpid. **2** *pellucid prose* clear, lucid, coherent, articulate, intelligible, understandable, comprehensible, straightforward, simple.

pelt verb **1** *pelt the strikebreakers with stones* bombard, shower, attack, assail, batter, pepper. **2** *rain came pelting down* pour, teem, bucket down, rain cats and dogs, come down like stair-rods. **3** *pelt along the road | came pelting down the hill* race, run, sprint, dash, rush, speed, charge, career, hare; *inf.* belt, tear, whiz.

pelt noun *a fox's/beaver's pelt* skin, hide, fleece, coat, fur, fell.

pen¹ noun *bring pen and paper* fountain-pen, ball-point, ball-point pen, felt-tip, felt-tip pen, marker; Biro™.

pen² verb *pen a note* write, write down, jot down, scribble, pencil, compose, draft, commit to paper.

pen³ noun *put animals in a pen* enclosure, fold, sheepfold, coop, hen-coop, pound, compound, corral.

pen⁴ verb **pen in, pen up** *pen in the animals for the night* shut up, enclose, confine, fence in, coop up, mew up, corral.

penal adjective **1** *a penal institution* disciplinary, punitive, corrective, retributive. **2** *a penal offence* punishable, indictable, chargeable, impeachable.

penalize verb **1** *penalized for arriving late* punish, discipline, castigate, correct. **2** *people penalized for being poor* handicap, inflict a handicap on, disadvantage, put at a disadvantage. **Opposites** REWARD.

penalty noun **1** *have to pay a penalty for his crime* punishment, punitive action, retribution, castigation, penance, fine, forfeit, sentence, mulct. **2** *one of the penalties of living in the city* handicap, disadvantage, drawback, snag, obstacle. **Opposites** REWARD; ADVANTAGE.

penance noun **1** *a penance imposed by the priest* punishment, penalty. **2** *carry out a penance for one's sins* self-punishment, atonement, reparation, amends, mortification.

penchant noun *a penchant for bright colours | has a penchant for spicy food* liking, fondness, preference, taste, partiality, soft spot, inclination, bent, proclivity, predilection, love, passion, desire, fancy, whim, weakness.

pencil noun **1** *pencil and paper* lead pencil, propelling pencil. **2** *a pencil of light* ray, beam, shaft, finger.

pencil verb **1** *pencil a note* write, write down, jot down, scribble, pen, compose, draft, commit to paper. **2** *pencil a likeness of the child* sketch, outline, draw, trace.

pendant noun *wear a silver pendant* necklace, locket, medallion. See table at JEWELLERY.

pendent adjective *a pendent light* hanging, suspended, dangling.

pending preposition **1** *receive bail pending trial* awaiting, waiting for, until. **2** *no action pending negotiations* during, throughout, in the course of, for the time/duration of.

pending adjective **1** *the lawsuit then pending* undecided, unsettled, unresolved, uncertain, awaiting action, undetermined, hanging fire, up in the air; *inf.* on the back burner. **2** *a decision is pending* imminent, impending, on the way, coming, approaching, forthcoming, near, nearing, close, close at hand, in the offing.

penetrate verb **1** *penetrate the skin* pierce, bore, perforate, stab, prick, gore, spike. **2** *penetrate the dense forest* go into, get in, enter, make one's way into/through, infiltrate. **3** *terror penetrated her whole being* permeate, pervade, fill, imbue, suffuse, seep through, saturate. **4** *we explained, but it didn't penetrate* be understood, be comprehended, be taken in, be grasped, register. **5** *the explanation did not seem to penetrate his mind* get through to, be understood/comprehended by, register on, make an impression on, have an impact on. **6** *unable to penetrate the mystery* understand, comprehend, apprehend, fathom, get to the bottom of, make out, solve, resolve, work out, figure out, unravel, decipher; *inf.* crack.

penetrating adjective **1** *a penetrating wind* sharp, keen, biting, stinging, harsh. **2** *a penetrating voice* shrill, loud, strong, carrying, piercing, ear-piercing, ear-splitting, intrusive. **3** *a penetrating mind* keen, sharp, sharp-witted, discerning, perceptive, percipient, intelligent, clever, smart, incisive, astute, shrewd, acute, discriminating. **4** *ask penetrating questions* penetrative, searching, sharp, incisive, inquisitive, analytic, in-depth. **Opposites** MILD; SOFT; DULL.

penetration noun **1** *the penetration of the skin* piercing, perforation, pricking. See PENETRATE 1. **2** *the penetration of the forest* entry, infiltration. See PENETRATE 2. **3** *the penetration of her being with terror* permeation, pervasion, imbuing, suffusion. See PENETRATE 3. **4** *the penetration of the mystery is taking a lot of time* understanding, comprehension, apprehension, fathoming, resolution; *inf.* cracking. See PENETRATE 6. **5** *impressed by the penetration of their minds* keenness, sharpness, sharp-wittedness, discernment, perception, perceptiveness, intelligence, cleverness, smartness, incisiveness, astuteness, shrewdness, acuteness, acuity, discrimination. **6** *admire the penetration of the questions* searchingness, sharpness, incisiveness. See PENETRATING 4.

penitence noun *show penitence for his sins* repentance, contrition, compunction, regret, remorse, remorsefulness, ruefulness, self-reproach, self-accusation, shame, sorrow.

penitent adjective *feel penitent about his sin | penitent pupils apologizing* repentant, contrite, regretful, remorseful, sorry, apologetic, conscience-stricken, rueful, ashamed, abject, sorrowful. **Opposites** IMPENITENT; UNREPENTANT.

pen-name noun pseudonym, nom de plume, nom de guerre, assumed name, allonym, alias. See table at PSEUDONYM.

pennant noun *pennants flying in the breeze* banner, banderole, streamer, flag, ensign, colours, bunting.

penniless adjective without a penny, without a penny to one's name, impecunious, penurious,

impoverished, indigent, poor, as poor as a church mouse, poverty-stricken, destitute, bankrupt, in reduced circumstances, in straitened circumstances, hard up; *inf.* broke, stony-broke, flat broke, skint, cleaned-out, strapped for cash, strapped.
Opposites WEALTHY; AFFLUENT.

penny *noun it costs one penny* pence; *inf.* p; *Am.* cent. **a bad penny** undesirable, *persona non grata*, rascal, scoundrel, rogue, good-for-nothing; *inf.* bad egg, bad news. **a pretty penny** *will cost a pretty penny* considerable sum of money; *inf.* lot of money, heaps of money, a mint, a bundle, a packet.

penny-pinching *adjective penny-pinching people refusing to give to charity* mean, miserly, parsimonious, niggardly, tight-fisted, close-fisted, cheese-paring, penurious, scrimping, skimping, close, near, grasping, money-grubbing, Scrooge-like, ungenerous; *inf.* stingy, tight, mingy.
Opposites GENEROUS; LIBERAL; MUNIFICENT.

pension *noun* **1** *draw one's pension at 60* retirement pension, old-age pension, superannuation. **2** *a disability pension* allowance, benefit, support, welfare.

pensioner *noun* retired person, old-age pensioner, OAP, senior citizen.

pensive *adjective in pensive mood* thoughtful, thinking, reflective, contemplative, musing, meditative, pondering, cogitative, ruminative, absorbed, preoccupied, serious, solemn, dreamy, dreaming, wistful, melancholy, sad.

pent-up *adjective pent-up feelings* bottled-up, repressed, suppressed, restrained, constrained, held in, kept in check, curbed, bridled.

penurious *adjective* **1** *penurious homeless people* penniless, without a penny, impecunious, impoverished, indigent, poor, poor as a church mouse, poverty-stricken, destitute, bankrupt, in reduced circumstances, in straitened circumstances, hard up; *inf.* broke, stony-broke, flat broke, skint, cleaned-out, strapped for cash, strapped. **2** *a penurious old skinflint* mean, miserly, parsimonious, niggardly, tight-fisted, cheese-paring, penurious, scrimping, skimping, close, Scrooge-like, ungenerous; *inf.* stingy, tight, mingy. *See* PENNY-PINCHING.
Opposites WEALTHY; GENEROUS.

penury *noun formerly wealthy but now reduced to penury* extreme poverty, pennilessness, impecuniousness, impoverishment, indigence, need, want, neediness, destitution, privation, pauperism, beggarliness, beggary, bankruptcy, insolvency, reduced circumstances, straitened circumstances.
Opposites WEALTH; AFFLUENCE.

people *noun* **1** *plural noun too many people in the hall/country* persons, individuals, human beings, humans, mortals, living souls, men women and children. **2** *a warlike people* race, tribe, clan, nation, country, population, populace. *See table.* **3** *plural noun issue to be decided by the people* the common people, the ordinary people, ordinary citizens, the general public, the public, the populace, electorate, the masses, the rank and file, commonalty, the

mob, the multitude, the *hoi polloi*, the rabble, the herd; *inf.* the plebs. **4** *plural noun her people live far away* family, relatives, relations, folk, kinsfolk, kin, kith and kin; *inf.* folks.

pep *noun full of pep after the holidays | a performance without pep* spirit, liveliness, animation, life, sparkle, effervescence, verve, ebullience, vivacity, fire, dash, zest, exuberance, élan, vigour, vim, brio; *inf.* zip.

pepper *noun* **1** *season the soup with pepper* white pepper, black pepper, peppercorns, cayenne pepper, cayenne. **2** *stuffed peppers* capsicum, red pepper, green pepper, yellow pepper.

pepper *verb* **1** *pepper the soup/sauce* add pepper to, season, flavour, spice, spice up. **2** *pepper his speech with quotations* sprinkle, intersperse, dot, bespatter, bestrew. **3** *pepper the new boy with paper pellets* pelt, bombard, shower, attack, assail, batter.

peppery *adjective* **1** *peppery food* peppered, hot, spicy, spiced, highly-seasoned, pungent, fiery. **2** *a peppery old man* hot-tempered, irascible, fiery, quick-tempered, irritable, touchy, testy, crabbed, crabby, crusty, splenetic, dyspeptic. **3** *give a peppery speech to the wrongdoers* caustic, acerbic, astringent, trenchant, cutting, sarcastic, stinging, biting, sharp.
Opposites MILD; BLAND; EASYGOING.

perceive *verb* **1** *perceive someone walking down the hill* see, catch sight of, spot, observe, glimpse, notice, make out, discern, behold, espy, detect, witness, remark. **2** *perceive the difference between right and wrong* discern, appreciate, recognize, be cognizant of, be aware of, be conscious of, know, grasp, understand, comprehend, apprehend, figure out, see, sense.

perceptible *adjective a perceptible change in her appearance | no perceptible improvement* perceivable, discernible, noticeable, detectable, distinguishable, appreciable, visible, observable, distinct, clear, plain, evident, apparent, obvious, manifest, conspicuous, patent, palpable, tangible.
Opposites IMPERCEPTIBLE; INCONSPICUOUS.

perception *noun* **1** *his perception of the magnitude of the problem* discernment, appreciation, recognition, cognizance, awareness, consciousness, knowledge, grasp, understanding, comprehension, apprehension, notion, conception, idea, sense. **2** *show great perception in his performance | his analysis shows great perception* perspicacity, discernment, perceptiveness, understanding, discrimination, insight, intuition, feeling, sensitivity.

perceptive *adjective* **1** *the fire noticed by the most perceptive* sharp-eyed, sharp-sighted, keen-sighted, observant, alert, vigilant. **2** *one of the more perceptive theatre critics* discerning, perspicacious, percipient, shrewd, understanding, discriminating, intuitive, responsive, sensitive. **3** *a perceptive analysis of the problem* discerning, perspicacious, percipient, penetrating, astute, shrewd.
Opposites HEEDLESS; OBTUSE; unobservant; DULL.

PEOPLES OF THE WORLD, ANCIENT AND MODERN

Africa
Afars
Afrikaners
Amharics
Bantu
Bemba
Beninese
Berbers
Biafrans
Bushmen
Carthaginians
Copts
Cushites
Dahomans
Damara
Danakil
Dinka
Edo
Efik
Ewe
Fan
Falla
Fingo
Fulah
Ganda
Griqua
Hausa
Herero
Hottentots
Hutu
Hyksos
Ibibio
Ibo/Igbo
Ijo
Ila
Issas
Kabyle
Kanuri
Khoisan
Kikuyu
Kongo
Kru
Luba
Lugbara/Lugwari
Luo
Maghribi
Malinke
Mande
Mandingo
Masai
Mende
Moors
Nago
Nama
Nandi
Negrillos
Nguni
Nubians
Numidians
Ovambo
Pondo
Pygmies
Samburu
Shona
Songhai
Soninke
Sotho

Tsonga
Tswana
Turkana
Tutsi
Twa
Ubangi
Watusi
Wolof
Xhosa
Yao
Yoruba
Zande
Zulus

Europe
Achaeans
Alsatians
Andalusians
Angevins
Anglo-Saxons
Apulians
Aragonese
Argives
Armoricans
Asturians
Athenians
Avars
Azeris
Basques
Batavians
Bavarians
Bessarabians
Boeotians
Bohemians
Bretons
Britons
Bulgars
Burgundians
Calabrians
Cantabrians
Castilians
Catalans
Caucasians
Celtiberians
Celts
Chechens
Cheremiss
Circassians
Corinthians
Corsicans
Cossacks
Cretans
Dacians
Dalmatians
Dorians
English
Etruscans
Faeroese
Flemings
Franks
Frisians
Friulians
Gaels
Galicians
Gauls
Ghegs
Goths
Gypsies

Helvetians
Herzegovinians
Hibernians
Hyrcanians
Iberians
Illyrians
Ingush
Ionians
Jutes
Kabardians
Karelians
Kashubians
Komi
Laconians
Lapps
Latins
Livonians
Lombards
Lusatians
Magyars
Manx
Mercians
Messenians
Mingrelians
Minoans
Moravians
Mordvins
Mycenaeans
Navarrese
Neapolitans
Normans
Norsemen
Northumbrians
Orcadians
Ossetes
Ostrogoths
Phocians
Picards
Picts
Piedmontese
Poitevins
Pomeranians
Provençals
Prussians
Rhinelanders
Rhaetians
Romans
Ruthenians
Saarlanders
Sabines
Salians
Sardinians
Savoyards
Saxons
Scandinavians
Scots
Shetlanders
Sicilians
Silesians
Slavs
Sorbs
Scythians
Spartans
Styrians
Swabians
Thracians
Thuringians

Tosks
Transylvanians
Tuscans
Tyroleans
Umbrians
Venetians
Viennese
Vikings
Visigoths
Vlachs
Wallachians
Walloons
Welsh
Wends
Westphalians

Middle East
Akkadians
Amalekites
Amorites
Anatolians
Arabs
Assyrians
Babylonians
Bedouin
Canaanites
Chaldaeans
Cilicians
Cumans
Edomites
Elamites
Ephesians
Galatians
Galileans
Himyarites
Hittites
Hurris
Judaeans
Kurds
Lycaonians
Lycians
Lydians
Mesopotamians
Moabites
Nabataeans
Palestinians
Paphlagonians
Parthians
Persians
Phoenicians
Phrygians
Sabaeans
Samarians
Samatians
Semites
Sidonians
Sumerians
Trojans
Tyrians

Asia (excluding the Middle East)
Ainu
Andamanese
Annamese
Assamese
Bactrians
Balinese

PEOPLES OF THE WORLD, ANCIENT AND MODERN *cont.*

Baluchis	Nagas	Ibanags	Caribs
Bashkirs	Nicobarese	Kamilaroi	Chibcha
Bengalis	Pathans	Kurnai	Guarani
Biharis	Punjabis	Maoris	Huastec
Dards	Rajasthanis	Melanesians	Huichol
Dravidians	Samoyeds	Micronesians	Incas
Dyaks	Shan	Moros	Lengua
Goanese	Sherpas	Pintupi	Maya
Gujeratis	Siamese	Polynesians	Mazahua
Hindustanis	Sindhis	Samals	Miskito
Huns	Sinhalese	Sulu	Mixtec
Javanese	Sumatrans	Tagalogs	Nahuatl
Kashmiris	Tajiks	**North**	Olmec
Kanarese	Talaings	**American Indian**	Otomi
Karens	Tamils	**Peoples**	Quechua
Kazakhs	Tatars/Tartars	*See table at* NORTH	Tarascans
Khmers	Tocharians	AMERICAN INDIAN.	Ticuna
Kyrgyz/Kirghiz	Turkmen	**Eskimo**	Tlapanec
Lushai	Uigurs	Aleut	Tlaxcalan
Maharashtrians	Uzbeks	Inuit	Toltec
Malays	Waziris	Yupik	Totonac
Malayalis	Yao	**South and**	Trique
Manchus	**Australasia and**	**Central America**	Tupi
Marathas	**Oceania**	**and the**	Tzeltal
Miao	Aborigines	**Caribbean**	Tzotzil
Moluccans	Aranda	Araucanians	Yaqui
Mon	Bajau	Arawaks	Yucatec
Mongols	Batak	Aymara	Yuma
Munda	Dyaks	Aztecs	Zapotec

perch *noun birds sitting on a perch* pole, rod, branch, roost, rest.

perch *verb birds perching on a branch* sit, rest, roost, settle, alight, land.

perchance *adverb* **1** *if perchance he arrives on time* by chance, by any chance, fortuitously. **2** *perchance we shall find the right book* perhaps, maybe, possibly, for all one knows; *lit.* peradventure.

percipient *adjective* **1** *a percipient commentator* perceptive, discerning, perspicacious, astute, shrewd, understanding, discriminating, intuitive, responsive, sensitive. **2** *a percipient summing-up* perceptive, discerning, perspicacious, penetrating, astute, shrewd.

percolate *verb* **1** *liquid percolating through the strainer* filter, filtrate, drain, drip, ooze, seep,

leach. **2** *percolate the coffee/liquid* strain, filter, filtrate, sieve, sift. **3** *coffee percolating in the pot* brew, bubble; *inf.* perk. **4** *information finally percolating through the department* go through, pass through, filter through, permeate, pervade.

percussion *noun instruments based on percussion* impact, collision, bang, clash, crash, striking, beating. *See table.*

perdition *noun cursed to perdition* damnation, hell-fire, hell, spiritual destruction.

peremptory *adjective* **1** *receive a peremptory request from the boss* imperious, high-handed, urgent, pressing, imperative, high-priority. **2** *behave in a peremptory manner to shop assistants* imperious, high-handed, overbearing, dogmatic, autocratic, dictatorial, domineering, arbitrary, tyrannical, despotic, arrogant, over-

PERCUSSION INSTRUMENTS

angel	chengcheng	gong	rommelpot	tabor	tubular
chimes	chime bar	gong	saron	taiko	bells
anvil	Chinese	chimes	scraper	tambour	Turkish
banana	block	handbell	sekere	tambourine	crescent
drum	clappers	hi-hat	shaker	tam-tam	tympani
barrel drum	claves	cymbals	side drum	tenor drum	vibraphone
bass drum	cowbell	idiophone	sistrum	temple	vibraslap
bells	crotals	jew's harp	sleigh bells	block	washboard
bhaya	cylindrical	kettledrum	slit drum	thumb	whip
bongo	drums	lithophone	snare drum	piano	wobble-
drums	cymbals	maracas	stamping	timbal	board
castanets	drum	mbila	tube	timpani	wood block
celesta	frame drum	piano	steel drum	tom-tom	xylophone
changko	glockenspiel	rattle	tabla	triangle	xylorimba

weening, supercilious, lordly. **3** *a peremptory judgement* incontrovertible, irreversible, binding, absolute, final, conclusive, decisive, definitive, categorical, irrefutable.

perennial *adjective* **1** *a subject of perennial interest | perennial favourite* perpetual, everlasting, eternal, unending, never-ending, endless, undying, ceaseless, abiding, enduring, lasting, persisting, permanent, constant, unfailing, unchanging. **2** *tired of their perennial complaining* constant, continual, continuous, continuing, uninterrupted, ceaseless, persistent, recurrent, chronic, never-ending; *inf.* eternal.

perfect *adjective* **1** *a perfect set of antique dinner plates* complete, full, whole, entire. **2** *this piece of work is now perfect* perfected, completed, finished. **3** *a perfect fool/disaster* absolute, complete, out-and-out, thorough, thoroughgoing, downright, utter, sheer, consummate, unmitigated, unqualified. **4** *a perfect performance | a perfect piece of work* flawless, faultless, unmarred, ideal, impeccable, consummate, immaculate, exemplary, superb, superlative, supreme, excellent, wonderful, **5** *a perfect mother/pupil* ideal, model, without fault, faultless, flawless, consummate, exemplary, excellent, wonderful. **6** *a perfect evening* superb, exquisite, superlative, excellent, wonderful, marvellous; *inf.* out of this world, terrific, fantastic, fabulous. **7** *a perfect copy* exact, precise, accurate, faithful, correct, right, close, true, strict; *inf.* spot on. **8** *the perfect present* ideal, just right, right, appropriate, fitting, fit, suitable, apt.
Opposites IMPERFECT; FAULTY; DEFECTIVE.

perfect *verb* *perfect the technique* make perfect, render faultless/flawless, improve, better, polish, refine, elaborate, complete, consummate, put the finishing touches to.

perfection *noun* **1** *working on the perfection of their technique* perfecting, improvement, betterment, polishing, refinement, completion, consummation. *See* PERFECT *verb.* **2** *try to achieve perfection in his work* perfectness, flawlessness, faultlessness, consummation, impeccability, immaculateness, exemplariness, superbness. *See* PERFECT *adjective* 4. **3** *as a singer she was perfection* paragon, one in a million; *inf.* the tops. **4** *the meal was perfection* ideal, acme, crown, peak of perfection.

perfectionist *noun* *writers who are perfectionists* stickler for perfection, precisionist, precisian, purist, formalist.

perfectly *adverb* **1** *perfectly happy/miserable* absolutely, utterly, completely, altogether, entirely, wholly, totally, thoroughly, fully. **2** *the cake turned out perfectly | he played perfectly* to perfection, flawlessly, faultlessly, without blemish, ideally, impeccably, immaculately, superbly, exquisitely, superlatively, wonderfully.

perfidious *adjective* *betrayed by perfidious allies* treacherous, traitorous, treasonous, false, untrue, disloyal, faithless, unfaithful, deceitful, double-dealing, duplicitous, dishonest, two-faced.

perfidy *noun* *captured because of the perfidy of his allies* perfidiousness, treachery, traitorousness, falseness, infidelity, disloyalty, faithlessness, unfaithfulness, deceitfulness, deceit, double-dealing, duplicity, dishonesty, two-facedness.

perforate *verb* **1** *perforate the skin* pierce, puncture, prick, stab, gore, bore, penetrate, spike. **2** *perforate paper* put holes in, make holes in, hole, punch holes in, punch, honeycomb.

perform *verb* **1** *perform acts of charity | could perform feats of skill* do, carry out, execute, discharge, conduct, effect, bring about, bring off, accomplish, achieve, fulfil, complete. **2** *perform in Hamlet* act, play, appear. **3** *perform a new symphony* play, execute. **4** *a car performing well* function, work, operate, run, go.
Opposites NEGLECT; OMIT.

performance *noun* **1** *faithful in the performance of his duty | performance of acts of charity* carrying out, execution, discharge, conducting, effecting, accomplishment, achievement, fulfilment. **2** *watch a musical performance* show, production, entertainment, act, presentation; *inf.* gig. **3** *his performance of Hamlet* acting, playing, representation, staging.

performer *noun* **1** *applaud the performers* actor/ actress, player, entertainer, artist, artiste, Thespian, trouper, musician, singer, dancer. **2** *performers of acts of charity | a performer of strange feats* doer, executor, worker, operator, architect, author.

perfume *noun* **1** *the perfume of roses | love the perfume of new-mown hay* scent, fragrance, aroma, smell, bouquet, redolence. **2** *buy some French perfume* scent, fragrance, eau de toilette, toilet water, eau-de-Cologne, cologne.

perfunctory *adjective* *take a perfunctory look at the contract* cursory, superficial, desultory, mechanical, automatic, routine, sketchy, brief, hasty, hurried, rapid, fleeting, quick, fast, offhand, casual, indifferent, careless, inattentive, negligent.

perhaps *adverb* *perhaps we may meet him on the way* it may be, maybe, possibly, it is possible that, conceivably, feasibly, for all one knows; *lit.* peradventure.

peril *noun* *abducted children in great peril* danger, jeopardy, risk, hazard, menace, threat.
Opposites SAFETY; SECURITY.

perilous *adjective* *a perilous journey through the mountains* dangerous, fraught with danger, menacing, risky, precarious, hazardous, chancy, threatening, unsafe.
Opposites SAFE; SECURE.

perimeter *noun* **1** *the perimeter of a circle* circumference. **2** *guards patrolling the perimeter of the estate* boundary, border, frontier, limits, outer limits, confines, edge, margin, fringe, periphery.

period *noun* **1** *during periods of peace | over a period of several years* time, space, spell, interval, term, stretch, span. **2** *absent for a period* time, while, spell. **3** *the post-war period | the period of the French Revolution* time, days, age, era, epoch, aeon. *See table at* AGE. **4** *he's going, period* finis, end, finish, conclusion, stop, halt, and that's that. **5** *put a period at the end of a sentence* full stop, full point, point, stop. **6** *irregular periods* menstruation, menstrual flow, monthly flow, menses; *inf.* the curse.

periodic *adjective periodic inspections | has periodic attacks of dizziness* periodical, at fixed intervals, recurrent, recurring, repeated, cyclical, cyclic, regular, intermittent, occasional, infrequent, sporadic, every once in a while, every so often.

periodical *noun consult a specialist periodical* journal, publication, magazine, review, organ, quarterly, monthly, weekly; *inf.* book, glossy.

peripatetic *adjective* **1** *peripatetic tribes* itinerant, travelling, wandering, roving, roaming, nomadic, migrant, migratory. **2** *peripatetic teachers* itinerant, travelling, mobile.

peripheral *adjective* **1** *peripheral zones of the city* outer, on the edge/outskirts, surrounding, neighbouring. **2** *waste time discussing peripheral matters* minor, lesser, secondary, subsidiary, ancillary, unimportant, superficial, irrelevant, beside the point.
Opposites CENTRAL; MAJOR; IMPORTANT; VITAL.

periphery *noun* **1** *on the periphery of the town* outskirts, boundary, border, limits, outer limits, edge, margin, fringe, perimeter. **2** *on the periphery of the group* edge, fringe, margin.

periphrastic *adjective a periphrastic style of prose* circumlocutory, redundant, tautological, pleonastic, roundabout, indirect, rambling, wandering, ambagious.

perish *verb* **1** *soldiers perishing in battle* die, lose one's life, be killed, lay down one's life, meet one's death, breathe one's last, draw one's last breath; *inf.* bite the dust, kick the bucket. **2** *the old theories/values having perished* come to an end, die away, disappear, vanish, disintegrate, go under, be destroyed. **3** *food perishing in the heat* go bad, go off, go sour, rot, decay, decompose.
Opposites LIVE; SURVIVE.

perjure *verb* **perjure oneself** *found guilty of contempt of court for perjuring herself* commit perjury, lie under oath, give false evidence/testimony, bear false witness.

perjury *noun* **1** *witnesses found guilty of perjury | committed perjury* lying under oath, violation of oath, giving false evidence/testimony, bearing false witness, false swearing. **2** *repeated her perjury* false oath, false statement, wilful/deliberate falsehood.

perk *verb* **perk up** **1** *children perking up at the promise of a treat* cheer up, become cheerful, brighten up, feel happy, be gladdened, take heart; *inf.* buck up, pep up. **2** *invalids perking up after treatment* brighten up, recover, recuperate, rally, revive. **3** *the holiday perked them up* cheer up, brighten up, raise someone's spirits, give someone heart, give someone a boost/lift; *inf.* buck up, pep up.

perk *noun. See* PERQUISITE.

permanence *noun* **1** *the permanence of their separation/disability* everlastingness, perpetuity, perpetualness, permanency, eternalness, eternality, endurance, constancy, persistence, endlessness, immutability, inalterability. *See*

PERMANENT 1. **2** *the permanence of the job/relationship* stability, lastingness, long-lastingness, fixedness, soundness, firmness.

permanent *adjective* **1** *the couple's separation is permanent | left with a permanent disability* everlasting, perpetual, eternal, enduring, perennial, lasting, abiding, constant, persistent, unending, endless, never-ending, immutable, unchangeable, inalterable, invariable. **2** *a permanent job/relationship* lasting, long-lasting, stable, fixed, established, sound, firm.
Opposites TEMPORARY; FLEETING; EPHEMERAL.

permanently *adverb permanently separated/disabled* everlastingly, perpetually, eternally, perennially, lastingly, constantly, persistently, unendingly, endlessly, immutably, inalterably, invariably, for all time, for good, for good and all, for ever and ever, for ever, evermore, for evermore, till the end of time, time without end; *inf.* till the cows come home, till hell freezes over.

permeate *verb* **1** *cooking smells permeating the whole house* spread through, be disseminated through, pass through, pervade, fill, diffuse through, be diffused through, extend throughout, imbue, penetrate, infiltrate, percolate through. **2** *water permeating the soil* spread through, pass through, penetrate, soak through, seep through, leak through, infiltrate, percolate through, leach through, saturate.

permissible *adjective driving with more than the permissible amount of alcohol* permitted, allowable, admissible, acceptable, tolerated, authorized, sanctioned, legal, lawful, legitimate, licit, within bounds; *inf.* legit.

permission *noun enter without permission | act with the permission of her mother* authorization, sanction, leave, licence, dispensation, empowerment, allowance, consent, assent, acquiescence, go-ahead, thumbs up, agreement, approval, approbation, tolerance, sufferance; *inf.* green light.

permissive *adjective a permissive parent/upbringing* liberal, tolerant, broad-minded, open-minded, easygoing, forbearing, latitudinarian, indulgent, lenient, unrestricted, overindulgent, lax, unprescriptive.
Opposites INTOLERANT; STRICT.

permit *verb* **1** *parents not permitting the children to go | not permit talking in class* give permission, allow, let, authorize, give leave, sanction, grant, license, empower, enable, consent to, assent to, acquiesce in, give the go-ahead to, give the thumbs up to, agree to, approve of, tolerate, countenance, suffer, brook; *inf.* give the green light to. **2** *if time permits* allow, make possible, allow the possibility of, give an opportunity.
Opposites BAN; FORBID; REFUSE.

permit *noun a permit to have a market stall* licence, authorization, warrant, sanction, pass, passport.

permutation *noun the system allows for permutation* variation, alteration, change, shift, transformation, transposition, transmutation.

pernicious · persistent

pernicious *adjective a pernicious influence on society* destructive, ruinous, injurious, damaging, harmful, hurtful, detrimental, deleterious, deadly, lethal, fatal, wicked, evil, bad, malign, malevolent, malignant, noxious, poisonous, venomous.
Opposites BENEFICIAL; FAVOURABLE.

pernickety *adjective* difficult to please, difficult, fussy, punctilious, finicky, over-fastidious, fastidious, over-particular, particular, nice, over-nice; *inf.* nit-picking, choosy, picky.
Opposites EASYGOING; LAID-BACK.

peroration *noun* **1** *give a peroration at the end of a speech* closing remarks, conclusion, summation, summing-up, recapitulation; *inf.* recapping. **2** *students wearying of the lecturer's peroration* lengthy talk/lecture/speech/address, rhetorical speech, bombastic oration, harangue, declamation, diatribe.

perpendicular *adjective* **1** *the perpendicular supports* upright, vertical, on end, standing, straight. **2** *a line perpendicular to another* at right angles to, at 90 degrees to. **3** *perpendicular cliffs* steep, sheer, precipitous, abrupt.
Opposites HORIZONTAL.

perpetrate *verb perpetrate a crime | has perpetrated an indiscretion* commit, carry out, perform, execute, do, effect, effectuate, bring about, be guilty of, be to blame for, be responsible for; *inf.* pull off.

perpetual *adjective* **1** *a state of perpetual bliss | the perpetual snow of the Arctic* everlasting, eternal, never-ending, unending, endless, undying, perennial, permanent, perdurable, lasting, abiding, persisting, enduring, constant, unfailing, unchanging, unvarying, invariable. **2** *work with perpetual noise* incessant, unceasing, ceaseless, unending, endless, never-stopping, non-stop, continuous, uninterrupted, unbroken, unremitting. **3** *tired of their perpetual complaints* interminable, persistent, frequent, continual, recurrent, repeated; *inf.* eternal.
Opposites TRANSITORY; FLEETING; INTERMITTENT.

perpetuate *verb* **1** *perpetuate the myth that he was a hero* keep alive, keep going, keep up, preserve, conserve, sustain, maintain, continue. **2** *perpetuate his memory with a statue* memorialize, commemorate, immortalize, eternalize, eternize.

perpetuity *noun* **in perpetuity** *land given in perpetuity to the family by the King* perpetually, permanently, perennially, for ever, for ever and ever, for all time, until the end of time, for good, eternally, for eternity, everlastingly.

perplex *verb* **1** *her behaviour perplexed him* puzzle, baffle, mystify, stump, keep someone guessing, bewilder, confound, confuse, nonplus, disconcert, dismay, dumbfound; *inf.* bamboozle. **2** *issues which perplex the situation* complicate, confuse, make involved, muddle, mix up, jumble, entangle, tangle, snarl up; *inf.* foul up.

perplexed *adjective explain the situation to her perplexed family | give a perplexed look* puzzled, baffled, mystified, bewildered, confused, nonplussed, disconcerted, dumbfounded; *inf.* bamboozled.

perplexing *adjective* **1** *her perplexing behaviour* puzzling, baffling, mystifying, mysterious, bewildering, confusing, disconcerting, unaccountable, strange, weird. **2** *a perplexing problem* complicated, involved, intricate, complex, difficult, thorny, knotty, taxing, trying, vexing.

perplexity *noun* **1** *filled with perplexity at her behaviour* puzzlement, bafflement, incomprehension, mystification, bewilderment, confusion, disconcertion, disconcertment, dismay; *inf.* bamboozlement. **2** *a problem of much perplexity* complication, involvement, intricacy, complexity, difficulty, muddle, jumble, entanglement. See PERPLEXING 2. **3** *the perplexities of the murder case* complication, intricacy, complexity, difficulty, mystery, puzzle, enigma, paradox.

perquisite *noun a perquisite of the job* fringe benefit, benefit, advantage, bonus, dividend, extra, plus; *inf.* perk, freebie.

persecute *verb* **1** *persecute people for their beliefs* oppress, tyrannize, abuse, mistreat, maltreat, ill-treat, molest, afflict, torment, torture, victimize, martyr. **2** *film stars persecuted by the press* harass, pester, hound, badger, vex, bother, worry, annoy; *inf.* hassle.

perseverance *noun to start with he wasn't very good but perseverance brought success* persistence, tenacity, pertinacity, determination, resolve, resolution, resoluteness, purposefulness, obstinacy, insistence, intransigence, patience, application, diligence, assiduity.

persevere *verb* **1** *persevere in his attempts to win* persist, go on, keep on, keep at, keep going, continue, carry on, struggle, work, hammer away, be tenacious, be persistent, be pertinacious, be resolute, be purposeful, be obstinate, be insistent, be intransigent, be patient, be diligent; *inf.* plug away. **2** *when you fail you must persevere* persist, go on, keep on, keep going, continue, carry on, be tenacious, be persistent, be pertinacious, be determined, be resolute, stand one's ground, stand fast, not give up; *inf.* stick to one's guns, stick at it.
Opposites give up (see GIVE); STOP; QUIT.

persist *verb* **1** *persist in his efforts to win* persevere, go on, keep on, keep going, continue, carry on; *inf.* plug away. See PERSEVERE 1. **2** *you must persist, not give up* persevere, keep going, carry on, be resolute, stand one's ground; *inf.* stick to one's guns, stick at it. See PERSEVERE 2. **3** *the cold weather persisted* carry on, keep on, keep up, continue, last, remain, linger, hold.
Opposites give up (see GIVE); STOP; DESIST.

persistence *noun with persistence he got a job* tenacity, determination, purposefulness, insistence, intransigence, patience, application. See PERSEVERANCE.

persistent *adjective* **1** *persistent people refusing to give up in their attempts* persevering, tenacious, pertinacious, determined, resolute, purposeful, obstinate, stubborn, insistent, intransigent, obdurate, intractable, patient, diligent. **2** *matches called off because of persistent rain* constant, continual, continuous, continuing, interminable, incessant, unceasing, endless, unremitting, unrelenting, relentless. **3** *a*

persistent cough chronic, frequent, repetitive, repititious.
Opposites IRRESOLUTE; INTERMITTENT; OCCASIONAL.

person noun *not a person was left alive* individual, human being, human, creature, living soul, soul, mortal; *inf.* character.

persona noun *seen to take on the persona of his dead brother* character, personality, role, part, public face.

personable adjective *a personable young man* pleasant, agreeable, amiable, affable, likeable, charming, nice, attractive, presentable, good-looking.

personage noun *events attended by royal personages* person, public figure, dignitary, notable, person of note, celebrity, personality, VIP, famous name, household name, luminary, worthy; *inf.* big shot, big noise, big gun, celeb.

personal adjective **1** *his reasons for leaving are personal* individual, private, confidential, secret, one's own business. **2** *a personal style of prose | a personal interpretation of the music* personalized, individual, idiosyncratic, characteristic, unique, peculiar. **3** *a personal letter to her boss* private, confidential, intimate. **4** *receive the personal attention of the manager* in person, individual, special. **5** *make personal remarks* insulting, slighting, derogatory, disparaging, pejorative, offensive.
Opposites PUBLIC; GENERAL.

personality noun **1** *of an unassuming personality* nature, disposition, character, temperament, temper, make-up, traits, psyche. **2** *an unassuming man with little personality* strength of personality, force of personality, personal identity, character, charisma, magnetism, powers of attraction, charm. **3** *several personalities attending charity events* celebrity, VIP, famous name, household name, dignitary, notable, person of note, personage, luminary, worthy. *See* PERSONAGE.

personalize verb **1** *he tends always to personalize issues* regard as personal, take personally, regard subjectively, be subjective about, interpret in terms of oneself. **2** *personalize his luggage | personalized number-plate* give a personal touch to, have one's initials engraved on, initial, monogram, customize.

personally adverb **1** *deal with the matter personally* in person, oneself/herself/themselves etc. **2** *personally speaking, I am opposed to the idea* for my etc. part, for my etc. own part, for myself etc., from my etc. own point of view, as far as I etc. am concerned. **take something personally** take as an insult, regard as a slight, take offence at, be offended by.

personification noun *he is the personification of politeness* embodiment, incarnation, epitome, quintessence, essence, symbol, representation, image, portrayal, likeness, semblance.

personify verb *personify all that was good about the country* embody, body forth, be the incarnation of, epitomize, typify, exemplify, symbolize, represent, mirror.

personnel noun *factory managers in charge of personnel* staff, employees, workers, workforce, labour force, manpower, human resources, liveware.

perspective noun **1** *young people have a different perspective of such matters* outlook, view, viewpoint, point of view, standpoint, vantage point, stand, stance, angle, slant, attitude, frame of mind. **2** *get a perspective of the whole valley from the tower* view, vista, bird's-eye view, prospect, scene, outlook, panorama, aspect, sweep.

perspicacious adjective *perspicacious of him to recognize her distress* discerning, perceptive, penetrating, percipient, sharp-witted, sharp, quick-witted, keen-witted, alert, clear-sighted, shrewd, acute, clever, intelligent, smart, judicious, wise, sagacious, sensitive, intuitive, understanding.
Opposites INATTENTIVE; DULL; STUPID.

perspicacity noun *admire his perspicacity in recognizing her distress* discernment, perception, perceptiveness, percipience, sharpness, sharp-wittedness, quick-wittedness, keen-wittedness, alertness, clear-sightedness, shrewdness, acuteness, acuity, cleverness, intelligence, smartness, judiciousness, sagacity, wisdom, sensitivity, intuition, intuitiveness, insight, understanding.

perspiration noun *perspiration running down his face* sweat, moisture; *tech.* sudor.

perspire verb *perspire in the heat* sweat, be dripping with sweat, be pouring with sweat, swelter, glow.

persuade verb *persuade her to go despite her disinclination* prevail upon, win over, talk someone into, bring round, induce, convince, influence, sway, prompt, coerce, inveigle, cajole, wheedle; *inf.* sweet-talk, soft-soap.
Opposites DISSUADE; DISCOURAGE; DETER.

persuasion noun **1** *their successful persuasion of the children to go* persuading, prevailing, winning over, inducement, convincing, coercion, inveiglement, cajolery, wheedling; *inf.* sweet-talking, soft-soaping. **2** *use their powers of persuasion* persuasiveness, inducement, influence, coercion, inveiglement, cajolery, wheedling, suasion. **3** *it is his persuasion that the decision was a mistake* belief, opinion, view, point of view, conviction. **4** *churchmen of different persuasions* denomination, belief, creed, credo, faith, school of thought, philosophy, sect, affiliation, camp, side, faction.

persuasive adjective *persuasive arguments* effective, effectual, convincing, cogent, plausible, compelling, forceful, eloquent, weighty, influential, telling.
Opposites INEFFECTIVE; WEAK.

pert adjective **1** *a pert young girl* impudent, impertinent, saucy, forward, presumptuous, audacious, bold, brash, brazen, bumptious. **2** *a pert little hat* jaunty, stylish, chic, trim, smart, spruce; *inf.* natty, saucy.

pertain verb **1** *evidence which does not pertain to the case* be connected with, relate to, be relevant to, have relevance to, concern, apply to, be pertinent to, have reference to, have a bearing upon. **2** *the manor-house and the land pertaining to it* belong to, be a part of, be an

adjunct of, go along with, be included in.
3 *the feeling of rebellion pertaining to youth* be appropriate to, be suited to, befit, fit in with, appertain to.

pertinacious *adjective* **1** *pertinacious people refusing to give up* persistent, persevering, tenacious, resolute, determined, purposeful, insistent, stubborn, obstinate, obdurate, strong-willed, headstrong, inflexible, intransigent, wilful, mulish, pig-headed, bull-headed, intractable, refractory, perverse. **2** *make pertinacious attempts to succeed* persistent, persevering, resolute, determined, dogged, purposeful, insistent.
Opposites IRRESOLUTE; TENTATIVE.

pertinent *adjective make a few pertinent comments* relevant, appropriate, suitable, fitting, fit, apt, apposite, to the point, applicable, material, germane, to the purpose, apropos, *ad rem.*
Opposites IRRELEVANT; INAPPROPRIATE.

perturb *verb* **1** *news of the war perturbed the King* disturb, make anxious, worry, alarm, trouble, upset, disquiet, discompose, disconcert, vex, bother, agitate, unsettle, fluster, ruffle, harass. **2** *perturb the smooth running of the office* throw into confusion, confuse, throw into disorder, disarrange, throw into disarray, muddle, jumble.

perturbed *adjective feel perturbed at the news* | *try to calm the perturbed people* disturbed, anxious, worried, alarmed, troubled, upset, disquieted, discomposed, disconcerted, vexed, agitated, unsettled, flustered, ruffled, harassed.
Opposites UNPERTURBED; CALM; TRANQUIL.

peruse *verb* **1** *peruse the document before signing* read carefully, read thoroughly, scrutinize, study, pore over, inspect, examine, scan. **2** *peruse the leaflets in the waiting-room* browse through, look through, glance through, leaf through, run an eye over, scan, skim through.

pervade *verb cooking smells pervaded the entire house* | *terror pervaded his whole being* spread through, be disseminated through, permeate, fill, pass through, extend throughout, suffuse, diffuse through, be diffused through, imbue, infuse, penetrate, infiltrate, percolate.

pervasive *adjective pervasive cooking smells* | *pervasive feelings of terror* pervading, permeating, prevalent, suffusive, extensive, ubiquitous, omnipresent, rife, widespread, universal.

perverse *adjective* **1** *perverse children* | *old people can be perverse* contrary, wayward, troublesome, unruly, difficult, awkward, unreasonable, disobedient, unmanageable, uncontrollable, rebellious, wilful, headstrong, capricious, stubborn, obstinate, obdurate, pertinacious, mulish, pig-headed, bull-headed, wrong-headed, querulous, fractious, intractable, refractory, intransigent, contumacious; *inf.* bolshie, stroppy. **2** *take a perverse delight in annoying her* contradictory, unreasonable, irrational, illogical, senseless, abnormal, deviant, excessive, undue, immoderate, inordinate, outrageous.
Opposites ACCOMMODATING; REASONABLE.

perversion *noun* **1** *a perversion of the truth* distortion, misuse, misrepresentation, falsifica-

tion, misinterpretation, misconstruction. **2** *the treatment of his sexual perversion* deviation, aberration, abnormality, irregularity, unnaturalness, corruption, debauchery, depravity, vice, wickedness; *inf.* kinkiness. **3** *such sexual perversions are very rare* deviation, aberration, abnormality, irregularity, depravity, vice, kink.

perversity *noun* **1** *the perversity of the children* | *the old man's perversity* perverseness, contrariness, troublesomeness, unruliness, difficulty, awkwardness, unreasonableness, disobedience, unmanageableness, unmanageability, rebelliousness, wilfulness, stubbornness, obstinacy, obduracy, pertinacity, mulishness, pig-headedness, querulousness, fractiousness, intractability, refractoriness, intransigence, contumaciousness. See PERVERSE 1. **2** *appalled at the perversity of his behaviour* unreasonableness, irrationality, abnormality, deviation, excessiveness, immoderateness, outrageousness. See PERVERSE 2.

pervert *verb* **1** *pervert the course of justice* turn aside, divert, deflect, avert, subvert. **2** *pervert common English expressions out of ignorance* misapply, misuse, distort, garble, warp, twist, misinterpret, misconstrue. **3** *pervert young minds* lead astray, corrupt, warp, deprave, debauch, debase, degrade, vitiate.

pervert *noun a sexual pervert* deviant, deviate, degenerate, debauchee; *inf.* perv, weirdo.

perverted *adjective a perverted old man abusing children* | *a perverted interest in young boys* corrupt, corrupted, depraved, debauched, debased, vitiated, deviant, abnormal, aberrant, warped, distorted, twisted, sick, unhealthy, immoral, evil, wicked, vile; *inf.* kinky.

pessimism *noun his pessimism made everyone gloomy* looking on the black side, expecting the worst, lack of hope, hopelessness, gloom, gloominess, gloom and doom, cynicism, defeatism, fatalism, distrust, doubt, suspicion, resignation, depression, dejection, despair.

pessimist *noun pessimists forecasting disaster* prophet of doom, cynic, defeatist, fatalist, alarmist, doubter, doubting Thomas; *inf.* doom merchant, gloom merchant, doomster.

pessimistic *adjective a pessimistic outlook on life* hopeless, gloomy, gloom-ridden, cynical, defeatist, fatalistic, distrustful, alarmist, doubting, suspicious, bleak, resigned, depressed, dejected, despairing.
Opposites OPTIMISTIC; HOPEFUL; CHEERFUL.

pest *noun regard the child as a pest* nuisance, bother, source of annoyance/irritation, vexation, irritant, thorn in the flesh, problem, trouble, worry, inconvenience, trial, tribulation, the bane of one's life; *inf.* pain, pain in the neck, aggravation.

pester *verb photographers pestering the film star* | *beggars pestering tourists for money* badger, hound, irritate, annoy, bother, irk, nag, fret, worry, harass, chivvy, get on someone's nerves, torment, plague, bedevil, harry; *inf.* get at, bug, hassle.

pestilence *noun* **1** *villagers dying from a/the pestilence* plague, bubonic plague, Black Death, epidemic, pandemic, disease, contagion, sickness. **2** *the pestilence of marauding neighbours* bane, blight, affliction, scourge, curse, torment.

pestilential *adjective* **1** *a pestilential infection* plague-like, contagious, communicable, catching, epidemic, dangerous, injurious, harmful, destructive, virulent, pernicious, toxic, venomous, malign, fatal, deadly. **2** *a pestilential creature wreaking havoc in their lives* annoying, irritating, irksome, vexatious, troublesome, bothersome, tiresome.

pet¹ *noun* *teacher's pet | she was a pet of the King* favourite, darling, idol, apple of one's eye; *inf.* blue-eyed boy/girl; *Am. inf.* fair-haired boy/girl.

pet² *adjective* **1** *a pet lamb* domesticated, domestic, house-trained, house-broken, tame, tamed. **2** *a pet theory/charity* favourite, favoured, cherished, prized, dear to one's heart, preferred, particular, special. **pet name** *call her daughter/husband by a pet name* affectionate name, term of endearment, endearment, nickname.

pet³ *verb* **1** *pet the cat* stroke, caress, fondle, pat, clap. **2** *young people petting in public* make love, kiss, cuddle, embrace, caress; *inf.* canoodle, neck, smooch, snog, bill and coo.

pet⁴ *noun* *in a pet at not getting her own way* sulk, the sulks, tantrum, bad mood, mood, bad temper, ill temper, temper, ill humour, fit of pique; *inf.* huff, paddy.

peter *verb* **peter out** *great enthusiasm which petered out* fade, die away, melt away, evaporate, wane, ebb, diminish, taper off, come to nothing, die out, fail, fall through, come to a halt, come to an end.

petition *noun* **1** *sign a petition to save the building from destruction* protest document, list of protesters, appeal, round robin. **2** *make a petition to God | made several petitions for mercy to the King* entreaty, supplication, plea, prayer, appeal, request, application, suit.

petition *verb* *petition God | petitioned the King for mercy* entreat, beg, beseech, plead with, make a plea to, pray, appeal to, request, ask, apply to, call upon, press, adjure, present one's suit to, sue.

petrify *verb* **1** *the thought of speaking in public petrified her | petrified at the strange sight* terrify, strike terror into, horrify, frighten, fill with fear, make terror-stricken, panic, alarm, scare out of his/her etc. wits, appal, paralyse, stun, stupefy, transfix. **2** *age had petrified the plant life* turn to stone, fossilize, calcify, ossify.

petticoat *noun* *a frilly petticoat* slip, underskirt, undergarment.

petty *adjective* **1** *waste time discussing petty matters/details* trivial, trifling, minor, small, slight, unimportant, inessential, inconsequential, inconsiderable, negligible, paltry, fiddling; *inf.* piffling. **2** *indulge in petty behaviour | do it out of petty spite* narrow-minded, narrow, small-minded, mean-minded, mean, ungenerous, grudging.
Opposites IMPORTANT; SERIOUS; MAJOR; MAGNANIMOUS.

petulant *adjective* *petulant children squabbling | children making petulant demands* querulous, complaining, peevish, fretful, impatient, cross, irritable, moody, crabbed, crabby, snappish, crotchety, touchy, bad-tempered, ill-tempered, ill-humoured, irascible, sulky, sullen; *inf.* ratty.
Opposites GOOD-NATURED; EASYGOING; AFFABLE.

phantom *noun* **1** *imagine he saw phantoms in the graveyard* ghost, apparition, spectre, shade, spirit, revenant, wraith, shadow, phantasm; *inf.* spook. **2** *dreams haunted by phantoms of evil* vision, hallucination, illusion, figment of the imagination, chimera.

phase *noun* **1** *the various phases of the reconstruction process | an exciting phase in history* stage, part, step, chapter, point, period, time, juncture. **2** *children going through a difficult phase* stage, time, period, spell. **3** *changing phases of the moon* aspect, facet, shape, form.

phase *verb* **phase in** *phase in new teaching methods* introduce gradually, incorporate by stages, begin using, ease in, start using. **phase out** *phase out the old machinery* withdraw/remove gradually, dispose of gradually, get rid of by stages, stop using, ease off, run down, wind down, wind up.

phenomenal *adjective* *enjoying phenomenal success* extraordinary, remarkable, exceptional, singular, uncommon, unheard-of, unique, unparalleled, unprecedented, amazing, astonishing, astounding, unusual, marvellous, prodigious, sensational, miraculous; *inf.* fantastic, fabulous, mind-boggling, mind-blowing.
Opposites ORDINARY; USUAL; RUN-OF-THE-MILL.

phenomenon *noun* **1** *a social phenomenon peculiar to our times* circumstances, fact, experience, occurrence, happening, event, incident, episode. **2** *the child is really a phenomenon | the child's compositions are regarded as something of a musical phenomenon* marvel, prodigy, rarity, wonder, sensation, miracle, nonpareil.

philander *verb* *always philandering | accused of philandering with the girls in the office* flirt, have an affair, have a love affair, womanize, dally with, trifle/toy with the affections of, play around, fool around, coquet with.

philanderer *noun* *marry a philanderer who would never be faithful* Casanova, Don Juan, womanizer, woman-chaser, ladies' man, flirt, Lothario, dallier, trifler; *inf.* lady-killer, wolf, stud.

philanthropic *adjective* **1** *a philanthropic concern for his fellow-men | charity work stemming from philanthropic motives* humanitarian, humane, public-spirited, socially-concerned, solicitous, unselfish, selfless, altruistic, kind-hearted. **2** *a philanthropic millionaire/organization* benevolent, beneficent, benignant, charitable, alms-giving, generous, kind, munificent, bountiful, bounteous, liberal, open-handed, giving, helping.
Opposites SELFISH; MEAN; MISERLY.

philanthropist *noun* **1** *philanthropists showing concern for their fellow-men* humanitarian, altruist. **2** *charitable organizations funded by philanthropists* alms-giver, benefactor, patron, sponsor, giver, donor, contributor, backer, helper.

PHILOSOPHERS

Abelard, Peter
(1079–1142; Fr.)

Adorno, Theodor
Wiesengrund
(1903–69; Ger.)

al-Farabi,
Mohammed ibn
Tarkhan (d. 950 A.D.;
Pers.)

al-Ghazālī, Abū
Hamid Muhammad
(1058–1111; Arab.)

Al-Kindi, Abu Yusuf
Ya'qub ibn Ishaq
(d. c. 870 A.D.; Arab.)

Althusser, Louis
(1919–90; Fr.)

Anaxagoras
(c. 500–428 B.C.; Gk)

Anaximander
(c. 610–c. 545 B.C.;
Gk)

Anaximenes
(d. c. 528 B.C.; Gk)

Anselm, St
(1033–1109; It.)

Aquinas, St Thomas
(c. 1225–74; It.)

Arendt, Hannah
(1906–75; Am., b. in
Germany)

Aristotle
(384–322 B.C.; Gk)

Augustine of Hippo,
St (354–430 A.D.;
North African)

Averroës (Ibn Rushd;
c. 1126–98; Arab.)

Avicenna (Ibn Sīnā;
980–1037; Arab.)

Ayer, Sir A(lfred)
J(ules) (1910–89;
Brit.)

Bacon, Francis
(1561–1626; Brit.)

Bacon, Roger
(c. 1214–94; Engl.)

Barthes, Roland
(1915–80; Fr.)

Beauvoir, Simone de
(1908–86; Fr.)

Bentham, Jeremy
(1748–1832; Brit.)

Bergson, Henri
(1859–1941; Fr.)

Berkeley, George
(1685–1753; Ir.)

Boethius, Anicius
Manlius Severinus
(c. 480–524 A.D.;
Rom.)

Carnap, Rudolf
(1891–1970; Am.)

Cassirer, Ernst
(1874–1945; Ger.)

Chomsky, Avram
Noam (b. 1928; Am.)

Cicero, Marcus
Tullius (106–43 B.C.;
Rom.)

Comte, Auguste
(1798–1857; Fr.)

Condillac, Étienne
Bonnot de
(1715–80; Fr.)

Confucius
(c. 551–479 B.C.;
Chin.)

Cousin, Victor
(1792–1867; Fr.)

Crescas, Hasdai ben
Abraham (d. 1412;
Jewish, b. in Spain.)

Croce, Benedetto
(1866–1952; It.)

Cudworth, Ralph
(1617–88; Brit.)

Democritus
(c. 460–370 B.C.; Gk)

Derrida, Jacques
(b. 1930; Fr.)

Descartes, René
(1596–1650; Fr.)

Dewey, John
(1859–1952; Am.)

Diderot, Denis
(1713–84; Fr.)

Diogenes Laertius
(3rd century A.D.;
Gk)

Diogenes of Sinope
(412–322 B.C.; Gk)

Empedocles
(c. 493–433 B.C.; Gk)

Engels, Friedrich
(1820–95; Ger.)

Epictetus
(c. 55–135 A.D.; Gk)

Epicurus
(341–270 B.C.; Gk)

Fichte, Johann Got-
tlieb (1762–1814;
Ger.)

Foucault, Michel
(1926–84; Fr.)

Frege, Gottlob
(1848–1925; Ger.)

Gentile, Giovanni
(1875–1944; It.)

Geulincx, Arnold
(1624–69; Belg.)

Habermas, Jürgen
(b. 1929; Ger.)

Han fei tzu
(d. 233 B.C.; Chin.)

Hegel, Georg
(1770–1831; Ger.)

Heidegger, Martin
(1889–1976; Ger.)

Helvétius, Claude
(1715–71; Fr.)

Heraclitus
(c. 535–c. 475 B.C.;
Gk)

Hobbes, Thomas
(1588–1679; Brit.)

Horkheimer, Max
(1895–1973; Ger.)

Hume, David
(1711–76; Scot.)

Husserl, Edmund
(1859–1938; Ger.)

Hypatia (d. 415 A.D.;
Gk)

Ibn al-'Arabi,
Muhyi-l-din
(1165–1240; Arab.,
b. in Spain)

Ibn Gabirol,
Solomon
(c. 1021–c. 58; Jew-
ish, b. in Spain)

Ibn Khaldūn, 'Abd al-
Rahmān
(1332–1406; Arab.)

Iqbal, Sir
Mohammed
(c. 1875–1938; Ind.)

James, William
(1842–1910; Am.)

Jaspers, Karl
(Theodor)
(1883–1969; Ger.)

Judah ha-Levi
(c. 1075–1141; Jew-
ish)

Kant, Immanuel
(1724–1804; Ger.)

Kierkegaard, Søren
(1813–55; Da.)

Kuhn, Thomas
(b. 1922; Am.)

Lacan, Jacques
(1901–81; Fr.)

Lakatos, Imre
(1922–74; Hungar-
ian)

Lao-tzu (6th
century B.C.; Chin.)

Leibniz, Gottfried
Wilhelm
(1646–1716; Ger.)

Leucippus (5th cen-
tury B.C.; Gk)

Locke, John
(1632–1704; Brit.)

Lucretius
(c. 95–55 B.C.; Rom.)

Maimonides, Moses
(Mosheh ben May-
mun; 1135–1204;
Jewish)

Marcuse, Herbert
(1898–1979; Am.)

Marx, Karl (1818–83;
Ger.)

Mencius
(c. 371–c. 289 B.C.;
Chin.)

Mill, John Stuart
(1806–73; Brit.)

Montesquieu,
Charles, Baron de
(1689–1755; Fr.)

Moore, G(eorge)
E(dward)
(1873–1958; Brit.)

Nagel, Ernest
(1901–85; Am., b. in
Czechoslovakia)

Nagel, Thomas
(b. 1937; Am.)

Nietzsche, Friedrich
(1844–1900; Ger.)

Ortega y Gasset, José
(1883–1955; Sp.)

Paine, Thomas
(1737–1809; Am.)

Parmenides
(c. 510–c. 450 B.C.;
Gk)

Pascal, Blaise
(1623–62; Fr.)

Peirce, Charles
(1839–1914; Am.)

Plato
(c. 429–c. 347 B.C.;
Gk)

Plotinus (205–70 A.D.;
Rom.)

Popper, Sir Karl
Raimund (1902–94;
Brit.)

Posidonius of
Apamea
(c. 135–51 B.C.; Gk)

Protagoras
(c. 485–415 B.C.; Gk)

Pyrrho
(c. 365–c. 270 B.C.;
Gk)

Pythagoras
(c. 560–480 B.C.; Gk)

Quine, Willard van
Orman (b. 1908;
Am.)

Ramanuja
(c. 1017–1137 A.D.;
Ind.)

Ramus, Petrus
(Pierre de la
Ramée; 1515–72;
Fr.)

Reid, Thomas
(1710–96; Scot.)

Roscelin (d. c. 1125;
Fr.)

Rousseau, Jean
Jacques (1712–78;
Fr.)

Russell, Bertrand,
3rd Earl
(1872–1970; Brit.)

Ryle, Gilbert
(1900–76; Brit.)

Saint-Simon, Claude-
Henri, Comte de
(1760–1825; Fr.)

PHILOSOPHERS *cont.*			
Sankara (8th century A.D.; Ind.)	Simplicius of Cilicia (4th century A.D.; Gk)	Swedenborg, Emanuel (1688–1772; Sw.)	Weil, Simone (1909–43; Fr.)
Santayana, George (1863–1952; Am.)	Smith, Adam (1723–90; Scot.)	Tarski, Alfred (1902–83; Am., b. in Poland)	Whitehead, A(lfred) N(orth) (1861–1947; Brit.)
Sartre, Jean-Paul (1905–80; Fr.)	Socrates (c. 469–399 B.C.; Gk)	Telesio, Bernardino (1509–88; It.)	William of Ockham (c. 1285–1349; Engl.)
Schelling, Friedrich (1775–1854; Ger.)	Solovyov, Vladimir (1853–1900; Russ.)	Thales (c. 624–545 B.C.; Gk)	Wittgenstein, Ludwig (1889–1951; Brit., b. in Austria)
Schlegel, Friedrich von (1772–1829; Ger.)	Sorel, Georges (1847–1922; Fr.)	Theophrastus (c. 370–287 B.C.; Gk)	Xenophanes of Colophon (c. 570–480 B.C.; Gk)
Schopenhauer, Arthur (1788–1860; Ger.)	Spengler, Oswald (1880–1936; Ger.)	Unamuno y Jugo, Miguel de (1864–1936; Sp.)	Zeno of Citium (c. 335–c. 263 B.C.; Gk)
Sextus Empiricus (2nd century A.D.; Gk)	Spinoza, Baruch (1632–77; Du.)	Vico, Giambattista (1668–1744; It.)	Zeno of Elea (b. c. 490 B.C.; Gk)
	Strawson, Sir Peter (b. 1919; Brit.)		
	Suárez, Francisco (1548–1617; Sp.)		

philanthropy noun **1** *look after his neighbours out of philanthropy* humanitarianism, humanity, humaneness, public-spiritedness, social concern, unselfishness, selflessness, altruism, kind-heartedness, brotherly love. **2** *organizations dependent on the philanthropy of the townspeople* benevolence, beneficence, benignity, charity, charitableness, generosity, alms-giving, kindness, munifence, bounty, bountifulness, bounteousness, liberality, open-handedness, patronage, sponsorship, giving, backing, help.

philippic noun *deliver a philippic against the state* diatribe, invective, tirade, harangue, verbal onslaught, fulmination, vituperation.

philistine adjective *a philistine attitude to the arts* uncultured, uncultivated, uneducated, unenlightened, unread, lowbrow, anti-intellectual, ignorant, bourgeois, boorish, barbaric.

philosopher noun **1** *the Greek philosopher* philosophizer, scholar, metaphysicist, metaphysician, sage, wise man, guru, pundit, seeker after truth. *See table.* **2** *a philosopher rather than a man of action* philosophizer, thinker, theorist, theorizer.

philosophical adjective **1** *read philosophical works* of philosophy, philosophic, metaphysical. **2** *in a philosophical mood* thoughtful, reflective, pensive, meditative, contemplative. **3** *remain philosophical in the face of failure* calm, composed, cool, collected, cool calm and collected, self-possessed, serene, tranquil, stoical,

impassive, phlegmatic, unperturbed, imperturbable, dispassionate, unruffled, patient, resigned, rational, logical, realistic, practical.
Opposites ACTIVE; PRACTICAL; EMOTIONAL; UPSET.

philosophy noun **1** *the philosophy of Aristotle | studying philosophy* thought, thinking, reasoning, logic, wisdom. *See table. See also table at* POLITICS. **2** *his philosophy of life* beliefs, convictions, ideology, ideas, doctrine, tenets, values, principles, attitude, view, viewpoint, outlook. **3** *admire their philosophy when disaster struck* philosophicalness, calmness, calm, coolness, composure, equanimity, aplomb, self-possession, serenity, tranquillity, stoicism, impassivity, phlegm, imperturbability, dispassion, dispassionateness, patience, resignation, rationality, logic, realism, practicality; *inf.* cool.

phlegm noun **1** *coughing up phlegm* mucus, catarrh. **2** *no crisis disturbs his phlegm* calmness, calm, coolness, composure, equanimity, serenity, tranquillity, placidity, placidness, impassivity, imperturbability, dispassionateness, philosophicalness; *inf.* cool. **3** *tire of the phlegm of most of her pupils* apathy, indifference, lack of interest, impassivity, sluggishness, lethargy, listlessness, languor, dullness, indolence, inertia, inactivity, stolidness, bovineness.

phlegmatic adjective **1** *a phlegmatic disposition | a phlegmatic attitude to every crisis* calm, cool, composed, cool calm and collected, serene, tranquil, placid, impassive, imperturbable, dispassionate, philosophical. **2** *tired of*

BRANCHES OF PHILOSOPHY			
aesthetics	gnosiology	metempirics	philosophy of mind
analytical philosophy	ideology	modal logic	
axiology	legal ethics	moral philosophy	philosophy of psychology
bioethics	linguistic philosophy	ontology	
cosmology	logic	phenomenology	philosophy of religion
deontology	mathematical philosophy	philosophy of language	
epistemology	metaethics	philosophy of law	philosophy of science
ethics	metaphysics	philosophy of mathematics	political philosophy
formal logic			teleology

PHOBIAS

Objects of Fear or Dislike	Phobia	Objects of Fear or Dislike	Phobia
air travel	aerophobia	foreigners	xenophobia
American people		freedom	eleutherophobia
and things	Americophobia	French people	
animals	zoophobia	and things	Francophobia/
bacteria	bacteriophobia		Gallophobia
beards	pogonophobia	fur	doraphobia
beating	mastigophobia	German people	
bed	clinophobia	and things	Germanophobia/
bees	apiphobia		Teutophobia
birds	ornithophobia	germs	spermophobia/
Black people and things	Negrophobia		bacteriophobia
blood	haemophobia	ghosts	phasmophobia
blushing	erythrophobia	giving birth to	
body odour	bromidrosiphobia	monsters	teratophobia
bridges	gephyrophobia	God	theophobia
bullets	ballistophobia	gold	chrysophobia/
cancer	carcinophobia		aurophobia
cats	ailurophobia	hair	trichophobia
childbirth	tocophobia	heart disease	cardiophobia
children	paedophobia	heat	thermophobia
Chinese people		heaven	uranophobia
and things	Sinophobia	hell	hadephobia/
church	ecclesiophobia		stygiophobia
clouds	nephophobia	heredity	patroiophobia
coitus	coitophobia	high buildings	batophobia
cold	cheimaphobia	high places	acrophobia/
colour	chromophobia		hypsophobia
comets	cometophobia	home	oikophobia
constipation	coprostasophobia	homosexuals	homophobia
corpses	necrophobia	horses	hippophobia
correspondence	epistolophobia	ice	cryophobia
crowds	demophobia/	ideas	ideophobia
	ochlophobia	idleness	thassophobia
dampness	hygrophobia	illness	nosophobia
darkness	scotophobia	imperfection	atelophobia
dawn	eosophobia	infinity	apeirophobia
death	thanatophobia	injury	traumatophobia
depth	bathophobia	inoculation	trypanophobia/
dirt	mysophobia		vaccinophobia
disease	pathophobia/	insanity	lyssophobia/
	nosophobia		maniphobia
dogs	cynophobia	insects	entomophobia
drink	potophobia	insect stings	cnidophobia
drugs	pharmacophobia	Italian people	
dust	koniophobia	and things	Italophobia
electricity	electrophobia	itching	acarophobia
enclosed places	claustrophobia	jealousy	zelotypophobia
English people		Jewish people	
and things	Anglophobia	and things	Judaeophobia
everything	panophobia/	justice	dikephobia
	pantophobia	lakes	limnophobia
eyes	ommetaphobia	leprosy	leprophobia
faeces	coprophobia	lice	pediculophobia
failure	kakorrhaphiaphobia	light	photophobia
fatigue	kopophobia	lightning	astrapophobia
fear	phobophobia	lists	pinaciphobia/
feathers	pteronophobia		katastichophobia
fever	febriphobia	loneliness	autophobia/
fire	pyrophobia		ermitophobia
fish	ichthyophobia	machinery	mechanophobia
floods	antlophobia	magic	rhabdophobia
flowers	anthophobia	marriage	gametophobia
fog	homichlophobia	men	androphobia
food	cibophobia/	metal	metallophobia
	sitophobia	mice	musophobia

PHOBIAS *cont.*

Objects of Fear or Dislike	Phobia	Objects of Fear or Dislike	Phobia
microbes	bacillophobia/ microbiophobia	sin	hamartophobia
mirrors	eisoptrophobia	skin disease	dermatosiophobia/ dermatopathophobia
mites	acarophobia	sleep	hypnophobia
mobs	ochlophobia	slime	blennophobia
money	chrematophobia	small things	microphobia
monsters	teratrophobia	smell	olfactophobia/ osmophobia
motion	kinetophobia		
music	musicophobia	snakes	ophidiophobia
names	onomatophobia	snow	chionophobia
narrowness	anginophobia	sound	acousticophobia
needles	belonephobia	sourness	acerophobia
new things	neophobia	speech	lalophobia/ glossophobia/ phonophobia
night	nyctophobia		
open places	agoraphobia		
pain	algophobia	speed	tachophobia
parasites	parasitophobia	spiders	arachnophobia
people	anthropophobia	standing	stasophobia
philosophy	philosophobia	stars	siderophobia
pins	enetophobia	stealing	kleptophobia
places	topophobia	string	linonophobia
pleasure	hedonophobia	sun	heliophobia
poison	toxiphobia	swallowing	phagophobia
politics	politicophobia	symmetry	symmetrophobia
Pope	papaphobia	taste	geumatophobia
poverty	peniaphobia	technology	technophobia
precipices	cremnophobia	teeth	odontophobia
priests	hierophobia	telephone	telephonophobia
punishment	poinephobia	thinking	phronemophobia
rabies	hydrophobophobia	thirteen	triskaidekaphobia
rail travel	siderodromophobia	thunder	brontophobia/ tonitrophobia/ keraunophobia
religious works of art	iconophobia		
reptiles	batrachophobia	time	chronophobia
responsibility	hypegiaphobia	touch	haptophobia
ridicule	katagelophobia	travel	hodophobia
rivers	potamophobia	tuberculosis	phthisiophobia
robbers	harpaxophobia	tyrants	tyrannophobia
ruin	atephobia	vehicles	ochophobia
Russian people and things	Russophobia	venereal disease	syphilophobia
		voids	kenophobia
saints	hagiophobia	vomiting	emetophobia
Satan	Satanophobia	water	hydrophobia
scabies	scabiophobia	waves	cymophobia
Scottish people and things	Scotophobia	weakness	asthenophobia
		wind	anemophobia
sea	thalassophobia	women	gynophobia
sex	erotophobia	words	logophobia
shadows	sciophobia	work	ergophobia
sharpness	acrophobia	worms	helminthophobia
shock	hormephobia	writing	graphophobia

the lack of interest of her *phlegmatic* pupils apathetic, indifferent, uninterested, impassive, sluggish, lethargic, listless, languorous, dull, indolent, inert, inactive, stolid, placid, bovine. **Opposites** EXCITABLE; QUICK-TEMPERED; ENTHUSIASTIC; ACTIVE.

phobia *noun a phobia about/towards rats | has a phobia about spiders* aversion, abnormal fear, irrational fear, obsessive fear, fear, dread, horror, terror, dislike, hatred, loathing, detestation, distaste, antipathy, revulsion, repulsion; *inf.* thing, hang-up. *See table.*

phone *noun* **1** *a public phone | spend hours on the phone* telephone, mobile phone, car phone, radio-telephone; *inf.* blower. **2** *give her a quick phone* phone call, telephone call, call, ring; *inf.* buzz, tinkle, bell.

phone *verb phone her mother for a chat* telephone, call, make/place a call to, give someone a call, ring, ring up, give someone a ring; *inf.* buzz, give someone a buzz/tinkle/bell, get on the blower to.

phonetic alphabet *noun. See table.*

PHONETIC ALPHABET

Alpha	Juliet	Sierra
Bravo	Kilo	Tango
Charlie	Lima	Uniform
Delta	Mike	Victor
Echo	November	Whisky
Foxtrot	Oscar	X-ray
Golf	Papa	Yankee
Hotel	Quebec	Zulu
India	Romeo	

phoney *adjective* **1** *old people taken in by phoney workmen* bogus, sham, fake, fraudulent, pseudo; *inf.* cod. **2** *phoney documents* bogus, sham, counterfeit, imitation, spurious, mock, ersatz, fake, forged, feigned, simulated, make-believe, false, fraudulent. **3** *a phoney American accent* bogus, sham, counterfeit, imitation, fake, feigned, assumed, simulated, affected, contrived, false, mock, pseudo; *inf.* cod.
Opposites AUTHENTIC; GENUINE.

phoney *noun* **1** *the doctor's a phoney* impostor, pretender, sham, fraud, fake, faker, charlatan, mountebank; *inf.* quack. **2** *the diamond's a phoney* counterfeit, fake, forgery, imitation, sham.

photocopy *noun* *take a photocopy of the documents* copy, photostat™, facsimile, fax; Xerox™.

photograph *noun* *show them a photograph of his children* | *take a photograph of the house* photo, snap, snapshot, picture, likeness, shot, print, slide, transparency.

photograph *verb* *photograph the film star* take a photograph/photo of, take a snapshot/snap of, snap, take a picture of, take a shot of, take a likeness of, shoot, capture on film.

photographer *noun.* See table.

photographic *adjective* **1** *a photographic record* pictorial, in photographs. **2** *a photographic description* detailed, graphic, exact, accurate, precise.

phrase *noun* **1** *in phrases and sentences* word group, group of words. **2** *a few well-chosen phrases* expression, idiomatic expression, idiom, remark, saying, utterance, witticism, tag. **3** *an elegant turn of phrase* phrasing, phraseology, way of speaking/writing, manner of speaking/writing, style of speech/writing, style, mode of speech/writing, usage, choice of words, idiom, language, diction, parlance.

phrase *verb* *phrase the instruction differently* put into words, put, word, express, formulate, couch, frame.

phraseology *noun* **1** *admire the writer's phraseology* way of speaking/writing, manner of speaking/writing, style of speech/writing, style, mode of speech/writing, phrasing, usage, idiom, language, diction, parlance. **2** *express it in simple phraseology* phrasing, wording, words, choice of words, language, vocabulary, terminology.

physical *adjective* **1** *physical and mental pain* | *physical well-being* bodily, non-mental, corporeal, corporal, somatic. **2** *the physical not spiritual considerations* non-spiritual, unspiritual, material, earthly, corporeal, carnal, fleshly, mortal. **3** *everything physical in the universe* material, substantial, solid, concrete, tangible, palpable, visible, real.
Opposites MENTAL; SPIRITUAL.

physician *noun* *treated by his own physician at home* doctor, doctor of medicine, medical practitioner, medical man, general practitioner, GP, specialist, consultant; *inf.* doc, medic, medico, quack. *See table at* DOCTOR.

physicist *noun.* *See table at* SCIENTIST.

physique *noun* *gymnasts having splendid physiques* body, body structure, build, shape, frame, form, figure.

pick *verb* **1** *pick a new television set from the range* | *pick him for the team* pick out, choose, select, opt for, plump for, single out, hand-pick, decide upon, settle upon, fix upon, sift out, prefer, favour, elect. **2** *get a job picking apples* harvest, gather, collect, take in, pluck, pull, cull. **3** *pick a safe* break into, break open, force open, prise open, crack. **pick at** *children picking at their food after eating sweets* nibble at, peck at, toy with, play with, eat like a bird, show no appetite for, eat sparingly of. **pick off** *soldiers picked off by a sniper* shoot, shoot down, gun down, fire at, hit, take out. **pick on** *a*

PHOTOGRAPHERS

Adams, Ansel (1902–84; Am.)	Cameron, Julia Margaret (1815–79; Brit., b. in India)	Kertész, André (1894–1985; Am., b. in Hungary)	Penn, Irving (b. 1917; Am.)
Jean-Eugène Auguste (1857–1927; Fr.)	Capa, Robert (1913–54; Hungarian)	Land, Edwin (1909–91; Am.)	Rodchenko, Alexander (1891–1956; Russ.)
Bailey, David (b. 1938; Brit.)	Cartier-Bresson, Henri (b. 1908; Fr.)	Lange, Dorothea (1895–1965; Am.)	Siskind, Aaron (1903–91; Am.)
Beaton, Sir Cecil (1904–80; Brit.)		Mapplethorpe, Robert (1946–89; Am.)	Steichen, Edward (1879–1973; Am., b. in Luxembourg)
Bourke-White, Margaret (1906–71; Am.)	Daguerre, Louis-Jacques-Mandé (1789–1851; Fr.)	McCullin, Don (b. 1935; Brit.)	Stieglitz, Alfred (1864–1946; Am.)
Brandt, Bill (1904–83; Brit.)	Doisneau, Robert (1912–94; Fr.)	Nadar (1820–1910; Fr.)	Talbot, William Henry Fox (1800–77; Brit.)
Brassaï (1899–1984; Fr., b. in Hungary)	Hine, Lewis (1874–1940; Am.)	Ray, Man (1890–1976; Am.)	Wolcott, Marion (1910–90; Am.)
		Parkinson, Norman (1913–90; Brit.)	

teacher accused of picking on a child punish repeatedly, blame regularly, constantly find fault with, criticize, badger. **pick out 1** *picked out from a huge list of applicants* pick, choose, select, single out, hand-pick. *See* PICK *verb* 1. **2** *pick out his face in the crowd* make out, distinguish, tell apart, discriminate, recognize, notice. **pick up 1** *pick up the case and leave* lift, take up, raise, hoist. **2** *business starting to pick up* improve, get better, recover, be on the road to recovery, rally, make a comeback, perk up, be on the mend, make headway, make progress, take a turn for the better. **3** *manage to pick up a first edition* find, discover, locate, come across, stumble across, happen upon, unearth, obtain, get, acquire, purchase, buy. **4** *pick up tomorrow where we left off today* take up, begin, begin again, start, start again, carry on, go on, continue. **5** *pick them up on the way to the station* collect, go to get, call for, fetch, give someone a lift, give someone a ride. **6** *picked up by the police for questioning* take into custody, arrest, apprehend; *inf.* collar, nab, run/pull in, nick, pinch. **7** *pick up a girl at the party* strike up an acquaintance with, take up with, fall in with, strike up a casual friendship with, strike up a sexual friendship with. **8** *pick up the basic skills* | *pick up the local language* learn, get to know, acquire a knowledge of, master; *inf.* get the hang of. **9** *pick up malaria abroad* catch, contract, get, become infected with, become ill with, go/come down with. **10** *pick up some interesting news* learn, hear, get to know, glean.
Opposites REJECT; DISCARD.

pick *noun* **1** *early purchasers have the pick of the range* choice, selection, option, preference. **2** *the pick of the crop/bunch* best, choicest, prime, cream, flower, prize, élite, *crème de la crème*.

picket *noun* **1** *line of pickets outside the factory* picketer, demonstrator, protester, objector, rebel, dissident. **2** *part of a picket on the look-out for the enemy* sentry, watch, guard, look-out, patrol, sentinel. **3** *drive pickets into the ground* stake, post, paling, pale, peg, upright, pike, stanchion, palisade.

picket *verb* **1** *picket the factory to keep out non-strikers* | *picket the laboratory in protest at research on animals* form a picket at, go on a picket line at, man the picket-line at, demonstrate at, launch a demonstration at, protest at, form a protest group at, blockade. **2** *picket the walls of the castle* form a sentry at, be part of the watch at, guard, patrol, form a sentinel at. **3** *picket the area where the animals were kept* enclose, fence off, box in, stake off, secure, rail off, palisade. **4** *picket the dog by the front door* tether, tie up, secure, fasten.

pickle *noun* **1** *serve pickle with the cold meat* relish, chutney. **2** *pickle in which vegetables are preserved* marinade, brine, vinegar. **3** *what a financial pickle to be in!* plight, predicament, mess, trouble, problem, straits, crisis, tight corner; *inf.* jam, fix, scrape, hole, hot water, tight spot, spot, pretty kettle of fish.

pickle *verb* *pickle vegetables* marinade, preserve, conserve.

pick-me-up *noun* **1** *invalids in need of a pick-me-up* tonic, restorative, energizer, bracer; *med.* roborant. **2** *the visit to the theatre was a real pick-me-up* boost, boost to the spirits, reviver, stimulus, invigoration; *inf.* shot in the arm.

pickpocket *noun* *a wallet snatched by a pickpocket* thief, purse-snatcher, petty thief; *inf.* dip.

picnic *noun* **1** *have a birthday picnic* | *a picnic on the mountainside/beach* outdoor meal, outdoor party, alfresco meal. **2** *persuading her to go was no picnic* easy task, child's play, walk-over; *inf.* piece of cake, pushover, cinch, doddle, breeze.

pictorial *adjective* **1** *a pictorial record of the holiday* in pictures, in picture form, in photographs, photographic, in snapshots. **2** *a pictorial calendar* illustrated, with illustrations, with pictures, with sketches.

picture *noun* **1** *paint a picture of the house* | *looked at the picture of the happy scene* painting, drawing, sketch, oil-painting, water-colour, print, canvas, delineation, portrait, portrayal, illustration, likeness, representation, similitude, semblance. **2** *take pictures at the wedding* | *keep her picture in his wallet* photograph, photo, snapshot, shot, snap, slide, print, still. **3** *his report painted a bleak picture* scene, view, image, impression, representation, vision, concept. **4** *write a graphic picture of his despair* description, portrayal, account, report, narrative, narration, story, tale, recital. **5** *the picture of health/happiness* personification, embodiment, epitome, essence, perfect example, model, exemplar, archetype. **6** *the child is the picture of his father* image, living image, double, exact likeness, duplicate, replica, carbon copy, twin; *inf.* spitting image, spit and image, spit, very/dead spit, ringer, dead ringer. **7** *see a picture starring Abbot and Costello* film, motion picture; *inf.* movie, flick. **put someone in the picture** *put him in the picture about the financial state of the firm* fully inform, give information to, give details to, explain the situation to, explain the circumstances to, describe the state of affairs to, bring up to date, update; *inf.* clue in/up. **the pictures** *have a night out at the pictures* cinema; *inf.* movies, flicks.

picture *verb* **1** *I can picture them still* see in one's mind, see in one's mind's eye, conjure up a picture of, conjure up an image of, imagine, call to mind, visualize, see, evoke. **2** *in the drawing they were pictured against a snowy background* paint, draw, sketch, depict, delineate, portray, illustrate, reproduce, represent. **3** *film stars pictured at a charity ball* photograph, snap, show. *See* PHOTOGRAPH *verb*.

picturesque *adjective* **1** *a picturesque old village* | *a picturesque setting* beautiful, pretty, lovely, attractive, scenic, charming, quaint, pleasing, delightful. **2** *write a picturesque description of the events* | *use picturesque language* vivid, graphic, colourful, impressive, striking.
Opposites UGLY; DRAB; DULL.

piddling *adjective* **1** *ignore the piddling details* trivial, trifling, minor, small, unimportant, insignificant, petty, paltry, worthless, useless, fiddling; *inf.* piffling. **2** *a piddling sum of money* meagre, trifling, paltry, derisory, negligible, small; *inf.* measly, piffling, Mickey Mouse.

pie *noun savoury and sweet pies* pastry, tart, tart-let, pasty, quiche. **pie in the sky** *their dreams of travel are pie in the sky* false hopes, illusions, delusions, unrealizable dreams, pipedreams, daydreams, castles in the air, castles in Spain.

piebald *adjective piebald horses* pied, skewbald, black and white, brown and white, dappled, brindled, spotted, mottled, speckled, flecked, variegated; *Am.* pinto.

piece *noun* **1** *a wardrobe delivered in several pieces* part, bit, section, segment, unit. **2** *a vase broken to pieces | a dress torn to pieces* bit, fragment, smithereens, shard, shred. **3** *buy a large piece of cheese/wood* bit, section, slice, chunk, lump, hunk, wedge. **4** *a piece of cloth* length, bit, remnant, scrap, snippet. **5** *a piece of his fortune | get a piece of the action* share, slice, portion, allotment, allocation, quota, percentage, fraction, quantity. **6** *a fine piece of early Victorian furniture* example, specimen, sample, instance, illustration, occurrence. **7** *write a piece on modern theatre | disagree with his latest piece* article, item, story, report, essay, review, paper, column. **8** *one of the finest pieces by the composer* musical work, work, composition, creation, opus. **9** *one of the artist's finest pieces* work of art, work, painting, canvas, composition, creation, opus. **all in one piece** *find the vase/car/child all in one piece* unbroken, undamaged, unhurt, uninjured, safe, sound, safe and sound. **fall/go to pieces** *people going to pieces in an emergency* panic, become agitated, lose control, lose one's head, fall apart, break down; *inf.* crack up.

piece *verb piece together the torn parts of the page | trying to piece together all the evidence* put together, assemble, join up, fit together, unite.

pièce de résistance *noun the pièce de résistance of the theatre group's performances* masterpiece, master-work, *chef d'oeuvre*, show-piece, jewel, jewel in the crown.

piecemeal *adverb put the story together piecemeal* piece by piece, bit by bit, gradually, in stages, in steps, little by little, by degrees, in fits and starts.

pied *adjective pied horses* piebald, black and white, dappled, brindled, spotted. *See* PIEBALD.

pier *noun* **1** *stand on the pier to watch the boats* jetty, quay, wharf, dock, landing, landing-stage, landing-place, promenade. **2** *the piers of the bridge damaged by storms* support, upright, pillar, post, column, pile, piling, buttress.

pierce *verb* **1** *arrows which pierced the skin | spear had pierced his shoulder* penetrate, puncture, perforate, prick, stab, spike, enter, pass through, transfix. **2** *pierce the leather to make a belt* make holes in, perforate, bore, drill. **3** *a heart pierced by the suffering of others* wound, hurt, pain, cut to the quick, affect, move, sting. **4** *torches piercing the darkness* penetrate, pass through, percolate, filter through, light up. **5** *shrill sounds piercing the air* penetrate, pervade, permeate, fill.

piercing *adjective* **1** *a piercing glance* penetrating, sharp, keen, searching, alert, shrewd, perceptive, probing. **2** *a piercing shriek* penetrating, shrill, ear-piercing, ear-splitting,

high-pitched, loud, air-rending. **3** *a piercing intelligence* perceptive, percipient, perspicacious, discerning, quick-witted, sharp, sharp-witted, shrewd, keen, acute, astute. **4** *a piercing pain* penetrating, sharp, stabbing, shooting, intense, severe, fierce, excruciating, agonizing, exquisite. **5** *frost-bitten in the piercing cold* biting, numbing, bitter, raw, keen, freezing, frigid, arctic.

piety *noun* **1** *a family noted for their piety* piousness, religiousness, religion, holiness, godliness, devoutness, devotion to God, devotion, veneration, reverence, faith, religious duty, spirituality, sanctity, religious zeal. **2** *children noted for their filial piety* obedience, duty, dutifulness, respect, respectfulness, deference, veneration.

pig *noun* **1** *farmers keeping pigs* hog, boar, sow, porker, grunter, swine, piglet; *inf.* piggy. *See table.* **2** *pigs who left hardly any food for the others* glutton, guzzler; *inf.* greedy pig, hog, greedy hog, greedy guts, guts. **3** *her boss is a real pig* boor, brute, swine, animal, monster; *inf.* bastard, beast, louse.

BREEDS OF PIG	
Berkshire	Pietrain
British Lop	Poland China
British Saddleback	Tamworth
Chester White	Vietnamese
Duroc	Pot-Bellied
Gloucester Old	Welsh
Spot	**Wild pigs**
Hampshire	babirusa
Landrace	hog
Middle White	peccary
Oxford Sandy and	warthog
Black	wild boar

pigeon *noun* **1** *feeding the pigeons* squab, homing pigeon, carrier pigeon. **2** *con men swindling pigeons* dupe, fool, simpleton, victim; *inf.* sucker, sap, sitting duck, sitting target, soft touch, pushover. **3** *sorting the problem out's your pigeon* responsibility, business, concern, worry, province; *inf.* look-out, baby.

pigeon-hole *noun* **1** *put the papers into the students' pigeon-holes* compartment, locker, cubbyhole, niche. **2** *apt to put people in pigeon-holes* compartment, category, class, classification, slot.

pigeon-hole *verb* **1** *pigeon-hole plans for reconstruction* postpone, put off, defer, shelve; *inf.* put on ice, put on the back burner. **2** *pigeon-hole her before she even started work* compartmentalize, categorize, classify, characterize, label, tag, slot.

pigheaded *adjective too pigheaded to take advice* obstinate, stubborn, stubborn as a mule, mulish, bull-headed, obdurate, tenacious, dogged, single-minded, inflexible, uncompromising, adamant, intractable, intransigent, unmalleable, headstrong, self-willed, wilful, perverse, contrary, stiff-necked.

pigment *noun use a red pigment for the wall-paint* | *natural pigments are used to dye the fabric* colouring matter, colouring agent, colourant, colour, tint, dye.

pile¹ *noun* **1** *a pile of clothes/logs/coins* heap, bundle, stack, mound, mass, accumulation, collection, assemblage, store, stockpile, hoard, load, mountain. **2** *a pile of work to do* great deal, quantity, abundance, mountain; *inf.* a lot, lots, heap, ocean, stacks, oodles, scuds. **3** *make a/his pile on the black market* fortune, money, wealth; *inf.* mint, packet, bomb, pots of money, stacks of money, tidy sum. **4** *the owner of a historical pile* edifice, impressive building/structure/erection.

pile² *verb* **1** *pile up the tins of vegetables* heap, stack. **2** *pile up logs for the winter* accumulate, amass, collect, gather, stockpile, hoard, store up, assemble, lay by/in. **3** *snow piled up by the roadsides* form piles, form heaps, heap up, amass, accumulate. **4** *pile his plate with food* heap, fill, load, stock. **5** *commuters piling on to the train* crowd, charge, tumble, stream, flock, flood, pack, squeeze, crush, jam. **pile it on** *it was a sad case but he really piled it on* exaggerate, overstate the case, overdraw the situation, make a mountain of a molehill, build up out of all proportion; *inf.* lay it on, lay it on with a trowel, blow up out of all proportion.

pile³ *noun the piles supporting the bridge collapsed* pillar, column, support, post, foundation, piling, pier, buttress, upright.

pile⁴ *noun* **1** *the pile of the carpet* soft surface, surface, nap. **2** *pile blocking up the vacuum cleaner* hair, fur, down, wool, fluff.

pile-up *noun a pile-up on the motorway* crash, multiple crash, collision, multiple collision, smash, smash-up, accident, road accident.

pilfer *verb pilfer money from the petty cash* steal, thieve, rob, take, filch, purloin, embezzle, misappropriate; *inf.* walk off/away with, pinch, swipe, nick, lift, knock off, snaffle, snitch.

pilgrim *noun pilgrims going to Bethlehem/Mecca* worshipper, devotee, shrine-visitor, traveller, palmer, hajji.

pilgrimage *noun make a pilgrimage to Bethlehem/Mecca* religious expedition, holy expedition, excursion, hajj.

pill *noun* **1** *take a pill for a headache* tablet, capsule, pellet, lozenge, bolus. **2** *she's a real pill* nuisance, pest, bore, trial; *inf.* pain, pain in the neck, drag.

pillage *verb rival tribes invading and pillaging* plunder, rob, raid, loot, maraud, sack, ransack, ravage, lay waste, despoil, spoil, spoliate, depredate, rape.

pillage *noun invaders guilty of pillage* pillaging, plunder, plundering, robbery, robbing, raiding, looting, marauding, sacking, ransacking, ravaging, rapine, despoiling, laying waste, spoliation, depredation.

pillar *noun* **1** *pillars supporting the temple* column, post, pole, support, upright, pile, piling, pilaster, stanchion, peristyle. **2** *a pillar of the community* mainstay, backbone, strength, tower of strength, support, upholder, rock.

pillory *noun put in the pillory for theft* stocks.

pillory *verb pilloried in the press for his treatment of children* brand, stigmatize, cast a slur on, denounce, show up, hold up to shame, hold up to ridicule, expose to ridicule, ridicule, heap scorn on.

pillow *noun lay one's head on the pillow* cushion, bolster, headrest.

pilot *noun* **1** *the pilot at the aircraft's controls* airman/airwoman, aviator, aeronaut, captain, commander, copilot, first/second officer; *inf.* flyer. *See table.* **2** *the pilot directing the ship into the harbour* navigator, guide, steersman, helmsman. **3** *act as his pilot through life* guide, leader, conductor, director.

pilot *verb* **1** *pilot the aircraft* fly, drive, operate, control, handle, manoeuvre. **2** *pilot the ship into the harbour* navigate, guide, steer. **3** *pilot the bill through Parliament* guide, steer, conduct, direct, shepherd.

pilot *adjective pilot scheme* trial, test, experimental, model.

pimple *noun put ointment on a pimple* spot, pustule, boil, swelling, papule; *inf.* whitehead, zit.

PILOTS, AVIATORS, AND ASTRONAUTS

Alcock, Sir John (1892–1919; Brit. aviator)	Curtiss, Glenn (1878–1930; Am. aviator)	Johnson, Amy (1903–41; Brit. aviator)	Savitskaya, Svetlana (b. 1948; Soviet astronaut)
Aldrin, Jr, Edwin "Buzz" (b. 1930; Am. astronaut)	Earhart, Amelia (1898–1937; Am. aviator)	Lindbergh, Charles (1902–74; Am. aviator)	Smith, Sir Keith (1890–1955; Austral. aviator)
Armstrong, Neil (b. 1930; Am. astronaut)	Gagarin, Yuri (1934–68; Soviet astronaut)	Nobile, Umberto (1885–1978; It. aviator)	Tereshkova, Valentina (b. 1937; Soviet astronaut)
Bader, Sir Douglas (1910–82; Brit. fighter pilot)	Glenn, John (b. 1921; Am. astronaut)	Richtofen, Manfred, Freiherr von (1892–1918; Ger. fighter pilot)	Wright, Orville (1871–1948; Am. aviator)
Batten, Jean (1909–82; NZ aviator)	Hinkler, Herbert (1892–1933; Austral. aviator)	Saint-Exupéry, Antoine de (1900–44; Fr. aviator)	Wright, Wilbur (1867–1912; Am. aviator)
Blériot, Louis (1872–1936; Fr. aviator)	Hughes, Howard (1905–76; Am. aviator)		

pin verb **1** *pin the pieces of cloth together* fasten, join, attach, secure. **2** *pin the notice to the board* attach, fasten, affix, fix, stick, tack, nail. **3** *pinned under the fallen tree | pinned against the wall* pinion, hold, press, restrain, constrain, hold fast, immobilize. **pin down 1** *bullies pinned the boy down | pinned down by the weight of the car* pinion, hold down, press down, restrain, constrain, hold fast, immobilize. **2** *he won't choose a date but you must pin him down* force, compel, make, pressure, put pressure on, pressurize, constrain, nail down. **3** *there's something I dislike about him but I can't pin it down* define, put one's finger on, put into words, put words to, express in words, express, designate, name, specify, identify, home in on. **pin something on someone** *try to pin the burglary on him* blame, blame something on someone, blame someone for something, lay the blame for something on someone, place the blame for something on someone, fix the responsibility for something on someone, attribute something to someone, impute something to someone, ascribe something to someone.

pin noun **1** *fasten the hem with a pin* dressmaking pin, safety pin. **2** *a broken pin in the machine* peg, bolt, rivet, screw, dowel, post.

pinch verb **1** *pinch her little brother's arm* nip, tweak, squeeze, compress. **2** *shoes pinching her feet* hurt, cause pain to, pain, crush, squeeze, cramp, confine. **3** *have to pinch and scrape to live* scrimp, skimp, stint, be sparing, be frugal, be economical, economize, be niggardly/tight-fisted/close; *inf.* be stingy, be tight, be mingy. **4** *pinch money from her mother's purse* steal, thieve, rob, take, pilfer, filch, purloin, embezzle, misappropriate; *inf.* walk away/off with, swipe, nick, lift, knock off, snaffle, snitch. **5** *burglars pinched by the police* arrest, take into custody, apprehend; *inf.* pick up, pull in, run in, nick, nab, collar, bust, do.

pinch noun **1** *give her arm a pinch* nip, tweak, squeeze. **2** *a pinch of salt* small quantity, bit, touch, trace, soupçon; *inf.* smidgen, tad. **at a pinch** *at a pinch we could accommodate five people* if necessary, in case of necessity, if need be, in an emergency, just possibly. **feel the pinch** *feel the pinch during a recession* be short of money, have less money, suffer hardship, suffer poverty, suffer adversity. **if it comes to the pinch** *if it comes to the pinch, he'll have to sell the car* if it comes to the push, in an emergency, in a crisis, if things get bad, in times of hardship, if one is in difficulty, in time of need, in case of necessity, if necessary.

pinched adjective *individuals looking pinched and tired* drawn, haggard, gaunt, worn, peaky, pale. **Opposites** HEALTHY; GLOWING; CHUBBY.

pine verb **1** *pine away with grief* decline, go into a decline, lose strength, weaken, waste away, wilt, fade, languish, droop. **2** *pine for her old way of life* long for, yearn for, ache for, sigh for, hunger for, thirst for, hanker for/after, crave, covet, lust after.

pinion verb **1** *pinion him to the ground* pin down, hold down, press down, restrain, constrain, hold fast, immobilize. **2** *pinion his arms to the wall* bind, tie, fasten, shackle, fetter, chain, manacle.

pink adjective **1** *pink dresses* rose, rose-coloured, salmon, salmon-pink, shell-pink, flesh-coloured, pale red. **2** *pink cheeks* rosy, flushed, blushing.

pink noun *the pink of condition* peak, best, height, culmination, acme, pinnacle, zenith, summit. **in the pink** *feeling in the pink after his holiday* in perfect health, in good health, very healthy, very well, hale and hearty, bursting with health, in rude health, bursting with rude health, in fine fettle.

pink verb **1** *pink the leather* pierce, punch, perforate, prick, stab, bore, drill. **2** *pink the edge of the cloth* scallop, serrate, notch, crenellate.

pinnacle noun **1** *the pinnacle of her success* peak, height, culmination, high point, acme, zenith, climax, crowning point, meridian, summit, apex, vertex, apogee. **2** *snow-covered pinnacles* peak, summit, top, crest, mountain, hill. **3** *pinnacles on the temple* turret, spire, obelisk, pyramid, cone. **Opposites** NADIR; trough.

pinpoint verb *pinpoint the cause of the trouble* identify, discover, distinguish, locate, spot, home in on, put one's finger on.

pioneer noun **1** *the pioneers of the Wild West* settler, colonist, colonizer, frontiersman/frontierswoman, explorer. *See table at* EXPLORER. **2** *the pioneers of television | a pioneer of cancer research* developer, innovator, ground-breaker, trail-blazer, front-runner, founder, founding father, architect.

pioneer verb *pioneer cancer research | pioneered the use of the drug* lay the groundwork for, lead the way for, prepare the way for, lay the foundations of, develop, introduce, launch, instigate, initiate, take the initiative in, institute, originate, set the ball rolling, create, open up, blaze a trail, break new ground.

pious adjective **1** *pious members of the community attending church regularly* religious, holy, godly, spiritual, devout, devoted, dedicated, reverent, God-fearing, righteous, faithful, dutiful. **2** *dislike being patronized by pious do-gooders* sanctimonious, hypocritical, self-righteous, unctuous, pietistic, religiose; *inf.* holier-than-thou, goody-goody. **3** *pious children performing filial duties* obedient, dutiful, respectful, reverent, righteous. **Opposites** IMPIOUS; IRRELIGIOUS; SINCERE.

pipe noun **1** *lay pipes under the street* tube, cylinder, conduit, main, duct, channel, conveyor, pipeline, drainpipe. **2** *smoke a pipe* brier, meerschaum, clay pipe, tobacco-pipe, peace-pipe, calumet, hookah. **3** *playing a pipe* whistle, penny-whistle, flute, recorder, fife, wind instrument. **pipes** plural noun *playing the pipes* bagpipes, pan-pipes.

pipe verb **1** *pipe the oil to the stove* convey, duct, channel, transmit, bring in, siphon. **2** *listen to him piping* play on a pipe, play the pipes, tootle. **3** *birds piping* tweet, cheep, chirp, chirrup, peep, twitter, sing, warble, whistle, squeak. **4** *'why?' the little girl piped* chirp, shrill, squeal, squeak. **pipe down** *children told to pipe* *down* be quiet, quieten down, be silent, hush, hold one's tongue; *inf.* shut up, button up one's lip, belt up.

pipedream *noun have pipedreams of winning the pools* fantasy, illusion, daydream, castle in the air, castle in Spain, pie in the sky, delusion.

pipeline *noun lay the pipeline under the street* pipe, conduit, main, duct, channel, conveyor. **in the pipeline** *price rises in the pipeline* on the way, under way, coming, imminent, about to happen, in preparation, being prepared.

piquancy *noun* **1** *the piquancy of the sauce/flavour* spice, spiciness, pepperiness, tang, pungency, sharpness, edge, tartness, zest, zip; *inf.* zing, kick, punch. See PIQUANT 1. **2** *the piquancy of the gossip* stimulation, intrigue, interest, fascination, allurement, raciness, saltiness, provocativeness. **3** *the piquancy of her wit* liveliness, sparkle, animation, spiritedness, sharpness, cleverness, quickness, raciness, saltiness.

piquant *adjective* **1** *a piquant sauce/flavour* spicy, highly-seasoned, flavoursome, peppery, tangy, pungent, sharp, tart, zesty, biting, stinging. **2** *a piquant piece of gossip* stimulating, intriguing, interesting, fascinating, alluring, racy, salty, provocative. **3** *a piquant wit* lively, sparkling, animated, spirited, sharp, clever, quick, racy, salty.
Opposites BLAND; INSIPID; DULL.

pique *verb* **1** *her lack of interest piqued him* irritate, annoy, anger, displease, affront, put out, offend, irk, peeve, vex, nettle, gall, wound; *inf.* aggravate, miff, rile. **2** *pique her curiosity* arouse, rouse, awaken, excite, stimulate, kindle, stir, whet.

pique *noun full of pique at his behaviour* irritation, annoyance, anger, displeasure, affront, offence, resentment, grudge, umbrage, vexation, gall.

piracy *noun* **1** *piracy on the high seas* buccaneering, freebooting. **2** *publishers guilty of piracy* copyright infringement, plagiarism.

pirate *noun* **1** *pirates boarded the ship* buccaneer, rover, sea rover, sea robber, corsair, freebooter. **2** *tapes/music/poems issued by pirates* copyright infringer, plagiarist, plagiarizer.

pirate *verb pirate his music/poetry* infringe the copyright of, plagiarize, illegally reproduce, copy, poach; *inf.* crib, lift.

pit¹ *noun* **1** *fall down a pit* abyss, chasm, crater, hole, cavity, excavation, quarry, coalmine, mine, diggings, working. **2** *pits in her skin* depression, hollow, dent, dint, indentation, dimple, pock-mark, pock, mark.

pit² *verb the disease had pitted her skin* depress, dent, dint, dimple, mark, pock-mark, scar. **pit against** *pit her wits against her enemy's* set against, match against, put in opposition to, oppose against.

pit³ *noun remove the pits from the cherries* stone, pip, seed, kernel.

pitch¹ *verb* **1** *pitch a stone in the water | pitch the bales on to the lorry* throw, cast, fling, hurl, toss, heave, launch; *inf.* chuck, lob, bung. **2** *pitch a tent* put up, set up, erect, raise. **3** *trip and pitch forwards into the lake* fall headlong, fall, tumble,

topple, plunge, dive. **4** *ships pitching in the storm* lurch, roll, reel, sway, rock, flounder, keel, list, make heavy weather. **pitch in 1** *everyone pitched in to finish the work* help, assist, lend a hand, join in, participate, play a part, do one's bit, cooperate, collaborate. **2** *everyone pitched in to buy a leaving present* contribute, make a contribution, make a donation, put money in; *inf.* chip in.

pitch² *noun* **1** *players leaving the pitch* field, ground, park, stadium, arena, sports field, playing-field. **2** *excitement reached such a pitch* level, point, degree, height, extent, intensity. **3** *the pitch of the roof* angle, slope, slant, tilt, cant, dip, inclination. **4** *get the right musical pitch* tone, timbre, sound, tonality, modulation. **5** *with one pitch* throw, cast, fling, hurl, toss, heave; *inf.* chuck, lob. **6** *the pitch of the ship* pitching, lurch, roll, reeling, swaying, rocking, keeling, list. **7** *taken in by the salesman's pitch* spiel, sales talk, patter; *inf.* line. **8** *the street vendor's pitch* place, station; *Scots* stance.

pitch³ *noun use pitch to make the barrels watertight* bitumen, asphalt, tar.

pitch-black *adjective pitch-black nights/eyes* pitch, pitch-dark, jet-black, jet, coal-black, inky, ebony, raven, sable.

pitcher *noun a pitcher of water* jug, ewer, jar, crock.

piteous *adjective hear a piteous cry/tale* pitiful, to be pitied, pitiable, pathetic, distressing, affecting. See PITIFUL 1.

pitfall *noun the pitfalls of running a small business* trap, snare, catch, stumbling-block, hazard, peril, danger, difficulty.

pith *noun* **1** *the pith of the argument* essence, essential part, main point, point, quintessence, gist, salient point, crux, heart, heart of the matter, nub, core, meat, kernel, marrow. **2** *make a speech that lacks pith* substance, weight, moment, significance, importance, import, depth, force, vigour, power, strength, cogency.

pithy *adjective a pithy remark | wrote a pithy piece of prose* terse, succinct, concise, condensed, compact, summary, epigrammatic, to the point, pointed, significant, meaningful, expressive, incisive, forceful.
Opposites VERBOSE; LONG-WINDED.

pitiful *adjective* **1** *in a pitiful condition | a pitiful sight* to be pitied, pitiable, piteous, pathetic, wretched, distressing, affecting, moving, sad, woeful, deplorable, heart-rending, heartbreaking, poignant, emotional, emotive. **2** *a pitiful excuse/coward* contemptible, despicable, poor, sorry, miserable, inadequate, worthless, base, shabby; *inf.* pathetic.

pitiless *adjective a pitiless tyrant* merciless, ruthless, relentless, cruel, severe, harsh, heartless, callous, brutal, inhuman, inhumane, coldhearted, hard-hearted, unfeeling, uncaring, unsympathetic.
Opposites MERCIFUL; COMPASSIONATE; KINDLY.

pittance *noun earn a pittance* insufficient amount, tiny amount; *inf.* peanuts, chickenfeed.

pity noun **1** *show pity for her situation* commiseration, condolence, sympathy, compassion, fellow feeling, understanding, forbearance, distress, sadness, emotion, mercy, clemency, kindness, charity. **2** *it's a pity that he left* shame, crying shame, misfortune, unfortunate thing, sad thing, sin; *inf.* crime. **take pity on** *take pity on the homeless child* show compassion towards, be compassionate towards, be sympathetic/charitable towards, show sympathy for, show charity/mercy to, help.
Opposites INDIFFERENCE; CRUELTY; SEVERITY.

pity verb *pity the poor orphans* feel pity for, feel sorry for, weep for, grieve for, commiserate with, feel sympathy for, be sympathetic towards, sympathize with, have compassion for, be compassionate towards, feel for, show understanding towards, show forbearance towards, show mercy to, be merciful towards.

pivot noun **1** *the machine turning on a pivot* axis, fulcrum, axle, swivel, spindle, central shaft. **2** *his job was the pivot of his life* central point, centre, focal point, focus, hub, heart, *raison d'être*. **3** *he was the pivot of the firm* key person, kingpin, key player, cornerstone, linchpin.

pivot verb **1** *the machine pivots on a central shaft* turn, revolve, rotate, spin, swivel, twirl. **2** *his whole future pivots on their decision* turn on, revolve around, depend on, hinge on, hang on, rely on, be contingent on.

pixie noun *children dressed up as pixies* elf, fairy, sprite, brownie.

placard noun *placards showing pictures of the wanted men* poster, notice, public notice, bill, sticker, advertisement; *inf.* advert.

placate verb *placate the angry customer* calm, calm down, pacify, soothe, appease, conciliate, propitiate, mollify, win over.
Opposites AGITATE; ANGER.

place noun **1** *the place where the accident happened* location, spot, scene, setting, position, site, situation, venue, area, region, whereabouts, locus. **2** *a sore place on her arm* spot, area, bit, part. **3** *the names of all the places in the region | visit a different place abroad each year* town, city, village, hamlet, district, locality, neighbourhood, quarter, country, state, area, region. **4** *have a place in town* house, flat, apartment, residence, home, accommodation, abode, dwelling, domicile, property, *pied-à-terre*; *inf.* pad. **5** *occupy a lowly place in the film | win first place* position, status, grade, rank, station, standing, footing, role, niche. **6** *find a place in a law firm* position, post, job, appointment, situation, office. **7** *children asked to go back to their places* seat, position, space. **8** *put the book back in its place* position, correct position, place. **9** *not your place to criticize* function, job, role, task, duty, responsibility, charge, concern, affair, prerogative. **in place** *everything must be in place before the meeting* in position, in order, set up, arranged. **in place of** *her sister went in place of her* instead of, in lieu of, in someone's place, in someone's stead, taking the place of, as a substitute for, as an alternative for, in exchange for. **out of place** **1** *with not a hair out of place* out of position, out of order, in disorder, disarranged, in disarray,

disorganized, in a mess, topsy-turvy. **2** *her remarks were quite out of place* inappropriate, unsuitable, inapposite, out of keeping, unseemly, improper, unfit. **3** *feel out of place at the party* out of one's element, uncomfortable, ill-at-ease, uneasy, like a fish out of water. **put someone in his/her place** *he was trying to flirt with her but she put him in his place* take down a peg or two, humble, humiliate, mortify, make someone eat humble pie; *inf.* cut down to size, settle someone's hash. **take place** *where did the murder take place?* happen, occur, come about, transpire, crop up, befall, come to pass. **take the place of** *trying to take the place of her mother* replace, substitute for, be a substitute for, act for, stand in lieu of, cover for.

place verb **1** *place the books on the shelves* put, put down, position, set down, lay down, deposit, rest, stand, install, establish, settle, station, situate. **2** *place the children according to their marks in the exam* order, rank, grade, group, arrange, sort, class, classify, categorize, bracket. **3** *place her trust in him* put, lay, set, invest, consign. **4** *I know his face but I can't place him* identify, recognize, know, remember, put one's finger on, locate. **5** *try to place school-leavers in local firms* find employment for, find a job for, find a home for, accommodate, find accommodation for, appoint, assign, allocate.

placid adjective **1** *the placid waters of the lake* still, calm, peaceful, at peace, pacific, tranquil, motionless, smooth, unruffled, undisturbed. **2** *remain placid throughout the disturbance | of a placid temperament* calm, cool, cool-headed, cool, calm and collected, composed, self-possessed, serene, tranquil, equable, even-tempered, peaceable, easygoing, unmoved, undisturbed, unperturbed, imperturbable, unexcited, unexcitable, unruffled, unemotional.
Opposites STORMY; EXCITED.

plagiarize verb *plagiarize part of his colleague's work* copy, pirate, poach, borrow, reproduce, appropriate; *inf.* rip off, crib, lift.

plague noun **1** *villagers dying from a/the plague* bubonic plague, Black Death, contagious disease, contagion, disease, pestilence, sickness, epidemic, pandemic. **2** *a plague of locusts ate the crops* huge number, miltitude, host, swarm, influx, infestation. **3** *famine and other plagues* affliction, evil, scourge, curse, blight, bane, calamity, disaster, trial, tribulation, torment, visitation. *See table.* **4** *that boy's a real plague* pest, nuisance, thorn in the flesh, problem, bother, source of annoyance/irritation, irritant, the bane of one's life; *inf.* pain, pain in the neck, aggravation.

THE SEVEN BIBLICAL PLAGUES

plague of frogs	plague of locusts
plague of lice	plague of
plague of disease	darkness
of animals	plague of death of
plague of hail	firstborn

---

plague verb **1** *plagued with/by poor health* afflict, cause suffering to, torture, torment, bedevil, trouble. **2** *plagued by her little brother* annoy, irritate, bother, disturb, worry, pester, vex, harass, torment, tease; *inf.* hassle, bug.

plain *adjective* **1** *it was plain that he was guilty* clear, clear as crystal, crystal-clear, obvious, evident, apparent, manifest, transparent, patent, unmistakable. **2** *plain indications of his guilt* clear, clear-cut, obvious, evident, apparent, manifest, visible, discernible, perceptible, distinct, transparent, patent, noticeable, pronounced, marked, striking, unmistakable, conspicuous. **3** *a plain statement of the facts* clear, clear-cut, simple, straightforward, uncomplicated, comprehensible, intelligible, understandable, lucid, unambiguous. **4** *live on a plain diet | have a plain lifestyle* simple, austere, stark, severe, basic, ordinary, unsophisticated, spartan. **5** *the plain furnishings | a plain style of decoration* restrained, muted, simple, austere, stark, bare, basic, unadorned, undecorated, unembellished, unornamented, unpatterned, spartan. **6** *rather a plain child* unattractive, ill-favoured, ugly, unprepossessing, unlovely; *Am.* homely. **7** *a plain man* simple, straightforward, ordinary, average, typical, unpretentious, unassuming, unaffected, artless, guileless, sincere, honest, plain-speaking, plain-spoken, frank, candid, blunt, outspoken, forthright, direct, downright.
Opposites OBSCURE; FANCY; ELABORATE; ATTRACTIVE.

plain *adverb that was just plain stupid* downright, utterly, completely, totally, thoroughly, positively, incontrovertibly, unquestionably, undeniably, simply.

plain *noun corn growing on the plain* flatland, lowland, grassland, prairie, steppe, tundra.

plain-spoken *adjective pride himself on being plain-spoken* plain-speaking, frank, candid, blunt, outspoken, forthright, direct, downright, unequivocal, unambiguous.
Opposites EVASIVE; GUARDED; AMBIGUOUS.

plaintive *adjective the plaintive cries of the lost* mournful, doleful, melancholy, sad, sorrowful, unhappy, disconsolate, wretched, woeful, grief-stricken, broken-hearted, heartbroken, pathetic, pitiful, piteous.

plan *noun* **1** *draw up an escape plan | think up a plan to make money* plan of action, scheme, system, procedure, method, programme, schedule, project, way, means, strategy, tactics, formula. **2** *our plan is to emigrate* idea, scheme, proposal, project, intention, intent, aim, hope, aspiration, ambition. **3** *look at the architect's plan for the new building* drawing, scale drawing, blueprint, layout, sketch, diagram, chart, map, illustration, representation, delineation.

plan *verb* **1** *plan a picnic for tomorrow* arrange, organize, line up, schedule, programme. **2** *plan the reconstruction of the company* devise, design, plot, formulate, frame, outline, sketch out, draft, prepare, develop, shape, build, concoct, contrive, think out. **3** *plan a garden* draw up a plan of, design, make a drawing of, draw up a layout of, sketch out, make a chart of, map out, make a representation of. **4** *we're planning to emigrate* make plans, intend, aim, propose, mean, purpose, contemplate, envisage, foresee.

plane *noun* **1** *objects standing on a plane* flat surface, level surface, the flat. **2** *on a different intellectual plane* level, stratum, stage, degree, position, rank, footing. **3** *planes taking off from the airport* aeroplane, aircraft, jet, jumbo jet; *Am.* airplane. *See table at* AIRCRAFT.

plane *adjective require a plane surface* flat, level, horizontal, even, flush, smooth, regular, uniform.

plane *verb* **1** *aircraft/seagulls planing through the air* glide, float, drift, volplane. **2** *boats planing across the water* glide, skim, skate.

planet *noun. See table.*

PLANETS AND THEIR SATELLITES	
Planet	**Moons**
Mercury	—
Venus	—
Earth	Moon
Mars	Phobos, Deimos
Jupiter	Metis, Adrastea, Amalthea, Thebe, Io, Europa, Ganymede, Callisto, Leda, Himalia, Lysithea, Elara, Ananke, Carme, Pasiphae, Sinope
Saturn	Atlas, Prometheus, Pandora, Epimetheus, Janus, Mimas, Enceladus, Tethys, Telesto, Calypso, Dione, Helene, Rhea, Titan, Hyperion, Iapetus, Phoebe
Uranus	Cordelia, Ophelia, Bianca, Cressida, Desdemona, Juliet, Portia, Rosalind, Belinda, Puck, Miranda, Ariel, Umbriel, Titania, Oberon
Neptune	Naiad, Thalassa, Despina, Galatea, Larissa, Proteus, Triton, Nereid
Pluto	Charon

plant *noun* **1** *buy plants for the garden | grow house-plants* flower, vegetable, herb, shrub, weed. *See tables. See also tables at* FLOWER, FRUIT, FUNGUS, GRASS, NUT, TREE, VEGETABLE. **2** *invest in new plant* machinery, equipment, apparatus,

PARTS OF A PLANT		
bark	phloem	tap root
flower	root	vascular
fruit	root cap	bundle
guard cell	root hair	xylem
lateral root	stem	
leaf	stoma	

TYPES OF PLANT	
algae	gymnosperms
angiosperms	hornworts
bryophytes	horsetails
conifers	lichens
cycads	liverworts
clubmosses	mosses
ferns	pteridophytes
fungi	vascular plants

gear. **3** *work in the office, not the plant* factory, works, foundry, mill, workshop, shop, yard.

plant *verb* **1** *plant sweet peas in the spring to flower in the summer* put in the ground, implant, set out, sow, scatter. **2** *plant his feet firmly on the ground* place, position, set, situate. **3** *plant an idea in his head* put, place, fix, establish, lodge, imbed, insert. **4** *plant a microphone in his bedroom* place secretly, hide, conceal, secrete.

plaque *noun a plaque on the wall where the hero died* plate, stone plate, metal plate, panel, slab, tablet, sign, brass.

plaster *noun* **1** *wait till the plaster is dry before painting the walls* stucco, plasterwork. **2** *ceiling decorations made of plaster* | *a broken leg in plaster* plasterwork, plaster of Paris, gypsum. **3** *put a plaster on the child's grazed knee* sticking plaster, adhesive dressing; Elastoplast™, Band-Aid™.

plaster *verb plaster her face with make-up* cover thickly, spread, coat, smear, overlay, bedaub. **plaster down** *plaster down his hair with gel* flatten, smooth down, sleek down.

plastic *adjective* **1** *plastic substances such as clay* mouldable, shapable, ductile, fictile, pliant, pliable, supple, flexible, soft. **2** *the plastic minds/ personalities of young children* impressionable, responsive, receptive, malleable, mouldable, ductile, pliable, supple, flexible, compliant, tractable, manageable, controllable, docile. **3** *a plastic charm* false, artificial, synthetic, spurious, sham, bogus, assumed, superficial, specious, meretricious, pseudo; *inf.* phoney. *Opposites* RIGID; INTRACTABLE; GENUINE.

plate *noun* **1** *serve food on plates* dish, platter, dinner plate, side plate. **2** *serve generous plates* plateful, helping, portion, serving. **3** *a plate on the church wall commemorating his heroism* plaque, tablet, sign, brass. **4** *a children's book with many coloured plates* illustration, picture, photograph, print, lithograph. **5** *steel plates used in shipbuilding* sheet, panel, slab.

plateau *noun* **1** *stand on the plateau to view the valley below* elevated plain, highland, upland, tableland. **2** *prices reaching a plateau after a period of high inflation* quiescent period, resting/ flat period, quiet time, let-up, break, respite, lull.

platform *noun* **1** *deliver a speech from the platform* dais, rostrum, podium, stage, stand. **2** *fight the election on a platform of improved welfare services* programme, policy, manifesto, party line, plan, plan of action, objectives, principles, tenets.

platitude *noun write in platitudes rather than in creative prose* cliché, truism, hackneyed expression, commonplace, stock expression, trite phrase, banal phrase, banality, stereotyped phrase, bromide, inanity.

platitudinous *adjective tired of his platitudinous remarks* hackneyed, overworked, clichéd, commonplace, stock, trite, banal, stereotyped, set, stale, well-worn, tired, vapid, inane; *inf.* corny.

platonic *adjective a platonic relationship* non-romantic, non-sexual, non-physical, friendly, spiritual, intellectual. *Opposites* PHYSICAL; sexual.

platoon *noun the officer in charge of the platoon* squadron, squad, company, patrol, group.

platter *noun serve the meal on a platter* serving plate, salver, plate, dish, tray.

plaudits *plural noun receive the plaudits of his colleagues* praise, acclaim, acclamation, applause, ovation, congratulations, compliments, cheers, bouquets, approval, approbation, commendation, accolade, pat on the back. *Opposites* CONDEMNATION; CRITICISM.

plausible *adjective an excuse that was far from plausible* | *put forward a plausible argument* tenable, cogent, reasonable, believable, credible, convincing, persuasive, likely, probable, conceivable, imaginable.

play *verb* **1** *time to play rather than work* amuse oneself, entertain oneself, enjoy oneself, have fun. **2** *children playing in the park* play games, frolic, frisk, gambol, romp, cavort, sport, disport oneself. **3** *play a musical instrument* perform on. **4** *play Ophelia in Hamlet* play the part of, act, act the part of, perform, portray, represent, execute. **5** *play a trick on* perform, carry out, execute, do, accomplish, discharge, fulfill. **6** *play football* take part in, participate in, engage in, be involved in. **7** *play against the neighbouring team* compete against, contend against, oppose, take on, challenge, vie with, rival. **8** *sunlight playing on the water* | *a smile playing on her lips* move lightly, dance, flit, dart. **play around** *accuse her husband of playing around* philander, womanize, have an affair, have a love affair, fool around; *inf.* mess about. **play at** *play at being a businesswoman* pretend to be, give the appearance of, assume/affect the role of; *inf.* make like. **play ball** *want to do business but they refused to play ball* cooperate, collaborate, play along, go along with the plan, show willing, be willing. **play down** *play down his part in the crime* make light of, make little of, gloss over, minimize, diminish, set little store by, underrate, underestimate, undervalue, think little of; *inf.* soft-pedal. **play for time** *try to play for time while his friend got away* stall, temporize, gain time, hang back, hang fire, procrastinate, delay, filibuster, stonewall. **play it by ear** *we have no plans - we're going to play it by ear* improvise, extemporize, ad lib, take it as it comes. **play on** *friends playing on his weakness for beautiful blondes* exploit, take advantage of, turn to one's account, profit by, capitalize on, impose on, trade on, milk, abuse, misuse; *inf.* walk all over. **play the fool** *always playing the fool even in serious situations* act the fool, fool about/around, monkey about/around, clown, clown around, act the clown, horse around; *inf.* act the goat, lark around, mess about/around. **play the game** *being honourable himself he expects everyone else to play the game* play fair, be fair, play by the rules, abide by the rules, follow the rules, be a good sport, toe the line. **play up 1** *this played up his eyes which are his best feature* emphasize, put/lay emphasis on, accentuate, bring/draw/call attention to, point up, underline, underscore, highlight, spotlight, give prominence to, bring to the fore, stress. **2** *children playing up when they have a new teacher* misbehave, be misbehaved, be naughty, be mischievous, be disobedient, be awkward, give trouble; *inf.* be stroppy, be bolshie. **3** *children playing the teacher up* be naughty/mischievous/disobedient/troublesome to, annoy, irritate, vex, be a nuisance to, be a thorn in the flesh/side of; *inf.* be a pain to, be a pain in the neck to. **4** *his injured leg was playing up* cause trouble, be painful, hurt, be sore, cause pain; *inf.* give someone gyp. **5** *the car is playing up* be not working properly, be malfunctioning, malfunction; *inf.* be on the blink, be wonky. **play up to** *she's always playing up to the boss so as to get her own way* flatter, ingratiate oneself with, try to get on the good side of, curry favour with, fawn over, toady to; *inf.* soft-soap, suck up to, butter up, be all over, lick someone's boots. **play with 1** *children told not to play with their pencils* fiddle with, toy with, fidget with, fool about/around with; *inf.* mess about/around with. **2** *he's only playing with her affections and isn't at all serious about their relationship* trifle with, toy with, dally with, amuse oneself with. **Opposites** WORK.

play *noun* **1** *children at play* | *prefer play to work* amusement, entertainment, recreation, diversion, leisure, enjoyment, fun, merrymaking, revelry. **2** *appear in a play by a local dramatist* drama, stage play, stage show, radio play, television play, teleplay, comedy, tragedy, farce. *See table. See also tables at* THEATRE. **3** *the play of supernatural forces* action, activity, operation, agency, working, functioning, exercise, interaction, interplay. **4** *need more play on the fishing line* movement, freedom of movement, free motion, slack; *inf.* give. **5** *give full play to her emotions* scope, range, latitude, liberty, licence, freedom, indulgence, free rein. **6** *injure the child accidentally in play* fun, jest, joking, sport, teasing.

TYPES OF PLAY AND DRAMA

antimasque	masque
burlesque	melodrama
closet play	mime
comedy	miracle play
comedy of manners	monodrama
commedia dell'arte	morality play
docudrama	mummers' play
dumbshow	mystery play
duologue	Nō play
fabula	pantomime
farce	passion play
Grand Guignol	psychodrama
Greek drama	sociodrama
harlequinade	teleplay
improvisation	tragedy
Kabuki	tragicomedy
kitchen-sink drama	two-hander
Kyōgen	verse drama

---

playboy *noun just a playboy without any interest in work* pleasure-seeker, man-about-town, socialite, rake, roué, womanizer, philanderer, ladies' man, ladykiller; *inf.* gay dog.

player *noun* **1** *one of the players in the tennis/football match* competitor, contestant, participant, team-member, sportsman/sportswoman.

2 *one of the players in the theatre company* actor/actress, performer, entertainer, artist, artiste, trouper, Thespian. **3** *several of the players in the orchestra* performer, musician, instrumentalist, artist, artiste, virtuoso.

playful *adjective* **1** *playful kitten* | *in playful mood* fun-loving, full of fun, high-spirited, frisky, skittish, coltish, frolicsome, sportive, mischievous, impish, puckish. **2** *a playful remark* in fun, in jest, joking, jesting, humorous, fun, facetious, waggish, tongue-in-cheek, arch, roguish. **Opposites** SOLEMN; SERIOUS.

playground *noun take the children to the playground* play area, park, playing field, recreation ground.

playwright *noun plays written by various playwrights* dramatist, dramaturge, dramturgist. *See table.*

plea *noun* **1** *make a plea to the King to save his mother's life* appeal, entreaty, imploration, supplication, petition, prayer, request, solicitation, suit, invocation. **2** *enter a plea of guilty* | *her plea was not guilty* answer, statement. **3** *produce evidence in support of his plea against the accused* allegation, case, suit, action, claim. **4** *ignore her pleas of another engagement* excuse, pretext, claim, vindication.

plead *verb* **1** *plead with the judge to show mercy* appeal to, beg, entreat, beseech, implore, petition, make supplication to, supplicate, importune, pray to, solicit, request, ask earnestly, present one's suit to. **2** *plead insanity as the reason for his crime* put forward, state, assert, argue, claim, allege.

pleasant *adjective* **1** *a pleasant experience* pleasing, pleasurable, agreeable, enjoyable, entertaining, amusing, delightful, satisfying, gratifying, nice, good, fine, welcome, acceptable; *inf.* lovely. **2** *a pleasant person/manner* agreeable, friendly, amiable, affable, genial, likeable, nice, good-humoured, charming, engaging, winning, delightful; *inf.* lovely. **Opposites** UNPLEASANT; DISAGREEABLE.

pleasantry *noun* **1** *exchange pleasantries with his neighbour every morning* good-natured remark, polite remark. **2** *try to laugh at the speaker's pleasantries* joke, jest, quip, witticism, bon mot, sally; *inf.* wisecrack.

please *verb* **1** *try to find a show that will please his mother* give pleasure to, be agreeable to, make pleased/happy/glad etc, gladden, delight, cheer up, charm, divert, entertain, amuse, tickle, satisfy, gratify, fulfil, content, suit; *inf.* tickle pink. **2** *do as one pleases* want, wish, see fit, will, like, desire, be inclined, prefer, opt. **Opposites** DISPLEASE; dissatisfy; ANNOY; BORE.

pleased *adjective give a pleased smile* happy, glad, cheerful, delighted, thrilled, elated, contented, satisfied, gratified, fulfilled, over the moon, as pleased as Punch; *inf.* on cloud nine.

pleasing *adjective* **1** *a pleasing experience* pleasant, pleasurable, agreeable, enjoyable, entertaining, amusing, delightful, satisfying, gratifying, nice, good, fine, welcome, acceptable; *inf.* lovely. **2** *he had/was a pleasing personality* pleasant, agreeable, friendly, amiable, affable, genial, likeable, nice, good-humoured, charming, engaging, winning, delightful; *inf.* lovely.

pleasure noun **1** *events which bring pleasure* happiness, gladness, delight, joy, enjoyment, entertainment, amusement, diversion, satisfaction, gratification, fulfilment, contentment. **2** *one of his pleasures was to play the piano* source of pleasure, delight, joy, enjoyment, diversion, recreation. **3** *the pursuit of pleasure* delight, joy, enjoyment, diversion, recreation. **4** *what is your pleasure?* wish, desire, will, inclination, preference, choice, option, purpose.
Opposites DISPLEASURE; SORROW; PAIN.

PLAYWRIGHTS

Aeschylus
(c. 525–c. 456 B.C.;
Gk)
Albee, Edward
(b. 1928; Am.)
Anouilh, Jean
(1910–87; Fr.)
Aristophanes
(c. 450–c. 385 B.C.;
Gk)
Ayckbourn, Alan
(b. 1939; Brit.)
Beaumarchais,
Pierre-Augustin
Caron de (1732–99;
Fr.)
Beaumont, Francis
(1584–1616; Brit.)
Beckett, Samuel
(1906–89; Ir.)
Behan, Brendan
(1923–64; Ir.)
Bennett, Alan
(b. 1934; Brit.)
Betti, Ugo
(1892–1953; It.)
Brecht, Bertolt
(1898–1956; Ger.)
Büchner, Georg
(1813–37; Ger.)
Bulgakov, Mikhail
(1871–1944; Soviet)
Calderón de la
Barca, Pedro
(1600–81; Sp.)
Chekhov, Anton
(1860–1904; Russ.)
Claudel, Paul
(1868–1955; Fr.)
Cocteau, Jean
(1889–1963; Fr.)
Congreve, William
(1670–1729; Brit.)
Corneille, Pierre
(1606–84; Fr.)
Cyrano de Bergerac,
Savinien (1619–55;
Fr.)
Dekker, Thomas
(c. 1570–1632; Engl.)
Dürrenmatt,
Friedrich (1921–90;
Swiss)
Euripides
(c. 480–406 B.C.; Gk)
Feydeau, Georges
(1862–1921; Fr.)

Fletcher, John
(1579–1625; Engl.)
Fo, Dario (b. 1926; It.)
Ford, John
(c. 1586–c. 1640;
Engl.)
Fry, Christopher
(b. 1907; Brit.)
Fugard, Athol
(b. 1932; S. Afr.)
Genet, Jean
(1910–86; Fr.)
Goethe, Johann
Wolfgang von
(1749–1832; Ger.)
Goldoni, Carlo
(1707–93; It.)
Goldsmith, Oliver
(1728–74; Ir.)
Gorky, Maxim
(1868–1936; Russ.)
Greene, Robert
(1558–92; Engl.)
Hauptmann, Ger-
hart (1862–1946;
Ger.)
Havel, Václav
(b. 1936; Cz.)
Hellman, Lillian
(1907–84; Am.)
Ibsen, Henrik
(1828–1906; Norw.)
Ionesco, Eugène
(1912–94; Fr., b. in
Romania)
Jarry, Alfred
(1873–1907; Fr.)
Jonson, Ben
(1572–1637; Engl.)
Kaiser, Georg
(1878–1945; Ger.)
Kaufman, George S.
(1889–1961; Am.)
Kotzebue, August
von (1761–1819;
Ger.)
Kyd, Thomas
(1558–94; Engl.)
Lorca, Federico Gar-
cía (1898–1936; Sp.)
Maeterlinck, Comte
Maurice
(1862–1949; Belg.)
Mamet, David
(b. 1947; Am.)
Marivaux, Pierre de
(1688–1763; Fr.)

Marlowe, Christo-
pher (1564–93;
Engl.)
Massinger, Philip
(1583–1640; Engl.)
Menander
(c. 342–c. 292 B.C.;
Gk)
Middleton, Thomas
(c. 1570–1627; Engl.)
Miller, Arthur
(b. 1915; Am.)
Molière (Jean-
Baptiste Poquelin;
1622–73; Fr.)
Montherlant, Henry
de (1896–1972; Fr.)
Musset, Alfred de
(1810–57; Fr.)
O'Casey, Sean
(1880–1964; Ir.)
Odets, Clifford
(1906–63; Am.)
O'Neill, Eugene
(1888–1953; Am.)
Orton, Joe (1933–67;
Brit.)
Osborne, John
(1929–94; Brit.)
Ostrovsky, Alek-
sandr (1823–86;
Russ.)
Pinero, Sir Arthur
Wing (1855–1934;
Brit.)
Pinter, Harold
(b. 1930; Brit.)
Pirandello, Luigi
(1867–1936; It.)
Plautus
(c. 259–184 B.C.;
Rom.)
Potter, Dennis
(1935–94; Brit.)
Pushkin, Aleksandr
(1799–1837; Russ.)
Racine, Jean
(1639–99; Fr.)
Rattigan, Sir
Terence (1911–77;
Brit.)
Rostand, Edmond
(1868–1918; Fr.)
Rowley, William
(c. 1585–1626; Engl.)
Saroyan, William
(1908–81; Am.)

Schiller, Friedrich
(1759–1805; Ger.)
Seneca, Lucius
Annaeus
(c. 4 B.C.–65 A.D.;
Rom.)
Shakespeare,
William
(1564–1616; Engl.)
Shaw, George
Bernard
(1856–1950; Ir.)
Shephard, Sam
(b. 1943; Am.)
Sheridan, Richard
Brinsley
(1751–1816; Ir.)
Simon, Neil (b. 1927;
Am.)
Sophocles
(c. 496–406 B.C.; Gk)
Stoppard, Tom
(b. 1937; Brit., b. in
Czechoslovakia)
Strindberg, August
(1849–1912; Sw.)
Sutherland, Efua
(b. 1924; Ghanaian)
Synge, J(ohn)
M(illington)
(1871–1909; Ir.)
Terence
(c. 185–159 B.C.;
Rom.)
Tourneur, Cyril
(c. 1576–1626; Engl.)
Vega, Lope de
(1562–1635; Sp.)
Vicente, Gil
(c. 1465–c. 1536;
Port.)
Webster, John
(c. 1580–c. 1625;
Engl.)
Wedekind, Frank
(1864–1918; Ger.)
Wesker, Arnold
(b. 1932; Brit.)
Wilde, Oscar
(1854–1900; Ir.)
Wilder, Thornton
(1897–1975; Am.)
Williams,
Tennessee
(1911–83; Am.)
Wycherley, William
(c. 1640–1716; Brit.)

plebeian *adjective* **1** *of plebeian origins* lower-class, low-class, low, low-born, working-class, proletarian, common, peasant, mean, ignoble. **2** *have plebeian tastes* uncultivated, uncultured, unrefined, coarse, common, base; *inf.* plebby.
Opposites ARISTOCRATIC; UPPER-CLASS.

plebeian *noun* *aristocrats looking down on the plebeians* common person, commoner, man/woman/person in the street, proletarian, working peasant; *inf.* pleb, prole.

pledge *noun* **1** *give his pledge to look after the children* promise, word, word of honour, vow, assurance, undertaking, oath, covenant, warrant. **2** *give his watch as a pledge that he would repay the loan* security, surety, guarantee, collateral, bond, earnest, gage, deposit, pawn. **3** *give her a ring as a pledge of his love* token, symbol, sign, mark, testimony, proof, evidence. **4** *drink a pledge to colleagues who were retiring* toast, health.

pledge *verb* **1** *he pledged that he would support the children* promise, give one's word, vow, give one's assurance, give an undertaking, undertake, take an oath, swear, swear an oath, vouch, engage, contract. **2** *pledge one's house as security for a personal loan* mortgage, put up as collateral, guarantee, plight, pawn. **3** *pledge the bride and groom* drink to the health of, drink to, toast.

plentiful *adjective* *plentiful supplies of food* abundant, copious, ample, profuse, lavish, liberal, generous, large, huge, bumper, infinite.
Opposites MEAGRE; SPARSE; SCANTY.

plenty *noun* *the years of plenty* plentifulness, plenteousness, affluence, prosperity, wealth, opulence, luxury, abundance, copiousness, fruitfulness, profusion. **plenty of** *have plenty of money* enough, sufficient, a good deal of, a great deal of, masses of; *inf.* lots of, heaps of, stacks of, piles of.

plethora *noun* *a plethora of good advice* overabundance, superabundance, excess, superfluity, surplus, surfeit, glut.
Opposites DEARTH; LACK.

pliable *adjective* **1** *a pliable substance* flexible, bendable, bendy, pliant, elastic, supple, stretchable, ductile, plastic. **2** *expect women to be pliable* malleable, yielding, compliant, docile, biddable, tractable, manageable, governable, controllable, amenable, adaptable, flexible, impressionable, influenceable, persuadable.
Opposites RIGID; INTRACTABLE; OBDURATE.

plight *noun* *the plight of the homeless* | *the plight they're in* unfortunate situation, sorry condition, predicament, trouble, difficulty, dire straits, extremity, tight corner; *inf.* hole, pickle, spot, jam.

plod *verb* *plod along the road* walk heavily, trudge, clump, stomp, lumber, tramp, drag oneself along, plough. **plod away** *plod away at/with one's work* toil away at, labour at, soldier on with, slog away at, drudge away at, persevere with, peg away at, grind away at; *inf.* plug away at.

plot *noun* **1** *grow vegetables in a plot* piece of ground, patch, allotment, lot, parcel. **2** *nobels*

planning a plot against the King conspiracy, intrigue, secret plan, secret scheme, stratagem. **3** *the plot of the novel/play* action, theme, subject, story line, story, scenario, thread.

plot *verb* **1** *plot the escape route* | *plot the new construction site* map out, make a plan/drawing of, draw, draw a diagram of, draw the layout of, make a blueprint/chart of, sketch out, outline. **2** *plot the battle-sites on the map* mark, chart, map. **3** *nobles plotting against the King* take part in a plot, scheme, conspire, participate in a conspiracy, intrigue, form an intrigue. **4** *plot the King's downfall* plan, hatch, scheme, construe, concoct, devise, frame, think up, dream up, conceive; *inf.* cook up.

plough *verb* *plough the field* till, work, cultivate, break up, turn up. **plough into** *the car ploughed into a crowd of people on the pavement* plunge into, lunge into, career into, crash into, smash into, bulldoze into, hurtle into, drive into. **plough through** *plough through the mud* plod through, trudge through, clump through, push one's way through, forge one's way through, wade through, flounder through.

ploy *noun* *a ploy to distract the teacher's attention* dodge, ruse, scheme, trick, stratagem, manoeuvre, move.

pluck *verb* **1** *pluck a rose from the bush* | *pluck the burning paper from the fire* pull, pull off/out, remove, extract. **2** *pluck flowers to make perfume* | *pluck blackberries for jam* gather, collect, harvest, take in, pull, cull. **3** *sit plucking nervously at his hair* | *plucking at her mother's skirt* tug at, pull at, clutch at, snatch at, catch at, tweak; *inf.* yank. **4** *pluck the string of the guitar* finger, strum, pick, plunk, thrum, twang.

pluck *noun* *require a lot of pluck to go into the jungle alone* courage, bravery, valour, heroism, intrepidity, fearlessness, mettle, nerve, backbone, determination, boldness, daring, spirit, audacity; *inf.* gumption, grit, guts, spunk, bottle.

plucky *adjective* *the plucky young man saved his friend from drowning* courageous, brave, valiant, valorous, heroic, intrepid, fearless, mettlesome, gritty, determined, bold, daring, spirited, audacious; *inf.* gutsy, spunky.
Opposites COWARDLY; TIMOROUS; TIMID.

plug *noun* **1** *put a plug in to prevent the water/oil escaping* stopper, bung, cork, stopple, seal. **2** *a plug of tobacco* cake, chew, twist, quid, wad. **3** *give him a free plug for his book on the television programme* publicity, advertisement, commercial, promotion, puff, push, mention; *inf.* advert, ad, hype.

plug *verb* **1** *plug the hole to prevent the water/oil escaping* stop up, close off, bung, cork, dam up, block, stopper, stopple, seal off, pack, stuff. **2** *arrested for plugging his enemy* shoot, shoot down, gun down, put a bullet in, hit, take out, pick off, pot. **3** *plug his new book on a television show* publicize, promote, give publicity to, advertise, give a puff to, puff up, push, give a push to, give a mention to, write up, build up; *inf.* hype, hype up. **plug away** *plug away at the investigation* | *must keep plugging away at his work* toil away at, labour at, soldier on with, slog away at, plod away at, drudge away at, persevere with, peg away at, grind away at.

plum *adjective get a plum job* prize, first-class, choice, best, excellent.

plumb *adverb* **1** *cliffs rising up plumb from the sea* vertically, perpendicularly, straight up, straight up and down. **2** *placed plumb in the centre* exactly, precisely, right, dead, slap; *inf.* bang, spot on. **3** *plumb crazy* utterly, absolutely, completely, totally, entirely, wholly, quite, stark.

plumb *verb plumb the mysteries of computer technology* probe, search out, delve into, explore, scrutinize, investigate, inspect, examine, sound out, go into, fathom, unravel. **plumb the depths of** *plumb the depths of despair | jokes which plumb the depths of bad taste* reach the lowest possible level of, reach the lowest point, reach the nadir of.

plummet *verb* **1** *the plane plummeted to the ground* fall perpendicularly, fall headlong, plunge, hurtle, nosedive, dive, drop. **2** *prices plummeted* fall steeply, plunge, tumble, nosedive, take a nosedive, drop rapidly, go down.

plump *adjective plump little girls | plump people trying to slim* chubby, round, rounded, well-rounded, of ample proportions, rotund, buxom, stout, fat, fattish, obese, corpulent, fleshy, portly, tubby, dumpy, podgy, roly-poly, well-covered; *inf.* well-upholstered, beefy. **Opposites** THIN; SLENDER; SKINNY.

plump *verb* **1** *plump down into a chair* fall, drop, flop, plonk, sink, collapse. **2** *plump the dish down on the table* set down, deposit, plonk, dump. **3** *children plumping for a day at the sea* decide on, choose, pick, select, opt for, vote for.

plunder *verb* **1** *enemy forces plundering the villages* rob, pillage, loot, raid, ransack, rifle, strip, fleece, ravage, lay waste, despoil, spoil, spoliate, depredate, harry, maraud, sack, rape. **2** *plunder food* steal, thieve, rob, purloin, filch, make off with; *inf.* walk away/off with, snaffle.

plunder *noun* **1** *the plunder of the village* plundering, robbery, robbing, pillaging, looting, raiding, ransacking, despoiling, laying waste, harrying, marauding, rapine. *See* PLUNDER *verb* 1. **2** *take their plunder back to their camp* stolen goods, loot, booty, spoils, prize, pillage, ill-gotten gains; *inf.* swag.

plunge *verb* **1** *plunge the dagger into his back* thrust, stick, jab, push, drive. **2** *the man on the deck plunged into the sea* dive, nosedive, jump, plummet, drop, fall, fall headlong, swoop down, descend. **3** *plunge the house into darkness* throw, cast, pitch. **4** *plunge his burnt hand into cold water* immerse, sink, dip, douse. **5** *the car plunged forward | plunge into matrimony* charge, lurch, rush, dash, hurtle, career. **6** *house prices plunged during the recession* fall steeply, drop rapidly, go down, plummet, tumble, nosedive, take a nosedive.

plunge *noun* **1** *witness his plunge into the sea* dive, nosedive, jump, fall, drop, swoop, descent. **2** *the car's sudden plunge forward* charge, lurch, rush, dash. **3** *an unexpected*

plunge in house prices fall, drop, tumble, nosedive.

plus *preposition* **1** *3 plus 3 makes 6* and, added to. **2** *we have to get four people plus their luggage into the car* as well as, in addition to, added to, and, coupled with, with.

plus *noun he likes the job - it's a plus that it's well paid* bonus, extra, added advantage, additional benefit, fringe benefit, perquisite; *inf.* perk.

plush *adjective plush furnishings* luxurious, luxury, de luxe, sumptuous, lavish, gorgeous, opulent, rich, costly; *inf.* ritzy, classy. **Opposites** PLAIN; AUSTERE; CHEAP.

plutocrat *noun plutocrats with plenty of money to spend* rich person, person of means, capitalist, tycoon, magnate, millionaire, billionaire, Midas, Croesus; *inf.* fat cat, moneybags.

ply *verb* **1** *a woodman plying his saw | plying the oars* wield, use, operate, work, utilize, employ, manipulate, handle. **2** *ply his trade as a street-merchant* carry on, practise, work at, engage in, pursue, follow, occupy oneself with, busy oneself with. **3** *ply them with questions* bombard, assail, besiege, beset, harass, importune; *inf.* hassle. **4** *ply them with food and drink* supply, provide, lavish, shower, load, heap. **5** *ships plying between England and France | buses plying between two cities* travel regularly, go regularly, ferry, shuttle.

poach *verb* **1** *poach rabbits/pheasants* hunt illegally, take illegally, kill illegally, trap illegally, steal. **2** *poach on his neighbour's property/ territory* trespass on, encroach on, infringe on, intrude on. **3** *poach his friend's ideas* steal, appropriate, misappropriate, copy, pirate; *inf.* lift, rip off.

pocket *noun* **1** *pockets on the side of the suitcase* pouch, compartment, receptacle. **2** *luxury goods beyond his pocket* budget, means, resources, finances, funds, capital, assets. **3** *isolated pockets of resistance to the government* small area, small region, small district, small zone.

pocket *adjective a pocket edition of the reference book* small, little, miniature, compact, concise, abridged, potted.

pocket *verb shop assistants pocketing part of the takings* take for oneself, appropriate, misappropriate, steal, thieve, purloin, filch; *inf.* lift, nick, swipe, snaffle.

pod *noun pea-pod | bean-pod* shell, husk, hull, shuck.

podgy *adjective* **1** *a podgy man with a long thin woman* small and fat/obese/corpulent, short and stout, round, rotund, roly-poly, dumpy, squat, stubby, stumpy, chubby, tubby; *inf.* pudgy. **2** *podgy fingers* short and fat, plump, fleshy, stubby, stumpy.

podium *noun deliver an address from the podium* platform, stage, dais, rostrum, stand.

poem *noun have a poem published in an anthology* verse composition, verse, verselet, song, rhyme, jingle. *See table. See also tables at* VERSE.

poet *noun an amateur poet* verse-maker, versifier, rhymer, rhymester, sonneteer, ballad-

TYPES OF POEM

ballad	lay
bucolic	limerick
chanson	lyric
clerihew	madrigal
dirge	nursery
dithyramb	rhyme
eclogue	ode
elegy	pastoral
encomium	prothalamion
epic	roundelay
epigram	saga
epithalamium	satire
epode	sonnet
georgic	tanka
haiku	threnody
idyll	vilanelle

monger, balladeer, lyricist, bard, minstrel. *See table.*

poetic *adjective* **1** *write poetic works* of poetry, poetical, metrical, rhythmical, lyrical, elegaic. **2** *poetic language* imaginative, creative, figurative, symbolic, flowery. **3** *a poetic rendering of the symphony* aesthetic, artistic, tasteful, graceful, elegant, sensitive.

poetry *noun write poetry rather than prose* poems, verse, verses, versification, metrical composition, rhythmical composition, rhymes, rhyming. *See tables at* VERSE.

pogrom *noun a pogrom ordered by the invading tyrant* massacre, wholesale slaughter, general slaughter, mass killing, mass murder, mass homicide, carnage, blood bath, genocide, ethnic cleansing, megadeath.

poignancy *noun* **1** *the poignancy of the farewell | the poignancy of her memories* tenderness, emotionalness, emotion, sentiment, feeling, pathos, sadness, sorrowfulness, tearfulness, evocativeness. *See* POIGNANT 1. **2** *the poignancy of the sight of the two orphans* pitifulness, piteousness, pathos, sadness, sorrow, misery, pain, distress, tragedy.

poignant *adjective* **1** *poignant farewell/memories* moving, affecting, touching, tender, emotional, sentimental, heartfelt, sad, heart-moving, sorrowful, tearful, evocative. **2** *the poignant sight of the weeping orphans* moving, affecting, touching, pitiful, piteous, pitiable, pathetic, sad, sorrowful, mournful, wretched, miserable, painful, distressing, upsetting, heart-moving, tragic.

point *noun* **1** *the point of the spear/tool* sharp end, tapered end, tip, top, extremity, prong, spike, tine. **2** *points at the end of sentences* full stop, full point, stop, period. **3** *ships sailing round the point* promontory, headland, head, foreland, cape, bluff. **4** *found dead at a point near her home* place, position, location, situation, site, spot, area, locality. **5** *abrupt to the point of rudeness* extent, degree, stage. **6** *reach an important point in her life* stage, position, circumstance, condition. **7** *have to die at some point* point/moment in time, time, juncture, stage, period, moment, instant. **8** *when it came to the point he couldn't face her* critical point,

decisive point, crux, moment of truth, point of no return. **9** *explain the situation point by point* detail, item, particular. **10** *get to the point | the point of the question* main point, central point, essential point, focal point, salient point, keynote, heart of the matter, essence, nub, core, pith, marrow, meat, crux. **11** *miss the point of the story* meaning, significance, signification, import, essence, gist, substance, drift, thrust, burden, theme, tenor, vein. **12** *raise various points during the discussion* subject, subject under discussion, issue, topic, question, matter, item. **13** *arguments that lack point* effectiveness, cogency, force, power, potency. **14** *the various points of the argument* part, element, constituent, component, ingredient. **15** *the point of the exercise is to make some money | what is the point of it?* aim, purpose, object, objective, goal, intention, reason for, use, utility. **16** *kindness is one of his strong points* characteristic, trait, attribute, quality, feature, property, predisposition, streak, peculiarity, idiosyncrasy. **17** *have more points than the other team* mark, score. **beside the point** *it's beside the point what he thinks - he's not on the deciding committee* irrelevant, immaterial, incidental, not to the point, not germane, not to the purpose. **in point of fact** *people think he's stupid but in point of fact he's brilliant* in fact, as a matter of fact, actually, really, in reality, in truth, truly. **point of view** **1** *listen to everyone's point of view before making a decision* view, viewpoint, opinion, belief, attitude, feeling, sentiment, stand, standpoint, stance, position. **2** *look at the situation from a different point of view* viewpoint, angle, slant, perspective, standpoint, outlook. **to the point** *his remarks were very much to the point* pertinent, relevant, germane, applicable, apropos, apposite, appropriate, apt, fitting, suitable. **up to a point** *I agree with you up to a point* to some extent, to some degree, in part, partly.

point *verb point the gun at his victim* direct, aim, level, train. **point out** *point out the disadvantages of the proposal* call attention to, draw attention to, indicate, show, specify, designate, identify, mention, allude to. **point to** *all the evidence points to the fact that he is the murderer* indicate, show, signify, suggest, be evidence of, evidence. **point up** *point up the difference between them* emphasize, put/lay emphasis on, stress, lay stress on, accentuate, underline, underscore, give prominence to, highlight, spotlight, play up, bring to the fore.

point-blank *adverb* **1** *shoot his victim point-blank* at close range, close up, close to. **2** *ask him point-blank for his reasons | refuse point-blank to go* directly, plainly, straight, straightfowardly, frankly, candidly, forthrightly, bluntly, openly, explicitly, unequivocally, unambiguously.

pointed *adjective* **1** *the pointed end of the stick* sharp, sharp-edged, edged, cuspidate, acicular. **2** *a pointed remark* cutting, trenchant, biting, incisive, penetrating, forceful, telling, significant. **3** *treat her with a pointed indifference* obvious, evident, conspicuous, striking, emphasized, unmistakable.

POETS

Akhmatova, Anna (1889–1966; Russ.)

Alcaeus (c. 620–c. 580 B.C.; Gk)

Anacreon (c. 570–478 B.C.; Gk)

Angelou, Maya (b. 1928; Am.)

Apollinaire, Guillaume (Wilhelm de Kostrowitzky; 1880–1918; Fr.)

Ariosto, Ludovico (1474–1533; It.)

Arnold, Matthew (1822–88; Brit.)

Auden, W(ystan) H(ugh) (1907–73; Am.)

Baraka, Imamu Amiri (b. 1934; Am.)

Bashō Matsuo (Matsuo Munefusa; 1644–94; Jap.)

Baudelaire, Charles (1821–67; Fr.)

Baxter, James (1926–72; NZ)

Belloc, Hilaire (1870–1953; Brit., b. in France)

Betjeman, Sir John (1906–84; Brit.)

Blake, William (1757–1827; Brit.)

Blok, Aleksandr (1880–1921; Russ.)

Bridges, Robert (1844–1930; Brit.)

Brodsky, Joseph (b. 1940; Russ.)

Brontë, Emily (1818–48; Brit.)

Brooke, Rupert (1887–1915; Brit.)

Browning, Elizabeth Barrett (1806–61; Brit.)

Browning, Robert (1812–89; Brit.)

Bunin, Ivan (1870–1953; Russ.)

Bürger, Gottfried (1747–94; Ger.)

Burns, Robert (1759–96; Scot.)

Butler, Samuel (1612–80; Brit.)

Byron, George Gordon, Lord (1788–1824; Brit.)

Caedmon (7th century A.D.; Anglo-Saxon)

Callimachus (c. 305–c. 240 B.C.; Gk)

Camões, Luís de (c. 1524–80; Port.)

Carew, Thomas (c. 1594–1640; Engl.)

Castilho, Antonio Feliciano de (1800–75; Port.)

Catullus (c. 84–c. 54 B.C.; Rom.)

Cavafy, Constantine (1863–1933; Gk)

Cavalcanti, Guido (c. 1255–1300; It.)

Celan, Paul (Paul Antschel; 1920–70; Jewish, b. in Romania)

Chapman, George (c. 1560–1634; Brit.)

Chatterton, Thomas (1752–70; Brit.)

Chaucer, Geoffrey (c. 1342–1400; Engl.)

Chrétien de Troyes (12th century A.D.; Fr.)

Clare, John (1793–1864; Brit.)

Clough, Arthur Hugh (1819–61; Brit.)

Coleridge, Samuel Taylor (1772–1834; Brit.)

Cowley, Abraham (1618–67; Brit.)

Cowper, William (1731–1800; Brit.)

Crabbe, George (1754–1832; Brit.)

cummings, e. e. (1894–1962; Am.)

Dafydd ap Gwilym (c. 1320–c. 80; Welsh)

D'Annunzio, Gabriele (1863–1938; It.)

Dante Alighieri (1265–1321; It.)

Day-Lewis, C(ecil) (1904–72; Brit.)

de la Mare, Walter (1873–1956; Brit.)

Dickinson, Emily (1830–86; Am.)

Donne, John (1572–1631; Engl.)

Doolittle, Hilda (1886–1961; Am.)

Dryden, John (1631–1700; Brit.)

Dunbar, William (c. 1456–c. 1513; Scot.)

Eliot, T(homas) S(tearns) (1888–1965; Brit., b. in America)

Éluard, Paul (1895–1952; Fr.)

Elytis, Odysseus (b. 1912; Gk)

Emerson, Ralph Waldo (1803–82; Am.)

Ennius (239–169 B.C.; Rom.)

Firdausi (Abu al-Qasim Mansur; c. 935–c. 1020; Pers.)

Fitzgerald, Edward (1809–83; Brit.)

Foscolo, Ugo (1778–1827; It.)

Freneau, Philip (1752–1832; Am.)

Frost, Robert Lee (1874–1963; Am.)

Gautier, Théophile (1811–72; Fr.)

Gay, John (1685–1732; Brit.)

Gibran, Khalil (1883–1931; Syrian/Lebanese)

Ginsberg, Allen (b. 1926; Am.)

Goethe, Johann Wolfgang von (1749–1832; Ger.)

Góngora y Argote, Luis de (1561–1627; Sp.)

Graves, Robert (1895–1985; Brit.)

Gray, Thomas (1716–71; Brit.)

Gunn, Thom(son William) (b. 1929; Brit.)

Haavikko, Paavo (b. 1931; Finn.)

Heaney, Seamus (b. 1939; Ir.)

Heine, Heinrich (1797–1856; Ger.)

Herbert, George (1593–1633; Engl.)

Herbert, Zbigniew (b. 1924; Pol.)

Herrick, Robert (1591–1674; Engl.)

Hesiod (8th century B.C.; Gk)

Homer (8th century B.C.; Gk)

Hopkins, Gerard Manley (1844–89; Brit.)

Horace (65–8 B.C.; Rom.)

Housman, A(lfred) E(dward) (1859–1936; Brit.)

Hughes, Ted (b. 1930; Brit.)

Iqbal, Sir Mohammed (1875–1938; Ind.)

Jonson, Ben (1572–1637; Engl.)

Kavanagh, Patrick (1905–67; Ir.)

Keats, John (1795–1821; Brit.)

La Fontaine, Jean de (1621–95; Fr.)

Laforgue, Jules (1860–87; Fr.)

Lamartine, Alphonse de (1790–1869; Fr.)

Landor, Walter Savage (1775–1864; Engl.)

Langland, William (c. 1330–c. 1400; Engl.)

Larkin, Philip (1922–85; Brit.)

Lawrence, D(avid) H(erbert) (1885–1930; Brit.)

Layamon (12th century; Engl.)

Leconte de Lisle, Charles (1818–94; Fr.)

Leopardi, Giacomo (1798–1837; It.)

Lermontov, Mikhail (1814–41; Russ.)

Li Po (701–62 A.D.; Chin.)

Longfellow, Henry Wadsworth (1807–82; Am.)

Lovelace, Richard (1618–57; Brit.)

Lowell, Amy (1874–1925; Am.)

Lowell, Robert (1917–77; Am.)

Lucan (39–65 A.D.; Rom.)

Lucretius (c. 95–c. 55 B.C.; Rom.)

Lydgate, John (c. 1370–c. 1450; Engl.)

Macdiarmid, Hugh (Christopher Grieve; 1892–1978; Scot.)

MacNeice, Louis (1907–63; Brit., b. in Northern Ireland)

POETS *cont.*			
Mallarmé, Stéphane (1842–98; Fr.)	Péguy, Charles (1873–1914; Fr.)	Sidney, Sir Philip (1554–86; Brit.)	Thomas, Dylan (1914–53; Welsh)
Mandelstam, Osip (1891–1938; Russ., b. in Poland)	Petrarch (1304–74; It.)	Simonides (c. 556–468 B.C.; Gk)	Thomas, Edward (1878–1917; Brit.)
Martial (c. 40–c. 104 A.D.; Rom.)	Pindar (c. 518–c. 438 B.C.; Gk)	Sitwell, Dame Edith (1887–1964; Brit.)	Thomas, R(onald) S(tuart) (b. 1913; Welsh)
Marvell, Andrew (1621–78; Brit.)	Plath, Sylvia (1932–63; Am.)	Skelton, John (c. 1460–1529; Engl.)	Tzara, Tristan (1896–1963; Fr.)
Masefield, John (1878–1967; Brit.)	Pope, Alexander (1688–1744; Brit.)	Smith, Stevie (1902–71; Brit.)	Ungaretti, Giuseppe (1888–1970; It.)
Mayakovsky, Vladimir (1893–1930; Russ.)	Porter, Peter (b. 1929; Brit. b. in Australia)	Southey, Robert (1774–1843; Brit.)	Valéry, Paul (1871–1945; Fr.)
Milosz, Czeslaw (b. 1911; Am., b. in Lithuania)	Pound, Ezra (1885–1972; Am.)	Spender, Sir Stephen (1909–95; Brit.)	Vaughan, Henry (1621–95; Welsh)
Milton, John (1608–74; Brit.)	Propertius, Sextus (c. 50–c. 16 B.C.; Rom.)	Spenser, Edmund (c. 1552–99; Brit.)	Verlaine, Paul (1844–96; Fr.)
Montale, Eugenio (1896–1981; It.)	Pushkin, Aleksandr (1799–1837; Russ.)	Statius, Publius Papinius (c. 45–96 A.D.; Rom.)	Virgil (70–19 B.C.; Rom.)
Moore, Marianne (1887–1972; Am.)	Rilke, Rainer Maria (1875–1926; Ger., b. in Czechoslovakia)	Stevens, Wallace (1879–1955; Am.)	Walcott, Derek (b. 1930; St Lucian)
Muir, Edwin (1887–1959; Scot.)	Rimbaud, Arthur (1854–91; Fr.)	Suckling, Sir John (1609–42; Brit.)	Whitman, Walt (1819–92; Am.)
Nash, Ogden (1902–71; Am.)	Rochester, 2nd Earl of (John Wilmet; 1647–80; Brit.)	Swinburne, Algernon Charles (1837–1909; Brit.)	Williams, William Carlos (1883–1963; Am.)
Neruda, Pablo (Neftalí Reyes; 1904–73; Chilean)	Rossetti, Christina (1830–94; Brit.)	Tagore, Rabindranath (1861–1941; Ind.)	Wordsworth, William (1770–1850; Brit.)
Omar Khayyam (c. 1048–c. 1122; Pers.)	Rossetti, Dante Gabriel (1828–82; Brit.)	Taliesin (6th century A.D.; Welsh)	Wright, Judith (b. 1915; Austral.)
Ovid (43 B.C.–c. 17 A.D.; Rom.)	Sappho (c. 610–c. 580 B.C.; Gk)	Tannhäuser (c. 1200–c. 70; Ger.)	Wyatt, Thomas (1503–42; Engl.)
Owen, Wilfred (1893–1918; Brit.)	Sassoon, Siegfried (1886–1967; Brit.)	Tasso, Torquato (1544–95; It.)	Yeats W(illiam) B(utler) (1865–1939; Ir.)
Pasternak, Boris (1890–1960; Russ.)	Shakespeare, William (1569–1616; Engl.)	Tennyson, Alfred, Lord (1809–92; Brit.)	Yesenin, Sergei (1895–1925; Russ.)
Paz, Octavio (b. 1914; Mex.)	Shelley, Percy Bysshe (1792–1822; Brit.)	Theocritus (c. 310–250 B.C.; Gk) Thespis (6th century B.C.; Gk)	Yevtushenko, Yevgenii (b. 1933; Russ.)

pointer *noun* **1** *the pointer on the speedometer* indicator, needle, hand. **2** *indicate the relevant place on a map with a pointer* stick, rod, cane. **3** *the older players will give the trainee a few pointers* tip, hint, piece of advice, suggestion, guideline, recommendation. **4** *some pointers to the likely text of the chairman's speech* indication, indicator, clue, sign.

pointless *adjective* **1** *it is pointless to try to go on in this bad weather* futile, useless, in vain, unavailing, to no purpose, valueless, unproductive, senseless, absurd, foolish, nonsensical, stupid, silly. **2** *a few pointless remarks* meaningless, insignificant, vague, empty, worthless, irrelevant, senseless, fatuous, foolish, nonsensical, stupid, silly, absurd, inane.
Opposites USEFUL; VALUABLE; SIGNIFICANT.

poise *noun* **1** *admire her poise in difficulties* composure, equanimity, self-possession, aplomb, presence of mind, self-assurance, self-control, calmness, coolness, collectedness, serenity, dignity, imperturbability, suaveness, urbanity,

elegance; *inf.* cool. **2** *admire the poise of the ballet dancers* balance, equilibrium, control, grace, gracefulness.

poise *verb* **1** *poise a jug of water on her head* balance, steady, position, support. **2** *poise oneself to jump* steady, get into position, brace, get ready, prepare. **3** *the hawk poised in mid-air ready to attack* hang, hang suspended, float, hover.

poised *adjective* **1** *a very poised young woman* composed, serene, self-possessed, self-assured, self-controlled, calm, cool, cool calm and collected, dignified, imperturbable, unperturbed, unruffled, suave, urbane, elegant; *inf.* unflappable. **2** *soldiers poised ready to attack | the deputy was poised ready to take over the president's job* ready, prepared, all set, standing by, waiting, waiting in the wings.
Opposites EXCITED; PERTURBED; flustered; INELEGANT.

poison *noun* **1** *kill them by means of poison* venom, toxin. *See table.* **2** *a poison in our society*

poison · polite

blight, bane, contagion, cancer, canker, malignancy, corruption, pollution.

HOUSEHOLD POISONS

alcohol	disinfectant	quinine
ammonia	fungicide	rat poison
antifreeze	hair dye	rust
bleach	iodine	remover
caustic	kerosene	strychnine
soda	methylated	turpentine
cyanide	spirit	warfarin
degreaser	paraquat	white spirit

poison verb **1** *a nurse who poisoned her patient* administer poison to, give poison to, kill by poison, murder by poison. **2** *his wound became poisoned* infect, make septic. **3** *poison the environment/soil* contaminate, pollute, blight, spoil. **4** *poison their minds* corrupt, warp, pervert, deprave, defile, debauch.

poisonous adjective **1** *poisonous snakes* venomous. **2** *poisonous plants/chemicals* toxic, venomous, deadly, fatal, lethal. **3** *a poisonous influence on society* cancerous, malignant, corrupting, polluting, harmful, injurious, noxious, pernicious, spiteful, malicious, rancorous, malevolent, vicious, vindictive, slanderous, libellous, defamatory.
Opposites HARMLESS; non-toxic; BENIGN.

poke verb **1** *poke him in the ribs* jab, prod, dig, elbow, nudge, butt. **2** *poke a pencil in his eye* jab, push, thrust, shove, stick. **poke around** *poke around among his possessions* rummage around, forage, rake around, ransack, nose around, pry into. **poke fun at** *children poking fun at the strangely dressed old woman* make fun of, laugh at, mock, jeer at, ridicule, deride, tease, chaff, taunt; *inf.* take the mickey out of, send up, rib, rag. **poke one's nose into** *poke one's nose into other people's affairs* pry into, interfere in, nose around in, intrude on, butt into, meddle with, tamper with; *inf.* snoop into. **poke out** *a letter poking out from her bag* stick out, jut out, protrude, project, extend.

poke noun **1** *give him a poke in the ribs* jab, prod, dig, nudge, elbow, butt. **2** *a poke in the eye with a stick* jab, push, thrust, shove.

poker noun. See table.

POKER HANDS

Hand	Odds Against
royal flush	649 739 to 1
straight flush	72 192 to 1
4 of a kind	4164 to 1
full house	693 to 1
flush	508 to 1
straight	254 to 1
3 of a kind	46 to 1
2 pairs	20 to 1
1 pair	1.37 to 1

poky adjective *a poky room* confined, cramped, narrow, cell-like, small, little, tiny.
Opposites SPACIOUS; ROOMY; PALATIAL.

polar adjective **1** *polar conditions* Arctic, Antarctic, frozen, freezing, icy, glacial, cold. **2** *polar political ideals* opposite, opposed, diametrically opposed, contrary, antithetical, antagonistic, conflicting.

polarity noun *the growing polarity between their political views* difference, separation, opposition, contrariety, antithesis, antagonism, conflict.

pole¹ noun **1** *poles supporting the bridge* post, upright, pillar, stanchion, standard, support, prop, rod, shaft, mast. **2** *jump over the pole* bar, rod, stick.

pole² noun *our points of view are at opposite poles* extremity, extreme, limit. **be poles apart** *be poles apart in their attitudes* be completely different, be widely separated, be incompatible, be worlds apart, be at opposite extremes, be like night and day.

polemics plural noun *skilled in polemics* argument, argumentation, dispute, disputation, discussion, controversy, wrangling.

police noun *send for the police | wanted by the police* police force, the law, constabulary; *inf.* the cops, the fuzz, the boys in blue, the Old Bill, the rozzers, the pigs.

police verb **1** *police the school buildings looking for intruders* patrol, make the rounds of, guard, keep guard over, keep watch on, protect. **2** *police the football match* keep in order, control, keep under control, regulate.

policeman, policewoman noun *a policeman directing the traffic | a policewoman arresting a criminal* police officer, PC, WPC; *inf.* bobby, copper, cop, rozzer, pig.

policy noun *the government's educational policy | not company policy* plan, scheme, programme, schedule, code, system, approach, procedure, guideline, theory.

polish verb **1** *polish the table* wax, buff, rub up, burnish, shine. **2** *polish one's French/etiquette* perfect, refine, improve, brush up, touch up, finish off. **polish off** *polish off his meal quickly* finish, eat up, consume, devour, eat greedily, wolf down, down, bolt.

polished adjective **1** *a polished table* waxed, buffed, burnished, shining, shiny, glossy, gleaming, lustrous, glassy, slippery. **2** *polished manners* refined, cultivated, civilized, well-bred, polite, well-mannered, genteel, courtly, urbane, suave, sophisticated. **3** *give a polished performance at the concert* expert, accomplished, masterly, skilful, proficient, adept, impeccable, flawless, faultless, perfect, consummate, exquisite, outstanding, remarkable.
Opposites DULL; tarnished; ROUGH; INEXPERT.

polite adjective **1** *teaching children to be polite | polite children giving up their seats in buses to elderly people* well-mannered, mannerly, courteous, civil, respectful, deferential, well-behaved, well-bred, genteel, polished, tactful, diplomatic. **2** *things not done in polite society* well-bred, civilized, cultured, refined, polished, genteel, urbane, sophisticated, elegant, courtly.
Opposites RUDE; IMPOLITE; UNMANNERLY; UNCOUTH.

politic *adjective decide on the most politic action* | *think it politic to leave* | *a politic young man* wise, prudent, sensible, advisable, judicious, well-judged, sagacious, expedient, shrewd, astute, discreet, tactful, diplomatic.

political *adjective* **1** *hold a political position in the country* governmental, ministerial, public, civic, administrative, bureaucratic. **2** *dismissed from the firm for political reasons* factional, partisan, bipartisan, power, status.

politician *noun politicians accused of running the country badly* Member of Parliament, MP, statesman, legislator, lawmaker, public servant; *Am.* senator, congressman; *inf.* politico.

politics *noun* **1** *a career in politics* government, local government, affairs of state, party politics. *See table at* GOVERNMENT. **2** *study politics* political science, civics, statecraft, statesmanship. *See table.* **3** *plural noun what are his politics?* party politics, political alliance, politic belief. **4** *plural noun resigned because the firm was full of politics* power struggle, manipulation, manoeuvring, jockeying for position, machiavellianism, opportunism, *realpolitik.*

POLITICAL PHILOSOPHIES	
absolutism	meritocracy
anarchism	monarchism
anarcho-syndicalism	nationalism
authoritarianism	pluralism
collectivism	plutocracy
communism	populism
conservatism	rightism
democracy	situationism
egalitarianism	socialism
Eurocommunism	Sovietism
fascism	Stalinism
federalism	syndicalism
imperialism	technocracy
individualism	Thatcherism
laissez-faire	theocracy
leftism	timocracy
Leninism	Titoism
liberalism	totalitarianism
libertarianism	Trotskyism
Maoism	utilitarianism
Marxism	Utopianism

poll *noun* **1** *organize a poll to decide on the best candidate* vote, ballot, vote-casting, canvass, headcount, show of hands, straw vote/poll. **2** *a heavy poll in favour of the present administration* voting figures, returns, count, tally. **3** *conduct a poll to investigate people's eating habits* opinion poll, Gallup poll, survey, market research, sampling.

poll *verb* **1** *poll more votes than his opponent* register, record, return, get, gain. **2** *poll one hundred people in a survey of eating habits* ballot, canvass, question, interview, survey, sample.

pollute *verb* **1** *pollute the water/soil with chemicals* | *pollute the environment* contaminate, adulterate, infect, taint, poison, befoul, foul, make dirty, make filthy. **2** *pollute the minds of the*

young corrupt, poison, warp, pervert, deprave, defile, debauch. **3** *pollute the good name of the family* besmirch, sully, taint, blacken, tarnish, dishonour, debase, vitiate, desecrate.
Opposites PURIFY; CLEAN; DISINFECT.

pollution *noun* **1** *chemicals involved in the pollution of our water* contaminating, contamination, adulteration, adulterating, infecting, tainting, befouling, fouling, dirtying. *See* POLLUTE 1. **2** *environmentalists trying to prevent pollution* contamination, adulteration, infection, impurity, foulness, dirtiness, filthiness; *inf.* muckiness. **3** *the pollution of young minds* corruption, corrupting, poisoning, warping, depraving. *See* POLLUTE 2. **4** *the pollution of their good name* besmirching, sullying, tainting, blackening. *See* POLLUTE 3. **5** *concerned about the pollution in our society* corruption, poison, blight, contagion, cancer, canker, malignancy, bane.

pomp *noun* **1** *the pomp expected at a coronation* ceremony, ceremoniousness, ritual, display, pageantry, pageant, show, spectacle, splendour, grandeur, magnificence, majesty, glory, brilliance, flourish, style. **2** *only interested in pomp rather than in the reason for the celebration* ostentation, exhibitionism, grandiosity, glitter, show, showiness, pomposity, vainglory, fanfaronade.

pomposity *noun* **1** *irritated by the pomposity of the official* pompousness, presumption, self-importance, presumptuousness, imperiousness, grandiosity, affectation, airs, pretentiousness, pretension, arrogance, vanity, haughtiness, pride, conceit, egotism, superciliousness, condescension, patronization; *inf.* uppishness. **2** *the pomposity of the language* pompousness, bombast, turgidity, portentousness, grandiloquence, magniloquence, euphuism, pedantry, stiltedness, fustian.

pompous *adjective* **1** *a pompous official who kept quoting the rules* self-important, presumptuous, imperious, overbearing, grandiose, affected, pretentious, arrogant, vain, haughty, proud, conceited, egotistic, supercilious, condescending, patronizing; *inf.* uppity, uppish. **2** *pompous language* high-sounding, high-flown, bombastic, turgid, grandiloquent, magniloquent, euphuistic, portentous, pedantic, stilted, fustian.
Opposites MODEST; HUMBLE; self-effacing; UNPRETENTIOUS.

pond *noun* pool, puddle, lake, tarn, mere, millpond, duck pond, fish pond, fish pool.

ponder *verb* **1** *take time to ponder his previous behaviour* think about, give thought to, consider, reflect on, mull over, contemplate, meditate on, deliberate about/on, dwell on, brood on/over, ruminate about/on/over, puzzle over, cogitate about/on, weigh up, review. **2** *sit in the dark and ponder* think, consider, reflect, meditate, contemplate, deliberate, brood, ruminate, cogitate, cerebrate.

ponderous *adjective* **1** *ponderous movements* heavy, slow, awkward, clumsy, lumbering, heavy-footed. **2** *a ponderous style* | *a piece of ponderous prose* heavy, awkward, clumsy, lumbering, heavy-footed, laboured, forced, stilted, turgid, stodgy, lifeless, plodding, dull, boring,

uninteresting, tedious, monotonous, dry, dreary, pedantic, verbose.
Opposites GRACEFUL; ELEGANT; LIVELY.

pontificate *verb pontificate about the rights and wrongs of the situation* hold forth, expound, declaim, preach, lay down the law, sound off, dogmatize, sermonize; *inf.* preachify.

pony *noun* Shetland pony, Iceland pony, Welsh pony, pit pony, polo pony.

pooh-pooh *verb pooh-pooh their attempts to raise money* ridicule, deride, disregard, brush aside, dismiss, make light of, belittle, hold up to scorn, treat with contempt, scoff at, sneer at.

pool¹ *noun* **1** *pools of water in the fields after the rain* pond, water hole, puddle, fish pool, lake, tarn, mere. **2** *a pool of blood* puddle. **3** *have a pool behind their house | go to the pool every day in summer* swimming pool, baths, swimming baths.

pool² *noun* **1** *a pool of parents to drive children to school | a pool of typists for the whole office | typing pool* consortium, syndicate, collective, combine, group, team. **2** *a pool of cars for use by all the firm's reps* common supply, supply, reserve. **3** *the pool in a gambling game* stakes, bank, kitty, purse, jackpot, ante, fund.

pool³ *verb pool their resources/ideas* put together, combine, amalgamate, merge, share.

poor *adjective* **1** *poor people with very few belongings | live in poor circumstances* badly off, poverty-stricken, penniless, hard up, needy, deprived, in need, needful, in want, indigent, impoverished, impecunious, destitute, penurious, beggared, in straitened circumstances, as poor as a church mouse, in the red, on one's beam-ends; *inf.* broke, stony-broke, flat broke, on one's uppers, on the rocks, skint. **2** *live in poor surroundings* humble, lowly, mean, modest, plain. **3** *a poor diet/performance* inadequate, deficient, insufficient, unsatisfactory, below standard, below par, inferior, imperfect, bad, low-grade. **4** *a poor crop of apples* sparse, scanty, meagre, scarce, skimpy, reduced, at a premium, paltry, miserable, exiguous. **5** *a diet poor in nutrients* deficient in, lacking in, wanting, insufficient in. **6** *poor furniture | goods of*

poor quality unsatisfactory, defective, faulty, imperfect, below standard, inferior, low-grade, second-rate, third-rate, jerry-built, rubbishy. **7** *poor soil* unproductive, barren, unyielding, unfruitful, uncultivatable, bare, arid, sterile, infecund. **8** *you poor thing* wretched, pitiable, pitiful, unfortunate, unlucky, luckless, unhappy, hapless, ill-fated, ill-starred. **9** *a poor specimen of a man* miserable, sad, sorry, spiritless, mean, low, base, disgraceful, despicable, contemptible, abject, pathetic.
Opposites WEALTHY; RICH; SUPERIOR; SATISFACTORY.

poorly *adjective too poorly to go to school* ill, unwell, sick, ailing, indisposed, below par, off colour, out of sorts; *inf.* under the weather, seedy.

poorly *adverb perform poorly in the competition* badly, inadequately, unsatisfactorily, unsuccessfully, incompetently, inexpertly.

pop *verb champagne corks popped | guns were popping* explode, go off, go off with a bang, go bang, bang, crack, burst, detonate. **pop in 1** *pop a coin in the phone box | popped the ticket into her handbag* insert, put in, place in, slip in, slide in, push in, stick in. **2** *pop in to see his mother on his way to work* visit, call in, go in, stop by; *inf.* drop in/by, nip in. **pop out, pop off** *just popping out to get a newspaper* go out quickly/briefly, leave quickly/briefly; *inf.* nip out/off. **pop up** *snowdrops popping up all over the garden | a new case popped up every few weeks* appear, appear suddenly/abruptly, occur suddenly/abruptly, crop up.

pop *noun* **1** *champagne opening with a pop | balloons bursting with a pop* bang, crack, boom, burst, explosion, report, detonation. **2** *serve biscuits and pop to the children* soft drink, fizzy drink, lemonade, cola, carbonated drink; *Am.* soda.

pope *noun an audience with the Pope in the Vatican* pontiff, Bishop of Rome, Holy Father, Vicar of Christ. *See table.*

populace *noun* **1** *the government seeking the view of the populace by a referendum* the general public, the public, the people, the population,

POPES SINCE 1492					
Name	**In Office**	**Name**	**In Office**	**Name**	**In Office**
Alexander VI	1492–1503	Clement VIII	1592–1605	Clement XIII	1758–69
Pius III	1503	Leo XI	1605	Clement XIV	1769–74
Julius II	1503–13	Paul V	1605–21	Pius VI	1775–99
Leo X	1513–21	Gregory XV	1621–3	Pius VII	1800–23
Adrian VI	1522–3	Urban VIII	1623–44	Leo XII	1823–9
Clement VII	1523–34	Innocent X	1644–55	Pius VIII	1829–30
Paul III	1534–49	Alexander VII	1655–67	Gregory XVI	1831–46
Julius III	1550–5	Clement IX	1667–9	Pius IX	1846–78
Marcellus II	1555	Clement X	1670–6	Leo XIII	1878–1903
Paul IV	1555–9	Innocent XI	1676–89	Pius X	1903–14
Pius IV	1559–65	Alexander VIII	1689–91	Benedict XV	1914–22
Pius V	1566–72	Innocent XII	1691–1700	Pius XI	1922–39
Gregory XIII	1572–85	Clement XI	1700–21	Pius XII	1939–58
Sixtus V	1585–90	Innocent XIII	1721–4	John XXIII	1958–63
Urban VII	1590	Benedict XIII	1724–30	Paul VI	1963–78
Gregory XIV	1590–1	Clement XII	1730–40	John Paul I	1978
Innocent IX	1591	Benedict XIV	1740–58	John Paul II	from 1978

popular · porter

the common people, common folk, the masses, commonalty, the mob, the multitude, the rabble, the rank and file, the *hoi polloi; inf.* the plebs. **2** *populace of the city* population, inhabitants, residents.

popular *adjective* **1** *a popular choice/teacher | teachers popular with the pupils | entertainers popular with the audience* well-liked, liked, favoured, in favour, favourite, well-received, approved, admired, accepted. **2** *the goods have proved so popular that we have run out* well-liked, liked, in favour, well-received, sought-after, in demand, desired, wanted, fashionable, in fashion, in vogue, in. **3** *popular film stars* well-known, famous, celebrated, renowned. **4** *for the popular market | a range of popular cars* inexpensive, budget, low-budget, low-priced, cheap, reasonable, reasonably-priced, moderately-priced, modestly-priced; *inf.* down-market. **5** *popular literature/music/science | the popular press* middle-of-the-road, middlebrow, lowbrow, accessible, simple, understandable, readily understood, easy to understand, readily comprehensible; *inf.* pop. **6** *issues of popular concern* public, general, civic. **7** *popular beliefs/myths* current, prevalent, prevailing, accepted, recognized, widespread, universal, general, common, customary, usual, standard, stock, conventional. **Opposites** UNPOPULAR; UNKNOWN; HIGHBROW.

popular music *noun.* See table.

popularity *noun* **1** *teachers gaining in popularity | teachers winning popularity with the pupils* favour, approval, approbation, admiration, acceptance. **2** *the popularity of their recent line of goods* demand, fashionableness, vogue. **3** *ideas gaining popularity | myths losing popularity* currency, prevalence, prevalency, recognition. **4** *the popularity of the film stars | film stars winning popularity* fame, renown, acclaim, esteem, repute.

popularize *verb* **1** *popularize classical music* simplify, make mass-market, give mass appeal to, make accessible to all. **2** *help to popularize the belief that the world was flat* give currency to, give credence to, universalize, generalize, spread, disseminate.

popularly *adverb* *it was popularly believed that every strange old woman was a witch | the EC, once popularly known as the Common Market* widely, generally, universally, commonly, usually, regularly, customarily, ordinarily, traditionally.

populate *verb* **1** *nomadic tribes populate the area | an area largely populated by nomadic tribes* inhabit, dwell in, occupy, people. **2** *newly discovered areas of the continent gradually populated by people from other countries* settle, colonize, people.

population *noun* **1** *the entire population of the town was affected by the closure of the factory* inhabitants, residents, community, people, citizenry, populace, society. **2** *the working population | the elderly population* people, folk, society. **3** *populations decreasing in rural areas* population count, numbers of inhabitants, census, headcount.

populous *adjective* *the populous urban areas of the country* densely populated, heavily popu-

lated, thickly populated, crowded.
Opposites EMPTY; UNINHABITED; DESERTED.

porcelain *noun.* See table at CERAMICS.

porch *noun* *leave wellingtons in the porch* vestibule.

pore *verb* **pore over** **1** *students poring over their books before the exams | poring over the map* study closely, read intently, peruse closely, be absorbed in, scrutinize, examine closely. **2** *sitting alone poring over his problem* meditate on, brood on/over, go over, ponder, reflect on, deliberate on, mull over, muse on, think about, contemplate.

pore *noun* *perspiration oozing from every pore | sap oozing through the plant's pores* opening, orifice, hole, outlet.

pornographic *adjective* *pornographic magazine/videos* obscene, blue, salacious, lewd, prurient, erotic, indecent, dirty, smutty, filthy; *inf.* porn, porno.
Opposites DECENT; PURE.

pornography *noun* **1** *make his money from pornography* obscenity, salaciousness, lewdness, prurience, erotica, indecency, smut, filth; *inf.* porn, porno, sexploitation. **2** *a shop selling pornography* pornographic literature, pornographic films/videos, erotica; *inf.* porn, hard porn, soft porn, porno, girlie magazines.

porous *adjective* **1** *porous soil | clothe made of porous material* absorbent, permeable, penetrable, pervious. **2** *a chunk of porous material* spongelike, spongy, sievelike, honeycomb, honeycombed, holey.
Opposites impermeable; IMPENETRABLE; IMPERVIOUS.

port *noun* **1** *ships seeking a port in a storm* harbour, harbourage, haven, anchorage, roads, roadstead. **2** *ports along the south coast* seaport.

portable *adjective* *portable radios/typewriters* transportable, movable, conveyable, easily carried, lightweight, compact, handy, manageable.

portend *verb* *the grey, angry sky portending a storm | his silence portends trouble* be a sign of, be a warning of, be an indication of, be a presage of, point to, be an omen of, herald, bode, augur, presage, forebode, foreshadow, foretell.

portent *noun* **1** *dark skies can be a portent of a storm | his silence was a portent of trouble* sign, indication, presage, warning, omen, harbinger, foreshadowing, augury. **2** *the lavish building was considered one of the portents of the modern world* marvel, wonder, prodigy, phenomenon, spectacle.

portentous *adjective* **1** *portentous events indicating that trouble was inevitable* ominous, warning, threatening, menacing, foreboding, foreshadowing, ill-omened. **2** *a portentous monument* marvellous, remarkable, prodigious, phenomenal, spectacular, wondrous, amazing, astounding. **3** *a portentous speech* pompous, pontifical, ponderous, solemn.

porter[1] *noun* *porters struggling with heavy baggage* carrier, bearer, baggage-carrier, stretcher-bearer, stretcher-carrier.

POPULAR MUSICIANS, SINGERS, AND BANDS

Abba
AC/DC
Adams, Bryan (b. 1959)
Alpert, Herb (b. 1935)
Animals, the
Ant, Adam (b. 1954)
Armatrading, Joan (b. 1950)
Bacharach, Burt (b. 1928)
Baez, Joan (b. 1941)
Band, the
Bassey, Shirley (b. 1937)
Beach Boys, the
Beatles, the
Bee Gees, the
Beck, Jeff (b. 1944)
Bennett, Tony (b. 1926)
Benson, George (b. 1943)
Berry, Chuck (b. 1926)
Black Sabbath
Blondie
Blur
Bon Jovi
Bowie, David (b. 1947)
Boy George (b. 1961)
Brown, James (b. 1928)
Browne, Jackson (b. 1948)
Bush, Kate (b. 1958)
Byrds, the
Campbell, Glen (b. 1936)
Carpenters, the
Cash, Johnny (b. 1932)
Charles, Ray (b. 1930)
Cher (b. 1946)
Chicago
Clapton, Eric (b. 1945)
Clash, the
Cline, Patsy (1932–63)
Cochran, Eddie (1938–60)
Cocker, Joe (b. 1944)
Cohen, Leonard (b. 1934)
Cole, Nat "King" (1917–65)
Collins, Phil (b. 1951)
Commodores, the
Como, Perry (b. 1912)
Cooder, Ry (b. 1947)
Cooke, Sam (1935–64)
Cooper, Alice (b. 1948)

Costello, Elvis (b. 1955)
Cream
Crosby, Bing (1904–77)
Crosby, Stills, and Nash
Cure, the
Deep Purple
Denver, John (b. 1943)
Diamond, Neil (b. 1941)
Diddley, Bo (b. 1928)
Dire Straits
Doobie Brothers, the
Doors, the
Drifters, the
Duran Duran
Dury, Ian (b. 1942)
Dylan, Bob (b. 1941)
Eagles, the
Earth, Wind and Fire
Emerson, Lake, and Palmer
Eno, Brian (b. 1948)
Enya
Eurythmics, the
Everly Brothers, the
Fairport Convention
Fame, Georgie (b. 1943)
Ferry, Bryan (b. 1945)
Flack, Roberta (b. 1939)
Fleetwood Mac
Four Seasons
Four Tops
Francis, Connie (b. 1938)
Frankie Goes to Hollywood
Franklin, Aretha (b. 1942)
Freddie and the Dreamers
Free
Fury, Billy (1941–83)
Gabriel, Peter (b. 1950)
Gallagher, Rory (1949–95)
Gaye, Marvin (1939–84)
Genesis
Gerry and the Pacemakers
Glitter, Gary (b. 1944)
Grateful Dead, the
Green, Al (b. 1946)
Guns 'n' Roses
Guthrie, Woody (1912–67)
Gypsy Kings, the
Haley, Bill (1925–81)
Hall and Oates

Harris, Emmylou (b. 1949)
Hendrix, Jimi (1942–70)
Hollies, the
Holly, Buddy (1936–59)
Houston, Whitney (b. 1963)
Iggy Pop (b. 1947)
INXS
Iron Maiden
Isley Brothers, the
Jackson Five, the
Jackson, Michael (b. 1958)
Jackson, Janet (b. 1966)
Jam, the
Jefferson Airplane
Joel, Billy (b. 1949)
John, Elton (b. 1947)
Jones, Grace (b. 1931)
Jones, Quincy (b. 1933)
Jones, Tom (b. 1936)
Joplin, Janis (1943–70)
Joy Division
Khan, Chaka (b. 1953)
King, B. B. (b. 1925)
Kinks, the
Knight, Gladys (b. 1949)
Kristofferson, Kris (b. 1936)
Led Zeppelin
Lee, Peggy (b. 1920)
Lewis, Jerry Lee (b. 1935)
Little Richard (b. 1935)
Los Lobos
Lulu (b. 1948)
Lynn, Loretta (b. 1935)
Lynyrd Skynyrd
Madness
Madonna (b. 1958)
Manfred Mann
Marley, Bob (1945–81)
Martin, Dean (b. 1917)
Masekela, Hugh (b. 1939)
Mathis, Johnny (b. 1935)
Mayall, John (b. 1933)
Meat Loaf
Michael, George (b. 1963)
Miller, Glenn (1904–44)

Minogue, Kylie (b. 1968)
Mitchell, Joni (b. 1943)
Monkees, the
Monro, Matt (1930–85)
Moody Blues, the
Morrison, Van (b. 1945)
Motorhead
Nelson, Willie (b. 1933)
New Order
Nirvana
Oasis
Orb, the
Orbison, Roy (1936–88)
Palmer, Robert (b. 1949)
Parton, Dolly (b. 1946)
Pet Shop Boys, the
Petty, Tom (b. 1953)
Pickett, Wilson (b. 1941)
Pink Floyd
Pogues, the
Police, the
Pretenders, the
Presley, Elvis (1935–77)
Prince (b. 1961)
Procul Harum
Public Enemy
Queen
Redding, Otis (1941–67)
Reed, Lou (b. 1944)
Reeves, Jim (1924–64)
R.E.M.
Richard, Sir Cliff (b. 1940)
Richie, Lionel (b. 1949)
Righteous Brothers, the
Robinson, Smokey (b. 1940)
Rogers, Kenny (b. 1938)
Rolling Stones, the
Ronstadt, Linda (b. 1946)
Ross, Diana (b. 1944)
Roxy Music
Run D.M.C.
Santana
Sedaka, Neil (b. 1939)
Sex Pistols, the
Shadows, the
Shaw, Sandie (b. 1947)
Simon and Garfunkel

POPULAR MUSICIANS, SINGERS, AND BANDS *cont.*

Simon, Paul (b. 1941)	Stewart, Rod	U2	Williams, Hank
Simone, Nina	(b. 1945)	Van Halen	(1923–53)
(b. 1933)	Sting	Velvet Underground,	Wilson, Jackie
Simple Minds	Stone Roses, the	the	(1934–84)
Simply Red	Streisand, Barbra	Vincent, Gene	Winwood, Steve
Sinatra, Frank	(b. 1942)	(1935–71)	(b. 1948)
(b. 1915)	Supremes, the	Waits, Tom (b. 1949)	Wonder, Stevie
Sledge, Percy	Talking Heads	Walker Brothers, the	(b. 1950)
(b. 1941)	Taylor, James	Waters, Muddy	Wynette, Tammy
Smiths, the	(b. 1948)	(1915–83)	(b. 1942)
Springfield, Dusty	Temptations, the	Weller, Paul (b. 1958)	Yardbirds, the
(b. 1939)	T. Rex	Wet Wet Wet	Yes
Springsteen, Bruce	Turner, Tina	Who, the	Young, Neil (b. 1945)
(b. 1949)	(b. 1938)	Williams, Andy	Zappa, Frank
Status Quo	UB40	(b. 1930)	(1940–93)

porter² *noun the porter refused to tell him which flat she lived in* door keeper, doorman, door-attendant, commissionaire, caretaker, janitor, concierge.

portion *noun* **1** *serve generous portions at the restaurant | children's portions available* helping, serving, piece, quantity. **2** *give a portion of his estate to each of his children* share, division, quota, part, bit, allocation, allotment, piece; *inf.* cut, whack. **3** *ask for three portions of cheese at the delicatessen* bit, section, segment, slice, wedge, lump, chunk, hunk. **4** *her portion in life to serve others* lot, fate, destiny, fortune, luck.

portion *verb portion the estate among his children* share, divide, split, partition, carve up, parcel out; *inf.* divvy up. **portion out** *portion out pieces of cake to the children* distribute, dispense, hand out, deal out, dole out, divide out, share out, allocate, apportion, allot, parcel out, mete out; *inf.* divvy up.

portly *adjective* stout, plump, fat, corpulent, obese, tubby, of ample build, stocky.

portrait *noun* **1** *portraits of his ancestors hung on the walls* painting, picture, drawing, sketch, portrayal, representation, likeness, image, study, portraiture, canvas. **2** *have the photographer take a portrait of his daughter* photograph, photo, picture, studio portrait, study, shot, snapshot, snap, still. **3** *the writer's portrait of his childhood* description, portrayal, depiction, account, story, chronicle, thumbnail sketch, vignette, profile.

portray *verb* **1** *the artist portrayed the girl in a simple blue dress* paint a picture of, paint, draw a picture of, draw, sketch, depict, represent, delineate. **2** *portray a scene of abject poverty in his novel* describe, depict, characterize, paint a word-picture of, paint in words, put into words. **3** *portray Hamlet's mother in the production* play, act the part of, play the part of, act, perform, represent, execute.

portrayal *noun* **1** *his portrayal of the girl in riding habit* painting, portrait, picture, drawing, sketch, representation, depiction, delineation, study. **2** *the writer's portrayal of scenes of poverty* description, depiction, characterization, word-picture, word-painting. **3** *her portrayal of the role of Hamlet's mother* acting, performance, representation, interpretation.

pose *verb* **1** *ask him to pose for a portrait* sit, model, take up a position. **2** *carefully pose the subjects for his still life* arrange, position, lay out, set out, dispose, place, put, locate, situate. **3** *she was always posing to try and impress the boys* strike an attitude, posture, put on an act, act, play-act, attitudinize, put on airs, show off. **4** *pose a question relating to finance* put forward, put, submit, set, advance, propound, posit. **5** *traffic conditions pose problems for drivers* present, set, create, cause, give rise to. **pose as** *the thief posed as a social worker* pretend to be, impersonate, pass oneself off as, masquerade as, profess to be, feign the identity of.

pose *noun* **1** *models asked to adopt a provocative pose for the swimsuit commercial* posture, stance, position, attitude, bearing, carriage. **2** *her shyness is only a pose, she's really brazen* act, playacting, pretence, façade, front, masquerade, posture, attitudinizing, affectation, airs.

poser *noun* **1** *how we're going to cope with him is a real poser* difficult question, awkward problem, vexed question, enigma, dilemma, puzzle, mystery, conundrum; *inf.* brain-teaser, facer. **2** *posers in the nude* model, sitter, subject. **3** *he's a real poser* See POSEUR.

poseur *noun he's not genuine - he's just a poseur* poser, attitudinizer, posturer, play-actor.

posh *adjective* **1** *a posh hotel* luxurious, luxury, de luxe, sumptuous, opulent, lavish, rich, elegant, ornate, fancy, plush; *inf.* plushy, ritzy, swanky. **2** *a posh accent* upper-class, aristocratic, fancy; *inf.* up-market, upper-crust.

position *noun* **1** *a house in an isolated position | plants in a sunny position* situation, location, site, place, spot, area, locality, locale, scene, setting. **2** *identify the ship's position* location, bearings, whereabouts. **3** *sitting/standing in an uncomfortable position | in an upright position* posture, stance, attitude, pose, bearing. **4** *in an unfortunate financial position* situation, state, condition, circumstance, predicament, plight, pass. **5** *several people jockeying for position in the race* advantageous position, favourable position, pole position, primacy, the upper hand, the edge, the whip hand. **6** *have to declare their position on privatization | speak from a position of knowledge* point of view, viewpoint, opinion, way of thinking, outlook, attitude, stand, standpoint, stance. **7** *apply for the vacant position of manager | his position as captain* post, job, situation, appointment, role, office, place, capacity, duty. **8** *what is his position in the class* place, level, grade, grading, rank, status, standing. **9** *people of position in society* rank, status, stature, standing, social standing, prestige, influence, reputation, importance, consequence.

position *verb position the building so that it faces south | position the soldiers in rows* place, locate, situate, put, arrange, set, settle, dispose, array.

positive *adjective* **1** *a set of positive rules | given positive instructions* clear, clear-cut, definite, precise, categorical, direct, explicit, express, firm. **2** *no positive proof of his guilt* real, actual, absolute, concrete, conclusive, unequivocal, incontrovertible, indisputable, undeniable, incontestable, unmistakable. **3** *they are positive that they have the solution* certain, sure, assured, confident, convinced. **4** *the results of the blood test are positive* affirmative. **5** *positive criticism/ proposals* constructive, productive, helpful, practical, useful, beneficial. **6** *a positive attitude to his work | positive thinking* confident, optimistic, assured, assertive, firm, forceful, determined, resolute, emphatic, dogmatic. **7** *positive developments have been made | positive progress* good, favourable, effective, promising, encouraging, heartening. **8** *he's a positive fool | it's a positive disgrace* utter, complete, absolute, perfect, out-and-out, outright, thoroughgoing, thorough, downright, sheer, consummate, unmitigated, rank.
Opposites VAGUE; UNCERTAIN; UNSURE; NEGATIVE.

positively *adverb* **1** *she assured us positively that he had gone | they were positively convinced that they were right* with certainty, definitely, emphatically, firmly, categorically, absolutely, without qualification, confidently, dogmatically. **2** *they were positively furious* absolutely, really, indeed, extremely, to a marked degree.

possess *verb* **1** *they possess two cars* own, be the owner of, have, be the possessor of, be the proud possessor of, count among one's possessions, have to one's name, hold, be blessed with, enjoy. **2** *possess a good mind* have, be endowed with, be gifted with. **3** *the invaders set out to possess all the castles* seize, take into possession, take possession of, take over, occupy. **4** *devils seemed to have possessed her | what possessed her?* influence, control, dominate, have mastery over, bewitch, enchant, put under a spell, obsess; *inf.* get into someone.

possessed *adjective* **1** *like someone possessed* bewitched, enchanted, under a spell, obsessed, haunted, bedevilled, crazed, mad, demented, berserk, frenzied. **2** *a very possessed young woman* self-possessed, poised, self-controlled, self-assured, self-confident, confident, calm, cool, even-tempered, composed, imperturbable; *inf.* unflappable.

possession *noun* **1** *her possession of the jewels* ownership, proprietorship, possessorship. **2** *their possession of the land/house* occupancy, occupation, holding, tenure, tenancy. **3** *a possession of which she was very fond* thing/article/item owned, asset. See POSSESSIONS.

possessions *plural noun thrown out of the flat with all her possessions* belongings, things, property, luggage, baggage, bags and baggage, personal effects, goods and chattels, accoutrements, paraphernalia, appendages, assets, impedimenta.

possessive *adjective* **1** *children possessive of their toys | a possessive attitude to toys | possessive children* acquisitive, greedy, grasping, covetous, selfish; *inf.* grabby. **2** *possessive parents* over-protective, clinging, controlling, dominating, jealous.

possibilities *plural noun the cottage is dilapidated but it has possibilities | see the possibilities of the run-down farm | have possibilities as an actress* potential, potentiality, promise, prospects, capability. See POSSIBILITY.

possibility *noun* **1** *beyond the bounds of possibility | discuss the possibility of the plan working* feasibility, practicability, attainability, likelihood, potentiality, conceivability, probability. See POSSIBLE. **2** *buying a smaller house is one possibility* likelihood, prospect, chance, hope, probability. **3** *a possibility of more violence* likelihood, prospect, chance, risk, hazard. See POSSIBILITIES.

possible *adjective* **1** *it is not humanly possible to get there on time | a dream that is not possible* feasible, able to be done, practicable, doable, attainable, achievable, realizable, within reach; *inf.* on. **2** *one of several possible outcomes* likely, potential, conceivable, imaginable, probable, credible, tenable, odds-on.
Opposites IMPOSSIBLE; IMPRACTICABLE; UNLIKELY.

possibly *adverb* **1** *he may possibly arrive tomorrow* perhaps, maybe, it may be, for all one knows, very likely; *lit.* peradventure. **2** *he will arrive if he possibly can | you can't possibly carry all that* conceivably, by any means, by any chance, at all.

post¹ *noun* **1** *put up the posts for the fence | posts supporting the wooden bridge* stake, upright, pole, shaft, prop, support, column, stanchion, standard, stock, picket, pillar, pale, palisade, baluster, newel. **2** *first past the post* finishing post, finishing tape. **3** *left at the post* starting post, finishing post.

post² *verb* **1** *post notices on the walls of the building* put up, stick, stick up, pin, pin up, tack, tack up, attach, affix, hang, display. **2** *details of the exams will be posted later* announce, make known, advertise, publish, publicize, circulate, broadcast.

post³ *noun* **1** *send the goods by post* postal service, mail. **2** *what time is the post?* postal delivery/collection, mail delivery/collection. **3** *got a lot of post this morning* mail, letters, correspondence. **4** *take the letters to the post* postbox, letter box, pillar box, post office, post room; *Am.* mailbox, mailroom.

post⁴ *verb* **1** *post the parcel early in the morning* send by post, dispatch by post, mail, transmit. **2** *post today's sales in the ledger* enter, write in, fill in, record, register, note. **keep someone posted** *the boss asked us to keep him posted while he was away* keep informed, keep briefed, brief, advise, notify, report to; *inf.* keep someone in the picture, keep someone up to date, fill someone in.

post⁵ noun **1** *advertise the post*|*three possible candidates for the post of manager* position, job, appointment, situation, place, office. **2** *soldiers at their posts* station, position, beat.

poster noun *posters advertising the amateur production*|*stick posters up all over his bedroom walls* placard, bill, notice, public notice, sticker, advertisement, announcement, bulletin, *affiche*; *inf.* advert.

posterity noun **1** *conserve the rain forests for posterity* future generations, succeeding generations. **2** *wish to keep his estate intact for posterity* descendants, heirs, successors, issue, offspring, progeny, children, seed.

post-mortem noun PM, autopsy, necropsy.

postpone verb defer, put off, put back, delay, hold over, adjourn, shelve, table, pigeon-hole; *inf.* put on ice, put on the back burner.
Opposites ADVANCE; bring forward.

postponement noun deferment, deferral, delay, adjournment, moratorium, stay. *See* POSTPONE.

postscript noun **1** *add a postscript to her letter* PS, subscript, afterthought. **2** *add a postscript to the essay* subscript, afterword, addendum, appendix, codicil, appendage, supplement.

postulate verb *postulate that the population will decrease by 10%* assume, presuppose, suppose, presume, take for granted, posit, hypothesize, theorize.

posture noun **1** *in a reclining posture* position, pose, attitude. **2** *have an elegant posture*|*stand with a hunched posture* carriage, bearing, stance. **3** *the parents adopted a critical posture towards the new educational policy* attitude, position, point of view, viewpoint, opinion, way of thinking, outlook, stand, standpoint, stance, angle, slant.

posture verb *posturing in front of the mirror admiring himself*|*girls posturing to attract the boys* pose, strike an attitude, put on an act, act, play-act, attitudinize, put on airs, show off.

potency noun **1** *the potency of the drugs* powerfulness, power, strength, effectiveness, efficacy. **2** *the potency of his influence in the land* power, powerfulness, force, forcefulness, strength, vigour, might, mightiness, influence, authoritativeness, authority, dominance, energy; *lit.* puissance. *See* POTENT 2. **3** *admire the potency of their arguments* power, powerfulness, force, forcefulness, strength, effectiveness, cogency, conviction, persuasiveness, impressiveness. *See* POTENT 3.

potent adjective **1** *potent drugs* powerful, strong, effective, efficacious. **2** *he was a potent force in the land* powerful, forceful, strong, vigorous, mighty, influential, authoritative, commanding, dominant, energetic, dynamic; *lit.* puissant. **3** *a potent argument* powerful, forceful, strong, effective, cogent, compelling, convincing, persuasive, eloquent, impressive, telling.
Opposites WEAK; POWERLESS; IMPOTENT.

potentate noun *the potentate of the neighbouring country* ruler, monarch, king/queen, emperor/empress, sovereign, mogul.

potential adjective **1** *a potential star* budding, embryonic, developing, promising, prospective, likely, possible, probable. **2** *his potential musical ability* latent, dormant, inherent, embryonic, developing, promising. **3** *a potential disaster* likely, possible, probable.

potential noun **1** *recognize the potential of the young singer* promise, capability, capacity, ability, aptitude, talent, flair. **2** *recognize the potential of the broken-down house* possibilities, promise, potentiality.

potion noun drink, beverage, brew, concoction, mixture, draught, elixir, philtre.

pot-pourri noun *a pot-pourri of children's poems and drawings* medley, miscellany, mélange, pastiche, collage, blend, mixture, hotchpotch, hodgepodge, mishmash, jumble, gallimaufry, farrago, olio, olla podrida.

potter verb *potter down the road* dawdle, loiter, dally, dilly-dally; *inf.* tootle. **potter about, potter around** *spend the weekend pottering about/around* mess about/around, dabble, fritter, tinker about/around, fiddle about/around.

pottery noun ceramics, earthenware, stoneware, terracotta.

pouch noun *carry money/tobacco in a pouch* bag, purse, wallet, container.

pounce verb **1** *the hawk pounced when it spied its prey* swoop down, drop down, descend. **2** *the fox pounced on the hen*|*the robbers pounced on the men carrying the gold* swoop on, spring on, lunge at, leap at, jump at/on, bound at, make a grab for, take by surprise, take unawares, attack suddenly.

pounce noun *the fox grabbed the hen at one pounce* swoop, spring, lunge, leap, jump, bound, grab, attack.

pound¹ verb **1** *pound the solid to powder*|*pound the garlic to a paste* crush, beat, pulverize, smash, mash, grind, comminute, triturate. **2** *pound his opponent with his fists* beat, batter, pummel, strike, belabour, hammer, pelt, thump. **3** *pound the streets* tramp, tread heavily on, trudge, walk heavily on, stomp along, clump along. **4** *with heart pounding* beat heavily, pulsate, pulse, throb, thump, pump, palpitate, go pit-a-pat.

pound² noun **1** *a pound of apples* pound avoirdupois, lb, pound troy, t. **2** *the cost in pounds* pound sterling, pound coin, pound note; *inf.* quid.

pound³ noun *stray dogs in a pound*|*cars in a pound* compound, enclosure, pen, yard.

pour verb **1** *she poured cream over the fruit* let flow, decant, splash, spill. **2** *water poured from the burst pipe*|*blood poured from the gunshot wound* gush, rush, stream, flow, course, spout, jet, spurt. **3** *it was pouring*|*it poured rain heavily/hard*, come down in torrents/sheets, rain cats and dogs, bucket, be bucketing, sheet-down, come down like stair-rods. **4** *people poured from the burning cinema*|*letters poured in* stream, swarm, crowd, throng, flood.

pout verb **1** *pout her lips provocatively/sullenly* push forwards, purse. **2** *pouting because she did not get her own way* sulk, look sullen, look petulant, scowl, glower, lour, make a moue.

poverty noun **1** *appalled at the poverty of the homeless people* pennilessness, neediness, need, want, hardship, deprivation, indigence, impoverishment, impecuniousness, destitution, penury, privation, beggary, pauperism, straitened circumstances. **2** *the poverty of their surroundings* humbleness, lowliness, meanness, modesty, plainness. **3** *poverty of resources | the poverty of their imagination* deficiency, dearth, shortage, scarcity, paucity, insufficiency, lack, want, meagreness. **4** *the poverty of the soil/land* poorness, barrenness, unfruitfulness, bareness, aridity, aridness, sterility, infecundity. *Opposites* WEALTH; LUXURY; ABUNDANCE.

powder noun *lumps of sugar crushed to powder | dry snow like powder* dust, fine grains, facepowder, talcum powder, talc, dusting powder, baby powder, soap powder, baking-powder, sleeping-powder, stomach-powder, pounce.

powder verb **1** *powder her face | powdered the baby* dust/sprinkle with powder, dredge/strew/scatter with powder. **2** *powder the coffee beans* crush, pound, pulverize, grind, granulate, comminute, triturate.

powdery adjective **1** *powdery snow* powder-like, fine, dry, dusty, chalky, floury, friable, granulated, ground, crushed, pulverized. **2** *her powdery face and reddened lips* powder-covered, powdered.

power noun **1** *the power to corrupt/inspire* ability, capability, capacity, potential, potentiality. **2** *lose the power of speech* ability, capability, faculty, competence. **3** *the power behind the blow | the sheer power of his arms* powerfulness, strength, force, forcefulness, might, weight, vigour, energy, potency. **4** *have him in her power | she fell into his power* control, authority, mastery, domination, dominance, rule, command, ascendancy, supremacy, dominion, sway, sovereignty, influence. **5** *have the power to veto the rule* authority, authorization, warrant, licence, right, prerogative. **6** *different kinds of power used for heating* energy, electrical power, nuclear power, solar power. **7** *the power of her oratory/argument* powerfulness, potency, strength, force, forcefulness, eloquence, effectiveness, cogency, conviction, persuasiveness. *Opposites* INABILITY; INCAPACITY; WEAKNESS; IMPOTENCE.

powerful adjective **1** *of powerful build | two powerful boxers* strong, sturdy, strapping, stout, stalwart, robust, vigorous, tough, mighty. **2** *powerful members of the committee | a country afraid of its powerful neighbours* influential, controlling, dominant, authoritative, commanding, forceful, strong, vigorous, potent, puissant. **3** *a powerful argument against leaving* forceful, strong, effective, cogent, compelling, convincing, persuasive, eloquent, impressive, telling. **4** *have powerful advertising appeal* strong, great, weighty, influential. *Opposites* POWERLESS; WEAK; INEFFECTIVE.

powerless adjective **1** *formerly influential members of the committee now totally powerless* without power, impotent. **2** *legs powerless after the accident* without power, without strength, paralysed, diasbled, incapacitated, debilitated, weak, feeble. **3** *powerless to give them any assistance* helpless, unfit, impotent, ineffectual, inadequate. *Opposites* POWERFUL; POTENT; STRONG.

practicability noun *question the practicability of the scheme* feasibility, possibility, viability, workability, achievability, attainability. *See* PRACTICABLE.

practicable adjective *find a practicable scheme* feasible, possible, within the bounds of possibility, within the realms of possibility, viable, workable, doable, achievable, attainable, accomplishable. *Opposites* IMPRACTICABLE; IMPOSSIBLE.

practical adjective **1** *practical tradesmen rather than graduates with academic qualifications* hands-on, active, trained, seasoned, experienced, skilled, practised, accomplished, proficient. **2** *a practical rather than theoretical knowledge* applied, empirical, pragmatic, workaday, hands-on; *inf.* nuts and bolts. **3** *practical clothing for hillwalking | the furniture is attractive but not very practical* functional, useful, utilitarian, sensible. **4** *he has a lot of theories but she is very practical* businesslike, sensible, down-to-earth, pragmatic, realistic, hard-headed; *inf.* hardnosed. **5** *find a practical solution* pragmatic, matter-of-fact, down-to-earth, hard-headed, sensible, businesslike, realistic, utilitarian, expedient. **6** *a practical atheist | in practical control* virtual, effective, in effect, essential. *Opposites* INEXPERIENCED; THEORETICAL; IMPRACTICAL.

practically adverb **1** *practically every day | practically unknown* almost, nearly, very nearly, well-nigh, virtually, all but, in effect; *inf.* pretty nearly/well. **2** *behave practically* sensibly, with common sense, realistically, reasonably, pragmatically.

practice noun **1** *put the plan into practice | it would never work in practice* action, operation, application, effect, exercise, use. **2** *go to tennis practice* training, preparation, study, exercise, drill, work-out, rehearsal. **3** *it is standard practice for shops to close on Wednesday afternoons* procedure, method, system, usage, tradition, convention. **4** *it was his practice to visit his mother on Sundays* habit, custom, routine, wont. **5** *he engaged in the practice of law/medicine* profession, career, business, work, pursuit. **6** *buy a medical/legal practice* firm, business.

practise verb **1** *to practise economy/self-control* carry out, perform, do, execute, follow, pursue, observe. **2** *practise her tennis strokes | practising a musical piece* work at, go through, run through, go over, rehearse, polish, refine. **3** *she must practise before the match/test* train, study, prepare, exercise, drill. **4** *practise medicine/law* work at, have a career in, pursue a career in, engage in, specialize in.

practised *adjective a practised liar* experienced, seasoned, skilled, skilful, accomplished, expert, proficient, able, adept, adroit.

pragmatic *adjective he has a lot of theories but she is very pragmatic | a pragmatic approach to the problem | a pragmatic solution* matter-of-fact, practical, down-to-earth, hard-headed, sensible, businesslike, realistic, utilitarian; *inf.* hard-nosed, nuts and bolts.
Opposites IMPRACTICAL; THEORETICAL; IDEALISTIC.

praise *verb* **1** *praise the musician's performance | praise him for his contribution* express approval of, express admiration for, applaud, acclaim, cheer, compliment someone on, congratulate someone on, pay tribute to, extol, laud, sing the praises of, eulogize about, cry up, throw bouquets at; *inf.* crack up. **2** *praise God* worship, glorify, honour, exalt, adore, laud, pay tribute to, give thanks to.
Opposites CRITICIZE; CONDEMN.

praise *noun* **1** *express praise for his efforts | work worthy of praise | receive praise for his efforts* approval, approbation, applause, acclaim, acclamation, cheers, compliments, congratulations, cómmendation, tributes, accolades, plaudits, eulogy, panegyric, encomium, extolment, laudation, ovation, bouquets. **2** *praise to God* worship, glory, honour, devotion, exaltation, adoration, tribute, thanks.

praiseworthy *adjective* commendable, laudable, admirable, honourable, estimable, creditable, deserving, meritorious, worthy, excellent, exemplary, sterling, fine.
Opposites DISGRACEFUL; DISHONOURABLE.

prance *verb* **1** *horses prancing round the field* leap, spring, jump, skip, cavort, caper, frisk, gambol. **2** *prancing along in her new shoes* parade, skip, cavort, strut, swagger; *inf.* swank.

prank *noun a childish prank | play a prank on his friend* trick, practical joke, joke, hoax, caper, stunt; *inf.* lark.

prattle *verb prattle on about the details of her wedding* chatter, jabber, babble, twitter, blather, blether, gabble, run on, rattle on; *inf.* rabbit on, witter on.

pray *verb* **1** *pray every night before going to bed* say one's prayers. **2** *pray to God* offer prayers to, say prayers to, commune with. **3** *pray the emperor to spare her husband's life* appeal to, call upon, beseech, entreat, ask earnestly, request, implore, beg, petition, solicit, plead with, importune, supplicate, sue, invoke, crave, adjure. **4** *pray for mercy* appeal for, call for, ask earnestly for, request earnestly, beg for, beg, petition for, solicit, plead for, crave, crave for, clamour for.

prayer *noun* **1** *say a prayer to God | say evening prayers* devotion, communion, litany, collect. **2** *prayers for mercy answered by the emperor* appeal, plea, beseeching, entreaty, petition, solicitation, supplication, suit, invocation, adjuration. *See* PRAY 3.

preach *verb* **1** *ministers preaching in Church on Sunday* give a sermon, deliver a sermon, sermonize, spread the gospel, evangelize. **2** *preach the word of God* make known, proclaim, teach, spread. **3** *preach economy* advocate, recommend, advise, urge, exhort. **preach at** *tired of being preached at by her father* lecture, moralize, admonish, harangue, sermonize.

preacher *noun* **1** *preachers giving sermons from the pulpit* minister, parson, clergyman, churchman, cleric, missionary, revivalist, evangelist, televangelist. **2** *preachers of economy* advocate, adviser, urger, exhorter. **3** *tired of preachers telling other people how to lead their lives* moralizer, sermonizer, homilist.

preaching *noun* **1** *inspired by the minister's preaching* sermon, homily, pulpitry, evangelism. **2** *tired of her father's preaching about her lifestyle* lecturing, moralizing, harangue, sermon, sermonizing, homily; *inf.* preachify.

preamble *noun begin his lecture without any preamble | a historical novel with a long preamble* opening statement, opening remarks, introduction, prefatory remarks, preface, prologue, front matter, forward matter, foreword, prelude, exordium, proem, prolegomenon; *inf.* prelims.

precarious *adjective* **1** *earn rather a precarious living | a precarious way of earning a living* uncertain, unsure, unpredictable, undependable, unreliable, risky, hazardous, chancy, doubtful, dubious, unsettled, insecure, unstable; *inf.* dodgy, dicey. **2** *sitting in rather a precarious position at the edge of the cliff | in rather a precarious legal position* risky, hazardous, insecure, unstable, shaky, tricky, perilous, dangerous, on a slippery slope, touch-and-go; *inf.* dicey, hairy.
Opposites SAFE; SECURE.

precaution *noun* **1** *take a few precautions to avoid being burgled* preventive measure, preventative measure, safety measure, safeguard, provision. **2** *a situation which demands precaution* foresight, foresightedness, forethought, far-sightedness, anticipation, prudence, circumspection, caution, care, attentiveness, chariness, wariness.

precede *verb* **1** *his father preceded him as chairman* go before, be the predecessor of. **2** *she preceded him into the room* go before, come before, go/come ahead of, lead, usher in. **3** *the events that preceded the murder/triumph* go before, go in advance of, antedate, antecede, lead to, lead up to, usher in, herald, pave the way for. **4** *precede her lecture with a few informal remarks* preface, prefix, introduce, begin, open, launch.
Opposites FOLLOW; SUCCEED.

precedence *noun a list of the nobles in order of precedence* rank, seniority, superiority, pre-eminence, eminence, supremacy, primacy, transcendence, ascendancy. **take precedence over** *educational considerations should take precedence over financial considerations* come before, take priority over, be considered more important/urgent than, take antecedence over.

precedent *noun is there a precedent for such a severe punishment? | the judge's ruling has created a precedent* previous case, prior case, previous instance, prior instance, pattern, model, example, exemplar, paradigm, criterion, yardstick, standard.

preceding adjective **1** as stated in the preceding paragraph above, foregoing, previous, earlier, prior, antecedent, anterior. **2** on the preceding day previous, earlier, prior.

precept noun **1** follow the precepts of one's religion/contract rule, guideline, principle, working principle, code, law, tenet, canon, ordinance, statute, command, order, decree, mandate, dictate, dictum, directive, direction, instruction. **2** precepts that her grandmother used to quote maxim, axiom, saying, law, adage, aphorism.

precinct noun **1** the cathedral/college precinct close, enclosure, court, courtyard, quadrangle. **2** a pedestrian/shopping precinct quarter, sector, zone, district, region.

precincts plural noun **1** the cottages within the precincts of his estate boundary, bounds, limits, confines. **2** visit the old city and its precincts surrounding area, surroundings, environs, neighbourhood, vicinity, purlieus.

precious adjective **1** precious metals valuable, high-priced, costly, expensive, dear, priceless, rare, choice. **2** precious souvenirs/memories valued, cherished, prized, treasured, favourite, dear, beloved, adored, revered, venerated. **3** poetry full of precious images | her manners are too precious for words affected, artificial, chichi, overrefined, effete; inf. twee.
Opposites WORTHLESS; CHEAP.

precipice noun cliff face, rock face, steep cliff, sheer drop, cliff, crag, bluff.

precipitate verb **1** precipitate the crisis hasten, accelerate, expedite, speed up, push forward, bring on, trigger. **2** the collision precipitated the car into the river | precipitated into economic disaster hurl headlong, hurl, throw headlong, fling, thrust, heave, propel.

precipitate adjective **1** his precipitate dash from the room hurried, rapid, swift, speedy, headlong, abrupt, sudden, unexpected, breakneck, violent, precipitous. **2** it was precipitate of him to act like that | his precipitate action landed him in trouble hasty, hurried, rash, heedless, reckless, impetuous, impulsive, precipitous, harebrained.

precipitous adjective **1** a precipitous cliff face steep, sheer, perpendicular, abrupt, high. **2** his precipitous exit from the room precipitate, hurried, rapid, headlong, abrupt, sudden, violent. See PRECIPITATE adjective 1. **3** precipitous of him to act like that | his precipitous action landed him in trouble precipitate, hasty, rash, heedless, impetuous. See PRECIPITATE adjective 2.

précis noun a précis of the report summary, synopsis, résumé, abridgement, abstract, outline, sketch, run-down, digest, epitome, compendium.

précis verb précis the monthly report summarize, sum up, abridge, condense, shorten, compress, abstract, outline.

precise adjective **1** a precise record of events exact, literal, actual, close, faithful, strict, express, minute, accurate, correct. **2** at that precise moment she saw him | articles found at the precise spot where they were left exact, very, actual, particular, specific, distinct. **3** she's a very precise person | precise attention to detail careful, exact, meticulous, scrupulous, conscientious, punctilious, particular, methodical, fastidious, finicky, rigid, strict, rigorous.
Opposites LOOSE; IMPRECISE; INACCURATE; CARELESS.

precisely adverb **1** at 6 o'clock precisely exactly, sharp, on the dot, dead, dead on; inf. bang on, spot on; Am. on the button. **2** write out instructions very precisely exactly, literally, strictly, minutely. See PRECISE 1.

precision noun **1** admire the precision of his prose carefulness, exactness, meticulousness, scrupulousness, conscientiousness, punctiliousness, methodicalness, rigour. **2** the precision of the mechanism accuracy, exactness, reliability, regularity.

preclude verb **1** the rules of the club preclude women from joining | the owners are precluded from altering the front of the house prevent, prohibit, debar, interdict, block, bar, hinder, impede. **2** the police findings preclude any doubt as to his guilt make impossible, rule out, eliminate.

precocious adjective precocious children in need of special schooling advanced, ahead, far ahead, forward, ahead of one's peers, gifted, brilliant, ultra-bright, quick, smart, adult-like.

preconception noun have a preconception that the solicitor would be a man preconceived idea, preconceived notion, assumption, presupposition, presumption, prejudgement, prejudice, bias.

precondition noun a degree in an appropriate subject is a precondition of the post prerequisite, essential condition, requirement, necessity, essential, sine qua non; inf. must.

precursor noun **1** the sporadic attacks proved to be the precursors of a full-scale war forerunner, prelude, harbinger, herald, curtain-raiser. **2** his precursor in the post predecessor, former/previous holder of the post etc, forerunner, antecedent. **3** a machine that was the precursor of the modern computer predecessor, forerunner, ancestor, forebear, antecedent, progenitor, pioneer.

predatory adjective **1** predatory birds of prey, hunting, predacious, rapacious, raptorial. **2** predatory tribes invading the country plundering, pillaging, marauding, ravaging, looting, robbing, thieving, rapacious. **3** her predatory relatives have left her without any money exploitative, exploiting, imposing, greedy, acquisitive, rapacious, vulturine.

predecessor noun **1** the success of the department is the result of the efforts of his predecessor former/previous holder of the post etc, precursor, forerunner, antecedent. **2** collect information on his predecessors for a family tree ancestor, forefather, forebear, progenitor, antecedent.
Opposites SUCCESSOR; DESCENDANT.

predestine verb he seemed predestined to lead a life of poverty | her success seemed predestined preordain, foreordain, predetermine, fate, destine, predestinate.

predetermined adjective everyone acted on a predetermined signal prearranged, pre-agreed, predecided, preplanned, agreed, settled, fixed, set.

predicament *noun* difficult situation, problematic situation, corner, plight, tight corner, mess, emergency, crisis, dilemma, quandary, trouble; *inf.* jam, sticky situation, hole, fix, pickle, scrape, tight spot, spot.

predict *verb predict future events | predict that something terrible would happen* forecast, foretell, prophesy, foresee, divine, prognosticate, forewarn, forebode, portend, presage, augur.

predictable *adjective a predictable reaction* foreseeable, to be expected, expected, anticipated, probable, likely, certain, sure; *inf.* on the cards.

prediction *noun* prophecy, forecast, divination, prognostication, forewarning, augury, soothsaying.

predilection *noun a predilection for spicy food | his predilection for intelligent women* liking, fondness, preference, love, partiality, taste, weakness, soft spot, fancy, inclination, leaning, bias, propensity, bent, proclivity, proneness, penchant, predisposition.

predispose *verb* **1** *his poverty-stricken childhood predisposed him to save* move, incline, dispose, persuade, influence, sway, induce, prompt. **2** *the child is predisposed to asthma* make susceptible to, make liable to, make subject to, make prone to, make vulnerable to, make open to.

predisposed *adjective before meeting her he was predisposed to believe her story* inclined, of a mind to, willing, biased, prejudiced.

predisposition *noun* **1** *a predisposition towards rheumatism/meanness* susceptibility, proneness, tendency, inclination, vulnerability. *See* PREDISPOSE. **2** *have a predisposition towards fast cars* predilection, inclination, leaning, bias, propensity, bent, proclivity, proneness, penchant. *See* PREDILECTION.

predominance *noun* **1** *try to avoid the predominance of one group over another in the alliance* dominance, control, ascendancy, leadership, mastery, supremacy, upper hand, edge, preponderance. **2** *a predominance of men on the staff | a predominance of blue in the room's colour-scheme* preponderance, dominance, prevalence, greater/greatest number/amount, majority, bulk.

predominant *adjective* **1** *the predominant member of the alliance* dominant, controlling, in control, ascendant, ruling, leading, principal, chief, main, supreme, more/most powerful, more/most important, superior, in the ascendancy. **2** *idleness is the predominant characteristic in that family* chief, main, principal, preponderant, most obvious, most noticeable, most prominent, prevailing, prevalent.

predominate *verb* **1** *the largest country predominates in the policy-making of the alliance* be dominant, be in control, rule, hold ascendancy, hold sway, have the upper hand, carry most weight. **2** *male members of staff predominate in the firm | blue predominates in the room's colour-scheme* be predominant, be greater/greatest in amount/number, be prevalent, preponderate, be most prominent. *See* PREDOMINANT 2.

pre-eminence *noun his pre-eminence as a poet* excellence, distinction, prestige, prominence, eminence, importance, fame, renown, supremacy, superiority, transcendence.

pre-eminent *adjective a pre-eminent scientist | a scientist pre-eminent in his field* outstanding, leading, foremost, chief, excellent, distinguished, prominent, eminent, important, famous, renowned, supreme, superior, unrivalled, unsurpassed, transcendent.
Opposites UNKNOWN; UNDISTINGUISHED; OBSCURE.

pre-empt *verb* **1** *pre-empt the sale of the building by buying it themselves* forestall, prevent, invalidate. **2** *the invading army pre-empted all the houses for their own use* take over, appropriate, acquire, commandeer, take possession of, occupy, seize, arrogate.

preen *verb birds preening their feathers with their beaks* clean, smooth, arrange, plume. **preen oneself** **1** *preening himself in front of the mirror* groom oneself, tidy oneself up, spruce oneself up, smarten oneself up, beautify oneself, prettify oneself, primp, primp oneself up, prink, prink oneself up, plume oneself; *inf.* titivate oneself, doll oneself up, tart oneself up. **2** *preen oneself on winning the prize* give oneself a pat on the back, congratulate oneself, be pleased with oneself, pride oneself, be proud of oneself.

preface *noun the preface explaining how to use the book* introduction, foreword, front matter, forward matter, preamble, prologue, prelude, proem, exordium, prolegomenon; *inf.* prelims, intro.

preface *verb preface her speech with a short introduction* precede, prefix, introduce, begin, open, launch.

prefatory *adjective made a few prefatory remarks before reading his poem* preliminary, introductory, opening, precursory, initial, preparatory.

prefer *verb* **1** *prefer cheese to dessert* like better, favour, be more partial to, incline towards, choose, select, pick, opt for, go for, plump for, single out; *inf.* fancy. **2** *prefer to go by bus* like better, would rather, would sooner, favour, choose, opt, elect, wish, want. **3** *prefer a proposal to the committee | prefer charges* put forward, proffer, present, offer, propose, tender, lodge, file, press. **4** *hope to be preferred in the near future* promote, upgrade, advance, move up, elevate, aggrandize.

preferable *adjective find going by train preferable to going by car* better, superior, more desirable, more suitable.

preferably *adverb looking for a cottage preferably a thatched one | preferably we would like to be paid in cash* for preference, by preference, from choice, by choice, much rather, rather, much sooner, sooner.

preference *noun* **1** *her preference is for a flat rather than a bungalow* choice, first choice, first option, liking, fancy, desire, wish, inclination, partiality, predilection, leaning, bias, bent. **2** *here are the cakes, what is your preference?* choice, selection, option, pick. **3** *applicants with experience will be given preference | show preference to members of her own family* preferential treatment, favoured treatment, favour, precedence, priority, advantage.

preferential *adjective preferential travel rates given to members of the group | members of the manager's family get preferential treatment* special, better, advantageous, favoured, privileged, partial, partisan.

preferment *noun hope for preferment in the firm* promotion, upgrading, advancement, moving up, elevation, aggrandizement.

pregnancy *noun* gestation, gravidity, parturiency.

pregnant *adjective* **1** *discover that she was pregnant* having a baby/child, expectant, with child, heavy with child, gravid, *enceinte*; *inf.* expecting, in the family way, preggers, in a delicate condition, in a certain condition, in the club, in the pudding club, in trouble, with a bun in the oven. **2** *a speech pregnant with menace | a situation pregnant with danger | an event pregnant with joy* full of, filled with, charged with, fraught with, abounding in, replete with, rich in. **3** *a pregnant pause following her surprise announcement* meaningful, significant, eloquent, expressive, suggestive, loaded, charged, pointed, telling.

prehistoric *adjective* **1** *prehistoric man* primeval, primordial, primitive, earliest. **2** *prehistoric attitudes to women | wear prehistoric clothes* out of date, old-fashioned, ancient, antiquated, superannuated; *inf.* out of the ark.

prejudice *noun* **1** *have a prejudice against young people | forget his prejudices against people from other countries* bias, partiality, jaundiced eye, preconceived idea, preconceived notion, preconception, prejudgement, predetermination. **2** *employers showing prejudice towards older people | found guilty of racial prejudice* bias, discrimination, partisanship, partiality, preference, one-sidedness, chauvinism, bigotry, narrow-mindedness, intolerance, unfairness, unjustness, racism, sexism, ageism, heterosexism. **3** *without prejudice to any future judgement | without prejudice to his claim* detriment, disadvantage, damage, injury, harm, hurt, loss.

prejudice *verb* **1** *wonder whether newspaper articles had prejudiced the attitude of the jury* bias, make partial, make partisan, colour, poison, jaundice, influence, sway, predispose. **2** *his conviction may prejudice his chances* be prejudicial to, be detrimental to, be deleterious to, be disadvantageous to, damage, injure, harm, hurt, mar, spoil, impair, undermine. *See* PREJUDICIAL.

prejudiced *adjective have a prejudiced attitude to others of a different race | be prejudiced against young people* biased, discriminatory, partisan, partial, one-sided, jaundiced, chauvinistic, bigoted, intolerant, narrow-minded, unfair, unjust, racist, sexist, ageist.
Opposites UNBIASED; IMPARTIAL.

prejudicial *adjective his conviction will be prejudicial to his chances of getting a job | actions prejudicial to the country's economy* detrimental, deleterious, disadvantageous, unfavourable, damaging, injurious, harmful, hurtful, inimical.

preliminary *adjective* **1** *preliminary training | a few preliminary remarks* introductory, prefatory, prior, precursory, opening, initial, beginning, preparatory, initiatory. **2** *preliminary heats/rounds/interviews* prior, precursory, qualifying, eliminating. **3** *preliminary experiments* introductory, early, exploratory, pilot, test, trial.

preliminary *noun dispense with the preliminaries and get on with the meeting | tired of preliminary after preliminary before their appeal was heard* preliminary measure, preliminary action, preparation, groundwork, first round, introduction, preamble, prelude, opening.

prelims *plural noun* **1** *got high marks in the prelims but not in the actual exam* preliminary exams, mock exams; *inf.* mocks. **2** *read the prelims at the start of the reference book* preliminary material, front matter, forward matter, introductory material, introduction, prefatory material, foreword, preface, preamble, proem, prolegomenon, exordium.

prelude *noun* **1** *the military skirmishes were a prelude to full-scale war* precursor, forerunner, curtain-raiser, harbinger, herald, preliminary, introduction, start, beginning. **2** *the prelude to the narrative poem* introduction, preface, prologue, preamble, proem, exordium, prolegomenon; *inf.* intro. **3** *the prelude to the fugue* overture, introductory movement, voluntary.

premature *adjective* **1** *his premature death/birth | the premature closing of the play because of lack of support* too soon, too early, early, untimely. **2** *it was premature of him to announce his plans* too soon, hasty, overhasty, precipitate, impulsive, impetuous, rash. **3** *announce premature plans* incomplete, undeveloped, immature, embryonic.

prematurely *adverb* **1** *leave prematurely* too soon, too early, before the usual time. **2** *announce his plans prematurely* too soon, too early, overhastily, precipately.

premeditated *adjective premeditated murder* planned, preplanned, prearranged, intentional, intended, deliberate, calculated, wilful.

premier *noun an international meeting of premiers* head of government, prime minister, PM.

premier *adjective the country's premier computer firm | a firm with a premier position in the computer industry* leading, foremost, chief, principal, head, top-ranking, top, prime, first, highest, main.

première *noun the première of the play/film* first night, first performance, first showing, opening, opening night, début.

premise, premiss *noun financial advice based on the premise that the recession was over* hypothesis, thesis, assumption, presupposition, presumption, argument, postulation.

premises *plural noun the firm has moved to new premises* building, property, establishment.

premiss *See* PREMISE.

premium *noun* **1** *monthly premiums for life insurance* insurance payment, insurance instalment. **2** *paid a premium of £3 on their investment* bonus, bounty. **3** *pay a premium for early delivery* additional payment, additional fee, surcharge. **4** *the boys received a premium for working late* reward, recompense, remuneration, perquisite, prize; *inf.* perk. **at a premium**

parking spaces are at a premium in the city centre rare, hard to come by, in short supply, scarce, in great demand, like gold dust, not to be had; *inf.* not to be had for love or money. **put a premium on 1** *the tutor puts a premium on creative work* set great store by, put a high value on, regard as valuable, hold in high regard, appreciate greatly, attach great importance to. **2** *the risk of disease puts a premium on hygiene* make invaluable, make valuable, put a high value on, make essential, make important.

premonition *noun* **1** *had a premonition that something terrible was going to happen* foreboding, presage, presentiment, intuition, feeling, hunch, suspicion, sneaking suspicion, misgiving, apprehension, fear, feeling in one's bones, funny feeling. **2** *given a premonition that all was not well in the firm* forewarning, warning, sign, pre-indication, indication, omen, portent.

preoccupation *noun* **1** *in his preoccupation he failed to notice her* abstraction, absorption, engrossment, concentration, brown study, deep thought, musing, pensiveness, reverie, absent-mindedness, absence of mind, distraction, inattentiveness, heedlessness, oblivion, wool-gathering, daydreaming. **2** *DIY is his major preoccupation* chief concern, obsession, fixation, hobby-horse, pet subject, bee in one's bonnet, *idée fixe; inf.* hang-up.

preoccupied *adjective she seemed rather preoccupied* lost in thought, deep in thought, immersed in thought, in a brown study, absorbed, engrossed, pensive, absent-minded, distracted, abstracted, *distrait*, oblivious, faraway, rapt.

preoccupy *verb his financial worries were preoccupying him* absorb, engross, take up one's whole attention, take up all one's time, distract, obsess.

preparation *noun* **1** *the preparation of their plans* making ready, arrangement, development, assembling, assembly, drawing up, production, construction, composing, composition, fashioning. See PREPARE 1. **2** *often preparations finalize their preparations for battle* arrangement, provision, preparatory measure, necessary step, groundwork, spadework. **3** *the preparation of the students for the exam/contest* coaching, training, grooming, priming. **4** *a preparation used as a tranquillizer* mixture, compound, concoction, composition, tincture. **5** *children complaining at doing preparation* homework, schoolwork; *inf.* prep.

preparatory *adjective a great deal of preparatory work to be done before the store opens* preliminary, introductory, prefatory, precursory, basic, elementary, fundamental, rudimentary, preparative. **preparatory to** *much to be done preparatory to the opening of the store* in preparation for, in advance of, before, prior to, in anticipation of, leading up to.

prepare *verb* **1** *prepare their plans* get ready, make ready, arrange, develop, put together, assemble, draw up, produce, construct, compose, concoct, fashion, work up. **2** *prepare for trouble* make preparations, get ready, arrange things, make provision, get everything set, take the necessary steps, lay the groundwork, do the spadework; *inf.* gear oneself up, psych oneself up, gird up one's loins. **3** *prepare for the sports event* train, get into shape for, practise, exercise, warm up. **4** *prepare for the exam* do preparation, revise, study, do homework; *inf.* swot. **5** *prepare the students for the exam/contest* coach, train, groom, prime. **6** *prepare her/oneself for a shock* make ready, brace, steel. **7** *prepare a meal* cook, make, put together, assemble; *Am. inf.* fix.

prepared *adjective* **1** *everything is prepared for the wedding* ready, in readiness, arranged, in order, set, all set, fixed, planned, primed. **2** *they are prepared to make peace* ready, disposed, predisposed, willing, inclined, of a mind, minded.

preponderance *noun* **1** *a preponderance of men over women on the staff | a preponderance of red in the room's decor* predominance, dominance, prevalence, greater number/quantity, majority, bulk. **2** *the preponderance of the group in the alliance* dominance, predominance, control, ascendancy, leadership, mastery, supremacy, upper hand, edge.

prepossessing *adjective a prepossessing child/manner* attractive, beautiful, pretty, handsome, good-looking, fetching, striking, pleasing, agreeable, appealing, likeable, lovable, amiable, charming, engaging, winning, winsome, taking, enchanting, captivating, bewitching, fascinating.
Opposites UGLY; REPULSIVE; unprepossessing.

preposterous *adjective what a preposterous idea!* absurd, ridiculous, foolish, ludicrous, farcical, asinine, senseless, unreasonable, irrational, outrageous, shocking, astonishing, unbelievable, incredible, unthinkable; *inf.* crazy, insane.

prerequisite *adjective tolerance is prerequisite when bringing up children* necessary, needed, required, called for, essential, requisite, vital, indispensable, imperative, obligatory, mandatory.

prerequisite *noun patience is a prerequisite for parenthood* requirement, requisite, necessity, essential, precondition, condition, *sine qua non; inf.* must.

prerogative *noun it's a woman's prerogative to change her mind | he thinks it's his prerogative to make all the decisions* right, birthright, privilege, due, entitlement, liberty, authority, licence, *carte blanche*.

presage *verb* **1** *clouds presaging a storm* be a sign of, be an indication of, be a presage of, be an omen of, be a warning of, give a warning of, portend, augur. **2** *she presaged that something terrible would happen* forecast, foretell, prophesy, predict, foresee, divine, prognosticate, forewarn.

prescribe *verb* **1** *the doctor prescribed antibiotics* write a prescription for, order, advise, direct. **2** *prescribe a holiday to cure her depression* advise, recommend, commend, suggest. **3** *the law prescribes strict penalties for drunk driving | school regulations prescribe that everyone must wear the uniform* lay down, require, direct, stipulate, specify, impose, decree, order, command, ordain, enjoin.

prescription *noun* **1** *the prescription of drugs is part of a doctor's job* prescribing, ordering, advising. *See* PRESCRIBE 1. **2** *the doctor wrote a prescription for antibiotics* instruction, order, direction. **3** *his prescription for long life was hard work* recipe, formula, direction, advice. **4** *ask the chemist to make up the prescription* medicine, drug, remedy, preparation, mixture.

presence *noun* **1** *the presence of too much acid in the soil* | *detect the presence of poison in the drink* existence, being. **2** *demand his presence at the meeting* attendance, company, companionship. **3** *they feel inadequate in the presence of such a great man* company, propinquity, proximity, neighbourhood, vicinity, closeness, nearness. **4** *a woman of presence* magnetism, aura, charisma, personality, attraction, poise, self-assurance, self-possession, self-confidence. **5** *impressed by her presence* dignified bearing, impressive carriage, dignified air/demeanour, dignity. **6** *she felt a presence in the castle* manifestation, apparition, supernatural being, spirit, ghost, spectre, wraith. **presence of mind** aplomb, level-headedness, sang-froid, phlegm, self-assurance, self-possession, composure, calmness, calm, coolness, imperturbability, alertness, quickness, quick-wittedness; *inf.* unflappability.
Opposites ABSENCE.

present¹ *adjective* **1** *establish that poison was present in the drink* existing, existent, extant. **2** *in the present climate* present-day, existing, current, contemporary. **3** *a doctor had to be present* in attendance, here, there, near, nearby, available, at hand, ready.
Opposites ABSENT.

present² *noun* *forget the past and think about the present* today, now, here and now, the present moment, the time being. **at present** *at present he's unavailable* just now, right now, at the moment, at this time, for the moment, at the present time, currently, at this moment in time; *Am. Scots* presently. **for the present** *for the present we must economize* for the moment, for the time being, for now, in the meanwhile, in the meantime. **the present day** *the old man is shocked by the morals of the present day* the present age/time, modern times, nowadays.
Opposites PAST; FUTURE.

present³ *verb* **1** *present a gift to the retiring chairman* give, hand over, confer, bestow, donate, award, grant, accord. **2** *present his proposals to the committee* submit, set forth, put forward, proffer, offer, tender, advance. **3** *present his apologies/greetings* give, offer, send, tender. **4** *may I present my daughter?* introduce, make known. **5** *present their new product to the trade/public* show, put on show, exhibit, display, put on display, demonstrate, introduce, launch. **6** *present a performance of Hamlet* put on, produce, perform, stage, mount. **7** *present a radio/television programme* be the presenter of, introduce, host, compère; *inf.* emcee. **present oneself** **1** *you must present yourself for interview at 11 a.m. tomorrow morning* be present, make an appearance, appear, attend, turn up. **2** *if the opportunity presents itself* occur, arise, happen, transpire, come about, appear.

present⁴ *noun* *a birthday present* | *the money was a present* gift, donation, offering, contribution, gratuity, hand-out, presentation, largesse, award, premium, bounty, boon, benefaction; *inf.* pressie, freebie.

presentable *adjective* *make yourself presentable for the interview* | *go to school looking presentable* well-groomed, smartly-dressed, tidily-dressed, tidy, spruce, of smart appearance, fit to be seen.

presentation *noun* **1** *the presentation of his retirement gift* presenting, giving, handing over, conferral, bestowal, donation, award, granting, according. **2** *hand over a presentation to mark his retirement* gift, present, donation, offering, contribution, gratuity. *See* PRESENT² *noun*. **3** *the presentation of their proposals to the committee* submission, proffering, offering. *See* PRESENT² *verb* 2. **4** *the presentation of his fiancée to his family* introduction, making known, acquainting. **5** *attend the presentation of their new product* launch, launching, show, exhibition, display, demonstration. **6** *attend the drama club's presentation of Hamlet* production, performance, staging, mounting, showing, rendition. **7** *improve the presentation of his material* arrangement, organization, ordering, disposition, layout, scheme, system, structure.

presentiment *noun* *a presentiment of impending doom* foreboding, premonition, presage, intuition, feeling, hunch, suspicion, sneaking suspicion, misgiving, fear, apprehension, feeling in one's bones, funny feeling.

presently *adverb* *he'll be here presently* soon, shortly, in a short time, in a short while, directly, in a moment, in a minute, before long, before you can say Jack Robinson; *inf.* in a jiffy, in a mo, in two shakes of a lamb's tail; *Am.* momentarily.

preservation *noun* **1** *the preservation of the wood* conservation, protection. *See* PRESERVE *verb* 1. **2** *the preservation of the town from danger* protection, defence, guarding, safeguarding, safe keeping, safety, security, salvation, shielding. *See* PRESERVE *verb* 2. **3** *the preservation of old traditions* conservation, keeping alive, maintenance, continuation, upholding, perpetuation. *See* PRESERVE *verb* 4. **4** *preservation of financial resources* conservation, keeping, saving, putting away. *See* PRESERVE *verb* 5.

preserve *verb* **1** *find a substance to preserve the wood* conserve, protect, safeguard, care for. **2** *preserve the town from danger* keep, protect, defend, guard, safeguard, secure, shelter, shield. **3** *preserve his work for posterity* conserve, save, keep, safeguard, maintain, perpetuate. **4** *preserve the old traditions* conserve, keep up, keep alive, keep going, maintain, continue with, uphold, prolong, perpetuate. **5** *preserve their financial resources until a rainy day* conserve, keep, save, retain, put away, put aside, store, hoard. **6** *preserve food* cure, smoke, dry, pickle, salt, marinate, kipper.
Opposites ATTACK; DAMAGE; NEGLECT; USE.

preserve *noun* **1** *an animal preserve* sanctuary, reserve, reservation, game reserve. **2** *he regards the family finances as his preserve* area, domain, field, sphere, realm; *inf.* thing. **3** *she* *usually makes strawberry preserve* jam, jelly, confiture, marmalade, conserve.

preside *verb* **1** *the committee members elected him to preside* chair, be in the chair, be chairman/chairwoman/chairperson, officiate. **2** *preside over a huge firm* be in charge of, be at the head/helm of, head, manage, administer, be in control of, control, be responsible for, direct, run, conduct, supervise, govern, rule, be boss of, head up, be in the driver's seat, be in the saddle, pull the strings, call the shots.

president *noun* **1** *terrorists have assassinated the president of a neighbouring country* chief of state, head of state. *See table.* **2** *the president of the society* head, chief, director, leader, captain.

press *verb* **1** *press the button/accelerator* press down, depress, push down, force down, bear down on. **2** *press grapes* crush, squeeze, compress, mash, reduce. **3** *press trousers* iron, smooth out, put creases in, calender, mangle. **4** *press flowers* | *press the soil down* flatten, make flat, smooth out. **5** *press the child to her bosom* clasp, enfold, hold close, clutch, grasp, embrace, hug, cuddle, squeeze, crush. **6** *press her hand/arm affectionately* squeeze, give something a squeeze, pat, caress. **7** *they are pressing him to make a decision* urge, entreat, exhort, implore, put pressure on, use pressure on, pressurize, force, compel, coerce, constrain. **8** *they are pressing for quick decision* call for, demand, insist on, clamour for. **9** *press a claim* plead, urge, push forward, advance insistently. **10** *press round the board to see the results* crowd, surge, cluster, mill, flock, gather, swarm, throng. **11** *the enemy are pressing our army* harass, besiege, attack, assail, beset, worry, torment. **be pressed for** *we are pressed for time* | *they are pressed for cash just now* be short of, have barely enough of, have too little of,

have an insufficiency of; *inf.* be strapped for. **be pressing** *other matters are pressing* be urgent, demand attention, require attention, call for action. **press on** *we must press on to reach the summit tonight* | *press on with the work* push on, make haste, hasten, hurry, proceed, continue, put one's nose to the grindstone, put one's shoulder to the wheel.

press *noun* **1** *usually the press the freedom of the press* | *advertise in the press* newspapers, papers, news media, journalism, the newspaper world, the media, Fleet Street, the fourth estate, newspapermen, newspaper women, reporters, pressmen, presswomen, gentlemen of the press. **2** *get a good/bad press* press treatment, press coverage, press reporting, newspaper articles, newspaper write-ups. **3** *go to press* | *the presses are running* printing-press, printing-machine. **4** *he has set up a small press* printing firm, publishing firm, publishing house. **5** *children getting lost in the press leaving the cinema* crowd, throng, multitude, mob, horde, swarm, herd, flock, pack, crush. **6** *the press of modern life* pressure, strain, stress, urgency, demands, hurry, hustle, hustle and bustle, flurry.

pressing *adjective* **1** *have a pressing engagement* urgent, vital, crucial, critical, demanding, important, high-priority, exigent, pivotal. **2** *a pressing invitation to dinner* insistent, persistent, determined, importunate, repeated, repetitive.

pressure *noun* **1** *have to exert pressure on the door to open it* | *the pressure of the crowd against the barriers* force, weight, heaviness. **2** *kill him by applying pressure to his neck and strangling him* compression, compressing, squeezing, crushing. **3** *parents exerting pressure to get her to marry him* force, compulsion, coercion, constraint, duress. **4** *have a breakdown because of*

PRESIDENTS OF THE U.S.A.

Number	Name	In Office	Number	Name	In Office
1	George Washington	1789–97	24	(Stephen) Grover Cleveland	1893–7
2	John Adams	1797–1801	25	William McKinley	1897–1901
3	Thomas Jefferson	1801–9	26	Theodore Roosevelt	1901–9
4	James Madison	1809–17	27	William Howard Taft	1909–13
5	James Monroe	1817–25	28	(Thomas) Woodrow Wilson	1913–21
6	John Quincy Adams	1825–9	29	Warren Gamaliel Harding	1921–3
7	Andrew Jackson	1829–37	30	Calvin Coolidge	1923–9
8	Martin Van Buren	1837–41	31	Herbert Clark Hoover	1929–33
9	William Henry Harrison	1841	32	Franklin Delano Roosevelt	1933–45
10	John Tyler	1841–5	33	Harry S. Truman	1945–53
11	James Knox Polk	1845–9	34	Dwight David Eisenhower	1953–61
12	Zachary Taylor	1849–50	35	John Fitzgerald Kennedy	1961–3
13	Millard Fillmore	1850–3	36	Lyndon Baines Johnson	1963–9
14	Franklin Pierce	1853–7	37	Richard Milhous Nixon	1969–74
15	James Buchanan	1857–61	38	Gerald Rudolph Ford	1974–7
16	Abraham Lincoln	1861–5	39	James Earl Carter, Jr.	1977–81
17	Andrew Johnson	1865–9	40	Ronald Wilson Reagan	1981–9
18	Ulysses Simpson Grant	1869–77	41	George Herbert Walter Bush	1989–93
19	Rutherford Birchard Hayes	1877–81	42	William Jefferson Clinton	from 1993
20	James Abram Garfield	1881			
21	Chester Alan Arthur	1881–5			
22	(Stephen) Grover Cleveland	1885–9			
23	Benjamin Harrison	1889–93			

pressure · pretentious

the pressures of modern life | unable to cope with the pressure of work strain, stress, tension, burden, load, weight, trouble; *inf.* hassle. **5** *find it difficult to work under pressure* adversity, difficulty, urgency, strain, stress, tension.

pressure, pressurize *verb pressure him into taking the job* put pressure on, use pressure on, press, force, compel, coerce, constrain, bulldoze, dragoon.

prestige *noun suffer a loss of prestige in the community when he lost his job* status, kudos, standing, stature, importance, reputation, fame, renown, esteem, influence, authority, supremacy, eminence, superiority, predominance.

prestigious *adjective* **1** *a prestigious school* reputable, respected, esteemed, eminent, distinguished, of high standing, well-known, celebrated, illustrious, renowned, famous. **2** *a prestigious job* conferring prestige, important, prominent, impressive, high-ranking, influential, glamorous.
Opposites UNKNOWN; OBSCURE; MINOR; HUMBLE.

presumably *adverb presumably he'll get the job* it is to be presumed, in all probability, probably, in all likelihood, all things being equal, all things considered, on the face of it, as likely as not; *inf.* as like as not.

presume *verb* **1** *I presume that your new partner is honest | presumed innocent until proved guilty* assume, take for granted, take it, take as read, suppose, presuppose, believe, think, imagine, judge, guess, surmise, conjecture, hypothesize, infer, deduce. **2** *don't presume to offer advice to a more experienced person* have the temerity, have the audacity, be so bold as, make so bold as, have the effrontery, go so far as, dare, venture.
presume on *presume on his good nature* take advantage of, take unfair advantage of, exploit, take liberties with.

presumption *noun* **1** *she was infuriated by his presumption in booking a seat next to her* confidence, arrogance, egotism, boldness, audacity, forwardness, insolence, impudence, bumptiousness, temerity, effrontery. **2** *our presumption is that he has run away* assumption, supposition, presupposition, belief, thought, guess, surmise, conjecture, hypothesis, premise, premiss, inference, deduction. See PRESUME 1. **3** *the presumption for their hypothesis* grounds, ground, basis, reason, evidence.

presumptive *adjective* **1** *the police lack any presumptive evidence* reasonable, plausible, feasible, likely, credible, believable, which holds water. **2** *the heir presumptive | the presumptive heir* probable, likely, assumed, supposed, expected.

presumptuous *adjective it was presumptuous of him to offer advice to someone of her age and experience | a presumptuous, overbearing young woman* presuming, ultra-confident, superconfident, overconfident, cocksure, self-confident, self-assured, arrogant, egotistical, conceited, overbold, bold, audacious, forward, insolent, impudent, bumptious, self-assertive, overbearing, overweening, haughty; *inf.* big-headed, swollen-headed, too big for one's boots, pushy.

presuppose *verb* **1** *they cannot presuppose the accuracy of his alibi* presume, assume, take for granted, take it, take as read, suppose. **2** *does their approval of the plan presuppose that funding is available* require, imply, assume, presume, take for granted.

presupposition *noun in the absence of evidence to the contrary their presupposition must be that he is innocent* presumption, assumption, preconception, supposition, thesis, theory, premise, premiss.

pretence *noun* **1** *she's not ill—it's just pretence* putting on an act, acting, dissembling, shamming, faking, dissimulation, make-believe, invention, imagination, posturing. See PRETEND 1. **2** *not taken in by their pretence of grief* false show, show, semblance, false appearance, appearance, false front, guise, façade, masquerade, mask, veneer, cover, charade. **3** *on the pretence that he was dying* pretext, false excuse, guise, sham, ruse, wile, trickery, lie, falsehood. See PRETEXT. **4** *make no pretence to expertness | I have no pretence to being expert* claim, aspiration, purporting, profession. **5** *lead humble lives without pretence* pretentiousness, display, ostentation, affectation, showiness, flaunting, posturing.
Opposites REALITY; FACT.

pretend *verb* **1** *she's not ill—she's only pretending* put on an act, act, play-act, put it on, dissemble, sham, feign, fake, fake it, dissimulate, make believe, put on a false front, posture, go through the motions. **2** *she is pretending that she knows nothing about the situation* make believe, affect, profess, make out, fabricate. **3** *pretend illness* sham, feign, fake, simulate, put on. **4** *pretend to the throne/title* claim, lay claim to, make a claim to, aspire to. **5** *pretend to be her friend* claim, profess, purport.

pretended *adjective* **1** *a pretended affection* alleged, avowed, professed, purported, spurious, insincere, sham, bogus, fake, faked, counterfeit, affected, put-on, pseudo; *inf.* phoney. **2** *a pretended friend* alleged, so-called, professed, ostensible, in name only, supposed, bogus, pseudo; *inf.* pretend.

pretender *noun a pretender to the throne* claimant, claimer, aspirant.

pretension *noun* **1** *make no pretensions to being an expert | a writer with pretensions to literary greatness* claim, aspiration, pretence, profession, purporting. **2** *dislike the pretension of her style | a life full of pretension* pretentiousness, affectation, ostentation, ostentatiousness, showiness, pomposity, floweriness, extravagance, flamboyance, grandiloquence, magniloquence, bombast. See PRETENTIOUS 1. **3** *the pretension of their lifestyle* affectation, ostentation, ostentatiousness, showiness, flaunting, flamboyance.

pretentious *adjective* **1** *a pretentious style of writing* affected, ostentatious, showy, overambitious, pompous, artificial, mannered, high-flown, high-sounding, flowery, grandiose, elaborate, extravagant, flamboyant, grandiloquent, magniloquent, bombastic, orotund; *inf.* highfalutin. **2** *a pretentious lifestyle* affected,

ostentatious, showy, flaunting, flamboyant.
Opposites PLAIN; SIMPLE; NATURAL; UNAFFECTED.

preternatural *adjective preternatural powers/ experience* extraordinary, out of the ordinary, exceptional, unusual, uncommon, singular, abnormal, supernatural, paranormal.

pretext *noun the thief got into the old lady's house on the pretext of reading the gas meter | find a pretext for getting into the house* pretence, false excuse, excuse, ostensible reason, alleged reason, alleged plea, supposed grounds, cover, guise, sham, ruse, wile, trickery, red herring, lie, falsehood, misrepresentation.

pretty *adjective* **1** *a pretty child* attractive, lovely, good-looking, nice-looking, comely, personable, prepossessing, appealing, charming, delightful, nice, engaging, pleasing, winning, winsome, cute, as pretty as a picture; *Scots* bonny. **2** *a pretty pattern* attractive, lovely, appealing, pleasant, pleasing, charming, delightful, nice; *Scots* bonny. **3** *a pretty turn of phrase* fine, neat, clever. **4** *cost a pretty penny | make a pretty profit* considerable, large, sizeable, substantial, appreciable, fair, tolerable, goodly, goodish; *inf.* tidy.
Opposites PLAIN; UGLY; UNPLEASANT.

pretty *adverb* **1** *a pretty large sum of money* moderately, reasonably, fairly. **2** *feeling pretty secure* quite, rather, somewhat; *inf.* kind of.

prevail *verb* **1** *in the end common sense prevailed* win, win out, win through, triumph, be victorious, be the victor, carry the day, prove superior, conquer, overcome, gain mastery, gain ascendancy, take the crown, gain the palm, rule. **2** *the economic conditions prevailing at the time* exist, be in existence, obtain, occur, be prevalent, be current, be widespread, abound, hold sway, predominate, preponderate. **prevail on, prevail upon** *try to prevail upon him to speak at the conference* persuade, induce, talk someone into, bring someone round, convince, sway, prompt, influence, urge, exhort, pressure, bring pressure to bear on, pressurize, cajole, coax; *inf.* sweet-talk.

prevailing *adjective* **1** *the prevailing attitude towards prisoners | the prevailing fashion in hats* prevalent, current, usual, common, general, widespread, set, established, accepted, popular, fashionable, in fashion, in style, in vogue. **2** *the prevailing political party* prevalent, dominant, predominant, predominating, preponderant, most influential, ruling, governing, ascendant, principal, chief, main, supreme. **3** *the prevailing wind in the area* most frequent, most common, commonest, most usual.

prevalence *noun* **1** *the prevalence of sexism in the firm | the prevalence of short skirts* currency, frequency, commonness, pervasiveness, universality, popularity, fashionableness. **2** *the prevalence of malaria in the region* commonness, universality, extensiveness, ubiquity, ubiquitousness, frequency, rifeness. **3** *the prevalence of the right wing of the party* dominance, predominance, preponderance, ascendancy, mastery, supremacy.

prevalent *adjective* **1** *the prevalent opinion in the country is against the war* prevailing, current, frequent, usual, common, general, widespread, pervasive, universal, set, established, accepted, popular, fashionable, in fashion, in style, in vogue. **2** *malaria is prevalent there* common, usual, endemic, widespread, universal, extensive, frequent, ubiquitous, rampant, rife. **3** *the prevalent political party* prevailing, dominant, predominant, predominating, preponderant, ruling, governing. See PREVAILING 2.
Opposites UNCOMMON; RARE; UNPOPULAR.

prevaricate *verb they tried to get him to commit himself to a course of action but he prevaricated* hedge, fence, beat about the bush, be evasive, shilly-shally, hum and haw, dodge the issue, dodge, sidestep the issue, sidestep, equivocate, quibble, tergiversate; *inf.* beg the question.

prevarication *noun* hedging, fencing, beating about the bush, evasion, evasiveness, shilly-shallying, humming and hawing, dodging, sidestepping, equivocation, quibbling, tergiversation. See PREVARICATE.

prevent *verb* **1** *prevent the spread of the fire | prevent further progress* stop, put a stop to, halt, arrest, avert, nip in the bud, fend off, turn aside, stave off, ward off, block, check, hinder, impede, hamper, obstruct, baulk, foil, thwart, frustrate, forestall, inhibit, hold back, restrain, prohibit, bar, deter. **2** *prevent his daughter from leaving school* stop, hinder, impede, hamper, obstruct, inhibit, hold back, restrain, prohibit, bar.
Opposites CAUSE; ENCOURAGE.

prevention *noun the prevention of the spread of the fire | the prevention of crime* stopping, halting, halt, arresting, staving off, warding off, checking, hindrance, hampering, obstruction, baulking, foiling, frustration, restraint, prohibition, barring, deterrence. See PREVENT 1.

preventive, preventative *adjective* **1** *preventive/preventative measures against crime* precautionary, protective, deterrent. **2** *preventive medicine* prophylactic, disease-preventing, precautionary, protective.

preventive, preventative *noun* **1** *a preventive/preventative against crime* preventive measure, precautionary/protective measure, safeguard, protection, deterrent, hindrance, obstruction. **2** *a preventive/preventative against disease* preventive, preventative drug, precautionary measure, prophylactic medicine, prophylactic device, prophylactic.

previous *adjective* **1** *the previous holder of the post* former, ex-, preceding, foregoing, past, sometime, one-time, quondam, erstwhile, antecedent, precursory. **2** *in previous paragraph* preceding, foregoing, earlier, prior, above, precursory, antecedent, anterior. **3** *on a previous occasion* prior, earlier, former, preceding. **4** *it was rather previous of him to assume he was in charge | you're rather previous in assuming you're in charge* premature, precipitate, hasty, overhasty, impetuous, too early, too soon, untimely, presumptuous; *inf.* ahead of oneself. **previous to** *previous to this everything was fine* before, prior to, until, up to, earlier than, preceding.
Opposites FOLLOWING; NEXT; CONSEQUENT.

previously adverb **1** *they now live locally but previously they lived in London* formerly, earlier on, before, until now, hitherto, heretofore, once, at one time, in the past, in years gone by. **2** *at that point he was a teacher but previously he had been in banking* formerly, earlier on, before, until then, once, at one time, in the past, in years gone by.

prey noun **1** *lions looking for prey* quarry, game, kill. **2** *a conman looking for prey | a prey for any dishonest salesman* victim, target, dupe; *inf.* sitting duck, sitting target, fall guy, mug.

prey verb **prey on 1** *lions preying on deer | hawks preying on small birds* live on, live off, eat, devour, hunt, catch, seize. **2** *unscrupulous conmen preying on old women* use as a victim, victimize, exploit, take advantage of, fleece, attack, terrorize, blackmail, bleed; *inf.* con. **3** *his crime preyed on his mind* weigh down on, weigh upon, weigh heavily on, lie heavy on, oppress, burden, be a burden on, hang over, trouble, worry, distress, haunt.

price noun **1** *what is the price of the table in the window? | with prices rising | charge a high price* cost, asking price, charge, fee, payment, rate, amount, figure, value, valuation, outlay, expenses, expenditure, bill. **2** *the price of breaking the law | being constantly photographed is the price that famous people have to pay* consequence, result, cost, penalty, sacrifice, forfeit, forfeiture, punishment. **3** *outlaws with a price on their heads* reward, bounty, premium, recompense, compensation. **at a price** *during the war most things were available on the black market—at a price* at a high price, at an expensive price, at a dear price, at a high cost, for a great deal of money, at considerable cost. **at any price** *they want that house at any price | the country wants peace at any price* whatever the price, whatever the cost, at whatever cost, no matter what the cost, no matter the cost, cost what it may, cost what it might, expense no object, regardless. **beyond price 1** *jewels/souvenirs beyond price* priceless, without price, of incalculable value, of incalculable worth, of inestimable value, invaluable, precious, rare, expensive, costly, irreplaceable, treasured, prized. See PRICELESS 1. **2** *a virtue beyond price* priceless, without price, of incalculable worth, of inestimable value, invaluable, precious, cherished. See PRICELESS 2.

price verb *price the items at £10 each* fix the price of, set the price of, cost, value, rate, evaluate, assess, estimate, appraise, assay.

priceless adjective **1** *priceless jewels* beyond price, without price, of incalculable value, of incalculable worth, of inestimable value, of inestimable worth, invaluable, precious, rare, incomparable, expensive, costly, rich, dear, irreplaceable, treasured, prized, worth its weight in gold, worth a king's ransom. **2** *honesty is a priceless virtue* beyond price, without price, of incalculable worth/value, of inestimable value/worth, invaluable, precious, rare, treasured, prized, cherished, worth its weight in gold, worth a king's ransom. **3** *his jokes are priceless* hilarious, extremely amusing, very funny, comic, riotous, side-splitting, rib-tickling; *inf.* killingly funny, a scream, a hoot.

4 *looking priceless in that hat* absurd, ridiculous, comical, hilarious, extremely amusing, very funny; *inf.* a scream, a hoot, killingly funny. **Opposites** WORTHLESS; CHEAP.

prick noun **1** *give his finger a prick with a sharp needle* jag, jab, stab, nick, wound. **2** *see the prick on the surface* puncture, perforation, hole, pinhole, nick, wound. **3** *feel a prick on the surface of the skin* prickle, sting, smarting, tingle, tingling, pain. **4** *the pricks of his conscience* pricking, pang, twinge, gnawing. **5** *a stick with a prick | rose-bushes with pricks* spike, thorn, barb, spine, prong, tine.

prick verb **1** *prick the balloon with a needle | prick the boil with a sterilized needle* pierce, puncture, perforate, make a hole in, put a hole in, stab, nick, gash, slit, bore, spike. **2** *she pricked her finger on a needle | thorns pricked her bare legs* jag, jab, stab, nick, wound. **3** *his eyes began to prick in the smoke* sting, smart, tingle. **4** *his conscience began to prick him* distress, cause distress to, trouble, worry, gnaw at, cause pain to. **5** *ambition pricked him on to greater effort* goad, prod, urge, spur, prompt, incite, push, propel.

prickle noun **1** *the prickles on the branches of the rose-tree* thorn, needle, barb, spike, point, spine, spur. **2** *feel a prickle on her skin* prickling sensation, tingle, tingling sensation, tingling, sting, stinging, smarting, itching, creeping sensation, goose-pimples, formication, paraesthesia, pins and needles.

prickle verb **1** *his scalp began to prickle* tingle, sting, smart, itch, have a creeping sensation, have goose-pimples, have pins and needles. **2** *the rough wool prickled his skin* make something, tingle, sting, make something smart, make something itch.

prickly adjective **1** *a prickly branch* spiky, spiked, thorny, barbed, bristly, spiny, pronged. **2** *a prickly feeling in his scalp* prickling, tingling, stinging, smarting, itching, itchy, creeping, crawling. **3** *the old man's rather a prickly character* cantankerous, irascible, irritable, bad-tempered, touchy, edgy, fractious, tetchy, peevish, grumpy, snappish, snappy; *inf.* ratty, stroppy, shirty. **4** *prickly issues | prickly problems* difficult, troublesome, vexatious, tough, complicated, complex, intricate, involved, knotty, thorny, ticklish, tricky.

pride noun **1** *his pride was hurt by her comments on his lack of ability* self-esteem, self-respect, ego, *amour propre*, self-worth, self-image, self-identity, feelings, sensibilities. **2** *guilty of pride | puffed with pride at his achievement* conceit, vanity, arrogance, haughtiness, self-importance, self-conceit, self-love, self-glorification, egotism, presumption, hauteur, superciliousness, disdain; *inf.* big-headedness, swollen-headedness. **3** *take/have pride in his work* satisfaction, gratification, pleasure, joy, delight. **4** *since she won the singing competition she is the pride of the school* pride and joy, prize, jewel, jewel in the crown, flower, gem, treasure, glory. **Opposites** MODESTY; HUMILITY.

pride verb **pride oneself on** *she prided herself on her punctuality* be proud of oneself for, take pride in, take satisfaction in, congratulate oneself on, flatter oneself on, preen oneself on, give oneself a pat on the back for, revel in, glory in, exult in, boast about, brag about, crow about.

priest *noun* clergyman, cleric, churchman, churchwoman, man/woman of the cloth, man/ woman of God, father, padre. *See table. See also table at* ECCLESIASTIC.

PRIESTS AND RELIGIOUS OFFICIALS

Arch Druid	guru	papaloi
Arch Druidess	haruspex	pongyi
	hazzan	priest
augur	hierophant	priestess
ayatollah	high priest	pundit
Brahman	houngan	purohita
Caliph	imam	qadi
chief rabbi	lama	qasisha
cohen	Levite	rabbi
Dalai Lama	mamaloi	rishi
dastur	muezzin	scribe
flamen	mullah	sheikh
Gosain	Panchen Lama	witch-doctor
Grand Lama		

---

prig *noun* prude, puritan, killjoy, Mrs Grundy, Grundy; *inf.* goody-goody, Goody Two-Shoes, holy Joe, holy Willie.

priggish *adjective* prudish, puritanical, prim, strait-laced, stuffy, starchy, self-righteous, sanctimonious, narrow-minded, censorious; *inf.* holier-than-thou, goody-goody, Grundyish.

prim *adjective too prim and proper to join in the fun of the party* proper, demure, formal, precise, stuffy, starchy, strait-laced, prudish, prissy, old-maidish, priggish, puritanical; *inf.* schoolmarmish, schoolmistressy.
Opposites INFORMAL; CAREFREE; LAID-BACK.

prima donna *noun* diva, leading lady, star.

primarily *adverb his role is primarily an administrative one* basically, essentially, in essence, fundamentally, in the first place, first and foremost, chiefly, mainly, in the main, principally, mostly, for the most part, on the whole, predominantly, predominately.

primary *adjective* **1** *the children's welfare is our primary consideration* prime, chief, main, principal, leading, predominant, most important, paramount. **2** *finding food to eat is a primary need* basic, fundamental, elemental, rudimentary, essential, prime. **3** *the primary stages of development | the primary stages of the disease* earliest, original, initial, beginning, first, opening, introductory. **4** *the primary stage of civilization* first, earliest, prehistoric, primitive, primeval, primal, primordial, autochthonal, pristine.
Opposites SECONDARY; SUBORDINATE.

prime *adjective* **1** *his prime motive was self-interest* chief, main, principal, leading, predominant, most important, major, paramount. **2** *the prime cause of the trouble* basic, fundamental, elemental, rudimentary, essential, primary. **3** *of prime quality | a prime site | prime meat* top-quality, highest, top, best, first-class, high-grade, grade A, superior, choice, select; *inf.*

A1. **4** *a prime example of what's wrong with modern society* classic, ideal, excellent, typical, standard.
Opposites MINOR; INFERIOR.

prime *noun* **1** *in the prime of his life* best part, peak, pinnacle, best days, height, zenith, acme, culmination, apex, heyday, full flowering. **2** *flowers in their prime* perfection, peak, full flowering, blossoming.

prime *verb* **1** *prime the machines for use* prepare, make ready, get ready, equip. **2** *prime the investigating officer* brief, give information to, inform, supply with facts; *inf.* clue in, clue up, give the low-down to, fill in, gen up. **3** *the solicitor was accused of priming the witness* instruct beforehand, coach, give information to, prepare. **4** *prime the travellers with food and drink* supply, provide, equip, furnish, provision, accommodate.

prime minister *noun See table.*

primeval *adjective primeval rocks* ancient, earliest, prehistoric, primitive, primordial, primal, autochthonal, pristine.

primitive *adjective* **1** *in primitive times | the primitive church* ancient, earliest, primeval, primordial, primal, autochthonal, pristine. **2** *primitive farming tools* crude, simple, rudimentary, undeveloped, unrefined, rough, unsophisticated, rude. **3** *primitive tribes* uncivilized, barbarian, barbaric, savage, wild. **4** *primitive art* simple, natural, unsophisticated, naive, undeveloped, childlike. **5** *primitive artists* unsophisticated, naive, untaught, untrained, untutored.
Opposites MODERN; ADVANCED; SOPHISTICATED.

primp *verb primp one's hair/clothes* groom, tidy, smarten, spruce, prink; *inf.* titivate. **primp oneself** groom oneself, tidy oneself up, smarten oneself up, spruce oneself up, preen oneself, prink, prink oneself up, plume oneself; *inf.* titivate oneself, doll oneself up, tart oneself up.

prince *verb the prince of a neighbouring state* ruler, lord, sovereign, potentate. *See table at* ROYALTY.

princely *adjective* **1** *a princely procession/array* regal, royal, stately, imposing, dignified, august, magnificent, majestic. **2** *give princely gifts | a princely sum of money* magnanimous, munificent, bounteous, bountiful, lavish, generous, open-handed, liberal.

principal *adjective* **1** *the principal members of the organization* chief, leading, pre-eminent, foremost, most important, most influential, dominant, controlling, ruling, in charge. **2** *the principal issues on the agenda | the principal points to be considered* chief, main, major, most important, leading, key, primary, prime, paramount. **3** *the principal cities of the world* capital, main, leading, major.
Opposites MINOR; SUBORDINATE; SUBSIDIARY.

principal *noun* **1** *the principals in the firm* chief, head, director, leader, manager, boss, ruler, controller; *inf.* honcho. **2** *the principal of the school* head teacher, headmaster, headmistress, head, rector. **3** *the principal of the college* head, master, dean, director, rector. **4** *the principals in the play* leading player, leading performer, leading man/lady, lead, star. **5** *lend him the* principal *to start up the firm* capital, capital sum, capital funds, working capital, financial resources.

principally *adverb he is interested principally in higher education* chiefly, above all, first and foremost, mainly, in the main, primarily, for the most part, mostly, particularly, especially.

principle *noun* **1** *the basic principles of geometry | understand the principles of monetarism* truth, philosophy, idea, theory, basis, fundamental, essence, assumption. **2** *believe in the principle of equal opportunity* rule, golden rule, law, canon, tenet, code, maxim, axiom, dictum, postulate. **3** *a woman of principle | a woman without principle* morals, ethics, integrity, uprightness, righteousness, probity, rectitude, sense of honour, honour, conscience, scruples. *See* PRINCIPLES. **in principle** **1** *there is no reason in principle why such a machine could not be built* in theory, theoretically. **2** *they agree in principle to the plan* in essence, in general.

principles *plural noun it is against his principles to lie | have no principles* moral code, code of ethics, code, morals, ethics, beliefs, credo. *See* PRINCIPLE 3.

print *verb* **1** *print books/newspapers* set in print, send to press, run off, put to bed. **2** *they have* printed thousands of copies publish, issue. **3** *print a design on the cloth* imprint, stamp, mark. **4** *events printed forever on her memory* imprint, impress, engrave, etch, stamp, mark.

print *noun* **1** *see the story in print | the print is too small to be legible* type, letters, lettering, typeface, newsprint. **2** *buy a print of one of Monet's works* copy, reproduction, replica. **3** *buy a set of prints showing the castles of Britain* picture, design, engraving, lithograph. **4** *get enlarged prints* photograph, photo, snap, snapshot. **5** *chairs covered in a print* printed material/cloth, patterned material/cloth, chintz. **6** *leave prints* fingerprint, footprint, mark, impression. **in print** **1** *she will believe it only if she sees it in print | likes to see his name in print* printed, in black and white, on paper. **2** *are her novels still in print?* published, printed, available in bookshops, obtainable in the shops, on the market. **out of print** *looking for a biography which is out of print* o.p., no longer published/printed, not on the market, unavailable, unobtainable.

printer *noun. See table.*

prior *adjective a prior claim | no prior knowledge required* earlier, previous, anterior. **prior to** *prior to the conference they had never met* before, until, up to, earlier than, preceding.
Opposites LATER.

PRIME MINISTERS OF THE U.K.

Prime minister	In Office	Prime minister	In Office
Sir Robert Walpole	1721–42	Viscount Palmerston	1859–65
Earl of Wilmington	1742–3	Earl Russell	1865–6
Henry Pelham	1743–54	Earl of Derby	1866–8
Duke of Newcastle	1954–6	Benjamin Disraeli	1868
Duke of Devonshire	1756–7	William Ewart Gladstone	1868–74
Duke of Newcastle	1757–62	Benjamin Disraeli	1874–80
Earl of Bute	1762–3	William Ewart Gladstone	1880–5
George Grenville	1763–5	Marquis of Salisbury	1885–6
Marquis of Rockingham	1765–6	William Ewart Gladstone	1886
Earl of Chatham	1766–8	Marquis of Salisbury	1886–92
Duke of Grafton	1768–70	William Ewart Gladstone	1892–4
Lord North	1770–82	Earl of Rosebery	1894–5
Marquis of Rockingham	1782	Marquis of Salisbury	1895–1902
Earl of Shelburne	1782–3	Arthur James Balfour	1902–5
Duke of Portland	1783	Sir Henry Campbell-Bannerman	1905–8
William Pitt	1783–1801	Herbert Henry Asquith	1908–16
Henry Addington	1801–4	David Lloyd George	1916–22
William Pitt	1804–7	Andrew Bonar Law	1922–3
Lord William Grenville	1806–7	Stanley Baldwin	1923–4
Duke of Portland	1807–9	James Ramsay MacDonald	1924
Spencer Perceval	1809–12	Stanley Baldwin	1924–9
Earl of Liverpool	1812–27	James Ramsay MacDonald	1929–35
George Canning	1827	Stanley Baldwin	1935–7
Viscount Goderich	1827–8	Neville Chamberlain	1937–40
Duke of Wellington	1828–30	Winston Spencer Churchill	1940–5
Earl Grey	1830–4	Clement Attlee	1945–51
Viscount Melbourne	1834	Sir Winston Spencer Churchill	1951–5
Duke of Wellington	1834	Sir Anthony Eden	1955–7
Sir Robert Peel	1834–5	Harold Macmillan	1957–63
Viscount Melbourne	1835–41	Sir Alec Douglas-Home	1963–4
Sir Robert Peel	1841–6	Harold Wilson	1964–70
Lord John Russell	1846–52	Edward Heath	1970–4
Earl of Derby	1852	Harold Wilson	1974–6
Earl of Aberdeen	1852–5	James Callaghan	1976–9
Viscount Palmerston	1855–8	Margaret Thatcher	1979–90
Earl of Derby	1858–9	John Major	from 1990

priority noun **1** *making sure the children are safe must be their priority* | *decide on a list of priorities* first/prime concern, most important thing/act, most pressing thing/act. **2** *give priority to homeless people* precedence, preference, urgency, highest place, top place. **3** *in terms of length of service he has priority* precedence, seniority, superiority, supremacy, paramountcy, prerogative. **4** *drive on—you have priority* right of way.

priory noun religious house, abbey, cloister, monastery, friary, convent, nunnery.

prise verb *prise the lid off* lever, force, pull; *inf.* yank; *Am.* pry.

prison noun jail, gaol, lock-up, penal institution, place of detention, place of confinement, dungeon; *inf.* clink, nick, cooler, quod, slammer, choky, stir, can, jug; *Am.* penitentiary; *Am. inf.* pen.

prisoner noun **1** *prisoners let out on parole* convict, jailbird; *inf.* con, lag, lifer. **2** *the kidnappers refused to release their prisoner* | *the invading army took many prisoners* prisoner of war, POW, hostage, captive, detainee, internee.

pristine adjective **1** *a pristine copy of the book* unmarked, unblemished, unspoilt, spotless, immaculate, clean, in mint condition, in perfect condition. **2** *pristine snow* unmarked, spotless, clean, fresh, virgin. **3** *remains of some pristine era* early, ancient, prehistoric, primeval, primordial, primal, primitive, autochthonal.

privacy noun **1** *enjoy the privacy of his study* | *the privacy of their walled garden* privateness, seclusion, solitude, isolation, retirement, sequestration, quietness, peace, lack of disturbance, lack of interruption, freedom from interference. **2** *accuse the press of invading her privacy* right to privacy, right to privateness, privateness, freedom from interference.

private adjective **1** *for her private use* personal, individual, own, particular, especial, special, exclusive. **2** *hold private talks* | *her private opinion* confidential, strictly confidential, not for publication, not to be made public, not to be disclosed, secret, unofficial, off-the-record, in camera, closet, privileged; *inf.* hush-hush. **3** *her private thoughts* personal, intimate, secret. **4** *a private place where the lovers meet* secluded, sequestered, quiet, secret, remote, out-of-the-way, withdrawn, retired. **5** *trespassing on private property* not open to the public, privately-owned, off-limits. **6** *wish to be private* undisturbed, without disturbance, uninterrupted, without interruption, alone, solitary. **7** *a private person* reserved, retiring, self-contained, uncommunicative, non-communicative, non-committal, diffident, secretive. **8** *the queen on a private visit* non-official, unofficial, non-

public, personal. **9** *private industry/education/medicine* non-state-controlled, non-state, private-enterprise, privatized, independent. **Opposites** PUBLIC; OPEN; GENERAL; SOCIABLE.

private noun *privates in the British army* private soldier, infantryman; *Am.* enlisted man; *inf.* Tommy, squaddie. **in private** *the talks were held in private* | *the legal case was heard in private* privately, in camera, in secret, secretly, in secrecy, behind closed doors, in confidence, confidentially, *sub rosa*.

privately adverb **1** *the talks were held privately* in private, in camera, in secret, behind closed doors. See PRIVATE noun, IN PRIVATE. **2** *privately she thought he was doing the wrong thing* personally, secretly, unofficially. **3** *they required somewhere to meet privately* out of public view, in seclusion, in solitude, alone, without being disturbed, without being interrupted.

privation noun *children suffering a life of privation* deprivation, want, need, neediness, disadvantage, poverty, penury, hardship, distress, indigence, destitution.

privilege noun **1** *parking in that area is the privilege of local residents* right, birthright, prerogative, entitlement, due, sanction, advantage, benefit. **2** *enjoy parliamentary privilege* immunity, exemption, dispensation, concession, liberty, freedom. **3** *has always led a life of privilege* advantage, social advantage, advantageousness, favour, favourable circumstances, superior situation. **4** *he felt that it had been a privilege to meet her* honour, special benefit.

privileged adjective **1** *coming from a privileged background* advantaged, socially advantaged, favoured, élite, indulgent, spoilt, protected, sheltered. **2** *that is certainly the law but MPs are privileged* immune, exempt, excepted. **3** *punished for revealing privileged information* confidential, private, not for publication, off-the-record, secret, top secret; *inf.* hush-hush.

privy adjective **privy to** *not privy to the plans of management* acquainted with, aware of, in on, informed of, apprised of, cognizant of; *inf.* in the know about, genned up on, clued in on.

prize noun **1** *win a prize in the lottery* winnings, jackpot, stakes, purse. **2** *win first prize in the track race* | *get second prize in the horticultural competition* trophy, medal, award, accolade, reward, premium, honour, laurels, palm, bays. **3** *he is studying for further qualifications with a higher salary* the prize goal, aim, desire, hope. **4** *the prizes of war* spoils, booty, plunder, loot, pillage, pickings, trophy, capture.

prize adjective *wind destroyed his prize roses* prize-winning, award-winning, winning, champion,

PRINTERS

bubble-jet printer	electrostatic printer	matrix printer
colour laser printer	golfball printer	parallel printer
colour printer	ink-jet printer	phase-change wax
daisywheel printer	ionographic printer	printer
dot-matrix printer	laser printer	serial printer
dye-sublimation printer	letter-quality printer	thermal ink jet printer
electrophotographic printer	line printer	thermal wax printer

best, top, choice, select, first-class, first-rate, excellent; *inf.* top-notch, A1.

prize *verb prize his few remaining possessions | she prizes his freedom* value, set a high value on, set great store by, treasure, cherish, hold dear, appreciate greatly, attach great importance to, esteem, hold in high regard.

prized *adjective have his prized stamp collection stolen* valued, treasured, cherished, precious, beloved.

probability *noun* **1** *what is the probability of the government losing the election? | there is little probability that we will be able to go* likelihood, likeliness, prospect, expectation, chance, chances, odds, possibility. **2** *snow at Christmas is a distinct probability* probable event, likelihood, prospect, possibility, reasonable bet.

probable *adjective the probable result is a win for the home team | it is probable that we will arrive late* likely, most likely, odds-on, expected, to be expected, anticipated, predictable, forseeable, on the cards, credible, quite possible, possible. **Opposites** IMPROBABLE; UNLIKELY.

probably *adverb they will probably win* in all probability, likely, most likely, in all likelihood, as likely as not, it is to be expected that, perhaps, maybe, it may be, possibly; *inf.* as like as not; *lit.* peradventure.

probation *noun new trainees must do a three-month period of probation* trial, trial period, test period, try-out, experimental period. **on probation** **1** *young offenders on probation* under official supervision. **2** *trainees on probation* on trial, on a trial period.

probe *noun order a probe into the company's accounting procedures* investigation, scrutiny, scrutinization, close inquiry, inquest, exploration, examination, study, research, analysis.

probe *verb* **1** *probing the patient's stomach looking for a lump | probe the tooth with his tongue* feel, feel around, prod, poke, explore, check. **2** *probe the financial state of the company* investigate, conduct an investigation into, scrutinize, inquire into, conduct, an inquiry into, carry out an inquest into, examine, subject to an examination, study, research, analyse.

problem *noun* **1** *face a seemingly impossible problem* difficulty, difficult situation, vexed question, complication, trouble, mess, predicament, plight, dilemma, quandary; *inf.* pickle, can of worms, facer. **2** *he has business problems | the car's mechanical problems* difficulty, difficult situation, trouble, complication. **3** *he and his wife have had a few problems* difficulty, dispute, subject of dispute, point at issue, bone of contention. **4** *solve the arithmetical problems | be baffled by the word problems* question, puzzle, poser, enigma, riddle, conundrum; *inf.* teaser, brain-teaser. **5** *the child's a real problem* source of trouble, source of difficulty, bother, pest, nuisance, vexation; *inf.* hassle, aggravation.

problem *adjective a problem child* difficult, troublesome, delinquent, unmanageable, unruly, uncontrollable, intractable, recalcitrant, nuisance.

problematic *adjective* **1** *a problematic situation* problematical, difficult, troublesome, complicated, puzzling, knotty, thorny, ticklish, tricky; *inf.* dodgy. **2** *the likely result is still problematic* doutful, open to doubt, uncertain, unsettled, questionable, open to question, debatable, arguable.
Opposites SIMPLE; STRAIGHTFORWARD; CERTAIN.

procedure *noun* **1** *the usual office procedure | pay due attention to procedure* course of action, line of action, plan of action, policy, system, method, methodology, *modus operandi*, technique, means, practice, operation, strategy, way, routine, wont, custom. **2** *essential procedures for setting up the new system* action, step, process, measure, move, operation, transaction.

proceed *verb* **1** *proceed along the platform with all possible haste | proceed upstairs slowly* make one's way, go, go on, go forward, go ahead, advance, carry on, move on, press on, progress. **2** *proceed to question him | how shall we proceed?* act, take action, take steps, take measures, go ahead, move, make a start, progress, get under way. **3** *noise proceeding from the floor below | the tragedy that proceeded from a family feud* arise, originate, spring, stem, come, derive, result, follow, ensue, emanate, issue, flow. **proceed against** *he decided to proceed against his employers for unfair dismissal* take proceedings against, begin an action against, start an action against, take to court, sue. **proceed with** *proceed with their work* go on with, continue with, continue, get on with, get ahead with.

proceeding *noun such a proceeding will have to be carefully considered* action, course of action, step, measure, move, manoeuvre, act, deed, operation, transaction, venture, procedure, process.

proceedings *plural noun* **1** *the evening's proceedings begin at 7 p.m. | the prize-giving proceedings were interrupted by someone fainting* activities, events, action, process, business, affairs, doings, happenings. **2** *the proceedings against him are likely to last several weeks* legal proceedings, legal action/case, case, lawsuit, litigation, trial. **3** *the proceedings of the meeting were made available to all society members* minutes, report, account, record, transactions.

proceeds *plural noun donate the proceeds of/from the fête to charity* takings, profits, returns, receipts, gain, income, earnings.

process *noun* **1** *damaged during the manufacturing process* operation, action, activity, steps, stages. **2** *develop a new process for cleaning old stone buildings* method, system, technique, means, practice, way, procedure. **3** *the ageing process* development, evolution, changes, stages, steps. **4** *in the process of time* course, advance, progress. **5** *legal processes can be very slow* proceedings, legal action, legal case, case, lawsuit, trial. **in the process of** *we are in the process of cataloguing our books* in the midst of, in the course of, in the performance of, in the execution of, at the stage of.

procession *noun* **1** *a torchlight procession as part of the town's centenary celebration* parade, march, column, file, train, cortège. **2** *a proces-*

sion of decorated lorries cavalcade, motorcade. **3** *a seemingly endless procession of house-guests* stream, steady stream, string, succession, series, sequence, run.

proclaim *verb* **1** *proclaim the news of a royal birth | proclaim a public holiday* announce, declare, make known, give out, notify, circulate, advertise, publish, broadcast, promulgate, pronounce, blazon, trumpet, shout something from the rooftops. **2** *proclaim him king* pronounce, announce, declare someone to be. **3** *her accent proclaimed that she was French* indicate, show, reveal, testify.

proclamation *noun* **1** *hear the proclamation of a royal birth* announcement, declaration, notification, circulation, advertisement, publishing, broadcasting, promulgation, pronouncement, blazoning. *See* PROCLAIM 1. **2** *the king's proclamation was posted in each town* announcement, declaration, pronouncement, decree, edict, order, command, rule, manifesto.

proclivity *noun* *a proclivity towards outbursts of rage | have peculiar sexual proclivities* tendency, inclination, leaning, propensity, bent, bias, proneness, penchant, predisposition, weakness.

procrastinate *verb* *procrastinate in the hope that someone else would do the work* delay, postpone action, defer action, be dilatory, use delaying tactics, stall, temporize, play for time, play the waiting game, dally, dilly-dally, drag one's feet/heels.

procreation *noun* *marriage regarded as being purely for procreation* sexual reproduction, generation, propagation, multiplication.

procure *verb* **1** *procure a copy of the book from the library* obtain, acquire, get, pick up, find, come by, get hold of, secure, get possession of, lay one's hands on, get one's hands on, gain. **2** *somehow procure the dismissal of his colleague* bring about, cause, contrive, manage, manipulate, rig; *inf.* fix. **3** *the police found that he was procuring* pimp, pander.

prod *verb* **1** *prod him in the ribs when pushing past* poke, jab, dig, nudge, elbow, butt, push, shove, thrust. **2** *try to prod the child into doing some work* urge, encourage, rouse, move, motivate, stimulate, incite, spur on, impel, actuate, goad.

prod *noun* **1** *get a prod in the ribs from someone in the crowd* poke, jab, dig, nudge, elbow, butt, push, shove, thrust. **2** *use a prod to get the cows to go back to the farm* goad, stick, spike. **3** *giving the child a prod to get him to do some work* encouragement, prompting, prompt, motivation, stimulus, incitement, spur, goad.

prodigal *adjective* **1** *a government accused of being prodigal | her prodigal catering* extravagant, spendthrift, squandering, improvident, imprudent, immoderate, profligate, excessive, wasteful, reckless, wanton. **2** *a philanthropist prodigal of his gifts to the poor | prodigal of compliments* lavish with, liberal with, generous with, bountiful with, bounteous with, abundant in, abounding in.
Opposites THRIFTY; FRUGAL; MEAN.

prodigious *adjective* **1** *a prodigious achievement* amazing, astonishing, astounding, staggering, stupendous, marvellous, wonderful, phenomenal, miraculous, impressive, striking, startling, extraordinary, remarkable, exceptional, unusual; *inf.* fantastic, fabulous, flabbergasting. **2** *children frightened by the prodigious creatures on the screen* enormous, huge, colossal, gigantic, giant, mammoth, immense, massive, vast, monumental, tremendous, inordinate, monstrous, grotesque, abnormal. **3** *charge a prodigious amount of money* huge, large, colossal, immense, massive, considerable, substantial, sizeable; *inf.* vast, tremendous.
Opposites ORDINARY; UNEXCEPTIONAL; NORMAL; TINY.

prodigy *noun* **1** *the child musician is a prodigy* genius, child genius, wonder child, wunderkind, gifted child, mastermind; *inf.* Einstein. **2** *the pyramids are among the prodigies of the world* wonder, marvel, phenomenon, sensation, miracle. **3** *the saint is a prodigy of patience* classic example, example, model, paragon, paradigm, epitome, exemplar, ideal.

produce *verb* **1** *a country which produces more goods than it can sell | a factory producing high-quality work* make, manufacture, create, construct, build, fabricate, put together, assemble, turn out. **2** *produce great works of art* compose, create, originate, prepare, develop, frame, fashion, turn out. **3** *produce new evidence* bring forward, set forth, present, offer, proffer, advance, show, exhibit, demonstrate, disclose, reveal. **4** *soil producing good crops | cows producing very little milk* yield, bear, give, bring forth, supply, provide, furnish. **5** *sows producing large litters of piglets* give birth to, bring forth, bear, breed, give life to, bring into the world, procreate. **6** *his speech produced an angry reaction* cause, give rise to, evoke, bring about, set off, occasion, generate, engender, induce, initiate, start, spark off. **7** *produce plays for television* mount, stage, put on, present, direct.

produce *noun* *organically-grown produce* crops, fruit and vegetables, fruit, vegetables, greengrocery, greens.

producer *noun* **1** *a country which is a major producer of cars | a factory noted as a producer of high-quality work* maker, manufacturer, creator, builder. *See* PRODUCE *verb* 1. **2** *producers of fine fruit and vegetables* grower, farmer. **3** *the producer of several major films* backer, impresario, casting-director, schedule-director; *inf.* angel. **4** *a producer of television/radio/amateur plays* director, stage-manager.

product *noun* **1** *a factory specializing in electronic products* commodity, artefact, manufactured item/article/thing. **2** *necessary for the firm to improve the image of its product* goods, wares, merchandise. **3** *good health is the product of good nutrition | he is a typical product of a Victorian upbringing* result, outcome, effect, consequence, upshot, fruit, spin-off, legacy.

production *noun* **1** *speed up the production of cars* producing, making, manufacture, manufacturing, creation, construction, building, fabrication, assembly. **2** *his production of great works of literature/work* composition, creation, origination, preparation, development, framing, fashioning. **3** *the production of new evidence* presenting, offering, proffering, advancement, exhibition, demonstration, disclosure. *See* PRO-DUCE *verb* 3. **4** *there has been a fall/increase in production* output, yield. **5** *go and see a production of Hamlet in modern dress* performance, staging, mounting. **6** *several productions staged by the company* play, film, concert, show, performance, presentation, piece. **7** *this is the writer's latest production* work, publication, book, volume, tome, novel, story, composition, piece, creation, opus. **8** *artist's latest production* work, work of art, painting, picture, piece, creation.

productive *adjective* **1** *productive soil* fertile, fruitful, fecund, rich, high-yielding. **2** *a productive worker* prolific, energetic, vigorous, efficient. **3** *not a very productive day's work* profitable, gainful, valuable, fruitful, useful, constructive, effective, worthwhile, beneficial, rewarding. **4** *an attitude scarcely productive of good labour relations* producing, causing, resulting in.
Opposites STERILE; BARREN; UNPRODUCTIVE.

productivity *noun* **1** *the productivity of the soil* productiveness, fertility, fecundity, fruitfulness, richness. **2** *improve the productivity of the workers/factory* productiveness, work-rate, output, yield, production, capacity, efficiency.

profane *adjective* **1** *their profane behaviour in setting fire to the altar* blasphemous, sacrilegious, impious, idolatrous, irreligious, ungodly, godless, irreverent, disrespectful. **2** *old ladies shocked by the man's profane language* blasphemous, obscene, foul, vulgar, crude, filthy, coarse. **3** *profane, not church music* lay, secular, non-religious, temporal, worldly.
Opposites RELIGIOUS; SACRED; DECOROUS.

profanity *noun* **1** *the profanity of drinking and brawling in church* profaneness, blasphemy, sacrilege, impiety, idolatry, irreligiousness, irreverence, disrespectfulness, disrespect. **2** *issue a stream of profanities* oath, swear-word, swearing, obscenity, four-letter word, curse, execration, imprecation.

profess *verb* **1** *profess satisfaction with his work* declare, announce, proclaim, assert, state, utter, affirm, avow, aver. **2** *professed undying love | he professed total ignorance of the situation but no one believed him* claim, lay claim to, allege, pretend, feign, make out, sham, fake, dissemble. **3** *profess one's Christian faith* declare publicly, make a public declaration of, avow, confess, confirm, declare one's allegiance to, acknowledge publicly.

professed *adjective* **1** *see through her professed love for children | deserted by her professed supporters* claimed, alleged, ostensible, supposed, so-called, pretended, feigned, sham, fake, would-be. **2** *he is a professed Christian/pacifist* declared, avowed, confessed, self-confessed, self-acknowledged, confirmed.

profession *noun* **1** *a teacher by profession | seek a profession in medicine* career, calling, vocation, occupation, line of work, line of employment, position, situation, post, job, office, appointment, métier. **2** *in the medical/legal profession* sphere of work, line of work, area of work, walk of life, business. **3** *they were relieved by his*

professions of satisfaction with their work declaration, announcement, proclamation, assertion, statement, affirmation, avowal, averment. **4** *were not taken in by his profession of ignorance | believed his profession of undying love* claim, allegation, pretence, feigning, shamming, faking, dissembling. **5** *his profession of his Christian faith* declaration, public declaration, avowal, confession, public acknowledgement, testimony.

professional *adjective* **1** *he is a professional man* white-collar. **2** *a very professional worker* skilled, skilful, proficient, expert, adept, competent, efficient, experienced. **3** *a very professional piece of work | such a professional performance* skilful, expert, adept, masterly, excellent, fine, polished, finished. **4** *a professional tennis player* non-amateur, paid. **5** *conduct that was hardly professional* ethical, fitting.
Opposites MANUAL; INEPT; AMATEURISH.

professional *noun* **1** *accommodation sought for young professionals* professional worker, white-collar worker. **2** *this tennis player is a professional now* professional player, non-amateur, paid player. **3** *the singer/tailor is a real professional* expert, skilled person, master, past master, adept, authority; *inf.* pro, dab hand.

professor *noun* **1** *professor of French at the local university* head of faculty, head of department, holder of a chair, chair, Regius professor. **2** *encouraged by the professors of satisfaction* declarer, proclaimer, asserter. *See* PROFESS 1. **3** *not deceived by the professors of total loyalty* claimant, alleger, pretender, dissembler. *See* PROFESS 2.

proffer *verb* *proffer assistance | decide to proffer one's resignation* offer, tender, present, extend, give, submit, volunteer, suggest.
Opposites REFUSE; WITHDRAW.

proficiency *noun* *their proficiency in keyboarding | acquired proficiency in the art of public speaking* skill, skilfulness, adeptness, aptness, expertise, expertness, adroitness, deftness, excellence, ability, ableness, capability, competence, experience, effectiveness, accomplishment, talent.

proficient *adjective* *a proficient keyboarder/swimmer | proficient at swimming | proficient in French* skilful (at), skilled (at/in), adept (at/in), apt (at), expert (at/in), adroit (at/in), deft (at), able (at), capable (at), competent (at/in), experienced (in/at), effective (at), accomplished (in/at), talented (at), gifted (at/in).
Opposites INEPT; INEXPERT; INCOMPETENT.

profile *noun* **1** *draw her profile | look better in profile* side-view, outline. **2** *the profile of the church against the sky* silhouette, outline, contour, lines, shape, form, figure. **3** *write a profile of the winner of the Booker prize* short biography, potted biography, sketch, thumbnail sketch, portrait, vignette.

profit *noun* **1** *the profit made from the sale of the house | the builder's annual profit* takings, proceeds, gain, yield, return, receipts, income, earnings, winnings. **2** *you could, with profit, take her advice | seem to gain little profit from the experience* gain, benefit, advantage, good, value,

use, avail.
Opposites LOSS; DISADVANTAGE.

profit verb it will not profit you to be openly critical of the firm benefit, be of benefit to, be of advantage to, be advantageous to, be of use/value to, be of service to, serve, do someone good, help, be helpful to, assist, aid, stand someone in good stead. **profit from** profit from his advice | try to profit from the experience derive benefit from, benefit from, reap the benefit of, gain from, derive advantage from, put to good use, learn from; inf. cash in on.

profitable adjective **1** a profitable venture profit-making, money-making, commercial, gainful, remunerative, paying, lucrative. **2** a profitable company profit-making, money-making, sound, solvent, in the black. **3** find it a profitable experience | think the conference profitable beneficial, advantageous, rewarding, helpful, productive, useful, worthwhile, valuable.

profligacy noun **1** the profligacy of her housekeeping | the profligacy of people who are always in debt extravagance, improvidence, prodigality, immoderateness, recklessness, wastefulness. See PROFLIGATE adjective 1. **2** tired of her husband's profligacy dissoluteness, dissipation, debauchery, corruption, degeneracy, depravity, immorality, promiscuity, looseness, wantonness, licentiousness, lasciviousness, lechery.

profligate adjective **1** a profligate housekeeper | a profligate young woman who is always in debt extravagant, spendthrift, improvident, prodigal, immoderate, squandering, reckless, wasteful. **2** a profligate cad dissolute, dissipated, debauched, abandoned, corrupt, degenerate, depraved, reprobate, unprincipled, immoral, promiscuous, loose, wanton, licentious, lascivious, lecherous.
Opposites THRIFTY; FRUGAL; MORAL.

profligate noun **1** the profligate soon got through his inheritance spendthrift, prodigal, squanderer, wastrel, waster. **2** he was a real profligate but he has reformed debauchee, degenerate, reprobate, roué, lecher.

profound adjective **1** a profound treatise/thinker discerning, penetrating, thoughtful, philosophical, deep, weighty, serious, learned, erudite, wise, sagacious. **2** unable to understand such profound doctrine learned, erudite, serious, deep, difficult, complex, abstract, abstruse, esoteric, impenetrable. **3** a profound love for his country deep, intense, keen, great, extreme, sincere, heartfelt. **4** a profound silence deep, pronounced, total, absolute, complete, utter. **5** profound changes taking place far-reaching, radical, extensive, exhaustive, thoroughgoing.
Opposites SHALLOW; SUPERFICIAL; SLIGHT.

profoundly adverb **1** speak very profoundly on the poet's philosophy discerningly, penetratingly, thoughtfully, philosophically, weightily, seriously, learnedly, eruditely, wisely, sagaciously. **2** profoundly disturbed by the news deeply, extremely, greatly, very, thoroughly, intensely, keenly, sincerely.

profuse adjective **1** give profuse apologies/thanks lavish, liberal, unstinting, generous, fulsome, extravagant, inordinate, immoderate, excessive. **2** a profuse harvest | profuse blossom on the trees abundant, copious, ample, plentiful, bountiful, luxuriant.
Opposites MEAGRE; SPARSE.

profusion noun a profusion of roses on the bushes abundance, superabundance, copiousness, quantities, scores, masses, multitude, plethora, wealth, plenitude, cornucopia; inf. heaps, stacks, piles, loads, mountains, tons, oodles.

progeny noun **1** the parents and all their progeny sitting round the table children, offspring, young ones, family, issue. **2** the progeny of William the Conqueror descendants, successors, lineage, scions, seed, posterity.

programme noun **1** what's on the programme for the first day of the conference? agenda, calendar, schedule, syllabus, list of events, order of the day. **2** buy a programme at the theatre list of performers, list of players, list of artistes. **3** the orchestra played a varied programme list of items, series of items. **4** watch several television programmes | listen to a radio programme production, presentation, show, performance, broadcast. **5** get the programme for the session's academic courses syllabus, prospectus, schedule, list, curriculum, literature. **6** organize a programme of financial investment schedule, scheme, plan, plan of action, project.

programme verb **1** a school trip programmed for next week schedule, plan, line up, map out, arrange, prearrange, organize. **2** programme the heating to come on at dawn set, fix, arrange.

progress noun **1** climbers making rapid progress towards the summit | drivers making slow progress on the icy roads forward movement, headway, advance, going, passage, advancement, advance, progression. **2** the company has made very little progress in the past few years advance, advancement, headway, steps forward, progression, improvement, betterment, upgrading, development, growth. **in progress** work in progress under way, going on, ongoing, happening, occurring, taking place, proceeding, being done, being performed.

progress verb **1** the climbers progressed up the mountain go forward, move forward/on, make one's way, advance, go on, continue, proceed, make progress, make headway, push forward, go/forge ahead. **2** the talks are progressing | science progresses all the time make progress, move forward, advance, make headway, take steps forward, make strides, develop, get better, improve. **3** the patient is progressing make progress, get better, improve, recover, recuperate.
Opposites RETURN; REGRESS; DETERIORATE.

progression noun **1** the progression from primary to secondary school | the progression from tea-boy to managing director progress, forward movement, upward movement, passage, advancement, advance, development. **2** a progression of unsuitable applicants | had a progression of dreary jobs succession, sequence, series, string, stream, steady stream, parade, chain, train.

progressive *adjective* **1** *progressive movement* forward, onward, advancing. **2** *a progressive improvement in the crime rate | a progressive amount of violence on the streets | a progressive disease* increasing, growing, intensifying, accelerating, escalating. **3** *a progressive firm | a progressive office system* modern, advanced, forward-looking, forward-thinking, go-ahead, enlightened, enterprising, up-and-coming, innovative, avant-garde. **4** *progressive ideas on education | progressive political views* radical, reforming, innovative, revolutionary, revisionist.
Opposites CONSERVATIVE; REACTIONARY.

prohibit *verb* **1** *a regulation to prohibit smoking in hospitals* forbid, ban, bar, disallow, proscribe, veto, interdict, outlaw. **2** *low salaries prohibit them from buying a house | the high cost of the medicine prohibits its universal use* prevent, stop, rule out, preclude, make impossible, hinder, impede, hamper, obstruct, restrict, constrain.
Opposites ALLOW; AUTHORIZE; FACILITATE.

prohibition *noun* **1** *vote for the prohibition of smoking in hospitals* forbidding, banning, barring, disallowing, proscription, vetoing, interdiction, outlawing. **2** *introduce a prohibition on the sale of cigarettes to children* ban, bar, interdict, veto, embargo, injunction, proscription.

prohibitive *adjective* **1** *introduce prohibitive measures on the employment of children* prohibitory, forbidding, banning, barring, disallowing, proscriptive, restrictive, suppressive, vetoing, interdicting, outlawing. **2** *the prohibitive cost of housing in that area of the city* exorbitant, extortionate, excessive, preposterous, high-priced, high-cost, sky-high; *inf.* steep.

project *noun* *a local authority project to build a community hall | initiate a project to conserve the environment* scheme, plan, programme, enterprise, undertaking, venture, activity, operation, campaign.

project *verb* **1** *they are projecting a visit to India | a projected new cinema complex* plan, propose, map out, devise, design, outline. **2** *project missiles into space* launch, discharge, propel, hurl, throw, cast, fling, shoot. **3** *a balcony that projects over the garden* jut, jut out, protrude, extend, stick out, stand out, hang over, bulge out, beetle, obtrude. **4** *project sales figures for next year* extrapolate, calculate, estimate, gauge, reckon, forecast, predict, predetermine.

projectile *noun* missile, rocket, shell, grenade, bullet. *See tables at* BULLET, MISSILE.

projection *noun* **1** *a projection of rock* overhang, ledge, shelf, ridge, protuberance, protrusion, jut, bulge. **2** *their sales projection for next year* extrapolation, calculation, computation, estimate, estimation, gauge, reckoning, forecast, prediction.

proletariat *noun* workers, working class, wage-earners, labouring classes, the common people, the ordinary people, the commonalty, lower classes, lower orders, the rank and file, the masses, the mob, the rabble, the *hoi polloi*; *inf.* the plebs, the proles, the great unwashed.
Opposites ARISTOCRACY; NOBILITY.

proliferate *verb* *the number of houses in the area has proliferated beyond belief* increase, grow rapidly, multiply, extend, expand, burgeon, accelerate, escalate, rocket, snowball, mushroom.
Opposites DECREASE; DWINDLE.

proliferation *noun* *the proliferation of new houses in the area* increase, growth, multiplication, spread, expansion, extension, burgeoning, acceleration, escalation, build-up, rocketing, snowballing, mushrooming.

prolific *adjective* **1** *prolific vegetation* fertile, fruitful, fecund, luxuriant, abundant, profuse, copious, rank. **2** *a prolific writer* productive.

prolix *adjective* over-long, lengthy, long-winded, long-drawn-out, prolonged, protracted, verbose, wordy, discursive, digressive, rambling, wandering, circuitous, ambagious, pleonastic.

prologue *noun* *the prologue to the play/poem/novel* introduction, foreword, preface, preamble, prelude, preliminary, exordium, proem, prolegomenon.
Opposites EPILOGUE.

prolong *verb* *mechanical problems with the car prolonged the journey by three hours* lengthen, make longer, elongate, extend, stretch out, draw out, drag out, protract, spin out.

prominence *noun* **1** *the prominence of her cheek-bones/eyes* protruding, protrusion, protuberance, protrusiveness, jutting out, standing out. *See* PROMINENT 1. **2** *a prominence on the flat countryside* protuberance, projection, jutting, swelling, bulge. **3** *a prominence overhanging the beach* promontory, pinnacle, projection, height, crest, cliff, crag. **4** *the prominence of the tower on the skyline* conspicuousness, obviousness, obtrusiveness. *See* PROMINENT 2. **5** *newspapers giving prominence to the political scandal* importance, weight, conspicuousness, precedence, top billing. **6** *men of prominence in the community* importance, eminence, pre-eminence, distinction, note, prestige, stature, illustriousness, celebrity, fame, renown, acclaim.

prominent *adjective* **1** *prominent cheek-bones/eyes* protruding, protuberant, protrusive, jutting, jutting out, projecting, standing out, sticking out, bulging. **2** *a prominent feature of the landscape* easily seen, conspicuous, noticeable, obvious, unmistakable, obtrusive, eye-catching, striking. **3** *a prominent member of the local community* leading, outstanding, chief, foremost, main, top, important, eminent, pre-eminent, distinguished, notable, noted, illustrious, celebrated, well-known, famous, renowned, acclaimed.
Opposites INCONSPICUOUS; OBSCURE.

promiscuity *noun* promiscuousness, dissoluteness, dissipation, licentiousness, looseness, profligacy, immorality, debauchery, wantonness.

promiscuous *adjective* *promiscuous people contracting sexually-transmitted diseases* sexually indiscriminating, dissolute, dissipated, fast, licentious, loose, profligate, abandoned, immoral, debauched, wanton, of easy

virtue, unchaste.
Opposites CHASTE; MORAL; PURE.

promise verb **1** *promise that he will be present* |
promise to go | *but you promised* give one's word
(that), give an undertaking (that/to), give one's
assurance (that), swear (that/to), vow that/to,
take an oath (that/to), pledge that/to, contract
that/to. **2** *skies which promise good weather* | *it
promises well for him that he has got an interview*
augur, indicate, denote, signify, be a sign of,
show signs of, hint at, suggest, betoken,
presage.

promise noun **1** *give a promise that he would be
there* word, word of honour, undertaking,
assurance, guarantee, commitment, vow, oath,
pledge, bond, contract, covenant. **2** *a promise
of spring in the air* indication, hint, suggestion,
sign. **3** *a young musician of promise* talent,
potential, flair, ability, aptitude, capability,
capacity.

promising adjective **1** *their first reactions to the
scheme are promising* | *it is promising that you have
a second interview* encouraging, hopeful,
favourable, auspicious, propitious, optimistic,
bright. **2** *a promising young writer* with potential, talented, gifted, able, apt; *inf.* up-and-
coming.
Opposites UNFAVOURABLE; UNPROMISING.

promontory noun headland, point, cape, head,
foreland, bluff, cliff, precipice, overhang,
height, projection, prominence.

promote verb **1** *the boss had promoted him* | *she
has been promoted to sales manager* give promotion to, upgrade, give a higher position to, give
a higher rank to, place in a higher rank, elevate, advance, move up, prefer, aggrandize.
2 *he promoted the cause of peace by his actions*
advance, further, assist, aid, help, contribute
to, foster, boost. **3** *the local council promotes
equal rights for all* advocate, recommend, urge,
support, back, endorse, champion, sponsor,
espouse. **4** *companies promoting their new products* advertise, publicize, push, puff, puff up,
beat the drum for; *inf.* plug, give a plug to,
hype, hype up.
Opposites DEMOTE; OBSTRUCT; IMPEDE.

promotion noun **1** *get promotion to a managerial post* upgrading, move up, elevation,
advancement, preferment, aggrandizement.
2 *his promotion of peace by his actions* advancement, furtherance, furthering, assistance, aid,
help, contribution to, fostering, boosting.
3 *the council's promotion of equal rights for all*
advocacy, recommendation, urging, support,
backing, endorsement, championship, sponsoring, espousal. **4** *the company's promotion of
their new products* advertising, advertising campaign, publicity, publicizing, push, pushing,
hard sell, puff, puffing; *inf.* plug, plugging,
hype, hyping.

prompt adjective **1** *receive a prompt reply* immediate, instant, instantaneous, swift, rapid,
speedy, quick, fast, expeditious, early, punctual, in good time, timely. **2** *she is prompt to
offer assistance* swift, rapid, speedy, quick, fast,
ready, willing, eager.
Opposites SLOW; LATE; tardy; UNWILLING.

prompt adverb *arrive at 9 a.m. prompt* sharp,
exactly, precisely, on the dot, dead, dead on,
promptly, punctually; *inf.* bang on, spot on;
Am. inf. on the button.

prompt verb **1** *what prompted them to join the
party?* cause, make, encourage, move, induce,
urge, incite, impel, spur on, motivate, stimulate, inspire, provoke. **2** *his actions prompted an
angry response* cause, give rise to, induce, call
forth, occasion, elicit, evoke, provoke. **3** *he forgot what he was going to say and she prompted him*
remind, jog someone's memory, refresh someone's memory, cue, give someone a cue, help
out.
Opposites DISCOURAGE; DETER; RESTRAIN.

promptly adverb **1** *arrive promptly* punctually,
on time, on the dot; *inf.* bang on, spot on; *Am.
inf.* on the button. **2** *reply to the letter promptly*
at once, directly, immediately, by return,
instantly, instantaneously, swiftly, rapidly,
speedily, quickly, fast, expeditiously; *inf.*
pronto.

promptness noun **1** *the promptness of his reply*
immediacy, immediateness, instantaneous-
ness, swiftness, rapidity, speediness, alacrity,
quickness, fastness, expeditiousness, expedition, earliness, punctuality. **2** *the promptness of
her offer to help* swiftness, rapidity, speediness,
alacrity, quickness, fastness, readiness, willingness, eagerness.

promulgate verb **1** *promulgate the information
about the project to the townspeople* make known,
make public, publicize, announce, spread,
communicate, disseminate, circulate, broadcast. **2** *promulgate the new law* proclaim,
announce, declare, herald, blazon, trumpet.

prone adjective **1** *suffocate on his pillow after
lying prone* face down, face downwards, in a
prone position, procumbent. **2** *after the party
the place was full of people in a prone position* | *peo-
ple lying prone on the battlefield* lying down, flat,
horizontal, full-length, supine, prostrate,
stretched out, recumbent, procumbent.
3 *prone to lose his temper* inclined, given, likely,
liable, apt, disposed, predisposed. **4** *prone to
headaches* inclined, liable, subject, susceptible,
disposed, predisposed.
Opposites UPRIGHT; VERTICAL; UNLIKELY; IMMUNE.

prong noun point, tip, spike, tine.

pronounce verb **1** *pronounce the words wrongly* |
have difficulty in pronouncing the letter 's' enunciate, articulate, say, utter, sound, voice, vocal-
ize. **2** *pronounce judgement* | *pronounce the patient
out of danger* announce, declare, proclaim,
assert, affirm, rule, decree.

pronounced adjective **1** *have a pronounced lisp*
marked, noticeable, obvious, evident, conspicuous, striking, distinct, unmistakable. **2** *have
pronounced views on the subject* decided, definite,
clear, strong, positive, distinct.
Opposites FAINT; INCONSPICUOUS; INDEFINITE; VAGUE.

pronouncement noun *wait for the consultant's
pronouncement on the patient's chances of survival*
formal statement, declaration, announcement,
judgement, decree, proclamation, assertion,
dictum.

pronunciation *noun have difficulty with the pronunciation of certain words* enunciation, articulation, saying, uttering, utterance, sounding, voicing, vocalization.

proof *noun* **1** *produce proof of your identity* evidence, certification, verification, authentication, validation, confirmation, attestation. **2** *produce proof of his guilt* evidence, demonstration, substantiation, corroboration, confirmation, attestation, testimony. **3** *send the novelist proofs of her book* galley proof, galley, page proof, pull, trial print.

proof *adjective roofing material proof against heavy winds* impervious, impenetrable, resistant, repellent, waterproof, windproof, bullet-proof, soundproof, childproof.

prop *noun* **1** *clothes prop | a prop holding up the side of the house* support, upright, brace, buttress, stay, bolster, stanchion, truss, column, post, rod, pole, shaft. **2** *a prop of the amateur theatrical society* pillar, mainstay, anchor, rock, backbone, supporter, upholder, sustainer.

prop *verb prop his bike/ladder against the wall* lean, rest, set, lay, stand, balance, steady. **prop up 1** *prop up the wall of the garage* hold up, shore up, bolster up, buttress, support, brace, underpin, reinforce, strengthen. **2** *prop up a firm in difficulties* support, give support to, bolster up, shore up, maintain, fund, finance, subsidize, underwrite.

propaganda *noun party members trying to recruit people by means of their propaganda* publicity material, publicity information, publicity, promotion, advertising, advertisement, information, agitprop; *inf.* hype.

propagate *verb* **1** *propagate plants/animals* grow, breed, multiply. **2** *animals propagating* reproduce, multiply, proliferate, breed, procreate. **3** *propagate new political ideas* spread, communicate, circulate, disseminate, transmit, distribute, broadcast, publish, publicize, proclaim, promulgate.

propel *verb propel the boat by means of oars | ambition propelling him to work long hours* move, set in motion, push forward, drive, thrust forward, force, impel.

propensity *noun a propensity to lie | a propensity for getting into trouble* tendency, inclination, leaning, bent, bias, disposition, predisposition, proneness, proclivity, penchant, susceptibility, weakness.

proper *adjective* **1** *the proper equipment for the sport | the proper qualifications for the job* right, suitable, fitting, appropriate, apt. **2** *the proper way to do things | doesn't know the proper way to address the queen* right, correct, precise, accepted, acceptable, established, orthodox, conventional, formal, *comme il faut.* **3** *put the books in their proper place* right, correct, own, individual, particular, respective, special, specific. **4** *have a very proper upbringing* seemly, decorous, respectable, decent, refined, genteel, gentlemanly/ladylike, formal, conventional, orthodox, strict, punctilious, sedate. **5** *have a proper holiday* real, actual, genuine, true. **6** *make a proper mess of things* real, actual, complete, thorough, thoroughgoing, utter.

Opposites INAPPROPRIATE; WRONG; IMPROPER; UNCONVENTIONAL.

property *noun* **1** *the books were her personal property* possessions, belongings, things, goods, effects, chattels, assets, resources. **2** *put his money in property* real estate, buildings, land, estates, acres. **3** *herbs with healing properties | the antiseptic properties of the susbtance* quality, attribute, characteristic, feature, power, peculiarity, idiosyncrasy, quirk.

prophecy *noun* **1** *her prophecy came true* prediction, forecast, prognostication, divination, augury. **2** *the gift of prophecy* prediction, foretelling the future, forecasting the future, fortune-telling, second sight, prognostication, divination, augury, soothsaying.

prophesy *verb the old woman prophesied his death* predict, foretell, forecast, foresee, forewarn of, presage, prognosticate, divine, augur.

prophet *noun* seer, soothsayer, fortune-teller, diviner, clairvoyant, forecaster of the future, prognosticator, prophesier, oracle, augur, sibyl, Cassandra. **prophet of doom** pessimist, Cassandra; *inf.* doom merchant, gloom merchant, doomster.

prophetic *adjective her pessimistic remarks proved prophetic—we did indeed fail* predictive, foretelling, forecasting, presaging, prognostic, divinatory, oracular, sibylline.

prophylactic *adjective prophylactic medicine* preventive, preventative, precautionary, protective, disease-preventing.

prophylaxis *noun advocate prophylaxis in medicine* prevention, protection.

propinquity *noun* **1** *dislike the propinquity of the two houses/families* closeness, nearness, proximity, adjacency, contiguity. **2** *the families have a propinquity with each other* close relationship, close kinship, blood ties, family connection, proximity, consanguinity.

propitiate *verb propitiate his angry mother* appease, conciliate, placate, mollify, pacify, soothe.

propitious *adjective not a propitious time to try to sell one's house* auspicious, favourable, promising, optimistic, bright, advantageous, fortunate, lucky, happy, rosy, beneficial, opportune, suitable, timely.
Opposites UNFAVOURABLE; INAUSPICIOUS; UNFORTUNATE.

proponent *noun a proponent of socialism* advocate, supporter, upholder, adherent, backer, promoter, endorser, champion, defender, sponsor, espouser, friend, well-wisher.

proportion *noun* **1** *the proportion of women to men on the staff* ratio, distribution, relative amount/number, relationship. **2** *give a large proportion of his income to the poor* portion, part, segment, share, quota, division, percentage, fraction, measure; *inf.* cut, whack. **3** *the pleasing proportions of the room | her features are in perfect proportion to each other* balance, symmetry, harmony, correspondence, congruity, agreement.

proportional *adjective have more work to do with a proportional increase in salary* proportionate, in proportion to, corresponding, commensurate, equivalent, comparable.

proportions *plural noun a man of huge proportions* dimensions, size, measurements, mass, bulk, expanse, magnitude, extent, width, breadth.

proposal *noun* **1** *the proposal of new terms of employment* putting forward, advancing, offering, proffering, presentation, submitting. *See* PROPOSE 1. **2** *study their proposals for expansion* | *draw up a financial proposal* scheme, plan, project, programme, motion, bid, proposition, presentation, suggestion, recommendation, tender, terms.

propose *verb* **1** *propose changes in legislation* | *propose that changes be made in the legislation* put forward, advance, offer, proffer, present, submit, tender, propound, suggest, recommend, advocate. **2** *they are proposing to leave now* intend, have the intention, mean, plan, have in mind, aim, purpose. **3** *propose his cousin as president of the society* put forward, put up, nominate, name, suggest, recommend. **4** *propose to his girlfriend* offer marriage to, ask for someone's hand in marriage to, pay suit to; *inf.* pop the question to.

proposition *noun* **1** *an attractive business proposition* proposal, scheme, plan, project, programme, motion, bid. *See* PROPOSAL 2. **2** *getting into the building unnoticed is not an easy proposition* | *it's a tough proposition* task, job, undertaking, venture, problem. **3** *make a proposition to the girl at the bar* sexual advance, sexual overture, indecent proposal, improper suggestion; *inf.* come-on.

proposition *verb* proposition *the girl/man at the bar* make sexual advances to, make sexual overtures to, make an indecent proposal to, make an improper suggestion to, accost; *inf.* make a proposition to, make a pass at.

propound *verb* propound *the theory that all men are equal* put forward, advance, offer, proffer, present, submit, tender, suggest, postulate, propose, advocate.

proprieties *plural noun expected to observe the proprieties* etiquette, social conventions, social graces, social niceties, protocol, civilities, formalities, rules of conduct, accepted behaviour, good manners, good form, the done thing, punctilio.

proprietor *noun* owner, possessor, title-holder, deed-holder, landowner, landlord/landlady.

propriety *noun* **1** *behave with propriety* seemliness, decorum, respectability, decency, correctness, appropriateness, good manners, courtesy, politeness, civility, refinement, gentility, breeding, conventionality, orthodoxy, formality, etiquette, protocol. **2** *question the propriety of your decision* | *I am uncertain of the propriety of the way he treats his staff* rightness, correctness, fitness, suitability, suitableness, appropriateness, aptness.
Opposites IMPROPRIETY; INDECORUM.

propulsion *noun fuel used for propulsion* | *jet propulsion* motive force, propelling force, drive, driving force, thrust, push, momentum, power.

prosaic *adjective* **1** *a prosaic style of writing* | *a prosaic decription of her experiences abroad* unimaginative, uninspired, matter-of-fact, dull, dry, humdrum, mundane, pedestrian, lifeless, spiritless, stale, bland, vapid, banal, hackneyed, trite, insipid, monotonous, flat. **2** *lead rather a prosaic life* ordinary, everyday, usual, common, routine, humdrum, commonplace, workaday, pedestrian, mundane, dull, tedious, boring, uninspiring, monotonous.
Opposites IMAGINATIVE; INSPIRED; INTERESTING.

proscribe *verb* **1** *proscribe the sale of alcohol on Sundays* prohibit, forbid, ban, bar, disallow, embargo, interdict, outlaw. **2** *he was proscribed for his part in the conspiracy* outlaw, exile, expel, expatriate, deport, boycott, blackball, ostracize, send to Coventry.
Opposites ALLOW; AUTHORIZE; ACCEPT.

proscription *noun* **1** *the proscription of the sale of alcohol on Sundays* prohibiting, prohibition, forbidding, banning, barring, embargo, interdicting. *See* PROSCRIBE 1. **2** *the proscription of her brother for his part in the conspiracy* outlawing, exiling, expelling, expulsion, expatriation, deporting. *See* PROSCRIBE 2. **3** *a proscription placed on the sale of alcohol* prohibition, ban, bar, embargo, interdict.

prosecute *verb* **1** *he was prosecuted for dangerous driving* bring a charge against, bring a criminal charge against, charge, prefer charges against, bring an action against, try, bring to trial, put on trial, sue, bring a suit against, interdict, arraign. **2** *prosecute an inquiry into the murder* carry on, conduct, direct, engage in, work at, proceed with, continue with. **3** *prosecute his prescribed tasks* accomplish, complete, finish, carry through, discharge, bring to an end.
Opposites PARDON; NEGLECT; OMIT.

proselyte *noun* convert, neophyte.

prosimian *noun. See table.*

PROSIMIANS AND RELATED ANIMALS	
angwantibo	lemur
aye-aye	loris
bushbaby	potto
colugo	sifaka
flying lemur	tarsier
galago	tree shrew
indri	

prospect *noun* **1** *there is little prospect of success* likelihood, likeliness, hope, expectation, anticipation, chance, chances, odds, probability, possibility. *See* PROSPECTS. **2** *the prospect of being unemployed frightens him* thought, idea, contemplation, outlook. **3** *admire the prospect from the hill* view, vista, outlook, perspective, panorama, scene, spectacle. **in prospect** *there are no jobs in prospect* in store, in the offing, on the horizon, on the cards, in the wind.

prospect *verb* prospect *an area for diamonds* explore, search, inspect, survey, examine, check out. **prospect for** *prospect for gold* search for, look for, seek, go after.

prospective *adjective* **1** *her prospective father-in-law* future, to-be, soon-to-be, intended, expected. **2** *attract prospective customers* would-be, potential, possible, likely, hoped-for, looked-for, awaited, anticipated. **3** *her prospective date with her friend's brother* coming, to come, approaching, about to be, forthcoming, imminent.

prospects *plural noun a job with few prospects* potential, promise, possibilities, expectations, scope.

prospectus *noun the prospectus from the college* brochure, literature, syllabus, programme.

prosper *verb the family/business is prospering* do well, get on well, thrive, flourish, be successful, succeed, get ahead, progress, advance, get on in the world, make headway, make good, become rich, be in clover; *inf.* be on Easy Street, live the life of Riley.
Opposites FAIL; COLLAPSE; CRASH.

prosperity *noun go from poverty to prosperity* prosperousness, success, good fortune, ease, plenty, affluence, wealth, riches, the good life, luxury, life of luxury.

prosperous *adjective prosperous young men working in the city* thriving, flourishing, successful, well-off, well-to-do, affluent, wealthy, rich, moneyed, opulent, in clover; *inf.* well-heeled, in the money, on Easy Street.
Opposites POOR; PENNILESS; IMPECUNIOUS.

prostitute *noun* call-girl, whore, woman of the streets, streetwalker, loose woman, woman of ill repute, fallen woman, courtesan, *fille de joie,* bawd; *inf.* tart, pro, hooker, hustler, moll.

prostitution *noun* whoredom, whoring, street-walking, the oldest profession, Mrs Warren's profession; *inf.* the game, hustling.

prostrate *adjective* **1** *people found prostrate on the floor after the fire* prone, lying down, flat, stretched out, horizontal, full-length, procumbent. **2** *prostrate before the emperor* bowed low, humbled. **3** *prostrate with grief* overcome by/with, overwhelmed by, overpowered by, brought to one's knees by, crushed by, helpless with, paralysed by, laid low by/with, impotent with. **4** *a country left prostrate after years of war | the old lady was prostrate after the long journey* worn out, exhausted, fatigued, tired out, dog-tired, spent, drained: *inf.* all in, done, fagged out, bushed, whacked, pooped.
Opposites UPRIGHT; VERTICAL; THRIVING.

prostrate *verb* **1** *the blow prostrated him* knock flat, flatten, knock down, floor, level. **2** *the heat prostrated them | prostrated by pain* overcome, overwhelm, overpower, bring to one's knees, crush, make helpless, paralyse, lay low, make powerless, make impotent. **3** *the long war prostrated the country | she was prostrated by the long journey* wear out, exhaust, tire out, fatigue, weary, drain, sap; *inf.* fag out, poop.

protagonist *noun* **1** *the protagonist in the new play* chief character, central character, leading/main character, principal, hero/heroine, leading man/lady, title role, lead. **2** *a protagonist of feminism* leader, leading supporter, prime mover, moving spirit, standard-bearer, mainstay, spokesman/woman/person, advocate, sup-

porter, upholder, adherent, backer, proponent, promoter, champion, exponent.

protean *adjective* ever-changing, variable, changeable, mutable, kaleidoscopic, mercurial, volatile, labile, versatile.

protect *verb* **1** *protect the child from would-be kidnappers | protect the house from burglars* keep safe, save, safeguard, shield, preserve, defend, shelter, secure. **2** *soldiers protecting the castle* guard, mount/stand guard on, defend, secure, watch over, look after, take care of. **3** *protect the surface of the table with a plastic sheet* preserve, shield, cover, cover up, conceal, mask.
Opposites ATTACK; HARM; ASSAULT; EXPOSE.

protection *noun* **1** *provide protection against violence* safe keeping, safety, shield, preservation, defence, security. **2** *under the protection of the police* safe keeping, care, charge, keeping, defence, protectorship. **3** *wear warm clothes as a protection against the cold | use a sun-block as a protection against the sun* safeguard, shield, barrier, buffer, screen, cover.

protective *adjective* **1** *wear a protective cream on her face in the sun | cyclists wearing protective headgear* protecting, safeguarding, shielding, covering. **2** *protective mother/parents* careful, watchful, vigilant, paternal/maternal, fatherly/motherly, over-protective, possessive, jealous, clinging.

protector *noun* **1** *his elder brother acted as his protector* defender, champion, bodyguard, guardian, knight in shining armour, guardian angel. **2** *wear shin protectors* guard, shield, pad, cushion.

protégé/protégée *noun* pupil, student, ward, dependant, charge.

protest *verb* **1** *protest at his treatment of his staff | protest against the government's economic police | protest about their low wages* make a protest at/against/about, object to, raise objections to, oppose, express opposition to, take issue about/on/over, make/take a stand against, put up a fight against, take exception to, complain about, express disapproval of, express disagreement with, demur at, remonstrate about, make a fuss about, demonstrate against; *inf.* kick up a fuss about, gripe about, grouse about, beef about, bitch about. **2** *protest his innocence* declare, announce, profess, proclaim, assert, affirm, argue, attest, testify to, maintain, insist on, aver, avow.
Opposites ACCEPT; SUPPORT.

protest *noun* **1** *register a protest at/against/about his treatment of the children* objection, opposition, exception, complaint, disapproval, disagreement, dissent, demurral, remonstration, fuss, outcry, demonstration, protestation. **2** *listen to his protests that he was innocent* protestation, declaration, announcement, profession, assertion, affirmation, attestation, assurance, avowal, proclamation.
Opposites SUPPORT; APPROVAL.

protestation *noun* **1** *not to believe his protestations of innocence/loyalty* protest, declaration, announcement, assertion, affirmation. *See* PROTEST *noun* 2. **2** *his protestations against his* *treatment in prison* protest, objection, opposition, exception, complaint. *See* PROTEST *noun* 1.

protester *noun a crowd of protesters gathered outside the embassy* objector, opposer, opponent, complainer, demonstrator, dissenter, dissident, rebel, protest marcher, striker, agitator.

protocol *noun observe the protocol associated with royal visits | guilty of a breach of protocol* etiquette, rules of conduct, code of behaviour, conventions, formalities, customs, propriety, proprieties, decorum, manners, courtesies, civilities, good form, *politesse.*

prototype *noun the prototype of the flying machine* original, first example, first model, pattern, paradigm, archetype.

protract *verb loves to talk at meetings and protract the discussions* prolong, extend, stretch out, draw out, lengthen, make longer, drag out, spin out, keep something going, continue.
Opposites CURTAIL; SHORTEN.

protracted *adjective tired of the protracted discussions* prolonged, extended, stretched out, drawn out, long-drawn-out, lengthened, lengthy, long, over-long, dragged out, spun out, interminable, never-ending, endless.

protrude *verb a piece of rock protruding from the cliff face | protruding front teeth* jut, jut out, stick out, stand out, project, extend, beetle, obtrude, bulge.

protrusion *noun* 1 *the protrusion of a piece of rock from the cliff face* jutting, sticking out, projection, projecting, obtrusion, obtruding. *See* PROTRUDE. 2 *rocky protrusions on the face of the cliff* projection, swelling, bulge, protuberance, lump, bump, knob.

protuberance *noun a protuberance on the trunk of the tree* swelling, bulge, lump, bump, protrusion, projection, knob, growth, outgrowth, tumour, excrescence.

protuberant *adjective protuberant stomach/eyes* bulging, swelling, swollen, jutting, jutting out, protruding, protrusive, prominent, bulbous, gibbous.
Opposites SUNKEN.

proud *adjective* 1 *proud parents | parents proud of their daughter's achievement* pleased (with), glad (about/at), happy (about/at/with), satisfied (with), gratified (at), content (at), appreciative (of). 2 *they were poor but proud* self-respecting, dignified, independent. 3 *he used to stop and speak to all the villagers but he has become very proud and passes them by* arrogant, conceited, vain, self-important, egotistical, boastful, haughty, disdainful, scornful, supercilious, snobbish, imperious, overbearing, lordly, presumptuous, overweening, high-handed; *inf.* high-and-mighty, stuck-up, uppity, snooty, toffee-nosed, highfalutin. 4 *it was a proud day when they won the cup* gratifying, satisfying, happy, memorable, notable, red-letter, glorious, marvellous. 5 *the ship was a proud sight sailing into harbour* magnificent, splendid, grand, noble, stately, imposing, majestic, august.
Opposites ASHAMED; MODEST; HUMBLE; SHAMEFUL.

prove *verb* 1 *prove that he was the murderer* produce/submit proof, produce/submit evidence, establish evidence, determine, demonstrate, show beyond doubt, substantiate, corroborate, verify, validate, authenticate, confirm. 2 *prove the new drug | young people having to prove themselves* put to the test, test, try out, put to trial. 3 *the rumour proved to be correct* be found, turn out. **be proved** *she was proved the winner* emerge, come out, end up.
Opposites DISPROVE; INVALIDATE.

proverb *noun* saying, adage, maxim, saw, axiom, aphorism, gnome, dictum, apophthegm.

proverbial *adjective in view of her proverbial meanness, we did not ask her for a contribution to the charity* legendary, notorious, infamous, famous, famed, renowned, well-known, acknowledged, accepted, traditional, time-honoured.

provide *verb* 1 *provide food and drink for the travellers | provide them with a car for their holiday* supply, furnish, equip, accommodate, provision, outfit. 2 *the job provides ample scope for promotion | the novel provides an insight into the problems of the age* give, bring, afford, present, offer, accord, yield, impart, lend. 3 *the contract provides that the tenants are responsible for house repairs* stipulate, lay down, give as a condition, require, state, specify. **provide against** *provide against a power cut by buying stocks of candles* make provision for, take precautions against, take steps/measures against, guard against, forearm oneself against. **provide for** 1 *provide for his wife and children* support, maintain, keep, sustain, take care of, care for, look after. 2 *the organizers of the fête tried to provide for every eventuality* allow for, prepare for, make preparations for, be prepared for, anticipate, arrange for, make arrangements for, get ready for, plan for, make plans for.
Opposites DEPRIVE; REFUSE; WITHHOLD.

provided, provided that *conjunction we are going on holiday, provided we have enough money | the party will be held out of doors, provided that it is not raining* providing that, on condition that, if, as long as, given, with the provision/proviso that, contingent upon, on the assumption that.

providence *noun* 1 *just have to trust in providence* God's will, divine intervention, destiny, fate, fortune. 2 *lack of providence has brought him to his present state* foresight, forethought, far-sightedness, prudence, judgement, judiciousness, shrewdness, circumspection, wisdom, sagacity, caution, care, carefulness, good management, careful budgeting, thrift, thriftiness, economy, canniness, frugality.

provident *adjective it was provident of them to take out accident insurance | provident people providing for their old age* far-sighted, prudent, judicious, shrewd, circumspect, wise, sagacious, cautious, careful, thrifty, canny, economical, frugal.

providing, providing that *conjunction* provided, provided that, on condition that, if. *See* PROVIDED.

province *noun* 1 *the administrative centre of the province* state, territory, region, area, district.

See table. **2** *that part of the business is not my province | its outside my province* area of responsibility, sphere of action, area of activity, field, business, line of business, line, charge, concern, duty; *inf.* pigeon. **3** *in the province of English literature* discipline, field, speciality, area.

PROVINCES AND TERRITORIES OF CANADA	
Province/Territory	**Capital**
Alberta	Edmonton
British Columbia	Victoria
Manitoba	Winnipeg
New Brunswick	Fredericton
Newfoundland and Labrador	St John's
Northwest Territories	Yellowknife
Nova Scotia	Halifax
Ontario	Toronto
Prince Edward Island	Charlottetown
Quebec	Quebec
Saskatchewan	Regina
Yukon Territory	Whitehorse

provincial *adjective* **1** *provincial rather than national/central government* state, regional. **2** *provincial newspapers/issues* non-national, local, parish pump. **3** *live in the city and look down on provincial areas* non-metropolitan, non-city, outlying, small-town, rural, country, rustic, backwood, backwater; *inf.* one-horse, hick. **4** *she regards herself as sophisticated and most of her colleagues as provincial* unsophisticated, parochial, limited, small-minded, insular, inward-looking, illiberal, narrow, narrow-minded, inflexible, bigoted, prejudiced, intolerant.
Opposites NATIONAL; URBAN; SOPHISTICATED.

provincial *noun city people looking down on people they regard as provincials* country cousin, rustic, yokel, peasant.

provision *noun* **1** *the provision of conference facilities | the provision of nursery schools* providing, supplying, supply, furnishing, equipping, outfitting, accommodation, giving, affording. **2** *make provision for their old age | make provision for a hard winter* preparation, plan, prearrangement, arrangement, precaution, precautionary steps/measures. **3** *the housing policy makes no provision for single people* arrangement, allowance, concession. **4** *under the provisions of his will his children inherit all his estate* term, requirement, specification, stipulation. **5** *the contract document has the provision that it must be reviewed annually* proviso, condition, stipulation, clause, rider, qualification, restriction, reservation, limitation, strings.

provisional *adjective a provisional contract | get provisional permission* provisory, temporary, interim, stopgap, transitional, to be confirmed, conditional, tentative, contingent; *inf.* pro tem.
Opposites PERMANENT; DEFINITE.

provisions *plural noun stock up with provisions for the Christmas holiday* supplies, food supplies, stores, groceries, food, food and drink, foodstuffs, staples, rations, provender, eatables, edibles, victuals, comestibles, viands.

proviso *noun they agreed to the change with the proviso that an investigation be held* condition, stipulation, provision, clause, rider, qualification, restriction, reservation, limitation, strings.

provocation *noun* **1** *the children's provocation of their mother* annoying, angering, incensing, enraging, irritating, irritation, exasperating, exasperation, infuriating, infuriation, maddening, vexing, harassing, harassment, irking; *inf.* riling, aggravation. See PROVOKE 1. **2** *hit him under provocation* incitement, rousing, stirring, stimulation, stimulus, motivation, prompting, inducement, goading. See PROVOKE 2. **3** *the provocation of the crowd's anger | the provocation of the audience's laughter* evocation, causing, occasioning, eliciting, inducement, inspiration, kindling, production, generation, instigation, precipitation, promotion. See PROVOKE 3. **4** *tired of his provocations | react to the slightest provocation* annoyance, irritation, vexation, harassment, affront, insult.

provocative *adjective* **1** *the fight was started by a provocative remark* provoking, annoying, irritating, exasperating, infuriating, maddening, vexing, galling, affronting, insulting, inflaming, goading; *inf.* aggravating. See PROVOKE 1,2. **2** *a provocative pout | wear a provocative, low-cut dress* sexually arousing, sexually exciting, alluring, seductive, sexy, tempting, suggestive, erotic, titillating.

provoke *verb* **1** *he's very irascible—don't provoke him | that child would provoke anyone* annoy, make angry, anger, incense, enrage, irritate, exasperate, infuriate, madden, pique, nettle, vex, harass, irk, gall, affront, insult; *inf.* rile, needle, make someone's blood boil, aggravate. **2** *provoke her into shouting at them* incite, rouse, stir, move, stimulate, motivate, excite, inflame, work/fire up, prompt, induce, spur, goad, prod, egg on. **3** *his speech provoked anger | his act provoked laughter* evoke, cause, give rise to, occasion, call forth, draw forth, elicit, induce, inspire, excite, kindle, produce, generate, engender, instigate, lead to, precipitate, promote, prompt.
Opposites PACIFY; APPEASE; DETER.

prow *noun the prow of the ship* bow, bows, nose, stem, fore, forepart, front, head.

prowess *noun* **1** *admire his prowess as a yachtsman | envied her prowess with a tennis-racket* skill, skilfulness, expertise, expertness, facility, ability, capability, talent, genius, adroitness, adeptness, aptitude, dexterity, deftness, competence, proficiency, know-how, savoir faire. **2** *the prowess of the soldiers in battle* courage, bravery, gallantry, valour, valiance, heroism, intrepidity, fearlessness, mettle, pluck, pluckiness, gameness, nerve, boldness, daring, fortitude, steadfastness, stoutness, sturdiness; *inf.* grit, guts, bottle, spunk.
Opposites INABILITY; ineptitude; COWARDICE.

prowl *verb prowling around the grounds looking for a way into the building* roam, range, move stealthily, slink, skulk, steal, sneak, stalk; *inf.* snoop.

proximity noun *live in proximity to a motorway | disturbed by the proximity of the railway to the house* closeness, nearness, propinquity, adjacency, contiguity.

proxy noun *send a proxy to vote at the annual general meeting* representative, deputy, substitute, agent, delegate, surrogate.

prude noun puritan, prig, Mrs Grundy, Grundy, old maid; *inf.* goody-goody, Miss Prim.

prudence noun **1** *question the prudence of his action* wisdom, judgement, good judgement, judiciousness, sagacity, shrewdness, common sense, sense, circumspection, far-sightedness, foresight, forethought. **2** *behave with prudence rather than rashness* caution, cautiousness, care, carefulness, discretion, wariness, vigilance, heedfulness. **3** *her prudence as a housewife* providence, good management, careful budgeting, thrift, thriftiness, economy, canniness, sparingness, frugality.

prudent adjective **1** *a prudent decision* wise, well-judged, judicious, sagacious, sage, shrewd, sensible, circumspect, far-sighted, politic. **2** *rash people always being advised to be prudent* cautious, careful, discreet, wary, vigilant, heedful. **3** *a prudent housewife* provident, thrifty,

economical, canny, sparing, frugal.
Opposites UNWISE; IMPRUDENT; INCAUTIOUS; RASH.

prudery noun *the prudery of the Victorian age* prudishness, puritanism, puritanicalness, priggishness, primness, strait-lacedness, prissiness, stuffiness, starchiness, Grundyism, old-maidishness; *inf.* school-marmishness.

prudish adjective *a prudish attitude towards sex* puritan, puritanical, priggish, prim, strait-laced, prissy, stuffy, starchy, Victorian, Grundyish, old-maid, old-maidish; *inf.* goody-goody, school-marmish, schoolmistressy.
Opposites PERMISSIVE; LIBERAL; BROAD-MINDED.

prune verb **1** *prune the roses* trim, thin, thin out, cut back, shape. **2** *prune branches from the bushes* cut, lop, chop, clip, snip, remove. **3** *prune the expenses budget | prune the over-long manuscript* cut back on, cut back, pare down, make cut-backs in, cut, trim, reduce, shorten, make reductions in, retrench, curtail.

prurient adjective *demonstrating a prurient interest in the details of the sex crimes* lascivious, lecherous, lustful, lewd, salacious, licentious, lubricious, libidinous.

pry verb *she was trying to help but they thought she was prying* be inquisitive, interfere, meddle, intrude, mind other people's business, be a

---

PSEUDONYMS AND ADOPTED NAMES

Pseudonym	Real Name	Pseudonym	Real Name
Arden, Elizabeth	Graham, Florence Nightingale	Markova, Dame Alicia	Marks, Alice
Bardot, Brigitte	Javal, Camille	Mata Hari	Zelle, Margaretha
Bell, Acton	Brontë, Anne	Meir, Golda	Mabovich, Goldie
Bell, Currer	Brontë, Charlotte	Melba, Dame Nellie	Mitchell, Helen
Bell, Ellis	Brontë, Emily	Mitchell, Joni	Anderson, Roberta
Boz	Dickens, Charles	Molière	Poquelin, Jean-Baptiste
Brassaï	Halasz, Gyula	Monroe, Marilyn	Mortenson, Norma Jean
Caine, Michael	Micklewhite, Maurice	Moravia, Alberto	Pincherle, Alberto
Carroll, Lewis	Dodgson, Charles Lutwidge	O'Brien, Flann	O'Nolan, Brian
Crawford, Joan	Le Sueur, Lucille	Orwell, George	Blair, Eric
Dietrich, Marlene	Losch, Maria Magdalene von	Pelé	do Nascimento, Edson Arantes
Dinesen, Isak	Blixen, Baroness Karen	Ray, Man	Rudnitsky, Emanuel
Dylan, Bob	Zimmerman, Robert	Richard, Cliff	Webb, Harry
El Greco	Theotocopoulos, Domenikos	Rob Roy	Macgregor, Robert
		Rogers, Ginger	McMath, Virginia
Eliot, George	Evans, Mary Ann	Saki	Munro, Hector Hugh
Erté	de Tirtoff, Romain	Sand, George	Dupin, Amandine
Firdausi	Mansur, Abdul al-Qasim	Stalin, Joseph	Dzhugashvili, Iosif Vissarionovich
Garland, Judy	Gumm, Frances		
Gorky, Maxim	Peshkov, Aleksey	Starr, Ringo	Starkey, Richard
Grant, Cary	Leach, Archibald	Stendhal	Beyle, Marie Henri
Hayworth, Rita	Cansino, Margarita	Sting	Sumner, Gordon
Henry, O.	Porter, William Sydney	Tito	Broz, Josip
Herriot, James	Wright, Alfred	Trotsky, Leon	Bronstein, Lev Davidovich
Holiday, Billie	Fagan, Eleanora		
Houdini, Harry	Weisz, Erik	Twain, Mark	Clemens, Samuel Langhorn
John, Elton	Dwight, Reginald		
Karloff, Boris	Pratt, William	Villa, Pancho	Arango Doroteo
Kaye, Danny	Kominski, David	Voltaire	Arouet, François-Marie
Le Carré, John	Cornwell, David	Waters, Muddy	Morganfield, McKinley
Le Corbusier	Jeanneret, Charles	Wayne, John	Morrison, Marion
Lenin, Vladimir Ilich	Ulyanov, Vladimir Ilich	Wonder, Stevie	Morris, Steveland
		Zeffirelli, Franco	Corsi, Gianfranco

busybody; *inf.* stick/poke one's nose in, stick one's oar in, snoop. **pry into** **1** *pry into her private affairs* be inquisitive about, nose into, inquire impertinently into, interfere in, meddle in; *inf.* be nosy about, stick/poke one's nose into, stick one's oar into, snoop into. **2** *pry into her possessions* peer into, peek into, scrutinize, probe into, ferret about in, nose into, nose around in, spy on; *inf.* stick/poke one's nose into, snoop into.

prying *adjective tired of their prying neighbours* inquisitive, curious, interfering, meddling, meddlesome, intrusive, probing, spying, impertinent; *inf.* nosy, snooping, snoopy.

psalm *noun* hymn, sacred song, song of praise, paean, religious song, chant, anthem.

pseudo *adjective his intellectualism is pseudo* | *a pseudo interest in the arts* feigned, pretended, simulated, imitation, false, artificial, ersatz, quasi-, spurious, fake, bogus, sham, mock, fraudulent, counterfeit, forged; *inf.* phoney. **Opposites** REAL; GENUINE; ACTUAL.

pseudonym *noun the pseudonym of the writer/actor nom de plume*, pen-name, stage name, professional name, assumed name, alias, allonym, false name, sobriquet, nickname, *nom de guerre. See table.*

psych *verb* **psych out** *try to psych out his opponent* unsettle, upset, agitate, disturb, make nervous, put off, put off balance, put off one's stroke, intimidate, frighten. **psych up** *have to psych himself up before the competition/interview* steel oneself, prepare, get ready, gird one's loins, get in the mood, get in the right frame of mind.

psyche *noun a disturbed psyche* soul, spirit, mind, intelligence, anima, self, essential nature, inner ego, man/woman, personality.

psychiatrist *noun* psychopathologist, psychotherapist, therapist, psychoanalyst, psychoanalyser; *inf.* shrink, head-shrinker, trick cyclist; *Am.* alienist.

psychic *adjective* **1** *people thought to be psychic* clairvoyant, telepathic, telekinetic, spiritualistic. **2** *psychic powers/influences/research* supernat- ural, supernormal, preternatural, preternormal, extrasensory, other-worldly, paranormal, occult. **3** *psychic analysis/disorder* spiritual, mental, psychological, psychogenic.

psychological *adjective* **1** *psychological studies* mental, of the mind, cerebral, psychic, psychical. **2** *her inability to work is thought to be psychological* in the mind, all in the mind, psychosomatic, emotional, irrational, imaginary, subconscious, unconscious.

psychology *noun* **1** *studying psychology* science of the mind, science of the personality, study of the mental processes. *See table.* **2** *the psychology of the typical burglar* mind, mind-set, mental processes, thought processes, way of thinking, attitude, make-up; *inf.* what makes one tick.

psychopathic *adjective murders carried out by psychopathic people* severely mentally ill, disturbed, insane, mad, maniac, maniacal, deranged, sociopathic, psychotic.

psychosomatic *adjective psychosomatic illnesses* stress-induced, stress-related, in the mind, all in the mind, psychological.

pub *noun* public house, bar, tavern, inn; *inf.* local, boozer.

puberty *noun young people reaching puberty* pubescence, sexual maturity, adolescence, young adulthood, teenage years, teens.

public *adjective* **1** *public health services* | *public law* state, national, civic, civil, social. **2** *public sentiment is against it* | *increase public awareness* popular, general, common, universal, widespread. **3** *public places/parks* not private, not exclusive, accessible to all, open to the public, of free access. **4** *make his views public* known, widely known, acknowledged, overt, in circulation, published, publicized, plain, obvious. **5** *scandals about public figures* in the public eye, prominent, well-known, important, eminent, respected, influential, prestigious, famous, celebrated, illustrious. **Opposites** PRIVATE; PERSONAL; SECRET.

public *noun* **1** *the public has/have a right to know about the claims* people, everyone, population,

---

BRANCHES OF PSYCHOLOGY

abnormal psychology	Freudianism	psychoanalysis
Adlerian psychology	gestalt psychology	psychobiochemistry
analytical psychology	group psychology	psychobiography
animal psychology	Horneyan psychology	psychobiology
apperceptionism	humanistic psychology	psychodynamics
applied psychology	industrial and organ-	psychogenetics
associationism	izational psychology	psychography
behaviourism	introspection psychology	psycholinguistics
child psychology	Jungian psychology	psychometry
clinical psychology	Lacanian psychology	psychopathology
cognitive psychology	metapsychology	psychopharmacology
comparative psychology	neuropsychology	psychophysiology
configurationism	object-relations theory	Reichian psychology
developmental	occupational psychology	Skinnerian
psychology	orgone theory	psychology
educational psychology	parapsychology	social psychology
ethology	Pavlovian psychology	structuralism
experimental psychology	physiological psychology	Watsonian psychology

country, nation, community, citizens, populace, ordinary people, the masses, commonalty, the multitude, the mob, the *hoi polloi*, electorate, voters. **2** *actors/authors worrying about what their public think* audience, spectators, readers, followers, following, fans, admirers, patrons, clientele. **in public** *refuse to appear in public after the scandal* publicly, openly, for all to see, in full view of the public.

publication *noun* **1** *the publication of the book/newspaper* publishing, production, issuing, issuance. **2** *a widely-read publication* book, newspaper, magazine, periodical, journal, daily, weekly, monthly, quarterly, booklet, brochure, leaflet, pamphlet, handbill. **3** *the publication of the committee's findings* publishing, announcement, notification, reporting, declaration, communication, imparting, proclamation, disclosure, divulgence, broadcasting, publicizing, distribution, spreading, dissemination, promulgation, issuance.

publicity *noun* **1** *film stars marrying amid a blaze of publicity* public attention, public interest, public notice. **2** *the publicity associated with the launch of the book* promotion, advertising, puff, push; *inf.* plug, hype, build-up.

publicize *verb* **1** *publicize a description of the wanted man* make public, make known, bring to public notice/attention, announce, publish, broadcast, distribute, disseminate, promulgate. **2** *publicize her new book* give publicity to, promote, advertise, give a puff to, puff, puff up, push, beat the drum for; *inf.* hype, plug.
Opposites CONCEAL; WITHHOLD.

publish *verb* **1** *a firm publishing reference books* produce, issue, print, bring out. **2** *publish the results/publish the committee's findings* make public, make known, announce, notify, report, declare, communicate, impart, proclaim, disclose, divulge, broadcast, publicize, distribute, spread, disseminate, promulgate.

pucker *verb* **1** *a dress puckered at the waist* gather, shirr, pleat, ruck, ruffle, wrinkle, crease. **2** *the unhappy child's face puckered/pucker her brows* screw up, wrinkle, crease, furrow, knit, crinkle, corrugate.

puckish *adjective* *a puckish sense of humour* mischievous, mischief-making, impish, imp-like, roguish, playful, arch, waggish.

pudding *noun* *soup, meat and pudding* dessert, sweet, sweet course/dish; *inf.* afters, pud. *See table at* DESSERT.

puddle *noun* *puddles of water/blood* pool.

puerile *adjective* *puerile behaviour/has a puerile sense of humour/piece of writing is so puerile* childish, immature, infantile, juvenile, adolescent, foolish, silly, inane, asinine.
Opposites MATURE; SENSIBLE.

puff *noun* **1** *a puff of wind* gust, blast, whiff, breath, flurry, draught. **2** *part of the puff given to his new book* promotion, publicity, advertising, advertisement, push; *inf.* hype, plug, build-up. **3** *give his new book a puff in her literary column* favourable mention, favourable review, good word, commendation, praise.

puff *verb* **1** *puffing while climbing the hill* breathe heavily/loudly/rapidly, pant, blow,

gasp, gulp. **2** *the drug seemed to have puffed him up* swell, distend, inflate, dilate, bloat. **3** *publishers puffing the latest works of their authors* promote, give publicity to, publicize, advertise, push, give a puff to, puff up; *inf.* hype, plug.

puffy *adjective* *puffy cheeks/eyes* puffed up, swollen, distended, inflated, dilated, bloated, bulging, oedematous.

pugilist *noun* boxer, fighter, prizefighter; *inf.* bruiser. *See table at* SPORT.

pugnacious *adjective* *a drunk in a pugnacious mood* belligerent, bellicose, combative, fighting, battling, aggressive, antagonistic, quarrelsome, argumentative, disputatious, hostile, threatening, irascible, ill-tempered, bad-tempered.
Opposites PEACEABLE; PACIFIC; FRIENDLY.

pull *verb* **1** *the child was pulling a toy behind him* haul, drag, draw, trail, tow, tug. **2** *pull the rope to straighten it* haul, tug, jerk; *inf.* yank. **3** *pull flowers* pluck, pick, gather, collect, cull. **4** *pull teeth* pull out, draw out, take out, extract, remove, root out. **5** *pull a muscle/ligament/has a pulled muscle* strain, sprain, wrench, stretch, tear, dislocate, damage. **6** *a new play that is pulling the audiences* pull in, draw, bring in, attract, lure, catch the eye of, entice. **pull apart 1** *children pulling apart their toys* take/pull to pieces, take/pull to bits, demolish, destroy, break. **2** *critics pulled apart her latest novel* take apart, take to pieces, criticize severely, find fault with, pick holes in, attack; *inf.* slate, pan, slam. **pull back** *the army pulled back after the defeat* withdraw, retreat, draw back, fall back. **pull down** *pull down old buildings to make way for new* take down, knock down, demolish, raze to the ground, level, destroy, bulldoze, dismantle. **pull in 1** *the car pulled in to the kerb* drive in, draw in, draw up, stop, park. **2** *plays pulling in large audiences* pull, draw, bring in, attract, lure, catch the eye of, entice. **3** *policeman pulling known criminals in for questioning* detain, take into custody, arrest; *inf.* run in, pinch, nab, collar, nail. **4** *he pulls in £50,000 a year* earn, take home, bring in, make, clear, net, gross, pocket. **pull off 1** *pull the top off the can* remove, detach, tear off, rip off, wrench off; *inf.* yank off. **2** *pull off the export deal* bring off, carry out, accomplish, execute, succeed in. **pull oneself together** regain one's composure/calm, get a grip on oneself; *inf.* snap out of it. **pull out 1** *pull out a gun* draw out, take out, bring out, withdraw. **2** *pull out of the agreement/contest* withdraw, retreat from, leave, quit, abandon, give up, stop participating in, renege on. **pull someone's leg** *she was upset but he was only pulling her leg* tease, make fun of, poke fun at, joke with, rag, chaff, twit; *inf.* rib, take the mickey out of. **pull through** *she was very ill but pulled through* get better, recover, rally, survive, come through, recuperate. **pull up 1** *pull up the weeds* root out, uproot, dig up, grub up, extract; *inf.* yank out. **2** *buses pulling up at the stop* stop, come to a stop, halt, come to a halt, brake. **3** *pull up the children for being cheeky* rebuke, scold, reprimand, admonish, reprove, take to task, castigate; *inf.* tell off, give someone a telling-off/dressing-down, tick off, give someone a ticking-off, carpet, give someone a carpeting.

pull *noun* **1** *give a pull at the bell-rope* tug, haul, yank, jerk; *inf.* yank. **2** *the pull of the current* tug, force, forcefulness, power, exertion, effort. **3** *the pull of the sea to sailors* attraction, lure, enticement, drawing power, draw, magnetism, influence. **4** *he could get you a job—he has a lot of pull with the boss | hasn't got much pull in the firm* influence, weight, leverage, muscle; *inf.* clout.

pulp *noun* **1** *the pulp of the fruit* soft part, fleshy part, flesh, marrow. **2** *reduce the mixture of vegetables to a pulp* paste, purée, mush, mash, pap, triturate. **3** *make a fortune out of writing pulp* pulp fiction, rubbish, trash, trivia, drivel, pap.

pulp *verb pulp the fruit to make jam* crush, squash, mash, purée, pulverize, triturate.

pulp *adjective pulp fiction* rubbishy, trashy, sensational, lurid.

pulsate *verb with hearts pulsating | loud music pulsating throughout the building* beat, throb, vibrate, pulse, palpitate, pound, thud, thump, drum.

pulse *noun* **1** *the compelling pulse of the music* beat, rhythm, throb, throbbing, vibration, pulsation, pounding, thudding, thud, thumping, thump, drumming. **2** *cooking with pulses* pea, bean. *See table at* BEAN.

pulse *verb loud music pulsing throughout the building* beat, throb, vibrate, pulsate, palpitate, pound, thud, thump, drum.

pulverize *verb* **1** *pulverize the solid foods* grind, crush, pound, crumble, powder, crunch, squash, pulp, purée, liquidize, mash, comminute, triturate. **2** *pulverize his opponent in the boxing ring* defeat utterly, overwhelm, trounce, rout, flatten, crush, smash, vanquish, destroy, annihilate; *inf.* hammer.

pump *verb* **1** *pump the bicycle tyres* pump up, blow up, inflate. **2** *pump blood through the body* drive, force, push, send. **3** *pump the child for information about his father* question closely, quiz, interrogate, cross-examine, give someone the third degree; *inf.* grill.

pun *noun amused by his puns* play on words, *double entendre*, paronomasia, calembour.

punch[1] *verb punch his opponent in the face* strike, hit, knock, thump, thwack, box, jab, cuff, slug, smash, bash, slam, batter, pound, pummel; *inf.* sock, biff, bop, wallop, whack, clout, plug.

punch[2] *noun* **1** *give his opponent a punch in the jaw/face* blow, hit, knock, thump, thwack, box, jab, cuff, slug, smash, bash, slam; *inf.* sock, biff, bop, wallop, whack, clout, plug. **2** *a speech which lacked punch* strength, vigour, vigorousness, force, forcefulness, verve, drive, impact, bite, effectiveness; *inf.* oomph, pizazz.

punch[3] *verb punch the paper/ticket/metal* make a hole in, put/punch holes in, perforate, puncture, pierce, prick, drill, bore, hole.

punctilio *noun* **1** *draw the organizers' attention to a punctilio relating to the coronation ceremony* fine point, nicety, detail, subtlety. **2** *observe the punctilio required by a royal visit* etiquette, conventions, formalities, code, protocol, propri-

eties, rules of conduct. **3** *organize the royal vist with punctilio | behave at the ceremony with punctilio* conformity, scrupulousness, meticulousness, conscientiousness, exactitude, precision, strictness, nicety.

punctilious *adjective a punctilious attention to detail | a punctilious observance of the convention* careful, scrupulous, meticulous, conscientious, exact, precise, particular, strict, nice, finicky, fussy; *inf.* pernickety.
Opposites CARELESS; SLAPDASH.

punctual *adjective they were always punctual at meetings | punctual arrivals* on time, on the dot, prompt, in good time, when expected, timely, well-timed, early.
Opposites LATE; BEHINDHAND.

punctuality *noun require punctuality of his employees* promptness, punctualness, promptitude, timeliness, earliness.

punctuate *verb* **1** *punctuate the piece of writing* put punctuation marks in, mark with punctuation marks. **2** *his speech was punctuated with coughs | punctuated his speech with thumps on the table* interrupt with/by, intersperse with, pepper with, sprinkle with.

punctuation *noun. See table.*

PUNCTUATION MARKS	
accent	hyphen
apostrophe	inverted comma
asterisk	obelus
asterism	omission mark
brace	parenthesis
bracket	period
caret	point
colon	printer's mark
comma	question mark
dagger	quotation mark
dash	semicolon
diacritical mark	solidus
ellipsis	square bracket
em dash/rule	stop
en dash/rule	stroke
exclamation mark	swung dash
full stop	virgule

puncture *noun* **1** *the puncture of the tyre* puncturing, holing, perforation, piercing, pricking, spiking, rupturing, cutting, nicking, slitting. **2** *get/mend a puncture in the tyre* hole, perforation, prick, rupture, cut, nick, slit, leak. **3** *get/mend a puncture* flat tyre; *inf.* flat.

puncture *verb* **1** *the piece of glass punctured the tyre* make a hole in, hole, perforate, pierce, bore, prick, spike, penetrate, rupture, cut, nick, slit. **2** *the news punctured his feeling of joy | puncture his conceit* prick, deflate, flatten, reduce.

punctured *adjective two punctured tyres* flat, deflated.

pundit *noun pundits disagreeing on the implications of the election results* expert, authority, master, guru, sage, highbrow.

pungent *adjective* **1** *a pungent smell* sharp, acrid, acid, sour, biting, stinging, burning,

smarting, irritating. **2** *a pungent taste* sharp, acid, sour, biting, bitter, tart, tangy, spicy, highly-flavoured, aromatic, piquant, peppery, hot, fiery. **3** *pungent remarks/wit* caustic, acid, biting, cutting, sharp, incisive, piercing, penetrating, scathing, pointed, acrimonious, trenchant, mordant, stringent.
Opposites BLAND; MILD.

punish *verb* **1** *punish the children* mete out punishment to, discipline, subject to discipline, take disciplinary action against, teach someone a lesson, penalize, castigate, chastise, smack, slap, beat, cane, whip, flog, lash, scourge. **2** *the boxer really punished his opponent* batter, thrash, beat up, knock about, thump, pummel, trounce; *inf.* wallop, bash, hammer, rough up. **3** *punish the car's engine by driving too fast* maltreat, mistreat, abuse, manhandle, damage, harm.
Opposites PARDON; EXONERATE.

punishing *adjective a punishing exercise routine| journey was extremely punishing* arduous, demanding, taxing, strenuous, hard, exhausting, fatiguing, wearing, tiring, gruelling, uphill, back-breaking.
Opposites EASY; EFFORTLESS.

punishment *noun* **1** *the punishment of the children* punishing, disciplining, penalizing, castigation, castigating, chastising, chastisement, smacking, slapping, beating, caning, whipping, flogging, lashing, scourging. **2** *children receiving a severe punishment* discipline, penalty, castigation, retribution, chastisement, smack, slap, beating, caning, whipping, flogging, lashing, scourging; *inf.* come-uppance. **3** *the punishment of his opponent in the ring* battering, thrashing, beating, thumping, pummelling, trouncing; *inf.* walloping, bashing, hammering, roughing up. **4** *the punishment given to the engine* maltreatment, mistreatment, abuse, manhandling, damage, harm.

punitive *adjective* **1** *take punitive measures against the culprits* punishing, penalizing, disciplinary, corrective, castigating, castigatory, chastising. **2** *punitive rates of taxation* harsh, severe, stiff, taxing, cruel, savage.

punning *noun there is a great deal of punning in the first scene* wordplay, playing on words.

puny *adjective* **1** *puny young men unable to do labouring work* weak, weakly, frail, feeble, undersized, underdeveloped, stunted, small, slight, little, dwarfish, pygmy. **2** *a puny contribution* paltry, petty, trifling, trivial, insignificant, inconsequential, minor, meagre; *inf.* piddling.
Opposites STRONG; STURDY; SUBSTANTIAL.

pupil *noun* **1** *all pupils wearing school uniform* schoolboy/girl, schoolchild, scholar, student. **2** *a pupil of Picasso* student, disciple.

puppet *noun* **1** *puppets amusing children* marionette, string-puppet, glove-puppet, finger-puppet. **2** *accused of being a puppet of management* tool, instrument, cat's-paw, pawn, poodle, creature, dupe, mouthpiece.

purchase *verb* **1** *purchase a new dress/car|purchased some shares* buy, pay for, acquire, pick up, obtain, invest in, put money into. **2** *pur-*

chase *victory with young lives* attain, achieve, gain, win.
Opposites SELL; MARKET.

purchase *noun* **1** *carry her purchases home| proud of her new purchase* buy, acquisition, investment. **2** *difficult to get any purchase on the slippery cliff face* grip, hold, foothold, footing, toehold, support, grasp, leverage, advantage.

pure *adjective* **1** *pure gold* unalloyed, unmixed, unadulterated, uncontaminated, flawless, perfect, genuine, real, true. **2** *pure air/water/food* clean, clear, fresh, unpolluted, untainted, unadulterated, uncontaminated, uninfected, wholesome, natural. **3** *insist on his bride being pure* virgin, virginal, chaste, maidenly, virtuous, undefiled, unsullied. **4** *clerics expected to be pure* uncorrupted, non-corrupt, moral, righteous, honourable, virtuous, honest, upright, decent, good, worthy, noble, blameless, guiltless, pious, sinless. **5** *of pure morals/character* stainless, spotless, unsullied, unblemished, impeccable, immaculate, blameless, sinless. **6** *pure madness* sheer, utter, absolute, downright, out-and-out, complete, total, perfect, unmitigated, unqualified. **7** *pure science of mathematics* theoretical, abstract, conceptual.
Opposites IMPURE; DIRTY; adulterated; IMMORAL.

purely *adverb find out purely by accident* entirely, completely, totally, wholly, solely, only, simply, just, merely.

purge *verb* **1** *purge their souls of sin* cleanse, clear, purify, make pure, shrive, lustrate. **2** *purge the party of dissidents* rid, clear, empty. **3** *purge the dissidents from the party* remove, clear out, expel, eject, dismiss, oust, depose, eradicate, root out, weed out. **4** *purge him of the charge* clear, absolve, pardon, forgive, exonerate, expiate.

purge *noun* **1** *the purge of their souls* purging, cleansing, purification. *See* PURGE *verb* 1. **2** *the purge of the dissidents from the party* removal, expulsion, ejection, dismissal, ousting, deposal, deposition, eradication, rooting out, weeding out. **3** *take a purge* purgative, aperient, laxative, enema, dose of salts.

purify *verb* **1** *purify the water* make pure, clean, cleanse, decontaminate, depollute, filter, filtrate. **2** *purify the air* make pure, clean, cleanse, freshen, deodorize, decontaminate, depollute, refine. **3** *purify the hospital after the cholera epidemic* make pure, clean, cleanse, decontaminate, depollute, disinfect, sterilize, sanitize, fumigate. **4** *purify their souls* purge, cleanse, clear, absolve, shrive, lustrate.
Opposites POLLUTE; CONTAMINATE; CORRUPT.

purist *noun purists disliking loose use of language* precisionist, formalist, stickler, dogmatist, pedant.

puritan *noun puritans who object to sex scenes in television plays* moral zealot/fanatic, moralist, pietist, prude, Mrs Grundy, Grundy; *inf.* goody-goody.

puritanical *adjective a puritanical view of life| her puritanical attitude to entertainment* puritan, ascetic, austere, strait-laced, narrow-minded, rigid, stiff, prudish, prim, priggish, prissy,

Grundyish; *inf.* goody-goody.
Opposites PERMISSIVE; LIBERAL; BROAD-MINDED.

purity *noun* **1** *test the purity of the gold* pureness, flawlessness, perfection, genuineness. *See* PURE 1. **2** *comment on the purity of the water* pureness, cleanness, clearness, freshness, lack of pollution, untaintedness, lack of contamination, wholesomeness. *See* PURE 2. **3** *formerly bridegrooms insisted on the purity of their brides* pureness, virginity, chasteness, chastity, virtue, virtuousness. *See* PURE 3. **4** *purity expected in churchmen* pureness, lack of corruption, righteousness, rectitude, morality, honour, virtuousness, honesty, integrity, uprightness, decency, goodness, worthiness, nobility, blamelessness, guiltlessness, piety, sinlessness. **5** *the purity of their morals* pureness, stainlessness, spotlessness, impeccableness, immaculateness, blamelessness, sinlessness.
Opposites IMPURITY; IMMORALITY.

purport *verb* **1** *he purports to be his firm's official representative | this report purports to be an official statement* claim, allege, profess, assert, proclaim, pretend, feign, pose as. **2** *the document purports that changes are to be made to the administration* mean, signify, indicate, denote, suggest, imply, state, convey, express, show, betoken.

purport *noun* **1** *the purport of his message is that he has gone permanently* gist, substance, drift, implication, meaning, import, tenor, thrust. **2** *his purport is to embarrass them* aim, intention, intent, object, objective, goal, plan, scheme, design, purpose.

purpose *noun* **1** *the purpose of his visit* reason, point, basis, motivation, cause, justification. **2** *his only purpose in life* aim, intention, object, objective, goal, end, target, ambition, aspiration, desire, wish, hope. **3** *their approach to the project lacks purpose* determination, resoluteness, resolution, resolve, firmness, steadfastness, single-mindedness, persistence, perseverance, tenacity, doggedness. **4** *to little purpose | not to much purpose* benefit, advantage, use, usefulness, value, gain, profit, avail, result, outcome, effect. **on purpose** *the driver hit our car on purpose* purposely, intentionally, deliberately, by design, wilfully, wittingly, knowingly, consciously.

purpose *verb* *they purposed to reach the summit that night* intend, have the intention, mean, decide, resolve, determine, plan, aim, have a mind, propose, set one's sights on, aspire.

purposeful *adjective* *attack the problem in a purposeful way* determined, resolute, resolved, firm, steadfast, single-minded, persistent, persevering, tenacious, dogged, unfaltering, unwavering.
Opposites AIMLESS; IRRESOLUTE.

purposely *adverb* *damage the car purposely* on purpose, intentionally, deliberately, by design, wilfully, wittingly, knowingly, consciously.

purse *noun* **1** *have her purse stolen* wallet, money, pouch. **2** *paid for from the public purse* funds, resources, money, coffers, exchequer.

3 *a purse of £50,000 won by the boxer* prize, award, reward, gift, present.

purse *verb* *purse her lips in disapproval* press together, compress, tighten, pucker.

pursuance *noun* *in the pursuance of his duties* execution, discharge, performance, carrying out, doing, pursuing, prosecution, following.

pursue *verb* **1** *the detective pursued the thief* go after, run after, follow, chase, give chase to, hunt, stalk, track, trail, shadow; *inf.* tail. **2** *decide not to pursue the line of inquiry* follow, go on with, proceed with, keep/carry on with, continue with, continue, persist in. **3** *pursue a career in science | a life in science* follow, engage in, be engaged in, be occupied in, work at, practise, prosecute, conduct, ply, apply oneself to. **4** *pursue his goal of happiness | pursue his ambition to be a doctor* strive towards, push towards, work towards, seek, search for, be intent on, aim at, have as a goal, have as an objective, aspire to. **5** *she pursued every eligible young man | he pursued all rich young women* chase after, chase, run after, woo, court, pay court to, pay suit to, make up to, set one's cap at.
Opposites FLEE; AVOID; SHUN; ESCHEW.

pursuit *noun* **1** *take part in the pursuit of the thief* pursuing, chasing, chase, hunt, stalking, tracking; *inf.* tailing. *See* PURSUE 1. **2** *give up the pursuit of that line of inquiry* pursuing, following, proceeding, continuance, persistence. *See* PURSUE 2. **3** *his pursuit of a life of crime | determined on his pursuit of a career in medicine* following, engagement, occupation, work, practising, prosecution, conducting, plying. *See* PURSUE 3. **4** *his pursuit of happiness | their pursuit of their ambitions* striving towards, search, aim, goal, objective, aspiration. *See* PURSUE 4. **5** *her relentless pursuit of eligible young men* chase, wooing, courting, suit, making up to. *See* PURSUE 5.

purvey *verb* **1** *purvey meat to the local schools* provide, supply, furnish, sell, retail, deal in. **2** *purvey information to the public about the drought* provide, supply, furnish, make available, pass on, spread, circulate, communicate, make known, publicize, publish, broadcast, disseminate.

pus *noun* *pus oozing from the wound* matter, suppuration, discharge; *Med.* sanies.

push *verb* **1** *push his friend into the swimming pool* shove, thrust, propel, drive, ram, jolt, butt, jostle. **2** *push one's way through the crowd* shove, thrust, force, press, squeeze, jostle, elbow, shoulder. **3** *push the bell* press, push down, press down, depress, exert pressure on. **4** *push him into applying for the job* encourage, prompt, press, urge, egg on, spur on, prod, goad, incite, impel, dragoon, force, coerce, constrain, browbeat, strong-arm. **5** *firms pushing their latest products* give a push to, promote, advertise, publicize, give a puff to, puff, puff up, boost, beat the drum for; *inf.* plug, hype.
push around *older boys pushing him around* bully, ride roughshod over, trample on, tread on, browbeat, tyrannize, intimidate, domineer.
push off *they told him to push off* go away, leave, depart, get out; *inf.* shove off, make oneself scarce, beat it, get lost, skedaddle, hit the road.
Opposites PULL; DETER; DISCOURAGE.

push *noun* **1** *the children gave his friend a push* shove, thrust, ram, jolt, butt, jostle. **2** *the general launched a big push* attack, assault, advance, onslaught, onset, charge, sortie, sally. **3** *looking for sales staff with push* drive, force, ambition, enterprise, initiative, energy, vigour, vitality, spirit, verve, enthusiasm, go, vim; *inf.* get-up-and-go, gumption, pizazz. **if it comes to the push** *See* IF IT COMES TO THE PINCH (PINCH).

pushover *noun* **1** *the task was a pushover* easy task, something easy, child's play, walk-over; *inf.* piece of cake, picnic, doddle, cinch, breeze. **2** *he'll lend you the money—he's a pushover* fool, dupe; *inf.* sucker, mug, soft touch, soft mark, easy mark, easy touch, walk-over, sap.

pushy *adjective* pushing, assertive, self-assertive, aggressive, forceful, forward, bold, brash, bumptious, presumptuous, cocksure, loud, obnoxious.

pusillanimous *adjective* cowardly, timorous, timid, fearful, faint-hearted, lily-livered, chicken-hearted, spineless, craven; *inf.* yellow, chicken, gutless.
Opposites BRAVE; FEARLESS; PLUCKY.

pussyfoot *verb* **1** *pussyfoot around the house so as not to wake people* creep, tiptoe, pad, steal, sneak, prowl, slink, tread warily. **2** *pussyfoot around instead of saying what he thought* equivocate, be evasive, evade the issue, dodge/sidestep the issue, prevaricate, hedge, fence, hum and haw, hem and haw, beat about the bush, sit on the fence, tergiversate.

pustule *noun* boil, spot, blister, pimple, abscess, papule; *inf.* whitehead, zit.

put *verb* **1** *put the books on the shelf | put him in a difficult situation* place, lay, lay down, set down, deposit, position, rest, stand, locate, situate, settle, emplace, install, posit. **2** *put them in the top grade* place, assign to, consign to, allocate to, rate, rank, grade, classify, categorize, catalogue, bracket. **3** *put the blame on the father/weather* place, attribute to, impute to, impose, fix, attach to, assign to, allocate to, lay, pin. **4** *put a tax on all travellers* impose, levy, demand, require, apply to, assign to, inflict, force, exact from. **5** *put into English* translate, transcribe, turn, render, construe, transliterate, interpret, word, express, phrase, frame, formulate, couch, say, utter, voice, speak, state, pronounce, proclaim. **7** *put to good use | put them to work* set, apply, employ, use, utilize, assign, allocate, devote. **8** *put to death* commit, consign, subject, condemn, sentence, convict, doom. **9** *I'd put it at five acres | put its worth at £500* assess, evaluate, value, estimate, calculate, reckon, guess, measure, establish, fix, place, set; *inf.* guesstimate. **10** *put money on a horse* place, bet, wager, gamble, stake, risk, chance, hazard. **11** *put it to the committee* set before, lay before, present, bring forward, forward, submit, tender, offer, proffer, put forward, set forth, advance, posit. **12** *put the shot* throw, toss, fling, pitch, cast, hurl, heave, lob, let fly, shy. **13** *put his fist through the window* thrust, drive, plunge, stick, push, force, lunge, knock, bang, smash, bash. **put about 1** *put a rumour about | put it about that he's bankrupt* spread, bandy about, circulate, disseminate, make public, make known, give out, publicize, broadcast, propagate, announce, bruit. **2** *ships putting about* come/go about, change course, alter course, change direction, turn round. **put across, put over** *successfully put across the message* get across/over, convey, communicate, make clear, explain, express, spell out, make understood, clarify. **put one across/over on** *succeed in putting one across on his rival* trick, deceive, hoodwink, mislead, delude, fool, take in, dupe, lead on, outwit, bamboozle, steal a march on; *inf.* pull a fast one on, con, make a sucker of. **put aside 1** *put aside food/money for a rainy day* put/lay by, put away, set/lay aside, save, reserve, keep in reserve, keep, put/lay down, store, stockpile, hoard, deposit, stow away, salt away, squirrel away. **2** *put aside the newspaper* set/lay aside, put to one side, move to one side, cast aside, delude, abandon, dispense with, drop. **3** *put aside their differences* set/lay aside, forget, disregard, ignore, forget, discount, bury, consign to oblivion. **put away 1** *put away food/money for a rainy day* put/lay aside, put/lay by, set/lay aside, save, keep in reserve, store, stockpile. **2** *put away the books* put back, replace, set back, return to its/their place, tidy away, tidy up, clear away. **3** *put away all thoughts of him* set/put/lay aside, discard, cast aside, forget, disregard, get rid of, rid oneself of, jettison, consign to oblivion. **4** *put the criminal/mental patient away* put in prison/mental hospital, confine, lock up, shut away/up, commit, imprison, hospitalize, institutionalize, certify; *inf.* bang up. **5** *put away quantities of food* consume, eat, eat up, swallow, gulp down, devour, down, get down, gobble up, bolt, wolf; *inf.* tuck away/into. **6** *put away the enemy | the injured dog had to be put away* kill, do away with, murder, slaughter, slay, dispatch, finish off, destroy, put down, put to sleep, put out of its misery; *inf.* bump off, wipe out. **put down 1** *put down a rebellion* crush, suppress, quash, quell, stamp out, stop, repress, smash, extinguish. **2** *put their names down* write down, put in writing, note down, make a note of, jot down, take down, set down, enter, list, record, register, log. **3** *put it down to experience* mark down, set down, attribute, ascribe, impute, chalk up to, blame on. **4** *put down cases of port* lay down/aside, put aside, set aside, save, store. **5** *put down the sick animal* put to sleep, put out of its misery, destroy, put away, do away with, kill. **6** *always putting down his wife* snub, disparage, deprecate, belittle, denigrate, deflate, slight, humiliate, crush, mortify. **put forward** *put forward a theory | his name was put forward for a life peerage* lay before, set before, submit, present, suggest, advance, tender, propose, move, introduce, offer, proffer, recommend, suggest, nominate, name. **put off 1** *put off the meeting* postpone, put back, defer, delay, adjourn, hold over, reschedule, shelve; *inf.* put on ice, put on the back burner. **2** *put off by his surly behaviour | the smell put her off* discourage, dissuade, dishearten, distress, dismay, discomfit, nonplus, daunt, repel, offend, disgust, revolt, sicken, nauseate. **3** *don't put the driver off* distract, divert the attention of, disturb the concentration of, draw away, sidetrack. **put it on** *he's not hurt—he's putting it on* pretend, play-act, make believe, exaggerate. **put on 1** *put on her new suit* dress in, get dressed in, clothe oneself in, change into, slip into, don. **2** *put on the light* switch on, turn on. **3** *put on transport for travellers to go to the airport* lay on, provide, supply, furnish, make available. **4** *put on a production of Hamlet* stage, mount, present, produce. **5** *she's not sad—she's putting on the grief* feign, fake, sham, simulate, affect. **6** *put money on a horse* place, lay, bet, wager. **put out 1** *she is easily put out* annoy, anger, irritate, exasperate, infuriate, provoke, irk, vex, gall, disturb, perturb, disconcert, agitate, harass. **2** *we don't want to put you out by staying to dinner | don't put yourself out* inconvenience, put (someone) to trouble, trouble, bother, impose upon, discommode, incommode. **3** *put out the fire* extinguish, quench, douse, stamp out. **4** *put out the candle* extinguish, blow out, snuff out, douse. **5** *put out a news report on the king's health* bring out, issue, circulate, release, disclose, make known, make public, publish, broadcast, publicize. **put up 1** *put up new houses/blocks of flats* build, construct, erect, raise. **2** *put up his friends for the night* give accommodation to, accommodate, provide with board and lodging, house, give a roof to, give a bed to, entertain. **3** *put up proposals for the expansion of the firm* put forward, propose, present, submit, recommend. **4** *put his friend up for chairman* put forward, nominate, propose, recommend. **5** *put up the money for the campaign* provide, supply, furnish, give, donate, pay, advance, pledge. **6** *put up prices* raise, increase; *inf.* jack up. **7** *put up notices advertising the event* stick up, post, display, exhibit. **put (someone) up to** *put his friend up to breaking into the house* egg on to, urge, encourage, persuade, incite, goad, spur. **put up with** endure, tolerate, bear, stand, abide, suffer, take, stomach, brook, accept, swallow. **put upon** *she is so obliging that she gets put upon* take advantage of, impose upon, take for granted, exploit, overwork, overburden,

saddle.
Opposites TAKE; REMOVE.

putative *adjective* **1** *the putative father of the baby* supposed, assumed, presumed, presumptive, acknowledged, accepted, recognized, commonly believed, commonly regarded, alleged, reputed.

put-down *noun regard his remark as a gross put-down* snub, rebuff, slight, disparagement, sneer, humiliation.

puzzle *verb he was puzzled by her behaviour* perplex, baffle, stump, beat, mystify, confuse, bewilder, nonplus, stagger, dumbfound, daze, confound; *inf.* flummox. **puzzle over** *puzzling over what she had said | puzzling over her motives* rack one's brains about, cudgel one's brains about, think hard about, give much thought to, mull over, muse over, ponder, brood about, wonder about. **puzzle out** *puzzle out the solution* find the answer to, work out, think out, think through, figure out, reason out, solve, resolve, decipher, find the key to, unravel; *inf.* crack.

puzzled *adjective the puzzled audience looked in amazement at the magician's tricks | despite all the information the police are still puzzled* perplexed, baffled, stumped, nonplussed, beaten, mystified, confused, bewildered, confounded, staggered, dumbfounded, dazed, at a loss, at sea; *inf.* flummoxed.

puzzling *adjective a puzzling situation* difficult, hard, unclear, perplexing, knotty, baffling, enigmatic, abstruse, nonplussing, mystifying, bewildering, unfathomable, inexplicable, incomprehensible, beyond one, above one's head.
Opposites CLEAR; STRAIGHTFORWARD; COMPREHENSIBLE; LUCID.

pygmy *noun* **1** *insultingly call the small man a pygmy* small man/woman/person, midget, dwarf; *inf.* shrimp, pint-sized person, Tom Thumb. **2** *a pygmy among intellectual giants* cipher, nonentity, nobody, lightweight; *inf.* pipsqueak.

pyromaniac *noun* arsonist, fire-raiser, incendiary; *inf.* firebug.

Qq

quack noun **1** *quacks selling fake medicines* charlatan, mountebank, impostor, fraud, fake, confidence trickster, pretender, humbug; *inf.* con man, phoney. **2** *get the quack to examine you* doctor, medical/general practitioner; *inf.* GP, doc, medic.

quack adjective *a quack cure for colds* fake, fraudulent, counterfeit, sham; *inf.* phoney.

quaff verb drink, swallow, gulp down, imbibe; *inf.* guzzle, swig.

quagmire noun **1** *birds on the quagmire* quag, bog, peat bog, marsh, swamp, morass, mire, slough, fen. **2** *in a quagmire with no place to live* difficulty, quandary, dilemma, predicament, plight, tight corner, muddle, entanglement, involvement, imbroglio, impasse, stalemate; *inf.* jam, scrape, pickle, fix, hot water, stew.

quail verb flinch, shrink, recoil, shy away, pull back, draw back, cower, cringe, shudder, shiver, tremble, shake, quake, blench, blanch.

quaint adjective pleasantly old-fashioned, old-fashioned, old-world, attractively unusual, unusual, droll, curious, whimsical, attractive, charming, sweet.
Opposites UGLY; MODERN; NEWFANGLED.

quake verb shake, tremble, quiver, shiver, shudder, rock, vibrate, pulsate, throb.

qualification noun **1** *qualification to be a teacher* certification, training, competence, competency, accomplishment, eligibility, acceptability, suitableness, preparedness, fitness, proficiency, skilfulness, adeptness, capability, aptitude; skill, ability, attribute, endowment. **2** *say what you mean without qualification* modification, limitation, restriction, reservation, stipulation, allowance, adaptation, adjustment; condition, proviso, provision, caveat.

qualified adjective **1** *a qualified doctor* certificated, trained, fitted, fit, equipped, prepared, competent, accomplished, proficient, skilled, skilful, adept, practised, experienced, expert, capable, able. **2** *a qualified approval* modified, limited, conditional, restricted, bounded, contingent, confined, circumscribed, reserved, guarded, equivocal, stipulated, adapted, adjusted.

qualify verb **1** *he qualified as a doctor* gain certification/qualifications, train, take instruction. **2** *his training qualifies him to teach* certify, license, empower, authorize, allow, permit, sanction, warrant, fit, equip, prepare, arm, make ready, ground, train, educate, coach, teach, instruct. **3** *qualify her statement* modify, limit, make conditional, restrict. **4** *qualify her criticism* modify, temper, soften, modulate, mitigate, reduce, lessen, diminish. **5** *not qualify as poetry* be characterizable as, meet the requirement of, be eligible, be designated.

quality noun **1** *the material is of poor quality* degree of excellence, standard, grade, level, make, sort, type, kind, variety. **2** *his quality has been recognized* excellence, superiority, merit, worth, value, calibre, talent, talentedness, eminence, pre-eminence, distinction. **3** *they have many good qualities* feature, trait, attribute, characteristic, aspect, property, peculiarity. **4** *differences in the quality of the two personalities* character, nature, constitution, make-up. **5** *the quality are not necessarily wealthy* aristocracy, nobility, upper class, gentry.

qualm noun **1** *have some qualms about going* doubt, misgiving, hesitation, hesitancy, reluctance, disinclination, anxiety, apprehension, disquiet, uneasiness, concern. **2** *have no qualms about having hurt them* pang/twinge of conscience, scruple, compunction, remorse.

quandary noun awkward situation, difficulty, dilemma, predicament, plight, tight corner/spot, cleft stick, state of uncertainty/perplexity, muddle, impasse; *inf.* jam, pickle, fix.

quantity noun **1** *what quantity of books/paper do you need?* number, amount, total, aggregate, sum, quota, weight. **2** *a quantity of books/paper has gone missing* number, quite a number, good number/few, several, numerous, many, amount, large amount, considerable amounts; *inf.* lot, lots. **3** *estimate the quantity* property, aspect; size, capacity, mass, volume, bulk, extent, length, area, time.

quark noun. See table.

ATTRIBUTES OF QUARKS AND ANTIQUARKS	
beauty	minus-green
blue	minus-red
bottom	red
charm	strangeness
down	top
green	truth
minus-blue	up

quarrel noun **1** *the lovers have had a quarrel* argument, row, fight, disagreement, difference of opinion, dispute, disputation, squabble, altercation, wrangle, tiff, misunderstanding, feud, vendetta; *inf.* spat, scrap. **2** *a quarrel developed in the pub* argument, row, fight, tussle, disturbance, altercation, clash, conflict, affray, fracas, fray, brawl, rumpus, brouhaha, commotion, uproar, tumult, scrimmage; *inf.* dust-up, set-to, shindig. **3** *I have no quarrel with him* bone of contention, complaint, grievance, resentment.
Opposites RECONCILIATION; AGREEMENT.

quarrel verb **1** *the lovers quarrelled* argue, have a row/fight, row, fight, dispute, squabble, bicker, spar, wrangle, have a misunderstand-

ing; *inf.* fall out. **2** *I cannot quarrel with his logic* find fault with, fault, criticize, object to, take exception to, complain about, cavil, carp; *inf.* pick holes in, nit-pick.
Opposites AGREE.

quarrelsome *adjective* argumentative, belligerent, disputatious, contentious, pugnacious, combative, ready for a fight, bellicose, litigious, hot-tempered, irascible, choleric, irritable.
Opposites PEACEABLE.

quarry *noun huntsmen stalking their quarry* prey, victim, prize.

quarter *noun* **1** *live in the Latin quarter of the city* district, area, region, part, side, neighbourhood, locality, zone, territory, province.
2 *accept help from any quarter* direction, place, point, spot, location. **3** *receive no quarter from the tyrant* mercy, leniency, clemency, lenity, compassion, pity, forgiveness, indulgence.

quarter *verb soldiers quartered in the town* put up, house, board, billet, accommodate, lodge, install, put a roof over someone's head.

quarters *plural noun* lodgings, rooms, chambers, barracks; accommodation, billet, residence, abode, dwelling, domicile, habitation, cantonment; *inf.* digs, pad.

quash *verb* **1** *quash the jail sentence* annul, declare null and void, nullify, invalidate, void, cancel, overrule, override, overthrow, reject, set aside, reverse, revoke, rescind, repeal.
2 *quash the rebellion* crush, put down, squash, quell, subdue, suppress, repress, quench, extinguish, stamp out, put a stop to, end, terminate, defeat, destroy.
Opposites VALIDATE; INCITE; PROVOKE; SUPPORT.

quasi- *prefix* **1** *quasi-scientific evidence* supposedly, seemingly, apparently, nominally, pseudo. **2** *a quasi-friend* supposed, so-called, would-be, pretended, pretend, sham, fake, pseudo.

quaver *verb his voice quavered* quiver, vibrate, tremble, shake, waver.

queasy *adjective* sick, nauseated, ill, indisposed, dizzy; *Am.* sick to one's stomach; *inf.* under the weather.

queen *noun* **1** *the queen reigned for 50 years* monarch, sovereign, ruler, king's consort. *See table at* ROYALTY. **2** *she was the queen of Wimbledon* pop star, prima donna, idol, ideal, doyenne.
Opposites KING.

queer *adjective* **1** *a queer fellow* | *queer behaviour* odd, strange, unusual, extraordinary, funny, curious, peculiar, weird, outlandish, singular, eccentric, unconventional, unorthodox, atypical, abnormal, irregular, anomalous, deviant, *outré*, offbeat; *inf.* off-the-wall. **2** *it's a queer story* | *something queer going on* strange, peculiar, suspicious, suspect, irregular, questionable, dubious, doubtful; *inf.* fishy, shady. **3** *feel a bit queer* ill, unwell, sick, queasy, faint, dizzy, giddy, light-headed.
Opposites ORDINARY; CONVENTIONAL; NORMAL; WELL.

queer *verb queer one's chances* spoil, damage, impair, mar, wreck, ruin, injure, harm, hurt,

jeopardize, threaten, put at risk, endanger, imperil.

quell *verb* **1** *quell the rebellion* | *quell rebellious forces* quash, defeat, conquer, vanquish, overpower, overcome, overwhelm, rout, crush, suppress, subdue, extinguish, stamp out, put down. **2** *quell their fears* allay, lull, put at rest, quiet, silence, calm, soothe, appease, assuage, abate, deaden, dull, pacify, tranquillize, mitigate, palliate.
Opposites AGITATE; EXCITE; PROVOKE.

quench *verb* **1** *quench one's thirst* satisfy, slake, sate, satiate. **2** *quench the candle* extinguish, put out, snuff out, blow out, douse. **3** *quench their desire* suppress, extinguish, stamp out, smother, stifle.

query *noun* **1** *raise a query* question, enquiry. **2** *his behaviour raises a query as to his sanity* question, question mark, doubt, uncertainty, reservation, suspicion; scepticism.

query *verb* **1** *"where are we?" he queried* ask, enquire, question. **2** *he queried their fitness for the job* call into question, question, raise/entertain doubts about, throw doubt on, doubt, have/harbour suspicions about, suspect, feel uneasy about, express reservations about, challenge, raise objections to.

quest *noun* **1** *in quest of a better life* search, seeking, pursuit, chase, hunt. **2** *their quest was the holy grail* goal, aim, objective, purpose, quarry, prey. **3** *knights setting out on a quest* adventure, expedition, journey, voyage, exploration, crusade.

question *noun* **1** *answer her questions* query, enquiry, interrogation. **2** *there is no question that he is ill* doubt, dubiety, dubiousness, dispute, argument, debate, controversy, reservation. **3** *there is the question of safety* issue, point at issue, problem, matter, point, subject, topic, theme, bone of contention. **beyond question** beyond doubt, without doubt, undoubtedly, indisputably, incontestably, incontrovertibly. **in question** *the matter in question* being discussed, under discussion/consideration, at issue, on the agenda. **out of the question** impossible, inconceivable, unthinkable, unimaginable, absurd, ridiculous, preposterous.
Opposites ANSWER; RESPONSE; CERTAINTY.

question *verb* **1** *question the witnesses* ask questions of, interrogate, cross-examine, cross-question, quiz, catechize, interview, sound out, examine, give the third degree to; *inf.* grill, pump. **2** *question his motives* call into question, query, raise doubts about, throw doubt on, have suspicions about, express reservations about, challenge, raise objections to. *See* QUERY *verb* 2.

questionable *adjective his motive/ability is questionable* open to question/doubt, doubtful, dubious, uncertain, debatable, in dispute, arguable, controversial, controvertible.
Opposites CERTAIN; INDISPUTABLE.

queue *noun join the queue* | *a queue of lorries* line, row, column, file, chain, string, train, succession, sequence, series, concatenation.

quibble noun **1** *raise quibbles over the cost* petty criticism/complaint, protest, trivial objection, niggle, cavil, nicety; *inf.* nit-picking. **2** *introduce the issue as a quibble* evasion, avoidance, equivocation, prevarication, dodge, hedging, fudging.

quibble verb **1** *quibble about a minor detail* raise petty objections (to), cavil, carp, pettifog, split hairs, chop logic; *inf.* nit-pick. **2** *he quibbles so that it is difficult to get a straight answer* be evasive, equivocate, avoid the issue, prevaricate, hedge, fudge, be ambiguous; *inf.* beat about the bush.

quick adjective **1** *a quick runner/worker/reader* fast, rapid, speedy, swift, fleet, express. **2** *a quick response* prompt, without delay, immediate, instantaneous, expeditious. **3** *a quick look at the map* brief, brisk, fleeting, momentary, hasty, hurried, cursory, perfunctory. **4** *the child is very quick* quick-witted, sharp-witted, alert, intelligent. *See* QUICK-WITTED. **5** *quick of temper* irascible, irritable. *See* QUICK-TEMPERED.
Opposites SLOW; SLUGGISH; LONG; DULL.

quicken verb **1** *his pulse quickened* become/ grow faster, speed up, accelerate. **2** *they quickened their steps/progress* speed up, accelerate, expedite, hasten, hurry, hurry up, precipitate. **3** *the film quickened his interest in wild life* stimulate, stir up, arouse, rouse, incite, instigate, whet, inspire, kindle, fan, refresh, strengthen, revive, revitalize, resuscitate, revivify.

quickly adverb **1** *run quickly* fast, rapidly, speedily, swiftly, with all speed, at speed, with all possible haste, at the double, posthaste; *inf.* at a rate of knots, hell for leather, like a bat out of hell, like an arrow from a bow. **2** *respond quickly* promptly, without delay, immediately, instantaneously, expeditiously. **3** *read the letter quickly* rapidly, briskly, hastily, hurriedly, cursorily, perfunctorily.
Opposites SLOWLY; THOROUGHLY.

quick-tempered adjective irascible, irritable, hot-tempered, fiery, hasty, impatient, touchy, testy, snappish, quarrelsome, petulant, choleric, splenetic, volatile; *inf.* on a short fuse.
Opposites PLACID; CALM; PHLEGMATIC.

quick-witted adjective quick, sharp-witted, nimble-witted, alert, intelligent, bright, lively, smart, perceptive, discerning, shrewd; *inf.* quick on the uptake.
Opposites STUPID; DULL.

quid pro quo noun exchange, substitution, trading, trade-off, barter, compensation, recompense, requital, reprisal, retaliation.

quiescent adjective inert, dormant, passive, inactive, idle, still, stagnant, torpid.
Opposites ACTIVE.

quiet adjective **1** *the house was quiet* silent, hushed, noiseless, soundless, peaceful. **2** *a quiet voice* soft, low, inaudible. **3** *she's a quiet person* calm, serene, composed, placid, untroubled, peaceful, tranquil, gentle, mild, temperate, unexcitable, restrained, phlegmatic, imperturbable, moderate, reserved, uncommunicative, taciturn, silent. **4** *quiet colours/clothes* unobtrusive, unostentatious, restrained, muted, understated, subdued, subtle, conserv-

ative, sober, modest, demure. **5** *live in a quiet village* peaceful, sleepy, undisturbed, unfrequented, private, secluded, sequestered, retired, isolated, out of the way; *inf.* off the beaten track. **6** *the shop/business is quiet today* inactive, not busy, sluggish. **7** *have a quiet word with him* private, confidential, secret, discreet, unofficial, off the record; *inf.* hush-hush. **8** *we kept his presence quiet* secret, unrevealed, undisclosed, uncommunicated; *inf.* hush-hush.
Opposites LOUD; NOISY; OBTRUSIVE; BUSY.

quiet noun *in the quiet of the evening* quietness, stillness, silence, hush, noiselessness, soundlessness, peace, peacefulness, calmness, tranquillity, serenity.

quieten verb **1** *quieten the noisy children* silence, hush, shush, quiet; *inf.* shut up. **2** *the children soon quieten* become quiet, grow silent, settle down; *inf.* shut up. **3** *quieten the frightened horse* calm, calm down, soothe, tranquillize. **4** *quieten their fears* allay, soothe, calm, tranquillize, appease, lull, pacify, mollify, palliate, suppress, quell, stifle, dull, deaden.

quietly adverb **1** *speak quietly* softly, in a low voice, in low/hushed tones, in a whisper, in an undertone, inaudibly. **2** *creep out quietly* silently, noiselessly, soundlessly. **3** *tell him quietly that he must leave* privately, confidentially, secretly, discreetly. **4** *she is quietly confident* calmly, patiently, placidly, serenely, undemonstratively, unemotionally. **5** *dress quietly* unobtrusively, unostentatiously, with restraint, conservatively, soberly, modestly, demurely.

quilt noun eiderdown, duvet, continental quilt.

quintessence noun **1** *the novel captures the quintessence of youth* essence, essentialness, core, heart, soul, spirit, quiddity. **2** *he is the quintessence of a gentleman* embodiment, personification, exemplar, perfect example, ideal, beau idéal.

quip noun *make witty quips* witticism, sally, wisecrack, joke, jest, *bon mot*, epigram, aphorism; *inf.* one-liner, crack.

quirk noun *it is one of his quirks to polish his car everyday* idiosyncrasy, peculiarity, oddity, eccentricity, foible, whim, vagary, caprice, kink, mannerism, habit, characteristic, trait, feature, obsession, passion, mania, fetish, *idée fixe*; *inf.* hang-up.

quit verb **1** *quit smoking* give up, stop, cease, discontinue, drop, leave off, abandon, abstain from, desist from. **2** *quit his job* leave, depart from, vacate, walk out on. **3** *he has decided to quit* leave, depart, go away, take off; *inf.* call it a day, call it quits, pack it in.
Opposites START; BEGIN; CONTINUE.

quite adverb **1** *he has quite recovered* completely, fully, entirely, totally, wholly, absolutely, in all respects. **2** *he is quite talented but not as good as his brother* fairly, relatively, moderately, reasonably, to some extent/ degree, to a certain extent, rather, somewhat.

quiver verb *quiver with fear* tremble, shiver, vibrate, quaver, quake, shudder, pulsate, convulse, palpitate.

quiver *noun a quiver of fear* tremble, tremor, shiver, vibration, quaver, shudder, pulsation, convulsion, palpitation, throb, spasm, tic.

quiz *noun* **1** *take part in a television quiz* test of knowledge, knowledge test. **2** *police subjecting them to a quiz* questioning, interrogation, cross-examination, cross-questioning, catechism, examination, third degree; *inf.* grilling, pumping.

quiz *verb quiz them about their movements* question, ask, interrogate, cross-examine, cross-question, catechize; *inf.* pump, grill.

quizzical *adjective a quizzical look/smile* questioning, puzzled, perplexed, baffled, mystified, mocking, teasing.

quota *noun* share, allowance, allocation, portion, ration, part, slice, measure, proportion; *inf.* cut, whack.

quotation *noun* **1** *full of quotations from Shakespeare* citation, reference, allusion, excerpt, extract, selection, passage, line; *inf.* quote. **2** *give them a quotation for the work* estimate, estimated price, cost, charge, figure; *inf.* quote.

quote *verb* **1** *quote verses from the Bible* repeat, iterate, recite, reproduce. **2** *he could not quote them an example of what he meant* cite, give, name, instance, mention, refer to, make reference to, allude to. **3** *quote for the job* estimate for, price, set a price for.

RABBITS AND HARES

angora	European
Arctic hare	rabbit
Belgian hare	jackrabbit
brown hare	mountain hare
cony	pika
cottontail	snowshoe hare

rabbit *noun. See table.*

rabble *noun* **1** *a rabble gathered round the accident* mob, horde, swarm, crowd, throng. **2** *noblemen despising the rabble* common people, populace, commonality, the mob, rank and file, peasantry, hoi polloi, riff-raff, canaille; the masses, lower classes, dregs of society; *inf.* great unwashed.
Opposites ARISTOCRACY; NOBILITY.

rabid *adjective* **1** *rabid dogs* rabies-infected, mad, foaming at the mouth, hydrophobic. **2** *rabid socialists/conservatives* fanatical, extreme, overzealous, overenthusiastic, fervent, perfervid, unreasonable, irrational, intolerant, bigoted, narrow-minded, narrow. **3** *rabid hatred/enemies* violent, wild, frenzied, frenetic, frantic, raging, raving, maniacal, distracted, beside oneself, berserk.
Opposites INDIFFERENT; HALF-HEARTED; MODERATE.

race¹ *noun* **1** *the competitors for the race* speed contest, competition, chase, pursuit, relay. **2** *the race for the presidency* contest, competition, rivalry, contention. **3** *drowned in the mill-race* channel, waterway, watercourse, sluice, spillway.

race² *verb* **1** *horses racing at Doncaster* run, take part in a race, contend, compete. **2** *race each other in the Olympics* run against, compete against, be pitted against. **3** *race to the finishing line* run, sprint, dash, dart, bolt, make a dash/bolt for, speed, hare, fly, tear, zoom, accelerate, career. **4** *you'll have to race to get there on time* hurry, hasten, make haste, rush; *inf.* get cracking, get a move on, step on it.

race³ *noun* **1** *humankind divided into races* racial division, people, ethnic group. **2** *discrimination on grounds of race* racial type, blood, bloodline, stock, line, lineage, breed, strain, stirps, extraction, ancestry, parentage. **3** *sailors are a race apart* group, type, class, species.

racial *adjective* race-related, ethnic, ethnological.

racism *noun* racialism, racial discrimination, racial prejudice/bigotry, apartheid.

racist *noun* racialist, bigot, illiberal.

racist *adjective* racialist, discriminatory, prejudiced, bigoted, intolerant, illiberal.

rack *noun* **1** *a clothes/luggage rack* frame, framework, stand, form, trestle, structure, holder, shelf. **2** *prisoners on the rack* instrument of torture, stretching instrument. **on the rack** in pain, in agony, in distress, suffering, in torture.

rack *verb* **1** *he was racked with pain* torture, agonize, afflict, torment, persecute, plague, distress, rend, tear, harrow, crucify, convulse. **2** *rack one's back/ankle* strain, wrench, rick, pull, stretch, put out of joint, disjoint, throw out, twist, sprain.

racket *noun* **1** *a racket coming from next door* noise, din, row, commotion, disturbance, uproar, hubbub, hullabaloo; clamour, pandemonium, tumult, shouting, yelling. **2** *he's involved in a drugs racket* criminal activity, illegal scheme/enterprise, fraud, fraudulent scheme, swindle. **3** *what racket is he in?* business, line of business, line, occupation, profession, job; *inf.* game.

raconteur *noun* storyteller, teller of tales, spinner of yarns, narrator, relater, romancer.

racy *adjective* **1** *a racy prose style* vigorous, lively, spirited, energetic, dynamic, animated, vivacious, enthusiastic, buoyant, sparkling, fast-moving, exciting, stimulating, entertaining, fascinating; *inf.* sexy, peppy. **2** *his racy jokes* risqué, suggestive, off-colour, ribald, bawdy, vulgar, coarse, crude, rude, smutty, dirty, blue, indecent, indelicate, immodest, naughty; *inf.* spicy, near the bone/knuckle. **3** *a racy wine/sauce* strong, strong-flavoured, distinctive, full-flavoured, flavoursome, tasty, rich, pungent, well-flavoured, piquant, spicy, tangy, peppery.

raddled *adjective* haggard, coarsened, the worse for wear, dishevelled, unkempt, dilapidated, run-down, broken-down, worn-out.

radiance *noun* **1** *the radiance of the sun* light, shining, brightness, brilliance, luminosity, effulgence, incandescence, glow, gleam, glitter, sparkle, shimmer, glare. **2** *the radiance of the bride* joyfulness, joy, elation, rapture, blitheness, happiness, delight, pleasure, gaiety, warmth. **3** *the radiance of her beauty* resplendence, splendour, dazzlingness.

radiant *adjective* **1** *the radiant sun/light* irradiant, shining, bright, illuminated, brilliant, luminous, luminescent, lustrous, lucent, effulgent, refulgent, incandescent, beaming, glowing, gleaming, glittering, sparkling, shimmering, glaring. **2** *the bride was radiant* joyful, elated, in raptures, ecstatic, blissfully happy, delighted, pleased, gay, happy, glowing; *inf.* in seventh heaven, on cloud nine. **3** *her radiant beauty* splendid, resplendent, magnificent, dazzling, glowing, vivid, intense.
Opposites DARK; DULL; GLOOMY.

radiate *verb* **1** *radiating heat/light* send out/forth, scatter, disperse, diffuse, spread, shed, give off/out, emit, emanate. **2** *radiate joy/hope* transmit, emanate, show, exhibit, demonstrate; *inf.* be the picture of. **3** *lines radiating* branch out, spread out, diverge, divaricate, issue.

radiation *noun* **1** *the radiation of light/X-rays* emission, emanation, propagation, transmission. **2** *ultraviolet/infrared radiation* waves, rays; transmitted energy. *See tables. See also table at* WAVE.

RADIOACTIVE ELEMENTS

actinides	francium	protac-
actinium	mendele-	tinium
americium	vium	radium
astatine	neptunium	radon
berkelium	nobelium	tech-
californium	plutonium	netium
curium	polonium	thorium
einsteinium	pro-	tritium
fermium	methium	uranium

TYPES OF RADIATION

alpha radiation	gravitational radia-
background radia-	tion
tion	infrared radiation
beta radiation	ionizing radiation
bremsstrahlung	microwaves
Cerenkov radia-	radio waves
tion	submillimetre radia-
coherent radia-	tion
tion	synchrotron radia-
cosmic rays	tion
electromagnetic	ultraviolet radiation
radiation	visible radiation
gamma radiation	X-rays

radical *adjective* **1** *radical issues/errors* fundamental, basic, rudimentary, elementary, elemental, constitutional. **2** *radical change needed* thorough, complete, total, entire, absolute, utter, comprehensive, exhaustive, sweeping, far-reaching, profound, drastic, stringent, violent. **3** *radical views/actions* extremist, extreme, immoderate, revolutionary, rebel, rebellious, militant, fanatic, leftist, left-wing. **Opposites** MINOR; SUPERFICIAL; CONSERVATIVE.

raffish *adjective* **1** *he has a raffish air* rakish, bohemian, jaunty, dashing, devil-may-care, casual, careless, disreputable, dissolute, dissipated, debauched, decadent, degenerate. **2** *raffish bars/decoration* tawdry, flashy, gaudy, loud, garish, showy, vulgar, tasteless, gross, coarse, meretricious; *inf.* flash.

raffle *noun* lottery, draw, sweepstake, sweep, tombola.

rag¹ *noun* **1** *a rag of cloth* remnant, fragment, worn/frayed piece. **2** *hand me the oil rag* cloth, duster.

rag² *noun* **1** *students holding a rag* fund-raising event, charity event, charitable event. **2** *just having a rag* prank, lark, caper, romp, joke, practical joke.

rag³ *verb* *other children ragging him* tease, poke fun at, make fun of, make a fool of, taunt; *inf.* rib, send up.

ragamuffin *noun* urchin, street arab, guttersnipe.

ragbag *noun* jumble, hotchpotch, mishmash, mixed bag, miscellany, medley, motley collection, pot-pourri, gallimaufry, salmagundi; *inf.* mix, omnium gatherum.

rage *noun* **1** *be filled with rage* fury, anger, wrath, ire, high dudgeon, frenzy, madness, raving. **2** *fly into a rage* fit of rage/fury, frenzy, tantrum, paroxysm of rage/anger, rampage. **3** *the rage of the storm* violence, turbulence, tumult, fire and fury. **all the rage** ultra-fashionable, ultra-popular, in demand; *inf.* trendy, latest thing/craze.

rage *verb* **1** *the teacher is raging* be furious, be infuriated, be angry, seethe, be beside oneself, lose one's temper, boil over, rant, rave, rant and rave, storm, fume, fulminate; *inf.* foam at the mouth, blow one's top, blow up, blow a fuse/gasket, hit the ceiling, flip one's lid, freak out. **2** *rage against the new rules* fulminate, complain vociferously, storm, inveigh against, rail. **3** *the storm is raging* be violent, be at its height, be turbulent, be tempestuous.

ragged *adjective* **1** *ragged clothes* tattered, in tatters, torn, rent, in holes, holey, worn to shreds, falling to pieces, threadbare, frayed, the worse for wear. **2** *ragged children* in rags, shabby, unkempt, down and out, down at heel, poor, destitute, indigent. **3** *a ragged coastline* jagged, notched, serrated, saw-toothed, craggy, rugged, uneven, irregular. **4** *a ragged prose style* rough, crude, unpolished, unrefined, faulty, imperfect, irregular, uneven. **5** *a ragged band of soldiers* in disarray, straggling, straggly, disorganized, fragmented.

raging *adjective* **1** *met by a raging teacher* enraged, furious, angry, infuriated, wrathful, incensed, seething, fuming, ranting, raving, mad. *See* RAGE *verb* 1. **2** *a raging storm* violent, strong, wild, stormy, turbulent, tempestuous, blustery. **3** *a raging toothache* agonizing, excruciating, painful, throbbing, aching, sore. **4** *a raging thirst* extreme, excessive, severe, very great, inordinate.

rags *plural noun* *dressed in rags* tatters, tattered/old clothes; torn clothing.

raid *noun* **1** *make a raid on the enemy* surprise attack, assault, onset, onslaught, invasion, incursion, foray, charge, thrust, sortie, sally. **2** *a bank raid* robbery, break-in; *inf.* smash and grab. **3** *a police raid* surprise search; *inf.* bust.

raid *verb* **1** *raid the enemy lines* make a raid on, attack, assault, invade, charge, assail, storm, rush, set upon, descend upon, swoop upon; *dial.* reive. **2** *raid the enemy supplies | raid the fridge* plunder, pillage, loot, rifle, forage, ransack, steal from. **3** *raid a bank* rob, break into. **4** *police raiding a house* make a raid on, search thoroughly, make a search of; *inf.* bust.

raider *noun* **1** *the enemy raiders* attacker, assaulter, invader, pillager, plunderer, marauder, ransacker, sacker; *dial.* reiver. **2** *the* *bank raiders | the raiders of the supplies* robber, burglar, thief; *inf.* crook.

rail *verb rail against the new rules* inveigh against, declaim against, rage against, protest strongly, complain bitterly, criticize severely, censure, condemn, castigate; *inf.* lambaste.

railing *noun* rails; balustrade, fencing, paling, barrier.

raillery *noun* banter, badinage, teasing, joking, japing, persiflage; *inf.* kidding, ragging, ribbing.

rain *noun* **1** *soaked in the rain* rainfall, precipitation, raindrops, drizzle, shower, rainstorm, cloudburst, torrent, downpour, deluge, thunderstorm. **2** *a rain of arrows* shower, hail, deluge, volley.

rain *verb* **1** *it is raining* pour, pour/come down, precipitate, shower, drizzle, rain hard, rain heavily; *inf.* rain cats and dogs, come down in buckets. **2** *contents rained from the suitcase | arrows rained down* fall, pour out/down, drop, shower. **3** *rain gifts on them* lavish, pour, give generously, bestow.

rainbow *noun.* See table.

COLOURS OF THE RAINBOW	
red	blue
orange	indigo
yellow	violet
green	

rainy *adjective* wet, showery, drizzly, damp.

raise *verb* **1** *raise one's eyes/hat | raise the ship* lift, lift up, raise aloft, elevate, uplift, upthrust, hoist, heave up. **2** *raise the fence* set up, set upright, put up, stand, up-end, stand on end. **3** *raise his offer/prices* increase, put up, escalate, inflate; *inf.* step up, hike, jack up. **4** *raise the volume/temperature* increase, heighten, augment, amplify, intensify; *inf.* step up. **5** *raise a block of flats | raise a statue* construct, build, erect, put up. **6** *raise money/troops* get/gather together, collect, assemble, muster, levy, accumulate, amass, scrape together. **7** *raise objections* put forward, introduce, advance, bring up, broach, suggest, moot, present. **8** *raise doubts/hopes* cause, set going, bring into being, engender, create, set afoot, kindle, arouse, awaken, excite, summon up, provoke, activate, evoke, incite, stir up, foment, whip up, instigate. **9** *raise three children* bring up, rear, nurture, educate. **10** *raise chickens* breed, rear. **11** *raise crops* grow, farm, cultivate, propagate, till, produce. **12** *raise him to captain/manager* promote, advance, upgrade, elevate, exalt. **13** *raise bread* cause to rise, leaven, puff up. **14** *raise a siege* end, bring to an end, put an end to, terminate, abandon, lift. **15** *raise the barriers* remove, get rid of, take away. **16** *raise a ghost* cause to appear, call up, call forth, summon up, conjure up. **17** *she must be away—we can't raise her* get hold of, reach, contact, communicate with. **18** *fail to raise him for work* awaken, wake, arouse, rouse, stir.
Opposites LOWER; DEMOLISH; END.

rake *verb* **1** *rake the dead leaves* scrape up, collect, gather. **2** *rake the soil* smooth, smooth out, level, even out, flatten. **3** *rake through her things* search, hunt, ransack, rummage, rifle, comb, turn upside down, scour. **4** *soldiers raking the line of prisoners with gunfire* sweep, enfilade, pepper. **5** *rake the side of the car* scratch, scrape, graze, bark. **rake in** *rake in money* gather in, earn, pull in, haul in, pile up, amass, accumulate. **rake up** *rake up the past | rake up old memories* revive, call to mind, reminisce about, recollect.

rake *noun* roué, debauchee, dissolute man, playboy, libertine, profligate.

rake-off *noun* share, cut, dividend, commission, half, portion, part.

rakish *adjective* **1** *a rakish young man in a sports car | at a rakish angle* dashing, jaunty, devil-may-care, sporty, breezy, debonair, smart, dapper, spruce; *inf.* natty. **2** *a rakish drunk* dissolute, debauched, dissipated, profligate, wanton, degenerate, depraved.

rally *verb* **1** *rally to support the king* come/get together, assemble, group, band together, convene, unite. **2** *rally the forces* call/bring together, assemble, summon, round up, muster, marshall, mobilize. **3** *they were defeated but they rallied* regroup, reassemble, reform, reunite. **4** *she was very ill but she rallied* recover, recuperate, revive, get better/well, improve, perk up, regain one's strength, pull through, take a turn for the better, turn the corner, be on the mend, get one's second wind.
Opposites DISPERSE; DETERIORATE.

rally *noun* **1** *a political rally* mass meeting, meeting, gathering, assembly, assemblage, convention, conference, congregation, convocation. **2** *a rally on the stock exchange* recovery, recuperation, improvement, revival, rehabilitation, comeback, resurgence.

ram *verb* **1** *ram the tobacco into the pipe | ram clothes into the case* force, cram, stuff, compress, jam, squeeze, thrust, tamp. **2** *ram piles into a river bed* drive, hammer, pound, beat, hit. **3** *his car rammed ours* strike, hit, dash against, run into, crash into, collide with, bump, slam.

ramble *verb* **1** *ramble through the countryside* take a walk, go for a walk, walk, hike, wander, stroll, saunter, amble, roam, range, rove, traipse, jaunt. **2** *the speaker rambled on | that writer rambles* digress, wander, speak/write discursively, go off at tangents, talk aimlessly, maunder, gibber, blather, blether, babble, chatter, gabble, rattle on; *inf.* rabbit on, witter on.

ramble *noun* walk, hike, wander, stroll, saunter, amble, roam, traipse, jaunt, trip, excursion, tour.

rambler *noun* walker, hiker, stroller, saunterer, wanderer, roamer, rover, drifter, traveller, wayfarer.

rambling *adjective* **1** *rambling holiday-makers* walking, hiking, strolling, roaming. *See* RAMBLE *verb* 1. **2** *rambling speeches/writings* digressive, wandering, roundabout, circuitous, diffuse, periphrastic, disconnected, disjointed, maun-

dering, long-winded, verbose, wordy, prolix.
3 *rambling suburbs* sprawling, spreading, unsystematic. **4** *rambling plants* straggling, trailing.

ramification *noun* **1** *the action had many ramifications* consequence, aftermath, outcome, result, upshot, issue, sequel, complication, implication. **2** *the ramifications of the structure* subdivision, offshoot, branch, outgrowth, limb, scion.

ramp *noun* a *ramp for wheelchairs* slope, sloping surface, incline, inclined plane, gradient, acclivity, rise; access ramp.

rampage *verb* **1** *animals/children rampaging about the woods* rush/run wildly, run riot, run amuck, charge, tear. **2** *parents rampaging at their children's behaviour* rage, rave, rant, rant and rave, storm, go berserk.

rampage *noun* uproar, furore, mayhem, turmoil. **on the rampage** running amuck, going berserk, out of control, rampaging.

rampant *adjective* **1** *rampant disease/crime* uncontrolled, out of control/hand, unrestrained, unchecked, unbridled, widespread, pandemic, epidemic, spreading like wildfire. **2** *rampant foliage* luxuriant, exuberant, rank, profuse, lavish. **3** *lion rampant* rearing, standing, upright, erect. **4** *rampant militancy* aggressive, vehement, violent, wild, fanatical.

rampart *noun* **1** *castle/town ramparts* embankment, earthwork, parapet, fortification, fort, stronghold, bulwark, bastion, barbican. **2** *a rampart against infection* protection, defense, guard, shield, barrier, buffer.

ramshackle *adjective* tumbledown, broken-down, run-down, dilapidated, derelict, gone to rack and ruin, falling to pieces, decrepit, neglected, crumbling, rickety, shaky, unsteady, tottering, unsafe, flimsy, jerry-built.

rancid *adjective* **1** *rancid butter* sour, turned, overripe, high, gamy, rotten, bad, off, tainted, putrid. **2** *a rancid smell* rank, sour, stale, fusty, musty, foul, stinking, malodorous, evil-smelling, fetid, offensive, obnoxious, noxious, noisome.
Opposites FRESH.

rancorous *adjective* resentful, malicious, spiteful, hateful, malevolent, malignant, antipathetic, hostile, acrimonious, venomous, vindictive.

rancour *noun* resentment, malice, spite, ill will, hatred, malevolence, malignancy, animosity, antipathy, enmity, hostility, acrimony, venom, vindictiveness.

random *adjective* haphazard, chance, accidental, fortuitous, serendipitous, adventitious, arbitrary, hit-or-miss, indiscriminate, sporadic, stray, spot, casual, unsystematic, unmethodical, orderless, disorganized, unarranged, unplanned, unpremeditated. **at random**
1 *chose numbers at random* randomly, haphazardly, arbitrarily, leaving things to chance, without method, without conscious choice, without pre-arrangement. **2** *trees planted at random* unsystematically, unmethodically, erratically, indiscriminately, sporadically, every now and then.
Opposites DELIBERATE; SYSTEMATIC; PREMEDITATED.

range *noun* **1** *range of vision | the range of his influence | range of ability* scope, compass, radius, span, scale, gamut, reach, sweep, extent, area, field, orbit, province, domain, latitude; limits, bounds, confines. **2** *a range of mountains* row, line, file, rank, string, chain, series, sequence, succession, tier. *See table.* **3** *a stock range of goods | a wide range of people* assortment, variety, kind, sort, type, class, rank, order, genus, species. **4** *cooking on the range* stove, cooking stove, oven; Aga™. **5** *animals on the range* pasture, pasturage, grass, grassland, grazing land.

range *verb* **1** *range from very hot to freezing | range from brilliant to poor* extend, stretch, reach, cover, go, run, pass, fluctuate between, vary between. **2** *range the goods on the shelves | soldiers ranged along the battlements* line up, align, draw up, put/set in order, order, place, position, arrange, dispose, array, rank. **3** *range the pupils according to ability* classify, class, categorize, bracket, group, grade, catalogue, file, pigeon-hole. **4** *children/sheep ranging over the hills* roam, rove, ramble, traverse, travel over, wander, meander, amble, stroll, stray, drift.

rank *noun* **1** *salary according to rank* grade, level, stratum, class, status, position, station, standing. **2** *persons of rank* nobility, aristocracy, high birth, eminence, distinction, influence, power, prestige, weight, importance. **3** *what is his rank in the organization?* grade, position, gradation, point on the scale, mark, echelon, rung on the ladder. **4** *a rank of people waiting/rank of mountains* line, file, column, row, range, series, succession, queue, string, train, procession. **5** *break rank* array, alignment, order, arrangement, organization. **rank and file 1** *the officers separated from the rank and file* other ranks, ordinary/private soldiers, soldiers, men, troops. **2** *directors/governments ignoring the wishes of the rank and file* ordinary members, non-office bearers; ordinary people, public, general public. **3** *the aristocracy despising the rank and file* common people, populace, commonality, rabble; the masses, lower classes. *See* RABBLE 2.

rank *verb* **1** *he ranks above a captain | rank with the best* have a rank, be graded, be placed, be positioned, have a status. **2** *rank their achievements | rank him a champion* classify, class, categorize, grade. **3** *rank the goods on the shelves | soldiers along the field* range, line up, align, set in order, place, arrange, dispose, array. *See* RANGE *verb* 2.

rank *adjective* **1** *rank vegetation* lush, luxuriant, abundant, dense, profuse, flourishing, exuberant, vigorous, productive, spreading, overgrown, jungly. **2** *a rank smell* strong, strong-smelling, pungent, acrid, malodorous, foul-smelling, evil-smelling, stinking, rancid, putrid, fetid, unpleasant, disagreeable, offensive, revolting, sickening, obnoxious, noxious, noisome, mephitic. **3** *condemn his rank behaviour/language* indecent, immodest, indecorous, coarse, gross, vulgar, shocking, outrageous, lurid, crass, scurrilous, abusive, nasty, foul, filthy, vile, obscene, smutty, risqué, profane, pornographic. **4** *a rank outsider | rank disobedi-*

ence utter, complete, total, absolute, out and out, downright, thorough, thoroughgoing, sheer, unqualified, unmitigated, arrant, flagrant, blatant, glaring, gross, egregious.

rankle *verb their insults still rankle* fester, cause resentment, cause annoyance, annoy, anger, irk, vex, peeve, irritate, rile, chafe, fret, gall, embitter; *inf.* get one's goat.

ransack *verb* **1** *raiders ransacking the area* plunder, pillage, raid, rob, loot, despoil, rifle, strip, fleece, sack, ravage, harry, maraud, devastate, depredate. **2** *ransack the house looking for the will* search, rummage through, rake through, scour, look all over, go through, comb, explore, turn inside out, turn over.

ransom *noun* **1** *pay the kidnappers a ransom* pay-off, payment, price. **2** *obtain the kidnapped child's ransom* release, freedom, deliverance, liberation, rescue, redemption, restoration.

ransom *verb* **1** *succeed in ransoming the kidnapped child* exchange for a ransom, buy the freedom of, release, free, deliver, liberate, rescue, redeem, restore to freedom. **2** *the kidnappers have ransomed the child* exchange for a ransom, release for money, release, free, set free, deliver, liberate, set loose.

rant *verb actors ranting | parents ranting with rage* declaim, hold forth, go on and on, bluster,

harangue, vociferate, shout, yell, roar, bellow, bawl, rave, rant and rave; *inf.* spout.

rant *noun tired of the actor's rant | his parents' rants* bombast, rhetoric, oration, declamation, discourse, harangue, tirade, diatribe, philippic, lecture, shouting, yelling, raving.

rap¹ *noun* **1** *a rap on the knuckles* tap, hit, blow, whack, bang, cuff, clip, clout. **2** *hear a rap at the door* knock, knocking, tap, bang, hammering, battering, ratatat. **3** *take/get the rap for the accident* blame, responsibility, accountability, punishment, penalty, castigation.

rap² *verb* **1** *rap him on the knuckles* tap, hit, strike, whack, bang, cuff, clip, clout, batter; *inf.* bash. **2** *rap at the door* knock, tap, bang, hammer, batter. **3** *rap him for his mistake* criticize, censure, reproach, scold, chide, castigate.

rap³ *noun not care/give a rap* little bit, whit, iota, jot; *inf.* damn.

rapacious *adjective* **1** *rapacious moneylender* grasping, acquisitive, greedy, avaricious, covetous, insatiable, predatory, usurious. **2** *rapacious invaders* plundering, pillaging, robbing, marauding, looting, piratical.

rape *noun* **1** *commit rape on the girl* sexual assault, ravishment, violation; date rape. **2** *the rape of their neighbour's territory* plundering, pillaging, ravaging, foraging, raiding,

MOUNTAIN RANGES

Range	Location	Range	Location
Alps	France/Switzerland/ Italy/Austria/ Liechtenstein	Himalayas	China/India/Pakistan/ Nepal/Bhutan
Altai	Kazakhstan/China/ Mongolia	Hindu Kush	Afghanistan/Pakistan
		Hoggar Mountains	Algeria
Andes	South America	Jura Mountains	France/Switzerland
Apennine Hills	Italy	Kaikoura Ranges	New Zealand
Appalachians	U.S.A.	Karakoram Range	Afghanistan/Pakistan/ China/India
Atlas Mountains	Morocco/Algeria/ Tunisia	Kunlun Shan	China
		Ladakh Range	India/Pakistan/China
Balkan Mountains	Bulgaria	MacDonnell Ranges	Australia
Bernese Alps	Switzerland	Middleback Ranges	Australia
Black Mountains	Wales, U.K.	Mourne Mountains	Northern Ireland, U.K.
Blue Mountains	Australia	Musgrave Ranges	Australia
Blue Ridge Mountains	U.S.A.	North West Highlands	Scotland, U.K.
Brecon Beacons	Wales, U.K.	Olympic Mountains	U.S.A.
Cairngorms	Scotland, U.K.	Pamir Mountains	Tajikistan/China/ Afghanistan
Cambrian Mountains	Wales, U.K.		
Cantabrian Mountains	Spain	Pennines	England, U.K.
Carpathians	Czech Republic/ Slovakia/Poland/ Romania/Ukraine	Pindus Mountains	Greece/Albania
		Pyrenees	France/Spain
		Rocky Mountains | Rockies	U.S.A./Canada
Caucasus Mountains	SE Russia/Georgia/ Azerbaijan/Armenia	Sayan Mountains	Russia
Cévennes	France	Sierra Madre Range	Mexico
Coast Mountains	Canada	Sierra Morena Range	Spain
Cumbrian Mountains	England, U.K.	Sierra Nevada Range	U.S.A.
Dolomites	Italy	Smoky Mountains | Smokies	U.S.A.
Drakensberg Mountains	Southern Africa		
Flinders Range	Australia	Snowy Mountains	Australia
Ghats Range	India	Taurus Mountains	Turkey
Golan Heights	Israel	Tien Shan	Kyrgyzstan/China/ Mongolia
Grampian Mountains	Scotland, U.K.		
Hamersley Range	Australia	Ural Mountains	Russia
Harz Mountains	Germany	Zagros Mountains	Iran

despoilment, despoliation, spoliation, marauding, sacking, sack, ransacking, rapine. **3** *the rape of the Sabine women* abduction, carrying off, kidnapping, seizure, capture. **4** *the rape of democracy* violation, abuse, defilement, desecration.

rape *verb* **1** *he raped the girl* sexually assault, ravish, violate. **2** *they rape their neighbour's territory* plunder, pillage, ravage, forage, raid, despoil, spoliate, maraud, ransack, sack. **3** *the Romans raped the Sabine women* abduct, carry off, kidnap, seize, capture. **4** *terrorists rape a national institution* violate, abuse, defile, desecrate.

rapid *adjective* quick, fast, swift, speedy, fleet, hurried, hasty, expeditious, express, brisk, lively, prompt, precipitate.
Opposites SLOW; LEISURELY.

rapidity *noun* quickness, fastness, swiftness, speed, speediness, fleetness, hurriedness, haste, hastiness, rush, expeditiousness, alacrity, dispatch, velocity, celerity, promptness, promptitude, precipitateness.

rapidly *adverb* quickly, fast, swiftly, speedily, at speed, hurriedly, in a hurry, hastily, in haste, in a rush, expeditiously, briskly, promptly, precipitately, hotfoot, at full tilt; *inf.* before one can say Jack Robinson, before the ink is dry on the page, like a bat out of hell, like greased lightning.

rapport *noun* affinity, bond, empathy, harmony, sympathy, understanding, close/special relationship, link.

rapt *adjective* **1** *rapt in thought | rapt attention* absorbed, engrossed, preoccupied, intent, concentrating, pensive, meditative. **2** *rapt by the music | a rapt smile* enraptured, enchanted, entranced, spellbound, bewitched, captivated, fascinated, charmed, thrilled, transported, blissful, ecstatic, ravished.
Opposites UNINTERESTED; INATTENTIVE.

rapture *noun* joy, ecstasy, elation, exaltation, exhilaration, bliss, euphoria, transport, rhapsody, ravishment, enchantment, delight, delectation, happiness, enthusiasm; *inf.* cloud nine, seventh heaven.

rapturous *adjective* joyful, joyous, ecstatic, elated, blissful, euphoric, transported, in transports, rhapsodic, ravished, enchanted, delighted, happy; *inf.* on cloud nine, in seventh heaven.

rara avis *noun* rarity, rare person/thing, anomaly, aberration, freak, freak of nature, wonder, marvel, nonpareil, nonsuch, one of a kind.

rare *adjective* **1** *a rare specimen* unusual, uncommon, out of the ordinary, exceptional, atypical, singular, remarkable, phenomenal, strange, recherché, unique. **2** *make a rare appearance* infrequent, few and far between, scarce, sparse, sporadic, scattered, thin on the ground. **3** *exhibit a rare skill* outstanding, superior, first-rate, special, choice, excellent, very fine, incomparable, unparalleled, peerless, matchless; *inf.* A1, top-notch.
Opposites COMMON; FREQUENT.

rarely *adverb* *she rarely visits* on rare occasions, seldom, infrequently, hardly/scarcely ever,

hardly, scarcely, almost never, little, once in a while, only now and then, not often; *inf.* once in a blue moon.

rarity *noun* **1** *the rarity of the specimen* rareness, unusualness, uncommonness, singularity, strangeness, uniqueness. See RARE 1. **2** *the rarity of the occurrences* infrequency, scarcity, sparseness, sporadicness. See RARE 2. **3** *the rarity of his skill* superiority, excellence, incomparability. See RARE 3. **4** *that book is a rarity* rare person/thing, rara avis, anomaly, freak, wonder, marvel, one of a kind. See RARA AVIS.

rascal *noun* **1** *the child's a little rascal* imp, scamp, scallywag, mischief-maker, little devil. **2** *that man is a real rascal* scoundrel, villain, rogue, blackguard, ne'er-do-well, good-for-nothing, wastrel, reprobate, cad; *inf.* rotter, bounder, creep, rat.

rash *adjective* **1** *a rash young woman* reckless, impetuous, hasty, impulsive, madcap, overadventurous, adventurous, overbold, audacious, brash, daredevil, foolhardy, harum-scarum, devil-may-care, headstrong, hot-headed, incautious, careless, heedless, thoughtless, imprudent. **2** *a rash act* reckless, impetuous, hasty, impulsive, incautious, careless, unthinking, ill-advised, ill-considered, foolish, imprudent, injudicious, hare-brained, unwary, unguarded.
Opposites CAREFUL; CAUTIOUS; PRUDENT.

rash *noun* **1** *a rash on his face* skin eruption, outbreak, breaking out; erythema, hives, heat rash, nettle rash, nappy rash. **2** *a rash of burglaries* outbreak, spate, torrent, flood, wave, plague, epidemic, succession, series, run.

rasp *noun* *the rasp of knives against plates* grating, grinding, scraping, scratching.

rasp *verb* **1** *rasp the surface smooth* abrade, file, sand, sandpaper, scrape, scratch. **2** *"Go away,"* *he rasped* screech, shrill, squawk, croak, stridulate. **3** *his behaviour really rasps | it rasps my nerves* grate (upon), jar (upon), irritate, irk, set one's teeth on edge, rub one up the wrong way.

rasping *adjective* *a rasping noise/voice* grating, scratchy, jarring, discordant, creaky, harsh, rough, gravelly, croaking, croaky, gruff.

rat *noun.* See table at RODENT.

rate *noun* **1** *rate of interest* percentage, ratio, proportion, scale, degree, standard. **2** *the rate per day* pay, payment, fee, remuneration, price, cost, charge, rent, tariff; *inf.* damage. **3** *walk at a great/swift rate* pace, stride, gait, motion, speed, tempo, velocity, measure. **at any rate** in any case, anyhow, anyway, nevertheless, at all events, in any event, no matter what happens.

rate *verb* **1** *how would you rate his performance?* adjudge, judge, assess, appraise, evaluate, value, put a value on, measure, weigh up, grade, rank, classify, class, categorize. **2** *I rate him as a complete fool* regard as, consider, count, deem, reckon, account, esteem. **3** *he rates respect* be worthy of, deserve, merit, be entitled to. **4** *I don't really rate him as a player* regard as good/talented, think highly of, hold in esteem, esteem, value, admire.

rather *adverb* **1** *I would rather not go* sooner, preferably, by preference, from choice, more willingly, more readily. **2** *she is tactless rather than rude* more, more truly. **3** *a leaflet rather than a book* correctly/strictly speaking, to be exact/precise. **4** *he is rather outspoken* quite, fairly, a bit, a little, slightly, somewhat, relatively, to some degree/extent; *inf.* sort of, kind of, pretty. **5** *he's not poor, rather he's very wealthy* on the contrary, instead.

ratify *verb* confirm, endorse, sign, countersign, corroborate, sanction, warrant, approve, authorize, authenticate, certify, validate, agree to, accept, consent to, uphold, bear out.
Opposites REJECT; REVOKE.

rating *noun* **1** *rating the competitors* adjudging, assessing, evaluating, grading, ranking, classifying. *See* RATE *verb* 1. **2** *his rating as a player has diminished* assessment, evaluation, value, appraisal, grading, grade, ranking, rank, classification, class, categorization, designation, standing, status, placing, position.

ratio *noun* proportion, comparative size/extent, correlation, correspondence, percentage, fraction, quotient.

ration *noun* *your ration of food/books/money for the week* allowance, quota, allotment, portion, share, measure, part, lot, amount, helping, proportion, percentage, budget.

ration *verb* **1** *ration the amount per person* limit, restrict, control, conserve, budget. **2** *ration out the week's supplies* distribute, issue, allocate, allot, divide out, apportion, give out, share out, deal out, hand out, pass out, dole out, measure out, mete out, parcel out.

rational *adjective* **1** *based on purely rational considerations* thinking, cognitive, mental, cerebral, reasoning, logical, analytical, conceptual. **2** *it seemed a rational decision | a rational course of action* sensible, reasonable, logical, sound, intelligent, wise, judicious, sagacious, prudent, circumspect, politic, astute, shrewd, perceptive, well-advised, well-grounded. **3** *the invalid does not always seem rational* able to think/reason, in sound mind, in one's right mind, *compos mentis*, lucid, coherent, well-balanced, sane, normal; *inf.* all there.
Opposites IRRATIONAL; ILLOGICAL; INSANE.

rationale *noun* theory, hypothesis, thesis, exposition, logic, philosophy, reason, *raison d'être*; grounds.

rationalize *verb* **1** *rationalize his behaviour* explain away, account for, make excuses/allowances for, make plausible, try to vindicate/justify. **2** *rationalize our research plans* apply logic/reasoning to, reason out, think through, elucidate, clarify, make consistent. **3** *rationalize workforce/work methods* streamline, trim, make more efficient/economic, make cuts in, cut back on, retrench on.

rations *plural noun* provisions, stores, supplies, victuals, commons; food, provender.

rattle *verb* **1** *the windows rattled* bang, clatter, clang, clank, jangle, clink. **2** *rattle the doorknocker* bang, knock, rap, clatter, clank. **3** *the car rattled along* bounce, bump, jiggle, jounce, shake, jolt, vibrate, jar. **4** *he rattled off their names* reel off, list/recite rapidly, run through. **5** *he rattled on about his job* go on, chatter, bab-

ble, gabble, prattle, jabber, gibber, blether, blather, prate; *inf.* rabbit, witter, yak, yakkety-yak. **6** *she was rattled by the experience* disconcert, disturb, fluster, upset, shake, perturb, discompose, discomfit, discountenance, put off one's stroke, frighten, scare; *inf.* faze.

raucous *adjective* strident, shrill, screeching, piercing, ear-piercing, harsh, sharp, grating, rasping, scratching, discordant, dissonant, jarring.
Opposites SWEET; DULCET.

ravage *verb* devastate, lay waste, leave desolate, lay/leave in ruins, ruin, wreak havoc on, destroy, level, raze, demolish, wreck, shatter, damage, pillage, plunder, despoil, harry, maraud, ransack, sack, loot.

ravages *plural noun* *the ravages of war* devastation, desolation, ruination, ruin, havoc, destruction, demolition, depredation, wreckage, damage, pillaging, plunder, spoliation, ransacking, looting.

rave *verb* **1** *the invalid is raving* talk wildly, be delirious, babble, ramble. **2** *her parents raved at her* rant and rave, rage, deliver a tirade/harangue, storm, fulminate, explode in anger, lose one's temper, lose control, go into a frenzy, run amuck; *inf.* fly off the handle, flip one's lid. **3** *rave about her performance | rave over his car* go into raptures over, rhapsodize over, enthuse about, praise extravagantly, praise to the skies, gush over, express delight over, acclaim, cry up; *inf.* go wild about, be mad about, throw bouquets at. **4** *going to rave after the exams* enjoy oneself with abandon, have a wild/good time, have a party, paint the town red; *inf.* let one's hair down.

rave *noun* **1** *receive a rave for her performance* lavish praise, acclaim, applause, encomium, rapturous welcome; *inf.* bouquets. **2** *teenagers attending a rave* warehouse party, acid house party. **3** *have a rave to celebrate the wedding* party, celebration; *inf.* do, bash, beanfeast, blow-out, knees-up. **4** *flared trousers are all the rave* fashion, vogue, trend, fad; *inf.* craze, rage.

rave *adjective* *rave reviews* rapturous, ecstatic, enthusiastic, laudatory, praising, excellent, favourable.

ravenous *adjective* **1** *ravenous after the day's march* very hungry, starving, starved, famished. **2** *a ravenous appetite* greedy, gluttonous, voracious, insatiable, insatiate, ravening, wolfish.

ravine *noun* chasm, gorge, canyon, abyss, gulf, gully, gulch, defile, pass, gap.

raving *adjective* **1** *raving patients* delirious, out of one's mind, irrational, frenzied, in a frenzy, deranged, hysterical, frantic, berserk, unbalanced, demented, insane, mad, crazed, wild; *inf.* crazy. **2** *a raving beauty* very great, considerable, remarkable, extraordinary, singular, striking, outstanding, stunning.

ravings *plural noun* *kept awake by his ravings* wild talk, babbling, rambling, gibberish.

ravish *verb* **1** *ravish the young girl* rape, sexually assault/abuse, violate. **2** *they were ravished by his performance* enchant, entrance, enthrall, captivate, bewitch, spellbind, fascinate, charm, enrapture, delight, transport, overjoy.

ravishing *adjective* beautiful, lovely, stunning, gorgeous, dazzling, radiant, enchanting, bewitching, charming.

raw *adjective* **1** *raw food* uncooked, fresh. **2** *raw sugar/silk* unrefined, crude, green, coarse, unprocessed, unprepared, untreated, unfinished, unmanufactured. **3** *raw recruits* inexperienced, untrained, unskilled, untutored, unschooled, unpractised, untried, untested, unseasoned, undisciplined, new, callow, immature, green, ignorant, naive, unsophisticated; *inf.* wet behind the ears. **4** *raw flesh/wounds* excoriated, skinned, grazed, abraded, scratched, chafed, open, exposed, unhealed, sore, tender. **5** *a raw day | raw weather* damp, wet, cold, chilly, chilling, chill, freezing, bitter, biting, nippy, nipping, piercing, penetrating. **6** *a raw literary style* unrefined, unpolished, unsophisticated, crude, rough, coarse. **7** *a raw portrayal of the miner's life* realistic, frank, candid, forthright, straightforward, blunt, outspoken, unembellished, unvarnished, naked, bare, brutal.

ray *noun* **1** *rays of light* beam, shaft, streak, stream, gleam, glint, flash, glimmer, flicker, twinkle. **2** *a ray of hope* flicker, glimmer, spark, trace, hint, indication, suggestion.

raze *verb* tear down, pull down, take down, knock down, knock to pieces, fell, level, lay low, bulldoze, flatten, demolish, ruin, wreck.

reach *verb* **1** *he reached out | reach out a hand* stretch, stretch out, outstretch, extend, hold out, thrust out, stick out. **2** *reach for the book* get hold of, grasp, seize, catch at, grab at, clutch at. **3** *reach one's destination* get as far as, get to, arrive at, come to, set foot on, land at/on. **4** *reach perfection* attain, achieve, gain, accomplish, make, get to. **5** *his land reaches ours* extend to, go as far as, stretch to, neighbour, touch, border on, abut. **6** *we could not reach him that day* contact, get in touch with, get hold of, get through to, communicate with. **7** *reach me that book* hand, pass, give.

reach *noun* **1** *the rope was beyond her reach | within reach of safety* grasp, stretch, spread, extension, extent, span, distance. **2** *within the reach of his influence* scope, range, compass, latitude, ambit, orbit, sphere, area, field, territory, authority, jurisdiction, sway, control, command.

react *verb* **1** *react to the drug* have a reaction/response to, respond, change/behave in response to. **2** *how did she react on hearing the news?* behave, act, conduct oneself, proceed, operate, function, cope. **3** *react against the new bill* rebel against, oppose, revolt against, rise up against.

reaction *noun* **1** *receive a reaction to their proposal* response, answer, reply, feedback. **2** *his harsh regime was a reaction to total disorder* counteraction, counterbalance, counterpoise, recoil, reversion, retroversion, reversal. **3** *they are people of political reaction* ultraconservatism, conservatism, obscurantism, the right, the right wing, the extreme right.

reactionary *adjective* ultraconservative, conservative, obscurantist, Colonel Blimp, diehard, rightist, right-wing.
Opposites RADICAL; PROGRESSIVE.

read *verb* **1** *read the words/book* peruse, study, scan, pore over, scrutinize, run one's eye over, look at, refer to, browse through; *inf.* wade through, dip into. **2** *read his silence as consent* interpret, construe, take to mean, decipher, deduce, understand, comprehend. **3** *the thermometer is reading zero* register, record, display, show, indicate. **4** *read the future* foresee, foretell, predict, forecast, prophesy, divine. **read into** *read too much into their statement/relationship* assume from, infer from, interpolate from, read between the lines.

read *noun* *a quick read of the book* perusal, study, scan, scrutiny, browse, reference.

readable *adjective* **1** *readable exam papers* legible, easy to read, decipherable, clear, intelligible, understandable, comprehensible. **2** *readable works of fiction* enjoyable, entertaining, interesting, gripping, enthralling, stimulating.
Opposites ILLEGIBLE; BORING; UNREADABLE.

readily *adverb* **1** *he will readily help you* willingly, without hesitation, gladly, happily, cheerfully, with pleasure, eagerly. **2** *the sofa readily converts into a bed* easily, with ease, without difficulty, effortlessly.

readiness *noun* **1** *the readiness of the troops for battle* preparedness, fitness. **2** *their readiness to help* willingness, inclination, aptness, eagerness, keenness, gladness; *inf.* gameness. See READY 3. **3** *the readiness of resources* availability, accessibility, handiness, convenience. See READY 4. **4** *the readiness of her answers* promptness, quickness, rapidity, swiftness, speed, speediness, punctuality, timeliness. **5** *the readiness of his wit/skill* alertness, resourcefulness, smartness, sharpness, astuteness, shrewdness, keenness, acuteness, discernment, cleverness, intelligence, brightness, aptness, adroitness, deftness, dexterity, skill, skilfulness. **in readiness** *reserves in readiness* ready, at the ready, available, on hand, accessible, handy, at one's fingertips, prepared, primed; *inf.* on tap.

reading *noun* **1** *his reading of the document* perusal, study, scan, scanning, scrutinization, scrutiny, browsing. See READ *verb* 1. **2** *a man of reading* book learning, learning, scholarship, knowledge, attainment, enlightenment, education, edification. **3** *his reading of the statement/situation* interpretation, construction, deciphering, deduction, understanding, comprehension, grasp, impression. **4** *several readings of the play in existence* version, edition, text, rendering. **5** *what's the reading on the gas meter?* measurement, indication.

ready *adjective* **1** *dinner is ready* prepared, completed, finished, organized. **2** *ready for battle | ready to go* prepared, equipped, organized, all set, in a fit state, fit. **3** *ready to help* willing, inclined, disposed, predisposed, minded, apt, prone, given, agreeable, eager, keen, happy, glad; *inf.* game. **4** *a ready source of income* within reach, available, on hand, present, near, near at hand, accessible, handy,

convenient, on call, at one's fingertips; *inf.* on tap. **5** *a ready answer* prompt, quick, rapid, swift, speedy, punctual, timely. **6** *a ready wit/skill* alert, resourceful, smart, sharp, astute, shrewd, keen, acute, perceptive, discerning, clever, intelligent, bright, apt, adroit, deft, dexterous, skilful. **7** *ready to collapse* about to, on the verge/brink/edge of, in danger of, liable to, likely to. **8** *ready for anything* prepared, eager, enthusiastic, anxious, keen; *inf.* psyched up, geared up.
Opposites INCOMPLETE; unprepared; RELUCTANT; INACCESSIBLE.

real *adjective* **1** *the real world/real fears/illnesses* actual, existent, occurring, factual, unimaginary, non-fictitious. **2** *real leather* authentic, genuine, *bona fide*, veritable, valid, legal, licit. **3** *real emotion/feelings* sincere, heartfelt, earnest, fervent, unfeigned, unpretended, unaffected, honest, truthful.
Opposites UNREAL; IMAGINARY; IMITATION; FALSE.

realistic *adjective* **1** *be realistic as to your prospects* practical, pragmatic, rational, down-to-earth, matter-of-fact, sensible, commonsensical, level-headed, hard-headed, business-like, hard-boiled, sober, unromantic, unsentimental, unidealistic; *inf.* with both feet on the ground, no-nonsense. **2** *a realistic model of a dinosaur* lifelike, true-to-life, true, faithful, close, representational, graphic, naturalistic, authentic, genuine.
Opposites UNREALISTIC; IDEALISTIC; IMPRACTICAL; ROMANTIC.

reality *noun* **1** *come back to reality* real/actual world, actuality, physical existence, corporeality, substantiality, materiality. **2** *the reality of his work* verisimilitude, lifelikeness, authenticity, genuineness, validity. *See* REALISTIC 2. **3** *the harsh realities of life/in reality the picture's a fake* fact, actuality, truth.

realization *noun* **1** *come to the realization that he is mad* understanding, awareness, consciousness, cognizance, appreciation, recognition, perception, discernment. **2** *the realization of one's hopes* fulfilment, achievement, accomplishment, fruition, consummation, effecting, actualization. *See* REALIZE 2. **3** *the realization of profits* making, clearing, obtaining. *See* REALIZE 3, 4.

realize *verb* **1** *realize that they are rich* understand clearly, grasp, take in, know, comprehend, apprehend, become aware, be conscious/cognizant of the fact, appreciate, recognize, perceive, discern, conceive; *inf.* twig, latch on. **2** *realize one's hopes/dreams* fulfil, achieve, accomplish, make happen, bring about, bring off, bring to fruition, consummate, effect, effectuate, perform, execute, actualize, reify. **3** *realize one's assets* convert into money. **4** *realize a profit* make, clear, acquire, gain, bring in, obtain, earn.

really *adverb* **1** *the comedienne is really a man* in reality, actually, in actuality, in fact, in truth. **2** *this is really useful* certainly, surely, truly, undoubtedly, without a doubt, indubitably, assuredly, unquestionably, indeed, absolutely, categorically. **3** *a really charming person* very, extremely, thoroughly, truly, decidedly. **4** *his

career is really over* to all intents and purposes, virtually, for all practical purposes, just about, almost.

realm *noun* **1** *when the Tudors ruled the realm* kingdom, country, land, state, province, empire, domain, monarchy, principality. **2** *the realm of the imagination/the realm of science* world, field, sphere, area, department, region, province, orbit, zone.

reap *verb* **1** *reap the corn* cut, crop, harvest, gather in, bring in, take in. **2** *reap the benefits of an education* realize, receive, obtain, get, acquire, secure, procure.

rear *noun* **1** *at the rear of the garage* back, back part, hind part, back end. **2** *at the rear of the queue* rear end, back end, end, tail, tail end.
Opposites FRONT; VANGUARD.

rear *verb* **1** *rear three children* bring up, raise, care for, nurture, parent, educate, train, instruct. **2** *rear chickens* breed, keep, tend. **3** *rear plants* grow, cultivate. **4** *rear one's head* raise, lift up, hold up, hoist, elevate, upraise. **5** *rear a ladder* set up, stand up, make upright, stand on end, up-end. **6** *rear a tower* erect, build, put up, construct. **7** *mountains rearing in the distance* tower, soar, loom, rise up.

reason *noun* **1** *the reason for his behaviour* grounds; ground, cause, basis, motive, motivation, impetus, actuation, instigation, inducement. **2** *give a reason for your absence* explanation, exposition, justification, argument, case, defence, vindication, apologia, rationalization, excuse, apology. **3** *follow reason not emotion* reasoning, intellect, intelligence, intellectuality, mind, judgement, logic, rationality, thought, understanding, apprehension, comprehension, ratiocination; brains. **4** *he has lost his reason* sanity, mind, soundness of mind; senses. **5** *keep a sense of reason in your expenditure* reasonableness, common sense, sense, good sense, practicality, practicability, shrewdness, wisdom, sagacity, moderation, propriety. **within reason** *have anything you like within reason* in moderation, within reasonable/sensible limits, within limits/bounds.

reason *verb* **1** *unable to reason when upset* use reason, think, think straight, use one's mind, use one's brain/head, analyse, cogitate, cerebrate, intellectualize, ratiocinate; *inf.* put on one's thinking cap. **2** *try reasoning with him* use logic on, apply argument to, argue with, debate with, dispute with, try to persuade, plead with. **3** *he reasoned that two could live as cheaply as one* deduce, infer, conclude, work out, reckon, be of the opinion, think, surmise. **4** *reason him out of that course of action/reason her into it* argue, persuade, talk, urge, coax. **5** *reason things out* think out, think through, consider, deliberate, analyse, come to a conclusion about.

reasonable *adjective* **1** *he's quite a reasonable man* open to reason, moderate, fair, just, equitable, impartial, dispassionate, unbiased, disinterested, above-board. **2** *it seemed a reasonable idea/plan* logical, practical, rational, sensible, intelligent, wise, sound, judicious, advisable, well-thought-out, admissible, tenable, plausible. **3** *reasonable prices* moderate, inexpensive,

low, modest, cheap, within one's means. **4** *his work is reasonable* tolerable, passable, acceptable, average; *inf.* OK.
Opposites UNREASONABLE; ILLOGICAL; EXPENSIVE.

reasoned *adjective reasoned arguments* logical, rational, well-thought-out, clear, systematic, methodical, organized, well-expressed, well-presented.

reasoning *noun* **1** *let reasoning not emotion dictate your actions* reason, thinking, thought, logic, rationalization, deduction, analysis, cerebration, ratiocination. **2** *his reasoning is faulty* argument, rationale, case, hypothesis, interpretation.

reassure *verb* put one's mind at rest, put at ease, settle doubts, restore/give confidence to, encourage, hearten, buoy up, cheer up, inspirit.
Opposites ALARM.

rebate *noun* refund, partial refund, repayment, deduction, discount, allowance, reduction, decrease.

rebel *noun* **1** *the government acting against the rebels* revolutionary, revolutionist, insurrectionist, insurgent, revolter, mutineer, seditionist, agitator, freedom/resistance fighter, anarchist, traitor. **2** *rebels not obeying rules/fashion* dissenter, nonconformist, heretic, apostate, schismatic, recusant.

rebel *verb* **1** *the troops are rebelling* mutiny, riot, revolt, rise up, rise up in arms, take to the streets. **2** *rebel against authority* defy, disobey, refuse to obey/follow. **3** *his stomach rebelled at the thought of food* recoil from, shrink from, flinch from, shy away from, pull back from, show repugnance/revulsion for/at.
Opposites ACQUIESCE; CONFORM.

rebel *adjective* **1** *the rebel troops* revolutionary, insurrectionary, insurgent, mutinous, mutinying. *See* REBEL *noun* 1. **2** *rebel schoolgirls* rebellious, defiant, disobedient, resistant, dissentient, recalcitrant, unmanageable.

rebellion *noun* **1** *troops putting down a rebellion* revolt, revolution, insurrection, insurgence, insurgency, uprising, rising, mutiny, riot, civil disobedience, resistance. **2** *rebellion against rules/fashion* defiance, disobedience, resistance, dissent, nonconformity, heresy, apostasy, schism, recusancy.

rebellious *adjective* **1** *rebellious tribes/schoolchildren* unruly, ungovernable, unmanageable, turbulent, disorderly, intractable, recalcitrant, incorrigible, contumacious. **2** *the rebellious group were imprisoned* rebelling, revolutionary, insurrectionary, insurgent, mutinous, mutinying, rioting. **3** *the rebellious pupils were expelled* defiant, disobedient, resistant, dissentient, nonconformist.
Opposites OBEDIENT; SUBSERVIENT.

rebound *verb* **1** *the ball rebounded off the wall* bounce, bounce back, spring back, recoil, ricochet, boomerang. **2** *the plan rebounded on her* misfire, backfire, have an adverse effect, come back on, redound on.

rebound *noun* **1** *the rebound of the ball* bounce, recoil, ricochet. *See* REBOUND *verb* 1. **2** *the*

rebound of her plans misfiring, backfiring, kickback, repercussion.

rebuff *noun* **1** *the rebuff of her suitor/request* rejection, refusal, spurning, repudiation, repulsion, cold shouldering, discouragement. **2** *upset by her rebuffs* snub, slight, repulse, cut, check, thumbs down; *inf.* brush-off, knockback, put-down, slap in the face.

rebuff *verb* *rebuff their advances | rebuff them* reject, refuse, decline, turn down, turn away, spurn, repudiate, repel, discourage, fend off, stave off, snub, slight, cold shoulder, give the thumbs down to; *inf.* brush off, knock back, put down.

rebuke *verb rebuke the children for their naughtiness* reprimand, scold, chide, admonish, reproach, reprove, remonstrate with, lecture, reprehend, censure, find fault with, berate, upbraid, castigate, take to task; *inf.* tell off, carpet, lambaste, haul over the coals, tear a strip off, tick off, bawl out.
Opposites PRAISE; APPLAUD.

rebuke *noun deliver a rebuke to the disobedient children/troops* reprimand, scolding, admonition, reproach, reproof, reproval, remonstration, lecture, censure, upbraiding, castigation; *inf.* telling-off, carpeting, lambasting, dressing-down, ticking-off, bawling-out, wigging.

rebut *verb rebut the charge/evidence* refute, disprove, negate, invalidate, deny, confute, contradict, discredit, give the lie to, drive a coach and horses through, explode; *inf.* shoot full of holes.

recalcitrant *adjective* intractable, refractory, unmanageable, ungovernable, disobedient, insubordinate, defiant, contrary, wayward, wilful, headstrong, perverse, contumacious, rebellious, mutinous, obstinate, obdurate.
Opposites AMENABLE; DOCILE; COMPLIANT.

recall *verb* **1** *recall parliament* summon back, call back, bring back. **2** *unable to recall his name* call to mind, remember, recollect, think of. **3** *sit recalling the old days* remember, recollect, reminisce about, look back on/to, think back on/to, hark back to. **4** *the sight of her recalled the old days* call/bring to mind, call up, summon up, evoke, put one in mind of. **5** *recall the verdict* revoke, retract, countermand, take back, withdraw, repeal, rescind, veto, overrule, override, invalidate, annul, nullify, cancel, recant.

recall *noun* **1** *the recall of parliament* summoning back. *See* RECALL *verb* 1. **2** *have total recall* memory, recollection, remembrance. **3** *the recall of the verdict | beyond recall* revocation, retracting, countermanding, withdrawal, repeal, rescinding, vetoing, veto, invalidation, annulment, cancellation. *See* RECALL *verb* 5.

recant *verb* **1** *recant his former beliefs* disavow, disclaim, disown, deny, renounce, relinquish, abjure, forswear, repudiate, renege on. **2** *he was a Catholic but he has recanted* change one's mind, apostatize, tergiversate, defect, renege. **3** *recant his evidence* recall, revoke, retract, countermand, take back, repeal, rescind, annul, cancel. *See* RECALL *verb* 5.

recapitulate *verb* restate, resay, repeat, re-iterate, go over, run over, summarize, sum up; *inf.* recap.

recede *verb* **1** *the water receded* go back, move back, move further off, move away, retreat, withdraw, fall back, ebb, abate, subside. **2** *the coastline receded as we rowed* grow less visible, become distant, become far off, fade into the distance, begin to disappear. **3** *danger receded in time* grow less, lessen, fade, diminish, decrease, dwindle, shrink, wane, fall off, taper off, peter out. **4** *his chin recedes* slope backwards, slant, fall away.

receipt *noun* **1** *the receipt of the goods | receipt of his apology* receiving, recipience, acceptance, getting, obtaining, taking. See RECEIVE 1, 2. **2** *get a receipt for the goods* till receipt, sales slip/ticket, proof of purchase, slip, stub, counterfoil, voucher. **3** *make a list of receipts for the tax inspector* money/payment received, financial return, income; takings, proceeds, profits, gains, earnings.

receive *verb* **1** *he did receive the goods* be in receipt of, accept delivery of, accept, take into one's possession. **2** *receive many benefits | receive good news* get, obtain, acquire, come by, gain, take, gather, collect. **3** *he received the news at home | received the news with fortitude* heard, be told, find out about, learn about, gather, be informed of, be notified of, take, react to. **4** *receive bad treatment* undergo, experience, meet with, encounter, go through, sustain, be subjected to, bear, suffer. **5** *the room/container will receive 20 people/tonnes* hold, contain, accommodate, admit, take. **6** *receive guests* welcome, greet, entertain, be at home to.
Opposites GIVE; SEND; PRESENT.

recent *adjective* **1** *recent developments* new, fresh, novel, latest, late, modern, contemporary, latter-day, current, up-to-date, up-to-the-minute. **2** *his recent illness* occurring/appearing recently, not long past.
Opposites OLD; FORMER.

recently *adverb* recently developed newly, freshly, lately, not long ago, of late.

receptacle *noun* container, holder, repository.

reception *noun* **1** *the reception of the goods* receiving, acceptance. See RECEIVE 1. **2** *the reception of the guests* welcoming, greeting, entertaining. **3** *the celebrity/show/news receiving a warm/cool reception* acceptance, response, acknowledgement, recognition, reaction, treatment, welcome. **4** *a wedding/graduation reception* party, formal party, function, social occasion, entertainment, soirée; *inf.* do, bash, beanfeast.

receptive *adjective* open, open to suggestions/ideas, flexible, willing, perceptive, sensitive, alert, bright, quick, keen.

recess *noun* **1** *books arranged in a recess* alcove, niche, nook, corner, cavity, bay, oriel. **2** *in the recesses of my memory* remote/secret/dark place, interior, heart, retreat, refuge, sanctum; depths; *inf.* innards. **3** *the children's recess | the parliamentary recess* break, respite, rest, interval, intermission, holiday, time off, vacation,

closure, cessation of work/business; *inf.* breather, time out.

recession *noun* **1** economic decline, downturn, depression, slump; hard times. **2** *the recession of flood waters* receding, retreat, withdrawal, ebbing, abatement. See RECEDE 1.

recipe *noun* **1** *follow the recipe for pancakes* directions, instructions; guide, cooking procedure. **2** *his suggestions are a recipe for a disaster* method, technique, system, procedure, *modus operandi*, process, means, way, formula, prescription.

reciprocal *adjective* **1** *a reciprocal favour* return, in return, returned, requited, retaliated. **2** *reciprocal affection* mutual, shared, common, reciprocative, reciprocatory, exchanged, give-and-take, complementary, corresponding, correlative.

reciprocate *verb* **1** *reciprocate his affection* return, requite, feel/give in return, repay, give back. **2** *I will take part if she reciprocates* respond, respond in kind, return the favour/compliment, do the same. **3** *reciprocate their ideas* interchange, exchange, give and take/receive, swap, barter, trade, bandy.

recital *noun* **1** *the recital of the poem* saying, rendering, declaiming, reading. See RECITE 1. **2** *the recital of the disasters* enumeration, detailing, itemizing, specification. See RECITE 3. **3** *a piano recital* musical performance, performance, solo performance, concert, show. **4** *listen to his recital of the events* account, report, recounting, telling, relation, description, detailing, rendering, narrative, record, story, tale, chronicle.

recitation *noun* **1** *the recitation of passages from John Donne* recital, saying, rendering, rendition, declaiming, reading. See RECITE 1. **2** *excellently chosen recitations* verse, poem, reading, passage, piece.

recite *verb* **1** *recite a poem/passage* say, repeat, read aloud, deliver, declaim, speak, render. **2** *ask the child to recite* say a poem, read a passage; *inf.* do one's party piece. **3** *recite a list of disasters* enumerate, detail, list, itemize, reel off, rattle off, specify, particularize, describe, recount, relate, narrate, recapitulate.

reckless *adjective* rash, careless, thoughtless, incautious, heedless, unheeding, inattentive, regardless, daredevil, devil-may-care, madcap, harum-scarum, wild, precipitate, headlong, hasty, irresponsible, hare-brained, foolhardy, overventuresome, ill-advised, imprudent, unwise, indiscreet, mindless, negligent, temerarious.
Opposites CAREFUL; CAUTIOUS; PRUDENT.

reckon *verb* **1** *he reckoned that she was lying* be of the opinion, think, believe, suppose, assume, surmise, conjecture, imagine, fancy, guess. **2** *she was reckoned a good painter* regard as, consider, judge, hold to be, think of as, look upon as, account, deem, rate, evaluate, gauge, count, estimate, appraise. **3** *reckon the cost* count, calculate, add up, compute, total, tally, put a figure on, give a figure to. **4** *reckon in the cost of the furnishings* count in, include, take into account. **5** *reckon on it being fine* count on, rely on, depend on, bank on, take for granted, trust. **6** *he will have her father to reckon with* cope with, deal with, contend with, handle, face. **7** *we did not reckon with his father's needs | we reckoned without the cost of the trip* anticipate, foresee, take into account/consideration, allow for, take cognizance of, take note of, bear in mind, not lose sight of; fail to anticipate, disregard, overlook.

reckoning *noun* **1** *according to my reckoning the total is wrong* counting, calculation, addition, computation, working out, total, tally, summation, score. **2** *according to their reckoning she is the best* opinion, judgement, evaluation, estimation, appraisal. **3** *deal with the reckoning of the account* settlement, paying, payment, discharging, defrayal, squaring, clearance. **4** *ask for the reckoning* bill, account, tally, amount due; *Am.* check; *Am. inf.* tab. **5** *the day of reckoning* settlement, retribution, judgement, fate, doom.

reclaim *verb* **1** *reclaim one's property* have returned, get back, take back, regain, retrieve, recover. **2** *reclaim the land from wilderness* retrieve, regain, reinstate, save, rescue, salvage. **3** *reclaim the criminals from vice* redeem, reform, regenerate, save, rescue.

recline *verb* lie, lie down, lean, be recumbent, rest, repose, loll, lounge, sprawl, stretch out, drape oneself over.

recluse *noun* hermit, anchorite, ascetic, eremite, monk, nun, solitary, lone wolf, loner.

recognition *noun* **1** *recognition of the criminal | recognition of an old friend* knowing, identification, spotting, recollection. *See* RECOGNIZE 1. **2** *his recognition of his defects/mistake* realization, awareness, consciousness, perception, appreciation, understanding, acknowledgement, acceptance, granting. *See* RECOGNIZE 2. **3** *their recognition of his claim* acknowledgement, acceptance, admittance, granting, endorsement, sanctioning, approval, validation, ratification. *See* RECOGNIZE 3. **4** *receive recognition as an artist* acknowledgement, appreciation, reward, honour, homage, applause; *inf.* bouquets.

recognize *verb* **1** *recognize the criminal | recognize an old friend* know, know again, identify, place, spot, recall, recollect, remember, call to mind. **2** *recognize his own defects/mistake | recognized that he was wrong* realize, see, be aware/conscious of, perceive, discern, appreciate, understand, apprehend, acknowledge, accept, admit, concede, allow, grant, confess, own. **3** *recognize his claim* acknowledge, accept, admit, concede, allow, grant, endorse, sanction, put the seal of approval on, approve, validate, ratify, uphold. **4** *recognize his achievement* show appreciation of, reward, honour, pay homage to, salute, applaud.
Opposites FORGET; OVERLOOK; IGNORE.

recoil *verb* **1** *recoil from him in terror/disgust* draw back, jump back, pull back, shrink, shy away, flinch, start, wince, cower, quail. **2** *recoil from/at the idea* feel revulsion at, baulk at, shrink from, shy away from, hesitate at, falter at. **3** *the spring recoiled* spring back, fly back, rebound, resile. **4** *the plan recoiled on the instigator* rebound, come back on, redound on,

misfire, backfire, go wrong, have an adverse effect, boomerang. **5** *the gun recoiled* kick back, jerk back.

recoil *noun* **1** *recoil of a gun* kickback, kick. **2** *the recoil from their plans* rebound, backlash; reaction; repercussions.

recollect *verb* **1** *as far as I recollect* remember, recall. **2** *I cannot recollect his name* remember, succeed in remembering, recall, call to mind, think of, summon up, place; *inf.* put one's finger on.
Opposites FORGET.

recollection *noun* **1** *the recollection of his name* remembering, recalling, calling to mind. *See* RECOLLECT 1. **2** *the photographs brought back happy recollections* memory, remembrance, reminiscence, mental image, impression. **3** *my recollection is that he was tall* memory, remembrance, power of recall.

recommend *verb* **1** *recommend this as a cure* advocate, commend, put in a good word for, speak favourably of, look with favour on, endorse, approve, vouch for, suggest, offer, put forward, propose, advance. **2** *I recommend caution | recommend that you go home* advise, counsel, guide, urge, exhort, enjoin. **3** *his plan has much to recommend it | his honesty recommended him to the board* make appealing/attractive/interesting, endow with appeal/attraction/interest, give an advantage to.
Opposites REJECT; VETO; DISAPPROVE.

recommendation *noun* **1** *the recommendation of the cure* advocacy, commendation, endorsement. *See* RECOMMEND 1. **2** *the recommendation of caution* advising, counselling, urging. *See* RECOMMEND 2. **3** *accept your recommendation as to the wine* commendation, endorsement, suggestion, tip, hint, proposal, good word, favourable mention, praise; words of approval; *inf.* plug. **4** *accept the judge's recommendation as to how to act* advice, counsel, guidance, exhortation, enjoinder. **5** *cheapness is the restaurant's only recommendation* good point, advantage, favourable aspect, benefit, blessing, boon.

reconcile *verb* **1** *mother and daughter have been reconciled | try to reconcile the feuders* make friendly gestures/overtures, reunite, bring together, restore harmony between, make peace between, resolve differences between, bring to terms, pacify, appease, placate, propitiate, mollify. **2** *reconcile themselves to her death | become reconciled to the unfortunate situation* come to accept, accept, accommodate, get used, resign, submit, yield, make the best of, grin and bear it. **3** *reconcile their differences* settle, resolve, square, put to rights, mend, remedy, patch up, heal, cure, rectify. **4** *reconcile his philosophy and his actions* harmonize, make compatible, put in agreement, adjust, attune, make coincide, make congruent.

reconciliation *noun* **1** *the reconciliation of the feuders* reuniting, bringing together, pacification, placating, propitiation, mollification. *See* RECONCILE 1. **2** *the reconciliation of differences* settling, settlement, resolving, resolution, mending, remedying. *See* RECONCILE 3. **3** *bring about a reconciliation* peace, end of hostilities, harmony, concord, amity. **4** *a reconciliation between his* *philosophy and his actions* harmonizing, adjustment. *See* RECONCILE 4.

recondite *adjective recondite information/texts* obscure, esoteric, abstruse, abstract, cryptic, incomprehensible, inscrutable, arcane, deep, profound, difficult, complex, involved, mysterious, dark.
Opposites STRAIGHTFORWARD; OPEN.

reconnaissance *noun* preliminary survey, survey, spying, exploration, scouting, probe, investigation, scrutiny, scan, inspection, observation; *inf.* recce.

reconnoitre *verb* survey, find out the lie of the land, see how the land lies, spy out, take stock of, explore, scout, investigate, scrutinize, scan, inspect, observe; *inf.* recce, case, check out.

reconsider *verb I ask you to reconsider your decision | please reconsider* think over, rethink, review, re-examine, re-evaluate, reassess, think better of; think again, think twice, have second thoughts, change one's mind.

reconstruct *verb* **1** *reconstruct the house* rebuild, remake, reassemble, refashion, recreate, remodel, revamp, renovate, recondition. **2** *reconstruct the scene* recreate, re-enact, piece together, build up, build up a picture/impression of. **3** *reconstruct society | reconstruct the firm* reorganize, rearrange, make over, redo, do over, overhaul, re-establish, reform.

record *noun* **1** *the records are missing* official document, register, log, logbook, file, official report/account, chronicle, diary, journal; documentation; documents, minutes, notes, annals, archives. **2** *play a record* gramophone record, disc, album, single, recording, release; vinyl; *inf.* platter. **3** *what do you know of his record?* employment/work history, employment/work performance, career to date, past performance, curriculum vitae, life history, history, background, reputation; *inf.* track record. **4** *does he have a record?* police/criminal record, history of crime; previous convictions. **5** *his jump was a record* best/star performance. **6** *this is a record of his achievement* memorial, remembrance, souvenir, token, testimony, testimonial, witness, trace; documentation, evidence. **7** *climate records* information, collected information; data, reports, accounts. **off the record** *this information is off the record* confidential, in confidence, unofficial, not for publication/circulation, private, secret, *sub rosa*. **on record** **1** *the wettest winter on record* recorded, registered, documented, officially noted. **2** *he is on record as promising improvements* recorded, officially noted, documented, publicly known.

record *verb* **1** *record the details* put on record, set down, write down, put in writing, take down, put down, enter, make a note of, document, minute, register, chronicle, file, put on file, docket, list, log, catalogue, inscribe, transcribe. **2** *record a very low temperature* register, read, indicate, show, display. **3** *record a song | record the wedding* make a record/recording of. **4** *record a disc/video* make, produce, cut, tape, videotape, video.

recorder *noun* **1** *purchase a recorder* tape recorder, video recorder. **2** *the documents com-*

piled *by the recorder* keeper of records, record keeper, registrar, archivist, annalist, chronicler, historian. **3** *the recorder noted down the details* scribe, clerk, secretary.

recording *noun* disc, record, gramophone record, tape recording, tape, video recording, video; vinyl, compact disc; *inf.* CD.

recount *verb* **1** *recount a tale* narrate, tell, relate, unfold, repeat. **2** *recount the events of the day* describe, detail, enumerate, list, specify, itemize, cite, particularize, catalogue.

recoup *verb* **1** *recoup the lost property* get back, win back, regain, recover, retrieve, repossess, redeem. **2** *recoup her for her losses* reimburse, pay back, repay, recompense, compensate, indemnify.

recourse *noun* **1** *their recourse to him was a last chance* resorting, turning to, looking to, appealing. *See* RESORT *verb* 1. **2** *their only recourse was private medicine* resort, way out, place/person to turn to, source of assistance, available resource, choice, option, possibility, alternative, expedient.

recover *verb* **1** *recover their stolen possessions* get back, win back, regain, recoup, retrieve, reclaim, repossess, redeem, recuperate, recapture. **2** *the invalid will recover in time* get better, get back to normal, get well, recuperate, convalesce, heal, get back on one's feet, feel oneself again, improve, mend, pick up, rally, revive, pull through, bounce back; *inf.* perk up. **3** *recover land from the sea | recover usable substances from waste* reclaim, retrieve, salvage, save, rescue, redeem, restore, recycle.
Opposites LOSE; DETERIORATE.

recovery *noun* **1** *the recovery of their goods* recouping, regaining, retrieval, reclamation, repossession, recapture. **2** *the invalid's recovery is slow* return to normal/health, recuperation, convalescence, healing, rallying, revival. *See* RECOVER 2. **3** *the recovery of the economy* improvement, betterment, amelioration, upturn, upswing. **4** *the recovery of land from the sea | recovery of material from waste* reclamation, retrieval, salvaging, rescue, recycling. *See* RECOVER 3.

recreation *noun* **1** *for recreation he rows* relaxation, refreshment, restoration, leisure, amusement, entertainment, distraction, diversion, pleasure, enjoyment, fun, play, sport. **2** *his recreations are all sport-based* leisure activity, pastime, hobby, diversion, distraction.
Opposites WORK.

recriminate *verb* counter-accuse, counter-charge, counter-attack, make mutual accusations, retaliate, take reprisals, exact retribution.

recrimination *noun* counter-accusation, counter-charge, counter-attack, retaliation, reprisal, retribution, vengeance; mutual accusations.

recruit *verb* **1** *recruit soldiers | recruit new members* enlist, enrol, sign up, draft, conscript, levy, engage, obtain, acquire, procure, take on, round up, muster. **2** *recruit an army* form, raise, gather/put together, muster, assemble. **3** *recruit his finances/membership* replenish, augment, increase, enlarge, add to, build up, strengthen, reinforce, fortify, shore up; *inf.* beef up.

recruit *noun* **1** *army recruits* enlistee, draftee, conscript. **2** *new recruits to the society/industry* new member, new entrant, newcomer, initiate, beginner, learner, trainee, apprentice, novice, tiro, neophyte, proselyte; *inf.* rookie, greenhorn.

rectify *verb* put/set right, right, correct, amend, emend, remedy, repair, fix, make good, redress, reform, improve, better, ameliorate, adjust, square.
Opposites DAMAGE; BREAK.

rectitude *noun* **1** *appoint a man of rectitude* righteousness, virtue, moral virtue, morality, honour, integrity, principle, probity, uprightness, good character, decency, honesty, upstandingness, scrupulousness, incomparability. **2** *the rectitude of the judgement/results* correctness, accuracy, exactness, precision, soundness, verity.
Opposites DISHONOUR; DISHONESTY; INACCURACY.

recuperate *verb* **1** *he is recuperating after an illness* recover, convalesce, get better, get back to normal, get well, regain one's strength/health, improve, mend, pick up, rally, revive, pull through, bounce back; *inf.* perk up. See RECOVER 2. **2** *recuperate costs* recover, recoup, get back, regain, retrieve, reclaim.

recur *verb* reoccur, happen/occur again, come back, return, reappear, be repeated, repeat itself, happen repeatedly.

recurrent *adjective* recurring, repeated, repetitive, reiterative, periodic, cyclical, regular, habitual, continual, frequent, intermittent, chronic.
Opposites ISOLATED; SINGLE; UNIQUE.

recycle *verb* reuse, reprocess, salvage, save.

red *adjective* **1** *red dresses/wallpaper/flowers* reddish, cherry, ruby, cardinal, carmine, ruby-coloured, wine, wine-coloured, claret, claret-coloured, coral, salmon-pink, cochineal, rose. See table at COLOUR. **2** *she had a red face* flushed, blushing, florid, ruddy, rubicund, roseate. **3** *with red eyes* bloodshot, red-rimmed, inflamed. **4** *red hair | horses with red coats* reddish, flaming-red, flame-coloured, auburn, Titian, chestnut, carroty, sandy, foxy, bay. **5** *soldiers with red hands* bloody, blood-stained, gory. **6** *red beliefs* Communist, ultra-left-wing, leftist; *inf.* commie, lefty.

red *noun* **1** *colour the walls with red* red colour/pigment. **2** *wearing red* red clothes/garments. **3** *suspecting them of being reds* Communist, socialist, leftist; *inf.* commie, lefty. **in the red** overdrawn, insolvent, in debt, in debit, owing money, showing a loss, bankrupt, in arrears; *inf.* on the rocks. **see red** be furious, be incensed, be infuriated, lose one's temper, become enraged, get mad, boil, seethe; *inf.* hit the roof, blow one's top, lose one's rag.

redden *noun* **1** *redden her lips* make/colour red. See RED *adjective* 1. **2** *she reddened in embarrassment* go red, blush, flush, colour, colour up, crimson.

redeem *verb* **1** *redeemed her gloves | redeem pawned goods* reclaim, get back, regain, recover,

retrieve, repossess, recoup, buy back, repurchase. **2** *redeem the vouchers* exchange, give in exchange, cash in, convert, turn in, trade in. **3** *Christ/missionaries redeeming sinners* free/save/deliver from sin, turn from sin, convert, purge/absolve of sin. **4** *his generosity redeems his bad temper* make up for, compensate for, atone for, offset, redress, outweigh. **5** *the wicked man redeemed himself by helping his neighbour* save/free from blame, vindicate, absolve, remove guilt from. **6** *redeem the slaves/hostages* free, set free, liberate, release, emancipate, ransom, rescue, save. **7** *redeem his promise/obligations* fulfil, discharge, make good, carry out, execute, keep, hold to, adhere to, abide by, obey, be faithful to, meet, satisfy.

redemption *noun* **1** *the redemption of possessions* reclamation, recovery, retrieval, recoupment, repurchase. See REDEEM 1. **2** *the redemption of his faults by his generosity* compensation, atonement, redress. See REDEEM 4. **3** *his redemption of himself by good works* freeing/saving from blame, vindication, absolution. **4** *the redemption of the slaves/hostages* freeing, liberation, release, emancipation, ransom, rescue, saving. **5** *the redemption of his promise/obligations* fulfilment, discharge, making good, execution, adherence, meeting, satisfying. See REDEEM 7.

redolent *adjective* **1** *films redolent of another age* evocative, suggestive, reminiscent. **2** *a room redolent of roses | breath redolent of garlic* smelling (of), scented (with), reeking (of). **3** *redolent flower gardens* sweet-smelling, fragrant, scented, perfumed, aromatic.

redoubtable *adjective* formidable, awe-inspiring, fearsome, mighty, powerful, dreadful, terrible, awful.

redound *verb* **1** *his action redounded to his credit* contribute to, conduce to, be conducive to, have an effect on, affect. **2** *your wicked actions will redound on you one day* come back on, recoil on, rebound on.

redress *verb* **1** *redress a wrong* rectify, remedy, put/set right, make amends for, compensate for, make up for, make reparation/restitution for, recompense for, atone for. **2** *redress the balance of power* put right, even up, regulate, adjust, correct.

redress *noun* **1** *make redress for the wrong* amends; compensation, reparation, restitution, recompense, atonement. **2** *the redress of wrongs* rectification, remedying, putting right, amending. See REDRESS *verb* 1.

reduce *verb* **1** *reduce the size of the garden | reduce the volume/speed/strength* make smaller, make less, lessen, lower, decrease, diminish, cut, curtail, contract, shorten, abbreviate, moderate, dilute, mitigate, alleviate, abate. **2** *they were reduced to tears/begging* bring to, bring to the point of, force to, drive to. **3** *they were reduced to a lower form/rank* demote, downgrade, lower, lower in rank/status, humble. **4** *reduced yesterday's stock* lower/cut in price, lower, make cheaper, cheapen, cut, mark down, slash, discount, put on sale. **5** *she is trying to reduce* get thinner, slim, slim down, lose/shed weight, go/be on a diet, diet, lose some

inches, shed some pounds; *Am.* slenderize.
6 *the army finally reduced the enemy/city* conquer, vanquish, overpower, subdue, subjugate, overcome, overrun. **7** *they have been reduced by the recession* bankrupt, make penniless/poor, impoverish, ruin, break.
Opposites INCREASE; ENLARGE.

reduction *noun* **1** *the reduction in size/volume/length/speed/strength* lessening, lowering, decrease, diminution, cut, contraction, abbreviation, moderation, dilution, alleviation, abatement. *See* REDUCE 1. **2** *their reduction to lower classes/ranks* demotion, downgrading, lowering, humbling. **3** *the reduction of goods* cheapening, discounting. *See* REDUCE 4. **4** *the reduction of the enemy/city* conquering, vanquishing, overpowering, subjugation, overrunning. *See* REDUCE 6. **5** *what reduction did you get on the car?* discount, deduction, cut, concession, allowance. **6** *the museum has some reductions of the artist's work* smaller copy, miniature, model.

redundant *adjective* **1** *his presence was redundant | redundant supplies* surplus to requirements, not required, unnecessary, inessential, unwanted, *de trop*, surplus, supernumerary, excessive, in excess, extra; *inf.* needed like a hole in the head. **2** *redundant passages/writings* unnecessary, inessential, padded, wordy, verbose, tautological, periphrastic, diffuse, pleonastic. **3** *declared redundant | redundant people seeking jobs* sacked, dismissed, disemployed, unemployed, jobless.
Opposites ESSENTIAL; VITAL.

reel *verb* **1** *drunks reeling down the street* stagger, lurch, sway, stumble, totter, wobble, falter, waver, pitch, roll. **2** *she was reeling from the blow* feel giddy/dizzy, feel confused, be shaken, be in shock, be upset. **3** *her mind was reeling | the room seemed to reel* go round, go round and round, whirl, spin, revolve, swirl, twirl, swim.

refer *verb* **1** *refer to a dictionary | refer to his notes* consult, turn to, look at, look up, seek information from, have recourse to. **2** *refer the question/person to a higher court* pass, hand on, send on, transfer, remit, direct. **3** *he referred to her death in his speech* mention, make mention of, make reference to, allude to, touch on, speak of, cite, advert to, hint at. **4** *these figures refer to last year* apply to, be relevant to, have relevance to, concern, relate to, belong to, pertain to, have a bearing on.

referee *noun* **1** *football referee | send the disputed matter to a referee* umpire, judge, adjudicator, arbitrator, arbiter, mediator; *inf.* ref. **2** *act as referee for his job application* character witness, commender, upholder, advocate, backer.

referee *verb* **1** *referee the match* umpire, judge, adjudicate. **2** *referee in the dispute* arbitrate, mediate, act as arbitrator/negotiator, intercede.

reference *noun* **1** *a reference to her death in his speech* mention, allusion, citation, hint. **2** *with reference to yesterday's meeting* regard, respect, relation, bearing, applicability, application, relevance, pertinence, connection, correlation. **3** *give a list of your references for the book* source, information source, citation, authority; bibliography. **4** *the teacher gave her a reference* character reference, testimonial, recommendation, good word; credentials.

referendum *noun* public vote, plebiscite, popular vote, poll.

refine *verb* **1** *refine sugar/flour* purify, rarefy, clarify, clear, cleanse, strain, sift, filter, distil, process. **2** *school refined her to some extent* civilize, make cultivated, polish, improve, make elegant. **3** *refine the art of conversation* improve, perfect, consummate, elaborate, hone, fine-tune, complete.

refined *adjective* **1** *refined sugar/flour* purified, pure, rarefied, clarified, clear, filtered, distilled, processed. **2** *a refined lady/gentleman* cultivated, cultured, polished, civilized, civil, gracious, stylish, elegant, sophisticated, urbane, courtly, well-mannered, well-bred, gentlemanly, ladylike, genteel. **3** *refined tastes/manners* discriminating, discerning, tasteful, sophisticated, fastidious.
Opposites CRUDE; COARSE; UNREFINED.

refinement *noun* **1** *the refinement of sugar* purification, processing. *See* REFINE 1. **2** *a person of refinement* cultivation, culture, taste, discrimination, polish, finish, civility, grace, graciousness, style, elegance, finesse, sophistication, urbanity, courtliness, good breeding, politeness, gentility, politesse; good manners. **3** *refinements of logic/language* subtlety, nicety, nuance, fine point.

reflect *verb* **1** *the surface reflects heat/light* throw back, cast back, send back, give back, scatter, diffuse. **2** *their faces reflected in the pool* mirror, image. **3** *reflect sound* send back, bounce back, echo, re-echo. **4** *their/a complexion reflecting his state of health* indicate, express, bespeak, communicate, show, display, demonstrate, exhibit, reveal, manifest, bear out, result from. **5** *it will reflect on the school if he does badly* discredit, put in a bad light, damage, damage the reputation of, detract from. **6** *reflect on her problems* think about, consider, give thought/consideration to, mull over, contemplate, deliberate over, ponder, meditate about, muse about, ruminate about, cogitate about, cerebrate, dwell on, brood about.

reflection *noun* **1** *the reflection of heat/sound/images* throwing back, sending back, echoing, mirroring. *See* REFLECT 1, 2, 3. **2** *look at her reflection* image, mirror image. **3** *his complexion is a reflection of the state of his health* indication, expression, display, demonstration, manifestation, result. **4** *his behaviour is a reflection on the school* imputation, slur, aspersion, source of discredit, derogation. **5** *on reflection, he decided to go* thought, thinking, consideration, contemplation, deliberation, meditation, rumination, cogitation, cerebration. **6** *write down your reflections on the subject* thought, opinion, view, idea, impression, comment; findings.

reflex *adjective* *a reflex action* automatic, involuntary, spontaneous; *inf.* knee-jerk.

reform *verb* **1** *reform the system* improve, make better, better, ameliorate, amend, mend, rectify, correct, rehabilitate, change, revise, revolutionize, reorganize, reconstruct, rebuild, refashion, remodel, remake, make over, revamp, renovate. **2** *he has reformed since you knew him* mend one's ways, change for the better, turn over a new leaf, improve; *inf.* go straight, get back on the straight and narrow. **Opposites** WORSEN.

reform *noun the reform of the system* improvement, betterment, amelioration, amendment, rectification, correction, rehabilitation, change, revision, reorganization, reconstruction, rebuilding, refashioning, remodelling, renovation.

refractory *adjective* intractable, recalcitrant, unmanageable, ungovernable, disobedient, insubordinate, defiant, contrary, wayward, wilful, headstrong, perverse, contumacious, rebellious, mutinous, obstinate, obdurate. **Opposites** OBEDIENT; MANAGEABLE.

refrain *verb refrain from drinking* desist, abstain, hold back, forbear, forgo, do without, avoid, eschew, cease, stop, give up, leave off, quit, renounce.

refresh *verb* **1** *refreshed by a long walk* freshen, invigorate, revitalize, revive, brace, fortify, enliven, stimulate, energize, exhilarate, reanimate, resuscitate, revivify, rejuvenate, regenerate, breathe new life into, inspirit; *inf.* perk up. **2** *refresh one's memory* stimulate, prompt, prod, jog, activate, rouse, arouse.

refreshing *adjective* **1** *a refreshing breeze* freshening, invigorating, revitalizing, reviving, bracing, stimulating, exhilarating, energizing. *See* REFRESH 1. **2** *a refreshing piece of writing | refreshing attitude* fresh, new, novel, original, different.

refreshment *noun* **1** *the refreshment of their system/ideas* freshening, invigoration, revitalizing, revival, stimulation, energizing, exhilaration, reanimation, rejuvenation. **2** *the guests took some refreshment | refreshments were available* food, food and drink, drink, sustenance; snacks, drinks; *inf.* eats, grub, nosh, chow.

refrigerate *verb* keep cold, cool, chill, freeze.

refuge *noun* **1** *seek refuge from the elements/danger* shelter, safety, security, protection, asylum, sanctuary. **2** *regard their house as a refuge* place of safety, safe house, shelter, haven, retreat, bolt-hole, sanctuary, harbour. **3** *borrowing money was his last refuge* resort, recourse, expedient, stopgap, tactic, stratagem, strategy.

refugee *noun* displaced/stateless person, émigré, exile, fugitive, escapee.

refund *verb refund her deposit* give back, return, repay, pay back, reimburse, make good, restore, replace.

refund *noun give the disappointed audience a refund* repayment, reimbursement.

refurbish *verb* renovate, revamp, make over, overhaul, redecorate, spruce up, recondition, refit, re-equip, remodel, repair, mend; *inf.* do up, fix up.

refusal *noun* **1** *the refusal of her invitation* turning down, declining, rejecting, spurning. *See* REFUSE *verb* 1. **2** *four acceptances and one refusal to the invitation* non-acceptance, dissent, no, demurral, negation, thumbs down, rebuff; regrets; *inf.* knock-back, brush-off. **3** *you can*

have first refusal option, choice, consideration, opportunity.

refuse *verb* **1** *refuse an invitation/offer* turn down, decline, say no to, reject, spurn, rebuff, repudiate; *inf.* pass up, knock back. **2** *refuse to go* decline, be unwilling, baulk at, demur at, avoid, resist, protest at. **3** *refuse permission to go* withhold, not grant. **Opposites** ACCEPT; CONSENT; GRANT.

refuse *noun* rubbish, waste, debris, litter, dross; dregs, leavings, sweepings; *Am.* garbage, trash; *inf.* junk.

regain *verb* **1** *regain one's property/composure* get back, win back, recover, recoup, retrieve, reclaim, repossess, redeem, recuperate, take back, retake, recapture. **2** *regain the shore* get back to, return to, reach again, reattain.

regal *adjective* royal, majestic, noble, proud, stately, magnificent, sumptuous; kingly, queenly, princely, fit for a king/queen/prince/princess.

regale *verb* **1** *regale their guests* entertain lavishly/sumptuously, ply with food and drink, wine and dine, feast, fête. **2** *regale his friends with stories of his travels* entertain, amuse, divert, delight, fascinate, captivate.

regard *verb* **1** *the security officer regarded them closely* watch, look at, gaze at, keep an eye on, stare at, observe, view, study, scrutinize, eye, mark, behold. **2** *he seldom regards her advice* heed, pay attention to, attend to, listen to, mind, take notice of, take into consideration/account. **3** *regard the prospect with horror* look upon, view, consider, contemplate, think of, weigh up, mull over, reflect on, deliberate on. **4** *his work/aunt is well/poorly regarded* judge, adjudge, rate, value, estimate, gauge, appraise, assess, account, deem, consider, look upon, hold. **5** *these figures do not regard the present project* apply to, relate to, concern, be relevant to, refer to, belong to, pertain to, have a bearing on.

regard *noun* **1** *she was aware of his steady regard* look, gaze, stare; observation, scrutiny. *See* REGARD *verb* 1. **2** *pay no regard to his warning* heed, attention, notice, consideration, thought, mind. **3** *looked upon with regard in the firm* respect, esteem, admiration, approval, approbation, appreciation, favour, deference, affection, love. **4** *in this regard I disagree with you | consider from all regards* respect, aspect, point, particular, detail, item, feature. **5** *this has no regard to the matter in question* application, relation, relationship, connection, relevance, reference, pertinence, bearing.

regarding *preposition* with/in regard to, as regards, as to, with reference to, on the subject/matter of, apropos, concerning, about, respecting.

regardless *adjective* **regardless of** without regard to, disregarding, unmindful of, heedless of, without consideration of, indifferent to, negligent of.

regardless *adverb he decided to go, regardless* anyway, anyhow, in any case, nevertheless, nonetheless, despite everything, for all that,

no matter what.
Opposites MINDFUL; HEEDFUL.

regards *plural noun send her my regards* best/
good wishes, greetings, salutations, respects,
compliments, remembrances.

regenerate *verb* **1** *he felt regenerated after his
holiday* renew, breathe new life into, restore,
invigorate, refresh, revitalize, revive, stimulate, energize, exhilarate, revivify, rejuvenate,
uplift, inspirit. **2** *regenerate the political party*
breathe new life into, change radically,
improve, amend, reorganize, reconstruct, overhaul.

regime *noun* government, system of government, rule, reign, control, command, administration, establishment, direction,
management, leadership.

regiment *verb regiment tourists into groups/regi-
mented school classes* organize/order rigidly, systematize, methodize, control strictly,
discipline, keep a tight rein on, bring into line,
run a tight ship, rule with a rod of iron.

region *noun* **1** *the western region of the country*
area, province, territory, division, section, sector, zone, tract, part, quarter, locality. *See
table.* **2** *the lumbar region of the body* part, place,
section, locality, site. **3** *work in the region of
metaphysics* field, sphere, orbit, ambit, realm,
domain, world. **in the region of** *in the region of
500 people/tonnes* approximately, about, roughly,
more or less, in the area/neighbourhood of.

REGIONS OF THE WORLD	
Africa	Meso-America
Antarctic	Middle East
Arctic	Micronesia
Asia	New World
Australasia	North Africa
Balkans	North America
Baltic States	Northern Europe
Caribbean	Occident
Central Africa	Oceania
Central America	Orient
Central Asia	Polynesia
Central Europe	Scandinavia
East Africa	South America
East Asia	Southeast Asia
Eastern Europe	Southern Africa
East Indies	Southern Asia
Eurasia	Southern Europe
Europe	South Pacific
Far East	Sub-Saharan Africa
Indian Subcontinent	Transcaucasia
Indochina	West Africa
Latin America	Western Europe
Melanesia	West Indies

regional *adjective* **1** *regional distinctions shown
on the map* geographical, topographical, zonal,
territorial. **2** *organized on a regional rather than
a national basis* local, localized, district, provincial, parochial.
Opposites NATIONAL.

register *noun* **1** *sign the register/be on the medical register* official list, listing, roll, roster,
index, directory, catalogue. **2** *historians consult-*

ing old parish registers record, chronicle, diary,
journal, log; annals, archives, files. **3** *the register of her voice* range, compass, scope, scale,
gamut, reach, sweep, spectrum.

register *verb* **1** *register a birth/register the date
of arrival* record, put on record, enter, set
down, chronicle, enrol, inscribe, write down,
put in writing, take down, note, minute, list,
catalogue. **2** *the speedometer registered 50 miles
per hour* read, record, indicate, show, display.
3 *her face registered surprise* show, express, display, exhibit, evince, betray, reveal, manifest,
demonstrate, reflect. **4** *his death/danger did not
register* make an impression, get through, sink
in, penetrate, have an effect.

registration *noun.* See table.

regress *verb he had improved but he has now
regressed* retrogress, revert, relapse, lapse, backslide, fall away, go backwards, degenerate,
retrograde, recidivate.
Opposites IMPROVE; PROGRESS.

regret *verb* **1** *she regrets her action* feel sorry/
contrite about, feel remorse about, wish
undone, have a conscience about, repent, rue.
2 *she regrets their going/regretting lost opportunities* feel sorry about, lament, bemoan, be upset/
disappointed about, mourn, grieve over, weep
over, fret about, pine over, deplore.

regret *noun* **1** *she looks upon her actions with
regret* sorrow, remorse, contrition, repentance,
pangs of conscience, compunction, ruefulness,
self-reproach, penitence. **2** *she regarded their
going with regret/regret at her lost opportunities*
sorrow, disappointment, lamentation, grief,
mourning, pining.

regretful *adjective* sorry, apologetic, remorseful, contrite, repentant, conscience-stricken,
rueful, penitent.
Opposites IMPENITENT; UNREPENTANT.

regrettable *adjective* deplorable, reprehensible, disgraceful, blameworthy, unfortunate,
unwelcome, distressing, ill-advised.

regular *adjective* **1** *his regular route to work*
usual, normal, customary, habitual, routine,
typical, everyday, daily, unvarying, common,
average, commonplace. **2** *regular breathing*
rhythmic, periodic, steady, even, uniform, constant, unchanging. **3** *trees placed at regular
intervals* even, uniform, consistent, orderly, systematic, fixed. **4** *build on a regular surface* level,
smooth, flat, uniform. **5** *apply through the regular channels* official, established, fixed, stated,
conventional, formal, proper, orthodox,
approved, sanctioned, bona fide, standard,
usual, traditional, classic, time-honoured.
6 *insist on regular office procedures* methodical,
systematic, well-organized, orderly, efficient,
smooth-running, streamlined. **7** *he's a regular
charmer/hero* real, thorough, absolute, utter,
complete.
Opposites IRREGULAR; UNUSUAL; ERRATIC; UNEVEN.

regulate *verb* **1** *regulate one's expenditure/
lifestyle/regulate the traffic* control, direct, guide,
govern, rule, manage, order, administer, handle, arrange, organize, conduct, run, supervise,
oversee, superintend, monitor. **2** *regulate the*

clock/mechanism adjust, balance, set, synchronize, modulate.

regulation *noun* **1** *the regulation of expenditure/lifestyles/traffic* control, direction, guidance, government, rule, management, administration, organization, conducting, handling, supervision, monitoring. See REGULATE 1. **2** *the regulation of the clocks/mechanisms* adjustment, balancing, synchronization, modulation. **3** *new government/school regulations* rule, ruling, order, directive, act, law, decree, statute, edict, ordinance, pronouncement, dictum, command, procedure, requirement, prescription, precept.

regulation *adjective regulation dress* official, prescribed, mandatory, required, set, fixed, standard, normal, usual, customary.

rehabilitate *verb* **1** *rehabilitate the wounded soldiers* restore to health/normality, get back to health/normality, reintegrate, readapt, retrain. **2** *rehabilitate slum areas/houses* restore, redevelop, recondition, renovate, renew, refurbish, redecorate, mend, repair, fix up, rebuild, reconstruct. **3** *rehabilitate the disgraced minister* reinstate, restore, bring back, re-establish.

rehearsal *noun* **1** *a rehearsal of the play/concert* practice, practice session, trial performance, run-through, going-over. **2** *weary of his rehearsal of the events* account, relating, recounting, narration, repeating, reiteration. See REHEARSE 4. **3** *listen to the rehearsal of their grievances* enumeration, listing, itemization, specification; list, catalogue. See REHEARSE 5.

rehearse *verb* **1** *rehearse the play/speech* practise, try out, run through, go over. **2** *actors rehearsing* practise, have a practice session, prepare, try out, have a trial performance, go through one's paces. **3** *rehearse the actors/children* drill, train, prepare. **4** *rehearse his adventures* relate, recount, narrate, describe, delineate, repeat, reiterate, recapitulate, go over. **5** *rehearse their grievances on paper* enumerate, list, itemize, detail, spell out, catalogue, recite.

reign *verb* **1** *the king/queen reigned for thirty years* be king/queen, be monarch/sovereign, sit on the throne, occupy the throne, wear the crown, wield the sceptre. **2** *the present committee has reigned for years* be in power, govern, be in government, rule, be in command/charge/control, administer, hold sway; *inf.* be at the

---

INTERNATIONAL CAR REGISTRATIONS (LETTERS AND NUMBERS)

Registration	Country	Registration	Country	Registration	Country
5	Russia	IND	India	RCB	Congo
A	Austria	IR	Iran	RCH	Chile
AL	Albania	IRL	Ireland	RH	Haiti
AUS	Australia	IRQ	Iraq	RI	Indonesia
B	Belgium	IS	Iceland	RIM	Mauritania
BD	Bangladesh	J	Japan	RL	Lebanon
BDS	Barbados	JA	Jamaica	RM	Malagasy
BG	Bulgaria	KWT	Kuwait		Republic
BR	Brazil	L	Luxembourg	RMM	Mali
BRG	Guyana	LAO	Laos	ROK	South Korea
BRN	Bahrain	LB	Liberia	RU	Burundi
BS	Bahamas	LS	Lesotho	RWA	Rwanda
C	Cuba	M	Malta	S	Sweden
CDN	Canada	MA	Morocco	SD	Swaziland
CH	Switzerland	MAL	Malaysia	SF	Finland
CI	Côte	MEX	Mexico	SGP	Singapore
	d'Ivoire	MS	Mauritius	SME	Surinam
CO	Colombia	MW	Malawi	SN	Senegal
CR	Costa Rica	N	Norway	SYR	Syria
CY	Cyprus	NIG	Niger	T	Thailand
D	Germany	NL	Nether-	TG	Togo
DK	Denmark		lands, the	TN	Tunisia
DZ	Algeria	NZ	New	TR	Turkey
E	Spain		Zealand	TT	Trinidad
EC	Ecuador	P	Portugal		and
F	France	PA	Panama		Tobago
FL	Liechten-	PAK	Pakistan	U	Uruguay
	stein	PE	Peru	USA	United
GB	Great	PI	Philippines		States of
	Britain	PL	Poland		America
GCA	Guatemala	PY	Paraguay	VN	Vietnam
GH	Ghana	R	Romania	WAL	Sierra Leone
GR	Greece	RA	Argentina	WAN	Nigeria
H	Hungary	RB	Botswana	WS	Western
HK	Hong Kong	RC	China		Samoa
HKJ	Jordan	RCA	Central	YV	Venezuela
I	Italy		African	Z	Zambia
IL	Israel		Republic	ZA	South Africa

helm. **3** *chaos reigned* prevail, predominate, obtain, hold sway, be supreme, be rife, be rampant.

reign *noun* **1** *during the reign of the king/queen* monarchy, sovereignty. *See table at* ROYALTY. **2** *under the reign of the present government* power, government, rule, command, control, administration, charge, influence, sway, ascendancy, dominion, supremacy.

rein *noun* *act as a rein on their expenditure* check, curb, restraint, constraint, restriction, limitation, control, bridle, brake.

rein *verb* *try to rein in his impatience | rein your expenditure* check, curb, restrain, constrain, hold back, restrict, control, bridle, put the brakes on, slow down.

reinforce *verb* **1** *reinforce the bridge | reinforce his argument* strengthen, fortify, bolster up, shore up, buttress, prop up, brace, support, back up, uphold, stress, underline, emphasize. **2** *reinforce the troops* augment, increase, add to, supplement.

reinforcement *noun* **1** *the reinforcement of the bridge/argument* strengthening, fortification, bolstering, propping up, supporting, stressing, emphasizing. *See* REINFORCE 1. **2** *the reinforcement of the troops* augmentation, increasing, supplementing. **3** *act as a reinforcement of his argument* fortification, buttress, prop, brace, support, emphasis.

reinforcements *plural noun* *armies sending for reinforcements* additional troops/supplies, supplementaries, reserves; support.

reiterate *verb* repeat, repeat/go over and over, say again, belabour, dwell on, harp on, hammer away at.

reject *verb* **1** *reject an offer/invitation* refuse, turn down, decline, say no to, give the thumbs down to, spurn, rebuff, repudiate, veto, deny; *inf.* pass up, knock back. **2** *reject the bill | reject his wife* cast out, cast aside, discard, jettison, renounce, abandon, forsake, scrap, exclude, eliminate.
Opposites ACCEPT; APPROVE.

reject *noun* **1** *a reject from the factory* substandard article, discard, second. **2** *one of society's rejects* failure, outcast, derelict; *inf.* drop-out.

rejection *noun* **1** *the rejection of their offer/invitation* refusal, turning down, declining, spurning; *inf.* knock-back, brush-off. *See* REJECT *verb* 1. **2** *the rejection of the bill | rejection of his wife* casting out, discarding, jettisoning, renunciation. *See* REJECT *verb* 2. **3** *receive a rejection* refusal, non-acceptance, no, demurral, negation, thumbs down; *inf.* knock-back, brush-off.

rejoice *verb* **1** *people rejoicing on hearing the good news* be joyful, be happy, be pleased, be glad, be delighted, be elated, be overjoyed, be jubilant, be euphoric, jump for joy, exult, glory, triumph, celebrate, revel, make merry, feast. **2** *rejoice in her new baby* take delight/pleasure in, find joy in.
Opposites MOURN; LAMENT.

rejoicing *noun* happiness, pleasure, gladness, delight, elation, jubilation, euphoria, exulta-

tion, glory, triumph, celebration, revelry, merry-making, feasting.

rejoinder *noun* answer, response, reply, riposte, retort; *inf.* comeback.

relapse *verb* **1** *the firm improved but then relapsed* lapse, regress, retrogress, revert, backslide, fall away, go backwards, slip back, degenerate, retrograde, recidivate. **2** *the patient relapsed* have/suffer a relapse, get ill/worse again, worsen, take a turn for the worse, sicken, deteriorate, sink.

relapse *noun* **1** *the firm had a relapse after its improvement* lapse, regression, retrogression, reversion, backsliding, recidivism. **2** *the patient suffered a relapse* reoccurence of illness, worsening of condition, turn for the worse, set-back, deterioration.
Opposites IMPROVEMENT; RECOVERY.

relate *verb* **1** *relate the story of the accident* recount, tell, narrate, describe, report, impart, communicate, recite, rehearse, present, detail, delineate, chronicle, set forth. **2** *it is sometimes difficult to relate cause and effect* connect, associate, link, correlate, ally, couple, join. **3** *this information does not relate to the matter in hand* apply to, be relevant to, have relevance to, concern, refer to, have reference to, belong to, pertain to, bear on.

related *adjective* **1** *related issues* connected, interconnected, associated, linked, correlated, allied, affiliated, accompanying, concomitant, akin. **2** *related through marriage* connected, akin, kindred, agnate, cognate, consanguineous.
Opposites UNCONNECTED; SEPARATE; UNRELATED.

relation *noun* **1** *the relation of the story* recounting, recountal, telling, narrating, narrative, description, reporting, rehearsal, reciting. *See* RELATE 1. **2** *the relation between cause and effect* connection, association, linking, tie-in, correlation, alliance, bond, interdependence. **3** *have no relation to the problem in hand* applicability, application, relevance, reference, pertinence, bearing. **4** *have relations in America* relative, member of the family, kinsman, kinswoman, connection; kin.

relations *plural noun* **1** *have business relations* connections, dealings, associations, communications; contact, interaction. **2** *suspected of having relations with each other* sexual intercourse, intimacy; sexual relationship, affair, liaison; *inf.* sex. **3** *have no relations in this country* family, kin, kinsfolk, kindred; connections, folks.

relationship *noun* **1** *the relationship between cause and effect* connection, association, link, correlation, alliance, bond, tie-up, parallel, correspondence, conjunction. **2** *enter in a new relationship* friendship, love affair, affair, liaison. **3** *I don't think there is a relationship between the families* family/blood ties, kinship.

relative *adjective* **1** *consider the relative merits of the candidates* comparative, comparable, respective, correlative, parallel, corresponding. **2** *the salary scale is relative to production* proportionate (to), in proportion/ratio (to), based (on). **3** *facts relative to the issue* applicable, relevant, pertaining, pertinent, germane, material, apposite, appropriate, apropos, appurtenant.

relative *noun a relative of his wife* relation, member of the family, kinsman, kinswoman, connection; kin, parent, sibling, grandparent; mother, father, brother, sister, son, daughter, stepmother, stepfather, stepchild, stepbrother, stepsister, aunt, uncle, niece, nephew, cousin, grandfather, grandmother.

relatively *adverb* **1** *for a car of this size it is relatively roomy* comparatively, in comparison, by comparison, proportionately. **2** *although ill he is relatively cheerful* quite, rather, reasonably, somewhat.

relax *verb* **1** *relax one's grip* loosen, slacken, weaken, untighten, lessen, let up, reduce, diminish. **2** *let her muscles relax* become less tense/stiff/rigid, loosen, slacken, untighten. **3** *relax the rules* moderate, make less strict/formal, soften, ease. **4** *relax one's efforts* lessen, reduce, diminish, decrease, ease off, slacken off, let up on, abate. **5** *tense people learning to relax* loosen up, ease up/off; *inf.* unwind, take it easy, let it all hang out, hang loose. **6** *this will relax you* loosen up, make less tense/uptight, calm, calm down, tranquillize, soothe, pacify; *inf.* unwind. **7** *he relaxes by playing the piano* be at leisure, take time off, enjoy oneself, amuse oneself, entertain oneself, rest; *inf.* let one's hair down. **8** *relax by the pool* rest, lounge, repose, take one's ease, idle, put one's feet up. **Opposites** TIGHTEN; INCREASE; INTENSIFY; EXERCISE.

relaxation *noun* **1** *the relaxation of his grip* loosening, slackening, weakening, letting-up. See RELAX 1. **2** *the relaxation of her muscles* loosening, slackening, untightening. See RELAX 2. **3** *relaxation of rules* moderation, softening, easing. See RELAX 3. **4** *relaxation of one's efforts* lessening, reduction, easing-off, abatement. See RELAX 4. **5** *tense people learning relaxation* loosening up. See RELAX 5. **6** *the relaxation of the patients* calming, tranquillization, soothing, pacification. See RELAX 6. **7** *for relaxation he plays the piano* leisure, recreation, enjoyment, amusement, entertainment, fun, pleasure, rest, refreshment.

relay *verb relay the information* pass on, hand on, communicate, send, transmit, broadcast, spread, circulate.

release *verb* **1** *release the prisoners* set free, free, let go, set/turn loose, let out, liberate, deliver, emancipate, manumit. **2** *release those who had been tied up* set free, free, untie, undo, unloose, unbind, unchain, unfetter, unshackle, extricate. **3** *release her from her promise/engagement* let off, let go, excuse, absolve, acquit, exonerate, exempt. **4** *release the news | release a bulletin* make public, make known, issue, break, announce, reveal, divulge, unveil, present, disclose, publish, broadcast, put out, circulate, disseminate, distribute, spread. **Opposites** IMPRISON; ENGAGE; SUPPRESS.

release *noun* **1** *the release of the prisoners* freeing, liberation, deliverance, emancipation, manumission. See RELEASE *verb* 1. **2** *prisoners obtaining their release* freedom, liberation, deliverance, emancipation, manumission. **3** *the release of the bound victims* freeing, untying,

unbinding, unchaining, extrication. See RELEASE *verb* 2. **4** *the release from her promise* excusing, absolution, acquittal, dispensation, exemption; *inf.* let-off. See RELEASE *verb* 3. **5** *the release of the news* issuing, breaking, announcement, divulging, publishing, publication, broadcasting, circulation. See RELEASE *verb* 4. **6** *write a press release* announcement, bulletin, publication, proclamation. **7** *the artist's latest release* record, disc, album, book, film.

relent *verb* **1** *the tyrant relented and released the child's mother* soften, become merciful/lenient, show mercy/pity, give quarter, melt, capitulate, yield, give way, give in, unbend, come round, forbear, change one's mind; *inf.* do a U-turn. **2** *the pace/wind relented* let up, ease, slacken, relax, abate, drop, fall off, die down, weaken.

relentless *adjective* **1** *a relentless tyrant* unrelenting, ruthless, merciless, uncompassionate, pitiless, remorseless, unforgiving, implacable, inexorable, cruel, grim, harsh, hard, cold-hearted, fierce, strict, obdurate, unyielding, unflexible, unbending. **2** *a relentless urge/ambition* unrelenting, unremitting, undeviating, persistent, unswerving, persevering, unflagging, punishing, unfaltering, unstoppable, incessant, unceasing, non-stop, unabated, unbroken.
Opposites LENIENT; MERCIFUL.

relevant *adjective* applicable, pertinent, apposite, material, appurtenant, to the point/purpose, germane, admissible, appropriate, apt, fitting.

reliable *adjective* **1** *a reliable friend* dependable, trustworthy, trusty, true, tried and true/tested, faithful, devoted, steady, steadfast, constant, unfailing, infallible, certain, sure, responsible. **2** *reliable evidence* dependable, trustworthy, well-founded, well-grounded, authentic, genuine, credible, sound. **3** *a reliable firm* dependable, trustworthy, reputable, established, safe, stable.
Opposites UNRELIABLE; UNTRUSTWORTHY; TREACHEROUS.

reliance *noun* **1** *place no reliance on what she says* confidence, trust, faith, belief, conviction. **2** *his total reliance on his colleagues* dependence, leaning.

relic *noun* **1** *relics on view in the museum* ancient/historical object, artefact, antique, heirloom. **2** *a tradition that is a relic of another age* vestige, trace, survivor, remnant. **3** *regard the ring as a relic of a former relationship* souvenir, memento, keepsake, remembrance, reminder.

relics *plural noun* **1** *looking for Roman relics* remains, reliquiae, fragments, shards. **2** *exhume the relics* corpse, dead body; remains.

relief *noun* **1** *the relief of the pain* relieving, alleviating, mitigating, assuaging, allaying, soothing, easing, dulling, lessening, reduction. See RELIEVE 1. **2** *the medicine brought relief* alleviation, mitigation, assuagement, palliation, ease, appeasement, abatement. **3** *the relief of the starving people/city* aiding, assisting, rescuing, saving. See RELIEVE 2. **4** *bring relief to the starving* *people* aid, help, assistance, succour. **5** *bring relief from the monotony* respite, remission, interruption, break, variation, diversion, lightening, brightening; *inf.* let-up. **6** *the soldier's/doctor's relief* replacement, substitute, stand-in, fill-in, locum, understudy. **7** *details bringing the story out in sharp relief* contrast, distinctness, vividness, intensity. **8** *relief from his burden* freedom, release, liberation, deliverance, exemption, extrication, discharge. *See* RELIEVE 5.

relieve *verb* **1** *relieve his pain/distress* alleviate, mitigate, assuage, allay, soothe, soften, palliate, appease, ease, dull, abate, reduce, lessen, diminish. **2** *relieve the starving people/city* bring aid to, aid, help, assist, rescue, save, succour. **3** *relieve the monotony* bring respite to, interrupt, break up, vary, lighten, brighten. **4** *relieve the soldier on guard* take over from, take the place of, stand in for, substitute for. **5** *relieve them of their burdens* free, release, liberate, deliver, exempt, extricate, discharge, unburden, disburden, disencumber, disembarrass.
Opposites EXACERBATE; AGGRAVATE; WORSEN.

religion *noun. See table. See also tables at* ANGEL, BIBLE, CHRISTIANITY, CHURCH, DEVIL, ECCLESIASTIC, FESTIVAL, GOD, POPE, PRIEST, SACRED TEXT, SAINT.

religious *adjective* **1** *religious festivals/discussions* church, holy, divine, theological, doctrinal, spiritual, sectarian. **2** *religious people* churchgoing, God-fearing, godly, pious, devout. **3** *pay religious attention to detail* scrupulous, conscientious, meticulous, zealous, strict, rigid, rigorous, exact, unfailing, unswerving, undeviating.
Opposites IRRELIGIOUS; IMPIOUS; UNGODLY.

relinquish *verb* **1** *relinquish her right to the title* give up, renounce, resign, abdicate, surrender, sign away. **2** *relinquish his position* depart from, leave, quit, vacate, pull out of, abandon, forsake. **3** *relinquish the habit* give up, discon-

tinue, stop, cease, drop, abstain from, forbear from, forgo, desist from. **4** *relinquish her grip* release, let go, loosen, unloose.
Opposites KEEP; RETAIN; CONTINUE.

relish *noun* **1** *eat/play with relish* enjoyment, delight, pleasure, satisfaction, gratification, appreciation, liking, zest, gusto. **2** *food with relish* flavour, taste, tang, piquancy, spiciness. **3** *serve relishes with the meat* condiment, sauce, chutney, pickle.
Opposites DISLIKE; DISTASTE.

relish *verb* **1** *the children relish a visit to the sea* enjoy, delight in, like, love, adore, appreciate, revel in, luxuriate in. **2** *they don't relish a visit from the doctor* look forward to, fancy, savour.
Opposites DETEST; LOATHE.

reluctance *noun* unwillingness, disinclination, hesitance, hesitancy, lack of enthusiasm, loathness, aversion, disrelish, distaste.

reluctant *adjective* **1** *a reluctant bride* unwilling, disinclined, hesitant, unenthusiastic, grudging. **2** *reluctant to go* unwilling, disinclined, loath, averse, slow, chary.
Opposites WILLING; EAGER; READY.

rely *verb* **1** *you can rely on him to help* depend on, count on, bank on, trust, be confident/sure of, swear by. **2** *he relies on his parents too much* depend on, lean on.

remain *verb* **1** *only a handful remained* be left, be left over, stay behind, survive, last, abide, endure, prevail. **2** *remain at home | remain in hospital* stay, wait, linger, tarry; *inf.* stay put. **3** *remain calm* stay, continue, persist in being.
Opposites GO; DEPART; LEAVE.

remainder *noun* remnant, residue, residuum, balance, surplus, excess, superfluity; remains, remnants, relics, vestiges, leavings, dregs.

remains *plural noun* **1** *the remains of a meal* remnants, leftovers, leavings, scraps; residue, debris, detritus. **2** *Roman remains* relics,

RELIGIONS			
Judaism	Shaktism	Mende	Ghost Dance
cabbalism	Tantrism	Nuer	Hopi
Conservative	Vedantism	Shilluk	Incan
Judaism	Vishnuism	Shona	Macumba
Essenes	Yogism	Voodoo	Manism
Falashas	**Sikhism**	Yoruba	Mayan
Hasidism	**Jainism**	Zande	Mithraism
Messianic Judaism	**Zoroastrianism**	**Christianity**	Navajo
Orthodox Judaism	Mazdaism	See table at CHRIS-	Norse
Pharisaism	Parseeism	TIANITY.	Orphism
Rabbinism	**Buddhism**	**Other**	Paganism
Reconstructionism	Lamaism	ancestor-worship	Phoenician
Reform Judaism	Mahayana Buddhism	animism	Rastafarianism
Zionism	Zen Buddhism	Aztec	Roman
Islam	**Taoism**	Babylonian	Sabaism
Shia Islam	**Shinto**	Bahaism	Scientology™
Sufism	**African**	cargo cult	Shamanism
Sunni Islam	Bantu	Celtic	Slavic
Hinduism	Dinka	Condomblé	Spiritualism
Brahmanism	Dogon	Confucianism	Sumerian
Hare Krishna	Fon	Druidism	Totemism
Sivaism	Gande	Eleusinianism	Umbanda
Saktism	Lovedu	Eskimo-Aleut	Vedic

reliquiae, fragments, shards. **3** *take his remains
to the cemetery* corpse, dead body, body, cadaver,
carcass.

remark *verb* **1** *she remarked that she had been ill*
mention, say, state, declare, pronounce, assert,
observe. **2** *she remarked on his appearance* comment on, pass comment on, mention.
3 *remark his resemblance to his father* note,
notice, observe, mark, perceive, discern.

remark *noun* **1** *ignore his nasty remarks* comment, statement, utterance, declaration, pronouncement, observation, reference, opinion.
2 *a performance worthy of remark* comment,
attention, mention, notice, observation, heed,
acknowledgement, recognition.

remarkable *adjective* **1** *a remarkable achievement* out of the ordinary, extraordinary,
unusual, uncommon, conspicuous, singular,
signal, rare, exceptional, outstanding, striking,
impressive, considerable, notable, noteworthy,
memorable, pre-eminent, significant, important, momentous, phenomenal, wonderful.
2 *he is remarkable for his calmness* noteworthy,
notable, conspicuous, distinctive, unusual,
uncommon, peculiar.
Opposites ORDINARY; COMMONPLACE; RUN-OF-THE-
MILL.

remedy *noun* **1** *given a remedy for asthma* cure,
treatment, medicine, medication, medicament,
therapy, antidote, specific, restorative, nostrum, panacea. **2** *find a remedy for the situation/
problem* corrective, solution, redress, panacea.

remedy *verb* **1** *unable to remedy her condition*
cure, heal, treat, counteract, control. **2** *remedy
the situation/problem* rectify, solve, set to rights,
put right, redress, fix, sort out.

remember *verb* **1** *I cannot remember his name*
recall, call to mind, recollect, think of.
2 *remember to go | remember that it's raining* keep/
bear in mind, not forget. **3** *sit remembering | sit
remembering the past* recall, recollect, reminisce;
reminisce about, look/think back on, hark
back to, summon up. **4** *remember the waiter*
tip, reward, recompense. **5** *remember me to
your parents* send greetings from, send one's
regards/compliments to.
Opposites FORGET; OVERLOOK.

remembrance *noun* **1** *their remembrance of
times past* remembering, recalling, recollecting,
recollection, reminiscing. **2** *I have a remembrance of seeing him once* memory, recollection.
3 *give her a remembrance of their meeting* keepsake, souvenir, memento, token, commemoration, memorial. **4** *send my remembrances to your
parents* greetings, regards, best wishes, compliments.

remind *verb* **1** *remind me to go* cause one to
remember, jog/refresh one's memory,
prompt. **2** *the village reminds me of home* cause
one to remember, awake one's memories of.

reminisce *verb* **1** *sit and reminisce* remember,
recollect, think back, look back, dwell on the
past. **2** *reminisce about the past* remember,
recall, recollect, call to mind, exchange memories.

reminiscences *plural noun* **1** *listen to her reminiscences about the old days* memories, recollec-

tions, anecdotes; review, retrospection. **2** *publish her reminiscences* memoirs, remembrances.

reminiscent *adjective reminiscent of an Italian
village* evocative, suggestive, redolent.

remiss *adjective* negligent, neglectful, lax,
slack, slipshod, careless, forgetful, inattentive,
heedless, thoughtless, unthinking, unmindful,
culpable, delinquent; *inf.* sloppy.
Opposites CAREFUL; DILIGENT; PAINSTAKING.

remission *noun* **1** *the remission of the penalty*
cancellation, revocation, repeal, rescinding.
2 *receive a remission for good behaviour* reduction
in sentence, reduced sentence. **3** *no remission
of our efforts* relaxation, slackening, weakening,
lessening, reduction, decrease, diminution,
dwindling, cessation, stopping, halt. **4** *the
remission of the storm/pain* easing, moderation,
abatement, lessening, decrease, dwindling,
wane, waning, ebb, ebbing, subsidence. **5** *the
remission of payment* sending, dispatch, forwarding, transmission, posting, mailing. **6** *the
remission of the matter to a committee* referral,
passing on, transfer, direction. *See* REMIT 5.
7 *the remission of the meeting/decision* postponement, deferral, shelving, delay, suspension. *See*
REMIT 6. **8** *given a remission for his offences/sins*
pardon, absolution, exoneration, forgiveness,
indulgence.

remit *verb* **1** *remit a punishment/penalty* cancel,
revoke, repeal, rescind, stop, halt. **2** *remit our
efforts* relax, slacken, weaken, lessen, reduce,
decrease, diminish, cease, stop, halt, desist
from. **3** *the storm/pain remitted* ease, moderate,
abate, lessen, decrease, dwindle, wane, ebb,
subside. **4** *remit payment* send, dispatch, forward, transmit, post, mail. **5** *remit the matter
to a committee | remit the case to another court*
refer, pass on, hand on, send on, transfer,
direct. **6** *remit the meeting/decision* postpone,
defer, put off, shelve, delay, hold off, suspend,
prorogue, reschedule. **7** *remit the offence/sin*
pardon, forgive, excuse, overlook, pass over.

remittance *noun* payment, fee, allowance.

remnant *noun* **1** *the remnant of the army*
remainder, residue, balance; remains,
vestiges. **2** *a remnant of material* piece, fragment, scrap, cut-off.

remonstrate *verb* **1** *remonstrate with them* take
issue with, argue with, dispute with, protest
to, complain to, expostulate with. **2** *remonstrate against cruelty to children* argue against,
protest against, object to, complain about,
take a stand against, oppose.

remorse *noun* regret, sorrow, sorriness, contriteness, compunction, penitence, repentance,
bad/guilty conscience, guilt, shame, self-
reproach, ruefulness; pangs of conscience.

remorseful *adjective* sorry, regretful, contrite,
apologetic, penitent, repentant, guilt-ridden,
conscience-stricken, ashamed, chastened,
rueful.

remote *adjective* **1** *the remote past | places remote
from each other* distant, far, far-off, far-away,
far-removed. **2** *in remote mountain villages* out
of the way, outlying, inaccessible, off the
beaten track, isolated, secluded, lonely, God-
forsaken. **3** *remarks remote from the subject* irrel-

evant, non-pertinent, inapposite, immaterial, unrelated, unassociated, unconnected, inappropriate, inapt. **4** *a remote possibility* outside, unlikely, improbable, implausible, negligible, insignificant, doubtful, dubious, meagre, inconsiderable, slight, slender, slim, small, poor. **5** *she is rather remote, although he is friendly* aloof, distant, detached, withdrawn, reserved, uncommunicative, unapproachable, standoffish, cool, haughty, uninvolved, indifferent, unconcerned.
Opposites NEAR; ACCESSIBLE; LIKELY.

removal *noun* **1** *the removal of dishes from the table to the sink* taking away, moving, shifting, conveying, conveyance, transfer, carrying away, transporting. **2** *his removal from office* dismissal, eviction, ejection, expulsion, ousting, dislodgement, deposition. *See* REMOVE 2. **3** *the removal of privileges* taking away, withdrawal, deprivation, abolition. **4** *removal of errors* deletion, elimination, erasure, effacing, obliteration. *See* REMOVE 5. **5** *the removal of weeds/opposition* uprooting, eradication, extirpation, destruction, extermination, annihilation. **6** *the removal of a limb/branch* cutting off, amputation, excision. *See* REMOVE 7. **7** *their removal to France* move, transfer, relocation; *Scots* flitting. **8** *the removal of a gang member by a rival* disposal, elimination, killing, murder, assassination, liquidation. *See* REMOVE 9.

remove *verb* **1** *remove the dishes from the table | remove them to the sink* take away, carry away, move, shift, convey, transfer, transport. **2** *remove him from office* get rid of, dismiss, evict, eject, expel, cast out, oust, throw out, thrust out, dislodge, relegate, unseat, depose, displace; *inf.* sack, fire. **3** *remove their coats/hats* take off, doff, pull off. **4** *remove their privileges* take away, withdraw, do away with, abolish. **5** *remove the errors* delete, eliminate, erase, rub out, cross out, strike out, blue-pencil, efface, obliterate. **6** *remove the weeds/opposition* take out, pull out, uproot, eradicate, extirpate, destroy, exterminate, annihilate. **7** *remove a limb/branch* cut off, amputate, lop off, chop off, excise. **8** *remove to France* move, move house to, transfer, relocate; *Scots* flit. **9** *hire an assassin to remove him* get rid of, dispose of, do away with, eliminate, kill, murder, assassinate, liquidate; *inf.* bump off, do in.
Opposites PLACE; INSTALL; put on (*see* PUT).

remuneration *noun* payment, pay, salary, fee, emolument, stipend, honorarium, income, profit, reward, recompense, reimbursement; wages, earnings.

remunerative *adjective* profitable, money-making, paying, lucrative, gainful, financially rewarding, rich.

renaissance, renascence *noun* rebirth, re-emergence, reappearance, resurgence, renewal, reawakening, revival, resurrection, rejuvenation, regeneration.

render *verb* **1** *render them helpless* make, cause to be/become, leave. **2** *pay for services rendered* give, contribute, make available, provide, supply, furnish. **3** *render good for evil | render insult for insult* give, exchange, trade, swap, return.

4 *render obedience* show, display, exhibit, evince, manifest. **5** *render an account* present, send in, submit, tender. **6** *the artist rendered her in a wistful mood* paint, portray, depict, represent. **7** *render the role of Macbeth* act, perform, play. **8** *the piano solo was well rendered* play, execute, perform, interpret. **9** *render the passage into Russian* translate, transcribe, construe, put, express. **10** *they rendered their land to the emperor* give, hand over, deliver, turn over, give up, yield, cede, surrender, relinquish. **11** *render the lands to the original owners* give back, return, restore.

rendezvous *noun* **1** *have a rendezvous with her lover* appointment, date, engagement, meeting, assignation. **2** *their rendezvous is the river-bank* meeting-place, venue, place of assignation.

rendezvous *verb* *we shall rendezvous at dawn* meet, come/gather together, gather, assemble.

renegade *noun* defector, deserter, turncoat, betrayer, traitor, dissenter, apostate, renouncer, recanter, revolutionary, rebel, mutineer.

renege *verb* go back on one's word, break one's promise, default, back out, pull out; *inf.* cop out, welsh.

renounce *verb* **1** *renounce his claim* give up, relinquish, resign, abdicate, abnegate, surrender, sign away, waive, forego. **2** *renounce his son* repudiate, disown, cast off, discard, reject, disinherit, wash one's hands of, spurn, shun. **3** *renounce strong drink* give up, abstain from, desist from, swear off, eschew. **4** *renounce one's friendship/religion* give up, abandon, forsake, renege on, turn one's back on, abjure.
Opposites CLAIM; MAINTAIN; EMBRACE.

renovate *verb* modernize, recondition, refurbish, rehabilitate, overhaul, restore, revamp, remodel, repair, redecorate, refit; *inf.* do up, fix up.

renown *noun* fame, repute, acclaim, celebrity, distinction, illustriousness, eminence, pre-eminence, prominence, mark, note, consequence, prestige.

renowned *adjective* famous, famed, well-known, of repute, acclaimed, celebrated, distinguished, illustrious, eminent, pre-eminent, prominent, noted, notable, of note, of consequence, prestigious.
Opposites UNKNOWN; OBSCURE; UNSUNG.

rent[1] *noun* *what is the rent of the house/boat?* rental, tenant's payment, hire fee.

rent[2] *verb* **1** *rent a house/boat from the owner* lease, hire, charter. **2** *they rent out houses/boats* let, lease, hire, hire/let out, farm out.

rent[3] *noun* *a rent in the material* tear, rip, split, gash, slash, hole, perforation, break, crack, fracture, crevice, fissure, cleft.

renunciation *noun* **1** *the renunciation of his claim* relinquishment, resignation, abdication, abnegation, surrender, waiving. **2** *the renunciation of his son* repudiation, disowning, discarding, rejecting, disinheriting, spurning. *See* RENOUNCE 2. **3** *the renunciation of strong drink* giving up, abstention. *See* RENOUNCE 3. **4** *the* renunciation of their friendship/religion abandonment, forsaking, reneging, abjuration.

repair¹ *verb* **1** *repair the machine* mend, fix, put right, restore, restore to working order, service, adjust, regulate, overhaul. **2** *repair the torn clothes* mend, darn, sew, patch. **3** *repair the rift in their friendship* mend, fix, patch up, heal, cure. **4** *repair the omission* make reparation for, put right, make good, rectify, correct, redress, compensate for.
Opposites BREAK; TEAR; HARM.

repair² *noun* **1** *the repair of the car* mending, fixing, restoration, servicing, overhaul. *See* REPAIR ¹ *verb* 1. **2** *you won't notice the repair* mend, darn, patch. **3** *the furniture/car is in good repair* condition, state, form, fettle, kilter; *inf.* shape, nick.

repair³ *verb repair to the library* go to, withdraw to, head for, betake oneself to, take off for, leave for, depart for.

reparation *noun demand reparation for wrongs* redress, atonement, restitution, satisfaction, compensation, recompense, indemnity; amends, damages.

repartee *noun* witty conversation, badinage, banter, raillery, wordplay, lively exchange.

repast *noun* meal, collation, refection, snack, feast; food, nourishment; *inf.* spread, feed.

repay *verb* **1** *repay him the money owed* pay back, refund, reimburse, recompense, remunerate, square accounts with, settle up with, indemnify. **2** *repay the money owed* pay back, give back, refund. **3** *repay him for the crime against her family* get back at, hit back, retaliate against, get even with, settle the score with; *inf.* get one's own back on, give just deserts, give comeuppance. **4** *repay the wrong* avenge, revenge, make reprisal for.

repeal *verb repeal the act/bill* revoke, rescind, abrogate, annul, nullify, declare null and void, make void, void, invalidate, quash, set aside, cancel, countermand, retract, withdraw, recall, abjure, overrule, override, reverse.
Opposites INTRODUCE; RATIFY.

repeal *noun the repeal of the act/bill* revocation, rescinding, rescission, abrogation, annulment, disannulment, nullification, voiding, invalidation, quashing, setting aside, cancellation, countermanding, retraction, withdrawal, recall, abjuration, overruling, overriding, reversal.

repeat *verb* **1** *repeat the statement/story* say again, restate, retell, iterate, recite, rehearse, recapitulate; *inf.* recap. **2** *she repeated his words* say again, restate, echo, parrot, quote, duplicate, copy, reproduce. **3** *repeat the task* do again, redo, duplicate. **4** *repeat the film/tape* rerun, replay. **repeat itself** *history repeated itself* occur again, reoccur, happen again, reappear.

repeat *noun* **1** *a repeat of his statement/story* repetition, restatement, retelling, iteration, recapitulation; *inf.* recap. **2** *a repeat of his words/actions* repetition, restatement, echoing, parroting, duplication, copy, reproduction. **3** *watch a repeat of the comedy* rerun, replay, rebroadcast.

repeated *adjective* recurrent, frequent, continual, incessant, constant, endless.

repeatedly *adverb* again and again, over and over, time and time again, time after time, frequently, often, many times.

repel *verb* **1** *repel attackers/invaders* repulse, drive back, push back, thrust back, force back, beat back, hold off, ward off, fend off, stave off, parry, keep at bay, keep at arm's length, foil, check, frustrate, put to flight. **2** *repel their advances* repulse, reject, decline, turn down, rebuff. **3** *the sight of blood repels her* revolt, disgust, sicken, nauseate, make one sick, turn one's stomach, be repugnant to, make one's flesh creep, put one off, offend, shock; *inf.* turn one off, give one the creeps/heebie-jeebies.
Opposites WELCOME; ATTRACT; DELIGHT.

repellent *adjective* repulsive, revolting, disgusting, sickening, nauseating, distasteful, repugnant, abhorrent, offensive, obnoxious, loathsome, off-putting, hateful, vile, nasty, shocking, despicable, reprehensible, contemptible, odious, abominable, horrible, horrid, foul, heinous, obscene.

repent *verb* regret, feel remorse for, rue; be penitent, be sorry, see the error of one's ways, be regretful, be contrite, feel remorse/remorseful, be conscience-stricken, reproach oneself, be ashamed, be guilt-ridden; *inf.* see the light.

repentance *noun* penitence, sorrow, sorriness, regret, contrition, contriteness, remorse, conscience, self-reproach, ruefulness, shame, guilt.

repentant *adjective* penitent, sorrowful, apologetic, regretful, contrite, remorseful, conscience-stricken, rueful, ashamed, guilt-ridden.

repercussion *noun* **1** *the repercussions of his action* effect, result, consequence, reverberation, backlash. **2** *he heard/felt the repercussion* echo, reverberation, reflection, recoil, rebound.

repetition *noun* **1** *a repetition of the statement/story* restatement, retelling, iteration, recital, rehearsal, recapitulation; *inf.* recap. **2** *her repetition of his words* repeating, restatement, echoing, parroting, quoting, copying. **3** *a repetition of his previous actions* repeat, redoing, duplication. **4** *a lot of repetition in the essay* repetitiousness, redundancy, tautology.

repetitive *adjective repetitive tasks/work* recurrent, unchanging, unvaried, undiversified, monotonous, tedious, boring, mechanical, automatic; *inf.* samey.

replace *verb* **1** *replace the book on the shelf* put back, return, restore. **2** *he will replace the retired teacher* take the place of, succeed, supersede, follow after, come after, supplant, substitute for, stand in for, act for, fill in for, cover for, act as locum for, understudy. **3** *replace the broken vase* give in place of, give as a replacement for, give in return/exchange for.

replacement *noun find a replacement for the retired teacher* successor, substitute, stand-in, fill-in, locum, understudy, proxy, surrogate.

replenish *verb* **1** *replenish one's glass/plate* refill, top up, fill up, recharge, reload. **2** *replenish* *stocks of food* stock up, fill up, make up, replace, renew.

replete *adjective* **1** *guests feeling replete* full, full up, full to bursting, satiated, sated, glutted, gorged, stuffed, well-fed. **2** *replete shelves* full, well-stocked, well-provided, brimful, brimming, chock-full, jam-packed, crammed, teeming.
Opposites HUNGRY; EMPTY.

replica *noun* copy, carbon copy, duplicate, facsimile, model, reproduction, imitation.

reply *verb* **1** *reply to his question/letter* answer, make answer, respond to, acknowledge, write back. **2** *"Not likely," she replied* answer, respond, rejoin, retort, return, riposte, come back, counter.
Opposites ASK.

reply *noun* answer, response, acknowledgement, rejoinder, retort, return, riposte, come back.

report *noun* **1** *a report of the accident* account, statement, record, exposition, delineation. **2** *newspaper/television reports* article, piece, account, story, write-up, communication, communiqué, dispatch, bulletin. **3** *a company's financial report* formal statement, record, register, chronicle. **4** *according to report he is a miser* rumour, hearsay, talk, gossip, tittle-tattle; *inf.* the grapevine. **5** *a person of good report* reputation, repute, regard, character, name. **6** *the report of a gun/explosion* bang, boom, crack, crash, rumble, reverberation, noise, sound, echo.

report *verb* **1** *report the latest findings* bring word about, announce, pass on, communicate, relay, relate, tell, recount, give an account of, set forth, document, narrate, describe, delineate, detail, divulge, disclose, circulate. **2** *journalists reporting on events in Russia* write, write an account of, broadcast. **3** *report the child for cheating* tell on, inform on, accuse, make a charge/complaint against; *inf.* grass on, squeal on, rat on. **4** *they will report at noon* present oneself, be present, appear, arrive, come, turn up, clock on/in; *inf.* show up. **5** *report the proceedings of the conference* record, document, minute, write up, chronicle, write down, take down.

reporter *noun* journalist, newsman, newswoman, pressman, correspondent, writer, broadcaster, announcer, presenter, news commentator; *inf.* newshound, hack.

repose *noun* **1** *seek repose after work* rest, relaxation, leisure, ease, inactivity, respite, time off, breathing-space, sleep, slumber. **2** *a place of repose in the mountains* quiet, quietness, quietude, calm, calmness, tranquillity, peace, peacefulness, stillness, silence, hush. **3** *her face looked sad in repose* relaxation, inactivity, stillness, idleness.
Opposites WORK; ACTIVITY.

repose *verb* **1** *workers reposing after their labours* rest, relax, take one's ease, take a break, sleep, slumber; *inf.* take it easy. **2** *reposing on couches* lie, lie down, recline, stretch out, sprawl.

repository *noun* store, storehouse, storeroom, reservoir, bank, safe, cache, receptacle, container.

reprehensible *adjective* blameworthy, blamable, reproachable, censurable, condemnable, reprovable, culpable, erring, errant, wrong, bad, shameful, disgraceful, discreditable, dishonourable, ignoble, objectionable, odious, opprobrious, unpardonable, indefensible, unjustifiable, inexcusable.

represent *verb* **1** *X represents the larger number | the tent represents home for them* stand for, correspond to, be the counterpart of, equal, be equivalent to, symbolize, mean, betoken. **2** *John Bull represents the spirit of Britain* stand for, symbolize, personify, epitomize, typify. **3** *the old man represents their idea of a Frenchman* embody, incorporate, typify, exemplify, be a sample/specimen of. **4** *the saint is usually represented as a young child* depict, portray, delineate, illustrate, picture, denote, paint, draw, sketch, exhibit, show, display, evoke. **5** *he represents Hamlet in the play* act, enact, portray, appear as, perform as. **6** *they represented Twelfth Night in Stratford* present, produce, put on, show, stage. **7** *he represented the children at the hearing* act for, appear for, speak for, be spokesperson for, be the representative of. **8** *he represents the constituency/ward* be the councillor/MP for, have the vote of. **9** *he represented himself as a qualified doctor* describe as, pass off as, pose as, pretend to be. **10** *represent their grievances to the committee* present, put/bring forward, set forth, state.

representation *noun* **1** *the representation of the saint as a young child* depiction, portrayal, portrait, delineation, illustration, picture, painting, drawing, sketch, image, model. **2** *their representation of Twelfth Night* presentation, production, performance, show, play, spectacle. **3** *have the best representation at the court/conference* spokesman, spokeswoman, spokesperson, representative, agent, deputy, ambassador, envoy, delegate; delegation, deputation. **4** *make representations to the court* statement, account, report, declaration, allegation, argument, protestation, remonstrance, expostulation.

representative *adjective* **1** *a representative specimen | a specimen representative of its genus* typical, archetypal, exemplary, characteristic, indicative, illustrative. **2** *John Bull is representative of Britain* emblematic, symbolic, evocative. **3** *a representative body* elected, elective, chosen, delegated, ambassadorial, authorized, accredited, official.
Opposites atypical; unrepresentative; EXTRAORDINARY.

representative *noun* **1** *a typical representative of its class* example, exemplification, exemplar, specimen, type, archetype, illustration, epitome, embodiment. **2** *he is the society's representative* spokesman, spokeswoman, spokesperson, agent, deputy, proxy. **3** *he is a sales representative* commercial traveller, travelling salesman, traveller, agent; *inf.* rep. **4** *our country's representative at the conference* delegate, commissioner, ambassador, envoy. **5** *the* town's representative in Parliament | our representative on the council Member of Parliament, MP, Member, deputy, councillor.

repress verb **1** *tyrants repressing the people* subjugate, conquer, vanquish, overpower, overcome, crush, master, dominate, domineer, bully, intimidate, oppress, tyrannize. **2** *repress a rebellion* put down, quell, quash, squash, subdue, suppress, extinguish, stamp out, stop, put an end to. **3** *repress a laugh | repress his desire* hold/keep back, hold in, bite back, restrain, suppress, keep in check, check, inhibit, bottle up, silence, muffle, stifle, smother.
Opposites ENCOURAGE; SUPPORT; RELEASE; EXPRESS.

repressed adjective **1** *a repressed people* subjugated, oppressed, tyrannized. See REPRESS 1. **2** *a repressed laugh* restrained, suppressed, muffled, smothered. **3** *a repressed child* inhibited, withdrawn, restrained.

repression noun **1** *the repression of the people* subjugation, domination, oppression, tyrannization. See REPRESS 1. **2** *the repression of the rebellion* quelling, quashing, suppression. See REPRESS 2. **3** *a regime of repression* tyranny, despotism, oppression, dictatorship, authoritarianism, domination, coercion, suppression, subjugation. **4** *the repression of a laugh* holding back, biting back, restraint, suppression, smothering. See REPRESS 3.

repressive adjective *a repressive regime* repressing, tyrannical, despotic, dictatorial, authoritarian, dominating, oppressive, coercive, suppressive, harsh, severe, strict, cruel.

reprieve verb **1** *reprieve the condemned man* postpone/delay punishment of, remit/cancel punishment of, grant a stay of execution to, let off, pardon; *inf.* let off the hook. **2** *the building has been reprieved for a while* give a respite to, save, rescue.
Opposites CHARGE; PUNISH.

reprieve noun *the condemned man has had a reprieve* postponement of punishment, remission/cancellation of punishment, stay of execution, pardon; *inf.* let-off.

reprimand noun *receive a reprimand from the teacher* rebuke, scolding, chiding, reproach, reproof, reproval, lecture, admonition, berating, upbraiding, castigation, tongue-lashing; *inf.* row, talking-to, telling-off, ticking-off, dressing-down, wigging, bawling-out.

reprimand verb *reprimand the pupils* rebuke, scold, chide, reproach, reprove, lecture, admonish, berate, upbraid, castigate, take to task, haul over the coals, blame, censure, check; *inf.* give a row to, give a talking-to, tell off, tick off, give a dressing-down/wigging to, bawl out.

reprisal noun retaliation, revenge, vengeance, retribution, redress, requital, recrimination, an eye for an eye, tit for tat.

reproach verb *reproach the government/pupils for their actions* criticize, find fault with, censure, blame, admonish, condemn, reprehend, disparage, abuse, reprimand, scold, chide, reprove, berate, upbraid, castigate, take to task, haul over the coals; *inf.* give a dressing-down to.

reproach noun **1** *words of reproach* criticism, fault-finding, censuring, admonition, condemnation, abuse, reprimand, scolding, reproof, reproval, upbraiding. See REPROACH verb. **2** *the ugly building is a reproach to the town* discredit, disgrace, shame, source of shame, stigma, blemish, stain, slur. **3** *her behaviour brought reproach to the family* discredit, disgrace, shame, dishonour, disrepute, ignominy, scorn, contempt, opprobrium, odium, obloquy.

reproachful adjective disapproving, disappointed, critical, censorious, admonitory, condemnatory, disparaging, reproving, castigatory.

reproduce verb **1** *the copier can reproduce colour photographs* copy, make a copy of, duplicate, replicate, photocopy, xerox, mimeograph, print, transcribe, clone. **2** *reproduce the effect* repeat, recreate, redo, remake, imitate, follow, emulate, echo, mirror, parallel, match, mimic, ape. **3** *the animals seen unable to reproduce* breed, procreate, bear young, produce offspring, give birth, multiply, propagate, proliferate, spawn.

reproduction noun **1** *the reproduction of colour photographs* copying, duplicating, photocopying, xeroxing, printing. See REPRODUCE 1. **2** *a reproduction of the painting* copy, duplicate, replica, facsimile, imitation, print. **3** *a reproduction of the photograph* copy, duplicate, facsimile, fax, photocopy, mimeograph, print; Xerox™. **4** *animal reproduction* breeding, procreation, producing young, multiplying, propagation, proliferation.

reproof noun **1** *without a word of reproof* reproval, disapproval, disapprobation, reproach, admonition, castigation, criticism, censure, blame, condemnation. **2** *ignore their reproofs* rebuke, scolding, chiding, reproach, lecture, admonition, berating, upbraiding, castigation, criticism, fault-finding, censure.
Opposites APPROVAL; PRAISE.

reprove verb *reprove the pupils* rebuke, scold, chide, reproach, reprove, lecture, admonish, berate, upbraid, castigate, take to task, haul over the coals, criticize, check, censure, blame, condemn; *inf.* give a row to, give a talking-to, tell off, tick off, give a dressing-down to, bawl out.

reptile noun. See table.

repudiate verb **1** *repudiate one's son/faith* disown, cast off, cut off, abandon, forsake, desert, discard, reject, renounce, disavow, abjure, turn one's back on, have nothing to do with, wash one's hands of. **2** *repudiate a charge/claim* deny, contradict, gainsay, disclaim, disavow. **3** *repudiate a treaty* reject, rescind, revoke, cancel, set aside, overrule, override, disregard, ignore, flout, spurn, dishonour, disobey.
Opposites EMBRACE; CONFIRM; ACCEPT.

repugnance noun abhorrence, aversion, revulsion, repulsion, disgust, nausea, distaste, antipathy, dislike, loathing, hatred, reluctance, contempt, odium.

repugnant adjective abhorrent, revolting, repulsive, repellent, disgusting, sickening, nauseating, disagreeable, distasteful, offensive,

objectionable, obnoxious, loathsome, off-putting, hateful, despicable, reprehensible, contemptible, abominable, horrible, horrid, foul, nasty, vile, ugly, odious, heinous.
Opposites ATTRACTIVE; AGREEABLE; PLEASANT.

repulsive adjective abhorrent, revolting, repellent, disgusting, sickening, nauseating, disagreeable, distasteful, offensive, objectionable, obnoxious, loathsome, off-putting, hateful, despicable, reprehensible, contemptible, abominable, horrible, foul, nasty, vile, ugly, odious, heinous.
Opposites ATTRACTIVE; AGREEABLE; PLEASANT.

reputable adjective of repute, of good repute, respectable, respected, well-thought-of, esteemed, estimable, worthy, creditable, reliable, dependable, conscientious, trustworthy, honest, honourable, above-board, legitimate, upright, virtuous, good, excellent.
Opposites DISREPUTABLE; UNTRUSTWORTHY.

reputation noun **1** have an honest/dishonest reputation name, estimation, character, repute, standing, position, status, station, rank. **2** she has lost her reputation good name, good character, good standing, respect, respectability, repute, esteem, fame, celebrity, renown. **3** the shop has lost its reputation as a good restaurant name, standing, position, status, stature.

repute noun **1** a house of ill repute reputation, name, character. See REPUTATION 1. **2** they are firms of repute good reputation, good name, high standing, stature, esteem, fame, renown, celebrity, distinction. See REPUTATION 2.

repute verb he is reputed to be a good player | reputed to be the father think, believe, consider, hold, suppose, reckon, judge, assume, presume.

reputedly adverb he is reputedly the father supposedly, allegedly, apparently, seemingly.

request noun **1** come at his request asking, entreaty, solicitation, petitioning, application, imploration, begging, pleading, behest, supplication, demand, summons, requisition. **2** make several requests entreaty, appeal, petition, plea, behest, demand, call, suit.

request verb request a favour ask for, solicit, seek, apply for, put in for, call for, entreat, beseech, beg for, plead for, pray for, petition, implore, sue for, supplicate for, requisition, demand, desire.

require verb **1** we require peace and quiet need, have need of, stand in need of, lack, be short of, be deficient in, want, wish, desire, crave, miss. **2** absolute obedience is required demand, order, command, call for, insist on, ask for, request. **3** they required him to go order, instruct, command, oblige, enjoin, bid, compel. **4** the job requires patience call for, demand, necessitate, involve, take.

required adjective required reading compulsory, obligatory, mandatory, prescribed, recommended, set, essential, necessary, vital.

requirement noun **1** list your travel requirements need, want, lack, must, necessity, necessary/essential item, demand. **2** what are the requirements for the job? prerequisite, requisite,

REPTILES

adder	crocodile	iguana	Russell's viper
agama	death adder	Indian python	sand lizard
alligator	diamondback	king cobra	scalyfoot
alligator lizard	rattlesnake	king snake	sea snake
amphisbaena	diamondback	Komodo dragon	sidewinder
anaconda	terrapin	krait	skink
anole	egg-eating snake	leatherback	slider
asp	fence lizard	legless lizard	slow-worm
bandy-bandy	fer-de-lance	legless skink	smooth snake
basilisk	flying lizard	lizard	snake
bearded dragon	flying snake	loggerhead turtle	snapping turtle
black snake	frilled lizard	mamba	soft-shelled turtle
blind snake	Gaboon viper	mangrove snake	spitting cobra
blindworm	Galapagos giant	matamata	taipan
bloodsucker	tortoise	milk snake	terrapin
boa constrictor	garter snake	moccasin	tiger snake
boomslang	gecko	moloch	tokay
box turtle	gharial	monitor lizard	tortoise
brown snake	giant tortoise	mugger	tree snake
bull snake	Gila monster	Nile crocodile	tuatara
bushmaster	glass lizard	pit viper	turtle
carpet python	glass snake	pond turtle	vine snake
cayman	goanna	puff-adder	viper
chameleon	grass snake	python	viviparous lizard
chuckwalla	green turtle	racer	wall lizard
cobra	harlequin snake	rat snake	wart snake
cooter	hawksbill turtle	rattlesnake	water moccasin
copperhead	hognose snake	reticulated python	water snake
coral snake	horned toad	rinkhals	whip snake
cottonmouth	horned viper	rock python	worm lizard

precondition, specification, qualification, *sine qua non*, stipulation.

requisite *adjective the requisite amount* required, prerequisite, needed, necessary, essential, indispensable, vital, called-for, demanded, obligatory, mandatory.

requisite *noun* **1** *list your holiday requisites* requirement, need, want. *See* REQUIREMENT 1. **2** *what are the requisites for the job?* requirement, prerequisite, precondition, specification, qualification. *See* REQUIREMENT 2.

requisition *noun* **1** *put in a requisition for supplies* application, order, claim, request, call, demand, summons. **2** *the requisition of their farm building* commandeering, appropriation, possession, occupation, seizure, confiscation.

requisition *verb* **1** *requisition for more books* apply for, order, put in a claim for, request, call for, demand. **2** *soldiers requisitioned the farm buildings* commandeer, appropriate, take over, take possession of, occupy, seize, confiscate.

rescind *verb* repeal, revoke, reverse, abrogate, retract, countermand, overturn, annul, disannul, nullify, declare null and void, void, quash, invalidate, cancel, set aside.

rescue *verb* save, save/deliver from danger, save the life of, come to the aid of, free, set free/loose, release, liberate, emancipate, get out, extricate, redeem, salvage, relieve. *Opposites* ENDANGER; JEOPARDIZE; IMPRISON.

rescue *noun* rescuing, saving, deliverance, delivery, freeing, release, liberation, emancipation, extrication, redemption, salvage, relief. *See* RESCUE *verb.*

research *noun carry out medical research* investigation, experimentation, fact-finding, testing, exploration, analysis, examination, scrutiny; experiment, assessment, study, review, inquiry, probe, inspection; tests.

research *verb research the new drug* do tests on, investigate, inquire into, look into, probe, explore, analyse, study, examine, scrutinize, review, inspect, experiment with, assess.

resemblance *noun* **1** *the resemblance between them* likeness, alikeness, similarity, similitude, semblance, identicalness, sameness, uniformity, correspondence, comparability, comparison, parallelism, parity, analogy, affinity, closeness, nearness, agreement, congruity, concurrence, conformity. **2** *this is a resemblance of their father* likeness, representation, image; photograph, painting.

resemble *verb he resembles his brother | his work resembles hers* be like, look like, bear a resemblance to, be similar to, put one in mind of, remind one of, take after, echo, mirror, parrot, duplicate, parallel; *inf.* favour.

resent *verb* feel aggrieved at, take offence/umbrage at, take exception to, take amiss, be annoyed/angry at, begrudge, feel bitter about, dislike.

resentful *adjective* aggrieved, offended, indignant, irritated, displeased, annoyed, angry, irate, incensed, piqued, in high dudgeon,

grudging, bitter, embittered, wounded; *inf.* huffed, huffy, in a huff, miffed, peeved.

resentment *noun* offence, indignation, irritation, displeasure, annoyance, anger, ire, pique, grudgingness, bitterness, animosity, hostility; hard feelings.

reservation *noun* **1** *the reservation of some supplies* putting aside, conservation, saving, retention, storing. *See* RESERVE *verb* 1. **2** *the reservation of a room* booking, engaging, prearranging. *See* RESERVE *verb* 2. **3** *make a reservation* advance booking, booking, engagement, prearrangement; charter/hire arrangements. **4** *have reservations concerning the plan | go ahead with some reservation* qualification, proviso, provision, condition, stipulation, limitation, qualm, scruple; hesitancy, doubt, demur. **5** *an American Indian reservation* reserve, preserve, enclave, sanctuary, tract, area, territory.

reserve *verb* **1** *reserve some food for later* put/set/lay aside, put away, keep back, keep, withhold, conserve, save, retain, store, hoard, stockpile; *inf.* hang on to. **2** *reserve a room* book, engage, arrange for, prearrange for, bespeak, charter, hire. **3** *reserve judgement* put off, postpone, defer, delay, withhold. **4** *reserve the right to refuse* keep, retain, secure; *inf.* hang on to.

reserve *noun* **1** *we have reserves of steel* store, stock, supply, reservoir, pool, cache, fund, stockpile, accumulation, backlog, hoard. **2** *agree with some reserve* reservation, qualification, proviso, condition, limitation, stipulation, qualm, scruple. *See* RESERVATION 4. **3** *her reserve puts people off* self-restraint, restraint, self-control, constraint, aloofness, detachment, distance, remoteness, formality, coolness, coldness, frigidity, reticence, unapproachability, uncommunicativeness, unresponsiveness, shyness, diffidence, secretiveness, taciturnity, silence. **4** *a nature reserve* preserve, reservation, sanctuary, park, tract, territory, area. **in reserve** available, at hand, to hand, obtainable, accessible, at one's disposal, on tap.

reserve *adjective a reserve player* in reserve, spare, extra, auxiliary, substitute, alternate.

reserved *adjective* **1** *reserved supplies* conserved, stored, stockpiled. *See* RESERVE *noun* 1. **2** *the table is reserved | reserved rooms* booked, engaged, prearranged, spoken for, chartered, hired. **3** *she is reserved but he is outgoing* self-restrained, aloof, detached, remote, formal, unemotional, undemonstrative, cool, cold, frigid, reticent, unapproachable, uncommunicative, unsociable, unfriendly, unresponsive, unforthcoming, shy, retiring, diffident, secret, secretive, taciturn, silent. *Opposites* OUTGOING; COMMUNICATIVE; SOCIABLE.

reservoir *noun* **1** *picnic by the reservoir* water source/supply; lake, loch, pool, pond. **2** *pour liquid into the reservoir* container, receptacle, holder, tank, cask, bowl, basin. **3** *reservoir of supplies/knowledge* reserve, store, stock, supply, pool, cache, fund, stockpile. *See* RESERVE *noun* 1.

reside *verb* **1** *he resides in London* live in, dwell in, stay in, sojourn in, inhabit, occupy, be settled in, lodge in; *inf.* hang out in. **2** *the* strength residing in his personality be inherent in, be intrinsic to, be contained/present in, lie in, dwell in, abide in, exist in. **3** the authority residing in him vested in, bestowed on, conferred on.

residence noun **1** his residence is in London house, home, place, dwelling, domicile, habitation; quarters, lodgings. **2** take up residence tomorrow | a residence of five years occupation, occupancy, habitation, inhabitation, tenancy, stay, sojourn.

resident noun all residents pay taxes inhabitant, occupant, occupier, householder, dweller, resider, sojourner, tenant, local, denizen.

resident adjective **1** a resident housekeeper live-in, living-in. **2** the resident population inhabiting, dwelling, neighbourhood, local.

residue noun residuum, remainder, remnant, rest, surplus, extra, excess, balance; remains, leftovers, dregs, lees.

resign verb **1** he resigned yesterday give notice, hand in one's notice, leave, quit. **2** resigned from his post give up, leave, quit, vacate, retire from. **3** resign his right to the title renounce, relinquish, give up, abdicate, surrender, cede. **4** resign oneself to losing reconcile oneself. See RESIGNED 1.

resignation noun **1** his resignation from his post leaving, quitting, vacating, retirement. **2** the resignation of his claim renunciation, relinquishment, abdication. See RESIGN 3. **3** hand over his resignation letter of resignation, notice, notice to quit. **4** accept the decision with resignation resignedness, acceptance, compliance, non-resistance, submission, passivity, patience, forbearance, sufferance, toleration, endurance.

resigned adjective **1** resigned to the fact that he would fail reconciled, acquiescent, submitting, yielding, bowing, acceding. **2** give a resigned shrug | take a resigned attitude compliant, unresisting, non-resistant, unprotesting, passive, submissive, subdued, docile, patient, long-suffering, forbearing, tolerant, enduring, stoical.

resilient adjective **1** a resilient material elastic, springy, rubbery, whippy, flexible, pliant, supple, pliable, plastic. **2** children are resilient after upsets quick to recover, quick to bounce back, difficult to keep down, irrepressible, tough, strong, hardy. **Opposites** INFLEXIBLE; SENSITIVE; DELICATE.

resist verb **1** material resisting the action of the rain withstand, be proof against, repel. **2** resist the march of progress stop, halt, prevent, check, stem, curb, obstruct, hinder, impede, block, thwart, frustrate, inhibit, restrain. **3** resist smoking abstain from, refrain from, keep from, forbear from, desist from, forgo, avoid. **4** resist the invading army fight, battle against, stand up to, withstand, stand one's ground against, hold out against, defy, oppose, confront, struggle against, contend with.

resistance noun **1** their resistance to progress curb, obstruction, hindrance, impediment, block. See RESIST 2. **2** their resistance against the invaders fight, battle, opposition, stand, defiance, confrontation, struggle, contention.

resistant adjective material resistant to water | diseases resistant to drugs proof against, impervious to, unaffected by, unsusceptible to, immune to.

resolute adjective determined, resolved, decided, firm, fixed, set, intent, steadfast, constant, earnest, staunch, bold, courageous, serious, purposeful, deliberate, inflexible, unyielding, unwavering, unfaltering, unhesitating, unswerving, unflinching, obstinate, obdurate, strong-willed, dogged, persevering, persistent, tenacious, relentless, unshakable, dedicated. **Opposites** IRRESOLUTE; DOUBTFUL.

resolution noun **1** admire the resolution of the competitors resolve, determination, firmness, intentness, steadfastness, constancy, staunchness, boldness, courage, seriousness, purpose, purposefulness, obstinacy, obdurateness, obduracy, will-power, doggedness, perseverance, persistence, tenacity, staying power, dedication. See RESOLUTE. **2** it is our resolution to proceed resolve, decision, aim, intent, intention, purpose, object, plan, design, aspiration. **3** the committee/court passed a resolution motion, declaration, decree, verdict, judgement. **4** the resolution of the problem/question will take time resolving, solving, solution, answer, sorting out, working out, unravelling, disentanglement, cracking.

resolve verb **1** he resolved to leave decide, make up one's mind, determine, settle on, undertake. **2** resolve the problem solve, answer, sort out, work out, clear up, fathom, unravel, disentangle, crack. **3** resolve their doubts dispel, remove, banish, clear up. **4** resolve the compound break down, break up, separate, divide, disintegrate, reduce, dissolve, analyse, anatomize, dissect.

resolve noun **1** their resolve is to win resolution, decision, aim, intent, intention, purpose. See RESOLUTION 2. **2** set out with resolve resolution, determination, firmness of purpose, staunchness, boldness, courage, purposefulness, obstinacy, perseverance, dedication. See RESOLUTION 1.

resort verb **1** resort to force fall back on, turn to, have recourse to, look to, make use of, use, utilize, avail oneself of, bring into play/service, exercise. **2** tourists resorting to the beaches head for, go to, repair to, visit, frequent, haunt.

resort noun **1** a beautiful resort | holiday/health resort holiday/tourist centre, haunt, centre, spot, retreat. **2** your only resort is to ask the police recourse, source of help, expedient, measure, alternative, choice, possibility, hope. **3** without resort to violence recourse, turning to, utilizing. See RESORT verb 1.

resound verb **1** caves resounding with the noise of waves reverberate, resonate, echo, ring. **2** her fame/discovery resounded throughout Europe be talked about, be made known, spread, circulate, be proclaimed, be famed, be celebrated, be glorified.

resounding adjective **1** resounding tones reverberating, resonating, resonant, echoing, ringing, sonorous, vibrant. **2** the fête was a resounding success very great, emphatic, striking, impressive, outstanding, notable, note-worthy.

resource *noun* **1** *use any resource to find help* expedient, resort, course, way, device; means. **2** *draw on one's coal resources* reserve, reservoir, store, stock, supply, pool, fund, stockpile, accumulation, hoard. **3** *person of resource* resourcefulness, initiative, ingenuity, inventiveness, quick-wittedness, cleverness, native wit, talent, ability, capability. **4** *rely on their country's resources* assets, reserves, materials; wealth.

resourceful *adjective* ingenious, inventive, creative, imaginative, quick-witted, clever, bright, sharp, talented, gifted, able, capable.
Opposites UNIMAGINATIVE.

respect *noun* **1** *their respect for their teacher* esteem, high regard, regard, high opinion, admiration, approbation, approval, appreciation, veneration, reverence, deference, honour, praise, homage. **2** *treat the old lady with respect* deference, consideration, thoughtfulness, attentiveness, politeness, courtesy, civility. **3** *without any respect for/to rhythm* heed, regard, consideration, attention, notice. **4** *correct in all respects* aspect, facet, feature, way, sense, characteristic, particular, point, detail, matter. **5** *with respect to the matter in hand* reference, relevance, regard, relation, connection, bearing.

respect *verb* **1** *they respect their teacher* esteem, have a high opinion of, think highly of, admire, approve of, appreciate, venerate, revere, honour, praise. **2** *they respect his judgement* think highly of, have a high opinion of, value, set store by. **3** *respect other people's privacy | respect the environment* show consideration/regard for, take into consideration, take cognizance of, observe, pay heed/attention to. **4** *respect her wishes | respect the treaty* heed, observe, comply with, follow, abide by, adhere to, obey.

respectable *adjective* **1** *a respectable woman/background* reputable, of good repute, upright, honest, honourable, trustworthy, above-board, worthy, decent, good, virtuous, admirable, well-bred, proper, decorous. **2** *a respectable effort* reasonable, fair, passable, tolerable, adequate, satisfactory; *inf.* not bad. **3** *earn a respectable salary* reasonable, fairly good, fair, considerable, ample, sizable, substantial; *inf.* not to be sneezed at.
Opposites DISHONOURABLE; UNWORTHY; SMALL; PALTRY.

respective *adjective* individual, separate, personal, own, particular, specific, various.

respects *plural noun* *send/pay one's respects* greetings, regards, best wishes, compliments, remembrances.

respite *noun* **1** *a respite from work* rest, break, breathing spell, interval, intermission, recess, lull, pause, hiatus, halt; relief, relaxation; *inf.* breather, let-up. **2** *a respite from the penalty* remission, reprieve, stay, stay of execution, suspension, postponement, adjournment, deferment, delay, moratorium.

respond *verb* **1** *respond to his question/letter* answer, reply to, say in response to, acknowledge. **2** *"No," she responded* say in response,

answer, reply, rejoin, retort, return, riposte, come back, counter. **3** *they responded to his action by hitting him* react to, act in response to.
Opposites ASK.

response *noun* **1** *the children gave no response to the question* answer, reply, acknowledgement, rejoinder, retort, return, riposte, comeback. **2** *receive a good response to their questionnaire* reply, reaction, feedback; *inf.* comeback.

responsibility *noun* **1** *it is his responsibility to get us there* charge, duty, onus, task, role, liability, accountability, answerability. **2** *the confusion was his responsibility* blame, fault, guilt, culpability. **3** *people of responsibility* maturity, adultness, reason, sanity, sense, common sense, soundness, stability, reliability, dependability, trustworthiness, competence, conscientiousness. *See* RESPONSIBLE 4. **4** *a post of responsibility* authority, control, power.

responsible *adjective* **1** *he is responsible for the production department* in charge/control of, accountable for, liable for; *inf.* at the helm of. **2** *who is responsible for the confusion?* accountable, answerable, to blame, blameworthy, at fault, guilty, culpable. **3** *he is responsible to the president* answerable to, accountable to. **4** *the children are very responsible* mature, adult, level-headed, rational, sane, reasonable, sensible, sound, stable, reliable, dependable, trustworthy, competent, conscientious, hard-working, industrious. **5** *a responsible position* authoritative, executive, decision-making, powerful, high, important.
Opposites IRRESPONSIBLE; UNTRUSTWORTHY.

responsive *adjective* *a responsive audience* quick to react, reactive, receptive, forthcoming, sensitive, perceptive, sympathetic, susceptible, impressionable, open, alive, awake, aware, sharp.
Opposites IMPASSIVE; APATHETIC; INSENSITIVE.

rest[1] *noun* **1** *seek rest after work* repose, relaxation, leisure, ease, inactivity, respite, time off, breathing-space, sleep, slumber. **2** *have a rest after work* sleep, nap, doze, slumber, siesta; *inf.* breather, snooze, forty winks, lie-down. **3** *go away for a rest* break, breathing-space, interval, interlude, intermission, lull, pause, holiday, vacation; time off. **4** *a place of rest in the mountains* repose, quiet, quietness, quietude, calm, calmness, tranquillity, peace, peacefulness, stillness, silence, hush. **5** *a rest for the vase* stand, base, holder, support, prop, shelf.

rest[2] *verb* **1** *invalids resting* take a rest, put one's feet up, relax, sit down, lie down, go to bed, sleep, take a nap, nap, catnap, doze, slumber; *inf.* take it easy, snooze. **2** *she rested her hands on the table* support, prop, steady, lie, place, position. **3** *the shelf rests on bricks* be supported by, be propped up by, lie on, be laid on, recline on, stand on, sit on. **4** *the result rests on the decision of the jury* depend, rely, hang, hinge, be based, be founded.

rest[3] *noun* *some will go; the rest will stay* remainder, residue, residuum, balance, remnant, surplus, excess, rump; those left, others, remains, leftovers.

rest⁴ *verb* **1** *you may rest assured* remain, stay, continue, be left. **2** *the arrangements rest with you* be the responsibility of, be down to, lie, reside.

restful *adjective* **1** *a restful effect* calming, relaxing, soothing, tranquillizing. **2** *a restful place* quiet, calm, tranquil, relaxed, peaceful, placid, still, languid, undisturbed, unhurried, sleepy.
Opposites EXCITING; NOISY.

restitution *noun* reparation, redress, atonement, recompense, compensation, indemnification, indemnity, requital, retribution, remuneration, reimbursement, repayment; amends.

restive *adjective* **1** *restive children on a Friday afternoon* restless, fidgety, fidgeting. **2** *the crowd grew restive* uneasy, ill at ease, edgy, on edge, tense, worked up, nervous, agitated, unquiet; *inf.* jittery, uptight. **3** *police trying to cope with restive demonstrators* unruly, unmanageable, uncontrollable, refractory, recalcitrant.
Opposites CALM; PEACEFUL.

restless *adjective* **1** *pass a restless night* sleepless, wakeful, tossing and turning, fitful. **2** *the crowd grew restless* uneasy, ill at ease, on edge, agitated. See RESTIVE 2. **3** *the restless sea* moving, in motion, on the move, changeable, changing. **4** *restless bands of people* unsettled, roaming, roving, wandering, itinerant, travelling, nomadic, peripatetic. **5** *restless children* restive, fidgety, fidgeting.
Opposites CALM; COMPOSED.

restoration *noun* **1** *the restoration of the building* renovation, repair, reconditioning, rehabilitation, refurbishment, rebuilding. See RESTORE 1. **2** *the invalid's restoration* recovery, resuscitation, revitalization. See RESTORE 2. **3** *the restoration of democracy* reinstitution, re-establishment, reinstatement, reinstallation. See RESTORE 5.

restore *verb* **1** *restore the building* renovate, repair, fix, mend, set to rights, recondition, rehabilitate, refurbish, rebuild, reconstruct, remodel, revamp, redecorate, touch up; *inf.* do up, fix up. **2** *a rest will help to restore him* build up, resuscitate, revitalize, refresh, revive, revivify. **3** *restore the dog to its owner* return, give back, hand back, send back. **4** *restore the vase to the shelf* put back, return, replace, reinstate. **5** *restore democracy* re-establish, reinstitute, reinstate, reinstall, reinforce, reimpose.

restrain *verb* **1** *restrain the unruly children/crowd* control, keep under control, hold in check, curb, keep within bounds, subdue. **2** *restrain one's anger* control, check, suppress, repress, contain, smother, stifle, bottle up, rein in; *inf.* keep the lid on. **3** *restrain the boy from jumping* prevent, hold back, hinder, impede, obstruct, delay, inhibit. **4** *restrain the thieves* tie up, bind, chain up, fetter, pinnion, confine, lock up, imprison, detain, arrest.

restrained *adjective* **1** *he's very restrained but she is outgoing* self-restrained, self-controlled, controlled, unemotional, undemonstrative, calm, reticent. **2** *restrained colours* muted, subdued, discreet, subtle, quiet, unobtrusive, understated, tasteful.
Opposites IMMODERATE; EMOTIONAL; GARISH; LOUD.

restraint *noun* **1** *he acts as a restraint on their impulsiveness* constraint, check, curb, barrier, block, hindrance, impediment, deterrent, inhibition. **2** *behave with restraint* self-restraint, self-control, self-discipline, moderation, temperateness, prudence, judiciousness. **3** *her restraint puts people off* self-restraint, self-control, self-possession, reserve, lack of emotion, coldness, formality, aloofness, detachment, reticence, uncommunicativeness. **4** *put the thieves under restraint* confinement, detention, imprisonment, incarceration, bondage, strait-jacket; bonds, chains, fetters, manacles. **5** *furnished with restraint* mutedness, discretion, subtlety, understatedness, taste, tastefulness, discrimination.

restrict *verb* **1** *restrict movement* hinder, impede, hamper, retard, handicap, cramp. **2** *restrict your food consumption* limit, set/impose limits on, keep within bounds, keep under control, regulate, control, moderate. **3** *restrict the prisoners* restrain, confine, lock up, imprison, wall up, hem in.

restricted *adjective* **1** *a restricted space* cramped, confined. **2** *a restricted intake* limited, controlled, regulated, moderate. **3** *a restricted area* out of bounds, off limits; private, closed off.

restriction *noun* **1** *impose currency restrictions* constraint, limitation, control, check, curb, regulation, condition, provision, proviso, stipulation, qualification, demarcation. **2** *the restriction of the space* confinement, crampedness, constraint. **3** *restriction of movement* hindrance, impediment, handicap.

result *noun* **1** *pleased with the result of the talks* outcome, consequence, issue, upshot, sequel, effect, reaction, repercussion, event, end, conclusion, termination, aftermath, product, byproduct; fruits. **2** *the wrong result to the addition* answer, solution.

result *verb* **1** *a fight resulted from the discussion* follow, ensue, issue, develop, stem, arise, evolve, emerge, emanate, occur, happen, come about, eventuate. **2** *it resulted in a draw* end in, culminate in, finish in, terminate in.

resume *verb* **1** *resume after lunch* take up, carry on, continue, proceed, go on, recommence, restart, start/begin again. **2** *resume negotiations* take up, carry on, continue, recommence, begin again, reopen, reinstitute. **3** *resume one's seat* take up again, reoccupy, occupy again. **4** *resume ownership* take up again, take back, recover, assume again.

résumé *noun* *present a résumé of the events* summary, précis, synopsis, abstract, epitome, outline, sketch, abridgement, digest.

resurrect *verb* **1** *Jesus was resurrected* raise from the dead, restore to life, bring back to life. **2** *resurrect old plans/practices* revive, breathe new life into, give new life to, bring back, restore, resuscitate, revitalize, reintroduce, reinstall, re-establish; *inf.* give the kiss of life to.

resurrection *noun* **1** *the resurrection of Jesus* raising from the dead, rising/return from the dead. **2** *the resurrection of old practices* revival, rebirth, renaissance, restoration, resuscitation, reintroduction, reinstallation, re-establishment, comeback.

resuscitate *verb* **1** *resuscitate him after his collapse* give artificial respiration to, bring round, revive, save; *inf.* give the kiss of life to. **2** *resuscitate old practices* revive, resurrect, breathe new life into, bring back, restore, reintroduce; *inf.* give the kiss of life to. See RESURRECT 2.

retain *verb* **1** *retain his job* | *retain the title* keep, keep possession/hold of, hold on/fast to; *inf.* hang on to. **2** *retain the old system* keep, maintain, continue, preserve, reserve. **3** *retain the facts* keep/bear in mind, memorize, remember, call to mind, recall, recollect. **4** *retain a gardener* hire, employ, engage, commission, pay.
Opposites give up (*see* GIVE); DISCONTINUE; DISMISS.

retainer *noun* **1** *pension off old retainers* attendant, servant, domestic; valet, footman. **2** *pay him a retainer in the holidays* retaining fee, partial payment, fee, deposit, advance.

retaliate *verb* return like for like, give tit for tat, give as good as one gets, get one's own back, get back at, make reprisal(s), take/exact/wreak revenge, avenge oneself, exact retribution, reciprocate, get even with, even the scores, settle a score.

retard *verb* slow down, slow up, hold back, set back, hold up, delay, hinder, hamper, obstruct, impede, decelerate, put a brake on, check, arrest, interfere with, interrupt, thwart, frustrate.
Opposites ACCELERATE; EXPEDITE.

retch *verb* gag, heave, dry-heave, vomit, be sick, spew; *Am.* keck; *inf.* throw up, puke.

reticence *noun* reserve, restraint, diffidence, uncommunicativeness, secretiveness, quietness, taciturnity, silence. See RETICENT.

reticent *adjective* reserved, restrained, diffident, uncommunicative, unforthcoming, secretive, tight-lipped, close-mouthed, quiet, taciturn, silent; *inf.* mum.
Opposites OUTGOING; TALKATIVE.

retire *verb* **1** *he retires at 65* give up work, stop working, be pensioned off; *inf.* be put out to grass. **2** *the jury retired* withdraw, go away, go out, depart, exit, take oneself off, leave, absent oneself. **3** *they retire at midnight* go to bed, go to one's room; *inf.* turn in, call it a day, hit the hay/sack. **4** *the troops retired, defeated* withdraw, pull back, fall back, pull out, give ground/way, retreat, decamp.

retirement *noun* **1** *happy in his retirement* retired years, post-work years. **2** *the retirement of the jury* withdrawal, exit. See RETIRE 2. **3** *they chose to live in retirement from the world* retreat, seclusion, solitude, loneliness, privacy, obscurity.

retiring *adjective* *a very retiring young woman* shy, diffident, bashful, self-effacing, shrinking, unassuming, unassertive, reserved, reticent, timid, timorous, nervous, modest, demure, coy, meek, humble.
Opposites BOLD; BRASH.

retract *verb* **1** *retract their horns* | *retracted his fishing line* draw in, pull in, pull back. **2** *retract one's statement* take back, withdraw, revoke, repeal, rescind, annul, cancel, abrogate, disavow, abjure, renounce, recant, disclaim, backtrack on, renege on, do an about-turn on.

retreat *verb* **1** *the army retreated* withdraw, pull back, fall back, back off, give way/ground, decamp, depart, leave, flee, take flight, turn tail, beat a retreat, beat a hasty retreat. **2** *the tide retreated* go back, recede, ebb.

retreat *noun* **1** *the retreat of the army* withdrawal, pulling back, decamping, departure, flight, evacuation. See RETREAT *verb* 1. **2** *he has a retreat in the mountains* refuge, haven, shelter, den, sanctuary, sanctum sanctorum, hideaway, resort, asylum. **3** *seek retreat from the world* retirement, seclusion, solitude, privacy, sanctuary.

retrench *verb* **1** *the firm must retrench* cut back, make cut-backs/savings/economies, economize, reduce expenditure, tighten one's belt, husband one's resources; *inf.* draw in one's horns. **2** *costs must be retrenched* curtail, limit, pare, prune, reduce, decrease, diminish.

retribution *noun* punishment, justice, nemesis, what is coming to one, reckoning, reprisal, requital, retaliation, revenge, vengeance, an eye for an eye, tit for tat, measure for measure, redress, reparation, recompense, restitution; just deserts.

retrieve *verb* **1** *retrieve one's property* get back, recover, regain, win back, recoup, redeem, reclaim, repossess, recapture, salvage, rescue. **2** *dogs retrieving sticks* fetch, bring back. **3** *difficult to retrieve the situation* set right, set/put to rights, repair, mend, remedy, rectify, redress, make good.

retrograde *adjective* **1** *retrograde motion* backwards, directed backwards, retreating, retrogressive, reverse. **2** *retrograde policy* worsening, deteriorating, declining, on the downgrade/wane.

retrospect *noun* **in retrospect** on looking/thinking back, on reflection, with hindsight.

return *verb* **1** *they returned at dawn* | *the symptoms returned* go back, come back, reappear, reoccur, come again, come round again. **2** *the ball/boomerang returned* rebound, recoil, boomerang. **3** *return milk bottles* | *return his love letters* give back, send back, take back, carry back, remit. **4** *return the books to the shelves* put back, replace, restore, reinstate, reinstall. **5** *return her greetings* reciprocate, repay, requite, send/give in response to. **6** *the firm returned a profit* yield, bring in, earn, make, net. **7** *"No, I won't," he returned* retort, reply, answer, respond, rejoin, riposte; *Am.* come back. **8** *return the ball* hit back, send back, throw back. **9** *return him as their candidate* elect, vote in, chose, select, pick. **10** *return a guilty verdict* bring in, deliver, announce, submit.
Opposites set off (*see* SET); KEEP; RETAIN.

return noun **1** look forward to their return home-coming, reappearance, reoccurrence. See RETURN verb **1**. **2** the return of the ball/boomerang rebound, recoil. **3** the return of the books to the shelf replacement, restoration, reinstatement, reinstallment. **4** there have been several returns from the bookshops thing returned, returned article, reject. **5** the return on the investment profit, yield, gain, income, revenue, interest, benefit. **6** fill in a tax return | the school attendance return statement, report, account, summary, form. **7** he gave a haughty return retort, reply, answer, response, rejoinder, riposte; inf. comeback. **8** done in return for your help reciprocation, repayment, response, exchange.

reveal verb **1** the coat blew back to reveal a red dress show, display, exhibit, expose to view. **2** examination revealed a deep cut bring to light, uncover, expose to view, lay bare, unearth, unveil, unmask. **3** reveal the details of the affair disclose, divulge, tell, let out, let on, let slip, give away, give out, leak, betray, make known/public, broadcast, publicize, publish, proclaim. **Opposites** CONCEAL; HIDE.

revel verb **1** party-goers revelling all night celebrate, make merry, have a party, party, carouse, roister; inf. live/whoop it up, go on a spree, have a fling, rave, paint the town red, push the boat out. **2** revel in her victory delight in, take pleasure in, bask in, rejoice in, relish, savour, gloat over, luxuriate in, wallow in.

revel noun noisy revels celebration, festivity, jollification, merrymaking, carousal, carouse, bacchanal; inf. spree, rave, bash, beanfeast, jag.

revelation noun **1** the revelation of the dress beneath show, display, exhibition, exposure. **2** the revelation of a deep cut bringing to light, uncovering, unearthing. See REVEAL 2. **3** the revelation of the details disclosure, divulgence, telling, leak, betrayal, broadcasting, publicizing, communication, publishing, proclamation. See REVEAL 3. **4** amazed at his revelations disclosure, divulgence; private/confidential information.

reveller noun celebrator, party-goer, merry-maker, pleasure-seeker, carouser.

revelry noun celebrations, festivities; jollification, merrymaking, carousal.

revenge noun **1** seek revenge vengeance, retaliation, retribution, reprisal, requital, redress, satisfaction, eye for an eye, tit for tat, measure for measure. **2** a heart full of revenge vengefulness, vindictiveness, spite, spitefulness, malice, maliciousness, ill will, animosity, hostility, hate, hatred, venom, rancour, bitterness.

revenge verb revenge an injustice | revenge oneself take revenge for, avenge, make retaliation for, retaliate, exact retribution for, take reprisals for, requite, get redress/satisfaction for.

revenue noun income, return, yield, interest, gain; profits, returns, receipts, proceeds, takings, rewards.

reverberate verb resound, echo, ring, vibrate.

revere verb look up to, think highly of, admire, respect, esteem, defer to, honour, reverence, venerate, worship, pay homage to, adore, hold in awe, exalt, put on a pedestal, idolize. **Opposites** DESPISE; SCORN.

reverence noun regard the leader with reverence high esteem, admiration, respect, deference, honour, veneration, worship, homage, adoration, devotion, awe, exaltation.

reverence verb reverence the leader revere, admire, respect, defer to, venerate, worship, adore, exalt, idolize. See REVERE.

reverent adjective reverential, admiring, respectful, deferential, worshipping, adoring, loving, devoted, awed, submissive, humble, meek.

reversal noun **1** policy reversal turn-round, turn-about, about-turn, about-face, volte-face, change of heart, tergiversation; inf. U-turn. **2** the reversal of roles change, exchange, trading, trade-off, swapping. **3** the reversal of the decision/verdict overturn, overthrow, revocation, repeal, rescinding, annulment, invalidation. See REVERSE verb **5**. **4** firms/families/armies suffering reversal failure, misfortune, adversity, vicissitude; reverse, upset, set-back, check, defeat. See REVERSE noun **3**.

reverse verb **1** reverse the collar turn round, put back to front. **2** reverse the barrel turn upside down, up-end, up-turn, invert. **3** reverse the car move/direct backwards, back. **4** reverse roles change, change round, exchange, trade, swap. **5** reverse the decision alter, change, countermand, undo, set aside, upset, overturn, overthrow, revoke, repeal, rescind, annul, nullify, declare null and void, void, invalidate, quash.

reverse adjective **1** a reverse trend opposite, contrary, converse, counter, inverse, contrasting, antithetical. **2** in reverse order reversed, backwards, inverted, transposed, turned round.

reverse noun **1** the reverse is the case opposite, contrary, converse, antithesis. **2** write on the reverse other side, back, rear, underside, wrong side, flip side, verso. **3** the firm/family/army has suffered reverses reversal, upset, set-back, check, non-success, failure, misfortune, mishap, misadventure, blow, disappointment; adversity, hardship, affliction, vicissitude, defeat, rout.

review noun **1** a review of the whole situation survey, study, analysis, examination, scrutiny, assessment, appraisal. **2** the salary structure is under review | undertake a salary review reconsideration, re-examination, reassessment, re-evaluation, reappraisal, revision, rethink, another look, fresh look. **3** the queen conducting a military review inspection, parade, display, procession, march past. **4** his review of the play criticism, critique, notice, assessment, evaluation, study, judgement, rating. **5** publish a learned review journal, periodical, magazine.

review verb **1** review the situation from their point of view survey, study, analyse, examine, scrutinize, assess, appraise. **2** it is more than time to review salaries reconsider, rethink, re-examine, re-evaluate, reassess, reappraise, revise. **3** review the past remember, recall, recollect, reflect on, look back on, call to mind, summon up, evoke. **4** review the troops inspect, view, scrutinize. **5** *review the play/book* criticize, evaluate, assess, appraise, judge, weigh up, discuss. *See* REVIEW *noun* 4.

reviewer *noun* critic, literary/arts critic, commentator.

revise *verb* **1** *revise the text* amend, emend, correct, alter, change, edit, rewrite, redraft, rework, update, revamp. **2** *revise our plans/opinions* reconsider, review, reassess, alter, change. **3** *revise the term's work* go over, reread, run through, study; *inf.* swot/bone up on.

revision *noun* **1** *the revision of the text* amendation, emendation, correction, alteration, editing, updating. *See* REVISE 1. **2** *the revision of our plans/opinions* reconsideration, alteration. **3** *get down to revision before the exam* studying; *inf.* swotting. *See* REVISE 3.

revival *noun* **1** *the revival of the collapsed man* resuscitation. *See* REVIVE 1. **2** *the revival of old traditions* resurrection, rebirth, renaissance, restoration, resuscitation, reintroduction, re-installation, re-establishment; *inf.* comeback.

revive *verb* **1** *revive the man who collapsed* bring round, resuscitate, give artificial respiration to, save, restore to health; *inf.* give the kiss of life to. **2** *the man soon revived* come round, recover consciousness, recover. **3** *a cup of tea revived her* refresh, restore, cheer up, comfort, enliven, revitalize. **4** *revive old traditions* breathe new life into, give a new lease of life to, bring back, restore, resuscitate, resurrect, revitalize, reintroduce, reinstall, re-establish.

revoke *verb* repeal, rescind, abrogate, countermand, annul, nullify, declare null and void, make void, void, invalidate, quash, set aside, cancel, retract, withdraw, recall, abjure, overrule, override, reverse.
Opposites ENACT; RATIFY.

revolt *verb* **1** *the citizens revolted against the army* rise up, rise, take to the streets, take up arms, rebel, mutiny, show resistance (to). **2** *the filthy sight revolted me* repel, disgust, sicken, nauseate, make sick, turn one's stomach, be repugnant to, make one's flesh creep, put one off, offend, shock; *inf.* turn one off, give one the creeps/heebie-jeebies.

revolting *adjective* repulsive, repellent, disgusting, sickening, nauseating, distasteful, repugnant, abhorrent, offensive, obnoxious, loathsome, off-putting, hateful, foul, vile, nasty, shocking, abominable, despicable, reprehensible, contemptible, odious, heinous, obscene.
Opposites ATTRACTIVE; PLEASANT; AGREEABLE.

revolution *noun* **1** *the French Revolution* rebellion, revolt, insurrection, uprising, rising, insurgence, mutiny, riot, coup, *coup d'état*, putsch. **2** *a revolution in the fashion industry* drastic change, radical alteration, complete shift, metamorphosis, sea change, upheaval, upset, transformation, innovation, reformation, cataclysm. **3** *a revolution of the wheel* rotation, single turn, whirl, round, spin, wheel. **4** *revolution of the planets round the sun* orbital motion; orbit.

revolutionary *adjective* **1** *revolutionary troops* rebellious, insurgent, insurrectionary, insurrectionist, mutinous, seditious, factious, insubordinate, subversive, extremist. **2** *revolutionary changes in education/revolutionary fashion* progressive, radical, innovative, new, novel, avant-garde, experimental, different, drastic.

revolutionary *noun* rebel, insurgent, insurrectionist, mutineer.

revolve *verb* **1** *the wheel revolved slowly* go round, turn round, rotate, spin, whirl, wheel. **2** *revolve round the sun* circle, orbit, gyrate, whirl. **3** *revolve the problem in her mind* turn over, think over, think about, deliberate, consider, reflect on, mull over, ponder, muse over, meditate, ruminate. **4** *her life revolves round her children* be concerned/preoccupied with, focus on, concentrate on.

revulsion *noun* repulsion, disgust, nausea, distaste, aversion, repugnance, recoil, abhorrence, loathing, hate, hatred, detestation, contempt.

reward *noun* **1** *a reward for your efforts/a reward for finding the wallet* recompense, payment, remuneration, bonus, bounty, present, gift, tip, gratuity, prize; *inf.* cut. **2** *the criminal got his just reward* punishment, penalty, retribution, requital, retaliation; just deserts, deserts; *inf.* comeuppance.

reward *verb* *reward them for their efforts* recompense, pay, remunerate, give a bounty/present to, tip.

rewarding *adjective* *taking the children out was a rewarding experience* satisfying, worthwhile, fulfilling, enriching, edifying, beneficial, profitable, advantageous, productive, valuable.

rhetoric *noun* **1** *the use of rhetoric to win over the crowd* oratory, eloquence, power of speech, delivery. *See table. See also table at* ORATOR. **2** *the literary work was spoiled by rhetoric* bombast, grandiloquence, magniloquence, hyperbole, pomposity, verbosity, long-windedness, wordiness, prolixity, turgidity, extravagant language, purple prose, fustian.

rhetorical *adjective* **1** *rhetorical language/passages* extravagant, pretentious, ostentatious, pompous, high-flown, flamboyant, showy, flowery, florid, oratorical, declamatory, bombastic, grandiloquent, magniloquent, hyperbolic, verbose, long-winded, wordy, prolix, turgid, periphrastic. **2** *rhetorical skills* oratorical, linguistic, verbal, stylistic.

rhyme *noun* *a nursery rhyme* verse, ditty, poem, song, ode.

rhythm *noun* **1** *musical rhythm* beat, cadence, tempo, pulse, throb, lilt. **2** *poetic rhythm* flow, cadence, metre. **3** *disturb the rhythm of their lives* flow, pattern, tempo, harmony.

ribald *adjective* bawdy, risqué, blue, smutty, broad, vulgar, coarse, earthy, off-colour, rude, naughty, racy, suggestive, indecent, indelicate, offensive, filthy, gross, lewd, salacious, licentious, concupiscent; *inf.* near the bone/knuckle.

rich *adjective* **1** *rich and powerful people* wealthy, affluent, well off, well-to-do, prosperous, moneyed, propertied; *inf.* well-heeled, filthy rich, loaded, made of money, rolling in it/money, flush, worth a packet/bundle, on

RHETORICAL DEVICES

alliteration	epizeuxis
anacoluthon	hendiadys
anadiplosis	hypallage
anaphora	hyperbaton
anastrophe	hyperbole
antiphrasis	hysteron
antistrophe	proteron
antithesis	isocolon
aporia	litotes
assonance	metaphor
catechresis	palindrome
chiasmus	paralipsis
diacope	periphrasis
enallage	polyptoton
epanalepsis	prosopopoeia
epanorthosis	simile
epiphora	symploce
epistrophe	trope

Easy Street. **2** *rich furnishings/surroundings* opulent, expensive, costly, precious, valuable, priceless, beyond price, lavish, luxurious, lush, sumptuous, palatial, splendid, superb, resplendent, elegant, fine, exquisite, magnificent, grand, gorgeous. **3** *rich in oil/talent* well-provided, well-supplied, well-stocked, abounding, overflowing, replete, rife. **4** *rich supplies of minerals/ideas* copious, abundant, ample, plentiful, plenteous, bountiful. **5** *a rich soil* fertile, productive, fecund, fruitful, lush. **6** *rich food* creamy, fatty, heavy, spicy, highly spiced. **7** *rich wines* full-bodied, heavy. **8** *rich colours* strong, deep, intense, vivid, brilliant, warm, vibrant. **9** *rich voices/music* full, sonorous, resonant, deep, mellow, mellifluous, melodious. **10** *that's rich, coming from you* preposterous, outrageous, ridiculous, laughable, risible. **11** *rich jokes* amusing, comical, funny, humorous, hilarious, side-splitting.
Opposites POOR; CHEAP; MEAGRE; PASTEL.

riches *plural noun* **1** *amass riches* money, gold, capital, property, treasure; assets, resources. **2** *a man of riches* wealth, affluence, opulence, prosperity.

richly *adverb* **1** *richly dressed/furnished* expensively, lavishly, luxuriously, sumptuously, palatially, splendidly, superbly, resplendently, magnificently. See RICH 2. **2** *an award/punishment richly deserved* fully, in full measure, well, thoroughly, completely, amply, utterly.

rid *verb* *rid the child/place of the pests* clear, cleanse, purge, purify, free, make free, relieve, deliver, unburden. **get rid of** dispose of, do away with, throw away, remove, dispense with, eliminate, dump, unload, jettison, expel, eject, weed out.

riddle *noun* puzzle, poser, conundrum, brain-teaser, Chinese puzzle, problem, enigma, mystery.

ride *verb* **1** *ride a horse* sit on, mount, be mounted on, bestride, manage, control. **2** *ride on a bus/ride in a car* travel, go, move, progress.

ride *noun* *a ride in a car/go for a ride* trip, outing, journey, jaunt; *inf.* spin.

ridicule *noun* *treat the old man with ridicule* derision, mockery, laughter, scorn, jeering, gibing, teasing, taunting, chaff, banter, badinage, raillery, satire, sarcasm, irony; *inf.* kidding, ribbing, ragging.

ridicule *verb* *ridicule the new pupil* deride, mock, laugh at, scoff at, scorn, jeer at, gibe at, make/poke fun at, make a fool of, tease, taunt, chaff, banter; *inf.* kid, rib, rag, take the mickey out of, send up.

ridiculous *adjective* **1** *wearing a ridiculous hat/telling ridiculous jokes* absurd, comical, funny, laughable, hilarious, humorous, droll, farcical, facetious, ludicrous, risible, derisory. **2** *what a ridiculous thing to do* pointless, senseless, foolish, inane, fatuous, nonsensical, mindless. **3** *it is ridiculous that he got away with it* unreasonable, illogical, unbelievable, incredible, outrageous, preposterous, shocking, monstrous.
Opposites SERIOUS; SENSIBLE; REASONABLE.

rife *adjective* **1** *disease is rife* prevalent, predominant, widespread, common, general, extensive, ubiquitous, universal, global, rampant. **2** *the territory is rife with disease/vermin* abounding, overflowing, alive, swarming, teeming.

riff-raff *noun* rabble, mob, commonality, *hoi polloi, canaille,* scum; dregs of society, undesirables.

rifle *verb* **1** *rifle through her belongings* ransack, rummage through, go through, rake through, search. **2** *rifle the contents of the safe* steal, rob, burgle, thieve. **3** *raiders rifling their neighbour's goods* plunder, pillage, loot, despoil, sack, ransack.

rift *noun* **1** *a rift in the rock* fault, split, break, breach, fissure, cleft, crevice, gap, crack, cranny, slit, chink, cavity, opening, space, hole, aperture. **2** *a rift between family members* breach, division, estrangement, schism, split, alienation, quarrel, disagreement, fight, row, altercation, conflict, feud; *inf.* falling-out.

rig *verb* **1** *rig the yacht with sails* equip, supply, furnish, provide, make ready. **2** *rigged out in silk* clothe, dress, attire, accoutre, array, deck, bedeck, drape, trick out. **3** *rig up a shelter* put together, erect/assemble hastily, throw together, cobble together, improvise. **4** *rig the results of the vote* falsify, fake, tamper with, doctor, engineer, manipulate, juggle, arrange, massage; *inf.* fix.

rigging *noun.* See table.

right *adjective* **1** *his actions were not right* just, fair, equitable, impartial, good, upright, righteous, virtuous, proper, moral, ethical, honourable, honest, principled, lawful, legal. **2** *the right answer/procedure/way* correct, accurate, without error, unerring, exact, precise, valid; *inf.* spot on, on the mark. **3** *he is the right owner—the other is a fraud* rightful, true, genuine, authentic, lawful, legal, legitimate; *inf.* legit. **4** *the right person for the job* suitable, appropriate, fitting, fit, proper, desirable, preferable, ideal. **5** *he came at the right moment* opportune, favourable, convenient, suitable, appropriate, propitious. **6** *in his right mind* sane, sound, rational, lucid, sensible, reason-

RIGGING		
backstay	gripe	shroud
bibb	hank	sling
bitt	hawser	snub
boom	horse	spar
bull's-eye	hound	spider
burton	jack	hoop
cable	jigger	spring
clamp	lanyard	stick
clinch	lead	stirrup
club	leader	stop
crossjack	mainstay	tabernacle
crowfoot	martingale	thimble
eye	mizzen-	topmast
fairlead	mast	traveller
foremast	messenger	trestle-
fore-	moorings	tree
topmast	mouse	truck
fox	pendant/	truss
gaff	pennant	warp
garland	pole	whelp
gasket	preventer	yardarm
gooseneck	service	yoke

able, clear-thinking; *inf.* all there. **7** *he was ill but he is all right now* | *the engine does not sound right* fine, healthy, in good health, well, fit, normal, sound, unimpaired, up to par; *inf.* up to scratch, in the pink. **8** *make a right mess* real, complete, thorough, thoroughgoing, absolute, utter, out-and-out. **9** *his politics are right but hers are left* Conservative, Tory, reactionary.
Opposites WRONG; UNJUST; INACCURATE.

right *adverb* **1** *go right on* straight, directly, in a straight line, as the crow flies. **2** *he'll be right down* immediately, instantly, promptly, quickly, straightaway, without delay. **3** *sink right to the bottom* | *come right off its hinges* all the way, completely, entirely, totally, wholly, altogether, utterly, quite. **4** *right in the middle* bang, exactly, precisely, just, squarely; *inf.* slapbang. **5** *if I remember right* aright, accurately, correctly, properly, exactly, precisely. **6** *you must behave/treat them right* justly, fairly, properly, righteously, virtuously, honourably, honestly, morally, ethically. **7** *it will come out right* well, for the better/best, favourably, advantageously, to one's advantage, beneficially. **right away** at once, immediately, right now, now, straight away, this instant, instantly, promptly, directly, forthwith, without delay/hesitation; *inf.* straight off.

right *noun* **1** *know the difference between right and wrong* lawfulness, legality, goodness, righteousness, virtue, virtuousness, integrity, rectitude, propriety, morality, truth, truthfulness, honesty, honour, honourableness, justice, justness, fairness, equity, equitableness, impartiality; ethics. **2** *his position gives him the right to dismiss people* prerogative, privilege, authority, power, licence, permission, warrant, sanction, entitlement. **by right/rights** in fairness, with justice, properly. **put to rights** right, put/set right, sort out, straighten out, rectify, fix, put in order, tidy up, repair.

right *verb* **1** *he righted himself* | *right the pole* stand/set upright. **2** *right the situation* put to rights, sort out, straighten out, rectify, fix, put in order, tidy up, repair. **3** *right a wrong* set/put right, rectify, compensate for, redress, vindicate.

righteous *adjective* **1** *righteous people outnumbering wrongdoers* good, virtuous, upright, moral, ethical, law-abiding, honest, innocent, faultless, honourable, blameless, guiltless, pure, noble, God-fearing. **2** *righteous indignation* rightful, justifiable, well-founded, defensible, admissible, allowable, reasonable.
Opposites BAD; DISHONEST; SINFUL.

righteousness *noun* goodness, virtue, virtuousness, uprightness, integrity, rectitude, probity, morality, ethicalness, honesty, honour, honourableness, innocence, purity; ethics. *See* RIGHTEOUS 1.

rigid *adjective* **1** *a rigid substance* stiff, hard, taut, inflexible, non-flexible, unbendable, unbending, unyielding, inelastic, non-pliant, unmalleable. **2** *a rigid schedule* fixed, set, firm, inflexible, unalterable, unchangeable, unvarying, invariable, hard and fast. **3** *a man of rigid principles* strict, severe, stern, stringent, rigorous, austere, spartan, harsh, inflexible, intransigent, uncompromising.
Opposites FLEXIBLE; LENIENT.

rigorous *adjective* **1** *a rigorous regime* | *rigorous discipline* strict, severe, stern, stringent, austere, spartan, tough, hard, harsh, rigid, inflexible, intransigent, uncompromising, demanding, exacting. **2** *rigorous attention to detail* | *a rigorous search* meticulous, punctilious, painstaking, thorough, laborious, scrupulous, conscientious, nice, exact, precise, accurate. **3** *rigorous weather* harsh, severe, bad, bleak, extreme, inclement.
Opposites GENTLE; MILD; SLAPDASH; LAX.

rigour *noun* **1** *the rigour of the regime* strictness, severity, sternness, stringency, austerity, toughness, hardness, harshness, rigidity, inflexibility, intransigence. *See* RIGOROUS 1. **2** *this job must be tackled with rigour* meticulousness, punctiliousness, thoroughness, exactness, exactitude, precision, accuracy. *See* RIGOROUS 2. **3** *the rigours of winter* hardship; adversity, harshness, severity.

rim *noun* **1** *the rim of a cup* brim, edge, lip, circumference. **2** *the rim of a lake* edge, border, verge, margin, brink, circumference.

rind *noun* outer layer, peel, skin, husk, crust, integument, epicarp.

ring¹ *noun* **1** *a wedding ring* | *she didn't wear a ring* band, gold band; wedding ring, marriage token. **2** *a ring round the moon* circle, circlet, round, loop, circuit, halo, disc. **3** *a circus/boxing ring* arena, enclosure, area. **4** *a ring of people stood around* circle, group, knot, gathering. **5** *a spy ring* gang, syndicate, cartel, mob, organization, confederacy, association, society, combine, alliance, league, fraternity, clique, cabal, junta.

ring² *verb* *a fence ringed the area* | *ring the correct answer* circle, encircle, circumscribe, encompass, loop, gird, enclose, surround, hem in, fence in, seal off.

ring³ *noun* **1** *the ring of the bells* ringing, tolling, peal, pealing, knell, chime, clang, tinkle. *See* RING⁴ *verb* 1,2. **2** *give her a ring* call, telephone call; *inf.* phone call, buzz.

ring⁴ *verb* **1** *ring the bells* toll, sound. **2** *the bells rang out* toll, peal, sound, chime, ding, ding-dong, clang, tinkle. **3** *the halls rang with music* resound, reverberate, resonate, echo, re-echo. **4** *bells ringing in the new year* | *ring in a new regime* herald, signal, announce, usher in. **5** *I shall ring you* call, telephone; *inf.* phone, buzz.

rinse *verb* *rinse the clothes by hand* | *rinse out the teapot* wash, wash out, wash lightly, clean.

riot *noun* **1** *there was a riot when he was arrested* rebellion, revolt, uprising, insurrection, insurgence, street fight, commotion, disturbance, uproar, tumult, mêlée, row, scuffle, fracas, fray, brawl, free-for-all. **2** *the young people's riot brought the police in* revelry, celebration, partying, merrymaking, festivity, jollification; revels; *inf.* high jinks, rave. **3** *the garden was a riot of colour* lavish display, splash, extravagance, flourish, show, exhibition. **run riot** **1** *children running riot* rampage, run/go wild, run amok, go berserk; *inf.* raise hell. **2** *flowers running riot in the wilderness* grow profusely, spread uncontrolled.

riot *verb* **1** *crowds rioting in the streets* rebel, revolt, mutiny, take to the streets, run riot, rampage, go on the rampage, run wild/amok, go berserk, fight, brawl. **2** *young people rioting* celebrate, party, make merry, revel, carouse, roister; *inf.* paint the town red, go on a spree/binge, let one's hair down, rave.

riotous *adjective* **1** *a riotous assembly* rebellious, mutinous, unruly, disorderly, uncontrollable, ungovernable, unmanageable, insubordinate, rowdy, wild, violent, brawling, lawless, anarchic. **2** *a riotous party* loud, noisy, boisterous, uproarious, rollicking, orgiastic. **3** *a riotous show* hilarious, uproarious, side-splitting, too funny for words; *inf.* screamingly funny.

ripe *adjective* **1** *ripe fruit/grain/cheese* mature, fully developed, full grown, ready to eat, ready, mellow, seasoned, tempered. **2** *our plans are now ripe* ready, all ready/set, developed, prepared, arranged, complete, finished. **3** *ripe in years* advanced, far on, old. **4** *sites ripe for development* ready, fit, suitable, right. **5** *the time is ripe* suitable, convenient, opportune, favourable, advantageous, auspicious.
Opposites IMMATURE; unripe; GREEN.

ripen *verb* **1** *fruit ripening on the trees* grow ripe, mature, come to maturity, mellow. **2** *ripen the fruit/cheese* make ripe, mature, bring to maturity, make mellow, season. **3** *our plans are ripening* develop, be in preparation, come to fruition.

riposte *noun* retort, rejoinder, answer, reply, response, return, sally; *inf.* comeback.

riposte *verb* retort, rejoin, answer, reply, respond, return; *Am.* come back.

rise *verb* **1** *the sun rose* | *a hand rose from the lake* arise, come/go up, move up, ascend, climb up. **2** *mountains rising above the town* rise up, tower, soar, loom, rear up. **3** *prices rose* go up, get higher, increase, soar, rocket, escalate. **4** *standards have risen* go up, get higher/better, improve, advance. **5** *her voice rose* | *noise levels rose* get higher, grow, increase, become louder, swell, intensify. **6** *the children rose on the arrival of the guest* stand up, get to one's feet, get up, jump up, leap up, spring up, become erect. **7** *he rose at dawn* arise, get up, get out of bed, wake up; *inf.* rise and shine, surface. **8** *the court rose at midday* adjourn, break off, be suspended, take a break. **9** *rise from the ranks* | *rise up the social ladder* climb, make progress, advance, get on, make/work one's way, be promoted. **10** *she won't rise to the bait* react to, respond to, take. **11** *Christ rose again* come to life, come back from the dead, be resurrected. **12** *dough rising* swell, expand, enlarge. **13** *citizens rising against the troops* rebel, revolt, mutiny, stage an insurrection, take up arms, mount the barricades. **14** *the river rises in the mountains* originate, begin, start, commence, issue from, spring from, flow from, emanate from. **15** *her spirits rose* become more cheerful, grow buoyant, become optimistic/hopeful. **16** *the ground rises here* slope/slant upwards, go uphill, climb, mount, get steeper.
Opposites SET; FALL; DECREASE; SIT.

rise *noun* **1** *the rise of the sun* rising, ascent. *See* RISE *verb* 1. **2** *the rise in prices* increase, upsurge, upswing. *See* RISE *verb* 3. **3** *a rise in standards* improvement, amelioration, advance, upturn. *See* RISE *verb* 4. **4** *his rise to power* | *his rise from the ranks* climb, progress, progression, advancement, promotion, aggrandizement. **5** *a rise in the ground* | *climb the rise* incline, elevation, upward slope, acclivity, rising ground, hillock, hill. **6** *workers seeking a rise* pay increase, salary/wage increase, increment; *Am.* raise.

risk *noun* **1** *there is a risk of fire* chance, possibility. **2** *put lives at risk* danger, peril, jeopardy. **3** *take a risk* | *an element of risk in the game* chance, hazard, uncertainty, speculation, venture.

risk *verb* **1** *risk his life* put at risk, endanger, imperil, jeopardize. **2** *risk getting wet* take the risk of, chance, venture; *inf.* grin and bear. **3** *risk £5 on the bet* gamble, hazard, chance, venture.

risky *adjective* dangerous, fraught with danger, hazardous, perilous, unsafe, precarious, touch-and-go, tricky, uncertain; *inf.* chancy, dodgy, dicey.
Opposites SAFE.

risqué *adjective* off-colour, indecent, indelicate, improper, suggestive, naughty, rude, coarse, earthy, crude, bawdy, smutty, dirty, spicy, racy, salacious, licentious, lewd, ribald.

rite *noun* ritual, ceremony, ceremonial, observance, service, sacrament, celebration, performance, act, practice, tradition, convention, formality, procedure, usage.

ritual *noun* **1** *the ritual of the Japanese tea ceremony* rite, ceremony, ceremonial, observance, celebration, act, practice, tradition, convention, procedure. *See* RITE. **2** *dislike ritual in public occasions* ceremony, tradition, convention, protocol, custom, habit, procedure, routine, stereotype.

rival *noun* **1** *he defeated his rival | they are rivals for her love* opponent, opposition, adversary, antagonist, contestant, competitor, challenger, vier, contender. **2** *in tennis she has no rival* equal, match, equivalent, fellow, peer.

rival *verb* *rival the south of France* compete with, vie with, match, equal, emulate, measure up to, compare with, bear comparison with, parallel.

rival *adjective* *rival teams* opposed, opposing, competing, in competition, contending, in conflict, conflicting.

rivalry *noun* *rivalry between brothers* opposition, competition, competitiveness, vying, contention, conflict.

river *noun. See table.*

road *noun* **1** *well-lit roads* street, thoroughfare, highway. **2** *this is the road to London* way, route, direction. **3** *ships in roads* roadstead, anchorage.

roam *verb* **1** *children/animals roaming around* wander, rove, ramble, meander, drift. **2** *roam the hills* wander through, range, travel, walk, tramp, traverse, trek, peregrinate.

roar *verb* **1** *the lion roared | the teacher roared at the children* bellow, yell, bawl, shout, howl, thunder, shriek, scream, cry, bay. **2** *roar at the comedian's jokes* roar/howl with laughter, laugh heartily, guffaw, hoot; *inf.* split one's sides, roll in the aisles.

roar *noun* **1** *the lion's/teacher's roar | the roar of the wind* bellow, growl, yell, bawl, shout, howl, rumble, shriek, scream, cry. **2** *his act was greeted with roars of laughter* guffaw, howl, hoot.

rob *verb* **1** *rob a bank* steal from, burgle, burglarize, hold up, break into. **2** *rob an old lady* steal from, mug; *inf.* rip off, jump. **3** *rob them of their savings* defraud, swindle, cheat, mulct, dispossess; *inf.* diddle, bilk, do out of. **4** *rob them of peace of mind* deprive.

robber *noun* burglar, thief, mugger, stealer, pilferer, housebreaker, looter, raider, bandit, brigand, pirate, highwayman.

robbery *noun* **1** *commit robbery* burglary, theft, thievery, stealing, housebreaking, larceny, pilfering, filching, embezzlement, misappropria-

LONGEST RIVERS IN THE WORLD	
River	**Location**
Amazon	South America
Amur	Asia
Congo/Zaire	Africa
Mississippi	North America
Nile	Africa
Ob	Russia
Paraná	South America
Yangtze	Asia
Yellow	Huang Ho	Asia
Yenisei	Russia

ROCKS AND MINERALS

Sedimentary				
arenite	gneiss	phonolite	diamond	periclase
argillite	granulite	picrite	dolomite	pitchblende
breccia	hornfels	porphyry	emery	plagioclase
chalk	marble	pumice	euxenite	polybasite
chert	phyllite	rhyolite	feldspar	pyrite
claystone	psammite	syenite	fluorspar	pyrites
coal	pyroxenite	tephrite	fool's gold	quartz
conglomerate	quartzite	tonalite	fulgurite	realgar
diatomaceous	schist	trachyte	galena	rutile
earth	slate	trap	garnet	saponite
dolomite	verdite	tuff	gypsum	sapphirine
flint	**Igneous**	variolite	haematite	scolecite
ironstone	andesite	vitrophyre	halite	serpentine
limestone	anorthosite	**Minerals**	harmotome	siderite
marl	aplite	anhydrite	hornblende	sodalite
mudstone	basalt	anorthoclase	hyacinth	sphalerite
oolite	breccia	apatite	illite	stannite
radiolarite	diorite	asbestos	ilmenite	talc
rag	dolerite	augite	kaolinite	thorite
rudite	dunite	beryl	lapis lazuli	topaz
sandstone	felsite	biotite	malachite	tourmaline
shale	gabbro	blackjack	marcasite	tungstite
siltstone	granite	borax	massicot	turquoise
tillite	kimberlite	cassiterite	meerschaum	vesuvianite
Metamorphic	lamprophyre	chalcopyrite	mica	water
amphibolite	lava	Chile	molybdenite	sapphire
eclogite	monzonite	saltpetre	mullite	wolframite
epidiorite	obsidian	chrysoberyl	oligoclase	zeolite
epidosite	pegmatite	cinnabar	opal	zincite
	peridotite	corundum	orthoclase	zircon

tion, swindling, fraud. **2** *a robbery at the bank* mugging, hold-up, break-in, raid; *inf.* rip-off.

robe *noun* **1** *wearing coronation robes* vestment, habit, costume, gown. **2** *wearing a robe over pyjamas* dressing-gown, housecoat, wrapper, peignoir.

robot *noun* automaton, android, machine.

robust *adjective* **1** *robust young athletes* healthy, strong, vigorous, hale and hearty, energetic, muscular, powerful, powerfully built, tough, rugged, sturdy, stalwart, strapping, brawny, burly. **2** *a robust sense of humour* earthy, crude, coarse, rough, raw, unsubtle, indecorous, unrefined. **3** *a robust attitude to life* sensible, common-sense, no-nonsense, down-to-earth, practical, realistic, pragmatic, hard-headed. *Opposites* WEAK; FEEBLE; FRAIL.

rock *noun* **1** *rocks dislodged from the cliff* boulder, stone. *See table.* **2** *that department is the rock on which the firm is built* foundation, cornerstone, support, prop, mainstay. **3** *he is her rock in an uncertain world* bulwark, anchor, tower of strength, protection, security.

rock *verb* **1** *the cradle/boat was rocking* move to and fro, swing, sway, roll, lurch, pitch, reel, wobble, undulate, oscillate. **2** *the world was rocked by his death* stun, shock, stagger, astound, astonish, amaze, dumbfound, surprise, shake, take aback, bewilder.

rocket *verb* **1** *it rocketed into the air* shoot up, take off, soar, zoom. **2** *prices have rocketed* soar, increase rapidly, escalate; *inf.* go through the ceiling, sky-rocket.

rocky¹ *adjective* **1** *a rocky shore* rock-strewn, stony, pebbly, rough.

rocky² *adjective* *he's a bit rocky after his illness* unsteady, unstable, shaky, tottering, teetering, wobbly, wobbling. **2** *their marriage is rather rocky* unsteady, unstable, uncertain, unsure; *inf.* iffy.

rod *noun* **1** *rods of iron* bar, stick, pole, baton, staff. **2** *spare the rod and spoil the child* cane, stick, birch, switch, wand.

rodent *noun. See table. See also table at* SQUIRREL.

rogue *noun* **1** *rogues who steal from their friends* villain, scoundrel, rascal, reprobate, swindler, fraudster, cheat, deceiver, confidence trickster, charlatan, mountebank, sharper, wretch, cad, blackguard, ne'er-do-well, wastrel, good-for-nothing; *inf.* rotter, bounder, con man, crook.

2 *the child's a rogue* scamp, imp, rascal, little devil, mischief-maker.

role *noun* **1** *play the role of King Lear* part, character, representation, portrayal. **2** *in his role as headmaster* capacity, function, position, place, situation, job, post, task.

roll *verb* **1** *the wheels rolled round* go round, turn, turn round, rotate, revolve, spin, whirl, wheel. **2** *roll up a newspaper* furl, coil, fold. **3** *as time rolls by | the bus rolled along* pass, go, flow, travel. **4** *roll the lawn/pastry* flatten, level, smooth, even, press down, crush. **5** *ships rolling on the ocean* toss, rock, pitch, lurch, sway, reel. **6** *waves rolling* billow, toss, tumble. **7** *drunks rolling home* lurch, stagger, reel, sway, waddle, wobble.

roll *noun* **1** *a roll of the wheel* turn, rotation, revolution, spin, whirl. **2** *a roll of film/tape* spool, reel, bobbin, cylinder. **3** *buy rolls for lunch* bread roll, bun, bap. **4** *on the electoral roll* register, list, file, index, roster, directory, catalogue. **5** *a roll of drums* boom, reverberation, thunder, rumble. **6** *the roll of the sea* undulation, billowing, swell, tossing, pitching, rocking.

romance *noun* **1** *live in a world of romance, not the real world* fantasy, fancy, whimsy, fabrication, glamour, mystery, legend, fairy tale, idyll. **2** *their romance is over* love affair, affair, liaison, attachment, intrigue, courtship, amour. **3** *write romances* love story; romantic fiction, melodrama; *inf.* tear-jerker. **4** *tired of the child's romances* lie, falsehood, fabrication, invention, trumped-up story, piece of fiction, fairy tale, flight of fancy, exaggeration; *inf.* tall story.

romance *verb* **1** *the young woman was romancing* fantasize, daydream. **2** *the child is romancing* lie, tell a lie, invent a story, exaggerate. **3** *he is romancing the girl next door* court, woo, go out with; *inf.* go steady with, date.

romantic *adjective* **1** *present a romantic picture of life today* unrealistic, idealistic, visionary, utopian, starry-eyed, optimistic, hopeful. **2** *romantic words* loving, amorous, passionate, fond, tender, sentimental; *inf.* soppy, mushy, sloppy. **3** *a romantic figure in black* fascinating, mysterious, glamorous, exotic, exciting. **4** *tell a romantic tale of his adventures* fantastic, fanciful, imaginative, extravagant, exaggerated, fic-

---

RODENTS

acouchi	climbing	hamster	mara	spring
agouti	mouse	harvest	mole rat	hare
bamboo rat	cotton rat	mouse	mouse	squirrel
bandicoot	coypu	house mouse	muskrat	steppe
rat	deer mouse	hutia	paca	lemming
bank vole	desert rat	jerboa	pocket	tuco-tuco
beaver	dormouse	jird	mouse	viscacha
black rat	field mouse	jumping	porcupine	vole
brown rat	field vole	mouse	pouched rat	water rat
cane rat	gerbil	kangaroo	rat	water vole
capybara	grasshopper	mouse	rice rat	wood mouse
cavy	mouse	kangaroo rat	spiny mouse	wood rat
chinchilla	guinea pig	lemming	springhaas	

titious, improbable, unlikely, implausible.
Opposites PRACTICAL; REALISTIC.

romantic *noun they are romantics but their child is practical* romanticist, dreamer, visionary, idealist, utopian.

room *noun* **1** *take up a lot of room* space, area, territory, expanse, extent, volume, elbow-room. **2** *room for improvement* scope, capacity, margin, leeway, latitude, occasion, opportunity. **3** *she has a room in that building* bedroom, apartment, office, bedsitting room; *inf.* bedsit.

room *verb room in the same building* have rooms, lodge, board, stay, dwell, reside.

rooms *plural noun* lodgings, quarters; apartment, residence, dwelling, abode; accommodation.

roomy *adjective* spacious, commodious, capacious, voluminous, ample, generous, sizable, large, broad, wide, extensive.
Opposites NARROW; TINY; POKY.

root *noun* **1** *the plant's roots* radicle, radix, rhizome, tuber, tap root. **2** *the root of the problem* source, origin, fountain-head, starting-point, basis, foundation, fundamental, seat, nucleus, kernel, nub, cause, reason, rationale, occasion, motivation; beginnings. **root and branch** completely, entirely, thoroughly, wholly, totally, utterly, radically.

root *verb* **1** *the seeds/idea rooted* take root, grow roots, become established, set. **2** *rooted to the spot | her fear was deeply rooted* fix, establish, embed, implant, entrench. **root around** *root around in the drawers* rummage, rifle, forage, search, shuffle through, ransack. **root out** **1** *root out the weeds* uproot, tear up by the roots. **2** *root out the evil* extirpate, weed out, eradicate, get rid of, remove, do away with, eliminate, abolish, destroy, erase, put an end to. **3** *root out the cause* dig out, unearth, turn up, dredge up, bring to light, discover.

rope *noun tie the logs with a rope | pin the clothes on a rope* cord, cable, line, strand, hawser.

rope *verb rope the logs together* bind, tie, fasten, lash, tether, pinion. **rope in** *rope us in to help* enlist, engage, inveigle, persuade, talk into, involve.

roster *noun* list, listing, rota, roll, register, schedule, agenda, calendar, directory, index, table.

rostrum *noun* dais, platform, stage, podium.

rosy *adjective* **1** *rosy cheeks* pink, pinkish, red, reddish, ruddy, rubicund, blushing, glowing, healthy looking. **2** *a rosy future* optimistic, promising, auspicious, hopeful, encouraging, bright, favourable, cheerful, happy, sunny.

rot *verb* **1** *the material is rotting* decompose, decay, crumble, disintegrate, corrode, perish. **2** *the food is rotting* go bad, spoil, go sour, moulder, putrefy, fester; *inf.* go off. **3** *moral standards are rotting away* degenerate, deteriorate, decline, break down, waste away, wither away.

rot *noun* **1** *material suffering from rot* decomposition, decay, disintegration, corrosion, putrefaction, mould, blight. See ROT *verb* 1. **2** *it was a thriving society but rot has set in* degeneracy, deterioration, decline, dissoluteness. **3** *talk rot* rubbish, nonsense, stuff and nonsense, bunkum, claptrap, twaddle, drivel, moonshine; *inf.* bosh, bunk, tommy-rot, gobbledegook, codswallop, hogwash, poppycock, guff, tosh.

rotary *adjective* rotating, rotational, revolving, turning, gyrating, gyratory, spinning, whirling.

rotate *verb* **1** *the wheels are rotating* go round, move round, turn, turn round, revolve, spin, whirl, swivel, reel, wheel, gyrate. **2** *the two doctors rotate | the directorship rotates* alternate, take turns, work/act in sequence, take place in rotation.

rotation *noun* **1** *the rotation of the wheel* revolving, spinning, whirling, gyration. See ROTATE 1. **2** *one rotation of the wheel* turn, revolution, spin, whirl, orbit. **3** *do the work in rotation* alternation, sequence, cycle. See ROTATE 2.

rotten *adjective* **1** *rotten food* bad, mouldy, mouldering, spoiled, tainted, sour, rancid, rank, decaying, decomposed, putrid, putrescent, festering, fetid, stinking; *inf.* off. **2** *rotten material* decomposing, decaying, crumbling, disintegrating, corroding, perishing. **3** *rotten teeth* decaying, crumbling, carious. **4** *he's a rotten creep* corrupt, dishonourable, dishonest, untrustworthy, immoral, unprincipled, unscrupulous, villainous, bad, wicked, evil, sinful, iniquitous, vicious, debauched, degenerate, dissolute, dissipated, perverted, wanton; *inf.* crooked, bent. **5** *that was a rotten thing to do* nasty, foul, mean, bad, dirty, filthy, contemptible, despicable, base, scurrilous. **6** *we had a rotten time* miserable, unpleasant, disagreeable, disappointing, regrettable, unfortunate, unlucky. **7** *it's a rotten idea* ill-considered, ill thought out, ill-advised, injudicious. **8** *what a rotten selection of goods* poor, inadequate, inferior, substandard, unsatisfactory, unacceptable; *inf.* lousy, crummy. **9** *feeling rotten with the flu* ill, sick, unwell, unhealthy, below par, off colour; *inf.* under the weather, poorly, rough, ropy.
Opposites FRESH; NICE; PLEASANT; GOOD.

rotter *noun* bad lot, blackguard, cad, swine; *inf.* bounder, creep, rat, louse.

rotund *adjective* **1** *rotund and jolly* plump, chubby, buxom, roly-poly, tubby, well-rounded, portly, stout, corpulent, podgy, fat, obese, heavy, fleshy. **2** *rotund vowels/speech* sonorous, full-toned, round, canorous, rich, mellow, resonant, orotund, magniloquent, grandiloquent.

rough *adjective* **1** *rough surfaces* uneven, irregular, bumpy, broken, stony, rugged, jaggy, craggy, lumpy, nodulous. **2** *dogs with a rough coat* shaggy, hairy, bushy, fuzzy, bristly, hirsute. **3** *get involved in some rough play* boisterous, rowdy, disorderly, wild, violent, savage. **4** *rough seas* turbulent, tumultuous, choppy. **5** *rough weather* inclement, stormy, squally, wild, tempestuous, wintry. **6** *he's a rough character* coarse, crude, uncouth, vulgar, unrefined, uncultured, loutish, boorish, churlish, brutish, ill-bred, ill-mannered, unmannerly, impolite, discourteous, uncivil, brusque, blunt, curt. **7** *a few rough words to say to him* curt, sharp, harsh, stern, unfeeling, insensitive. **8** *have a rough time | receive rough treatment* harsh, severe,

hard, tough, difficult, unpleasant, disagreeable, nasty, cruel. **9** *had rough luck* unfortunate, undeserved. **10** *he was rough on his son* harsh, hard, stern, unrelenting, merciless, unfeeling, unfair, unjust. **11** *rough wood/flour* crude, raw, unpolished, undressed, uncut, rough-hewn, unrefined, unprocessed. **12** *rough voices* husky, gruff, hoarse, harsh. **13** *rough sounds* discordant, inharmonious, cacophonous, harsh, grating, jarring, strident, raucous. **14** *rough wines* harsh, sharp, unrefined. **15** *a rough sketch* rough-and-ready, hasty, quick, sketchy, cursory, crude, incomplete, rudimentary, basic, unpolished, unrefined. **16** *a rough estimate* approximate, inexact, imprecise, vague, hazy. **17** *feeling rather rough* ill, sick, unwell, unhealthy, below par, off colour; *inf.* hung-over, under the weather, poorly, rotten, ropy.
Opposites SMOOTH; GENTLE; REFINED; PRECISE.

rough noun **1** *make a rough of your plan* draft, sketch, outline, mock-up, model. **2** *mugged by a gang of roughs* ruffian, thug, bully-boy; *inf.* tough, roughneck, bruiser, bovver boy.

rough verb roughen, make rough. **rough out** *rough out your ideas* draft, sketch out, outline, block out, adumbrate. **rough up** *the children were roughed up by their father | old men roughed up by muggers* maltreat, mistreat, abuse, manhandle, batter, beat up, knock about; *inf.* bash.

rough-and-tumble noun horseplay; scuffle, struggle, fight, brawl, fracas, mêlée; *inf.* scrap, dust-up, rough house.

round adjective **1** *a round shape* circular, ring-shaped, hooplike, annular, cycloid, discoid, disklike, cylindrical, spherical, spheroid, ball-shaped, globelike, globular, globate, globose, orblike, orbicular, orbiculate, bulb-shaped, balloon-like, convex, curved. **2** *a round dozen* complete, entire, whole, full, undivided, unbroken. **3** *a round figure* well-rounded, ample, rotund, chubby, buxom, roly-poly, tubby, portly, stout, corpulent, podgy, fat, obese. **4** *use round language | she was round with him* blunt, candid, outspoken, frank, direct, plain, straightforward; *inf.* not pulling any punches. **5** *the round tones of the singer* sonorous, resonant, rich, full, mellow, flowing, orotund.

round noun **1** *shaped in a round | cut it in rounds* circle, circlet, ring, hoop, band, disk, cylinder, sphere, ball, globe, orb. **2** *a round of parties* succession, sequence, series, cycle. **3** *the milkman's/ doctor's round* circuit, course, ambit, beat, routine, schedule. **4** *two rounds left in the gun* bullet, cartridge, shell. **5** *the first round of the competition* stage, level, division, lap, heat, game.

round verb *round Cape Horn* go round, move round, travel round, sail round, circumnavigate. **round off 1** *round off the evening | round off his career* finish off, crown, cap, top off, complete, conclude, close, bring to a close/end, end, terminate. **2** *round off the edges* smooth, plane, level, sand. **round on** *she suddenly rounded on her tormentor* attack, set upon; *inf.* lay into, light into, lace into, tear into, lambaste. **round up** bring together, gather together, drive

together, assemble, collect, group, muster, marshal, rally.

roundabout adjective **1** *a roundabout route* indirect, circuitous, meandering, winding, tortuous. **2** *a roundabout way of saying it* indirect, circuitous, discursive, oblique, circumlocutory, periphrastic.

rouse verb **1** *rouse the sleeping children* wake, wake up, call, get up. **2** *he finds it difficult to rouse* wake up, awaken, get up, get out of bed, rise. **3** *rouse the crowds to protest | rouse himself to participate* stir up, bestir, excite, incite, egg on, induce, impel, inflame, agitate, whip up, galvanize, stimulate. **4** *the teacher was really roused* anger, annoy, infuriate, incense, exasperate, work up. **5** *rouse feelings of guilt* stir up, kindle, touch off, provoke, induce, evoke, call up, conjure up.

rousing adjective **1** *a rousing speech* inspiring, stimulating, exciting, stirring, inflammatory, moving, exhilarating, inspiriting, encouraging, vigorous, energetic, lively, spirited, enthusiastic, fervent. **2** *three rousing cheers* hearty, vigorous, loud, strong, great, tremendous.

rout noun **1** *troops put to rout* disorderly retreat, retreat, flight, headlong flight. **2** *suffer a rout at the hands of the enemy/opponents* crushing defeat, defeat, drubbing, trouncing, conquest, subjugation, overthrow, beating, thrashing; *inf.* licking, pasting.

rout verb **1** *they routed the enemy troops and chased them* put to rout/flight, drive off, dispel, scatter. **2** *they easily routed their enemy/opponents* defeat, drub, trounce, worst, conquer, subjugate, overthrow, crush, beat, thrash; *inf.* lick, give a pasting to.

route noun course, way, itinerary, road, path.

routine noun **1** *he hates to upset his routine* pattern, procedure, practice, custom, habit, wont, programme, schedule, formula, method, system, order, way. **2** *have heard the comic's routine before* act, performance, piece, line; *inf.* spiel.

routine adjective **1** *carry out routine procedure* usual, normal, everyday, workaday, common, ordinary, typical, customary, habitual, wonted, scheduled, conventional, standard. **2** *he finds the work too routine* boring, tedious, tiresome, monotonous, humdrum, run-of-the-mill, hackneyed, predictable, unexciting, uninspiring.
Opposites UNUSUAL; EXCITING.

row[1] noun **1** *a row of people* line, column, queue, procession, chain, string; *inf.* crocodile. **2** *a row of vegetables* line, column, sequence, series. **3** *a row of seats* line, tier, rank, bank.

row[2] noun **1** *the two brothers had a row* argument, dispute, disagreement, controversy, quarrel, squabble, tiff, fight, conflict, altercation, brawl, affray, wrangle, scuffle, free-for-all, fracas, mêlée; *inf.* falling-out, set-to, scrap. **2** *the row coming from the party* noise, din, clamour, commotion, rumpus, uproar, tumult, hubbub, babel, pandemonium. **3** *the children got a row* reprimand, reproof, scolding, chiding, lecture, castigation; *inf.* dressing-down, telling-off, ticking-off, talking-to, rollicking, flea in one's ear, bawling-out.

row³ *verb the brothers are rowing again* argue, quarrel, squabble, fight, wrangle, brawl; *inf.* scrap.

rowdy *adjective rowdy drunks* unruly, disorderly, noisy, boisterous, loud, obstreperous, wild, rough, unrestrained, lawless.
Opposites PEACEFUL; QUIET; LAW-ABIDING.

rowdy *noun police arresting rowdies* ruffian, thug, hooligan, troublemaker, brawler; *inf.* tearaway, tough, rough.

royal *adjective* **1** *a royal wave* kingly, queenly, kinglike, queenlike, princely, regal, monarchical, sovereign. **2** *royal surroundings* majestic, magnificent, impressive, glorious, splendid, imposing, grand, superb. **3** *have a royal time* excellent, fine, first-rate, first-class, marvellous, wonderful.

royalty *noun. See table.*

ROYALTY OF THE WORLD

Reigning Monarch	Country
Sheikh al-Khalifa	Bahrain
King Albert II	Belgium
H.M. Jigme Singye Wangchuck	Bhutan
H.M. Sultan Haji Hassanal Bolkiah	Brunei
King Sihanouk	Cambodia
Queen Margrethe II	Denmark
Emperor Akihito	Japan
King Hussein ibn Talal	Jordan
Sheikh Al-Sabah	Kuwait
King Moshoeshoe III	Lesotho
Prince Hans Adam II	Liechtenstein
Grand Duke Jean	Luxembourg
Sultan Tuanku Abdul Rahman (until 1999)	Malaysia
Prince Rainier III	Monaco
King Hassan II	Morocco
King Birendra Bir Bikram Shah Dev	Nepal
Queen Beatrix	Netherlands
King Harald V	Norway
Sultan Qaboos bin Said	Oman
Sheikh al-Thani	Qatar
King Fahd ibn Abdul Aziz	Saudi Arabia
King Juan Carlos I	Spain
King Mswati III	Swaziland
King Carl XVI Gustaf	Sweden
King Bhumibol Adulyadej	Thailand
King Taufa'ahau Tupou IV	Tonga
Queen Elizabeth II	U.K.

---

rub *verb* **1** *rub her sore neck* massage, knead, embrocate. **2** *rub the cat's back* stroke, caress, fondle, pat. **3** *rub the silver lamp* polish, buff up, burnish. **4** *rub the dirty mark/floor* scrub, scour, wipe, clean. **5** *rub in the ointment* apply, put on, smear, spread, work in. **6** *rub off/out the message* erase, wipe off, efface, obliterate, expunge, remove, cancel, delete.

rub *noun* **1** *give her neck a rub* massage, kneading, embrocation, friction. **2** *give the cat's back a rub* stroke, caress. *See* RUB *verb* 2. **3** *give the lamp a rub* polish, buffing, burnishing. **4** *give*
the floor a rub scrub, scour, wipe, clean. **5** *there's the rub* difficulty, problem, trouble, drawback, snag, hitch, hindrance, obstacle, obstruction, impediment.

rubbish *noun* **1** *put the rubbish in bins* waste, refuse, litter, lumber, junk, debris, detritus, dross, rubble, scrap, flotsam and jetsam; sweepings, leavings, dregs, offscourings, odds and ends; *Am.* garbage, trash. **2** *talking rubbish* nonsense, stuff and nonsense, drivel, gibberish, balderdash, bunkum, twaddle, moonshine; *Scots* havers; *inf.* rot, tommy-rot, bunk, gobbledegook, bosh, piffle, hogwash, codswallop, guff, tosh.

ruddy *adjective* **1** *a ruddy complexion* red, reddish, pink, pinkish, rosy, rosy-cheeked, rubicund, flushed, blushing, glowing, fresh, healthy. **2** *what a ruddy cheek!* damnable, abominable, diabolical, flaming; *inf.* bloody.

rude *adjective* **1** *rude children | being rude to old people* ill-mannered, bad-mannered, mannerless, impolite, discourteous, impertinent, insolent, impudent, cheeky, uncivil, disrespectful, churlish, curt, brusque, blunt, offhand, short, offensive. **2** *rude tools* primitive, crude, rudimentary, rough, rough-hewn, simple. **3** *rude peasants* simple, artless, uncivilized, uneducated, untutored, ignorant, illiterate, uncultured, unrefined, rough, coarse, uncouth, oafish, loutish. **4** *rude jokes* vulgar, coarse, indelicate, smutty, dirty, naughty, risqué, blue, ribald, bawdy, licentious. **5** *a rude awakening* sudden, abrupt, sharp, violent, startling, harsh, unpleasant, disagreeable, nasty.
Opposites POLITE; SOPHISTICATED; CLEAN.

rudimentary *adjective* **1** *rudimentary arithmetic* elementary, basic, fundamental, introductory, early. **2** *rudimentary tools* primitive, crude, rough, simple. **3** *a rudimentary organ* undeveloped, immature, incomplete, vestigial.
Opposites ADVANCED; SOPHISTICATED.

rudiments *plural noun* basics, fundamentals, beginnings, elements, essentials; foundation; *inf.* nuts and bolts.

rue *verb live to rue her actions* regret, be sorry about, feel apologetic/remorseful about, feel remorse for.

rueful *adjective* regretful, apologetic, sorry, remorseful, contrite, repentant, penitent, conscience-stricken, self-reproachful, woebegone, woeful, plaintive.

ruffian *noun* thug, villain, scoundrel, hoodlum, hooligan, rogue, rascal, miscreant; *inf.* rough, tough, rowdy.

ruffle *verb* **1** *ruffle feathers* disarrange, discompose, disorder, derange, rumple, dishevel, tousle, tangle, mess up; *inf.* muss up. **2** *she gets ruffled in a crisis* annoy, irritate, irk, vex, nettle, rile, anger, exasperate, fluster, agitate, harass, upset, disturb, discompose, perturb, unsettle, disconcert, worry, alarm, trouble, confuse; *inf.* rattle, shake up, hassle.

Rugby *noun. See table. See also table at* SPORT.

rugged *adjective* **1** *rugged terrain* rough, uneven, irregular, bumpy, rocky, stony, broken up, jagged, craggy, precipitous. **2** *rugged features* wrinkled, furrowed, lined, gnarled, irreg-

ular, weather-beaten, leathery. **3** *rugged manners | a rugged beauty* unrefined, unpolished, uncultured, crude, unsophisticated, graceless, inelegant. **4** *you have to be rugged to survive there* tough, hardy, robust, sturdy, strong, vigorous, stalwart, hale and hearty, muscular, brawny, solid, mighty, burly, well-built; *inf.* husky, beefy. **5** *a rugged way of life* tough, harsh, austere, spartan, exacting, taxing, demanding, difficult, hard, arduous, rigorous, strenuous, onerous.
Opposites SMOOTH; REFINED; FEEBLE.

ruin *noun* **1** *cities in a state of ruin | his plans in ruin* ruination, destruction, devastation, havoc, wreckage, demolition, disintegration, dilapidation, desolation, decay, disrepair. **2** *the ruin of the army | the ruin of his hopes* ruination, downfall, overthrow, defeat, undoing, conquest, elimination, termination, end. **3** *firms facing ruin* ruination, loss, failure, bankruptcy, insolvency, financial failure, deprivation, penury, impoverishment, indigence, destitution, calamity, disaster. **4** *castle ruins | the ruins of our hopes* remains, relics, remnants, vestiges; wreckage, wreck, remainder, debris, detritus.

ruin *verb* **1** *the rain ruined the crops/dresses | it ruined our plans* damage, spoil, wreak havoc on, mar, injure, wreck, botch, make a mess of, mess up, smash, shatter. **2** *the recession ruined him* bring to ruin, bankrupt, make insolvent, impoverish, pauperize. **3** *invading armies ruining cities | decisions ruining our hopes | armies leaving ruined cities* destroy, devastate, lay waste, raze, demolish, crush.
Opposites CREATE; RESTORE; ENHANCE; ENRICH.

ruinous *adjective* **1** *a ruinous agreement | ruinous expenses* disastrous, devastating, calamitous, catastrophic, cataclysmic, dire, injurious, damaging, crippling, destructive. **2** *ruinous old buildings* in ruins, ruined, dilapidated, decaying, in disrepair, derelict, ramshackle, brokendown, decrepit.

rule *noun* **1** *obey the rules of the realm/society* ruling, law, by-law, regulation, statute, ordinance, tenet, canon, order, court order, decree, commandment, directive, guideline. **2** *it is a good rule to wait for others to speak* principle, precept, standard, axiom, truth, truism, maxim, aphorism, motto. **3** *as a general rule children are not allowed* practice, procedure, routine, custom, habit, wont, convention, standard, form. **4** *under the rule of the Tudors | the rule of the present government* reign, dominion, sovereignty, kingship, queenship, regime, government, administration, jurisdiction, authority, control, direction, mastery, leadership, command, ascendancy, supremacy, power, sway, influence. **as a rule** generally, in general, usually, normally, ordinarily, for the most part, on the whole, mainly.

rule *verb* **1** *the king/president/administration rules over a wide area* preside over, govern, control, have control of, dominate, direct, administer, manage, regulate. **2** *the king ruled for ten years* reign, sit on the throne, wear the crown, wield the sceptre. **3** *the last administration ruled for only a few months* be in power, be in control, be in authority, be in command, be in charge, govern; *inf.* be at the helm. **4** *the judge ruled that he be released* order, decree, direct, pronounce, make a judgement, judge, adjudge, adjudicate, lay down, decide, determine, resolve, settle, establish. **5** *let common sense rule* prevail, obtain, hold sway, predominate, preponderate. **rule out** *rule out the possibility of arson* preclude, exclude, eliminate, reject, dismiss, disregard, ignore.

ruler *noun* sovereign, monarch, king, queen, emperor, empress, head of state, head, governor, president, overlord, chief, chieftain, lord, commander, leader.

ruling *noun* judgement, adjudication, finding, verdict, resolution, decree, pronouncement.

ruling *adjective* **1** *the ruling monarch* reigning, regnant, on the throne. **2** *the ruling classes* dominant, controlling, governing, commanding, leading, in charge, upper. **3** *the ruling theory* prevalent, predominant, main, chief, principal, widespread, general, popular, universal.

ruminate *verb* **1** *sit and ruminate | ruminating on her problems* think, contemplate, deliberate, ponder, brood, meditate, muse, cogitate; think about, think over, give thought to, consider, mull over, brood about, chew over; *inf.* put on one's thinking cap. **2** *cows ruminating* chew the cud.

rummage *verb* *rummage through drawers/papers* search through, hunt through, forage through, rifle, ransack, turn over, pry into.

rumour *noun* **1** *rumour has it that he has gone* gossip, hearsay, talk; *inf.* the grapevine. **2** *hear a rumour that he has gone* report, story, whisper, canard; information, word, news; tidings; *inf.* buzz.

rumour *verb* *it is rumoured that they are wealthy | they are rumoured to be wealthy* say, report,

---

RUGBY POSITIONS AND ROLES

attacker	front row	lock (forward)	second row
back row	front-head forward	loose head (prop)	second-row forward
back-row forward	full-back	loose forward	stand-off half
ball carrier	half-back	number eight	three-quarter
blocker	hooker	prop (forward)	tight end
centre	jumper	right centre three-	tight head (prop)
defender	left centre three-	quarter	try scorer
flanker	quarter	right wing three-	winger
fly-half	left wing three-	quarter	wing forward
forward	quarter	scrum half	wing (three-quarter)

think, give out, put about, circulate, spread, pass around, noise abroad, disseminate, gossip, hint, suggest.

rumple verb **1** *rumple clothes* crumple, crease, wrinkle, crush, crinkle. **2** *rumple hair* disarrange, tousle, dishevel, ruffle, mess up; *inf.* muss up.

rumpus noun disturbance, row, uproar, commotion, brouhaha, fracas, brawl, free-for-all, mêlée, riot.

run verb **1** *she ran to catch the bus* race, rush, hasten, hurry, dash, sprint, bolt, dart, gallop, career along, tear along, charge along, speed along, jog along, scurry, scamper, scramble; *inf.* scoot, hare, step on it, get a move on, hotfoot it, stir one's stumps. **2** *the prisoners ran from the camp* abscond, flee, take flight, take oneself off, make off, decamp, bolt, beat a retreat, make a run for it, show a clean pair of heels, clear out, make one's getaway, escape; *inf.* beat it, scarper, vamoose, skedaddle, split, cut and run, do a runner, hightail it. **3** *trains run on tracks* move, go, get along, travel. **4** *the river runs by* glide, course, roll, slide. **5** *leave the engine running* go, operate, function. **6** *the lease runs for 20 years* operate, be in operation, be valid, be current, continue. **7** *the play is running at the Empire Theatre* be staged, be presented, be performed, be on, be put on. **8** *the road runs along the coast | the path runs from the lake to the village* go, continue, proceed, extend, stretch. **9** *prices/tempers are running high* get, go, reach, stretch. **10** *he has decided not to run in a race* compete, take part, enter, be in the race. **11** *run for president* stand for, stand for election as, stand as candidate for, be a contender for, put oneself forward for. **12** *water running* flow, issue, stream, pour, gush, cascade, spurt, jet, trickle, leak. **13** *walls running with water* be wet with, stream with, flow with, drip with, be flooded by. **14** *run the water* turn on, switch on. **15** *ink ran over the surface* spread, spread over, be diffused, extend, stretch. **16** *the dye from the shirt ran on to the trousers* spread, be diffused, bleed, mix with. **17** *the butter ran* melt, dissolve, liquefy, thaw. **18** *he'll never run the course* travel, traverse, go over, complete, finish. **19** *run an errand* go on, do, carry out, perform, fulfil, execute. **20** *the newspaper ran a story about the accident* publish, print, feature, carry. **21** *run a business | run the firm* own, operate, conduct, carry on, direct, manage, administer, be in charge/control of, control, head, lead, look after, organize, coordinate, supervise, superintend, oversee; *inf.* boss. **22** *run a car* drive, own, possess, have. **23** *run the children to school* drive, transport, convey. **24** *run guns* smuggle, traffic in, deal in, bootleg. **25** *run them out of town* chase, drive, propel, hunt, put to flight. **26** *ideas running through my mind* go, pass, dart, flow, slide. **27** *run your eye over the page* pass, slide, flick. **28** *tights/stockings running* ladder, unravel, tear, be snagged. **29** *her eyes are running because of the cold* stream, exude/secrete/ooze liquid. **run across** *run across an old friend* run into, come across, chance upon, stumble upon; *inf.* bump into. **run away 1** *the prisoners have run away* abscond, flee, make off, bolt,

decamp, clear out, escape. See RUN verb 2. **2** *he tries to run away from the problems* avoid, evade, disregard, ignore, take no notice of, pay no attention to, put to the back of one's mind, turn one's back on. **run away with 1** *run away with his daughter* run off with, elope with, abduct, make off with. **2** *run away with the firm's takings* run off with, make off with, abscond with, snatch, steal, purloin; *inf.* pinch, nick, swipe. **3** *run away with the race* win easily; *inf.* win hands down, win by a mile, walk it. **run down 1** *the driver ran down an old woman* knock down, knock over, knock to the ground. **2** *run down the workforce* cut back on, cut, curtail, pare down, trim, reduce, decrease. **3** *my watch has run down* stop, halt, cease to function/operate. **4** *the British manufacturing industry has been running down for years* decline, wane, diminish, dwindle, become less effective; *inf.* lose steam. **5** *she finally ran down the book in a second-hand shop* run to earth, unearth, track down, ferret out, hunt out, dredge up, find, discover, locate. **6** *she's always running down her neighbour* speak ill/badly of, disparage, denigrate, criticize, decry, belittle, revile, vilify; *inf.* knock. **run high** *feelings are running high* be strong, be vehement, be fervent/fervid, be passionate. **run in 1** *run in a new car* drive gently/slowly, break in. **2** *the police finally ran him in* arrest, apprehend, take into custody, jail; *inf.* pull in, collar, nab, nick, bust. **run into 1** *another car ran into ours* bump into, knock into, collide with, crash into, hit, strike, ram. **2** *I ran into an old friend* run across, chance on; *inf.* bump into. See RUN verb run across. **3** *the cost runs into thousands of pounds* reach, extend to, be as high/much as. **run low** *supplies are running low* dwindle, diminish, get less, become depleted, become exhausted. **run off 1** *the children/dog ran off* run away, flee, make off, bolt, beat a retreat, show a clean pair of heels, make one's getaway, clear out, escape; *inf.* beat it, scarper, hightail it. **2** *run off several copies* copy, duplicate, xerox, mimeograph. **run off with 1** *run off with her daughter* run away with, elope. See RUN verb run away with 1. **2** *run off with the takings* run away with, abscond with, snatch, steal. See RUN verb run away with 2. **run on 1** *I hope the meeting will not run on into the afternoon* go on, continue, carry on, keep going, last. **2** *she does run on* talk a lot, talk incessantly, chatter on, ramble on; *inf.* rabbit on, witter on, natter on. **run out** *supplies have run out | run out of food* be finished, give out, dry up, fail, be exhausted; exhaust. **run out on** *he has run out on his wife* desert, abandon, forsake, jilt; *inf.* leave high and dry, leave in the lurch, leave holding the baby, rat on. **run over 1** *run over a rabbit* run down, knock down, knock over, hit. **2** *the bath water's running over* overflow, overbrim, spill over. **3** *run over a speech | run over the figures for tomorrow* run through, look over, go over, go through. **4** *could you run over yesterday's work?* run through, go over, repeat, iterate, recapitulate; *inf.* recap. **run through 1** *run through the speech/figures for tomorrow* run over, go over, look over, look through. **2** *could you run through yesterday's work?* run over, go over, repeat, recapitulate. **3** *run through money* go

through, squander, fritter away, dissipate, waste; *inf.* blow. **4** *an air of sadness runs through the book* go through, pervade, permeate, suffuse. **5** *the knight ran through his enemy with his spear* pierce, transfix, stab. **run to 1** *the cost runs to thousands* run into, reach, extend to, be as high/much as. **2** *we can't run to a new car* afford, have/be sufficient for. **3** *the family runs to fat* tend to, be disposed/inclined to.
Opposites WALK; CRAWL.

run noun **1** *go for a run | break into a run* jog, sprint, dash, gallop, canter, headlong rush, scamper. *See* RUN *verb* 1. **2** *go for a run in the car/bus* drive, ride, trip, outing, excursion, jaunt, short journey; *inf.* spin, tootle. **3** *the train-driver operates on the Edinburgh to London run* route, way, course, itinerary. **4** *a run of fine weather | a run of luck/disasters* period, spell, stretch, streak, chain, string, round, cycle, sequence, series, succession. **5** *a run on sterling/ice-cream* demand, rush, clamour. **6** *different from the general run of applicants* kind, variety, type, sort, class, category, order. **7** *against the run of play | the recent run of events* tendency, trend, tide, course, direction, movement, drift, current, stream. **8** *the chickens' run* enclosure, pen, coop. **9** *a run in her tights* ladder, rip, tear, snag. **in the long run** *he will have to pay in the long run* eventually, in the end, ultimately, when all is said and done, in the final analysis. **on the run** *prisoners on the run* running away, fleeing, in flight, bolting, escaping.

runaway noun *runaways from the children's home* absconder, deserter, escapee, fugitive, truant.

runaway adjective **1** *a runaway horse* escaped, loose, on the loose, uncontrolled, out of control, wild. **2** *runaway children from the home* absconding, escaping, fugitive. **3** *a runaway victory* effortless, easy; *inf.* peasy, easy as pie.

rundown noun **1** *been a rundown in the workforce* cut, curtailment, reduction, decrease. *See* RUN *verb* run down 2. **2** *a rundown in British industry* decline, waning, diminution. *See* RUN *verb* run down 4. **3** *give them the rundown on/of the situation* analysis, briefing, brief, review, summary, résumé, sketch, outline; *inf.* lowdown.

run-down adjective **1** *run-down property* dilapidated, tumbledown, ramshackle, broken-down, decaying, decayed, in ruins, ruined, gone to wrack and ruin, seedy, shabby, slummy. **2** *feel run-down after an illness* debilitated, out of condition, below par, drained, exhausted, fatigued, tired, enervated, worn-out, unhealthy; *inf.* not oneself, under the weather, pooped.
Opposites FIT; WELL.

runner noun **1** *twenty runners in the field* racer, sprinter, hurdler, harrier, jogger, athlete. **2** *runners from the plant* branch, shoot, offshoot, tendril. **3** *give the message to the runner* messenger, courier, dispatch rider, bearer, errand boy/girl.

running noun **1** *take part in the running* racing, race, sprinting, sprint, jogging. **2** *his running of the firm* direction, administration, controlling, organization, coordination, supervision.

See RUN *verb* 21. **3** *the smooth running of the business* operation, working, functioning, performance. **4** *out of the running for the job* competition, contest, contention.

running adjective **1** *a running battle* continuous, unceasing, incessant, ceaseless, uninterrupted, constant, perpetual. **2** *three weeks running* in a row, in succession, one after the other; *inf.* on the trot. **3** *running water* flowing, streaming, gushing. *See* RUN *verb* 12.

run-of-the-mill adjective ordinary, average, common, middling, mediocre, commonplace, everyday, undistinguished, unexceptional, passable, tolerable, acceptable, fair, not bad; *inf.* common or garden, nothing special, so-so.
Opposites EXTRAORDINARY; EXCEPTIONAL.

rupture noun **1** *a rupture in the defences* break, fracture, crack, split, burst, rent, tear, rift, fissure. **2** *the rupture of the defences/artery* breaking, fracture, cracking, splitting, bursting. *See* RUPTURE *verb* 1. **3** *there has been a rupture in their relationship | ruptures exist within the party* rift, estrangement, schism, break-up, breach, division, alienation, variance, disagreement, quarrel, feud; *inf.* falling-out. **4** *an operation for a rupture* hernia.

rupture verb **1** *rupture the defences | rupture an organ* break, fracture, crack, split, breach, burst, rend, tear, puncture. **2** *rupture East-West relations* sever, cut off, break off, disrupt, breach.

rural adjective country, countryside, pastoral, rustic, agricultural, agrarian, Arcadian.
Opposites URBAN; CITY; TOWN.

ruse noun trick, stratagem, subterfuge, artifice, device, wile, dodge, ploy, machination, manoeuvre, tactic, deception, hoax, blind.

rush verb **1** *rush to the door* hurry, make haste, hasten, run, race, dash, sprint, bolt, dart, gallop, career, tear, charge, speed, scurry, scamper; *inf.* step on it, get a move on, hotfoot it. **2** *rush the enemy* attack, assault, charge, storm, take by storm, capture, seize. **3** *rush the job through* hurry, hasten, expedite, speed up, accelerate, advance, hustle, press, push.
Opposites DAWDLE; DELAY.

rush noun **1** *make a rush on the enemy* onslaught, attack, assault, charge. **2** *a rush of water/blood* surge, flow, gush, stream, flood. **3** *no rush for the goods* hurry, haste, speed, swiftness, rapidity, dispatch. **4** *a rush for toys* demand, clamour, run (on). **5** *the Christmas rush* activity, bustle, hubbub, flurry. **6** *rushes growing by the stream* bulrush. *See table at* GRASS.

rushed adjective *a rushed job* hurried, hasty, speedy, quick, fast, swift, rapid, expeditious, prompt.

rustic adjective **1** *rustic scenes* country, countryside, rural, pastoral, agricultural, agrarian, Arcadian, bucolic. **2** *rustic pleasures* unsophisticated, plain, simple, homely, homespun. **3** *rustic peasants* artless, plain, simple, homely, unassuming, guileless, naive, ingenuous, unsophisticated, uncultured, unrefined, unpolished, homespun, coarse, rough, indelicate, uncouth, graceless, awkward, clumsy, inept,

maladroit, blundering, lumbering, clod-hopping, churlish, boorish.
Opposites URBAN; CITY; TOWN.

rustic noun countryman, countrywoman, countryperson, peasant, son/daughter of the soil, country cousin/bumpkin, yokel; Am. inf. hillbilly, hayseed.

rustle verb 1 silk rustling | trees rustling in the wind swish, whisper, whoosh. 2 rustle cattle steal, purloin, filch, plunder, abduct, kidnap.

rusty adjective 1 rusty parts on the car rusted, rust-covered, corroded, oxidized. 2 a rusty dress rust-coloured, reddish, reddish-brown, russet, brick-red, brick. 3 his French is a bit rusty deficient, impaired, diminished, weak,

below par, unpractised, out of practice, neglected, not what it was. 4 his voice is a bit rusty hoarse, croaking, cracked.

rut noun 1 farm roads full of ruts furrow, groove, track, crack, hollow, hole, pothole, trough, gutter, ditch. 2 in a rut in his job humdrum existence, routine job, boring routine; inf. daily grind, treadmill, dead end.

ruthless adjective merciless, unmerciful, pitiless, compassionless, relentless, unrelenting, remorseless, unforgiving, unsparing, inexorable, implacable, heartless, unfeeling, hard, harsh, severe, stern, grim, cruel, vicious, brutal, barbarous, callous, savage, fierce, ferocious.
Opposites MERCIFUL; COMPASSIONATE; GENTLE.

S s

sable *adjective* black, jet-black, jet, pitch-black, pitch, black as pitch, raven, ink-black, inky, black as ink, coal-black, black as coal, black as night.

sabotage *noun* **1** *the fire at the factory was an act of sabotage* deliberate destruction/damage/ wrecking, impairment/incapacitation, subversive destruction, vandalism. **2** *the sabotage of our plans* disruption, spoiling, ruining, wrecking; *inf.* fouling up.

sabotage *verb* **1** *sabotage the factory machinery* deliberately destroy/damage/wreck, impair, incapacitate, cripple, vandalize; *inf.* foul up. **2** *sabotage our plans* disrupt, spoil, ruin, wreck; *inf.* throw a spanner in the works of, put the kibosh on, foul up.

saccharine *adjective* **1** *saccharine desserts* oversweet, cloying. **2** *saccharine words of farewell* | *saccharine novels* mawkish, maudlin, sentimental; *inf.* soppy, mushy, schmaltzy.

sack¹ *noun* **1** *sacks of coal/flour* bag, pack. **2** *get the sack* dismissal, discharge, redundancy, termination of employment; *inf.* one's cards, one's marching orders, the boot, the old heave-ho, the push, the chop, the axe. **3** *longing for one's sack after a hard day* bed, bunk; *inf.* pit, kip. **hit the sack** go to bed, retire, go to sleep; *inf.* turn in, hit the hay, go to one's pit, go to one's kip.

sack² *verb* *sack workers for stealing* discharge, dismiss, terminate someone's employment, declare redundant, give the sack; *inf.* kick out, give someone his/her cards, give someone his/ her marching orders, boot out, give the boot to, give someone the old heave-ho, give someone the push/chop/axe.

sack³ *verb* *enemy soldiers sacking the city* plunder, ransack, raid, loot, strip, rob, rifle, pillage, maraud, harry, forage, lay waste, wreak havoc on, destroy, ruin, devastate, ravage, vandalize, despoil, rape.

sack⁴ *noun* *the sack of the city* plunder, ransack, raid, looting, stripping, robbing, pillage, marauding, harrying, destruction, ruin, devastation, ravaging, vandalization, vandalism, despoliation, rape, rapine. *See* SACK ² *verb.*

sackcloth *noun* **1** *aprons of sackcloth* sacking, hopsacking, ginny, burlap. *See table at* FABRIC. **2** *wearing sackcloth* mourning, funeral garments, penitential garments. **in sackcloth and ashes** penitent, penitential, repentant, contrite, sorry, remorseful, regretful, conscience-stricken, guilt-ridden, ashamed, chastened, compunctious.

sacred *adjective* **1** *a sacred place* holy, blessed, blest, hallowed, consecrated, sanctified. **2** *sacred music* religious, spiritual, devotional, church, churchly, ecclesiastical. **3** *sacred beings* godly, divine, deified, supreme, venerated. **4** *in Hinduism the cow is sacred* sacrosanct, inviolable, inviolate, unimpeachable, invulnerable, protected, defended, secure, safe, unthreatened.
Opposites PROFANE; SECULAR; TEMPORAL.

sacred text *noun. See table. See also table at* BIBLE.

SACRED TEXTS AND HOLY BOOKS	
Text	**Religion**
Analects of Confucius	Confucianism
Atharva-veda	Hinduism
Bhagavadgita	Hinduism
Bible	Christianity
Guru Granth Sahib	Sikhism
I Ching	Confucianism
Koran	Islam
Li Chi	Confucianism
Mahabharata	Hinduism
Ramayana	Hinduism
Rig-veda	Hinduism
Sama-veda	Hinduism
Shih Ching	Confucianism
Shu Ching	Confucianism
Talmud	Judaism
Tao Te Ching	Taoism
Torah	Judaism
Tripitaka	Buddhism
Yajur-veda	Hinduism

sacrifice *noun* **1** *the job wasn't worth the sacrifice of her principles* giving up, renunciation, abandonment, surrender, relinquishment, yielding, ceding, forfeiture. **2** *make many sacrifices to educate their children* renunciation, relinquishment, loss, self-sacrifice. **3** *give the goat as a sacrifice to their god* offering, gifts, oblation, burnt offering. **4** *the sacrifice of the goat to their god* offering, immolations, hecatomb.

sacrifice *verb* **1** *sacrifice her principles for the job* give up, forgo, renounce, abandon, surrender, relinquish, yield, cede, forfeit. **2** *sacrifice the goat to the god* offer up, offer, immolate.

sacrilege *noun* *sacrilege to vandalize the cross* desecration, profanity, profaneness, profanation, blasphemy, impiety, irreverence, irreligion, godlessness, disrespect.

sacrilegious *adjective* profane, blasphemous, impious, irreverent, irreligious, godless, disrespectful.

sad *adjective* **1** *feeling/looking sad about his departure* unhappy, miserable, sorrowful, gloomy, melancholy, blue, mournful, woebegone, wretched, dejected, downcast, despondent, in low spirits, low-spirited, low, downhearted, depressed, doleful, glum, cheerless, dispirited, disconsolate, heart-broken, broken-hearted, sick at heart, grief-stricken,

grieving; *inf.* down, down in the dumps, down in the mouth, in the pits. **2** *the sad events of the past* unhappy, unfortunate, sorrowful, miserable, sorry, depressing, upsetting, distressing, dispiriting, heart-breaking, heart-rending, pitiful, pitiable, grievous, tragic, disastrous, calamitous. **3** *the country is in a sad state* sorry, wretched, deplorable, lamentable, regrettable, unfortunate, pitiful, pitiable, pathetic, shameful, disgraceful.
Opposites HAPPY; CHEERFUL; FORTUNATE.

sadden *verb* cast down, deject, depress, dishearten, dispirit, dampen one's spirits, cast a gloom upon, desolate, upset, distress, grieve, break one's heart, make one's heart bleed. *See* SAD 1.

sadness *noun* *she was full of sadness* unhappiness, misery, sorrow, gloom, melancholy, wretchedness, dejection, despondency, low spirits, depression, dolefulness, glumness, cheerlessness, disconsolateness, brokenheartedness, heartache, grief. *See* SAD 1.

safe *adjective* **1** *the children are safe in bed | the jewels are safe in the bank* safe and sound, secure, protected, sheltered, guarded, defended, free from harm/danger, out of harm's way. **2** *the kidnapped children are safe* unharmed, all right, alive and well, well, unhurt, uninjured, unscathed, undamaged, out of danger; *inf.* OK, out of the woods. **3** *the place/building is quite safe* secure, sound, riskfree, riskless, impregnable, unassailable.
4 *he's a safe person to leave the children with* reliable, dependable, responsible, trustworthy, tried and true, reputable, upright, honest, honourable. **5** *he's a safe driver | on the safe side* reliable, cautious, circumspect, prudent, unadventurous, conservative, timid, unenterprising. **6** *these drugs are quite safe for children* harmless, innocuous, non-toxic, non-poisonous, wholesome.
Opposites INSECURE; DANGEROUS; UNRELIABLE; HARMFUL.

safe *noun* *put money/jewellery in the safe* strongbox, safety-deposit box, safe-deposit box, cash-box, repository, depository, locker, vault, crypt.

safeguard *noun* *they need to have some safeguard against fraud* protection, defence, preventive, precaution, security, surety.

safeguard *verb* *you must safeguard your investment in the firm* protect, look after, defend, guard, preserve, secure.
Opposites ENDANGER.

safekeeping *noun* *leave the children in her safekeeping* protection, care, charge, keeping, surveillance, custody, guardianship, trusteeship, wardship.

safety *noun* **1** *worry about the safety of the children/jewels* safeness, security, secureness. *See* SAFE *adjective* 1. **2** *worry about the safety of the place/building* security, secureness, soundness, riskiness, impregnability, assailability. **3** *check her safety as a baby-sitter* reliability, dependability, responsibility, trustworthiness, reputableness. *See* SAFE *adjective* 4. **4** *ships/refugees reaching safety* shelter, sanctuary, refuge.

sag *verb* **1** *the ceiling sags | the cake sags in the middle* sink, subside, curve down, slump. **2** *the hem of the skirt sags* hang unevenly, droop. **3** *his spirits sagged as the bus passed him by* fall, flag, fail, wilt, falter, weaken, languish. **4** *industrial production has sagged* fall, decline, decrease, diminish, sink, plummet, tumble; *inf.* take a nose-dive.

saga *noun* epic, chronicle, legend, history, romance.

sage *adjective* **1** *give sage advice* wise, judicious, prudent, sensible, shrewd, politic. **2** *he's a sage old man* wise, sagacious, learned, intelligent, acute, shrewd, discerning, perspicacious; *lit.* sapient.

sage *noun* wise man/woman, learned man/woman, man/woman of letters, philosopher, thinker, savant, pundit, authority, expert, guru.

sail *verb* **1** *learn to sail* boat, cruise, yacht, ride the waves, go by water, go on a sea voyage, voyage. **2** *we sail tonight* set sail, embark, put to sea, leave port/dock, hoist sail, raise sail, put off, shove off. **3** *he is sailing the ship* steer, captain, pilot, navigate. **4** *swans/clouds sailing by* glide, drift, float, slide, sweep, skim. **5** *sail into the air* soar, wing, fly. **sail into** *he really sailed into the driver of the other car* attack, set about, fall upon, belabour; *inf.* lay into, lambaste. **sail through** *sail through the exams* pass easily, gain success in easily; *inf.* walk.

sail *noun. See table. See also table at* RIGGING.

SAILS		
Bermuda rig	gaff-topsail	royal sail
canvas	Genoa jib	skysail
course	headsail	spanker
fore-and-aft	jib	spinnaker
sail	jigger	spritsail
fore-course	kite	square
fore-royal	lateen sail	sail
foresail	lugsail	staysail
forestaysail	main-course	studding-
fore-	mainsail	sail
topgallant	maintopsail	topgallant
fore-topsail	mizzen	topsail
gaff foresail	moonraker	trysail

sailing ship *noun. See table.*

sailor *noun* seaman, seafaring man, seafarer, mariner, marine, salt, sea dog, boatman, yachtsman/woman; *inf.* tar, Jack Tar, matelot.

saint *noun. See table.*

saintly *adjective* saintlike, sainted, holy, godly, pious, God-fearing, religious, devout, blessed, virtuous, righteous, good, moral, ethical, unworldly, innocent, sinless, blameless, pure, angelic.

sake *noun* **1** *pardon her for her mother's sake* good, wellbeing, welfare, behalf, benefit, advantage, interest, gain, profit, consideration, regard, concern, account, respect. **2** *for the sake of peace we agreed* cause, reason, purpose, aim, end, objective, object, goal, motive.

salacious *adjective* **1** *salacious literature* lewd, obscene, pornographic, crude, ribald, blue, smutty, filthy, dirty, indecent, indelicate. **2** *he's a salacious young rascal* lustful, lecherous, randy, libidinous, licentious, lascivious, promiscuous, loose, wanton.

salary *noun* pay, earnings, remuneration, fee, emolument, stipend, honorarium.

sale *noun* **1** *not concerned in the actual sale of the cars* selling, vending, bargaining. **2** *she gets commission on all sales* deal, transaction. **3** *a ready sale for high-quality furniture* markets, outlet, demand, buyers, purchasers, customers, consumers. **for sale** *cars/flowers for sale* on sale, on offer, to be bought/purchased, purchasable. **on sale** **1** *videos on sale now* for sale, in stock, on the market, purchasable, available, obtainable. **2** *end-of-season clothes on sale* reduced, marked down, discounted.

salient *adjective* *discuss the salient points* important, main, prominent, conspicuous, striking, noticeable, obvious, remarkable, pronounced, signal, arresting.
Opposites UNIMPORTANT; INCONSPICUOUS.

sallow *adjective* *looking rather sallow in the winter* yellowish, jaundiced-looking, pallid, wan, pale, waxen, anaemic, colourless, pasty, pasty-faced, unhealthy-looking, sickly-looking.
Opposites ROSY; GLOWING.

sally *noun* **1** *enemy troops making a sally into our territory* charge, sortie, foray, thrust, offensive, drive, attack, raid, assault, onset, rush, onrush. **2** *taking a quick sally to the seaside* trip, excursion, expedition, outing, jaunt, visit, tour, airing. **3** *coming out with a series of quick sallies* witticism, smart remark, bon mot, quip, joke, jest, barb; *inf.* wisecrack, crack.

salon *noun* *a hairdressing salon* shop, small shop, boutique.

salt *noun* **1** *salt added to the dish* sodium chloride, table salt, sea salt, rock salt. **2** *conversation in need of a little salt* spice, spiciness, flavour, piquancy, pungency, zest, bite, liveliness, vigour; *inf.* zing, zip, zap. **3** *old salts sitting by the harbour* sailor, seaman, mariner, seafarer; *inf.* tar, limey, matelot. **with a grain/pinch of salt** with reservations, sceptically, cynically, doubtfully, suspiciously, disbelievingly.

salt *adjective* *salt water* salted, salty, saline, briny, brackish.

salty *adjective* **1** *salty water* salted, saline, briny, brackish. **2** *a salty after-dinner speech* spicy, piquant, pungent, biting, zestful, tangy, lively, vigorous.

salubrious *adjective* *living in a not very salubrious place/climate* healthy, health-giving, healthful, beneficial, good for one's health, wholesome, salutary, refreshing, invigorating, bracing.
Opposites UNHEALTHY.

salutary *adjective* **1** *learn a salutary lesson* good, beneficial, good for one, advantageous, profitable, helpful, useful, valuable, practical, timely. **2** *salutary conditions* healthy, health-giving, healthful, wholesome. See SALUBRIOUS.

salutation *noun* greeting, salute, address, welcome.

salute *noun* **1** *raise his hat as a friendly salute* greeting, salutation, address, welcome. **2** *in salute of his services to the country* tribute, testimonial, honour, homage, recognition, acknowledgement.

salute *verb* **1** *salute one's neighbour in passing* greet, address, hail, acknowledge, pay one's respects to. **2** *salute the old man's achievement* pay tribute to, pay homage to, honour, recognize, acknowledge; *inf.* take one's hat off to.

salvage *noun* **1** *the salvage of the ship* rescue, saving, recovery, reclamation, salvation. **2** *council workers collecting salvage for recycling* waste material, waste paper, scraps, remains.

salvage *verb* **1** *succeed in salvaging the ship* rescue, save, recover. **2** *salvage valuable articles from the fire* | *salvage her pride* rescue, save, recover, retrieve, reclaim, get back.

salvation *noun* **1** *the salvation of sinners* redemption, deliverance, saving, rescue. **2** *regard his work as his salvation* lifeline, preservation, conservation.
Opposites DAMNATION; DOWNFALL; DESTRUCTION.

same *adjective* **1** *the same person I saw yesterday* identical, the very same, selfsame, one and the same, the very. **2** *family members having the same mannerisms* identical, alike, duplicate, twin, indistinguishable, interchangeable, corresponding, equivalent. **3** *this same man later died* selfsame, aforesaid, aforementioned. **4** *the same old food/story* unchanging,

---

SAILING SHIPS AND BOATS

barque	dromond	junk	nuggar	skipjack
barquentine	felucca	ketch	outrigger	sloop
brigantine	frigate	lateen	pink	sloop of war
caique	full-rigger	lighter	pinnace	smack
caravel	gaff cutter	longboat	polacre	snekkja
carrack	galleon	long-ship	proa	square-rigger
catamaran	galley	lugger	razee	tall ship
catboat	galliot	man-of-war	rigger	tartan
clipper	hermaphrodite	merchantman	sabot	trimaran
cutter	brig	merchant	schooner	windjammer
dhow	hooker	ship	scow	xebec
dinghy	in-rigger	monohull	shallop	yacht
dragon boat	jolly boat	multihull	skiff	yawl

SAINTS

Saint	Feast Day	Saint	Feast Day
Agnes of Bohemia	March 2	Gregory the Great	March 12
Agnes of Rome	January 21	Helena	May 21 (E. Ch.), August 18 (W. Ch.)
Aidan	August 31		
Alban	June 22	Hilary	January 13, January 14 (R.C. Ch.)
Albertus Magnus	November 15		
Alexander Nevsky	August 30, November 23	Ignatius Loyola	July 31
		Irenaeus	August 23 (E. Ch.), June 28 (W. Ch.)
Aloysius	June 21		
Ambrose	December 7	Isidore of Seville	April 4
Andrew	November 30	James the Great	July 25
Anne	July 26	James the Just	May 1
Anselm	April 21	James the Less	October 9 (E. Ch.), May 1 (W. Ch.)
Anthony	January 17		
Anthony of Padua	June 13	Jerome	September 30
Athanasius	May 2	Joan of Arc	May 30
Augustine (of Canterbury)	May 26	John of Damascus	December 4
		John of the Cross	December 14
Augustine (of Hippo)	August 28	John the Baptist	June 24
Barnabas	June 11	John the Evangelist	December 27
Bartholomew	August 24	Joseph	March 19
Basil	January 2, June 14	Joseph of Arimathea	March 17
Bede	May 27	Jude	October 28
Benedict	July 11	Justin	June 1
Bernadette of Lourdes	February 18	Ladislaus I	June 27
Bernard	August 20	Lawrence	August 10
Birgitta	October 8	Leo I	February 18 (E. Ch.), April 11 (W. Ch.)
Bonaventura	July 15		
Boniface	June 5	Louis	August 25
Bridget of Ireland	July 23	Lucy	December 13
Bridget of Sweden	February 1	Luke	October 18
Bruno	October 6	Margaret	November 16
Campion	December 1	Mark	April 25
Catherine (of Alexandria)	November 25	Martha	July 29
Catherine of Siena	April 29	Martin	November 11
Cecilia	November 22	Mary	January 1 (R.C. Ch.), March 25, August 15, September 8
(John) Chrysostom	January 27		
Clare of Assisi	August 11		
Clement of Alexandria	December 5	Mary Magdalene	July 22
Clement (of Rome)	November 23	Matthew	September 21
Columba	June 9	Matthias	May 14 (W. Ch.), August 9 (E. Ch.)
Crispin	October 25		
Cuthbert	March 20	Michael	September 29
Cyprian	September 16, 26	Monica	August 27
Cyril	February 14	Nicholas	December 6
Cyril of Alexandria	February 9	Olaf II	July 29
David	March 1	Oliver Plunket	July 11
Denis	October 9	Oswald of York	February 28
Dominic	August 8	Patrick	March 17
Dunstan	May 19	Paul	June 29
Edmund	November 16	Peter	June 29
Edmund the Martyr	November 20	Philip	June 6
Edward the Confessor	October 13	Polycarp	February 23
Edward the Martyr	March 18	Sebastian	January 20
Elizabeth	November 5	Sergius	September 25
(John) Fisher	June 22	Simeon Stylites	January 5
Francis of Assisi	October 4	Simon	October 28
Francis of Sales	January 24	Stanislaus	April 11
Francis Xavier	December 3	Stephen	December 26 (W. Ch.), December 27 (E. Ch.)
Geneviève	January 3		
George	April 23		
Giles	September 1	Stephen of Hungary	September 2
Gregory of Nazianzus	January 25 and 30 (E. Ch.), January 2 (W. Ch.)	Swithin	July 15
		Teresa of Ávila	October 15
		Thérèse	October 3
Gregory of Nyssa	March 9	Thomas	December 21
Gregory of Tours	November 17	Thomas à Becket	December 29

SAINTS *cont.*			
Saint	**Feast Day**	**Saint**	**Feast Day**
Thomas Aquinas	January 28	Vitus	June 15
Thomas More	June 22	Vladimir I	July 15
Timothy	January 26, January 22	Wenceslas	September 28
		Wilfrid	October 12
Titus	August 23 (E. Ch.), February 6 (W. Ch.)		
Ursula	October 21	E. Ch. = Eastern Church	
Valentine	February 14	R.C. Ch. = Roman Catholic Church	
Vincent de Paul	July 19	W. Ch. = Western Church	

unchanged, changeless, unvarying, unvaried, invariable, unfailing, constant, consistent, uniform. **all the same 1** *all the same, I've got to go* nevertheless, nonetheless, still, yet, be that as it may, in any event, anyhow, notwithstanding. **2** *all the same to them whether he stays or goes* immaterial, irrelevant, of no importance, unimportant, of no consequence, inconsequential.
Opposites DIFFERENT; DISSIMILAR.

sameness *noun complain about the sameness of the work* monotony, lack of variety, identicalness, similarity, uniformity, tedium, tediousness, routine, humdrum, predictability, repetition.

sample *noun* **1** *a sample of his handwriting* specimen, example, instance, illustration, exemplification, representative type, model, pattern. **2** *the votes of a sample of the population* cross-section, sampling, test.

sample *verb sample the wine* try, try out, test, examine, inspect, taste, partake of.

sample *adjective* **1** *a sample section of people* representative, illustrative, typifying. **2** *a sample size of perfume bottle* test, trial, pilot.

sanctify *verb* **1** *sanctify the building* consecrate, make holy/sacred, bless, hallow, set apart, dedicate. **2** *sanctify sinners* free from sin, absolve, purify, cleanse, wash someone's sins away. **3** *a practice sanctified by tradition* sanction, ratify, confirm, warrant, legitimize, legitimatize.

sanctimonious *adjective* self-righteous, holier-than-thou, over-pious, pietistic, unctuous, smug, mealy-mouthed, hypocritical, Pharisaic, Tartuffian; *inf.* too good to be true, goody-goody, pi.

sanction *noun* **1** *receive the sanction of the church/authorities* authorization, warrant, accreditation, licence, endorsement, permission, consent, approval, seal of approval, stamp of approval, go-ahead, approbation, acceptance, thumbs up; *inf.* backing, support; *inf.* the green light, OK. **2** *laws receiving sanction* ratification, validation, confirmation. **3** *sanctions imposed against certain crimes* penalty, punishment, penalization, penance, sentence. **4** *impose trade sanctions on the enemy country* embargo, ban, boycott.

sanction *verb* **1** *unwilling to sanction the sale* authorize, warrant, accredit, license, endorse, permit, allow, consent to, approve, accept, give the thumbs up to, back, support; *inf.* give the green light to, OK. **2** *sanction the new law* rat-

ify, validate, confirm.
Opposites PROHIBIT; BAN; REJECT.

sanctity *noun* **1** *the sanctity of the altar | the sanctity of marriage* sacredness, holiness, inviolability. **2** *the sanctity of the priest* holiness, godliness, saintliness, spirituality, religiosity, piety, devoutness, devotion, righteousness, goodness, virtue, purity.

sanctuary *noun* **1** *priests standing in the sanctuary* holy place, church, temple, shrine, altar, sanctum. **2** *find a sanctuary from his pursuers* refuge, haven, shelter, retreat, hide-out, hiding place. **3** *seek sanctuary in the church* safety, safekeeping, protection, shelter, security, immunity. **4** *a bird sanctuary* preserve, reserve, wildlife reserve, reservation.

sane *adjective* **1** *patients not absolutely sane* of sound mind, in one's right mind, *compos mentis*, rational, lucid, in possession of one's faculties; *inf.* all there. **2** *a sane decision | a sane course of action* sensible, reasonable, sound, balanced, level-headed, judicious, responsible, prudent, wise, politic, advisable.
Opposites INSANE; MAD; FOOLISH.

sang-froid *noun* composure, coolness, calmness, self-possession, self-control, presence of mind, poise, equanimity, equilibrium, aplomb, nerve, imperturbability, unflappability.

sanguine *adjective* **1** *not sanguine of their chances of success* optimistic, confident, assured, hopeful, buoyant, cheerful, spirited. **2** *a sanguine complexion* florid, ruddy, red, rubicund.
Opposites PESSIMISTIC; GLOOMY.

sanitary *adjective scarcely sanitary conditions in the hotel kitchens* hygienic, clean, germ-free, antiseptic, aseptic, sterile, unpolluted, salubrious, healthy.

sanity *noun* **1** *question the patient's sanity* saneness, soundness of mind, mental health, reason, rationality, lucidness. **2** *acknowledge the sanity of the decision* sense, sensibleness, common sense, good sense, reasonableness, rationality, soundness, judiciousness, prudence, wisdom, advisability.

sap *noun* **1** *the sap rising in the plants* vital fluids, life fluid, juice. **2** *people full of sap and ready to go* vigour, energy, vitality, vivacity, enthusiasm, spirit; *inf.* pep, zip, oomph. **3** *a poor sap taking all the blame* fool, idiot, simpleton, nincompoop, ninny; *inf.* twit, nitwit, chump, jerk, drip, wet.

sap *verb* **1** *completely sapped by the heat* drain, enervate, exhaust, weaken, enfeeble, debilitate, devitalize. **2** *sap their confidence* erode, wear away, deplete, impair, drain, bleed.

sarcasm *noun* derision, scorn, mockery, ridicule, sneering, scoffing, gibing, taunting, irony, satire, lampoon, causticness, trenchancy, acerbity, acrimony, asperity, mordancy, bitterness, spitefulness.

sarcastic *adjective* derisive, derisory, scornful, mocking, sneering, jeering, scoffing, taunting, ironic, sardonic, satirical, caustic, trenchant, acerbic, acrimonious, mordant, bitter, spiteful; *inf.* sarky.

sardonic *adjective* dry, wry, derisory, scornful, mocking, cynical, sneering, jeering, scoffing, contemptuous, ironic, sarcastic, caustic, trenchant, acerbic, mordant, bitter, spiteful.

Satan *noun. See table at* DEVIL.

satanic *adjective* diabolical, fiendish, devilish, demonic, demoniac, demoniacal, hellish, infernal, accursed, wicked, evil, sinful, iniquitous, malevolent, vile, foul.

satellite *noun* **1** *launch a satellite into space* spacecraft, space capsule, space station, communications satellite, weather satellite. **2** *satellites requesting independence* protectorate, dependency, colony, dominion. **3** *the star and his satellites have arrived* henchman, hanger-on, lackey, flunkey, minion, underling, toady, sycophant, follower, dependent, retainer, dependant. **4** *the satellites of Mars* moon. *See table at* PLANET.

satellite *adjective a satellite state* dependent, tributary, subordinate, puppet, vassal.

satiate *verb satiated with food/pleasure* sate, fully satisfy, overfill, surfeit, stuff, glut, gorge, cloy.

satire *noun* **1** *write a satire* burlesque, parody, travesty, caricature, lampoon, skit, pasquinade; *inf.* take-off, spoof, send-up. **2** *treat them with satire* mockery, ridicule, irony, sarcasm.

satirical *adjective* mocking, ridiculing, taunting, ironic, sarcastic, sardonic, caustic, biting, cutting, stinging, trenchant, mordant, acerbic, pungent, critical, censorious, cynical.

satirize *verb* mock, ridicule, hold up to ridicule, deride, make fun of, poke fun at, parody, lampoon, burlesque, travesty, criticize, censure; *inf.* take off, send up.

satisfaction *noun* **1** *derive satisfaction* fulfilment, gratification, pleasure, enjoyment, delight, happiness, pride, comfort, content, contentment, smugness. **2** *the satisfaction of her desires/demands* fulfilment, gratification, appeasement, assuagement, achievement. **3** *demand satisfaction for the trouble caused* damages, compensation, recompense, amends, reparation, redress, indemnity, restitution, requital, atonement, reimbursement, remuneration, payment.
Opposites DISSATISFACTION; DISCONTENT; LOSS.

satisfactory *adjective* adequate, all right, acceptable, fine, good enough, sufficient, competent, up to standard, up to the mark, up to par, up to scratch, passable, average; *inf.* OK, okay.

Opposites INADEQUATE; UNACCEPTABLE; POOR; unsatisfactory.

satisfied *adjective* **1** *satisfied desires* fulfilled, gratified, appeased, assuaged. **2** *satisfied with the results of their work* pleased, happy, content, smug; *inf.* like the cat that swallowed the cream/canary. **3** *satisfied that he is telling the truth* convinced, persuaded, sure, positive, certain, easy in one's mind.
Opposites DISSATISFIED; UNHAPPY; UNCERTAIN.

satisfy *verb* **1** *satisfy their appetites/thirst* satiate, sate, slake, quench. **2** *satisfy their desires/demands* fulfil, gratify, appease, assuage, meet, indulge. **3** *satisfy the heating needs* solve, resolve, answer, be the answer to, meet, serve the purpose of, be sufficient/adequate/good enough for. **4** *satisfy the qualification requirements* fulfil, meet, comply with, answer. **5** *satisfy a debt* pay, settle, discharge, square up. **6** *satisfy old scores* make reparation for, atone for, compensate for, recompense. **7** *satisfy the police that he is innocent* convince, persuade, assure, reassure, remove/dispel doubts, put one's mind at rest.

satisfying *adjective* **1** *a satisfying job* fulfilling, gratifying, pleasing, enjoyable, pleasurable. **2** *give a satisfying reason* satisfactory, reasonable, convincing, reassuring.

saturate *verb* **1** *saturate the garment* wet through, wet, soak, souse, steep, douse. **2** *the rain saturated us* wet through, soak, drench. **3** *bodies saturated with sunshine* permeate, imbue, pervade, suffuse. **4** *saturate the market* overfill, surfeit, glut, satiate, sate.

saturated *adjective* wet through, soaked, soaked to the skin, soaking, soaking wet, drenched, sodden, dripping wet, wringing wet.

sauce *noun* **1** *salt and sauce | a red-wine sauce* relish, dressing, condiment, flavouring. *See table.* **2** *annoyed at the sauce of the girl* impudence, cheek, impertinence, insolence, rudeness, disrespect, audacity, presumption, temerity, boldness, brazenness, gall, pertness, brashness; *inf.* sauciness, brass, lip, freshness, backchat.

saucy *adjective* **1** *older people complaining about saucy girls* impudent, cheeky, impertinent, insolent, rude, disrespectful, audacious, presumptuous, bold, brazen, pert, brash; *inf.* fresh. **2** *hats worn at a saucy angle* jaunty, dashing, rakish, sporty, gay, dapper; *inf.* natty.

saunter *verb* stroll, amble, wander, meander, walk, ramble, roam, promenade; *inf.* mosey.

saunter *noun* stroll, amble, wander, meander, walk, ramble, turn, roam, airing, promenade, constitutional.

savage *adjective* **1** *a savage blow | savage criticism* vicious, ferocious, fierce, brutal, cruel, bloody, murderous, bloodthirsty, inhuman, harsh, grim, terrible, merciless, ruthless, pitiless, sadistic, barbarous, fell. **2** *a savage animal* fierce, ferocious, wild, untamed, undomesticated, feral. **3** *attacked by a savage gang* fierce, ferocious, wild, rough, rugged, uncivilized, barbarous, barbaric. **4** *explorers encountering savage tribes in the jungle* primitive, uncivilized, uncultivated, wild.

Opposites MILD; TAME; CIVILIZED.

savage *noun* **1** *sailors attacked by island savages* barbarians, wild man/woman, native, primitive, heathen. **2** *calling the children savages* barbarian, boor, churl, yahoo; *inf.* yobbo. **3** *her attacker was a savage* brute, beast, monster, barbarian, ogre.

savage *verb* **1** *lambs savaged by a wild dog* maul, lacerate, mangle, tear to pieces, attack. **2** *plays savaged by critics* criticize severely, tear to pieces, take apart; *inf.* knock, slate, slam.

save *verb* **1** *save the children from death/danger* rescue, free, set free, liberate, deliver, snatch, bail out, salvage, redeem. **2** *save them from their sinful desires* protect, safeguard, guard, keep, keep safe, shield, screen, preserve, conserve. **3** *save a lot of trouble* prevent, obviate, forestall, spare, make unnecessary, rule out. **4** *save some money/supplies* put aside, set aside, put by, put away, lay by, keep, reserve, conserve, salt away, stockpile, store, hoard. **5** *time to save not spend* economize, practise economy, be thrifty, be frugal, budget, husband one's resources, cut costs, cut expenditure, draw in one's horns.

Opposites ENDANGER; CAUSE; WASTE; SPEND.

savings *plural noun* capital, assets, resources, reserves, funds, nest-egg.

saviour *noun* *rescued children thanking their saviour* rescuer, liberator, deliverer, emancipator, champion, knight in shining armour, Good Samaritan, friend in need.

Saviour *noun* *worshipping the Saviour* Christ, Jesus, Jesus Christ, the Redeemer, the Messiah, Our Lord.

savoir faire *noun* finesse, poise, aplomb, social graces, social skill, adroitness, accomplishment, style, tact, tactfulness, diplomacy, discretion, smoothness, urbanity, suaveness; *inf.* savvy.

savour *noun* **1** *the savour of fresh raspberries in her mouth* taste, flavour, tang, relish, smack. **2** *the savour of freshly baked bread in the air* smell, aroma, fragrance, scent, perfume, bouquet, odour. **3** *a smile with a savour of menace/politics with a savour of fanaticism* hint, suggestion, touch, vein, tone. **4** *a life deprived of some of its*

savour enjoyment, joy, excitement, interest, zest, spice, piquancy.

savour *verb* **1** *savour the taste of home-made soup | savour the joys of freedom* taste, enjoy, enjoy to the full/to the hilt, appreciate, delight in, take pleasure in, relish, revel in, smack one's lips over, luxuriate in. **2** *a situation savouring of dishonesty* smack of, show signs of, exhibit traces of, suggest, be suggestive of, be indicative of, bear the hallmark of.

savoury *adjective* **1** *savoury smells from the kitchen | tables laden with savoury delights* appetizing, mouth-watering, fragrant, flavoursome, palatable, tasty, delicious, delectable, luscious, toothsome; *inf.* scrumptious. **2** *preferring savoury snacks to sweets* salty, piquant, tangy, spicy.

Opposites UNPALATABLE; SWEET.

saw *noun* *a book of old saws* saying, proverb, maxim, aphorism, axiom, adage, epigram, dictum, gnome, apothegm, platitude, cliché.

say *verb* **1** *refuse to say his name* speak, utter, mention, voice, pronounce, put into words, give utterance to, give voice to, vocalize. **2** *"It's too expensive," he said* state, remark, announce, affirm, assert, maintain, declare, aver, allege, profess, avow; *lit.* opine; *inf.* come out with. **3** *finding it difficult to say how one feels* express, put into words, tell, phrase, articulate, communicate, make known, convey, reveal, divulge, disclose. **4** *say a short poem* recite, repeat, deliver, declaim, orate, read, perform, rehearse. **5** *What do the instructions say?* indicate, specify, designate, tell, give information, suggest. **6** *I would say it's four miles from here* estimate, judge, guess, hazard a guess, predict, speculate, conjecture, surmise, imagine, assume, suppose, presume. **7** *old people said to be dying* state, suggest, allege, claim, put about, report, rumour, bruit, noise abroad. **8** *much to be said in favour of the idea* propose, advance, bring forward, offer, introduce, adduce, plead.

say *noun* **1** *everyone being entitled to a say* opinion, view, right to speak, chance to speak, turn to speak, vote, voice; *inf.* twopence worth. **2** *people having no say in the decision* share, part, influence, sway, weight, input. **that is to say** *a*

SAUCES, DIPS, AND DRESSINGS

aioli	cheese sauce	mousseline	skordalia
apple sauce	chilli sauce	sauce	soy sauce
baba ghanoush	cranberry sauce	mustard sauce	sweet and sour
barbecue sauce	demi-glace	onion sauce	sauce
Béarnaise sauce	French dressing	parsley sauce	Tabasco sauce
béchamel sauce	gravy	pebre	taramasalata
blue cheese dressing	guacamole	pepper sauce	tartare sauce
bolognese sauce	harissa	pesto	Teriyaki sauce
bordelaise sauce	hoisin sauce	pizzaiola sauce	Thousand Island
bread sauce	hollandaise sauce	ragù	dressing
brown sauce	horseradish sauce	salad dressing	tomato ketchup
carbonara sauce	hummus	salsa de ají	tzatziki
catsup	mayonnaise	salsa verde	velouté
chasseur sauce	milanese sauce	satay sauce	vinaigrette
chaud-froid	mint sauce	sauce ravigote	white sauce
chawan mushi	mornay sauce	sauce remoulade	Worcester sauce

fortnight, that is to say fourteen days in other words, to put it another way, to rephrase it. **to say the least** *to say the least he is not a good worker* to put it mildly, without any exaggeration, at the very least.

saying noun *old sayings about the weather* proverb, maxim, aphorism, axiom, adage, saw, epigram, dictum, gnome, apothegm, platitude, cliché. **it goes without saying** *it goes without saying that he will pay* of course, naturally, it is taken for granted, it is understood/assumed, it is taken as read, it is accepted, it is unquestionable.

scaffold noun **1** *painters standing on a scaffold* scaffolding, frame, framework, gantry. **2** *murderers going to the scaffold* gallows, gibbet.

scale¹ noun **1** *scales on a fish* lamella, lamina, plate, squama. **2** *a disease causing scales on the skin* flake, scurf, furfur. **3** *scale on a kettle* coating, coat, crust, incrustation, covering.

scale² noun *weigh it on the scale* scales, weighing machine, balance.

scale³ noun **1** *on the Richter scale | social scale* graduated system, calibrated system, measuring system, progression, succession, sequence, series, ranking, register, ladder, hierarchy; *inf.* pecking order. *See table.* **2** *a scale of a hundred miles to the centimetre* ratio, proportion. **3** *entertain on the grand scale* extent, scope, range, degree, reach.

THE MUSICAL SCALE IN TONIC SOL-FA

doh	soh
ray	lah
mi	te
fah	

---

scale verb *scale the high wall* climb, ascend, go up, clamber, mount, clamber up, escalade. **scale down** *scale down the extent of the alterations* reduce, cut down, cut back on, decrease, lessen, lower, trim.

scaly adjective **1** *scaly creatures* squamate, squamose, squamous. **2** *scaly patches on the skin* flaky, scurfy, rough, scabrous, furfuraceous.

scamp noun rascal, rogue, imp, devil, monkey, wretch, scallywag, mischief-maker, troublemaker, prankster, miscreant, tyke, scapegrace.

scamper verb scurry, scuttle, dart, run, rush, dash, race, sprint, hurry, hasten, scramble; *inf.* scoot.

scan verb **1** *scan the horizon/evidence* study, examine, scrutinize, survey, inspect, take stock of, search, scour, sweep. **2** *scan the pages of the document* skim, look over, have a look at, glance over, run one's eye over, read through, leaf through, thumb through, flick through, flip through.

scandal noun **1** *corruption scandals destroying political careers* wrongdoing, impropriety, misconduct, offence, transgression, crime, sin. **2** *caused a scandal in the village* outrage, disgrace, embarrassment. **3** *bring scandal on the family* disgrace, shame, dishonour, disrepute, discredit, odium, opprobrium, censure, obloquy. **4** *spread scandal about the politician* scandalmongering, slander, libel, calumny, defamation, aspersion, gossip, malicious rumours, dirt, muck-raking, smear campaign. **5** *his treatment of her was a scandal* disgrace, shame, pity, crying shame.

scandalize verb *scandalized by their unethical behaviour* shock, appal, outrage, horrify, affront, disgust, offend, insult, cause raised eyebrows.

scandalous adjective **1** *public figures, guilty of scandalous behaviour* disgraceful, shameful, dishonourable, outrageous, shocking, monstrous, disreputable, improper, unseemly, discreditable, infamous, opprobrious. **2** *spread scandalous rumours* slanderous, libellous, defamatory, scurrilous, malicious, gossiping.

scant adjective *pay scant attention* little, minimal, limited, barely sufficient, insufficient, inadequate, deficient.
Opposites ABUNDANT; AMPLE; SUFFICIENT.

scanty adjective *scanty supplies of food* meagre, scant, sparse, small, paltry, slender, negligible, skimpy, thin, poor, insufficient, inadequate, deficient, limited, restricted, exiguous.
Opposites ABUNDANT; AMPLE; COPIOUS.

scapegoat noun whipping-boy; *inf.* fall guy.

scar noun **1** *a scar left by the knife-wound* mark, blemish, blotch, discoloration, cicatrice, disfigurement, defacement. **2** *child abuse leaving a permanent emotional scar* damage, trauma, shock, injury, suffering, upset.

scar verb **1** *scarred for life by the knife attack* mark, blemish, blotch, discolour, disfigure, deface. **2** *emotionally scarred for life* damage, traumatize, shock, injure, upset.

scarce adjective **1** *money being scarce* in short supply, short, meagre, scant, scanty, sparse, paltry, not enough, too little, insufficient, deficient, inadequate, lacking, at a premium, exiguous. **2** *red squirrels being scarce* rare, infrequent, few and far between, seldom seen/found, sparse, uncommon, unusual.
Opposites PLENTIFUL; ABUNDANT; FREQUENT.

scarcely adverb **1** *I scarcely know them* hardly, barely, only just. **2** *I can scarcely expect them to believe that* hardly, certainly not, definitely not, surely not, not at all, on no account, under no circumstances, by no means.

scarcity noun **1** *scarcity of money in the recession* dearth, shortage, undersupply, paucity, scantness, meagreness, sparseness, insufficiency, deficiency, inadequacy, lack, exiguity. **2** *the scarcity of red squirrels* rarity, rareness, infrequency, sparseness, uncommonness, unusualness.

scare verb frighten, make afraid, alarm, startle, make fearful, make nervous, terrify, terrorize, petrify, horrify, appal, shock, intimidate, daunt, awe, cow, panic, put the fear of God into, scare stiff, make one's blood run cold, make one's flesh creep, make one's hair stand on end; *inf.* put the wind up, scare the living daylights out of, scare the pants off.

scare *noun children recovering from a scare* fright, alarm, start, fearfulness, nervousness, terror, horror, shock, panic.

scared *adjective scared children running away* frightened, afraid, alarmed, shaken, fearful, nervous, terrified, petrified, horrified, cowed, panic-stricken, panicky.

scarf *noun* muffler, neckerchief, kerchief, cravat, bandanna, headscarf. *See table at* HAT.

scary *adjective a scary experience* scaring, frightening, alarming, startling, nerve-racking, terrifying, petrifying, hair-raising, horrifying, appalling, daunting.

scathing *adjective scathing criticism* virulent, savage, fierce, ferocious, brutal, stinging, biting, mordant, trenchant, caustic, vitriolic, withering, scornful, harsh, severe, stern. *Opposites* MILD.

scatter *verb* **1** *scatter seed | scatter breadcrumbs for birds* disseminate, diffuse, spread, sow, sprinkle, strew, broadcast, fling, toss, throw. **2** *the crowd scattered | police scattered the crowd* break up, disperse, disband, separate, dissolve. *Opposites* COLLECT; GATHER; ASSEMBLE.

scatterbrained *adjective* irresponsible, forgetful, dreamy, wool-gathering, with one's head in the clouds, feather-brained, hare-brained, erratic, giddy.

scavenge *verb scavenging on the beach for food* search, look for, hunt, forage for, rummage for, scrounge.

scavenger *noun scavengers looking for goods in dustbins* forager, rummager, scrounger.

scenario *noun* **1** *discuss the scenario with the producer* plot, outline, synopsis, summary, précis, rundown, storyline, structure, scheme, plan. **2** *predict a depressing scenario* sequence of events, future situation.

scene *noun* **1** *the scene of the accident* place, location, site, position, spot, setting, locale, whereabouts, arena, stage. **2** *against a scene of confusion* background, backdrop, setting, set, *mise en scène.* **3** *witnessing scandalous scenes* event, incident, happening, situation, episode, affair, moment, proceeding. **4** *look out on beautiful rural scenes* scenery, view, outlook, landscape, vista, panorama, prospect. **5** *the embarrassing scene created by his wife* fuss, exhibition, outburst, commotion, to-do, row, upset, tantrum, furore, brouhaha. **6** *football not being his scene* area of interest, field of interest, field, interest, sphere, world, milieu. **7** *appearing in every scene of the play* division.

scenery *noun* **1** *tourists admiring the scenery* view, outlook, landscape, vista, panorama, prospect. **2** *helping to shift/paint the scenery* set, stage set, setting, background, backdrop, *mise en scène.*

scenic *adjective* **1** *the scenic route* picturesque, pretty, beautiful, pleasing. **2** *the scenic advantages of the area* landscape, panoramic.

scent *noun* **1** *the scent of new-mown hay* aroma, perfume, fragrance, smell, bouquet, redolence, odour. **2** *dogs losing the scent of the fox* track, trail, spoor. **3** *a scent of scandal about the affair* hint, suggestion, whiff, implication. **4** *wearing*

an expensive scent perfume, fragrance, toilet water, *eau de Cologne.*

scent *verb* **1** *dogs scenting the fox* smell, sniff, be on the track/trail of, track, trail. **2** *scenting danger/redundancy* detect, discern, recognize, become aware of, sense, get wind of, sniff out, nose out.

scented *adjective scented paper* perfumed, sweet-smelling, fragrant, aromatic.

sceptic *noun* **1** *supporters of his theories arguing with the sceptics* questioner, doubter, doubting Thomas, disbeliever, dissenter, scoffer, cynic. **2** *ministers of the church challenging sceptics* agnostic, unbeliever, doubter, doubting Thomas.

sceptical *adjective trying to convince sceptical opponents* doubting, doubtful, dubious, questioning, distrustful, mistrustful, suspicious, hesitant, disbelieving, misbelieving, incredulous, unconvinced, scoffing, cynical, pessimistic, defeatist. *Opposites* CERTAIN; CREDULOUS; OPEN-MINDED.

scepticism *noun* **1** *persist in the face of scepticism* doubt, doubtfulness, dubiety, distrust, mistrust, suspicion, hesitancy, disbelief, misbelief, incredulity, scoffing, cynicism, pessimism, defeatism. **2** *religious scepticism* agnosticism, unbelief, doubt.

schedule *noun* **1** *projects going according to schedule* timetable, plan, scheme, programme. **2** *a busy schedule* appointment list, list of appointments, diary, calendar, social calendar, itinerary, agenda. **3** *a schedule of services/equipment* list, catalogue, syllabus, inventory.

schedule *verb schedule the meeting for tomorrow* time, timetable, arrange, organize, plan, programme, book, slot in.

scheme *noun* **1** *a scheme for recycling paper* plan, programme, project, course of action, line of action, system, procedure, strategy, design, device, tactics, contrivance. **2** *an attractive colour scheme* arrangement, system, organization, disposition, schema. **3** *produce the scheme for the new shopping centre* outline, blueprint, design, delineation, diagram, layout, sketch, chart, map, schema. **4** *police discovering his little scheme* plot, ruse, ploy, stratagem, manoeuvre, machinations, subterfuge, intrigue, conspiracy; *inf.* game, racket.

scheme *verb rebels scheming to overthrow the government* plot, conspire, intrigue, manoeuvre, plan, lay plans.

scheming *adjective* calculating, designing, conniving, wily, crafty, cunning, sly, tricky, artful, foxy, slippery, underhand, duplicitous, devious, Machiavellian. *Opposites* INGENUOUS; HONEST; ABOVE-BOARD.

schism *noun* division, breach, split, rift, break, rupture, separation, splintering, disunion, scission, severance, detachment, discord, disagreement.

scholar *noun* **1** *scholars giving expert opinions on texts* man/woman of letters, learned person, academic, intellectual, pundit, savant; *inf.* bookworm, egghead, highbrow. **2** *quick schol-*

ars | a school of 500 scholars learner, student, pupil, schoolboy, schoolgirl.

scholarly *adjective* learned, erudite, academic, well-read, intellectual, scholastic, literary, studious, bookish, lettered; *inf.* egghead, highbrow. **Opposites** ILLITERATE; IGNORANT.

scholarship *noun* **1** *works showing scholarship* learning, book-learning, knowledge, education, erudition, letters. **2** *people of great scholarship* learning, book-learning, letters, erudition, education, academic achievement/attainment/accomplishment. **3** *on a scholarship to the school/college* bursary, fellowship, endowment, grant.

scholastic *adjective her scholastic record* academic, educational, school.

school *noun* **1** *attend the local school* educational institution, nursery school, primary school, secondary school, comprehensive school, grammar school, high school, academy, seminary, public school, private school. **2** *the music school at the university* department, faculty, division. **3** *belonging to the Impressionist school of art* group, set, proponents, adherents, devotees, circle, class, sect, clique, faction, followers, following, disciples, admirers, votaries, pupils, students. **4** *teachers belonging to the old school* school of thought, outlook, persuasion, opinion, point of view, belief, faith, creed, credo, doctrine, stamp, way of life.

school *verb* **1** *schooled locally* educate, teach, instruct. **2** *school a horse/oneself in patience* train, coach, instruct, drill, discipline, direct, guide, prepare, prime, verse.

schooling *noun* **1** *refuse to continue with his schooling* education, instruction, teaching, tuition, learning, book-learning. **2** *the schooling of a horse* training, coaching, instruction, drill, discipline. *See* SCHOOL *verb* 2.

schoolteacher *noun* schoolmaster/mistress, instructor, tutor, pedagogue.

science *noun* **1** *the science of the universe* body of knowledge/information/facts, branch of knowledge, area of study, discipline. **2** *study science rather than the arts* physical science, physics, chemistry, biology. *See table. See also tables at* ENGINEERING, MATHEMATICAL, PSYCHOLOGY. **3** *pursuits requiring a certain science* skill, art, expertise, expertness, proficiency, dexterity, deftness, facility.

scientific *adjective* **1** *scientific discoveries* chemical, biological, medical, technical, technological. **2** *requiring a scientific approach* systematic, methodical, orderly, regulated, controlled, exact, precise, mathematical.

scientist *noun. See table. See also tables at* DOCTOR, ENGINEER, INVENTOR.

scintillate *verb* **1** *diamonds scintillating* sparkle, twinkle, flash, gleam, glitter, glint, glisten, coruscate. **2** *scintillating at the dinner party* be sparkling, be vivacious, be lively, be witty. *See* SCINTILLATING.

scintillating *adjective scintillating companions/conversation* sparkling, dazzling, vivacious, effervescent, lively, animated, ebullient, bright, brilliant, witty, exciting, stimulating, invigorating. **Opposites** BORING; DULL; PEDESTRIAN.

scion *noun* **1** *a scion of a noble family* descendant, heir, offspring, issue, child. **2** *planting scions* shoot, offshoot, cutting, graft.

BRANCHES OF SCIENCE

acoustics	endocrinology	mechanics	photochemistry
aerodynamics	engineering	medical physics	physics
anatomy	entomology	medicine	physiography
astronomy	epidemiology	metallurgy	physiology
astrophysics	ethnology	meteorology	phytology
atomic physics	exobiology	microbiology	phytopathology
bacteriology	fluid mechanics	mineralogy	psychiatry
behavioural science	genetic engineering	molecular biology	psychology
biochemistry	genetics	mycology	quantum
biology	geochemistry	nephology	mechanics
botany	geochronology	neurology	radiochemistry
chemistry	geography	neuroscience	radiology
climatology	geology	nuclear chemistry	robotics
computer science	geomorphology	nuclear physics	seismology
conchology	geophysics	oceanography	sociobiology
cosmology	glaciology	oncology	soil science
cryogenics	haematology	ophthalmology	spectroscopy
crystallography	herpetology	optics	stratigraphy
cybernetics	histology	ornithology	taxonomy
cytology	holography	palaeobotany	tectonics
dendrology	hydrodynamics	palaeoclimatology	thermodynamics
dynamics	hydrology	palaeontology	toxicology
earth science	hydrostatics	palynology	veterinary medicine
ecology	ichthyology	parasitology	virology
electrical engineer-	immunology	particle physics	vulcanology
ing	limnology	pedology	zoogeography
electrodynamics	marine biology	petrology	zoology
electronics	mathematics	pharmacology	zymurgy

SCIENTISTS

Agricola, Georgius (George Bauer; 1494–1555; Ger. physician/mineralogist)

Al-Battani (c. 858–929 A.D.; Arab. astronomer)

Alfvén, Hannes (1908–95; Sw. theoretical physicist)

Ampère, André-Marie (1775–1836; Fr. physicist/mathematician)

Ångström, Anders (1814–74; Sw. physicist/astronomer)

Aristarchus of Samos (c. 310–230 B.C.; Gk astronomer)

Arrhenius, Svante (1859–1927; Sw. physicist/chemist)

Avery, Oswald (1877–1955; Can. bacteriologist)

Avogadro, Amedeo, Conte di (1776–1856; It. physicist/chemist)

Becquerel, Antoine-Henri (1852–1908; Fr. physicist)

Bell Burnell, (Susan) Jocelyn (b. 1943; Brit. astronomer)

Bergius, Friedrich (1884–1949; Ger. chemist)

Berthollet, Claude, Comte (1748–1822; Fr. chemist)

Berzelius, Jöns, Baron (1779–1848; Sw. chemist)

Bichat, Marie (1771–1802; Fr. pathologist)

Bjerknes, Vilhelm (1862–1951; Norw. meteorologist/geophysicist)

Bohr, Niels (1885–1962; Da. physicist)

Boltzmann, Ludwig (1844–1906; Austrian physicist)

Bondi, Sir Hermann (b. 1919; Brit. cosmologist/physicist)

Bonnet, Charles (1720–93; Swiss naturalist)

Bordet, Jules (1870–1961; Belg. bacteriologist/immunologist)

Born, Max (1882–1970; Brit. physicist)

Bosch, Carl (1874–1940; Ger. chemist)

Bose, Sir Jagdis (1858–1937; Ind. physicist/plant physiologist)

Bovet, Daniel (1907–92; Swiss pharmacologist)

Boyle, Robert (1627–91; Ir. physicist/chemist)

Brahe, Tycho (1546–1601; Da. astronomer)

Bunsen, Robert (1811–99; Ger. chemist)

Calvin, Melvin (b. 1911; Am. biochemist)

Cannon, Annie (1863–1941; Am. astronomer)

Cannizzaro, Stanislao (1826–1910; It. chemist)

Carnot, Nicolas (1796–1832; Fr. scientist)

Cavendish, Henry (1731–1810; Brit. physicist/chemist)

Chadwick, Sir James (1891–1974; Brit. physicist)

Chain, Sir Ernst (1906–79; Brit. biochemist, b. in Germany)

Chamberlain, Owen (b. 1920; Am. physicist)

Chandrasekhar, Subrahmanyan (1910–95; Am. astronomer, b. in India)

Cherenkov, Pavel (1904–90; Soviet physicist)

Cockcroft, Sir John (1897–1967; Brit. physicist)

Copernicus, Nicolaus (1473–1543; Pol. astronomer)

Coulomb, Charles-Augustin de

(1736–1806; Fr. physicist)

Crick, Francis (b. 1916; Brit. biophysicist)

Culpeper, Nicholas (1616–54; Brit. herbalist)

Curie, Marie (1867–1934; Fr. physicist, b. in Poland)

Curie, Pierre (1859–1906; Fr. physicist)

Dalton, John (1766–1844; Brit. chemist)

Darwin, Charles (1809–1882; Brit. naturalist/geologist)

Davy, Sir Humphry (1778–1829; Brit. chemist)

Dawkins, Richard (b. 1941; Brit. biologist)

de Broglie, Louis-Victor, Prince (1892–1987; Fr. physicist)

de Vries, Hugo (1848–1935; Du. physiologist/geneticist)

Diels, Otto (1876–1954; Ger. chemist)

Doppler, Christian (1803–53; Austrian physicist)

Einstein, Albert (1879–1955; Am. physicist, b. in Germany)

Eratosthenes of Cyrene (c. 276–c. 194 B.C.; Gk astronomer)

Faraday, Michael (1791–1867; Brit. chemist/physicist)

Fermi, Enrico (1901–54; Am. physicist)

Feynman, Richard (1918–88; Am. physicist)

Fitzgerald, George (1851–1901; Ir. physicist)

Fleming, Sir Alexander (1881–1955; Scots. bacteriologist)

Foucault, Jean (1819–68; Fr. physicist)

Franklin, Rosalind (1920–58; Brit. crystallographer/chemist/molecular biologist)

Fraunhofer, Joseph von (1787–1826; Ger. physicist)

Fresnel, Augustin (1788–1827; Fr. physicist)

Frisch, Karl von (1886–1982; Austrian zoologist)

Frisch, Otto (1904–79; Brit. physicist, b. in Austria)

Galileo Galilei (1564–1642; It. physicist/astronomer)

Gassendi, Pierre (1592–1655; Fr. physicist/astronomer)

Gay-Lussac, Joseph (1778–1850; Fr. chemist/physicist)

Geber (14th century; Sp. alchemist)

Geiger, Hans (1882–1945; Ger. physicist)

Gell-Mann, Murray (b. 1929; Am. physicist)

Guericke, Otto von (1602–86; Ger. physicist)

Haber, Fritz (1868–1934; Ger. chemist)

Halley, Edmond (1656–1742; Brit. astronomer/mathematician)

Heaviside, Oliver (1850–1925; Brit. physicist)

Heisenberg, Werner (1901–76; Ger. physicist)

Herschel, Caroline (1750–1848; Brit. astronomer, b. in Germany)

Herschel, Sir William (1738–1822; Brit. astronomer, b. in Germany)

Hertz, Heinrich (1857–94; Ger. physicist)

SCIENTISTS cont.

Hevesy, George de (1885–1966; Sw. radiochemist, b. in Hungary)

Hipparchus (b. c. 170 B.C.; Gk astronomer)

Hodgkin, Dorothy (1910–94; Brit. bio-chemist)

Hoff, Jacobus van't (1852–1911; Du. chemist)

Hooke, Robert (1635–1703; Brit. physicist)

Hoyle, Sir Fred (b. 1915; Brit. astro-physicist)

Hubble, Edwin (1889–1953; Am. astronomer)

Huygens, Christiaan (1629–95; Du. astronomer/ physicist/ mathematician)

Joule, James Prescott (1818–89; Brit. physicist)

Kekulé von Stradonitz, Friedrich (1829–96; Ger. chemist)

Kelvin, William, 1st Baron (1824–1907; Scot. physicist)

Kepler, Johannes (1571–1630; Ger. astronomer)

Kinsey, Alfred (1894–1956; Am. zoologist/sociolo-gist)

Krebs, Sir Hans (1900–81; Brit. bio-chemist, b. in Ger-many)

Kurchatov, Igor (1903–60; Russ. physicist)

Lamarck, Jean-Baptiste de Cheva-lier de (1744–1829; Fr. naturalist)

Langley, Samuel (1834–1906; Am. astronomer)

Lavoisier, Antoine (1743–94; Fr. chemist)

Leavitt, Henrietta (1868–1921; Am. astronomer)

Liebig, Justus, Baron von (1803–73; Ger. chemist)

Linnaeus, Carolus (Carl Linné; 1707–78; Sw. botanist)

Lockyer, Sir Joseph (1836–1920; Brit. astronomer)

Lonsdale, Dame Kathleen (1903–71; Ir. physicist)

Lorenz, Konrad (1903–89; Austrian zoologist)

Lumière, Auguste (1862–1954; Fr. photographer)

Lysenko, Trofim (1898–1976; Soviet biologist/ geneticist)

McClintock, Barbara (1902–92; Am. geneticist)

Mach, Ernst (1838–1916; Aus-trian physicist)

Maxwell, James Clerk (1831–79; Scot. physicist)

Meitner, Lise (1878–1968; Sw. physicist, b. in Austria)

Mendel, Gregor (1822–84; Austrian botanist)

Mendeleyev, Dmitri (1834–1907; Russ. chemist)

Mercator, Gerardus (Gerhard Kremer; 1512–94; Flem. geographer/ cartographer)

Meyerhof, Otto (1884–1951; Am. biochemist, b. in Germany)

Millikan, Robert (1868–1953; Am. physicist)

Morgan, Thomas (1866–1945; Am. geneticist/zoologist)

Muller, Hermann (1890–1967; Am. geneticist)

Needham, Dorothy (1896–1987; Brit. biochemist)

Newton, Sir Isaac (1642–1727; Brit. physicist/mathe-matician)

Nobel, Alfred Bern-hard (1833–96; Sw. chemist)

Ohm, Georg (1787–1854; Ger. physicist)

Oppenheimer, J. Robert (1904–67; Am. physicist)

Pasteur, Louis (1822–95; Fr. chemist/ bacteriologist)

Pauli, Wolfgang (1900–58; Am. physicist, b. in Austria)

Pauling, Linus (1901–94; Am. chemist)

Planck, Max (1858–1947; Ger. physicist)

Porter, George, Baron (b. 1920; Brit. chemist)

Proust, Joseph-Louis (1754–1826; Fr. chemist)

Purcell, Edward (b. 1912; Am. physi-cist)

Raman, Sir Chandrasekhara (1888–1970; Ind. physicist)

Regiomontanus (Johannes Müller; 1436-76; Ger. astronomer/ mathematician)

Röntgen, Wilhelm (1845–1923; Ger. physicist)

Rutherford, Sir Ernest, 1st Baron (1871–1937; NZ physicist)

Ryle, Sir Martin (1918–84; Brit. astronomer)

Sabatier, Paul (1854–1941; Fr. chemist)

Sakharov, Andrei (1921–89; Soviet physicist)

Salam, Abdus (b. 1926; Pakistani physicist)

Sandage, Allan (b. 1926; Am. astronomer)

Schrödinger, Erwin (1887–1961; Austrian physicist)

Seaborg, Glenn (b. 1912; Am. nuclear chemist)

Segrè, Emilio (1905–89; Am. physicist, b. in Italy)

Sosigenes of Alexan-dria (1st century B.C.; Gk astronomer)

Spallanzani, Lazzaro (1729–99; It. physi-ologist/biologist)

Swammerdam, Jan (1637–80; Du. natu-ralist/microscopist)

Swan, Sir Joseph (1828–1914; Brit. physicist/chemist)

Teller, Edward (b. 1908; Am. physi-cist, b. in Hungary)

Tinbergen, Niko(laas) (1907–88; Du. zoologist/ ethologist)

Torricelli, Evange-lista (1608–47; It. physicist/mathe-matician)

Tull, Jethro (1674–1741; Brit. agriculturalist)

Tyndall, John (1820–93; Ir. physi-cist)

Ulugh Beg (1394–1449; Pers. astronomer)

Van Allen, James (b. 1914; Am. physi-cist)

Volta, Alessandro, Count (1745–1827; It. physicist)

Watson, James (b. 1928; Am. geneticist/biologist)

Watson-Watt, Sir Robert (1892–1973; Scot. physicist)

Wigner, Eugene (1902–95; Am. physicist)

Wilkins, Maurice (b. 1916; Brit. bio-chemist/molecular biologist, b. in New Zealand)

Yukawa, Hideki (1907–81; Jap. physicist)

Zeeman, Pieter (1865–1943; Du. physicist)

Zworykin, Vladimir (1889–1982; Am. physicist, b. in Russia)

scoff[1] *verb upset by other children scoffing at his size* jeer at, mock at, sneer at, gibe at, taunt, laugh at, ridicule, poke fun at, make a fool of, make sport of, rag, revile, deride, belittle, pooh-pooh, scorn; *inf.* knock.

scoff[2] *verb scoff all the biscuits* guzzle, gulp down, devour, finish off.

scold *verb* **1** *children scolded for being late* rebuke, reprimand, chide, reprove, reproach, remonstrate with, upbraid, berate, censure, lecture, castigate, haul over the coals, read the riot act to, rap over the knuckles, bring to book; *inf.* tell off, give a telling-off to, give a talking-to to, give a dressing-down to, tick off, give a ticking-off to, carpet, give a carpeting to, bawl out. **2** *a wife always scolding* nag, lay down the law, rail, carp, criticize, find fault, complain; *inf.* go on.

scold *noun married to a scold* nag, shrew, termagant; *inf.* battleaxe.

scolding *noun* rebuke, reprimand, chiding, reproach, upbraiding, lecture, rap over the knuckles; *inf.* telling-off, talking-to, ticking-off, row, carpeting, bawling-out, wigging.

scoop *noun* **1** *a scoop of ice-cream* ladle, spoon, dipper. **2** *reporters getting a scoop* exclusive story, revelation, exposé.

scoop *verb* **1** *scoop out the hole* hollow out, gouge out. **2** *scoop out the earth from the site* hollow out, gouge out, dig, excavate. **3** *scoop up the leaves* gather up, pick up, lift.

scope *noun* **1** *within the scope of the inquiry* extent, range, sphere, area, field, realm, compass, orbit, reach, span, sweep, confine, limit. **2** *a job with much scope | scope for improvement* opportunity, freedom, latitude, capacity, room to manoeuvre, elbow-room.

scorch *verb* **1** *scorched by an iron* burn, singe, char, sear, discolour. **2** *grass scorched by the sun* burn, dry up, wither, discolour, brown.

scorching *adjective* **1** *a scorching day* very hot, unbearably hot, sweltering, torrid; *inf.* boiling, broiling, sizzling, baking. **2** *scorching criticism* stringent, scathing, caustic, mordant, trenchant, biting, harsh, severe.
Opposites FREEZING.

score *noun* **1** *enter their score* number of points/goals, record of points/goals, total. **2** *a score of five-nil* result, outcome. **3** *rejected on several scores* basis, grounds, reason, account, count. **4** *a score on the table/wall* notch, mark, scratch, mark, groove, cut, nick, chip, gouge, incision, slit, gash. **5** *money to pay the score* bill, tally, reckoning, amount due, debt, obligation; *inf.* tab. **6** *a score to settle* dispute, grievance, grudge, injury, a bone to pick, a bone of contention. **know the score** be aware of the situation, be aware of the facts, know the truth of the matter, know the true state of affairs; *inf.* know what's what.

score *verb* **1** *score a point/goal* win, gain, achieve; *inf.* chalk up, notch up. **2** *yet to score* win a point/goal, gain a point. **3** *scoring for the two teams* keep count, keep a record, keep a tally. **4** *least likely to score* achieve success, win, triumph, gain an advantage, make an impression; *inf.* be a hit. **5** *score the paintwork* notch,

make a notch in, mark, scratch, scrape, make a groove in, cut, nick, chip, gouge, slit, gash. **score off** *score points off his opponent in public* get the better of, humiliate, make a fool of, have the last laugh; *inf.* be one up on. **score out/through** *score out his name* cross out, strike out, put a line through, delete, obliterate.

scores *plural noun scores of people at the concert* crowds, throngs, multitudes, droves, swarms, armies, legions.

scorn *noun treat the poor with scorn* contempt, contemptuousness, disdain, haughtiness, disparagement, derision, mockery, contumely.
Opposites ADMIRATION; PRAISE.

scorn *verb* **1** *scorn their attempts at playing* be contemptuous, hold in contempt, look down on, disdain, disparage, slight, deride, mock, scoff at, sneer at. **2** *scorn his invitation/advice* rebuff, spurn, shun, refuse, reject, turn down.

scornful *adjective* contemptuous, disdainful, haughty, supercilious, disparaging, slighting, scathing, derisive, mocking, scoffing, sneering, contumelious.

scoundrel *noun* villain, rogue, rascal, miscreant, reprobate, scapegrace, cad, good-for-nothing, ne'er-do-well, wastrel; *inf.* rotter, bounder.

scour *verb* **1** *scour the bath* scrub, rub, clean, cleanse, abrade, wash, wipe, polish, buff, burnish. **2** *scour the countryside | scour the newspaper* search, comb, go over, look all over, ransack, hunt through, rake through, rummage through, leave no stone unturned.

scourge *noun* **1** *her employer/backache regarded as the scourge of her life* bane, curse, affliction, plague, trial, trial and tribulation, torment, torture, suffering, burden, cross to bear, thorn in one's flesh/side, nuisance, pest, punishment, penalty, visitation. **2** *punished with a scourge* whip, horsewhip, bullwhip, switch, lash, cat o' nine tails, thong, flail, strap, birch.

scourge *verb* **1** *scourge the offenders* whip, horsewhip, flog, lash, strap, birch, cane, thrash, beat, leather; *inf.* belt, wallop, lambaste, tan someone's hide. **2** *scourge by guilt* curse, afflict, plague, torment, torture, suffer from, burden, punish.

scout *noun* **1** *scouts returning with no information* advance guard, vanguard, look-out man/woman, outrider, spy. **2** *a scout in the audience* talent scout, talent spotter, recruiter.

scout *verb* **1** *scout for information* search for, search out, look for, seek, hunt for, look around for, cast around for, ferret around for. **2** *scout out the territory* reconnoitre, make a reconnaissance of, spy out, survey, make a survey of, inspect, investigate, examine, scan, study, observe; *inf.* check out, case, make a recce of.

scowl *verb old men scowling at the noisy children* frown, glower, glare, lower, look daggers at, look angry/disapproving, give black looks, give dirty looks.

scowl noun frown, glower, glare, black look, dirty look.

scraggy adjective scrawny, thin, thin as a rake, skinny, gaunt, bony, angular, raw-boned. **Opposites** FAT; PLUMP.

scramble verb **1** *scramble over the fence* clamber, climb, crawl. **2** *scramble to get there on time* hastily struggle, hurry, hasten, rush, race, scurry. **3** *scramble for a place in the final* jockey, struggle, jostle, strive, contend, compete, vie. **4** *her sewing things were scrambled* mix up, jumble, tangle, throw into confusion, disorganize.

scramble noun **1** *go for a scramble over the hills* clamber, climb, trek. **2** *a scramble to get there on time* hurry, rush, race, scurry. **3** *a scramble to get/reach the final* jockeying, struggle, tussle, jostle, competition, vying.

scrap[1] noun **1** *a scrap of material* fragment, piece, bit, snippet, remnant, tatter. **2** *a scrap of food* piece, bit, morsel, particle, sliver, crumb, bite, mouthful. **3** *not a scrap of truth in it* bit, grain, iota, trace, whit, snatch. **4** *collect scrap* waste, junk, rubbish, scrap metal.

scrap[2] verb *scrap the van/plans* throw away, get rid of, discard, toss out, abandon, jettison, dispense with, shed; *inf.* ditch, junk, throw on the scrap-heap. **Opposites** KEEP; RETAIN; RESTORE.

scrap[3] noun *children having a scrap* fight, row, quarrel, argument, squabble, wrangle, tiff, fracas, brawl, scuffle, disagreement, clash; *inf.* set-to, dust-up, run-in, barney.

scrap[4] verb *children scrapping* fight, row, quarrel, bicker, argue, squabble, wrangle, brawl, disagree; *inf.* fall out, have a set-to/dust-up.

scrape verb **1** *scrape the surface to level it* scour, rub, scrub, file, sandpaper. **2** *scrape food from the pans* clean, remove, erase. **3** *a child scraping a knife across metal* grate, rasp, grind, scratch. **4** *gates scraping in the wind* creak, grate, squeak, screech, set one's teeth on edge. **5** *fall and scrape one's knee* graze, scratch, abrade, skin, cut, lacerate, bark. **6** *scrape the side of a car* damage, deface, spoil, mark. **scrape by/along** *scrape by on his earnings* barely manage to live, barely have enough to live on, keep the wolf from the door, scrape a living. **scrape through** *scrape through exams* just pass, pass and no more, pass by a narrow margin, just succeed, narrowly achieve.

scrape noun **1** *the scrape of a knife on metal* grating, rasping, grinding, scratching, creaking, squeaking. **2** *wash the scrape on the child's knee* graze, scratch, abrasion, cut, laceration, wound. **3** *a scrape on the paintwork* scratch, mark, defacement. **4** *getting into scrapes at school* trouble, mischief. **5** *in a bit of a financial scrape* trouble, difficulty, straits, distress, mess, muddle, predicament, plight, tight spot, tight corner; *inf.* fix.

scraps plural noun leftovers, leavings, scrapings, remains, residue, bits and pieces, odds and ends.

scratch verb **1** *skin scratched by rose bushes* graze, scrape, abrade, skin, cut, lacerate, bark. **2** *scratch an itchy part* rub, scrape, tear at. **3** *scratch a knife over metal* scrape, grate,

rasp, grind. **4** *scratch his name from the list* cross out, strike out, delete, erase, remove, eliminate. **5** *runners scratching from the race* withdraw, pull out, stand down. **scratch about/around** *scratch about for proof* search, hunt, cast about, rummage around, forage about, poke about.

scratch noun **1** *a scratch on the skin* graze, scrape, abrasion, cut, laceration, wound. **2** *a scratch on the paintwork* scrape, mark, line, defacement. **up to scratch** up to standard, up to par, satisfactory, acceptable, passable, sufficient, adequate, competent; *inf.* OK.

scrawl verb *scrawl his name* scribble, scratch, dash off.

scrawl noun *unable to read his scrawl* scribble, illegible handwriting.

scrawny adjective scraggy, thin, skinny. *See* SCRAGGY.

scream noun **1** *a scream of pain* shriek, howl, shout, yell, cry, screech, yelp, squeal, wail, squawk, bawl; *inf.* holler. **2** *the entertainer's a scream* comedian, comic, joker, laugh, wit, clown; *inf.* hoot, riot, barrel of laughs, card, caution.

scream verb **1** *scream in pain* shriek, howl, shout, cry out, call out, yell, screech, yelp, squeal, wail, squawk, bawl; *inf.* holler. **2** *the true facts screamed at one* be obvious, be glaringly obvious, be blatant, be apparent. **3** *the colours screamed* clash, not go together, jar.

screech noun *a screech of fright* shriek, howl, shout, yell, squeal, squawk, bawl; *inf.* holler.

screech verb *screeching in pain* shriek, howl, shout, yell. *See* SCREECH *noun.*

screen noun **1** *washing facilities behind a screen* partition, room-divider. **2** *a screen on a window* mesh, net, netting, curtain, blind. **3** *act as a screen from the wind/sun* shelter, shield, protection, guard, safeguard, buffer. **4** *the shop was a screen for his drug-dealing* concealment, cover, cloak, veil, mask, camouflage, disguise, façade, front, blind. **5** *coal put through a screen* sieve, riddle, strainer, colander, filter, winnow.

screen verb **1** *screen off the washing area* partition off, divide off, conceal, hide. **2** *screen them from the wind* shelter, shield, protect, guard, safeguard. **3** *their activities screened by darkness* conceal, hide, cover, cloak, veil, mask, camouflage, disguise. **4** *employees screened by the security service* vet, check, test. **5** *screen people for cancer* check, test, examine, investigate, scan. **6** *screen coal* sieve, riddle, sift, strain, filter, winnow.

screw noun **1** *loose screws in the door* bolt, pin, fastener. **2** *tighten with two or three screws* turn, twist, twirl. **put the screws on** *put the screws on them to get the money* put pressure on, pressurize, bring force to bear on, force, coerce, compel, constrain, hold a pistol to someone's head.

screw verb **1** *screw in the nail* tighten, turn, twist, work in. **2** *screw the planks down* fasten, clamp, rivet, batten. **3** *screw money out of her* force, extort, extract, wrest, bleed, wring. **screw up 1** *screw up one's face in the sun* wrinkle up, pucker, crumple, contort, distort, twist. **2** *screw up a business deal* make a mess of, bungle, botch, make a botch of, ruin, spoil.

scribble *verb scribble a note* dash off, jot down, scrawl.

scribble *noun unable to read the scribble* scrawl, illegible handwriting.

scribe *noun* **1** *scribes taking dictation* amanuensis, copyist, transcriber, secretary, recorder. **2** *describes himself as a scribe* writer, author, journalist, reporter.

scrimp *verb* skimp, economize, be frugal, be thrifty, husband one's resources, tighten one's belt, draw in one's horns.

script *noun* **1** *written in a careful script* handwriting, writing, hand, pen, calligraphy. **2** *read over the script of the play* text, book, libretto, score, lines, words, manuscript.

Scripture *noun* Holy Writ, the Bible, the Holy Bible, the Gospel, the Good Book, the Word of God, the Book of Books. *See tables at* BIBLE, SACRED TEXT.

scrounge *verb scrounge money* cadge, beg, borrow; *inf.* sponge, bum.

scrounger *noun* cadger, beggar, borrower, parasite; *inf.* sponger, freeloader.

scrub *verb* **1** *scrub the floor/bath* rub, scour, clean, cleanse, wash, wipe. **2** *scrub the plans* cancel, drop, discontinue, abandon, call off, give up, do away with, discard, forget about, abort.

scrub *noun land covered in scrub* brushwood, brush, copse, coppice, thicket.

scruffy *adjective* untidy, unkempt, dishevelled, ungroomed, ill-groomed, shabby, down-at-heel, ragged, tattered, slovenly, messy, slatternly, sluttish.
Opposites TIDY; NEAT; CHIC; SPRUCE.

scrumptious *adjective* delicious, tasty, mouthwatering, palatable, delectable, delightful.

scruple *verb not scruple about lying* have qualms about, hesitate to, stick at, think twice about, balk at, demur about, boggle at, be reluctant to, recoil from, shrink from, waver about, vacillate about.

scruples *plural noun have no scruples about stealing food* qualms, twinge of conscience, compunction, hesitation, second thoughts, doubt, misgivings, uneasiness, reluctance, restraint, wavering, vacillation.

scrupulous *adjective* **1** *pay scrupulous attention to detail | a scrupulous inspection* meticulous, careful, painstaking, thorough, rigorous, strict, conscientious, punctilious, exact, precise, fastidious. **2** *scrupulous in his business dealings* honest, honourable, upright, righteous, rightminded, moral, ethical.
Opposites CARELESS; SLAPDASH; DISHONEST; UNSCRUPULOUS.

scrutinize *verb* examine, study, inspect, survey, scan, look over, investigate, go over, peruse, probe, inquire into, sift, analyse, dissect.

scrutiny *noun* examination, study, inspection, survey, scan, perusal, investigation, exploration, probe, inquiry, analysis, dissection.

scuffle *noun involved in a bar-room scuffle* struggle, fight, tussle, row, quarrel, fracas, brawl, clash, affray, rumpus, disturbance, brouhaha, commotion; *inf.* scrap, set-to, dust-up, barney, ruction.

scuffle *verb arrested for scuffling in the street* struggle, fight, exchange blows, come to blows, tussle, row, brawl, clash; *inf.* scrap, have a set-to/dust-up.

sculptor *noun. See table.*

sculpture *noun purchase a sculpture of Churchill* statue, statuette, bust, figure, figurine.

sculpture *verb sculpture his head in bronze* sculpt, sculp, chisel, model, fashion, shape, cast, carve, cut, hew.

scum *noun* **1** *scum forming on coffee* film, layer, froth, foam. **2** *scum forming on a pond* film, crust, algae, filth, dirt. **3** *regard his neighbours as scum* lowest of the low, dregs of society, riffraff, rabble, *canaille*, rubbish.

scupper *verb* **1** *scupper a ship* sink, submerge. **2** *scupper their plans* ruin, defeat, demolish, wreck, smash.

scurrilous *adjective a scurrilous attack on her character* abusive, vituperative, insulting, offensive, disparaging, defamatory, slanderous, gross, foul, scandalous.

scurry *verb scurry home in the rain* hurry, hasten, make haste, rush, race, dash, run, sprint, scuttle, scamper, scramble.

scurry *noun the scurry of the homeward-bound crowds* hurry, haste, rush, bustle, racing, dashing, scuttling, scampering. *See* SCURRY *verb.*

sea *noun* **1** *sail on the sea* ocean, brine; *lit.* the deep, main; *inf.* the brink, the drink. *See table at* OCEAN. **2** *experience rough seas* waves, swell, breakers, rollers, billows. **3** *a sea of daffodils* expanse, sheet, mass, multitude, host, profusion, abundance, plethora. **at sea** *at sea as to the cause of their behaviour* confused, perplexed, bewildered, puzzled, baffled, at a loss, mystified.

seal *noun* **1** *carry the king's seal* emblem, symbol, insignia, badge, crest, token, mark, monogram. **2** *the seal round the bath* sealant, sealer, adhesive. **3** *receive their seal of approval* assurance, attestation, confirmation, ratification, guarantee, proof, authentication, warrant, warranty. **4** *seals swimming near the coast* seal cub. *See table.*

seal *verb* **1** *seal the parcel* fasten, secure, shut, close up. **2** *seal the jars* seal up, make airtight, make watertight, close, shut, cork, stopper, stop up. **3** *seal off the area* close off, shut off, cordon off, fence off. **4** *seal the bargain* secure, clinch, settle, decide, complete. **5** *seal his appointment* confirm, guarantee, ratify, validate.

seam *noun* **1** *the seam between the lengths of material/wood* joint, join, junction. **2** *seams of coal* layer, stratum, vein, lode. **3** *seams on her brows* furrow, line, ridge, wrinkle, scar.

sear *verb* **1** *cloth seared by an iron* burn, singe, scorch, char. **2** *grass seared by the sun* burn, dry up, wither, discolour, brown. **3** *a soul seared by an unhappy love affair* anguish, torture, torment, wound, distress, harry.

search *verb* **1** *search the house* go through, look through, hunt through, rummage through, forage through, rifle through, scour, ransack, comb, go through with a fine-tooth comb, sift through, turn upside down, turn inside out, leave no stone unturned in. **2** *search for clues* look for, seek, hunt for, look high and low for, cast around for, ferret about for, scout out. **3** *search one's soul* examine, explore, investigate, inspect, survey, study, pry into. **4** *search the prisoner* examine, inspect, check; *inf.* frisk. **search me!** I don't know, how should I know?, why ask me?, it beats me, it's a mystery.

search *noun* **1** *conduct a search of the house* hunt, rummage, forage, rifling, scour, ransacking. *See* SEARCH *verb* 1. **2** *a search for truth* exploration, pursuit, quest, probe. **in search of** *in search of happiness* looking for, on the lookout for, seeking, hunting for, in pursuit of, on the track of, questing after.

searching *adjective* **1** *a searching look* penetrating, piercing, discerning, keen, alert, sharp, observant, intent. **2** *searching questions* probing, penetrating, analytic, quizzical, inquiring, inquisitive.

seashell *noun. See table.*

season *noun* *in the warm season of the year* period, time, time of year, spell, term. **in season** *when strawberries are in season* available, obtainable, readily available/obtainable, common, plentiful.

season *verb* **1** *season the sauce* flavour, add flavouring to, add salt/pepper/herbs to, spice, add spices to, pep up; *inf.* add zing to. **2** *letters seasoned with gossip* enliven, leaven, add spice to, pep up; *inf.* add zest/zing to. **3** *season the wood* mature, mellow, prime, prepare. **4** *sea-*

SEALS, SEA LIONS, AND SEA COWS

Baikal seal	leopard seal
bearded seal	manatee
crabeater seal	monk seal
dugong	ringed seal
elephant seal	Ross seal
fur seal	sea cow
grey seal	sea elephant
harbour seal	seal
harp seal	sea lion
hooded seal	walrus
	Weddell seal

SCULPTORS

Aaltonen, Wäinö (1894–1966; Finn.)	Daumier, Honoré (1808–79; Fr.)	woodcarver, b. in the Netherlands)	Oldenburg, Claes (b. 1929; Am., b. in Switzerland)
Andre, Carl (b. 1935; Am.)	della Quercia, Jacopo (c. 1374–1438; It.)	Gill, Eric (1882–1940; Brit. engraver)	Orcagna, Andrea (c. 1308–c. 68; It.)
Appel, Karel (b. 1921; Du.)	della Robbia, Luca (1400–82; Florentine)	Goujon, Jean (c. 1510–68; Fr.)	Paolozzi, Sir Eduardo (b. 1924; Brit.)
Archipenko, Aleksandr (1887–1964; Am., b. in Russia)	Donatello (c. 1386–1466; Florentine)	Hepworth, Dame Barbara (1903–75; Brit.)	Pevsner, Antoine (1886–1962; Fr., b. in Russia)
Arp, Jean (1887–1966; Alsatian)	Dubuffet, Jean (1901–85; Fr.)	Leighton, Frederic, 1st Baron (1830–96; Brit.)	Phidias (c. 490–c. 417 B.C.; Athenian)
Barlach, Ernst (1870–1938; Ger.)	Duchamp, Marcel (1887–1968; Am., b. in France)	Lysippus (4th century B.C.; Gk)	Pisano, Andrea (c. 1290–1348; It.)
Bernini, Gian Lorenzo (1598–1680; It.)	Epstein, Sir Jacob (1880–1959; Brit.)	Maillol, Aristide (1861–1944; Fr.)	Pisano, Nicola (c. 1220–c. 78; It.)
Bourdelle, Émile (1861–1929; Fr.)	Flaxman, John (1755–1826; Brit.)	Marini, Marino (1901–80; It.)	Polyclitus (5th century B.C.; Gk)
Brancusi, Constantin (1876–1957; Romanian)	Frink, Dame Elisabeth (1930–93; Brit.)	Meštrović, Ivan (1883–1962; Am., b. in Croatia)	Praxiteles (mid-4th century B.C.; Gk)
Butler, Reginald (1913–81; Brit.)	Gabo, Naum (1890–1977; Am., b. in Russia)	Michelangelo Buonarroti (1475–1564; It.)	Rodin, Auguste (1840–1917; Fr.)
Calder, Alexander (1898–1976; Am.)	Gaudier-Brzeska, Henri (1891–1915; Fr.)	Michelozzo di Bartolommeo (1396–1472; Florentine)	Roubiliac, Louis-François (1702–62; Fr.)
Canova, Antonio (1757–1822; It.)	Ghiberti, Lorenzo (1378–1455; It.)	Moholy-Nagy, László (1895–1946; Am., b. in Hungary)	Sluter, Claus (c. 1345–1406; Du.)
Cato, Sir Anthony (b. 1924; Brit.)	Giacometti, Alberto (1901–66; Swiss)	Moore, Henry (1898–1986; Brit.)	Stoss, Veit (c. 1447–1533; Ger.)
Cellini, Benvenuto (1500–71; Florentine)	Giambologna (1529–1608; It.)	Myron (c. 480–440 B.C.; Gk)	Thorvaldsen, Bertel (c. 1770–1844; Da.)
Clodion (1738–1814; Fr.)	Gibbons, Grinling (1648–1721; Brit.		Verrocchio, Andrea del (c. 1435–88; It.)
			Zadkine, Ossip (1890–1967; Fr.)

son *one's language* temper, moderate, qualify, tone down.

seasonable *adjective* **1** *seasonable weather* usual, appropriate to the time of year. **2** *seasonable advice* opportune, timely, well-timed, appropriate, suitable, apt.

seasoned *adjective seasoned travellers* experienced, practised, well-versed, established, habituated, long-serving, time-served, veteran, hardened, battle-scarred.
Opposites INEXPERIENCED; CALLOW; GREEN.

seasoning *noun add seasoning to the sauce* flavouring, salt and pepper, herbs, spices, condiments, dressing, relish.

seat *noun* **1** *enough seats for the audience/spectators* chair, bench, settle, stool, stall. *See table at* CHAIR. **2** *the seat of government* headquarters, location, site, whereabouts, place, base, centre, hub, heart. **3** *fall on one's seat* bottom, buttocks, posterior, rump, hindquarters; *inf.* behind, backside, bum; *Am. inf.* butt, tail, fanny; *vulg.* arse. **4** *the seat of his anxiety* grounds, cause, reason, basis, source, origin. **5** *the family seat in Suffolk* family residence, ancestral home, mansion, stately home.

seat *verb* **1** *seat them next to each other* place, position, put, situate, deposit. **2** *the hall seats 500* hold, take, have room for, accommodate.

seating *noun* seats, room, places, chairs, accommodation.

secede *verb secede from the organization* withdraw from, break away from, break with, separate oneself from, sever relations with, quit, split with, resign from, pull out of, drop out

of, have nothing more to do with, turn one's back on, repudiate, reject, renounce.

secluded *adjective a secluded place* sheltered, concealed, hidden, private, unfrequented, solitary, lonely, sequestered, retired, out-of-the-way, remote, isolated, off the beaten track, tucked-away, cut-off.
Opposites PUBLIC; BUSY; ACCESSIBLE.

seclusion *noun former film stars now living in seclusion* privacy, solitude, retreat, retirement, withdrawal, sequestration, isolation, concealment, hiding, secrecy.

second¹ *adjective* **1** *on the second day of the trial* next, following, subsequent, succeeding. **2** *a second helping | a second pair of boots* additional, extra, further. **3** *take a second pair of climbing boots* extra, additional, other, alternative, back-up, substitute. **4** *move from the second team to the first* secondary, lower, subordinate, lesser, lower-grade, inferior. **5** *regarded as a second Churchill* other, duplicate, replicate. **second to none** *as a player he is second to none* unparalleled, without parallel, unequalled, without equal, unmatched, unique, in a class of one's own.

second² *noun act as second to the boxer/duellist* assistant, attendant, helper, supporter, backer, right-hand man/woman.

second³ *verb* **1** *seconded in his research by a student* assist, help, aid, support. **2** *second the proposal* formally support, give one's support to, back, approve, give one's approval to, endorse, promote.

SEASHELLS

abalone	flamingo tongue	nutmeg shell	sunset shell
angel wing	frog shell	nut shell	tellin
ark shell	furrow shell	olive	thorny oyster
auger	gaper	ormer	tiger cowrie
basket shell	giant clam	otter shell	tooth shell
bonnet	hard clam	oyster	top-shell
bubble shell	harp	oyster drill	tower shell
canoe shell	heart cockle	partridge shell	triton
carpet shell	helmet	pearly nautilus	triton's trumpet
carrier shell	hoof shell	pelican's foot	trough shell
cask shell	horn shell	pen shell	trumpet shell
chambered nautilus	horse mussel	periwinkle	tulip shell
chank	jewel box	pheasant shell	tun
clam	jingle shell	piddock	turban
coat-of-mail	junonia	pyramid shell	turkey wing
cockle	keyhole limpet	quahog	turret shell
cock's-comb oyster	lima	queen scallop	tusk shell
conch	limpet	razor-shell	umbrella shell
cone	lion's paw	rock shell	vase shell
cowrie	lucine	saddle oyster	venus
cup-and-saucer	marginella	scallop	Venus clam
date mussel	mitre	sea snail	violet sea snail
dog whelk	money cowrie	slipper limpet	volute
dove shell	moon shell	slit limpet	wedge shell
drill	murex	slit shell	wentletrap
drupe	mussel	spider conch	whelk
ear shell	nautilus	spindle shell	wing oyster
fig shell	necklace shell	spire shell	winkle
fighting conch	nerite	staircase shell	worm shell
file shell	Noah's ark	sundial	zebra mussel

second⁴ verb second staff to another department transfer, move, shift, assign.

second⁵ noun I'll be with you in a second | disappear in a second moment, minute, instant, trice, twinkling, twinkling of an eye; inf. sec, jiffy, jif, tick, mo, two shakes of a lamb's tail, two shakes.

secondary adjective 1 ignore the secondary issues lesser, subordinate, minor, ancillary, subsidiary, non-essential, unimportant. 2 patients with secondary infections non-primary, derived, derivative, indirect, resulting, resultant. 3 a secondary line of action second, back-up, reserve, relief, auxiliary, extra, alternative, subsidiary. **Opposites** PRIMARY; PRIME; MAIN.

second-class adjective treated as second-class citizens second-rate, low-class, inferior, lesser, unimportant.

second-hand adjective second-hand goods/clothes used, worn, nearly-new, handed-down; inf. hand-me-down, reach-me-down.

second hand adverb hear the news second hand at second hand, indirectly; inf. on the grapevine, on the bush telegraph.

second-in-command noun deputy, number two, substitute, subordinate, right-hand man/woman.

secondly adverb second, in the second place, next.

second-rate adjective 1 regarded as second-rate citizens second-class, low-class, inferior, lesser, unimportant. 2 try to give us second-rate goods inferior, sub-standard, poor-quality, low-quality, low-grade, shoddy, rubbishy, tawdry; inf. tacky.

seconds plural noun 1 children asking for seconds second helping, further helping, more. 2 a shop selling seconds rejects, imperfect goods, faulty/flawed goods, inferior goods.

secrecy noun 1 the secrecy of the information confidentiality, privateness. See SECRET adjective 1. 2 the secrecy of their love affair clandestineness, furtiveness, surreptitiousness, stealth, covertness. See SECRET adjective 3. 3 appreciate the secrecy of their meeting-place seclusion, concealment, privacy, solitariness, retirement, sequestration, remoteness. See SECRET 5.

secret adjective 1 keep the matter secret confidential, private, unrevealed, undisclosed, under wraps, unpublished, untold, unknown; inf. hush-hush. 2 a secret drawer in the table hidden, concealed, camouflaged, disguised. 3 a secret love affair | secret political activities hidden, clandestine, furtive, conspiratorial, undercover, surreptitious, stealthy, cloak-and-dagger, covert; inf. hole-and-corner, closet. 4 a secret code/message hidden, mysterious, cryptic, abstruse, recondite, arcane. 5 a secret place secluded, concealed, hidden, sheltered, private, unfrequented, solitary, lonely, sequestered, retired, out-of-the-way, remote, tucked-away. See SECLUDED. 6 a secret person secretive, reticent, uncommunicative. See SECRETIVE. **Opposites** PUBLIC; OPEN; OBVIOUS.

secret noun 1 unable to keep a secret confidential matter, confidence, private affair. 2 the

secrets of nature mystery, enigma, puzzle, riddle. 3 the secret of their success recipe, formula, key, answer, solution. **in secret** 1 talks held in secret secretly, behind closed doors, in camera. See SECRET adjective 1. 2 conduct their love affair in secret privately, discreetly, furtively, stealthily, covertly.

secrete verb 1 secrete a watery discharge discharge, emit, excrete, exude, ooze, leak, give off, send out. 2 secrete the package in a hidden drawer hide, conceal, cover up, stow away, sequester, cache; inf. stash away. **Opposites** ABSORB; REVEAL; SHOW.

secretion noun discharge, emission, excretion, exudate, oozing, leakage.

secretive adjective a secretive person/nature secret, reticent, uncommunicative, unforthcoming, reserved, taciturn, silent, quiet, tight-lipped, close-mouthed, close, playing one's cards close to one's chest, clamlike; inf. cagey. **Opposites** OPEN; COMMUNICATIVE; CHATTY.

secretly adverb 1 committees meeting secretly/married secretly in secret, confidentially, privately, behind closed doors, in camera, sub rosa. 2 conducting their love affair secretly in secret, clandestinely, furtively, conspiratorially, surreptitiously, stealthily, on the sly, covertly; inf. on the q.t. 3 secretly she admired him privately, in one's heart, in one's innermost thoughts.

sect noun 1 a strange religious sect religious cult, religious group, religious denomination, religious order. See tables at CHRISTIANITY, RELIGION. 2 the organization split by warring sects faction, camp, splinter group, wing, division.

sectarian adjective sectarian groups in conflict | sectarian views doctrinaire, partisan, bigoted, prejudiced, narrow-minded, insular, hidebound, extreme, fanatic, fanatical. **Opposites** TOLERANT; LIBERAL; BROAD-MINDED.

section noun 1 divide the wood/fruit/material into sections part, segment, division, component, piece, portion, bit, slice, fraction, fragment. 2 the various sections of the book part, division, component, chapter. 3 the reference section of the library part, division, department, branch.

sector adjective 1 the manufacturing sector of the economy part, division, area, branch, category, field. 2 forbidden to enter the military sector zone, quarter, district, area, region.

secular adjective secular music/matters lay, non-religious, non-spiritual, non-church, laical, temporal, worldly, earthly. **Opposites** HOLY; RELIGIOUS; SACRED.

secure adjective 1 the children/jewels will be quite secure there safe, free from danger, out of harm's way, invulnerable, unharmed, undamaged, protected, sheltered, shielded. 2 the windows are quite secure fastened, closed, shut, locked, sealed. 3 secure steps leading to the attic stable, fixed, steady, strong, sturdy, solid. 4 children feeling secure | feeling secure in his job safe, unworried, at ease, comfortable, confident, assured. 5 look forward to a secure future safe, reliable, dependable, settled, fixed,

established, solid.
Opposites INSECURE; PRECARIOUS.

secure verb **1** *secure the building from attack* make safe, make sound, fortify, strengthen, protect. **2** *secure the doors and windows* fasten, close, shut, lock, bolt, chain, seal. **3** *secure the boat* tie up, moor, anchor. **4** *secure their rights* assure, ensure, insure, guarantee, underwrite, confirm, establish. **5** *finally secure all they needed* acquire, obtain, gain, get, get hold of, procure, get possession of, come by; *inf.* get one's hands on, land.

security noun **1** *the security of the children/jewels* safety, freedom from danger, invulnerability, protection, safe-keeping, shielding. *See* SECURE *adjective* 1. **2** *seek security from their pursuers* protection, refuge, sanctuary, asylum, safety. **3** *children losing their feelings of security* safety, lack of worry/anxiety, freedom from doubt, certainty, feeling of ease, confidence, assurance. **4** *the security of the future/job* safety, reliability, dependability. *See* SECURE *adjective* 5. **5** *tight security for the queen's visit* safety measures, safeguards, guards, surveillance, defence, protection. **6** *use one's house as security for a loan* collateral, surety, guarantee, pledge, gage.

sedate adjective **1** *too sedate a way of life for the teenagers* calm, tranquil, placid, dignified, formal, decorous, proper, demure, sober, earnest, staid, stiff. **2** *sedate old ladies untroubled by the excitement* calm, composed, tranquil, placid, serene, unruffled, imperturbable, unflappable. **3** *move at a sedate pace* slow, slow-moving, leisurely, measured, deliberate, dignified, staid.
Opposites EXCITING; WILD; EXCITABLE; FAST.

sedate verb *sedate the patient* give a sedative to, put under sedation, calm down, tranquillize.

sedative noun tranquillizer, calmative, depressant, sleeping pill, narcotic, opiate; *inf.* downer.

sedative adjective *drugs/voices with a sedative effect* calming, tranquillizing, soothing, calmative, relaxing, assuaging, lenitive, soporific, narcotic.

sedentary adjective *sedentary workers/people* sitting, seated, desk-bound, desk, inactive.
Opposites ACTIVE; MOBILE.

sediment noun lees, dregs, grounds, deposit, residue, precipitate, settlings.

sedition noun **1** *speakers accused of sedition* incitement to riot/rebellion, agitation, rabble-rousing, fomentation. **2** *advocating sedition* civil disorder, rebellion, insurrection, insurgence, uprising, mutiny, rioting, subversion, treason.

seditious adjective **1** *a seditious speech* inciting, rabble-rousing, agitating, fomenting. **2** *a seditious element at court* rebellious, insurrectionist, insurgent, mutinous, subversive, dissident, disloyal, treasonous.

seduce verb **1** *men seducing young girls* lead astray, corrupt, deflower, ravish, violate. **2** *seduced into the industry by high salaries* attract, allure, lure, tempt, entice, beguile, ensnare.

seductive adjective **1** *seductive smiles/dresses* attracting, alluring, tempting, provocative, exciting, arousing, sexy. **2** *seductive music/salaries* attractive, appealing, inviting, alluring, tempting, enticing, beguiling.

see verb **1** *I can see the house* make out, catch sight of, glimpse, spot, notice, observe, view, perceive, discern, espy, descry, distinguish, identify, recognize. **2** *see that man over there* look at, regard, note, observe, heed, mark, behold, watch; *inf.* get a load of. **3** *see the comedy programme last night* watch, look at, view. **4** *see what they mean* understand, grasp, get, comprehend, follow, take in, know, realize, get the drift of, make out, fathom; *inf.* latch on to. **5** *go and see what he wants* find out, discover, learn, ascertain, determine, ask, enquire, make enquiries, investigate. **6** *we'll have to see* think, consider, reflect, deliberate, give thought, have a think. **7** *see that the door is locked* see to it, take care, mind, make sure, make certain, ensure, guarantee. **8** *see trouble ahead* foresee, predict, forecast, anticipate, envisage, imagine, picture, visualize. **9** *see an old friend in the street* meet, encounter, run into, stumble upon, chance upon, recognize. **10** *see the doctor* visit, pay a visit to, consult, confer with. **11** *they see each other from time to time* meet, have meetings, arrange to meet, meet socially. **12** *he's seeing someone else now* go out with, take out, keep company with, court; *inf.* go steady with, date. **13** *see her to her car* escort, accompany, show, lead, take, usher, attend. **see about 1** *see about travel arrangements* see to, deal with, attend to, cope with, look after, take care of. *See* SEE TO. **2** *see about what's happening* look into, investigate, enquire about, make enquiries about, ask about. **see over** *see over the house* see round, look round, have a look around, go on a tour of, tour, inspect. **see through 1** *see through his disguise | see through their attempts to charm* be undeceived by, not be taken in by, be wise to, get the measure of, fathom, penetrate; *inf.* not fall for, have someone's number. **2** *see the job through* keep at, persevere with, persist with; *inf.* stick out. **3** *see a friend through misfortune* support, help, assist, back up, stand by, stick by. **see to** *see to the travel arrangements* see about, deal with, arrange, organize, attend to, cope with, look after, take care of, be in charge of, be responsible for.

seed noun **1** *growing plants from seeds* ovule, germ. **2** *issue of his seed* sperm, spermatic fluid, semen, spermatozoa. **3** *the seed of her discontent* source, origin, root, cause, reason, grounds, basis, motivation, motive. **4** *seed of the royal house* child, offspring, progeny, issue, descendants, scions. **go/run to seed** *the farm has gone to seed* deteriorate, decline, degenerate, decay, go to rack and ruin, become dilapidated; *inf.* go downhill, go to pot, go to the dogs.

seedy adjective **1** *seedy little hotels* shabby, scruffy, shoddy, run-down, dilapidated, squalid, mean, sleazy, sordid, tatty; *inf.* crummy. **2** *feeling rather seedy* unwell, ill, poorly, out of sorts, off-colour, indisposed; *inf.* under the weather.

seek *verb* **1** *seek up-to-date information* search for, try to find, look for, be on the look-out for, be after, hunt for, be in quest of, be in pursuit of. **2** *seek help from a counsellor* ask for, request, solicit, entreat, beg for. **3** *seek to please* try to, attempt to, endeavour to, strive to, aim to, aspire to.

seem *verb seem a pleasant place* appear, appear to be, have the appearance of being, give the impression of being, look, look like, look to be, have the look of.

seeming *adjective his seeming charm* apparent, ostensible, outward, external, surface, superficial, pretended, feigned, assumed, supposed. **Opposites** ACTUAL; REAL; GENUINE.

seemly *adjective seemly behaviour/dress* decorous, proper, decent, becoming, fitting, suitable, appropriate, apt, apposite, meet, *comme il faut*, in good taste. **Opposites** UNSEEMLY; UNBECOMING; UNSUITABLE.

seep *verb pus seeping from the wound* ooze, leak, exude, drip, drain, percolate.

seer *noun* prophet, soothsayer, augur, sibyl.

seesaw *verb emotions seesawing* fluctuate, go from one extreme to the other, swing, oscillate.

seethe *verb* **1** *liquid seething in the pan* boil, bubble, fizz, foam, froth, ferment, churn. **2** *seething at the lateness of the bus* be furious, be livid, be incensed, be in a rage, rant and rave, storm, fume, foam at the mouth, breathe fire.

segment *noun divide the fruit into segments* section, part, division, component, piece, portion, slice, wedge.

segregate *verb* separate, set apart, isolate, dissociate, cut off, sequester, ostracize, discriminate against.

segregation *noun* separation, setting apart, isolation, dissociation, sequestration, discrimination, apartheid, partition. See SEGREGATE.

seize *verb* **1** *a drowning man seizing an overhanging branch* grab, grab hold of, take hold of, grasp, take a grip of, grip, clutch at. **2** *police seizing a haul of drugs* confiscate, impound, commandeer, appropriate, take possession of, sequester, sequestrate. **3** *criminals seizing a child/van* snatch, abduct, take captive, kidnap, hijack. **4** *police seizing the criminals* catch, arrest, apprehend, take into custody, take prisoner; *inf.* collar, nab. **5** *seize upon the meaning of the message* grasp, understand, comprehend, discern, perceive, get the drift of.

seizure *noun* **1** *the police's seizure of the drug haul* confiscation, commandeering, appropriation, sequestration. See SEIZE 2. **2** *the seizure of the child/van* snatching, abduction, kidnapping, hijacking. **3** *the seizure of the criminals* arrest, apprehension; *inf.* collaring, nabbing. See SEIZE 4.

seldom *adverb* rarely, hardly ever, scarcely ever, infrequently, only occasionally, not ever; *inf.* once in a blue moon. **Opposites** OFTEN; FREQUENTLY.

select *verb* choose, pick, hand-pick, single out, opt for, decide on, settle on, prefer, favour.

select *adjective* **1** *a select range of goods* choice, hand-picked, prime, first-rate, first-class, finest, best, high-quality, top-quality, supreme, superb, excellent. **2** *a select club* exclusive, elite, limited, privileged, cliquish; *inf.* posh. **Opposites** INFERIOR; SECOND-RATE; COMMON.

selection *noun* **1** *offer a wide selection of goods* choice, pick, option. **2** *publish a selection of his works* choice, anthology, variety, assortment, miscellany, collection, range.

selective *adjective able to be selective about houses* particular, discriminating, discriminatory, discerning, fussy, careful, cautious; *inf.* choosy, picky.

self-assurance *noun* self-confidence, confidence, assertiveness, positiveness.

self-centred *adjective* egocentric, egotistic, egotistical, self-absorbed, self-seeking, wrapped up in oneself, selfish, narcissistic.

self-confidence *noun* self-assurance, confidence, self-reliance, self-dependence, self-possession, poise, aplomb, composure, *sang froid*.

self-conscious *adjective* awkward, shy, diffident, bashful, blushing, timorous, nervous, timid, retiring, shrinking, ill-at-ease, embarrassed, uncomfortable.

self-control *noun* self-restraint, restraint, self-discipline, will-power, strength of will.

self-denial *noun* self-discipline, asceticism, self-abnegation, self-deprivation, abstemiousness, temperance, abstinence, self-sacrifice, selflessness, unselfishness, altruism.

self-esteem *noun* self-respect, self-regard, pride in oneself/one's abilities, faith in oneself, *amour propre*.

self-important *adjective* pompous, vain, conceited, arrogant, swollen-headed, egotistical, presumptuous, overbearing, overweening, haughty, swaggering, strutting.

self-indulgence *noun* self-gratification, lack of self-restraint, unrestraint, intemperance, immoderation, excess, pleasure-seeking, pursuit of pleasure, sensualism, dissipation.

selfish *adjective* self-seeking, self-centred, egocentric, egotistic, egoistic, self-interested, self-regarding, self-absorbed; *inf.* looking out for number one. **Opposites** UNSELFISH; ALTRUISTIC; SELFLESS.

selfless *adjective* unselfish, altruistic, generous, self-sacrificing, self-denying, magnanimous, liberal, ungrudging. **Opposites** SELFISH; SELF-CENTRED; EGOISTIC.

self-possessed *adjective* self-assured, confident, sure of oneself, composed, cool, cool as a cucumber, cool, calm, and collected; *inf.* together.

self-respect *noun* self-esteem, self-regard, pride in oneself, pride in one's abilities, belief in one's worth, faith in oneself, *amour propre*.

self-righteous *adjective* sanctimonious, holier-than-thou, over-pious, pietistic, too good to be true, Pharisaic, unctuous, mealy-mouthed; *inf.* goody-goody.

self-sacrifice *noun* self-denial, selflessness, self-abnegation, unselfishness, altruism.

self-satisfied *adjective* pleased with oneself, well-pleased, proud of oneself, flushed with success, self-approving, complacent, smug, like the cat that swallowed the cream/canary.

self-seeking *adjective* self-interested, opportunistic, looking out for oneself, ambitious, mercenary, out for what one can get, fortune-hunting, gold-digging; *inf.* on the make, looking out for number one.

self-styled *adjective* would-be, so-called, self-named, self-titled.

self-willed *adjective* wilful, contrary, perverse, uncooperative, wayward, recalcitrant, refractory, intractable, stubborn, pig-headed, mulish, intransigent, difficult, disobedient; *inf.* cussed.

sell *verb* **1** *sell their house* put up for sale, put on sale, dispose of, vend, auction off, trade, barter. **2** *traders selling fruit and vegetables* trade in, deal in, be in the business of, traffic in, stock, carry, offer for sale, market, handle, peddle, hawk. **3** *goods selling well* be bought, be purchased, go, go like hot cakes, move, be in demand. **4** *selling for £5* retail, go for, be, be found for. **5** *sell the idea of self-support* get acceptance for, win approval for, get support for, get across, promote. **6** *you won't sell the workforce that* persuade of, convince of, talk someone into, bring someone round to, induce to, win someone over to. **7** *You've been sold!* sell down the river, betray, cheat, swindle, defraud, fleece, deceive, trick, double-cross, bilk, gull; *inf.* diddle, con, stab someone in the back. **sell out 1** *bakers sold out of bread* be out of stock of, run out of, dispose of, have none left. **2** *supplies of tickets all sold out* be bought up, be depleted, be exhausted. **3** *he used to have principles but he sold out for a huge salary* prostitute oneself, sell one's soul, betray one's cause/ideals, go over to the other side, play false.
Opposites BUY; PURCHASE.

seller *noun* vendor, retailer, salesman/woman/person, shopkeeper, trader, tradesman, merchant, dealer, agent, representative, traveller, commercial traveller; *inf.* rep.

selling *noun* **1** *the selling of property* vending, trading. See SELL 1. **2** *a career in selling* sales, salesmanship, marketing, merchandising.

semblance *noun* only a semblance of honesty appearance, outward appearance, show, air, guise, pretence, façade, front, veneer, mask, cloak, disguise, camouflage, pretext.

send *verb* **1** *send a letter* dispatch, forward, mail, post, remit. **2** *send a message* transmit, convey, communicate, broadcast, televise, telecast, radio. **3** *send a stone skimming over the water* throw, fling, hurl, cast, let fly, propel, project. **4** *send one mad* drive, make, cause one to be/become. **5** *the music sent him* excite, stimulate, titillate, rouse, stir, thrill, intoxicate, enrapture, enthral, ravish, charm, delight; *inf.* turn one on. **send for** *send for a doctor/plumber* call for, summon, request, order. **send off** *send off evil-smelling fumes* give off, discharge, emit, exude.
Opposites RECEIVE; GET.

senile *adjective* doddering, decrepit, failing, in one's dotage, in one's second childhood, mentally confused.

senior *adjective* **1** *senior officer* high-ranking, higher-ranking, superior. **2** *the senior of the staff | James Black senior* older, elder.
Opposites JUNIOR; SUBORDINATE; INFERIOR.

sensation *noun* **1** *awake with a sensation of fear* feeling, sense, awareness, consciousness, perception, impression. **2** *their affair caused a sensation* stir, excitement, agitation, commotion, furore, scandal. **3** *the new show's a sensation* great success; *inf.* hit, smash hit, wow.

sensational *adjective* **1** *a sensational news story* spectacular, stirring, exciting, startling, staggering, dramatic, amazing, shocking, scandalous, lurid. **2** *looking sensational in the evening dress* marvellous, superb, excellent, exceptional, remarkable; *inf.* fabulous, fab, out of this world.
Opposites RUN-OF-THE-MILL; DULL; ORDINARY.

sense *noun* **1** *a sense of touch* feeling, sensation, faculty, sensibility. **2** *detect a sense of hostility* feeling, atmosphere, impression, aura. **3** *a sense of guilt* feeling, sensation, awareness, consciousness, perception. **4** *a sense of humour* appreciation, awareness, understanding, comprehension. **5** *have the sense to keep quiet* common sense, practicality, wisdom, sagacity, sharpness, discernment, perception, wit, intelligence, cleverness, understanding, reason, logic, brain, brains; *inf.* gumption, nous. **6** *a word with several senses* meaning, definition, import, signification, significance, implication, nuance, drift, gist, purport, denotation. **7** *no sense in what she said/did* intelligibility, coherence, comprehensibility, logic, rationality, purpose, point.

sense *verb* sense their hostility feel, get the impression of, be aware of, be conscious of, observe, notice, perceive, discern, grasp, pick up, suspect, divine, intuit; *inf.* have a feeling about.

senseless *adjective* **1** *a senseless act/comment* nonsensical, stupid, foolish, silly, inane, idiotic, mindless, unintelligent, unwise, irrational, illogical, meaningless, pointless, absurd, ludicrous, fatuous, asinine, moronic, imbecilic, mad; *inf.* daft. **2** *knocked senseless by the blow* unconscious, insensible, out cold, out, cold, stunned, numb, numbed, insensate.
Opposites SENSIBLE; WISE; CONSCIOUS.

sensibilities *plural noun* offend older people's sensibilities moral sense, finer feelings, susceptibilities, sense of outrage.

sensibility *noun* a coarse man without sensibility sensitivity, sensitiveness, finer feelings, delicacy, taste, discrimination, discernment.

sensible *adjective* **1** *a sensible person/approach* practical, realistic, down-to-earth, wise, prudent; judicious, sagacious, sharp, shrewd, discerning, perceptive, far-sighted, intelligent, clever, rational, logical; *inf.* brainy. **2** *a sensible rise in temperature* perceptible, discernible, appreciable, noticeable, visible, observable, tangible, palpable. **3** *sensible of his inadequacies* aware of, conscious of, mind-

ful of, sensitive to, alive to, cognizant of, acquainted with.
Opposites FOOLISH; SILLY; UNAWARE.

sensitive adjective **1** *sensitive to unfriendly atmospheres* responsive to, easily affected by, susceptible to, reactive to, sentient of. **2** *sensitive skin* delicate, fine, soft, easily damaged, fragile. **3** *sensitive rather than coarse people* responsive, receptive, perceptive, discerning, discriminatory, sympathetic, understanding, empathetic. **4** *too sensitive for a competitive industry* over-sensitive, easily upset, thin-skinned, touchy, temperamental. **5** *a sensitive issue* delicate, difficult, problematic, ticklish.
Opposites INSENSITIVE; COARSE; TOUGH.

sensitivity noun **1** *the sensitivity of her skin* sensitiveness, delicacy, fineness, softness, fragility. **2** *the sensitivity of the artist* sensitiveness, responsiveness, receptiveness, perceptiveness, discernment, discrimination. See SENSITIVE 3. **3** *unable to cope with her sensitivity* over-sensitivity, touchiness. See SENSITIVE 4.

sensual adjective **1** *sensual rather than spiritual pleasures* physical, carnal, bodily, fleshly, animal, voluptuous, non-spiritual, epicurean, sybaritic. **2** *sensual curves/lips* voluptuous, sexual, sexy, erotic.
Opposites SPIRITUAL; ASCETIC.

sensuous adjective *sensuous music* | *the sensuous feel of satin* aesthetic, pleasing, pleasurable, gratifying.

sentence noun **1** *listen to the judge delivering the sentence* judgement, verdict, pronouncement, ruling, decision, decree. **2** *serve a three-year sentence* prison sentence, jail sentence, penal sentence, prison term; *inf.* time, porridge.

sentence verb **1** *hear the judge sentencing the prisoners* impose a sentence on, pass judgement on, mete out punishment to, punish. **2** *sentenced to a life of pain* condemn, doom, punish, penalize.

sententious adjective **1** *always making sententious remarks about their neighbour's behaviour* moralistic, moralizing, judgemental, sanctimonious, canting, pompous. **2** *a sententious style of prose* concise, succinct, terse, compact, epigrammatic, pithy, axiomatic, aphoristic.

sentiment noun **1** *no room for sentiment in business* emotion, emotionalism, finer feelings, tender feelings, tenderness, softness. **2** *a revolutionary sentiment obvious in her writings* feelings, attitude, belief, opinion, view, point of view. See SENTIMENTS. **3** *romantic novels full of sentiment* sentimentality, emotionalism, over-emotionalism, mawkishness. See SENTIMENTALITY.

sentimental adjective **1** *singing sentimental love songs* emotional, overemotional, romantic, mawkish, maudlin, soppy; *inf.* mushy, slushy, soppy, schmaltzy, corny. **2** *a sentimental attachment to the town* emotional, nostalgic, affectionate, loving, tender, warm.
Opposites DISPASSIONATE; PRACTICAL; HARD-HEADED; DOWN-TO-EARTH.

sentimentality noun *criticizing the sentimentality of the novels* emotionalism, overemotionalism,

romanticism, mawkishness, soppiness; *inf.* mush, slush, soppiness, corniness.

sentiments plural noun *my sentiments exactly* feeling, attitude, belief, thoughts, way of thinking, opinion, view, point of view, idea, judgement, persuasion.

sentry noun guard, lookout, watch, watchman, sentinel.

separate adjective **1** *have separate residences* individual, distinct, different, particular, autonomous, independent. **2** *the problems being quite separate* unconnected, unattached, distinct, different, disconnected, unrelated, detached, divorced, divided, discrete.
Opposites UNITED; SAME.

separate verb **1** *separate the joined pieces of wood* disconnect, detach, sever, uncouple, divide, disjoin, sunder. **2** *old pipes separating at the joints* come apart, come away, break off, divide, disunite. **3** *the fence separating the two gardens* divide, come between, stand between, keep apart, partition. **4** *the roads separated at the foot of the hill* part, part company, go their separate ways, go different ways, diverge, split, divide. **5** *the couple separated last year* officially separate, obtain an official separation, break up, split up, part, become estranged, divorce. **6** *a splinter group separating from the society* break away from, break with, secede from, withdraw from, sever relations with. **7** *separate the items according to size* divide, sort, sort out, classify, categorize. **8** *separate the naughty children from the rest* set apart, segregate, single out, put to one side, isolate.
Opposites JOIN; UNITE; MARRY; MIX.

separately adverb **1** *all four living separately* apart, individually, independently, autonomously. **2** *the members of the group left separately* individually, one by one, one at a time, singly, severally, independently.

separation noun **1** *the separation of the pieces* disconnection, detachment, severance, uncoupling, division, disjunction, disunion, dissociation, segregation. **2** *upset by her parents' separation* break-up, split-up, split, parting, estrangement, parting of the ways, rift, divorce.

septic adjective infected, festering, pussy, poisoned, putrefying, putrefactive, putrid.

sepulchre noun tomb, vault, burial place, grave.

sequel noun *an unfortunate sequel of/to the party* follow-up, development, result, consequence, outcome, issue, upshot, end, conclusion.

sequence noun *sequence of events/movements/numbers* chain, course, cycle, series, progression, succession, set, arrangement, order, pattern.

sequester verb **1** *nuns sequestered from the world* isolate, seclude, withdraw, retire, cut off, set apart, segregate, shut off. **2** *sequester a debtor's funds* sequestrate, confiscate, take possession of, seize, appropriate, expropriate, impound, commandeer.

seraphic adjective **1** *seraphic beings* angelic, celestial, heavenly, holy. **2** *a seraphic smile* blissful, beatific, rapt, joyful, serene.

serendipity *noun* chance, mere chance, happy chance, luck, good fortune, fortuity, fortuitousness, accident, coincidence.

serene *adjective* **1** *remain serene throughout the trouble* calm, composed, tranquil, peaceful, placid, still, quiet, unperturbed, imperturbable, undisturbed, unruffled, unworried, unexcited, unexcitable, unflappable. **2** *a serene sky* cloudless, unclouded, clear, bright, sunny.

serenity *noun* **1** *admire her serenity in face of trouble* calm, calmness, composure, tranquillity, peace, peacefulness, peace of mind, placidity, placidness, stillness, quietness, quiet, quietude, imperturbability. **2** *the serenity of the sky* cloudlessness, clearness, brightness, sunniness.

series *noun* *a series of events/people/numbers* succession, progression, sequence, chain, course, string, train, run, cycle, set, row, arrangement, order.

serious *adjective* **1** *serious expressions* solemn, earnest, unsmiling, unlaughing, thoughtful, preoccupied, pensive, grave, sombre, sober, long-faced, dour, stern, grim, poker-faced. **2** *serious problems/trouble* important, significant, consequential, of consequence, momentous, of moment, weighty, far-reaching, urgent, pressing, crucial, vital, life-and-death. **3** *serious injuries* acute, grave, bad, critical, alarming, grievous, dangerous, perilous. **4** *serious about reforming* earnest, in earnest, sincere, honest, genuine, firm, resolute, resolved, determined, fervent.
Opposites CHEERFUL; TRIVIAL; MINOR; FLIPPANT.

seriously *adverb* **1** *nodding seriously* solemnly, earnestly, unsmilingly, with a straight face, thoughtfully, pensively, gravely, sombrely, soberly, dourly, sternly, grimly. **2** *seriously injured* severely, acutely, gravely, badly, critically, alarmingly, grievously, dangerously, perilously. **3** *seriously, you'll like it here* to be serious, without joking, no joking, truthfully, I mean it.

seriousness *noun* **1** *the seriousness of their expressions* solemnity, solemnness, thoughtfulness, preoccupation, pensiveness, graveness, gravity, sombreness, soberness, sobriety, dourness, sternness, grimness. **2** *the seriousness of the problem* importance, significance, consequence, momentousness, moment, weightiness, weight, urgency, crucialness, vitalness. **3** *the seriousness of the injuries* severity, severeness, acuteness, gravity, graveness, badness, criticalness, grievousness, danger, dangerousness, peril, perilousness. **4** *acknowledge their seriousness about reforming* sincerity, earnestness, honesty, genuineness, firmness, resolution, resolve, determination, fervour.

sermon *noun* **1** *sermons from the pulpit* preaching, teaching, speech, homily, address, oration. **2** *she listened to a sermon on lateness by her father* lecture, moralizing, declamation, tirade, harangue, ranting, diatribe, reprimand, reproof, remonstrance, castigation; *inf.* talking-to, dressing-down.

serrated *adjective* serrate, serrulate, serrulated, serriform, saw-toothed, notched, jagged.

servant *noun* *kitchen servants* domestic, help, domestic help, helper, maid, charwoman, char, handyman, menial, drudge; scullion, slave, vassal, serf, retainer, attendant, lackey, flunkey; *inf.* Mrs Mop.

serve *verb* **1** *serve two masters* be in the service of, work for, be employed by, have a job with. **2** *willing to serve his fellow men* be of service for, be of use to, help, give help to, assist, give assistance to, aid, lend a hand to, do a good turn to, benefit, support, foster, minister to, succour. **3** *serve on the committee* have/hold a place on, be on, perform duties, carry out duties, fulfil duties. **4** *sofas serving also as beds* act as, do duty as, function as, fulfil the function of, do the work of, be suitable for. **5** *Will the car serve us for another year?* be useful, be all right, be good, be adequate, suffice, serve a purpose, meet requirements; *inf.* fill the bill, do. **6** *serve three years as an apprentice/prisoner* spend, go through, carry out, fulfil, complete, discharge. **7** *serve food* dish up, give out, distribute, set out, present, provide. **8** *serve at table* wait, act as waiter/waitress, distribute food/refreshments, deal out food. **9** *serve a customer* attend to, attend to the wants of, look after, take care of, assist. **10** *it has served them well* treat, act towards, behave towards, conduct oneself towards, deal with, handle.

service *noun* **1** *conditions of service in the factory* work, employment, labour, duty, business. **2** *retire after fifty years' service* work, employment, period of employment, labour, duties. **3** *do him a service by telling him* good turn, assistance, help, advantage, benefit. **4** *wedding service | service of baptism* ceremony, ritual, rite, sacrament. **5** *cars due for a service* servicing, overhaul, check, maintenance check, repair. **6** *pay extra for service in a restaurant* serving, waiting at table, waiting, waitressing, serving food and drink. **7** *have had good service from it* treatment, behaviour, conduct, handling.

service *verb* *service the washing machine* check, go over, overhaul, give a maintenance check to, repair.

serviceable *adjective* **1** *serviceable rather than fashionable shoes* functional, utilitarian, practical, non-decorative, plain, useful, durable, hard-wearing, tough, strong. **2** *machinery no longer serviceable* usable, of use, functioning, operative, repairable.
Opposites DECORATIVE; IMPRACTICAL.

services *plural noun* **1** *go into the services* armed services, forces, armed forces. **2** *require the services of a lawyer* work, labour, duties, assistance, ministrations.

servile *adjective* **1** *made to do servile tasks* menial, low, lowly, humble, mean, base. **2** *a rich man surrounded by servile employees* subservient, obsequious, sycophantic, fawning, toadying, grovelling, submissive; *inf.* bootlicking.

serving *noun* *dish up six servings of soup* helping, portion, plateful.

servitude *noun* slavery, enslavement, thraldom, subjugation, subjection, domination, bondage, bonds, chains, fetters, shackles, serfdom, vassalage.

session *noun* **1** *a recording session* period, time, spell, stretch; *inf.* get-together. **2** *the afternoon sessions of the summit talks* meeting, sitting, assembly, conference, discussion. **3** *pupils at the start of the session* school year, school term, term; *Am.* semester.

set *verb* **1** *set the books down there | a house set in parkland* put, put down, place, lay, lay down, deposit, position, rest, locate, lodge, situate, station, posit; *inf.* stick, park, plonk. **2** *set the post in the ground | set a jewel in the ring* fix, embed, insert, lodge, mount, arrange, install. **3** *set pen to paper* put, apply, lay, place, bring into contact with, touch. **4** *set your mind to it* apply, direct, aim, turn, address, focus, concentrate, zero in on. **5** *set one's watch* adjust, regulate, synchronize, coordinate, harmonize, collimate, calibrate, rectify, set right. **6** *set the machine to start* fix, make ready, prepare, arrange, organize. **7** *set the table* lay, make ready, prepare, arrange. **8** *set her hair* fix, style, arrange, curl, wave. **9** *the sky set with stars | a dress set with sequins* decorate, adorn, ornament, deck, bedeck, embellish, furbish, bejewel. **10** *set things in motion | set it on fire* put, cause to be, start, actuate, instigate. **11** *the jelly/concrete won't set* solidify, stiffen, thicken, jell, harden, cake, congeal, coagulate, crystallize, gelatinize. **12** *the sun setting* go down, sink, dip below the horizon, vanish, disappear, subside, decline. **13** *set them thinking* set off, start, begin, motivate, cause. **14** *set a new record* set up, establish, fix, create, bring into being, bring into existence, institute. **15** *set a date/time for the meeting* fix, fix on, settle, agree on, appoint, decide on, name, specify, stipulate, determine, designate, select, choose, arrange, schedule, confirm. **16** *set down rules* lay down, impose, establish, define, determine, stipulate, prescribe, ordain, allot. **17** *set them tasks* assign, allocate, allot, give, give out, distribute, dispense, mete out, deal out, dole out, prescribe. **18** *set her services at naught* evaluate, valuate, value, assess, price, rate, estimate, reckon, calculate. **19** *faces/footsteps set towards home* direct, steer, orientate, point, incline, bend, train, aim. **set about 1** *set about clearing up* begin, start, make a start on, commence, set to, get to work, get down to, get going, tackle, undertake, address oneself to, attack, enter upon, put the wheels in motion, set in motion, set the ball rolling, lead off, put into execution, put one's shoulder to the wheel, put one's hand to the plough; *inf.* get cracking, get weaving, sail into, wade into. **2** *set about the intruders with a stick* attack, assault, assail, belabour; *inf.* sail into. **set apart 1** *behaviour setting him apart from the rest* differentiate, mark off, distinguish, single out, demarcate, characterize. **2** *set apart some logs for winter* lay aside, put aside, reserve. **set aside 1** *set aside money/food for later* lay aside, lay by, put away, put aside, set apart, save, reserve, keep in reserve, keep, put down, store, stockpile, hoard, deposit, stow away, salt away,

squirrel away; *inf.* stash away **2** *set aside the newspaper* put aside, put to one side, move to one side, cast aside, discard, abandon, dispense with, drop. **3** *set aside our differences for now* put aside, forget, disregard, ignore, discount, bury, consign to oblivion. **4** *set aside the judge's ruling* overrule, overturn, reverse, nullify, render null and void, annul, quash, dismiss, reject, cancel, repudiate, abrogate. **set back** *set back their progress* hinder, impede, obstruct, hold up, delay, slow down, retard, check, thwart. **set down 1** *set down a list of requirements* write down, write out, put in writing, commit to writing, put down, mark down, jot down, note down, record, register, tabulate, catalogue. **2** *set his incompetence down to inexperience* put down, attribute, ascribe, assign, lay at the door of, charge. **set forth 1** *set forth for the city* set out, start out, depart. *See* SET OUT 1. **2** *set forth their demands* declare, state, expound, describe, detail, delineate, submit, present, bring forward, advance. **set in** *winter has set in* begin, start, commence, arrive, come, come into being. **set off 1** *set off for the city* set out, start out, set forth, depart. *See* SET OUT 1. **2** *set off a bomb* detonate, explode, blow up, ignite, light. **3** *set off a flurry of selling on the stock market* cause, begin, start, commence, initiate, set in motion, prompt, touch off, incite, stimulate, encourage. **4** *a dress setting off the blue of her eyes* enhance, bring out, heighten, intensify, increase, emphasize, show off, throw into relief. **set on** *thugs setting on the old man* attack, assault, strike, beat, beat up, fall upon, pounce on, go for, fly at; *inf.* mug, sail into. **set out 1** *they set out for the city early* set off, set forth, start out, depart, leave, take one's departure, get under way, embark, sally forth; *inf.* hit the road. **2** *I didn't set out to hurt them* intend to, have the intention of, aim to, have the aim of, mean to, have in mind, set one's sights on, aspire to. **3** *set out goods on a counter* lay out, arrange, dispose, present, exhibit, display, array, expose to view. **4** *they will set out their demands* set forth, declare, state, describe, detail, submit, present. *See* SET FORTH 2. **set up. 1** *they set up a statue in his memory* put up, erect, raise, elevate, construct, build, assemble. **2** *we set up a business/scholarship* establish, institute, found, create, bring into being, start, begin, initiate, inaugurate, institute, organize, set going, get going, lay the foundations of. **3** *we must set up a meeting* arrange, prearrange, organize, prepare, plan, devise, fix. **4** *the country air will soon set the invalid up* make better, make stronger, strengthen, build up, restore, invigorate, energize, fortify, rehabilitate.

set *noun* **1** *a set of articles for sale* collection, group, assemblage, series, batch, arrangement, array, succession, progression, assortment, selection. **2** *the golfing set* circle, crowd, clique, group, gang, coterie, faction, band, company, sect; *inf.* crew. **3** *the set of his shoulder/eyes* bearing, carriage, cast, posture, position, altitude, turn, inclination. **4** *paint the set* stage set, stage setting, setting, stage scene,

scene, scenery, backdrop, wings, flats, *mise en scène*.

set adjective **1** *set texts/meals* fixed, prescribed, scheduled, specified, predetermined, prearranged, determined, arranged, appointed, established, decided, agreed. **2** *her set routine* customary, regular, normal, usual, habitual, accustomed, everyday, common. **3** *give a set speech* stock, standard, habitual, routine, rehearsed, unspontaneous, hackneyed, conventional, stereotyped. **4** *people of set opinions | set in their ways* fixed, firm, rooted, immovable, deep-seated, ingrained, entrenched, rigid, inflexible, hidebound. **5** *all set for the journey* ready, prepared, equipped, primed, fit. **6** *set on getting his own way* intent, resolved, determined, bent on, resolute about, earnest about.
Opposites UNUSUAL; FLEXIBLE; OPEN-MINDED.

setback noun *their progress/plans suffered a setback* reversal, reverse, upset, check, stumbling block, hitch, hold-up, hindrance, impediment, obstruction, disappointment, misfortune, blow.

setting noun **1** *houses in rural settings | animals in their natural settings* environment, surroundings, milieu, background, location, place, site. **2** *a modern setting for the play* stage setting, set, scene, stage, scenery, backdrop, back-cloth, flats, *mise en scène*. **3** *an unusual setting for the jewel* mounting, frame.

settle verb **1** *settle in America* make one's home, set up home, take up residence, put down roots, establish oneself, go to live, move to, emigrate to. **2** *an area settled by Scots* establish/found a colony, colonize, occupy, people, inhabit, populate. **3** *the children will not settle after the excitement* calm down, quieten down, be quiet, be still, relax. **4** *the sedative will settle her* calm, calm down, tranquillize, quieten, quiet, soothe, compose, pacify, lull, sedate, quell. **5** *settle the patients for the night* make comfortable, bed down, tuck in. **6** *a butterfly settling on the leaf* alight, light, land, come down, descend, repose, rest. **7** *settle on a date* decide on, agree on, determine, confirm, arrange, fix, choose, appoint, select. **8** *settle a dispute* resolve, clear up, make peace, patch up, reconcile, conclude, bring to an end. **9** *settle one's affairs* put in order, order, arrange, set to rights, straighten out, organize, regulate, adjust, clear up, systematize. **10** *settle for a smaller sum* compromise on, submit to, accept, agree to, accede to, acquiesce in, assent to. **11** *settle one's bills/debts* pay, discharge, square, clear, liquidate. **12** *dregs settled at the foot of the cup* sink, subside, fall, gravitate.
Opposites AGITATE; DISTURB.

settlement noun **1** *the settlement of the area* establishing, founding, pioneering, peopling, colonization. See SETTLE 2. **2** *a remote settlement* community, colony, village, hamlet, encampment, outpost. **3** *the settlement of the dispute* resolution, patching up, reconciliation, conclusion. See SETTLE 8. **4** *reach a financial settlement with management* agreement, contract, pact, compact. **5** *the settlement of his financial affairs* ordering, arrangement, organization, regulation, adjustment, systematization. See SETTLE 9.

6 *in settlement of debts* payment, discharge, defrayal, liquidation. See SETTLE 11.

settler noun colonist, colonizer, pioneer, frontiersman/woman, immigrant.

set-to noun argument, quarrel, row, disagreement, fight, squabble, wrangle, fracas; *inf.* dust-up, scrap, slanging-match, spat, barney.

set-up noun system, organization, structure, arrangement, framework, format, composition, procedure.

sever verb **1** *sever a limb/branch* cut off, chop off, lop off, hack off, break off, tear off. **2** *sever the log in two pieces* divide, split, cleave, rive, dissect, halve. **3** *sever relations with them* break off, discontinue, suspend, dissolve, end, bring to an end, terminate, stop, cease, conclude.
Opposites JOIN; MAINTAIN; BEGIN.

several adjective **1** *several people came* some, a number of, a few. **2** *go their several ways* separate, different, diverse, disparate, divergent, respective, individual, own, particular, specific, various, sundry.

severe adjective **1** *severe criticism/punishment* harsh, hard, stringent, rigorous, unsparing, relentless, merciless, ruthless, painful, sharp, caustic, biting, cutting, scathing, serious, extreme. **2** *a severe regime* harsh, hard, stern, rigorous, stringent, strict, grim, inflexible, uncompromising, inexorable, implacable, relentless, unrelenting, merciless, pitiless, ruthless, brutal, inhuman, cruel, savage, hard-hearted, iron-fisted, iron-handed, autocratic, tyrannical, despotic. **3** *a severe shortage of food* extreme, very bad, serious, grave, acute, critical, dire, dangerous, perilous. **4** *severe storms/headaches* fierce, strong, violent, intense, powerful, forceful, very bad. **5** *a severe test of their stamina* demanding, taxing, exacting, tough, difficult, hard, fierce, arduous, rigorous, punishing, onerous, burdensome. **6** *a severe expression* stern, grim, cold, chilly, austere, forbidding, dour, disapproving, tight-lipped, unsmiling, sombre, grave, sober, serious. **7** *a severe style of decoration* austere, stark, ultraplain, spartan, ascetic, plain, simple, modest, bare, blank, unadorned, undecorated, unembellished, restrained, functional, classic. **8** *a severe winter* harsh, extreme, inclement, cold, freezing, frigid.
Opposites MILD; LENIENT; ORNATE.

severely adjective **1** *treat the culprits severely | speak severely to them* harshly, stringently, unsparingly, relentlessly, painfully, sharply, with an iron hand, with a rod of iron, caustically, scathingly. See SEVERE 1. **2** *injured severely* very badly, extremely badly, seriously, gravely, acutely, critically. **3** *severely dressed* austerely, starkly, spartanly, plainly, simply, without adornment, restrainedly, classically. See SEVERE 7.

severity noun **1** *the severity of the criticism* harshness, stringency, rigorousness, relentlessness, painfulness, sharpness, causticness. See SEVERE 1. **2** *the severity of the regime* harshness, hardness, sternness, rigorousness, stringency, strictness, inflexibility, relentlessness, pitilessness, ruthlessness, brutality, cruelty, savagery, tyranny, despotism. *See* SEVERE 2. **3** *the severity of the storm/pain* fierceness, strength, violence, intensity. *See* SEVERE 4. **4** *the severeness of her expression* sternness, graveness, gravity. *See* SEVERE 6. **5** *the severity of the decoration* austerity, starkness, spartanism, asceticism, plainness, simplicity, bareness, lack of adornment, restraint, functionalism. *See* SEVERE 7. **6** *the severity of the winter* severeness, harshness, extremity, inclemency, coldness.

sew *verb* stitch, machine stitch, seam, embroider, mend, darn. *See table. See also tables at* KNIT, STITCH.

sex *noun* **1** *identify the sex of the animal* gender. **2** *attraction based on sex* sexuality, sexual attraction, sexual chemistry, sexual desire, desire, sex drive, sexual appetite, libido. **3** *lessons in sex | sex education* facts of life, sexual reproduction, reproduction; *inf.* the birds and the bees. **4** *have sex with him | a relationship without sex* intimacy, coitus, coition, coupling, copulation, carnal knowledge, making love, mating, fornication.

sexuality *noun* **1** *differences based on sexuality* sex, gender, sexual characteristics. **2** *famous for her sexuality* sexual desire, sexual appetite, sexiness, carnality, physicalness, eroticism, lust, sensuality, voluptuousness; sexual orientation, sexual preferences.

sexy *adjective* **1** *sexy films* erotic, titillating, suggestive, arousing, exciting, stimulating. **2** *sexy clothes* titillating, arousing, provocative, seductive, sensuous, slinky. **3** *sexy women/men* sexually attractive, alluring, seductive, shapely. **4** *a sexy new project* exciting, stimulating, stirring, interesting, intriguing, trendy, fashionable.

shabby *adjective* **1** *shabby furniture/houses* dilapidated, broken-down, run-down, tumbledown, ramshackle, in disrepair, scruffy, dingy, seedy, squalid, tatty, slum-like, slummy; *inf.* tacky. **2** *shabby clothes* worn, worn-out, threadbare, ragged, frayed, tattered, faded, scruffy, tatty, the worse for wear. **3** *shabby treatment of the old lady* contemptible, despicable, dishonourable, disreputable, mean, base, low, dirty, odious, shameful, ignoble, unworthy, cheap, shoddy; *inf.* rotten, low-down.
Opposites SMART; NEAT; HONOURABLE.

shackle *verb* **1** *shackle the prisoner* chain, fetter, put in irons, manacle, tie up, bind, tether, hobble, handcuff. **2** *no longer shackled by convention* deter, restrain, restrict, limit, impede, hinder, hamper, obstruct, encumber, check, curb, constrain, tie the hands of.

shackles *plural noun* **1** *prisoners in shackles* chains, fetters, bonds, irons, manacles, tethers,

ropes, handcuffs; *inf.* cuffs. **2** *throw off the shackles of convention* deterrent, restraint, impediment, hindrance, obstruction, obstacle, check, curb, constraint.

shade *noun* **1** *sit in the shade of a tree* shadiness, shadow, shadowiness, shadows, shelter, cover. **2** *in the shade of evening* dimness, dusk, semi-darkness, twilight, gloaming, darkness, gloom, gloominess, murkiness, murk. **3** *a darker shade for the carpets* colour, hue, tone, tint, tinge. **4** *act as a shade against the light* screen, shield, curtain, blind, canopy, veil, cover, covering. **5** *in the shade compared to his brother* obscurity, shadow, inconspicuousness, unrecognition. **6** *a word with several shades of meaning* nuance, degree, gradation, difference, variety. **7** *imagined he saw the shade of his father* ghost, spectre, phantom, apparition, spirit, manes. **a shade** *a shade better* a little, a bit, a trace, a touch, a dash, a modicum, a soupçon, slightly, marginally. **put one in the shade** *her dress put all the others in the shade* outshine, outclass, overshadow, eclipse, surpass, excel, transcend, cap, top, outstrip, outdo, outrival, put to shame. **shades of** *shades of Napoleon* reminder of, memories of, intimations of, suggestions of, hints of.
Opposites SUNLIGHT; LIGHT.

shade *verb* **1** *trees shading the garden* shut out the light from, block off light to, cast a shadow over, screen, darken, dim. **2** *shading the light* cover, obscure, mute, hide, conceal, veil, curtain.

shadow *noun* **1** *sit in the shadow of the building* shade, shadowiness, shadows. *See* SHADE *noun* 1. **2** *in the shadow of evening* dimness, dusk, semi-darkness, twilight, gloaming, darkness, gloom. *See* SHADE *noun* 2. **3** *their shadows on the wall* silhouette, outline, shape. **4** *cast a shadow on their happiness* gloom, gloominess, cloud, blight, sadness, unhappiness. **5** *her younger sister was her shadow* constant companion, inseparable companion, close friend, bosom friend, intimate, alter ego; *lit.* Achates; *inf.* sidekick. **6** *the policewoman acting as a shadow* watch, follower, detective; *inf.* tail. **a shadow of** **1** *not a shadow of a doubt* a little, a bit, a shade, a trace, a touch, a dash, a modicum, a soupçon, slightly, marginally. **2** *a shadow of a smile* a trace, a hint, a suggestion, a suspicion, a ghost. **3** *a shadow of his former self* a ghost, a spectre, a phantom, a remnant, a poor imitation.

shadowy *adjective* **1** *shadowy parts of the garden/house* shady, shaded, dim, dark, gloomy, murky, crepuscular, tenebrous, tenebrious. **2** *shadowy shapes on the horizon* indistinct, indeterminate, indefinite, unclear, vague, nebu-

---

SEWING TECHNIQUES

appliqué	darning	gathering	oversewing	scalloping
basting	drawn-work	laid work	patchwork	shirring
binding	embroidery	mitring	pleating	smocking
couching	facing	needlepoint	quilting	topstitching
crocheting	faggoting	overcasting	ruching	tucking
cutwork	fine-drawing	overlocking	ruffling	whitework

lous, ill-defined, indistinguishable, unsubstantial, ghostly, phantom, spectral.
Opposites BRIGHT; SUNNY; DISTINCT.

shady *adjective* **1** *shady parts of the garden* shaded, shadowy, screened, sheltered, covered, dim, dark, leafy, bowery, umbrageous, tenebrous, tenebrious. **2** *shady character* disreputable, of dubious character, suspicious, suspect, questionable, dishonest, dishonourable, untrustworthy, devious, shifty, slippery, tricky, underhand, unscrupulous; *inf.* crooked, fishy.
Opposites BRIGHT; SUNNY; REPUTABLE; ABOVE-BOARD.

shaft *noun* **1** *the shafts of the mine* passage, duct, tunnel, well, flue. **2** *shafts of light* ray, beam, gleam, streak, pencil. **3** *the shaft of a spade* pole, stick, rod, staff, shank, stem, handle, upright. **4** *his cruel shafts of sarcasm* barb, gibe, thrust, dart, sting, cutting remark, cut.

shaggy *adjective* hairy, hirsute, long-haired, rough, coarse, matted, tangled, unkempt, untidy.

shake *verb* **1** *the cart shaking on the rough roads* rock, bump, jolt, bounce, roll, sway, swing, oscillate, wobble, rattle, vibrate, jar, jerk, judder, joggle, jounce. **2** *children shaking with fear/cold* shiver, tremble, quiver, quake, shudder. **3** *shake the can of coins* jiggle, joggle, jolt, jerk, rattle, agitate, jounce. **4** *people shaken by the accident/news* agitate, upset, distress, shock, alarm, disturb, perturb, fluster, unsettle, discompose, disquiet, disconcert, unnerve, ruffle, jolt, flurry, confuse, muddle; *inf.* rattle. **5** *shake her confidence* undermine, weaken, lessen, impair, harm, hurt, injure. **6** *shake a fist/stick at them* brandish, wave, flourish, swing, wield, raise. **shake off** *shake off their pursuers* escape, elude, get away from, leave behind, give the slip to, throw off, get rid of, rid oneself of, extricate oneself from; *inf.* get shot of. **shake up 1** *shake up the dressing/cocktail* mix, churn up, agitate. **2** *passengers shaken up by the accident* shake, agitate, upset, disturb, unsettle, discompose. **3** *shake up the system/firm* reorganize, rearrange, revolutionize, rouse, stir up.

shake *noun* **1** *upset by the shakes of the cart on the rough road* shaking, rocking, bump, jolt, bounce, roll, swaying, rattle, jarring, jerk. *See* SHAKE *verb* 1. **2** *the children had the shakes* shaking, shivering, trembling, tremor, quiver, quivering, convulsion. *See* SHAKE *verb* 2. **3** *with one shake of the can* jiggle, joggle, jolt, jerk, rattle. *See* SHAKE *verb* 3. **4** *give quite a shake from the accident/news* upset, shock, jolt. *See* SHAKE *verb* 4. **5** *with a shake of his fist/stick* brandish, wave, flourish, swing.

shaky *adjective* **1** *with shaky limbs* shaking, trembling, tremulous, quivering, quivery, unsteady, wobbly, weak. **2** *take a few shaky steps* shaking, unsteady, faltering, wobbly, tottering, teetering, doddering, staggering. **3** *still a bit shaky after the illness* infirm, unsound, unwell, ill, below par, indisposed; *inf.* under the weather. **4** *rather shaky reasoning/grounds* questionable, dubious, tenuous, unsubstantial, flimsy, weak, nebulous, unsound, unreliable, undependable,

ungrounded, unfounded. **5** *shaky bits of furniture* rickety, wobbly, flimsy, ramshackle, dilapidated, gimcrack, jerry-built.
Opposites STEADY; SOUND; STABLE.

shallow *adjective* **1** *a shallow person* frivolous, foolish, unintelligent, unthinking, trivial, insincere, superficial. **2** *shallow ideas/attitudes/remarks* frivolous, superficial, unsubstantial, trifling, trivial, petty, empty, meaningless.
Opposites SERIOUS; PROFOUND.

sham *verb* **1** *sham illness* fake, pretend, feign, counterfeit, put on, simulate, affect, imitate. **2** *he's only shamming* fake, feign, pretend, counterfeit, dissemble, malinger, make believe.

sham *noun* **1** *his charm is only a sham* fake, pretence, feint, feigning, counterfeit, imposture, simulation. **2** *he's not a doctor – he's a sham* impostor, fake, fraud, pretender, masquerader, dissembler, wolf in sheep's clothing, charlatan; *inf.* phoney, pseudo. **3** *the document's a sham* counterfeit, fake, forgery, imposture, copy, imitation, hoax.

sham *adjective* **1** *sham sympathy* pretended, pretend, feigned, fake, contrived, put-on, simulated, affected, artificial, insincere, ungenuine, false, bogus, spurious; *inf.* phoney, pseudo. **2** *sham gold watches* fake, counterfeit, imitation, simulated, artificial, synthetic, ersatz; *inf.* phoney, pseudo.
Opposites REAL; GENUINE; AUTHENTIC.

shamble *verb* shuffle, hobble, limp, falter, totter, dodder, toddle.

shambles *plural noun* chaos, muddle, mess, confusion, disorder, disarray, disorganization, anarchy; *inf.* disaster area.

shame *noun* **1** *feel shame at being imprisoned* humiliation, ignominy, mortification, loss of face, remorse, guilt, compunction, shamefacedness, embarrassment, discomfort, discomposure. **2** *bring shame on the family* disgrace, dishonour, scandal, discredit, degradation, ignominy, disrepute, infamy, odium, opprobrium, condemnation, reproach. **3** *he's a shame to the family* disgrace, discredit, blot, smirch, stain, blemish, stigma. **4** *a shame he couldn't be there* pity, misfortune, bad luck, ill luck, source of regret. **put to shame** *put their efforts to shame* outshine, outclass, overshadow, eclipse, surpass, excel, outstrip, outdo, outrival, put in the shade.
Opposites PRIDE; HONOUR; CREDIT.

shamefaced *adjective* **1** *too shamefaced to appear after his crime* ashamed, embarrassed, guilty, conscience-stricken, remorseful, contrite, penitent, regretful, humiliated, mortified, shamed. **2** *shamefaced children hiding behind their mothers* shy, bashful, timid, timorous, shrinking, coy, sheepish.

shameful *adjective* **1** *shameful behaviour* disgraceful, base, mean, low, vile, outrageous, shocking, dishonourable, unbecoming, unworthy, discreditable, deplorable, despicable, contemptible, reprehensible, scandalous, atrocious, heinous. **2** *shameful secrets* shaming, humiliating, mortifying, embarrassing; *inf.* blush-making.
Opposites ADMIRABLE; HONOURABLE; LAUDABLE.

shameless *adjective* **1** *shameless about his prison sentence* unashamed, without shame, unabashed, uncontrite, unpenitent, impenitent, unregretful. **2** *the shameless behaviour of the girls* brazen, impudent, bold, brash, forward, audacious, immodest, unseemly, improper, unbecoming, indecorous, wanton, abandoned, indecent.

shape *noun* **1** *clouds of different shapes | pieces of plastic in all shapes and sizes* form, figure, configuration, formation, conformation, contour, outline, silhouette, profile, outward form, external appearance. *See table. See also table at* TRIANGLE. **2** *in the shape of the devil* form, guise, appearance, likeness, look, semblance, image, aspect. **3** *business in poor shape | athletes in good shape* condition, state, health, trim, fettle, kilter. **4** *make out shapes in the distance* figure, form, outline, shadow, body, apparition. **5** *jelly/cement in a shape* mould, frame. **6** *dressmaking shapes* pattern, model.

GEOMETRICAL SHAPES

circle	pentangle
decagon	polygon
diamond	quadrangle
dodecagon	quadrant
ellipse	quadrilateral
hendecagon	rectangle
heptagon	rhomboid
hexagon	rhombus
kite	semicircle
lozenge	square
nonagon	tetragon
oblong	trapezium
octagon	trapezoid
parallelogram	triangle
pentagon	trigon
pentagram	undecagon

---

shape *verb* **1** *shape the clay into a figure* form, fashion, make, create, design, mould, model, cast, frame, block, carve, sculpt, sculpture. **2** *attitudes shaped by childhood experiences* form, fashion, mould, create, produce, influence, guide, determine, define. **3** *shape a secret plan* plan, devise, prepare, develop, organize, line up. **4** *shape the dress to her figure* adjust, adapt, accommodate, alter, modify, tailor. **shape up 1** *new recruits shaping up* improve, show improvement, get better, make progress, progress, make headway, show promise. **2** *plans shaping up* take form, take shape, develop, crystallize, fall into place, come along, go forward, progress, make headway.

shapeless *adjective* **1** *shapeless hunks of plastic* amorphous, formless, unformed, unshaped, unfashioned, undeveloped, embryonic. **2** *shapeless clothes* formless, badly cut, sack-like, ill-proportioned, inelegant. **3** *shapeless old hats* misshapen, battered, deformed.

shapely *adjective* *shapely legs* well-formed, well-shaped, well-proportioned, elegant, curvaceous, curvy.

shard *noun* fragment, piece, particle, scrap, bit, chip, sliver, splinter, paring, shaving, remnant.

share *noun* *each receiving a fair share* division, quota, allowance, ration, allocation, allotment, portion, part, lot, measure, helping, serving; *inf.* cut, whack, rake-off, piece of the cake, piece of the action.

share *verb* **1** *share a job/costs* divide, split, use/ have in common, go halves in; *inf.* go fifty-fifty in, go Dutch. **2** *share the profits* divide, distribute, apportion, parcel out, deal out, dole out, give out. **3** *everyone sharing in their good fortune* have a share in, have a part in, participate in, take part in, partake of, have a percentage of, have a stake in.

sharp *adjective* **1** *a sharp utensil* cutting, serrated, knife-like, edged, razor-edged, keen. **2** *a sharp length of metal* pointed, needle-like, spear-shaped, barbed, spiky. **3** *a sharp drop to the sea* steep, sheer, abrupt, precipitous, vertical. **4** *come to a sharp stop* sudden, abrupt, rapid, unexpected. **5** *a sharp difference between the two* clear, clear-cut, distinct, marked, well-defined, crisp. **6** *a sharp pain* intense, acute, keen, piercing, cutting, extreme, severe, stabbing, shooting, stinging. **7** *a sharp taste* pungent, biting, bitter, acid, sour, tart, vinegary. **8** *a sharp smell* acrid, pungent, burning. **9** *a sharp noise* piercing, shrill, high-pitched, ear-splitting, harsh, strident. **10** *exchange sharp words* harsh, curt, brusque, bitter, hard, cutting, scathing, caustic, biting, barbed, acrimonious, trenchant, sarcastic, sardonic, venomous, malicious, vitriolic, hurtful, unkind, cruel. **11** *a sharp pupil* sharp-witted, intelligent, bright, clever, quick. **12** *sharp intelligence/wits* keen, acute, quick, ready, smart, knowing, comprehending, shrewd, discerning, perceptive, penetrating. **13** *sharp practices | a sharp customer* unscrupulous, dishonest, cunning, wily, crafty, artful; *inf.* fly. **14** *move at a sharp pace* brisk, rapid, quick, fast, swift, vigorous, spirited, animated. **15** *a sharp dresser* smart, stylish, fashionable, chic, elegant; *inf.* dressy, snappy, natty.
Opposites BLUNT; GENTLE; INDISTINCT; MILD.

sharp *adjective* **1** *arrive at 9 a.m. sharp* promptly, punctually, on time, on the dot; *inf.* on the nose. **2** *pull up sharp* abruptly, suddenly, all of a sudden, unexpectedly, without warning.

sharpen *verb* put an edge on, edge, whet, hone, strop, grind.

shatter *verb* **1** *shatter the windscreen* smash, smash to smithereens, break, break into pieces, splinter, fracture, shiver, pulverize, crush, crack; *inf.* bust. **2** *shatter one's hopes/ dreams* destroy, demolish, wreck, ruin, dash, blight, wipe out, overturn, blast, bring to naught, devastate, torpedo. **3** *shattered by their betrayal* break one's heart, devastate, crush, upset, distress, dumbfound; *inf.* knock the stuffing out of.

shave *verb* **1** *shave his beard* cut off, trim, snip off, crop. **2** *shave off pieces of wood* pare, plane, shear. **3** *shave the fence with his car* brush, graze, touch, scrape, rub.

sheath noun **1** *a sheath from a sword* scabbard, case. **2** case, casing, cover, covering, envelope, wrapper. **3** *a contraceptive sheath* condom, contraceptive; *Am.* rubber.

shed noun *a garden shed* hut, outhouse, lean-to, shack.

shed verb **1** *trees shedding their leaves* let fall, let drop. **2** *snakes shedding their skins* cast off, slough off. **3** *shed clothes* take off, remove, strip off, doff. **4** *shed blood* pour forth, let flow, spill, discharge, exude. **5** *shed light* diffuse, send forth, radiate, disperse, scatter. **6** *companies shedding workers* discard, get rid of, dispense with, drop, declare/make redundant, dismiss; *inf.* sack, fire.

sheen noun shine, lustre, gleam, sparkle, gloss, burnish, polish, patina.

sheep noun. See table.

sheepish adjective embarrassed, uncomfortable, ashamed, shamefaced, blushing, abashed, shy, bashful, diffident, foolish, silly.

sheer adjective **1** *sheer folly/magic* utter, complete, thoroughgoing, total, absolute, veritable, downright, out-and-out, unqualified, unconditional, unmitigated, unalloyed, unadulterated. **2** *a sheer cliff/drop to the sea* steep, abrupt, sharp, precipitous, vertical, perpendicular. **3** *sheer silk* diaphanous, transparent, see-through, translucent, filmy, gossamer,

gauzy, ultra-fine, fine, thin.
Opposites QUALIFIED; GRADUAL; THICK.

sheer verb **1** *ships sheering* swerve, change course, slew, veer, drift, yaw. **2** *sheer away from the topic* turn away from, change the subject from, avoid, evade, dodge, deviate from.

sheet noun **1** *sheets and blankets* bed-sheet, bed-linen. **2** *a sheet of lacquered veneer on the table* layer, statum, overlay, surface, lamina, covering, coating, coat, facing, veneer, film. **3** *sheets of glass/plastic* piece, pane, panel, plate, slab. **4** *sheet of paper* piece of paper, leaf, page, folio. **5** *sheets of water* expanse, stretch, span, reach, sweep, covering, blanket, carpet.

shelf noun **1** *putting books/cards on shelves* ledge, bracket, mantelshelf, mantelpiece. **2** *shelves in the sea* sandbank, sand bar, reef, shoal.

shell noun **1** *the shell of a crab* carapace, case. See table at SEASHELL. **2** *the shell of a nut* casing, case, husk, pod, integument. **3** *shells in the army magazine* bullet, grenade, shot, shrapnel. See tables at BULLET, EXPLOSIVE. **4** *the shell of a car/ship under construction* framework, frame, structure, chassis, hull, skeleton.

shell verb **1** *shell peas* husk, shuck. **2** *troops shelling the city* bomb, bombard, blitz, torpedo, strafe, fire on, open fire on. **shell out** *shell out money* pay out, spend, lay out, disburse, squander; *inf.* fork out.

BREEDS OF SHEEP

Abyssinian	Dorper	Masai	Spanish Merino
Africander	Dorset Down	Merino	Suffolk
Altai	Dorset Horn	Mongolian	Swaledale
Askanian	Dubrovnik	Mug	Swedish Landrace
Australian Merino	English Longwool	Norfolk Horn	Swiss White Alpine
Awassi	Exmoor Horn	North Country	Swiss White Moun-
Berber	Finnish Landrace	Cheviot	tain
Bergamo	French	North Ronaldsay	Talavera
Beulah Speckled	Blackheaded	Old Norwegian	Targhee
Face	Galway	Orkney	Teeswater
Biella	Greek Zackel	Oxford Down	Texel
Blackface	Hampshire Down	Panama	Tibetan
Blackhead Persian	Hebridean	Poll Dorset	Tsigai
Black Welsh Moun-	Herdwick	Polwarth	Tyrol Mountain
tain	Hill Radnor	Portland	Welsh Mountain
Bluefaced Leicester	Icelandic	Précoce	Wensleydale
Border Leicester	Ile-de-France	Radnor	Whiteface
Bosnian Mountain	Island Pramenka	Rambouillet	Dartmoor
Brazilian Woolless	Jacob	Red Karaman	Whiteface Wood-
Campanian Barbary	Karakachan	Rhiw Hill	lands
Cannock Chase	Karakul	Romanov	Wicklow
Castlemilk Moorit	Kent	Romeldale	Mountain
Caucasian	Kerry Hill	Romney Marsh	Wiltshire Horn
Cheviot	Kivircik	Rough Fell	**Wild Sheep**
Chios	Lacaune	Ryeland	aoudad
Clun Forest	Lacho	Sardinian	argali
Colbred	Lamon	Scottish Blackface	barbary sheep
Columbia	Leicester	Shetland	bharal
Corriedale	Lincoln Longwool	Shropshire	bighorn
Cotswold	Llanwenog	Sicilian	blue sheep
Dales-Bred	Lleyn	Soay	dall sheep
Dartmoor	Lonk	South Devon	mouflon
Derbyshire Gritstone	Lourdes	Southdown	mountain sheep
Devon Closewool	Manech	South Wales	urial
Devon Longwool	Manx Loghtan	Mountain	white sheep

shelter noun **1** *provide shelter from danger/cold* protection, shield, cover, screen, safety, security, defence, refuge, sanctuary, asylum. **2** *a shelter for battered wives* refuge, sanctuary, retreat, haven, harbour.

shelter verb **1** *shelter them from the weather* protect, provide protection from, shield, cover, screen, safeguard. **2** *shelter the criminal from the police* protect, shield, screen, safeguard, provide refuge/sanctuary from, guard, harbour, conceal, hide. **3** *shelter from the elements/pursuers in a barn* take shelter, take refuge, seek protection, seek refuge/sanctuary.
Opposites EXPOSE; ENDANGER.

sheltered adjective **1** *a sheltered spot for the picnic* shady, shaded, protected, screened, shielded, secluded. **2** *lead a sheltered life* secluded, quiet, withdrawn, retired, isolated, protected, cloistered, reclusive.

shelve verb *shelve expansion plans* put to one side, lay aside, put off, postpone, defer, delay, suspend, mothball, pigeon-hole, put on ice, put in cold storage, put on the back-burner; *Am.* table.

shepherd verb *shepherd the children to their classes* escort, conduct, usher, convoy, guide, marshal, steer.

shield noun **1** *using his shield to fend off blows* buckler; *lit.* targe; *Herald.* escutcheon. *See table at* HERALDRY. **2** *act as a shield against bullies* protection, defence, guard, safeguard, support, bulwark, screen, protector.

shield verb *shield one's eyes from the dust | shield the child from the facts* protect, screen, defend, guard, safeguard, shelter.
Opposites EXPOSE; ENDANGER.

shift verb **1** *shift the furniture from the house to the van* move, carry, transfer, switch, transpose, relocate, reposition, rearrange. **2** *shift one's position on the new project* change, alter, vary, modify, reverse, do an about-turn; *inf.* do a U-turn. **3** *unable to shift the stain* remove, take out, get rid of, budge. **shift for oneself** manage by oneself, manage without help/assistance, make it on one's own, fend for oneself,

take care of oneself, make do, get by, scrape by; *inf.* stand on one's own two feet, paddle one's own canoe.

shift noun **1** *a shift of people from the country areas* move, movement, transference, switch, transposition, relocation, repositioning. **2** *a shift in public opinion* change, alteration, variation, modification, about-turn, reversal, sea-change; *inf.* U-turn. **3** *an eight-hour shift* work period, stint, spell of work. **4** *resort to dubious shifts to make money* expedient, scheme, strategy, stratagem, device, plan, subterfuge, dodge, trick, ruse, wile, artifice, deception.

shiftless adjective lazy, idle, indolent, slothful, inefficient, unambitious, unenterprising, worthless, good-for-nothing, ne'er-do-well.

shifty adjective evasive, slippery, devious, duplicitous, deceitful, underhand, untrustworthy, double-dealing, dishonest, wily, crafty, artful, sly, scheming, contriving.
Opposites HONEST; OPEN; TRUSTWORTHY.

shilly-shally verb be indecisive/irresolute, vacillate, waver, hesitate, hem and haw, oscillate, fluctuate; *inf.* blow hot and cold.

shimmer verb *light shimmering on the water* glisten, glint, flicker, twinkle, sparkle, gleam, glow, scintillate, dance.

shimmer noun *the shimmer of light on water* glistening, glint, flicker, twinkle, sparkle, gleam, glow, lustre, iridescence, scintillation.

shine verb **1** *the sun/torch shining* emit light, give off light. **2** *with shoes/glasses shining* gleam, sparkle, glisten. **3** *lights shining in the distance* gleam, glow, glint, sparkle, twinkle, flicker, glitter, glisten, shimmer, flash, dazzle, beam, radiate, illuminate, luminesce, incandesce. **4** *with face shining* glow, beam, radiate, bloom, look healthy, look good. **5** *shine the shoes* polish, burnish, buff, wax, gloss, brush, rub up. **6** *shine at tennis* excel, be expert, be brilliant, be very good, be outstanding. **7** *shine in a crowd* stand out, be outstanding, be conspicuous, be pre-eminent, excel, dominate, star.

SHIPS AND BOATS

amphibious	dinghy	inflatable	paddle steamer	shell
landing craft	dory	dinghy	passenger ship	ship's boat
barge	dredger	jet-boat	pilot boat	side-wheeler
battleship	drifter	kayak	pinnace	speedboat
botel	DUKW/duck	keelboat	pirogue	steamboat
bulk carrier	E-boat	launch	pontoon	steamship
bumboat	factory ship	lifeboat	powerboat	sternwheeler
cabin cruiser	flagship	lighter	punt	supertanker
cable ship	flat boat	longboat	Q-ship	surfboat
canal boat	freighter	mailboat	raft	tanker
canoe	galley	monkey-boat	randan	tender
cargo ship	gig	mosquito	revenue	torpedo boat
coal ship	gondola	boat	cutter	tramp
collier	houseboat	motor-boat	roll-on roll-off	steamer
container ship	hovercraft	narrow boat	rowing boat	trawler
coracle	hydrofoil	oil tanker	sailing ship	troop carrier
crabber	ice-boat	outboard	sampan	tugboat
cruiser	ice-breaker	outrigger	school-ship	whaleboat
cruise ship	Indiaman	paddle boat	sculler	wherry

shine noun **1** the shine of the street lights light, brightness, gleam, glow, glint, sparkle, twinkle, flicker, glitter, glisten, shimmer, flash, dazzle, glare, beam, radiance, illumination, luminescence, luminosity, lambency, effulgence. **2** put a shine on the polished table polish, burnish, gleam, gloss, lustre, sheen, patina.

shining adjective **1** shining lights gleaming, glowing, glinting, sparkling, twinkling, flickering, glittering, flashing, dazzling, incandescent, effulgent. See SHINE verb 3. **2** with shining, happy faces glowing, beaming, radiant, blooming, healthy. **3** a shining example | shining stars in the theatre outstanding, pre-eminent, leading, illustrious, brilliant, splendid. **4** shining tables/glasses shiny, polished, burnished, gleaming, glossy, satiny, lustrous; lit. nitid.

shiny adjective shiny tables/glasses shining, polished, burnished, gleaming, glossy, satiny, lustrous; lit. nitid.
Opposites DULL.

ship noun. See tables. See also table at SAILING SHIP.

shirk verb shirk work avoid, evade, dodge, sidestep, shrink from, shun, get out of, slide out of, play truant from; inf. funk, skive off.

shirker noun dodger, slacker, truant, habitual absentee, malingerer, layabout, loafer, idler; inf. skiver.

shirt noun. See table.

shiver¹ verb shiver with cold/fear tremble, quiver, shake, shudder, quaver, quake, vibrate.

shiver² noun give a shiver of fear tremble, quiver, shake, quaver, shudder.

shiver³ noun cut by a shiver of glass splinter, sliver, fragment, shard, shaving.

SHIRTS	
aloha shirt	olive-drab shirt
boiled shirt	overblouse
choli	polo shirt
dashiki	short-sleeved
dress shirt	shirt
evening shirt	smock
grandad shirt	sports shirt
long-sleeved shirt	sweatshirt
middy blouse	T-shirt

shiver⁴ verb the window shivered into thousands of pieces shatter, smash, splinter, fragment, explode, crack, break.

shivery adjective feeling shivery in the cold | be shivery from the fever trembling, trembly, quivering, quivery, shaking, shaky, shuddering, quavering, quaking.

shock¹ noun **1** the shock of the two cars hitting each other impact, blow, collision, crash, clash, jolt, bump, jar, jerk, shake. **2** the news of the murder came as a shock | he gave the villagers a shock blow, upset, disturbance, state of agitation/perturbation, source of distress, source of amazement/consternation, revelation, bolt from the blue, bombshell, eye-opener. **3** suffering from shock after the accident state of shock, trauma, traumatism, prostration, stupor, stupefaction, collapse.

shock² verb shocked by the housing conditions | shocked by the battle scenes appal, horrify, scandalize, outrage, repel, revolt, disgust, nauseate, sicken, offend, traumatize, make one's blood run cold, distress, upset, perturb, disturb, disquiet, unsettle, discompose, agitate, astound,

PARTS OF A SHIP				
after deck	companion	hatch	planking	stack
anchor	ladder	hatchway	Plimsoll line	stanchion
berth	companionway	hawsehole	poop	starboard
bilge	counter	hawse-pipe	poop deck	state-cabin
bilge keel	crow's nest	hawser	porthole	stateroom
bitt	daggerboard	head	portside	stern
board	davit	hold	promenade	sternpost
boat deck	engine room	keel	deck	strake
boiler room	false keel	keelson	propeller	stretcher
bollard	figurehead	larboard	propeller	stringer
bow	fin keel	lazaretto	shaft	thole
bridge	flight deck	limber	prow	tiller
brig	forecastle/	limber hole	quarter rail	transom
bulkhead	fo'c'sle	mainmast	quarters	trunnion
bull's-eye	freeboard	maintop	radio room	turtleback
bulwarks	futtock	mizzen-mast	rail	wardroom
cabin	galley	mizzentop	riding lamp	washboard
capstan	gangplank	monkey rail	rigger	washstrake
carline	gangway	oar	round house	waterline
cathead	glory-hole	orlop deck	rowlock	weather-
cat hole	guard-rail	outboard	rudder	board
centreboard	gudgeon	outrigger	rudderpost	weather
chain	gun-deck	paddle wheel	scupper	deck
locker	gunwale/	painter	skeg	wheel
chart room	gunnel	pilot house	spanker	winch
cleat	half-deck	pintle	stabilizer	windlass

dumbfound, stagger, amaze, astonish, stun, flabbergast, stupefy, overwhelm, bewilder.

shock³ *noun a shock of red hair* mass, mop, mane, thatch.

shocking *adjective shocking conditions | a shocking sight* appalling, horrifying, horrific, dreadful, awful, frightful, terrible, horrible, scandalous, outrageous, disgraceful, vile, abominable, ghastly, foul, monstrous, unspeakable, abhorrent, hideous, atrocious, repellent, revolting, odious, repulsive, repugnant, disgusting, nauseating, sickening, grisly, loathsome, offensive, distressing, upsetting, perturbing, disturbing, disquieting, unsettling, agitating, staggering, amazing, astonishing, stupefying, overwhelming, bewildering.
Opposites ADMIRABLE; WONDERFUL; DELIGHTFUL.

shoddy *adjective* poor-quality, inferior, second-rate, cheapjack, tawdry, rubbishy, trashy, junky, gimcrack, jerry-built; *inf.* tacky, tatty.

shoe *noun. See table at* FOOTWEAR.

shoot *verb* **1** *shoot a deer* hit, wound, injure, shoot down, bring down, pick off, bag, fell, kill, slay; *inf.* pump full of lead, plug, zap. **2** *shoot at the fugitives* fire at, open fire on, aim at, snipe at, shell. **3** *shoot a round of bullets/arrows* fire, discharge, launch, let off, let fly, send forth, emit. **4** *athletes shooting past* race, dash, sprint, bound, charge, dart, fly, hurtle, bolt, streak, flash, whisk, run, speed, hurry, hasten; *inf.* scoot. **5** *plants shooting* put forth buds, bud, burgeon, sprout, germinate, appear, spring up. **6** *shooting animal scenes* film, photograph, take photographs of.

shoot *noun shoots of a plant/tree* bud, offshoot, slip, scion, sucker, sprout, branch, twig, sprig, cutting, graft.

shop *noun* **1** *purchase goods at a shop* store, retail outlet, trading post. **2** *cars worked on at the shop* workshop, plant, factory.

shop *verb* **1** *shop for essential goods* go shopping, look to buy, be in the market for. **2** *shop his fellow bank-raiders* inform against, tell tales on, impeach; *inf.* grass on, rat on, blow the whistle on, put the finger on, squeal on, peach on, sing about.

shore *noun* seashore, seaside, beach, coast, seaboard, waterside, foreshore, strand.

shore *verb shore up the broken wall* prop up, support, hold up, underpin, strengthen, brace, buttress.

short *adjective* **1** *short people* small, little, slight, petite, tiny, squat, stubby, dwarfish, diminutive, dumpy, Lilliputian; *Scots* wee; *inf.* pint-sized, pocket-sized, knee-high to a grasshopper. **2** *short bushes* low, stubby, miniature; *Scots* wee. **3** *a short piece of string* small, little, tiny, minuscule. **4** *a short report* brief, concise, succinct, to the point, compact, terse, summary, crisp, pithy, epigrammatic, abridged, abbreviated, condensed, summarized, contracted, curtailed, truncated. **5** *a short affair* brief, momentary, temporary, short-lived, impermanent, short-term, cursory, fleeting, passing, transitory, transient, ephemeral, fugacious, evanescent, meteoric. **6** *the short route* direct, straight. **7** *money/food is a bit short*

deficient, lacking, wanting, insufficient, inadequate, scarce, scanty, meagre, sparse, unplentiful, tight, low. **8** *he was short with her | give rather a short reply* curt, sharp, abrupt, blunt, brusque, terse, gruff, surly, testy, tart, rude, discourteous, uncivil, impolite. **9** *short pastry* short-crust, crumbly, crispy, crisp, brittle, friable.
Opposites TALL; LONG; ABUNDANT.

short *adverb stop short* abruptly, suddenly, all of a sudden, unexpectedly, without warning, out of the blue. **cut short** shorten, curtail, truncate, abbreviate, reduce, bring to an untimely end, terminate, end, stop, halt, arrest, cut off, interrupt, break up. **fall short** be deficient, be insufficient, be inadequate, disappoint, fail, not fulfil expectations; *inf.* not come up to scratch. **in short** briefly, to put it briefly, in a word, in a nutshell, in essence, to cut a long story short, to come to the point. **sell short** **1** *always selling herself short* undervalue, underrate, underestimate, disparage, deprecate, belittle, detract from, derogate. **2** *shopkeepers selling people short* cheat, swindle, defraud, fleece, short-change, over-charge. **short of** **1** *short of eggs/brains* deficient in, lacking, wanting, in need of, low on, missing. **2** *short of killing him how will you get rid of him?* other than, apart from, aside from, besides, except, without, excluding, leaving out, not counting, disregarding.

shortage *noun* dearth, scarcity, lack, deficiency, insufficiency, paucity, deficit, inadequacy, shortfall, want, poverty.
Opposites ABUNDANCE; SURFEIT; SURPLUS.

shortcoming *noun forgive his shortcomings* defect, fault, flaw, imperfection, failing, drawback, weakness, weak point, foible, frailty, infirmity.

shorten *verb* **1** *shorten the text* abbreviate, condense, abridge, cut, cut down, contract, compress, reduce, lessen, decrease, diminish, curtail, duck, trim, pare down. **2** *the days are shortening* get shorter, grow shorter, grow less.
Opposites LENGTHEN; EXTEND; ELONGATE.

short-lived *adjective short-lived happiness* brief, momentary, temporary, impermanent, fleeting, transitory, ephemeral. *See* SHORT *adjective* 5.

shortly *adverb* **1** *she will be with you shortly* soon, in a short while, in a little while, presently, before long, directly; *inf.* before you know it, before you can say Jack Robinson. **2** *he replied shortly* curtly, sharply, abruptly, bluntly, brusquely, tersely, gruffly, surlily, testily, tartly, rudely, discourteously, uncivilly, impolitely.

short-sighted *adjective* **1** *wear spectacles because of being short-sighted* myopic, near-sighted. **2** *a short-sighted attitude to business* lacking foresight, uncircumspect, ill-considered, unwary, imprudent, injudicious, unwise, ill-advised, thoughtless, unthinking, heedless, rash, incautious.

short-staffed *adjective* under-staffed, short-handed, undermanned, below strength.

731

short-tempered · showing

short-tempered *adjective* quick-tempered, hot-tempered, irascible, touchy, testy, fiery, peppery, choleric; *inf.* on a short fuse, ratty.

shot *noun* **1** *hear a shot* gun-fire, report of a gun, crack, bang, blast, explosion. **2** *shot for the guns* pellet, bullet, slug, projectile, ammunition. See table at BULLET. **3** *hit the target with one shot* throw, lob, fling, hurl, shot-put. **4** *a better shot than his brother* shooter, marksman, rifleman. **5** *take a shot of the house* photograph, photo, film, snap, snapshot. **6** *have a shot at getting there* attempt, try, effort, endeavour, essay; *inf.* go, stab, crack, bash, whack. **7** *it's your shot now* turn, chance, opportunity; *inf.* go. **8** *have shots before going to the tropics* injection, vaccination. **9** *a nasty/cheap shot* comment, remark, statement, utterance; *inf.* crack. **a shot in the arm** *a shot in the arm for the tourist industry* boost, fillip, lift, encouragement, stimulus. **a shot in the dark** *her answer was right but it was a shot in the dark* wild guess, random guess, guess, pure conjecture. **like a shot** *he would take the job like a shot* without hesitation, unhesitatingly, very willingly, eagerly, immediately, instantly, right away, at once, like a flash. **not by a long shot** by no means, not at all, not in the least, on no account, under no circumstances.

shot *adjective* *shot silk* variegated, multicoloured, many-coloured, varicoloured.

shoulder *verb* **1** *shoulder a heavy burden/responsibility* bear, carry, support, be responsible for, take on, take upon oneself. **2** *shoulder his way to the front* push, shove, thrust, jostle, elbow, force. **give someone the cold shoulder** ostracize, shun, snub, ignore, rebuff, send someone to Coventry; *inf.* cut, cut dead. **put one's shoulder to the wheel** apply oneself, exert oneself, get down to work, set to work, make an effort, strive; *inf.* buckle down, give it one's best shot. **rub shoulders with** associate with, mix with, socialize with, consort with, fraternize with, hobnob with. **shoulder to shoulder** side by side, cheek by jowl, together, united, jointly, in partnership, in cooperation, in unity, in unison, as one. **straight from the shoulder** directly, frankly, candidly, forthrightly, bluntly, plainly, explicitly, outspokenly, unequivocally, unambiguously; *inf.* pulling no punches, with no holds barred.

shout *verb* "Help," *he shouted* cry out, call out, yell, roar, howl, bellow, scream, bawl, call at the top of one's voice, raise one's voice; *inf.* holler.

shout *noun* **1** *a shout of pain* cry, call, yell, roar, howl, bellow, scream, bawl; *inf.* holler. **2** *your shout* turn to pay, round, treat.

shove *verb* *shove forward|shove her out of the way* push, thrust, drive, force, shoulder, elbow, jostle, jolt.

shove *noun* *give the child a shove* push, thrust, jostle, jolt.

shovel *noun* *move coal with a shovel* spade, scoop. See table at TOOL.

shovel *verb* *shovel coal* scoop up, spade, dig, excavate.

show *verb* **1** *grey hairs beginning to show* be visible, be seen, be in view, appear, put in an appearance. **2** *show the toys to the children* exhibit, display, present, demonstrate, set forth, uncover, reveal. **3** *show his grief* indicate, express, manifest, reveal, make known, make plain, make obvious, evince, evidence, disclose, betray, divulge. **4** *show them the new procedures* demonstrate, point out, explain, expound, clarify, elucidate, teach, instruct in, give instructions in, tutor in, indoctrinate in. **5** *show them to their seats* escort, accompany, usher, conduct, attend, guide, lead, direct, steer. **6** *he didn't show* appear, put in an appearance, make an appearance, turn up, come, arrive, be present. **show off 1** *models showing off the dresses* show to advantage, display, exhibit, demonstrate, parade, flaunt. **2** *children showing off about their new clothes* put on airs, give oneself airs, boast, brag, swagger around. **show up 1** *sunshine showing up the dust* expose, reveal, bring to light, lay bare, make visible, make obvious, highlight, pinpoint, put the spotlight on. **2** *the red showing up well against the grey* be visible, be obvious, be conspicuous, stand out, catch the eye. **3** *show him up in front of his rich friends* expose, show in a bad light, shame, put to shame, mortify, humiliate, embarrass. **4** *the guest didn't show up* appear, make an appearance, put in an appearance, turn up, come, get here/there, be present; *inf.* show.

Opposites CONCEAL; SUPPRESS; WITHHOLD.

show *noun* **1** *a brilliant show of flowers* display, array, arrangement, exhibition, presentation, exposition, spectacle. **2** *a clothes show* exhibition, demonstration, display, exposition, presentation; *inf.* expo. **3** *put on a musical show* performance, public performance, theatrical performance, production; *inf.* gig. **4** *a show of courage although terrified* appearance, outward appearance, air, guise, semblance, pretence, illusion, pose, affectation, profession, parade. **5** *only doing it for show* display, ostentation, affectation, window-dressing. **6** *run the show* organization, establishment, undertaking, enterprise, business, venture. **steal the show** be the main attraction, be the centre of attraction, get all the attention, have all eyes upon one, be the cynosure.

showdown *noun* confrontation, open conflict, clash, face-off, moment of truth, crisis, culmination, climax.

shower *noun* **1** *a shower of rain/snow* fall, drizzle, flurry, sprinkling. **2** *a shower of arrows* volley, raining, barrage, fusillade. **3** *a shower of gifts* abundance, profusion, plethora, flood, deluge.

shower *verb* **1** *arrows showered on them* rain, fall. **2** *shower them with gifts* deluge, inundate, overwhelm. **3** *shower gifts on them* lavish, pour, load, heap.

showing *noun* **1** *a private showing* show, exhibition, display, exposition; *inf.* expo. **2** *on the firm's/employee's present showing* performance, track record, record, results.

show-off *noun* exhibitionist, extrovert, swaggerer, bragger, braggart, boaster, braggadocio; *inf.* blow-hard.

showy *adjective showy clothes/lifestyle* ostentatious, flamboyant, elaborate, fancy, pretentious, overdone, glittering.
Opposites DISCREET; RESTRAINED; PLAIN.

shred *noun* **1** *shreds of material* scrap, fragment, wisp, sliver, bit, piece, remnant, snippet, tatter. **2** *not a shred of evidence* scrap, bit, iota, whit, particle, atom, modicum, trace, speck.

shred *verb shred paper/cabbage* cut up, tear up, rip up, grate.

shrew *noun married to a real shrew* virago, termagant, fury, harpy, nag.

shrewd *adjective* **1** *a shrewd businessman* astute, sharp, clever, intelligent, smart, alert, quick-witted, discerning, perspicacious, perceptive, discriminating, wise, sagacious, farseeing, canny, cunning, artful, crafty, wily, calculating; *inf.* with all one's wits about one. **2** *a shrewd plan* astute, clever, wise, judicious, far-sighted, cunning, artful, crafty, wily, calculated.
Opposites STUPID; UNWISE; INGENUOUS.

shrewdness *noun* acumen, astuteness, sharpness, cleverness, smartness, alertness, quick-wittedness, discernment, perspicacity, perceptiveness, wisdom, sagacity, canniness, cunning, artfulness, craftiness, wiliness, calculation, calculatedness.

shriek *verb shriek with laughter/terror* scream, screech, squeal, yell, howl, shout, cry out, call out, whoop, wail; *inf.* holler.

shriek *noun a shriek of laughter/terror* scream, screech, squeal, yell, howl, shout, cry, call, whoop, wail; *inf.* holler.

shrill *adjective* high-pitched, high, sharp, piercing, ear-piercing, penetrating, ear-splitting, screeching, shrieking.
Opposites LOW; SOFT; DULCET.

shrine *noun* **1** *a shrine in memory of the dead soldiers* memorial, monument, cenotaph. **2** *worship in the shrine* holy place, temple, church. **3** *the relics of the saint in a shrine* reliquary, burial chamber, tomb, sepulchre.

shrink *verb* **1** *shirts shrinking in the wash* get smaller, become/grow smaller. **2** *markets shrinking* get smaller, become/grow smaller, contract, diminish, lessen, reduce, dwindle, narrow, decline, fall off, drop off, shrivel. **3** *children shrinking from the bully | shrink from admitting the truth* draw back, pull back, start back, back away, shy away, recoil, retreat, withdraw, flinch, cringe, wince.
Opposites STRETCH; EXPAND; CONFRONT.

shrivel *verb leaves shrivelled by the sun* dry up, wither, desiccate, dehydrate, wrinkle, pucker up.

shrivelled *adjective shrivelled leaves/skins* dried up, withered, desiccated, dehydrated, wrinkled, puckered, wizened; *lit.* sere.

shroud *noun* **1** *corpses in shrouds* winding-sheet, grave-clothes, burial clothes, cerements. **2** *a shroud of mist over the hills* cover, covering, pall, cloak, mantle, blanket, cloud, veil, screen.

shroud *verb hills shrouded in mist* cover, enshroud, swathe, envelop, cloak, blanket, cloud, veil, screen, conceal, hide.

shrub *noun. See table at* TREE.

shrug *verb shrug off failure* disregard, take no notice of, not trouble about, dismiss, gloss over, play down, make light of, minimize.

shudder *verb shudder in horror* shake, shiver, tremble, quiver, quaver, quake, convulse.

shudder *noun a shudder of horror* shake, shiver, tremor, tremble, quiver, quaver, convulsion, spasm.

shuffle *verb* **1** *shuffle along the road* shamble, hobble, limp, drag one's feet, scuff one's feet. **2** *the audience shuffling their feet* scrape, scuff, drag. **3** *shuffle cards/papers* mix, intermix, shift about, rearrange, reorganize, jumble. **4** *shuffling and refusing to give a straight answer* hedge, equivocate, be evasive, prevaricate, fence, parry, beat about the bush, beg the question; *inf.* pussyfoot around.

shun *noun shun the ex-convict/publicity* avoid, evade, eschew, steer clear of, shy away from, recoil from, keep away from, keep one's distance from, cold-shoulder, give a wide berth to.

shut *verb shut the doors* draw to, pull to, close, fasten, bar, lock, secure, seal. **shut down 1** *shut down the factory* close, close down. **2** *the factory has shut down* close, close down, cease productions, come to halt, cease operating, go on strike. **3** *shut down the machinery* switch off, stop, halt. **shut in** *shut in the dogs/prisoners* lock in, keep in, enclose, confine, restrain, imprison, hem in, fence in, corral. **shut out 1** *shut out intruders* lock out, keep out. **2** *shut him out of their negotiations/club* exclude, leave out, omit, keep out, bar, debar, ostracize, blackball, banish, exile, outlaw. **3** *shut out the light* keep out, block out, screen, cover up. **shut up 1** *shut the child up in a wardrobe* lock in, confine, imprison, coop up, box in, cage in. **2** *criminals shut up for life* imprison, jail, incarcerate, intern, immure. **3** *children asked to shut up* keep quiet, be quiet, keep silent, fall silent; *inf.* hold one's tongue, keep one's lips sealed, keep mum, pipe down, keep one's trap shut. **4** *shut the children up* quieten, silence, hush, shush, gag; *inf.* button the lip of.
Opposites OPEN; UNLOCK.

shutter *noun* blind, shade.

shuttle *verb shuttle between the two cities* go back and forth between, alternate between, commute between, shunt between, ply between.

shy *adjective* bashful, diffident, reserved, reticent, retiring, self-effacing, shrinking, withdrawn, timid, timorous, fearful, nervous, hesitant, wary, suspicious, chary, unconfident, self-conscious, embarrassed, abashed, modest.
Opposites BOLD; BRASH; CONFIDENT.

shy *verb shy a stone at the tree* throw, fling, cast, pitch, toss, hurl, propel; *inf.* chuck. **fight shy of** *fight shy of getting involved* shy away from, recoil from, flinch from, back away from. *See*

SHY AWAY FROM. **shy away from** *shy away from trouble* fight shy of, shrink from, recoil from, flinch from, balk at, quail at, draw back from, back away from.

shyness *noun* bashfulness, diffidence, reserve, reservedness, reticence, timidity, timorousness, fearfulness, nervousness, hesitancy, hesitation, wariness, suspicion, chariness, lack of confidence, self-consciousness, embarrassment, modesty. *See* SHY *adjective*.

sick *adjective* **1** *off work sick* unwell, ill, ailing, indisposed, poorly, below par, out of sorts, laid up; *inf.* under the weather, on the sick list. **2** *feel sick on a boat* nauseated, queasy, bilious; *inf.* green about the gills. **3** *be sick on the boat* vomit, retch; *Am.* be sick to one's stomach; *inf.* throw up, puke. **4** *sick of that music* tired, weary, bored, jaded, surfeited, satiated, glutted; *inf.* fed up, have had something up to here. **5** *be sick about losing* angry, annoyed, displeased, disgruntled, distressed, disgusted; *inf.* fed up, cheesed off. **6** *a sick joke | sick humour* morbid, macabre, ghoulish, gruesome, sadistic, perverted, cruel.
Opposites WELL; HEALTHY; fond of (*see* FOND).

sicken *verb* **1** *sickened by the sight of the mangled corpse* make sick, nauseate, turn one's stomach, make one's gorge rise, revolt, disgust, repel, shock, appal. **2** *sicken for something/flu* show symptoms of, take ill with, become ill with, fall ill with, become infected with, contract, be stricken with; *inf.* come down with. **3** *begin to sicken of that type of music* tire, weary, become bored with/of, feel jaded with, have a surfeit of, be satiated with, have a glut of; *inf.* be fed up with, have had something up to here.

sickening *adjective the sickening sight of the mangled corpse* nauseating, nauseous, revolting, disgusting, repellent, repulsive, loathsome, off-putting, distasteful, stomach-turning, stomach-churning, shocking, appalling, offensive, vile, foul.

sickly *adjective* **1** *a sickly child* unhealthy, in poor health, chronically ill, delicate, frail, weak, feeble, puny. **2** *look sickly | a sickly complexion* pale, wan, pallid, peaky, anaemic, bloodless, languid, listless; *inf.* washed-out. **3** *sickly love songs* sentimental, cloying, mawkish, maudlin, slushy, mushy, syrupy; *inf.* soppy, schmaltzy. **4** *sickly colours* pallid, insipid, wan, pale, washed-out, faded; *inf.* bilious.

sickness *noun* **1** *suffering from a terminal sickness* illness, disease, disorder, ailment, complaint, affliction, malady, infirmity, indisposition; *inf.* bug. *See table at* ILLNESS. **2** *a bout of sickness* vomiting, retching, upset stomach, stomach upset; *inf.* throwing up, puking. **3** *a feeling of sickness on the swaying boat* nausea, queasiness, biliousness.

side *noun* **1** *by the side of the lake/road* edge, border, verge, boundary, margin, rim, fringe, skirt, flank, brink, brim, periphery. **2** *on the east side of the city* part, quarter, section, sector, neighbourhood. **3** *the upper side of the paper/wood* surface, face, part, facet. **4** *both sides of the question/problem* aspect, angle, facet, point of view, viewpoint, view, opinion, standpoint,

position, slant. **5** *on the chairman's side in the dispute* camp, faction, caucus, party, wing, splinter group, sect. **6** *left out of the football side* team, squad, line-up. **7** *no side about the aristocratic family* airs, airs and graces, pretentiousness, arrogance, superciliousness; *inf.* snootiness. **side by side** *walk/fight side by side* close together, together, alongside each other, shoulder to shoulder, cheek by jowl, arm in arm. **take the side of** *take the side of the likely winner* side with, take the part of, support, give one's support to, favour.
Opposites CENTRE; HEART.

side *adjective* **1** *on the side position of the battle* lateral, wing, flank. **2** *a side issue/road* minor, lesser, secondary, subordinate, subsidiary, ancillary, marginal. **3** *a side look* sidelong, oblique, indirect. *See* SIDELONG.
Opposites CENTRAL; MAJOR; PRIMARY.

side *verb* *side with his brother against his sister* take the side of, be on the side of, take the part of, support, give one's support to, back, give one's backing to, ally with, associate oneself with, join with, favour.
Opposites OPPOSE.

sidelong *adjective* side, sideways, oblique, indirect, covert.

sidestep *verb* *sidestep the problematic issue* avoid, skirt round, evade, dodge, circumvent, bypass, steer clear of; *inf.* duck.

sidetrack *verb* *get sidetracked from the main issue* divert, deflect, distract, lead away from.

sideways *adverb* **1** *walk sideways* crabwise, to the side. **2** *bring the table in sideways* side first, edgeways, edgewise. **3** *look sideways at her* obliquely, indirectly, sidelong.

sideways *adjective* *a sideways glance* sidelong, side, oblique, indirect.

siege *noun* blockade, besiegement, beleaguerment, investment. *See table. See also tables at* BATTLE, WAR.

siesta *noun* nap, sleep, rest, catnap, doze; *inf.* forty winks, snooze.

sieve *noun* *use a sieve to strain the mixture* strainer, sifter, filter, colander, riddle, screen.

sieve *verb* **1** *sieve the mixture* strain, sift, filter, riddle, screen. **2** *sieve the lumps from the sauce* separate out, remove, winnow.

sift *verb* **1** *sift the flour* filter, strain, riddle, screen. **2** *sift flour onto a board* shake, sprinkle, distribute, scatter, strew. **3** *sift the lumps from the flour* separate out, remove, winnow. **4** *sift through the evidence* examine, scrutinize, study, pore over, investigate, analyse, screen, review, probe. **5** *sift through the debris* search through, look through, rummage through, ransack.

sigh *verb* **1** *sigh with tiredness/boredom* breathe out, exhale. **2** *the wind sighing through the trees* whisper, rustle. **3** *sigh for times past* yearn for, pine for, long for, weep for, mourn for.

sight *noun* **1** *have excellent sight* eyesight, vision, eyes, faculty of sight, power of sight. **2** *within sight of her father* range of vision, field of vision, view. **3** *our first sight of the building* view, glimpse, seeing, glance at. **4** *in her father's sight she was perfect* opinion, view, point of view, judgement, estimation, feeling, observation, perception. **5** *the town's historic sights* spectacle, scene, display, show, exhibition, curiosity, rarity, marvel; *inf.* something to write home about. **6** *a sight in those clothes* spectacle, eyesore, monstrosity, mess; *inf.* fright, blot on the landscape. **catch sight of** glimpse, get a glimpse of, see, spot, sight, descry, espy, set eyes on, have sight of. **set one's sights on** aim at/for, aspire to, strive towards, work towards, be after, seek.

sight *verb sight land* catch sight of, see, behold, spot, make out, descry, espy, perceive, observe, discern.

sign *noun* **1** *a sign of weakness/strength* indication, symptom, hint, suggestion, trace, mark, clue, manifestation, token, evidence, proof. **2** *signs indicating the various shops in the complex* signpost, notice, placard, board, marker. **3** *make a sign to follow him* gesture, signal, motion, movement, wave, gesticulation. **4** *mathematical signs | signs instead of language* symbol, mark, cipher, code, hieroglyph, hieroglyphics. **5** *look for a sign that the Messiah will come* omen, portent, warning, forewarning, augury, presage.

sign *verb* **1** *sign one's name* write, inscribe. **2** *sign the letter* write one's name on, autograph, initial. **3** *sign the agreement* write one's name on, initial, endorse, certify, validate, authenticate. **4** *sign to her to follow* signal, indicate, beckon, gesture, motion, gesticulate, wave, nod. **sign on/up** **1** *soldier signing on for five years* enlist, join up, join the services. **2** *sign on for music classes* enrol, register, put one's name down for, enlist, become a member of. **3** *sign on new employees* employ, take on, engage, hire, recruit, take into one's employ. **sign over** *sign over the estate to his son* transfer, make over, hand over, turn over, assign, consign.

SIEGES		
City	**Fighters**	**Date**
Alamo, Texas	Americans besieged by Mexicans	1836
Alesia	Gauls besieged by Romans	46 B.C.
Antioch	Muslims besieged by Crusaders	1098
Antwerp	Belgians besieged by Spanish	1585
Calais	French besieged by English	1346–7
Charleston	Americans besieged by British	1780
Constantinople	Byzantines besieged by Ottoman Turks	1453
Dien Bien Phu	French besieged by Vietnamese	1954
Grozny	Chechens besieged by Russians	1994–5
Jerusalem	Muslims besieged by Crusaders	1099
Khartoum	British and Egyptians besieged by Sudanese	1885
Kiev	Russians besieged by Germans	during World War II
Ladysmith	British besieged by Boers	1899–1900
Lamia	Macedonians besieged by Greeks	323–322 B.C.
La Rochelle	Huguenots besieged by French Catholics	1627
Leiden	Dutch besieged by Spanish	1574
Limerick	Irish besieged by English	1691
Londonderry	Protestants besieged by Catholics	1688–9
Lucknow	Indians besieged by British	1857–8
Madrid	Spanish Republicans besieged by Spanish Nationalists	1937–9
Mafeking	British besieged by Boers 1899–1900	
Malta	Maltese besieged by Turks	1530
Masada	Jews besieged by Romans	71–73 A.D.
Metz	French besieged by Prussians	1870–1
Montcalm	French besieged by British	1759
Montpellier	Huguenots besieged by Catholics	1622
Orléans	French besieged by English	1428–9
Paris	French besieged by Prussians	1870–1
Plataea	Boeotians besieged by Spartans	429–427 B.C.
Leningrad (St Petersburg)	Russians besieged by Germans	1941–4
Sarajevo	Bosnians besieged by Serbs	from 1992
Sebastopol	Russians besieged by the British and French	1854–5
Syracuse	Greeks besieged by Romans	215–212 B.C.
Troy	Trojans besieged by Greeks	?c.1200 B.C.
Tyre	Phoenicians besieged by Greeks	322 B.C.
	besieged by Romans	68 B.C.
Vicksburg	Confederates besieged by Federals	1863
Venice	Venetians besieged by Austrians	1848–9
Verdun	French besieged by Germans	1916
Vienna	Austrians besieged by Ottoman Turks	1529, 1532, 1683
Warsaw	Germans besieged by Soviets	1945
Yorktown	British besieged by American Revolutionaries	1781
Zaragoza	Spanish besieged by French	1808–9

signal noun **1** *the signal to stop | a signal that someone was coming* sign, indicator, cue. **2** *a signal that winter was coming* sign, indication, token, evidence, hint. **3** *the arrival of the star was the signal for applause* incentive, impetus, stimulus, motive, cause, reason.

signal verb **1** *signal to her to follow* sign, give a sign to, indicate, beckon, gesture, motion, gesticulate, nod. **2** *signal his displeasure with silence* indicate, show, express, communicate. **3** *the sudden cold weather signalled the start of a hard winter* be a sign of, mark, signify, designate.

signal adjective *a signal achievement* exceptional, conspicuous, notable, noteworthy, significant, memorable, outstanding, striking, remarkable, distinguished, eminent.

significance noun **1** *not comprehend the significance of his remark* meaning, sense, import, signification, purport, point, gist, essence, implications. **2** *the significance of the medical discovery* importance, consequence, moment, momentousness, weight, weightiness, magnitude, impressiveness, seriousness.

significant adjective **1** *a significant few words* meaningful, eloquent, expressive, indicative, pregnant, knowing. **2** *make significant progress* important, of importance, of consequence, momentous, of moment, weighty, material, impressive, serious, vital, critical.
Opposites INSIGNIFICANT; MEANINGLESS; MINOR.

signify verb **1** *dark clouds signifying rain* be a sign of, indicate, mean, denote, betoken, suggest, point to, portend. **2** *What do the symbols signify?* mean, denote, represent, symbolize, stand for. **3** *signify one's agreement* indicate, show, exhibit, express, communicate, intimate, announce, proclaim, declare, pronounce. **4** *his opinion doesn't signify* matter, be of importance, be of consequence, be important, be significant, be of significance, carry weight, count.

silence noun **1** *in the silence of the night* still, stillness, quiet, quietness, hush, peace, peacefulness, tranquillity, noiselessness, soundlessness. **2** *their behaviour reduced him to silence* speechlessness, wordlessness, voicelessness, dumbness, muteness, taciturnity, reticence, uncommunicativeness. **3** *the need for silence about their whereabouts* secrecy, secretiveness, concealment, reticence, taciturnity, uncommunicativeness.
Opposites NOISE; SPEECH; COMMUNICATION.

silence verb **1** *silence the noisy children* quiet, quieten, hush, still, calm, pacify, subdue, quell. **2** *silence the noise of the engine* muffle, deaden, abate, extinguish. **3** *silence their complaints* put an end to, put a stop to, cut short, gag, prevent.

silent adjective **1** *in their silent surroundings* still, quiet, hushed, peaceful, tranquil, noiseless, soundless. **2** *silent in the face of the opposition* speechless, unspeaking, wordless, voiceless, dumb, mute, taciturn, reticent, uncommunicative, mum, tight-lipped, tongue-tied; *inf.* struck dumb. **3** *silent criticism* unspoken, wordless, unvoiced, unsaid, unexpressed, unpronounced, tacit, implicit, under-

stood, implied.
Opposites NOISY; LOQUACIOUS; SPOKEN.

silhouette noun *see her silhouette on the wall* outline, contour, profile, delineation, form, shape.

silhouette verb *silhouetted against the sky* outline, stand out, etch, delineate.

silky adjective silken, smooth, sleek, velvety, diaphanous.

silly adjective **1** *a silly person* foolish, stupid, unintelligent, idiotic, brainless, witless, unwise, imprudent, thoughtless, reckless, foolhardy, irresponsible, mad, erratic, unstable, scatter-brained, feather-brained, flighty, frivolous, giddy, fatuous, inane, immature, childish, shallow, naive; *inf.* daft, crazy, dotty, scatty, loopy, screwy. **2** *silly actions* foolish, stupid, unintelligent, senseless, mindless, idiotic, unwise, imprudent, inadvisable, injudicious, ill-considered, misguided, unsound, impractical, pointless, meaningless, purposeless, inappropriate, illogical, irrational, unreasonable, thoughtless, reckless, foolhardy, irresponsible, erratic, hare-brained, absurd, ridiculous, ludicrous, laughable, risible, farcical, preposterous, fatuous, asinine; *inf.* half-baked, daft, crazy, dotty, loopy, screwy, for the birds. **3** *knocked silly by the blow* dazed, in a daze, stunned, stupefied, groggy, muzzy, benumbed.
Opposites SENSIBLE; CLEVER; RATIONAL.

silly noun *accused of being a silly* fool, ninny, nincompoop, idiot, simpleton, dolt, scatterbrain, halfwit; *inf.* nitwit, twit, clot, dope, goose, silly-billy.

similar adjective **1** *have similar houses* like, alike, much the same, comparable, corresponding, analogous, parallel, equivalent, kindred, approximate. **2** *ideas similar to his* resembling, like, much the same as, comparable to, corresponding to, close to.
Opposites DISSIMILAR; UNLIKE; DIFFERENT.

similarity noun *a degree of similarity* resemblance, likeness, sameness, similitude, comparability, correspondence, analogy, parallel, parallelism, equivalence, approximation, closeness, affinity, kinship.

similarly adverb likewise, in the same way, in like matter, correspondingly, by the same token.

similitude noun *a marked degree of similitude in their views* resemblance, likeness, similarity, sameness, comparability, correspondence, closeness, analogy. *See* SIMILARITY.

simmer verb **1** *a stew simmering on the stove* cook gently, boil gently, bubble, stew, poach, seethe. **2** *simmering with rage* fume, seethe, smoulder, chafe, smart, be angry, be furious.

simple adjective **1** *a simple task* easy, uncomplicated, straightforward, uninvolved, effortless, manageable, elementary, facile; *inf.* like falling off a log, a piece of cake, a cinch, easy-peasy, no sweat. **2** *simple instructions | in simple language* clear, plain, intelligible, comprehensible, understandable, lucid, direct, straightforward, uncomplicated, uninvolved. **3** *simple clothes* plain, classic, clean-cut, unelaborate, unadorned, undecorated, without ornament/

simpleton · sincerity

ornamentation, unembellished, unfussy, uncluttered, austere, stark, spartan, unpretentious, restrained, natural, casual, informal. **4** *simple chemical substances* non-complex, non-compound, uncompounded, uncombined, unmixed, unblended, unalloyed, pure, basic, single, elementary, fundamental. **5** *the simple truth/facts* plain, straightforward, frank, direct, candid, honest, sincere, absolute, unqualified, unvarnished, bald, stark, unadorned, unembellished. **6** *a simple country girl* unsophisticated, natural, unaffected, wholesome, innocent, artless, guileless, childlike, naive, ingenuous, gullible, inexperienced; *inf.* green. **7** *lead a simple life* ordinary, commonplace, unpretentious, modest, homely, humble, lowly, rustic. **8** *too simple to have committed the crime* simple-minded, feeble-minded, mentally retarded, retarded, backward, slow-witted, slow, dull-witted.
Opposites DIFFICULT; COMPLICATED; FANCY; COMPOUND.

simpleton *noun* idiot, halfwit, dolt, fool, ninny, nincompoop; *inf.* nitwit, twit, clot, dope.

simplicity *noun* **1** *the simplicity of the task* simpleness, easiness, lack/absence of complication, straightforwardness, effortlessness, elementariness, facility. *See* SIMPLE 1. **2** *the simplicity of the directions/language* simpleness, clarity, clearness, plainness, intelligibility, lucidity, lucidness, directness, straightforwardness; *inf.* calling a spade a spade, telling like it is. *See* SIMPLE 2. **3** *the simplicity of the clothes* simpleness, classic lines, clean lines, non-elaborateness, lack/absence of adornment/decoration/ornament/ornamentation/embellishment, unfussiness, plainness, lack/absence of clutter, austereness, starkness, unpretentiousness, restraint, naturalness, casualness, informality. **4** *the simplicity of the statement* simpleness, plainness, straightforwardness, frankness, directness, candidness, candour, honesty, sincerity, baldness, starkness, lack of embellishment. **5** *the simplicity of their lifestyle* ordinariness, unpretentiousness, modesty, homeliness, humbleness, lowliness.

simplify *verb* **1** *simplify the complicated instructions* make simple/simpler, make easy/easier, make plainer, clarify, decipher, disentangle, explain, paraphrase, translate, abridge, shorten, condense. **2** *simplify the procedure/method* make simple/simpler, make easy/easier, streamline, reduce to essentials.

simplistic *adjective* *a simplistic solution/attitude* oversimple, oversimplified, facile, shallow, superficial, naive.

simply *adverb* **1** *try to express oneself simply* clearly, plainly, intelligibly, lucidly, directly, straightforwardly. **2** *dress simply* plainly, classically, unelaborately, without adornment/decoration/ornament/ornamentation/embellishment, unfussily, without clutter, austerely, starkly, spartanly, with restraint, naturally, casually, informally. **3** *live simply* unpretentiously, modestly, humbly. **4** *break windows simply to gain attention* purely, solely, merely, only, just. **5** *simply the best painting*

he had ever seen absolutely, unreservedly, positively, certainly, unconditionally, categorically, utterly, completely, altogether, totally, wholly.

simulate *verb* **1** *simulate grief* feign, pretend, fake, sham, affect, fake the appearance of. **2** *simulate flight landing conditions* reproduce, mimic, parallel, do a mock-up of.

simultaneous *adjective* *simultaneous disasters in different parts of the country* concurrent, contemporaneous, concomitant, coinciding, coincident, synchronous, coexistent, parallel.

simultaneously *adverb* *twins giving birth simultaneously* | *scream simultaneously* at the same time, concurrently, concomitantly, together, all together, in unison, in concert, in chorus.

sin *noun* **1** *commit a sin in the eyes of the church* wrong, wrongdoing, act of evil/wickedness/badness, crime, offence, misdeed, misdemeanour, transgression, error, lapse, fall from grace; *lit.* trespass. *See table.* **2** *guilty of sin* wrongdoing, wrong, evil, evildoing, wickedness, badness, iniquity, crime, immorality, transgression, error, unrighteousness, ungodliness, irreligiousness, irreverence, profanity, blasphemy, impiety, sacrilege.
Opposites VIRTUE; GOOD.

SEVEN DEADLY SINS	
anger	lust
covetousness	pride
envy	sloth
gluttony	

sin *verb* **1** *sin against the church/family* commit a sin, do wrong, commit a crime, offend, commit an offence, transgress. **2** *punish people who sin* commit a sin, do wrong, commit a crime, commit an offence, break the law, misbehave, transgress, go astray, stray from the straight and narrow, go wrong, fall from grace.

sincere *adjective* **1** *sincere affection/beliefs* genuine, real, true, honest, unfeigned, unaffected, *bona fide*, honest, wholehearted, heartfelt, serious, earnest, fervent. **2** *sincere people* honest, above-board, trustworthy, frank, candid, straightforward, plain-dealing, no-nonsense, genuine, undeceitful, artless, guileless, ingenuous; *inf.* up-front.
Opposites INSINCERE; FALSE; DISHONEST.

sincerely *adverb* **1** *thank them sincerely* with all sincerity, wholeheartedly, with all one's heart, earnestly, fervently. **2** *mean it most sincerely* genuinely, really, truly, in truth, without pretence, without feigning, honestly, in good faith.

sincerity *noun* **1** *doubt the sincerity of his affections/beliefs* genuineness, truth, honesty, good faith, wholeheartedness, seriousness, earnestness, fervour. **2** *misled by their seeming sincerity* openness, honesty, trustworthiness, frankness, candour, candidness, straightforwardness, genuineness, lack of deceit, artlessness, guile-lessness, ingenuousness.

sinecure noun easy job, soft option, cinch; inf. cushy number, money for old rope, money for jam, picnic, gravy train.

sinewy adjective muscular, brawny, burly, powerfully-built, stalwart, strapping.

sinful adjective **1** sinful deeds/thoughts wrong, evil, wicked, bad, iniquitous, criminal, immoral, corrupt, unrighteous, ungodly, irreligious, irreverent, profane, blasphemous, impious, sacrilegious. **2** sinful people wrongdoing, evil, evildoing, wicked, bad, criminal, erring, immoral, dissolute, corrupt, depraved.

sing verb **1** children singing happily carol, trill, warble, pipe, quaver, croon, chant, yodel. **2** birds singing trill, warble, chirp. **3** sing to the police inform, act as informer, tell tales, rat; inf. grass, squeal, blow the whistle, spill the beans, fink, peach. **sing out** "We're here," he sang out call, call out, cry, cry out, shout, yell, bellow; inf. holler.

singe verb singe the cloth/bread scorch, burn, sear, char, blacken.

singer noun vocalist, soloist, songster, songstress, chorister, crooner, warbler, chanteuse, minstrel; ballad-singer, opera-singer, diva, pop singer. See tables at JAZZ, MUSICIAN, OPERA, POPULAR MUSIC, VOICE.

single adjective **1** a single apple on the tree | send a single rose one, one only, sole, lone, solitary, unique, isolated, by itself, unique, exclusive. **2** the single most important event | remove every single item individual, particular, separate, distinct. **3** men preferring to remain single unmarried, unwed, unwedded, wifeless/husbandless, spouseless, partnerless, a bachelor, a spinster, unattached, free. **single out** single out the best/worst pupil separate out, set apart, put to one side, pick, choose, select, fix on, decide on, winnow.
Opposites DOUBLE; MARRIED.

single-handed adverb sail the Atlantic single-handed by oneself, alone, on one's own, solo, independently, unaided, unassisted, without help.

single-minded adjective too single-minded to be distracted from their aim unswerving, unwavering, undeviating, set, fixed, devoted, dedicated, committed, determined, dogged, tireless, purposeful, obsessive, monomaniacal.

singly adverb guests arriving singly one by one, one at a time, individually, separately, by oneself.

singular adjective **1** a singular talent extraordinary, exceptional, rare, unusual, unique, remarkable, outstanding, notable, noteworthy, striking, conspicuous, distinctive. **2** singular occurrences happening in the village strange, unusual, odd, peculiar, curious, queer, bizarre, weird, abnormal, atypical.
Opposites ORDINARY; COMMON; RUN-OF-THE-MILL.

sinister adjective **1** a sinister figure evil-looking, wicked-looking, villainous, malevolent, menacing, threatening, frightening, terrifying. **2** sinister motives evil, wicked, bad,

criminal, base, vile, vicious, cruel, malicious, malign. **3** sinister signs ominous, ill-omened, inauspicious, portentous.
Opposites BENEVOLENT; GOOD; INNOCENT; AUSPICIOUS.

sink verb **1** sink to one's knees | watch the sun sinking fall, drop, descend, go down, go lower, plunge, plummet, slump. **2** ships sinking go under, submerge, founder, capsize. **3** feel the ground sinking collapse, cave in, fall in. **4** empires/invalids sinking rapidly decline, fade, fail, deteriorate, weaken, grow weak, flag, degenerate, decay; inf. go downhill. **5** would not sink to that level stoop, lower oneself, debase oneself, be reduced to. **6** voices sinking lower, become/get lower, drop, become softer. **7** sink a well/shaft dig, bore, drill, excavate. **8** sink posts in the earth drive, place, put down, plant, position. **9** sink hopes of winning | sink the opposition's plans destroy, ruin, cause the downfall of, be the ruin/ruination of, demolish, devastate; inf. put the kibosh on, scupper, put the skids under. **10** having sunk their savings in the venture invest, put into, venture, risk. **11** sink their differences overlook, disregard, ignore, forget.
Opposites RISE; ASCEND; IMPROVE.

sinner noun wrongdoer, evildoer, criminal, offender, miscreant, transgressor, reprobate; lit. trespasser.

sinuous adjective winding, curving, twisting, turning, bending, curling, coiling, undulating, serpentine.

sip verb sip the drink drink slowly, sup, taste, sample.

sip noun take a sip of the drink mouthful, swallow, drink, drop, thimbleful, sup, taste.

siren noun **1** police sirens alarm, alarm bell, warning bell, danger signal, tocsin. **2** attracted by the siren at the bar seductress, temptress, femme fatale; lit. Circe, Lorelei; inf. vamp.

sit verb **1** children asked to sit sit down, take a seat, settle down, be seated; inf. take the load/weight off one's feet. **2** the books sitting on the mantelpiece be placed, be positioned, be situated, rest, perch. **3** sit the package on the table set down, place, put, deposit, rest, position, situate. **4** tables sitting twelve people seat, have space for, have room for, accommodate, hold. **5** committees sitting until midnight be convened, meet, assemble, be in session. **6** sit for her neighbours babysit, babymind, childmind.
Opposites STAND; RISE; LIFT.

site noun **1** the site of the battle location, situation, position, place, locality, setting, scene. **2** the building site ground, plot, lot.

site verb site the garage to the right of the house place, put, install, position, situate, locate.

sitting noun during a sitting of the council meeting, session, assembly, hearing.

situate verb companies situating their headquarters out of town | schools situated near the city centre place, position, locate, site.

situation noun **1** houses in a rural situation place, position, location, site, setting, milieu, environment. **2** their financial situation circumstances, affairs, state, state of affairs, condition, case, predicament, plight; *inf.* kettle of fish, ball-game. **3** *from a lowly situation in life* status, station, standing, footing, rank, degree. **4** *apply for a situation in the new firm* post, position, place, job, employment.

size *noun the size of his feet/car* dimensions, measurements, proportions, bigness, largeness, magnitude, vastness, bulk, area, expanse, extent.

size *verb size the eggs* sort, categorize, classify. **size up** *size up the opposition* appraise, assess, judge, evaluate, gauge, estimate, rate.

skeleton *noun* **1** *the skeleton of the building/car* framework, frame, structure, shell, chassis, support. **2** *give the skeleton of the argument* outline, sketch, bones, bare bones, draft, rough draft, plan, blueprint. **3** *the human skeleton* bones. *See table at* BONE.

skeleton *adjective skeleton staff* minimum, minimal, essential.

sketch *noun* **1** *draw a rough sketch of the house* drawing, preliminary drawing, outline, diagram, plan, representation, delineation. **2** *give a sketch of his plans* outline, summary, abstract, précis, résumé, sketch, skeleton, bones, bare bones, draft, plan. **3** *the theatre company performing a comic sketch* short play, skit, act, scene.

sketch *verb* **1** *sketch the subject of the portrait* draw, rough out, outline, pencil, represent, delineate, depict. **2** *sketch out his plans* outline, rough out, give a summary of, summarize, give an abstract/précis/résumé of, précis, draft.

sketchy *adjective* **1** *plans still a bit sketchy* preliminary, provisional, unfinished, unrefined, unpolished, rough, crude. **2** *sketchy knowledge/information* slight, superficial, cursory, perfunctory, meagre, scrappy, skimpy, bitty, insufficient, inadequate, imperfect, incomplete, deficient, defective.

skilful *adjective* **1** *a skilful performer* skilled, able, good, accomplished, adept, competent, efficient, adroit, deft, dexterous, masterly, expert, first-rate, experienced, trained, practised, professional, talented, gifted, clever, smart. **2** *a skilful performance* skilled, able, accomplished, competent, masterly, deft, expert, first-rate, talented, clever.
Opposites INCOMPETENT; INEPT; AMATEURISH.

skill *noun the skill of the performer/performance* skilfulness, ability, accomplishment, adeptness, competence, efficiency, adroitness, deftness, dexterity, aptitude, expertise, expertness, art, finesse, experience, professionalism, talent, cleverness, smartness.

skilled *adjective* **1** *a skilled performer* skilful, able, good, accomplished, adept, competent, masterly, expert, talented. *See* SKILFUL 1. **2** *a skilled performance* skilful, able, accomplished, competent, masterly, expert, first-rate. *See* SKILFUL 2. **3** *jobs for skilled workers* trained, qualified, expert, experienced, practised.

skim *verb* **1** *skim the milk* cream. **2** *skim the greasy liquid* scum, despumate. **3** *birds skimming the surface of the lake* glide over, move lightly over, brush, graze. **4** *skim pebbles across the lake* throw, pitch, skip, bounce. **5** *time only to skim through the report* read quickly, glance at, scan, run one's eye over, flip through, leaf through, thumb through.

skimp *verb* **1** *skimp on food/material* be sparing with, be economical with, economize on, be sparing with, be frugal with, be mean with, be parsimonious, be niggardly with, scrimp on, stint on, cut corners with, limit; *inf.* be stingy with. **2** *skimp a piece of work* do hastily, do carelessly, dash off, cut corners with.
Opposites SQUANDER; LAVISH.

skimpy *adjective* **1** *skimpy meals* small, meagre, scanty, insubstantial, insufficient, inadequate, sketchy, paltry. **2** *skimpy dresses* short, brief, scanty, insubstantial, sketchy.

skin *noun* **1** *damage the skin* integument, epidermis, cuticle, corium, derma. **2** *fair skins* complexion, colouring. **3** *animal skin* hide, pelt, fleece, fell, integument, tegument. **4** *banana/orange skin* peel, rind, hull, husk. **5** *a skin forming on the coffee* coating, coat, layer, crust. **6** *the skin of a rocket* casing, cover, covering, pod. **by the skin of one's teeth** *catch the train by the skin of one's teeth* only just, narrowly, barely, by a hair's-breadth; *inf.* by a whisker. **get under one's skin** **1** *noisy neighbours getting under her skin* irritate, annoy, irk, vex, grate on, rub up the wrong way, chafe, gall, nettle; *inf.* needle. **2** *computer games getting under children's skins* interest, absorb, engross, rivet, grip, attract, charm, enchant, mesmerize, hypnotize. **no skin off one's nose** *it's no skin off my nose if they leave* of no concern to, of no importance to, of no relevance to, of no interest to.

skin *verb* **1** *skin the fruit* peel, pare, hull, decorticate. **2** *skin one's knee* scrape, graze, abrade, cut, bark, excoriate.

skinflint *noun* miser, niggard, penny-pincher, Scrooge.

skinny *adjective* thin, thin as a rake, lean, scraggy, scrawny, emaciated, skeletal; *inf.* skin and bone.
Opposites FAT; PLUMP; OBESE.

skip *verb* **1** *children skipping along in the sunshine* bound, jump, leap, spring, hop, bounce, dance, caper, prance, trip, cavort, gambol, frisk, bob. **2** *skip from subject to subject/city to city* move quickly, go rapidly, pass quickly, flit, dart, zoom. **3** *skip the more boring parts of the text* omit, leave out, miss out, pass over, bypass, skim over. **4** *skip lectures* play truant from, miss, not attend, dodge; *inf.* cut, play hookey from, skive off from, wag.

skirmish *noun* battle, fight, clash, conflict, encounter, confrontation, engagement, combat, contest, tussle, scrimmage, fracas, affray, mêlée, quarrel, altercation, argument, dispute; *inf.* set-to, scrap, dust-up.

skirmish *verb skirmishing with the enemy* fight, engage with, combat with, clash, collide, have a confrontation, come to blows, tussle, quarrel, argue, have a dispute.

skirt *noun* **1** *growing round the skirt of the lake* edge, border, boundary, margin, fringe, rim. **2** *on the skirts of the town* outskirts, outer area,

outer limits, outlying districts, periphery, suburbs, purlieus. **3** *wearing a red skirt* long skirt,
short skirt. *See table.*

SKIRTS	
A-line skirt	kilt
ballet skirt	lungi
crinoline	maxi-skirt
dirndl	miniskirt
divided skirt	overskirt
filibeg	piupiu
flared skirt	pleated skirt
full skirt	puffball skirt
fustanella	rah-rah skirt
gathered skirt	sarong
ghagra	slit skirt
gored skirt	sports skirt
grass skirt	straight skirt
hakama	tennis skirt
hobble skirt	tutu
hoop skirt	underskirt
hula skirt	wrap skirt

skirt *verb* **1** *flowers skirting the lake* border,
edge, flank. **2** *people skirting the lake* go round,
move round, walk round, circle, circumnavigate. **3** *skirt the issue* evade, avoid, dodge, steer
clear of, sidestep, circumvent, bypass.

skit *noun* burlesque, parody, travesty; *inf.*
spoof, take-off, send-up.

skittish *adjective* **1** *get skittish on a few drinks*
playful, lively, frolicsome, frisky, sportive, mischievous, flirtatious. **2** *skittish horses* highly-
strung, nervous, restive, jumpy, fidgety,
excitable.
Opposites SOLEMN; STAID; CALM.

skulk *verb* lurk, loiter, prowl, creep, sneak,
slink, steal, sidle.

sky *noun* *fly off into the sky* upper atmosphere,
heaven, the firmament, the blue, the blue yonder; *lit.* welkin, the ether. **to the skies** *praise
them to the skies* unreservedly, without reserve,
very much, very greatly, highly, profusely, ful-
somely, extravagantly, inordinately, excessively, immoderately.

slab *noun* **1** *a slab of cake/cheese* hunk, chunk,
lump, slice, wedge, piece, portion; *inf.* wodge.
2 *a slab of wood/stone* plank, hunk, chunk,
lump, piece.

slack *adjective* **1** *slack clothes* not tight, loose,
baggy, bagging, easy, hanging, flapping.
2 *slack muscles* not taut, relaxed, limp, flaccid,
flabby. **3** *a slack rope* not taut, not rigid,
relaxed, flexible, pliant. **4** *business a bit slack*
not busy, slow, quiet, inactive, sluggish.
5 *rather slack about punctuality* lax, negligent,
remiss, neglectful, careless, inattentive, offhand, slapdash, slipshod, sloppy, disorderly,
disorganized, tardy.
Opposites TIGHT; TAUT; METICULOUS.

slack *noun* **1** *take up the slack of the rope* looseness, play; *inf.* give. **2** *no more slack left in the
staffing situation* surplus, excess, inessentials,
leeway.

slack *verb* *workers slacking when the boss is away*
idle, shirk, be inactive, be lazy, be indolent, be
neglectful; *inf.* skive. **slack off 1** *business slacks
off in the winter* get less, lessen, fall off, drop
off, taper off, let up, decrease, dwindle, ebb,
recede, wane. **2** *children slacking off after the
exams* relax, let up, take things easy, be less
active. **3** *drivers slackening off at the corner* slow
down, slow, decelerate, drop speed.

slacker *noun* idler, shirker, loafer, dawdler,
dallier, layabout, work-dodger, malingerer,
good-for-nothing; *inf.* clock-watcher, skiver.

slake *verb* *slake one's thirst/desire* satisfy, quench,
assuage, relieve, take the edge off, gratify, satiate.

slam *verb* **1** *slam the door | the door slammed*
bang, shut/close with a bang, shut/close with a
crash, shut/close noisily, shut/close with
force. **2** *slam the money on the table* slap, bang,
thump, crash, smash, dash, hurl, fling, throw.
3 *a play slammed by the critics* criticize, attack,
pillory, vilify, damn; *inf.* slate, pan, lambaste,
shout down, blast. **4** *slam the opposition* defeat
utterly, rout, trounce, thrash, vanquish, conquer, crush, overwhelm, give a drubbing to;
inf. wipe the floor with, clobber, slaughter,
hammer.

slander *noun* *gossips guilty of slander* defamation, misrepresentation, calumny, libel, aspersion, vilification, verbal abuse, muck-raking,
smear campaigning, backbiting, obloquy, disparagement, denigration.

slander *verb* *slander his neighbour by lying about
her being in prison* defame, blacken the name of,
libel, cast aspersions on, malign, vilify, verbally abuse, muck-rake about, smear, slur,
backbite, calumniate, disparage, denigrate,
decry, run down.

slanderous *adjective* defamatory, damaging,
libellous, abusive, muck-raking, malicious,
backbiting, calumnious, disparaging, denigrating.

slang *noun* **1** *use slang rather than formal language* colloquialism, informal language, lingo.
2 *outsiders failing to understand the technicians'
slang* jargon, cant, argot; *inf.* gobbledegook,
technospeak, mumbo-jumbo.

slant *verb* **1** *the old floor/picture on the wall slants*
slope, tilt, be askew, lean, dip, shelve, list.
2 *accuse the newspaper of slanting the news* give a
slant to, give a bias to, bias, angle, distort,
twist.

slant *noun* **1** *the slant of the floor/picture* slope,
tilt, dip, leaning, inclination, shelving, listing.
2 *accused of giving a political slant to the news*
bias, leaning, one-sidedness, prejudice, angle,
distortion, twist. **3** *require a woman's slant on
the new product* angle, point of view, view, opinion, attitude.

slanting *adjective* slanted, aslant, at an angle,
sloping, oblique, tilting, tilted, askew, leaning,
dipping, shelving, listing, diagonal.
Opposites STRAIGHT.

slap *noun* *a slap across the ears* smack, blow, hit,
whack, thump, cuff, punch, spank, buffet, rap,
bang; *inf.* wallop, clout, clip, biff, swipe, belt,
sock. **a slap in the face** *their giving the job to his*

assistant was a slap in the face to him snub, insult, rebuff, put-down, repulse, humiliation, blow to one's pride.

slap verb **1** slap the man's face smack, strike, hit, whack, cuff, spank, bang; inf. wallop, clout, biff, swipe, belt, sock. **2** slap the money on the table plonk, plop, slam, bang, fling, hurl, toss, throw. **3** slap paint on daub, plaster, spread. **slap down** slap down the protesters squash, put down, bring to heel, put someone in his/her place, rebuke, reprimand. **slap on** slap on a service charge put on, add, append, tack on.

slap adverb run slap into the policeman smack, headlong, right, straight, directly, exactly, precisely, suddenly, bang, plumb; inf. slap-bang.

slapdash adjective careless, slipshod, sloppy, untidy, messy, hasty, hurried, cursory, perfunctory, disorganized, slipshod, offhand, thoughtless, heedless, negligent, neglectful, remiss.
Opposites CAREFUL; METICULOUS; PAINSTAKING.

slash verb **1** slash the cloth cut, gash, lacerate, hack, rip, rend, slit, score, knife. **2** slash prices reduce/lower/decrease drastically, cut/drop/ mark down greatly.

slash noun the slashes in the garment cut, gash, laceration, hack, rip, rent, slit, score, incision.

slate verb critics slating the performance criticize harshly/severely; inf. tear to pieces/shreds, pan, slam, hammer, lambaste.

slaughter verb **1** slaughter animals for food kill, butcher. **2** slaughter the enemy soldiers massacre, murder, butcher, kill, put to death, do to death, put to the sword, slay, assassinate, liquidate, exterminate, annihilate. **3** slaughter the opposition defeat utterly, rout, trounce, thrash, vanquish, conquer, crush, overwhelm, give a drubbing to; inf. wipe the floor with, clobber, slam, hammer.

slaughter noun **1** the slaughter of the innocent children massacre, murder, butchery, killing, putting to death, slaying, liquidation, extermination, annihilation. **2** a scene of slaughter massacre, murder, bloodshed, carnage.

slaughterhouse noun abattoir, butchery, shambles.

slave noun **1** the master and his slaves bondsman/bondswoman, bondservant, serf, vassal. **2** slaves in the kitchen drudge, labourer, menial worker, servant; lit. scullion; inf. skivvy.

slave verb slave away at the stove toil, drudge, slog, labour, grind, work one's fingers to the bone, work day and night, work like a Trojan.

slaver verb slobber, drool.

slavery noun **1** sold into slavery enslavement, bondage, servitude, subjugation, thraldom, thrall, serfdom, vassalage. **2** working there is sheer slavery drudgery, toil, slog, hard labour, grind.
Opposites FREEDOM; LIBERTY; EMANCIPATION.

slavish adjective **1** slavish followers/admiration servile, subservient, obsequious, sycophantic, deferential, grovelling, fawning, cringing, menial, abject. **2** slavish imitation imitative, unoriginal, uninspired, unimaginative.

slay verb **1** slay his enemy kill, murder; slaughter, put to death, do to death, assassinate, do away with; inf. rub out. **2** the comedian's act slayed them convulse with mirth/laughter, amuse greatly, entertain greatly; inf. have one rolling in the aisles, be a hit with, wow.

sleek adjective **1** sleek hair smooth, glossy, shiny, lustrous, silken, silky, satiny, burnished. **2** sleek businessmen well-fed, thriving, prosperous, well-groomed; inf. well-heeled.
Opposites DULL; ROUGH; UNKEMPT.

sleep verb sleep for a few hours be asleep, slumber, doze, nap, drowse; lit. rest in the arms of Morpheus; inf. snooze, have forty winks, be in the land of Nod.

sleep noun have a short sleep slumber, doze, nap, rest, siesta, drowse; inf. snooze, forty winks, a bit of shut-eye.

sleepiness noun drowsiness, tiredness, somnolence, somnolency, languor, languidness, lethargy, sluggishness, inactivity, heaviness, lassitude, torpor, torpidity, comatoseness.

sleepless adjective **1** sleepless nights without sleep, wakeful, restless, disturbed. **2** sleepless people unsleeping, wakeful, insomniac.

sleeplessness noun suffer from sleeplessness insomnia, wakefulness.

sleepwalking noun somnabulism, somnambulation, noctambulism, noctambulation.

sleepy adjective **1** feeling sleepy | sleepy children drowsy, tired, somnolent, languid, languorous, lethargic, sluggish, inactive, heavy, torpid, comatose. **2** sleepy little villages inactive, quiet, peaceful, slow-moving, slumberous.
Opposites AWAKE; ALERT; ACTIVE.

slender adjective **1** slender figures slim, thin, slight, lean, narrow, svelte, willowy, sylphlike. **2** people of slender means slight, small, little, meagre, scanty, paltry, insubstantial, inadequate, insufficient, deficient, negligible, trifling. **3** a slender hope of success small, slight, slim, faint, remote, feeble, flimsy, tenuous, fragile.
Opposites FAT; SUBSTANTIAL; CONSIDERABLE.

sleuth noun detective, private detective, investigator, private investigator; inf. private eye, dick, gumshoe.

slice noun **1** a slice of cake piece, portion, segment, sliver, wedge, chunk, hunk; inf. wodge. **2** a slice of the action share, part, proportion, allotment, allocation.

slice verb **1** slice the cake/apple/meat cut up, cut through, carve, divide, segment. **2** slice a piece from the apple cut, sever, separate.

slick adjective **1** a slick presentation smooth, smooth-running, well-organized, streamlined, efficient, polished. **2** a slick reply smooth, glib, fluent, plausible, specious. **3** a slick performer/ operator smooth, efficient, skilful, deft, adroit, masterly, professional, smart, sharp, shrewd. **4** slick businessman suave, urbane, sophisticated, polished, smooth-speaking, glib, smarmy, unctuous.
Opposites CLUMSY; INEPT; UNSOPHISTICATED.

slick verb *slick one's hair down* smooth, flatten, plaster down.

slide verb **1** *slide on the ice* slip, skid, slither, skate, glissade. **2** *drawers sliding in easily* slip, glide, slither. **3** *they slid from the room* pass/ move quickly, slip, steal, slink. **let slide** *let the housework slide* neglect, forget, ignore, pass over, gloss over, push to the back of one's mind.

slight adjective **1** *a slight change* small, little, tiny, minute, inappreciable, imperceptible, subtle, modest. **2** *of slight importance* little, minor, unimportant, petty, inconsiderable, insignificant, inconsequential, negligible, irrelevant, trivial, trifling, paltry, meagre, scant. **3** *a slight girl/figure* slightly built, slim, slender, small, spare, delicate, frail. **4** *a slight structure* fragile, frail, flimsy, rickety, jerry-built.
Opposites LARGE; SUBSTANTIAL; CONSIDERABLE.

slight verb *slight him by not inviting him* snub, insult, affront, rebuff, treat disrespectfully, give the cold shoulder to, cold-shoulder, keep at arm's length, disregard, ignore, neglect, take no notice of, disdain, scorn.

slight noun *upset by her slights* snub, insult, affront, rebuff, cold-shouldering, disregard, neglect, inattention, scorn, disdain; *inf.* a slap in the face.

slighting adjective *a slighting remark* snubbing, insulting, disrespectful, uncomplimentary, abusive, offensive, disparaging, belittling, derogatory, disdainful, scornful.

slightly adverb *slightly hurt* a little, a bit, somewhat, rather, to some degree.

slim adjective **1** *slim girls/ankles* slender, thin, slight, lean, narrow, svelte, willowy, sylphlike. **2** *slim hopes of success* slight, small, slender, faint, remote, feeble, flimsy, tenuous, fragile.
Opposites FAT; THICK; SUBSTANTIAL; STRONG.

slim verb *trying to slim* lose weight, shed weight, lose pounds, reduce, diet, go on a diet.

slime noun sludge, muck, ooze, mud; *inf.* goo, gunk.

slimy adjective **1** *slimy surfaces* sludgy, mucky, oozy, muddy, slippery, sticky, viscous, mucous. **2** *distrust the slimy creature* oily, unctuous, obsequious, sycophantic, toadying, ingratiating, servile, grovelling, forelock-tugging, creeping; *inf.* smarmy.

sling verb **1** *sling it into the rubbish bag* toss, fling, throw, cast, hurl, heave, pitch, shy, lob; *inf.* chuck. **2** *sling it from a hook* hang, suspend, dangle, swing.

sling noun *have one's arm in a sling* support bandage, support, bandage, strap.

slink verb **1** *culprits slinking from the room* steal, sneak, creep, slip, slide. **2** *strange figures slinking around in the garden* skulk, lurk, sneak, creep.

slip¹ verb **1** *slip on the ice* slip, skid, slither, lose one's footing, lose one's balance. **2** *slip from her hands* fall, slide, drop. **3** *slip from the room unnoticed* steal, slide, creep, sneak, slink. **4** *officials having slipped up* make a mistake, blunder, make a blunder, miscalculate, err, go

wrong; *inf.* boob, make a bloomer, make a boo-boo, slip one's mind, screw up. **5** *slip through the police net* break free from, escape, get away from, break away from, evade, dodge. **6** *slip the knot* untie, unfasten, undo, unbind, untangle, unsnarl. **7** *slip on a jersey* put on, pull on, don. **8** *the value of the pound slipped* go down, decline, decrease, lessen, depreciate, sink, slump, plummet. **9** *the standard of the student's work slipped* drop, fall off, decline, deteriorate, degenerate; *inf.* go downhill, go to the dogs. **let slip** *let slip the secret* let out, reveal, disclose, divulge, give away, leak, blurt out, come out with.

slip² noun **1** *one slip and she fell* slide, skid, slither. **2** *an accountant accused of making a slip* slip-up, mistake, error, blunder, miscalculation, oversight; *inf.* boob, bloomer, boo-boo. **3** *a silk slip* underskirt, petticoat. **give the slip** *the pickpocket eventually gave the policeman the slip* escape from, get away from, get free from, break away from, lose, evade, dodge, elude, shake off, get rid of, outwit.

slip³ noun **1** *written on a slip* slip of paper, piece of paper, paper, note, card; Post-it note™. **2** *a slip from the plant* cutting, off-shoot, scion, sprout, sprig. **a slip of a** *a slip of a girl* small, slender, delicate, young.

slipper noun **1** *housecoat and slippers* bedroom slipper, mule, houseshoe, moccasin. See table at FOOTWEAR. **2** *evening slippers* pump, soft shoe.

slipperiness noun **1** *the slipperiness of the surface* greasiness, oiliness, sliminess, iciness; *inf.* slippiness. See SLIPPERY 1. **2** *the slipperiness of the criminal* shiftiness, deviousness, deceit, deceitfulness, duplicitousness, craftiness, cunning, sneakiness, treachery, dishonesty, untrustworthiness. See SLIPPERY 2.

slippery adjective **1** *slippery surfaces* greasy, oily, slimy, icy, glassy, smooth, soapy; *inf.* slippy, skiddy. **2** *a slippery customer/creature* shifty, devious, deceitful, duplicitous, crafty, cunning, foxy, tricky, sneaky, treacherous, perfidious, two-faced, dishonest, false, unreliable, untrustworthy.

slipshod adjective *slipshod methods* careless, slovenly, untidy, sloppy, slapdash, disorganized, unsystematic, unmethodical.

slip-up noun slip, mistake, error, blunder. See SLIP¹ noun 2.

slit verb *slit the material* cut, split open, slash, gash, rip, make an incision in, tear, rend, pierce, knife, lance.

slit noun *make a slit in the material* cut, split, slash, gash, rip, incision, tear, rent, fissure, opening.

slither verb *slither about on the ice* slide, slip, skid.

sliver noun chip, flake, splinter, shred, fragment, scrap.

slobber verb slaver, drool, dribble, splutter.

slog verb **1** *slog his opponent* hit, strike, thump, whack; *inf.* hit for six, slug, wallop, sock, slosh. **2** *slog away at homework* work, labour, toil, slave, drudge, plough. **3** *slog up the hill* trudge, tramp, hike, plod, trek.

slog noun **1** *knock out his opponent with one slog* hit, stroke, thump, whack; *inf.* slug, wallop, sock. **2** *regard homework as a slog* labour, Herculean task, hard task. **3** *a slog up the hill* trudge, tramp, hike, plod, trek.

slogan noun motto, logo, catchword, jingle, rallying cry, shibboleth.

slop verb *water slopping over* spill, overflow, splash, slosh, splatter, spatter.

slope verb *gardens sloping down to the river | handwriting sloping* drop away, fall way, slant, incline, lean, tilt, dip. **slope off** *pupils sloping off before the class* go away, slip away, steal away, slink off; *inf.* make oneself scarce.

slope noun **1** *floors on a slope* slant, inclination, angle, skew, tilt, dip, gradient. **2** *grassy slopes* hill, hillside, hillock, bank, rise, scarp, mountain.

sloping adjective slanting, oblique, leaning, inclining, inclined, angled, askew, tilting, dipping.
Opposites STRAIGHT.

sloppy adjective **1** *a sloppy mixture* watery, wet, soggy, splashy, slushy, sludgy. **2** *sloppy work* careless, slapdash, slipshod, disorganized, unmethodical, untidy, messy, slovenly, hasty, hurried, offhand. **3** *sloppy verses* sentimental, overemotional, mawkish, maudlin, gushing, gushy, effusive, banal, trite; *inf.* soppy, mushy, wet, schmaltzy.
Opposites DRY; CAREFUL; METICULOUS; UNEMOTIONAL.

slot noun **1** *money in the slot* slit, crack, hole, opening, aperture, groove, notch. **2** *a slot in the programme* place, position, niche, space, opening, time, period.

sloth noun laziness, indolence, idleness, sluggishness, inertia, inactivity, lethargy, langour, slothfulness, torpor, torpidity, fainéance.

slothful adjective lazy, indolent, idle, workshy, sluggish, inert, inactive, lethargic, languorous, torpid, fainéant.
Opposites INDUSTRIOUS; ACTIVE.

slouch verb slump, hunch, stoop, droop, bend.

slovenly adjective **1** *of slovenly appearance* slatternly, untidy, dirty, unclean, messy, unkempt, dishevelled, bedraggled, tousled, rumpled. **2** *slovenly methods* careless, sloppy, slapdash, slipshod, disorganized, unmethodical.
Opposites TIDY; NEAT; CAREFUL.

slow adjective **1** *at a slow pace* slow-moving, unhurried, leisurely, measured, deliberate, ponderous, creeping, dawdling, loitering, lagging, laggard, sluggish, snail-like, tortoise-like. **2** *slow pupils* backward, retarded, slow-witted, dull-witted, dull, unintelligent, stupid, thick, dense; *inf.* dumb, dopey; slow on the uptake. **3** *the service being a bit slow* slow-moving, delayed, dilatory, unpunctual, tardy. **4** *a slow process* long-drawn-out, drawn-out, time-consuming, protracted, prolonged, interminable. **5** *a slow play* dull, uninteresting, tedious, boring, tiresome, wearisome, monotonous, uneventful. **6** *a slow part of the world* sleepy, unprogressive, behind-the-times, backward, stagnant; *inf.* not with it, one-horse,

dead-and-alive. **7** *business being slow* not busy, slack, quiet, sluggish, slow-moving, dead. **slow to** *slow to anger* reluctant, hesitant, loath, unwilling, disinclined, averse.
Opposites FAST; QUICK; BRISK; BRIGHT.

slow verb **1** *slow down at the corner* reduce speed, decelerate, relax speed, put the brakes on. **2** *weather slowed the runners down* hold back, keep back, delay, detain, restrain. **3** *businessmen told to slow down* take it easy, ease up, relax; *inf.* let up.

slowly adverb **1** *walk slowly* at a slow pace, without hurrying, unhurriedly, at a leisurely pace, steadily, ploddingly, taking one's time, in one's own good time, with heavy steps, at a snail's pace. **2** *improve slowly* at a slow pace, gradually, bit by bit, by degrees.

sluggish adjective **1** *feeling sluggish with a hangover* inactive, inert, heavy, lifeless, apathetic, listless, lethargic, languid, languorous, torpid, phlegmatic, indolent, lazy, slothful, drowsy, sleepy. **2** *business being sluggish* slow, slow-moving, slack, inactive, stagnant.
Opposites ACTIVE; ENERGETIC; BUSY.

sluggishness noun **1** *sluggishness caused by overeating* inactivity, inertia, heaviness, lifelessness, apathy, listlessness, lethargy, languidness, languor, lassitude, torpidity, torpor, indolence, laziness, sloth, slothfulness, drowsiness, sleepiness, somnolence. **2** *the sluggishness of business* slowness, slackness, inactivity, stagnation.

slumber verb sleep, be asleep, doze, nap, drowse; *lit.* rest in the arms of Morpheus; *inf.* snooze, have forty winks, be in the land of Nod.

slumber noun sleep, doze, nap, rest, siesta, drowse; *inf.* snooze, forty winks, a bit of shut-eye.

slump noun *a slump in share prices* plummeting, plunge, nosedive, collapse, fall, falling-off, drop, downturn, downswing, slide, decline, decrease, lowering, devaluation, depreciation, depression.

slump verb **1** *slump into a chair* collapse, sink, fall, subside. **2** *prices slumped* plummet, plunge, nosedive, fall, drop, go down, slide, decline, decrease, devalue. **3** *standards slumped* plummet, plunge, nosedive, fall, drop, decline, deteriorate, degenerate; *inf.* go downhill, go to the dogs.
Opposites RISE; SOAR; IMPROVE.

slur verb *slur his words* mumble, stumble over, stammer, drawl.

slur noun **1** *upset by the slurs made by the opposition on her character* insult, slight, aspersion, imputation, slanderous statement, libellous statement, misrepresentation, smear, stain, stigma. **2** *avoid all suggestion of a slur* insult, affront, defamation, slander, libel, calumny.

slush noun **1** *slush thrown up by cars* melting snow, muck, mud. **2** *the slush of romantic songs* sentimentality, overemotionalism, mawkishness, maudlinism, effusiveness, banality, triteness; *inf.* sloppiness, soppiness, mush, mushiness, schmaltz.

slut noun **1** *a slut who rarely washes* slattern, sloven, trollop. **2** *a slut seducing men* loose woman, hussy, wanton; prostitute, harlot, whore, street-walker; *inf.* tart, floozie, hooker.

sly adjective **1** *a sly creature* cunning, crafty, wily, artful, foxy, tricky, conniving, scheming, devious, underhand, shrewd, smart, astute. **2** *in a sly manner* furtive, insidious, underhand, shifty, stealthy, sneaky, secret, surreptitious, covert, under-cover, clandestine. **3** *a sly smile* roguish, impish, mischievous, playful, arch, knowing. **on the sly** *have another job on the sly* in secret, secretly, furtively, stealthily, sneakily, surreptitiously, covertly, under cover, clandestinely.
Opposites FRANK; HONEST; ABOVE-BOARD.

smack¹ noun **1** *a smack on the face* slap, blow, hit, whack, thump, cuff, punch, spank, buffet, rap, bang; *inf.* wallop, clout, clip, biff, swipe, belt, sock. **2** *the object hit the car with a smack* thud, thump, bang, wham; *inf.* wallop. **a smack in the eye** rebuff, repulse, snub, setback, slight, cold shoulder; *inf.* brush-off.

smack² verb *smack the child* slap, hit, strike, whack, thump, cuff, punch, rap, bang; *inf.* wallop, clout, clip, biff, swipe, belt, sock.

smack³ adverb *run smack into the police* slap, headlong, right, straight, directly, bang, plumb, exactly, precisely, suddenly.

smack⁴ verb **1** *a sauce smacking of garlic* taste of, have the flavour of. **2** *actions smacking of treachery* suggest, hint at, have overtones of, have the hallmark of, resemble, seem like, have the air of.

smack⁵ noun **1** *dishes having a smack of garlic* taste, flavour, savour. **2** *have a smack of treachery* suggestion, hint, trace, tinge, touch, overtone, hallmark, resemblance, air.

small adjective **1** *a small toy* little, tiny, teeny, teeny-weeny, petite, slight, minute, miniature, mini, minuscule, diminutive, under-sized, puny; *inf.* pocket-size, pint-sized, teensy-weensy; *Scots* wee. **2** *a small change/mistake* slight, minor, unimportant, trifling, trivial, insignificant, inconsequential, inappreciable. **3** *from small beginnings* humble, modest, lowly, simple, unpretentious, poor, inferior. **4** *a small mind/man* narrow, narrow-minded, mean, petty.
Opposites BIG; LARGE; SUBSTANTIAL.

small-minded adjective narrow-minded, bigoted, prejudiced, intolerant, hidebound, rigid, ungenerous, illiberal.

small-time adjective *small-time crooks* petty, minor, unimportant, insignificant, of no account, of no consequence, inconsequential.

smart adjective **1** *wedding-guests looking smart* well-dressed, well-turned-out, fashionably-dressed, fashionable, stylish, modish, elegant, chic, neat, spruce, trim; *inf.* natty, snappy, out of a bandbox. **2** *smart children* clever, bright, intelligent, gifted, sharp, quick-witted, nimble-witted, shrewd, ingenious. **3** *at a smart pace* brisk, quick, fast, swift, lively, energetic, spirited, vigorous, jaunty; *inf.* cracking, spanking.
Opposites SCRUFFY; STUPID; SLOW.

smart verb *eyes smarting with the smoke* sting, nip, burn, bite, pain.

smash verb **1** *smash the crockery* break, shatter, crash, shiver, pulverize, splinter, crack. **2** *smash the car* crash, smash, collide, wreck. **3** *smash their hopes* destroy, ruin, shatter, devastate.

smash noun **1** *hear the smash of crockery* breaking, shattering, crashing, crack. **2** *involve in a smash* car smash, car crash, car accident, traffic accident, collision; *inf.* pile-up. **3** *survive the smash of their plans* destruction, ruin, ruination, failure, shattering, devastation.

smashing adjective *a smashing time at the fair* marvellous, magnificent, sensational, stupendous, superb, wonderful, excellent, first-rate; *inf.* terrific, fantastic, super, great, fabulous, fab.

smattering noun *a smattering of French* bit, modicum, dash, rudiments, elements.

smear verb **1** *children smearing paint on the walls* spread, daub, slap, plaster. **2** *smear the windows* smudge, streak, blur. **3** *smear his reputation* sully, tarnish, blacken, taint, stain, slur, defame, defile, vilify, slander, libel, calumniate.

smear noun **1** *a smear of paint on the walls* daub, spot, patch, splotch. **2** *smears on the windows* smudge, streak. **3** *the smears on their reputation* taint, stain, slur, blot.

smell verb **1** *smell something rotten/pleasant* scent, sniff, get a sniff of, get a whiff of, nose. **2** *drains smelling* have a bad smell, stink, be stinking, reek, be malodorous; *inf.* stink to high heaven, pong, hum.

smell noun **1** *the smells of the countryside* odour, scent, whiff. **2** *the smell of new-mown hay* scent, aroma, perfume, fragrance, bouquet, redolence. **3** *What a smell from the drains!* stink, stench, reek; *inf.* pong, hum.

smelly adjective *smelly drains* smelling, evil-smelling, foul-smelling, stinking, high, malodorous, fetid, mephitic; *lit.* noisome; *inf.* ponging, humming, whiffy.

smirk verb leer, sneer, simper, grin.

smitten adjective **1** *smitten with flu* suffering from, affected by, laid low with, struck down with, afflicted by. **2** *smitten with the pretty girl/ the new fashion* taken with, infatuated with, enamoured of, attracted by, charmed by, captivated by, enchanted by, bewitched by, beguiled by; *inf.* bowled over by, swept off one's feet by.

smog noun haze, fog, pollution.

smoke verb **1** *fires smoking* smoulder, reek. **2** *smoke the salmon* cure, dry, preserve.

smoky adjective **1** *a smoky atmosphere* smoke-filled, reeky, hazy, foggy, smoggy, murky. **2** *smoky walls* begrimed, grimy, smoke-stained, smoke-darkened, sooty. **3** *smoky glass* dark, grey, black.

smooth adjective **1** *paint smooth surfaces* even, level, flat, plane, flush, unrough, unwrinkled. **2** *smooth hair/table-tops* glossy, shiny, sleek, silky, satiny, velvety, polished, burnished. **3** *smooth sea* calm, still, tranquil, flat, glassy, mirrorlike. **4** *smooth progress* easy, effortless,

trouble-free, simple, plain sailing. **5** *the smooth running of the machine* steady, regular, rhythmic, uninterrupted, flowing, fluid. **6** *smooth sounds* soft, soothing, mellow, dulcet, mellifluous, melodious, musical. **7** *smooth face* clean-shaven, smooth, shaven, hairless. **8** *smooth young men* smooth-tongued, suave, urbane, sophisticated, courteous, gracious, glib, persuasive, slick, oily, ingratiating, unctuous; *inf.* smarmy.
Opposites UNEVEN; ROUGH; IRREGULAR.

smooth verb **1** *smooth the surface* level, even, flatten, plane, press down, steamroll.
2 *smooth the troubled situation* ease, soothe, pacify, calm, tranquillize, alleviate, assuage, appease, palliate. **3** *smooth out/away the difficulties* get rid of, remove, eliminate. **4** *smooth his promotion* ease, make easy/easier, facilitate, clear the way for, pave the way for, open the door for, expedite, assist, aid, help, help along.

smoothness noun **1** *the smoothness of the road surfaces* evenness, levelness, flatness. *See* SMOOTH *adjective* 1. **2** *the smoothness of her hair* glossiness, gloss, shininess, sleekness, silkiness. *See* SMOOTH *adjective* 2. **3** *the smoothness of the sea* calmness, stillness, tranquillity, flatness. *See* SMOOTH *adjective* 3. **4** *the smoothness of the progress* ease, easiness, effortlessness, simplicity. *See* SMOOTH *adjective* 4. **5** *the smoothness of the engine's running* steadiness, regularity, rhythm, fluidity. *See* SMOOTH *adjective* 5. **6** *the smoothness of the sounds* softness, mellowness, mellifluousness, melodiousness. *See* SMOOTH *adjective* 6. **7** *the smoothness of his face* clean-shavenness, smooth-shavenness, hairlessness. **8** *the smoothness of the salesman* suaveness, urbaneness, urbanity, sophistication, courteousness, glibness, slickness; *inf.* smarminess. *See* SMOOTH *adjective* 8.

smother verb **1** *smother the old woman with a pillow* suffocate, stifle, asphyxiate, choke. **2** *smother them with kindness* overwhelm, shower, inundate, envelop, surround, cocoon. **3** *smother the pudding in cream* cover, pile with, heap with. **4** *smother a fire* extinguish, dampen, damp down, put out, snuff out, stamp out. **5** *smother a laugh* stifle, muffle, repress, suppress, keep back, conceal, hide.

smoulder verb **1** *fires smouldering* smoke, reek. **2** *hate smouldering in her* burn, seethe, simmer, fester. **3** *she was smouldering with resentment* seethe, fume, burn, boil, foam, rage, smart.

smudge noun *smudges on the walls* dirty mark, mark, spot, smear, streak, stain, blotch, blot, blur, smut, splotch.

smudge verb **1** *walls smudged with children's finger marks* mark, dirty, soil, blacken, smear, streak, daub, stain, besmirch. **2** *smudge the wet paint/lipstick* smear, streak, blur.

smug adjective self-satisfied, complacent, content, pleased with oneself, superior, proud of oneself, conceited.

smuggler noun contrabandist, runner; *inf.* boot-legger.

snack noun *a snack between meals* light meal, refreshments, bite, nibbles, titbit; *inf.* elevenses, bite to eat, little something.

snack verb *snack between meals* eat between meals, nibble, munch; *inf.* graze.

snag noun **1** *discover a snag about the seemingly attractive job* catch, drawback, hitch, stumbling-block, obstacle, disadvantage, inconvenience, unseen problem, problem, complication. **2** *a snag in her tights* rip, tear, run, hole.

snag verb *snag one's tights* catch, rip, tear.

snap verb **1** *the rod/rope snapped* break, break into two, fracture, splinter, separate, come apart, crack. **2** *suddenly snap after years of being abused* have a nervous breakdown, break down, collapse, lose one's mind, lose one's reason, go mad, go insane. **3** *snap one's fingers* crack, click, crackle. **4** *dogs snapping* bite, gnash the teeth. **5** *snapping irritably at the children* speak sharply/brusquely/curtly/abruptly/angrily, bark, snarl, growl, lash out at; *inf.* jump down the throat of, fly off the handle at. **6** *snap into action* hurry, hasten, rush, race. **7** *snap the children at play* take a snap of, photograph, take a photograph of, take a shot of, film, capture. **snap out of it** *she's been miserable but she's snapped out of it* get over it, recover, get better, cheer up, become cheerful, perk up; *inf.* pull oneself together, get a grip on oneself, become one's old self. **snap up** *snap up the bargain* offers snatch at, accept eagerly, take advantage of, grab, seize, grasp, pounce upon, swoop down upon; *inf.* nab.

snap noun **1** *with a snap of one's fingers* crack, click, crackle. **2** *with a snap of its teeth* bite, gnashing, clenching. **3** *a snap of cold weather* spell, period, time, stretch, interval. **4** *put a bit of snap into the production* liveliness, animation, sparkle, verve, vitality, vivacity, spirit, vigour, sprightliness, zest; *inf.* pizzazz, zip, zing, pep, oomph. **5** *a snap of the children at play* photo, photograph, picture.

snappy adjective **1** *a snappy mood/reply* irritable, irascible, ill-tempered, cross, touchy, testy, crabbed, crotchety, grumpy, grouchy, peppery. **2** *a snappy dresser* smart, fashionable, up-to-date, stylish, chic, up-to-the-minute, modish, dapper; *inf.* natty, trendy. **look snappy/make it snappy** hurry up, be quick, make haste, look lively; *inf.* get a move on, get one's skates on, step on it, move it, buck up.

snare verb **1** *snare rabbits* trap, entrap, catch, springe, net. **2** *snare a rich husband* ensnare, trap, catch, get hold of, seize, capture.

snare noun **1** *rabbits caught in a snare* trap, gin, springe, net, noose. **2** *unaware of the snares set by the opposition* trap, pitfall, trick, catch, danger, hazard, peril.

snarl[1] verb **1** *dogs snarling* show one's teeth, growl. **2** *snarling at everyone first thing in the morning* snap, growl, bark, lash out at; *inf.* jump down the throat of, fly off the handle at.

snarl[2] verb **1** *ropes getting snarled up* tangle, entangle, entwine, ravel, twist, knot. **2** *snarl up plans for reorganization* complicate, confuse, muddle, jumble; *inf.* mess up.

snatch *verb* **1** *snatch the last sandwich from the plate* seize, grab, take hold of, pluck. **2** *snatch the old lady's handbag* grab, steal, make off with, appropriate; *inf.* nab, swipe. **3** *snatch the millionaire's child* kidnap, abduct, grab, hold to ransom, take as hostage. **4** *snatch victory towards the end of the game* pluck, wrest, wring, seize, secure. **snatch at** **1** *a drowning man snatching at the branch* grab at, make a grab for, grasp at, catch at, clutch at, grope for, reach for. **2** *snatch at the bargain/opportunity* snap up, accept eagerly, grab, seize, pounce upon. *See* SNAP UP.

snatch *noun* **1** *at one snatch* grab, pluck, grip, clutch. **2** *a snatch of song/a broadcast* fragment, snippet, bit, scrap, piece, part. **3** *a snatch of sleeplessness* spell, period, time, fit, bout.

sneak *verb* **1** *sneak out of the lecture* steal, creep, slip, slide, slink, sidle. **2** *hear people sneaking around outside* creep, skulk, lurk, prowl, pad. **3** *sneak a quick look* snatch, take, catch. **4** *sneak on friends* tell tales on, inform on, report; *inf.* tell on, grass on, squeal on, blow the whistle on, peach on.

sneak *noun* informer, tell-tale; *inf.* grass, squealer, whistle-blower, snitch.

sneak *adjective* *a sneak look* secret, stealthy, furtive, clandestine, surprise.

sneaking *adjective* *a sneaking desire to be chairman* secret, private, hidden, concealed, unexpressed, unvoiced, undisclosed, undivulged, unconfessed, unavowed.

sneer *verb* **1** *sneering rather than smiling* curl one's lip, smirk, snicker, snigger. **2** *sneer at their unsuccessful attempts* scoff at, scorn, be contemptuous of, hold in contempt, disdain, mock, jeer at, gibe at, ridicule, deride, taunt, insult, slight.

sneer *noun* **1** *give a sneer* smirk, snicker. **2** *endure the sneers of her enemies* jeer, jibe, taunt, insult, slight.

sneeze *verb* **not to be sneezed at** *a salary not to be sneezed at* be taken seriously, not be taken lightly, not be scoffed at, not be laughed at.

snicker *verb* snigger, sneer, smirk, titter, giggle, chortle.

snicker *noun* snigger, sneer, smirk.

sniff *verb* **1** *people with colds sniffing* snuffle, inhale, breathe in. **2** *sniff the aroma of newly made bread* smell, detect the smell of, catch the scent of, scent, get a whiff of. **sniff at** *sniffing superiorly at their ragged children* scoff at, show contempt for, scorn, mock, disdain, turn up one's nose at, look down one's nose at, look down on.

sniff *noun* **1** *the sniffs of people with colds* snuffle. **2** *take a sniff of the sea air* smell, scent, whiff.

snip *verb* **1** *snip the piece of cloth* cut, cut into, nick, slit, notch, incise, snick. **2** *snip off a lock of hair* cut, clip, dock, trim, crop, prune.

snip *noun* **1** *cut it with one snip* cut, nick, slit, notch, incision, snick. **2** *snips of cloth* scrap, cutting, bit, piece, fragment, remnant, tatter. **3** *the dress was a snip* bargain, good buy, cheap buy; *inf.* giveaway, steal. **4** *the job was a snip*

easy task, child's play; *inf.* picnic, cinch, pushover.

snippet *noun* *snippets of information* bit, piece, scrap, fragment, particle, shred, snatch.

snivel *verb* **1** *children snivelling with disappointment* weep, cry, sob, whimper; *inf.* blub, blubber. **2** *children snivelling with colds* sniffle, snuffle, run at the nose, have a runny/running nose.

snobbery *noun* snobbishness, social arrogance, pride, airs, airs and graces, condescension, haughtiness, superiority, disdain, disdainfulness, superciliousness; *inf.* snootiness, uppishness, side.

snobbish *adjective* snobby, arrogant, proud, condescending, haughty, disdainful, supercilious, patronizing; *inf.* snooty, uppity, stuck-up, hoity-toity, toffee-nosed.

snoop *verb* *snoop into another's affairs* pry into, spy on, interfere with, meddle with; *inf.* poke one's nose into.

snoop *noun* **1** *a snoop into another's affairs* pry, poke. **2** *accused of being a snoop* snooper, pryer, interferer, meddler; *inf.* nosy parker, sticky beak, Paul Pry.

snooze *verb* *snooze in front of the fire* doze, nap, catnap, drowse, sleep, slumber; *inf.* take forty winks, have a kip, kip.

snooze *noun* *a snooze after lunch* doze, nap, catnap, siesta, sleep, slumber; *inf.* forty winks, kip.

snub *verb* *snub him in public* ignore, disregard, take no notice of, shun, rebuff, repulse, spurn, slight, give the cold shoulder to, cold-shoulder, insult, affront; *inf.* cut dead, give the brush-off to, give a slap in the face to, give the go-by, put down.

snub *noun* *embarrassed by the snub* rebuff, repulse, slight, insult, affront; *inf.* brush-off, slap in the face, put-down.

snug *adjective* **1** *a snug little house* cosy, comfortable, warm, homelike, homely, sheltered; *inf.* comfy. **2** *a snug fit* close-fitting, tight, skin-tight.

snuggle *verb* nestle, cuddle, curl up, nuzzle.

soak *verb* **1** *soaked by the rain* drench, wet through, saturate, make sopping. **2** *soak the soiled dress in soapy water* steep, immerse, souse. **3** *ink soaking through the paper* permeate, penetrate, infuse, imbue.

soaking *adjective* *dry off the soaking children/soaking wet clothes* soaked, soaked to the skin, wet through, drenched, sodden, saturated, sopping wet, dripping wet, wringing wet, streaming wet.

soar *verb* **1** *birds/planes soaring into the air* fly, take flight, take off, ascend, climb, rise, mount. **2** *prices soaring* rise, go up, increase, climb, rapidly, spiral.

sob *verb* *sobbing at the funeral* weep, cry, shed tears, blubber, snivel, howl, bawl; *Scots* greet; *inf.* boohoo.

sober *adjective* **1** *he was drunk but is now sober* not drunk/intoxicated, abstemious, teetotal, abstinent, temperate, moderate; *inf.* on the

wagon, dry, having signed the pledge. **2** *both sober and light-hearted people* serious, solemn, thoughtful, grave, earnest, calm, composed, sedate, staid, dignified, steady, level-headed, self-controlled, strict, puritanical. **3** *discuss sober matters* serious, solemn, grave, important, crucial, weighty, ponderous. **4** *a sober account* factual, low-key, dispassionate, objective, rational, logical, well-considered, circumspect, lucid, clear. **5** *wearing sober clothes/colours* dark, dark-coloured, sombre, quiet, restrained, drab, severe, austere. **sober up 1** *sober up after the party* become sober, become clear-headed, be cured of one's hangover; *inf.* dry out. **2** *sober him up after all the excitement* make sober, make serious, subdue, calm down, quieten, make reflective/pensive, make one stop and think, give pause for thought.
Opposites DRUNK; LIGHT-HEARTED; FLAMBOYANT.

sobriety *noun* **1** *impressed by the sobriety of the former drunks* soberness, teetotalism, abstemiousness, abstinence, non-indulgence, temperance, moderation, moderateness. **2** *his sobriety and studiousness* soberness, seriousness, solemnness, solemnity, thoughtfulness, gravity, graveness, earnestness, calmness, composure, sedateness, staidness, dignity, dignifiedness, steadiness, level-headedness, practicality, practicalness, self-control, self-restraint, strictness, puritanism. **3** *the sobriety of the subject* soberness, seriousness, solemnness, solemnity, gravity, graveness, importance, crucialness, weightiness, ponderousness. **4** *the sobriety of the account* soberness, factualness, dispassionateness, objectivity, rationality, logicality, circumspection, lucidity, clarity. **5** *the sobriety of the clothes/colours* soberness, darkness, sombreness, quietness, restraint, drabness, severity, austerity.

so-called *adjective* **1** *so-called professional people* self-styled, professed, *soi-disant*. **2** *so-called friendship* supposed, alleged, ostensible, pretended.

soccer *noun. See table.*

WORLD CUP WINNERS			
Team	**Date**	**Team**	**Date**
Uruguay	1930	Brazil	1970
Italy	1934	West	
Italy	1938	Germany	1974
Uruguay	1950	Argentina	1978
West		Italy	1982
Germany	1954	Argentina	1986
Brazil	1958	West	
Brazil	1962	Germany	1990
England	1966	Brazil	1994

sociability *noun* friendliness, affability, cordiality, neighbourliness, companionability, gregariousness, convivialness, conviviality. *See* SOCIABLE.

sociable *adjective* social, friendly, affable, cordial, neighbourly, companionable, gregarious, convivial, communicative, conversable, genial, outgoing, approachable, accessible.

Opposites UNSOCIABLE; UNFRIENDLY; UNCOMMUNICATIVE; SOLITARY.

social *adjective* **1** *social problems* community, civil, civic, public, societal. **2** *social clubs/evenings* entertainment, recreation, amusement. **3** *not a very social person* friendly, affable, cordial, companionable, gregarious, convivial, communicative. *See* SOCIABLE.

socialize *verb* lonely people not socializing with colleagues be social, be sociable, mix, mingle, keep company, fraternize, consent, hobnob, get together, get out and about.

society *noun* **1** *enemies of society* mankind, humanity, civilization, the public, the general public, the people, the population, the world at large, the community. **2** *urban and rural societies* community, group, culture, civilization. **3** *leaders of society | marry into society* high society, polite society, aristocracy, gentry, nobility, upper classes, the elite, the smart set, beau monde, haut monde; *inf.* privileged classes, the upper crust, the top drawer, toffs, nobs, swells. **4** *enjoy the society of friends* company, companionship, fellowship, friendship, camaraderie. **5** *join a society* association, club, group, band, circle, body, fraternity, brotherhood, sisterhood, league, union, alliance, federation.

sodden *adjective* **1** *sodden clothes* soaked, soaking wet, drenched, saturated, sopping, dripping, wringing wet. **2** *sodden ground* saturated, sopping, soggy, boggy, swampy, miry, waterlogged.

soft *adjective* **1** *soft clay/mud* mushy, squashy, pulpy, doughy, spongy; *inf.* gooey. **2** *soft ground* spongy, swampy, boggy, miry, quaggy. **3** *pieces of a soft substance* pliable, pliant, supple, elastic, flexible, ductile, malleable, plastic. **4** *the soft surface of the curtains* smooth, velvety, cushiony, fleecy, downy, leathery, furry, silky, silken, satiny; *inf.* like a baby's bottom. **5** *soft winds blowing* gentle, light, mild, moderate, calm, balmy, delicate. **6** *soft lights* low, faint, dim, shaded, subdued, muted, mellow. **7** *soft colours* pale, light, pastel, subdued, muted, understated, restrained, dull. **8** *he spoke in soft tones* hushed, whispered, murmured, stifled, inaudible, low, faint, quiet, mellow, melodious, mellifluous. **9** *soft outlines* vague, blurred, fuzzy, ill-defined, indistinct, flowing, fluid. **10** *soft words* sympathetic, kind, gentle, soothing, tender, affectionate, loving, warm, sweet, sentimental, romantic; *inf.* mushy, slushy, schmaltzy. **11** *teachers too soft with the pupils* easygoing, tolerant, forgiving, forbearing, lenient, indulgent, permissive, liberal, lax. **12** *too soft to kill the chicken* tender-hearted, docile, sensitive; spineless, feeble; *inf.* soppy. **13** *soft muscles* flabby, flaccid, limp, out of condition. **14** *lead a soft life* easy, comfortable, cosy; pampered, privileged, indulged; *inf.* cushy. **15** *soft in the head* feeble-minded, simple, silly; *inf.* daft, nutty.
Opposites FIRM; HARD; HARSH; STRICT.

soften *verb* **1** *soften the blow* ease, cushion, temper, mitigate, assuage. **2** *the winds softened* abate, moderate, lessen, diminish, calm down. **3** *they softened their harsh approach* modify, moderate, temper, tone down. **soften up** *soften him up until he agrees* work on, persuade, win over, disarm.

soggy *adjective* soft, soaking, saturated, sodden, sopping wet, boggy, swampy, miry, waterlogged, over-moist.

soil *noun* **1** *plant in a light soil* earth, ground, clay, dirt. **2** *on British soil* land, country, terra firma.

soil *verb* **1** *soil her white gloves* dirty, stain, muddy, spot, smear, splash, smudge. **2** *soil his reputation* sully, stain, taint, besmirch, blot, smear.

sojourn *noun* stay, visit, stop, stopover; holiday, vacation.

solace *noun* **1** *bring solace to the bereaved* comfort, consolation, condolence, support. **2** *solace for their pain* mitigation, alleviation, assuagement, amelioration.

soldier *noun* fighter, warrior, trooper, warmonger; *inf.* cannon fodder. *See table at* MILITARY. **soldier on** *soldier on through hard times* persevere, keep going; *inf.* plug away, stick it out.

solecism *noun* **1** *an essay full of solecisms* mistake, error, blunder; *inf.* howler, boob. **2** *she was embarrassed by her solecism at the dinner party* breach of etiquette, inappropriate behaviour, impropriety, social indiscretion, faux pas.

solemn *adjective* **1** *a solemn occasion* serious, grave, important, profound; formal. **2** *a solemn procession* dignified, ceremonious, stately, majestic, imposing, impressive, grand. **3** *a solemn child* serious, sombre, unsmiling; pensive, thoughtful; gloomy, glum, grim; *inf.* moody, blue. **4** *a solemn promise* earnest, sincere, honest, genuine, committed, heartfelt.
Opposites FRIVOLOUS; LIGHT-HEARTED; INSINCERE.

solemnity *noun* **1** *the solemnity of the occasion* solemness, graveness, gravity; dignity, formality. **2** *the solemnity of the procession* formality, ceremoniousness, dignity, stateliness, majesty. **3** *the solemnity of the child* solemness, gravity, thoughtfulness, sombreness, gloominess. **4** *the solemnity of his promise* seriousness, formality, earnestness, sincerity, fervour. **5** *attend the coronation solemnities* ceremony, proceedings, rite, ritual, formalities, celebration.

solicit *verb* **1** *solicit information/assistance* ask for, request, apply for, seek, beg, plead for, crave. **2** *solicit him for financial help* ask, beg, beseech, implore, entreat, petition, importune, supplicate. **3** *women soliciting in the streets* work as a prostitute, engage in prostitution, accost people, make sexual advances; *inf.* hustle.

solicitous *adjective* **1** *solicitous enquiries about his health/solicitous about your health* concerned, caring, attentive, considerate, anxious, worried, nervous, uneasy, apprehensive. **2** *solicitous to be successful* eager, keen, anxious, desirous, enthusiastic, avid, zealous.

solicitude *noun* show solicitude for his sick wife/ solicitude for her health concern, care, caringness, regard, attentiveness, consideration, considerateness, anxiety, worry, nervousness, uneasiness, apprehensiveness.

solid *adjective* **1** *a solid rather than liquid substance* firm, hard, thick, dense, concrete, compact, compressed, condensed. **2** *made of solid silver* complete, pure, unalloyed, unmixed, unadulterated, genuine. **3** *solid houses* sound, substantial, strong, sturdy, stout, durable, well-built, well-constructed, stable. **4** *solid arguments* sound, well-founded, well-grounded, concrete, valid, reasonable, logical, cogent, weighty, authoritative, convincing, plausible, reliable. **5** *a solid friendship* reliable, dependable, trustworthy, stable, steadfast. **6** *solid citizens* sensible, level-headed, down-to-earth, decent, law-abiding, upright, upstanding, worthy. **7** *good solid work* sound, worthy, staid, unexciting, unimaginative, uninspired. **8** *a solid company* financially sound, sound, solvent, creditworthy, in good standing, in the black, secure. **9** *a solid line of people/a solid hour* continuous, uninterrupted, unbroken, undivided. **10** *political support that remained solid* unanimous, united, undivided, of one mind, of the same mind, in unison, consentient.
Opposites LIQUID; HOLLOW; FLIMSY; UNSOUND.

solidarity *noun* the success of the strike relies on the solidarity of the workers unity, unification, union, unanimity, singleness of purpose, likemindedness, team spirit, camaraderie, harmony, esprit de corps.

solidify *verb* leave the jelly/toffee mixture to solidify harden, go hard, set, jell, congeal, cake.

solitary *adjective* **1** *forced to lead a solitary life* lonely, lonesome, companionless, friendless, antisocial, unsocial, unsociable, withdrawn, reclusive, cloistered, introverted, hermitical. **2** *seek a solitary spot for holidays* loney, remote, out-of-the-way, isolated, secluded, hidden, concealed, private, unfrequented, unvisited, sequestered, retired, desolate. **3** *a solitary tree on the horizon* lone, single, sole, alone, by oneself/itself.
Opposites SOCIABLE; BUSY.

solitary *noun* a solitary living in the forest loner, lone wolf, introvert, recluse, hermit, eremite, anchorite, stylite, cenobite.

solitude *noun* **1** *the solitude of the place* loneliness, remoteness, isolation, seclusion, privacy, retirement, desolation. *See* SOLITARY *adjective* 1. **2** *few solitudes left* wilderness, wasteland, desert, vast expanse.

solution *noun* **1** *the solution to the mathematical problem* answer, result, key, resolution. **2** *the solution of the problem will take years* solving, resolving, explanation, clarification, elucidation, unravelling, unfolding. **3** *a solution of brine* suspension, emulsion, mixture, mix, blend, compound.

solve *verb* solve the problem find the solution to, answer, find the answer to, resolve, work out, figure out, fathom, find the key to, decipher, clear up, get to the bottom of, unravel, disentangle, unfold; *inf.* crack.

solvent *adjective* financially sound, debt-free, creditworthy, in the black.

sombre *adjective* **1** *dress in sombre clothes* dark, dark-coloured, dull, dull-coloured, drab, dingy. **2** *in a sombre mood/a sombre expression*

gloomy, depressed, sad, melancholy, dismal, doleful, mournful, joyless, cheerless, lugubrious, funereal, sepulchral.
Opposites BRIGHT; CHEERFUL.

somebody *noun her father's a somebody on the local council* VIP, person of note, notable figure, notable, public figure, dignitary, celebrity, name, luminary, personage, household name; *inf.* bigwig, big noise, big shot, big wheel, big cheese.

someday *adverb they'll get there someday* sometime, one day, one of these days, at some time in the future, at a future time/date, one of these fine days, sooner or later, by and by, eventually, ultimately.

somehow *adverb get there somehow* by some means, in some way, in one way or other, no matter how, come what may, be fair means or foul, by hook or by crook; *inf.* come hell or high water.

sometime *adverb we must visit her sometime* someday, one day, one of these days, at some time in the future, at a future time/date, by and by. *See* SOMEDAY.

sometimes *adverb we see her sometimes* occasionally, on occasion, on occasions, now and then, now and again, from time to time, once in a while, every so often, off and on.

somnolent *adjective* **1** *feeling somnolent* sleepy, drowsy, half-asleep, heavy-eyed, dozy, groggy, comatose; *inf.* dopey. **2** *a somnolent drug* soporific, sleep-inducing.

song *noun* **1** *a beautiful song* ballad, popular song, pop song, ditty, chorus, shanty, carol, anthem, hymn, psalm, chant, canticle, lay. **2** *the song of the birds* warble, chirp, trill, whistle, pipe.

sonorous *adjective* **1** *the sonorous tones of the minister* deep, rich, full, round, resonant, resounding, booming, ringing, reverberating, vibrating, pulsating. **2** *a sonorous style of prose* impressive, imposing, majestic, lofty, high-sounding, grandiloquent, declamatory, orotund, euphuistic, fustian.

soon *adverb* **1** *be there soon* shortly, in a short time, in a little while, before long, in a minute, in a moment, any minute, in the near future, in a twinkling, in the twinkling of an eye; *inf.* before you know it, before you can say Jack Robinson, pronto, in two shakes of a lamb's tale. **2** *How soon can you get here?* quickly, promptly, speedily, punctually, early.

soothe *verb* **1** *soothe the baby* quieten, quiet, calm, calm down, pacify, settle, settle down, hush, lull, tranquillize, mollify. **2** *soothe the pain* ease, assuage, alleviate, allay, moderate, mitigate, temper, palliate, soften, lessen, reduce.
Opposites AGITATE; DISTURB; AGGRAVATE.

soothsayer *noun* seer, augur, prophet, diviner, sibyl.

sophisticated *adjective* **1** *sophisticated city-dwellers* worldly-wise, worldly, experienced, seasoned, suave, urbane, cultured, cultivated, polished, refined, elegant, stylish, cosmopolitan, blasé. **2** *sophisticated production techniques*

advanced, highly-developed, ultra-modern, complex, complicated, elaborate, intricate.
Opposites UNSOPHISTICATED; NAIVE; CRUDE.

sophistication *noun the sophistication of the city-dwellers* worldliness, experience, suaveness, urbanity, urbaneness, culture, refinement, elegance, poise, finesse, savoir faire.

sophistry *noun* casuistry, quibbling, equivocation, fallaciousness, fallacy.

soporific *adjective soporific drugs* sleep-inducing, somnolent, sedative, tranquillizing, narcotic, opiate, somniferous.

soporific *noun given a soporific* sleeping potion, sleeping pill, sedative, tranquillizer, narcotic, opiate.

soppy *adjective* **1** *soppy love films* mawkish, maudlin, sentimental, oversentimental, over-emotional, slushy, mushy, sloppy; *inf.* schmaltzy, corny. **2** *boys thinking girls soppy* silly, foolish; *inf.* daft, wet, soft. **3** *soppy about the boy next door* infatuated with, in love with, enamoured of, smitten with, keen on; *inf.* sweet on, wild about, crazy about, stuck on.

sorcerer *noun* magician, wizard, enchanter, warlock, necromancer, magus, thaumaturgist.

sorceress *noun* magician, witch, enchantress, necromancer, thaumaturgist.

sorcery *noun* black magic, magic, witchcraft, witchery, wizardry, necromancy, black art, enchantment, thaumaturgy.

sordid *adjective* **1** *sordid hovels* filthy, dirty, foul, unclean, grimy, sooty, soiled, stained, mucky, squalid, shabby, seedy, seamy, slummy, sleazy. **2** *a sordid creature* vile, foul, base, low, debased, degenerate, dishonourable, disreputable, despicable, ignominious, ignoble, abhorrent, abominable. **3** *sordid money-lenders* mean, greedy, avaricious, covetous, grasping, mercenary, miserly, niggardly, stingy; *inf.* grubby.
Opposites IMMACULATE; HONOURABLE; NOBLE; GENEROUS.

sore *adjective* **1** *a sore leg* painful, in pain, aching, hurting, tender, inflamed, raw, smarting, stinging, burning, irritated, bruised, wounded, injured. **2** *feel sore about her treatment of him* distressed, upset, resentful, vexed, aggrieved, offended, hurt, pained, annoyed, angry, irritated, irked, nettled; *inf.* peeved. **3** *in sore need of some food* dire, urgent, pressing, desperate, critical, acute, extreme.

sore *noun a sore on his leg* wound, scrape, abrasion, cut, laceration, graze, boil, abscess, swelling, gathering.

sorrow *noun* **1** *the sorrow of the widow* sadness, unhappiness, grief, misery, distress, heartache, heartbreak, anguish, suffering, pain, woe, affliction, wretchedness, dejection, heaviness of heart, desolation, depression, disconsolateness, mourning. **2** *one of the great sorrows of his life* trouble, worry, woe, misfortune, affliction, trial, tribulation.
Opposites JOY; DELIGHT; PLEASURE.

sorrow *verb* **1** *children sorrowing at the departure of their mother* be sad, feel sad, be miserable, suffer, be wretched, be dejected, be heavy of heart, pine, weep. See SORROW *noun* 1. **2** *the bereaved sorrowing* grieve, mourn, lament, wail.

sorrowful *adjective* **1** *sorrowful expressions* sad, unhappy, tearful, heartbroken, wretched, woebegone, miserable, dejected, desolated, depressed, disconsolate, mournful, doleful, melancholy, lugubrious. **2** *a sorrowful sight before their eyes* sorry, wretched, miserable, pitiful, piteous, pitiable, moving, affecting, pathetic, heart-rending, deplorable, lamentable.

sorry *adjective* **1** *sorry for his actions* regretful, apologetic, repentant, penitent, remorseful, contrite, ashamed, conscience-stricken, guilt-ridden, in sackcloth and ashes, compunctious. **2** *feel sorry for the child* sympathetic, pitying, full of pity, compassionate, moved, commiserative, empathetic. **3** *sorry to hear about his accident* sad, unhappy, distressed, grieved, regretful, sorrowful, miserable, wretched. **4** *a sorry sight* wretched, miserable, pitiful, piteous. See SORROWFUL 2.
Opposites IMPENITENT; UNREPENTANT; SHAMELESS.

sort *noun* **1** *a new/different sort of plant/car* kind, type, variety, class, category, style, variety, group, set, genre, genus, family, order, breed, make, brand, stamp. **2** *a good sort* person, individual, soul; *inf.* fellow, chap, bloke, guy, character, customer. **out of sorts** **1** *having been out of sorts with a bad cold* unwell, unhealthy, sick, ill, indisposed, off colour, poorly, below par, not up to the mark; *inf.* seedy, under the weather. **2** *avoid his father when he's out of sorts* in a bad mood, in a bad temper, ill-tempered, irritable, cross, crabbed, touchy, testy, crotchety, grumpy, snappish. **3** *out of sorts after her broken engagement* in low spirits, dejected, depressed, downcast, gloomy, glum, melancholy, unhappy, miserable, wretched; *inf.* down, down in the mouth, down in the dumps.

sort *verb* **1** *sort the potatoes according to size | sort out the books in piles* classify, class, categorize, catalogue, grade, rank, group, divide, arrange, order, put in order, organize, assort, systematize, methodize. **2** *teachers asked to sort out the problem/mess* clear up, tidy up, put straight, put in order, deal with. **sort out** **1** *sort the books out into piles* sort, classify, class, categorize, grade, arrange, organize. **2** *sort out the weaker plants and dispose of them* separate out, put to one side, segregate, sift, pick out, select. **3** *sort out the problem* sort, clear up, put straight, put right, solve, find a solution to.

sortie *noun a sortie into enemy territory* sally, foray, charge, rush, onrush, raid, attack.

so-so *adjective* mediocre, average, indifferent, unexceptional, undistinguished, uninspiring, tolerable, passable; *inf.* fair to middling, no great shakes, nothing to write home about.

soul *noun* **1** *the soul as opposed to the body* spirit, psyche, inner self, true being, vital force, animating principle. **2** *the soul of discretion* personification, embodiment, incarnation, essence, epitome. **3** *not a soul in sight* person, human being, being, individual, creature. **4** *the life and soul of the party* essential part, essence, heart, core, centre, vital force, driving

force. **5** *play the piece without soul* feeling, emotion, intensity, fervour, ardour, vitality, animation, vivacity, energy, inspiration.

sound¹ *noun* **1** *not a sound was heard* noise. **2** *she made not a sound* utterance, cry. **3** *the sound of the flute* noise, music, note, chord. **4** *they do not like the sound of her plans* impression, idea, thought, concept. **5** *within the sound of the church bells* hearing, distance, earshot, range.
Opposites SILENCE; HUSH.

sound² *verb* **1** *sound the trumpet/bugle* play, blow. **2** *the trumpet sounded* resound, reverberate, resonate. **3** *sound the alarm* operate, set off, ring. **4** *sound the letter "f" or "t"* pronounce, utter, voice, enunciate, articulate, vocalize. **5** *it sounds as though he's mad* appear, look, seem, give/create the impression that, strike one that, have every indication that. **6** *sound a word of warning* utter, express, voice, pronounce, declare, announce.

sound³ *adjective* **1** *sound lungs | sound in limb* healthy, in good health, in good condition, physically fit, disease-free, hale and hearty, undamaged, uninjured, unimpaired, in good shape, in fine fettle. **2** *sound rafters in the building* solid, substantial, sturdy, well-constructed, intact, whole, undamaged, unimpaired. **3** *sound policies/arguments* solid, well-founded, well-grounded, concrete, valid, reasonable, logical, cogent, weighty, authoritative, convincing, plausible, reliable, orthodox. **4** *a sound judge of character* reliable, dependable, trustworthy, fair, good, sensible, intelligent, wise, judicious, sagacious, astute, shrewd, perceptive, foresighted. **5** *sound business* solvent, creditworthy, in good financial standing, in the black, solid, secure. **6** *a sound sleep* deep, undisturbed, unbroken, uninterrupted, untroubled, peaceful. **7** *a sound thrashing/ telling-off* thorough, complete, without reserve, unqualified, out-and-out, drastic, severe.
Opposites UNSOUND; UNHEALTHY; FLIMSY.

sound⁴ *verb* **1** *sound the river depths* plumb, fathom, probe. **2** *sound the patient's chest* examine, do tests on, investigate, inspect. **sound out** *sound out popular opinion* investigate, carry out an investigation of, conduct a survey of, research, carry out research into, explore, look into, examine, probe, canvass.

sour *adjective* **1** *sour substances* acid, acidy, acidlike, acetic, aciduous, tart, bitter, sharp, vinegary, vinegarlike, unpleasant, distasteful, pungent. **2** *sour milk/butter* turned, curdled, fermented, give off, rancid, bad. **3** *a sour old man* embittered, nasty, unpleasant, disagreeable, bad-tempered, ill-tempered, ill-natured, sharp-tongued, irritable, crotchety, cross, crabbed, testy, touchy, snappish, peevish, churlish, grumpy; *inf.* grouchy.
Opposites SWEET; FRESH; AMIABLE.

sour *verb people soured by his treatment of them* embitter, make bitter, disenchant, alienate; *inf.* turn off.

source *noun* **1** *the source of the river* wellspring, well-head, headspring. **2** *the source of the rumour* origin, derivation, commencement, beginning, start, rise, cause, wellspring, fountainhead, provenance, author, originator, begetter. **3** *sources listed in the essay* reference, authority, informant.

souse *verb* **1** *souse the herring* pickle, marinade, soak, steep. **2** *souse the garment in the dye solution* plunge, immerse, dip, submerge, sink, dusk, dunk, soak, steep, douse, drench, saturate. **3** *set out to get his friend soused* become drunk, intoxicate, inebriate, befuddle.

souvenir *noun* memento, keepsake, token, reminder, relic, memorabilia.

sovereign *noun* ruler, monarch, supreme ruler, king, queen, emperor, empress, tsar, crowned head, potentate. *See table at* ROYALTY.

sovereign *adjective* **1** *sovereign power* supreme, absolute, unlimited, chief, paramount, principle, dominant, predominant, ruling. **2** *a sovereign state* independent, self-ruling, self-governing, autonomous. **3** *our sovereign lord* ruling, kingly, queenly, princely, royal, regal, majestic, noble. **4** *a sovereign remedy* efficient, effective, efficacious, effectual, excellent, outstanding.

sovereignty *noun* **1** *hold sovereignty over adjoining states* supremacy, dominion, power, ascendancy, jurisdiction, control, sway. **2** *an island sovereignty* kingdom, realm, country.

sow *verb* **1** *sow seed* scatter, disperse, strew, bestrew, disseminate, distribute, spread, broadcast. **2** *sow a field with wheat* plant. **3** *sow doubt in their minds* implant, plant, lodge, initiate, instigate, foster, promote, foment, invite.

space *noun* **1** *houses taking up a lot of space | not enough space for them all* room, expanse, extent, capacity, area, volume, amplitude, spaciousness, scope, elbow-room, latitude, margin, leeway. **2** *a large space between houses* interval, gap, opening, interstice, break. **3** *write your name in the space provided* blank, empty space, gap. **4** *no spaces left in the theatre* empty seat, seat, place, berth, accommodation. **5** *green spaces at the edge of the city* unoccupied area, empty area, expanse, stretch, sweep. **6** *within the space of three hours* time, duration, period, span, stretch, interval. **7** *staring into space* empty space, the blue, vacuum, void. **8** *travel in space* outer space, the universe, the galaxy, the solar system; infinity.

space *verb* **1** *space the trees out around the garden* place at intervals, arrange, line up, range, order. **2** *space out the plans* interspace, set apart.

spacious *adjective* **1** *a spacious house* roomy, commodious, capacious, sizable, large, big, ample. **2** *spacious grounds* extensive, broad, wide, expansive, ample, large, vast.
Opposites CRAMPED; POKY.

span *noun* **1** *the span of the bird's wings* length, extent, reach, stretch, spread, distance. **2** *within a short span of time* time, duration, period, space, stretch, interval.

span *verb* **1** *a life spanning almost a century | knowledge spanning many areas* extend over, stretch across, cover, range over. **2** *bridges spanning the Thames | planks spanning the river* bridge, cross, traverse, pass over, arch over, vault over.

spank *verb* smack, slap, put over one's knee; *inf.* tan someone's hide, give someone a hiding, warm someone's bottom, wallop, belt, give someone a licking.

spar *verb* *children who are always sparring* argue, bicker, squabble, wrangle, fight, quarrel, skirmish, have a tiff; *inf.* fall out, have a spat.

spare *adjective* **1** *a spare blanket* extra, additional, reserve, supplementary, auxiliary, surplus, supernumerary. **2** *have little spare time* free, leisure, unoccupied. **3** *a spare figure | of spare build* lean, thin, slim, slender, without an ounce of fat, skinny, wiry, lank; *inf.* skin and bones. **4** *a spare helping* meagre, frugal, scanty, skimpy, modest. **5** *spare with money* sparing, economical, frugal. *See* SPARING. **to spare** *a few plants to spare* left over, superfluous, surplus, surplus to requirements; *inf.* going a-begging. **go spare** *father going spare at the damage* go into a rage, lose one's temper, be furious, be angry; *inf.* go mad, have a fit, blow one's top, hit the ceiling/roof, go up the wall, do one's nut.
Opposites ESSENTIAL; OCCUPIED; FAT.

spare *verb* **1** *Can you spare a few pounds for charity?* afford, part with, give, provide. **2** *no staff to spare* dispense with, do without, manage without, get along without. **3** *spare the culprit* be merciful to, show mercy to, be lenient to, deal leniently with, pardon, leave unpunished; *inf.* let off, unhurt, go easy on, uninjured. **4** *spare the tree from destruction* save, protect, guard, defend.

sparing *adjective* *be sparing with money/food* economical, frugal, thrifty, careful, saving, prudent, cautious, parsimonious, niggardly; *inf.* stingy, tight-fisted.
Opposites EXTRAVAGANT; LAVISH.

spark *noun* **1** *sparks of light* flicker, flash, flare, glint. **2** *not a spark of interest* bit, flicker, glimmer, trace, scrap, vestige, touch, hint, suggestion, suspicion, jot, whit, iota. **3** *require some spark in his employees* sparkle, vivacity, liveliness, animation, energy, spirit, enthusiasm, wit. *See* SPARKLE *noun* 2.

spark *verb* **spark off** *incidents sparking off wars* set off, start off, trigger off, touch off, precipitate, provoke, stir up, incite.

sparkle *verb* **1** *lights/diamonds sparkling* twinkle, flicker, shimmer, flash, glitter, glint, blink, wink, dance, shine, gleam, glow, coruscate. **2** *people sparkling at the party* be sparkling, be vivacious, be lively, be animated, be ebullient, be effervescent, be witty, be brilliant. **3** *wine sparkling* bubble, give off bubbles, effervesce.

sparkle *noun* **1** *the sparkle of lights on the river* twinkle, flicker, shimmer, flash, glitter, glint, blinking, winking, dancing, shining, gleam, glow, coruscation. **2** *require employees with some sparkle* vivacity, liveliness, life, animation, energy, vitality, spirit, enthusiasm, dash, élan, panache; *inf.* pizzazz, vim, zip, zing.

sparse *adjective* *a sparse population | sparse coverage of the news* scanty, meagre, slight, thinly

distributed.
Opposites ABUNDANT; PLENTIFUL.

spartan *adjective a spartan life* austere, harsh, frugal, stringent, rigorous, strict, severe, bleak, grim, ascetic, abstemious, self-denying.

spasm *noun* **1** *stomach spasms* contraction, convulsion, cramp, twitch. **2** *a spasm of coughing/laughter* fit, paroxysm, convulsion, attack, bout, seizure, outburst, access.

spasmodic *adjective spasmodic fits of repentance* intermittent, fitful, irregular, sporadic, erratic, periodic, recurring, recurrent.

spate *noun a spate of burglaries* rush, flood, deluge, torrent, outpouring, outbreak, cluster.

spatter *verb cars spattering mud up on pedestrians* bespatter, splash, spray, shower, daub.

spawn *verb governments spawning committees* create, bring into being, give rise to, cause, originate.

speak *verb* **1** *speak the truth* utter, voice, express, say, pronounce, articulate, enunciate, state, tell. **2** *she spoke to him angrily* address, talk to, converse with, communicate with, have a discussion with, chat with, have a chat with, have a word with, accost, apostrophize; *inf.* have a confab with, have a chinwag with, chew the fat/rag with, pass the time of day with. **3** *the lecturer spoke for two hours* give a speech, give a talk, talk, lecture, deliver an address, hold forth, discourse, orate, harangue, sermonize; *inf.* spout, spiel, speechify. **4** *speak volumes|actions speak louder than words* mean, convey, signify, impart, suggest, denote, indicate, demonstrate. **speak for 1** *a lawyer speaking for the accused* represent, act for, act on behalf of, intercede for, act as spokesman/woman/person. **2** *speak for the motion* support, uphold, defend, stand up for, advocate. **speak of** *speak of his faults* talk about, discuss, mention, make mention of, refer to, make reference to, allude to, comment on, advert to. **speak out/up 1** *speak out/up to be heard in the crowd* speak loudly, speak clearly, raise one's voice, make oneself heard, make oneself audible. **2** *speak out/up against the cruelty* speak boldly, speak frankly, speak openly, speak one's mind, sound off, stand up and be counted. **speak to 1** *speaking angrily to him* address, talk to, converse with, communicate with. **2** *speak to the naughty children* reprimand, rebuke, scold, lecture, admonish; *inf.* tell off, give a telling-off, talk to, give a talking to, give a dressing-down to, tick off, give a ticking-off to, carpet. **3** *speak to the motion* comment on, give information about, say something about, say a word about, touch upon, remark on.

speaker *noun an accomplished speaker* public speaker, speech-maker, lecturer, orator, declaimer, haranguer, demagogue; *inf.* tub-thumper, spieler.

spearhead *noun the spearhead of the opposition to the plan* vanguard, van, forefront, driving force.

spearhead *verb spearhead the opposition to the plan* lead, head, be in the van/vanguard of, set in motion, initiate, launch, pioneer.

special *adjective* **1** *have a special talent|be a special person* exceptional, remarkable, unusual,

rare, out-of-the-ordinary, extraordinary, singular, distinctive, notable, outstanding, unique. **2** *words with a special meaning* specific, particular, individual, distinctive, exact, precise, definite. **3** *take special care of it* especial, extra special, particular, exceptional, out-of-the-ordinary. **4** *a special occasion* significant, momentous, memorable, festive, gala, red-letter. **5** *a special tool* specific, particular, custom-built. **6** *his special interest/subject* particular, chief, main, major, primary.
Opposites ORDINARY; USUAL; RUN-OF-THE-MILL.

specialist *noun a specialist in electronics* expert, authority, professional, consultant, master.

speciality *noun* **1** *many specialities in the field of medicine* specialty, area of specialization, field of study. **2** *putting people at ease is her speciality* distinctive feature, forte, métier, talent, gift, pièce de résistance, claim to fame. **3** *the restaurant's speciality* speciality of the house, house special, spécialité de la maison, chef's special, particular product.

species *noun a species of plant* sort, kind, type, variety, class, category, group, genus, breed, genre.

specific *adjective* **1** *give very specific instructions* well-defined, clear-cut, unambiguous, unequivocal, exact, precise, explicit, express, detailed. **2** *for a specific purpose* particular, specified, fixed, set, determined, distinct, definite.
Opposites VAGUE; GENERAL.

specification *noun* **1** *the specification of your housing requirements* stating, statement, naming, itemizing, designation, detailing, cataloguing. *See* SPECIFY. **2** *a house built to their specifications* instructions, description, details, delineation, conditions, stipulations.

specify *verb specify your housing requirements* state, mention, name, stipulate, define, set out, itemize, designate, detail, list, spell out, enumerate, particularize, catalogue, be specific about.

specimen *noun collect specimens of the soil|dry plant specimens* sample, representative, example, illustration, exemplification, instance, type, exhibit.

specious *adjective arguments found to be specious* plausible, seemingly correct, misleading, deceptive, fallacious, unsound, casuistic, sophistic.

speck *noun* **1** *specks of soot on the white sheets* spot, fleck, dot, speckle, stain, mark, smudge, blemish. **2** *not a speck of food left* particle, bit, piece, atom, iota, grain, trace.

speckled *adjective speckled eggs/birds* mottled, flecked, spotted, dotted, dappled, brindled, stippled.

spectacle *noun* **1** *the spectacle of brilliantly-clad skiers against the snow* sight, vision, scene, picture. **2** *spectacles organized as part of the celebrations* display, show, exhibition, pageant, parade, extravaganza. **3** *a drunk making a spectacle of himself* laughing stock, fool, curiosity.

spectacles *noun* glasses, eye-glasses; *inf.* specs.

spectacular *adjective* **1** *a spectacular display/view* striking, picturesque, impressive, magnifi-

cent, splendid, eye-catching, breathtaking, glorious, dazzling, sensational, stunning, dramatic; *inf.* out of this world. **2** *a spectacular victory* striking, impressive, remarkable, outstanding, extraordinary, sensational, dramatic, astonishing, singular.
Opposites ORDINARY; RUN-OF-THE-MILL; SIMPLE.

spectacular *noun a Christmas spectacular* extravaganza, display, exhibition, performance.

spectator *noun* watcher, beholder, viewer, observer, onlooker, looker-on, witness, eye-witness, bystander; *inf.* rubber-neck.

spectre *noun* apparition, ghost, phantom, wraith, spirit, shade, vision, revenant, manes; *inf.* spook.

speculate *verb* **1** *speculate on their chances of success | speculate that he left unwillingly* conjecture about, theorize about, hypothesize about, guess about, take a guess about, surmise about, muse on, reflect on, mediate about, deliberate about, cogitate about, consider, think about. **2** *speculate on the stock market* gamble, take a risk on, venture on, take a venture on; *inf.* have a flutter on.

speculation *noun* **1** *much speculation about the creation of the universe* conjecture, theorizing, hypothesizing, supposition, guessing, surmising, musing, reflection, meditation, cogitation. See SPECULATE 1. **2** *unfounded speculation* conjecture, theory, hypothesis, supposition, guess, guesswork, surmise, opinion, reflection, meditation, deliberation, cogitation. **3** *his speculation on the stock market* gambling, gamble, venture, risk; *inf.* flutter.

speculative *adjective* **1** *conclusions which are purely speculative* conjectural, theoretical, hypothetical, suppositional, notional, academic, tentative, unproven, vague, indefinite. **2** *speculative dealings on the stock market* gambling, risky, hazardous; *inf.* chancy, dicey.

speech *noun* **1** *the power of speech | express opinions in speech* communication, talk, conversation, discussion, dialogue, colloquy. **2** *slurred speech* diction, articulation, enunciation, pronunciation. **3** *give an after-dinner speech* talk, lecture, address, discourse, oration, sermon, harangue, diatribe, tirade, philippic. **4** *the speech of Southern Germany* language, tongue, idiom, dialect, parlance; *inf.* lingo. **5** *given to obscene speech* utterance, remarks, comments, observations, declarations, assertions.

speechless *adjective* **1** *speechless with rage* rendered speechless, struck dumb, dumb-struck, dumbfounded, astounded, thunder-struck. **2** *speechless with modesty* tongue-tied, inarticulate, dumb, struck dumb. **3** *speechless disappointment* silent, unspoken, unexpressed, unsaid, unvoiced, tacit.
Opposites LOQUACIOUS; VERBOSE.

speed *noun* *move with great speed* rapidity, swiftness, quickness, fastness, haste, hurry, hurriedness, expeditiousness, expedition, alacrity, promptness, fleetness, celerity, velocity.

speed *verb* **1** *workers speeding homewards* hurry, hasten, make haste, rush, race, dash, sprint, scurry, scamper, charge; *inf.* tear, scoot. **2** *a*

driver speeding drive too fast, break the speed limit, exceed the speed limit; *inf.* put one's foot down, step on it. **3** *speed their recovery* expedite, hasten, hurry up, accelerate, advance, further, forward, facilitate, promote, boost, aid, assist. **speed up 1** *need to speed up to win the race* make haste, hurry up, rush, increase speed, accelerate; *inf.* get moving, get a move on, step on it. **2** *speed up the process* speed, expedite, hasten, hurry, accelerate. See SPEED verb 3.

speedy *adjective* **1** *a speedy form of transport* rapid, swift, quick, fast, expeditious, fleet, high-speed. **2** *a speedy reply* rapid, swift, quick, fast, prompt, immediate, express.
Opposites SLOW; LEISURELY; DILATORY.

spell¹ *verb the storm spelt disaster for farmers* mean, signify, amount to, add up to, signal, denote, result in, cause, bespeak, portend, augur, presage. **spell out** *spell out their reasons for leaving* specify, set out, itemize, detail, enumerate, particularize, stipulate, make clear, make plain, elucidate, clarify.

spell² *noun* **1** *recite a spell* incantation, conjuration, charm, abracadabra. **2** *put under a spell* trance, state of enchantment, entrancement, enthrallment, bewitchment. **3** *fall under the spell of an evil man* irresistible influence, fascination, magnetism, allure, charm, attraction, pull, draw, enticement, beguilement.

spell³ *noun* **1** *a spell of warm weather* time, period, interval, stretch, course, extent, span, patch. **2** *a spell of coughing* bout, fit, access. **3** *do a spell at the wheel* turn, stint, term, stretch, shift.

spellbinding *adjective a spellbinding tale* riveting, entrancing, enthralling, bewitching, fascinating, captivating, mesmerizing, mesmeric, hypnotic.

spellbound *adjective an audience spellbound by the actor's performance* riveted, entranced, enthralled, enraptured, transported, rapt, bewitched, fascinated, captivated, mesmerized, hypnotized; *inf.* hooked.

spend *verb* **1** *spend a great deal of money on clothes* pay out, lay out, expend, disburse; *inf.* fork out, shell out, dish out, splash out, splurge. **2** *spend hours on the task* occupy, fill, take up, use up, pass, while away. **3** *spend a lot of effort* use, use up, employ, put in, apply, devote. **4** *the storm spent its force | soldiers having spent all their ammunition* exhaust, finish off, deplete, drain.
Opposites SAVE; KEEP; HOARD.

spendthrift *noun spendthrifts getting into debt* squanderer, prodigal, profligate, wastrel; *inf.* big spender.

spendthrift *adjective spendthrift habits* extravagant, thriftless, squandering, prodigal, profligate, wasteful, improvident.

spent *adjective* **1** *a spent force/talent* used up, consumed, exhausted, finished, depleted, drained, emptied; *inf.* played-out, burnt-out. **2** *feeling spent after the long walk* exhausted, worn-out, tired-out, fatigued, weary, wearied, weakened; *inf.* all in, done in, dead beat, dead on one's feet, shattered, knackered, bushed, whacked, fagged out, had it.

spew verb **1** *passengers spewing up on the sea voyage* vomit, be sick, retch, heave; *inf.* puke, throw up. **2** *lava spewing from the volcano* gush, pour, spurt, issue, discharge, spout, rush.

sphere noun **1** *ornaments in the shape of glass spheres* globe, bull, orb, globule. **2** *spheres in the sky* planet, star, moon, celestial body. **3** *a limited sphere of influence* area, field, range, scope, extent, compass, jurisdiction. **4** *in the sphere of economics* field, area of interest, area of study, discipline, speciality, specialty, domain, realm, province. **5** *marry out of his sphere* social class, social level, social stratum, station, rank, status, social circumstances, walk of life.

spherical adjective *spherical ornaments* globe-shaped, globular, globoid, round, orb-like, orbicular.

spice noun **1** *add spices to food* flavouring, seasoning, herb, condiment, relish. *See table. See also table at* HERB. **2** *add a bit of spice to food* spiciness, flavouring, flavour, seasoning, piquancy, pungency, relish, tang, bite, zest, savoir; *inf.* punch, kick. **3** *add spice to life* excitement, interest, colour, piquancy, zest, gusto, pep; *inf.* zip, zing, zap.

SPICES	
allspice	garam masala
black pepper	garlic
capers	ginger
caraway seeds	ginseng
cardamom	green pepper
cassia	juniper berries
cayenne pepper	mace
chilli	mustard
cinnamon	nutmeg
cloves	paprika
coriander	pimento
cumin	turmeric
curcuma	vanilla
five spices	white pepper

spicy adjective **1** *spicy sauces* spiced, seasoned, flavoursome, well-seasoned, sharp, tart, hot, peppery, piquant, pungent. **2** *spicy stories about her colleagues* lively, spirited, suggestive, risqué, racy, off-colour, improper, indecent, offensive; *inf.* raunchy.
Opposites BLAND; TASTELESS; BORING.

spider noun. *See table at* ARACHNID.

spike noun *spikes on top of a fence* prong, barb, stake, spine, point, projection.

spike verb **1** *spike one's foot on a nail* pierce, penetrate, prick, impale, injure. **2** *spike their drinks* lace, adulterate, contaminate, drug. **3** *spike their efforts to win* frustrate, foil, check, thwart, balk, hinder, obstruct, defeat, crush, destroy, eradicate.

spill verb **1** *milk spilling from the jug* pour, pour out, flow, overflow, brim over, run over, slop over, well over. **2** *spill the scandalous details*

reveal, disclose, divulge, leak, make known; *inf.* let out, blab.

spill noun *take a spill from a horse* fall, tumble, accident; *inf.* header, nosedive, cropper.

spin verb **1** *wheels spinning* revolve, rotate, turn, turn round, circle, whirl, gyrate. **2** *spin around to face him* wheel, whirl, twirl, turn, twist, swivel, pirouette. **3** *spin the plate* revolve, rotate, turn, whirl. **4** *spin a yarn about his successes* tell, unfold, relate, narrate, recount, concoct, make up, invent, fabricate. **5** *her head was spinning* go round, whirl, reel, swim, be giddy. **spin out** *have to spin out his lecture* protract, draw out, stretch out, drag out, prolong, extend, expand, enlarge, fill out, pad out.

spin noun **1** *a spin of the coin* turn, revolution, rotation, whirl, gyration. **2** *a spin in the car* drive, ride, trip, run, jaunt, journey, outing, turn; *inf.* joyride, tool. **in a flat spin** agitate, flustered, in a panic, overwrought, in a dither, frantic, frenzied; *inf.* in a flap, in a state, in a tizz, in a tiz-woz.

spine noun **1** *injure his spine* spinal column, vertebrae, vertebral column, backbone, dorsum. *See table at* VERTEBRA. **2** *a weak man lacking spine* mettle, grit, pluck, pluckiness, spirit, firmness of purpose, determination, resolution, fortitude, courage, braveness, valour, manliness. **3** *the hedgehog's/shrub's spines* needle, spike, barb, quill, rachis.

spine-chilling adjective terrifying, horrifying, blood-curdling, hair-raising; *inf.* scary, spooky.

spineless adjective *spineless people not fighting back* weak, weak-willed, feeble, spiritless, irresolute, indecisive, cowardly, timorous, timid, submissive, unmanly, lily-livered, white-livered; *inf.* chicken, yellow, yellow-bellied, gutless.
Opposites BOLD; BRAVE; STRONG-WILLED.

spiral adjective *spiral staircases | spiral columns of smoke* coiled, corkscrew, winding, twisting, whorled, helical, cochlear, cochleate, voluted.

spiral noun *a spiral of smoke* coil, twist, whorl, corkscrew, wreathe, curlicue, helix, volute.

spiral verb **1** *smoke spiralling from the chimney* coil, wind, twist, swirl, wreathe. **2** *prices spiralling* soar, rocket, rise, go up, mount, increase.

spire noun **1** *a church spire* steeple, belfry. **2** *mountain spires* peak, pinnacle, crest, top, tip.

spirit noun **1** *a healthy body but a troubled spirit* soul, psyche, inner self, ego. **2** *the spirit of nature* breath of life, vital spark, animating principle, life force. **3** *haunted by spirits* apparition, ghost, phantom, spectre, wraith, shade, revenant, manes; *inf.* spook. **4** *a person of determined spirit* character, temperament, temper, disposition, humour, complexion, quality, constitution, make-up. **5** *take the criticism in the wrong spirit* attitude, way, state of mind, mood, frame of mind, point of view, reaction, feeling, humour. **6** *the spirit of the age* prevailing tendency, motivating force, animating principle, dominating characteristic, ethos, essence,

quintessence, embodiment, personification, quiddity. **7** *lack the spirit to carry out the task* courage, bravery, braveness, valour, mettle, pluck, grit, pluckiness, willpower, motivation, backbone, stout-heartedness, manliness, vigour, energy, determination, firmness of purpose, resoluteness; *inf.* guts, spunk. **8** *play the song with spirit* animation, liveliness, vivacity, enthusiasm, fervour, fire, passion, energy, verve, zest, dash, élan; *inf.* pizzazz, zing, zip, zap. **9** *the spirit of the new rule* implication, underlying message, essence, gist, tenor, drift, meaning, sense, purport. *See* SPIRITS. **spirit away** *spirit away the pop star from the photographers* whisk away, carry off, steal away with, make off with, snatch, seize.
Opposites BODY; FLESH.

spirited *adjective* **1** *put up a spirited defence* courageous, brave, valiant, valorous, heroic, mettlesome, plucky, gritty, determined, resolute. **2** *a spirited playing of the song* animated, lively, vivacious, enthusiastic, fervent, fiery, passionate, energetic.
Opposites TIMID; APATHETIC; LIFELESS.

spiritless *adjective* **1** *spiritless creatures putting up no defence* weak, feeble, spineless, irresolute, indecisive, cowardly, timorous, timid, submissive, unmanly, lily-livered, white-livered; *inf.* chicken, yellow, yellow-bellied, gutless. **2** *a spiritless performance* lacklustre, dull, colourless, passionless, bland, insipid, vapid, indifferent, prosaic. **3** *seeming spiritless after their defeat* depressed, dejected, disconsolate, downcast, listless, languid, lethargic, sluggish, inert, lifeless.

spirits *plural noun* **1** *in low spirits | raise one's spirits* mood, humour, temperament, temper, feelings, morale, frame of mind. **2** *wine and spirits* liquor, strong liquor; *inf.* hard stuff, hooch, fire-water.

spiritual *adjective* **1** *spiritual needs* non-material, incorporeal, ethereal, intangible, other-worldly, unworldly. **2** *spiritual music* religious, sacred, divine, holy, non-secular, churchly, ecclesiastic, devotional, devout.
Opposites MATERIAL; corporeal; SECULAR.

spit[1] *verb* **1** *not allowed to spit in public* expectorate, hawk. **2** *spit blood* discharge, issue, eject. **3** *"Get out," he spat* hiss, rasp, snort.

spit[2] *noun* *clean the spit from the floor* spittle, saliva, sputum. **the spit/the very spit** the spitting image, exact likeness, the very image, mirror image, clone, identical twin, duplicate, copy; *inf.* ringer, dead ringer.

spit[3] *noun* *cook the meat on a spit* turnspit, roasting rod, skewer, rotisserie.

spite *noun* *say it out of spite* malice, maliciousness, ill-will, malevolence, venom, malignance, hostility, evil, resentment, resentfulness, snideness, rancour, grudgingness, envy, hate, hatred, vengeance, vengefulness, vindictiveness. **in spite of** *happy in spite of being poor* despite, despite the fact, notwithstanding, regardless of.
Opposites BENEVOLENCE; GOODWILL; CHARITY.

spite *verb* *do it to spite her sister* injure, harm, hurt, wound, annoy, harass, irritate, vex,

offend, provoke, peeve, pique, thwart, foil, frustrate.

spiteful *adjective* *spiteful comments/behaviour* malicious, ill-natured, malevolent, venomous, poisonous, malignant, malign, hostile, resentful, snide, rancorous, grudging, envious, vengeful, vindictive, splenetic; *inf.* bitchy, catty.

splash *verb* **1** *splash water/paint around* spatter, sprinkle, spray, shower, splatter, squirt, slosh, slop, splodge. **2** *splash clothes with mud* spatter, bespatter, spray, shower, splatter. **3** *waves splashing against the rocks* dash, beat, batter, buffet, break, wash, surge. **4** *children splashing about in water* paddle, wade, wallow, dabble. **5** *his name splashed across the newspapers* blazon, display, exhibit, plaster, publicize, broadcast, headline, flaunt, trumpet. **splash out** *splash out on new clothes after being paid* be extravagant, go on a spending spree, splurge, spare no expense; *inf.* lash out, push the boat out.

splash *noun* **1** *the splash of water against the rocks* splashing, dashing, beating, battering. **2** *splashes of mud on the walls* spot, splotch, daub, smudgy, smear, murk, stain. **3** *the scandal made a front-page splash* display, exhibition, splurge, sensation, impact. **4** *a splash of colour* patch, burst, streak. **make a splash** *make a splash with her first novel* cause a sensation, cause a stir, cut a dash, attract attention, get noticed.

spleen *noun* *vent one's spleen on the innocent* bad temper, ill-temper, ill-nature, ill-humour, irritability, irascibility, peevishness, petulance, pique, querulousness, crossness, crabbedness, testiness, touchiness, cantankerousness, moodiness, sullenness, resentment, spite, spitefulness, bitterness, hostility, rancour, malice, maliciousness, malevolence, malignity, acrimony, animosity, bile.

splendid *adjective* **1** *splendid furnishings* magnificent, imposing, superb, grand, sumptuous, resplendent, opulent, luxurious, plush, deluxe, rich, costly, lavish, ornate, gorgeous, glorious, dazzling, brilliant, showy, elegant, handsome. **2** *a splendid reputation* distinguished, impressive, glorious, illustrious, brilliant, notable, noted, remarkable, outstanding, eminent, celebrated, renowned, noble, venerable. **3** *splendid colours* glorious, brilliant, bright, gleaming, glowing, lustrous, radiant, dazzling, refulgent. **4** *a splendid meal/holiday* excellent, fine, first-class, first-rate, marvellous, wonderful; *inf.* fantastic, terrific, great, fabulous, fab.
Opposites DRAB; INFERIOR; ORDINARY; UNDISTINGUISHED.

splendour *noun* **1** *the splendour of the furnishings* magnificence, grandeur, sumptuousness, opulence, luxury, luxuriousness, richness, lavishness, gloriousness, elegance. *See* SPLENDID 1. **2** *the splendour of his reputation* illustriousness, brilliance, notability, eminence, renown, venerableness. *See* SPLENDID 2. **3** *the splendour of the colours* gloriousness, brilliance, brightness, gleam, glow, lustre, radiance. *See* SPLENDID 3.

splice *verb* **1** *splice the rope ends* interweave, braid, plait, intertwine, interlace, join, unite, connect, bind, fasten. **2** *splice the tapes* join, unite, connect, overlap. **get spliced** *get spliced in a registry office* get married, marry, get wed, wed, become man and wife, tie the knot.

splinter *noun splinters of wood* sliver, fragment, shiver, shard, chip, shaving, shred, piece, bit.

splinter *verb the glass splintered* break into pieces, break into fragments, break into smithereens, shatter, shiver, fracture, split, disintegrate, crumble.

split *verb* **1** *split the material in two* break, chop, cut, hew, lop, cleave, rend, rip, tear, slash, slit, splinter, snap, crack, rive. **2** *split the party in two* divide, separate, sever, sunder, bisect, partition. **3** *split up the twins at birth* divide, separate, set apart, disunite. **4** *split the money/profits* share, divide, halve, apportion, distribute, dole out, parcel out, allot, allocate, carve up, slice up; *inf.* divvy. **5** *the road splits over the hill* divide in two, divide, fork, bifurcate. **6** *split with his partner* break up with/from, separate from, part from, part company with, reach the parting of the ways, dissociate oneself from. **7** *the couple split up* break up, separate, part, part company, become estranged, reach the parting of the ways, divorce, get a divorce. **8** *her husband split* leave, depart, take off, decamp, exit; *inf.* push off, shove off. **9** *children splitting on their friends* inform on, tell tales on, report, give away; *inf.* grass on, squeal on, blow the whistle on, rat on, peach on.

split *noun* **1** *a split in the material* break, cut, rent, rip, tear, slash, slit, crack, fissure, breach. **2** *a split in the political party* division, rift, schism, rupture, division, partition, separation, break-up, alienation, estrangement.

split-up *noun after the split-up of her parents* break-up, separation, parting, estrangement, divorce.

spoil *verb* **1** *spoil the material by washing it* damage, impair, mar, blemish, disfigure, deface, injure, harm, ruin, destroy, wreck. **2** *spoil our plans* upset, mess up, disorganize, ruin, destroy, wreck. **3** *spoil her little boy* pamper, overindulge, mollycoddle, cosset, coddle, baby, spoonfeed, featherbed, wait on hand and foot, kill with kindness. **4** *the food will spoil* go bad, turn, go sour, become rotten, rot, become tainted, decompose, decay; *inf.* go off. **spoiling for** *spoiling for a fight* eager for, anxious for, keen to have, desirous of, bent on, longing for, on the lookout for.

spoils *plural noun* **1** *the spoils of high rank* benefit, advantage, gain, profit. **2** *divide up the spoils from the burglary* booty, loot, plunder, pickings, pillage; *inf.* swag, boodle.

spoilsport *noun* killjoy, damper, dog in the manger; *inf.* wet blanket, party-pooper, misery.

spoken *adjective spoken judgement* oral, verbal, uttered, voiced, expressed, by word of mouth, unwritten.

spokesman *noun* spokeswoman, spokesperson, mouthpiece, voice, negotiator, mediator, representative.

sponge *verb sponge the walls* clean, wash, wipe, mop, rub, swab. **sponge off/on** live off, impose on, be a parasite on, scrounge from, beg from,

borrow from; *inf.* freeload on, cadge from, mooch from; *Am. inf.* bum from.

sponger *noun* parasite, hanger-on, scrounger, beggar, borrower; *inf.* freeloader, cadger, moocher; *Am. inf.* bum.

spongy *adjective spongy material/ground* soft, cushiony, squashy, springy, resilient, elastic, porous, absorbent.

sponsor *noun a sponsor of the new art gallery* patron, backer, promoter, subsidizer, guarantor, supporter; *inf.* angel.

sponsor *verb companies sponsoring the sports meeting* be a patron of, back, put up the money for, fund, finance, promote, subsidize, act as guarantor of, support, lend one's name to.

spontaneous *adjective* **1** *spontaneous offers of help* voluntary, unforced, unconstrained, uncompelled, unprompted. **2** *a spontaneous vote of thanks* unplanned, unpremeditated, unrehearsed, impromptu, extempore, spur-of-the-moment, extemporaneous; *inf.* off-the-cuff. **3** *a spontaneous smile* natural, instinctive, involuntary, automatic, impulsive, impetuous. **Opposites** FORCED; PREMEDITATED.

spoonfeed *verb* pamper, mollycoddle, cosset, coddle, featherbed, wait on hand and foot, kill with kindness, overindulge, spoil.

sporadic *adjective sporadic showers* irregular, intermittent, scattered, random, infrequent, occasional, on and off, isolated, spasmodic. **Opposites** FREQUENT; REGULAR; STEADY.

sport *noun* **1** *the world of sport* physical activity, physical exercise, physical recreation, athletics. **2** *play a variety of sports* physical activity, competitive game, pastime. *See tables. See also tables at* ATHLETICS, BALL, BASEBALL, BOXING, CARD, CRICKET, FENCING, FOOTBALL, GOLF, HORSE, MARTIAL ARTS, OLYMPIC GAMES, RUGBY, SOCCER, SWIMMING, TEAM, TENNIS. **3** *torment the animal for sport* amusement, entertainment, diversion, play, fun, pleasure, enjoyment. **make sport of** *children making sport of the new boy* make fun of, laugh at, poke fun at, mock, jeer at, ridicule, taunt, gibe at, sneer at.

sport *verb* **1** *children sporting in the water* play, have fun, amuse oneself, entertain oneself, divert oneself, frolic, gambol, frisk, romp, cavort, caper, disport oneself. **2** *sport a new tie* wear, exhibit, display, have on show, show off.

sporting *adjective a sporting gesture* sportsmanlike, fair, just, honourable, generous.

sportive *adjective students in sportive mood* playful, frolicsome, high-spirited, sprightly, jaunty, rollicking, frisky, skittish, mischievous, waggish, prankish, gamesome.

spot *noun* **1** *black spots on the white cloth* mark, dot, speck, speckle, fleck, smudge, stain, blotch, splotch, patch. **2** *a spot on her face* pimple, pustule, papule, boil, pock, whitehead, blackhead, blemish. **3** *a black spot on her reputation* stain, taint, blemish, defect, flaw, brand, stigma. **4** *a picnic spot* area, place, site, location, scene, locate, setting, situation. **5** *a regular spot on the programme* place, position, niche. **6** *a spot of lunch* little, bit, morsel, smidgen, bite. **7** *a spot of whisky* little, splash, smidgen. **8** *in rather a spot* difficulty, mess, trouble, plight, predicament, quandary, tight corner; *inf.* hot water, fix, jam.

spot *verb* **1** *spot someone following him* catch sight of, see, notice, observe, espy, discern, descry, detect, make out, pick out, recognize, identify. **2** *the material spots easily* mark, stain. **3** *the mud spotted her dress* mark, stain, dirty, soil, spatter, besmirch. **4** *spot her reputation* stain, sully, blacken, taint, blemish.

spotless *adjective* **1** *spotless sheets/houses* clean, ultra-clean, snowy-white, whiter-than-white. **2** *spotless houses* clean, ultra-clean, spick-and-span, immaculate, shining, gleaming. **3** *of spotless character* pure, flawless, faultless, blameless, unstained, unsullied, untainted, unblemished, unimpeachable, above reproach. **Opposites** DIRTY; FILTHY; BLAMEWORTHY; tainted.

spotlight *noun celebrities always in the spotlight* limelight, public eye, glare of publicity, publicity, public attention, public interest.

spotlight *verb a report which spotlights the financial problems* highlight, point up, draw attention to, focus on, zero in on, accentuate, underline, stress, emphasize, give prominence to, bring to the fore.

spotted *adjective* **1** *a spotted dog/horse* dappled, mottled, pied, piebald, speckled. **2** *a spotted dress* polka-dot, spotty, flecked.

spotty *adjective* **1** *a spotty face/youth* pimply, acned. **2** *a spotty dog* spotted, dappled, mottled. *See* SPOTTED 1. **3** *a spotty dress* spotted, polka-dot, flecked. **4** *the standard of the quality being spotty* patchy, irregular, non-uniform.

spouse *noun* husband/wife, partner, mate, companion, consort, helpmate; *inf.* better half, old man/woman/lady, missis.

spout *verb* **1** *oil spouting from the well* spurt, gush, spew, squirt, jet, spray, emit, erupt, disgorge, pour, stream, flow, spray. **2** *tired of politicians spouting* declaim, orate, hold forth, ramble, rant, harangue, speechify, sermonize; *inf.* spiel.

sprawl *verb* **1** *people sprawling on the sofa* stretch out, lounge, lie around, repose, recline, slump, flop, loll, slouch. **2** *suburbs sprawling out into the countryside* spread, stretch, spill over, ramble, straggle, trail.

SPORTS

aerobatics	discus throwing	marathon running	skateboarding
aerobics	diving	match fishing	skibob racing
aikido	drag racing	motorcycle	skiing
American football	falconry	racing	ski jumping
angling	fencing	motor racing	skittles
archery	field hockey	mountain biking	skydiving
Association Football	figure skating	mountaineering	sled-dog racing
athletics	fly-fishing	netball	snooker
Australian Rules	fox hunting	orienteering	snorkelling
football	freestyle skiing	parachuting	soccer
autocross	French cricket	paragliding	softball
badminton	Gaelic football	parascending	speedball
bandy	game fishing	pelota	speed skating
baseball	gliding	pigeon racing	spelunking
basketball	golf	pistol shooting	sprinting
beagling	greyhound	pool	squash
billiards	racing	potholing	stock car racing
bobsleighing	hammer	powerboat	stoolball
boccie/boules	throwing	racing	surfing
bowls	handball	racquetball	swimming
boxing	hang-gliding	rallycross	synchronized
bull fighting	hiking	rollerblading	swimming
bungee jumping	hurling	roller hockey	table tennis
caber tossing	ice dancing	roller skating	tae kwon do
Canadian football	ice hockey	roller skiing	tennis
canoe racing	jai alai	rounders	tobogganing
caving	jet skiing	rowing	trampolining
clay pigeon shooting	judo	Rugby Fives	tug-of-war
climbing	kabaddi	Rugby League	volleyball
coarse fishing	karate	Rugby Union	water polo
coursing	karting	sailing	water-skiing
court handball	kayaking	sailplaning	weightlifting
cricket	kendo	scuba-diving	white water
croquet	korfball	sculling	rafting
crossbow archery	kung fu	sea fishing	wildfowling
cross-country run-	lacrosse	shinty	wild water
ning	langlauf	shooting	racing
curling	lawn tennis	short tennis	windsurfing
cycle racing	gymnastics	shot-putting	wrestling
darts	luge	sidecar racing	yacht racing

SPORTSPEOPLE

Abrahams, Harold (1899–1978; Brit. athlete)

Agassi, Andre (b. 1970; Am. tennis player)

Agostini, Giacomo (b. 1944; It. racing motorcyclist)

Akabusi, Kriss (b. 1958; Brit. runner)

Ali, Muhammad (Cassius Clay; b. 1942; Am. boxer)

Aouita, Saïd (b. 1960; Moroccan runner)

Ashe, Arthur (1943–93; Am. tennis player)

Ballesteros, Severiano (b. 1957; Sp. golfer)

Bannister, Sir Roger (b. 1929; Brit. runner)

Beckenbauer, Franz (b. 1945; Ger. footballer)

Becker, Boris (b. 1967; Ger. tennis player)

Belmonte y García, Juan (1892–1962; Sp. matador)

Best, George (b. 1946; Brit. footballer, b. in Northern Ireland)

Border, Allan (b. 1955; Austral. cricketer)

Borg, Björn (b. 1956; Sw. tennis player)

Botham, Ian (b. 1955; Brit. cricketer)

Boycott, Geoffrey (b. 1940; Brit. cricketer)

Brabham, Jack (b. 1926; Austral. motor-racing driver)

Bradman, Sir Donald (b. 1908; Austral. cricketer)

Bristow, Eric (b. 1957; Brit. darts player)

Broome, David (b. 1940; Brit. showjumper)

Brough, Louise (b. 1923; Am. tennis player)

Bruno, Frank (b. 1961; Brit. boxer)

Bubka, Sergey (b. 1963; Ukrainian pole-vaulter)

Bueno, Maria (b. 1939; Brazilian tennis player)

Burrell, Leroy (b. 1967; Am. runner)

Busby, Sir Matt (1909–94; Brit. footballer)

Carling, Will (b. 1965; Brit. Rugby Union player)

Carson, Willie (b. 1942; Scot. jockey)

Chappell, Greg (b. 1948; Austral. cricketer)

Chappell, Ian (b. 1943; Austral. cricketer)

Charlton, Bobby (b. 1937; Brit. footballer)

Charlton, Jack (b. 1935; Brit. footballer)

Christie, Linford (b. 1960; Brit. runner, b. in Jamaica)

Coe, Sebastian (b. 1956; Brit. runner)

Comaneci, Nadia (b. 1961; Am. gymnast, b. in Romania)

Compton, Denis (b. 1918; Brit. cricketer)

Connors, Jimmy (b. 1952; Am. tennis player)

Constantine, Learie, Baron (1902–71; West Indian (Trinidadian) cricketer)

Cowdrey, Sir Colin (b. 1932; Brit. cricketer)

Cruyff, Johann (b. 1947; Du. footballer)

Culbertson, Ely (1891–1955; Am. bridge authority/player)

Curry, John (1949–94; Brit. iceskater)

Dalglish, Kenny (b. 1951; Scot. footballer)

Davis, Steve (b. 1957; Brit. snooker player)

Dean, Christopher (b. 1958; Brit. iceskater)

Dempsey, Jack (1895–1983; Am. boxer)

Devoy, Susan (b. 1954; NZ squash player)

DiMaggio, Joe (b. 1914; Am. baseball player)

Duke, Geoffrey E. (b. 1923; Brit. racing motorcyclist)

Edberg, Stefan (b. 1966; Sw. tennis player)

Edwards, Gareth (b. 1947; Welsh Rugby Union player)

Evert, Chris(tine) (b. 1954; Am. tennis player)

Faldo, Nick (b. 1957; Brit. golfer)

Fangio, Juan Manuel (1911–95; Argentinian motor-racing driver)

Fittipaldi, Emerson (b. 1946; Brazilian motor-racing driver)

Foreman, George (b. 1948; Am. boxer)

Fosbury, Richard (b. 1947; Am. athlete)

Frazier, Joe (b. 1944; Am. boxer)

Fry, C. B. (1872–1956; Brit. cricketer/athlete)

Gascoigne, Paul (b. 1967; Brit. footballer)

Gibson, Althea (b. 1927; Am. tennis player)

Grace, W(illiam) G(ilbert) (1848–1915; Brit. cricketer)

Graf, Steffi (b. 1969; Ger. tennis player)

Greaves, Jimmy (b. 1940; Brit. footballer)

Griffith Joyner, Florence (b. 1959; Am. runner)

Gunnell, Sally (b. 1966; Brit. hurdler)

Hadlee, Sir Richard (b. 1951; NZ cricketer)

Hailwood, Mike (1940–81; Brit. racing motorcyclist)

Heyhoe-Flint, Rachel (b. 1939; Brit. cricketer)

Higgins, Alex (b. 1949; Brit. snooker player, b. in Northern Ireland)

Hill, Damon (b. 1962; Brit. motor-racing driver)

Hill, Graham (1929–75; Brit. motor-racing driver)

Hoad, Lewis (1934–94; Austral. tennis player)

Hobbs, Sir Jack (1882–1963; Brit. cricketer)

Hogan, Ben (b. 1912; Am. golfer)

Hunt, James (1947–93; Brit. motor-racing driver)

Hutton, Sir Len (1916–90; Brit. cricketer)

Illingworth, Ray (b. 1932; Brit. cricketer)

Jackson, Colin (b. 1967; Brit. hurdler)

Jeeps, Dickie (b. 1931; Brit. Rugby Union player)

John, Barry (b. 1945; Welsh Rugby Union player)

Johnson, Earvin "Magic" (b. 1959; Am. basketball player)

Johnson, Jack (1878–1946; Am. boxer)

Jones, Bobby (1902–71; Am. golfer)

Jordan, Michael (b. 1963; Am. basketball player)

Joselito (José Gómez; 1895–1920; Sp. matador)

Kapil Dev (b. 1959; Ind. cricketer)

Karpov, Anatoly (b. 1951; Russ. chess player)

Kasparov, Gary (b. 1963; Azerbaijani chess player)

758

SPORTSPEOPLE cont.

Keegan, Kevin (b. 1951; Brit. footballer)

Khan, Hashim (b. 1916; Pakistani squash player)

Khan, Imran (b. 1952; Pakistani cricketer)

Khan, Jahangir (b. 1963; Pakistani squash player)

King, Billie Jean (b. 1943; Am. tennis player)

Korbut, Olga (b. 1955; Soviet gymnast)

Korchnoi, Victor (b. 1931; Soviet-born chess player)

Lara, Brian (b. 1969; West Indian (Trinidadian) cricketer)

Lasker, Emanuel (1868–1941; Ger. chess player)

Lauda, Niki (b. 1949; Austrian motor-racing driver)

Laver, Rod (b. 1938; Austral. tennis player)

Law, Denis (b. 1940; Scot. footballer)

Lendl, Ivan (b. 1960; Am. tennis player, b. in Czechoslovakia)

Leonard, Sugar Ray (b. 1956; Am. boxer)

Lewis, Carl (b. 1961; Am. athlete)

Liddell, Eric (1902–45; Brit. athlete)

Lillee, Dennis (b. 1949; Austral. cricketer)

Lindwall, Raymond (b. 1921; Austral. cricketer)

Lineker, Gary (b. 1960; Brit. footballer)

Llewellyn, Harry (b. 1911; Welsh showjumper)

Lloyd, Clive (b. 1944; West Indian (Guyanese) cricketer)

Louis, Joe (Joseph Barrow; 1914–81; Am. boxer)

Lyle, Sandy (b. 1958; Scot. golfer)

McBride, Willie (b. 1940; Ir. Rugby Union player)

McEnroe, John (b. 1959; Am. tennis player)

Mansell, Nigel (b. 1953; Brit. motor-racing driver)

Mantle, Mickey (b. 1931; Am. baseball player)

Maradona, Diego (b. 1960; Argentinian footballer)

Marciano, Rocky (1923–69; Am. boxer)

Matthews, Sir Stanley (b. 1915; Brit. footballer)

May, Peter (1929–94; Brit. cricketer)

Meads, Colin (b. 1935; NZ Rugby Union player)

Merckx, Eddy (b. 1945; Belg. cyclist)

Milo of Croton (6th century B.C.; Gk wrestler)

Montana, Joe (b. 1956; Am. footballer)

Moore, Bobby (1941–93; Brit. footballer)

Morphy, Paul (1837–84; Am. chess player)

Moss, Stirling (b. 1929; Brit. motor-racing driver)

Navratilova, Martina (b. 1956; Am. tennis player, b. in Czechoslovakia)

Newcombe, John (b. 1944; Austral. tennis player)

Nicklaus, Jack (b. 1940; Am. golfer)

Norman, Greg (b. 1955; Austral. golfer)

Nurmi, Paavo (1897–1973; Finn. runner)

Ovett, Steve (b. 1955; Brit. runner)

Owens, Jesse (John Cleveland Owens; 1913–80; Am. athlete)

Palmer, Arnold (b. 1929; Am. golfer)

Pelé (Edson Arantes do Nascimento; b. 1940; Brazilian footballer)

Perry, Fred (1909–95; Am. tennis/table-tennis player, b. in Britain)

Piggott, Lester (b. 1935; Brit. jockey)

Player, Gary (b. 1935; S. Afr. golfer)

Prost, Alain (b. 1955; Fr. motor-racing driver)

Puskas, Ferenc (b. 1927; Hungarian footballer)

Ramsey, Sir Alf (b. 1922; Brit. footballer)

Ranjitsinhji Vibhaji, Kumar Shri, Maharajah (1872–1933; Ind. cricketer)

Reardon, Ray (b. 1932; Welsh snooker player)

Rhodes, Wilfred (1877–1973; Brit. cricketer)

Richards, Viv (b. 1952; West Indian (Antiguan) cricketer)

Robinson, Sugar Ray (Walker Smith; 1920–89; Am. boxer)

Robson, Bryan (b. 1957; Brit. footballer)

Ruth, Babe (1895–1948; Am. baseball player)

Sampras, Pete (b. 1971; Am. tennis player)

Sánchez-Vicario, Arantxa (b. 1971; Sp. tennis player)

Scudamore, Peter (b. 1958; Brit. jockey)

Seles, Monica (b. 1973; Am. tennis player, b. in Yugoslavia)

Senna, Ayrton (1960–94; Brazilian motor-racing driver)

Sheene, Barry (b. 1950; Brit. racing motorcyclist)

Simpson, O. J. (b. 1947; Am. football player)

Smith, Harvey (b. 1938; Brit. showjumper)

Sobers, Sir Gary (b. 1936; West Indian (Barbadian) cricketer)

Spassky, Boris (b. 1937; Russ. chess player)

Spitz, Mark (b. 1950; Am. swimmer)

Stewart, Jackie (b. 1939; Scot. motor-racing driver)

Surtees, John (b. 1934; Brit. motor-racing driver)

Szewinska, Irena (b. 1946; Pol. athlete)

Thompson, Daley (b. 1958; Brit. decathlete)

Todd, Mark (b. 1956; NZ equestrian)

Torvill, Jayne (b. 1957; Brit. ice-skater)

Trevino, Lee (b. 1939; Am. golfer)

Trueman, Freddy (b. 1931; Brit. cricketer)

Turishcheva, Ludmilla (b. 1952; Soviet gymnast)

Tyson, Mike (b. 1966; Am. boxer)

Viren, Lasse (b. 1949; Finn. runner)

Wade, Virginia (b. 1945; Brit. tennis player)

Watson, Tom (b. 1949; Am. golfer)

Williams, J(ohn) P(eter) R(hys) (b. 1949; Welsh Rugby Union player)

Wills (Moody), Helen (b. 1905; Am. tennis player)

Winkler, Hans (b. 1926; Ger. showjumper)

Worrell, Sir Frank (1924–67; West Indian (Barbadian) cricketer)

Zátopek, Emil (b. 1922; Cz. runner)

spray[1] *noun* **1** *a spray from the sea* shower, jet, mist, drizzle, spindrift, foam, froth. **2** *buy a deodorant spray* atomizer, vaporizer, aerosol, sprinkler, sprinkling can.

spray[2] *verb* **1** *spray scent/insecticide* disperse, disseminate, sprinkle, shower. **2** *water sprayed from the sea* jet, spout, gush.

spray[3] *noun* *a spray of flowers* sprig, posy, bouquet, nosegay, corsage, wreath, garland.

spread *verb* **1** *spread its wings/spread the map out* stretch, extend, open out, unfurl, unroll. **2** *the town is spreading out* stretch out, extend, enlarge, grow bigger, widen, broaden, grow, develop, branch out. **3** *the view spread out before them* stretch out, unfold, be on display, be exhibited, be on show, uncover, be unveiled, be revealed. **4** *spread manure on the fields* lay on, put on, apply, smear on; *inf.* plaster on. **5** *spread the bread with butter* cover, coat, layer. **6** *the disease/influence is spreading* mushroom, extend, increase, advance, proliferate, escalate. **7** *spread rumours* disseminate, circulate, transmit, make public, make known, broadcast, publicize, propagate, promulgate, bruit. **8** *spread a table* set, lay, arrange, order.

spread *noun* **1** *measure the spread of the bird's wings* extent, stretch, span, reach, compass, sweep. **2** *a spread of three decades* period, time, term. **3** *the spread of the disease* increase, advance, expansion, mushrooming, proliferation, escalating, diffusion. **4** *the spread of rumours* dissemination, circulation, transmission, broadcasting, publicizing, propagation. See SPREAD *verb* 7. **5** *a brightly-coloured spread* bedspread, bedcover, cover, coverlet, counterpane, throw. **6** *lay on a birthday spread* feast, banquet, repast; *inf.* blow-out.

spree *noun* **1** *go out on a spree to celebrate* enjoyable outing, fling, revel, junketing, jollification, drinking bout, orgy, debauch, bacchanal, bacchanalia; *inf.* binge, bender, jag. **2** *a shopping spree* buying orgy; *inf.* shopping splurge.

sprig *noun* *a sprig of lilac* spray, branch, bough, twig, shoot.

sprightly *adjective* *sprightly elderly people* spry, lively, energetic, active, agile, nimble, supple, animated, vivacious, spirited, brisk, vital, light-hearted, cheerful, merry, jolly, blithe, jaunty, perky, frisky, frolicsome, playful, sportive. **Opposites** DODDERING; SLUGGISH; LETHARGIC; INACTIVE.

spring *verb* **1** *springing to his feet/cats springing from the trees* jump, leap, bound, vault, hop. **2** *her family springs from a relative of Queen Anne* be described from, descend from, have its/their origins in, originate in, derive from, issue from. **3** *disapproval springs from ignorance* originate, have its origins in, derive from, stem from, arise in, emanate from, proceed from, start from. **4** *Where did you spring from?* appear, come into view, crop up; *inf.* pop up. **5** *spring his resignation on them* present unexpectedly, introduce suddenly, reveal suddenly, announce without warning. **spring back** *the branch sprang back* rebound, recoil, fly back. **spring up** *new houses springing up everywhere* appear, make a sudden appearance, come into

being, come into existence, shoot up, develop quickly, mushroom, burgeon.

spring *noun* **1** *reach her in one spring* jump, leap, bound, vault, hop. **2** *injured by the spring of the branch* rebound, recoil. **3** *a mattress with little spring* springiness, bounciness, elasticity, resilience, flexibility, stretch, stretchiness, tensility. **4** *put a spring in his step* bounce, bounciness, buoyancy, liveliness, light-heartedness, merriment. **5** *get married in the spring* springtime, springtide. **6** *mineral springs* well, wellspring, source. **7** *the springs of their behaviour* origin, source, cause, root, basis.

spring *adjective* *spring weather* springlike, vernal.

springy *adjective* **1** *springy mattresses* bouncy, elastic, resilient, flexible, stretchy, tensile. **2** *a springy step* bouncy, lively, light-hearted, merry.

sprinkle *verb* **1** *sprinkle water on the grass* spray, shower, splash, trickle, spatter. **2** *sprinkle icing sugar on the cake* scatter, strew. **3** *sprinkle the cake with icing sugar* dust, powder, dredge.

sprinkling *noun* **1** *a sprinkling of snow on the ground* scattering, dusting. **2** *only a sprinkling of people in the audience* few, handful, trickle.

sprint *verb* *sprinting for the bus* run, race, rush, dash, put on a turn/burst of speed; *inf.* scoot, tear, hare, hotfoot it.

sprite *noun* fairy, elf, pixie, nymph, dryad, imp, goblin, kelpie, leprechaun.

sprout *verb* **1** *deer sprouting antlers* send forth, put forth, grow, develop. **2** *potatoes sprouting* bud, germinate, put forth shoots. **3** *weeds sprouting up everywhere* shoot up, spring up, grow, develop, appear, mushroom, proliferate.

spruce *adjective* neat, well-groomed, well-turned-out, smart, trim, dapper, elegant, chic, looking as though one has just stepped out of a bandbox; *inf.* natty. **Opposites** SCRUFFY; UNTIDY; DISHEVELLED.

spry *adjective* sprightly, lively, energetic, active, agile, nimble, quick.

spume *noun* foam, froth, head, lather, surf, spindrift.

spunk *noun* courage, bravery, valour, pluck, pluckiness, mettle, gameness, daring, spirit, backbone; *inf.* guts.

spur *noun* **1** *the use of spurs to speed up the animals* goad, prick, prod. **2** *act as a spur to his ambition* stimulus, stimulant, incentive, inducement, encouragement, impetus. **on the spur of the moment** *make his decision on the spur of the moment* impulsively, on impulse, impetuously, impromptu, on the spot, unpremeditatedly, without thinking, without planning, suddenly, all of a sudden, unexpectedly, out of the blue.

spur *verb* **1** *spur the animal to go faster* goad, prick, prod. **2** *his early success spurred him on to try hard* stimulate, give the incentive to, induce, encourage, prompt, urge, impel.

spurious *adjective* *spurious excuses/research* counterfeit, fraudulent, fake, bogus, sham, mock, feigned, pretended, make-believe, imitation,

contrived, fictitious, deceitful, specious; *inf.* phoney, pseudo.
Opposites AUTHENTIC; GENUINE; REAL.

spurn *verb* spurn her lover/his advances reject, turn away, repulse, rebuff, repudiate, snub, slight, cold-shoulder, treat with contempt, disdain, look down one's nose at, scorn, despise, condemn; *inf.* kick in the teeth, give the go-by.

spurt *verb* oil/water spurting from the well gush, squirt, shoot, surge, well, jet, spring, pour, stream, flow, issue, emanate.

spurt *noun* **1** a spurt of oil/water gush, surge, jet, spray, outpouring. **2** a sudden spurt of energy/speed burst, outburst, fit, surge, access. **3** put on a spurt at the end burst of speed, turn of speed, increase of speed, burst of energy, sprint, rush.

spy *noun* government documents stolen by an enemy spy enemy agent, foreign agent, secret agent, undercover agent, secret service agent, intelligence agent, double agent, fifth columnist; *inf.* mole, spook.

spy *verb* spy someone on the horizon catch sight of, spot, see, notice, observe, glimpse, make out, discern, descry, espy. **spy on** spy on the rival firm | spy on his neighbours keep under surveillance, watch, keep a watch on, keep an eye on, observe, keep under observation, follow, shadow, trail; *inf.* tail.

squabble *noun* a squabble over money quarrel, fight, row, dispute, argument, difference of opinion, dispute, tiff, wrangle, brawl; *inf.* scrap, set-to, dust-up, barney, run-in, spat.

squabble *verb* children squabbling constantly quarrel, fight, row, argue, bicker, have a dispute/difference of opinion, have a tiff, have words, wrangle, brawl; *inf.* fall out, scrap.

squad *noun* **1** a squad of soldiers company, platoon, troop, unit. **2** a squad of workmen gang, band, group.

squalid *adjective* **1** squalid hovels dirty, filthy, dingy, grubby, grimy, mucky, slummy, slum-like, foul, vile, low, wretched, mean, nasty, seedy, sordid, sleazy, slovenly, repulsive, disgusting, neglected, dilapidated, ramshackle, broken-down, tumble-down; *inf.* grungy, grotty. **2** squalid tales of corruption sordidly, vile, nasty, repulsive, horrible, disgraceful, shameful, abominable, odious, filthy, indecent, depraved.
Opposites CLEAN; SPOTLESS; PLEASANT.

squalor *noun* the squalor of slums squalidness, dirt, dirtiness, filth, filthiness, dinginess, grubbiness, grime, griminess, muckiness, foulness, vileness, lowness, wretchedness, meanness, nastiness, seediness, sordidness, dilapidation; *inf.* grunge, grottiness.

squander *verb* squander his savings on alcohol waste, misspend, dissipate, fritter away, run through, lavish, splurge, be prodigal with, spend like water, pour down the drain; *inf.* blow.

square *noun* **1** a band playing in the square town square, village square, market square, quadrangle. **2** regard parents as old squares fogy, old fogy, conservative, traditionalist,

conventionalist, die-hard, conformist; *inf.* stick-in-the-mud, fuddy-duddy.

square *adjective* **1** the teams are all square equal, even, level-pegging, drawn; *inf.* even-steven. **2** a businessman square in all his dealings fair, just, equitable, honest, straight, upright, above board, ethical; *inf.* on the level. **3** a square refusal direct, straight, straightforward, explicit, unequivocal. **4** regard her parents as being square old-fashioned, behind the times, conservative, ultra-conservative, traditionalist, conventional, conformist, bourgeois, strait-laced, stuffy, unadventurous; *inf.* fuddy-duddy.

square *verb* **1** the two accounts do not square with each other tally, agree, be consistent with, correspond, fit, conform, be in harmony with, harmonize, be congruous with. **2** square the score level, even, make equal. **3** square the bill settle, settle up, pay, pay in full, discharge, make good. **4** square the doorman to let them in bribe, suborn, corrupt; *inf.* buy off. **5** square matters before we go straighten out, set straight, set right, put in order, arrange.

squash *verb* **1** squash the beetle with his foot | squash the berries with a wooden spoon crush, squeeze, flatten, compress, press, smash, pulp, mash, pulverize, macerate. **2** the audience were squashed into the hall crowd, crush, cram, pack tight, pack like sardines, jam, squeeze, wedge. **3** squash him in front of the class humiliate, mortify, deflate, repress, put in his/her place, take the wind out of someone's sails, take down a peg or two, intimidate, bully; *inf.* put down. **4** squash the rebellion put down, quash, quell, crush, suppress, scotch, squelch, nip in the bud; *inf.* put the kibosh on.

squashy *adjective* pulpy, mushy, spongy, squishy, oozy, pappy.

squat *verb* squat behind the hedge crouch, sit on one's haunches, sit on one's heels.

squat *adjective* a squat figure dumpy, stubby, chunky, flattet, thickset, stocky, short.

squawk *noun* **1** the squawk of the hens screech, cackle, shriek, scream, yelp. **2** squawking about the high prices complain, protest, grumble, moan; *inf.* grouse, kick up a fuss, gripe, beef, bitch, bellyache.

squeak *noun* the squeak of the mice squeal, peep, pipe, yelp, whimper.

squeak *verb* **1** mice squeaking squeal, peep, pipe, yelp, whimper. **2** gates squeaking in the wind creak, scrape, grate.

squeal *noun* the squeals of the children shriek, yell, scream, screech, howl, shout, cry, wail.

squeal *verb* **1** children squealing with pain/excitement shriek, yell, scream, howl, shout, cry, shrill, wail. **2** the burglar squealing on his associates inform, tell tales on; *inf.* grass, blow the whistle on, rat, peach, snitch, put the finger on. **3** squealing about the prices complain, protest, grumble, moan; *inf.* grouse, kick up a fuss, gripe, beef, bitch, squawk, bellyache.

squeamish *adjective* **1** feeling squeamish on the sea voyage queasy, nauseous, sickish, sick, queer. **2** squeamish with regard to etiquette and morals fastidious, particular, punctilious, finicky, fussy, scrupulous, prudish, straight-laced; *inf.* pernickety, prissy.

squeeze *verb* **1** *squeeze the sweater to remove moisture* wring, twist, press. **2** *squeeze the water from the sweater | squeeze the juice from the orange* extract, press, force, express. **3** *squeeze the oranges* compress, crush, squash, mash, pulp. **4** *squeeze his arm* grip, clutch, pinch, press, compress. **5** *the audience were squeezed into the hall* crowd, crush, cram, pack tight, pack like sardines, jam, squash, wedge. **6** *squeeze his fiancée* embrace, hug, cuddle, clasp, hold tight. **7** *squeeze money out of them* extort, wring, wrest, extract, tear from, milk; *inf.* bleed. **8** *squeeze them for money* bring pressure to bear on, pressure, pressurize, strong-arm, blackmail; *inf.* put the squeeze on, lean on, bleed, put the screws on, put the bite on.

squeeze *noun* **1** *give his fiancée a squeeze* embrace, hug, cuddle, clasp, hold. **2** *give her hand a squeeze* clasp, grip, grasp, clutch. **3** *it was a bit of a squeeze in the hall* crowd, crush, jam, squash, press, congestion. **4** *a squeeze of lemon juice* drop, droplet, dash, spot, bit.

squire *noun* *country squires* landowner, land-holder, country gentleman.

squire *verb* *squire her to the dance* escort, accompany, be someone's partner, be someone's companion, attend, usher, guide, conduct, lead.

squirm *verb* *squirm in their seats | squirm in embarrassment* wriggle, wiggle, writhe, twist, turn, shift.

squirrel *noun.* See table. See also table at RODENT.

SQUIRRELS AND RELATED RODENTS

chickaree	mountain beaver
chipmunk	palm squirrel
flying squirrel	pocket gopher
giant squirrel	prairie dog
gopher	red squirrel
grey squirrel	scaly-tailed squirrel
groundhog	souslik
ground squirrel	sun squirrel
marmot	woodchuck

---

squirt *verb* **1** *squirt water from a water pistol* discharge, expel, shoot, spurt. **2** *water squirting from the water pistol* eject, emit, discharge, spew out, spurt, spout, jet, stream, spray, gush, surge, pour, flow, issue. **3** *squirting people with water* splash, wet, spray, bespatter, shower, sprinkle, besprinkle.

squirt *noun* **1** *a squirt of water/cream* jet, stream, spray, flow. **2** *a nasty little squirt* insignificant person; *inf.* pipsqueak, twerp.

stab *verb* *stab him in the heart* knife, pierce, puncture, run through, stick, skewer, gash, slash, wound, injure. **stab in the back** betray, break faith with, be a traitor to, play false, double-cross, sell out, give a Judas kiss to; *inf.* sell down the river.

stab *noun* **1** *receive a stab in the leg* puncture, gash, slash, incision, wound, injury. **2** *feel a stab of pain in the chest* pain, shooting pain, pang, twinge, ache, throb, spasm. **3** *have a stab at writing a novel* try, attempt, endeavour, essay, effort, venture; *inf.* go, shut, crack.

stability *noun* **1** *the stability of the structures* firmness, solidity, steadiness, secureness, strength, fastness, stoutness, sturdiness. See STABLE 1. **2** *the stability of their relationship* secureness, solidity, strength, steadiness, firmness, sureness, durability, constancy, permanence, reliability, dependabilty. See STABLE 2. **3** *question her stability* soundness, sense, responsibility, self-control, sanity. See STABLE 3.

stable *adjective* **1** *stable structures* firm, solid, steady, secure, fixed, strong, fast, stout, sturdy, moored, anchored, immovable. **2** *a stable relationship* secure, solid, strong, steady, firm, sure, steadfast, unwavering, unfaltering, unswerving, established, long-lasting, long-lived, deep-rooted, well-founded, well-grounded, abiding, durable, enduring, lasting, constant, permanent, reliable, dependable, true. **3** *a stable person* well-balanced, balanced, sound, mentally sound, steady, reasonable, sensible, responsible, equable, self-controlled, sane.
Opposites rickety; INSECURE; UNSTABLE.

stack *noun* **1** *a stack of logs* heap, pile, mass, accumulation, collection, hoard, store, stock, stockpile, mound, mountain. **2** *put hay into stacks* haystack, rick, hayrick, cock, shock. **3** *a stack of money | stacks of money* abundance, amplitude; *inf.* a great deal, a lot, lots, bags, loads, heaps, tons, oodles, scads.

stack *verb* *stack logs* heap, pile, pile up, amass, accumulate, collect, hoard, store, stockpile.

stadium *noun* *sports stadium*, arena, sports field, athletic field, football field, football pitch.

staff *noun* **1** *the lame man leaning on a staff* walking stick, stick, cane, crook, crutch, prop. **2** *hit him with a staff* stick, cane, rod, pole, baton, truncheon. **3** *the staff of office* rod, mace, sceptre. **4** *reduce staff in the office* employees, workers, workforce, personnel.

staff *verb* *staff the factory with school-leavers* man, people, equip, fit out, supply, furnish, provide.

stage *noun* **1** *a stage in the development* point, period, step, juncture, time, division, level. **2** *the last stage of a race/journey* lap, leg, phase, step. **3** *stand on a stage in the theatre* platform, dais, rostrum, podium. **4** *the stage for many international meetings* setting, scene, site, arena, background, backdrop. **the stage** *a career connected with the stage* the theatre, drama, show business, the footlights, the boards.

stage *verb* **1** *stage a production of Shakespeare* put on, produce, direct, perform, mount, present. **2** *stage a protest rally* arrange, organize, engineer, orchestrate, put together, lay on.

stagger *verb* **1** *stagger drunkenly up the road* reel, sway, teeter, totter, wobble, lurch, pitch, roll. **2** *staggered by the price of the toys* amaze, astound, dumbfound, astonish, flabbergast, shock, shake, confound, nonplus, take aback, take one's breath away, stupefy, stun; *inf.*

stagnant · stand

strike dumb. **3** *stagger the lines of bricks* alternate, step.

stagnant *adjective* **1** *stagnant water* still, unflowing, motionless, standing, foul, stale, dirty, filthy, polluted, putrid, putrefied, brackish. **2** *stagnant business economy* sluggish, slow-moving, quiet, inactive, dull, static.
Opposites FLOWING; FRESH; ACTIVE.

stagnate *verb* **1** *water stagnating in weed-covered pools* stand, vegetate; become stagnant/still/foul/stale/dirty/filthy; fester, putrefy. *See* STAGNANT 1. **2** *businesses/economies stagnating* become stagnant, do nothing, be sluggish, lie dormant, be inert. *See* STAGNANT 2. **3** *stagnating waiting for a job to turn up* vegetate, idle, be idle, laze, loaf, hang about, languish.

staid *adjective* *staid old gentleman/ladies* sedate, quiet, serious, serious-minded, grave, solemn, sombre, sober, proper, decorous, formal, prim, demure, stiff, starchy; *inf.* stuffy, stick-in-the-mud.
Opposites FRIVOLOUS; FLIGHTY; INFORMAL.

stain *verb* **1** *material permanently stained with blood/rust* soil, mark, discolour, dirty, spot, blotch, blemish, smudge, smear, besmirch, begrime. **2** *stain her reputation* blacken, tarnish, sully, blemish, damage, mar, injure, defame, denigrate, dishonour, besmirch, defile, taint, blot, slur. **3** *stain the wood* varnish, dye, paint, colour.

stain *noun* **1** *unable to remove the stains made by the blood* mark, spot, blotch, blemish, smudge, smear. **2** *stains on her character* blemish, damage, injury, taint, blot, slur, stigma. **3** *use a brown stain on the wood* varnish, dye, paint, colourant.

stake¹ *noun* *stakes for plants to grow up* post, pole, stick, upright, rod, spike, pale.

stake² *verb* **1** *stake the rose bushes* support, prop up, hold up, brace, tether. **2** *stake off his garden with posts* mark off, mark out, separate off, demarcate, define, delimit, bound, circumscribe. **3** *stake a claim to part of the estate* establish, declare, state, lay claim to.

stake³ *noun* **1** *card-players laying down £50 stakes each* wager, bet, ante. **2** *have a stake in the firm* financial interest, interest, share, investment, involvement, concern.

stake⁴ *verb* *stake £10 on the race | stake his life on the outcome* wager, bet, place a bet of, put on, gamble, pledge, chance, venture, risk, hazard.

stakes *plural noun* *the stakes in a horse-race* prize-money, purse, winnings.

stale *adjective* **1** *stale bread/cheese* unfresh, dry, dried-out, hard, hardened, mouldy, decayed. **2** *stale air* unfresh, stuffy, close, musty, fusty. **3** *stale beer* flat, sour, turned, spoiled; *inf.* off. **4** *stale jokes* hackneyed, tired, worn-out, threadbare, banal, trite, stock, stereotyped, clichéd, run-of-the-mill, commonplace, platitudinous, unoriginal, unimaginative, uninspired, flat, insipid, vapid; *inf.* old hat.
Opposites FRESH; ORIGINAL.

stalemate *noun* *reach stalemate in their talks* deadlock, impasse, standstill, stand-off.

stalk *noun* *the stalk of a plant* stem, branch, shoot, twig.

stalk *verb* **1** *hunters stalking deer* pursue, chase, give chase to, follow, shadow, trail, track down, creep up on, hunt; *inf.* tail. **2** *stalk haughtily out of the room* stride, march, flounce, strut, prance. **3** *raiders stalking the land* move threateningly through, pervade, permeate.

stall *noun* **1** *stalls in a market* booth, stand, table, counter. **2** *animals in their stalls* pen, coop, sty, corral, compartment, cubicle.

stall *verb* **1** *stall until he thinks of the answer* play for time, use delaying tactics, delay, beat about the bush, hem and haw; *inf.* drag one's feet. **2** *stall his creditors* hold off, stave off, keep at bay, keep at arm's length, evade, avoid.

stalwart *adjective* **1** *healthy stalwart young men* strong, sturdy, robust, hardy, muscular, brawny, strapping, powerfully built, burly, rugged, lusty; *inf.* husky. **2** *stalwart adventurers* brave, courageous, valiant, valorous, intrepid, fearless, manly, heroic, indomitable, bold, daring, plucky, spirited, adventurous; *inf.* gutsy.
Opposites PUNY; FRAIL; TIMID.

stamina *noun* endurance, staying power, indefatigability, resistance, resilience, fortitude, strength, vigour, energy, staunchness, robustness, toughness; *inf.* grit, guts.

stammer *verb* *stammer nervously* stutter, stumble, mumble, splutter, hesitate, falter, pause.

stammer *noun* *have a stammer when he's nervous* stutter, speech impediment, speech defect.

stamp *verb* **1** *stamp on the poisonous insect* trample, step on, tread on, trample on, crush, squash. **2** *stamp his name on the book* imprint, inscribe, engrave, emboss, mark, sign. **3** *her last words stamped on her mind* imprint, impress, fix. **4** *he was stamped as a criminal* brand, characterize, designate, identify, categorize, style, term, label, dub, name, tag. **stamp out** *stamp out the rebellion* quash, suppress, put down, quell, crush, squelch, extinguish, scotch, put an end to, eradicate, eliminate.

stamp *noun* **1** *have the stamp of genius* mark, hallmark, label, brand, tag, characteristics, quality. **2** *a man of a different stamp* kind, sort, type, variety, class, classification, form, breed, kidney, mould, cast, cut.

stampede *noun* *run over by the stampede of the cattle* charge, rush, flight, scattering.

stampede *verb* *the animals stampeded in fear | shoppers stampeded to the sales* charge, rush, flee, take flight, dash, race, run.

stance *noun* *take up a liberal stance on the issue* stand, standpoint, position, line, policy, attitude, angle, slant, viewpoint, point of view, opinion.

stand *verb* **1** *ask the children to stand* be upright, be erect, rise, rise to one's feet, get to one's feet, get up. **2** *a village once stood there* be situated, be located. **3** *stand the ladder against the wall* set, place, put, position. **4** *stand and listen* stop, halt, come to a halt, come to a standstill. **5** *their offer/orders stand* remain/be in force, remain/be valid, remain/be effective, hold, hold good, obtain, prevail, be the case.

6 *unable to stand his attitude* put up with, tolerate, bear, take, endure, abide, suffer, brook, countenance, cope with, handle; *inf.* stomach, wear. **stand by 1** *stand by his friend* stand up for, support, be supportive of, back, uphold, be loyal to, defend, come to the defence of, stick up for, champion, take someone's part, take the side of, side with. **2** *stand by his word* adhere to, hold to, stick to, observe. **3** *soldiers asked to stand by* wait, be prepared, be ready for action. **stand for 1** *What do the initials stand for?* represent, mean, signify, denote, indicate, betoken, imply, symbolize, exemplify, illustrate. **2** *he stands for all that is good* advocate, favour, support, back, uphold, promote, argue for, speak in favour of, subscribe to. **3** *refuse to stand for her behaviour* put up with, tolerate, bear, take, endure, suffer, brook, countenance; *inf.* stomach, wear. **stand in for** *stand in for the headmaster when he was ill* | *stand in for the leading lady* deputize for, act as deputy for, take the place of, replace, act as substitute for, do duty for, cover for, hold the fort for, act as understudy, understudy, act as locum for. **stand out 1** *sculptures standing out from the building project*, jut out, protrude, extend, stick out, poke out. **2** *in that dress she stood out in the crowd* be noticeable, be noticed, be conspicuous, be striking, be distinctive, be prominent, attract attention, catch the eye; *inf.* stick out a mile, stick out like a sore thumb. **stand up 1** *that argument will not stand up in court* be valid, be sound, have force, be well-founded, be well-grounded, be effective, be plausible. **2** *stand her up on a date* fail to meet, fail to keep an appointment with, fail to turn up for, let down. **stand up for 1** *stand up for his friend in his trouble* stand by, support, be supportive of, defend, come to the defence of, stick up for, champion. See STAND BY 1. **2** *stand up for what one believes* uphold, promote, argue for, speak in favour of. **stand up to** *stand up to the bully* confront, face up to, oppose openly, show resistance to, brave, defy, challenge.
Opposites SIT; LIE.

stand *noun* **1** *come to a stand* standstill, halt, stop, stoppage, rest. **2** *take up a stand against the new policies* firm stand, defensive position, resistance, opposition. **3** *take a liberal stand* stance, standpoint, position, line, policy, attitude. See STANCE. **4** *stands in the market-place* stall, booth, table, counter. **5** *put books in stands* display case, shelf, rack, frame, base. **6** *give a speech from the stand in the hall* platform, stage, staging, dais, rostrum. **7** *a taxi stand* rank, station, place.

standard *noun* **1** *a standard by which quality is judged* yardstick, benchmark, gauge, measure, criterion, guide, guideline, norm, touchstone, model, pattern, example, exemplar, paradigm, ideal, archetype, specification, requirement, rule, principle, law, canon. **2** *works of a low standard* level, grade, quality, evaluation, worth, merit. **3** *raise the battle standard* flag, banner, pennant, streamer, ensign, colours. **4** *trees supported by standards* support, prop, post, pole, cane, upright. **5** *maintain old-fashioned standards* principle, code of behaviour, code of honour, morals, ethics, ideals.

standard *adjective* **1** *standard behaviour* | *standard shoe sizes* usual, ordinary, average, normal, habitual, common, regular, stock, set, fixed, conventional. **2** *the standard work on Shakespeare* definitive, established, classic, recognized, approved, accepted, authoritative, official.
Opposites ABNORMAL; UNUSUAL; UNCOMMON.

standardize *verb* *standardize procedures* make uniform, regulate, systematize, normalize, homogenize, regiment, bring into line.

stand-in *noun* *act as a stand-in for the teacher/ actor/doctor* representative, deputy, substitute, second, proxy, understudy, locum, right-hand man/woman/person.

standing *noun* **1** *his standing in the community* status, rank, ranking, social position, position, station, footing, place, circumstances. **2** *people of standing in the community* reputation, good reputation, repute, eminence, prominence, note, noteworthiness. **3** *her husband of many years standing* duration, length of time, existence, continuance, endurance.

standing *adjective* **1** *standing stones* upright, erect, vertical, upended, perpendicular; *Herald* rampant. **2** *standing water* still, stagnant, static, motionless. **3** *a standing army/invitation* permanent, fixed, regular, perpetual, constant.

stand-off *noun* *the two sides have reached a stand-off* deadlock, impasse, stalemate.

standoffish *adjective* aloof, distant, cold, cool, reserved, withdrawn, remote, detached, unapproachable, unfriendly, unsociable, haughty, disdainful.

standpoint *noun* *from the standpoint of the customer* point of view, viewpoint, opinion, perspective, angle, slant, frame of reference.

standstill *noun* *factories/talks coming to a standstill* halt, stop, dead stop, stoppage, rest, pause, cessation, stand.

staple *adjective* *staple foods* chief, primary, main, principal, foremost, leading, basic, fundamental, essential, indispensable, necessary, important, vital.

star *noun* **1** *stars in the sky* heavenly body, celestial body; planet, planetoid, asteroid. *See tables. See also tables at* ASTEROID, GALAXY, METEOR, MOON, PLANET. **2** *born under a lucky star* astral influence, destiny, fate, fortune, lot. **3** *read his stars* horoscope, forecast, augury. *See table at* ZODIAC. **4** *one of the stars of the film* principal, leading lady, leading man, lead, name, superstar. **5** *some of the stars on the local council* celebrity, dignitary, notable, name, somebody, VIP; *inf.* bigwig, big shot, big cheese, big wheel.

star *adjective* *one of her star pupils* brilliant, great, talented, gifted, celebrated, illustrious, renowned, famous, distinguished, prominent, eminent, pre-eminent, principal, chief, leading, major.

stare *verb* **1** *stare into space* gaze, gape, goggle, look; *inf.* gawp, gawk. **2** *the solution was staring them in the face* be conspicuous, be obvious, be blatant, stand out, be prominent, stick out, glare.

stark *adjective* **1** *in stark contrast* sharp, sharply delineated, sharply defined, obvious, evident, clear, clear-cut. **2** *a stark landscape* desolate, bare, barren, arid, vacant, empty, forsaken, bleak, dreary, depressing, grim, harsh; *lit.* drear. **3** *stark attire* austere, severe, plain, simple, unadorned, unembellished, undecorated. **4** *stark madness* sheer, utter, absolute, downright, out-and-out, outright, total, complete, thorough, thoroughgoing, pure, unmitigated, unqualified, consummate, unmissable, patent, palpable, rank, arrant. **5** *the stark facts* bald, bare, simple, blunt, straightforward, unadorned, unembellished, harsh, grim. **6** *the stark figure of a man* naked, nude, bare, stark naked. *See* STARK NAKED.

stark *adverb* *stark staring mad* completely, totally, entirely, wholly, altogether, utterly, absolutely, quite. **stark naked** naked, nude, in the nude, bare, stripped, undressed, unclad, as naked as the day one was born, in a state of nature; *inf.* in the buff, in the altogether, in the raw, in one's birthday suit, starkers.

start *verb* **1** *events starting in the morning* begin, commence, get underway, get going; *inf.* kick off. **2** *when her illness started* commence, get underway, get going, begin, commence, appear, come into being, come into existence, arise, originate, crop up, first see the light of day. **3** *have to start now to finish the job in time* begin, commence, make a start, make a beginning, get going, go ahead, set things moving, buckle to/down, turn to, put one's shoulder to the wheel, put one's hand to the plough, start the ball rolling; *inf.* get moving, get down to it, get down to business, get one's finger out, get the show on the road, take the plunge, kick off, pitch in, get off one's backside. **4** *start*

CONSTELLATIONS			
Astronomical Name	**Common Name**	**Astronomical Name**	**Common Name**
Andromeda	—	Lacerta	Lizard
Antlia	Air Pump	Leo	Lion
Apus	Bird of Paradise	Leo Minor	Little Lion
Aquarius	Water Bearer	Lepus	Hare
Aquila	Eagle	Libra	Balance/Scales
Ara	Altar	Lupus	Wolf
Aries	Ram	Lynx	—
Auriga	Charioteer	Lyra	Lyre
Boötes	Herdsman | Bear Driver	Mensa	Table
		Microscopium	Microscope
Caelum	Chisel	Monoceros	Unicorn
Camelopardalis	Giraffe	Musca	Fly
Cancer	Crab	Norma	Level/Rule
Canes Venatici	Hunting Dogs	Octans	Octant
Canis Major	Great Dog	Ophiuchus	Serpent Bearer
Canis Minor	Little Dog	Orion	Hunter
Capricornus	Goat | Sea Goat	Pavo	Peacock
Carina	Keel	Pegasus	—
Cassiopeia	—	Perseus	—
Centaurus	Centaur	Phoenix	—
Cepheus	—	Pictor	(Painter's) Easel
Cetus	Whale	Pisces	Fishes
Chamaeleon	Chameleon	Piscis Austrinus	Southern Fish
Circinus	Compasses	Puppis	Stern/Poop
Columba	Dove	Pyxis	Compass (Box)
Coma Berenices	Berenice's Hair	Reticulum	Net
Corona Australis	Southern Crown	Sagitta	Arrow
Corona Borealis	Northern Crown	Sagittarius	Archer
Corvus	Crow	Scorpius	Scorpion
Crater	Cup	Sculptor	—
Crux (Australis)	(Southern) Cross	Scutum	Shield
Cygnus	Swan	Serpens	Serpent
Delphinus	Dolphin	Sextans	Sextant
Dorado	Swordfish/Goldfish	Taurus	Bull
Draco	Dragon	Telescopium	Telescope
Equuleus	Little Horse | Foal	Triangle	Triangulum
Eridanus	River	Triangulum Australe	Southern Triangle
Fornax	Furnace		
Gemini	Twins	Tucana	Toucan
Grus	Crane	Ursa Major	Great Bear
Hercules	—	Ursa Minor	Little Bear
Horologium	Clock	Vela	Sails
Hydra	Sea Serpent	Virgo	Virgin
Hydrus	Water Snake	Volans	Flying Fish
Indus	Indian	Vulpecula	Fox

now to be there by tonight start out, set out, set off, depart, leave, make a start; *inf.* hit the road, hit the trail, push off, get the show on the road. **5** *start the machine* set in motion, set moving, turn on, start functioning, start operating, activate. **6** *the machine started up* begin working, start functioning, start operating. **7** *start up the business* set up, establish, found, lay the foundations of, lay the cornerstone of, create, institute, initiate, launch, get going, originate, pioneer, organize. **8** *start in pain* jump, leap up, jerk, twitch, recoil, shrink, flinch, blench, wince, shy. **9** *animals suddenly starting out of the bushes* jump, leap, spring, bound, dart.
Opposites FINISH; END; STOP; ARRIVE.

start *noun* **1** *present at the start of the event* beginning, commencement, opening, inception, inauguration, dawn, birth; *inf.* kick-off. **2** *at the start of her illness* beginning, commencement, onset, emergence, first appearance. **3** *the start of the trouble* origin, source, root, basis, derivation, wellspring. **4** *at the start of the campaign* establishment, foundation, institution, launch, origination. *See* START *verb* 7. **5** *get a start in the race* head start, advantage, advantageous position. **6** *get a start in life* good start, advantageous beginnings, opening, opportunity, chance, helping hand, encouragement, introduction, embarking, sponsorship, patronage; *inf.* break. **7** *give a start in pain* jump, leap, jerk, twitch, flinch, blench, wince, spasm, convulsion.

startle *verb* *a loud noise startled the children* | *startled by the news* make one jump, disturb, agitate, perturb, unsettle, scare, frighten, alarm, surprise, astonish, shock; *inf.* give one a turn.

startling *adjective* *some starling news* | *a startling result* disturbing, unsettling, alarming, surprising, unexpected, unforeseen, astonishing, amazing, staggering, shocking, extraordinary, remarkable.

starvation *noun* extreme hunger, lack of food, death from lack of food, fasting, famine, undernourishment, malnourishment.

starving *adjective* starved, famished, ravenous, very hungry, faint from lack of food, dying from lack of food, fasting; *inf.* able to eat a horse.

state *noun* **1** *in a state of readiness* | *in its previous state* condition, shape, situation, circumstances, position, predicament, plight. **2** *in a calm/nervous state* condition, mood, humour, spirits, frame of mind, attitude. **3** *she often gets into a state* state of agitation, anxiety, nerves, panic, distressed state, fluster, pother; *inf.* flap, tizzy, tiz-woz. **4** *look at the state of this room* untidy state, untidiness, mess, chaos, disorder, disarray, disorganization, confusion, clutter. **5** *a meeting of the world's states* country, nation, land, realm, kingdom, republic, territory, federation, commonwealth, body politic. *See table at* COUNTRY. **6** *Alaska is the largest American state* federal state, province, region. *See table. See also table at* PROVINCE. **7** *feel the state is too powerful* government, parliament, the administration, the establishment. **8** *occasions of state* pomp, cere-

STARS			
Star	**Constellation**	**Star**	**Constellation**
Achernar	Eridanus	Dog Star	Canis Major
Acrux	Crux	Dubhe	Ursa Major
Adhara	Canis Major	Elnath	Taurus
Alcor	Ursa Major	Fomalhaut	Piscis Austrinus
Alcyone	Taurus	Gacrux	Crux
Aldebaran	Taurus	Garnet star	Cepheus
Algenib	Pegasus	Hadar	Centaurus
Algieba	Leo	Hamal	Aries
Algol	Perseus	Markab	Pegasus
Alioth	Ursa Major	Merak	Ursa Major
Alkaid/Benatnasch	Ursa Major	Mira	Cetus
Almach	Andromeda	Mirach	Andromeda
Alnilam	Orion	Mirfak	Perseus
Alnitak	Orion	Mirzam	Canis Major
Alpha Centauri | Rigil Kentaurus	Centaurus	North Star	Ursa Minor
Alphard	Hydra	Nunki	Sagittarius
Altair	Aquila	Peacock	Pavo
Antares	Scorpius	Polaris	Ursa Minor
Arcturus	Boötes	Pollux	Gemini
Barnard's Star	Ophiuchus	Procyon	Canis Minor
Becrux Mimosa	Crux	Proxima Centauri	Centaurus
Bellatrix	Orion	Regulus	Leo
Betelgeuse	Orion	Rigel	Orion
Canopus	Carina	Shaula	Scorpius
Capella	Auriga	Sirius	Canis Major
Castor	Gemini	Spica	Virgo
Deneb	Cygnus	Tau Ceti	Cetus
Denebola	Leo	Tycho's star	Cassiopeia
		Vega	Lyra

mony, display, dignity, majesty, grandeur, glory, splendour.

state verb state one's objections express, voice, utter, say, tell, declare, set out, lay down, affirm, assert, announce, make known, reveal, disclose, divulge, pronounce, articulate, aver, proclaim, present, expound, promulgate.

stated adjective at the stated times set, settled, fixed, agreed, declared, determined, approved, authorized, ruled, ordained, accredited, official.

stately adjective stately occasions ceremonial, dignified, solemn, majestic, royal, regal, magnificent, grand, glorious, splendid, elegant, imposing, impressive, august, lofty, pompous; slow-moving, measured, deliberate.

statement noun a statement of one's views declaration, account, recitation, report, affirmation, assertion, announcement, revelation, disclosure, divulgence, pronouncement, articulation, averment, proclamation, presentation, expounding, promulgation.

static adjective static house prices/pressure unmoving, unvarying, undeviating, changeless, constant, stable, steady, stationary, motionless, at a standstill, frozen.
Opposites MOBILE; VARIABLE.

station noun 1 trains stopping at several stations stop, stopping-place. 2 get the bus at the bus station terminus, terminal, depot. 3 police station depot, base, office, headquarters, seat. 4 security staff at their appointed stations post, place,

position, location, site. 5 from different stations in life class, level, rank, grade, standing, status, caste.

stationary adjective 1 stationary traffic unmoving, motionless, at a standstill, parked. 2 stationary price patterns changeless, unchanging, constant, unvarying, invariable, undeviating.
Opposites MOVING; VARIABLE.

statue noun statuette, sculpture, effigy, figure, figurine, representation, likeness, image, bust, head.

statuesque adjective statuesque figures/woman dignified, stately, majestic, noble, magnificent, splendid, imposing, impressive, regal, well-proportioned, handsome, beautiful.

stature noun 1 ill-developed in stature height, tallness, size, altitude. 2 post demanding people of stature status, importance, import, standing, consequence, eminence, pre-eminence, prominence, note, fame, renown.

status noun of uncertain social status standing, rank, level, grade, degree, position, importance, reputation, consequence.

staunch adjective staunch supporters loyal, faithful, dependable, reliable, steady, constant, stable, firm, steadfast, unswerving, unwavering, unhesitating, unfaltering.
Opposites DISLOYAL; UNFAITHFUL; UNRELIABLE.

stave verb **stave in** stave in the side of door break in, smash in, put a hole in, push in, cave in, splinter, shiver, fracture. **stave off** stave off their

---

STATES AND TERRITORIES

State/Territory	Capital	State/Territory	Capital
States of America		New Mexico	Santa Fe
Alabama	Montgomery	New York	Albany
Alaska	Juneau	North Carolina	Raleigh
Arizona	Phoenix	North Dakota	Bismarck
Arkansas	Little Rock	Ohio	Columbus
California	Sacramento	Oklahoma	Oklahoma City
Colorado	Denver	Oregon	Salem
Connecticut	Hartford	Pennsylvania	Harrisburg
Delaware	Dover	Rhode Island	Providence
Florida	Tallahassee	South Carolina	Columbia
Georgia	Atlanta	South Dakota	Pierre
Hawaii	Honolulu	Tennessee	Nashville
Idaho	Boise	Texas	Austin
Illinois	Springfield	Utah	Salt Lake City
Indiana	Indianapolis	Vermont	Montpelier
Iowa	Des Moines	Virginia	Richmond
Kansas	Topeka	Washington	Olympia
Kentucky	Frankfort	West Virginia	Charleston
Louisiana	Baton Rouge	Wisconsin	Madison
Maine	Augusta	Wyoming	Cheyenne
Maryland	Annapolis	**States/Territories of Australia**	
Massachusetts	Boston	New South Wales	Sydney
Michigan	Lansing	Queensland	Brisbane
Minnesota	St Paul	South Australia	Adelaide
Mississippi	Jackson	Tasmania	Hobart
Missouri	Jefferson City	Australian Capital	
Montana	Helena	Territory	Canberra (federal capital)
Nebraska	Lincoln	Northern Territory	Darwin
Nevada	Carson City	Victoria	Melbourne
New Hampshire	Concord	Western Australia	Perth
New Jersey	Trenton		

attack ward off, fend off, evade, avert, avoid, dodge, keep at bay, keep at arm's length, repel, repulse, rebuff.

stay *verb* **1** *stay there till we call you* remain, wait, stay put, continue, linger, pause, rest, delay, tarry. **2** *stay loyal to him* remain, continue, go on. **3** *stay at a hotel|stay with her mother for a few days* lodge at, take a room at, put up at, be accommodated at, sojourn at, visit, reside at, take up residence, dwell at, live at. **4** *stay judgement until tomorrow* put off, postpone, suspend, adjourn, defer, hold over, hold in abeyance, delay, prorogue. **5** *stay the progress of the disease* check, curb, arrest, stop, delay, hold, prevent, hinder, impede, obstruct.
Opposites LEAVE; DEPART.

stay *noun* **1** *a brief stay at a hotel* visit, sojourn, stop, stopover, holiday, vacation. **2** *a stay of judgement* postponement, suspension, adjournment, deferment, delay. **3** *a stay in his old age* prop, underprop, support, brace, bolster, buttress.

staying power *noun* endurance, stamina, resistance, resilience, fortitude, strength, vigour, energy, staunchness, robustness, toughness; *inf.* grit, guts.

steadfast *adjective* **1** *a steadfast friend* faithful, loyal, true, constant, devoted, dedicated, trustworthy, dependable, reliable, staunch. **2** *a steadfast refusal to help|steadfast in his views* steady, firm, determined, resolute, unchanging, unwavering, unfaltering, unswerving, unyielding, inflexible, uncompromising, relentless, implacable. **3** *a steadfast gaze* steady, fixed, intent, immovable, unwavering, unfaltering.
Opposites DISLOYAL; IRRESOLUTE.

steady *adjective* **1** *make the posts steady* firmly fixed, firm, fixed, stable, secure, immovable. **2** *a steady hand* still, unshaking, motionless, unmoving, sure. **3** *a steady gaze* steadfast, fixed, immovable, unwavering, unfaltering. **4** *a steady faith* constant, unchanging, changeless, unvarying, invariable, undeviating, continuous, continual, unceasing, ceaseless, perpetual, persistent, unremitting, unwavering, unfaltering, unfluctuating, undying, unending, endless. **5** *walk at a steady pace* uniform, even, regular, rhythmic, consistent. **6** *a steady boyfriend* regular, habitual, usual, customary. **7** *a steady young man* well-balanced, balanced, sensible, level-headed, rational, settled, down-to-earth, calm, equable, imperturbable, reliable, dependable, serious-minded, serious.
Opposites INSECURE; INCONSTANT; UNEVEN; SPORADIC.

steady *verb* **1** *steady the ladder* make steady, hold steady, stabilize, secure, balance, support. **2** *steady one's nerves* calm, calm down, settle, compose, tranquillize, control, get a grip on.

steal *verb* **1** *steal money from the old lady* thieve, take, appropriate, misappropriate, pilfer, purloin, filch, walk off with, embezzle, pocket, abstract, shoplift, peculate; *inf.* pinch, nick, snitch, swipe, lift, rip off. **2** *steal someone else's work* plagiarize, copy, pirate, appropriate,

poach; *inf.* lift, crib. **3** *steal a child* kidnap, snatch, abduct, carry off, make off with, seize, shanghai. **4** *steal a kiss|steal a few hour's sleep* snatch, obtain stealthily, get surreptitiously. **5** *steal out of the room* slip, slide, tiptoe, sneak, creep, slink, slither, flit, glide.

steal *noun* **1** *taking that money was a steal* theft, robbery, misappropriation, pilfering, larceny; embezzlement, peculation; *inf.* pinching, nicking. See STEAL *verb* 1. **2** *her new dress was a steal* bargain buy, bargain, good buy, cheap buy; *inf.* giveaway. **3** *getting into the house secretly was a steal* easy job, simple task; *inf.* cinch, piece of cake, child's play, picnic, pushover.

stealing *noun* **1** *found guilty of stealing* theft, thieving, thievery, robbery, larceny, burglary, appropriation, misappropriation, pilfering, pilferage, purloining, filching, embezzlement, shoplifting, peculation; *inf.* pinching, nicking, swiping. See STEAL *verb* 1. **2** *guilty of the stealing of other people's work* plagiarizing, copying, piracy, appropriation, poaching; *inf.* lifting, cribbing. **3** *the stealing of children* kidnapping, snatching, abduction, seizure, shanghaiing. See STEAL *verb* 3.

stealth *noun* *get into the house by stealth* stealthiness, secrecy, furtiveness, surreptitiousness, slyness, sneakiness, clandestineness, covertness, shadiness.

stealthy *adjective* *stealthy movements/manoeuvres* secret, furtive, surreptitious, sly, sneaky, clandestine, covert, shady, underhand, undercover.
Opposites ABOVE-BOARD; OPEN.

steam *noun* **1** *boiling water giving off steam* vapour, fume, smoke, exhalation. **2** *run out of steam|have no steam left* energy, vigour, vigourousness, vitality, stamina, power, force. **let off steam** use up energy, release surplus energy, give vent to one's feelings, lose one's inhibitions, let oneself go; *inf.* let it all hang out. **under one's own steam** *get the job under one's own steam* unaided, unassisted, without help, by oneself, by one's own efforts, on one's own two feet.

steam *verb* *steaming along the road to the bus stop* rush, race, run, dash, charge, sprint, hurry, speed, hasten; *inf.* tear, zoom, zip. **get all steamed up** get agitated, get excited, get flustered, get hot and bothered, get angry, get annoyed, get furious; *inf.* lose one's cool. **steam up** *windscreens steaming up* become misty/misted, become blurry/blurred, become cloudy/clouded.

steamy *adjective* **1** *a steamy atmosphere* humid, muggy, sticky, moist, damp, sweltering, boiling, like a Turkish bath, like a sauna. **2** *steamy love scenes in the film* erotic, sexy, passionate, tempestuous, sensuous, lustful, wanton.

steel *noun* **1** *men of steel* strength, fortitude, hardiness, courage, bravery, valour, intrepidity, pluck, mettle, nerve; *inf.* grit, guts. **2** *a grip of steel* firmness, solidity, hardness. **steel oneself** *steel herself to have the operation* brace oneself, harden oneself, nerve oneself, get up courage, screw up courage, screw one's courage to the sticking point.

steely *adjective* **1** *a steely colour* steel-coloured, grey, blue-grey, steel-grey, iron-grey. **2** *steely eyes* hard, harsh, severe, unfeeling, unsympathetic, cruel, ruthless, pitiless. **3** *steely determination* firm, determined, resolute, undaunted, unyielding, inflexible, unwavering, unfaltering.

steep *adjective* **1** *steep cliffs* sheer, abrupt, precipitous, sudden, sharp, perpendicular, vertical, declivitous, acclivitous. **2** *a steep rise in share prices* sharp, rapid, sudden, precipitate. **3** *prices at that restaurant are a bit steep* high, dear, costly, expensive, unreasonable, excessive, exorbitant; *inf.* over the top, OTT. **4** *demands considered too steep* unreasonable, excessive, exorbitant, immoderate, inordinate, unwarranted; *inf.* over the top, OTT.
Opposites GRADUAL; GENTLE; REASONABLE.

steep *verb* **1** *steep the stained clothes in cold water* soak, saturate, immerse, submerge, wet through, drench, souse, macerate. **2** *steep the meat in wine* marinade, marinate, soak, souse. **3** *a family steeped in misery* imbue, permeate, pervade, infuse, suffuse, fill. **4** *they were steeped in the classics* submerge, immerse, saturate, make thoroughly conversant with, make closely acquainted with.

steeple *noun* spire, tower, church tower, bell tower, campanile, turret, minaret.

steer *verb* **1** *steer the car/boat* guide, navigate, drive, pilot, be in the driver's seat of, be at the wheel of. **2** *steer the guests to the garden | steer the conversation back to the subject* guide, lead, direct, conduct, usher. **steer clear of** *steer clear of his ex-wife* keep away from, keep one's distance from, keep at arm's length, give a wide berth to, avoid, evade, dodge, eschew, shun.

stem *noun* **1** *the stem of a bush* trunk, stock, peduncle. **2** *flowers/foliage on a stem* stalk, shoot, branch, twig. **stem from** *troubles stemming from poverty* arise from, originate from, have its origins in, be rooted in, derive from, spring from, emanate from, issue from, proceed from, be caused by, be brought about by.

stem *verb* *stem the flow of blood* check, stop, halt, hold back, contain, curb, dam, staunch.

stench *noun* stink, foul smell, foul odour, reek, mephitis; *lit.* noisomeness; *inf.* pong, whiff, niff.

stentorian *adjective* stentorious, booming, roaring, thundering, thunderous, trumpeting, ear-splitting, resonant, vibrant, powerful, loud, strong, full.

step *noun* **1** *reach her in one step* stride, pace. **2** *hear steps on the stairs* footstep, footfall, tread, tramp. **3** *police examining steps in the mud* footstep, footprint, print, impression, track. **4** *walk with a cheerful step* walk, gait, bearing, carriage. **5** *live just a step away* short distance, pace, stone's throw, spitting distance. **6** *the steps of a ladder* rung, tread. **7** *take a foolish step* course of action, move, act, action, deed, measure, manoeuvre, procedure, expedient, effort. **8** *another step towards international peace* step forward, advance, advancement, development, progression, stage, move. **9** *another step in his promotion* stage, level, grade, rank, degree. **in**

step *in step with the views of the committee* in agreement, in accord with, in harmony with, in line with, in concurrence with, in conformity with, in consensus with, in unison with. **mind/watch one's step 1** *mind/watch your step on the broken pavement* step carefully, walk carefully, tread cautiously. **2** *mind/watch your step when doing business with him* be careful, be cautious, be wary, be circumspect, be chary, take care, take heed, be attentive, be on one's guard, look out, have one's wits about one, mind how one goes. **out of step** *out of step with modern thinking* in disagreement with, at odds with, out of line with, at variance with, in opposition to, at loggerheads with. **step by step** *follow the instructions step by step* by stages, by degrees, progressively, through all the gradations, gradually, bit by bit, slowly. **take steps** *take steps to control expenditure* take action, take measures, act, take the initiative, prepare, get ready.

step *verb* *step lightly down the street* walk, tread, stride, pace, move, advance, proceed; *inf.* hoof it. **step down** *step down to make way for a younger person* resign, give up one's post/job, retire, abdicate. **step in** *the police had to step in to prevent a murder* intervener, intercede, become involved, act, take action, take measures, take a hand; *inf.* clip on. **step on** *step on dog dirt* walk on, tread on, tramp on, trample on. **step up 1** *police stepping up their efforts* increase, boost, augment, intensify, escalate. **2** *step up the pace of production* increase, speed up, accelerate, raise up.

stereotype *noun* *the stereotype of a sergeant major* conventional type, received idea, standardized image, hackneyed conception, cliché.

stereotype *verb* *stereotype librarians as being serious people* typecast, pigeon-hole, conventionalize, standardize, label, tag, categorize.

stereotyped *adjective* *stereotyped images of a woman's role* typecast, conventional, conventionalized, standardized, hackneyed, clichéd, banal, trite, platitudinous.

sterile *adjective* **1** *sterile women* infertile, barren, infecund, unprolific. **2** *sterile soil/land* infertile, unproductive, unfruitful, unyielding, arid, dry, barren, unprolific. **3** *sterile discussions* unproductive, unfruitful, fruitless, useless, futile, vain, idle, unsuccessful, ineffectual, ineffective, worthless, abortive, unprofitable, unrewarding. **4** *sterile conditions in the operating theatre* sterilized, germ-free, germless, antiseptic, disinfected, aseptic, uninfected, uncontaminated, unpolluted, pure, clean.
Opposites FERTILE; FRUITFUL; SEPTIC.

sterility *noun* **1** *the sterility of the woman* sterileness, infertility, barrenness, infecundity, unprolificness. **2** *the sterility of the soil/land* sterileness, infertility, non-productivity, unproductiveness, unfruitfulness, aridness, aridity. See STERILE 2. **3** *the sterility of the discussions* sterileness, unproductiveness, unfruitfulness, fruitlessness, uselessness, futility, unsuccessfulness, ineffectualness, ineffectiveness, worthlessness, abortiveness. See STERILE 3. **4** *the sterility of the operating theatre* sterileness, freedom from germs, asepticism, lack of infection/contamination/pollution, purity, cleanliness.

sterilize verb **1** *sterilize surgical instruments* disinfect, purify, fumigate. **2** *sterilize a woman* make infertile, make barren, make infecund. **3** *sterilize a man* make infertile, castrate, vasectomize. **4** *sterilize male animals* castrate, geld, neuter, emasculate; *inf.* fix. **5** *sterilize female animals* make infertile, spay; *inf.* fix.

sterling adjective **1** *have done sterling service* excellent, first-rate, first-class, exceptional, outstanding, splendid, superlative; *inf.* A1. **2** *sterling friends* genuine, real, true, reliable, dependable, trustworthy, faithful, loyal.

stern adjective **1** *stern treatment | a stern regime* strict, harsh, hard, severe, rigorous, stringent, rigid, exacting, demanding, cruel, relentless, unsparing, inflexible, unyielding, authoritarian, tyrannical, despotic, Draconian. **2** *look very stern | a stern expression* severe, forbidding, frowning, unsmiling, sombre, sober, austere. **Opposites** LENIENT; LAX; FRIENDLY.

stern noun *the stern of the ship* back, rear, tail, poop.

stew verb **1** *stew the meat* simmer, boil, casserole, fricassee. **2** *be stewing waiting for the results* be anxious, be nervous, be agitated, worry, fret, agonize, get in a panic, get worked up, get overwrought; *inf.* get in a flap, get in a tizzy, get in a tiz-woz. **3** *people stewing in the heat* swelter, be very hot, perspire, sweat; *inf.* be boiling.

stew noun **1** *make a beef stew* casserole, ragout, fricassee. **2** *get in a stew about the lost document* state of agitation, nervous state, fluster, panic, dither, pother; *inf.* flap, tizz, tiz-woz.

steward noun **1** *air stewards* cabin attendant, member of cabin staff. **2** *stewards at the horse show* official, functionary, organizer. **3** *club/bar stewards* caterer, catering manager/manageress, housekeeper, major-domo, butler. **4** *the steward of the estate* property manager, agent, bailiff, caretaker; *Scots* factor.

stick noun **1** *throw a stick for the dog | burn sticks and leaves from the garden* piece of wood, branch, twig, switch. **2** *old men leaning on sticks* walking stick, cane, crutch, staff, crook, alpenstock. **3** *sticks supporting plants* cane, pole, post, stake, upright. **4** *punish the boy with a stick* cane, birch, switch, rod. **5** *mug the old man with a stick* cosh, cudgel, truncheon, baton. **6** *get stick for his handling of the situation* criticism, abuse, blame, censure, reproach, reproof, condemnation. **7** *get stick from the headmaster* punishment, chastisement, discipline, beating. **the sticks** *bored with living in the sticks* remote area, rural districts, backwoods, hinterland, backwater; *inf.* the middle of nowhere, boondock.

stick verb **1** *stick a fork in the potato* thrust, push, insert, jab, poke. **2** *stick his head out the window* thrust, push, poke. **3** *a nail sticking into the tyre | a needle sticking into his finger* pierce, penetrate, puncture, prick, spear, stab. **4** *stick him through with a sword* stab, spear, run through, transfix, impale. **5** *stick the pictures to a sheet of paper* glue, paste, gum, tape, sell-

otape, fasten, attach, fix, pin, tack. **6** *events which stick in the mind* remain, stay, linger, dwell, lodge, persist, continue. **7** *the car stuck in the mud* become bogged down, become embedded, become lodged, become clogged up, be mixed, become immobilized, be unable to move. **8** *machines sticking* jam, become jammed, come to a standstill, stop, halt, come to a halt, cease to work, become inoperative. **9** *stick the books over there* put, set down, place, lay, deposit, drop, position, locate, site, plant; *inf.* plonk, stuff. **10** *make the accusation stick* be valid, be sound, be well founded, be well grounded, be convincing, be cogent, be persuasive, be relevant. **11** *she can't stick his behaviour* put up with, tolerate, bear, stand, take, abide, endure, stomach. **stick at** **1** *you'll have to stick at it to finish the job today* keep at, persist with, persevere with, work at; *inf.* put one's back into. **2** *he would stick at walking out* draw back from, recoil from, shrink from, balk at, demur, have scruples about. **stick by** *stick by his friend in his misfortune* stand by, be loyal to, remain faithful to, support, be supportive of, back, defend. **stick it out** *the work's hard but he'll stick it out* see it through, see it through to the end, last out, put up with it, endure it, grin and bear it, soldier on; *inf.* take it, hang in there, tough it out. **stick out** **1** *sculptures sticking out from the wall* stand out, jut out, project, extend, protrude, poke out, bulge. **2** *she stuck out in the crowd* stand out, be noticeable, be obvious, be obtrusive.

sticky adjective **1** *sticky tape* adhesive, adherent, gummy, gluey, tacky. **2** *sticky substances* gluey, treacly, glutinous, viscous, viscoid; *inf.* gooey. **3** *a sticky summer day* close, humid, muggy, clammy, sultry, sweltering, oppressive. **4** *a sticky situation* awkward, difficult, tricky, ticklish, delicate, thorny, touch-and-go, embarrassing; *inf.* hairy.

stiff adjective **1** *stiff cardboard/substance* rigid, inflexible, unyielding, inelastic, firm, hard, hardened, brittle. **2** *stiff muscles* unsupple, tight, tense, taut, aching, arthritic, rheumatic; *inf.* creaky. **3** *a stiff climb/task* difficult, hard, arduous, tough, laborious, exacting, demanding, formidable, challenging, tiring, fatiguing, exhausting, Herculean. **4** *a stiff penalty* severe, harsh, hard, stringent, rigorous, drastic, strong, heavy, Draconian. **5** *put up a stiff resistance* strong, vigorous, determined, resolute, dogged, tenacious, unflagging, stubborn, obdurate. **6** *a stiff occasion* formal, ceremonial, ceremonious, dignified, proper, decorous, pompous. **7** *stiff behaviour* formal, unrelaxed, prim, punctilious, chilly, cold; *inf.* starchy. **8** *a stiff drink* strong, potent, alcoholic. **9** *a stiff breeze* strong, vigorous, powerful, brisk, fresh. **Opposites** FLEXIBLE; SUPPLE; LENIENT; MILD.

stiffen verb **1** *the mixture needs time to stiffen* become stiff, thicken, set, jell, solidify, harden, congeal, coagulate. **2** *need something to stiffen their resolve* strengthen, harden, fortify, brace, steel, reinforce. **3** *his muscles have stiffened* tighten, become stiff, tense, become taut, begin to ache, become arthritic/rheumatic; *inf.* become creaky.

stifle verb **1** *stifle a yawn* smother, check, restrain, keep back, hold back, hold in, withhold, choke back, muffle, suppress, curb, silence, prevent. **2** *stifle a rebellion* suppress, quash, quell, put an end to, put down, stop, extinguish, stamp out, crush, subdue, repress. **3** *stifle the old lady with a pillow* suffocate, smother, asphyxiate, choke. **4** *it's stifling in here* suffocating, very hot, sweltering, airless, close.

stigma noun *the stigma formerly associated with illegitimacy* shame, disgrace, dishonour, slur, stain, taint.

still adjective **1** *completely still bodies | asked to be still* motionless, unmoving, without moving, immobile, unstirring, inert, lifeless, stock-still, stationary, static. **2** *the house was completely still at night* quiet, silent, hushed, soundless, sound-free, noiseless, undisturbed. **3** *a still evening* calm, mild, tranquil, peaceful, serene, restful, windless, wind-free, halcyon. **4** *a still pool/sea* calm, stagnant.
Opposites MOVING; NOISY; WINDY.

still noun *in the still of the night* quietness, quiet, silence, hush, soundlessness, noiselessness, calmness, calm, tranquillity, peace, peacefulness, serenity.

still adverb **1** *they are still here* at this time yet, up to this time, even now, until now. **2** *he was badly injured but he's still getting better* nevertheless, however, in spite of that, notwithstanding, for all that.

still verb **1** *try to still her fears* quiet, quieten, calm, settle, lull, pacify, soothe, allay, assuage, appease, silence, hush, subdue. **2** *the wind stilled* abate, die down, grow less, lessen, moderate, slacken, weaken.

stilted adjective **1** *a stilted manner | a stilted way of speaking* stiff, unnatural, wooden, forced, laboured, constrained, unrelaxed, awkward. **2** *stilted prose* pompous, pretentious, high-flown, high-sounding, grandiloquent, pedantic, bombastic.
Opposites NATURAL; SPONTANEOUS; UNPRETENTIOUS.

stimulant noun **1** *act as a stimulant to the system* tonic, restorative, reviver, energizer, excitant, analeptic; *inf.* pep pill, upper, pick-me-up, bracer. **2** *act as a stimulant to further economic growth* stimulus, incentive, impetus, fillip, spur. *See* STIMULUS.

stimulate verb *stimulate economic activity* act as a stimulus/incentive/impetus/fillip/spur to, encourage, prompt, spur on, activate, stir up, excite, whip up, kindle, incite, instigate, foment, fan.

stimulating adjective **1** *a stimulating drug* tonic, restoring, restorative, reviving, energizing, analeptic; *inf.* pick-me-up. **2** *a stimulating lecture* interesting, exciting, stirring, thought-provoking, inspiring, exhilarating, rousing, intriguing, provoking, provocative.
Opposites SEDATIVE; UNINTERESTING; BORING.

stimulus noun *act as a stimulus to economic growth* stimulant, incentive, fillip, spur, push, drive, encouragement, inducement, incitement, goad, jog, jolt; *inf.* shot in the arm.

sting noun **1** *get a sting from a nettle* prick, inflamed area, wound, injury. **2** *take the sting out of the burns* irritation, smarting, tingling, tingle, pain, hurt. **3** *the sting of unrequited love* pain, hurt, distress, anguish, agony, torture, torment. **4** *a sharp sting in his wit* sharpness, bite, edge, pungency, causticity, acrimony, malice, spite, venom. **5** *crooks bringing off a sting* swindle, fraud, cheating, fleecing; *inf.* rip-off. *See* STING verb 5.

sting verb **1** *stung by a nettle/jelly-fish* prick, wound, injure, hurt. **2** *wounds stinging from the antiseptic solution | eyes stinging in the smoke* smart, tingle, burn, be irritated by. **3** *parents stung by their son's treatment of them* hurt, wound, distress, grieve, vex, pain, anguish, torture, torment, harrow. **4** *stung to shout about his rudeness* provoke, incense, anger, annoy, vex, rouse, stir up, drive, spur on, goad, move, motivate. **5** *stung by the dishonest dealer* swindle, defraud, cheat, fleece, gull, overcharge; *inf.* do, rip off, take for a ride.

stingy adjective mean, miserly, parsimonious, niggardly, tight-fisted, cheese-paring, penny-pinching; *inf.* tight, cheap.
Opposites GENEROUS; LIBERAL; MAGNANIMOUS.

stink verb **1** *the rotten meat stinks* smell bad, give off a bad smell, reek; *inf.* smell to high heaven. **2** *his behaviour stinks* be very bad, be unpleasant, be nasty, be vile, be foul, be abhorrent, be despicable, be dishonest, be corrupt. **3** *his name stinks around here* be disreputable, be in disrepute, have a bad reputation, be in disgrace, be infamous, be tainted.

stink noun **1** *rotten meat giving off a stink* bad smell, foul smell, stench, reek, malodour, malodorousness. **2** *the parents raised a stink about the teacher's behaviour* row, fuss, trouble, to-do, commotion, outcry, uproar, brouhaha; *inf.* dust-up.

stint verb *not to stint on the wine* skimp on, limit, restrict, hold back on, be sparing with, be economical with, be frugal with, be mean with, be parsimonious with, be niggardly with; *inf.* be stingy with, be mingy with.

stipulate verb *stipulate a delivery date as part of the argument* specify, set down, lay down, state clearly, demand, require, insist upon, make a condition of, make a point of, make a precondition/proviso of.

stipulation noun *make several stipulations before signing the contract* specification, demand, requirement, condition, precondition, provision, proviso, prerequisite.

stir verb **1** *stir the mixture* mix, blend, beat, whip. **2** *the child stirred in his sleep* move, quiver, tremble, twitch. **3** *the wind stirring the leaves* move, disturb, agitate, rustle. **4** *refuse to stir from the fireside* move, move an inch, budge, get up, leave, depart from. **5** *everyone stirring early on Christmas Day* get up, get out of bed, rise, rouse oneself, bestir oneself, move about, be up and about, be active; *inf.* be up and doing, shake a leg, look lively. **6** *stir his imagination* stimulate, excite, rouse, awaken, waken, kindle, quicken, electrify, inspire. **7** *speakers stirring the men to action* stir up, rouse, incite, provoke, inflame, goad, spur, egg on, urge, encourage, motivate, drive, impel.

stir *noun their arrival caused quite a stir in the village* excitement, commotion, disturbance, fuss, uproar, to-do, bustle, flurry, ferment, brouhaha.

stirring *adjective a stirring tale of adventure* exciting, dramatic, thrilling, gripping, riveting, spirited, rousing, stimulating, moving, lively, animated, heady, passionate, impassioned.
Opposites BORING; PEDESTRIAN.

stitch *noun* **1** *get a stitch after running* sharp pain, stabbing pain, stab of pain, shooting pain, pang, twinge, spasm. **2** *decorate the cloth with fancy stitches* sewing stitch. *See table.*

stitch *verb* **1** *stitch the cloth* sew, baste, seam. **2** *stitch the tear* sew, sew up, repair, mend, darn. **stich up** *stitched up by his fellow criminals* betray, cheat, trick, deceive, hoodwink, defraud, cozen, swindle.

SEWING STITCHES

backstitch	lazy daisy stitch
blanket stitch	lock stitch
blind stitch	needlepoint
buttonhole stitch	petit point
chain stitch	running stitch
cross stitch	satin stitch
crow's foot	stay stitch
feather stitch	stem stitch
Florentine stitch	tack
French knot	tailor's tack
gros point	tent stitch
hemstitch	topstitch
herringbone stitch	whipstitch

stock *noun* **1** *a stock of goods for sale* store, supply, range, selection, assortment, variety, collection, quantity. **2** *run out of stock before Christmas* supplies, goods, merchandise, wares, items/articles for sale, commodities. **3** *lay in a stock of wood for the winter* store, supply, stockpile, reserve, reservoir, accumulation, pile, heap, load, hoard, amassment, cache. **4** *rolling stock* equipment, apparatus, machinery, implements, appliances. **5** *employed to look after the farm stock* farm animals, livestock, cattle, cow, beasts, herds, sheep, flocks, pigs. **6** *the stock of the business* capital, funds, assets. **7** *have stock in the company* shares, investment, holding, money. **8** *his stock in the company is rising* standing, status, reputation, repute, position. **9** *of good peasant stock* descent, line of descent, lineage, ancestry, extraction, family, parentage, relatives, pedigree, genealogy, strain, breed, background. **10** *stock for soup/stews* bouillon. **11** *the stock of a tree* trunk, tree-trunk, stalk, stem, caudex. **12** *the stock of an implement* handle, haft, grip, shaft, shank. *See* STOCKS. **in stock** *a range of goods always in stock* for sale, on sale, available. **take stock of** *take stock of the situation before proceeding* review, weigh up, appraise, make an appraisal of; *see how the land lies; inf.* size up.

stock *adjective* **1** *stock sizes of clothes* standard, regular, average, readily available, widely available. **2** *stock items in a kitchen cupboard* regular, common, customary, staple, basic, fundamental, necessary, essential, indispensable. **3** *stock responses to his requests | stock jokes* usual, routine, run-of-the-mill, commonplace, conventional, traditional, stereotyped, clichéd, hackneyed, overused, worn-out, banal, trite.
Opposites IRREGULAR; UNCOMMON; ORIGINAL.

stock *verb* **1** *shops stocking children's clothes* sell, trade in, deal in, market, handle, supply, keep. **2** *stock the factory with modern machinery* equip, fit, outfit, kit out, furnish, accoutre, supply, provide. **stock up 1** *stock up the shelves* fill, fill up, load, replenish. **2** *stock up with logs for the winter* get in supplies of, obtain a store of, buy up, collect, gather, accumulate, amass, lay in, put away, put down, deposit, store up, stockpile, hoard; *inf.* squirrel away, salt away.

stockings *plural noun* hosiery, hose, nylons.

stockpile *verb stockpile logs for the winter* collect, gather, accumulate, amass, pile up, store, lay in, put away, put down, deposit; *inf.* put away for a rainy day, squirrel away, salt away, stash.

stocks *plural noun a ship still on the stocks* supporting structure, support, framework, frame, timbers. **on the stocks** *the car he designed is still on the stocks* in preparation, under construction.

stock-still *adverb stand stock-still* motionless, unmoving, without moving, immobile, immobilized, inert.

stocky *adjective* heavy-set, thick-set, dumpy, stubby, stumpy, squat, chunky, solid, sturdy, mesomorphic.
Opposites SLENDER.

stodgy *adjective* **1** *stodgy food* heavy, solid, substantial, filling, starchy, leaden, indigestible. **2** *a stodgy young man* dull, uninteresting, boring, staid, sedate, stuffy; *inf.* fuddy-duddy. **3** *stodgy prose* dull, dull as ditchwater, uninteresting, boring, tedious, dry, wearisome, heavy-going, unimaginative, uninspired, monotonous, laboured, wooden, turgid.
Opposites LIGHT; INTERESTING; LIVELY.

stoical *adjective remain stoical in misfortune | stoical attitude to misfortune* impassive, dispassionate, unimpassioned, unemotional, self-controlled, self-disciplined, forbearing, patient, long-suffering, resigned, philosophical, fatalistic, imperturbable, calm, cool, unexcitable, unflappable, phlegmatic.
Opposites EMOTIONAL; IMPASSIONED; MELODRAMATIC.

stoicism *noun admire his stoicism in misfortune* impassivity, dispassion, self-control, self-discipline, forbearance, patience, long suffering, fortitude, endurance, resignation, acceptance, fatalism, philosophicalness, imperturbability, calmness, coolness, cool, phlegm.

stolid *adjective difficult to engage the interest of the stolid child* impassive, unemotional, apathetic, uninterested, unimaginative, indifferent, dull, stupid, bovine, lumpish, wooden, doltish, thick, dense.
Opposites EMOTIONAL; LIVELY; IMAGINATIVE.

stomach noun **1** *a pain in the stomach* abdomen, belly, paunch, potbelly; *inf.* tummy, gut, insides, pot, corporation, breadbasket. **2** *have no stomach for rich food* appetite, taste, hunger. **3** *have no stomach for the battle* appetite, inclination, desire, liking, fancy, mind, taste, fondness, relish, zest, gusto.

stomach verb **1** *unable to stomach rich food* eat, digest, swallow, find palatable. **2** *unable to stomach his arrogance* stand, put up with, bear, take, tolerate, abide, endure, suffer, swallow, submit to; *inf.* weather.

stone noun **1** *throwing stones on the road before* pebble, rock, boulder. *See table at* ROCK. **2** *an engagement ring set with three stones* precious stone, jewel, gem, brilliant; *inf.* rock. *See table at* GEM. **3** *erect a stone in his memory* tombstone, gravestone, headstone, memorial stone, monument. **4** *remove the stones from the fruit before cooking* kernel, pit, nut, seed, pip.

stony adjective **1** *stony ground* rocky, pebbly, gravelly, shingly, gritty, rough, hard. **2** *a stony stare* cold, chilly, frosty, icy, frigid, hard, stern, severe, rigid, fixed, expressionless, blank, poker-faced, deadpan, sphinxlike. **3** *a stony heart | a stony attitude to the poor* unfeeling, uncaring, unsympathetic, insensitive, callous, heartless, tough, unmoved, unemotional, dispassionate, unresponsive, stern, severe, harsh, hard, cruel, cold-hearted, merciless, pitiless, ruthless, unforgiving, inflexible, unbending, unyielding, adamant, obdurate. **Opposites** SMOOTH; FRIENDLY; SYMPATHETIC.

stooge noun **1** *the comedian's stooge* butt, foil. **2** *he gets his stooges to do all the work* dogsbody, underling, subordinate, assistant, deputy, right-hand man/woman, girl/man Friday; *inf.* sidekick, skivvy.

stoop verb **1** *stoop to pick something up* bend down, lean over, lean down, crouch down. **2** *stoop his head to get into the car* bend, bend down, bow, lower, duck. **3** *very tall people often stoop* walk with a stoop, be round-shouldered, hunch one's shoulders, bend one's head forward. **4** *never stoop to talk to her inferiors* condescend, deign, lower oneself to, humble oneself to, demean oneself to. **5** *refuse to stoop to crime* sink to, descend to, lower oneself to, demean oneself to, resort to.

stoop noun **1** *with a slight stoop of her head* bending, bow, lowering, ducking. **2** *have a scholarly stoop* round-shoulderedness, hunch, droop/sag of the shoulders.

stop verb **1** *stop the fight* bring to a stop, halt, bring to a halt, end, bring to an end, put an end to, finish, bring to a close, terminate, bring to a standstill, wind up, discontinue, cut short, interrupt, nip in the bud. **2** *unable to stop laughing* discontinue, cease from, refrain from, desist from, leave off, break off, quit, forbear from, abandon; *inf.* knock off, pack in. **3** *work has stopped for the day* come to a stop, come to a halt, end, come to an end, finish, come to a close, be over, cease, conclude, terminate, come to a standstill, pause. **4** *stop the crooks from getting away* prevent, hinder, obstruct, impede, block, check. **5** *stop their getaway flight* prevent, hinder, obstruct, impede,

hamper, block, check, curb, frustrate, thwart, foil, stall, restrain, bar; *inf.* put the kibosh on. **6** *stop up a leak* plug, seal, block, bung, staunch, stem. **7** *stop off/over at York on the way to London* break one's journey, stay, remain, sojourn, put up, lodge, rest. **Opposites** START; BEGIN; CONTINUE; EXPEDITE.

stop noun **1** *come to a stop* halt, end, finish, close, cessation, conclusion, termination, standstill, stoppage, discontinuation, discontinuance. **2** *there are ten stops on the bus route* stopping-place, halt, stage, fare stage, terminus, terminal, depot. **3** *stops on the railway line* stopping-place, station, halt, terminus, terminal, depot. **4** *put a stop at the end of the sentence* full stop, period, point. **5** *a stop in the leaking pipe* plug, bung, cork, stopper. **6** *aim for a stop at York* journey-break, break, stop-off, stopover, stay, sojourn, overnight, rest.

stopgap noun temporary substitute, substitution, fill-in, makeshift, improvisation, expedient, last resort.

stop-over noun *a stop-over halfway through the journey* stop, break, stop-off, stay. *See* STOP noun 6.

stoppage noun **1** *the stoppage of some forms of welfare benefit* stopping, halting, end, discontinuation, discontinuance, finish, cessation, termination. **2** *another stoppage at the factory* strike, walk-out, industrial action, shut-down. **3** *a stoppage in the pipe* blockage, obstruction, occlusion. **4** *a stoppage in the supply* obstruction, obstacle, impediment, check, snag. **5** *stoppages from their salaries* deduction, charge, subtraction.

stopper noun **1** *the stopper in a bottle* cork, lid, cap, top. **2** *put a stopper in the leak* stop, plug, bung, cork.

store noun **1** *a store of logs for the winter* supply, stock, stockpile, reserve, accumulation, pile, heap, load, amassment, cache, deposit, reservoir. *See* STORES. **2** *get supplies from the store* storeroom, storehouse, warehouse, repository, depository. **3** *build new houses and stores* shop, department store, chain store, supermarket, retail outlet, emporium. **set store by** think highly of, hold in regard, hold in high regard, hold in high esteem, admire, appreciate, value, prize, esteem.

store verb **1** *store food in case of a shortage* stock up with, get in supplies of, stockpile, collect, gather, accumulate, amass, lay in, put away, put down, deposit, hoard; *inf.* put away for a rainy day, squirrel away, salt away, stash. **2** *store furniture* put into storage, put in store. **Opposites** USE; DISCARD; SCRAP; JETTISON.

stores plural noun *get low on stores* supplies, provisions, rations, food, provender.

storm noun **1** *ships damaged in the storm | children soaked in the storm* gale, hurricane, cyclone, tempest, squall, cloudburst, downpour, torrent. **2** *a storm of protest at the decision* outcry, outburst, commotion, furore, brouhaha, clamour, tumult, row, disturbance, fight, trouble; *inf.* to-do, rumpus, dust-up. **3** *engage in a storm on the castle* assault, attack, offensive, onslaught, charge, raid, foray, sortie, siege.

4 *a storm of missiles* shower, spray, deluge, volley, salvo, discharge.

storm *verb* **1** *storm the castle* attack, conduct an offensive on, make an onslaught on, charge, rush, make a raid/foray/sortie on, take by storm. **2** *storm out of the room* charge, rush headlong, flounce, stake, stride, stamp; *inf.* stomp. **3** *storming at the children because of their behaviour* rage, rant, rave, rant and rave, fume, bellow, thunder, shout, fly into temper; *inf.* fly off the handle, blow one's top, blow up, raise the roof, raise hell.

stormy *adjective stormy weather | a stormy day* blustery, blustering, windy, gusty, squally, rainy, wild, tempestuous, turbulent.
Opposites CALM; STILL.

story *noun* **1** *have a story published | read the children a story* short story, tale, fairy tale, fable, myth, legend, anecdote, novel, novella, romance, narrative, chronicle; *inf.* yarn. *See table at* NOVEL. **2** *their stories of the accident did not tally* account, report, recital, record. **3** *the novel's complicated story* storyline, plot, plot development. **4** *journalists looking for a story* news item, news report, article, feature; *inf.* scoop. **5** *told a story when she was caught* lie, white lie, untruth, falsehood, fib, piece of fiction; *inf.* terminological inexactitude.

stout *adjective* **1** *stout people advised to lose weight* fat, fattish, plump, portly, tubby, obese, corpulent, rotund, big, heavy, thick-set, overweight, bulky, burly, brawny, fleshy; *inf.* beefy. **2** *a stout stick* strong, heavy, solid, substantial, sturdy. **3** *a stout defender of the city* stout-hearted, brave, courageous, valiant, valorous, gallant, fearless, unafraid, intrepid, bold, plucky, manly, heroic, lion-hearted, daring, tough, doughty; *inf.* gutsy, spunky. **4** *put up a stout resistance* firm, determined, resolute, staunch, steadfast, unyielding, unbending, unfaltering, unswerving, unwavering.
5 *launch a stout attack on the enemy* vigorous, forceful, spirited, energetic, strenuous.
Opposites THIN; COWARDLY; WEAK.

stout-hearted *adjective stout-hearted defenders of the city* stout, courageous, valiant, valorous, gallant, fearless, plucky. *See* STOUT 3.

stove *noun* oven, range, furnace, cooker.

stow *verb stow one's hand luggage in the rack* place, deposit, put, put away, pack, store, load, bundle, stuff. **stow away** *stow away on the yacht* travel secretly, hide, conceal oneself, secrete oneself.

straddle *verb* **1** *straddle the fence/horse* bestraddle, sit/stand astride. **2** *the town straddles the border* be situated on both sides of, lie on each side of. **3** *straddle an issue* be undecided about, be non-committal about, equivocate about, vacillate about, waver about, sit on the fence about, hem and haw about.

strafe *verb* **1** *the enemy strafing the city* bombard, bomb, shell, fire on, open fire on, shout at, machine-gun, rake with gun-fire. **2** *children getting strafed for their wicked behaviour* punish/chastise/discipline severely, reprimand/scold/upbraid harshly; *inf.* carpet.

straggle *verb* **1** *sheep struggling across the moors* wander, ramble, stray, roam, meander, rove, range, spread out. **2** *some of the runners are straggling* trail behind, fall behind, lag, string out, linger, loiter. **3** *hair straggling to her shoulders* grow untidily, be messy, be dishevelled, be unkempt.

straight *adjective* **1** *in a straight line/course* direct, undeviating, unswerving, uncurving, unbent, straight as an arrow. **2** *three straight wins* successive, consecutive, in a row, running, uninterrupted, solid, non-stop. **3** *Is the picture straight?* level, symmetrical, even, true, in line, aligned. **4** *get the room/things straight* in order, orderly, neat, tidy, spruce, shipshape, in place, organized, arranged, sorted out; *inf.* shipshape and Bristol fashion. **5** *a straight answer* direct, honest, faithful, sincere, frank, candid, forthright, straightforward, plain-spoken, plain-speaking, plain, matter-of-fact, outspoken, straight from the shoulder, unequivocal, unambiguous, unqualified, unmodified. **6** *incapable of straight thinking* logical, rational, sound, intelligent, unemotional, dispassionate. **7** *a straight and valued colleague* respectable, upright, upstanding, honourable, honest, sincere, decent, fair, just, righteous, right-minded, law-abiding, conventional, orthodox. **8** *straight spirits* unmixed, undiluted, unadulterated, pure, neat.
Opposites BENT; INDIRECT; ASKEW; EVASIVE.

straight *adverb* **1** *go straight there* directly, by a direct route, without deviating; without delay. **2** *tell them straight* straight out, directly, honestly, frankly, candidly, outspokenly, plainly, straight from the shoulder, with no holds barred, unequivocally, unambiguously; *inf.* pulling no punches. *See* STRAIGHT *adjective* 5. **3** *not thinking straight* logically, rationally, intelligently, unemotionally, dispassionately.
straight away, straightaway *the work must be done straight away* right away, immediately, at once, instantly, without delay, without hesitation, straight off; *inf.* pronto, PDQ (= pretty damned quickly). **straight out** *tell him straight out that he is disliked* straight, directly, honestly, frankly, candidly, outspokenly.

straighten *verb* **1** *straighten the carpet* make straight, adjust, arrange, put in order, make tidy, tidy up, neaten, put to rights. **2** *have her hair straightened* uncurl, untangle. **straighten out** *straighten out the mess his affairs are in* put in order, put right, sort out, clear up, tidy up, settle, resolve, regulate, rectify, disentangle, unsnarl. **straighten up** *she was bending down but she suddenly straightened up* stand up, stand up straight, stand upright, become erect, straighten one's back.

straightened *adjective live in straightened circumstances* poverty-stricken, poor, destitute, impoverished, penniless, impecunious, penurious, beggared, pauperized; *inf.* on one's uppers.

straightforward *adjective* **1** *a straightforward answer* straight, direct, honest, frank, candid, forthright, plain-speaking, unambiguous, straight from the shoulder. *See* STRAIGHT *adjective* 5. **2** *a straightforward task* uncomplicated, easy, simple, elementary, effortless, undemanding, unexacting, routine; *inf.* easy as falling off a log, easy as pie. **Opposites** EVASIVE; DEVIOUS; INDIRECT; COMPLICATED.

strain¹ *verb* **1** *strain a rope till it snaps* draw tight, tighten, make taut, tauten, stretch, extend, elongate, distend. **2** *strain a muscle* pull, wrench, twist, sprain, rick, wrick, injure, hurt, damage, weaken, impair. **3** *strain one's eyes by reading too much* | *strain every nerve* tax, overtax, exert to the limit, exert something excessively, overwork, push to the limit, fatigue, tire. **4** *strain to win* make every effort, make a supreme effort, strive one's utmost, push/drive oneself to the limit, struggle, labour; *inf.* pull out all the stops, go all out, give it one's all. **5** *strain at the rope* pull, tug, heave, haul, jerk; *inf.* yank. **6** *an account which strained the truth* distort, falsify, garble, misrepresent, invert, stretch, exaggerate, embroider, overdraw. **7** *his account strained the credulity of his listeners* tax, overtax, be too much for, go beyond the limit of, exceed the range/scope of, overstep. **8** *strain the coffee* sieve, filter, percolate. **9** *strain the mixture* sieve, sift, screen, riddle, separate. **10** *strain her to his bosom* clasp, press, clutch, embrace, hug, squeeze, enfold, envelop.

strain² *noun* **1** *the rope snapped under the strain* tightness, tautness, tension, tensity, distension. **2** *his injury is just a strain* | *suffer muscle strain* wrench, twist, sprain, rick. *See* STRAIN *verb* 2. **3** *the strain of his job* demands, exertions, burdens, pressure, stress, tension. **4** *suffer from strain* stress, pressure of work, tension, overwork, exhaustion, anxiety.

strain³ *noun* **1** *people coming from a hardy strain* stock, descent, lineage, ancestry, family, extraction, blood, breed. **2** *a new strain of flu* variety, kind, type, sort. **3** *a strain of madness in the family* trait, disposition, characteristic, tendency, susceptibility, proclivity, proneness, inclination. **4** *a strain of cruelty in an otherwise kindly man* streak, vein, element, strand, trace, indication, suggestion, suspicion. **5** *the speaker went on in the same strain for more than an hour* vein, way, tone, style, manner. **6** *the strains of a boys' choir* music, tone, melody, air, song. **7** *remember a strain of an old poem* snatch, line, snippet, fragment, scrap, bit.

strained *adjective* **1** *a strained smile/laugh* forced, artificial, unnatural, false, constrained, laboured, wooden, stiff, self-conscious. **2** *a strained silence* awkward, embarrassed, uneasy, uncomfortable, tense, unrelaxed. **3** *strained relations* | *relations between them are strained* under a strain, tense, troubled, uneasy, hostile. **Opposites** NATURAL; relaxed; FRIENDLY.

strainer *noun* *put the food through a strainer* sieve, colander, filter, sifter, screen, riddle.

strait *noun* *the boat crossing the strait* sound, narrows, channel, inlet, arm of the sea. *See* STRAITS.

strait-laced *adjective* puritanical, prudish, prim, proper, priggish, moralistic, narrow, narrow-minded, stuffy; *inf.* fuddy-duddy. **Opposites** PERMISSIVE; BROAD-MINDED.

straits *plural noun* *in dire straits* predicament, plight, difficulty, trouble, crisis, mess; *inf.* pretty kettle of fish, tight corner, hot water, jam, hole, scrape, stew.

strand¹ *noun* **1** *the strands of the wool/rope* thread, fibre, filament, length. **2** *curling strands of hair* lock, wisp, tress. **3** *the last volume drawing together the strands of the trilogy* element, component, strain, storyline, theme.

strand² *noun* *walk on the strand* shore, seashore, foreshore, beach, coast, seaside, waterfront.

stranded *adjective* **1** *left stranded when her purse was stolen* left helpless, without help/assistance, left penniless, in dire straits, in difficulties, left in the lurch, left high and dry, abandoned, forsaken. **2** *stranded ships* grounded, beached, shipwrecked, wrecked, marooned.

strange *adjective* **1** *he had a strange expression on his face* peculiar, odd, bizarre, unusual, atypical, abnormal, surprising, weird, funny, unfamiliar. **2** *a strange land* previously unencountered, unknown, unfamiliar. **3** *a strange phenomenon* inexplicable, anomalous, unexpected, extraordinary. **4** *he was strange to the business of window cleaning* unused to, inexperienced, unaccustomed, unfamiliar. **5** *strange people from across the sea* alien, foreign. **6** *his manner was strange* shy, distant, reserved, withdrawn, introverted. **Opposites** NORMAL; ORDINARY; FAMILIAR.

stranger *noun* **1** *he was a complete stranger to her* unknown person, alien. **2** *strangers not being welcome in the village* new person, new arrival, newcomer, incomer, foreigner. **a stranger to** *a stranger to the area* unfamiliar with, unacquainted with, unaccustomed to, new to, fresh to, unused to, inexperienced in, unpractised in, unversed in, unconversant with.

strangle *verb* **1** *he strangled his victim with a scarf* throttle, choke, strangulate, garrotte. **2** *strangle artistic expression* suppress, inhibit, repress, check, restrain, hold back, curb, stifle, gag.

strap *noun* *straps fastening the trunk* band, belt, thong, cord, tie.

strap *verb* **1** *strap the trunk with leather thongs* fasten, secure, tie, bind, lash, truss, pinion. **2** *strap her strained ankle* bind, bandage. **3** *strap the naughty children* flog, lash, whip, scourge, beat; *inf.* belt.

stratagem *noun* *only win by means of a stratagem* trick, ruse, plot, cunning/crafty plan, scheme, manoeuvre, plan, tactic, artifice, machination, wile, subterfuge, dodge, deception.

strategic *adjective* **1** *strategic schemes* tactical, diplomatic, politic, calculated, planned, plotted, cunning, wily. **2** *strategic bases in the war* crucial, key, vital, critical, essential, important.

strategy *noun* **1** *the government's economic strategy* policy, approach, programme, scheme, plan of action, master plan, schedule, blueprint, game plan. **2** *the general's strategy* art of war, martial art, military science, military tactics.

stratum *noun* **1** *the top stratum of rock* layer, tier, scum, vein, lode. **2** *belong to the same stratum of society* class, level, grade, status, station, gradation.

stray *verb* **1** *children straying from home | cows straying from the field* wander, roam, rove, go astray from. **2** *walkers straying over the hills* wander, roam, ramble, meander, drift, range, stroll, amble, saunter, straggle. **3** *stray from the point* digress from, wander from, deviate from, get off the subject of, get sidetracked from, go off at a tangent from, lose the thread of. **4** *good children who strayed in later life* go astray, go wrong, do wrong, stray from the straight and narrow, err, sin, transgress, go down the primrose path.

stray *noun* *give strays a home* homeless animal, stray dog/cat, homeless person, waif, foundling.

stray *adjective* **1** *a stray dog* strayed, gone astray, lost, homeless, wandering, vagrant, abandoned, unclaimed. **2** *a stray customer or two | a stray bullet* odd, random, isolated, scattered, occasional, incidental, accidental, chance, freak.

streak *noun* **1** *a streak of light in the dark sky* line, band, strip, stripe, slash, smear. **2** *a streak of cowardice in him* strain, vein, element, trace, touch, dash. **3** *a streak of lightning* bolt, flash, beam. **4** *streaks on the windows when he cleaned them* smear, smudge, mark. **5** *on a winning streak* spell, period, course, stretch, series.

streak *verb* **1** *a blue sky streaked with white* band, stripe, mark, slash, striate, fleck, daub, smear. **2** *dirty cloths streaking the glass* smear, smudge, mark. **3** *runners streaking past* race, rush, speed, dash, sprint, hurtle, scurry, fly, flee, flash, whistle, zoom, zip; *inf.* tear, whiz, go hell for leather.

stream *noun* **1** *mountain streams* river, brook, rivulet, rill, freshet; *dial.* beck; *Scots* burn; *Am.* creek. **2** *a stream of blood* flow, rush, gush, surge, jet, outpouring, efflux, current, cascade. **3** *people going with the stream* flow, current, tide, course, drift.

stream *verb* **1** *water streaming from the pipe | tears streaming down his face* flow, run, pour, course, spill, gush, surge, flood, cascade, well. **2** *wound streaming blood* emit, issue, shed, spill. **3** *hair/flags streaming in the breeze* flow, float, swing, flap, flutter. **4** *people streaming out of the building* surge, pour, crowd.

streamer *noun* flag, pennant, banner, standard, ensign, gonfalon.

streamlined *adjective* **1** *streamlined cars* smooth, sleek, elegant. **2** *streamlined production methods* efficient, smooth-running, well-run, modernized, rationalized, slick.

street *noun* **1** *lighted streets* road, thoroughfare. **2** *live in a suburban street* road, terrace, avenue, drive, row, crescent.

strength *noun* **1** *men of great physical strength | the strength to break the door* power, might, force, brawn, muscle, muscularity, sturdiness, robustness, vigour, toughness, stamina. **2** *regain his strength* health, robustness, healthiness, vigour. **3** *adversity gave him inner strength* fortitude, courage, bravery, pluck, firmness, stamina, backbone; *inf.* grit, guts. **4** *test the strength of the castle doors* solidity, toughness, resistance, impregnability. **5** *the strength of the feeling against him* force, forcefulness, intensity, vehemence, ardour, fervency. **6** *the strength of their argument* cogency, potency, weight, effectiveness, efficacy, soundness, validity. **7** *workers who are the strength of the firm* mainstay, chief support, tower of strength, anchor, foundation stone. **8** *the firm's reliability is its main strength* advantage, asset, strong point, forte. **9** *the strength of the workforce* size, extent, magnitude, bigness, largeness, greatness. **on the strength of** *he got the job on the strength of his qualifications* on the basis of, based on, because of, on the grounds of.
Opposites FRAILTY; INFIRMITY; WEAKNESS; FAILING.

strengthen *verb* **1** *strengthen children's bones* make strong, make stronger, give strength to, make healthy, nourish, build up. **2** *the wind strengthened* grow strong, grow stronger, gain strength, intensify, heighten. **3** *strengthen their determination* make stronger, give strength to, fortify, give a boost to, harden, stiffen, toughen, steel. **4** *his evidence strengthened their argument* give strength to, reinforce, support, back up, bolster, authenticate, confirm, substantiate, corroborate.

strenuous *adjective* **1** *a strenuous task* arduous, laborious, taxing, demanding, difficult, hard, tough, uphill, heavy, weighty, burdensome, exhausting, tiring, fatiguing. **2** *make strenuous efforts to reach the top* energetic, active, vigorous, forceful, strong, spirited, bold, determined, resolute, tenacious, earnest, keen, zealous.
Opposites EASY; EFFORTLESS; HALF-HEARTED.

stress *noun* **1** *the stress of his new job | suffer from stress* strain, pressure, tension, worry, anxiety. **2** *in times of stress* worry, anxiety, trouble, difficulty, distress, trauma. **3** *place stress on education* emphasis, priority, importance, weight, significance, value, worth, merit. **4** *place stress on the first syllable* emphasis, accent, accentuation. **5** *wire unable to bear stress* strain, tension, tensity, tightness, tautness, stretching.

stress *verb* **1** *stress the importance of education* lay stress on, emphasize, place emphasis on, give emphasis to, accentuate, underline, underscore, point up, highlight, spotlight, press home, dwell on, harp on, belabour. **2** *stress the first syllable* lay stress on, emphasize, place emphasis on, give emphasis to, place the accent on, accentuate. **3** *discover that the workers have been stressed for years* subject to stress/strain/tension, tax, overtax, pressurize, overwork, overstretch, overburden, push to the limit, push too far.

stretch *verb* **1** *the material stretches* be stretchy, be elastic, be tensile. **2** *stretch the piece of elastic/rope* extend, elongate, lengthen, expand, draw out, pull out. **3** *sweaters stretching in the wash* get larger, get bigger, enlarge, expand, pull out of shape. **4** *stretched a hand out* reach out, hold out, put forth, proffer, offer. **5** *stretch one's arms* unbend, extend, elongate. **6** *the forests stretched for miles* extend, spread,

unfold, cover, range. **7** *a job that will stretch her* be a challenge to, challenge, extend, tax, push to the limit. **8** *stretch the truth* strain, overstrain, exaggerate, overdraw, push too far. **9** *stretch out on the sofa* lie down, recline, sprawl, lounge.
Opposites SHORTEN; CONTRACT; WITHDRAW.

stretch noun **1** *stretches of forest* expanse, area, tract, extent, spread, sweep. **2** *a four-hour stretch* period, time, spell, term, space, run, stint.

strict adjective **1** *a strict interpretation of the rules* precise, exact, close, faithful, true, accurate, scrupulous, meticulous, conscientous, punctilious. **2** *a strict regime/upbringing* | *strict parents* stringent, rigorous, severe, harsh, hard, stern, authoritarian, rigid, narrow, austere, illiberal, inflexible, unyielding, uncompromising. **3** *in strict confidence* absolute, utter, complete, total, perfect. **4** *strict members of the religious sect* orthodox, fundamentalist.
Opposites LOOSE; MODERATE; LIBERAL; LENIENT.

stricture noun **1** *pass strictures on the children's behaviour* criticism, censure, blame, condemnation; *inf.* flak. **2** *be able to do what they like without strictures* restriction, limitation, control, constraint, restraint, curb, check. **3** *a stricture in the wind-pipe* narrowing, constriction, strangulation.

stride verb *stride along swinging their arms* step, pace, walk, stalk.

stride noun *take huge strides* long/large step, pace.

strident adjective *strident music/voices* harsh, raucous, rough, grating, discordant, rasping, jarring, shrill, loud, screeching, unmelodious, unmusical, stridulous, stridulant, stridulatory.
Opposites SOFT; MUSICAL; DULCET.

strife noun *a country suffering from industrial strife* conflict, friction, discord, disagreement, dissension, dispute, argument, quarrelling, wrangling, bickering, controversy, contention, ill feeling, hostility, animosity.
Opposites PEACE; HARMONY.

strike verb **1** *strike the gong at lunch-time* bang, beat, hit, pound, batter. **2** *strike the child for misbehaving* hit, slap, smack, beat, batter, thrash, thump, thwack, punch, cuff, box, knock, rap, buffet, smite, cane, lash, whip; *inf.* wallop, belt, tan someone's hide, clout, whack, bash, clobber, bop, biff, lambaste, sock, plug. **3** *the ship struck a rock* run into, knock into, bang into, bump into, smash into, collide with, be in collision with, dash against. **4** *strike the ball a good distance* hit, drive, propel; *inf.* swipe. **5** *strike his arm away* push, thrust, shove, force. **6** *strike a match* light, ignite. **7** *the enemy struck our army at dawn* attack, launch an attack upon, charge, make an assault on, assault, storm, set upon, fall upon. **8** *disease struck the town* | *disaster struck the family* hit, come upon, affect, afflict, smite. **9** *strike a balance* reach, achieve, arrive at, find, attain, effect. **10** *strike a bargain* agree on, come to an agreement on, settle on, sign, endorse, ratify, sanction. **11** *strike a dramatic pose* assume, adopt, take on, affect, feign.

12 *strike oil/gold* | *strike a new source of information* discover, find, come upon, light upon, chance upon, happen upon, stumble upon, unearth, uncover, turn up. **13** *an idea struck him* occur to, come to, come to the mind of, dawn on, hit. **14** *the house strikes me as unfriendly* seem, appear, impress, affect, have an impact on. **15** *workers striking for higher wages* go on strike, take industrial action, down tools, walk out. **16** *strike a tent* take down, pull down, knock down, level, take apart. **17** *strike a flag* lower, take down, let down, bring down. **18** *strike north* go, make one's way, set out, direct one's footsteps. **strike out** *strike out the disputed clause* delete, cross out, erase, rub out, obliterate.
strike up 1 *the band struck up* begin/start/commence playing, begin/start to play. **2** *he struck up an acquaintance with his fellow-passenger* begin, start, commence, embark on, set going, initiate.

strike noun **1** *kill the boy with one strike* hit, slap, smack, thump, thwack, punch, cuff, box, knock; *inf.* wallop, clout, whack, bop, biff, plug. *See* STRIKE *verb* 2. **2** *a lucky strike* discovery, find, unearthing, uncovering. **3** *killed during an enemy strike* air strike, air attack, attack, assault, bombing, blitz. **4** *workers on strike* | *declare a strike* industrial action, walk-out.

striking adjective **1** *a striking resemblance* noticeable, obvious, conspicuous, evident, visible, distinct, prominent, clear-cut, unmistakable, remarkable, extraordinary, incredible, amazing. **2** *a striking floral display* impressive, imposing, grand, splendid, magnificent, superb, marvellous, wonderful, dazzling; *inf.* great, smashing. **3** *married to a striking woman* attractive, good-looking, beautiful, glamorous, stunning, gorgeous.
Opposites INCONSPICUOUS; ORDINARY; unremarkable.

string noun **1** *tie the package with string* twine, cord, yarn, rope, cable, line. **2** *own a string of shops/houses* chain, series, succession. **3** *a string of people waiting to get in* queue, line, row, procession, file, column, stream, succession, sequence. **4** *a string of coloured beads* strand, necklace. **5** *the musician broke a string* guitar string, violin string; piano wire. *See table.*

string verb **1** *string decorations from the branches of the tree* hang, suspend, sling. **2** *string the washing line from pole to pole* stretch, sling, run, fasten, tie, secure together. **3** *string the beads* thread. **string along 1** *she won't marry him — she's just stringing him along* make use of, take advantage of, mislead, deceive, make a fool of, fool, lead up the garden path. **2** *string along with them for want of anything else to do* go along, go with, accompany, join up with. **string out 1** *string out the seats across the lawn* spread out, space out, set apart, place at intervals. **2** *speakers stringing out their material as much as possible* draw out, stretch, protract, spin out. **string up** *his fellow prisoners decided to string him up* hang, lynch; *inf.* make swing.

stringent adjective **1** *a stringent ban on smoking* strict, firm, rigid, rigorous, severe, harsh, tough, tight, exacting, demanding, inflexible, hard and fast, uncompromising. **2** *stringent economic conditions* difficult, tight, hard, harsh,

tough.
Opposites LENIENT; MILD; EASY.

strings *plural noun she got the job but there were strings attached* conditions, qualifications, provisions, provisos, stipulations, contingencies, limitations.

stringy *adjective* **1** *stringy hair* lank, straggly, straggling. **2** *stringy young men* lanky, gangling, spindly, skinny, wiry. **3** *stringy meat* tough, fibrous, gristly, leathery.

strip *verb* **1** *they stripped and got into dry clothes* strip naked, undress, take one's clothes off, remove one's clothes, disrobe. **2** *strip the soaking wet child* undress, unclothe. **3** *strip the bark from the tree* peel, pare, skin, excoriate. **4** *strip paint from the doors* remove, take off, peel off, flake off. **5** *strip him of his rank/honours* take away, dispossess of, deprive of, confiscate. **6** *strip a machine* dismantle, take to pieces, take to bits, take apart. **7** *the burglars stripped the house* clear out, empty out, clean out, plunder, ransack, rob.

strip *noun strips of paper* piece, bit, band, belt, ribbon, stripe, bar, swathe, slip, fillet.

stripe *noun a white stripe on a black background* strip, band, belt, bar.

striped *adjective wear a striped dress* stripy, banded, barred, striated, variegated.

stripling *noun his father died when he was just a stripling* youth, adolescent, youngster, boy, lad, teenager, child, juvenile, minor, young man; *inf.* kid, young'un.

strive *verb* **1** *strive to succeed* try, try hard, attempt, endeavour, make an effort, make every effort, exert oneself, do one's best, do all one can, do one's utmost, labour, toil, strain, struggle, bend over backwards; *inf.* go all out, give it one's best shot. **2** *had to strive all his life against poverty/oppression* struggle, fight, battle, combat, contend with, grapple with.

stroke *noun* **1** *kill him with one stroke* blow, hit, slap, smack, thump, thwack, punch, cuff, box, knock, rap, buffet, smite; *inf.* wallop, clout, whack, bop, biff. **2** *swimming/rowing strokes* movement, action, motion. **3** *a stroke of genius/diplomacy* accomplishment, achievement, feat, attainment, coup. **4** *with one stroke of the pen/brush* movement, action, mark, line. **5** *put the finishing strokes to the plan* touch, detail, bit, addition. **6** *hear five strokes of the church bell* striking, peal, ring, knell, ding-dong, boom.

7 *in hospital since he had a stroke* thrombosis, embolism, cerebral vascular accident, CVA, seizure, shock, apoplexy.

stroke *verb stroke the cat* caress, fondle, pat, touch, rub, massage, soothe.

stroll *verb stroll along in the sunshine* saunter, amble, wander, meander, ramble, dawdle, promenade, go for a walk, take a walk, stretch one's legs, take the air; *inf.* mosey along.

stroll *noun go for a stroll in the sunshine* saunter, walk, amble, wander, turn, airing, constitutional, promenade, perambulation.

strong *adjective* **1** *strong men lifting heavy weights* powerful, mighty, brawny, muscular, well-built, strapping, sturdy, burly, robust, vigorous, tough, rugged, stalwart, hardy, lusty, Herculean, strong as an ox/horse/lion. **2** *invalids becoming strong again* healthy, well, robust, vigorous, hale and hearty. **3** *strong enough to refuse the blackmailer's demands* courageous, brave, plucky, firm, resolute, strong-minded; *inf.* gutsy. **4** *nervous of strong women* determined, forceful, high-powered, self-assertive, tough, formidable, aggressive, redoubtable. **5** *strong castle doors* solid, well-built, heavy, tough, secure, well-fortified, well-defended, well-protected, impregnable, impenetrable. **6** *strong material* heavy-duty, solid, sturdy, durable, hard-wearing, long-lasting, enduring. **7** *a strong interest in local history* keen, eager, deep, acute, dedicated, passionate, fervent, zealous. **8** *arouse strong feelings against him* forceful, intense, vehement, passionate, fervent. **9** *a strong supporter of the local team* keen, eager, enthusiastic, dedicated, staunch, loyal, steadfast, passionate, fierce, fervent. **10** *a strong argument* powerful, cogent, potent, weighty, compelling, convincing, plausible, effective, efficacious, sound, valid, well-founded. **11** *a strong resemblance* marked, pronounced, distinct, definite, clear-cut, obvious, evident, unmistakable, notable, remarkable. **12** *strong colours* deep, intense, vivid, graphic. **13** *in strong light* bright, brilliant, intense, radiant, gleaming, dazzling, glaring. **14** *strong measures required to reduce crime* firm, energetic, active, forceful, severe, drastic, extreme, Draconian. **15** *strong coffee* concentrated, undiluted, highly flavoured. **16** *strong drink* alcoholic, spiritous, intoxicating, heady. **17** *strong cheese/garlic/sauces* highly

---

STRINGED INSTRUMENTS

acoustic	bass viol	gusli	mandolin	vina
guitar	bouzouki	harp	psaltery	viol
aeolian/wind	cello	Hawaiian	rebec	viola
harp	Celtic harp	guitar	saz	viola bastarda
archlute	chitarrone	hurdy-gurdy	sitar	viola da
balalaika	classical	kanoon	steel guitar	gamba
banjo	guitar	kantele	steel-string	viola d'amore
banjolele	contrabass	kithara	guitar	violetta
banjolin	double bass	electric	theorbo-lute	violin
banjulele	fiddle	guitar	twelve-string	violoncello
bass guitar	gamba	lute	guitar	violone
bass lute	guitar	lyre	ukulele	zither

flavoured, sharp, pungent, biting, spicy.
Opposites WEAK; FRAIL; TIMID; MILD.

strongbox *noun put the jewels in the strongbox* safe, safe-deposit box, vault.

stronghold *noun* **1** *launch an assault on the enemy stronghold* fortress, fort, castle, keep, citadel, fastness. **2** *a conservative stronghold at the last election* bastion, centre, refuge, hotbed.

strong-minded *adjective strong-minded enough to give up smoking* determined, firm, resolute, resolved, self-disciplined, uncompromising, unyielding, unbending.

strong-willed *adjective too strong-willed to take others' advice* determined, resolute, stubborn, obstinate, headstrong, self-willed, inflexible, intractable, recalcitrant, refracting.

structure *noun* **1** *wooden structures* building, edifice, construction, erection, pile, complex. **2** *the structure of the body/firm/sentence* construction, form, configuration, conformation, shape, constitution, composition, make-up, organization, system, arrangement, design, frame, framework,

structure *verb structure the timetable to suit the students* construct, build, put together, assemble, shape, design, organize, arrange, order.

struggle *verb* **1** *struggle to obtain power* strive, try hard, endeavour, make every effort, exert oneself, do one's best, do all one can, do one's utmost, battle, labour, toil, strain, bend over backwards; *inf.* go all out, give it one's best shot. **2** *boys struggling with each other* fight, grapple, wrestle, scuffle, brawl; *inf.* scrap. **3** *rivals struggling with each other for supremacy* fight, compete, contend, vie, clash, lock horns, cross swords. **4** *struggling up the hill* make one's way with difficulty, battle, battle one's way, fight one's way.

struggle *noun* **1** *his struggles to obtain power* striving, battle, endeavour, effort, exertion, labour, toiling, pains. **2** *boys engaging in a struggle in the playground* fight, wrestling match, wrestling-bout, scuffle, brawl, tussle; *inf.* scrap, set-to, dust-up. **3** *opposing armies engaged in a struggle* battle, fight, combat, conflict, contest, hostilities, clash, skirmish, brush. **4** *a struggle on the committee for supremacy* battle, fight, competition, contention, vying, rivalry. **5** *a struggle just to survive* battle, fight, trial, labour, problem, trouble; *inf.* grind, hassle.

strumpet *noun* **1** *earn a living as a strumpet* prostitute, sex worker, call-girl, streetwalker; *derog.* harlot, whore; *derog. inf* tart, hooker. **2** *the nobleman's strumpet* mistress, paramour, kept woman, concubine, courtesan.

strut *verb strutting around in his new suit* swagger, prance, parade, flounce, peacock; *Am.* sashay.

stub *noun* **1** *cigarette stubs* end, butt, tail-end, remnant; *inf.* dog-end, fag-end. **2** *ticket stubs* counterfoil. **3** *the stub of a tree* stump, remnant.

stubborn *adjective* obstinate, headstrong, wilful, strong-willed, pig-headed, mulish, dogged, persistent, adamant, inflexible, uncompromis-

ing, unbending, unyielding, unmalleable, obdurate, intractable, refractory, recalcitrant, contumacious.
Opposites COMPLIANT; DOCILE; MALLEABLE.

stubby *adjective clothes making her look stubby* dumpy, squat, stumpy, stocky, chunky, thickset, chubby.

stuck *adjective* **1** *posters stuck to the wall* glued, fixed, fastened. **2** *stuck in the mud* immovable, immobile, fast, fixed, rooted. **3** *she cannot solve the problem – she's stuck* baffled, beaten, stumped, at a loss, perplexed, nonplussed, at one's wits ends; *inf.* up against a brick wall. **get stuck into** *get stuck into some work* get down to, make a start on, make a beginning on, set about, tackle. **stuck on** *he's stuck on the new girl* attracted to, infatuated with, keen on, enthusiastic about, fond of, in love with, obsessed by; *inf.* mad about, wild about, hung up on. **be stuck with** *he was stuck with his young sister for the day* left with, made responsible for, lumbered with.

stuck-up *adjective* conceited, proud, arrogant, haughty, condescending, disdainful, patronizing, snobbish; *inf.* high-and-mighty, snooty, uppity, uppish, big-headed, swollen-headed, toffee-nosed, hoity-toity.
Opposites MODEST; HUMBLE; UNASSUMING.

student *noun* **1** *college students* undergraduate. **2** *students at the high school* pupil, schoolboy, schoolgirl. **3** *nursing students on the wards* trainee, apprentice, probationer.

studied *adjective with studied indifference* deliberate, wilful, conscious, calculated, purposeful, studious, contrived, affected, forced, feigned, artificial.
Opposites UNPREMEDITATED; NATURAL; SPONTANEOUS.

studio *noun the artist's studio* workshop, workroom, atelier.

studious *adjective* **1** *a studious pupil* scholarly, academic, intellectual, bookish, book-loving, serious, earnest. **2** *the studious checking of detail* diligent, careful, attentive, industrious, assiduous, painstaking, thorough, meticulous, punctilious, zealous, sedulous. **3** *with studious indifference* deliberate, wilful, conscious, calculated, purposeful, contrived. *See* STUDIED.
Opposites IDLE; CARELESS; NEGLIGENT.

study *noun* **1** *a life devoted to study* learning, scholarship, education, academic work, research, book work, reading; *inf.* swotting, cramming. **2** *make a study of rural transport* investigation, inquiry, research, examination, analysis, review, survey, scrutiny. **3** *writing in his study* office, workroom, studio, library. **4** *write a study on/of Shakespeare's late plays* paper, work, essay, review. **in a brown study** lost in thought, in a reverie, thinking, reflecting, pondering, contemplating, deliberating, ruminating.

study *verb* **1** *study hard before the exams* apply oneself, revise, burn the midnight oil; *inf.* swot, cram, mug up. **2** *study history* learn, read up on, read, work at; *inf.* mug up on. **3** *study the effects of sleeplessness* investigate, inquire into, research, conduct research into, look into, examine, analyse, review, survey, conduct a survey of, scrutinize. **4** *study the suspect's movements* watch, keep watch on, look at, observe, keep an eye on, keep under surveillance.

stuff noun **1** *make out of hard-wearing stuff* material, fabric, matter, substance. **2** *get rid of the stuff in the hall* things, objects, articles, items. **3** *leave your stuff in the left-luggage office* things, luggage, baggage, belongings, possessions, goods, goods and chattels, paraphernalia. **4** *know one's stuff* facts, information, data, subject, discipline; *inf.* onions. **stuff and nonsense** nonsense, rubbish, twaddle, balderdash, bunkum; *inf.* poppycock, rot, tommyrot, tripe, bunk, piffle, bosh.

stuff verb **1** *stuff a pillow* fill, pack, pad. **2** *too much furniture stuffed into the room* pack, load, cram, squeeze, crowd, stow, press, force, compress, jam, wedge. **3** *stuff the money into his wallet* thrust, shove, push, ram. **4** *stuff themselves with turkey* fill, gorge, overindulge, satiate; *inf.* make a pig of oneself. **5** *his nostrils are stuffed because of the cold* block, stop up, bung up, obstruct, choke.

stuffing noun **1** *stuffing for cushions* filling, filler, packing, padding, wadding. **2** *stuffing for the duck* filling, forcemeat, farcemeat, farce.

stuffy adjective **1** *a stuffy atmosphere* airless, close, muggy, fuggy, stifling, suffocating, musty, stale. **2** *a stuffy young man* dull, boring, dreary, staid, sedate, stiff, formal, pompous, starchy, prim, priggish, strait-laced, conventional, conservative, stodgy; *inf.* fuddy-duddy, square. **3** *a stuffy nose* stuffed-up, blocked, bunged-up.
Opposites AIRY; EXCITING; INFORMAL.

stultify verb **1** *stultify their efforts to escape* thwart, frustrate, foil, impede, obstruct, hamper, suppress, repress, nullify, negate. **2** *a mind stultified by a boring job* dull, numb, benumb, stupefy, make bored.

stumble verb **1** *stumble and fall* trip, lose one's balance, slip. **2** *drunks stumbling home* blunder, lumber, lurch, stagger, reel. **3** *stumble a little when giving her speech* stammer, stutter, hesitate, falter; *inf.* fluff one's lines. **stumble upon** *stumble upon an unpublished work of the novelist* chance upon, happen upon, light upon, hit upon, come across, run across, find, discover, encounter.

stump noun **1** *a tree stump* end, stub, remnant, remains. **2** *a pencil stump* end, tail-end, butt, remnant.

stump verb **1** *the last question stumped him* baffle, be too much for, put at a loss, nonplus, mystify, outwit, foil, perplex, puzzle, confound, bewilder; *inf.* flummox, stymie. **2** *stumping around in a bad temper* clomp, clump, stamp, stomp, lumber, blunder. **stump up** *stump up his share of the bill* pay up, pay, hand over, part with, contribute, donate; *inf.* fork out, shell out, come across with, cough up, chip in.

stun verb **1** *the blow stunned him* daze, stupefy, knock senseless, knock unconscious, knock out, lay out, knock stupid. **2** *stunned by the news of his death* shock, astound, dumbfound, stupefy, overwhelm, overcome, overpower, devastate, stagger, amaze, astonish, take one's breath away, confound, bewilder, confuse; *inf.* flabbergast, knock for six, hit one like a ton of bricks.

stunning adjective **1** *a stunning range of electronic equipment* impressive, imposing, remarkable, extraordinary, staggering, incredible, amazing, astonishing, marvellous, splendid; *inf.* mind-boggling, mind-blowing. **2** *looking stunning in a new evening dress* sensational, ravishing, dazzling, wonderful, marvellous, magnificent, glorious, exquisite, impressive, splendid, beautiful, lovely; *inf.* gorgeous, out of this world, fabulous, smashing.
Opposites ORDINARY; RUN-OF-THE-MILL; AVERAGE.

stunt verb *stunt the child's growth* retard, slow, impede, hamper, hinder, check, curb, restrict, arrest, stop.

stunt noun *children amazed at the acrobat's stunts* feat, exploit, trick, *tour de force*, act, action, deed.

stunted adjective *a stunted tree* dwarf, dwarfish, undersized, diminutive, tiny, small, little, baby.

stupefaction noun **1** *stupefaction caused by a blow to the head* daze, senselessness, state of unconsciousness, insensibility, oblivion, blackout, coma. **2** *his stupefaction at the news of his redundancy* shock, devastation, amazement, astonishment, bewilderment, confusion.

stupefy verb **1** *a boxer stupefied by the first blow* stun, daze, knock senseless, knock unconscious, knock out, lay out. **2** *stupefied by the news of his redundancy* stun, shock, astound, dumbfound, overwhelm, shake, devastate, stagger, amaze. See STUN 2.

stupendous adjective **1** *a stupendous achievement* amazing, astounding, astonishing, extraordinary, remarkable, wonderful, prodigious, phenomenal, staggering, breathtaking; *inf.* fantastic, mind-boggling, mind-blowing. **2** *a stupendous beast* colossal, immense, vast, gigantic, massive, huge, enormous, mighty.
Opposites RUN-OF-THE-MILL; ORDINARY; SLIGHT.

stupid adjective **1** *a stupid fellow* unintelligent, foolish, dense, brainless, mindless, dull-witted, dull, slow-witted, slow, duncelike, doltish, simple-minded, half-witted, gullible, naive; *inf.* thick, dim, dumb, dopey, dozy, crazy, moronic, imbecilic, cretinous. **2** *stupid error* foolish, silly, unintelligent, idiotic, brainless, mindless, crackbrained, nonsensical, senseless, irresponsible, unthinking, ill-advised, ill-considered, inept, unwise, injudicious, indiscreet, short-sighted, inane, absurd, ludicrous, ridiculous, laughable, fatuous, asinine, pointless, meaningless, futile, fruitless, mad, insane, lunatic; *inf.* crazy, cock-eyed. **3** *knocked stupid by the blow* dazed, stupefied, unconscious.
Opposites INTELLIGENT; SENSIBLE; PRUDENT; CONSCIOUS.

stupidity noun **1** *the unbelievable stupidity of the fellow* lack of intelligence, unintelligence, foolishness, denseness, brainlessness, mindlessness, dull-wittedness, dullness, slow-wittedness, slowness, doltishness; *inf.* thickness, dimness, dumbness, dopiness, doziness, craziness. *See* STUPID 1. **2** *the stupidity of his actions* foolishness, folly, silliness, idiocy, brainlessness, senselessness, irresponsibility, injudiciousness, ineptitude, inaneness, inanity, absurdity, ludicrousness, ridiculousness, fatuousness, fatuity, asininity, pointlessness, meaningfulness, futility, fruitlessness, madness, insanity, lunacy; *inf.* craziness. *See* STUPID 2.

stupor *noun in a drunken stupor* daze, state of stupefaction/senselessness/unconsciousness, insensibility, oblivion, coma, black-out.

sturdy *adjective* **1** *sturdy young men* well-built, well-made, muscular, athletic, strong, strapping, brawny, powerfully built, powerful, solid, substantial, robust, vigorous, tough, hardy, stalwart, mighty, lusty. **2** *put up a sturdy resistance* strong, vigorous, stalwart, firm, determined, resolute, tenacious, staunch, steadfast, unyielding, unwavering, uncompromising.
Opposites PUNY; FRAIL; WEAK.

stutter *verb stutter nervously as she gave the speech* stammer, stumble, speak haltingly, hesitate, falter, splutter.

style *noun* **1** *an unusual style of house* kind, type, variety, sort, design, pattern, genre. **2** *try to copy the style of her favourite novelist* technique, method, methodology, approach, manner, way, mode, system. **3** *launch the new product in/with style* stylishness, smartness, elegance, polish, suaveness, urbanity, chic, flair, dash, panache, élan; *inf.* pizzazz, ritziness. **4** *used to living in style* comfort, elegance, chic, affluence, wealth, luxury. **5** *styles popular in the 1920s* fashion, trend, vogue, mode. **6** *criticize both the content and style of the novel* mode of expression, phraseology, wording, language.

style *verb* **1** *style the clothes to suit a warm climate* design, fashion, tailor, make, produce. **2** *he styled himself professor* designate, call, term, name, entitle, dub, address, denominate, label, tag.

stylish *adjective* **1** *stylish clothes* fashionable, smart, elegant, chic, modish, à la mode, voguish, modern, up-to-date; *inf.* trendy. **2** *a stylish dresser* fashionable, smart, elegant, chic; *inf.* dressy, trendy, natty, classy, nifty, ritzy, snazzy, snappy, with it.
Opposites UNFASHIONABLE; DOWDY.

suave *adjective* smooth, smooth-tongued, glib, bland, sophisticated, urbane, worldly, charming, polite, civil, courteous, affable, tactful, diplomatic, civilized, polished, worldly.
Opposites UNSOPHISTICATED; DISCOURTEOUS; ROUGH.

subconscious *adjective subconscious images/ fears* subliminal, latent, suppressed, repressed, hidden, underlying, innermost, deep, intuitive, instinctive.

subdue *verb* **1** *subdue the rebel forces* conquer, defeat, vanquish, get the better of, overpower, overcome, overwhelm, subjugate, master, gain the upper hand at, triumph over, crush, quash, quell, tame, humble, bring to his/her knees, hold in check. **2** *subdue one's desire to hit him* control, curb, restrain, check, hold back,

inhibit, rein in, repress, suppress, stifle.
Opposites AROUSE; INCITE; PROVOKE.

subdued *adjective* **1** *subdued lighting* dim, muted, toned down, softened, soft, lowered, shaded, low-key, subtle, unobtrusive. **2** *a subdued atmosphere in the hall* quiet, hushed, noiseless, soundless, silent, still, calm. **3** *children seeming very subdued* low-spirited, downcast, dejected, depressed, down in the mouth, restrained, repressed, inactive, spiritless, lifeless, dull, passive, unexcited, unemotional, unresponsive.
Opposites BRIGHT; NOISY; LIVELY.

subject *noun* **1** *the subject of the talk/discussion* subject matter, topic, theme, question, substance, gist, text, thesis. **2** *subjects studied at university* branch of study, branch of knowledge, course of study, course, discipline. **3** *a suitable subject for hypnosis* case, client, patient, participant; *inf.* guinea pig. **4** *his disappearance was the subject of much speculation* occasion, basis, grounds, source. **5** *a British subject* citizen, national. **6** *the king's subjects* liege, liegeman, subordinate, underling, vassal.

subject *adjective* **subject to** **1** *the house is yours, subject to the contract being signed* conditional upon, contingent upon, dependent on. **2** *children subject to colds in the winter* susceptible to, liable to, prone to, apt/likely to suffer from, in danger of, vulnerable to. **3** *subject to the laws of the land* bound by, constrained by, answerable to, accountable to.

subject *verb subject prisoners of war to torture* submit, put through, expose to, lay open to, treat one to.

subjective *adjective present a highly subjective view of the situation* personal, personalized, individual, biased, prejudiced, bigoted.
Opposites OBJECTIVE; IMPARTIAL.

subjugate *verb subjugate a people* gain mastery over, gain ascendancy over, gain control of, bring one to his/her knees, bring to heel, bring under the yoke, conquer, vanquish, defeat, crush, quell, quash, overpower, overcome, subdue, tame, break, humble, tyrannize, oppress, enslave.

sublime *adjective* **1** *sublime devotion/beauty* noble, exalted, lofty, awe-inspiring, majestic, imposing, glorious, supreme, grand, great, virtuous, high-principled. **2** *a sublime meal* excellent, outstanding, first-rate, first-class, superb, perfect, ideal, wonderful, marvellous; *inf.* fantastic, fabulous, fab. **3** *a sublime lack of concern for the truth* supreme, total, complete, utter, arrogant.

submerge *verb* **1** *watch the submarines submerging* go under water, dive, sink, plummet. **2** *submerge the dress in soapy water* immerse, dip, plunge, duck, dunk. **3** *flood water submerged the streets* flood, inundate, deluge, engulf, swamp, overflow. **4** *submerged in a backlog of correspondence* overwhelm, inundate, deluge, swamp, bury, engulf. **5** *submerge his true feelings* hide, conceal, veil, cloak, repress, suppress.
Opposites SURFACE.

submission *noun* **1** *despise their submission to his demands* yielding, capitulation, agreement, acceptance, consent, accession, compliance. *See* SUBMIT 1. **2** *the submission of our army to the enemy forces* surrender, yielding, laying down one's arms. *See* SUBMIT 2. **3** *resent their submission to discipline* observance, adherence, regulation, subjection. *See* SUBMIT 3. **4** *the submission of a planning proposal* presentation, presenting, proffering, tendering, proposal, proposing, tabling, introduction. *See* SUBMIT 4. **5** *reject his submission for planning permission* presentation, tender, proposal, suggestion. **6** *the submission of his claim* sending in, entry, referral. *See* SUBMIT 5. **7** *accept his submission that his client was innocent* argument, assertion, contention, statement, averment, claim. **8** *he expects submission from women* submissiveness, yielding, compliance, malleability, acquiescence, tractability, manageability, unassertiveness, non-resistance, passivity, obedience, biddability, dutifulness, docility, meekness, patience, resignation, humility, self-effacement, deference, subservience, obsequiousness, servility, subjection, self-abasement; *inf.* boot-licking.

submissive *adjective* *he expects women to be submissive* yielding, compliant, malleable, acquiescent, accommodating, tractable, manageable, unassertive, non-resisting, passive, obedient, biddable, dutiful, docile, meek, patient, resigned, subdued, humble, self-effacing, deferential, obsequious, servile, self-abasing; *inf.* boot-licking.
Opposites HEADSTRONG; OBSTINATE; INTRACTABLE.

submit *verb* **1** *refuse to submit to his demands* give in to, yield to, give way to, bow to, capitulate to, defer to, agree to, accept, consent to, accede to, acquiesce in, comply with, conform to. **2** *submit to the enemy forces* surrender to, give in to, yield to, lay down one's arms to, raise/show the white flag to, knuckle under to, humble oneself to, bend the knee to. **3** *submit to discipline* observe, adhere, abide by, be governed by, be regulated by, be subject to. **4** *submit a planning proposal* put forward, present, proffer, tender, advance, propose, suggest, table, introduce, move. **5** *submit a claim* put in, send in, hand in, enter, refer. **6** *submit that his client was innocent* argue, assert, contend, state, claim, aver, propound.

subnormal *adjective* **1** *subnormal temperatures* below normal, below average, too low, very low. **2** *educationally subnormal | subnormal pupils* slow, retarded, backward, of low intelligence.

subordinate *adjective* **1** *his subordinate officers* lower-ranking, junior, lower, lesser, inferior. **2** *subordinate issues* lesser, minor, secondary, subsidiary, ancillary, auxilliary, subservient.
Opposites SUPERIOR; MAJOR; CENTRAL.

subordinate *noun* *be patronizing to his subordinates* junior, assistant, second, deputy, aide, subaltern, underling, inferior, second fiddle; *inf.* sidekick.

sub rosa *adverb* *the discussion was sub rosa* in secret, secret, private, in confidence, confidential, behind closed doors, in camera.

subscribe *verb* **1** *subscribe to several learned journals* pay a subscription to, buy regularly,

take regularly, contract to buy. **2** *subscribe to several charities* make a subscription to, make a donation to, donate to, give to, give money to, make a contribution to, contribute towards; *inf.* chip into. **3** *subscribe to the theory that he was murdered* agree with, be in agreement with, accede to, consent to, accept, believe in, endorse, back, support. **4** *subscribe one's name to the petition* sign, initial, write, inscribe, undersign, add, append.

subscription *noun* **1** *pay one's annual subscription to the club* fee, membership fee, dues, annual payment. **2** *make a subscription to the charity* donation, contribution, offering. **3** *his subscription on the document* signature, initials, undersigning, addition, appendage. **4** *his subscription to an old-fashioned theory* subscribing, agreement with, acceding to, consent to, acceptance of, belief in, endorsement of, backing for, support of.

subsequent *adjective* *on subsequent visits to the house* following, ensuing, succeeding, later, future. **subsequent to** *subsequent to his illness* following, after, in the wake of.
Opposites PREVIOUS; PRIOR; FORMER.

subservient *adjective* **1** *a powerful man surrounded by subservient people* servile, submissive, deferential, obsequious, sycophantic, grovelling, fawning, ingratiating, toadying, unctuous, truckling; *inf.* boot-licking. **2** *workers regarded as being subservient to profits* subordinate to, secondary to, subsidiary to, less important than, of lesser importance than, ancillary to. **3** *his friendship with the manager was subservient to his promotion* conducive to, instrumental to, contributory to, helpful to, useful to, advantageous to, beneficial to, valuable to.
Opposites OVERBEARING; DOMINEERING; SUPERIOR.

subside *verb* **1** *storms subsiding* abate, let up, moderate, quieten down, calm, slacken, die out, peter out, taper off, recede, lessen, diminish, dwindle. **2** *water levels subsiding* go down, get lower, sink, fall back, recede. **3** *houses subsiding* sink, settle. **4** *land near old mines subsiding* sink, cave in, fall in, collapse.
Opposites INTENSIFY; RISE.

subsidiary *adjective* *discuss subsidiary issues after the main one* subordinate, secondary, ancillary, auxilliary, lesser, minor, subservient, supplementary, additional.
Opposites CENTRAL; PRINCIPAL; MAJOR.

subsidize *verb* *ask the local council to subsidize the project* pay a subsidy to, give a grant to, contribute to, make a contribution to, give money to, back, support, invest in, sponsor, finance, fund, underwrite, foot the bill for; *inf.* pick up the tab for.

subsidy *noun* *government subsidies for the arts* grant, contribution, backing, support, aid, investment, sponsorship, finance, funding, subvention.

subsist *verb* **1** *subsist on bread and water* live on, exist on, eke out an existence on, survive on. **2** *old customs still subsist | animals thought to be extinct still subsisting* be in existence, exist, be alive, live, survive, continue, last. **3** *her attrac-*

tiveness subsists in her personality lie in, reside in, have its being in, be attributable to, be ascribable to.

subsistence *noun* **1** *their subsistence on bread and water* existence, survival. See SUBSIST 1. **2** *be unaware of the subsistence of such old customs* existence, survival, continuance. See SUBSIST 2. **3** *contribute to the child's subsistence* keep, support, maintenance, livelihood; sustenance, provisions, food, aliment.

substance *noun* **1** *a hard substance* matter, material, stuff, medium, mass, fabric. **2** *he saw ghostly figures with no substance* solidity, body, corporeality, reality, actuality, materiality, concreteness, tangibility. **3** *an argument with little substance* solidity, meaningfulness, significance, weight, power, soundness, validity, pith. **4** *a person of very little substance* character, backbone, mettle, strength of character. **5** *the substance of the novel as opposed to the style* subject matter, subject, theme, topic, content, text, burden, essence, gist, sense, import. **6** *born poor, he became a man of substance* wealth, affluence, prosperity, money, capital, means, resources, assets, property.

substantial *adjective* **1** *confuse the substantial world with the world of the imagination* real, true, actual, existing, material, concrete. **2** *make a substantial contribution to the project* real, material, weighty, sizeable, considerable, meaningful, significant, important, notable, major, marked, valuable, useful, worthwhile. **3** *pay substantial damages* sizeable, considerable, significant, large, ample, goodly; *inf.* tidy. **4** *substantial houses* solid, sturdy, stout, strong, well-built, durable. **5** *a substantial figure of a man* large, big, solid, sturdy, stout, hefty, bulky. **6** *put forward a substantial argument* solid, meaningful, significant, weighty, powerful, sound, valid, pithy. **7** *run a substantial business | a substantial businessman* successful, profit-making, prosperous, wealthy, affluent, moneyed, well-to-do. **8** *in substantial agreement* essential, basic, fundamental.
Opposites INSUBSTANTIAL; SLIGHT; PALTRY; FLIMSY.

substantially *adverb* **1** *standards have improved substantially* considerably, significantly, greatly, to a great extent, to a marked extent, markedly. **2** *a report that is substantially accurate* largely, for the most part, by and large, in the main, in essence, essentially, materially, basically, fundamentally.

substantiate *verb* *substantiate their accusation against him* give substance to, prove, support, uphold, back up, bear out, validate, corroborate, verify, authenticate, confirm.

substitute *noun* *act as a substitute for the manager/actor/doctor* replacement, deputy, relief, proxy, reserve, surrogate, fill-in, stand-in, standby, locum, locum tenens, stopgap.

substitute *verb* **1** *substitute sparkling wine for champagne* use as a replacement for, replace with, use instead of, exchange, switch; *inf.* swap. **2** *she substituted for him when he was ill* take the place of, replace, deputize for, act as deputy for, relieve, fill in for, act as stand-in for, cover for, take over from, act as locum for, hold the fort for. See SUBSTITUTE *noun.*

substitute *adjective* acting, replacement, deputy, relief, reserve, surrogate, fill-in, stand-in, temporary, standby, locum, stopgap.

subterfuge *noun* **1** *think of a subterfuge to get past the doorman* trick, ruse, wile, ploy, stratagem, artifice, dodge, manoeuvre, pretext, expedient, intrigue, scheme, deception. **2** *use subterfuge to gain entry* trickery, intrigue, deviousness, evasion, deception, duplicity.

subtle *adjective* **1** *a subtle flavour* elusive, delicate, faint, understated, low-key, muted, toned down. **2** *a subtle distinction* fine, fine-drawn, nice, slight, minute, tenuous, indistinct, indefinite. **3** *a subtle intelligence* perceptive, discerning, sensitive, discriminating, penetrating, astute, keen, acute, shrewd, sagacious. **4** *subtle devices to trap the unwary* clever, ingenious, skilful, adroit, complex, intricate, strategic, cunning, crafty, wily, artful, devious.
Opposites OBVIOUS; OBTRUSIVE; CRUDE; ARTLESS.

subtlety *noun* **1** *the subtlety of the flavour* subtleness, elusiveness, delicacy, delicateness, faintness, understatedness, understatement, mutedness. See SUBTLE 1. **2** *the subtlety of the distinction* subtleness, fineness, niceness, nicety, slightness, minuteness, tenuousness, indistinctness, indefiniteness, lack of definition. **3** *the subtlety of his mind* perceptiveness, perception, discernment, sensitivity, discrimination, astuteness, keenness, acuteness, shrewdness, sagacity. **4** *the subtlety of the devices* cleverness, ingenuity, skilfulness, adroitness, complexity, intricacy, cunning, guile, craftiness, wiliness, artfulness, deviousness.

subtract *verb* *subtract 5 from 20* take away, take from, deduct; *inf.* knock off.

suburb *noun* *a suburb of Glasgow* outlying district, residential area, dormitory area, purlieus.

suburban *adjective* *suburban housewives/attitudes* provincial, unsophisticated, parochial, insular.
Opposites SOPHISTICATED; COSMOPOLITAN.

subversive *adjective* *spread subversive rumours about the abilities of his boss* undermining, discrediting, destructive, disruptive, troublemaking, inflammatory, seditious, revolutionary, treasonous.

subvert *verb* **1** *subvert the government* overthrow, overturn, wreak havoc on, sabotage, ruin, destroy, demolish, wreck, upset, disrupt, undermine, weaken. **2** *subverted by gifts from the enemy* corrupt, pervert, warp, deprave, contaminate, vitiate.

subway *noun* **1** *cross the road by the subway* underground road, pedestrian tunnel. **2** *go by subway* underground railway, underground, metro; *inf.* tube.

succeed *verb* **1** *succeed in his endeavour/ambition* be successful, gain success, accomplish, achieve, bring off, carry out, attain, reach, arrive at, complete, fulfil, realize, be victorious in, triumph in. **2** *he succeeded in life* achieve success, be successful, do well, make good, prosper, flourish, thrive, triumph; *inf.* make it, do all right for oneself, arrive. **3** *plans that succeed* be successful, turn out well, work, work out; *inf.* pan out, do the trick. **4** *as day suc-*

ceeded day come after, follow, follow after.
5 *he succeeded him as chairman* come after, follow, replace, take the place of, supplant, supersede. **6** *succeed to the throne* accede to, inherit, assume, take over, come into, be elevated to.
Opposites FAIL; FLOP; PRECEDE.

succeeding *adjective grow weaker in the succeeding days* subsequent, following, ensuing, next.
Opposites PRECEDING; PREVIOUS.

success *noun* **1** *gain success in his endeavour/aim* accomplishment, achievement, attainment, fulfilment, victory, triumph. *See* SUCCEED 1. **2** *plans meeting with success* successful outcome, favourable result, positive result, victory. **3** *envy his success* prosperity, affluence, wealth, life of ease, fame, eminence. **4** *the book/play was a success* best-seller, winner; *inf.* hit, sensation. **5** *the play was a success* box-office success, winner, sell-out, triumph; *inf.* hit, box-office hit, smash hit, sensation. **6** *a former pupil who was a success* celebrity, big name, somebody, VIP, star.
Opposites FAILURE; FLOP; DISASTER; POVERTY.

successful *adjective* **1** *successful in his endeavour/aim* victorious, triumphant. **2** *envying successful people* prosperous, affluent, wealthy, well-to-do, famous, eminent, at the top, top. **3** *a successful business* flourishing, thriving, booming, profitable, profit-making, money-making, lucrative.
Opposites UNSUCCESSFUL; VAIN; INEFFECTIVE; POOR.

succession *noun* **1** *a succession of events leading to disaster* sequence, series, progression, course, cycle, chain, train, run, continuation. **2** *his succession to the throne* accession, inheritance, assumption, elevation. *See* SUCCEED 6. **3** *the succession is through his eldest son* line of descent, descent, ancestral line, dynasty, lineage. **in succession** *several firms closed in quick succession* successively, running, one after the other, one behind the other; *inf.* on the trot.

successor *noun* **1** *the successor to the throne* heir, heir apparent, next-in-line. **2** *select the chairman's successor* heir, replacement, supplanter.
Opposites PREDECESSOR.

succinct *adjective a succinct report* short, brief, concise, compact, condensed, crisp, terse, tight, to the point, pithy, summary, short and sweet, in a few well-chosen words.
Opposites LENGTHY; LONG-WINDED; VERBOSE.

succour *noun give succour to the wounded/bereaved* assistance, aid, help, comfort, relief, support.

succour *verb succour the wounded* give assistance to, render assistance to, assist, aid, bring aid to, help, give help to, minister to, comfort, bring comfort to, bring relief to, support.

succulent *adjective succulent fruit/steak* juicy, moist, luscious, mouthwatering.
Opposites DRY.

succumb *verb* **1** *succumb to temptation* give in to, give way to, yield to, submit to, surrender to, capitulate to, be overcome by, be overwhelmed by, fall victim to. **2** *succumb to his injuries* die from/of, pass away as a result of, be

a fatality of.
Opposites RESIST; WITHSTAND; CONQUER.

suck *verb* **suck in** **1** *suck in one's cheeks* draw in, pull in. **2** *material sucking in liquid* suck up, draw up, absorb, soak up, blot up. **3** *sucked in to the whirlpool* draw in, pull in, engulf, swallow up, swamp, drown. **4** *sucked into the conspiracy against his will* draw in, involve, implicate; *inf.* mix up. **suck up** **1** *materials sucking up liquid* suck in, absorb. **2** *sucking up to the teacher* toady to, fawn upon, be obsequious/servile/sycophantic to; *inf.* boot-lick.

suckle *verb mothers suckling their young* feed, breastfeed, nurse, give suck to.

sudden *adjective* **1** *a sudden change in the temperature* immediate, instantaneous, abrupt, unexpected, unforeseen, unanticipated, unlooked-for, without warning. **2** *his sudden rise to fame* rapid, swift, speedy, fast, quick, meteoric.
Opposites GRADUAL; GENTLE; DELIBERATE.

suddenly *adverb suddenly it began to rain* all of a sudden, all at once, instantaneously, abruptly, unexpectedly, without warning; *inf.* out of the blue.

suds *plural noun soap suds* foam, lather, froth, bubbles.

sue *verb* **1** *sue him for libel* take one to court, take legal action against, bring an action against, prefer/bring charges against, charge, bring a suit against, prosecute, bring to trial, summons, indict; *inf.* have the law on. **2** *sue for peace* petition for, appeal for, solicit, request, ask for, beg for, plead for, entreat for, beseech.

suffer *verb* **1** *she suffered greatly before she died* be in pain, feel pain, be racked with pain, endure agony, hurt, ache. **2** *children who suffer when parents divorce* be distressed, be in distress, experience hardship, be upset, be miserable, be wretched, be hurt, hurt, be handicapped. **3** *suffer from headaches* affected by, be afflicted by, be troubled with. **4** *suffer loss* experience, undergo, sustain, encounter, meet with, endure. **5** *his work suffered because of emotional problems* be impaired, deteriorate, fall off, decline, get worse. **6** *she cannot suffer his arrogance* put up with, tolerate, bear, stand, abide, endure, stomach, support. **7** *suffer them to approach* allow, permit, let, give leave to, sanction.

suffering *noun* **1** *distressed by the suffering of the dying woman* pain, agony, torment, torture, hurting. **2** *children who endure suffering when parents divorce* distress, hardship, misery, wretchedness, hurt, pain, anguish.

suffice *verb* **1** *a sandwich will suffice for lunch* be enough, be sufficient, be adequate, do, serve, meet requirements, satisfy demands, answer/fulfil/meet one's needs; *inf.* fill the bill, hit the spot. **2** *two will suffice him* be enough/sufficient/adequate for, do, satisfy, meet the requirements of, answer/fulfil/meet the needs of.

sufficient *adjective sufficient stocks of food* enough, adequate, plenty of, ample; *inf.* plenty.
Opposites INSUFFICIENT; INADEQUATE; SPARSE.

suffocate verb **1** kill the child by suffocating him smother, stifle, asphyxiate. **2** she was suffocating in the heat be suffocating, be stifling, be breathless, be short of air, be too hot.

suffrage noun right to vote, voting rights, franchise.

suffuse verb a blush suffusing her cheeks | the evening sky suffused with crimson spread over, cover, bathe, mantle, permeate, pervade, imbue.

sugar noun. See table.

TYPES OF SUGAR

arabinose	maltose
deoxyribose	mannose
dextrose	raffinose
fructose	rhamnose
fucose	ribose
galactose	saccharose
glucose	sorbose
lactose	sucrose
laevulose	xylose

---

sugary adjective **1** sugary tea sugared, sweet, over-sweet. **2** sugary love songs over-sweet, syrupy, sentimental, maudlin, mawkish, sloppy, slushy, mushy; inf. schmaltzy.
Opposites SOUR; TART.

suggest verb **1** suggest that they go by bus | suggest him as a replacement propose, put forward, move, submit, recommend, advocate; inf. throw out. **2** an aroma suggesting home-baked cakes put one in mind of, bring to mind, evoke. **3** an appearance suggesting that he lived rough indicate, lead to believe, give the impression, give the idea. **4** a letter suggesting that he is lying insinuate, hint, imply, intimate.

suggestion noun **1** put forward a suggestion that we leave proposal, proposition, plan, motion, submission, recommendation. **2** a suggestion of a French accent in her speech hint, trace, touch, suspicion. **3** object to the suggestion that he was making insinuation, hint, implication, intimation.

suggestive adjective make suggestive remarks provocative, titillating, sexual, sexy, indecent, indelicate, improper, off-colour, smutty, dirty, ribald, bawdy, racy, blue, risqué, lewd, salacious. **suggestive of** an aroma suggestive of newly cut grass redolent of, indicative of, evocative of, reminiscent of.

suicide noun self-destruction, felo de se, hara-kiri, suttee; inf. topping oneself.

suit noun **1** a woman wearing a blue suit set of clothes, outfit, costume, ensemble. **2** bring a suit against his employers lawsuit, court case, action, proceedings, prosecution. **3** take one's suit to the king petition, appeal, request, plea, entreaty. **4** pay suit to his friend's sister courtship, wooing, addresses, attentions. **5** cards in the same suit ordinary suit, trumps.

suit verb **1** a colour which suits her become, look attractive on, enhance the appearance of, go well with, look right on. **2** the suggested date does not suit him be suitable for, be convenient for, be acceptable to, meet requirements, satisfy demands, be in line with the wishes of. **3** rich food does not suit him be agreeable to, agree with, be good for, be healthy for. **4** suit your speech to the occasion make appropriate to, make fitting to, tailor, fashion, accommodate, adjust, adapt, modify.

suitable adjective **1** find a suitable date convenient, acceptable, satisfactory. **2** wear suitable shoes | shoes suitable for dancing right, appropriate, fitting, apt. **3** a speech suitable for the occasion suited to, befitting, appropriate to, relevant to, pertinent to, apposite to, in keeping with, in character with, tailor-made for. **4** not suitable behaviour appropriate, fitting, becoming, seemly, decorous, proper. **5** a suitable candidate for the post right, appropriate, fitting, apt, well qualified, ideal.
Opposites UNSUITABLE; UNFIT; INAPT.

suitcase noun case, travel bag, travelling bag, holdall, grip, valise, overnight case, vanity case.

suite noun **1** reserve a suite at a central hotel suite of rooms, set of rooms, apartment. **2** the suite of the king retinue, entourage, train, escort, attendants, retainers, followers.

suitor noun **1** unable to choose among her suitors admirer, beau, wooer, boyfriend; lit. follower. **2** the king giving audience to several suitors petitioner, supplicant, beseecher, plaintiff, appellant.

sulk verb sulking after losing the contest mope, pout, be sullen, have a long face, be in a bad mood, be put out, be out of sorts, be out of humour, be grumpy; inf. be in a huff.

sulk noun have a sulk | be in the sulks pout, bad mood, bad humour, ill humour, pique; inf. huff.

sulky adjective a sulky young woman | sulky because of losing moping, pouting, moody, sullen, piqued, disgruntled, ill-humoured, out of humour, bad-tempered, grumpy, churlish, glowering.

sullen adjective difficult to communicate with the sullen girl morose, unresponsive, uncommunicative, unsociable, resentful, sulky, sour, glum, gloomy, dismal, cheerless, surly, cross, angry, frowning, glowering, grumpy.
Opposites OUTGOING; SOCIABLE; RESPONSIVE.

sultry adjective **1** a sultry day/atmosphere close, airless, stuffy, stifling, suffocating, oppressive, muggy, humid, sticky, hot, sweltering. **2** a sultry singer sensual, sexy, voluptuous, seductive, provocative, alluring, tempting, passionate, erotic.

sum noun **1** find the sum of the line of figures sum total, grand total, tally, aggregate, answer. **2** a large sum of money amount, quantity. **3** get the children to do sums arithmetical problem, problem, calculation, reckoning, tally. **4** look at the problem in its sum entirety, totality, total, whole; inf. whole shebang, whole caboodle, whole shooting match. **sum up 1** when the judge sums up give a summing-up, summarize the evidence, review the evidence, summarize the argument. **2** *sum up the situation* form an opinion of, form an impression of, make one's mind up about, get the measure of, form a judgement of; *inf.* size up. **3** *sum up the facts of the situation* give a summary of, summarize, précis, give an abstract of, encapsulate, put in a nutshell.

summarily *adverb summarily dismissed when caught stealing* immediately, instantly, right away, straight away, at once, on the spot, directly, forthwith, promptly, speedily, swiftly, rapidly, without delay, suddenly, abruptly, peremptorily, without discussion, without formality.

summarize *verb summarize the plot of the novel in a short essay | summarize recent events* give/make a summary of, sum up, give a synopsis of, précis, give a précis of, give a résumé of, give an abstract of, abridge, condense, epitomize, outline, sketch, give the main points of, give a rundown of, review.

summary *noun give a summary of the plot of the novel* synopsis, précis, résumée, abstract, abridgement, digest, epitome, outline, sketch, rundown, review, summing-up.

summary *adjective* **1** *summary dismissal/justice* immediate, instant, instantaneous, direct, prompt, speedy, swift, rapid, without delay, sudden, abrupt, hasty, peremptory, without discussion, without formality. **2** *a summary account of the long debate* abridged, abbreviated, shortened, condensed, short, brief, concise, succinct, thumbnail, cursory.
Opposites DILATORY; SLOW; LENGTHY.

summerhouse *noun* pavilion, gazebo, arbour, bower, pergola.

summit *noun* **1** *the summit of the mountain* top, peak, crest, crown, apex, vertex, apogee. **2** *the summit of her stage career* peak, height, pinnacle, culmination, climax, crowning point, zenith, acme.
Opposites BOTTOM; BASE; NADIR.

summon *verb* **1** *summoned by the headmaster* send for, call for, bid, request the presence of, demand the presence of. **2** *summon a committee meeting* order, call, convene, assemble, convoke, muster, rally. **3** *summon a witness* summons, serve with a summons, cite, serve with a citation, serve with a writ, subpoena.
summon up **1** *summon up the courage to act* gather, collect, muster, rally, call into action, mobilize. **2** *summon up half-forgotten memories* call to mind, bring to mind, call up, conjure up, evoke, recall, revive. **3** *summon up evil spirits by magic* call up, conjure up, invoke, rouse up.

summons *noun* **1** *a summons to give evidence in court* citation, writ, subpoena. **2** *obey the headmaster's summons to attend* order, directive, command, instruction, dictum, demand.

summons *verb summons him to appear in court* serve with a summons, summon, serve with a citation/writ, subpoena.

sumptuous *adjective sumptuous furnishings* lavish, luxurious, de luxe, opulent, magnificent, gorgeous, splendid, rich, costly, expensive,

dear, extravagant; *inf.* plush, ritzy.
Opposites HUMBLE; PLAIN; CHEAP.

sunburnt *adjective* **1** *soothe her sunburnt shoulders* sunburned, burnt, peeling, inflamed, blistering. **2** *showing off her sunburnt arms* suntanned, tanned, brown, bronzed.

sunder *verb sunder the beam* separate, divide, split, sever, cleaver, rend.

sundry *adjective* **1** *sundry items* several, various, varied, miscellaneous, assorted, diverse. **2** *on sundry occasions* several, some, various, different.

sunken *adjective* **1** *a sunken terrace* at a lower level, below ground level, lowered. **2** *the sunken cheeks of the invalid* hollow, hollowed, concave, drawn, haggard.

sunless *adjective* **1** *a sunless day* overcast, dark, grey, gloomy, murky. **2** *a sunless spot* dark, shady, shadowy, dim, gloomy, murky, bleak.

sunlight *noun sunlight does not penetrate the forest* sun, sunshine, light, daylight, light of day.

sunny *adjective* **1** *a sunny day* sunshiny, sunlit, bright, clear, fine, cloudless, unclouded, without a cloud in the sky. **2** *a sunny nature* happy, cheerful, cheery, light-hearted, bright, glad, gay, merry, joyful, buoyant, bubbly, blithe. **3** *look on the sunny side* bright, cheerful, hopeful, optimistic.
Opposites DULL; SHADY.

sunrise *noun* dawn, crack of dawn, daybreak, morning, cock-crow; *lit.* peep of day, aurora; *Am.* sunup.

sunset *noun* nightfall, close of day, evening, twilight, dusk, gloaming; *Am.* sundown.

sunshine *noun* **1** *sit and enjoy the sunshine* sun, sunlight, sun's rays. **2** *a life devoid of sunshine* happiness, laughter, cheerfulness, gladness, gaiety, merriment, joy, joyfulness, blitheness.

superannuated *adjective* **1** *superannuated ex-employees* pensioned, pensioned off, retired, elderly. **2** *a superannuated bicycle* old, old-fashioned, antiquated, obsolete, broken-down; *inf.* clapped-out.

superb *adjective* **1** *dancers giving a superb performance* superlative, excellent, first-rate, first-class, of the first water, outstanding, remarkable, dazzling, brilliant, marvellous, magnificent, wonderful, splendid, exquisite; *inf.* fantastic, fabulous, A1. **2** *superb furnishings* magnificent, gorgeous, splendid, sumptuous, opulent, lavish, luxurious, de luxe; *inf.* plush, ritzy.
Opposites POOR; INFERIOR; DREADFUL.

supercilious *adjective* arrogant, haughty, conceited, proud, vain, disdainful, scornful, condescending, superior, patronizing, imperious, overbearing, lofty, lordly, snobbish, snobby; *inf.* hoity-toity, high-and-mighty, uppity, snooty, stuck-up, toffee-nosed.

superficial *adjective* **1** *superficial damage/wounds only* surface, exterior, external, outer, outside, peripheral, slight. **2** *a superficial examination* cursory, perfunctory, hasty, hurried, casual, sketchy, desultory, slapdash. **3** *a superficial similarity* outward, apparent, evident,

ostensible. **4** *rather a superficial person* shallow, empty-headed, trivial, frivolous, silly. **5** *a superficial book* lightweight, sketchy, slight, insignificant, trivial.
Opposites DEEP; PROFOUND; THOROUGH.

superfluous *adjective* **1** *sell off the superfluous furniture* spare, to spare, surplus, surplus to requirements, extra, unneeded, unrequired, excess, in excess, supernumerary. **2** *their presence was superfluous* unnecessary, needless, unneeded, inessential, uncalled-for, unwarranted, gratuitous.
Opposites NECESSARY; ESSENTIAL.

superhuman *adjective* **1** *require a superhuman effort* Herculean, phenomenal, prodigious, stupendous, heroic, extraordinary. **2** *superhuman intervention* divine, god-like, holy. **3** *a cry that seemed superhuman* supernatural, preternatural, preterhuman, paranormal, other-worldly.

superintend *verb superintend the factory* be in charge of, be in control of, preside over, direct, administer, manage, run, look after, supervise, oversee.

superintendent *noun* director, administrator, manager, supervisor, overseer, controller, boss, chief; *inf.* honcho.

superior *adjective* **1** *the superior player* better, greater, better-class, more expert, more skilful, more advanced. **2** *hold a superior position* higher, higher-ranking, higher-up. **3** *of superior quality* better, higher-grade, greater, surpassing. **4** *goods of superior leather* good-quality, high-quality, first-rate, top-quality, high-grade, of the first water, of the first order, choice, select, prime, up-market, fine. **5** *live in a superior area* high-class, up-market, select, exclusive, snobby. **6** *act superior|give her a superior look* haughty, disdainful, condescending, supercilious, patronizing, lofty, lordly, snobbish, snobby; *inf.* high-and-mighty, hoity-toity, uppity, snooty, stuck-up, toffee-nosed.
Opposites INFERIOR; LOW.

superior *noun* get a warning from his superior boss, manager, chief, supervisor, foreman.
Opposites INFERIOR; SUBORDINATE; ASSISTANT.

superiority *noun* **1** *the superiority of their performance* better quality, supremacy. **2** *their superiority in numbers* advantage, lead, dominance.

superlative *adjective superlative players|of superlative quality* best, greatest, supreme, consummate, first-rate, first-class, of the first water, of the first order, of the higher order, brilliant, excellent, magnificent, outstanding, unsurpassed, unparalleled, unrivalled, peerless, matchless, transcendent; *inf.* crack, ace.
Opposites POOR; MEDIOCRE; UNEXCEPTIONAL.

supernatural *adjective* **1** *supernatural beings* otherworldly, unearthly, spectral, ghostly, phantom, magical, mystic, unreal. **2** *supernatural powers* paranormal, supernormal, hypernormal, psychic, miraculous, extraordinary, uncanny.

supersede *verb* **1** *workers superseded by machines* take the place of, replace, take over from, displace, supplant, oust, usurp. **2** *supersede him as chairman* replace, take the place of,

take over from, succeed. **3** *the office equipment was superseded when it became obsolete* discard, cast aside, throw out, dispose of, abandon, jettison; *inf.* chuck out.
Opposites PRECEDE.

supervise *verb* **1** *supervise the factory* superintend, be in charge of, direct, administer, manage, run. *See* SUPERINTEND. **2** *supervise the work of trainees/the trainees* oversee, keep an eye on, watch, observe, inspect, be responsible for, guide.

supervision *noun* **1** *the supervision of the factory* administration, management, direction, control, charge, superintendence. **2** *children playing under supervision* observation, inspection, guidance.

supervisor *noun* **1** *the supervisor of the factory* director, administrator, manager, overseer, controller, boss, chief, superintendent; *inf.* honcho. **2** *the supervisors of the children/trainees* overseer, observer, inspector, guide, advisor.

supine *adjective* **1** *supine on the floor* flat on one's back, prone, prostrate, horizontal. **2** *rather a supine individual* weak, feckless, spineless, idle, inactive, indolent, lazy, slothful, languid, apathetic, indifferent; *inf.* laid-back.
Opposites ERECT; VERTICAL; ENERGETIC.

supper *noun* **1** *invite guests to supper* dinner, evening meal. **2** *have toasted cheese for supper* evening snack.

supplant *verb a nobleman plotting to supplant the king* take the place of, take over from, replace, displace, supersede, oust, usurp, overthrow, remove, unseat.

supple *adjective* **1** *supple gymnasts* lithe, loose-limbed, limber. **2** *supple leather* pliant, pliable, flexible, bendable, stretchable, elastic.
Opposites STIFF; RIGID.

supplement *adjective* **1** *dietary supplement* addition, supplementation, additive, extra, add-on. **2** *add a supplement to the book/document* appendix, addendum, end-matter, tail-piece, codicil, rider. **3** *a newspaper supplement* pull-out, insert, special-feature section, magazine section.

supplement *verb supplement his salary with an evening job* add to, augment, increase, top up, complement.

supplementary *adjective* **1** *a supplementary payment* supplemental, additional, extra, add-on, complementary. **2** *a supplementary section* added, appended, attached, extra.

suppliant *noun suppliants asking the king for mercy* supplicant, petitioner, pleader, beseecher, applicant, suitor, beggar, appellant.

supplicate *verb supplicate for a pardon* plead, entreat, beseech, beg, implore, petition, appeal, solicit, ask, request, pray, invoke.

supplication *noun ignore the poor man's supplication* plea, pleading, entreaty, beseeching, begging, imploration, petition, appeal, solicitation, request, prayer, invocation.

supplies *noun army supplies running out* provisions, stores, rations, food, victuals, provender.

supply verb **1** *supply the necessary money* provide, give, furnish, contribute, donate, grant, come up with; *inf.* fork out, shell out. **2** *supply him with food/tools* provide, furnish, equip, kit out, outfit. **3** *supply all their needs* satisfy, meet, fulfil.

supply noun **1** *difficult to organize the supply of wood* supplying, providing, provision, furnishing. **2** *build up a supply of logs* stock, store, reserve, reservoir, stockpile, heap, pile, mass, hoard, cache. *See* SUPPLIES.

supply adjective *a supply teacher* substitute, stand-in, fill-in, locum, temporary, stopgap.

support verb **1** *beams supporting the roof* bear, carry, hold up, prop up, bolster up, brace, keep up, shore up, underpin, buttress. **2** *work to support his family* maintain, provide for, provide sustenance for, sustain, take care of, look after. **3** *support him in his hour of need* give moral support to, give strength to, be a source of strength to, comfort, help, sustain, encourage, buoy up, hearten, fortify; *inf.* buck up. **4** *bring evidence to support his argument* back up, substantiate, give force to, bear out, corroborate, confirm, verify, validate, authenticate, endorse, ratify. **5** *support several charities/new enterprises* back, contribute to, give a donation to, give money to, subsidize, fund, finance. **6** *support the youngest candidate* back, champion, give help to, help, assist, aid, be on the side of, side with, vote for, stand behind, stand up for, take one's part, take up the cudgels for; *inf.* stick up for. **7** *support conservation of the countryside* back, advocate, promote, further, champion, be on the side of, espouse, espouse the cause of, be in favour of, recommend, defend. **8** *cannot support his behaviour* bear, put up with, tolerate, stand, abide, suffer, stomach, brook. **Opposites** NEGLECT; ABANDON; OPPOSE; CONTRADICT.

support noun **1** *the supports of the bridge* base, foundations, pillar, post, prop, underprop, underpinning, substructure, brace, buttress, abutment, bolster, stay. **2** *pay towards his family's support* keep, maintenance, sustenance, food and accommodation, subsistence, aliment. **3** *in need of support in his hour of need* moral support, friendship, strengthening, strength, encouragement, buoying up, heartening, fortification; *inf.* bucking up. **4** *give support to charities/enterprises* backing, contribution, donation, money, subsidy, funding, funds, finance, capital. **5** *give his support to the youngest candidate* backing, help, assistance, aid, votes. *See* SUPPORT *verb* 6. **6** *in support of conservation of the countryside* backing, advocacy, promotion, championship, espousal, recommendation. **7** *he was a great support to his widowed mother* help, assistance, comfort, tower of strength, prop, backbone, mainstay.

supporter noun **1** *supporters of the charity* backer, contributor, donor, sponsor, patron, friend, well-wisher. **2** *the candidate's supporters* backers, helper, adherent, follower, ally, voter, apologist. **3** *supporters of the cause of animals* backer, adherent, advocate, promoter, champion, defender, apologist. **4** *football supporter* fan, follower.

supportive adjective *need supportive friends when in trouble* helpful, encouraging, caring, sympathetic, understanding.

suppose verb **1** *I suppose you're right* dare say, assume, take for granted, take as read, presume, expect, imagine, believe, think, fancy, suspect, guess, surmise, reckon, conjecture, theorize, opine. **2** *suppose we arrive late* take as a hypothesis, hypothesize, postulate, posit. **3** *creation supposes a creator* presuppose, require, imply.

supposed adjective *his supposed brother* presumed, assumed, believed, professed, so-called, alleged, putative, reputed. **be supposed to** *they are not supposed to know* meant, intended, expected.

supposition noun **1** *his suppositions proved correct* assumption, presumption, suspicion, guess, surmise, conjecture, speculation, theory. **2** *on the supposition that he is right* assumption, hypothesis, postulation.

suppress verb **1** *suppress the rebellion* conquer, vanquish, put an end to, crush, quell, squash, stamp out, extinguish, put out, put an end to, crack down on, clamp down on. **2** *suppress his anger/laughter* restrain, keep a rein on, hold back, control, keep under control, check, keep in check, curb. **3** *suppress the information/truth* keep secret, conceal, hide, keep hidden, keep silent about, withhold, cover up, smother, stifle, muzzle.
Opposites ENCOURAGE; INCITE; PUBLICIZE.

suppression noun **1** *the suppression of the rebellion* conquering, crushing, extinction, crackdown, clampdown. *See* SUPPRESS 1. **2** *the suppression of his anger* restraint, holding back, curbing. *See* SUPPRESS 2. **3** *the suppression of the information/truth* concealment, withholding, cover-up, smothering, stifling, muzzling. *See* SUPPRESS 3.

suppurate verb fester, matter, maturate, gather, come to a head, discharge.

supremacy noun **1** *a country holding supremacy over its neighbours* ascendancy, predominance, paramountcy, dominion, sway, authority, mastery, control, power, rule, sovereignty, lordship. **2** *challenge her supremacy as top tennis player* pre-eminence, dominance, superiority, ascendancy, incomparability, inimitability, matchlessness, peerlessness.

supreme adjective **1** *the supreme commander* highest-ranking, highest, leading, chief, foremost, principal. **2** *supreme bravery | a supreme effort* extreme, greatest, utmost, uttermost, maximum, extraordinary, remarkable. **3** *the supreme sacrifice/judgement* final, last, ultimate. **reign supreme** *the athlete still reigns supreme* be superlative, be unsurpassed, be the best, be the greatest, be unrivalled, be matchless, be peerless, be pre-eminent, be excellent, be first-rate.
Opposites SUBORDINATE; MINIMUM.

sure adjective **1** *we cannot be sure that he is honest* certain, definite, positive, convinced, confident, decided, assured, free from doubt, unhesitating, unwavering, unfaltering, unvacillating. **2** *sure of success* assured of, certain of,

surely · surrender

confident of, with no doubts about. **3** *a sure success/failure* assured, certain, guaranteed, inevitable, irrevocable; *inf.* in the bag. **4** *in the sure knowledge* true, certain, undoubted, absolute, categorical, well-grounded, well-founded, proven, unquestionable, indisputable, incontestable, irrefutable, incontrovertible, undeniable. **5** *a sure remedy* certain, unfailing, infallible, never-failing, reliable, dependable, trustworthy, tested, tried and true, foolproof, effective, efficacious; *inf.* sure-fire. **6** *sure friend* true, reliable, dependable, trusted, trustworthy, trusty, loyal, faithful, steadfast. **7** *with a sure hand* firm, steady, stable, secure, confident, unhesitating, unfaltering, unwavering. **be sure of** *be sure to arrive on time* be certain to, be careful to, take care to, remember to.
Opposites UNSURE; UNCERTAIN; DOUBTFUL.

surely *adverb* **1** *they will surely fail* for certain, certainly, definitely, assuredly, undoubtedly, without doubt, beyond the shadow of a doubt, indubitably, unquestionably, incontestably, irrefutably, incontrovertibly, undeniably, without fail, inevitably, unavoidably. **2** *walk slowly but surely* firmly, steadily, confidently, unhesitatingly.

surety *noun* **1** *use the house as surety for the loan* security, indemnity, collateral, guarantee, pledge, bond. **2** *he acted as surety for her loan* guarantor, sponsor.

surface *noun* **1** *the surface of the wood* outside, exterior, top. **2** *look beneath the surface to appreciate his vulnerability* outward appearance, superficial appearance, façade. **on the surface** *on the surface the firm seems profitable* at first glance, to the casual eye, outwardly, to all appearances, apparently, superficially.

surface *adjective* *a surface scratch* superficial, external, exterior, outward.

surface *verb* **1** *the submarine surfaced* come to the surface, come up, come to the top. **2** *the old rumours have surfaced again* reappear, appear, come to light, come up, emerge, crop up. **3** *he won't surface till lunch-time* get up, get out of bed, rise, wake, awaken.

surfeit *noun* **1** *a surfeit of food and drink* excess, surplus, oversupply, superabundance, superfluity, glut, too much. **2** *ill from a surfeit of chocolates* over-indulgence, satiety, satiation.
Opposites DEARTH; LACK.

surfeit *verb* *be surfeited with food/pleasure* satiate, gorge, overfeed, overfill, glut, cram, stuff, overindulge.

surge *noun* **1** *a surge of water* gush, rush, outpouring, stream, flow, sweep, efflux. **2** *a sudden surge in prices* upsurge, increase, rise, upswing, escalation. **3** *the surge of the sea* rise, swell, swelling, heaving, billowing, rolling, eddying, swirling.

surge *verb* **1** *the water surged from the broken pipe/crowds surging from the hall* gush, rush, stream, flow. **2** *the sea surged in the storm* rise, swell, heave, billow, roll, eddy, swirl.

surgery *noun.* See tables at DOCTOR, INSTRUMENT, OPERATION.

surly *adjective* bad-tempered, ill-natured, crabbed, grumpy, crotchety, grouchy, cantankerous, irascible, testy, crusty, gruff, abrupt, brusque, churlish, uncivil, morose, sullen, sulky.
Opposites GOOD-NATURED; FRIENDLY; PLEASANT.

surmise *verb* *she surmised that he was lying* guess, conjecture, suspect, deduce, assume, presume, gather, feel, be of the opinion, think, believe, imagine.

surmount *verb* **1** *many problems/obstacles to surmount* get over, overcome, conquer, triumph over, prevail over, get the better of, beat. **2** *climbers struggling to surmount the mountain* climb, ascend, scale, mount. **3** *snow surmounting the hills* top, cap, crown. **4** *mountains surmounting the houses* rise above, tower above, overtop, dominate.

surname *noun* last name, family name, patronymic.

surpass *verb* *her beauty/work surpasses that of the others* be greater than, be better than, beat, exceed, excel, transcend, outdo, outshine, outstrip, overshadow, eclipse.

surpassing *adjective* exceptional, extraordinary, remarkable, outstanding, striking, phenomenal, rare, supreme, incomparable, inimitable, unrivalled, matchless.

surplus *noun* *get rid of the surplus after the sale* excess, remainder, residue, surfeit.
Opposites DEARTH; SHORTAGE; LACK.

surplus *adjective* *surplus food going to waste* excess, in excess, superfluous, leftover, unused, remaining, extra, spare.

surprise *verb* **1** *their sudden appearance surprised him* astonish, amaze, nonplus, take aback, startle, astound, stun, flabbergast, stagger, leave open-mouthed, take one's breath away; *inf.* bowl over, blow one's mind. **2** *surprise the burglars opening the safe* take by surprise, catch unawares, catch off guard, catch red-handed, catch in the act, catch napping, burst in on, spring upon, catch with his/her trousers down, catch on the hop.

surprise *noun* **1** *look up in surprise* astonishment, amazement, incredulity, wonder. **2** *it was a surprise when she left* shock, bolt from the blue, bombshell, revelation.

surprised *adjective* *a surprised look/the surprised children* astonished, amazed, nonplussed, startled, astounded, stunned, flabbergasted, staggered, open-mouthed, speechless, thunderstruck. See SURPRISE *verb* 1.

surprising *adjective* astonishing, amazing, startling, astounding, staggering, incredible, extraordinary, remarkable; *inf.* mind-blowing.

surrender *verb* **1** *surrender his right to the title* give up, relinquish, renounce, forgo, forsake, cede, abdicate, waive. **2** *surrender the keys of the car* hand over, give up, deliver up, part with, let go of, relinquish. **3** *surrender to the enemy* give in, give oneself up, yield, submit, capitulate, lay down one's arms, raise/show the white flag, throw in the towel, throw in the sponge. **4** *surrender to his old habits* give way to, yield to, succumb to, capitulate to. **5** *sur-*

render all hope give up, abandon, leave behind, lose.
Opposites RESIST; WITHSTAND; DEFY.

surrender *noun* **1** *the surrender of his title* surrendering, relinquishment, renunciation, forgoing, ceding, cession, abdication. *See* SURRENDER *verb* 1. **2** *witness their surrender to the enemy* yielding, capitulation, submission. *See* SURRENDER *verb* 3.

surreptitious *adjective* *find the information by surreptitious means* stealthy, clandestine, secret, sneaky, sly, cunning, furtive, underhand, undercover, covert.
Opposites OPEN; HONEST; BLATANT.

surround *verb* *a fence surrounds the lake* go around, encircle, enclose, encompass, ring, gird, girdle, fence in, hem in, confine.

surrounding *adjective* *the surrounding countryside* neighbouring, nearby.

surroundings *plural noun* *brought up in squalid surroundings* environment, setting, milieu, element, background.

surveillance *noun* *under surveillance* observation, watch, scrutiny, spying, espionage.

survey *verb* **1** *survey the burnt building* look at, take a look at, observe, view, contemplate, regard, examine, inspect. **2** *survey the evidence* look at, look over, scan, study, consider, review, examine, inspect, scrutinize, take stock of; *inf.* size up. **3** *survey a building* make a survey of, value, carry out a valuation of, estimate the value of, appraise, assess, prospect, triangulate.

survey *noun* **1** *undertake a survey of the evidence* study, consideration, review, overview, examination, inspection, scrutinization, scrutiny. *See* SURVEY *verb* 2. **2** *carry out a survey of the building* valuation, appraisal. *See* SURVEY *verb* 3. **3** *carry out a survey into TV viewing habits* investigation, inquiry, research, study, review, probe, questionnaire.

survive *verb* **1** *old customs surviving in the village* live on, be extant, continue, remain, last, persist, endure, exist, be. **2** *fathers surviving their sons* outlive, outlast, live after, remain alive after. **3** *people surviving in the freezing conditions* remain alive, live, hold out, pull through, cling to life.

susceptibility *noun* **1** *the young woman's susceptibility* impressionability, credulity, credulousness, gullibility, defencelessness, vulnerability, responsiveness, sensitivity, emotionalism. *See* SUSCEPTIBLE. **2** *their susceptibility to his charm* openness, responsiveness, receptiveness, vulnerability, defencelessness. **3** *their susceptibility to colds* liability, proneness, predisposition, propensity. *See* SUSCEPTIBLE.

susceptible *adjective* *protect susceptible young girls* impressionable, likely to be taken in, credulous, gullible, innocent, defenceless, vulnerable, easily led, responsive, sensitive, thin-skinned, highly-strung, emotional. **susceptible to 1** *susceptible to his charm* open to, responsive to, receptive to, vulnerable to, defenceless against. **2** *susceptible to colds/disease* subject to, liable to, prone to, inclined to, pre-

disposed to, disposed.
Opposites SCEPTICAL; IMMUNE; RESISTANT.

suspect *verb* **1** *I suspect you could be right* feel, have a feeling, be inclined to think, fancy, surmise, guess, conjecture, have a suspicion that, speculate, have a hunch, suppose, believe, think, conclude. **2** *suspect the truth of his statement* doubt, have doubts about, harbour suspicions about, have misgivings about, be sceptical about, distrust, mistrust. *See* SUSPICION 1. **3** *police suspect her brother* regard as guilty, regard as a wrongdoer.

suspend *verb* **1** *suspend a light from the tree* hang, put up, swing, dangle, sling. **2** *suspend the proceedings* adjourn, interrupt, cut short, bring to an end, cease, discontinue, break off, arrest, put off, postpone, delay, defer, shelve, pigeon-hole, table, put on the back burner; *inf.* put on ice. **3** *suspend him from his job/membership* debar, shut out, exclude, keep out, remove.
Opposites CONTINUE; RESUME.

suspense *noun* *in a state of suspense about the outcome* uncertainty, doubt, doubtfulness, anticipation, expectation, expectancy, excitement, tension, anxiety, nervousness, apprehension, apprehensiveness.

suspension *noun* **1** *the suspension of talks* adjournment, interruption, cessation, postponement, delay, deferment, shelving. *See* SUSPEND 2. **2** *his suspension from office* debarment, exclusion, removal, temporary removal.

suspicion *noun* **1** *have suspicions about his motives* doubts, misgivings, qualms, wariness, chariness, scepticism, distrust, mistrust; *inf.* funny feeling. **2** *his suspicion is that she will appear* feeling, surmise, guess, conjecture, speculation, hunch, supposition, belief, notion, idea, conclusion; *inf.* gut feeling. **3** *a suspicion of liqueur in the dessert* trace, touch, suggestion, hint, soupçon, tinge, shade.

suspicious *adjective* **1** *give him suspicious looks* doubtful, unsure, wary, chary, sceptical, distrustful, mistrustful, disbelieving. **2** *police observing a suspicious character* guilty-looking, dishonest-looking, strange-looking, queer-looking, funny-looking; *inf.* shifty, shady. **3** *suspicious circumstances* questionable, doubtful, odd, strange, irregular, queer, funny; *inf.* fishy, shady.
Opposites TRUSTFUL; UPRIGHT; ORDINARY; INNOCENT.

sustain *verb* **1** *beams sustaining the weight of the roof* bear, support, carry, keep something up, prop up, shore up. **2** *sustain one's courage* keep something up, keep something going, continue, carry on, maintain, prolong, protract. **3** *sustain him in his hour of need* support, give strength to, be a source of strength to, be a tower of strength to, comfort, help, assist, encourage, buoy up, cheer up, hearten; *inf.* buck up. **4** *not enough to sustain her* keep alive, keep going, maintain, continue, preserve. **5** *enough food to sustain them* feed, nourish, keep going, nurture. **6** *sustain defeat/injury* experience, undergo, go through, suffer, endure. **7** *the court sustained his claim* uphold, validate, ratify, vindicate. **8** *evidence sustaining his allega-*

tions confirm, verify, corroborate, substantiate, bear out, prove, authenticate, validate.

sustained *adjective a sustained interest in the firm* continuing, steady, continuous, constant, prolonged, perpetual, unremitting.
Opposites BROKEN; INTERMITTENT; SPORADIC.

sustenance *noun* **1** *enough money to buy sustenance for his family* food, nourishment, daily bread, provisions, victuals, rations, aliment, comestibles; *lit.* provender; *inf.* grub, chow, scoff. **2** *try to earn enough for sustenance* living, livelihood, means of support, maintenance, support, subsistence.

swagger *verb* **1** *swagger down the street in his new coat* strut, parade, prance. **2** *swaggering about her recent victory* boast, bray, bluster; *inf.* show off, swank.

swagger *noun* **1** *walk with a swagger* strut, parading, prancing. **2** *tired of his swagger* boasting, bragging, bluster, swashbuckling, braggadocio, vainglory; *inf.* showing-off, swank.

swallow *verb* **1** *swallow the meat with difficulty* gulp down, eat, consume, devour, ingest; *inf.* scoff. **2** *swallow two drinks in quick succession* gulp down, drink, swill down; *inf.* swig. **3** *unable to swallow her treatment of him* put up with, tolerate, endure, stand, bear, suffer, abide, stomach, brook. **4** *expect him to swallow their story* believe, accept; *inf.* fall for, buy. **5** *swallow one's pride/anger* repress, restrain, hold back, choke back, control, rein in. **swallow up** **1** *the waves swallowed him up* engulf, swamp, flood over, overwhelm. **2** *big companies swallowing up small ones* engulf, take over, absorb, assimilate, overrun, overwhelm, swamp.

swamp *noun* *get stuck in a swamp* marsh, bog, quagmire, mire, morass, fen, quag.

swamp *verb* **1** *heavy rains swamping the town* flood, inundate, deluge, wash out, soak, drench, saturate. **2** *swamped with applications* inundate, flood, deluge, overwhelm, engulf, snow under, overload, overburden, weight down, besiege, beset.

swampy *adjective* marshy, boggy, soggy, soft, spongy, waterlogged, miry, fenny, quaggy.

swap *verb* **1** *children swapping toys with each other* exchange, interchange, trade, barter, switch. **2** *swap jokes/insults* exchange, trade, bandy.

swarm *noun* **1** *a swarm of bees* hive, flight. **2** *a swarm of people* crowd, multitude, horde, host, mob, throng, stream, mass, body, army, flock, herd, pack, drove.

swarm *verb* **1** *shoppers swarming to the sales* flock, crowd, throng, stream, surge. **2** *rats swarming all over the floor* run, crawl, crowd. **be swarming with** be crowded with, be thronged with, be overrun with, abound in, be teeming with, be bristling with, be alive with, be crawling with, be infested with.

swarthy *adjective* dark, dark-coloured, dark-skinned, dark-complexioned, dusky, tanned.
Opposites PALE; FAIR.

swashbuckling *adjective* swaggering, dashing, daring, adventurous, bold, gallant.

swathe *verb* *swathed in bandages* wrap, envelop, bind, swaddle, bandage, bundle up, muffle up, cover, shroud, drape.

sway *verb* **1** *trees swaying in the breeze* swing, shake, bend, lean, incline. **2** *drunks swaying on their way home* roll, stagger, wobble, rock. **3** *swaying her hips* swing, oscillate, shake. **4** *swaying between emigrating and staying* waver, hesitate, fluctuate, vacillate, oscillate. **5** *swayed by their arguments* influence, affect, persuade, prevail on, bring round, win over, induce. **6** *swayed by ambition* rule, govern, dominate, control, direct, guide.

sway *noun* **1** *countries under the sway of Rome* jurisdiction, rule, government, sovereignty, dominion, control, command, power, authority, ascendancy, domination, mastery. **2** *under the sway of her husband* control, domination, power, authority, influence, guidance, direction. **hold sway** *the same political power still holds sway* be most powerful, hold power, rule, be in control, predominate, have ascendance, have the greatest influence.

swear *verb* **1** *swear to take care of the child | swear that he would take care of the child* promise, promise under oath, solemnly promise, pledge oneself, vow, give one's word, take an oath, swear on the Bible. **2** *he swore that he was fit to drive* vow, insist, be emphatic, pronounce, declare, assert, maintain, contend, aver. **3** *he swore when he hit his finger | swear at the other driver* curse, blaspheme, be blasphemous, utter profanities, be foul-mouthed, use bad language, take the Lord's name in vain, swear like a trooper; *inf.* cuss, turn the air blue. **swear by** **1** *swear by Almighty God* call as one's witness, appeal to, invoke. **2** *swear by her remedy for colds* have confidence in, have faith in, have trust in, place reliance on, depend on, believe in.

swearing *noun* *disapprove of swearing* cursing, blaspheming, profanity, imprecation, bad language.

sweat *noun* **1** *sweat pouring from his brow* perspiration; *Tech.* sudor, diaphoresis. **2** *in a sweat until the results came through* fluster, fret, dither, fuss, panic, state of anxiety/agitation/nervousness/worry; *inf.* state, flap, tiz-woz, stew, lather. **3** *it was a sweat to finish on time* labour, effort, chore, back-breaking task.

sweat *verb* **1** *sweating in the heat* perspire, exude perspiration, drip with perspiration/sweat, break out in a sweat. **2** *they were sweating until the results came through* be flushed, fret, dither, fuss, panic, be on tenterhooks, be in a state of anxiety/agitation/nervousness, worry, agonize, lose sleep; *inf.* be on pins and needles, be in a state of anxiety/agitation/nervousness, worry, agonize, lose sleep, be in a state/flap/tiz-woz/stew/lather. **3** *sweat to get the work done* work hard, work like a Trojan, labour, toil, slog.

sweaty *adjective* *sweaty hands* sweating, perspiring, clammy, sticky.

sweep verb **1** *sweep the floor* brush, vacuum, clean. **2** *sweep up the dust* brush up, clean up, clear up, remove. **3** *sweep aside the rest of the queue* push, thrust, shove, force, elbow, jostle, make a path through. **4** *sweep away/aside their objections* cast aside, discard, disregard, ignore, take no notice of, dismiss. **5** *swept away by the waves* carry, pull, drag, drive. **6** *sweep from the room* glide, sail, stride, flounce. **7** *fire sweeping through the building* race, hurtle, streak, whip, spread like lightning; *inf.* tear. **8** *cars sweeping up the drive* glide, sail, zoom, swoop.

sweep noun **1** *with one sweep of her hand* gesture, movement, move, action, stroke, wave. **2** *the sweep of the road* curve, curvature, bend, arc. **3** *within the sweep of his power* range, span, scope, compass, reach. **4** *a sweep of pasturelands* stretch, expanse, extent, vastness.

sweeping adjective **1** *sweeping reforms* extensive, wide-ranging, global, broad, wide, comprehensive, all-inclusive, all-embracing, thorough, radical, far-reaching. **2** *make sweeping statements* blanket, wholesale, over-general, unqualified, indiscriminate. **3** *a sweeping victory* decisive, overwhelming, thorough, complete, total, absolute, out-and-out, thoroughgoing.
Opposites RESTRICTED; LIMITED; INDECISIVE.

sweet adjective **1** *sweet types of food* sweetened, sugary, sugared, honeyed, syrupy, saccharine. **2** *sweet fruit* ripe, mellow, luscious. **3** *the sweet smell of roses* sweet-smelling, fragrant, aromatic, perfumed, scented, balmy. **4** *the sweet sound of children's voices* sweet-sounding, musical, tuneful, dulcet, mellifluous, soft, harmonious, euphonious, silvery, silver-toned. **5** *sweet foodstuffs* not sour, not rotten, wholesome, palatable, pure. **6** *the sweet sight of home* pleasant, pleasing, agreeable, delightful, welcome. **7** *have a sweet nature* good-natured, amiable, pleasant, agreeable, friendly, kindly, charming, likeable, appealing, engaging, winning, winsome, taking. **8** *sweet girls* attractive, beautiful, lovely, comely, glamorous. **9** *his sweet wife* dear, dearest, darling, beloved, loved, cherished, precious, treasured. **sweet on** *sweet on the boy next door* fond of, taken with, in love with, enamoured of, infatuated with, keen on; *inf.* gone on, mad about.
Opposites SOUR; HARSH; DISAGREEABLE.

sweet noun **1** *have fruit for sweet* sweet course, dessert, pudding; *inf.* afters. *See table at* DESSERT. **2** *suck a sweet* bonbon, sweetmeat; *Am.* candy; *inf.* sweetie. *See table.*

sweeten verb **1** *sweeten the tea* make sweet, add sugar to, sugar, add honey to, add sweetener to. **2** *sweeten an unpleasant situation* make agreeable, soften, ease, alleviate, relieve, mitigate. **3** *sweeten her father before asking for a loan* soften, soften up, mellow, pacify, appease, mollify. **4** *sweeten the air* purify, fresh, ventilate, deodorize.

sweetheart noun **1** *his teenage sweetheart* girlfriend, boyfriend, lover, suitor, admirer, beau, paramour, inamorato, inamorata; *lit.* swain, follower; *inf.* steady, flame. **2** *goodbye, sweetheart* dear, dearest, darling, love, beloved; *inf.* honey, sweetie, sugar, baby.

TYPES OF SWEET	
acid drop	jelly baby
aniseed ball	jelly bean
barley sugar	jujube
boiled sweet	lemon sherbert
bon-bon	liquorice
bull's-eye	liquorice
butterscotch	allsort
candy	lollipop
candyfloss	marshmallow
caramel	marzipan
chocolate	nougat
coconut ice	peardrop
comfit	peppermint
crystallized fruit	praline
fondant	rock
fruit gum	sherbert
fruit pastille	sherbert dip
fudge	sugared almond
gobstopper	toffee
gumdrop	toffee apple
humbug	wine gum

swell verb **1** *his stomach/ankle swelled up* expand, bulge, distend, become distended, inflate, become inflated, dilate, become bloated, blow up, puff up, balloon, tumefy, intumesce. **2** *the numbers have swelled* increase, grow larger, grow greater, rise, mount, escalate, accelerate, step up, snowball, mushroom. **3** *the music swelled* grow loud, grow louder, intensify, heighten.
Opposites SHRINK; CONTRACT; DECREASE.

swell noun **1** *the swell of the sea* billowing, undulation, surging. **2** *a swell in numbers* increase, rise, escalation, acceleration, stepping-up, snowballing, mushrooming. **3** *think himself a bit of a swell* dandy, fop, beau; *inf.* fashion plate, trendsetter, nob.

swell adjective **1** *have a swell time* enjoyable, marvellous, wonderful, first-rate, excellent. **2** *a swell hotel* expensive, luxurious, deluxe, fashionable, elegant, grand; *inf.* posh, plush, ritzy.

swelling noun *treat the swelling on his head* bump, lump, bulge, blister, inflammation, protuberance, tumescence.

sweltering adjective *a sweltering day | sweltering conditions* too hot, hot, torrid, tropical, stifling, suffocating, humid, sultry, sticky, muggy, clammy, close, stuffy; *inf.* boiling, baking.
Opposites FREEZING; COLD; CHILLY.

swerve verb *swerve to avoid an oncoming car* change direction, go off course, veer, turn aside, skew, deviate, sheer, twist.

swift adjective **1** *a swift runner* fast, rapid, quick, speedy, fleet-footed, fleet, swift as an arrow; *inf.* nippy. **2** *at a swift pace* fast, rapid, quick, brisk, lively, speedy, expeditious, express; *inf.* spanking, nippy. **3** *a swift change of plan* rapid, sudden, abrupt, hasty, hurried, meteoric. **4** *a swift reply* rapid, prompt, immediate, instantaneous.
Opposites SLOW; LEISURELY; UNHURRIED.

swiftness noun **1** *the swiftness of the runners* fastness, rapidity, rapidness, quickness, speediness, fleetness; *inf.* nippiness. **2** *the swiftness of the race* fastness, rapidity, rapidness, quickness, briskness, liveliness, speed, speediness, expeditiousness. **3** *the swiftness of the change of plan* rapidity, rapidness, suddenness, abruptness, haste, hastiness, hurriedness. **4** *the swiftness of the reply* rapidity, rapidness, promptness, immediateness, immediacy, instantaneousness.

swill verb *swill pints of beer* gulp down, drink, quaff, swallow, down, drain, guzzle; *inf.* swig, knock off. **swill out** *swill out the stables* sluice, wash down, wash out, clean out, flush out, rinse out.

swill noun **1** *take a swill from the beer mug* gulp, drink, swallow; *inf.* swig. **2** *remove the swill from the pigsties* pigswill, waste matter, waste, slop, refuse, scourings.

swim verb **1** *children swimming in the pond* float, tread water. **2** *food swimming in grease* be saturated in, be drenched in, be soaked in, be steeped in, be immersed in.

swimming noun. See table.

SWIMMING STROKES AND KICKS

Australian crawl	fishtail kick
back crawl	frog kick
backstroke	front crawl
breaststroke	overarm stroke
butterfly	recovery
crawl	stroke
dog-paddle	scissors kick
dolphin kick	sidestroke

---

swimmingly adverb *things going swimmingly* very well, smoothly, effortlessly, like clockwork, with no hitch, without difficulty, as planned; *inf.* like a dream.

swindle verb *swindle the old lady* defraud, cheat, trick, fleece, dupe, deceive, rook, exploit; *inf.* do, con, diddle, rip off, take for a ride, pull a fast one on, bilk.

swindle noun *get the money through a swindle* fraud, trick, deception, exploitation, sharp practice; *inf.* con-trick, con, diddle, rip-off, fiddle.

swindler noun *done out of her money by a swindler* fraudster, cheat, trickster, rogue, mountebank, exploiter; *inf.* con-man, con artist, shark, bilker.

swing verb **1** *lights swinging from the roof* hang, be suspended, dangle, be pendent. **2** *the pendulum swings* move back and forth, sway, oscillate, wag. **3** *the road swings to the right* curve, veer, turn, lean, incline, wind, twist. **4** *swing down the road* march, stride, stroll. **5** *he swings from optimism to despair* change, fluctuate, oscillate, waver, see-saw, yo-yo. **6** *manage to swing an interview with the chairman* achieve, obtain, acquire, get, manoeuvre.

swing noun **1** *the swing of the pendulum* swaying, oscillation, wagging. **2** *music with a swing* rhythm, beat, pulse. **3** *a swing to the left at the election* move, change, variation, turnaround.

swirl verb *water swirling round and round* whirl, eddy, circulate, revolve, spin, twist, churn, swish.

switch noun **1** *a switch from a tree* shoot, twig, branch. **2** *hit the child with a switch* cane, rod, stick, whip, thong, cat-o'-nine-tails. **3** *a sudden switch in direction* change, change of direction, shift, reversal, turnaround, about-turn, swerve, U-turn. **4** *the switch from one method to another* change, changeover, transfer, conversion. **5** *get a new book in a switch with his friend* exchange, trade; *inf.* swap.

switch verb **1** *switch the naughty child* cane, whip, lash, birch, scourge, flagellate. **2** *switch directions* change, shift, reverse. **3** *switch cars* exchange, interchange, trade, barter; *inf.* swap.

swollen adjective *a swollen stomach* expanded, bulging, distended, inflated, dilated, bloated, blown-up, puffed-up, puffy, tumescent.

swoop verb *hawks swooping on their prey* pounce, dive, descend, sweep down on, drop down on. **swoop up** *swoop up the baby in her arms* take up, lift up, pick up, scoop up, seize, snatch, grab.

sword noun blade, steel; *lit.* brand. See tables at KNIFE, WEAPON. **cross swords** fight, do battle, quarrel, have a dispute, engage in conflict, wrangle, bicker, lock horns; *inf.* have a dust-up, have a scrap, have a barney. **put to the sword** *put the traitor to the sword* put to death, execute, kill, slay, murder.

sybaritic adjective *sybaritic tastes* luxurious, self-indulgent, pleasure-seeking, sensual, voluptuous, hedonistic, epicurean, debauched, dissolute.
Opposites ASCETIC; ABSTEMIOUS.

sycophant noun *a great man surrounded by sycophants* toady, fauner, flatterer, truckler, Uriah Heep; *inf.* bootlicker, yes-man.

sycophantic adjective servile, subservient, obsequious, toadying, fauning, flattering, ingratiating, unctuous, truckling, Uriah Heepish; *inf.* bootlicking.

syllabus noun *introduce a new syllabus to the schools* course of study, educational programme, course outline.

symbol noun **1** *the dove is the symbol of peace* emblem, token, sign, badge, representation, figure, image, type. **2** *mathematical/chemical symbol* sign, character, mark. See tables. See also table at ELEMENT. **3** *the symbol of the firm* stamp, emblem, badge, trade mark, logo, logotype, monogram.

symbolic adjective **1** *the dove being symbolic of peace* emblematic, representative, typical. **2** *a symbolic dance* representative, illustrative, emblematic, figurative, allegorical.

symbolize verb *the dove symbolizing peace* be a symbol of, stand for, be a sign of, represent, personify, exemplify, typify, betoken, denote, signify, mean.

symmetrical adjective **1** *symmetrical features* balanced, well-proportioned, proportional, in proportion, regular, even, harmonious. **2** *the two sides of the building must be symmetrical* regu-

lar, even, uniform, consistent, in agreement.
Opposites ASYMMETRICAL; UNEVEN; DISPROPORTION-
ATE.

symmetry *noun* **1** *the symmetry of her features*
balance, proportions, regularity, evenness of
form, harmony. **2** *the symmetry of the two sides
of the building* regularity, evenness, uniformity,
consistency, congruity, conformity, agreement,
correspondence.

sympathetic *adjective* **1** *be sympathetic when
she lost | give the losers a sympathetic look* compas-
sionate, commiserating, commiserative, pitying, condoling, consoling, comforting,
supportive, caring, concerned, solicitous, considerate, kindly, kind, kind-hearted, warm,
warm-hearted, understanding, charitable,
empathetic. **2** *she's a very sympathetic person/
character* pleasant, agreeable, likeable, congenial, friendly, sociable, companionable, neighbourly, easy to get along with; *inf.* simpatico.
3 *not very sympathetic to their cause* in sympathy
with, well-disposed to, favourably disposed to,
favourable to, in favour of, approving of, pro,
on the side of, supporting of, encouraging of.
Opposites UNSYMPATHETIC; UNFEELING; INDIFFERENT;
UNFRIENDLY.

sympathize *verb* **1** *sympathize with the bereaved*
show sympathy for, be sympathetic towards,
show compassion for, be compassionate
towards, commiserate with, pity, offer condolences to, console, offer consolation to, comfort, be supportive of, show understanding to,
empathize with. **2** *sympathize with their cause/
aims* be in sympathy with, be sympathetic
towards, be in favour of, be well-disposed to,
approve of, commend, back, side with, support, encourage.
Opposites DISREGARD; DISAPPROVE.

sympathizer *noun* **1** *the bereaved being comforted by sympathizers* commiserater, condoler,
consoler, comforter, empathizer. **2** *sympathizers of their cause* advocate, supporter, backer,
well-wisher, ally, partisan, fellow-traveller.

sympathy *noun* **1** *express their sympathy to the
bereaved* compassion, commiseration, pity, condolence, consolation, comfort, solace, support,
caring, concern, solicitude, solicitousness, consideration, kindness, kind-heartedness,

warmth, warm-heartedness, charity, charitableness, understanding, empathy. **2** *a bond of
sympathy between them* affinity, empathy, rapport, fellow-feeling, harmony, accord, compatibility, closeness, friendship. **3** *show sympathy
for their cause* favour, approval, approbation,
good will, commendation, support, encouragement.
Opposites INDIFFERENCE; HOSTILITY; DISAPPROVAL.

symptom *noun* **1** *a symptom of the disease* sign,
indication, signal, warning, mark, characteristic, feature. **2** *his bad behaviour was a symptom
of his unhappiness* expression, sign, indication,
signal, mark, token, evidence, demonstration,
display.

symptomatic *adjective pains symptomatic of
heart disease* indicative of, signalling, characteristic of, suggesting, suggestive of.

synthesis *noun* **1** *the synthesis of several elements into a whole* combination, combining,
union, unification, merging, amalgamation,
fusion, coalescence, integration. **2** *a synthesis
of two substances* combination, union, amalgam,
blend, compound, fusion, coalescence.

synthetic *adjective synthetic leather* manufactured, man-made, fake, artificial, mock, ersatz.
Opposites REAL; GENUINE; NATURAL.

syrupy *adjective* **1** *syrupy desserts* over-sweet,
sugary, sweet, honeyed, saccharine, sticky; *inf.*
gooey. **2** *syrupy love stories* sentimental, oversentimental, mawkish, maudlin, mushy,
slushy, sloppy; *inf.* soppy, schmaltzy.

system *noun* **1** *the railway/digestive system*
structure, organization, order, arrangement;
inf. set-up. **2** *a new system for teaching languages*
method, methodology, technique, process, procedure, approach, practice, line, attack, means,
way, modus operandi. **3** *absolutely no system in
his accounting methods* systematization, methodicalness, orderliness, planning, logic, tightness, routine.

systematic *adjective a systematic approach to the
problem* structured, organized, methodical,
orderly, well-ordered, planned, systematized,
logical, efficient, business-like.
Opposites DISORGANIZED; HAPHAZARD; CHAOTIC.

SYMBOLS

Symbol	Meaning	Symbol	Meaning	Symbol	Meaning
<	less than	∞	infinity	£	pound
>	greater than	±	plus or minus	©	copyright
=	equal to	≡	identical to	&	and
≤	less than or equal to	∝	proportional to	@	at
		∂	partial differential	∴	therefore
≥	greater than or equal to	∫	integral	¶	paragraph
		°	degree	™	trade mark
≠	not equal to	%	per cent	𝄞	treble clef
≈	approximately equal to	π	pi	𝄢	bass clef
		Σ	sum	#	sharp
+	plus	√	square root	♭	flat
−	minus	!	factorial	♮	natural
÷	divide	$	dollar	✓	tick
×	multiply	¢	cent	✆	telephone

Tt

tab *noun hang the jacket up by the tab* loop, flap, tag.

table *noun* **1** *put the plates on the table* counter, bar, buffet, bench, stand. *See table.* **2** *provide an excellent table* food, fare, diet, board; meals, victuals; *inf.* spread, nosh, grub, chow. **3** *terrain characterized by tables* tableland; plateau, elevated plain, flat, mesa, steppe. **4** *a table of contents | table of geographical data* list, catalogue, tabulation, inventory, digest, itemization, index. **5** *leave room in the scientific text for tables* chart, diagram, figure, graph, plan.

TABLES AND DESKS	
bedside table	kneehole desk
bureau	lectern
card table	library table
coffee table	pedestal table
console table	Pembroke
Davenport	table
desk	pier table
dining table	reading desk
dressing table	roll-top desk
drop-leaf table	secretaire
end table	side table
escritoire	tea table
gaming table	work table
gateleg table	writing desk
kitchen table	writing table

table *verb table a question/motion* submit, put forward, propose, suggest, move, enter.

tableau *noun* **1** *paint evocative tableaux of village life* picture, painting, representation, portrayal, illustration. **2** *the children's tableau was part of the show* human representation, tableau vivant, pageant. **3** *admire the tableau below from the mountain top* spectacle, scene, sight.

tablet *noun* **1** *the dedication inscribed on the stone tablet* slab, panel, stone. **2** *prescribed tablets for headaches* pill, capsule, lozenge. **3** *a tablet of soap* bar, cake.

taboo *adjective such practices are taboo | taboo language* forbidden, prohibited, banned, proscribed, vetoed, ruled out, outlawed, not permitted, not acceptable, frowned on, beyond the pale.
Opposites ACCEPTABLE.

taboo *noun such practices are subject to taboo* prohibition, proscription, veto, interdiction, non-acceptance; interdict, ban.

tabulate *verb* tabularize, chart, systematize, systemize, arrange, order, dispose, organize, catalogue, list, classify, class, codify, group, range, grade.

tacit *adjective by tacit agreement* implicit, understood, implied, taken for granted, unstated, undeclared, unspoken, unexpressed, unmentioned, unvoiced, silent, wordless.
Opposites EXPLICIT.

taciturn *adjective* unforthcoming, uncommunicative, reticent, untalkative, tight-lipped, close-mouthed, quiet, silent, mute, dumb, reserved, withdrawn, antisocial, unsociable, distant, aloof, cold, detached, dour, sullen.
Opposites COMMUNICATIVE; LOQUACIOUS.

tack *noun* **1** *attach the notice to the wall with a tack* drawing pin, nail, pin, staple, rivet. **2** *try a different tack if that one is unsuccessful* course/line of action, method, approach, process, way, policy, tactic, plan, strategy, attack.

tack *verb* **1** *tack the picture to the wall | tack the carpet to the floor* nail, pin, staple, fix, fasten, affix, put up/down. **2** *tack up the hem* stitch, baste, sew. **3** *in politics it is necessary to know when to tack* change course/direction, alter one's approach, change one's mind/attitude, have a change of heart, do an about-turn; *inf.* do a U-turn. **4** *tack a postscript on the letter | tack a conservatory to the house* add, attach, append, tag, annex.

tackle *noun fishing tackle* gear, equipment, apparatus, outfit; tools, implements, accoutrements, paraphernalia, trappings; *inf.* things, stuff.

tackle *verb* **1** *tackle the task/problem* undertake, attempt, apply/address oneself to, get to grips with, set/go about, get to work at, busy oneself with, embark on, set one's hand to, take on, engage in. **2** *tackle the intruder* grapple with, seize, take hold of, confront, face up to; *inf.* have a go at. **3** *tackle him on the subject of his lateness* speak to, confront, accost, waylay, remonstrate with.

tacky¹ *adjective the paint/surface is tacky* sticky, gluey, gummy; *inf.* gooey.

tacky² *adjective tacky souvenirs on sale* tawdry, tasteless, kitsch, vulgar, crude, garish, gaudy, flashy; *inf.* flash.

tact *noun* diplomacy, discretion, savoir faire, sensitivity, understanding, thoughtfulness, consideration, delicacy, subtlety, finesse, skill, adroitness, dexterity, discernment, perception, judgement, prudence, judiciousness; *inf.* savvy.
Opposites INDISCRETION; tactlessness.

tactful *adjective* diplomatic, politic, discreet, sensitive, understanding, thoughtful, considerate, delicate, subtle, skilful, adroit, discerning, perceptive, prudent, judicious.
Opposites TACTLESS; INDISCREET.

tactic *noun try a different tactic to achieve success* manoeuvre, expedient, device, stratagem, trick, scheme, plan, ploy, course/line of action, method, approach, tack; means. *See also* TACTICS.

tactical *adjective effect the takeover by tactical means* strategic, politic, planned, shrewd, skilful, adroit, clever, smart, cunning, artful.

tactics *plural noun military tactics|his clever tactics secured the takeover bid* strategy, campaign, policy; plans, battle/game plans, manoeuvres.

tactless *adjective* undiplomatic, impolitic, indiscreet, insensitive, inconsiderate, indelicate, unsubtle, rough, crude, unskilful, clumsy, awkward, inept, bungling, maladroit, gauche, undiscerning, imprudent, injudicious.
Opposites TACTFUL; DIPLOMATIC; DISCREET.

tag *noun* **1** *a tag showing the price* label, ticket, sticker, docket. **2** *hang the jacket up by its tag* tab, loop, flap. **3** *tags of wool at the end of the sleeves* end, snippet, tatter, rag, remnant, shred, clipping. **4** *Latin tags* quotation, stock phrase, platitude, cliché, epithet.

tag *verb* **1** *tag the items* label, put a ticket/sticker on, mark. **2** *tag him Lanky* name, call, nickname, title, entitle, label, dub, term, style, christen. **3** *tag a postscript to the letter* add, attach, append, affix, tack. **4** *children tagging along with their parents* go with, accompany, follow, trail behind, tread on the heels of, dog.

tail *noun* **1** *the tail of the animal* brush, scut, dock; *Tech.* cauda. **2** *hurt one's tail* bottom, rump; buttocks; *inf.* backside, rear, bum, sit-upon, arse. **3** *the tail of the queue* rear, end, back, extremity. **4** *the tail of the shirt* bottom, lowest part, extremity. **5** *a tail of traffic stretching from the accident* tailback, queue, line, file, train. **6** *at the tail of the storm* tail-end, close, end, conclusion, termination. **7** *the pursuers are on his tail* track, trail, scent. **8** *put a tail on the crook* detective, investigator, private investigator, shadow; *inf.* sleuth, private eye; *Am. inf.* gumshoe. **turn tail** run away, flee, retreat, take to one's heels, cut and run; *inf.* skedaddle, vamoose.
Opposites HEAD; FRONT.

tail *verb detectives tailing the crooks* follow, shadow, stalk, trail, track, dog the footsteps of, keep under surveillance. **tail off/away** *business tails off in the winter* dwindle, decrease, drop off, fall away, peter out, fade, wane, die away, die out, come to an end.

tailor *noun* outfitter, dressmaker, couturier, clothier, costumier. *See table at* FASHION.

tailor *verb tailor the holiday to your needs* fit, suit, fashion, style, mould, shape, adapt, adjust, modify, convert, alter, accommodate.

taint *verb* **1** *the water/meat had become tainted* contaminate, pollute, adulterate, infect, blight, befoul, spoil. **2** *taint his reputation* tarnish, sully, blacken, stain, besmirch, smear, blot, blemish, muddy, damage, injure, harm.

taint *noun* **1** *food poisoning caused by the taint of the water* contamination, pollution, adulteration, infection, contagion. **2** *a taint on his character* stain, smear, blot, blemish, stigma. **3** *a taint of insanity in the family* trace, touch, suggestion, hint.

take *verb* **1** *take the book from the woman* get/lay hold of, get into one's hands, grasp, grip, clutch. **2** *take first prize* get, receive, obtain, gain, acquire, secure, procure, come by, win,

earn. **3** *take several prisoners* seize, catch, capture, arrest, carry off, abduct. **4** *who took my pen/savings?* remove, appropriate, make off with, steal, filch, pilfer, purloin, pocket; *inf.* pinch, swipe, nick. **5** *take a pound of apples* buy, purchase, pay for. **6** *take a single room | take a boat for the day* reserve, book, engage, rent, hire, lease. **7** *she showed me several dresses but I took the blue one* pick, choose, select, decide on, settle on, opt for. **8** *take the bus/motorway* use, make use of, utilize. **9** *take some bread and wine* consume, eat, devour, swallow; drink, imbibe. **10** *the vaccination did not take* be effective, have/take effect, be efficacious, work, operate, succeed. **11** *the journey takes three hours* use, use up, require, call for, need, necessitate. **12** *take the box home with you* carry, fetch, bring, bear, transport, convey, cart, ferry; *inf.* tote. **13** *will you take his sister home?* escort, accompany, conduct, guide, lead, usher, convoy. **14** *take measles* catch, become infected/ill with. **15** *take fright | take pleasure in acting* experience, be affected by, undergo. **16** *take the child's temperature* find out, discover, ascertain, determine, establish. **17** *I take it that you agreed | she took his silence to mean agreement* understand, interpret as, grasp, gather, comprehend, apprehend, assume, believe, suppose, consider, presume. **18** *take the news badly* receive, deal with, cope with. **19** *she took him for a fool* regard as, consider as, view as, look upon as. **20** *take the offer* accept, receive, adopt. **21** *take a course of study* enter upon, undertake, begin, set about. **22** *take French at school* study, learn, be taught, take up, pursue. **23** *take an oath/look* perform, execute, effect, do, make, have. **24** *take a nap* engage in, occupy oneself in. **25** *the bucket takes three litres* hold, contain, have the capacity for, have space/room for, accommodate. **26** *I cannot take his rudeness* bear, tolerate, stand, put up with, stomach, brook. **27** *the machine takes its name from the inventor* derive, obtain, come by. **28** *the passage is taken from Hamlet* extract, quote, cite, excerpt, derive. **29** *take three from five* subtract, deduct, remove. **30** *we were quite taken with the little girl | taken by her beauty* captivate, enchant, charm, delight, please, attract, win over, fascinate. **31** *do you think the idea will take?* catch on, become popular, gain popularity, be successful, succeed. **take after** resemble, look like, be like, favour; *inf.* be a chip off the old block, be the spitting image of. **take against** take a dislike to, feel hostile towards, view with disfavour. **take back 1** *take back the accusing statement* retract, withdraw, renounce, disclaim, unsay, disavow, recant. **2** *take the book back to its owner* carry back, bring back, fetch back, return. **3** *his stories took me back to my youth* awaken/evoke one's memories of, put one in mind of, remind one of. **4** *the shop won't take the goods back* accept back, give a refund for, exchange, trade, swap. **5** *his wife has taken him back* accept back, welcome, forgive. **6** *take back the land won by the enemy* get back, regain, repossess, reclaim, recapture, reconquer. **take down 1** *take down the details* write down, note down, make a note of, jot down, set down, record, put on record, commit to paper, document, minute. **2** *take down* *the marquee/scaffolding/fence* remove, dismantle, disassemble, take apart, take to pieces, demolish, tear down, level, raze. **3** *take down the flag* | *took down his trousers* pull down, let down, haul down, lower, drop. **4** *that should take him down a bit* humble, deflate, humiliate, mortify, take down a peg or two; *inf.* put down. **take in** **1** *take in the homeless child* | *take in paying guests* take, admit, let in, receive, welcome, accommodate, board. **2** *take the skirt in* make smaller/narrower, reduce in size. **3** *he didn't seem to take the news in* grasp, understand, comprehend, absorb, assimilate. **4** *the child said nothing but took everything in* observe, see, notice, take note of, note, perceive, regard. **5** *the old lady was completely taken in by the con man* deceive, delude, hoodwink, mislead, trick, dupe, fool, cheat, defraud, swindle, gull; *inf.* con, bilk, pull the wool over someone's eyes, do. **6** *the school catchment area takes in these three districts* include, encompass, embrace, contain, comprise, cover. **7** *try to take in a concert/film when you are there* go to, go to see, attend, visit. **take off** **1** *take the lid off the jar* remove, detach, pull off. **2** *take off one's clothes* remove, discard, strip off, peel off, throw off, divest oneself of, doff. **3** *take the show off after three weeks* remove, withdraw, retract. **4** *take money off the bill for poor service* deduct, subtract, take away. **5** *the children took off when they saw the police* | *she took off for Australia* run away, take to one's heels, flee, decamp, disappear, leave, go, depart; *inf.* split, beat it, skedaddle, vamoose, hightail it. **6** *the child takes off the teacher very cleverly* mimic, impersonate, imitate, parody, mock; *inf.* send up, spoof. **7** *the plane took off* become airborne, leave the ground, lift off. **8** *the business/scheme has really taken off* succeed, do well, become popular, catch on. **9** *it's time I took myself off* take one's leave, make one's departure. **take on** **1** *take on extra work* undertake, accept, tackle, turn one's hand to; *inf.* have a go at. **2** *take on extra staff* employ, engage, hire, enroll, enlist; *inf.* take on board. **3** *take him on at chess* compete against, oppose, challenge, face, pit/match oneself against, contend with, vie with, fight. **4** *suddenly his words/situation took on a new meaning* acquire, come to have, assume. **5** *don't take on so* get upset, make a fuss, break down, get excited, overreact; *inf.* lose one's cool, get in a tizzy. **take out** **1** *take out a tooth* remove, extract, pull out, yank out. **2** *take out the girl next door* go out with, escort; *inf.* date. **take over** *take over the business* | *take over the running of the household* take/assume/gain control of, take charge/command of, assume responsibility for. **take to** **1** *she's taken to smoking* begin, start, commence, make a habit of, resort to. **2** *he didn't take to her friend* develop a liking for, like, get on with, become friendly with. **3** *he has really taken to swimming* become good at, develop an ability/aptitude for, develop a liking for, like, enjoy, become interested in. **take up** **1** *take up the carpets/pen* lift up, raise. **2** *take up surfing* become involved/interested in, engage in, begin, start, commence. **3** *practising the piano takes up a great deal of time* use, use up, occupy, fill, consume, absorb, cover, extend over. **4** *take up the story where they left off* resume,

recommence, restart, begin again, carry on, continue, pick up. **5** *take up an offer* accept, say yes to, agree to, accede to, adopt. **6** *take up a skirt/hem* shorten, make shorter; raise. **7** *take up with the wrong sort of people* become friendly/friends (with), go around (with); *inf.* knock about (with), hang around (with).
Opposites GIVE; REFUSE.

take *noun* **1** *fishermen/hunters assessing the take* catch, haul, bag. **2** *counting the take after the sale/match* takings, proceeds, returns, receipts, profits, winnings, pickings, earnings; gain, income, revenue.

take-off *noun* **1** *the take-off of the plane* taking-off, lift-off, departure, ascent, climbing, mounting, soaring, flying. **2** *admire his take-off of the celebrity* mimicry, impersonation, imitation, parody, mockery; *inf.* send-up, spoof.

taking *adjective a taking child* captivating, enchanting, beguiling, bewitching, fascinating, charming, delightful, pleasing, engaging, attractive, winning, lovable, winsome, prepossessing; *inf.* fetching.
Opposites REPULSIVE; UNPLEASANT.

takings *plural noun* proceeds, returns, receipts, earnings, winnings, pickings; profit, gain, income, revenue.

tale *noun* **1** *a fairy tale* story, short story, narrative, anecdote, legend, fable, myth, parable, allegory, epic, saga; *inf.* yarn. **2** *hear tales of her wild behaviour* talk, rumour, gossip, hearsay; report, allegation. **3** *the child didn't see the burglar—that was a tale* lie, fib, falsehood, untruth, fabrication, piece of fiction; *inf.* story, tall story, cock-and-bull story, whopper, terminological inexactitude.

talent *noun* gift, flair, aptitude, facility, knack, bent, ability, capacity, faculty, aptness, endowment, strong point, forte, genius.

talented *adjective* gifted, accomplished, able, capable, apt, deft, adept, proficient, brilliant, expert, artistic.
Opposites INCAPABLE; HOPELESS; INEPT.

talk *verb* **1** *talk incessantly* speak, give voice/utterance, chat, chatter, gossip, natter, prattle, prate, gibber, jabber, babble, rattle on, gabble; *inf.* rabbit, yak, witter, gab. **2** *talk rubbish* speak, say, utter, voice, express, articulate, pronounce, enunciate, verbalize. **3** *they don't talk any more* communicate, converse, speak to each other, discuss things, confer, consult each other, have negotiations, have a tête-à-tête, parley, palaver, confabulate; *inf.* have a confab, chew the fat/rag, jaw, rap. **4** *if you tell her your secret she'll talk* tell, reveal all, tell tales, give the game away, open one's mouth, let the cat out of the bag; *inf.* blab, squeal, spill the beans, grass, sing. **5** *people will talk if they live together* gossip, spread rumours, pass comment, make remarks, criticize. **6** *the professor is talking tonight* give a talk, give/make/deliver a speech, speak, lecture, discourse. **7** *after years of silence the spy has decided to talk* speak, speak out, speak up, give voice, tell the facts, divulge information, reveal all. **talk back** *children reprimanded for talking back to their parents* answer defiantly/impertinently, answer back. **talk big**

brag, boast, crow, exaggerate; *inf.* blow one's own trumpet, shoot one's mouth. **talk down 1** *hecklers talking down the speaker* out-talk, drown, silence, override. **2** *talk down to young people* speak condescendingly to, condescend to, speak haughtily to, patronize. **3** *talk the pilot down* give landing instructions to, bring to land. **talk into** *talk him into buying the car* persuade to, cajole to, coax into, influence. **talk of** *they talked of going away* speak about, discuss, mention, make mention of, refer to, make reference to. **talk out of** dissuade from, persuade against, discourage from, deter from, stop.

talk *noun* **1** *their noisy talk kept me awake* talking, speaking, chatter, chatting, gossiping, nattering, prattling, gibbering, jabbering, babbling, gabbling; *inf.* rabbiting, yakking, wittering, gabbing. *See* TALK *verb* 1. **2** *baby/seamen's talk* words; speech, language, dialect, jargon, cant, slang, idiom, idiolect, patois; *inf.* lingo. **3** *have a talk about their future* conversation, chat, discussion, tête-à-tête; dialogue; *inf.* confab, jaw, rap. **4** *give a talk to the society* lecture, speech, address, discourse, oration, sermon, disquisition. **5** *there is talk of a merger* gossip, rumour, hearsay, tittle-tattle. **6** *the talk in the pub was of the footballer's accident* chat, conversation, discussion, gossip, subject, theme.

talkative *adjective* loquacious, garrulous, voluble, chatty, gossipy, conversational, long-winded, gushing, effusive; *inf.* gabby, mouthy, big-mouthed.
Opposites TACITURN; UNCOMMUNICATIVE.

talker *noun* **1** *the talker bored the audience* speaker, speech-maker, lecturer, orator. **2** *the child is a good talker* speaker. **3** *they are a family of talkers* conversationalist, chatter, chatterbox, gossip.

talking-to *noun* *give the naughty children a talking-to* lecture, scolding, row, reprimand, rebuke, reproof, reproach; *inf.* telling-off, ticking-off, wigging, carpeting.

talks *plural noun* *talks to try stop the war* conference, summit, meeting, consultation, discussion, dialogue, negotiation, symposium, seminar, conclave, colloquy, palaver, parley, confabulation; *inf.* pow-wow.

tall *adjective* **1** *tall people* big, colossal, gigantic, lanky, rangy, gangling. **2** *three feet tall in height*, high. **3** *tall buildings* high, lofty, towering, soaring, sky-high, sky-scraping. **4** *a tall story* exaggerated, unlikely, incredible, far-fetched, implausible. **tall order** demanding/exacting/difficult task, unreasonable demand/request.
Opposites SHORT; SMALL; LOW.

tally *noun* **1** *keep a tally of the number of visitors* count, record, running total, reckoning, enumeration, register, roll, census, poll. **2** *what was the tally at the end of the game?* score, count, result, total, sum. **3** *produce as a tally for identification* ticket, label, sticker, stamp, tab. **4** *his tally in the other team | the glove's tally* counterpart, match, mate, duplicate.

tally *verb* *the two accounts don't tally | his story doesn't tally with hers* agree, accord, concur,

coincide, conform, correspond, match, fit, harmonize.

tame *adjective* **1** *tame animals* domesticated, not wild, not fierce, gentle, used to humans. **2** *find the supposedly rebellious children quite tame* subdued, docile, submissive, compliant, meek, obedient, tractable, amenable, manageable, unresisting. **3** *we have a tame joiner* available, willing, amenable. **4** *the horror film turned out to be quite tame* unexciting, uninteresting, uninspired, dull, bland, flat, insipid, vapid, run-of-the-mill, mediocre, prosaic, humdrum, boring, tedious, wearisome.
Opposites WILD; FIERCE.

tame *verb* **1** *tame the wild cat* domesticate, break, train, gentle. **2** *tame the unruly element in the class/party* subdue, discipline, curb, control, master, bring to heel, overcome, suppress, repress, humble.

tamper *verb* **tamper with 1** *tamper with the exam papers* meddle with, interfere with, monkey around with, mess about with, tinker with, fiddle with, alter/change/adjust illegally; *inf.* fool about with, muck about with, poke one's nose into, stick one's oar into. **2** *tamper with the jury* influence, get at, rig, manipulate, bribe, corrupt; *inf.* fix.

tan *adjective* *tan shoes* yellowish-brown, brownish-yellow, light brown, pale brown, tawny.

tan *verb* **1** *they tan easily* become suntanned, take a suntan/tan, brown, go brown. **2** *the hot sun tanned their skins* suntan, brown, turn brown, darken. **3** *the father tanned his son* beat, thrash, wallop, whip, lash, leather, lambaste.

tang *noun* **1** *the tang of orange* flavour, taste, savour. **2** *the tang of the sea* smell, odour, aroma. **3** *add some tang to the food/occasion* spice, spiciness, piquancy, relish, sharpness, zest; *inf.* ginger, punch, zip.

tangible *adjective* **1** *tangible changes to the skin* touchable, palpable, tactile, visible. **2** *tangible proof* concrete, real, actual, solid, substantial, hard, well-documented, well-defined, definite, clear, clear-cut, distinct, unmistakable, positive, discernible.
Opposites INTANGIBLE; ABSTRACT.

tangle *verb* **1** *her hair became tangled in the rose bush | the rain had tangled her hair* entangle, intertwine, intertwist, twist, snarl, ravel, knot, mat. **2** *don't tangle with the authorities* become involved, come into conflict, have a dispute, dispute, argue, quarrel, fight, row, wrangle, squabble, contend, cross swords, lock horns.
Opposites UNTANGLE; UNRAVEL.

tangled *adjective* **1** *tangled wool/hair* entangled, twisted, snarled, ravelled, knotted, knotty, matted, tousled, messy; *inf.* mussed-up. **2** *tangled affairs* confused, jumbled, mixed-up, messy, chaotic, complicated, involved, convoluted, complex.

tank *noun* **1** *water tank* container, receptacle, vat, cistern. **2** *soldiers in tanks* armoured car, combat vehicle.

tantalize *verb* *tantalize them with a sight of the unobtainable gold* tease, torment, torture, frustrate, disappoint, thwart, make one's mouth water, lead on, entice, titillate, allure, beguile.

tantamount *adjective his statement was tantamount to a confession* equivalent (to), equal (to), as good as, synonymous (with).

tantrum *noun* fit of temper/rage, fit, outburst, flare-up, pet, paroxysm; *inf.* paddy, wax.

tap[1] *noun* **1** *turn the tap off* spigot, stopcock, valve; *Am.* faucet. **2** *put a tap on their telephone* listening device; *inf.* bug, bugging device. **on tap 1** *beer on tap* on draught, not bottled/canned. **2** *extra supplies on tap* at/on hand, available, ready, in reserve, standing by.

tap[2] *verb* **1** *tap cider from a cask* draw off, siphon off, drain, bleed. **2** *tap a cask* draw liquid from, broach, open, pierce. **3** *tap sources of information* use, make use of, put to use, utilize, draw on, exploit, milk. **4** *tap mineral resources* extract, obtain, open up, explore, probe. **5** *tap their telephone* wire tap; *inf.* bug. **6** *tap their telephone calls* wire tap, listen in to, eavesdrop on; *inf.* bug, get on record.

tap[3] *noun* **1** *give a tap at the window* knock, rap, beat. **2** *give a tap on the shoulder* touch, pat, light blow/slap.

tap[4] *verb* **1** *tap on the window | tap the table* knock, rap, strike, beat, drum. **2** *tap him on the shoulder* touch, pat, strike/slap lightly.

tape *noun* **1** *tie a tape round the parcel* band, strip, string, ribbon. **2** *use tape to repair the crack/tear* adhesive tape, insulating tape, masking tape, parcel tape; Sellotape™. **3** *play a tape* tape recording, cassette, videotape, video cassette, video, audiotape, audiocassette.

tape *verb* **1** *tape the pieces together* bind, tie, fasten, stick, seal, secure; Sellotape™. **2** *tape the concert/conversation* record, tape-record, video-record, video. **3** *tape off the area* seal, mark with tape. **have taped** *have the situation/patient taped* understand fully, know all about, have all the details of, know the ins and outs of.

taper *verb* **1** *the candles taper at the top* narrow, thin, become narrow/thinner, come to a point. **2** *sales tend to taper off at this time of year* dwindle, diminish, lessen, decrease, reduce, subside, die off, die away, fade, peter out, wane, ebb, wind down, slacken off, thin out.

target *noun* **1** *fail to hit the target in the shooting gallery* mark, bull's-eye. **2** *the injured bird was an easy target* prey, quarry, game. **3** *our target is £50,000 | their target is the European market* objective, goal, object, aim, end, intention, desired result. **4** *she is the target of their jokes* butt, victim, scapegoat.

tariff *noun* **1** *the tariff is on display* price list/schedule, list of charges. **2** *ask the waitress for the tariff* menu, bill of fare. **3** *pay a tariff on imports* tax, duty, toll, excise, levy, impost.

tarnish *verb* **1** *time had tarnished the brass* dull, dim, discolour, rust. **2** *silver tarnishes easily* lose its shine/lustre, become dull, discolour, rust. **3** *tarnish his reputation* sully, besmirch, blacken, stain, blemish, blot, taint, befoul, drag through the mud.
Opposites BRIGHTEN; POLISH; ENHANCE.

tarnish *noun* **1** *remove the tarnish from the silver* discoloration, oxidation, rust. **2** *survive the tarnish on his reputation* black mark, slur, stain, blemish, blot, taint, stigma.

tart[1] *noun* *a fruit/meat tart* pastry, tartlet, pie, quiche, strudel.

tart[2] *noun* **1** *he picked up a tart* prostitute, whore, call girl, harlot, streetwalker, fallen woman, woman of easy virtue, woman of the night, *fille de joie*; *inf.* hooker. **2** *his wife's just a tart* loose woman, slut, trollop, wanton.

tart[3] *verb* **tart up 1** *tart oneself up* dress (oneself) up, make (oneself) up, smarten (oneself) up. **2** *tart up the old café* renovate, refurbish, redecorate, modernize, smarten up.

tart[4] *adjective* **1** *rather a tart apple/dessert* sharp, sharp-tasting, sour, tangy, piquant, pungent, bitter, acid, acidulous, vinegary. **2** *a tart remark/wit* astringent, caustic, sharp, biting, cutting, stinging, mordant, trenchant, incisive, piercing, acrimonious, barbed, scathing, sarcastic, sardonic.
Opposites SWEET; KIND.

task *noun* job, duty, chore, charge, odd job, piece of work/business, assignment, commission, mission, engagement, occupation, undertaking, exercise, errand, quest. **take to task** rebuke, reprimand, reprove, reproach, upbraid, scold, berate, lecture, castigate, censure, criticize, blame; *inf.* tell off.

taste *noun* **1** *the taste of fresh raspberries* flavour, savour, relish, tang. **2** *have a taste of the pudding/sauce* bit, morsel, bite, mouthful, spoonful, sample, sip, drop, swallow, touch, soupçon. **3** *have a taste for the unknown | expensive tastes* liking, love, fondness, fancy, desire, preference, penchant, predilection, inclination, partiality, leaning, bent, hankering, appetite, palate, thirst, hunger. **4** *furnish the house with taste* discrimination, discernment, judgement, cultivation, culture, refinement, polish, finesse, elegance, grace, stylishness. **5** *her remark lacked taste* decorum, propriety, correctness, etiquette, politeness, tact, tactfulness, diplomacy, delicacy, nicety, discretion.

taste *verb* **1** *taste the pudding while cooking it* sample, test, try, nibble, sip. **2** *I can't taste the garlic* make out, perceive, discern, distinguish, differentiate. **3** *not to taste food for days* eat, partake of, consume, devour. **4** *taste of onions* have a flavour of, savour of, smack of. **5** *taste success/defeat* experience, undergo, encounter, meet, come face to face with, come up against, know.

tasteful *adjective* **1** *a tasteful display/room* in good taste, aesthetic, artistic, harmonious, pleasing, elegant, graceful, beautiful, pretty, charming, handsome, discriminating, refined, restrained. **2** *tasteful behaviour/manners* decorous, proper, seemly, correct, polite, fitting, fit, appropriate, refined, cultured, cultivated.
Opposites TASTELESS; TACKY; GARISH; IMPROPER.

tasteless *adjective* **1** *tasteless food* flavourless, unflavoured, savourless, bland, insipid, watery, watered-down, weak, thin, unappetizing, uninteresting, vapid. **2** *tasteless decorations* vulgar, crude, tawdry, garish, gaudy, loud, flashy,

showy, cheap, gross, meretricious. **3** *tasteless behaviour* indecorous, improper, unseemly, incorrect, impolite, rude, unfitting, inappropriate, unrefined, uncultured, uncultivated. **4** *tasteless remarks* vulgar, crude, low, gross, indelicate, uncouth, crass, tactless, undiplomatic, indiscreet.
Opposites SPICY; APPETIZING; TASTEFUL; SEEMLY.

tasty *adjective* flavoursome, flavourful, full-flavoured, appetizing, palatable, toothsome, delectable, delicious, luscious, mouth-watering, piquant, pungent, spicy; *inf.* scrumptious, yummy, finger-licking.
Opposites BLAND; INSIPID.

tatter *noun* rag, torn/ragged piece. **in tatters 1** *clothes in tatters* ragged, torn, in shreds, in bits. **2** *his career/argument in tatters* in ruins, ruined, destroyed, demolished.

tattle *verb tattling about their friend's affairs* gossip, tittle-tattle, chatter, natter, prattle, prate, babble, rattle on; *inf.* rabbit on, witter on, gab.

taunt *noun ignore the taunts of the opposition* gibe, jeer, sneer, insult, barb, catcall, brickbat; teasing, provocation, ridiculing, derision, mockery, sarcasm; *inf.* dig, put-down.

taunt *verb rich children taunting the poor* gibe at, jeer at, sneer at, insult, chaff, tease, torment, provoke, ridicule, deride, mock, poke fun at.

taut *adjective* **1** *taut ropes* tight, tightly stretched, stretched, rigid. **2** *taut muscles* tightened, flexed, tensed. **3** *a taut expression* tense, strained, stressed, drawn; *inf.* uptight. **4** *run a taut ship* in good order/condition, orderly, in order, shipshape, tight, trim, neat, well-ordered, well-regulated, tidy, spruce, smart.
Opposites LOOSE; SLACK.

tautology *noun* repetition, repetitiveness, repetitiousness, reiteration, redundancy, pleonasm, wordiness, long-windedness, verbosity, prolixity.

tawdry *adjective* showy, gaudy, flashy, garish, loud, tasteless, cheap, cheapjack, shoddy, meretricious, Brummagem; *inf.* flash, tatty, tacky, kitsch.
Opposites TASTEFUL; REFINED.

tax *noun* **1** *income tax | charge a tax on imports* levy, charge, duty, toll, excise, tariff, impost, tribute; customs. **2** *they became a tax on her health/resources* burden, load, weight, encumbrance, strain, pressure, stress, drain.

tax *verb* **1** *tax his salary at source | tax imports* levy a tax on, impose a toll on, charge duty

on. **2** *work taxing his strength* make demands on, weigh heavily on, weigh down, burden, load, encumber, overload, push, push too far, stretch, strain, try, wear out, exhaust, sap, drain, enervate, fatigue, tire, weary, weaken. **3** *tax him with his unpunctuality* confront, call to account, charge, blame, censure, accuse, impeach, indict, arraign.

taxing *adjective a taxing job* demanding, exacting, burdensome, onerous, difficult, hard, tough, heavy, tiring, exhausting, enervating, draining, sapping, stressful, wearing, trying, punishing.
Opposites EASY; EFFORTLESS.

tea *noun.* See table.

TYPES OF TEA	
Assam	Indian tea
blackcurrant tea	jasmine tea
black tea	Keemun
camomile tea	Lapsang
Ceylon tea	Souchong
China tea	lemon tea
Darjeeling	orange pekoe
Earl Grey	pekoe
fruit tea	peppermint tea
green tea	rosehip tea
gunpowder tea	Russian tea
herbal tea	tisane
iced tea	yerba maté

teach *verb* **1** *teach children* give lessons to, instruct, educate, school, tutor, coach, train, drill, ground, enlighten, edify. **2** *teach French to children* give lessons/instruction in, instil, inculcate. **3** *teach them how to ride a bike* instruct, train, show, guide.

teacher *noun* schoolteacher, schoolmaster, schoolmistress, master, mistress, instructor, educator, tutor, coach, trainer, lecturer, professor, don, pedagogue, guide, mentor, guru.

team *noun* **1** *a team of workers/players* group, band, bunch, company, party, gang, crew, troupe, set, squad, side, line-up. See table. **2** *a team of horses* pair, span, yoke.

team *verb team up with his friend to do the project* join (with), get/come/band together (with), work together (with), unite (with), cooperate (with), form an alliance (with).

tear[1] *noun* **1** *a tear in the material* rip, split, hole, rent, run, rupture. **2** *bandage the tear in*

TEAMS			
Sport	**Number of Players**	**Sport**	**Number of Players**
American football	11	netball	7
baseball	9	polo	4
basketball	(men) 5	rounders	9
	(women) 6	Rugby League	13
cricket	11	Rugby Union	15
curling	4	shinty	12
field hockey	11	soccer	11
ice hockey	6	team handball	4
lacrosse	(men) 10	volleyball	6
	(women) 12	water polo	7

his arm laceration, gash, slash, scratch, cut, mutilation, injury, wound.

tear² *verb* **1** *tear the paper/cloth* rip, pull apart, pull to pieces, split, rend, sever, rive, sunder, rupture. **2** *tear the flesh* lacerate, gash, slash, pierce, stab, scratch, cut, claw, mangle, mutilate, hack, injure, wound. **3** *tear the painting from the wall | tear off the cover* rip, pull, wrench, yank, wrest, extract, peel, snatch, pluck, grab, seize. **4** *torn between going and staying* divide, split, rend, disrupt, break apart. **5** *torn by guilt* disrupt, distress, upset, harrow, torture, torment. **6** *children tearing down the street* run, race, sprint, gallop, rush, dash, bolt, career, dart, fly, shoot, hurry, speed, hasten; *inf.* belt, hotfoot it, whiz, zoom, zip, zap.

tear³ *noun* **1** *tears ran down her cheeks* teardrop. **2** *tears of perspiration/resin* drop, droplet, globule, bead. **in tears** tearful, crying, weeping, sobbing, blubbering, wailing; upset.

tearful *adjective* **1** *in a tearful state* in tears, crying, weeping, sobbing, blubbering, snivelling, whimpering, wailing; emotional, upset, distressed; *inf.* weepy, blubbing. **2** *a tearful parting/event* emotional, upsetting, distressing, heartbreaking, heart-rending, sad, sorrowful, piteous, pitiful, pitiable, pathetic, poignant, mournful, melancholy, lamentable, dolorous.

tease *verb* **1** *tease the cat | tease the new boy* torment, provoke, badger, bait, goad, needle, pest, bother, worry, vex, irritate, annoy, gibe, mock, ridicule, poke fun at; *inf.* aggravate. **2** *he didn't mean to upset her; he was only teasing her* joke (with), fool (with), chaff, rag, twit; *inf.* kid, rib, have on.

technical *adjective* **1** *technical training/applications* mechanical, practical, scientific, applying science, non-theoretical. **2** *technical terms* specialist, specialized, scientific.

technique *noun* **1** *new business techniques* method, method of working, *modus operandi*, system, procedure, style of approach, manner, way, course of action, mode, fashion; means. **2** *admire the violinist's technique* execution, performance, skill, skilfulness, proficiency, expertise, expertness, mastery, artistry, art, craftsmanship, craft, ability, adroitness, deftness, dexterity, knack. **3** *admire his technique in dealing with management* skill, ability, capability, proficiency, capacity, aptitude, expertise, knack, talent, gift, genius; *inf.* know-how.

tedious *adjective* wearisome, wearying, tiresome, tiring, fatiguing, soporific, long-drawn-out, overlong, long-winded, prolix, dull, deadly dull, boring, uninteresting, dry, dreary, drab, unexciting, lifeless, uninspired, flat, banal, vapid, insipid, monotonous, unvaried, prosaic, humdrum, run-of-the-mill, routine. *Opposites* EXCITING; INTERESTING.

tedium *noun* tediousness, wearisomeness, tiresomeness, prolixity, dullness, boredom, ennui, uninterestingness, dryness, lifelessness, dreariness, drabness, flatness, banality, vapidity, insipidity, monotony, sameness.

teem *verb* **1** *fish teem in these waters* abound, be abundant, be plentiful, be copious. **2** *rivers*

teeming with fish | teeming with ideas abound, swarm, crawl, bristle, seethe, brim.

teenage *adjective* adolescent, youthful, young, juvenile.

teenager *noun* young person, adolescent, youth, minor, juvenile; *inf.* teeny-bopper.

teeter *verb* **1** *teeter down the street on high heels* totter, wobble, stagger, stumble, reel, sway, roll, lurch. **2** *teeter between accepting and refusing* waver, vacillate, fluctuate, oscillate, dither, hesitate, shilly-shally, see-saw.

teetotalism *noun* abstinence, abstention, temperance, sobriety, Rechabitism.

teetotaller *noun* abstainer, non-drinker, Rechabite.

telegram *noun* telemessage, cable, telex; *inf.* wire.

telepathy *noun* thought transference, mind-reading, extrasensory perception, ESP, psychometry.

telephone *noun* **1** *speak on the telephone* telephone set; car phone, cellular telephone, cellphone, cordless telephone, videophone; *inf.* phone, blower. **2** *lift the telephone* handset, receiver.

telephone *verb* *I'll telephone you tomorrow* call, call up, ring up, ring; *inf.* phone, give someone a ring/tinkle/buzz, get on the blower, buzz.

telescope *noun* glass, spyglass. *See table.*

TYPES OF TELESCOPE

astronomical telescope	Newtonian telescope
Cassegrain telescope	radio telescope
	reflecting telescope
coudé telescope	refracting telescope
Galilean telescope	Schmidt telescope
	terrestrial telescope

---

telescope *verb* **1** *the two parts of the instrument telescope* slide into each other, slide together. **2** *the front two carriages were telescoped together in the crash* concertina, crush, squash, squeeze, compress, compact. **3** *telescope the long novel into a one-act play* reduce, condense, boil down, compress, compact, consolidate, shorten, abbreviate, abridge, truncate, curtail, cut, trim. *Opposites* ELONGATE; EXTEND; AMPLIFY.

television *noun* television set; *inf.* TV, telly, the box, gogglebox, small screen, the tube, idiot box, talking head. *See table.*

PARTS OF A TELEVISION RECEIVER

aerial	luminance signal amplifier
amplifier	phosphor dots
cathode-ray tube	scanning current generator
chrominance signal extractor	screen
colour decoder	shadow mask
control	sound demodulator
deflector coil	synchronizing pulse separator
electron gun	tuner
loudspeaker	

tell verb **1** *tell the news to everyone* | *tell the truth* make known, impart, communicate, announce, proclaim, broadcast, divulge, reveal, disclose, declare, state, mention, utter, voice, say, speak. **2** *tell a story* narrate, relate, recount, give an account of, report, chronicle, recite, rehearse, describe, portray, sketch, delineate. **3** *tell them tomorrow that you are going* inform, let know, make aware, apprise, notify. **4** *he's guilty, I tell you* assure, promise, guarantee, warrant. **5** *tell them to go home* instruct, bid, order, give orders, command, direct, charge, enjoin, dictate to, call upon, require. **6** *he knows her secret but he promised not to tell* talk, tell tales, blab, give the game away, open one's mouth, let the cat out of the bag; *inf.* squeal, spill the beans, grass, sing, rat. **7** *his friend told on him* report (on), inform (on); *inf.* squeal (on), rat (on), grass (on), blow the whistle (on), pull the plug (on). **8** *his expression told how he felt* reveal, disclose, show, display, exhibit, indicate. **9** *unable to tell his reaction from his expression* deduce, make out, discern, perceive, see, identify, recognize, discover, understand, comprehend. **10** *unable to tell one from the other* distinguish, differentiate, discriminate. **11** *breeding tells* have an effect, make its presence felt, count, carry weight, have influence/force, register; *inf.* have clout. **12** *the strain told on him* have an effect on, affect, take its toll of. **13** *tell the votes* count, calculate, tally, estimate, compute, number, reckon.

telling adjective *make a telling contribution* | *telling evidence* marked, significant, substantial, considerable, sizeable, solid, weighty, important, striking, impressive, potent, powerful, forceful, effective, effectual, cogent, influential, decisive.
Opposites UNIMPORTANT; INSIGNIFICANT.

tell-tale noun *the tell-tale reported his friend to the teacher/authorities* talebearer, blabbermouth, blabber; *inf.* loud mouth, squealer, grass.

tell-tale adjective *children stealing raspberries with tell-tale signs round their mouths* revealing, revelatory, suggestive, meaningful, significant, indicative; *inf.* give-away.

temerity noun *have the temerity to call him a liar* effrontery, impudence, audacity, cheek, gall, presumption, presumptuousness, brazenness, rashness, recklessness, foolhardiness.

temper noun **1** *he is of an equable temper* temperament, disposition, nature, humour, mood, character, frame of mind, cast of mind, mind, attitude, stamp. *See* TEMPERAMENT 1. **2** *the temper of the times* tenor, tone, attitude, vein. **3** *he is in a temper* bad mood, ill humour, fury, rage, passion, fit of temper/pique, tantrum; *inf.* paddy, wax. **4** *a display of temper* ill humour, anger, annoyance, fury, rage, irritation, irritability, irascibility, hot-headedness, petulance, peevishness, resentment, surliness, churlishness. **5** *lose one's temper* composure, equanimity, self-control, coolness, calm, calmness, tranquillity, good humour; *inf.* cool.

temper verb **1** *temper the metal* toughen, anneal, harden, strengthen, fortify. **2** *temper justice with mercy* moderate, soften, tone down,

modify, mitigate, alleviate, allay, palliate, mollify, assuage, lessen, weaken.

temperament noun **1** *of an equable/nervous temperament* disposition, nature, humour, mood, character, personality, make-up, constitution, complexion, temper, spirit, mettle, frame of mind, cast of mind, mind, attitude, outlook, stamp, quality. **2** *actors often are people of temperament* excitability, emotionalism, volatility, mercurialness, capriciousness, moodiness, oversensitivity, touchiness, hot-headedness, impatience, petulance; moods.

temperamental adjective **1** *temperamental differences between them* | *a temperamental dislike of parties* constitutional, inherent, innate, inborn, congenital, deep-rooted, ingrained. **2** *actors are often temperamental people* excitable, emotional, volatile, mercurial, oversensitive, capricious, erratic, touchy, moody, hot-headed, explosive, impatient, petulant.
Opposites CALM; STABLE; EASYGOING.

temperance noun **1** *now leading a life of temperance after his excesses* moderation, self-restraint, self-control, abstemiousness, continence, abstinence, austerity, self-denial. **2** *former alcoholics now practising temperance* teetotalism, abstinence, abstention, sobriety, prohibition.

temperate adjective **1** *lead a temperate life* moderate, self-restrained, restrained, abstemious, self-controlled, continent, austere, self-denying. **2** *the temperate members of the party* teetotal, abstinent, sober. **3** *temperate winds/climates* moderate, mild, gentle, clement, balmy, pleasant, agreeable.
Opposites INTEMPERATE; IMMODERATE; EXTREME.

tempest noun **1** *ships/houses buffeted by the tempest* storm, gale, hurricane, squall, cyclone, tornado, typhoon, whirlwind. **2** *a tempest broke out when the star lost her necklace* storm, uproar, commotion, furore, disturbance, tumult, turmoil, upheaval.

tempestuous adjective **1** *tempestuous weather* stormy, turbulent, blustery, squally, windy, gusty, breezy. **2** *a tempestuous affair* stormy, turbulent, boisterous, violent, wild, uncontrolled, unrestrained, passionate, impassioned, emotional, intense, fierce, heated, feverish, hysterical, frenetic.

temple noun place of worship, holy place, shrine, sanctuary.

tempo noun **1** *the lively tempo of the music* beat, rhythm, cadence, throb, pulse, pulsation. **2** *the tempo of life today* pace, rate, speed, measure.

temporal adjective **1** *temporal affairs* secular, non-spiritual, worldly, material, earthly, carnal. **2** *temporal measurements* of time, time-related.
Opposites SPIRITUAL.

temporarily adverb **1** *temporarily out of order* for the time being, for the moment, for now, for the nonce, pro tem. **2** *he was temporarily in love with her* briefly, fleetingly, for a short time, for a little while, momentarily, transiently.

temporary adjective **1** *just a temporary job* short-term, impermanent, interim, provi-

sional, pro tem, *pro tempore*. **2** *a temporary infatuation* brief, fleeting, passing, momentary, short-lived, here today and gone tomorrow, transient, transitory, ephemeral, fugitive, evanescent, fugacious.
Opposites PERMANENT; CONSTANT.

tempt verb **1** *tempt him to break the law by bribing him* | *she is tempted to run away* try to persuade, entice, incite, induce, egg on, urge, goad, prompt, sway, influence, persuade, cajole, coax. **2** *rows of glamorous gifts to tempt buyers* allure, lure, entice, attract, whet the appetite of, make one's mouth water, captivate, appeal to, beguile, inveigle, woo, seduce, tantalize. **3** *tempt fate* fly in the face of, risk, bait, provoke.

temptation noun **1** *subject the jury to temptation* enticement, incitement, inducement, urging, influence, persuasion, cajolery, coaxing. **2** *sweets acting as a temptation to children* allurement, lure, attraction, draw, bait, pull, enticement, inducement, invitation, decoy, snare; *inf.* come-on. **3** *the temptation of the array of sweets* allure, attractiveness, appeal, fascination, tantalization.

tempting adjective *a tempting array of goods* alluring, enticing, attractive, captivating, appealing, beguiling, fascinating, tantalizing, appetizing, mouth-watering.
Opposites OFF-PUTTING.

tenable adjective **1** *tenable theories/objections* justifiable, defensible, defendable, arguable, maintainable, supportable, plausible, credible, reasonable, rational, sound, viable. **2** *positions tenable only for a year* holdable, occupiable, available.
Opposites INDEFENSIBLE; UNTENABLE.

tenacious adjective **1** *the eagle held its prey in a tenacious grip* clinging, firm, fast, tight, strong, forceful, powerful, unshakable, iron. **2** *we tried to get rid of her but she's so tenacious* | *tenacious efforts* persistent, pertinacious, determined, dogged, resolute, firm, steadfast, purposeful, unshakable, unswerving, relentless, inexorable, unyielding, inflexible, stubborn, obstinate, intransigent, obdurate, strong-willed, contumacious. **3** *a tenacious memory* retentive, retaining, remembering, unforgetful. **4** *tenacious clay* sticky, gluey, adhesive, clinging.
Opposites LOOSE; IRRESOLUTE; HESITANT.

tenacity noun **1** *the tenacity of its grip* firmness, fastness, tightness, strength, force, forcefulness, power. **2** *admire her tenacity in seeing it through until the end* persistence, pertinacity, determination, doggedness, resolution, resoluteness, resolve, firmness, steadfastness, purposefulness, purpose, strength of purpose, application, diligence, relentlessness, inexorableness, inflexibility, stubbornness, obstinacy, intransigence, obduracy, strong will. *See* TENACIOUS 2. **3** *the tenacity of his memory* retentiveness. **4** *the tenacity of the clay* stickiness, glueyness, adhesiveness.

tenancy noun **1** *disapprove of his tenancy of the flat* occupancy, occupation, residence, habitation, inhabitance, renting, leasing, lease, holding, possession. **2** *his tenancy is for three years* period of occupancy/occupation, lease, tenure.

tenant noun occupier, occupant, resident, inhabitant, renter, leaseholder, lessee, holder, possessor.

tend[1] verb **1** *he tends to lose his temper easily* have/show a tendency to, incline towards, be apt/disposed/liable to, be likely to. **2** *the graph tends upwards* move, go, head, point, gravitate.

tend[2] verb *tend the sick/cows* look after, take care of, care for, attend to, minister to, see to, cater to, nurse, wait on, watch over, watch, guard, keep an eye on, keep.

tendency noun **1** *he has a tendency to dishonesty* inclination, disposition, predisposition, proclivity, propensity, proneness, aptness, bent, leaning, penchant, susceptibility, liability. **2** *the upward tendency of the graph* movement, direction, course, drift, bias, trend.

tender adjective **1** *tender meat* not tough, easily chewed, succulent, juicy, soft. **2** *tender blossoms/shoots* easily damaged, breakable, fragile, frail, delicate, sensitive, slight, feeble. **3** *they are still of tender years* | *a tender youth* young, youthful, early; immature, callow, inexperienced, green, raw. **4** *have a tender heart* compassionate, soft-hearted, kind, kindly, sympathetic, warm, caring, humane, gentle, solicitous, generous, benevolent, sentimental, emotional, susceptible, vulnerable. **5** *have tender feelings for her* fond, loving, affectionate, warm, emotional, amorous. **6** *awake tender memories* warm, fond, emotional, touching, moving, poignant, evocative. **7** *a tender spot on her arm* sore, painful, aching, smarting, throbbing, inflamed, irritated, red, raw, bruised. **8** *a tender subject requiring tact* delicate, sensitive, difficult, tricky, ticklish, risky.
Opposites TOUGH; DURABLE; CRUEL.

tender verb **1** *tender assistance* | *tender a proposal* offer, proffer, present, extend, give; volunteer, put forward, propose, suggest, advance, submit. **2** *tender for the job* put in a bid, bid, give an estimate, propose a price.

tenderness noun **1** *the tenderness of the meat* succulence, softness. *See* TENDER *adjective* 1. **2** *the tenderness of the blossoms/shoots* fragility, frailness, frailty, delicacy, sensitivity, sensitiveness, slightness, feebleness. *See* TENDER *adjective* 2. **3** *the tenderness of their years* youthfulness, immaturity, callowness, inexperience, greenness. *See* TENDER *adjective* 3. **4** *the tenderness of her heart* compassion, compassionateness, softheartedness, kindness, kindliness, sympathy, warmth, humaneness, gentleness, solicitousness, generosity, benevolence, sentimentality, emotionalism, vulnerability. **5** *the tenderness of his feelings for her* fondness, love, affection, affectionateness, warmth, emotion, amorousness. **6** *the tenderness of the topic* delicacy, delicateness, sensitivity, sensitiveness, difficulty, trickiness, ticklishness, riskiness. **7** *the tenderness of the wounded area* soreness, pain, painfulness, ache, aching, smarting, throbbing, inflammation, irritation, redness, rawness, bruising.

tenet noun doctrine, creed, credo, principle, belief, conviction, persuasion, view, opinion, theory, thesis, hypothesis, postulation.

tennis noun. See table. See also table at SPORT.

TENNIS STROKES	
ace	half volley
backhand drive	lob
backhand volley	overhead smash
drive	serve
drop shot	slice service
forehand drive	smash
forehand volley	swing
ground stroke	volley

tenor noun **1** the tenor of his speech drift, gist, essence, import, vein, meaning, purport, intent. **2** follow the even tenor of his ways settled course, prevailing trend, movement, current, flow, direction, drift.

tense adjective **1** tense ropes pulled tight, tight, taut, rigid, stretched, strained. **2** feeling tense about the interview strained, under a strain, under pressure, nervous, keyed up, worked up, overwrought, distraught, anxious, uneasy, worried, apprehensive, agitated, jumpy, edgy, on edge, restless, jittery, fidgety; inf. uptight, wound up, strung up. **3** there were some tense moments in the negotiations/film nerve-racking, stressful, worrying, fraught, exciting, cliff-hanging **Opposites** SLACK; CALM; COOL; relaxed.

tension noun **1** the tension of the ropes tightness, tautness, rigidity, stretching, straining. **2** the tension of waiting for the interview strain, stress, stressfulness, suspense, pressure, anxiety, unease, disquiet, worry, apprehensiveness, agitation, jumpiness, edginess, restlessness; nerves; inf. butterflies in the stomach. **3** the tension between the two sides grew strain, unease, ill feeling, hostility, enmity.

tentative adjective **1** a tentative proposal/plan speculative, conjectural, experimental, exploratory, trial, provisional, test, pilot, untried, unproven, unconfirmed, unsettled, indefinite. **2** take a few tentative steps hesitant, hesitating, faltering, wavering, uncertain, unsure, doubtful, cautious, diffident, timid. **Opposites** DEFINITE; CONFIDENT.

tenterhooks plural noun **on tenterhooks** in suspense, on edge, edgy, jumpy, jittery, keyed up, overwrought, anxious, apprehensive, uneasy, worried; inf. uptight, waiting for the axe to fall.

tenuous adjective **1** a tenuous connection between the two events slight, flimsy, weak, insubstantial, shaky, sketchy, doubtful, dubious, nebulous, hazy, vague, unspecific, indefinite. **2** a tenuous thread fine, thin, slender.

tepid adjective **1** tepid water lukewarm, warmish. **2** he's rather tepid about the idea | a tepid reaction unenthusiastic, apathetic, half-hearted, indifferent, cool. **Opposites** HOT; COLD; ENTHUSIASTIC.

term noun **1** fail to understand the technical term word, expression, phrase, name, title, denomination, appellation, designation. **2** the chairman's term of office period, time, spell, interval, stretch, span, duration, space. **3** a pregnancy reaching term | a life cut off before its natural term fruition, culmination, limit, termination, close, end, conclusion.

term verb what do they term the process? call, name, entitle, style, dub, label, tag, designate, denominate.

terminal adjective **1** a terminal illness fatal, deadly, mortal, lethal, killing, incurable. **2** a terminal patient dying, on one's deathbed, near death, in the throes of death, incurable. **3** terminal markers boundary, bounding, limiting, confining, end, ending. **Opposites** INITIAL.

terminal noun **1** the terminals of the estate extremity, end, boundary, bound, limit, edge. **2** the terminal of the railway line terminus, last stop, depot. See TERMINUS. **3** collect one's luggage at the terminal air/sea terminal. **4** seated at the computer terminal workstation, visual display unit, input/output device; inf. VDU.

terminate verb **1** terminate the meeting as soon as you can bring to a close/end/conclusion, close, end, conclude, finish, stop, wind up, discontinue. **2** the meeting terminated at midnight come to a close/end, close, end, conclude, finish, stop. **3** they terminated his contract end, bring to an end, stop, cease, discontinue, cancel. **4** the match terminated in a draw end, finish, conclude, result. **5** his contract terminated last week end, come to an end, stop, cease, expire, run out, lapse. **6** terminate a pregnancy abort, end, put an end to, stop. **Opposites** BEGIN; START; COMMENCE; INITIATE.

termination noun **1** the termination of the meeting closing, close, ending, end, conclusion, finish, stopping, winding-up, discontinuance; inf. wind-up. **2** the termination of his contract end, stopping, cessation, discontinuance, expiry, lapse, cancellation. **3** the termination of the match was a draw end, finish, conclusion, result, issue, denouement. **4** the pregnant woman underwent a termination abortion.

terminology noun legal terminology language, phraseology, vocabulary, nomenclature, jargon, cant, argot; terms, expressions, words; inf. lingo.

terminus noun the bus/railway terminus last stop, depot, garage, station, end of the line.

terms plural noun **1** tell them in no uncertain terms words, phrases, expressions; language, mode of expression, manner of speaking. **2** be on good/friendly/unfriendly terms with their neighbours relations; standing, footing, relationship. **3** under the terms of the will/treaty stipulations, specifications, conditions, provisions, provisos, particulars, premises, details, points, clauses. **4** offer reduced terms in the winter prices, rates, charges, costs, fees. **come to terms 1** they finally came to terms with the neighbours about the dividing wall reach agreement, come to an agreement/understanding, reach a compromise. **2** come to terms with her loss become reconciled, reach an acceptance (of), learn to live (with). **in terms of** *in terms of worldly wealth he is poor* with regard to, as regards, regarding, with reference to, as to, in respect of.

terrible *adjective* **1** *he's a terrible bore/flirt* great, extreme, incorrigible, outrageous; *inf.* awful, dreadful, frightful, impossible. **2** *he's a terrible tennis player* bad, poor, incompetent, useless, talentless; *inf.* rotten, duff. **3** *hostages enduring terrible experiences* dreadful, terrifying, frightening, frightful, horrifying, horrible, horrific, horrendous, terrific, harrowing, hideous, grim, unspeakable, appalling, awful, gruesome. **4** *the terrible heat/pain* extreme, severe, harsh, unbearable, intolerable, insufferable. **5** *what's that terrible smell?|he's a terrible creature* nasty, foul, offensive, odious, obnoxious, vile, revolting, repulsive, abhorrent, loathsome, hateful, unpleasant, disagreeable; *inf.* dreadful, awful, horrible, horrid.
Opposites BRILLIANT; WONDERFUL; PLEASANT.

terribly *adverb terribly good/sad* very, extremely, exceedingly, decidedly, thoroughly; *inf.* awfully, dreadfully, frightfully, terrifically.

terrific *adjective* **1** *a terrific bang/speed* tremendous, great, very great, very big, huge, sizeable, considerable, intense, extreme, extraordinary, excessive. **2** *she's a terrific singer* very good, excellent, superb, remarkable, magnificent, wonderful, marvellous, great, super, sensational; *inf.* fantastic, fabulous, fab, A1, ace, wizard, unreal, awesome. **3** *there's been a terrific accident* dreadful, frightful, horrible, horrific, hideous, grim, appalling, awful.
Opposites AWFUL; DREADFUL; USELESS.

terrified *adjective* terror-stricken, terror-struck, terrorized, frightened out of one's wits/skin, frightened to death, frightened, scared stiff, scared, petrified, horrified, horror-struck, alarmed, panic-stricken, intimidated, dismayed, appalled, shocked, paralysed with fear; *inf.* spooked.

terrify *verb* terrorize, frighten to death, frighten, scare stiff, scare, petrify, horrify, make one's blood run cold, make one's flesh creep, make one's hair stand on end, alarm, panic, intimidate, dismay, appal, shock, paralyse with fear, put the fear of God into; *inf.* spook.

territory *noun* **1** *territories governed by the same ruler* country, state, domain, county, district. *See tables at* PROVINCE, STATE. **2** *an unexplored territory* region, area, terrain, tract. **3** *the financial affairs of the firm are her father's territory* area, area of concern/activity, province, field, sector, department. **4** *a salesman's territory* area, section, route, beat, ambit. **5** *an animal defending its territory* area, domain, space.

terror *noun* **1** fright, fear, fear and trembling, dread, alarm, panic, intimidation, dismay, consternation, shock, horror; *inf.* heebie-jeebies. **2** *imagining all manner of terrors* bogeyman, bugbear, monster, demon, fiend, devil. **3** *that child's a little terror* hooligan, ruffian, hoodlum, villain, rogue, rascal, troublemaker; *inf.* holy terror.

terrorize *verb* **1** *terrorize the children* strike terror in/into, terrify, frighten to death, scare stiff, petrify, horrify. *See* TERRIFY. **2** *terrorize them into leaving their homes* coerce, browbeat, bully, intimidate, menace, threaten; *inf.* bulldoze, strong-arm.

terse *adjective* **1** *a terse description of the event* concise, succinct, compact, brief, short, to the point, crisp, pithy, elliptical, epigrammatic. **2** *she sounded terse on the phone* abrupt, curt, brusque, laconic, short, clipped, blunt.
Opposites LONG-WINDED; VERBOSE; POLITE.

test *noun* **1** *a test to distinguish the competent from the incompetent* examination, check, assessment, evaluation, appraisal, investigation, inspection, analysis, scrutinization, scrutiny, study, probe, exploration. **2** *take the bike out for a test* trial, try-out, try, probation, assay. **3** *the children are sitting a test tomorrow* exam, examination, quiz, set of questions, questionnaire. **4** *the test of a good cake|the test by which a good cake is judged* criterion, touchstone, yardstick, standard, measure, model, pattern.

test *verb* **1** *test the children's knowledge of local history* put to the test, examine, check, assess, evaluate, appraise, investigate, scrutinize, study, probe. **2** *their behaviour really tested his patience* try, tax, strain, put a strain on. **3** *test the bike for oneself* try, try out, put to the test. **4** *test the water for pollution* analyse, assay, check, investigate, scrutinize, explore, probe.

testament *noun* **1** *left her his estate by testament* will. **2** *the sculpture was a testament to his skill* attestation, testimony, evidence, proof, witness; demonstration, indication, exemplification, tribute.

testify *verb* **1** *asked to testify in court* give evidence, bear witness, attest, be a witness. **2** *she testified to his honesty* swear to, attest to, corroborate, substantiate, verify, vouch for, endorse, support, back up, uphold. **3** *testify that she had witnessed the accident* swear, declare, assert, affirm, state, allege, pledge, profess, avow. **4** *tears that testified to her guilt* be evidence/proof of, confirm, corroborate, bear out, prove, show, demonstrate, establish, indicate.
Opposites DENY; BELIE.

testimonial *noun* **1** *a testimonial from his previous employer* reference, character reference, recommendation, letter of recommendation, commendation, credential, endorsement, certificate of competence. **2** *given as a testimonial to him* gift, tribute, trophy, memento, souvenir.

testimony *noun* **1** *challenge the testimony of the witness* evidence, attestation, sworn statement, deposition, affidavit. **2** *he stuck to his testimony that he had seen her before* statement, declaration, assertion, protestation, affirmation, profession, submission, allegation. **3** *her academic record was a testimony to her ability* proof, evidence, verification, corroboration, support; demonstration, manifestation, indication.

testy *adjective* tetchy, touchy, irritable, irascible, petulant, cross, ill-tempered, crotchety, crabbed, snappish, querulous. *See* TETCHY.

tetchy *adjective* touchy, irritable, irascible, petulant, peevish, cross, ill-tempered, crotchety, grouchy, grumpy, crabbed, testy, cantankerous, crusty, peppery, snappish, querulous, fractious.

tête-à-tête noun chat, dialogue, conversation, duologue; inf. confab, rap.

tether noun the goat broke free from its tether rope, cord, chain, lead, leash, line.

tether verb tether the goat to a stake tie, tie up, fasten, secure, chain, rope.

text noun **1** references in the text of the book to the index main body, content, main matter. **2** responsible for the text of the book, not for the illustrations words; wording. **3** the speaker took covetousness as his text theme, subject matter, subject, matter, topic, issue, point, motif. **4** the texts chosen for the funeral service passage, verse, paragraph. **5** familiarize yourself with some of the texts before term begins textbook, book, set book.

texture noun **1** the texture of her skin feel, touch, appearance, surface, grain. **2** fabrics of varying texture weave, structure, composition, constitution, constituency.

thank verb thank them for their present/help offer/ extend thanks to, express/show gratitude to, show appreciation to.

thankful adjective **1** she was thankful to reach home safely grateful, appreciative, pleased, relieved. **2** she was thankful to them for taking her in grateful, indebted, obliged, under an obligation, beholden.
Opposites UNGRATEFUL.

thankless adjective **1** thankless children ungrateful, unthankful, unappreciative, ungracious, unmannerly. **2** thankless tasks unappreciated, unrewarded, unrewarding, unacknowledged, vain, in vain, fruitless, useless.

thanks plural noun express thanks for their help gratitude, gratefulness, appreciation, acknowledgement, recognition. **thanks to** thanks to his late arrival we missed the bus as a result of, because of, owing to, due to, through, by reason of.

thanks interjection thank you, many thanks, thank you kindly, much obliged, much appreciated; inf. ta, cheers.

thaw verb **1** the frozen juice thawed defrost, unfreeze, melt, soften, liquefy. **2** at first she was very aloof but she soon thawed become friendly/genial/sociable, relax, loosen up, become responsive.
Opposites FREEZE; CHILL; SOLIDIFY.

theatre noun **1** study theatre at college drama, dramatic art, dramaturgy, the stage, show business, thespian art; inf. show biz. See tables. See also tables at ACTOR, PLAY, PLAYWRIGHT. **2** the lecture theatre hall, room. **3** the theatre of war | the theatre of civil discord scene, field, place of action.

theatrical adjective **1** theatrical performances/ careers dramatic, stage, dramaturgical, showbusiness, thespian; inf. show-biz. **2** theatrical gestures dramatic, melodramatic, histrionic, emotional, exaggerated, overdone, ostentatious, showy, affected, mannered, stilted,

---

THEATRICAL MOVEMENTS

Chicana	Symbolism
documentary drama	Theatre of Cruelty
epic theatre	Theatre of Fact
expressionism	Theatre of Silence
Little Theatre	Theatre of the
naturalism	Absurd
realism	total theatre
ritual drama	Verfremdung (alienation)
Shingeki	ation)
Sturm und Drang	Verismo

PARTS OF A THEATRE

acting area	iron
apron stage	lighting gallery
auditorium	lighting rig
backstage	orchestra pit
bridge	picture-frame stage
curtain	prompter's box
dais	proscenium arch
dressing room	proscenium stage
fire curtain	revolving stage
float	rostrum
fly gallery	slip stage
fly tower	stage
footlights	stage door
forestage	thrust stage
front of house	trap
green room	wings

---

unreal, forced, stagy; inf. hammy.
Opposites NATURAL; UNAFFECTED; LOW-KEY.

theft noun done for theft | a theft at the bookshop stealing, robbery, thieving, thievery, burglary, larceny, misappropriation, pilfering, purloining, shoplifting, embezzlement, swindling, fraud; inf. swiping, nicking, rip-off, knocking-off.

theme noun **1** the theme of the speech topic, subject, subject matter, matter, thesis, text, argument, burden, idea, keynote. **2** play the theme from the TV series theme song, melody, tune, air, leitmotif. **3** the theme of the fancy dress ball motif, leitmotif, unifying idea. **4** students writing themes in French essay, composition, paper, dissertation.

then adverb **1** we went home then at that point, at that time/moment, on that occasion. **2** from then on he was ill that point, that time/ moment, that occasion. **3** she went and then he went next, after that, afterwards, subsequently, later. **4** she has the washing to do and then there's the cooking in addition, also, besides, as well, moreover. **5** you're tired? then you must go home in that case, that being the case, that being so, under those circumstances. **6** our hero then received the hand of the princess so, therefore, thus, consequently.

theological adjective religious, scriptural, divine, holy, ecclesiastical, doctrinal, dogmatic.

theoretical adjective **1** theoretical sciences not practical, conceptual, abstract. **2** a theoretical situation hypothetical, conjectural, suppositional, speculative, notional, postulatory,

assumed, presumed.
Opposites PRACTICAL; CONCRETE; ACTUAL; REAL.

theorize *verb* form/evolve a theory, speculate, conjecture, suppose, hypothesize.

theory *noun* **1** *one of my pet theories* hypothesis, thesis, conjecture, supposition, speculation, guess, notion, postulation, assumption, presumption, opinion, view. **2** *all very well in theory* abstract knowledge, speculative thought, hypothetical situation, the abstract. **3** *scientific theory* system, scheme, philosophy.

therapeutic *adjective* curative, curing, healing, restorative, remedial, health-giving, sanative, reparative, corrective, ameliorative, beneficial, good, advantageous, salutary.

therapy *noun* **1** *limbs responding to therapy* treatment, remedy, cure. **2** *receiving therapy for depression* psychotherapy, psychoanalysis. *See table.*

TYPES OF THERAPY

acupuncture	mechanotherapy
aromatherapy	megavitamin
art therapy	therapy
aversion therapy	metrazol shock
behaviour therapy	therapy
chiropractic	music therapy
cognitive therapy	narcotherapy
colour therapy	naturopathy
confrontation	occupational therapy
therapy	osteopathy
crystal therapy	play therapy
drama therapy	primal therapy
electroconvulsive	psychotherapy
therapy	rational-emotive
electroshock therapy	therapy
electrotherapy	recreational therapy
family therapy	reflexology
Gerson cure	regression therapy
Gestalt therapy	relaxation therapy
group therapy	release therapy
homoeopathy	Rogerian therapy
humanistic therapy	sex therapy
hydrotherapy	shiatsu
hypnotherapy	shock therapy
insulin shock	sleep therapy
therapy	sound therapy

thereabouts *adverb* **1** *it's over there or thereabouts* about there, near there, around there, around that place. **2** *we'll need two hundred or thereabouts* about that, approximately that number/quantity, roughly that number/quantity.

thereafter *adverb* afterwards, after that, then, next, subsequently.

therefore *adverb* and so, so, then, thus, accordingly, consequently, as a result, for that reason.

thesis *noun* **1** *his thesis is that the territory is uninhabited* theory, hypothesis, contention, argument, proposal, proposition, premiss, postulation, opinion, view, idea. **2** *present a thesis for his doctorate* dissertation, paper, treatise, disquisition, essay, composition, monograph.

thick *adjective* **1** *walls/concrete/trees a metre thick* across, in extent/diameter, wide, broad, deep; of great extent/diameter. **2** *thick legs* broad, wide, large, big, bulky, solid, substantial, fat; *inf.* beefy. **3** *the ground thick with ants | thick with dust* teeming, swarming, crawling, alive, abounding, overflowing, covered. **4** *the room thick with smoke* full (of), filled; *inf.* chock-full. **5** *a thick forest* dense, close-packed, concentrated, crowded, condensed, compact, impenetrable, impassable. **6** *thick cream* clotted, coagulated, heavy, firm. **7** *thick mists* dense, heavy, opaque, smoggy, soupy, murky, impenetrable. **8** *he's too thick to understand* stupid, dense, unintelligent, dull-witted, dull, slow-witted, slow, doltish, blockish; *inf.* dim, dim-witted, boneheaded, wooden-headed. **9** *a thick voice | a voice thick with emotion* husky, hoarse, throaty, guttural, rough, indistinct, muffled. **10** *a thick accent* broad, pronounced, marked, strong, rich, obvious, distinct, decided, very great, extreme. **11** *those two are very thick these days* friendly, on friendly/good terms, intimate, close, devoted, hand-in-glove, inseparable, familiar; *inf.* pally, palsy-walsy, chummy, matey, well in. **a bit thick** excessive, unreasonable, unfair, unjust.
Opposites THIN; SPARSE; CLEVER.

thicken *verb* **1** *the jelly/cream would not thicken* set, gel, solidify, congeal, clot, coagulate, cake. **2** *the plot thickens* deepen, get more profound, become more involved/complicated/intricate.
Opposites DILUTE; thin down (*see* THIN).

thicket *noun* dense growth, tangle, copse, grove, wood.

thickness *noun* **1** *two metres in thickness* width, breadth, depth, diameter, extent. **2** *the thickness of their legs* breadth, broadness, width, wideness, largeness, bigness, bulkiness, solidness, fatness; *inf.* beefiness. **3** *the thickness of the mist* denseness, heaviness, opacity, opaqueness, soupiness, murkiness, impenetrability. **4** *his thickness is unbelievable* stupidity, denseness, dull-wittedness, dullness, slow-wittedness, doltishness, blockishness; *inf.* dimness, dim-wittedness, boneheadedness, wooden-headedness. **5** *the thickness of her voice* huskiness, hoarseness, throatiness, gutturalness, roughness, gravelliness, indistinctness. **6** *the thickness of his accent* broadness, pronouncedness, markedness, richness, obviousness, decidedness.

thickset *adjective* **1** *thickset countrymen* heavily/solidly built, powerfully built, well-built, heavy, burly, brawny, muscular, bulky, sturdy, stocky; *inf.* beefy. **2** *a thickset hedge/forest* dense, close-packed, crowded, compact.

thick-skinned *adjective* insensitive, unfeeling, tough, unsusceptible, impervious, invulnerable, hardened, case-hardened, callous; *inf.* hard-boiled.
Opposites SENSITIVE; THIN-SKINNED.

thief *noun* robber, burglar, housebreaker, larcenist, pilferer, stealer, purloiner, filcher, shoplifter, pickpocket, embezzler, bandit, swindler, fraudster; *inf.* mugger, swiper, nicker.

thieve verb steal, rob, pilfer, purloin, shoplift, filch, run off with, embezzle, swindle; inf. swipe, nick, rip off, knock off, lift, snitch.

thin adjective **1** thin lines narrow, fine, attenuated. **2** thin materials fine, light, delicate, flimsy, diaphanous, gossamer, unsubstantial, sheer, transparent, see-through, gauzy, filmy, translucent. **3** trying to be thin | models have to be thin slim, slender, lean, slight, svelte, light, spare. **4** thin and ill-looking thin as a rake, skinny, spindly, lank, lanky, scrawny, scraggy, bony, skeletal, wasted, emaciated, shrunken, anorexic, undernourished, underweight. **5** thin hair sparse, scanty, wispy, skimpy. **6** the audience was rather thin sparse, scarce, scanty, meagre, paltry, scattered. **7** a thin mixture dilute, diluted, weak, watery, runny; inf. wishy-washy. **8** a thin voice weak, small, low, soft, faint, feeble. **9** a thin excuse flimsy, unsubstantial, weak, feeble, lame, poor, shallow, unconvincing, inadequate, insufficient.
Opposites THICK; FAT; ABUNDANT.

thin verb **1** she has thinned down a lot become thinner/slimmer, slim down, lose weight, reduce. **2** thin down the mixture dilute, water down, weaken. **3** thin out the plants/population reduce in number, lessen, decrease, diminish. **4** the mist/traffic thinned out become less dense, decrease, diminish, dwindle.

thing noun **1** people matter more than things object, article. **2** a few things to buy item, article. **3** where did you get that thing? object; inf. what-d'you-call-it, what's-its-name, what's-it, thingummy, thingumabob, thingumajig. **4** what a silly/difficult thing to do action, act, deed, exploit, feat, undertaking, task, job, chore. **5** what a silly thing to think idea, thought, notion, concept, theory, conjecture. **6** say silly things statement, remark, comment, declaration, utterance, pronouncement. **7** a terrible thing to happen event, happening, occurrence, incident, episode. **8** patience is a useful thing quality, characteristic, attribute, property, trait, feature. **9** the poor/little thing has no home poor soul, creature, wretch. **10** there's another thing you should know fact, point, detail, particular, aspect. **11** have a thing about spiders phobia, fear, dislike, aversion, horror, obsession, fixation; inf. hang-up. **12** have a thing about champagne liking, love, fancy, predilection, penchant, preference, taste, particularity, inclination, obsession, fixation, idée fixe. **13** the latest thing in swimwear style, fashion, specimen, example. **the thing 1** the thing is to avoid annoying him aim, intention, idea, objective, object, purpose. **2** I've found just the thing for a wedding present something ideal/appropriate/desirable, something necessary, right thing, very thing. **3** the thing is that he has no money fact, fact of the matter, point, issue, problem.

things plural noun **1** put on dry things | take night things clothing, attire, apparel; clothes, garments; inf. gear, togs, clobber. **2** I'll watch your things while you get a ticket belongings, possessions, paraphernalia; inf. stuff, bits and pieces. **3** her painting things equipment, apparatus, gear, tackle; implements, tools. **4** things

are getting worse matters, affairs, circumstances, conditions, relations; state of affairs, situation.

think verb **1** I think they will come believe, suppose, expect, imagine, surmise, conjecture, guess, fancy. **2** he is thought to be clever consider, deem, hold, reckon, regard as, assume, presume, estimate. **3** he is sitting thinking ponder, meditate, deliberate, contemplate, muse, cogitate, ruminate, cerebrate, concentrate, brood, rack one's brains, be lost in thought, be in a brown study. **4** he is thinking about his career contemplate, consider, deliberate about, muse on, mull over, reflect on, weigh up, review. **5** she's thinking about her youth think back to, call to mind, recall, remember, recollect. **6** he's thinking about what it would be like to be wealthy imagine, picture, visualize, envisage, dream. **7** I think I'll go have a mind to, consider possible, intend possibly. **8** who'd have thought she would be there expect, anticipate, imagine, surmise. **think better of** have second thoughts about, reconsider, change one's mind about, decide against. **think nothing of** regard as quite usual/normal, consider routine, take in one's stride. **think over** think over the implications contemplate, consider, deliberate about, muse over, mull over, ponder, reflect on, weigh up, consider the pros and cons of. **think up** think up an advertising slogan dream up, come up with, devise, invent, create, concoct.

think noun have a think about the situation consideration, contemplation, deliberation, muse, reflection.

thinker noun among the world's great thinkers philosopher, scholar, sage, theorist; inf. intellect, brain.

thinking noun what's the latest thinking on the effects of the drug? view, opinion, outlook, judgement, assessment, appraisal, evaluation, position, theory, reasoning; conclusions, thoughts.

thinking adjective a thinking person rational, reasoning, logical, sensible, intelligent, philosophical, contemplative, reflective, meditative.

thin-skinned adjective sensitive, oversensitive, hypersensitive, supersensitive, easily offended/hurt, touchy, temperamental.
Opposites INSENSITIVE; UNFEELING; THICK-SKINNED.

third-rate adjective inferior, poor-quality, low-quality, low-grade, poor, bad, shoddy, mediocre; inf. duff, ropy.

thirst noun **1** dying of thirst in the desert thirstiness, dryness, parchedness, dehydration. **2** a thirst for knowledge/novelty desire, craving, longing, hankering, yearning, avidity, keenness, eagerness, hunger, lust, appetite, passion, covetousness; inf. yen.

thirst verb **1** thirsting for a drink feel/have a thirst. **2** thirsting for revenge | thirsted after knowledge desire, crave, long for, hanker after, yearn for, hunger after, lust after, covet.

thirsty adjective **1** thirsty people having a thirst, parched, dehydrated; inf. dry. **2** thirsty land dry, droughty, parched, dehydrated. **3** thirsty for knowledge thirsting, avid, keen, eager, hungry, greedy, covetous. See THIRST noun 2.

thong *noun* strip, belt, strap, cord, lash, rope, tie, tether.

thorn *noun* prickle, spike, barb, spine, bristle.

thorny *adjective* **1** *thorny branches* prickly, spiky, barbed, spiny, spined, spinose, bristly, sharp, pointed. **2** *a thorny situation/issue* problematic, awkward, ticklish, difficult, tough, troublesome, bothersome, trying, taxing, irksome, vexatious, worrying, harassing, complicated, convoluted, involved.

thorough *adjective* **1** *a thorough investigation* in-depth, exhaustive, complete, comprehensive, full, intensive, extensive, widespread, sweeping, all-embracing, all-inclusive, detailed. **2** *he is slow but thorough* meticulous, scrupulous, assiduous, conscientious, painstaking, punctilious, methodical, careful. **3** *he's a thorough villain* thoroughgoing, out and out, utter, downright, sheer, absolute, unmitigated, unqualified, complete, total, perfect.
Opposites SUPERFICIAL; CURSORY; CARELESS.

thoroughbred *adjective* **1** *thoroughbred horses* pure-bred, pure, pure-blooded, full-blooded, pedigreed, pedigree. **2** *thoroughbred young women* well-bred, high-born, aristocratic, blue-blooded, elegant, graceful, refined, cultivated; *inf.* classy.

thoroughfare *noun* **1** *police directing traffic on the thoroughfare* road, roadway; main road, motorway, street; *Am.* highway, freeway, throughway. **2** *no thoroughfare* passageway, passage, way, access.

thoroughly *adverb* **1** *search the place thoroughly | investigate the matter thoroughly* exhaustively, from top to bottom, completely, comprehensively, fully, intensively, extensively, meticulously, scrupulously, assiduously, conscientiously, painstakingly, methodically, carefully, in detail, detailedly. **2** *she is thoroughly spoilt* completely, utterly, absolutely, totally, entirely, unreservedly, positively, dead.

though *conjunction* **1** *he went though he did not want to* although, despite the fact that, in spite of the fact that, notwithstanding that. **2** *he will go though he has to walk* even if, even supposing, despite the possibility that.

though *adverb* *you'll probably be right; I'll find out though* even so, however, but, still, yet, be that as it may, for all that, nonetheless, all the same, notwithstanding.

thought *noun* **1** *incapable of thought* powers of thinking, faculty of reason, power of reasoning. **2** *lost in thought* thinking, reasoning, pondering, meditation, deliberation, cogitation, rumination, musing, mulling, reflection, introspection, contemplation, consideration, cerebration. **3** *a thought came to me as to how we should proceed* idea, notion, line of thinking, theory, opinion. **4** *I had no thought of going* intention, plan, design, purpose, aim. **5** *what are your thoughts on the matter?* judgement, conclusion, appraisal, assessment, estimation, opinion, point of view, position, stance, stand, feeling, sentiment, belief, conviction. **6** *act without thought | give the matter thought* consideration, attention, heed, regard, scrutiny, care, carefulness. **7** *give up all thought of winning* expectation, anticipation, hope, prospect, aspiration, dream. **8** *he has no thought for his widowed mother* thoughtfulness, consideration, care, regard, concern, solicitude, kindness, kindliness, compassion, tenderness. **9** *he could be a thought more helpful* little, touch, bit, dash, jot, tinge, trace; *Am. inf.* tad.

thoughtful *adjective* **1** *he seems thoughtful | in a thoughtful mood* pensive, reflective, introspective, meditative, contemplative, ruminative, cogitative, absorbed, rapt/lost in thought, in a brown study. **2** *a thoughtful book/essay* profound, deep, serious, pithy, meaty, weighty. **3** *every action he takes is thoughtful* considered, circumspect, prudent, careful, cautious, heedful, wary, guarded. **4** *he is a thoughtful son | thoughtful acts* considerate, attentive, caring, solicitous, helpful, kind, kindly, compassionate, tender, charitable.
Opposites SUPERFICIAL; CARELESS; INCONSIDERATE; THOUGHTLESS.

thoughtless *adjective* **1** *she is a very thoughtless person | thoughtless remarks* tactless, undiplomatic, indiscreet, insensitive, inconsiderate, careless, selfish, impolite, rude. **2** *his thoughtless actions* unthinking, heedless, careless, unmindful, absent-minded, injudicious, ill-advised, ill-considered, imprudent, unwise, foolish, silly, stupid, reckless, rash, precipitate, negligent, neglectful, remiss.
Opposites THOUGHTFUL; SENSITIVE; CONSIDERATE; CAREFUL.

thrash *verb* **1** *masters thrashing boys* beat, whip, horsewhip, flog, lash, birch, cane, flagellate, scourge, leather, spank, chastise, belt, wallop, lambaste; *inf.* tan, give a hiding/pasting to. **2** *the home team thrashed the opposition* trounce, rout, vanquish, drub, give a drubbing to, defeat, beat, worst, crush; *inf.* beat hollow, lick, clobber, hammer, slaughter, wipe the floor with. **3** *thrashing around unable to get to sleep* thresh, flail, toss and turn, jerk, twitch, squirm, writhe. **thrash out** *thrash out their differences* discuss, talk over, debate, air, argue out, resolve, settle.

thread *noun* **1** *embroidered with gold thread | needles and thread* yarn, cotton, filament, fibre. **2** *a thread of white through the dark background* strand, line, streak, strip, seam. **3** *lose the thread of the story* train of thought, story line, drift, theme, plot, subject, subject matter, motif, tenor.

thread *verb* **1** *thread film into a projector* pass, string, ease. **2** *thread beads* string. **3** *she threaded her way through the crowds* inch, wind, push, squeeze, shoulder, elbow.

threadbare *adjective* **1** *threadbare clothes/upholstery* worn, frayed, tattered, ragged, holey, shabby; *inf.* tatty. **2** *threadbare imagery/jokes/arguments* hackneyed, tired, stale, worn-out, trite, banal, platitudinous, clichéd, cliché-ridden, stock, stereotyped; *inf.* old-hat, corny, played-out.

threat *noun* **1** *issue threats* threatening remark, warning, menace, menacing, intimidating remark; *lit.* commination. **2** *a threat of rain in the air | under threat of war* warning, menace, risk, danger, omen, foreboding, portent.

3 *she is a threat to the smooth running of the company* menace, danger, risk, hazard.

threaten verb **1** *bullies threatening younger children* make threats, menace, intimidate, browbeat, bully, pressurize; *inf.* lean on. **2** *threaten to tell* announce one's intention. **3** *rain is threatening* be imminent, impend, hang over, loom, foreshadow. **4** *a sky threatening rain* warn of, give warning of, presage, portend, augur. **5** *pollution threatening the environment* be a threat to, menace, endanger, imperil, put at risk, put in jeopardy, jeopardize.

threatening adjective **1** *make threatening gestures* menacing, warning, intimidating, bullying, minacious, minatory. **2** *threatening signs of a storm* ominous, inauspicious, foreboding.

threesome noun trio, triumvirate, triad, trinity, troika, triunity; triplets.

threshold noun **1** *guests standing on the threshold* doorway, doorstep, entrance, entry. **2** *on the threshold of a new era* beginning, commencement, start, outset, inception, opening, dawn, brink, verge, debut; *inf.* kick-off. **3** *threshold of pain* lower limit, minimum.

thrift noun thriftiness, good husbandry, economy, economicalness, economizing, carefulness, frugality, frugalness, sparingness, scrimping, parsimony, penny-pinching, miserliness.

thrifty adjective economical, economizing, careful, frugal, sparing, scrimping, parsimonious, penny-pinching, miserly.
Opposites EXTRAVAGANT; WASTEFUL; SPENDTHRIFT.

thrill noun **1** *seeing his hero gave him a thrill* feeling of excitement/stimulation, sensation of joy, wave of pleasure, glow, tingle; *inf.* buzz, charge, kick. **2** *it was a thrill to see the baby take her first steps* thrilling experience, joy, delight, pleasure, adventure. **3** *a thrill of terror ran through him* throb, tremble, tremor, quiver, flutter, shudder, vibration.

thrill verb **1** *seeing the air display thrilled him* excite, stimulate, arouse, stir, electrify, move, give joy/pleasure to; *inf.* give a buzz/charge/kick. **2** *she thrilled to hear the music* tingle, be excited, feel joy; *inf.* get a buzz/charge/kick. **3** *his body thrilled with fear* throb, tremble, quiver, shiver, flutter, shudder, vibrate.

thrilling adjective **1** *a thrilling experience* exciting, stirring, stimulating, electrifying, rousing, moving, gripping, riveting, joyful, pleasing; *inf.* hair-raising. **2** *a thrilling sensation through the body* throbbing, trembling, tremulous, quivering, shivering, fluttering, shuddering, vibrating.
Opposites BORING; DULL; MONOTONOUS.

thrive verb **1** *the business/family is thriving* flourish, prosper, do/go well, boom, burgeon, succeed, advance, get ahead, make progress. **2** *plants thriving* flourish, burgeon, grow vigorously, do well, shoot up.
Opposites FAIL; DECLINE; WITHER.

thriving adjective **1** *a thriving business* flourishing, prosperous, prospering, booming, burgeoning, successful, advancing, progressing; *inf.* going strong. **2** *thriving plants* flourish,

burgeoning, growing, healthy, luxuriant, lush, prolific.

throat noun gullet, oesophagus.

throb verb *his pulse throbbed rapidly | her wound throbbed* beat, pulse, pulsate, palpitate, pound, vibrate, go pit-a-pat, thump.

throb noun *the throb of her pulse/wound* beating, beat, pulse, pulsating, palpitation, pounding, vibration, pit-a-pat, pitter-patter, thumping.

throes plural noun **1** *the throes of childbirth | death throes* agony, suffering, excruciation, pain, torture, distress; pangs. **2** *in the throes of moving house* turmoil, upheaval, disruption, tumult, hurly-burly, confusion, chaos, pandemonium.

throne noun **1** *a golden throne* royal seat, seat of state. **2** *succeed to the throne* sovereignty, rule, command, dominion.

throng noun *a throng of fans* crowd, horde, mob, mass, host, multitude, swarm, flock, pack, herd, drove, press, assemblage, gathering, congregation.

throng verb **1** *people thronged to see the play | they thronged forward* flock, troop, swarm. **2** *fans thronging round the star* crowd round, press round, mill around, congregate round, converge round, hem in, jostle. **3** *fans thronging the stadium* pack, cram, jam, fill.

throttle verb **1** *the attacker throttled him* choke, strangle, strangulate, garrotte. **2** *governments trying to throttle opposition* gag, muzzle, silence, stifle, suppress, control, inhibit.

through preposition **1** *go through the building* into and out of, to the other/far side of, from one side to the other of, from end to end of. **2** *he got the job through an advertisement/friend* by means/way of, through the agency of, via, using, with the help/aid/assistance of, under the aegis of, by virtue of, as a result/consequence of, on account of, owing to, because of. **3** *he worked through the night* throughout, during, until the end of. **4** *Monday through Friday* up to and including.

through adverb **1** *just walk through* from one end to another, from end to end. **2** *the baby slept through | we worked through* all the time, without a break, without an interruption, nonstop. **3** *it was a struggle but we got through* to the end/finish/termination, to the completion, to the culmination. **through and through** *he's a villain through and through* thoroughly, completely, utterly, altogether, totally, to the core, entirely, wholly, fully, unreservedly, out and out.

through adjective **be through 1** *I'm through and I'm going home* finished, finished work, reached the end. **2** *the job is through now* completed, done, finished, ended, terminated; *inf.* washed-up. **3** *she says she's through with acting/boyfriends* finished with, no longer involved with, tired of.

throughout preposition **1** *throughout the world/house* all over, all round, in every part of, everywhere in. **2** *working throughout the night* through, all through, for the duration of, until the end of.

throughout *adverb* **1** *the house is carpeted throughout | they painted the house throughout* all through, right through, in every part, all over, everywhere. **2** *we loved the performance; we were riveted throughout* all the time, until the end, for the duration.

throw *verb* **1** *throw a brick* hurl, toss, cast, sling, pitch, shy, lob, propel, launch, project, send; *inf.* heave, chuck. **2** *throw his arms in the air* move quickly/suddenly, turn quickly/suddenly. **3** *throw a shadow* cast, project, send. **4** *throw a glance/smile at him* cast, send, dart, bestow on, give. **5** *the wrestler threw his opponent* throw/hurl to the ground, fell, floor, prostrate. **6** *the horse threw his rider* unseat, dislodge. **7** *his question threw me* disconcert, discomfit, disturb, confound, astonish, surprise, dumbfound, discountenance. **8** *threw the lever* operate, switch on, move. **9** *throw a vase* shape, form, mould, fashion. **10** *she threw on her clothes* pull on, put on quickly, don quickly, slip into. **throw away** **1** *throw away his textbooks* throw out, discard, get rid of, dispose of, jettison, scrap, reject, dispense with; *inf.* dump, ditch. **2** *throw away a good opportunity | actresses throwing away their lines* fail to exploit, make poor use of, waste, squander, fritter away, lose; *inf.* blow. **throw off** **1** *throw off their shackles* cast off, discard, shake off, drop, jettison, free/rid oneself of, abandon. **2** *throw off one's pursuers* shake off, outdistance, outrun, evade, escape from, get away from, elude, give someone the slip, lose, leave behind. **throw out** **1** *throw out old letters* throw away, discard, get rid of, dispose of, jettison, scrap. **2** *throw the drunk out of the house* eject, evict, expel, show the door to, put out; *inf.* kick out, turf out. **3** *throw out a proposal* reject, give the thumbs down to, turn down, dismiss, disallow. **4** *fires throwing out heat* emit, radiate, give off, diffuse, disseminate.

throw *noun* **1** *hit the coconut in the fair at one throw* hurl, toss, cast, sling, pitch, shy, lob; *inf.* heave, chuck. **2** *jackets at £50 a throw* each, apiece, per item, for one.

thrust *verb* **1** *thrust the money at the taxi-driver* push, shove, ram. **2** *thrust open the door* push, shove, drive, press, prod, propel. **3** *thrust responsibility on him* force, impose, push, press, urge. **4** *thrust him through the heart* stab, pierce, stick, jab, lunge at. **5** *thrust their way through the crowd* push, shove, press, force, shoulder, elbow, jostle.

thrust *noun* **1** *with one thrust of his fist* push, shove, ram, drive, press, prod. **2** *killed by his opponent's thrust* stab, jab, lunge. *See* LUNGE *noun.* **3** *surprised by the enemy's sudden thrust* advance, push, drive, attack, offensive, assault, charge, onslaught, incursion, raid. **4** *upset by her nasty thrust* verbal attack/assault, criticism, censure, hostile remark. **5** *a man with thrust* drive, push, force, impetus, energy, assertiveness, aggression, ambition; *inf.* get-up-and-go. **6** *the thrust of the engine | the thrusts in the bridge* motive force, propulsive force, force, pressure. **7** *they failed to grasp the thrust of the speech* gist, drift, substance, essence, theme, subject, thesis.

thrusting *adjective* *a thrusting young salesman* forceful, pushing, forward, energetic, assertive, aggressive, insistent, ambitious; *inf.* pushy. **Opposites** RETICENT; MEEK.

thud *noun* *fall with a thud* thump, clunk, clonk, crash, smack, wham, bang, wallop.

thud *verb* **1** *thudding around in heavy boots* thump, clump, clunk, clonk, crash. **2** *branches thudding against the window* thump, clunk, clonk, crash, smack, knock, bang.

thug *noun* ruffian, tough, rough, hoodlum, bully-boy, hooligan, villain, gangster, robber, bandit, murderer, killer, assassin; *inf.* heavy, bovver boy, hit-man.

thumb *noun* *an injured thumb* pollex. **all thumbs** clumsy, awkward, maladroit, inept; *inf.* butter-fingered, cack-handed, ham-fisted. **thumbs down** rejection, refusal, no, negation, rebuff, disapproval. **thumbs up** acceptance, affirmation, yes, approval, encouragement; *inf.* go-ahead, OK, green light.

thumb *verb* **1** *thumb through the book* leaf through, flick through, flip through, riffle through, browse, skim, scan. **2** *thumb a book badly* soil, mark, make dog-eared. **3** *thumb a lift* signal for, obtain; *inf.* hitch.

thumbnail *adjective* *a thumbnail sketch* succinct, concise, compact, short, brief, pithy, quick, rapid.

thump *verb* **1** *he thumped the girl's attacker* strike, hit, punch, thwack, wallop, smack, slap, batter, beat, cudgel, knock, thrash; *inf.* whack, belt, clout, lambaste. **2** *my heart/head is thumping* pound, thud, pulse, pulsate, throb, palpitate. **3** *thumping on the table* bang, batter, beat, crash, knock, rap.

thump *noun* **1** *give the attacker a thump* blow, punch, thwack, wallop, smack, slap; *inf.* whack, belt, clout, lambasting. **2** *give the table a thump* bang, knock, rap. **3** *the shoe landed with a thump* thud, clunk, clonk, crash, smack, wham, bang, wallop.

thumping *adjective* **1** *hear a thumping noise* thudding, clunking, clonking, crashing, banging. **2** *a thumping lie/majority* huge, massive, enormous, immense, vast, colossal, gigantic, mammoth, monumental, great, tremendous, impressive, extraordinary; *inf.* whopping, thundering.

thumping *adverb* *a thumping great house/present* extremely, very, extraordinarily, remarkably, uncommonly; *inf.* thundering.

thunder *noun* **1** *we could hear thunder* thunder crack, thunder clap. **2** *the thunder of guns/applause* boom, booming, rumble, rumbling, outburst, roar, roaring.

thunder *verb* **1** *his voice thundered in my ear* boom, rumble, roar, blast, resound, reverberate. **2** *workers thundering against management* fulminate against, rail against, denounce, curse, threaten. **3** *"Get back," he thundered* roar, bellow, bark, declaim, yell, shout.

thundering *adjective* *a thundering lie/majority* huge, massive, enormous, immense, vast, colossal, great, tremendous; *inf.* thumping. *See* THUMPING *adjective* 2.

thundering *adverb a thundering great house/present* extremely, very, extraordinarily; *inf.* thumping.

thunderous *adjective thunderous voices/applause* booming, rumbling, roaring, resounding, reverberating, deafening, ear-splitting, loud, noisy, tumultuous.

thunderstruck *adjective* amazed, astonished, dumbfounded, astounded, speechless, struck dumb, open-mouthed, at a loss for words, aghast, stunned, staggered, startled, taken aback, surprised, disconcerted, shocked, non-plussed, bewildered; *inf.* flabbergasted, bowled over, knocked for six, floored, flummoxed.

thus *adverb* **1** *hold the apparatus thus* like this, in this way, so, like so. **2** *he is the eldest son and thus inherits the estate* so, that being so, therefore, accordingly, hence, consequently, as a result, for this/that reason, on this/that account, *ergo*. **3** *having come thus far* so, to this extent.

thwack *verb thwack the child | thwack his attacker* hit, strike, slap, smack, wallop, thump, punch, box, knock, beat, batter, pound, pummel; *inf.* whack, belt, clout, bush, bop, slug, lambaste.

thwack *noun give the child/attacker a thwack* hit, slap, smack, wallop, thump, punch, box, knock; *inf.* whack, clout, bop, slug. *See* THWACK *verb.*

thwart *verb thwart their plans | he was thwarted in his aims* frustrate, foil, baulk, check, block, stop, prevent, defeat, impede, obstruct, hinder, hamper, stymie.
Opposites ASSIST; HELP; FACILITATE.

tic *noun a tic in his eye/face* twitch, spasm, jerk.

tick *noun* **1** *the tick of a clock/taximeter* ticking, click, beat, tap, tapping, tick-tock. **2** *I'll be there in a tick* moment, second, instant, minute, flash, trice, in no time at all, twinkling, the twinkling of an eye; *inf.* sec, jiffy, shake, two shakes of a lamb's tail, half a mo. **3** *put a tick at the correct answer* affirmative mark, stroke, mark, dash, line.

tick *verb* **1** *the clock/meter was ticking* click, beat, tap, sound, tick-tock. **2** *tick the items you want | tick the items present* put a tick at, mark, mark off, check off, indicate. **tick off** **1** *tick off the items present* put a tick at, mark, mark off, check off, indicate. **2** *she ticked the children off for being late* scold, reprimand, chide, rebuke, lecture, reproach, reprove, upbraid, berate, censure, take to task; *inf.* tell off, carpet, give a dressing-down to, haul over the coals, tear into.

ticket *noun* **1** *show your ticket to enter* pass, token, stub, coupon, card. **2** *there's no price ticket on this label* tag, tally.

tickle *verb* **1** *tickle the child under the chin* stroke, pet, touch. **2** *tickle the fancy* interest, excite, stimulate, arouse, captivate, please, gratify, delight. **3** *we were tickled by the antics of the children* amuse, entertain, divert, cheer, gladden.

ticklish *adjective a ticklish situation* difficult, problematic, awkward, delicate, sensitive,

tricky, thorny, knotty, touchy, risky, uncertain, precarious; *inf.* sticky.

tide *noun* **1** *sailing times dependent on the tide* tidal flow, tidewater, tide race, ebb, current, stream. **2** *the tide of events* course, movement, direction, trend, current, drift, run, tendency, tenor.

tide *verb* **tide over** *the extra money will tide us over until pay day* help out, assist, aid, keep one going, see one through, keep one's head above water, keep the wolf from the door.

tidings *plural noun good tidings | hear tidings of his death* news, notification, word, communication, information, intelligence, advice; reports; *inf.* info, low-down, dope.

tidy *adjective* **1** *a tidy room/garden* neat, trim, orderly, in order, in good order, well-ordered, spruce, shipshape, well-kept, clean, spick and span. **2** *children looking tidy* neat, well-groomed, spruce. **3** *people who are tidy by nature* neat, orderly, organized, well-organized, methodical, systematic, business-like. **4** *leave a tidy sum* considerable, sizeable, substantial, goodly, handsome, generous, ample, largish, large, respectable, fair, decent, healthy.
Opposites UNTIDY; MESSY; SCRUFFY; UNKEMPT.

tidy *verb* **1** *tidy up the living room | tidy your desk* clean, clean up, put to rights, put in order, straighten, make shipshape. **2** *tidy oneself up for the interview* spruce up, groom, smarten, neaten, brush down.

tie *verb* **1** *tie the dog to the tree | the boat was tied fast to the jetty* tie up, fasten, attach, fix, bind, secure, tether, moor, lash, join, connect, link, couple, rope, chain. **2** *tie the string/knot* knot, make a bow/knot in. **3** *having a young child rather tied her* tie down, restrict, confine, curb, limit, constrain, restrain, hamper, hinder, impede, cramp. **4** *the two teams tied* draw, be equal, be even, be neck and neck. **tie in** *her evidence doesn't tie in with that of other people | the new evidence just does not tie in fit* in with, correspond to, tally with, concur with, conform with, dovetail with. **tie down** *children/petty rules tied her down* tie, restrict, confine, curb, limit, constrain, hinder. **tie up** **1** *tie up the dog/boat* fasten, attach, bind, secure, tether, moor, connect, rope, chain. *See* TIE *verb* 1. **2** *the robbers tied up the guard* bind, truss up. **3** *tie up the parcel* wrap, wrap up, bind, truss. **4** *his capital is tied up* invest, commit. **5** *the meeting will tie him up all morning* occupy, engage, keep busy, engross, take up one's attention. **6** *we should tie up the meeting/arrangements/contract* finalize, conclude, bring to a conclusion, wind up, complete, finish off; *inf.* wrap up.
Opposites UNTIE; LOOSEN.

tie *noun* **1** *rubbish bags fastened with a tie* bond, ligature, link, fastening, fastener, clip, catch. **2** *men wearing ties* necktie, bow-tie, cravat, neckerchief. **3** *family/business ties* bond, connection, relationship, kinship, affiliation, allegiance, liaison, friendship. **4** *owning a restaurant can be a tie* restriction, curb, limitation, constraint, restraint, hindrance, impediment, encumbrance. **5** *the game ended in a tie* draw, dead heat, deadlock, stalemate. **6** *the* team have two ties this week fixture, game, match, contest.

tier noun **1** *tiers of seats* row, rank, bank, line. **2** *the tiers of a wedding cake* layer, level. **3** *the tiers of the underground garage* level, storey. **4** *the tiers of the hierarchy in the firm* layer, level, echelon, rank.

tight adjective **1** *keep a tight grip* fast, secure, fixed, clenched, clinched. **2** *tight ropes/muscles* taut, rigid, stiff, tense, stretched, strained. **3** *a tight skirt rather than a full one* tight-fitting, close-fitting, figure-hugging, narrow. **4** *a tight mass of fibres* compact, compacted, compressed. **5** *space was a bit tight with so many people* cramped, restricted, limited, constricted. **6** *the box must be tight* impervious, impenetrable, sound, sealed, hermetic; watertight, airtight. **7** *money is a bit tight just now* scarce, scant, sparse, in short supply, limited, insufficient, inadequate. **8** *security was tight at the president's talk* strict, rigorous, stringent, tough, rigid, uncompromising, exacting. **9** *in a tight situation* problematic, difficult, precarious, hazardous, dangerous, perilous, tricky, ticklish, worrying, delicate; *inf.* sticky. **10** *a piece of tight prose* concise, succinct, terse, crisp, straightforward, pithy, epigrammatic. **11** *it was a tight race* close, even, evenly matched, neck and neck. **12** *he got tight at the party* drunk, intoxicated, inebriated, tipsy; *inf.* tiddly, under the influence, bevvied, plastered, smashed, legless, paralytic, wasted, wrecked, pickled, sozzled, steaming, stewed, out of it, blotto, pie-eyed, half-cut, three sheets to the wind, pissed. **13** *the old man's so tight he won't buy food* tight-fisted, mean, miserly, parsimonious, stingy, niggardly.
Opposites LOOSE; SLACK; GENEROUS.

tighten verb **1** *she tightened her grip* secure, make fast, make more secure. **2** *tighten the rope* tauten, make tight/taut, stretch, make rigid, rigidify, stiffen, tense. **3** *tighten the lid* screw on, close. **4** *tighten security* increase, make stricter, make rigorous/stringent/rigid. *See* TIGHT 8. **5** *his throat tightened* narrow, constrict, contract.
Opposites LOOSEN; slacken; RELAX.

till preposition **1** *he played till six o' clock | playing till they went home* until, up to, as late as, up to the time that/of. **2** *we hadn't seen him till then* before, prior to, previous to, earlier than.

till noun *money in the till* cash register, cash box, cash drawer, strong box.

till verb *till the soil/field* cultivate, work, farm, plough, dig, turn over.

tilt verb **1** *the building tilts a bit* lean, list, slope, slant, incline, tip, cant. **2** *tilt at the other knight* charge against, rush at, run at. **3** *tilt with the other knight* joust with, clash with, contend with, fight with.

tilt noun **1** *the building/picture is at a tilt | with a tilt of his head* angle, slant, slope, incline, inclination, cant. **2** *knights taking part in a tilt* joust, tournament, tourney, combat, contest, fight, duel; lists. **at full tilt** at full speed/pelt, at breakneck speed, headlong, very rapidly/quickly/swiftly, with great force.

timber noun **1** *timber for building the house* wood; *Am.* lumber. **2** *the ceiling/ship's timbers* beam, spar, pole. **3** *timber for the fire* wood, firewood; logs.

time noun **1** *in the time of the dinosaurs* age, era, epoch, period. *See table at* AGE. **2** *he worked there for a time* while, spell, stretch, span, period, term. **3** *the last time I saw him* occasion, point, juncture. **4** *now is the time to act/leave* moment, point, instant, stage. **5** *the house will last his time* lifetime, life, life span, allotted span. **6** *have a hard time | endure hard times* conditions, circumstances; situation, experience. **7** *beat time | in waltz time* rhythm, measure, tempo, beat, metre. **8** *he never has any time to himself* freedom, leisure, leisure time, spare time; moments, odd moments. **ahead of time** early, earlier than expected, in good time, with time to spare. **all the time 1** *they chattered all the time he was speaking* throughout, for the duration. **2** *he works all the time* constantly, always, at all times, perpetually, continuously, continually. **at one time 1** *at one time he worked there* at one point, once, time was when, in the past, previously, formerly, hitherto. **2** *several matches going on at one time* simultaneously, concurrently, at once, at the same time, together. **at the same time 1** *they arrived at the same time* simultaneously, together, concurrently. **2** *he's wealthy; at the same time he lives frugally* nevertheless, nonetheless, however, but, still, yet, just the same. **at times** from time to time, every now and then, periodically, on occasion, occasionally. **behind time** late, running late, behind schedule. **behind the times** old-fashioned, out of date/fashion, dated, outmoded, obsolete, passé, antiquated; *inf.* old hat. **for the time being** for now, for the moment/present, in the meantime, meantime, meanwhile, temporarily, pro tem. **from time to time** now and then, every so often, once in a while, at times, periodically, on occasion, occasionally, sometimes. **in no time 1** *your mum will be here in no time* very soon, any moment/minute now, before one knows it, in a trice; *inf.* in a jiffy. **2** *he did the job in no time* very rapidly/quickly/swiftly, speedily, at great speed, expeditiously, with dispatch. **in good time** punctually, on time, early, ahead of time, with time to spare. **in time 1** *he didn't reach the station in time* early enough, punctually, in good time, at the appointed/right time, on schedule. **2** *they will forget in time* eventually, ultimately, as time goes on/by, by and by, one day, someday, sooner or later, in the long run. **many a time** often, frequently, many times, on many occasions. **on time** punctually, early enough, in good time, sharp; *inf.* on the dot. **time after time** again and again, many times over, repeatedly, time and again, time and time again, recurrently, frequently, often, on many occasions.

time verb **1** *time the meeting for the afternoon* schedule, fix, set, arrange, timetable, programme. **2** *time his progress | time the race* clock, measure, calculate, regulate, count. **3** *time the film exposure | time his entrance* regulate, adjust, set, synchronize.

timeless *adjective* ageless, enduring, lasting, permanent, abiding, unending, ceaseless, undying, deathless, eternal, everlasting, immortal, changeless, immutable, indestructible.
Opposites EPHEMERAL; FLEETING.

timely *adjective their timely intervention* opportune, well-timed, at the right time, convenient, appropriate, seasonable, felicitous.
Opposites ILL-TIMED; INCONVENIENT.

timetable *noun bus timetables | the timetable for the conference* schedule, programme, calendar, list, agenda.

timetable *verb timetable the appointment for tomorrow* schedule, fix, set, programme.

timid *adjective* **1** *too timid to stand up to the bully* easily frightened, timorous, fearful, apprehensive, afraid, frightened, scared, faint-hearted, cowardly, pusillanimous; *inf.* chicken, yellow, lily-livered. **2** *too timid to speak to strangers* shy, diffident, bashful, reticent, unselfconfident, timorous, shrinking, retiring, coy, demure.
Opposites BOLD; BRAZEN.

timorous *adjective* **1** *too timorous to fight* easily frightened, timid, fearful, apprehensive, afraid, frightened, scared, cowardly; *inf.* chicken. *See* TIMID 1. **2** *too timorous to introduce herself* timid, shy, diffident, bashful, reticent, retiring, coy. *See* TIMID 2.
Opposites BRAVE; BOLD.

tincture *noun* **1** *tincture of iodine* solution, suspension, infusion. **2** *a tincture of pink in the material* tint, colour, shade, tinge. **3** *a tincture of garlic* flavour, taste, smell, aroma, trace. **4** *a tincture of heresy in their attitude* hint, suggestion, trace, touch, dash, soupçon.

tinge *verb* **1** *wallpapers tinged with silver* colour, tint, shade, dye, stain, suffuse, imbue. **2** *admiration slightly tinged with envy* affect by, flavour with, colour with, suffuse, imbue.

tinge *noun* **1** *a tinge of silver in the wallpaper* colour, tint, shade, tone, tincture, cast, dye, stain, wash. **2** *a tinge of sadness in her attitude* hint, suggestion, trace, touch, bit, dash, tincture, soupçon.

tingle *verb my fingers were tingling* prickle, prick, tickle, itch, sting, quiver, tremble.

tingle *noun* **1** *the tingle in her fingers* tingling, prickling, pricking, tickle, itch, quiver, trembling; *inf.* pins and needles. **2** *feel a tingle of excitement* quiver, tremor, thrill, throb.

tinker *verb tinker with the engine | tinker at computers* fiddle with, play with, toy with, tamper with, fool around with, mess about with.

tinkle *verb the bell tinkled* ring, chime, peal, ding, jingle.

tinkle *noun* **1** *the tinkle of the doorbell* ring, chime, peal, ding, jingle. **2** *give her a tinkle* telephone call, call; *inf.* phone, phone call, ring, buzz, bell. **3** *go for a tinkle* urination; *inf.* pee.

tinsel *noun* **1** *Christmas trees decorated with tinsel* metallic yarn, spangle, clinquant. **2** *dislike the tinsel of the occasion* ostentation, showiness, flashiness, pretentiousness, display, glitter, ornateness, flamboyance, gaudiness, garishness, tawdriness, meretriciousness.

tinsel *adjective tinsel clothes/furnishings/occasions* ostentatious, showy, flashy, pretentious, glittering, ornate, flamboyant, gaudy, garish, trashy, meretricious, tawdry; *inf.* flash.

tint *noun* **1** *several tints to chose from* shade, colour, tone, tinge, cast, tincture. **2** *strong colours contrasting with tints* pastel, pale colour, soft colour. **3** *a hair tint* dye, colourant, colouring, wash.

tiny *adjective* minute, diminutive, miniature, mini, minuscule, infinitesimal, microscopic, dwarfish, midget, pocket-sized, Lilliputian, wee, *petite*, small, little, insignificant, trifling, negligible, inconsequential; *inf.* teeny, teeny-weeny, itsy-bitsy, pint-sized.
Opposites HUGE; ENORMOUS; GIGANTIC.

tip¹ *noun* **1** *the tip of an iceberg | the mountain tip* point, peak, top, summit, apex, crown. **2** *the tip of the fingers* end, extremity. **3** *the tip of an umbrella* point, end. **4** *the chair legs have rubber tips* cap, cover.

tip² *verb they tipped the cigarettes with filters | warriors tipping their spears with poison* cap, top, crown.

tip³ *noun take the rubbish to the tip* rubbish dump, dump, refuse dump, rubbish heap; *dial.* midden.

tip⁴ *verb* **1** *the wardrobe tends to tip* tilt, lean, list, cant, slant. **2** *the chair/boat tipped over* topple, overturn, fall over, turn topsy-turvy, capsize. **3** *he tipped over the rubbish bin* upset, overturn, topple, upend, capsize. **4** *tip the water into the bath | tip rubbish onto the dump* pour, empty, unload, dump.

tip⁵ *noun* **1** *give the waiter a tip* gratuity, pourboire, baksheesh. **2** *tips on how to take out stains* hint, suggestion, piece of advice; advice. **3** *a tip for the 3.30 racing* tip, recommendation.

tip⁶ *verb* **1** *tip the waiter* give a tip to, reward, remunerate. **2** *tip the grey horse | the older candidate to win* recommend, back.

tip⁷ *verb the ball tipped the edge of the racket* touch, tap, strike/hit lightly.

tip-off *noun the police received a tip-off about the murderer's whereabouts* warning, forewarning, hint, clue; advice, information, notification.

tipple *verb* **1** *began to tipple on his wife's death* drink, take alcohol regularly, have a drink problem; *inf.* indulge, booze. **2** *tipple whisky* drink, sip, swig, quaff, imbibe.

tipple *noun what's your tipple?* regular/usual drink, favourite drink; *inf.* poison. *See tables at* ALCOHOL, BEER, WHISKY.

tippler *noun* drinker, hard/problem drinker, drunk, drunkard, inebriate, toper, sot, imbiber; *inf.* boozer, soak, lush.

tipsy *adjective* drunk, intoxicated, inebriated; *inf.* tiddly, tight, under the influence, merry, bevvied, half-cut.
Opposites SOBER.

tirade *noun* diatribe, harangue, stream of abuse, verbal onslaught, lecture, upbraiding, denunciation, obloquy, philippic; invective, vituperation, fulmination, censure, vilification.

tire *verb* **1** *climbing the mountain tired him* tire out, fatigue, wear out, weary, exhaust, drain, enervate, debilitate, jade; *inf.* fag out, take it out of, whack, bush, knacker, poop. **2** *he tires easily* get/grow/become tired, get fatigued, flag, droop. **3** *their constant boasting tires me* bore, weary, irk, irritate, get on one's nerves, annoy, exasperate; *inf.* get to. **4** *he never tires of hearing the story | she tired of her lover* grow bored, become weary, be fed up; *inf.* be sick (of).

tired *adjective* **1** *feel tired after the climb* fatigued, worn out, weary, wearied, exhausted, drained, enervated, debilitated, jaded; *inf.* fagged, done, done in, all in, dead beat, dog-tired, whacked, bushed, knackered, pooped, dead on one's feet, ready to drop. **2** *tired children anxious for bed* sleepy, drowsy, weary; *inf.* asleep on one's feet. **3** *tired jokes* stale, hackneyed, familiar, worn-out, outworn, well-worn, clichéd, stock, platitudinous, trite, banal; *inf.* corny. **4** *made tired by their chatter* bored, wearied, irked, irritated, annoyed, exasperated. **5** *tired of listening to the story* bored, weary, wearied, fed up; *inf.* sick.
Opposites ENERGETIC; LIVELY; FRESH.

tireless *adjective* *tireless workers/efforts* untiring, unwearied, unflagging, indefatigable, energetic, industrious, vigorous, determined, resolute, dogged.

tiresome *adjective* **1** *tiresome work* wearisome, laborious, wearing, tedious, boring, monotonous, dull, uninteresting, unexciting, humdrum, routine. **2** *she's a tiresome child* troublesome, irksome, vexatious, irritating, annoying, exasperating, trying.
Opposites INTERESTING; EXCITING; PLEASANT.

tiring *adjective* *a tiring journey/job* wearying, wearing, fatiguing, exhausting, draining, enervating, arduous, laborious, strenuous, exacting, taxing, tough.

tissue *noun* **1** *coverings made of tissue* gauze, gossamer, netting, webbing. **2** *wrap the china in tissue* tissue paper. **3** *pass the child a tissue* paper handkerchief, disposable handkerchief, paper towel; Kleenex™. **4** *a tissue of lies* web, network, nexus, mass, conglomeration, set, series, chain.

titbit *noun* **1** *keep some titbits for the children/dogs* tasty morsel, treat, snack, delicacy, dainty, bonne bouche; *inf.* goody. **2** *neighbours passing on titbits* piece of gossip, bit of scandal, juicy/spicy scrap.

titillate *verb* *titillated by the pornographic film* excite, arouse, stimulate, provoke, thrill, interest, fascinate, tantalize, seduce; *inf.* turn on.
Opposites BORE; turn off (*see* TURN).

titillating *adjective* *titillating pictures* exciting, arousing, stimulating, provocative, thrilling, interesting, fascinating, tantalizing, suggestive, seductive, erotic.

titivate *verb* *titivate herself to go out* groom, smarten up, spruce up, make up, prink, preen, primp; *inf.* doll up, do up, tart up.

title *noun* **1** *what is the title of the book/musical?* name. **2** *picture/illustration titles* credit, caption,

legend, inscription, heading. **3** *what is the title of the queen's niece?* form of address, designation, appellation, name, denomination, epithet, sobriquet, style; *inf.* moniker, handle. **4** *disputing his title to the land* entitlement, right, claim, ownership, proprietorship, possession, holding. **5** *lose the titles to the land* title-deed, deed, ownership document, proof of ownership. **6** *boxers contending for the title* championship, first place, crown; laurels.

title *verb* *they titled the book Sunburst* entitle, name, call, designate, label, tag, style, term.

titter *noun* snicker, snigger, giggle, tee-hee, laugh, chuckle, cackle; *inf.* chortle.

tittle-tattle *noun* *you shouldn't listen to tittle-tattle* gossip, idle talk, chit-chat, prattle, hearsay.

titular *adjective* **1** *a titular description* naming, designative, appellative, denominative, identifying, labelling. **2** *the titular head of state* nominal, in title/name only, so-called, self-called, self-styled, soi-disant, token, puppet, putative.

toad *noun*. See table at AMPHIBIAN.

toadstool *noun*. See table at FUNGUS.

toady *noun* *the boss and a couple of his toadies* sycophant, fawner, flatterer, groveller, kowtower, lackey, flunkey, minion, lickspittle, truckler, hanger-on, parasite, leech, jackal, spaniel; *inf.* yes-man, crawler, bootlicker.

toady *verb* *he toadies to his superiors* bow and scrape to, be obsequious to, fawn on, flatter, grovel to, kowtow to, curry favour with, truckle to; *inf.* butter up, fall all over, suck up to.

toast *verb* **1** *toast the bread/crumpets* brown, crisp. **2** *toast oneself at the fire* warm, warm up, heat, heat up. **3** *toast the winner* drink the health of, drink to, pledge, salute.

toast *noun* **1** *drink/make a toast to the winner* health, pledge, salutation, salute, tribute; compliments, greetings. **2** *she was the toast of the town* celebrity, darling, favourite, heroine, hero.

today *noun* **1** *today is his birthday* this day, this very day. **2** *today is all that matters to the young* the present, the present time, now, the here and now, this moment, this time, this period, this age.

toddle *verb* **1** *children toddling down the road* totter, teeter, wobble, falter, dodder. **2** *we must be toddling off* go, leave, depart.

to-do *noun* commotion, fuss, fuss and bother, bother, trouble, disturbance, uproar, tumult, hurly-burly, brouhaha, bustle, hustle and bustle.

together *adverb* **1** *friends who work together* with each other, in conjunction, jointly, conjointly, in cooperation, as one, in unison, side by side, hand in hand, hand in glove, shoulder to shoulder, cheek by jowl. **2** *they arrived/shouted together* simultaneously, concurrently, at the same time, at once, all at once, in unison, with one accord, synchronously. **3** *it rained for days together* in a row, in succession, successively, consecutively, on end, one after the other, continuously, without a break, without interruption. **4** *they've got it/things together* *at last* organized, sorted out, straight, to rights, settled, fixed, arranged.

together *adjective she seems very together* composed, calm, cool, well-balanced, stable, well-adjusted, well-organized, efficient.

toil *verb* **1** *they toiled away on the land | toiling at their books* labour, slog, slave, push oneself, drive oneself, strive, drudge, work, work doggedly, work like a dog/slave/Trojan; *inf.* work one's fingers to the bone, sweat, grind, graft. **2** *they toiled up the hill* labour, struggle, drag oneself; *inf.* sweat, make heavy weather.

toil *noun years of toil wore him out* hard/heavy work, labour, slog, slaving, striving, donkey-work, drudgery, application, industry, effort, exertion, travail, sweat of one's brow; *inf.* elbow-grease, grind, graft.

toilet *noun* **1** *public toilets* lavatory, bathroom, ladies' room, powder room, convenience, outhouse, urinal, latrine, privy; *Am.* washroom; *inf.* loo, bog, gents, ladies, WC; *Am. inf.* john, can. **2** *attending to his toilet* bathing, washing, grooming, dressing; ablutions.

toils *plural noun caught in the toils of the law* net, snare, trap.

token *noun* **1** *a white flag being a token of surrender | a token of friendship* symbol, sign, emblem, badge, representation, indication, mark, manifestation, expression, demonstration, recognition, index; evidence. **2** *keep the menu as a token of the celebration* memento, souvenir, keepsake, remembrance, reminder, memorial. **3** *slot machine tokens* disc, substitute, substitute coin. **4** *book tokens* voucher, coupon.

token *adjective* **1** *a token strike to emphasize union solidarity* symbolic, emblematic. **2** *offer token resistance* perfunctory, superficial, nominal, minimal, slight, hollow.

tolerable *adjective* **1** *the pain/noise level was scarcely tolerable* endurable, bearable, sufferable, supportable, brookable, acceptable. **2** *his work was tolerable but far from brilliant* fairly good, fair, all right, passable, adequate, satisfactory, good enough, average, mediocre, middling, fair to middling, ordinary, run-of-the-mill, indifferent, unexceptional; *inf.* not bad, OK, so-so, nothing to write home about.
Opposites INTOLERABLE; UNBEARABLE; INSUFFERABLE.

tolerance *noun* **1** *treat the young with tolerance* toleration, open-mindedness, lack of prejudice/bias, broad-mindedness, liberalism, forbearance, patience, magnanimity, understanding, charity, lenience, lenity, indulgence, permissiveness, complaisance, laxness. **2** *his tolerance of pain | accept the situation with tolerance* toleration, endurance, sufferance, acceptance, fortitude, stamina, hardiness, resilience, toughness.

tolerant *adjective tolerant people accepting the beliefs of others | tolerant of the views of others* open-minded, unprejudiced, unbiased, unbigoted, broad-minded, liberal, catholic, forbearing, patient, long-suffering, magnanimous, sympathetic, understanding, charitable, lenient, indulgent, permissive, free and easy, easy-

going, complaisant, lax.
Opposites INTOLERANT; NARROW-MINDED.

tolerate *verb* **1** *tolerate opposition | tolerate other people's views* permit, allow, admit, sanction, warrant, countenance, brook, recognize, acknowledge. **2** *unable to tolerate the pain/noise* endure, bear, suffer, take, stand, put up with, abide, accept, stomach, submit to. **3** *able to tolerate the new drug/treatment* take, receive, be treated with.

toleration *noun* **1** *treat the young with toleration* tolerance, open-mindedness, lack of prejudice/bias, broad-mindedness, liberalism, patience, understanding, charity, indulgence. See TOLERANCE 1. **2** *his toleration of the noise levels | accept it with toleration* tolerance, endurance, sufferance, acceptance, fortitude, stamina, hardiness. See TOLERANCE 2. **3** *countries which do not practise religious toleration* freedom of worship, religious freedom, freedom of conscience.

toll *noun* **1** *pay a toll to use the bridge/road* charge, fee, payment, levy, tariff. **2** *the fever took a heavy toll of her health | the death toll* cost, damage, loss; inroads.

toll *verb* **1** *bells tolling in the distance* sound, ring, peal, knell, clang. **2** *toll the bells* sound, ring. **3** *bells tolling for his death | tolling the outbreak of war* announce, herald, signal, warn of. **4** *clocks tolling 6 o'clock* strike, chime.

tomb *noun* grave, burial place/chamber, sepulchre, vault, crypt, catacomb, mausoleum.

tombstone *noun* headstone, gravestone, grave marker, memorial, monument.

tome *noun* volume, book, work, opus.

tomfool *adjective what a tomfool thing to do* foolish, stupid, idiotic, silly, insane, mad, irresponsible.

tomfoolery *noun children told to stop their tomfoolery* horseplay, mischief, fooling, foolery, clowning, skylarking, buffoonery, nonsense; pranks, tricks, capers, antics, larks; *inf.* shenanigans, monkey tricks.

tone *noun* **1** *the pleasant tone of the flute* sound, sound quality, colour, pitch, timbre, tonality. **2** *speak in an angry tone | whisper in soft tones* tone of voice, mode of expression, expression, intonation, inflection, modulation, accentuation. **3** *the tone of his letter was optimistic* mood, air, attitude, character, manner, spirit, temper, tenor, vein, drift, gist. **4** *lower the tone of the place* style, quality, high quality. **5** *decorated in tones of pink* tint, shade, tinge, cast, tincture.

tone *verb the curtains tone with the bedspread* harmonize with, go with, go well with, blend with, match, suit. **tone down 1** *tone down the brightness of the wall colours* soften, lighten, subdue, mute. **2** *tone down your aggressive approach* moderate, soften, modulate, play down, temper, subdue, dampen, restrain, soft-pedal.

tongue *noun* **1** *speak in a foreign tongue* language, speech, parlance, dialect, idiom, patois, vernacular; *inf.* lingo. See table at LANGUAGE. **2** *he has a glib tongue* way of speaking, mode of expression.

tongue-tied *adjective tongue-tied in the presence of her hero* at a loss for words, wordless, speech-

less, bereft of speech, struck dumb, dumb, silent, mute, taciturn, inarticulate.
Opposites LOQUACIOUS; GARRULOUS.

tonic *noun* **1** *prescribe a tonic for the invalid* restorative, stimulant, analeptic, pick-me-up. **2** *the good news was a tonic to the depressed woman* stimulant, boost, fillip, pick-me-up; *inf.* shot in the arm.

too *adverb* **1** *the dog came too | think, too, of her age* as well, also, in addition, besides, furthermore, moreover, to boot. **2** *she is too busy* excessively, overly, unduly, inordinately, unreasonably, extremely, very; *inf.* too-too.

tool *noun* **1** *the tools of his trade | kitchen tools* implement, instrument, utensil, device, apparatus, gadget, appliance, machine, contrivance, contraption, aid. *See table.* **2** *he is the manager's tool* creature, cat's-paw, puppet, pawn, minion, lackey, flunkey, henchman, toady; *inf.* stooge.

tool *verb* **1** *tool leather* shape, work, cut, chase, decorate, ornament. **2** *tooling along the motorway* bowl, drive, ride, motor.

tooth *noun. See tables.*

HUMAN TEETH

canines	molars
eye teeth	permanent teeth
incisors	premolars
milk teeth	primary teeth

PARTS OF A HUMAN TOOTH

cementum	nerve
crown	periodontal membrane
dentine	
enamel	pulp cavity
gingiva	root
neck	root canal

top *noun* **1** *the top of the mountain/hill* highest point/part, summit, peak, pinnacle, crest, crown, tip, apex, vertex, apogee. **2** *he's at the top of his career* height, high point, peak, pinnacle, zenith, acme, culmination, climax, crowning point, prime, meridian. **3** *the top of the table/milk* upper part, upper surface, upper layer. **4** *put the top on the bottle/jar* cap, lid, stopper, cork, cover. **5** *she wore a blue top* sweater, jumper, jersey, sweat shirt, T-shirt, blouse, shirt. **6** *turnip tops* leaves, shoots, stem, stalk. **over the top** *his criticism of the play was over the top | her budget/dress for the party was over the top* excessive, inordinate, immoderate, over the limit, exaggerated, too much, uncalled-for, going too far; *inf.* a bit much, OTT.

top *adjective* **1** *the top drawer/floor* topmost, uppermost, highest. **2** *top scientists* foremost, leading, principal, pre-eminent, greatest, finest; *inf.* top-notch. **3** *the top men/positions in the firm* leading, chief, principal, main, highest, ruling, commanding. **4** *top goods* top-quality, top-grade, best, finest, prime, choicest, quality, excellent; *inf.* A1, top-notch. **5** *at top speed* maximum, maximal, greatest, utmost.

top *verb* **1** *icecream topped with chocolate sauce* cap, cover, finish, garnish. **2** *top the list of candidates* head, lead, be first in. **3** *donations have topped the £1,000 mark | topped our expectations | he topped his previous record* surpass, exceed, go beyond, transcend, better, best, beat, excel, outstrip, outdo, outshine, eclipse. **4** *top the mountain* reach the top of, climb, scale, ascend, mount, crest.

topcoat *noun* overcoat, greatcoat. *See table at* COAT.

topic *noun* subject, subject matter, theme, issue, matter, point, question, argument, thesis, text.

topical *adjective* *write about topical issues* newsworthy, in the news, current, up-to-date, up-to-the-minute, contemporary, popular.
Opposites OUT-OF-DATE, OUTDATED.

topmost *adjective* **1** *the topmost drawer* top, uppermost, highest. **2** *the topmost authority on the subject* top, foremost, leading, principal, pre-eminent. *See* TOP *adjective* 2. **3** *the topmost people/positions in the organization* leading, chief, principal, highest, ruling. *See* TOP *adjective* 3.

TOOLS

adze	crowbar	hedge clipper	pliers	shears
auger	cultivator	hoe	pruning hook	shovel
awl	dibber	jack	punch	sickle
axe	drill	jemmy	rake	sledge-hammer
beetle	edging shears	jigsaw	ram	soldering iron
bevel	file	knife	rasp	spade
billhook	fork	lawn mower	riddle	spanner
blowlamp	fretsaw	lever	ripsaw	spokeshave
blowtorch	gavel	mallet	roller	swage
brace bit	glass cutter	mattock	sander	trowel
bradawl	grinder	mitre	sandpaper	tweezers
burnisher	hacksaw	nippers	saw	vice
chainsaw	hammer	perforator	scraper	wedge
chisel	hammer drill	pickaxe	screwdriver	wire cutter
clamp	hand-axe	pincers	scribe	wire stripper
claw hammer	handsaw	pitchfork	scythe	wrench
clough	handspike	plane	secateurs	

top-notch *adjective* first-rate, top-grade, excellent, choice, superior, superb; *inf.* A1, ace, crack, top-hole, tiptop, wizard.

topple *verb* **1** *the load was unstable and toppled* fall over, tip over, keel over, overturn, overbalance, capsize. **2** *his kick toppled the dustbin* upset, knock over, push over, tip over, capsize. **3** *the rebels toppled the tyrant* overthrow, oust, unseat, overturn, bring down, bring low.

topsy-turvy *adverb/adjective* **1** *children turning topsy-turvy on the climbing frame* upside down, wrong side up, head over heels. **2** *turn the house topsy-turvy looking for the documents* in disorder, in confusion, in a muddle, in a jumble, in chaos, in disarray, in a mess, upside down.

torment *noun* **1** *endure torment at the hands of his captors* agony, suffering, torture, pain, excruciation, anguish, hell, misery, distress, affliction, wretchedness. **2** *the ill-behaved children were a torment to him* scourge, curse, plague, bane, affliction, thorn in the flesh, irritation, irritant, vexation, annoyance, worry, nuisance, bother, trouble, pest; *inf.* pain in the neck.

torment *verb* **1** *he was tormented by his captors/ wound/conscience* cause agony/suffering/pain to, inflict anguish on, afflict, harrow, plague, torture, distress, worry, trouble. **2** *the children tormented the new teacher* tease, irritate, vex, annoy, pester, harass, badger, plague, worry, be a nuisance to, bother, trouble, be a pest to.

torn *adjective* **1** *torn clothes* ragged, tattered, ripped, split, slit, cut, lacerated, rent. **2** *I am torn between the two dresses* divided, split, wavering, vacillating, irresolute, uncertain, unsure, undecided.

tornado *noun* cyclone, whirlwind, wind storm, storm, hurricane, gale, squall, typhoon; *Am. inf.* twister.

torpid *adjective* sluggish, slow-moving, slow, dull, lethargic, heavy, inactive, stagnant, inert, somnolent, sleepy, languorous, languid, listless, apathetic, passive, slothful, indolent, lazy. **Opposites** ENERGETIC; ACTIVE.

torpor *noun* torpidity, sluggishness, slowness, dullness, lethargy, heaviness, inactivity, stagnation, inertia, somnolence, sleepiness, languor, languidness, listlessness, apathy, passivity, sloth, slothfulness, indolence, laziness.

torrent *noun* **1** *torrents of flood water pouring down the streets* flood, deluge, inundation, spate, cascade, rush, stream, current. **2** *get soaked in the torrent* downpour, deluge, rainstorm. **3** *a torrent of abuse* outburst, stream, volley, outpouring, barrage, battery.

torrid *adjective* **1** *the torrid conditions in the desert* hot, arid, sweltering, scorching, boiling, parching, sultry, stifling. **2** *torrid love scenes* passionate, impassioned, ardent, fervent, fervid, amorous, erotic; *inf.* steamy. **Opposites** COLD; PASSIONLESS; UNEMOTIONAL.

tortuous *adjective* **1** *a tortuous mountain path* twisting, winding, curving, curvy, sinuous, undulating, coiling, serpentine, snaking, snaky, zigzag, convoluted, meandering, spir-

alling, anfractuous. **2** *a tortuous description of the incident* convoluted, roundabout, circuitous, indirect, unstraightforward, involved, complicated, ambiguous. **3** *his tortuous policy* devious, cunning, tricky, deceitful, deceptive, guileful. **Opposites** STRAIGHT; STRAIGHTFORWARD.

torture *noun* **1** *use torture to extract a confession* persecution, pain, suffering, abuse, ill-treatment, punishment, torment. **2** *the torture of toothache | the torture of watching his friend die* torment, agony, suffering, pain, excruciation, anguish, misery, distress. *See* TORMENT *noun* 1.

torture *verb* **1** *torture the hostages* persecute, inflict pain/suffering on, abuse, ill-treat, punish, torment; *inf.* work over. **2** *he was tortured by the pain of his wound | tortured by his conscience* torment, rack, cause agony/suffering/pain to, inflict anguish on, afflict, harrow, plague, distress, worry, trouble.

toss *verb* **1** *toss the book over here* throw, hurl, cast, sling, pitch, shy, lob, propel, launch, project; *inf.* heave, chuck. **2** *tossing and turning restlessly | tossing around unable to sleep* thrash, wriggle, writhe, squirm, roll, tumble. **3** *ships tossing around on the waves* rock, roll, sway, undulate, pitch, lurch, heave. **4** *toss one's head* throw back, throw up, jerk, jolt.

tot *noun* **1** *mothers and tots* baby, infant, toddler, child, little one, mite. **2** *a tot of whisky* measure, dram, nip, slug; *inf.* shot, finger.

tot *verb* **1** *tot up the costs* add, count, calculate, total, sum, reckon, tally. **2** *it's surprising how the costs tot up* add up, mount up. **tot up to** *the bill tots up to £2000* amount to, total, come to.

total *noun* *the total of those figures is 500 | score a total of six goals* sum, sum total, aggregate, whole, entirety, totality.

total *adjective* **1** *the total number of votes | the total amount spent* complete, entire, whole, full, comprehensive, combined, aggregate, composite, integral. **2** *he's a total idiot | it was a total disaster* complete, thorough, thoroughgoing, all-out, utter, absolute, downright, out and out, outright, sheer, rank, unmitigated, unqualified.

total *verb* **1** *these figures total more than £1000* add up to, come to, tot up to, amount to. **2** *total these figures rapidly* add up, sum, count up, count, reckon, tot up. **3** *total a car* wreck, crash, destroy, demolish, write off.

totalitarian *adjective* totalitarian government one-party, monocratic, undemocratic, autocratic, authoritarian, absolute, despotic, dictatorial, tyrannical, oppressive, fascist. **Opposites** DEMOCRATIC; AUTONOMOUS.

totality *noun* **1** *the grant in its totality will not cover the expense* entirety, entireness, wholeness, fullness, completeness, inclusiveness. **2** *the totality was less than expected* total, sum, aggregate, whole, entirety; all, everything.

totally *adverb* totally blind | forget totally completely, entirely, wholly, fully, thoroughly, utterly, absolutely, quite.

totter *verb* **1** *babies tottering about | women tottering on high heels* teeter, wobble, stagger, stumble, reel, sway, roll, lurch. **2** *tables/buildings* tottering in the explosion shake, sway, rock, lurch, shudder, judder. **3** the regime is tottering be unstable, be unsteady, be shaky, be on the point of collapse, falter.

touch verb **1** the wires are touching be in contact, come into contact, come together, meet, converge, be contiguous, adjoin, abut. **2** he touched her arm press lightly, tap, brush, graze, feel, stroke, pat, fondle, caress. **3** don't touch her things handle, hold, pick up, move, play with, toy with, fiddle with, interfere with. **4** she didn't touch her meal | never touch alcohol eat, consume, drink, take, partake of. **5** they were touched by the child's sad plight affect, move, make an impression on, have an impact on, influence, upset, disturb, make sad, arouse sympathy; inf. get to. **6** the recession did not touch him have an effect on, affect, concern, involve, have a bearing on, be relevant/pertinent to. **7** they wouldn't touch anything illegal be associated with, concern/involve oneself in, have dealings with, deal with, handle, be a party to. **8** no-one can touch him at tennis come near, come up to, compare with, be on a par with, equal, match, be a match for, be in the same league as, parallel, rival; inf. hold a candle to. **9** their speed touched 100 miles per hour | they touched rock bottom reach, get up/down to, attain, arrive at, come to. **10** touch his father for money ask, beg, borrow from. **touch down** the plane touched down at midnight land, alight, arrive. **touch off** **1** touch off the explosive set alight, set off, ignite, trigger, explode, detonate. **2** the statement touched off a storm of protest set off, start, begin, set in motion, initiate, instigate, trigger off, launch. **touch on/upon** **1** touch on the financial situation in his speech refer to, mention, comment on, remark on, allude to, bring in, speak of, talk about, write about, deal with. **2** his actions touched on treason come close to, verge on, incline to, be tantamount to. **touch up** **1** touch up the paintwork of the house patch up, fix up, repair, refurbish, renovate, revamp, give a face-lift to. **2** touch up a photograph improve, enhance. **3** accused of touching up women fondle, molest.

touch noun **1** feel a touch on his arm pressure, tap, strike, hit, blow, brush, stroke, pat, caress. **2** sense its presence by touch feel, feeling, sense of touch, tactile sense, tactility. **3** the material has a velvety/steely touch feel, texture, grain, finish, surface, coating. **4** a touch of garlic/professionalism | a touch down-hearted small amount, bit, trace, dash, taste, spot, drop, pinch, speck, smack, suggestion, hint, soupçon, tinge, tincture, whiff, suspicion. **5** admire the player's/artist's touch craftsmanship, workmanship, artistry, performance, dexterity, deftness, skill, virtuosity, adroitness. **6** the room needs a few extra touches detail, feature, addition, accessory, fine point. **7** I think the teacher is losing his touch skill, skilfulness, expertise, technique, knack, adeptness, ability, talent, flair. **8** the house needs a woman's touch influence, effect, hand, handling, direction, management, technique, method. **9** be/get in touch with old friends | lose touch contact, communication, correspondence.

touch-and-go adjective a touch-and-go situation | it was touch-and-go whether he got the job uncertain, precarious, risky, hazardous, dangerous, critical, suspenseful, cliff-hanging, hanging by a thread.

touched adjective **1** he was touched by their thoughtfulness moved, impressed, affected, softened, warmed. **2** he must be a bit touched to do that unbalanced, unhinged, deranged, demented, crazed, mad, insane; inf. daft, barmy, batty, dotty, nutty, screwy.

touching adjective **1** a touching act of kindness moving, impressive, affecting, warming, heart-warming. **2** a touching story of a sad childhood affecting, moving, emotive, stirring, upsetting, disturbing, saddening, pitiful, piteous, poignant, pathetic, heartbreaking, heartrending.

touchstone noun criterion, yardstick, benchmark, norm, standard, gauge, guide, exemplar, model, pattern.

touchy adjective **1** he's very touchy about his lack of height/results sensitive, oversensitive, hypersensitive, easily offended, thin-skinned; tetchy, testy, irascible, irritable, grouchy, grumpy, peevish, querulous, bad-tempered, captious, crabbed, cross, surly. **2** a touchy situation tricky, ticklish, delicate, precarious, chancy, risky, uncertain.
Opposites CALM; AFFABLE; GOOD-HUMOURED.

tough adjective **1** a tough substance strong, durable, resistant, resilient, sturdy, firm, solid, hard, rigid, stiff. **2** tough meat chewy, leathery, gristly, stringy, fibrous, sinewy. **3** explorers/children have to be tough to survive those conditions hardy, strong, fit, sturdy, rugged, stalwart, vigorous, strapping, robust, resilient. **4** it's a tough job managing the firm difficult, hard, arduous, onerous, heavy, uphill, laborious, strenuous, exacting, taxing, stressful. **5** teachers getting tough with the children | police getting tough with criminals firm, strict, stern, severe, harsh, hard-hitting, adamant, inflexible. **6** tough exam questions difficult, hard, knotty, thorny, baffling, perplexing, ticklish. **7** a tough way of life hard, harsh, austere, rugged, bleak, grim, dire, rough, taxing, exacting. **8** led astray by tough kids rough, rowdy, unruly, disorderly, violent, wild, lawless, lawbreaking, criminal. **9** it was tough that he had to lose unfortunate, unlucky, hard, regrettable; inf. too bad.
Opposites SOFT; TENDER; WEAK; EASY.

tough noun set on by a gang of toughs ruffian, rowdy, thug, hoodlum, hooligan, bully; inf. hard man, roughneck, bruiser.

toughen verb **1** toughen the glass strengthen, fortify, reinforce, harden, rigidify. **2** toughen the laws stiffen, tighten, make stricter, make severe; inf. beef up.

tour noun **1** a world tour | a coach tour through France trip, excursion, journey, expedition, jaunt, outing, peregrination. **2** give the visitors a tour of the new building guided tour, walk round, visit, inspection. **3** on a golfing tour circuit, ambit, round, course, beat. **4** troops doing a tour in Northern Ireland tour of duty, duty, stint, stretch, turn.

tour *verb* **1** *touring the world | touring France* travel round/through, journey through, explore, holiday in. **2** *tour the new building/ estate* go round, walk/drive round, visit, sightsee, inspect.

tourist *noun* visitor, sightseer, holiday-maker, traveller, tripper, excursionist, journeyer; *inf.* globe-trotter.

tournament *noun* **1** *a tennis tournament* competition, contest, series, meeting, event, match. **2** *knights competing in a tournament* joust, jousting, tourney; lists.

tousled *adjective* *tousled hair* rumpled, dishevelled, uncombed, unkempt, disordered, disarranged, untidy, messy; *inf.* mussed up.

tout *verb* **1** *tout for business* ask for, solicit, seek, petition for, appeal for, beg for. **2** *tout customers* solicit, seek, petition, importune, accost, approach; *inf.* hustle. **3** *tout their wares/ tickets* hawk, peddle, sell, offer for sale.

tow *verb* *towing a car/sledge* pull, draw, drag, haul, tug, trail, lug.

tow *noun* *gave the car a tow* towing, haul. *See* TOW *verb.* **in tow** *he had the family/girlfriend in tow* in attendance, by one's side, in one's charge, under one's protection.

towards *preposition* **1** *walk towards the door/ town* in the direction of, to, on the way to, en route for. **2** *his attitude towards her success* with regard to, as regards, regarding, with respect to, respecting, in relation to, concerning, about, apropros. **3** *working towards a degree* for, with the aim of, in order to obtain/ achieve. **4** *the money will go towards the hospital appeal fund* as a contribution, for, to help, to assist. **5** *towards the end of the day/journey* near, nearing, around, close to, coming to, getting on for, just before, shortly before.

tower *noun* **1** *the tower at the top of the church/ castle* steeple, spire, belfry, bell tower, turret, column, pillar, obelisk, minaret. **2** *soldiers manning the tower* fortress, fort, citadel, stronghold, fortification, keep, castle.

tower *verb* **1** *mountains towering into the skies | he towers above the children* soar, rise, ascend, mount, rear, reach/stand high. **2** *he towers above the rest of the modern poets | his writing towers above the rest* surpass, excel, outshine, outclass, overshadow, cap, top, transcend, eclipse, be head and shoulders above, put in the shade; *inf.* run circles around.

towering *adjective* **1** *towering mountain peaks | towering skyscrapers* high, tall, lofty, elevated, sky-high. **2** *in a towering rage* extreme, mighty, fierce, terrible, intense, violent, vehement, passionate, frenzied, frantic. **3** *one of the towering intellects of his age* outstanding, extraordinary, pre-eminent, surpassing, superior, great, incomparable, unrivalled, peerless.

town *noun* borough, municipality, township, urban area.

toxic *adjective* poisonous, venomous, virulent, noxious.
Opposites non-toxic; HARMLESS; SAFE.

toy *noun* **1** *children's toys* plaything, game. **2** *the rich woman surrounds herself with toys* trinket, bauble, knick-knack, gewgaw, trifle, triviality.

toy *adjective* **1** *a toy car | toy soldiers* model, miniature, imitation, make-believe. **2** *toy breeds of dog* small, tiny, miniature, diminutive.

toy *verb* **1** *he's just toying with the girl* amuse oneself with, play around with, flirt with, dally with, sport with, trifle with. **2** *the child was toying with his food* play around with, fiddle with, fool around with, mess about with. **3** *he's toying with the idea of leaving* play with, think idly about, have thoughts about.

trace *noun* **1** *there was no trace left of the picnic* mark, sign, vestige, indication; evidence; remains, remnants, relics. **2** *traces of poison in the drink | no trace of emotion in his voice* bit, touch, hint, suggestion, suspicion, trifle, drop, dash, tinge, tincture, shadow, jot, iota. **3** *follow the burglar's/bear's traces* track, trail, spoor, scent; marks, tracks, prints, imprints, footprints, footmarks, footsteps.

trace *verb* **1** *unable to trace the letter* find, discover, detect, unearth, uncover, track down, turn up, dig up, ferret out, hunt down. **2** *trace the bear to the forest* follow, pursue, track, trail, tail, shadow, stalk, dog. **3** *trace the river back | trace his ancestry back* find the origins/source/ roots of. **4** *trace out the route they would take | trace out the policies for the year* draw, draw up, sketch, draft, outline, mark out, delineate, rough out, map, chart, record, indicate, show, depict.

track *noun* **1** *follow the tracks of the burglar/bear/ motor-bike* marks, traces, impressions, prints, imprints, footprints, footmarks, footsteps; trail, spoor, scent. **2** *follow in the track of the great explorers* trail, path, pathway, way, course, route. **3** *the track of the hurricane/satellite* path, line, course, orbit, route, trajectory, flight path. **4** *follow the track through the forest* path, trail, route, way. **5** *the train left the track* rail, line; railway line, tramline; rails. **6** *run round the track* course; running track, racetrack. **keep track of** keep up with, follow, monitor, record. **lose track of** forget about, be unaware of, misplace, lose/cease contact with.

track *verb* *track the bear to the forest* follow, pursue, trail, trace, tail, shadow, stalk, dog. **track down** *track down the necessary information* hunt down, hunt out, run to earth, unearth, uncover, turn up, dig up, ferret out, nose out, bring to light, expose, discover, find out, detect.

tract[1] *noun* *tracts of forest/desert* area, region, zone, stretch, expanse, extent, plot.

tract[2] *noun* *religious tracts* pamphlet, booklet, leaflet, brochure, monograph, essay, treatise, disquisition, dissertation, thesis, lecture, homily, sermon.

tractable *adjective* malleable, controllable, manageable, governable, amenable, complaisant, compliant, submissive, yielding, docile, dutiful, obedient.
Opposites DEFIANT; OBSTINATE; RECALCITRANT.

trade *noun* **1** *he's in the export trade* commerce, buying and selling, dealing, traffic, trafficking, business, marketing, merchandizing; transactions. **2** *what trade is his father in?* line of work/ business, line, occupation, job, career, profession, craft, vocation, calling, *métier*; work, employment. **3** *I'll do a trade of my car with yours* swap, trade-off, exchange, switch, barter.

trade *verb* **1** *the firm is trading at a loss* do business, deal, run, operate. **2** *they trade in diamonds | they trade with France* buy and sell, deal, traffic, market, merchandise. **3** *he traded his stamp collection for the collection of comics* swap, exchange, switch, barter. **trade on** *he trades on his father's reputation | trading on her kind nature* take advantage of, make use of, exploit, capitalize on, profit from; *inf.* cash in on.

trade mark *noun* **1** *a trade mark for a kind of cleaner* stamp, symbol, logo, sign, emblem, badge, crest, trade name, brand name, proprietary name. **2** *killing dogs is the burglar's trade mark* characteristic, speciality, feature, trait, penchant, proclivity, peculiarity, idiosyncrasy.

trader *noun* merchant, dealer, buyer, seller, buyer and seller, marketer, merchandiser, broker.

tradesman, tradeswoman *noun* **1** *high-street tradesmen protesting against a sales tax* shopkeeper, retailer, storekeeper, vendor, merchant, dealer. **2** *require skilled tradesmen to renovate the old house* workman, craftsman, skilled worker, artisan.

tradition *noun* **1** *keep up the old traditions* custom, belief, practice, convention, ritual, observance, habit, institution, usage, praxis. **2** *handed on by tradition* historical convention, unwritten law, oral history, lore, folklore.

traditional *adjective* **1** *traditional Christmas fare* customary, accustomed, conventional, established, ritual, ritualistic, habitual, set, fixed, routine, usual, wonted, old, time-honoured, historic, folk, familial, ancestral. **2** *keeping alive traditional customs* handed-down, folk, unwritten, oral.
Opposites NOVEL; UNCONVENTIONAL.

traduce *verb* *accused of traducing his neighbour* defame, slander, speak ill/evil of, misrepresent, malign, vilify, calumniate, blacken the name of, cast aspersions on.

traffic *noun* **1** *noisy traffic rushing past* vehicles, cars. **2** *a move to attract traffic to the railways from the roads* transport, transportation, movement of goods/people, freight, conveyancing. **3** *the traffic in diamonds has decreased | drug traffic* trafficking, trade, trading, dealing, commerce, business, peddling, smuggling, bootlegging. **4** *he has little traffic with his neighbours* contact, communication, intercourse; dealings, relations.

traffic *verb* *arrested for trafficking in drugs* trade in, deal in, do business in, peddle, smuggle.

tragedy *noun* **1** *some tragedy had blighted his youth* disaster, calamity, catastrophe, misfortune, misadventure, affliction, adversity, sad event, serious accident, shock, blow. **2** *the play was a tragedy* tragic drama; *lit.* buskin.
Opposites FORTUNE; JOY; COMEDY.

tragic *adjective* **1** *a tragic accident | a tragic end to the day* disastrous, calamitous, catastrophic, fatal, terrible, dreadful, appalling, dire, awful,

miserable, wretched, unfortunate. **2** *listen to her tragic tale* sad, unhappy, pathetic, moving, distressing, disturbing, pitiful, piteous, melancholy, doleful, mournful, dismal, gloomy. **3** *it is tragic what they have done to the village* dreadful, terrible, awful, deplorable, lamentable, regrettable.
Opposites FORTUNATE; HAPPY; JOYFUL.

trail *noun* **1** *follow the trail left by the leader | police on the trail of the criminal* track, scent, spoor; traces, marks, signs, footprints, footmarks. **2** *follow the trail through the forest* path, beaten path, pathway, footpath, track, road, route. **3** *the rock star had a trail of young admirers* line, queue, train, file, column, procession, following, entourage. **4** *leave a trail of disaster behind them* train, chain, series, sequence, aftermath. **5** *vapour trail* stream, tail, appendage.

trail *verb* **1** *the child trailed the toy behind him* tow, pull, drag, draw, haul. **2** *her long skirt trailing on the floor* drag across, sweep, dangle, hang down, droop. **3** *children trailing along | trailing behind their parents* trudge, plod, drag oneself, dawdle, straggle, loiter, linger, lag, fall behind. **4** *plants/creatures trailing along the ground* creep, crawl, slide, slink. **5** *they trailed him to his lair* follow, pursue, track, trace, tail, shadow, stalk, dog. **6** *the team is trailing by five points* lose, be down, be behind. **7** *their enthusiasm gradually trailed off | his voice trailed away* fade, fade away/out, disappear, vanish, peter out, die away, melt away.

train *noun* **1** *the dress had a long train* tail, appendage. **2** *leaving a train of vapour* trail, stream, track, path, wake, wash. **3** *a train of disasters followed* trail, chain, string, series, sequence, set, progression, order, concatenation. **4** *a train of people climbing the mountain* procession, line, file, column, convoy, caravan. **5** *having to accommodate the princess and her train* retinue, entourage, cortège, following, staff, household, court; followers, attendants. **6** *they travel by train* railway train. *See table.*

TRAINS, ENGINES, AND CARRIAGES

baggage car *Am.*	luggage van
buffet car	mail coach
caboose *Am.*	mail train
carriage	observation car
couchette	parlor car *Am.*
diesel-electric	passenger train
diesel locomotive	Pullman
dining car	railcar
express	restaurant car
freight car	roomette *Am.*
freight train	shunter
goods train	sleeper
goods wagon	sleeping car
guard's van	slow train
jerkwater engine *Am.*	steam locomotive
	stopping train
light engine	traction unit

train *verb* **1** *train the young pupils in reading/ musical skills* instruct, teach, coach, tutor, give lessons to, school, educate, drill, prepare, ground, guide, indoctrinate, inculcate. **2** *she is training to be a teacher* study, qualify, learn, prepare. **3** *athletes having to train each night* exercise, do exercises, work out, practise, prepare. **4** *train the football team | /train the horse for the race* coach, drill, exercise. **5** *train the gun/binoculars on the distant figure* aim, point, focus, direct, level, line up.

trainer *noun the trainer of the team* coach, instructor.

trainers *plural noun wearing trainers* training/ sports shoes.

training *noun* **1** *pupils getting training in the social skills* instruction, teaching, coaching, tutoring, schooling, education, drilling, preparation, grounding, guidance, indoctrination, inculcation; lessons. **2** *undergo training for the race* exercise, working out, body-building, practice, preparation; exercises, physical exercises.

trait *noun one of her annoying/endearing traits* characteristic, attribute, feature, quality, property, idiosyncrasy, peculiarity, quirk.

traitor *noun* betrayer, back-stabber, turncoat, double-crosser, double-dealer, renegade, defector, deserter, apostate, Judas, quisling, fifth columnist; *inf.* snake in the grass, two-timer.

traitorous *adjective* treacherous, back-stabbing, double-crossing, double-dealing, disloyal, faithless, unfaithful, perfidious, false-hearted, false, untrue, renegade, seditious, apostate; *inf.* two-timing.
Opposites LOYAL; FAITHFUL.

trajectory *noun* path, track, line, course, orbit, route, flight path.

trammel *noun coping with the trammels of ill health* restraint, constraint, obstacle, bar, block, curb, check, barrier, hindrance, handicap, impediment, drawback, snag; stumbling-block, shackles, fetters, bonds.

trammel *verb mothers trammelled by young children* restrict, restrain, constrain, shackle, fetter, curb, check, hinder, handicap, impede, obstruct, thwart, frustrate.

tramp *verb* **1** *hear him tramping upstairs | workmen tramping in and out of the kitchen* trudge, march, plod, stamp, stump, stomp; *inf.* traipse. **2** *spend the day tramping over the hills* trek, trudge, hike, march, slog, footslog, plod, walk, ramble, roam, range; *inf.* traipse, yomp. **3** *tramp down the corn* trample, tread on, step on, stamp on, squash, crush, flatten.

tramp *noun* **1** *tramps sleeping rough* vagrant, vagabond, derelict, down-and-out, itinerant, drifter; *Am.* hobo; *inf.* dosser. **2** *hear the tramp of the soldiers approaching* heavy step, footstep, footfall, tread, stamp, stomping. **3** *go for a tramp over the hills* trek, hike, march, walk, ramble, roam, wander, range; *inf.* traipse, yomp. **4** *she's just a tramp* loose woman, slut, wanton, trollop, prostitute, whore; *inf.* tart.

trample *verb* **1** *trample on the corn | people trampled to death* tramp on, tread on, walk over, stamp on, squash, crush, flatten. **2** *trample on other people | trample on other people's feelings/ rights* ride roughshod over, treat with con-

tempt, disregard, set at naught, show no consideration for, encroach on, infringe.

trance *noun* daze, stupor, hypnotic state, half-conscious state, dream, reverie, brown study.

tranquil *adjective* **1** *a tranquil life* peaceful, restful, reposeful, calm, quiet, still, serene, placid, undisturbed. **2** *she's a tranquil person* calm, placid, pacific, composed, cool, calm, cool and collected, serene, even-tempered, unexcitable, unflappable, unruffled, unperturbed.
Opposites NOISY; DISTURBED; EXCITABLE.

tranquillity *noun* **1** *love the tranquillity of the place* peace, peacefulness, restfulness, reposefulness, calm, calmness, quiet, quietness, quietude, stillness, serenity, placidity. **2** *her tranquillity is never disturbed* calm, calmness, placidity, composure, coolness, serenity, equanimity, even-temperedness, unexcitability, unflappability.

tranquillize *verb tranquillize the excited animal/ anxious woman* sedate, calm, calm down, soothe, quiet, quieten down, pacify, compose, settle someone's nerves, lull, relax.

tranquillizer *noun* sedative, opiate; *inf.* downer.

transact *verb transact business in private* carry out, conduct, do, perform, execute, enact, manage, handle, negotiate, take care of, see to, conclude, discharge, accomplish, settle.

transaction *noun* **1** *the transaction took less than an hour* business, deal, undertaking, affair, bargain, negotiation; proceedings. **2** *the transaction of business in private* conducting, performance, execution, enactment, handling, negotiation, conclusion, discharge, settlement. *See* TRANSACT.

transactions *plural noun publish the transactions of the Royal Society* records, proceedings, affairs, concerns, dealings; *inf.* doings, goings-on.

transcend *verb* **1** *transcend human belief* go beyond, exceed, overstep, rise above. **2** *her performance transcended that of her opponents* surpass, excel, be superior to, outdo, outstrip, leave behind, outrival, outvie, outrank, outshine, eclipse, overshadow, throw into the shade.

transcendence, transcendency *noun acknowledge his transcendence* excellence, greatness, magnificence, superiority, supremacy, predominance, pre-eminence, ascendency, paramountcy, incomparability, matchlessness.

transcendent *adjective his transcendent talent* excellent, excelling, great, magnificent, superior, supreme, consummate, predominant, pre-eminent, ascendent, paramount, unsurpassed, incomparable, matchless, unrivalled, unequalled, unparalleled.

transcendental *adjective a transcendental experience* mystical, mystic, mysterious, preternatural, supernatural, otherworldly, transmundane.

transcribe *verb* **1** *students transcribing rough notes* copy out, write out, copy/write in full, type/print out. **2** *transcribe the symbols* interpret, translate, transliterate, render. **3** *tran-*

scribe the performance | *now transcribed to compact disc* record, rerecord, transfer.

transcript *noun a transcript of the trial* written/ recorded copy, copy, record, written/printed version, documentation.

transfer *verb* **1** *transfer the material from the house to the garage* convey, move, shift, remove, take, carry, transport. **2** *transfer the pupils to a different school* move, shift, remove, change, relocate. **3** *transfer his property/share to his son* make over, turn over, sign over, hand on, hand down, pass on, transmit, convey, devolve, assign, delegate.

transfer *noun* **1** *teachers/footballers asking for a transfer* move, shift, relocation, change. **2** *the property transfer has been drawn up* transfer document, conveyance; papers, deeds.

transfix *verb* **1** *a fish transfixed with a harpoon* run through, transpierce, impale, stab, spear, prick, stick, spike, skewer. **2** *the onlookers were transfixed with/in terror* root to the spot, paralyse, petrify, stop dead, hypnotize, mesmerize, rivet, spellbind, fascinate, engross, stun, astound.

transform *verb transform the girl's appearance* | *transform his outlook on life* change, alter, convert, metamorphose, revolutionize, transfigure, remodel, redo, reconstruct, rebuild, reorganize, rearrange, renew, translate, transmute; *inf.* transmogrify.

transformation *noun* change, radical change, alteration, conversion, metamorphosis, sea change, revolutionization, revolution, transfiguration, remodelling, reconstruction, reorganization, renewal, transmutation; *inf.* transmogrification. *See* TRANSFORM.

transgress *verb* **1** *transgress the bounds of decency* | *transgress the laws of the land* go beyond, overstep, exceed, infringe, breach, break, contravene, violate, defy, disobey. **2** *they transgressed and were punished* do wrong, go astray, misbehave, break the law, err, lapse, fall from grace, stray from the straight and narrow, sin, trespass.

transgression *noun* **1** *their transgression of the bounds of taste* | *transgression of the law* overstepping, infringement, breach, breaking, contravention, violation, defiance, disobedience. **2** *punished for their transgressions* wrong, misdemeanour, misdeed, law-breaking, crime, offence, lapse, fault, sin; wrongdoing, misbehaviour.

transgressor *noun transgressors will be punished* wrongdoer, law-breaker, criminal, miscreant, delinquent, villain, felon, offender, culprit, sinner, trespasser, malefactor.

transience *noun* short-livedness, transitoriness, impermanence, temporariness, brevity, briefness, shortness, evanescence, momentariness, fugitiveness, mutability. *See* TRANSIENT.

transient *adjective* transitory, short-lived, short-term, impermanent, temporary, brief, short, ephemeral, evanescent, momentary, fleeting, flying, passing, fugitive, fugacious, mutable, here today and gone tomorrow. *Opposites* PERMANENT; CONSTANT; PERPETUAL.

transit *noun* **1** *troop transit* movement, travel, journeying, passage, transfer, crossing. **2** *city councils budgeting for modern transit* transport, transportation, conveyance, haulage, freightage. **in transit** *goods lost in transit* en route, on the journey, on the way, on the road, during transport.

transition *noun the transition from childhood to adulthood* | *the transition to foreign currency* move, passage, change, transformation, conversion, change-over, metamorphosis, shift, switch, jump, leap, progression, gradation, development, evolution, transmutation.

transitional *adjective* **1** *the transitional period* transition, changing, change-over, conversion, developmental, evolutionary, intermediate, fluid, unsettled. **2** *the transitional government* transition, provisional, temporary.

transitory *adjective* transient, short-lived, short-term, impermanent, temporary, brief, short, ephemeral, evanescent, momentary, fleeting, flying, passing, fugitive, fugacious, mutable, here today and gone tomorrow. *Opposites* PERMANENT; PERPETUAL.

translate *verb* **1** *translate the French passage into English* construe, interpret, render, convert, transcribe, transliterate. **2** *translate the legal jargon into plain English* render, paraphrase, reword, convert, decipher, decode, explain, elucidate. **3** *translate his silence as agreement* interpret, take, construe, understand, read, judge, deem. **4** *translate ideas into action* turn, change, convert, transform, alter, metamorphose, transmute; *inf.* transmogrify. **5** *translate the children from the country to the city* transfer, move, remove, shift, relocate, convey, transport.

translation *noun* **1** *the translation of the French passage into English* interpretation, construing, rendering, rendition, conversion, transcription, transliteration. **2** *unable to follow the rough translation* interpretation, rendition, transcription, transliteration. **3** *the translation of the legal jargon into plain English* rendering, rendition, paraphrasing, rewording, conversion, deciphering, decoding, explanation, elucidation. **4** *the translation of ideas into action* change, conversion, transformation, alteration, metamorphosis, transmutation; *inf.* transmogrification. **5** *the translation of the children from the country to the city* transfer, transferral, move, removal, shift, relocation, conveyance, transportation.

transmission *noun* **1** *the transmission of mail* sending, conveyance, transport, dispatch, remission. **2** *the transmission of information/disease* transference, transferral, passing on, communication, imparting, dissemination, spreading. *See* TRANSMIT 2. **3** *the transmission of late-night programmes* broadcasting, relaying, sending out. **4** *a live transmission* broadcast, programme.

transmit *verb* **1** *transmit the package by air* send, convey, transport, dispatch, forward, remit. **2** *transmit information/disease to others* transfer, pass on, hand on, communicate, impart, disseminate, spread, carry, diffuse.

3 *transmit late-night programmes* broadcast, relay, send out, put on air.

transparency *noun* **1** *the transparency of the plastic/streams* clarity, clearness, translucency, lucidity, pellucidity, limpidness, limpidity, glassiness, transpicuousness. **2** *the transparency of the material* sheerness, diaphanousness, diaphaneity, filminess, gauziness. **3** *the transparency of his lies* obviousness, patentness, unmistakableness, clearness, plainness, distinctness, apparentness, perceptibility, discernibility. *See* TRANSPARENT 3. **4** *appreciate her transparency* frankness, openness, candidness, directness, forthrightness, ingenuousness, artlessness. **5** *the transparency of the prose* clarity, clearness, lucidity, straightforwardness, plainness, explicitness, unambiguousness. **6** *transparencies of their holiday* slide, photograph.

transparent *adjective* **1** *transparent plastic/streams* clear, see-through, translucent, lucid, pellucid, crystal-clear, crystalline, limpid, glassy, transpicuous. **2** *blouses made of transparent material* see-through, sheer, diaphanous, filmy, gauzy. **3** *his transparent dishonesty* obvious, patent, manifest, undisguised, unmistakable, clear, plain, visible, noticeable, recognizable, distinct, evident, apparent, perceptible, discernible. **4** *preferring transparent people to dissembling people* frank, open, candid, direct, forthright, plain-spoken, straight, ingenuous, artless. **5** *a transparent account of the events* clear, lucid, straightforward, plain, explicit, unambiguous, unequivocal. **Opposites** OPAQUE; CLOUDY.

transpire *verb* **1** *it transpired that he had been married before* become known, be revealed, be disclosed, come to light, emerge, come out. **2** *tell me what transpired at the meeting* come about, take place, happen, occur, turn up, arise, chance, befall.

transplant *verb* **1** *transplant seedlings* replant, repot, relocate. **2** *transplant organs* transfer, graft. **3** *he hated being transplanted to a different region* transfer, move, remove, shift, relocate.

transport *verb* **1** *transport the goods to the warehouse* convey, take, transfer, move, shift, bring, fetch, carry, bear, haul, lug, cart, run, ship. **2** *transport criminals to an island* banish, exile, deport, drive away, expatriate. **3** *she was transported by his piano-playing* enrapture, entrance, enchant, enthrall, captivate, bewitch, fascinate, spellbind, charm, overjoy, thrill, delight, ravish, carry away.

transport *noun* **1** *road and rail transport* transportation, conveyance, transit, carriage, freight. **2** *our transport has not yet arrived* transportation, conveyance, vehicle, car, carriage. *See tables at* BICYCLE, CAR, CARRIAGE, TRAIN, VEHICLE. **3** *a transport of joy/rage* strong emotion. *See* TRANSPORTS.

transports *plural noun* **1** strong emotion, intense feeling, passion, fervour, vehemence. **2** *in transports over her engagement/promotion* rapture, ecstasy, elation, exaltation, exhilaration, euphoria, bliss, seventh heaven, heaven, paradise; *inf.* cloud nine.

transpose *verb* *transpose the middle letters of the word* interchange, exchange, switch, swap, transfer, reverse, invert, rearrange, reorder, change, alter, convert, move.

transverse *adjective* *transverse beams* crosswise, crossways, cross, athwart.

trap *noun* **1** *rabbits caught in a trap* snare, net, mesh, gin, springe, ambush, pitfall, booby trap. **2** *the question was a trap to get him to confess* stratagem, play, artifice, ruse, wile, trick, device, deception, subterfuge. **3** *lay a trap for the criminal* ambush, lure, decoy, bait. **4** *regard marriage as a trap* snare, net, cage, prison.

trap *verb* **1** *trap the rabbits* snare, ensnare, enmesh, entrap, catch, corner. **2** *trapped into making a confession* trick, dupe, deceive, lure, inveigle, beguile. **3** *they were trapped in the burning building* cut off, corner, confine, imprison.

trappings *plural noun* *all the trappings necessary for the coronation | the trappings of power* accoutrements, appurtenances, appointments, trimmings, paraphernalia, fittings, things; equipage, equipment, apparatus, gear, livery, adornment, ornamentation, decoration, finery, frippery; panoply.

trash *noun* **1** *talk trash* rubbish, garbage, nonsense, drivel, balderdash, bunkum, twaddle; *inf.* rot, tommy-rot, bunk, tripe, bilge, poppycock. **2** *empty out the trash* rubbish, waste, refuse, litter, garbage. **3** *he regards his neighbours as trash* riff-raff, scum, rabble, *canaille*, vermin; dregs, good-for-nothings.

trauma *noun* **1** *the trauma caused by the accident/surgery* injury, wound, lesion. **2** *suffering from trauma after the attack | the trauma of divorce* shock, disturbance, disorder, distress, pain, anguish, suffering.

traumatic *adjective* **1** *a traumatic injury/attack* painful, agonizing, shocking, scarring, disturbing, distressing, damaging, injurious, harmful. **2** *a traumatic journey home* unpleasant, disagreeable, irksome, troublesome, vexatious, irritating, distressing.

travel *verb* **1** *he travels a lot in connection with his work | she plans to travel after she retires* use transport, journey, take a trip, tour, voyage, sightsee. **2** *light travels faster than sound | news travels fast* proceed, progress, advance, be transmitted, carry. **3** *travel the length of the country* journey, cross, traverse, cover, wander, ramble, roam, rove, range, wend, make one's way over. **4** *the driver/car was certainly travelling* speed, go fast/rapidly, drive fast, go at breakneck speed; *inf.* go hell for leather, go like a bat out of hell, tear up the miles. **5** *he travels in perfume* sell, be a representative/agent for; *inf.* rep for.

travel *noun* *the cost of travel* travelling, journeying, touring.

traveller *noun* **1** *holiday/foreign travellers* tripper, journeyer, tourer, tourist, excursionist, explorer, passenger, voyager, holiday-maker, sightseer, globe-trotter. **2** *have a job as a traveller* sales representative, agent, travelling salesman, commercial traveller; *inf.* rep, sales rep. **3** *travellers moving from camp to camp* gypsy, nomad, migrant, wanderer, wayfarer, tramp, vagrant; travelling people/folk.

travelling adjective **1** *a travelling circus* itinerant, peripatetic, moving, mobile. **2** *a travelling people/tribe* itinerant, peripatetic, nomadic, migratory, migrating, wandering, roaming, roving, wayfaring, unsettled, restless, on the move/go.

travels plural noun *she wrote about her travels* journey, journeying, trip, tour, expedition, excursion, voyage, sightseeing, exploration, wandering, roaming, ramble, rambling, peregrination, *inf.* globe-trotting.

traverse verb **1** *traversing the desert* cross, go across, travel over, journey over, make one's way across, pass over, wander, roam, range. **2** *beams traversing the ceiling* go across, lie across, stretch across, extend across, cross, cut across, bridge. **3** *traverse all aspects of the subject* consider, examine, check, study, review, investigate, inspect, scrutinize, look into, look over, scan, pore over, take stock of.

travesty noun *the trial was a travesty of justice* misrepresentation, distortion, perversion, corruption, poor imitation, mockery, parody, caricature, sham, burlesque, satire, lampoon, take-off; *inf.* send-up, spoof.

travesty verb *travesty the solemn occasion* misrepresent, distort, pervert, mock, ridicule, deride, make fun of, parody, caricature, burlesque, satirize, lampoon, take off; *inf.* send up, spoof.

treacherous adjective **1** *betrayed by a treacherous follower* traitorous, back-stabbing, double-crossing, double-dealing, disloyal, faithless, unfaithful, perfidious, duplicitous, deceitful, false-hearted, false, untrue, untrustworthy, unreliable, undependable; *inf.* two-timing. **2** *the weather conditions can be treacherous* precarious, unreliable, undependable, unstable, unsafe, risky, hazardous, dangerous, perilous, deceptive; *inf.* dicey. **3** *roads which are treacherous in winter* hazardous, dangerous, unsafe; flooded, icy, ice-covered, slippery.
Opposites LOYAL; FAITHFUL; RELIABLE.

treachery noun *the treachery of his best friend* traitorousness, back-stabbing, double-crossing, double-dealing, disloyalty, faithlessness, unfaithfulness, perfidy, perfidiousness, treason, duplicity, deceit, deceitfulness, deception, false-heartedness, falseness, untrustworthiness; *inf.* two-timing.

tread verb **1** *tread softly so as not to wake the baby* walk, step, go, pace, march, tramp. **2** *tread the long road home* walk, hike, tramp, stride, step out, trek, march, trudge, plod. **3** *tread grapes | tread the corn down* trample, tramp on, step on, stamp on, squash, crush, flatten, press down. **4** *tread mud into the carpet* trample, tramp, stamp, press. **5** *aristocrats tread on the villagers* ride roughshod over, oppress, repress, suppress, subdue, subjugate, quell, crush.

tread noun *walk with a heavy/soft tread | hear the tread of the people upstairs* step, footstep, footfall, walk, tramp.

treason noun *high treason;* betrayal, traitorousness, treachery, disloyalty, faithlessness, perfidy, disaffection, sedition, subversion, mutiny, rebellion, lese-majesty.

treasonable adjective traitorous, treacherous, disloyal, faithless, perfidious, seditious, subversive, mutinous, rebellious.

treasure noun **1** *find buried treasure | a miser gloating over his treasure* riches, valuables; wealth, fortune, hoard; jewels, gems, coins, gold, money, cash. **2** *art treasures* valuable, masterpiece. **3** *she's her father's treasure* darling, pride and joy, apple of one's eye, jewel, jewel in the crown, gem, pearl, precious, prize, paragon. **4** *advertising for a treasure* paragon, household/domestic help, housekeeper.

treasure verb **1** *she treasures their friendship* value, place great value on, prize, set great store by, think highly of, hold dear. **2** *he treasures his children* adore, cherish, love, worship, revere, venerate, dote on, prize, hold dear. **3** *treasure the souvenirs of holidays* value, prize, save, collect, accumulate, hoard, store up, lay

TREATIES			
Treaty	**Date**	**Treaty**	**Date**
Aix-la-Chapelle, Treaty of	1748	Nuclear Non-proliferation	
Anglo-Egyptian Treaty	1936	Treaty	1968
Anglo-Irish Treaty	1921	Outer Space Treaty	1967
Antarctic Treaty	1959	Paris, Treaties of	1763, 1783, 1856,
Breda, Treaty of	1667		1898, 1919–20
Brest-Litovsk, Treaties of	1918	Peace of Cateau Cambrésis	1559
Brétigny, Treaty of	1360	Peace of Westphalia	1648
Camp David Agreement	1978	Pressburg Treaties	1491, 1805
Geneva Convention	1864, 1906,	Pretoria Convention	1881
	1929, 1949	Rome, Treaty of	1957
Guadelupe Hidalgo,		Strategic Arms Limitation	
Treaty of	1848	Treaty	1972
Hague Agreement	1949	Strategic Arms Reduction	
Intermediate-range Nuclear		Treaty	1991
Forces Treaty	1987	Test-Ban Treaty	1963
Lateran Treaty	1929	Utrecht, Treaties of	1713–4
Maastricht Treaty	1993	Versailles, Treaty of	1783, 1919
North American Free Trade		Waitangi, Treaty of	1840
Agreement	1994	Westphalia, Treaty of	1840

by, stow away, squirrel away, salt away; *inf.* stash away.

treat *noun* **1** *think of a treat for her birthday* surprise, celebration, entertainment, amusement, diversion, party, feast, banquet. **2** *grandmother bringing a treat for the child* gift, present, titbit, delicacy; *inf.* goodie. **3** *it was a treat to see her again* pleasure, delight, thrill, joy, gratification, satisfaction; fun. **4** *the drinks are his treat* gift, present, one's turn to pay; *inf.* shout.

treat *verb* **1** *treat his wife badly | treat his car recklessly* act towards, behave towards, deal with, handle, cope with, contend with, manage, use. **2** *treat his remarks as jokes* regard, consider, view, look upon, deal with. **3** *treat the sick patient* give treatment to, medicate, doctor, nurse, care for, attend to, minister to, cure, heal. **4** *treat the wood with creosote | treat the stain with chemicals* apply to, put on, use on, ply with. **5** *treat them to dinner* pay for, buy for, pay/foot the bill for, stand, finance, entertain, take out. **6** *we were treated to the unusual sight of him letting his hair down* entertain, amuse, divert, cheer, gratify, delight, regale. **7** *the general treating with the enemy* have talks with, talk with, confer with, negotiate with, parley with, bargain with, make terms with, come to terms with. **8** *she treats the question of incest in her books | her essay treats of religious doubt* deal with, discuss, go into, write/speak/talk about, discourse upon, be concerned with, touch upon, refer to, consider, study, review, analyse.

treatise *noun* discourse, exposition, disquisition, dissertation, thesis, study, essay, paper, monograph, tract, pamphlet, work, piece of writing.

treatment *noun* **1** *his treatment was cruel* action, behaviour, conduct, handling, management, use; dealings. **2** *patients/wounds responding to treatment* medical care, medication, medicament, therapy, doctoring, nursing, first aid, care, ministration; cure, remedy; drugs, therapeutics.

treaty *noun* agreement, pact, deal, compact, covenant, bargain, pledge, contract, alliance, concordat, convention, entente. *See table.*

tree *noun. See table.*

trek *verb* *trek across the rough terrain* trudge, tramp, hike, march, slog, footslog, plod, walk, ramble, roam, range, rove, travel, journey; *inf.* traipse, yomp.

trek *noun* *a trek across the desert | it's quite a trek to the village* expedition, trip, journey, trudge, tramp, hike, march, slog, walk, odyssey.

TREES AND SHRUBS

acacia	cornel	juniper	mulberry	sandarac	tamarisk
alder	cypress	kaffirboom	myrtle	sandbox	tawa
almond	deodar	kahikatea	ngaio	tree	teak
apple	dhak	kalmia	nipa	sapele	tea-tree
araucaria	divi-divi	kamala	nux vomica	sappan-	terebinth
arbutus	dogwood	karri	oak	wood	thorn tree
ash	dragon tree	kauri	ocotillo	saskatoon	thuja
aspen	eaglewood	kawakawa	osier	sassafras	toothache
assegai	ebony	kiaat	pagoda tree	savin	tree
balsa	elder	kingwood	palm	sequoia	totara
banksia	elm	koa	palmyra	seringa	tuart
banyan	eucalyptus	kowhai	paulownia	service tree	tupelo
baobab	fever tree	kurrajong	peepul	shagbark	turpentine
bay tree	fir	lacquer tree	pepper tree	shea	tree
bebeeru	flame tree	lantana	pine	silk-cotton	umbrella
beech	fringe tree	larch	plane	tree	tree
belah	Gaboon	laurel	pohutu-	simarouba	varnish
birch	gidgee	lemonwood	kawa	sneezewood	tree
blackthorn	ginkgo	lilly-pilly	poplar	snowball	walnut
bo tree	gomuti	lime	privet	tree	wandoo
bottle-brush	guaiacum	linden	puriri	soapbark	wattle
bottle tree	guayule	logwood	pyinkado	sorb	wayfaring
box	gum tree	macrocarpa	quassia	sorrel tree	tree
buckthorn	hawthorn	madroño	quebracho	sourwood	welling-
cacao	hazel	mahogany	rain tree	spindle	tonia
calabash	hickory	maidenhair	redbud	spruce	whitebeam
camphor	holly	tree	redwood	stinkwood	wilga
tree	hornbeam	mako	rewarewa	strawberry	willow
cassia	iroko	mangrove	rhododen-	tree	wine palm
cedar	ironwood	manna-ash	dron	styrax	witch
champac	ivorywood	maple	ribbonwood	sumach/	hazel
chestnut	jacaranda	matai	robinia	sumac	yarran
coco-de-mer	jarrah	maté	rosewood	sycamore	yaupon
coffee tree	jelutong	may	rowan	tallow tree	yew
coolabah	jojoba	mesquite	rubber	tallow wood	ylang-ylang
coral tree	Joshua tree	monkey	plant	tamarack	yucca
corkwood	Judas tree	puzzle	sandalwood	tamarind	zebrawood

trellis noun lattice, network, mesh, fret, grille, grid, grating.

tremble verb **1** *fingers trembling with excitement* shake, quiver, shiver, quake, twitch, wiggle. **2** *buildings trembling in the earthquake* shake, shudder, judder, teeter, totter, wobble, rock, vibrate, oscillate, rattle. **3** *she trembles for the safety of her children* fear, be afraid, be fearful, be frightened, be apprehensive, worry, be anxious.

tremendous adjective **1** *animals of a tremendous size* | *people of tremendous girth* great, huge, enormous, immense, massive, vast, colossal, prodigious, stupendous, gigantic, gargantuan, mammoth, giant, titanic; *inf.* whopping. **2** *it made a tremendous difference to his lifestyle* great, huge, enormous, immense, colossal, prodigious, stupendous; *inf.* whopping. **3** *there was a tremendous noise* loud, deafening, ear-splitting, booming, thundering, roaring, resounding, crashing. **4** *she's a tremendous player/cook* excellent, very good, great, marvellous, remarkable, extraordinary, exceptional, wonderful, incredible; *inf.* fabulous, fantastic, terrific, super, ace, wizard.
Opposites TINY; SMALL; SLIGHT; POOR.

tremor noun **1** *notice the tremor of her hands* | *a tremor of fear* tremble, trembling, shake, shaking, shiver, quiver, quaver, vibration, twitch, judder, spasm, paroxysm. **2** *villages damaged by a tremor* earth tremor, earthquake; *inf.* quake. *See table at* EARTHQUAKE.

tremulous adjective **1** *a tremulous voice* trembling, shaking, shaky, quivering, quavering, vibrating, nervous, weak. **2** *with tremulous hands* trembling, shaking, shaky, quivery, twitching, twitchy, jittery, shuddering, juddering, jerky, spasmodic. **3** *give a tremulous look* timid, diffident, shy, timorous, fearful, frightened, scared, nervous, anxious, apprehensive, alarmed, cowardly.

trench noun ditch, excavation, earthwork, furrow, duct, trough, channel, conduit, cut, drain, waterway, moat, fosse. *See table.*

DEEPEST OCEAN TRENCHES

Trench	Ocean
Bonin	Pacific
Izu	Pacific
Java	Indian
Kermadec	Pacific
Kuril	Pacific
Mariana	Pacific
New Britain	Pacific
Philippine	Pacific
Puerto Rico	Atlantic
South Sandwich	Atlantic
Tonga	Pacific

trenchant adjective **1** *a trenchant wit/criticism* incisive, cutting, pointed, sharp, biting, pungent, caustic, piercing, penetrating, razor, razor-edged, mordant, scathing, acrid, acid, tart, acidulous, acerbic, astringent, sarcastic. **2** *trenchant divisions between the political parties* clear, clear-cut, distinct, defined, well-defined, sharp, crisp, unequivocal, unambiguous.
Opposites DULL; KIND; ILL-DEFINED; FUZZY.

trend noun **1** *an upward trend in prices* | *votes showing a trend towards the right* tendency, drift, course, direction, bearing, current, inclination, bias, leaning, bent, swing. **2** *teenagers like to follow the trend* fashion, vogue, style, mode, look, craze; *inf.* fad.

trend verb *prices trending upwards* | *political opinions trending to the left* move, go, tend, head, drift, turn, incline, lean, shift, veer, swing.

trepidation noun fear, fearfulness, alarm, fright, apprehensiveness, apprehension, terror, panic, anxiety, worry, uneasiness, disquiet, unrest, agitation, trembling, nervousness, jumpiness, perturbation, discomposure, dismay, consternation; *inf.* butterflies, cold feet, jitters, cold sweat, blue funk, heebie-jeebies, willies.
Opposites CALM; EQUANIMITY; COMPOSURE.

trespass verb **1** *trespass on his land/privacy* intrude on, encroach on, infringe on, poach on, invade, obtrude on. **2** *trespass on their hospitality* take advantage of, impose upon, exploit, abuse, make use of. **3** *punished for having trespassed* do wrong, err, go astray, fall from grace, stray from the straight and narrow, sin, transgress. **4** *punished for trespassing against his neighbours* do wrong to, wrong.

trespass noun **1** *the laws of trespass* | *found guilty of trespass* unlawful entry, intrusion, encroachment, infringement, invasion, obtrusion. **2** *forgive their trespasses* wrongdoing, wrong, misdemeanour, misdeed, crime, offence, transgression, sin, malefaction.

trespasser noun **1** *trespassers will be prosecuted* intruder, interloper, unwelcome visitor, encroacher, infringer, invader, obtruder. **2** *trespassers asking for forgiveness* wrongdoer, evildoer, criminal, offender, transgressor, sinner, malefactor.

tresses plural noun hair; locks, curls, ringlets, braids, plaits.

trial noun **1** *the murder trial lasted several days* court case, case, hearing, inquiry, tribunal, litigation, judicial examination, legal investigation. **2** *give the applicant a trial* trial period, probation, test, test/testing period, audition. **3** *put a car through safety trials* test, testing, tryout, trial/test run, check, assay, experiment; *inf.* dry run. **4** *climb the mountain at the third trial* try, attempt, endeavour, effort, venture; *inf.* go, shot, stab, crack. **5** *she's a trial to her mother* nuisance, pest, bother, worry, vexation, annoyance, irritant, irritation, bane, affliction, curse, burden, cross to bear, thorn in one's flesh; *inf.* pain in the neck, hassle, plague. **6** *the trials of life* trouble, worry, anxiety, vexation, load, burden, cross to bear, blow, affliction, tribulation, adversity, hardship, ordeal, pain; suffering, distress, misery, wretchedness, unhappiness, sadness, woe, grief. **7** *football trials* selection contest, preliminary match, audition. **8** *motorbike/sheepdog trials* contest, competition.

trial *adjective trial period* testing, experimental, pilot, probationary, provisional.

triangle *noun. See table.*

TYPES OF TRIANGLE	
acute-angled	obtuse-angled
circular	right
congruent triangles	right-angled
	scalene
equilateral	similar triangles
isosceles	spherical

tribe *noun* **1** *the tribes of Israel* ethnic group, family, dynasty, clan, sept. *See table.* **2** *meet a tribe of doctors at the conference* group, crowd, company, party, band, number, gang, assembly, collection; *inf.* bunch.

THE TWELVE TRIBES OF ISRAEL		
Asher	Issachar	Naphtali
Benjamin	Judah	Reuben
Dan	Levi	Simeon
Gad	Manasseh	Zebulun

tribulation *noun* trouble, worry, anxiety, vexation, load, burden, cross to bear, blow, affliction, trial, adversity, hardship, ordeal, pain; suffering, distress, misery, wretchedness, unhappiness, sadness, woe, grief.

tribunal *noun* **1** *members of a rent tribunal* court, forum, arbitration board. **2** *hold a tribunal* hearing, court case, judicial examination.

tributary *noun tributaries of the Thames* branch, feeder, confluent.

tribute *noun* **1** *give tributes to the heroes* gift, present, accolade, commendation, testimonial, paean, eulogy, panegyric, encomium; gratitude, applause, praise, homage, honour, exaltation, laudation, extolment, glorification; congratulations, compliments; *inf.* bouquets. **2** *the success is a tribute to their hard work* acknowledgement, recognition, testimonial, indication, manifestation; evidence, proof. **3** *kings paying tributes to the emperor* homage; payment, contribution, offering, gift, donation, charge, tax, duty, levy, tariff, ransom. **Opposites** BLAME; CRITICISM; REPROACH; condemnation.

trick *noun* **1** *he got the job by a trick* stratagem, ploy, artifice, ruse, dodge, wile, device, manoeuvre, trick of the trade, deceit, deception, subterfuge, swindle, fraud; *inf.* con. **2** *a trick of the light* illusion, mirage. **3** *he has the trick of making guests feel welcome* knack, art, gift, talent, technique, ability, skill, expertise; *inf.* know-how. **4** *play tricks on the old man | tired of the children's tricks* hoax, practical joke, joke, prank, jape, antic, caper, frolic, lark, gambol; *inf.* leg-pull, gag, put-on. **5** *artists demonstrating their tricks* sleight of hand, legerdemain; juggling, prestidigitation. **6** *he has an annoying trick of repeating himself* idiosyncrasy, habit, mannerism, quirk, peculiarity, foible, eccentricity, characteristic, trait, practice.

trick *verb he wasn't a policeman—you've been tricked* deceive, delude, mislead, take in, cheat, hoodwink, fool, outwit, dupe, hoax, gull, cozen, defraud, swindle; *inf.* con, pull a fast one on, put one over on; *Am. inf.* shaft. **trick out** *they were tricked out in their finery* dress up, deck out, array, attire, adorn, decorate, embellish, ornament.

trickery *noun use trickery to get the job* guile, artifice, wiliness, deceit, deception, cheating, subterfuge, craft, craftiness, chicanery, pretence, dishonesty, fraud, swindling, imposture, double-dealing, duplicity; *inf.* conning, monkey/funny business, hanky-panky, jiggery-pokery. **Opposites** HONESTY; CANDOUR.

trickle *verb* **1** *water trickled from the tap | blood trickled from the wound* drip, dribble, leak, ooze, seep, exude, percolate. **2** *information trickled out | people trickled into the meeting* come/go/pass gradually. **Opposites** POUR; GUSH.

trickster *noun* cheat, swindler, fraud, fraudster, defrauder, confidence man, deceiver, deluder, dissembler, hoodwinker, hoaxer, phoney, charlatan, rogue, scoundrel; *inf.* con man.

tricky *adjective* **1** *a tricky situation* difficult, problematic, awkward, delicate, sensitive, ticklish, thorny, knotty, touchy, risky, uncertain, precarious; *inf.* sticky. **2** *he's a tricky character* cunning, crafty, wily, artful, devious, scheming, foxy, sly, slippery, subtle, deceitful, deceptive. **Opposites** STRAIGHTFORWARD; HONEST.

tried *adjective tried remedies | friends who are tried and true* tried out, tested, put to the test, proved, proven, established, sure, certain, true, dependable, reliable, trustworthy, reputable.

trifle *noun* **1** *her mind is occupied with trifles* trivia, inessentials; triviality, unimportant thing, thing of no consequence, bagatelle, nothing. **2** *buy a few trifles for Christmas* bauble, trinket, knick-knack, gimcrack, gewgaw, toy, doodah, whatnot. **3** *I paid a mere trifle for it* next to nothing, hardly anything, pittance; *inf.* piddling amount, row of beans. **4** *he's a trifle confused* bit, small amount, touch.

trifle *verb* **1** *stop trifling and do some work* idle, do nothing, potter about, fiddle about, fool about, mess around, hang around, loiter, waste time, fritter away one's time. **2** *he's just trifling with the young woman | trifle with her affections* amuse oneself with, toy with, play around with, flirt with, dally with, sport with. **3** *he's not a man to be trifled with* treat lightly, deal with casually, treat in a cavalier fashion, dismiss.

trifling *adjective* **1** *discuss trifling matters* petty, trivial, unimportant, insignificant, inconsequential, shallow, superficial, frivolous, silly, idle, foolish, empty. **2** *cost a trifling amount* trivial, small, tiny, miniscule, infinitesimal, negligible, insignificant, paltry, nominal, worthless, valueless; *inf.* piddling. **Opposites** IMPORTANT; WEIGHTY; CONSIDERABLE.

trigger *verb it triggered the riot | her behaviour triggered off his fit of rage* set off, set in motion, spark off, activate, give rise to, generate, start, cause, bring about, prompt, provoke.

trim *adjective* **1** *looking trim in her uniform* neat, tidy, neat and tidy, smart, spruce, well-groomed, well-dressed, well-turned-out, dapper, elegant, soigné/soignée; *inf.* natty. **2** *trim gardens* neat, tidy, orderly, in good order/condition, well-maintained, shipshape, well-looked-after, well-cared-for, spick and span. **3** *have a trim figure | keep trim* slim, slender, lean, svelte, streamlined, willowy, lissom, sleek, shapely, in good shape, fit, physically fit. **Opposites** UNTIDY; MESSY; FAT.

trim *verb* **1** *trim one's hair/beard* cut, clip, snip, shear, prune, pare, even up, neaten, tidy up. **2** *trim the fat from the meat | trim the branches from the tree* cut, chop, hack, remove, take off. **3** *trim the annual budget* cut down, decrease, reduce, diminish, cut back on, curtail, dock, retrench. **4** *trim the Christmas tree | trim her evening dress* decorate, adorn, ornament, embellish, trick out, festoon. **5** *trim the dress with lace* decorate, adorn, ornament, embellish, edge, pipe, border, fringe, embroider, bespangle. **6** *the father trimmed his son* scold, chide, rebuke, reprimand, reproach, reprove, admonish; *inf.* give a dressing-down to, tell off. **7** *schoolmasters were not allowed to trim pupils* beat, thrash, leather, cane, whip, flog, spank; *inf.* tan someone's hide, thump, lambaste. **8** *they trimmed them at football* trounce, rout, give a drubbing to, worst, vanquish, conquer, defeat thoroughly, beat soundly.

trim *noun* **1** *admire the trim on the dress* trimming, decoration, adornment, ornamentation, embellishment, edging, piping, border, fringe, frill, embroidery. **2** *have a trim at the hairdressers* haircut, cut, clip, snip, shearing, pruning, paring, tidy-up. **3** *the old man's still in trim* good health, good condition, in good shape/ form, fine fettle, shape.

trimming *noun admire the trimming on the dress* trim, decoration, adornment, ornamentation, edging, piping, fringe, fringing, frill, embroidery. *See* TRIM *noun* 1.

trimmings *plural noun* **1** *turkey with all the trimmings* accompaniments, frills, extras, accessories, accoutrements, trappings, paraphernalia; garnishing, garnish. **2** *hedge/pastry trimmings* cuttings, clippings, parings, shavings.

trinket *noun buy a trinket as a souvenir* bauble, ornament, knick-knack, trifle, gimcrack, gew-gaw, piece of bric-à-brac, bibelot, doodah, whatnot.

trio *noun* threesome, triumvirate, triad, trine, trinity, triunity, triple, trilogy, triptych; triplets.

trip *noun* **1** *go on a trip to China/town* excursion, tour, expedition, voyage, jaunt, outing, run. **2** *just one trip crippled her for life* stumble, misstep, false step, slip, slide, fall, tumble, spill. **3** *one more trip and you're sacked* mistake, error, blunder, slip, lapse, *faux pas*, indiscretion, oversight, bungle, botch; *inf.* slip-up, booboo, boob.

4 *have a bad trip* hallucination, drug experience, vision.

trip *verb* **1** *she tripped on the broken pavement* stumble, lose one's footing/balance, stagger, totter, slip, slide, misstep, fall, tumble. **2** *she tripped up when she tried to alter the accounts* make a mistake, blunder, go wrong, err, lapse, bungle, botch; *inf.* slip up, boob. **3** *the defending lawyer tripped the witness up* catch out, trap, outwit, outsmart, put off one's stride, confuse, disconcert, unsettle, discountenance; *inf.* throw, wrong-foot. **4** *she tripped upstairs* skip, dance, hop, prance, bound, spring, gambol, caper, frisk, cavort, waltz. **5** *he trips at least once a week* hallucinate; *inf.* get stoned/high.

tripe *noun he's talking tripe* nonsense, rubbish, drivel, twaddle, bunkum, balderdash; *inf.* rot, tommy-rot, poppycock, claptrap, bunk, garbage, trash, hogwash, guff.

triple *adjective* **1** *a triple alliance* three-way, threefold, tripartite. **2** *a triple whisky | at triple the recommended speed* three times, three times as much as, threefold, treble.

triple *noun* trio, threesome, triumvirate, triad, trine, trinity, triunity.

tripper *noun* tourist, holiday-maker, sightseer, excursionist, traveller, journeyer, voyager.

trite *adjective* hackneyed, banal, commonplace, ordinary, common, platitudinous, clichéd, stock, stereotyped, overused, overdone, stale, worn-out, threadbare, unimaginative, unoriginal, uninspired, dull, pedestrian, run-of-the-mill, routine, humdrum. **Opposites** ORIGINAL; FRESH; IMAGINATIVE.

triumph *noun* **1** *his triumph over his opponent* conquest, victory, win, ascendancy, mastery, success; *inf.* walk-over. **2** *it was a triumph of engineering* coup, tour de force, feat, masterstroke, achievement, attainment, accomplishment, supreme example, sensation; *inf.* hit. **3** *expressions of triumph on their faces* exultation, jubilation, jubilance, elation, rejoicing, joy, joyfulness, pride. **Opposites** DEFEAT; FAILURE; DISASTER.

triumph *verb* **1** *the better team triumphed* win, succeed, come first, be the victor, be victorious, gain a victory, carry the day, take the honours/prize/crown. **2** *triumph over his opponent/ disability* beat, defeat, conquer, vanquish, best, worst, overcome, overpower, get the better of, gain ascendancy over, gain mastery of, prevail against. **3** *the defeated team watching the winners triumph* exult, rejoice, jubilate, celebrate, revel, glory, gloat, swagger, brag, boast.

triumphant *adjective* **1** *the triumphant team took a bow* winning, victorious, successful, undefeated, unbeaten, prize-winning, trophy-winning. **2** *wearing triumphant expressions | giving triumphant shouts* exultant, jubilant, elated, rejoicing, joyful, joyous, proud, cock-a-hoop, gloating, boastful. **Opposites** UNSUCCESSFUL; defeated; DEPRESSED.

trivia *plural noun ignore the trivia and address the main issue* petty details, details, minutiae, trivialities, trifles, technicalities.

trivial *adjective* **1** *raise trivial objections* unimportant, insignificant, inconsequential, flimsy,

insubstantial, petty, minor, of no account/matter, negligible, paltry, trifling, foolish, worthless; *inf.* piddling. **2** *he's a trivial young man* frivolous, small-minded, feather-brained, giddy, silly.
Opposites IMPORTANT; SIGNIFICANT; PROFOUND.

triviality noun **1** *the triviality of the objections* unimportance, insignificance, inconsequence, flimsiness, insubstantiality, pettiness, paltriness, foolishness, worthlessness. **2** *the triviality of the young man* frivolousness, small-mindedness, feather-brainedness, giddiness, silliness. **3** *do not wish to discuss trivialities* petty/mere detail, thing of no importance, trifle, technicality.

troop noun *a troop of people surged forward* band, group, company, assemblage, gathering, body, crowd, throng, multitude, horde, host, mob, squad, pack, drove, flock, swarm, stream; *inf.* gang, crew.

troop verb *the audience trooped out* flock, stream, swarm, surge, crowd, throng, mill.

troops plural noun *call in the troops* armed forces, army, military, services, soldiers, soldiery, fighting men/women.

trophy noun **1** *win the sports trophy* cup, prize, award; laurels. **2** *trophies of his time as a hunter* spoil, booty, souvenir, memento, keepsake, relic.

tropical adjective *tropical weather* hot, torrid, sweltering, boiling, sultry, steamy, humid, sticky.
Opposites COLD; ARCTIC.

trouble noun **1** *his car is causing him trouble | having trouble with the computer* worry, bother, anxiety, disquiet, unease, irritation, vexation, inconvenience, annoyance, agitation, harassment, difficulty, distress; problems. **2** *there has been a lot of trouble in her life* difficulty, misfortune, adversity, hardship, bad luck, ill luck, burden, distress, pain, suffering, affliction, torment, woe, grief, unhappiness, sadness, heartache; problems. **3** *please don't go to any trouble | our hostess went to a lot of trouble* bother, inconvenience, disturbance, fuss, effort, exertion, work, labour, attention, care, thoughtfulness; *inf.* hassle. **4** *the girl was no trouble | it was no trouble to collect the mail* nuisance, bother, inconvenience, problem, pest; *inf.* headache, pain in the neck, pain. **5** *the trouble with her is she's too old-fashioned | his trouble is he's too nice* problem, difficulty, failing, weakness, shortcoming, fault, imperfection, defect, blemish. **6** *he has stomach trouble* disorder, disease, illness, dysfunction. **7** *the barman doesn't want any trouble* disturbance, disorder, unrest, fighting, rowing, strife, conflict, tumult, commotion, turbulence, law-breaking. **in trouble 1** *he's in trouble financially | in trouble with the police* in difficulty, having problems, in dire straits, in a predicament; *inf.* in a tight corner, in hot water, in a jam/pickle, in a mess/spot. **2** *the girl's in trouble* pregnant while unmarried, having a baby; *inf.* expecting.
Opposites LUCK; PLEASURE; PEACE.

trouble verb **1** *he's troubled by neighbours/ finances* worry, bother, disturb, annoy, irritate, vex, irk, fret, pester, torment, plague, inconvenience, upset, perturb, agitate, discompose, harass, distress; *inf.* hassle. **2** *don't trouble to see me out* take the trouble/time (to), bother, make the effort (to), exert/disturb oneself, go out of one's way. **3** *he is troubled by back pain* afflict, oppress, weigh down, burden, incapacitate. **4** *I'm sorry to trouble you but may I use your phone* bother, disturb, inconvenience, put out, impose upon, discommode, incommode.

troublemaker noun mischief-maker, inciter, agitator, instigator, *agent provocateur*, rabble-rouser, demagogue, storm petrel.

troublesome adjective *troublesome neighbours/ problems* worrying, worrisome, bothersome, tiresome, disturbing, annoying, irritating, irksome, upsetting, perturbing, harassing, distressing, difficult, problematic, demanding, taxing.
Opposites EASY; PLEASANT.

trough noun **1** *animals feeding from a trough* feeding box, feedbox, manger, rack, crib. **2** *troughs to drain away water* channel, conduit, duct, flume, gutter, drain, culvert, trench, ditch, furrow, groove, depression.

trounce verb **1** *they trounced the other team* defeat utterly, beat soundly, rout, drub, thrash, crush, overwhelm; *inf.* make mincemeat of, walk all over, wipe the floor with, hammer, clobber, slaughter, give a pasting to. **2** *the father trounced his son for breaking the window* thrash, beat, whip, flog, lash, birch, cane, leather, spank, chastise; *inf.* belt, wallop, lambaste, give a hiding to, tan the hide of.

troupe noun *a troupe of artistes* company, band, cast.

trousers plural noun slacks, legwear; *Am.* pants. *See table.*

TROUSERS

bell-bottoms	knickerbockers
Bermuda shorts	knickers *Am.*
bloomers	lederhosen
breeches	overalls
buckskins *Am.*	Oxford bags
Capri pants	palazzo pants
chaps	pantaloons
cords	pedal pushers
culottes	pegged pants
cycling shorts	*Am.*
denims	plus fours
dhoti	riding breeches
dungarees	riding pants *Am.*
flannels	shalwar
galligaskins	short pants *Am.*
gym pants *Am.*	shorts
hip-huggers *Am.*	short trousers
hipsters	ski pants
hot pants	slacks
jeans	toreador pants
jodhpurs	Turkish trousers

truancy noun absenteeism, absence, French leave, shirking, malingering; *inf.* skiving, bunking-off.

truant *noun* absentee, dodger, malingerer, shirker, deserter.

truant *verb* play truant, dodge, malinger, shirk; *inf.* skive, play hooky, bunk off, be AWOL.

truce *noun* cease-fire, armistice, suspension/cessation of hostilities, peace, respite, moratorium, lull; *inf.* let-up.

truck[1] *noun* *trucks racing down the motorway* lorry, articulated lorry, heavy goods vehicle, van; *inf.* HGV.

truck[2] *noun* *refuse to have any truck with them* association, contact, communication, connection, business, trade; dealings, relations.

truculent *adjective* aggressive, antagonistic, belligerent, pugnacious, bellicose, combative, contentious, hostile, obstreperous, violent, fierce, defiant, sullen, surly, cross, bad-tempered, ill-natured.
Opposites FRIENDLY; AMIABLE; PLACID.

trudge *verb* *trudge through the deep snow* plod, lumber, shuffle, drag one's feet, clump, slog, footslog, trek, tramp, hike; *inf.* yomp.

true *adjective* **1** *what you say is true | it's true that he's dead | a true account* truthful, accurate, correct, right, valid, factual, exact, precise, faithful, genuine, reliable, veracious, honest. **2** *a true witchdoctor* real, genuine, authentic, actual, *bona fide*, valid, legitimate; *inf.* honest-to-goodness. **3** *a true friend* loyal, faithful, trustworthy, trusty, reliable, dependable, staunch, firm, fast, steady, constant, unswerving, unwavering, devoted, sincere, dedicated, supportive, dutiful. **4** *give a true picture of Victorian times* exact, precise, perfect, faithful, close, accurate, correct, unerring; *inf.* spot-on.
Opposites UNTRUE; FALSE; DISLOYAL; INACCURATE.

true *adverb* **1** *tell me true* truly, truthfully, honestly, sincerely, candidly, veraciously. **2** *the arrow flew true* accurately, unerringly, unswervingly, without deviating, on target; *inf.* spot on.

truly *adverb* **1** *she is truly his daughter* in truth, really, in reality, actually, in fact, genuinely, certainly, surely, definitely, decidedly, positively, absolutely, unquestionably, undoubtedly, beyond doubt/question, indubitably, beyond the shadow of a doubt. **2** *tell me truly what you think* truthfully, honestly, frankly, candidly, openly; *inf.* with no punches pulled. **3** *truly, I did not know* honestly, truthfully, genuinely, really, indeed, veritably. **4** *they are truly grateful* really, genuinely, sincerely, very, extremely, exceptionally. **5** *the old man served his master truly* loyally, faithfully, reliably, staunchly, firmly, steadily, constantly, unswervingly, devotedly, with all one's heart, sincerely, dedicatedly, dutifully. **6** *the novel does not truly depict the era* exactly, precisely, faithfully, closely, accurately, correctly, unerringly.

trump *verb* *she trumped her sister's record/rival* surpass, outperform, outdo. **trump up** *trump up an excuse for not going* invent, make up, fabricate, devise, concoct, hatch, contrive, fake; *inf.* cook up.

trumpery *noun* *wanton women in their trumpery* cheap finery, flashy ornamentation; baubles, trinkets, gewgaws.

trumpery *adjective* *trumpery decorations/furnishings* worthless, valueless, showy, flashy, tawdry, shoddy, meretricious, Brummagem; *inf.* flash.

trumpet *verb* **1** *trumpet in rage* bellow, roar, bay, shout, yell, cry out, call out. **2** *trumpet the news of his appointment* proclaim, announce, herald, broadcast, promulgate, noise abroad.

truncate *verb* *truncate the time allotted | truncate the length/essay* shorten, reduce, diminish, decrease, cut short, prune, trim, lop, curtail, abbreviate.
Opposites LENGTHEN; EXTEND.

truncheon *noun* club, staff, stick. *See table at* WEAPON.

trunk *noun* **1** *the trunk of a tree* main stem, bole. **2** *find the trunk of the murdered man* torso. **3** *the animal's trunk* proboscis, snout. **4** *put the linen in a trunk* chest, case, portmanteau, crate, storage box, box, coffer.

truss *verb* **1** *truss a fowl* tie up, wrap up, bind up, bundle up. **2** *the thieves trussed up the guard* tie up, bind, tether, chain up, secure.

truss *noun* **1** *the truss of the bridge* support, brace, prop, strut, buttress. **2** *a truss for a hernia* support, pad. **3** *a truss of hay* bundle, bunch, bale.

trust *noun* **1** *have trust in the surgeon | take it on trust* faith, confidence, belief, conviction, credence, assurance, certainty, reliance, hope, expectation. **2** *a position of trust* responsibility, duty, obligation, commitment. **3** *the money is kept in trust for her* trusteeship, guardianship, safe keeping, protection, charge, care, custody.

trust *verb* **1** *I do not trust him | trust his judgement* put/place one's trust in, have faith/confidence in, be convinced by, pin one's hopes on. **2** *you can trust him to behave well* rely on, depend on, bank on, count on, be sure of, swear by. **3** *I trust you will come | trust everything is all right* hope, assume, presume, expect, believe, suppose. **4** *he trusted his son to her | trust them with his life* entrust, put in the hands of, turn over, assign, consign, commit, delegate.
Opposites DISTRUST; MISTRUST; DOUBT.

trustful *adjective* trusting, unsuspicious, unguarded, unwary, unsuspecting, unquestioning, credulous, gullible, ingenuous, naive, innocent.
Opposites SUSPICIOUS; WARY.

trustworthy *adjective* *trustworthy employees* reliable, dependable, stable, staunch, loyal, faithful, trusty, responsible, sensible, level-headed, honest, honourable, upright, ethical, righteous, principled, virtuous.
Opposites UNTRUSTWORTHY; UNRELIABLE; UNFAITHFUL.

trusty *adjective* *his trusty steed/valet* trustworthy, reliable, dependable, staunch, faithful, loyal, responsible. *See* TRUSTWORTHY.

truth *noun* **1** *no truth in what she says* truthfulness, accuracy, correctness, rightness, validity, fact, factualness, factuality, genuineness, veracity, verity, honesty. **2** *truth is stranger than fiction* reality, actuality, factuality. **3** *he is a man of truth* truthfulness, honesty, integrity, uprightness, righteousness, honour, honourableness, sincerity, candour. **4** *cite an old truth* truism, axiom, maxim, proverb, adage, aphorism, saw.

truthful *adjective* **1** *a truthful child* honest, trustworthy, veracious, candid, frank, open, forthright, straight. **2** *a truthful account* true, accurate, correct, right, valid, factual, exact, faithful, precise, genuine, reliable, veracious, honest.
Opposites UNTRUTHFUL; LYING; DISHONEST; INACCURATE.

try *verb* **1** *try to do well* attempt, aim, endeavour, make an effort, exert oneself, undertake, strive, assay, seek, struggle, do one's best; *inf.* have a go/shot/crack/stab. **2** *try a new brand | try something new* try out, test, put to the test, experiment with, assay, investigate, examine, appraise, evaluate, assess, experience, sample; *Am.* check out. **3** *the children try her patience* tax, strain, make demands on, sap, drain, exhaust. **4** *she has been sorely tried by the children* trouble, bother, irk, vex, annoy, irritate, harass, afflict, nag, pester, plague, torment; *inf.* drive mad. **5** *try the case* hear, adjudge, adjudicate, examine. **try out** *try out a new product/restaurant* try, test, put to the test, experiment with, appraise, evaluate, sample; *Am.* check out. See TRY 2.

trying *adjective* **1** *the children were very trying* troublesome, bothersome, tiresome, irksome, vexatious, annoying, irritating, exasperating. **2** *have a trying day* taxing, demanding, stressful, difficult, arduous, hard, tough, tiring, fatiguing, exhausting, upsetting.
Opposites ACCOMMODATING; EASY.

tuck *verb* **1** *tuck the shirt into the skirt* gather, push, ease, insert, stuff. **2** *tuck the material* gather, fold, ruck, ruffle, pleat. **tuck in/into 1** *tuck the child in* tuck up, cover up, wrap up, put to bed, make snug/comfortable. **2** *tuck into a large meal* eat heartily, gobble up, wolf down, *inf.* get stuck into. **tuck away** *houses tucked away under the mountain* hide, conceal, secrete, stow away.

tuck *noun* **1** *tucks in the fabric* gather, fold, ruck, ruffle, pleat. **2** *children asking for tuck* food; victuals, comestibles; *inf.* eats, grub, nosh, scoff.

tug *verb* **1** *tug the rope hard | tug her hair* pull, jerk, yank, wrench, wrest. **2** *the dog was tugging him along the road* pull, draw, drag, haul, tow, trail.

tug *noun* *give the gate a good tug* pull, jerk, yank, wrench, haul.

tuition *noun* teaching, instruction, coaching, education, schooling, training, drill, direction, guidance.

tumble *verb* **1** *the toddler tumbled suddenly* fall over, fall down, fall headlong, topple, fall head over heels, fall end over end, lose one's footing/balance, stumble, stagger, trip up. **2** *acrobats tumbling* somersault, go head over heels. **3** *share prices have tumbled* plummet, plunge,

slump, dive, drop, slide, fall, decrease, decline. **4** *ships tumbling about on the waves* roll, toss, pitch, heave, thrash about. **5** *tumble out of bed | tumble into the car* fall headlong, move hurriedly, blunder, stumble. **6** *the wind had tumbled her hair* tousle, dishevel, ruffle, disarrange, disorder, mess up, rumple; *inf.* muss up. **7** *suddenly tumble to what he meant | tumble to his motive* grasp, realize, understand, comprehend, apprehend, perceive; *inf.* latch on to, suss.

tumble *noun* **1** *the toddler took a tumble* fall, stumble, trip, spill; *inf.* nosedive, header. **2** *the tumble of the share index* plummeting, plunge, slump, dive, drop, fall, decline, failure, collapse. **3** *acrobats demonstrating tumbles* somersault, acrobatic feat. **4** *clothes in a tumble on the floor* jumble, clutter, mess, confusion; chaos, disorder, disarray.

tumbledown *adjective* dilapidated, ramshackle, crumbling, disintegrating, falling to pieces/bits, decrepit, ruined, in ruins, rickety, shaky, tottering, teetering.

tumid *adjective* *limbs looking tumid* swollen, enlarged, puffy, puffed up, bloated, distended, tumescent, turgid, oedematose.

tumour *noun* **1** *benign tumours* lump, growth, swelling, excrescence, protuberance, tumefaction, intumescence. **2** *die of a lung tumour* cancerous/malignant growth, carcinoma, cancer, malignancy.

tumult *noun* **1** *we cannot hear you above the tumult* din, uproar, commotion, racket, hubbub, hullabaloo, clamour, shouting, yelling, pandemonium, babel, bedlam, noise. **2** *the meeting ended in tumult* disorder, disarray, disturbance, confusion, chaos, upheaval, uproar. **3** *police sent to deal with a tumult* riot, protest, insurrection, rebellion, breach of the peace, row, brawl, fight, quarrel, altercation, affray, fracas, mêlée, brouhaha; *inf.* ruction, free-for-all. **4** *emotions in tumult* turmoil, upheaval, confusion, ferment.

tumultuous *adjective* **1** *tumultuous applause* loud, noisy, clamorous, ear-shattering, deafening, ear-piercing, blaring, uproarious, unrestrained, boisterous. **2** *a tumultuous crowd* rowdy, unruly, boisterous, disorderly, disturbed, restless, agitated, excited, fierce, obstreperous, wild, violent, lawless, vociferous, noisy, rioting. **3** *tumultuous emotions* passionate, vehement, fervent, violent, raging, unrestrained, uncontrolled, frenzied, in turmoil, turbulent.

tune *noun* **1** *play a folk tune* melody, air, song, theme, strain, motif. **2** *his ideas are not in tune with modern thinking* agreement, accord, accordance, harmony, correspondence, congruence, conformity, sympathy. **3** *changed his tune* mind, attitude, view, opinion.

tune *verb* *tune the instrument* adjust, regulate, pitch, bring into harmony, attune.

tuneful *adjective* melodious, melodic, musical, rhythmical, mellifluous, sweet-sounding, dulcet, euphonious, lyrical, harmonious, pleasant, agreeable, catching, foot-tapping,

tunnel · turn

Opposites DISCORDANT; HARSH.

tunnel noun **1** *miners crawling along the tunnel* underground/subterranean passage, underpass, subway. *See table.* **2** *moles/rabbits making tunnels* burrow, underground passage.

TUNNELS	
Tunnel	**Location**
Cascade	U.S.A.
Channel Tunnel	U.K./France
Chesapeake Bay Bridge Tunnel	U.S.A.
Connaught	Canada
Delaware Aqueduct	U.S.A.
Flathead	U.S.A.
Great St Bernard	Switzerland
Kanmon	Japan
Lincoln	U.S.A.
Lötschberg	Switzerland
Mont Blanc	Italy/France
Mont Cenis	Italy
Rokko	Japan
St Gotthard	Switzerland
San Bernardino	Switzerland
Seikan	Japan
Simplon Tunnels	Switzerland/Italy

tunnel verb **1** *prisoners tunnelling under the prison* dig, excavate, burrow, mine. **2** *tunnel a way out* dig, excavate, cut, scoop out.

turbulence noun **1** *the turbulence of the seas* tempestuousness, storminess, roughness, choppiness, agitation. **2** *experience turbulence on the flight* irregular atmospheric motion, uneven air movement, rough air currents. **3** *the turbulence of the crowds* rowdiness, unruliness, disorderliness, restlessness, agitation, wildness, violence, noisiness. *See* TURBULENT 2. **4** *the turbulence of her emotions* agitation, instability, troubledness, turmoil.

turbulent adjective **1** *turbulent seas* tempestuous, stormy, raging, foaming, rough, choppy, agitated. **2** *turbulent crowds* rowdy, unruly, boisterous, disorderly, restless, agitated, obstreperous, wild, violent, lawless, noisy. *See* TUMULTUOUS 2. **3** *affected by turbulent emotions/moods* disturbed, agitated, unsettled, unstable, troubled, distraught, in turmoil.
Opposites CALM; PEACEFUL; QUIET.

turf noun **1** *lay new turf in the garden* grass, patch of grass, lawn, green; *lit.* sward. **2** *replace a damaged turf* divot, clod, sod. **3** *he is a fan of the turf* racing, horse-racing; racecourses.

turf verb *turf the garden* lay grass, grass. **turf out 1** *turf out old clothes* throw out, fling out, dispose of, get rid of, discard, scrap; *inf.* chuck out, dump. **2** *turf out the intruder* throw out, fling out, eject, evict, oust, dismiss, discharge, expel; *inf.* chuck out, bounce, show someone the door, sack, fire.

turgid adjective **1** *turgid ankles* swollen, enlarged, puffy, puffed up, bloated, distended, tumescent, oedematose. **2** *turgid prose* bom-

bastic, high-flown, high-sounding, rhetorical, oratorical, grandiloquent, magniloquent, extravagant, pretentious, pompous, flowery, fulsome, orotund, fustian.
Opposites SIMPLE; PLAIN.

turmoil noun *the house was in turmoil just before the wedding* agitation, ferment, confusion, disorder, disarray, upheaval, chaos, pandemonium, bedlam, tumult; disturbance, bustle, flurry, commotion.

turn verb **1** *the wheel is turning* go round, rotate, revolve, circle, roll, spin, wheel, whirl, twirl, gyrate, swivel, pivot. **2** *he turned in the driveway | they turned for home* turn round, change direction/course, go back, return, reverse direction, make a U-turn. **3** *the tide is turning* change direction/course. **4** *he turned towards her* change position, veer, wheel round, swing round. **5** *turn the meat* turn over, reverse, invert, flip over, turn topsy-turvy. **6** *turn the hose on them* aim, direct, point, train, level, focus. **7** *his expression turned from amusement to horror* change, alter, transform, metamorphose, mutate. **8** *turn to the next task* turn one's attention to, attend to, address/apply/devote oneself to, set about, take up, undertake. **9** *he turned nasty* become, come to be, get, go. **10** *the milk/butter turned* go/turn sour, sour, curdle, become rancid, go bad; *inf.* go off. **11** *the heat turned the milk/butter* turn sour, sour, curdle, make rancid, spoil, taint. **12** *my stomach is turning* be nauseated, be upset, be unsettled. **13** *the sight turned my stomach* nauseate, sicken, upset, unsettle. **14** *my head is turning* go round, spin, feel dizzy/giddy. **15** *turn the corner* go/come round, round, pass round, negotiate, take. **16** *turn 40 | turn 5 o'clock* become, reach, get to, pass. **17** *turn on/off/out the light* put, switch. **18** *turn somersaults* perform, execute, do, carry out. **19** *turn a profit* make, bring in, gain, acquire, obtain, get, procure, secure. **20** *turn a pot* shape, mould, fashion, form, cast, construct. **21** *he used to be a loyal follower but he turned* change sides, go over, defect, desert, renege, turn renegade, break faith, apostatize, tergiversate. **turn against 1** *he suddenly turned against his old friend* become unfriendly/hostile to, take a dislike to. **2** *he turned her against her old friend* set against, make hostile to, cause to be unfriendly, prejudice against, influence against. **turn away** *turn away the beggar | turn away those without tickets* send away, refuse admittance/entrance to, reject, rebuff, repel, cold-shoulder; *inf.* give the brush-off to. **turn back** *turn back if the weather is bad* go back, retrace one's steps, return, retreat. **turn down 1** *he turned down the applicant/proposal* reject, decline, give the thumbs down to, rebuff, repudiate, spurn, veto; *inf.* give the red light to. **2** *turn down the volume/gas* lessen, lower, reduce, decrease, diminish. **turn in 1** *turn in your homework/uniform before you leave* hand in, give in, submit, tender, hand over, deliver, return, give back, surrender. **2** *they turned in high scores* register, record, reach, achieve, attain. **3** *it's time to turn in* go to bed, retire, call it a day, go to sleep; *inf.* hit the hay/sack. **4** *her feet turn in* curve in, bend in/inwards.

5 *turn him in to the police* hand over, turn over, deliver, inform on, betray; *inf.* grass on, squeal on, blow the whistle on, rat on, finger, put the finger on. **turn off 1** *turn off the electricity/heater* put off, turn out, switch off, shut off, flick off, unplug. **2** *the driver suddenly turned off the main road* branch off, leave, quit, depart from, deviate from. **3** *she turned off before the town* branch off, take a side road, take another road. **4** *he was turned off geography by the boring lessons | she was turned off by his table manners* put off, turn against; disenchant, alienate, repel, disgust, nauseate, sicken. **turn on 1** *turn on the electricity/heater* put on, switch on, flick on, plug in, operate. **2** *she turned on her husband when he criticized her friend | the dog turned on his master* attack, launch an attack on, fall on, round on, set upon, become hostile to; *inf.* lay into, tear into, light into, lace into. **3** *the result turns on the number of people voting* depend on, hang on, hinge on, pivot on, rest on, be contingent on, be decided by. **4** *she is turned on by muscular men* arouse, sexually arouse, excite, titillate, stimulate, thrill, attract, please. **turn out 1** *turn her out of her house* put out, throw out, kick out, eject, evict, oust; *inf.* chuck out, turf out, bounce. **2** *turn her out of her job* eject, dismiss, discharge, axe; *inf.* fire, sack, give the sack to, boot out. **3** *turn out the light/gas* turn off, put off, switch off, shut off, flick off, unplug. **4** *turn out thousands of books/toys per year* bring out, put out, produce, make, manufacture, fabricate, yield, process. **5** *turn out the cupboards* clear out, clean out, empty. **6** *a big crowd turned out to hear him* go, come, be present, attend, put in an appearance, appear, turn up, arrive, assemble, gather; *inf.* show up, show. **7** *as it turned out we were safe | it turned out that she was right* happen, occur, come about, end up, prove to be the case, emerge, eventuate; *inf.* transpire, pan out. **8** *she turned out a beautiful girl* become, grow/come/get to be, develop into, end up, emerge as. **turn over 1** *the boat turned over* overturn, topple, upturn, capsize, keel over, turn turtle. **2** *they turned the boat over* overturn, upturn, upend, capsize, upset. **3** *turn over the pages* flick over, flip over, leaf over. **4** *turn over the pros and cons* consider, think about, ponder, reflect on, mull over, muse on, ruminate about. **5** *turn over the estate to his brother* hand over, transfer, consign, assign, commit. **turn to 1** *turn to drink* have recourse to, resort to, take to. **2** *turn to him for help* look, apply to, approach, appeal to, have recourse to. **3** *arrived and soon turned to* set about one's work/task. **turn up 1** *turn up the volume* increase, raise, amplify, make louder, intensify. **2** *turn up some interesting information* uncover, unearth, discover, bring to light, find, hit upon, dig up, ferret out, root out, expose. **3** *he's mislaid the book but it'll turn up* be found, be located, come to light. **4** *they didn't turn up at the party* arrive, appear, put in an appearance, present oneself, be present; *inf.* show up, show. **5** *he hopes a job will turn up* present itself, occur, happen, crop up, pop up, arise, come on the scene, come to light, manifest itself; *inf.* transpire. **6** *turn up the garment* take up, raise, shorten.

turn *noun* **1** *give the wheel a few turns* rotation, revolution, circle, spin, whirl, twirl, gyration, swivel. **2** *take a turn to the left* change of direction/course, deviation, divergence, veer. **3** *a road full of turns* turning, bend, curve, corner, twist, winding. **4** *dislike the turn of events* trend, tendency, bias, leaning, direction, drift. **5** *a turn for the better/worse* change, alteration, variation, difference, deviation, divergence, shift. **6** *he is of an academic turn of mind* bent, tendency, inclination, bias, propensity, affinity, leaning, aptitude, talent, gift, flair, knack. **7** *it is your turn to play* time, opportunity, chance, stint, spell, move, try, attempt; *inf.* go, shot, crack. **8** *take a turn in the park* walk, stroll, saunter, amble, airing, constitutional, promenade, drive, ride, outing, excursion, jaunt; *inf.* spin. **9** *a comedy turn in the show* performance, act, routine, appearance, show. **10** *do him a good/bad turn* act, action, deed, service, gesture, favour. **11** *you gave me quite a turn* shock, start, surprise, fright, scare. **12** *it served my turn* purpose, objective, object, aim, end.

turning-point *noun the turning-point in their fortunes* crossroads, crisis, crisis point, critical period, crux, decisive point, moment of truth/decision.

turnout *noun* **1** *there was a good turnout at the meeting* number, gathering, crowd, assembly, assemblage, audience, attendance, gate. **2** *dressed in a smart turnout* outfit, costume, ensemble, attire; *inf.* rig-out, get-up, gear.

turnover *noun* **1** *the company's annual turnover is two million dollars* gross revenue, volume of business, business, financial flow; sales figures. **2** *aim for a quick turnover in the shop* buying and selling, movement of goods. **3** *the turnover of staff is very high* change, coming and going, movement, replacement.

tussle *noun* **1** *in the tussle to get the gun from him* struggle, wrestle, conflict, fight, battle, skirmish, scuffle, affray, brawl; *inf.* set-to, scrap. **2** *we had a tussle to finish the work on time* struggle, effort, exertion, labour, toil, strain.

tutor *noun tutors marking exams* teacher, instructor, coach, lecturer, educator.

tutor *verb tutor him in maths* teach, instruct, coach, educate, school, train, drill, direct, guide.

TV *noun* television set, television; *inf.* telly, the box, gogglebox, small screen, the tube, idiot box, talking head. *See table at* TELEVISION.

twaddle *noun* nonsense, rubbish, garbage, trash, drivel, blather, balderdash, bunkum, hogwash, gibberish, gobbledegook; *inf.* hot air, waffle, bunk, tosh, bosh, poppycock, piffle.

tweak *verb tweak the child's ear* twist, pinch, nip, twitch, squeeze, pull, jerk.

tweak *noun give his ear a tweak* twist, pinch, nip, twitch, squeeze, pull, jerk.

twig *noun* branch, stick, offshoot, shoot, spray, stem.

twilight *noun* **1** *walk home at twilight* dusk, late afternoon, early evening; *lit.* crepuscule; *Scots* gloaming. **2** *scarcely able to see her in the twilight* half-light, semidarkness, dimness. **3** *in the twi-*

light of his career decline, ebb, waning, closing years.

twin noun **1** he and his brother are twins identical twin, non-identical twin. See table. **2** where is the twin of that glove? mate, fellow, match, counterpart, complement. **3** she's an absolute twin for the queen double, look-alike, likeness, image, duplicate, clone; inf. spitting image, spit, dead spit, ringer, dead ringer.

TWINS
Aegyptus and Danaus
Artemis and Apollo
Auguste and Jean Piccard
Castor and Pollux
Esau and Jacob
Polyneices and Eteocles
Romulus and Remus

twin verb twin the two firms join, link, couple, pair, yoke.

twine noun **1** a ball of twine cord, string, yarn, thread. **2** vines in a twine coil, spiral, whorl, convolution, twist, tangle.

twine verb **1** the plant had twined itself round the tree entwine, coil, twist, wind, weave, wrap. **2** twine a garland weave, plait, braid, twist. **3** the path twines up the mountain twist, twist and turn, wind, curve, zigzag, meander, snake, worm.

twinge noun **1** a twinge of rheumatism stab of pain, spasm, pain, pang, ache, throb, tweak, tingle, cramp, stitch. **2** a twinge of conscience pang, uneasiness, discomfort, qualm, scruple, misgiving.

twinkle verb **1** stars twinkling glitter, glint, sparkle, flicker, shimmer, glimmer, gleam, dazzle, flash, wink, blink, shine, scintillate, coruscate. **2** her eyes twinkled with amusement sparkle, gleam, shine. **3** her feet twinkled upstairs dart, glide, dance, flit.

twinkle noun **1** the twinkle of stars twinkling, glitter, glint, sparkle, flicker, shimmer, glimmer, gleam, dazzle, flash, wink, blink, shining, scintillation, coruscation. **2** with a twinkle of her eyes sparkle, gleam, shining. **3** the twinkle of her feet darting, gliding, dancing, flitting. **4** she'll be with you in a twinkle twinkling, instant, second, moment, flash. See TWINKLING.

twinkling noun **1** the twinkling of the stars twinkle, glitter, glint, sparkle, flicker, shimmer. See TWINKLE noun 1. **2** I'll be there in a twinkling twinkle, instant, second, split second, moment, flash; inf. jiffy, tick, shake, two shakes of a lamb's tail.

twirl verb **1** twirl the cane spin, whirl, twist. **2** she twirled round to the music spin, whirl, turn, pirouette, wheel, gyrate, revolve, rotate, pivot. **3** twirl a curl of hair round her finger twist, coil, wind, curl.

twirl noun **1** give the cane a twirl spin, whirl, twist. **2** a series of twirls round the room spin, whirl, turn, pirouette, gyration, revolution, rotation. **3** a twirl of chocolate twist, coil, whorl, curl.

twist verb **1** twist the metal rod | twist it off the wall bend, warp, misshape, deform, contort, distort; wrench, wrest. **2** his face twisted in agony contort, screw up. **3** he twisted his ankle wrench, turn, sprain, rick. **4** the plant had twisted itself round the tree twine, entwine, coil, wind, weave, wrap. **5** twist a garland twine, weave, plait, braid. **6** twist a curl of hair round her finger twirl, coil, wind, curl. **7** the path twisted round the mountain wind, curve, bend, twine, zigzag, meander, snake, worm. **8** the child twisted out of his grasp wriggle, writhe, squirm, wiggle. **9** twist their words distort, pervert, warp, garble, misrepresent, falsify, misquote, misreport, change, alter. **10** she twisted her head round swivel, screw, turn, rotate. **11** she twisted round to look at him swivel, turn, spin, pivot, rotate, revolve. **Opposites** STRAIGHTEN; UNWIND.

twist noun **1** with a twist of his arm wrench, wrest, turn, contortion, pull, jerk, yank. **2** try to repair the twist in the metal bar bend, warp, kink, deformity, contortion, distortion, defect, flaw, imperfection. **3** a painful twist of the ankle wrench, turn, sprain, rick. **4** a twist of hair coil, twirl, curl, braid. **5** a twist of tobacco roll, plug, quid. **6** the twists in the mountain path bend, turn, curve, winding, arc, zigzag, meander, undulation. **7** a slight twist to his character aberration, peculiarity, quirk, oddity, eccentricity, idiosyncrasy, foible. **8** upset by the twist of events development, turn, change, alteration, variation, slant.

twit noun fool, idiot, ass, blockhead, nincompoop, ninny, simpleton, clown; inf. chump, halfwit, dope.

twitch verb **1** with limbs twitching move spasmodically, jerk, jump, quiver, shiver, quaver. **2** her eye twitched blink, flutter, jump. **3** twitch the rug into place | twitch at his tie pull, tug, pluck; inf. yank.

twitch noun **1** his leg gave a twitch spasm, jerk, jump, quiver, tremor, shiver, quaver. **2** a twitch in her eye blink, flutter, jump, tic. **3** adjust the rug with a twitch pull, tug; inf. yank.

twitter verb **1** birds twittering chirrup, cheep, tweet, trill, warble, whistle, sing. **2** stand twittering in the bus queue chatter, jabber, prattle, babble, gossip.

twitter noun **1** the twitter of the birds trill, chirrup, cheep, tweet, warble, whistle, song. **2** in a twitter about her exam results flutter, flurry, state of excitement/agitation; inf. tizzy, state, dither.

two-edged adjective a two-edged remark double-edged, ambiguous, equivocal, ambivalent.

two-faced adjective hypocritical, insincere, deceitful, deceiving, dissembling, duplicitous, false, untrustworthy, treacherous, perfidious, double-dealing, Janus-faced. **Opposites** SINCERE; HONEST.

tycoon noun magnate, baron, big businessman, captain of industry, industrialist, financier, merchant prince, mogul; inf. fat cat.

type noun **1** a nasty type of person | a rare type of plant kind, sort, variety, form, class, classification, category, group, order, set, genre, strain, species, genus; *inf.* ilk. **2** *he's a nasty type* person, individual, specimen, character. **3** *they regard her as the very type of womanhood* example, exemplar, model, pattern, essence, personification, epitome, quintessence, archetype, prototype. **4** *set in a different kind of type* print, fount, face, character. *See table.*

TYPEFACES	
Aldine	Gill Sans
American Typewriter	Gondy
Antique Olive	Gothic
Arial	Grotesque
Avant Garde	Helvetica
Balmoral	Hobo
Baskerville	Korinna
Bauhaus	Melior
Bembo	Novarese
Bodoni	Old English
Bookman	Optima
Boston	Palatino
Broadway	Peignot
Caslon	Perpetua
Century Gothic	Photina
Century School-	Plantin
book	Prestige
Clarendon	Rockwell
Clearface	Serifa
Colonna	Showbill
Cooper Black	Souvenir
Courier	Stone
Flash	Times New Roman
Folio	Trump
Fraktur	Univers
Franklin Gothic	University Roman
Futura	Vivaldi
Galliard	Windsor
Garamond	Zapf Chancery

typhoon *noun* cyclone, tornado, tropical storm, hurricane, squall, tempest.

typical *adjective* **1** *a typical English pub* representative, classic, standard, stock, orthodox, conventional, true-to-type, quintessential, archetypal. **2** *what would be your typical day?* normal, average, ordinary, regular, general, customary, habitual, routine, run-of-the-mill. **3** *it is typical of him to be rude* characteristic, in character, in keeping, to be expected, usual, normal.
Opposites atypical; EXCEPTIONAL; UNORTHODOX; SINGULAR.

typify *verb* **1** *he typifies the self-made man* exemplify, characterize, personify, epitomize, symbolize, embody, sum up, incarnate. **2** *they have tried to typify the various sectors of society* exemplify, represent, indicate, illustrate, denote.

tyrannical *adjective* despotic, autocratic, dictatorial, absolute, arbitrary, authoritarian, high-handed, imperious, oppressive, coercive, domineering, bullying, harsh, strict, severe, cruel, brutal, unjust, unreasonable.
Opposites DEMOCRATIC; LIBERAL; GENTLE.

tyrannize *verb* *tyrannize over the peasants|tyrannize the children* rule despotically, rule with a rod of iron; oppress, suppress, repress, crush, subjugate, dominate, domineer, order around, browbeat, intimidate, bully, ride roughshod over, lord it over.

tyranny *noun* **1** *the tyranny of the country's/school's regime* despotism, absolutism, authoritarianism, arbitrariness, high-handedness, imperiousness, oppressiveness, oppression, coercion, bullying, harshness, strictness, severity, cruelty, brutality, unjustness, unreasonableness. **2** *government by tyranny rather than democracy* despotism, autocracy, dictatorship, absolute power, authoritarianism.

tyrant *noun* despot, autocrat, dictator, absolute ruler, authoritarian, oppressor, martinet, slave-driver, bully.

Uu

ubiquitous *adjective* everywhere, omnipresent, ever-present, in all places, all-over, all over the place, pervasive, universal.

ugly *adjective* **1** *ugly people/buildings* ill-favoured, hideous, plain, unattractive, unlovely, unprepossessing, unsightly, displeasing; *Am.* homely; *inf.* not much to look at. **2** *an ugly sight met their eyes* hideous, horrible, horrid, frightful, terrible, disagreeable, unpleasant, foul, nasty, vile, shocking, distasteful, disgusting, revolting, repellent, repugnant, loathsome, hateful, nauseating, sickening. **3** *he is an ugly character* horrible, disagreeable, unpleasant, nasty, objectionable, offensive, obnoxious, foul, vile, base, dishonourable, dishonest, rotten. **4** *an ugly situation* threatening, menacing, ominous, sinister, dangerous, nasty, unpleasant, disagreeable. **5** *the crowd grew ugly* nasty, angry, bad-tempered, ill-natured, hostile, surly, sullen, mean, sour. **6** *gave them ugly looks* dark, threatening, menacing, hostile, spiteful, malevolent, evil.
Opposites BEAUTIFUL; ATTRACTIVE; PLEASANT; FRIENDLY.

ulcer *noun* ulceration, sore, open sore, abscess, gathering, boil, carbuncle, pustule.

ulterior *adjective* *an ulterior motive* hidden, concealed, unrevealed, undisclosed, undivulged, unexpressed, secret, covert, unapparent.
Opposites OVERT; OBVIOUS.

ultimate *adjective* **1** *the ultimate outcome/take ultimate responsibility* last, final, eventual, concluding, conclusive, terminal, end, furthest. **2** *ultimate truths* basic, fundamental, primary, elemental, radical. **3** *the ultimate gift/luxury* topmost, utmost, maximum, supreme, superlative, paramount, greatest, highest, unsurpassed, unrivalled.
Opposites FIRST; SECONDARY; MINIMUM.

ultimate *noun* *the ultimate in luxury* last word, utmost, height, peak, culmination, perfection, epitome, nonpareil.

ultimately *adverb* **1** *he is bound to win ultimately* in the end, in the long run, eventually, finally, sooner or later. **2** *ultimately he is an honourable person* basically, fundamentally, at heart, deep down.

ultramodern *adjective* ahead of its/one's time, futuristic, avant-garde, modernistic, advanced, progressive, forward-looking.

umbrage *noun* offence, pique, chagrin, vexation, irritation, exasperation, indignation, annoyance, anger, ire, high dudgeon, hurt, resentment, bitterness; *inf.* huff.
Opposites PLEASURE; GOODWILL.

umbrella *noun* *under the umbrella of the parent organization* agency, aegis, cover, protection, support, patronage, backing.

umpire *noun* *the umpire in the dispute/match* adjudicator, arbitrator, arbiter, judge, moderator, referee; *inf.* ref.

umpire *verb* *umpire in the dispute | umpire the match* adjudicate, arbitrate, judge, moderate, referee; *inf.* ref.

umpteen *adjective* countless, numerous, very many, ever so many.

unable *adjective* *unable to get about | unable to reach the standard* not able, incapable, powerless, impotent, not up/equal to, inadequate, ineffectual, incompetent, unfit, unfitted, unqualified.

unabridged *adjective* uncut, unshortened, unreduced, uncondensed, unexpurgated, full-length, complete, entire, whole, intact.

unacceptable *adjective* **1** *unacceptable terms of agreement* unsatisfactory, inadmissible, unsuitable. **2** *unacceptable behaviour* insupportable, intolerable, objectionable, offensive, obnoxious, undesirable, disagreeable, distasteful, improper.

unaccompanied *adjective* *go unaccompanied | unaccompanied people* alone, on one's own, by oneself, partnerless, unescorted, solo, lone, solitary, single.

unaccomplished *adjective* **1** *unaccomplished tasks* unfinished, uncompleted, incomplete, undone, half-done, unperformed, unexecuted. **2** *unaccomplished players* inexpert, unskilful, unskilled, without finesse, blundering, talentless, amateur, dilettante.

unaccountable *adjective* **1** *an unaccountable increase in births | for some unaccountable reason* inexplicable, unexplainable, insoluble, unsolvable, incomprehensible, beyond comprehension/understanding, unfathomable, puzzling, baffling, mysterious, inscrutable, peculiar, unusual, curious, strange, queer, bizarre, extraordinary, astonishing; *inf.* weird. **2** *she is unaccountable for the error* not responsible, not answerable, not liable, free, clear, exempt, immune.

unaccustomed *adjective* **1** *unaccustomed to public speaking* unused (to), not used (to), new (to), unpractised, unfamiliar, inexperienced, unversed. **2** *the unaccustomed luxury* unusual, unfamiliar, uncommon, unwonted, new, exceptional, out of the ordinary, extraordinary, special, remarkable, singular, rare, surprising, strange.

unaffected *adjective* **1** *unaffected by the events* unchanged, unaltered, uninfluenced, untouched, unmoved, unimpressed, proof (against), impervious, unresponsive. **2** *unaffected young girls* artless, guileless, ingenuous, naive, unsophisticated, unassuming, unpretentious, down-to-earth, without airs, natural, plain, simple. **3** *unaffected sincerity* unfeigned, unpretended, genuine, real, sincere, honest, true, candid, frank; *inf.* up-front.

unanimity *noun* **1** *the unanimity of the committee* agreement, accord, concord, unity, consensus, like-mindedness. **2** *the unanimity of the vote* solidity, concertedness, consensus, uniformity, consistency, congruence.
Opposites DISAGREEMENT; DIVISION.

unanimous *adjective* **1** *the committee was unanimous* in complete agreement/accord, of one mind, like-minded, totally in harmony, at one, of a piece, with one voice, united, concordant. **2** *a unanimous vote* solid, united, concerted, uniform, consistent, congruent.

unanswerable *adjective* **1** *an unanswerable case* irrefutable, inarguable, indisputable, undeniable, incontestable, incontrovertible, conclusive, absolute, positive. **2** *unanswerable questions* insoluble, unsolvable, insolvable, unresolvable, unexplainable, inexplicable.
3 *unanswerable for the error* not answerable, not responsible, unaccountable. *See* UNACCOUNTABLE 2.

unapproachable *adjective* **1** *unapproachable places* inaccessible, remote, out of the way, out of reach, unreachable; *inf.* off the beaten track, unget-at-able. **2** *the new head teacher is unapproachable* aloof, standoffish, distant, remote, detached, reserved, withdrawn, uncommunicative, unresponsive, unfriendly, unsociable, cool, chilly, frigid.

unarmed *adjective* without arms/weapons, weaponless, open to attack, defenceless, unprotected, vulnerable, exposed, pregnable.

unassailable *adjective* **1** *an unassailable stronghold* impregnable, invulnerable, invincible, secure, well-defended. **2** *their unassailable right to vote* indisputable, undeniable, unquestionable, incontestable, incontrovertible, irrefutable, conclusive, absolute, positive, proven.

unassuming *adjective* modest, self-effacing, humble, meek, retiring, demure, restrained, reticent, diffident, shy, bashful, unassertive, unobtrusive, unostentatious, unpretentious, unaffected, natural, genuine, simple, artless, ingenuous.
Opposites BOLD; BRAZEN; PRETENTIOUS.

unattached *adjective* **1** *she is still unattached* unmarried, unwed, unwedded, unengaged, unbetrothed, wifeless, husbandless, spouseless, uncommitted, free, available, footloose and fancy free, partnerless, single, on one's own, by oneself, unescorted. **2** *the firm is still unattached to any other organization* independent of, unaffiliated, unassociated, autonomous, non-aligned, self-governing, self-ruling.

unattended *adjective* **1** *an unattended garden* untended, neglected, ignored, disregarded, forgotten, forsaken, abandoned. **2** *an unattended vehicle* by itself, left alone, unguarded, unwatched. **3** *unattended young women* unaccompanied, alone, lone, on one's own, by oneself, partnerless, unescorted. *See* UNACCOMPANIED.

unauthorized *adjective* uncertified, unaccredited, unlicensed, unofficial, unsanctioned,

unwarranted, unapproved, disallowed, prohibited, forbidden, illegal.

unavailing *adjective* vain, futile, useless, ineffective, ineffectual, unsuccessful, failed, fruitless, unproductive, pointless, to no avail/purpose, abortive, for nought.

unavoidable *adjective* inescapable, inevitable, bound to happen, inexorable, ineludible, ineluctable, certain, fated, predestined, necessary, compulsory, required, obligatory, mandatory.

unaware *adjective* **1** *unaware of what is going on | unaware that they have gone* unknowing, unconscious, ignorant, heedless, unmindful, oblivious, uninformed (about), unenlightened (about); *inf.* in the dark. **2** *politically unaware* not perceptive, undiscerning, incognizant, nondiscriminating, unresponsive.

unawares *adverb* **1** *come upon him unawares* unexpectedly, by surprise, without warning, suddenly, abruptly, unprepared, off-guard; *inf.* with one's trousers down. **2** *I must have dropped my keys unawares* unknowingly, unwittingly, unintentionally, unconsciously, inadvertently, without noticing, accidentally, by accident, by mistake, mistakenly.

unbalanced *adjective* **1** *unbalanced since the death of her husband* unstable, of unsound mind, mentally ill, deranged, demented, crazed, distracted, insane, mad, lunatic; *inf.* crazy, not all there, off one's head. **2** *an unbalanced report of the events* one-sided, biased, prejudiced, partisan, partial, inequitable, unjust, unfair.

unbearable *adjective* intolerable, insufferable, unsupportable, unendurable, unacceptable, more than flesh and blood can stand; *inf.* too much, enough to try the patience of a saint.

unbeatable *adjective* invincible, indomitable, unconquerable, unstoppable, unsurpassable, excelling.

unbecoming *adjective* **1** *an unbecoming hat* unflattering, unattractive, unsightly. **2** *behaviour unbecoming in a young girl | unbecoming behaviour* unfitting, inappropriate, unsuitable, inapt, improper, indecorous, unseemly, unladylike, ungentlemanly, indelicate, tasteless.

unbelief *noun* non-belief, atheism, disbelief, incredulity, scepticism, doubt, agnosticism.

unbelievable *adjective* beyond belief, incredible, unconvincing, far-fetched, implausible, improbable, inconceivable, unthinkable, unimaginable, impossible, astonishing, astounding, staggering, preposterous.

unbeliever *noun* non-believer, atheist, disbeliever, infidel, sceptic, doubter, doubting Thomas, agnostic.

unbend *verb* **1** *unbend the twisted pole* straighten, align, flatten. **2** *she unbent enough to smile* relax, become less formal, become informal, unwind, loosen up, let oneself go; *inf.* let one's hair down, let up, let it all hang out, hang loose.

unbending *adjective* **1** *an unbending material* rigid, stiff, inflexible, unpliable, inelastic, unmalleable. **2** *she is a very unbending old lady* formal, stiff, aloof, reserved; *inf.* up-tight. **3** *an* *unbending regime* inflexible, hard-line, uncompromising, tough, harsh, strict, stern, severe, firm, resolute, determined, unrelenting, relentless, inexorable.

unbiased *adjective* impartial, unprejudiced, non-partisan, neutral, objective, disinterested, dispassionate, detached, even-handed, open-minded, equitable, fair, fair-minded, just.

unbidden *adjective* **1** *unbidden guests* unasked, uninvited, unrequested, unwanted, unwelcome. **2** *memories coming unbidden to mind* spontaneous, voluntary, unprompted, unforced, uncompelled.

unbind *verb* **1** *unbind the hostages* release, free, set free/loose, liberate, untie, unchain, unfetter. **2** *unbind the ropes* untie, unfasten, undo, loosen, unloose.

unborn *adjective* **1** *her unborn child* expected, awaited, *in utero*, embryonic. **2** *unborn generations* future, to come, coming, subsequent, hereafter.

unbounded *adjective* boundless, unlimited, limitless, illimitable, infinite, unrestrained, unconstrained, uncontrolled, unchecked, unbridled, vast, immense, immeasurable. **Opposites** LIMITED; RESTRICTED.

unbreakable *adjective* non-breakable, shatterproof, infrangible, indestructible, toughened.

unbridled *adjective* unrestrained, unconstrained, uncontrolled, unchecked, uncurbed, ungoverned, rampant, excessive, intemperate.

unbroken *adjective* **1** *unbroken china/sets* intact, whole, undamaged, unimpaired, complete, entire. **2** *an unbroken horse* untamed, unsubdued. **3** *an unbroken series* uninterrupted, continuous, unremitting, ceaseless, unceasing, endless, incessant, constant, nonstop. **4** *unbroken sleep* uninterrupted, undisturbed, untroubled, sound. **5** *unbroken records* unbeaten, unsurpassed, unrivalled.

unburden *verb* **1** *unburden the horse* unload, disburden, unpack, disencumber. **2** *unburden one's sins/guilt* confess, confide, acknowledge, disclose, reveal, divulge, expose, lay bare, make a clean breast of; *inf.* come clean.

uncalled-for *adjective* **1** *uncalled-for advice* unsought, unasked, unsolicited, unrequested, unprompted, unwelcome, gratuitous. **2** *uncalled-for rudeness* unnecessary, needless, undeserved, unmerited, unjustified, unreasonable, inappropriate.

uncanny *adjective* **1** *uncanny happenings in the old house* strange, mysterious, odd, queer, weird, eerie, unnatural, preternatural, supernatural, unearthly, ghostly; *inf.* creepy, spooky. **2** *bear an uncanny resemblance to the king* remarkable, striking, extraordinary, exceptional, astounding, astonishing, incredible. **Opposites** ORDINARY; RUN-OF-THE-MILL; USUAL.

unceremonious *adjective* **1** *his unceremonious departure* abrupt, sudden, hasty, hurried, undignified, rude, impolite, uncivil, discourteous, unmannerly. **2** *an unceremonious occasion* informal, without ritual, casual, simple, relaxed, easy.

uncertain *adjective* **1** *the outcome is uncertain* unknown, undetermined, unsettled, pending, in the balance, up in the air. **2** *feel uncertain about what to do* unsure, doubtful, dubious, undecided, unresolved, indecisive, irresolute, hesitant, wavering, vacillating, equivocating, vague, hazy, unclear, ambivalent, in two minds. **3** *the future is uncertain* unpredictable, unforeseeable, incalculable, speculative, unreliable, untrustworthy, undependable, risky, chancy. **4** *uncertain weather* changeable, variable, irregular, fitful, unpredictable, unreliable. **5** *in an uncertain voice* hesitant, hesitating, tentative, halting, unsure, unconfident.

uncertainty *noun* **1** *full of uncertainty about the future* unsureness, indecision, irresolution, hesitancy, vacillation, equivocation, doubt, doubtfulness, vagueness, ambivalence. *See* UNCERTAIN 2. **2** *the uncertainty of the future* unpredictability, unreliability, riskiness, chanciness. *See* UNCERTAIN 3. **3** *give voice to a few uncertainties* doubt, qualm, misgiving, quandary, dilemma. **4** *the uncertainty of the weather* changeableness, variability, irregularity, fitfulness, unpredictability, unreliability. **5** *the uncertainty in her voice | uncertainty of the baby's steps* hesitancy, tentativeness, unsureness, lack of confidence.

unchangeable *adjective* changeless, immutable, unalterable, incommutable, invariable, firm, fixed, established, permanent, deep-rooted, enduring, abiding, lasting, indestructible, unfading, constant, perpetual, eternal.

uncharitable *adjective* *uncharitable in judging other's faults* harsh, severe, stern, hard, hard-hearted, censorious, uncompromising, inflexible, unforgiving, merciless, ruthless, uncompassionate, unsympathetic, ungenerous, unfeeling, unkind, unchristian.

uncharted *adjective* *uncharted territory* unmapped, unsurveyed, unexplored, unresearched, unplumbed, unfamiliar, unknown, strange.

uncivil *adjective* discourteous, rude, impolite, unmannerly, bad-mannered, ill-bred, ungallant, unchivalrous, ungracious, disrespectful, brusque, curt, gruff, surly, boorish, churlish, uncouth.

uncivilized *adjective* **1** *uncivilized tribes* barbarian, barbarous, barbaric, primitive, savage, wild. **2** *some of their friends are so uncivilized* uncouth, coarse, rough, boorish, vulgar, philistine, uneducated, uncultured, uncultivated, unsophisticated, unrefined, unpolished.

unclean *adjective* **1** *unclean water* dirty, filthy, polluted, fouled, impure, adulterated, tainted. **2** *unclean hands/houses* dirty, filthy, grubby, grimy, stained, besmirched, smeared, unwashed. **3** *unclean people corrupting the innocent* unchaste, impure, lustful, licentious, lewd, corrupt, sullied, degenerate, bad, wicked, evil, sinful. **4** *unclean food* forbidden, impure.

uncomfortable *adjective* **1** *uncomfortable chairs/shoes/houses* not comfortable. **2** *feel uncomfortable in their presence* uneasy, ill-at-ease, nervous, tense, edgy, self-conscious, awkward, embarrassed, discomfited, disturbed, troubled, worried, anxious, apprehensive. **3** *an uncomfortable silence* awkward, uneasy, unpleasant, disagreeable, painful, distressing, disturbing.

uncommitted *adjective* **1** *uncommitted young people* unpledged, unpromised, unengaged, unbetrothed, unmarried, free, available, unattached, single. **2** *uncommitted politically* non-aligned, non-partisan, neutral, undecided, floating, undeclared, sitting on the fence.

uncommon *adjective* **1** *an uncommon name* unusual, rare, uncustomary, unfamiliar, strange, odd, curious, out of the ordinary, novel, singular, peculiar, queer, bizarre; *inf.* weird. **2** *those birds are uncommon here* rare, scarce, infrequent, few and far between, occasional. **3** *an uncommon resemblance/appetite* remarkable, extraordinary, exceptional, singular, outstanding, notable, noteworthy, distinctive, striking.

uncommonly *adverb* *uncommonly talented* unusually, remarkably, extraordinarily, exceptionally, singularly, particularly, strikingly, extremely, inordinately, incredibly, amazingly.

uncommunicative *adjective* taciturn, reserved, shy, retiring, diffident, reticent, quiet, unforthcoming, unconversational, untalkative, silent, tight-lipped, secretive, unresponsive, close, distant, remote, aloof, withdrawn, standoffish, unsociable, antisocial.

uncompromising *adjective* rigid, stiff, inflexible, unbending, unyielding, hard-line, tough, immovable, firm, determined, dogged, obstinate, obdurate, tenacious, relentless, implacable, inexorable, intransigent.

unconcern *noun* indifference, apathy, lack of interest, uninterestedness, nonchalance, insouciance, lack of involvement, passivity, dispassionateness, detachment, aloofness, remoteness.

unconcerned *adjective* **1** *unconcerned with political issues* indifferent, apathetic, uninterested, uninvolved, dispassionate (about), detached (from), aloof (from), remote (from). **2** *she is completely unconcerned despite her difficulties* unworried, untroubled, unperturbed, unruffled, unanxious, insouciant, nonchalant, carefree, blithe, without a care in the world, serene, relaxed, at ease.

unconditional *adjective* complete, total, entire, full, plenary, outright, absolute, downright, out and out, utter, all-out, thoroughgoing, unequivocal, conclusive, definite, positive, indubitable, incontrovertible, categorical, unqualified, unlimited, unreserved, unrestricted.

unconnected *adjective* **1** *the two houses are unconnected* unjoined, detached, independent, separate. **2** *the two events are unconnected* unassociated, unrelated, separate. **3** *his prose style is unconnected* | *unconnected prose* disconnected, disjointed, rambling, diffuse, ununified, disorderly, haphazard, disorganized, incoherent, meaningless.

unconscionable *adjective* **1** *an unconscionable criminal* amoral, immoral, unethical, unprincipled, unscrupulous, dishonourable, dishonest, corrupt. **2** *an unconscionable length of time* excessive, unwarranted, uncalled-for, unreasonable, inordinate, immoderate, undue, outrageous, preposterous, inexcusable.
Opposites MORAL; ACCEPTABLE; MODERATE.

unconscious *adjective* **1** *fall unconscious* senseless, insensible, comatose, knocked out, stunned, dazed; *inf.* blacked out, KO'd, out like a light, laid out, flaked-out, out cold, out. **2** *unconscious of the noise* unaware, heedless, ignorant, in ignorance, incognizant, oblivious, insensible. **3** *deliver an unconscious insult* unintentional, unintended, accidental, unthinking, unwitting, inadvertent, unpremeditated. **4** *unconscious prejudice* instinctive, automatic, reflex, involuntary, inherent, innate, subliminal, subconscious, latent.

uncontrollable *adjective* **1** *uncontrollable children* out of control, unmanageable, ungovernable, wild, unruly, disorderly, restive, recalcitrant, refractory, intractable, incorrigible, contumacious. **2** *uncontrollable rages* ungovernable, unrestrained, wild, violent, frantic, frenzied, raging, raving, mad.

unconventional *adjective* unorthodox, irregular, informal, unusual, uncommon, uncustomary, unwonted, rare, out of the ordinary, atypical, singular, individual, individualistic, different, original, idiosyncratic, nonconformist, bohemian, eccentric, odd, strange, bizarre; *inf.* offbeat, freakish, way-out.

uncoordinated *adjective* *uncoordinated people always dropping things* clumsy, awkward, inept, maladroit, bungling, blundering, bumbling, lumbering, heavy-footed, clodhopping, graceless, ungainly; *inf.* butter-fingered, all thumbs, like a bull in a china shop; *Am. inf.* klutzy.

uncouth *adjective* rough, coarse, uncivilized, uncultured, uncultivated, unrefined, unpolished, unsophisticated, provincial, crude, gross, loutish, boorish, oafish, churlish, uncivil, rude, impolite, discourteous, unmannerly, bad-mannered, ill-bred, vulgar.
Opposites REFINED; CULTIVATED; SOPHISTICATED.

uncover *verb* **1** *uncover the wound/food* expose, lay bare, bare, reveal, unwrap. **2** *uncover a plot against the president* discover, detect, unearth, dig up, expose, bring to light, unmask, unveil, reveal, lay bare, make known, divulge, disclose.

unctuous *adjective* **1** *unctuous followers at court* | *unctuous behaviour* sycophantic, ingratiating, obsequious, fawning, servile, toadying, insincere, flattering, honey-tongued, gushing, effusive, suave, urbane, glib, smooth. **2** *unctuous substance* oily, oleaginous, greasy, soapy, saponaceous.

undaunted *adjective* undismayed, unalarmed, unafraid, unflinching, unfaltering, indomitable, resolute, unflagging, intrepid, bold, valiant, brave, courageous, heroic, doughty, plucky; *inf.* spunky.

undeceive *verb* *undeceive her of the error* put right, set straight, disabuse, enlighten, be honest with, disillusion, disenchant.

undecided *adjective* **1** *the result is as yet undecided* uncertain, unsettled, unresolved, indefinite, unknown, unestablished, unascertained, pending, in the balance, up in the air. **2** *they are undecided as to what to do* unsure, uncertain, doubtful, dubious, unresolved, indecisive, irresolute, hesitant, wavering, vacillating, equivocating, dithering, vague, hazy, unclear, ambivalent, in two minds.

undefined *adjective* **1** *an undefined reason/plan* unexplained, non-specific, unspecified, indeterminate, unclear, vague, imprecise, inexact. **2** *undefined shapes* indefinite, indistinct, vague, hazy, nebulous, dim, obscure, blurred, shadowy, formless.
Opposites SPECIFIC; DEFINITE; CLEAR.

undemonstrative *adjective* unemotional, impassive, restrained, self-contained, reserved, uncommunicative, unresponsive, stiff, reticent, aloof, distant, remote, withdrawn, cool, cold, unaffectionate.

undeniable *adjective* indisputable, indubitable, unquestionable, beyond doubt/question, inarguable, incontrovertible, incontestable, irrefutable, unassailable, certain, sure, definite, positive, proven, clear, obvious, evident, manifest, patent.

under *preposition* **1** *under the tree* below, beneath, underneath, at the foot/bottom of. **2** *prices under £5 | numbers under 20* below, less than, lower than, smaller than. **3** *ranks under major* below, lower than, inferior to, subordinate to, junior to, secondary to, subservient to, reporting to, subject to, controlled by, at the mercy of, under the heel of. **4** *under repair* undergoing, receiving, in the process of. **5** *under water* submerged by, immersed in, sunk in, engulfed by, inundated by, flooded by, drowned by. **6** *it is under his mother's name* listed under, classified under, categorized under, placed under, positioned under, included under, subsumed under. **7** *living under threat* subject to, liable to, bound by.

under *adverb* **1** *if you cannot go over the bridge go under* below, beneath, underneath. **2** *his father kept him under* down, in an inferior position, in a subordinate position; *inf.* under someone's thumb. **3** *the swimmer went under* underwater, to the bottom, downward.

underclothes *plural noun* undergarments; underclothing, underwear, lingerie, underlinen; *inf.* underthings, undies, smalls, unmentionables.

undercover *adjective* **1** *an undercover operation | undercover behaviour* secret, hidden, concealed, masked, veiled, shrouded, private, confidential, covert, clandestine, underground, surreptitious, furtive, stealthy, sly, underhand; *inf.* hush-hush. **2** *undercover agents* spying, espionage.
Opposites OPEN; OVERT.

undercurrent *noun* **1** *boats affected by the undercurrent* undertow, underflow. **2** *an undercurrent of discontent in the firm* undertone, overtone, hint, suggestion, implication, whisper, murmur, atmosphere, aura, tenor, flavour; vibrations; *inf.* vibes.

undercut *verb* **1** *undercut their competitors* charge less than, undersell. **2** *undercut the ore*

vein cut out, cut away, gouge out, scoop out, hollow out, excavate. **3** *laws undercutting democracy* undermine, weaken, impair, damage, injure, sap, threaten, subvert, sabotage.

underdog *noun* weaker party, loser, victim, prey, scapegoat; *inf.* little fellow, fall guy, stooge.

underestimate *verb* **1** *underestimate the cost* miscalculate, misjudge, set too low. **2** *underestimate the opposition* underrate, rate too low, undervalue, set little store by, not do justice to, misprize, minimize, hold cheap, belittle, disparage, look down on, deprecate, depreciate; *inf.* sell short.

undergo *verb* *undergo surgery/hardship* go through, experience, sustain, be subjected to, submit to, endure, bear, tolerate, stand, withstand, put up with, weather.

underground *adverb* **1** *animals going underground* below ground, below the surface. **2** *criminals going underground* into secrecy, into seclusion, into hiding, behind closed doors.

underground *adjective* **1** *underground shelters* subterranean, subterrestrial, below-ground, buried, sunken, hypogean. **2** *an underground organization* secret, clandestine, surreptitious, covert, undercover, concealed, hidden. **3** *underground literature* unconventional, unorthodox, experimental, avant-garde, alternative, radical, revolutionary, subversive.

underground *noun* **1** *go round London by underground* metro, subway; *inf.* tube. **2** *the army executing members of the underground* resistance, opposition; partisans.

undergrowth *noun* underwood, thicket, brushwood, brush, scrub; *Am.* underbrush, underbush.

underhand *adjective* deceitful, devious, crafty, cunning, scheming, sneaky, furtive, secret, clandestine, surreptitious, covert, dishonest, dishonourable, unethical, immoral, unscrupulous, fraudulent, dirty, unfair, treacherous, double-dealing, below the belt, two-timing; *inf.* crooked.
Opposites HONEST; HONOURABLE; FAIR; ABOVE-BOARD.

underline *verb* **1** *underline the word* underscore, emphasize. **2** *underline the importance of seat belts* emphasize, stress, highlight, point up, accentuate, call attention to, give prominence to.
Opposites play down (*see* PLAY); MINIMIZE.

underling *noun* subordinate, deputy, junior, inferior, minion, lackey, flunky, menial, retainer, hireling, servant.
Opposites BOSS; LEADER.

underlying *adjective* **1** *underlying issues* basic, basal, fundamental, primary, prime, root, elementary, elemental. **2** *an underlying hostility amid all the friendliness* latent, lurking, concealed, hidden, veiled, masked.
Opposites SUBORDINATE; OVERT.

undermine *verb* **1** *undermine their authority* weaken, impair, damage, injure, sap, threaten, subvert, sabotage; *inf.* throw a spanner in the works of, queer the pitch of, foul up. **2** *undermine the foundations* tunnel under, dig under, burrow under, excavate. **3** *undermine the river banks* wear away, erode, eat away at.

underprivileged *adjective* disadvantaged, deprived, in need, needy, in want, destitute, in distress, poor, impoverished, impecunious, badly off.

underrate *verb* underestimate, undervalue, set little store by, rate too low, not do justice to, belittle, disparage; *inf.* sell short. *See* UNDERESTI-MATE.

undersized *adjective* undersize, underdeveloped, stunted, atrophied, dwarf, dwarfish, pygmy, runtish, short, small, little, tiny, minuscule, stubby, squat; *inf.* pint-sized, pocket-sized, knee-high to a grasshopper.

understand *verb* **1** *understand his meaning* | *understand what he says* comprehend, apprehend, grasp, see, take in, perceive, discern, make out, glean, recognize, appreciate, get to know, follow, fathom, get to the bottom of, penetrate, interpret; *inf.* get the hang/drift of, catch on, latch on to, tumble to, twig, figure out. **2** *I understand your feelings/position* appreciate, accept, commiserate with, feel compassionate towards, sympathize with, empathize with. **3** *I understand that he has left* gather, hear, be informed, learn, believe, think, conclude.
Opposites MISUNDERSTAND; be ignorant of (*see* IGNORANT); IGNORE.

understanding *noun* **1** *it depends on your understanding of his meaning* comprehension, apprehension, grasp, perception, discernment, appreciation, interpretation. *See* UNDERSTAND 1. **2** *his powers of understanding are limited* | *use your understanding* intelligence, intellect, mind, brainpower; brains, powers of reasoning; *inf.* grey matter. **3** *it is my understanding that he has gone* belief, perception, view, notion, idea, fancy, conclusion, feeling. **4** *treat the difficult problem with understanding* compassion, sympathy, empathy, insight. **5** *we have an understanding although not a signed contact* agreement, gentleman's agreement, arrangement, bargain, pact, compact, contract.
Opposites IGNORANCE; MISUNDERSTANDING; INDIFFERENCE.

understanding *adjective* an understanding boss to give him time off compassionate, sympathetic, sensitive, considerate, kind, thoughtful, tolerant, patient, forbearing, lenient, merciful, forgiving.

understate *verb* understate the difficulties downplay, play down, make light of, minimize, de-emphasize; *inf.* soft-pedal.

understudy *noun* substitute, replacement, reserve, stand-in, fill-in, locum, backup, relief.

undertake *verb* undertake the job/responsibility take on, set about, tackle, shoulder, assume, enter upon, begin, start, commence, embark on, venture upon, attempt, try.
Opposites NEGLECT; FORGO.

undertaker *noun* funeral director; *Am.* mortician.

undertone *noun* **1** *speak in an undertone* low tone/voice, murmur, whisper. **2** *undertones of unrest in their seemingly peaceful life* undercurrent, hint, suggestion, intimation, inkling, insinuation, trace, tinge, touch, atmosphere, aura, tenor, flavour.
Opposites SHOUT.

undervalue *verb* underestimate, underrate, set little store by, rate too low, think too little of, not do justice to, belittle, disparage; *inf.* sell short. *See* UNDERESTIMATE.

underwater *adjective* submarine, subaqueous, undersea, submerged, immersed.

underwear *noun* underclothes, undergarments; underclothing, lingerie, underlinen; *inf.* underthings, undies, smalls, unmentionables.

underworld *noun* **1** *police trying to arrest members of the underworld* | *the underworld revenged his death* criminal world, world of crime, organized crime; criminals, gangsters; *inf.* gangland, mob. **2** *Orpheus in the underworld* abode of the dead, nether/infernal regions, hell, Hades, Avernus.

underwrite *verb* **1** *underwrite the official document* sign, countersign, endorse, initial. **2** *underwrite the agreement* agree to, approve, sanction, confirm, ratify, validate; *inf.* okay, OK. **3** *underwrite the new project* fund, finance, back, support, sponsor, subsidize, contribute to, insure.

undesirable *adjective* **1** *the undesirable side-effects of the drug* unpleasant, disagreeable, nasty, unacceptable, unwanted, unwished-for. **2** *he's a most undesirable character* unpleasant, disagreeable, nasty, foul, objectionable, offensive, obnoxious, disliked, hateful, repugnant, repellent, distasteful, unsavoury.

undisciplined *adjective* **1** *undisciplined pupils* unruly, disorderly, disobedient, obstreperous, recalcitrant, refractory, uncontrolled, unrestrained, wild, wilful, wayward, capricious, unsteady, untrained, unschooled. **2** *undisciplined office methods* unsystematic, unmethodical, disorganized, unorganized, erratic, lax.

undisguised *adjective* undisguised envy open, obvious, evident, patent, manifest, transparent, overt, unconcealed, unhidden, unmistakable.

undisputed *adjective* uncontested, unchallenged, unquestioned, not in question, undoubted, not in doubt, certain, accepted, acknowledged, recognized, incontestable, unquestionable, indubitable, incontrovertible, irrefutable.

undistinguished *adjective* ordinary, common, plain, simple, commonplace, everyday, mediocre, run-of-the-mill, pedestrian, prosaic, unexceptional, indifferent, unimpressive, unremarkable, unnoticeable, inconspicuous; *inf.* nothing special, no big deal, no great shakes, nothing to write home about.

undo *verb* **1** *undo buttons/laces/bonds/locks* unfasten, unhook, unbutton, untie, unlace, unbind, unfetter, unshackle, loosen, loose, disentangle, release, free, open, unlock. **2** *undo the arrangement/agreement* cancel, annul, nullify, invalidate, revoke, repeal, rescind, reverse, set aside, wipe out. **3** *undo all his work/hopes* destroy, ruin, wreck, smash, shatter, annihilate, eradicate, obliterate, defeat, conquer, overthrow, overturn, topple, upset, quash, squelch, crush.

undoing noun **1** *the undoing of all his work/hopes* destruction, ruin, ruination, downfall, defeat, overthrow, collapse. *See* UNDO 3. **2** *his drunkenness was his undoing* fatal flaw, weakness, blight, misfortune, affliction, trouble, curse.

undone *adjective* *leave tasks undone* not done, unfinished, incomplete, unaccomplished, unperformed, unfulfilled, unattended to, omitted, neglected, passed over, disregarded, ignored, left, outstanding.

undoubted *adjective* undisputed, not in doubt, uncontested, unquestioned, not in question, certain, unquestionable, indubitable, incontrovertible, irrefutable. *See* UNDISPUTED.

undoubtedly *adverb* indubitably, doubtless, doubtlessly, beyond a doubt, unquestionably, beyond question, undeniably, positively, absolutely, certainly, with certainty, decidedly, definitely, assuredly, of course.

undress *verb* **1** *they undressed quickly* take off one's clothes, remove one's clothes, strip, disrobe; *inf.* peel off. **2** *undress her daughter* unclothe, take off clothes from, remove clothes from, strip.

undress *noun* *a state of undress* nakedness, nudity, *déshabillé*.

undue *adjective* unwarranted, unjustified, unreasonable, inappropriate, unsuitable, unseemly, unbecoming, improper, ill-advised, excessive, immoderate, disproportionate, inordinate, fulsome, superfluous, too much, too great, uncalled-for, unneeded, unnecessary, non-essential, unrequired.
Opposites DUE; APPROPRIATE; PROPER.

unduly *adverb* *not unduly worried* excessively, overly, over-much, disproportionately, out of all proportion, immoderately, inordinately, unnecessarily, unreasonably, unjustifiably.

undying *adjective* deathless, immortal, eternal, infinite, perpetual, unending, never-ending, never dying, unceasing, ceaseless, incessant, permanent, lasting, endurable, abiding, continuing, constant, unfading, undiminished, imperishable, indestructible, undestroyed, inextinguishable.
Opposites TRANSIENT; EPHEMERAL.

unearth *verb* **1** *dogs unearthing bones* dig up, excavate, exhume, disinter, unbury. **2** *unearth new evidence* uncover, discover, find, come across, hit upon, bring to light, reveal, expose, turn up, root up, dredge up, ferret out.
Opposites BURY; COVER.

unearthly *adjective* **1** *unearthly manifestations/ sounds/happenings* otherworldly, not of this world, supernatural, preternatural, ghostly, spectral, phantom, haunted, uncanny, eerie, strange; *Scots* eldritch; *inf.* spooky, creepy. **2** *come home at an unearthly hour* unreasonable, preposterous, abnormal, extraordinary, absurd, ridiculous; *inf.* ungodly, unholy.
Opposites NORMAL; ORDINARY; REASONABLE.

uneasy *adjective* **1** *feel uneasy about what was happening* ill at ease, troubled, worried, anxious, apprehensive, alarmed, disturbed, agitated, nervous, on edge, edgy, restive, restless, unsettled, discomposed, discomfited, perturbed, upset; *inf.* jittery, nervy. **2** *an uneasy peace* strained, constrained, tense, awkward, precarious, unstable, insecure. **3** *an uneasy suspicion that all was not well* worrying, alarming, dismaying, disturbing, perturbing, disquieting, unsettling, upsetting.
Opposites CALM; COMPOSED; TRANQUIL; STABLE.

uneconomic *adjective* *uneconomic industries | uneconomic to sell goods at that price* unprofitable, non-profit-making, non-paying, unremunerative, non-viable, loss-making.

unemotional *adjective* undemonstrative, passionless, cold, frigid, cool, reserved, restrained, self-controlled, unfeeling, unresponsive, unexcitable, unmoved, impassive, apathetic, indifferent, phlegmatic, detached.

unemployed *adjective* jobless, out of work, out of a job, workless, redundant, laid off, idle; *inf.* on the dole.

unending *adjective* endless, never-ending, interminable, perpetual, ceaseless, incessant, unceasing, non-stop, uninterrupted, continuous, continual, constant, unremitting, relentless.

unenviable *adjective* *an unenviable task* undesirable, unpleasant, disagreeable, nasty, painful, thankless.

unequal *adjective* **1** *unequal in size/talent/difficulty* different, differing, dissimilar, unlike, unalike, disparate, unidentical, varying, variable, not uniform, unmatched. **2** *unequal to the task* not up to, inadequate, insufficient, found wanting. **3** *the sides of the box are unequal* uneven, asymmetrical, unsymmetrical, unbalanced, lopsided, irregular, disproportionate, not matching. **4** *unequal contest* unfair, unjust, inequitable, uneven, one-sided, ill-matched.

unequalled *adjective* without equal, peerless, unmatched, unrivalled, unparalleled, without parallel, unsurpassed, incomparable, beyond compare, inimitable, perfect, supreme, paramount, second to none, nonpareil, unique.

unequivocal *adjective* *an unequivocal statement/ demand* unambiguous, clear, clear-cut, crystal-clear, unmistakable, plain, well-defined, explicit, unqualified, categorical, outright, downright, direct, straightforward, blunt, point-blank, straight from the shoulder, positive, certain, decisive.

unethical *adjective* immoral, unprincipled, unscrupulous, dishonourable, dishonest, disreputable, dirty, unfair, underhand, bad, wicked, evil, sinful, iniquitous, corrupt, depraved; *inf.* shady.

uneven *adjective* **1** *uneven surfaces* rough, bumpy, lumpy. **2** *his work is uneven* variable, varying, changeable, irregular, fluctuating, erratic, patchy. **3** *the sides of the box are uneven* unequal, asymmetrical, unsymmetrical, unbalanced, lopsided, irregular, disproportionate, not matching. **4** *an uneven contest* unequal, unfair, unjust, inequitable, one-sided, ill-matched.

843

uneventful · unguarded

uneventful *adjective* unexciting, uninteresting, monotonous, boring, dull, tedious, routine, unvaried, ordinary, run-of-the-mill, pedestrian, commonplace, everyday, unexceptional, unremarkable, unmemorable; *inf.* common or garden.

unexceptional *adjective* ordinary, usual, regular, normal, average, typical, common, everyday, run-of-the-mill, mediocre, pedestrian, unremarkable, undistinguished, unimpressive; *inf.* nothing special, nothing to write home about.

unexpected *adjective* unforeseen, unanticipated, unlooked-for, unpredicted, not bargained for, sudden, abrupt, surprising, startling, astonishing, out of the blue, chance, fortuitous.

unfair *adjective* **1** *an unfair judgement | receive unfair treatment* unjust, inequitable, partial, partisan, prejudiced, biased, one-sided, unequal, uneven, unbalanced. **2** *the punishment was unfair* undeserved, unmerited, uncalled-for, unreasonable, unjustifiable, unwarrantable, out of proportion, disproportionate, excessive, extreme, immoderate. **3** *unfair play* foul, unsporting, unsportsmanlike, dirty, below-the-belt, underhand, unscrupulous, dishonourable; *inf.* crooked.

unfaithful *adjective* **1** *unfaithful friends* disloyal, false, false-hearted, faithless, perfidious, treacherous, traitorous, untrustworthy, unreliable, undependable, insincere. **2** *unfaithful spouses* faithless, adulterous, fickle, untrue, inconstant; *inf.* cheating, two-timing.

unfamiliar *adjective* **1** *an unfamiliar face | this work is unfamiliar* unknown, new, strange, alien, unaccustomed, uncommon. **2** *I am unfamiliar with this method* unacquainted, unused to, unaccustomed, unconversant, unpractised, inexperienced, unskilled, uninformed, uninitiated.

unfashionable *adjective* out of fashion/date, old-fashioned, outmoded, *démodé*, outdated, dated, behind the times, *passé*, archaic, obsolete, antiquated.

unfasten *verb* undo, open, loose, detach, disconnect, untie, unwrap, unbind, unlace, unhitch, untether, unlock, unbolt.

unfavourable *adjective* **1** *an unfavourable report | unfavourable reviews* adverse, critical, hostile, inimical, unfriendly, negative, discouraging, poor, bad. **2** *unfavourable circumstances* disadvantageous, adverse, unfortunate, unhappy, detrimental. **3** *come at an unfavourable moment* inconvenient, inopportune, untimely, untoward.

unfeeling *adjective* *unfeeling people ignoring the poor* uncaring, unsympathetic, hard-hearted, hard, harsh, heartless, apathetic, cold, callous, cruel, pitiless, inhuman.

unfit *adjective* **1** *she is unfit for the task* unsuited, ill-suited, unsuitable, unqualified, ineligible, unequipped, unprepared, untrained, incapable, inadequate, incompetent, not up to, not equal to; *inf.* not cut out for. **2** *food unfit for human consumption* unsuitable, inappropriate, not good enough. **3** *unfit people taking up sport* out of condition, in poor condition/shape, out of kilter, flabby, unhealthy, debilitated, weak.

unflattering *adjective* **1** *unflattering remarks* uncomplimentary, critical, blunt, candid, honest, straight from the shoulder. **2** *an unflattering hat* unbecoming, unattractive, unsightly.

unfold *verb* **1** *unfold the map* open out, spread out, stretch out, flatten, straighten out, unfurl, unroll, unravel. **2** *unfold a tale of horror | unfold the events of the night* narrate, relate, recount, tell, reveal, make known, disclose, divulge, present. **3** *when our plans unfold* develop, evolve, grow, mature, bear fruit.

unforeseen *adjective* unpredicted, unexpected, unanticipated, unlooked-for, not bargained for, sudden, abrupt, surprising, startling, astonishing, out of the blue.

unforgettable *adjective* memorable, impressive, striking, outstanding, extraordinary, exceptional, remarkable.

unforgivable *adjective* inexcusable, unpardonable, unwarrantable, unjustifiable, indefensible, reprehensible, deplorable, despicable, contemptible, disgraceful, shameful.

unfortunate *adjective* **1** *unfortunate circumstance* adverse, disadvantageous, unfavourable, unlucky, untoward, unpromising, hostile, inimical, disastrous, calamitous. **2** *the unfortunate girl* unlucky, out of luck, luckless, ill-starred, star-crossed, hapless, wretched, miserable, unhappy, poor. **3** *an unfortunate remark* regrettable, deplorable, ill-advised, inappropriate, unsuitable, inapt, tactless. *See* UNHAPPY 4.

unfounded *adjective* *unfounded rumours* without basis/foundation, groundless, baseless, unsubstantiated, unproven, unsupported, uncorroborated, speculative, conjectural, spurious.

unfriendly *adjective* **1** *unfriendly neighbours/looks* unamicable, uncongenial, unsociable, inhospitable, unneighbourly, unkind, unsympathetic, aloof, cold, cool, distant, disagreeable, unpleasant, surly, sour, hostile, inimical, antagonistic, aggressive, quarrelsome. **2** *an unfriendly climate/atmosphere* unfavourable, disadvantageous, unpropitious, inauspicious, hostile, inimical, alien.

ungainly *adjective* awkward, clumsy, ungraceful, graceless, inelegant, gawky, gangling, maladroit, inept, bungling, bumbling, lumbering, uncoordinated, hulking, lubberly. *Opposites* GRACEFUL; ELEGANT.

ungodly *adjective* **1** *ungodly people/acts* godless, irreligious, impious, blasphemous, profane, immoral, sinful, wicked, iniquitous. **2** *come home at an ungodly hour* unreasonable, preposterous, outrageous, abnormal, extraordinary, absurd, ridiculous; *inf.* unholy, unearthly.

ungrateful *adjective* unthankful, unappreciative, impolite, uncivil, rude.

unguarded *adjective* **1** *an unguarded comment* careless, ill-advised, ill-considered, incautious, thoughtless, rash, foolhardy, indiscreet, imprudent, unwise, uncircumspect, undiplomatic. **2** *in an unguarded moment* off guard, unwary,

inattentive, unobservant, unmindful, unheeding, heedless, distracted, absent-minded.
3 *unguarded fortresses* undefended, unprotected, defenceless, vulnerable, open to attack.

unhappy *adjective* **1** *feeling unhappy* sad, miserable, sorrowful, dejected, despondent, disconsolate, broken-hearted, down, downcast, dispirited, crestfallen, depressed, melancholy, blue, gloomy, glum, mournful, woebegone, long-faced, joyless, cheerless. **2** *an unhappy girl* unfortunate, unlucky, luckless, hapless, ill-starred, ill-fated, star-crossed, wretched, miserable. **3** *unhappy circumstances* unfortunate, disadvantageous, unlucky, adverse, miserable, wretched. **4** *an unhappy choice of phrase* unfortunate, regrettable, inappropriate, unsuitable, inapt, tactless, untactful, ill-advised, injudicious, awkward, clumsy.

unhealthy *adjective* **1** *unhealthy children* in poor health, unwell, ill, ailing, sick, sickly, poorly, indisposed, unsound, weak, feeble, frail, delicate, debilitated, infirm. **2** *an unhealthy diet/climate* unwholesome, unnourishing, detrimental, injurious, damaging, deleterious, noxious, insalubrious. **3** *show an unhealthy interest in death* unwholesome, morbid, undesirable.

unheard-of *adjective* **1** *unheard-of authors* unknown, little-known, undiscovered, obscure, nameless, unsung. **2** *unheard-of levels of radiation* unprecedented, unexampled, exceptional, extraordinary, out of the ordinary, uncommon, unusual, unparalleled, unrivalled, unmatched, unequalled, singular, unique, unbelievable, inconceivable.
Opposites FAMOUS; COMMON.

unheeded *adjective* disregarded, ignored, neglected, overlooked, unobserved, unnoted.

unhinged *adjective* unbalanced, deranged, demented, out of one's mind, crazed, mad, insane; *inf.* crazy.
Opposites SANE; STABLE.

unholy *adjective* **1** *unholy people/acts* ungodly, godless, irreligious, impious, blasphemous, profane, immoral, sinful, wicked, iniquitous. **2** *an unholy row* unreasonable, preposterous, outrageous, appalling, shocking, dreadful; *inf.* ungodly.

unhoped-for *adjective* unexpected, unanticipated, unlooked-for, undreamed of, beyond one's wildest dreams, like a dream come true.

unhurried *adjective* leisurely, leisured, easy, slow, slow-moving, slow-going, slow and steady, deliberate, sedate, lingering, loitering.

unidentified *adjective* *an unidentified donor/spot* nameless, unnamed, unknown, anonymous, incognito, obscure, unmarked, undesignated, unclassified.

unification *noun* union, junction, merger, fusion, alliance, amalgamation, coalition, combination, consolidation, confederation.

uniform *adjective* **1** *a uniform temperature* constant, consistent, invariable, unvarying, unvaried, unchanging, undeviating, stable, regular, even, equal, equable. **2** *all of uniform length* same, alike, like, selfsame, identical, similar, equal.

Opposites CHANGEABLE; VARIABLE; VARIED; DIFFERENT.

uniform *noun* livery, regalia, habit, suit, dress, costume, garb; regimentals.

uniformity *noun* **1** *the uniformity of the temperature is important* constancy, consistency, lack of variation/change, stability, regularity, evenness, equality, equability. **2** *uniformity of length of all the garments* sameness, likeness, identicalness, similarity, equalness, equality. **3** *tired of the uniformity of the days* sameness, monotony, tedium, dullness, drabness.

unify *verb* unite, bring together, merge, fuse, amalgamate, coalesce, combine, blend, mix, bind, link up, consolidate.
Opposites SEPARATE; SPLIT; SEVER.

unimaginable *adjective* unthinkable, inconceivable, incredible, unbelievable, unheard-of, unthought-of, implausible, improbable, unlikely, impossible, undreamed of, fantastic, beyond one's wildest dreams; *inf.* mind-boggling, mind-blowing.

unimaginative *adjective* *an unimaginative description* unoriginal, uninspired, uncreative, commonplace, pedestrian, mundane, matter-of-fact, ordinary, usual, routine, humdrum, prosaic, stale, hackneyed, derived, dull, monotonous, lifeless, vapid, insipid, bland, dry; *inf.* common or garden.

unimportant *adjective* of little/no importance, insignificant, of little/no consequence, inconsequential, of no account/moment, non-essential, immaterial, irrelevant, not worth mentioning, not worth speaking of, minor, slight, trifling, trivial, petty, paltry, insubstantial, inferior, worthless, nugatory; *inf.* small-fry, no great shakes; *Am. inf.* dinky.

uninhabited *adjective* *uninhabited houses/places* vacant, empty, unoccupied, untenanted, unpopulated, unpeopled, unsettled, abandoned, deserted, forsaken, unfrequented, barren, desert, desolate.

uninhibited *adjective* **1** *her sister is completely uninhibited* unreserved, unrepressed, unconstrained, unselfconscious, spontaneous, free and easy, relaxed, informal, open, candid, outspoken. **2** *uninhibited behaviour* unrestrained, unrestricted, unrepressed, unconstrained, uncontrolled, uncurbed, unchecked, unbridled.

unintelligible *adjective* **1** *unintelligible ramblings* incomprehensible, meaningless, unfathomable, incoherent, indistinct, inarticulate, confused, muddled, jumbled. **2** *unintelligible handwriting* illegible, indecipherable.

unintentional *adjective* unintended, accidental, inadvertent, unplanned, unpremeditated, uncalculated, chance, fortuitous, unconscious, involuntary, unwitting, unthinking.

uninterested *adjective* **1** *uninterested in other people's problems* indifferent, unconcerned, uninvolved, apathetic, blasé, unresponsive, impassive, dispassionate, aloof, detached, distant. **2** *uninterested in the lecture* bored, incurious.

uninteresting *adjective* unexciting, dull, unentertaining, boring, tiresome, wearisome, tedious, dreary, flat, monotonous, humdrum, uneventful, commonplace, dry, pedestrian, prosaic, hackneyed, stale.

uninterrupted *adjective* unbroken, undisturbed, continuous, continual, constant, steady, sustained, non-stop, unending, endless, ceaseless, unceasing, incessant, interminable, unremitting.

uninviting *adjective* unappealing, untempting, undesirable, unattractive, unappetizing, unpleasant, disagreeable, distasteful, unpalatable, repellent, revolting, repugnant, sickening, nauseating, offensive; *inf.* off-putting.

union *noun* **1** *the union of three firms into one* joining, junction, merging, merger, fusion, amalgamating, amalgamation, blend, mixture, coalition, combining, combination, consolidation, confederation. **2** *the union is made up of several organizations* association, alliance, league, coalition, consortium, syndicate, guild, confederation, federation, confederacy. **3** *the union of the man and the woman* marriage, wedding; coupling, intercourse, coition, coitus, copulation. **4** *we are all in union about the plans* agreement, accord, concurrence, unity, unison, unanimity, harmony, concord.
Opposites SEPARATION; PARTING; DIVORCE; DISAGREEMENT.

unique *adjective* **1** *a unique specimen* only, one and only, single, sole, lone, solitary, *sui generis,* exclusive, in a class by itself. **2** *a unique opportunity/beauty* unequalled, without equal, unparalleled, unexampled, unmatched, matchless, peerless, unsurpassed, unexcelled, incomparable, beyond compare, inimitable, second to none.
Opposites COMMON; ORDINARY; USUAL.

unison *noun the committee was in unison* agreement, accord, harmony, concord.

unit *noun* **1** *the family regarded as a unit* entity, whole. **2** *the course is divided into units* component, part, section, element, constituent, subdivision, portion, segment, module, item, member. **3** *a unit of length* measurement, measure, quantity. *See tables.*

unite *verb* **1** *unite the two parties/firms* join, link, connect, combine, amalgamate, fuse, weld. **2** *unite the two substances* combine, mix, commix, admix, blend, mingle, homogenize. **3** *unite this man and this woman* marry, wed, join in wedlock, tie the knot between; *inf.* splice. **4** *they united to fight the common enemy* join together, join forces, combine, amalgamate, band/club together, ally, cooperate, work/act/pull together, work side by side, pool resources.
Opposites SEPARATE; SPLIT; DIVORCE.

united *adjective* **1** *a united force/effort* combined, amalgamated, allied, cooperative, concerted, collective, pooled. *See* UNITE 4. **2** *united in their opinion of the plan* in agreement, agreed, in unison, of the same opinion/mind, of like mind, like-minded, at one, in accord, unanimous.

United Nations *noun. See table.*

unity *noun* **1** *detract from the unity of the painting* oneness, singleness, wholeness, entity,

integrity. **2** *their strength lies in their unity* union, unification, amalgamation, coalition, alliance, cooperation, undividedness. **3** *strive for political unity* | *live in unity* agreement, harmony, accord, concord, concurrence, unanimity, consensus, concert, togetherness, solidarity.
Opposites DIVISION; DISCORD; disunity.

universal *adjective* general, all-embracing, all-inclusive, comprehensive, across the board, worldwide, global, widespread, common, predominant, preponderate, omnipresent, ubiquitous, catholic.
Opposites PARTICULAR; RESTRICTED; LOCAL.

universally *adverb* without exception, in all instances/cases, everywhere, comprehensively, uniformly, invariably.

universe *noun* **1** *the wonders of the universe* cosmos, totality, whole world, Creation. **2** *the achievements of the universe* mankind, humankind, human race, humanity, people, society.

unjust *adjective* **1** *an unjust verdict* unfair, inequitable, prejudiced, biased, partisan, partial, one-sided. **2** *an unjust accusation* unfair, wrongful, wrong, undue, undeserved, unmerited, unwarranted, uncalled-for, unreasonable, unjustifiable.

unjustifiable *adjective* **1** *unjustifiable behaviour* indefensible, inexcusable, unforgivable, unpardonable, uncalled-for, blameworthy, culpable, unwarrantable. **2** *unjustifiable fears/accusations* groundless, unfounded, without foundation, baseless, without basis, unsupported, unsubstantiated, unreasonable.

unkempt *adjective* *unkempt hair/people* untidy, dishevelled, disordered, disarranged, tousled, rumpled, windblown, uncombed, ungroomed, messy, messed up, scruffy, slovenly; *inf.* sloppy; *Am. inf.* mussed up.
Opposites TIDY; NEAT; TRIM.

unkind *adjective* **1** *unkind people/remarks* unkindly, unfriendly, unamiable, uncharitable, unchristian, inhospitable, ungenerous, nasty, mean, cruel, vicious, spiteful, malicious, malevolent, harsh, pitiless, ruthless, unsympathetic, unfeeling, hard-hearted, heartless, cold-hearted. **2** *an unkind climate* inclement, harsh, intemperate.

unknown *adjective* **1** *the results of the test are as yet unknown* untold, unrevealed, undisclosed, undivulged, undetermined, undecided, unestablished, unsettled, unascertained, in the balance, up in the air. **2** *the donor is unknown* unidentified, unnamed, nameless, anonymous, incognito. **3** *unknown territory* unfamiliar, unexplored, uncharted, untravelled, undiscovered. **4** *unknown poets* unheard-of, little-known, obscure, undistinguished, unrenowned, unsung.

unlawful *adjective* against the law, illegal, illicit, illegitimate, criminal, felonious, actionable, prohibited, banned, outlawed, proscribed, unauthorized, unsanctioned, unwarranted, unlicensed.

unlike *adjective* unalike, dissimilar, different, distinct, disparate, contrastive, contrasted,

GENERAL UNITS

acre	degree	hour	minute	quart
air mile	denier	hundred-	nail	quarter
are	em	weight	nautical	quartern
barleycorn	en	inch	mile	quintal
barrel	fathom	kilderkin	noggin	rod
bushel	firkin	kilometre	ounce	rood
butt	foot	kip	peck	scruple
cable	furlong	knot	perch	span
carat	gallon	last	pica	stone
cental	gill	lea	pint	tog
centiare	grain	league	pipe	ton
chain	hank	link	point	tonne
cord	hogshead	litre	pole	troy ounce
cup	Hoppus foot	mile	pound	yard
day	horsepower	minim	puncheon	year

SI UNITS

Unit	Symbol	Physical Quantity	Unit	Symbol	Physical Quantity
ampere	A	electric current	hertz	Hz	frequency
candela	cd	luminous intensity	joule	J	energy
kelvin	K	thermodynamic	lumen	lm	luminous flux
		temperature	lux	lx	illuminance
kilogram	kg	mass	newton	N	force
metre	m	length	ohm	Ω	electric resistance
mole	mol	amount of	pascal	Pa	pressure
		substance	siemens	S	electric
radian	rad	plane angle			conductance
second	s	time	sievert	Sv	dose equivalent
steradian	sr	solid angle	tesla	T	magnetic flux
Derived Units					density
becquerel	Bq	activity	volt	V	electric potential
coulomb	C	electric charge			difference
farad	F	electric capacitance	watt	W	power
gray	Gy	absorbed dose	weber	Wb	magnetic flux
henry	H	inductance			

SCIENTIFIC AND TECHNICAL UNITS

ampere	coulomb	gauss	line	phon
amu	curie	gilbert	lumen	phot
angstrom	cusec	grade	Mach	poise
astronomical	cycle	gram/	number	poundal
unit	dalton	gramme	magneton	rad
atmosphere	daraf	gram-atomic	maxwell	radian
atomic mass	darcy	weight	megaton	roentgen/
unit	decibel	gram-	metre	röntgen
baud	degree-day	molecular	mho	rutherford
becquerel	dioptre	weight	micrometre	sabin
bel	dyne	gray	micron	siemens
bit	electron-	henry	mil	sievert
Board of Trade	volt	hertz	millibar	slug
Unit	epoch	jansky	millimicron	steradian
British thermal	erg	joule	mole	stilb
unit	farad	kelvin	morgan	stokes
byte	faraday	kilocycle	neper	tesla
calorie	fathom	kilogram/	nit	therm
candela	fermi	kilogramme	oersted	torr
candle	fresnel	kiloton	ohm	var
centner	gal	kilowatt-	okta/octa	volt
chronon	gallon	hour	parsec	weber
circular mil	gamma	light year	pascal	x-unit

contrary, diverse, divergent, incompatible, ill-matched, incongruous; *inf.* like chalk and cheese.

unlike *preposition* not like, not typical of, differently from.

unlikely *adjective* **1** *an unlikely chance of success* improbable, doubtful, dubious, faint, slight, remote. **2** *it is unlikely that he will win* not likely, improbable, unexpected. **3** *an unlikely excuse* improbable, implausible, questionable, unconvincing, incredible, unbelievable, inconceivable, unimaginable.

unlimited *adjective* **1** *unlimited freedom | unlimited room for manoeuvre* unrestricted, unconstrained, uncontrolled, unrestrained, unchecked, unhindered, unhampered, unimpeded, unfettered, untrammelled. **2** *unlimited power* unrestricted, absolute, total, unqualified, unconditional. **3** *unlimited supplies of money* limitless, illimitable, boundless, unbounded, immense, vast, great, extensive, immeasurable, incalculable, untold, infinite, endless.

unload *verb* *unload the horse/lorry* unburden, unlade, empty, unpack.

unlock *verb* unbolt, unlatch, unbar, undo, unfasten.

unlooked-for *adjective* unforeseen, unexpected, unanticipated, not bargained for, unhoped for, undreamed of, unpredicted, sudden, abrupt, surprise, surprising, startling, astonishing, out of the blue.

unloved *adjective* unbeloved, uncared-for, uncherished, unwanted, unpopular, forsaken, rejected, jilted, disliked, hated, detested, loathed.

unlucky *adjective* **1** *an unlucky young man* luckless, out of luck, down on one's luck, unfortunate, hapless, ill-fated, ill-starred, star-crossed, wretched, miserable. **2** *an unlucky attempt* unsuccessful, failed, ill-fated. **3** *an unlucky set of circumstances* adverse, disadvantageous, unfavourable, unfortunate, untoward, unpromising, inauspicious, unpropitious, doomed, ill-fated, ill-omened.

unmanageable *adjective* **1** *an unmanageable load* unwieldy, unmanoeuvrable, awkward, inconvenient, cumbersome, bulky, incommodious. **2** *unmanageable children* unruly, disorderly, uncontrollable, ungovernable, out of hand, wild, difficult, refractory, recalcitrant, intractable, obstreperous, wayward, incorrigible, contumacious; *inf.* stroppy.

unmanly *adjective* **1** *an unmanly way of walking* effeminate, womanish; *inf.* sissy. **2** *too unmanly to fight* timid, timorous, fearful, cowardly, craven, pusillanimous; *inf.* yellow.

unmannerly *adjective* ill-mannered, mannerless, impolite, uncivil, discourteous, disrespectful, rude, ill-bred, uncouth.

unmarried *adjective* single, unwed, unwedded, spouseless, partnerless, divorced, unattached, bachelor, celibate; husbandless, wifeless.

unmistakable *adjective* *the unmistakable noise of a train* clear, plain, obvious, evident, manifest, apparent, patent, palpable, distinct, distinctive, conspicuous, well-defined, pronounced, striking, glaring, blatant, undoubted, indisputable, indubitable, beyond a doubt, unquestionable, beyond question.

unmitigated *adjective* *an unmitigated disaster* absolute, unqualified, unconditional, categorical, complete, total, thorough, thoroughgoing, downright, utter, out and out, veritable, perfect, consummate.

unmoved *adjective* **1** *unmoved furniture* in place, in position, unchanged. **2** *unmoved from their purpose* firm, steadfast, unshaken, staunch, unwavering, unswerving, undeviating, determined, resolute, decided, resolved. **3** *unmoved by the sad sight* unaffected, untouched, unstirred, unconcerned, uncaring, indifferent, impassive, unfeeling, impervious.

unnatural *adjective* **1** *his face turned an unnatural colour* unusual, uncommon, extraordinary, strange, queer, odd, bizarre, preternatural. **2** *unnatural mothers* inhuman, heartless, uncaring, unconcerned, unfeeling, soulless, cold, hard, hard-hearted, callous, cruel, brutal, merciless, pitiless, remorseless, evil, wicked. **3** *an unnatural laugh | unnatural behaviour* affected, artificial, feigned, false, self-conscious, contrived, forced, laboured, studied, strained, insincere, theatrical, stagy, mannered.

unnecessary *adjective* **1** *it is unnecessary to come early* needless, inessential. **2** *unnecessary expense/supplies* needless, unneeded, inessential, non-essential, uncalled-for, unrequired, gratuitous, useless, dispensable, expendable, redundant, superfluous.

unnerve *verb* unman, discourage, dishearten, dispirit, deject, demoralize, daunt, alarm, frighten, dismay, disconcert, discompose, perturb, upset, throw off balance, unsettle, disquiet, fluster, agitate, shake; *inf.* rattle. **Opposites** ENCOURAGE; HEARTEN; EMBOLDEN.

unobtrusive *adjective* **1** *an unobtrusive person* self-effacing, retiring, unassuming, modest, quiet, meek, humble, unaggressive, unassertive, low-profile. **2** *unobtrusive decorations/colours* low-key, restrained, subdued, quiet, unostentatious, unshowy, inconspicuous, unnoticeable.

SECRETARY-GENERALS OF THE UNITED NATIONS			
Name	**Dates**	**Nationality**	**In Office**
Trygve Halvdan Lie	(1896–1968)	Norwegian	1946–52
Dag Hammarskjöld	(1905–61)	Swedish	1953–61
U Thant	(1909–74)	Burmese	1962–71
Kurt Waldheim	(b. 1918)	Austrian	1972–81
Javiar Pérez de Cuéllar	(b. 1920)	Peruvian	1982–91
Boutros Boutros-Ghali	(b. 1922)	Egyptian	from 1992

unoccupied *adjective* **1** *unoccupied houses* vacant, empty, uninhabited, untenanted, tenantless. **2** *unoccupied territory* uninhabited, unpopulated, unpeopled, depopulated, deserted, forsaken, desolate, God-forsaken. **3** *he is unoccupied just now* not busy, at leisure, idle, inactive, unemployed.

unofficial *adjective* **1** *an unofficial meeting* informal, casual, unauthorized, unsanctioned, unaccredited, wildcat. **2** *an unofficial rumour* unconfirmed, unauthenticated, uncorroborated, unsubstantiated.

unorthodox *adjective* **1** *unorthodox beliefs* heterodox, uncanonical, heretical, nonconformist. **2** *unorthodox methods* unconventional, unusual, uncommon, uncustomary, unwonted, out of the ordinary, nonconformist, unconforming, irregular, abnormal, divergent, aberrant, anomalous.

unpalatable *adjective unpalatable food/suggestions* unsavoury, unappetizing, uneatable, inedible, undelectable, nasty, disgusting, repugnant, revolting, nauseating, sickening, distasteful, disagreeable, unpleasant, offensive, obnoxious, unattractive, repulsive, repellent.

unparalleled *adjective* without parallel, unequalled, without equal, matchless, unmatched, peerless, unrivalled, unprecedented, unsurpassed, unexcelled, incomparable, beyond compare, singular, unique. **Opposites** ORDINARY; RUN-OF-THE-MILL.

unperturbed *adjective* calm, composed, cool, collected, serene, tranquil, self-possessed, placid, unruffled, unflustered, unexcited, undismayed, untroubled, unworried; *inf.* laid-back.

unpleasant *adjective* **1** *an unpleasant taste* disagreeable, unpalatable, unsavoury, unappetizing, disgusting, repugnant, revolting, nauseating, sickening. **2** *an unpleasant smell* disagreeable, offensive, obnoxious, foul, smelly, stinking. **3** *unpleasant person/personality* disagreeable, unlikable, unlovable, unattractive, nasty, ill-natured, cross, bad-tempered. **4** *an unpleasant task* disagreeable, irksome, troublesome, annoying, irritating, vexatious.

unpopular *adjective* disliked, unliked, unloved, friendless, unwanted, unwelcome, avoided, ignored, rejected, shunned, out in the cold, cold-shouldered, unattractive, undesirable, out of favour, not in the swim; *inf.* sent to Coventry.

unprecedented *adjective* unparalleled, unequalled, unmatched, unheard-of, extraordinary, uncommon, out of the ordinary, unusual, exceptional, abnormal, singular, anomalous, atypical, remarkable, novel, original, unique; *inf.* one of a kind. **Opposites** USUAL; NORMAL; RUN-OF-THE-MILL.

unpredictable *adjective* **1** *unpredictable results* unforeseeable, undivinable, doubtful, dubious, uncertain, unsure, in the balance, up in the air; *inf.* iffy. **2** *unpredictable people/behaviour* erratic, fickle, capricious, whimsical, mercurial, volatile, unstable, undependable, unreliable.

unpremeditated *adjective* unplanned, unarranged, unprepared, unintentional, extempore, impromptu, ad lib, spontaneous, spur of the moment, on the spot, impulsive, hasty; *inf.* off the cuff.

unpretentious *adjective* **1** *an unpretentious house/lifestyle* simple, plain, modest, ordinary, humble, unostentatious, unshowy, unimposing, homely. **2** *an unpretentious person* unassuming, modest, unaffected, natural, straightforward, honest.

unprincipled *adjective* immoral, amoral, unethical, dishonourable, dishonest, unprofessional, deceitful, devious, unscrupulous, corrupt, crooked, bad, wicked, evil, villainous.

unproductive *adjective* **1** *an unproductive exercise* fruitless, futile, vain, idle, useless, worthless, valueless, ineffective, ineffectual, inefficacious, unprofitable, unremunerative, unrewarding. **2** *unproductive soil* barren, sterile.

unprofessional *adjective* **1** *unprofessional methods/conduct* unethical, unprincipled, improper, unseemly, indecorous, lax, negligent. **2** *unprofessional workers* amateur, amateurish, unskilled, inexpert, untrained, unqualified, inexperienced, incompetent.

unpromising *adjective unpromising prospects* unfavourable, adverse, unpropitious, inauspicious, gloomy, black, discouraging, portentous, ominous.

unqualified *adjective* **1** *unqualified teachers* uncertificated, unlicensed, untrained. **2** *unqualified to do the job | unqualified to comment* ineligible, unfit, incompetent, incapable, unequipped, unprepared, not equal/up to, not cut out. **3** *unqualified approval* unconditional, unreserved, without reservations, categorical, unequivocal, positive, unmitigated, complete, absolute, thorough, thoroughgoing, total, utter, outright, out and out, perfect, consummate.

unquestionable *adjective his honesty is unquestionable* beyond question/doubt, indubitable, undoubted, indisputable, undeniable, irrefutable, uncontestable, incontrovertible, certain, sure, definite, positive, conclusive, self-evident, obvious.

unravel *verb* **1** *unravel knots* untangle, disentangle, straighten out, separate out, unknot, undo. **2** *unravel the problem* solve, resolve, work out, clear up, puzzle out, get to the bottom of, fathom; *inf.* figure out. **Opposites** ENTANGLE; TANGLE; COMPLICATE.

unreal *adjective unreal characters/situation* imaginary, make-believe, fictitious, mythical, fanciful, fantastic, fabulous, hypothetical, non-existent, illusory, chimerical, phantasmagoric.

unrealistic *adjective* **1** *an unrealistic plan* impractical, impracticable, unworkable, unreasonable, irrational, illogical, improbable, foolish, wild, absurd, quixotic; *inf.* half-baked. **2** *an unrealistic model* unreal-looking, unlifelike, non-naturalistic.

unreasonable *adjective* **1** *unreasonable demands* excessive, immoderate, undue, inordinate, outrageous, extravagant, preposterous, unconscionable. **2** *unreasonable prices* exorbitant, extortionate, expensive; *inf.* steep. **3** *unreasonable people* irrational, illogical, opinionated, biased, prejudiced, blinkered, obstinate, obdurate, wilful, headstrong, temperamental, capricious. **4** *unreasonable behaviour* unacceptable, preposterous, outrageous, ludicrous, absurd, irrational, illogical.

unrefined *adjective* **1** *unrefined flour* crude, raw, unpurified, unprocessed, untreated. **2** *unrefined guests/manners* uncultured, uncultivated, unsophisticated, inelegant, ungraceful, boorish, loutish, coarse, vulgar, rude, uncouth.

unrelenting *adjective* **1** *unrelenting demands/ rain* relentless, unremitting, continuous, continual, constant, incessant, unceasing, nonstop, endless, unending, perpetual, unabating. **2** *unrelenting judge* relentless, merciless, pitiless, unforgiving, unsparing, ruthless, implacable, inexorable, inflexible, rigid, hard, strict, harsh, stern.
Opposites INTERMITTENT; LENIENT.

unreliable *adjective* **1** *unreliable friends* undependable, irresponsible, untrustworthy, erratic, fickle, inconstant. **2** *unreliable evidence* suspect, questionable, open to question/doubt, doubtful, unsound, implausible, unconvincing, fallible, specious.

unrepentant *adjective* impenitent, unrepenting, unremorseful, shameless, unregenerate, abandoned.

unreserved *adjective* **1** *unreserved seats* unbooked, unhired, unchartered. **2** *unreserved young women* uninhibited, extrovert, outgoing, unrestrained, demonstrative, bold, communicative, outspoken, frank, open. **3** *unreserved approval* without reservations, unqualified, unconditional, categorical, unequivocal, positive, unmitigated, absolute, complete, thorough, thoroughgoing, wholehearted, total, utter, outright, out and out, perfect, consummate.

unresolved *adjective* undecided, to be decided, unsettled, undetermined, pending, unsolved, unanswered, debatable, open to debate/question, doubtful, in doubt, moot, up in the air; *inf.* iffy.

unrest *noun* *industrial unrest* dissatisfaction, discontent, discontentment, unease, disquiet, dissension, dissent, discord, strife, protest, rebellion, agitation, turmoil, turbulence.
Opposites PEACE; CALM.

unrestricted *adjective* *unrestricted access* unlimited, open, free, unhindered, unchecked, unbounded; *inf.* free for all, with no holds barred.

unrivalled *adjective* unparalleled, unequalled, without equal, matchless, unmatched, peerless, unsurpassed, unexcelled, incomparable, beyond compare, singular, unique.

unruly *adjective* disorderly, unmanageable, uncontrollable, rowdy, wild, irrepressible, obstreperous, refractory, recalcitrant, intractable, contumacious, disobedient, rebellious, mutinous, insubordinate, defiant, way-

ward, wilful, headstrong.
Opposites ORDERLY; OBEDIENT; DOCILE.

unsaid *adjective* unspoken, unvoiced, unpronounced, unuttered, unstated, unmentioned, untold, untalked-of, tacit, suppressed, unrevealed.

unsavoury *adjective* **1** *unsavoury food/smell* unpalatable, unappetizing, unpleasant, disagreeable, disgusting, loathsome, repugnant, revolting, nauseating, sickening. **2** *unsavoury characters* unpleasant, disagreeable, nasty, objectionable, offensive, obnoxious, repellent, repulsive, disreputable, degenerate, coarse, gross, vulgar, boorish, churlish, rude, uncouth.

unscrupulous *adjective* unprincipled, unethical, amoral, immoral, conscienceless, shameless, corrupt, dishonest, dishonourable, deceitful, devious, exploitative, wrongdoing, bad, evil, wicked; *inf.* crooked.
Opposites ETHICAL; HONEST.

unseat *verb* **1** *unseat the MP/king* depose, oust, remove from office, dislodge, discharge, dethrone; *inf.* drum out. **2** *the horse unseated the rider* throw, dismount, unsaddle, unhorse.

unseemly *adjective* unbecoming, unfitting, unbefitting, indecorous, improper, unsuitable, inappropriate, undignified, unrefined, indelicate, tasteless, in poor taste, coarse, crass.

unselfish *adjective* altruistic, self-sacrificing, selfless, kind, self-denying, open-handed, generous, liberal, unsparing, ungrudging, unstinting, charitable, philanthropic.

unsettle *verb* **1** *the move unsettled the children* upset, disturb, discompose, throw off balance, confuse, perturb, discomfit, disconcert, trouble, bother, agitate, ruffle, shake; *inf.* rattle. **2** *unsettle the smooth workings of the firm* throw into confusion/disorder, disorder, disorganize, disarrange, derange.

unsettled *adjective* **1** *the children are unsettled* restless, restive, fidgety, flustered, agitated, ruffled, uneasy, anxious, edgy, on edge, tense, troubled, perturbed, shaken; *inf.* thrown, rattled. **2** *the weather is unsettled* changeable, changing, variable, inconstant, erratic, undependable, unreliable, uncertain, unpredictable. **3** *several issues are still unsettled* undecided, to be decided, unresolved, undetermined, pending, open to debate/question, doubtful, in doubt, moot, up in the air; *inf.* iffy. **4** *unsettled accounts* unpaid, payable, outstanding, owing, due, in arrears. **5** *unsettled territories* uninhabited, unpopulated, unpeopled, unoccupied.

unshakable *adjective* firm, steadfast, resolute, staunch, constant, unswerving, unwavering, unfaltering.

unsightly *adjective* ugly, unattractive, unprepossessing, hideous, horrible, repulsive, revolting, offensive, distasteful.
Opposites ATTRACTIVE; BEAUTIFUL.

unskilled *adjective* untrained, unqualified, inexpert, inexperienced, amateurish, unprofessional.

unsociable *adjective* unfriendly, unamiable, unaffable, uncongenial, unneighbourly, inhospitable, reclusive, solitary, misanthropic, uncommunicative, unforthcoming, reticent, withdrawn, aloof, distant, remote, standoffish, cold, cool, chilly.

unsolicited *adjective* unsought, unasked-for, unrequested, undemanded, uncalled-for, unrequired, uninvited, unwelcome, gratuitous, volunteered, voluntary, spontaneous.

unsophisticated *adjective* **1** *unsophisticated country girls* unworldly, naive, simple, innocent, inexperienced, childlike, artless, guileless, ingenuous, natural, unaffected, unpretentious, unrefined, unpolished, gauche, provincial. **2** *unsophisticated tools* crude, unrefined, basic, rudimentary, primitive, undeveloped, homespun. **3** *unsophisticated methods*| *unsophisticated approach to the problem* simple, straightforward, uncomplicated, uninvolved, unspecialized.

unsound *adjective* **1** *in unsound health* unhealthy, unwell, ailing, delicate, weak, frail. **2** *of unsound mind* disordered, diseased, deranged, demented, unbalanced, unhinged. **3** *unsound furniture* defective, disintegrating, broken, broken-down, rotten, rickety, flimsy, shaky, wobbly, tottery, insubstantial, unsafe, unreliable, dangerous. **4** *unsound reasoning* flawed, defective, faulty, ill-founded, weak, shaky, unreliable, illogical, unfounded, ungrounded, untenable, specious, spurious, false, fallacious, erroneous.

unspeakable *adjective* **1** *unspeakable joy* beyond words, inexpressible, unutterable, indescribable, undefinable, beggaring description, ineffable, unimaginable, inconceivable, unthinkable, unheard-of, overwhelming, marvellous, wonderful. **2** *an unspeakable scoundrel/crime* indescribable, indescribably bad/wicked/evil, unmentionable, appalling, shocking, horrible, frightful, terrible, dreadful, abominable, deplorable, despicable, contemptible, repellent, loathsome, odious, monstrous, heinous, execrable.

unspoilt *adjective* **1** *unspoilt countryside* preserved, intact, as good as new/before, perfect, unblemished, unimpaired, undamaged, untouched, unaffected, unchanged. **2** *unspoilt young girls*|*unspoilt despite her success* innocent, wholesome, natural, simple, artless, unaffected, pure, uncorrupted, undefiled, unblemished.

unspoken *adjective* **1** *unspoken criticism* unexpressed, unstated, undeclared, not spelt out, tacit, implicit, implied, understood, taken for granted. **2** *unspoken plea for mercy* mute, silent, wordless, unuttered.

unstable *adjective* **1** *unstable chairs* unsteady, infirm, rickety, shaky, wobbly, tottery, unsafe, unreliable, insecure, precarious. **2** *unstable people likely to kill* unbalanced, unhinged, irrational, deranged, mentally ill, crazed, insane, mad. **3** *emotionally unstable* unbalanced, volatile, moody, mercurial, capricious, giddy, erratic, unpredictable. **4** *unstable prices* changeable, variable, unsettled, fluctuating, inconstant, unpredictable.

unstudied *adjective* *unstudied grace* natural, unaffected, unpretentious, without airs, artless, guileless, informal, casual, spontaneous, impromptu.
Opposites STUDIED; AFFECTED; PRETENTIOUS.

unsubstantial *adjective* **1** *unsubstantial furniture* insubstantial, flimsy, fragile, frail, slight, puny, inadequate, insufficient; *inf.* jerry-built. **2** *unsubstantial arguments/evidence* insubstantial, flimsy, tenuous, weak, lame, poor, unsound, faulty, ungrounded, groundless, unfounded, baseless, unsupported. **3** *unsubstantial figures* insubstantial, imaginary, unreal, impalpable, incorporeal, illusory, chimerical, hallucinatory, phantom, ghostly.

unsubstantiated *adjective* unconfirmed, uncorroborated, unproven, not validated, unestablished, questionable, open to question, disputable.

unsuccessful *adjective* **1** *an unsuccessful attempt* without success, failed, vain, unavailing, futile, useless, worthless, abortive, nugatory, ineffective, ineffectual, inefficacious, fruitless, unproductive, unprofitable, baulked, frustrated, thwarted, foiled. **2** *an unsuccessful businessman* failed, losing, unprosperous, unlucky, luckless, out of luck, unfortunate, ill-starred, ill-fated.

unsuitable *adjective* inappropriate, inapt, inapposite, unfitting, unbefitting, incompatible, incongruous, out of place/keeping, ineligible, unacceptable, unbecoming, unseemly, indecorous, improper.

unsung *adjective* unacclaimed, unapplauded, uncelebrated, unhonoured, unpraised, unlauded, unhailed, unacknowledged, unrecognized, unrenowned, neglected, disregarded, unknown, anonymous, nameless.
Opposites FAMOUS; CELEBRATED.

unsure *adjective* **1** *he was a bit unsure at first*| *unsure of himself* lacking self-confidence, unselfconfident, not confident, not self-assured, lacking assurance, insecure, hesitant, diffident. **2** *unsure what to do* undecided, irresolute, in two minds, in a dilemma/quandary, ambivalent. **3** *unsure about his motive* uncertain, unconvinced, dubious, doubtful, sceptical, distrustful, suspicious.

unsuspecting *adjective* unsuspicious, unwary, off guard, trusting, trustful, overtrustful, gullible, credulous, ingenuous, naive, innocent, dupable, exploitable.
Opposites SUSPICIOUS; WARY.

unsympathetic *adjective* **1** *unsympathetic parents* unsympathizing, unkind, uncompassionate, compassionless, unpitying, pitiless, uncommiserating, uncaring, unfeeling, insensitive, unconcerned, indifferent, unresponsive, apathetic, unmoved, untouched, heartless, cold, hard-hearted, stony-hearted, hard, harsh, callous, cruel. **2** *unsympathetic to his cause* disapproving of, opposed to, against, anti.

untangle *verb* **1** *untangle the knotted wool* disentangle, unravel, unsnarl, straighten out. **2** *untangle the complications* straighten out, sort out, clear up.

untenable *adjective* indefensible, undefendable, insupportable, unmaintainable, unsustainable, refutable, unsound, weak, flawed, defective, faulty, implausible, specious, groundless, unfounded, baseless, unacceptable, unadmissible.

unthinkable *adjective* **1** *it is unthinkable that the territory is unexplored* inconceivable, unimaginable, unbelievable, beyond belief, impossible, beyond the bounds of possibility, implausible. **2** *it is unthinkable that he should represent us* not to be considered, out of the question, absurd, preposterous, outrageous; *inf.* not on.
Opposites IMAGINABLE; PLAUSIBLE; CONCEIVABLE.

unthinking *adjective* **1** *hurt by an unthinking remark* thoughtless, inconsiderate, tactless, undiplomatic, injudicious, indiscreet, insensitive, blundering, careless, rude. **2** *an unthinking kick of the ball* inadvertent, unintentional, unintended, mechanical, automatic, instinctive, involuntary.

untidy *adjective* **1** *untidy children* dishevelled, unkempt, bedraggled, rumpled, messy, slovenly, slatternly; *inf.* mussed up, sloppy. **2** *untidy desks/rooms* disordered, disorderly, disarranged, disorganized, chaotic, confused, muddled, jumbled, topsy-turvy, at sixes and sevens; *inf.* higgledy-piggledy, like a dog's breakfast, every which way.

untie *verb* undo, loose, unbind, unfasten, unwrap, unlace, untether, unhitch, unknot.

untimely *adjective* **1** *an untimely visit* ill-timed, mistimed, inconvenient, inopportune, inappropriate, inapt, awkward, unsuitable, infelicitous. **2** *his untimely death* premature, early.

untiring *adjective* tireless, indefatigable, unfailing, unfaltering, unwavering, unflagging, unremitting, constant, incessant, unceasing, dogged, determined, resolute, steady, persistent, staunch.

untold *adjective* **1** *her untold story | untold secrets* unrecounted, unrelated, unnarrated, unreported, unmentioned, unstated, unspoken, unrevealed, undisclosed, undivulged, unpublished, secret. **2** *the untold horrors of the war | untold joy* unspeakable, indescribable, inexpressible, unutterable, ineffable, unimaginable, inconceivable. **3** *untold millions/damage* countless, innumerable, myriad, incalculable, immeasurable, measureless.

untoward *adjective* **1** *untoward developments delayed us* unfortunate, inconvenient, inopportune, untimely, awkward, annoying, troublesome, vexatious. **2** *do their best in untoward circumstances* unfortunate, unlucky, adverse, disadvantageous, inauspicious, unpropitious, hostile, inimical. **3** *see nothing untoward in his reaction* unusual, uncommon, abnormal, atypical, out of the way, out of place. **4** *find nothing untoward in his behaviour at the party | the teacher's treatment of the child was untoward* unsuitable, inappropriate, unbefitting, unseemly, improper, indecorous.
Opposites TIMELY; ADVANTAGEOUS; USUAL; APPROPRIATE.

untroubled *adjective* unperturbed, undisturbed, unworried, unruffled, unagitated, unbothered, unconcerned, calm, cool, collected, composed, serene.

untrue *adjective* **1** *untrue stories/accounts* false, fallacious, fictitious, fabricated, erroneous, in error, wrong, incorrect, inaccurate, economical with the truth, inexact, flawed, unsound, distorted, misleading. **2** *untrue friends* disloyal, faithless, unfaithful, false, treacherous, perfidious, deceitful, untrustworthy, double-dealing, insincere, unreliable, inconstant. **3** *his aim was untrue* inaccurate, wide of the mark, wide, off, out of true.

untrustworthy *adjective* treacherous, not to be trusted, two-faced, double-dealing, duplicitous, deceitful, dishonest, dishonourable, unreliable, undependable; *inf.* slippery.

untruth *noun* **1** *a story full of untruth* lying, falsehood, falsity, fiction, mendacity, fabrication, inaccuracy; lies. **2** *tell an untruth* lie, falsehood, piece of fiction, fabrication, fib, white lie; *inf.* whopper, terminological inexactitude.

untruthful *adjective* **1** *an untruthful account* false, fictitious, fabricated, fallacious, erroneous, wrong, economical with the truth, inaccurate, inexact, flawed, unsound. **2** *an untruthful person* lying, mendacious, dishonest, deceitful.

unusual *adjective* **1** *unusual behaviour/reactions* uncommon, out of the ordinary, atypical, abnormal, rare, singular, odd, strange, curious, queer, bizarre, surprising, unexpected, different, unconventional, uncustomary, unwonted, unorthodox, irregular; *inf.* weird. **2** *an unusual talent* extraordinary, exceptional, singular, rare, remarkable, outstanding.

unutterable *adjective* **1** *unutterable joy* unspeakable, inexpressible, indescribable, beyond words/description, ineffable, unimaginable, inconceivable, overwhelming. *See* UNSPEAKABLE 1. **2** *unutterable cad* indescribable, indescribably bad, appalling, shocking, frightful, dreadful, deplorable. *See* UNSPEAKABLE 2.

unveil *verb* *unveil the facts | unveiled their plans* uncover, reveal, lay open/bare, expose, bring to light, disclose, divulge, make known/public.

unwarranted *adjective* **1** *an unwarranted entry into the palace | unwarranted market traders* unauthorized, uncertified, unaccredited, unlicensed, unsanctioned, unapproved. **2** *unwarranted behaviour | an unwarranted intrusion into our affairs* unjustifiable, unjustified, indefensible, inexcusable, unforgivable, unpardonable, uncalled-for, gratuitous.

unwelcome *adjective* **1** *unwelcome visitors* unwanted, undesired, uninvited, unpopular. **2** *unwelcome news | the unwelcome truth* unpleasant, disagreeable, unpalatable, displeasing, distasteful, undesirable.

unwell *adjective* ill, sick, sickly, ailing, in poor health, unhealthy, off-colour, run-down, below par; *inf.* out of sorts, poorly, under the weather.

unwieldy *adjective* cumbersome, unmanageable, unmanoeuvrable, awkward, clumsy, massive, hefty, bulky, ponderous; *inf.* hulking.
Opposites MANAGEABLE; GRACEFUL; DAINTY.

unwilling *adjective* **1** *an unwilling guest | their unwilling presence* reluctant, disinclined, unenthusiastic, grudging, involuntary, forced. **2** *unwilling to go* reluctant, disinclined, averse, loth, opposed, not in the mood.

unwind *verb* **1** *unwind the balls of wool | unwind the roll of bandage* undo, unravel, uncoil, unroll, untwine, untwist, disentangle. **2** *unwind by watching television* wind down, relax, calm down, slow down; *inf.* loosen up, let oneself go, take it easy, let one's hair down.

unwise *adjective* imprudent, injudicious, inadvisable, ill-considered, ill-judged, ill-advised, impolitic, indiscreet, short-sighted, irresponsible, foolhardy, rash, reckless, foolish, silly, unintelligent, mindless.

unwitting *adjective* **1** *an unwitting offender* unknowing, unconscious, unaware, ignorant. **2** *an unwitting slight* unintentional, unintended, inadvertent, unmeant, unplanned, accidental, chance.
Opposites CONSCIOUS; DELIBERATE.

unwonted *adjective* unusual, uncommon, uncustomary, out of the ordinary, exceptional, atypical, abnormal, irregular, anomalous.
Opposites USUAL; CUSTOMARY; HABITUAL.

unworldly *adjective* **1** *unworldly considerations* spiritual, spiritualistic, non-material, religious. **2** *too unworldly to cope on her own* naive, inexperienced, green, raw, uninitiated, unsophisticated, gullible, ingenuous, trusting, credulous, idealistic. **3** *unworldly beings* otherworldly, unearthly, extraterrestrial, ethereal, ghostly, spectral, phantom, preternatural, supernatural.

unworthy *adjective* **1** *conduct unworthy of a teacher | unworthy conduct* unsuitable in, inappropriate in, unbefitting, unfitting, unseemly in, improper in, incompatible with, incongruous in, inconsistent with, out of keeping with, out of character, out of place in, degrading, discreditable. **2** *he is unworthy of her | she is unworthy of the honour conferred on her* not worthy, not good enough for, undeserving, ineligible for, unqualified for. **3** *an unworthy cause* worthless, inferior, second-rate, undeserving, ignoble, disreputable; *inf.* lousy, crappy. **4** *an unworthy wretch* disreputable, dishonourable, base, contemptible, reprehensible.

upbraid *verb* scold, rebuke, reproach, reprove, chide, reprimand, berate, remonstrate with, castigate, criticize, censure.

upbringing *noun* bringing up, rearing, raising, nurture, care, tending, training.

upgrade *verb* **1** *upgrade the facilities/building* improve, better, ameliorate, reform, enhance, touch up, rehabilitate, refurbish. **2** *upgrade the teacher | upgrade him to a higher position* promote, advance, elevate, raise.
Opposites DOWNGRADE; DEMOTE.

upheaval *noun* disruption, disturbance, revolution, disorder, confusion, turmoil, chaos, cataclysm.

uphill *adjective* **1** *an uphill path* upward, ascending, climbing, mounting, rising. **2** *an uphill job* arduous, difficult, laborious, strenuous, hard, tough, burdensome, onerous, tax-

ing, punishing, gruelling, exhausting, wearisome, Herculean, Sisyphean.

uphold *verb* **1** *uphold the committee's decision | uphold his right to refuse* confirm, endorse, support, back up, stand by, champion, defend. **2** *uphold the old traditions* maintain, sustain, hold to, keep.
Opposites OPPOSE; DISCARD.

upkeep *noun* **1** *pay for the upkeep of the house* maintenance, running, preservation, conservation; repairs. **2** *pay for the child's upkeep* keep, maintenance, support, subsistence, sustenance. **3** *the upkeep is deducted from his salary* outlay, running/operating costs, costs, overheads, expenses.

uplift *verb* **1** *uplift the load* raise, upraise, lift, hoist up, heave up, elevate. **2** *uplift his spirits* raise, improve, edify, inspire.

upper *adjective* **1** *the upper shelf/storey* higher, further up, loftier. **2** *the upper ranks* superior, higher-ranking, elevated, greater.
Opposites LOWER; INFERIOR.

upper-class *adjective* aristocratic, noble, highborn, patrician, blue-blooded; *inf.* top-drawer.

upper hand *noun* advantage, edge, whip hand, ascendancy, superiority, supremacy, sway, control, mastery, dominance, command.

uppermost *adjective* **1** *the uppermost shelf/floor* highest, furthest up, loftiest, top, topmost. **2** *the uppermost consideration | uppermost in our minds* foremost, greatest, predominant, dominant, principal, chief, main, paramount, major.

uppish *adjective* conceited, arrogant, overweening, self-important, self-assertive, presumptuous, supercilious, snobbish, disdainful, hoity-toity; *inf.* uppity, high and mighty, stuck-up, toffee-nosed.

upright *adjective* **1** *upright posts* erect, on end, vertical, perpendicular, standing up, rampant. **2** *upright members of the community* honest, honourable, upstanding, decent, respectable, worthy, reputable, good, virtuous, righteous, law-abiding, ethical, moral, high-principled, of principle, high-minded.
Opposites HORIZONTAL; DISHONOURABLE; CROOKED.

uprising *noun* rising, rebellion, revolt, insurrection, insurgence, mutiny, riot, revolution, coup, coup d'état, overthrow, putsch; fighting in the streets.

uproar *noun* **1** *the place was in uproar* tumult, turmoil, turbulence, disorder, confusion, commotion, mayhem, pandemonium, bedlam; din, noise, clamour, hubbub, racket. **2** *there was an uproar when he was dismissed* outburst, row, rumpus, brouhaha, hullabaloo, affray, furore, fracas, brawl, scuffle, conflict, struggle, free-for-all; howls of protest; *inf.* ruckus.

uproarious *adjective* **1** *an uproarious party* noisy, loud, rowdy, disorderly, unruly, boisterous, wild, unrestrained, rollicking. **2** *an uproarious show* hilarious, hysterically/riotously funny, side-splitting; *inf.* killingly funny, killing, too funny for words, too much, rip-roaring, rib-tickling.
Opposites QUIET; BORING; SOLEMN.

upset *verb* **1** *upset the bucket/boat* overturn, knock over, push over, upend, tip over, topple, capsize. **2** *upset the old lady* perturb, disturb, discompose, unsettle, disconcert, dismay, disquiet, trouble, worry, bother, agitate, fluster, ruffle, shake, frighten, alarm, anger, annoy, distress, hurt, grieve. **3** *upset the smooth running of the firm* disturb, throw into disorder/confusion, disorganize, disarrange, mess up, mix up, jumble, turn topsy-turvy. **4** *upset Napoleon's army* defeat, beat, conquer, vanquish, rout, overthrow, overcome, triumph over, be victorious over, get the better of, worst, thrash, trounce.

upset *noun* **1** *cause a great deal of upset | emotional upset* perturbation, discomposure, dismay, disquiet, trouble, worry, bother, agitation, fluster, alarm, distress, hurt. *See* UPSET *verb* 2. **2** *cause upset to the running of the firm | an upset of our plans* disturbance, disorder, confusion, disorganization, disarrangement. *See* UPSET *verb* 3. **3** *a stomach upset* disorder, disturbance, complaint, ailment, illness, sickness, disease, malady; *inf.* bug. **4** *the upset of the army* defeat, conquering, rout, overthrow, worsting. *See* UPSET *verb* 4.

upset *adjective* **1** *the upset bucket* overturned, upturned, up-ended, toppled, capsized, upside down. **2** *the old lady was upset by the attack/news* perturbed, disturbed, discomposed, unsettled, disconcerted, dismayed, disquieted, troubled, worried, bothered, anxious, agitated, flustered, ruffled, shaken, frightened, alarmed, angered, annoyed, distressed, hurt, saddened, grieved. **3** *an upset stomach | feeling upset in the boat* disordered, disturbed, queasy, ill, sick; *inf.* gippy. **4** *our upset plans* disturbed, disordered, in disorder, confused, in confusion, disarranged, in disarray, jumbled up, messed up, chaotic, in chaos, topsy-turvy; *inf.* at sixes and sevens, higgledy-piggledy.
Opposites CALM; COMPOSED; UNPERTURBED; ORDERLY.

upshot *noun* result, outcome, conclusion, issue, end, end result, denouement, effect, repercussion, reaction; *inf.* pay-off.
Opposites ORIGIN.

upside down *adjective* **1** *the bucket was upside down* upturned, up-ended, bottom up, wrong side up, inverted. **2** *the house is upside down | our plans are upside down* in disorder, in disarray, jumbled up, in a muddle, messed up, chaotic, in chaos, topsy-turvy; *inf.* at sixes and sevens, higgledy-piggledy.

upstanding *adjective* **1** *ask the congregation to be upstanding* in a standing position, on one's feet, erect, vertical. **2** *a fine upstanding young man* healthy, hale and hearty, strong, sturdy, robust, vigorous, hardy, stalwart, well-made, well-built. **3** *upstanding members of the community* upright, honest, honourable, decent, worthy, respectable, good, virtuous, righteous, law-abiding. *See* UPRIGHT 2.

upstart *noun* parvenu, parvenue, would-be, social climber, status seeker, nouveau riche, arriviste.

up-to-date *adjective* *up-to-date clothes | she's so up to date* modern, current, prevalent, prevailing, present-day, recent, up-to-the-minute, fashion-able, in fashion, in vogue, voguish; *inf.* all the rage, in the swim, trendy, with it, now.
Opposites OUT OF DATE; OUTDATED; OLD-FASHIONED.

upturn *noun* **1** *an upturn in sales* upswing, increase, rise, upsurge, boost, acceleration, escalation; *inf.* step-up. **2** *an upturn in the economy* upswing, improvement, advancement, betterment, recovery, revival.

upward *adjective* *the upward slope/trend* rising, climbing, mounting, ascending, on the rise.
Opposites DOWNWARD.

upward, upwards *adverb* **1** *going upward* up, uphill, to the top, straight up. **2** *prices spiralling upward* towards a higher level/standing.
upwards of *upwards of 100 miles* more than, above, over, beyond.

urban *adjective* city, cityish, citified, inner-city, town, townish, metropolitan, municipal, civic, oppidan.

urbane *adjective* suave, debonair, sophisticated, smooth, worldly, elegant, cultivated, cultured, civilized, polished, refined, gracious, charming, agreeable, affable, courtly, civil, polite, courteous, well-mannered, mannerly.
Opposites UNCOUTH; UNSOPHISTICATED; BOORISH.

urbanity *noun* suaveness, sophistication, smoothness, worldliness, cultivation, culture, polish, refinement, graciousness, charm, affability, courtliness, civility, politeness, mannerliness.

urchin *noun* ragamuffin, gamin, guttersnipe, waif, stray, imp, rogue, brat.

urge *verb* **1** *urge the horses on | urge the children up the hill* push, drive, propel, impel, force, hasten, hurry, speed up. **2** *urge the contestants to greater effort* spur, incite, stir up, stimulate, prod, goad, egg on, encourage, prompt; *inf.* psych up. **3** *urged him to go | "Go," he urged* entreat, exhort, implore, appeal, beg, beseech, plead. **4** *urge caution upon them* advise, counsel, advocate, recommend, suggest, support, endorse, back, champion.
Opposites DISSUADE; DETER; DISCOURAGE.

urge *noun* *a sudden urge to travel | sexual urge* desire, need, compulsion, longing, yearning, wish, fancy, impulse, itch; *inf.* yen.

urgency *noun* **1** *a matter of urgency* imperativeness, exigency, top priority, importance, necessity, seriousness, gravity, extremity, hurry, haste. **2** *the urgency in her voice* importunateness, insistence, clamorousness, earnestness, pleading, begging.

urgent *adjective* **1** *it is urgent that we operate* imperative, vital, crucial, critical, essential, exigent, top-priority, high-priority, important, necessary. **2** *urgent matters* vital, crucial, exigent, top-priority, high-priority, important, pressing, serious, grave. **3** *an urgent whisper/demand* importunate, insistent, clamorous, earnest, pleading, begging.
Opposites UNIMPORTANT; TRIVIAL; CASUAL.

urinate *verb* pass water, micturate; *inf.* spend a penny, pee, wee-wee, wee, have a tinkle/slash/leak.

usable *adjective for use*, to be used, utilizable, available, ready/fit for use, in working order, functional.

usage *noun* **1** *damaged by rough usage* use, treatment, handling, management, running, operation, manipulation, manoeuvring. **2** *old usages now forgotten* custom, practice, habit, way, procedure, method, mode, form, tradition, convention. **3** *study English usage* manner of speaking/writing, mode of expression, phraseology, phrasing, idiom, idiolect.

use *verb* **1** *use tools* make use of, utilize, employ, work, operate, wield, ply, manoeuvre, manipulate, avail oneself of, put to use, put into service. **2** *use tact* employ, exercise, apply. **3** *use him roughly* treat, handle, deal with, act/behave towards. **4** *he just uses people for his own ends* make use of, exploit, manipulate, take advantage of, impose upon, abuse; *inf.* walk all over, play for a sucker. **5** *have you used any eggs?* | *we have used up all the food* consume, get through, exhaust, deplete, expend, spend, waste, fritter away. **used to** accustomed to, familiar with, at home with, in the habit of, given to, prone to, wont to, habituated to, addicted to, inured to.

use *noun* **1** *for external use* usage, application, utilization, employment, operation, manipulation, manoeuvring. **2** *fall to pieces from use* using, usage, wear, wear and tear. **3** *he has the use of the garden* right, privilege, prerogative, usufruct. **4** *his use of other people for his own ends* exploitation, manipulation. *See* USE *verb* 4. **5** *what use is this to you?* usefulness, good, advantage, benefit, service, help, gain, profit, avail. **6** *established by long use* usage, practice, custom, habit, wont. **7** *we have no use for this machine* need, necessity, call, demand, purpose, reason.

used *adjective used car/clothing* second-hand, nearly new, cast-off; *inf.* hand-me-down.
Opposites NEW; PRISTINE.

useful *adjective* **1** *a useful tool* of use, functional, utilitarian, of service, practical, convenient. **2** *a useful experience* beneficial, advantageous, of help, helpful, worthwhile, profitable, rewarding, productive, valuable. **3** *he's a useful player* effective, efficacious, effectual, competent, capable, able.
Opposites USELESS; DISADVANTAGEOUS; INEFFECTIVE.

useless *adjective* **1** *a useless attempt* | *useless meetings* vain, in vain, to no avail/purpose, unavailing, unsuccessful, futile, purposeless, ineffectual, inefficacious, fruitless, unprofitable, unproductive, abortive. **2** *he's a useless player/salesman* worthless, ineffective, ineffectual, incompetent, incapable, inadequate; *inf.*

no good.
Opposites USEFUL; BENEFICIAL; EFFECTIVE.

usher *noun* escort, guide, attendant.

usher *verb* **1** *usher the people to their seats* escort, show, conduct, direct, guide, lead. **2** *usher in new methods* herald, precede, pave the way for, give notice of, announce, introduce, bring in, get going, get under way, launch.

usual *adjective* **1** *his usual route* habitual, customary, accustomed, wonted, normal, regular, routine, everyday, established, set, familiar. **2** *not usual behaviour* common, typical, ordinary, average, run-of-the-mill, expected, standard, stock, regular.
Opposites UNUSUAL; UNCOMMON; EXTRAORDINARY.

usually *adverb usually he works late* generally, as a rule, normally, by and large, in the main, mainly, mostly, for the most part, on the whole.

usurp *verb usurp the throne/position* take over, seize, expropriate, take possession of, appropriate, commandeer, lay claim to, assume.

utilitarian *adjective* practical, functional, useful, to the purpose.

utility *noun* use, usefulness, service, serviceableness, advantageousness, benefit, helpfulness, profitability, convenience, practicality, practicability, effectiveness, efficacy.

utilize *verb* use, put to use, make use of, employ, avail oneself of, have recourse to, resort to, take advantage of, turn to account.

utmost *adjective* **1** *have the utmost confidence in them* maximum, supreme, paramount, greatest, highest, most. **2** *the utmost ends of the earth* uttermost, furthest, farthest, remotest, outermost, extreme, ultimate.

utmost *noun to the utmost* maximum, most, uttermost, top, pinnacle, peak, best, finest.

utter *adjective an utter cad* | *feel utter happiness* absolute, complete, total, thorough, thoroughgoing, positive, downright, out and out, sheer, unmitigated, categorical, unqualified, unconditional, perfect, consummate.

utter *verb* **1** *utter a sound* emit, let out, give. **2** *utter threats* voice, say, speak, pronounce, express, put into words, enunciate, articulate, verbalize, vocalize.

utterance *noun* **1** *give utterance to his thoughts* voice, expression, articulation, enunciation, verbalization, vocalization. **2** *his prophetic utterances* remark, word, comment, statement, opinion.

utterly *adverb utterly delightful* absolutely, completely, totally, entirely, thoroughly, positively, extremely, categorically, perfectly, consummately, to the core.

vacancy *noun* **1** *the vacancy of the place* emptiness, voidness. **2** *a vacancy in the firm* opening, position, post, job, opportunity, slot. **3** *no vacancies in the hotel* unoccupied room, room. **4** *the vacancy of his expression* blankness, lack of expression, expressionlessness, lack of emotion/interest, emotionlessness, vacuousness. **5** *his vacancy is unbelievable* lack of thought/ intelligence, brainlessness, denseness, thickness, vacuousness, vacuity, inaneness, inanity, stupidity.

vacant *adjective* **1** *a vacant space* empty, void, without contents. **2** *a vacant position* unoccupied, unfilled, free, empty, available. **3** *a vacant seat* empty, unoccupied, free, unengaged, not in use, unused, available; *inf.* up for grabs. **4** *a vacant house* empty, unoccupied, uninhabited, untenanted, tenantless, to let, abandoned, deserted. **5** *how to spend his vacant time* free, leisure, idle, unemployed. **6** *a vacant expression/countenance* blank, expressionless, inexpressive, deadpan, poker-faced, emotionless, uninterested, vacuous, inane. **7** *he seems to be completely vacant* without thought, unintelligent, brainless, dense, dull-witted, thick, vacuous, inane, stupid.
Opposites FULL; OCCUPIED; EXPRESSIVE.

vacate *verb* *vacate the house/post* leave, quit, depart from, evacuate, abandon, desert.
Opposites OCCUPY; INHABIT.

vacation *noun* **1** *take a vacation* holiday, break, recess, furlough, rest, respite; leave, time off. **2** *the vacation of the post* quitting, departure, evacuation. See VACATE.

vacillate *verb* shilly-shally, waver, dither, be irresolute/indecisive, hesitate, equivocate, hem and haw, keep changing one's mind, beat about the bush; *inf.* blow hot and cold.

vacuous *adjective* **1** *a vacuous expression* vacant, blank, expressionless, deadpan, inane. See VACANT 6. **2** *he seems to be completely vacuous* unintelligent, brainless, vacant, inane, stupid. See VACANT 7.

vacuum *noun* **1** *create a vacuum* emptiness, void, empty, space, nothingness, vacuity. **2** *a vacuum in his life* gap, empty space, lacuna, vacuity, hollowness, need, want. **3** *plug in the vacuum* vacuum cleaner; Hoover™.

vagabond *noun* *vagabonds living rough* wanderer, itinerant, nomad, wayfarer, traveller, rover, tramp, vagrant, derelict, beachcomber, down-and-out, beggar, person of no fixed address, knight of the road, bird of passage, rolling stone; *Am.* hobo; *Am. inf.* bum.

vagabond *adjective* *a vagabond existence* wandering, nomadic, itinerant, peripatetic, travelling, journeying, roving, roaming, vagrant, drifting, unsettled, transient, footloose.

vagary *noun* caprice, whim, whimsy, fancy, notion, crotchet.

vagrancy *noun* nomadism, peripateticism, itineracy, vagabondism, wandering, roving, roaming, drifting, homelessness.

vagrant *noun* *vagrants sleeping rough* tramp, beggar, person of no fixed address, itinerant, nomad, wanderer, vagabond; *Am.* hobo; *Am. inf.* bum. See VAGABOND *noun*.

vagrant *adjective* *a vagrant existence* tramplike, itinerant, nomadic, peripatetic, wandering, roving, vagabond, homeless. See VAGABOND *adjective*.

vague *adjective* **1** *a vague shape* indistinct, indeterminate, ill-defined, unclear, nebulous, amorphous, shadowy, hazy, dim, fuzzy, foggy, blurry, bleary, out of focus. **2** *a vague description* imprecise, inexact, unexplicit, nonspecific, loose, generalized, ambiguous, equivocal, hazy, woolly. **3** *have only a vague idea of what is involved* imprecise, ill-defined, hazy, nebulous. **4** *she is rather vague about her plans* uncertain, unsure, hesitant, wavering, shilly-shallying; *inf.* blowing hot and cold. **5** *her plans are rather vague* uncertain, undecided, indefinite, indeterminate, doubtful, open, speculative, conjectural; *inf.* up in the air. **6** *she is rather vague* absent-minded, abstracted, dreamy, vacuous; *inf.* with one's head in the clouds.
Opposites DISTINCT; PRECISE; CLEAR; CERTAIN.

vaguely *adverb* **1** *she looks vaguely familiar* in a general way, in a way, somehow, slightly, obscurely. **2** *point vaguely in her direction* approximately, roughly, imprecisely. **3** *smiling vaguely* absent-mindedly, abstractedly, vacantly, vacuously.

vain *adjective* **1** *vain people* conceited, self-loving, narcissistic, self-admiring, peacockish, egotistical, proud, haughty, arrogant, boastful, swaggering, imperious, overweening, cocky, affected; *lit.* vainglorious; *inf.* stuck-up, big-headed, swollen-headed. **2** *vain triumphs* futile, worthless, insignificant, pointless, meaningless, nugatory, valueless, meritless, empty, hollow, insubstantial, idle, vapid. **3** *vain attempts* unsuccessful, futile, useless, unavailing, to no avail, ineffective, inefficacious, fruitless, unproductive, abortive, unprofitable, profitless. **in vain 1** *try in vain to save him* unsuccessfully, without success, to no avail/purpose, ineffectually, with no result, fruitlessly. **2** *his efforts were in vain* unsuccessful, unavailing, to no avail/purpose, ineffectual.
Opposites MODEST; SIGNIFICANT; SUCCESSFUL.

valedictory *adjective* farewell, parting, final.

valiant *adjective* brave, courageous, valorous, heroic, stout-hearted, lion-hearted, gallant,

manly, intrepid, fearless, undaunted, undismayed, bold, daring, audacious, staunch, stalwart, indomitable, resolute, determined.
Opposites COWARDLY; TIMOROUS.

valid *adjective* **1** *valid reasons/objections* sound, well-founded, well-grounded, substantial, reasonable, logical, justifiable, defensible, vindicable, authentic, bona fide, effective, cogent, powerful, convincing, credible, forceful, weighty. **2** *the ruling is still valid* lawful, legal, licit, legitimate, legally binding, binding, contractual, in force, in effect, effective.
Opposites INVALID; NULL; VOID; ILLEGAL.

validate *verb* **1** *validate the contract | validate his appointment* ratify, legalize, legitimize, authorize, sanction, warrant, license, approve, endorse, set one's seal to. **2** *validate a statement* verify, prove, authenticate, substantiate, confirm, corroborate, justify.
Opposites INVALIDATE; REVOKE; DISPROVE.

valley *noun* dale, dell, hollow, coomb, vale, depression; *Scots* glen, strath.

valour *noun* bravery, courage, heroism, stout-heartedness, gallantry, manliness, intrepidity, fearlessness, boldness, daring, staunchness, fortitude.

valuable *adjective* **1** *a valuable watch* costly, high-priced, expensive, priceless, precious. **2** *a valuable contribution/lesson* useful, helpful, beneficial, advantageous, worthwhile, worthy, important.
Opposites WORTHLESS; CHEAP; USELESS.

valuables *plural noun* treasures, costly articles.

value *noun* **1** *place a value on the ring* monetary value, face value, price, market price, cost. **2** *the value of a healthy diet | his advice is of great value* worth, merit, usefulness, advantage, benefit, gain, profit, good, avail, importance, significance.

value *verb* **1** *value the watch | value his worth to the firm* set a price on, price, evaluate, assess, appraise. **2** *we value his contribution greatly* rate highly, appreciate, esteem, hold in high regard, think highly of, set store by, respect, admire, prize, cherish, treasure.

valued *adjective* *a valued contribution/friendship* esteemed, highly regarded, respected, prized, cherished, treasured.

values *plural noun* *moral values* code of behaviour; principles, ethics, morals, standards.

vamp[1] *verb* *vamp up old property* renovate, restore, rehabilitate, recondition, refashion, repair, mend, patch up.

vamp[2] *verb* *girls trying to vamp older men* seduce, tempt, lure, beguile, flirt with, make up to.

vamp[3] *noun* *vamps seducing men in bars* seductress, siren, temptress, loose woman, adventuress.

van[1] *noun* *drive a van* lorry, truck, pantechnicon, camper.

van[2] *noun* *in the van of the new fashion* vanguard, forefront, front, front line, leading position.
See VANGUARD.
Opposites REAR; END; TAIL.

vanguard *noun* advance guard, forefront, front, front line, front rank, leading position, van; leaders, spearheads, trail-blazers, trend-setters.

vanish *verb* **1** *she vanished in the mist* disappear, be lost to sight/view, be/become invisible, evaporate, dissipate, disperse, fade, fade away, evanesce, melt away, recede from view, withdraw, depart, leave. **2** *a way of life that has vanished | hopes of success have vanished* cease to exist/be, pass away, die out, come to an end, end, be no more, become extinct/obsolete.
Opposites APPEAR; MATERIALIZE.

vanity *noun* **1** *his vanity about his looks/achievements* conceit, conceitedness, self-conceit, self-admiration, self-love, narcissism, egotism, pride, haughtiness, arrogance, boastfulness, braggadocio, pretension, affectation, ostentation, show, vainglory; airs; *inf.* stuck-upness, big-headedness, swollen-headedness, showing-off. **2** *the vanity of human triumphs* worthlessness, futility, futileness, insignificance, pointlessness, meaninglessness, emptiness, hollowness, insubstantiality, vapidity. *See* VAIN 2.
Opposites MODESTY; HUMILITY; WORTH.

vanquish *verb* conquer, defeat, triumph over, beat, overcome, best, worst, master, subdue, subjugate, put down, quell, quash, repress, rout, overwhelm, overrun, overthrow, crush, trounce, thrash, drub; *inf.* clobber.

vapid *adjective* insipid, flat, lifeless, colourless, bland, dull, trite, uninteresting, zestless.
Opposites LIVELY; COLOURFUL; EXCITING.

variable *adjective* varying, variational, changeable, changeful, changing, mutable, chameleonic, protean, shifting, fluctuating, wavering, vacillating, inconstant, unsteady, unstable, fitful, capricious, fickle; *inf.* blowing hot and cold.
Opposites CONSTANT; UNIFORM; STEADY.

variance *noun* *an obvious variance between statements* discrepancy, disagreement, diverging. **at variance** *they are at variance about his suitability* in disagreement, in dissent, in opposition, in conflict, at odds.

variant *adjective* *variant spellings* alternative, divergent, derived, modified.

variant *noun* *a variant of the normal spelling* variation, alternative, derived form, development, modification, mutant.

variation *noun* **1** *subject to variation* change, alteration, modification, diversification. **2** *noted for its variation* variability, changeability, fluctuation, vacillation, vicissitude. **3** *a variation in sizes* varying, difference, dissimilarity. **4** *show variation from the norm* deviation, divergence, departure, difference. **5** *a variation on a theme* diversification, innovation, novelty.

varied *adjective* *a varied selection* diversified, diverse, assorted, miscellaneous, mixed, motley, heterogeneous.
Opposites UNIFORM.

variegated *adjective* multicoloured, particoloured, prismatic, rainbow-like, kaleidoscopic, marbled, streaked, striated, mottled, speckled, flecked.

variety noun **1** *introduce variety into your selection* variation, diversification, diversity, multifariousness, many-sidedness, change, difference. **2** *a variety of flowers were exhibited* assortment, miscellany, range, mixture, medley, motley, collection, multiplicity. **3** *a variety of rose/humour* strain, breed, kind, type, sort, class, category, classification, brand, make.

various adjective **1** *come in various shapes* varying, diverse, different, differing, dissimilar, unlike, disparate, many, assorted, mixed, miscellaneous, variegated, heterogeneous. **2** *for various reasons* numerous, many, several, varied, sundry, divers.

varnish verb **1** *varnish the table* lacquer, japan, shellac, enamel, glaze, veneer. **2** *varnish the truth* embellish, smooth over, cover up, gloss over, mask, disguise.

varnish noun *apply a varnish to the surface* coating, lacquer, shellac, enamel, glaze, veneer.

vary verb **1** *they tend to vary in size* differ, be different, be unlike, be dissimilar. **2** *the sky varies constantly* change, be transformed, alter, metamorphose, suffer a sea change, vacillate, fluctuate. **3** *our opinions vary* be at variance, disagree, be in disagreement, differ, conflict, clash, be at odds, be in opposition, diverge. **4** *vary the speed/appearance* change, alter, modify, transform, permutate. **5** *vary from the norm* deviate, diverge, depart, differ.

vast adjective **1** *a vast shape loomed* immense, huge, enormous, massive, bulky, tremendous, colossal, prodigious, gigantic, monumental, elephantine, Brobdingnagian; *inf.* hulking. **2** *vast forests* immense, extensive, broad, wide, expansive, boundless, limitless, infinite. **Opposites** TINY; MINUTE.

vault noun **1** *look up at the vault* arched roof/ceiling, arch. *See table.* **2** *hide in the vault* cellar, basement, underground chamber, tomb. **3** *valuables stored in the vault* strongroom, repos-

---

VAULTS

barrel vault	quadripartite
cross vault	vault
domical vault	ribbed vault
fan vault	Romanesque
Gothic vaulting	vaulting
groin vault	segmental vault
intersecting vault	sexpartite vault
lierne vault	tunnel vault
palm vault	underpitch vault
parabolic vault	wagon vault

---

itory, depository. **4** *take a vault over the fence* jump, leap, spring, bound.

vault verb *vault the fence* jump, leap, jump over, leap over, spring over, bound over.

vaunt verb *always vaunting his achievements* boast about, brag about, make much of, crow about, give oneself airs about, exult in; *inf.* show off about.

veer verb change course/direction, shift direction, turn, swerve, swing, sidestep, sheer, tack, be deflected.

vegetable noun. See table.

vegetate verb **1** *vegetating at home without a job* do nothing, idle, be inactive, laze around, lounge around, loaf around, languish, stagnate, moulder; *inf.* go to seed. **2** *plants vegetating* grow, sprout, shoot up, burgeon, flourish.

vegetation noun plant life, herbage, greenery, verdure; plants, flora. *See tables at* GRASS, PLANT, TREE.

vehemence noun passion, ardour, fervour, strength, force, forcibleness, forcefulness, emphasis, vigour, intensity, violence, earnestness, keenness, enthusiasm, zeal, zealousness, spirit, spiritedness, gusto, verve.

vehement adjective passionate, ardent, impassioned, fervent, fervid, strong, forceful, forcible, powerful, emphatic, vigorous,

---

VEGETABLES

artichoke	chayote	kohlrabi	salsify
asparagus	chervil	leek	savoy
aubergine	chicory	lentil	scallion
avocado pear	Chinese cabbage	lettuce	scorzonera
bamboo shoots	Chinese leaves	mangetout	sea kale
bean	collard	manioc	shallot
beet	corn on the cob	marrow	spinach
beetroot	courgette	marrow squash	spinach beet
breadfruit	cress	mustard	squash
broccoli	cucumber	okra	succory
Brussels sprout	curly kale	onion	swede
cabbage	dishcloth gourd	orache	sweet corn
calabrese	eggplant	oyster plant	sweet potato
capsicum	endive	pak-choi	taro
cardoon	fennel	parsnip	tomato
carrot	gherkin	pepper	turnip
cassava	gourd	pimiento	water
cauliflower	gumbo	potato	chestnut
celeriac	Jerusalem	pumpkin	watercress
celery	artichoke	radish	yam
chard	kale	rutabaga	zucchini

intense, violent, earnest, keen, enthusiastic, zealous, spirited.
Opposites APATHETIC; INDIFFERENT.

vehicle noun **1** *park the vehicle* means of transport, transportation, conveyance; car, bus, lorry. *See table. See also tables at* CAR, CARRIAGE, TRAIN. **2** *a vehicle for their propaganda* channel, medium, means, means of expression, agency, instrument, mechanism, organ, apparatus.

veil noun **1** *her face covered by a veil* face covering, mantilla, yashmak, purdah. **2** *a veil of mist covered the mountain | under a veil of secrecy* covering, cover, screen, curtain, film, mantle, cloak, mask, blanket, shroud, canopy, cloud.

veil verb **1** *try to veil his contempt | did not veil his threats* hide, conceal, cover up, camouflage, disguise, mask, screen. **2** *mist veiling the mountains* cover, envelop, mantle, cloak, blanket, shroud, canopy.

veiled adjective *thinly veiled threats* hidden, concealed, covert, disguised, camouflaged, masked, suppressed.

vein noun **1** *sever a vein* blood vessel. *See table.* **2** *a vein of ore* lode, seam, stratum. **3** *veins of blue in the white marble* streak, stripe, line, thread, marking. **4** *there was a vein of wickedness in him* streak, strain, trait, dash, hint. **5** *he was in humorous vein* humour, mood, temper, temperament, disposition, frame of mind, attitude, inclination, tendency, tenor, tone.

velocity noun speed, swiftness, fastness, quickness, rapidity, celerity.

venal adjective corrupt, corruptible, bribable, open to bribery, purchasable, buyable, mercenary, greedy, avaricious, grasping, rapacious.
Opposites HONOURABLE; HONEST.

vendetta noun feud, blood feud, quarrel, war, conflict, rivalry, enmity.

vendor noun seller, salesperson, dealer, trader, merchant, pedlar, hawker.

veneer noun **1** *a veneer of mahogany* facing, covering, coat, finishing coat, finish. **2** *a veneer of politeness* façade, front, false front, show, outward display, appearance, semblance, guise, mask, pretence, camouflage.

MAIN HUMAN VEINS AND ARTERIES	
aorta	median cubital vein
axillary artery	mesenteric artery
axillary vein	ovarian artery
basilic vein	ovarian vein
brachial artery	palmar network
brachial vein	popliteal artery and
carotid artery	vein
coeliac artery	pulmonary artery
cephalic artery and	pulmonary vein
vein	renal artery
coronary artery	renal vein
crural artery and	saphenous vein
vein	subclavian artery
femoral artery	subclavian vein
femoral vein	superior vena cava
hepatic artery and	suprarenal vein
vein	testicular artery
iliac artery	testicular vein
iliac vein	ulnar artery and
inferior vena cava	vein
jugular vein	vena cava
long thoracic artery	vertebral artery

venerable adjective *venerable scientist/traditions* venerated, respected, revered, reverenced, worshipped, honoured, esteemed, hallowed.
Opposites DISREPUTABLE.

veneration noun respect, reverence, worship, adoration, honour, esteem.

vengeance noun revenge, retribution, requital, retaliation, reprisal, an eye for an eye, tit for tat, measure for measure, blow for blow, quid pro quo. **with a vengeance 1** *the rain came down with a vengeance* forcefully, violently, vehemently, furiously, wildly. **2** *go at the job with a vengeance* to the utmost, to the greatest extreme, to the full, to the limit, all out, flat out.

venial adjective *a venial offence* pardonable, forgivable, excusable, allowable, tolerable, slight, minor, unimportant, insignificant, trivial.

venom noun **1** *suck the venom of the snake bite* poison, toxin, toxicant. **2** *speak with venom about his rival* spite, spitefulness, rancour, vindictiveness, malice, malevolence, malignity, ill

MOTOR VEHICLES				
ambulance	car transporter	float	mammy	shooting
armoured car	Caterpillar™	fork-lift truck	wagon	brake
articulated	charabanc	garbage truck	milk float	single-decker
lorry	coach	*Am.*	mobile home	bus
automobile	crash wagon	go-kart	motor	snowmobile
beach buggy	*Am.*	golf cart	caravan	snowplough
bloodmobile	crawler tractor	gritter	omnibus	steamroller
Am.	delivery truck	hackney cab	pick-up truck	taxi
bookmobile	digger	half-track	public service	tracklayer
Am.	Dormobile™	hearse	vehicle/PSV	tractor
bowser	double-decker	HGV	recreational	trailer
bulldozer	bus	JCB™	vehicle/RV *Am.*	tram
bus	dragster	Jeep™	refrigerated	transporter
cab	DUKW/duck	juggernaut	van	trolleybus
camper	dune buggy	kart	removal van	truck
car	dustcart	lorry	runabout	van
carryall *Am.*	fire engine	low-loader	semitrailer	wagon/waggon

will, animosity, bitterness, resentment, grudgingness, acrimony, virulence, antagonism, hostility, enmity, hatred, viciousness.

venomous *adjective* **1** *a venomous snake/bite* poisonous, toxic, lethal, deadly, fatal, noxious. **2** *a venomous remark/look* spiteful, rancorous, vindictive, malicious, malevolent, malignant, baleful, bitter, resentful, grudging, virulent, antagonistic, hostile, hate-filled, vicious.

vent *noun* **1** *an air vent* opening, outlet, aperture, hole, gap, orifice, duct, flue. **2** *give vent to his anger* outlet, free passage, expression, release.

vent *verb* *vent his anger on his children* give vent/expression to, express, air, utter, voice, verbalize, let out, release, pour out, emit, discharge, come out with.

ventilate *verb* **1** *ventilate a room* air, aerate, oxygenate, air-condition, freshen, cool, purify. **2** *ventilate one's views* air, give an airing to, bring into the open, discuss, debate, talk over, give expression to, express.

venture *noun* **1** *explorers engaged in a new venture* adventure, exploit, mission, risky undertaking. **2** *a business venture* enterprise, undertaking, project, speculation, fling, plunge, gamble.

venture *verb* **1** *venture to voice an opinion* dare, take the liberty of, make so bold as to, presume to. **2** *venture an opinion* volunteer, advance, put forward, chance, risk. **3** *venture his life for her* risk, put at risk, endanger, hazard, put in jeopardy, jeopardize, imperil, chance, gamble. **4** *it's now possible to venture out/forth* go, set forth, embark (on).

veracious *adjective* **1** *a veracious person* truthful, honest, sincere, frank, candid, honourable, upright, upstanding, ethical, moral, righteous, virtuous, decent, good. **2** *a veracious statement* true, truthful, accurate, exact, precise, factual, literal, realistic.
Opposites DISHONEST; UNTRUE.

verbal *adjective* **1** *a verbal account* oral, spoken, said, uttered, articulated. **2** *a verbal translation* word for word, verbatim, literal, close, faithful, exact, precise.

verbatim *adjective* *a verbatim translation* word for word, literal, exact. *See* VERBAL 2.

verbatim *adverb* *translate his statement verbatim* word for word, literally, to the letter, closely, faithfully, exactly, precisely.

verbose *adjective* wordy, loquacious, garrulous, long-winded, prolix, diffuse, pleonastic, circumlocutory, periphrastic, tautological.
Opposites SUCCINCT; TACITURN.

verbosity *noun* verboseness, wordiness, loquacity, garrulity, long-windedness, logorrhoea, verbiage, prolixity, diffuseness, circumlocution, periphrasis, tautology.

verdict *noun* decision, judgement, adjudication, finding, conclusion, ruling, opinion.

verge *noun* **1** *the verges of the lake* edge, border, margin, rim, limit, boundary, end, extremity. **2** *on the verge of a breakdown/discovery* brink, threshold.

verge *verb* *it verges on the ridiculous* approach, incline to/towards, tend towards, border on, come near.

verification *noun* *ask for verification of his statement* confirmation, substantiation, corroboration, attestation, validation, authentication, endorsement, accreditation, ratification; evidence, proof.

verify *verb* **1** *ask the witness to verify his statement* confirm, substantiate, prove, corroborate, attest to, testify to, validate, authenticate, endorse, accredit, ratify. **2** *our suspicions were verified* bear out, justify, give credence to, confirm, prove, substantiate.

vernacular *noun* everyday/spoken language, colloquial/native speech, conversational language, common parlance, non-standard language, jargon, cant, patois; *inf.* lingo, patter.

versatile *adjective* **1** *a versatile member of staff* adaptable, flexible, all-round, multifaceted, resourceful, ingenious, clever. **2** *a versatile tool* adaptable, adjustable, multipurpose, all-purpose, handy.
Opposites INFLEXIBLE.

verse *noun* **1** *write verse rather than prose* poetry; poems. *See tables.* **2** *a poem in several verses* stanza, strophe, canto, couplet. **3** *read out a verse about the countryside* poem, lyric, sonnet, ode, limerick, piece of doggerel, ditty, song, lay, ballad.

VERSE FORMS

Alcaics	blank verse	haiku	ritornello	Spenserian
alexandrine	clerihew	limerick	rondeau	stanza
alliterative verse	doggerel	macaronic	Sapphics	terza rima
Anacreontics	epigram	ottava rima	sequidilla	triolet
ballade	fixed form	Pindaric	sestina	triplet
	free verse	rhyme royal	sonnet	vilanelle

METRES AND METRICAL FEET

alexandrine	cretic	elegiac couplet	iambic	pyrrhic
amphibrach	dactyl	elegiac distich	pentameter	spondee
amphimacer	dimeter	heptameter	ionic	tetrameter
anapaest	dipody	heroic couplet	octameter	tribrach
choree	distich	hexameter	paeon	trimeter
choriamb	duple metre	iamb	pentameter	trochee

version noun **1** *tell us your version of the events* account, report, story, rendering, interpretation, construction, understanding, reading, impression, side. **2** *published in several versions* adaptation, interpretation, translation. **3** *there are several versions of the song going around* variant, variation, form, copy, reproduction.

vertebra noun. *See table.*

VERTEBRAE	
Vertebra	**Number**
cervical	7
coccyx	4 fused
lumbar	5
sacral	5
thoracic	12

vertical adjective upright, erect, on end, perpendicular.
Opposites HORIZONTAL.

vertigo noun dizziness, giddiness, lightheadedness, loss of balance/equilibrium; *inf.* wooziness.

verve noun enthusiasm, vigour, force, energy, vitality, vivacity, liveliness, animation, sparkle, spirit, life, *élan*, dash, brio, fervour, gusto, passion, zeal, feeling, fire; *inf.* zing, zip, vim, punch, get-up-and-go, pizzazz.

very adverb *very pretty | done very easily* extremely, exceedingly, to a great extent, exceptionally, uncommonly, unusually, decidedly, particularly, eminently, remarkably, really, truly; *inf.* awfully, terribly, jolly.

very adjective **1** *his very words* actual, exact, precise, unqualified. **2** *that is the very thing for the task* ideal, perfect, appropriate, suitable, fitting, right, just right. **3** *its very simplicity appeals* sheer, utter, simple, pure, plain, mere. **4** *at the very beginning* extreme, absolute.

vessel noun **1** *a sea-going vessel* ship, boat, yacht, craft; *lit.* barque. *See tables at* SAILING SHIP, SHIP. **2** *pour the milk into several vessels* container, receptacle.

vest verb *he has the power to execute vested in him* bestow, confer, endow, entrust, invest, lodge, place, put in the hands of.

vestibule noun entrance hall, hall, porch, portico, foyer, lobby, anteroom.

vestige noun **1** *see vestiges of a pack of wolves* trace, mark, sign, indication, print, imprint, impression, track. **2** *vestiges of a lost civilization* remains, relics; evidence. **3** *not a vestige of proof* scrap, hint, suggestion, touch, tinge, suspicion, soupçon, inkling, drop, dash, jot, iota.

vestigial adjective **1** *vestigial signs of an extinct civilization* remaining, surviving. **2** *a vestigial tail* rudimentary, non-functional, undeveloped.

vet verb *vet their qualifications | vet the staff* check, check out, investigate, examine, appraise, look over, review, scrutinize; *inf.* give the once-over, size up.

veteran noun *veterans of the acting profession* old hand, old-timer, old stager, past master, master; *inf.* pro, warhorse.
Opposites NOVICE; APPRENTICE.

veteran adjective *a veteran member of the committee* long-serving, seasoned, old, adept, expert; *inf.* battle-scarred.

veto verb *veto the tax cuts | veto the candidate for membership* reject, turn down, give the thumbs down to, prohibit, forbid, interdict, proscribe, disallow, outlaw, embargo, ban, bar, preclude, rule out; *inf.* kill, put the kibosh on.
Opposites APPROVE; ALLOW; ENDORSE; AUTHORIZE.

veto noun *the right of veto | have a veto over any proposal* rejection, prohibition, interdict, proscription; embargo, ban.

vex verb anger, annoy, irritate, incense, irk, enrage, infuriate, exasperate, pique, provoke, nettle, disturb, upset, perturb, discompose, put out, try one's patience, try, bother, trouble, worry, agitate, pester, harass, fluster, ruffle, hound, nag, torment, distress, tease, fret, gall, molest; *inf.* peeve, miff, bug, hassle, aggravate, rile, get one's goat, drive up the wall, get to.

vexation noun **1** *her vexation at his behaviour* anger, annoyance, irritation, rage, fury, exasperation, pique, provocation, perturbation, discomposure, worry, agitation, harassment, gall. *See* VEX. **2** *the child is a vexation to them* nuisance, pest, problem, trouble, worry, bother, irritant, thorn in one's flesh; *inf.* headache, pain, pain in the neck.

vexatious adjective annoying, irritating, irksome, infuriating, exasperating, provoking, upsetting, perturbing, bothersome, troublesome, worrying, worrisome, trying, distressing; *inf.* aggravating.

vexed adjective **1** *vexed about his behaviour | his vexed parents* annoyed, irritated, incensed, irked, enraged, infuriated, exasperated, upset, perturbed, bothered, troubled, worried, agitated, harassed, flustered, distressed; *inf.* aggravated, peeved, miffed. *See* VEX. **2** *the vexed question* disputed, in dispute, contested, in contention, debated, controversial, moot.

viable adjective *a viable plan/operation* workable, sound, feasible, practicable, applicable, usable.
Opposites IMPRACTICABLE; non-viable.

vibrant adjective **1** *vibrant pendulums* vibrating, vibratory, oscillating, swinging. **2** *vibrant music* throbbing, pulsating, resonant, reverberating, ringing, echoing. **3** *vibrant with excitement* trembling, quivering, shaking, shivering. *See* VIBRATE 3. **4** *a vibrant personality* lively, energetic, spirited, vigorous, animated, sparkling, vivacious, dynamic, electrifying. **5** *vibrant colours* vivid, bright, strong, striking.

vibrate verb **1** *the pendulum vibrated* oscillate, swing, move to and fro. **2** *the noise vibrated through the house* throb, pulsate, resonate, resound, reverberate, ring, echo. **3** *vibrating with excitement* pulsate, tremble, quiver, shake, quaver, shiver, shudder.

vibration noun **1** *the vibration of the pendulum* oscillation, swinging. **2** *the musical vibration* throb, pulsation, resonance, reverberation. *See* VIBRATE 2. **3** *the vibration of the engine | vibration of the bird's wings* pulsating, trembling, tremble, quivering, quiver, shake, shaking, quaver, shiver, shivering; *inf.* judder.

vicar *noun* minister, clergyman, cleric, church-man, ecclesiastic. *See table at* ECCLESIASTIC.

vicarious *adjective vicarious pleasure from another's joy* indirect, second-hand, surrogate, by proxy, at one remove.

vice *noun* **1** *vice is rampant* sin, sinfulness, wrong, wrongdoing, wickedness, badness, immorality, iniquity, evil, evildoing, venality corruption, depravity, degeneracy. **2** *enumer-ate his vices* sin, wrongdoing, transgression, offence, misdeed, error, violation. **3** *chocolate/ shopping is one of her vices* failing, flaw, defect, imperfection, weakness, foible, shortcoming. **Opposites** VIRTUE.

vice versa *adverb* conversely, inversely, the other way round, contrariwise.

vicinity *noun* **1** *he lives in the vicinity* surround-ing district, neighbourhood, locality, area, dis-trict; environs, precincts, purlieus; *inf.* this neck of the woods. **2** *the village's vicinity to Lon-don* nearness, closeness, proximity, propin-quity. **in the vicinity** *in the vicinity of £3000* in the neighbourhood (of), near (to), close (to).

vicious *adjective* **1** *attacked by vicious dogs* fierce, ferocious, savage, dangerous, ill-natured, bad-tempered, surly, hostile. **2** *vicious gossip/remarks* malicious, malevolent, malignant, spiteful, vindictive, venomous, catty, backbiting, rancorous, caustic, mean, cruel, defamatory, slanderous; *inf.* bitchy. **3** *a vicious attack* violent, savage, brutal, fierce, ferocious, inhuman, barbarous, fiendish, sadis-tic, monstrous, heinous, atrocious, diabolical. **4** *fall in with a vicious band of people* corrupt, degenerate, depraved, debased, wicked, evil, sinful, bad, wrong, immoral, unprincipled, abandoned, unscrupulous, disreputable, dis-solute, dissipated, debauched, profligate, liber-tine, vile, infamous, notorious. **Opposites** GENTLE; KINDLY; VIRTUOUS.

vicissitude *noun the vicissitudes of a writer's life* change, alteration, transformation, incon-stancy, instability, uncertainty, unpredictabil-ity, chanciness, fickleness; ups and downs.

victim *noun* **1** *victims of the attack* injured party, casualty, sufferer. **2** *they were victims of his sales patter* dupe, easy target/prey, fair game, sitting target, everybody's fool; *inf.* sit-ting duck, sucker, sap, fall guy, pushover. **3** *track down their victims* prey, quarry, game, the hunted, target. **4** *a sacrificial victim for the gods* offering, sacrifice, scapegoat. **Opposites** ATTACKER; ASSAILANT.

victimize *verb* **1** *bullies victimizing young chil-dren* persecute, pick on, discriminate against, punish unfairly; *inf.* have it in for, have a down on. **2** *unscrupulous men victimize old ladies* exploit, prey on, take advantage of, swindle, dupe, cheat, trick, hoodwink.

victor *noun* conqueror, vanquisher, winner, champion, prizewinner, conquering hero; *inf.* champ, top dog, number one. **Opposites** LOSER; vanquished.

victorious *adjective* conquering, vanquishing, triumphant, winning, champion, successful,

prizewinning, top, first. **Opposites** UNSUCCESSFUL; losing.

victuals *plural noun* food, food and drink; eatables, foodstuffs, viands, comestibles, food supplies, provisions, rations, stores; *inf.* eats, grub, nosh.

vie *verb vie with her for first place* compete, con-tend, contest.

view *noun* **1** *come into view* sight, field/range of vision, vision, eyeshot. **2** *the view from the mountain* outlook, prospect, scene, spectacle, vista, panorama; landscape, seascape. **3** *his view is that we should wait/have radical views* point of view, viewpoint, opinion, belief, judgement, way of thinking, thinking, thought, notion, idea, conviction, persuasion, attitude, feeling, sentiment, impression. **4** *a private view of the exhibition* viewing, sight, look, contemplation, observation, study, survey, inspection, scrutiny, scan. **in view of** *in view of his political opinions* considering, taking into consideration, bearing in mind, taking into account, in the light of. **on view** *pictures on view* on display, on exhibition, on show.

view *verb* **1** *view the birds through binoculars* look at, watch, observe, contemplate, regard, behold, scan, survey, inspect, gaze at, stare at, peer at. **2** *view the house* see over, be shown over, survey, examine, scrutinize, take stock of. **3** *view the prospect with dismay* look on, con-sider, contemplate, think about, reflect on, ponder. **4** *view himself as an upright man* see, consider, judge, deem.

viewer *noun* television watcher, watcher, spec-tator, onlooker, member of the audience.

viewpoint *noun* point of view, way of thinking, frame of reference, perspective, angle, slant, standpoint, position, stance, vantage point.

vigilance *noun* watchfulness, observation, sur-veillance, attentiveness, attention, alertness, guardedness, carefulness, caution, wariness, circumspection, heedfulness, heed.

vigilant *adjective* watchful, on the lookout, observant, sharp-eyed, eagle-eyed, attentive, alert, on the alert, on the qui vive, awake, wide awake, unsleeping, on one's guard, care-ful, cautious, wary, circumspect, heedful. **Opposites** HEEDLESS; NEGLIGENT; INATTENTIVE.

vigorous *adjective* **1** *vigorous children brought up in the country* robust, healthy, in good health, hale and hearty, strong, sturdy, fit, in good condition/shape/kilter, tough. **2** *feel much more vigorous after a holiday* energetic, lively, active, spry, sprightly, vivacious, animated, dynamic, full of life, sparkling. **3** *a vigorous attempt at winning* powerful, potent, strenuous, forceful, forcible, spirited, mettle-some, plucky, determined, resolute, aggres-sive, eager, keen, enthusiastic, zealous, ardent, fervent, vehement, intense, passionate. **4** *use vigorous arguments* strong, forceful, effective, cogent, valid, pointed, to the point, striking, graphic, vivid. **Opposites** FRAIL; FEEBLE; WEAK.

vigorously *adverb defend himself vigorously/argue vigorously* strongly, powerfully, strenuously, forcefully, energetically, aggressively, eagerly, enthusiastically, with might and main, all out, with a vengeance, hammer and tongs; *inf.* like mad.

vigour *noun* **1** *the natural vigour of country children* robustness, healthiness, strength, sturdiness, fitness, toughness. **2** *return to work with renewed vigour* energy, activity, liveliness, spryness, sprightliness, vitality, vivacity, verve, animation, dynamism, sparkle, zest, dash, *élan*, gusto, pep; *inf.* zip, zing, oomph, vim.

vile *adjective* **1** *a vile taste/smell* foul, nasty, unpleasant, disagreeable, horrid, horrible, offensive, obnoxious, odious, repulsive, repellent, revolting, repugnant, disgusting, distasteful, loathsome, hateful, nauseating, sickening. **2** *he's a vile creature | a vile thing to do* base, low, mean, wretched, foul, nasty, horrible, horrid, dreadful, disgraceful, appalling, shocking, ugly, abominable, monstrous, wicked, evil, iniquitous, sinful, vicious, corrupt, depraved, perverted, debased, reprobate, degenerate, debauched, dissolute, contemptible, despicable, reprehensible. **3** *vile weather* foul, nasty, unpleasant, disagreeable. **Opposites** PLEASANT; AGREEABLE; ADMIRABLE.

vilify *verb* defame, run down, impugn, revile, berate, denigrate, disparage, speak ill of, cast aspersions at, criticize, decry, denounce, fulminate against, malign, slander, libel, conduct a smear campaign against, blacken the name/reputation of, calumniate, traduce; *inf.* badmouth, do a hatchet job on, pull to pieces, throw mud at, drag through the mud. **Opposites** PRAISE; COMMEND; EXALT.

villain *noun* **1** *he pretends to be honest but he's a real villain* rogue, scoundrel, blackguard, wretch, cad, reprobate, evildoer, wrongdoer, ruffian, hoodlum, hooligan, miscreant; *inf.* baddy, crook, rat, louse. **2** *the police chasing the villains* criminal, miscreant, jailbird; *inf.* crook. **3** *the child's a little villain* rascal, rogue, imp, monkey, scamp, brat; *inf.* scallywag.

villainous *adjective* **1** *a villainous attack* wicked, evil, iniquitous, sinful, nefarious, vile, foul, monstrous, shocking, outrageous, atrocious, abominable, reprehensible, hateful, detestable, horrible, heinous, diabolical, fiendish, vicious. **2** *a villainous wretch* wicked, evil, sinful, bad, base, dishonourable, dishonest, unscrupulous, scoundrelly, unprincipled, criminal, lawless, corrupt, degenerate, reprobate, depraved, dissolute; *inf.* crooked. **Opposites** GOOD; VIRTUOUS.

villainy *noun* wickedness, badness, evil, sin, iniquity, wrongdoing, roguery, rascality, vice, criminality, delinquency, vileness, viciousness, degeneracy, depravity, turpitude; crime, offence, misdeed.

vindicate *verb* **1** *he was vindicated when his alibi was proved* acquit, clear, absolve, free from blame, exonerate, exculpate. **2** *time vindicated his suspicions* justify, warrant, substantiate, testify to, verify, confirm, corroborate. **3** *vindicate his claim* defend, support, back, fight for, champion, uphold, maintain, sustain, stand by. **Opposites** BLAME; CONVICT; INCRIMINATE.

vindictive *adjective* vengeful, out for revenge, revengeful, avenging, unforgiving, grudge-bearing, resentful, ill-disposed, implacable, unrelenting, unconciliative, spiteful, rancorous, venomous, malicious, malevolent, malignant. **Opposites** FORGIVING; MERCIFUL; GENEROUS.

vintage *noun* **1** *the vintage was ruined by storms* grape harvest, grape gathering, grape crop. **2** *what vintage is this wine?* year. **3** *the furniture is of 18th century vintage* era, epoch, period, time. **4** *his parents are of the same vintage as mine* generation, period, time.

vintage *adjective* **1** *vintage wines* high-quality, quality, prime, choice, select, superior, best. **2** *vintage comedy* classic, ageless, enduring. **3** *this is vintage Sharon* characteristic, most typical, supreme, at his/her/its best.

violate *verb* **1** *violate a law/treaty* break, breach, infringe, contravene, infract, transgress, disobey, disregard, ignore. **2** *violate a grave* desecrate, profane, defile, blaspheme. **3** *violate their privacy* disturb, disrupt, intrude on, interfere with, encroach on, invade. **4** *violate the peace* disturb, disrupt, break into, upset, shatter, destroy. **5** *he was accused of violating his niece* rape, ravish, indecently assault, abuse, deflower, molest, seduce.

violence *noun* **1** *the violence of his temper* strength, forcefulness, lack of control/restraint, wildness, passion. See VIOLENT 1. **2** *the violence of the blow* forcefulness, powerfulness, might, savagery, ferocity, destructiveness, brutality. **3** *the violence of the storm* wildness, tempestuousness, turbulence. See VIOLENT 4. **4** *the violence of his dislike* strength, intensity, vehemence. See VIOLENT 5. **5** *the violence of the pain* sharpness, acuteness, intensity. See VIOLENT 6. **6** *use violence to get his way* force, brute force, roughness, ferocity, brutality, savagery; strong-arm tactics.

violent *adjective* **1** *a violent temper* strong, powerful, forceful, uncontrolled, unrestrained, unbridled, uncontrollable, ungovernable, wild, passionate, raging. **2** *he's a violent person* brutal, vicious, destructive, savage, fierce, wild, intemperate, hot-headed, hot-tempered, bloodthirsty, homicidal, murderous, maniacal. **3** *a violent blow* forceful, powerful, mighty, savage, ferocious, destructive, damaging, brutal. **4** *a violent storm* wild, blustery, boisterous, raging, tempestuous, turbulent, tumultuous. **5** *a violent dislike* strong, great, intense, extreme, vehement, inordinate, excessive. **6** *a violent pain/toothache* sharp, acute, intense, excruciating, agonizing, biting.

virgin *adjective* **1** *virgin snow/territory* pure, immaculate, unblemished, spotless, stainless, unused, untouched, untainted, unspoilt, untarnished, unadulterated. **2** *virgin young girls*. See VIRGINAL.

virginal *adjective* *virginal young girls* pure, chaste, virtuous, uncorrupted.

virile *adjective* **1** *a virile man* manly, all-male, strong, vigorous, robust, powerfully built, muscular, rugged, strapping, sturdy, red-blooded; *inf.* macho. **2** *virile enough to procreate*

young sexually potent. **3** *virile rather than femi-nine/effeminate* manly, masculine, male.
Opposites UNMANLY; EFFEMINATE.

virility *noun* **1** *the virility of the body-building enthusiasts* manliness, strength, vigour, robustness, muscularity, ruggedness; *inf.* machismo. See VIRILE 1. **2** *impaired virility* sexual potency, potency, sexuality. **3** *question his virility* manliness, masculinity, maleness, manhood.

virtual *adjective* **1** *traffic at a virtual standstill* more or less, near, effective, in effect, tantamount to, for all practical purposes. **2** *he is the virtual manager* in all but name, functioning as, operating as, for all practical purposes.

virtually *adverb traffic virtually at a standstill | he is virtually in charge* more or less, nearly, practically, as good as, effectively, in effect, essentially, in essence, for all practical purposes, to all intents and purposes, in all but name.

virtue *noun* **1** *admire the virtue of the hard-working men* goodness, righteousness, morality, ethicalness, uprightness, upstandingness, integrity, rectitude, honesty, honourableness, honour, incorruptibility, probity, decency, respectability, worthiness, worth, trustworthiness. *See tables.* **2** *admire virtue in a young girl* virginity, celibacy, purity, pureness, chastity, chasteness, innocence, modesty. **3** *generosity is one of her virtues | reliability is one of the car's virtues* good quality/point, merit, asset, credit, attribute, advantage, benefit, strength; *inf.* plus. **4** *there is no virtue in the use of such drugs* merit, advantage, benefit, usefulness, efficacy, efficaciousness, power, potency. **by virtue of** *win by virtue of his talent* by reason of, by dint of, on account of, as a result of, owing to, thanks to.
Opposites VICE; SIN; FAILING; DISADVANTAGE.

VIRTUES

faith	**Cardinal virtues**
fortitude	fortitude
hope	justice
justice	prudence
love/charity	temperance
prudence	
temperance	

---

virtuosity *noun* skill, skilfulness, mastery, expertise, prowess, excellence, craftsmanship, flair, finish, polish, panache, brilliance, éclat, wizardry.

virtuoso *noun a virtuoso on the piano* master, genius, expert, artist, maestro, wizard.

virtuoso *adjective a virtuoso performance* skilful, masterly, impressive, outstanding, dazzling, bravura.

virtuous *adjective* **1** *virtuous hard-working people* good, righteous, moral, ethical, upright, upstanding, honest, honourable, incorruptible, decent, respectable, worthy, trustworthy. **2** *virtuous young girls* virginal, celibate, pure, chaste, innocent, modest.
Opposites EVIL; SINFUL; PROMISCUOUS.

virulent *adjective* **1** *using virulent substances as weed-killers* poisonous, toxic, venomous, deadly, lethal, fatal, noxious, harmful. **2** *a virulent form/strain of the disease* severe, extreme, violent, rapidly spreading, highly infectious/contagious, harmful, lethal. **3** *a virulent attack | virulent forms of abuse* hostile, spiteful, venomous, vicious, vindictive, malicious, malevolent, malignant, bitter, rancorous, acrimonious, abusive, aggressive, violent.

virus *noun. See table.*

VIRUSES

adenovirus	parainfluenza virus
arbovirus	paramyxovirus
arenavirus	parvovirus
bacteriophage	picornavirus
Coxsackie virus	poliovirus
cytomegalovirus	polyomavirus
echovirus	polyoma virus
enterovirus	poxvirus
Epstein-Barr virus	reovirus
herpesvirus	retrovirus
HIV/human immuno-	rhabdovirus
deficiency virus	rhinovirus
influenza virus	Ross River virus
Lassa virus	rotavirus
lentivirus	Sendai virus
leukovirus	Shope virus
Marburg virus	slow virus
mengovirus	tobacco mosaic
morbillivirus	virus
myxovirus	togavirus
oncornavirus	tumour virus
orbivirus	ultravirus
papillomavirus	varicella virus
papovavirus	West Nile virus

---

visible *adjective* **1** *hills scarcely visible in the mist* in view, perceptible, perceivable, discernible, detectable, seeable. **2** *his distress was visible to all* apparent, evident, noticeable, observable, detectable, recognizable, manifest, plain, clear, obvious, patent, palpable, unmistakable, unconcealed, undisguised, conspicuous, distinct, distinguishable.
Opposites INVISIBLE; HIDDEN.

vision *noun* **1** *have good vision* eyesight, sight, power of seeing; eyes. **2** *the saint saw a vision* apparition, spectre, phantom, ghost, wraith, phantasm, chimera, revelation. **3** *see his late mother in one of his visions* dream, hallucination, chimera, optical illusion, mirage, illusion, delusion, figment of the imagination. **4** *have visions of a juicy steak* dream, daydream, pipe-dream, fantasy, image, mental picture. **5** *artists must have vision* perception, perceptiveness, insight, intuition, imagination. **6** *in need of political vision* foresight, far-sightedness, prescience, breadth of view, discernment. **7** *she was a vision in white* dream, spectacle, picture, feast for the eyes, beautiful sight; *inf.* sight for sore eyes.

visionary *adjective* **1** *too visionary to make a success of business* idealistic, impractical, unrealistic, utopian, romantic, quixotic, dreamy, dreaming; *inf.* starry-eyed. **2** *visionary artists* perceptive, intuitive. *See* VISION 5. **3** *visionary politicians* far-sighted, discerning, wise. *See* VISION 6. **4** *visionary figures* unreal, imaginary, imagined, fanciful, fancied, illusory, delusory, figmental, phantasmal, phantasmagoric, spectral, ghostly, wraithlike. **5** *visionary schemes* impractical, unrealistic, unworkable, unfeasible, theoretical, hypothetical, idealistic, utopian.

visionary *noun* **1** *ancient visionaries* mystic, seer, prophet. **2** *too much of a visionary to run a business* dreamer, daydreamer, idealist, romantic, romanticist, fantasist, theorist, utopian.

visit *verb* **1** *visit his aunt | visit a friend in hospital* pay a visit to, go/come to see, pay a call on, call on, call/look in on, stop by; *inf.* pop/drop in on, look up. **2** *he is visiting his aunt this week* stay with, be the guest of. **3** *inspectors visiting the school* pay a call on, inspect, survey, examine. **4** *a city visited with the plague* attack, assail, afflict, smite, descend on, trouble, harrow, torture.

visit *noun* **1** *pay a visit to the new tenants* call, social call. **2** *their visit lasted three days* stay, sojourn, stopover.

visitation *noun* **1** *school inspectors making their annual visitation* official visit, inspection, tour of inspection, survey, review, scrutiny, examination. **2** *the peasants regarded the earthquake as a divine visitation* affliction, scourge, plague, pestilence, blight, disaster, tragedy, calamity, catastrophe, cataclysm.

visitor *noun* **1** *a visitor to the house* caller, guest. **2** *a visitor to the country* tourist, traveller, pilgrim.

visual *adjective* **1** *visual problems* seeing, optical, ocular. **2** *have visual appeal | the visual arts* to be seen, seeable, perceivable, discernible.

visualize *verb* conjure up, envisage, picture in the mind's eye, picture, envision, imagine, conceive.

vital *adjective* **1** *the heart performs a vital function | the vital organs* life-giving, life-preserving, life-sustaining, basic, fundamental, essential. **2** *matters of vital importance* essential, necessary, needed, indispensable, key, important, significant, imperative, urgent, critical, crucial, life-and-death. **3** *such a vital person* lively, animated, spirited, vivacious, vibrant, zestful, dynamic, energetic, vigorous, forceful. **4** *a vital error* deadly, lethal, fatal, fateful.
Opposites UNIMPORTANT; DISPENSABLE; PERIPHERAL; LISTLESS.

vitality *noun* *children full of vitality* life, liveliness, animation, spirit, spiritedness, vivacity, vibrancy, zest, zestfulness, dynamism, energy, vigour, forcefulness.

vitamin *noun. See table.*

vitriolic *adjective* *vitriolic criticism* caustic, mordant, acrimonious, bitter, acerbic, astringent, acid, acidulous, acrid, trenchant, virulent, spiteful, venomous, malicious, scathing, withering, sarcastic, sardonic; *inf.* bitchy.

vituperate *verb* revile, rail against, inveigh against, fulminate against, condemn,

VITAMINS	
Letter	**Chemical Name**
A	retinol
B_1	thiamine
B_2	riboflavin
B_3	niacin
B_6	pyridoxine
B_{12}	cyanocobalamin
B complex	folic acid, pantothenic acid, biotin, inositol, choline, pteroylglutamic acid
C	ascorbic acid
D_2	calciferol
D_3	cholecalciferol, lumisterol
E	tocopherol
H	biotin
K_1	phyllaquinone
K_2	menaquinone, menadione
P	citrin, bioflavonoid

denounce, upbraid, berate, reprimand, castigate, chastise, rebuke, scold, chide, censure, find fault with, take to task, abuse, vilify, denigrate; *inf.* slate.

vituperation *noun* revilement, invective, condemnation, denunciation, blame, reprimand, admonition, castigation, chastisement, rebuke, scolding, fault-finding, abuse, vilification, denigration; *inf.* flak.

vivacious *adjective* lively, full of life, animated, effervescent, bubbling, ebullient, sparkling, scintillating, light-hearted, spirited, high-spirited, gay, merry, jolly, vibrant, vivid, dynamic, vital.
Opposites DULL; LANGUID; LISTLESS.

vivacity *noun* liveliness, animation, effervescence, ebullience, sparkle, scintillation, spiritedness, spirit, high-spiritedness, sprightliness, gaiety, merriment, jollity, vibrancy, vividness, dynamism, vitality.

vivid *adjective* **1** *vivid colours* strong, intense, colourful, rich, glowing, bright, brilliant, clear. **2** *a vivid description* graphic, clear, lively, stirring, striking, powerful, impressive, highly coloured, dramatic, memorable, realistic, life-like, true to life. **3** *a vivid personality* strong, striking, flamboyant, memorable, dynamic, lively, animated, spirited, vibrant, vital.
Opposites DULL; COLOURLESS; NONDESCRIPT.

vocabulary *noun* **1** *have a limited vocabulary* word stock, lexicon, lexis. **2** *there's a vocabulary at the back of the book* word list, dictionary, glossary.

vocal *adjective* **1** *vocal noises* voiced, vocalized, spoken, said, uttered, expressed, articulated, oral. **2** *people vocal in their criticism* vociferous, outspoken, forthright, plain-spoken, free-spoken, blunt, clamorous, strident, loud, noisy.
Opposites TACITURN; RETICENT.

vocation *noun* profession, calling, occupation, walk of life, career, life's work, métier, trade, craft, job, work, employment, business, line, speciality.

vociferous *adjective* **1** *vociferous complaints* loud, noisy, clamorous, vehement, insistent.

2 *vociferous people complaining* vocal, outspoken, forthright, plain-spoken, strident, loud, noisy. *See* VOCAL 2.
Opposites SILENT; QUIET.

vogue *noun* **1** *the vogue for short skirts* fashion, mode, style, trend, taste, fad, craze, rage, latest thing, last word, *dernier cri*; *inf.* the thing. **2** *that hairstyle had a vogue in the '20s* fashionableness, modishness, popularity, currency, prevalence, favour, acceptance.

voice *noun* **1** *lose her voice* power of speech; powers of articulation. *See table.* **2** *give voice to her feelings* expression, utterance, verbalization, vocalization, airing. **3** *listen to the voice of the people* opinion, view, comment, feeling, wish, desire, vote. **4** *he is the voice of the people* spokesman, spokeswoman, spokesperson, mouthpiece, organ, agency, medium, vehicle.

TYPES OF SINGING VOICE	
baritone	falsetto
bass	mezzo-soprano
castrato	soprano
contralto/alto	tenor
counter-tenor	treble

voice *verb* *voice one's displeasure* put in words, express, give utterance to, utter, articulate, enunciate, mention, talk of, communicate, declare, assert, divulge, air, ventilate; *inf.* come out with.

void *adjective* **1** *a void space* empty, emptied, vacant, without contents, bare, clear, free, unfilled, unoccupied, uninhabited, untenanted, tenantless. **2** *void of people* devoid of, lacking, wanting, without, destitute of. **3** *the contract/ticket is now void* null and void, nullified, invalid, cancelled, inoperative, ineffective, not binding, not in force, non-viable, useless, worthless, nugatory.
Opposites FULL; OCCUPIED; VALID.

void *noun* **1** *stare into a void* empty space, emptiness, blank space, blankness, vacuum. **2** *a void left by the death of his wife* space, gap, lacuna, hole, hollow, chasm, abyss.

void *verb* **1** *void the decision* annul, nullify, disallow, invalidate, quash, cancel, repeal, revoke, rescind, reverse, abrogate. **2** *void the bucket/bowels* empty, drain, evacuate. **3** *void faeces* eject, expel, emit, discharge.

volatile *adjective* **1** *a volatile person* mercurial, changeable, variable, capricious, whimsical, fickle, flighty, giddy, inconstant, erratic, unstable. **2** *volatile trading conditions* changeable, variable, inconstant, erratic, unsteady, unstable, irregular, fitful. **3** *a volatile international situation* explosive, eruptive, charged, inflammatory, tense, strained. **4** *volatile substances* evaporative, vaporous, vaporescent.
Opposites STABLE; CONSTANT; CALM.

volition *noun* **of one's own volition** of one's own free will, of one's own choice, by one's own preference, voluntarily.

volley *noun* **1** *the police fired a volley of plastic bullets* barrage, cannonade, battery, broadside,

salvo, fusillade, shower. **2** *a volley of questions/insults* barrage, battery, stream, deluge.

volubility *noun* talkativeness, loquaciousness, loquacity, chattiness, articulacy, eloquence, fluency, glibness; *inf.* gift of the gab.

voluble *adjective* talkative, loquacious, garrulous, chatty, gossipy, chattering, articulate, eloquent, forthcoming, fluent, glib.
Opposites TACITURN; UNCOMMUNICATIVE.

volume *noun* **1** *publish a volume on butterflies* book, publication, tome. **2** *measure the volume* enclosed space, bulk, capacity. **3** *a volume of water escaped* quantity, amount, mass. **4** *turn down the volume | the volume of the music is too loud* loudness, sound, amplification.

voluminous *adjective* *a voluminous cape* capacious, roomy, commodious, ample, full, big, vast, billowing.

voluntarily *adverb* of one's own free will, freely, of one's own volition/accord, willingly, by choice, by preference, spontaneously, without being asked.

voluntary *adjective* **1** *attendance is voluntary* of one's own free will, volitional, of one's own accord, optional, discretional, at one's discretion, elective, non-compulsory, non-mandatory. **2** *undertake voluntary work* unpaid, without payment, honorary, volunteer.
Opposites COMPULSORY; OBLIGATORY.

volunteer *verb* **1** *volunteer one's services* offer, tender, proffer, present, put forward, advance. **2** *he volunteered as a helper* offer one's services, present oneself, step forward.

voluptuous *adjective* **1** *voluptuous pleasures* hedonistic, sybaritic, epicurean, pleasure-loving, self-indulgent, sensual, carnal, licentious, lascivious. **2** *a voluptuous woman* curvy, shapely, full-figured, ample, buxom, seductive; *inf.* curvaceous.

vomit *verb* **1** *he suddenly vomited* be sick, spew; *inf.* throw up, puke; *Am. inf.* barf. **2** *vomit blood* bring up, regurgitate, spew up, spit up. **3** *chimneys vomiting smoke* belch, eject, emit, send forth, eruct.

voracious *adjective* **1** *a voracious eater* gluttonous, greedy, ravenous, ravening, starving, hungry. **2** *a voracious appetite* insatiable, insatiate, unquenchable, prodigious, uncontrolled. **3** *a voracious reader* compulsive, enthusiastic, eager.

vortex *noun* whirlpool, maelstrom, eddy, swirl, whirlwind.

vote *noun* **1** *have a vote on who should lead* ballot, poll, election, referendum, plebiscite. **2** *get the vote* right to vote, franchise, suffrage.

vote *verb* **1** *vote for a new president* cast one's vote, go to the polls, mark one's ballot paper. **2** *vote the government in* elect, opt for, return. **3** *I vote that we go home* suggest, propose, recommend, advocate.
Opposites ABSTAIN.

vouch *verb* **vouch for** **1** *vouch for his honesty* attest to, bear witness to, give assurance of, answer for, be responsible for, guarantee, go/stand bail for. **2** *vouch for the painting's authenticity* certify, warrant, confirm, verify, validate, substantiate.

voucher *noun* chit, slip, ticket, token, document.

vouchsafe *verb* **1** *vouchsafe them a free pardon* | *vouchsafe a reply* grant, give, accord, confer on, yield to, cede to, favour with. **2** *vouchsafe to reply* deign, condescend.

vow *noun take a vow of silence* | *wedding vows* oath, pledge, promise.

vow *verb vow to be true* swear, state under oath, pledge, promise, undertake, give one's word of honour.

voyage *noun* **1** *a sea voyage* crossing, cruise, passage. **2** *voyage by land and sea* journey, trip, expedition; travels.

voyage *verb* **1** *voyage across the Atlantic* sail, cruise. **2** *voyage through space* travel, journey, take a trip.

vulgar *adjective* **1** *vulgar language/jokes* rude, indecent, indecorous, indelicate, unseemly, offensive, distasteful, obnoxious, risqué, suggestive, off-colour, blue, ribald, bawdy, obscene, lewd, salacious, licentious, concupiscent, smutty, dirty, filthy, pornographic, scatological; *inf.* raunchy. **2** *vulgar table manners* rude, impolite, ill-mannered, unmannerly, ill-bred, common, coarse, boorish, rough, crude. **3** *vulgar decorations* tasteless, gross, crass, unrefined, tawdry, ostentatious, showy, flashy, gaudy; *inf.* flash. **4** *the vulgar herd* common, ordinary, low, low-born, ignorant, unsophisticated, unrefined, uneducated, illiterate, uncultured, uncultivated, uncouth, crude.
Opposites DECOROUS; GENTEEL; MANNERLY; TASTEFUL.

vulgarity *noun* **1** *the vulgarity of the language/jokes* rudeness, indelicacy, offensiveness, suggestiveness, ribaldry, obscenity, smuttiness; *inf.* raunchiness. *See* VULGAR 1. **2** *the vulgarity of his table manners* rudeness, impoliteness, ill manners, coarseness, crudeness. *See* VULGAR 2. **3** *the vulgarity of the decorations* tastelessness, grossness, crassness, tawdriness, ostentation, gaudiness. *See* VULGAR 3. **4** *the vulgarity of the common herd* commonness, lowness, ignorance, unsophisticatedness, lack of refinement, uncouthness, crudeness. *See* VULGAR 4.

vulnerable *adjective* **1** *vulnerable armies/children* open to attack, attackable, assailable, exposed, unprotected, unguarded, defenceless, easily hurt/wounded/damaged, powerless, helpless, weak, sensitive, thin-skinned. **2** *vulnerable to criticism/temptation* open to, wide open to, exposed to, liable to, subject to.
Opposites INVULNERABLE; IMMUNE.

wad noun **1** *a wad of putty* | *wads of cotton wool* lump, mass, chunk, hunk, ball, plug, block. **2** *a wad of bank notes* bundle, roll.

wadding noun stuffing, filling, packing, padding, lining.

waddle verb sway, wobble, totter, toddle, shuffle.

wade verb **1** *wade the stream* | *wade across the snow* ford, cross, traverse. **2** *children wading in the stream* paddle, splash about. **3** *wade through piles of papers* proceed with difficulty, work one's way, plough (through), labour (through), toil/plug/peg away. **wade in** *if we all wade in we'll soon get finished* set to, set to work, pitch in, buckle down, go to it, put one's shoulder to the wheel; *inf.* get cracking, get stuck in. **wade into** *wade into the boy who hit/criticized his sister* attack, set about, assault, launch oneself at; *inf.* light into, tear into.

waffle noun *it was all waffle so we didn't learn anything* meaningless talk/writing, padding, equivocation, prattle, jabbering, verbiage, logorrhoea; *inf.* wittering.

waffle verb *speakers waffling on to a bored audience* | *waffle without getting to the point* ramble, prattle, jabber, babble; *inf.* rabbit, witter.

waft verb **1** *leaves wafting down the river* | *smells wafting from the kitchen* float, glide, drift, be carried/borne/conveyed. **2** *the wind wafted the leaves towards us* carry, bear, convey, transport, transmit.

wag[1] noun **1** *a wag of the tail* swing, sway, vibration, quiver, shake. **2** *a wag of the finger* wiggle, wobble, wave. **3** *a wag of the head* nod, bob.

wag[2] verb **1** *the dog's tail wagged* swing, sway, vibrate, quiver, shake, rock, twitch. **2** *wag one's finger* waggle, wiggle, wobble, wave. **3** *wag one's head* nod, bob.

wag[3] noun *he's quite a wag* wit, humorist, jester, joker, jokester, comic, comedian, comedienne, wisecracker, punner.

wage noun *on a low wage* pay, remuneration; wages, earnings. *See* WAGES 1.

wage verb *wage war* carry on, conduct, execute, engage in, pursue, undertake, devote oneself to, practise.

wager noun *lay a wager that he will win* bet, gamble, stake, pledge, hazard; *inf.* flutter.

wager verb *I wager that he will win* lay a wager, bet, place/make/lay a bet, lay odds, put money on, speculate.

wages plural noun **1** *low wages* | *collect one's wages* pay, payment, fee, remuneration, salary, emolument, stipend; earnings. **2** *the wages of sin* recompense, requital, retribution; returns, deserts.

waggish adjective playful, roguish, impish, mischievous, joking, jesting, jocular, jocose, facetious, witty, amusing, entertaining, droll, whimsical.

waggle verb *waggle one's finger/ears/bottom* wiggle, wobble, shake, sway, wag, quiver.

waif noun stray, foundling, orphan.

wail noun *the wails of the bereaved/abandoned children* cry of grief/pain, lament, lamentation, weeping, sob, moan, groan, whine, complaint, howl, yowl, ululation.

wail verb *widows/children wailing* cry, lament, weep, sob, moan, groan, whine, complain, howl, yowl, ululate.

wait verb **1** *wait here* stay, remain, rest, linger, tarry, abide. **2** *you'll just have to wait and see* | *wait until you hear from him* be patient, hold back, stand by, bide one's time, hang fire, mark time, cool one's heels; *inf.* sit tight, hold one's horses, sweat it out. **3** *wait his arrival* await, wait for, look/watch out for, anticipate, expect, be ready for, be in readiness for. **4** *wait dinner for him* delay, postpone, put off, hold off, hold back, defer. **5** *wait for him* | *wait for his arrival* be ready, anticipate, expect. **wait on** *wait on the dinner guests* act as a waiter/waitress to, serve, attend to. **wait up** *wait up until his daughter returns* stay up, stay awake, keep vigil.

wait noun *have a wait of two hours for the bus* period of waiting, interval, stay, delay, hold-up.

waiter, waitress noun steward, stewardess, server, attendant.

waive verb **1** *waive one's right to appeal* relinquish, renounce, give up, abandon, surrender, yield, cede. **2** *waive the rules* set aside, forgo, disregard, ignore. **3** *waive the decision until tomorrow* postpone, defer, put off, delay, shelve; *inf.* put on the back-burner.
Opposites CLAIM; UPHOLD; PURSUE.

wake verb **1** *wake at dawn* awake, awaken, waken, wake up, waken up, rouse, stir, come to, get up, arise. **2** *wake the children* wake up, waken, rouse. **3** *wake him out of sloth* rouse, stir up, activate, stimulate, spur, prod, galvanize, provoke. **4** *wake to the fact that he is dishonest* become aware/conscious, become alert, become mindful/heedful. **5** *wake old memories* awaken, evoke, call up, conjure up, rouse, stir, revive, resuscitate, revivify, rekindle, reignite.
Opposites SLEEP; SNOOZE; DOZE.

wake noun *hold a wake for his dead mother* vigil, death-watch, watch.

wakeful adjective **1** *wakeful children* unsleeping, restless, tossing and turning, insomniac. **2** *wakeful security staff* alert, on the alert, vigilant, on the lookout, on one's guard, on the qui vive, watchful, observant, attentive,

heedful, wary.
Opposites ASLEEP; INATTENTIVE.

waken *verb* **1** *waken at dawn* wake, awaken, stir. *See* WAKE *verb* 1. **2** *waken the children* wake, rouse. *See* WAKE *verb* 2. **3** *waken old memories* wake, awaken, evoke, call up, stir, revive, rekindle. *See* WAKE *verb* 5.

walk *verb* **1** *we walked rather than take the car* go by foot, travel on foot, foot it; *inf.* go by shank's pony, hoof it. **2** *walk, don't run* stroll, saunter, amble, plod, trudge, hike, tramp, trek, march, stride, step out. **3** *walk her home* accompany, escort, convoy. **walk off/away with 1** *walk off with the firm's takings* make/run off with, carry off, snatch, steal, filch, pilfer, embezzle. **2** *walk off with the match/prize* win easily, win hands down. **walk out 1** *he had a row with the boss and walked out* leave suddenly, make a sudden departure, get up and go, storm out, flounce out; *inf.* take off. **2** *the workers walked out at lunch-time* go on strike, call a strike, withdraw one's labour, down tools, stop work, take industrial action. **walk out on** *walk out on his wife and children* desert, abandon, forsake, leave, leave in the lurch, run away from, throw over, jilt; *inf.* chuck, dump.
Opposites RUN; DRIVE.

walk *noun* **1** *go for a walk* stroll, saunter, amble, promenade, ramble, hike, tramp, march, constitutional, airing. **2** *he has a distinctive walk* manner of walking, gait, pace, step, stride. **3** *the walk up to the house* road, avenue, drive, promenade, path, pathway, footpath, track, lane, alley. **4** *the postman's usual walk* route, beat, round, run, circuit. **walk of life** social rank/status, sphere, area, line of work, profession, career, vocation, job, employment, trade, craft, *métier*.

walker *noun* pedestrian, hiker, rambler, wayfarer, footslogger.

walk-out *noun* strike, industrial action, stoppage.

walk-over *noun winning the prize was a walk-over* easy victory; *inf.* piece of cake, child's play, doddle, push-over.

wall *noun* **1** *areas of the house separated by walls* partition, room divider. **2** *the area had a wall around it* enclosure. **3** *the city walls are still standing* fortification, rampart, barricade, parapet, bulwark, stockade, breastwork. **4** *create new tariff walls* barrier, obstacle, impediment, block.

wallet *noun* pocket book, notecase, purse, pouch; *Am.* billfold.

wallow *verb* **1** *the hippopotamus was wallowing in mud* roll, tumble about, lie around, splash around. **2** *wallow in luxury/self-pity* luxuriate in, bask in, take pleasure/satisfaction in, indulge oneself in, delight in, revel in, glory in, enjoy.

wan *adjective* **1** *looking wan after illness* pale, pallid, ashen, white, white as a sheet/ghost, anaemic, colourless, bloodless, waxen, pasty, peaky, tired looking, washed out, sickly. **2** *a wan light* dim, faint, weak, feeble, pale.
Opposites FLUSHED; RUDDY; BRIGHT.

wand *noun* baton, stick, staff, twig, sprig, withe, withy.

wander *verb* **1** *wander over the hills* ramble, roam, meander, rove, range, prowl, saunter, stroll, amble, peregrinate, drift; *inf.* traipse, mooch. **2** *rivers wandering along* wind, meander, curve, zigzag. **3** *wander from the path/point | wander from the straight and narrow* stray, depart, diverge, veer, swerve, deviate. **4** *the child has wandered off* lose one's way, get lost, go off course, go astray, go off at a tangent. **5** *the old man is wandering* be incoherent, ramble, babble, talk nonsense, rave, be delirious.

wander *noun have a wander in the hills | a wander round the shops* ramble, saunter, stroll, amble.

wanderer *noun* rambler, roamer, rover, drifter, traveller, itinerant, wayfarer, nomad, bird of passage, rolling stone, gypsy; vagabond, vagrant, tramp, derelict; beggar, homeless/displaced person; *Am.* hobo; *inf.* bum.

wandering *adjective* **1** *wandering bands of people* rambling, roaming, roving, drifting, travelling, itinerant, peripatetic, nomadic, gypsy, vagabond, vagrant, migrant, transient, homeless. **2** *wandering rivers/paths* winding, meandering, curving, bending, zigzagging.

wane *verb* **1** *the moon has waned* pass full moon, decrease, diminish, dwindle. **2** *his power/importance is waning* decrease, decline, diminish, dwindle, shrink, contract, taper off, subside, sink, ebb, dim, fade away, vanish, die out, draw to a close, evanesce, peter out, wind down, be on the way out, abate, fail, become weak, deteriorate, degenerate.
Opposites WAX; INCREASE; GROW.

wane *noun the wane of his power/importance* decline, decrease, diminution, dwindling, contraction, subsidence, ebb, vanishing, evanescence, abatement, failure, weakening, deteriorating, degenerating. *See* WANE *verb* 2.

want *verb* **1** *children wanting sweets* wish, wish for, desire, demand, call for, long for, hope for, yearn for, pine for, fancy, crave, hanker after, hunger for, thirst for, lust after, covet, need; *inf.* have a yen for. **2** *he wants to emigrate* wish, desire, long, yearn. **3** *the garden wants weeding | the car wants petrol* need, be/stand in need of, require. **4** *poor people wanting food* have need of, lack, be lacking, be without, be devoid of, be bereft of, be short of, be deficient in, have insufficient.

want *noun* **1** *for want of time* lack, absence, dearth, deficiency, inadequacy, insufficiency, shortness, paucity, shortage, scarcity, scarceness, scantiness. **2** *children expressing their wants* wish, desire, demand, longing, yearning, fancy, craving, hankering, hunger, thirst, lust, covetousness; *inf.* yen. **3** *give aid to people in want* need, neediness, privation, poverty, destitution, penury, indigence.
Opposites PRESENCE; ABUNDANCE; WEALTH.

wanting *adjective* **1** *find the service wanting* lacking, deficient, inadequate, imperfect, not up to standard/par, not good enough, disappointing, not acceptable, not up to expectations, flawed, faulty, defective, unsound, substandard, inferior, second-rate, patchy,

sketchy. **2** *something wanting in the machine/ organization* lacking, missing, absent, not there, short.
Opposites SUFFICIENT; ADEQUATE; ACCEPTABLE.

wanting *preposition a car wanting an engine* lacking, in need of, without, sans; *inf.* minus.

wanton *adjective* **1** *wanton women seducing the soldiers* promiscuous, fast, immoral, loose, immodest, shameless, unchaste, unvirtuous, of easy virtue, impure, abandoned, lustful, lecherous, lascivious, libidinous, licentious, libertine, dissolute, dissipated, debauched, degenerate. **2** *wanton destruction* wilful, malicious, malevolent, spiteful, wicked, evil, cruel, unmotivated, motiveless, arbitrary, groundless, unjustifiable, unjustified, needless, unnecessary, uncalled-for, unprovoked, gratuitous, senseless, pointless, purposefulness. **3** *a wanton wind* capricious, playful, sportive, careless, heedless, impulsive, rash, reckless, devil-may-care. **4** *weeds growing in wanton profusion* wild, unrestrained, uncontrolled, immoderate, lavish, extravagant, abundant, profuse, luxuriant.
Opposites MORAL; CHASTE; JUSTIFIABLE.

wanton *noun wantons out to seduce the men in the bar | wantons seducing older women* loose woman, woman of easy virtue, slut, trollop, harlot, strumpet, prostitute, whore; lecher, Casanova, libertine, debauchee, rake.

war *noun* **1** *a state of war between the nations* conflict, strife, hostility, enmity, antagonism, animus, ill will, bad blood. **2** *the war lasted five years | take part in many wars* warfare, conflict, strife, combat, fighting, struggle, armed conflict, battle, fight, confrontation, skirmish;

hostilities. *See table. See also tables at* BATTLE, SIEGE. **3** *the war against poverty* battle, fight, campaign, crusade.
Opposites PEACE; HARMONY; TRUCE.

war *verb nations warring with nations* wage/make war, be at war, conduct a war, do combat/battle, fight, take up arms, cross swords, quarrel, wrangle.

ward *noun* **1** *a hospital ward* room, compartment, cubicle. **2** *counting the votes in the various wards* administrative district, district, division, quarter, zone. **3** *his niece is his ward* charge, protégé, dependant, pupil.

ward *verb* **ward off** **1** *ward off a blow* fend off, stave off, parry, avert, deflect, turn aside. **2** *ward off intruders* drive back, repel, repulse, beat back, rout, put to flight, scatter, disperse; *inf.* send packing. **3** *ward off the attack* fend off, stave off, keep at bay, keep at arm's length, avert, rebuff, foil, frustrate, thwart, checkmate.

warden *noun* **1** *traffic warden* supervisor, superintendent, steward, overseer. **2** *game wardens* custodian, keeper, guardian, protector, guard, watchman. **3** *a prison warden* prison officer, guard.

warder, wardress *noun* prison officer, guard, warden, jailer, gaoler; *inf.* screw.

wardrobe *noun* **1** *put the suits in the wardrobe* clothes cupboard; *Am.* closet. **2** *she has a huge wardrobe | her summer wardrobe* collection/set of clothes, trousseau.

warehouse *noun* store, storehouse, depot, depository, stockroom.

WARS

War	Dates	War	Dates
American Civil War	1861–5	Peninsular War	1808–14
Balkan Wars	1912–3	Persian Wars	5th century B.C.
Boer War	1880–1, 1899–1902	Punic Wars	264–241 B.C.,
Bosnian Civil War	from 1992		218–201 B.C.,
Crimean War	1853–6		149–146 B.C.
English Civil War	1642–9	Russian Civil War	1918–21
Falklands War	1982	Russo-Japanese War	1904–5
First World War	1914–8	Samnite Wars	343–341 B.C.,
Franco-Prussian War	1870–1		316–314 B.C.,
French and Indian			298–290 B.C.
War	1754–63	Second World War	1939–45
French Indochina War	1946–54	Seven Years War	1756–63
French Wars of Religion	1562–98	Sino-Japanese Wars	1894–5, 1937–45
Gallic Wars	58–51 B.C.	Six Day War	1967
Great Northern War	1700–21	Spanish-American War	1898
Gulf War	1991	Spanish Civil War	1936–9
Hundred Years War	1337–1453	Thirty Years War	1618–48
Iran-Iraq War	1980–8	Vietnam War	1954–75
Korean War	1950–3	War of 1812	1812–4
Macedonian Wars	214–205 B.C.,	War of American	
	200–196 B.C.,	Independence	1775–83
	171–168 B.C.,	War of the Austrian	
	149–148 B.C.	Succession	1740–8
Mexican War	1846–8	War of the Spanish	
Napoleonic Wars	1805–15	Succession	1701–14
Opium Wars	1839–42, 1856–60	Wars of the Roses	1455–85
Peloponnesian Wars	431–404 B.C.	Yom Kippur War	1973

wares *plural noun* goods, products, commodities, lines; merchandise, produce, stuff, stock.

warfare *noun* armed conflict, combat, strife, fighting, battle, campaigning, passage at arms; hostilities.

warily *adverb* **1** *tread warily* carefully, with care, cautiously, gingerly, circumspectly, guardedly, on one's guard, on the alert, on the qui vive, watchfully, vigilantly. *See* WARY 1. **2** *treat him warily* cautiously, suspiciously, distrustfully, mistrustfully, charily; *inf.* cagily.

wariness *noun* **1** *tread with wariness* care, carefulness, caution, circumspection, alertness, attention, heedfulness, watchfulness, vigilance. **2** *treat the stranger with wariness* caution, circumspection, suspicion, distrust, mistrust.

warlike *adjective* aggressive, belligerent, bellicose, pugnacious, combative, militaristic, militant, martial.
Opposites PEACEFUL; PEACEABLE; PACIFIC; CONCILIATORY.

warlock *noun* sorcerer, wizard, male witch, magician.

warm *adjective* **1** *warm water* heated, tepid, lukewarm. **2** *a warm day* sunny, balmy. **3** *a warm person/personality | a warm heart* kindly, kind, friendly, affable, amiable, genial, cordial, sympathetic, affectionate, loving, tender, caring, charitable, sincere, genuine. **4** *receive a warm welcome* hearty, cordial, genial, friendly, hospitable, enthusiastic, eager, sincere, heartfelt, ardent, vehement, passionate, intense, fervent, effusive. **5** *the international situation is getting rather warm* heated, hostile, tense, strained, explosive, dangerous, perilous, hazardous, tricky, difficult, unpleasant, uncomfortable, disagreeable. **6** *players of the guessing game getting warm* close, near.
Opposites COLD; COOL; UNFRIENDLY.

warm *verb* **1** *warm the food in the oven* warm up, make warm, heat, heat up, reheat. **2** *feel themselves warming to her | warm to the idea* feel well-disposed, feel sympathetic, feel a liking (for), feel attracted. **warm up 1** *warm up the food* heat up. *See* WARM *verb* 1. **2** *warm the party up* liven, enliven, put some life into, cheer up, animate; *inf.* get going. **3** *warm up for the race* loosen up, limber up, prepare, exercise, practise, train.

warmed up *adjective* **1** *warmed up food* reheated, heated up. **2** *warmed up ideas/prose* repeated, unoriginal, derivative, stale, hackneyed, trite, stock, banal; *inf.* old hat.

warmth *noun* **1** *feel the warmth of the fire/sun* warmness, heat, hotness. **2** *the warmth of her personality* kindness, kindliness, friendliness, affability, amiability, geniality, cordiality, sympathy, sympatheticness, affectionateness, affection, lovingness, love, tenderness, care, charitableness, charity, sincerity, genuineness. **3** *the warmth of the welcome* heartiness, cordiality, geniality, friendliness, hospitableness, hospitality, enthusiasm, eagerness, sincerity, ardour, vehemence, passion, intensity, fervour, effusiveness.
Opposites COOL; CHILL; APATHY.

warn *verb* **1** *write to warn them of the approaching confrontation/danger* inform, notify, give notice, give prior notice/tell, let know, acquaint, give fair warning, forewarn; *inf.* tip off, put wise. **2** *warn them to be careful* advise, exhort, urge, counsel, caution, forewarn, prewarn, put on the alert, make aware. **3** *the headmaster warned the unruly pupils* give a warning to, admonish, remonstrate with.

warning *noun* **1** *send them a warning of the approaching confrontation* information, notification, notice, word, forewarning; *inf.* tip-off. **2** *deliver a warning that they should be careful* caution; advice, exhortation, counselling. **3** *get a warning from the headmaster* admonition, remonstrance. **4** *he regarded it as a warning of things to come* omen, premonition, foretoken, token, augury, signal, sign, threat, caveat.

warrant *noun* **1** *they are acting under warrant of the king* authorization, consent, sanction, permission, validation, licence, imprimatur, seal of approval. **2** *a warrant for his arrest | a death warrant* authorization, official document, written order; papers. **3** *a sales warrant* voucher, chit, slip, paper.

warrant *verb* **1** *the law warrants the procedure* authorize, consent to, sanction, permit, license, approve of. **2** *her interference was not warranted* justify, vindicate, excuse, be a defence of, explain away, account for, be a reason for, offer grounds for, support. **3** *unable to warrant the truth of the statement* guarantee, swear to, answer for, vouch for, testify to, bear witness to, support, endorse, underwrite, back up, stand by.

warrantable *adjective* **1** *his action was warrantable by the king* authorizable, sanctionable, approvable. *See* WARRANT *verb* 1. **2** *his interference was scarcely warrantable* justifiable, vindicable, excusable, explainable, explicable, reasonable, supportable.

warring *adjective* *warring factions* conflicting, opposing, clashing, hostile, rival; *inf.* at each other's throats.

warrior *noun* fighter, fighting man, combatant, soldier, champion. *See table at* MILITARY.

wary *adjective* **1** *be wary when you walk alone at night* careful, cautious, circumspect, chary, on one's guard, alert, on the alert/look out, on the qui vive, attentive, heedful, watchful, vigilant, observant; *inf.* wide awake, on one's toes. **2** *you should be wary of strangers* careful, cautious, chary, suspicious, distrustful, mistrustful; *inf.* leery.
Opposites unwary; UNSUSPECTING; INATTENTIVE; TRUSTFUL.

wash *verb* **1** *I must wash before breakfast* wash oneself, have a wash, bath, shower, have a bath/shower. **2** *wash one's face | wash the floor* clean, cleanse, sponge, scrub. **3** *wash one's clothes* launder, clean. **4** *wash one's hair* shampoo, clean. **5** *waves washing against the rocks* splash against, dash against, break against, beat against. **6** *his story just won't wash* be accepted, be plausible, be convincing, hold up, hold water, stand up, bear scrutiny; *inf.* stick. **7** *the current washed the boat away* carry off, bear away, sweep away, convey, transport. **8** *wash away the river bank* erode, abrade, wear, denude. **9** *wash off/out the stain* remove by washing, sponge, scrub.

wash noun **1** *have a wash | in need of a wash* clean, cleaning, cleansing, bath, shower. **2** *I must do the wash* washing, laundry. **3** *put the wash in the basket* dirty washing, dirty clothes, soiled linen. **4** *the wash of the waves against the rocks | the ship's wash* surge, swell, roll, flow, splash. **5** *antiseptic wash* liquid, lotion, salve, application, preparation. **6** *put a yellow wash on the walls* paint, stain, varnish, coat, layer, film, overlay, screen.

washed out adjective **1** *washed-out jeans* faded, blanched, bleached. **2** *always wear washed-out colours* pale, flat, lacklustre. **3** *a washed-out complexion* pale, wan, pallid, white, anaemic, etiolated, colourless, drawn, haggard. **4** *feeling washed out after a hard day* exhausted, tired out, worn out, weary, fatigued, spent, drained; *inf.* all in, done in, dead on one's feet, dead, dog-tired, played out, pooped, knackered.
Opposites BRIGHT; RUDDY; ENERGETIC; perky.

waspish adjective petulant, peevish, querulous, touchy, testy, irritable, irascible, cross, snappish, cantankerous, splenetic, short-tempered, ill-tempered, bad-tempered, crabbed, crotchety, grumpy.

waste verb **1** *waste resources/money | jokes wasted on the audience* squander, dissipate, fritter away, misspend, misuse, spend recklessly, throw away, go through, run through; *inf.* blow. **2** *his legs are gradually wasting away* grow weak, wither, atrophy, become emaciated. **3** *the disease had wasted his legs* weaken, enfeeble, sap the strength of, wither, debilitate, atrophy, emaciate, shrivel, shrink. **4** *the invading army wasted the land* destroy, devastate, wreak havoc on, pillage, plunder, sack, spoliate, loot, maraud, harry.
Opposites CONSERVE; SAVE; STRENGTHEN.

waste noun **1** *a waste of money/time* squandering, dissipation, frittering away, misspending, misuse, prodigality, unthriftiness. **2** *dispose of the waste* rubbish, refuse, debris, dross; dregs, leavings; *Am.* garbage, trash. **3** *lost in the wastes of Antarctica* desert, wasteland, wilderness, barrenness, emptiness, vastness.

waste adjective **1** *waste material* left over, unused, superfluous, supernumerary, unwanted, worthless, useless. **2** *waste land* desert, barren, uncultivated, unproductive, arid, bare, desolate, solitary, lonely, empty, void, uninhabited, unpopulated, wild, bleak, cheerless.

wasted adjective **1** *wasted resources* squandered, dissipated, exhausted, used up, misspent, misused. **2** *wasted opportunities* missed, lost, past, bungled. **3** *wasted limbs* weakened, weak, withered, atrophied, emaciated, shrivelled, shrunken.

wasteful adjective *wasteful use of the supplies* prodigal, profligate, thriftless, spendthrift, extravagant, lavish.
Opposites THRIFTY; FRUGAL; ECONOMICAL.

wastrel noun **1** *a wastrel getting through a fortune* waster, spendthrift, prodigal, squanderer, big spender. **2** *she's hard-working but he's a complete wastrel* good-for-nothing, layabout, ne'er-do-well, idler, drone, loafer, shirker, malingerer.

watch verb **1** *watch the moon* look at, observe, view, eye, gaze at, stare at, gape at, peer at, contemplate, behold, inspect, scrutinize, survey, scan, examine. **2** *watch his movements | watch the man next door* keep watch on, keep an eye on, keep in sight, follow, spy on; *inf.* keep tabs on. **3** *watch and don't get mugged* look out, pay attention, take heed/care, be on the alert/lookout, be watchful. *See* WATCH *verb* watch out. **4** *could you watch the children for me* mind, take care of, look after, supervise, superintend, tend, guard, protect; *inf.* keep an eye on. **watch out 1** *watch out and don't get mugged* watch, watch oneself, be watchful, be on the watch, mind out, look out, pay attention, take heed/care, be careful, have a care, be on the alert/lookout, keep a sharp lookout, be vigilant, be wary, be on the qui vive; *inf.* keep an eye open, keep one's eyes peeled/skinned. **2** *watch out for the postman* look out for, wait for; *inf.* keep an eye open for. **watch over** *shepherds watch over the sheep | lawyers watching over our interests* look after, tend, take care of, guard, protect, shield, preserve.
Opposites IGNORE; DISREGARD; NEGLECT.

watch noun **1** *the time by my watch* wristwatch, pocket watch, timepiece, chronometer. **2** *on watch at night* guard, vigil.

watchdog noun **1** *a watchdog guarding the premises at night* guard dog. **2** *a watchdog of consumers' interests* custodian, guardian, protector, monitor, scrutineer, inspector.

watcher noun spectator, onlooker, looker-on, observer, viewer, witness, spy.

watchful adjective *keep a watchful eye on the building* observant, alert, vigilant, attentive, heedful, sharp-eyed, eagle-eyed, wary, circumspect.
Opposites INATTENTIVE; CARELESS.

watchman noun security guard/man, guard, custodian, caretaker.

watchword noun **1** *quality is meant to be the watchword of the firm* slogan, motto, maxim, catchphrase, catch-phrase, byword, battle/rallying cry. **2** *unable to gain entry without the correct watchword* password, magic word, sign, shibboleth.

water noun **1** *drink water* Adam's ale; tap water, mineral water, bottled water. *See table at* DRINK. **2** *have a picnic by the water* aquatic region; sea, river, lake, loch, pool, reservoir. **hold water** *your theory won't hold water* be tenable, ring true, bear examination, work out.

water verb **1** *water the garden* sprinkle, moisten, dampen, wet, water down, douse, hose, spray, drench, saturate, sodden, flood. **2** *his eyes are watering* exude water, moisten, leak. **3** *water the drinks* add water to, water down, dilute, thin, weaken, adulterate. **water down 1** *water down the drinks* water, add water to, dilute. *See* WATER *verb* 3. **2** *water down the*

WATERFALLS	
Waterfall/Falls	**Country**
Angel	Venezuela
Augrabies	South Africa
Cauvery	India
Cuquenán	Venezuela
Della	Canada
Grande Cascade	France
Iguaçu	Argentina/Brazil
Jog	India
Kabalega	Uganda
Kalambo	Tanzania/Zambia
Kapachira	Malawi
Kegon	Japan
Mardalsfossen	Norway
Niagara	Canada/U.S.A.
Ruacana	Angola
Sutherland	New Zealand
Takakkaw	Canada
Tugela	South Africa
Victoria	Zimbabwe/Zambia
Wallaman	Australia
Yosemite	U.S.A.

TYPES OF ELECTROMAGNETIC WAVE	
gamma rays	submillimetre
infrared (IR)	radiation
radiation	ultraviolet (UV)
light	radiation
microwaves	visible radiation
radar waves	X-rays
radio waves	

hem and haw, vacillate, beat about the bush; *inf.* shilly-shally, pussyfoot around, blow hot and cold. **3** *lights wavering* flicker, quiver, tremble. **4** *drunks wavering down the road* weave, reel, totter, teeter, stagger, wobble.

wavy *adjective* undulating, curvy, curling, squiggly, rippled, curving, winding. *Opposites* STRAIGHT.

wax *verb* **1** *the moon was waxing* approach full moon, get bigger, increase in size, enlarge. **2** *his power waxed in time of war* increase, grow, develop, enlarge, magnify, extend, widen, broaden, spread, mushroom. **3** *wax lyrical about his achievements* become, grow. *Opposites* WANE; DECREASE; FADE.

way *noun* **1** *walk along the paved way* road, roadway, street, thoroughfare, track, path, pathway, lane, avenue, drive. **2** *is this the way to London?* route, road, course, direction. **3** *the right way to cook the meat* method, course of action, process, procedure, technique, system, plan, scheme, manner, *modus operandi*; means. **4** *admire the way in which she dresses* manner, style, fashion, mode. **5** *dislike his brusque way* conduct, behaviour, practice, wont, manner, style, nature, personality, temperament, disposition, character; habit, custom, characteristic, trait, attribute, mannerism, peculiarity, idiosyncrasy. **6** *a long way from here to London* distance, length, stretch, journey. **7** *make way for the children* room, elbowroom, space. **8** *we've got some way to winning* | *under way* headway, progress, advance. **9** *things are in a bad way* state, condition, situation; *inf.* shape. **10** *in some ways it will be useful* | *can I help you in any way?* feature, aspect, detail, point, particular, respect, sense. **by the way** incidentally, by the by, in passing, *en passant*. **give way 1** *the bridge gave way* collapse, give, fall to pieces, crumble, cave in. **2** *he refused to help but finally gave way* yield, back down, make concessions, concede defeat, acquiesce. **on the/one's way** coming, going, proceeding, journeying, travelling.

extent of the disaster play down, downplay, tone down, soft-pedal, understate, underemphasize.

waterfall *noun* cascade, cataract; falls. *See table.*

watertight *adjective* **1** *the boat/jacket is watertight* waterproof, sound. **2** *a watertight excuse* sound, flawless, incontrovertible, indisputable, foolproof, unassailable, impregnable.

watery *adjective* **1** *a watery substance* aqueous, liquid, liquefied, fluid, hydrous. **2** *watery terrain* wet, damp, moist, sodden, soggy, squelchy, saturated, waterlogged, marshy, boggy, swampy, miry. **3** *a watery soup/batter* thin, runny, weak, dilute, diluted, watered down, adulterated, tasteless, flavourless; *inf.* wishy-washy. **4** *watery colours* pale, wan, insipid; *inf.* wishy-washy. **5** *watery eyes* moist, tearful, teary, weeping, weepy, lachrymose. *Opposites* SOLID; DRY; THICK.

wave *verb* **1** *corn waving in the breeze* undulate, ripple, stir, flutter, flap, sway, swing, shake, quiver, oscillate. **2** *wave one's hand/flag* move up and down, move to and fro, wag, waggle, flutter. **3** *wave a sword in the air* brandish, swing, shake. **4** *wave to them to follow* gesture, gesticulate, signal, sign, beckon, indicate. **5** *her hair waves beautifully* undulate, curl, kink. **wave aside** *wave aside his objections* set aside, dismiss, reject, disregard, ignore.

wave *noun* **1** *children playing in the waves* breaker, billow, roller, comber, ripple, white horse, white cap; swell, surf. **2** *a wave of visitors* stream, flow, rush, surge, flood. **3** *the waves in her hair* undulation, curl, kink. **4** *a wave of enthusiasm* | *a crime wave* surge, upsurge, ground-swell, welling up, rush, outbreak, rash. **5** *waves in the water* | *light waves* ripple, vibration, oscillation, undulation. *See table.*

waver *verb* **1** *his gaze did not waver* | *his courage began to waver* become unsteady, falter, wobble, hesitate. **2** *we wavered and someone else got in first* | *waver between staying and leaving* be irresolute/indecisive, hesitate, dither, equivocate,

wayfarer *noun* traveller, walker, hiker, rambler, wanderer, roamer, rover, nomad, gypsy, vagabond, vagrant.

wayfaring *adjective* travelling, journeying, walking, hiking, wandering, roaming, roving, drifting, nomadic, itinerant, peripatetic, on the move/go.

waylay *verb* **1** *the highwaymen waylaid them* lie in wait for, ambush, hold up, attack. **2** *she waylaid the teacher to ask about her child* accost, stop and talk to, intercept, pounce on, swoop down on.

wayward *adjective* **1** *wayward children* wilful, self-willed, headstrong, stubborn, obstinate, obdurate, perverse, contrary, uncooperative, refractory, recalcitrant, contumacious, unruly, ungovernable, unmanageable, incorrigible, intractable, difficult, fractious, disobedient, insubordinate. **2** *wayward fancies/youngster* capricious, whimsical, fickle, inconstant, changeable, changeful, variable, erratic, unpredictable, unstable, mercurial, volatile, flighty. **Opposites** TRACTABLE; DOCILE; STABLE.

weak *adjective* **1** *feeling weak after illness | too weak to walk* weakly, frail, fragile, delicate, feeble, infirm, shaky, debilitated, incapacitated, ailing, indisposed, decrepit, puny, faint, enervated, tired, fatigued, exhausted, spent, worn out. **2** *too weak to stand up to his enemies/wife* cowardly, pusillanimous, timorous, timid, spineless, ineffectual, useless, inept, effete, powerless, impotent, namby-pamby, soft; *inf.* yellow, weak-kneed. **3** *weak eyes/eyesight* defective, faulty, poor, inadequate, deficient, imperfect, substandard, lacking, wanting. **4** *weak excuses* unsound, feeble, flimsy, lame, hollow, pathetic, unconvincing, untenable, implausible, unsatisfactory. **5** *a weak sound/signal* faint, low, muffled, stifled, muted, scarcely audible. **6** *a weak light* faint, dim, pale, wan. **7** *weak coffee* understrength, dilute, diluted, watery, waterish, thinned down, thin, adulterated, tasteless, flavourless, insipid; *inf.* wishy-washy. **Opposites** STRONG; POWERFUL; FLAWLESS; CONVINCING.

weaken *verb* **1** *the illness had weakened her* enfeeble, debilitate, incapacitate, sap one's strength, enervate, tire, exhaust, wear out. **2** *weaken the force of the argument* lessen, reduce, decrease, diminish, moderate, temper, sap. **3** *the force of the storm weakened* abate, lessen, decrease, dwindle, diminish, ease up, let up. **4** *weaken the argument* impair, undermine, invalidate. **5** *they first refused to help but weakened later* relent, give in, acquiesce, yield, give way, accede, come round. **6** *too much milk weakened the coffee* dilute, water down, thin, adulterate.

weakling *noun* coward, mouse, milksop, namby-pamby; *inf.* wimp, sissy, drip, wet, doormat, chicken, yellow-belly, fraidy-cat, scaredy-cat.

weakness *noun* **1** *the weakness of the invalid* frailty, fragility, delicateness, delicacy, feebleness, infirmity, debility, incapacity, indisposition, decrepitude, puniness, enervation, fatigue. *See* WEAK 1. **2** *despise his weakness* cowardliness, timidity, spinelessness, ineffectuality, ineptness, powerlessness, impotence. *See* WEAK 2. **3** *the weakness of her eyesight* defectiveness, faultiness, inadequacy, deficiency. *See* WEAK 3. **4** *the weakness of the excuses* unsoundness, feebleness, flimsiness, lameness, untenability, implausibility. *See* WEAK 4. **5** *the weakness of the sound/signal* faintness, low intensity, mutedness. *See* WEAK 5. **6** *the weakness of the light* faintness, dimness. *See* WEAK 6. **7** *the weakness of the coffee* diluteness, wateriness, thinness, tastelessness, flavourlessness; *inf.*

wishy-washiness. **8** *extravagance is one of her weaknesses* weak point, failing, foible, fault, flaw, defect, shortcoming, imperfection, blemish, Achilles' heel, chink in one's armour. **9** *she has a weakness for chocolate* soft spot, fondness, liking, love, passion, partiality, preference, penchant, predisposition, predilection, leaning, inclination, proneness, proclivity. **Opposites** STRENGTH; POWER; FORTE.

wealth *noun* **1** *amass wealth* money, cash, capital, treasure, fortune, finance, property; riches, assets, possessions, resources, goods, funds; *inf.* wherewithal, dough, bread. **2** *people of wealth* richness, money, affluence, prosperity, substance; means. **3** *a wealth of beautiful pictures | a wealth of opportunities* mass, abundance, profusion, copiousness, plenitude, amplitude, bounty, cornucopia. **Opposites** POVERTY; DEARTH.

wealthy *adjective* **1** *wealthy people travelling abroad* rich, well off, well-to-do, moneyed, affluent, prosperous, of means, of substance; *inf.* well-heeled, rolling in it/money, in the money, made of money, filthy/stinking rich, loaded, flush, on easy street, quids in. **2** *wealthy surroundings* rich, opulent, lavish, luxurious, sumptuous, splendid, magnificent. **Opposites** POOR; PENNILESS; IMPOVERISHED.

weapon *noun.* See table. See also tables at BULLET, GUN, EXPLOSIVE, MISSILE.

PERSONAL WEAPONS

assegai	dagger	machete
axe	dirk	panga
battering	épée,	parang
ram	falchion	partisan
battleaxe	flick knife	pike
bayonet	foil	poleaxe
bilbo	gisarme	quarterstaff
bill	halberd	rapier
blade	hanger	sabre
bludgeon	harpoon	scimitar
bowie knife	hatchet	shillelagh
brass	javelin	skean-dhu
knuckles	jerid	staff
broadsword	knife	stave
cavalry	knobkerrie	stick
sword	knuckle-	stiletto
chopper	duster	sword
claymore	kris	swordstick
club	kukri	Toledo
cosh	lance	tomahawk
cudgel	lathi	truncheon
cutlass	mace	yataghan

wear *verb* **1** *wear beautiful clothes* be dressed in, dress in, be clothed in, cloth oneself in, have on, put on, don, sport. **2** *she wore an anxious expression* have, assume, present, show, display, exhibit. **3** *he wants to leave school but his parents won't wear it* tolerate, stand for, put up with, countenance, accept, allow, permit, brook; *inf.* stomach. **4** *wind and rain have worn the rock* erode, corrode, abrade, wash away, rub away, rub down, grind away, wear down. **5** *the carpet is starting to wear* become worn, show signs of wear, wear thin, fray, become threadbare, go into holes. **6** *she is worn by the whole experience* fatigue, tire, weary, exhaust. *See* WEAR *verb* wear out 2. **7** *this carpet has worn well* last, endure, hold up, survive, bear up, stand up to wear, prove durable. **wear away** *the steps have become worn away* wear, erode, corrode, abrade, rub away. *See* WEAR *verb* 4. **wear down** **1** *the steps have become worn down* wear, wear away, erode, corrode, abrade, rub down. *See* WEAR *verb* 4. **2** *wear down their resistance/opposition* gradually overcome, slowly reduce/diminish, erode, undermine; *inf.* chip away at. **wear off** **1** *wear the pattern off the plates* rub away, efface, fade. **2** *the novelty will soon wear off* lose effectiveness/effect, lose intensity/strength, fade, peter out, dwindle, decrease, diminish, disappear, subside, ebb, wane. **wear on** *as time wore on* pass, go by, move on, roll on. **wear out** **1** *children wear out their clothes quickly* wear thin, make threadbare, fray. *See* WEAR *verb* 5. **2** *the children/job has quite worn her out* wear, fatigue, tire, weary, exhaust, drain, strain, stress, weaken, enfeeble, prostrate, enervate; *inf.* knacker, wear to a frazzle, poop.

wear *noun* **1** *clothes/items for everyday wear* use, service, employment. **2** *pack away her winter wear* clothing, attire, apparel, wardrobe; clothes, garments, outfits; *inf.* gear, clobber. **3** *showing signs of wear and tear* use, friction, erosion, detrition, attrition, corrosion, abrasion, deterioration, degeneration, damage.

weariness *noun suffering from weariness* fatigue, tiredness, exhaustion, enervation, lassitude, languor, listlessness, lethargy.

wearing *adjective have a wearing day | find the children wearing* fatiguing, tiring, wearying, exhausting, draining, stressful, enervating.

wearisome *adjective wearisome tasks/journeys* fatiguing, tiring, exhausting, draining, wearing, trying, irksome, boring, tedious, dull, uninteresting, monotonous, humdrum, routine.
Opposites REFRESHING; INTERESTING; ENJOYABLE.

weary *adjective* **1** *weary at the end of a hard day's work* fatigued, tired, exhausted, drained, worn, worn out, spent, wearied; *inf.* dead tired/ beat, dead on one's feet, dog-tired, all in, done in, fagged out, pooped, whacked, bushed, knackered. **2** *the last weary hours/tasks | a weary journey* wearisome, fatiguing, tiring, exhausting, wearing, trying, taxing, irksome, tiresome, laborious, boring, tedious, dull. *See* WEARISOME. **3** *she is weary of the job | the dull job makes her weary* bored, fed up, discontented, jaded, uninterested, listless, lethargic; *inf.* browned-off, cheesed-off, sick and tired.
Opposites ENERGETIC; refreshed; REFRESHING; ENTHUSIASTIC.

weary *verb* **1** *the hard work wearies them* fatigue, tire, exhaust, drain, wear out; *inf.* knacker, wear to a frazzle. **2** *the repetitive job wearies him* bore, irk, make fed up, make discontented/jaded. *See* WEARY *adjective* 3. **3** *she wearied of living abroad* grow weary, tire, get bored, have enough, grow discontented/jaded. *See* WEARY *adjective* 3.
Opposites REVIVE; REFRESH; INVIGORATE.

WEASELS AND RELATED ANIMALS

badger	mink
beech marten	mongoose
civet	otter
cusimanse	palm civet
ermine	pine marten
ferret	polecat
fisher	ratel
fossa	sable
genet	sea otter
glutton	skunk
grison	stoat
honey badger	suricate
kolinsky	tayra
linsang	toddy cat
marbled polecat	weasel
marten	wolverine
meerkat	zorilla

weasel *noun. See table.*

weather *noun what's the weather like?* meteorological/atmospheric conditions; temperature, raininess, cloudiness, dryness, humidity, windiness. *See table.* **under the weather** below par, unwell, not well, off colour, out of sorts, indisposed, ailing, ill, sick; *inf.* poorly, seedy, groggy, hung over.

METEOROLOGICAL PHENOMENA

anticyclone	ridge
blocking high	shallow
cold front	depression
cyclone	stationary
deep depression	depression
depression	stationary high
filling depression	temperature
frontal system	inversion
high pressure	thermal
jet stream	trough
low pressure	turbulence
occlusion	warm front
pressure system	warm sector

weather *verb* **1** *weather the wood* dry, season, expose, expose to the elements. **2** *wood weathering well | rocks weathered by storms* be exposed, undergo change, erode, wear, bleach, colour, become discoloured. **3** *weather the storm/recession* come/get through, survive, withstand, live/ pull through, bear up against, stand, endure, ride out, rise above, surmount, overcome, resist; *inf.* stick out.

weave *verb* **1** *weave thread into cloth | weave flowers into garlands* interlace, intertwine, interwork, intertwist, twist together, entwine, braid, plait, interknit. *See table.* **2** *weave a story to account for his movements* make up, fabricate, put together, construct, invent, create, contrive. **3** *weave in and out of the crowds* zigzag, wind, criss-cross.

web *noun* **1** *a design composed of webs* interlacing, lacework, lattice, latticework, mesh, net, netting. **2** *a web of lies/deceit* network, tissue, tangle, knot, complex.

WEAVING TERMS

bobbin	leno weave	twill
hand loom	list	weave
interlocking	loom	warp
weave	plain weave	weaving
jacquard	satin weave	frame
jacquard	selvedge	web
loom	shuttle	weft
lace	tapestry	woof

wed *verb* **1** *they wed tomorrow* get married, marry, become man and wife; *inf.* get hitched/spliced, tie the knot. **2** *she weds him tomorrow* marry, take as one's wife/husband. **3** *the local minister wed them* marry, join in matrimony, make one, unite; *inf.* hitch. **4** *the two firms have been virtually wedded for years* unite, join, merge, amalgamate, fuse, link, ally. **5** *he is wedded to his work* dedicate, devote.
Opposites DIVORCE; SEPARATE.

wedded *adjective wedded bliss* married, marital, matrimonial, connubial, conjugal, nuptial.

wedding *noun* wedding/marriage ceremony, marriage; nuptials, espousals. *See table.*

WEDDING ANNIVERSARIES

paper	1st	lace	13th
cotton	2nd	ivory	14th
leather	3rd	crystal	15th
fruit/flowers	4th	china	20th
wood	5th	silver	25th
iron	6th	pearl	30th
wool/copper	7th	coral	35th
bronze/pottery	8th	ruby	40th
pottery/willow	9th	sapphire	45th
tin/aluminium	10th	gold	50th
steel	11th	emerald	55th
silk/linen	12th	diamond	60th

wedge *noun* **1** *insert a wedge* tapered block. **2** *a wedge of cheese/cake* tapered piece, chunk, lump, block; *inf.* wodge.

wedge *verb* **1** *wedge packing material round the vase in the box* thrust, stuff, pack, ram, force, cram, squeeze, jam. **2** *the adults wedged the child in* block, jam, squeeze, crowd, pack. **3** *wedge the door open* secure, fasten.

weed *verb weed out the less able candidates* separate out, get rid of, remove, dispense with, eliminate, shed, root out, eradicate, extirpate.

weekly *adverb the paper is published weekly* once a week, every week, by the week, hebdomadally.

weep *verb* cry, shed tears, sob, blubber, snivel, whimper, whine, moan, lament, grieve, mourn, keen, wail; *inf.* boo-hoo, blub.
Opposites LAUGH; REJOICE.

weepy *adjective* tearful, teary, lachrymose, close to tears, whimpering, crying, sobbing, blubbering.

weigh *verb* **1** *weigh the potatoes* measure/gauge the weight of, put on the scales. **2** *the child weighs 25 kilograms* have a weight of; *inf.* tip the scales at. **3** *weigh one plan against the other* balance, compare with, evaluate. **4** *weigh up the situation | weigh up his chances of success* consider, contemplate, think over, mull over, ponder, deliberate upon, meditate on, muse on, brood over, reflect on. **5** *his previous record will weigh with the committee* carry weight with, have influence with, be influential to, count with, tell with, matter to, be important/significant to. **6** *his guilt weighs on his conscience* bear down, burden, oppress, prey on. **weigh down 1** *he was weighed down by/with heavy luggage* load, overload, burden, overburden. **2** *his responsibilities weighed down on him* weigh, bear down, press down, burden, be a burden to, oppress, prey on, trouble, worry, get one down.

weight *noun* **1** *what is the weight of the flour?* heaviness; poundage, tonnage, avoirdupois. **2** *a weight of potatoes was delivered to everyone* load, quantity. **3** *a weight fell on his head* heavy object. **4** *the weights in the machine* ballast. **5** *lack of money is a real weight on his mind* burden, load, onus, millstone, albatross, oppression, trouble, worry, strain, millstone round one's neck, cross to bear. **6** *how much weight is attached to his statement?* importance, significance, consequence, value, substance, force, influence; *inf.* clout. **7** *the weight of the evidence is against him* preponderance, main force, onus.

weighty *adjective* **1** *weighty loads* heavy, massive, burdensome, cumbersome, ponderous; *inf.* hefty. **2** *weighty responsibility* burdensome, onerous, oppressive, troublesome, worrisome, stressful, taxing, vexatious. **3** *weighty matters* important, of great import, significant, momentous, of moment, consequential, of consequence, vital, crucial, serious, grave, solemn. **4** *weighty arguments* cogent, powerful, potent, forceful, effective, effectual, persuasive, authoritative, influential.
Opposites LIGHT; UNIMPORTANT; TRIVIAL; WEAK.

weird *adjective* **1** *weird things were happening* strange, queer, uncanny, eerie, mysterious, mystifying, supernatural, preternatural, unnatural, unearthly, ghostly; *Scots* eldritch; *inf.* spooky, creepy. **2** *she wears weird clothes* strange, queer, odd, eccentric, bizarre, outlandish, freakish, grotesque; *inf.* off-beat, far-out, way-out, out on a limb.
Opposites NORMAL; ORDINARY; CONVENTIONAL.

welcome *noun receive a welcome from their hostess* greeting, salutation, reception, warm reception.

welcome *verb* **1** *welcome the guests* bid welcome, greet, receive, embrace, receive with open arms, roll out the red carpet for, meet, usher in. **2** *welcome the news of his release* receive with gladness, be pleased by, take pleasure in, feel satisfaction at.
Opposites SHUN; SPURN; REJECT.

welcome *adjective* **1** *welcome guests* wanted, appreciated, popular, desirable. **2** *welcome news* gladly received, pleasant, pleasing, agreeable, cheering, to one's liking, to one's taste.
Opposites UNWELCOME; UNPOPULAR; UNPLEASANT.

welfare *noun* **1** *concern for the welfare of the children/firm* well-being, health, good health, soundness, happiness, comfort, security, prosperity, success, fortune, good fortune. **2** *poor families on welfare* state aid/benefit, public assistance; social security, sickness/unemployment benefit, income support, retirement pension.

well *adverb* **1** *behave well* satisfactorily, in a satisfactory manner/way, correctly, rightly, properly, fittingly, suitably, nicely. **2** *get on well* agreeably, pleasantly, happily; *inf.* famously, capitally. **3** *he plays the piano well* ably, competently, proficiently, adeptly, skilfully, with skill, effectively, expertly, with expertise, admirably, excellently. **4** *treat their guests well* kindly, in a kind/kindly way, genially, affably, generously, hospitably, civilly, politely. **5** *polish it well* thoroughly, completely, efficiently, effectively, conscientiously, industriously, carefully. **6** *know the subject well | we don't know her well* thoroughly, fully, deeply, profoundly, intimately, personally. **7** *look at it well | listen to it well* closely, attentively, carefully, conscientiously. **8** *speak well of him* highly, admiringly, with admiration, with praise, glowingly, approvingly, favourably, warmly. **9** *live well* comfortably, in comfort, prosperously. **10** *you may well be right | I can't very well go now* probably, possibly, likely, undoubtedly, certainly, unquestionably, justifiably, reasonably. **11** *he is well over forty* very much, considerably, to a great/marked extent/degree, markedly, substantially. **12** *it bodes well for the future* fortunately, luckily, auspiciously, propitiously. **as well** *she left and he went as well* too, also, in addition, besides, into the bargain, to boot. **as well as** *John went as well as Peter | take champagne as well as wine* in addition to, besides, along with, over and above.
Opposites BADLY; POORLY.

well *adjective* **1** *the former invalid is quite well now | a clinic for well babies/woman* healthy, in good health, fit, strong, robust, hale and hearty, able-bodied, up to par. **2** *all is well now* satisfactory, all right, fine, good, thriving, flourishing; *inf.* OK, fine and dandy. **3** *it would be well to leave early* advisable, fitting, proper, wise, prudent, sensible.
Opposites ILL; POORLY; INADVISABLE.

well *noun* **1** *a land rich in oil wells | get water from the well* sunken/drilled shaft, borehole. **2** *well of knowledge* source, well-spring, fount, reservoir, repository, mine. **3** *hot wells are to be found there* spring, fountain, water-hole, pool.

well *verb* *blood welled from the wound | tears welled from her eyes* flow, stream, run, ooze, seep, trickle, pour/rush forth, issue, gush, surge, spurt, spout, jet.

well-advised *adjective* sensible, wise, prudent, judicious, circumspect, far-sighted, sagacious.

well-balanced *adjective* **1** *well-balanced people/personalities* well-adjusted, sensible, reasonable, rational, level-headed, sound, practical, discerning, logical, sane, in one's right mind. **2** *a well-balanced diet* balanced, well-proportioned, well-ordered. **3** *a well-balanced exhibition/room* balanced, symmetrical, well-proportioned, proportional, well-ordered, well-arranged, graceful, elegant.

well-being *noun* welfare, health, good health, happiness, comfort, prosperity, security.

well-bred *adjective* well brought up, mannerly, well-mannered, courteous, polite, civil, ladylike, gentlemanly, gallant, chivalrous, cultivated, refined, polished, cultured, debonair, urbane.
Opposites RUDE; DISCOURTEOUS; ILL-BRED.

well-built *adjective* strongly built, strong, muscular, brawny, sturdy, robust, strapping, burly, big; *inf.* hulking, husky, hefty, beefy.
Opposites PUNY; SLIGHT.

well-groomed *adjective* neat, neatly dressed, tidy, smart, spruce, well turned out, trim, dapper; *inf.* natty, without a hair out of place, out of a bandbox.
Opposites UNTIDY; UNKEMPT; SCRUFFY.

well-known *adjective* **1** *well-known facts | a well-known figure around the village* known, widely known, familiar, common, usual, everyday. **2** *a well-known artist* famous, famed, renowned, celebrated, noted, notable, illustrious, eminent.
Opposites UNKNOWN; OBSCURE; UNSUNG.

well-nigh *adverb* *well-nigh impossible* virtually, next to, practically, all but, just about, almost, nearly, more or less.

well off *adjective* **1** *his parents are poor but he is very well off | well-off people* wealthy, rich, well-to-do, moneyed, affluent, prosperous, of means, of substance; *inf.* well-heeled, rolling in it/money, in the money, made of money, filthy/stinking rich, loaded, flush, on easy street, quids in. **2** *he doesn't know when he is well off* fortunate, lucky, comfortable, thriving, successful, flourishing. **3** *we are well off for logs this winter* well-supplied, well-furnished, well-equipped, well-stocked.
Opposites POOR; BROKE; badly off; UNFORTUNATE.

well-read *adjective* highly literate, literate, well-educated, educated, well-informed, knowledgeable, erudite.
Opposites ILLITERATE; IGNORANT.

well-spoken *adjective* articulate, eloquent, fluent, silver-tongued, smooth-talking; *inf.* having the gift of the gab.

well-thought-of *adjective* highly thought-of, highly regarded, esteemed, respected, looked up to, acclaimed, revered, venerated.

well-to-do *adjective* *his parents are well-to-do | well-to-do parents* wealthy, rich, moneyed, well off, affluent, prosperous, of means, of substance; *inf.* well-heeled, in the money, made of money, loaded. *See* WELL OFF.

wet *adjective* **1** *wet clothes/ground* damp, dampened, moist, moistened, wet through, soaked, drenched, saturated, sopping/dripping/wringing wet, sopping, dripping, soggy, waterlogged. **2** *a wet day* rainy, raining, pouring, showery, drizzling, damp, humid, dank, misty. **3** *a wet mixture* aqueous, watery, watered, sloppy. **4** *he's a wet creature* feeble, weak, inept, ineffective, ineffectual, effete, timid, timorous, cowardly, spineless, soft; *inf.* namby-pamby, weedy.
Opposites DRY; FINE; STRONG.

wet *noun* **1** *the wet damaged the table/land* wet-ness, damp, dampness, moisture, moistness, condensation, humidity, water, liquid. **2** *get in out of the wet | the wet affects his rheumatism* wet/rainy weather, rain, showery/damp weather, drizzle, damp; rains. **3** *he's a real wet* weakling, milksop; *inf.* namby-pamby, wimp, weed, drip.

wet *verb* **1** *wet the clothes before ironing them* dampen, damp, moisten, sprinkle, spray, splash. **2** *wet the soil* water, irrigate, sprinkle, spray, douse. **3** *the rain really wet them* wet through, dampen, soak, saturate.
Opposites DRY.

whale *noun*. See table. See also table at SEAL.

WHALES AND DOLPHINS

beaked whale	narwhal
beluga	orca
blue whale	pilot whale
bottlenose dolphin	porpoise
bottlenose whale	right whale
bowhead	Risso's dolphin
cachalot	river dolphin
fin whale	rorqual
grampus	sei whale
grey whale	sperm whale
humpback whale	spinner dolphin
killer whale	white-sided dolphin
minke whale	white whale

---

wharf *noun* pier, quay, dock, landing stage, jetty.

wheedle *verb* coax, cajole, beguile, charm, flatter, inveigle, win over, talk into, persuade, induce, entice, influence; *inf.* butter up.

wheel *noun* **1** *the wheels of the machine* circular frame, disc. **2** *soldiers making a right-hand wheel* turn, revolution, rotation, circle, pivot, gyration, spin, roll, twirl, whirl. **at the wheel 1** *he was at the wheel when the accident happened* driving, steering, in the driving-seat. **2** *a new man at the wheel in the firm* in charge, in command, in control; *inf.* at the helm, in the driving-seat.

wheel *verb* **1** *discs/birds wheeling around* turn, go round, circle, rotate, revolve, spin. **2** *soldiers wheeling round* swivel round, pivot, whirl/twirl round, make a U-turn. **3** *wheel a pram* push, shove, trundle.

wheeze *verb* *asthmatics wheezing* breathe audibly/noisily, gasp, whistle, hiss, rasp.

wheeze *noun* **1** *give a painful wheeze* gasp, whistle, hiss. See WHEEZE *verb.* **2** *the school girls thought fooling the teacher was a good wheeze* joke, trick, ruse, ploy, scheme, prank, stunt.

whereabouts *noun* *I don't his whereabouts | the whereabouts of his cottage* location, site, position, situation, place.

wherewithal *noun* *he doesn't have the wherewithal to travel* means, resources, funds, reserves; money, ready money, cash, capital, finance; *inf.* dough, bread, loot.

whet *verb* **1** *whet a blade* sharpen, put an edge on, edge, hone, strop, file, grind, rasp. **2** *whet*

the curiosity/appetite stimulate, excite, arouse, rouse, kindle, quicken, stir, titillate, tempt.
Opposites BLUNT.

whiff *noun* **1** *a whiff of air/smoke* puff, breath, gust, draught. **2** *catch a whiff of her perfume* smell, scent, odour, aroma, stink, reek. **3** *a whiff of scandal* hint, suggestion, trace, suspicion, soupçon.

while *noun* *wait for a while* time, spell, period, interval.

while *verb* *while away the hours* laze, idle, loaf, lounge, loiter.

whim *noun* **1** *have a sudden whim to go to the fair* notion, fancy, idea, impulse, urge, caprice, vagary, craze, passion, inclination, bent. **2** *behaviour ruled by whim* whimsy, capriciousness, caprice, volatility, fickleness.

whimper *verb* *dogs/children whimpering* whine, cry, sniffle, snivel, moan, wail, groan; *inf.* grizzle.

whimper *noun* *a whimper of fear* whine, cry, moan, wail, groan.

whimsical *adjective* *a whimsical sense of humour | a whimsical children's story* capricious, fanciful, fantastical, playful, mischievous, waggish, quaint, unusual, curious, droll, eccentric, peculiar, queer, bizarre, weird, freakish.

whine *verb* **1** *a dog/child was whining* whimper, cry, wail, groan; *inf.* grizzle. See WHIMPER *verb.* **2** *he's always whining about the state of the country* complain, grumble, moan, groan, fuss, lament; *inf.* grouse, gripe, whinge, bellyache, go on, beef.

whine *noun* **1** *listen to the dog's whines* whimper, cry, wail, groan. **2** *his constant whines about prices* complaint, grumble, moan, groan, fussing, lamenting; *inf.* grouse, gripe, whinging, bellyache, beefing.

whip *verb* **1** *whip the naughty children | whip the reluctant horse* lash, flog, scourge, flagellate, birch, switch, strap, cane, thrash, beat, strike, leather, spank, punish, castigate; *inf.* belt, tan, lay into, give a hiding to, beat the living daylights out of. **2** *whip cream* beat, whisk, mix. **3** *whip a handkerchief from his pocket* whisk, flash, snatch, pull, yank, jerk, produce, remove. **4** *he whipped round the corner* whisk, dart, dash, dive, dodge, shoot, tear, rush, fly, bolt, zoom. **5** *he whipped the money* steal, thieve, pilfer, purloin, filch, snatch, seize, pocket; *inf.* pinch, swipe, nick, nab. **6** *whip the opposition at football* beat, defeat, overcome, overpower, overwhelm, thrash, trounce, crush, rout. **7** *whip them into a frenzy* rouse, stir up, incite, goad, prod, spur, prompt, agitate. **whip up** *whip up enthusiasm* rouse, stir up, provoke, excite, incite, instigate, work up.

whip *noun* *use a whip on the criminal/horse* lash, scourge, flagellum, horsewhip, bull whip, cat o'nine tails, knout, birch, switch, thong, crop, riding crop, cane.

whipping *noun* **1** *give the child a whipping* lashing, flogging, scourging, flagellation, birching, caning, thrashing, beating, leathering, spanking, castigation; *inf.* belting, tanning, hiding. See WHIP *verb* 1. **2** *give the opposition a whipping* beating, thrashing, trouncing, routing. *See* WHIP *verb* 6.

whirl *verb* **1** *wheels/dancers whirling* turn round, circle, spin, rotate, revolve, wheel, twirl, swirl, gyrate, reel, pirouette, pivot. **2** *buses whirling past* speed, rush, race, shoot, tear, charge, whip. **3** *my head/brain is whirling* go round, spin, reel, feel dizzy/giddy.

whirl *noun* **1** *give the wheel a whirl | the whirls of the dancers* turn, spin, rotation, revolution, wheel, twirl, swirl, gyration, reel, pirouette, pivot. **2** *the social whirl* activity, bustle, flurry, to-do, hurly-burly. **3** *a whirl of parties* round, merry-go-round, succession, series, sequence, progression, string, chain, cycle. **4** *with heads in a whirl* spin, dither, state of confusion, daze, muddle, jumble. **5** *give the new game a whirl* try, try-out, test; *inf.* go, shot, stab.

whirlpool *noun* vortex, maelstrom.

whirlwind *noun* tornado; *inf.* dust devil.

whirlwind *adjective* *a whirlwind romance* lightning, swift, rapid, quick, speedy, hasty, headlong, impulsive.

whisk *verb* **1** *the horse whisked its tail* wave, flick, brandish. **2** *whisk the table clean | whisk away the crumbs* brush, sweep, wipe. **3** *whisk a handkerchief out of his pocket* whip, snatch, pull, yank, jerk, produce, remove. **4** *the cat whisked round the corner* dart, dash, dive, dodge, whip, shoot, tear, rush, fly, bolt, zoom. **5** *whisk the guest away* whirl, whip, snatch. **6** *whisk eggs* whip, beat, mix.

whisk *noun* **1** *with a whisk of the tail* wave, flick brandish. **2** *clean the table with a few whisks* brush, sweep, wipe. **3** *beat eggs with a whisk* beater.

whisky *noun. See table.*

TYPES OF WHISKY

bourbon *Am.*	rye whiskey *Am.*
corn whisky	Scotch whisky
Irish whiskey	usquebaugh

---

whisper *verb* **1** *whisper to her friend* murmur, mutter, speak softly, speak in muted/hushed tones. **2** *whisper endearments* murmur, mutter, breathe, say/utter softly, say/utter under the breath. **3** *trees whispering in the wind* murmur, rustle, sigh, sough, swish.
Opposites SHOUT; YELL.

whisper *noun* **1** *speak in a whisper* murmur, mutter, low voice, hushed tone, undertone. **2** *the whisper of trees in the wind* murmur, rustle, sigh, sough, swish. **3** *there's a whisper that he has been promoted* rumour, report, insinuation, suggestion, hint; gossip, word. **4** *a whisper of perfume/hostility about the room* whiff, trace, tinge, hint, suggestion, suspicion.

whit *noun* *not give a whit | not a whit better* particle, bit, jot, iota, mite, little, trifle.

white *adjective* **1** *a white face* white as a ghost/sheet, chalk-white, pale, wan, pallid, ashen, anaemic, colourless, bloodless, waxen, pasty, peaky, whey-faced, grey. **2** *white hair* grey, sil-

ver, hoary, snowy-white, grizzled.
Opposites RUDDY; BLACK.

white-collar *adjective* *white-collar workers* non-manual, office, clerical, professional, executive, salaried.

whiten *verb* *clothes whitened by the sun* make white, make pale, bleach, blanch, fade, wash out, etiolate.

whitewash *noun* *regard the report on the accident as a whitewash* cover-up, concealment, camouflage, mask.

whitewash *verb* *try to whitewash his role in the accident* cover up, gloss over, conceal, camouflage, suppress, downplay, make light of, soft-pedal, minimize.

whittle *verb* **1** *whittle wood from the block* cut, hew, pare, shave, trim. **2** *whittle a tent peg from the wood* carve, shape, model. **3** *inflation whittled away their savings* wear away, eat away, erode, consume, use up, undermine, destroy. **4** *the number of employees has been whittled away* reduce, lessen, decrease, diminish, cut back.

whole *adjective* **1** *three whole days | the whole book | a whole cake* entire, complete, full, total, solid, integral, unabridged, unreduced, undivided, uncut. **2** *no glasses left whole | he came home whole* intact, sound, flawless, in one piece, unimpaired, undamaged, unharmed, unhurt, uninjured, unmutilated.
Opposites PART; PARTIAL; INCOMPLETE; BROKEN.

whole *adverb* *eat/cook it whole* in one piece, in one.

whole *noun* **1** *parts making up a whole* entity, unit, ensemble, totality, entirety. **2** *the whole of the year | the whole country rejoiced* all, every part, every person/member/inhabitant. **on the whole 1** *on the whole he is perfect for the job* all in all, all things considered, taking everything into consideration, by and large. **2** *on the whole he works late* as a rule, as a general rule, generally, in general, in the main, for the most part.

wholehearted *adjective* **1** *a wholehearted fan of the group* devoted, dedicated, enthusiastic, eager, keen, zealous, earnest, serious, committed. **2** *give the movement their wholehearted support* unreserved, unqualified, unstinting, complete, committed, hearty, emphatic, real, sincere, genuine.
Opposites APATHETIC; HALF-HEARTED; QUALIFIED.

wholesale *adjective* *the wholesale destruction of animals* indiscriminate, mass, all-inclusive, total, comprehensive, extensive, wide-ranging, sweeping, broad.
Opposites PARTIAL; SELECTIVE.

wholesale *adverb* *destroy the animals wholesale | throw all the furniture out wholesale* indiscriminately, all at once, in a mass, without exception, on a large scale, comprehensively, extensively.

wholesome *adjective* **1** *wholesome food* nutritious, nourishing, health-giving, healthful, good, good for one, strengthening. **2** *wholesome air/climate* salubrious, invigorating, bracing, stimulating, refreshing. **3** *wholesome literature/advice* moral, ethical, non-erotic, non-violent, uplifting, edifying, helpful, beneficial, prudent. **4** *wholesome country children* healthy, fit, in good health, robust, vigorous, lusty, hale and hearty, ruddy-cheeked, innocent, virtuous, righteous, pure.

wholly adverb **1** *wholly in favour of the scheme* completely, fully, entirely, totally, utterly, thoroughly, altogether, comprehensively, in every respect, perfectly, enthusiastically, with total commitment, unreservedly, heart and soul; *inf.* one hundred per cent. **2** *the burden rests wholly on his shoulders* only, solely, exclusively, purely.

whoop noun *whoops of excitement/admiration* cry, call, shout, yell, scream, shriek, hoot, cheer, hurrah; *inf.* holler.

whoop verb *whoop with excitement/admiration* cry, call, shout, yell, scream, shriek, hoot, cheer; *inf.* holler.

whore noun **1** *earn her living as a whore* prostitute, call girl, streetwalker, harlot, lady of the night, *fille de joie*, woman of ill repute, fallen woman, strumpet, courtesan, *demi-mondaine*; *inf.* tart, hooker, hustler. **2** *he's very respectable but she is a whore* loose woman, harlot, wanton; *inf.* tart.

wicked adjective **1** *an evil man* evil, sinful, bad, black-hearted, villainous, base, vile, vicious, dishonourable, unprincipled, unrighteous, criminal, lawless, perverted, immoral, amoral, unethical, corrupt, dissolute, abandoned, dissipated, degenerate, reprobate, debauched, depraved, unholy, impious, irreligious, ungodly, godless, devilish. **2** *his wicked deeds* evil, sinful, iniquitous, wrong, bad, vile, foul, base, mean, gross, odious, obnoxious, nefarious, heinous, flagitious, infamous, dreadful, dire, grim, horrible, hideous, gruesome, monstrous, atrocious, abominable, abhorrent, loathsome, hateful, detestable, reprehensible, dishonourable, disgraceful, shameful, ignoble, ignominious, lawless, unlawful, illicit, illegal, villainous, dastardly, blackguardly, unholy, impious, impure, ungodly, godless, profane, blasphemous, irreverent, irreligious, damnable, devilish, demonic, diabolic. **3** *hurt by her wicked remarks* spiteful, malicious, malignant, nasty, offensive, hurtful, distressing, galling, vexatious. **4** *aim a wicked blow* dangerous, perilous, destructive, harmful, injurious, hurtful, painful, agonizing, ferocious, fierce, terrible, mighty. **5** *give a wicked smile | have a wicked sense of humour* mischievous, impish, roguish, arch, rascally, naughty. **6** *the weather has been wicked* bad, nasty, unpleasant, disagreeable; *inf.* dreadful, terrible, awful. **7** *he's a wicked player* excellent, expert, masterly, skilful, proficient, deft, adept, dexterous, first-rate, outstanding, superior, superlative; *inf.* top-notch.
Opposites VIRTUOUS; GOOD; RIGHTEOUS.

wide adjective **1** *a wide river/building* broad, extensive, spacious. **2** *wide hips* broad, large, outspread, spread out, ample. **3** *wide eyes* fully open, dilated. **4** *a wide range of subjects | a wide knowledge* ample, broad, extensive, large, large-scale, vast, far-ranging, immense, wide-ranging, expansive, sweeping, encyclopedic, comprehensive, general, all-embracing, catholic, compendious. **5** *wide trousers* full, loose, baggy, capacious, roomy, generous, commodious. **6** *his shot was wide | his guess was wide of the mark* off target, off course.
Opposites NARROW; LIMITED; RESTRICTED; TIGHT.

wide adverb **1** *open your mouth wide* to the fullest/furthest extent, as far as possible, fully, completely. **2** *he shot wide* wide of the mark/target, off target, off course, astray.

wide awake adjective **1** *still wide awake at dawn* fully awake, awake, conscious, open-eyed, not asleep. **2** *you have to be wide awake to do business with them* alert, on the alert, on the qui vive, vigilant, wary, chary, watchful, observant, attentive, heedful, aware; *inf.* on one's toes, on the ball, keeping a weather eye open.

wide-eyed adjective **1** *children wide-eyed at the antics of the clown* surprised, amazed, astonished, astounded. **2** *taking advantage of wide-eyed young girls* naive, impressionable, ingenuous, credulous, trusting, unsuspicious, innocent, simple, unsophisticated, inexperienced, green; *inf.* wet behind the ears.

widen verb **1** *widen the road* make wider, broaden. **2** *widen her knowledge* broaden, expand, extend, enlarge, increase, augment, add to, supplement. **3** *her eyes widened in surprise* open wide, dilate.
Opposites NARROW; RESTRICT; LIMIT.

wide open adjective **1** *with eyes wide open* open wide, fully open, dilated, gaping. **2** *with legs wide open* open wide, outspread, spread open, outstretched, splayed open, fully extended. **3** *wide open to attack/criticism* exposed, vulnerable, unprotected, unguarded, defenceless, at risk, in danger. **4** *the outcome of the game was wide open* uncertain, unsure, indeterminate, unsettled, unpredictable, in the balance, up in the air; *inf.* anyone's guess.

widespread adjective *widespread terror/confusion* universal, common, general, far-reaching, far-flung, prevalent, rife, extensive, sweeping, pervasive, epidemic.
Opposites LOCAL; LIMITED; RARE.

width noun **1** *the width of the river/cloth* wideness, breadth, broadness, span, diameter. **2** *the width of her hips* wideness, broadness, breadth, largeness, thickness, ampleness. **3** *impressed by the width of his knowledge* wideness, broadness, breadth, scope, range, span, extensiveness, vastness, immensity, immenseness, expansiveness, comprehensiveness, catholicity, compendiousness. *See* WIDE *adjective* 4.

wield verb **1** *come out wielding a sword* brandish, flourish, wave, swing, shake, use, put to use, employ, handle, ply, manipulate. **2** *wield the power in the country* exercise, exert, be possessed of, have, have at one's disposal, hold, maintain, command, control, manage, be in charge of.

wife noun spouse, mate, consort, woman, helpmate, squaw, bride; *inf.* better/other half, missus, missis, old woman/lady, the little woman, the lady of the house, 'er/her indoors.

wild *adjective* **1** *wild cats/horses* untamed, undomesticated, unbroken, feral, savage, fierce, ferocious. **2** *wild flowers* uncultivated, natural, native, indigenous. **3** *wild peoples/tribes* uncivilized, primitive, ignorant, savage, barbaric, barbarous, brutish, ferocious, fierce. **4** *wild country/countryside* uncivilized, uncultivated, unpopulated, uninhabited, unsettled, unfrequented, empty, barren, waste, desolate, forsaken, God-forsaken, isolated. **5** *a wild night* stormy, tempestuous, turbulent, blustery, howling, violent, raging, furious, rough. **6** *lead a wild life* | *wild confusion/delight* undisciplined, unrestrained, unconstrained, uncontrolled, out of control, uncurbed, unbridled, unchecked, chaotic, disorderly. **7** *a wild football crowd* rowdy, unruly, disorderly, noisy, turbulent, violent, lawless, riotous, out of control, uncontrolled, unmanageable, ungovernable, unrestrained, excited, passionate, frantic. **8** *when he was killed the crowd went/were wild* beside oneself, berserk, frantic, frenzied, in a frenzy, hysterical, crazed, mad, distracted, distraught, irrational, deranged, demented, raving, maniacal, rabid; *inf.* crazy. **9** *the teacher was wild at the children* angry, infuriated, incensed, exasperated, in a temper, seething; *inf.* mad. **10** *wild schemes* extravagant, fantastical, impracticable, foolish, ill-advised, ill-considered, imprudent, unwise, madcap, impulsive, reckless, rash, outrageous, preposterous. **11** *wild about rock music* enthusiastic, eager, avid, agog; *inf.* crazy, mad, nuts, potty, daft. **12** *a wild guess* arbitrary, random, hit-or-miss, haphazard, uninformed, unknowledgeable. **13** *wild hair* uncombed, unkempt, dishevelled, tousled, wind blown, disarranged, untidy. **run wild 1** *weeds running wild* grow unchecked, spread like wildfire, ramble, straggle. **2** *children running wild* run free, go undisciplined/unchecked. **3** *demonstrators running wild* run riot, go on the rampage, go berserk, get out of control, cut loose.
Opposites TAME; CIVILIZED; CALM; RESTRAINED.

wilderness *noun* **1** *the Arctic wilderness* desert, wasteland, waste, jungle, no-man's land; wilds. **2** *a wilderness of abandoned cars* confusion, tangle, jumble, muddle, clutter, miscellany, hotchpotch, bewilderment, maze, labyrinth.

wile *noun* **1** *make use of wile to get her own way* trickery, craftiness, craft, cunning, artfulness, slyness, guile, chicanery, fraud, deception, cheating. **2** *use all her wiles to get her own way* trick, dodge, ruse, subterfuge, ploy, stratagem, lure, artifice, manoeuvre, device, contrivance.

wilful *adjective* **1** *wilful neglect/murder* deliberate, intentional, intended, conscious, purposeful, premeditated, planned, calculated. **2** *coping with wilful children* headstrong, strong-willed, obstinate, stubborn, stubborn as a mule, mulish, pig-headed, bull-headed, obdurate, intransigent, adamant, dogged, determined, persistent, unyielding, uncompromising, intractable, refractory, recalcitrant, disobedient, contrary, perverse, wayward, self-willed.
Opposites ACCIDENTAL; UNINTENTIONAL; DOCILE.

will¹ *verb* **1** *come when you will* wish, want, desire, please, see/think fit, think best, choose, prefer, opt, elect. **2** *accidents will happen* do, have a tendency to, have a habit of.

will² *verb* **1** *will him to live* impose one's will on, try to make/cause. **2** *God willed it* decree, order, ordain, command, direct, bid, intend, wish, desire. **3** *will him all her books* bequeath, leave, give, hand/pass down, pass on, transfer.

will³ *noun* **1** *freedom of the will* volition, choice, option, decision, discretion, prerogative. **2** *he has the will to live* desire, wish, preference, inclination, fancy, mind. **3** *it is the will of God* decree, ordinance, dictate, wish, decision. **4** *he lacks the will to succeed* will-power, determination, resolution, resolve, firmness of purpose, purposefulness, doggedness, single-mindedness, commitment, moral fibre, pluck, mettle, grit, nerve. **5** *draw up his will* last will and testament, testament; last wishes. **6** *bear him ill will* feeling, disposition, attitude. **at will** *come and go at will* as one wishes/pleases, as one thinks fit, to suit oneself, at one's inclination/discretion.

willing *adjective* **1** *willing helpers* ready, eager, keen, enthusiastic, avid. **2** *willing to accept responsibility* prepared, ready, disposed, content, happy, so-minded, consenting, agreeable, amenable, in the mood, compliant; *inf.* game. **3** *willing help* cooperative, gladly given, cheerful, accommodating, obliging.
Opposites UNWILLING; RELUCTANT.

willingly *adverb* **1** *she went with him willingly— she was not forced* voluntarily, of one's own free will, of one's own accord, by choice, by volition, spontaneously, unforced. **2** *I'll willingly help you* cheerfully, happily, with pleasure, readily, without hesitation, ungrudgingly, with all one's heart.

willingness *noun* **1** *their willingness to learn* readiness, eagerness, keenness, enthusiasm, avidity. **2** *their willingness to accept responsibility* readiness, preparedness, consent, agreeableness, amenability. *See* WILLING 2.

will-power *noun* will, strength of will, determination, resolution, resolve, firmness of purpose, purposefulness, doggedness, commitment, single-mindedness, moral fibre, self-discipline, pluck, mettle, grit, nerve.

wilt *verb* **1** *plants wilting* droop, wither, shrivel, lose freshness, sag. **2** *people wilting in the heat* droop, sag, feel weak/faint, languish. **3** *their courage/determination/strength wilted when faced by the enemy* diminish, dwindle, lessen, grow less, flag, fade, melt away, ebb, wane, weaken, fail.
Opposites GROW; THRIVE.

wily *adjective* crafty, cunning, artful, sharp, astute, shrewd, scheming, intriguing, shifty, foxy, sly, guileful, deceitful, deceptive, fraudulent, cheating, underhand; *inf.* crooked, fly.

win *verb* **1** *win first prize* achieve, attain, earn, gain, receive, obtain, acquire, procure, get, secure, collect, pick up, come away with, net; *inf.* bag. **2** *win the battle/contest* be victorious in, be the victor in, achieve success in, come first in. **3** *may the best side win* be victorious, be the victor, gain the victory, overcome, achieve

mastery, carry the day, carry all before one, finish first, come out ahead, come out on top, succeed, triumph, prevail; *inf.* win out. **4** *she won them by her beauty | win their hearts* charm, attract, lure, disarm. **win over/round** *win over the opposition | win them round to our way of thinking* talk/bring round, persuade, induce, influence, sway, prevail upon, convert.
Opposites LOSE; FAIL; REPEL.

win *noun their side needs a win* victory, conquest, success, triumph.

wince *verb wince in pain/embarrassment* grimace, start, flinch, blench, shrink, recoil, cringe, squirm.

wince *noun give a wince of pain* grimace, start, flinch.

wind¹ *noun* **1** *a day almost entirely without wind* air current, current/stream of air; puff of wind, light air/wind, zephyr, breeze, gust, strong wind, blast, gale, storm, hurricane. *See tables.* **2** *need a lot of wind to play the bagpipes* breath, respiration; *inf.* puff. **3** *a pompous fool full of wind* empty talk, talk, babble, blather, blether, boasting, bluster, braggadocio; *inf.* hot air, baloney, twaddle, gab, gas. **4** *suffer from wind after a meal* flatulence, flatus, gas. **5** *the deer have got our wind* scent, smell, odour. **6** *there's wind of a pay increase | wind of a scandal* rumour, gossip, hint, suggestion, inkling, intimation; news, information, report, intelligence. **in the wind** *sense that redundancies were in the wind* about to happen, in the offing, on the way, coming near, close at hand, approaching, impending, looming; *inf.* on the cards.

wind² *noun the path has many winds* winding, twist, turn, curve, bend, loop, coil, whorl, convolution.

wind³ *verb* **1** *the road winds up the hill* twist, twist and turn, curve, bend, loop, zigzag, snake, spiral, meander, ramble. **2** *smoke wind-ing up into the sky* curl, spiral, wreathe, snake. **3** *wind the wool into a ball* twist, twine, coil, wrap, roll. **wind down 1** *the competitors need to wind down after a race* unwind, relax, become less tense, ease up, calm down, cool off. **2** *we are winding the firm down* bring to a close/end, make less active. **3** *school-work is winding down for the summer* slacken off, ease up, taper off, dwindle, diminish, lessen, decline, come to an end/close. **wind up 1** *the events of the evening really wound her up | she gets wound up easily* make tense, strain, make nervous, work up, put on edge, agitate, fluster, disconcert, discompose. **2** *they aren't serious—they're winding her up* tease, chaff, make fun of; *inf.* kid, have one on, pull one's leg, rib, rag, get a rise out of. **3** *it's time to wind up the meeting* bring to an end/conclusion, end, conclude, terminate, finish; *inf.* wrap up. **4** *he has wound up his business* close down, dissolve, liquidate, put into liquidation. **5** *we wound up in a small village* end up, finish, find oneself.

winded *adjective* breathless, out of breath, gasping for breath, panting; *inf.* puffed out, out of puff.

windfall *noun* piece/stroke of good luck, unexpected gain, godsend, manna from heaven, bonanza, jackpot.

winding *adjective a winding road* twisting, twisting and turning, curving, bending, looping, tortuous, zigzagging, snaking, spiralling, meandering, serpentine, sinuous, rambling.

winding *noun the road had many windings* wind, twist, turn, bend, loop, coil, curve, convolution, meander.

window *noun* opening, aperture. *See table.*

windy *adjective* **1** *a windy day* breezy, blowy, blustery, blustering, gusty, gusting, boisterous, squally, stormy, wild, tempestuous, turbulent. **2** *a windy speech* long-winded,

BEAUFORT SCALE

Number	Wind Force	Wind Speed	Number	Wind Force	Wind Speed
0	Calm	<1 mph	7	Near gale	32–38 mph
1	Light air	1–3 mph	8	Gale	39–46 mph
2	Light breeze	4–7 mph	9	Strong gale	47–54 mph
3	Gentle breeze	8–12 mph	10	Storm	55–63 mph
4	Moderate breeze	13–18 mph	11	Violent storm	64–72 mph
5	Fresh breeze	19–24 mph	12–17	Hurricane	≥73 mph
6	Strong breeze	25–31 mph			

WINDS

Wind	Location	Wind	Location
bise	Central Europe	levanter	W. Mediterranean
bora	Central Europe	meltemi	E. Mediterranean
buran	Central Asia	mistral	Mediterranean
Cape doctor	South Africa	monsoon	S. Asia
chinook	Rocky Mountains, U.S.A.	nor'wester	New Zealand
el Niño	E. Pacific	simoom/samiel	N. Africa
etesian	E. Mediterranean	sirocco	N. Africa
Föhn/Foehn	Central Europe	southerly buster	SE Australia
ghibli/gibli	N. Africa	tramontana	W. Mediterranean
harmattan	W. Africa	wet chinook	NW U.S.A.
khamsin	Egypt	williwaw	U.S.A./Canada

TYPES OF WINDOW

bay window	oeil-de-boeuf
bow window	oriel window
bull's-eye	picture window
casement	quarter-light
Catherine wheel	rose window
compass window	roundel
deadlight	sash window
dormer window	sidelight
double window	skylight
fanlight	stained-glass
fenestella	window
gable window	storm window
garret window	transom *Am.*
guichet	wheel window
lancet window	windscreen
lucarne	windshield *Am.*

loquacious, wordy, verbose, rambling, meandering, prolix, diffuse, turgid, bombastic.
3 *she's a bit windy about living alone* nervous, scared, frightened, alarmed, fearful, timid, timorous, cowardly; *inf.* nervy.

wine *noun. See table.*

wing *noun* **1** *a bird's wings* pennate limb, organ of flight; *lit.* pinion. **2** *the extreme wing of the party* arm, side, branch, section, segment, group, grouping, circle, faction, clique, set, coterie, cabal. **3** *the east wing of the house* side piece, extension, annex, addition; *Am.* ell.

wing *verb* **1** *birds winging through the air* fly, glide, soar. **2** *she winged to the top of her profession | winged to the finishing tape* soar, zoom, speed, race, hurry, hasten. **3** *the bullet winged the bird/soldier* wound, hit, clip.

wink *verb* **1** *wink an eye* blink, flutter, bat, nictate, nictitate. **2** *lights winking across the water* flash, twinkle, sparkle, glitter, gleam. **wink at** *wink at the junior's mistakes* turn a blind eye to, close/shut one's eyes to, blink at, ignore, overlook, disregard, let pass, connive at, condone, tolerate.

wink *noun* **1** *the wink of an eye* blink, flutter, bat, nictation. **2** *the winks of the lights* flash, twinkle, sparkle, glitter, gleam. **3** *I'll be with you in a wink* moment, minute, second, instant; *inf.* jiffy, mo, two shakes of a lamb's tail.

winkle *verb* **1** *winkle the splinter out of her hand | winkle the children out of their hiding place* prise out, dig out, extricate, extract, dislodge, remove. **2** *winkle the information from him* draw out, prise out, worm out, extract, extricate.

winner *noun* champion, victor, vanquisher, conqueror, conquering hero; cup winner, prizewinner.

winning *adjective* **1** *the winning team* victorious, successful, triumphant, vanquishing, conquering. **2** *a winning smile/child* captivating, enchanting, bewitching, beguiling, disarming, taking, engaging, endearing, winsome, charming, attractive, fetching, alluring, sweet, lovely, delightful, darling, amiable, pleasing.

winnings *plural noun* proceeds, spoils, profits, takings, gains; booty.

winnow *verb* **1** *winnow the grain* blow, fan. **2** *winnow the chaff from the grain* remove, get rid of, divide, separate, part, sort out. **3** *winnow the evidence* sift, go through, examine, comb, sort out.

wintry *adjective* **1** *a wintry day | wintry showers* cold, chilly, icy, frosty, freezing, frozen, snowy, arctic, glacial, biting, piercing, nippy. **2** *a wintry smile/look* unfriendly, cool, chilly, cold, distant, remote, bleak, cheerless.

wipe *verb* **1** *wipe the table* rub, brush, dust, mop, sponge, swab, clean, dry. **2** *wipe the dirt off* rub off, brush off, mop up, sponge off, clean off, remove, get rid of, take off, take away, erase, efface. **wipe out** destroy, demolish, annihilate, exterminate, eradicate, eliminate, extirpate, obliterate, expunge, erase, blot out, extinguish.

wipe *noun* *give the table a wipe* rub, brush, dust, mop, sponge, swab, clean.

wiry *adjective* **1** *wiry children/youths* lean, spare, sinewy, tough, strong. **2** *wiry hair* strong, coarse, tough. **3** *wiry brushes* bristly, prickly, thorny, stiff, rigid.
Opposites FRAIL; STRAIGHT; SMOOTH.

wisdom *noun* **1** *admire the wisdom of the old man/sayings* sageness, sagacity, cleverness, intelligence, erudition, learning, education, knowledge, enlightenment, reason, philosophy, discernment, perception, insight. **2** *admire their wisdom in leaving early | the wisdom*

GRAPE VARIETIES

White wine grapes	Muscadelle	Vermentino	Lambrusco
Blanc Fumé	Muscat	Vernaccia	Malbec
Bual	Pinot Blanc	Viognier	Mammolo
Chardonnay	Pinot Gris	**Red wine grapes**	Mandelaria
Chenin Blanc	Riesling	Aleatico	Manseng
Colombard	Sauvignon Blanc	Barbera	Merlot
Fumé Blanc	Sémillon	Cabernet Franc	Meunier
Furmint	Sylvaner	Cabernet	Montepulciano
Gewürztraminer	Tocai Friulano	Sauvignon	Mourvedre
Grüner Veltliner	Trebbiano	Carignan	Nebbiolo
Kerner	Verdejo	Cinsaut	Pinot Noir
Malvasia Bianca	Verdelho	Dolcetto	Sangiovese
Manseng	Verdello	Gamay	Shiraz/Syrah
Marsanne	Verdicchio	Grenache	Tempranillo
Müller-Thurgau	Verduzzo	Grignolino	Zinfandel

of her decision sense, common sense, prudence, judiciousness, judgement, shrewdness, astuteness, smartness, circumspection, strategy, foresight, reasonableness, rationality, logic, soundness, saneness.
Opposites FOLLY; STUPIDITY.

wise *adjective* **1** *he's a wise old man | wise sayings* sage, sagacious, clever, intelligent, learned, educated, well-read, knowledgeable, informed, enlightened, philosophic, deep-thinking, discerning, perceptive, experienced; *lit.* sapient. **2** *it was wise to leave early | you were wise to leave | a wise decision* sensible, prudent, well-advised, judicious, politic, shrewd, astute, smart, strategic, reasonable, rational, logical, sound, sane.
Opposites STUPID; SILLY; FOOLISH.

wisecrack *noun* quip, witticism, joke, jest, smart remark; *inf.* gag, funny.

wish *verb* **1** *wish for a long life* want, desire, long for, hope for, yearn for, pine for, have a fancy for, fancy, crave, hunger for, thirst for, lust after, covet, sigh for, set one's heart on; *inf.* hanker after, have a yen for. **2** *wish to die* want, desire, long, yearn, aspire, have an inclination. **3** *they wish you to go now* desire, demand, bid, ask, require, instruct, direct, order, command. **4** *I wish you goodbye* bid.

wish *noun* **1** *satisfy her wish to travel* desire, liking, fondness, longing, hope, yearning, want, fancy, aspiration, inclination, urge, whim, craving, hunger, thirst, lust; *inf.* hankering, yen. **2** *you must obey their wishes* want, desire, demand, bidding, request, requirement, instruction, direction, order, command.

wishy-washy *adjective* **1** *he's a bit wishy-washy* weak, feeble, puny, ineffectual, effete, spineless, irresolute; *inf.* weak-kneed. **2** *wishy-washy colours* pallid, pale, wan, sickly. **3** *wishy-washy soup* tasteless, flavourless, insipid, watery, weak, diluted.

wistful *adjective* yearning, longing, forlorn, disconsolate, melancholy, sad, mournful, dreaming, dreamy, daydreaming, in a reverie, pensive, reflective, musing, contemplative, meditative.

wit *noun* **1** *he didn't have the wit to understand the position* intelligence, intellect, cleverness, wisdom, sageness, sagacity, judgement, common sense, understanding, comprehension, reason, sharpness, astuteness, shrewdness, acumen, discernment, perspicacity, perception, percipience, insight, ingenuity; brains; *inf.* nous. **2** *entertained by a person of great wit* wittiness, humour, jocularity, funniness, facetiousness, drollery, waggishness, repartee, badinage, banter, raillery. **3** *one of the great wits of his time* humorist, wag, funny person, comic, jokester, banterer, *farceur*; *inf.* card.
Opposites STUPIDITY; GRAVITY.

witch *noun* sorceress, enchantress, magician, necromancer, hex.

witchcraft *noun* witchery, sorcery, black art/magic, magic, necromancy, wizardry, occultism, the occult, sortilege, thaumaturgy, wonder-working.

withdraw *verb* **1** *withdraw her son from the school | withdraw the poker from the fire* take back, pull back, take away, extract, remove. **2** *asked to withdraw their remarks* take back, retract, recall, unsay. **3** *parliament withdrew the bill* revoke, annul, disannul, nullify, declare void, rescind, repeal, abrogate. **4** *she withdrew into the shadows | withdraw from the group* draw back, go back, absent oneself, detach oneself. **5** *the troops/spectators withdrew* pull back, fall back, retire, retreat, disengage, depart, go, leave; *inf.* make oneself scarce.
Opposites KEEP; PROFFER; STAY; PROCEED.

withdrawal *noun* **1** *his withdrawal from the school | withdrawal of the poker from the fire* extraction, removal. See WITHDRAW 1. **2** *the withdrawal of their remarks* retraction, recall, unsaying. **3** *the withdrawal of the bill* revocation, nullification, rescinding, repeal, abrogation. *See* WITHDRAW 3. **4** *the withdrawal of the troops/spectators* falling back, retiral, retreat, disengagement, departure, leaving, exit, exodus, evacuation. **5** *withdrawal from drugs* cessation (of), abstention, deprivation, absence.

withdrawn *adjective* *a withdrawn person/personality* retiring, reserved, uncommunicative, non-forthcoming, unsociable, taciturn, silent, quiet, introverted, detached, aloof, self-contained, distant, private, shrinking, timid, timorous, shy, bashful, diffident.
Opposites OUTGOING; SOCIABLE.

wither *verb* **1** *flowers withering in the heat* dry up/out, shrivel, go limp, wilt, die. **2** *heat withering the flowers* dry up/out, desiccate, kill off. **3** *time withered their enthusiasm/hopes* destroy, ruin, kill off, blight, blast. **4** *gradually their enthusiasm/dreams withered* wilt, decline, fade, ebb, wane, disintegrate, die, perish.

withhold *verb* **1** *unable to withhold their laughter* hold back, keep back, restrain, hold/keep in check, check, curb, repress, suppress. **2** *withhold permission* refuse to give/grant/allow, refuse, decline, keep back.

within *preposition* **1** *within the walls of the city* inside, in, within the confines of, enclosed by. **2** *within the speed limit* inside, inside the range/limits of, in the bounds of. **3** *come back within half-an-hour* before, not after, not exceeding, not more than, in the compass of.

without *preposition* **1** *they were three days without food* lacking, short of, wanting, requiring, in want/need of, deprived of, destitute of. **2** *he arrived without her* unaccompanied by, unescorted by, in the absence of. **3** *that is the price without service charge* exclusive of, excluding, not including, not counting.

withstand *verb* *withstand attack/pressure* hold out against, stand up to, stand firm against, resist, fight, combat, oppose, endure, stand, tolerate, bear, put up with, take, cope with, weather, brave, defy.
Opposites SURRENDER; YIELD.

witness *noun* **1** *taking statements from witnesses | a witness to the accident* eyewitness, observer, spectator, onlooker, looker-on, viewer, watcher, beholder, bystander. **2** *witnesses giving evidence in court* testifier, attestant, deponent. **3** *his ragged clothes were witness of his poverty* evidence, testimony, confirmation, corroboration, proof. **bear witness 1** *several people were asked to bear witness* give evidence, testify, give testimony. **2** *her bruises bore witness to her claim that she had been attacked* testify to, attest to, be evidence of, confirm, corroborate, be proof of, prove, bear out, vouch for, betoken.

witness *verb* **1** *the children witnessed the accident* see, observe, view, watch, look on at, behold, perceive, be present at, attend. **2** *witness his will/signature* endorse, countersign, sign. **3** *his ragged clothes witnessed to his poverty* bear witness to, testify to, attest to, be evidence of, confirm, corroborate, be proof of, prove. **4** *she was asked to witness to the truth of the statement* testify to, give testimony to, attest to, bear witness to, give evidence about.

wits *plural noun he didn't have the wits to understand the position* wit, intelligence, brains, intellect, cleverness, judgement, common sense, shrewdness, perspicacity; *inf.* nous.

witticism *noun* witty remark, clever saying, flash of wit, *bon mot*, quip, sally, pleasantry, riposte, joke, jest, epigram; *inf.* wisecrack, crack, one-liner.

witty *adjective* clever, original, ingenious, sparkling, scintillating, humorous, amusing, jocular, funny, facetious, droll, waggish, comic.
Opposites BORING; DULL.

wizard *noun* **1** *wizards casting spells* sorcerer, warlock, enchanter, witch, necromancer, magician, magus. **2** *he's a wizard at the piano* expert, master, adept, genius, virtuoso, maestro, star; *inf.* dab hand, ace, whiz, wiz.

wizened *adjective* withered, shrivelled, dried-up, shrunken, wasted, wrinkled, lined, gnarled, worn.

wobble *verb* **1** *the table/boat wobbled* rock, sway, see-saw, teeter, shake, vibrate. **2** *she wobbled down the road on high heels* teeter, totter, stagger, waddle, waggle. **3** *her voice wobbled with emotion* shake, tremble, quiver, quaver. **4** *the politicians were wobbling* be undecided, be uncertain, waver, vacillate, hesitate, dither, shilly-shally.

wobble *noun* **1** *try to prevent the wobble of the table/boat* rocking, swaying, teetering, shaking. See WOBBLE *verb* 1. **2** *walk with a wobble* teeter, totter, stagger. See WOBBLE *verb* 2. **3** *a wobble of emotion in her voice* shaking, trembling, tremor, quiver, quaver.

woe *noun* **1** *a tale of woe* misery, wretchedness, misfortune, disaster, grief, anguish, affliction, suffering, pain, agony, torment, sorrow, sadness, unhappiness, distress, heartache, heartbreak, despondency, desolation, dejection, depression, gloom, melancholy. **2** *she told everyone her woes* trouble, misfortune, adversity, trial, tribulation, ordeal, burden, affliction, suffering, disaster, calamity, catastrophe; trials and tribulations.
Opposites HAPPINESS; JOY; LUCK.

woebegone *adjective a woebegone face/expression* miserable, sad, unhappy, sorrowful, sorrowing,

disconsolate, mournful, downcast, dejected, doleful, desolate, depressed, despairing, tearful.

woeful *adjective* **1** *telling woeful tales of poverty* sad, saddening, unhappy, sorrowful, miserable, dismal, wretched, doleful, gloomy, tragic, pathetic, grievous, pitiful, plaintive, heart-rending, heartbreaking, distressing, anguished, agonizing, dreadful, terrible. **2** *the army will meet a woeful fate* sad, miserable, wretched, harsh, tragic, disastrous, ruinous, calamitous, catastrophic. **3** *a woeful piece of work* poor, bad, inadequate, substandard, lamentable, deplorable, disgraceful, wretched, disappointing, feeble; *inf.* rotten, appalling, terrible, lousy, shocking, duff.

wolf *noun* **1** *the wolf killed a sheep* wild dog. See table. **2** *a wolf trying to seduce the young girl* lady-killer, ladies' man, philanderer, womanizer, seducer, lecher, Casanova, Don Juan, Lothario.

WOLVES AND WILD DOGS		
bush dog	jackal	Simian
coyote	maned wolf	jackal
dhole	raccoon dog	timber
dingo	red dog	wolf
grey wolf	red wolf	wild dog
hunting dog		zorro

wolf *verb wolf his food* devour, gulp down, bolt, gobble, cram down, stuff down, gorge oneself with; *inf.* scoff, pack away.

woman *noun* **1** *women and children first* female, lady, girl, she, member of the fair/gentle sex; *derog. inf.* bird, chick, dame. **2** *he has a new woman* girlfriend, female friend, lady love, sweetheart, partner, lover, wife, spouse. **3** *employ a woman to help in the house* charwoman, domestic help, domestic, maid, maidservant; *inf.* char, Mrs Mop.

womanhood *noun* **1** *reach womanhood* maturity, muliebrity. **2** *appreciate her warmth and womanhood* womanliness, feminineness, femininity. **3** *considering the role of womanhood* womankind, women, woman, female sex, womenfolk.

womanish *adjective laugh at his womanish ways* effeminate, effete, unmanly; *inf.* sissy.

womanizer *noun* lady-killer, ladies' man, philanderer, seducer, lecher, Casanova, Don Juan, Lothario; *inf.* wolf.

womankind *noun* women, woman, female sex, womanhood, womenfolk.

womanly *adjective* woman-like, female, feminine, matronly, motherly.

wonder *noun* **1** *children gazing with wonder at the Christmas tree* wonderment, awe, surprise, astonishment, amazement, bewilderment, stupefaction, fascination, admiration. **2** *one of the wonders of the world* marvel, phenomenon, miracle, prodigy, curiosity, rarity, nonpareil, sight, spectacle. See table.

SEVEN WONDERS OF THE WORLD
Pyramids of Egypt
Colossus of Rhodes
Hanging Gardens of Babylon
Mausoleum of Halicarnassus
Statue of Zeus at Olympia
Temple of Artemis at Ephesus
Pharos/Lighthouse of Alexandria

WIND AND WOODWIND INSTRUMENTS	
alpenhorn	heckelphone
altohorn	kazoo
bagpipes	mouth organ
barrel organ	oboe
bassoon	ocarina
bombard	piccolo
clarinet	piffero
contrabassoon	pipe
crumhorn	recorder
fife	saxophone
fipple flute	shawm
flageolet	stock-and-horn
flute	tin whistle
harmonica	whistle

wonder *verb* **1** *she wondered what to do next | he wondered where she came from* think, speculate, conjecture, ponder, meditate, reflect, deliberate, muse, ask oneself, puzzle, be curious about, be inquisitive about; *inf.* cudgel one's brains about. **2** *I wonder you didn't walk out* be surprised, express surprise, find it surprising, be astonished/amazed. **3** *they wondered at the beauty of the church* marvel, stand amazed, stand in awe, be dumbfounded, gape, stare, goggle, look agog; *inf.* be flabbergasted, gawk, boggle.

wonderful *adjective* **1** *the church ceiling was wonderful to behold* marvellous, awe-inspiring, awesome, remarkable, extraordinary, phenomenal, prodigious, miraculous, fantastic, amazing, astonishing, astounding, surprising, incredible, unprecedented, unparalleled, unheard-of; *lit.* wondrous. **2** *a wonderful mother/piano-player* superb, marvellous, magnificent, brilliant, sensational, stupendous, excellent, first-rate, outstanding, terrific, tremendous, admirable, very good; *inf.* great, super, fantastic, smashing, ripping, fabulous, tiptop, ace, A1, wizard, bad, wicked.
Opposites ORDINARY; INDIFFERENT; AWFUL; DREADFUL.

wont *adjective* *wont to get up late* accustomed, in the habit (of), used, given.

wont *noun* *it is their wont to rise late* custom, habit, routine, practice, way, rule, convention.

wonted *adjective* *work with his wonted industriousness* customary, accustomed, habitual, usual, normal, routine, regular, common, frequent, familiar, conventional.

woo *verb* **1** *woo the daughter of a millionaire* court, pay court/suit to, seek the hand of, pursue, chase after, set one's cap at, make love to. **2** *woo fame* seek, seek to win/gain, pursue, chase after. **3** *woo the voters* seek the support/favour of. **4** *salesmen wooing householders into buying their goods* importune, press, urge, entreat, beg, implore, supplicate, solicit, coax, wheedle.

wood *noun* **1** *goods made of wood* timber. **2** *wood for the fire* firewood, kindling, fuel. **3** *go for a walk in the wood/woods* forest, woodland, copse, thicket, coppice, grove; trees.

wooded *adjective* woody, forested, tree-covered, tree-clad, timbered, sylvan.

wooden *adjective* **1** *wooden furniture/houses* made of wood, of wood, wood, woody, timber. **2** *give a wooden performance* stiff, stolid, stodgy, expressionless, graceless, inelegant, ungainly, gauche, awkward, clumsy, maladroit. **3** *wearing a wooden expression | give him a*

wooden look expressionless, inexpressive, blank, deadpan, empty, vacant, vacuous, glassy, impassive, lifeless, spiritless, unanimated, emotionless, unemotional, unresponsive. **4** *children seeming completely wooden* stupid, thick, dense, dull, dull-witted, slow, slow-witted, doltish, witless, obtuse, bovine; *inf.* dim, dim-witted.

woodwind *noun. See table.*

wool *noun* **1** *sheep with dirty wool* fleece, hair, coat. **2** *knit the wool into a sweater* yarn. *See table at* FABRIC.

wool-gathering *noun* daydreaming, dreaming, reverie, musing, abstraction, preoccupation, absent-mindedness, inattention.

woolly *adjective* **1** *animals with woolly coats* fleecy, fluffy, shaggy, hairy, furry, flocculent. **2** *wearing woolly garments* woollen, made of wool, of wool, wool. **3** *a woolly TV picture* fuzzy, blurred, hazy, cloudy, foggy, indistinct, unclear, ill-defined. **4** *a woolly description | woolly thoughts* vague, hazy, indefinite, muddled, confused, disorganized.

word *noun* **1** *what's another word for fame?* term, expression, name. **2** *he said not a word* remark, comment, statement, utterance, expression, declaration. **3** *she gave him her word that she would be present* word of honour, solemn word, promise, pledge, assurance, guarantee, undertaking, vow, oath. **4** *have a word with the teacher* chat, talk, conversation, discussion, tête-à-tête, consultation, exchange of views; *inf.* confab, chit-chat, pow-wow. **5** *they have had word of his death* news, intimation, notice, communication, information, intelligence; tidings; message, report, account, communiqué, dispatch, bulletin; *inf.* gen, low-down. **6** *word has it that he is a spy* rumour, talk, hearsay, gossip; *inf.* grapevine. **7** *give the word to begin* command, order, signal, go-ahead, thumbs up; *inf.* green light. **8** *the king's word is law* command, order, decree, edict, mandate, bidding, will. **9** *our word now must be success* slogan, watchword, password, catchword. **in a word** *in a word he's mad* in short, in a nutshell, briefly, to put it briefly, succinctly, concisely. **word-for-word** verbatim, literal, exact, precise, accurate, close, faithful, strict, undeviating.

word *verb* *word the account differently* express, phrase, couch, put, say, utter, state.

words · workshop

words *plural noun* **1** *write the words of the song/ opera/play* lyrics, libretto, book, text, script. **2** *she has had words with her sister* angry talk, argument, disagreement, row, altercation.

wordy *adjective a wordy description* long-winded, verbose, loquacious, garrulous, voluble, prolix, protracted, discursive, diffuse, rambling, digressive, maundering, tautological, pleonastic.

work *noun* **1** *building a house involves a lot of work* effort, exertion, labour, toil, slog, sweat, drudgery, trouble, industry; *lit.* travail; *inf.* grind, elbow-grease. **2** *your work is to answer the phone* job, task, chore, undertaking, duty, charge, assignment, commission, mission. **3** *engaged in financial work | out of work | what is his work?* employment, occupation, business; job, profession, career, trade, vocation, calling, craft, line, field, *métier*, pursuit. **4** *he regards it as his life's work* achievement, accomplishment, deed, feat, handiwork, fulfilment, performance, production. **5** *a work of art* composition, creation, opus, piece, oeuvre, masterpiece. **6** *admire the work that has gone into the stained-glass window* workmanship, art, craft, skill.
Opposites LEISURE; PLAY; HOLIDAY; RETIREMENT.

work *verb* **1** *he works in industry* be employed, have a job, hold down a job, be engaged, earn one's living, do business, follow/ply one's trade. **2** *you will really have to work to build the house | work hard to pass the exam* exert oneself, put in effort, make efforts, labour, toil, slog, sweat, drudge, slave, peg away; *inf.* grind, plug away, knock oneself out. **3** *work the machine* operate, control, drive, manage, direct, use, handle, manipulate, manoeuvre, ply, wield. **4** *this machine won't work* go, operate, function, perform, run. **5** *your idea/plan won't succeed* be successful, have success, go well, be effective, be effectual. **6** *work the land* cultivate, till, dig, farm. **7** *they can work miracles* bring about, achieve, accomplish, perform, carry out, execute, create, cause, contrive, effect, implement. **8** *they worked it so that the criminal got off* arrange, handle, manipulate, manoeuvre, contrive, bring off, carry off, pull off; *inf.* fix, fiddle, swing. **9** *work the clay* knead, shape, form, mould, fashion, model. **10** *work the peg into the hole* manoeuvre, manipulate, negotiate, guide, engineer, direct, edge. **11** *work one's way through the crowd* manoeuvre, progress, penetrate, move, make, push, elbow. **12** *screws working loose* come, become, move. **13** *his face worked* twitch, convulse, writhe, twist. **work on** *work on your mother to let you go* coax, cajole, wheedle, pester, press, nag, importune, persuade, influence, sway. **work out 1** *work out the puzzle/problem* solve, resolve, puzzle out, figure out. **2** *work out the answer* puzzle out, figure out, find out, calculate. **3** *the bill works out at £50* come to, add up to, amount to, total up to. **4** *work out a plan* develop, evolve, formulate, devise, arrange, organize, elaborate, construct, put together, plan, contrive. **5** *the plan did not work out* work, succeed, be successful, go well, go as planned/arranged/wished, be effective, be effectual. **6** *things worked out well/badly* go,

turn out, come out, develop, evolve, result; *inf.* pan out. **7** *work out to keep fit* exercise, do exercises, train, drill, practise, warm up. **work up 1** *work up to a climax* advance, progress, proceed, make headway. **2** *work up an appetite* cause, create, whet, stimulate, arouse, awaken. **3** *unable to work up any enthusiasm* stir up, arouse, rouse, awaken, excite, instigate, prompt, generate, kindle, foment. **4** *the speaker succeeded in working up the crowd* agitate, stir up, arouse, excite, animate, inflame; *inf.* get worked up, wind up.
Opposites REST; PLAY; FAIL; PREVENT.

workable *adjective* practicable, practical, viable, doable, feasible, possible.

workaday *adjective* ordinary, everyday, average, commonplace, mundane, run-of-the-mill, routine, humdrum, prosaic.

worker *noun* **1** *workers and employers* employee, hand, workman, workwoman, working man/ woman/person, blue-collar worker, white-collar worker, labourer, artisan, craftsman, craftswoman, wage-earner, proletarian. **2** *workers of miracles* doer, performer, perpetrator, executor, operator. **3** *he's a real worker* hard worker, toiler, workhorse, busy bee; *inf.* workaholic.

working *adjective* **1** *working mothers* in work, employed, in a job, waged. **2** *working models/ machines* functioning, operating, going, running, in working order. **3** *a working majority/ plan* effective, viable.
Opposites UNEMPLOYED; BROKEN.

working *noun* **1** *understand the working of the machine* functioning, operation, running process, method of working, *modus operandi*. **2** *the working of miracles* doing, performing, performance, perpetration, execution, operation. **3** *the children fell down the disused workings* mine, pit, quarry, shaft; diggings, excavations. **4** *mend the workings of the clock* mechanism, machinery; works. *See* WORKS 4.

workman, workwoman *noun workmen mending the roof* worker, employee, hand, labourer, artisan, tradesman, tradeswoman, operative.

workmanship *noun admire the workmanship of the tapestry/carpentry* craftsmanship, craft, artistry, art, handicraft, handwork, expertise, skill, technique, work.

workout *noun* training/practice session; physical exercise, drill, training; exercises, gymnastics, aerobics; *inf.* daily dozen.

works *plural noun* **1** *busy at the works* factory, plant, mill, workshop. **2** *the author's complete works* writings, productions; *oeuvre*, output. **3** *doing good works* deeds, acts, actions. **4** *the works of the clock/engine* workings, working parts, parts; mechanism, machinery, action, movement; *inf.* innards, insides, guts. **the works 1** *get the works at the beauty saloon* full treatment, everything available/required; *inf.* the lot. **2** *the enemy gave the prisoners the works* harsh treatment, physical beating, torture.

workshop *noun* **1** *the car's still in the workshop* factory, plant, mill, garage. **2** *craftsmen at work in their workshop* workroom, studio, atelier, shop. **3** *hold a workshop in self-assertiveness* seminar, study/discussion group, class.

world *noun* **1** *the mountains of the world | travel round the world* earth, globe, sphere, planet. **2** *the world was shocked by the nuclear attack* whole world, world at large, mankind, man, humankind, humanity, people everywhere, people, everyone, everybody, public, general public. **3** *God created the world* universe, creation, cosmos, all existence. **4** *the earth and other worlds* planet, satellite, moon, star, heavenly body, orb. **5** *the academic world disliked the novel* society, sector, section, group, division. **6** *he works in the world of finance* area, field, department, sphere, province, domain, realm. **7** *the world of the dinosaurs/Tudors* age, epoch, era, period; times. **8** *it made a world of difference* vast/huge amount; *inf.* great deal, immensity. **9** *renounce the world | not interested in the world* secular interests, earthly concerns, human existence.

worldly *adjective* **1** *worldly considerations/pleasures* earthly, terrestrial, secular, temporal, material, materialistic, human, carnal, fleshly, corporeal, physical. **2** *she is worldly but her sister is innocent* worldly-wise, experienced, knowing, sophisticated, cosmopolitan, urbane.
Opposites SPIRITUAL; NAIVE; UNSOPHISTICATED.

worldwide *adjective* universal, global, international, pandemic, general, ubiquitous, extensive, widespread, far-reaching, wide-ranging.

worm *noun*. See table.

worn *adjective* **1** *worn carpets/clothes* worn-out, threadbare, tattered, in tatters, ragged, frayed, shabby, shiny. **2** *worn furniture* worn-out, dilapidated, crumbling, broken-down, run-down, tumbledown, decrepit, deteriorated, on its last legs; *inf.* clapped-out. **3** *mothers looking worn* haggard, drawn, strained, careworn; *inf.* all in, done in, dog-tired, dead on one's feet, fit to drop, played-out, bushed, knackered, pooped. **4** *mothers worn by child-bearing* worn out, exhausted, overtired, tired out, fatigued, weary, wearied, spent. See WORN-OUT. **5** *worn ideas/jokes* well-worn, worn-out, obsolete, antiquated, old, hackneyed, stale; *inf.* played-out, clapped-out.
Opposites NEW; MINT; ENERGETIC; FRESH.

worn-out *adjective* worn, dilapidated, exhausted. See WORN 1, 5.

worried *adjective* anxious, disturbed, perturbed, troubled, bothered, distressed, concerned, upset, distraught, uneasy, ill at ease, disquieted, fretful, agitated, nervous, edgy, on edge, tense, overwrought, worked-up, distracted, apprehensive, fearful, afraid, frightened; *inf.* uptight, on tenterhooks; *Am. inf.* antsy.
Opposites CAREFREE; CALM; UNCONCERNED.

worry *verb* **1** *she worries too much* be worried, be anxious, fret, brood. See WORRIED. **2** *his absences worry her* cause anxiety, make anxious, disturb, trouble, bother, distress, upset, concern, disquiet, discompose, fret, agitate, unsettle. See WORRIED. **3** *stop worrying your mother about new clothes* pester, harass, vex, irritate, annoy, nag, importune, plague, torment, harry, persecute; *inf.* hassle. **4** *dogs worrying sheep* tear at, bite, gnaw at, lacerate, savage, go for, attack, shake, pull at.

worry *noun* **1** *the children are a worry to their father* nuisance, pest, plague, trial, trouble, problem, irritation, irritant, vexation, thorn in one's flesh. **2** *their disappearance/behaviour caused him a lot of worry* anxiety, disturbance, perturbation, trouble, bother, distress, concern, care, upset, uneasiness, unease, disquiet, disquietude, fretfulness, agitation, edginess, tenseness, apprehension, fearfulness. See WORRIED.

worsen *verb* **1** *his statement simply worsened the situation* make worse, aggravate, exacerbate, damage, intensify, increase, heighten. **2** *the financial situation worsened* get/grow/become worse, take a turn for the worse, deteriorate, degenerate, retrogress, decline, sink, slip, slide; *inf.* go downhill.
Opposites IMPROVE; ameliorate.

worship *noun* **1** *worship of God | acts of worship* reverence, veneration, homage, respect, honour, adoration, devotion, praise, prayer, glorification, exaltation, laudation, extolment. **2** *attend morning worship* service; religious rites/ acts. **3** *the fan's worship of the rock star* adulation, admiration, adoration, devotion, idolization, hero-worship.

WORMS				
acorn worm	eye-worm	horseshoe	peacock worm	spiny-headed
annelid	fanworm	worm	peanut worm	worm
arrow worm	feather-duster	kidney worm	pinworm	spoonworm
ascarid	filaria	leech	platyhelminth	tapeworm
bamboo worm	fireworm	liver fluke	polychaete	thorny-headed
beard worm	flatworm	lobworm	pot worm	worm
bladder worm	fluke	lugworm	proboscis	threadworm
blood fluke	gapeworm	lungworm	worm	tongue-worm
bloodworm	gordian worm	nematode	ragworm	toxocara
bootlace worm	Guinea worm	nemertean	rainworm	trematode
bristle worm	hairworm	nereid	ribbon worm	trichina
catworm	heartworm	oligochaete	roundworm	tube worm
chaetognath	helminth	paddle worm	scaleworm	tubifex
dung-worm	hookworm	palolo worm	sea mouse	vinegar eel
earthworm	horsehair	parchment	serpulid	whipworm
eelworm	worm	worm	sipunculid	white worm

worship verb **1** *worship God* revere, venerate, pay homage to, honour, adore, praise, pray to, glorify, exalt, laud, extol. **2** *worship at the local church* attend a service, pray. **3** *he worships his wife | the fans worship the rock star* adore, be devoted to, cherish, treasure, admire, adulate, idolize, hero-worship, lionize; *inf.* be wild about.
Opposites BLASPHEME; LOATHE; DESPISE.

worst verb defeat, beat, best, get the better of, gain the advantage over, trounce, rout, thrash, whip, drub, vanquish, conquer, master, overcome, overwhelm, overpower, overthrow, crush, subdue, subjugate.

worth noun **1** *the jewels are of little worth* financial value, value, price, cost. **2** *put a low worth on the house* value, valuation, price, assessment, appraisal. **3** *his advice is of little worth to you* value, use, usefulness, advantage, benefit, service, gain, profit, avail, help, assistance, aid. **4** *persons of great worth in the community* worthiness, merit, credit, value, excellence, eminence, importance.

worthless adjective **1** *the jewels are worthless* valueless, of little/no financial value, rubbishy, trashy. **2** *his advice was worthless | worthless attempts* valueless, useless, no use, of no benefit, to no avail, futile, ineffective, ineffectual, pointless, nugatory. **3** *their worthless son ended up in prison* good-for-nothing, useless, despicable, contemptible, base, low, vile, corrupt, depraved; *inf.* no-good, no-account.
Opposites VALUABLE; PRECIOUS; USEFUL.

worthwhile adjective worth it, worth the effort, valuable, of value, useful, of use, beneficial, advantageous, helpful, profitable, gainful, productive, constructive, justifiable.
Opposites WORTHLESS; USELESS; POINTLESS.

worthy adjective **1** *worthy people not receiving recognition | lead worthy but boring lives* virtuous, good, moral, upright, righteous, honest, decent, honourable, respectable, reputable, trustworthy, reliable, irreproachable, blameless, unimpeachable, admirable, praiseworthy, laudable, commendable, deserving, meritorious. **2** *worthy of respect* deserving, meriting.
Opposites DISREPUTABLE; UNWORTHY.

worthy noun local worthies dignitary, notable, celebrity, personage, luminary, official; *inf.* VIP, big shot, bigwig, big cheese, big gun.

wound noun **1** *a wound in the leg that is not healing* lesion, cut, graze, scratch, gash, laceration, tear, puncture, slash, injury, sore. **2** *a wound to his pride* blow, injury, insult, slight, offence, affront; hurt, harm, damage. **3** *suffering from mental/emotional wounds* injury, hurt, pain, pang, ache, distress, grief, trauma, anguish, torment, torture.

wound verb **1** *the shot wounded his arm* cut, graze, scratch, gash, lacerate, tear, puncture, pierce, stab, slash, injure, hurt, damage, harm. **2** *their words wounded his pride* hurt, harm, damage, injure, insult, slight, offend, affront. **3** *his actions wounded her feelings* hurt, distress, grieve, mortify, pain, shock, traumatize.
Opposites HEAL; BOOST; GLADDEN.

wraith noun ghost, spectre, shade, phantom, apparition, spirit.

wrangle noun *neighbours involved in a wrangle about the upkeep of a dividing wall* dispute, disagreement, argument, quarrel, row, fight, bickering, squabble, altercation, angry exchange, controversy, tiff, tussle, brouhaha, rumpus, brawl; *inf.* falling-out, set-to, dust-up, spat.

wrangle verb *wrangle over custody of the children* have a disagreement, argue, quarrel, row, bicker, fight, clash, squabble, have words, brawl; *inf.* fall out. *See* WRANGLE *noun*.

wrap verb **1** *wrap the child in blankets* envelop, enfold, encase, enclose, cover, swathe, bundle up, swaddle. **2** *wrap the shawl round her* fold, swathe, bundle, draw, arrange. **3** *wrap the present* wrap up, parcel up, package, do up, tie up, gift-wrap. **wrap up 1** *wrap up the present* wrap, parcel up, gift-wrap. *See* WRAP *verb* 3. **2** *try to wrap up the meeting early* finish, end, bring to an end/close, conclude, terminate, wind up. **3** *you must wrap up well in the winter* dress warmly, wear warm clothes. **4** *tell that child to wrap up* be quiet, be silent, hold one's tongue, stop talking; *inf.* shut up, shut one's mouth/face/trap, put a sock in it.

wrap noun shawl, stole, cloak, cape, mantle.

wrapper noun **1** *sweet wrapper* wrapping, cover, covering, packaging, paper. **2** *book wrappers* cover, jacket, casing. **3** *hot-water tank wrapper* cover, covering, case, casing, sheath, jacket, capsule, pod, shell. **4** *wearing a wrapper and slippers* housecoat, bathrobe, dressing-gown, robe, kimono, negligée, peignoir.

wrath noun anger, ire, rage, fury, annoyance, indignation, exasperation, dudgeon, high dudgeon, bad temper, ill humour, irritation, crossness, displeasure, irascibility.

wrathful adjective angry, irate, raging, enraged, incensed, infuriated, furious, fuming, ranting, raving, beside oneself, indignant, exasperated, bad-tempered, ill-humoured, irritated, cross, displeased, irascible; *inf.* on the warpath.
Opposites CALM; GOOD-HUMOURED.

wreath noun **1** *wreaths of flowers* garland, chaplet, circlet, coronet, crown, diadem, festoon, lei. **2** *wreaths of smoke* ring, loop, circle.

wreathe verb **1** *the display was wreathed in flowers | her face was wreathed in smiles* cover, envelop, festoon, garland, adorn, decorate. **2** *the snake wreathed itself round the tree trunk* twist, wind, coil, twine, entwine, curl, spiral, wrap. **3** *smoke wreathing from the chimneys* coil, wind, spiral, curl.

wreck noun **1** *the divers failed to salvage the wreck* shipwreck, sunken ship/vessel, derelict. **2** *the wreck of the car/house/dreams* wreckage, debris, rubble, detritus; ruins, remains, remnants, fragments, pieces, relics. **3** *upset by the wreck of their car/house/dream* wrecking, wreckage, destruction, devastation, ruination, ruin, demolition, smashing, shattering, disruption, disintegration, undoing.

wreck *verb* **1** *wreck the car* smash, demolish, ruin, damage; *inf.* write off. **2** *wreck their plans/ hopes* destroy, devastate, ruin, demolish, smash, shatter, disrupt, undo, spoil, mar, play havoc with. **3** *the new crew wrecked the ship* shipwreck, sink, capsize, run aground. **4** *the liner wrecked on its first voyage* founder, run aground, sink.
Opposites BUILD; CREATE; SAVE; REPAIR.

wreckage *noun* **1** *clear away the wreckage of the car/house/accident* wreck, debris; ruins, remains, remnants, fragments. *See* WRECK *noun* 2. **2** *upset by the wreckage of their car/house/dream* wreck, wrecking, destruction, ruination, ruin, demolition, smashing. *See* WRECK *noun* 3.

wrench *noun* **1** *remove the root at one wrench* twist, pull, tug, yank, wrest, jerk, jolt. **2** *have a wrench in the tool-box* spanner, adjustable spanner; monkey wrench. **3** *the wrist injury is just a wrench* sprain, twist, strain, rick. **4** *leaving home was a wrench* painful parting, distressing separation. **5** *the wrench caused by parting from her children* pain, ache, pang, anguish, distress, trauma.

wrench *verb* **1** *wrench the root from the ground* twist, pull, tug, yank, wrest, jerk, tear, rip, force. **2** *wrench one's ankle/wrist* sprain, twist, strain, rick.

wrest *verb* *wrest the gun from him* twist, wrench, pull, snatch, take away, remove.

wrestle *verb* **1** *men wrestling in the ring* grapple, contend. **2** *wrestle with one's conscience* struggle, grapple, fight, contend, battle, combat. **3** *wrestle with the problem* struggle, contend, come to grips with, face up to, pit oneself against; *inf.* plug away at.

wretch *noun* **1** *pity wretches sleeping rough* poor creature/soul/thing, miserable creature, unfortunate, poor devil. **2** *that's the wretch that mugged the old lady* scoundrel, villain, ruffian, rogue, rascal, blackguard, reprobate, criminal, delinquent, miscreant; *inf.* rotter, creep, jerk, louse, rat, swine, skunk.

wretched *adjective* **1** *feeling wretched at leaving home* miserable, unhappy, sad, broken-hearted, sorrowful, sorry, distressed, disconsolate, downcast, down, downhearted, dejected, crestfallen, cheerless, depressed, melancholy, gloomy, mournful, doleful, forlorn, woebegone, abject. **2** *feeling wretched during the sea voyage* ill, unwell, sick, sickly, ailing, below par; *inf.* under the weather, out of sorts. **3** *lead a wretched existence* miserable, unhappy, poor, hard, harsh, grim, difficult, unfortunate, sorry, pitiful, tragic. **4** *wretched creatures sleeping rough* miserable, poor, unhappy, unfortunate, unlucky, hapless, pitiable. **5** *the wretched burglar is back in prison* contemptible, despicable, base, low, vile. **6** *the food was wretched* poor, bad, substandard, low-quality, inferior, pathetic, worthless.
Opposites HAPPY; WELL; FORTUNATE.

wriggle *verb* **1** *children wriggling in their seats* twist, squirm, writhe, jiggle, jerk. **2** *wriggle along the ground* twist and turn, zigzag, wiggle, snake, crawl, slink. **3** *wriggle out of the task* avoid, evade, dodge, duck, extricate oneself.

wriggle *noun* *the wriggles of the children* squirming, writhing, jiggling, jerk.

wriggly *adjective* *a wriggly line* wiggly, wiggling, twisting, zigzag, zigzagging.

wring *verb* **1** *wring the clothes* twist, squeeze. **2** *wring the information from him* extract, force, coerce, exact, extort, wrest, wrench, screw. **3** *her poverty wrung their hearts* pierce, stab, wound, harrow, tear at, lacerate, rack, distress, pain, hurt.

wrinkle *noun* *wrinkles in her face | wrinkles in the material* crease, fold, pucker, gather, furrow, ridge, line, corrugation, crinkle, crumple, rumple.

wrinkle *verb* *time had wrinkled her face | sitting wrinkled the dress* crease, pucker, gather, furrow, line, corrugate, crinkle, crumple, rumple.

writ *noun* court order, summons, decree.

write *verb* **1** *write their names* write down, put in writing, put in black and white, commit to paper, jot down, note, set down, take down, record, register, list, inscribe, scribble, scrawl. **2** *write an essay/letter* compose, draft, create, pen, dash off. **3** *don't forget to write* write a letter, correspond, communicate; *inf.* drop a line/ note. **write down** put in writing, jot down, note, set down, take down, record, register, list. **write off 1** *write off the debt* forget about, disregard, give up for lost, cancel, annul, nullify, wipe out, cross out, score out. **2** *write off the car* damage beyond repair, wreck, smash, crash, destroy, demolish; *Am. inf.* total. **3** *don't write off your opponent* disregard, regard as finished, dismiss.

writer *noun* author, wordsmith, penman, hack; novelist, essayist, biographer, journalist, columnist, scriptwriter; *inf.* scribbler, penpusher. *See table. See also tables at* PLAYWRIGHT, POET.

writhe *verb* twist about, twist and turn, roll about, squirm, wriggle, jerk, thrash, flail, toss, struggle.

writing *noun* **1** *the writing is illegible* handwriting, hand, penmanship, script, print, calligraphy, chirography scribble, scrawl. **2** *have his writings published* work, *opus*, book, volume, publication, composition.

wrong *adjective* **1** *the wrong answer | he is wrong in his calculation* incorrect, inaccurate, in error, erroneous, mistaken, inexact, imprecise, unsound, faulty, false, wide of the mark, off target; *inf.* off beam, barking up the wrong tree. **2** *chose the wrong moment to speak* unsuitable, inappropriate, inapt, inapposite, undesirable, infelicitous. **3** *the wrong way to behave on such an occasion* unsuitable, inappropriate, undesirable, unacceptable, unfitting, improper, unseemly, indecorous, unconventional. **4** *it is wrong to steal* unlawful, illegal, illicit, lawless, criminal, delinquent, felonious, dishonest, dishonourable, corrupt, unethical, immoral, bad, wicked, evil, sinful, iniquitous, blameworthy, culpable; *inf.* crooked. **5** *he's a wrong 'un* criminal, dishonest, dishonourable, corrupt, bad, wicked, evil, sinful, nasty, vile, base, despicable, contemptible, reprehensible. **6** *something wrong with the phone/heart* amiss,

WRITERS

Achebe, Chinua (b. 1930; Nigerian)

Addison, Joseph (1672–1719; Brit.)

Aesop (6th century B.C.; Gk)

Alain-Fournier (1886–1914; Fr.)

Alcott, Louisa May (1832–88; Am.)

Aldiss, Brian (b. 1925; Brit.)

Amis, Martin (b. 1949; Brit.)

Amis, Sir Kingsley (b. 1922; Brit.)

Andersen, Hans Christian (1805–75; Da.)

Andrić, Ivo (1892–1975; Serbian)

Angelou, Maya (b. 1928; Am.)

Asimov, Isaac (1920–92; Am.)

Asturias, Miguel (1899–1974; Guatemalan)

Atwood, Margaret (b. 1939; Can.)

Austen, Jane (1775–1817; Brit.)

Baldwin, James (1924–87; Am.)

Ballard, J(ames) G(raham) (b. 1930; Brit.)

Balzac, Honoré de (1799–1850; Fr.)

Bates, H(erbert) E(rnest) (1905–74; Brit.)

Beauvoir, Simone de (1908–86; Fr.)

Beckford, William (1759–1844; Brit.)

Beerbohm, Sir Max (1872–1956; Brit.)

Behn, Aphra (1640–89; Brit.)

Belloc, Hilaire (1870–1953; Brit., b. in France.)

Bellow, Saul (b. 1915; Am., b. in Canada)

Bennett, Arnold (1867–1931; Brit.)

Blackmore, Richard (1825–1900; Brit.)

Boccaccio, Giovanni (1313–75; It.)

Böll, Heinrich (1917–85; Ger.)

Borges, Jorge Luis (1899–1986; Argentinian)

Boswell, James (1740–95; Scot.)

Boyd, Martin (1893–1972; Austral.)

Bradbury, Malcolm (b. 1932; Brit.)

Braine, John (1922–86; Brit.)

Brink, André (b. 1935; S. Afr.)

Broch, Hermann (1886–1951; Austrian)

Brontë, Anne (1820–49; Brit.)

Brontë, Charlotte (1816–55; Brit.)

Brontë, Emily (1818–48; Brit.)

Brookner, Anita (b. 1928; Brit.)

Browne, Sir Thomas (1605–82; Brit.)

Buchan, John, 1st Baron Tweedsmuir (1875–1940; Scot.)

Bunyan, John (1628–88; Brit.)

Burgess, Anthony (John Burgess Wilson; 1917–93; Brit.)

Burroughs, Edgar Rice (1875–1950; Am.)

Burroughs, William S. (b. 1914; Am.)

Butler, Samuel (1835–1902; Brit.)

Byatt, A(ntonia) S(usan) (b. 1936; Brit.)

Calvino, Italo (1923–85; It.)

Camus, Albert (1913–60; Fr.)

Canetti, Elias (1905–94; Brit., b. in Bulgaria)

Capote, Truman (1924–84; Am.)

Carroll, Lewis (Charles Dodgson; 1832–98; Brit.)

Carter, Angela (1940–92; Brit.)

Cartland, Dame Barbara (b. 1901; Brit.)

Cary, (Arthur) Joyce (1888–1957; Brit.)

Cather, Willa (1876–1974; Am.)

Cela, Camilo José (b. 1916; Sp.)

Céline, Louis (L. F. Destouches; 1884–1961; Fr.)

Cervantes, Miguel de (1547–1616; Sp.)

Chandler, Raymond (1888–1959; Am.)

Chateaubriand, Vicomte de (1768–1848; Fr.)

Chesterton, G(ilbert) K(eith) (1874–1936; Brit.)

Christie, Dame Agatha (1890–1976; Brit.)

Clarke, Arthur C(harles) (b. 1917; Brit.)

Coetzee, J(ohn) M(ichael) (b. 1940; S. Afr.)

Colette (Sidonie Gabrielle Colette; 1873–1954; Fr.)

Collins, (William) Wilkie (1824–89; Brit.)

Compton-Burnett, Ivy (1884–1969; Brit.)

Conrad, Joseph (Teodor Korzeniowski; 1857–1924; Brit., b. in Poland)

Cookson, Dame Catherine (b. 1906; Brit.)

Cooper, James Fenimore (1789–1851; Am.)

Crompton, Richmal (1890–1969; Brit.)

Dahl, Roald (1916–90; Brit.)

Defoe, Daniel (c. 1660–1731; Brit.)

Deighton, Len (b. 1929; Brit.)

De Quincey, Thomas (1785–1859; Brit.)

Dickens, Charles (1812–70; Brit.)

Dinesen, Isak (Karen Blixen, Baroness; 1885–1962; Da.)

Dos Passos, John (1896–1970; Am.)

Dostoevsky, Feodor (1821–81; Russ.)

Doyle, Sir Arthur Conan (1859–1930; Brit.)

Drabble, Margaret (b. 1939; Brit.)

Dumas, Alexandre (1802–70; Fr.)

Du Maurier, Daphne (1907–89; Brit.)

Durrell, Lawrence (1912–90; Brit.)

Eco, Umberto (b. 1932; It.)

Edgeworth, Maria (1767–1849; Ir.)

Ehrenberg, Ilya (1891–1967; Russ.)

Eichendorff, Josef, Freiherr von (1788–1857; Ger.)

Eliot, George (Mary Ann Evans; 1819–80; Brit.)

Evelyn, John (1620–1706; Brit.)

Farrell, J(ames) G(ordon) (1935–79; Brit.)

Faulkner, William (1897–1962; Am.)

Fielding, Henry (1707–54; Brit.)

Fitzgerald, F. Scott (1896–1940; Am.)

Flaubert, Gustave (1821–80; Fr.)

Fleming, Ian (1908–64; Brit.)

Forester, C(ecil) S(cott) (Cecil Lewis Troughton Smith; 1899–1966; Brit.)

Forster, E(dward) M(organ) (1879–1970; Brit.)

Forsyth, Frederick (b. 1938; Brit.)

Fowles, John (b. 1926; Brit.)

Frame, Janet (b. 1924; NZ)

France, Anatole (Jacques Anatole François Thibault; 1844–1924; Fr.)

Francis, Dick (b. 1920; Brit.)

Fuentes, Carlos (b. 1928; Mex.)

Galsworthy, John (1867–1933; Brit.)

García Márquez, Gabriel (b. 1928; Colombian)

Gaskell, Mrs (Elizabeth Cleghorn Stevenson; 1810–65; Brit.)

Genet, Jean (1910–86; Fr.)

Gide, André (1869–1951; Fr.)

Gissing, George (1857–1903; Brit.)

WRITERS *cont.*

Gogol, Nikolai
(1809–52;
Russ.)

Golding, Sir William
(1911–93; Brit.)

Goldsmith, Oliver
(1730–74; Ir.)

Goncharov, Ivan
(1812–91; Russ.)

Goncourt, Edmond
de (1822–96; Fr.)

Goncourt, Jules de
(1830–70; Fr.)

Gordimer, Nadine
(b. 1923; S. Afr.)

Gorky, Maksim
(Aleksei Maksim-
ovich Peshkov;
1868–1936; Russ.)

Grahame, Kenneth
(1859–1932; Scot.)

Grass, Günter
(b. 1927; Ger.)

Graves, Robert
(1895–1985; Brit.)

Greene, Graham
(1904–91; Brit.)

Haggard, Sir H(enry)
Rider (1856–1925;
Brit.)

Hall, Radclyffe
(1883–1943; Brit.)

Hammett, Dashiell
(1894–1961; Am.)

Hamsun, Knut
(1859–1952; Norw.)

Hardy, Thomas
(1840–1928; Brit.)

Hašek, Jaroslav
(1883–1923; Cz.)

Hawthorne,
Nathaniel (1804–64;
Am.)

Hazlitt, William
(1778–1830; Brit.)

Heller, Joseph
(b. 1923; Am.)

Hemingway, Ernest
(1899–1961; Am.)

Henry, O. (William
Porter; 1862–1910;
Am.)

Hesse, Hermann
(1877–1962; Ger.)

Heyer, Georgette
(1902–74; Brit.)

Highsmith, Patricia
(1921–94; Am.)

Holmes, Oliver Wen-
dell (1809–94; Am.)

Hugo, Victor
(1802–85; Fr.)

Huxley, Aldous
(1894–1963; Brit.)

Irving, Washington
(1783–1859; Am.)

Ishiguro, Kazuo
(b. 1954; Brit., b. in
Japan)

James, P(hyllis)
D(orothy), Baroness
(b. 1920; Brit.)

James, Henry
(1843–1916; Brit.)

Jerome, Jerome
K(lapka)
(1859–1927; Brit.)

Joyce, James
(1882–1941; Ir.)

Kadare, Ismail
(b. 1936; Albanian)

Kafka, Franz
(1883–1924; Cz.)

Keneally, Thomas
(b. 1935; Austral.)

Kerouac, Jack
(1922–69; Am.)

Kingsley, Charles
(1819–75; Brit.)

Kipling, Rudyard
(1865–1936; Brit.,
b. in India)

Koestler, Arthur
(1905–83; Brit., b. in
Hungary)

Kundera, Milan
(b. 1929; Cz.)

La Bruyère, Jean de
(1645–96; Fr.)

Laclos, Pierre
Choderlos de
(1741–1803; Fr.)

Lagerkvist, Pär
(1891–1974; Sw.)

Lampedusa,
Giuseppe Tomasi di
(1896–1957; It.)

Lawrence, D(avid)
H(erbert)
(1885–1930; Brit.)

Lawrence, T(homas)
E(dward)
(1888–1935; Brit.)

Le Carré, John
(David Cornwell;
b. 1931; Brit.)

Le Fanu, Sheridan
(1814–73; Ir.)

Lessing, Doris
(b. 1919; Brit.)

Levi, Carlo (1902–75;
It.)

Levi, Primo (1919–87;
It.)

Lewis, C(live)
S(taples)
(1898–1963; Brit.)

Lewis, Sinclair
(1885–1951; Am.)

Lindsay, Norman
(1879–1969; Aus-
tral.)

Lowry, Malcolm
(1909–57; Brit.)

McCarthy, Mary
(1912–89; Am.)

McEwan, Ian
(b. 1948; Brit.)

Mackenzie, Sir
Compton
(1883–1972; Brit.)

Maclean, Alistair
(1922–87; Brit.)

Mahfouz, Naguib
(b. 1911; Egypt.)

Mailer, Norman
(b. 1923; Am.)

Malamud, Bernard
(1914–86; Am.)

Malory, Sir Thomas
(c. 1400–71; Engl.)

Malraux, André
(1901–76; Fr.)

Mann, Thomas
(1875–1955; Ger.)

Manning, Olivia
(1911–80; Brit.)

Mansfield, Katherine
(Kathleen Mansfield
Beauchamp;
1888–1923; NZ)

Manzoni, Alessandro
(1785–1873; It.)

Marsh, Dame Ngaio
(1899–1982; NZ)

Maugham,
W. Somerset
(1874–1965; Brit.)

Maupassant, Guy de
(1850–93; Fr.)

Mauriac, François
(1885–1970; Fr.)

Melville, Herman
(1819–91; Am.)

Meredith, George
(1828–1909; Brit.)

Mérimée, Prosper
(1803–70; Fr.)

Miller, Henry
(1891–1980; Am.)

Milne, A(lan)
A(lexander)
(1882–1956; Brit.)

Mishima, Yukio
(Kimitake Hiraoka;
1925–70; Jap.)

Mitford, Nancy
(1904–73; Brit.)

Monsarrat, Nicholas
(John Turney;
1910–79; Brit.)

Montaigne, Michel
de (1533–92; Fr.)

Moravia, Alberto
(Alberto Pincherle;
1907–90; It.)

Morrison, Toni
(b. 1931; Am.)

Murdoch, Dame Iris
(b. 1919; Brit.)

Musil, Robert
(1880–1942; Aus-
trian)

Mutanabbi, Abu al-
(915–65 A.D.; Pers.)

Nabokov, Vladimir
(1899–1977; Am.,
b. in Russia)

Naipaul, Sir V(idiad-
har S(urajprasad)
(b. 1932; Brit., b. in
Trinidad)

Narayan,
R(asipuram)
K(rishnaswami)
(b. 1906; Ind.)

Nesbit, Edith
(1858–1924; Brit.)

O'Brien, Edna
(b. 1932; Ir.)

O'Brien, Flann
(Brian O'Nolan;
1911–66; Ir.)

Oë, Kenzaburo
(b. 1935; Jap.)

Orwell, George (Eric
Blair; 1903–50;
Brit.)

Parker, Dorothy
(1893–1967; Am.)

Pasternak, Boris
(1890–1960; Russ.)

Pater, Walter
(1839–94; Brit.)

Pavese, Cesare
(1908–50; It.)

Paz, Octavio (b. 1914;
Mex.)

Peacock, Thomas
Love (1785–1866;
Brit.)

Peake, Mervyn
(1911–68; Brit.)

Pepys, Samuel
(1633–1703; Brit.)

Perec, Georges
(1936–82; Fr.)

Perrault, Charles
(1628–1703; Fr.)

Pliny the Younger
(c. 61–c. 113 A.D.;
Rom.)

Plutarch
(c. 46–c. 120 A.D.;
Gk)

Poe, Edgar Allan
(1809–49; Am.)

Potter, Beatrix
(1866–1943; Brit.)

Powell, Anthony
(b. 1905; Brit.)

Priestley, J(ohn)
B(oynton)
(1894–1984; Brit.)

WRITERS *cont.*

Pritchett, Sir V(ictor) S(awdon) (b. 1900; Brit.)

Proust, Marcel (1871–1922; Fr.)

Pym, Barbara (1913–80; Brit.)

Pynchon, Thomas (b. 1937; Am.)

Queneau, Raymond (1903–76; Fr.)

Rabelais, François (c. 1494–1553; Fr.)

Radcliffe, Ann (1764–1823; Brit.)

Ransome, Arthur (1884–1967; Brit.)

Renault, Mary (Mary Chalans; 1814–84; S. Afr., b. in Britain)

Rendell, Ruth (b. 1930; Brit.)

Richardson, Samuel (1689–1761; Brit.)

Richler, Mordecai (b. 1931; Can.)

Robbe-Grillet, Alain (b. 1922; Fr.)

Roth, Philip (b. 1933; Am.)

Runyon, Damon (1884–1946; Am.)

Rushdie, Salman (b. 1947; Brit.)

Sackville-West, Vita (1892–1962; Brit.)

Saki (H. H. Munro; 1870–1916; Scot., b. in Burma)

Salinger, J. D. (b. 1919; Am.)

Sand, George (Aurore Dupin, Baronne Dudevant; 1804–76; Fr.)

Sargeson, Frank (1903–82; NZ)

Sarraute, Nathalie (b. 1902; Fr.)

Sartre, Jean-Paul (1905–80; Fr.)

Sayers, Dorothy L. (1893–1957; Brit.)

Scott, Sir Walter (1771–1832; Scot.)

Shadbolt, Maurice (b. 1932; NZ)

Shelley, Mary (1797–1851; Brit.)

Sholokhov, Mikhail (1905–84; Russ.)

Shute, Nevil (1899–1960; Brit.)

Simenon, Georges (1903–89; Belg.)

Singer, Isaac Bashevis (1904–91; Am., b. in Poland)

Sitwell, Dame Edith (1887–1964; Brit.)

Smollett, Tobias (1721–71; Scot.)

Snow, C(harles) P(ercy), Baron (1905–80; Brit.)

Solzhenitsyn, Aleksandr (b. 1918; Russ.)

Soyinka, Wole (b. 1934; Nigerian)

Spark, Dame Muriel (b. 1918; Brit.)

Stein, Gertrude (1874–1946; Am.)

Steinbeck, John (1902–68; Am.)

Stendhal (Henri Beyle; 1783–1842; Fr.)

Sterne, Laurence (1713–68; Brit., b. in Ireland)

Stevenson, Robert Louis (1850–94; Scot.)

Stoker, Bram (1847–1912; Ir.)

Stowe, Harriet Beecher (1811–96; Am.)

Strachey, Lytton (1880–1932; Brit.)

Surtees, Robert (1805–64; Brit.)

Sutherland, Efua (b. 1924; Ghanaian)

Svevo, Italo (Ettore Schmitz; 1861–1928; It.)

Swift, Jonathan (1667–1745; Ir.)

Symons, Julian (b. 1912; Am., b. in Britain)

Thackeray, William Makepeace (1811–63; Brit., b. in India)

Theroux, Paul (b. 1941; Am.)

Thoreau, Henry (1817–62; Am.)

Tolkien, J(ohn) R(onald) R(euel) (1892–1973; Brit., b. in South Africa)

Tolstoy, Leo, Count (1828–1910; Russ.)

Trollope, Anthony (1815–82; Brit.)

Turgenev, Ivan (1818–83; Russ.)

Twain, Mark (Samuel Clemens; 1835–1910; Am.)

Updike, John (b. 1932; Am.)

Vargas Llosa, Mario (b. 1936; Peruvian)

Verne, Jules (1828–1905; Fr.)

Vidal, Gore (b. 1925; Am.)

Voltaire (François-Marie Arouet; 1694–1778; Fr.)

Vonnegut, Kurt (b. 1922; Am.)

Walker, Alice (b. 1944; Am.)

Wallace, Edgar (1875–1932; Brit.)

Walpole, Horace (1717–97; Brit.)

Walton, Izaak (1593–1683; Brit.)

Warren, Robert Penn (1905–89; Am.)

Waugh, Evelyn (1903–66; Brit.)

Wells, H(erbert) G(eorge) (1866–1946; Brit.)

West, Dame Rebecca (Cicely Fairfield; 1892–1983; Brit.)

Wharton, Edith (1862–1937; Am.)

White, Patrick (1912–90; Austral.)

Wilder, Thornton (1897–1975; Am.)

Wilson, Sir Angus (1913–91; Brit.)

Wodehouse, Sir P(elham) G(renville) (1881–1975; Am., b. in Britain)

Wolf, Christa (b. 1929; Ger.)

Wolfe, Tom (b. 1931; Am.)

Woolf, Virginia (1882–1941; Brit.)

Wright, Richard (1908–60; Am.)

Wyndham, John (1903–69; Brit.)

Zola, Émile (1840–1902; Fr.)

---

awry, out of order, not right, faulty, defective. **7** *iron the dress on the wrong side* inside, reverse, opposite, inverse.

Opposites RIGHT; CORRECT; APPROPRIATE; LEGAL.

wrong *adverb* **1** *guess wrong* wrongly, incorrectly, inaccurately, erroneously, mistakenly, inexactly, imprecisely, falsely. **2** *things went wrong* badly, amiss, awry, astray. **get wrong** *get the message wrong* misunderstand, misinterpret, misapprehend, misconstrue. **go wrong** **1** *you can't go wrong if you follow the instructions* make a mistake, go astray, err; *inf.* slip up, boob, make a booboo. **2** *things went wrong from the start* go badly, go amiss, go awry. **3** *their plans/marriage went wrong* fail, fall through, come to nothing, misfire, miscarry; *inf.* come to grief, flop. **4** *the machine's gone wrong* break down,

malfunction, fail, stop working/functioning; *inf.* be on the blink, conk out, go phut, go kaput. **5** *young people who go wrong* go astray, err, commit a crime/sin, stray from the straight and narrow, fall from grace; *inf.* go to the dogs.

wrong *noun* **1** *not know right from wrong* badness, immorality, sin, sinfulness, wickedness, evil, iniquity, unlawfulness, crime, dishonesty, dishonour, injustice, transgression, abuse; *inf.* crookedness. **2** *commit a wrong | do us a wrong* bad deed/act/action, misdeed, offence, injury, crime, infringement, infraction, injustice, grievance, outrage, atrocity. **in the wrong** *you were in the wrong to accuse him* in error, mistaken, at fault, to blame, blameworthy, culpable, guilty, off course, off target, wide of the

mark; *inf.* off beam.
Opposites RIGHT; VIRTUE; HONOUR.

wrong *verb* **1** *he wronged his wife* abuse, mistreat, maltreat, ill-treat, ill-use, harm, hurt, do
injury to. **2** *you wrong him by calling him a thief*
misrepresent, malign, dishonour, impugn, vilify, defame, slander, libel, denigrate, insult;
Am. inf. bad-mouth.

wrongdoer *noun* lawbreaker, criminal, delinquent, culprit, offender, felon, villain, miscreant, evildoer, sinner, transgressor, malefactor;
inf. wrong 'un.

wrongful *adjective wrongful dismissal/arrest*
unfair, unjust, improper, unjustified, unwarranted, unlawful, illegal, illegitimate, illicit.

wry *adjective* **1** *make/pull a wry face* twisted,
distorted, contorted, crooked, lopsided,
askew. **2** *a wry wit/remark* ironic, sardonic,
mocking, sarcastic, dry, droll, witty, humorous.

Xx Yy Zz

xerox *verb xerox the document* photocopy, copy, duplicate, reproduce, photostat.

Xerox™ *noun get a Xerox of the document* photocopy, copy, duplicate, photostat™.

X-ray *noun* X-ray image, radiogram, radiograph.

yank *verb yank the weeds out* pull, tug, jerk, wrench.

yank *noun remove the tooth with one yank* pull, jerk, wrench.

yap *verb* **1** *dogs yapping* yelp, bark. **2** *people yapping when we're trying to read* chatter, gossip, jabber, prattle, gibber, babble, gabble, clack.

yardstick *noun* measure, standard, gauge, scale, guide, guideline, touchstone, criterion, benchmark, model, pattern.

yarn *noun* **1** *use a fine yarn* thread, fibre, strand. *See table at* FABRIC. **2** *tell a good yarn* story, tale, anecdote, fable, traveller's tale; *inf.* tall tale/story, cock and bull story.

yawning *adjective a yawning gap* wide, wide open, gaping, cavernous, chasmal.

year *noun have a good year|the academic year* twelve-month period/session; calendar year, fiscal year. *See table at* MONTH. **year in, year out** regularly, without a break, unfailingly.

yearly *adjective a yearly event* annual, once a year, every year.

yearly *adverb published yearly* annually, once a year, per annum.

yearn *verb yearn for a child|yearn to go abroad* long, pine, have a longing, crave, desire, want, wish for, hanker after, covet, fancy, hunger for, thirst for; *inf.* have a yen for.

yearning *noun* longing, craving, desire, want, wish, hankering, fancy, hunger, thirst, lust, ache, burning; *inf.* yen.

yell *verb children yelling a warning to their friends* shout, cry out, howl, scream, shriek, screech, squeal, roar, bawl, whoop; *inf.* holler.

yell *noun give a yell of pain* shout, cry, howl, scream, shriek, screech, squeal, roar, bawl, whoop; *inf.* holler.

yen *noun* hankering, desire, want, wish, fancy, longing, craving, hunger, thirst, lust.

yes *adverb yes, I'll come* all right, of course, by all means, sure, certainly, in the affirmative; *dial.* aye; *inf.* yeah, yah, yep, uh-huh, righto.

yet *adverb* **1** *he hasn't appeared yet* as yet, so/thus far, up till/to now, until now. **2** *he is poor, yet he gives to charity* nevertheless, nonetheless, however, still, notwithstanding, despite that, for all that, just the same. **3** *there is yet more to come* still, in addition, additionally, besides, also, too, as well, further, into the bargain, to boot. **4** *I wasn't expecting him yet* now, just/right now, by now, already, so soon.

yield *verb* **1** *fields yielding a good crop* produce, bear, give, give forth, supply, provide. **2** *investments yielding a good return* give, return, bring in, fetch, earn, net, produce, supply, provide, generate, furnish. **3** *yield one's place in the team to another|yield the crown to the conqueror* give up, surrender, relinquish, part with, deliver up, turn over, give over, remit, cede, renounce, resign, abdicate, forgo. **4** *the army yielded after a long battle* admit/concede defeat, surrender, capitulate, submit, lay down one's arms, give in, give up the struggle, succumb, raise/show the white flag; *inf.* throw in the towel/sponge, cave in. **5** *yield to their demands* submit to, bow down to, comply with, accede to, agree to, consent to, go along with, grant, permit, allow, sanction, warrant. **6** *the material yields*

YOUNG OF ANIMALS			
Young	**Animal**	**Young**	**Animal**
calf	buffalo/camel/cattle/elephant/elk/ giraffe/hartebeest/rhinoceros/ whale	foal	horse/zebra
		fry	fish
		gosling	goose
cheeper	grouse/quail/partridge	joey	kangaroo
chick	chicken/hawk/pheasant	kid	antelope/goat/roedeer
colt	horse	kit	beaver/fox/weasel
cub	badger/bear/fox/leopard/lion/tiger/ walrus/wolf	kitten	bobcat/cat/cougar/jackrabbit/skunk
		lamb	sheep
cygnet	swan	leveret	hare
duckling	duck	piglet	pig
eaglet	eagle	pup	seal
elver	eel	puppy	coyote/dog
eyas	hawk	tadpole	frog/toad
fawn	caribou/deer	squab	pigeon
filly	horse	whelp	dog/wolf

on pressure give, bend, stretch, be flexible/pliant.
Opposites RESIST; WITHSTAND; DEFY.

yoke *noun* **1** *the yoke of the oxen* harness, collar, coupling. **2** *under the yoke of the tyrant* oppression, tyranny, enslavement, slavery, servitude, bondage, thrall. **3** *the yoke of marriage* tie, link, bond.

yoke *verb* **1** *yoke the oxen* harness, hitch up, couple, join up. **2** *yoked in marriage* join, unite, link, bond, tie.

yokel *noun* rustic, countryman, countrywoman, peasant, country bumpkin, provincial; *inf.* country cousin; *Am. inf.* hayseed, hill-billy.

young *adjective* **1** *young people* youthful, juvenile, junior, adolescent, in the springtime of life, in one's salad days. **2** *young industries* new, recent, undeveloped, fledgling, in the making.
Opposites OLD; ELDERLY; MATURE.

young *noun bear young* offspring, progeny, family, issue; little ones, babies, *inf.* sprogs. *See table.*

youngster *noun* young adult/person, youth, juvenile, teenager, adolescent, young hopeful; lad, boy, young man/woman, lass, girl; *inf.* kid, shaver, young 'un.

youth *noun* **1** *in their youth they were beautiful* young days, early years, teens; early life, adolescence; boyhood, girlhood. **2** *a youth has been killed* boy, young man, lad, youngster, juvenile, teenager, adolescent; *inf.* kid. **3** *the youth of today* young people, the young, younger/rising generation; *inf.* kids.
Opposites AGE; old age.

youthful *adjective* **1** *both youthful and elderly dancers* young, juvenile. *See* YOUNG *adjective* 1. **2** *grannies looking very youthful* fresh-faced, young-looking. **3** *he's a youthful sixty-five* young, active, vigorous, spry, sprightly.
Opposites OLD; ELDERLY; DODDERING.

zany *adjective a zany sense of humour | a zany personality* eccentric, peculiar, odd, ridiculous, absurd, comic, clownish, madcap, funny, amusing; *inf.* weird, wacky, daft, screwy; *Am. inf.* kooky.
Opposites ORDINARY; RUN-OF-THE-MILL; CONVENTIONAL.

zap *verb* **1** *ordered to zap the enemy* kill, slay, murder, put to death, liquidate, destroy; *inf.* do in, knock off. **2** *zap the ball/fly* hit, strike, slap; *inf.* whack. **3** *they were zapped by the invading army | zap the opposing team* defeat, beat, conquer, vanquish, trounce, rout, overcome, overpower, overthrow, crush. **4** *zap from place to place* rush, dash, pelt, race, sprint, tear, shoot,

fly, scurry, speed, hurry, hasten; *inf.* whiz, hare, zoom, zip.

zeal *noun* **1** *his zeal for life/sport* ardour, fervour, fervency, passion, fire, devotion, vehemence, intensity, enthusiasm, eagerness, keenness, earnestness, vigour, energy, verve, gusto, zest, fanaticism; *inf.* zing. **2** *upset by their religious/political zeal* zealotry, fanaticism, extremism. *See* ZEALOTRY.
Opposites APATHY; INDIFFERENCE.

zealot *noun a religious/political zealot* enthusiast, fanatic, extremist, radical, militant, bigot; *inf.* fiend.

zealotry *noun religious/political zealotry* zeal, fanaticism, extremism, single-mindedness, radicalism, militancy, dogmatism, bigotry.

zealous *adjective zealous athletes/stamp-collectors* ardent, fervent, fervid, passionate, impassioned, devoted, intense, enthusiastic, eager, keen, earnest, vigorous, energetic, zestful, fanatical.
Opposites APATHETIC; INDIFFERENT.

zenith *noun zenith of his achievement/powers* highest/high point, crowning point, height, top, acme, peak, pinnacle, climax, prime, meridian, apex, apogee, vertex; *inf.* high noon.
Opposites NADIR; BOTTOM.

zero *noun* **1** *a series of zeroes* nought, nothing, cipher. **2** *win absolutely zero* nothing, naught, nil; *inf.* zilch, not a sausage. **3** *economic growth is at zero* lowest point, nadir, rock bottom.

zero *verb zero the stopwatch* adjust to zero point. **zero in on** *his talk zeroed in on the economy* focus on, centre on, concentrate on, home in on, pinpoint.

zero hour *noun* appointed hour/time, crucial/vital/crisis moment, moment of truth.

zest *noun* **1** *approach the project with zest* relish, gusto, enthusiasm, eagerness, zeal, vigour, liveliness, energy, enjoyment, joy, delectation, appetite; *inf.* zing, oomph. **2** *add zest to the dish/occasion* piquancy, spice, pungency, flavour, relish, tang, savour, interest; *inf.* kick.
Opposites APATHY; INDIFFERENCE; DISTASTE.

zing *noun* zest, enthusiasm, eagerness, gusto, zeal, life, liveliness, spirit, animation, vitality,

SIGNS OF THE CHINESE ZODIAC

rat	horse
ox	sheep/goat
tiger	monkey
rabbit	rooster
dragon	dog
snake	boar/pig

SIGNS OF THE ZODIAC

Sign	Dates
Aries	March 21 – April 19
Taurus	April 20 – May 20
Gemini	May 21 – June 21
Cancer	June 22 – July 22
Leo	July 23 – August 22
Virgo	August 23 – September 22
Libra	September 23 – October 23
Scorpio	October 24 – November 21
Sagittarius	November 22 – December 21
Capricorn	December 22 – January 19
Aquarius	January 20 – February 18
Pisces	February 19 – March 20

vivacity, sparkle, vigour, pep, energy, vim, *élan*, dash, brio; *inf.* go, oomph, zip, pizzazz.

zip *noun a bit of zip to your playing* zest, enthusiasm, eagerness, gusto, life, liveliness, spirit, animation, sparkle, pep, *élan*, brio; *inf.* oomph, zing. *See* ZING.

zip *verb he zipped off before I could speak* rush, dash, pelt, race, tear, shoot, fly, scurry, speed, hurry, hasten; *inf.* whiz, hare, zoom, zap.

zodiac *noun. See tables.*

zone *noun* area, sector, section, belt, district, region, province. *See table. See also tables at* PROVINCE, REGION, STATE.

zoom *verb* **1** *planes/flies zooming around* fly, buzz. **2** *they zoomed off before he could question them* rush, dash, pelt, race, tear, shoot, fly, scurry, speed, hurry, hasten; *inf.* whiz, hare, zip, zap.

CLIMATIC ZONES			
arid	highland	polar	trade-wind
boreal	ice cap	semi-arid	littoral
continental	Marine West	steppe	tropical savannah
humid	Coast	subarctic	tropical wet
desert	Mediterranean	subtropical humid	tropical wet-dry
equatorial rainforest	monsoon	temperate rainy	tundra